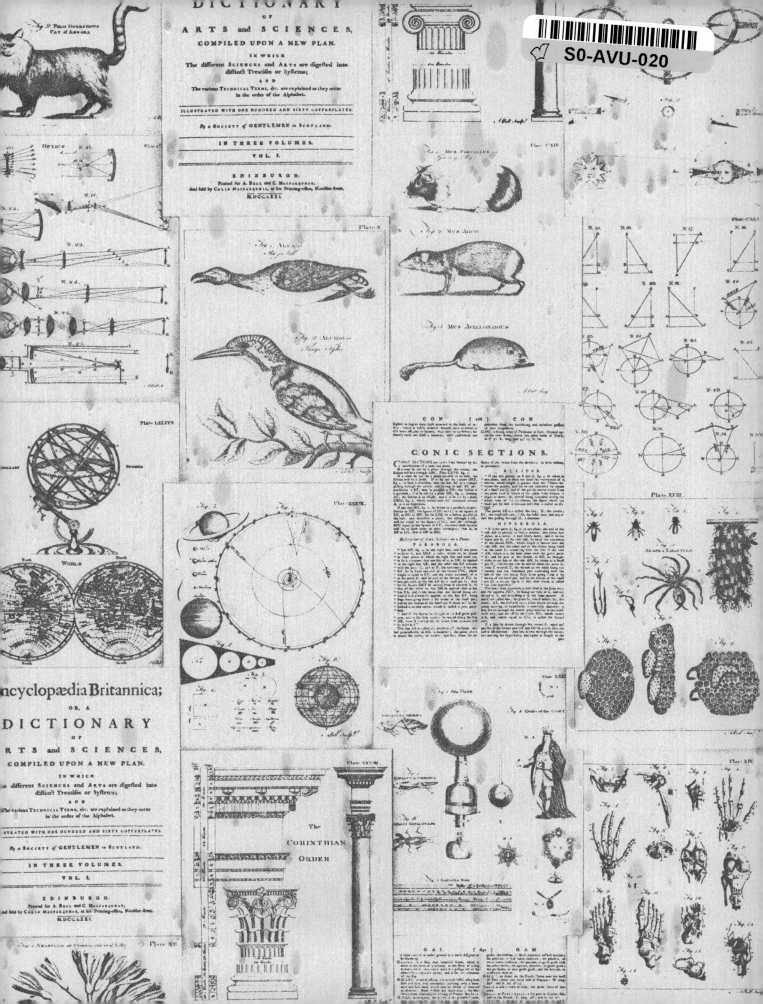

BRITANNICA

Book of the Year

1972

Encyclopaedia Britannica, Inc.

WILLIAM BENTON

Publisher

Chicago, Toronto, London, Geneva, Sydney, Tokyo, Manila, Johannesburg

THE UNIVERSITY OF CHICAGO

The Britannica Book of the Year is published with the editorial advice
of the faculties of The University of Chicago

The Publisher's Message

Of Man and His Ideas: The Essence of History

William Benton, publisher of "Encyclopædia Britannica."

The excitement of our time is not only in its events but also in our unparalleled opportunity to deal with and think about them—in short, its ideas. "Ideas rule the world," as the philosopher Auguste Comte remarked over a century ago. And human history, H. G. Wells reminded us, "is in essence a history of ideas."

Perhaps never before has a generation embodied so many ideas in the events of everyday happenings. The history of our time is to be seen not only in the way we deal with events but also in the ideas that give them substance and meaning. The *Britannica Book of the Year* is a creative construction of a brief moment in man's unending struggle with his fate. The yearbook is thus a reflection of life, an enlargement of the perspective of the individual on a world that can at best be incompletely known. It is a venture into the meaning of history, an inquiry into the nature of society, an exploration of the whimsy, duty, and purpose of man. It is an effort to see this moment in the light of the past and to stress the supremacy of man over the remorseless horizons of time.

This 1972 *Book of the Year* is an opportunity—for me as its publisher, for you as its reader—to try to see things whole, to pursue perspective and understanding of the shifting, contradictory happenings of our times. This is not an easy goal. The rapid accumulation of knowledge is dividing history, even current history—as it has already divided science—into a thousand specialities. These isolated insights into modern civilization are enlarged in the yearbook by special reports and feature articles. These help show how, in this particular year, man has applied some of his ideas. And they suggest how much more lies before him. "Our minds are infinite," said Alfred North Whitehead. "We are surrounded by possibilities that are infinite, and the purpose of human life is to grasp as much as we can out of that infinitude."

A man uniquely qualified to provide us with perspective is Theodore H. White, widely regarded as America's outstanding political journalist. His 1972 article is a follow-up on his feature article in the 1971 yearbook. During World War II, White spent six years as *Time*'s correspondent in China. This helped prepare him to give us insight into the monumental series of events during the past year involving that giant nation.

In his current article, White views 1971 as the year in which the postwar era came to an abrupt end—with the U.S. diplomatic initiatives toward China, admission of China to the United Nations, and the upheaval in the world monetary and trade situation. You will understand better the coming political events of 1972 with the insight White provides.

Another subject of continuing concern worldwide is poverty in the less developed nations and the imperatives facing civilized man in combating it. You will find in this volume a prescient article on world poverty by Gunnar Myrdal, the renowned Swedish economist who achieved international acclaim for his book on the Negro, *An American Dilemma*. Myrdal embraces the dilemma that arises between the visceral instinct of man—to save himself and his countrymen first—and his humanitarian instinct: to offer in a warm and enlightened spirit the help that is needed so desperately by the disadvantaged.

A third major feature article is by Sir Robert Menzies, for many years prime minister of Australia. He describes the complexities of development for a people tied politically and culturally to one race in a distant hemisphere, and tied geographically and economically to another race in its own hemisphere. When one considers how violent and difficult was the loosening of England's ties to some parts of its empire—Rhodesia, South Africa, India—one can sense the historic uniqueness in the subtle manner through which Australia loosened its links and attempted to find its identity in a new economic relationship with the East. (You will note in the Menzies article how upset Sir Winston Churchill was when Australia first entered into a treaty to which Great Britain was not a party!) But Australia was able to make this move toward Japan—despite the simmering enmities of World War II—because of idioms it inherited from the past: the insistence of Sir Winston and an earlier prime minister of England, William Pitt the Younger, that—as Sir Robert reminds us—"hatred must not be perpetuated if international life is to have an opportunity to become civilized."

Sir Robert's article helps dramatize the fact that one of the nations most deeply affected by the turbulence of world monetary conditions in 1971 was Japan. Indeed, I think it's a fair guess that the most important aspect of America's foreign policy in the '70s may be our relations with Japan. Its astonishing economic development since the end of World War II is outlined in a special report on the changing perspectives that have turned the attention of the world so compellingly toward Asia. We must learn to look at the totality of Asia and the relationships that bind its peoples together. Accordingly, we examine Japan as the dramatic representation of the Orient's adjustment to the modern world. Australia, of course, shows the West's adjustment to the East. These two nations are opposites that have much in common: their trade with each other, their abrupt separation from their past. The article on Japan and Sir Robert Menzies' article should be read together.

In two other special reports we are reminded of the continuing conflict over one of the most ancient concerns of man: the relationship between the individual and his government.

If we can see in the *Book of the Year* the imperatives of change today, we can see in history the benefits of change in the past. The idea of democracy was still young, for example, when—as Plutarch has recorded of the Athens of 594 B.C.—"the disparity of fortune between the rich and the poor had reached its height so that the city seemed to be in a dangerous condition, and no other means for freeing it from disturbances . . . seemed possible but despotic power." That would mean the end of democracy—and there were many who clamoured for that end. The poor, sensing that their status was worsening each year and despairing because the government seemed to be in the hands of their masters, began to talk of violent revolt. The rich, outraged at the challenge to their status and property, were ready to defend themselves by force. The violence that brings an end to reason, and to ideas, was averted only because the institution could accept change. The moderate elements in the city secured the election of Solon, a businessman of aristocratic lineage, to the highest civic office. He then undertook those reforms that preserved not only the government of Athens but the idea of democracy. Does not this lesson from the past seem relevant to the present? Does it not indicate directions in which our institutions might flow in the future? It is the cutting edge of the present that puts the past into perspective—and the future.

In Robert Sherrill's special report on the invasion of privacy we see the newest dimension of the age-old effort of government to gather information that extends its domination in ways that are not allowed by law. The use of government agents to spy on a nation's own citizenry is alien to democracy but not to history. That such spying is being used in our time in our country —under the rationale that the people can profit enormously from the planning and policy-making made possible by the gathering of relevant data—is a shocking and sobering commentary on the continuing contest between the people and those who would rule them, according to Sherrill. Frankly, I think such dangers to our way of life are exaggerated. I don't think we've reached a point to warrant Sherrill's fears, but read his article and decide for yourself.

It is the same with the government's challenge to the right of free flow of information to the people, as discussed in Fred W. Friendly's special report about political pressures on television. Friendly is a former executive of CBS and was an associate of my friend Ed Murrow. He is now a professor in the Columbia School of Journalism and a key adviser on television to the Ford Foundation. He gives us a reprise on a fight that was an issue as far back as the 1780s—whether the press can and should be free, whether the people can and should have free access to the secret decisions of their governors. Today this involves not only television but issues arising out of the publication of the Pentagon papers. (The government's effort to suppress those papers was rejected by the U.S. Supreme Court.) But the issue surfaces in other forms and in other forums—through criticism of the press by individual officeholders, through investigation by governmental bodies, through restrictive regulations resting in the hands of government. Some feel that one can see in this struggle not merely a conflict of ideas but a combat between the institutions that reflect them. Some claim that the Government and the Press are locked in a battle to see which institution will win ultimate power in the nation—the Government through suppression of free information, or the Press through dissemination of information that elected officials regard as prejudicial to their own rights—and hopes of being reelected.

When I was in the U.S. Senate in the early 1950s, I proposed in a speech on the floor that the Senate authorize the appointment by the president of a high level official whose job would be to fight for the people's "right to know." He would seek to force government departments to disgorge material like the Pentagon papers. I still think this is a good idea. However, as with the right to privacy, I am not seriously alarmed about any danger to freedom of the press. I think the danger always has been, as it is now, greatly exaggerated.

In all of this, the saving element seems to be neither government nor the press. It is the individual in pursuit of ideas. His major source will be, significantly, that medium that baffles one institution and angers the other: books. This is Britannica's business; we are the world's largest publisher of books. Governments traditionally have hated books and the ideas they perpetuate. Many know that the Library of Congress originated with the purchase of Thomas Jefferson's library from his bankrupt estate for $25,000, but few realize that every graduate of Yale, Harvard, and Princeton in the Congress voted against the appropriation because so many books in Jefferson's library were deemed to be dangerous. Books are the repository of man's free thoughts, and free thinking often is feared. As individuals, we respond instinctively to the importance of books in our lives: we deplore the mindless habit of watching television for two, three, four, or five hours a day while we envy the man who reads a significant book a day or book a week—the person who spends an hour or two a day in communion with his own mind.

It is in that recognition that UNESCO is sponsoring 1972 as International Book Year (IBY). This is clearly as important an event culturally as was the International Geophysical Year scientifically. Only rarely since the invention of movable type has the reading of books been the subject of such a genuinely dramatic gesture as IBY—or so meaningful a one. "Dreams, books are each a world," wrote William Wordsworth, "and books we know are a substantial world, both pure and gold."

The individual who reads the great or provocative books with zest and an aggressive drive is one who is immersed not only in the abstractions of wisdom but also in the uses of ideas. "Knowledge is a treasure," wrote Thomas Fuller, "but practice is the key to it." It is the high privilege and unwavering aspiration of the *Book of the Year* not only to express our times in terms of ideas and events but to seek that connective tissue within human events that helps translate thought into action.

Wm Benton

Editorial Staff

Editor in Chief: DEAN H. SCHOELKOPF

Editors: DAPHNE DAUME; J. E. DAVIS, London

Classification Advisers: A. G. Armstrong, Morris Fishbein, M.D., Edwin W. Goodpaster, Miroslav Kriz, D. A. Pyke, M.D., M.R.C.P., John Kerr Rose, Harvey Sherman

Copy Editors: Judy Booth, David Calhoun, Conrad Chyatte, Vanessa Clarke, Ray Dennerstein, R. M. Goodwin, Mary Alice Molloy, Dorothy M. Partington, Basil H. Tripp, Richard York

Consulting Editor: Jacques Havet, Paris

Latin America Editor: Cesar A. Ramos, Mexico City

Art Director: Will Gallagher

Associate Art Director: Cynthia Peterson

Picture Staff: James Sween, Senior Editor; Florence Scala, Adelle Weiner; Elisabeth West, London

Layout Artist: Mark Cowans

Cartographers: Chris Leszczynski, Supervisor; Eugene Tiutko

Art Staff: Martina Daker, Bernard Holliday

Geography Editor: Frank J. Sutley

Assistant Geography Editor: Olga A. Titelbaum

Geography Staff: William A. Cleveland, Supervisor; Janet Feller, Juanita Bartholomew, Gerald E. Keefe, Charlene R. Neidlinger, Marino P. PeBenito, David L. Schein, Joseph R. Sturgis. Copy Correspondents: Peggy Clark, Naomi Gralnek

Editorial Production Manager: J. Thomas Beatty

Production Coordinator: Lorene Lawson

Assistant Coordinators: Barbara W. Cleary, Ruth Passin

Staff: John Atkinson, Necia Brown, Susan Alison Bush, Charles Cegielski, Rama Deva, Robin Fink, Gerald M. Fisher, Emily A. Friedman, Barbara Wescott Hurd, Marilyn Klein, Lawrence Kowalski, Lois C. Lantz, Winifred Laws, Lynn K. McEwan, Lila H. Morrow, Richard O'Connor, Mary Reardon, Julian Ronning, Madolynn Scheel, Linda G. H. Schmidt, Harry Sharp, Elliott Major Singer, Carol Kalata Smith, Cheryl M. Trobiani, Valerie Walker, Penne L. Weber, Anita K. Wolff

Copy Control: Felicité Buhl, Supervisor; Mary K. Finley, Recorder; Gurtha McDonald, Shirley Richardson Barbara Chandler, Pat Woodgate, London

Index Staff: Frances E. Latham, Supervisor; Virginia Palmer, Assistant Supervisor; Grace R. Lord, Mary L. Reynolds, Rosalba Rueda

Editorial Assignments: Mary Hunt, Allena McCorvey

Secretary: Judith Lukens

Executive Vice-President Editorial, Encyclopædia Britannica, Inc.: HOWARD L. GOODKIND

Contents

1971: The End of the Postwar World

by THEODORE H. WHITE

It was a year of watershed events; only 1945 and 1948 could match its panorama of upheavals; history would be decades trying to weigh its impact.

China was to be accepted back into the community of nations; proud Great Britain was to be absorbed in the Common Market; Berlin, the swollen pressure head of postwar Europe, was to be lanced. Gold itself, the magic metal of all time, was to be stripped of meaning; a trading world that had endured a generation was to collapse with a shivering fall whose end result no one could predict.

On the periphery of the main arena of action, violence, sputtering, and commotion continued. More than a dozen coups or attempted coups would roil the African states. Tyranny would stain Bengal with murder, then bring war, and the swift collapse of the state of Pakistan which knew neither how to govern nor how to fight.

Yet, when it was over, a story came clear: In 1971 the postwar world came to its end. The settlements of the great wars of the '40s had outlived their times—and were now as obsolete as the Peace of Westphalia.

A giant paradox governed world politics. The postwar world had been one which the United States policed and patrolled against revolution—and, for a decade, it had been steadily losing its power to control events. In 1971 the U.S. recognized this—and, by so doing, paradoxically regained a long-forgotten initiative of action. For years, the U.S. as patron-protector of the "free world" had subordinated its needs to the needs of those it claimed to protect; in 1971 other nations were forced to adjust their needs to America's recalculation of its needs. For at home, as abroad, the postwar world was over: ungovernable cities, uncontrollable inflation, hitherto-unimagined citizen actions were making Americans rethink the role of government in a free society. Revolutions abroad would have to be let go their own course: Americans had enough to do managing their own revolution.

Thus, though this American recapture of initiative was as impossible to predict at the beginning of the year as its results were to predict at the end, it is in the U.S. that the story of 1971 must start.

The Year of the Dollar. No drama stirred American imagination in the dull headlines of New Year's Day, 1971. Congress, after 11 months of foot-dragging, had once again, as it had for 24 years, unhappily passed a foreign aid bill. Environment, as always, was front-page news: the president had just signed the Clean Air Act, which insisted that in six years the pollutants in auto fumes be cut by 90%. Public concern was about to entertain the Great Phosphate Scare as phosphates in detergents were indicted as prime pollutants of America's beautiful rivers and lakes. (By fall the federal government would be reversing itself

Pulitzer Prize winner Theodore H. White is the author of the "Making of the President" books, Thunder Out of China *(a study of the Chinese revolution), and* Fire in the Ashes *(a history of European postwar recovery). He has been a foreign correspondent in both China and Europe, and is now a historian, novelist, playwright, and television writer.*

—yielding a reluctant acquiescence to phosphates because the caustic soda replacing them was seen as more dangerous.) On New Year's Day all cigarette advertising, with its jingles and faceless horsemen, was removed from television—yet, in the next six months, cigarette consumption was to go up by 10%. The best-seller lists at year's opening ran more heavily than ever to sex and romance.

For anyone seeking a clue to the way the world might move, the more serious items had to be sought in the back pages. For example: the ritual year-end conferences of professors and academic societies provoked recognition that, at least momentarily, the public lust for education was slackening. Hopeful scholars were facing a new world in which the services of plumbers, carpenters, structural steel workers were sought far more widely than their own. A great building boom was approaching, and construction workers were demanding, and receiving, three-year increases of 50 to 60% in hourly wage rates. While assistant professors of philosophy went begging at $9,000 a year, sheet-metal workers, electricians, plasterers were demanding $20,000 a year.

The dollar was clearly at the centre of things as 1971 opened. But whatever was ailing the dollar was considered chiefly a domestic problem—something to be controlled by the interacting decisions of banks, corporations, consumer choice, the Federal Reserve Board, the budget and the Treasury. Only later would events demonstrate that what ailed the dollar was the agony of an era that did not know how to die gracefully, and the dollar was cracking in the general crack-up of the postwar world.

In the spring of 1971, however, the unhappiness of Americans about their dollar—whether the soiled bills peeled over by the housewife at the supermarket checkout line or the endless digits in economists' calculations—was the underlying discontent against which episodes echoed; and one should examine the Americans' attitude to their dollar in those early months.

Dollars—just like marks, pounds, yen, rubles—are a way government has of issuing tickets for goods and services. This is an immensely delicate and complicated process, for when too many tickets are issued by government for limited services, spaces, or command of goods, orderly economic procedures become a mob action.

In January of 1971, the pressure for dollar-tickets threatened to become just such a mob action. At the point of greatest commotion in this mob action were the clashes within government itself: city officials argued with state officials and both turned to argue with federal officials. The nation wanted services more than goods, and the chief giver of services was local government. But no city in the country any longer commanded the resources to meet the needs that social conscience required—for better health care, better police, better schools, better fire protection, and growing welfare demands. From New York to California, local officials were to squeeze welfare rolls throughout the year; yet their service burdens kept rising.

The Wage-Price Squeeze. There followed, in the jostle for dollars, the conflict between the great unions and the great employing groups. Terrified by inflation, having watched seemingly generous union settlements melt in purchasing power as the value of the dollar itself melted, the unions were entering 1971 prepared to leapfrog the great inflation. But their demands were so huge that they could be met only by price rises that, if passed on to ordinary people, would cripple the family budgets of the vast majority of the unorganized.

As for this great majority—they seemed helpless. The abstractions of the higher theological economics were brought down to them as biting daily and weekend reality. For the first time in a decade, so reported economists in 1971, there had been no real gain in the purchasing power of the average American family. Six percent of all Americans, as the year opened, could find no work, the highest number in 12 years. The ripples of worry spread far beyond the 4.6 million actual jobless—to their merchants, their families, their friends. Moreover, though the pace of inflation seemed statistically to be slowing in the early months, inflation as felt by common people was swinging. For the last 25 years, ever since 1946, prices had gone up every year with the single exception of 1949. And now all the homely indices seemed set for another sprint. The two-cent stamp of prewar years had gently risen to three, four, five, then six cents as Richard Nixon took office—and was about to be hiked, in 1971, to eight cents. In New York the nickel subway fare of postwar years had gone to 30 cents—and leaders talked of jumping it to 50 cents. The 15 cent milk bottle of the postwar years had become a 30 cent carton—and its price was climbing. Fear, fostered by rising prices, gripped every family trying to plan its future.

Hypersensitive to politics, the Nixon administration recognized the fear. Yet, in January, with remarkable stubbornness, Nixon clung to his "game plan." There would be no government intervention in the wage-price spiral; adopting the Keynesian economics so long derided by orthodox Republicans, he would rest his hopes on stimulating the economy by letting the budget spin free and unbalanced until full employment was restored. In only one area of economics did he offer a major novelty, and that was tied to a philosophy called the "New American Revolution." Too much power was concentrated in Washington, he felt, and with that power too much of the nation's revenues. Thus, he proposed to Congress that the federal government share its revenues with those states and cities where the people's hunger for services was most acute. The proposal lived for several weeks in public discussion, then vanished in the ambuscades of Congress while the nation's pocketbook nerve ached. All through spring Nixon remained firm: no tax cuts as some demanded, no tax raises as others insisted, and no intervention. "Steady as you go," was the White House word, as the administration grimly prepared to withstand the present public unhappiness, looking forward to the payoff, politically, in stable prosperity in 1972, the election year.

The War in Vietnam. But politics are not quite as neat a science as, say, chemistry, where given inputs can be controlled by formulas to yield given results. Politics move by the impact of episodes on the minds of hundreds of millions of people of different emotional background. Thus, though the apparent indifference of the administration to the economic hurts of the American people might have been sustained politically, its politics could not, at the same time, absorb another new set of unanticipated emotional impacts and remain viable. And these new impacts, in the spring months, began to jolt in from Vietnam.

It was in his foreign policy that Nixon had been at his strongest—and strongest of all in his persuasion of the American people that his slow, costly disengagement of U.S. forces from Vietnam was not only working but working because it rested on the steady turnover of that war to the Vietnamese.

Thus, then, in February and March, the people along with their president witnessed betrayal of their common hopes in Vietnam. A year earlier Nixon had ordered the invasion of Cambodia where, in cooperation with U.S. troops, the Army of South Vietnam—ARVN—had performed with spectacular élan and efficiency. Denounced, despised, and derided by U.S. public opinion at the time, the Cambodian foray had been one of the rare, solid victories of the Vietnam war.

Now, in winter 1971, came the crucial test—could ARVN go it alone? So, the plan—the ARVN would mass its troops in the northern provinces of South Vietnam, then hack across the Laotian border and cut the strands of the Ho Chi Minh Trail, vital to the enemy effort.

Secrecy is as essential to successful military assault as night is to sleep. In conventional Asian politics, secrecy is as difficult to keep as water in a sieve. Nonetheless, even in Asia, few critical offensives had been heralded with as much public fanfare and lack of security as was ARVN's thrust into Laos. Two weeks in advance, public dispatches reported the preparations; correspondents wired the day they expected the invasion to start. And the North Vietnamese concentrated for resistance.

When, then, on February 8, the ARVN offensive did get under way—with ground troops provided by South Vietnam and air

Construction workers protest in Newport, R.I. Early in 1971
Pres. Richard M. Nixon faced growing discontent among Americans as the value of their dollar declined and wage increases for most brought no increase in purchasing power.

cover provided by the U.S., the action was anticipated almost as if it were a scheduled football game. And within ten days, disaster had overtaken the venture. Badly commanded, ARVN battalions penetrated 11 mi. across the border; then, in many cases, meeting resistance and massed artillery fire, they stalled, in some cases panicking, as soldiers scrambled and fought to cling to the skids of U.S. helicopters sent to evacuate them. By mid-March it was abundantly clear that the blow which, it was hoped, could settle the war then and there was more than a failure—it was a catastrophe. The ARVN forces simply were not ready to carry an offensive war and win against the combat-hardened Communist veterans of Hanoi; nor could anyone venture to say when they would be ready. The diplomacy of the Vietnam war, the extrication of U.S. troops and the freeing of U.S. prisoners continued in its bleak perspective.

The disaster in Laos, as it seeped in over five winter-spring weeks, was simultaneous with an even more emotional impact on the U.S. mind and conscience: the My Lai episode.

Tragedy at My Lai. Ever since Nov. 12, 1970, there had been proceeding at Ft. Benning, Ga., the trial of a short, stumpy, rather unintelligent Army first lieutenant named William L. Calley, Jr. Day by day, for almost five months, in testimony eventually reaching 5,000 pages of transcript, a military court—and the nation—had been learning of the massacre three years earlier of unarmed women and children at a village called My Lai in Quang Ngai Province of South Vietnam. And what was being described, day by day, was an abomination, a hideous act of evil perpetrated by a platoon of the U.S. Army.

On March 16, 1968—so the trial record made clear—C Company of the 1st Battalion, 20th Infantry, 11th Light Infantry Brigade of the Americal Division, had been ordered to purge My Lai, in the Communist-raddled strip of the panhandle of South Vietnam. Calley's platoon of 100 men had landed by helicopter at 7:30 A.M. and moved on target. No resistance was encountered; no hostile gunfire; the armed Viet Cong units that had been operating out of the village had fled. Nonetheless,

Calley, then only 24 years old, had rounded up the remaining villagers, old men, women, and children. Thirty were herded together and Calley gave orders to kill them. Another 100 villagers were herded to a ditch and these, too, were murdered, Calley firing at point-blank range, as he testified himself. Women with babes in arms were killed by single shots. Old men were clubbed to death. Wounded were dispatched, said one of the participants, "to help them . . . out of their misery."

Three years later, in March of 1971, after four months of trial, the full story finally was told. Americans in uniform were the undoubted executioners of anonymous human beings. It mattered little that the enemy Viet Cong had been guilty of far graver massacres of civilians in larger batches in the course of the savage war. The hidden beast in every man, *"das innere Schweinhund,"* whom Kurt Schumacher had described in the Nazi nightmare, lurked within Americans, too.

No court hearing such testimony could do else but convict. Thus, on March 29, 1971, the military court at Ft. Benning—six officers, all combat veterans—found Calley guilty, personally, of the premeditated murder of at least 22 unarmed civilians. And with that, what had been an episode that every American wished could not be true became more than episode—it became a national sin for which every American held himself responsible. If the Army itself, by its own military justice, had found Calley guilty, then—as every editorialist, every politician, every observer hastened to say—all Americans shared the guilt.

Few controversies of 1971 prickled more quickly into emotional turbulence—flags flown half-staff across the nation, draft boards resigning, impassioned defense and denunciation of the

First Lieut. William L. Calley, Jr. (left), leaves the courtroom at Ft. Benning, Ga., where on March 29, 1971, he was found guilty of the premeditated murder of 22 unarmed civilians at the village of My Lai, South Vietnam.

hapless Calley himself. Few such isolated emotional episodes were more likely to have permanent effects.

For Americans the spirit had gone out of the Vietnam war. It was over. However short or long it took Nixon to get U.S. forces out of Vietnam—it was all too long. The war had lost its meaning and its grip on the residual loyalties of those who salute the flag by reflex. Politically, the draft now was doomed. Politically, too, in the next few weeks, the last congressional bases of support for the war crumbled as the most ardent Southern senators and congressmen, reflex supporters of the armed forces, abandoned the enterprise.

By mid-April 1971 the presidency of Richard Nixon had reached its low point.

His conduct of Vietnamese affairs, among other passages of his superlative foreign policy, always had been the president's strongest claim on public support. (The high point of his popularity, as measured by the Gallup Poll, had been 68%, reached after his first major statement, on television, in November 1969 when he had promised orderly liquidation of the war along with a transfer of combat responsibilities to the Vietnamese). Now, in early 1971, as the economy sluggishly failed to respond to his direction, as prices rose, as defeat became clear in Laos, as the squalor of the My Lai massacre pressed in on the American mind, his standing crumbled. Both major national polling organizations, despite their differences, traced the downward course. The Gallup Poll, with a Republican skew, held him at 56% in national popularity at the beginning of 1971; the same poll showed him at 51% in February, 50% in March, 49% in April. The Harris Poll, with a Democratic skew, consistently paired the president against his chief Democratic rival, Edmund Muskie. In January, Muskie had led Nixon in the Harris Poll by 43 to 40. In February by 44 to 39, and in April by an astonishing 47 to 39! In the spring months of the year, Nixon's popularity had fallen to a lower level, as measured by the Gallup Poll, than that of any U.S. president since Harry Truman at a comparable point in his administration.

Yet it was precisely at this low point in April that the president's fortunes turned—faint, yet sharp as the sound of a Ping-Pong ball on a Ping-Pong table, came the first response of China to the tentacular groping of U.S. power as initiated by Richard Nixon. The bamboo curtain was splitting—but, more importantly, so too was the bedrock of the postwar world's diplomacy.

CHINA SHAKES THE WORLD

The world that had set in its jagged antagonisms after the war against fascism was like a body, broken by multiple fractures, then set again in permanently crippled postures.

South Vietnamese troops at Ham Nghi after their evacuation from Laos. In February 1971 ARVN troops invaded Laos in an attempt to cut the flow of military supplies along the Ho Chi Minh Trail. After penetrating only 11 mi., they were halted and forced to retreat.

Of all these, none was more grotesque, for Americans, than the locked hates that set the U.S. so rigidly against China.

It had been to save China that the U.S. originally was drawn into the Great War—Franklin D. Roosevelt's refusal to cooperate in imperial Japan's conquest of China had directly brought about the Japanese attack on Pearl Harbor. Yet now, as 1971 opened, 30 years later, China had become America's most impassioned self-proclaimed enemy.

Shock had gripped the U.S. immediately after the war when Americans first realized that China's future lay with the Communists, not with Chiang Kai-shek's Nationalists. And following shock came paranoia as, for years, witch-hunters and demagogues pursued the spoor of those U.S. leaders who, they claimed, "had lost China to the Reds." Purging the State Department of its finest Oriental expertise, wrecking the careers of all who sought a reasoned response to Asia's revolution, the paranoids froze America's posture to a rigidity totally contradictory to perceived reality. In August 1958 the U.S. government described the Chinese government as a vassal of the Soviet Union and then declared *officially*, "The United States holds the view that Communism's rule in China is not permanent and that it one day will pass. By withholding diplomatic recognition from Peiping it seeks to hasten that passing." This declaration, one step short of war, remained official U.S. policy for more than a decade. And, by then, in order to halt what Americans thought was the expansion of Chinese Communism, the U.S. had plunged its men into Vietnam, in one of the bloodiest of all wars, which was to cost over $100 billion and some 50,000 lives.

The intensity of this paranoia was rooted in the very special attitude of Americans to China—an international love-hate syndrome rare in international diplomacy. History had fashioned this syndrome: for thousands of years China had lived in isolation from the Western world. China was, to the Chinese, Tien-Hsia—All Under Heaven. Foreign relations had been unknown; strangers were all barbarians; isolation had been the great formula of traditional Chinese diplomacy in its millennia of pride. In this grand stretch of time, the period occupied by U.S. history was, to the Chinese, but an eye blink—an eye blink that smarted with a century of catastrophic humiliation, when China was blasted open and foreigners looted its treasures. For Chinese, this time span of the 19th and 20th centuries was remembered as an abnormality that had to be erased. But to Americans, with their short time span of national history, it was the way things always were in the Orient, and the U.S. had a special mission of guardianship for the suffering Chinese.

In those 19th-century years and until but recently, the U.S. was a predominantly Protestant country, and the energy of the Protestant ethic found one of its finer expressions in missionary enterprise abroad, particularly in China. China thus entered U.S. diplomatic history not only as a trade and power problem, but as a moral problem. In the contending rapacities of the Western imperialisms that sought to carve up China, the U.S. was not only the most moderate but, under missionary influence, the most protective. It was the U.S., foremost among all powers, that prevented the dismemberment of China by its Open Door policy and the U.S., foremost among all others, that implanted universities, hospitals, schools in that land. China was America's ward.

Yet China had a life of its own. The culture of its philosophers, its craving for order, the savagery of daily life, the scatological and vituperative common talk of Chinese, the ribald overtones of its popular writings, as well as the torment and suffering that ensued from 1911 to 1940 when orderly traditional government dissolved to leave all life at the mercy of random gunmen called warlords—these basically were unknown to U.S. policy-makers and the U.S. public at large. In the American mind, China and the U.S. were friends forever—until the seizure of power on the mainland of China by the Communists in 1949, which set off a paranoia of love betrayed or denied; in American eyes, an ungrateful people had repudiated U.S. friendship.

The paranoia of the Communists was at least equal to that of

the U.S. demagogues as both powers in the early postwar years, before the set of history, sought to adjust their relations.

The Chinese had been humiliated by white men. White men had invaded their country, for a century had patrolled and gunned their rivers, had exploited their resources, had treated natives as beasts, had set themselves above Chinese law by the colour of their skin. It mattered little that Americans had, certainly, been the least offensive among foreigners in this century of humiliation. The U.S., in the Chinese Communist view of the world, was the heartland of capitalism and imperialism; the U.S. military presence during the war had made theirs the most familiar, and thus the most hated, white faces; and U.S. support of Chiang had scorched the Communists with untold deaths as the civil war of Nationalists and Communists wore on to its bloody conclusion in 1949. Before then, in the presidency of Harry Truman, the wise U.S. decision had been taken in 1948 to abandon the Nationalists to their fate; in the last year of their guttering agony, no further U.S. support was forthcoming. And, with the ultimate triumph of the Communists in 1949, the U.S. signed off from involvement on the mainland of Asia, helping the Nationalists only to move to Taiwan, where for the next year they were left marooned, to wither away.

A year later, however, all things changed. With the invasion of South Korea in June 1950, the U.S. found itself at war with a Communist aggressor, and by fall of that year Chinese and U.S. soldiers were killing each other. After the Korean truce of 1953, all dialogue between China and the U.S. government ended, hatred frozen.

It is one of the great paradoxes of history that few men more eloquently spoke this hatred than Richard Nixon, then vice-president (1953–61); and part of the essential drama of 1971 is the personal drama of Richard Nixon.

Wounded ARVN airborne troops make their way to a first-aid station at Khe Sanh, South Vietnam, after their evacuation from Laos on March 10, 1971. The troops, part of the ill-fated invasion force, were hit by shrapnel and later removed by helicopter.

Nixon had, in his youth, as congressman and senator, believed that China had been lost to the Reds by conspiracy within the State Department. (So, too, at that time, had John F. Kennedy.) Nixon had helped purge and lent his name to the hysteria of anti-Communism in the early 1950s. He had advocated, at one time, the nuclear bombing of Hanoi to prevent the spread of Asian Communism. Yet he was, above all, a thoughtful and pragmatic man. While his early perception of domestic life in the U.S. was encased in the political orthodoxy of southern California, his perception of foreign affairs had come later, when he was vice-president and sat in the Cabinet. There, in maturity, approaching foreign affairs around the long table of the dark Victorian Cabinet room, he had found them both fluid and fascinating. The experience remained with him. By 1967, after seven years of reflection out of public office, his attitude to China had changed. Both privately and publicly, he made clear his feeling, as he prepared for his 1968 campaign, that the lack of dialogue between the world's most populous and ancient civilization and the world's richest and most powerful civilization was an absurdity. If ever he became president, he averred, the overriding priority of his administration would be to set these two civilizations to talking.

The first two years of his presidency were marked by a system of public, private, and secret signals to Peking—and all seemed signals into a void, from which no echo returned. Yet there were listeners; how they would respond, no one could tell.

There is an unquenchable sense of humour in the Chinese tradition, however, familiar to all who have lived there or savoured its popular culture. Thus, then, when the first response of China to the U.S. overtures came in April 1971, it came almost as a drollery. On April 7 the world read that a team of U.S. Ping-Pong players had been invited to match strokes against Chinese Ping-Pong players. More importantly: a handful of U.S. newsmen would be invited to accompany the Ping-Pong players and be allowed to observe what was happening in China. The result of the Ping-Pong tourney is of scant interest (Americans were defeated by 5–3 and 5–4). Ping-Pong experts might debate whether the American grip on the paddle (thumb over forefinger, as in tennis technique) was really inferior to Maoist technique (thumb straight down over the paddle trunk, as in the Chinese calligraphic brushstroke). But such discussion was beside the point. What had happened was the first official opening for dialogue. And in the months that followed, as carefully screened U.S. correspondents filtered into China, one had the impression of a darkened stage slowly, ever so slowly, opening to light.

In the Light of Recognition. At least two historic acts of recognition developed in this first rekindling of light in a generation. One was that of a new China, almost completely rewired in its human emotions, panting from internal exertion—but momentarily held in a balance of tensions. And the second, which came more slowly, was of China's fears and concerns, and its view of its own place in the world.

The dozen or more U.S. correspondents, and the scores of scholars and guests of the Peking government, who made the journey in 1971 reported the new China much as Marco Polo had reported the domain of Kublai Khan. Whether peering down from plane windows on the green half-moon paddy fields below, or traveling by the immaculate blue express train that ran from Canton to Peking, or being led through the lanes of villages and communes—China was even to those most familiar with it a mysteriously transformed society.

First, there was the apparent quiet—a social quiet—the absence of a turbulence that had roiled Chinese for half a century. The filth that had so smeared the beauties of prewar China, the stench of sewage in gutters and rotting refuse that once had mixed with the fragrance of flowers and incense—this was gone. China was clean—its streets swept, its procedures orderly, its buildings shabby but neatly painted. And, apparently, where Westerners were allowed to go, China was thriving. Caravans and red-tasseled Mongolian ponies still traversed the roads of the north; carts still hauled by humans mingled in traffic flow; but bicycles now were everywhere, and the strollers were neat, well dressed or well patched, and apparently healthy. There were no flies in China, reported some of the earlier travelers, nor were there any beggars; and, in many regions, even the familiar Chinese dogs were absent. In Peking, the imperial city of the Manchus, a new subway was being dug, and the tawny crenellated walls of the Mongols had been torn down; the T'ien-an Men, Gate of Heavenly Peace, remained, but it opened on the Great Red Square, surrounded by its neo-Stalinist block architecture. Shanghai, that glittering citadel of the Western presence, had been transformed. Once the purveyor of every luxury and depravity known to man, Shanghai had now not only been purged—but purified. Bars were proscribed, prostitution outlawed, gunslingers vanished, waterfront gangs gone. Tips were refused, theft was unknown, lost and forgotten articles were recovered immediately. Shanghai bustled, as did Peking and Canton, with the same old unforgettable Chinese energy of muscle and nerves. But where once it had bustled to no larger purpose than getting and selling, now it bustled with a purpose imposed on it by the new faith of China.

It was difficult to describe this new faith—for no correspondent, even the oldest and wisest of the visitors, could find the proper words to describe the transformation of people. Yet, collectively, what they reported—if it were to last—amounted to one of the most spectacular conversions of spirit since Christianity, ages ago, had subverted the pagan spirit of Rome and then transformed the state. Those who remembered China as a land of poverty, hunger, and disease remembered the dazzling contrasts of the generation past—remembered when the cadavers of child labourers were collected outside their factory gates each morning with the rubbish; remembered days of famine when dogs roamed the fields chewing at bodies of peasants dead of starvation; remembered the warlords with their wolfish soldiers and retinues of concubines; remembered sybaritic peaks of delight China could deliver either in its great homes or at commercial emporiums of flesh and food and gaiety; remembered occasionally the art and the beauties hoarded privately by collectors against the barbarism of the times.

That prewar China had disappeared; a vast monotony of colour in dress, of conformity in behaviour, in phrases of speech and greeting, had replaced the phantasmagoria of remembered contrasts. A far older Chinese past than the one remembered by foreigners had surfaced in new and hyperbolic form. China had recovered order—and the new order, reported the correspondents, was working: the grain crop, 240 million metric tons of it, was the highest on record; cloth production was not only the highest in China's history but the highest in the world; Chinese satellites bleeped aloft; Chinese nuclear physicists produced bombs; China was producing its own new jet fighter; atomic missiles were ready; biological research proceeded. And all of this progress, apparently, flowed from the order that Chinese political thinking had sought to impose on society since the time of Confucius—and that, after a century of unrest, Mao Tse-tung had indeed imposed as no other man in his country's history had done before.

It was hard to distinguish this new Maoist order from a religion. Mao had become both godhead and teacher. The country lived, beat, pulsed apparently as Mao desired. When hundreds of thousands on parade brandished the Little Red Book that held Mao's thought, they were brandishing their catechism, an object of worship. Mao's statue stood in every public place; his image hung in homes; loudspeakers blared his praise on train, in plane, on buses. Ballistic missile scientists claimed that Mao-thinking had illuminated their way to China's satellites; peasants in the field held that Mao-thinking taught them to raise better crops; engineers, doctors, patients, soldiers all had been taught, and apparently believed, that whether it came to the redesign of a steam engine, the endurance of pain, the assault on a hill or a mythical American invading army—Mao's thoughts held the solution.

The world would remember Mao, certainly, as one of the authentic geniuses of the 20th century, and the career that had made his thinking the bible of a nation was one of the marvels of the human story. A peasant's son, a passionate intellectual, a didactic and sometimes explosive debater, a man of inflexible will and purpose, a self-recruited revolutionary who had lifted his first gun at the age of 18 to join the insurrection against the Manchu empire in 1911—this man had examined China by himself, with his own ideas, for decades, and then made these ideas doctrine for 700 million people.

At the heart of Maoism—though Chinese theoreticians certainly would denounce this analysis—was the erasure of the individual personality. Phrased otherwise, this root-thought could be made more understandable: the people en-masse were ALL. The second tenet was the power of the will—willing could make it so, and the will of the individual harnessed to improve the masses could change the very nature of those masses. If properly trained to exploit their inner energies, the people could reach undreamed-of achievements. In Mao-thought, not guns, not massed firepower, not atomic weaponry, not artillery decided battles but will—the spirit, the skill, the response of masses to trained leadership. Perhaps the most original military thinker of the 20th century, Mao by his thinking on irregular and partisan warfare had frustrated the forces first of the Chinese Nationalists, then of the Japanese, then of the Americans. Yet always at the heart of this thinking remains the subordination of the individual to the needs of the masses and the training of a leadership that makes of its lives a flare for the masses to follow.

Classless himself, Mao in his thinking brooks no classes, no privileged groups, no layers or tiers of independent authority or free will within the ultimate state he envisages. Students and professors alike must, if the party demands, go to the fields and hoe with the peasantry, must accept life careers in distant rural places. Marriages must be shaped as the state wills, and so the state sets the age of marriage for young men and women; no cranny is left in the new life for selfishness, personal ambition, or romance. At every level of enterprise the collective will must be supreme—in factory or ship, in communes, in military units. Those who subordinate themselves to Mao's guidance, who absorb in their reflexes Mao's thinking, demonstrate it by success at their work; and as they reach higher and higher levels of leadership they become, in the terminology of their state, "leading responsibles," responsible only to the judgments of Maoism.

The transformation of China by this unbending thinking was only part of the story brought to the world in 1971 by some of the most sober and thoughtful minds of U.S. journalism. Neither they nor anyone else could be sure that their observations told the whole story of China. Limited in the range of their travels, they were even more limited by courtesy and good taste in their exploration of China's politics, or its recent past. There they reached a blank wall.

The Great Proletarian Cultural Revolution. From behind this blank wall of time, which they could not explore, came however, the echo of blood and battle in a recent upheaval that the Chinese "responsibles" styled the "Great Proletarian Cultural Revolution." Of the dimensions of this Cultural Revolution, we in the West are still ignorant. Yet from the tales of the reporters of 1971, and from fragments put together by intelligence analysts from the Chinese press and refugees, one could piece together this account:

At some point in 1966, the hardening bureaucracy of the revolution in China had thrust Mao from his unchallenged supremacy to recognition of a threat to both his person and his philosophy. Under then-president Liu Shao-ch'i, Mao had perceived his revolution casing itself once more in class distinctions, bureaucratic forms, and government structures offensive to his revolutionary mind. Perhaps it was a classic case of spiritual power challenged by temporal power, a pope finding lip service, not loyalty, from those he himself had chosen to be his executives of state.

When, thus, in 1966 Mao found himself unable to express his *own* ideas in state-controlled organs, he appealed to the most

Yeh Chien-ying (light-rimmed glasses), vice-chairman of the Military Affairs Commission of the Chinese Communist Party, greets Henry Kissinger upon his arrival in Peking to discuss a visit to China by Pres. Richard Nixon.

easily mobilized "mass" he could reach—in this case, the student masses of the universities, who had grown up in his perfect faith. Accepting the call for a Great Proletarian Cultural Revolution, the students took to the streets, savaging any bureaucrat or bureaucracies they could reach. Riots became the order of the day. From the fall of 1966 to the fall of 1970, all Chinese universities suspended classes as students by the hundreds of thousands first shattered their own academic leadership, then, chanting Mao's phrases, took to the road to shatter the other "malicious" bureaucracies.

Of the fighting and bloodshed in China, there is no accurate account. Men of great dignity were humiliated, expelled from office, subjected to abuse, exile, and in some cases violence. Swinging to its own rhythm of direct action, the Maoist youth revolution split and splintered, as student bands began to purge not only the "new-olds" but the ancient monuments and art objects of Chinese history; then, finally, turned to attack one another, killing in the name of Mao.

What happened in the deep interior we do not know. Most of what the West knows has seeped through that traditional eyelet city, Canton. There, at least, the violence, confrontations, and countermassacres within the Cultural Revolution could not be concealed. The Pearl River floated out to Hong Kong the bodies of those who were killed and cast to the streams. Gruesome accounts by Western intelligence of events in Canton—of bodies hanging from lampposts, of baskets of punched-out human eyes being paraded by student bands like trophies—might have been exaggerated; but the tingle of horror they conveyed was real.

By 1969, apparently, the worst of the combat crisis had passed; by 1970 students were back in schools. Yet the internal Chinese politics that Western observers attempted to define in their visits of 1971 remained obscured by the murk of a power struggle that seemed as unending as it was incomprehensible. Liu had disappeared, as had previously such other revolutionary heroes of the romantic past as P'eng Teh-huai, their fate unknown. Briefly, the new China of the post-Cultural Revolution seemed to be ruled by a triumvirate of Mao; Lin Piao, commander of the People's Liberation Army, which had restored order in the cities; and Chou En-lai, premier and foreign minister. Yet as 1971 wore on it became apparent that even these three comrades-in-arms, blood brothers for 40 years, who had shared the Long March in 1934 and the mountain refuges of Yenan later, could not see eye to eye on the future direction of their country or the successor to the aging Mao. By December 1971 Lin Piao had fallen from eminence and any public place—whether permanently or temporarily, Western intelligence could not guess—and what China had to say was being said by Chou, its premier.

Sightseers visit the Great Wall of China. The soldier is an officer but bears no sign of his rank in keeping with China's egalitarian social order. In the foreground a civilian adjusts his Chinese-made camera.

MARC RIBOUD—MAGNUM

There could be no doubt that Chou spoke for Mao, for Mao remained supreme, enshrined in both power and theology. Yet Chou was Chinese Communism's most civilized and sensitive leader, always the aperture into Communist thinking of Western influence. Grandson of a mandarin himself, European-trained, one-time favourite of the U.S. diplomatic and press corps, dark-eyed, pungently witty, graceful in phrase, Chou was as dedicated a Communist and fighter as Mao himself. What he had to say, therefore, had to be taken seriously. His message to the American people, however tough it was, would be the best description of Chinese hopes and fears the Americans could expect to get. The public message was delivered in fragments, stretched over months, as Chou received a succession of American visitors.

There was, first, the absolute head-on confrontation between China and the U.S. over Taiwan. Nothing, in any statement of Chou's, reflected the slightest give or softness in the main Chinese demand of the U.S.: that it abandon, once and for all, Chiang's Nationalist regime on Taiwan and yield it to the People's Republic in Peking, unconditionally. Until that day came, according to Chou, there could be no normal relations between the two countries.

There followed shortly, in other interviews, a larger view of China's place in the world as Chou detailed for visitors whom he trusted the menace to China of the Soviet Union. A million Soviet troops, he said, with nuclear weapons and guided missiles, lay along the 4,000-mi. frontier that separated the two countries. In the rhetoric of their state, Chinese made little distinction between the social revisionist imperialism of the Soviets and the capitalist-aggressive imperialism of America.

Then Chou made a final point, most notably in his interview with James Reston of the *New York Times*. The third point was Japan. The U.S. diplomatic thrust in Asia had, since the war, rested on Japan's vitality. Now Chou made the point that the vitality of Japan—its rearmament, its economic power, its renascent nationalism and military tradition—made it a threat to both China *and* to America. Here, skillfully, Chou was touching a nerve. U.S.-Japanese relations had been deteriorating for several years and were to worsen sharply in the late summer of 1971. And, for America, the memory of Pearl Harbor, along with the war that followed, was an emotional scar on both the old who had fought the war and the young who had learned of its glories and horror on television. Could there possibly be some rapprochement with China on the basis of mutual interests? In short, did geography and history ordain, as they had in the first 150 years of the American republic, a community of interdependence between the two powers?

An Opening for Dialogue. These then were the atmospherics of diplomacy when, in mid-July, came the stroke of action, and events began to move. On the evening of July 8 the urbane and polished presidential counselor for foreign affairs, Henry Kissinger, had disappeared from public view in Pakistan, where he had paused in a worldwide survey of global problems. Supposedly ill with diarrhea, he had slipped away with three aides to an airfield outside Rawalpindi and then, in a Pakistan Airlines 707 jet, had flown to Peking. There, for a full day and a half, he had conferred with Chou, flown back secretly to Pakistan and thence to Paris and the U.S., where on July 15 the world learned of his mission. Kissinger, announced Nixon in a television statement to the nation, had journeyed to China to arrange for a visit by the president himself. Not since the Cairo conference of 1943 had a U.S. president and a Chinese sovereign met face to face; no president ever had visited China; no president ever had set out to discuss matters at the summit with a nation his government did not recognize. Yet now, declared the president, he was prepared for the long journey, with no preconditions, on an open agenda by which both sides would seek "normalization of relations."

The world gasped at this stroke of diplomacy—and then the parade of realignment began. By the time Kissinger had flown to Peking for the second time—in the last week of October—to arrange detailed planning for the president's trip, the UN was already in session. And if the U.S. was on the point of recognizing China, few wished to be left behind. Thus, in a clangorous, emotional session in New York, the General Assembly by a vote of 76 to 35 brutally dismissed Chiang Kai-shek's China from its midst and, to the sound of cheers and laughter, installed the China of Mao as the only true China in its stead, proprietor of China's seat on the Security Council and its membership in the world community of nations.

At year's end, the world was readying for the presidential mission, which would open 1972. What the Chinese and Americans would talk about no one knew. The urbane Kissinger titillated the world's appetite for news with traveler's tales and commented on the nature of Chinese cuisine and banqueting, but his inner counsel and the report of his two trips was reserved for the president alone. One could only speculate: at the very minimum the two great powers were seeking to dissolve the hatreds of the postwar world to which they had contributed so much. At the most, if China's fears of the U.S.S.R., Japan, and Taiwan could be satisfied without creating new enemies, and the U.S. exertion in South Vietnam could be wound down to a close without surrendering the Saigon regime to extermination—then, indeed, in 1972 the world could get down to the task of exploring a new order among nations.

Long before Mao-thought had become the doctrine of all China, the Chinese had enjoyed an aphorism that dated back to Confucius. The longest journey, read the old aphorism, begins with a single step. In 1971 that first step had been taken.

In the Cradle of New Europe. The recognition of the new China rose, like a Matterhorn, above the other major events of international diplomacy in 1971—but in any other year these events, too, would have seemed like climactic episodes, worthy of long and dramatic telling. Yet all of them beat on the main theme of the year: that the postwar world was over, and it behooved the great powers—all of them—to recognize the new realities.

In Europe, for example, at least two events of titanic significance marked this recognition:

• The British Parliament, by a vote of 356 to 244, on October 28 voted the United Kingdom into the Common Market. Englishmen ever since World War II had been aware with growing melancholy that their stature as one of the three great victors of the war against fascism could be sustained only with greater and greater strain—until finally the strain was recognized as unendurable. Only continental blocs like the U.S. or the Soviet Union or China could swing power in the modern world. For years Britain had sought a "special relationship" with its cultural ally, the U.S. By the end of the 1960s British leaders—if not ordinary Englishmen in the street—had given up on that hope, and turned their aspirations to the continent to which geography bound them: Europe. In February 1971, almost as symbolic as a heraldic *annunciamento* of things to come, the English announced the abandonment of their medieval currency system. Twelve pence would no longer count to a shilling, 20 shillings would no longer count to a pound—farthings, ha'pennies, tuppences, and half crowns all were consigned to the museum of history and replaced by a new decimal system—100 new pence to a pound worth about $2.60 at year's end. And, in October, joining the Common Market of Europe, merging its economic future with a continent of aliens, Britain joined itself as a seventh partner to countries in which its troops had fought in a great war only 26 years before.

• No less important, certainly, was the apparent agreement on Berlin between West Germany and the Soviet Union, blessed by the U.S. and all the world. Lodged as a garrison city within East Germany, patrolled by British, French, and U.S. troops, surrounded by the overwhelming power of the Soviet Army, Berlin had been the sorest inflammation of central Europe since the end of the war. An outpost of freedom, subject to Communist whim and harassment, it had been tweaked to aggravation by the Soviets and East Germans whenever it seemed possible to win some momentary advantage by extortion. The Berlin blockade of 1948 had stimulated the creation of NATO and brought about the reentry of the U.S. Army as a permanent garrison of the Thuringian ridges. Again and again, through fruitless negotiations and half a dozen crises threatening war, Berlin had been Europe's flash point. Yet now, in 1971, came direct agreement between the Soviet Union and West Germany on a normal and civilized status for the isolated one-time German capital.

In international diplomacy, all great movements set up rhythms that interlock with other rhythms. The crescent strength of China, its apparent first step to rapprochement with the U.S., its entry into the UN—all these brought alive in the Soviet mind the potential threat from a hostile China along their border in Asia. Thus, prudence and foresight urged the Soviets to induce a climate of relaxation on their western and Atlantic fronts. In late fall Soviet Premier Aleksei Kosygin traveled not only to Berlin but also to France and Canada as he tried to erase, by smiling, the scowl that had been characteristic of Soviet diplomacy. And on October 12 it was announced jointly in Moscow and Washington that this new turn of diplomacy would be capped by a visit of Nixon to the Soviet capital in May 1972.

No overview of the grand diplomacy of 1971 can close except with the bloody events of December on the subcontinent of India. There, the year ended with the final dismemberment of the totally artificial state of Pakistan by the superior forces of India. Pakistan had been arbitrarily drawn on a map in 1947 not by history but by British imperial indifference as it abandoned empire. The archetype of a fictional postwar state, Pakistan had been doomed from birth and the events of 1971 simply buried it.

If a balance of war and peace had to be struck as the world entered 1972, Pakistan was a clear negative. Yet the balance on the positive side clearly outweighed the negative. The Middle East remained quiet; the U.S. was winding down its war in Vietnam—the battle casualties in one December week dropping to only two Americans killed in action; central Europe was hushed; China was returning to participation in world affairs; nuclear disarmament talks between the Soviet Union and the U.S. held more promise than at any time since the atomic bomb was first detonated. Despite the Pakistan affair, peace seemed closer at the end of the year than at its beginning; and in this achievement the U.S. had played a proud and leading role.

Members of a Chinese family enjoy a quiet Sunday afternoon relaxing and taking pictures in a Shanghai park. Quotations from Mao Tse-tung adorn the pillar in the background.
MARC RIBOUD—MAGNUM

VESPERS FOR THE AGE OF GOLD

Attention had barely absorbed the U.S. announcement of the presidential visit to Peking when, only four weeks later, on August 15, came the shattering of another bedrock assumption of the postwar world. The U.S., declared Richard Nixon on television, no longer would freely convert dollars into gold. Nor would it any longer accept the flow of trade around the world in the grand pattern that the U.S. had blueprinted 30 years ago and that it had sustained ever since.

One must go back a long way—even beyond the beginning of the modern world—to understand the drama of this climactic action.

Since the earliest of records, gold always had been the miser's metal—the measure of value of land, of bridal dowries, of cattle, of the exchange of goods. But only in the 19th century, the high golden summer of Western expansion, did it reach its peak of authority. In that century of imperial buccaneering, as the powers of Western Europe opened the globe, financed the building of the U.S. and Latin America, subdued Africa and raided Asia, gold attained an almost mystic quality. Gold governed all commerce in a theological fancy that viewed it as the essential automatic balancing mechanism of trade among nations. When a nation's merchants could not sell enough abroad to pay for what they imported, so ran the theory, they must pay in gold. And if they lacked gold, that nation was in trouble—its imports were choked off, its export prices were squeezed down, millions went without or saw their wages drop, until somehow the nation's merchants earned enough gold to balance its trading account abroad.

Two members of a Chinese ballet company dance in "The White Hair Girl," a revolutionary ballet scheduled for its Western debut in Paris in the winter of 1971. As is the case with all arts in China, dance is used to bring the teachings of Chairman Mao to the people.

MARC RIBOUD—MAGNUM

The weakness of this automatic function of gold was quite simple: when a national trading account was out of balance, poor and ordinary people suffered most. If gold, by its scarcity, caused the prices of imported raw materials to rise, workers in the mills lost their jobs or saw the price of bread rise, their white dhoti or colourful calico become scarce, and the price of tea, coffee, and jam from overseas soar to exorbitant levels.

It was the rise of social conscience in the countries of the West, and the unmasking of the gold superstition by the work of 20th-century economists, that brought an end to the cruelties imposed on world trade by the blind devotion of its bankers to one single metal as a measure of all value. With the despair of the depression of the 1930s visible in the streets, governments were persuaded they must manage their economies to do what was best for their people, and they began to shrug off the financial morality that insisted only gold measured true value for all actions. But during the hunger decade of the '30s, the effort of each government to so manage its own currency and its own trade in the interests of its own people brought vicious trade wars that contributed to both the rise of fascism and World War II.

Thus during the war the U.S., at one of its crests of idealism, summoned its allies to a conference at Bretton Woods, N.H., to plan a new, more civilized way of regulating world trade. And, with the war over, the new blueprint of world trade was accepted not only by the free-world victors, but was offered to and accepted by the vanquished powers, Germany and Japan.

One must grasp the nature of the postwar monetary agreements to understand how startling was Nixon's action in August 1971. In simplest terms, those agreements had tried to abolish such trade wars as come from currency juggling and trade quotas. The value of every currency in the world was pegged to the value of the U.S. dollar. Other nations' money might fluctuate in value with the tides of world trade, but they would fluctuate only in relation to each other, while at the centre stood the U.S. dollar, rigid, its strength firmly socketed in gold. If anywhere in the world a trading firm could convert yen, francs, marks, or pounds into dollars—then those dollars, as of yore, could be converted by their central banks into gold.

For 25 years—from 1945 to 1970—this new system of international exchange permitted a growth in volume of trade unparalleled in history. It ushered in a period when more common people, around the globe, learned to eat better, dress better, shelter better, learn better as their governments explored the opportunities of this new system. The fact that it could work so well depended, however, on a passing condition that both the U.S. and the rest of the world misunderstood: it was the episode of American power.

The U.S. had emerged from the war against fascism with a momentary dominance of world trade such as no other nation had ever known before. Asia—Japan and China—had been ravaged. Europe was in collapse. The Soviets had been reduced to a primitive scratching for survival. The world hungered, the world shivered in the cold of the early postwar winters, the world was ill. And there stood the U.S.: only the U.S. could provide the surplus coal, the grain, the foodstuffs, the airplanes, the sulfur, the tobacco, the machinery, the medicinals the world craved and needed. During those early postwar years, the problem of world trade always was referred to as "the dollar gap." How could nations in distress around the globe find the necessary dollars, or the goods to earn dollars, in order to buy those vital necessities without which hunger, pestilence, and political upheaval might upset their governments?

In those years, starting with emergency aid and the Marshall Plan, in a policy combining enlightened commercial pragmatism and idealism, the U.S. set out to cure the dollar gap in two ways: by giving away almost $45 billion in civilian aid (plus $100 billion in military aid) to encourage other nations to rebuild their society, industry, and technologies; and by urging those nations, down into the 1960s, to compete with the U.S. in world markets in order to earn their own dollars to buy U.S. goods. So strong was America that nothing, it appeared in those days, could weaken it, and the vast U.S. investment in science and fundamental research was thrown open to all the world.

Thus the first postwar strip-steel mills were implanted in Europe and Japan by U.S. gifts; so too came the mechanization of European farming and the spread of tractors from France to Italy; so too came the revival of Japanese science and technology; so too were anemic industries abroad urged to invade the U.S. market. As they moved to compete, however, counterpart adjustments were forced on the U.S., noted only sporadically and locally, voiced only by individual congressmen, whose hometown constituents could not understand that their jobs were being sacrificed for the greater good of world peace and flourishing world trade.

The Vanishing Trade Surplus. It was not until the late 1960s that those Americans most pinched began to receive a national hearing on their complaint that the Bretton Woods-Marshall Plan-foreign aid model of trade was no longer working as its designers had planned. For one thing, the brains and science and gift of innovation, on which Americans had preened themselves, were not theirs alone. The vitality of other technologies began to press in on the long U.S. lead—as did the enormous disparity in standards of living and low wages abroad. By 1970 it was apparent that not only were such low-wage U.S. industries as shoes, textiles, and garments being imperiled by foreign competitors. So, too, was the U.S. steel industry—pressed by European and Japanese exports. So, too, was the proud aviation industry. So, too, was the electronics industry—and the U.S., which had pioneered both radio and television, found its markets commanded by imported products selling below any possibility of competition. By 1971 the manufacture of black and white television sets in the U.S. had all but ceased, and major U.S. manufacturers of radio and television were, in many instances, simply assemblers of Asian-made components. The same situation prevailed in the U.S. photographic industry. Even more unsettling was the threat to the U.S. automobile industry, the most romantic and quintessentially American industry. That industry had absorbed the first penetration of the German Volkswagen soon after the war; then absorbed the invasion of its markets by French, Italian, and British products. But in 1971 it was being punished savagely by an exponential jump in cheap Japanese automotive imports. From an import total of 63,000 in 1966, the Japanese had pushed the total to 415,-000 in 1970, and in 1971 Japanese imported cars were entering at the rate of 700,000!

These were more than threats to nationalist pride or local jobs. These were threats to the U.S. position in the world, for that position rested on two legs: its military might and its excess economic energy.

The translation of the economic threat came in those abstract figures of balance of trade that had perplexed economists since David Ricardo and sovereigns since George III. Ever since 1893, the U.S. had enjoyed a current trade surplus—that is, it earned more abroad by its sales than it spent on its imports. This trade surplus had reached a peak of over $7 billion in 1964. But this balance of trade was only part of what economists call the balance of accounts or the balance of payments.

The balance of accounts includes not only the trading surplus, but also "invisible" factors that channel the flow of money around the world. When "invisibles" were included, the U.S. balance of accounts had been running for more than a decade at a deficit. The sums spent by tourists abroad, dividends paid to foreign investors, transport charges to foreign shipping lines, above all the immense expenditures flushed away in Vietnam and the huge sums of military and civilian aid granted to other nations drained more gold and dollars out than trade brought in.

As this balance of accounts showed red year after year, the gold hoard at Ft. Knox, Ky., dropped from its postwar high of $25 billion to a low of $10.5 billion in mid-1971. Moreover, foreign central banks now held reserves of $40 billion and foreign individuals $30 billion, which they considered as good as gold be-

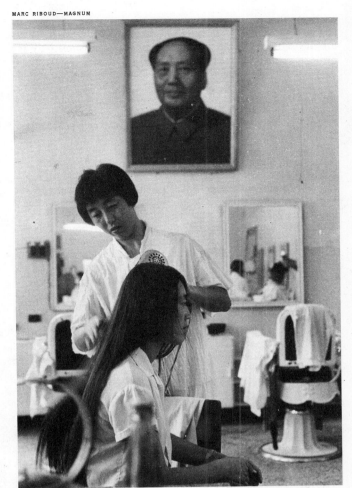

Beauty shop aide dries and combs the hair of a young Chinese girl under the ubiquitous portrait of Mao Tse-tung. Western visitors to China in 1971 found the citizens well dressed, neatly groomed, well fed, and healthy.

cause the U.S. would cash them for gold. It was true that if all cashed their money claims at once, the dollar would become a fiction; but as long as the solid old-fashioned U.S. balance of trade, which had run in America's favour since 1893, showed its usual husky profit, other nations would be content to continue in the postwar system.

In 1971, for the first time in almost 80 years, this trading balance turned against the U.S. The nation had ended 1970 with a diminished trade balance of $2.7 billion—$42.7 billion of exports, $40 billion of imports. Then, in 1971, matters turned as if on a pivot. U.S. goods had for years become more and more expensive on world markets as inflation forced their prices up. Foreign goods had for years become cheaper and better. In a time of inflation and unemployment, millions sought bargains. Nor could they individually determine what their collective appetites were doing to the figures of national trade.

In April 1971 a morbid figure was posted—the first monthly deficit in trading balance in two years; in May came a repeat—another deficit, the first two-month-in-a-row deficit in 22 years; in June came another deficit, in July a fourth—and the secretary of commerce warned the nation that, for the first time since it had ceased being a colony of European industry in the 1890s, it appeared that the U.S. would have a trade deficit in 1971.

Already the speculators of the world had taken notice of what was happening. In early May, with the first announcement of the April deficit, had come a ripple of financial panic in Europe and a major run on the U.S. dollar. The central bankers of the Western world concerted action to support the dollar; the West Germans let their mark float free and upward in value as against the dollar; momentarily the panic was stanched. But only momentarily. As the balance of payments worsened, as the summer outflow of U.S. tourists drained balances even further, the panic refueled itself—art dealers abroad selling their treasures only for Swiss or German marks, wary of accepting dollars; U.S. corporations abroad converting their own huge dollar balances to foreign currencies; speculators liquidating dollar holdings for a flight to the stronger Japanese yen or German mark; the gold outflow steadily accelerating.

If the postwar system of 1944–45 were not to collapse in chaos, if there were to be any chance of reasonably reordering a new world trading system for another generation, someone had to act. And thus in mid-August, Richard Nixon did.

The Game Plan Is Changed. Two streams of pressure had been converging on the president since the early months of the year. There was, immediately, as we have seen, the international gold crisis, the sharpest instant provocation to action.

But there was also the internal situation. At home, Nixon's "game plan" for prosperity was simply not working. The fairly stable price situation of the early months had given way by summer to price rises at a 6% annual rate, as had been characteristic of 1970. Unemployment remained obdurate, rising to 6.1% in April, to 6.2% in May. Nixon had embraced Keynesian economics early in the year—but with no anticipation of embracing such a budget deficit as was now apparent. The budget surplus for fiscal 1971, originally estimated at $1.3 billion, had become, by July of 1971, an estimated *deficit* of $35 billion!

There was no way out of a simple intellectual realization: Keynesian economics, which had dominated the thinking of governments since the end of the great war, was as obsolete as all the other postwar imperatives. Keynesian economics gave the government, as one economist put it, only a pendulum push—shove the budget one way, and one had full employment at the cost of inflation; shove it the other way and one had stable prices at the cost of unemployment. And now the U.S. had both at once. Keynesian thinking, which had been valid in a world of scarcities of goods, simply did not fit the realities of U.S. economic life.

No president, however brilliant his record in foreign policy, could be reelected if prices were rising and jobs falling at the same time. Ever since January, the president's mind had been the arena of debate between his key economic advisers. On the one hand were the classicists, led by George Shultz, director of the Office of Management and Budget, insisting that policy must remain "steady-as-you-go." On the other hand were some of the president's closest political friends, notably Arthur Burns, chairman of the Federal Reserve Board, who sensed early the ending of an era and who mused publicly that economics simply no longer worked by old laws or theories. However abhorrent in theory a wage-price freeze, some "incomes policy," Burns insisted, was inescapably necessary.

There was, to be sure, substantial good news: the U.S. was about to set an all-time harvest record—an estimated 1.6 billion bu. of wheat, 5.5 billion bu. of corn—and with such a harvest one could look forward to lower prices at the supermarket food counters. The housing industry was also setting a new record. Yet the climate was wrong. The business recovery to which the White House had looked forward, on which it had projected its gross national product estimate of $1,065,000,000,000 was stumbling. Summer employment was low. Teachers, telephone men, longshoremen, railway crewmen, steelworkers, copper workers, and a score of lesser craft groups were either already on strike or threatening to strike. The stock market reflected the dismal mood of 30 million American investors, and the Dow Jones average had fallen from a 1971 peak of 950.80 on April 28 to a summer low of 839.5 on August 10.

It was three days later, on Friday, August 13, that Nixon decided the time had come to act. To his weekend retreat at Camp David, Md., he summoned his Big Four economic advisers—Secretary of the Treasury John Connally; Burns; Paul McCracken, chairman of the Council of Economic Advisers; and Shultz. With them were his personal counselors and several government economists, in all, ten men. Earlier in the year, the president had made up his mind to persist in his game plan at least until October, to see whether classical and Keynesian economics together could right the helm. In June he and Connally had discussed emergency measures privately—if they had to, if affairs insisted, they would be ready to take drastic measures by fall.

Now their hand was being forced from abroad.

The uncertainties in the U.S.; the shifting trade balance (it had run to a deficit of $3.4 billion in the second quarter alone); the sadness of the New York Stock Exchange, which is the world's bourse—all these had accelerated concern abroad to panic. All over the world, men and traders who held dollars were getting rid of them in a financial hemorrhage not known since the British Treasury was forced to the wall in 1967. The Belgian National Bank had been forced to accept the dumping of $11 million on its accounts the Friday of the meeting. The Bank of France had been forced to receive approximately $300 million dumped in the previous week. The Bank of England, as the panic grew, reported to the U.S. it might have to cover $3 billion dumped in the next week. The Bank of Japan was forced to cover first $600 million and then $690 million on successive days. And all these dollars, dumped by frightened traders on their own central banks, were gold claims against the rapidly shrinking hoard at Ft. Knox. Later, Nixon was to say privately that if he had not acted to save the dollar over the weekend, there might not have been a dollar.

On Sunday night, therefore, before the world's trading centres opened for business on what might have been remembered for generations as the Black Monday of the Dollar, the president announced that the U.S., the world's last champion of gold as the measure of value, no longer would redeem its currency in gold.

The shock of this statement set off tidal quakes in the world's trading centres the next morning.

Yet the statement was bundled with other statements that, if conceivable, were of even greater significance in marking 1971 as a terminal year for one era of Western culture.

One must review the package that came to be known as the New Economic Policy (NEP): not only would the dollar no longer be convertible into gold; all imports to the U.S. would be subject to a 10% surcharge. At home there would be a 90-day wage-price freeze while the government tried to make up its mind, under pressure, how to reorganize the entire economy. Tax cuts would be urged on Congress to stimulate sluggish consumer buying. Automobile sales would be stimulated by eliminating the 7% excise tax. Investment tax credits for business were to begin immediately (if Congress approved) to stimulate the technological progress in production that remained the chief hope for retaining U.S. industrial preeminence among nations.

Nothing in Nixon's administration, save the journey to China, was more enthusiastically applauded than his NEP, from near-left to near-right. The president had acted; the government was offering leadership, promising a control of events. Euphoria swept the stock market, as the Dow Jones average soared on the Monday after Nixon's statement to a record gain of 32.93 points, simultaneously setting a volume record of 31,730,000 shares.

Groping to a New World. It is difficult in a year of such joltings as 1971 to weigh and measure the significance of passing events. The great realignments in foreign affairs could be sensed immediately. But what lay tangled in Nixon's NEP would take months to unravel—and, when unraveled, might be of even more importance than the other great events of the year. Somewhere, philosophically, buried in his wage-price freeze, Nixon had taken a first step on another long journey. The journey, if pursued, might remake American domestic life and politics as drastically and profoundly as Roosevelt's New Deal revolution of the 1930s.

The statements, pronunciamentos, decrees, protests, and dictates that followed the August 15 statements gave contemporaries little sense of the profound nature of the issue. The statements were long, detailed, and administrative: the superefficient Internal Revenue Service would become a national police force not only for taxes, but for prices and wages; a Cost of Living Council was established in August to which was added, in November, two other organs, a National Pay Board and a National Price Board; these, together, would lay down rules to govern the way Americans worked and shared in the sum total of the national product, both by wage and by price.

It was like a giant hinge turning in a giant gate. One door was closing, another was opening. It had been almost 40 years since Roosevelt had last reshaped the U.S. economy and, by so doing, changed the nature of free-enterprise economy as practiced in the heartland of capitalism. Roosevelt had found that enterprise system in collapse. He had reinvigorated it by restraining the corporate profit-making centres of power and balancing them with an equal potential power of workingmen gathered in great national unions; and then patrolled both by such devices as the National Labor Relations Board and the Securities and Exchange Commission. Now Nixon presided over a nation where the free bargaining of both these enterprise groups had combined to manipulate a price system of which the general public was the victim, and which provided better and better jobs only for those in organized collectives. Knowingly or not, the president had embarked on a passage of leadership where the government would decide, henceforward and indefinitely, on what wages workers would get and what prices shoppers would pay. If war were too important to be left to generals, then business and labour were too important to be left to the decisions of business and labour leaders. *Rien,* say the French, *ne dure que le provisoire* ("Nothing lasts as long as the makeshift"). The government, having replaced Phase One by Phase Two, hopefully looked forward to a return to unrestrained economics. But that would be a long time in coming.

The thought of government presiding over what is "fair" in the trading and selling of works and goods has recurred again and again in history—from Hammurabi of Babylonia through the Sung dynasty of China through the Europe of the medieval Catholic kings. U.S. enterprise had been born free of such restraints in an intellectual revolt against the fiat of kings. This American freedom has been increasingly defined and reduced by governmental restraint for almost two centuries—yet it still remained free to take its own major decisions, to build, to plan, to invest, to shape everyday life until 1971. Now, as 1971 entered on 1972, a great debate was beginning as to how much freedom would be left to unions to wring the last top dollar out of a settlement, and to corporations to wring the last top percentile out of its sales package. Unions protested and wrangled about the sanctity of contracts as corporations had done generations before; financiers and investors worried about how far the government's decrees might curb their control of profits, interest, marketing. But they, along with the rest of the American people and their president, were on a voyage from which there could be no return.

At year's end, vague shapes, vague promises, vague threats floated daily across the American marketplace, as the new organs of economic governance groped for a philosophy. Quite clearly, it appeared, the great national unions now would have to submit their wage claims to national judgment. Equally clearly, the great corporations—those employing more than 5,000 workers or grossing more than $100 million annually—would have to submit to government control of their profit margins. The seeds of free enterprise still would be allowed to grow and flourish—but only up to a given ceiling set by government.

This realization, and its attendant uncertainties, depressed investors all through the fall months as the Dow-Jones average dropped, and dropped again. It reached its year's low, 797.97, in mid-November and then turned up again under stimulus from abroad. The giant U.S. economy was still the world's greatest—but it was no longer the world's master; and thus the international agreements of December 18, which Nixon hailed as "the most significant monetary agreement in the history of the world," provided the prod that sent the market up simply because they recognized new realities.

Two months of negotiation, led by the shrewd and swashbuckling Connally, had preceded the December agreements. By

Customers of Merrill Lynch, Pierce, Fenner and Smith watch New York Stock Exchange prices being posted on Aug. 16, 1971. On that day stock prices registered huge gains in response to Pres. Richard Nixon's new economic policies.

WIDE WORLD

these agreements, the nature and role of gold remained to be defined. Although to please the French a new technical value was set for gold, this value was fictitious—for the dollar, which had protected the majesty of gold for so many years, remained unconvertible into gold into the indefinite future. Henceforward, the value of the dollar was to be set by international agreement as yen, marks, pounds, francs, lire, and all other major trading currencies measured against each other and the dollar as well. The interim December measurement of the dollar technically devalued its worth by 8.57%—and in terms of volume of U.S. trade, by a drop of some 12%. This new adjustment would make U.S. goods more salable abroad; foreign products, particularly Japanese, would be more expensive in the United States. The impact, said the U.S. government, might increase the number of jobs in the U.S. by a half-million. In return, the U.S. government pleased its trading partners by eliminating the emergency 10% surcharge on imports it had imposed in August. Such a devaluation would, 20 years earlier, have been interpreted at home and abroad as evidence of U.S. weakness—which, indeed, it was. At the end of 1971, it was received by Americans as good common sense; they and their government had begun to learn to live with the changing world.

It was good that 1972 was to be an election year. Nixon, whether he knew it or not, was reshaping U.S. life. In presenting its new shape to the American people and the voters, he would be forced to define a philosophy. So, too, would he have to define the foreign policy that had brought about the sweeping new world attitudes of the last year. So, too, would the Democrats have to define their alternatives. If the issues were sharply met, the election of 1972 might be a watershed comparable to 1932 or 1860.

SNAPSHOT OF A CHANGING NATION

The political rhetoric of 1972 was only vaguely shaping its phrases at the end of 1971.

What muffled and blurred the early rhetoric was quite simple: all such rhetoric would flourish, or fall sterile, before an electorate changed from any in the past, whose response was impossible to predict. For, among its other contributions to history, the year 1971 finally had delivered a new profile of the nation. This profile first had been caught, as in a snapshot, by the 1970 census. But the picture in all its detail had taken months to develop, and it was not until mid-1971 that clear results had begun to emerge.

In 1970 the census offered only first coarse figures: the U.S. had grown in the decade of the 1960s from 179 million to 203 million in population—a jump roughly half the size of the population of Great Britain. It had been the second largest growth in numbers in U.S. history—yet, contrariwise, if the growth were read in percentiles, it had shown a jump of only 13.3%, the smallest growth in U.S. population percentages since the depression decade. Of these 203 million Americans counted, 22.6 million, or 11% of the total, were black.

Now, in 1971, the analysts were telling politicians what the figures meant, for buried in them were a new set of dynamics they must understand and master in 1972.

One might start anywhere in the output of the computers of the Census Bureau. But, historically, one marker, shrunken so small that it was generally overlooked in public comment, provoked a beginning reflection on how the country had changed: America's farmers, said the census, were vanishing faster than ever. In 1960, ten years earlier, 15,635,000 Americans had still lived and worked on farms. By 1970 their number had fallen by 38% to 9.7 million. Among these, the flight of blacks had been even more pronounced than that by whites. In April of 1960, 2.5 million black people still lived and worked on farms. Ten years later only 900,000 blacks still lived on farms—60% had given up! All in all, U.S. history had come full circle. At the founding of the republic, the first census had shown only 5% of Americans living in towns and cities, the rest on farms or in villages. By 1970 less than 5% still lived down on the farm—and they had produced, as we have seen, all-time record crops of corn and wheat. For politicians, the traditional farm vote would in 1972 be a romantic abstraction. Except in a few prairie states, the farm problem was no longer people—it was a tangle of agribusiness, exports, imports, macroeconomics, pollution problems.

The geographic patterns of the census traced another change. Of America's 3,124 counties, two-fifths showed absolute declines in population; two-thirds had suffered a net out-migration of people, as their young sought fame and fortune in the cities. A map published by the Census Bureau in 1971 showed matters graphically in varying shades of red and blue—red for loss, blue for gain. Like an inverted triangle, the red wedge of declining population ran from a broad base on the Canadian border, narrowing as it thrust down through the Plains states west of the Mississippi, throwing off red spurs east in Appalachia and the old Black Belt of the South, then falling south to Texas. North Dakota, South Dakota, and West Virginia were the only three states to show absolute losses in total population—but the rural counties stained every state with huge areas of population loss down to the Gulf.

A third intriguing change showed the massive reverse effect of rural depopulation.

Only 955 counties had succeeded in attracting newcomers, net in-migrants; but these counties clustered overwhelmingly in the swollen cities that make up the 243 standard metropolitan statistical areas (SMSAs) of the U.S. Almost three-quarters of all Americans now lived in these metropolitan areas while the countryside was returning to scrub, thorn, and thistle. These clusters, moreover, lay preponderantly by the shores of the oceans or the Great Lakes—indeed, more than half of all Americans now lived within 50 mi. of these shores. Eighty-five percent of the 24 million gain in U.S. population had come in these sprawling belts of touching cities, towns, suburbs that created the dominant new form of American civilization. And within these areas, 80% of that gain had come in the suburbs. Their problems would be cardinal in the politics of 1972.

The Black Migration. Within the new geographic patterns, there were other signals of change. There was, for example, the growth of the South. For the first time in a full century, the South overall was gaining population by in-migrations. Not only such traditional gainers as Florida and Texas, but also such states as Georgia, Alabama, North Carolina, and Virginia. The growth in this migration into the South would give the old states of the Confederacy a net gain of two seats in Congress in 1972; but more important was the growing impact this South would have on the presidential election.

What was happening was quite simple—whites were moving from North to South, in such numbers as to overbalance the huge, continuing black migration from South to North.

The black migration from the South to the North continued at its overall rate of 150,000 a year, but in some states it traced outlines of drama. In Mississippi, for example, the number of young black men between the ages of 15 and 24 had been 70,000 in 1960—and had fallen, unbelievably, to only 30,324 in 1970! Overall, the change in black life in the South could be simply described. In 1940, before the war, the 11 states of the old Confederacy held 69% of all the black people in the U.S.; in 1970, they held only 45%.

The 1970 census told where the blacks were going. Of the 1.5 million black out-migrants from the South, no less than one million had concentrated on just five states—New York, California, Michigan, Illinois, and New Jersey. Where the climate of tolerance invited black migration, Southern blacks moved in greatest numbers. Boston's black population gained 29% by in-migration, New York's 28%. Only one major central city had counted a black majority in 1960—Washington, D.C. By 1970 at least four major central cities—Washington, Gary, Ind., Newark, N.J., Atlanta—had black majorities, as did 12 other cities that counted more than 25,000 in population.

Such black concentrations were power. In 1960 white politicians had courted such black power blocs in an advocate-client relation. Now, as 1972 approached, black politicians sought to manage their power on their own. All over the country, black political leaders had begun to form in black officeholder blocs. There were now 13 black congressmen as against 4 in 1960; by 1970, 8 black mayors had been elected; black state legislators had grown in number from 52 to 198. Whether black leaders meant to wield their power outside traditional political parties in separatist groups, as had the Irish MPs in Victorian England, or whether they meant to act within the traditional parties—no one could predict until the presidential campaign actually opened.

Youth: A Political Imponderable. Most important of what the census told politicians about what they must face in 1972 was what it said of America's youth. For what might have been considered in other years as analysis of purely sociological interest had become the most critical political imponderable of 1972.

Youth, and its qualification for voting, had been thrust centrestage by one of the more bizarre decisions of the Supreme Court. In December 1970 the court had ruled that 18-year-olds must be allowed to vote in federal elections, yet need not be permitted to vote in local elections. This imposed enormous administrative confusion on those 47 states that did not already permit 18-year-olds to vote. (In the previous eight years, no less than 22 of the 29 states that put the question to the polls had voted *against* lowering the voting age.) Congress thus rushed through to passage on March 23, 1971, with only one hour of debate and no committee hearings at all, the Twenty-sixth Amendment to the Constitution, empowering 18-year-olds to vote anywhere, in any election, throughout the U.S. Even before the amendment had been embossed and sent to the secretary of state, the legislatures of Minnesota, Connecticut, Delaware, Tennessee, and Washington had approved it. Then, in a spring rush, all the other states followed as local politicians, recognizing the inevitable, hastened to join it. In less time than was required for the passage of any other amendment, with no national discussion, in two months and seven days, the Twenty-sixth Amendment had been ratified. Thus, 11 million Americans between the ages of 18 and 21 were qualified to vote, along with 14 million other Americans between the ages of 21 to 25 who also would be eligible to vote for the first time in 1972.

What were these new potential voters like? How would they affect the politics of 1972?

The census gave only crude answers:

First, said the census, their numbers bulged on the age profile of the U.S. like an orange passing down the throat of an ostrich. They represented the postwar baby boom, and in 1970 Americans between the ages of 14 to 24 were a larger proportion of the population than at any time since 1910. There had been only 27 million in this age group when John F. Kennedy was elected in 1960; in 1970 there were 40 million of them. U.S. national elections count, usually, about 70 million voters; the huge increment of 25 million potential new voters made old-fashioned politics unpredictable.

Next, reported the census of American youth, was their degree of education. As national defense had been the sacred issue of the 1950s, and environment promised to be the sacred issue of the 1970s, so had education been the sacred issue of the 1960s. Federal, state, and local governments, seized by the spirit of the 1960s, had pumped such funds into education as to change the character of U.S. society. Of all high-school-age youngsters, 94% were enrolled in high school. Of the 18–19-year-olds, 50% were still in school; and in the 20–24-year-old age bracket, 23% were still in college (versus only 13% a decade earlier). Refining the figures to count only the newly enfranchised voters, one found that in the 18–21-year-old bracket, there were 14.3 million Americans of college age (up 52% from the 1960 figure), and of these approximately half, or 7.8 million, were actually in college.

The cleavage between the higher educated and lesser educated always has been one of the sharpest lines of social distinction. The 1971 analysis of youth characteristics gave this distinction a cutting political edge—for what most people spoke of as the generation gap was an education gap. Of all college students in 1971, for example, 61% of the whites came from homes where the father had never gone to college; among blacks the figure was 71%. Politically, such young people simply had to have different reflexes to political rhetoric, and to reality as they perceived it, than their parents. The life-style of such people, their dress, their mobility, their rhetoric, even the remembered phrases and songs of such people, were different from those of their parents. Television had changed their vision of war and of glory. The drug culture had blurred their perception of rights and wrongs.The pill had changed their attitude to sex and family life. (In the single decade of the 1960s, said the census, the number of children under five born to 24-year-old women who had finished college dropped by 55%.) They were more mobile than any group in history—of those 22 to 24 years old counted in the 1970 census, no less than 45% had changed their address that year. With the new amendment they threatened a take-over of local government in college towns, from Berkeley to Cambridge.

In earlier times, when education was delivered to the young in their neighbourhood schools, when culture was shaped in homes without television, when the church polished moralities with ritual and piety, such new voters might have conformed in future behaviour to the conventional wisdom of politicians. This wisdom still held in 1971 that the young voters would vote largely as their parents would—splitting along lines of class, ethnic origin, income brackets, tradition, occupation.

But 1972 would test this conventional wisdom. Any number of voters always can be unified, cutting across traditional bloc lines, by specific interests. As coal miners are unified to vote the miners' interests, doctors to vote the doctors' interests, farmers to vote the farmers' interests—so too might young people be unified by a special appeal to their specific interests. And young people so far outweighed the farmers' vote as to make their collective impulse the supreme political target for those who sought to challenge Nixon for the presidency.

What apparently unified young people in 1971 was their own stake in life. And the greatest threats to their life and freedoms were the draft and the war in Vietnam. A biological urge caused them to cherish life above the hazard of death; if, by voting against the draft, they could vote dissolution of the armed forces upon which the U.S. role in the world depended, they could in 1972 write not only a coda to the End of the Postwar World, but make the next stage of that world unmanageable. How much the vocal coastal leadership of the elite students who stretched from Yale to Berkeley represented the will of all youth, no one knew. Nor could any politician measure how tenacious were the old loyalties and willingness to serve—even in stupid causes—of the nonvocal youth; nor could he judge how the surge of joblessness after a decade of prosperity might engage the attention of the largest class of job seekers.

Two young men take the voter registration oath at a Pittsburgh, Pa., rally where more than 4,000 registered after the 26th Amendment had been ratified. Better educated as a group than their elders, the new young voters posed a perplexing riddle to politicians facing the elections of 1972.

It remained to be seen, looking forward to 1972, how the political contenders would judge the mood of a generation invited to pass judgment on its fathers.

PERSPECTIVES: THE ELECTIONS OF 1972

The election campaign of 1972 would open with Richard Nixon as the candidate of the Republican Party—and barring tragedy, his candidacy was the only certain thing predictable.

Whether he could win or not, and by a margin sufficient to give him the power to govern, was another matter entirely.

In the first three quarters of the 20th century, only three U.S. presidents had managed to win at least two successive national elections—Woodrow Wilson, Franklin D. Roosevelt, and Dwight D. Eisenhower. Nixon hoped to be the fourth; yet a marginal victory scarcely would elevate him to the company of such political greats. The political technology and trickery that could shift a few hundred thousand votes might, indeed, be vital. But no marginal manipulation of votes could roll up the national mandate for which he yearned. Nixon had been an activist and innovative president; his record in foreign affairs had turned U.S. diplomacy about in the most considerable performance since the foreign policy of Truman and Dean Acheson. His war record was impressive—he had captained the greatest retreat in American history, reducing American forces in Vietnam from a peak of 543,000 in 1969 to less than 158,000 by the end of 1971 with no loss of prestige at home. But his largest, and equally innovative, domestic programs—from welfare reform to the reorganization of the Cabinet—had been stalled in Congress. He was a minority president, with neither authority nor control of a Democratic Congress. If he could not roll up a national mandate of the dimensions of a Roosevelt or Eisenhower or Johnson majority, he was doomed to remain, even if he won in 1972, a minority president—with little chance of blueprinting for the future what must come after the postwar world.

His only strategy was, therefore, clear. He would have to play the game called "Presidency." If he could turn the economy around and incubate rising employment; if he could liquidate the war in Vietnam and abolish the draft; if he could maintain the truce in the Middle East; if his dialogues in Peking and Moscow brought China and the Soviet Union to postures of tolerance or, hopefully, friendship—if he could achieve these, then no matter how deep the dry rot in the Republican Party which he was indifferently guiding, history would wring reelection for him. And if he could generate enough emotion in his campaign, he might—conceivably but unlikely—carry with him a Republican-controlled Senate and House. Then, and then only, could history fairly judge him.

The Democrats in Turmoil. For those, however, who loved politics as politics, the action at the end of 1971 centred clearly in the Democratic Party. One overwhelming fact remained permanent—the Democratic Party was still, after all its brawls, dissensions, and internal dissonances, the enduring majority party. It had lost its executive grip on the presidency in 1968 because it had led the U.S. into a futile war; but it still held, by a wide margin in every sounding of public opinion, its grip on the loyalties of the American people; and it still held, apparently unshakably, its control of Congress which disposes of what presidents propose.

The specific charge of the Democratic Party in 1972, by the binding unwritten laws of politics, was to carry the challenge for national leadership directly to Nixon—and replace him.

Yet the party—the oldest continuing political institution in the world—was itself in turmoil. Racked by internal conflict, experimenting with a basic and radical reconstruction of its own structure, seething with a clamour of new voices and new phrases, the traditional Democratic Party had become a party in search of its own identity. In this quest, and in its own way, it was simply reflecting inwardly what we have noted on the grand international scale—the End of the Postwar World.

One might describe the turmoil in the Democratic Party as the clash of the structured blocs that had once formed the Rooseveltian coalition. One might describe it as an expression of guilt for war, or the result of the vast domestic reforms it had pioneered for a generation. One might describe it as a conflict of old and new; or simply as a struggle of personalities. Yet basically it was a struggle over what should be the nature of a political party in a democracy and how such a party should offer citizens a voice in leadership. It is best, therefore, to begin a look at its problems by glancing at the new "reform" rules of the party, adopted in 1971. Rooted in the violence and turbulence of the 1968 Democratic convention in Chicago which had authorized them, the new rules would shape the Democratic campaign in 1972.

These rules had a covering phrase: the party was to be "opened" to all who wished to participate. Old tradition had made the Democratic Party a "leaders'" party; bosses of ethnic groups, big city mayors, labour union chieftains, the intellectual elite of the academies, courthouse bands bound in fealty to Southern senators, had gathered once every four years, shepherding and bargaining their delegate blocs for choice of candidate. It was a party of professional politicians, whose pros felt they knew best what was best for their troopers.

Now the Democratic convention of 1972, and thus the party, was to be "democratized." The new rules insisted that all delegates would have to be elected in "timely" fashion—which meant they must be chosen in 1972 and not, as in the past, by closed procedures that had begun two or even three years before. Except for a handful of delegates left to be chosen by a few state committees, all delegates must win their authority directly by open voting. No longer could a single boss, mayor, or governor choose the entire slate of delegates from his state. Moreover, and most importantly, the new party rules required that each delegation from each state properly and "reasonably" reflect its ethnic minorities, its youth, its women; and, if they did not, such delegates could be expelled for noncompliance.

On paper, no fairer set of election practices could be blueprinted. But this wrenching of the base of party decision could not help but set up an entirely new system of dynamics in the party—indeed, it had been rammed through for this purpose. Yet these new dynamics might make of the new rules a set of booby traps that could explode with total surprise in 1972.

For example:

• In mandating the composition of each delegation, the new rules were, in effect, predetermining how voters should vote. What if, in the process of new "open" selection, the voters of a given state simply refused to vote into being precisely the kind of delegation the new rules required? Could the party's credentials committee exclude a delegation because its voters had failed to elect the proper proportion of blacks, women, and youth? Could party mandate take precedence over delegates elected lawfully under the laws of their states?

• The new rules already had provoked for 1972 a schedule of 23 state primaries, the largest number in recent history. How would so long and so exhausting a string of primary contests affect the energies and vitality of the contestants? How much more money would it require beyond the already scandalous outlay needed for presidential primaries? Would it free delegates from traditional control by leaders and bosses, only to make them figurines merchandised by the media, the word-masters, the image-makers, commercial advertising men?

• Above all: how would the courts react to all the built-in conflicts the new reform rules seemed to promise? It was already certain, in 1971, that political lawyers were planning a busy spring of appeals of their clients' cases from party decision to federal law. And the Supreme Court, if it continued in its penchant for reviewing the political process, would be called upon, in a whole new set of decisions, to define, once and for all, the legal nature and authority of a national party.

Three Kinds of Candidates. Against this background of change within the party, the figures of the aspirants for the Democratic candidacy were sometimes sharp, sometimes blurred, but one could encompass them all by a rough division into traditionalists, moralists, and romantics.

• Among the traditionalists, clearly the front-runner at the end of 1971 was Sen. Edmund Muskie of Maine. The soft-spoken Muskie had, with full faith, supported the reform rules of 1971 and put his strength behind the moralists in their early struggle to control the new machinery. Yet his strategy as a campaigner was otherwise. Ever since the elections of 1970, Muskie had been slowly putting together a nationwide network of Democratic veterans, state by state, who embraced, wherever they operated, the full spectrum of traditional leadership. Superlatively organized at the end of 1971, the Muskie campaign lacked only that fire, that emotional kindling which fuels the drive of great presidential campaigns. Muskie, among the traditionalists, was playing the role of healer, doing his best to preempt the crowded centre of the party without giving offense to anyone, right or left, whom he might later need for the final drive against Nixon.

The greatest challenge to Muskie's control of the centre came from his one-time sponsor, ex-Vice-Pres. Hubert Humphrey, the candidate of 1968. The shape of Humphrey's campaign still was unclear—his resources within the party of loyalty, affection, and in some cases downright love were immense. But those fondest of him seemed anxious to promote Humphrey as a grandfather figure in the party, while Humphrey could not see himself as anything but an active contender for the prize he had sought for 16 years.

There remained, then, a third contender as a serious figure among the traditionalists, Sen. Henry Jackson of Washington. His traditional Rooseveltian-Trumanesque liberalism had made him by 1971 the sole voice that urged the party to continue with the international diplomacy—and the sustaining armament—which for 25 years had been wedded to its policies of domestic reform. His marginal chance lay in whether he could reach traditional voters across the sound barrier of the media—and whether they would respond.

• Challenging the traditionalists for the party nomination were two men who could be styled moralists or "issue" candidates. The hopes of both—Sen. George McGovern of South Dakota and Mayor John Lindsay of New York—lay in the reform rules of the party, in the anticipated surge of youth voting, in the new ideologies by which the Democratic Party was being increasingly influenced. Of these two, clearly the best organized was McGovern. Where Muskie sought to preempt the party's centre, McGovern sought to preempt the party's left. McGovern, the most eloquent of the peace spokesmen of 1971, a gentle and thoughtful man, pressed his appeal to the youth of the college campuses, to the ghettos and minorities, to the concerned conscience of suburbia. Where Muskie was organized from the top down, McGovern was organized from the bottom up.

Chief challenger to McGovern among the moralists was the charismatic Lindsay. Handsome, tall, and fair haired, Lindsay combined the manners of a patrician consul with the emotions of a tribune of the people. If any candidate was an issue candidate it was Lindsay—and his issue was the condition of American cities, their desperate entrapment by a constitution that they had outgrown, and their impoverishment by a society that seemed witlessly to be depriving them of the right to live. As McCarthy had, in 1968, caused the election of that year to turn on the Vietnam war, so Lindsay now sought to make the election of 1972 a confrontation between the American past and the needs of its new urban civilization.

• Beyond the traditionalists and moralists, one could discern the romantics, none of whom had any serious chance for the presidency, but whose power to sway the politics of 1972 was immeasurable.

There was Eugene McCarthy, the insurgent of 1968, the melancholy poet, speaking with all his remembered eloquence about the nation's destiny, not sure whether he should make his challenge again within the party—or from outside it.

There was George Wallace, the primitive of Alabama, nominally still a Democratic governor but almost certain to launch another national drive as the American Independent Party candidate.

Black leaders debated intensely among themselves whether to swing their clout within the Democratic Party—or blackmail it by running an independent black candidate for president to demonstrate their strength.

The Democrats might, in 1972, find that they had fathered not only a third party, but a fourth and fifth, too—and if all of these came to pass, then the reelection of Nixon was assured.

One last figure gave a final tonal quality to the Democratic condition as 1971 turned the corner into 1972—the figure of Sen. Edward M. Kennedy of Massachusetts. Kennedy brooded, no man knowing his inner thoughts; he did not himself want to make the race in 1972. But his name and his office were the centre of a convergence of forces. From roughhewn Mayor Richard Daley of Chicago, last and mightiest of the old-time urban bosses, through the most indignant of the black leadership to the most innocent and hopeful of student leaders, the Kennedy name had magic. It was not so much the personality who bore the name that gripped their imagination as the memory and magic that went with the name. The name bore history; and it was history itself that haunted the Democratic Party.

Off and Running. What the Democrats lacked as they entered 1972 was a name of any grandeur and a philosophy with any new perspective.

It was sad that this should be so, for in the history of the 20th century only two other political parties—the Communist parties of the Soviet Union and China—could match the imprint of the Democratic Party on world affairs. This party had in the 1930s proven that a great industrial state could reasonably and with no loss of freedom reorganize its entire economy. In the 1940s it had proven that a great democracy could organize for war and conquer with no loss of freedom. The party had shown the world how to harness science to state in freedom; had fostered the explosion of education; had written the constitutions of West Germany and Japan; had aided the hungering and the underprivileged around the world; had withstood aggression everywhere around the world until, overestimating U.S. strength, it had let itself be provoked into Vietnam.

The party still was virile and combat-ready as the U.S. pre-

pared for the election of 1972. Yet its voice was a babble and its challenge to Nixon was quantitative—not qualitative. Nixon was evacuating Vietnam—the Democrats agreed, but wanted it to go quicker. He was piloting a welfare bill through Congress—the Democratic opposition wanted it bigger and more generous. Nixon was trying to stabilize prices by wage-price controls—the Democrats sought controls at once stricter and more generous.

Nowhere yet, by the end of 1971, had the Democrats challenged Nixon by offering, as they had in 1932 and again in 1960, a change in national directions.

But this, after all, was what campaigns were all about. From March through July of 1972, the Democratic candidates, traditionalist, moralist, and romantic, would roam the country, challenging each other for the right to challenge Nixon. In the process they would be seeking to redefine the identity of a party that had, more than any other, shaped the world that was ending.

This was the best experience the open democracy of the U.S. provided its citizens. If, in their internal wars, the Democrats could find their own sense of direction without destroying themselves, if they could give Americans a clear choice between what they offered and what Nixon offered—then they might make the election of 1972 the milestone from which the next generation would date the beginning of the history of its time.

Pres. Richard Nixon relaxes in the White House office at the end of a day. At the close of 1971 he faced an undefined challenge from the Democratic Party, which had yet to formulate a unified program for a nation at the beginning of a new era.

The World Poverty Problem

by GUNNAR MYRDAL

IT IS THE AUTHOR'S firm conviction that progress in the social sciences can be achieved only by continual and searching criticism of approaches and methods. The quality and relevance of the swelling volume of research on the underdeveloped countries since World War II have suffered seriously from the lack of such criticism. This is, in particular, true of the valiant efforts of economists to tackle the problems of planning for development of those countries.

In this article an attempt is made to carry out a critical analysis of these research efforts—in general terms, without reference to sources, so that it can be grasped by the knowledgeable layman. Since, besides tradition and conservatism, the source of bias in economic science is the intellectual milieu in which researchers live and work, a measure of success in making this important fraction of the general public watchful and suspicious could contribute to making the economists themselves more critical.

A "NEW" PROBLEM

Like the nuclear armament race, the pollution of soil, water, and air, and the rapid spread of the use of harmful drugs, the abject poverty of that great majority of the world's population who live in underdeveloped countries now unfolds itself as a threatening new problem. But while the first three of these stupendous dangers for the well-being of mankind reflect real trends of change in conditions and human actions, the fourth danger is not new; only our awareness of it is new.

Economic conditions in the non-Communist underdeveloped countries are not fundamentally different today from what they were in the colonial period before World War II. Then, as now, there was a huge income gap between developed and underdeveloped regions. And even at that time, the gap was continuously widening, as indeed it had been for a century and more, without any great concern being expressed about it. The only major change that has occurred in those "backward regions" since the war has been the recent acceleration in the rate of population increase. But our awareness of the problem of world poverty preceded this change, which only came to light with the censuses around 1960.

In the prewar period, very little research was directed toward the social and economic conditions of the masses of people living in underdeveloped regions. Cultural anthropologists, sent out from the Western centres of learning and working with the indulgence of colonial and indigenous holders of power,

Gunnar Myrdal, economist and writer, is professor of international economy at the University of Stockholm. His books include An American Dilemma: The Negro Problem and Modern Democracy; The Political Element in the Development of Economic Theory; *and, more recently,* Economic Theory and Underdeveloped Regions; Asian Drama: An Inquiry into the Poverty of Nations; *and* The Challenge of World Poverty. *Professor Myrdal has held several governmental positions in Sweden and was executive secretary of the United Nations Economic Commission for Europe.*

focused interest on the way people lived. With few exceptions, their approach was static, and changes ordinarily were dealt with as "disturbances" of established social relations. They were sympathetic to the peoples they studied, and they reacted to European ethnocentrism by attempting to ascribe purpose to the social organization of even the most primitive peoples. But this inclination, and the generally static approach that corresponded to it, tended to draw attention away from the poverty problem.

More astonishing was the lack of interest shown by most economists of that era. Poverty falls in our field of study: all the traditions of our profession should have led us to inquire into what could be done about it. Had we devoted more interest to the backward regions, we could not have avoided raising the issue of poverty there as a policy problem.

Under the prewar colonial and quasi-colonial power system, there was little demand for such an approach. And economists, even more than other social scientists, always have been sensitive to what is practical and politically opportune. The fact that we mostly avoided research on conditions in the backward regions reflected the lack of political importance given to such research in colonial times. We may note in passing that even the highly idealistic Charter of the United Nations, drawn up toward the end of the war, did not focus on the plight of the underdeveloped regions and made no special provision for promoting their development.

The Great Awakening. All this has now radically changed. Today the poverty of underdeveloped countries is a problem of which everyone who is at all alert has been made aware. We have been living through one of history's most abrupt reversals of political climate. The social sciences, and most especially economics, have as usual responded to this change. In turn, scientific research itself has contributed to the accelerating awareness of the world poverty problem. A sizable proportion of our research resources today are employed in the study of underdeveloped countries. The tide is still rising, and we economists are riding the crest of the wave.

But this tremendous redirection of research, particularly in economics, has not been an autonomous or spontaneous development of our sciences. The cue to the reorientation of our work has come, as always, from the sphere of politics. The political changes on the international scene that have effected this redirection are clear.

First, we have the rapid dissolution of the colonial power structure which, beginning with the decolonization of the British dependencies in South Asia, has swept over the globe like a hurricane, creating a great number of new, politically independent countries, all of them underdeveloped. In Latin America political independence was won long ago, but these countries have joined in the decolonization movement by demanding "real" (meaning, particularly, economic) independence as well.

Second, demands for development in the now politically independent underdeveloped countries themselves are raised by the alert elite groups there who think, speak, and act on their countries' behalves, even though they do not arouse much response among the masses.

Third, international tensions, culminating in the Cold War, have created a competitive situation in which not only the foreign policy but also the internal affairs of underdeveloped countries are of political concern to the developed countries.

The United Nations and its specialized agencies have been made into sounding boards for the underdeveloped countries' demands for aid and commercial considerations from the developed countries. Underdeveloped countries did not carry much weight when the UN system of intergovernmental organizations was planned and set up, and their particular interests were not brought into focus. Since then, as a direct effect of the decolonization movement, UN membership has risen from the original 51 to 131. The great majority in all the UN organizations is now made up of the governments of underdeveloped countries.

While, on the whole, the effectiveness of the UN and its affiliated organizations has tended to deteriorate in recent years, particularly in the field of security and, more generally, on all issues in which the developed countries feel they have a stake, this whole system of intergovernmental organizations has been turned more and more into an instrument for discussing, analyzing, and promoting development in underdeveloped countries.

This is part of the process through which awareness of the world poverty problem has been engendered in the postwar period. Thus, an age-old problem abruptly came to figure as a "new" problem when it became politically important and, as a result, the object of large-scale research and worldwide debate.

BIASES IN PUBLIC DISCUSSION AND RESEARCH

A basic fact that is systematically neglected by almost all participants in the debate on the world poverty problem, whether they are speaking as scientists or as men of affairs, is that all knowledge, like all ignorance, tends to deviate from truth in an opportunistic direction—if not critically scrutinized.

Our views—from popular beliefs to the most sophisticated theories—tend to be influenced by interests as commonly, though often mistakenly, perceived by the dominant groups in the society where we are all living. This is taken for granted when we look back at an earlier period in history. We say about an author or statesman that, of course, he was "a product of the age in which he lived."

But in our own intellectual endeavours, we are ordinarily unaware of such influences—as, indeed, was true of people in every earlier epoch of history. A disturbing fact is that social scientists, and economists in particular, are usually naïve in this respect, and do not even consider the possibility that they may be so influenced. We believe—as our predecessors did, and with equal firmness—that we are simply factual and rational.

The Colonial Theory. In retrospect it is clear that, in the colonial era, remaining unaware of the problem of poverty in the underdeveloped regions and being satisfied by the paucity of research on their social and economic conditions were opportune reactions. It is equally clear that both the popular and the more sophisticated beliefs of that era were plainly apologetic. They were fashioned so as to relieve the colonial powers, and developed nations generally, from moral and political responsibility by proving that poverty and the lack of development in backward regions were natural and impossible to change.

It was taken as established by experience that peoples in backward regions were so constituted that they reacted differently from people of European stock. Their tendency toward idleness and inefficiency, and their reluctance to venture into new enterprise and often even to seek wage employment, were seen as expressions of their lack of ambition, limited economic horizons, survival-mindedness, carefree disposition, and preference for a leisurely life.

In more sophisticated writings, these mental traits were seen to be rooted in the entire system of social relations, upheld by attitudes and institutions and fortified by religious taboos and other prescriptions based in superstitious beliefs. These attitudinal and institutional conditions were taken to form a static system rather beyond any large-scale changes induced by policy measures, which might instead create "disturbances." On this score, the anthropologists' static bias was a convenient support.

Particularly in the discussion of economic matters, climate was given a dominant role in explaining low productivity and, in particular, low levels of labour input and efficiency of work. Also, the idea that people in these regions were hereditarily less well endowed than Europeans was never far below the surface, even if it was somewhat suppressed in later decades.

Occasionally it was noted that malnutrition, and inferior levels of living generally, lowered stamina and thereby affected willingness and ability to work and to work hard. But since productivity was so low and since there were all these other powerful and unchangeable causes preventing higher labour input and efficiency, combating underdevelopment and poverty by raising incomes and levels of living was seen as an unrealistic policy.

Young Vietnamese boy carries water to his home in a Saigon slum. War in Southeast Asia has accentuated problems of the rural poor, many of whom have moved to cities, where they have no marketable skills.

PHILIP JONES GRIFFITHS—MAGNUM

The Indigenous Protest. The colonial theory was not flattering to the indigenous peoples in the backward regions. To the upper strata of alert and educated persons among them it was felt to be condescending and humiliating. Furthermore, after the war and the wave of decolonization, it discouraged efforts toward development in "the underdeveloped countries," as they were now beginning to be called. In a sense, this had been its apologetic purpose.

It is understandable that the colonial theory gave rise to an indigenous protest. Indeed, the protest antedated, to some extent, the downfall of the colonial power system in those colonies where there had been a liberation movement. After political independence had been won, the intellectuals in the new countries were released from the inhibitions many of them had felt as officeholders and, more generally, as belonging to a privileged class in a foreign-controlled dependency. The protests against the colonial theory then rang out clearly and, in fact, became the official creed.

It is important to discuss the intellectual content of this protest. The colonial theory had alleged the existence of certain peculiarities of the indigenous peoples and of the conditions in which they lived and worked, including the structure of their societies. The indigenous protest simply denied the existence of these peculiarities. Although it had been largely suppressed, the racial inferiority doctrine was suspected, on good grounds, of living on surreptitiously and was condemned as "racialism." Differences in climate simply were disregarded, as were the alleged differences in social structure, attitudes, and institutions. Only differences in "culture" were recognized, and it was implied that they were not obstacles to development.

This position was shared by those intellectuals who identified themselves with the Western world and by more aggressive anti-Western nationalists. Both groups insisted that the development problem was essentially the same in underdeveloped and developed countries. From this assertion, it followed that underdevelopment had to be blamed on the colonial regimes. In those countries, particularly in Latin America, that had been politically independent long before World War II, the doctrine tended to be similar, except that it was directed against foreign economic domination and the political influence based on it.

Adjustment in the Developed Countries. Those who shape and express public opinion in the developed countries—including politicians, officials, journalists, writers of popular tracts, and social scientists—proved receptive to this ideology. For one thing, in the Western tradition we all feel sympathy for the underdog. Furthermore, independence relieved the people in the former metropolitan countries of responsibility for ruling these peoples, and thus of the need to explain, to themselves and others, why they were so poor. When the dependent peoples were thrown abruptly on their own, there was every reason to wish them well.

The experience of ideological competition with the Communists, intensified by the Cold War, contributed to this sudden conversion in the Western world. Ever since the time of Marx, Communists had condemned colonialism. They had never shared in the colonial theory, but had blamed the poverty in the backward regions on colonial exploitation. They could agree wholeheartedly with the indigenous protest and could even express the opinion that the former colonial powers and, indeed, all developed countries had a debt to repay. But aside from these ideological tenets, which were genuinely held and in line with their traditional thinking, they had, of course, opportunistic reasons for backing up the protest ideology. And the easiest way for the Western nations to take the air out of Communist propaganda in the underdeveloped countries was to give up the colonial theory as rapidly and completely as possible and accept a new theory cleansed from all the old offensive elements.

This new theory will be set out below. At this stage in our argument, it should only be asserted that even research tended to become "diplomatic," forbearing, and generally overoptimistic, bypassing facts that raised awkward problems, concealing them in unduly technical terminology, or treating them in an excusing and "understanding" way. While the "white man's burden" in colonial times had been to rule those who supposedly could not rule themselves, it now became a felt need to be diplomatic in research as well as in public debate.

This tendency even involved terminology. In colonial times a common expression had been the static "backward regions." It reflected the fact that most of these regions were not countries, and it also gave no support to the idea that conditions in them could be changed. After decolonization, the term became the dynamic "underdeveloped countries." This expressed a recognition of their present state of underdevelopment, but it also implied the valuations that this was undesirable, that they should plan for development, and that they should be helped to succeed in doing so by the developed countries.

But that term soon was felt to be insufficiently polite. By a common conspiracy guided by diplomatic considerations, it gave way to various euphemistic expressions. One such expression is "developing countries," which for many years has been given official sanction in all documents emanating from the UN. This term is, of course, illogical, since it begs the question of whether a country is developing or not. Moreover, it does not express the thought that is really relevant: that a country is underdeveloped, that it wants to develop, and that it should be planning to develop.

This overoptimistic approach also served opportunistic interests. When awareness of the world poverty problem was once created, people in developed countries were brought to recognize—though still only in general and noncommittal terms—that they should aid the underdeveloped countries in their development efforts. If the overoptimistic approach were realistic, effective aid could be cheaper.

In the underdeveloped countries, both conservatives and radicals had opportunistic reasons to adhere to it. If it were realistic, the privileged classes could hope to achieve development without giving up their privileges. They would not have to permit radical domestic reforms. And it is natural that they, and conservative persons generally, would want to hear as little as possible about all that had been thrown out with the old theory—climate, social structure, attitudes and institutions, and the adverse effects on productivity of very low levels of living.

The radicals were inclined to hope for rapid and effective development as a result of planning. It also should be recalled that Marx had assumed that the effects of industrialization, and of investments generally—changes in the "modes of production" —would spread quickly to other sectors of the economy and would determine the whole "superstructure" of culture, social structure, attitudes, and institutions. In underdeveloped countries most intellectuals had been under "Marxist" influence—far more than those who are now in the Communist fold—and Western economists, usually without referring to the source and often without being aware of it, have now widely accepted Marx's overoptimistic views on the rapid "spread effects" of economic changes and many other elements of "Marxism" as well.

THE POSTWAR THEORY

By all our traditions, ambitions, and working habits, we economists were destined to dominate the rising tide of research on the postwar problems of underdeveloped countries. Economists are accustomed and trained to lay a dynamic policy perspective on problems and also to seek out for study problems where that approach is required. In a sense, ours has been, and is, a "political science" in the proper sense of the term. In principle, we are planners, even those of us whose planning prescriptions conclude by advising nonintervention. And we do not shy away from constructing theoretical macromodels, applicable to whole countries or to the entire world. This was exactly what was required when backward regions became politically independent and faced the problem of planning for development.

Unfortunately, our profession also happened to have at hand

a body of theory that, when applied to underdeveloped countries, perfectly answered to the postcolonial system of opportune bias. It was natural that the economists, on undertaking massive research on conditions in underdeveloped countries, came to rely on the theoretical tools they had perfected and made such good use of in the developed countries. But by so doing, they strengthened and fortified the tendency to over-optimism. Since conditions in underdeveloped countries are vastly and systematically unlike those in developed countries, the result was disastrous to realism and relevance.

It could not be expected that economists in the underdeveloped countries should take another approach. Besides the opportune interests working on the minds of both conservative and radical intellectuals, most of them had been trained either at Western universities or by teachers who had acquired their training in the West. All of them had been exposed to the great economic literature in the Western tradition. And familiarity with, and ability to work in accordance with, the concepts and theoretical models developed in that tradition were apt to give status in their native countries as well as abroad.

The Unrealistic Assumptions. With all the variations between different authors and schools of thought, the whole body of Western economic theories had certain important common assumptions that simply did not fit conditions in underdeveloped countries. Generally speaking, this approach abstracts from most of the conditions that are not only peculiar to the underdeveloped countries but are largely responsible for their underdevelopment and for the particular difficulties they meet when attempting to develop.

Thus, climatic conditions have never been very important for economic development in the developed countries, which are all situated in the temperate zones. But most underdeveloped countries are in the tropical and subtropical zones. It is a fact that all successful industrialization and economic development has taken place in the temperate zones. In colonial times, this was not taken as an accident of history; climatic conditions were given an important role in explaining underdevelopment in the backward regions. In the postwar economic literature they are either ignored or casually dismissed as being of no importance.

From the point of view of making scientific study realistic and relevant this is, of course, unwarranted. Even if little research has been carried out in this field, it is clear that, generally speaking, the extremes of heat and humidity in most underdeveloped countries contribute to a deterioration of soil and many kinds of material goods. They bear a partial responsibility for the low productivity of certain crops, forests, and animals. Not only do they cause discomfort to workers, but they also impair health by favouring the existence, multiplication, and spread of various microorganisms that give rise to parasitic and infectious diseases. In these and other ways, climatic conditions decrease participation in and duration of work and its efficiency.

Overcoming these unfavourable effects—and occasionally turning some of them into advantages (which in regard to agriculture in several countries is quite possible)—requires expenditures, often of an investment type. Since capital and all other real cost elements, such as effective administration, put demands on scarce resources in underdeveloped countries, climatic conditions often impose serious obstacles to development. To abstract from climatic conditions in the study of underdeveloped countries represents, therefore, a serious bias.

In a crude way the colonial theory also laid stress on various aspects of the social organization, institutions, and attitudes in underdeveloped countries. By the static assumption that these conditions were practically immutable, the colonial theory had undoubtedly been biased in a pessimistic direction. But to study the underdeveloped countries' planning problems in purely "economic" terms, completely ignoring these "noneconomic" factors, was a contrary and most serious bias in the opposite direction. In developed countries, institutions and attitudes are usually already highly rationalized in the sense that they do not block

Labourers line up with their meagre food purchases at a market in Peru. Even in areas of Latin America where there has been some industrial development, the living standard for many workers remains at the poverty level.

development impulses, but this cannot be assumed in underdeveloped countries that have been stagnant for a long time.

Again, the relatively higher levels of living and income and the social security measures in developed countries make it possible to consider nutrition and, more generally, levels of living merely from the point of view of people's welfare interest. They are largely inconsequential as regards willingness and ability to work and efficiency when working. In Western growth models consumption is, therefore, usually left out. This simplification is not permissible when analyzing underdeveloped countries. Incomes and levels of living do have effects on productivity. Furthermore, the situation is complex, since some consumption items —for instance, food and educational facilities—are more important for productivity than others.

In one respect, however, the assumptions taken over from the economists' body of theories for the developed countries did work for rationality and realism. Ever since its origin in the Enlightenment, economic thinking has kept extraordinarily free from speculation about hereditary differences in regard to intelligence and other aptitudes between groups of people. In that respect the economists were on the side of the angels.

Differences in Initial Conditions. The distortions caused by the uncritical transference of the basic assumptions of economic analysis to the underdeveloped countries leads to the view that

Elderly woman in central India hobbles through railroad yards on her way to the marketplace to beg. Life for many of the nation's teeming millions is precarious; death from starvation is not uncommon.

differences in the level of development have only a "dimensional," not a "qualitative," character. More specifically, it is assumed that there is only a "time lag" between developed and underdeveloped countries. This thesis had been pronounced by Marx who wrote, in the preface to *Das Kapital:* "The country that is more developed industrially only shows, to the less developed, the image of its own future." Particularly in the United States, it has been popularized in simplified theories of "stages of growth," usually without accounting for their origin in old-fashioned Marxism.

Within this general framework, it was natural that views tended to become distorted in the same direction, even with regard to conditions that, by themselves, should not be conceptually difficult to include in an "economic" theory. This would, indeed, apply to climatic conditions, although by tradition they have been disregarded in economic analysis.

In the same way, economists, at least until recently, have not attached enough importance to population density and the increasingly rapid population growth in most underdeveloped countries. As a matter of fact, most people live in crowded circumstances, and there is "overpopulation" even in those countries that have large land reserves and an abundance of other natural resources. Spreading out population, however, would often demand, in addition to large investments and effective administrative exertions, domestic institutional reforms, especially in land ownership and tenancy, and a hospitable political climate. Going deeper into such matters was not in the tradition of Western economic theory.

Proper consideration of politics and political development lies even further outside the traditional economic approach. Well before industrialization, the developed countries were fairly consolidated nation-states, able to pursue national policies. The underdeveloped countries—and not only those that are newly independent—have to plan for bringing about and speeding up development while still striving to become consolidated as states.

With regard to international trade, being a latecomer in the small developed world of the 19th century was not a disadvantage, but often quite the opposite. When huge backward regions try to emerge from political and economic dependency today, they cannot simply repeat the trade experience of the developed countries. They also lack the easy access to low-interest capital from abroad that the developed countries had in earlier times. The trading position of the underdeveloped countries as a group is steadily weakening, and they are driven to rely on investment in industries for import substitution—a development that cannot be planned too well because the primary cause is usually exchange difficulties, bringing about import restrictions that tend to give highest protection to less necessary production. These phenomena have been analyzed, of course, but it is not unfair to reproach economists for generally tending to underestimate the inhibitions and obstacles that prevent underdeveloped countries from turning trade into an "engine of growth." The exceptionally successful development in a few smaller countries cannot be generalized.

It is commonly assumed that, in one respect at least, underdeveloped countries today should be in a better position than the presently developed countries were when they started out. There exists a much more highly developed technology, which they can make use of without having the burden of inventing it. This, however, is a static view. The rapid and steadily accelerating scientific and technological advance in the developed countries has had, and is now having, an effect on underdeveloped countries' economies that, on balance and with many exceptions, is detrimental to their prospects. In the developed countries we will continue to raise agricultural productivity and protect our own farmers, make savings in the use of raw materials, and develop substitute products for traditional imports from underdeveloped countries. Scientific and technological advance in developed countries is also partly responsible for the difficulty underdeveloped countries have in increasing their production and export of industrial goods. All this is well known and commented upon in specialized fields; however, the cumulative adverse effect on development usually is not accounted for in the literature.

More generally—and contrary to a common misconception—change was not rapid in the countries that are developed today. The underdeveloped countries lack time for the gradual transition experienced by the developed countries. The need for modernization, accentuated by the population explosion, leads to a situation where elements of modernism are sprinkled throughout a society in which many conditions have remained almost the same for centuries. As Jawaharlal Nehru said for India, "We have atomic energy and we also use cow dung."

To take the view that spurts of modernism are important "growing points" is to assume a number of things: not only that the hampering effects of the population explosion at home and of the ever more rapid technological advance in the developed countries can be overcome, but also, more specifically, that the "spread effects" within the underdeveloped countries can be made to operate more effectively than, in most of them, they have done up to the present time. This, in turn, presupposes policies initiated to influence attitudes and institutions directly. But these "noneconomic" factors were kept outside economic analysis and the planning of policies made on the basis of that analysis.

These reminders are apt to be characterized as "pessimistic," which is natural in the intellectual milieu of "optimism" created by the postwar approach to development. Both "optimism" and "pessimism," however, are nothing but biases, from which scientific analysis should free itself. When a realistic study of the conditions in underdeveloped countries leads to a more sober view of their prospects, this should not result in defeatism. Instead, it should motivate increased and, in many respects, more radical efforts. A realistic view of the world poverty problem must rightly demand a courage and determination that can never be inspired by opportunistic optimism.

Criticism of the Economic Models. Every scientific approach must simplify. This is especially necessary on that macro-level where conditions pertinent to planning for development of an entire country are being studied. But it is not permissible to abstract from conditions that are crucially important in the society under study. The theory must work with concepts that are adequate to reality in underdeveloped countries from the very approach in the analysis of their problems.

The growth models implied in conventional economic analysis of the development problems in underdeveloped countries—in terms of demand, supply and prices, and employment, unemployment, savings, investment, gross national product or income—are based on certain unwarranted assumptions. One is that it is possible to reason in terms of aggregates for an entire underdeveloped country. In turn, this assumes, among other things, the prevalence of markets—and fairly effective markets at that. A third assumption is that it is realistic to exclude consumption from a growth model. And there are others.

This might be the place to insert a few remarks on the economists' use of statistics in the analysis of underdeveloped countries. In the beginning, the very fact that our knowledge of conditions in these countries was so extremely scant encouraged, or at least did not discourage, a careless use of the Western models. This was particularly true for those many economists who were content to construct models in the air and to insert Greek characters when data were missing. When data were then obtained they were assembled by utilizing the conceptual categories implied in the models. The resulting mountains of figures have, therefore, little or no meaning or validity.

Thus the gross national product or income and its growth have

Two-year-old girl suffering from severe malnutrition in the Venezuelan Andes weighed 11.5 lb. when this picture was taken. After ten months of care in a rehabilitation centre, she was on her way to recovery.

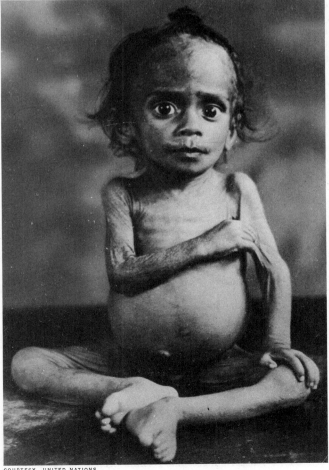

PER GUNVALL

Young boy drinks from a pipe that is the only water supply for an entire slum neighbourhood in Dacca. In such cases the water often is contaminated because of overcrowding and lack of adequate waste-disposal facilities.

been permitted to play a most important role in all discussions of development. Even in developed countries we are becoming aware that these concepts are flimsy. They take no account of distribution. Pollution and resource depletion are usually not accounted for. It is not clear exactly what is supposed to be growing, or whether it is real growth in any sense or merely reflects the costs caused by undesirable developments, or conspicuous public and private consumption and investments. And there are other insufficiencies. To this is added, in underdeveloped countries, the absence of effective markets over wide areas of the economy and many other conceptual difficulties, not to mention the usually extreme weaknesses in the operation of the statistical services. Accordingly, the figures on national product or income so confidently quoted must be deemed almost valueless.

The same holds true of the figures quoted for other "economic" concepts in the macromodels, for instance the figures for savings. Quite aside from the general weakness in the primary observations and the virtual impossibility of accounting properly for direct investments in agriculture and many other parts of the economy, the clear conceptual distinction in developed countries between two parts of an individual's income—the part that is consumed and that which is saved—has no counterpart in underdeveloped countries, where some consumption is akin to direct investment.

Statistics on international trade and capital movements should be more reliable. The concepts are clear-cut, and since political boundaries are crossed, there is a double check on accuracy. In spite of large-scale smuggling in some underdeveloped countries, underdeclaration of exported merchandise in order to acquire foreign exchange outside the national controls, and undeclared capital flights, these figures should be better than most.

But unemployment defined as an aggregate of workers, seeking but not finding employment for the ruling wages in a market they know, is a concept that fits conditions in underdeveloped countries only for a very minor part of the labour force and even for them very imperfectly. The term "underemployment," invented to fit conditions there better, has, when critically scrutinized, no definite meaning at all. The actual and apparent underutilization of the labour force in underdeveloped countries has to be studied in purely behavioural terms that relate to observable facts: which people work at all; for what periods during

Ancient automobiles and makeshift shacks indicate the standard of living in a slum on the outskirts of Buenos Aires, Arg. In spite of the level of poverty, a few of the homes boast television sets.
PAUL CONKLIN—PIX

the day, week, month, and year they work; and with what intensity and effectiveness.

The list of criticisms cannot be extended in the context of this article. Let me merely assert that, when beginning massive research on conditions in underdeveloped countries, economists commonly have shown great carelessness in their use of statistics. The articles and books are punctuated by figures, most of which are not worth the paper they are printed on. A basic cause is undoubtedly the approach, implying an overstraining of the theoretical models when uncritically applied to underdeveloped countries. From what has already been said, it is to be expected that this use, or rather misuse, of grossly defective statistics has generally supported the optimistic bias. One flagrant example is the use of figures for school enrollment. These figures are extremely bad by themselves, but they are, moreover, rather commonly used as if they measured what we are really interested in—namely whether children attend school, which they often do not. The statistics on literacy are likewise generally very weakly founded and exaggerated.

The Master Model. The archetype of theoretical growth models, which in the beginning dominated the literature and which has continued to determine the very structure of the plans, is the one in which aggregate output is related to physical investment by the capital/output ratio. Designed originally as a theoretical tool for dealing with the problems of economic stagnation and instability in developed countries, this one-factor model was applied to the utterly different development problems of underdeveloped countries. Thus used, it implied on a gross scale an unwarranted abstraction from other relevant relationships, misplaced aggregation even in regard to the factors highlighted in the model, and an illegitimate isolation from other changes, induced or spontaneous. It should be added that these critical points are equally valid when the model is broken up into separate models for two or more sectors in an economy.

The capital/output approach had gained popularity among economists after World War II because of several studies in Western countries that purported to show a close relationship between physical investment and economic growth. In fact, for a time the capital/output ratio came to be regarded as akin to the constants that have made it possible to advance knowledge of the physical universe by purely abstract mathematical reasoning.

In recent years, however, more intensive studies in some highly developed Western countries have revealed that even there only a part of economic growth could be explained by the amount of investment in physical capital. While estimates of the unexplained residual vary widely, they generally support the view that it is considerably bigger than that part of economic growth explained by capital investment.

This important negative finding demolished—even in regard to developed countries—the foundation of the model cast in terms of physical investment alone, and threw the door open to speculation about other operative factors in development: education, health, research, technology, organization, management, administration, and so on. Interest, however, has mainly focused on education. At least the more elaborate models all reduce what came to be called "investment in man" to this one factor. The importance of education for development is nothing new, of course; it had been appreciated by the classical and neoclassical economists from Adam Smith on. If it was announced as a new discovery by economists, the explanation is simply that it had been forgotten by members of our profession. More striking, however, is the conservatism of even this newest school of economists. They restrict themselves merely to widening the abstract concept of investment in the capital/output model to include investment in the educational sector.

Adam Smith and Alfred Marshall would never have thought of theorizing along this line. Marshall even warned against treating education in terms of input and output. It can only conceal the real problems of the role of education in development, which are all related to the content and direction of education, its effects on attitudes and institutions, particularly those of economic and social stratification, and the effects of these factors back upon education. As we shall see, much education in underdeveloped countries has negative effects on development, and where the effects are positive they have no simple relation to input, however it is accounted for.

Before leaving the master model, it should be noted that it is in accordance with that model that plans are regularly presented, discussed, and later evaluated, as fiscal plans for public investment. Since most of the policy measures needed for engendering development—besides physical investments—have only the most incidental relation to costs and returns in financial terms and even less to a fiscal budget, this permits presenting the appearance of a plan without much real planning. Of course a fiscal budget is needed for the orderly conduct and control of public administration and public expenditure. But that type of "planning" cannot serve as a rational coordination of, or even as a basis for, real planning, which should encompass induced changes in all sorts of economic and social conditions carried out in a coordinated fashion.

Trends. Even when the flimsy figures for gross national product or income have indicated successful development—"more rapid than ever in the now developed countries," it is often asserted—there are many other signs well calculated to dampen overoptimism. Partly because economists cannot keep themselves entirely unaware of this, they have become ever more eager to make the most generous reservations and qualifications—indeed, to emphasize that in the last instance development is a "human problem" that must aim at "changing man." But having made their bow to the "noneconomic" factors, all too many of them proceed as if those factors did not exist. Not even the most empty model-building, devoid of any real attempt to relate it to observable facts, is missing. High respect is paid to mathematical "sophistication" without much scrutiny of the concepts employed and the assumptions implied. An appearance of precision and rigour is created, and the basic logical confusion is hidden by a common lack of conceptual clarity.

But the more empirically inclined economists increasingly attempt to reach realism. Enlarging their vista, they seek to encompass more and more of all that is excluded from the simplified economic models. It must be admitted that the literature is now giving us much factual information about reality in the underdeveloped countries. As the models representing the scientific approach are found to lack realism, the idea is spreading that we "do not yet have a theory of development." However, the use of statistics by even the empirically inclined economists is open to severe criticism. Even when they have been made aware that concepts like national output or income, savings, or unemployment are inadequate to describe reality in underdeveloped countries, they continue uncritically to use these terms and also the statistics collected and aggregated under these categories, as if they were proper categories.

And when the point is made that an opportune bias has been permeating not only the public debate but also the scientific economic analysis of development problems, this is met by blunt silence. The thought that we economists, like other human beings, are influenced by the tradition in which we are working and the inclinations prevalent in the society of which we are part is taboo to the ordinary economist. Meanwhile, the thousands of economists working on development problems have become an establishment with vested interests, shared by the great majority of others who are involved in these problems, politically and practically or as experts of various types.

Nevertheless, the very fact that thousands of researchers are now wrestling with development problems will in 10 or 15 years' time necessitate a change of scientific approach in the direction of institutional economics. It is already on its way. In time, this will be as radical a change as that from the colonial theory to the postwar approach. All honest research has an inbuilt, self-cleansing capacity. Facts kick, even though with a delay.

I have no doubt that the main responsibility for research pertinent to development and planning of underdeveloped countries will continue to rest on us economists. We naturally accept the responsibility for taking a broad view of an entire country and for thinking in terms of national planning. Place any economist in the capital city of an underdeveloped country and give him the necessary assistance, and in no time he will produce a Plan. No anthropologist, sociologist, or psychologist would ever think of trying to do such a thing.

What a state needs, and what politics is about, is precisely a macro-plan for inducing changes simultaneously in a great number of conditions, not only the economic ones, and for doing it so as to coordinate all these changes to reach maximum de-velopment effect of efforts and sacrifices. We need to retain our tradition to take the broad perspective of a macro-plan for an entire country, but at the same time we need to become better informed and incorporate in our analysis the social structure and the political forces, attitudes and institutions, and also the productivity consequences of very low levels of living.

THE NEED FOR RADICAL DOMESTIC REFORMS

So far, this article has focused on the world poverty problem from the viewpoint of how it has been approached in public debate and in economic research. Now an attempt will be made to state positively some main facts of the underdeveloped countries' actual situation and, in particular, to characterize the types of policies that must be applied in order to engender rapid and sustained development. It is in the nature of things that the text must be utterly condensed, in fact consisting only of an assortment of *obiter dicta,* the evidence for which must be sought elsewhere.

When I laboured on a comprehensive study of South Asia, I made it a strict rule to stress that my generalizations and inferences related only to that very large region which I had studied intensively. But later, when I elaborated my policy conclusions and then tried to look a little more closely at other underdeveloped regions, I was surprised to find conditions and, in particular, the need for specific domestic reforms much more similar than I had expected. This will be stressed as we now attempt to view the world poverty problem from the angle of the planned policy measures needed in order to meet the quest for development.

Inequality. In spite of the radical premises that they inherited from the philosophers of natural law and utilitarianism, economists in all generations have shown an inclination to assume that there is a conflict between egalitarian reforms and economic growth, in the sense that the price of a somewhat lower growth rate must be paid for these reforms. This bias has been broken only in very recent times and in the most advanced welfare states. The conventional view was argued consistently in speculative terms. We still largely lack detailed studies of how, even in developed countries, "economic" factors such as the sav-

Tailor works at his sewing machine outside his hut in a Ujamaa village in the Rufiji district of Tanzania. In this area development remains at a primitive level.

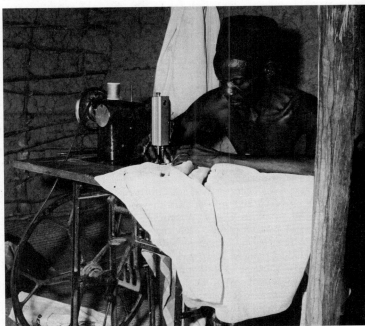

PER GUNVALL

ings ratio, labour input, and labour efficiency react to a changed degree of inequality in the distribution of income and wealth.

When, after World War II, economists came to direct their research interests toward underdeveloped countries, it was almost self-evident to most of them that these extremely poor countries could not afford to think in terms of social justice. There are a number of reasons why, contrary to this conception of a conflict between the two goals of economic growth and greater economic equality, the latter is almost a condition for rapid and sustained growth in underdeveloped countries.

First, large masses of people in underdeveloped countries suffer from undernutrition, malnutrition, lack of elementary health and educational facilities, extremely bad housing conditions and sanitation, and other serious defects in their levels of living; this impairs their preparedness and ability to work and to work intensively and thus holds down production. It implies that measures to raise income levels for the masses of people would raise productivity. In the opposite direction, forced saving on the part of these masses, brought about by inflation and the usually highly regressive taxation in underdeveloped countries, may make possible some more physical investments, but at the same time it holds down or even decreases labour input and efficiency.

Second, social inequality is tied to economic inequality in a mutual relationship, each being both cause and effect of the other. As social inequality, by decreasing mobility and free competition in the widest sense of the term, is quite generally detrimental to development, so it is clear that greater economic equality would lead to higher productivity.

Third, the usual argument that economic inequality enriches an upper class that is able to save more of its income has little relevance in most underdeveloped countries, where landlords and other rich people are known to squander their incomes in conspicuous consumption, conspicuous investments, and sometimes —and not only in Latin America—in capital flights. Because of extreme deficiencies in the assessment and tax collection, inequality of incomes does not contribute to public savings either.

Fourth, all underdeveloped countries have to strive for national consolidation. Great and, particularly, growing inequality is a serious obstacle to this goal.

We face a strange paradox in regard to the quest for greater equality in underdeveloped countries. On the one hand, the policy declarations in all underdeveloped countries stress the need for greater equality and, in particular, for raising the levels of living for the masses. On the other hand, economic as well as social inequality is not only very gross and harsh in most of these countries but seems generally to be increasing. Most policy measures said to be taken in the interest of the poor are either not implemented or they turn out in practice to favour the not-so-poor. Whatever development there has been has mostly enriched only the top strata, the urban "middle class" of "educated," and what in South Asia is called the "rural elite."

This cannot be unrelated to the fact that almost all underdeveloped countries are ruled by varying constellations of people in the upper class, taken in this wider sense. This is true even in countries such as India, where free discussion and other civil liberties are guaranteed and which has a system of government built upon universal suffrage, but it is usually an even more firmly set pattern in those underdeveloped countries under a more authoritarian rule.

The masses generally are not informed enough to be aware of their interests, and still less are they organized to stand up for them in an effective way. When they break out of inarticulateness and passivity, too often they are driven by religious or ethnic fanaticism, combined with impulses to steal land and household property from each other. That type of "rebellion" not only is useless but it inhibits rational and organized mass action to defend real and common interests.

Under these circumstances, egalitarian reforms are not initiated or, if initiated or even legislated, they are not implemented or they are distorted. The upper class, however, is in a serious ideological dilemma and its moral position is weak. Its members were the harbingers of the modernizing ideals from the West and from the Communist countries, among which egalitarianism held a prominent place. To a large extent, they still hold to these ideals in their hearts. But in the absence of determined and organized pressure from below, they permit their own interests, often shortsightedly perceived, to block egalitarian reforms.

Industry and Agriculture. From the beginning, industrialization has been a primary goal for the development efforts of underdeveloped countries. Indeed, it is impossible to conceive that countries like India and Pakistan will be able to retain even the present low levels of living, still less to raise them, if at the end of this century a much larger proportion of their labour force is not employed in industry. With few exceptions, this holds true for most underdeveloped countries.

But what was not seen—and is not often seen even today— is that, for the near future, the growth of modern industry will not create much new employment. This is because of the low level from which industrialization starts and because modern industry is not labour-intensive. In fact, because crafts and traditional industry generally may be put out of business, the growth of modern industry might for a time actually decrease the total demand for labour. This is particularly important since, whatever is happening in regard to the spread of birth control among the masses, the labour force will be increasing by 2 to 3% annually or more till at least toward the end of this century.

For this reason alone, the trend to attach greater importance to agriculture is well warranted. This does not often involve a question of "priorities" even in regard to the disposal of resources. First, most of what, besides labour, is needed for raising agricultural yields is locally available and in any case does not require much foreign exchange. Second, industrialization may be directed toward serving agricultural advance by producing fertilizers, tools, and other implements for agricultural production.

Land Reform. With few exceptions, agricultural yields are very low in underdeveloped countries. This is related to the fact that agriculture is not intensive, as is commonly assumed because of the very large part of the labour force tied to it. It is, instead, extensive. Labour utilization is extremely low because of the very low input of the labour force and very low labour intensity. The low yields, and the fact that almost every improvement in production techniques that is not merely labour-saving is bound to increase the demand for labour, should motivate some hopefulness with regard to the possibilities of raising productivity. There are many inhibitions and obstacles in the way, but the main difficulties undoubtedly are rooted in the systems of land ownership and tenancy.

Land reform can take various forms adapted to the conditions of the several countries and districts. A more egalitarian redistribution among the cultivators, including the labourers and other landless groups, is one possibility. Cooperative farming is another. Municipal or state ownership is a third. It is even possible that in some countries capitalist farming, cleansed of patterns of absentee land ownership and sharecropping, could have an important role to play. What is commonly needed is the creation of a new relationship between man and land that gives opportunities and creates incentives for a man to work more and more effectively and to invest whatever he can to improve the land—in the first place, his own labour.

Land reform has been on the political agenda in practically all underdeveloped countries. And almost everywhere governments have made a sham of it. When legislated, it has been a mini-reform, and even that has not been carried out effectively. Quite generally the interests of the landless labourers have been totally neglected. The supplementary reforms—community development, agricultural extension, credit and other cooperatives —have had an easier passage. But in the absence of effective land reform, they have rather tended to assist the upper strata in the villages and thus actually increased inequality.

The recent availability of high-yielding varieties of grain

seeds is by itself a most important innovation. But it cannot be a substitute for land reform. In its absence, this development tends, on the contrary, to increase inequality. It draws into agriculture a new group of capitalist entrepreneurs who can afford to buy irrigated land, fertilizers, and other implements for intensive agriculture. Their profits are largely untaxed. This development becomes most serious when they begin to use laboursaving equipment, speeding up the exodus to the slums of the cities. But the general euphoria surrounding the Green Revolution has given an excuse to researchers as well as politicians to let the need for land reform fade from their thoughts.

Population Policy. In practically all underdeveloped countries, populations are increasing at an unprecedented rate. The blunt fact is that no advance in the spread of birth control among the masses, if it could be brought about, would have much effect on the growth of the labour force for a long time to come. The new age-groups that will be entering the labour force for decades ahead have been born already or will be born soon.

This will steadily increase the difficulties in agriculture, where even at present there is vast underutilization of the labour force. The economic and social structure will become still more inegalitarian as farmers who own some land are reduced to sharecroppers or landless labourers and the small farm units tend to become still smaller. Under these conditions, the stream of refugees to urban slums will continue to swell, increasing there the number of seriously underutilized and poverty-stricken people.

On the other hand, the spread of birth control would have an immediate and favourable effect on the age distribution of the population. There would be fewer children to support. In many direct and indirect ways, a higher level of living would increase the productivity of labour. In the next generation both the reproduction potentialities and the rate of increase of the labour force would be lowered. For these reasons, all underdeveloped countries have the strongest interest in spreading birth control as soon and as effectively as possible.

In the now developed countries, both Western and Communist, birth control had to spread by "private enterprise" in individual families—in fact, through "subversive activity," since it was against public policy. Today the underdeveloped countries can make the spread of birth control public policy. Further, while birth control in the developed countries did not depend much upon contraceptive techniques, the underdeveloped countries can utilize a vastly improved birth-control technology that is continually improving further.

Nevertheless, the task is immensely difficult: to cause millions of individual couples to change their most intimate sexual behaviour. And this must occur in populations that are very poor, illiterate or semi-illiterate, often with impaired health and vigour, and mostly living in traditional and stagnant communities with an inegalitarian and rigid social and economic structure, all of which breeds fatalism and apathy. To succeed, a government must, against prevalent prejudices, make a firm decision to take action. Then it must build up an administrative apparatus for the purpose, reaching out to the individual families in the villages and the city slums. It must employ a large staff of medical and paramedical personnel under conditions where such staff is extremely scarce and badly needed for other duties. It is not difficult to explain why family planning has mostly not been very successful up till now, but there is no alternative. Failure would be a serious blow to the hopes for development everywhere, and in many large countries it would be simply calamitous.

Educational Reform. Even in the developed countries, education still tends to favour the upper class, thus contributing to a class ranking that becomes almost hereditary. Reform activity stretching back over generations has, in general, diminished this effect, but in underdeveloped countries this mechanism of preventing social and economic mobility is much more blatant. After World War II, leaders in many underdeveloped countries raised the demand for a radical reform of the educational system, but in most cases that is exactly what did not happen. The school system has been allowed to follow a conservative laissez-faire line, passing a swelling stream of pupils through the established channels without interference, except to enlarge those channels where the pressure in society is greatest. And the effective demand for education comes from the educated and articulate upper strata that have retained most of the political power.

One revolutionary idea that was widely accepted was the abolition of illiteracy. This was a rational policy choice. But actual policies have not adhered to this position. For one thing, in non-Communist countries adult education has been neglected in an almost scandalous way, even though adult education is needed in order to reach general literacy within a reasonably short time

Below, Nigerian children sit on a dirt floor in a classroom equipped with a television set. Below, right, an instructor conducts an adult literacy class that emphasizes the occupational needs of the population in the village of Weyebo, Eth.

period and, even more basically, in order to make school education of children effective.

The literacy goal became translated into merely a program for rapidly enlarging the enrollment of children in primary schools. And although the declared purpose was to give priority to the increase of elementary schools, what has actually happened almost everywhere is that secondary schooling has been rising much faster and tertiary schooling still more rapidly. This has happened in spite of the fact that secondary schooling seems to be some three to five times more expensive than primary schooling, and schooling at the tertiary level five to seven times more expensive than at the secondary level. Furthermore, despite all the efforts to make secondary and tertiary schools practical, technical, and job-directed, the bulk of them have remained "academic," "literary," and general.

On the whole, primary schools have been kept on a very low standard, particularly in the poorest countries and the poorest regions. The enrollment figures, again particularly in the poorest countries and regions, are entirely unreliable because of the prevalence of irregular attendance, repeating, and dropping out. This represents a huge waste of resources. If expenditures were expressed in costs per child who successfully completes primary school, the cost per pupil would be much greater than is commonly reported. Unfortunately, this cost would be particularly high in the poorest countries and the poorest districts. The wastage is greatest where it can be least afforded.

Behind these various developments lie common causes. The winning of political independence did not work great changes in the peoples or their society. The educational establishment embodies strong vested interests on the part of administrators, teachers, students, and, above all, the families in the powerful upper class who do not want to undermine the support given to their positions by the inherited school system. The fact that a more practical and vocational orientation in the secondary schools would often require participation in manual work makes such schools less popular than the traditional ones. Generally, what is sought is status and degrees and some preparation for desk jobs. The whole school system is thus antidevelopmental. It swells the ranks of administrative personnel, particularly in the lower brackets, and the "educated unemployed," who do not want to soil their hands.

Radical reforms are needed. First, stress should be placed on adult education. The universities should be engaged in the effort. This, incidentally, would benefit both students and teachers by bringing them nearer to the acute problems of their countries and thus giving more purpose and meaning to both their studies and their lives. The high priority of primary schooling should be carried out in practice, but even expansion on the primary level should not be so fast as to decrease quality. And the competence and status of teachers should be raised.

In many underdeveloped countries, the expansion of secondary and still more tertiary schooling should be halted or even reversed for some time. This would make it possible to raise quality standards and, in particular, to increase the number of those schools giving technical, vocational, and professional training— providing, instead of generalists, more and better trained teachers, agricultural extension workers, medical and paramedical personnel, to point out only a few of the fields where trained personnel are urgently needed.

Greater Social Discipline. In varying degrees, all the underdeveloped countries are "soft states." There are deficiencies in their legislation, providing loopholes and leading to widespread arbitrariness, particularly in law observance and enforcement. Public officials on all levels disregard rules and directives that they should follow. Often they act in collusion with powerful persons and groups of persons whose conduct they should regulate. All this acts as an impediment to policy making and policy implementation.

Laxity and licentiousness in any state can be, and are, exploited for unjust enrichment by persons who have economic, social, and political power, but in a soft state the general inclination to resist public controls will be much more widespread. This has little to do with form of government. A country under authoritarian rule, such as Pakistan, Thailand, or Indonesia, can be as soft as, or more soft than, India and Ceylon with their functioning parliamentary systems. Despite major differences resulting from their historical legacy, all underdeveloped countries today show a remarkable similarity in the main features of softness in their states. Everywhere it is clear that, without more social discipline, development efforts are being frustrated.

Corruption is a significant element in the life of a soft state, crucially important by itself as well as for its generally demoralizing effects on all social, economic, and political relations. It is not only extraordinarily widespread in all underdeveloped countries but seems to be on the increase.

Corruption introduces an element of irrationality into all planning. Since the method of exploiting a position of public responsibility for private gain is the threat of obstruction and delay, it impedes the processes of decision-making and execution on all levels. It increases the need for controls to check the dishonest officials and makes the honest officials reluctant to take decisions on their own. It decreases respect for and allegiance to the government and, indeed, endangers political stability. Wherever a political regime has crumbled, a major and often a decisive cause has been the prevalence of misconduct among politicians and administrators and the concomitant spread of unlawful practices among businessmen and the general public. A common pattern is that the new regime soon becomes equally corrupt or more so.

One important causal factor in promoting corruption is the practice on the part of Western business firms of bribing politicians and officials. This is damaging not only to development but also to the long-term interests of Western businesses and Western countries themselves. Western businesses are already stigmatized in the eyes of many intellectuals in underdeveloped countries as being associated with exploitation, colonialism, and imperialism; the observation that they undermine the integrity of politicians and administrators is now added to these sources of resentment. And it gives rise to unfair competition. But quite aside from Western interests, abstention by Western business firms from such practices in the underdeveloped countries would be a very substantial form of "aid."

Common Traits. These conditions in underdeveloped countries have one trait in common: they concern crucial aspects of inequality of opportunity. And the suggested reforms are all intended to work toward creating greater equality. The underlying thesis is that bringing about greater justice by wisely planned egalitarian reforms, exemplified above for several important fields, also would enhance the possibilities for growth and development. Indeed, domestic reforms along these lines are a far more important requisite for rapid and sustained development than any favours obtained from abroad.

But all these things concern "noneconomic" factors and therefore are easily excluded from conventional development analysis. In the literature on planning for development, land reform, as a condition for raising productivity in agriculture, has generally been either disregarded entirely or dealt with in a superficial and prejudiced way. Education has been hedged into "investment in man" and dealt with in aggregate terms. Corruption and, more generally, the soft state are usually not mentioned. A few economists even suggest that corruption acts as a lubricant in a cumbersome administration, while the truth is that corruption is a major reason why administration becomes cumbersome.

All these reforms must be carried out by the governments in the underdeveloped countries. And when economists shy away from dealing with these immensely important problems, they also meet and satisfy the opportunistic interests of the ruling upper strata that everywhere stand against reforms. That these interests are shortsightedly perceived, even from the point of view of these strata, does not make this approach less biased.

THE RESPONSIBILITY OF THE DEVELOPED COUNTRIES

The egalitarian reforms dealt with in the preceding section are all in line with the cherished ideals of the developed Western countries. With individual variations of timing and accomplishment these countries all have now become democratic welfare states. Reforms of this type have become part of their economic, social, and political history—in some respects for a century and more. Rationally, it should be in line with their ideals to support the liberal forces in underdeveloped countries that are now fighting for domestic reforms.

There is hardly a single member of the legislative assembly in any Western country who would not welcome an underdeveloped country's taking effective action for land reform, spreading birth control among the masses, democratizing its educational system, and enforcing more social discipline. Very generally the influence exerted by developed countries has nevertheless worked to support reaction in these countries. Why is this so?

The colonial power system as it functioned up to World War II had a built-in mechanism that almost automatically led the colonial power to ally itself with the privileged groups. To support its reign, the colonial government would thus feel an interest in upholding or even strengthening the inegalitarian social and economic structure in a colony. There is no doubt that a similar mechanism has been operating since the liquidation of colonialism or that, now as before, it has its counterpart in those underdeveloped countries that were politically independent before the war, primarily in Latin America. This is the main justification for the use of the term "neocolonialism."

It is understandable that Western business interests would be more willing to invest in an underdeveloped country where rule was tightly held by an oligarchic regime bent upon preserving the status quo. It was also natural that they preferred to deal with the rich and powerful there. Indeed they had to. That this, in turn, strengthened the rich and powerful in their own countries is equally self-evident. And these are exactly the groups who raised the resistance to domestic reforms or saw to it that they became ineffective or even distorted. The governments in developed countries naturally had to take into account the interests of their business firms operating in underdeveloped countries. In their aid policies they also had to deal with the groups in power. I have stressed this development as the almost automatic unfolding of a mechanism that operates when very rich countries have economic relations with very poor ones. Events would tend to take this course rather independently of any policy inclinations in the developed Western countries.

The operation of this mechanism was, however, given an extra impetus by the Cold War. The United States, which felt its responsibility as leader of the "free world," used state policy as a powerful engine to support that mechanism, especially during the long Dulles-McCarthy era when anti-Communism was the determining motive in its foreign policy. With great determination, aid was, and still continues to be, awarded to utterly reactionary regimes.

All in all, it must be concluded that the developed Western countries have not used their influence in underdeveloped countries to spur them to develop their societies in line with Western liberal ideals. Rather, on balance, they have supported economic, social, and political reaction, sometimes of the most sinister character. Thus, when economists shunned analysis of the importance of radical domestic reforms for development, they not only pleased the ruling oligarchies in underdeveloped countries but also came in line with the policies actually pursued by the developed countries.

Trade and Capital Movements. The inherited theory of international trade never was worked out to explain the reality of underdevelopment and the need for development. While international inequality has been increasing steadily for a century and more and is still increasing, this imposing structure of abstract reasoning was directed toward showing that international trade initiates a tendency toward a gradual equalization of incomes among different countries.

The fact is that, contrary to theory, unhampered international trade—and capital movements—will generally tend to breed inequality, and will do so the more strongly when great inequalities are already established. A country that is superior in productivity will tend to become more superior, while a country on an inferior level will tend to be kept at that level or even to deteriorate further—as long as matters are left to the free unfolding of the market forces. Here we face another built-in mechanism, automatically working to the disadvantage of the underdeveloped countries. As in the earlier case, it has been strengthened by the commercial policies of developed countries, which discriminate against the trading interests of underdeveloped countries.

After independence, underdeveloped countries gained the opportunity to plan their own commercial policies purposively in order to break this vicious circle. But even if their planning and its implementation were better than they usually are, they can interfere only with their own underdeveloped economy, which does not take them very far. Such an economy is very dependent on the rest of the world and, in particular, on the market conditions and policies of the developed countries that dominate world commerce and finance. Therefore, the underdeveloped countries must press for changed policies on the part of the developed countries: not only for their abstention from discriminatory commercial policies but for their positively promoting the underdeveloped countries' export interests. This is what the great movement of the underdeveloped countries that led to the UN Conference on Trade and Development (UNCTAD) is all about.

One major reason why great results have not been achieved is the wide spread, among broad layers of the population in developed countries, of vested interests in preserving policies injurious to the underdeveloped countries. These policies are mostly shortsighted. The industries where the underdeveloped countries could compete are resource-based and labour-intensive, not usually the industries that it is in the developed countries' long-term interest to promote or even to preserve at home. They are most often low-wage industries, while rational planning in developed countries should regularly attempt to keep labour resources scarce and move them to high-productivity industries. A similar criticism can be made of developed countries' agricultural protection. The blame should ordinarily not be put on the "capitalist system." On these points, it is more often the people who are reactionary and have the narrow vision.

Aid: Juggling the Statistics. Development of underdeveloped countries depends first of all upon what these countries themselves do in order to engender it. This generally accepted view stands out even more importantly when, as is done in this article, the crucial role of egalitarian domestic reforms is recognized and duly accounted for. Nevertheless, considering the desperately difficult position in which these countries find themselves, not only more commercial considerations but also financial assistance could play a significant role.

On the whole, aid as measured in real terms has been decreasing in recent years. It never has been great enough to imply sacrifices for people in developed countries. Loans increasingly have been substituted for grants, and both types of beneficent capital transferences have been tied to exports from the "donor countries." The political interests of those countries have continuously been allowed to play a major role. In this situation, aid statistics, as published by the developed countries, have been juggled. The figures as presented usually have not even taken account of rising prices. By lumping loans and grants together, the aid element in capital transfers has been exaggerated. Tying both loans and grants to exports favours private industries at home but restricts the receiving countries' freedom of choice and often considerably increases costs.

The United States has taken the lead both in decreasing its aid and in juggling the statistics in the ways hinted at. And between a quarter and a third of what is accounted for as foreign aid is simply part of the U.S. military involvement in Indochina. Making an honest account would, for the United States, decrease the official aid figures by more than half, perhaps by almost two-thirds. The figures presented by most other developed countries also contain a lot of misrepresentation, although generally not as much—which is important in that it gives a false view of the U.S. share in global aid-giving. These twisted figures then are accepted uncritically and presented in annual reports by the Development Assistance Committee (DAC) of the Organization for Economic Cooperation and Development (OECD), which includes practically all of the developed non-Communist countries.

Besides these "public flows," DAC also presents statistics for "net private flows." These private flows are a mixed bag of business transactions, ranging from direct investments to short-term and often expensive export credits, which never would be reckoned as aid or assistance when made between developed countries. Moreover, profits, interest payments, payments for licenses, etc., are not included in the "backflows," and neither is the capital sent out by residents of an underdeveloped country.

But when DAC's figures for public and private flows are computed and published, they are accepted widely as measuring "development assistance" or "development aid." This mutation occurs in scholarly as well as popular and political writings and pronouncements. Pertinent to the problems discussed in this article is the fact that the economic profession on the whole has not criticized these manipulations of the data. The experts of underdeveloped countries acquiesce in this deceptive practice.

Now that the defects of the DAC statistics have been revealed, I am informed that the DAC Secretariat will gradually try to improve its statistics as much and as rapidly as the vested interests of the member governments will permit.

Aid: Motivation. Even though the economists have been less than careful in regard to the definition of aid and have accepted and used statistics in an uncritical way, as a group they have generally favoured increased aid in the whole postwar era. Indeed, much of the economic literature on development has the character of pleas to the peoples and governments in developed countries to be prepared to do more for the underdeveloped countries. In doing this, economists have followed a pattern common to all who have argued for aid: that aid is also in the self-interest of developed countries.

Hardly any public person will make a statement about the world situation that does not contain the glib assertion that the underdeveloped countries must be aided in order to preserve peace in the world. The assumption is that reasonable progress in economic development will make the underdeveloped countries less rebellious and more peaceful toward each other and toward the developed countries. But this is an entirely unsupported rationalization based on how people who are well-off think they would feel and act if they lived in misery and saw no hope for improvement. Known facts do not provide any proof of this rationalization. If any generalization can be made, it is rather that people become restless and rebellious when they are getting a little better off, but not enough so. Equally unsupported by research is the idea that an underdeveloped country would become more "democratic" if it had a little economic progress, and that this would promote more peaceful attitudes.

These lofty ideas about the developed countries' self-interest also have been given a much coarser interpretation. When aid is justified as being "in the best interest of the United States," these interests have been defined primarily in terms of political, strategic, and military advantages in the Cold War. In the United States and in most other developed countries, additional interests propounded as reasons for giving aid are those of continued cultural domination (France, in particular) and, even more generally, commercial advantages. Economists who have been writing about aid have ordinarily listed their "national interests."

In recent years willingness to give aid has been faltering, in the United States and in most other developed countries. The explanation is, I believe, that these arguments focused on self-interest do not appeal to the common people who make up the bulk of the electorate in all these countries. It is only natural that the disastrous course of U.S. foreign and military policies toward some underdeveloped countries, particularly in Asia and Latin America, has made the reduction of U.S. aid particularly steep. On the other hand, in a few, mostly smaller, countries where aid has instead been increasing, these arguments in terms of self-interest have been given less weight or have been totally absent. Aid has been argued for more simply as motivated by human solidarity with, and compassion for, the needy. It is my firm conviction, not only as a moralist but as an economist, that this is the only motivation that holds. It is unrealistic and self-defeating to distrust the moral forces in a nation. Americans are basically not less charitable than Swedes. But, as an American writer rightly observes, when the American public appears "massively indifferent to the aid program," it may be because "its humanitarian and fundamental decency have not been properly appealed to."

Before leaving this problem of motivation, a crucial relationship to the internal development in underdeveloped countries should be stressed. As long as they show great and increasing inequalities, as long as they are ruled by rich oligarchies, as long as corruption is widespread and increasing, it will be more difficult to argue for aid in terms of solidarity and compassion. The ordinary man will ask: why do they not tax their own rich and reform their own countries before they come to us with the begging bowl? This points to the necessity for setting moral and political conditions for aid, if we want to increase it substantially. No aid can be neutral. Preference should be given to underdeveloped countries that are trying to carry out reform. If aid is given to other countries, it should be given with such precautions that it promotes internal equality. Otherwise the moral basis for aid will falter.

CONCLUDING OBSERVATIONS

The colonial power system served as a protective shield for consciences in Western developed countries. There was no political basis for the peoples there to feel any degree of collective responsibility for what happened in underdeveloped countries. When we criticize the developed countries' policies in regard to trade and aid, we should remind ourselves how very new the idea of such collective responsibility is. Before World War II the idea was simply not yet born. Now it is becoming recognized as a general proposition, and this has happened within a time period that is very short, historically speaking. Perhaps for this reason we should not feel disheartened.

Neither is there reason to mistrust the future progress of economic science in the many areas where this article has found it faltering so severely. As we all labour on with the problems and are compelled to check our hypotheses and findings with actual facts, a new, truly institutional approach will gradually be established. As in all scientific progress, new perspectives will open up through controversy and through more careful investigation into the facts.

Rectification of the present situation in both theoretical speculation and empirical research is needed for three reasons. It is needed because what is presented in our literature as facts and interrelations between facts should be true: this is a general requirement of our scientific endeavour. It is also urgently needed if we want to succeed in impressing upon the peoples of developed countries the necessity of exerting themselves, and even undertaking sacrifices, in order to help underdeveloped countries to advance. Last but not least, it is needed to give the support that true knowledge can give to the liberal forces in underdeveloped countries which, against heavy odds, are struggling for domestic reforms.

Australia Enters the '70s

by SIR ROBERT MENZIES

Australia is geologically an old continent. Within 30 miles of where I live in Melbourne, in the southern state of Victoria, plain physical signs can be observed of the Volcanic Age and of the later Ice Age. There large glaciers moved inexorably toward the sea, leaving their marks upon the basaltic rock produced by earlier volcanoes. We no longer have glaciers, and the remaining signs of volcanic action are to be seen mainly in age-old, broken-down lava that has produced an immensely fertile soil in some areas, and in outcrops of basaltic rock, particularly in the southern parts of the continent. For countless centuries no record was left to tell us whether people lived here at all, but later the aboriginal natives arrived and began their wandering existence.

As far as the Western world was concerned, Australia was indeed an unknown land, a great southern land, largely guessed at by the old cartographers. In the 17th century Spanish navigators touched on the north coast of Australia. One of them, Luis de Torres, gave his name to the strait that lies between the Australian continent and what is now called New Guinea. Dutch navigators in the same century skirted the northerly shores of Australia, while other navigators discovered the coast of Australia from Cape York in the northeast right around the west to the Great Australian Bight, which lies south of Western Australia. The most celebrated of these, Abel Tasman, gave his name to the island of Tasmania, lying off the southern coast of the mainland, which is now one of the six states of the Australian Commonwealth.

French navigators made contact with the eastern coast of Australia and they left their names at various points, but none of these explorers appears to have conceived any notion of starting settlement on the continent. They came and they went. The first settlement of Europeans arose from the work of the famous Capt. James Cook who, in 1770, traced various sections of the east coast and actually landed in Botany Bay, now a southerly suburb of the city of Sydney. On Aug. 23, 1770, the history of Australia was brought into definite political association with Western civilization, for it was on that date that Captain Cook dashingly took possession of the whole eastern coast of the continent in the name of King George III.

Even then, nothing much might have happened had it not been for the American Revolution. Great Britain, with a large supply of people convicted of crimes great or small, had been easing the burden upon its own prisons by sending convicts to the eastern colonies of America. When the Americans by force of arms established their own independence and proceeded to set up the United States, this avenue for transportation of criminals was no longer open. So the authorities in Great Britain turned to the new world and decided that they would establish a convict settlement at Botany Bay, in the great unknown land in the south. Thus, though nobody could have foreseen it at the time, the American Revolution created two nations: one the United

Steel framework of a modern building rises in downtown Sydney. Increases in almost all phases of building construction have accompanied gains in other sectors of Australia's economy.
KEYSTONE

States, the other Australia. In 1786, Capt. Arthur Phillip was put in charge of a fleet of ships containing convicts and their military guards and some administrative personnel. On arrival, he discovered Sydney Harbour, sailed in, and established the new colony.

I need not belabour subsequent history. In due course transportation was abolished and the number of free immigrants into Australia grew steadily and then rapidly. Internal exploration began, over the mountains and along the rivers. Settlement spread very widely. Looking back over our history, one can see the pastoral age ushering in the first great rural industries. There followed the gold discoveries, particularly in Victoria, the development of agriculture, the discovery of iron ore and coal and the institution of what is now a powerful and progressive iron and steel industry, the growth of manufactures, the intense development of means of transport, and, in quite recent years, the great outcropping of mineral discoveries that are in process of revolutionizing the Australian balances of trade and payments and, therefore, the Australian economy.

Modern National Development. If we are to appreciate the scope and significance of the great period of development that has been going on in Australia for the last 20 years, it must be realized that the population of the country, which in 1951 stood at 8.5 million, is now nearly 13 million and has been increasing at the rate of over 2% a year. The high rate of natural increase is, of course, materially assisted by the immigration program, to which I shall refer later. It is substantially correct to say that the post-World War II immigration intake in Australia, in relation to the preexisting population, is probably as great as it was

Sir Robert Gordon Menzies served as prime minister of Australia during 1939–41 and from 1949 until 1966. During the latter period he was also leader of the Liberal Party, which he had helped to organize. Born in rural Victoria, he graduated with first-class honours from Melbourne University. After a brief but highly successful career in the law, he was elected to the Victoria state legislature and, in 1934, to the federal House of Representatives.

in the United States during the great immigration movements of the late 19th century.

There is virtually no unemployment. On the public registers, unfilled vacancies in the whole continent range between 40,000 and 50,000, while persons registered for employment run at about 60,000. There are only about 15,000 who are in receipt of government unemployment benefit. These are overall figures. It will be readily understood that in many industries there is overfull employment in the sense that the supply of workers falls short of the demand. This state of affairs has led to an inevitable upward pressure upon wage rates as well as to much working of overtime.

Numerous important industries have been developed in recent times. To give but one example, it is not so long since the establishment of a motor-vehicle manufacturing industry in Australia was regarded as of doubtful practicability. Today the position has changed. New motor-vehicle registrations in Australia run in excess of 400,000 annually, of which a large majority have been locally produced. There is a substantial export of motor vehicles to New Zealand and various Eastern countries.

But mineral development has been the outstanding feature of recent years in Australia. Iron ore in a natural or semitreated state has generated an enormous export income. Valuable deposits of nickel, bauxite, uranium, and copper also have been discovered, and each of these either produces export income or, what is almost as important, serves as a replacement for imports. Notably, the big mineral developments, with all their ancillary railways, ports, and port facilities, could not have occurred without a substantial inflow of capital from overseas.

I know that in Australia we have some reputation for being thriftless gamblers, but this, like so many sweeping generalizations, is substantially untrue. Of all the capital needed in Australia for investment purposes both public and private, we generate about 90% ourselves. Of course, this vast total is distributed over a host of capital requirements, many of them very small and local in their effect. So when we consider overall development, the other 10% becomes immensely important, since it is needed for large capital-intensive schemes that require an outlay no government could be expected to meet but that can be provided from overseas for propositions holding out the prospect of future growth. This is where the mineral development and a great influx of capital come in. Australia is seen abroad as a country of great resources and possibilities, possessing a stable government and willing to treat imported capital fairly, that is to say, to enable the net earnings of that capital to be used from time to time not only for further developmental purposes in Australia but also for remitting dividends overseas. Further, Australian policy over the years has been not to stand in the way of the repatriation of foreign capital should this be sought.

Naturally, this has given rise to local controversy. Some people, including some who are influential, believe that, in effect, we are mortgaging or even selling out many of our national assets. But I think most people in Australia agree that, on balance, the importation of capital weighs heavily in our favour, since exports generated by the application of this capital have enhanced our international solvency and added to our international reserves. True, it is easy to imagine that at some time or other, well in the future, we might find that these investments were taking more out of the country than they were putting into it. If such a state of affairs emerged, it would not be beyond the powers of government to cope with it. It is very far from emerging as yet, however. During the past ten years, income payable abroad on overseas investment in Australia, as a proportion of net national product, has ranged from 1.8 to 2.3%. The broad picture is that big overseas-financed projects now in train will add directly and substantially to our export earnings and to local construction and employment, and that, as our economy grows, we can expect the import-replacement and the export capacity of our secondary industries to grow with it. As was said in an authoritative Treasury paper:

. . . reliance upon overseas capital is a necessity for countries like Australia. There are industrial projects which cannot be undertaken economically, if at all, except on a comparatively big scale and with heavy initial outlays. There are also forms of development which, though of undoubted promise in the long run, require the promoters to see out long periods without profits and at times to carry losses before returns come in. Our capital situation and stage of growth being what they are, it is often not possible to obtain from local sources adequate amounts of that sort of venture capital. In this our case is no different from that of many other countries. There are countries in Europe far larger and industrially more advanced than Australia which have to look abroad when really big undertakings have to be financed.

Immigration and the Problems of Race. When Australia was first settled, in 1788, the indigenous inhabitants, whom we call Aborigines, were a largely nomadic people living in a primitive fashion upon native game and the natural products of the soil. In the early days of white settlement, there were many disastrous conflicts between the settlers and the Aborigines. What the native population was in 1788 is, of course, impossible to ascertain in the absence of records.

Today, out of a total population of over 13 million, the aboriginal population has been established as about 80,000, of whom 60,000 live in the north and west, in the subtropical and tropical areas. Thus, numerically, the indigenous racial problem is of no great magnitude, though it does give rise to a good deal of debate and to constant demands for improvement in the status and treatment of the native people. But there is no internal racial problem, either quantitative or qualitative, in the sense that such a problem exists in the United States or South Africa or, recently, in England.

It is a long-established feature of Australian immigration policy that it should be based on the need to maintain a predominantly homogenous population, it being fundamental to the policy that people coming to Australia for residence should be capable of ready integration into the community. Our national policy is not based upon an idea that, in their very nature, white people are superior to black or brown or yellow people. Rather, it is based upon a recognition that they are in many respects fundamentally different, and that to ignore that fact would be to invite the acute divisions in society and the resultant problems that other countries have found to be almost insoluble.

Very few Australians would wish to reproduce in our country the political and social problems of race with which the United States has to struggle, problems that exist between people of predominantly European stock and a very large and increasingly active Negro population. South Africa is, of course, a classic example of what happens when the government of a country industrially and commercially established by white settlers finds itself with a majority of a different race, most of whom are either descendants of immigrants who came after the Dutch or recent immigrants. Many years ago the South African government under Jan Christiaan Smuts decided against integration and equal political rights and in favour of separate development or apartheid. Later governments now are encountering much world hostility as a consequence. The position in England has become so difficult that special legislation has been passed and tribunals have been set up, with what success I do not think anybody can, as yet, be certain.

To repeat, the simple fact is that we do not want to reproduce these conditions in Australia if we can avoid it. We believe the immense social problems that would arise from an "open door" policy for all immigrants would impair the sense of nationhood and of common institutions and interests to which, I think rightly, we attach great importance. This does not mean that no non-Europeans are admitted to Australian citizenship. Individual cases of persons with special qualifications are dealt with on their merits. Some thousands are admitted to permanent citizenship each year, but the numbers are comparatively small. We also have about 10,000 private students from Asia and the Pacific area and from Africa who attend our universities and other educational establishments, obtain qualifications, and return to their homelands to aid in their development.

The Organic Structure of Government. As the settlement of Australia proceeded, the various colonies that were established, first on the seaboard and then spreading inland, came to achieve self-government. They were Queensland, New South Wales, Victoria, South Australia, Western Australia, and Tasmania. Inevitably, each of these colonies developed a strong local patriotism and pride. Each obtained its own government and parliament on the Westminster system. But the time came when it was seen that Australia needed, not six separate colonies, but a strong and united nation in which each colony would be a state but the government and Parliament of the nation would have far-reaching powers and authority. So the Commonwealth of Australia came into existence, with a federal system of government that can usefully be compared with that of the United States.

Such a comparison will reveal many points of similarity, but there are two material differences that must be clearly understood. The American Constitution was, of course, the direct creation of the people themselves following a declaration of independence from Great Britain and a successful revolutionary war. In Australia there were six self-governing British colonies, and the federation, which through long discussions and peaceful processes was put into constitutional form, required legislation

from Westminster. Thus the Australian Constitution emerged in 1901 as a schedule to an act of the British Parliament. It does, however, contain provisions for amendment by act of the Australian federal Parliament, submitted to and approved by the people at a referendum. Amendment is therefore a matter for the Australian people and not for the British Parliament.

When the founders and draftsmen of the Australian Constitution were working out its form, they adopted many aspects of the American precedent but departed from it in certain important particulars. In Australia we have inherited and practice the British system of responsible government. Shortly put, this means that the prime minister of Australia and his ministers (and the premiers of the states and their ministers) must be members of Parliament, sit in Parliament, be questioned by and accountable to Parliament, and will go out of office if they forfeit the support of Parliament. The American system is quite different. Their Constitution attaches great importance to the separation of the powers of the executive, legislature, and judiciary. In Australia a prime minister who loses the support of the House of Representatives will resign and his ministers with him. This will commonly lead to a new general election or at least a change in government. In the United States the president

Distribution of agricultural and mineral resources and major manufacturing facilities in Australia. Recent years have brought rapid expansion of Australia's industrial capacity, and minerals may become the nation's most important export commodity.

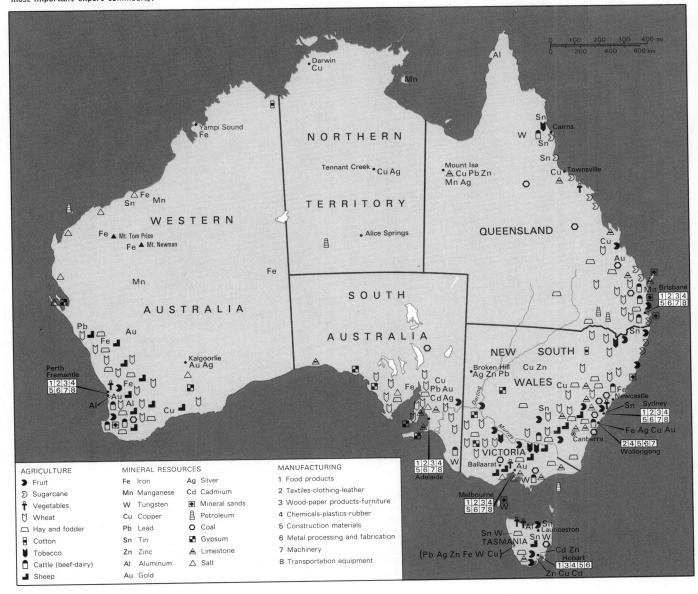

Technician adjusts a valve at the plant that processes natural-gas liquids from the Bass Strait offshore fields. Capacity of the plant, 45 mi. from Melbourne, is 17,000 bbl. per day of propane and butane, and 6,000 bbl. per day of ethane.

and what we would call his "ministers" do not sit in Congress, and for all practical purposes the president has an assured four years in office. The "merging" of the powers of the executive and the legislature in Australia reveals a fundamental difference from the American situation, where conflict between the executive and the legislature is not only possible but quite frequent.

The other material difference between the Australian and American systems is that the American Constitution and particularly its earliest amendments exhibit a distrust of officials, no doubt derived from the Americans' own turbulent history. Thus, the first ten amendments are called the Bill of Rights and are principally concerned with restricting the powers of the legislature. Like all such provisions, they are necessarily couched in fairly broad political terms: "Congress shall make no law . . . abridging the freedom of speech, or of the press"; "cruel and unusual punishments" are forbidden. A later amendment (the Fourteenth) provides that "no State shall make or enforce any law which shall abridge the privileges or immunities of citizens of the United States."

Both constitutions provide for a Supreme Court (in the United States) or High Court (in Australia), one of whose functions it is to pass upon the validity of laws made by the legislature. In Australia the High Court is strictly a court of law which applies the established rules of legal interpretation to the cases coming before it, and this sometimes requires a decision as to whether an act passed by an Australian Parliament falls within the legislative powers of that Parliament. But the court is not a political body. The justices are there not to give political expression to their views but legal expression to a decision based upon purely legal considerations. To a distant observer, the Supreme Court of the United States seems to act in quite a different way. The very generality and, therefore, vagueness of some of the provisions it has to enforce mean that there is much room for the application of social or sociological ideas held by the individual justices.

I frequently have thought that the Supreme Court of the United States is a legislative body rather than a purely legal one. I am not concerned to criticize this, for I think that it arises inevitably from the use in the American Constitution of generalities that can be interpreted broadly or narrowly. For example, an absolute guarantee of the freedom of speech, taken by itself, would appear to render unlawful any form of censorship in time of war or any statutory punishment of or remedy for seditious or defamatory speech or writing. It is true that over the years some practical compromises have been arrived at in the interests of the safety of the country and the preservation of the basic constitutional structure, but the point is that they have been arrived at by the justices, not by Congress.

In Australia the draftsmen of the Constitution rejected the idea of a Bill of Rights; except for one or two minor provisions, there is no formal constitutional guarantee of the rights enumerated in the American document. The reason for this attitude on the part of the draftsmen—a reason that up to now has been strongly sustained by the people—is that they regarded responsible government in a democracy as the ultimate guarantee of justice and individual rights. The best guarantee, they felt, was to have a parliament that represented public opinion and a government that could be put out of office if it substantially violated these rights. They felt that checks on legislative action such as we see in the American Constitution were actually undemocratic, since they indicated a want of confidence in the elected legislature and its capacity to reflect healthy public opinion.

When there is a vacancy on the Supreme Court of the United States, the president nominates a person to fill it but the actual appointment requires the "advice and consent" of the Senate. The Senate Judiciary Committee examines the nominee. As far as my observation has taken me, few questions are put to the nominee to elicit his qualifications and eminence as a lawyer; instead, much of the questioning and discussion seem to centre around his political views. And the political views inquired into are usually matters that give rise to a good deal of emotion— problems of race relations, industrial problems, and other hotly contested social questions which in our opinion are matters for the elected and responsible Parliament to deal with and not for judges whose training, for the most part, has been in entirely different fields.

Another aspect of constitutional comparison concerns the position of the Senate. In the United States the Senate has powers, such as those relating to the appointment of ambassadors, justices of the Supreme Court, and so on, that are not possessed by the Senate in Australia. The result is that in the United States the Senate is regarded as more powerful than the House of Representatives, and its leading members are among the most prominent politicians in the country. In Australia the House of Representatives, which under our system of responsible government can make or unmake governments, is regarded as the more significant house. True, the Australian Senate has broad legislative powers, but while it can reject a money bill it cannot amend one, and it cannot by some adverse vote directly get rid of a prime minister and his Cabinet.

On any matter declared by the government of the day to be vital, an adverse vote in the House of Representatives will send the prime minister to the governor-general to recommend either that somebody else in the House be called to form a government or that a general election be held. The Senate could not produce a general election unless, by rejecting the government's annual financial budget, it rendered government financially impossible. Such an event has not as yet occurred. Another point to be noted is that although the Commonwealth House of Representatives is elected for a term of three years, it does not always run its course. For various reasons the prime minister may decide to have an early election and to advise the governor-general that he should dissolve the House. Thus, in my more recent period in office, the House of Representatives went to election in 1949, 1951, 1954, 1955, 1958, 1961, 1963, and 1966. In other words, there were eight elections in 17 years.

For the rest, it is true that, as in the United States, the Australian Constitution grants a series of specific powers to the Commonwealth legislature—most, if not all, concerning matters of national importance—while the residue of power is left with the parliaments of the states. It should be observed, however, that most of the powers granted to the Commonwealth are concurrent with powers of the states, subject to a very important provision that when the Commonwealth passes legislation on a matter falling within its grant of powers and a state passes or has a law that is inconsistent with the Commonwealth law, the Commonwealth law is to prevail.

The Party Structure. Into our political system has been woven the party system. Without it no newly elected prime minister could be sure whether he had a majority or not.

The principal parties represented in the Australian Commonwealth Parliament are the Australian Liberal Party, which I had a good deal to do with establishing in 1944; the Australian Country Party (the Liberal Party's partner in all material respects); the Australian Labor Party, deeply rooted in the trade union movement; and the Democratic Labor Party, which broke away from the Labor Party when Herbert Evatt was leader of the opposition. The DLP is represented in Parliament by only a few members, but under our system of voting it can influence the election of a number of other members. The Australian voting system is what we call the preferential system. That is to say, the voter is required (voting is compulsory) to put the candidates for his electoral division into his order of preference— 1, 2, 3, and so on. In the count, candidates who have the lowest number of first preferences go out. The second preferences on those ballots are then distributed, and so on. "First past the post" has been rejected, the idea of a preferential system being that the person declared elected is the one who on the whole, and after eliminating the lower candidates, is found to be the ultimate choice of the electorate.

The Country Party, while having some special claims upon a number of rural electorates, has found it possible for many years to be an ally of the Liberal Party—a sort of junior partner —and to sit in composite governments under (except for a few days) a Liberal prime minister. This great alliance has held the reins of government in the Commonwealth since 1949. The Labor Party, which has been seriously divided in recent years, has been in opposition over the same period.

There are several other small splinter parties that put up candidates, but so far they have not been able to effect an entry into the Commonwealth Parliament. This leaves the Communist Party. An attempt to outlaw it was rejected by the people almost 20 years ago. Though it puts up candidates in a number of constituencies, it has not been able to secure a seat in the Commonwealth Parliament. Its influence is to be found largely in the industrial world and not in Parliament itself.

The distinction between the Labor Party and the Liberal Party-Country Party coalition is clear. Labor adheres to its old policy of state socialism. For many years its principal objective was "the socialization of the means of production, distribution and exchange." This has been somewhat modified by a series of interpretations and verbal changes, but it is still true that Labor looks to government as the prime means of solving new problems and dealing with old ones. Liberalism, on the other hand, believes in private enterprise as the principal creator of wealth and therefore as the chief means whereby standards of living can be raised.

This does not mean that Liberals see no scope for government action. The fact is that in Australia, and in each of its states, the railways are owned by government. Education is to a large extent provided by government. Each of the universities is primarily dependent upon government for its funds. There are great housing projects carried out by government authorities. The generation and distribution of electric light and power and of the water supply are chiefly government tasks. Indeed, one could make a detailed list of government activities that might almost lead the reader to conclude that Australia is a socialist country. But this would be a false picture. In our country, governments have undertaken these important functions because they rightly felt such activities were not suitable for private enterprise in a young, scattered, and growing country. To take a single example,

the railway systems of Australia never would have extended as far inland as they do or opened up so much new country but for the fact that governments, accepting a general responsibility for the development of the land, were prepared to construct initially unprofitable lines.

When it comes to basic production, manufacturing operations, and wholesale and retail business, however, Liberal philosophy has held that these things are best attended to by competitive private enterprise, actuated by the much-debated profit motive. We believe that the best incentive to a forward drive in all these general business activities is to hold out the prospect of profit. This does not mean, of course, that there is a sort of "open go" for profit. Income tax and company tax are fairly high. Death duties are substantial though by no means confiscatory. There is a system of industrial law which ensures that people shall be paid adequate wages, and there are an increasing number of statutory provisions laying down fair trading practices.

Labor does not accept all of these views. Over 30 years ago the then Labor government in the Commonwealth made an attempt to nationalize the entire banking system and failed only because the High Court and the Judicial Committee of the Privy Council found that it had exceeded its constitutional powers. The same government attempted to nationalize the internal air services and again failed. Today we have what we call a two-airline policy, with two major operators on the internal air routes, one owned by the Commonwealth government and the other by private enterprise. This has produced healthy competition and highly efficient aviation services.

Current Political Trends. Against this inevitably sketchy account of the party structure, I turn to trends that have been discernible in recent years. The Australian Labor Party has made some political advances. During the last few years there has been a perceptible reaction against the long Liberal-Country Party dominance in government. This swing of the pendulum is something well known in other democracies. In mid-1969, Labor controlled no government, federal or state. Today Labor has achieved state office in South Australia and Western Australia, and has reduced substantially the Liberal-Country governments' majorities in both the Commonwealth Parliament and the state parliament of New South Wales. This movement is either the symptom or the cause of leadership disputes in Canberra.

Harold Holt, who succeeded me on my retirement early in

Power shovel loads a truck with high-grade iron ore at the Koolanooka mine. Potential production from the mine has been estimated at 7.5 million tons of ore, yielding 60.3% iron.

1966, gained a smashing victory in the Commonwealth general election at the end of that year. It is interesting to recall that Labor, at that time, made an issue of our involvement in Vietnam and was overwhelmingly rejected. But in 1967 Holt was attacked from various sectors, and I think it is correct to say that in the event the government's stocks began to fall. At the end of the year a great tragedy occurred. Holt, who was a keen skin diver, was taking a short holiday at a seaside resort some 30 miles south of Melbourne. In the course of this he ventured into an ocean surf, disappeared, and was never seen again.

This was not only a great blow to his family and his friends—indeed, to the whole nation—it also produced a sequel of political disorder. After a brief interregnum, a senator, John Gorton, became prime minister. At the general election of 1969 his government lost many seats and was left with a much diminished majority. In 1971, after a considerable disturbance within the Liberal Party, he resigned and was succeeded by William McMahon, the present incumbent. The new government was confronted by many difficult domestic problems, including a serious inflation accompanied, and to some extent caused, by large increases in wages. At the same time the government was to find that, as in the United States, the long-drawn-out character of the Vietnam war was beginning to tell against it.

It is clear, I think, that the government of Australia will have quite a battle on its hands before the next election. This will be the product of three things. First, the Liberal Party is exhibiting strong symptoms of disunity, with sometimes bitter conflicts over leadership. Second, the Vietnam war is becoming increasingly unpopular. And third, the country faces domestic economic problems brought on by the inflationary condition to which I have already referred and by the grim fact that in the last year or two our great staple industry, wool, has suffered very low world prices. This has been accompanied by a general decline in the income of primary industry, consequent political dissatisfaction, and a feeling of frustration in the rural areas.

For many years wool has been Australia's chief export. During much of this time it had a world market, for Australia is the greatest producer of fine wool in the world. The demand for it was so constant and, on the whole, the prices paid for it were so adequate that the sheep farmer (or grazier) was envied by the wheat grower, the dairy farmer, and most others engaged in rural activities. In my earlier years the common phrase was that "Australia rides on the sheep's back."

With the advent of man-made fibres the position began to change. Despite the great promotional and research efforts of the international wool industry, demand and prices have both fallen steadily. Most other Australian industries, both rural and manufacturing, have enjoyed government help, through protective tariffs, "stabilization" schemes, and the like, but wool, we proudly boasted, asked for and received no government assistance. In the last few years this has changed. The Commonwealth government has decided to supplement the wool prices obtained at auction by over A$100 million. Whether this will continue to be a feature of the economic landscape remains to be seen; the government doubtless hopes that it will not. But clearly wool is no longer the predominant export staple it once was, making its great independent contribution to the balances of trade and payments and to our international reserves. Under these circumstances, it is a stroke of fortune for Australia that mineral discoveries have been so dramatic in terms of national production, development, and export income.

Foreign Policy. There are critics who say that Australia has had no foreign policy of its own but has merely "tagged along," first with Great Britain and now, increasingly, with the United States. This allegation misconceives the purpose of foreign policy which, as I see it, is to maintain, as far as possible, good relations with other countries, particularly with neighbours, but to take care that if, contrary to our wish, a war breaks out we will go into it with powerful allies on our side.

The first thing, of course, is to maintain an attitude of friendliness and, if possible, of understanding. Like the inhabitants of Great Britain, we are not good haters except in the very throes of war, when an element of hatred may prove to be a stimulus to morale. When the war is over, we agree with the Younger Pitt and with Winston Churchill, two of the greatest British wartime leaders, that hatred must not be perpetuated if international life is to have an opportunity to become civilized. In my own time we had to give effect to these views in relation to Japan. Japan had fought a war that began with the sudden and dreadful treachery of Pearl Harbor, a war in which inhuman atrocities were committed by Japanese forces, many of them against our own Australians. It followed that when the war was over there was great anti-Japanese feeling among Australians.

But, as a relatively isolated neo-European country, we saw before long that the current facts of international life must be recognized. Looking to the future, we realized that we must learn to cooperate with Japan. Here was a great Pacific power, with people of remarkable skill and industry, a country sure to develop economically and internationally very rapidly. My government saw—and the people came to support us—that a great industrial nation in the Western Pacific would be an important international trader and that, having relatively few natural resources, Japan would be a large importer of the primary products and minerals of which we were and are surplus producers. We also saw that if, for any reason, Japan decided to move into the Communist area, the western defense of the United States would be materially weakened and Australia's own security gravely imperiled.

In short, it was essential to encourage Japan to become a friendly member of the free world community. This is why we not only accepted a "soft" treaty of peace but also made the first of several trade treaties with Japan. In the event, our trade to and from Japan has increased enormously. Japan is easily our largest export customer. Furthermore, it has been a considerable factor in the growth of an export market and of local development plans for our new minerals industries, many of which have represented something revolutionary in modern Australian history. We made these trading arrangements of our own volition and not as the humble, obedient servant of any of the great powers. The policy was an independent one.

Later on, we were active participants in the ANZUS Treaty and the Southeast Asia Treaty. It is interesting to recall that after we had executed the ANZUS Treaty I was in London, and was taken severely to task by no less a person than Winston Churchill for having entered into a treaty that omitted Great Britain. My answer was quite plain. I pointed out that ANZUS was a treaty between three Pacific powers. As a result of the war and of the events in Southeast Asia, Great Britain was, unhappily, a diminishing force in that part of the world. But it had, of course, taken its full share of the arrangements under NATO and was already carrying more foreign burdens than almost any other country. We felt that in Southeast Asia and the Southwest Pacific we had primary liabilities that we must, in our own capacity, be prepared to accept.

Australian Participation in Southeast Asia. The two outstanding documents that were negotiated during my term of office as Australian prime minister were the ANZUS Pact and the Southeast Asia Treaty, SEATO. It is important that their nature and terms be clearly understood.

The ANZUS Pact was signed at San Francisco on Sept. 1, 1951, was duly ratified by each of the contracting parties, and came into force on April 29, 1952. The parties were the United States, Australia, and New Zealand. The agreement demonstrated, as perhaps nothing else could have done, the willingness of the United States after World War II to accept great responsibilities for resisting aggressive Communism. Obviously, Australia and New Zealand could do comparatively little to assist the United States while the United States could do a great deal for us. But the Americans still made the treaty. A few quotations from its preamble should be given.

Desiring to declare publicly and formally their sense of unity, so that no potential aggressor could be under the illusion that any of them stand alone in the Pacific Area, and

Desiring further to co-ordinate their efforts for collective defence for the preservation of peace and security pending the development of a more comprehensive system of regional security in the Pacific Area.

The most important operative clause is in Article IV:

Each Party recognizes that an armed attack in the Pacific Area on any of the Parties would be dangerous to its own peace and safety and declares that it would act to meet the common danger in accordance with its constitutional processes.

Article V provided:

For the purpose of Article IV, an armed attack on any of the Parties is deemed to include an armed attack on the metropolitan territory of any of the Parties, or on the island territories under its jurisdiction in the Pacific or on its armed forces, public vessels or aircraft in the Pacific.

The importance of this treaty is obvious and I need not elaborate it.

Two years later, the Southeast Asia Collective Defense Treaty, commonly known as SEATO, was executed on Sept. 8, 1954, by the plenipotentiaries of Australia, France, New Zealand, Pakistan, the Philippines, Thailand, the United Kingdom, and the United States. Having been duly ratified, it is a binding and authoritative treaty in each of the countries concerned.

Once again, its purpose is established by its preamble:

Reaffirming that, in accordance with the Charter of the United Nations, they uphold the principle of equal rights and self-determination of peoples, and declaring that they will earnestly strive by every peaceful means to promote self-government and to secure the independence of all countries whose people desire it and are able to undertake its responsibilities.

Intending to declare publicly and formally their sense of unity, so that any potential aggressor will appreciate that the Parties stand together in the area, and

Desiring further to co-ordinate their efforts for collective defence for the preservation of peace and security.

Article II provided:

In order more effectively to achieve the objectives of this Treaty, the Parties, separately and jointly, by means of continuous and effective self-help and mutual aid will maintain and develop their individual and collective capacity to resist armed attack and to prevent and counter subversive activities directed from without against their territorial integrity and political stability.

It will be noted that the phrase "separately and jointly" involves individual responsibility. Unanimity in any particular decision is legally irrelevant. The United States and Australia accepted and accept this view and are at this very time acting under it in Vietnam.

The words "to resist armed attack and to . . . counter subversive activities directed from without against their territorial integrity and political stability" are still a precise statement of the events that have occurred and are occurring in Vietnam. The parties, by unanimous agreement and acting in accordance with the terms of the treaty, designated South Vietnam as a "protocol State," thus bringing it within the protection of the treaty. When the United States went with armed forces into South Vietnam, it did so at the invitation of the government of that country. The same procedure was followed when Australia participated.

At the time this treaty was executed, some minor criticism was voiced in the Australian Parliament and in the United States Congress, but there was overwhelming support for the treaty and its implications. I am, of course, not unaware that this support has dwindled and it is now becoming the fashion among demonstrators to denounce intervention in Vietnam as "wicked," "immoral," "cruel," and "unjust," but I do not recall such statements being made when the treaty was executed. Nobody said then that it was an immoral or wicked treaty. On the contrary, its great significance and utility were freely recognized. It must be left to the historians to trace how a good and moral treaty becomes immoral and wicked when its obligations are performed.

The simple truth that the war has dragged on so long and has not led to a conclusive victory has weakened the national will and has persuaded many people that the treaty was wrong from

Drovers bring in a herd of cattle during the annual roundup. Though relatively less in value than in previous years, meat and dairy products still comprise a substantial share of Australia's foreign trade.

GEORGE LIPMAN—CAMERA PRESS FROM PIX

the beginning. Perhaps democracies expect results too quickly and are not, in their nature, capable of weathering long-drawn-out and sustained crises. I for one hope not, because, if the termination of our activities in Vietnam leaves South Vietnam as exposed as ever to external attack and to internal revolution, many lives will have been fruitlessly sacrificed, the danger against which SEATO was set up will be triumphant, and the whole position in Southeast Asia will be rendered extraordinarily precarious. This may seem a rather remote problem to the citizen of Oklahoma, but it is of tremendous importance in Australia.

It will be seen from this that I am a believer in the "domino theory," as it has been called—the theory that the loss of one Southeast Asian country to the Communists would probably, and perhaps certainly, threaten the independent position of others. We can see this in the Communist activities in Laos, in the disturbed position of Cambodia, and in the establishment of something like a "National Liberation Front" in Thailand. I know that this view is rejected in certain academic circles where some people insist that communism in Asia does not possess a monolithic character or a common purpose. I believe (but I cannot prove) that Communist China is at the back of these excursions and is conducting aggression by deputy. All I can say under these circumstances is that politics is an essentially pragmatic business and that statesmen cannot afford the luxury of treating theories as facts.

Indeed, these problems are intimately associated with the problems of Australian defense. In Australia there is a school of thought that believes our defense ought to be based upon some notion of a "Fortress Australia." This view, which sees defense as a local matter, is, of course, at odds with the policy we have pursued of having our defense "in depth," of keeping the enemy as far away from our shores as possible and of entering into regional treaties, such as SEATO, that tend to achieve this objective. We still maintain some forces in Malaysia and Singapore to assist in preserving stability and security. Our intervention in South Vietnam was made not only as a matter of obligation under SEATO but with the hard practical realization, of which SEATO is the expression, that winning the contest in South Vietnam is of importance to the defense of Australia itself.

Current Economic Trends. Current trends in the economy are sufficiently clear to be broadly described. In 1929, when Australia, in common with other countries, entered the great depression, it was primarily dependent for export income on what we call primary industries; *i.e.*, wool, wheat, meat, dairy products, and sugar. In the late 1920s a slump in world prices for most, if not all, of these commodities wrought havoc with Australia's balances of trade and payments and called for very stringent internal economic decisions. Manufacturing industries, including basic iron and steel, were growing but were by no means fully developed.

This state of affairs was to change drastically, partly under the impetus of World War II and also because of Australia's realization that it must have a balanced economy if it was to survive external shocks. Over the last 20 years the average gross national product at constant prices has increased by from 4 to 5% annually. Even these figures do not reveal the full extent to which the nonfarming sector has been strengthened, because droughts and floods and marketing problems in the rural sector have acted as a brake on overall growth. It has been officially calculated that, in this period, growth in the nonfarming sector has been above 6% per annum in constant-price terms.

Unemployment ran fantastically high during the depression period, but, under the impetus of modern developments, it has practically disappeared. Indeed, in many sectors of industry there is what we call "overfull" employment which, for obvious reasons, produces its own problems. Apart from natural increase, the chief sources of growth of the work force have been immigration and the entrance of married women into employment. Before World War II there was little popular demand for an immigration program. There was, in fact, great and understandable objection on the part of the trade unions to bringing in people to add to the work force at a time of substantial unemployment. But after the war the atmosphere changed. The Labor government, acting through A. A. Calwell, adopted a policy of substantial assisted immigration and secured the necessary support of the trade union movement.

Arthur Calwell is, in this sense, the father of the modern immigration drive in Australia, a drive that has continued under succeeding governments. Immigrants are actively sought, and their movement to Australia is facilitated by a policy of charging them nominal transport costs, the great burden of fares being borne by the government. In the last four years net immigration has been 87,000, 93,000, 126,000, and 127,000, respectively. There can be no doubt that the initial effect of such immigration is inflationary, since it adds to the demand for such public works as schools, roads, water supply, and housing. But before very long the contribution of migrants begins to outstrip the increase in demand. At least half of the net number of migrants enter the work force. Within a measurable period of time, their contribution to national production has become very large and very welcome. This is particularly true in the basic manufacturing industries. There has also been a remarkable increase in the proportion of married women entering the work force. By February 1970 the percentage of married females in the civilian work force had risen to 33.

In the event, there has been a rapid enlargement both of industrial capacity and of the general infrastructure of the economy. This is evidenced by the greatly increased outlay on building construction and capital equipment. In addition, there has been a strong growth of exports, which reached an all-time record in 1969–70, despite drought, low wool prices, and the marketing difficulties that affected most rural products. These things are not without their disadvantages. For example, the overstraining of capacity in the building industry and of the resources available to it can be seen in the scarcity of skilled labour, some shortages of materials, and, of course, a considerable increase in both wages and prices. In spite of the notable growth in employment and outlook, there has been a still larger rise in overall demand for goods and services, which has contributed powerfully to an inflationary movement. This problem is still with us, but I do not believe it is of unmanageable proportions.

But the greatest factor in this modern improvement in national income and buoyant trade balances has been the development of mining. Mining has produced the most spectacular industrial revolution in Australia's recent history. Phenomenal gains have been made in iron ore, copper, nickel, lead-zinc, bauxite, and uranium. I can remember a time in my political life when nobody imagined such developments to be possible. Take iron ore, for example. Just before World War II the J. A. Lyons government, of which I was a member, prohibited the export of iron ore for what seemed to us to be a compelling reason. The experts of the day had told us that the ascertained resources of iron ore in Australia would be sufficient to maintain our own iron and steel industry, then firmly established, for only about 40 years. In recent years geologists and the geophysicists have exploded that finding. They have discovered workable and rich iron ore over vast areas in Australia, and the decision against export has had to be abandoned. In the event, a tremendous iron-ore industry has been established, with railways constructed to the seaboard by the great companies concerned and port facilities built where there were none before.

To make all this possible, it was quite clear that large sums of capital and substantial quantities of expertise would have to be imported from abroad. The inflow of capital has continued and, indeed, without it these developments would have been impossible or, at any rate, considerably delayed. The production of copper has increased. New nickel deposits are being discovered. We are a net exporter of bauxite and are at least self-sufficient in uranium. As a consequence, our overseas balances are at record levels. The net capital inflow heavily outweighs the deficit on current account. The latest recorded figures show that our exports for the nine months ended March 1971 totaled A$3,187,000,000 while our imports over the same period were A$2,745,000,000. These figures do not mean that our imports are falling—they are, in fact, rising under the stimulus of increasing personal demand—but our exports have outstripped them.

When Great Britain goes into the European Economic Community, some aspects of Australian export trade will be adversely affected and some new markets will have to be developed. We retain our pride in our British inheritance and our intimate and affectionate relations with Great Britain and its people. But we have become a modern economy in our own right, a balanced nation, a great country of the present, with even greater promise for the future.

I write about Australia with pride in its past and optimism for its future. That it confronts economic problems domestically cannot be denied, but we have energy and great resources and resourcefulness, and I feel confident that the future is bright. That we confront external problems in relation to Southeast Asia is also obvious, but we will assist in their solution in no spirit of isolation but by increasing understanding and constructive aid.

1971 Chronology of major events

JANUARY

2

Final session of the 91st U.S. Congress adjourned after the Senate extended funding of the supersonic transport program for three months.

Steel barrier collapsed after a soccer game in Glasgow, Scot., causing 66 deaths and scores of injuries.

3

Swiss Supreme Court authorized tax officials to give the U.S. information on bank dealings of U.S. citizens suspected of tax fraud.

East Pakistani leader Sheikh Mujibur Rahman pledged to seek full autonomy for East Pakistan in the constitution to be written by the new National Assembly.

4

Four separatists were held criminally responsible for the death of Quebec Labour Minister Pierre Laporte by a Montreal court.

Lord Robens resigned as chairman of the U.K. National Coal Board to protest government plans to sell parts of nationalized industries to private investors.

U.S.S.R. charged the U.S. with "conniving" with "Zionist extremists" to interfere with normal activities of Soviet citizens in the U.S.

5

Chile established diplomatic relations with China.

Egypt, Israel, and Jordan resumed indirect peace talks with UN mediator Gunnar Jarring.

6

Hormone responsible for human growth was reported to have been synthesized by University of California scientists.

U.S. Command in Saigon announced a drive to combat the abuse of drugs among U.S. military personnel in Vietnam.

7

French Pres. Georges Pompidou announced Cabinet changes including the establishment of a new environmental ministry.

8

U.K. Ambassador to Uruguay Geoffrey Jackson was kidnapped in Montevideo by Tupamaro guerrillas.

Bomb exploded outside a U.S.S.R. cultural building in Washington, D.C.

9

UN mediator Jarring concluded a two-day visit to Jerusalem for talks on a new peace proposal.

10

Egypt and Jordan reportedly urged UN and Big Four efforts to prevent Israel from settling permanently in occupied territories.

11

Bolivian Pres. Juan José Torres announced he had crushed a rightist military coup.

U.S. Navy Secy. John H. Chafee signed an agreement to end the Navy's use of Culebra Island off Puerto Rico as a missile target area.

U.S. and U.K. withdrew from the UN colonialism committee.

U.S. Pres. Richard M. Nixon announced rules that would liberalize depreciation standards and reduce business taxes in 1971.

12

Six persons, including three Roman Catholic priests and a nun, were indicted on charges of conspiring to kidnap U.S. presidential adviser Henry A. Kissinger and to bomb heating systems of federal buildings in Washington, D.C.

British workers staged a one-day strike protesting proposed industrial regulations legislation.

Petroleum exporting countries and representatives of Western oil companies began meetings in Teheran, Iran, to discuss demands for higher payments.

Two bombs exploded at the home of U.K. Minister of Employment Robert Carr.

13

U.S. Interior Department released a study approving construction of an oil pipeline across Alaska despite environmental consequences.

14

Commonwealth heads of state conference opened in Singapore.

Truce agreement ended a week of clashes between Jordanian troops and Palestinian commandos north of Amman, Jordan.

Israeli helicopter force attacked a Palestinian commando base 28 mi. inside Lebanon.

15

Aswan High Dam was formally dedicated by Egyptian Pres. Anwar as-Sadat and Soviet Pres. Nikolai Podgorny.

U.S. Sen. Robert J. Dole (Rep., Kan.) succeeded Rep. Rogers C. B. Morton (Rep., Md.) as chairman of the Republican National Committee.

16

Swiss Ambassador to Brazil Giovanni Enrico Bucher was released 40 days after being kidnapped by Brazilian terrorists.

17

Baltimore Colts defeated the Dallas Cowboys, 16 to 13, to win the U.S. professional football championship.

Israel officially condemned the use of terrorist activities to force the U.S.S.R. to permit Jews to emigrate.

18

Bethlehem Steel Corp. reduced its previously announced steel price increases from 12.5 to 6.8%.

Northern Ireland Prime Minister James D. Chichester-Clark met with U.K. Home Secy. Reginald Maudling to request more help in curbing disorders.

U.S. State Department announced the suspension of arms sales to Ecuador in retaliation for the seizure of U.S. tuna boats fishing within 200 mi. of the Ecuadorian coast.

19

Pres. Nixon ordered a halt in construction of the Cross-Florida Barge Canal to prevent environmental damage.

New York City police ended their six-day walkout over wages.

20

U.K. postal workers began the first nationwide postal strike in the nation's history.

21

First session of the 92nd U.S. Congress convened with Rep. Carl Albert (Dem., Okla.) as the new speaker of the House and Rep. Hale Boggs (Dem., La.) as House majority leader; Sen. Mike Mansfield (Dem., Mont.) was reelected Senate majority leader and Sen. Edward M. Kennedy (Dem., Mass.) was replaced as assistant majority leader by Sen. Robert C. Byrd (Dem., W.Va.).

22

Commonwealth heads of state conference ended in Singapore with the adoption of a resolution that served as a compromise between nations backing and opposing the U.K. decision to resume arms sales to South Africa.

Pres. Nixon delivered to Congress his state of the union message dealing with domestic matters.

South Vietnamese and Cambodian forces were reported to have met in Pich Nil Pass, Cambodia, completing a drive to clear Route 4 of Communist control; Communist forces shelled the Phnom Penh airport for the first time.

23

Egypt disclosed it had formally rejected a U.S. proposal that the Suez Canal cease-fire be continued beyond the February 5 expiration date.

25

West German Chancellor Willy Brandt and French Pres. Pompidou began their semiannual meetings in Paris.

Coup d'etat led by Maj. Gen. Idi Amin deposed Uganda's Pres. Milton Obote as he was returning from the Commonwealth heads of state conference.

Charles Manson and three female followers were convicted of first-degree murder in the slayings of actress Sharon Tate and six other persons.

26

U.S. Defense Department admitted that a U.S. force in civilian clothes had landed at Phnom Penh airport to retrieve damaged helicopters.

27

South Africa reported its willingness to permit a plebiscite to determine the future status of South West Africa.

Cambodian troops launched a drive against Communist concentrations west and northwest of Phnom Penh.

Organization of American States (OAS) Council called for a foreign ministers' conference to discuss charges by Ecuador that U.S. fishing boats were violating its territorial waters.

U.S. embassy in Moscow delivered its second protest in three days against the harassment of U.S. newsmen.

28

Pres. Nixon asked Congress for pay increases and other benefits for servicemen as a step toward creation of an all-volunteer army.

29

East German Pres. Walter Ulbricht rejected the appeal made by West German Chancellor Brandt the previous day for German unity and an end to harassment of civilians traveling West Berlin access routes.

Pres. Nixon sent to Congress an "expansionary but not inflationary" budget for fiscal 1972.

30

Reports of a massive incursion into southern Laos by South Vietnamese troops with U.S. air support were unconfirmed because of an embargo imposed on news from the area.

31

U.S. Apollo 14 manned spacecraft was launched toward the moon.

Telephone service between East and West Berlin was established for the first time in 19 years.

FEBRUARY

1

Pres. Nixon called for decreased unemployment and inflation in his annual economic message to Congress.

2

OAS foreign ministers' conference passed a convention condemning political kidnapping.

3

U.S.S.R. accused the U.S. of negotiating in bad faith by refusing to include certain curbs on fighter-bombers in discussions at the strategic arms limitation talks (SALT) in Helsinki, Fin.

Clashes between Roman Catholics and British troops broke out in Belfast, N.Ire.

French Pres. Pompidou began a tour of five former French colonies in West Africa.

4

Egyptian Pres. Sadat confirmed his nation's acceptance of a 30-day extension of the Suez Canal cease-fire and proposed to reopen the canal if Israel agreed to begin partial troop withdrawals from the canal's east bank in that period.

Rolls-Royce Ltd. declared bankruptcy citing losses on a jet engine contract.

5

Apollo 14 landed on the moon after a flight marked by engineering problems.

7

Wladyslaw Gomulka, former first secretary of the Polish Communist Party, was suspended from membership on the party's Central Committee.

Swiss male voters approved a referendum giving women the right to vote in federal elections and to hold federal office.

8

South Vietnamese troops with U.S. air support swept into Laos in a move to cut North Vietnamese supply routes into South Vietnam.

UN mediator Jarring reportedly proposed his own plan for Middle East peace in a memorandum submitted to Egyptian and Israeli representatives.

U.S. Senate confirmed the nomination of John B. Connally as U.S. treasury secretary.

9

Israeli Prime Minister Golda Meir asserted her country's willingness to support the reopening of the Suez Canal to all ships and to discuss "mutual de-escalation" with Egypt.

EEC member nations agreed to move toward the establishment of a single currency area in the next ten years.

10

Cambodian Premier Lon Nol was reported to have suffered a paralyzing stroke.

11

Ceremonies in London, Moscow, and Washington marked the signing by over 60 nations of the treaty banning nuclear weapons from the ocean floor.

Jordanian troops and Palestinian guerrillas were reported to be fighting near Amman.

U.S. Conference of Mayors charged that Pres. Nixon's revenue sharing plan was "misleading" because funds for previously approved projects were being canceled.

14

Persian Gulf oil producing nations and Western oil companies signed an agreement settling their dispute over oil prices and marketing conditions.

15

Polish government announced that the food price increases that had precipitated rioting in December 1970 would be withdrawn on March 1.

Israel announced its intention to build housing projects on land seized in the 1967 war despite international objections.

Britain adopted a decimal currency system.

16

Highway between West Pakistan and China was formally opened.

Regional assembly of Calabria, Italy, confirmed Catanzaro as the region's capital and made Reggio Calabria the seat of the assembly by approving compromise legislation intended to settle nine months of unrest in Reggio Calabria.

17

Pres. Nixon indicated at a news conference that he ruled out use of tactical nuclear weapons in Indochina, but no limits had been placed on U.S. air support of South Vietnamese offensives.

Israeli Foreign Minister Abba Eban said his country's retention of some occupied territory would be a condition of any peace settlement.

U.S. administration requested from Congress a $40 billion increase in the statutory debt limit and a repeal of the 4¼% interest ceiling on government bonds.

18

Egypt reportedly was willing to sign a peace treaty if Israel withdrew from all occupied Arab territory.

North Vietnamese delegation to the Paris peace talks charged that recent U.S. moves in Indochina threatened North Vietnam and China.

Big Four meetings on the status of Berlin were reported to be moving into a "new stage."

Italian Premier Emilio Colombo met with Pres. Nixon in Washington.

Warsaw Pact foreign ministers met in Bucharest, Rom.

20

Heavy ground fighting stalled the South Vietnamese advance in Laos for the third day; a battalion was driven from its hilltop position as heavy antiaircraft fire thwarted U.S. support efforts.

Emergency warning of a nuclear attack was broadcast by mistake in the U.S. in place of the usual Saturday morning test alert.

Tuanku Abdul Halim Shah was installed as *yang di-pertuan agong* (chief of state) of Malaysia.

21

Israeli Foreign Ministry issued a statement describing Egypt's expressed willingness to reach a peace settlement as opening the way to "meaningful negotiations."

Brazilian diplomat Aloysío Dias Gomide was released by Uruguayan Tupamaros almost seven months after he had been kidnapped.

22

Egypt warned the Big Four that Israel's refusal to withdraw from occupied territories created a "dangerous situation."

U.K. Foreign Secy. Sir Alec Douglas-Home announced the government planned to sell helicopters to South Africa under terms of a 1955 agreement.

23

U.S. sources reported the South Vietnamese incursion into Laos had not seriously lessened the flow of supplies on the Ho Chi Minh Trail.

Pres. Nixon suspended regulations calling for the payment of union scale wages to workers on federally assisted construction projects.

Conference of the Committee on Disarmament reconvened in Geneva.

24

U.K. government proposed legislation restricting the right of Commonwealth citizens to settle in Britain.

Algerian Pres. Houari Boumédienne announced the take-over of 51% interest in French oil companies and the nationalization of natural gas facilities.

Spain and Tunisia announced agreement to plan to reestablish diplomatic relations.

25

Pres. Nixon delivered his second state of the world message to Congress.

U.S.S.R. denounced U.S. vietnamization policy and said increased fighting in Indochina would affect U.S.-Soviet relations.

East Germany, in a letter to West Berlin Mayor Klaus Schütz, proposed negotiations to permit West Berliners to visit East Berlin and East Germany.

Three-day conference on the problems of Soviet Jews closed in Brussels.

Yemen (San'a') government resigned in anticipation of national elections.

26

Colombian government declared a state of siege after rioting broke out in the city of Cali.

28

U.S. tanks assumed positions along the Laos-South Vietnam border to block the expected advance of a North Vietnamese tank force into South Vietnam.

Male voters in Liechtenstein defeated a referendum granting women voting rights.

MARCH

1

National Assembly meeting to draft a new constitution for Pakistan was postponed indefinitely; East Pakistani leader Mujibur called a general strike in protest.

U.K. government announced its intention to withdraw from the Persian Gulf area in 1971.

Bomb exploded in the Senate wing of the U.S. Capitol.

2

Norwegian Prime Minister Per Borten and his coalition government resigned following a political scandal.

Soviet Jews who had taken part in sit-ins in Moscow were reportedly told they could emigrate to Israel.

3

China was reported to have launched its second earth satellite.

4

Canadian Prime Minister Pierre Elliott Trudeau married Margaret Sinclair in North Vancouver, B.C.

5

UN Secy.-Gen. U Thant urged Israel to "respond favourably" to Jarring's request that it commit itself to complete withdrawal from occupied Egyptian territory.

6

South Vietnamese troops entered Tchepone, Laos, a major objective of the drive to cut North Vietnamese supply routes.

7

Egyptian Pres. Sadat said the cease-fire with Israel would not be extended.

8

Four U.S. airmen kidnapped on

March 4 by Turkish leftists were freed unharmed.

U.S. Army Capt. Ernest L. Medina was ordered court-martialed on murder charges in connection with the My Lai incident of March 1968.

Strike of British postal workers ended.

10

Supreme Soviet office building in Moscow was occupied for several hours by about 100 Soviet Jews demanding permits to emigrate to Israel.

William McMahon was sworn in as prime minister of Australia following a parliamentary Liberal Party vote of no confidence in Prime Minister John Gorton.

11

Pres. Nixon rejected a Japanese plan to limit textile exports and indicated he would support pending legislation setting import quotas.

South Vietnamese troops were reported withdrawing from Tchepone in the face of advancing North Vietnamese forces.

Egyptian and Israeli representatives met separately with UN mediator Jarring.

12

Israeli Prime Minister Meir said Israel would keep various occupied sites around Jerusalem and demand the demilitarization of the Sinai Peninsula in any peace settlement.

Turkish Prime Minister Suleyman Demirel and his government resigned following a demand for a strong government by armed forces chiefs.

Syrian Premier Hafez al-Assad was elected president of Syria in a national referendum.

14

West German Social Democratic Party of Chancellor Brandt retained control of the West Berlin Parliament by a narrow margin in local elections.

15

Heavy rocket and mortar attack hit Khe Sanh, the support base for the South Vietnamese Laotian operation.

U.S. government lifted restrictions on travel to China by U.S. citizens.

Fourth round of SALT meetings resumed in Vienna.

East Pakistanis assumed administrative control of their province; Pakistani Pres. Agha Muhammad Yahya Khan arrived in Dacca for talks on self-rule.

Mexico charged that North Korea had trained a group of Marxist guerrillas to overthrow the Mexican government.

16

State of emergency was declared in Ceylon.

Motion of no confidence in Israeli Prime Minister Meir's views on occupied territory was defeated in the Knesset.

17

Minority government under Prime Minister Trygve Bratteli took office in Norway.

Finnish Prime Minister Ahti Karjalainen announced the resignation of his government after the Communist faction of the coalition voted against a government bill.

18

Indian Cabinet based on results of general elections in which the Ruling Congress Party of Prime Minister Indira Gandhi won a large majority was sworn in.

20

Northern Ireland Prime Minister Chichester-Clark resigned under pressure from Protestants demanding stronger action against Roman Catholics.

22

U.S. command indicated no action would be taken against 53 U.S. soldiers who had refused to carry out an order to retake a damaged helicopter and an armoured vehicle on the Laotian frontier.

Argentine Pres. Roberto Marcelo Levingston was deposed in a bloodless coup d'etat by armed forces chiefs.

Zambian Pres. Kenneth Kaunda accused Portugal of imposing an economic blockade on Zambian goods.

North Vietnamese missile sites were bombed for the second day in retaliation for attacks on U.S. reconnaissance planes and bombers in Laos.

23

U.S. Congress gave its approval to a constitutional amendment lowering the voting age to 18 in all elections.

Brian Faulkner won leadership of Northern Ireland's Unionist Party and was asked to form a government.

Sierra Leone government reported that an attempted coup led by the army commander in chief had been thwarted.

24

South Vietnamese incursion into Laos ended after 44 days with the removal of all but about 500 of the 20,000-man task force.

U.K. Parliament approved legislation to regulate labour-management relations.

U.S. Senate voted to end all further funding of the development of the supersonic transport.

25

EEC nations agreed on a program of higher farm prices and modernization in response to protests by farmers.

South Vietnamese retreat from Laos . . . March 24

Fighting between Pakistani Army units and East Pakistanis broke out in East Pakistan following the collapse of talks on self-rule.

26

Finnish Prime Minister Karjalainen withdrew his government's resignation.

Alejandro Agustín Lanusse was sworn in as president of Argentina.

Turkish Pres. Cevdet Sunay announced a new government under Nihat Erim as prime minister.

27

Pakistani Army was reported to have killed more than 10,000 East Pakistanis and to have arrested East Pakistani leader Mujibur.

28

North Vietnamese force raided a fire base south of Da Nang killing 33 U.S. military personnel, the highest death toll for a single attack since July 1970.

Ramón Ernesto Cruz was elected president of Honduras.

29

U.S. Army court-martial found 1st Lieut. William L. Calley, Jr., guilty of the premeditated murder of at least 22 South Vietnamese civilians at My Lai in March 1968.

Pres. Nixon signed an executive order establishing "constraints" on construction industry wages and prices and reinstating federal support of the union wage structure.

30

Pakistan central government announced the East Pakistan independence movement was crushed.

Twenty-fourth Congress of the Soviet Communist Party opened in Moscow.

U.K. Chancellor of the Exchequer Anthony Barber presented a budget for fiscal 1972 that included tax cuts and a major reform of the tax system.

South African Prime Minister B. J. Vorster announced his willingness to discuss his country's policies with black African leaders.

31

Indian Parliament accused Pakistan of genocide in East Pakistan.

APRIL

1

Egyptian Pres. Sadat offered to reinstate the Suez Canal cease-fire and permit reopening of the canal if Israel would agree to a partial withdrawal of troops from the east bank of the canal.

Argentina announced the legalization of political parties outlawed since 1966.

2

Palestinian guerrillas announced their intention to fight in Jordan until King Husain I replaced Prime Minister Wasfi at-Tal and army officers hostile to their cause.

Pakistan issued a formal protest of Indian support of the East Pakistan independence movement.

Increase in the delivery of Soviet weapons to Egypt, especially for air defense, was reported.

3

Soviet Foreign Minister Andrei A. Gromyko urged the U.S. to take seriously a call to improve world relations.

Pres. François Duvalier of Haiti dies . . . April 22

4

Israeli Prime Minister Meir said Israel would be willing to negotiate the reopening of the Suez Canal when Arabs showed a willingness to bargain.

U.S. Sen. J. W. Fulbright (Dem., Ark.) asserted that the U.S. obsession with Communism permitted countries such as Israel and South Vietnam to manipulate U.S. foreign policy.

Municipal elections in Chile indicated a major victory for the coalition government of Pres. Salvador Allende Gossens.

5

U.S. Rep. Boggs called for the resignation of Federal Bureau of Investigation (FBI) Director J. Edgar Hoover, citing the tapping of telephones of members of Congress.

6

Soviet Premier Aleksei N. Kosygin called for closer economic ties with Western Europe and increased living and cultural standards in the announcement of a new five-year plan.

Letter to Pres. Nixon from U.S. Army Capt. Aubrey M. Daniel III, prosecutor in the Calley trial, said the president's interference in the case compromised the judicial process.

Ceylon Prime Minister Mme Sirimavo Bandaranaike announced the imposition of a nationwide curfew after the start of armed rebellion the previous day by a Marxist liberation front.

7

Pres. Nixon announced a further 100,000-man reduction in U.S. troops in South Vietnam by December 1.

U.S. table tennis team an-

nounced it had accepted an invitation to visit China.

U.S. Defense Secy. Melvin R. Laird announced plans to increase substantially U.S. military aid to Jordan.

8

Pakistani troops were reported on the offensive against independence forces in western East Pakistan.

Paris peace talks, suspended since March 18, resumed.

9

Truce between Jordan and Palestinian commandos arranged by Syrian mediators was announced.

12

Chinese Premier Chou En-lai endorsed Pakistani Pres. Yahya Khan's efforts to curb the East Pakistan independence movement.

Bangla Desh government proclaimed its sovereignty over East Pakistan.

13

Relief forces reached Fire Base 6 in the South Vietnamese Central Highlands, which had been under siege for two weeks.

U.S. Council of Economic Advisers issued its third inflation alert, warning the steel industry against excessive wage and price increases.

14

Pres. Nixon announced a relaxation of restrictions on trade with China.

OAS General Assembly opened its annual meeting in San José, Costa Rica.

Chinese Premier Chou met with the visiting U.S. table tennis team and the first U.S. newsmen admitted to China since 1949.

15

North Vietnamese chief delegate Xuan Thuy ended a seven-week boycott of the Paris peace talks.

Yugoslav Ambassador to Sweden Vladimir Rolovic died of gunshot wounds received a week earlier when he was attacked by Croatian separatists.

16

Pres. Nixon said U.S. air power would continue to be used in Vietnam as long as North Vietnam held U.S. prisoners.

New pact providing for the defense of Malaysia and Singapore was signed in London.

17

Egypt, Libya, and Syria announced agreement to form a federation of Arab republics.

19

Israel submitted to the U.S. a plan for reopening the Suez Canal.

Sierra Leone declared itself a republic within the British Commonwealth.

Unemployment in the U.K. was reported to have reached 3.4%, the highest level since May 1940.

20

U.S. Supreme Court issued four unanimous decisions supporting school desegregation.

Cambodian Premier Lon Nol resigned for reasons of health, launching a government crisis.

22

Death of Haitian Pres. François Duvalier was announced; his son Jean-Claude was sworn in as "president for life."

23

U.S. Vietnam veterans tossed their combat medals toward the Capitol at the close of their week of antiwar demonstrations in Washington, D.C.

U.S. jets carried out their sixth attack in six days on North Vietnamese missile sites, the heaviest series of such bombings since 1968.

24

Mass rallies calling for an immediate end to the Indochina war were held in Washington, D.C., and San Francisco.

Soyuz 10, Soviet spacecraft carrying three cosmonauts, docked in space with Salyut, a previously launched space station.

25

Franz Jonas was reelected as president of Austria.

26

U.S. presidential commission recommended admission of China to the UN.

U.K. government announced a new London airport would be built at Foulness, ruling out inland sites for environmental reasons.

27

U.S. Secy. of State William P. Rogers, at the annual meeting of the Southeast Asia Treaty Organization in London, called on China to play a constructive role in Southeast Asia.

South Korean Pres. Park Chung Hee won reelection to a third term.

Japan announced plans to more than double its defense spending in the next five years.

28

U.S.S.R. was reported to have proposed at SALT meetings a five-year treaty limiting missile defenses.

Ivory Coast Pres. Félix Houphouët-Boigny appealed for a dialogue between black African nations and South Africa.

29

North Vietnamese delegate Thuy proposed negotiations on a date for U.S. total withdrawal from South Vietnam at the Paris peace talks.

U.S. death toll in combat in Viet-

nam was reported to have passed 45,000 men.

Canadian Communications Minister Eric Kierans resigned in disagreement over government economic policies.

Coalition government of Netherlands Prime Minister Piet J. S. de Jong lost its parliamentary majority in national elections.

30

U.S. Air Force reported the F-111 aircraft was being grounded during an inquiry into crashes.

Canadian government allowed antiterrorist legislation to expire.

MAY

1

Egyptian Pres. Sadat said his demand that Israel pull back from the Suez Canal would have to be met for the canal to reopen.

Pres. Nixon said at a news conference that he would ask for a tax cut if it were needed to keep the economy moving upward.

Yugoslav Pres. Tito announced that political leaders had agreed on a government reorganization aimed at strengthening unity.

Amtrak, the National Railroad Passenger Corp., took over operation of most U.S. passenger trains.

U.S. Secy. of State Rogers arrived in Riyadh, Saudi Arabia, at the start of a five-nation tour designed to assess possibilities for Middle East peace.

2

Dismissal of Egyptian Vice-Pres. Ali Sabry was announced in Cairo.

3

Erich Honecker was named first secretary of the East German Communist Party, replacing Ulbricht, who resigned citing old age and ill health.

Cambodian government crisis was resolved with an agreement that Lon Nol would serve as titular premier and Sirik Matak would hold the principal executive power.

Antiwar protesters in Washington, D.C., failed in their attempt to close down the U.S. government; more than 7,000 arrests were made, a record for the city.

Vatican announced that Polish and Vatican officials had met to discuss church-state relations for the first time since World War II.

4

Mexico urged nonaligned members of the Geneva Disarmament Conference to draft their own ban on biological and chemical warfare.

Ceylon government reported that more than 1,700 rebels had surrendered during a four-day amnesty.

5

West German Bundesbank, followed by central banks in four other European countries, withdrew support of the U.S. dollar on the second day of massive speculation against the dollar.

6

U.S. Food and Drug Administration advised against eating swordfish because of mercury contamination.

Greece and Albania resumed diplomatic relations, broken since 1940.

8

Demonstration calling for military victory in Vietnam was led in Washington, D.C., by the Rev. Carl McIntire.

9

West Germany, Switzerland, the Netherlands, Austria, and Belgium announced either upward revaluations of their currencies or their floating against the fixed gold price of the U.S. dollar in moves to stem the monetary crisis.

10

Robert Bradshaw won a fifth term as prime minister in elections in St. Kitts and Nevis; Anguilla boycotted the election.

11

U.K. Prime Minister Edward Heath ordered an investigation of reports that businesses and foreign embassies were buying confidential government information.

13

Six Egyptian Cabinet members and three officials of the Arab Socialist Union resigned.

North Vietnamese forces were reported to have made two strong attacks on South Vietnamese forces in the A Shau Valley.

Paris peace talks began their fourth year.

U.K. and the EEC announced agreement on major issues regarding U.K. membership.

U.K. Labour Party candidates made sweeping gains in local elections.

14

Egyptian Pres. Sadat announced the foiling of an attempted coup and the formation of a new Cabinet.

Soviet Communist Party General Secy. Leonid I. Brezhnev asked Western nations to begin negotiations on troop reductions in Europe.

Indian government warned that the influx of East Pakistani refugees into India, which it estimated at 2.6 million, could endanger peace in southern Asia.

Pope Paul VI issued an apostolic letter warning against both Marxism and the excesses of capitalism.

17

Laos reported the loss of its last major positions on the Boloven Plateau to North Vietnamese forces.

18

U.S. Congress passed legislation ending a two-day nationwide strike of railroad signalmen.

19

U.S. Senate defeated legislation calling for the withdrawal of 150,-000 U.S. troops from Europe by the end of 1971.

Soviet Premier Kosygin and Canadian Prime Minister Trudeau signed an agreement in Moscow to improve relations.

U.S.S.R. launched a space probe toward Mars.

20

Nine Soviet Jews were found guilty of anti-Soviet activity in Leningrad.

U.S. and U.S.S.R. announced they had agreed at SALT meetings to seek a treaty limiting offensive as well as defensive weapons.

21

French Pres. Pompidou and U.K. Prime Minister Heath ended two days of summit talks in Paris with an agreement to promote U.K. entry into the EEC.

22

North Vietnamese rockets hit U.S. bases near the demilitarized zone for the fourth straight night.

23

Viet Cong infiltrators blew up aviation fuel supplies at the U.S. air base at Camranh Bay, South Vietnam.

Body of Ephraim Elrom, Israeli consul general in Istanbul, was found six days after Turkish left-

ists had kidnapped him and demanded the release of political prisoners.

24

Mistrial was declared in the kidnap and murder trial of Black Panther Party Chairman Bobby G. Seale and Mrs. Ericka Huggins in New Haven, Conn.

Trinidad and Tobago Prime Minister Eric Williams won a fourth five-year term in national elections.

25

Czechoslovak Communist Party First Secy. Gustav Husak and Pres. Ludvik Svoboda, at the opening of the Czechoslovak Communist Party Congress, praised the 1968 Soviet-led invasion of their country as "international assistance."

Soviet supersonic jetliner, the Tu-144, made its Western debut, arriving in Paris for an air show.

27

Soviet Pres. Podgorny and Egyptian Pres. Sadat signed a treaty of friendship and cooperation after two days of talks in Cairo.

Lithuanian Supreme Court sentenced Simas Kudirka, a Soviet seaman who tried to defect to the U.S. in November 1970, to ten years in prison on charges of treason.

28

U.S.S.R. launched a second spacecraft toward Mars.

Fourth round of SALT meetings concluded in Vienna.

Residents of Filicudi Island, Sicily, began leaving the island rather than remain with Mafia leaders exiled there by the Italian government.

30

South Vietnamese and U.S. spokesmen in Saigon reported 48 incidents of enemy attacks in 24 hours.

U.S. launched the Mariner 9 spacecraft toward Mars.

Mass rally in Rome called upon the Italian government to institute social reforms.

31

North Vietnamese troops were reported to have driven South Vietnamese forces from Snoul, Cambodia, a major base for control of supply routes through Cambodia.

Jordan accused Palestinian guerrillas of sabotage to undermine the Jordanian economy and provoke the Army.

South African Prime Minister Vorster offered to discuss peace on equal terms with any African state.

Cambodian Chief of State Cheng Heng proposed talks to end fighting in Cambodia if the Viet Cong and North Vietnamese would withdraw their forces.

JUNE

1

Romanian Pres. Nicolae Ceausescu began state visits to China, North Vietnam, and North Korea.

Palestinian refugees charged Jordanian police fired on demonstrators at a refugee camp in Amman, killing ten persons.

Antiwar protesters arrested in Washington, D.C. . . . May 3

UPI COMPIX

Chronology
of Events

2

U.S. bombers and helicopters attacked North Vietnamese troops in Cambodia in response to a South Vietnamese call for help in preventing an invasion of South Vietnam.

U.S. Treasury Secy. Connally presented the government's revenue sharing program to Congress.

Yuba City, Calif., court arraigned Juan V. Corona on murder charges in connection with the slayings of 23 men whose bodies had been found in nearby orchards.

3

U.S. Senate completed congressional action on the reorganization of federally financed volunteer service programs.

South Vietnamese National Assembly passed election reform legislation requiring presidential candidates to have the endorsement of a specific number of legislators and councillors.

North Vietnam officially refused to accept the return of 13 prisoners, the only prisoners of the 570 South Vietnam had offered to release who wished repatriation.

4

NATO foreign ministers' meeting in Lisbon approved U.S.S.R. proposals for talks on troop reductions in Central Europe.

7

Soyuz 11, Soviet spacecraft, docked in earth orbit with the Salyut space station, and its three cosmonauts began laboratory experiments.

U.S. Senate met in secret session to review the U.S. role in the war in northern Laos.

EEC accepted a U.K. pledge to reduce the role of the pound as a reserve currency.

World Health Organization reported 3,000 cholera deaths in the India-East Pakistan border area.

8

Chilean Pres. Allende imposed a state of emergency on Santiago Province after the assassination of former Cabinet minister Edmund Pérez Zukovic.

9

Big Four negotiators were reported to have reached a consensus on controls over traffic between West Berlin and West Germany.

Israeli Prime Minister Meir called on the U.S. to provide Israel with armaments to match the increasing strength Egypt would have because of its friendship treaty with the U.S.S.R.

10

Pres. Nixon removed the 21-year-old embargo on trade with China.

Tricia Nixon and Edward Cox wed . . . June 12

11

Pres. Nixon issued a major policy statement supporting existing bans on racial discrimination in housing.

12

Tricia Nixon, elder daughter of Pres. Nixon, was married to Edward Finch Cox in the White House Rose Garden.

UN Command proposed clearing the Korean demilitarized zone of military installations to lessen tensions.

13

New York Times began publishing papers from a secret Pentagon study on the history of U.S. involvement in Vietnam.

Oil tanker bound for Israel was reported to have been shelled by an unmarked boat in international waters off the entrance to the Red Sea.

Pres. Nixon ordered a drive to secure jobs and job training for Vietnam veterans.

14

Iceland Prime Minister Johann Hafstein announced the resignation of his Independence Party-Social Democratic coalition government following loss of its majority in

the Althing (parliament) in general elections June 13.

15

New York Times complied with a court order to halt temporarily publication of the Pentagon papers.

West German Chancellor Brandt met with Pres. Nixon at the White House as part of his week-long visit to the U.S. and Caribbean.

U.S.S.R. formally proposed a five-power nuclear disarmament conference to include China.

16

U.S. Senate defeated two amendments that would have set deadlines on withdrawal of U.S. troops from Indochina.

Canadian federal-provincial conference completed drafting a proposed constitutional charter.

17

U.S. and Japan signed a treaty to return Okinawa and the southern Ryukyus to Japan in 1972.

Pres. Nixon requested funds to combat drug abuse and named Jerome H. Jaffe to head the campaign.

Dom Mintoff was sworn in as prime minister of Malta after his

Labour Party's victory in weekend parliamentary elections.

18

Washington Post began publishing articles based on the Pentagon papers.

Canadian Finance Minister Edgar Benson submitted a new federal budget including proposals to reform the tax structure.

20

U.K. government announced that Soviet scientist Anatoli Fedoseyev, who had defected during the Paris Air Show, was given permission to stay in Britain.

21

International Court of Justice at The Hague advised that South Africa's administration of South West Africa (Namibia) was illegal and should be surrendered to the UN.

Chinese Premier Chou told U.S. newsmen that U.S. military support of Taiwan was a major obstacle to easing U.S.-Chinese relations.

22

U.S. Senate adopted an amendment calling for withdrawal of U.S. troops from Indochina in nine months if prisoners of war were released.

Bolivian Pres. Torres declared a state of emergency following reports of a right-wing coup attempt.

U.S. military personnel in the Mekong Delta were being confined to base during a massive narcotics crackdown.

23

U.S.S.R. and Israel were reported to be studying the possibility of resuming diplomatic relations.

U.K. and EEC reached final agreement on the major issues related to U.K. Market membership.

Organization of African Unity (OAU) annual heads of state conference ended in Addis Ababa, Eth., with passage of a resolution opposing dialogue with South Africa.

24

Columbia Broadcasting System (CBS) refused to give Congress material used in making a documentary film, "The Selling of the Pentagon."

North Vietnamese special adviser Le Duc Tho returned to the Paris peace talks for the first time in over a year.

25

Pathet Lao proposal to end fighting in Laos was renewed at the Paris peace talks.

26

Cambodian troops reported the capture of an enemy command post protecting infiltration routes to South Vietnam.

27

Saigon military sources reported at least two North Vietnamese regiments had infiltrated into South Vietnam across the demilitarized zone and were contributing to a series of attacks.

U.S. Vice-Pres. Spiro Agnew began a month-long round-the-world tour.

Japanese Prime Minister Eisaku Sato's Liberal-Democratic Party retained control of the parliamentary upper house in nationwide elections.

28

Joseph A. Colombo, a reputed crime syndicate leader, was critically wounded at a New York City rally.

Pakistani Pres. Yahya Khan outlined proposals for the return of a civilian government.

Richard Helms, U.S. Central Intelligence Agency (CIA) director, arrived unannounced in Israel.

29

U.S. Treasury Secy. Connally announced Pres. Nixon's decision not to alter his economic policy.

30

U.S. Supreme Court ruled 6–3 that the government had failed to prove that reasons for suppressing publication of the Pentagon papers outweighed the constitutional guarantee of freedom of the press.

Soyuz 11 cosmonauts were found dead in their reentry capsule after completing a flight that set a new space endurance record.

Twenty-sixth Amendment to the U.S. Constitution, extending full voting rights to 18-year-olds, received necessary 38 ratifications when Ohio legislature approved it.

JULY

1

North Vietnamese and Viet Cong delegates to the Paris peace talks offered a seven-point peace plan including release of U.S. prisoners by the end of 1971 if all U.S. troops were withdrawn from Indochina by then.

U.S. Postal Service was inaugurated as a semi-independent government agency.

U.S. military draft law expired after a House-Senate conference failed to agree on the Mansfield amendment calling for withdrawal from Indochina if U.S. prisoners were released.

3

Maltese Chief Justice Sir Anthony Mamo was named governor-general for Malta, replacing Sir Maurice Dorman, who had resigned following Malta's request that a Maltese hold the post.

Government-backed candidates won a landslide victory in Indonesian general elections.

4

Hijackers of a passenger airliner from Mexico surrendered in Argentina after the government refused to allow refueling of the plane for a flight to Algeria.

Egypt and Soviet Union, in a communiqué from Moscow, maintained the Suez Canal would reopen only if Israel withdrew from all occupied territories.

5

Former West German Chancellor Kurt Georg Kiesinger announced he would not seek reelection as chairman of the Christian Democratic Union.

6

Hastings Kamuzu Banda was sworn in as Malawi's "president for life."

Barend W. Biesheuvel was sworn in as prime minister of the Netherlands, heading a right-of-centre coalition.

Louis Armstrong, famed jazz trumpeter, died in New York City.

7

U.K. government issued a White Paper urging public approval of EEC membership.

West German Foreign Minister Walter Scheel began a visit to Israel, becoming the highest ranking German official to do so.

Arab terrorists fired rockets into a Tel Aviv suburb killing four persons.

Laotian Meo tribesmen were reported to have seized complete control of the Plaine des Jarres.

8

North Vietnam rejected a U.S. proposal that the recent peace offer be discussed in a restricted session.

South Vietnamese troops were airlifted into the Parrot's Beak section of Cambodia in a new drive against enemy troops and supply lines.

Ugandan Pres. Amin ordered that any plane crossing the Tanzanian border be shot down.

Fifth round of SALT began in Helsinki.

Negotiations on an EEC-Japan trade agreement were suspended in Brussels.

Severe earthquake struck north central Chile.

9

U.S. Rep. Paul N. McCloskey (Rep., Calif.) announced he would seek the Republican presidential nomination.

South Vietnamese troops assumed responsibility for defense of the demilitarized zone.

10

Three Moroccan generals and the Belgian ambassador were killed during an attempted coup attack on the summer palace of King Hassan II.

11

Chilean Congress approved a constitutional amendment permitting the government to nationalize copper interests.

U.S. labour leader George Meany indicated his support of direct controls on wages and prices to curb inflation.

12

Pres. Nixon signed the Emergency Employment Act of 1971 designed to provide 150,000 government jobs.

13

U.S. House refused to approve a contempt citation against CBS.

Jordanian Army began a campaign to remove Palestinian guerrillas from their bases in northern Jordan.

14

Australian embassy in Washington reported China had indicated it would participate in an international conference on Indochina.

Coalition government with Progressive Party leader Olafur Johannesson as prime minister took office in Iceland.

15

Pres. Nixon announced he would visit China before May 1972.

Portuguese National Assembly convened for a special session ordered by Premier Marcello Caetano to consider constitutional reforms.

16

U.S. Agriculture Secy. Clifford M. Hardin promised federal aid to help halt the spread of Venezuelan equine encephalomyelitis in the southwestern U.S.

Belgian Parliament approved two constitutional reform bills recognizing three national language communities.

United Transportation Union began selective strikes against U.S. railroads.

Northern Ireland opposition party members announced they would boycott Parliament because the U.K. government refused to inquire into the July 8 killings in Londonderry of two civilians by U.K. troops.

17

Italy and Austria signed a treaty stipulating that disputes over the South Tirol border would be referred to the International Court of Justice.

U.S. Vice-Pres. Agnew said at an African news conference that "querulous" U.S. blacks could learn from African leaders.

18

Iraq closed its border with Jordan and asked for the withdrawal of the Jordanian ambassador.

19

Leftist Sudanese Army officers seized power in Khartoum.

U.K. Chancellor of the Exchequer Barber announced sales tax cuts and the elimination of consumer credit controls.

20

U.S.S.R. stated its support of China's admission to the UN and its opposition to an international conference on Indochina.

Syria and Jordan reported artillery attacks across their common border.

21

William F. Buckley, Jr., disclosed that "secret papers" published in his *National Review* were a hoax.

22

Gaafar Nimeiry was reported restored to power in the Sudan; Libya forced down a U.K. airliner carrying Sudanese coup leaders.

Coup leaders arrested in the Sudan . . . July 22

U.S. negotiators at SALT were reported to have proposed a halt in the construction of both land-based missiles and missile submarines and the limiting of anti-missile missiles.

23

Egyptian Pres. Sadat warned he would not allow 1971 to pass without decisive action against Israel unless agreement was reached on withdrawal from Arab territories.

Uruguay's Chamber of Deputies voted to impeach Pres. Jorge Pacheco Areco for restoring security measures the General Assembly had repealed.

Liberian Pres. William V. S. Tubman died in London; Vice-Pres. William R. Tolbert, Jr., was sworn in as his successor.

26

Apollo 15, U.S. manned lunar spacecraft, was launched.

27

U.S. Commerce Secy. Maurice H. Stans warned Congress that the U.S. might experience a balance of trade deficit in 1971 for the first time in this century.

28

U.K. Labour Party Executive Committee voted to oppose U.K.

membership in the EEC on the terms negotiated.

Cyprus government reported the first exchange of gunfire between Turkish and Greek Cypriots in four years.

William J. Porter replaced David K. E. Bruce as chief U.S. delegate to the Paris peace talks.

29

Yugoslav Pres. Tito was re-elected to a new five-year term.

Comecon agreed in Bucharest on plans for economic integration and a convertible currency.

30

Japanese Air Force fighter collided with a passenger jetliner killing 162 persons, the worst air disaster toll on record.

31

Apollo 15 astronauts made the first of three planned excursions on the moon in their lunar rover.

AUGUST

1

U.S. steel companies and the United Steelworkers reached a contract agreement.

2

U.S. announced its support for Chinese membership in the UN and its continued opposition to the removal of Taiwan.

Sudan declared persona non grata a U.S.S.R. embassy counselor and the Bulgarian ambassador; Warsaw Pact countries denounced the anti-Communist campaign in the Sudan.

Apollo 15 astronauts blasted off from the moon's surface.

United Transportation Union and U.S. railroads reached an agreement ending strikes against ten railroads.

U.S. Senate completed congressional action on legislation aimed at saving Lockheed Aircraft Corp. from bankruptcy.

5

U.S. and U.S.S.R. submitted a draft treaty to the Geneva Disarmament Conference to ban biological weapons.

Sweden, U.S., and North Vietnam denied a Swedish newspaper report that a Scandinavian airline had been asked to fly 187 released U.S. prisoners from Laos to Rome.

U.S. Assistant Secy. of State Joseph J. Sisco ended six days of talks in Jerusalem in a new initiative to reopen the Suez Canal.

South Vietnamese Supreme Court approved the applications for presidential candidacy of Pres. Nguyen Van Thieu and Gen. Duong Van Minh and rejected that of Vice-Pres. Nguyen Cao Ky.

U.K. Parliament enacted the Conservative government's labour relations bill.

7

Four Cabinet members resigned in Chile in disagreements over party policies.

9

Northern Ireland invoked emergency powers of preventive detention without trial and began arresting suspected leaders of the outlawed Irish Republican Army (IRA); at least 12 persons were killed in rioting.

U.S.S.R. and India signed a 20-year friendship treaty during the visit to India of U.S.S.R. Foreign Minister Gromyko.

10

Pakistan canceled permission for U.S. Sen. Kennedy to visit refugee camps in East Pakistan.

11

White House warned that federal officials could lose their jobs if they tried to impose extensive busing to desegregate school systems.

New York City Mayor John V. Lindsay announced he was switching from the Republican to the Democratic Party.

East Pakistani leader Mujibur went on trial for treason.

12

Australian Prime Minister McMahon dismissed Defense Minister Gorton following a political controversy.

Syria severed diplomatic relations

Rioting in Northern Ireland . . . August 9

IAN BERRY—MAGNUM

with Jordan citing Jordan's crackdown on guerrilla activities.

Alabama Gov. George Wallace launched a challenge of the U.S. administration busing policy.

Irish Prime Minister John Lynch called for replacement of the Northern Ireland government with one in which Roman Catholics would share power.

13

NATO announced its Mediterranean naval headquarters would be moved from Malta in compliance with Maltese wishes.

14

Bahrain declared its independence from Britain.

15

Pres. Nixon announced a series of economic moves including a 90-day freeze on wages and prices, tax reductions, an import surcharge, and suspension of the dollar's convertibility into gold.

Opposition legislators in Northern Ireland began a campaign of civil disobedience protesting internment laws.

Massive air and artillery assault on North Vietnamese concentrations near the demilitarized zone was reported.

16

European governments closed their foreign exchanges; U.S. financial markets experienced record trading and price rises; Japanese stocks recorded the worst decline in their history.

Daniel Ellsberg pleaded not guilty in a Los Angeles federal court to charges of illegal use of the secret Pentagon papers.

17

Australian Prime Minister McMahon survived a vote of no confidence in his handling of recent dismissals of two Cabinet members.

18

New Zealand and Australia announced withdrawal of their combat forces from Vietnam by about the end of the year.

Greece announced revisions of a recently issued code of ethics for all newsmen in response to worldwide protest.

19

Irish Prime Minister Lynch announced he would support the passive resistance campaign in Northern Ireland unless the U.K. gave up attempting military solutions to the problem.

Israeli Defense Minister Moshe Dayan called for the immediate establishment of permanent governments in occupied territories.

20

Gen. Minh withdrew his presidential candidacy, charging South Vietnamese Pres. Thieu with rigging the election.

Malawi Pres. Banda ended an official five-day visit to South Africa and urged other black leaders to make similar trips.

Chiefs of state of Egypt, Syria, and Libya signed in Damascus a constitution forming the Confederation of Arab Republics.

North and South Korean Red Cross representatives established the first direct contact between the two countries since 1950.

Pres. Nixon announced he would meet with Japanese Emperor Hirohito in Anchorage, Alaska.

Life sentence of Lieut. Calley was reduced to 20 years by a reviewing general.

Proposed constitution for Sweden called for retaining the king only as a ceremonial chief of state.

21

U.K. announced it would investigate charges its troops had beaten and terrorized political prisoners in Northern Ireland.

Grenades thrown during a Liberal Party rally in Manila killed ten persons.

China issued a statement that it would not accept UN membership unless Taiwan was expelled.

South Vietnamese Supreme Court reversed its decision excluding Vice.-Pres. Ky from the presidential ballot.

Israel announced a 20% devaluation of its pound.

22

Hugo Banzer Suárez took office as president of Bolivia, ending four days of civil war.

23

European foreign exchange markets opened for the first time since August 15.

Big Four representatives agreed on a draft of principles for settling the status of Berlin.

South Vietnamese Vice-Pres. Ky withdrew his presidential candidacy.

Philippine Pres. Ferdinand E. Marcos suspended habeas corpus rights of persons involved in what he described as armed leftist rebellion sanctioned by an unnamed foreign power.

24

Emergency meeting of the General Agreement on Tariffs and Trade council opened to study whether the U.S. import surcharge was a violation of GATT's fair trade rules.

Cook County (Ill.) State's Attorney Edward V. Hanrahan and 13 others were indicted on charges of conspiring to obstruct justice in connection with a Chicago police raid in December 1969 in which two Black Panthers were killed.

Border clashes between Uganda and Tanzania were reported.

26

Netherlands Queen Juliana be-

Prisoners riot at Attica, N.Y. . . . September 13

came the first ruling sovereign of the House of Orange to visit Indonesia.

27

Japan announced provisional floating of the yen.

Chad reported an attempt to overthrow the government and broke relations with Libya.

29

South Vietnamese Pres. Thieu retained control of the House of Representatives despite substantial gains by opposition party candidates in elections to the lower house.

30

Israel announced the end of its month-long evacuation of Arab refugees from the Gaza Strip.

31

Cuba was reported to have notified the U.S. of its intention to end the airlift of refugees to the U.S.

Pres. Nixon invoked executive privilege, refusing to give the Senate Foreign Relations Committee information on foreign military aid plans.

U.S. Chief Justice Warren E. Burger said courts ordering busing to achieve racial balance in all schools were misreading Supreme Court opinions.

Pakistani Pres. Yahya Khan appointed a civilian to replace the military governor of East Pakistan.

Israeli Ambassador to the U.S. Itzhak Rabin said the U.S. was impeding Middle East peace by refusing to supply Israel with jet warplanes.

SEPTEMBER

1

Referendums in Egypt, Syria, and Libya approved the Confederation of Arab Republics.

3

Big Four representatives signed an agreement on the status of Berlin to take effect when East and West Germany reached agreement on its implementation.

4

U.S.S.R. called for heightened "political vigilance" to prevent China from extending its influence in the Communist movement.

South Vietnamese Vice-Pres. Ky's office denied Ky had threatened to overthrow the government if the presidential election was not postponed.

6

Young girl caught in a gun battle between U.K. troops and snipers became the 100th person to be killed in sectarian violence in Northern Ireland since 1969.

Uruguayan Tupamaros freed 111

WIDE WORLD

prisoners from the Punta Carretas maximum security prison.

South Vietnamese troops launched a major sweep against North Vietnamese positions near the Laotian border.

7

Irish Prime Minister Lynch and U.K. Prime Minister Heath ended two days of talks on Northern Ireland's problems without reaching agreement.

Canadian government submitted to Parliament a bill to create an $80 million emergency fund for businesses forced to lay off workers because of the U.S. import surcharge.

8

U.S. Sen. Edmund Muskie (Dem., Me.) said that having a black as vice-presidential candidate would defeat the Democratic ticket.

9

West Germany broke off talks with East Germany on the implementation of the Big Four Berlin agreement.

Pres. Nixon said in a speech to Congress that the wage-price freeze would be replaced by temporary controls after November 13.

Tupamaros released U.K. Ambassador to Uruguay Geoffrey Jackson in Montevideo.

10

Japanese Foreign Minister Takeo Fukuda, after two days of talks with U.S. Secy. of State Rogers, announced Japan would not co-sponsor the U.S. resolution to retain Taiwan's UN seat; the talks also failed to achieve agreement on trade and monetary problems.

11

South Vietnamese Pres. Thieu opened his presidential campaign by declaring he would resign if he received less than 50% of the vote.

Luna 18, U.S.S.R. lunar probe, was reported to have lost contact with earth after landing on the moon.

12

All military flights and most commercial flights over China were suspended.

13

EEC finance ministers agreed on a trade and monetary policy intended to get the U.S. to devalue the dollar and revoke the import surcharge.

Nine hostages and at least 28 prisoners were killed when about 1,500 state troopers, sheriff's deputies, and guards regained control of Attica (N.Y.) prison, held for four days by 1,200 inmates.

14

Sir Alec Douglas-Home ended three days of talks on Middle East peace prospects during the first formal visit to Cairo of a U.K. foreign secretary in over 15 years.

15

Northern Ireland Prime Minister Faulkner announced he had authorized the indefinite internment without trial of 219 persons.

16

Pres. Nixon announced at a news conference that the U.S. would vote to seat China on the UN Security Council.

Group of Ten ministers ended a two-day meeting in London without resolving their position on the dollar crisis.

GATT council adopted a report urging that the U.S. repeal the import surcharge "within a short time."

17

U.S. Supreme Court Associate Justice Hugo L. Black retired for health reasons after 34 years.

Argentine Pres. Lanusse announced that general elections would be held in March 1973, the first to be held in ten years.

18

Egypt and Israel exchanged rocket fire across the Suez Canal for the first time since the August 1970 cease-fire.

West German Chancellor Brandt and Soviet Communist Party General Secy. Brezhnev concluded two days of talks in the Crimea.

20

EEC foreign ministers decided in Brussels not to invoke immediate reprisals against U.S. trade policies.

Representatives of Jordan and Palestinian guerrillas began talks in Saudi Arabia aimed at resolving their differences.

Inter-American Economic and Social Council ended its eight-day meeting in Panama City without any resolution of Latin-American objections to U.S. trade policies.

21

Chinese Foreign Ministry announced cancellation of the annual National Day parade in Peking and denied reports that Chairman Mao Tse-tung was seriously ill or dead.

UN General Assembly 26th session opened in New York; Indonesian Foreign Minister Adam Malik was elected president, and Bhutan, Bahrain, and Qatar were admitted.

U.S. jets staged a massive raid inside North Vietnam.

U.S. Senate completed congressional action on a bill extending military conscription for two years.

22

Malta accepted the offer of $22.8 million a year to permit U.K. and NATO forces to continue using military facilities on Malta.

U.K. Home Secy. Maudling, at the opening of a two-day House of Commons emergency debate, proposed granting major political concessions to Roman Catholics in Northern Ireland.

U.S. Ambassador to the UN George Bush submitted two resolutions bearing on the seating of China; Japanese Prime Minister Sato announced Japan would co-sponsor the U.S. resolutions.

U.S. Army court-martial acquitted Capt. Medina of all charges in connection with civilian deaths at My Lai.

South Vietnamese Senate passed a resolution calling on Pres. Thieu to postpone the presidential election.

23

Canadian Prime Minister Trudeau warned that Canada would be forced to reassess its relations with the U.S. if current U.S. economic measures became permanent.

Fifth round of SALT ended in Helsinki.

U.S. Supreme Court Associate Justice John M. Harlan retired after 16 years because of ill health.

24

U.K. government ordered the permanent expulsion of 105 Soviet representatives in Britain, charging them with espionage activity.

King Baudouin I of Belgium dissolved Parliament in anticipation of general elections.

25

Soviet Communist Party General Secy. Brezhnev concluded a three-day, unofficial visit to Yugoslavia.

Italian police recovered more than 40 stolen works of art in a nationwide effort against gangs that had been looting churches and private collections.

26

Group of Ten ministers meeting in Washington agreed on a program of negotiations for ending the monetary crisis.

North Vietnamese forces launched heavy attacks on South Vietnamese positions along the Cambodian border.

Japanese Emperor Hirohito was greeted in Anchorage, Alaska, by Pres. Nixon on the first stop of the first trip abroad by a Japanese emperor.

Israel announced it would ignore the UN Security Council call for a halt in the development of occupied Jerusalem.

27

Danish Prime Minister Hilmar

Baunsgaard and his centre-right coalition government resigned six days after losing its parliamentary majority in national elections.

28

Jozsef Cardinal Mindszenty arrived at the Vatican, after 15 years spent in the U.S. embassy in Hungary.

Prime Ministers of U.K., Northern Ireland, and Ireland ended two days of talks without agreeing on measures to halt violence in Northern Ireland.

Twelve nations, led by the U.S. and U.S.S.R., submitted to the Geneva Disarmament Conference a final draft of a convention prohibiting biological weapons.

Greek military court found five persons, including Lady Amalia Fleming, guilty of plotting the escape of a Greek prisoner.

Chilean Pres. Allende announced he would deduct "excess profits" from the compensations paid to U.S. copper companies for nationalized properties.

29

Pres. Nixon and Soviet Foreign Minister Gromyko conferred at the White House.

30

U.S. Treasury Secy. Connally told the International Monetary Fund (IMF) annual meeting the U.S. would remove the import surcharge if other nations would relieve barriers to trade and allow their currencies to float freely upward.

U.S. Secy. of State Rogers and Soviet Foreign Minister Gromyko signed agreements on preventing nuclear accidents and modernizing the Moscow–Washington "hot line."

OCTOBER

1

IMF annual meeting ended in Washington after passing a nonbinding resolution calling for a return to relatively fixed currency exchange rates and nonrestrictive trade practices.

U.K. Defense Secy. Lord Carrington issued orders permitting U.K. troops to use automatic weapons against terrorists in Northern Ireland.

Stalemate ended in East and West German negotiations to implement the agreement on Berlin.

Soviet Pres. Podgorny visited India overnight en route to an official visit to North Vietnam.

3

South Vietnamese Pres. Thieu won uncontested reelection to a second four-year term.

4

U.S. Secy. of State Rogers addressed the UN General Assembly urging that Israel and Egypt reach an interim agreement on reopening the Suez Canal and that Taiwan be retained in the General Assembly.

U.K. Labour Party conference voted to oppose EEC entry on existing terms.

Egyptian Pres. Sadat was selected to be the first president of the Confederation of Arab Republics.

5

Soviet Premier Kosygin began an official visit to Algeria.

6

NATO foreign ministers appointed former NATO Secy.-Gen. Manlio Brosio to explore with the U.S.S.R. the possibility of mutual troop reductions in Europe.

7

Pres. Nixon outlined Phase Two of his program of wage and price controls in a televised address.

U.K. government announced an additional three battalions would be sent to Northern Ireland to tighten border controls.

8

U.S.S.R. ordered the expulsion of five British subjects, prevented the return of 13 others, and canceled high-level exchange visits including one planned by U.K. Foreign Secy. Sir Alec Douglas-Home.

Argentine Pres. Lanusse ordered the Army to crush a revolt by two regiments.

Chinese Chairman Mao greeted Ethiopian Emperor Haile Selassie on his arrival in Peking for a state visit.

U.S. Army Secy. Robert F. Froehlke ordered a damaging efficiency report removed from the file of Lieut. Col. Anthony B. Herbert, who had accused his superior officers of covering up atrocities in Vietnam.

10

Soviet Premier Kosygin ended a three-day visit to Morocco.

Austrian Chancellor Bruno Kreisky received in parliamentary general elections the first majority to be held by an Austrian government since World War I.

11

U.K. Prime Minister Heath asserted his government's intention to maintain control of Northern Ireland.

Minority government with Social Democratic leader Jens Otto Krag as prime minister took office in Denmark.

12

Simultaneous announcements in Moscow and Washington stated Pres. Nixon would visit Moscow in May 1972.

U.S. labour leaders pledged support of Phase Two economic programs after receiving assurances that decisions of the Pay Board would not be subject to veto by the Cost of Living Council.

Celebration of the 2,500th anniversary of the Persian Empire began in Persepolis, Iran.

13

A new arms agreement was announced after three days of talks between Egyptian Pres. Sadat and Soviet leaders in Moscow.

U.K. troops destroyed roads from Ireland into Northern Ireland in an attempt to curb arms flow.

U.K. Conservative Party conference endorsed the government's commitment to EEC entry.

14

Canadian Finance Minister Benson announced a program of government spending and tax cuts to counteract unemployment.

15

Three-year agreement to limit the export of Japanese textiles to the U.S. was initialed by Japan.

U.K. Parliament passed legislation curbing nonwhite immigration into England.

East German Council of Ministers sent a memorandum to UN Secy.-Gen. U Thant and to more than 100 member states proposing membership in the UN for both Germanys.

16

U.S. Vice-Pres. Agnew began an official visit to Greece.

Yugoslav Pres. Tito began a four-day state visit to India.

17

U.K. Prime Minister Heath ordered an official inquiry into allegations of torture of internees in Northern Ireland.

Jean-Jacques Servan-Schreiber was elected president of the French Radical Party, ousting incumbent Maurice Faure.

Pittsburgh Pirates won the baseball World Series by defeating the Baltimore Orioles, 2–1, in the seventh game.

18

Soviet Premier Kosygin was assaulted on the Parliament grounds in Ottawa during his eight-day tour of Canada.

Knapp Commission opened public hearings on police corruption in New York City.

U.K. Conservative government released its members of Parliament to vote as they chose on the EEC-membership issue.

19

Japanese Prime Minister Sato announced a new effort to open contacts with China in a speech to the Diet.

U.S. Congress received legislation to implement Phase Two.

20

Nobel Peace Prize was awarded to West German Chancellor Brandt for his efforts to lessen East-West tensions.

Cambodian Premier Lon Nol declared a state of emergency and named a new government to rule by "ordinance."

U.S. presidential adviser Kissinger arrived in Peking for talks to arrange an agenda and itinerary for Pres. Nixon's China visit.

Denmark imposed a 10% tariff surcharge to improve its balance of payments position.

21

Pres. Nixon announced his surprise choices of Lewis F. Powell, Jr., and Asst. U.S. Atty. Gen. William H. Rehnquist as associate justices of the U.S. Supreme Court.

UN Secy.-Gen. U Thant offered his good offices to help avoid an India-Pakistan conflict.

22

U.S.-U.S.S.R. agreement on preventing accidents at sea was announced following 11 days of talks in Moscow.

24

South African police staged predawn searches of 115 homes of prominent persons, many critical of apartheid policies.

25

UN General Assembly approved, 76–35, an Albanian resolution calling for the admission of China to the UN and expulsion of Taiwan; earlier the assembly defeated a U.S. resolution to call expulsion of Taiwan an important question requiring a two-thirds majority vote.

Pakistan reported killing 501 "Indians and Indian agents" in East Pakistan.

26

Israeli Prime Minister Meir told the Knesset that the proposal made by U.S. Secy. of State Rogers at the UN constituted a switch of U.S. support to the Egyptian position on reopening the Suez Canal.

2,500th anniversary of the Persian Empire . . . October 12

KEYSTONE

Soviet Premier Kosygin received a warm welcome on his arrival in Cuba.

EEC agriculture ministers concluded two days of meetings without agreeing on implementation of the Mansholt plan for agricultural reform.

27

Turkish Pres. Sunay refused to accept the resignation of the government of Prime Minister Erim.

Congo (Kinshasa) government announced the country was to be known as the Republic of Zaire.

28

U.K. Parliament approved plans for membership in the EEC by 112-vote margin.

Irish troops confronted U.K. troops attempting to blow up a bridge on the Ireland-Northern Ireland border.

Yugoslav Pres. Tito received a warm official welcome on his first state visit to the U.S.

29

U.S. Senate refused to authorize funds to continue the foreign aid program, effectively ending the program.

U.S.S.R. military delegation arrived in India to study defense needs in fighting with Pakistan.

Finnish coalition government of Prime Minister Karjalainen resigned in a dispute among coalition partners over agricultural policy.

30

Major document of Franco-Soviet cooperation and European détente was signed at Versailles by Soviet Communist Party General Secy. Brezhnev and French Pres. Pompidou.

NOVEMBER

1

South African court sentenced the Anglican dean of Johannesburg cathedral, Gonville A. ffrench-Beytagh, to five years in prison on charges of subversion.

Egyptian Pres. Sadat took personal command of his country's armed forces.

3

Northern Ireland announced the arming of the Royal Ulster Constabulary reserve forces, which had threatened to strike in the face of mounting terrorist attacks.

4

Romanian Pres. Ceausescu announced a program to strengthen Communist Party control.

Pittsburgh Pirates win World Series . . . October 17
UPI COMPIX

5

Cuban sugar technicians returned to Havana ten days after landing unannounced in New Orleans, La., to attend a conference for which they had been denied visas.

EEC foreign ministers agreed to hold a summit conference to include candidate members to spur economic and monetary union and seek a common front on major international issues.

6

Roman Catholic Synod of Bishops ended in Rome having generally reaffirmed papal policies.

U.S. Atomic Energy Commission conducted a controversial hydrogen bomb test on Amchitka Island hours after a special session of the U.S. Supreme Court denied an appeal for an injunction against the test.

Turkish Justice Party reversed its decision to withdraw from the Cabinet, ending a government crisis.

7

Belgian coalition government retained its majority in parliamentary elections, although militant French- and Flemish-language parties gained substantially.

Four African presidents representing an OAU committee ended talks in Israel and Egypt in an effort to reach a Middle East solution.

8

Reports of a reshuffle of the Chinese leadership raised speculation that Defense Minister Lin Piao had been ousted and possibly slain.

Philippine opposition Liberal Party scored several victories in midterm elections marked by violence.

U.S. announced the cancellation of licenses for export of military equipment to Pakistan.

9

U.K. troops swept through three Roman Catholic sections of Belfast, arresting 43 suspected IRA members.

10

U.S. Senate ratified the treaty returning Okinawa and the southern Ryukyus to Japan.

Cuban Prime Minister Fidel Castro arrived in Chile on his first visit to a Latin-American country since 1959.

11

Chilean Pres. Allende sent Congress a constitutional reform bill that included replacement of the two-house Congress with a unicameral "People's Assembly" and increased presidential powers.

Japan reported its first official overture to open communications with China had been spurned by Chinese Premier Chou.

Pres. Nixon nominated Earl L. Butz as secretary of agriculture to replace Hardin, who had resigned, and announced that plans to reorganize the department had been dropped.

12

Pres. Nixon announced U.S. troops in Vietnam would be reduced by 45,000 additional men by February 1972.

Joint declaration ending a two-day visit to the U.K. by French Foreign Minister Maurice Schumann announced a "new and yet closer relationship" between the two countries.

13

Military sources in Saigon said the North Vietnamese were massing supplies for a major push down the Ho Chi Minh Trail into Laos and Cambodia.

Indian Prime Minister Gandhi completed a three-week tour of Western nations, calling problems with Pakistan "less and less tolerable."

Mariner 9, unmanned U.S. spacecraft, went into orbit around Mars, the first man-made object to orbit another planet.

14

Phase Two of the new U.S. economic program went into effect.

15

Chinese delegation headed by Deputy Foreign Minister Chiao Kuan-hua took their seats in the UN General Assembly.

South Vietnamese Pres. Thieu announced an economic reform program that included a devaluation of the piastre.

Sixth round of SALT opened in Vienna.

French counterespionage official and one of his former aides were indicted by a U.S. grand jury on charges of conspiracy to smuggle $12 million worth of heroin into the U.S.

16

U.K. commission cleared U.K. troops of charges of torturing and brainwashing internees in Northern Ireland but reported some evidence of ill treatment.

17

Pres. Nixon signed a weapons procurement authorization bill stating he would disregard the Mansfield amendment attached to it.

Thai Prime Minister Thanom Kittikachorn and a "revolutionary" council seized full power in a bloodless coup d'etat.

18

U.S. Congress extended until December 8 funding for the foreign aid program, which had expired at midnight November 15.

Indian Prime Minister Gandhi reported she had rejected UN Secy.-Gen. U Thant's proposal to help relieve tensions between India and Pakistan saying Thant should work toward ending Pakistan's civil war.

19

Pres. Nixon received a chilly response from the AFL-CIO convention in Bal Harbour, Fla., as he sought labour support for his new economic policy.

Israeli Prime Minister Meir said she would "demand" that the U.S. supply Israel with more jet fighter-bombers to correct the military imbalance in the Middle East.

20

Adolf von Thadden resigned the chairmanship of West Germany's extreme-right National Democratic Party.

Egyptian Pres. Sadat warned his troops that war with Israel was "at hand."

22

Pakistan claimed Indian divisions had launched a four-pronged attack on East Pakistan.

South Vietnamese troops began a major drive into eastern Cambodia.

U.S. announced it had suspended its Middle East mediation efforts.

23

Rhodesian Prime Minister Ian Smith and U.K. Foreign Secy. Sir Alec Douglas-Home reached an agreement settling Rhodesian independence.

U.K. Chancellor of the Exchequer Barber announced accelerated public works spending aimed at curbing the highest unemployment rate in 32 years.

24

Soviet Premier Kosygin presented a new five-year economic plan to the Supreme Soviet stressing rivalry with the U.S.

Japanese lower house approved the Okinawa treaty, adding resolutions to reduce U.S. military bases and ban nuclear weapons on the island.

Hijacker parachuted from a U.S. jetliner over Washington state after collecting a $200,000 ransom.

25

Denmark and Norway became the first NATO members to establish full diplomatic relations with North Vietnam.

26

GATT annual conference ended in Geneva after failing to agree on a 1972 program.

Czechoslovak voters approved a slate of unopposed candidates in the first parliamentary elections held since 1964.

27

Three men were killed in more than 30 incidents of violence throughout Northern Ireland.

Israel agreed to the reactivation of UN envoy Jarring's Middle East peace mission.

Chilean congressional committee rejected Pres. Allende's reform legislation and moved to prevent Allende from dissolving the Congress.

28

Jordanian Prime Minister Tal was shot to death in Cairo by Palestinian guerrillas.

Juan Maria Bordaberry won a narrow victory in Uruguayan presidential elections as voters also rejected a constitutional amendment to permit Pres. Pacheco to succeed himself.

29

Soviet Foreign Minister Gromyko was reported to have insisted in talks with visiting West German Foreign Minister Scheel that West Germany must ratify the 1970 Moscow pact simultaneously with Big Four ratification of the 1971 agreement on Berlin.

Simultaneous announcements in Washington and Peking said Pres. Nixon would begin his China visit on Feb. 21, 1972.

Jordanian King Husain appointed Ahmed al-Lawzi as prime minister.

30

Iranian forces seized Abu Musa and two British protectorate islands, Greater and Lesser Tumbs, in the Persian Gulf; Iraq broke diplomatic relations with Iran and the U.K. because of the take-over.

DECEMBER

2

Cambodian defenses near Phnom Penh were reported to have collapsed in the face of a heavy North Vietnamese thrust.

Israeli Prime Minister Meir conferred with Pres. Nixon at the White House.

U.K. committee recommended doubling Queen Elizabeth II's allowance and increasing annuities to other members of the royal family.

Six Persian Gulf sheikhdoms proclaimed their independence as the Union of Arab Emirates.

3

India declared that full-scale war with Pakistan had begun in response to Pakistani air strikes on Indian airfields.

4

Two Germanys announced agreement on transit arrangements through East Germany to Berlin; parallel talks on visiting rights to East Berlin were deadlocked.

6

India recognized the Bangla Desh rebel government as the government of East Pakistan; Pakistan broke diplomatic relations with India.

Canadian Prime Minister Trudeau met with Pres. Nixon at the White House in the first of several meetings scheduled between Nixon and Western leaders prior to his planned trips to China and the U.S.S.R.

U.S. Senate confirmed the nomination of Powell to the Supreme Court.

UN debate on the India-Pakistan war was transferred to the General Assembly after two U.S.S.R. vetoes had deadlocked Security Council action.

South Korean Pres. Park proclaimed a national emergency to cope with a possible invasion by North Korea.

7

India reported its troops had taken the city of Jessore, East Pakistan, after heavy fighting, giving India control of half of East Pakistan.

Pakistani troops surrender to Indian Army . . . December 16

European NATO members announced in Brussels that they would increase their national defense budgets by over $1 billion.

U.S.S.R. announced a capsule launched from its Mars 3 space probe on December 2 had soft-landed on Mars.

All charges were dropped for lack of evidence against 20 defendants in Kent (O.) State University trials.

8

Chilean Pres. Allende announced the government would take control of food distribution in the wake of demonstrations protesting food shortages.

9

Former Egyptian Vice-Pres. Sabry and three others were sentenced to death for conspiring to seize power; Pres. Sadat commuted the sentences to life imprisonment.

Pres. Nixon vetoed legislation to set up a national system of day-care centres for children.

10

West Germany agreed to increase its payments toward maintaining U.S. troops in West Germany.

U.S. Senate confirmed the appointment of Rehnquist to the Supreme Court.

Pres. Nixon signed the tax reduction bill requested under the New Economic Policy.

Portugal and the U.S. announced an agreement permitting continued U.S. use of air and naval bases in the Azores.

11

Two agreements implementing the Big Four Berlin settlement were initialed by East Germany, West Germany, and West Berlin.

Turkish Prime Minister Erim named a new Cabinet, ending a political crisis sparked by the resignations of several Cabinet members critical of the government's ability to implement reforms.

EEC Council of Ministers said it would not negotiate trade conces-

sions until after the U.S. dollar had been devalued and currencies realigned.

12

U.S. naval task force was reported in the Bay of Bengal as the U.S.S.R. was reportedly increasing its naval strength in the Indian Ocean.

Northern Ireland Unionist Party Sen. John Barnhill was killed and his home bombed.

U.K., Ireland, and Denmark reached agreement with the EEC on fishing rights in the last of the major negotiations leading to their EEC membership.

China released from prison two U.S. citizens and reduced the sentence of a third.

13

UN General Assembly approved a resolution calling on Israel to withdraw from occupied territory and for the resumption of indirect negotiations by UN envoy Jarring; U.S.S.R. vetoed for the third time a Security Council resolution aimed at halting India-Pakistan fighting.

West German Chancellor Brandt submitted for legislative ratification the nonaggression treaties signed with the U.S.S.R. and Poland in 1970.

14

East Pakistan government in Dacca resigned, dissociating itself from any further actions of the central Pakistan government.

Pres. Nixon, in joint statement following talks in the Azores with French Pres. Pompidou, expressed U.S. willingness to devalue the dollar.

U.S. Congress completed action on the Economic Stabilization Act extending presidential authority over wages, prices, and rents until April 1973.

15

Pakistani Foreign Minister Zulfikar Ali Bhutto walked out of the UN Security Council protesting its failure to take effective action to halt the India-Pakistan war.

U.S.-based freighter radioed it was sinking in Bahamian waters

after being fired on and rammed by a Cuban gunboat.

16

Pakistani Army commander in East Pakistan surrendered to Indian troops; India ordered a unilateral cease-fire on the West Pakistan front.

China filed a protest charging India with incursions into Tibet.

17

Pakistan accepted a cease-fire along its West Pakistan-India border, ending 15 days of war.

First session of the 92nd U.S. Congress adjourned after passage of a resolution continuing foreign aid funding until Feb. 22, 1972.

Canadian Parliament passed major tax reform legislation after six months of debate.

18

Pres. Nixon announced that agreement on a general realignment of currency exchange rates had been concluded by the Group of Ten ministers meeting in Washington.

North Vietnamese Foreign Ministry claimed three U.S. planes had been shot down over North Vietnam.

Greek Prime Minister Georgios Papadopoulos announced that martial law, in force since the 1967 coup, would be eased beginning Jan. 1, 1972.

20

Pakistani Pres. Yahya Khan resigned and was replaced immediately by Bhutto, returning Pakistan to civilian rule for the first time since 1958.

North Vietnamese troops were reported to have captured the Plaine des Jarres in northern Laos.

Pres. Nixon, in Bermuda for talks with U.K. Prime Minister Heath, announced termination of the U.S. 10% import surcharge.

21

UN Security Council nominated Austrian Kurt Waldheim to succeed Secy.-Gen. U Thant when China abstained after casting vetoes in two earlier votes.

22

East Pakistani leader Mujibur

was released from prison and transferred to house arrest in West Pakistan.

24

Giovanni Leone was elected sixth president of Italy on the 23rd ballot after a 15-day deadlock.

26

U.S. aircraft launched massive, sustained air strikes against North Vietnamese military installations.

Soviet trade mission employee Anatoly Chebotarev, who defected to the West in Brussels in October, returned to the U.S.S.R. from the U.S.

27

Pakistani Pres. Bhutto met with East Pakistani leader Mujibur.

28

Pres. Nixon signed legislation requiring able-bodied welfare recipients to register for jobs or job training.

North Vietnamese and Pathet Lao forces attained virtual control of the Boloven Plateau in southern Laos.

29

U.K. Foreign Office ordered the withdrawal of U.K. forces from Malta rather than pay an additional $11 million demanded by the Maltese government.

Two-day meeting in Key Biscayne, Fla., ended between Pres. Nixon and West German Chancellor Brandt.

Italian Pres. Leone rejected the resignation of Premier Emilio Colombo and his Cabinet.

30

U.S. Command in Saigon announced the end of intensified bombing of North Vietnam after five days; South Vietnamese offensive in eastern Cambodia ended after 39 days.

Anglican-Roman Catholic International Commission announced agreement on essential teachings about the Eucharist.

31

Maltese Prime Minister Mintoff extended to Jan. 15, 1972, the deadline for the withdrawal of U.K. forces from the island.

1971

Advertising

Sensitive as always to the general economic climate, the advertising business continued to reflect the lack of confidence brought about by the world trade recession, and growth was not sustained at the usual high level during 1970 and 1971. Western industrial countries, already troubled by inflationary pressures, were shaken by the world monetary crisis that followed U.S. efforts to correct the imbalance of the dollar with other currencies, notably the Japanese yen. Difficulties of companies of the stature of Rolls-Royce, uncertainties attending Britain's entry into the EEC, and continuing labour unrest on both sides of the Atlantic did nothing to help.

According to the latest figures available, in 1970 the 100 largest advertisers in the U.S. cut advertising and promotion expenditures by nearly one-half of 1%, from the 1969 figure of $4,640,000,000 to $4,620,000,-000 (see below). In Britain during the same period, total expenditure rose by only £10 million, an increase of less than 2% at a time when the price level went up by 8%. Net profits of advertising agencies before taxes were down to 1.5% on turnover in 1970, as against 1.79% in 1969. Pretax profits fell to 9.28%, compared with 11.2%. Gross income on turnover rose to 16.17% from 15.96%, and the number of employees was 15,600, or 1,600 fewer than a year earlier. However, forecasts for 1971 suggested that there would be an improvement.

The advertising business faced other problems. As part of the general selling process, it had come under increasing pressure from the consumer protection movement, whose growing strength led to an awareness among advertisers, media owners, and agencies of the need for more self-discipline. There was concern that failure to act would encourage the introduction of arbitrary legislation that could work against the interests of both advertisers and consumers. The

Advertisement urging withdrawal of U.S. forces from Vietnam appeared in many publications in the spring of 1971.

MEDALS FOR PEACE
Thousands of Viet Nam veterans marched in Washington this April—against the war. Hundreds turned in their hard-won medals. Because medals were meant to be worn proudly and these men could no longer feel proud. Could anything tell us more loudly and clearly that it's time not just to "wind down" the war, but to end it completely?

Strike one blow for peace. Write or wire your Congressman. Urge him to work for total withdrawal this year.

COURTESY, HELP UNSELL THE WAR

Aden:
see Yemen, People's Democratic Republic of

British Advertising Standards Authority and the European Association of Advertising Agencies were especially active in this regard, mounting presentations in the U.S., France, Belgium, Switzerland, Finland, Lebanon, and South Africa during the year.

The main purpose was to encourage the enforcement of codes of practice whereby truth and accuracy in advertisements were assured by means of voluntary control within the industry. Following one of these presentations, the French Bureau de Vérification de la Publicité was reconstituted. In the U.S. a new self-regulatory body, the National Advertising Review Board, was established with Charles W. Yost, former U.S. ambassador to the UN, as its chairman. The NARB was to look into complaints of deceptive advertising from the public, media, and manufacturers.

The Council of Europe's working party on "misleading advertising," which was set up in 1968, prepared a report; a second committee was still examining consumer education and information. In January 1971 the Consultative Assembly adopted a recommendation, prepared by the Legal Affairs Committee, on the legal protection of consumers; it called for a full and comparative study of the subject in member states with a view to arriving at common measures and standards. In India, which might have been thought to be far removed from these pressures, the minister for information told the seventh Asian Advertising Conference, meeting in New Delhi, "I would earnestly call upon you who are experts in the field of advertising to work at this aspect of the problem so that a socially meaningful code of conduct may be evolved by you for rigid adherence by all advertisers."

The threat of taxation was another source of anxiety. On July 1 the Swedish government introduced a controversial tax on advertisements in the press, the purpose of which was partly to subsidize publications handicapped by lack of advertising revenue. The Vatican, in a pastoral instruction on the subject of social communications, appeared to support the Swedish view in recommending that "a variety of independent means of social communication must therefore be carefully safeguarded even if this requires legislative action. This will ensure that there is an equitable distribution of advertising revenue among the most deserving media of communication and prevent the lion's share from going to those that are already the most powerful." Earlier, the Mexican government established a precedent by including, for taxation purposes, advertising within the nomenclature of investment. The American Advertising Federation reported that tax measures involving advertising were pending in a number of states, and radio and television had been included in Indiana's 0.5% gross receipts tax.

J. Walter Thompson, with worldwide billings of $764 million in 1970, maintained the position it had held since World War II as the world's leading advertising agency. It was followed in 1970 by McCann-Erickson ($546.9 million); Dentsu Advertising ($522.3 million); Young & Rubicam ($520.2 million); Ted Bates & Co. ($414.2 million); Leo Burnett International ($389 million); Benson Needham Univas ($357.4 million); Batten Barton Durstine & Osborn ($350.4 million); SSC & B-Lintas International ($318.6 million); and Doyle Dane Bernbach ($291.4 million).

In the 1960s there had been a consolidation of television as an advertising medium in Britain and Western Europe; by the end of the decade only Belgium, Sweden, and Denmark were without commercial TV

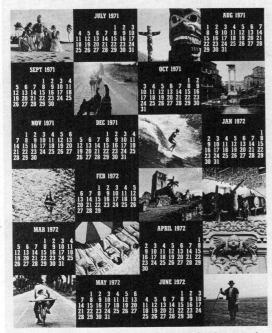

Pick the time. Pick the place.

Your choice. Go on active duty up to six months after you enlist. Head for 16 months in either Hawaii, Europe, Alaska or Panama. Time and place guaranteed. **Today's Army wants to join you.**

U.S. Army-sponsored advertisement attempts to stimulate enlistments by stressing the glamour of foreign travel as pressures to end the draft increased in 1971.

service. Britain, Belgium, Denmark, Finland, and Switzerland still had no commercial radio. The distribution of advertising among the various media in Western European countries other than Britain in 1970 is shown in the table; in comparing the figures, it should be kept in mind that much depends on availability and restrictions on usage rather than on effectiveness.

The growth of advertising in Western Europe during the '60s was lowest in Britain (just over 3%) and highest in Greece and Denmark (nearly 14%). Advertising expenditure in West Germany grew more than $12\frac{1}{2}\%$ during the decade, outstripping France and Britain combined. Total advertising expenditure in West Germany in 1970 amounted to £1,146,460,000.

In Britain advertising expenditure in 1971 was forecast at £550 million, £21 million more than was spent in 1970. The press led all other media in 1970, with £207 million spent on display advertising, compared with £202 million in 1969; if classified, financial, and trade and technical advertising were included, the total expenditure for print advertising was £375 million. Television advertising was down slightly, from £129 million to £125 million, while outdoor and transport, at £22 million, and motion picture and radio, at £7 million, remained about constant.

With advertising expenditure increasing only marginally while operating costs rose 15% between January 1970 and June 1971, a number of well-known British agencies disappeared or were absorbed through take-overs or mergers; among them were Pritchard Wood, Dorland, Crawford, Street, Horniblow Cox-Freeman, Alexander Butterfield & Ayer, and S. H. Benson. J. Walter Thompson was the leading agency

in Britain with billings of £26,159,000, followed by Ogilvy Benson & Mather, Masius Wynne-Williams, Young & Rubicam, and Hobson Bates.

During the year the Newspaper Publishers' Association in Britain introduced regulations whereby agencies were required to settle accounts not later than the last day of the month following the month of the appearance of the advertisement. Thereafter a surcharge of 3% on the gross rate would be levied and another 2% after the elapse of a further month, making 5% in all. The agencies, in turn, protested that they were unable to carry the burden of interest-free loans while awaiting repayment, and sought to tighten financial arrangements with their clients.

On the media side, the Conservative government committed itself to commercial radio. One of the Independent Television Authority's subcontracting companies, London Weekend, had the distinction of running up the highest media rate yet seen in Britain: £2,625 for 30 seconds of peak TV time in the Greater London area.

Lever Brothers & Associates was Britain's leading advertiser in 1970, with expenditures of £6,801,000, £6,480,000 of which went to television. Following in order were Imperial Tobacco, the Central Office of Information, Procter & Gamble, and the Beecham Group.   (G. DE.)

Advertising volume in the U.S. increased in 1970 for the tenth consecutive year, but the gain was minimal: 1.6%, or $330 million, to a total of $20.8 billion. At the same time, the gross national product rose 5%. Some experts expected that volume in 1971 would rise as much as 4%, but predictions made in the fall by organizations representing the nine biggest carriers of national advertising were not so sanguine.

Network television expected to end 1971 with $1,470,000,000 in national advertising dollars, a decline from the medium's actual result of $1,650,000,000 in 1970. Spot television also forecast a drop, to $1,040,000,000 from $1.2 billion. Direct mail looked to a $2.8 billion year, off from 1970's $2,850,000,000. Six media were expecting gains: newspapers anticipated a rise from $1,080,000,000 to $1.2 billion; magazines from $1,190,000,000 to $1,250,000,000; business publications from $807.4 million to $810 million; network radio from $48.4 million to $49.9 million; spot radio from $350 million to $365.8 million; and outdoor advertising from $145 million to $160 million. Together, the nine media expected to end the year with a combined $9,140,000,000 worth of national advertising, a decline from 1970's actual total of $9,320,000,000.

Attacks on the advertising industry multiplied during the year—so much so that Thomas R. Shepard, Jr., publisher of *Look* magazine (which folded in October), charged the existence of a "disaster lobby." An *Advertising Age* editorial assailed the Federal Trade Commission for demanding that General Electric substantiate an advertising claim that its air-conditioner provides "the clean freshness of clear, cool mountain air." The editorial said: "This is the kind of tortured action . . . that has business men tearing their hair out wondering what directions the commission is going to move next."

Seemingly, the FTC was moving in many directions. It challenged ITT Continental Baking for saying that Wonder bread "Helps build strong bodies 12 ways" and got the same company to agree to devote 25% of its media advertising budget for one year to FTC-approved advertisements saying that, contrary to pre-

"Mao Tse-tung" and "Fidel Castro" appear on posters for Red Barrel ale produced by Watney Mann, one of Britain's largest brewers.

vious ads, its Profile bread was not effective for weight reduction. In another move against claims of "uniqueness," the commission called on the Amstar Corp. to devote 25% of its advertising for a year to correcting the claim that its Domino and Spreckles sugars are different from other refined sugars in that they assimilate into the body faster and enable professional athletes to perform better. The FTC called on seven automobile manufacturers to document their advertising claims (the manufacturers initially replied that the order would pose no difficulty since all the documentation was available anyway). It further indicated it planned to take a look at testimonial advertising.

In the sweepstakes area, Procter & Gamble agreed to an FTC consent order since it had "no desire to engage in a prolonged controversy over a type of promotion which we are no longer using." At the same time it denied a charge that it had withheld prizes from the public. *Reader's Digest* also agreed to a consent order restriction after the FTC said its sweepstakes promotions had sought to interest prospects by listing neighbours' names in direct mail pieces without their knowledge. The order required the awarding of all prizes and the listing of numerical odds for winning. A sweepstakes case involving Coca-Cola and Glendinning, partners in a "Big Name Bingo" contest, moved into federal district court in an effort to bar the FTC from proceeding with its action.

In July, Senate and government agency leaders turned their attention to what was being described as a national over-the-counter drug binge created by advertising for "mood" drugs, such as sleeping pills and tranquilizers. The Food and Drug Administration indicated that it intended "to make the wording on [mood-drug] labeling specific enough so that we will have a solid basis on which to prevent the kind of

over-promotion and exaggerated advertising that so plagues and bewilders and mystifies the consumer today."

Meanwhile, the subject of advertising television shows aimed at children was becoming heated. A group called Action for Children's Television called for banning all advertising in such programs. Various television officials suggested that the amount of commercial time might be reduced. Toy and game advertisers, after a year of criticism, started moving away from children's shows and into sports and prime time programs. Environmentalists, parents, and ghetto dwellers were becoming quite effective in challenging commercials and programs. Government hearings were planned to look into children's programs and into the "fairness" doctrine, including the drafting of guidelines that would define when a broadcaster must give free time to those who want to reply to commercials.

The cigarette industry, which had been banned from advertising its products on television and radio after 1970, reported a 2.5% increase in cigarette consumption during 1971. The TV and radio ban had turned the companies to various special promotions, sweepstakes, couponing, and sampling, and to introducing new brands.

In the magazine field, the year's biggest news was the suspension of *Look.* (*See* PUBLISHING.) Perhaps the most important development of the advertising year was an FTC decision to start a lengthy and unprecedented examination of modern advertising practices. The ostensible aim was to provide the commissioners with an opportunity to get a fuller understanding of the business they are empowered to regulate, but some advertising men feared that the end result would be to open the gates to further and perhaps even more restrictive regulations.

The 100 leading national advertisers in the U.S. in 1970, as compiled by *Advertising Age,* reduced their advertising and promotional investment by nearly one-half of 1%, the first such decrease in at least 16 years. By far the largest advertiser was Procter & Gamble, with an expenditure of $265 million, a reduction of $10 million from its 1969 investment. In second place was General Foods, followed by Sears, Roebuck & Co., General Motors (which lost its long-time hold on second place in a lagging sales year), Warner-Lambert, Colgate-Palmolive, Bristol-Myers, American Home Products, Ford, and American Telephone & Telegraph.

The 615 advertising agencies covered in *Advertising Age*'s annual compilation had combined billings of $10,158,133,000 in 1970, a record total and about $300 million above the 1969 level. There were 60 agencies that succeeded in billing $25 million or more, six less than in 1969. J. Walter Thompson billed $764 million, a gain of $24 million over 1969. The other top agencies were: McCann-Erickson ($546.9 million); Young & Rubicam ($520.2 million); Ted Bates & Co. ($414.2 million); Leo Burnett Co. ($389 million); Batten Barton Durstine & Osborn ($350.4 million); Doyle Dane Bernbach ($291.4 million); Grey Advertising ($251.4 million); Ogilvy & Mather ($250.2 million); and Foote, Cone & Belding ($240.6 million).

The average net profit of advertising agencies declined to 3.11% in 1970, down from 4.03%. The 60 largest agencies reduced their domestic payrolls by 1,561 people—an average of 26 employees per agency. Even J. Walter Thompson reduced its U.S. staff by 72 people, apparently because its billings in the U.S.

Distribution of Advertising in Western Europe, 1970 In percent							
Country	News-papers	Maga-zines	TV	Radio	Motion pictures	Out-door	Others
France	18.3	42.5	13.7	12.8	2.1	10.6	
Italy	25.6	37.0	20.6	10.0	6.8		
Netherlands	82.0*		11.0	2.0	1.0	4.0	
Spain	36.0	7.2	21.1	6.7	4.1	6.7	18.2
Belgium	47.0	28.0		2.0	1.5	21.5	
Switzerland	22.0	16.0	3.0		1.0	6.0	37.0
Denmark	26.0	18.0			1.0	2.0	53.0
Austria	63.3*		22.7	8.2	1.2	4.4	
West Germany	25.7	51.3	17.4	5.6			

*Newspapers/magazines combined total.

declined by $9 million (although it gained billings overseas).

Canadian advertising billings were expected to reach a record $1.2 billion in 1971, a 6% gain over the 1970 estimate. National advertising amounted to $500 million, about 37% of which was handled by U.S.-owned agencies. In June the government introduced a bill to prohibit all advertising and promotion of cigarettes, effective Jan. 1, 1972. The measure would also require that every package of cigarettes carry a health warning. With the rate of government prosecutions for false or misleading advertising almost doubled, Canadian admen were considering the establishment of a panel of lawyers to pass judgment on advertising material. (J. J. Gм).

See also Consumer Affairs; Industrial Review; Merchandising; Telecommunications; Television and Radio.

Afghanistan

A constitutional monarchy in central Asia, Afghanistan is bordered by the U.S.S.R., China, West Pakistan, and Iran. Area: 250,775 sq.mi. (649,508 sq.km.). Pop. (1971 est.): 17,480,280, including (1961 est.) Pathan 54%; Tadzhik 20%; Uzbek 9%; Hazara 8%. Cap. and largest city: Kabul (pop., 1971 est., 318,094). Language: Dari (Persian) and Pashto. Religion: Muslim. King, Mohammad Zahir Shah; prime ministers in 1971, Noor Ahmad Etemadi and, from June 9, Abdul Zahir.

Political life in the capital during the spring and summer of 1971 was dominated by squabbles between

AFGHANISTAN
Education. (1969–70) Primary, pupils 500,665, teachers 11,523; secondary, pupils 83,529, teachers 3,352; vocational, pupils 6,138, teachers 578; teacher training, students 9,491, teachers 589; higher, students 5,680, teaching staff 881.
Finance. Monetary unit: afghani, with a par value of 45 afghanis to U.S. $1 (108 afghanis = £1 sterling) and a free rate (Sept. 27, 1971) of 85 afghanis to U.S. $1 (210 afghanis = £1 sterling). Budget (1969–70 est.): revenue 6,796,000,000 afghanis; expenditure 7,419,000,000 afghanis (excluding development expenditure financed by foreign aid). Money supply: (March 1971) 7,383,000,000 afghanis; (March 1970) 7,011,000,000 afghanis.
Foreign Trade. (1969–70) Imports 9,410,000,000 afghanis; exports 6,161,000 afghanis. Import sources: U.S.S.R. 33%; Japan 12%; India 9%; China 8%; U.S. 6%; West Germany 6%. Export destinations (1968–69): U.S.S.R. 38%; India 19%; U.K. 16%; Pakistan 7%; Switzerland 6%. Main exports: fruit and nuts 35%; karakul (Persian lamb) skins 16%; wool 8%; carpets 8%; cotton 7%.
Transport and Communications. Roads (all weather; 1968) *c.* 6,700 km. Motor vehicles in use (1969): passenger 30,800; commercial (including buses) 18,200. Air traffic (1969): 84,888,000 passenger-km.; freight 7,325,000 net ton-km. Telephones (Jan. 1969) *c.* 10,000. Radio receivers (Dec. 1967) 248,000.
Agriculture. Production (in 000; metric tons; 1970; 1969 in parentheses): wheat *c.* 2,500 (2,401); corn *c.* 812 (785); rice *c.* 415 (407); barley *c.* 380 (365); cotton, lint *c.* 33 (29); sugar, raw value (1970–71) *c.* 21, (1969–70) *c.* 19; wool, greasy (1969) 29, (1968) 27. Livestock (in 000; 1969–70): cattle 3,608; sheep 21,880 (including *c.* 6,000 karakul); horses *c.* 415; asses *c.* 1,350; goats *c.* 3,150; camels 301.
Industry. Production (in 000; metric tons; 1969–70): coal 136; electricity (kw-hr.) 325,000; cement 180; salt 37; cotton yarn 0.4; cotton fabrics (m.) 49,000.

the administration and the People's Council. The 1969 elections had returned assembly members who were for the most part quite unfamiliar with parliamentary methods and procedure, at least as laid down in the constitution. The final brush came over a widely supported demand that questions concerning the administration be dealt with by the minister concerned at the time they were asked. This might not have been serious, but it followed a series of deliberate refusals to pass bills that the government regarded as essential. These refusals were based less on any difference over principles than on the rivalry between groups headed by individual parliamentarians, who, in the absence of political parties, formed cabals linked by a determination to promote local interests. To secure the passage of essential legislation, the king was obliged to intervene, with a threat to dissolve Parliament.

Prime Minister Noor Ahmad Etemadi, after being continually frustrated in his efforts to modernize the administration and bring the country forward, resigned on May 17 but was persuaded to continue as head of the government until his successor, Abdul Zahir, who had been ambassador in Rome, was confirmed as prime minister on June 9. Zahir made earnest efforts to reach a good understanding with Parliament; and when he presented his list of ministers to the king in July, he was able to put forward the general desire that the administration concentrate attention on the difficulties of low-income groups. The king gave an assurance that the wishes of the legislators would be respected.

The economic life of the country was severely affected by the most serious drought in its history; it was feared that almost three-quarters of the nation's sheep, the main meat staple, might have perished. Large numbers of people crossed into Pakistan and Iran in search of food; and the government took the unprecedented step of launching a worldwide appeal. The response, especially from Pakistan and Iran, was generous. The government undertook a massive campaign of relief operations to deal with the emergency, but was hampered by the traditionally independent attitude of remote outlying areas.

Afghanistan's alignments in external affairs remained unchanged, but its ties with the Muslim world were strengthened by participation in the Islamic conference of foreign ministers that met in Kabul in September. (L. F. R. W.)

Africa

The patterns of recent years were substantially repeated in Africa during 1971 as the continent witnessed an assortment of abortive coups, slow but visible economic growth, the retention of white dominance in the south, and the maintenance elsewhere of one-party states. Echoing the nationalism of the past decade, the Democratic Republic of the Congo (Kinshasa) changed its name to the Republic of Zaire on October 27, and Sierra Leone became a republic on April 19.

Attempted Coups. More than a dozen countries reported unsuccessful attempts at overthrowing their regimes. The only successful one, black Africa's 27th coup in a little more than a decade, occurred in Uganda. There, Pres. Milton Obote, who had been in power since 1962 and who had sought to make his land a pillar of socialism, was deposed by Maj. Gen.

Aerospace Industry:
see Astronautics; Defense; Industrial Review; Transportation

Maj. Gen. Idi Amin
(wearing dark glasses)
drives through
the streets of Kampala
in January 1971
after leading the coup
that succeeded in toppling
the Uganda government
led by Milton Obote.

Idi Amin (*see* BIOGRAPHY) on January 25. Obote received sanctuary in neighbouring Tanzania and vigorous support from its president, Julius Nyerere, who called the coup "an act of treason to the whole course of African progress and freedom." General Amin, formerly the boxing champion of Uganda, said that elections would be held as soon as possible but not before two years.

Evidence of the different tone of the new regime was seen in the curbing of the extensive nationalization plans of its predecessor. Amin pleased the Baganda tribe by bringing back the body of the late kabaka, Sir Edward Mutesa II, who had died in England in 1969, but he did not restore the kabakaship. With some reluctance the Organization of African Unity (OAU) accepted the new regime. In late September Amin announced that he would send a delegation to South Africa. This caused an upsurge in border friction with Tanzania, which was one of the centres in the struggle against South Africa.

The Sudan went through three days of turmoil in July when a coup by leftist forces was reversed by a successful countercoup. Prime Minister Gaafar Nimeiry (*see* BIOGRAPHY), who had seized power in 1969, was deposed on July 19. Earlier in the year he had called for the ending of subversive activities by Communists. Supported by the considerable influence in the country of the Soviet bloc nations, the Communists took control of the government only to be defeated in turn by Nimeiry, who forthwith hanged the leading Communist, Abdul Khalik Mahgoub. Hundreds of the revolutionaries were arrested, and relations with the Soviet Union and Bulgaria were subsequently strained. In September Nimeiry was chosen president by 98.6% of the vote in an uncontested election.

In Morocco, while King Hassan II (*see* BIOGRAPHY) was host to a lavish birthday party for hundreds of guests, the royal palace was attacked. Thirty-two guests were killed and 130 wounded. The coup, ostensibly, was designed to fight corruption. After it had been put down with the support of loyal troops, Hassan struck quickly, and summary executions, including those of ten high army officers followed. Hassan bitterly denounced Libyan encouragement of the revolt. Later he dismissed his Cabinet and promised to fight corruption.

In the aftermath of the unsuccessful invasion of Guinea in November 1970 by disaffected Guineans led by Portuguese officers, Guinea announced that 92 persons were sentenced to death on January 24. Disregarding the pope's plea for clemency, Guinean Pres. Sékou Touré pointed out that over 200 Guineans had been killed in the invasion.

Other countries, too, reported that they had thwarted attempts to seize power. In Cameroon, where a ten-year-old insurrection existed but seemed to be no great threat to the government, three leaders of banned groups were executed on January 15 for plotting to assassinate Pres. Ahmadou Ahidjo the previous year. Bishop Albert Ndongmo, who was also convicted, had his death sentence commuted to life imprisonment. Most of the opposition to Ahidjo came from the Bamiléké people in southern Cameroon. In Sierra Leone, which in recent years had gone through several political upheavals, army officers on March 23 arrested their commander hours after he had taken power from Prime Minister Siaka Stevens. Five days later, armed forces from neighbouring Guinea came into the country at the request of Stevens and in conformance with an agreement signed on March 26.

In Mali, Moussa Traoré on April 7 said that his government had foiled a plot to overthrow it. Malagasy Vice-Pres. André Resampa was arrested on June 1 for alleged involvement in a scheme to depose Pres. Philibert Tsiranana. The foreign minister on June 27 charged the United States with complicity in the conspiracy. In Kenya, although Pres. Jomo Kenyatta freed his former vice-president Oginga Odinga, of the banned Kenya Peoples' Union, 12 men who pleaded guilty to sedition were sentenced on June 8.

Two generals in Somalia were accused of trying to assassinate government leaders and reinstate a capitalist regime. The coup, planned for May 25, was averted. Charging that the Egyptian government was behind a coup that failed on August 27, Chad broke off diplomatic relations with that country and, on the next day, with Libya. In Zambia, 75 opposition United Progressive Party members were arrested on September 20, charged with having the backing of the South African government. And in Zaire three ministers, including Justin-Marie Bomboko, foreign minister in six Cabinets, were arrested on October 5 on charges of trying to kill Pres. Joseph Mobutu. In Egypt more than 90 officials were tried for allegedly plotting against Pres. Anwar as-Sadat (*see* BIOGRAPHY) in May. Four, including the former vice-president, Aly Sabry, were given death sentences, but these subsequently were commuted to life imprisonment.

Organization of African Unity (OAU). Though no unusually dramatic step was taken during the year by the assembled African states, the OAU did reaffirm earlier positions. Because of disagreements over the coup in Uganda, the OAU did not meet at Kampala, Uganda, as originally planned, even though former president Obote had built a $17 million meeting hall to house the delegates. Despite the change of site, the OAU's Council of Ministers, meeting ten days earlier, did accept General Amin's new Ugandan regime.

In perhaps its most significant action, the OAU rejected the "outward diplomacy" of South Africa. At the OAU's eighth Assembly of Heads of State and Government held in Addis Ababa, Eth. (June 21–23), the policy of having a dialogue with South Africa was rejected 28–6. Those believing that more could be gained by talking with the white-dominated land than by the present policy of opposition included Ivory Coast, Gabon, Lesotho, Malagasy, Malawi, and Mauritius with abstentions by Upper Volta, Dahomey,

Niger, Togo, and Swaziland. All others bitterly denounced what seemed an unnecessary concession to South Africa that was unlikely to change its program of racial separation.

Diallo Telli, secretary-general of the OAU, sought the support of the major powers at the UN to use all means to carry out the UN resolutions concerning Namibia (South West Africa). On June 21 the World Court had ruled 13–2 that "the continued presence of South Africa in Namibia being illegal, South Africa is under obligation to withdraw its administration from Namibia immediately." The power to enforce the court's wishes was, however, lacking.

Mokhtar Ould Daddah, president of the OAU (and also president of Mauritania), told the UN General Assembly in September that by aiding Portugal NATO was responsible for the long wars in Mozambique, Angola, and Portuguese Guinea and for the continued subjection of the people of southern Africa. He planned to tour the NATO countries, Switzerland, and Japan in order to persuade them to stop arms shipments to South Africa.

In an attempt to mediate the dispute between Egypt and Israel the OAU sent a four-man delegation (Léopold Senghor, Yakubu Gowon, Joseph Mobutu, and Ahmadou Ahidjo) in early November to try to unscramble the knotty problems of a "trilogy of suffering peoples, the Africans, Arabs and Jews." Little came of the mission.

Intra-African Unity. On September 1 a loose union of Egypt, Libya, and Syria, called the Confederation of Arab Republics, received overwhelming popular approval in referendums in the involved nations. Afterward, Egypt changed its name from the United Arab Republic to the Arab Republic of Egypt.

Several meetings indicative of African cooperation took place during the year. The first all-African seminar on the Human Environment in Africa was held in Addis Ababa during August, with 33 countries in attendance. Meeting ten years after the first conference, the second conference on hydrology in the economic development of Africa sat for ten days in September. Jointly sponsored by the OAU and the UN Economic Commission for Africa (ECA), it attracted 34 African countries and 60 international experts. The ECA also brought together eight Western industrial nations and African states at Addis Ababa on October 1 to discuss a proposed trans-African highway from Mombasa to Lagos. On July 19 the first scientific advisory panel set up by the OAU began work in Addis Ababa, focusing upon disease.

A Pan-African Women's Conference, held in Brazzaville, Congo, July 17–24, was attended by representatives of 16 African countries. Among other requests was one asking for professional training for women. The eighth conference of the General Association of French-speaking Psychologists of Africa and Malagasy was held in Dakar July 8–13, with representatives from 13 states. Questions of learning and associated matters were discussed. In the north, Algeria, Morocco, and Tunisia sent delegates to the first Maghrebine conference on archaeology, held in Rabat, July 2–8. African cooperation was also evident in the joint Pan-African track team, sponsored by the Supreme Council for Sport in Africa, which performed creditably in a dual meet with a U.S. team in North Carolina, July 16–17.

In an attempt to make West Africa self-sufficient in rice, 14 African nations attended the first West African Rice Development Association meeting in

Monrovia, Lib., on September 20. Cooperation also existed on a bilateral scale as Ghana and Upper Volta signed an agreement on May 28 to coordinate their efforts in various fields. And in a mood of reconciliation, Nigeria exchanged ambassadors with Ivory Coast, Tanzania, and Zambia—links broken during the Nigerian civil war. On the other hand, friction existed between Chad and Libya, Congo and Zaire, Uganda and Tanzania, and Senegal and Guinea. And internal strife beset Ethiopia, Sudan, and Chad.

The Economy. In a conference in Rabat of the Association of African Central Banks it was noted that, taken as a whole, the average annual per capita growth of the gross domestic product in Africa during the UN Development Decade (the 1960s) had been less than 2%. This was below the level of other less developed countries. Of the 25 countries listed by the UN with unusually low per capita incomes, 16 were in Africa. The diversity of the African economic picture could be illustrated by the optimistic prediction that there would be 800 new retail food outlets in Ivory Coast within five years and by the fact that drought had forced the government of Kenya to feed 120,000 people to prevent starvation.

The Algerian government on February 24 took 51% control of French-owned oil holdings; France had controlled two-thirds of the Algerian oil production, with an investment since 1954 of $1,350,000,000. Unsuccessful talks having gone on since 1969, the Algerians seized the companies and demanded the payment of tax arrears. The French preferred 100% nationalization and a just compensation. On June 30 a ten-year accord (amplified on September 21) was signed by Sonatrach (the Algerian oil trust) and the Compagnie Française des Pétroles, one of the two main companies whose assets had been taken. The French firm was to receive a $50 million indemnity to be paid over a seven-year period, and in turn would pay back taxes of $27 million. The second major company, Elf-Erap, settled with Sonatrach in December. Similarly, Libya was able to gain an extra $620 million a year in an oil agreement signed on April 2 which would give it annual revenues of $2 billion. Libya in December nationalized the holdings of British Petroleum Co. in retaliation for Britain's support of Iran in a Persian Gulf dispute.

Nigeria, which in November 1970 had announced a four-year plan (including rebuilding war-torn areas of the country) with an overall investment of $4.5 billion, received a World Bank loan of $50 million. Yakubu Gowon, Nigeria's chief of state, reported good progress in the first year of the plan, with gross domestic product for 1970–71 increasing at 9.6%. The World Bank also granted a loan to Guinea of $64.5 million (its third largest in Africa), which provided a considerable stimulus to the development of the rich bauxite mines of Boké. Despite his continual protestations of socialism, President Touré believed that his country's 49% ownership in an international consortium would prove mutually advantageous. In Ghana, a U.S.-owned company was awarded rights to prospect for bauxite on August 3, and a month later the U.S. granted Ghana a $20 million loan. In Tanzania President Nyerere reported that during the nation's ten years of independence net per capita income had increased more than 40%.

Against this mixed picture of economic growth must be noted the migration into the cities, where many could not find jobs. A curious illustration of both the prosperity of the new Africa and the poverty of the

Bishop Albert Ndongmo is under heavy guard in Yaoundé, Cameroon, during his trial in January 1971. He was sentenced to death for plotting to overthrow the government, but his sentence later was commuted to life imprisonment.
ABBAS/GAMMA—
PHOTOREPORTERS

old could be seen in the expulsion by Zaire of several thousand "foreign" Africans, including many alleged diamond smugglers.

External Relations. African nations, led by Tanzania, played an important role in the admission of China to the UN and the expulsion of Taiwan (Nationalist China), 26 voting for the resolution and 15 opposed. On September 13, Togo became the sixth African state in less than a year to recognize China, the others being Equatorial Guinea, Nigeria, Cameroon, Sierra Leone, and Ethiopia. The last-named, after a visit to Peking by Emperor Haile Selassie in October, received an $84 million loan from China for farm development. The Chinese in August also provided the Sudan with a $35 million loan for highways, bridges, and a textile factory. Lesser aid projects and economic agreements were signed with other nations. The Chinese, in addition, provided military training as well as small arms in Tanzania and Guinea. Contrary to their policy of several years before, the Chinese in 1971 maintained a "low profile" in foreign relations with more effective results. The Soviet Union, after the formal opening on January 15 of the massive Aswan High Dam that it helped finance in Egypt, signed a pact with Egypt on March 20, involving more than $400 million. After a visit to Algeria in October, Soviet Premier Aleksei N. Kosygin pledged aid to that country and later to Morocco.

U.S. visitors to Africa included Vice-Pres. Spiro T. Agnew and the chairman of the House of Representatives' subcommittee on Africa, Charles C. Diggs, Jr. After returning from South Africa, Diggs wrote "I have . . . the conviction that majority rule in South Africa is inevitable. . . . The U.S. has no choice but to get on the side of freedom."

Southern Africa. No fundamental shift in attitude or power occurred during the year in southern Africa. The reaching out for "dialogue" with other African states, though rebuffed by the OAU (*see* above), was moderately successful in a handful of countries. On August 16 the first black chief of state ever to visit South Africa, Pres. H. Kamuzu Banda (*see* BIOGRAPHY) of Malawi, was given a warm diplomatic reception. Such collaboration could be simply explained by the fact that impoverished Malawi exported its labour to work in South African mines. Delegates also came from Malagasy and the Ivory Coast, and contacts were made with Uganda. As expressed by Ivory Coast Pres. Félix Houphouët-Boigny, those nations favouring dialogue believed that it was preferable to work within the existing, realistic framework to try to effect change in South African policies. Other

Africans were highly skeptical of altering South Africa's racial policy in that way.

Meanwhile, South Africa increased its defense budget by $83 million and welcomed the decision of the British government to sell it helicopters. South Africa also developed air-to-air missiles during the year. In late October, the homes of churchmen, university teachers, students, and newsmen were raided, and on November 1, the dean of Johannesburg's Anglican cathedral, the Rev. Gonville Aubrey ffrench-Beytagh, was sentenced to five-years' imprisonment under an act to combat terrorism. For the immediate future, apartheid seemed less likely to be challenged by the UN condemnation of it (109–2) on November 9 than by a shortage of skilled labour. In February some jobs in the construction field previously reserved for whites were opened to Africans.

In November, Britain and Rhodesia agreed to a settlement of their dispute, including an end to British sanctions. The accord, which provided for gradual political progress for Africans, was denounced by the OAU as an "outright sellout . . . of five million Africans to 243,000 white Rhodesians committed to white rule and apartheid."

Miscellany. Zambia in September agreed to set up a 2,400-sq.mi. wildlife refuge. Nigeria began the switch from driving on the left to the right side of the road. In Nairobi, Kenya, authorities began slum clearance of shantytowns as health hazards. For robbers who injure victims, the Kenyan legislature voted the death penalty. Great Britain announced that it was doubling the quota of those East African Asians who had English citizenship and wished to enter Britain. Tanzania prescribed standards of correct dress and required Swahili to be used in mosques. Pres. Habib Bourguiba of Tunisia relented in his campaign to get Muslims to work in the daytime during the holy month of Ramadan. Pres. William Tubman of Liberia, in power since 1944, died on July 23. It was reported on February 18 that a jawbone had been found in Kenya which, according to Harvard University scholars, represented the oldest member of the human family ever found.

The International Scientific Committee of UNESCO authorized work on a *General History of Africa* in eight volumes (in French and English) and an abridged volume in various African languages to be completed in 1978.   (W. So.)

ENCYCLOPÆDIA BRITANNICA FILMS. *Africa: Living in Two Worlds* (1970); *Boy of Botswana* (1970); *City Boy of the Ivory Coast* (1970); *A Family of Liberia* (1970); *Two Boys of Ethiopia* (1970); *Youth Builds a Nation in Tanzania* (1970); *Elephant* (1971); *Giraffe* (1971); *Lion* (1971); *Zebra* (1971).

Agriculture

The world's farmers experienced a highly productive year in 1971. In general, nature cooperated. Production of livestock and major crops reached new record levels in important producing areas, while production per capita appeared to have kept pace with expanding population overall. Wide discrepancies still existed, however, especially between developed and less developed areas. The Green Revolution proceeded, with notable results in such areas as India, which set new records in food grains. Only in a few areas—notably East Pakistan and East Africa, where uncommonly refractory weather compounded problems of economic disorganization—did famine and near famine occur.

In fact, many of the agricultural problems of the year were created by man. Though the value of world agricultural trade increased by an exceptional 15%, trade barriers, monetary and foreign exchange factors, and strikes at ports proved disruptive. In many parts of the world, agricultural products did not fully participate in price inflation, and the producer was caught in a severe price-cost squeeze.

NORTH AMERICA

United States. For feed-grain producers, 1971 was a year of "watch and wait" to see whether the corn (maize) crop would be adequate to maintain livestock production at high levels and thus damp the fires of food-price inflation or so abundant as to depress the price below the cost of production. The crop proved to be a record large 5,551,769,000 bu., and the price declined to about two-thirds the level of the first half of 1971. Consumers would be abundantly fed, but the cost-price squeeze would tighten further for many of the 5% of the U.S. population still living on farms. Net income would be as much as $1 billion less than in 1970. It appeared that price controls would not affect many agricultural products directly but, with the price of processed items controlled, there would be reluctance on the part of processors to bid up for the raw materials.

Crops. The somewhat relaxed acreage controls of the Agricultural Act of 1970, plus an early and generally favourable crop season, resulted in record large production. The production index of all crops was 113 (1967 = 100), compared with 100 in 1970 and a previous record of 104 in 1969. Despite severe drought in the southern plains, the yield index of 28 major crops was a record high 110. Crops were planted for harvest on 314 million ac., about 4% more than in 1970. Actual crop acreage harvested was estimated at 303 million, up 5% from 1970 and the largest since 1960.

Despite fears to the contrary, seed-corn supplies proved sufficient, and corn acreage planted for harvest was indicated at 64,470,000 ac., 12.4% above 1970. Southern leaf blight (race T strain of *Helminthosporium maydis*), which had seriously affected the 1970 crop, was apparently controlled by the increased planting of resistant varieties and by drier, cooler weather. The result, the first corn crop ever to exceed 5,000,000,000 bu., was forecast at 5,265,641,000 bu., 35% above 1970 and 15% larger than the 1969 record. The average yield per acre was 86.6 bu., compared with 71.7 bu. in 1970. Iowa was the leading producing state, followed by Illinois and Indiana.

Members of a task force charged with wiping out hog cholera in the Dismal Swamp area of North Carolina quarantine a suspected herd until the diagnosis can be confirmed.
AUTHENTICATED NEWS INTERNATIONAL

Grain sorghum acreage for harvest was indicated at 16,649,000, about 21% more than in 1970. Yield per acre averaged 53.9 bu., and the crop, at 889,894,000 bu., was 28% above a year earlier. The oat crop of 884,642,000 bu. was 3% below 1970, but a record yield of 56.4 bu. per ac. was achieved. The barley crop totaled 469,879,000 bu., 14% above a year earlier. Total production of the four feed grains was about 206 million tons, 30% more than the 159 million tons of 1970. Other livestock feeds, pasture, hay, and meal concentrates were also abundant. All hay totaled a record 131,081,000 tons, of which alfalfa provided 76,445,000 tons.

Food-grain production (wheat, rye, and rice) was about 54.5 million tons, 17% more than in 1970. Indicated production of all wheat was a record 1,627,575,000 bu.; acreage was only 9% above 1970, but the average yield was 33.7 bu. per ac., compared with about 31 bu. in the two preceding years. The 1,162,660,000-bu. winter wheat crop did not fully reflect the new farm program, but farmers growing spring wheat had ample time to respond. The durum crop was estimated at 87,038,000 bu., 72% more than the small crop of 1970 but 18% below the 1969 record. Other spring wheat was forecast at 377,877,000 bu. from 12,620,000 ac., compared with 209,904,000 bu. from 8,835,000 ac. in 1970. Early indications were that acreage sown to wheat in 1972 would probably be even greater. The 1971 rye crop, the largest since 1942, was estimated at 52,306,000 bu., compared with 38,552,000 bu. in 1970. Rice totaled 84,213,000 cwt., more than in 1970 but below the 90,838,000-cwt. crop of 1969.

The cotton crop was estimated at 10,718,000 bales, for an index of 143. Average lint yield was 444 lb. per ac., against 437 lb. in 1970. World cotton production also rose, to 53,140,000 bales, compared with 51,254,000 in 1970–71. U.S. cottonseed production, estimated at 4,449,000 tons, was up 11%. U.S. oilseed crops totaled 42.5 million tons, 5% more than in 1970. Soybean production was a record 1,200,201,000 bu., but this was one of the few 1971 crops for which it appeared that demand might exceed supply. Peanuts were expected to total a record 2,992,724,000 lb. The flaxseed crop of 20,011,000 bu. was one-third below 1970; acreage was reduced from 2,888,000 to 1,630,000, largely because of unfavourable prices.

The production index for all sugar crops was 121, compared with 118 in 1970 and a previous record of 120 in 1969. The sugar-beet crop was forecast at 26,-

339,000 tons, 1% more than in 1970, while the sugar-cane harvest was expected to total 25,770,000 tons, up 7%. Cold weather delayed the start of the 1971 maple season in most producing states. Syrup production was estimated at 954,000 gal., 14% below the 1970 output.

Production of all tobacco was indicated at an index of 92, compared with 96 in 1970. The forecast was for 1,803,871,000 lb. from 850,840 ac. Flue-cured production was estimated at 1,101,962,000 lb., and Burley production at 545,425,000 lb.

Fresh vegetable crops were moderately short in 1971, and prices during the first half of the year averaged 9% higher than in the corresponding period of 1970. Summer vegetable supplies were down about 2%, with melon production down substantially. Estimated fall-vegetable production (excluding melons) was 6% below 1970. Acreage planted to vegetables for processing rose about 2% over 1970; early indications were that the pack of six major vegetables for freezing might be 5 to 10% larger than in 1970. Potato production was estimated at 318,462,000 cwt., compared with 325,588,000 cwt. a year earlier, and sweet potatoes, at an estimated 12.2 million cwt., were down by 10%. Dry beans fell 6% to 16,413,000 cwt. The dry field pea crop, at 5,228,000 cwt., was up 33%.

The 1971 pecan crop was forecast at 251.8 million lb., nearly two-thirds larger than in 1970. Filberts totaled 11,560 tons, compared with 9,510 tons in 1970, and walnuts rose to 125,100 tons from 111,800. California almond production was down 2%.

Production of deciduous fruits in 1971 totaled about 10.5 million tons, 9% more than in 1970. The commercial apple crop was slightly smaller, however, and peach production was 7% below 1970, largely because the California clingstone crop was reduced under a supply adjustment program. The pear crop was up 37%. California prune production was down 34%, but prunes and plums in other areas rose 96%. Grape production was 26% above the previous year, and sweet cherries were up 12%.

Early, midseason, and navel oranges were forecast at 93.6 million boxes for 1971–72, 11% below the previous crop. Florida's Valencia crop was expected to be 64 million boxes, 6% more than the previous season. Grapefruit, excluding some California production, was indicated at 58.7 million boxes, slightly below 1970–71 but 14% above 1969–70. The lemon crop, excluding California production, was forecast at 17.3 million boxes.

Livestock. Output of all livestock and products in 1971 was indicated at an index of 106, the same as in 1970. The value of all livestock and poultry

on farms and ranches as of Jan. 1, 1971, totaled a record $23.8 billion, with cattle and calves accounting for $21.1 billion. All types except sheep and lambs increased in numbers over a year earlier; hogs and pigs were up 19%.

All cattle and calves on farms were estimated at 114,568,000 head at the beginning of 1971, an increase of 2% over 1970. However, early returns from the 1969 U.S. census of agriculture indicated that such estimates might be 4½% too high. Beef cows and heifers that had calved rose 3% to 37,557,000 head in 1971. Average value per head of all cattle and calves rose to $185, from $180 in 1970. The 1971 calf crop was estimated at 47.1 million head; beef calves were up about 4% while the dairy calf crop fell 1%. Calf slaughter declined 8% in the first half of the year, reflecting not only the reduction in dairy calves, the usual source of veal, but also the strong demand for cattle for further feeding to early maturity. Lighter-weight feeder cattle and calves continued to bring higher prices than fat cattle. The Western states gained in relative importance in cattle feeding and were approaching one-half the total.

Milk cow numbers continued to decline, falling 1% to 12,445,000 head at the beginning of 1971. Milk cow replacement heifers were indicated at 3,939,000 head. Output per cow during the first seven months of 1971 rose 2% over a year earlier. The favourable milk-feed price ratio during the second half of 1971 encouraged heavier grain feeding to dairy cows, and in spite of the freeze on dairy prices, 1971 production was forecast at about 119,000,000,000 lb., as compared with 117,400,000,000 lb. in 1970.

Hogs and pigs on farms on Dec. 1, 1970, were uncommonly numerous, totaling 67,540,000 head or 19% more than a year earlier. The average value per head was only $23.40, compared with $39 a year earlier, and the total value was down 29%. As of September 1 indications were that the June–August pig crop in ten Corn Belt states was 9% below the corresponding period of 1970, and that farrowing intentions for September–November and for December 1971–February 1972 were down 11%. By the second half of 1971, however, hog prices had recovered from less than $16 per hundredweight late in 1970 to nearly $20, and corn prices had fallen. The hog-corn price ratio improved from a very unfavourable 11 early in the year to more than 16, raising prospects that the pig crop would be increased late in 1972.

All sheep and lambs on farms and ranches in early 1971 numbered 19,560,000 head, down 4% from the previous year. Total value also declined, to $462,-906,000, compared with $506,816,000 in 1970. Of these totals, stock sheep (mostly breeding stock) numbered 16,937,000 head, 3% fewer than a year earlier; another 2,623,000 head (mostly lambs) were being fattened for market. Prices after March were more than $2 per hundredweight higher than a year earlier. Shorn wool production was estimated at 154.7 million lb. (greasy basis), 4% below a year earlier and 42% below 1960.

The Jan. 1, 1971, inventory indicated chicken numbers at 442,783,000 (excluding commercial broilers), 2% more than a year earlier. Hens and pullets of laying age totaled 335,079,000, up 3% from January 1970. Egg output continued well above 1970, largely because of a higher laying rate. Commercial broilers totaled about 3,000,000,000; prices averaged 14 cents per pound to producers, slightly higher than the average for 1970. There were 7,462,000 turkeys valued at

Table I. Index Numbers of Volume of Agricultural Production

Average 1952–56 = 100

Region	Total agricultural production			Per capita food production		
	1970*	1969	1948–52	1970*	1969	1948–52
Western Europe	145	145	84	128	129	87
North America	124	124	93	102	105	99
Latin America	156	153	87	104	102	97
Oceania	160	163	89	117	121	102
Far East (excl. China and Japan)	160	154	87	110	108	94
Near East (excl. Israel)	163	164	82	104	104	90
Africa (excl. South Africa)	149	146	85	95	96	94
Eastern Europe and U.S.S.R.	177	168	82	147	141	87
Other developed countries (Japan, South Africa, and Israel)	166	166	81	141	142	87
All above regions	151	148	87	112	112	93

*Preliminary.

Source: Food and Agriculture Organization of the United Nations, *Monthly Bulletin of Agricultural Economics and Statistics* (July and August 1971).

nearly $40 million on farms at the beginning of 1971, 10% more than a year earlier. Reduced honey production was indicated, compared with the 234,791,000 lb. harvested in 1970 from 4,639,000 honeybee colonies. World production was also expected to decline. The problem of the vicious "African" hybrid bees migrating northward from Brazil received increased attention.

Many thousands of horses and mules in the U.S. were inoculated against Venezuelan equine encephalomyelitis in a midsummer emergency. (*See* VETERINARY MEDICINE.) At the end of July the 345 ac. on Chicago's South Side that had housed the city's famous stockyards became available for other uses.

Farm Prices, Costs, Income, and Finances. In October 1971 prices received by U.S. farmers stood at a composite index of 113, compared with 108 a year earlier. The price picture by commodity groups was very mixed. The index for all crops was 106, up from 102 a year earlier, but such large segments as food grains and feed grains registered sharp declines. Oil-bearing crops, cotton, and fresh fruits and vegetables were sharply higher. Livestock and livestock product prices rose as a group, while poultry and eggs fell slightly.

The parity index of production costs paid by farmers for commodities and services, interest, taxes, and wages stood at 121, 5% above a year earlier. Larger increases were recorded for taxes, interest, wage rates, and feeder livestock. The nation's farm labour force totaled 5,251,000 workers in late August 1971, nearly 2% below August 1970. The composite per-hour wage rate was $1.54 on October 1, compared with $1.46 a year earlier; farmhands were receiving an average of $338 per month with housing and other allowances, up from $325 in October 1970. Sales of most major types of farm equipment during the first half of 1971 sagged below the low levels of a year earlier.

The parity ratio, an overall measure of farmers' purchasing power, was 93, compared with 94 a year earlier. The farmers' share of the retail all-food "market basket" remained at approximately the 1970 level of 38%. The index of retail food costs was 120, while the more inclusive consumer price index stood at 122.2. Cash receipts from farm marketings during the first half of 1971 were at an annual rate of about $50.1 billion, approximately the same as a year earlier. Nonmoney income and government payments of $7 billion raised realized gross farm income to more than $57 billion, but farm production expenses of at least $42.5 billion left farmers' realized net income at about $14.7 billion, some $1 billion below 1970.

The estimated value of farm assets in 1970 was $311.4 billion, of which real estate accounted for $208.9 billion. The national index of farmland value per acre rose to 121 in March 1971, 3% above a year earlier. The farm real estate market was described as sluggish. Farm mortgage debt increased to $29,562,000,000, a rise of $1.2 billion in one year, while short-term debt of farmers rose from $27,044,-000,000 to $29,738,000,000. Interest rates charged on Federal Land Bank loans increased from 6 to 6.4%.

Trade and Stocks. Although the U.S. trade balance was described as the worst since 1893, U.S. agricultural exports advanced to a new record of $7,752,-000,000 in 1970–71, 15% above the previous year. U.S. purchases of foreign farm products also increased, but the trade balance in agricultural products was a "favourable" $1,919,000,000. All major export commodity groups registered increases, but there was concern that Pres. Richard Nixon's new economic policies might lead to protectionist reactions in importing countries. (*See* COMMERCIAL POLICIES.)

Inventories declined in the first half of 1971, but it was anticipated that large amounts of some over-abundant 1971 crops would come under the shelter of Commodity Credit Corporation programs, especially as dock strikes prevented shipment at the height of the harvest season. As of July 31, 1971, the total investment of the CCC in commodity loans and inventory was $3,046,810,000, compared with $4,590,-816,000 a year earlier.

Legislation and Administration. The Sugar Act of 1948, as amended and extended for three years, revised quotas that foreign sugar producers were authorized to supply to the U.S. Domestic producers were authorized to supply about 62% of approximately 11 million tons of sugar consumed annually in the U.S.; the remaining 38% was allocated to various foreign countries.

The tobacco marketing quota provisions of the Agricultural Adjustment Act of 1938 were further amended to provide for poundage quotas, without acreage allotments, for Burley tobacco.

Other acts approved during the 1971 session of Congress covered expansion of agricultural exports; new farm peanut allotments; and paid advertising under marketing orders for California peaches.

Among administrative actions, milk prices were increased and a new regulation that would have ended diversion of marginal land was rescinded for 1971.

In November the resignation of Secretary of Agriculture Clifford M. Hardin was accepted by the president. He was succeeded by Earl L. Butz of Purdue University (*see* BIOGRAPHY).

Canada. The Prairie Provinces returned to more normal production in 1971, ending the emergency program of 1970, which had been designed to reduce the burdensome wheat surplus and encourage diversification. In 1970 wheat acreage had been reduced to 12,483,000 from 24,967,000 in 1969, and the 1970 harvest was only 338,336,000 bu., compared with 684,278,000 bu. a year earlier. Exports in 1970–71 proved to be larger than anticipated, and by July

Top, veterinarian draws a blood sample from a colt suspected of having Venezuelan equine encephalomyelitis, which swept through Texas in the summer of 1971. Bottom, highway crew removes the carcass of a horse that died from the disease.

COURTESY, U.S. DEPARTMENT OF AGRICULTURE

UPI COMPIX

31, 1971, carry-over stocks had declined from about 1,000,000,000 bu. to 685 million. With the carry-over situation eased, it was possible to permit more nearly normal production in 1971. The federal government discontinued payments to farmers to convert wheatland to summer fallow, though it did continue payments for land turned to grassland. Wheat acreage rose to 19,222,000 and about 507.4 million bu. were harvested.

World production of wheat was estimated at 304 million metric tons, 3% more than in 1970 and second only to the 308 million-ton harvest of 1968. Larger crops were indicated in all major areas except the U.S.S.R., and the increase in the European crop appeared to foreshadow a reduction in demand for import grains of as much as 10%. In June it appeared that Canada had successfully negotiated an agreement with the U.S.S.R. for cash wheat sales amounting to $235 million for 3.5 million tons. In September it was announced that China had contracted to buy about 20 million bu., in addition to the 98 million bu. contracted for a year earlier. Some 3.7 million bu. were sold to North Korea in April.

In 1971 a new plan was proposed that would, in effect, attempt to ensure that in any particular year the cash receipts from wheat, oats, barley, rye, flaxseed, and rapeseed would not be less than the preceding five-year average. Opposition to the plan was strong, however, and in mid-October the government withdrew the proposed payments, which would have totaled about $100 million on 1971 crops. Under existing legislation, payments on 1971 crops would be about $62 million.

Feed-grain acreage was increased to 24,588,000 in 1971, compared with 19,404,000 the previous year. The large 1971 barley harvest totaled 656.1 million bu.; the oat crop, at 371.4 million bu., was slightly larger than in 1970; and rye production was 25.3 million bu., compared with 22.4 million bu. a year earlier. The rapeseed crop set a new record of 72.2 million bu., and special delivery quotas were established for rapeseed low in erucic acid.

The number of cattle and calves reached a record high, estimated at 13.7 million head on June 1, 1971. Marketings and inspected slaughter increased in the early part of 1971, and prices averaged higher than a year earlier. Hog and sheep numbers also rose.

LATIN AMERICA

Among the more encouraging developments in Latin America in 1971 were gains in the production of some crops important to both the domestic market and the export trade. Coffee production appeared to have recovered; record sugar production was registered in some countries; and Argentina harvested its largest corn crop in 30 years. Total agricultural production throughout the region in 1970 reached an index of 162 (1952–56 = 100), according to the Food and Agriculture Organization of the United Nations (FAO); this was somewhat less than 4% above a year earlier.

Mexico. Midyear prospects indicated an increase in Mexico's overall agricultural output, although livestock production, which had improved in 1970 after an 18-month drought, was again threatened by a resurgence of dry weather. The 1970–71 corn crop was estimated at 8.7 million metric tons, reflecting increases in both yields and acreages. Production of cotton, once Mexico's leading foreign exchange earner, was estimated at 1.4 million bales in 1970–71, continuing a three-year decline attributed to insect damage, insufficient water, and competition from more profitable food crops. Beans—one of the country's main food staples—were forecast at between 850,000 and 900,000 metric tons, a low level that would probably necessitate imports from the U.S.

Fearing the application of import restrictions, Mexican producers of winter fruits and vegetables, particularly strawberries and tomatoes, attempted voluntary restraints on shipments to the U.S. in the 1970–71 season.

A new agrarian code, passed in early 1971, was expected to speed up distribution of land and halt further illegal occupation. Incorporating the first changes in Mexico's agrarian law in 29 years, the new act provided for streamlining court processes in land transactions, regulating land tenure and the distribution of rural property, new economic and agrarian planning programs, and the establishment of a National Ejido Development Fund and a Rural Industries Development Organization.

Central America. Midyear forecasts for the production of sugar, rice, coffee, and cotton promised a continuation of upward trends in the region. Cotton production in 1970–71 was expected to be about 3% above that for 1969–70, and Central America's keen competition in world cotton markets appeared likely to continue into 1972. Increased sugar production was forecast in all countries except British Honduras. Guatemala, the region's leading sugar producer, expected a 1970–71 output of 207,000 metric tons, compared with 178,000 tons a year earlier. Coffee production continued to expand, with moderate increases forecast for nearly all countries in 1971–72.

Table II. Cotton Production of the Principal Producing Countries

In 000 480-lb. bales net

Country	Indicated 1971	1970	Average 1965–69	Average 1960–64
Argentina	575	400	484	552
Brazil	2,900	2,250	2,720	2,235
China	6,900	6,900	6,740	5,040
Colombia	580	540	479	335
Egypt	2,400	2,335	2,198	2,037
Greece	540	505	406	377
India	4,800	4,500	4,900	4,741
Iran	650	690	618	494
Mexico	1,560	1,440	2,215	2,206
Pakistan	2,650	2,425	2,262	1,656
Peru	400	395	455	632
Spain	200	240	338	427
Sudan	1,150	1,150	918	675
Syria	600	685	694	656
Turkey	2,150	1,835	1,777	1,091
U.S.S.R.	9,800	10,800	9,140	7,370
United States	10,701	10,166	10,589	14,795

Source: U.S. Department of Agriculture, Foreign Agricultural Service.

Table III. Orange (including Tangerine) Production in Principal Producing Countries

In 000 boxes

Country	1970*	1969	Average 1960–64
Algeria	14,000	13,900	11,647
Argentina	38,266	34,382	21,540
Brazil	65,130	63,140	27,020
Greece	12,519	14,607	7,646
Israel	32,565	28,572	16,536
Italy	51,629	53,427	30,650
Japan	95,837	76,328	38,314
Mexico	32,124	29,510	23,478
Morocco	23,709	25,800	15,493
South Africa	16,692	15,924	13,939
Spain	63,618	67,248	51,191
Turkey	15,747	14,928	8,522
United States	249,651	241,193	145,937

*Preliminary.
Source: U.S. Department of Agriculture.

El Salvador's 1971–72 crop was estimated at 2,350,-000 bags (132.3 lb. each), compared with 2 million bags in 1970–71.

Livestock production continued to supply a large percentage of the region's exports, but pressure on the industry as a source of foreign exchange led to a reduction in domestic supplies. A World Bank Group loan of $4 million was announced early in 1971 to assist Guatemalan cattle ranchers to increase beef output by improving pastures and cattle-raising techniques; the $7.8 million project was the first stage of a broader livestock development project.

South America. Prospects in Brazil were uncertain at midyear. A severely reduced cotton crop, lower rice production, and a slightly smaller corn crop might be offset by improved output of sugar, dry edible beans, and wheat. The cotton crop was estimated at only 2.2 million bales, compared with 3.1 million in 1969–70; severe drought in the northeast had lowered the crop there by 50%. Sugar production in 1970–71 rose 18% to an estimated 5,431,-000 metric tons. At midyear the Brazilian Sugar and Alcohol Institute approved the Sugar Production Plan for the 1971–72 marketing year; production of 5.1 million metric tons was authorized, 75% of which was to be for domestic consumption.

Livestock numbers rose moderately in 1970, but production of 3,628,800,000 lb. of beef and veal was nearly 10% below a year earlier. Exports of beef—a record 114,862 tons in 1970—were expected to be 40% lower in 1971, largely as a result of government efforts to retain supplies for domestic use.

Drought in Brazil's northeast exacerbated the social and political unrest endemic in the area. SUDENE, the government agency established to develop the 600,000-sq.mi. region, was reported to have created only 11,000 new jobs in agriculture by 1970, when the drought struck. Pres. Emílio Garrastazú Médici's relief-work program, inaugurated in 1970, appeared to have been cut back in early 1971 in favour of such longer-range programs as low-interest loans to small farmers and irrigation projects. Work progressed on the trans-Amazon highway, one of the reported purposes of which was to encourage subsistence farmers to emigrate from the northeast to new lands in the Amazon Basin.

Brazilian coffee production appeared to have recovered from the effects of the 1969 freeze and drought. Production for 1971–72 was estimated at 23.6 million bags, compared with only 9,750,000 bags in the preceding crop year. Reflecting Brazil's recovery, the U.S. Department of Agriculture (USDA) September estimate placed the 1971–72 world crop at 71,685,000 bags (of which some 52,883,000 bags were expected to be available for export), compared with 56,980,000 bags in 1970–71. The estimated South American crop was up 64% to 34,729,000 bags, while African production, at 19,459,000 bags, showed a slight improvement.

The future of the International Coffee Agreement was open to question as the U.S. Congress failed to renew implementing legislation; congressional inaction was attributed to Brazilian actions against U.S. fishermen accused of operating within that country's territorial waters. Earlier in the year, a long-standing disagreement between the U.S. and Brazil was resolved when Brazil agreed to drop export taxes on coffee to be shipped to U.S. instant coffee manufacturers and, in exchange, was permitted to drop its 13-cents-per-pound export tax on soluble coffee. In

Bagged fish meal awaits export from a Peruvian dock. Peru was expected to substantially increase fish-meal exports in 1971.

August the International Coffee Council set the world coffee trade quota for the 1971–72 coffee year (October–September) at 47 million bags, a reduction of 2.5 million bags from the previous year. The reduced quota was designed to raise coffee prices, which declined in the first quarter of 1971.

Drought reduced the area planted for the 1970–71 wheat harvest in Argentina to 3,313,000 ha. (8,183,-110 ac.), more than a third below a year earlier; production of 4,215,000 metric tons of wheat was 40% less than in 1969–70, and it was expected that exports would be reduced by two-thirds. Planting intentions for 1971–72-crop wheat were high, but might be reduced if dry weather persisted in La Pampa Province. Heavy rains favoured the corn-producing areas, however, and the 1970–71 crop was estimated at 9,360,000 metric tons.

A sharp decline in meat production reduced beef exports in the first half of 1971 to only 123,000 metric tons, compared with 220,000 tons in the corresponding period a year earlier. In an attempt to increase exports, the government resorted to restrictions on domestic consumption.

Reinterpretation of agrarian reform by Chile's new socialist government created uncertainty among farmers in 1971. Basic government policies contemplated the expropriation of all farms—except those classified as medium and small—within the shortest possible time.

Agricultural production in Paraguay suffered from heavy rains and flooding early in 1971. The 1970–71 corn crop, expected to be about 180,000 metric tons, was 10% less than a year earlier.

Coffee and rice production declined in the Andean nations in 1970–71, but gains were shown for cocoa beans, sugar, and corn. Coffee production in Colombia was estimated at 7.8 million bags, a slight increase over 1969–70, and production of cocoa beans in Ecuador was expected to rise 18%. Redistribution of farmland began under Peru's agrarian reform program, which contemplated the expropriation of every large hacienda by 1975. Production of bananas, which accounted for about 45% of Ecuador's export income, was estimated at some 2.7 million tons in 1971.

Cuba. Cuba's 1971 sugar harvest was a disappointing 6.5 million short tons, a reduction of more than 30% from the 9.4 million tons produced in 1970. The new crop failed to reach either the preharvest goal of

Table IV. Honey Production in Specified Countries
In 000,000 lb.

Country	1970*	Average 1960–64
Argentina	55	47
Australia†	49	41
Austria	11	10
Brazil	15	17
Bulgaria	13	5
Canada	51	35
Chile	12	14
China	37	6
Czechoslovakia	16	9
France	22	32
Germany, West	40	26
Greece	15	13
Guatemala	6	6
Hungary	15	12
Italy	14	15
Japan	16	15
Mexico	66	60
New Zealand	13	12
Poland	19	10
Romania	13	15
Spain	20	20
Turkey	28	20
United Kingdom	9	8
United States	235	253
U.S.S.R.	237	234
Yugoslavia	12	8

*Preliminary.
†Crop year beginning July of previous year.
Source: U.S. Department of Agriculture.

World Production and Trade of Principal Grains

In 000 metric tons

	Wheat Production 1948-52 average	Wheat Production 1970	Wheat Imports— Exports+ 1967-70 average	Barley Production 1948-52 average	Barley Production 1970	Barley Imports— Exports+ 1967-70 average	Oats Production 1948-52 average	Oats Production 1970	Oats Imports— Exports+ 1967-70 average	Rye Production 1948-52 average	Rye Production 1970	Rye Imports— Exports+ 1967-70 average	Corn (Maize) Production 1948-52 average	Corn (Maize) Production 1970	Corn Imports— Exports+ 1967-70 average	Rice Production 1948-52 average	Rice Production 1970	Rice Imports— Exports+ 1967-70 average
World total	171,151	316,582	-44,687* / +45,404*	59,323	138,637	-6,848* / +6,900*	61,725	52,611	-1,192* / +1,072*	36,967	30,753	-644* / +640*	139,851	259,425	-27,334* / +27,528*	167,349	308,214	-6,668* / +6,745*
EUROPE																		
Austria	348	810	-19 / +11*	210	913	-118	274	271	-37	343	363	-23	120	612	-103 / +1*	—	—	-36*
Belgium	525	727	-834† / +168*†	244	525	-611† / +56*†	483	190	-76† / +1*†	221	65	-11† / +3*†	3	9	-1,140† / +290†	—	—	-45* / +10*†
Bulgaria	1,776	3,032	-226* / +379*	332	1,167	-25* / +1*	148	c.98	-1*	240	c.29	—	720	2,375	-49* / +242*	37	66	-19* / +1*
Czechoslovakia	1,493	3,174	-1,273*	1,046	2,280	-168* / +21*	961	943	-8‡	1,110	575	-127*	316	c.520	-207* / +5‡	—	—	-64‡ / +1‡
Denmark	285	512	-12 / +14*	1,708	4,813	-183 / +251	922	631	-19 / +17	365	c.120	-26	—	—	-214	—	—	-7*
Finland	263	409	-38* / +22*	201	933	-15 / +7*	718	1,330	+6*	201	131	-26	—	—	-15	—	—	-15*
France	7,791	12,922	-531 / +4,022	1,534	8,009	-4* / +2,915	3,392	2,070	+123	573	302	+28	452	7,431	-489 / +1,993	46	101	-111 / +36
Germany, East	1,243	2,132	-1,191* / +8*	593	1,926	-197*	1,188	558	-2*	2,516	1,483	-59*	5	c.3	-353*	—	—	-47*
Germany, West	2,669	5,662	-2,051 / +383*	1,402	4,754	-1,571 / +184	2,523	2,484	-446* / +16	3,066	2,663	-87* / +5*	20	507	-2,343 / +54	—	—	-145 / +21*
Greece	894	1,930	-41* / +192*	211	718	-8* / +45*	119	c.105	—	47	c.7	—	225	c.527	-233*	39	c.79	-4* / +8*
Hungary	1,909	2,742	-276* / +225*	654	558	-43* / +1*	216	64	—	732	160	-20* / +15*	2,081	4,072	-27* / +45*	40	45	-20* / +1*
Ireland	327	c.368	-181	163	c.800	-46 / +1*	616	c.210	-9	4	c.1	—	—	—	-125*	—	—	-3*
Italy	7,170	9,630	-1,199 / +181	258	315	-987	495	486	-206	123	69	—	2,306	4,729	-4,667 / +9	723	819	-6* / +214
Netherlands	324	643	-1,218 / +498	201	334	-185 / +135	419	201	-84* / +87	455	172	-37 / +37	26	c.4	-2,290 / +215*	—	—	-65 / +20*
Norway	58	12§	-360 / +1*	109	581	-118	170	140§	-8	2	c.4	-35	—	—	-98	—	—	-6
Poland	1,833	4,616	-1,177	1,061	2,148	-608 / +71	2,238	3,205	+8*	6,374	5,455	-45* / +53*	4	c.12	-257*	—	—	-62
Portugal	499	516	-307	96	54	-8*	124	76	—	162	150	-3*	421	586	-336 / +1*	114	198	-30*
Romania	2,778	3,351	+805*	412‖	511	+4*	369‖	c.150	—	177‖	c.45	+13*	2,495‖	6,395	+483*	35‖	c.70	-31*
Spain	3,625	4,064	-1* / +509*	1,909	3,092	-123 / +84*	519	409	-1* / +4*	482	250	—	520	1,868	-2,301	280	388	+2* / -99
Sweden	677	965	-47 / +269	231	1,904	-8 / +160*	804	1,686	+139	258	211	-17 / +21	—	—	-40	—	—	-12*
Switzerland	260	370	-423	55	c.143	-424	68	c.32	-162	34	c.40	-7	6	c.63	-200	—	—	-26* / +1*
U.S.S.R.	35,759¶	99,500	-1,069* / +5,206*	6,354¶	38,100	+605*	13,005¶	14,100	+8*	17,961¶	13,000	+260*	5,751‖	9,400	-373* / +207*	202¶	1,280	-328* / +4*
United Kingdom	2,397	4,174	-4,398 / +4*	2,061	7,496	-539 / +413	2,852	1,233	-16 / +6*	52	14	-11*	—	—	-3,445 / +14*	—	—	-118 / +1*
Yugoslavia	2,171	3,795	-172* / +1*	323	402	-11* / +41*	286	309	-3* / +2*	248	127	—	3,078	6,928	-3* / +498*	5	c.27	-36*
ASIA																		
Burma	4	c.90	—	—	—	—	—	—	—	—	—	—	30	c.150	+9*	5,481	c.8,300	+514
Cambodia	—	—	—	—	—	+1*	—	—	—	—	—	—	57	137	+71*	1,635¶	3,814	+117
China	15,913‖	c.28,500§	-3,908*	c.12,360	c.15,000	+1*	c.1,540	c.2,400	—	—	—	—	c.14,082	c.25,000§	-45* / +63‡	58,188‖	c.95,000§	-20* / +916*
India	6,087	20,093	-4,734*	2,384	2,716	-2*	—	—	—	—	—	—	2,165	c.6,500	-37*	33,383	c.64,500	-398* / +7*
Indonesia	—	—	—	—	—	—	—	—	—	—	—	—	1,535¶	2,433	—	9,441¶	18,090	-553*
Iran	1,879‖	c.3,800	-298‡ / +144‡	767	c.200	+5*	—	—	—	—	—	—	6	c.35	-40‡	424	1,060	-20* / +1‡
Iraq	448	1,059	-128* / +6*	722	691	+44*	—	—	—	—	—	—	14	c.6	-2*	203	203	-3* / +1*
Japan	1,375	474	-4,304	2,020	573	-670	119	61	-67	6	c.1	-67	57	148	-5,152 / +3*	12,736	16,479	-214 / +121*
Korea, South	139	357	-993	c.846	1,974	-88*	—	—	—	36	c.27	—	14	c.63	-45*	3,385	5,515	-339*
Lebanon	51	c.50	-280	25	c.8	-71 / +1*	2	c.2δ	-3*	—	—	—	12	c.1	-63‡ / +1*	—	—	-20*
Malaysia	—	—	-311*	—	—	—	—	—	-6*	—	—	—	8	c.10	-97*	670□	c.1,488	-342* / +6*
Pakistan	3,685	c.7,399	-1,377* / +1*	150	128	—	—	—	—	—	—	—	384	c.676	-72*	12,399	c.21,000	-81* / +121
Philippines	—	—	-510*	—	—	—	—	—	-2*	—	—	—	695	2,005	-25*	2,767	5,343	-97* / +13*
Syria	761	625	-213 / +2*	321	235	-3* / +147	6	2	-1* / +3*	—	—	—	31	c.9	-2*	13	c.3	-37*
Thailand	—	—	-43*	—	—	—	—	—	—	—	—	—	31	1,600	-2* / +1,349*	6,846	13,400	+1,149
Turkey	4,770	10,081	-287 / +1*	2,270	3,250	—	326	400	—	500	630	—	747	1,040	—	109	257	-4* / +1*
Vietnam, South	—	—	—	—	—	-1*	—	—	—	—	—	—	30¶	c.31	-48*	2,395□	5,716	-590*
AFRICA																		
Algeria	996	c.1,500	-597*	808	c.465	-24* / +2*	137	c.30	+3*	—	—	—	6	c.7	-8*	—	c.5	-3*
Egypt	1,111	1,516	-1,335	123	83	—	—	—	—	—	—	—	1,378	2,359	-112	971	2,605	+608
Kenya	101	c.220	-516* / +43*	8	c.12	—	5	c.4	—	—	—	—	93°	c.1,350	+185*	c.6	c.22	-1* / +2*
Morocco	786	1,801	-516* / +1*	1,483	1,753	-2* / +48*	51	c.16	+2*	4	c.2	—	302	456	-6* / +6*	8¶	c.51	+8*
South Africa	555°	1,358°	-163*	41‖°	30°	-3*	79‖	122	-6* / +1*	10‖	8	-1*	2,629	6,133	-113* / +1,904*	c.6	c.2▲	-77* / +1*
Tunisia	452	c.450	-301*	218	c.150	-48*	14	6▲	—	—	—	—	—	—	-17*	—	—	-1*
NORTH AND CENTRAL AMERICA																		
Canada	13,443	9,023	+9,054	4,245	9,051	+1,379	6,220	5,673	+88	469	570	+138	388	2,549	-672 / +3*	—	—	-42*
Mexico	534	2,436	+144	160	212	-2*	47	c.47	-1*	—	—	—	3,090	c.9,100	-195 / +735	173	383	-2* / +15*
United States	31,065	37,516	-26 / +15,779+	5,843	8,937	-545 / +325	18,970	13,201	-32 / +102	524	979	-21 / +45	74,308	104,393	-40 / +14,064*	1,925	3,758	+1,852
SOUTH AMERICA																		
Argentina	5,175	4,230	-56* / +2,164	656	367	+152*	743	c.600	+214*	526	c.375	+12*	2,839	9,360	+3,745*	137	407	+59*
Bolivia	37□	62	-37‡	39¶	c.55	-91*	2¶	11δ	-1‡	—	—	—	163	c.370	—	20¶	c.60	-1‡
Brazil	498	1,657	-2,474*	15	c.30	-36*	9	c.27	-15*	17	c.19	—	5,841	15,381	-4* / +949	2,921	7,482	+88
Chile	928	1,307	-292*	79	97	—	80	c.100	+1‡	5	c.10	—	68	239	-98*	75	c.78	-12*
Colombia	124	c.80	-230*	50	c.84	-10*	—	—	-7*	—	—	—	753	c.850	-4* / +2*	248	673	+5*
Peru	146	c.150	-577*	208	c.180	-13*	c.2	c.2	-3*	—	—	—	275	c.630	-4* / +1*	191	607	-41*
Uruguay	469	388	+30*	23	50	+1*	44	c.62	—	—	—	—	141	139	—	41	142	+44* / +1*
Venezuela	5¶	c.1	-718*	—	—	—	—	—	-8*	—	—	—	303	710	-77*	41	226	-5* / +35*
OCEANIA																		
Australia	5,161	7,511	+6,739	531	2,177	-11* / +457	560	1,270	+289	12	c.19	—	126	239	-1* / +2*	63	243	-2* / +105
New Zealand	139	287	-51*	49	174	—	49	55	—	—	—	—	10	57	—	—	—	-4*

Note: (—) indicates quantity nil or negligible; (c.) indicates provisional or estimated. *1967-69 average. †Belgium-Luxembourg economic union. ‡1967-68 average. §1969. ‖Average of 4 years. ¶Average of 3 years. °1950. δ1965. □Average of 2 years. °Farms and estates only. ▲1966. +Including foreign aid shipments.

Sources: FAO *Production Yearbook 1970;* FAO *Trade Yearbook 1970;* FAO *Monthly Bulletin of Agricultural Economics and Statistics.*

(M. C. Mac D.)

7.7 million tons or the revised goal of 7.3 million tons set by Prime Minister Fidel Castro early in May. The reduced crop was attributed to a variety of reasons, not the least being the decision not to commit the heavy component of labour that was used in the 1970 harvest. A severe drought in western Pinar del Rio Province reduced Cuba's production of tobacco in 1971 by 40%. It was reported that the deadly and highly contagious African swine fever had been discovered in Cuba; 30,000 hogs were slaughtered by late July in an effort to control the disease.

World production of centrifugal sugar in 1970–71 was estimated at 78,416,000 short tons, a decrease of about 1% from the record harvests of a year earlier. Production in Western Hemisphere countries of an estimated 29,394,000 tons was 3.6% below 1969–70. South American production was up 13%; production in Western Europe declined fractionally; and production in Africa, at an estimated 4,962,000 tons, was down slightly. The U.S. Congress agreed on a bill extending the sugar program for three years. The measure provided for the distribution of 11.2 million tons of sugar for the U.S. domestic market; 6,285,000 tons were allocated to domestic production areas, and the balance was divided among 32 foreign suppliers. In October the International Sugar Organization announced a 5% reduction in basic export tonnages for 1971–72; in December it suspended all sugar quotas to free markets, as of Jan. 1, 1972. The quotas would be reestablished if the prevailing price rose above 5.25 cents per pound.

WESTERN EUROPE

Weather in most areas of Western Europe was satisfactory during the 1971 growing season, although severe drought during the latter half of the year was experienced in parts of France and much of the Rhine Valley. The total wheat crop of 48,994,000 metric tons from 42,491,410 ac. was 12% larger than in 1970 and 10% above the 1965–69 average. Barley production rose 9% to 40,037,000 metric tons from 31,727,-150 ac., and feed grains, fruit crops, and livestock products were at high levels. The agricultural worries of 1971 were largely economic—unrest associated with the severe cost-price squeeze, trade barriers, and instability in national and international monetary relations.

United Kingdom and Ireland. An excellent grain crop was harvested in the U.K.; wheat set a new record of 4.5 million metric tons, and the barley crop

totaled 7,950,000 tons, compared with 7,496,000 tons in 1970. The oat crop fell, however—to 1.2 million tons from 1,233,000. Cattle numbers rose to 12,469,-000 head from 12,295,000 a year earlier, and hogs to 8,565,000 head from 8,127,000. As in some other parts of the world, sheep numbers declined—to 18,690,000 head from 19,157,000.

In March, U.K. Minister of Agriculture James Prior announced details of the 1971 annual price review. Increased costs for the whole agricultural sector were computed at £217 million, while net farm income had risen only 2.5%. The new price guarantees would total £138 million, not quite offsetting the £141 million cost increase on review commodities. Fat cattle prices were raised 11% from the March 1970 review level; milk was raised by 12.8%, and the price for fat sheep and lambs was increased to 53.5 cents per pound. The guaranteed price of wheat was raised 8% and of oats, 3.5%, but no increase was made for rye. Some minor subsidies were ended.

To some it appeared that U.K. entry into the EEC would reinforce trends already present, since for some years there had been a shift toward an EEC type of policy and away from deficiency payments. Agricultural negotiations between the U.K. and the EEC were directed to two main points: Britain's contribution to the EEC common agricultural fund for price supports, export subsidies, and farm structural adjustments; and access of New Zealand's dairy products to the U.K. markets. It was agreed that Britain would pay 8.4% of the total fund in 1973, increasing progressively to 18.92% in 1977. New Zealand would continue to sell its dairy products to the U.K. during the transitional period at gradually decreasing guaranteed minimum prices and quantities. There were also broad commitments to safeguard other Commonwealth agricultural markets in Britain, especially for sugar.

Ireland's wheat crop totaled 330,000 metric tons, compared with a 1965–69 average of 265,000 tons. Cattle numbers increased to 5,405,000 head from 5,229,000 a year earlier, and hog numbers rose about 10%. Exports of livestock products reached a record 107,000 long tons, mostly in carcass form and very largely to the U.K. Under the Beef Cattle Incentive Scheme, subsidies of about $11 million were paid to farmers for not producing commercial milk.

EEC Countries. In March 1971 perhaps as many as 100,000 farmers from the EEC countries protested in Brussels, where the EEC agriculture ministers were

Table V. Poultry Meat Production in Selected Countries*
In 000,000 lb.

Country	1969†	1968	1967	Average 1955–59
Belgium-Luxembourg	194	200	223	95
France	1,280	1,199	1,129	511
Germany, West	508	463	450	172
Italy	1,197	1,173	829	215
Netherlands	540	470	441	96
Total EEC	3,719	3,505	3,071	1,089
Austria	81	80	76	4
Canada	903	807	818	428
Denmark	145	142	146	58
Greece	125	113	102	36
Japan	741	606	529	—
Poland	265	251	236	109
Spain	628	566	567	—
United Kingdom	1,246	1,160	1,062	455
United States	9,728	9,145	9,410	5,480

*On ready-to-cook basis (70% of live weight).
†Preliminary.
Source: U.S. Department of Agriculture, Foreign Agricultural Service.

Table VI. Egg Production in Specified Countries
In 000,000

Country	1969*	1968	1967
Argentina	2,940	2,880	2,640
Australia	2,380	2,328	2,554
Belgium-Luxembourg	3,900	3,438	3,083
Brazil	9,670	9,480	8,750
Canada	5,655	5,436	5,306
Czechoslovakia	3,410	3,270	3,110
France	11,200	10,800	10,300
Germany, East	4,050	4,046	3,995
Germany, West	14,400	14,076	13,802
Hungary	2,600	2,792	2,750
Italy	10,281	9,450	10,465
Japan	27,565	24,390	23,307
Mexico	5,657	5,375	5,356
Netherlands	4,370	3,969	3,695
Poland	6,400	6,315	6,348
Romania	3,200	3,113	2,900
U.S.S.R.	37,000	35,522	33,921
United Kingdom†	15,036	14,814	14,916
United States	68,700	69,324	70,161

*Preliminary.
†Year beginning June 1 of year shown.

Table VII. Milk Cows and Milk Production in Specified Countries

Country	Number of milk cows in 000			Milk production in 000,000 lb.		
	1970*	1969	Average 1961–65	1970*	1969	Average 1961–65
Australia	2,677	2,701	3,190	17,002	16,573	15,244
Austria	1,085	1,085	1,122	7,326	7,366	6,743
Belgium	1,033	1,066	1,024	8,386	8,642	8,664
Canada	2,471	2,526	2,930	18,279	18,698	18,404
Denmark	1,153	1,233	1,428	10,214	10,754	11,713
France	9,550	9,639	9,409	65,525	66,206	54,162
Germany, West	5,593	5,878	5,852	48,184	48,977	45,368
Greece	460	478	434	1,276	1,217	1,159
Ireland	1,669	1,655	1,373	7,987	8,122	6,458
Italy	3,500	3,715	3,448	20,613	20,051	21,872
Japan	1,067	967	717	10,500	9,940	5,976
Netherlands	1,920	1,904	1,701	18,164	17,582	15,578
New Zealand	2,363	2,304	2,007	13,023	14,625	12,302
Norway	424	436	568	3,979	4,030	3,666
Sweden	746	802	1,180	6,512	7,035	8,446
Switzerland	901	908	926	6,909	6,993	6,837
United Kingdom	4,471	4,432	4,202	27,314	26,784	24,791
United States	12,509	12,693	16,195	117,436	116,345	125,660

*Preliminary.
Source: U.S. Department of Agriculture, Foreign Agricultural Service.

Butter pours from a giant churn in a Danish dairy-products plant. High dairy prices in the European Community were expected to stimulate dairy production in Denmark, Great Britain, and Ireland.

COURTESY, "FOREIGN AGRICULTURE"

meeting, to express their anger at the EEC Commission in general and at Sicco Mansholt, the Commission's agricultural expert, in particular. The farmers complained especially of low incomes and high and constantly rising costs. The "parity ratio," even for the comparatively well-off Belgian farmer, declined to 68% in 1970.

At the Brussels meeting the EEC Council of Agricultural Ministers revised prices for major farm products upward for the first time in three years, and instituted a $1,480,000,000 program to reform and modernize farm structure. Various types of assistance would be provided to prevent further expansion of the agricultural production area and to encourage larger, modernized farms with fewer farmers. Efforts to correct the EEC's troublesome butter surplus were finally overeffective, bringing sharply higher prices and a shortage in some markets. In June the Council of

Agricultural Ministers decided that free trade in liquid milk for direct human consumption would be permitted among the member states on March 31, 1972, with Italy having a waiver until the end of 1973.

The mixed feed industry of Belgium reached a new record of 4.9 million tons, and even a pause in the upward trend of the hog cycle failed to dampen the estimated expansion for 1971. Dutch poultry meat exports in 1970 rose 16% to about 420 million lb. Egg supplies were in surplus and prices were depressed.

As West Germany moved toward greater emphasis on livestock and products, it became increasingly dependent on grain imports. Though support for high grain prices caused a large part of the $3 billion annual cost of the EEC agricultural program, West Germany in 1970 produced only 24.4% of the Community's grain output. Within this context, 1971 grain production was high, with wheat (14,566,000 metric tons), barley (5.7 million metric tons), and oats (2,930,000 tons) all setting new records.

French grain crops were also substantially larger than in 1970. Under the Sixth Economic Plan, grain production in 1975 was projected at about 40 million tons, compared with 32.4 million tons in 1969–70. Livestock and meat output were expected to expand substantially, while the Sixth Plan for Poultry (1971–75) forecast broiler output of 575,000 tons against 470,000 tons in 1970.

Italy produced an above average wheat crop of 9,852,000 metric tons. A large filbert crop was reported, despite adverse weather during March. Output of meats was lagging behind consumer demand, giving rise to imports that accounted for half of Italy's negative trade balance. Meat consumption had increased by 900% over the preceding 15 years, while domestic production had risen only 230%.

Other Countries. The important Danish barley crop totaled a record 5.5 million metric tons in 1971. Milk production in 1970 fell 5% to 4.6 million metric tons; a further reduction was expected in 1971 as

Table VIII. Cattle and Buffalo Numbers in Major Producing Areas

In 000

Area	Estimated 1971*	1970†	Average 1961–65
North America	172,538	169,078	151,359
Canada	12,217	11,828	11,332
Mexico	25,374	25,123	20,210
United States	114,568	112,303	103,892
South America	201,358	198,154	168,937
Argentina	49,633	49,429	43,341
Brazil	97,122	95,258	78,718
Colombia	21,173	20,359	15,780
Uruguay	8,600	8,500	8,526
Venezuela	8,850	8,631	6,943
Western Europe	88,246	88,825	83,469
France	21,621	21,719	20,131
Germany, West	13,995	14,286	13,115
Italy	9,324	9,612	9,292
United Kingdom	12,469	12,295	11,610
Eastern Europe	33,939	34,044	32,964
Poland	10,400	10,844	9,697
Yugoslavia	5,149	5,075	5,509
U.S.S.R.	99,100	95,162	83,493
Africa	135,047	134,007	124,478
South Africa	12,557	11,682	12,514
Asia	449,242	447,379	405,551
Iran	5,865	5,960	4,782
Japan	3,650	3,593	3,327
Philippines	6,125	6,050	4,849
Turkey	14,600	14,367	13,783
Oceania	32,147	31,411	25,325
Australia	22,637	22,162	18,357
New Zealand	9,100	8,839	6,646
World total‡	1,211,617	1,198,060	1,075,576

*Forecast.
†Preliminary.
‡Includes allowance for any missing data for countries shown and for other producing countries not shown.
Source: U.S. Department of Agriculture.

Table IX. Hog Numbers in Major Producing Areas

In 000

Area	Estimated 1971*	1970†	Average 1961–65
North America	98,810	82,668	74,911
Canada	7,701	6,458	5,220
Mexico	12,424	11,721	7,969
United States	67,540	56,655	55,544
South America	83,483	82,014	66,681
Argentina	4,500	4,400	3,388
Brazil	67,000	65,867	53,126
Western Europe	87,839	81,778	66,189
Denmark	8,733	8,361	7,284
France	11,306	10,462	8,982
Germany, West	20,915	19,323	16,933
Italy	9,530	9,224	4,787
Spain	...	6,400	5,659
United Kingdom	8,565	8,127	7,098
Eastern Europe	52,159	47,321	47,004
Germany, East	...	9,237	8,654
Hungary	...	5,970	6,216
Poland	14,333	13,446	13,080
Yugoslavia	6,655	5,544	5,815
U.S.S.R.	67,200	56,055	57,808
Africa	6,127	6,076	5,300
South Africa	1,280	1,250	1,321
Asia	218,631	212,107	126,449
Japan	6,800	6,335	3,474
Philippines	12,500	12,000	9,236
Taiwan	...	3,048	2,917
Oceania	3,314	3,194	2,463
Australia	2,500	2,398	1,567
World total‡	617,563	571,213	446,805

*Forecast.
†Preliminary.
‡Includes allowance for any missing data for countries shown and for other producing countries not shown.
Source: U.S. Department of Agriculture, Foreign Agricultural Service.

Table X. Sheep Numbers in Major Producing Areas

In 000

Area	Estimated 1971*	1970†	Average 1961–65
North America	26,629	27,463	37,500
Canada	652	598	911
Mexico	5,161	5,321	6,305
United States	19,560	20,288	29,023
South America	118,129	118,420	121,256
Argentina	42,000	43,000	48,127
Brazil	25,500	24,449	19,997
Peru	...	14,500	14,454
Uruguay	19,000	18,900	21,860
Western Europe	76,969	77,331	81,486
France	10,106	10,037	8,876
Greece	7,500	7,449	8,775
Italy	8,125	8,137	7,956
Spain	...	18,800	21,116
United Kingdom	18,690	19,157	20,689
Eastern Europe	42,525	42,551	42,834
Bulgaria	...	9,223	10,070
Romania	13,813	13,836	12,217
Yugoslavia	8,693	8,974	10,232
U.S.S.R.	137,800	130,700	133,860
Africa	129,729	131,967	125,747
South Africa	38,332	40,415	39,661
Asia	258,531	257,188	221,063
Iran	34,000	35,000	21,445
Turkey	36,500	36,351	32,863
Oceania	246,403	240,368	211,474
Australia	185,640	180,079	160,924
New Zealand	60,750	60,276	50,536
World total‡	1,036,715	1,025,988	975,220

*Forecast.
†Preliminary.
‡Includes allowance for any missing data for countries shown and for other producing countries not shown.
Source: U.S. Department of Agriculture, Foreign Agricultural Service.

cow numbers declined, largely as a result of labour problems. Butter output fell 9% to 131,000 tons, and exports were 13% below those of 1969.

Norway became the world's first country to finance paid vacations to farmers receiving 80% or more of their total income from farming. The compensation would be $140 for a two-week period. Sweden reported a record barley crop of 2,075,000 metric tons. Swiss cattle numbers were at an all-time high, and official efforts were being made to shift emphasis from dairy to beef.

The grain harvest in Greece was about the same as in 1970, but above the 1965-69 average. An attempt was being made to reach self-sufficiency in livestock and dairy production by increasing production of feed grains and by expansion of small farms and development of new large-scale units for both beef and dairy cattle. Spain experienced its most acute drought in five years in 1970; livestock, grains, and olives were severely damaged, and there was considerable distress in rural communities. Both wheat and barley appeared to have recovered in 1971. The virus disease called tristeza had spread to about 30% of Spain's citrus area, with Valencia the hardest hit. Growers who bulldozed diseased trees and replaced them with resistant varieties were eligible for official compensation of $290 to $433 per acre. Oilseeds continued to replace olive oil; in 1969-70 nearly half of the oil consumed in Spain was from seed.

AFRICA

There was some progress among the diverse agricultural economies of Africa in 1971. Record production of wheat in Morocco, recovery of the corn crop in South Africa and Rhodesia, and good cereal crops in North African countries were reported. A record cotton harvest in Sudan and an improved peanut harvest in Senegal added to the favourable outlook in those areas. There were reverses, however. Cotton production declined in Egypt; both crops and livestock were threatened by prolonged drought in East Africa; and South Africa's important wool clip was sharply reduced as a result of drought in 1970. According to the USDA Foreign Agricultural Service, the index of total agricultural production in 1970 was 113 (1961-65 = 100), only 1 point above 1969 and representing a 2% loss on a per capita basis.

North Africa. A record wheat crop in Morocco, estimated at 2,155,000 metric tons, and prospects for good crops in other North African countries in 1971 held out the hope for an unusually productive agricultural year. At midyear the first official estimate of the harvest of four principal grains in Morocco set production at 4.3 million metric tons, 19% above a year earlier. Citrus production in Morocco in 1970-71 declined more than 8%, primarily because of the cyclical downturn following the 1969-70 bumper crop. Algeria's 1970-71 citrus harvest rose to 466,000 metric tons from 461,000 tons in 1969-70.

The Moroccan cotton crop was 20% larger than in 1969-70, and the government's guaranteed price program for domestic sugar resulted in a 1970 sugar-beet harvest of 1.1 million tons from 84,000 ac., sufficient to produce 150,000 tons of raw sugar. The 1970-71 Tunisian olive harvest was estimated at 425,000 metric tons. Production of dates in Algeria rose to an estimated 100,000 metric tons in 1970 from 85,000 tons a year earlier.

Cotton production in Egypt fell to 2.3 million bales (480 lb. each) in 1970-71 from 2.5 million a year

earlier; average yields fell from 714 lb. per ac. in 1969-70 to 669. A further decrease was expected in 1971-72 as a result of government action to reduce acreage. Wheat imports in 1970-71 were nearly double those of 1969-70. It was reported that new water supplies from the Aswan High Dam would be used to increase acreage for crops by about 2 million, of which 1.3 million ac. would be new land brought under cultivation for the first time and the remainder would be accounted for by production of two or more crops per year on land that formerly yielded only one. Production of cotton and peanuts in Sudan appeared to have reached a high level in 1970-71. Cotton production was estimated at a record 1,150,-000 bales while peanut production, at an estimated 353,000 metric tons, was second only to 1969-70.

West Africa. Total agricultural production in the West African nations appeared to have remained essentially unchanged in 1970-71. Reduced production of coffee, peanuts, and cotton was offset to some degree by increases in cocoa and some food crops. The important Nigerian cotton harvest fell to an estimated 175,000 bales in 1970-71 from the exceptional 420,000 bales of a year earlier; losses were attributed to inadequate early rain followed by too much moisture in midseason. Cotton production was also down in Cameroon and Chad. Palm oil continued to gain in importance; Nigeria's production rose to 500,000 metric tons from 488,000, and slight increases were forecast for Cameroon, Dahomey, Ghana, Ivory Coast, Liberia, and Sierra Leone. The 1970-71 West African coffee crop was estimated at 4 million bags (132.3 lb. each), about 13% less than in 1969-70.

Nigeria's peanut crop was estimated at a sharply reduced 825,000 metric tons in 1970, resulting from both unfavourable weather and dissatisfaction with prices to producers. Senegal's 1970-71 peanut harvest was drastically reduced to an estimated 660,000 metric tons, compared with 800,000 tons in 1969-70 and a

Table XI. Centrifugal Sugar Production in Principal Producing Countries
In 000 short tons, raw value

Country	1970-71	1969-70	Average 1961/62 1965/66
Argentina	1,061	1,059	1,053
Australia	2,614	2,314	1,943
Brazil	5,987	5,063	4,121
China	2,300	2,200	1,236
Colombia	762	774	440
Cuba	6,500	9,400	5,094
Czechoslovakia	850	800	1,142
Denmark	321	335	346
Dominican Republic	1,200	1,118	808
France	2,971	2,974	2,225
Germany, East	600	575	847
Germany, West	2,270	2,280	1,894
India	5,033	5,520	3,788
Indonesia	800	700	686
Iran	660	642	206
Italy	1,323	1,526	1,136
Jamaica	448	414	537
Mauritius	745	635	660
Mexico	2,746	2,587	2,043
Netherlands	773	845	595
Peru	882	816	880
Philippines	2,334	2,124	1,709
South Africa	1,542	1,788	1,206
Spain	863	876	565
Taiwan	819	668	1,004
Turkey	610	773	709
United Kingdom	1,090	1,033	978
U.S.S.R.	10,000	9,755	8,443
United States	5,802	5,558	5,047
U.S. dependencies*	400	460	964
Yugoslavia	424	545	424
World total	78,416	79,251	62,746

*Puerto Rico and Virgin Islands of the U.S.
Source: U.S. Department of Agriculture, Foreign Agricultural Service.

Table XII. Coffee Production (Green) in Principal Producing Countries
In 000 bags, 132.3 lb. each

Country	1971-72*	1970-71	1969-70	Average 1962/63 1966/67
Angola	3,400	3,300	3,300	3,017
Brazil	23,600	9,750	19,000	24,580
Cameroon	1,250	1,150	1,200	939
Colombia	7,800	7,500	8,450	7,820
Congo (Kinshasa)	1,250	1,200	1,100	1,005
Costa Rica	1,330	1,250	1,400	1,043
Ecuador	1,200	1,200	660	833
El Salvador	2,350	2,000	2,500	1,898
Guatemala	2,000	1,840	1,750	1,808
India	1,325	1,800	1,150	1,181
Indonesia	2,250	2,350	2,200	2,016
Ivory Coast	4,000	4,000	4,600	3,565
Malagasy Republic	850	950	830	915
Mexico	3,300	3,000	3,075	2,671
Peru	1,030	990	940	835
Philippines	840	840	815	679
Tanzania	900	900	775	653
Uganda	3,050	3,000	3,350	2,669
Venezuela	920	900	900	809
Total North America	12,304	11,442	11,921	10,488
Total South America	34,729	20,501	30,189	35,017
Total Africa	19,459	19,279	19,659	16,419
Total Asia and Oceania	5,193	5,758	4,866	4,316
World total	71,685	56,980	66,635	66,240

*Second estimate.
Source: U.S. Department of Agriculture, Foreign Agricultural Service.

record 1,170,000 tons in 1964–65; poor quality seed, the most widespread drought in recent years, as well as the possibility that up to 50,000 tons of Senegalese peanuts were smuggled into The Gambia to take advantage of higher prices, were given as reasons.

Early estimates placed the 1971–72 world cocoa crop at 1,532,000 metric tons, compared with 1,497,-600 tons produced in 1970–71. The forecast for the 1971–72 crop represented a 2.3% increase over the record 1970–71 harvest. According to the forecast, production in African countries would reach 1,113,600 tons, led by Ghana, with a forecast crop of 445,000 tons. South American production of 1971–72 cocoa beans was forecast at 300,800 metric tons, an improvement of 5% over 1970–71, when 286,800 metric tons were produced. Cocoa prices through mid-1971 continued to weaken and prospects for improvement were not good. In mid-September the six-nation Cocoa Producers Alliance adopted a draft agreement on an export quota plan and a buffer stock arrangement designed to maintain a satisfactory balance between supply and demand. Earlier, members of the Alliance had agreed to withhold forward sales of 1971–72-crop cocoa until market conditions improved.

East Africa. The "short" rains that usually fall in October and November failed in late 1970, with disastrous consequences. In Kenya, especially, crops failed, cattle starved, and by April some 150,000 of the population were being fed by the government and by voluntary relief agencies. By early April even the "long" rains, which usually begin in March, had been only fitful, and prospects for 1971 crops were dim in some areas. Even so, some East African crops, such as sugar, coffee, and, in some places, wheat and cotton, improved over a year earlier. Coffee production in East African nations overall showed a slight improvement, as did wheat production in Kenya and Ethiopia. Kenya's important corn crop was estimated at 1.5 million tons in 1970–71, compared with 1,433,000 tons a year earlier. Cotton production for the region as a whole was unchanged.

Tea production in 1970 reached record levels, reflecting increases in Kenya, but drought dimmed the outlook for the 1971 tea harvest there. Uganda's 1971 tea harvest was also affected. Tobacco production in East Africa continued to increase in 1970; Malawi's crop was nearly double that of 1969. Exports of vanilla beans from the Malagasy Republic in 1970 rose 11% to 2,680,000 lb., and clove exports rose sharply to 11.6 million lb.

Tanzania was the world's second leading producer of sisal in 1970, with 445.7 million lb. Brazil was first with 463 million lb.; Angola was third with 124 million lb.; and Kenya, fourth with 107.5 million lb. World production of hard fibres—sisal, henequen, and abaca—was estimated at 1,892,000,000 lb. in 1970, about 1% more than in 1969. Of this, sisal accounted for about 1,366,600,000 lb. Abaca, chiefly from the Philippines, totaled 199 million lb., and henequen production, dominated by Mexico, amounted to 321 million lb. Low sisal prices continued to depress production in most areas except Brazil. Representatives from sisal- and henequen-producing countries met at Rome in May 1971 to revive the informal export quota and minimum price arrangements that had been in force in 1968 and 1969, and agreement was reached on a global export quota for fibre and cordage totaling 605,000 metric tons.

Central and South Africa. Several areas in southern Africa showed signs of recovery from the di-

sastrous drought of February–September 1970. South Africa's corn crop, which fell to 6,135,000 metric tons in 1969–70, was estimated at 8,750,000 tons for 1970–71; this would provide an export surplus of 2.5 million tons or more. The 1970–71 sorghum harvest was expected to provide exports of 400,000 tons. The wheat harvest showed a slight improvement over 1969–70; acreage was up by a third, but yields declined more than 20%. Drought affected sugar production in the principal sugarcane area around Natal; the 1970–71 harvest was estimated at 1,399,000 metric tons, compared with 1,622,000 tons in 1969–70.

South Africa's livestock numbers—except sheep—continued an upward trend in 1971; cattle were up 7.5% to 12,557,000 head and hog numbers rose about 2.5% to 1,280,000 head. Sheep numbers declined nearly 5%, and the 1970–71 wool season was described as the most disappointing in the post-World War II period; production in 1971 was forecast at 6.5% below the 278 million lb. produced in 1970 and 20% below 1969. Furthermore, the full effects of the 1970 drought were not expected to be felt for two or three years.

Exports of tobacco from Rhodesia rose to 70 million lb. in 1970 from 50 million lb. a year earlier; nevertheless, 1970 exports were far below the 1960–64 average of 178,730,000 lb. At midyear Rhodesia announced an increased tobacco target of 132 million lb. for 1971–72 at a guaranteed average price of 32.2 cents per pound—less than half the annual production of that country in the period prior to its declaration of independence. Large holdover stocks continued to be held in government warehouses. Drought in 1970 exacerbated the already serious agricultural situation in Zambia, which was forced to import more than 400,000 metric tons of corn in 1970–71.

EASTERN EUROPE AND THE U.S.S.R.

The grain harvest appeared to be substantially more favourable than in 1970, especially in Eastern Europe. Early indications were that oilseed crops, especially rape and sunflower, would be larger than the small crops of the preceding year.

Eastern Europe. Wheat production was estimated at 27,565,000 metric tons in 1970, compared with 22,720,000 tons in 1970. The rye crop of 10,540,000 metric tons, more than one-third of the world total, was 36% above 1970. Barley totaled 9,928,000 metric tons, compared with 8,856,000 metric tons a year earlier, but the oat crop fell to 5,097,000 metric tons from 5,302,000. Cattle and sheep numbers were down moderately in early 1971, while hog numbers increased to 52,159,000 head from 47,321,000.

A steep rise in Poland's food prices following two lean years appeared to have been a basic cause of the unrest and disorders of December 1970. Grain production had declined 4 million tons in 1970, and meat animal numbers had also decreased. In the wake of the riots, higher retail prices were largely rescinded, with some meat prices reduced 15 to 25%. Prices to farmers for milk and livestock were raised somewhat after March 24, and other incentives were offered to increase production, especially of meats. Despite some worry about drought in early summer, grain production, other than oats, did rise substantially in 1971.

Unlike most of Eastern Europe, East Germany suffered a severe spring drought that resulted in the worst harvest since World War II.

In Hungary an examination of the larger collective

farms after three years of economic reform revealed that about two-thirds of the country's 2,700 collective farms were profitable. Within the framework of official policies, farm managers were able to base decisions on economic factors.

After a short crop in 1970, Yugoslavia achieved a needed gain in farm production. Wheat set a new record of 5.3 million metric tons, while barley, rye, and oats increased moderately. In an effort to assure adequate sugar-beet plantings minimum purchasing prices to growers were raised from 0.18 dinars per kilo ($12 per ton) to 0.22 dinars. Total poultry numbers were up 10% over the previous year, and further increases were anticipated. Some 80 Holstein-Friesian dairy heifers, the first commercial shipment of U.S. dairy cattle to Yugoslavia, were displayed in May at the Novi Sad Agricultural Trade Fair.

U.S.S.R. Having completed the eighth five-year plan with record large grain production in 1970, the U.S.S.R. started the ninth plan with good, but smaller, grain crops. Wheat was forecast at 70 million metric tons from 64.5 million ha. (159,315,000 ac.), compared with 80 million tons in 1970 and an average crop of 66.9 million tons. The barley crop was estimated at 27 million tons, compared with 29.5 million tons in 1970, but oats increased to 12 million tons, up from 10.5 million tons. Rye declined to 11 million tons; even so, the U.S.S.R. and Poland together accounted for about two-thirds of world rye production, which in 1971 totaled 29,661,000 tons.

Although the 1970 grain output had been the largest in history, grain purchases, especially of wheat, continued. In June an agreement was announced to buy as much as 130 million bu. of Canadian wheat valued at about $235 million, and in November 80 million bu. of corn, 28 million bu. of barley, and 21 million

COURTESY, "FOREIGN AGRICULTURE"

Herder in the Soviet Union moves sheep to summer pasture. Agricultural production in the U.S.S.R. was moving back toward record levels after a setback in 1969 due to unfavourable weather conditions.

bu. of oats, valued at about $135 million, were purchased from the U.S. Exports of wheat, largely to Eastern Europe, rose to about 7 million tons in 1970–71. The corn crop was not up to planned levels, and additional feed grains would probably be imported to take care of larger livestock herds. The goal of 15 million tons of corn for 1971 would require an increase in acreage of approximately 50% over 1970.

The new five-year plan called for raising the average annual output of meat to not less than 14.3 million tons (slaughter weight), of milk to 98 million tons, of eggs to 51,000,000,000, and of wool to 464,000 tons. The meat goal in particular was challenged by USDA scientists as representing an improbable increase of 26.8% in five years. Cattle at the beginning of 1971 numbered 99.1 million head, up from 95,162,000 head a year earlier. Hog numbers had increased at an even more rapid rate, and even sheep numbers had risen. The plan target for sunflower seed, 8.1 million tons (gross), compared with 5.6 million tons in 1970, was also questioned. The plan did not call for any major increase in sugar-beet production.

The five-year plan also indicated a doubling in consumption of electricity for agricultural production and communal needs. Agriculture would receive 1.7 million tractors, 1.1 million trucks, and 15 billion rubles worth of other agricultural machinery. In all, some 82.2 billion rubles would be invested in agricultural production. A growing flight from the countryside to the cities, not unknown in the Western world, was reported to be causing official concern.

MIDDLE EAST AND INDIA

Middle East. After a comparatively poor harvest in 1970, 1971 provided a record wheat outturn in Turkey of 10 million metric tons. The barley crop, at 4 million tons, was also a record, and rye rose to 760,000 tons from 680,000. The filbert harvest was far below the 1970 record, however; exports in 1970–71 declined to 165,000 tons, and an unusually large carry-over was anticipated. Some 55,000 tons of the 1970 raisin pack remained unsold in August 1971. The International Raisin Agreement between Turkey, Greece, and Australia, which had existed since 1963, was terminated in June when no formula could be

Table XIII. World Cocoa Production in Leading Areas*

In 000 metric tons

Area	Forecast 1971–72	1970–71	1969–70	Average 1962/63–1966/67
North and Central America	76.2	72.0	88.8	80.7
Dominican Republic	29.0	26.0	43.0	32.8
Mexico	25.0	25.0	24.0	21.5
South America	300.8	286.2	293.5	222.2
Brazil	200.0	182.4	201.6	139.3
Ecuador	60.0	65.0	55.0	42.8
Africa	1,113.6	1,098.6	1,007.4	956.1
Ghana	445.0	396.0	414.3	446.8
Nigeria	265.0	323.0	225.0	229.7
Ivory Coast	200.0	178.0	180.7	122.3
Cameroon	110.0	108.0	108.0	83.1
Asia and Oceania	41.4	40.8	34.8	30.0
New Guinea and Papua	29.0	29.0	22.3	18.4
World total	1,532.0	1,497.6	1,424.5	1,289.0

*Crop year, October 1 to September 30.
Source: U.S. Department of Agriculture, Foreign Agricultural Service.

Table XIV. Tea Production in Principal Producing Areas

In 000 metric tons

Area	Forecast 1971	1970*	1969	1968	Average 1960–64
World total†	1,090	1,092	1,060	1,035	869
Asia†	944	948	924	917	797
Ceylon	214	212	220	225	211
India	425	422	396	403	348
Indonesia	44	43	41	41	44
Japan	92	91	90	85	80
Pakistan	20	31	30	28	24
Taiwan	28	28	26	24	19
U.S.S.R.	60	60	60	56	44
Africa	115	119	110	95	57
South America	30	25	26	23	15

*Preliminary.
†Excluding China.
Source: U.S. Department of Agriculture, Foreign Agricultural Service.

found to resolve the problems of countries with large surpluses. The Turkish government gave top priority to the development of the fresh fruit and vegetable export trade; to some degree, such products might replace the intensive cultivation of the opium poppy, officially banned after June 1972.

Wheat and barley crops were up throughout the region. Cyprus produced 90,000 tons of wheat against 49,000 in 1970, and Syria's wheat crop was estimated at a normal 600,000 tons, 100,000 tons more than a year earlier. Israel's wheat crop reportedly rose 60,000 tons to 180,000 tons and barley totaled 25,000 tons, against 13,000 tons the preceding year. Israeli citrus exports were up about 12% and earnings rose 25% to about $110 million.

To the east, drought was a serious problem. Iraq was expected to require imports of some 600,000 tons of wheat, even more than the abnormally high 500,000 tons imported in 1970–71. Iran, in some recent years a wheat exporter, would need imports of 1 million tons. Even the Iranian dried fruit crop declined to an estimated 379,400 short tons, 10% below 1970. Many sheep deaths were reported, especially in southeastern Iran, and water for irrigation was restricted. Drought also affected Afghanistan, where the wheat deficit was estimated at 250,000 tons.

Pakistan. Famine, possibly involving millions of people, was reported in East Pakistan despite food assistance from foreign sources. Information on the important 1971–72 rice crop, grown largely in East Pakistan, was unavailable, but it was presumed to have suffered severely from the heavy floods of late 1970 and from disorganization associated with the political disorders and military action. Earlier, the outlook had been described as promising, but typhoon damage alone was estimated to have reduced the potential rice crop by 2.5 million tons. The 1971–72 East Pakistani jute crop was also thought to be substantially smaller than in the previous year. Raw jute exports were suspended for a time, but were resumed in mid-May with little increase in prices.

Factory workers can pineapples in Taiwan. U.S. exports of fruits and vegetables have faced increasing competition from many other countries.

COURTESY, "FOREIGN AGRICULTURE"

The 1971 wheat crop, grown largely in West Pakistan, totaled 6,808,000 metric tons, compared with 7,399,000 tons in 1970, and the barley crop of 132,000 tons was slightly larger than a year earlier.

India. Indian wheat production set a new record in 1971 for the second successive year; the harvest totaled 23,247,000 metric tons, compared with an average of 13,860,000 tons in 1965–69. The barley crop was a large 2,865,000 tons, and these, plus a large crop of corn and a somewhat improved rice crop, indicated that India was near if not at self-sufficiency in food. In total the food-grain harvest amounted to some 110 million–113 million tons, despite floods in the north and drought in the southern areas. The Agricultural Prices Commission recommended a reduction in the procurement prices of wheat during the 1971–72 marketing season and that the price be uniform in all the states. Even so, a recent study reported that 40% of India's rural population and 50% of its urban population—some 225 million persons in all—could not afford a minimally adequate diet.

With the sugar surplus from previous crops at 2 million tons, acreage under sugarcane was decreased about 10%; early estimates of 1970–71 production were 3.8 million tons, against 4.2 million in 1969–70. Cashew output, largely for export, was increased; it was reported from Madras that 100,000 ac. of forest were being cleared for additional cashew cultivation. Jute production was pushed up 25% during the period of temporary suspension of production and shipment by Pakistan. Despite estimates of a larger 1971–72 cotton crop, some 1 million bales of imports would be needed. Pepper exports rose 13% in 1970.

India accounted for about 425,000 metric tons of the world's tea production total of 1,090,000 tons. The tea industry faced many problems. A multinational agreement was reached in New Delhi in December 1970 to limit world tea exports, but demand and prices had both been trending downward and, at the same time, investment capital was opening new gardens, mostly in East Africa. Indian tea exports in the first half of 1971 were 7,000 tons larger than for the same period of 1970. Ceylon's tea exports were reported to have been badly disrupted by the revolt of early 1971.

FAR EAST

Though little firm information was available on large parts of this highly diverse area, 1971 appeared to have been a good—if not, indeed, an excellent—agricultural year.

The USDA estimated that some 210 million metric tons of grains had been produced in China in 1970, including 24.5 million tons of wheat—substantially above the 1965–69 average of 21,920,000 tons. Some estimates put the 1970 total as high as 240 million tons, probably by including sweet potatoes. The 1971 harvest was also believed to have been excellent, though there were no firm reports that crops had reached new record levels. It was thought that 1971–72 wheat imports might be reduced below the 3.6 million tons imported from Canada and Australia in 1970–71. Oilseed production was also reported to be making a strong comeback, with rapeseed in some areas 20% above the previous crop and deliveries exceeding set quotas. Livestock, especially hogs and perhaps chickens, were produced in larger numbers. A fourth five-year farm plan was begun with recommendations directed toward improvement in fertilization, water conservancy, seed selection, close planting, pesticides, and care of tools.

Japan's 1971 wheat crop of 470,000 tons was slightly smaller than that of 1970 and far less than the 1,016,000-ton average for 1965–69. Barley, at 512,000 tons, was also considerably below average. There were few indications of the quantity or quality of the rice crop, but plans called for a reduction of perhaps 500,000 ha. (1,235,000 ac.) in the area planted. Carry-over stocks from previous bumper crops were large, and some 400,000 metric tons of rice were provided on a long-term-credit basis to South Korea. The dairy industry continued to expand, and new grasslands accelerated the growth in the small beef industry. Nevertheless, there were some indications that, in view of the disturbed foreign trade and monetary situation, imports of wheat and feed grains might be reduced in late 1971 and 1972.

Following a disappointing crop season in 1970, South Korea planned to produce about 15% more staple foods, primarily rice, barley, and wheat. Rice would account for about 55% of the total increase. Tobacco exports were reduced to 15,600 tons from 19,000 tons as Korean farmers devoted their land and labour more fully to other crops. The booming mushroom industry exceeded its export goal by 10% during the first half of 1971. A new five-year plan provided for major investment in irrigation facilities.

Overall agricultural production continued to increase in the Philippines, although severe economic problems had been experienced after 1969. The 1971 copra crop was a large 1.6 million metric tons. World production was estimated at 3.7 million tons, 12% above 1970 and slightly above the 1964 record. Total world trade in 1971 involved 1,085,000 tons (oil basis), of which exports from the Philippines accounted for 820,000 tons (oil equivalent). The rice crop was a large 5,443,000 metric tons, but about 300,000 tons were imported from Japan on a concessionary price basis to increase stocks and deflate prices. Sugar totaled 2,334,000 short tons in 1970–71, compared with 2,124,000 tons the previous year and an average crop of about 1.7 million tons. New U.S. sugar legislation accorded the Philippines a somewhat reduced annual quota of about 1,314,000 tons, primarily because, before the larger production of 1970 and 1971, it had apparently been unable to provide the full amount permitted.

Sugar production in Taiwan totaled 819,000 short tons in 1970–71, up from 668,000 tons the previous year. In September 10% of the North Vietnamese rice crop, or about 800,000 tons, was reported to have been destroyed by floods. Following an above-average corn crop of 2 million metric tons in 1970, Thailand was said to be pushing the export of both corn and rice; an agreement to sell 1 million tons of corn to Japan was announced in September, and Thai rice exports were expected to be 50% above 1970. Thailand withdrew from the International Sugar Agreement after requesting an export quota of 120,000 metric tons and receiving one of 36,000 tons. It was reported that Cambodia would have to import as much as 200,000 tons of rice to avert starvation. The world rice crop appeared to be at record levels of about 294,645,000 metric tons for 1970, compared with a 1964–68 average of 259,036,000 tons; the non-Communist countries produced some 198,055,000 tons of the total.

In West Malaysia the issuing of land titles to Chinese farmers in 500 "new" villages with about 700,000

inhabitants was expected to reduce insecurity. Palm oil exports rose sharply to 197,600 metric tons in early 1971. Commercial production of copra in Indonesia reached a post-World War II high of 1,834,000 metric tons (oil equivalent), up from 1,688,000 tons a year earlier.

OCEANIA

Internal economic difficulties, as well as major changes in external trading patterns, brought the surplus productivity of Australian and New Zealand agriculture into sharper focus in 1971. Australia's reliance on wheat exports to China appeared not to have been fully justified. The wool market continued to decline, and falling prices forced measures to subsidize producers. At the same time, British entry into the EEC threatened disruption of the preferred trading status in agricultural commodities long enjoyed by both Australia and New Zealand.

Australia. Australia's important wheat harvest was reduced in 1970–71 by dry weather in northern New South Wales, parts of Queensland, and Western Australia. Lower yields, as well as reduced acreages resulting from government action, cut total output to an estimated 7,987,000 metric tons, compared with 10,835,000 tons a year earlier.

Given domestic requirements of about 2 million tons and a carry-over of 7.2 million tons, Australia's Wheat Board launched a vigorous export program. Success hinged on the uncertain prospect of heavy sales to China, which had taken more than 30% of Australia's wheat exports in 1969–70. Some observers attributed China's seeming preference for Canadian wheat to that country's recognition of the Communist government, whereas Australia's government had continued to withhold recognition, but China's reluctance to maintain high-level imports from Australia could also be attributed to good grain crops in that country, as well as to the improved world rice situation. Even so, Australia was reported to have exported 6,340,000 tons during the first nine months of 1971. Traditional markets, such as Hong Kong, Taiwan, and the Philippines, took large amounts, but increased sales to Japan, as well as to relatively new markets in Egypt, Iraq, and Iran, also accounted for the export gain.

Australian livestock numbers increased in 1971: cattle numbers, at 22,637,000 head, were 2% above

Table XV. Production of Meats in Principal Producing Countries
In 000,000 lb., carcass-meat basis

Country	Beef and veal 1970*	1969	Average 1961–65	Pork (excluding lard) 1970*	1969	Average 1961–65	Mutton, lamb, and goat meat 1970*	1969	Average 1961–65
Argentina	5,710	6,356	4,913	463	462	384	348	426	345
Australia	2,230	2,061	1,941	385	358	257	1,670	1,500	1,310
Belgium-Luxembourg	591	567	482	961	781	508	8	16	6
Brazil	3,629	4,028	3,095	1,356	1,340	1,030	121	123	106
Canada	1,907	1,909	1,618	1,349	1,135	1,002	18	18	31
Colombia	944	909	837	...	...	117	5	5	5
Denmark	423	427	357	1,578	1,509	1,466	4	6	3
France	3,450	3,422	3,166	2,721	2,601	2,534	267	257	237
Germany, West	2,998	2,795	2,541	4,927	4,775	3,979	27	24	30
Italy	1,722	1,767	1,388	1,001	1,065	887	103	101	86
Japan	562	476	400	1,424	1,121	649	2	3	6
Mexico	1,332	1,250	1,045	575	549	452	124	124	129
Netherlands	714	630	590	1,488	1,300	923	24	18	18
New Zealand	867	830	614	85	82	94	1,250	1,241	1,039
Poland	...	1,248	878	...	1,994	1,826	...	58	57
South Africa	978	971	998	185	171	115	464	367	282
Spain	606	560	404	1,047	963	608	305	284	276
U.S.S.R.	11,305	11,084	7,135	6,216	6,323	5,858	2,094	2,094	2,220
United Kingdom	2,090	1,920	1,978	2,085	2,034	1,796	500	457	559
United States	22,272	21,831	17,862	13,434	12,953	11,863	551	550	755
Yugoslavia	643	641	529	882	782	844	132	136	117

*Preliminary.
Source: U.S. Department of Agriculture, Foreign Agricultural Service.

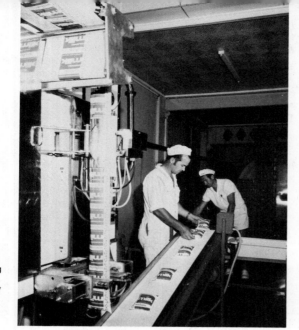

Plastic milk packets, expected to revolutionize the packaging and selling of fresh milk, move down a conveyor belt in a dairy plant in Hamilton, N.Z.
AUTHENTICATED NEWS
INTERNATIONAL

a year earlier, while hog numbers rose 4% to 2.5 million. Sheep numbers were reported to be 179.2 million head on March 31, 1971, compared with 180.1 million head in March 1970. Production of red meat in 1970 exceeded that of 1969 by 9%, but with reduced supplies of Argentine beef on the world market, the Australian high commissioner warned that Australia might not be able to fill all its overseas orders in 1971.

Wool production in Australia and New Zealand was estimated at 2,661,400,000 lb. in 1971, a reduction from 2,670,900,000 lb. produced in the region a year earlier. Reflecting the generally declining profitability of sheep farming, world production of wool in 1971 was estimated at 6,068,400,000 lb. (greasy basis), the third consecutive decline from the 1968 high of 6,270,800,000 lb. World mill consumption was estimated at 3,465,000,000 lb. (clean content) in 1970, a reduction of 2% from a year earlier. It was suggested that lower prices in 1971 might increase mill consumption in the latter half of the year, but total use was expected to be less in 1971 than a year earlier. Exports of raw wool from surplus-producing countries in the Southern Hemisphere through most of the 1970–71 trade year appeared to have declined by as much as 11% from 1969–70.

New Zealand. Prospects for recovery from the severe drought conditions of 1969–70 were not bright by mid-1971. The livestock industry, source of nearly 85% of the country's exports, continued to feel the effect of falling wool prices and of reduced production of butter resulting from the drought. Production of butter declined about 13% in 1970, and New Zealand butter prices on the London market rose to a record 45 cents per pound by midyear. The 1970 dairy herd totaled 2,363,000 head, only fractionally larger than a year earlier, while milk production per cow fell to 5,511 lb. from 6,348. Sheep numbers on June 30, 1971, totaled some 59.5 million head, compared with 60,276,000 head a year earlier.

(J. K. R.; H. R. Sh.)

See also Alcoholic Beverages; Commercial Policies; Commodities, Primary; Cooperatives; Fisheries; Food; Gardening; Industrial Review; Prices; Tobacco.

ENCYCLOPÆDIA BRITANNICA FILMS. *The Orange Grower* (1967); *The Sheep Rancher* (1967); *Midwest—Heartland of the Nation* (1968); *Produce—From Farm to Market* (1968); *Problems of Conservation—Soil* (1969); *Problems of Conservation—Our Natural Resources* (1970).

Albania

A people's republic in the western Balkan Peninsula, Albania is on the Adriatic Sea, bordered by Greece and Yugoslavia. Area: 11,100 sq.mi. (28,748 sq.km.). Pop. (1970 est.): 2,168,000. Cap. and largest city: Tirana (pop., 1967 est., 169,300). Language: Albanian. Religion: Muslim, Orthodox, Roman Catholic. First secretary of the Albanian (Communist) Party of Labour in 1971, Enver Hoxha; president of the Presidium of the People's Assembly, Haxhi Leshi; chairman of the Council of Ministers (premier), Mehmet Shehu.

On Oct. 25, 1971, Albania stood in the limelight of the world scene when its resolution to admit China to the UN and expel Taiwan was accepted by 76 votes to 35 with 17 abstentions.

Following the example of friendly China, Albania continued a policy of cautious reconciliation with its chief neighbour, Yugoslavia, during 1971. On February 5 both countries agreed to raise their diplomatic missions to embassy level.

On May 6 Greece and Albania agreed to exchange ambassadors although technically the two countries had been at war since 1940. This rapprochement was interpreted in Tirana as Greece's desistance from its claim to the so-called Northern Epirus with the Gjinikaster and Korce areas.

During the year, Belgium, the Netherlands, Norway, and Iran also established diplomatic relations

ALBANIA
Education. (1968–69) Primary, pupils 473,687, teachers 16,872; secondary, pupils 20,657, teachers 915; vocational, pupils 29,822, teachers 819; teacher training, students 2,216, teachers 93; higher (including University of Tirana with 7,300 full-time students in 1970–71), students 16,649, teachers 614.
Finance. Monetary unit: new lek, with an official exchange rate of 5 leks to U.S. $1 (12 leks = £1 sterling) and a tourist rate of 12.5 leks to U.S. $1 (30 leks = £1 sterling). Budget (1968 est.): revenue 4,025,000,000 new leks; expenditure 3,985,000,000 new leks.
Foreign Trade. (1964) Imports U.S. $98 million; exports U.S. $66 million. Import sources: China 63%; Czechoslovakia 10%; Poland 8%; East Germany 5%. Export destinations: China 40%; Czechoslovakia 19%; East Germany 10%; Poland 10%. Main exports: fuels, minerals, and metals (including crude oil, iron ore, chrome ore, and copper) 54%; foodstuffs (including vegetables, wine, and fruit) 21%; tobacco; wool.
Transport and Communications. Roads (motorable; 1960) 3,100 km. Motor vehicles in use (1960 est.): passenger 1,900; commercial (including buses) 3,400. Railways: (1968) 205 km.; traffic (1967) 146 million passenger-km., freight 123 million net ton-km. Shipping (1970): merchant vessels 100 gross tons and over 17; gross tonnage 56,472; goods loaded (1967) *c.* 1.3 million metric tons, unloaded *c.* 575,000 metric tons. Telephones (Dec. 1963) 10,150. Radio receivers (Dec. 1969) 160,000. Television receivers (Dec. 1969) 2,500.
Agriculture. Production (in 000; metric tons; 1970; 1969 in parentheses): wheat *c.* 200 (*c.* 200); corn *c.* 240 (*c.* 240); oats *c.* 17 (*c.* 17); cotton, lint *c.* 8 (*c.* 8); sugar, raw value (1970–71) *c.* 17, (1969–70) *c.* 16; potatoes *c.* 118 (*c.* 118); tobacco *c.* 13 (*c.* 13). Livestock (in 000; Dec. 1969): sheep *c.* 1,610; cattle *c.* 435; pigs *c.* 150; goats *c.* 1,330; poultry (Oct. 1969) *c.* 1,790.
Industry. Production (in 000; metric tons; 1969): crude oil 1,147; lignite *c.* 640; petroleum products *c.* 520; chrome ore (oxide content) 172; iron ore *c.* 400; copper ore (metal content) 6; cement 220; electricity (kw.-hr.) 788,000.

with Albania, and Iran and Finland raised their missions to embassy status. Albania's relations were friendly with Romania but not with Bulgaria, whose leader, Todor Zhivkov, speaking in April in Sofia at the Bulgarian Communist Party congress, described First Secretary Enver Hoxha as a man "sunk in anti-Soviet mud."

When the Presidium of the Supreme Soviet of the U.S.S.R. sent good wishes to the Albanian National Assembly on January 11 on the 25th anniversary of the proclamation of the People's Republic of Albania, no reply was sent to Moscow. Shortly afterward, on the 53rd anniversary of the formation of the Soviet Red Army (January 28), *Luftetari,* the organ of the Albanian Ministry of Defense, described the Soviet Army as "an instrument of imperialist oppression." On April 17, the 14th anniversary of the Soviet-Albanian friendship agreement of 1957, Moscow radio broadcast a bitter talk on Albania's ingratitude.

Chinese influence remained dominant and China was financing about 33 industrial enterprises under the 1971–75 five-year plan. Many hundreds of Chinese technicians remained in the country, though their numbers had diminished during recent years. The railway connecting Durres with Elbasan was being extended under Chinese direction to Pishkashi. A Chinese military delegation headed by Gen. Li Teh-sheng visited Albania in September.   (K. Sм.)

Alcoholic Beverages

Beer. World beer production rose to some 630 million hectolitres (hl.) in 1970, an increase of slightly more than 4% over the previous year. A total of some 660 million hl. was anticipated for 1971. The increase in European production from 330 million to 344 million hl. corresponded roughly to the average; North America's share (210 million hl.) was lower; while in Asia (41 million hl.) and Africa (15 million hl.) the rates of growth were naturally somewhat higher because of the early stage of development of many brewing industries. Development was also above average in Oceania (19 million hl.).

While in many parts of the world, including Eastern Europe, consumption continued to be determined by productive capacity, in Western Europe and North America there was surplus capacity, and buyers' markets predominated. According to some estimates, West Germany's total brewing capacity exceeded actual output by 15 million to 20 million hl. Mergers did not generally lead to large-scale shutdowns. On the contrary, new premises were often built on a generous scale in order to avoid shortages later on.

The three principal beer-producing countries—the U.S. (143 million hl.), West Germany (87 million hl.), and Great Britain (55 million hl.)—continued to account for some 45% of world production. These three countries, together with the U.S.S.R. (an estimated 40 million hl.) and Japan (30 million hl.), were still the only individual countries whose total output exceeded that of the world's largest brewery concern, Anheuser-Busch Inc., based in St. Louis, Mo.

Enzyme preparations permitting the use of unmalted barley, as well as preisomerized hop extracts, continued to attract interest, although in the traditional beer-producing countries there was a marked disinclination to use such substances except where a shortage of raw materials was a compelling factor (for instance, in Yugoslavia and East Germany). In West Germany their use was prohibited by law.

Interbrau 1971, which took place September 13–18 in Munich, W.Ger., included the largest exhibition of brewery equipment ever shown. Noticeable trends in brewing techniques included increasing automation; new ways of streamlining and accelerating all stages of production; greater emphasis on very large outdoor tanks (with a working capacity of 5,000–10,000 hl. or more); European interest in the keg system; and increasingly complex and varied possibilities for packaging. Bottling plants with an hourly capacity of 100,000 bottles and more were anticipated in the near future, a precondition of these high capacities being containers conforming to very close dimensional tolerances.

There was a tendency for breweries to include their own packing stations, run either by themselves or by outside firms. Some West German breweries spent

Table I. Estimated Consumption of Beer in Selected Countries
In litres* per capita of total population

Country	1967	1968	1969
Belgium†	140	140	140
Germany, West	127.2	129.4	135.8
Czechoslovakia	129.3	132.8	...
Luxembourg	121.4	116.1	124.6
Australia‡	113.1	116.8	120.4
New Zealand	109.9	110.4	111.1
Denmark	91.5	94.4	102.2
Austria	102.6	98.2	99
United Kingdom	93.2	96.5	98.4
Germany, East	84.5	86.3	92
Ireland	62.2	85.1	...
Switzerland	76.2	73.7	...
Canada	69.5	71	71.2
United States	63.2	65.2	67.4
Sweden	45.5	51.8	58.4
Hungary	49.9	51.2	54
Finland	29.9	32.6	52.2
Netherlands§	44.3	45.4	51.4
France	40.8	40	40.7
Venezuela	35	35	...
Norway	30	32.5	34.7
Spain	30.4	32.9	32
Colombia	30	31	...
Poland	27.7	28.9	30.4
Bulgaria	25.5	27.6	...

*One litre = 1.0567 U.S. quarts = 0.8799 imperial quart.
†Including so-called "household beer."
‡Years ending June 30.
§Excluding ships' supplies.

Table II. Estimated Consumption of Potable Distilled Spirits in Selected Countries
In litres* of 100% pure spirit per capita of population

Country	1967	1968	1969
Poland	3	3.3	3.4
United States	2.67	2.82	2.91
Germany, West	2.23	2.59	2.75
Yugoslavia	2.6	2.6	...
Sweden	2.70	2.55	2.60
Cyprus	1.56	2.85	2.60
Spain	2.3	2.3	2.5
Germany, East	2.2	2.2	2.5
Hungary	1.86	1.95	2.35
France†	2.5	2.2	2.2
Canada	2.16	2.26	2.2
Italy	1.60	1.8	2
Netherlands	1.63	1.76	1.88
Bulgaria	1.7	1.8	...
Switzerland	1.8	1.8	...
Peru	1.5	1.7	1.7
Czechoslovakia	1.32	1.64	...
Finland	1.4	1.4	1.6
Norway	1.42	1.47	1.48
Austria	1.8	2	1.2
Ireland	1.97	1.19	...
South Africa	1.11	1.07	1.13
Luxembourg	1.14	1.8	1.1
Belgium	0.96	1.10	1.08
Australia‡	0.78	1.04	1.04

†Including alcohol- and wine-based aperitifs and liqueur wines.
‡Years ending June 30.

Table III. Estimated Consumption of Wine in Selected Countries
In litres* per capita of total population

Country	1967	1968	1969
Italy†	109.7	114.2	115.3
France†	113.0	113.0	115
Portugal	92.3	93.2	...
Argentina	82.8	87.5	...
Spain	61.0	62.1	62.5
Chile	44.6	48.9	...
Switzerland‡	38.5	38.6	...
Hungary	34.2	34.8	38
Greece	36.7	36.7	35
Luxembourg	33.8	35.9	32
Austria	31.9	29.7	31
Yugoslavia	26.5	26.3	...
Romania	20.0	26.9	25
Uruguay	25.0	25	...
Bulgaria	18.5	21.7	...
Germany, West	15.6	15.3	15.9
Czechoslovakia	18.6	15.8	...
Belgium	10.6	11.9	12.1
U.S.S.R.	8.9	12.0	...
South Africa	9.2	9.1	9.4
Australia§	6.8	7.7	8.2
Cyprus	10.4	11.2	8
Sweden	5.0	5.3	5.8
Poland	4.7	5.0	5.6
Germany, East	4.7	4.6	5.2

†Excluding cider (20.4 litres per capita in 1966).
‡Excluding cider (annual average 8.3 litres per capita, 1965–68).
§Years ending June 30.

Source: Produktschap voor Gedistilleerde Dranken, *Hoeveel alcoholhoudenden dranken worden er in de wereld gedronken?*

Electra-Bar,
a computerized liquor
dispensing and control
system, automatically
prepares a cocktail (top)
at the touch of a single
register key (above).
Simultaneously, the device
records the sale
on a guest check
and updates the inventory.

tion increases of this magnitude. Nevertheless, spirits consumption in the U.K. was still only about 3–3½ bottles per head per annum, ranking the U.K. 33rd among spirit-consuming countries.

The international trend toward lighter spirits continued and was expected to grow still more with the advent, from July 1, 1972, of the new light American whiskey. About 50 million gal. were expected to be ready for sale by that date. Some adjustments, particularly in prices, were expected as a result of British entry into the EEC. The introduction of the value-added tax in Community countries was also causing some concern. The 10% import duty imposed by the U.S., while unwelcome, was not regarded as catastrophic, since it was levied on import value, not duty-paid value. High taxation and import controls led some distributors to seek substitutes. For example, bulk exports of Scotch malt whisky to such countries as Japan, Argentina, and Brazil had been growing rapidly. They could be blended with locally produced neutral spirits, and sold as a national whiskey.

(J. W. MA.)

Apparent consumption of distilled spirits in the U.S. in 1970 reached a record high of 370.1 million gal., 2.3% above 1969. Per capita consumption rose 1.7% to 1.83 gal. Prohibition was eliminated in 33 areas in 12 states by local option. Four more states lowered the drinking age below 21; eight states lessened or removed the ban on serving liquor on election days; and liquor by the drink became legal in Texas. Consumer expenditure for alcoholic beverages for 1970 was $22.4 billion, compared with $20.6 billion in 1969. Federal excise tax on alcoholic beverages totaled $4,800,482,000 in fiscal 1971, 73.2% of which was accounted for by distilled spirits. During fiscal 1971, U.S. agents seized 3,327 stills producing illicit spirits.

A total of 759,250,572 gal. of distilled spirits were produced in the U.S. in fiscal 1971, 17% less than in 1970. This included industrial alcohol. Whiskey production was down 20.6% to 127,220,443 tax gallons. U.S. bottlings rose 0.5% to 312,194,048 gal. in 1970, with whiskey accounting for 61% of the total. Vodka bottlings rose 10.7%, while gin, cordials, and brandy remained steady. There was a distinct trend to larger bottles, with quarts increasing 3.1% and half gallons, 28.6%.

At 90,902,977 tax gallons, total imports of spirits into the U.S. were up 7.9% in 1970. They were valued at $530 million, or 75% of alcoholic beverage imports. The percentage of bulk to total whiskey rose from 30.7 to 36.8% for Canadian whiskey and from 29.7 to 30% for Scotch. Tequila imports rose 9.1%.

Public revenue from alcoholic beverage taxes in Canada rose 7.8% to Can$913,536,000 in fiscal 1970. Consumption of spirits in the same year climbed 4.3% to 23,899,000 imperial gallons. Production rose 10.2% to 84,650,000 imperial tax gallons, imports rose 20.5%, and exports increased 23.1%. (JU. W.)

Wine. When complete statistics became available in 1971, it was established that the 1970 harvest had been the largest of the century. The world total exceeded 300 million hl. Europe was the biggest producer with 245 million hl., followed by North America with 35 million hl. Estimates of the 1971 harvest suggested that it would fall short of the previous year by 10 to 15%. All the Mediterranean countries produced less, notably France (−8 million hl.), Spain (−6 to 7 million hl.), Portugal (−2 to 3 million hl.), and Italy (−2 million hl.). However, in

over three times as much on packaging materials as on raw materials. The use of containers manufactured wholly of plastics or other synthetics was under discussion. However, developments in packaging were increasingly inhibited by the proliferating regulations aimed at protecting the environment and seeking to impose bans on the use of throwaway containers and nonreturnable bottles. One such set of regulations was due to come into operation in Oregon on Oct. 1, 1972. Manufacturers of drinks and packaging materials were taking legal steps in an attempt to protect themselves, but many were also investigating means of bringing their operations into line with the current concern about environmental pollution and were examining, for example, the possibility of using returnable containers and setting up collection centres for their return. (T. Sc.)

Spirits. World production and consumption of potable spirits in 1970–71 showed no great change, the pattern of modest growth being repeated practically everywhere. Increases in taxation occurred in several countries, as an almost inevitable result of currency inflation, but there was a welcome reduction in the differential duty on bulk and bottled spirits in West Germany. Attacks on the spirits trade were noticeably fewer, the drug and tobacco problems being of more immediate public interest.

Consumption in Great Britain recovered strongly after a long, dull period caused by excessive taxation. Scotch whisky, gin, and British vodka increased by about 14% and imported spirits by up to 18%. These were mainly rum and brandy, but there was an increase of over 16% in other spirits, chiefly imported whiskies. This increase, largely a release of pent-up demand, was gratifying to both the distributors and the Inland Revenue, but it raised social problems since no government was prepared to see regular consump-

all these countries the quality of the wine produced was good, and in certain areas it was excellent.

After reaching the extraordinarily high level of 74 million hl. in 1970, French wine production fell in 1971 to a more average 65 million hl. All wine-producing regions had lower harvests, but everywhere the wine was better and the alcoholic content more than satisfactory. The decrease in volume was more noticeable in the Bordeaux region than elsewhere, but the red wines promised extremely well, with sufficient colour, a good bouquet, and in some cases a slightly higher level of acidity than usual. In Burgundy, where the harvest was down by two-thirds, 1971 would no doubt stand out in the records as a first-rate vintage. The quality of the Beaujolais wines was decidedly above the average. In Champagne and in Alsace production was only about one-half that of the previous year, but there also the quality was excellent.

In Italy the 1971 harvest totaled 66 million hl., compared with 68.9 million hl. in 1970. The decrease was more marked in the north of the country, the south—especially Sicily—having obtained fairly large harvests. The quality was uneven in the northern vineyards, while in Puglia and Sicily it was equal or superior to that of 1970.

Serious ravages by mildew were mainly responsible for the decrease in the 1971 harvest in Spain. In certain regions this had reached catastrophic proportions; for example, in León, Lugo, and Orense the harvest was 70 to 80% below that of 1970. Fortunately, a few districts showed improvement; Cádiz (a sherry-producing region) experienced a rise of 10%; Ciudad Real was also up 10%; and Toledo, up 5%. On the average, the harvest fell 30 to 35% below the 25.5 million hl. of a year earlier. Portugal also suffered serious losses. Its production in 1971 was around 8 million hl., or about 70% of that in 1970.   (R. Pn.)

In contrast to Europe, the 1971 U.S. grape harvest and vintage established a number of new records. Just under 4 million tons of grapes were harvested in the dozen principal vineyard states, with California responsible for 3,475,000 tons of the total. In order of crop size, the next three grape-producing states were New York (180,000 tons), Washington (80,000), and Michigan (68,000). In all three states, the harvest set new tonnage marks.

In California the big (but not record) crop was particularly welcome. The comparatively short crop of 1970 had resulted in a crush that was well under the tonnage needed to supply the rapidly expanding U.S. wine market, but the 1971 California crush of 2.2 million tons exceeded the 1965 record by some 10%. American wines produced in 1971 were expected to be of good to superior quality. In certain areas of California the sugar content was not ideally high, but it was well above the level that makes production of good wines possible.

There was increasing interest in the wine industry on the part of nonwine firms seeking areas of expansion. This was particularly true of the California industry, where a number of outside firms or individuals purchased part-ownerships in existing wineries, began building their own wineries, or set out vineyards. Sales of 255 million gal. of U.S.-produced wines in fiscal 1971 were well above the 1970 record. Table wines continued as the sales leader with 124 million gal. sold; second place went to dessert wines with 71 million gal.; the so-called flavoured wines were in third place with 34 million gal., while sparkling wine sales reached 21 million gal.   (I. H. M.)

Algeria

A republic on the north coast of Africa, Algeria is bounded by Morocco, Mauritania, Mali, Niger, Libya, and Tunisia. Area: 896,588 sq.mi. (2,322,164 sq.km.). Pop. (1970 est.): 13,547,000. Cap. and largest city: Algiers (pop., 1970 est., 1,839,000). Language: Arabic, Berber, French. Religion: Muslim. President in 1971, Col. Houari Boumédienne.

Algeria imposed state control on its oil industry on February 24 at the cost of ending the country's special relationship with France. In achieving this take-over of a major industry without any prospect of long-term detriment to the economy, President Boumédienne's regime showed itself a step ahead of other Arab oil-producing countries and seemed well set to prove that Algeria could become a significant industrial nation on the basis of its own natural and financial resources.

Negotiations with France, which had dragged on intermittently since Algeria unilaterally imposed a new price structure in July 1970, reached a crisis point in January, and French companies were prevented from loading Saharan crude oil at Arzew. In February 51% of all French oil companies' Algerian interests were taken over by the state and vested in its own oil corporation, Sonatrach. The French companies, which controlled two-thirds of Saharan crude production and supplied 27% of France's needs, resisted the nationalization measures and sought to prevent their application by withdrawal of technical staff and an attempt to blacklist Algerian oil on the international market.

ALGERIA
Education. (1968–69) Primary, pupils 1,585,682, teachers (public only) 36,255; secondary, pupils 130,-960, teachers (public only) 5,384; vocational, pupils 40,684, teachers (public only) 2,752; teacher training, students 5,738, teachers (public only) 380; higher (including 3 universities), students 10,681.

Finance. Monetary unit: dinar, with a par value of 4.94 dinars to U.S. $1 (11.85 dinars = £1 sterling) and a free rate (Sept. 27, 1971) of c. 4.78 dinars to U.S. $1. Gold, SDRs, and foreign exchange, central bank: (June 1971) U.S. $420 million; (June 1970) U.S. $317 million. Budget (1969 est.) balanced at 3,890,000,000 dinars.

Foreign Trade. (1969) Imports 4,981,000,000 dinars; exports 4,611,000,000 dinars. Import sources: France 44%; West Germany 9%; U.S. 9%; Italy 8%. Export destinations: France 54%; West Germany 15%. Main exports: crude oil 64%; wine 14%.

Transport and Communications. Roads (1970) 75,953 km. Motor vehicles in use (1969): passenger 121,151; commercial (including buses) 70,776. Railways: (1968) 3,951 km.; traffic (state only; 1970) 1,016,000,000 passenger-km., freight 1,391,000,000 net ton-km. Air traffic (1969): 417,515,000 passenger-km.; freight 3,548,000 net ton-km. Shipping (1970): merchant vessels 100 gross tons and over 9; gross tonnage 28,929; goods loaded 43,824,000 metric tons, unloaded 8,069,000 metric tons. Telephones (Dec. 1969) 169,188. Radio receivers (Dec. 1969) 700,000. Television receivers (Dec. 1969) c. 100,000.

Agriculture. Production (in 000; metric tons; 1969; 1968 in parentheses): wheat c. 1,100 (1,534); barley c. 465 (538); oats c. 30 (42); potatoes 224, (272); dates c. 85 (161); figs 21 (45); oranges (1970) 470, (1969) 410; tomatoes c. 85 (84); onions c. 35 (30); tobacco c. 5 (4.6); olive oil (1970) c. 18, (1969) c. 24; wine 874 (995). Livestock (in 000; Nov. 1969): sheep c. 7,400; goats c. 2,200; cattle c. 870; asses c. 310; horses c. 125; camels c. 170.

Industry. Production (in 000; metric tons; 1970): crude oil 47,224; natural gas (cu.m.) 2,900,000; electricity (excluding most industrial production; kw-hr.) 1,702,000; iron ore (metal content; 1969) 1,599; phosphate rock (1969) 420.

Alcoholism:
see Medicine

Algeria responded by suspending production at some oil fields and banning oil exports to France. By the end of June, however, Compagnie Française des Pétroles (CFP) had accepted its role as a minority partner in its Algerian operations in return for compensation payable over seven years, had agreed to pay substantial tax arrears, and had perforce to agree to a much higher tax reference price for the future. Entreprise de Récherches et d'Activités Pétrolières (ERAP), the other major French group involved, came to similar terms on September 21. On December 15 the dispute officially ended with the signing of an agreement under which compensation claimed by the oil companies was canceled out by back taxes claimed by the Algerian Treasury. Future disputes would be settled in the Algerian courts rather than by international arbitration.

For Boumédienne Algerian oil had "regained its national character," and the take-over was but the most important sign of a trend away from dependence on and association with France. The extensive vineyards were for most Algerians the most visible remaining evidence of this former dependence and, with the end of the grape harvest in August, a start was made on converting the "colonialist" vineyards to the growing of other food crops. The French share in Algerian trade, as high as 80% at the time of independence, was down to 45%. Also, in what was described as a cultural revolution, French was eliminated as the language of the law courts in September.

With economic development the preoccupation of the regime, little attention was given to the political life of the country. Only the students of Algiers University demonstrated their militancy—against the regime—and the students' union was dissolved for "counterrevolutionary activity." Municipal elections were carried out, with a choice between candidates all nominated by the National Liberation Front (FLN), the sole political organization, but a general apathy toward the FLN continued.

With half the period of the 1970–73 four-year plan completed, the plan's development projects were on schedule. The annual budget, with expenditure 10% over the previous year, concentrated, like the overall plan, on industry and infrastructure to the neglect of agriculture, a sector in which mismanagement was evident.

The loss in revenue from a cut in oil production as a result of the dispute with France caused a decline in foreign currency reserves, but this was expected to be offset by increased oil revenue after full production was resumed in the last quarter. Over the longer term, the prospect of natural gas sales to the United States promised enough funds to ensure financing of the next development plan.

The eighth International Algiers Fair was held in September after being relocated at a cost of $22 million, largely paid for by the Chinese. Following the break with France, a large number of newcomers were among the 35 countries represented. Companies from the U.S. and West Germany, neither of which maintained diplomatic relations with Algeria, took an increasing share in development projects, and the success of Italian companies (one of which had completed the Annaba steel rolling mill well ahead of schedule) was recognized with the award to an Ente Nazionale Idrocarburi subsidiary of the contract for a 510-km. pipeline to supply the natural-gas liquefaction plant at Arzew.

Trade and aid ties with the Soviet Union and East-

ern Europe were maintained, if on a muted scale, and Algeria remained dependent on the U.S.S.R. for arms, aircraft, and other military equipment. Soviet Premier Aleksei N. Kosygin underlined this continuing cooperation with a visit to Algiers in October, but Boumédienne's declared Mediterranean policy seemed to preclude the provision of any permanent facilities for the Soviet fleet.

Maghreb cooperation—between Algeria and its immediate neighbours—was not significantly advanced in 1971 and, while promising fullest support to the Palestinian guerrillas and suspending all relations with Jordan, Algeria stood somewhat aloof from the chronic Arab-Israeli crisis. Col. Muammar al-Qaddafi, the Libyan leader, took Algeria to task for this attitude in a speech in October; he was promptly invited to a meeting with Boumédienne, who held to the view that Algeria's economic gains had won "one of the greatest battles waged by the Arab nation."

(PR. K.)

Andorra

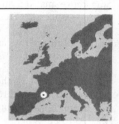

An independent principality of Europe, Andorra is in the Pyrenees Mountains between Spain and France. Area: 180 sq.mi. (465 sq.km.). Pop. (1971): 20,550. Cap.: Andorra la Vella (Catalan; Andorra la Vieja, Spanish) (pop., 1971 parish, 8,062). Language: Catalan, French, Spanish. Religion: predominantly Roman Catholic. Co-princes: the president of the French Republic and the bishop of Urgel, Spain, represented by their *vegeurs* (provosts) and *batlles* (prosecutors). An elected Council General of 24 members elects the first syndic; in 1971, Francesc Escudé-Ferrero.

The February 1971 census revealed that native Andorrans constituted a minority in their own nation, numbering a mere 6,234 of the total population of 20,550. Spanish citizens formed the majority.

The new bishop of the see of Urgel, Bishop Martí, was installed as the 80th co-prince of Andorra. The bishop was expected to interest himself in his role as co-prince to a greater degree than had his predecessor, the bishop of Lérida.

The government maintained its active program to attract winter tourists. It was believed that the winter trade would spend more per capita than the summer tourists, many of whom were campers.

Elections for half of the members of the Council General were held in December 1971, with the younger generation casting ballots for the first time. Their influence on future political trends in Andorra had yet to be gauged, however. (R. D. Ho.)

ANDORRA
Education. (1968–69) Primary, pupils 814, teachers 32; secondary, pupils 191, teachers 11.
Finance and Trade. Monetary units: French franc and Spanish peseta. No income tax, death duty, or customs; public treasury is funded by a 3% levy on gasoline and liquor. Exchange and deposit banking is important. Foreign trade (1970): imports from France Fr. 149,560,000 (U.S. $26.9 million), from Spain 983,-931,000 pesetas (U.S. $14.1 million). Tourism (1970) c. 1.5 million visitors.
Communications. Radio receivers (Dec. 1969) 6,000. Television receivers (Dec. 1969) 1,700.
Agriculture and Industry. Production: cereals, potatoes, tobacco, wool. Livestock (in 000; 1969): sheep c. 25; cattle c. 3; horses c. 1.

Antarctica

In 1971, 10 of the 16 Antarctic Treaty nations occupied 43 stations in Antarctica; Norway and Belgium, while not having bases of their own, participated in research programs of other nations. A broad scientist-exchange program was carried out between most nations. Pollution and conservation on the continent and surrounding waters continued to be of serious concern.

At its meeting in Moscow, Aug. 2–5, 1971, the Executive Committee of the Scientific Committee on Antarctic Research (SCAR) considered reports from its ten working groups, symposia on Antarctic research, exchanges of data and scientists between Antarctic Treaty nations, the multinational Antarctic Glaciological and Ross Ice Shelf projects, relationships with other international scientific bodies, and recommendations to the Antarctic Treaty nations.

A study of the August 1970 volcanic eruption on Deception Island by a group of scientists from seven nations determined that the eruption was the most violent of several that had occurred over the past three years. It altered the shoreline, erased the three-crater island of cinder cones that emerged during the 1967 eruption, shifted the intertidal zone upward, and destroyed subtidal life to a depth of 120 ft. Whaling was outlawed by the U.S. and other countries were urged to follow suit. At its meeting in Washington, D.C., in June 1971, the International Whaling Commission postponed action on the issue despite warnings that many species of whales were facing extinction.

Scientific Programs. Unusually warm weather hampered scientific studies during the austral summer. A high of 44° F was recorded, causing melting of ice runways and snow cover to such an extent that supply planes were unable to land and programs were delayed for a full month. Meteorologists suggested that melting was due to black volcanic ash from the latest Deception Island volcanic eruption, which drifted onto the mainland and caused increased absorption of solar energy and heat.

Argentina. The Argentine Antarctic research program was carried out by 19 institutions at seven permanent and two temporary stations, all but one of which were located on the Antarctic Peninsula. The icebreaker "General San Martin" made two cruises into the Weddell Sea and one into the Bellingshausen Sea. Three over-ice traverses were launched for glaciologic, geologic, and cartographic observations.

Australia. Australian activities in Antarctica were focused on four permanent and two temporary stations, where 78 men spent the winter. The Danish ice-strengthened motor vessels "Nella Dan" and "Thala Dan" were again contracted to resupply the Australian stations. A team of 25 men, supported by three helicopters and one small aircraft, spent four weeks in the Prince Charles Mountains conducting geophysical studies and surveying control points for aerial photographic mapping. Instrumental rafts were used to study sea ice in Mawson Harbor. A summer party again visited the Amery Ice Shelf, using a radar unit mounted on a motor toboggan to measure ice strain, thickness, accumulation, and movement. Ice cores were drilled in Wilkes Land for glaciologic studies, and rock outcrops around Casey Station and offshore islands were mapped and specimens collected for laboratory analysis. Work continued on the preparation of over 30 maps showing some physical parameters of the Antarctic ice sheet.

Belgium. Although Belgium did not maintain stations, Belgian scientists participated in expeditions of other nations. Leon Lambrecht and Josef Sekyra (Czech.) spent two months investigating the stratigraphy and sedimentology of the coal-bearing Permian formation that extends from Victoria Land to the Horlick Mountains. Roland R. Poepe and Etienne L. Paulissen studied periglacial features in the ice-free valleys with a U.S. party.

Chile. Chileans carried on a broad research program at three permanent stations on the Antarctic Peninsula and at several summer sites. The vessels "Piloto Pardo" and "Yelcho" helped resupply Palmer Station (U.S.). Helicopters from "Piloto Pardo" supported geologic studies in and around Deception Island by a party under Francisco Muniazga. Supported by the research ship "Hero," Chilean and U.S. scientists joined in a study of marine mammals and birds along the Antarctic Peninsula.

France. The French maintained one permanent base on the continent, Dumont d'Urville, and three others in the sub-Antarctic islands of Kerguelen, Crozet, and Amsterdam. Approximately 60 personnel operated in and around Dumont d'Urville Station, with 30 of them remaining for the winter. The first phase of a centralized data-collection centre was completed.

Japan. The 12th Japanese Antarctic Research Expedition, composed of 40 members, was centred at the permanent Showa Station, Japan's only base in Antarctica. An eight-man party made observations along a 1,000-mi. over-ice traverse from Showa Station to the Sandercock Nunataks and back. At Vanda Station (N.Z.), three scientists conducted limnological, chemical, and energy-flux studies of nearby Lake Vanda. Sadao Kawaguchi spent the winter at McMurdo Station and remained through the summer to continue meteorological observations. The icebreaker "Fuji," providing annual relief for the Antarctic program, was trapped in the ice while trying to reach Showa Station, causing a delay of over a month in the summer program.

New Zealand. Over 70 personnel, including 3 women, participated in the year's Antarctic program, which was focused largely at Scott Base and nearby Vanda Station. Fourteen separate projects were fielded in remote areas in cooperation with three other nations. Most of the fieldwork was conducted in the Dry Valleys near Vanda Station. The richest deposit of fossil fishes ever to be found in Antarctica was discovered in the upper Wright Valley. Complete

U.S. Navy personnel of the Operation Deep Freeze task force prepare the site of a new South Pole station in January 1971. The task force handles procurement and transportation of supplies for scientific programs conducted by the National Science Foundation.

AUTHENTICATED NEWS INTERNATIONAL

specimens of fish and plants dating back to the Devonian Period (340 million to 405 million years ago) were uncovered. As a result of the unseasonably warm weather, the Onyx (the largest known river on the continent) discharged ten times its normal flow into Lake Vanda, which has no outlet. On returning to McMurdo Station from Vanda Station, U.S. helicopters airlifted refuse in order to minimize possible pollution of the somewhat sterile dry valley area. A geologic party of eight from Victoria University was flown to Skelton Névé by U.S. aircraft, then on to the Horseshoe and Darwin mountains.

Norway. While Norway did not maintain stations in Antarctica, its scientists often participated in research programs of other nations. A party of six scientists, with U.S. logistic support, undertook studies in the Sverdrup Mountains of Dronning Maud Land. Plants, insects, and birds were collected for study, and two glaciologic traverses were made across the Jutulstraumen Glacier.

South Africa. South Africa maintained two permanent bases on the continent and two others on sub-Antarctic islands. The 12th South African National Antarctic Expedition was centred at the main SANAE Station on Queen Maud Land. Five men wintered at Borga Station, situated about 230 mi. from SANAE. Paleontologist James Kitching participated in the U.S. geologic expedition to the Central Transantarctic Mountains.

United Kingdom. The British Antarctic Survey conducted research programs at nine stations on the continent, the Antarctic Peninsula, and islands in Antarctic seas; six bases were occupied throughout the winter, including a new one at Fossil Bluff on the Antarctic Peninsula. A total of 92 personnel spent the winter in Antarctica. A new ship, the "Bransfield," joined three others in resupplying Antarctic stations. Two traverses were run from Halley Bay Station to collect snow samples for chemical studies. A wide range of geophysical studies was carried out at Halley Bay, Argentine Islands, and South Georgia. Geologic work was carried out in the Shackleton Range, where specimens were collected for isotope dating and paleomagnetic studies. R. J. Adie and O. G. Edholm received the Soviet Bellingshausen Medal, awarded to commemorate the 150th anniversary of Capt. Fabian von Bellingshausen's circumnavigation of Antarctica.

U.S.S.R. The 16th Soviet Antarctic Expedition was centred at four permanent stations along the East Antarctic Coast and at Vostok I, an inland station. A lesser program was carried out at Bellingshausen Station off the Antarctic Peninsula Coast. A new permanent base, Leningradskaya, was established on the Oates Coast, and a new meteorological centre was opened at Molodezhnaya Station, replacing the old facility at Mirnyy. The ships "Ob," "Professor Vize," and "Professor Zubov" participated in the annual resupply.

For the first time, Soviet scientists used laser beams to study glacier movements in Antarctica. An eight-inch-diameter mirror was placed on a glacier and tracked by a reflected laser beam. It was concluded that the glacier moved at random, and that movement occurred sometimes within seconds and other times over a period of hours. A 12-vehicle tractor-train again resupplied Vostok I Station from the base at Mirnyy. A geophysicist, Aleksandr Shirochkov, wintered at Byrd Station (U.S.) and an upper-atmosphere physicist, Dale Vance (U.S.), spent the winter

at Vostok Station. Sergei Miagkov, who wintered at McMurdo Station (U.S.), did geomorphologic and glaciologic studies of Ross Island and glaciers in the nearby Dry Valleys. A biologist, John Croom (U.S.), spent the winter at Bellingshausen Station.

United States. Over 200 scientists and technicians from more than 50 universities, government agencies, and industrial firms participated in the United States Antarctic Research Program during the year. Logistic support was provided by ships, aircraft, helicopters, and over 1,000 personnel at five permanent stations and several summer sites. The field-party staging centre at McMurdo Station was named after Thomas E. Berg, a geologist, who was killed in an aircraft accident in Antarctica in 1969.

A group of scientists from South Africa, the U.S.S.R., New Zealand, and the U.S. studied geology, geophysics, and paleontology in the Central Transantarctic Mountains. The party discovered fossils of the mammal-like reptile *Thrinaxodon,* including a nearly complete skeletal impression. This find, along with earlier related fossil discoveries in the same general area, added further support for the theory of continental drift, which suggests the existence of a former great southern continent of Gondwanaland. Studies were made on chaenichthyids or "icefish," the only adult vertebrates known to lack hemoglobin in their blood. A helicopter with four men aboard crashed into the summit of the 12,450-ft. Mt. Erebus; all were rescued 12 hours later with only minor injuries. The Academy of Sciences of the U.S.S.R. awarded Bellingshausen Medals to L. M. Gould, C. Craddock, M. J. Rubin, V. P. Hessler, and F. M. Maish.

Other Activities. Women biologists, geologists, technicians, and media representatives from Japan, Latin America, Australia, New Zealand, and the U.S. visited the continent during the 1970–71 summer season.

The tourist ship "Lindblad Explorer" carried 85 tourists on two trips of three weeks' duration to McMurdo and Hallett stations, stopping at several islands en route. Trips were launched from Hobart, Tasmania, and Bluff, N.Z., and cost around $4,000 for each traveler. Air New Zealand announced plans to initiate commercial air service to Antarctica sometime after 1973, when accommodations for tourists and adequate navigation and safety aids might be made available.

The annual Ice Bowl football game between scientists and U.S. Navy personnel at Byrd Station was won by the Navy. The game was played on ice 7,000 ft. thick, in temperatures of −20° F, and with winds between 25 and 30 mph. This tied the series at 5–5.

(L. M. Gd.)

See also Oceanography.

Anthropology

The dominant theme in anthropology in 1971 could best be expressed in the simple query: "Whither anthropology?" The question was reflected both in positive intellectual developments and in the turmoil and self-evaluation that reached a peak in 1970–71. This mood of doubt and uncertainty mirrored the temper of the times. It was also a response to the increased difficulty anthropologists were experiencing in engaging in traditional ethnographic fieldwork, derived in part from the rising opposition to such work in new nations, growing resentment of such investigations by the tribal peoples themselves, and the curtailment of financial support.

The best evidence of intellectual reexamination and ferment was the initiation of a number of new publishing ventures reaching out to other fields of study. The anthropological interest in ecology received expression in the *Journal of Human Ecology,* edited by the anthropologist Andrew P. Vayda. A second interdisciplinary journal, *Ethos,* scheduled to begin publication under the aegis of the University of California Press in 1972, had as its purpose the examination of the interrelationships between culture, society, and personality. It was jointly edited by Walter Goldschmidt, an anthropologist, and Douglass Price-Williams, a psychologist. A third journal, *Urban Anthropology,* edited by Jack R. Rollwagen, demonstrated the rebirth of anthropological interest in modern American culture. Each of these three areas was an active anthropological interest in the 1930s but fell into abeyance with the intensive concentration on less developed areas after World War II.

These were positive signs, but the discipline was also undergoing a period of introspection and torment in which it faced political and ethical issues of great complexity. Probably more than any other scholarly group, anthropologists have reason to be identified with the less developed areas of the world and the native populations of those countries. The problem of responsibility that this entails first emerged in 1965 with the disclosure of anthropologists' involvement in Project Camelot, a U.S. Defense Department-sponsored research program on insurgency and counterinsurgency in Chile. The affair had repercussions throughout Latin America, and anthropologists were made aware that their's had become a policy science.

This led, among other things, to the establishment of a special Ethics Committee of the American Anthropological Association. In 1970 a student activist newspaper published an accusation against a group of anthropologists working in Thailand, and individual members of the Ethics Committee made supportive public statements regarding this before investigating the charges.

The resulting controversy reached its peak at the association's November 1970 meetings. For the first time the presidency was contested by a candidate proposed by members other than those who constituted the nominating committee. This effort was defeated when two of the committee's candidates withdrew in favour of the third. Extensive debate appeared in the association's newsletter, as well as in sessions of the council of the association at the annual meetings in San Diego, Calif. A special committee of inquiry to investigate the Thailand affair was appointed, with Margaret Mead as chairman. Mead's report absolved the anthropologists in Thailand, but it was rejected at the November 1971 annual meeting and the matter was referred back to the board.

Aside from these immediate policy matters, deeper ethical issues captured the attention of anthropologists and were the subject of public discussion. As anthropology plays an increasing role in practical affairs and as anthropologists serve governments and private corporations in addition to engaging in pure research, they must consider their obligation to the native people who have been their hosts, friends, and colleagues, as against the interests of their employers and the demands of scientific inquiry.

Several symposia were held on these issues. The first, an all-day session at the San Diego meetings, involved a dialogue between anthropologists and American Indians (mediated by two Indian anthropologists). It was sparked, in part, by the castigation of the profession by Vine Deloria, Jr., a Sioux (who participated in the discussion), in his best-selling *Custer Died for Your Sins.* The second, international in scope, was a symposium on "The Anthropologist and His Constituency," sponsored by the American Ethnological Society at its spring meeting in May 1971 and chaired by Philleo Nash, former U.S. commissioner of Indian affairs. The third, a published discussion in the June issue of *Current Anthropology,* included an argument for a professional code of ethics by Joseph G. Jorgensen, a statement on the responsibility of the anthropologist to his host country by Richard N. Adams, and extensive comments by several contributors. Finally, a symposium was held in Barbados, under the sponsorship of the University of Bern, Switz., and financed by the World Council of Churches, on the topic of interethnic friction in South America. It produced a document condemning the activities of missionaries in particular, but also those of social scientists (including anthropologists) and of South American governments with regard to indigenous cultures.

The American Anthropological Association initiated an annual distinguished lectureship as a means of honouring persons of high scholarly calibre who, for one reason or another, cannot accept the increasingly onerous association presidency. Joseph H. Greenberg, Ray Lyman Wilbur professor at Stanford (Calif.) University, was the first recipient of this award. He addressed the association on "Is Language Like a Game of Chess?" The editorship of the *Ameri-*

Tasaday children, members of a primitive tribe found living in a Philippine rain forest in 1971, play in front of their hut. Studies of the tribe were expected to challenge widely accepted theories of prehistoric cultures.

can *Anthropologist,* the official organ of the association, was transferred to Laura Bohannan, the first woman to serve in this capacity since the journal was founded over 70 years earlier. The president of the association was Charles Wagley and the president-elect, A. F. C. Wallace.

A Philippine governmental survey conducted on the island of Mindanao discovered a hitherto unknown tribe of forest-dwelling natives living in a Stone Age style. According to the report, the timid tribe, called Tasaday and numbering no more than 100 persons, had been cut off from all outside contact for at least 400 years and perhaps as much as 2,000. The Tasaday were said to be ignorant of pottery, rice, corn, salt, sugar, and tobacco. The survey team was made aware of the existence of the Tasaday by local tribes, who referred to them as "the bird who walks the forest like the wind." To protect this remnant of an earlier era, the team asked the government to set aside the forest areas as a preserve out of bounds to commercial exploitation.

Further discoveries of early man were reported from East Africa. In addition to new finds at Olduvai Gorge in Tanzania and at Omo in Ethiopia, 16 fossil fragments were discovered east of Lake Rudolf in Kenya by Richard Leakey, making a total of 19 individuals discovered there. Preliminary reports suggested that this new evidence might help to resolve some controversies with respect to early man. Leakey believed that the coexistence of the robust and slender forms of *Australopithecus* at Lake Rudolf makes it unlikely that these are separate species; more probably, they represent sexual dimorphism within a single species. His classification of the shaft of a femur as belonging to an individual of the genus *Homo,* if correct, would serve to extend backward in time the origin of the genus to which modern man belongs and establish beyond doubt the contemporary existence of the two genera *Homo* and *Australopithecus.* Preliminary indications suggested that the Lake Rudolf materials date back to 2.6 million years.

An australopithecine jaw fragment (with one molar in place), found on Lothagam Hill in northern Kenya in 1967, was assigned an age of 5.5 million years by Bryan Patterson of the Harvard University Museum of Comparative Zoology. He considered the specimen to be a representative of *Australopithecus africans.* The date assigned to this specimen, which extends the antiquity of this genus from a previous maximum of 4 million years, was established by utilizing radioactive isotopes from nearby volcanic formations and in relation to its association with the fossil elephant remains for which dating had been established.

(W. R. G.)

See also Archaeology.

ENCYCLOPÆDIA BRITANNICA FILMS. *The Egyptologists* (1967).

Archaeology

Eastern Hemisphere. There were significant signs of change in Old World archaeology during 1971, although some of the change might be more apparent than real. Thus the "new archaeology," which claims for itself the discovery of emphasizing "the anthropological dimensions of archaeology," had begun to gather some enthusiasm, especially among younger archaeologists in Europe.

At the same time, in the U.S., where the movement

first developed, it appeared to be subdividing itself into a variety of often conflicting schools of thought as to how archaeology could most effectively be made a "science." It seemed improbable that the movement would gain quite such popularity in the Old World, where the time span is much longer than in the New World, where the image (real or imaginary) of direct descent from a national ancestral group pertains, and where the academic training of archaeologists more characteristically includes a disciplined study of history.

During the year there was further professional concern with destruction of sites and cultural contexts brought about by activities of illicit diggers for the commercial antiquities market. A committee of 17 states of the Council of Europe was formed for the protection of sites and monuments, and 63 countries adopted a firm UNESCO resolution to combat the looting of archaeological sites, the smuggling of stolen antiquities, and their irresponsible purchase by museums and private collectors. Most professional archaeological associations and university-based research museums had adopted similar and even stronger resolutions. Happily a growing number of "antiquities" purchased on the "art market" by both fine arts museums and private collectors were proving to be fakes, and this might tend to dampen the enthusiasm for such purchases.

New means of analyzing archaeological materials were noted. An important symposium on application of the physical sciences in archaeology was reported in *Science* (Feb. 26, 1971). Dexter Perkins and colleagues suggested ways of studying the structure of animal bones in order to distinguish wild from domestic species. There was intensified study of the culture-historical consequences of the so-called bristlecone pine calibration corrections, which (for certain ranges of time) suggest earlier real dates than those supplied by radioactive carbon (^{14}C) age determinations. (See *Western Hemisphere,* below.)

Further calls were made for aid in archaeological salvage work in areas to be flooded by dams and irrigation works. A substantial first report on salvage excavations in the Keban flood basin of the Euphrates in Turkey appeared, and work continued there. Farther south on the Euphrates, in Syria, more salvage was under way and the Syrian government appealed for added help. Pakistan sought aid in preserving the great Indus Valley site of Mohenjo-Daro, where a new irrigation system had induced a rise in ground-water level and soil salt endangered the site. A second interesting new site, Vlasac, was exposed in the Iron Gate gorge of the Danube in Yugoslavia, soon to be inundated by the pool of a new hydroelectric station. Vlasac appears to have been a fishing-hunting settlement, somewhat earlier than the first Iron Gate site, Lepenski Vir.

Pleistocene Prehistory. Glynn Isaac, Richard Leakey, and Anna Behrensmeyer reported the finding of stone artifacts sealed within a bed of tuff east of Lake Rudolf in Kenya. The tuff is dated at 2.6 million years ago, and similar nearby deposits yielded australopithecine fossils. Thus, this may be the oldest known hominid occupation site. New animal paintings were discovered in further explorations of the Niaux cave in France. Near Mezhirichi in the Ukraine, Ivan Pidoplichko cleared the remains of late Paleolithic huts framed of mammoth bones and suggested his finds are evidence of a permanent village of hunter-collectors of some 20 years' duration. Remains of a subhuman skull of a previously unknown type, possibly some 200,000 years old (pre-Neanderthal man), were found in a cave in the French Pyrenees.

The Near East. Because of the general Near Eastern political situation, archaeologists in Egypt remained restricted to relatively urban areas. Thus, for example, the Chicago Oriental Institute's copying of the temple reliefs at Luxor continued, but there were no excavations in the countryside. Some 29 royal mummies of pharaohs and their queens had been X-rayed in the Cairo Museum.

In contrast, Israel saw a great amount of digging activity, over 25 sites being under clearance by Israeli, European, and American archaeologists. The find of a burial near Jerusalem was announced, one heel bone of which had been pierced by an iron nail. Although the find was the first of its kind, it has long been known through literary sources that crucifixion was a common method of execution. A Herodian street was cleared along the south and west walls of the Second Temple, and walls of the "Nea" basilica—the emperor Justinian's A.D. 542 gift to the Jerusalem Christian community—were located.

Important French excavations proceeded at Tell Ramad, an early village site in southern Syria, and at the great coastal site of Ras Shamra in the north. A University of Pennsylvania expedition, digging on Phoenician ruins in Lebanon, recovered a seal positively identifying the site as Sarepta.

It was known that both foreign and government archaeologists were at work in Iraq, but news of their results was scanty. Fuad Safar of the Iraqi Antiquities Directorate announced the recovery of 20 large stone panels with Assyrian paintings at Nimrud, from what appears to have been the private bathroom of King Ashurnasirpal II. News was also tardy from Iran, except as concerns the Harvard University excavations of C. C. Lamberg-Karlovsky at Tepe Yahya. The site yielded clay tablets inscribed in the script known as Proto-Elamite and dated to *c.* 3500 B.C., and much evidence of trade with Sumerian Mesopotamia.

For Turkey, the first report of the international salvage effort in the Keban Dam area accounted for work by teams representing Istanbul University, Amsterdam and Chicago universities, the British School of Archaeology in Ankara, and the German Archaeological Institute. Among other levels, each expedition encountered particularly rich establishments of the 3rd millennium B.C. Farther south in the headwaters of the Tigris region, the Joint Istanbul-Chicago Prehistoric Project expanded its architectural clearances of Cayonu, an important early village site of *c.* 7000 B.C.

The Greco-Roman Regions. Detailed news summaries on Asia Minor, Italy, and Greece appeared in the 1971 issues of the *American Journal of Archaeology.* On the extreme fringe of archaeology proper came an overpublicized dispute on the attribution of a battered sculptured head in a basement storeroom of the British Museum. The Athens Archaeological Museum opened a spectacular exhibit of frescos and painted pottery recovered from the island of Thera, destroyed by a volcanic eruption *c.* 1500 B.C. In Athens itself, a large limestone slab near the Acropolis was identified as that upon which the city's archons (elected leaders) stood to be sworn to office.

News from Italy underlined the continuing struggle to speed construction of Rome's subway while at the same time salvaging traces of the past. Only 14 mi.

of the first of three projected lines had been completed since 1964, and it was planned to tunnel the second and third lines some 60 ft. underground in order to miss buried archaeological evidence. A joint Smithsonian Institution-Archaeological Institute of Belgrade expedition excavated an imperial Roman city under the Yugoslav market town of Sremska Mitrovica.

Late Prehistoric and Historic Europe. In several easily available studies (*e.g., New York Times,* May 19, 1971; *Scientific American,* Oct. 1971), Colin Renfrew called attention to the effect of the new calibration corrections on the ^{14}C based late prehistoric European chronology. Certain antiquities, such as the megalithic monuments and henges of Western Europe and certain Balkan assemblages, were now seen as being too early to depend for their origin on influences from the Near East. The origins of some general developments such as copper metallurgy may also have been independently achieved in Europe, but it was still too early for such broad generalizations as that "civilization" itself was independently achieved in Europe.

No very startling discoveries appeared in the available summaries on post-Paleolithic investigations in Europe. The finds from thousands of Bronze Age graves in Slovakia were reported, and new evidence for a long development within the Koros assemblage was discovered in Hungary. A new Viking-style boat appeared during drainage work in the Graveney Marshes in Britain.

Africa and Asia. Desmond Clark reported briefly on a rather hurried British survey in the Aïr Mountains of the Nigerian Sahara. In addition to Paleolithic tools, a microlithic assemblage with coarse pottery and an assemblage of the "Ténérian Neolithic" type appeared. J. E. Vogel of the Livingston Museum in Zambia continued the clearances of Iron Age sites, leading to "a quite comprehensive picture of the Victoria Falls regional succession."

In India, H. D. Sankalia finished his third season's work at Inamgaon east of Poona, recovering—for the first time—secure evidence of village and house plans and the general inventory of metalworking farmers of *c.* 1500–700 B.C. Further details had not yet appeared in support of W. G. Solheim's new thesis that the polishing of stone tools, cord-marked pottery, and the domestication of certain plants first took place in southeastern Asia prior to 10,000 B.C.

Excavations were conducted by C. C. Lamberg-Karlovsky at the Tepe Yahya site in southeastern Iran. The site yielded clay tablets dated c. 3500 B.C.

COURTESY, PEABODY MUSEUM, HARVARD UNIVERSITY

Archaeological assistant examines the skeleton of an Iron Age chieftain discovered between the wheels of his chariot during excavations at Garton, Yorkshire.

THE PRESS AGENCY (YORKSHIRE) LTD.

Solheim noted that a Thai-Danish expedition interpreted its data in contrary fashion, suggesting diffusion from north China.　　　　　　　　　　(R. J. B.)

Western Hemisphere. Although financial support for archaeological investigations continued to decrease in 1971, the funding loss was in small part offset by an increase in the number of New World field schools. The Archaeological Institute of America and the Society for American Archaeology approved resolutions condemning the illegal excavation and export of antiquities, for reasons that included both the loss of historical and scientific information that such actions bring about and the loss of important cultural and historical resources for the nation from which the antiquities are illegally obtained. Both organizations called upon members and museums to refrain from purchasing or accepting donations of artifacts unethically or illegally acquired.

Computer analysis of the results of microscopic studies of the long-lived bristlecone pine allowed C. W. Ferguson, University of Arizona, to establish a precise tree-ring chronology extending back more than 8,000 years. Direct use of this chronology had already been made by archaeologists, such as D. A. Graybill, who dated several tree-ring specimens from a previously undated prehistoric rock shelter in the White Mountains of California. Of greater significance, however, was the comparison of ages of wood samples that had been dated by both the tree-ring method and the radiocarbon technique. The results supported other data indicating that the amount of ^{14}C in the atmosphere has not been constant in the past, an assumption of the radiocarbon method. The bristlecone pine studies provided a method for converting radiocarbon ages into true dates, thus refining the radiocarbon dating procedure. It had been shown that in some cases a single radiocarbon age may correlate with as many as five true dates, and that radiocarbon ages are consistently more recent than true ages in the period prior to 800 B.C.

John Noakes and Kent A. Schneider, University of Georgia, developed and field tested a mobile archaeological laboratory with capabilities for flotation recovery of microsamples and radiocarbon dating. Work in progress included developing capabilities for neutron activation analysis, gas-liquid chromatography, and thermoluminescence analysis. At the State University of New York, Oswego, the Lake Ontario Environmental Laboratory, directed by Richard B. Moore, was developing an automated system of similar analytical procedures. The Wenner-Gren Foundation for Anthropological Research supported a meeting of the Arkansas Archaeological Survey to explore the problems of establishing a computerized archaeological data bank.

Far North. John P. Cook, University of Alaska, and William B. Workman, Alaska Methodist University, directed an archaeological reconnaissance of a portion of the right-of-way of the proposed Alaskan pipeline, which would extend about 800 mi. from Prudhoe Bay to Valdez. More than 100 sites representing a wide array of time periods and cultural affiliations were discovered, with additional findings expected as the survey continued. Investigations along the eastern coast of the Ungava Peninsula, sponsored by the National Research Council of Canada, revealed evidence of early Norse activity radiocarbon dated at A.D. 1050. Remnants of a bow and an iron ax, both unique for this portion of Canada, were found in association with stone beacons and house ruins.

Studies of the Franchthi cave site in southern Greece continued during 1971. Finds reported included Middle Neolithic vases (above) and the oldest complete skeleton from Greece (below).

The remains were believed to represent a hunting outpost of Norsemen whose major settlement was in Greenland.

Eastern United States. The first indisputable evidence of Adena culture maize farming was reported by James L. Murphy, Case-Western Reserve University, Cleveland, O. The find, a carbonized ear of maize closely resembling the variety common from the Hopewell culture to the east, was recovered from a site at Athens, O. A radiocarbon date of 280 B.C. for the context of the Adena maize was earlier than any similar context for Hopewell maize. Frank B. Fryman, Jr., Bureau of Historic Sites and Properties, Florida, reported that the state of Florida had acquired a major portion of the Lake Jackson site, north of Tallahassee, for conversion into a park area with public facilities and a museum. Available archaeological evidence indicated that the Lake Jackson site was a major ceremonial centre of the Fort Walton period, dated A.D. 1300–1500.

Western North America. A field school party from Sonoma (Calif.) State College, in cooperation with the California Department of Parks and Recreation, completed the second year of long-term investigations at Ft. Ross, the site of a 19th-century Russian colony north of San Francisco Bay. While no Russian material had yet been found, material dating from the subsequent American period was common.

Gardiner F. Dalley, University of Utah, conducted excavations at seven rock shelters in the mountains of northwestern Utah in order to determine the pattern of prehistoric usage of the high elevation environments. All the shelters appeared to have functioned primarily as hunting camps. A joint operation of Prescott (Ariz.) College, the University of Arizona, and the Museum of Northern Arizona investigated Stanton's Cave in the Grand Canyon in order to obtain biological materials for a paleoclimatological study. Cultural material was restricted to the uppermost stratum, which dated 1000 to 2000 B.C. Extinct goat and sheep remains dated about 10,000 B.C. were recovered from the second stratum, while driftwood dating back to 36,000 B.C. was found in the deepest stratum excavated.

Rainer Berger, UCLA, and associates reported radiocarbon ages determined from organic bone collagen for a number of human remains found in California during past years and for which adequate dating had not yet been obtained. Of greatest significance was the date of 15,200 B.C. for the so-called Laguna skull, originally discovered in 1933 in Laguna Beach. The remarkably early date, the oldest yet determined for human bone in the New World, prompted an intensive examination of the discovery locale, but with negative results.

Mesoamerica. Systems analysis techniques were employed by investigators headed by Kent Flannery, University of Michigan, in a study of the beginnings of social stratification and the rise of the state in the Oaxaca Valley, Mexico. Initial results indicated that canal irrigation, which appears to have been initiated about 500 B.C., and state organization, which seems to have been achieved between 100 B.C. and A.D. 1, developed in an interdependent manner.

Gordon R. Willey, Harvard University, and Demitri B. Shimkin, Center for Advanced Study in the Behavioral Sciences, Stanford, reported the results of a symposium, held at Santa Fe, N.M., that reviewed new data and interpretations on the decline and collapse of Maya civilization. Shortly after A.D. 770, after almost 500 years of Classic period growth and elaboration in the tropical lowlands of southern Mexico and adjacent Central America, the initial signs of slowdown appeared in Maya culture. By A.D. 830 most of the ceremonial centres were seriously affected, and by A.D. 950 outlying farming villages, as well as the great Maya centres themselves, were almost totally abandoned. The symposium gained general consensus for the hypothesis that the downward trend of Classic Maya culture was precipitated by contacts and pressures along its western boundaries, where long-distance trade contacts had been established with militarily backed professional groups from the dynamic and aggressive nations of the central Mexican uplands. Internal stress related to social class, health, and food production also were believed to have contributed to the decline.

Central America. An important figurine complex was discovered in the vicinity of Chalchuapa, El Salvador, by Stanly H. Boggs, Universidad Nacional de El Salvador. Solid hand-formed figurines of the expected late Preclassic type constituted the bulk of the collection, but a number of unique larger specimens with hollow torsos were also discovered. An archaeological survey in the region between the Coclé del Sur and Santa María rivers, Panama, conducted by Richard S. Cooke, University of London, revealed a total of 37 habitation and cemetery sites. Results of the survey suggested a relatively dense prehistoric population along the lower reaches of the two rivers.

South America. In a worldwide study of prehistoric metallurgical processes, utilizing precise determinations of trace impurities and crystalline structure in ancient metal artifacts, Clair C. Patterson, California Institute of Technology, demonstrated that the Mochi of Peru were smelting, melting, alloying, and casting metals at about A.D. 200. The development of metallurgy in the Andean region between A.D. 200 and 1500 was shown to have progressed through a complex series of steps similar to those that occurred in southwest Asia between 5500 and 3800 B.C. The parallel development, coupled with the significant difference in time, indicated a lack of Old World influence upon New World metallurgy.

The earliest occurrence of gold work in the Andean area was discovered during investigations directed by Joel W. Grossman, University of California, Berkeley, at the deeply stratified early ceramic site of Waywaka in the south central Peruvian highlands. A tool kit for working gold was recovered, as well

as a human grave with gold foil in association. Previously, the earliest gold work in Peru dated back to the Chavín Cult of about 800 B.C. Dating based upon ceramic styles placed the Waywaka gold work as early as 1200–1500 B.C. (D. A. F.)

See also Anthropology.

Encyclopædia Britannica Films. *The Egyptologists* (1967).

Architecture

Despite the economic recession and growing inflation of 1971, which were reflected in the world of architecture, many stimulating and worthwhile projects were completed, notably in the fields of commercial and educational buildings, and particularly in the United States.

School and University Architecture. One of the most exciting new buildings to be erected on a campus was the huge new athletics facility at Phillips Exeter Academy, Exeter, N.H. The architects were Kallmann and McKinnell, best known as the designers of the new Boston City Hall. The most striking features of the building from the outside were the enormous three-dimensional steel trusses supporting the roofs of the gymnasium, swimming pool, and skating rinks. The trusses were built outside rather than inside to leave the building free of interior supports that would hinder the sporting activities it was designed to house. The interior of the building, which expressed its complex circulation pattern and structure, was dominated by a structural spine with a continuous skylight. The roof was framed with precast concrete struts. The building cost more than $5 million.

The new gymnasium for the Japan Dental College in Tokyo by architect Shin'ichi Okada represented a very different solution to the challenge of designing a building for sports. The structure was composed of a see-through glass cage supported by concrete service towers at the ends. The various activities were "stacked" vertically to make the most of a restricted city site. The glass cage made sport an urban event, giving pleasure not only to the participants but to outside spectators as well.

The new building for the College of Fine and Applied Arts and College of Graphic Arts and Photography for Rochester (N.Y.) Institute of Technology was one of the largest academic buildings in the state of New York, covering an area of 425,000 sq.ft. De-

Headquarters complex of the Denver Technological Center was dedicated on Oct. 2, 1971. The five buildings of the complex, designed by Carl Worthington Associates, surround a plaza used for sculpture displays, promenading, relaxing, and eating.

TED EDEEN—PICTORIAL PARADE

A new Vatican audience hall, designed by Pier Luigi Nervi, was inaugurated by Pope Paul VI on June 30, 1971.

signed by Hugh Stubbins and Associates, it was spatially organized to act as an "anchor building" within the academic core. The L-shaped structure was conceived as a series of terraces, and housed offices, laboratories, studios, and workshops. The new teaching and research centre at Washington University School of Medicine, St. Louis, Mo., was designed by the firm of architects Murphy, Downey, Wofford & Richmond. The nine-story, block-long centre presented a facade dominated by external circular utility shafts, which gave it a corrugated effect.

In England the first stage of a series of residential buildings for Christ's College, Cambridge, by Denys Lasdun and Partners was completed, adding yet another fine example of modern architecture to a town that already had more excellent modern buildings than almost any other in Britain. The new Christ's building was based on a scheme of stepped construction and interlocking spaces similar to that developed by Lasdun for the University of East Anglia, in Norwich. A low-rise, high-density project, the building was of precast concrete.

Also in England, a new comprehensive school in Pimlico, London, stirred comment. The controversial brutalist building, designed by John Bancroft for the architects' department of the Greater London Council, was built of concrete, but its extensive use of glass skylights and clerestories made it look almost like a series of greenhouses. Occupying a restricted 4½-ac. site in central London, the school building was designed to accommodate 1,725 students, and emphasis was on ease of circulation. To compensate for the lack of outdoor play space, two large gymnasiums and a 66-ft. by 24-ft. indoor swimming pool were included.

Office Buildings. The new headquarters of the American Can Co. at Greenwich, Conn., was designed by architect Gordon Bunshaft of Skidmore Owings & Merrill on a beautifully landscaped 175-ac. site. American Can was one of the growing number of U.S. companies to move out of expensive and crowded quarters in Manhattan. The new headquarters consisted of a main office block and a smaller "executive complex." Underground parking lots on five levels for employees' cars were a feature of the design. The problem of integrating office development with residential areas in the suburbs, and increased concern with environmental problems in general, had led to a new concern with the problems of unsightly acres of parking lots. At a new office complex by architect Paul Rudolph at Haupauge, Long Island, each office unit was raised on stilts above a parking area for 360 cars.

The Westcoast Building in Vancouver, B.C., by architects Rhone & Iredale won the award for the best engineering in high-rise construction in the 1970–71 Design in Steel program of the American Iron and Steel Institute. Twelve floors of the building were suspended from steel bridge cables over a central core, leaving a large open plaza below. The engineers for the project were Bogue Babicki & Associates.

The new Five Cents Savings Bank in Boston by Kallmann and McKinnell was constructed as a columnless banking hall with three floors of offices above on a fan-shaped site in the historic downtown area. The glass facade of the banking hall was protected by giant five-story columns which formed a colonnade at ground level. The new Penn Mutual Building in Philadelphia was planned to rise to a height of 21 stories across from the historic Independence Hall. The four-story facade of an existing 19th-century building in the Egyptian style was to be preserved and incorporated into the new building, forming part of the lobby entrance. In addition, there was to be a glass-enclosed elevator to carry visitors to the observation deck. Architects for the project were Mitchell/Giurgola Associates.

The new headquarters for Ralston Purina at St. Louis was designed as a showplace for visitors by Hellmuth, Obata & Kassabaum. The 15-story structure was of concrete with a pyramidal base, and the total cost of the building was more than $10 million. Architect Jasper D. Ward designed the building for the City Blue Print Co. of Louisville, Ky., as a sort of visual joke. The playful design featured an enormous bright blue cube at the corner. The exterior volume was broken by huge circular windows on one facade.

The new concrete and glass West German headquarters for Rank-Xerox was designed by German architects Hentrich-Petschnigg & Partner. Situated in a suburb of Düsseldorf, the building was composed of three hexagons grouped around a central service core. The new Standard Bank Centre in Johannesburg, S.Af., also by Hentrich-Petschnigg & Partner, was the largest suspended-floor structure in the world. The building was 430 ft. high and had a two-story banking hall at ground level surrounded by a plaza.

A year-long effort to save the Old Stock Exchange building in Chicago from demolition failed. The Landmarks Preservation Council Inc. of Chicago was not able to raise enough money to acquire the historic structure, the largest ever designed by Louis Sullivan, and wreckers began their work in October. The 13-story, 77-year-old building, the first to use caisson foundations in Chicago, was to be replaced by a 43-story office tower. Mayor Richard J. Daley of Chicago announced that the city would attempt to preserve the building's main entrance arch and such parts as the balustrades and the column capitals for display in Chicago museums.

Civic and Cultural Buildings. The new Ohio Historical Centre at Columbus was hailed by the *Architectural Record* as "the most architecturally significant public structure built in Ohio since the state capitol building of 1841." The building was designed primarily as a teaching tool by architects Ireland and Associates. The bulk of the centre hovered over an entrance-level podium and housed the state archives and historical library. The construction was reinforced concrete, with the exterior walls sheathed in the native Ohio salt-glazed chute tile commonly used on Ohio farm buildings.

Paul Rudolph was the architect for the new Orange County Government Center at Goshen, N.Y. Although small in scale in keeping with its setting, the building nevertheless achieved a sense of monumentality. The design was based on a carefully worked out system of intersecting planes and parallel surfaces. It housed a complex variety of interior spaces, including separate courtrooms for adults and juveniles, assembly spaces, and various offices. The three distinct areas were grouped around a central court, and an elaborate system of clerestories admitted natural light. The construction was of exposed concrete with split-rib concrete block, and the cost was more than $5.8 million.

The new City Hall for St. John's, Nfd., was designed by John B. Parkin Associates. The exterior was of concrete striated vertically, but inside wood and bright colours were used to contrast with the starkness of the concrete. The City Hall was an integral part of a new complex that was to include shops, apartments, a hotel, and a bus terminal.

The new Denver (Colo.) Art Museum was one of the largest museums in the western U.S. Designed by architects John S. Sudler of Denver and Gio Ponti of Italy, the structure was composed of two six-story cubes and cost $6 million. Where the cubes joined were the main entrance, lobbies, and utility core. Inside, the mezzanine was designed with a double-height gallery to house such artifacts as 28-ft. Indian totem poles. The new museum had a sparkling glass chip facade.

The John F. Kennedy Center for the Performing Arts on the Potomac River in Washington, D.C., was opened officially in September. Designed by Edward Durell Stone, the 630-ft.-long, 300-ft.-wide, and 100-ft.-high marble-clad structure housed three separate theatres, one for opera, one for concerts, and one for drama. The theatres were connected by two 250-ft.-long halls, while a 600-ft.-long "grand foyer" stretched along the front of the building. Architecturally, the $66.4 million centre drew considerable condemnation. One critic called it a "cross between a concrete candy box and a marble sarcophagus in which the art of architecture lies buried." Its supporters praised it for its "magnificence" and "timelessness."

Several noteworthy new libraries were completed in the U.S. in 1971. The Brighton Branch Library, near Boston, was the first of a group of small regional libraries planned for the Boston Public Library system. Designed by The Architect's Collaborative Inc., it was an attractive building composed of three polygonal wings on three different levels for adults, children, and community service. The construction was of reinforced concrete, and the total cost came to just over $1.5 million.

The Mount Angel Abbey Library, St. Benedict, Ore., was designed by the famous Finnish architect Alvar Aalto and was only his third American building. Built for a Benedictine monastery on a beautiful country site, the library was characterized by simple, elegant brickwork and traditional use of wood. The desks and chairs were also designed by Aalto. The new Lyndon Baines Johnson Library, in Austin, Tex., with Gordon Bunshaft of Skidmore Owings & Merrill as chief architect, was planned "to express through monumentality the importance of its historical treasures." The main mass of the tomblike library rested upon a podium and was defined by two vast 65-ft.-high parallel walls, 90 ft. apart and 200 ft. long.

The Veteran's Memorial Auditorium, which formed part of the Marin County Civic Center, in San Rafael,

Calif., was designed by William Wesley Peters of the Taliesin Associated Architects of the Frank Lloyd Wright Foundation. Wright had been the original architect for the Civic Center. Dominated by a shallow-domed scalloped roof, the structure had a seating capacity of 2,000 and cost $2.5 million. The Mummers Theatre in Oklahoma City by architect John Johansen represented a new departure in theatre design. The astonishing and controversial building incorporated grain elevator tubes of brightly painted steel. The helter-skelter expressive form, akin to the sets for some contemporary plays, was composed of three volumes connected by "people tubes."

A new cathedral at Kasama in northern Zambia included residential accommodations and was designed by Julian Elliott to be built by unskilled local labour. It consisted of a conglomeration of small vaults in local oatmeal-coloured brick with the church itself roofed by a concrete shell.

A "capsule" office-apartment building in Tokyo was designed by Noriaki Kurokawa to nest factory-made modular apartment units into 175-ft. shaft frames. Each steel module would have built-in furniture, bathroom, and air-conditioning. They would sell for $10,000 to $13,000 each.

The American Institute of Architects awarded its Gold Medal for 1971 to architect Louis I. Kahn. The Royal Institute of British Architects Royal Gold Medal for the year went to Hubert de Cronin Hastings, chairman of the Architectural Press and an editor of the *Architectural Review.* (S. MI.)

See also Cities and Urban Affairs; Engineering Projects; Housing; Industrial Review.

Encyclopædia Britannica Films. *The Medieval Mind* (1969).

Arctic Regions

Actual production of oil and gas resources failed to materialize in the North American Arctic in 1971 on the scale predicted by past exploration activities. Nevertheless, considerable progress was made in resolving environmental and native land claims problems and in developing the necessary infrastructure. The state of Alaska began seriously dipping into the $900 million nest egg resulting from the 1969 sale of North Slope land leases. Based on current projections, the lease funds would last until fiscal 1977.

In midyear it was announced that Canada and the U.S. had signed a cooperative agreement for combating forest fires along the Yukon-Alaska border. At the request of the U.S. government, exploratory discussions were held in Ottawa during July on a proposal to pave the Canadian portion of the Alaska Highway. The highway, built in 1942–43, was 1,523 mi. in length, of which 302 mi. were in Alaska. Fewer than 110 mi. of the Canadian portion were paved; the remainder consisted of an all-weather gravel surface. Alaska announced plans to seek a right-of-way for construction of a road from the Yukon River to Prudhoe Bay on the Arctic Ocean. In Canada priority was being given to a final 450-mi. link of all-weather gravel-topped road leading to Inuvik in the Northwest Territories.

The Canadian government's White Paper on Defence stated that one of the primary responsibilities of the Canadian Forces in the 1970s would be surveillance of Canada's own northern territory and coastlines. Recruiting officers visited Arctic communities during the year to interest young northerners in a career with the Forces. Increased Forces responsibilities in Canada's north created a need for people having an intimate familiarity with local conditions.

In February the Canadian government announced an agreement between Canada and the Soviet Union concerning cooperation in the industrial application of science and technology; identified for further study were problems arising from severe northern climatic and permafrost conditions in the construction, electrical, and oil and gas industries. During his official visit to the Soviet Union in May, Canadian Prime Minister Pierre Trudeau visited Murmansk and Norilsk, two of the largest communities within the Arctic Circle.

A dog team expedition led by an Italian author reached the North Pole on May 10. During the trek, Interior Airways in Fairbanks airlifted 300 dogs, 35 sleds, and about 40 expedition members and supplies from Thule, Greenland, to Alert, Can. From there, the group was airlifted to a base camp 60 mi. out of Alert at Cape Columbia. On April 6 the dash to the pole began.

Protests by conservation groups, as well as the Canadian and Japanese governments, failed to stop a U.S. underground test of a five-megaton nuclear weapon on Amchitka Island in the Aleutian chain. (*See* ENVIRONMENT.)

The Alaska Slope Native Association filed suit in U.S. District Court in October against the U.S. Interior Department seeking a court ruling that tentative approval of state-selected lands on the Arctic Slope in 1964 violated the natives' aboriginal rights. The suit also requested an accounting for all funds received by Alaska, including those from the 1969 land-lease sale. The association claimed title to 56 million ac. from the Canadian border to Port Hope and from the summit of the Brooks Range to the Arctic Ocean. Congress, meanwhile, acted quickly on Alaskan native claims legislation. A bill passed in December granted Alaska's natives 40 million ac. and specified payment of $962.5 million, including $462.5 million from the Treasury and $500 million from mineral revenues from state and federal lands. The money would be distributed to 12 regional corporations, in which the natives would hold shares, for purposes of investment in such projects as education and housing.

In July *Alaska from the Inside* reported that uncertainty over the construction of pipelines and the question of native land settlements had brought exploration-drilling activity on the North Slope almost to a halt. A final decision on construction of the trans-Alaska pipeline from Prudhoe Bay to Valdez was expected early in 1972. A controversial study of the economic consequences of the pipeline through the year 2000, released in October by the University of Alaska's Institute of Social, Economic, and Government Research, predicted that pipeline construction would not ease unemployment in the state.

The Alyeska Pipeline Service Co. announced plans to build a 140-mi. gas pipeline from Prudhoe Bay to the foot of the Brooks Range to parallel the trans-Alaska line. The Gas Arctic Systems Study Group, a consortium of Canadian and U.S. companies, estimated that natural gas could be moving through Canada via a 1,550-mi., 48-in. pipeline from Prudhoe Bay to U.S. markets by late 1975 or 1976.

A second discovery of oil in a test well in the Northwest Territories by Imperial Oil was described by a company spokesman in July as "fantastic." The strike was at Tuktoyaktuk, just east of the mouth of the Mackenzie River. The discovery was made on the heels of an initial find in the same well in May, when it was announced that the company had recovered oil and gas during a test at a 3,800-ft. level. The Canadian government increased its investment in Panarctic Oils Ltd. to just over $34 million. Panarctic Oils, a consortium of 20 companies, was formed in 1967 to ex-

Crewmen from the nuclear-powered submarine HMS "Dreadnought," the first British submarine to surface at the North Pole, leave the ship during their voyage in March 1971.

CENTRAL PRESS—PICTORIAL PARADE

Areas:
see Populations and Areas; *see also the individual country articles*

plore for oil and gas in the Canadian Arctic and to maintain national equity interest in northern resource development.

The possible use of icebreaker supertankers to move Alaskan oil was under continued investigation during the year. It was estimated that 20 vessels costing up to $2 billion would be required. According to *Alaska News Review,* two Canadian researchers concluded that an ice-breaking cargo vessel the size of the "Manhattan," which navigated the Northwest Passage in 1969, would have to generate between 1.3 million and 13 million hp. to move through certain conditions of sea ice. The "Manhattan," one of the most powerful commercial ships of its size ever built, generated 43,-000 hp.

Late in the year the Canadian Institute of Guided Ground Transport announced plans for a feasibility study of a railway to move oil from the Alaskan and Canadian western Arctic oil fields. The Canadian Ministry of Transport initiated an interim federal contingency plan for handling oil and other toxic material spilled in Canada's northern waters. Under the plan, the Canadian government would assume full responsibility for responding to pollution incidents in the Canadian Arctic.

The Soviet periodical *Vodnyy Transport* reported that, according to Soviet scientists, in 1,000 years vessels will be able to navigate in the area of the North Pole all year round if Arctic ice continues to thaw at the present rate. In January it was reported that the U.S.S.R. drifting scientific station North Pole 16 was nearly 2,000 km. away from the coastline of Siberia. No other Soviet drifting station had ever traveled so far from the mainland. The station was nearing the halfway mark of its circular journey and it was believed that the ice floe would return to its starting point within two or three years.   (K. DE LA B.)

Argentina

The federal republic of Argentina, occupying the southeastern section of South America, is bounded by Bolivia, Paraguay, Brazil, Uruguay, Chile, and the Atlantic Ocean. It is the second largest Latin-American country, after Brazil, with an area of 1,072,-157 sq.mi. (2,776,888 sq.km.). Pop. (1970): 23,364,-431. Cap. and largest city: Buenos Aires (pop., 1970, 2,972,453). Language: Spanish. Religion: mainly Roman Catholic. Presidents in 1971, Brig. Gen. Roberto Marcelo Levingston and, from March 26, Lieut. Gen. Alejandro Agustín Lanusse.

Domestic Affairs. The overthrow of President Levingston on March 22, after only nine months in office, was followed by the appointment of the army commander in chief, Lieut. Gen. Alejandro Lanusse (*see* BIOGRAPHY), as the new president. The growing antipathy between Levingston and Lanusse and the deteriorating economic situation were the principal factors behind Levingston's downfall. The commanders in chief of the Army, Navy, and Air Force initially stated that they would jointly assume the powers of government, but on March 26 Lanusse was sworn in as president to exercise the executive and legislative functions of government. However, legislation on matters of national importance was to be submitted to the military junta for approval.

Although Lanusse inherited an unstable economic situation, emphasis was placed from the outset on solving the country's political problems. Through his minister of the interior, Lanusse frequently stressed that the government's primary objective was to achieve a national consensus as a first step toward a return to constitutional rule. With this declared objective in mind, the government in September announced details of the political timetable whereby elections would take place in March 1973 and the elected government would be installed on May 25, 1973. In the meantime, legislation governing the electoral process was passed, and the institutional framework of political parties formed after July 1, 1971, was settled.

Lanusse's commitment to a return to representative democracy aroused considerable opposition among certain elements of the military, and early in October a section of the Army attempted to oust the president. The movement, led by Col. Manuel García, commanding officer of a tank regiment, and supported by ex-president Levingston, accused Lanusse of "counter-revolution," that is, of the betrayal of the original aims of the 1966 military take-over, which were to put the country in order before allowing elections to be held. The ouster attempt failed as support anticipated from the Air Force did not materialize—both the Air Force and the Navy reaffirmed their support for Lanusse—and the revolt was confined largely to the army garrisons at Azul and Olavarría. The two garri-

Lieut. Gen. Alejandro Agustín Lanusse was inaugurated as president of Argentina on March 26, 1971.

ARGENTINA

Education. (1968) Primary, pupils 3,238,936, teachers 165,130; secondary, pupils 197,571, teachers 30,137; vocational, pupils 485,724, teachers 67,921; teacher training, students 203,-941, teachers 24,336; higher (including 29 universities and technical institutes), students 265,-303, teaching staff 19,788.

Finance. Monetary unit: new peso, with a free rate (Sept. 27, 1971) of 5 new pesos to U.S. $1 (12.37 new pesos = £1 sterling). Gold, SDRs, and foreign exchange, central bank: (March 1971) U.S. $495 million; (March 1970) U.S. $501 million. Budget (1969 est.): revenue 9,773,-000,000 new pesos; expenditure 10,205,000,000 new pesos. Gross national product: (1969) 69,-510,000,000 new pesos; (1968) 61.1 billion new pesos. Money supply: (March 1971) 18,110,-000,000 new pesos; (March 1970) 15,260,000,-000 new pesos. Cost of living (Buenos Aires; 1963 = 100): (May 1971) 483; (May 1970) 366.

Foreign Trade. (1970) Imports 6,382,800,000 new pesos; exports 6,502,900,000 new pesos. Import sources (1969) U.S. 22%; Brazil 11%; West Germany 11%; Italy 7%; U.K. 6%. Export destinations (1969): Italy 14%; Netherlands 11%; U.K. 10%; U.S. 9%; Brazil 8%; Chile 5%; Spain 5%; West Germany 5%. Main exports: meat 25%; corn 15%; wheat 7%; hides and skins 5%.

Transport and Communications. Roads (1970) 201,059 km. Motor vehicles in use (1969): passenger 1,390,000; commercial 722,000. Railways (1969): 39,546 km.; traffic 14,146,000,000 passenger-km., freight 12,949,-000,000 net ton-km. Air traffic (1969): 2,127,-600,000 passenger-km.; freight 58,228,000 net ton-km. Shipping (1970): merchant vessels 100 gross tons and over 327; gross tonnage 1,265,510. Telephones (Dec. 1969) 1,668,426. Radio receivers (Dec. 1968) 9 million. Television receivers (Dec. 1969) 3.1 million.

Agriculture. Production (in 000; metric tons; 1970; 1969 in parentheses): wheat 4,230 (7,020); corn 9,360 (6,900); sorghum 4,068 (2,616); barley c. 580 (570); oats c. 600 (425); potatoes 2,336 (2,340); sugar, raw value (1970–71) 979, (1969–70) 978; linseed 702 (640); sunflower seed 1,140 (876); cotton, lint 140 (112); oranges 1,086 (1,038); apples 446 (436); wine 2,000 (1,792); tobacco 71 (52); beef and veal c. 2,930 (2,884); cheese (1969) 179, (1968) 178; wool, greasy c. 175 (c. 175); quebracho extract (1968) 123, (1967) 119. Livestock (in 000; June 1970): cattle c. 48,000; sheep c. 43,900; pigs c. 4,250; horses c. 3,620; chickens c. 33,000.

Industry. Fuel and power (in 000; metric tons; 1970): coal 616; crude oil 19,891; natural gas (cu.m.) 6,016,000; electricity (excluding most industrial production; kw-hr.) 16,891,000. Production (in 000; metric tons; 1970): cement 4,769; crude steel 1,825; cotton yarn (1969) 76; passenger cars (including assembly; units) 169; commercial vehicles (including assembly; units) 51.

sons were quickly surrounded by loyalist forces and in less than 24 hours the rebellion had collapsed with the surrender and imprisonment of the rebel leaders and the arrest of Levingston. Perhaps encouraged by the lack of support for the rebels, Lanusse felt his position secure enough to leave a few days later to visit Peru and Chile.

In December, Isabel Martínez de Perón, wife of the former dictator, arrived in Argentina to coordinate the activities of his still active following, with the supposed intention of paving the way for his return from Spain.

The Economy. Against the background of political uncertainty and experimentation, the economic situation deteriorated substantially in 1971. The expansionist policies pursued by Aldo Ferrer, who had replaced Carlos Moyano Llerena as economy and labour minister in October 1970, proved unsuited for the relief of inflationary pressures and for the resolution of numerous short-term economic problems. In spite of the deterioration in the principal economic indicators, notably the burgeoning crisis in the meat industry, the disappointing wheat harvest, the large treasury deficit, and the poor export performance, no significant attempt was made by the government to shift the basis of its economic policies. In May Ferrer was forced to resign, and the all-powerful Ministry of Economy and Labour was abolished.

By the end of July, the rise in the cost-of-living index, which reached 21.7% in 1970, was running at about 40%, and by September an increase of more than 45% was generally estimated for the year as a whole. An additional inflationary factor was the large fiscal deficit. By mid-1971 the treasury deficit had reached 427 million pesos, representing an increase of 174% over the first half of 1970. In an attempt to improve the government's finances, the minister of treasury and finance, Juan Quilici, announced a 10% reduction in public expenditure without, however, cutting down on the public works program.

On April 3 the Banco Central introduced a "crawling peg" exchange rate system and raised the exchange rate from 4 to 4.04 pesos to the U.S. dollar. By August 25, after five further adjustments, the exchange rate stood at 5 new pesos to the U.S. dollar. When this failed to improve the investment situation, the government introduced a two-tier exchange-rate system with a commercial rate for trade operations and a financial rate for all other operations. By October the peso had fallen to a new low of 8.25 to the dollar on the official exchange market. In July, in a somewhat belated attempt to reduce the trade deficit, the government imposed a one-year ban on imports of luxury goods, and in September a general import ban was imposed until October 31. The controversy over the role of private foreign investment in Argentina led to the passing of a new foreign investment code under which preference would be granted to the setting up of joint ventures. Foreign investments approved and registered under the law would be able to transfer profits after the first year of operation. However, companies with a majority foreign-capital participation could only obtain short-term loans on the local market.

On July 1 Argentina signed a three-year nonpreferential trade agreement with the EEC. Under its terms the EEC would apply to imports of frozen meat from Argentina a maximum duty of 55% of the tariff levied on similar imports from third countries, the maximum level of duty to be revised every three months. The agreement would enable Argentina to increase its exports of frozen meat by 30%. In return, Argentina agreed not to discourage investments by EEC member countries.　　　　　　　　　　　　　(W. Bn.)

Art Exhibitions

The 500th anniversary of the birth of the German Renaissance painter Albrecht Dürer was the occasion for several major exhibitions in 1971. The largest of these was the loan exhibition held at the Germanisches Nationalmuseum at Nürnberg, W.Ger. Although some of the artist's most famous paintings are too delicate to travel, a representative selection of Dürer's work was assembled that allowed visitors to assess and appreciate his excellence. Works by his contemporaries also were included, thus putting him into the perspective of his own time. The show included prints and drawings as well as paintings. In the U.S. the National Gallery of Art in Washington, D.C., mounted an exhibition of prints and drawings by Dürer from North American collections. Almost every Dürer drawing in a North American collection was included. An exhibition of Dürer prints was shown at the Philadelphia Museum of Art, and in the fall the Boston Museum of Fine Arts organized a print exhibition that compared different impressions of the same Dürer prints. Although the majority of Dürer paintings are in European museums, American collections are particularly rich in drawings and prints.

The 90th birthday of Pablo Picasso was marked by exhibitions of his paintings and engravings throughout the Western world. His native Málaga, Spain, decided to commission the sculptor Ortiz Berrocal to design a monument in his honour.

The many difficulties involved in organizing loan exhibitions were highlighted by the show "Art in Revolution," organized by the Arts Council of Great Britain and held at the Hayward Gallery, London, in the spring. The show originally was planned to chronicle avant-garde Russian art of the 1920s, and the Soviet government promised to lend a large number of important items. However, when the Soviets discovered that works by El Lissitzky and Kazimir Malevich, borrowed from private sources in the West, were to be included, they threatened to withdraw the promised loan; since the work of these artists was not approved of by the Soviet Union, they did not feel able to participate in the show unless they were removed. This, of course, changed the character of the exhibition, and at the last minute emphasis had to be shifted from painting to architecture and the theatre. Included were models of Constructivist stage sets and a large, spiraling model of Vladimir Tatlin's unexecuted Monument to the Third International, set up on the terrace of the gallery.

Later in the summer the Hayward Gallery was the scene of a retrospective exhibition devoted to the English "Op" artist Bridget Riley. Riley, whose optical paintings are concerned with visual sensations, was influenced in her early work by the pointillist artist Georges Seurat. The exhibition included many of her most recent canvases in which she had begun to experiment with colour. Her best-known works were in black and white. The attendants at the gallery all wore dark glasses, presumably to protect their eyes from too much visual stimulation. The retrospective was also seen in Bern, Switz.; Hanover and Düsseldorf, W.Ger.; and Turin, Italy.

Also in London, the Queen's Gallery at Buckingham Palace held an exhibition devoted to Dutch pictures in the Royal Collection. Paintings included six Rembrandts, a Vermeer, and almost a hundred other masterpieces. The exhibition was confined to the 17th century, the golden age of Dutch painting. It was interesting to see how the Dutch pictures reflected the taste of English monarchs over 400 years. Many of the finest examples, including three of the Rembrandts, were acquired by George IV.

In the spring the Victoria and Albert Museum, London, held an exhibition entitled "The Ceramic Art of China" to mark the 50th anniversary of the Oriental Ceramic Society. It was the first such large-scale show since 1935, and pieces were lent from as far afield as Japan, the Philippines, and the U.S. The exhibition traced the development of Chinese ceramics over 3,000 years from the unglazed earthenware of the Neolithic period to the sophisticated, elegant porcelain of the 18th century. Over 250 fine specimens were assembled.

Later in the summer the Victoria and Albert mounted an imaginative show entitled "Covent Garden: Twenty-five Years of Opera and Ballet." It took the form of a tour of the Royal Opera House and used music, film, models, scenery, and lighting to create the effect that the visitor was actually at Covent Garden. Included in the show were reconstructions of actual sets for famous productions and designs for costumes and sets, including work by Cecil Beaton, Franco Zeffirelli, and Osbert Lancaster.

"Shock of Recognition" was the startling title of an exhibition of British and Dutch landscape paintings and drawings shown at the Mauritshuis in The Hague, Neth., in late 1970 and at the Tate Gallery, London, in January and February. The point of the show was to indicate the debt owed by English landscape painters to the Dutch 17th-century masters. A similarity of approach was evident in Dutch works by such artists as Cuyp, Hobbema, and Ruisdael and English masters including Gainsborough, Constable, and Turner.

Another show devoted to landscape was that given over to the work of the English 18th-century watercolourist John Cozens and shown at the Whitworth Art Gallery, Manchester, and then at the Victoria and Albert. It was the first show on such a scale devoted to this romantic landscape artist in 40 years and included 100 drawings and watercolours.

The Royal Academy's Winter Exhibition for 1971 was devoted to the work of the Vienna Secession, an Austrian movement in architecture and the decorative arts roughly corresponding to Art Nouveau. At the Tate Gallery "Léger and Purist Paris" concentrated on work done between 1912 and the late 1920s in Paris. Over half the works were by the artist Fernand Léger, who celebrated the machine age in his mechanical-looking compositions of figures and objects.

The Tate Gallery was also the scene of a popular show of works by the pop artist Andy Warhol. Confined to work done since 1962, the exhibition included his famous themes such as soup cans and Brillo boxes.

As always, Paris was the scene of many provocative art exhibitions in 1971. The Musée des Arts Décoratifs held a show, "Pioneers of 20th-Century Architecture," covering the work of four great architects of the period: the Spaniard Antonio Gaudí (1852–1926), the Frenchman Hector Guimard (1867–1942), and the Belgians Victor Horta (1861–1947) and Henry

Van de Velde (1863–1957). The show was comprised largely of sculptures, photographs, and audiovisual aids.

The Musée du Petit Palais mounted "The Golden Age of Holland," an exhibition of 241 canvases borrowed from public collections in France and covering the period from Mannerism to the early Rococo. The high spots of the exhibition were 20 canvases by Rembrandt.

The first of a series of exhibitions to be devoted to a single famous work of art was held at the Louvre and centred on the famous painting by Ingres, "The Turkish Bath." Intended to document the work as fully as possible, the show comprised preliminary studies, drawings, photographs, sources, and material showing how it had influenced later works.

"A Thousand Years of Japanese Theatre" was the title of an exhibition at the Musée de l'Homme in January. Devoted to the evolution of the Japanese theatre to the present day—including traditional and avant-garde aspects—it included prints, dolls, masks, and costumes.

The Armenian S.S.R. lent an exhibition of Armenian art to the Musée des Arts Décoratifs in the winter. It included almost 500 objects from the Paleolithic era to the present day and was composed of tools, pottery, jewels, ceramics, bronzes, and models of architecture. In return the French government compiled an exhibition of 100 French Impressionist masterpieces which it lent to the U.S.S.R. The whole collection, which included important works by Manet,

Giant portrait of Albrecht Dürer dominates the announcement of an exhibition in Nürnberg, W.Ger., commemorating the 500th anniversary of his birth.

DIGNE MELLER MARCOVICZ

Spectator sits among paintings by Bernard Buffet during an exhibition of the painter's work at the Garnier Gallery in Paris.

Monet, Renoir, and Degas, was valued at Fr. 100 million. It was shown at the Hermitage, Leningrad, and the Pushkin Museum, Moscow. Later in the summer the same canvases were lent to the Prado in Madrid.

An exhibition at the Uffizi Gallery in Florence entitled "Firenze e Inghilterra" ("Florence and England") put on view the English paintings in this famous Italian museum. Many visitors were surprised to discover that Florence has one of the largest collections of English paintings on the continent. The show included a remarkable group of 55 self-portraits by English artists. Paintings by Lely, Zoffany, Kneller, Millais, and Watts and drawings by Gainsborough, Constable, and Blake were among the exhibits.

The Albertina Gallery in Vienna marked the third centenary of the death of Rembrandt (1969) in March with an exhibition entitled "Rembrandt, His Family, and Friends," providing a new and little-known picture of the great artist's private life.

Once again American museums mounted a number of large and important exhibitions. "Zen Painting and Calligraphy" was one of the major shows mounted at Boston to celebrate the centennial year of the Boston Museum of Fine Arts in 1970. The largest exhibition of Zen Buddhist painting and calligraphy ever assembled, it included over 80 Chinese and Japanese paintings borrowed from temples, museums, and private collections in Japan and ranged from 12th-century China to early 19th-century Japan. Two of the items in the exhibition were classified by the Japanese government as national treasures. It was estimated that a visitor to Japan would require 15 years to see all of the works gathered in Boston.

Another major exhibition was "Four Americans in Paris: The Collections of Gertrude Stein and Her Family" at the Museum of Modern Art, New York, in the winter. The show later traveled to Baltimore, San Francisco, and Ottawa. There were 225 paintings, drawings, prints, and sculptures, many of which had never before been seen in the U.S. A particularly fine group included works by such artists as Matisse, Picasso, and Gris.

Duncan Phillips, founder of the Phillips Collection in Washington, D.C., was also an eminent collector of French 19th-century paintings. The Collection marked the occasion of its 50th anniversary with a great Cézanne exhibition, also seen in Chicago and

Boston. A fine group of paintings was borrowed to complement Phillips' own collection.

The Baltimore Museum of Art celebrated the centennial of the birth of the French artist Henri Matisse with an important exhibition of his drawings from the museum's own superb Matisse collection. They covered every aspect of his varied career, and about one-third had not been seen previously in the U.S. The exhibition later traveled to the California Palace of the Legion of Honor in San Francisco and to the Art Institute of Chicago.

Another French painter, Francis Picabia (1879–1953), a pioneer of abstraction whose work is little known by the general public, was the subject of a show at the Solomon R. Guggenheim Museum, New York, in late 1970. It was the first American retrospective of Picabia's work and included 139 paintings, drawings, documents, and mixed media works.

The Whitney Museum of American Art organized the most important exhibition ever held of the work of the influential modern American artist Georgia O'Keeffe. The show consisted of 121 paintings, watercolours, and drawings selected from 55 years of her creative career, many of which were lent by the artist for the first time. The show was seen in New York in late 1970 and then moved on in 1971 to the Art Institute of Chicago and the San Francisco Museum of Art.

Another important show organized by the Whitney was the comprehensive exhibition of the work of the American realist Thomas Eakins (1844–1916). It was the first major Eakins show in New York in 53 years and included 153 oils, watercolours, drawings, sculptures, and photographs taken by Eakins.

An exhibition on a little-known subject, "German Painting of the 19th Century," toured the U.S. in late 1970 and 1971. Assembled from a number of West German collections, the paintings, of a type that strongly influenced English and American art in the 19th century, were seen at the Yale University Art Gallery, New Haven, Conn.; the Cleveland (O.) Museum of Art; and the Art Institute of Chicago.

The first major American show of the work of the contemporary German sculptor Gerhard Marcks was organized by the UCLA Art Galleries, Los Angeles, for circulation to various museums across the United States. Sculpture, drawings, and prints were included.

"Man-Eaters and Pretty Ladies" was the provocative title of an exhibition at the Montreal Museum of Fine Arts devoted to the art of Mexico from 1200 B.C. to A.D. 100. Few of the 950 objects had ever been on public view. "Man-eaters" referred to the jaguar-worshiping Olmec peoples. "Pretty ladies" is the archaeological term for the clay figures of women found in graves at the Aztec site of Tlatilco.

Finally, an exhibition at the Philadelphia Museum of Art devoted to multiple art pointed the way to future directions in collecting. A multiple was defined as "a work of art designed by the artist to be produced in sizable or even unlimited editions, hence aimed at the collector whose income is limited." The artist creates a prototype which is then mass-produced in a factory. The show included work by Marcel Duchamp, Andy Warhol, Claes Oldenburg, and Victor Vasarely.   (S. MI.)

See also Museums and Galleries; Photography.

ENCYCLOPÆDIA BRITANNICA FILMS. *Meaning in Modern Painting* (1967); *The Artist at Work—Jacques Lipchitz Master Sculptor* (1968); *Henry Moore—The Sculptor* (1969); *Siqueiros—"El Maestro"* (1969); *Richard Hunt—Sculptor* (1970); *Interpretations* (1970).

Art Sales

The combined firm of Sotheby of London and Parke-Bernet of New York announced total net sales for the 1970–71 season of £35,795,211, having for the first time deducted all unsold items. Christie's of London once more included unsold lots, for which bids did not reach the reserve price, in their greatly increased total for the year of £25,291,951.

Christie's sold some outstanding pictures, jewelry, and furniture during the season, accounting for much of the increase, but many items were "bought in" unsold at large sums. For instance, in the big sale of June 25 a so-called Caravaggio was bought in at £136,500 and a Rembrandt at £168,000, among others. This sale was the big event of the art sales year, when Lord Harewood's Titian "The Death of Actaeon" was sold to the London dealer Julius Weitzner for £1,680,000. Shortly afterward the painting was resold to the J. Paul Getty Museum in Malibu, Calif., through French & Co. of New York. However, the National Gallery, London, announced its interest in acquiring the painting, and the granting of an export license was delayed while attempts were made to raise the money to keep the painting in Britain.

At the same sale French & Co. also acquired for the Getty museum an exceptionally interesting Van Dyck study of four Negro heads for £420,000 and two large panels by Boucher, sold together for £420,-000. These had belonged to the late Anna Thomson Dodge, widow of the U.S. automotive pioneer, as had some extremely valuable jewelry sold in Geneva by Christie's. A highlight was a splendid emerald and diamond necklace sold for £123,800. Mrs. Dodge's furniture was sold by Christie's in London, the highest price ever paid for a single piece of furniture, £173,250, being given by Henri Sabet, an Iranian oil magnate, for an exquisite Louis XVI writing table attributed to Martin Carlin. Sabet was bidding against the Detroit Museum for this *bureau plat,* which once belonged to the Tsaritsa Maria Fedorovna of Russia.

With such extremely important items to sell over the year, Christie's was able to reduce the number of sales held. For the rarest and finest specimens prices rose steeply, while mediocre examples generally brought no more than they had two years before. Excepting the occasional rarity, sales of silver did not do particularly well, although £24,000 was paid at Christie's for a coffeepot made by Paul de Lamerie in London in 1738.

Fine drawings and prints rose in price. A 1631 drawing of "A Bearded Man Seated in an Armchair" by Rembrandt brought £55,000 at Sotheby's, which sold many other drawings of various dates at high prices, including Ben Nicholson's "Wicca, March 1953" for £16,500, "The Sick Child" by Edvard Munch for £13,200, and "Knieender Akt" by Egon Schiele for £8,700. In New York many valuable drawings changed hands, including "Avant l'Audience" by Honoré Daumier for $85,000, and "Portrait of Mrs. Charles Badham" by J. A. D. Ingres for $65,000.

New high prices were paid in New York for modern American paintings and sculpture: $60,000 for "Indian Red and Black" by Clifford Still; $75,000 for "Big Painting No. 6" by Roy Lichtenstein; and $45,000 for Claes Oldenburg's "Stove." Antique American furniture brought new high prices, the peak being $102,000 paid at Parke-Bernet's in May for the Hazard family bonnet-top highboy, made by John Goddard in Newport, R.I., in the 1780s. Although $150,000 was paid in New York for the painting "Summertime" by Mary Cassatt, in general the market in Impressionist paintings was noticeably quieter than in recent years, probably because of a lack of U.S. bidders in the international auction rooms. Collectors from Japan, however, were bidding in Europe and the U.S. for Chinese and Japanese works of art. A T'ang dynasty pottery glazed jar brought £20,800, and an early 15th-century blue and white Ming stem cup was sold for £44,000, both in a sale at Sotheby's in March.

That fashions change was demonstrated in the Dodge sale of Chinese works of art. Mrs. Dodge was 103 when she died in 1970, and she had paid high prices for ornate *famille rose* and *famille noire* vases 40 to 50 years earlier. Since then their value had slumped, and a *yen-yen* vase that cost $38,000 went for £504 at Christie's in June. In contrast, Mrs. Dodge's collection of jade, for which she had paid an average of $400 to $500 per piece, sold for much more, a large mutton fat jade jar fetching £10,500.

In a sale of Oriental art at Kunsthaus Lempertz, Cologne, W.Ger., a T'ang figure went for DM. 12,-000. In May, Lempertz sold works from the Jakob Johann Lyversberg collection, including a triptych of 1500 fetching DM. 180,000. Paul Brandt's in Amsterdam sold an important "Riverscape" by Jan van Goyen for 110,000 guilders, "View of a Village on a River" by Jan Brueghel for 83,000 guilders, and "Dutch Riverscape" by Salomon van Ruysdael for 132,000 guilders. (WA. LS.)

Book Sales. There was no weakness in prices or the supply of rare books in 1971. Some fine and unexpected items were unearthed and met with encouraging responses. At Sotheby's in March, 19th-century English poets did well at the Britwell sale, which contained two star items of quite different description: William Blake's illuminated *The First Book of Urizen,* which brought £24,000; and a beautiful vellum copy of the Ulm Ptolemy *Cosmographia* of 1482, which went for £34,000. In April, a rare flower

During its June art sale, Christie's of London sold Rembrandt's etching "Christ Presented to the People" for £33,600—a record price for a print.

COURTESY, CHRISTIE'S

book, Fontaine's *Collection de cent espèces . . . Camelia*, 1845, was sold for £2,800.

Twenty-nine duplicates from the Pierpont Morgan Library sold by Sotheby's in June featured two Caxtons which remained in England: Boethius' *De Consolatione Philosophique, c.* 1478, fetched £25,000 and *The Game and Playe of Chesse*, 1475, £44,000. At the same sale the first book entirely printed in italics, the Aldine Vergil, reached the astounding price of £8,500 and crossed the Atlantic. A fine collection of Aldine books also appeared at Christie's.

A Latin Pontifical was found in 1970 in limp wrappers consisting of leaves from printed books pasted together. Written in England around the year 1000, with a few glosses in Anglo-Saxon, it failed to make the reserve price at Sotheby's and was subsequently sold to the British Museum for £14,000.

Fine books on travel and voyages appeared for sale with the Boies Penrose library, of which the first part was dispersed in June at Sotheby's. At a sale of duplicates from the Chatsworth library, Christie's sold some fine incunabula. A 1742 first Nicolas Jenson *Pliny* brought £11,000. At the sixth portion of Major J. R. Abbey's library, sold by Sotheby's in October, one of Humphrey Repton's original manuscript Red Books, showing alterations to be made at Newton Park, sold for £1,200. From the sale of the same library's manuscripts, held in December, the *Ruskin Hours, c.* 1312, sold for £28,000.

An illuminated manuscript on vellum of Horace's *Works*, Florence, *c.* 1460, went for £10,000 at Sotheby's in December; and a *Book of Hours* in Dutch in the style of *Hours of Catherine of Cleves, c.* 1440–50, brought £7,000. An elaborately illuminated French *Book of Hours, c.* 1470, went for £3,200 and another, thought to have been written for a knight of the Golden Fleece, 1440–50, was sold for £2,000. An illuminated manuscript on vellum of Cicero's *Orations*, once in the collection of William Morris, went for £5,500.

At Sotheby's in November John Gould's *The Birds of Europe*, 1832–37, was bought by Smidt van Gelder for £5,000; Anna Maria Sibylla Merian's *Disertation sur la Génération et les Transformations des Insectes de Surinam*, The Hague, 1726, went to Israel for £3,600. Gould's *The Birds of Great Britain*, 1862–73, brought £2,800 and John Speed's *Theatre of the Empire of Great Britain*, 1676, went for £2,500.

Out-of-the-way items did not always do well. The first part of the Cornelius Greenway collection offered for sale at Parke-Bernet in New York in November displayed nearly 300 autographed photo-

graphs of 19th-century celebrities. Prices did not reward what must have been for the collector a most difficult pursuit. The highest price, $1,000, was given for a *carte de visite* signed portrait of U.S. President Franklin Pierce, whereas Victor Hugo's was given away at $25.

Hauswedell in Hamburg displayed the second part of King Ernst Augustus of Hanover's library. In Paris the Jean Pozzi sales featured material from various fields of interest: books having belonged to the French 19th-century poet Leconte de Lisle (Baudelaire, *Les Fleurs du mal*, 1857, inscribed, Fr. 22,500) and to Catherine Pozzi, one of Paul Valéry's most important women friends; and some beautiful Oriental manuscripts collected by Pozzi.　　(P. Bs.)

Astronautics

Tragedy marred the end of an otherwise highly successful Soviet space mission in 1971. The three cosmonauts of Soyuz 11 were found dead upon returning to earth on June 30 after their 23-day mission aboard the Salyut space station. However, proponents of manned space flight were elated by the successful Apollo 15 lunar mission to Hadley Rille in July.

The success of Apollo 15 notwithstanding, the American space program continued to decline. There was a 15.7% drop in employment in the aerospace industry between March 1970 and March 1971. Further reductions in the nation's aerospace workers were predicted for the remainder of the year and for 1972 as well. The National Aeronautics and Space Administration (NASA) also was required by Congress to reduce its payroll by 1,500 employees on October 1. The $3,298,035,000 budget approved for 1972 by Congress was again a holding action with no funds for long-range developments.

NASA gained its fourth administrator on May 1. James C. Fletcher, former president of the University of Utah, accepted the position after it had been offered to and declined by a number of prominent men in the aerospace field. While gaining an administrator, the agency lost astronaut Walter Cunningham, who resigned on August 1 to become vice-president of Century Development Corp., a nonspace company in Houston, Tex. Neil A. Armstrong, the first man to walk on the moon, also resigned from NASA. After little more than a year as NASA's deputy associate administrator for aeronautics, Armstrong on October 4 became professor of engineering at the University of Cincinnati, O. His fellow Apollo 11 astronaut Edwin

Association Football:
see Football

Aldrin returned to duty with the U.S. Air Force. Further shifts among NASA astronauts during the year found Alan B. Shepard, returned from Apollo 14, assuming his former position as chief of the Astronaut Office at the Manned Spacecraft Center in Houston. Astronaut Thomas Stafford, who had held the job during the Apollo 14 mission, was assigned as deputy director of flight crew operations, assisting Donald K. Slayton, former Mercury astronaut. Astronaut James Lovell removed himself from flight status to become deputy director of science and applications at the Manned Spacecraft Center.

In Europe, interest in space continued to increase. The budget for the European Launcher Development Organization (ELDO) was fixed at $88 million. It included approval for the development of the Europa II space carrier vehicle. Generally, there seemed to be a growing tendency for Western European space organizations to rely more on the European Space Research Organization (ESRO) and ELDO and to cooperate less with NASA. Sweden recommended increased support for ESRO and the development of a Swedish scientific satellite. The nation expressed a coolness toward participation in the U.S. post-Apollo space program. Joining Sweden in this respect was Great Britain, which made it clear that it would have no part in financing a post-Apollo (space shuttle) program. Denmark, on the other hand, announced that it would withdraw from ESRO by the end of the year. France continued to strengthen its domestic space program by increasing its space budget by 23%. Significantly, the greatest amount went to the nation's commitment to ELDO. However, the country did not rule out participation with the U.S. in the post-Apollo project.

ESRO in April received a new director general when Hermann Bondi, after $3\frac{1}{2}$ years, was replaced by A. Hocker of West Germany. Bondi resigned in order to accept the position of chief scientific adviser to the Ministry of Defence in London.

Cooperation between the U.S. and U.S.S.R. increased considerably during the year. The two nations exchanged lunar soil samples for analysis in each other's scientific institutions. Soviet scientists on June 10 presented U.S. space officials in Moscow with three grams of material returned to earth by the Luna 16 probe. In return, they received three grams of soil each from the Apollo 11 and 12 missions.

On the technological level, the two nations took the first steps toward joint manned space flight programs in the late 1970s. On Oct. 26, 1970, representatives of the two countries met in Moscow to discuss a common design for docking mechanisms on spacecraft. Thus, the way was opened to permit rescue operations as well as joint manned operations in earth-orbiting space stations, possibly by 1976. The talks continued through 1971.

Acutely aware of congressional concern for safety in manned space flight operations, NASA revealed in March a rescue plan for the astronauts of the Skylab, to be launched in 1973. The plan called for an Apollo command module modified to carry five men instead of three. It would be launched in case the conventional Apollo spacecraft used with the Skylab for some reason became inoperable.

Manned Space Flight. Apollo 14 continued the success of the American lunar landing series that had been marred only by the failure of Apollo 13. Its crew consisted of mission commander Shepard, America's first man in space; command module pilot Stuart A.

Roosa, a rookie astronaut on his first space flight; and lunar module pilot Edgar D. Mitchell, also a novice. Lifting off from Cape Kennedy, Fla., on January 31, the mission soon proved to be exciting. After the spacecraft achieved a parking orbit around the earth, it seemed as if the mission would have to be aborted. The Kitty Hawk command module refused to dock with the Antares lunar module. For almost two hours the crew attempted to join the two. Finally, on the sixth try, the two craft achieved a "hard dock" and the mission proceeded.

During the voyage to the moon, the crew engaged in a series of technological experiments that gave engineers on the earth the basic data for designing more comprehensive experiments of a similar nature for the Skylab program. One experiment demonstrated the feasibility of producing composite metal castings under weightless conditions—a process impossible on the earth because gravitational forces cause sedimentation of the different metals.

With Shepard at the controls the lunar module landed on the moon on February 5 within 60 ft. of its designated target in Fra Mauro. On their first excursion from the landing craft, Shepard and Mitchell spent 4 hours and 49 minutes on the lunar surface. They set up the Apollo lunar surface experiments package (ALSEP) approximately 500 ft. west of the landing craft, collected 43 lb. of rocks and soil, deployed a solar wind experiment and a laser-beam reflector, and performed the traditional implanting of the American flag. In addition, Mitchell operated a pyrotechnic "thumper" that sent shock waves to a depth of 60 to 70 ft. into the moon. The signals were recorded by geophones in the ALSEP and transmitted to the earth for seismological interpretation. For the first time in the Apollo program, Shepard and Mitchell used the modular equipment transporter (MET), a two-wheeled cart to carry tools, scientific instruments, and rocks and soil samples.

A second period of lunar exploration on February 6 found Mitchell and Shepard struggling toward the rim of Cone Crater with the MET loaded with photographic equipment and a magnetometer. However, they never reached this objective because the condition of the soil impeded their progress to the point that they might not have had enough oxygen left in their portable life support systems to make it back to the spacecraft. On returning to Antares for lift-off and rendezvous with Kitty Hawk, they had spent 9 hours and 42 minutes exploring the moon.

For the first time, geologists on the earth had the opportunity of studying a man-made seismic event on the moon by means of two seismometers on the moon. The 5,200-lb. Antares was deliberately crashed into the moon on February 6, impacting about 42 mi. from the Apollo 14 landing site and some 68 mi. from the Apollo 12 landing site at a velocity of 3,850 mph. The moon "rang" for about $1\frac{1}{2}$ hours after the impact. Earlier, on February 4, the 26,300-lb. third stage of the Saturn V that boosted the Apollo 14 to the moon crashed onto the lunar surface some 100 mi. away from the Apollo 12 seismometer, and the moon "rang" for almost 3 hours.

From the time of their deployment on the lunar surface the Apollo 12 and 14 seismometers recorded a rather large number of moonquakes. Many of them occurred at the time of the lunar perigee, and this was interpreted as indicating that they resulted from the earth's gravitational pull and that the moon is not intrinsically highly tectonically active. Other possible

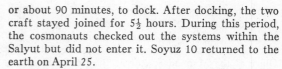

Above, cosmonauts Vladislav N. Volkov, Viktor I. Patsayev, and Georgi T. Dobrovolsky before their tragic space flight. Below, Soyuz 11 is launched.

sources for the moonquakes are meteoroid impacts and strong tidal loading. In October scientists reported that other instruments left on the moon by Apollo 12 and 14 astronauts had detected geysers of water vapour erupting through cracks in the lunar surface. This was the first evidence that there might be subsurface pools of water on the moon.

In summary, the Apollo 14 mission was marred by several unexplainable malfunctions in equipment; but it largely succeeded in its objectives of evaluating the role of man in lunar exploration and of implanting scientific instruments on the moon. It also succeeded in returning approximately 100 lb. of rocks and soil samples to the earth. Furthermore, it demonstrated the high degree of accuracy with which spacecraft could be returned to a predetermined location on the earth. On February 9 Kitty Hawk landed only four nautical miles from the recovery ship USS "New Orleans." Its crew was the last to be quarantined for two weeks in the Lunar Receiving Laboratory at the Manned Spacecraft Center.

On April 19 the Soviet Union launched an unmanned space station into orbit from Tyuratam. Salyut was placed into a near-circular orbit about 167 mi. above the earth. With typical caution, Tass, the Soviet news agency, described its purpose as being for "perfecting the elements of the design and the onboard systems and for conducting scientific research and experiments in space." Western observers were not misled, however. They anticipated a manned rendezvous and docking and were proved correct on April 23 when Soyuz 10 was launched and subsequently docked with Salyut. Soyuz 10 was manned by cosmonauts Vladimir Shatalov, a veteran of Soyuz 4 and 8; Aleksei S. Yeliseyev, also a veteran of Soyuz 8; and Nikolai N. Rukavishnikov, a novice.

The mission was declared a success by the Soviet Union, but Western space officials were skeptical. The objective seemed to have been to demonstrate the rendezvous and docking of a small manned spacecraft with a very large, passive, unmanned space station. However, the cosmonauts had difficulty in making the requisite maneuvers. With the Soyuz only 550 ft. from the Salyut, Shatalov needed an entire orbit,

or about 90 minutes, to dock. After docking, the two craft stayed joined for 5½ hours. During this period, the cosmonauts checked out the systems within the Salyut but did not enter it. Soyuz 10 returned to the earth on April 25.

The ill-fated Soyuz 11 mission began with a perfect lift-off from Tyuratam on June 6. The crew consisted of the flight commander, Lieut. Col. Georgi T. Dobrovolsky, a native of Odessa who became a cosmonaut in 1963; Vladislav N. Volkov, a native Muscovite and veteran flight engineer on Soyuz 7; and Viktor I. Patsayev, a design engineer who had become a cosmonaut in 1968.

On the following day, Soyuz 11 docked with the Salyut. The crew then transferred into the Salyut vehicle and powered down the Soyuz 11. On the next day, the main-stage engine of the Salyut was fired to raise the vehicle into an orbit with an apogee of 164 mi. and a perigee of 144 mi. On June 9, the orbit was again adjusted to raise the apogee to 173 mi. and the perigee to 161 mi.

During the third day of the mission, the crew began wearing a special pressure suit called the Penguin that had been designed by aerospace medical specialists to maintain muscle tone and to counteract the debilitating effects of weightlessness on the cardiovascular system. Medical and biological experiments were prominent among those conducted by the crew. Among the former were a special instrument for studying human adaptation to weightlessness and another for determining bone density. Typical of the latter was the hatching of tadpoles under conditions of weightlessness and their preservation at varying stages of development so that biologists could study the effects of weightlessness on the formation of the vestibular apparatus of their inner ear. Experiments in meteorological photography were also made; and plants such as flax, cabbage, and onions were grown in hydroponic solutions. In addition, certain experiments of a military nature were reportedly conducted.

A 24-hour work schedule was instituted for the crew. For example, on June 11, Volkov started to work at 9:30 P.M.; Dobrovolsky began at 1:50 A.M. on June 12; and Patsayev followed him at 6 A.M. An integral part of each man's work session was a long period of physical exercise, including walking on a treadmill. On June 24, after 18 days in orbit, the crew set a new endurance record, breaking the record of 17 days, 16 hours, and 59 minutes set by their fellow cosmonauts of Soyuz 9 a year earlier.

The crew continued to perform its experiments and maintain its rigid physical training program. At no time was there any indication of illness or lack of adaptation to weightlessness. On June 29, the crew entered the Soyuz 11 and checked it out preparatory to undocking it from Salyut. The undocking itself was performed uneventfully that day. On June 30, Soyuz 11 was oriented for reentry into the earth's atmosphere and the retrorockets were fired for the necessary period of time.

The official news release from Tass (as quoted in *Soviet Report,* July 8, 1971) chillingly summed up what followed:

"On completion of the braking engine operations, communications with the crew ceased. In conformance with the schedule after aerodynamic braking in the atmosphere, the parachute system was deployed and immediately before touchdown the soft-landing engines were switched on. The descent module made a smooth landing in the assigned area. Landing at the same time as the ship, the rescue party from a helicopter after opening the hatch found Lieut. Col. Georgi Timofeyevich Dobrovolsky, Flight Engineer Vladislav Nikolayevich Volkov, and Test Engineer Viktor Ivanovich Patsayev at their duty stations without any signs of life. The causes of death will be investigated." (*See* OBITUARIES.)

It later was reported by the Soviet government that the cosmonauts of Soyuz 11 had died when their reentry craft suddenly lost cabin pressure. Since there was no rupture of the cabin structure itself, the failure must have been in a pressure seal of the hatch or perhaps a valve.

One month later, America's manned spaceflight program produced its most spectacularly successful mission since the first landing of man on the moon. First of the J-series of spacecraft (designed for periods of 16 days in space), Apollo 15 lifted off from Cape Kennedy on July 26. For this mission the Endeavor command module weighed 2,640 lb. more than usual, while the Falcon lunar module was 2,470 lb. heavier, caused in part by a 480-lb. lunar roving vehicle folded up and stored in the descent stage. The lunar "dune buggy" was equipped with a colour television camera that provided spectacular views of the moon's surface for television watchers on the earth. The crew consisted of mission commander David R. Scott, a veteran of the Gemini 8 and Apollo 9 missions; command module pilot Alfred M. Worden, who was making his first space flight; and lunar module pilot James B. Irwin, also making his first flight. They were wearing a new type of space suit that permitted greater mobility and flexibility on the moon.

Shortly after Apollo 15 left earth orbit for the moon, the first of several minor equipment malfunctions occurred. A short-circuit caused a light to indicate that the main propulsion engine of the Endeavor was firing. When Scott tapped it, the light went out. Later tests proved that the engine was operating properly. On July 27, Scott and Irwin entered the Falcon to check it out and found that the glass cover over a dial had been broken. However, it did not present a problem.

Apollo 15 entered lunar orbit on July 29. An hour later, the spent S IVB stage of their Saturn V booster crashed onto the lunar surface about 186 mi. east of the Apollo 14 landing site, giving valuable scientific data to geologists on the earth who recorded the event on the seismometers left on the moon by the crews of Apollo 12 and 14.

On July 30 the lunar module Falcon landed on the moon near the Hadley Rille at the base of the Apennine Mountains in the Sea of Rains, at a site in the Marsh of Decay. About 15 hours later Scott climbed down the ladder of Falcon and stepped onto the moon. After some difficulty in releasing their balky lunar roving vehicle from its storage bay in the Falcon, Scott and Irwin extracted it and set off to put 17.4 mi. on it during their weekend on the moon. The astronauts checked out the rover and found that the front wheels did not steer. While annoying, the situation was not serious since the car was designed to steer with the rear wheels as well.

Leaving Hadley Base and the Falcon, Scott and Irwin drove to the edge of Hadley Rille and then up the slope of St. George Crater. They covered five miles, returning to their base after about 2¼ hours. During the excursion the lunar rover averaged a speed of five miles per hour, but Scott "opened it up" to ten

miles per hour at one point. On this first exploration, the astronauts spent 6½ hours collecting rock and soil samples, taking photographs, and deploying scientific instruments. The day ended with a fatiguing task, the deployment of the ALSEP. Scott, in particular, had trouble using a drill in an attempt to make holes for special temperature sensors beneath the soil. Because of the energy expended, Mission Control cut 30 minutes off the seven-hour work period.

On August 1, Scott and Irwin again left the Falcon and climbed aboard their lunar rover for the slopes of the Apennine Mountains. The high point of this exploration was the discovery of a rock that was later dubbed the "Genesis" rock. It appeared to be an anorthosite, or fragment of the original crust of the moon. Preliminary analysis of the half-pound rock after the mission left in doubt whether it was indeed such a primeval building block, but it appeared to be about 4,150,000,000 years old (±200 million). The oldest rock previously returned from the moon was 3,600,000,000 years old.

The following day's excursion in the lunar rover to the northern edge of Hadley Rille found the crew outside Falcon for 4 hours and 45 minutes. Their first task was to check the nuclear power supply for the ALSEP, and they succeeded in removing from the ground a balky drill core that had proved intractable the day before. With the aid of the lunar rover, they returned to the rim of Hadley Rille. Dismounting, they walked about 30 ft. down its slope and picked up rock samples. They also photographed the far side of the rille with a telephoto lens to record the stratification of the rock.

After 66 hours and 15 minutes on the moon, Scott and Irwin lifted off in the ascent stage of Falcon on August 2. With them were 171 lb. of lunar rocks and soil samples and hundreds of photographs, both in black and white and in colour. The docking with Worden in the command module was accomplished without difficulty. There was some consternation later, however. With the memory of Soyuz 11 in everyone's mind, the crew reported an unusually high pressure in the tunnel between the Endeavor and the Falcon. The situation could have meant a leak in either spacecraft. The tunnel was vented to 1.6 lb. per sq.in. (psi). Mission controllers and astronauts watched their meters and displays with apprehension, but the pressure did not rise. There was no leak in the Endeavor. Two hours later, the Falcon was jettisoned to crash into the moon at 3,890 mph, providing geologists on earth with their first chance to measure seismic events to a depth of 150 mi. into the moon's interior.

On August 4, while Apollo 15 was still circling the moon, the crew ejected into lunar orbit a subsatellite from the scientific-instrument bay of the service module. Weighing 78½ lb., the satellite had instruments aboard that would gather data on the moon's gravitational field, the earth's magnetosphere, and the moon's magnetic field. Two days later, on the return journey to the earth, Worden left the command module and took a 16-minute "walk" in space to the instrument bay of the service module to recover film from its cameras.

On August 7 the Apollo 15 command module splashed down in the Pacific Ocean, with only two of its three parachutes fully open. While the crew experienced a somewhat harder impact than usual, they suffered no discomfort, and there was no structural damage to the spacecraft. They were only 12 seconds late and only 6.6 mi. from the planned impact point.

Major Satellites and Space Probes Launched Oct. 1, 1970–Sept. 30, 1971

Name/country/ launch vehicle/ scientific designation	Launch date, lifetime*	Physical characteristics					Initial orbital data			
		Weight (kg.)†	Shape	Diameter	Length or height	Experiments	Perigee (km.)†	Apogee (km.)†	Period (min.)	Inclination to Equator (degrees)
Intercosmos 4/U.S.S.R./B I/ 1970-084A	10/14/70 1/17/71	350 (770)	Octahedron with 8 solar panels	1.4 m.	1.5 m.	Investigations of the ionosphere with instruments supplied by several Soviet bloc nations	263 (163)	668 (415)	93.6	48.5
Meteor 6/U.S.S.R./A I/1970-085A	10/15/70	‡	Cylinder	1.5 m.	4.8 m.	Weather satellite	626 (389)	644 (400)	97.3	81.2
Cosmos 373/U.S.S.R./‡/ 1970-087A	10/20/70	‡	‡	~2 m.	~4 m.	Inspector-killer satellite	422 (262)	588 (365)	94.7	92.9
Cosmos 374/U.S.S.R./‡/ 1970-089A	10/23/70 10/23/70	‡	‡	~2 m.	~4 m.	Target satellite destroyed by Cosmos 373	514 (319)	2,131 (1,323)	112.0	62.9
Cosmos 375/U.S.S.R./‡/ 1970-091A	10/30/70 10/30/70	‡	‡	~2 m.	~4 m.	Target satellite destroyed by Cosmos 373	517 (321)	2,104 (1,307)	111.8	62.7
OFO A/U.S./Scout/ 1970-094A	11/9/70 5/9/71	133 (293)	Octahedron with 4 booms	0.8 m.	1.2 m.	Carried two live frogs to study effects of weightlessness on the vestibular apparatus of the inner ear	304 (189)	518 (322)	96.2	37.4
Molniya 1/U.S.S.R./A IIe/ 1970-101A	11/27/70	1,100 (2,420)	Cylinder with conical ends	1.6 m.	3.4 m.	Communications satellite, 16th in a series	843 (524)	39,502 (24,543)	717.5	65.4
NOAA 1/U.S./Scout/ 1970-106	12/11/70	312 (687)	Rectangular box with three panels	1.2 m.	1 m.	Improved Tiros weather satellite	1,425 (885)	1,476 (917)	114.8	101.9
Explorer 42/U.S./Scout/ 1970-107A	12/12/70	143 (315)	Cylinder	0.7 m.	0.6 m.	Small astronomy satellite for measurement of high-energy X rays	526 (327)	565 (351)	95.6	3.0
Peole/France/Diamant B/ 1970-109A	12/12/70	70 (154)	Octahedron with cone and 8 panels	0.7 m.	0.6 m.	Experimental weather satellite	505 (314)	731 (454)	97.1	15.0
Molniya 1/U.S.S.R./A IIe/ 1970-114A	12/25/70	1,100 (2,420)	Cylinder with conical ends	1.6 m.	3.4 m.	Communications satellite, 17th in a series	599 (372)	39,755 (24,700)	717.7	65.0
Meteor 7/U.S.S.R./A I/ 1971-03A	1/20/71	‡	Cylinder	1.5 m.	4.8 m.	Weather satellite	627 (390)	656 (408)	97.5	81.2
Intelsat 4(F 2)/U.S./Atlas Centaur/1971-06A	1/26/71	707 (1,555)	Cylinder	2.4 m.	2.8 m.	Communications satellite	35,774 (22,226)	35,786 (22,234)	1,435.8	0.4
Apollo 14/U.S./Saturn V/ 1971-008A	1/31/71 2/9/71	44,200 (97,240)	Cylinder with conical end	3 m.	9 m.	Third successful lunar landing mission in Apollo program	Landed on moon February 5			
NATO 2/NATO/Thor Delta/ 1971-09A	2/3/71	129 (284)	Cylinder	1.4 m.	0.8 m.	Military communications satellite	34,429 (21,390)	35,860 (22,280)	1,403.4	2.8
Tansei/Japan/Mu IVS/ 1971-011A	2/16/71	81.9 (180)	Cylinder	0.7 m.	0.8 m.	Test satellite for future scientific satellite	983 (611)	1,103 (685.2)	106.0	29.6
China 2/China/‡/ 1971-018A	3/3/71	221 (486)	‡	1 m.	‡	Engineering and test satellite	262 (163)	1,770 (1,100)	105.4	69.9
Explorer 43/U.S./Scout/ 1971-019A	3/13/71	288 (634)	Cylinder	1.4 m.	1.8 m.	Interplanetary monitoring platform	5,233 (3,251)	200,000 (124,260)	5,968.6	33.8
Tournesol/France/Diamant B 1971-030A	4/15/71	96 (211)	Octahedron	0.9 m.	1 m.	Measure cosmic radiation for period of six months	457 (284)	692 (430)	96.1	46.3
Meteor 8/U.S.S.R./A I/ 1971-031A	4/17/71	‡	Cylinder	1.5 m.	4.8 m.	Weather satellite	609 (378)	633 (393)	97.0	81.2
Salyut/U.S.S.R./Proton/ 1971-032A	4/19/71	19,000 (41,800)	Cylinder in 3 sections	4 m.	10 m.	First manned space station in orbit around earth	280 (174)	309 (192)	90.4	51.5
Soyuz 10/U.S.S.R./A II/ 1971-034A	4/23/71 4/24/71	6,600 (14,520)	Cylinder with spherical end	3.1 m.	10.7 m.	Manned spacecraft which docked with Salyut 1	208 (129)	246 (153)	88.9	51.6
San Marco/Italy/Scout/ 1971-036A	4/24/71	172 (378)	Sphere	0.7 m.	‡	Scientific satellite to measure density of upper atmosphere	210 (130)	560 (348)	92.3	3.2
Mars 2/U.S.S.R./Proton/ 1971-045A	5/19/71	4,650 (10,230)	‡	‡	‡	Unmanned scientific probe to Mars	Entered orbit about the sun after passing Mars			
Mars 3/U.S.S.R./Proton/ 1971-049A	5/28/71	4,650 (10,230)	‡	‡	‡	Unmanned scientific probe to Mars	Entered orbit about the sun after passing Mars			
Mariner 9/U.S./Atlas Centaur 1971-051A	5/30/71	1,000 (2,200)	Octahedron with 4 solar panels	0.9 m.	1.4 m.	Unmanned scientific probe to Mars	Entered orbit about Mars on November 12			
Soyuz 11/U.S./A II/ 1971-053A	6/6/71 6/29/71	6,600 (14,520)	Cylinder with spherical end	3.1 m.	10.7 m.	Ferried first crew to Salyut space station	185 (115)	217 (135)	88.3	51.6
Explorer 44/U.S./Scout/ 1971-058A	7/8/71	115 (253)	12-sided box	0.8 m.	0.7 m.	Monitor solar electromagnetic radiation	433 (269)	632 (393)	95.2	51.0
Meteor 9/U.S.S.R./A I/ 1971-059A	7/16/71	‡	Cylinder	1.5 m.	4.8 m.	Weather satellite	614 (381)	642 (399)	97.2	81.2
Apollo 15/U.S./Saturn V/ 1971-063A	7/26/71 8/7/71	33,803 (74,367)	Cylinder with conical end	3 m.	9 m.	Fourth successful lunar landing mission in the Apollo program	Landed on the moon July 30			
Molniya 1/U.S.S.R./A IIe/ 1971-064A	7/28/71	1,100 (2,420)	Cylinder with conical ends	1.6 m.	3.4 m.	Communications satellite, 18th in a series	478 (297)	39,863 (24,767)	714.4	65.4
EOLE 1/France/Scout/ 1971-071A	8/17/71	84 (185)	Octahedron with 8 solar panels	0.7 m.	0.6 m.	Meteorological satellite to control weather balloons	677 (421)	904 (562)	100.6	50.1
Luna 18/U.S.S.R./‡/ 1971-073A	9/2/71 9/11/71	‡	‡	‡	‡	Unmanned lunar probe that crashed into moon	‡	‡	‡	‡
Luna 19/U.S.S.R./‡/ 1971-082A	9/28/71 10/3/71	‡	‡	‡	‡	Unmanned lunar probe	Entered lunar orbit October 3			
OSO 7/U.S./Thor Delta/ 1971-003A	9/29/71	636 (1,400)	Decahedron with solar panel	1.4 m.	2.4 m.	Orbiting solar observatory Number 7	329 (204)	575 (357)	93.6	33.1
TETR 3/U.S./Thor Delta/ 1971-083B	9/29/71	21 (46)	Octahedron	0.3 m.	0.3 m.	Test satellite for Apollo tracking stations launched piggyback with OSO 7	391 (243)	571 (345)	94.3	33.0

*All dates are in universal time (UT).
†English units in parentheses: weight in pounds, apogee and perigee in statute miles.
‡Not available.

(M. R. S.)

Unmanned Satellites. In late 1970 and 1971 there was a general increase in activity concerning military satellites. The Soviet Union clearly demonstrated that it had an advanced reconnaissance satellite capable of matching U.S. counterparts in longevity if not in quality and quantity of intelligence sensed and transmitted. During the first six months of 1971, all the recoverable Soviet reconnaissance satellites remained in orbit for 12–14 days. As a result, the U.S.S.R. realized an economy in such launchings: it was able to reduce their number by 15% during the year.

The U.S. Air Force began studies with the aerospace industry to develop a maneuverable inspection satellite, a weapons system in which the Soviet Union had a clear lead. The studies were to determine the feasibility of developing a satellite capable of making orbital plane changes and rendezvousing with an enemy satellite to determine whether it was armed with a nuclear warhead.

As early as 1968, the U.S.S.R. proved with Cosmos 248, 249, and 252 that it had under development a satellite with rendezvous and inspection capabilities. In October 1970, the Soviet Union again demonstrated that it had such a weapons system. On October 23, Cosmos 374 was launched from Plesetsk into an orbit with a perigee of 312.6 mi. and an apogee of 1,284 mi. Within four hours, it was maneuvered into close proximity to Cosmos 373, which had been launched three days earlier. Suddenly, Cosmos 374 appeared as a number of fragments on radar tracking screens monitoring the event. This occurred as both satellites were almost directly over Leningrad. On October 30, Cosmos 375 was launched into an orbit closely resembling that of Cosmos 374. In less than four hours after launch it also passed near Cosmos 373, over Leningrad, and just as suddenly fragmented, too.

On Nov. 6, 1970, the U.S. Air Force launched a pair of Project 647 early warning satellites from the Eastern Test Range. They went into an elliptical orbit with a perigee of 16,200 mi. and an apogee of 22,400 mi. The 2,400-lb. satellites were instrumented to detect the launching of large missiles from the Soviet Union and China by means of infrared emissions from their exhausts. An additional pair was launched on May 5 from the Western Test Range and went into orbit over the Indian Ocean. The complete system was to consist of six satellites in orbit: two over the western end of the Indian Ocean, two in a spot over Singapore, and one each at a point over mid-Atlantic and mid-Pacific.

The Air Force also launched a "mystery" satellite on March 20 with a Titan IIIB-Agena D, indicating a very heavy payload. It was officially said to be "an advanced experimental communications satellite." One of the possible explanations for the satellite is that it might receive data from other military satellites and store it on tape for relay to ground stations when they come in view.

The year was an active one for nonmilitary satellites as well. Meteor 7, a weather satellite, was launched from Plesetsk by the U.S.S.R. on January 20; and five days later Intelsat 4 (F 2) was orbited from the U.S. The new communications satellite was equipped with a special antenna that provided a capacity of 3,000 to 9,000 simultaneous telephone circuits. By comparison, the fifth transatlantic cable, placed in service in 1970, could handle only 750 circuits.

Japan launched its second satellite on February 16. Named Tansei ("Sky Blue"), it was boosted into orbit from the Uchinoura Space Center by a four-stage Mu IVS launch vehicle. It weighed 139 lb. and was a test device for a future scientific satellite.

On March 3, China launched its second satellite. Weighing 486 lb., it was 106 lb. heavier than the first satellite, launched on April 24, 1970. Unlike the first, however, the second did not broadcast "The East Is Red." It appeared to be a purely scientific satellite.

Canada's Isis 2 was launched from Cape Kennedy on March 31. The scientific satellite was a joint venture with the U.S. Of its 12 experiments, 8 were Canadian and 4 were American. Isis 2 featured two antennas, each 240 ft. in length, and two others, each 62 ft. long. It was the last satellite in the series sponsored by the two nations.

Early Bird, the apparently immortal communications satellite, was activated briefly on April 6, its sixth birthday in orbit. It transmitted from Hawaii to the East Coast of the U.S. the first message ever sent by satellite.

France launched its seventh satellite with a Diamant B on April 15 from its new space centre at Kourou in French Guiana. Named Tournesol ("Sunflower"), the 211-lb. satellite carried five scientific experiments for studying hydrogen distribution in solar rays and for studying the earth's atmosphere by analyzing the Lyman-alpha spectral lines.

Italy's third satellite, San Marco 3, was orbited by a Scout on April 24 from a Texas Tower launching site off Kenya. The 360-lb. scientific satellite was designed to study the upper atmosphere by measuring its drag on the satellite.

On September 29, NASA launched its Orbiting Solar Observatory. However, the second stage of the launch vehicle malfunctioned slightly, and the satellite did not achieve the circular orbit desired. Instead, it was placed into a slightly elliptical orbit, where NASA scientists believed that it could still perform its mission of studying and photographing the sun's corona by producing artificial eclipses mechanically. Riding piggyback into orbit with OSO 7 was a TETR 3, a smaller satellite that simulates radio signals from Apollo spacecraft. It was used to check out ground tracking stations.

Interplanetary Probes. As 1970 drew to a close, several significant events took place in the field of interplanetary probes. On October 27, the Soviet Union returned to the earth Zond 8, which had been launched on October 20 to circle the moon. Thus closed a program that had begun with Zond 1 in September 1968. It was largely a biological program to study the effects of the space environment on a variety of life forms, including turtles, algae, wheat, barley, and other plants. However, the program also gave the Soviets a chance to check out a spacecraft that could be used for manned lunar missions in the future.

Lunokhod 1, the Soviet Union's unmanned lunar rover, continued to amaze scientists and engineers with its technological longevity. For months the vehicle traveled back and forth within its landing area making tests of the lunar soil and measuring radiation. Laser beams fired from the Crimean Astrophysical Observatory near Yalta and the Pic du Midi observatory in the Pyrenees tracked the vehicle.

On Dec. 13, 1970, a gigantic flare occurred on the sun. The radiometer on board the Lunokhod detected and measured it at the same time as did the Soviet

James C. Fletcher, formerly president of the University of Utah, was appointed to succeed Thomas O. Paine as administrator of the National Aeronautics and Space Administration.

COURTESY, NASA

Above, the lunar module is photographed against a brilliant sun while Apollo 14 astronauts Alan B. Shepard and Edgar D. Mitchell explore the moon. Right, astronaut David R. Scott performs a task during the first Apollo 15 lunar surface extravehicular activity.

The modular equipment transporter and an Apollo 35-mm. stereo camera near a shadow of the erectable S-band antenna are viewed from the lunar module following the second Apollo 14 extravehicular activity.

probe Venera 7, some 180 million mi. away. The event was also detected and measured by the Soviet-East European scientific satellite Intercosmos 4. Thus, for the first time such a cosmic occurrence was measured simultaneously from several points in space.

During the lunar day (equal to about 14 earth days) the Lunokhod 1 roamed about performing its experiments, which included climbing slopes as steep as 20°. At night, it was parked and its solar-cell lid folded down to wait out the two-week period of darkness and temperatures of −245° F. Incredibly, as the astronauts of Apollo 15 were making their last excursion aboard their lunar rover on Hadley plain, the solar-cell lid of Lunokhod 1 opened, and the rover prepared to undertake a series of measurements on its tenth lunar day. However, its performance was degraded, and it could no longer move about; but it had amazed the world by operating for more than ten months after having been designed to last but three.

On Dec. 15, 1970, Venera 7 made its rendezvous with Venus, after having been launched on August 17 from Tyuratam. It ejected a landing pod as had the earlier Veneras 4, 5, and 6. However, this pod had been built to withstand pressures as great as 2,645 psi and temperatures as high as 986° F. The trip to the surface took 36 minutes and 32 seconds. Once there, the pod's instrumentation telemetered data to the earth for 23 minutes. It reported a stable temperature of 887° F and a pressure of 1,136 psi.

May 1971 saw a veritable volley of probes fired toward Mars by the U.S. and U.S.S.R. Both countries experienced failures in the effort. The opening round was an attempted launch of Mariner 8 by an Atlas Centaur from Cape Kennedy on May 8. However, a failure in the Centaur stage of the vehicle caused it to plunge into the Atlantic Ocean some 450 mi. north of Puerto Rico. This failure caused a delay of several weeks in launching the second Mariner. Two days later, on May 10, the U.S.S.R. also had an aborted Mars mission when a probe failed to leave its parking orbit around the earth.

More successful were the Soviet Union's Mars 2 and Mars 3, launched on May 19 and May 28, respectively, from Tyuratam using Proton boosters. Both craft were instrumented to measure solar wind and cosmic radiation between the earth and Mars. Three of these instruments were provided by French scientists in a cooperative space venture. The Soviet Union announced on November 30 that Mars 2 had gone into a highly elliptical orbit around Mars and also had ejected a capsule that became the first man-made object to land on the Martian surface. Mars 3, which went into Martian orbit shortly thereafter, ejected a capsule that soft landed on the planet's surface and emitted radio and television signals.

Mariner 9 was successfully launched from Cape Kennedy on May 30. The 2,200-lb. probe was designed to enter an orbit about Mars and perform television mapping of its surface. Following the unsuccessful Mariner 8 mission, Mariner 9 was reprogrammed to accomplish some of the tasks that had been assigned to its predecessor.

A midcourse correction was made on June 4 to ensure that the probe would approach Mars and hopefully enter an orbit with a perigee of 750 mi. and an apogee of 10,700 mi. at an angle of 65° to the Martian equator. The path traced over the planet should result in the mapping of some 70% of its surface. Also, the probe was designed to pass repeatedly over areas of the surface that are known to change with time. Thus, every 17 days the probe would again be over the same feature, permitting scientists to study the surface variations. Mariner 9 reached Mars on November 12 and went into an elliptical orbit that ranged from 868 to 11,135 mi. above the planet's surface. The spacecraft took pictures that showed a huge dust storm on Mars and also photographed the planet's two tiny moons.

The Soviet Union returned to the moon with its Luna 18 probe, which was launched from Tyuratam on September 2. It entered a lunar orbit on September 7 at an altitude of about 63 mi. On September 11, after making 54 lunar orbits, the probe failed in an attempted soft landing and crashed into the Sea of Fertility. Luna 19 was launched from Tyuratam on September 28, apparently headed for another orbital mission of the moon with no landing expected. It went into lunar orbit on October 3.

Space-Shuttle Vehicles. The U.S. space-shuttle picture moved from confusion to near chaos as 1971 progressed. In March requests for proposals for the main engine for the shuttle were issued to three U.S. rocket engine companies. In the same month, in Phoenix, Ariz., the American Institute of Aeronautics and Astronautics Space Shuttle Development, Testing, and Operations Conference met jointly with NASA's Space Shuttle Technology Conference. NASA's plans for the shuttle were announced as: beginning of unmanned testing in 1976, manned tests in 1977, and an operational vehicle in 1979. The U.S. Air Force stated that it was basing all its future space operations on the shuttle and would cease to develop expendable rockets beyond the Titan III. However, it did not announce that it was not going to fund any of the development work on the shuttle.

NASA and the Air Force announced their agreement on the configuration and characteristics of the shuttle. In general, there would be an orbital vehicle and a booster vehicle, both equipped with the same rocket engine and as many other common subsystems as possible. Each would have a lifetime of ten years and be capable of 100 missions. On June 10, NASA announced that overall program management for the shuttle would be invested with the Manned Spacecraft Center, which would also manage development of the orbital vehicle. The booster vehicle and main engines would be the responsibility of the George C. Marshall Space Flight Center, Huntsville, Ala. The Kennedy Space Center, Fla., would be responsible for the design of launch and recovery facilities.

In July, the main shuttle engine contract was awarded to the Rocketdyne Division of the North American Rockwell Corp. This award was immediately protested by Pratt & Whitney Inc., an unsuccessful bidder, and a reconsideration ensued.

In August several aerospace contractors further complicated the shuttle picture by suggesting that an expendable launch vehicle should be considered as an interim measure while the development of the orbiter was receiving full attention. NASA immediately began investigating the possibility and was still doing so as the year ended, with consideration being

The Apollo 15 command and service modules orbit the moon with astronaut Alfred M. Worden aboard. The scientific instrument module bay, containing eight orbital science experiments, is clearly exposed on the right side of the service module.

COURTESY, NASA

given to modified boosters such as the Titan III and the S IC stage of the Saturn V.   (M. R. S.)

See also Astronomy; Defense; Industrial Review; Meteorology; Telecommunications; Television and Radio.

Encyclopædia Britannica Films. *Controversy over the Moon* (1971); *Man Looks at the Moon* (1971).

Astronomy

Until very recently, observational astronomy was ground-based and, therefore, restricted to the few "windows" in the earth's atmosphere in which electromagnetic radiation is not strongly absorbed. During the 1960s efforts were made, largely with balloons and sounding rockets, to extend the spectral range over which astronomical observations could be made. The result was the birth of X-ray, ultraviolet, and far infrared astronomy, each producing important and often completely unexpected results. The events of 1971—in particular the overwhelming success of the Explorer 42 X-ray satellite, the continued operation of the Orbiting Astronomical Observatory (OAO 2), and the remarkably successful Apollo 15 mission (*see* Astronautics)—demonstrated that space astronomy has come of age.

X-Ray Astronomy. Explorer 42, dubbed Uhuru (Swahili for "freedom"), the first of a series of Small Astronomy Satellites sponsored by the U.S. National Aeronautics and Space Administration (NASA), was launched by the Aerospace Research Centre of Italy from the San Marco platform off the coast of Kenya on Dec. 12, 1970. Designed by a group at American Science and Engineering, Inc., under the leadership of R. Giacconi, the satellite was intended both to survey the sky for cosmic X-ray sources in the range of 2–20 Kev (thousand electron volts) and to analyze with higher spatial and time resolution those sources suspected to be variable or to have interesting structures. The instrument was more successful than perhaps even

Maffei 1 and Maffei 2, discovered by Italian astronomer Paolo Maffei in 1968, were identified as galaxies in 1971 from observations made at the Mount Wilson and Palomar Observatories. Neighbours to the Milky Way, the new galaxies were estimated to be three million light years from earth.

Eclipses, 1971

Jan. 16	Sun, annular (begins 3:46 A.M.*), visible extreme Southern Hemisphere — Antarctica, Argentina, S. Indian O.
Jan. 30	Moon, total (begins 5:36 A.M.*), visible N.E. Asia, E. Australasia, Arctic, N. & S. America
July 10	Sun, total (begins 2:32 P.M.*), visible W. Pacific O., N. Alaska, N. & E. Canada, N. Atlantic O.
July 26	Moon, partial (umbral begins 1:56 A.M.*), visible New Zealand, Antarctica, E. Pacific O., N. & S. America, Atlantic O., N.W. Africa

Equinoxes and Solstices, 1972

March 20	Vernal equinox (7:22 A.M.*)
June 21	Summer solstice (2:06 A.M.*)
Sept. 22	Autumnal equinox (5:33 P.M.*)
Dec. 21	Winter solstice (1:13 P.M.*)

Earth Perihelion and Aphelion, 1972

Jan. 3	Perihelion, 91.4 million mi. from the sun
July 5	Aphelion, 94,510,000 mi. from the sun

*Eastern Standard Time.

Source: *American Ephemeris and Nautical Almanac, 1972.*

its designers could have hoped. As expected, a large number of new sources were discovered, and the locations of others were determined with much greater accuracy. More surprising, however, was the discovery of rapid periodic intensity variations in the galactic sources Cygnus X-1 and Centaurus X-3.

In the case of Centaurus X-3 the pulsations were of large amplitude and had a period of roughly 5 sec. The mean intensity of Centaurus X-3 varied strongly, on one occasion increasing by a factor of 10 in about an hour. In Cygnus X-1 the situation was more complicated. After the original discovery by American Science and Engineering, other groups also found evidence for periodic variations in this source but they were unable to agree on the period. It seemed probable, therefore, that the period, which appears to be in the range 1–5 sec., was changing on a time scale of several minutes.

The origin of the X-ray pulsations in Cygnus X-1 and Centaurus X-3 remained a mystery, although the existence of pulsed X-ray emission from the Crab pulsar suggested that a similar mechanism may be responsible. Unfortunately, Cygnus X-1 and Centaurus X-3 had very little else in common with the Crab pulsar and differed from it strongly in the following respects: the X-ray sources were not associated with supernova remnants; they emitted comparatively little energy at radio frequencies; and, if detectable, this radio emission was not strongly pulsed. In addition, the X-ray spectrum of Centaurus X-3 indicated that the pulsations had a thermal rather than a synchrotron origin. (Synchrotron radiation is generated by electrons moving at speeds near that of light spiraling about the lines of force of a magnetic field.) From the observed periods, it may safely be deduced that the pulsating X-ray sources are associated with white dwarfs or neutron stars, but beyond this very little is understood about these objects.

The Uhuru satellite also produced exciting information on extragalactic objects. X-ray emission was detected from the Seyfert galaxies NGC 1275 (also detected by the group at the Naval Research Laboratory, Washington, D.C.) and NGC 4151, both of which, incidentally, showed evidence of mass outflow. No emission was, however, detected from NGC 1068, which is visually the brightest Seyfert galaxy. The quasar 3C 273 was also detected by Uhuru, confirming an earlier identification by a group at the University of California, Berkeley. The similarity between the quasars and the nuclei of Seyfert gal-

axies, apparent in both their radio and optical emissions, thus may extend to the X-ray region as well.

The nearest galaxies to our own are the Magellanic Clouds, and they were the subject of much interest to X-ray astronomers during 1971. X-ray emission from these irregular galaxies was first reported by investigators at the Lawrence Radiation Laboratory, Berkeley, Calif., and was confirmed by Uhuru. The satellite data indicated the presence of a single strong variable source in the Small Magellanic Cloud. In the Large Cloud three strong sources were detected; two of them were probably single objects, while the third was rather diffuse and probably consisted of many weaker sources. These results were particularly important because there was no ambiguity in the distance and, hence, in the intrinsic strength of the sources. In particular, the Small Cloud variable source confirmed the existence of single, compact sources emitting at least 10^{38} ergs/sec. in the 2–7 Kev band, a result that should help resolve the uncertainty in the distance to many sources in our own galaxy.

Observations of the Magellanic Clouds by a group of scientists at the University of Wisconsin also furnished new insights into the origin of the excess background radiation at lower X-ray energies. It had been known for some time that the flux of background radiation at $\sim$0.25 Kev was considerably larger than would be expected by extrapolation from higher energies. By observing in the galactic plane, where low-energy X-rays can propagate without attenuation for up to 200 parsecs (1 parsec = 19.2 trillion mi.), the Wisconsin group was able to demonstrate that at least some of the 0.25 Kev background was coming from comparatively nearby. Because the 0.25 Kev flux increases substantially toward the galactic pole, it had been surmised that most of this excess is extragalactic in origin as is the case at the higher energies. Indeed, it had even been proposed as evidence for the existence of a hot intergalactic gas. Recent observations in the direction of the Small Magellanic Cloud, however, failed to show any measurable absorption ($\lesssim 25\%$) in the 0.25 Kev background. This was contrary to the findings that were expected if the radiation had originated beyond the clouds. It is, therefore, almost certain that the excess radiation arises in our own galaxy in material that is not highly concentrated in the galactic plane.

A major difficulty in X-ray astronomy has been to determine accurate positions of sources in order to facilitate optical identification. This problem is particularly acute for the galactic sources, which are confined to the crowded fields along the Milky Way. Recently, however, R. Hjellming and C. Wade at the National Radio Astronomy Observatory, Green Bank, W.Va., were able to identify variable radio sources with the X-ray sources Scorpius X-1, Cygnus X-1, and GX 17 + 2. Since the radio positions can be determined to a very high accuracy, this should provide a powerful method of identifying X-ray sources. The position of Cygnus X-1, which was also determined independently by L. Braes and G. Miley using the new Westerbork interferometer in the Netherlands, led to a possible identification of the source with a blue supergiant (or its invisible companion).

Orbiting Astronomical Observatory. Astronomers at the University of Wisconsin and the Smithsonian Astrophysical Observatory were responsible for the experiments aboard the first successful Orbiting Astronomical Observatory (OAO 2), which was launched into earth orbit in the late 1960s. The results were slowly being made known to the astronomical community but, unfortunately, little detail was yet available. The purpose of the OAO 2 was to investigate the wavelength region between the point where the earth's atmosphere absorbs radiation (about 3000 Å) and the Lyman limit (912 Å), beyond which hydrogen absorption precludes further observation until the soft X-ray region. This region is of special interest because hot stars, about which we are best able to make theoretical predictions, emit most of their energy in this range.

Among the most important achievements of the OAO 2 was the measurement for the first time of the ultraviolet flux from an active nova (Nova Serpentis 1970). These stars may reach 10^4 times their normal luminosity in a single day as a result of explosive events that cause ejection of their surface layers. The ultraviolet flux in Nova Serpentis continued to rise for more than a month after the visual emission had begun its characteristic decay. Continuous observations of this kind were expected to be of immense value in understanding the processes leading to nova outbursts. Even in the optical range there are advantages to satellite observations when continuous surveillance is required, since there are no interruptions for daytime or weather.

The OAO 2 also provided new material on interstellar extinction at short wavelengths, which should help determine the properties of the particles causing this attenuation. Perhaps most interesting, however, was the discovery of excess emission at wavelengths shorter than 2000 Å in the centres of globular clusters and in galaxies. This is almost certainly caused by very hot stars whose presence, at least in the globular clusters, was quite unexpected. In elliptical galaxies the ultraviolet flux rises too steeply to be attributable to stars alone but may result from subsequent distortion of the spectrum by dust absorption. If, as is likely, the hot stars are also young, these observations imply the existence of substantial quantities of gas in the centres of globular clusters and elliptical galaxies, contrary to previous supposition. Astronomers eagerly awaited further details of the OAO 2 observations.

Infrared Astronomy. The wavelength region between 1 mm. (1,000 μ) and 20 μ, commonly referred to as the far infrared, is inaccessible to ground-based telescopes. By using a balloon-borne 12-in. telescope, however, W. Hoffman, C. Frederick, and R. Emery at the Goddard Institute for Space Studies, New York City, were able to obtain a detailed map of the galactic centre region at 100 μ. They confirmed the existence of a diffuse source extending approximately 3.6° along the galactic plane and 2° perpendicular to it. They also found structure in the form of four intensity peaks, two of which are associated with the radio sources Sagittarius A and Sagittarius B2 (see *Interstellar Molecules*, below). The total emission at 100 μ from this region corresponds to 3.5×10^8 solar luminosities, which represents a significant proportion of the total output of our galaxy.

Observations between 50 μ and 300 μ were also made by F. Low (University of Arizona) and D. Harper and H. Aumann (Rice University) with a 12-in. telescope mounted in a jet aircraft. They were able to verify their earlier suggestion that a wide variety of celestial objects ranging from H II regions (ionized gas clouds) in our own galaxy to nuclei of Seyfert galaxies emit most of their radiation in the neighbourhood of 100 μ, as is the case for the centre of our own galaxy. These results, which came as a complete surprise to the astronomical community, clearly demonstrated the necessity of making observations from above the earth's atmosphere.

Interstellar Molecules. At wavelengths longer than 2 mm. it once again becomes possible to observe with ground-based equipment. The part of this "radio window" between 2 mm. and 20 cm. was particularly interesting to astronomers since a number of the simple molecules have transitions (abrupt changes in energy levels) at these wavelengths. During recent months transitions associated with at least 13 new molecules were detected. These range from simple diatomic molecules like carbon monoxide (CO) and silicon monoxide (SiO) to fairly complex structures such as methyl cyanide (CH_3CN) and formamide ($HCONH_2$). These discoveries were, in the main, made with the 140-ft. dish at Green Bank, W.Va., and the 36-ft. dish at Kitt Peak, Ariz., both of which were operated by the National Radio Astronomy Observatory. The molecules were usually found in dense clouds either near the galactic centre (Sagittarius A, Sagittarius B2), in association with OH (hydroxyl) sources (W 51) or infrared sources (IRC + 10216), or in regions of known star formation (Orion A).

Studies of the composition of the interstellar medium, at least in dense clouds, were expected to become possible for the first time. In particular, the large relative wavelength shifts (for microwave transitions) due to differences in molecular weight would allow accurate measurement of interstellar isotope abundances. In addition, studies of the excitation of the observed microwave transitions yield estimates of the densities in the molecular clouds which, in some cases, are as high as 10^6 particles per cc. The results also implied that most of the hydrogen in the dark clouds must be in molecular form, which, unfortunately, cannot be observed directly in the microwave region. The existence of large amounts of molecular hydrogen in regions of high visual extinction was, however, demonstrated by G. Carruthers at the Naval Research Laboratory during observations in the ultraviolet part of the spectrum with rocket-borne detectors. Thus, even where direct evidence was lacking, it appeared that the molecular clouds must be regions of rapid star formation. The presence of so many molecules in nebulae surrounding these young stars is clearly of major importance in connection with theories of the formation of the solar system and of the origin of life.

Radio studies of interstellar material in external galaxies were until 1971 confined to the 21-cm. neutral hydrogen line. However, L. Weliachew (Observatoire de Meudon, France), working at the Owens Valley Radio Observatory in California, was able to detect absorption lines of the hydroxyl radical (OH) in the galaxies NGC 253 and M 82. His observations clearly demonstrated the possibility of extending radio-line astronomy and, perhaps, interstellar abundance analysis well beyond the confines of our own galactic system.

Galaxies and Quasars. In 1968 the Italian astronomer P. Maffei noted the existence of two infrared objects lying near the plane of the galaxy in the direction of IC 1805. More recently, a group of astronomers at the University of California, Berkeley, and the California Institute of Technology suggested that the brighter object, known as Maffei 1, is a giant elliptical galaxy at a distance of about 1 megaparsec. On this interpretation Maffei 1 is unlikely to be gravitationally bound to the Local Group (those galaxies, including the Andromeda Nebula, the Magellanic Clouds, and our own, which form a loose clustering approximately one megaparsec in diameter) although it would appear to be within its confines. The object is, however, heavily reddened by dust in our galaxy so that an accurate determination of its luminosity, mass, or distance is not possible at present. Similar remarks hold true for Maffei 2 about which less had been discovered but which is probably a nearby spiral galaxy. A number of other highly reddened distended objects were subsequently discovered in the galactic plane, but some of these, at least, are probably globular clusters.

Dwarf emission-line galaxies were the subject of a study by P. Chamaraux, J. Heidmann, and R. Lauqué (Observatoire de Meudon, France) and W. Sargent and L. Searle (Hale Observatories). From 21-cm. hydrogen-line measurements and an analysis of their optical spectra, these objects appeared to be dense intergalactic clouds in which the formation of massive stars is proceeding rapidly while the formation of low-mass stars is suppressed. A number of interpretations were possible. Most conservatively, one could simply infer that the stellar birthrate function varies substantially among the galaxies. The result could, however, be an indication that galaxies themselves are still forming, a point of considerable potential importance in determining the way in which the universe is evolving.

Quasars continued to be the subject of intense study. Observations by J. Gunn (Hale Observatories) of PKS 2251 + 11 showed it to have approximately the same red shift ($z = 0.32$) as the brightest galaxy of a cluster within which it appears when projected on the celestial sphere. This finding was widely acclaimed as proof that the quasar is at the same distance as the cluster and, hence, that the quasar red shifts do indeed indicate a true cosmological distance. The evidence was indeed impressive, but for the following reasons fell short of proving the cosmological hypothesis. The essence of the method was to find an apparent physical connection between quasars and galaxies (in this case, superposition on the sky) and to demonstrate that their red shifts are equal. Since it is widely believed that galaxy red shifts indicate distance, the same should follow for the particular quasar in question. This method was then applied to other quasars, besides PKS 2251 + 11, that were also apparently associated with clusters. In each case there was a considerable discrepancy between the red shifts of the quasar and the cluster, a result usually attributed to chance projection and therefore discarded.

In an effort to avoid this projection difficulty H. Arp (Hale Observatories) looked for evidence of a real physical connection between the quasar and galaxy before determining the red shift. A particularly good example is Markarian 205, a quasar connected by a luminous jet to the galaxy NGC 4319. The red shifts for the two are very different and, on the cosmological interpretation, suggested that Markarian 205 is more than ten times the distance of NGC 4319. Arp, however, provided further evidence which suggested that even certain galaxies may have a substantial noncosmological component to their red shift. A similar conclusion could be reached from the various chains of galaxies, such as Stephan's quintet, in which one member has a highly discrepant red shift. In each case it

was possible to argue that, despite the strong circumstantial evidence of physical connection, the objects were merely the products of chance superposition. The number of such chance superpositions was, however, becoming somewhat too large for comfort and suggested that an alternative approach to the quasar distance problem be tried. (P. A. St.)

See also Astronautics.

Australia

A federal parliamentary state and a member of the Commonwealth of Nations, Australia occupies the smallest continent and, with the island state of Tasmania, is the sixth largest country in the world. Area: 2,967,909 sq.mi. (7,686,849 sq.km.). Pop. (1971 est.): 12,794,164. Cap.: Canberra (pop., 1970 est., 130,250). Largest city: Sydney (metro. pop., 1970 est., 2,780,310). Language: English. Religion: (1966) Church of England 34%; Roman Catholic 26%; Methodist 10%; Presbyterian 9%. Queen, Elizabeth II; governor-general in 1971, Sir Paul Hasluck; prime ministers, John Grey Gorton and, from March 10, William McMahon.

Domestic Affairs. During 1971 almost continual crisis beset the Liberal-Country Party (LCP) coalition government of Australia. The most important event was the removal from the prime ministership, in March, of John Grey Gorton. Gorton was voted out of office by the parliamentary Liberal Party after an attack on his methods of direction by the minister of defense, Malcolm Fraser. Fraser delivered a violent attack on Gorton in the House of Representatives, saying that since being elected prime minister Gorton had seriously damaged the Liberal Party and cast aside the stability and sense of direction of earlier times. Gorton, said Fraser, had "a dangerous reluctance to consult the Cabinet" and "an unreasoned drive to get his own way," ridiculing the advice of the public service unless it supported his own view. The prime minister's "obstinacy" and "impetuous and emotional reactions" had "imposed strains on the Liberal Party, the government, and the public service." Since Fraser did not consider Gorton fit to hold the office of prime minister, he could not serve in Gorton's government, and accordingly resigned.

The Liberal Party met on March 10 and in a confidence motion on Gorton's leadership the vote stood at 33–33. In this deadlock Gorton cast his vote against himself. Subsequently a ballot was held for party leader and William McMahon (*see* BIOGRAPHY), the minister for foreign affairs, defeated Billy Mackie Snedden, minister for labour and national service. There were three candidates for the post of deputy leader of the Liberal Party—Gorton, Fraser, and David Fairbairn. Gorton won this contest and also took up the portfolio of defense vacated by Fraser.

On August 12, Gorton was relieved as minister for defense. Prime Minister McMahon demanded Gorton's resignation following an article Gorton had written in a Sunday newspaper, saying "I did it my way." McMahon maintained that Gorton had reflected on the integrity of some Cabinet members by alleging that they had leaked confidential material to the press. Gorton's purpose in writing the article was, as he put it, to refute the "libelous scribblings" against him in a book, *The Gorton Experiment,* published by political journalist Alan Reid. The Australian Labor Party (ALP) opposition was unable to force an election over either issue, since the LCP closed ranks when the votes were needed in the federal Parliament. It was generally agreed that McMahon possessed qualities that Gorton lacked, being less impulsive and less addicted to the one-man-band style.

John McEwen, leader of the Australian Country Party, the junior member in the ruling Liberal-Country coalition, retired after 37 years in Parliament. He was replaced by John Douglas Anthony, who took over the portfolio of trade and industry from McEwen.

There was considerable division within the Australian community as a result of a tour of Australia by the South African Rugby union team, the Springboks. Violent clashes took place between supporters and opponents of the tour, and hundreds were arrested in demonstrations against South African apartheid. The premier of Queensland, J. Bjelke-Petersen, declared a state of emergency during the Springboks' tour of his state. The Australian Council of Trade Unions (ACTU) tried unsuccessfully to stop the tour by withholding transportation, but the Springboks chartered aircraft to fly from state to state. In Queensland it appeared that Bjelke-Petersen had correctly judged the climate of public opinion over the Rugby tour. His LCP won two by-elections in the wake of the Springboks' tour, one of them a seat held by the ALP since the 1930s. Bjelke-Petersen described the LCP victory as a triumph for common sense, showing that the people of Queensland would not accept dictatorial tactics from union leaders. Subsequently, in September, a proposed tour by a South African cricket team was canceled by Australian cricket authorities.

Aboriginal and land rights continued to be a thorny issue. In April the aborigines at Yirrkala on the Gove Peninsula in Arnhem Land lost their test case in the Northern Territory Supreme Court. Eleven tribes had claimed legal title to the Gove Peninsula, where a Swiss-Australian aluminum company was mining. The aborigines' legal expenses had been paid by the Methodist Christian Citizenship Council in Melbourne, and the unsuccessful proceedings took over 12 months to complete. Aborigines believed that the Yirrkala mission station was endangered by blasting. They feared that their mission would close and their town be removed.

Foreign Affairs. During the period that William McMahon was minister for foreign affairs he made several important changes. The first, in November 1970, involved changing the title of his department from external affairs to foreign affairs. This was not merely a minor alteration; it reflected changing patterns in Australian foreign policy, and was accompanied by a new administrative structure. The departmental section dealing with Asia, the Pacific, and defense was upgraded, a "think tank" of experienced diplomats was organized to originate policies, and a new division was created to deal with overseas aid. The changes were part of McMahon's long-term aim that the Australian foreign office should play a more important role in Cabinet decisions. The reorganization involved an increase in the number of foreign affairs divisions from four to seven.

The chief problems facing Australian diplomats and political leaders were those involving Vietnam and the People's Republic of China. The commander of the Australian force in Vietnam, Maj. Gen. C. A. E. Fraser, released the information that the South Vietnamese, at their own request, wished some areas of Australian civil action in their country to be reduced. Major General Fraser said that it had been assumed for planning purposes that in 1971–72 the South Vietnamese would take up responsibility for health, education, and welfare. Subsequently, in August, the prime minister announced that he expected most of the 6,000 Australian troops in Vietnam to be home by Christmas, leaving only a small group of training personnel. At the same time the government intended to give South Vietnam aid worth A$25 million over a three-year period.

McMahon also announced that the number of men serving in the Australian Army was to be reduced by 4,000 and the period of national service changed from two years to 18 months. The number of men called up remained at 8,000 a year. These men would continue as national servicemen for five years, but more of this time (three and a half years instead of three) was to be spent in the reserve Citizens Military Forces. The ALP opposition argued that Australia was only withdrawing from Vietnam because the U.S. was getting out. The leader of the Democratic Labor Party (DLP) minority in the Senate criticized McMahon for reducing the strength of the Army and not providing Australian naval ships for the Indian Ocean.

WIDE WORLD

Neville Bonner became the first aborigine ever to sit in the Australian Parliament when he took his place in the Australian Senate in August 1971.

AUSTRALIA
Education. (1968) Primary, pupils 1,768,060, teachers 64,900; secondary, pupils 890,539, teachers 53,600; vocational, pupils 189,985; higher (including 14 universities), students 164,528, teaching staff (at universities only) 6,487.
Finance. Monetary unit: Australian dollar, with a par value of A$0.89 to U.S. $1 (A$2.14 = £1 sterling) and a free rate (Sept. 27, 1971) of A$0.87 to U.S. $1. Gold, SDRs, and foreign exchange, reserve bank: (June 1971) U.S. $2,345,-000,000; (June 1970) U.S. $1,480,000,000. Commonwealth budget (1970–71 est.): revenue A$7,722,000,000; expenditure A$7,087,000,000. Gross national product: (1969–70) A$29,460,-000,000; (1968–69) A$26,720,000,000. Money supply: (March 1971) A$5,415,000,000; (March 1970) A$5,337,000,000. Cost of living (1963 = 100): (Jan.–March 1971) 128; (Jan.–March 1970) 122.
Foreign Trade. (1970) Imports A$4,054,600,-000; exports A$4,259,500,000. Import sources: U.S. 25%; U.K. 21%; Japan 13%; West Germany 7%. Export destinations: Japan 26%; U.S.

13%; U.K. 11%; New Zealand 5%. Main exports: wool 15%; meat 10%; wheat 9%; iron ore 8%; nonferrous metals 7%.
Transport and Communications. Roads (1968) 903,139 km. (including 97,883 km. main roads). Motor vehicles in use (1970): passenger 3,836,000; commercial (including buses) 963,000. Railways: (government; 1970) 40,330 km.; freight traffic (1968–69) 21,463,000,000 net ton-km. Air traffic (1969): 7,404,000,000 passenger-km.; freight 250,885,000 net ton-km. Shipping (1970): merchant vessels 100 gross tons and over 344; gross tonnage 1,074,112; goods loaded (1968–69) 57,229,000 metric tons, unloaded 33.3 million metric tons. Telephones (Dec. 1969) 3,-598,692. Radio licenses (Dec. 1970) 2,678,000. Television licenses (Dec. 1970) 2,557,000.
Agriculture. Production (in 000; metric tons; 1970; 1969 in parentheses): wheat 7,511 (10,-834); barley 2,177 (1,789); oats 1,270 (1,452); sorghum 572 (299); corn 239 (188); potatoes 762 (811); sugar, raw value (1970–71) 2,524,

(1969–70) 2,214; apples 424 (422); oranges c. 305 (255); wine c. 275 (236); wool, greasy 947 (927); milk 7,640 (7,807); butter (1969) c. 224, (1968) 201; beef and veal 1,078 (1,029); mutton and lamb 760 (779). Livestock (in 000; March 1970): sheep 181,387; cattle c. 20,700; pigs 2,392; horses c. 474; chickens c. 22,900.
Industry. Fuel and power (in 000; metric tons; 1970): coal 49,481; lignite 24,203; crude oil 8,-292; natural gas (cu.m.) 1,503,000; manufactured gas (cu.m.; 1967–68) 3,466,000; electricity (kw.-hr.) 56,156,000. Production (in 000; metric tons; 1970): iron ore (65% metal content) 50,-990; bauxite 9,390; pig iron 6,149; crude steel 6,822; zinc 260; aluminum 204; copper 105; lead 180; tin 5.2; nickel concentrates (metal content; 1969) 11; sulfuric acid 1,681; cement 4,-599; cotton yarn 29; wool yarn 27; gold (troy oz.; 1969) 702; passenger cars (including assembly; units) 392; commercial vehicles (including assembly; units) 81. Dwelling units completed (1970) 143,000.

As newly elected leader of the Liberal Party, William McMahon became prime minister of Australia on March 10, 1971. McMahon replaced John Grey Gorton, who received a vote of no confidence from the Liberal Party.

AUTHENTICATED NEWS INTERNATIONAL

The export wharf at Weipa, Austr., was being doubled in size to increase its annual capacity from 7 million to 10.5 million tons by 1972.

The question of the recognition of China replaced involvement in Vietnam as the major issue of Australian foreign policy. Canadian recognition of the Peking government in October 1970 sparked the controversy. Two weeks after Canada announced its intention to recognize the regime of Mao Tse-tung, the Canadian Wheat Board sold 98 million bushels of wheat to the Chinese, the largest sale the Canadian board had made to a single country over a 12-month period. The value of the crop sale was $160 million. R. A. Patterson, the ALP spokesman on primary industry, pointed out in Parliament that if Australia wished to continue to sell its wheat to China it too would have to recognize the Peking government. John Douglas Anthony, minister for trade and industry, said he was not prepared to sacrifice political principles to economic expediency, adding that he did not believe that recognition was a significant factor in selling wheat to China.

The Australian government then received a note from the British government saying that China intended to make no further wheat purchases from Australia following a recent statement by a senior Australian Cabinet minister. Opposition leader E. Gough Whitlam announced that if the ALP won the 1972 general election it would establish diplomatic relations with China. Whitlam also headed an ALP delegation to China in July, and was received by Premier Chou En-lai in a trip that marked the first high-level diplomatic contact with the People's Republic since 1949.

Australia faced criticism in the United Nations over its administration of Papua New Guinea, the largest territory outside the continent of Africa that remained dependent. A UN mission visited the area in 1971 to see how Australia was going about drawing a fragmented society into an identifiable nation. The task, said McMahon, was extremely difficult because of the exceptionally rugged terrain, the successive waves of migration that had occurred over the centuries, and ethnic and tribal differences.

The Economy. The Australian economy was pulled in two directions in 1971 as the government tried to halt inflation caused by a decision of the Wage Arbitration Commission. On Dec. 14, 1970, the full bench of the commission granted Australian industrial workers a 6% pay raise, the largest awarded by the commission since it began operating in 1956. The increase was payable from the first pay period in the new year. The president of the Arbitration Court explained that the decision had been reached after examining the economy over the past year, as well as prospects for the ensuing one. The court concluded that the 6% increase was economically sustainable and industrially just.

The main issue the court had to decide was how to implement, in a sensible way, a combination of flat money increase and percentage increase, but no solution was found. The 6% increase represented a compromise. The president of the ACTU, Robert J. Hawke, had asked for A$9 a week extra, white-collar workers wanted a 16% rise, and employers had asked that the rise be limited to 2%. The ACTU was unsuccessful in its application for restoration of quarterly cost of living adjustments. Employers were told that if the arbitration court was not realistic in its attitude toward wage fixing, those who looked to it as the main source of wage increases would be treated inequitably and those who were strong enough would seek increases by other means. The government was faced with an additional A$720 million annually on the national wage bill and consequent inflation.

Australia found great difficulty in selling the country's wheat and wool crops. There were two alterations in the wool industry. An Australian Wool Commission was set up to purchase wool when its price fell below a reserve price. During the first week of the Wool Commission's operation it bought 5% of the 136,000 bales offered at auction. The chairman of the Wool Board, Sir William Gunn, was satisfied with the first week's result, which showed a 3½% price rise, but the Australian Wool Growers and Graziers Council was afraid the commission might not be able to sell the wool it bought. The government and trading banks provided A$56 million to the Wool Commission for 1970–71, but decided that further assistance was necessary. A one-year scheme of deficiency payments was, therefore, introduced for the 1971–72 wool clip. Deficiency payments were to give growers a return of 36 cents a pound for their wool.

The wool industry was the first to be hit by the U.S. dollar crisis. Japanese wool buyers immediately informed the Australian Wool Board that they could not buy wool during the international currency crisis as this was impossible during a situation in which buyers were uncertain of the exchange rate of the yen and the Australian dollar.

State-federal financial arrangements were improved by an agreement to transfer payroll tax to the states to aid their capacity for raising their own revenues. While the payroll tax was a useful addition to resources, the states still were unable to meet costs of the abnormally high wage increases awarded to employees. The federal government made an additional payment of A$40 million for this purpose.

The main feature of government economic policy in 1971 was the attempt to restrain demand. The

treasurer, Billy Snedden, announced in August that the $2\frac{1}{2}\%$ personal income tax levy would be increased to 5%. The rate of duty on cigarettes and tobacco rose by 50 and 25 cents a pound, respectively, and excise duties on gasoline and aviation fuel were increased by 2 cents a gallon. (A. R. G. G.)

See also Dependent States.

Austria

A republic of central Europe, Austria is bounded by West Germany, Czechoslovakia, Hungary, Yugoslavia, Italy, Switzerland, and Liechtenstein. Area: 32,374 sq.mi. (83,850 sq.km.). Pop. (1971): 7,443,809. Cap. and largest city: Vienna (pop., 1971, 1,603,400). Language: German. Religion: Roman Catholic 89%. President in 1971, Franz Jonas; chancellor, Bruno Kreisky.

AUSTRIA

Education. (1968–69) Primary, pupils 862,193, teachers 39,033; secondary, pupils 147,543, teachers 9,170; vocational, pupils 226,505, teachers 12,532; teacher training, students 3,701, teachers 499; higher (including 6 universities), students 52,527, teaching staff 6,334.

Finance. Monetary unit: schilling, with a par value (following revaluation of May 9, 1971) of 24.75 schillings to U.S. \$1 (59.40 schillings = £1 sterling) and a free rate (Sept. 27, 1971) of 24.13 schillings to U.S. \$1 (59.85 schillings = £1 sterling). Gold, SDRs, and foreign exchange, central bank: (June 1971) U.S. \$1,759,000,000; (June 1970) 1,369,000,000. Budget (1971 est.): revenue 101,574,000,000 schillings; expenditure 111,118,000,000 schillings. Gross national product: (1969) 323.3 billion schillings; (1968) 295.1 billion schillings. Money supply: (March 1971) 70.8 billion schillings; (March 1970) 66,240,000,000 schillings, Cost of living (1963 = 100): (May 1971) 132; (May 1970) 127.

Foreign Trade. (1970) Imports 92,278,000,000 schillings; exports 74,274,000,000 schillings. Import sources: EEC 56% (West Germany 41%, Italy 7%); Switzerland 7%; U.K. 7%. Export destinations: EEC 39% (West Germany 23%, Italy 10%); Switzerland 10%; U.K. 6%; Yugoslavia 5%. Main exports: machinery 20%; iron and steel 14%; textile yarns and fabrics 12%; timber 7%; paper and board 5%. Tourism (1969): visitors 7,842,000; gross receipts U.S. \$785 million.

Transport and Communications. Roads (1970) 94,831 km. (including 478 km. expressways). Motor vehicles in use (1970): passenger 1,196,584; commercial 120,857. Railways: state (1969) 5,908 km.; private (1968) 636 km.; traffic (state only; 1970) 6,-316,000,000 passenger-km., freight 9,781,000,000 net ton-km. Air traffic (1970): 452.2 million passenger-km.; freight 8,860,000 net ton-km. Telephones (Dec. 1969) 1,334,339. Radio receivers (Dec. 1969) 2,044,-000. Television receivers (Dec. 1969) 1,277,000.

Agriculture. Production (in 000; metric tons; 1970; 1969 in parentheses): wheat 810 (950); barley 913 (934); rye 363 (440); oats 271 (288); corn 612 (698); potatoes 2,704 (2,941); sugar, raw value (1970–71) c. 324, (1969–70) 349; apples 309 (327); wine 252 (227); meat 501 (510); timber (cu.m.; 1969) 12,000, (1968) 11,200. Livestock (in 000; Dec. 1969): cattle 2,418; sheep 121; pigs 3,422; horses 53; goats 69; chickens 11,543.

Industry. Fuel and power (in 000; metric tons; 1970): lignite 3,672; crude oil 2,798; natural gas (cu.m.) 1,897,000; electricity (kw-hr.) 30,024,000 (64% hydroelectric in 1969); manufactured gas (Vienna only; cu.m.) 677,000. Production (in 000; metric tons; 1970): iron ore (30% metal content) 3,996; pig iron 2,965; crude steel 4,080; magnesite (1969) 1,608; aluminum 129; copper 22; lead 8; zinc 16; cement 4,806; paper (1969) 943; nitrogenous fertilizers (N content; 1969–70) 248; cotton yarn 20; woven cotton fabric 18; wool yarn 12; rayon fibres (1969) 67.

In the Austrian presidential election held on April 25, 1971, incumbent Franz Jonas, the candidate of the Socialist Party of Austria (SPÖ), defeated Kurt Waldheim, Austrian ambassador to the UN and candidate of the conservative Austrian People's Party (ÖVP), and was thus confirmed in his post for a further six years.

Meanwhile, the Socialist minority administration under Chancellor Kreisky was forced to seek the support of one or the other of the opposition parties in Parliament in order to legislate. Out of the 165 parliamentary seats, 81 were held by the SPÖ, 78 by the ÖVP, and 6 by the Austrian Freedom Party (FPÖ). Anxious to try to achieve an overall majority, the SPÖ decided in July, with the help of the FPÖ, upon a premature dissolution of Parliament and a general election to be held on October 10.

The October elections were the first to be held under the 1971 Electoral Regulations Act, which modified the electoral system in various ways. Under the new law the number of electoral districts was reduced from 25 to 9. The difference between "cheap" and "expensive" seats was substantially lessened by the new regulations. Previously the number of parliamentary seats had been fixed at 165 and the number of votes required for a particular seat was a function of the size of the electorate. However, under the new regulations the number of parliamentary seats was to be calculated from the size of the electorate, giving a total of 183 seats to be contested.

After a very close finish, Kreisky's party gained an absolute majority of seats and could thus form a one-party SPÖ government to take office for the next four years. This was the first time since the foundation of the Republic of Austria that one political party had succeeded in winning more than 50% of the total votes cast. With an electoral turnout of over 90%, the final figures were as follows: SPÖ, 93 seats (50.04%); ÖVP, 80 seats (43.12%); and FPÖ, 10 seats (5.45%). Since the Socialists would provide the nonvoting speaker, Kreisky's new government had an overall majority of two. The Austrian Communist Party (KPÖ) increased its support from 0.98% in 1970 to 1.35%, but under regulations excluding splinter parties from Parliament it did not gain a seat.

Few changes were made in the composition of the Cabinet that had taken office in April 1970. In his preliminary statements, Kreisky stressed that the Socialists would endeavour to secure parliamentary cooperation with other parties, expressing the belief that the chance of such cooperation would be enhanced by the fact that the other parties now knew it was no longer indispensable. However, he also emphasized that the Socialists would make use of their parliamentary majority if need be.

Prior to the elections, Kreisky's minority government had sought to accomplish as much as possible of its reform program. New legislation during the year included various reforms of the Austrian criminal code; the abolition of certain privileges for civil servants; the legalization of homosexuality between consenting adults; and an improvement in the legal status of illegitimate children. Stricter penalties were introduced for cruelty to children and animals. The distribution of the contraceptive pill and the relaxation of penalties with regard to abortion provoked heated debate both in and outside Parliament. A comprehensive reform program for the educational system was introduced, and an agency was appointed to act as ombudsman in cases where all other possibilities for appeal had been exhausted. In July, after much debate, an amendment of the national defense regulations was passed, cutting national service from nine to six months with 60 days of refresher courses.

In November 1970 the Austrian foreign minister had made a statement on Austria's position to the EEC Council of Ministers, supporting an agreement in accordance with article 24 of GATT and suggesting an interim trade agreement. Further discussions took place in January and March of 1971. Austria and China agreed on mutual recognition and the exchange of ambassadors, and on September 15 the Chinese ambassador presented his credentials.

The Austrian economy was at the height of boom. In 1970 the gross national product rose by over 7%, the highest growth rate of any Western industrialized country. Full employment reigned, and there were few strikes. However, prices rose by over 5% for the first time, despite intensive efforts at control by the government.

In May the Austrian currency was revalued by 5.05%, setting the new exchange rate at 24.75 schillings to the U.S. dollar. The dollar crisis later in the year and the subsequent economic measures taken by the U.S. brought difficulties for Austria, since the U.S. import surcharge considerably affected Austrian exports. It was decided that the issuing bank should no longer be obliged to intervene to maintain the parity of the dollar. This meant floating the schilling against the dollar, and by the end of September the prevailing rate was about 24.13 schillings to U.S. $1.

The 1971 census gave the population of Austria as 7,443,809, an increase of 4.8% (of which 0.4% were immigrants) over the 1961 figures. The population of Vienna had decreased by 1.5%, the increase having taken place in western Austria. (E. Di.)

Bahrain

An independent emirate, Bahrain consists of a group of islands in the Persian Gulf, lying between the Qatar Peninsula and Saudi Arabia. Total area: 256 sq.mi. (662 sq.km.). Pop. (1971): 216,078. Cap.: Manama (pop., 1970 est., 80,000). Language: Arabic (official), Persian. Religion: Muslim. Emir, Isa ibn Sulman al-Khalifah.

After Iran's renunciation of its claim on Bahrain in 1970 and continued failure of British-initiated efforts to establish a federation linking the sheikhdom with Qatar and the seven Trucial States, Bahrain became a fully independent state on Aug. 15, 1971, and the title of the ruler was changed to emir. The decision ended 151 years of political and military de-

pendence on Britain, and the special treaty relationship dating back to 1820 was replaced by a new treaty of friendship. It contained no British commitment to defend the island but did provide for "consultation in time of need." (X.)

Barbados

The parliamentary state of Barbados is a member of the Commonwealth of Nations and occupies the most easterly island in the southern Caribbean Sea. Area: 166 sq.mi. (430 sq.km.). Pop. (1970): 238,000, predominantly Negro. Cap. and largest city: Bridgetown (pop., 1970, 8,790). Language: English. Religion: Christian, with Anglicans in the majority. Queen, Elizabeth II; governor-general in 1971, Sir Winston Scott; prime minister, Errol Walton Barrow.

At the general election in September Errol Barrow and his Democratic Labour Party were returned to power with 18 out of 24 House of Assembly seats, three more than they had previously held. Barrow had warned the governments of the U.S., the U.K., and Guyana against intervention on behalf of the opposition, alleging that the U.S. Central Intelligence Agency had made such attempts.

During the year the government announced its intention of establishing a central bank and introducing its own currency. Barbados became a member of the International Monetary Fund on Dec. 29, 1970. Because of its high growth rate Barbados had a tax-free budget for the first time in ten years.

Tourism, Barbados' major foreign-exchange earner, suffered from overfast expansion, high prices, tougher competition from cheaper European resorts for the North American tourist trade, and apprehensions aroused by Black Power and other radical manifestations. There was evidence of an increase in black American tourism, and Barbados was promoting tourism from Europe, aided by a new airline, International Caribbean Airways.

In attempts by the Commonwealth sugar-producing countries to gain assurances that they would not suffer unduly by U.K. entry into the EEC, only Barbados remained unconvinced by placatory promises that the EEC would "take their interests to heart." Neither was it satisfied with suggestions from the Commonwealth Caribbean Secretariat that after the end of the Commonwealth Sugar Agreement in 1974, CARIFTA members should seek common associate status within the EEC. (SH. P.)

BAHRAIN
Education. (1968–69) Primary, pupils 35,875, teachers (public only) 1,048; secondary, pupils 10,503; vocational, pupils 877; higher, students 191, teaching staff 24.
    Finance and Trade. Monetary unit: Bahrain dinar, with a par value of 0.48 dinars to U.S. $1 (1.14 dinars = £1 sterling) and a free rate (Sept. 27, 1971) of 0.46 dinars to U.S. $1. Budget (1969 est.): revenue 12,750,000 dinars; expenditure 12,580,000 dinars. Foreign trade (1970): imports 80,127,000 dinars (31% from U.K., 12% from Japan, 7% from U.S., 5% from China); exports (excluding oil) 25,156,000 dinars (50% to Saudi Arabia, 12% to Kuwait, 6% to Dubai, 5% to Qatar). Main exports: crude oil and petroleum products.
    Industry. Production (in 000; metric tons): crude oil (1970) 3,834; petroleum products (1969) 11,433.

BARBADOS
Education. (1966–67) Primary, pupils 40,712, teachers 1,163; secondary, pupils 25,136, teachers 1,074; vocational, pupils 2,362, teachers 141; teacher training, students 300, teachers 30; higher, students 373, teaching staff 85.
    Finance and Trade. Monetary unit: East Caribbean dollar, with a par value of ECar$2 to U.S. $1 (ECar$4.80 = £1 sterling) and a free rate (Sept. 27, 1971) of ECar$1.94 to U.S. $1. Budget (1969–70 est.): revenue ECar$57,768,000; expenditure ECar$62,061,000. Foreign trade (1969): imports ECar$194,554,000 (29% from U.K., 22% from U.S., 11% from Canada); exports ECar$74,255,000 (37% to U.K., 21% to U.S.). Main exports: sugar 36%; petroleum products 12%; shellfish 10%; molasses 5%. Tourism (1969) 138,000 visitors.
    Agriculture. Sugar production, raw value (metric tons; 1970–71) c. 168,000, (1969–70) 157,000.

Baseball

The Pittsburgh Pirates dethroned world champion Baltimore by edging the Orioles, 2–1, in the seventh game of the World Series. Roberto Clemente (*see* BIOGRAPHY) of Pittsburgh was adjudged the Series' most valuable player. The 37-year-old right fielder from Puerto Rico got a record-tying 12 hits en route to a .414 average. He hit safely in all seven games, just as he had done when the Pirates last ruled the baseball world in 1960.

Pittsburgh had entered the World Series after beating the San Francisco Giants, three games to one, in the best-of-five divisional play-offs for the National League pennant. The Pirates lost the opener to the Giants, 5–4, then took three straight by scores of 9–4, 2–1, and 9–5. Baltimore required only three games to eliminate the Oakland Athletics in the American League play-offs. The Orioles prevailed by margins of 5–3, 5–1, and 5–3.

It was a season of bizarre happenings. California Angels outfielder Alex Johnson, American League batting champion in 1970, was suspended without pay by the Angels in June for "not hustling and not showing the proper mental attitude." But in what was termed by some sources a landmark decision, an impartial arbitration board ruled in late September that an emotional disturbance should be treated no differently than a physical ailment in baseball and ordered the Angels to restore Johnson's back pay of $29,970. The board upheld 29 disciplinary fines against Johnson totaling an estimated $3,750. Johnson was traded to Cleveland at the season's end.

Chicago Cubs' owner Phil Wrigley made headlines on September 3 when he took out advertisements in four Chicago newspapers in support of Cubs' manager

Pirates' Gene Clines (left), covered by Roberto Clemente and Jackie Hernandez, attempts to field a single by Dave Kingman during the first inning of a National League play-off game between the San Francisco Giants and the Pittsburgh Pirates on Oct. 3, 1971.

Leo Durocher. The ad was published following a stormy clubhouse meeting in which Durocher feuded with some of his star players. Wrigley's message warned that players who let down on the job would be traded in the off-season. The Cubs, who had made a bid for divisional honours late in August, wound up in a third-place tie with the New York Mets. Durocher later was retained as manager for 1972.

American League owners, by a vote of 10 to 2, gave Washington Senators' owner Bob Short permission to move his financially troubled franchise to Dallas-Fort Worth in time for the 1972 season. The nation's capital had been the site of an American League franchise since 1901.

Baseball's Hall of Fame at Cooperstown, N.Y., inducted eight new members: LeRoy "Satchel" Paige, Dave Bancroft, Jacob Beckley, Charles "Chick" Hafey, Harry Hooper, Joseph James Kelley, Richard "Rube" Marquard, and George Weiss. Paige was named by the new Hall of Fame Committee on Negro Baseball Leagues. The others were chosen by the Veterans' Committee.

Baltimore's pitching staff produced four 20-game winners: Dave McNally, Mike Cuellar, Jim Palmer, and Pat Dobson. It was the second such pitching accomplishment in major league history. The 1920 Chicago White Sox turned the trick behind Urban ("Red") Faber, Claude Williams, Dickie Kerr, and Ed Cicotte.

Spectacular Oakland pitcher Vida Blue (*see* BIOGRAPHY), in his first full major league season, electrified the baseball world by winning 17 games before the All-Star break. His final record was 24–8. Three National Leaguers—Ken Holtzman of Chicago, Rick Wise of Philadelphia, and Bob Gibson of St. Louis—pitched no-hit, no-run games. It was Holtzman's second masterpiece.

Atlanta's Hank Aaron joined Babe Ruth and Willie Mays in hitting 600 home runs. Harmon Killebrew of Minnesota and Frank Robinson of Baltimore both delivered their 500th homers, the 10th and 11th to reach that plateau. Ron Hunt, the Montreal second baseman, set a major league record when he was hit by pitched balls 50 times.

The National League established a new attendance record of 17,333,371 as 11 of its 12 teams topped the million mark. The American League dropped off somewhat to 11,870,557.

Major Leagues. A frenzied finish in the National League's Western Division highlighted regular-season competition. The San Francisco Giants took over first place on April 12 and stayed there for the rest of the year, but they had to win their final game to outlast onrushing Los Angeles. The Dodgers staged a blistering rally after trailing by 8½ games early in September only to lose out by the margin of one game. The Giants beat San Diego, 5–1, in their finale to preserve their one-game edge over the Dodgers, whose 2–1 victory over Houston thereby became meaningless. Pittsburgh captured the Eastern Division convincingly with a seven-game margin over St. Louis.

Both American League races developed into runaways. Baltimore ran up 101 victories in the Eastern Division to shake off Detroit by 12 games. Oakland gathered the same win total in the Western Division and finished 16 games in front of Kansas City.

The World Series opened in Baltimore, and the Orioles responded by winning 5–3. Left-hander Dave McNally survived early problems to post a three-hit victory. McNally pitched hitless ball for 6⅔ innings,

Fans crowd the streets of downtown Pittsburgh, Pa., to celebrate victory after the Pirates clinched the 1971 World Series. Reports of fighting and looting caused the police to institute special riot procedures.

Oakland's Vida Blue, recipient of the 1971 Cy Young Award, demonstrates his winning pitching style. In his first full major league season, Blue had an impressive 24–8 record.

The Orioles won the second game in a runaway, 11–3, after rain forced postponement of the Series for one day. Baltimore got 14 hits, all singles, and ran up an 11–0 lead for pitcher Jim Palmer before Richie Hebner's three-run homer put Pittsburgh on the scoreboard in the eighth. The loser was Bob Johnson.

The Series moved to Pittsburgh's Three Rivers Stadium for the third game, and the Pirates grabbed their first victory, 5–1, behind the three-hit pitching of Steve Blass. Pittsburgh led, 2–1, in the seventh when Bob Robertson, after missing a bunt sign, smashed a home run with two on off loser Mike Cuellar to put the game out of Baltimore's reach. Frank Robinson's homer accounted for the Orioles' lone run.

The first night game in World Series history unfolded at Three Rivers Stadium on October 13, and a record Pittsburgh baseball crowd of 51,378 saw the Pirates beat Baltimore, 4–3, to tie the Series at two games apiece. The Orioles took a 3–0 lead in the top of the first inning, but 21-year-old rookie pitcher Bruce Kison came on in relief to halt Baltimore on no runs and one hit over the next 6⅓ innings. Ironically, Kison walked none but hit three batters, a World Series record. He was credited with the win when pinch-hitter Milt May singled home the tie-breaking run in the seventh.

Nelson Briles handed Pittsburgh the Series lead, three games to two, by pitching a brilliant two-hitter to shackle the Orioles, 4–0, in the fifth contest. Bob Robertson homered off Dave McNally in the second inning to provide Briles with the only offensive support he needed.

The Series switched back to Baltimore for the sixth game, and Baltimore rebounded from a 2–0 deficit to survive, 3–2, in ten innings and square the fall classic at three games apiece. Brooks Robinson's sacrifice fly in the bottom of the tenth brought in the run to make a winner out of McNally in relief and a loser out of Bob Miller in relief. Clemente and Buford hit home runs.

Four-hit pitching by Blass carried Pittsburgh to the championship in the seventh game. The Pirates' 2–1 win upset earlier conjecture that the Orioles had built a long-term dynasty. Clemente's fourth-inning home run was the first hit off the loser, Cuellar, and established the trend. Jose Pagan's double in the eighth drove home Willie Stargell from first and boosted the Pirates' advantage to 2–0. Ellie Hendricks and Mark Belanger singled off Blass to lead off the Baltimore eighth, but the Orioles' budding rally produced only one run. Blass made it look easy in the ninth and Pittsburgh thus emerged as champion.

Ten American League pitchers won 20 or more games in 1971, highest total in the majors since 1920. Detroit's Mickey Lolich (25–14) and Oakland's Vida Blue (24–8) led the way in wins. In addition to Baltimore's "big four" of McNally, Cuellar, Palmer, and Dobson, the select group included Wilbur Wood of the Chicago White Sox, Jim Hunter of Oakland, Andy Messersmith of California, and Joe Coleman of Detroit. Blue paced the earned run averages with 1.82, while Lolich struck out 308.

Minnesota's Tony Oliva won the American League batting title with .337. Bill Melton became the first White Sox player ever to grab home run honours with 33. Harmon Killebrew of Minnesota drove in the most runs, 119.

Oakland's Vida Blue, 22, became the youngest player to win the most valuable player award as he

retiring 19 straight batters in one stretch. Pittsburgh struck first. The Pirates, helped along by two errors, piled up a 3–0 lead in the second inning. Frank Robinson's home run off loser Dock Ellis reduced the deficit to 3–1 in the bottom of the second. Merv Rettenmund then homered with two on in the third to put the Orioles on top to stay. Don Buford hit a fifth inning homer for Baltimore's final run.

Table I. Final Major League Standings, 1971

American League
Eastern Division

Club	W.	L.	Pct.	G.B.	Balt.	Det.	Bos.	N.Y.	Wash.	Clev.	Cal.	Chi.	K.C.	Mil.	Minn.	Oak.
Baltimore	101	57	.639	—	—	8	9	11	13	13	7	8	6	9	10	7
Detroit	91	71	.562	12	10	—	6	10	14	12	6	5	8	10	6	4
Boston	85	77	.525	18	9	12	—	7	12	11	6	10	1	6	8	3
New York	82	80	.506	21	7	8	11	—	7*	10	6	7	7	10	4	5
Washington	63	96	.396	38½	3	4	6	11	—	11	8	2	3	6	6	3
Cleveland	60	102	.370	43	5	6	7	8	7	—	4	9	2	4	4	4

Western Division

Club	W.	L.	Pct.	G.B.	Oak.	K.C.	Chi.	Cal.	Minn.	Mil.	Balt.	Bos.	Clev.	Det.	N.Y.	Wash.
Oakland	101	60	.627	—	—	13	7	11	10	15	4	9	8	8	7	9
Kansas City	85	76	.528	16	5	—	9	10	9	8	5	11	10	4	5	9
Chicago	79	83	.488	22½	11	9	—	10	7	11	4	2	3	7	5	10
California	76	86	.469	25½	7	8	8	—	12	6	5	6	8	6	4	4
Minnesota	74	86	.463	26½	9	9	11	6	—	7	2	4	8	6	8	5
Milwaukee	69	92	.429	32	3	10	7	12	10	—	3	6	8	2	2	6

*Includes forfeit awarded in game of September 30.

National League
Eastern Division

Club	W.	L.	Pct.	G.B.	Pitt.	St. L.	Chi.	N.Y.	Mon.	Phil.	Atl.	Cin.	Hou.	L.A.	S.D.	S.F.
Pittsburgh	97	65	.599	—	—	11	12	8	11	12	8	7	8	8	9	3
St. Louis	90	72	.556	7	7	—	9	8	14	11	6	4	10	6	8	7
Chicago	83	79	.512	14	6	9	—	11	8	11	7	6	5	8	9	3
New York	83	79	.512	14	10	10	7	—	9	13	5	4	7	7	7	4
Montreal	71	90	.441	25½	7	4	10	9	—	6	5	5	8	4	6	7
Philadelphia	67	95	.414	30	6	7	7	5	12	—	4	7	4	5	4	6

Western Division

Club	W.	L.	Pct.	G.B.	S.F.	L.A.	Atl.	Hou.	Cin.	S.D.	Chi.	Mon.	N.Y.	Phil.	Pitt.	St.L.
San Francisco	90	72	.556	—	—	6	11	9	9	13	9	5	8	6	9	5
Los Angeles	89	73	.549	1	12	—	9	10	11	13	4	8	5	7	4	6
Atlanta	82	80	.506	8	7	9	—	9	9	11	5	7	7	8	4	6
Houston	79	83	.488	11	9	8	9	—	13	10	7	4	5	8	4	2
Cincinnati	79	83	.488	11	9	7	9	5	—	10	6	3	8	5	5	8
San Diego	61	100	.379	28½	5	5	7	8	8	—	3	5	5	8	3	4

Tie: Montreal 1, St. Louis 1.
Source: The Sporting News.

dominated post-season individual honours in the American League. He also captured the Cy Young award for pitching excellence, while Chris Chambliss, first baseman of the Cleveland Indians, was rookie of the year.

In the National League, Ferguson Jenkins of the Chicago Cubs collected a league-high total of 24 wins. It was his fifth straight 20-game season. Three other pitchers won 20—Al Downing of Los Angeles, Steve Carlton of St. Louis, and Tom Seaver of the New York Mets. Seaver rated first in both earned run averages, 1.76, and strikeouts, 289.

Joe Torre of St. Louis hit .363 and produced 137 runs batted in for National League leadership in both categories. Pittsburgh's Willie Stargell hammered 48 home runs to capture the fight for individual home run laurels from Atlanta's Hank Aaron, who had 47.

Torre was named most valuable player in the National League, and Ferguson Jenkins of the Chicago Cubs won the Cy Young award. Earl Williams, catcher for the Atlanta Braves, was rookie of the year.

The American League broke an 8-game losing streak to beat the National League, 6–4, in the All-Star Game at Detroit. A prodigious home run by Reggie Jackson of the American League was one of the game's six homers, tying an All-Star record. Frank Robinson and Harmon Killebrew also connected for the Americans, while Johnny Bench, Hank Aaron, and Roberto Clemente homered for the Nationals. Robinson's two-run home run climaxed the American League's four-run third to rub out the Nationals' 3–0 lead and bring the victory to the starter, Vida Blue. The Americans thus triumphed for the 18th time against 23 losses and 1 tie.

In post-season developments Danny Murtaugh retired as manager of the Pirates and was replaced by batting coach Bill Virdon. Del Rice, a former major league catcher, replaced Lefty Phillips as manager of the Angels. Frank Robinson and Pete Richert of Baltimore were traded to the Los Angeles Dodgers for four young players.

Amateur. Southern California repeated as champion of the college baseball World Series at Omaha, Neb., in 1971, thereby dominating the National Collegiate Athletic Association (NCAA) tournament for the seventh time, four more than any other school. The Trojans clinched the title with a 7–2 win over Southern Illinois University on the eight-hit pitching of Steve Busby. Frank Alfano accounted for three USC runs with a homer and single and his teammate, Craig Perkins, also homered.   (J. Be.)

Japanese. The Yomiuri Giants of Tokyo, the first professional baseball club organized in Japan (1934), won the 1971 pennant of the Central League for an unprecedented seventh straight year, largely through the batting of third baseman Shigeo Nagashima and first baseman Sadaharu Oh. In the rival Pacific League, the Hankyu Braves of Osaka captured the pennant for the fourth time in five years.

The Central League, which is more popular than the Pacific because of the presence of the Yomiuri Giants, drew an attendance past the 6 million mark for the fourth straight season. Average attendance per game was 15,000.

The Giants had a wobbly pitching staff but won the Central League pennant when Nagashima took the league batting crown for an unprecedented sixth time with a .320 average and Oh hit 39 homers to lead the league in this category for the tenth straight year.

The Giants defeated the Braves, four games to one,

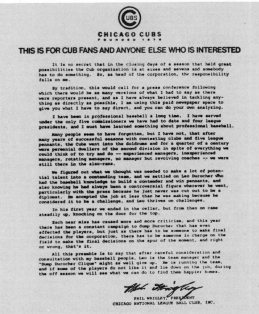

In an attempt to thwart a "dump Durocher" campaign sponsored by dissatisfied fans, Phil Wrigley, owner of the Chicago Cubs, declared support for manager Leo Durocher in an advertisement that appeared in Chicago newspapers.

in Japan's version of the World Series for their seventh straight Japanese baseball championship. The Giants had previously triumphed over the Braves, four games to two, in 1967, 1968, and 1969.

First baseman Shinichi Eto of the Lotte Orions won the Pacific League batting crown with a .337 average and became the first player to have won the batting championship in both leagues. He was the Central League batting champion in 1964 and 1965 as a player on the Chunichi Dragons.

The 1971 final standings were: Central League (1) Yomiuri Giants (Tokyo), (2) Chunichi Dragons (Nagoya), (3) Hiroshima Carp (Hiroshima), (4) Taiyo Whales (Kawasaki), (5) Hanshin Tigers (Osaka), (6) Yakult Atoms (Tokyo); Pacific League (1) Hankyu Braves (Osaka), (2) Lotte Orions (Tokyo), (3) Kintetsu Buffaloes (Osaka), (4) Nankai Hawks (Osaka), (5) Toei Flyers (Tokyo), (6) Nishitetsu Lions (Fukuoka).   (X.)

Table II. Minor League Champions, 1971

League	Pennant winner	Play-off winner
American Association	Denver (East)	Denver
	Indianapolis (West)	
International	Rochester	Rochester
Rochester defeated Denver for Junior World Series title		
Mexican	Saltillo (Northern)	Jalisco
	Jalisco (Southern)	
Pacific Coast	Tacoma (Northern)	Salt Lake City
	Salt Lake City (Southern)	
Dixie Association	Amarillo (Western)	
	Arkansas (Central)	Charlotte
	Charlotte (Eastern)	
Eastern	Elmira (American)	Elmira
	Three Rivers (National)	
California	Fresno (1st half)	Visalia
	Visalia (2nd half)	
Carolina	Kinston (1st half)	Peninsula
	Peninsula (2nd half)	
Florida State	Miami (Eastern)	Miami
	Daytona Beach (Western)	
Mexican Center	Ebano (Gulf)	Ebano
	San Luis Potosí (Central)	
Midwest	Appleton (Northern)	Quad Cities
	Quad Cities (Southern)	
New York-Pennsylvania	Oneonta	No play-off
Northern	St. Cloud	No play-off
Northwest	Tri-City	No play-off
Western Carolinas	Greenwood	No play-off
Appalachian	Bluefield	No play-off
Gulf Coast	Royals	No play-off
Pioneer	Great Falls	No play-off

Source: *The Sporting News.*

Basketball

United States. *Collegiate.* The University of California at Los Angeles (UCLA), again emphasizing team balance and a relentless pressing defense, continued its remarkable domination of U.S. collegiate basketball. Coached by Johnny Wooden (*see* BIOGRAPHY), the Bruins finished with a 29–1 record, losing only a mid-season game to Notre Dame, and for the fifth consecutive year won top honours in the National Collegiate Athletic Association (NCAA) tournament.

It was the first time a school had won five successive NCAA championships—UCLA having the previous record of four—and was the seventh title for the Bruins in the last eight years. In those eight seasons, the Bruins had a combined 221–15 record; they were 203–7 in the seven years they won NCAA championships. Additionally, the Bruins, as a result of their latest success, finished with 28 successive NCAA tournament victories, also a record.

As in the past, UCLA stressed team balance. The Bruins had four starters who averaged 11 points per game or higher, and had an especially outstanding front line of Sidney Wicks, Curtis Rowe, and Steve Patterson. Together, the three averaged 32.6 rebounds and 51.7 points a game. Wicks, chosen the player of the year by the United States Basketball Writers Association, led the Bruins with a 20.3-point average.

Only two major schools, Marquette and Pennsylvania, were undefeated going into NCAA tournament play. Marquette, rated no. 1 during much of the season, was upset by Ohio State 60–59 in the Mideast Regional. Pennsylvania was also eliminated, bowing 90–47 to a Villanova team that grew stronger as the season progressed and reached the finals before losing to UCLA.

UCLA entered NCAA tournament play in the Western Regional and won its opener 91–73 over Brigham Young University. The next tournament opponent for the Bruins was California State of Long Beach, champion of the Pacific Coast Athletic Association. UCLA edged Long Beach 57–55 in a tough game. The Bruins then went on to Houston for the NCAA finals and marched to the title with victories over Kansas, 68–60, and Villanova, 68–62.

The title game against Villanova was close throughout. Villanova, in the championship game for the first time in the school's history, trailed by eight points, 45–37, at the half, but in the final minutes twice drew to within three points of a tie, first at 61–58 and later at 63–60. Patterson, who averaged only 12.9 points for the season, led the Bruins in this game with a 29-point performance, his best of the season. He sank 13 of 18 field-goal attempts and was also a major factor in the Bruins' full-court press defense.

Villanova star Howard Porter, voted the tournament's most outstanding player, subsequently was found to have been ineligible for college competition with the discovery that he had signed a professional contract some three months before the season's end. This voided Villanova's second-place finish.

North Carolina won the championship in the annual National Invitational Tournament (NIT) by defeating Georgia Tech 84–66. Bill Chamberlain led North Carolina with 34 points, scoring 18 in one nine-minute stretch in the second half when Georgia Tech was trying to rally. Chamberlain was voted the tournament's most valuable player.

Milwaukee's Kareem Jabbar sinks the ball in an over-the-shoulder shot during a successful game against the Baltimore Bullets in the 1971 NBA championship play-off finals. The Milwaukee Bucks became the second team ever to sweep the NBA championship round in four straight games.

HEINZ KLUETMEIER FOR SPORTS ILLUSTRATED © TIME INC.

Johnny Neumann, a University of Mississippi sophomore, won the major division scoring title with 923 points for a 40.1 game average. Austin Carr of Notre Dame played in six more games and scored 1,101 points but was second to Neumann in game average with 38. John Belcher of Arkansas State finished with the best shooting percentage, making good on 174 of 275 field-goal attempts for a .633 average. Belcher shot a remarkable .746 in his last six games.

Artis Gilmore of Jacksonville, a 7-ft. 2-in. centre, retained the rebounding title with an average of 23.2 rebounds per game. This enabled Gilmore to finish his collegiate career with a 22.7 average, breaking the previous career record of 21.8 by Marshall's Charlie Slack in 1953–56. Greg Starrick of Southern Illinois won the free-throw percentage title by converting 119 of 132 penalty shots for a .902 average.

Players chosen on the All-American team, as published in the *Official NCAA Basketball Guide,* were: Howard Porter of Villanova; Austin Carr of Notre Dame; Johnny Neumann of Mississippi; Ken Durrett of LaSalle; Sidney Wicks and Curtis Rowe of UCLA; Jim McDaniels of Western Kentucky; John Roche of South Carolina; Dean Meminger of Marquette; and Artis Gilmore of Jacksonville.

Evansville (Ind.) won the championship in the NCAA's college division (limited to smaller schools) by defeating Old Dominion University (Norfolk, Va.) 97–82. It was the fifth college division title for Evansville in the tournament's 15-year history. Don Buse, a 6-ft. 4-in. guard from Holland, Ind., led Evansville in the championship game with 23 points and was named the tournament's outstanding player.

Professional. In its 25th anniversary season the National Basketball Association (NBA) continued to boom in popularity. New franchises were opened in Buffalo, Cleveland, and Portland, raising league membership from 14 to 17 teams and causing a new geographic alignment of four divisions, replacing the old Eastern and Western divisions. The result was another highly successful season and a record league attendance of 6,194,606, an increase of approximately 20% over the previous season when paid admissions had exceeded 5 million for the first time.

The Milwaukee Bucks, led by second-year man Lew Alcindor and veteran playmaker Oscar Robertson, won the league title. An expansion team, the Bucks entered the NBA in 1968 and set several major records en route to the championship. Their 20 consecutive victories bettered by 2 the previous league mark for successive wins; additionally, they had a .509 team field-goal percentage, the first team in the NBA's 25-year history to score on more than half of its shots.

Alcindor, a 7-ft. 2-in. centre, was the league's dominant figure. He led the NBA in scoring with a 31.7 average, was second in field-goal percentage, and fourth in rebounding. He was a near-unanimous choice for the All-Star team and won the Podoloff Cup, which goes to the league's most valuable player. After the season Alcindor officially changed his name to Kareem Abdul Jabbar (*see* BIOGRAPHY).

The combination of Alcindor and Robertson, who was acquired in a trade with Cincinnati, made Milwaukee an easy winner in the Midwest Division. Robertson, a perennial All-Star selection, averaged 19.4 points per game and was third in the league in assists with an 8.2 average and second in free-throw percentage. It was the first time in his brilliant 11-year professional career that Robertson helped lead a team to the league championship.

Milwaukee had a 66–16 record during the regular season and set records for the most games won at home (38) and also for the most games won on the road (28). The Bucks were the most accurate shooters in NBA history, with all five starters ranking among the league's top ten players in field-goal percentage.

In the championship play-offs Milwaukee and Baltimore advanced to the finals. Baltimore eliminated New York's defending league champions in the semifinals, winning an exciting series four games to three. New York was weakened in rebounding as a result of a knee injury suffered by Willis Reed, its star centre and the NBA hero of the previous season. Milwaukee eliminated Los Angeles in five games in the other semifinal series and then breezed to the title by knocking off Baltimore in four straight games, an accomplishment last achieved in 1959 when Boston whipped Minneapolis.

Alcindor's season-long effectiveness was such that he won the Podolof Cup by the biggest margin in history. There were 156 voters who were allowed to select three players, in 1–2–3 order. Alcindor received 133 first-place votes, 10 seconds, and 3 thirds. Only one other player, Dave Bing of Detroit, won as many as six first-place votes. Robertson earned five first-place votes and finished fifth in the balloting.

Alcindor also dominated the voting in the selection of the mid-season All-Star team, winning almost unanimous recognition. Other players honoured with first-team All-Star berths were forwards John Havlicek of Boston and Billy Cunningham of Philadelphia and guards Jerry West of Los Angeles and Bing of Detroit.

To celebrate the league's 25th year of competition a silver anniversary All-Star team was selected. Players eligible for this recognition were those who had completed their playing careers and who had won All-Star

Chris Ford from Villanova University and Terry Schofield from UCLA race for the ball during the NCAA championship game in Houston, Tex., on March 27, 1971. UCLA won 68–62, capturing the NCAA title for the fifth straight season.

status at least once. Ten players were selected: forwards Bob Pettit, Dolph Schayes, Paul Arizin, and Joe Fulks; centres Bill Russell and George Mikan; and guards Bob Cousy, Bill Scharman, Bob Davies, and Sam Jones. Arnold (Red) Auerbach was chosen as the coach.

The rival American Basketball Association (ABA) also had a successful season and continued to approach the standards achieved by the NBA. The ABA, with 11 teams, drew more than 2 million paid admissions and continued signing many of the top college stars. Officials from both the NBA and ABA agreed to a merger and sought congressional approval. However, the NBA Players Association opposed the merger, and both leagues were still operating independently when the 1971–72 season began. The Utah Stars, led by Zelmo Beaty, won the 1971 ABA championship. (JE. HO.)

World Amateur. In May 1971, at the sixth women's world championship, held at São Paulo, Braz., teams competed for the Ivan Raposo Gold Cup for the first time. (The cup commemorated the former Brazilian associate general secretary of the International Basketball Federation, who died in January 1970.) The Soviet Union had little difficulty in retaining the title, its closest match being against Czechoslovakia, 88–69. Czechoslovakia defeated Brazil 68–59 to be runner-up.

Soviet superiority in women's basketball had previously been demonstrated in the 12th European championship for women, held in Rotterdam and Leeuwarden, Neth., in September 1970. Throughout the championship there was little doubt who the eventual winners would be. France, which eventually finished second, met the Soviet Union toward the end of the tournament and was decisively beaten 94–33. Yugoslavia, Bulgaria, and Czechoslovakia finished third, fourth, and fifth, respectively, among the 12 competing teams.

The Great Britain four-country senior men's tournament, staged during April 1971 in the Meadowbank Stadium, Edinburgh, gave an opportunity to the home team, Scotland, to retain the title. The championship rested on the outcome of the final game in the series, Scotland v. England. At half-time Scotland had man-

Table I. Major College Champions, 1971

League	Team and location	League record	All games
Eastern (Ivy)	Pennsylvania (Philadelphia)	14-0	28-1
Yankee	Massachusetts (Amherst)	10-0	23-4
Atlantic Coast	North Carolina (Chapel Hill)	11-3	26-6
Southeastern	Kentucky (Lexington)	16-2	22-6
Southern	Davidson (N.C.)	9-1	15-11
Ohio Valley	Western Kentucky (Bowling Green)	12-2	24-6
Big Ten	Ohio State (Columbus)	13-1	20-6
Mid-American	Miami (Oxford, O.)	9-1	20-5
Big Eight	Kansas (Lawrence)	14-0	27-3
Missouri Valley	*Drake (Des Moines, Ia.)	9-5	21-8
	Louisville (Ky.)	9-5	20-9
	St. Louis (Mo.)	9-5	17-12
Southwest	Texas Christian (Fort Worth)	11-3	15-12
AAWU (Pacific Eight)	UCLA (Los Angeles, Calif.)	14-0	29-1
West Coast	Pacific (Stockton, Calif.)	12-2	22-6

*Won play-off for national championship berth.

Table II. NBA Final Standings and Play-offs, 1971

Team	W	L	Pct.	Team	W	L	Pct.
Atlantic Division				**Central Division**			
New York	52	30	.634	Baltimore	42	40	.512
Philadelphia	47	35	.573	Atlanta	36	46	.439
Boston	44	38	.537	Cincinnati	33	49	.402
Buffalo	22	60	.268	Cleveland	15	67	.183
Midwest Division				**Pacific Division**			
Milwaukee	66	16	.805	Los Angeles	48	34	.585
Chicago	51	31	.622	San Francisco	41	41	.500
Phoenix	48	34	.585	San Diego	40	42	.488
Detroit	45	37	.549	Seattle	38	44	.463
				Portland	29	53	.354

Play-offs, quarterfinal series

Atlantic v. Central	Midwest v. Pacific
New York 4, Atlanta 1	Milwaukee 4, San Francisco 1
Baltimore 4, Philadelphia 3	Los Angeles 4, Chicago 3

Semifinal series

Baltimore 4, New York 3	Milwaukee 4, Los Angeles 1

Championship series
Milwaukee defeated Baltimore 4 games to 0
Milwaukee 98, Baltimore 88
Milwaukee 102, Baltimore 83
Milwaukee 107, Baltimore 99
Milwaukee 118, Baltimore 106

Kentucky's Dan Issel scores against the Utah Stars in the American Basketball Association championship game on May 18, 1971. Utah defeated Kentucky for the title.
WIDE WORLD

aged to secure a six-point lead, 48–42. At the start of the second half Scotland raced 12 points ahead and it looked like an easy Scottish victory. England, however, edged slowly back into the picture and at the end of the second half the game was tied 73–73. In the extra period W. McInnes and W. Cameron for Scotland eventually gave Scotland the game and the championship, 83–75. Ireland finished third and Wales fourth.

In the finals of the European Cup competitions it was the Soviet Union matched against Italy for both men's and women's championship honours. The European Club Championship final was played off at Antwerp, Belg., and it was the TSSKA Red Army Club of Moscow that met the Italian champions, Ignis, Varese. A capacity crowd of 6,000 watched the Soviet team triumph 67–53. The prestige of Italian basketball recovered on the occasion of the final of the Cup Winners' Cup, which was played in two legs. In the first, Simmenthal went to Leningrad to play the Soviet club, Spartak, and lost 66–56. But in the second leg, in Milan, Simmenthal won 71–52, thereby winning the championship on an aggregate point score. The Women's Cup went to Daugava Riga of the U.S.S.R. for the 11th time. On this occasion their victims in the final were the French champions, Clermont Ferrand, whom they beat 72–59 and 62–56.   (K. K. Mɪ.)

Belgium

A constitutional monarchy on the North Sea coast of Europe, Belgium is bordered by the Netherlands, West Germany, Luxembourg, and France. Area: 11,781 sq.mi. (30,514 sq.km.). Pop. (1970): 9,690,991. Cap.: Brussels (pop., 1970, 161,089). Largest city: Antwerp (pop., 1970, 226,570). Language: French and Dutch. Religion: predominantly Roman Catholic. King, Baudouin I; prime minister until Nov. 7, 1971, Gaston Eyskens.

During 1971 there was hard bargaining between the two coalition parties with respect to the introduction of cultural autonomy for the two linguistic communities, economic planning, and decentralization measures. Since cultural autonomy involved constitutional amendments, a two-thirds majority in Parliament was required, and the government was forced to seek opposition support. In return for their votes, the Liberals (PLP) insisted on a cultural pact by all three national parties to protect ideological and philosophical minorities. The government finally agreed, and cultural autonomy became effective on Dec. 1, 1971. Two cultural councils, one comprising all French-speaking and the other all Dutch-speaking members of Parliament, were entitled to issue decrees regarding matters considered to be the exclusive province of each language community.

In September the government decided to dissolve Parliament and hold the general election that would have been due in the spring of 1972. The outcome of the election, held on November 7, was that the Social Christians held 67 seats (1968; 69), the Socialists 61 (1968; 59), and the Liberals 34 (1968; 47). The majority, therefore, remained in the hands of the Social Christians and Socialists. However, both the Social Christians and the Liberals had lost seats, while the two French-speaking federalist parties, the Front Démocratique des Francophones and the Rassemblement Wallon, between them doubled their strength with 24 seats as opposed to 12 in 1968. The Volksunie (Flemish nationalists) increased their total from 20

Farmers demonstrate with staves in Brussels to demand higher prices for EEC farm produce. Beginning as a peaceful march, the demonstration ended in tragedy as a farmer was mortally wounded by a tear-gas grenade.
CAMERA PRESS—PIX

Beekeeping:
see Agriculture

Beer:
see Alcoholic
Beverages

to 21 seats. The dramatic swing toward the French-speaking groups, largely at the expense of the Liberals, meant that for the first time there would be more French-speaking federalists in the chamber than Flemish ones, a fact that boded ill for future relations between the two linguistic communities. The risk of Flemish discontent was further increased on November 21 when the French-speaking parties gained absolute control of the Greater Brussels councils. Repeated efforts to form a new Social Christian-Socialist Cabinet had not succeeded by year's end.

The introduction of the value-added tax on January 1, one year behind schedule, caused much apprehension because of the unique automatic link between prices and wages. Fearing unbridled inflation, the government ordered compulsory price reductions and an almost universal price freeze. Moreover, Parliament was invited to reactivate a World War II law providing for strict price controls. The new legislation gave the minister the power to close for a period of up to five days any firm raising its prices without official blessing; workers would continue to be paid. The bill met with strong opposition, as did a provision of the value-added tax statute that made compulsory a large

deposit for due taxes. After a national demonstration, the government backed down on the latter issue.

As the year progressed, signs of stagnation in the economy began to appear: industrial production slowed down; balance of trade deficits were registered; home building declined sharply. A Kredietbank report in August warned that only about one-third of all Belgian firms still showed a net profit of more than 10%. In March Belgian farmers demonstrated throughout the country in protest against the EEC prices policy. Following the December 18 agreement settling the monetary crisis, the fixed exchange rate of the franc with respect to the U.S. dollar was altered from BFr. 50 to BFr. 44.81.

Despite strict government control over most prices, the retail price index climbed 3.82% during the first eight months of 1971. The unions claimed that it no longer truly represented the real cost-of-living increases. Wildcat strikes proliferated, and union leaders requested an early new agreement with industry.

Parliament approved bills creating a complete university at Antwerp and a University Centre at Hasselt (Limburg). On February 2 King Baudouin laid the foundation stone of "Louvain la neuve" University, the independent French section of the Catholic University of Louvain (Leuven).   (JA. R. E.)

Bhutan

A monarchy situated in the eastern Himalayas, Bhutan is bounded by China, India, and Sikkim. Area: 18,000 sq.mi. (47,000 sq.km.). Pop. (1970 est.): 836,000. Cap.: Thimphu (no population total available). Language: Dzongkha (official). Religion: approximately 75% Buddhist, 25% Hindu. Druk gyalpo (king) in 1971, Jigme Dorji Wangchuk.

In September the UN General Assembly unanimously approved Bhutan's membership, and plans were announced for a permanent Bhutanese mission in New York. Earlier, Bhutan had for the first time exchanged ambassadors with India, which "guides" the Himalayan kingdom in foreign affairs, defense, and communications. This put relations between the two countries on a new basis befitting Bhutan's independent status.

Bhutan's third five-year development plan, involving approximately $44 million, was officially launched in 1971. India would again provide the bulk of the funds, earmarked mainly for the improvement of agriculture, irrigation, communications, and education, and would also provide training personnel.

King Jigme Dorji Wangchuk made an official visit to India in April. Before leaving, the king expressed satisfaction with the working of the 1949 treaty with India and dismissed reports that Bhutan might seek a revision of it.   (G. U.)

ABZUG, BELLA SAVITSKY

When Bella Abzug walked onto the floor of the U.S. House of Representatives for the first time on Jan. 21, 1971, representing the 19th congressional district of New York, members were soon aware of her presence. She introduced a resolution calling for the withdrawal of all troops from Indochina by July 4, and she demanded appointment to the House Armed Services Committee, on the ground that no woman had served on the panel since 1949.

She achieved neither the troop withdrawal nor the appointment, but Washington felt her impact. Ignoring the tradition that freshmen in Congress should be neither seen nor heard, she introduced or co-sponsored more than 100 bills, dealing with a spectrum of controversial topics ranging from women's rights to crime and narcotics control.

Not content to use the legislative mill to achieve her goals, she addressed peace demonstrators on the Capitol steps, spoke out on behalf of Soviet Jews in direct communications to the Soviet government, and led a sidewalk demonstration of senior citizens on New York City's West Side to protest the raising of rents in residential hotels. When she read that the president had joked with his staff about the newly formed National Women's Political Caucus, in which she held office, she fumed: "Nixon will find out in 1972 that the Caucus is no laughing matter. . . . Women will no longer let themselves be consigned to . . . the sidelines of political power." Perhaps her most unorthodox proposal during the year was to make New York City the 51st state.

Although Washington was sometimes amused by her flamboyant personality, earthy language, and the broad-brimmed hats that quickly became a trademark, no one underestimated her sincerity or effect. Born in 1920 in the Bronx, Bella Savitsky Abzug attended local schools and graduated in 1942 from Hunter College. She received her law degree from Columbia in 1947 and specialized in labour law, as well as championing the rights of tenants and minority groups. A Democrat, she was elected to Congress by a decisive margin, 47,128 votes to 38,438 for her opponent.   (T. R. T.)

ALBERT, CARL BERT

Carl Albert had walked a careful political road and acquired a minimum of enemies during his 24-year career as a U.S. representative. His reward came in January 1971, when he was elected speaker of the House. The only opposition to the Oklahoma Democrat in the Democratic caucus came from Rep. John Conyers, Jr., of Michigan, a black. The caucus vote was 220 for Albert, 20 for Conyers.

A small, quiet-spoken man, Albert moved to the top leadership post in the House from the number-two position as majority leader, a job he had held since 1962. Before that, he had spent seven years as assistant majority leader. In the speakership, he replaced John W. McCormack of Massachusetts, who retired at age 79 after 42 years in the House. Albert's style differed markedly from that of McCormack. He spent much of his time in a private office in the Capitol, some distance from the speaker's larger but more public quarters, where McCormack had held forth with his friends in the manner of a Boston ward politician.

Despite his good personal relations with the warring factions in his party, Albert was criticized by some Democrats for failing to provide stronger leadership. "The Speaker gets blamed for everything," he complained midway through his first year. "It's awfully hard to walk the tightrope when you've got so many points of view." But Albert advanced the views of House Democrats by issuing news releases and holding news conferences at which he did not hesitate to attack the Republican administration. He also instituted a series of press briefings on important legislation by Democratic House committee chairmen.

Albert learned much of his skill at political accommodation in his poor, rural district in southeastern Oklahoma, where conservatism on racial questions coexisted with a populist tradition on economic matters. His voting record had become more liberal since his election in 1946. Albert was born May 10, 1908, in a miner's shack in McAlester, Okla., and worked his way through the University of Oklahoma. After graduating with a Phi Beta Kappa key in 1931, he went to Britain on a Rhodes scholarship and earned his law degree there.   (M. Cs.)

AMIN, IDI

Gen. Idi Amin became president of Uganda in January 1971 after a military coup that he led ousted Pres. Milton Obote, whose army commander he had been since 1966. A devout Muslim from the small Kakwa tribe, Amin was largely self-taught, having joined the British colonial army as a young man. He saw service in the Burma campaign in World War II with the King's African Rifles, an East African regiment. Subsequently, he fought against the Mau Mau rebellion in Kenya. Under the colonial regime he rose to the highest noncommissioned rank and became an officer only a year before Uganda achieved its independence in 1962. Four years later he was made army commander, after having led the government forces against the kabaka of Buganda, who fled to safety in exile. Amin became the centre of a controversy in 1966 when a judicial inquiry was appointed to examine the roles that he and others had played in the Congolese rebellion. He admitted at the hearings that he had used a considerable sum of gold smuggled from the Congo to assist the revolutionary leaders.

Amin was born about 1925 in the village of Koboko. A burly, extroverted soldier, most at ease with the rank and file of the Army with whom he spent the greater part of his career, he was for ten years heavyweight boxing champion of Uganda and an enthusiastic Rugby player. He was closely involved with Obote in dealing with previous attempts at coups and assassinations in Uganda. But the two men became increasingly estranged after 1969, when Obote decided on changes in the army structure to which Amin was opposed. These disagreements later turned into hostility, and Amin —who had lost some of his authority in the Army as a result of changes in 1969—was on the point of being dismissed when he staged his successful coup.   (Co. L.)

ASSAD, HAFEZ AL-

After taking power in Syria in November 1970, Gen. Hafez al-Assad radically modified the form and style of Syria's Baathist regime. He introduced a more personalized rule, liberalized the government in a number of ways, and reduced Syria's former isolation by improving relations with other Arab countries, notably Lebanon, Egypt, and Saudi Arabia (although remaining hostile toward the rival Baathist regime in Iraq and highly critical of Jordan's actions against the Palestinian guerrillas). He rapidly established close relations with Egypt and in September 1971 led Syria into a federal union with Egypt and Libya. Although maintaining Syria's close relationship with the Soviet Union, he consistently rejected Soviet advice to accept the UN Security Council resolution of November 1967 as a basis for a political settlement in the Middle East.

Hafez al-Assad was born in the Latakia province of Syria in 1928 to a poor family of Alawites, a minority Islamic sect. He was graduated from the Homs Military Academy in 1955 as a pilot officer and was sent to the Soviet Union in 1958 for training in night warfare. He was later promoted to squadron leader but was dismissed from the armed forces in 1961 because of his opposition to Syria's secession from the union with Egypt. He then devoted his activities to the Baath Party, which he had joined as a student in indignation against social conditions in Syria, and became one of the key figures in the party's military wing when it took power in 1963. In 1964 he was made commander in chief of the Air Force and in February 1966 he became minister of defense after the radical Baathists' overthrow of the moderate international Baath leadership in Syria. In 1969–70 he was involved in a power struggle with the party's civilian wing that came to a head after Syria's intervention (to which he was opposed) in the Jordanian civil war. When the civilian Baathists refused cooperation, he formed his own government and in March 1971 was elected president for a seven-year term by 99.2% of the votes cast in a national plebiscite.   (P. MD.)

BANDA, HASTINGS KAMUZU

Malawi's strongly independent-minded president, H. Kamuzu Banda, defied the majority of the leaders of independent African nations in 1971 to become the first head of a black state ever to be received with full state honours in South Africa. Ignoring the strict boycott maintained by the Organization of African Unity, Banda had established formal diplomatic relations with South Africa in 1970 and played host to its prime minister. He also established close relations with his Portuguese neighbours in Mozambique.

Banda was born in Nyasaland in 1905, and the last time he had visited South Africa was in the early 1920s when, as a young migrant, he had worked for a time as a clerk and interpreter in the gold mines of the Witwatersrand. Helped by a grant from an American Methodist bishop, he went to Indiana University, where he majored in history and political science, and subsequently took degrees at the University of Chicago and Meharry Medical College, Nashville, Tenn. After 12 years in North America he went to Britain in 1937 to get his medical degree at Edinburgh University.

For the next 15 years he practiced successfully as a doctor in northern England and London, meanwhile working closely with Pan-Africanist leaders in developing the early black independence movements. He became the leading opponent in Britain of the Central African Federation, which had sought to link Nyasaland (later Malawi) with Southern and Northern Rhodesia. When his campaign against the establishment of a new white-dominated regime in central Africa failed in 1953, he left England to work in Kwame Nkrumah's Ghana. In 1958 he returned home to lead the nationalist movement, helping to destroy the Central African Federation and opening the way for the emergence of Malawi as an independent black republic, with himself as its first president.

Firmly committed to the ideals of non-racialism and to the Church of Scotland, of which he was an elder, President Banda believed that the best hope of changing the political systems of his white-ruled neighbour states was through political and social contacts. He established himself as leader of a small group of African heads of state who favoured the policy of a dialogue with South Africa. (Co. L.)

BANZER SUÁREZ, HUGO

After a whirlwind coup d'etat that ousted the leftist military regime, Col. Hugo Banzer Suárez, a career army officer, emerged in August as president of a new revolutionary government in Bolivia. Banzer raised the standard of revolt because the government of Pres. Juan José Torres Gonzales had fallen into a state of disorder bordering on anarchy. Even though Torres was himself a general in the Bolivian Army, the armed forces rallied to Banzer and toppled the leftist government in 48 hours. More than 100 persons were killed in the coup.

The coup that brought Banzer to the presidency may have paved the way for the eventual return to power of Víctor Paz Estenssoro, who led Bolivia to its great revolutionary reform in 1952 but had lived in exile in recent years. The alliance of the Bolivian armed forces with the left-centre Nationalist Revolutionary Movement (MNR) party of Paz and the conservative Bolivian Socialist Falange Party might give the Andean nation its first viable coalition since 1964.

Banzer's ascension to power was by no means a development of one-man rule. The small, mustachioed colonel maintained his power base through influential army officers, such as Col. Andres Selich, a tough Ranger Regiment commander, and most of the anti-left officer corps. His greatest bastion of strength was the Military Academy in La Paz, where Banzer was something of a hero to the cadet corps.

The deteriorating trend of United States-Bolivian relations was reversed after Banzer became president. Under Banzer's two military predecessors, Gen. Alfredo Ovando Candía and Torres, the Bolivian government nationalized Gulf Oil Corp. properties and became vociferously "anti-Yanqui." Banzer's relations with the U.S. were excellent and heralded a return to the close association of the past.

Born May 10, 1926, in the eastern province of Santa Cruz, Banzer was educated in Bolivian and U.S. military schools. His main support came from the country's small farmers and from the rich eastern region where he was born, while his principal enemies were leftist unionists and students in La Paz and miners in the bleak Altiplano region. Banzer did not say when he would call for elections, but experts believed he would do so before the end of 1972. He was considered more likely to throw his considerable support to a civilian rather than seek the office himself. (J. A. O'L.)

BARZEL, RAINER

As parliamentary floor leader of the Christian Democratic Union and its Bavarian sister party, the Christian Social Union, Rainer Barzel in 1971 staked his claim as candidate for the West German chancellorship in the federal election in 1973. There appeared to be no other contenders for the post. At the CDU conference in Saarbrücken in October, Barzel was elected chairman with 344 votes. His opponent,

Saul Bellow

Bella Abzug

Carl Albert

Rainer Barzel

Helmut Kohl, minister-president of Rhineland-Palatinate, polled only 174. Since Barzel had insisted that the positions of party chairman and candidate for chancellor be filled by one and the same man, his election was tantamount to saying that he would lead the party in 1973. Adroit and ambitious, his main disadvantage was probably a lack of public appeal, due perhaps to a too evident smoothness of manner, particularly on television.

Born on June 20, 1924, at Braunsberg in East Prussia, Barzel was brought up in Berlin. During World War II he served with the German naval air arm and, after the war, studied law at the University of Cologne. His first political experience was as a supporter, though not a member, of a newly formed Catholic Centre Party, which had a list toward the left, but later, during the cold war, he became the joint founder of a body called "Save Freedom," which organized a pale version of U.S. Sen. Joseph McCarthy's witch-hunt for Communists. In 1949 he was appointed an official with the

state government of North Rhine-Westphalia and rapidly became a prominent member of the CDU. He was elected to the Bundestag in 1957 and became floor leader of the joint CDU-CSU parliamentary group in 1963.

Barzel led the parliamentary group, particularly through the period of its "grand coalition" with the Social Democrats (1966–69), with great skill. He claimed that his political position was middle-of-the-road, but he depended for support on the Christian Social Union and consequently was subject to the influence of its chairman, Franz Josef Strauss. Barzel was a strong critic of the Brandt government's Ostpolitik. (N. Cr.)

BELLOW, SAUL

When Saul Bellow won the National Book Award in 1971 for *Mr. Sammler's Planet,* he became the first novelist to receive the prize three times, having taken it for *The Adventures of Augie March* in 1954 and *Herzog* ten years later.

His latest best seller was unanimously chosen by the NBA judges for its superb characterization of an aging intellectual Everyman, a half-blind Jewish refugee lurking out his life in the microcosm of Manhattan. The award panel said it comprised "a strain of speculation, both daring and serene, on the future of life." Bellow himself believed it was the least contrived of his works. "Here I'm baring myself naked," he said.

Such exposure might seem de rigueur in an era of chic self-popularizers, but Bellow had never been of their number. Rather, he was the most private of writers. He scoffed at "those long isolated writers who yearn to become part of the cultural furniture . . . like King Kong." The novelist, he believed, has a more crucial and less commercial raison d'être: to be the spokesman through which "the community comes to know its heart."

Consonant with this view, Bellow had reduced more than one student group to sullen or chagrined silence by criticizing such vogues as women's liberation and political militance. "A radical stance is the ultimate luxury for those who already have everything else," he told a group at Yale, where he was once a visiting professor. His permanent academic affiliation was with the University of Chicago, where he served on the august Committee on Social Thought.

Born in Lachine, Que., July 10, 1915, he was nine when his family moved to Chicago, where he lived most of his life. He studied anthropology and sociology, earned a bachelor's degree at Northwestern University in 1937, and had begun graduate work at the University of Wisconsin when he turned to writing fiction. Before publishing his first novel, *Dangling Man*, in 1944, he worked on the WPA Writers' Project, served in the wartime merchant marine, and helped edit the *Encyclopædia Britannica*'s series of Great Books. His other major works include *The Victim* (1947), *Seize the Day* (1956), and *Henderson the Rain King* (1959). A play, *The Last Analysis* (1964), was not a notable success. (Ph. K.)

BENTON, WILLIAM

During 1971 publisher William Benton was honoured by his Yale class and by the Connecticut Bar Association for his distinguished record of public service. At their 50th reunion, his classmates presented him with a silver cup as "the most distinguished member of the class." On October 19, he received the Connecticut Bar Association's Distinguished Public Service Award at a banquet in New Haven. Benton served as U.S. senator from Connecticut from 1949 to 1952. As a "founding father" of UNESCO, he went to Paris in November as a member of the U.S. delegation to ceremonies marking the 25th anniversary of the founding of the organization.

The William Benton Foundation, of which he was president and chairman, continued during 1971 to give major support to innovative research and experimentation in the field of mass communications. A substantial grant was made to the Broadcasting Foundation of America to obtain significant foreign programs and make them available to U.S. radio stations. Other grants went to the National Citizens Committee for Broadcasting and to Connecticut Public Television to stimulate programs in the pub-

lic interest. In addition, the foundation provided support for the Aspen Institute for Humanistic Studies to examine the public aspects of the mass media and for the Open University in England to help develop alternative methods for higher education through the use of radio, television, and home study.

Born in Minneapolis, Minn., April 1, 1900, Benton was graduated from Yale in 1921. He and Chester Bowles founded the advertising agency of Benton and Bowles in 1929. Benton became vice-president of the University of Chicago in 1937. In 1943, in partnership with the university, Benton became owner and publisher of *Encyclopædia Britannica* and chairman of its board. He was named U.S. assistant secretary of state by Pres. Harry S. Truman in 1945 and served until 1947. During that time he was instrumental in developing the first U.S. peacetime international information and educational exchange. Appointed to the U.S. Senate as a Democrat in 1949 and elected for a two-year term in 1950, Benton was a victim of the Eisenhower sweep in 1952. Benton traveled widely and wrote extensively. He is the subject of a biography, *The Lives of William Benton*, by Sidney Hyman, published in 1970 by the University of Chicago Press. (Mx. H.)

BERRIGAN, DANIEL J. and PHILIP FRANCIS

Daniel and Philip Berrigan, brothers, both Roman Catholic priests, spent 1971 in U.S. federal prisons, serving sentences imposed for their part in the burning of draft board records at Catonsville, Md., in May 1968. To some they symbolized the leading edge of a movement that might, at long last, make the church meaningful to modern society. For others, they had sold the church's birthright for a mess of relevancy.

Both men had come to the antiwar movement through civil rights activism. Daniel was born May 9, 1921, in Virginia, Minn.; Philip on Oct. 5, 1923, at Two Harbors, Minn.; and the two boys grew up in Syracuse, N.Y., where their father, a militant socialist and union business agent, had moved during the Depression. Dedicated to priestly service from his youth, Daniel was admitted to the Society of Jesus and, after his ordination in 1952, served one year in a small town near Lyons, France, where he encountered the worker-priest movement. Later he became a teacher and gained a considerable following as a writer—especially of poetry—and as a leader of social causes. As the focus of ethical concern shifted from civil rights to peace, he became preoccupied with antiwar work, traveling to Hanoi to try to arrange the release of prisoners.

Meanwhile, Philip, having served in Europe during World War II, was ordained and entered the Society of St. Joseph, an order dedicated to the urban poor. He worked with such groups as CORE and SNCC and in 1967, having become primarily concerned about the war, entered a Baltimore draft board with three associates and poured blood on the files.

Both Berrigans were members of the Catonsville Nine, who burned the records of a suburban Baltimore draft board with home-made napalm and then waited for police to arrest them. Sentenced to three years in prison for destruction of government property, Daniel went underground, surfacing now and then—to the embarrassment of the FBI—to appear at a peace rally or give an interview. It was four months before FBI agents posing as bird watchers

captured him on Block Island, R.I., and sent him to join his brother in Danbury penitentiary. His play, *The Trial of the Catonsville Nine*, opened Feb. 7, 1971, in a New York church. A book, *The Dark Night of Resistance*, won the Thomas More Medal.

In January 1971 Philip and five others—two priests, a former priest, a nun, and a college professor—were indicted for conspiracy to kidnap presidential aide Henry Kissinger and to blow up heating systems in federal buildings. (Daniel was first named as a co-conspirator, but he was omitted from later indictments.) The crux of the matter involved correspondence which an FBI informer smuggled between Philip Berrigan and Sister Elizabeth McAlister. In it they discussed a symbolic kidnapping of Kissinger—in which he would be given moral lectures but not harmed—but bits of the letters published in national magazines seemed to suggest idle speculation rather than a serious plot. In August Philip Berrigan and some other prisoners began a hunger strike, and shortly thereafter Philip was temporarily moved from Danbury to Springfield, Mo. (Ph. K.)

BIESHEUVEL, BAREND WILLEM

On July 6, 1971, Barend Biesheuvel became the 35th prime minister of the Netherlands. The appointment symbolized the personal success of the leader of the Antirevolutionary Party (ARP) and also the peculiarities of the Dutch party system. The three main confessional parties—Catholic People's Party, Christian Historical Union, and the ARP—had declared prior to the general election on April 28 that they would cooperate in the new legislature, either as governmental parties or as oppositional parties. In the elections, however, the three parties suffered a considerable loss of votes, but the ARP's relative position in the combination was strengthened. In spite of the setback, the three confessional parties remained the strongest coalition in the second chamber and, supported by two other parties, formed the new government.

Biesheuvel's public career started just after World War II. After being appointed secretary to the food supplies directorate in the province of Noord-Holland in 1945, he became secretary-general of the Christian League of Farmers and Horticulturalists (an effective pressure group in agricultural affairs) in 1952. In 1959 he was appointed chairman of this body, becoming an expert on national and international agrarian affairs. From 1961 to 1963 he was chairman of the International Federation of Agricultural Producers, and a member of the European Parliament at Strasbourg. After becoming minister of agrarian affairs and vice-prime minister in 1963, Biesheuvel participated actively in the meetings of the European Economic Community.

After the ARP's successes in the 1967 general election, Biesheuvel was asked by Queen Juliana to form a government, but on that occasion he did not succeed.

Born in Haarlemmerliede on April 5, 1920, Biesheuvel was proud of his farming background (he was the fourth son of a farmer). He was educated at schools in Haarlem, studied law at the Free University of Amsterdam, and graduated in 1945. (D. Bo.)

BLANDA, GEORGE

In professional sports the race usually is to the young. But in 1971 George Blanda of the Oakland Raiders, a backup quarterback and kicking specialist, brought joy to middle-aged egos everywhere. At the age of

44 and in his 22nd season as a pro football player, Blanda was still on the field and lengthening an impressive string of records and accomplishments.

On October 31 in a game against Kansas City Blanda scored 8 points, kicking two field goals and two extra points. This increased his career total to 1,609 points, breaking the previous record held by Lou Groza. It also reinforced Blanda's stature as a most unusual athlete, who, in 1970 at the age of 43, won such honours as male athlete of the year, outstanding pro football player of the year, and player of the year in the National Football League's American Football Conference.

Blanda insisted that his remarkable longevity was essentially the result of his competitive desire, which he traced to his boyhood in Youngwood, Pa., a coal-mining town. Born on Sept. 19, 1927, he is from a family of 11 children and the 4th of 7 sons. Says Blanda: "Those six brothers of mine kept the pressure on [me] all through childhood and helped to make me as competitive as I am today."

In high school Blanda was all-county in basketball, football, and track. He concentrated on football at the University of Kentucky, winning considerable recognition. Blanda began his professional career in 1949 when he signed for a $6,600 a year salary with the Chicago Bears of the National Football League (NFL). With the Bears, he did not reach stardom, serving mostly as a reserve quarterback and kicker. In the latter capacity he kicked 156 consecutive extra points.

Blanda's retirement from the Bears after the 1958 season did not cause much of a stir. He stayed out of football the next season but returned in 1960, joining the Houston Oilers of the newly formed American Football League. He set scoring records at Houston and was later traded to Oakland. There, in 1970, he had his most outstanding season, accounting for five successive last-quarter victories with his field-goal kicking and passing, and leading the Raiders to the championship of the Western Division in the American Football Conference.

(Je. Ho.)

BLUE, VIDA

When Pres. Richard Nixon, an enthusiastic sports fan, gave a White House reception for the Oakland baseball team in mid-August, he told star pitcher Vida Blue: "I'll give you a challenge. Every year until you reach 30, you've got to win as many games as your age."

Southpaw Blue was equal to this challenge in 1971, his first full year in the major leagues. At the age of 22, he won 24 games, two more than the presidential mandate, and led the Oakland Athletics to the championship in the Western Division of the American League. For this performance he won the Cy Young award, given annually to the best pitcher in each major league, and was named the American League's most valuable player.

That Blue became a star was not altogether a surprise. An all-around athlete as a schoolboy, he attracted both football and baseball scouts while attending DeSoto High School in Mansfield, La. During his senior year he led the football team by throwing 35 touchdown passes. He was equally outstanding in baseball and once struck out 21 batters in a seven-inning game.

Born June 28, 1949, in Mansfield, Blue signed with Oakland for an estimated $30,-000 bonus after finishing high school. In his first year as a professional, in 1968, he led the Midwest League in strikeouts with

WIDE WORLD

Vida Blue

BOB FITCH—BLACK STAR

Daniel J. Berrigan

BOB FITCH—BLACK STAR

Philip Berrigan

George Blanda

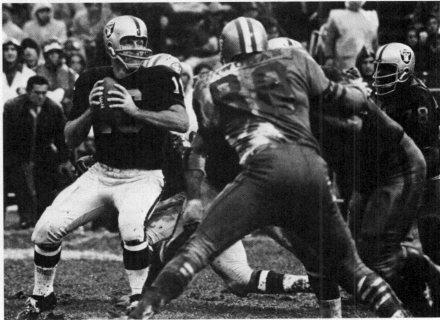

WIDE WORLD

Leonid Ilyich Brezhnev

Jorge Luis Borges

231 while pitching only 152 innings. He advanced through Oakland's farm system and in his second major league appearance, on Sept. 11, 1970, pitched a one-hitter. Ten nights later he pitched a no-hitter against the powerful Minnesota Twins.

Blue proved in 1971 that he had not been a mere late-season flash. After losing the season's opening game in Washington, D.C., he reeled off ten successive victories. Then after losing one game, he won six more in a row and on June 25 had a 16–2 record, a remarkable achievement considering the season still had not reached the halfway point. Most experts predicted he would finish with 30 victories, but he was unable to maintain the pace and won only three games in July, four in August, and one in September.

(JE. HO.)

BOK, DEREK C.

Though his intellectual and personal credentials were immaculate, the installation of Derek C. Bok as the 25th president of Harvard University on Oct. 11, 1971, represented something of a heresy for more than one old grad: Bok was the first president in two centuries not to have attended Harvard as an undergraduate. He was, however, a magna cum laude graduate of Harvard Law School and, as its dean since 1968, was known as a popular teacher and liberal administrator. Confronted with demonstrating law students, he had initiated an optional pass/fail marking system; he had mobilized Harvard's distinguished law alumni to challenge U.S. Pres. Richard M. Nixon's nomination of G. Harrold Carswell to the U.S. Supreme Court; and, when student disorders disrupted Harvard, he opposed Pres. Nathan M. Pusey's invitation to police to summarily restore order.

A pragmatic liberal, Bok was committed to innovative solutions to university problems; he instituted basic curriculum changes and considered untraditional approaches to the position of the independent university in an increasingly fettered society.

Bok was born March 22, 1930, scion of an old Main Line Philadelphia family. His father was a justice on the Pennsylvania Supreme Court, his grandfather a Pulitzer prizewinning biographer and editor of the *Ladies' Home Journal,* his great grandfather the founder of the Curtis Publishing Com-

pany. After his parents were divorced he moved with his mother to California. He earned a bachelor's degree at Stanford University in 1951 and was elected to Phi Beta Kappa. After considering a career in the Foreign Service, he chose Harvard Law School, graduating in 1954. While on a Fulbright grant at the Sorbonne he met Sissela Ann Myrdal, daughter of Swedish economist Gunnar Myrdal. They were married by Pierre Mendès-France, a former French premier.

In 1958 a law school professor, Kingman Brewster, Jr., persuaded Bok to join the Harvard Law School faculty. Bok became an expert in collective bargaining; he later taught at the John F. Kennedy School of Government and served on Pres. Lyndon Johnson's Committee on Labor Management. When he was invited to consider the university presidency he again consulted Brewster, now president of Yale.   (PH. K.)

BORDABERRY AROCENA, JUAN MARIA

Juan Bordaberry Arocena was elected president of Uruguay in national voting that took place on Nov. 28, 1971, though the outcome of the close race was not known for more than a week. The 43-year-old Colorado Party candidate received only 10,000 votes more than Sen. Wilson Ferreira Aldunate of the Blanco Party, who demanded a recount. The new president's inauguration for a five-year term, succeeding Jorge Pacheco Areco, was scheduled for March 1972.

In the election, 1.6 million Uruguayan voters not only continued the rule of the Colorado Party of the liberal and democratic left but decisively repudiated a candidate representing a coalition of Marxists and members of the far left. Gen. Liber Seregni, running as the Frente Amplio (Broad Front) candidate, failed even to carry the capital city of Montevideo, supposedly his stronghold. Seregni also had the backing of the Tupamaro urban guerrilla organization, which had ceased all terrorist activities for three months to give their candidate a better chance.

Bordaberry's victory signified to most political observers that Uruguay's people preferred a continuation of democratic life, as well as indicating support for President Pacheco's hard-line policies against the militant left. Bordaberry was Pacheco's desig-

nated alternate in Uruguay's complex electoral system, whereby the top vote-getter in each party gets all the votes of his party. Pacheco failed to win a constitutional amendment that would have permitted him to succeed himself, so all his votes went to Bordaberry and Bordaberry in turn got all the Colorado votes.

Bordaberry was born June 17, 1928, in Montevideo. He left law school on his father's death to take over management of the family ranch—one of the largest in Uruguay. He began his political life as a Blanco Party member and won a Senate seat in 1962, but in 1965 he broke with the Blanco leadership, which supported the collegiate system of government then used in Uruguay. He led the Rural League, a powerful pressure group representing Uruguayan agricultural interests, in support of the 1966 referendum that switched the nation to a one-man presidency. Pacheco named him minister of agriculture and livestock on Oct. 3, 1969.   (J. A. O'L.)

BORGES, JORGE LUIS

Jorge Luis Borges, born in Argentina in 1899 but a citizen of the world, was considered by many critics in 1971 to be the greatest living Latin-American author and one of the foremost living writers in any language. Unlike the majority of writers to whom Spanish is the mother tongue, Borges was unbelievably facile in English. He also had the virtue of translating well into other languages, so that his influence and fame were not limited to Hispanic readers.

Blind since 1955, Borges was director of Argentina's national library and taught English at the University of Buenos Aires when he was not traveling, lecturing, or continuing his own prodigious output. His milieu was the short story and poetry, and the subjects that preoccupied him were the vagaries of time and the attributes of courage, of mythological beasts, and metaphysics. Although he was an old-fashioned and conservative man who abhorred the crowd-pleasing dictator Juan Perón, Borges had the facility of appealing to the young and rebellious. He became a celebrated figure in Harvard Yard when he was Charles Eliot Norton professor of poetry in 1967–68. In 1961 he shared the International Publishers Prize with Samuel Beckett.

The young Borges was educated in Geneva, Switz., because his father was an anarchist who objected to the government having a hand in his schooling. Borges' father had written a novel, while his mother was a translator of Herbert Read, Hawthorne, Melville, Faulkner, and Virginia Woolf. Both parents encouraged him in the pursuit of a purely literary life, and it was not until the '30s that he became a librarian in Argentina to earn his living. Borges lost that job when Perón seized power. He was made librarian for the national library after the dictator was overthrown.

Some of his better-known writings include *The Aleph and Other Stories, Ficciones, Labyrinths, Dreamtigers, A Personal Anthology,* and *The Book of Imaginary Beings.* His own autobiography, written in English, demonstrates his bilinguality. Borges long had been considered a possible candidate for the Nobel Prize for Literature. When the 1971 prize went to Chilean poet Pablo Neruda, Borges commented: "In spite of our political differences, I think the Academy has been very wise." (J. A. O'L.)

BRATTELI, TRYGVE

After the resignation of Norway's nonsocialist coalition government on March 2, 1971, Trygve Bratteli, 61-year-old chairman of the Norwegian Labour Party, was entrusted with the task of forming a new government on March 10. While it was the largest single party in the Storting (parliament), Labour was still in a minority, with only 74 of the total of 150 seats. But even though it could not command a clear majority, Bratteli's government in its first few months put forward a number of relatively controversial and unpopular proposals, including recognition of North Vietnam and a sharp increase in state expenditure. The Bratteli administration clearly worked on the principle that it could count on votes for particular measures from various segments of the nonsocialist parties.

Bratteli had taken over the leadership of the Labour Party from Einar Gerhardsen, who served as premier of a Labour government almost continuously from 1945 to 1965. For almost ten years Bratteli was minister of finance, and from 1960 to 1964 he was minister of communications. Elected a member of the Storting in 1950, he had been vice-chairman of the Labour Party from 1945 until 1965.

Born Jan. 11, 1910, Bratteli was a builder by trade. However, after holding various positions in the Labour youth organizations in his home county of Vestfold in southern Norway, in 1934 he became editor of the Labour newspaper in Kirkenes, in the far north, and later editor of the Labour youth magazine and secretary of the nationwide youth organization. He held these posts until 1940 when Norway was invaded by Germany. Bratteli was an active member of the resistance movement until his arrest in 1942. He spent the rest of World War II in various German prisons. (O. F. K.)

BREZHNEV, LEONID ILYICH

In 1971 Leonid I. Brezhnev was seen to be (in the Orwellian phrase) "more equal" than his colleagues in the Soviet collective leadership. He also revealed (during a six-day visit to France) an almost Khrushchevian ability to quip, and confided that he was a heavy smoker, had an insomnia problem, and felt most relaxed behind the wheel of a car.

Reelected general secretary of the Communist Party of the Soviet Union (CPSU) on April 9, Brezhnev immediately stepped into the lead of the Soviet diplomatic peace offensive. In April he addressed the tenth congress of the Bulgarian Communist Party in Sofia; in May, the 14th congress of the Communist Party of Czechoslovakia in Prague; and in June, the eighth congress of the Socialist Unity (Communist) Party of Germany in East Berlin. On all these occasions he spoke of the urgency of strengthening European security.

On August 2, at Oreanda in the Crimea, he conferred with the leaders of the member countries (Romania excepted) of Comecon. From September 22 to 25 he was in Yugoslavia as unofficial guest of President Tito and used the opportunity to deny the existence of any "Brezhnev Doctrine" (despite the Soviet-Czechoslovak treaty of 1970). Brezhnev's direct contacts with statesmen of Western Europe began on September 16 when Willy Brandt, chancellor of West Germany, arrived at Oreanda for a three-day visit. The crowning event of his peace offensive was his official visit to France (October 25-30), although its outcome was merely a "common declaration" on mutual cooperation rather than the treaty of friendship that the Soviets had wanted.

Brezhnev was born on Dec. 19, 1906, at Kamenskoye (now Dneprodzerzhinsk) in the Ukraine. He joined the Communist Party in 1931, and rose through its ranks, becoming first secretary of the Kazakh Communist Party in 1954. On May 7, 1960, he was elected chairman of the Presidium of the Supreme Soviet (titular chief of state), a position in which he was succeeded by A. I. Mikoyan on July 15, 1964. Shortly afterward he took part in the conspiracy that prepared N. S. Khrushchev's downfall, and on October 14 of that year he became first secretary of the CPSU (the title being changed to general secretary on April 8, 1966). (K. Sм.)

BUTZ, EARL L.

"An educator keenly attuned to politics," as the *New York Times* called him, Earl L. Butz was confirmed as U.S. secretary of agriculture by a Senate vote of 51–44 on Dec. 2, 1971. The vote was unusually close for confirmation of a Cabinet appointee, and the preceding debate had been heated. Some senators from farm states had objected to Butz's close ties with big agriculture—"agribusiness" as it was called. The practice whereby giant companies controlled vast farms meant greater efficiency, but critics had charged for decades that agribusiness was forcing independent farmers to leave the land, rendering obsolete the "family farm" that has been a socioeconomic mainstay of America since colonial times.

Born on a farm near Albion, Ind., on July 3, 1909, Butz graduated from Purdue University in 1932 and earned a doctorate there in 1937. He stayed on to teach agricultural economics, and in time became head of the department. In 1954 he joined Pres. Dwight D. Eisenhower's administration as assistant secretary of agriculture for marketing and foreign agriculture. In that position he spent three years serving under Ezra Taft Benson, probably the most unpopular secretary of agriculture since the 1930s.

After leaving Washington, Butz returned to Purdue as dean of agriculture. In 1968 he became dean of continuing education, the post he held when Pres. Richard Nixon announced his nomination. He was also a director of the Ralston Purina Co., the General Motors of the grain industry. His predecessor as agriculture secretary, Clifford M. Hardin, quit the job to become Ralston's vice-chairman.

A political conservative, Butz once ran unsuccessfully for governor of Indiana. He never had been a strong supporter of large commodity programs, but he did agree with farmers that "the price of corn is too low." It was low farm prices, combined with rising farm costs, that had prompted the Cabinet change. At the same time, Nixon announced he had abandoned his plan to abolish the Agriculture Department. Noting the discontent among farmers, many observers had felt that Nixon might face a farmers' revolt in 1972, similar to the one that helped defeat Thomas Dewey in 1948. (PH. K.)

CALLEY, WILLIAM L.

U.S. Army Lieut. William L. Calley, Jr., became a celebrity in 1971, but whether as martyred hero or war criminal was unclear. His apotheosis began when a military jury of army combat veterans convicted him of the premeditated murder of 22 civilians at My Lai, South Vietnam, in 1968.

Until months of gruesome court-martial testimony proved that some 122 old men, women, and children had been massacred by U.S. troops at My Lai, many Americans believed that GIs were simply incapable of atrocity. After the verdict, a few clung to that belief—or sloughed off the incident as an inevitable by-product of war—but far more defended Calley on the ground that he was a scapegoat. If he was culpable, then his superiors—including the commander in chief—shared his guilt. The more learned invoked the post-World War II Nürnberg trials, where the U.S. had insisted that guilt for war crimes reaches to the highest levels.

A massive public outcry followed Calley's sentencing to life imprisonment. Letters and phone calls deluged the White House and the Capitol. One Southern sheriff declared he would stop arresting AWOL servicemen. Several veterans surrendered themselves to random police, claiming they were guilty of equal crimes in combat. A heroic ballad sold 200,000 copies in a fortnight. Nor were all Calley's sympathizers conservatives, military personnel, or apologists for the Johnson and Nixon administrations. Many antiwar leaders argued the scapegoat theory. The index of this war's immorality, they said, was that ordinary men like Calley were forced to commit such crimes.

In the face of this furor, Pres. Richard Nixon took an extraordinary step. He ordered the convict returned from the Ft. Benning stockade to his bachelor apartment and held under house arrest until all his appeals were exhausted. Then, the president said, he would personally review the case. In an open reply, Capt. Aubrey M. Daniel III, the brilliant young prosecutor at the court-martial, accused the president of undermining public confidence in American justice in general and military courts in particular for the sake of political expediency. Subsequently, Calley's sentence was reduced to 20 years' imprisonment, and further appeals were pending.

One of the little men of history, Calley was a symbol, an "unlikely villain"—a somewhat pathetic, dull, insecure young man who had failed in civilian life and might not have risen so high in the Army but for the shortage of willing soldiers during the Vietnam years. Born in 1943, he had joined the Army in 1966. He admitted shooting some of My Lai's dead, but claimed he had been ordered by Capt. Ernest Medina to annihilate everyone his platoon encountered there. (Medina denied such an order. He was acquitted in a later court-martial and subsequently resigned his commission.)

(Ph. K.)

CHOU EN-LAI

The end of China's cataclysmic Cultural Revolution was also the beginning of a new era for the country. During 1971 the most dramatic aspect of the change manifested itself—a return to active diplomacy based on a foreign policy of pragmatism. As the bamboo curtain opened to admit first U.S. table-tennis players and then journalists, as a historic invitation was issued to U.S. Pres. Richard M. Nixon, and as the People's Republic took over China's UN seat, world attention turned to the man who was widely credited as the architect of the new policy, Premier Chou En-lai.

Chou was identified as leader of a moderate group that had gained ascendancy over the extreme left-wing group associated with the Cultural Revolution. During that upheaval Chou apparently was unaffected. During the "Peking mystery" that developed after cancellation of traditional ceremonials connected with China's National Day on October 1, he again was conspicuous as the only top leader to be seen publicly. The popular description of Chou as China's "man for all seasons" gained even wider currency.

Also known as Chou Shao-shan and Chou Wu-hao, Chou was born of a literary family in 1898 in Shaohsing. After a traditional education in the Chinese classics he went to Japan for higher studies. Returning to China, he began participating in student activities and was jailed for six months for his part in an anti-Japanese student demonstration in 1919. He then went to France, where he became one of the founders of the European Headquarters, Chinese Communist Party. He returned to China in 1924 and three years later was elected a member of the Communist Party Politburo. He accompanied Mao Tse-tung on the Long March to northwest China in 1934–35 to escape the Nationalists and later represented the Communist Party in negotiations with the Nationalists.

During World War II Chou was the principal Communist Party liaison officer in Chungking. When the Communists formed the central people's government in 1949, he became premier and minister for foreign affairs. It seemed likely that his past achievements might be dwarfed by the diplomatic successes of 1971.

(T. J. S. G.)

CLEMENTE, ROBERTO

Knowledgeable baseball fans long had known that Roberto Clemente of the Pittsburgh Pirates was the complete baseball player. Yet it was not until the 1971 World Series, when Clemente led the Pirates to victory over Baltimore, that he gained full acceptance as a genuine superstar, deservedly ranking with such contemporaries as Willie Mays and Hank Aaron.

That Mays and Aaron previously had overshadowed Clemente was principally because they hit more home runs. Clemente had the highest lifetime batting average of the three (.318), was as outstanding as Mays on defense, and without question had the strongest and most accurate arm. Many experts regarded Clemente as the best defensive right fielder in baseball history. In the 1971 World Series, Clemente was the dominant player. He led all Series hitters

with a .414 average; 5 of his 12 hits were for extra bases, including 2 home runs.

Born Aug. 18, 1934, in Carolina, Puerto Rico, Clemente played all sports in high school and was outstanding in both baseball and track and field. He won local championships in the javelin, the high jump, and the hop, step, and jump, and most likely would have qualified for the U.S. Olympic track team if he had not signed a baseball contract with the Brooklyn Dodgers.

The Dodgers, at the time surfeited with talent, had Clemente for only one year, 1954, when he hit .257 with their Montreal farm club in the International League. Instead of promoting him to Brooklyn, the Dodgers kept him on the Montreal roster, confident that he would not be chosen in the winter draft. But the Pirates acquired him for the then $4,000 draft price, one of the best bargains in recent baseball history.

Clemente immediately earned a place in Pittsburgh's starting lineup and in his second major league season batted .311. He hit over .300 in 12 of his 17 major league seasons and four times won the National League batting championship. Not a power hitter, Clemente averaged only 13 home runs a season. However, he maintained an exceptionally high ratio of extra-base hits to singles and led all active players in triples with 159.

(Je. Ho.)

COLOMBO, JOSEPH ANTHONY, SR.

Joseph A. Colombo, Sr., nearly robbed the vocabulary of "Mafia" and "Cosa Nostra" in 1971 because (he said) the words described a fiction defamatory to all Italian-Americans. But he was shot in the brain and permanently disabled in July because (police officials said) he chaired one of New York's five Mafia or Cosa Nostra branches and another mobster coveted his empire.

Colombo organized the Italian-American Civil Rights League in 1970, ostensibly to convince the FBI, policemen, and citizens everywhere to stop identifying organized crime with patriotic Americans of Italian extraction. The League's accomplishments were impressive: It gathered 100,000 people at Columbus Circle rallies. It packed Madison Square Garden for a benefit starring Frank Sinatra that raised $500,000. It persuaded Alka-Seltzer to shelve a prizewinning television commercial that featured the line "Mamma mia, that's a spicy meatball." It talked Paramount Pictures into excising the offensive nouns from its forthcoming film *The Godfather*. After it picketed FBI offices in New York, Attorney General John Mitchell ordered federal press officers to use a new terminology when discussing organized crime.

But the League's influence could not eradicate Colombo's earlier criminal record of 13 arrests and three convictions, or his current conviction for perjury and indictments for income tax evasion, grand larceny, and conspiracy to commit extortion in connection with a $750,000 jewel robbery.

Colombo was shot at the League's second annual rally by Jerome Johnson, who police theorized was hired by rival Mafia chieftain Joseph Gallo. Ironically, Gallo was trying to expand his influence within the syndicate by recruiting non-Italian personnel. Johnson was gunned down immediately after shooting Colombo. As for the League, it was barred from New York's official Columbus Day Parade.

Colombo was the son of a mobster who was garrotted with a girl friend in the '30s. He reportedly gained power in the organization in return for a double cross

during the chaos that followed Albert Anastasia's murder. Elevated to head a "family" in 1963, he was the youngest Mafia chief in the U.S., albeit not a widely respected one.

(Ph. K.)

CONNALLY, JOHN BOWDEN, JR.

When Pres. Richard M. Nixon decided that strong measures would be necessary to cure the ailing U.S. economy, he also decided that mild-mannered, soft-spoken David Kennedy would have to be replaced as secretary of the treasury by a politically astute, tough salesman. To the surprise of many, including some recently defeated Republican governors, Nixon chose Democrat John Connally, secretary of the navy in John Kennedy's administration and a political protégé of former Pres. Lyndon Johnson.

Sworn in on Feb. 11, 1971, Connally took over the Treasury Department in a time of unemployment, inflation, and a floundering balance of payments. In keeping with the flamboyant style he had developed as a three-term governor of Texas, he quickly turned the dollar crisis into a major offensive. He bluntly told congressional leaders and top industrialists that "The simple fact is . . . others are outproducing us, outthinking us, outworking us, and outtrading us." Just as tough with foreign officials, on May 28 he told bankers from 20 nations meeting in Munich, W.Ger.: "No longer can considerations of friendship or need or capacity justify the U.S. carrying so heavy a share of the common burdens." Even after the international monetary agreement in December had ended the immediate crisis, Connally cautioned that this by itself would not cure the U.S. balance of payments deficit.

Connally's stature within the administration became apparent when Nixon put him in charge of the (narrowly successful) fight to get congressional approval of the controversial $250 million loan guarantee designed to save the Lockheed Corporation from bankruptcy. And it was Connally who explained the wage-price freeze and other sweeping economic policies in nationally televised news conferences. All this sparked speculation that Connally would replace Vice-Pres. Spiro Agnew on the 1972 Republican presidential ticket. Connally would not comment, though his wife, Idanell, told reporters such talk was "nonsense."

Connally was born in Floresville, Tex., on Feb. 27, 1917, and received his law degree from the University of Texas. He managed Lyndon Johnson's successful 1948 campaign for the Senate, and in 1949 went to Washington as Johnson's administrative assistant. Appointed secretary of the navy in 1961, he served as governor of Texas from 1962 to 1968. He was riding with President Kennedy in the motorcade in Dallas, Tex., on Nov. 22, 1963, when the president was assassinated, and was himself critically wounded.

(J. F. Ba.)

COX, MR. and MRS. EDWARD FINCH

Patricia Nixon and Edward Cox were married on June 12, 1971. She was the 8th presidential daughter to be married at the White House and the first to exchange vows in its Rose Garden. He was clearly the most liberal member of Pres. Richard Nixon's family.

The wedding was dampened by rain that delayed it 30 minutes, and attended by dignitaries including FBI Director J. Edgar Hoover, Attorney General John Mitchell, Supreme Court Chief Justice Warren Bur-

John B. Connally, Jr.

Joseph Colombo, Sr.

Walter Cronkite

ger, and consumer advocate Ralph Nader, who as Cox's friend and former boss sat on the groom's side of the aisle. The couple honeymooned at Camp David, the presidential retreat in Maryland. In the fall they took up residence in Cambridge, Mass., while Cox completed his senior year at Harvard Law School.

Patricia Nixon was born in Whittier, Calif., on Feb. 21, 1946, nine days after her father announced his first candidacy for a congressional seat. A diminutive ash blonde given to size three party dresses of pastel hues, she was never a favourite among the press corps, who dubbed her "Little Bo Peep." Her inclination for privacy was so strong that her younger sister, Mrs. David Eisenhower, called her "the Howard Hughes of the White House." Tricia also was considered by many the most politically conservative Nixon. She had praised segregationist Lester Maddox for refusing to serve Negroes in his restaurant and Vice-Pres. Spiro T. Agnew for his attacks on the press.

Cox, who was born on Oct. 2, 1946, in Southampton, N.Y., was a descendant of Robert R. Livingston, a signer of the Declaration of Independence who administered the presidential oath to George Washington and served as envoy to Napoleon. His mother was chairman of the International Debutante Ball at which Tricia was presented to society in 1964; Cox was Tricia's escort.

He graduated from Princeton University in 1968, and studied architecture at Yale for a year before entering Harvard Law School. He spent the summer of 1968 as one of Nader's Raiders, investigating the Federal Trade Commission and writing a scathing report on its practices. The following summer he wrote articles on cigarette advertising, pesticides, and the United Mine Workers union for the liberal weekly *The New Republic.* A friend called him "a left leaner from the right side of the tracks."

(PH. K.)

CRONKITE, WALTER

CBS News's preeminent chronicler of national and world events, Walter Cronkite won the George Polk Freedom of the Press Award in 1971 and was named Broadcaster of the Year by the International Radio and Television Society. Perhaps more significant than these fraternal plaudits was the observation in a *Life* cover story that a na-

Chou En-lai

tional election, state funeral, or moon shot without Cronkite would be as unbelievable to millions of Americans as "a World Series without an umpire."

Longevity on the protean screen of nightly network newsdom is certainly one factor of his prestige. Another is the hallmark of his telecasting since the national conventions of 1952: nearly constant total objectivity. Cronkite rarely expresses an opinion or a bias. (In one memorable exception he read a massive governmental hyperbole of self-serving public information policy prompted by the embarrassment of the Pentagon papers. His opinion, an incredulous "Oh.")

His habitual noninvolvement lent extra weight to his words when, in a May 1971 speech, he castigated the Nixon administration for "a grand conspiracy to destroy the credibility of the press." The Polk Award was bestowed in February for his dedication to that credibility; he was cited specifically for "resisting a reported attempt by the White House to discredit" the network. And he reportedly was determined to be jailed rather than submit to censorship or journalistic review by Justice Department witch-hunters.

Cronkite was born in St. Joseph, Mo., Nov. 4, 1916. He studied at the University of Texas in Austin while covering the state legislature as a stringer for the *Houston*

(Tex.) *Post.* After two years of college, he went to work full-time for the *Houston Press,* then moved to a Kansas City, Mo., radio station, and then to United Press. At the outbreak of World War II, he was one of the first correspondents accredited to cover Allied operations. After the war he covered the Nürnberg trials, and then went to Moscow as United Press bureau manager. In 1950 he joined the Washington, D.C., news staff of CBS-TV. "The elder statesman of television news" has also won the Peabody Award, the William Allen White journalism prize, and several honorary degrees. (PH. K.)

CRUZ UCLÉS, RAMÓN ERNESTO

A lawyer, diplomat, and teacher, Ramón Cruz was elected president of Honduras in March and began his six-year term on June 6. He was the first president of Honduras to serve under the new national unity system, in which the National and Liberal parties shared congressional seats, Cabinet posts, and judicial positions. Cruz defeated Liberal candidate Jorge Bueso Arias for the presidency.

Honduras had been under the military rule of Gen. Osvaldo López Arellano since a revolution overthrew Pres. Ramón Villeda Morales in 1963. The election of Cruz represented a return to constitutional government, although as commander of the armed forces General López remained in a position of ultimate power. López, however, was the instigator of the national unity plan, and it was presumed that he would defend it.

Cruz was born in San Juan de Flores in the department of Francisco Morazán on Jan. 4, 1903. He earned a master's degree in juridical and social science and a law degree from the Central University of Honduras. After a long career as lawyer and magistrate, Cruz became a member of the nation's Supreme Court in 1949. He also served almost continuously either on the faculty or in the administration of the university. From 1946 to 1948 he represented his country in El Salvador.

From 1958 to 1960, Cruz served as Honduran representative before the International Court of Justice at The Hague, Neth., in the border dispute with Nicaragua. He was the National Party candidate for president in the 1963 election that was forestalled when a military coup propelled General López into the presidency.

Cruz characterized his philosophy of government as social democracy as practiced in West Germany. His principal problems were restoration of relations with El Salvador, with which Honduras had recently fought a small but exhausting war, and the issue of the Central American Common Market, from which Honduras in effect had withdrawn.   (J. A. O'L.)

DALEY, RICHARD JOSEPH

Richard J. Daley, considered by many observers to be the last of the big city Democratic bosses, was elected to an unprecedented fifth term as mayor of Chicago on April 6, 1971. He had served 16 consecutive years in office, longer than any man in the city's 134-year history. In the 1971 election he won 70% of the vote, defeating Richard E. Friedman, an independent Democrat running as the Republican nominee.

Despite the victory, there were signs that Daley faced grave problems ahead. Chicago's black population had increased by nearly 300,000 between 1960 and 1970, while the city lost 505,000 white residents. A symptom of the pressures being created was the protracted struggle between the city and the federal courts over delays in the city's selection of public housing sites outside the ghetto.

A more immediate threat concerned the 1972 elections. Led by Daley in his role as Cook County Democratic chairman, the county slate-making committee first endorsed incumbent Edward V. Hanrahan for the politically sensitive office of state's attorney, even though he was under indictment on charges stemming from a 1969 police raid on a Black Panther apartment. When it appeared that Hanrahan might actually be tried, the committee reneged and named a traffic court judge, but Hanrahan, defying the machine, said he would run anyway. Compounding Daley's difficulties were racetrack-stock scandals involving prominent Illinois Democrats and a new party rule that loosened his control over the Illinois delegation to the 1972 national convention. But Daley continued to play the role of kingmaker, and as the year wore on, party leaders and presidential hopefuls began the usual round of courtesy calls at City Hall.

Controversy surrounded publication dur-

Richard J. Daley

ing the year of *Boss: Richard J. Daley of Chicago* by *Chicago Daily News* columnist Mike Royko, a best-selling account of Daley's use of machine politics. In a bizarre episode in September, the mayor's wife, Eleanor "Sis" Daley, reportedly demanded that copies of the book be removed from a Chicago chain food store. The chain complied, according to news accounts, but later backed down.

Born in Chicago's Bridgeport section on May 15, 1902, Daley received a law degree from DePaul University in 1933 and served in the Illinois legislature from 1936 to 1946. He was state director of revenue in 1948–50 and clerk of Cook County for the next five years until election to his first term as mayor of Chicago in 1955.   (T. R. T.)

DAVIS, COLIN

In September 1971 Colin Davis became musical director of the Royal Opera, Covent Garden, a post for which his gifts and experience were well suited. Davis' career as an international conductor really began to take shape when he replaced an ailing Otto Klemperer at a concert performance of *Don Giovanni* at London's Royal Festival Hall in 1959. Since then he had been musical director of the Sadler's Wells Opera Company and chief conductor of the BBC Symphony Orchestra. He also had conducted most of the world's major orchestras, scoring such a success with the Boston Symphony that he was asked to become that orchestra's principal guest conductor, a post he continued to hold. During June 1971 he was acclaimed by the Berlin public when he conducted the Berlin Philharmonic.

Davis was born at Weybridge, Surrey, Eng., on Sept. 25, 1927, and was educated at the Royal College of Music (RCM) in London. He decided, secretly, that he wanted to become a musician when he heard a performance of Beethoven's Eighth Symphony at the age of 14. At first he expected to be a clarinetist and in fact began his career as one after World War II. His conducting began in the late 1940s when he directed the Kalmar Orchestra and the Chelsea Opera Group, formed from RCM students and ex-students.

Disheartening years followed until his luck changed in 1957 when he became assistant conductor of the BBC Scottish Orchestra. He began to get to know the music of Berlioz and gradually built a reputation as the

world's leading interpreter of the French composer. At Sadler's Wells from 1960 he won a growing reputation as an opera conductor while continuing his orchestral development with the London Symphony Orchestra on tours of Europe, Japan, Australia, and the U.S. As conductor of the BBC Symphony Orchestra he was popular with young audiences at the traditional Henry Wood Promenade concerts.

He made many recordings, specializing in the four composers whom he loved most—Mozart, Berlioz, Stravinsky, and Sir Michael Tippett. During 1970 he conducted notable revivals of *Così fan tutte* and *Peter Grimes* at Covent Garden.   (A. G. BL.)

DRYDEN, KEN

Goalie Ken Dryden, a scholar-athlete who believes in education first and sports second, added a new and exciting dimension to the National Hockey League (NHL) in 1971: a college student who stepped off the campus to lead his team to victory in the Stanley Cup play-offs. This done, he joined consumer advocate Ralph Nader, working with other Nader's Raiders in helping organize a clean-water crusade.

A student at Montreal's McGill University Law School, Dryden joined the Montreal Canadiens in the final stages of the 1970–71 season. He appeared in only six of their regular games and then played in every minute of 20 Stanley Cup play-off struggles, winning the Conn Smythe Trophy as the most valuable player in the play-offs and also setting a record of 1,221 minutes played, most ever by a goalie in the play-offs.

Born on Aug. 7, 1947, at Islington, Ont., Dryden played hockey from an early age. He enrolled at Cornell University believing he had sacrificed his hockey career but discovered instead that the 24-game U.S. college season—roughly a third of the Canadian junior league's 70-game marathons—sharpened his concentration and made winning more important. During his college career he led Cornell to a 76–4–1 record and a national championship.

After graduation, Dryden enrolled at McGill and joined the Canadian national team. When the team disbanded, he turned professional and signed as a part-time goalie with the Montreal Canadiens' farm club, the Voyageurs. In December 1970, Dryden agreed to play hockey full-time. He was called up by the Canadiens in March and immediately led them to their upset Stanley Cup victory.

Dryden planned to continue studying for a law degree and hoped to inspire more young Canadian players to mix education with their hockey. In 1971 only about 25% of the players in the NHL, almost all of whom were native Canadians, had high school diplomas. (JE. HO.)

DUVALIER, JEAN-CLAUDE

Twenty-year-old Jean-Claude Duvalier, president-for-life of the republic of Haiti, was in 1971 one of the most extraordinary chiefs of state in the world. The son of one of the bloodiest dictators of modern times, Duvalier was nominally the president of the 5 million Haitians but in reality was only a figurehead for a regency that ruled the country under the magic aegis of the Duvalier name. This regency included his mother, Mme Simone Ovide Duvalier; Minister of Defense and Interior Luckner Cambronne; Gen. Claude Raymond, commander of the Haitian Army; his brother, Foreign Minister Adrien Raymond; and Minister of Côordination and Information Fritz Cinéas. Mme Marie Denise Dominique, the president's sister and private secretary, also was an influential figure.

Early in 1971 when he began to sense that his illness was terminal, Duvalier's father, François Duvalier, announced he would be succeeded by Jean-Claude. When the old dictator died on April 21, 1971, Jean-Claude immediately took over his father's role in the National Palace.

However, where François Duvalier was as absolute a monarch as ever reigned, Jean-Claude seemed the antithesis of power. An introverted, overweight, and somewhat glum youth, he appeared to prefer driving his stable of fast cars to presiding over affairs of state. In fact, he presided in name only.

The regency counted heavily, and accurately, on the power of the Duvalier name as its only hope of holding Haiti against enemies of the regime. To the rural peasants of Haiti, "Papa Doc" Duvalier was a demigod and his son inherited the mantle. The presence in the palace of "Baby Doc," as he was sometimes called, tended to lend both continuity and stability to the regime.

Moreover, young Duvalier's advisers soon concluded that Haiti needed a new image to attract economic assistance, tourism, and investment, and they acted to clean up the appearance if not the substance of the Haitian reality. Young Duvalier's government thus presented at least outward evidence of having reformed. The once-dreaded Tontons Macoutes, a strong-arm organization that had terrorized the nation with the blessing of "Papa Doc," was relegated to the role of an auxiliary labour force.

Jean-Claude was born in Haiti in 1951. He received most of his schooling in Roman Catholic and Protestant schools in Port-au-Prince and was studying law when his father fell ill. (J. A. O'L.)

ELLSBERG, DANIEL

As a brilliant Defense Department analyst and consultant, Daniel Ellsberg had studied military options and helped shape the bloody strategies of the Vietnam war. In 1971, in a startling about-face, he released to the nation's press the "Pentagon papers," a mammoth secret official study of the decisions that led the U.S. into that Asian quagmire.

When the *New York Times* and then the *Washington Post* began publishing the documents, the Justice Department sought to block them with injunctions. After some two

Colin Davis

Daniel Ellsberg

weeks of legal skirmishing, the Supreme Court decided that "prior restraint" in this case was inappropriate and illegal. (*See* LAW; PUBLISHING.)

The source of the papers soon became known. Ellsberg, on the Massachusetts Institute of Technology faculty, vanished from his Cambridge home for a few days, then surrendered to a federal court. He was indicted in July by a federal grand jury in California for unauthorized possession of national defense documents (although, ironically, they were documents he had written in part) and again in December on more serious charges, including theft of government property and conspiracy. He said that if his actions could help end the war, it would be worth the penalties.

Born in Chicago on April 7, 1931, Ellsberg was third out of 1,147 graduates in the Harvard class of 1952. He studied at Cambridge, then returned to Harvard for his master's and doctorate. Commissioned as a Marine, he extended his stint when it appeared that Middle East troubles might enable him to see combat. In 1959 he joined the Rand Corporation, and at that "think tank" he applied sophisticated systems analysis to military matters. Five years later he was made an assistant to the assistant secretary of defense for international security affairs. In 1967, when Defense Secretary Robert McNamara ordered a top secret study of how the nation became involved in Indochina, Ellsberg became an original member of the team that compiled it.

There was no doubt that Ellsberg once enthusiastically favoured the war, but he began changing his mind when he saw—and reported to McNamara—the failure of the "pacification" program in the Vietnamese countryside. He returned to Rand, resigning in 1970 so he could speak out publicly against the war. He also took photocopies of the report with him and, after vainly trying to interest various Senate "doves" in them, gave them to the press. (PH. K.)

ERIM, NIHAT

In March 1971 Nihat Erim emerged as the one man in Turkey trusted simultaneously by the armed forces and the main political parties. Nominated prime minister after the ouster of Justice Party leader Suleyman Demirel, Erim was confirmed in office on April 7 by the biggest majority that the Turkish Parliament had ever awarded a new government since the introduction of party politics.

For Erim, a 59-year-old jurist, it was the continuation, after a 21-year gap, of a political career that had seemed full of promise. In 1949 he had become deputy prime minister of the last administration formed by the Republican People's Party (RPP), which had been created by Kemal Ataturk as the instrument for modernizing and ruling Turkey. Erim's job was to draw up a new electoral law that would usher in genuine democracy. He did this at the cost of his job, for under the new law the RPP was swept from power.

Erim became editor of the opposition organ *Ulus*. He acted as a link between an

Bobby Fischer

Walter E. Fauntroy

Indira Gandhi

FAUNTROY, WALTER EDWARD

For the first time in a century, residents of the District of Columbia elected a delegate to the U.S. House of Representatives in 1971. He was Walter E. Fauntroy, 38, a Democrat, a black Baptist minister, and a civil rights leader.

Fauntroy's election on March 23 brought self-government, long coveted by the citizens of a capital controlled by Congress, a notch closer to reality. But, unlike full-fledged representatives, the delegate had no vote on the House floor, although he had the right to participate in debate. He ranked 437th in seniority—behind all full members and the nonvoting delegate from Puerto Rico—although he drew the full salary, $42,500 a year, and was permitted to have a complete staff. Most important to Fauntroy, he was appointed to the House District of Columbia Committee, where he had a vote and was able to pursue his two principal goals for Washington: home rule and full congressional representation.

Fauntroy's constituency was more than 70% black in 1971—the largest black population of any major American city. He was elected, despite lack of financing, partly because of his David versus Goliath image and partly because of support from other black ministers, an influential group in the District. In addition, his name was familiar to many voters. Pres. Lyndon Johnson had appointed him vice-chairman of the newly established District of Columbia City Council in 1967. A year later, Fauntroy had resigned that job to work on his favourite project, the federally funded Model Inner City Community Organization.

His campaign had emphasized his close relationship with the late civil rights leader Martin Luther King, Jr. Fauntroy directed the Washington bureau of King's Southern Christian Leadership Conference. He was a coordinator for the 1963 civil rights march on Washington, for the Selma to Montgomery, Ala., march of 1965, and for the Poor People's Campaign of 1968.

Fauntroy was born on Feb. 6, 1933, in the section of Washington he later worked to rebuild. He was graduated, cum laude, from Virginia Union University in 1955 and from Yale Divinity School in 1958. After graduation, he became pastor of Washington's New Bethel Baptist Church. He continued to hold the pastorate after he was elected to the House.   (M. Cs.)

FISCHER, BOBBY

"I'm tired of being the unofficial champion," said U.S. chess player Bobby Fischer. "I should have been world champion ten years ago." His chance to make up that lag would come in 1972, when he would challenge Boris Spassky for the world championship. No U.S. master had ever held the title, and it had been 23 years since a non-Soviet player had even challenged.

According to many experts (Bobby Fischer among them), Bobby Fischer was the best chess player in the world and perhaps the greatest of the century. In the course of the elimination rounds to select the challenger, the 28-year-old American won 20 consecutive games, an unprecedented winning streak that could be compared to a quarterback throwing 20 consecutive touchdown passes in the Super Bowl. Fischer's feat was all the more remarkable when the conventions of international chess competition are considered. The majority of official games end in ties, which earn each player half a point (a full point is credited for a clear victory). As New York chess columnist Al Horowitz noted, "To win one game

experienced opposition and an inexperienced democratic government, but as relations between the two worsened he found it increasingly difficult to keep the confidence of his own political chief, Ismet Inonu. Erim then returned to his original specialty, international and constitutional law.

The return to power of the RPP after the 1960 military coup did not bring political preferment to Erim. It became gradually clear that he was more in the party than of it. He had started his political career as an independent in 1945, in which year he was a member of the Turkish delegation to the conference in San Francisco that established the UN. In 1971 he became an independent once again, as leader of a government above the parties, but briefly acceptable to them all. The task that he shouldered was that of re-laying the foundations of Turkish democracy in such a way that military coups would become both unnecessary and impossible. That this would not be easy was indicated in October, when the Justice Party withdrew its participation in the government. Erim remained in office when Pres. Cevdet Sunay refused to accept his proffered resignation. He resigned again in December after 13 ministers left the Cabinet, but once again he was asked to continue and his new Cabinet was announced December 11.   (A. J. A. M.)

FAULKNER, (ARTHUR) BRIAN (DEANE)

Brian Faulkner became prime minister of Northern Ireland on March 23, 1971, at the age of 50. He succeeded James Chichester-Clark, who resigned in response to growing pressure within the Unionist Party for a more aggressive policy to restore law and order in a country torn by the feud between Protestants and Roman Catholics. Faulkner

was elected leader of the Unionist MPs in Stormont (the Ulster Parliament) by 26 votes to 4 for William Craig, who represented the more extreme Protestant opinion.

Faulkner was perhaps the most fully professional of all the Northern Ireland politicians. When elected to Stormont in 1949 he was the youngest MP. He held office in Northern Ireland governments from 1956, first as chief whip (1956–59), then as minister of home affairs (1959–63) and minister of commerce (1963–69). He resigned over disagreement with the then prime minister Terence O'Neill, only to return to the Chichester-Clark government as minister of development.

On his appointment as prime minister, Faulkner said law and order was the central problem. He also promised to continue with reforms, offered to have talks with all shades of opinion, and appointed a member of the Northern Ireland Labour Party, David Bleakley, to his Cabinet in the post of minister for community relations. In spite of the emphasis on law and order, violence increased in the first months of the Faulkner government, and it was he who persuaded the United Kingdom government to back the internment of suspected terrorists in August. "We are quite simply at war with the terrorists," he said. Yet he tried to promote sectarian tolerance and joined in talks with the prime minister of the Republic of Ireland, Jack Lynch, and the U.K. prime minister, Edward Heath, at Chequers in September.

A small, quiet, resolute man, Faulkner was born in Northern Ireland on Feb. 18, 1921. He was educated there and in Dublin and joined the family textile firm in Belfast, later resisting any temptation he may have felt to branch out into British politics.   (W. H. Ts.)

and draw the rest . . . is, of course, amply sufficient to win" in a 12-game match—and not unusual.

Fischer's winning streak ended during his match with former world champion Tigran Petrosian in the fall of 1971. The Soviet grand master won the second game, and the next three were drawn. But then Fischer rebounded to beat the demoralized Petrosian four in a row, giving him the 6½ points needed for victory. The next match would be with Spassky.

Fischer, who was born in Chicago on March 9, 1943, started playing chess at the age of 6. At 13 he became the youngest national junior champion and in 1958, when he was 14, he won the first of his five U.S. championships. When he was 15 he became the youngest international grand master in history. He also earned a reputation for being an enfant terrible, and for a time he withdrew from competition. When he did return, his game had been tempered. Always known as a daringly aggressive player, he had become slightly less willing to surrender minor pieces to develop a commanding position. But he had not totally mellowed. "The Russians . . . play for draws with each other but play to win against the Western masters," he said. "Draws make for dull chess." (PH. K.)

FITZSIMMONS, FRANK E.

Although he had been in federal prison since 1967 for jury tampering and mail fraud, James R. Hoffa continued to hold the title of president of the International Brotherhood of Teamsters during his elected term of office. That term expired in July 1971, and the union, at its convention in Miami Beach, faced the sticky problem of whether to reelect him or turn to acting president Frank Fitzsimmons. Shortly before the convention a parole board turned down Hoffa's application for freedom, and Fitzsimmons announced he would run for the office. He won over only token opposition. Pres. Richard Nixon commuted Hoffa's sentence just before Christmas, but the former leader was freed on the condition that he take no part in union management.

Fitzsimmons had been handpicked by Hoffa to serve as his surrogate while he was in prison. The two had worked together since 1937, when Hoffa, then president of Detroit Local 299, had selected Fitzsimmons as the local's business agent. Born April 7, 1908, in Jeannette, Pa., Fitzsimmons had left high school at 17 to help support his family. Before entering union work, he had been a Detroit bus and truck driver and a dock worker.

In July, Fitzsimmons took formal control of the two million-member union, the largest in the non-Communist world. Less than half of its members were truck drivers. In an era when many unions seemed content to conserve past gains, the Teamsters were known as an aggressive union with superior organizing talent. Among their numbers were warehouse and office workers, airline employees, clerks, zookeepers, and meter maids.

The Teamsters' reputation had a less attractive side, however. In 1957, long before Hoffa was imprisoned, they had been expelled from the AFL-CIO for corruption. One of Fitzsimmons' jobs was to regain respectability for the big union and an indication of success came with the surprise visit by President Nixon to a union board meeting in midsummer. This was followed by Secretary of Labor James Hodgson's appearance at the union's national convention.

In contrast to his most recent predeces-

sors, Frank Fitzsimmons was a mild, soft-spoken, almost shy man. He did not like the spotlight, and some observers guessed that, with the king gone, the power would pass to the princes at the district and local levels.
(M. B. SU.)

FRAZIER, JOE

At the age of 14 Joe Frazier, wanting to lose weight, began to work out in a Philadelphia Police Athletic League gym. Yancey (Yank) Durham, a trainer, saw Frazier there, recognized his potential as a boxer, and encouraged him to pursue a career in the ring. That was in 1958. On March 8, 1971, Frazier defeated Muhammad Ali (formerly Cassius Clay) to become the world's undisputed heavyweight champion.

The Frazier-Ali match was billed "The Fight of the Century" and in terms of money was easily the biggest single boxing event in history. It grossed an estimated $25 million and was seen by approximately 300 million people, most of whom watched via satellite television. For their efforts, Frazier and Ali each were rewarded with a record-breaking purse of $2.5 million.

Born Jan. 17, 1944, in Beaufort, S.C., where his family owned a small farm, Frazier was the second youngest of 13 children. His late father, Rubin, had lost his left arm in an accident, and so Joe "became his left arm." Said Joe, years later: "He'd hold a bolt with his right hand and I'd screw it. By the time I was seven I could drive a tractor and when I was eight I was driving an automobile."

When he was 14, Frazier got into a fight with a white man who had called him "nigger." He then dropped out of school on his mother's advice and traveled north, settling in Philadelphia where he found a job as a meatcutter. After working hours he went to the gymnasium.

Under Durham's direction, Frazier began his boxing career. He won a gold medal for the United States in the 1964 Olympic Games and the next year turned professional. In March 1968—after Muhammad Ali had been stripped of his title because he had refused induction into the armed forces—Frazier knocked out Buster Mathis to win recognition in New York, Massachusetts, Illinois, and Maine as the heavyweight champion.

Total recognition came after his 1971 triumph over Ali. This win gave Frazier an unbroken string of 27 professional victories, 23 by knockouts, which was the highest knockout percentage in the history of modern boxing. (JE. HO.)

GANDHI, INDIRA PRIYADARSHINI

In May 1971 a Gallup poll in the United States found Mrs. Indira Gandhi, India's prime minister, to be "the most admired person in the world." This clearly was not an opinion endorsed by U.S. Pres. Richard Nixon, whose stance in the Indo-Pakistani conflict appeared to reflect a degree of personal animosity toward her. Within India, however, Mrs. Gandhi enjoyed not only admiration but also undisputed political power. At the end of the year the swift victory over Pakistan and the liberation of East Bengal, subsequently recognized by India as independent Bangla Desh, left her in a stronger position than ever.

In the country's fifth general election, which she had called in March, a year ahead of time, an alliance of four main opposition parties went to the polls united on a slogan of "Remove Indira." The Ruling Congress Party replied with "Remove poverty," and as the party's chief campaigner Mrs. Gandhi traveled 36,000 mi. in 45 days and addressed

Joe Frazier

some 20 million people. In the outcome the Ruling Congress won more than two-thirds of the seats in the Lok Sabha.

The emergence of a strong central government raised hopes of new initiatives in foreign policy, but possibilities of an improvement of relations with Pakistan were ruled out by the political upheaval there. National sentiment in India was largely in favour of giving active help to the freedom fighters in East Pakistan, but Mrs. Gandhi resisted any irrevocable action. On August 9 she signed a 20-year treaty of friendship with the Soviet Union. Then, during September–November, she undertook journeys to the U.S.S.R., the United States, and the leading countries of Western Europe in the hope of mobilizing international pressure on Pakistan to reach a political settlement with the people of East Bengal. When these efforts failed the decision to resort to open warfare followed inevitably.

The only child of India's first prime minister, Jawaharlal Nehru, Indira Gandhi was born at Allahabad on Nov. 19, 1917. Educated mainly in Europe, in 1942 she married a lawyer, Feroze Gandhi (d. 1960), by whom she had two sons. President of the Congress Party in 1959, she was minister for information and broadcasting from 1964 until 1966, when she became prime minister. (H. Y. S. P.)

GIEREK, EDWARD

Succeeding Wladyslaw Gomulka as first secretary of the Polish United Workers' Party (PZPR) on Dec. 20, 1970, in the midst of industrial unrest, Edward Gierek immediately changed both the style and language of government by visiting the struck shipyards in Gdansk, Gdynia, and Szczecin to seek the trust and cooperation of the workers. As first secretary of the party organization in the highly industrialized Katowice province, Gierek had been a popular figure with miners and steelworkers and was respected by managers and the people at large. Under his 13-year-long rule, the province had flourished and the city of Katowice had changed beyond recognition.

Gierek was born on Jan. 6, 1913, at Porabka in the industrial district of Bedzin, then part of Russian Poland. His father perished in a mining accident, and in 1923 his mother emigrated to France, taking him with her. He started work as a coal miner in the Pas-de-Calais and in 1931 joined the

French Communist Party. In 1934 he helped organize a sit-down strike in the mines, for which he was expelled from France. After his return to Poland he was called up for military service. In 1937 he emigrated to Belgium and worked as a miner in the newly developed Limbourg coalfields. During the German occupation of Belgium he lay low until 1943, when he joined the Belgian resistance. In 1945 he founded, in Belgium, the Union of Polish Patriots and became the leader of the Polish section of the Belgian Communist Party.

Gierek returned to Poland in 1948 and the next year began working in Katowice province as a PZPR organizer. In 1952 he was elected a member of the Polish Sejm (parliament). He enrolled as an extramural student at the Mining and Metallurgical Academy of Cracow, receiving a diploma in mining engineering in 1951. In March 1954 he was elected to the Central Committee of the PZPR and to its Secretariat. He was a member of the Politburo for a short time in 1956, and in March 1957 was appointed first secretary at Katowice; in March 1959 he again became a member of both the Politburo and the Secretariat.   (K. Sm.)

GOODMAN, ARNOLD
ABRAHAM GOODMAN, BARON

Although he enjoyed the company of a wide range of friends, many of them in positions of power, Lord Goodman himself avoided personal publicity—so successfully, in fact, that he could fly on a "secret" mission to Rhodesia in May 1971 without being noticed. He accomplished this despite the Dickensian bulk of his physique, which made him unmistakable, and despite his position as the outstanding chairman of British public life.

In 1971 he was chairman of the Arts Council, chairman of the Observer Newspaper Trust, chairman of the Newspaper Publishers Association, chairman of British Lion Films Ltd., and a member of the British Council and of the National Theatre board. He had won a reputation as a great conciliator, having helped to sort out a television strike in 1964 and a number of tangles in the newspaper industry, including national stoppages in 1970 and 1971. He was used by both the Wilson and the Heath governments to make confidential approaches to Ian Smith, leader of the breakaway regime in Rhodesia. His negotiations in Salisbury in 1971 paved the way for the November agreement in which Britain and Rhodesia agreed to settle their differences.

On the Arts Council, Goodman showed himself adroit at raising funds from private sources for good causes. He was also responsible for a report on censorship that was marked by wit as well as a liberal attitude. His relaxed tolerance could be seen in the administration of Arts Council grants to young writers and artists, whom he did not expect to conform with his standards or confirm his expectations.

Arnold Goodman was born into a prosperous London Jewish family in Aug. 21, 1913. From the time he gained a double first in law at Cambridge, he was a lawyer of outstanding ability, but it was only in his 50s that he began, with some suddenness, to make a mark on British public life. His legal business had brought him into touch with some leading Labour politicians in the 1950s and he became Harold Wilson's solicitor. In 1965 Wilson, then prime minister, chose him to be chairman of the Arts Council and made him a life peer. Goodman remained unmarried and nonpartisan in politics, claiming to be "the last democrat."   (W. H. Ts.)

GOOLAGONG, EVONNE

Winner of the women's singles in both the French and Wimbledon championships in 1971 was 19-year-old Evonne Goolagong of Australia, a novice in international tennis competition. She was remarkable not only for her talent for the game but also, as part Aboriginal by race, in being the first of her blood to become a leading player.

Born on July 31, 1951, at Barellan, a small township in New South Wales, about 400 mi. from Sydney, Evonne was one of eight children of Linda and Ken Goolagong (the name, according to an Australian anthropologist, could be translated as "nose of kangaroo"), her father being a part-time fruit picker, sheep shearer, and wheat grader. Her talent for tennis was spotted when she took part in a traveling "clinic" organized by Vic Edwards, a well-known Sydney coach. Edwards took Miss Goolagong at age 14 to live at his home in Roseville, a Sydney suburb, where she was educated with his own daughters and treated as one of his family.

After conspicuous success in Australian junior tournaments, Miss Goolagong was taken by Edwards for her first overseas tour in 1970. Her success was immediate, although it fell short of the highest achievements. She won 7 out of 21 tournaments she entered, including the Welsh and Bavarian championships, and also took the women's consolation plate at Wimbledon. Edwards predicted when Miss Goolagong was 16 that she could win the Wimbledon singles by 1974. She did so in 1971 when still short of her 20th birthday, and with the French championship also to her credit she established herself as the outstanding woman player of the year.

In the last two rounds at Wimbledon Miss Goolagong first defeated Billie Jean King of the U.S., the champion in 1966, 1967, and 1968, and then her fellow Australian Margaret Court, the champion in 1963, 1965, and 1970.   (L. O. T.)

GREEN, JULIEN

In June 1971 an American had the privilege of being the first of his nationality to be elected to the French Academy. Julien Green, winner of the Academy's 1970 Grand Prix for literature, a writer obsessed with the struggle between good and evil, seemed the only possible successor to the chair of François Mauriac, the great Catholic novelist who died in 1970.

Born in Paris on Sept. 6, 1900, one of eight children of parents from the American South, he went to the Lycée Janson de Sailly in Paris and was brought up bilingually. During World War I, he served with the U.S. Army as an ambulance driver and later in the French artillery. He was 19 when he first set foot on American soil, to spend three years at the University of Virginia. In 1922 he returned to France, but although a Parisian by birth and habit and European in spirit, he remained at heart an American and never wished to give up his U.S. citizenship. He revisited the United States in 1933 and in 1940, when he again joined the Army. Strictly Protestant by upbringing, he was converted to Catholicism in 1916, but his first published work was a *Pamphlet contre les catholiques de France* (1924).

The struggle between the soul and the flesh permeates Green's writing, sometimes driving his characters to the point of madness, suicide, or crime, as in the novels *Mont-Cinère* (1926), *Adrienne Mesurat* (1927), and *Moïra* (1950), or the play *Sud* (1953). His most recent novel, *L'Autre* (1971), mirrors the same world of morbid anguish haunted by the shades of desire and shame, the same violence, and the same struggle between grace and sin. The eight volumes of his *Journal* (1938–58) and his three autobiographical volumes (1963–66) are uncompromisingly explicit, yet reveal little of the mysterious depths of personality from which the novels spring. Linking two literary epochs, Green appeared to stand apart from contemporary preoccupations. Between the great generation of French pre-World War II novelists and the *nouveau roman,* he continued to examine the adventures of the soul. Green's only book written in English, *Memories of Happy Days* (1942), won him the Harper 125th Anniversary Award.   (S. Ls.)

GREER, GERMAINE

Germaine Greer leavened and enlivened the women's liberation movement in 1971 by injecting it with some wit and some ribaldry. She was the first feminist to frankly enjoy her own (hetero)sexual appeal, if not the traditional allocation of male-female roles. *Newsweek* called her "a dazzling combination of erudition, eccentricity and eroticism whose passionate treatise entitled *The Female Eunuch* may well be women's liberation's most realistic and least anti-male manifesto." Her thesis: "We [women] suffer not from penis envy, as Freud would have us believe, but from the castration of our true female personality; this is not the fault of men, but our own, and history's."

She believes women are blessedly different from men and must work creatively to reassert themselves and their equality. In an interview she argued: "It is important that women should see that they have connived in the situation, that they have consented in the streamlining of themselves into the role of super chattels." In her view the traditional role of the housewife is degrading and dull.

Now a confirmed nonconformist, Germaine Greer was born in middle-class circumstances in Melbourne, Austr., and educated in convents. She studied at the university there, earning honours, went on to Sydney for a master's degree and to Cambridge for her doctorate. She was an actress on British television, a star of the pop scene, and a "groupie" (a camp follower of rock musicians), a columnist in the conservative weekly *Spectator,* a contributor to a pornographic underground journal published in the Netherlands, *Suck,* and a popular, respected lecturer at Warwick University in the English Midlands, where she specialized in Shakespeare.

Six feet tall, 32, and openly promiscuous, she was called "a super heroine" by *Vogue.* But an activist writing in the *Nation* sneered that she is everything other feminists aren't: "pretty, . . . aggressively heterosexual, mediawise, clever, foreign, and exotic. . . . She has always been treated [by men] as an equal. That good fortune just about disqualifies her for writing a feminist book." Thinking like that led the *Vogue* writer to say: "We need more like her."   (Ph. K.)

HAGGARD, MERLE

"Merle sings like every other country singer wants to, or thinks he does." Another country singer said that about Merle Haggard, casting him in a role like the one Ella Fitzgerald filled so long in jazz: the singer's singer. But Haggard's was no esoteric talent recognizable only by the initiated. His songs and lyrics, his strong but intimate voice, and his direct masculinity made him "entertainer of the year" and "male vocalist of the year," and his recording of "Okie from Muskogee" was both the single record and the album of the year when the Country Music Association presented its 1970 awards. A gold album that year, rare in country music, was testimony to his wide appeal.

Haggard's life was like not one, but a collection, of tales out of country music lyrics, and he plowed it back into his own works, giving them an authenticity amplified by his heartfelt delivery. His parents left Oklahoma in the 1930s and were living in a converted boxcar outside Bakersfield, Calif., when Merle was born in 1937. His father died when he was nine, and soon Merle's rowdiness flared into drinking, burglary, armed robbery, and assorted other adventures as he rambled the Southwest, picking a guitar in between times. After spending two years and nine months in prison at San Quentin, Calif., he returned to Bakersfield in 1960.

Haggard worked at first as an electrician's helper, while playing guitar weekends, but in 1962 went to Las Vegas, Nev., to play backup for singer Wynn Stewart. The next year he cut his first records. His success was steady but unspectacular until 1969 when he wrote "Okie from Muskogee," which became the anthem of those who objected to the anti-Establishment, longhaired culture that was dominating the media. It began "we don't smoke marijuana in Muskogee, we don't take our trips on LSD . . ." and proudly endorsed flying the flag "down at the courthouse." "Okie" was followed by "The Fightin' Side of Me" (". . . when you're runnin' down our country, hoss, you're walkin' on the fightin' side of me"). The short, wiry Haggard was the first country artist to appear at the John F. Kennedy Center for the Performing Arts in Washington, D.C., when it opened in September 1971.   (C. Th.)

HASSAN II

The soldier holding King Hassan II at gunpoint in a small room at the beach palace on July 10, 1971, suddenly realized who his captive was and knelt down to kiss the king's hand. Thus ended the bizarre but bloody attempt at a revolution against the Moroccan monarchy. The attempt was made while King Hassan was giving a party, celebrating his birthday, for government officials and foreign diplomats at Skhirat, on the coast south of Rabat. Its prime instigator was Gen. Muhammad Madbouh, head of the king's personal military staff. The coup plan was executed by army noncommissioned officer cadets, who had been told that their king's life was in danger and who directed sporadic fire at the royal guests, killing 32 of them including the Belgian ambassador and General Madbouh himself.

When his two-hour detention was ended, King Hassan reasserted his authority and appointed his interior minister, Gen. Muhammad Oufkir, to clear up the mess. Four army generals were executed for their involvement; five more generals had been killed during the coup attempt. Hassan quickly set about reforming the administration and promised to eliminate the corruption that had been the apparent main cause of the abortive coup.

Born July 9, 1929, at Rabat, Hassan II was the eldest son of Sultan (later King) Muhammad V, who led Morocco to independence from France in 1956. After taking a law degree at Bordeaux University, France, Hassan was appointed commander in chief of the Army (1957) and deputy premier (1960) before succeeding his father as king in February 1961. He served as his own prime minister during 1961–63 and from

Germaine Greer

Hugh Hefner

1965, when he dissolved Parliament, to 1967. Regarded as a descendant of the Prophet Muhammad and "commander of the faithful," Hassan had been able to command the unswerving allegiance of the rural bulk of Morocco's 15 million people and, by the careful manipulation of political and economic patronage, had been able to nullify serious opposition from the educated classes. He had also relied on the Army, and the dissent evidenced in July led to his reorganization of its command structure to ensure its loyalty to the throne.   (Pr. K.)

HEATH, EDWARD RICHARD GEORGE

In his first year as prime minister of the United Kingdom, Edward Heath consolidated his hold on the leadership of the Conservative Party. He did so in a year of difficulty and disappointment in many fields. Prices continued to rise rapidly—and the promise to stop the rise in prices had been a key factor in the Conservative election campaign in June 1970. The period was the worst for labour unrest since World War II. Unemployment rose to nearly a million. Industrial firms as notable as Rolls-Royce and Upper Clyde Shipbuilders came close to collapse. The government's most important achievement was the 356–244 House of Commons vote approving Britain's entry into the EEC. This did not appear to be welcomed by the majority of British voters, but Heath's "outstanding services to . . . European unification" won for him the first award of a $90,000 prize for European statesmanship, established in 1969 by the FVS Foundation (set up by Alfred Töpfer, a Hamburg, W.Ger., merchant).

Heath's own personal popularity as measured by opinion polls was not high. Yet there was no doubt about the authority and firmness with which he headed his government. He pursued what he called a quiet revolution in domestic and foreign policy with a persistence that some critics called stubbornness and obstinacy. In an important keynote speech to the Conservative Party conference on October 16, Heath stressed his belief that the task of his government was to find new ways in a new world, and that this involved a radical change from the past. In pursuit of this goal, he held talks with French Premier Georges Pompidou in Paris in May, during which essential agreement was reached on the conditions of British entry into the EEC. In late December, Heath journeyed to Bermuda for talks on a wide range of subjects with U.S. Pres. Richard M. Nixon.

Born at Broadstairs, Kent, on July 9, 1916, the son of a carpenter who later became a builder, Heath went to a Ramsgate grammar school and then to Oxford University with the help of scholarships. Elected to Parliament from Bexley in 1950, he advanced rapidly in the Conservative Party, and by 1955 he had the influential post of chief whip. In the Harold Macmillan government he took charge of Britain's first application to join the EEC, an experience that left him convinced of the rightness of a European future for Britain. He was elected leader of the Conservative Party in July 1965.   (W. H. Ts.)

HEFNER, HUGH

Hugh Hefner considered going public in 1971—that is, he took steps to offer a portion of his $127 million empire to investors who might want to own a piece of *Playboy* and its chattels. According to *Forbes* magazine, which rarely notices such things, that

Emperor Hirohito and Empress Nagako

empire showed signs of exploding into a $1 billion conglomerate from its more modest beginnings as the most successful girlie and gewgaw magazine in history.

Playboy's very success, of course, was what interested the staid financial magazine. Hefner, who still owned 80% of the entire operation, began it in 1953 with $10,-000 raised from friends and all his own assets, which then amounted to $600. In 1970 the magazine had a circulation of six million, ad revenues of nearly $33 million, and profits of $8.5 million. The parent company also owned nightclubs and resort hotels and peddled such products as costume jewelry. Said *Forbes,* "Now *Playboy* wants to sell its fantasy *as a way of life,*" marketing Playboy clothes to tenants of Playboy apartments who listen to Playboy educational tape cassettes and read Playboy books when they are not vacationing in Playboy resorts.

Actually it was a playpen in the sky that attracted the most attention during the year. Hefner spent $5.5 million on a DC-9, painted black, bearing the famous bunny emblem on the tail, and fitted with such extras as a round bed covered with Tasmanian opossum pelts and a discotheque. It represented a new departure for Hefner, who for years rarely left the boudoir-office of his $800,000, 48-room mansion on Chicago's North Side from which he masterminded his empire, working 36 hours at a stretch while living on stimulants and Pepsi-Cola, waited on hand and foot by round-the-clock chefs, secretaries, and "playmates" who lived in a dormitory upstairs.

Born in Chicago, April 9, 1926, Hefner was raised by devout Methodist parents. He studied psychology at the University of Illinois and sought his fortune first as the personnel director of a cardboard-box company, later as a subscription promoter for *Esquire* before he hit on the idea of his own magazine. Ultimately *Playboy* published some of the nation's most polished fiction and popular essays—admittedly somewhat overshadowed by the foldout photograph of the month's "Playmate," smiling, wholesome, and undressed.   (PH. K.)

HIROHITO, EMPEROR

Never before had a Japanese emperor left his country during his reign, but on Sept. 26, 1971, Emperor Hirohito and Empress Nagako flew out of Tokyo for an 18-day tour of Europe. Since the Japanese aircraft had to stop at Anchorage, Alaska, for refueling, Pres. Richard M. Nixon flew there to greet on U.S. soil the former "son of heaven," who at the end of World War II "de-godded" himself at the request of Gen. Douglas MacArthur. Hirohito then flew on to Copenhagen and later visited Belgium, the Netherlands, Switzerland, France, West Germany, and the U.K.

While the visits of the Japanese imperial pair to other capitals of Europe had been described as private, that to London was a state one, with all the traditional English pomp and pageantry. At the state banquet at Buckingham Palace, Queen Elizabeth II said, "We cannot pretend that the relations between our two peoples have always been peaceful and friendly," and added, "It is precisely this experience which should make us all the more determined never to let it happen again." There were no public demonstrations in London against Hirohito's visit, but war veterans from the Far Eastern campaigns protested when the queen reinstated the emperor as a knight of the Garter.

After frozen politeness in England and unveiled hostility in the Netherlands, Hirohito found a friendlier atmosphere in West Germany (October 12–13), especially among the older generation, when he spoke about "bitter experiences" which the Germans and the Japanese "had to suffer during and after the last war." For the first time criticisms of the way the tour had been managed were voiced in the Japanese press. It was stated that the advisers underestimated the strength of lingering anti-Japanese feelings in Europe, and that the speeches prepared for the emperor had been perfunctory.

Hirohito was born on April 29, 1901, at the Tokyo Imperial Palace, the son of Emperor Yoshihito. He was educated at the Peers' School. In 1921 he became the first heir to the Japanese throne to leave his country and to visit Europe. Five years

later he was crowned emperor. His reign, although designated Showa ("bright peace"), was characterized by aggressive and warlike policy. A book published during the year, *Japan's Imperial Conspiracy,* charged that Hirohito encouraged and helped lead Japan into World War II. On November 16, in his first on-the-record press conference since he became emperor, he denied the charges and insisted that, throughout the war, he had acted only as a constitutional monarch.   (K. SM).

HONECKER, ERICH

Erich Honecker succeeded Walter Ulbricht as first secretary of the East German Sozialistische Einheitspartei Deutschlands (Socialist Unity Party of Germany, or SED) on May 3, 1971. He had been groomed for this post, the most powerful in the East German Communist hierarchy, for several years. Faster progress was made in the four-power negotiations on Berlin after he assumed office, and it was assumed that he was more responsive to Moscow's Central European policy than Ulbricht had been. Honecker was uncompromising in his first policy speech, however. Although he agreed that peaceful coexistence between the two German states was necessary, he said that East Germany must fence itself off completely from the "imperialist" Federal Republic.

Born in Neunkirchen (Saarland) on Aug. 25, 1912, Honecker was the son of a miner who was an official of the Communist Party. At the age of 14 he joined the Communist Youth Movement and in 1929 became a full party member. By trade he was a slater. After the Nazis came to power in 1933 he organized illegal activities by young Communists in various parts of Germany. He was arrested by the Gestapo in 1935, and sentenced to ten years' hard labour for "preparing treason." He told the court that he would not change his Communist convictions.

In 1945 he was freed by the Soviet Army, and he quickly caught up with the "Ulbricht group" of Communists trained in the Soviet Union to set up a Communist government in the Soviet-occupied zone. He was one of the founders of the Freie Deutsche Jugend (Free German Youth movement, or FDJ), and was its chairman from 1946 to 1955.

He was elected a member of the Central Committee of the Communist Party in 1946 and was one of the prime movers behind the fusion of the Communist and Social Democratic parties in East Germany into the SED. After leaving the FDJ, he spent two years in Moscow at the party's training school. His influence in the SED grew rapidly, and in 1967 he was designated as Ulbricht's successor. His wife, Margot, was minister of education in the East German government.   (N. CR.)

HOOVER, J. EDGAR

In the twilight of an FBI career spanning a half century of distinction and controversy, J. Edgar Hoover worked increasingly under a cloud of criticism that spread to previously friendly quarters. His feuds with top aides and the resultant schisms in lower ranks hampered the efficiency of the bureau, according to FBI watchers in and outside government, and some believed that his jealous guarding of power undermined the entire U.S. intelligence effort.

At immediate issue in 1971 was the forced retirement of William C. Sullivan, formerly the third-ranking man in the FBI. As early as 1960 Sullivan had contended that the Ku Klux Klan was a more serious threat to U.S. internal security than Hoover's candidate, the American Communist Party. Sullivan in 1970 publicly minimized the danger of the Communists, suggesting instead that militant New Left tactics might trigger a dangerous avalanche of rightist reaction among the nation's moderates. Outraged at his former favourite for contradicting him, Hoover effectively demoted him by reorganizing top-echelon responsibilities.

Sullivan's ouster focused national attention on internal FBI affairs. There were reports that morale was at an unprecedented low and that many officials were resigning. It also was revealed that as a result of a minor breach of confidence, Hoover had terminated liaison between the FBI and the Central Intelligence Agency.

There was published speculation that the Nixon administration would ease Hoover out of office as gracefully and swiftly as possible. Department of Justice sources tried to quash articles about this, and many observers believed that Hoover was too powerful a public figure to be forced from office. Indeed, former President Lyndon Johnson had approved special legislation exempting Hoover from mandatory retirement at age 70. In December, Hoover stated that he had never considered stepping down.

Born in Washington, D.C., Jan. 1, 1895, Hoover was educated in public schools in the nation's capital and at George Washington University there. A lawyer, he was a special assistant to the attorney general for two years, then named assistant director of the demoralized and corrupt Bureau of Investigation from 1921 to 1924. In the latter year he was named director of the reorganized and politically insulated FBI, and he built it into an effective national law enforcement agency that became world famous as a bulwark against professional crime in peacetime and espionage during World War II.   (Ph. K.)

HUGHES, HOWARD

The most famous little-known man in the world was an apt description of Howard Hughes—a hermit with the resources of Midas. A billionaire commanding what was probably the largest private fortune in America, he had been an industrialist, philanthropist, aviator, movie magnate, and national hero before becoming a recluse. In recent years he had lived in an aerie above a Las Vegas casino, seen only by five male secretary/valets and running his considerable empire by memo and telephone. In 1970 he made headlines when holes appeared in the curtain of corporate secrecy surrounding him.

In 1966, due largely to management pressure, he liquidated 6.6 million shares of TWA stock for $546,549,771, which he was pressed to reinvest. A bacteriophobe if not a hypochondriac, he moved to Las Vegas because of its healthy air and turned the top floor of the Desert Inn into a cloister. He bought the hotel, and in time he controlled 17% of Nevada's gambling business, became the area's largest real estate owner, bought the commercial airline Air West, and spent nearly $40 million in mining claims and options. In all, he invested perhaps $200 million in Nevada alone in three years—and began losing money.

He had told top echelon employees—who never met him—that he intended to spend the rest of his life in Las Vegas, but he also planned "a vacation," and for 13 months two jet transports with crack crews were held on 48-hour call. Then, on Thanksgiving Eve, 1970, he abruptly flew to the Bahamas under such extraordinary security precautions that only the personal aides traveling with him were aware of the move.

In the following weeks Robert A. Maheu,

WIDE WORLD

Howard Hughes (in 1947)

the manager of Hughes's Nevada interests, became alarmed, especially when officers of the Hughes Tool Co. tried to oust him, armed with a handwritten document signed with Hughes's name. Rumours flew: the document was forged; the Man might be seriously ill, dead, or kidnapped. The governor became involved, and the Nevada courts. In the end, however, one of the secretary/valets swore the scrawled proxy was genuine, and Maheu was out, fired by his eccentric boss. The possibility of further revelations arose in December, when McGraw-Hill announced that it planned to publish Hughes's purported autobiography, said to have been transcribed from taped reminiscences by novelist Clifford Irving.

Hughes was born in Houston, Tex., Dec. 24, 1905, set several speed records piloting Hughes Aircraft planes, won the Collier Trophy, and produced such films as *Scarface* and *The Outlaw*.   (Ph. K.)

ILLICH, IVAN

Ivan Illich, a controversial and free-thinking Roman Catholic priest, founder and head of the Center for Intercultural Documentation at Cuernavaca, Mex., was in 1971 a major thorn in the side of political and clerical conservatives. Born in Vienna, Sept. 4, 1926, the son of a Spanish-Jewish mother and a Yugoslav-Catholic father, he received a thoroughly orthodox Catholic upbringing. At an early age he displayed a brilliant and restless mind that led him to a doctorate in history at Salzburg when he was 24, studies in theology at Rome's Pontifical Gregorian University, and ordination to the priesthood in 1951. By the time he was 31, Illich had become vice-rector of the Catholic University of Puerto Rico and a monsignor.

Illich first ran afoul of the church authorities in 1960 when he disagreed with the political intervention of a bishop who opposed Gov. Luis Muñoz Marín's position on birth control. The late Francis Cardinal Spellman brought him to New York, but the next year Illich went to Mexico to start his centre. The original concept was to train a new breed of missionary for Latin America, where priests are scarce, but soon the

centre became a gathering place for intellectuals, reformers, and students of many faiths. When Illich began to speak out against North American domination and declared that social reform had to come from outside the church, he attracted the suspicion and animosity of the hierarchy.

The Mexican Bishops Conference tried to get Illich recalled to New York, but Spellman refused. Shortly after Spellman's death, Illich was summoned to appear in Rome before the Congregation for the Doctrine of the Faith, where he was handed 85 questions that he found too vague to answer. In the end, the Congregation forbade all members of Catholic religious orders to attend the centre. Illich then asked for lay status.

Though still loyal to basic doctrine, Illich continued to write against clericalism and colonialism. His articles on educational reform often appeared in intellectual publications. He most recently attracted the attention of educators by criticizing the educational ethic by which attendance at college is equated with preparation for a successful life. Illich did not believe that every boy or girl is better served by passing four years in a university and, indeed, felt that many would be better off without conventional education at all.   (J. A. O'L.)

JABBAR, KAREEM ABDUL

The dominant figure in professional basketball in 1971 was Kareem Abdul Jabbar, formerly Lew Alcindor, a 7-ft. 2-in. centre with the Milwaukee Bucks. Throughout his playing career wherever Jabbar went, basketball championships followed, and in 1971, his second season as a professional, he led Milwaukee to the title in the National Basketball Association.

Though raised as a Roman Catholic, Jabbar, who once called the autobiography of Malcolm X the most significant book he had ever read, converted to Islam while a student at UCLA. Following a U.S. Department of State tour of Africa in June, he had his name legally changed. His name in Islam translates freely into "servant of Allah," "generous," and "powerful."

The only child of Ferdinand and Cora Alcindor, Jabbar was born in New York City on April 16, 1947. At birth he weighed 13 lb. and measured about 22 in. His father, a native of Trinidad, was 6 ft. 2 in., and his mother 6 ft. 1 in.

By the time Jabbar was 13 his height had reached 6 ft. 8 in., and he was a basketball player of unusual ability. He attended Power Memorial Academy in New York City, leading the varsity team to a four-year record of 95–6 and scoring 2,067 points, a New York City record.

At graduation the most publicized high-school player in the country, Jabbar received more than 100 college scholarship offers and chose UCLA. He enrolled there in the fall of 1965 and led the Bruins to three consecutive NCAA championships. A three-time collegiate All-American, Jabbar set a college career field-goal percentage record of .641.

The Milwaukee Bucks, winning a special coin flip, gained the no. 1 draft choice and selected Jabbar prior to the 1969–70 season. As had been expected, he was an immediate sensation as a professional, averaging 28.8 points per game and winning the rookie-of-the-year trophy. The next season he averaged 31.7 points and won the most valuable player award.   (Je. Ho.)

JACKSON, GLENDA

By the time she won an Oscar in 1971 for her performance as D. H. Lawrence's man-eating heroine in Ken Russell's screen version of *Women in Love,* Glenda Jackson had appeared in four previous films and had a successful stage career behind her.

Born at Hoylake, near Liverpool, Eng., in 1937, Miss Jackson won a scholarship to the Royal Academy of Dramatic Art and then spent six years in repertory, mostly in character parts. In 1964 Peter Brook chose her for his "Theatre of Cruelty" group attached to the Royal Shakespeare Company. She remained with the company for three years, playing a variety of parts including an abrasive Ophelia to David Warner's Hamlet and Charlotte Corday in Peter Weiss's *Marat/Sade* in London and New York (Variety Poll Award for the most promising new actress of the Broadway season).

She repeated this performance in 1966 in Brook's film of the play—a shocking and terrifying study of a lunatic playing a murderess that set the pattern for a long line of neurotic roles. Another Brook film, *Tell Me Lies,* followed in 1967, and in 1968, *Negatives* (more neurotic sexual fantasies). She played Tchaikovsky's pitiful nymphomaniac bride in Russell's *The Music Lovers* (1970) and would have been in his *The Devils* (as the sex-crazed nun) but for a previous commitment to John Schlesinger's *Sunday, Bloody Sunday.* Here at last she played a comparatively normal woman caught in an unconventional relationship, and her capacity for humour and tenderness were allowed to appear.

Meanwhile she had a great success in a BBC television series as Queen Elizabeth I. Although she had broken away from the unbalanced parts that she had come to hate, she now seemed to be in danger of being typed in regal history. She played Elizabeth I again in Hal Wallis' production of *Mary Queen of Scots* and was due to appear as Isabella of Spain in a new film by Ronald Neame.

Highly intelligent and unusually honest, Glenda Jackson had neither the obvious beauty nor the conventional glamour of the old-style star. She preferred the immediacy of the cinema to the long-term drudgery of the theatre. (B. D.)

JACKSON, HENRY MARTIN

Sen. Henry M. Jackson of Washington became known during the year as the "different" candidate for the 1972 Democratic presidential nomination. This label was applied by those, including some of his opponents, who regarded him as the contender farthest to the right on the party's political spectrum.

Jackson, who officially announced his candidacy on November 19, gained this reputation largely because of his record on national security matters. A veteran member of the U.S. Senate Armed Services Committee, he always strongly supported military preparedness. He thereby frequently found himself in opposition to most other prospective Democratic presidential nominees, many of whom took the position that national priorities had to be rearranged in favour of meeting domestic social needs.

Jackson, however, was proud of his stand, declaring in campaign speeches that "world peace, if we ever achieve it, will be achieved by strength and not by weakness." He also jabbed at opponents who he believed spent too much time cataloging the ills of the nation. "I think we are a great and generous and often noble nation and not a sick, guilty or oppressive one," he told his audiences.

But on many issues, Jackson voted consistently with his rivals for the nomination. Throughout his 30 years in Congress, he was solidly pro-labour and pro-civil rights. His image as a hawk was softened when he voted in 1970 for the Cooper-Church amendment to limit U.S. military involvement in Cambodia. He said he stood "proudly and squarely in the mainstream of the progressive Democratic tradition."

Despite his long service on Capitol Hill, Jackson was virtually unknown nationally. His standings during 1971 in the public opinion polls often were so low that he was relegated to the anonymous category of "others." "This is one of my main problems," he acknowledged. Although his standing remained low, it did improve enough during the year so that his candidacy was being taken seriously as a possible long shot.

Jackson was born May 31, 1912, in Everett, Wash. After receiving a law degree from the University of Washington in 1935, he practiced law until 1940 when he was elected to the House of Representatives from Washington. He served in the House until 1952 when he was elected a senator. (F. Wt.)

KEELER, RUBY

In 1971, Ruby Keeler was the Woman of the Yesteryear, the dancing revivalist par excellence, and star of *No, No, Nanette,* a 1925 hit that took Broadway by atavistic storm nearly half a century later. The show, winner of four Tony Awards, exemplified a trend that saw the resurrection of old chestnuts and renewed popularity of the passé, the glorious, and the romantic.

Miss Keeler and the original Vincent Youmans musical were contemporaries. She was born in Halifax, Nova Scotia, Aug. 25, 1909 or 1910. The fabled Flo Ziegfeld gave her a break in 1927, a tour opposite Eddie Cantor in *Whoopee.* But she left the show in Pittsburgh and eloped with Al Jolson. Her talents were such that Ziegfeld forgave her and starred her in *Show Girl* in 1929.

But it was Hollywood and the massive choreographies in Busby Berkeley extravaganzas like *Gold Diggers of 1933, Dames,* and *Flirtation Walk* that made her famous. She was never much of a singer, nor, by her own admission, an actress: "You certainly can't call what I did on the screen acting," she declared. But a dancer she was, and she became one again when Berkeley, himself coming out of retirement to help with the *Nanette* revival, suggested that she star as the title character's aunt.

She had not set foot on New York boards in 40 years, a period in which Jolson had died and she married John Lowe, a socially prominent stockbroker, settling down to raise children and horses for 27 years. Widowed now, she confessed to being nervous about returning to Broadway, but that feeling dated back to the archetypal moment in her first film, *42nd Street,* when she was the chorus girl about to stand in for the leading lady. "Sawyer, you're going out a youngster," the director confides, "but you've got to come back a star!" That was in 1933. "I was scared to death," she recalled before the *Nanette* opening. "I'm scared to death now."

She noted, "The audiences have been having fun; in the 'I Want to be Happy' number at the end, they're smiling and singing and swaying along with us. It's like having a party in your own living room." Better than television. (Ph. K.)

KISSINGER, HENRY

The prestige and power of Henry Kissinger within the U.S. administration emerged beyond question during 1971. When Pres. Richard M. Nixon needed someone who could, in absolute secrecy and confidence, arrange a precedent-shattering presidential visit to China, he turned to Kissinger. And the assistant to the president for national security affairs was widely credited with being one of the movers behind the U.S. hard line toward India during the December Indo-Pakistani war. Earlier, Sen. Stuart Symington (Dem., Mo.) had quipped that it was obvious that Kissinger was secretary of state in everything but name. Nixon accused Symington of "taking a cheap shot" at the secretary, William P. Rogers.

Kissinger's mission to Peking proved to be the best kept secret of an administration that had more than its share of leaks of highly classified information.

Kissinger left Washington in late June, ostensibly on a visit to South Vietnam, Thailand, India, Pakistan, and France. While in Pakistan, he was reported to have contracted a stomach ailment and to be recuperating in the mountain resort of Nathia Gali. Instead, Kissinger and three aides boarded a plane for Peking and Chinese officials respected his wishes for absolute secrecy throughout a series of meetings held there with Premier Chou En-lai.

News of the visit was successfully kept secret until Nixon announced in a nationally televised statement on July 15 that he had been invited to visit Peking sometime before May 1972 as a result of the Kissinger trip. Kissinger made a second, well-publicized trip to China in late October to head a team working out technical arrangements and an agenda for the presidential visit, later scheduled to begin on Feb. 21, 1972.

Kissinger was born in Fürth, Ger., on May 27, 1923, and emigrated to the U.S. with his parents in 1938 in order to escape persecution under Hitler. After serving in World War II, he entered Harvard University, received his doctorate in 1954, became a professor of government there and a consultant to Presidents Eisenhower, Kennedy, and Johnson. He severed his connections with Harvard in 1971 to remain at the White House. He seemed to enjoy a reputation as the sort of man beautiful women seek out at social events. (J. F. Ba.)

LANUSSE, ALEJANDRO AGUSTÍN

After leading a bloodless military coup against Roberto Levingston, the incumbent he had installed, Lieut. Gen. Alejandro Lanusse assumed the presidency of Argentina on March 26, 1971. The new president had a paradoxical political record. He had taken part in or led no less than five military coup attempts, yet in 1971 was the leading proponent of returning Argentina to elected government. He was probably the stoutest enemy of former dictator Juan Perón, yet also recognized that Argentina could not have any semblance of democratic government without the participation of the neo-Peronists, who were the most cohesive element on the national political scene.

Lanusse was born Aug. 28, 1918, to an aristocratic family of landowners in Buenos Aires. He graduated from the National Military School in 1938 and was a captain and a student in the Superior War School when he took part in an abortive attempt to overthrow General Perón. The Peronists jailed him for four years until the eventual overthrow of Perón in 1955. Lanusse swore that if Perón ever returned to Argentina from exile one or the other of them would die within 24 hours. As commander of the presidential palace guard, Lanusse helped in the overthrow of Gen. Eduardo Lonardi, Perón's successor, in 1955. In June 1966, Lanusse joined with Gen. Juan Carlos Onganía and other officers in ousting constitutional president Arturo Illía.

Onganía appointed Lanusse commander of the Army in 1968. In June 1970, Lanusse joined with the Navy and Air Force commanders to oust Onganía. The basic reason for Onganía's downfall was his increasing penchant for making decisions without consulting with the armed forces. The replacement selected by Lanusse and his cohorts was Brig. Gen. Roberto Marcelo Levingston, who was serving as military attaché in the U.S. When Lanusse and the other military leaders decided the time had come for a staged return to democratic rule, Levingston defied and tried to fire them. Lanusse and the military leaders then deposed Levingston on March 22, and two weeks later Lanusse ordered the Interior Ministry to begin preparations for return to civil rule by means of elections in 1973. Lanusse later successfully suppressed an uprising of two regiments led by rightist officers on October 8. (J. A. O'L.)

LINDSAY, JOHN VLIET

Rumours persisted during early 1971 that John V. Lindsay, mayor of New York City, would switch from the Republican to the Democratic Party and that he would seek the Democratic nomination for the presidency. He announced the shift in parties on August 11. "Whether this means I'll run for president, I do not know," he said. He maintained that his main objective was to fight for new national leadership to turn the country around in 1972.

Within a few weeks, however, he was on the road, meeting with Democratic leaders in New Hampshire, California, and other states, looking very much the candidate. He told newsmen he went to New Hampshire because a "bachelor assistant" was getting married. He added that he had other "bachelor assistants" active in Wisconsin, California, and Oregon, which, like New Hampshire, have presidential primaries. Late in September Lindsay estimated his chances for the Democratic nomination were 100 to 1 and added that if the chances did not improve by January "it's damn doubtful I'd run." Finally, in a press conference held in Miami on December 28, he dropped the other shoe, announcing that he was a candidate for the Democratic nomination and that he would enter the Florida presidential primary. The following day he entered the presidential primary in Wisconsin.

Lindsay's switch to the Democratic Party had long been expected. In his contest for a second four-year term as mayor in 1969, he was defeated in the Republican primary. He ran successfully, however, as the candidate of the Liberal Party and the newly organized Independent Party. In 1970 he supported Democratic candidate Arthur J. Goldberg for the governorship of New York against Nelson A. Rockefeller. In announcing the changeover, Lindsay said "there was . . . no flash of lightning," but a gradual realization that the Republican Party "has finally become a closed institution."

Lindsay was born Nov. 24, 1921, in New York City. He was graduated from Yale University in 1944 and served in the Navy during World War II before entering law school. He represented New York's 17th congressional district (the "Silk Stocking district") in the U.S. House of Representatives from 1959 until his election as mayor in 1965. (Mx. H.)

John V. Lindsay

Glenda Jackson

Ruby Keeler with Busby Berkeley

Henry Kissinger

Carl McIntire

George McGovern

Joseph Losey

LOSEY, JOSEPH

Like several other successful film makers who helped raise the British cinema's international status, Joseph Losey, director of *The Go-Between,* which won the Grand Prix at the 1971 Cannes Film Festival, was an expatriate American.

Losey was born in La Crosse, Wis., on Jan. 14, 1909. He studied medicine at Dartmouth College where his interest in the theatre was aroused, leading him to spend a year studying literature at the Harvard Graduate School of Arts and Sciences. Throughout the 1930s he wrote and directed in the theatre in Europe as well as the United States. His first film, a puppet short feature on the history of oil, was made in 1939, and this was followed in 1943 by two shorts for the U.S. Army made while he was in the Signal Corps.

Losey's first feature film, *The Boy with Green Hair,* was made in Hollywood in 1948. A slightly naïve political fantasy, it was followed by four more American films, all socially conscious but of variable quality. In the early 1950s Losey was blacklisted from working in Hollywood for alleged Communist sympathies and returned to Europe where he made a feature film in Italy and two in England under pseudonyms. By 1957 he had settled in England, which was the scene of his subsequent career and became his permanent home.

In the early 1960s Losey directed such films as *The Criminal, These Are the Damned,* and *Eva.* They attracted attention, although their baroque and overemphatic style irritated some critics. It was *The Servant* (1963), Losey's first collaboration with playwright Harold Pinter, that finally established him not only as a film maker of distinction but as an intelligent observer of the English social scene. His obsession with the class structure in Britain and its effects on personal lives continued in *Accident* and *The Go-Between,* both also scripted by Pinter. Losey's films seemed to fall into two distinct categories: the restrained, meticulously observed social studies made with Pinter and embodying a sort of love-hate relationship with the recent English past; and extravaganzas such as *Modesty Blaise, Boom,* and *Secret Ceremony,* in which he gave full rein to his taste for the baroque. Both were enjoyable in their different ways and all bore the mark of a master film maker. (B. D.)

LUNS, JOSEPH MARIE ANTOINE HUBERT

Doyen of Western European foreign ministers, Joseph Luns left his country's government in 1971 to become secretary-general of the North Atlantic Treaty Organization, a position to which he was elected by the NATO Council of Ministers on June 4. He succeeded Manlio Brosio of Italy.

Luns had headed the Netherlands Ministry for Foreign Affairs continuously from 1956. During his 19 years as Cabinet minister he had exerted considerable influence on the foreign policy of the Netherlands and of Western Europe as a whole. He was a staunch supporter of consolidation of the Atlantic alliance and of U.S. policy toward Southeast Asia. He also played an active part in attempts to bring about European unification and expansion of the European Economic Community. Although he had great respect for Charles de Gaulle (whom he was said to resemble not only in being very tall but also in obstinacy), he resolutely opposed him with regard to France's position in the EEC and the question of Britain's admission to membership —for which he was an enthusiastic and consistent advocate.

When Luns became foreign minister in 1956 the Netherlands was in the throes of a confrontation with Indonesia over the future of Netherlands New Guinea (West Irian) in which emotions ran high. Luns had to preside over a complete reversal of Dutch policy when in 1962 agreement was reached by which the territory was to be transferred to Indonesia under UN auspices.

Born in Rotterdam on Aug. 28, 1911, Luns was educated at Amsterdam and Brussels. He studied law at the University of Leiden and graduated at the University of Amsterdam. Before entering the Netherlands foreign service in 1938, he continued his studies abroad, at the London School of Economics and Political Science and elsewhere. After holding several diplomatic posts (Bern, 1940–41; Lisbon, 1941–43; London, 1943–49; United Nations, New York, 1949–52), he entered the Cabinet in 1952, when the Catholic People's Party appointed him minister without portfolio. He was awarded the Prix Charlemagne in 1967 and the Gustav Stresemann Medal in 1968. (D. Bo.)

McGOVERN, GEORGE STANLEY

On Jan. 18, 1971, more than 21 months before the election, Sen. George McGovern of South Dakota officially announced his candidacy for the 1972 Democratic presidential nomination. The announcement made him the first to formally enter the field. Not since Andrew Jackson 145 years earlier had anyone declared himself so far in advance.

McGovern had little choice, however. He was too far behind to wait. According to the public opinion polls, only 2% of the nation's Democrats said they wanted him as their nominee. He also felt that, with his well-spoken but low-key style, he could not gain ground quickly. The 49-year-old son of a Methodist minister said of his personality, "People think I come across like a Sunday School teacher."

McGovern had little trouble forming an organization of high calibre and raising at least sufficient money for his 1971 effort. Many of his staff members were professionals, 1968 supporters of the late Robert F. Kennedy and former senator Eugene McCarthy, who joined up because McGovern, an air force veteran who flew 35 combat missions in World War II, had been outspokenly opposed to the war in Vietnam longer than anyone else in the Senate.

Money was available because McGovern had carefully maintained lists of contributors to his highly successful effort to raise funds for congressional peace candidates in 1970.

The war remained a prominent issue for McGovern in 1971. Along with Sen. Mark Hatfield (Rep., Ore.), he reintroduced a resolution in the Senate to pull U.S. troops out of Indochina. He also visited the Paris peace talks and made a trip to Vietnam. But to prove he was not a one-issue candidate, he attacked the Nixon administration's economic policies, called for less military spending, and urged more federal emphasis on domestic problems.

McGovern was born July 19, 1922, at Avon, S.D. He received his B.A. from Dakota Wesleyan University at Mitchell, S.D., and, after obtaining a Ph.D. at Northwestern University, returned to Dakota Wesleyan to teach history and political science. He was elected to the House of Representatives in 1956 and to the Senate in 1962. In 1968 he campaigned briefly for the presidential nomination after Robert Kennedy, whom he supported, was assassinated.

(F. Wt.)

McINTIRE, CARL

Preacher Carl McIntire, long defrocked but undeterred, tried to boost his brand of rabidly political Christianity with two Marches for Victory in Vietnam in 1971. One, in the spring on the Washington Monument grounds, was to feature South Vietnam's Vice-Pres. Nguyen Cao Ky. The visit never came to pass, possibly because the Nixon administration prevailed on Ky to stay away; his appearance certainly would have sparked a riot. Veteran demonstration watchers in Washington termed the rally little more than pathetic. It was not eclipsed in October by the gathering of barely 2,500 faithful who joined McIntire to oppose Pres. Richard Nixon's proposed visit to China.

The self-styled "Number One anti-Communist of American Protestantism" fared better at Cape Kennedy, Fla. There he established the Reformation Freedom Center at a multimillion dollar, 300-ac. resort complex. Some local residents and businessmen welcomed McIntire's invasion as a new magnet for tourist dollars to replace dwindling revenues from U.S. space activity. Others feared the area would become a "camp of ultraconservatism."

Born in Ypsilanti, Mich., May 17, 1906, McIntire was reared in Oklahoma where his father was a Presbyterian minister. He took a degree at Westminster Theological Seminary in Philadelphia, Pa., and was ordained as a Presbyterian. But missionary policies of the church were too liberal for him and he withheld funds from the national organization. An ecclesiastical court defrocked him in 1935 for "sowing dissension within the church." In retaliation, he founded the Bible Presbyterian Church, a fundamentalist sect that had about 35 congregations in the U.S. in 1971.

McIntire's religious operations, including a daily radio program that was syndicated throughout the Bible Belt of the South, and a newspaper with a circulation of 134,000, were supported by donations from his followers. Recently, however, the college he ran at his Twentieth Century Reformation Center in Collingswood, N.J., to educate "Christian warriors" lost its state accreditation. The license of his nearby radio station was revoked after the Greater Philadelphia Council of Churches complained that its programming was blatantly "anti-Semitic, anti-Negro, and anti-Roman Catholic."

(Ph. K.)

Norman Mailer

McMAHON, WILLIAM

Sworn in as prime minister of Australia on March 10, 1971, William McMahon emerged as his country's leader as a result of a crisis within the Liberal Party, senior partner in the Liberal-Country Party coalition that had ruled Australia since 1949. Before taking office McMahon had been elected leader of the parliamentary Liberal Party, and at that time he stated that his main stance as a politician was anti-Communist and anti-socialist. His task was to stop the widespread dissatisfaction with the coalition and revitalize his party for the 1972 elections.

The party crisis had grown out of a dispute between the previous prime minister, John Grey Gorton, and the minister for defense, Malcolm Fraser. McMahon's task was made more difficult by Gorton's election as deputy leader and his decision to take up the defense portfolio vacated by Fraser. On August 12 McMahon dismissed Gorton from the Cabinet after Gorton was charged with breaching its solidarity by writing newspaper articles alleging widespread leakage of information by ministers; he was replaced as defense minister by David Fairbairn. A week later Fraser was reinstated in the Cabinet as minister for education and science following the reshuffle necessitated by Gorton's departure to the back benches.

During the year McMahon tried to counter the diplomatic initiatives of the Australian Labor Party opposition toward China. He took a hard line on the South African Rugby tour of Australia, and lost ground when the South African cricket tour had to be canceled. He was extremely critical of the activities of the president of the Australian Council of Trade Unions, R. J. Hawke. His most important decision was to remove Australian troops from Vietnam by the end of 1971. In November he journeyed overseas for talks with Pres. Richard Nixon and Prime Minister Edward Heath.

Born on Feb. 23, 1908, McMahon was educated at Sydney University, graduating in law. After serving in the Australian Army during World War II he traveled in Europe and North America and on his return to Australia obtained a degree in economics. As a member of the House of Representatives for Lowe, New South Wales, from 1949 he held the portfolios of navy and air, social services, labour and national service, primary industry, the treasury, and foreign affairs (1969–71).

(A. R. G. G.)

MAILER, NORMAN

Norman Mailer's name was mud among women's liberationists in 1971. First he had the "sexist" audacity to publish a lengthy essay entitled "The Prisoner of Sex" in *Harper's;* feminists labeled it outrageous male chauvinism (coincidentally, it was said to have brought on editor Willie Morris' departure from the magazine). Then he challenged some women's liberationists to debate in New York's Town Hall, where he called their philosophy "Diaper Marxism." One of his distaff antagonists, who had a pistol permit, threatened to shoot him.

The coolest adversary there, Germaine Greer, responded to his *Harper's* article with one of her own in *Esquire.* "For Mailer, Women's Liberation had become simply another battle of the books in a war in which he had been campaigning all his life," she wrote. Greer went on to question his essential masculinity and to warn: "In challenging the women's movement he put himself in danger, for theirs is a fight for life, no holds barred."

Autobiographical essay had been Mailer's literary preoccupation in recent years, and the *Harper's* piece was only the latest example. He won the National Book Award, the Pulitzer and Polk prizes in 1969 for *Armies of the Night,* a personal account of a peace march in Washington, D.C., and chronicled several national political conventions and manned moon missions. His last novel was the 1967 *Why Are We in Vietnam?,* which he called an exercise in comic obscenity. Still his career was founded in fiction.

Born in Long Branch, N.J., Jan. 31, 1923, he was raised in Brooklyn and entered Harvard as an engineering student at 16. Drafted for army duty in the Pacific, he drew on that experience for his masterful World War II novel, *The Naked and the Dead* (1948). *Barbary Shore,* a novel of political ideology, followed to little acclaim in 1951; then came *The Deer Park* (1955) and *An American Dream,* written in installments for *Esquire.* Boisterous, bawdy, and a man of eclectic energies, Mailer was a founder of the *Village Voice* and once ran for mayor of New York, pledging to turn the city into the 51st state. He also made several movies, shot à la cinéma vérité with scant planned script and said to be interesting if rambling and self-indulgent.

(Ph. K.)

MALIK, ADAM

In his acceptance speech after being elected president of the 26th session of the United Nations General Assembly on Sept. 21, 1971, Adam Malik expressed the hope that the session would be remembered as "an assembly of universality." He urged that it achieve universality of membership by including all the divided nations without prejudice "as to political ideology, social system or legal recognition." On another occasion, he told newsmen he believed China should be seated in the world organization while permitting Taiwan to retain its seat. Malik, speaking as foreign minister of Indonesia, noted that his country was the only one that had left the UN and returned to it. "We must come to the realization," he said, "that at some point every nation, big or small, strong or weak, will need the United Nations."

Malik was born in Pematangsiantar in North Sumatra on July 22, 1917. His formal education was limited to attending a Dutch-run primary school for Indonesians and a religious school. He became involved in the nationalist movement at an early age and at the age of 17 was chairman of the Partai Indonesia (Indonesia Party) in Pematangsiantar. In 1937 he founded the Antara press bureau, which later became the national Antara News Agency. Antara was taken over during the Japanese occupation in World War II, and Malik continued to work there while maintaining close contact with the underground nationalist movement.

When Indonesia was struggling to maintain its independence after the war, Malik served as third deputy chairman of the first Indonesian Parliament and as a member of its Daily Executive Board. He began his career in foreign affairs as Indonesian ambassador to the U.S.S.R. and Poland in 1959. He represented Indonesia in the 1962 negotiations that led to the transfer of West Irian (West New Guinea) from the Netherlands to Indonesia. In November 1963, Malik was appointed minister of commerce, and in 1965 he became minister-coordinator for the implementation of "guided economy." As foreign minister since 1966, Malik had been the architect of his country's nonalignment policy and had led Indonesia back into the UN after former president Sukarno had withdrawn from the world organization in 1965 because Malaysia was elected to the Security Council.   (Mx. H.)

MATAK, SISOWATH SIRIK

The paralytic stroke that felled Cambodia's premier, Gen. Lon Nol, in February 1971 put the spotlight on Sirik Matak, the man who always had been credited as the brain behind the coup d'etat against Prince Norodom Sihanouk the previous year. Known as an ambitious and skillful political operator and the power behind Lon Nol, he should have been a natural successor to the premier. But the fact that he also made powerful political enemies stood in the way.

During the two months Lon Nol underwent treatment in Hawaii, Sirik Matak acted as premier, but when Lon Nol resigned on his return to Phnom Penh there was no automatic transfer of power. In the end Sirik Matak's opponents failed to keep him down only because he was strongly backed by the U.S. establishment in Cambodia. Lon Nol returned as premier with Sirik Matak, designated premier-delegate, wielding effective power.

Born on Jan. 22, 1914, Sirik Matak was a member of the Khmer royal family and a cousin of the prince he helped overthrow. He belonged to the Sisowath branch of the family, Sihanouk to the Norodom branch. The ruler before Sihanouk, King Monivong, was a Sisowath and the line of succession was broken because the French thought Monivong's eldest son, Sisowath Monireth, was too blunt a nationalist. It was believed that Sirik Matak bore a grudge against Sihanouk because of the circumstances under which the French gave him the throne. In the Khmer royal tradition of intricate intermarriages, Sirik Matak married Norodom Kathneari. They had six children.

Educated at Saigon and Phnom Penh, Sirik Matak started his career in the administrative service, and his royal blood helped him rise to be governor of various provinces. His political career began in 1952, and he was six times national defense minister and four times education minister. He also held the portfolios of foreign affairs, communications, information, and interior at various times, and had been Cambodian ambassador to China, Japan, and the Philippines. He was currently a three-star general. He was first deputy premier in the "salvation government" formed by Sihanouk in August 1969, seven months before the coup.

(T. J. S. G.)

MEANY, GEORGE

As the economy replaced Vietnam in the forefront of problems facing the United States in 1971, organized labour's voice in opposition to Pres. Richard M. Nixon's domestic programs became louder and more critical. Chief spokesman for the 20 million union members in the U.S. was George Meany, since 1952 head of the American Federation of Labor and since 1955 president of the combined AFL-CIO labour federation.

Meany, a gruff, white-haired, one-time plumber from New York City, criticized the Nixon administration's economic policy through midsummer as unemployment rose to 5.8% and inflationary pressures continued. Then, on August 15, in a dramatic nationwide television address, Nixon announced a "new economic policy," calling for a 90-day wage-price freeze, import taxes, and tax adjustments for individuals and business.

Meany promptly charged that the new program favoured business and discriminated against the working man. He was joined by United Auto Workers Pres. Leonard Woodcock and Teamsters Pres. Frank Fitzsimmons, heads of the two largest unions not affiliated with the AFL-CIO. The three announced that they would defer support for the president's program until actual plans for its administration had been drawn up.

On October 7 Nixon announced his plans, including a tripartite Pay Board of which labour would be a working member. Meany's 35-member executive council, meeting in special session (with the Teamsters and UAW attending in a show of labour solidarity), agreed to participate in the Pay Board only after being assured that it would be autonomous, restricted only by overall administration policy.

But the reconciliation was far from complete. Making a last-minute appearance before the AFL-CIO convention in Miami, Fla., Nixon was greeted coolly and without the usual playing of "Hail to the Chief." His speech was angry and, when it was over, his attempt to greet the delegates was cut short when Meany abruptly called the meeting to order. Later, the convention voted to raise Meany's salary from $70,000 a year to $90,000—a 28% hike, compared with the admin-

istration's 5.5% guideline—though it was not clear at year's end whether the Pay Board would allow it or not.

Meany was born Aug. 16, 1894, in New York City. After attending public schools in the city he worked as a plumber. In 1922 he became business representative of his local union. He served as president of the New York State Federation of Labor from 1934 to 1939 and as secretary-treasurer of the AFL from 1940 to 1952.   (M. B. Su.)

MEIR, GOLDA

In 1971 Israel's prime minister, Golda Meir, faced a degree of domestic unrest, discontent, and malaise that seriously threatened the tremendous popularity she had achieved the previous year, when her firm refusal to move from Israel's stated position echoed the popular mood. The policy of *immobilisme* had begun to exact its price on the home front, and as the pressures of inflation, taxation, and social discrimination built up, some observers doubted Mrs. Meir's ability to retain the reins of power throughout 1972—her announced final year of office. The lack of initiative in foreign policy and the involvement of two of her ministers in a public inquiry made the challenge of Defense Minister Moshe Dayan all the more serious.

When Mrs. Meir was sworn in as Israel's fourth prime minister on March 17, 1969, following the sudden death of Levi Eshkol, it was a choice that few Israelis outside the inner circle of the establishment had anticipated. She was then 71, and an opinion poll on the eve of her appointment had given her only a 1% vote. Once in office, she set her objectives in precise terms. She was above all concerned that Israel's security should remain in its own hands, and that neither the UN nor the great powers should become the arbiters of its fate. She also set out to ensure a united country.

She courted unpopularity among friends abroad in the pursuit of her policy, and rejected any separate accommodation with the Palestinians because she feared this might upset the security equilibrium. Her unwillingness to trade Israeli positions for hypothetical peace offers strained relationships with Washington, which spent much of the year searching for a Middle East peace formula. Her December trip to the U.S. for talks with Pres. Richard Nixon appeared to have eased the situation if it did not totally resolve the differences between the two leaders.

Golda Meir was born in Kiev, Russia, on May 3, 1898. She emigrated to Milwaukee, Wis., in 1906 and settled in Palestine with her Russian-born husband in 1921. Her increasing involvement in politics led to the directorship of the political department of the Jewish Agency for Israel in 1946. She was minister of labour (1949–56), foreign minister (1956–66), and secretary-general of Mapai (the Labour Party) until July 1968.

(J. K.)

MILLS, WILBUR DAIGH

"Wilbur watching" was the phrase coined to describe the pastime of trying to figure out what was happening behind the inscrutable features of Wilbur D. Mills, chairman since 1958 of the powerful U.S. House Ways and Means Committee. And 1971 was a banner year for Wilbur watchers. Because his committee handled money bills, Pres. Richard Nixon's new economic measures thrust him automatically into the spotlight. With increasing seriousness, the taciturn Arkansas Democrat was being mentioned as a presidential possibility for 1972.

As usual, he kept his own counsel, but the signals grew that he, too, took the idea seriously. Contrary to his custom, he took on an active and wide-ranging speaking schedule. He broke precedent and consented to appear on nationally televised interview shows. He accepted—but did not encourage—the opening of a Draft Mills for President headquarters in downtown Washington. His hand was reported to be behind action by the Arkansas legislature that would allow a person to run for Congress and be a national candidate at the same time.

The whole nation had indeed been touched by the important legislation considered by Ways and Means—taxation, tariffs, social security, health insurance, welfare reform. Mills also was chairman of the Democratic Committee on Committees, the group that controlled the committee assignments of all House Democrats. Whether liked or disliked, Mills was respected by his fellow representatives, regardless of party. A conservative both personally and politically, he shunned Washington social life, concentrating on his legislative homework and acquiring a reputation for encyclopaedic knowledge of the bills before his committee. Bills approved by Ways and Means were virtually assured of passage in the House.

Mills was born on May 24, 1909, in Kensett, Ark. He was graduated from Hendrix College, Conway, Ark., in 1930 and from Harvard Law School in 1933. Elected to the House in 1938, Mills was never opposed in a general election and he had primary opponents only three times. His dominant position was recognized in 1971 by another House member who asked him, "Wilbur, why do you want to run for President and give up your grip on the country?"

(M. Cs.)

MILNES, SHERRILL

"The best American baritone to have appeared since the young Robert Merrill" and "another Leonard Warren" were among the accolades awarded to Sherrill Milnes after his debut at the Metropolitan Opera, New York, in 1965, only five years after embarking on his operatic career. On April 22, 1971, he made his debut at the Royal Opera, Covent Garden, as Renato in *Un Ballo in Maschera,* and won further laurels.

Born at Downers Grove, Ill., on Jan. 10, 1935, Milnes began singing as a boy in local choirs at his home just outside Chicago, where he had a farming-cum-musical upbringing ("I was brought up to milk cows and to have an interest in music; it was an odd combination"). Music was eventually the winner, and he enrolled at Drake University in Des Moines, Ia., to study and train as a music teacher. He joined the Chicago Symphony Orchestra Chorus and by 1959 thought his voice was about ready to face professional competition. Engagements came quickly, and he decided to join the Boris Goldovsky touring company. Between 1960 and 1965 he sang some 500 performances with the group.

After winning one of the prizes in the American Opera Auditions in 1964, he sang in *Il Barbiere di Siviglia* at the Teatro Nuovo in Milan. The same year he appeared with the New York City Opera Company as Valentin in *Faust,* and in 1965 graduated to the Met in the same role. At the Met he sang a succession of parts with increasing success. His debut in Britain was delayed until 1969 when he appeared in a concert performance of *La Gioconda.* He sang in the complete recordings of many operas, including Rodrigo in a much-praised 1971 recording of Verdi's *Don Carlos.*

Milnes's voice was a strong, exciting Verdian baritone in the tradition established by Lawrence Tibbett and Leonard Warren.

George Meany

Adam Malik

Golda Meir

He wanted to add Don Giovanni in Italian to his repertory (he sang it in English with Goldovsky), and he hoped to improve his other portrayals, particularly Iago in *Otello.*

(A. G. Bl.)

MINDSZENTY, JOZSEF CARDINAL

On Sept. 28, 1971, Jozsef Cardinal Mindszenty, archbishop of Esztergom and primate of Hungary, emerged from 15 years' refuge in the U.S. embassy in Budapest, where he had sought asylum in 1956. Until then he had been serving a life sentence imposed by Hungary's Communist regime in 1949. During World War II he had been imprisoned by the Nazis. He was a tragic figure not only because of his sufferings and long isolation but also because his strength of character had made him an embarrassment to his church.

Jozsef Mindszenty was born on March 29, 1892, at Csehimindszent, near Szombathely. Ordained priest on June 12, 1915, he was appointed bishop of Veszprem on March 3, 1944. In October he was arrested by the Germans because he refused to recognize the authority of the Fascist puppet regime. Liberated by Soviet troops in April 1945, he was appointed archbishop of Esztergom and primate of Hungary by Pope Pius XII on October 2 and named cardinal on Feb. 18, 1946.

In 1948, when the Communist Hungarian government undertook to nationalize all Catholic schools, Mindszenty strongly protested. On December 26 he was arrested on a charge of treason, including espionage for the West. His show trial, staged in typically Stalinist style, opened on Feb. 3, 1949. He "confessed," and on February 8 was sentenced to life imprisonment. More than seven years later, on Oct. 30, 1956, Hungarian freedom fighters released the cardinal from confinement and brought him to his palace at Buda. After the suppression of the revolt by Soviet armour early in November, Mindszenty took asylum in the then U.S. legation (Nov. 4, 1956).

From 1963 the Vatican made many efforts to persuade the cardinal that in the interest of Hungarian Catholics he should leave the country, but he insisted that the Hungarian government should proclaim his complete rehabilitation and assure him the right to reenter the country. The government was ready only to give him a free pardon on leaving the country forever. In mid-September 1971 Pope Paul VI sent to Budapest a member of the Curia, Msgr. Giovanni Cheli; bowing to higher church considerations, Mindszenty finally obeyed, and on September 28 arrived in Rome.

(K. Sm.)

MINTOFF, DOMINIC

Returning to power in June 1971, after 13 years in opposition to the Nationalist government, Dom Mintoff, leader of the Maltese Labour Party, immediately asserted his bad temper. He demanded replacement of the British governor-general by a Maltese and revision of the ten-year Anglo-Maltese de-

Edmund S. Muskie

Ralph Nader

fense agreement signed in 1964. He also declared the Italian NATO naval commander posted at Valletta persona non grata and stated that no treaty existed permitting the U.S. 6th Fleet to use Maltese harbours.

Under the 1964 agreement with Great Britain, Malta was receiving £5 million yearly; in return, it agreed to the stationing of a British infantry battalion on the island and the operation of Royal Air Force and Royal Navy installations. Mintoff wanted Great Britain to pay a rent of £30 million yearly.

Lord Carrington, the British defense secretary, visited Mintoff on July 20–21 and told him that his demands were unrealistic. On August 7–8 Mintoff received Jörg Kastl, NATO acting secretary-general, and on August 20 it was announced that NATO Mediterranean naval headquarters had been transferred to Naples. While bargaining with London, Mintoff visited Col. Muammar al-Qaddafi, the Libyan leader, and was visited by the Soviet ambassador to the U.K. Moscow announced on August 20 that Soviet ships would henceforth be repaired in Maltese dry docks.

After all these soundings, Mintoff went to London on September 17 and stayed at Chequers with Prime Minister Edward Heath. It was disclosed that he had accepted an offer of £6 million in cash and £3.5 million in development aid annually, and half this amount (£4,750,000) was paid in advance on September 30. However, when in December Mintoff demanded an immediate additional payment of £4,250,000, the British government announced that it would withdraw all personnel and equipment from the base. At year's end, with the British withdrawal under way, Mintoff was again negotiating with Libya.

Mintoff was born on Aug. 6, 1916, at Kospikwa, Malta. After becoming prime minister in 1955, he first asked for Malta's integration with the U.K., but when he and London disagreed over financial aid, he resigned in April 1958 and then agitated for complete independence. (K. Sм.)

MONOD, JACQUES

An unexpected best seller, *Le Hasard et la nécessité* (*Chance and Necessity*), and his appointment as head of the Pasteur Institute

in Paris put molecular biologist and Nobel prizewinner Jacques Monod in the public eye in 1971. His theories were vehemently discussed in drawing rooms and universities, as Existentialism had been a few years earlier.

Monod's researches into molecular biology, undertaken jointly with François Jacob and André Lwoff in the late 1940s and 1950s, led to the award of the 1965 Nobel Prize for Medicine or Physiology to the trio for discoveries that obliged scientists to revise their conceptions of the origins and mechanisms of life. In 1967, in a sensational inaugural lecture as professor of metabolic chemistry at the Collège de France, Monod clearly defined his stand on the problems facing contemporary man. In *Chance and Necessity* he developed his ideas further.

From the discovery that the living being's faculty for reproducing itself derives entirely from the particular structure of a chemical molecule, deoxyribonucleic acid (DNA), which serves to store hereditary information, Monod concluded that matter and life are only different arrangements of the same atoms. Nature proposes groupings of molecules: some are ephemeral; others perpetuate and reproduce themselves. As a result, man is seen as the simple product of chance and necessity, an accident in the universe. Hence values, which are given their meaning by man, no longer can be founded on religions and mythologies, but on objective knowledge alone. Monod himself calls this "an austere, abstract, and arrogant morality," attainable only by an elite since, in the consumer society, men have become alienated from science.

Born in Paris on Feb. 9, 1910, Monod went to school in Cannes, then to the University of Paris. He won a Rockefeller Foundation grant in 1936. After service in World War II, for which he received French and U.S. decorations, he joined the Pasteur Institute in 1945, becoming head of its cellular biochemistry department in 1953.

(S. Ls.)

MORTON, ROGERS CLARK BALLARD

When the U.S. Senate confirmed Rogers C. B. Morton as the new secretary of the interior on Jan. 28, 1971, misgivings al-

ready had appeared in the press about his ability to be as effective a conservationist as Walter J. Hickel, whom he replaced. Morton soon reassured the doubters. In mid-February he announced that the government would not grant oil or gas drilling rights in Los Padres National Forest in California because it was the nesting ground of most condors, an endangered species. That was only the first of several strong conservationist actions.

In the same month, Undersecretary of the Interior Fred J. Russell resigned. Reportedly, he had been asked to leave because of his pro-business philosophy and his reversal of environmental protection orders previously issued by Hickel. Morton also told a Senate Appropriations subcommittee in February he was a "long way" from approving the controversial 800-mi. oil pipeline through Alaska.

In March, Morton testified before the House Interior Committee that the U.S. had "dragged its feet" in its relations with the Pacific trust territories. In April, Pres. Richard Nixon sent to Congress a bill, drawn up by Morton, to settle the claims of Alaska's 60,000 Eskimos, Aleuts, and Indians; as passed by Congress in December, the law would give the Alaskan natives 40 million ac. of land and $962 million, including $462 million from the U.S. Treasury. Morton also announced moves to improve the treatment of Indians.

Born in Louisville, Ky., Sept. 19, 1914, Morton received an A.B. from Yale in 1937. He became a gentleman farmer in Maryland in the 1950s and was elected to Congress for five consecutive terms. He was Nixon's floor manager at the 1968 GOP national convention and served as Republican national chairman for two years before being named to head the Interior Department.

(T. R. T.)

MURDOCH, KEITH RUPERT

Arriving in England from Australia in 1968 almost unknown to the British public, Rupert Murdoch took only a couple of years to establish himself as the most dynamic of Fleet Street's newspaper tycoons. He came in October 1968 to help the family proprietors of the Sunday *News of the World* thwart a take-over bid by Pergamon Press publisher Robert Maxwell. Appointed managing director in January 1969, he quickly raised the paper's circulation by 500,000, partly by serializing the memoirs of Christine Keeler (a central figure in a scandal that had rocked the Conservative government in 1963), a stroke that was condemned by the Press Council as unethical.

In June 1969 the chairman of the company, Sir William Carr, retired, and Murdoch, at the age of 38, succeeded him. In August he made a successful bid for the ailing *Sun*, but not before clashing once again with Maxwell, who had plans to run the *Sun* as a nonprofit-making paper in support of the Labour Party. Murdoch more than doubled the *Sun*'s circulation in under two years, having turned the paper into a tabloid run on an unabashed formula of sexual titillation and sports backed up with sharp news presentation. Murdoch then widened his interests to take in television. Chipping in more than £500,000 to help out the flagging London Weekend Television (in which David Frost held a large stake), he became its majority shareholder and effective boss.

Born in Australia on March 11, 1931, Murdoch inherited a relatively small newspaper property, based on an Adelaide evening paper, from his father, Sir Keith Murdoch, in 1952. By 1968 he had added papers in Sydney, Perth, Melbourne, and Brisbane, and Adelaide's principal TV station. In 1964 he launched the *Australian* (Melbourne), planned as Australia's first national paper. His experience in Australia had made him a practical newspaperman and editor as well as proprietor. Admittedly, his target sometimes seemed to be the lower end of the mass audience, to be won by appealing to the lowest common denominator of taste. He also had a left-of-centre view of politics, and as a student had been president of the Oxford University Labour Club. The latest of his newspaper ventures was the *Sunday Australian*, to be run on the lines of Britain's quality Sunday papers.   (W. H. Ts.)

MUSKIE, EDMUND SIXTUS

Maine's Sen. Edmund S. Muskie spent 1971 nurturing his position as front-runner for the 1972 Democratic presidential nomination. Although Muskie had been in politics since the 1940s, when he first was elected to the state House of Representatives, two much more recent events had moved him to the fore. His 1968 candidacy for vice-president made him well known nationally and gave him a reputation for independence and coolness. In 1970 his stature was enhanced by his nationally televised election eve speech chastising Pres. Richard Nixon and the Republican Party for practicing what Muskie called the "politics of fear."

At the start of 1971 the public opinion polls showed Muskie well ahead, but numerous problems soon arose. His staff, initially devoted to developing positions on issues, had to be revamped to put more emphasis on political organization in the states. Money became difficult to find as potential contributors held back, many of them waiting to see whether an old friend, Sen. Hubert Humphrey of Minnesota, the 1968 nominee, would run again.

As 1972 grew closer, Republicans and some of Muskie's Democratic competitors began to attack him. They accused him of being indecisive. He replied that he felt it necessary to consider all sides of a question before taking a stand. He was accused of dashing the hopes of black people by saying that he could not be elected with a black running mate. He replied that he was trying only to be candid. In all things, he clung closely to the political centre, hoping that his moderately liberal views and subdued approach would project him as a unity candidate who could be supported by all.

Muskie was born March 28, 1914. He attended Bates College, Lewiston, Me., and received a degree from Cornell Law School in 1939. In 1954 he was elected governor of Maine, the first Democrat to hold that office in 20 years, and in 1958 he became the first popularly elected Democratic senator in the state's history.   (F. Wt.)

NADER, RALPH

Throughout 1971 Ralph Nader testified often before committees of the U.S. Congress, arriving in a rumpled suit, his hair uncombed, looking as if he had been up all night working. Chances are that he had. For by the end of the year Nader and his group of dedicated young consumer advocates, known as Nader's Raiders, had prepared and presented scores of studies investigating and attacking policy on such widely divergent topics as pipeline safety, baby food, insecticides, mercury poisoning, pension reform, land use, banking, the century-old practice of dumping human wastes from moving railroad trains, and the stuffing of frankfurters with fat. Nader was credited with being the prime moving force in new legislation calling for stricter regulation of meat- and poultry-processing plants, coal mine safety and health, radiation emissions from television sets, and tire and auto safety standards.

When Nader's book *Unsafe at Any Speed* first appeared in 1965, the author was so unknown that General Motors, whose Corvair automobile was the target of the attack, hired a special investigator to determine who he was and what he was really up to. He was found to be a modest young bachelor and recent graduate of Harvard Law School, who appeared to be up to nothing more than being concerned over the safety, health, and rights of individual citizens living in a world dominated by business and government interests. Corvair sales dropped after Nader's book was published and the car was discontinued entirely in 1969.

If that had been his sole accomplishment Nader would have carved a niche for himself in history. However, it was only the beginning. Nader used royalties from the book and his fees for lecturing to finance other investigations probing into the government's regulatory agencies, which he charged were tools of the industries they were supposed to police.

Nader was born on Feb. 27, 1934, the son of Lebanese immigrants who operated a restaurant and bakery in Winsted, Conn. He recalled he was taught as a child to search for freedom and to question injustices. His decision to go into public service in a private way grew out of what he found at law school. "All the courses," Nader said, "trained us how to defend corporations. I wondered where the lawyers for the ordinary people were being trained, and discovered that they weren't."   (M. B. Su.)

NIMEIRY, GAAFAR

Maj. Gen. Gaafar Nimeiry, chairman of Sudan's Revolutionary Council, survived a three-day pro-Communist counterrevolution in July 1971 to emerge as the country's sole leader. In October he was elected president of Sudan in a popular referendum.

Nimeiry had headed the group of army officers that seized power in May 1969, toppling Sudan's parliamentary democracy. The revolutionary government that he installed was an uneasy alliance of Nasser-type Arab

DENNIS BRACK—BLACK STAR

Rogers Morton

nationalists and Communist sympathizers. The Sudan Communist Party (SCP) stood aloof, but Nimeiry took individual SCP members into his Cabinet.

Tension came to a head in November 1970 when Nimeiry dismissed three members of his Revolutionary Council for leaking Cabinet secrets to the SCP executive, and in February 1971 he pledged to "crush and destroy" the SCP. In July the three dismissed council members staged a coup with the support of the SCP and—Nimeiry later alleged—the Soviet Union and Bulgaria. Nimeiry was held prisoner for three days but, after an epic escape, reestablished his regime. Twelve army officers and three members of the SCP executive were executed for their part in the coup, and more than 1,000 Communists or sympathizers were detained.

Right-wing opposition to the Nimeiry regime had been eliminated with the crushing of the Mahdist movement in March 1970 and so, with the destruction of his Communist collaborators, Nimeiry sought to find a wider popular base for his rule. He formed the Sudanese Socialist Union on the Egyptian model, tried to establish confidence in the war-torn southern provinces by appointing southerners to top posts, and conducted a nationwide personal campaign leading to his election as president in October. He was the only candidate and received 98.6% of the vote. After the election the Revolutionary Council was dissolved.

Born Jan. 1, 1930, at Omdurman, Nimeiry was educated at Hantoub Secondary School and was commissioned in the Sudan Defence Force in 1952, four years before the country gained its independence. He had three times been suspended from active command for political activities.   (Pr. K.)

NIXON, RICHARD MILHOUS

The third year of U.S. Pres. Richard Nixon's administration was one of major policy reversals and surprises. On July 15 the president stunned the world by announcing that he would soon visit the People's Republic

Pope Paul VI

of China, though it had long been an article of faith of U.S. foreign policy that the mainland Communist regime was a pariah among nations. A month later, reversing his well-known aversion to economic controls, he announced an economic policy package that included a 90-day wage-price freeze. In December he announced plans to devalue the dollar.

The administration had been making conciliatory gestures toward Peking for some time. Even so, nothing had prepared either the U.S. public or foreign governments for the presidential visit, which was scheduled to begin Feb. 21, 1972. Given the drama of the Peking trip, the October announcement that Nixon would visit Moscow in May 1972 was almost anticlimactic.

Nixon's "new economic policy" came at a time when the U.S. balance of trade was in deficit and the dollar was under fire in the world's money markets. Perhaps almost as important, high unemployment and continuing inflation were threatening to make the economy a pivotal issue in the 1972 presidential election. Meanwhile, the president continued to defuse the other key issue by diminishing the U.S. presence in Vietnam.

The goal of a "Nixon court" came closer in 1971 when Lewis Powell and William Rehnquist, the third and fourth Supreme Court justices to be appointed by the president, were confirmed by the Senate. In other respects, however, relations between the Democratic-controlled Congress and the president were somewhat strained.

Nixon made a number of political and quasi-political trips during the year, becoming the first president to have visited all 50 states. In September he journeyed to Alaska to greet the emperor and empress of Japan during a stopover on their trip to Europe. Then, in December, he began a round of talks with the heads of allied governments. Canadian Prime Minister Pierre Trudeau came to Washington, after which Nixon met French Premier Georges Pompidou in the Azores, British Prime Minister Edward Heath in Bermuda, and West German Chancellor Willy Brandt in Key Biscayne, Fla.

On the lighter side, Nixon became the seventh president to see a daughter married at the White House (Woodrow Wilson had seen two). The wedding of Patricia Nixon and Edward Finch Cox (*q.v.*) took place on June 12.

Born on Jan. 9, 1913, in Yorba Linda, Calif., Nixon was graduated from Whittier

College and from Duke University Law School. After serving in the Navy during World War II, he won election in 1946 as a U.S. representative from California. He was elected to the U.S. Senate four years later, and in 1952 won election as vice-president on the ticket headed by Dwight D. Eisenhower. He was defeated by John Kennedy in the 1960 presidential election. (J. F. BA.)

PAHLAVI ARYAMEHR, MOHAMMED REZA

"O most noble ancestor, rest in peace, we are here!" proclaimed Mohammed Reza Pahlavi, shah-in-shah (emperor) of Iran, on Oct. 12, 1971, at Pasargadae, when he laid a wreath at the tomb of Cyrus the Great, who 2,500 years before founded the Persian Empire. These lofty words were pronounced near the ruins of Cyrus' palace in the presence of more than 3,000 guests, including 69 heads of state or their representatives.

Two days later the shah-in-shah offered his foreign guests a fabulous banquet in tents near the ruins of Persepolis, the second Persian capital city, built by Darius some 25 mi. SW of Pasargadae. The climax of the celebrations, on October 15, was a splendid military pageant depicting 25 centuries of the Persian Empire, a spectacle surpassing anything Cecil B. DeMille ever mounted. More than 3,000 troops—foot, horse, and camel—paraded in historic uniforms with authentically reproduced weapons, chariots, and other equipment, with tough looking units of the modern Iranian Army bringing up the rear. In connection with the celebration, "Aryamehr," meaning "Light of the Aryans," was added to the shah's name.

These ostentatious and expensive festivities had a clear meaning: after its political and economic transformation under the ruling dynasty, Iran was once more a power to be reckoned with—a power able to take over the British role in the Persian Gulf area. This was demonstrated more concretely when, the day before British withdrawal, Iran forcibly occupied three islands in the Gulf. Iran's strength lay in its immense oil revenues, which had grown steadily since 1954, when a favourable settlement was reached with the foreign oil companies, and which by 1963 enabled the shah to launch the "white revolution" of economic development and agrarian and social reforms.

Mohammed Reza Pahlavi was born in Teheran on Oct. 26, 1919, the eldest son of Reza Shah Pahlavi, who proclaimed himself shah in 1925. He succeeded to the throne on his father's forced abdication, Sept. 16, 1941, while his country was occupied by Soviet, British, and later U.S. troops. His first two wives, Princess Fawzieh, daughter of King Fuad I of Egypt, and Soraya Bakhtiari, were divorced after they failed to produce an heir to the throne. In December 1959 he married Farah Diba, the daughter of an Iranian army captain. A crown prince, Reza, was born on Oct. 31, 1960. The coronation of the shah-in-shah and the empress took place on Oct. 26, 1967. (K. SM.)

PAUL VI

Determination to improve his church's relations with Eastern European governments and to maintain traditional religious values in the face of liberalizing influences marked Paul VI's efforts as Roman Catholic pontiff in 1971. The thaw in relations with Communist governments began in January when Poland announced it would return to the church the lands and buildings confiscated at the end of World War II. In March, Yugoslav President Tito became the first Communist chief of state to pay an official visit to a pope and Paul's unofficial foreign

minister, Archbishop Agostino Casaroli, headed the Vatican's first high-level mission to the U.S.S.R. The Vatican's Eastern policy produced its most dramatic results on September 28, when the pontiff received the primate of Hungary, Jozsef Cardinal Mindszenty, at the Vatican. Mindszenty had acceded to the pope's personal plea that he give up his demand that the Hungarian government withdraw his 1949 treason conviction and exchange his 15-year voluntary asylum in the U.S. embassy in Budapest for exile.

Two days later, on September 30, Pope Paul, with Mindszenty at his side, opened the third synod of bishops. He warned the bishops to beware of "outside influences," particularly opinions of "doubtful conformity with the teachings of the faith" and "accusations of anachronism."

This exhortation reflected much of what the pontiff urged elsewhere during the year. In an apostolic letter issued in May he warned of the danger of "forgetting the intimate link" between Marxist ideology and the "violent society" to which it leads. Commenting on another occasion on priests who broke vows of celibacy, he deplored "the moral mediocrity by which they pretend it is natural and logical to break a long premeditated promise." And, in January, he warned bishops against permitting theologians or psychologists to be the arbiters of Roman Catholic doctrine.

Rumours surfaced throughout the year that the pope might retire in 1972 in compliance with his order that church officials retire by age 75. Pope Paul, born Giovanni Battista Montini on Sept. 26, 1897, in Concesio, Italy, was 74. He was elected pope on June 21, 1963. (*See* RELIGION.)

(J. F. BA.)

POMPIDOU, GEORGES JEAN RAYMOND

On Dec. 12, 1971, French Pres. Georges Pompidou rounded off a year of summit diplomacy with considerable panache by flying off in France's prototype of the Anglo-French Concorde supersonic airliner to the Azores, where he convinced U.S. Pres. Richard Nixon that the dollar should be devalued. The international monetary crisis had also been the topic of Pompidou's conversations with the West German chancellor, Willy Brandt, who had visited Paris earlier in the month. Before that, Pompidou was host to the general secretary of the Soviet Communist Party, Leonid I. Brezhnev, on October 25–30. More significant in its outcome was British Prime Minister Edward Heath's meeting with Pompidou in Paris on May 20–21, when terms were agreed by which France would support Britain's admission to the EEC. Still earlier in the year Pompidou had toured five French-speaking African states, and had also visited Brussels and Bonn, in May and July, respectively.

In his third year as chief of state Pompidou seemed much more relaxed and firmly settled in power than he had prior to the death of his predecessor, Charles de Gaulle, in November 1970. He had begun to assert himself, deviating in some cases from the policies of the Fifth Republic's founder. In internal affairs he sought for a relaxation of tension, for appeasement and order; he succeeded to a great extent in defusing the "leftism" that led to the student upheavals of May 1968, and in avoiding new social crises. His economic administration was considerably less successful: major reforms were either abandoned or rendered ineffectual; relative prosperity led to speculation and financial scandals; and monetary policy was confined to narrow classicism. In the international field Pompidou accepted something de Gaulle always had rejected—British membership in the EEC. He also stressed rapprochement with the U.S. and he pursued a more active policy of détente with the East.

Pompidou was born on July 5, 1911, at Montboudif in the Cantal. In 1958 de Gaulle made him director of the Cabinet during the transition between the Fourth and Fifth Republics and in 1962 he became premier. Dismissed after the disturbances of May 1968, he stood successfully for the presidency in 1969 after de Gaulle's resignation. (P. V.-P.)

POWELL, LEWIS FRANKLIN, JR.

The nomination of Lewis Powell to the U.S. Supreme Court in 1971 came as a surprise. A long list of possible nominees to fill the seats left vacant by the retirement of John Marshall Harlan and Hugo Black had been submitted to the American Bar Association for investigation, leaked to the press, and widely criticized before Pres. Richard Nixon, in a radio and TV address on October 21, named as his choices Powell and Assistant U.S. Attorney General William Rehnquist (*q.v.*), neither of whom had been on the original list. Powell, a corporation lawyer from Richmond, Va., widely respected in legal circles, proved to be the less controversial of the two. While the liberals' fire concentrated on Rehnquist, the Senate confirmed Powell's nomination December 6 by a vote of 89–1.

Powell's stand on civil rights was considered moderate. In 1959, while he was chairman of the Richmond public school board, Negroes were admitted to white schools there with none of the bitter disruption that marked integration in other Virginia districts. He also served on the National Advisory Committee on Legal Services to the Poor and helped establish the Legal Services to the Poor of the Office of Economic Opportunity.

In announcing the nomination, the president said, "Excellence had marked his career since his days as a student at Washington and Lee, where he was Phi Beta Kappa and first in his class at law school." Powell received his master's degree from Harvard Law School. The choice fitted Nixon's concept of balancing the court toward conservatism, with emphasis on law and order. Powell was considered a strict constructionist in his interpretation of legal questions. In an article that appeared in the *Richmond Times Dispatch* of August 1, he was highly critical of the radical left. He also viewed the wiretapping issue as a tempest in a teapot, declaring that the innocent have nothing to worry about. The article was later reprinted in the FBI *Law Enforcement Bulletin*.

Powell was born Sept. 19, 1907, in Suffolk, Va. From 1932 he was with the Richmond firm of Hunton, Williams, Gay, Powell and Gibson. He served as president of the American Bar Association (1964–65), president of the American College of Trial Lawyers (1969–70), and president of the American Bar Foundation (1969–71). (B. S. KA.)

QADDAFI, MUAMMAR AL-

Muammar al-Qaddafi was an unknown captain in the Libyan Army when he came to prominence in September 1969 as the leader of the coup that overthrew the Libyan monarchy. Following the coup he was promoted to colonel and became commander in chief of the Libyan armed forces as well as chairman of the otherwise anonymous Revolutionary Command Council. In January 1970 the names of the other members of the council were revealed, and Colonel

Georges Pompidou

al-Qaddafi headed a new government as prime minister and defense minister.

The young colonel rapidly made his mark in Middle Eastern and Mediterranean politics, and it was widely believed that he aspired to the position of Arab leadership that had been occupied by the late Egyptian president Gamal Abd-an-Nasser. While his brand of revolutionary nationalism had much in common with the Nasserism of the 1950s, Qaddafi was also deeply religious and socially conservative. Among his first acts were the banning of alcohol, the enforced use of Arabic in all street signs and public notices, and the prohibition of expatriates from working in Libya.

Qaddafi initiated negotiations with Britain and the U.S. that led to the removal of their military bases in 1970, and in July 1970 he expropriated the holdings of the Jewish and Italian communities. Although his nationalism led Libya into more anti-Western attitudes, his Islamic piety made him strongly anti-Communist and he kept his distance from the Soviets. In June 1971 he recognized Communist China, though he stated that China was a country on which "atheism has been imposed and is a stranger to Libya."

Qaddafi's diplomacy was adventurous to the point of rashness. In July 1971 Libya was the only Arab country to express immediate support for the Moroccan rebels in their unsuccessful coup against King Hassan (*q.v.*). Shortly afterward he helped to ensure the failure of the pro-Communist coup against Pres. Gaafar Nimeiry (*q.v.*) in the Sudan by arresting two of the coup's leaders who were en route from London to Khartoum. Overruling his colleagues' doubts, he led Libya into a federal union with Syria and Egypt. In December he nationalized British Petroleum's Libyan operations in retaliation for Britain's alleged connivance in Iran's occupation of three Persian Gulf islands.

Qaddafi was born in 1942 and educated in Libya. In 1966 he attended a course at Sandhurst Military College in Britain. (P. MD.)

Mujibur Rahman

Lewis F. Powell, Jr.

RAHMAN, MUJIBUR

Sheikh Mujibur Rahman emerged at the beginning of 1971 as the favourite candidate to become the first democratically elected prime minister of Pakistan since the country came under military rule in 1958. At year's end, following the Indo-Pakistani war of December 3–16, it seemed beyond all doubt that he would become the head of a new independent state, Bangla Desh (formerly East Pakistan).

In December 1970 Mujibur's Awami League—a Bengali nationalist movement operating exclusively among the 75 million people in East Pakistan—had won a clear majority in the first free national elections since the country's independence.

"Mujib," as he was commonly called, expressed his willingness to form a new national democratic government provided his party's six-point program for constitutional autonomy could be met through negotiations with Pres. Agha Muhammad Yahya Khan. When these efforts ended in failure and violence, martial law was proclaimed in East Pakistan and Mujib was arrested. His supporters then proclaimed the independent republic of Bangla Desh. He was placed on trial for treason. After Pakistan's defeat in the brief war with India into which the East Pakistan situation eventually erupted, the new Pakistani president, Zulfikar Ali Bhutto, ordered Mujib released from prison and placed under house arrest. At the end of the year his return to free Bangla Desh appeared imminent.

Mujib, a tall, handsome but unsmiling man, was a nationalist radical reformer rather than a revolutionary. He was born of middle-class landowning parents at Tongipara in the district of Faridpur in 1920. After matriculating from a Christian mission school, he went to the University of Calcutta and then on to the University of Dacca where he studied law. His political activities brought his expulsion from the university and the first of many prison sentences.

When the Awami League was formed to oppose the dominant Muslim League, Mujib became its first secretary. He was elected to the East Pakistan Assembly in 1954 and briefly held ministerial posts. He became a forthright opponent of Field Marshal Muhammad Ayub Khan when the military took power in 1958. In 1968 student demonstrations against his trial for conspiracy to overthrow the regime spilled over into large-scale violence and conflict with the Army, which ended in Ayub Khan's abdication as president. Before the turbulent events of 1971 he was not an advocate of secession for East Pakistan. (Co. L.)

REHNQUIST, WILLIAM HUBBS

At 47, William Rehnquist became the youngest member of the U.S. Supreme Court on Dec. 10, 1971, when the Senate confirmed his nomination, 68–26. The assistant attorney general was the fourth Supreme Court justice to be appointed by Pres. Richard Nixon. Observers believed that he would join the others—Chief Justice Warren Burger, Harry Blackmun, and Lewis Powell (q.v.)—in a conservative bloc. The liberal side was represented by three holdovers from the activist Warren court, William Brennan, Jr., William O. Douglas, and Thurgood Marshall, while Potter Stewart and Byron White were expected to be the "swing men."

Rehnquist's nomination had been more controversial than that of Powell, whom Nixon had named at the same time and who had been confirmed a few days earlier. As assistant attorney general, Office of Legal Counsel, Rehnquist had helped to prepare many of the controversial documents issued by the Nixon administration. He had irritated some congressional liberals with his constitutional defense of the Cambodia invasion of May 1970, his defense of two previous Nixon nominees to the court—Clement Haynsworth and G. Harrold Carswell, both of whom had been rejected—and his suggestion that government workers might be restricted in their right to criticize government actions. He had also been the administration's spokesman on police handling of demonstrations, notably the May 3, 1971, "Mayday" demonstrations in Washington, D.C., when wholesale arrests had been made.

Pointing to this background, various liberal groups claimed that he was unsympathetic to the problems of minorities and favoured "law and order" above individual rights. Unlike Haynsworth and Carswell, however, he was not vulnerable on grounds of either financial interests or legal ability. In the end, several liberal Democratic senators voted for him, saying that a president has the right to pick appointees with a congenial philosophy and that Rehnquist was suitable in all other respects.

Rehnquist was born Oct. 1, 1924, in Milwaukee, Wis. After graduating first in his class from the Stanford (Calif.) University Law School, he served as law clerk to the late Justice Robert Jackson in 1952. He practiced law in Phoenix, Ariz., for 16 years before Nixon appointed him assistant attorney general in 1969. (B. S. KA.)

RUCKELSHAUS, WILLIAM DOYLE

William D. Ruckelshaus entered 1971 with less than a month's experience as administrator of the newly formed U.S. Environmental Protection Agency, but he had wasted no time putting its powers to work. Within a week after EPA began operating, he had brought action against the cities of Atlanta, Ga., Detroit, and Cleveland, O., for violations of water-quality standards. In January he filed suits against Armco Steel Corp. in Houston, Tex., and ITT Rayonier's pulp mill on Juan de Fuca Strait. In the ensuing months there was a veritable drumfire of similar actions.

Other federal agencies did not escape his attention. In March, Ruckelshaus requested the Interior Department to call a halt to the Alaskan oil pipeline pending further study. Friction with the Food and Drug Administration arose in August when the two agencies failed to reach agreement on possible regulation of bottled water.

By August the inevitable had occurred: a backlash from industry, with mounting political pressures for Ruckelshaus to ease up on the antipollution campaign. Indiana & Michigan Electric Co. sued EPA to eliminate a requirement for cooling towers on a nuclear power plant, and Kennecott Copper Corp. also sued, claiming sulfur dioxide standards were overly harsh and not founded on sound data. Other agencies and some members of Congress sought to weaken EPA's powers by providing that environmental reports include consideration of economic effects—i.e., costs of the cleanup. Ruckelshaus was said to be undeterred.

Born July 24, 1932, in Indianapolis, Ind., Ruckelshaus graduated from Princeton in 1957 and received a law degree from Harvard in 1960. He served as deputy attorney general for Indiana, 1960–65, drafting the state's Air Pollution Control Act. He was elected to the Indiana House of Representatives in 1967 and became majority leader his first term. After running unsuccessfully for the U.S. Senate on the Republican ticket in 1968, he served as an assistant attorney general and head of the U.S. Justice Department's Civil Division. (T. R. T.)

SADAT, ANWAR AS-

In 1971 Anwar as-Sadat emerged from the shadow of his predecessor, Gamal Abd-an-Nasser, as a strong and independent-minded president of Egypt. In May, following criticism within the Arab Socialist Union (ASU) of his moves to join an Arab federation, he abruptly dismissed the left-wing vice-president, Ali Sabry. Within two weeks, after the mass resignation of senior ministers and officials, he announced that Sabry and his associates had been plotting against him and that court proceedings against them would be begun. He also promised free elections for the National Assembly and ASU, the dismantling of police-state apparatus, and establishment of the rule of law.

To counteract Soviet disquiet over his actions Sadat concluded a 15-year treaty of friendship and cooperation with the U.S.S.R. In September he led Egypt into a federal union with Syria and Libya, and in October became its first president. Egypt's first permanent constitution since the 1952 revolution, giving strong powers to the presidency, was overwhelmingly approved by a plebiscite in September. While broadly pursuing Nasser's domestic and foreign policies, Sadat placed greater emphasis on Islam and achieved a rapprochement with conservative forces in the Arab world. Toward year's end, his attitude toward Israel appeared to become more belligerent.

Born Dec. 25, 1918, in the Al Minufiyah Governorate of the Nile Delta, Sadat was educated at the Cairo Military Academy, graduating in 1938. During World War II he was one of a group of Egyptian officers who plotted to end the British occupation of Egypt with Axis assistance. Captured by British intelligence in 1942, he was interned but escaped in 1944 and remained in hiding until after the war. In 1950 his army commission was restored, and he at once joined Nasser's Free Officers, who were planning to overthrow the monarchy. After the 1952 revolution he was successively member of the Revolutionary Command Council, secretary general of the National Union (1957–61), president of the National Assembly (1961–69), and vice-president of the nation (1964–66). In December 1969 Nasser made him his only vice-president, and as such Sadat became acting president on Nasser's death. He was unanimously nominated for the presidency by the ASU and National Assembly, and he was elected overwhelmingly in a national plebiscite. (P. MD.)

SAINT LAURENT, YVES HENRI DONAT MATHIEU

With 17 years' experience behind him—including 10 with his own fashion house—Yves Saint Laurent, at 35 one of the most influential couturiers, upset the already tottering high fashion world by announcing that his July 1971 haute couture collection would be his last. From now on, he said, he would devote himself to ready-to-wear clothes.

The decision seemed a logical development, given the doubtful profitability of couture collections (largely loss leaders to boost the perfume and other interests behind the fashion houses) and the $6 million annual turnover of Saint Laurent's ready-to-wear. At year's end it seemed that he might be backtracking. A couture showing was announced for January 1972, though only buyers and representatives of two fashion magazines would be admitted. It was rumoured that Saint Laurent's U.S. backers, Squibb Beech-Nut, Inc., had insisted he continue his couture collections for prestige reasons. Other fashion houses, notably Cardin and Nina Ricci, seemed similarly confused, caught between the profitability of ready-to-wear and the dependence of that profitability on the haute couture magic.

Born in Oran, Algeria, on Aug. 1, 1936, Saint Laurent was a shy boy of 17 when he won first prize in a fashion-drawing competition organized by the International Wool Secretariat. On the strength of this, he was presented by Michel de Brunhoff, editor of French Vogue, to Christian Dior, with whom he worked closely until the famous designer's death in 1957. The following year his first collection as Dior's successor, in which he stressed the "trapeze" line, was a triumph.

In 1961 the contract with the House of Dior was broken and, after a short interval, Saint Laurent opened his own establishment

in the rue Spontini. His reputation grew steadily, and in 1966 the first ready-to-wear boutique was opened in the rue de Tournon under the Saint Laurent-Rive Gauche label. By 1971 there were some 40 boutiques spread around the world, selling the clothes Saint Laurent really enjoyed designing for the young and active career woman.

(T. Sw.)

SARTRE, JEAN-PAUL

For 30 years Sartre had felt the need to combine thought and action, and in 1971 he did so in exemplary fashion. Since May 1968 he had been involved in the leftist movement, and on June 18, 1971, he was summoned to the Palais de Justice in Paris and charged with slandering the police and prison administration. The offending articles had appeared in two Maoist newspapers for which he had assumed nominal responsibility when their young editors were arrested. A few weeks earlier he had published *L'Idiot de la famille*—the first 2,000 pages of a monumental study of Gustave Flaubert, on which he had been working for 15 years.

As one who favoured political commitment by intellectuals, Sartre, with his friend Simone de Beauvoir, had taken a public stand on all the great ideological issues since World War II. Active in the peace movement, a member of the Russell War Crimes Tribunal, he was the first signatory of the *Manifeste des 121* that demanded the right for French citizens to refuse service in the Algerian war. Although a Marxist fellow traveler, he never belonged to the Communist Party and had remained out of line with it since the 1956 Hungarian revolt. The May 1968 upheaval in France brought another personal reappraisal. The new-style intellectual, he held, must give everything to the people, and toward this end he sold Maoist newspapers in the streets, founded a press agency for the defense of truth, and presided from time to time over "people's tribunals."

Sartre was born in Paris on June 21, 1905, and in the beginning followed a classic career in the humanities through the École Normale Supérieure and *agrégation* (the highest professional examination for teachers). After teaching for 12 years in lycées, from 1944 he devoted himself to literature, founding the review *Les Temps modernes*. By then he had already published three basic works: a novel, *La Nausée* (1938); a play, *Les Mouches* (1943); and *L'Être et le néant* (1943), his summation of Existentialist philosophy. In 1964 he refused the Nobel Prize for Literature.

(S. Ls.)

SCHILLER, KARL

Already minister of economics, in 1971 Karl Schiller became without question the most important member of the West German Cabinet after Chancellor Willy Brandt. Following the resignation of the finance minister, Alex Möller, on May 13, he became economics "overlord," taking over the combined finance and economics ministries.

It was above all Schiller's decision to allow the mark to "float," which had the effect of revaluing the currency upward by some 10%. This did not endear him to the French, but it strengthened his reputation at home as a man who put national interests first. Throughout the year—not least following U.S. Pres. Richard M. Nixon's August economic measures—Schiller remained a central figure in the continuing world monetary crisis. He was present at the Washington meeting in December of the Group of Ten that agreed on a solution to the crisis.

Born in Breslau on April 24, 1911, Schiller went to grammar school in Kiel and later studied economics and sociology

George C. Scott

Jean-Paul Sartre
ROBERT COHEN—AGIP FROM
PICTORIAL PARADE

Yves Saint Laurent

at the universities of Kiel, Frankfurt am Main, and Heidelberg. He became a member of the Nazi Party, and during World War II served in the Army. In 1946 he joined the Social Democratic Party (SPD). A year later he became professor of economics at the University of Hamburg (of which he was rector, 1956–58), and he was economics senator for the city-states of Hamburg (1948–53) and West Berlin (1961–65). But his main contribution to party thinking was to turn it away from Marxism. As early as 1954 he developed the slogan "As much competition as possible, as much planning as necessary." This remained his watchword.

The background was Keynesian, but it also echoed Ludwig Erhard and other German apostles of the social market economy —the free market economy with a social conscience. Some critics said that he was in the wrong party, but he answered that he was a Social Democrat because he had more interest than the Christian Democrats in a fairer distribution of wealth. He also admitted the need for an element of overall planning, which the old Christian Democrats did not. Schiller was appointed minister of economics on the formation of the "grand coalition" of the Christian Democratic Union (CDU) and the SPD in 1966.

(N. Cr.)

SCOTT, GEORGE C.

For portraying the titanic World War II general in *Patton*, George C. Scott was named best actor of the year in 1971. But

Scott refused to accept the Oscar and had asked that his name be withdrawn from the balloting because he considered the annual Academy Awards ritual so much self-serving hokum for the movie industry. "What I hate," he said, "is that whole superstructure and the phony suspense and the crying actor clutching the statue to his bosom and all of that crap. It's all such a bloody bore." He had acquiesced in 1960, when he was nominated for his role in *Anatomy of a Murder,* but had found the intramural politics demeaning and concluded that the competition was "a beauty contest in a slaughterhouse." When he was nominated again two years later for his gangster-gambler role in *The Hustler,* he shunned the distinction—but did not win.

Scott was an actor's actor, practicing his craft tooth and claw. Witness Judith Crist's appraisal of *Patton,* which took best-picture honours: "All the glory emanates from Scott, who dominates the large screen as no single actor has, in my memory, making us party to the very depths of the soldier's soul. It is a stunning accomplishment from an actor who has never been less than excellent but proves perpetually that he can be better than ever." It was an accomplishment, incidentally, that won him a host of other plaudits, including the coveted New York Film Critics prize.

Scott was born in Wise, Va., on Oct. 18, 1927, the son of a coal-mine surveyor who resettled in Michigan during the Depression. After a stint in the Marines, he enrolled in journalism school at the University of Missouri. On a lark, he tried out for a role in a campus play and was hooked. His performance in 1957 of "the meanest Richard III ever seen by human eyes" in one of Joseph Papp's Shakespeare productions in New York's Central Park launched his stardom. He went on to Neil Simon comedies, Chekhov, more Shakespeare (notably Shylock in *The Merchant of Venice*), and O'Neill's *Desire Under the Elms,* in which he played opposite his wife, Colleen Dewhurst. His distinguished film work included Stanley Kubrick's epic satire *Dr. Strangelove* and Richard Lester's psychological study *Petulia.*   (Ph. K.)

SHEARES, BENJAMIN HENRY

A gynecologist of international repute, Benjamin Sheares was installed as president of the Republic of Singapore on Jan. 2, 1971, for a four-year term. The first Eurasian to attain such high office in an Asian country, he had been elected by Parliament on Dec. 30, 1970, to succeed Inche Yusof bin Ishak, who died on Nov. 23, 1970, after two and a half terms as Singapore's chief of state.

Born on Aug. 12, 1907, of a Eurasian father and a Japanese mother, Sheares studied at St. Andrew's School and Raffles Institution before joining the King Edward VII College of Medicine where he qualified in 1929. He was the first Singapore-born doctor to be appointed acting professor in the college, where he was a tutor for several years before the Japanese occupation. The ability of his generation of graduates largely influenced the decision to raise the college to the status of University of Singapore.

Sheares was also the first Singapore- or Malaysian-born obstetrician to obtain membership in the Royal College of Obstetricians and Gynaecologists of England, and the first Singapore doctor to be made a fellow of the American College of Surgeons. A modest and warmhearted man with a distinguished record of service to the republic and its people, Sheares was a skilled surgeon and researcher who developed, among other things, a new surgical technique—the "Sheares operation" —in the field of corrective gynecological plastic surgery.

From 1946 until he retired to go into private practice in 1961, Sheares was solely responsible for the development of his department in the medical faculty of the University of Singapore. After his retirement, he continued his association with the Kandang Kerbau Maternity Hospital as honorary consultant, and retained close contact with the teaching of both undergraduate and postgraduate students. As a gynecologist, he had been directly associated with the problems of family planning in Singapore, and as early as 1953 had advocated voluntary sterilization for people with three children. As chairman of the Medical Specialties Board, he helped to draw up a plan for the future development of Singapore's medical services.   (M. S. R.)

SINATRA, FRANK

The voice that lulled a thousand sips was stilled. Frank Sinatra gave his farewell performance on June 14, 1971.

For a generation he had been the romantic troubadour to much of America: to those bobby soxers who swooned at New York's Paramount Theater in the 1940s; to Ivy Leaguers who spun his LPs on new stereos in the late '50s; to middle-class marrieds swinging in the suburbs of the '60s; and certainly to almost every over-30 sibling-in-spirits of a man The Man himself recalled before his farewell performance: "A fella came up to me the other day with a nice story. He was in a bar somewhere and it was the quiet time of night. Everybody's staring down at the sauce and one of my saloon songs comes on the jukebox. 'One for My Baby,' something like that. After a while a drunk at the end of the bar looks up and says . . . 'I wonder who *he* listens to?'"

"Frankie" was born of immigrant Italian parents in Hoboken, N.J., Dec. 12, 1917. He won first prize on the "Major Bowes Amateur Hour," went on to sing with Dorsey and James in the Big Band era, starred in the sequined Hollywood spectaculars of the period, and crooned ballads on radio's old "Lucky Strike Hit Parade." Then, in the early '50s, his vocal chords hemorrhaged and his agent dropped him like a secondhand Band-Aid. Somehow he rustled a supporting role in a dramatic movie—and won an Oscar for playing Maggio in *From Here to Eternity* (1953).

It was the beginning of one of the most notable comebacks in show biz. He made personal appearances and movies—musical movies like *Guys and Dolls,* dramatic movies like *The Man with the Golden Arm,* soapy films like *Not as a Stranger,* and cops-and-robbers adventures like *Ocean's 11.* He was presumed to be the real-life model of the singer in Mario Puzo's novel about the Italian-American underworld, *The Godfather,* and rumour gave him sinister underworld connections. Socially he ran with the self-styled "rat pack" of Hollywood friends, among them Sammy Davis, Jr., Dean Martin, Peter Lawford. His private life, bittersweet as the lyrics he sang, included three divorces and three children, two of whom, Nancy and Frank, Jr., were singers themselves. Then, in the spring of 1971, he sang some of the old songs at a Hollywood benefit, finishing with the line, " 'Scuse me while I disappear."   (Ph. K.)

SKINNER, B(URRHUS) F(REDERIC)

Described as one of the most influential of living psychologists by his colleagues, B. F. Skinner became one of the most talked about in 1971 after his latest book, *Beyond Freedom and Dignity,* was published in September. On October 17, the book made its first appearance on the *New York Times* nonfiction best-seller list. Its author made the cover of *Time,* was interviewed repeatedly on television, and was subjected to critical reviews.

The book declared that freedom as Western man had known it was now obsolete and that in its stead a new society was needed, based on a technology of behaviour that will shape man to act in ways that will serve the group's interests. The traditional concepts of freedom and dignity must be discarded if we are to survive, and for Skinner survival was most important: "The only value according to which a culture eventually can be judged." He maintained that behaviour must be controlled by subtle conditioning techniques that will encourage man to take the proper actions. The environment would have to provide the rewards to reinforce socially beneficial actions that would allow mankind to live happily, without crises.

In September, Skinner received the annual award of the American Psychological Association, and in October, was one of nine persons honoured with a Kennedy International Award for his work on operant conditioning as applied to the field of mental retardation. His laboratory experiments with pigeons and rats had shown that certain kinds of behaviour can be produced in a subject by proper stimuli and by reinforcing the desired actions by rewards. His results and techniques were being used in behaviour therapy in mental institutions and served as the basis for programmed instruction and teaching machines.

As one of the leading exponents of behaviourism, Skinner had given free rein to his ideas of a utopian community in his 1948 novel, *Walden Two.* He joined the Harvard University department of psychology in 1948 and became the Edgar Pierce professor of psychology there in 1958. He was born in Susquehanna, Pa., on March 20, 1904. While at Indiana University in 1945–48, he designed his Air Crib, which provided a glassed-in, temperature-controlled environment for his infant daughter.   (B. S. Ka.)

STEWART, JOHN YOUNG

World champion racing driver in 1971 for the second time, Jackie Stewart, with 18 Grand Prix victories to his credit, was a race winner who ranked with such legendary figures of the sport as Juan Fangio (five times world champion; 24 Grand Prix wins). Stewart also attracted attention as an outspoken campaigner for more stringent safety precautions in automobile racing. He himself escaped unhurt from a 140-mph crash in the 1971 Austrian Grand Prix.

Born in Scotland on June 11, 1939, Stewart grew up around cars, his father being an automobile dealer and his elder brother Jimmy becoming a proficient racing driver in the mid-1950s until he had a serious accident at Le Mans. Jackie had reached Olympic Games standards in trapshooting before turning to motor racing. After performing well in sports cars at club races, he became a member of the Tyrrell Cooper-BMC Formula Three team and scored successes that led to his acceptance in the BRM Formula One (F1) team for 1965. That year he followed in the wheeltracks of Jim Clark, winning at Monza, Italy, and placing third in the world championship. A serious accident on the Spa circuit in Belgium set his career back and turned his thoughts to safety precautions.

At the Indianapolis 500 in 1966 Stewart led to within ten miles of the finish, when engine failure forced him to retire. In 1967 he continued his association with the Tyrrell Matra Formula Two (F2) team and was more successful in this field than with the F1 BRMs. In 1968 this great Anglo-French combination bore full fruit: Ken Tyrrell built the Matra F1 cars, using Ford-Cosworth V-8 engines, and signed on Stewart as his driver. Stewart broke a bone in his wrist in an F2 race at Jarama, Spain, but nevertheless won the Netherlands, German, and U.S. Grand Prix. In 1969 he dominated Grand Prix racing—six major races being won by the invincible Stewart-Matra-Cosworth combination—and became world champion for the first time. He was less in the lead in 1970 with the new Tyrrell-March cars but in 1971 was back in full form, the fastest driver of them all. He clinched the 1971 championship before the season ended, driving the Ford V-8-powered Tyrrell cars.   (W. C. Bo.)

TEMIN, HOWARD MARTIN

While the U.S. Congress worked on legislation to expand research on cancer (finally approving, in December 1971, a $1.6 billion three-year program), individual researchers already working under government grants continued to make progress toward the fundamentals of understanding the disease. Among those researchers was Howard M.

Temin, a virologist at the McArdle Cancer Research Laboratories, University of Wisconsin. With co-worker Satoshi Mizutena, Temin demonstrated that the cell chemical RNA (ribonucleic acid) could serve as a blueprint for the synthesis of the master chemical of genes, DNA (deoxyribonucleic acid), found in the nucleus of cells. The results were corroborated at about the same time by a Massachusetts Institute of Technology biologist, David Baltimore.

Temin had theorized this possibility in 1964, but it was not until 1970 that he was able to offer experimental proof. His findings showed that certain viruses with an RNA core contain an enzyme, or catalyst, that can reverse the pattern of genetic information channeling, which was previously thought to go only one way—from DNA to RNA. This reverse transcription, as the process is called, may allow a cancer-associated RNA strand to alter the hereditary DNA of a normal cell and transform that cell to a cancerous state.

Temin's discovery opened the way to the possibility of diagnosing certain types of cancer and of developing selective drugs to block the causative factors. However, Temin was extremely cautious about the chances of finding an applicable cure through this discovery.

Temin was born Dec. 10, 1934, in Philadelphia, Pa. After graduation from Swarthmore College in 1955, he was a National Science Foundation fellow at California Institute of Technology (1955–56) and then received a fellowship from the U.S. Public Health Service (1957–60). He joined the faculty of the University of Wisconsin in 1960.   (B. S. Ka.)

THIEU, NGUYEN VAN

South Vietnamese Pres. Nguyen Van Thieu was reelected October 3 in a controversial election in which he was the sole candidate. The South Vietnamese government claimed that Thieu received 91% of the votes cast, but diplomats in Saigon expressed skepticism, particularly since the official results showed Thieu won heavily even in areas known to be strongly opposed to him. Gen. Duong Van Minh, who had led the 1963 coup against Pres. Ngo Dinh Diem, and Vice-Pres. Nguyen Cao Ky both withdrew from the campaign on grounds that Thieu had rigged the election. Although U.S. officials did not publicly criticize Thieu's handling of the campaign, which discouraged any competition, they did little privately to mask their disappointment. The single-candidate election generally was regarded by U.S. policy makers as a major setback.

Thieu said he would step down if he received less than 50% of the vote in the election. He claimed that if any voter opposed him, the person could express disapproval by disfiguring the ballot. Foreign newsmen reported, however, that few voters appeared aware of such an alternative on election day.

Also during the year, Thieu ordered about 20,000 South Vietnamese forces, under U.S. air cover, to invade Laos to wipe out Communist North Vietnamese supply camps and routes there. Although both South Vietnamese and U.S. officials subsequently described the operation as a success, it was generally regarded as a failure since South Vietnamese forces had to withdraw under heavy Communist fire.

Thieu was born April 5, 1923, in Phan Rang, the capital of Ninh Thuan, a province in the central lowlands of southern Vietnam. During the Japanese occupation of Vietnam in World War II, he joined the Viet Minh, fighting first against the Jap-

Tito

Frank Sinatra

anese and later against the French. Eventually, he quit the Viet Minh because of its Communist leanings.

Thieu entered the Merchant Marine Academy in Saigon and later transferred to the newly established Vietnamese National Military Academy, graduating with the first class in 1949. He then rose rapidly in the Vietnamese Army. When President Diem was assassinated in a coup in 1963, Thieu was a general and commander of the division that defeated Diem's guards. Thieu became South Vietnam's chief of state on June 19, 1965, when a ten-member military junta took command of the nation.

(J. F. Ba.)

TITO (JOSIP BROZ)

Marshal Tito, 79, became Yugoslavia's president for the sixth time on July 29, 1971. But in his acceptance speech before the Federal Assembly in Belgrade, Tito, the country's leader since 1945, indicated that this would have to be his last five-year presidential term, and he declined the offer to remain president for life. His reelection was welcomed by Communists and non-Communists alike. Within the Communist Party, the liberals saw it as a guarantee for implementation of the bold reform program initiated by Tito in 1970. The conservatives believed that he would not allow the country to become too liberal at home or too pro-Western in its foreign policies. Earlier in the year, at a dramatic meeting of party leaders from Yugoslavia's six republics and two autonomous provinces, Tito had powerfully reasserted his leadership and ended months of tension within the party.

As an international statesman, Tito scored something of a record in 1971 by meeting such diverse figures as Pope Paul VI in March, Soviet party leader L. I. Brezhnev in September, the shah of Iran and U.S.

Pres. Richard M. Nixon in October, and the queen of England in November. The concessions he made to Brezhnev in September in the matter of renewed contacts with the Soviet Communist Party provoked misgivings in Yugoslavia and abroad. Coming so soon after Soviet military exercises around Yugoslavia's frontiers and strong propaganda attacks on Yugoslavia in Warsaw Pact capitals, the renewal of direct contacts looked too much like a one-sided concession to the U.S.S.R. Spectacular Yugoslav military maneuvers in October seemed to reaffirm an independent, nonaligned position. Trouble soon erupted in another area, however, as unrest in Tito's native Croatia led to a drastic purge of the Croatian party.

Tito was born at Kumrovec, near Zagreb, Croatia (then part of the Austro-Hungarian empire), on May 25, 1892. Early in World War I he was captured by the Russians and in 1917 he joined the Red Army. Returning home in 1920, he joined the Yugoslav Communist Party, of which he became secretary-general in 1937. During World War II he organized and led the Yugoslav partisans against the German occupiers and in 1945, by then a legendary figure, he became prime minister. Subsequently he developed a "Yugoslav brand of Communism," and in 1948 Yugoslavia was expelled from the Cominform. Tito then became increasingly identified with a policy of nonalignment.

(K. F. Cv.)

TREVINO, LEE

Emerging as golf's newest superstar in 1971 was the ebullient son of poor Mexican-American farmers, Lee Trevino. "Supermex," as he called himself, scored an unprecedented sweep by winning the United States, Canadian, and British Open tournaments. His earnings on the 1971 pro golf tour totaled $231,202.

Trevino was born in Dallas, Tex., Dec. 1, 1939, and was raised on a small farm by his grandfather. When he was six, he found a golf club in a field and made himself a two-hole course in a pasture, where he began to practice the sport. His self-instruction was still evident in 1971, especially in his flat swing.

Trevino worked in the maintenance crew at a local golf course until joining the U.S. Marines at 17. While in service he polished his golf game at Okinawa, where he played golf with officers. After completing four years in the Marines, Trevino returned to Dallas, where he operated a pitch-and-putt course and, to pick up extra money, won bets from customers by playing the game with a large soft-drink bottle. He wrapped the bottle with adhesive tape, giving it a good hitting surface, and was able to drive a ball with it accurately to distances of 150 yd. He also putted with the bottle, using it in the manner of a cue stick.

Later, Trevino worked as an assistant professional at an El Paso club, earning $30 a week. He began competing on the Professional Golfers' Association tour in 1966, when he won only $600. The next year he increased his earnings to $26,472 and, in 1968, leaped into prominence by winning the U.S. Open with four sub-par rounds, the first golfer in history to achieve this distinction. He soon became one of the most popular players on the golf tour, delighting the galleries with his exuberant personality, his jaunty stride, and his lucky coin to which he attributed his good fortune. (JE. HO.)

TRUDEAU, PIERRE ELLIOTT

One of the world's most eligible bachelors, Canadian Prime Minister Pierre Elliott Trudeau gave the world one of the brightest love stories of 1971 when he married Margaret Sinclair, 29 years his junior, in private religious services in North Vancouver, B.C., on March 4. The courtship between Trudeau, who had been linked romantically with many actresses and socialites, and Miss Sinclair, daughter of a top-ranking Liberal Party official, had gone on quietly for three years, making it perhaps the best-kept secret of the flamboyant prime minister's private life. A son, Justin, was born to the couple on Christmas Day.

On May 17 the newlywed Trudeaus flew to Moscow with an entourage of 21 officials and 40 reporters for an 11-day official visit to the U.S.S.R. Trudeau had three private meetings with Premier Aleksei N. Kosygin and joined in signing a pact that provided for regular high-level consultations between Moscow and Ottawa. To the concern of U.S. officials, Trudeau asserted independence in foreign affairs by telling his Soviet hosts that Canada and the U.S. were good friends "but Canada has found it increasingly important to diversify its channels of communications because of the overpowering presence of the United States."

Coping with the "overpowering presence" also flavoured Trudeau's activities at home. In February he was accused of uttering an obscenity toward an opposition member during a House of Commons debate on unemployment, one of the more pressing problems aggravated by Canada's ties to the U.S. economy. In September, angered by the unwillingness of the U.S. to grant Canada an exemption from its surcharge on imports, Trudeau wondered seriously if the U.S. was "really trying to rearrange the North American continent so that we are

just a supplier of natural resources," and this was the chief topic of talks between Trudeau and U.S. Pres. Richard Nixon in Washington in December. One of Trudeau's proposals for eliminating Canada's dependence on the U.S., the establishment of a separate defense role, took shape in a White Paper issued on August 24.

A wealthy French-Canadian born in Montreal on Oct. 18, 1919, Trudeau sought and won his first elective office, a seat in the House of Commons, in 1965. Despite a reputation as a political dilettante, three years later, on April 6, 1968, he defeated six other candidates for leadership of the Liberal Party and, on April 20, became prime minister when Lester B. Pearson retired. That June Trudeau led his party to a decisive victory in national elections. (J. F. BA.)

VORSTER, BALTHAZAR JOHANNES

South Africa's prime minister from 1966, John Vorster always had been a controversial political figure. In 1971 he emerged successfully from a bitter struggle with the more inward-looking section (the *verkramptes*) of his ruling Afrikaner National Party in which one of the major issues was his new foreign policy. The goals of this policy were winning back friends among Western nations and establishing normal relations with Africa's independent states to overcome the republic's relative isolation in the world community, and especially in Africa.

Vorster had militantly pursued the idea of engaging in a dialogue with the black African states, arguing that the racial aspects of his white-supremacist government did not preclude establishing diplomatic and economic relations based on terms of equality between South Africa and the rest of the continent. He became the first South African prime minister to pay an official visit to an independent African country when he visited Malawi in 1970, and in 1971 he established a new precedent by receiving Malawi's Pres. H. Kamuzu Banda (*q.v.*) on a return state visit. Complementary to his policy of winning black friends abroad, Vorster promised independence to the eight black homelands, or Bantustans, whenever their leaders chose to ask for it.

Vorster's policies produced divisions even within his own Cabinet and ruling party, but he had never shirked unpopular measures. In World War II he broke from the Afrikaner nationalist ranks to become a leader of a militant antiwar movement, the Stormjaers, who both worked for the defeat of the Allies' cause and embraced the teachings of Nazism. He was one of the leaders interned during the war by the then prime minister, Field Marshal J. C. Smuts. After the war he won a seat in the House of Assembly and became minister of justice in 1961, gaining a reputation as an exceptionally tough law-and-order man.

Vorster was born at Jamestown, Cape Province, in 1915. He took his law degree at Stellenbosch University and, until his internment, practiced as a lawyer in the Transvaal. (Co. L.)

WALDHEIM, KURT

On Dec. 21, 1971, his 53rd birthday, Kurt Waldheim won the approval of the UN Security Council as the fourth secretary-general of the United Nations, succeeding U Thant of Burma. The General Assembly formalized the appointment by acclamation the following day, and he was sworn in immediately for a five-year term beginning Jan. 1, 1972. For Waldheim, a career diplomat, it had been a year of defeat and triumph. In April he made an unsuccessful bid, as the candidate of the conservative

Austrian People's Party, for the presidency of Austria, losing to Pres. Franz Jonas by 260,000 votes.

Waldheim long had had his eye on the post of UN secretary-general, but he never formally announced his candidacy. He received the approval of the Security Council after being vetoed twice by the People's Republic of China in secret balloting. On the third ballot, the Peking representative responded to backstage urging and withheld the veto.

In his acceptance speech before the Assembly, Waldheim noted that he came from a neutral country and promised to follow a path of strict neutrality in the performance of his new tasks. He acknowledged that one of his major jobs would be to find a formula to solve the organization's financial problems. He also welcomed the seating of the People's Republic of China and expressed the hope that the dual governments in Germany, Vietnam, and Korea would be brought into the world organization in the near future.

Waldheim was born Dec. 21, 1918, in St. Andrea-Wördern in lower Austria, attended the Vienna consular academy, and received a doctor of laws degree at Vienna University in 1944. His first diplomatic assignment was in the Paris embassy. After serving in the Foreign Ministry from 1951 to 1955, he became Austria's first minister to Canada. He came to the UN in 1964 as permanent representative of his country and remained until 1968, when he became minister of foreign affairs. At the time of his appointment as secretary-general he was once more Austria's permanent UN representative. (Mx. H.)

WILSON, FLIP

In a time when Black Panthers and other militants promoted the feeling that for any black American to smile at a white was Uncle Tomism, Flip Wilson made both black and white fans laugh and like it. Without apologies to the militants, the 38-year-old comedian blended a whole cast of fabricated characters and impersonations, all with unblushing black accents, into a weekly hour of television that was one of the most popular shows of the 1970–71 season.

He rolled his eyes and did shuffles that physically were reminiscent of Bert Williams and Stepin Fetchit, black comedians of another day. Yet his spirit was different. It was confident, even tough, but the ingredient that conquered fans was a friendliness so infectious that a studio audience was likely to give him a prolonged standing ovation at the end of a show. Wilson himself was disdainful of the comparisons of his style with that of the "Amos 'n' Andys," and also criticized reviews that dealt with the racial aspects of his work. " 'The funny' has no color," he said.

The reappearing characters he played included Reverend Leroy, the preacher at the Church of What's Happening Now; Geraldine, the falsetto-voiced soul sister who swings her way through life; Charlie, who runs a hamburger joint where Wilson's guest stars are always dropping in off the road; and Queen Isabella, who is overjoyed when she finds out from Christopher Columbus that "Chris gon' find Ray Charles!"

It was his Discovery of America routine, along with his own engaging attitude, that brought Clerow "Flip" Wilson the first big break of his career. Born in Jersey City, N.J., in 1933, one of 18 surviving children, he lived in and out of foster homes and schools from the age of 7 until he was 16. Then he lied about his age to enlist in the U.S. Air Force, and later was working as a bellboy in San Francisco when he did his first nightclub comedy act as a fill-in. But fame came slowly. Studiously he honed his style at small nightclubs before moving up a rung to the Apollo Theater in Harlem. In 1965 he was invited onto Johnny Carson's "Tonight Show" and did the Christopher Columbus routine. His fortunes took off from there. (C. Th.)

WILSON, (JAMES) HAROLD

Soon after losing office in the general election of June 1970, Harold Wilson, leader of the British Labour Party from 1963, set to work on writing his account of his years as prime minister of the United Kingdom. Published in July 1971, *The Labour Government 1964–70: A Personal Record* ran to more than 300,000 words, which Wilson wrote in longhand in the space of only five months. The book gave an inside account of many notable episodes in the history of the 1960s, among them his confrontations with Ian Smith over the status of Rhodesia, the sterling crisis of 1966 and 1967, and his unsuccessful attempt to negotiate an end to the Vietnam war during the visit of Aleksei N. Kosygin to London in February 1967.

Wilson was severely criticized for his conduct of the 1970 election campaign in which he played down controversial issues and behaved as though a Labour victory was a foregone conclusion. After his defeat there was some talk of possible retirement, but in fact he kept his grip on the leadership of his party. This he did partly by changing his stand on British entry into the EEC. As prime minister he had revived the British application in 1967 with a considerable show of enthusiasm, saying "this time we mean business," but he kept his options open by emphasizing the need to get the right terms. When Geoffrey Rippon had completed the negotiation of terms for entry on behalf of Edward Heath's Conservative government, Wilson argued that the terms were unacceptable. Despite his opposition, EEC entry was approved by the Commons on October 28 by 356–244, with 69 Labour members defying Wilson to vote with the government. In November Wilson again made headlines by putting forth a 15-year plan for a united Ireland.

Born on March 11, 1916, in Huddersfield, Wilson was educated in Yorkshire and Cheshire grammar schools and won his way to Oxford University on scholarships. Elected to Parliament in 1945, he was brought into Clement Attlee's Cabinet as president of the Board of Trade at the age of 31. (W. H. Ts.)

WOODEN, JOHN

The nation's most successful collegiate basketball coach in 1971, as in many of the years before, was John Wooden of UCLA. Prior to his arrival at the school in 1949, UCLA had never had a winning season. The transformation was remarkable. Under his direction, the Bruins had 15 seasons in which they won, at the minimum, a conference championship. They first became a national power in the early 1960s, winning their first National Collegiate Athletic Association (NCAA) title in 1964 and repeating as champions in 1965. Then, in 1967, UCLA began putting together an unprecedented string of five NCAA titles.

In his 36 years of college coaching, Wooden's teams won 779 games and lost only 196, a victory ratio of 80%. More remarkable yet was that going into the 1971–72 season UCLA had won 149 of its last 154 games, including a record 28 successive victories in NCAA tournament play.

Wooden was born on Oct. 14, 1910, on a

Pierre Trudeau

Flip Wilson (as Geraldine)

Elmo Zumwalt

farm eight miles from Martinsville, Ind. He began playing basketball in grade school, at Centerton, Ind., and was an all-around athlete and star basketball player at Martinsville High School. Winning a scholarship to Purdue University, he was a three-time All-American guard there and also won a Big Ten medal for combined proficiency in athletics and scholarship.

Wooden's first coaching assignment was at Dayton (Ky.) High School, where he remained for two years. He then coached at South Bend (Ind.) Central High School for nine seasons. During World War II he served in the Navy, with the rank of lieutenant. After his discharge and before going to UCLA, he was the athletic director and basketball coach at Indiana State Teachers College in Terre Haute. (Je. Ho.)

ZUMWALT, ELMO RUSSELL

The U.S. Navy's chief of naval operations, Adm. Elmo Zumwalt, brought a new look to the most conservative of the armed forces—bringing beer into the barracks, permitting beards, and abolishing the time-honoured bell-bottom uniforms. But in one respect, at least, he acted in the tradition of all naval leaders before him by urging throughout 1971 that the U.S. fleet be rebuilt in the next ten years at an estimated cost of $50 billion.

Warning that Soviet naval power was being increased, particularly in the Mediterranean, at a time when Congress was reducing U.S. strength, Zumwalt strongly recommended that the U.S. build an all-nuclear carrier force with enough nuclear-powered frigates to escort all the carriers.

During February, Zumwalt toured Brazil, Argentina, and Chile, making him the first high-ranking U.S. official to visit Chile's Marxist president, Salvador Allende. The Chilean visit became controversial when Zumwalt tentatively accepted Allende's invitation to have the USS "Enterprise" call at a Chilean port. Zumwalt's recommendation that the invitation be accepted was overturned by State Department and White House officials, publicly embarrassing Allende, who had already announced the visit.

Zumwalt continued his efforts to improve the Navy's image. On February 11 he ordered that Filipino enlistees no longer would be restricted to positions as stewards and mess attendants.

During a trip to South Vietnam on May 30, he announced that the Navy would adopt the drug amnesty program already in operation for the Army. Zumwalt, who liked to send memos that had become known as "Z-Grams," sent one during the summer that abolished the traditional bell bottoms, bibbed jumper, and black kerchief (which legend says mourns the death of the British hero Horatio Nelson). The old outfit was officially replaced by a double-breasted suit.

Zumwalt was born in San Francisco, Calif., on Nov. 29, 1920, and graduated from the Naval Academy at Annapolis in 1942. He served in World War II, Korea, and Vietnam. Zumwalt was nominated by Pres. Richard Nixon as chief of naval operations in the spring of 1970, and took his oath of office at Annapolis on July 1 of that year. (J. F. Ba.)

See also Nobel Prizes.

Bolivia

A landlocked republic in central South America, Bolivia is bordered by Brazil, Paraguay, Argentina, Chile, and Peru. Area: 424,162 sq.mi. (1,098,581 sq.km.). Pop. (1971 est.): 5,062,500, of whom more than 50% were Indian. Language: Spanish (official). Religion: Roman Catholic. Judicial cap.: Sucre (pop., 1971 est., 69,800). Administrative capital and largest city: La Paz (pop., 1971 est., 850,000). Presidents in 1971, Gen. Juan José Torres Gonzales and, from August 22, Col. Hugo Banzer Suárez.

For Bolivia 1971 was yet another year of political intrigue and a military coup that added one more former president to the list of Bolivian exiles and left the fortunes of the people relatively unchanged. General Torres, who had become president following a coup and countercoup in October 1970, remained in power until August 1971 when his fellow generals, supported by Bolivia's businessmen and allegedly by the U.S. Central Intelligence Agency, moved against him. Col. Hugo Banzer Suárez (*see* BIOGRAPHY), formerly head of the military academy, was proclaimed chief of state on August 22.

The businessmen's dissatisfaction had resulted from Torres' implementation of a program directed largely against foreign monopolies. Business leaders were extremely unhappy with the nationalization of the Bolivian Gulf Oil Co. (a subsidiary of U.S. Gulf Oil), expropriation of the sugar industry, the surrender to workers' demands for higher wages and greater control over working conditions, and expulsion of the U.S. Peace Corps.

For the military, traditionally the most powerful entity in Bolivian politics, the dilemma was more acute. Torres had come to power voicing suitably left-wing proposals to gain the somewhat begrudging support of the labour unions and students. To keep that support he was forced to appear the instigator rather than the slave of events. As his administration proceeded it began to appear that the power of the military might be eclipsed by left-wing elements to whom the president was increasingly bowing. In an attempt to break his dependence on both the left and the military establishment, Torres tried, like his former chief, ex-Pres. René Barrientos Ortuño, to form an effective political base, but with little success.

There were persistent rumours of imminent coups from the day Torres came to power, and Banzer himself, with Col. Edmundo Valencia, attempted one in January. The event that most incensed the military and drew Torres' downfall much closer was the institution in February of the Asamblea del Pueblo (People's Assembly) headed by the Army's archenemy, Juan Lechín Oquendo, the miners' leader and a former vice-president of the republic. Nominally an advisory body, it contained most of the country's hardline radical leaders and appeared a direct threat to the preeminence of the Army.

The change in administration in August was preceded by four days of bloody fighting between the Colorado regiment manned by left-wing students and workers on the one hand, and Army detachments led by right-wing officers, later reinforced by the Air Force, on the other. In his first press conference after the coup Banzer described his government as a "revolutionary nationalist" one that would reestablish "respect for the law" and safeguard foreign investments. Initially, his administration had a firm political base in the armed forces and two largest political parties, the Nationalist Revolutionary Movement (MNR) and the Bolivian Socialist Falange (FSB), which combined together to form the Nationalist Popular Front (FPN). Later, however, internal dissensions began to show when the MNR felt its role was being deliberately minimized.

Col. Hugo Banzer Suárez was sworn in as president of Bolivia on Aug. 22, 1971, after a rebellion overthrew the government of Juan José Torres.

Troops loyal to the regime that overthrew Pres. Juan José Torres stand guard in La Paz.

BOLIVIA

Education. (1968) Primary, pupils 612,629, teachers 22,438; secondary, pupils 114,185, teachers 4,551; vocational, pupils 10,648, teachers 1,276; teacher training, students 8,321, teachers 431; higher (including 8 universities; 1966), students 13,312.

Finance. Monetary unit: peso boliviano, with a free rate (Sept. 27, 1971) of 11.47 pesos to U.S. $1 (28.45 pesos = £1 sterling). Gold, SDRs, and foreign exchange, central bank: (June 1971) U.S. $39.1 million; (June 1970) U.S. $51.2 million. Budget (1969 rev. est.) balanced at 1,265,300,000 pesos. Gross national product: (1969) 10,822,000,000 pesos; (1968) 9,-939,000,000 pesos. Money supply: (March 1971) 1,449,500,000 pesos; (March 1970) 1,321,300,000 pesos. Cost of living (La Paz; 1963 = 100): (March 1971) 153; (March 1970) 149.

Foreign Trade. (1969) Imports U.S. $166.9 million; exports U.S. $209.3 million. Import sources (1968): U.S. 43%; West Germany 12%; Japan 11%; Argentina 7%; U.K. 5%. Export destinations (1968): U.K. 45%; U.S. 35%; Argentina 5%. Main exports: tin 49%; tungsten 5%; antimony 5%; silver 5%.

Transport and Communications. Roads (1968) 24,985 km. (including 11,324 km. all-weather). Motor vehicles in use (1969): passenger 17,700; commercial (including buses) 23,700. Railways: (1970) 3,524 km.; traffic (1968) 249 million passenger-km., freight 316 million net ton-km. Air traffic (1970): 109 million passenger-km.; freight 1,730,000 net ton-km. Telephones (Jan. 1970) 37,551. Radio receivers (Dec. 1968) 1,350,000.

Agriculture. Production (in 000; metric tons; 1970; 1969 in parentheses): corn *c.* 370 (393); wheat 62 (47); barley *c.* 55 (55); potatoes *c.* 620 (642); cassava *c.* 160 (*c.* 150); oranges *c.* 40 (*c.* 40); sugar, raw value (1970–71) 134, (1969–70) 135; rubber (exports) *c.* 3 (*c.* 3). Livestock (in 000; Oct. 1969): sheep *c.* 6,800; cattle *c.* 3,000; pigs *c.* 900; horses *c.* 290; asses *c.* 650; goats *c.* 2,400; llamas *c.* 1,500; chickens *c.* 3,150.

Industry. Production (in 000; metric tons; 1969): cement 80; crude oil (1970) 1,128; electricity (kw-hr.) 731,000 (82% hydroelectric); gold (troy oz.) 51; other metal ores and concentrates (exports; metal content) tin 30, lead 25, antimony 13, zinc 26, tungsten (oxide content) 2.3, copper 8, silver 0.19.

Economic progress over the year was not as favourable as in 1970. The left-wing stance of the Torres administration had undermined business confidence. However, a long-term industrialization program which, it was hoped, would double industry's contribution to the gross domestic product within 20 years was announced in December; investments totaling $600 million would be needed. A $12 million tin smelter was opened by President Torres at Vinto in January, and a Czechoslovakian state firm was financing the installation of an antimony smelter.

(D. K. Da.)

Botswana

A landlocked republic of southern Africa, Botswana, a member of the Commonwealth of Nations, is bounded by South Africa, South West Africa, and Rhodesia. Area: 220,000 sq.mi. (570,000 sq.km.). Pop. (1971 est.): 667,000, almost 99% African. Capital: Gaborone (pop., 1971 est., 14,467). Largest city: Serowe (pop., 1969 est., 34,186). Language: English (official) and Tswana. Religion: Christian 60%; animist. President in 1971, Sir Seretse Khama.

In 1971 Botswana continued to strike a balance between economic dependence on South Africa and political allegiance to black Africa. Pressure increased for africanization of the civil service, and in August police command was transferred to the country's first African commissioner. Work permits were granted less freely to expatriates, who were encouraged to seek citizenship.

Game park tourism, with South Africa as a main customer, developed rapidly, although the economy remained dominated by huge mining projects. De Beers, with the largest single investment of R 21.5 million (in which the government held a 15% interest), began diamond production at Orapa in July. The huge copper-nickel Shashi project continued to absorb more than half the R 100 million 1970–75 National Development Plan and Botswana RST Ltd., the mining company, was negotiating with a West German firm that wanted to obtain marketing rights.

South Africa remained Botswana's main trading partner and increased its exports following Botswana's ban on Rhodesian tobacco and beer. The trade deficit continued to be made up by money brought in by miners working in neighbouring countries, revenue from South Africa, and British aid. (M. Mr.)

BOTSWANA

Education. (1969) Primary, pupils 82,214, teachers (1968) 1,791; secondary (1968), pupils 2,299, teachers 131; vocational (1968), pupils 592; teacher training, students 303, teachers (1968) 22.

Finance and Trade. Monetary unit: South African rand, with a par value of R 0.71 to U.S. $1 (R 1.71 = 1£ sterling) and a free rate (Sept. 27, 1971) of R 1.77 to £1 sterling. Budget (1969–70 est.): revenue R 21,404,000; expenditure R 20,394,000. Foreign trade (1969): imports R 30,833,000 (65% from South Africa in 1966); exports R 13,060,000 (18% to South Africa in 1966). Main exports (1967): meat 42%; hides and skins 18%; meat extract 14%; other meat products 11%; live cattle 5%.

Agriculture. Production (in 000; metric tons; 1970; 1969 in parentheses): sorghum 8 (30); corn 5 (18). Livestock (in 000; 1969–70): cattle 1,481; sheep 418; goats 1,152; poultry 400.

Bowling and Lawn Bowls

The greatest event in the history of amateur tenpin bowling, the seventh World Bowling Championships of the Fédération Internationale des Quilleurs (FIQ), took place in Milwaukee, Wis., in August 1971. A record total of 268 men and 103 women amateur bowlers from 32 countries crowded the 28 bowling lanes specially installed in the Milwaukee Arena, and 16 world championship records fell. The United States won five gold medals, Puerto Rico two, and Japan's ladies one.

Ed Luther of Wisconsin won the individual champion's title with a record of 5,963 pins. The women's individual title was won by Ashie Gonzales from San Juan, P.R. The men's division winners were: teams of eight, (1) U.S., 12,691, (2) Mexico, 12,502, (3) Venezuela, 12,470; doubles, (1) Puerto Rico, 2,520, (2) U.S., 2,478, (3) Australia, 2,474; teams of five, (1) U.S., 6,194, (2) Belgium, 5,980, (3) Italy, 5,948; individual, all events, (1) Ed Luther, U.S., 5,963, (2) Edmond Clauws, Belgium, 5,825, (3) Bob Glaser, U.S., 5,779. In the women's division the winners were: teams of four, (1) U.S., 4,656, (2) Australia, 4,530, (3) Mexico, 4,317; doubles, (1) Japan, 2,302, (2) U.S., 2,215, (3) U.S., 2,194; teams of five, (1) U.S., 5,474, (2) Australia, 5,322, (3) Venezuela, 5,283; individual, all events, (1) Ashie Gonzalez, Puerto Rico, 4,535, (2) Dixie Burmeister, U.S., 4,514, (3) Penny McClain, U.S., 4,471.

The first official FIQ Asian Bowling Championships took place late in 1970 in Singapore with participants from all major Asian bowling countries. The men's division winners were: teams of eight, (1) Malaysia, 11,785, (2) Philippines, 11,719, (3) Singapore, 11,670; doubles, (1) Singapore, 2,301, (2) Japan, 2,226, (3) Philippines, 2,209; teams of five, (1) Singapore, 5,537, (2) Hong Kong, 5,518, (3) Malaysia, 5,438; individual, all events, (1) M. Nava, Philippines, 5,446, (2) Yu Fook On, Hong Kong, 5,412, (3) Allan Lee, Malaysia, 5,390. Women's division winners were: teams of four, (1) Japan, 4,135, (2) Hong Kong, 4,032, (3) Singapore, 3,969; doubles, (1) Japan, 2,102, (2) Singapore, 2,033, (3) Philippines, 2,032; teams of five, (1) Philippines, 5,244, (2) Japan, 5,040, (3) Hong Kong, 4,706; individual, all events, (1) Shimizu, Japan, 4,251, (2) Bong Coo, Philippines, 4,230, (3) Ido, Japan, 4,164.

In October 1970 the second Europe Bowling Cup was contested at Breda, Neth., by five-man teams from 12 countries. France won, with a score of 10,639. Great Britain (10,500) and Sweden (10,488) finished second and third. The finals of the World Bowling Cup were held at Copenhagen, Den., in November 1970. Klaus Müller of West Germany brought the amateur singles crown back to Europe, defeating Henry Tan of Singapore 606–561.

The Tournament of the Americas drew participants from 20 countries in 1971. The best bowlers and teams were: mixed foursomes, U.S., 4,777; mixed doubles, U.S., 2,445; men's doubles, U.S., 3,621; women's doubles, U.S., 3,553; men's singles, Bill Stearns, Bermuda, 3,009; women's singles, Virginia Speights, U.S., 2,923; women's all events, Lorrie Koch, U.S., 7,111; men's all events, Larry Turner, U.S., 7,245. (Y. S.)

United States. The "left-handed problem," a phrase created by the right-handed majority, became

---

The 1971 American Bowling Congress tournament begins on March 6. More than 6,000 teams competed in the 79-day event held in Detroit's Cobo Hall.
UPI COMPIX

the dominant topic among members of the Professional Bowlers Association (PBA) in 1971. A change in the type of dressing applied to most bowling lanes in recent years, making the dressing longer-lasting and more resistant to fire, was the apparent cause of a situation that frequently seemed to give left-handed bowlers an advantage in the professional tournaments. Right-handers claimed that their side of the lanes deteriorated under heavy tournament play, while the less-used left side remained relatively constant. Evidence included the fact that left-handers won 6 of the 13 nationally televised PBA meets on the winter portion of the tour. Johnny Petraglia, a 24-year-old resident of Brooklyn, won four of these events, including the last three.

In the $100,000 Tournament of Champions at Akron, O., the last of the televised meets, Petraglia scored a 245–169 victory over Don Johnson of Akron in the final game to win $25,000. Johnson, who placed second, was the only right-hander among the five bowlers who qualified for the final round.

Petraglia brought his total of PBA championships for 1971 to five when he won the meet at Houston, Tex., in midsummer. He established a record for one-year earnings by going past the $78,000 mark with several tournaments still to be rolled. Petraglia's only challenger for bowler-of-the-year honours appeared to be Johnson, who won three PBA events but was approximately $15,000 behind the New Yorker in earnings.

In the American Bowling Congress (ABC) meet held in Detroit, Mich., over a 79-day period in the spring, Al Cohn, a 43-year-old furniture salesman from Chicago, Ill., was the only double winner. Cohn won the Regular Division singles title with a three-game total of 738 and the nine-game all-events with 2,063. The Carter Tool & Die Corp. team of Rochester, N.Y., won the five-man title with 3,236, and in the Regular Division doubles the champions were Tony Maresca and Bill Haley, Mesa, Ariz., with 1,330. The winners in the Classic Division (for professionals) were: singles, Victor Iwlew, Kalamazoo, Mich., 750; doubles, Bill Zuben and Barry Warshafsky, Cranston, R.I., 1,357; all-events, Gary Dickinson, Fort Worth, Tex., 2,000; team, Chester Iio Investments, Houston, Tex., 3,081.

In the Masters Tournament, held on the same lanes used for the ABC meet, right-handed Jim Godman, Lorain, O., rolled a 300 game as he defeated Don Johnson in two four-game matches, 992–864 and 922–880, to capture the title. Johnson was second.

In the Women's International Bowling Congress (WIBC) tournament, held in Atlanta, Ga., the big-

gest surprise was the victory by 19-year-old Lorrie Koch, Carpentersville, Ill., in the Open Division all-events. Miss Koch totaled 1,840 for nine games. Other Open Division winners: team, Koenig & Strey, Wilmette, Ill., 2,891; doubles, Dotty Fothergill, North Attleboro, Mass., and Millie Martorella, Rochester, N.Y., 1,263; singles, Ginny Younginer, Winnsboro, S.C., 667. In Division One the winners were: all-events, Joyce Mooney, Pittsburgh, Pa., 1,721; team, Peeples, Detroit, Mich., 2,659; doubles, Judy Bell, Lithonia, Ga., and Daisy Trout, Marietta, Ga., 1,194; singles, Mary Scruggs, Richmond, Va., 698. Millie Martorella won the WIBC Queens tournament for the third time, defeating 19-year-old Katherine Brown, Columbus, O., in two four-game matches, 837–763 and 809–778.

The 1971 National Duckpin Tournament took place in Hagerstown, Md., April 3–May 9, and Hagerstown entrants won two of the men's titles. The Auto Electric Service took the team championship with 2,114, and Joe Bitner had the high singles total of 488. Ed Brown and Paul Sharpe of Wheaton, Md., took the doubles honours with 871, and Don Meyd of Baltimore, Md., had the best all-events score with 1,336. The women's champions were: team, Overlea Catering, Baltimore, Md., 1,861; doubles, Betty Stevens and Allena Roberts, Suitland, Md., 826; singles, Sue Marxhone, Washington, D.C., 460; all-events, Peggy Nichols, Washington, D.C., 1,236. The mixed doubles title went to Kathy Vail and Alan Hickox, Glastonbury, Conn., with 843.   (J. J. A.)

Lawn Bowls. Planning for the second World Championships, to be held at Worthing, Eng., in June 1972, tended to overshadow events in 1971. In New Zealand the growth of sponsored tournaments continued, and there was an increase in this aspect of the game in Britain, with whisky distillers, manufacturers of lager, cigarette manufacturers, and others generously sponsoring the game. A new venture over the New Year period, staged by the Indoor Centre at Teesside, Eng., was a Masters Tournament to which the sponsor, a newspaper, invited stars from all over the British Isles; but because its prizes seemed modest when compared with those of the Open golf tournament running concurrently, the promoters began a quiet campaign to have bowls made a game in which professionals and amateurs could compete side by side and for their 1971–72 repeat offered the most substantial prizes ever known in the game, namely two 14-day foreign holidays for the winner and his wife or other nominee.

In the international team series Scotland won the championship for the seventh successive year, a new record, while in individual competition David Bryant continued to dominate the world scene. Winner of the Sydney International Masters Tournament in Australia early in the year, he returned to England and qualified for three out of the four English Bowling Association Championship events, winning the singles and foursomes and so taking his total to a record-breaking ten, three more than the seven collected by the illustrious Percy Baker during a career spanning 40 years.

The New Zealand Championships, staged at Wellington under the sponsorship of a cigarette manufacturer, resulted in victory for Phil Skoglund—his record-breaking fourth win. In Australia perhaps the most heartening feature was the Limbless Bowlers Carnival, staged at the Belfield and Earlwood clubs in Queensland. The standard of play reached a high level and demonstrated that such handicapped men could, in bowls, find an outlet in which they could compete on something like equal terms with fully able colleagues. In Hastings, Eng., the annual blind bowlers tournament was no less successful.

In the United States Ezra Wyeth, an Australian, won the American Lawn Bowls Association's Singles Championship and, with Neil McInnes, the Pairs Championship. Wyeth's success perhaps stemmed from research he had conducted into the techniques of bowls. From these he had evolved a special mirror that could be set on a green so the player could study his delivery while actually playing.

(C. M. Jo.)

Boxing

The world heavyweight championship was settled beyond all dispute when Joe Frazier of the United States (*see* BIOGRAPHY) scored a unanimous decision over 15 rounds against Muhammad Ali (Cassius Clay) at Madison Square Garden, New York City, on March 8, 1971. Though Frazier had been accepted as official champion by all U.S. states, Europe, and the Orient when he stopped Jimmy Ellis (U.S.) in four rounds in New York City in February 1970, the general pub-

lic would not accept him as champion until he had proved himself the victor over Ali. Ali had made his last previous appearance as official champion in March 1967, but the title was declared vacant after he had refused to be inducted into the U.S. Army. Frazier's victory was convincing, as he floored Ali in the final round to win the decision on points. Frazier did not fight again in 1971, but Ali had two more bouts, stopping Ellis in 12 rounds at Houston, Tex., in July and outpointing Buster Mathis (U.S.) over 12 rounds, also at Houston, in November.

Bob Foster (U.S.) successfully defended the world light-heavyweight championship four times, beating U.S. challengers Hal Carroll in 4 rounds, Ray Anderson over 15, Tommy Hicks in 8, and Brian Kelley in 3. The World Boxing Association (WBA) light-heavyweight champion, Vicente Rondon (Venez.), beat Jimmy Dupree (U.S.) in 6 rounds, Piero Del Papa (Italy) in 1, Eddie Jones (U.S.) over 15, Gomeo Brennan (Bahamas) in 13, and Doyle Baird (U.S.) in 8.

Carlos Monzon (Arg.) retained the middleweight championship, beating Nino Benvenuti (Italy) in 3 rounds and Emile Griffith (U.S.) in 14. The junior middleweight title changed hands. After retaining it by drawing with José Hernandez (Spain), Carmelo Bossi (Italy) lost it in Tokyo to Koichi Wajima (Jap.).

José Napoles (Mex.) surprisingly dropped the welterweight championship in four rounds to Billy Backus (U.S.) but later recaptured it, stopping Backus in eight rounds. After this, Napoles retained the championship, stopping Jean Josselin (France) in 5 rounds and Hedgemon Lewis (U.S.) over 15. Bruno Arcari (Italy) retained the World Boxing Council (WBC) junior welterweight crown, outpointing João Henrique (Brazil), and stopping Enrique Jana (Arg.) in nine rounds and Domingo Barrera Corpas (Spain) in ten. Nicolino Loche (Arg.) successfully defended the WBA junior welterweight crown, stopping Barrera Corpas in two rounds.

Ken Buchanan (Scot.), who had won the WBA lightweight title by beating Ismael Laguna (Pan.), was recognized by the WBC and British Boxing Board

Joe Frazier drops Muhammad Ali with a left hook in the 15th round of their world heavyweight title bout on March 8, 1971. Frazier won the championship by a unanimous decision.

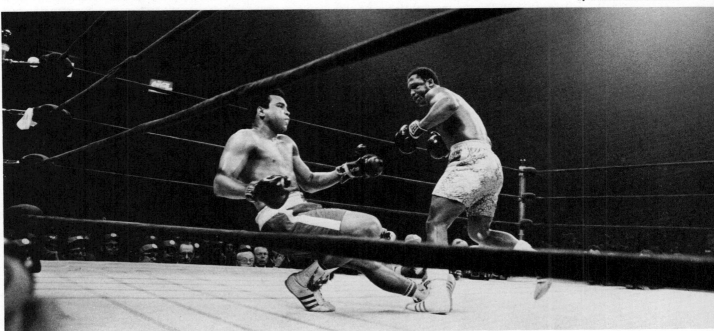

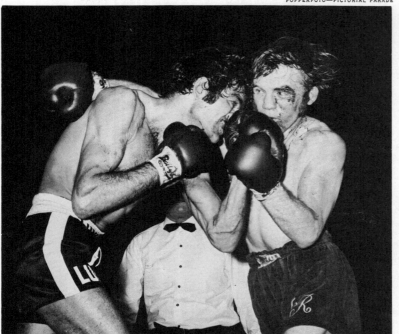

Alan Rudkin (right)
of Great Britain batters
Italy's Franco Zurlo
during their European
bantamweight title
fight on Feb. 16, 1971.
Rudkin scored
an 11th-round
technical knockout
to win the title.

Ruben Olivares (Mex.) regained the bantamweight championship from Chucho Castillo (Mex.) and then retained it by beating Kazuyoshi Kanazawa (Jap.) in 14 rounds and Jesús Pimentel (Mex.) in 11. Masao Ohba (Jap.) retained the WBA flyweight championship, outpointing Betulio Gonzalez (Venez.) and Fernando Cabanela (Phil.). In WBC flyweight competition Erbito Salavarria (Phil.) was involved in a controversy after drawing with Gonzalez, the WBC disqualifying him for allegedly drinking from a bottle of "sugar water." The title was awarded to Gonzalez pending further investigation.

In Europe, Henry Cooper (Eng.) lost the European heavyweight title on a hotly disputed decision to Joe Bugner (Eng.), on points after 15 rounds. The British and Commonwealth championships were also at stake. Cooper, who had first won the British title in 1959, announced his retirement after the fight. Bugner successfully retained the European championship against Jurgen Blin (W.Ger.) but later lost all three titles to Jack Bodell (Eng.). Bodell's venture among higher-rated Americans ended disastrously when he was knocked out in 64 seconds by Jerry Quarry at Wembley, 49 days after becoming triple champion.

European championships changed hands frequently. Apart from the heavyweight title passing from Cooper to Bugner to Bodell and then to José Urtain (Spain), there were other changes. Conny Velensek (W.Ger.) became light-heavyweight champion, outpointing Piero Del Papa (Italy) in Berlin, and was later given a drawn decision against Chris Finnegan (Eng.), also in Berlin. France claimed two titles in one week. Jean-Claude Bouttier won the middleweight title with a unanimous decision over Carlos Duran (Italy), while Roger Menetrey took over the welterweight championship, knocking out Ralph Charles (Eng.) in seven rounds at Geneva. France, however, lost a title when Pedro Carrasco (Spain) won the junior welterweight crown from René Roque.

A new European lightweight champion was crowned when Antonio Puddu (Italy) stopped Miguel Velazquez (Spain) in four rounds. Puddu retained the title against Claude Thomias (France). Augustin Senin (Spain) was hailed as one of the best of the new champions when he took the bantamweight title from England's veteran champion, Alan Rudkin, who had gained the title in February. The junior lightweight championship, which had been vacant, was won by Tommaso Galli (Italy), who outpointed Alca Marin (Spain) and later retained the title against Lothar Abend (W.Ger.).

Chris Finnegan (Eng.) won the Commonwealth and British light-heavyweight titles from Eddie Avoth (Wales).   (F. Br.)

of Control after outpointing Ruben Navarro (Mex.) at Los Angeles. When he successfully defended the championship against Laguna again in New York City, the WBA, the New York State Athletic Commission, and the British Boxing Board of Control recognized Buchanan as champion, but the WBC declared the title vacant because he had declined to meet Mando Ramos (U.S.). Ramos was matched for the WBC title against Pedro Carrasco (Spain) in Madrid: uproar followed when Nigerian referee Samuel Odubote disqualified Ramos in the 11th round after he had knocked Carrasco down four times. Later the WBC declared the championship fight "null and void."

Japan lost the WBC and WBA junior lightweight titles. Yoshiaki Numata, after retaining the WBC version against Rebe Barrientos (Phil.) and Lionel Rose (Austr.), was beaten in ten rounds by Ricardo Arredondo (Mex.). Hiroshi Kobayashi had earlier retained the WBA version of the title by outpointing Arredondo, but surprisingly lost the championship in ten rounds to the unrated Alfredo Marcano from Venezuela. Japan lost another title when Antonio Gomez (Venez.) took over the WBA featherweight crown at the expense of Shozo Saijo, but Kuniaki Shibata (Jap.), who had won the WBC championship from Vicente Saldivar (Mex.), retained it by knocking out Raúl Cruz (Mex.) in the first round.

Boxing Champions
As of Dec. 31, 1971

Division	World	Europe	Commonwealth	Britain
Heavyweight	Joe Frazier, U.S.	José Urtain, Spain	Jack Bodell, Eng.	Jack Bodell, Eng.
Light heavyweight	Bob Foster, U.S.	Conny Velensek, W.Ger.	Chris Finnegan, Eng.	Chris Finnegan, Eng.
	Vicente Rondon, Venez.*			
Middleweight	Carlos Monzon, Arg.	Jean-Claude Bouttier, France	Bunny Sterling, Jam.	Bunny Sterling, Jam.
Junior middleweight	Koichi Wajima, Jap.	José Hernandez, Spain		
Welterweight	José Napoles, Mex.	Roger Menetrey, France	Ralph Charles, Eng.	Ralph Charles, Eng.
Junior welterweight	Nicolino Loche, Arg.*	Pedro Carrasco, Spain	. . .	. . .
	Bruno Arcari, Italy			
Lightweight	Ken Buchanan, Scot.	Antonio Puddu, Italy	Percy Hayles, Jam.	Vacant
Junior lightweight	Alfredo Marcano, Venez.*	Tommaso Galli, Italy	. . .	. . .
	Ricardo Arredondo, Mex.			
Featherweight	Kuniaki Shibata, Jap.	José Legra, Spain	Toro George, N.Z.	Evan Armstrong, Scot.
	Antonio Gomez, Venez.*			
Bantamweight	Ruben Olivares, Mex.	Augustin Senin, Spain	Alan Rudkin, Eng.	Alan Rudkin, Eng.
Flyweight	Betulio Gonzalez, Venez.	Fernando Atzori, Italy	Henry Nissen, Austr.	John McCluskey, Scot.
	Masao Ohba, Jap.*			

*Recognized as champions only by the World Boxing Association.

Brazil

A federal republic in eastern and central South America, Brazil is bounded by the Atlantic Ocean and all the countries of South America except Ecuador and Chile. Area: 3,286,470 sq.mi. (8,511,965 sq.km.). Pop. (1970): 93,204,379, including (1960 census) Caucasians 60%; mulattoes 26%; Negroes 11%; Amerindians 2%; Asians 1%. Principal cities (pop., 1970): Brasília (cap.) 272,002; Rio de Janeiro 4,252,009; São Paulo 5,186,752. Language: Portuguese. Religion: Roman Catholic 93%. President in 1971, Gen. Emílio Garrastazú Médici.

Domestic Affairs. At the end of 1970 the Swiss ambassador, Giovanni Enrico Bucher, was kidnapped

BRAZIL

Education. (1968) Primary, pupils 11,943,506, teachers 423,145; secondary, pupils 2,318,456, teachers 134,070; vocational, pupils 542,418, teachers 43,798; teacher training, students 344,815, teachers 33,272; higher (including 47 universities), students 282,653, teaching staff 46,322.

Finance. Monetary unit: cruzeiro, with a free rate (Sept. 27, 1971) of 5.44 cruzeiros to U.S. $1 (13.50 cruzeiros = £1 sterling). Gold, SDRs, and foreign exchange, official: (June 1971) U.S. $298 million; (June 1970) U.S. $999 million. Budget (1970 rev. est.): revenue 16,830,000,000 cruzeiros; expenditure 19,-703,000,000 cruzeiros. Gross national product: (1968) 98,957,000,000 cruzeiros; (1967) 70,698,000,000 cruzeiros. Money supply: (Dec. 1970) 35,920,000,000 cruzeiros; (Dec. 1969) 28,670,000,000 cruzeiros. Cost of living (São Paulo; 1963 = 100): (May 1971) 1,250; (May 1970) 1,023.

Foreign Trade. Imports (1970) 12,903,400,000 cruzeiros; exports (1969) 8,282,500,000 cruzeiros. Import sources (1969): U.S. 30%; West Germany 13%; Argentina 7%. Export destinations: U.S. 26%; West Germany 10%; Argentina 7%; Netherlands 6%. Main exports: coffee 28%; raw cotton 9%; iron ore 7%; cocoa 5%.

Transport and Communications. Roads (1969) 1,089,000 km. (including 64,000 km. main roads). Motor vehicles in use (1969): passenger c. 1,650,000; commercial (including buses) c. 1.1 million. Railways: (1968) 32,182 km.; traffic (1969) 13,338,000,000 passenger-km., freight 25,207,000,000 net ton-km. Air traffic (1970): 4,620,000,000 passenger-km.; freight 181,480,000 net ton-km. Shipping (1970): merchant vessels 100 gross tons and over 422; gross tonnage 1,721,608; goods loaded 39,970,000 metric tons, unloaded 28,043,000 metric tons. Telephones (Dec. 1969) 1,787,000. Radio receivers (Dec. 1969) 5,575,000. Television receivers (Dec. 1969) 6.5 million.

Agriculture. Production (in 000; metric tons; 1970; 1969 in parentheses): corn 15,381 (12,693); rice 7,482 (6,394); cassava (1969) 30,074, (1968) 29,203; potatoes c. 1,571 (1,507); sweet potatoes (1969) 2,173, (1968) 2,120; wheat c. 1,800 (1,374); cotton, lint 717 (697); coffee 863 (1,283); cocoa (1970–71) 187, (1969–70) 211; bananas (1969) c. 6,023, (1968) c. 5,484; oranges 3,339 (3,126); sisal 325 (311); tobacco c. 265 (250); peanuts 905 (754); sugar, raw value (1970–71) c. 5,400, (1969–70) 4,543; dry beans 2,305 (2,284); soybeans c. 1,500 (1,057); rubber c. 25 (24); timber (cu.m.; 1969) 167,100, (1968) 163,200; fish catch (1968) 495, (1967) 419. Livestock (in 000; Dec. 1969): cattle 95,008; horses 9,116; pigs 65,734; sheep 24,333; goats 14,744; chickens 275,880.

Industry. Fuel and power (in 000; metric tons; 1970): crude oil 8,009; coal (1969) 2,364; natural gas (cu.m.) 1,260; electricity (kw-hr.; 1969) 41,648,-000 (78% hydroelectric). Production (in 000; metric tons; 1970): pig iron 4,202; crude steel 5,389; iron ore (1969) c. 33,000; bauxite (1969) 348; manganese ore (metal content; 1968) 922; gold (troy oz.; 1969) 194; cement 9,000; asbestos (1968) 345; wood pulp (1969) c. 701; paper (1969) 849; passenger cars (including assembly; units) 459; commercial vehicles (including assembly; units) 147.

in Rio de Janeiro. The kidnappers killed a Brazilian security agent accompanying the ambassador and left a leaflet identifying themselves as members of the Popular Revolutionary Vanguard, a guerrilla organization that had been responsible for two similar kidnappings since 1969.

The kidnappers informed the authorities by indirect means that they wanted the release of 70 prisoners (68 Brazilian and 2 foreign) as ransom. The released prisoners were to be flown to Chile, Algeria, or Mexico. After the government of Chile had been consulted and agreed to receive the prisoners, President Médici signed a decree on January 13 banishing them from Brazil; they were flown to Santiago, Chile, where they arrived on January 14. Two days later Bucher was released.

The country seemed engulfed in a wave of violence and crime. In retaliation for the killing of a state policeman in São Paulo in 1968 a secret society which became known as the Death Squad had sprung up in that city, allegedly to avenge the murder. It rapidly spread to Rio de Janeiro and other cities. Reprisal killings followed and bullet-riddled bodies (some say 180) were found frequently in remote areas. Usually a skull picture, the trademark of the group, was left with the corpse. Alarmed at such developments, church leaders, the press, and other leading groups and individuals clamoured for government action against the Death Squad. Eventually, President Médici intervened, demanding full prosecution of those found guilty of murder and other barbarous acts.

At the beginning of 1971 action against the Death Squad was taken by the courts. On January 29 two policemen were each sentenced to 65 years in jail on charges of murder. These were said to be the first members of the Squad so condemned. On March 9 an additional 15 policemen were indicted on murder charges. At about the same time, a military court sentenced to death by a firing squad a man convicted of fatally shooting a policeman. This was the first instance of such a sentence since the restoration of the death penalty in September 1969. However, in June the federal court of appeals declared unanimously that civil instead of military courts would henceforth try cases arising from Death Squad executions. The military courts continued to try persons accused of subversive activities.

The Brazilian authorities were criticized both within the country and abroad for the alleged inhuman treatment of the nation's Indian population, especially those in the Amazon Basin. The authorities acknowledged that in the last 20 years with the connivance of some officials Indians had been murdered and their lands stolen, but claimed that the responsible parties had been prosecuted. A three-man surveying team sent in May 1970 by the International Committee of the Red Cross to investigate the matter, after traveling some 14,000 mi. in the interior of Brazil with permission from the government, reported on February 23 that the Indian population in Brazil was in danger of extinction but that they had seen no evidence of massacre or signs of physical illtreatment.

Early in 1971 the nation was elated with the news that Brazilian consul Aloysio Dias Gomide (kidnapped by the terrorist group known as Tupamaros in Montevideo, Uruguay, on July 31, 1970) had been released (February 21). The Tupamaros released the diplomat after receiving a payment to them of between $250,000

Pres. Emílio Garrastazú Médici's government set up a social security plan for rural workers and announced further plans for redistributing national income in 1971.

Judith Malina and Julian Beck and 13 other members of the Living Theater group were jailed in Belo Horizonte after their arrest for possession of marijuana.

and $650,000 from the consul's wife. She had raised the money privately, the Brazilian government having declared that it would not pay ransom.

The federal Congress reopened on March 31 for its seventh session. On that day, the seventh anniversary of the revolution, former vice-president Pedro Aleixo formally announced the creation of a third political party to be known as the Democratic Republican Party (PRD). Its declared purpose was not to oppose the current military-backed government but to support and promote the ideals of the 1964 revolution. Apparently the government took no official action against the new party, although the minister of justice declared that it was unnecessary.

Addressing the Congress on March 31, President Médici declared himself satisfied with the progress made in all sectors of national life. He stressed, however, the need to redistribute the national income and to correct the economic imbalance between rural and urban areas. Two days earlier he had announced the setting up of a social security program for rural workers. This plan included the expropriation of about 15,000 sq.mi. of land along the trans-Amazon highway for the settlement of drought-impoverished farmers from the northeastern area.

The Economy. Economically, despite unrest, the nation continued to progress. According to reports of the U.S. Commerce and Agriculture departments (July 12 and Oct. 4, 1971) the Brazilian economy was booming with an extremely healthy market. Exports increased from $1.4 billion in 1963 to $2.7 billion in 1970, and they included an ever increasing amount of industrial products. Coffee declined as the principal export of Brazil, contributing only about one-third of the total. Foreign direct investments had increased at the rate of 8% annually during the last few years, with the investment of U.S.-based companies reaching $2 billion.

The optimistic opinions regarding the Brazilian economy were expressed in the continued loans from foreign banking institutions. The World Bank approved a loan of $130 million for road construction, and the Inter-American Development Bank a loan of $30 million for construction of water supply and sanitary facilities.

The government embarked on an ambitious road construction plan estimated to cost $1 billion for the 1970–73 period. The National Integration plan, adopted in 1970, included the construction of approximately 3,000 km. of new roads in the Amazon Basin with the gradual resettlement of farmers from the impoverished northeast along the roadway.

International Relations. On March 25, 1970, President Médici signed a decree extending the territorial waters under Brazilian sovereignty to 200 mi. off the coast. Another decree on March 29, 1971, prohibited all foreign vessels from fishing within the 100 mi. nearest to the coast and required a special license for fishing within the outer 100 mi. The new regulations went into effect on June 1. It was announced that warships, planes, and submarines would patrol the area. Several foreign countries protested this unilateral decision that changed the traditional offshore sovereignty rule of 12 mi. On June 18 the U.S. Department of State issued a communiqué declaring that it would protest if rumours that Brazilian gunboats fired over U.S. shrimpers fishing 40 mi. off the coast of Brazil were found to be true. It was reported that the State Department had advised the owners of the vessels that Brazil's unilateral decision was not to be respected. The firing was denied by the Brazilian authorities. Apparently, Brazil's decision arose from the desire to protect the rich fishing area off the coast and also to defend its right to sole exploitation of oil resources on the continental shelf.

When it was reported that a U.S. congressional committee had decided to postpone its approval of the International Coffee Agreement of 1970, requesting at the same time that the U.S. Department of State find a solution for Brazil's refusal to allow foreign vessels to fish within the 200-mi. claimed area, the Brazilian foreign ministry issued a communiqué expressing shock and added that the Brazilian government did not accept linking the coffee agreement with a subject touching the sovereignty of the nation. The communiqué added that such linking of the two questions constituted an "intolerable economic pressure." However, President Médici's talks with U.S. Pres. Richard Nixon during his visit to Washington in December were described as "cordial."   (R. D'E.)

Bulgaria

A people's republic of Europe, Bulgaria is situated on the eastern Balkan Peninsula along the Black Sea, bordered by Romania, Yugoslavia, Greece, and Turkey. Area: 42,823 sq.mi. (110,912 sq.km.). Pop. (1970 est.): 8,-490,000. Cap. and largest city: Sofia (pop., 1969 est., 848,049). Language: chiefly Bulgarian. First secretary of the Bulgarian Communist Party in 1971 and chairman of the Council of State from July 7, Todor Zhivkov; chairmen of the Council of Ministers (premiers), Zhivkov and, from July 7, Stanko Todorov.

The major event of 1971 was the tenth congress of the Bulgarian Communist Party, held in Sofia from April 20 to 25. Speaking in the presence of over 1,500 delegates, Todor Zhivkov, first secretary of the Bulgarian Communist Party from 1954, read a traditionally lengthy report, concluding that "the eternal friendship with the U.S.S.R. was the unshakable base of Bulgarian foreign policy."

Presenting an optimistic picture of the economy, Zhivkov forecast that during the sixth five-year development plan (1971–75) national income would rise by 47–50% while real income per capita would grow by 25–30%. Rapid industrialization by a purely agrarian state within 25 years could not have been

achieved without Soviet aid, which from 1947 to 1970 amounted to 2.2 billion rubles, more than any other Comecon country had received from Moscow; for the current five-year plan another 350 million rubles were available. By 1975, 82% of Bulgaria's foreign trade would be with the socialist bloc, 58% of this with the U.S.S.R. Having imaginatively planned its new seaside resorts, Bulgaria had considerably increased its income from tourism: a total of 1,050,000 foreign visitors entered Bulgaria in 1970—another Comecon record.

The party congress discussed and approved the draft of a new constitution to supersede that of 1947 and elected a new 147-member Central Committee, which reappointed the old 11-member Politburo. The new constitution, adopted by the Bulgarian Communist Party congress and by the National Assembly, was approved in a national referendum on May 16 by 99.7% of the electorate.

Under the new constitution Bulgaria was defined as "a socialist state of the working people in towns and countryside, headed by the working class"; this state was "a part of the world socialist community," and it was "its duty to develop and strengthen friendship, cooperation, and mutual assistance with the U.S.S.R. and other socialist countries." The party was "the leading force in society and the state." In place of the old Presidium of the National Assembly, the new Council of State of 23 members was the "supreme organ of state power."

The new constitution downgraded the position of national minorities by giving them only "the right to study their mother tongues"; the 1947 constitution gave them "the right to be educated in their mother tongues and to develop their national cultures."

A new National Assembly was elected on June 27. There were only single lists presented by the Otechestven (Patriotic) Front, comprising 400 candidates, including 266 Communists, 100 members of the Agrarian Union, and 34 nonparty men. All were

Workmen in Varna erect the steel framework of a new calcinated soda plant in April 1971. The project was being built with aid from the Soviet Union, Czechoslovakia, and Hungary.
UPI COMPIX

elected by 99.9% of the voters. The new assembly met on July 7, reelected Georgi Traikov as its speaker, elected Zhivkov (who resigned as premier) as chairman of the Council of State, and appointed Stanko Todorov as premier. The following day the assembly approved the composition of the Council of Ministers submitted by Todorov.

Military maneuvers of Bulgarian and Soviet armed forces planned in Bulgaria for mid-August were abandoned because of strong objections by Romania and Yugoslavia.

Maurice Schumann, French foreign minister, visited Sofia on September 10–11 and discussed with Zhivkov, Todorov, and Ivan Bashev, Bulgarian foreign minister, the possibility of convoking a European security conference.

(K. Sm.)

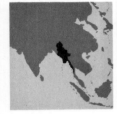

Burma

A republic of Southeast Asia, Burma is on the Indochinese Peninsula, bordered by East Pakistan, India, Tibet, China, Laos, and Thailand. Area: 261,789 sq.mi. (678,034 sq.km.). Pop. (1970 est.) 27.6 million. Cap. and largest city: Rangoon (pop., 1969 census, 1,733,000). Language: Burmese 66%. Religion: Buddhist 84%. Chairman of the Revolutionary Council and prime minister in 1971, Gen. Ne Win.

Gen. Ne Win's Burmese Way to Socialism took a leap forward in 1971 with the holding of the first congress of the Burma Socialist Program Party (BSPP) during June–July. The congress marked the transition of BSPP from a cadre party to a broadly based popular party in keeping with the general's desire to introduce an element of democracy into the Burmese system. Other tasks he listed as urgent were drafting a new constitution based on democratic socialism and uniting the nation's various races. In his inaugural address to the congress, whose convening was delayed by his protracted illness and treatment in London, Ne Win directed that the constitution must embody "prohibition of exploitation of man by man or one national group by another and the guarantee of the birth rights of every citizen." He set no deadline for completion of the drafting nor did he say specifically how the constitution would be brought into force or amended.

A political report submitted to the congress by the BSPP Central Committee underlined the two threats still facing Burma—right-wing reaction backed by the exiled former prime minister U Nu and left-wing action from rebels comprising the "Red Flag" (Trotskyist) and "White Flag" (pro-Peking) Communists. The committee approved a reconstituted 15-man Revolutionary Council, which for the first time included four civilians. As chairman of the council Ne Win also formed a new national government with few changes from the previous cabinet. He assigned himself the portfolios of prime minister and minister of defense.

The arrival of the new Chinese ambassador, Chen Chao-yuan, in Rangoon in February continued the trend of gradually improved relations with China, which had become strained during the anti-Chinese riots of 1967. Ne Win visited Peking in early August and during a week-long stay met Chairman Mao Tsetung and talked at length on bilateral relations with Premier Chou En-lai. There was no official indication as to the subjects discussed or progress achieved, but observers in Rangoon concluded that Ne Win had been able to persuade the Chinese to withhold support from the pro-Peking "White Flag" Communist rebels. Resumption of Chinese economic aid in the near future and revival of the ten-year-old friendship and nonaggression treaty also were considered likely.

The Burmese economy continued to stagnate, the fiscal year 1970–71 showing a record deficit of 518.8 million kyats. The Central Committee, in a report submitted to the congress, noted that agriculture was still subject to violent annual fluctuations and that industry remained sluggish. The government appeared to pin all hope for recovery on the four-year development plan, which the BSPP was entrusted to make ready for launching in October 1971.

Both Japan and West Germany provided loans for offshore oil exploitation ($60 million and DM. 22 million respectively), while the former also sent a high-level trade and economic delegation to improve trade relations.

Significant victories were achieved by the armed forces against rebels in various areas. Following the capture of Thakin Soe, "Red Flag" Communist leader, in November 1970, an army battalion smashed the headquarters of the Karen National Union Front in April. Kyin Pe, general secretary and Politburo member of the front, was fatally wounded in action, and several of his lieutenants along with a large quantity of arms were captured. In May the Army also claimed the elimination of 44 "U Nu emigré infiltrators" in the southeast; 8 were listed as killed, 5 captured, and 31 surrendered.

(G. U.)

BURMA

Education. (1967–68) Primary, pupils 2,791,190, teachers 50,449; secondary, pupils 586,306, teachers 15,321; vocational, pupils 3,662, teachers 304; teacher training, students 3,155, teachers 180; higher (including 2 universities), students 28,890, teaching staff 2,339.

Finance. Monetary unit: kyat, with a par value of 4.76 kyats to U.S. $1 (11.43 kyats = £1 sterling) and a free rate (Sept. 27, 1971) of 4.61 kyats to U.S. $1. Gold, SDRs, and foreign exchange, official: (June 1971) U.S. $59.3 million; (June 1970) U.S. $103 million. Budget (1970–71 est.): revenue 8,841,-000,000 kyats; expenditure 9,359,000,000 kyats. National income: (1966–67) 7,283,000,000 kyats; (1965–66) 7,058,000,000 kyats. Money supply: (Sept. 1969) 2,480,000,000 kyats; (Sept. 1968) 2,372,000,-000 kyats.

Foreign Trade. (1970) Imports 686 million kyats; exports 492 million kyats. Import sources (1969): Japan 22%; West Germany 13%; India 12%; U.K. 10%; Czechoslovakia 7%; U.S. 7%. Export destinations (1969): India 24%; Singapore 9%; U.K. 8%; Japan 8%; Hong Kong 7%; Indonesia 5%. Main exports: rice 52%; teak 23%; oilcakes 6%.

Transport and Communications. Roads (1970) c. 25,000 km. (including 13,174 km. all-weather). Motor vehicles in use (1969): passenger 29,400; commercial (including buses) 30,000. Railways: (1970) 3,100 km.; traffic (1969) 2,016,000,000 passenger-km., freight 808 million net ton-km. Air traffic (1970): 168,840,000 passenger-km.; freight 3,192,000 net ton-km. Shipping (1970): merchant vessels 100 gross tons and over 35; gross tonnage 51,221. Telephones (Dec. 1969) 24,754. Radio receivers (Dec. 1969) 399,000.

Agriculture. Production (in 000; metric tons; 1970; 1969 in parentheses): rice c. 8,300 (7,985); rubber (exports) c. 10 (12); sesame c. 102 (102); peanuts c. 460 (440); dry beans c. 140 (c. 140); cotton, lint c. 20 (25); jute c. 24 (23); tobacco 61 (57); sugar, raw value (1970–71) c. 238, (1969–70) c. 233; timber (cu.m.; 1969) 4,900, (1968) 4,800. Livestock (in 000; March 1970): cattle c. 7,000; buffaloes c. 1,450; pigs c. 1,320; goats c. 750; sheep c. 190.

Industry. Production (in 000; metric tons; 1969): cement 182; crude oil 746; electricity (excluding most industrial production; kw-hr.) 442,000; lead concentrates (metal content) 11; zinc concentrates (metal content) 4.7; tin concentrates (metal content) 0.3.

Burundi

A republic of eastern Africa, Burundi is bordered by the Congo (Kinshasa), Rwanda, and Tanzania. Area: 10,759 sq.mi. (27,865 sq.km.). Pop. (1970 est.): 3,600,000, mainly Hutu, Tutsi, and Twa. Cap. and largest city: Bujumbura (pop., 1970 est., 110,000). Language: Kirundi and French. Religion (1964): Roman Catholic 51%; Protestant 4%; animist 45%. President in 1971, Michel Micombero.

On Nov. 28, 1970, the fourth anniversary of the republic, President Micombero announced the promulgation of its first constitution, to be submitted for referendum during 1971. Extensive presidential powers were provided for, and the president was empowered to bypass the constitution in times of crisis. The guiding principle was the preeminence of the Unity and National Progress Party, the sole political party, which through its Central Committee was to recommend a single presidential candidate and also nominate all members of Parliament. The president would hold the offices of premier and party leader. As premier, he would control all measures for external defense and internal security and could appoint and dismiss ministers, who were accountable to him. Liberty for the individual and independence for the judiciary were guaranteed, and discrimination against race or tribe was prohibited.

In February diplomatic relations were established with Romania, and in April Emperor Haile Selassie of Ethiopia paid a state visit to Bujumbura. While condemning any dialogue with South Africa, the two leaders agreed their "historic and fraternal ties" should be extended. The discovery of an alleged antigovernment plot in July led to the arrest of former finance minister L. Ndabakwaje and former minister of information J. Ntungumburanye.

During the year a second contingent of military personnel was sent for training to Congo (Brazzaville), although the defense agreement with France of April 1970 was maintained. France presented three aircraft for the national airline, which became operational in April 1971. Aid from the UN Development Program included a new water research project at Lake Tanganyika, while in June Burundi joined with Rwanda and Tanzania in a UNDP river project taking in the Kagera River basin to Lake Victoria and including a mineralogical survey. (M. MR.)

Cambodia

A republic of Southeast Asia, Cambodia (officially known as the Khmer Republic) is the southwest part of the Indochinese Peninsula. Area: 69,898 sq.mi. (181,035 sq.km.). Pop. (1970 est.): 6,818,200, including (1962 est.) Khmer 93%; Vietnamese 4%; Chinese 3%. Cap.: Phnom Penh (pop., 1970 est., 468,900). Language: Khmer and French. Religion: Buddhism. Chief of state in 1971, Cheng Heng; premier, Gen. Lon Nol.

By the end of 1970 the "vietnamization" of Cambodia was so complete that what the Cambodians did or did not do hardly seemed to matter; the conduct of the war was largely in the hands of the Vietnamese (South and North) and the U.S. The fighting in Cambodia was only secondary to the main war in Vietnam, and the Cambodians were used merely as supplementary forces.

The Communists began 1971 with a spectacular show of strength. On the night of January 21–22 a suicide squad staged a daring raid on Phnom Penh's international airport, turned almost every plane in Cambodia's minuscule Air Force into a rubble of twisted steel, and killed at least 39 Cambodians before withdrawing with only one or two casualties. Simultaneously, the Communists shelled central Phnom Penh for the first time since the war began. U.S. military analysts saw the unexpected Communist attack as a direct response to the increasing U.S. involvement in Cambodia.

The U.S. involvement was by that time wide open. On the ground American soldiers appeared only in civilian clothes and only as advisers directing Cam-

BURUNDI
Education. (1968–69) Primary, pupils 180,419, teachers 4,787; secondary, pupils 3,652, teachers 295; vocational, pupils 2,194, teachers (1967–68) 204; teacher training, students 2,523, teachers 176; higher (including University of Bujumbura), students 361, teaching staff 87.
Finance. Monetary unit: Burundi franc, with a par value of BurFr. 1.75 to Belgian Fr. 1 (BurFr. 87.50 = U.S. $1; BurFr. 210 = £1 sterling) and a free rate (Sept. 27, 1971) of BurFr. 123 to U.S. $1 (BurFr. 305 = £1 sterling). Gold, SDRs, and foreign exchange, central bank: (June 1971) U.S. $14,390,000; (June 1970) U.S. $8,770,000. Budget (1970 est.) balanced at BurFr. 2,080,000.
Foreign Trade. (1970) Imports BurFr. 1,956,000,-000; exports BurFr. 2,132,000,000. Import sources (1968): Belgium-Luxembourg 26%; Japan 12%; West Germany 12%; U.S. 7%; Iran 6%; France 5%; U.K. 5%. Export destinations (1968): U.S. 72%; Belgium 11%. Main exports: coffee 84%; cotton 9%.
Agriculture. Production (in 000; metric tons; 1969; 1968 in parentheses): cassava 1,024 (940); corn 237 (120); sweet potatoes 874 (758); dry beans 311 (121); dry peas 20 (36); coffee 146 (165). Livestock (in 000; Dec. 1969): cattle c. 670; sheep c. 235; goats c. 470.

CAMBODIA
Education. (1967–68) Primary, pupils 934,292, teachers 20,048; secondary, pupils 99,574, teachers 3,886; vocational, pupils 5,787, teachers 464; teacher training (1966–67), students 1,751, teachers 104; higher (including 10 universities), students 8,929, teaching staff 874.
Finance. Monetary unit: riel, with a free rate (Sept. 27, 1971) of 55 riels to U.S. $1 (136.36 riels = £1 sterling). Budget (1969 est.): revenue 6,250,000,000 riels; expenditure 7,565,000,000 riels.
Foreign Trade. (1969) Imports 2,191,000,000 riels; exports 2,242,000,000 riels. Import sources: Japan 27%; France 24%; U.S. 11%; China 9%; Singapore 7%. Export destinations (1968): France 23%; South Vietnam 17%; Hong Kong 11%; China 10%; Singapore 8%. Main exports: rubber 49%; rice 22%; cattle 9%; corn 8%; timber 6%.
Transport and Communications. Roads (1967) 10,826 km. (including 2,600 km. all-weather). Motor vehicles in use (1968): passenger 23,100; commercial (including buses) 10,700. Railways: (1970) 655 km.; traffic (1969) 170 million passenger-km., freight 71 million net ton-km. Air traffic (1969): 68,350,000 passenger-km.; freight 810,000 net ton-km. Inland waterway (Mekong River; 1970) c. 1,400 km. Telephones (Jan. 1970) 8,024. Radio receivers (Dec. 1968) 1 million. Television receivers (Dec. 1969) 50,000.
Agriculture. Production (in 000; metric tons; 1970; 1969 in parentheses): rice 3,814 (2,503); corn 137 (118); rubber c. 20 (52); bananas (1969) 141, (1968) 136; dry beans c. 37 (37); jute c. 11 (9). Livestock (in 000; Dec. 1969): cattle c. 2,420; buffalo c. 900; pigs c. 1,200.

Business Review:
see Economy, World

Butter:
see Agriculture

Cambodian soldiers carry a wounded companion out of the line of fire during a battle with Vietnamese and Viet Cong troops near Saang, Cambodia, on Jan. 29, 1971. This battle was part of a Cambodian offensive to rout Communists from key towns around the capital.

UPI COMPIX

bodian troops in combat. In the air U.S. planes were out in force. In January, as battles raged to free Phnom Penh's lifeline to the seaport of Kampong Saom (formerly Sihanoukville) from Communist control, the U.S. committed its Strategic Air Command B-52 bombers in widespread raids in Cambodia.

South Vietnamese troops, although officially allies of the Cambodians, continued to cause considerable dismay in Phnom Penh. Their reported atrocities against Cambodians made the Phnom Penh government highly resentful. A joint Cambodian-South Vietnamese military commission was set up to inquire into allegations of burning, looting, and rape by the South Vietnamese against civilians, but the South Vietnamese authorities maintained that these charges were exaggerated. In August the Cambodian high command said it was planning to withdraw the South Vietnamese troops from their principal base at Neak Leung, a ferry point 35 mi. SE of Phnom Penh. However, with the coming of the dry season in the late fall, the Communists opened a new major offensive, threatening Phnom Penh and cutting Route 6 to the northern provinces. The Cambodian Army was unable to counter the threat, and additional South Vietnamese troops were brought into the country.

Early in the year the government in Phnom Penh came under a sudden threat of collapse. On February

South Vietnamese troops near Krek, Cambodia, fire a flamethrower mounted atop an armoured personnel carrier. The new weapon was intended for use against bunker complexes.

WIDE WORLD

8, shortly after he finished a three-hour speech to a National Assembly committee on the military situation, Premier Lon Nol suffered a stroke that paralyzed him on the right side. Being the only universally respected figure in post-Sihanouk Cambodia, Lon Nol was the indispensable unifying force in the government. He was taken to Honolulu for treatment and remained there for two months. During that period Deputy Premier Lieut. Gen. Sisowath Sirik Matak (see BIOGRAPHY) acted as premier. But Sirik Matak, known as a canny politician, had powerful enemies. In March there were reports that a group of army officers had tried to stage a coup and restore the monarchy. One or more generals, a colonel, and a dozen other officers were said to have been involved. Sirik Matak was able to crush the plot in time.

But the issue of succession defied settlement. On returning to Phnom Penh in April, Lon Nol formally resigned, with a grateful National Assembly promoting him to marshal of the Cambodian armies and giving him the title of national hero. On April 21 the four special advisers of Lon Nol proposed that he remain premier in name with three deputy ministers who would carry on the government. Lon Nol accepted this, and Sirik Matak, National Assembly President In Tam, and the chief political adviser, Song Ngok Thanh, were named deputy premiers.

The arrangement apparently did not work because of internal feuds. It was reported at the time that the U.S. favoured Sirik Matak as premier. The job was offered to him a week after the three-man arrangement was made. In a surprise move—interpreted by analysts as calculated to consolidate his position—Sirik Matak declined. This led to unsuccessful attempts by some others to form a government. Eventually the ailing Lon Nol again was asked to become the titular premier with Sirik Matak as his "premier-delegate" wielding the real power. The announcement of this compromise was made by Lon Nol's influential brother, Lieut. Col. Lon Non.

Lon Nol returned to the political forefront in October when he allowed the National Assembly to expire as a law-making body. Rather than extend its term for another year, the premier converted it into a constituent assembly and charged it with the responsibility of drafting a new constitution. Many protested this action, and on October 20 Lon Nol declared a national state of emergency and appointed a new government to rule by "ordinance" rather than by constitutional law. He said that he would no longer "play the game of democracy and freedom" because it interfered with winning the war. The next day, however, Information Minister Long Boret issued a formal statement that denied any intention of the government to abandon democracy permanently. The constituent assembly, meeting in November for the first time, elected as its president In Tam, who had been dismissed as deputy premier in September.

During a three-week visit to the U.S. in August, Sirik Matak met Pres. Richard M. Nixon in Washington. Their talks mostly centred on U.S. aid to Cambodia. According to the U.S. embassy in Phnom Penh, the country needed $200 million in military aid alone. This was in addition to substantial economic aid without which Cambodia could not avoid bankruptcy.

The economic situation was dangerous indeed. The riel had declined from the official rate of 55 to 200–220 to the U.S. dollar. A headlong flight of capital from the country only intensified following the death sentence passed on two Chinese merchants in August on charges of "economic sabotage." Late in October the government announced a stringent anti-inflationary program, worked out with the U.S. and the International Monetary Fund, the principal feature of which was a flexible exchange rate between the riel and the dollar. (T. J. S. G.)

Cameroon

A federal republic of west equatorial Africa on the Gulf of Guinea, Cameroon borders on Nigeria, Chad, the Central African Republic, the Congo (Brazzaville), Gabon, and Equatorial Guinea. Area: 179,557 sq.mi. (465,054 sq.km.). Pop. (1970 est.): 5,836,000, mainly Negro. Cap.: Yaoundé (pop., 1970 est., 178,000). Largest city: Douala (pop., 1970 est., 250,000). Language: English and French (official), Bantu, Sudanic. Religion: mainly animist; some Christian and Muslim. President in 1971, Ahmadou Ahidjo.

International opinion, often indifferent to events in Africa, was stirred deeply by the conspiracy trials held in Yaoundé in January. A tribunal in the federal capital sentenced to death six men accused of attempting to overthrow the government. Among them were Ernest Ouandié, leader of the illegal opposition party, the Union of the Cameroon Peoples (UPC), and Albert Ndongmo, Roman Catholic bishop of Nkongsamba. While President Ahidjo denounced the "vile smear campaign" he considered had been waged against his government over the trials, Pope Paul VI and UN Secretary-General U Thant intervened on behalf of the condemned men, and demonstrations aimed at putting pressure on the Cameroon authorities multiplied throughout the world. Ndongmo's sentence

was commuted, but Ouandié was shot publicly at Bafoussam, in the home territory of the dissident Bamiléké population, presumably as a public demonstration of the government's power.

The death of Ouandié marked the end of the last of the "historic leaders" of the Cameroon revolution. Ruben Um Nyobe had been killed by a French patrol in Sanaga Maritime in 1958, and Félix Moumié poisoned with thallium at Geneva in 1960. Shortly after Ouandié's execution, Pres. Georges Pompidou of France paid an official visit to Cameroon, his fourth stop on a long African tour, beginning in Mauritania and ending in Gabon.

In March the Cameroon government recognized China, accused several years earlier by President Ahidjo of supplying financial and military aid to the revolutionary guerrillas of the UPC.

Dissatisfied with the running of the multinational airline Air Afrique, Cameroon withdrew from the company in 1971 and founded its own airline company, Cameroon Airlines. On October 1 the country celebrated the tenth anniversary of its establishment as a federal state. (PH. D.)

CAMEROON
Education. (1968–69) Primary, pupils 879,048, teachers 18,534; secondary, pupils 41,768, teachers 1,839; vocational, pupils 13,060, teachers 689; teacher training, students 3,328; higher (including university at Yaoundé), students 1,899, teaching staff 154.
Finance. Monetary unit: CFA franc, with a parity of CFA Fr. 50 to the French franc (CFA Fr. 277.71 = U.S. $1; CFA Fr. 666.50 = £1 sterling) and a free rate (Sept. 27, 1971) of CFA Fr. 276.50 to U.S. $1 (CFA Fr. 685.75 = £1 sterling). Federal budget (1969–70 est.) balanced at CFA Fr. 31.5 billion.
Foreign Trade. (1970) Imports CFA Fr. 67,160,-000,000; exports CFA Fr. 62,780,000,000. Import sources (1968): France 53%; West Germany 9%; U.S. 6%; U.K. 5%. Export destinations (1968): France 34%; Netherlands 21%; West Germany 11%; U.S. 10%. Main exports: cocoa 24%; coffee 23%; aluminum 9%; cotton 8%; timber 7%.
Transport and Communications. Roads (main; 1969) 9,300 km. Motor vehicles in use (1969): passenger 28,200; commercial (including buses) 30,000. Railways: (1968) 868 km.; traffic (1970) 220 million passenger-km., freight 271 million net ton-km. Telephones (Dec. 1969) 12,303. Radio receivers (Dec. 1969) c. 210,000.
Agriculture. Production (in 000; metric tons; 1969; 1968 in parentheses): corn c. 349 (c. 457); sweet potatoes 330 (304); cassava c. 1,100 (c. 1,074); coffee c. 88 (82); cocoa (1970–71) 115, (1969–70) 110; bananas c. 120 (c. 120); peanuts c. 188 (188); rubber (exports) 12 (13); cotton, lint (1970) c. 28, (1969) 34; millet and sorghum 38 (350); palm kernels 52 (51); palm oil c. 50 (46); timber (cu.m.; 1968) c. 7,100, (1967) c. 7,000. Livestock (in 000; Dec. 1969): cattle c. 2,100; pigs c. 360; sheep c. 1,700; goats c. 2,200; chickens c. 8,800.
Industry. Production: aluminum (1970) 52,000 metric tons; gold (1968) 965 troy oz.

Canada

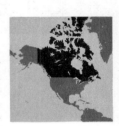

Canada is a federal parliamentary state and member of the Commonwealth of Nations covering North America north of conterminous United States and east of Alaska. Area: 3,851,809 sq.mi. (9,976,196 sq.km.). Pop. (1971 est.): 21,688,243, including (1961) British 43.8%; French 30.4%; other European 22.6%; Indian and Eskimo 1.2%. Cap.: Ottawa (metro. pop., 1971, 596,176). Largest city: Montreal (metro. pop., 1971, 2,720,413). Language (1961): English only 67.4%; French only 19.1%; both 12.2%; neither 1.3%. Religion: Roman Catholic 45.7%; Protestant 47.7%. Queen, Elizabeth II; governor-general in 1971, D. Roland Michener; prime minister, Pierre Elliott Trudeau.

Canadians shifted their attention during 1971 from the terrorist crisis of October 1970 in Quebec to the urgent problem of relations with the United States. The economic measures imposed by Pres. Richard Nixon on August 15 created immediate difficulties for the Canadian economy, which was already performing well below capacity. The need to reestablish a healthy economic relationship with the U.S. was the most critical challenge facing the government of Pierre Elliott Trudeau (*see* BIOGRAPHY). The $22 billion flow of trade across the Canadian-U.S. border represented the largest movement of commodity trade between any two nations. But, while U.S.-Canada trade represented about 60% of Canada's total foreign trade, it was only 20% of U.S. trade.

Canada's first reaction to the Nixon announcement was to claim exemption from the 10% import surcharge. A delegation led by Minister of Finance Edgar Benson visited Washington on August 19 and pointed out that because the Canadian dollar had been floating freely since May 1970, there was no question of an artificial valuation having been placed upon it. The group also asserted that Canada had not imposed any discriminatory tariff and nontariff barriers against U.S. exports and, in fact, had experienced a deficit in its commercial transactions with the U.S. of almost $14 billion in 1950–69, compared with the $1.7 billion deficit the U.S. had accumulated since 1969.

On August 19, Trudeau interrupted a visit to Yugo-

Left, an assailant attempts to jump on Soviet Premier Aleksei N. Kosygin in Ottawa on Oct. 18, 1971, as he walks with Canadian Prime Minister Pierre Trudeau; above, Kosygin struggles to free himself.

slavia to deal with the crisis. He provided a further rationale to Canada's argument by pointing out that reductions in production and employment in Canada would result from application of the surcharge, which would mean a weaker Canadian economy that could not absorb U.S. exports. Canada was currently buying about one-quarter of all U.S. exports, almost as much as the U.S.'s other leading industrial customers, Japan, West Germany, the U.K., and France, combined.

Much of Canada's exports to the U.S. entered under duty-free, quota, or special arrangements that were not subject to the surcharge. But the exports of its growing secondary manufacturing industry, which successive governments had encouraged in an attempt to diversify the country's economy and which constituted 25% of Canada's exports to the U.S., would be penalized. Disruption of the markets for these labour-intensive industries would create unemployment in Canada's most populous province, Ontario, where these industries were concentrated.

In negotiations to resolve the world trade crisis it became clear that there were specific items in Canadian-U.S. trade that were causing the U.S. concern. Perhaps the most pressing was the Automotive Agreement of 1965, which had brought about free trade in automobiles and component parts between the two countries. Safeguards had been written into the pact to protect Canada's automotive industry during a transitional period. The U.S. wanted these safeguards modified and wished to see an end to the 15–17% duty that individual Canadians were obliged to pay on U.S. automobiles. The U.S. government was also anxious to bring about a free movement in automobile replacement parts and in used cars, and was apparently interested in removing snowmobiles from the operations of the pact. Another item on the U.S. "list of particulars" was the Defence Production Sharing Agreement, which allowed Canadian firms to compete on equal terms for U.S. defense orders.

Canada's Minister of External Affairs, Mitchell Sharp, stated some of the Canadian grievances. He singled out the U.S. ban on importing uranium (re-

cently confirmed); the manufacturers' clause in the U.S. copyright law, which effectively prevented Canadian printers from selling their product in the U.S.; the U.S. government's restrictions on immigrants from Canada; and artificial U.S. selling prices on chemicals.

An Employment Support Bill, introduced in Parliament in early September, was the Trudeau government's first measure to counteract the effect of the surcharge. It provided $80 million over the following seven months to allow production and employment to be maintained in affected companies.

In December, Trudeau traveled to Washington for talks with President Nixon and received assurances that the U.S. respected Canadian independence and had no desire to assert economic domination over Canada. Nixon also indicated that the 10% surcharge would be rescinded as soon as the international monetary crisis had been settled satisfactorily. This was borne out later in the month, when the surcharge was, in fact, lifted following agreement on currency realignment by the Group of Ten principal trading nations, although numerous other problems relating to U.S.-Canadian economic relations remained to be resolved. Alone among the Group of Ten currencies, the Canadian dollar continued to float after the agreement.

Domestic Affairs. The Liberal Party lost a little ground in the House of Commons as the New Democratic Party captured two seats in by-elections in 1971. Party standings on November 8 were: Liberals 150; Conservatives 71; New Democratic Party 25; Social Credit (Ralliement Créditiste) 13; Independents 2; Independent Liberal 1; and two vacancies in a 264-seat House.

The Trudeau government's legislation program for the 1970–71 session (28th Parliament, third session), which opened on Oct. 8, 1970, consisted of 68 bills. The legislative schedule was upset by the kidnapping by Quebec terrorists of British trade commissioner James Cross, which led to the introduction of a measure to cope with civil disturbances. The government replaced its original weapon against the Front de Libération du Québec (FLQ), the War Measures Act, with the less drastic Public Order (Temporary Measures) Act of 1970. The new order outlawed the FLQ and gave the police special powers to deal with groups advocating political violence. It was passed, after a bitter debate, in early December. When the act expired on April 30 the subject of measures to deal with terrorism was referred to a joint parliamentary committee. For the interim the FLQ would be considered an illegal organization under the seditious conspiracy sections of the Criminal Code.

The legislative process moved slowly through the early part of the session, with only 13 bills passed by January. When a summer recess began on June 30, 48 bills had been approved, 17 bills were under consideration by committees, and one had been withdrawn by the government. The House resumed on September 7.

An important innovation in economic development was embodied in the Canada Development Corporation Act, which established a public corporation capitalized at $2 billion to initiate and finance large-scale Canadian-owned enterprises. Air contamination and the pollution of navigable waters were dealt with in legislation paralleling the Canada Water Act (1970). A packaging and labeling bill was approved to bring about uniform standards and to ensure accurate statements of essential information on packages. Veterans' pensions and unemployment insurance benefits were increased. Old age pensions were readjusted to provide support on a selective rather than a universal basis; the basic pension was frozen but guaranteed income supplements were provided in case of need. Salaries of members of Parliament and senators were raised for the first time since 1963. In October the government discovered it could not muster sufficient support to win approval for a new grain stabilization bill intended to provide a more uniform return to prairie farmers. The opposition claimed that by basing payments on agricultural returns of the last five years the bill would provide farmers with abnormally low incomes. The government had to fall back on payments authorized under the Wheat Reserves Act of 1956.

Two pieces of major legislation were introduced in 1971 but were not approved by the end of the year. Debate on one, the tax reform proposals first announced by Finance Minister Benson in 1969, began after the summer recess, but the complexity of the

measure meant that its progress was slow. A new Competition Act, creating a powerful tribunal to review mergers and take-overs, also came under discussion.

In federal-provincial constitutional relations it seemed possible for a moment that an end was in sight to the long impasse over amending power. At a preliminary conference in Ottawa on February 8–9, Premier Robert Bourassa of Quebec offered to agree to a formula for amending the constitution if Quebec could be guaranteed full jurisdiction over all social programs. The formula included the entrenchment of basic rights in the constitution and a plan that divided Canada into four regions and required consent for constitutional change from the federal government and six of the provinces, as long as the six included Ontario and Quebec, two of the four Atlantic provinces, and two Western provinces having 50% of the West's population.

The formula was further discussed at a federal-provincial conference held in Victoria, B.C., on June 14–16 and referred to the ten provinces for acceptance or rejection by June 28. The package also gave Quebec an expanded jurisdiction in the social security field; provided a guarantee of equality across Canada for the French and English languages; gave the provinces a voice in the appointment of Supreme Court judges; and ended the power of Ottawa to disallow provincial legislation. On June 23 Premier Bourassa dashed hopes that the agreement would be accepted by stating that he and his Cabinet had decided to reject it because it was "unclear." Prime Minister Trudeau expressed his disappointment but indicated his willingness to pursue bilateral talks with Quebec over the points of difficulty.

Three provinces changed their governments in 1971; a fourth gave a new premier a resounding vote of confidence. Saskatchewan began the trend toward overturning governments on June 23 when its voters gave their support to the New Democratic Party headed by a Regina lawyer, Allan Blakeney. The New Democrats captured 45 of the 60 seats in the legislature. A month after the election the former premier, Ross Thatcher, died of a heart attack.

A more startling upset occurred in next-door Alberta on August 30 when the Social Credit Party, which had held office for 36 years (the longest period for any government in Canadian history), was over-

---

CANADA

Education. (1968–69) Primary, pupils 3,832,-309, teachers (including preprimary) 153,762; secondary, pupils 1,428,226, teachers 99,606; vocational, pupils 188,694; higher (including 61 universities), students 477,967, teaching staff (full time) 26,661.

Finance. Monetary unit: Canadian dollar, with a free rate (Sept. 27, 1971) of Can$1.01 to U.S. $1 (Can$2.50 = £1 sterling). Gold, SDRs, and foreign exchange, official: (June 1971) U.S. $4,-347,000,000; (June 1970) U.S. $3,810,000,000. Budget (1969–70, est.): revenue Can$12,313,-000,000; expenditure Can$11,938,000,000. Gross national product: (1970) Can$86,470,000,000; (1969) Can$78,560,000,000. Money supply: (May 1971) Can$15.2 billion; (May 1970) Can $12.8 billion. Cost of living (1963 = 100): (May 1971) 129; (May 1970) 126.

Foreign Trade. (1970) Imports Can$13,935,-000,000; exports Can$17,666,000,000. Import sources: U.S. 71%; EEC 6%; U.K. 5%. Export destinations: U.S. 65%; U.K. 9%; EEC 7%; Japan 5%. Main exports: motor vehicles 20%; machinery 11%; nonferrous metals 10%; metal ores 9%; newsprint 6%; timber 6%.

Transport and Communications. Roads (1970) 810,144 km. (including 2,759 km. expressways). Motor vehicles in use (1969): passenger 6,433,283; commercial (including buses) 1,682,515. Railways (1969): 72,932 km.; traffic 3,891,000,000 passenger-km., freight 140,830,-000,000 net ton-km. Air traffic (1970): 15,111,-000,000 passenger-km.; freight 412,295,000 net ton-km. Shipping (1970): merchant vessels 100 gross tons and over 1,266; gross tonnage 2,399,-949; goods loaded 83,404,000 metric tons, unloaded 67,463,000 metric tons. Telephones (Dec. 1969) 9,303,000. Radio receivers (Dec. 1969) 14,740,000. Television receivers (Dec. 1968) 6.1 million.

Agriculture. Production (in 000; metric tons; 1970; 1969 in parentheses): wheat 9,023 (18,-623); barley 9,051 (8,238); oats 5,673 (5,728); rye 570 (419); corn 2,549 (1,865); potatoes 2,428 (2,362); rapeseed 1,617 (758); linseed 1,243 (700); tobacco c. 98 (112); butter (1969) 162, (1968) 156; cheese (1969) 112, (1968) 106; beef and veal c. 900 (901); pork c. 587 (516); timber (cu.m.; 1968) 111,900, (1967) 107,600); fish catch (1969) 1,408, (1968) 1,499.

Livestock (in 000; Dec. 1969): cattle 11,836; sheep 616; horses (June) 344; pigs 6,460; chickens (June) 83,269.

Industry. Labour force (excluding agriculture; June 1971) 8,304,000. Unemployment: (May 1971) 6.3%; (May 1970) 6.1%. Index of industrial production (1963 = 100): (1970) 147; (1969) 144. Fuel and power (in 000; metric tons; 1970): coal 11,702; lignite 3,463; crude oil 62,332; natural gas (cu.m.) 67,653,000; electricity (kw-hr.) 203,740,000 (78% hydroelectric in 1969). Metal and mineral production (in 000; metric tons; 1970): iron ore (shipments; 55% metal content) 47,178; crude steel 11,201; copper ore (metal content) 613; nickel ore (metal content; 1969) 194; zinc ore (metal content) 1,240; lead ore (metal content) 358; aluminum (1969) 978; asbestos (1969) 1,448; gold (troy oz.) 2,340; silver (troy oz.) 44,620; uranium oxide (1969) 3.5. Other production (in 000; metric tons; 1970): wood pulp 17,524; newsprint 7,808; sulfuric acid 2,409; synthetic rubber 205; passenger cars (units) 941; commercial vehicles (units) 253. Dwelling units completed (1970) 175,800.

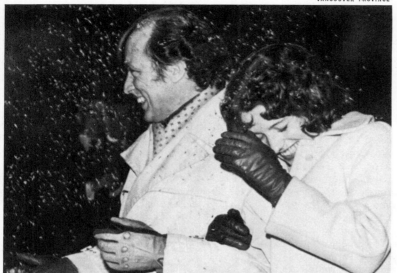

Prime Minister Pierre
Elliott Trudeau
and his young bride,
the former Margaret
Sinclair, receive
a shower of rice
after their wedding
in Vancouver
on March 4, 1971.

William Davis became
premier of Ontario
on Feb. 13, 1971,
when he defeated Allan
Lawrence.

thrown. The Conservatives, under a vigorous 43-year-old lawyer, Peter Lougheed, captured the urban vote to win 49 of the 75 seats in the legislature, a result that few observers had predicted.

Another surprising election result occurred in Newfoundland on October 28 when Joseph R. Smallwood, who had led the island into Confederation in 1949 and had been premier ever since, suffered a narrow defeat. Smallwood's Liberals captured 20 seats in the 42-seat House, the Conservatives won 21, and the remaining seat was held by an independent from Labrador. When the independent member announced his support for the Conservatives, Smallwood conceded defeat and resigned as premier. The new premier, Frank Moores, had been a member of the federal house before taking over the leadership of the Newfoundland Conservatives.

In Ontario the ruling Conservative Party picked as leader William Davis, 41, who had been minister of education in the Cabinet of J. P. Robarts. On March 1 Davis was sworn in as Ontario's 18th premier and submitted himself and his government for a vote of confidence on October 21. The Conservatives increased their strength in the 117-seat legislature from 68 to 78 seats while the Liberals won 20 seats and the New Democratic Party 19.

Canada received its first award of a Nobel prize in the natural sciences field in 1971. Gerhard Herzberg of the National Research Council was given the award in chemistry in recognition for outstanding contributions in molecular spectroscopy (*see* NOBEL PRIZES).

Foreign Affairs. Canadian foreign policy reached out in a new direction in 1971 as closer relations were established with the U.S.S.R. The approach was initiated by Prime Minister Trudeau in May when, accompanied by his wife of less than three months, he paid an 11-day official visit to the Soviet Union. The two countries signed an agreement by which they promised to hold high-level talks at least once a year. In addition, they agreed to look into the possibilities of increasing Soviet-Canadian trade, which up to this point had run strongly in Canada's favour, and agreed to the exchange of information of a scientific character on development in the Arctic.

Trudeau's visit was returned by Soviet Premier Aleksei Kosygin, who visited Canada for eight days beginning October 17. A four-year renewable agree-

ment to expand relations between the two countries in many fields was signed during his visit. On October 18, at a state dinner for Kosygin, Trudeau commented that "Canada and Canadians want very much to be able to look to the north, as they long have looked to the south, and see friends in each direction." Afterward he denied vigorously that this statement had implied an anti-U.S. attitude.

Another distinguished visitor was French Foreign Minister Maurice Schumann, who spent a busy day in Ottawa on September 22. Schumann's round of talks with Canadian ministers on subjects ranging from the international monetary crisis to Canada's involvement in French-speaking Africa showed that relations between France and Canada had improved markedly since 1967 when French Pres. Charles de Gaulle had been reprimanded severely by Canadian Prime Minister Lester Pearson for his "Vive le Québec libre" outburst in Montreal.

In early November, President Tito of Yugoslavia and his wife arrived on a six-day tour of eastern Canada. The visit returned the one that the Trudeaus had cut short in August because of the economic crisis. Tito signed a scientific and technical agreement with Canada and the two countries agreed to investigate the possibilities of a direct air link between them.

The first Canadian ambassador to China, Ralph Collins, took up his post in June 1971. His counterpart in Ottawa, Huang Hua, an experienced diplomat, arrived in Canada some time afterward and, after China's admission to the UN, also was named China's permanent representative on the Security Council. In July, Jean-Luc Pepin, Canada's minister of industry, trade, and commerce, led a strong trade mission to Peking in the first of a series of exchange visits by commercial groups. Pepin announced that more Canadian grain sales to China were in the offing and China expressed interest in the Canadian market to dispose of metals, light manufactures, and textiles. Trade with China was very much in Canada's favour: $141 million (mostly in wheat sales) in exports, with only $19 million in imports.

At the conference of Commonwealth heads of government in Singapore on January 14–22, Trudeau attempted to mediate between Britain and the African member states in the clash of views that developed over Britain's proposed sale of arms to South Africa. The Canadian prime minister insisted that the arms issue should be looked at in the context of the future development of the entire continent of Africa, a point of view that headed off a walkout of the African members. In private discussions an agreement was worked out under which Britain was to consult with Commonwealth states on the proposed sale and an eight-member study group, which included Canada, was set up to consider the security of ocean trade routes in the Indian Ocean and the South Atlantic. Nigeria, however, withdrew from the group in February, leaving the issue a potentially explosive one in the Commonwealth association. The Canadian delegation also made a significant contribution to the drafting of a momentous declaration of principles for the Commonwealth. This document emphasized the diversity of peoples and cultures in the international organization and rejected coercion as a means of enforcing collective decisions. It also recognized, however, that measures taken by a nation to guarantee its security were inevitably of concern to other members of the organization. (*See* COMMONWEALTH OF NATIONS.)

On his way to Singapore Trudeau spent some time in India and Pakistan. After the conference, he visited parts of Malaysia, Indonesia, Ceylon, and Iran. In these countries he announced increased levels of external aid from Canada.

A White Paper on Defence issued in August amplified objectives spelled out by Trudeau in 1969 during his first year in office. The White Paper confirmed Canada's partnership with the U.S. in North American defense arrangements and its continued participation in NATO. But surveillance and control over Canadian territory was reemphasized as the chief function of Canada's integrated defense forces, which would also have the responsibility of enforcing regulations such as those passed in 1970 relating to Arctic pollution. The report also suggested a more active role for the defense forces in supporting the civil power, a function they had successfully performed during the FLQ crisis in Quebec in 1970.

The report also outlined changes in Canada's contribution to North American defense. Two squadrons of Bomarc nuclear-tipped missiles located in eastern Canada would be phased out of service, but 48 interceptor aircraft of the CF 101-Voodoo type and carrying nuclear weapons would be maintained at three Canadian bases. U.S. tanker aircraft were to be allowed continued refueling facilities at Goose Bay, Labrador, while U.S. Strategic Air Command training exercises could be carried out in Canadian airspace if nuclear weapons were not being carried. Canada would take over and operate the radar station at Melville, Labrador, that U.S. forces were vacating. Minister of National Defence Donald Macdonald stated that the U.S. had not requested Canadian cooperation in the installation of an antiballistic missile system for North America; Canadian territory was not needed for these defenses.

The Canadian air force in Europe would abandon its nuclear strike role at the end of the year. By the end of the year the strength of the Canadian Forces would be set at 83,000 and the freeze on military spending imposed in mid-1969 would be lifted.

The Economy. Although long-term prospects were felt to be favourable, the Canadian economy suffered short-term difficulties in 1971. The gross national product was expected to rise to $91,010,000,000, representing an 8–9% increase over 1970 in market prices. Real output was expected to grow at a rate of 5.5%, a significant improvement over 1970. Capital spending, estimated to increase 11% over 1970, was a major stimulant in the economy, joined with higher consumer spending and a strong demand for housing.

Exports and imports both increased although imports grew more strongly. The U.S. market remained strong for lumber, petroleum, natural gas, and aluminum. Commodity exports to all countries for the first nine months of 1971 rose 4.6% to a new total of $13.1 billion. This growth was the more remarkable in view of the 7% upward revaluation of the Canadian dollar in May 1970. Global imports rose 6.8% over 1970, to reach the figure of $11,290,000,000.

Unemployment continued to be the most unsatisfactory feature in the performance of the economy. In September it reached the rate, on a seasonally adjusted basis, of 7.1%, the highest level since 1961. The labour force grew to 8,622,000, a larger increase than had been expected. Although the unemployment rate turned down slightly in the last months of the year, it was still a cause of grave concern. More suc-

cess was achieved by the Trudeau government in its fight against inflation. The consumer price index was held to a rise of about 3.5% for the year.

Three budget statements were made between December 1970 and October 1971, reflecting the uncertain economic conditions. A standpat budget announced by Finance Minister Benson on Dec. 3, 1970, produced a deficit of $417.6 million by the end of the fiscal year on March 31, 1971. On June 18, with the unemployment rate still climbing, Benson brought in more sweeping changes. About one million low-income and elderly taxpayers were taken off the rolls and about five million more persons in middle-income brackets were assessed lower taxes by reducing their taxable income and eliminating a 3% surcharge on personal income taxes. Individuals with higher incomes were given notice of increased taxes through the application of a capital gains tax after Jan. 1, 1972. Revenues for the fiscal year 1971–72 were estimated at $13,660,000,000, while expenditures were expected to reach $14,410,000,000, leaving a deficit of $750 million. On October 14 Benson presented Parliament with a third budget, cutting personal income taxes by another 3% retroactive to July 1 and reducing corporation taxes by 7%. Federal spending on new capital projects and vocational training was also announced. These measures were expected to cost $1,070,000,000; the new total revenues were $13,580,000,000 and expenditures were $14,580,000,000.   (D. M. L. F.)

ENCYCLOPÆDIA BRITANNICA FILMS. *The Legend of the Magic Knives* (1970).

Central African Republic

The landlocked Central African Republic is bounded by Chad, Sudan, the Congo republics, and Cameroon. Area: 240,377 sq.mi. (622,577 sq.km.). Pop. (1970 est.): 1,522,000. Cap. and largest city: Bangui (pop., 1968, 298,579). Language: French (official). Religion: mainly animist. President and premier in 1971, Jean-Bédel Bokassa.

The whimsical behaviour of President Bokassa continued to be a major factor in the political life of the Central African Republic. The head of state reshuffled his government several times during the course of the year, dismissing such ministers as no longer pleased

CENTRAL AFRICAN REPUBLIC
Education. (1968–69) Primary, pupils 156,178, teachers, 2,662; secondary, pupils 5,730, teachers 237; vocational, pupils 1,341, teachers 99; teacher training, students 211, teachers 18. The University of Bangui was founded in 1970.
Finance. Monetary unit: CFA franc, with a parity of CFA Fr. 50 to the French franc (CFA Fr. 277.71 = U.S. $1; CFA Fr. 666.50 = £1 sterling) and a free rate (Sept. 27, 1971) of CFA Fr. 276.50 to U.S. $1 (CFA Fr. 685.75 = £1 sterling). Budget (1969–70 est.): revenue CFA Fr. 10,749,000,000; expenditure CFA Fr. 11,450,000,000.
Foreign Trade. (1970) Imports CFA Fr. 9,492,000,-000; exports CFA Fr. 8,494,000,000. Import sources (1969): France 55%; West Germany 7%; U.S. 5%. Export destinations (1969): France 51%; Israel 15%; U.S. 9%. Main exports: diamonds 41%; cotton 22%; coffee 22%.
Agriculture. Production (in 000; metric tons: 1969; 1968 in parentheses): cassava c. 1,000 (1,000); peanuts 75 (75); sweet potatoes 47 (42); bananas c. 170 (c. 170); coffee 11 (9); cotton, lint 22 (22). Livestock (in 000; 1969–70): cattle c. 470; pigs c. 54; sheep c. 64; goats c. 520; chickens c. 1,070.
Industry. Diamond production (1969) 646,000 metric carats.

him, concentrating ever wider powers in his own hands, and suppressing all opposition.

Despite the appointment of a new ambassador in January, relations with France remained chaotic. In June and September the Bangui authorities expelled various French personnel without convincing reason. In July, France returned the base at Bangui to the Central African Army, retaining the use of certain barracks for technical advisers and medical personnel. Later in the summer, Bokassa demanded sovereignty in monetary matters but expressed the wish that the Central African Republic should remain within the franc area. The head office of the Central African Bank was to be transferred from Paris to Bangui.

In August, the Central African Republic ostentatiously withdrew from the multinational airline company Air Afrique, having contracted considerable debts in this enterprise, and set up its own airline company.

President Bokassa established close relations with the military-sponsored regime in Greece, and in May received an official visit from the Greek deputy prime minister, Stylianos Patakos. Also, Bokassa, subject to ever more rapidly changing moods, periodically would announce a rapprochement with the East, whereas his first action on seizing power in 1966 had been to break off diplomatic relations with China.

One comic incident kept the president in the limelight for several months. This was the "two Martines" affair. A young Vietnamese girl by the name of Martine falsely claimed to be Bokassa's daughter. Having discovered and recognized the "true Martine," born while he was serving with the French forces in Indochina, the president then placed the "false Martine" under house arrest, accused of espionage. However, he then relented and decided to pardon the "impostor," and adopted her as well.   (PH. D.)

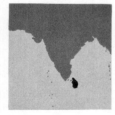

Ceylonese soldiers hold a captured rebel flag at Deniyaya in southern Ceylon in May 1971 during a four-day period in which the government offered amnesty to rebels who surrendered.

Central America: see Inter-American Affairs; *articles on the various countries*

Ceylon

An Asian parliamentary state of the Commonwealth of Nations, Ceylon occupies an island off the southeast coast of peninsular India. Area: 25,332 sq.mi. (65,610 sq.km.). Pop. (1970 est.): 12,514,000, including (1963) Sinhalese about 71%; Tamil, 22%; Moors 6%. Cap. and largest city: Colombo (pop., 1970 est., 582,767). Language: Sinhalese and Tamil (official), English. Religion: mainly Buddhist, with Hindu, Christian, and Muslim minorities. Queen,

Elizabeth II; governor-general in 1971, William Gopallawa; prime minister, Mme Sirimavo Bandaranaike.

The most significant event of 1971 was an armed rebellion against Mme Bandaranaike's left-wing coalition by the People's Liberation Front, or "Che Guevarists," led by Rohana Wijeweera, a graduate of the revolutionary Lumumba University in Moscow. Participants were mainly unemployed graduates, school dropouts, and young Buddhist *bhikkus* (monks). The rebellion stemmed from the disappointed expectations of the People's Liberation Front and the Maoist section of the Communist Party, who had hoped for extreme radical measures, such as the complete nationalization of the press, plantations, and banks, when Mme Bandaranaike's government came to power. Some government ministers originally had sympathized with such measures, but soon found them economically impracticable.

The rebellion, which had been well planned and armed, began in March with an attack on the U.S. embassy in Colombo, in which a police inspector was killed. In early April attacks were made on several police stations and public buildings, from some of which arms were seized; several individuals were murdered. The government, which had already declared a state of emergency, then called out the armed forces. These numbered only 18,000; the rebels were more numerous. The Army was short of arms and ammunition, and the government appealed abroad for supplies. These were furnished quickly by several countries, among them the U.K., India, and the U.S.S.R., and included some helicopters. There was no evidence that the rebels had sympathy or support from any foreign countries, but the government took the step of advising the recently established mission from North Korea to close.

CEYLON

Education. (1967–68) Primary, secondary, and vocational, pupils 2,594,072, teachers 94,113; teacher training, students 5,570, teachers 438; higher (including 3 universities; 1966–67), students 16,098, teaching staff 1,064.

Finance. Monetary unit: Ceylonese rupee, with a par value of CRs. 5.95 to U.S. $1 (CRs. 14.29 = £1 sterling) and a free rate (Sept. 27, 1971) of CRs. 5.74 to U.S. $1. Gold, SDRs, and foreign exchange, official: (June 1971) U.S. $53 million; (June 1970) U.S. $41 million. Budget (1969–70 est.): revenue CRs. 2,834,000,000; expenditure CRs. 2,883,000,000. Gross national product: (1969) CRs. 11,661,000,000; (1968) CRs. 10,596,000,000. Money supply: (Feb. 1971) CRs. 1,955,000,000; (Feb. 1970) CRs. 1,866,-000,000. Cost of living (Colombo; 1963 = 100): (May 1971) 129; (May 1970) 127.

Foreign Trade. (1970) Imports CRs. 2,313,000,-000; exports CRs. 2,021,000,000. Import sources: U.K. 14%; China 12%; India 10%; Japan 8%; West Germany 6%; U.S. 6%. Export destinations: U.K. 23%; China 13%; U.S. 7%. Main exports: tea 55%; rubber 22%; coconut products 12%.

Transport and Communications. Roads (1970) 21,291 km. Motor vehicles in use (1970): passenger 87,344; commercial 32,952. Railways: (1968) 1,515 km.; traffic (1968–69) 2,867,000,000 passenger-km., freight 337 million net ton-km. Air traffic (1970): 109,470,000 passenger-km.; freight 2,461,000 net ton-km. Telephones (Dec. 1969) 60,215. Radio receivers (Dec. 1969) 500,000.

Agriculture. Production (in 000; metric tons; 1970; 1969 in parentheses): rice 1,514 (1,374); cassava (1969) 403, (1968) 425; sweet potatoes (1969) 66, (1968) 76; onions (1969) 49, (1968) 35; tea 212 (220); rubber *c.* 157 (151); copra *c.* 210 (*c.* 210). Livestock (in 000; June 1970): cattle *c.* 1,580; sheep *c.* 29; buffalo *c.* 750; goats *c.* 535; pigs *c.* 107; chickens *c.* 6,600.

Industry. Production (in 000; metric tons; 1969): cement 283; graphite (exports) 11; electricity (kw-hr.) 752,000.

The revolt was crushed and at least 1,200 persons killed, 60 of them from the Army and police; 14,000 were taken into custody. About 2,000 were subsequently released, 5,000 were to face trial, and the rest were put in detention camps for "rehabilitation." Curfews and strict censorship were imposed.

Despite the government's failure to live up to extremist expectations, many radical changes were introduced. The Petroleum Corporation took charge of the distribution and sale of gasoline; a corporation was established with powers to carry on the export-import business and the sale of any kind of goods and produce; and an act was passed enabling the government to take over any business undertaking and "property necessary for the purpose of that undertaking." In addition, trade-union rights were conceded to nearly all public employees, and workers' councils were started in some departments. In the higher ranges of the administrative service several permanent secretaries to ministries were replaced by others more acceptable to the government. The same was the case with ambassadors and high commissioners abroad. In local government People's Committees (*Janata*) were created to watch against corruption.

The new constitution was expected to be brought before the House of Representatives for formal approval early in 1972. Although the document was not yet in its final form, several "basic resolutions" were passed by the Constituent Assembly, including one to make Ceylon a republic and another extending the duration of a one-chamber parliament to six years.

The economic situation remained precarious, partly because of the low world market price of Ceylon's main export, tea, partly because of the high price of rice, and partly as a result of commercial and industrial inefficiency. Far too many foodstuffs that could be produced at home were being imported, and unemployment was chronic. Despite massive aid from the International Monetary Fund, Europe, and China, and a strict limitation on most imports, the government was finding it increasingly difficult to finance its policies. (S. A. P.)

Chad

A landlocked republic of central Africa, Chad is bounded by Libya, the Sudan, the Central African Republic, Cameroon, Nigeria, and Niger. Area: 495,750 sq.mi. (1,284,-000 sq.km.). Pop. (1970 est.): 3,706,000, including Saras, other Africans, and Arabs. Cap. and largest city: Fort-Lamy (pop., 1968, 132,502). Language: French (official). Religion (1964): Muslim 41%; animist 30%; Christian 29%. President and premier in 1971, François Tombalbaye.

In August, President Tombalbaye's regime survived an attempted coup, which was immediately suppressed. After the coup was put down, Tombalbaye accused Libya of interfering in his country's affairs and broke off diplomatic relations with the government in Tripoli. In September the president of Niger, Hamani Diori, visited Fort-Lamy in the role of mediator in the dispute.

Despite the adherence to the government of a few isolated elements, rebellion continued in the central

and northern areas of the country. The leader of the illegal opposition party, the Chad National Liberation Front (Frolinat), Abba Sidick, officially refused to negotiate with Tombalbaye. Operating from Tripoli with the help of the Libyans, he continued to direct Frolinat in the armed struggle it had been engaged in for the previous three years.

At the beginning of June, the French expeditionary force in Chad returned home, although in fact almost 2,000 French personnel remained in Chadian territory: some 600 marines stationed at Fort-Lamy in accordance with Franco-Chadian cooperation agreements; approximately 700 air force personnel with helicopters and aircraft; and about 700 officers and enlisted men on detachment to the Fort-Lamy government, serving in Chadian uniform as technical assistants. During the year, about a dozen French troops were killed in the fighting in Chad, increasing the hostility of public opinion in France toward the French intervention. This hostility was reinforced by the strained relations between Paris and Fort-Lamy. On several occasions Tombalbaye expelled French nationals from his country, and also, paradoxically, made periodic accusations of imperialism against the French government, although never making the allegation explicit.

Despite his steadfastly conservative internal policies, in foreign matters the president made broad advances toward the East. In July, Chad officially recognized East Germany, and a broadly based dialogue was commenced with China.

Of all the nations of black Africa affected by the 1971 cholera epidemic, Chad suffered most, with more than 3,000 deaths from the disease. (Ph. D.)

Chemistry

Physical and Inorganic. *Analyses of Atmospheric Pollutants by Infrared Spectroscopy with Tunable Diode Lasers.* Scientists at the Lincoln Laboratory, Massachusetts Institute of Technology, used variable frequency semiconductor diode lasers consisting of compounds of lead, tin, and tellurium ($Pb_{1-x}Sn_xTe$) to detect gaseous molecular pollutants in the atmosphere. In one application, remote sensing was achieved by measurement of the infrared absorption or emission lines characteristic of a particular contaminant at atmospheric pressure. Another technique involved gas sampling at a particular point: the gas pressure was reduced until the Doppler-broadened infrared absorption spectrum was obtained, thereby minimizing overlap with neighbouring spectral lines. This method makes possible high specificity in the

Cheese:
see Agriculture
Chemical Industry:
see Industrial Review

170

Chemistry

parts-per-hundred million range of contamination.

A typical monitoring application involved several $Pb_{1-x}Sn_xTe$ diode lasers of varying composition, each emitting in a strongly absorbing infrared region of one of the pollutant gases. At atmospheric pressure, the collision-broadened spectral line widths for typical gases were well below the limit of resolution of infrared spectrometers previously available. The resolution with a tunable diode laser was imposed by the pressure-broadened line width of the gas itself, to yield all the available optical information within the tuning range. Monitoring of atmospheric pollutant gases by long-path transmission had the advantage over point sampling of producing an average value of the pollutant concentration over the path; this value was of higher overall significance in ambient air analyses.

Synthesis of Hypofluorous Acid. Isolation of the first oxyacid of fluorine, HOF, was achieved by chemists at the Argonne National Laboratory in Illinois. First detected in 1968 at the University of California in a low-temperature matrix, HOF was at that time thought to be too unstable for isolation. Milligram quantities of the acid were prepared by passing a low-pressure stream of F_2 gas over water at 0° C in a vessel made of Kel-F, a compound containing fluorine, chlorine, and carbon. The products were HOF, HF, O_2, and OF_2, and the HOF was trapped from the F_2 stream at $-183°$ C and detected with a time-of-flight mass spectrometer. It was a white solid that melted at $-117°$ C and had a half-life for decomposition varying from 5 min. to 1 hr. at room temperature.

Ion Cyclotron Resonance Mass Spectrometry. After the recent advent of commercial instruments, considerable interest was shown in ion cyclotron resonance

mass spectrometry, which offered the unique feature of sufficient sensitivity to detect both positive and negative ions. The ions were produced by electron impact in a uniform magnetic field (B). The motion of the ions in a plane perpendicular to B was constrained to a circular path of angular frequency ω_c but was not restricted in the direction parallel to B. The cyclotron resonance frequency, ω_c, was dependent upon the mass-to-charge ratio of an ion, m/e, and was given by $\omega_c = eB/m$. By applying an alternating electric field of frequency ω_1, absorption of energy by the ions took place when $\omega_1 = \omega_c$. A spectrum, linear in mass, was obtained by applying a fixed frequency and scanning the magnetic field, so that ions of different m/e fulfilled the above equation.

The absorption of energy by the ions was detected with a radiofrequency marginal oscillator to supply the alternating electric field, the energy absorption changing the Q-factor (ratio of reactance to resistance) of the oscillator and producing a signal. Double-resonance and multiple-pulse techniques made the instrument particularly suitable for studying ion-molecule reactions. Other applications included the measurement of energy levels in neutral species, proton and electron affinities, and the structures and relative acidities of ions in the gas phase.

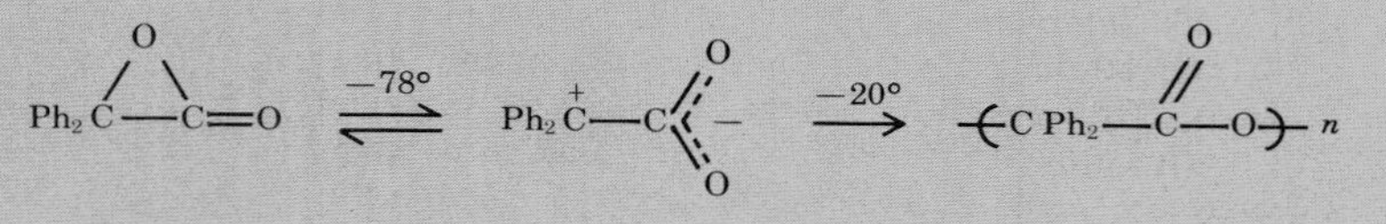

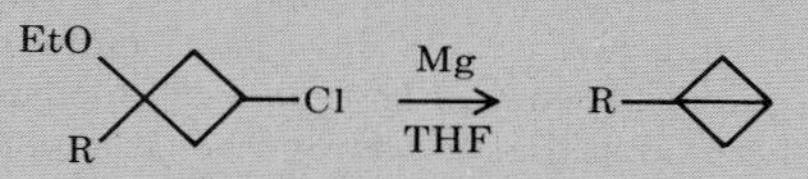

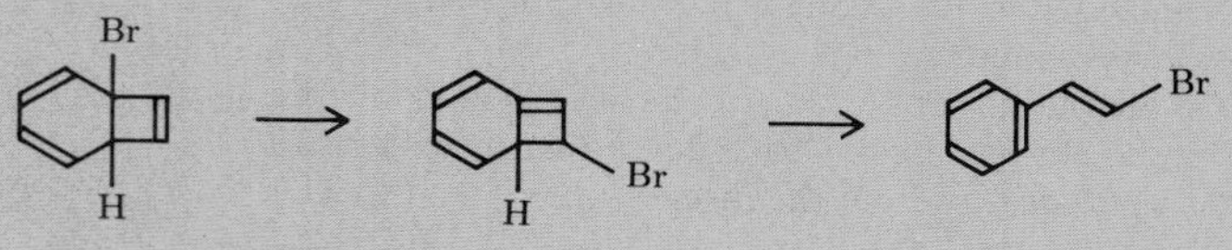

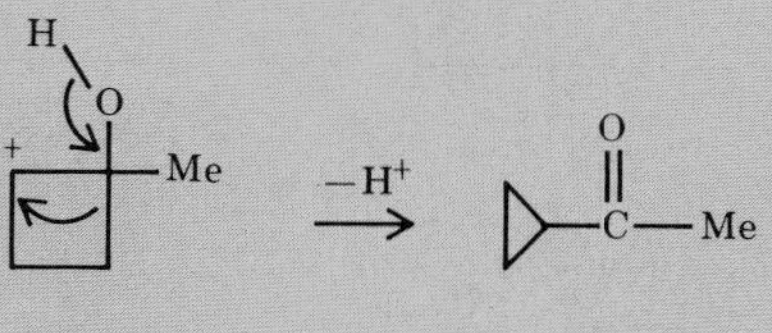

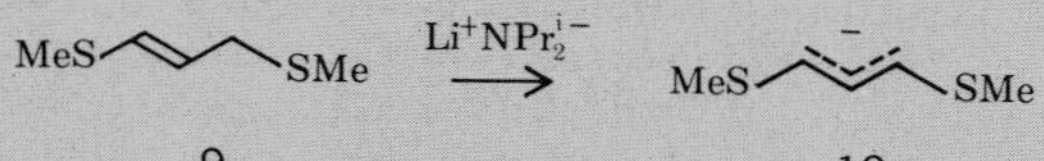

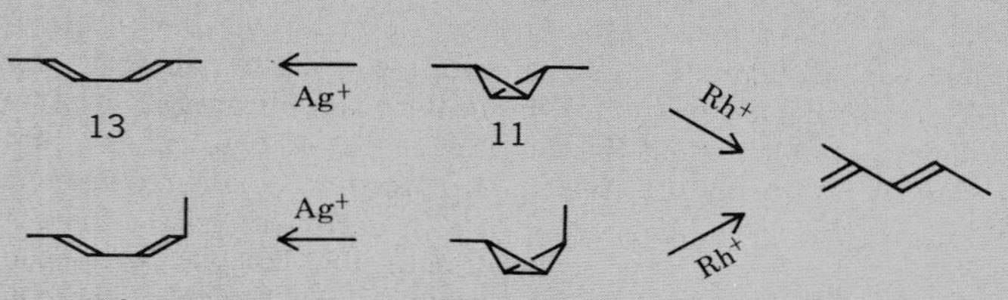

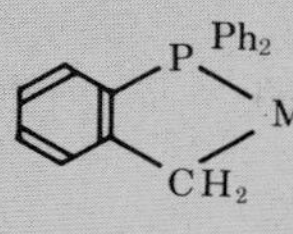

Astrochemistry: First Molecule Containing Four Different Elements. A team of astronomers and chemists, working at the observatory at Green Bank, W. Va., discovered the molecule formamide, $HCONH_2$, in two stellar clouds, Sagittarius A and B_2, which lie toward the centre of the Milky Way. The spectrum was recorded with a 140-ft. radiotelescope. Formamide was the most complex substance so far identified in space, but the list of more than a dozen molecules was growing rapidly. The molecules occurred in the ultrahigh vacuum of space, at unknown relative concentrations. (J. A. Kr.)

Organic. The preparation and some properties of α-lactones were reported during the year. Low-temperature treatment of diphenylketene with ozone, or of diphenyldiazomethane with carbon dioxide, gave the lactone **1a,** apparently in equilibrium with the zwitterionic (characterized by a dipolar ion) form **1b,** for on allowing the fluorotrichloromethane solution to warm up a precipitate of the polyester **2** appeared. A similar zwitterionic structure was implicated in the solvolysis of α-halocarboxylate ions.

Cyclodecanol was found to undergo ring-closure (the closing of an open chain of atoms) with loss of hydrogen when treated with antimony pentafluoride in fluorosulfonic acid, to give a bicyclic alcohol. Homologous monocyclic alcohols gave only n-alkyl cyclohexanols. Bicyclobutane and some of its derivatives were prepared as shown from 3-ethoxychlorocyclobutanes **3** with magnesium in tetrahydrofuran. Rearrangement of bromocyclooctatetraene to *trans* ω-bromostyrene **6** was found to proceed via the bicyclic valence tautomer **4,** which on ionization and recombination gave **5.** Electrocyclic ring-opening then yielded compound **7** stereospecifically (formed a specific stereoisomer). The action of the thallium III ion on methylcyclobutene provoked ring contraction, with oxidation to cyclopropyl methyl ketone **8.** The intermediate hydroxycarbonium ion **7** was clearly involved. Other chemists detected the formation of cyclopentane aldehyde from cyclohexene oxide, a similar but entirely unexpected rearrangement. This required for its initiation the particular combination of lithium bromide with a dipolar aprotic solvent such as triphenylphosphine oxide.

New cyclic ketones prepared included cyclobutenone and cyclobutenedione, the latter by the photochemical addition reaction of acetylene with dichlorovinylidene carbonate followed by hydrolysis in aqueous acetone. Cyclobutenedione was found to be markedly polar and, though stable as a solid, it decomposed slowly in methanol solution.

Some transition metal ions in low oxidation states were found to facilitate the recovery from ketoximes of the parent ketones under very mild conditions. Titanium III chloride in buffered acetic acid catalyzed the hydrolysis of oximes themselves, while chromium II acetate, also buffered at pH 5 (slightly acid; the pH scale is a numerical measure of hydrogen ion concentration), promoted the decomposition of ketoxime acetates. New methods for the synthesis of aldehydes were described. α,β-unsaturated aldehydes were obtained from the dithioether **9,** which could be converted to the anion **10** by lithium di-isopropyl amide, thus effectively equivalent to the unknown species $-CH = CH \cdot CHO$. Coupling with a halide RX and subsequent treatment with a mercuric salt gave the aldehyde $R \cdot CH = CH \cdot CHO$. Another preparative reaction utilized the iron tetracarbonyl dianion $Fe(CO)_4{}^{2-}$ as the source of the carbonyl group. Primary alkyl bromides yielded in the presence of triphenylphosphine the acyl derivative $RCOFe(CO)_3$ PPh_3^-, which liberated the aldehyde RCHO on acidification with acetic acid.

Such reactions involving metal ions or organometallic compounds emphasized the extent to which the traditionally distinct areas of organic and inorganic chemistry had merged, extending the range

of synthetic methods at the service of the organic chemist.

Many highly strained polycyclic molecules (in which the bond angles are much reduced by the geometry of the carbon framework from the normal tetrahedral angle of 110°) owe their stability to kinetic factors, since isomerization to forms of lower energy is symmetry-forbidden. They may, however, react rapidly in the presence of metal ions, and the influence of silver I, rhodium I, and palladium II in particular was actively investigated. Typical examples noted were the isomerization by silver I of *cis* (but not *trans*) tricyclooctane to 1,5-cyclooctadiene and of cubane to cuneane. Often the product differed according to the metal; thus, treatment of cubane with rhodium I yielded tricyclooctadiene; and the bicyclobutanes **11** and **12,** which gave the hexadienes **13** and **14** stereospecifically with silver I, gave the methylpentadiene **15** as well as both **13** and **14** on treatment with rhodium I or palladium II. The explanation of these differences was not clear, and though it was agreed that the metal ions provided an alternative pathway of lower activation energy for the isomerization, both carbonium ions and carbene intermediates were proposed.

A novel example of the influence of chelation (combining with a metal to form a ring of five or six atoms with a central metallic ion) in enhancing stability was found in compounds of the type **16** (M = Ni, Pd, or Pt) in which the metal atom is σ-bonded to the benzyl group. (J. C. Y.)

See also Industrial Review; Life Sciences; Physics.

Chess

Major interest in 1971 centred around the candidates series of matches to determine who would challenge world champion Boris Spassky (U.S.S.R.) in a match for the title in 1972. Bobby Fischer (U.S.; *see* Biography) emerged as the victor after an easy $6\frac{1}{2}$–$2\frac{1}{2}$ win over Tigran Petrosian (U.S.S.R.) in the final of the series, held in Buenos Aires, Arg., in October.

Fischer scored a runaway victory at the Interzonal Tournament held at Palma de Mallorca, Spain, Nov. 8–Dec. 13, 1970, to decide the six qualifiers who would join Petrosian and V. Korchnoi (U.S.S.R.) in the candidates series. In addition to Fischer, whose

U.S. chess player Bobby Fischer ponders opening move in his victorious match with the Soviet player Tigran Petrosian at candidates' tournament in Buenos Aires, Arg., in October 1971. Fischer won the privilege of challenging the world champion, Boris Spassky, in the spring of 1972.

KEYSTONE

score was 18½, the qualifiers were E. Geller (U.S.S.R.), R. Hübner (W.Ger.), and Bent Larsen (Den.), 15; M. Taimanov (U.S.S.R.) and W. Uhlmann (E.Ger.), 14. A tie for the reserve place between L. Portisch (Hung.) and V. Smyslov (U.S.S.R.) was to have been resolved by a match in April 1971 at Portoroz, Yugos. This ended in a 3–3 draw, however, so Portisch was adjudged the winner on account of his superior Sonneborn-Berger score at Mallorca.

The candidates series began in May. In the quarter-finals Petrosian beat Hubner at Seville, Spain, 4–3, the latter retiring on losing the seventh game; Korchnoi beat Geller 5½–2½ in Moscow; Larsen beat Uhlmann 5½–3½ at Las Palmas in the Canary Islands, and Fischer created a sensation by beating Taimanov in Vancouver, B.C., 6–0. Fischer was to underline this superiority by beating Larsen 6–0 in a semifinal match at Denver, Colo., in July. In the other semifinal match, Petrosian beat Korchnoi in Moscow 5½–4½.

In October 1970 Larsen was first in a strong international tournament at Vinkovic, Yugos. Korchnoi easily won the 38th Soviet championship at Riga in December. The European Ladies Championship at Vrnjacka Banja, Yugos., was won by Nana Alexandria (U.S.S.R.). Over the turn of the year Portisch won first prize at the Hastings (Eng.) Premier Tournament for the second year in succession. B. Ivkov (Yugos.) was first at an international tournament in Stockholm.

Korchnoi scored a narrow victory in a strong Hoogoven tournament, at Wijk aan Zee, Neth., in January 1971.

First prize at the annual Málaga, Spain, international tournament went to A. Pomar (Spain). A strong international tournament at Tallinn in February and March ended in a tie for first place between P. Keres and M. Tal (both U.S.S.R.). The Netherlands won the Clare Benedict International Team Tournament in March in Madrid. L. Polugaievsky (U.S.S.R.) was first by a margin of 3 points at the Mar del Plata, Arg., international tournament. V. Hort (Czech.) was first at the Capablanca Memorial Tournament in Havana, and the woman world champion, Nona Gaprindashvili (U.S.S.R.), was first in a women's international tournament at Belgrade, Yugos.

The Women's Interzonal Tournament was held in May at Ohrid, Yugos., and won by Alexandria. The other two players to qualify for the candidates women's matches were T. Zatulovskaia (U.S.S.R.) and M. Lazarevic (Yugos.). The 20-year-old Soviet master R. Vaganian was first in an international tournament at Vrnjacka Banja. There was a tie for first place at the annual Sarajevo, Yugos., international tournament between M. Bobotsov (Bulg.), D. Bronstein (U.S.S.R.), and M. Matulovic (Yugos.). Hort won an easy victory in an international tournament at Luhacovice, Czech. In June, G. Forintos (Hung.) scored a good first at an international tournament at Baja, Hung. First place in an international tournament at Bucharest, Rom., was shared by Y. Averbach (U.S.S.R.) and M. Hennings (E.Ger.).

At the annual IBM international tournament in July at Amsterdam, Smyslov was first. Spassky was a disappointing third at an international tournament at Göteborg, Swed., first place being shared by Hort and the young Swede Ulf Andersson. Another surprise came in the World Junior Championship at Athens, which was won by the young Swiss Werner Hug. The World Students Team Championship in Mayagüez, P.R., was won easily by a powerful Soviet team. There was a tie for first place at the annual international tournament at Natanya, Israel, between L. Kavalek (Czech.) and B. Parma (Yugos.).

Former world champion Max Euwe (Neth.) was elected president of the World Chess Federation. He succeeded Folke Rogard of Sweden, who had held the post for 21 years. (H. Go.)

Queen's Pawn, King's Indian defense (played in the IBM Grandmasters' Tournament at Amsterdam, July 1971)

White R. G. Hartoch	Black V. Smyslov	White R. G. Hartoch	Black V. Smyslov
1 P—Q4	Kt—KB3	17 P—Q5	Kt—Q5
2 Kt—KB3	P—KKt3	18 B—K5	Kt—K7ch
3 P—B3(a)	B—Kt2	19 K—R1	Q×Q
4 B—B4	P—Kt3	20 R×Q	Kt—Q6(d)
5 QKt—Q2	B—QR3	21 P—KKt3	Kt×B
6 P—QR4(b)	P—B4	22 Kt×Kt	B×QKtP
7 P—R5	Kt—B3	23 R—K1(e)	B×QKtP
8 P×P	P×P	24 R×Kt	B—B3
9 P—K3	B×B	25 Kt—Kt3	R—B1
10 Kt×B	O—O	26 R—B2	P—Q3
11 Kt(B1)—Q2	P×P	27 K—Kt2	K—B2
12 KP×P	Kt—Q4	28 K—B3	P—KKt4
13 B—Kt3	P—B4	29 K—K2	P—Kt5(f)
14 O—O	R×R	30 Kt—B1	P—Kt4
15 Q×R	Q—R1	31 K—Q3	R—B4
16 P—B4(c)	Kt(Q4)—Kt5	resigns (g)	

(a) An inelastic and somewhat old-fashioned move; better is the normal 3 P—B4. (b) This advance merely reacts to his eventual disadvantage; now was the time for aggression on the other flank by P—KR3, preparing to play P—KKt4. (c) Seriously weakening his hold on the central black squares; but if he does nothing, then Black attacks on the King side by P—KR3, threatening P—B5, etc. (d) The knights have developed a marvelous activity and now threaten mate. To avert this, White proceeds to surrender material. (e) Or 23 R—Kt1, R—R1; followed by 24 . . ., R—R7. (f) Note the skill with which Black is putting his pawns on the White squares so as to increase the scope of action for his bishop. (g) The threat of P×Pch and R×P cannot be averted.

Sicilian defense (played in the Interzonal Tournament at Palma de Mallorca, December 1970)

White R. Fischer	Black J. Rubinetti	White R. Fischer	Black J. Rubinetti
1 P—K4	P—QB4	13 P×Pdis ch	K—Q2(e)
2 Kt—KB3	P—Q3	14 P—QKt4	Kt—R5
3 P—Q4	P×P	15 Kt×Kt	P×Kt
4 Kt×P	Kt—KB3	16 P—QB4	K—B1
5 Kt—QB3	P—K3	17 Q×P(f)	Q—Q2
6 B—QB4	P—QR3	18 Q—Kt3	P—Kt4
7 B—Kt3	P—QKt4	19 B—Kt3	Kt—R4
8 O—O	B—Kt2(a)	20 P—B5	P×P
9 R—K1	QKt—Q2(b)	21 P×P	Q×P(g)
10 B—Kt5	P—R3(c)	22 R—K8ch	K—Q2
11 B—KR4	Kt—B4(d)	23 Q—R4ch	B—B3
12 B—Q5	P×B	24 Kt×B	resigns (h)

(a) This is a most dangerous way of playing since it is risky to leave the king too long in the centre; more prudent was 8 . . ., B—K2; 9 P—B4 O—O. (b) Whereas now after 9 . . ., B—K2; White has the stunning rejoinder 10 B×P! (c) This, in conjunction with his new move, leads to a speedy loss. Q—R4 was the indicated move. (d) The logical continuation was 11 . . ., P—Kt4; 12 B—Kt3, Kt—K4; after which he might still hope to defend himself. But it would seem he has overlooked White's next move. (e) Or 13 . . ., B—K2; 14 Kt—B5; winning back the piece with advantage both in position and material. (f) White has only two pawns for the piece, but what pawns! Their advance is irresistible. (g) If 21 . . ., B×QP; 22 Q—Kt6, threatening P—B6. (h) Because of 25 . . ., K×R; 26 R—K1ch, K—Q2; 27 Kt—Q4dis ch, followed by mate in a few moves.

Chile

A republic extending along the southern Pacific coast of South America, Chile has an area of 292,256 sq.mi. (756,945 sq.-km.), not including its Antarctic claim. It is bounded by Argentina, Bolivia, and Peru. Pop. (1970): 8,853,140. Cap. and largest city: Santiago (metro. pop., 1970, 2,661,920). Language: Spanish. Religion: predominantly Roman Catholic. President in 1971, Salvador Allende Gossens.

The newly elected coalition government of President Allende introduced economic and social reforms designed to change the basic structure of Chilean society along socialist lines. The president announced his intention to achieve these changes within the framework of Chile's tradition of respect for due process of law and of individual liberties.

The most far-reaching reforms were directed at the organization of the economy and particularly at the ownership of the means of production. The government declared its intention to create three economic "areas": the state-owned area, which would include all major industries; the mixed area in which the majority ownership of the companies was by the state, but with minority private participation; and the private area of small and medium-sized enterprises. To be completely state-owned were nitrate, iron, coal, and copper mining; the steel, pulp and paper, cement, petrochemical, and heavy chemical industries; the banking system; transportation; communications; public utilities; and foreign trade. In practice, however, the new government intervened with and expropriated companies in many industries not included in the above list. For example, textile mills and metal-working and fishing companies were intervened with and expropriated, or both.

In January, the government took over the Lota-Schwager coal mine by buying out the owners. Also during the year the government development corporation, CORFO, bought the Anglo-Lautaro nitrate mine, the Bethlehem Steel Corporation's iron mine, and the Northern Indiana Brass Company's Chilean affiliates. The CORFO also bought the remaining pri-

A constitutional amendment authorized nationalization of major U.S. copper producers in Chile. Above, men work at the largest underground copper mine in the world; prior to expropriation the mine was 49% U.S. owned.
UPI COMPIX

vately held shares of the state-controlled steel monopoly, the Compañía de Acero del Pacífico. Systematically bought out by the government were the privately owned shares of the country's commercial banks. Foreign banks operating in Chile were bought out through direct negotiations.

In September, Allende announced expropriation of the remaining U.S. ownership in the large copper mines. The legal basis for expropriation was a constitutional amendment passed unanimously by both houses of Congress on July 16 which authorized the president to deduct from the adjusted book value of the U.S. investments any "excess profits" earned by those companies since 1955. The amendment did not define the term "excess profits," but Allende declared that any return in excess of 10% of book value would be deducted. Thus, neither Anaconda Co. nor Kennecott Copper Corp. received compensation when their property was expropriated.

Chile's economic policies were guided by political as well as economic considerations. At the beginning of 1971 the government authorized a 35% average pay increase to compensate wage earners for the previous year's inflation. Price increases were not allowed except in a few cases. The foreign exchange rate was frozen at its pre-election level as an anti-inflationary move. Large amounts of currency were printed to pay for the fiscal deficit and to pay for the expropriations. These policies were designed to achieve several purposes, including an economic recuperation from the recession that set in after the September 1970 presidential elections, an increase in employment, and a redistribution of income. The short-term effects of these policies proved them reasonably successful in that industrial production rose at least 4% during the first six months of the year over the corresponding period of 1970. Unemployment fell, at least in Santiago. Inflation was reduced to about half the previous year's rate, although the artificially low foreign exchange rate and higher domestic subsidies made it difficult to measure the true impact of the government's policies.

Indicators of future growth were less favourable. Foreign exchange reserves fell from their record levels under the prior government. Exports fell, partly because of lower copper prices and partly because copper production failed to increase as planned. Investment in production facilities was at a near standstill. The confidence of the private sector in its future was generally low.

CHILE

Education. (1968) Primary, pupils 1,934,478, teachers (public only) 34,069; secondary, pupils 153,114, teachers 10,242; vocational, pupils 73,142, teachers (1967) 7,398; teacher training, students 6,493, teachers 1,000; higher (including 8 universities; 1967), students 57,146, teaching staff (1965) 8,835.

Finance. Monetary unit: escudo, with (Sept. 27, 1971) a brokers' free market rate of 27 escudos to U.S. $1 (67 escudos = £1 sterling). Gold, SDRs, and foreign exchange, central bank: (May 1971) U.S. $308.8 million; (May 1970) U.S. $442.9 million. Budget (1970 est.): revenue 17,465,000,000 escudos; expenditure 17,250,000,000 escudos. Gross national product: (1969) 61,447,000,000 escudos; (1968) 42,-882,000,000 escudos. Money supply: (June 1970) 7,651,000,000 escudos; (June 1969) 5,225,000,000 escudos. Cost of living (Santiago; 1963 = 100): (May 1971) 707; (May 1970) 585.

Foreign Trade. (1969) Imports U.S. $909.1 million; exports U.S. $1,069,200,000. Import sources: U.S. 38%; West Germany 10%; Argentina 10%; U.K. 5%. Export destinations: U.S. 17%; U.K. 14%; Japan 14%; Netherlands 11%; West Germany 9%; Italy 8%; Argentina 6%; France 6%. Main exports: copper 76%; iron ore 7%.

Transport and Communications: Roads (1970) 70,549 km. Motor vehicles in use (1969): passenger 207,846; commercial 59,418. Railways (1969): 8,960 km.; traffic (principal railways) 2,217,000,000 passenger-km., freight 2,652,000,000 net ton-km. Air traffic (1970): 842 million passenger-km.; freight 43,-832,000 net ton-km. Shipping (1970): merchant vessels 100 gross tons and over 134; gross tonnage 307,-560. Telephones (Dec. 1969) 334,415. Radio receivers (Dec. 1969) c. 1,375,000. Television receivers (Dec. 1969) c. 400,000.

Agriculture. Production (in 000; metric tons; 1970; 1969 in parentheses): wheat 1,250 (1,214); barley c. 95 (80); oats c. 100 (95); corn 239 (154); potatoes c. 650 (603); rapeseed c. 71 (64); dry beans c. 70 (47); onions (1969) c. 80, (1968) 81; sugar, raw value (1970–71) c. 221, (1969–70) c. 191; apples c. 65 (c. 70); wine c. 400 (482); wool, greasy c. 26 (25); timber (cu.m.; 1969) 7,000, (1968) 7,077; fish catch (1969) 1,077, (1968) 1,376. Livestock (in 000; 1969–70): cattle c. 2,911; sheep c. 6,758; pigs c. 1,105; horses c. 450.

Industry. Production (in 000; metric tons; 1970): crude oil 1,620; coal (1969) 1,560; electricity (kw-hr.) 7,484,000; iron ore (65% metal content) 11,110; pig iron 456; crude steel (ingots) 547; copper 461; nitrate of soda (1969) 657; manganese ore (1969) 24; iodine (1969) 2.4; molybdenum (metal content; 1969) 4.8; silver (troy oz.; 1969) 3,133; gold (troy oz.; 1969) 59; woven cotton fabrics (m.) 110,000; fish meal (1969) 180.

On the political scene, the country changed little. The government ruled by a coalition of six parties, called the Unidad Popular (UP). The opposition parties, however, controlled the Congress. The trend toward smaller parties continued, with major splits in the Christian Democratic, Radical, and MAPU parties.

In April the ruling coalition of six parties received almost 50% of the votes in the municipal elections. The pro-government vote was substantially higher than that received by Allende in the presidential election and was widely interpreted as an indication of popular support, but signs of unrest surfaced later in the year. Pro-government candidates lost a by-election in Congress and key positions in labour unions and the University of Chile. More serious was a protest march on the presidential palace early in December, staged by some 5,000 women beating pots and pans and shouting slogans of complaint about the high price of food and opposing the visit to Chile of Cuban Prime Minister Fidel Castro. The march was broken up by police firing tear-gas grenades, but the disorders spread and President Allende was forced to declare a state of emergency. (R. L. Ro.)

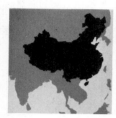

China

The most populous country in the world and the third largest in area, China is bounded by the U.S.S.R., Mongolia, North Korea, North Vietnam, Laos, Burma, India, Bhutan, Sikkim, Nepal, Pakistan, and Afghanistan. From 1949 the country has been divided into the People's Republic of China (Communist) on the mainland and on Hainan and other islands, and the Republic of China (Nationalist) on Taiwan (*see* TAIWAN). Area: 3,691,500 sq.mi. (9,561,000 sq.km.), including Tibet but excluding Taiwan. Pop. of the People's Republic (1970 est.): 827 million. Cap.: Peking (metro. pop., 1967–68 est., 7 million). Largest city: Shanghai (metro. pop., 1968 est., 10 million). Language: Chinese (varieties of the Mandarin dialect). Chairman of the Communist Party in 1971, Mao Tse-tung; premier, Chou En-lai.

In 1971 moderate leaders in Peking continued to seek a return to more normal conditions after the turbulence and disruption of the Cultural Revolution, and more rational domestic and foreign policies prevailed. The year's developments included China's admittance to the UN and the improved relations with the U.S. Premier Chou En-lai (*see* BIOGRAPHY) emerged as the central figure in much of the diplomatic activity.

Chou's Ping-Pong diplomacy in receiving U.S. table-tennis players and press reporters in response to U.S. overtures led to a relaxation of Chinese restrictions on American visitors and to a thaw in Sino-American relations. On July 15—four days after Henry A. Kissinger, national security affairs adviser to U.S. Pres. Richard Nixon, paid a secret visit to Peking—Nixon stated in a nationwide broadcast that he would visit China at Chou's invitation "to seek the normalization of relations between the two countries" and as "a journey for peace."

Although Nixon's announcement did not reveal the content of the Chou-Kissinger secret talks, the meetings constituted one of the major events of the year in international relations. They signified a sudden change in the U.S. policy in Asia, affecting not only the position of the two Chinese republics and Japan and Korea but also that of the Soviet Union. In mainland China Nixon's new policy might have precipitated a power struggle within the Peking leadership, as some considered Chou's invitation to Nixon an abandonment of the revolutionary principles proclaimed by Peking.

Signs of a leadership struggle and political crisis were evident two weeks before the 22nd anniversary of the founding of the Chinese People's Republic on October 1. Troop movements and army leaves were suspended and military and commercial flights were canceled between September 13–15. Especially surprising was the cancellation of the annual October 1 National Day parades on T'ien-an Men (Gate of Heavenly Peace) Square in Peking. On this occasion, for 21 years, Chairman Mao and other top leaders customarily had lined up in order of rank to display unity, deliver speeches, and review giant military and mass parades. Preparations for the traditional celebration of the anniversary had been reported, and the sudden cancellation of the parade gave rise to speculation on the state of health of Chairman Mao and his heir apparent, Defense Minister Lin Piao. The ill health or incapacity of the 77-year-old Mao and the 64-year-old Lin, who had not been seen in public since June, could give rise to the serious problem of succession. Either circumstance would create problems of reshuffling top positions and power roles.

The Foreign Ministry in Peking announced that the parade had been canceled for reasons of economy and also declared that Chairman Mao was in good health. But no mention was made of Lin Piao. On September 29 Radio Peking announced that National Day celebrations would take place in parks, but would be confined to dancing and other entertainment.

CHINA

Education. Primary (1959–60), pupils 90 million, teachers (1964) *c.* 2.6 million; secondary (1958–59), pupils 8,520,000; vocational (1958–59), pupils 850,000; teacher training (1958–59), students 620,000; higher (1962–63), students 820,000.

Finance. Monetary unit: jen min piao or people's bank dollar, also called the yuan, with an official exchange rate of 2.46 yuan to U.S. $1 (5.90 yuan = £1 sterling). Budget (1960 est.; latest published) balanced at 70,020,000,000 yuan. Latest five-year plan began in 1971. Gross domestic product (1965 est.) 130 billion yuan.

Foreign Trade. (1969) Imports *c.* U.S. $1.5 billion; exports *c.* U.S. $1,850,000,000. Import sources: Japan *c.* 26%; West Germany *c.* 11%; U.K. *c.* 9%. Export destinations: Hong Kong *c.* 24%; Japan *c.* 13%; U.K. *c.* 5%. Main exports: textiles and clothing, metal ore and nonferrous metals, rice, tea, coal.

Transport and Communications. Roads (1969) *c.* 800,000 km. (including *c.* 300,000 km. all-weather). Motor vehicles in use (1969): passenger *c.* 60,000; commercial *c.* 409,000. Railways: (1970) *c.* 35,000 km.; traffic (1959) 45,670,000,000 passenger-km., freight 265,260,-000,000 net ton-km. Air traffic (1960): 63,882,-000 passenger-km.; freight 1,967,000 net ton-km. Inland waterways (including Yangtze River; 1969) *c.* 150,000 km. Shipping (1970): merchant vessels 100 gross tons and over 248; gross tonnage 867,994. Telephones (1951) 255,000. Radio receivers (Dec. 1966) *c.* 8 million. Television receivers (Dec. 1969) *c.* 3 million.

Agriculture. Production (in 000; metric tons; 1969; 1968 in parentheses): rice *c.* 95,000 (*c.* 91,000); corn *c.* 26,000 (*c.* 25,000); wheat *c.* 28,500 (*c.* 27,000); barley *c.* 17,500 (*c.* 17,000); potatoes *c.* 31,000 (*c.* 30,000); soybeans (1970) *c.* 11,500, (1969) *c.* 10,920; peanuts *c.* 2,300 (*c.* 2,150); cotton, lint *c.* 1,518 (*c.* 1,474); jute *c.* 500 (*c.* 495); rapeseed *c.* 940 (*c.* 1,070);

sugar, raw value (1970–71) *c.* 3,900, (1969–70) *c.* 3,700; tobacco *c.* 776 (*c.* 848); tea *c.* 169 (*c.* 167); pears *c.* 850 (*c.* 890); oranges *c.* 670 (*c.* 650); timber (cu.m.; 1969) 169,000, (1968) 158,000; fish catch (1960) 5,800, (1959) 5,020. Livestock (in 000; 1969–70): cattle *c.* 63,100; sheep *c.* 70,600; pigs *c.* 220,000; goats *c.* 57,000; buffalo *c.* 29,300; horses *c.* 7,300; asses *c.* 11,620.

Industry. Fuel and power (in 000; metric tons; 1969): coal (including lignite) *c.* 330,000; coke 17,000; crude oil *c.* 20,000; electricity (kw-hr.; 1960) *c.* 58,500,000. Production (in 000; metric tons; 1968): iron ore (metal content) *c.* 20,900; pig iron *c.* 19,000; crude steel *c.* 15,000; lead (1969) *c.* 100; copper (1969) *c.* 100; aluminum (1969) *c.* 120; tungsten concentrates (oxide content; 1969) *c.* 10; cement *c.* 9,000; salt *c.* 15,000; sulfuric acid (1966) *c.* 2,500; chemical fertilizers (1966) *c.* 5,500; cotton yarn 1,453; woven cotton fabrics (m.; 1966) *c.* 5,900,000; paper (1969) 3,550.

Members of the U.S. table tennis team visit the Great Wall of China in April 1971. The team and three reporters who accompanied them were the first group of U.S. citizens to visit China in nearly 25 years.

Although Mao and Lin failed to appear, Premier Chou showed up at a National Day celebration with U.S. Black Panther Party co-founder Huey Newton. On October 8, Mao reappeared in public without Lin to greet Emperor Haile Selassie of Ethiopia. But in spite of this appearance many observers believed that Mao's central role in Chinese politics was diminishing and that Lin was losing in his rivalry with Chou for leadership. Unsubstantiated stories appearing in the West claimed that Lin, after making three unsuccessful attempts on Chairman Mao's life, had fled with his wife and some associates, and that their plane had been shot down over Mongolia with the loss of all on board.

These unusual developments in Peking caused concern in the U.S. On October 2, U.S. Secretary of State William Rogers expressed the hope that events in China "do not signal any change in the possibility of President Nixon's visit to Peking." Three days later, however, the White House and Radio Peking announced simultaneously that the two governments had agreed on Kissinger's return trip to Peking to make concrete arrangements for Nixon's visit. Kissinger and a team of specialists were in China from October 16 to October 22. In November it was announced that Nixon would begin his trip on Feb. 21, 1972. The visit would last a week, and would include Shanghai and Hangchow as well as Peking.

Internal Politics. The Cultural Revolution had decimated the Communist Party as an effective civilian organ of power and authority. During the latter part of the revolution three components of the Revolutionary Committees (armed forces, Red Guards, and cadres of the party and government) were established to carry out the functions of government in China's 29 administrative areas (26 provinces and 3 special municipalities). Military leaders came to dominate the organs of authority in the provinces, while representatives of the party and mass organizations occupied subsidiary positions.

The first important step in the reconstruction of the Communist Party was the convocation in April 1969 of the long-postponed ninth congress, which elected a large Central Committee of 279 members, 118 of whom were in military service. In turn, the Central Committee elected a 25-member Politburo, 12 of whom were military men. A Politburo standing committee of five members was formed with Chairman Mao and Defense Minister Lin on top of the list, followed by Ch'en Po-ta, Chou En-lai, and K'ang Sheng. Ch'en, editor of *Red Flag* and ghost writer for Mao, and K'ang, chief of the Intelligence Service, were both right-hand men of Chiang Ch'ing (Mao's third wife) in the Cultural Revolution group.

Mao's goal was to reorganize and revitalize the party by purging his opponents who had followed the capitalist road, and by instituting proletarian leadership. His directives for party building emphatically stated that the party organization should be composed of the advanced proletariat. But the influence of regional army commanders and moderate administrators made it impossible for the Maoists to stop internal splits, severely affecting Mao's plans for rebuilding the party. In the ensuing factional struggle for power, staunch Maoist leftists suffered a defeat. Ch'en Po-ta was not seen in public after Aug. 1, 1970, and was in disgrace. K'ang Sheng and Hsieh Fu-chi, minister of public security, also disappeared from the spotlight for a considerable time. Also, Yao Teng-shen, a radical leader in the Cultural Revolution, was denounced at a public rally in June and later put in prison. All these developments showed that the extreme-left faction, some members of which had been very close to Chairman Mao and his wife, was on the wane and that Mao seemed to have lost control of events.

The rebuilding of the party structure at the provincial level was impeded by factional rivalries and the protracted nature of electing "old, middle-aged, and young people" to the new party committees. It was not until August 1971 that the process of rebuilding was completed. In the majority of cases, leaders of the Revolutionary Committees became principal offi-

Henry Kissinger (left), assistant to Pres. Richard Nixon, dines with Chou En-lai in the Great Hall of the People in Peking on Oct. 20, 1971. The visit was to plan Nixon's trip to China.

WIDE WORLD

cers of the party committees. With the exception of the Peking and Shanghai party committees, military membership predominated in the upper ranks.

The slow pace of party reconstruction and the difficult problem of succession delayed the convening of the long-overdue fourth National People's Congress. Since the old constitution adopted in 1954 had been discarded and numerous members of the party and government had been purged, the fourth congress was expected to adopt a new constitution, elect a new chief of state, and approve government structure and personnel.

Economic Development. Political turmoil and the emphasis on ideological indoctrination during the Cultural Revolution retarded economic advancement. The gross national product for 1970 was estimated at between $75 billion and $90 billion, although Premier Chou said that it was the equivalent of $120 billion. The New China News Agency claimed that a bumper grain harvest was expected in 1971 and that the country had become self-sufficient in grain. Without disclosing information on the result of the third five-year plan (1965–70) or on future economic goals

Martial dancers perform a patriotic dance of revolution during May Day celebrations in Peking.

LONDON "DAILY EXPRESS"—PICTORIAL PARADE

and priorities, Chou announced the inception of China's fourth five-year plan.

The recovery of the domestic economy resulted in an increase in China's foreign trade to more than $4.2 billion in 1970, about equal to the previous record years of 1959 and 1966. Non-Communist countries remained the chief trading partners of China, accounting for approximately 80% of the total foreign trade. Japan continued to be the largest trading partner, followed by Hong Kong and West Germany. To encourage exports, trade fairs were held and trade missions were dispatched to a number of countries, including Ceylon, Malaysia, Sudan, Morocco, Romania, Yugoslavia, France, Italy, and the Scandinavian nations.

Foreign Relations. As the moderates took greater control of internal affairs, they began to assert their influence in improving China's international position by means of conventional diplomacy. Early in 1971 Chinese diplomats who had been recalled during the Cultural Revolution were being sent back to their posts in more than 40 countries. Following the recognition of the People's Republic by Canada and Italy in late 1970 as the sole legal government of China, more than ten additional countries had followed suit by October 1971.

In order to win China greater influence in world affairs, Premier Chou called upon small and medium-sized nations to unite in resistance to bullying by the superpowers. China's bid for leadership in the third world was clearly demonstrated by the joint communiqué against big-power chauvinism signed on June 9 in Peking by Chou and Romania's chief of state, Nicolae Ceausescu. In signing the document, Chou stated that "we will always stand together with oppressed countries and peoples in firmly opposing power politics of superpowers." Speaking through its closest ally, Albania, China demanded the "restoration of the lawful rights of the People's Republic of China in the United Nations." In its efforts to normalize relations with other countries irrespective of their political leanings, Peking demonstrated an increasing degree of moderation and flexibility.

Sino-American Rapprochement. The war in Indochina constituted one of the important problems affecting Sino-American relations. As President Nixon's vietnamization program to end U.S. involvement in

Chinese youths present
a concert with stringed
instruments in Shanghai.
Young people
are encouraged
to learn Chinese folk
and traditional music
rather than Western-style
popular music.

Vietnam advanced, and because U.S. actions in Laos in the spring were not directed at China, China's realistic new leadership no longer feared American expansion of the war close to Chinese borders. It therefore appeared to consider it excessive and dangerous to intervene militarily in Vietnam in order to give all-out support to North Vietnam. This lack of military intervention in Vietnam in turn lessened American fear of Chinese military expansion in Southeast Asia, which had motivated the U.S. policy of containment. China began to show conciliatory gestures toward the U.S. and expressed interest in an international conference to settle the conflict in Indochina. Also, Peking's fear of the Soviet military threat on the long Sino-Soviet borders, the revival of militarism in Japan, and the importance of eliminating U.S. opposition to seating Peking in the UN further prompted the Chinese leaders to seek better relations with Washington. President Nixon's desire for negotiation instead of confrontation with China was conveyed to the leaders in Peking through carefully chosen third countries friendly to both Peking and Washington.

A dramatic thaw in relations between Peking and Washington began on February 25 with Nixon's "state of the world" message to Congress, in which he declared that there would be no more important challenge to the United States in the 1970s than that of drawing China into a constructive relationship with the world community, and particularly with the rest of Asia. On March 15 the U.S. Department of State lifted its ban on travel by Americans to China. Next came the surprise invitation to the U.S. table-tennis team, then in Japan, to visit China. On April 10 the Americans (nine players, four officials, and two wives), later joined by American correspondents, crossed from Hong Kong to China for a one-week stay. In receiving the team, Chou stated that a new page in the relations of the Chinese and American peoples had been opened.

To strengthen his policy of seeking normal ties with China, Nixon announced on April 14 a series of measures to remove trade barriers. Early in May, implementing Nixon's decision to relax financial and commercial restrictions, the U.S. Department of the Treasury removed curbs on the use of dollars in trade

with China; the Commerce and Transportation departments granted authorization to U.S. ships and aircraft to transport commodities to China by way of ports and airfields not on Chinese territory. On June 10 Nixon lifted the 21-year embargo on nonstrategic items and permitted imports from China under general license. The climax came with Nixon's acceptance of Chou's invitation to visit Peking.

The radical reversal of U.S.-China policy added prestige and respectability to Peking, caused shock and anger in Taiwan, jolted Asian allies of the U.S., and fed the fear of Soviet leaders concerning a possible Sino-American deal against the Soviet Union. Since in mainland China the people had been urged for years by the government to unite and defeat the "United States aggressors and all their running dogs," the announcement of Nixon's visit to China evoked surprise, curiosity, and ideological confusion. Belatedly, Chou revealed that it had been Chairman Mao's quick decision to invite the American table-tennis team, and in a special combined issue of *Red Flag*, Mao's policy to negotiate with Nationalist leaders during the civil war was cited as a precedent.

Bayonets and rifles
provide the props
for a ballet group
celebrating May Day
in an open-air performance
in Peking.

Sino-Soviet Relations. Relations between China and the U.S.S.R. showed improvement with the exchange of new ambassadors and the conclusion of a new trade agreement toward the end of 1970, but talks to settle border issues stalled over the scope of the negotiations. China wanted to limit the discussion relating to the frontier and sought Soviet acknowledgment in principle that the Soviets had gained much of their Far Eastern territories through unequal treaties with China under the tsarist regime. The Soviet Union refused to discuss the question of legitimacy of territories under its control, but wanted to expand the talks to include economic, cultural, and political matters. China's demand for an immediate pullback of troops on both sides of the border met no response. Consequently, tensions on the borders intensified with heavy deployment of troops on both sides.

In March, on the occasion of the centenary of the Paris Commune, Peking launched a bitter ideological attack on Moscow, and the exchange of polemics between the two Communist giants continued almost unabated throughout the year. In the midst of this ideological conflict, Moscow became extremely sensitive about U.S. overtures to China and Peking's invitation to President Nixon. Ten days after the announcement of Nixon's planned trip to China, the Soviet Communist Party newspaper *Pravda* published a long article accusing the Chinese leadership of splitting the ranks in world Communism.

Immediately after the visit of a high-ranking Chinese military delegation to Albania and Romania in August, Hungary and Poland charged Peking with building an anti-Soviet "Balkan axis." On September 3 the Soviet government news agency Tass distributed a lengthy article in English attacking China for trying to disrupt the Communist movement by sowing seeds of tension in the Balkans and blaming Peking for rejecting Moscow's efforts to end their border disputes. In reply the official Chinese news agency criticized Tass for "odious fabrications and lies." Shortly before the convocation of the 26th General Assembly of the UN, however, the Soviet newspaper *Izvestia* paused in its attack on the Chinese leadership and stressed the mutual benefits of a Moscow-Peking reconciliation. At the General Assembly the Soviet Union affirmed its support for Peking's membership.

China's Representation in the UN. The proposal for admitting China into the UN, which had failed to be accepted even on the General Assembly agenda during 1949–60 and had been rejected between 1961 and 1970 due to the lack of a two-thirds majority, became an overriding item for the 26th General Assembly in 1971. The central issue was whether to replace Nationalist China (Taiwan) with Communist China or admit Communist China while retaining Nationalist China. In his "state of the world" message of February 25, President Nixon declared that the U.S. policy was to find a solution that would admit Peking without expelling Taipei. In April a presidential commission headed by Henry Cabot Lodge formally recommended a two-China doctrine.

When Nixon announced his projected visit to China, the U.S. holding action against the entry of Peking into the UN came to an end for all practical purposes. On the same day Albania submitted a resolution to the General Assembly proposing the expulsion of Nationalist China and the seating of Communist China as one of the five permanent members of the Security Council. On August 2 Secretary Rogers formally announced that the U.S. would support the admission of

KEYSTONE

The last link of a railroad, built to serve an oil refinery in Liaoning Province, is placed in position. Construction of the railroad through mountainous terrain was a difficult feat.

Peking but would oppose the expulsion of Taipei. Peking declared on August 20 that China would not take a seat at the UN unless Taiwan was expelled.

In order to obtain adequate co-sponsorship for its efforts to prevent the expulsion of Taiwan, the U.S. decided on September 15 to support the assignment of China's permanent seat on the Security Council to Peking. The failure of the U.S. to consult its close allies on Nixon's new China policy had caused some resentment, and, in particular, delayed Japan's decision to co-sponsor the two-China resolution. Rogers urgently warned that Japan's failure to be a co-sponsor would be detrimental to the cause of keeping Taiwan in the UN. On the eve of the convocation of the General Assembly on September 21, the governments of Australia, New Zealand, and Japan announced that they would co-sponsor the two American resolutions designed to seat China in the UN as a permanent member of the Security Council and to save Nationalist China's membership in the General Assembly by treating the proposal for its expulsion as an important question requiring a two-thirds majority.

The tardiness in submitting the American resolutions gave the Albania resolution a procedural and psychological advantage. On October 25 the General Assembly defeated the crucial important-question resolution by a vote of 59–55 with 15 abstentions, and adopted the Albania resolution by a vote of 76–35 with 17 abstentions. Thus, China was admitted to the UN and Taiwan expelled. On November 2 Chiao Kuan-hua, vice-minister of foreign affairs, was named as head of the delegation to the General Assembly and Huang Hua, ambassador to Canada, was appointed deputy to Chiao and permanent representative on the Security Council. The delegation arrived at UN headquarters on November 11. In China's first address to the General Assembly on November 15,

Chiao strongly attacked U.S. policy in Asia and said that his government would oppose efforts by the superpowers to dominate the UN. (H.-T. Ch.)

See also Propaganda; Taiwan.

Encyclopædia Britannica Films. *China: A Portrait of the Land* (1967); *China's Industrial Revolution* (1967); *China's Villages in Change* (1967).

Cities and Urban Affairs

As cities around the world continued to grow in size and complexity, their function was increasingly seen as not only the provision of urban services and amenities but also the creation of man-centred living milieus. Although citizen expectations were firmly rooted in the social values of the 1970s, cities often were operating within governmental and organizational systems created half a century earlier in predominantly agricultural times. The next decade, therefore, would be characterized by new governmental configurations that would take into account the interdependence of cities and their rural hinterlands, as well as by a reversal of the proliferation of governmental jurisdictions within a single region.

Concomitant with this restructuring at the metropolitan level would be a continuation of already existing—or the initiation of new—evaluations of total governmental systems and of the interrelationships of tasks and finances between the different governmental levels, with due consideration being given to the social implications of economic planning and investment decisions. Increasingly, attention would be given to strengthening existent means whereby citizens could influence the making of policies and decisions affecting their daily lives, and to devising new forms of citizen participation.

Urbanization Policies. It was estimated that by 1995 two-thirds of the world's population would be urban residents, and that the larger the city, the more rapid would be its growth. In addition, a document prepared by the Centre for Housing, Building and Planning of the United Nations stated that each year for the next 30 years the equivalent of 86 new cities of one million population would need to be built to cope with normal population increase plus migration of rural residents to urban areas. Urbanization clearly required direction if cities of the future were to provide the kind of overall environment and quality of living that their citizens expected. Since cities formed integral parts of national governmental systems, all levels of government were accepting the necessity of drawing up, within the scope of their given competences, policy guidelines for the further development of existing cities and the shape and nature of those yet to be built.

Thus, national governments were devising policies concerning the growth and distribution of population, the economic and social development of the country, and the division of powers, functions, and resources among the various levels of government. State or provincial governments drew up policy statements regarding economic and social development within their geographic borders, as well as indicating general land use throughout their territories. They were also devising means of providing technical assistance for those cities and other local governments whose own financial and manpower resources were inadequate to the task, and adopting policies of administrative coordination.

Firemen, gathered from cities and towns in the provinces, demonstrate in front of the Ministry of Finance in Paris on March 18, 1971, to call attention to their unsatisfactory working conditions.

At the urban regional, or metropolitan, level, governments were further defining the economic and social development within their territories and establishing policies concerning use of land, transportation, utilities, disposal of wastes, housing, air and water pollution, and social and recreational facilities. Local communities adopted policies regarding urban renewal, housing, citizen participation, and the provision of a wide range of governmental services. Increasingly, they also were evaluating their organizational structures and adopting new policies of internal coordination and external cooperation with other governments, both horizontally and vertically.

Metropolitan Areas. An important aspect of urbanization policies is a coordinated governmental structure, particularly in larger cities and metropolitan areas covering a multitude of overlapping jurisdictions performing parallel tasks. Undertaken on an area-wide basis, such coordination can produce significant savings in finances, manpower, and time.

In some countries, chiefly in Scandinavia but to a lesser extent in West Germany and the Netherlands, overall amalgamations were bringing together small,

		City proper				Metropolitan	
Rank	City and country	Most recent census	Year	Estimate	Year	Census or Estimate	Year
1	Tokyo, Japan	8,840,942	1970	8,787,249	1971	22,082,044	1970
2	New York, U.S.	7,895,563	1970	...	...	11,575,740	1970
3	Shanghai, China	—	—	—	—	10,000,000*	1967–68
4	London, U.K.	—	—	—	—	7,379,014†	1971
5	Peking, China	—	—	—	—	7,061,000	1970
6	Moscow, U.S.S.R.	6,942,000	1970	...	...	...	...
7	Bombay, India	4,152,056	1961	5,700,358	1970	5,931,989	1971
8	Seoul, S. Korea	5,536,337	1970	...	...	...	...
9	São Paulo, Brazil	5,186,752	1970	...	...	5,921,796	1970
10	Cairo, Egypt	4,219,853	1966	4,961,000	1970	6,255,000	1970
11	Jakarta, Indonesia	2,973,052	1961	4,542,146	1971	5,899,000	1971
12	Rio de Janeiro, Brazil	4,252,009	1970	...	...	...	...
13	Leningrad, U.S.S.R.	3,513,000	1970	...	...	3,950,000	1970
14	Teheran, Iran	2,719,730	1966	3,378,000	1970	...	...
15	Chicago, U.S.	3,369,359	1970	...	...	6,978,733	1970
16	Delhi, India	2,061,758	1961	3,349,942	1970	3,629,842	1971
17	Tientsin, China	2,693,831	1953	3,278,000	1958	3,800,000	1958
18	Madrid, Spain	3,146,071	1970	...	...	7,040,345	1971
19	Calcutta, India	3,141,180	1971	—	—	8,352,900	1970
20	Buenos Aires, Argentina	2,972,453	1970	...	...	14,886,005	1970
21	Osaka, Japan	2,980,487	1970	2,953,164	1971	8,589,631	1970
22	Mexico City, Mexico	2,902,969	1970	...	...	7,036,887	1970
23	Los Angeles, U.S.	2,809,596	1970	...	...	...	...
24	Rome, Italy	2,188,160	1961	2,778,872	1970	...	...
25	Lima, Peru	1,547,370	1961	2,673,400	1971	3,131,853	1971

*Municipality. †Greater London.
Ranking based on latest estimates of city proper population. Berlin, both sectors combined 1970 population 3,219,166, is excluded due to the political as well as physical division of the city.

financially weak local governments into bigger, more viable units. In other countries the trend was toward cooperative arrangements for the provision of one or several tasks. In France multipurpose syndicates and urban districts provided a framework for undertaking services on a region-wide basis. Joint committees in Great Britain, the *consortia* in Italy, the *Gemeindeverbände* in West Germany, and the proposed federation of communes in Belgium all had a similar purpose. In the United States councils of government had been formed in several metropolitan areas to undertake such tasks as physical planning, the provision of sewers and water, control of air, water, and soil pollution, and the designing of an area-wide road network.

In several Canadian provinces, regional councils executed a variety of tasks. In the Netherlands regional structures had been created to coordinate mandatorily certain activities in the Rhine Estuary communities and, on a voluntary basis, to provide for services and amenities in the agglomeration centred on the city of Eindhoven and 35 other such regions. One of the oldest regional arrangements was the 50-year-old Siedlungsverband Ruhrkohlenbezirk, undertaking primarily spatial planning and the designation of green belts and recreational areas in the Ruhr area of West Germany. In many of these cooperative arrangements the regional body had only advisory powers; in others it had a legal personality and powers equal to those of other local government bodies. Cooperation was sometimes voluntary, sometimes compulsory.

A further step in coordinating activities on an area-wide basis was the formation of a comprehensive metropolitan government. Several well-known efforts had been made toward this end; *e.g.*, the *Communautés Urbaines* in France, Metropolitan Toronto in Canada, and the Greater London Council in Britain.

The French Communautés Urbaines. Under a law put into effect in 1968, the formation of metropolitan authorities was mandatory in the agglomerations centred around Lyons, Lille, Bordeaux, and Strasbourg, and might be adopted in any other similar areas hav-

After traditional fining procedures failed, the city administration in Hanover, W.Ger., installed a maze of "pedestrians only" signs to prevent motorists from parking on the pavement in front of the Opera House.

UPI COMPIX

ing a population of 50,000 inhabitants or more. Since the introduction of the law, Le Creusot and Dunkerque also had adopted the system of urban communities on a voluntary basis. Each authority had a two-tier form of government, both levels being governed according to current French municipal law. The metropolitan authority was responsible for such transferred functions as town planning; infrastructure investments over the major part of the territory, and the corresponding public services of roads (and eventually their maintenance), water, sanitation, transport, secondary schools, housing, industrial parks, etc.; capital investments in hospitals and sport, social, educational, and cultural facilities; and other tasks not explicitly laid down by law for which the member-municipalities might give their agreement.

Member municipalities retained responsibility for local day-to-day administration, contact with the public, and tasks of a purely local nature. The governing body of the metropolitan authority consisted of 50 to 90 members, depending on the total number of inhabitants concerned and the number of local municipalities included. Each local council directly elected its representatives to the metropolitan council, according to its population. Municipalities with populations too small to warrant a seat on the council were grouped into electoral districts, with representatives being elected by an electoral college composed of the mayors of these municipalities. The metropolitan council elected its own chairman, who in turn could call meetings of all the mayors for purposes of consultation and information.

Metropolitan Toronto. In April 1953 Metropolitan Toronto became the first federated urban structure in the Western Hemisphere. Its original council consisted of 25 members, of whom 12 were from the city of Toronto and 12 were mayors, aldermen, or controllers from the 12 other member municipalities. The 25th member, the chairman, was at first appointed by the provincial government, but later he was elected annually by the council. Primarily, the metropolitan government concentrated on infrastructure investments; *e.g.*, for water, sewers, roads and expressways, and public transport—particularly the subway—as well as for overall physical planning, the construction of schools, and tax assessments. The 13 member municipalities retained responsibility for police, licensing, fire protection, libraries, and local taxes.

In 1967 Metropolitan Toronto was reorganized to provide for representation on a population basis. The 13 municipalities were reduced to 6, and the metropolitan council was reconstituted with 33 members—the chairman plus 12 members representing the city of Toronto and 20 representing the suburban communities, of whose councils they were leaders. All would serve three-year terms of office. The chairman was elected by the metropolitan council, either from among its own members or from outside. An executive committee composed of the metropolitan chairman, five members from the city of Toronto, and five from the boroughs was set up to make policy recommendations to the council. New tasks given to the metropolitan council included the complete financing of school construction and operation, social welfare services, waste disposal, the Canadian National Exhibition, the establishment of a metropolitan-wide public ambulance service, and the financing of regional libraries. The metropolitan council was also authorized to participate in urban renewal in conjunction with the municipalities.

Greater London Council. A two-tier system of government was also in operation in the London metropolitan area, the upper level being the Greater London Council (GLC) and the lower level the councils of the 32 London boroughs and the City of London. Six-sevenths of the council members were directly elected, the remaining one-seventh being aldermen selected by the councillors from among their own number or from suitable outside candidates. Here, too, tasks were divided between the metropolitan and local councils. The former dealt with overall planning, metropolitan roads, fire protection, ambulance service, regional open spaces, and sewage and refuse disposal, as well as education within the area of the old London County Council. It operated an intelligence unit collecting statistical and other data concerning metropolitan-wide governmental services, and had coextensive powers with the boroughs in respect to housing. All other services were provided by the borough councils and the City of London, including planning (to conform with the GLC's overall plan); education in the outer London boroughs; personal and environmental health; care of the aged, the sick, and the mentally ill; services for children; parks and open spaces; collection of refuse; sewers; and highways other than metropolitan roads.

Citizen Participation. The two-tier structure adopted in many metropolitan areas indicated local governments' concern that enlargement should not result in increased distance between administration and citizens. In addition to such institutionalized forms of participation as council membership, advisory committees, hearings (particularly in regard to master and other physical plans), political party activities, elections, referendums, initiatives, and recalls, city governments were experimenting with other means of encouraging citizen interest in local affairs. Various forms of neighbourhood management were being initiated, such as little city halls, multiservice centres, branch city offices, community corporations, and neighbourhood advisory committees.

In the U.S., citizen participation in neighbourhood affairs was initially stimulated by federally funded programs related to urban renewal and other improvement programs. In 1971 many cities were adopting their own programs. In Dayton, O., for instance, a city-financed program distributed local funds on a per capita basis to six geographic areas covering the entire city, with the exception of the central business district. To qualify for funds, neighbourhood programs had to meet three requirements: general neighbourhood consensus on the proposed project or activity; the establishment of a neighbourhood priority board; and a project that would help to fulfill a previously designated neighbourhood goal.

Yugoslavia had begun experiments with the "delegate system." In addition to geographic and functional representation on city councils, there was also representation by interest groups, such as students, civil servants, apprentices, and pensioners. Each of these had a delegate acting on his group's specific directives, thus providing a channel of communication between the administration and the citizen group.

There were also many instances of citizens organizing outside institutional channels to bring pressure to bear on local government decisions. Such actions were primarily ad hoc and short-term, pertaining mainly to planning decisions felt to be harmful to the local environment, but they also fulfilled a useful function in arousing often intense interest, which might then also be directed to other matters. They also served to remind city administrations that decisions must have regard for human factors and not merely technical or financial considerations.

Urban Land Use. A livable environment continued to be of vital concern to citizens and administrations in all countries, and increased attention was being given to problems of urban land use. Over the years, a variety of regulatory devices had been adopted to control land use, and these were coming under ever closer scrutiny.

In North America criticism was mounting against the inflexibility of the traditional zoning system, whereby land was divided into various districts, in each of which the use of buildings, structures, and land was uniformly regulated and restricted. The zoning ordinance thus served as a tool for implementing the city's master plan. However, change being characteristic of the modern city, zoning too often had proved an impediment to meeting new land use requirements and to the use of modern building techniques and styles. It also had served to strengthen racial and economic segregation through the establishment of exclusive residential zones, thus leading to leap-frog development beyond suburban boundaries or to the bottling up of residents and commercial and industrial enterprises in often deteriorated inner city pockets. Finally, since each city had control over land use within its boundaries, too little thought had been given to the regional effects of many individual land-use decisions.

Various innovations had been introduced to deal with these problems. Among them were: classification according to performance standards, whereby the criterion for allowing industries or workshops to locate in an area was their actual effect, rather than the product manufactured; delineation of environmental zones, with land identified on the basis of best use according to quality; designation of special districts where development was exempt from uniform standards; and incentive zoning, whereby permission was granted for development if certain advantages to the city were built in. A classic case of the latter could be seen in New York City, where extra floor space was granted to builders in the theatre district if they included live theatre facilities in their projects. As for the regional effect of individual land-use decisions, there was a call for criteria to be established at a higher level, which would apply to all municipalities and thereby assure a region-wide approach to land use and development.

In Europe, where development was undertaken through the issuance of planning or building permits, strict control was exercised over land resources. In Sweden permission from the local building committee was needed not only for new building but for changing the colour of a facade or erecting a sign, the object being to prevent the harmony of a neighbourhood from being endangered by individual decisions and actions that might have a deleterious effect on nearby landowners. Not unexpectedly, such strict controls tended to lead to dissatisfaction, primarily centred on arbitrariness and delay. There was inevitable disagreement over matters of personal taste, and the length of time involved in the granting of permissions often seemed unreasonably long to those involved.

It might be argued that rational use of scarce land could best be realized if all land were in public ownership. In practice, however, problems of misal-

The Lambeth town crier, riding with his bell strapped to his pillion, hurries to catch a train.

continued on page 184

THE FUTURE OF AMERICAN CITIES

By John V. Lindsay

It is time we rethought the role of cities in the American governmental system. It is time, because our present federal system, which makes literally no provision for cities, threatens the very life of the urban nation we have become. Today, the great urban centres have a national role. They are financial, commercial, and communication centres for whole regions or for the nation itself. They are, in fact, "national cities" and not only merit but require a more realistic political status if they are to survive.

The failure of our present federal system to provide proper powers for cities did not result from any oversight on the part of the nation's early leaders. Quite the contrary, our first statesmen deliberately chose to discourage the creation of large urban centres. They regarded their society as materially, morally, and aesthetically superior to Europe's and attributed much of this superiority to the fact that 95% of the American population lived in rural areas. Thomas Jefferson wrote to James Madison in 1787 that: "Our governments will remain virtuous for centuries as long as they are chiefly agricultural. . . . When they get piled upon one another in large cities, as in Europe, they will become corrupt as Europe." That same year, the Northwest Ordinance of 1787, one of our first declarations of national policy, encouraged westward migration and fulfilled the provision of an earlier federal ordinance providing free land for schools. New York City, however, could not establish a public-school system until more than 50 years later—with no federal assistance at all.

The Growth of Urban Centres.
Even though the authors of the Constitution hoped America would remain rural and omitted from their great document any reference to cities, we have become an urban nation. One can no longer think of America without thinking of its major cities. Our commerce and industry exist almost completely within cities like New York, and our system of urban centres is larger and more complex than anything imaginable during the nation's formative years.

From a population that was 95% rural, we have become a population that is 73.5% urban. A colonial nation of only six cities with more than 8,000 people has grown into 26 central cities of more than 500,000 people, each of which is the core of an even larger metropolitan area. While all our urban centres once contained only 5% of our population, the 29 largest metropolitan areas now hold more than one-third of our people. From an overwhelmingly agricultural economy we have changed—despite the most productive agriculture in world history—into an economy that concentrates the bulk of its productive capacity in metropolitan areas, half of it in the 29 largest.

Every major city reaches beyond the state that contains it, controlling vital services for whole sections of the nation. The Federal Reserve Banks are located in 12 major cities, and federal circuit Courts of Appeals in ten. Such cities are regional centres for the distribution of money, credit, and justice. Similarly, cities like Atlanta, Denver, and Boston are regional hubs of transportation, communications, and commerce. They perform economic and social functions for a much broader geographic area than the states in which they are located. It is no longer reasonable to say that cities like Chicago and Baltimore and Philadelphia—whose budgets are each larger than 15 of the 50 states—must still be treated as inferiors by their state governments.

Moreover, the major cities carry the nation's heaviest burden because they contain and must deal with most of America's social problems. During the past century, the Industrial Revolution concentrated job opportunities in the central cities, thereby attracting to the cities the people most desperately in need of work—but also most unlikely to find it. The poor, the unskilled, the immigrants, and the victims of discrimination came to the cities because that is where the most jobs were. Many of them came because mechanization and agricultural controls wiped out farm employment. The most recent arrivals often lacked the skills needed in cities or were barred from jobs by discrimination. They and their families often fell into the cycle of unemployment and welfare that now threatens to create in our cities a permanent underclass.

By the late 1960s the Industrial Revolution had created in our cities the kinds of problems that the Constitution's authors had hoped to avoid when they reserved all powers not specifically designated as federal to the states. Still, the law said that the great cities existed solely at the mercy of the states, and had no right to national power or authority.

City-State Relations.
Denying cities a place in the federal system did not, of course, stop the growth of the cities. What it did accomplish was to give power over the cities to state legislatures dominated by rural interests and often unwilling to understand, much less deal with, the complex problems common to every city. The states hold the power to tax, to borrow, to lend, to impose fees, to negotiate with neighbouring jurisdictions, to deal with the federal government, to set priorities, to regulate commerce and public service utilities, to establish civil service rules, and even to manage municipal services. Most cities are not allowed to perform any of these essential functions without specific state legislative approval. Few have ever won an increase in local power without a battle against rural, and sometimes suburban, state representatives who are hostile to urban needs, goals, and residents, and are capable of using their leverage to block action or to exact major concessions from urban legislators.

The absurdities of city-state relations are legion. In one major city, all police policy—including hiring, promotion, and pay—is set by a commission named by the governor of the state. Another city must get state approval to shift the responsibility for sidewalk inspection from one city agency to another. Just recently, my state legislature eliminated our city's careful system of rent controls while strengthening similar controls elsewhere in the state.

By the time the national government awoke to the problems in our cities, the weaknesses of the present federal system were painfully evident. Under the domestic thrust of Pres. Lyndon B. Johnson's administration in the 1960s, some 180 federal programs to aid cities were started, ranging from education to sewage treatment. The new legislation encouraged greater state-city cooperation, metropolitan integration, and more cooperation between separate taxing authorities (such as school districts) and local governments. Federal financing of some of these programs was channeled through state governments, so that states frequently became involved in urban problems for the first time.

But, for any number of reasons—the war in Vietnam and the accompanying cuts in domestic spending, racial tension, urban racial disorders, and the tangle of federal, state, and local bureaucracies—the great federal initiative faltered by the end of the decade. And, by that time, the inflationary recession of 1969–71 had imposed on the cities rising expenditures with little increase in revenue from their principal taxes. State and local

John V. Lindsay is the mayor of New York City. (See BIOGRAPHY.)

governments depend upon a brisk growth in the national economy to meet their fiscal needs. When that growth ceased at the same time that unemployment and inflation increased the need for revenue, the cities were the prime victims. Faced with the same pressures as the cities, states cut back their budgets, and the first item to go was usually aid to localities.

The "National Cities" Charter. Taken together, these events of the past decade clearly show the need for a new look at the cities' role in the federal system. I have proposed that the federal government charter a certain number of "national cities," granting them the power to act independently on critical issues of local concern and urban development.

These national cities should have essential economic powers—to raise taxes, to set fees, and to issue bonds and notes. They should have the right to chart their own financial courses. National cities should have the freedom to deal directly with the federal government and to cooperate on joint federal-city programs in such areas as manpower training, child care, education, and health. Under the present system, federal programs in these vital areas go through the state governments with city officials and Washington agencies dealing through remote state bureaucrats.

National cities should have additional powers: the right to manage and direct urban services; the right to a voice, at least equal to the state's, in the regulation of local industry; collective bargaining, utility monopolies, and franchised public services; the right to decentralize certain functions to local neighbourhoods; and the right to resist unjustified mandated state costs. These are the rights and powers that cities must have if they are to deal decisively with the problems of urban America today. The national cities charter would constitute a direct grant of national home rule in those areas where state governments have failed to act.

National cities would create a new federal-city relationship alongside the present federal-state system. These national cities would still remain politically part of their states but they would have a relationship with the national government consistent with their national responsibilities.

There need be no set size for national cities, although the 25 largest urban centres with populations greater than 500,000 seem logical choices for that designation. However, national functions and national responsibilities, not size, should make cities worthy of national status.

The pressure of the past few years has given many of us the sense that the futures of our cities are linked one to another. We only recently have discovered that Seattle and Baltimore, Atlanta and Phoenix, San Francisco and Pittsburgh have inherited a common national legacy. Despite state differences—despite a long history of regional competition for national resources—we have learned that the things that unite us in the cities are more important than the things that divide us. The mayors of America's major cities have thus mounted an unprecedented campaign to persuade the Congress and the public of the priority of urban needs.

Regard for Urban Needs. There is sound precedent for a national charter for major cities. In the past, the government has granted similar special status and corporate charters to other bodies from the Tennessee Valley Authority to the Federal Deposit Insurance Corporation to AMTRAK. The creation of national cities with substantial powers might require a Constitutional amendment, though careful legislation might accomplish the task. Most important, it demands a concentrated national focus on urban needs. The National Commission on the Causes and Prevention of Violence, chaired by Milton Eisenhower, called for an Urban Constitutional Convention to consider such questions. But that suggestion went almost unnoticed.

The notion of national cities is hardly radical. In 1937, the National Resources Committee, headed by Secretary of the Interior Harold Ickes, sent a brief for city home rule to Pres. Franklin D. Roosevelt. The committee concluded: "In spite of

this vital and growing significance as the principal instrument of public service and community control, the American city is still the legal creature of higher authorities, subject to their fiat for the most minor power and procedures, reaching out in one state to legislature to perform the peddling of peanuts on a municipal pier. The city is in many ways the ward of a guardian who refuses to function."

The committee recommended the establishment of a direct relationship between the federal government and the major cities. But like so many other important, farsighted reports, it was ignored—and only now, over 30 years later, have we come to appreciate its wisdom.

The national cities proposal is susceptible to great improvement, refinement, and elaboration. But a change of this scale is essential—and even that is no guarantee that our cities will be free or able to do what they must. The national functions and national burdens of our major cities also demand much greater national financial support: the cities must receive more federal assistance for the unique burden of caring for so many of our country's poor, untrained, and uneducated. Only a meaningful program of federal revenue sharing directly with cities, and a national reform of our archaic welfare system, will meet that national obligation. These would be long overdue responses to national conditions of poverty, unemployment, discrimination, and migration that have so burdened our cities.

The Need for Commitment. Of course, there has always been one "national city," Washington, D.C., directly run by the federal government. Unhappily, the kind of support and leadership provided that city by successive Congresses has been as backward and antiurban as that of any state legislature in the nation. So the national cities idea by itself is no cure-all. A new national attitude and new national commitment to our great cities will be required if it is to have real impact.

For years now, the U.S. has poured billions of dollars into cities and villages and jungles in all parts of the world under the guise of protecting our national security. It is time for us to admit that the greatest threat to American stability in the 1970s comes from within our own borders. Continued neglect of our cities can only lead to more despair and bitterness and violence. Today our national security demands the same kind of multi-billion-dollar commitment at home that we gave the great cities of Europe through the Marshall Plan after World War II.

The very survival of this nation depends upon a willingness to innovate and act on our urban crisis. We have only just emerged from almost two centuries of neglecting urban problems. We must, as a nation, be willing to make changes in our most basic arrangements if we are to deal with the urban civilization we have created.

continued from page 181

location of land, excessive industrial use, and pollution of air, water, and soil were just as grave in those countries where private landownership had been abolished as in market economies. The only solution seemed to be for cities to continue devising various control measures, aimed at encouraging developments that would make life more stimulating and satisfying.

Municipal Finances. Insufficient finances continued to be a major source of concern to most of the world's cities, holding back the provision of basic infrastructure and modern governmental services. The almost exclusive use of the tax on property (in North America, the United Kingdom, and countries with similar governmental systems) tended to encourage the very symptoms—deterioration and monotony in construction and design—that cities were attempting to alleviate since it led to competition for new tax sources among neighbouring governmental jurisdictions. It also proved a negative factor in regional planning and development schemes.

Property taxes or rates were thus under close review in many countries. It seemed unlikely that legal limitations would be raised by state or national legislatures. The alternatives were to improve administrative practices, particularly as regards assessments; to make other sources of income available to local governments, especially the hard-pressed metropolitan areas; and to offer various incentives to developers for providing public facilities. It also seemed likely that in many countries a careful examination would be requested of the total distribution of tasks and of tax resources over all governmental levels. Income or retail sales taxes, equalization grants, grants-in-aid, or subsidies could serve to bridge serious financial gaps, but they could be no more than a first step in coming to grips with the basic cause of the crisis currently besetting cities—a disharmony between tasks and revenue.   (IULA)

A thorough reevaluation of tasks and revenues was expected in the United States, where critical revenue shortages continued to plague the cities. Municipalities for the fiscal year 1970, as reported by the Bureau of the Census, spent $1.5 billion in excess of their receipts, a gap between expenditures and revenues greater than in previous years. During the preceding year expenditures increased by 12%, whereas revenues rose by only 10%. The greater financial deficit

occurred despite the fact that many cities curtailed or failed to increase essential services such as police protection, education, health services, garbage collection, and welfare. Moreover, the financial plight of the central cities in metropolitan areas was understated by these statistics since they included municipalities in suburbia.

These figures substantiated the claims of mayors about the worsening of municipal finances, as the influx of a poor minority group population, mainly black, and the exodus of middle-class and upper-income whites to the suburbs increased the need for urban services while the tax base eroded. Although mayors, especially of the larger cities, intensified their pressures for more federal and state aid, most of the increase in their funds came from their own sources. Municipal sources of revenue provided an increase of 11%, while federal and state moneys to cities rose by only 8%. A report by a special commission appointed by the National Urban Coalition stated that "most cities by 1980 will be preponderantly black and brown, and totally bankrupt."

The financial plight of the cities and the prospect that it would worsen rather than improve led the Nixon administration, in 1971, to propose a "revenue sharing" program. In a publication of the Domestic Council in the Executive Office of the President, in which the proposed program was explained, an introductory statement read: "State and local governments are facing a crisis today. We can no longer avoid this fact. The crisis exists here and now—and must be met head on." The administration's plan would provide state and local governments with a total of $16 billion in federal funds. Of this amount, $6 billion would be new money, that is, above that which state and local governments were already receiving for specific programs. The plan was designed to achieve the following objectives:

Alleviate the fiscal problems of state and local governments by providing unrestricted additional revenues;

Eliminate the present matching requirements and narrow purposes of categorical grants-in-aid which will be absorbed into the new revenue sharing funds;

Allow more spending priorities to be set at those levels of government closest to the problems and the people;

Reinforce both the responsibility and responsiveness of government by providing state and local officials with both the flexibility and the funds to carry out their duties effectively.

The administration viewed its revenue sharing program as the "cornerstone" of the president's plan to revitalize the U.S. system of government—"to reverse the trend by which the Federal Government's awesome revenue-raising powers have given rise to an awesome, centralized government bureaucracy . . . to restore a proper balance to our Federal system."

The plan, as proposed, had two major elements. One was general revenue sharing, which entailed the granting of unencumbered funds for state and local use. The second, special revenue sharing, would provide state and local governments with funds for specified program areas, within which localities would have flexibility in expenditures. General revenue sharing would represent a step in the direction of closing the revenue gap of state and local governments, estimated at $10 billion for 1971. That revenue gap had widened despite the increases in state and local taxes—mainly property and consumer taxes which, during the preceding two decades, had risen from $105 to $380 per capita—and despite the rise in state and local government debt from $19 billion in 1948 to $135 billion in 1969. Federal revenues, based on the graduated income tax, increase with national economic growth and,

Empty taxicabs line the streets of New York City in March 1971 as cab passengers staged a boycott to protest a 50% rise in taxicab fares.

therefore, can meet new expenditure requirements more readily.

Special revenue sharing would provide state and local governments with greater discretion than they currently had under categorical grant programs. In lieu of 130 separate grant programs, $11 billion of shared revenues would be placed under six broad headings within which local priorities could be followed. The six categories would be: rural community development, urban community development, education, manpower training, law enforcement, and transportation.

The direct recipients of shared revenues under the administration plan would be the general purpose units of government: states, counties, cities, and towns. To improve the ability of these governmental units to manage their own affairs and to use the federal funds effectively, the federal government would greatly increase funds for a planning-management program for state and local officials and for relevant research. To begin with, the federal moneys would be distributed on the basis of population and "revenue effort," the latter referring to the extent to which a state had effectively used its own revenue-raising powers. Within the state, funds could be distributed on the basis of the formula in the General Revenue Sharing Act, based on the portion of general revenues raised by each unit; or the state, in consultation with local governments, could work out its own distribution system.

The federal government would retain the responsibility of ensuring equal treatment and opportunities for all, including safeguards against discrimination. Procedures would be provided to deal with noncompliance, which could result in a cutoff of funds, and to assure appropriate accounting. No matching of funds would be necessary. It was estimated that under general revenue sharing, a typical city of 70,000 people in a metropolitan area of 150,000 would receive a grant of about 7% of its annual budget, plus benefits from the approximately 6% increase in the budget of the surrounding county area. Furthermore, under special revenue sharing such a city would be spared the preparation of lengthy and costly applications for special program funds. It would receive funds for projects under the six program categories much more promptly than under the existing system, and would be in a position to exercise more choice with respect to its programs.

The administration's plan immediately stimulated widespread debate. Although governors, mayors, and hard-pressed taxpayers favoured revenue sharing in principle, many did not agree with the administration's specific proposals. The Democrats, as the opposition party, attacked the plan, and it soon became apparent that Congress, with a Democratic majority in each house, was loath to increase federal funds to state and local governments while relaxing control over their use. The administration itself, in response to the stubborn recession and inflation, adopted economic policies that called for a huge federal deficit and asked Congress to defer the consideration of revenue sharing. (*See* GOVERNMENT FINANCE.)

Opponents of the administration's revenue sharing plan developed the following objections to it:

1. The federal government is also hard pressed for funds and is operating with huge annual deficits.

2. Since a state's present tax effort is one element in the proposed distribution of federal funds, many of the neediest states and Western states with large tracts of federal land would be relatively adversely affected.

3. Under the formula for the distribution of funds some

Policemen question
streetwalkers
during a massive campaign
launched during 1971
by Mayor John Lindsay
to keep prostitutes
off the streets of New
York City.

states would get less money from the federal government than they currently received under the grant-in-aid programs.

4. The funds proposed for revenue sharing were obtained mainly from already existing programs, and the new moneys proposed were inadequate to meet the state and local government revenue gap.

5. State governments, which historically have been dominated by rural areas and which were increasingly dominated by a coalition of rural and suburban populations, would not readily meet the needs of the largest cities with the most severe problems.

6. State and city governments are more corrupt than is the federal government.

7. The decrease in federal control over funds would weaken standards of performance and certainly make them uneven.

8. It would be unwise to divorce the control of expenditures from the responsibility of revenue raising.

9. Minority groups in the inner cities have more confidence in the government in Washington than in state capitols or city halls.

10. It is doubtful that revenue sharing would increase the ability of the citizen to cope with the power of government.

11. Funds for dealing with social problems might decrease as specific programs lost their identities.

The focus of national attention on the financial distress of the cities and the debate on the administration's revenue sharing proposals led to the consideration of alternatives. Undoubtedly, this would include serious exploration of how to achieve a better allocation of sources of revenue for state and local governments. Currently, cities and other local units of government obtained about 85% of their revenues from property taxes and the states got about 60% of their revenues from sales taxes. Although all but ten states had some form of income tax, the rates were so low that this tax generated only 15% of the states' revenues. The federal government obtained about two-thirds of its revenues from the income tax. Local taxes about doubled during the 1960s as property and sales levies were increased to painful and politically dangerous levels. Moreover, in contrast to the progressive federal income tax, state and local taxes tended to be regressive, falling most heavily on low-income groups. It seemed certain that there would be pressure to increase the tax burden of the middle-

Noteworthy winners of 1971 mayoral contests include (from top to bottom) Richard J. Daley in Chicago, Warren Widener in Berkeley, Frank Rizzo in Philadelphia, and Joseph Alioto in San Francisco.

income and wealthy elements of the population and decrease that of the poor.

Among the alternatives to the proposed revenue sharing plan were:

1. Extension of state income taxes and increased tax rates, with credits for state income tax payments in the federal income tax.

2. Imposition of a federal consumption tax such as the "value-added" tax—a tax on a product at each stage of fabrication and sale. Such a tax would be regressive but it could raise substantial revenue.

3. Allocation of all costs of welfare, including present and possible future public medical costs, to the federal government.

4. Allocation to state governments of all costs of public education. A 1971 decision of the California Supreme Court, declaring the use of the property tax for local public education unconstitutional because of the educational inequities it generated, might accelerate this trend.

5. Increase of federal grant-in-aid programs, with improved distribution of funds to assure adequate flow to the most needy areas.

Quality of Life. Urban conditions during the year showed little evidence of improvement. Although the summer of 1971 did not bring widespread riots in the U.S., some cities experienced serious racial incidents. Increasingly it was Chicanos (Mexican-Americans), Puerto Ricans, and American Indians, rather than blacks, who openly revolted. According to the Department of Justice, there were 11 major disorders and 32 serious disturbances in the first eight months of 1971 (through August), compared with 19 major disorders and 49 serious disturbances for the same period in 1970. The consensus of observers seemed to attribute this not to improved living conditions for minority groups but, rather, to the fact that blacks had found more productive ways to express their frustration and alienation. Blacks and other minority groups were increasing their community organization efforts and political activity in an attempt to bring about change within the system. Other factors in the decrease in violence were the greater sophistication of police and government officials in dealing with episodes and more reasoned coverage of episodes by the mass media.

In general, then, decreased riots and arson could not be interpreted to mean that conditions had improved or that frustration and hostility had diminished. On the contrary, a Harris Poll reported on Oct. 4, 1971, that the attitudes of blacks were becoming increasingly hostile toward whites, even while white perceptions of blacks were improving with the deterioration of distorted stereotypes from the past. Guerrilla warfare, aimed particularly at the police, and bombings had not decreased, and pent-up inner city hostility continued to be a major threat to the viability of American society.

As to the actual conditions within cities, the evidence was that they had probably worsened. According to the FBI, violent crimes—murder, forcible rape, aggravated assault, and robbery—rose by 11% during the first six months of 1971. The FBI also reported that 80 law enforcement officers were killed in the first eight months of 1971, compared with 67 for the corresponding period in 1970.

A National Urban Coalition task force reported that the condition of U.S. cities has generally worsened in the three years following the report of the National Advisory (Kerner) Commission on Civil Disorders. The 12-member task force, of which Sen. Fred R. Harris (Dem., Okla.) and Mayor John V. Lindsay of New York were co-chairmen, issued a report entitled *The State of the Cities*, which assessed the progress made since the 1968 Kerner report. The National Urban Coalition report concluded

that the races had become more polarized and that American institutions, public and private, were losing the confidence of the public. Sol M. Linowitz, the Coalition chairman, stated that "The cities have not cooled off. The basic causes that sparked the tragic ghetto rebellions of the nineteen-sixties are still there —worse, in most cases, than ever. And the people are angry."

The finding was that, in the main, the Kerner Commission recommendations for improvements in housing, employment, welfare, and education had not been carried out. Comparing the situation with that at the end of 1967, the Coalition report stated: "Housing is still the national scandal it was then. Schools are more tedious and turbulent. The rates of crime and unemployment and disease and heroin addiction are higher. Welfare rolls are larger. And, with few exceptions, the relations between minority communities and the police are just as hostile." With respect to the white racism stressed in the Kerner report, the Coalition report said: "Separation and inequality have proceeded apace. In every major central city, the new census shows blacks and Chicanos comprise a bigger proportion of the population today than they did 10 years ago." The only optimistic trend the Coalition report noted was the increasing grass roots organization for self-help.

Another indication of the worsening quality of life in urban U.S. was given by the Gallup Poll, which found that public discontent increased between 1969 and 1971. Although most Americans continued to express satisfaction with their condition of life, dissatisfaction with jobs, income, and housing increased during the two years, and dissatisfaction with the future facing the person and his family also rose. The level of dissatisfaction among blacks was, without exception, higher than that among whites in 1971: 25% of blacks were dissatisfied with their work, compared with 9% for whites; for family income, the figures were 57% for blacks and 33% for whites; for housing, 46% for blacks and 19% for whites; for children's education, 29% for blacks and 26% for whites; for quality of community life, 44% for blacks and 18% for whites; and for the future facing the person and his family, 45% for blacks and 29% for whites. (P. M. HA.)

See also Architecture; Crime; Environment; Historic Buildings; Housing; Police; Transportation.

ENCYCLOPÆDIA BRITANNICA FILMS. *The Northeast—Headquarters for a Nation* (1967); *Operation Bootstrap* (1968); *Problems of Conservation—Air* (1968); *The House of Man, Part II—Our Crowded Environment* (1969); *Manuel from Puerto Rico* (1969); *The South: Roots of the Urban Crisis* (1969); *Chicano from the Southwest* (1970); *The Garbage Explosion* (1970); *The Industrial City* (1970); *Linda and Billy Ray from Appalachia* (1970); *The Rise of the American City* (1970); *What Is a Community?* (1970); *Jesse from Mississippi* (1971); *Noise—Polluting the Environment* (1971); *Turn off Pollution* (1971).

Colombia

A republic in northwestern South America, Colombia is bordered by Panama, Venezuela, Brazil, Peru, and Ecuador and has coasts on both the Caribbean Sea and the Pacific Ocean. Area: 439,735 sq.mi. (1,138,914 sq.km.). Pop. (1971 est.): 21,785,700. Cap. and largest city: Bogotá (pop., 1971 metro. est., 2,664,800). Language: Spanish. Religion: Roman

Catholic (91%). President in 1971, Misael Pastrana Borrero.

President Pastrana, who took office on Aug. 7, 1970, was committed not only to consolidating the economic gains made under the previous president, Carlos Lleras Restrepo, but also to reducing unemployment and improving social conditions. To this end, in December 1970 the government submitted to Congress a three-year economic and social development plan. This postulated an average annual increase in employment of 4.3% over the period 1971–73 and a reduction in unemployment from 8.4 to 6.4% by the end of 1973. To obtain this expansion of employment, the plan estimated that the gross national product (GNP) must grow by 7.5% yearly, necessitating an estimated total investment of 77 billion pesos with foreign financing of at least $300 million a year. At its meeting in Paris on Feb. 16–17, 1971, the Credit Consultative Group for Colombia declared that the Colombian government's economic performance and development programs justified continued assistance on the scale and terms requested.

Unfortunately, coffee prices fell steadily from 51.78 cents per pound in January to 47.57 cents in July, leading the government to declare that its public investment expenditure would have to be cut and the growth target of 7.5% abandoned. President Pastrana also expressed concern about the country's external indebtedness, warning that total debt service payments would reach $150 million from 1971 onward, compared with $87.2 million in 1970. The decline in coffee receipts combined with increased import expenditures produced a fall in exchange reserves of $37.7 million in the first half of 1971. The consequent deterioration in the balance of payments, together with other unfavourable factors such as reduced public and private investments and a rise in the cost of living of 9% in the first seven months of 1971 (compared with an average of 7% in the previous three years), led to forecasts that GNP growth for 1971 would be only 6.5–7%.

President Pastrana seemed to lack the firm control over ministers and the influence in Congress that marked the Lleras administration. Despite plans to combat unemployment and introduce urban reforms, the National Front government faced serious social unrest and increased opposition in 1971. On February 26 student demonstrations in Cali, where eight people were killed and about 50 injured, caused a state of siege to be declared throughout Colombia, with strict press and radio censorship. But a 24-hour general strike called by the Union de Trabajadores de Colombia on March 8, to protest rising living costs and the slow pace of social reforms, was almost completely unsuccessful. The failure of the strike was attributed to sudden government action in settling the long-outstanding pay claims of some 65,000 schoolteachers and 20,000 rail, steel, and cement workers. At the end of April, further serious unrest culminated in a 48-hour student strike and the closing of the National University.

The national conventions of the Conservative and Liberal parties, held in May, were characterized by dissension between progressive and traditional wings. At the Liberal Party convention, the new executive council was elected by followers of Sen. Julio Turbay Ayala (a firm supporter of President Pastrana), after a walkout by supporters of Lleras and Alfonso Lopez Michelsen. At the same time, the Conservative minister of agriculture, Emilio Valderrama, resigned to join the progressive sector of the party. In the midst of sharp clashes between Conservative and Liberal members, the entire Cabinet, with the exception of the minister of defense, resigned on June 1 to enable President Pastrana to carry out a reshuffle and settle differences. Pastrana appointed a new Cabinet almost entirely from right-wing sectors of the Conservative and Liberal parties. (R. B. Le.)

COLOMBIA

Education. (1967) Primary, pupils 2,586,288, teachers 70,235; secondary, pupils 376,718, teachers 24,942; vocational, pupils 137,274, teachers 9,553; teacher training, students 63,425, teachers 4,434; higher (including 31 universities), students 58,417, teaching staff 9,526.

Finance. Monetary unit: peso, with a free rate (Sept. 27, 1971) of 20 pesos to U.S. $1 (50 pesos = £1 sterling). Gold, SDRs, and foreign exchange, central bank: (June 1971) U.S. $165 million; (June 1970) U.S. $280 million. Budget (1970 est.): revenue 11,030,800,000 pesos; expenditure 12,132,500,000 pesos. Gross national product: (1969) 108,280,000,-000 pesos; (1968) 94,420,000,000 pesos. Money supply: (June 1970) 19,640,000,000 pesos; (June 1969) 15,737,000,000 pesos. Cost of living (Bogotá; 1963 = 100): (June 1971) 214; (June 1970) 202.

Foreign Trade. (1969) Imports 11,813,000,000 pesos; exports 8,879,000,000 pesos. Import sources: U.S. 46%; West Germany 10%; Spain 7%; Japan 5%. Export destinations: U.S. 39%; West Germany 13%; Netherlands 6%. Main exports: coffee 54%; crude oil 6%.

Transport and Communications. Roads (1967) c. 45,000 km. (including 7,200 km. with improved surface). Motor vehicles in use: passenger (1969) c. 150,500; commercial (including buses; 1968) 123,200. Railways: (1969) 3,483 km.; traffic (1970) 223 million passenger-km., freight 1,180,000,000 net ton-km. Air traffic (1970): 2,030,000,000 passenger-km.; freight 71,008,000 net ton-km. Shipping (1970): merchant vessels 100 gross tons and over 49; gross tonnage 234,526. Telephones (Dec. 1969) 542,765. Radio receivers (Dec. 1969) 2,214,000. Television receivers (Dec. 1969) 622,000.

Agriculture. Production (in 000; metric tons; 1970; 1969 in parentheses): Corn c. 850 (850); rice 673 (695); wheat c. 70 (68); barley c. 84 (76); potatoes c. 1,100 (1,000); cassava (1969) c. 920, (1968) 900; coffee c. 507 (c. 474); bananas (1969) c. 800, (1968) 770; cotton, lint c. 134 (125); cane sugar, raw value (1970–71) c. 787, (1969–70) c. 677; sugar, panela (1970–71) c. 680, (1969–70) c. 670; tobacco 44 (44). Livestock (in 000; Dec. 1969): cattle c. 19,576; sheep c. 1,850; pigs c. 2,000; goats c. 900; horses c. 1,050; poultry (Oct.) c. 25.300.

Industry. Production (in 000; metric tons; 1970): crude oil 11,071; natural gas (cu.m.; 1969) 1,338,000; coal (1969) 3,317; electricity (excluding most industrial production; kw-hr.; 1969) 7,344,000; crude steel (ingots) 239; gold (troy oz.; 1968) 219; salt (1969) 637; cement 2,763.

Commercial Policies

During 1971 the world trade and monetary system that had contributed so much to the expansion of exchange and economic growth since World War II faced its most serious trials. The crisis was not unforeshadowed. In spite of such encouraging milestones as the Kennedy Round (1967) and the general progress in the removal of trade restrictions, the system had been increasingly weakened by a persistent and partly latent growth of protectionist practices and sentiments.

Import Levies and Restrictions. With the world's attention focused on the British negotiations for entry into the EEC, few commercial policy measures of significant dimensions were encountered up to the middle of the year. On the tariff side, another step in the implementation of the Kennedy Round was taken on

Jan. 1, 1971, when the participating governments—apart from those that had already acted—put into effect the fourth of five installments of the negotiated concessions.

In December 1970, Argentina revoked all the tariff reductions it had made upon the devaluation of the peso six months earlier. In July 1971 the government imposed restrictions on a wide range of luxury and nonessential products for a period of one year, and this was followed by an increase in the customs duties on certain industrial products and equipment. A further step was taken in September when all imports were suspended for a six-week period. Toward the end of 1970, Colombia modified its customs tariff and reduced rates of its prior deposit on imports. A tariff reduction was made in Honduras.

In April 1971, a substantial liberalization of imports took place in Nigeria, as a result of which only some 12 items of essential foodstuffs remained under licensing control. At the same time, import duties were lowered for certain essential supplies, notably flour. As from July 1, New Zealand freed a number of imports from licensing control. In March, Peru introduced import licensing for all agricultural products. New regulations were issued in July under which local producers of industrial products were required to register their products, and imports were to be allowed only if the goods were not available in sufficient quantities from domestic production.

Spain's import deposit was reduced from 20 to 10% at the beginning of the year. In November 1970, Uruguay introduced an additional import surcharge of 5% applying to most imports, which had already been subject to a levy at a wide range of rates. The import surcharge rates were further increased in May 1971. As an emergency measure, imports of capital goods were suspended for a three-month period. At the beginning of the year, Yugoslavia abolished its import deposit and reduced its import surcharge from 5 to 2%. In order to avoid a worsening of the balance of payments position, the surcharge rate was raised to 6% in September. The measure was to be terminated by the end of the year.

Japan continued its policy of liberalizing imports by steps. On January 1, ten items, including whisky, antibiotics, and colour film, were freed from restrictions. Another installment followed at the beginning of July, and a further 30 items were liberalized at the end of September.

Beginning in mid-1969, the Nixon administration had taken a series of minor steps relating to trade or travel regulations to demonstrate its desire to improve U.S. relations with China. In June 1971 the U.S. finally abandoned its general ban on commercial and financial dealings with China, and a long list of nonstrategic goods was freed from export control. In July, Export-Import Bank facilities were made available for financing trade with Peking.

U.S. Import Surcharge. The drastic and far-reaching monetary and financial measures that U.S. Pres. Richard Nixon announced on August 15, the long-smoldering dollar crisis, and the internal measures taken to deal with the obdurate problems of the U.S. economy are discussed elsewhere. (*See* Economy, World; Government Finance; Payments and Reserves, International.) Directly affecting international trade and giving rise to apprehensions as to U.S. intentions in the domain of commercial policy was the import surcharge imposed as part of the "interrelated and integrated programs."

This surcharge, of up to 10%, applied to all dutiable goods not subject to import limitations pursuant to U.S. statutes. It did not apply to cotton textiles (or, later, other textiles), petroleum, petroleum products, sugar, certain meat and certain other agricultural products, mainly dairy products, which were subject to statutory import limitations of one kind or another. Nor did it affect imports of most tropical products and many industrial raw materials.

The principal purpose of the surcharge, as stated by U.S. officials, was to afford relatively rapid relief for the U.S. balance of trade and payments while more fundamental measures took effect. The position taken by the U.S. was that, for the first time in nearly a hundred years, the U.S. was to be faced with a trade deficit; that the dismal outlook for the U.S. balance of trade was a critical element in the international pressure against the dollar; that the U.S. needed to earn a trade surplus in order to offset deficits on the invisible account, net private capital outflow, and foreign aid and governmental expenditure abroad; and that the U.S. was, therefore, justified in limiting the growth of imports.

The position taken by the United States' trading partners was that, while the U.S. was admittedly in a serious balance of payments situation, the surcharge was clearly inappropriate, since the problems lay mainly in the domain of capital movement and foreign investment rather than in international trade. There was also a general feeling that the surcharge, if not removed within a short time, would have far-reaching and detrimental repercussions on the world economy.

Particularly disconcerting were the uncertain terms in which U.S. officials subsequently commented on the conditions under which the U.S. would remove this new impediment to trade. Mention was made of the undervaluation of certain foreign currencies and, in general, the unfair exchange-rate structure; unfair trade barriers or practices adversely affecting U.S. exports; and the uneven sharing among Western nations of their common defense expenditure. Certain U.S. officials stated that the realization, or assured prospect, of a $13 billion favourable swing in the overall U.S. balance of payments was considered a prerequisite.

The repeated assurances offered by U.S. officials that the import surcharge in no way presaged a resurgence of protectionism failed to dispel general doubt about U.S. intentions. Apart from the shifting positions mentioned above, and the uncompromising attitude adopted by certain U.S. officials at later international gatherings on monetary and related matters, the fact that the import surcharge was supported and welcomed by large sectors of U.S. industry and labour was considered ominous. International attention was also directed to other steps taken by the Nixon administration in the context of the national emergency, notably its recommendation to Congress of a "job development tax credit" that, in limiting the tax benefit to purchases of domestically produced capital equipment, contained an element of discrimination against imports. Another proposed measure was the creation of a new type of "domestic international sales corporation" enjoying certain tax privileges that would have an incentive effect on exports.

Removal of the surcharge was given high priority by the United States' principal trading partners in the negotiations concerned with ending the international monetary crisis, and in late December the U.S. announced that it would take this step as part of the general settlement agreed to by the Group of Ten.

At the same time, other major steps, chiefly devaluation of the dollar and revaluation of certain other currencies, would in effect raise the price of U.S. imports. The settlement was generally believed to mark the end of the postwar international monetary system. The effect this would have on world trade remained to be seen.

In October, Denmark introduced a similar temporary 10% surcharge on about two-thirds of its imports, mainly industrial products, also as part of a general economy program. The Danish surcharge was to be applied until mid-1972 and, thereafter, at a reduced rate up to March 1973.

Trade Restraints on Textiles. For nearly ten years Western developed countries had relied on a multilateral intergovernmental arrangement, made within the framework of the General Agreement on Tariffs and Trade (GATT), to check any excessively rapid growth of exports of cotton textiles from Japan and certain less developed countries. During this period, however, there had been a gradual but accelerating switch in textile production from cotton to man-made fibres, and exports of man-made and mixed-fibre textiles and garments from Japan, Hong Kong, South Korea, and Taiwan had risen by leaps and bounds.

In the U.S., especially, the threat of market disruption in these products had become a leading political issue. A trade bill presented to Congress in 1970 by Wilbur D. Mills (Dem., Ark.), chairman of the House Ways and Means Committee, had as its principal provision the restriction of textile imports. To head off such restrictions, the Japanese textile industry implemented as from July 1971 a program of voluntary restraints on textile exports to the U.S., which it had negotiated with Mills in March. These restraints, consisting of an overall ceiling for all textiles, were considered insufficient by the U.S. administration, which demanded a government-to-government agreement providing for ceilings on particularly sensitive product categories.

On the heels of the 10% surcharge, which was particularly damaging to Japanese exports, the U.S. informed the Japanese government that unless a satisfactory agreement was reached by October 15, the U.S. would impose unilateral import quotas on textiles. Against overwhelming opposition from the textile industry, and at great political risk, the Sato government accepted the terms. Japanese exports of wool and man-made textiles to the U.S. would be subject to quantitative limitations for some 18 specified groups and subgroups, based on actual imports in the 12-month period ending March 31, 1971, to be raised by 5% (1% for wool) per year during a three-year period. Similar agreements were entered into between the U.S. and Hong Kong, South Korea, and Taiwan.

Upon conclusion of these agreements, the U.S. import surcharge was removed for the products covered. Owing to the rapid expansion of U.S. imports of these products in 1970–71, the base quotas (trade during the 12-month period ended March 31, 1971) seemed fairly generous, although the subdivision into 18 groups with individual ceilings and the strict limits on intergroup switching meant more severe control for individual lines of products. Meanwhile, there was serious concern among European producers that the excluded Asian exports would be massively diverted to their markets.

Britain's Entry into the EEC. Certain main issues had emerged in the negotiations for British entry into the EEC in 1970, the most important being related to

Community finance, a large share of which, at least in the near future, would be devoted to schemes of agricultural support in the interest of less efficient agricultural producers. The other points considered essential by Britain were New Zealand dairy products and sugar from Australia and the less developed countries of the Commonwealth. By December agreement had been reached on certain crucial points. To cushion the shock of entry, a five-year period was agreed upon for the alignment of both the industrial and the agricultural sectors, although Britain insisted on a much longer period for making full payment to the EEC budget. The Commonwealth countries in Africa and most of the British overseas territories would be offered association arrangements.

The negotiations reached an impasse on March 11, 1971, marked by a strong statement by the British negotiator, Geoffrey Rippon. Shortly before a summit meeting between French Premier Georges Pompidou and British Prime Minister Edward Heath, however, a breakthrough was achieved on May 13 when agreement was reached on another range of subjects. Included were tariff quotas for a number of industrial materials entering the U.K. duty-free, agricultural transitional arrangements regarding horticulture and modalities of changeover to the continental system, and association arrangements for Caribbean, Indian Ocean, and Pacific Commonwealth countries, regarding which the Community also declared its intention to safeguard traditional trade interests, particularly in relation to sugar. A new proposal was presented by the Six on the budget question. On June 7 agreement was reached on sterling.

On June 23, Britain and the EEC reached agreement on the major outstanding questions, notably New Zealand's dairy products and Britain's contribution to the Community budget. Special arrangements would be made to guarantee New Zealand a market for agreed quantities of dairy products up to 1977. Britain's contribution to the budget would amount to 8.4% of the total in the first year, rising by steps to 18.92% in the fifth year; there would be special rules for the calculation of its contribution in 1977 and 1978. At some stages of the subsequent debate in Britain, the fundamental issues of economic integration and the geopolitical implications of a unified Europe in an emerging world of multiple giants seemed to have been lost amid a welter of mutterings concerning food prices. However, when the vote in Parliament was taken, the motion to decide in principle to accede to the EEC on the terms negotiated was carried by a comfortable margin of 112 votes. (*See* EUROPEAN UNITY.)

Parallel to the British negotiations, talks were opened between the EEC and the other applicants for accession, as well as those members of EFTA that did not wish to become members of the Community but desired to establish other forms of cooperation. There was general agreement that all such arrangements should come into effect at the same time and, as a result, progress was accelerated after the settlement of the British case. By mid-July all major problems had been resolved concerning Danish accession.

International Organizations. The atmosphere of crisis did not seem to have disturbed the routine pursuits of international bureaucracy. GATT plodded on with its tariff study and stocktaking of nontariff trade barriers in preparation for further concerted international action to liberalize trade, which it was hoped might resume once the dust had settled. GATT also made further progress in its *Ostpolitik* when Romania, after three years of discussion, was finally admitted as a full contracting party.

The General System of Preferences in favour of less developed countries, which had been formulated in the Organization for Economic Cooperation and Development and agreed upon in the UN Conference on Trade and Development, received the necessary blessing in GATT. Also in GATT, a long-drawn-out series of tariff negotiations among less developed countries, known as the "mini Kennedy Round," was concluded in October.   (Co. S.)

See also Agriculture; Commodities, Primary; Development, Economic; Trade, International.

Commodities, Primary

Trends in World Production. Combined world production of agricultural, fishery, and forest products in 1970 continued to increase according to UN Food and Agriculture Organization estimates (*see* Table I). The 1970 increase of 2%, while up from a rise of less than 1% in 1969, was below the 1968 upturn of 3.5%. World agricultural production was up 2%, rising in the less developed countries as a whole but standing still in developed market economies for the second consecutive year. Fishery production, the growth of which slowed down in 1969, again accelerated in 1970. However, the direct impact on the nutritional situation was somewhat limited since most of the increase was in fish not used for food. Forest production also continued to grow but at a slower rate.

The stationary level of agricultural production in the developed countries largely resulted from policies designed to reduce surplus stocks of wheat, dairy products, and rice, but output was also held down by unfavourable weather in some areas. Particularly drastic cuts were made in wheat production in Canada and Australia. A 6% increase in agricultural production in Eastern Europe and the U.S.S.R. was due mainly to a sharp recovery in the latter country, especially of cereals.

In the less developed countries of the Far East, total agricultural output and production of foodstuffs rose by 4%, while in Latin America, agricultural production rose well over 3% and output of food products increased by more than 5½%. However, much of the latter reflected a sharp increase in Cuba's 1970 sugar production, which was mainly for export. In the rest of the region combined, food production increased by 3%, or roughly in line with population growth. For the less developed countries of Africa, overall agricultural production increased only slightly although there was a considerable but still incomplete recovery of production in the Maghreb countries (Morocco, Algeria, and Tunisia). No increase in agricultural production occurred in the countries of the Middle East, where output in all major countries except Turkey and Afghanistan remained stationary or fell.

In regard to other primary commodities—excluding agricultural, fishery, and forest products—production of crude petroleum, cement, pig iron, and crude steel continued upward in 1970 (*see* Table II). With demand not keeping pace, sizable increases in inventories occurred with cutbacks in production becoming more frequent late in the year. The situation in nonferrous metals was mixed, with output of aluminum and copper rising to new peaks with a resultant

marked increase in stocks despite relatively good demand. Production of lead rose only moderately, while the output of zinc, which rose sharply in 1969, fell nearly 3%. Tin production declined for the second consecutive year. The increase in natural rubber production in 1970 was less than 1%, leveling off from a rise of nearly 10% in 1969.

Prices and Terms of Trade. Table III shows trends in primary commodity prices in recent years. Although there was considerable variation among the different products, rises and declines were about equal in 1970. The prices of butter, coffee, newsprint, peanuts, tea, and tin showed the largest advances. Declines were most noticeable in 1970 for cocoa, copper, jute, rice, rubber, and wool. For cocoa, copper, rice, rubber, and wool, further weakness occurred in 1971, which also brought considerable weakness in prices of coffee, copra, cotton, and tin. On the other hand, 1971 prices of beef, butter, hides, jute, newsprint, peanuts, sugar, tea, and zinc displayed a marked increase over 1970.

Import prices in the less developed countries rose, largely as a result of the recent acceleration of inflation, but there was no evidence of a general speeding up of prices. In individual countries where inflation had been quite rapid, such as Argentina, Brazil, Peru, and Uruguay, it slowed noticeably and in some cases virtually stopped. But growing food shortages in many countries and the increasing use of price incentives exerted upward pressure on food prices, and in many countries such prices had risen more rapidly during the 1960s than the general level of consumer prices. It was encouraging to note, however, that efforts made by many less developed countries to increase their grain production contributed to an easing of price pressures in recent years. While not decreasing in absolute terms, increases in grain prices were smaller than those of other items in the cost of living; thus, grain prices declined in relative terms.

The value of world exports of agricultural, fishery, and forest products combined increased by about 12% in 1970. Although the expansion in agricultural and fishery products was larger, the 1970 rise in exports of forestry products fell below that of 1968 and 1969. Prices of commodity exports by the less developed countries in 1968, 1969, and 1970 were in line with prices of exports from the developed countries. However, in early 1971 the advantage was with the developed countries, mainly because of higher prices for cattle, corn, dairy products, newsprint, and oilseeds.

World agricultural exports in 1970 increased 14% in value over 1969. As in 1969 higher prices contributed to the increase, but a 10% rise in volume of shipments was mainly responsible. The expansion involved most major commodities except for some raw materials of agricultural origin, and coffee and tobacco. For several commodities, including sugar, meat, corn, oils and oilseeds, dairy products, and tea, the greater volume coincided with higher prices. For other commodities, including rubber, rice, and wheat, prices were lower but were partly or fully compensated for by the volume expansion.

Available data suggested that the agricultural trade of the less developed countries in 1970 rose by approximately 10%, about double the rate of 1969. The largest gains were made by Latin America and Africa. In Latin America the concentration of exports on commodities for which prices were higher in 1970—grains, sugar, bananas, beef and veal, cotton, and coffee—was largely responsible for the sharp rise in earnings. For only a few—sugar, bananas, and coarse grains—were shipments also larger. In Africa both prices and volume contributed to the increased earnings, mainly from exports of beverage crops, sugar, and cotton. The value of exports from the Middle and Far East also increased in 1970, but by considerably less than in other regions. In the Middle East the expansion in the volume of cotton exports was the only positive item, as shipments of other commodities were smaller and prices were generally lower. In the Far East higher prices were received for exports of oils and oilseeds, sugar, coffee, and tea, but these were partly offset by the sharp reduction in rice and rubber prices and by the failure of most exports (except rice and tea) to increase more than marginally.

For the developed regions 1970 brought a sharp recovery in the agricultural exports of North America, which reached their 1966 level after three successive years of decline. The increase, which resulted in higher earnings for both Canada and the U.S., reflected larger shipments of wheat, coarse grains, and soybean oil. For Western Europe the rapid growth over the long term was maintained, while 1970 earnings for Oceania increased somewhat less than in 1969, when they were recovering from the low level of 1968.

The value of world trade in fishery products in 1970 increased at the extremely rapid rate of 16% and exceeded $3 billion for the first time. The virtually uninterrupted upward trend of volume since World War II continued, but high prices during most of the year contributed to the greater part of the rise in value. The value of world trade in fishery products nearly doubled during the 1960s, and 40% of the world catch entered international trade, compared with about 30% a decade earlier.

World trade in forest products continued to expand in 1970, although both volume and value growth was somewhat less than in 1968 and 1969. This deceleration, which apparently continued into 1971, affected both the developed and the less developed countries. It was more pronounced in the case of the latter, where growth had been particularly dynamic in 1968 and 1969. Earnings in 1970 were estimated to have been smaller in all the less developed regions except the Far East, where they rose by about 4%, compared with nearly 30% in each of the two preceding years.

Commodity Policies. *National Policies.* There were few significant changes in policies concerning agriculture or other commodities in 1970. The main emphasis in most countries was on efforts to implement and improve policies that had been adopted in recent years. The new five-year plan (1971–75) of the U.S.S.R., for example, was evolutionary rather than radical in approach. Like its predecessor, it was based on a more realistic appraisal of possibilities than had been the case in the past. The planned increase was 20 to 22% in agricultural production, the same as actually achieved in 1966–70 and less than the 25% target for those years. Within a total increase in investment of 40%, agricultural investment was to go up by 60%.

France in 1970 passed two important laws that aimed at facilitating the modernization of farm enterprises. One, which provided incentives for longer leases (of at least 18 years) by offering landowners tax advantages and better rents, was designed to help alleviate farmers' indebtedness by making them less inclined to buy the land they farmed. The other law

Table 1. Indexes of World Production* of Agricultural, Fishery, and Forestry Products

1952–56 average=100

Item	1960	1964	1968	1969	1970
Total production	119	131	147	148	151
Agriculture	119	132	148	148	151
Fisheries	121	147	177	181	192
Forestry	112	121	128	130	131
Population	112	122	132	134	137
Per capita production	106	108	111	110	110
Agriculture	106	108	112	110	110
Fisheries	107	121	134	135	140
Forestry	100	99	97	97	96

*Excluding China and other Asian centrally planned countries.
Source: Food and Agriculture Organization of the United Nations, *The State of Food and Agriculture* (1971).

Table II. Indexes of World Production of Certain Raw Materials

1963 average=100

Raw material	1961	1965	1968	1969	1970
Coal*	94	105	105	106	109
Crude petroleum	86	116	147	158	173
Cement	89	115	137	143	152
Pig iron†	91	120	138	150	156
Crude steel	91	118	137	148	153
Copper (smelter)‡	95	109	118	128	134
Zinc‡§	93	113	133	144	140
Lead‡§	96	105	115	128	130
Tin‖	95	103	128	124	123
Aluminum‡§	83	120	155	176	187
Natural rubber	101	113	125	137	138

*Including coal equivalent of brown coal and lignite.
†Including ferroalloys.
‡Excluding the U.S.S.R., East Germany, and North Korea.
§Excluding Czechoslovakia and Romania.
‖Excluding the U.S.S.R. and Eastern Europe.
Source: United Nations, *Monthly Bulletin of Statistics* (November 1971).

granted tax privileges to groups engaged in the collective farming of private holdings. It also extended the right to participate in such groups to persons contributing only cash (previously membership was conditional on the ownership of land or real estate), with the aim of slowing down or even reversing the movement of capital out of agriculture.

As specified under art. 39 of the Treaty of Rome, one of the objectives of the common agricultural policy of the EEC was to give the agricultural population an equitable living standard. In 1971 this had not yet been accomplished. Although agriculture in 1969 employed 14% of the total labour force in the EEC, it contributed only 6% of the Community's gross national product. An EEC memorandum in 1968 cited the need for structural reform and social assistance, and in April 1970 firm proposals were made. Although inflation accentuated the relative de-

Table III. Changes in International Prices of Selected Major Commodities

Commodity, unit, country of origin, and market	Wholesale price in U.S. dollars				
	1963	1968	1969	1970	July 1971
Beef (100 lb.) U.K. (London)	27.26	37.78	40.56	41.26	58.56*
Butter (100 lb.) New Zealand (London)	40.88	32.14	32.14	33.49	45.00
Cocoa (100 lb.) Ghana (N.Y.)	25.33	34.40	45.59	34.17	28.35
Coffee (100 lb.) Brazil (N.Y.)	34.11	37.48	40.27	53.57	42.71
Copper (100 lb.) U.K. (London)	29.26	56.09	66.54	64.17	50.56
Copra (100 lb.) Philippines (London)	8.65	10.54	9.23	10.13	8.71*
Cotton (100 lb.) Egypt (Liverpool)	41.81	58.66	63.20	62.60	60.90
Hides (100 lb.) Argentina (London)	21.70	18.00	21.81	21.42	23.95*
Jute (short ton) Pakistan (London)	278.00	290.00	315.00	304.00	309.00*
Lead (100 lb.) U.K. (London)	8.00	10.91	13.14	12.72	11.86
Newsprint (short ton) Canada (Quebec)	116.70	124.00	128.20	131.90	136.70
Peanuts (100 lb.) Nigeria (London)	7.78	7.49	9.38	10.39	11.44*
Petroleum (bbl.) Venezuela (La Cruz)	2.80	2.80	2.80	2.80	2.80
Rice (100 lb.) Thailand (Bangkok)	6.56	9.14	8.30	6.53	5.85
Rubber (100 lb.) Malaysia (Singapore)	23.66	17.33	22.81	18.49	15.02
Sugar (100 lb.) Caribbean (N.Y. for exp.)	8.50	1.98	3.45	3.76	4.20
Tea (100 lb.) Ceylon-India (N.Y.)	53.10	46.00	42.60	45.83	48.10
Tin (100 lb.) Malaysia (Penang)	111.60	138.60	153.40	163.30	156.50
Tobacco (100 lb.) U.S. (U.S.)	58.00	66.50	69.33	n.a.	71.87
Wheat (bu.) Canada (Fort William)	1.83	1.82	1.76	1.71	1.79
Wool (100 lb.) Australia (Sydney)	60.50	51.70	49.50	40.50	34.20
Zinc (100 lb.) U.K. (London)	9.72	11.91	12.69	13.41	14.39

*May 1971.
n.a.=not available.
Source: International Monetary Fund, *International Financial Statistics.*

cline in agricultural incomes in the year following, surpluses were eliminated. Therefore, despite, or perhaps because of, possible accession to the EEC of countries with lower prices, the organization's governing Commission proposed the raising of prices that had remained unchanged for three or four years. But in granting the price hikes, the Commission requested that they be tied to a decision on structural and social programs.

Early in February 1971 the Chilean Senate passed a constitutional amendment granting Pres. Salvador Allende full power to take over the copper interests of U.S. companies. As a result the interest of U.S. companies in Chile's copper properties was completely wiped out. (*See* CHILE.)

After being passed on October 4 by the U.S. House of Representatives (it had previously received Senate approval), a compromise sugar bill was signed a few days later by Pres. Richard Nixon. This new law, entitled the Sugar Act Amendments of 1971, extended the Sugar Act of 1948, as amended, for three years ending Dec. 31, 1974. It continued the division of the U.S. sugar market among domestic and foreign suppliers.

The new sugar law was based on an annual U.S. sugar consumption of 11.2 million short tons, raw value, 100,000 tons below the final adjusted quota for 1971. Of this total, domestic suppliers were allocated 6,910,000 tons, with foreign suppliers getting the balance of 4,290,000 tons.

International Policies. The International Coffee Council met in London from August 16 to 30 to fix quotas and price ranges for the 1971–72 (October–September) coffee year under the International Coffee Agreement. About 98% of the coffee moving in world trade was shipped by members of this pact. The initial overall export quotas were set at a total of 47 million bags (132.3 lb. each), as compared with the 1970–71 final total of 49.5 million bags, which represented several downward adjustments from an initial 54 million bags. These downward adjustments were triggered by declining market prices early in the 1970–71 season. There was a sizable buildup of stocks in consuming countries during 1970–71, but the reverse was expected in 1971–72. Most of the stock changes in both seasons were attributed to the U.S., the world's leading coffee consumer.

The fourth International Tin Agreement became effective July 1, 1971, for a five-year period. Major objectives of this pact (similar to those of its predecessors) were to: (1) prevent surpluses or shortages of tin; (2) prevent wide price fluctuations (largely through the operations of a "buffer" stocks manager who traded in world markets); (3) increase export earnings of tin-producing nations; (4) secure fair prices for consumers while allowing a remunerative return to producers; and (5) take steps (such as increasing or decreasing export quotas of its producer members) to alleviate serious supply or shortage problems. Of the world's tin-consuming countries, 22 had ratified the new agreement by its opening date, including West Germany and the U.S.S.R. for the first time. However, the U.S., the world's largest user of tin, remained outside the pact.

Strong demand for tightening world sugar supplies in late 1971 drove the world free market spot price of sugar up to 7.05 cents per pound, f.o.b. stowed, Caribbean ports, well above the International Sugar Agreement ceiling of 5.25 cents per pound and the highest in more than seven years. As recently as

Common Market:
see Commercial
Policies; European
Unity; *see also* Index
*for information on
specific common
markets*

mid-September, the spot world sugar price was below the set minimum of 3.25 cents per pound.

Most world trade in sugar was protected by such measures as the U.S. sugar quota law, the British tariff preferential for Commonwealth producers, and other forms of subsidies. The rest of the world sugar trade, which accounted for 10 to 15% of world output, moved through the so-called world free market. It was in this market that the International Sugar Agreement attempted to stabilize prices through an export quota system.

Attempting to halt the upsurge in prices, the International Sugar Organization (ISO) on December 21 suspended all agreement quotas, effective Jan. 1, 1972. Previously, the ISO had set 1972 initial export quotas under the agreement at 105% of basic export tonnages. While of the opinion that supplies were sufficient to meet requirements, the ISO stated that it suspended quotas because it believed that the price rises were of a speculative and transient character. The ISO announced that quotas would again be established if the daily price over five days within a period of 17 consecutive market days was at or below the ceiling of 5.25 cents a pound.

Late in September the Cocoa Consultative Committee of the United Nations Conference on Trade and Development met in Geneva to consider a revised draft of an International Cocoa Agreement and to evaluate the feasibility of a full-scale negotiating conference in 1972. The meeting produced no conclusive results, but another meeting was scheduled for January 1972.

Late in 1970 and early in 1971, the Intergovernmental Council of Copper Exporting Countries—Chile, Zambia, the Congo (Kinshasa; now Zaire), and Peru—expressed concern about sagging prices and implied that the countries involved were considering several undisclosed price support plans. These countries accounted for about 80% of the primary copper sold in export markets, and copper provided a major share of their export earnings. Methods of supporting copper prices included: (1) production cutbacks; (2) selling at a fixed price instead of relying on the London Metal Exchange as a pricing basis; (3) export controls; and (4) support buying on the London Metal Exchange. The producers, however, were reluctant to implement any of these price-propping measures and there was serious doubt that they could get together to make them work.

The new International Wheat Agreement, composed of leading wheat-exporting and wheat-importing countries, went into force on July 1, 1971. Unlike the International Grains Arrangement which expired June 30, the new pact contained no minimum and maximum price provisions or related obligations. The old arrangement had called for minimum wheat prices well above quotations on world wheat. However, unable to prevent world prices of wheat from falling below the prescribed minimum levels, it proved to be a failure. Some exporters felt that tighter controls would be required to maintain an acceptable price level, but no agreement could be reached on this principle in the new pact. In view of uncertainties in the outlook for wheat trade, no agreement could be reached either on the range of prices to be established or on the definition of a reference wheat to which prices of other wheats would be related.   (N. R. U.)

See *also* Agriculture; Commercial Policies; Development, Economic; Food; Mining; Payments and Reserves, International; Trade, International.

Commonwealth of Nations

Full members of the Commonwealth at the end of 1971 included: United Kingdom, Australia, Barbados, Botswana, Canada, Ceylon, Cyprus, Fiji, The Gambia, Ghana, Guyana, India, Jamaica, Kenya, Lesotho, Malawi, Malaysia, Malta, Mauritius, New Zealand, Nigeria, Pakistan, Sierra Leone, Singapore, Swaziland, Tanzania, Tonga, Trinidad and Tobago, Uganda, Western Samoa, and Zambia.

At the 1971 meeting of Commonwealth heads of government, held in Singapore, the dominant themes were economic anxieties caused by Britain's proposed membership in the EEC, and concern with policy toward white supremacist southern Africa. It was the first major Commonwealth conference outside London and the largest, with all 31 members represented. Only the skill of Chairman Lee Kuan Yew, prime minister of Singapore, aided by senior members, prevented its degeneration from a unique "body of friends" into a forum for national propaganda. African insistence concentrated attention on southern African problems, particularly the sale of arms to South Africa. British Prime Minister Edward Heath's judgment that Britain must act in its own interests met with vigorous denials from some Afro-Asian members. However, the conference maintained the British view that legal obligations under the Simonstown naval agreement included the supply of limited categories of equipment to South Africa for the defense of sea lanes threatened by the Soviet naval buildup in the Indian Ocean. Three factors emerged from the conference: the agreed value of the association and the need for its existence; agreement that no member should dictate policy to another; and the need to revert to the "no vote, no veto" informality and privacy of early Commonwealth meetings.

Africa. Repercussions of the South African dispute were felt by African leaders who returned home to pressure for and against a policy of "dialogue" with the white-dominated republic. Though denounced by a divisive meeting of the Organization of African Unity, Malawi Pres. H. Kamuzu Banda made history in August as the first black head of state to visit South Africa (returning South African Prime Minister B. J. Vorster's 1970 visit). At about the same time Malawi's Joe Kachingwe became the first black ambassador to the republic.

In Sierra Leone the government moved leftward toward accommodation with Guinea. Nigeria and Ghana, though competing for African leadership, remained bound by domestic problems: Nigeria, despite peace, faced the questions of the return to civilian government and the absorption of a swollen army; Ghana remained bowed by the burden of its external debts and the resultant political and economic frustrations. East African leaders, most vehement against South Africa, faced increasing domestic problems. Pres. Milton Obote of Uganda was deposed in January on his way home from the Commonwealth conference and took refuge in Tanzania, while Gen. Idi Amin, head of the armed forces, took over Uganda's administration. His rightist revolution altered the East African balance of power, though Tanzania refused to recognize the new regime and reports of border fighting between Uganda units and Chinese-led Tanzanians were widespread later in the year.

Construction of the Tanzam (Tanzania-Zambia)

The Rt. Rev. Ambrose Reeves begins a vigil of protest against the imprisonment of the dean of Johannesburg cathedral. The vigil was maintained by relays of clergymen outside the South African embassy in London.

Railway continued with the aid of a £169 million Chinese loan and the importation of 13,000 Chinese personnel by June. The loan was to be repaid by Zambia and Tanzania in equal shares of about £2,750,000 per annum over a period beginning in 1985 and extending into the 21st century. Zambia experienced economic deterioration through a fall in copper production and prices and, with the expansion of nationalization, the loss of foreign confidence and exchange. Former Vice-Pres. Simon Kapwepwe formed a new opposition party against the alleged corruption and the tribal discrimination of Pres. Kenneth Kaunda's UNIP administration. He demanded immediate elections, a new constitution (the old one was suspended in 1969), and economic independence. A decline in corn (maize) production resulted in the humiliation of having to buy 1.5 million bags from Rhodesia.

The long-standing dispute between the U.K. and Rhodesia was finally settled on November 24, when agreement was reached in Salisbury. Relations were to be normalized and sanctions lifted; proportional representation for the African population was deferred, though there were guarantees of political progress. No major guerrilla incidents occurred during the year. The Rhodesian economy prospered both by agricultural diversification and major nickel discoveries, but remained limited by scarcity of foreign exchange and the need to provide for the fastest growing black African population on the continent.

Far East. In April 1971 a conference on Far Eastern defense was held in London between representatives of Australia, Malaysia, New Zealand, Singapore, and the U.K., resulting in a five-power defense agreement for Malaysia and Singapore (effective from November 1971). It was designed to replace the Anglo-Malaysian Defence Agreement and to establish an integrated air defense system for the area and an Air Defence Council responsible for its operation.

In August a South Pacific forum was held in New Zealand, with Australia, Fiji, Western Samoa, Tonga, and Nauru present. The meeting concentrated on interregional trade, the population explosion in relation to resources, and joint diplomatic representation.

Canada and the Mediterranean. Canada, also increasingly aware of its Pacific involvements, was deeply torn by the violence of the Quebec secessionists, though the brilliance of Prime Minister Pierre Trudeau's diplomacy made it the trusted ally of developing Commonwealth nations. At home, concern for Canada's aboriginal Indians resulted in the 1970 Red and Brown papers on the settlement of Indian land claims and in the National Indian Brotherhood Assembly in March 1971, which demanded the right of Indians to decide their own future.

Commonwealth islands in the Mediterranean also reflected increasing violence and instability in world affairs. The Cyprus situation of "negative stability," according to a UN May report, showed no hope for a withdrawal of the 3,000-man UN peacekeeping force and its replacement by an intercommunal political settlement. Increased economic cooperation and the extension of public services to Turkish Cypriots were the most encouraging features of the situation. In the western Mediterranean, Dom Mintoff's Labour Party won victory by one seat in Malta and he threatened to abrogate the Anglo-Maltese agreement unless much larger amounts of aid were provided. NATO's Mediterranean headquarters moved from Malta at Mintoff's request, and the British—possibly spurred by the interest shown by the U.S.S.R. and Libya in replacing British influence in the island—agreed to increase their payments to the Maltese government.

Economic Affairs. The economic future of the Commonwealth was dominated by fears concerning the effect of proposed British membership in the EEC. Those in favour saw a strong Britain within the EEC able to extend greater aid to less developed countries, while others believed British membership to be synonymous with Commonwealth dissolution and economic disaster. To the latter, while the disadvantages to the Commonwealth were seen clearly and specifically (eventual British payment to the EEC of considerably more money than the total aid to the Commonwealth; reduction by 1977 of New Zealand's exports of butter and cheese to Britain to 80 and 20%, respectively), the possible advantages appeared nebulous. Offers of associate status for Commonwealth countries similar to that given the African members of the Yaoundé Convention did not meet a favourable reception. India was not satisfied that Britain's offer of £10 million aid would compensate for its abrogation of the textile trade agreement, and the 17 sugar-producing countries foresaw economic and political disaster should Britain drastically reduce its imports.

Despite long-term eroding influences, Commonwealth trade maintained more than a one-fifth share of the world total. At the June 1971 meeting of Commonwealth trade ministers a Commonwealth Export Market Development Fund was agreed upon as a measure of collective self-help. Private British investment in the Commonwealth was estimated to have reached the target of 1% of the country's gross national product during 1969–70. Though the necessity to collate aid with need was recognized, 1971 showed increasing political pressures on the direction of that aid (as in the case of Pakistan). This was underlined by the merging of the Overseas Development Ministry with the Foreign and Commonwealth Office as the Overseas Development Administration. British aid during 1970–71 totaled about £225 million. The

Commonwealth Development Corporation's gross revenue expanded sharply to £10.4 million, with the largest operating surplus yet recorded at £9.4 million. Nonetheless, nationalization of foreign assets by less developed countries and their seeming refusal or inability to equalize benefits and prevent aid from being swamped by population expansion made Western sources less amenable to their demands.   (M. Mr.)

See also articles on the various political units.

Communist Movement

In the world Communist movement, 1971 was marked by a concerted effort on the part of the Soviet Communist Party and most of the Moscow-oriented parties to strengthen what was left of the movement's unity and to consolidate domestic bases of support. Although this Soviet-inspired attempt met with moderate success, it once again ran afoul of the obstacles that had frustrated similar efforts in the past: the continuing antagonism of the Chinese Communists and other "left-revisionist" elements; the appeal for many Communists of the libertarian "right-revisionist" ideas that had inspired the Czechoslovak reformers in 1968; nationalism within the movement; and, outside, the lingering mistrust of Communist intentions by various allied anti-imperialist and national liberation movements.

Soviet Efforts at Consolidation. The need to submerge differences and to achieve a more disciplined unity was the major theme of the uneventful 24th congress of the Soviet Communist Party, which finally assembled in Moscow in March–April 1971. The tone was set by the party's general secretary, Leonid I. Brezhnev, who emerged from the congress with his authority in the Soviet collective leadership considerably enhanced. He indicated that whereas certain economic concessions should be made to the population in order to maintain domestic support, any manifestations of ideological dissent would be combated, and that whereas a certain degree of diversity could exist within the Communist movement, anti-Soviet activity or the questioning of fundamental tenets could not be permitted. Brezhnev pledged full support to the anti-imperialist struggles in Indochina and the Middle East, but also reiterated the Soviet desire for peaceful coexistence with capitalist states.

The 24th congress of the CPSU represented the largest international gathering of Communist and allied leaders since the 1969 Moscow World Conference of Communist and Workers' Parties; 101 foreign delegations from 90 countries were present, and most of the assembled leaders demonstrated their willingness to contribute to the spirit of solidarity and "normalization." Even the Japanese party, which had banned the representatives of both Moscow and Peking from its own congress in 1970, was sufficiently reconciled to send a delegation. However, the underlying differences within the movement could not be totally submerged. Neither the Chinese nor the Albanians attended the congress; pro-Chinese parties, such as those of Thailand, Burma, and Malaysia, were absent; and neither the divided Philippine party nor the decimated Indonesian party sent representatives. On the other side of the political spectrum, the parties of the Netherlands and Iceland both boycotted the congress, and the Yugoslavs sent only a second-rank leader. Nicolae Ceausescu, the general secretary of the Romanian party, pointedly restated his party's belief

Communications:
see
Telecommunications;
Television and Radio

in the principle of noninterference in the internal affairs of one party by another. The Italian party representative similarly called for full independence of each party and country.

Following the congress, the Soviet leadership vigorously set about furthering consolidation of the pro-Moscow forces. Brezhnev personally traveled to the 10th congress of the Bulgarian party in April, to the 14th congress of the Czechoslovak party in May, and to the 8th congress of the East German party in June, and other party congresses were visited by lesser functionaries. However, by early summer these efforts began to sour. In June, Ceausescu dramatically reiterated his party's neutrality in the Sino-Soviet dispute by embarking on a widely publicized trip to China, North Vietnam, and North Korea. On top of this came the surprise announcement in July of a forthcoming visit by U.S. Pres. Richard Nixon to China, an event that could not fail to exacerbate the already tense relations between the two largest Communist states. Only a few weeks later the Soviet leaders experienced another embarrassing setback when an attempt by pro-Moscow Communists to seize power in Sudan ended with the execution of several Sudanese Communist leaders.

In August the Soviet leaders summoned the leaders of the Eastern European Communist parties (except Ceausescu) to a conference with Brezhnev in the Crimea. Pressures, such as military maneuvers by Warsaw Treaty forces in Hungary, were used to bring the Romanians into line, and Soviet polemics against the Chinese were increased. In a flurry of activity, the U.S.S.R. signed an accord with the U.S., Britain, and France on the status of Berlin; Brezhnev met with West German Chancellor Willy Brandt to discuss the improvement of Soviet-West German relations and then traveled to Paris to meet French leaders; and Soviet Premier Aleksei N. Kosygin scheduled trips to Canada, Norway, and Denmark. In October an invitation was issued to President Nixon to come to Moscow in May 1972. On its southern flank the Soviets signed a 20-year friendship treaty with India and, in October, Soviet Pres. Nikolai V. Podgorny traveled to North Vietnam with promises of aid. At the same time, promises of aid were given to Pres. Anwar as-Sadat of Egypt. By the end of the year it could be said that, although Soviet hopes for greater unity within the Communist movement were still far from fulfillment, their actions in countering the midyear reversals had been moderately successful.

The Communist Movement in Europe. In mid-August warnings appeared in the Hungarian press asserting that Peking planned to form a pro-Chinese entente in the Balkans composed of Albania, Yugoslavia, and Romania. At the time a high-ranking Chinese delegation was visiting Albania and Romania, and the Soviet-inspired "war of nerves" designed to bring the Romanian party into line was at its height.

That Albania was named a part of this alleged entente came as no surprise, since that tiny Communist country has been China's one outpost in Europe for a decade. However, the inclusion of nonaligned, "right-revisionist" Yugoslavia could only have been a reflection of Soviet bloc resentment at Yugoslavia's neutral stance in the Sino-Soviet dispute, its backing of Romania, and its strong insistence on noninterference in interparty affairs. Yugoslavia's relationship with China had improved considerably since 1968, but in 1971 Marshal Tito and his associates

were far too preoccupied with internal problems to become seriously entangled in the Sino-Soviet rivalry. Of particular concern were the twin problems of national disunity within the multinational republic and an ever worsening inflationary spiral. In April and May the aging President Tito angrily reasserted his authority, and in July, despite earlier announcements that a collective presidency should be formed to succeed him, he accepted reelection as president for a five-year term at the head of an enlarged 22-man presidency.

In fact, the maneuvers and warnings were primarily aimed at Romania, even though, in 1971, Ceausescu's regime had demonstrated a greater willingness to cooperate with its Soviet bloc neighbours than had previously been the case. In January, Romania finally agreed to participate with other Comecon members in their international investment bank. In the spring Ceausescu accepted a visit from Czechoslovak party leader Gustav Husak, sent the Romanian defense minister to a Warsaw Pact meeting, and joined the other Communist states in blaming Israel for the Middle East situation. Undoubtedly it was such compromises, combined with conservative internal policies, that kept Soviet hostility to Romania's external policies, particularly in regard to China, from assuming a more dramatic form.

Hungary, in many ways the reverse image of Romania, remained the most politically, economically, and culturally liberal regime in the Soviet bloc, purchasing its controlled reformism at the expense of conformity to Soviet wishes in external matters. It was not surprising, therefore, that the Hungarians should have played an active role in the midyear "war of nerves" against Romania. More surprising was the fact that the Bulgarian Communists did not take a more active part. Under Todor Zhivkov's leadership, Bulgaria continued to give the appearance of being Moscow's most loyal adherent, with the possible exception of Mongolia. However, certain differences on questions of economic priorities and of relations with Bulgaria's rival, Yugoslavia, might indicate that strains were developing in the relationship.

With an estimated 80,000 Soviet troops stationed in his country and with ultraconservative rivals eager to replace him, Czechoslovakia's Husak had little choice but to tailor both his domestic and foreign policies to Soviet specifications. Throughout 1971, literally every other month, Husak either journeyed to the Soviet Union or received a high-level Soviet delegation in Prague. At the Czechoslovak party's 14th congress in May, with Brezhnev looking on, Husak announced that the post-invasion "normalization" was now completed, but that vigilance was still required to forestall any recurrence of "revisionism." There was considerable evidence that, despite some improvement in economic conditions, the Czechoslovak regime still lacked the support of a majority of the population, and that apathy and cynicism remained widespread, particularly among the youth.

A similar preoccupation with domestic problems was to be found among the Polish and East German Communists. Spurred by the disastrous Gdansk riots that had toppled Polish party chief Wladyslaw Gomulka from power in December 1970, Gomulka's successor, Edward Gierek, tried to regain popular support for his regime and to stimulate economic growth. (See POLAND: *Special Report.*)

As in Poland, it was the deteriorating economic

Membership of the Major Communist Parties of the World*

Countries with a membership of 2,000 or more persons

Country	Membership
Albania	75,670†
Argentina	60,000
Australia	3,900
Austria	25,000
Belgium	12,500
Bolivia‡	4,500
Brazil‡	14,000
Bulgaria	637,300†
Burma‡	§
Canada	2,000
Ceylon	2,300
Chile	45,000
China	17,000,000†
Colombia	9,000
Cuba	125,000†
Cyprus	13,000
Czechoslovakia	1,200,000
Denmark	5,000
Finland	47,000†
France	275,000
Germany, East	1,900,000†
Germany, West	28,500
Greece‡	28,000
Hungary	662,400†
India	144,500
Iraq‡	2,000
Israel	2,000
Italy	1,500,000
Japan	300,000
Korea, North	1,600,000†
Laos	13,000
Malaysia‡	2,000
Mexico	5,000
Mongolia	48,600†
Nepal‡	9,000
Netherlands	11,000
Norway	2,000
Paraguay‡	4,500
Peru	3,200
Philippines‡	2,000
Poland	2,296,000†
Portugal‡	2,000
Romania	1,999,700†
Spain‡	5,000
Sudan	7,500
Sweden	17,000
Switzerland	3,500
Syria‡	3,000
U.S.S.R.	14,254,000†
United Kingdom	32,000
U.S.	§
Uruguay	20,000
Venezuela	8,000
Vietnam, North	1,100,000†
Vietnam, South‡	§
Yugoslavia	1,146,100†

*Estimated from figures available December 1970.
†Official claim.
‡Communist Party illegal.
§No estimate available.
Source: U.S. Department of State, Bureau of Intelligence and Research, "World Strength of the Communist Party Organizations" (May 1971).

Leonid Brezhnev (centre),
general secretary
of the Soviet Communist
Party, and Czechoslovak
leaders Gustav Husak
(left) and Ludvik Svoboda
(right) accept greetings
at the 14th Czechoslovak
Communist Party Congress
in Prague in May 1971.

Canadians parade
on Parliament Hill
in Ottawa to support
a statement
by the Communist Party
of Canada that the U.S.
had declared economic war
on the rest of the world.

situation in East Germany that provided the impetus to retire Walter Ulbricht, who had headed the Communist Party there for a quarter of a century. The transfer of power was carried out in a far more orderly fashion, however, with an announcement at a session of the party's Central Committee in early May that the aging Ulbricht had decided to step down as first secretary in favour of his close associate Erich Honecker. Reports that high-level discord had accompanied Ulbricht's ouster received greater credibility later in the year as new measures were introduced to deal with "distortions" that had been allowed to develop in the economy. It also became clear that Honecker would be more compliant than Ulbricht in acceding to Soviet policy concerning Berlin, West Germany, and the European détente.

Soviet attempts to impose unity among the Western European Communist parties were only partially successful. The two largest parties, those of Italy and France, persisted in criticizing some aspects of the Soviet system, even at the height of the Soviet efforts to smooth over differences during the spring. The Italian party was especially emphatic in its insistence on polycentrism within the movement and on respect for the principle of noninterference in interparty affairs. This led the Italian Communists, in spite of their problems with the Italian Maoists, to join the Romanians and others in remaining neutral in the Sino-Soviet dispute. The death in September of former Soviet Premier Nikita Khrushchev, the initiator of destalinization, provided yet another occasion for divergence to be expressed. While many parties in Eastern Europe and some in the West followed the Soviet lead in giving only a delayed and perfunctory announcement of the death, a number of Western parties, including the British and Italians, produced considerable praise for the former Soviet leader.

Communism in Asia. In 1971 the Chinese Communists continued to pursue their post-Cultural Revolution policies of general intransigence toward Soviet "revisionism," political and economic stabilization at

home, and new diplomatic initiatives abroad. Although formal state relations had been resumed between the Soviet Union and China in October 1970, during 1971 the Chinese disdainfully rebuffed several Soviet offers to take positive steps toward reconciliation. The internal political situation in China remained cloudy and there were indications of a major political crisis at the highest levels. At the provincial level, however, party committees reportedly had been reestablished with strong military participation, and the economic situation was well on the way to recovery. The figure of Premier Chou En-lai loomed large, particularly in international relations where the process of breaking out of the self-imposed isolation of the Cultural Revolution was epitomized by China's acceptance by the UN. (*See* UNITED NATIONS.)

According to a statement made by Chou En-lai in June, the aim of most of the Chinese diplomatic offensive was the formation of a "united front" of small and medium-sized powers that could resist the political, economic, and military hegemony of the U.S. and the U.S.S.R. In fact, Chinese foreign policy seemed to be aimed primarily against the Soviet Union, particularly as China moved from personal and Ping-Pong diplomacy to the announcement of President Nixon's visit. Advantageous as this move toward a Sino-American détente may have been for China, it clearly disturbed the Communist leaders of Vietnam, North Korea, the Pathet Lao, and other Chinese allies.

The North Vietnamese continued their skillful efforts to maintain the support of both China and the Soviet Union without becoming dependent on either. In March, soon after Chou En-lai visited Hanoi, the North Vietnamese party leader, Le Duan, arrived in Moscow to deliver a speech at the 24th party congress. However, en route to and from the congress, Le Duan and the Viet Cong and Pathet Lao delegations were careful to stop in Peking for discussions. The North Koreans had tried to maintain a similar balance between the two Communist giants. Although they were implicated in the Chinese-style insurrection in Ceylon in May, which was suppressed with Soviet assistance, they signed a new trade agreement with the U.S.S.R. early in the year and exchanged high-level visits with Moscow.

Communism in Latin America. In past years the Soviet emphasis on peaceful coexistence and the possibility of Communists gaining power through peaceful means had come under severe attack from those Latin-American Communists who subscribed to the more violent revolutionary outlook of the Cubans or the Chinese. Such attacks subsided considerably in 1971, even though many Latin-American Communist parties continued to suffer from intense factionalism. This came about for a variety of reasons, including the lack of visible success encountered by rural-based guerrilla movements and the emergence of left-wing anti-American military regimes such as the one in Peru. At the same time, some of the lustre of the Cuban model had worn off as Fidel Castro was forced to devote his primary energies to his overwhelming domestic economic problems.

Another cause of the decline in criticism was the success achieved in 1970 by the Chilean Communists in winning power by legal means in alliance with the Socialist Party of Salvador Allende Gossens. As the policies of the Allende government, particularly the nationalization of American businesses in Chile, led to a steady worsening of relations with the U.S. during 1971, Chilean trade, aid, and diplomatic contacts with Communist states expanded. The Chilean model was attractive to many nonruling Communists, particularly in Western Europe, as an example of a popularly elected Marxist government that permitted opposition parties and newspapers to function. Nevertheless, the alternative model of the urban guerrillas continued to attract the interest of a small but active segment of the Latin-American movement.

(D. Ws.)

See also China; Czechoslovakia; Defense; Intelligence Operations; Soviet Bloc Economies; and articles on the various countries.

ENCYCLOPÆDIA BRITANNICA FILMS. *China: A Portrait of the Land* (1967); *China's Industrial Revolution* (1967); *China's Villages in Change* (1967).

Computers

The computer industry was shaken in September, when RCA Corp. announced its withdrawal from computer manufacturing. Not even the announcement in May 1970 that General Electric would be selling its computer business to Honeywell, Inc. caused such reverberations—General Electric, at least, had a buyer when it made the announcement.

RCA had hoped to dispose of its entire computer business in a single package, but in late November Sperry Rand Corp. agreed in principle to acquire the RCA customer base for its UNIVAC division for up to $130 million to be paid over five years. Sperry Rand would also hire about 2,500 former RCA employees. The agreement left RCA with two plants to sell and several foreign trade agreements to settle.

Following RCA's withdrawal, computer users faced a sharply increased risk if they made long-term commitments with any other computer manufacturer but International Business Machines Corp. (IBM), in the judgment of most observers. RCA had endeavoured to make its machines as nearly compatible with IBM's as possible and had failed, in spite of its position as one of the largest and strongest companies in the U.S. General Electric suffered a similar fate, without trying to be compatible. Therefore, the reasoning went, many customers would desert the remaining smaller companies in favour of IBM. Thus, customers who stayed with the smaller companies ran the risk of being left with an "orphan" computer and no source of parts or service, if its maker followed General Electric and RCA out of the business, or merged with another company.

RCA's announcement involved three major decisions: to discontinue "the manufacture and marketing of general-purpose central processors"; to concentrate effort in the development, manufacture, and marketing of specialized data communications systems; and to continue maintaining previously installed computers and other equipment through its subsidiary, the RCA Service Co.

In other developments during the year IBM continued an aggressive price adjustment policy that it had begun in 1970. These adjustments were widely interpreted as moves to counter increasing competition from a number of independent manufacturers who were offering equipment that could replace IBM's directly but at much lower prices. These companies were doing well in spite of the general economic recession because customers hard hit by the recession were cutting costs by installing their less expensive equipment.

At first, IBM's price adjustments took the form of a three-pronged attack: the company introduced new peripherals—primarily magnetic tape and disk storage units—offering much higher performance than existing models at only slightly higher prices; it announced new models that were essentially identical to existing ones but were priced much lower; and it began to permit 24-hour, 7-day use of some leased peripheral equipment at the same charges as for 8-hour, 5-day-per-week use. Later, IBM began offering long-term leases on such equipment at substantially lower monthly rates than it had previously offered on month-to-month leases—a policy the independents had employed extensively. Then IBM increased lease and purchase prices from 3 to 8% on its principal central processor models, saying that they reflected the increased cost of doing business. Purchase prices went up immediately upon the announcement, at the end of June; the lease price increase was scheduled for November 1, but did not go into effect then because of the administration's wage-price freeze.

Minicomputers. During 1971 the first units of IBM's smallest computers, announced late in 1970, were shipped to customers. These were the System 3 model 6, a small general-purpose machine, and the System 7, for such applications as process control, data acquisition, and laboratory instrumentation. The advent of these machines was expected to intensify the shake-out of small firms making minicomputers, many of which had been forced into merger or bankruptcy by the economic recession of 1970. Availability of the small machines from IBM was expected to increase the pressure on such small firms, although the brightening economic picture was encouraging to them. Also encouraging to the minicomputer market was the appearance in late 1970 and during 1971 of low-cost peripheral equipment designed specifically for use with minicomputers—as opposed to cheap versions of large computer peripherals. These included small printers and machines for handling punched cards, as well as magnetic tape and disk units.

But the improvement in the economy came too late for Viatron Computer Systems Corp., a company established in 1968 to build and sell very small computers interlinked with communication lines for the extremely inexpensive price of $39 a month. Viatron had hoped to make this low price possible by building its machines with the latest large-scale integrated circuits, and by leasing them in very large quantities to businesses of all kinds and sizes. But although the initial response to its efforts was good, it encountered serious technical and financial problems and was forced into bankruptcy in April.

Considerable interest was expressed during the year in networks of interconnected minicomputers—said to be as effective for many purposes as a single large computer, and much less expensive. One estimate, for example, proposed that a network of eight machines with 16-bit word lengths and 1-microsecond cycle times, costing $10,000 each, could equal the performance of a $1 million machine operating twice as fast with words four times as long.

A new approach to minicomputer marketing was undertaken in the early spring of 1971 with the introduction by Computer Automation, Inc. of a "naked" minicomputer consisting only of a processor, a small core memory, and normally available software; it had no power supply, console, or chassis. These machines were offered as subassemblies to manufacturers of other equipment which already incorporated the nec-

Design model of the new
IBM 3270 information
display station
is operated
with an electronic pen.

essary power supplies and other accessories. Some other manufacturers followed Computer Automation's lead with their own stripped-down versions.

But Digital Equipment Corp., the largest company in the minicomputer field, countered with its own version of its two main minicomputer lines, the PDP-11/05 and the PDP-8/M. These machines, like Computer Automation's, also were offered to manufacturers of other equipment but were supposed to overcome the hidden overhead in the stripped-down versions.

Displays. Several significant new developments in plasma display panels occurred in 1971. The panels, invented in 1966 at the University of Illinois, were flat and only about $\frac{1}{2}$ in. thick; they were potentially much less expensive than cathode-ray tubes, yet were suitable for many similar display applications. The simplest kind of plasma panel presented an image made up of yellowish-red dots that were either on or off (lighted or dark); it retained an image indefinitely without external refreshing as long as the power was on. Owens-Illinois Corp. marketed this form of the panel under a license from the University of Illinois. An alternative form, introduced by the Burroughs Corp. in 1969 under the trade name Self-Scan, required refreshing but was much more economical to build because it needed considerably less external electronic circuitry to control it.

In 1971 Owens-Illinois developed a version of the monochrome panel that would display up to seven discrete colours; and Burroughs described an experimental variation of the Self-Scan design that permitted the colour of the display to vary continuously from yellowish-red to green. Burroughs, Bell Laboratories, and Zenith Radio Corp. developed ways of adding a "gray scale" to the display, which would permit halftone-like images to be displayed. For the University of Illinois the Magnavox Corp. developed a full display unit using Owens-Illinois-produced monochrome non-gray-scale panels.

Progress was made during the year on two rather advanced methods of displaying information in a computer. One was the head-mounted display, being developed as a research project at the University of

Utah. The other was a tactile display, also a research project, at the University of North Carolina.

The head-mounted display consists of two small cathode-ray tubes that simultaneously display computer-generated images, each slightly different so as to preserve a stereoscopic effect. The tubes are mounted on the sides of a headset that the user wears like a hat; prismatic goggles on the helmet permit the wearer to observe the image on the cathode-ray tube screens while he also sees his surroundings. The system includes a means by which the position and orientation of the headset, and thus of the wearer's head, is continuously transmitted to the computer. With this information, the computer continually updates the stereoscopic display, so that the headset wearer has the impression that he is inside the display and can walk around and look at it from various angles.

At the University of North Carolina, the tactile display was the outgrowth of the concept that one's eyes need not be the only means of receiving information from a computer. A common means of putting information into a computer is by means of a "joystick," a small lever that can be tilted in various directions and which, as it tilts, operates potentiometers or digital shaft encoders that transmit information about the angle of the lever into the computer. Often this information is processed to alter the position of a spot, or cursor, on the display screen of a cathode-ray tube. If a pattern is displayed on the screen that represents, for example, an electric field, and if the cursor represents a charged particle, then the motions imparted to it via the joystick may be resisted by the forces in the electric field. The tactile display is a means by which the human operator feels these forces in his fingertips. They are transmitted to him through computer-driven servomotors connected to the joystick mechanism along with the shaft encoders.

The first attempts to design such a tactile display used a two-dimensional input quite similar to the ordinary input device often used with displays. Also being developed was a seven-dimensional unit, being converted from a pair of remote manipulators ordinarily used for handling radioactive material; its seven dimensions are the three linear coordinate directions, rotations around them, and a grasping motion.

Other Developments. In the spring of 1971 the Federal Aviation Administration (FAA) installed a prototype associative processor as part of the air traffic control equipment at the Knoxville, Tenn., airport. The processor was Goodyear Aerospace Corp.'s Staran 4, which in full-fledged form would be able to keep track of hundreds of aircraft, isolate those on collision courses or in other potentially hazardous situations, and provide information for display, at perhaps 200 times the speed of conventional machines. A single module in the Staran computer contained 256 words of 256 bits each; Goodyear engineers, investigating various applications for the computer, found none that would require more than 16 of these modules. At Knoxville only one module, operating at only one-quarter of its capacity, was sufficient for the traffic density at that airport and for the FAA's tests. By early fall the computer had passed its initial tests and was being used operationally for tracking, while the conflict-prediction software (programs and procedures) was still being developed; Goodyear Aerospace was looking forward to building more and larger systems for use in larger airports.

Early in the year a computer called Symbol, which had a high-level programming language implemented directly in the hardware, was completed, following an eight-year development project. The computer, quite different in concept from conventional machines, was built at the Digital Systems Research department of Fairchild Camera and Instrument Co., Palo Alto, Calif. It represented an important advance by hardware into a previously all-software realm.

Illiac 4, the giant array processor conceived at the University of Illinois, sponsored by the Advanced Research Projects Agency of the U.S. Department of Defense and built in the laboratories of Burroughs Corp., neared completion in 1971. It was scheduled for shipment to the Ames Research Laboratory of the National Aeronautics and Space Administration (NASA), Moffett Field, Calif., in the spring of 1972, where it would be used largely for research into the aerodynamics of high-performance aircraft.

(W. B. Rɪ.)

Congolese Pres. Joseph Mobutu (right) and French Foreign Minister Maurice Schumann sign an agreement for cultural and technical cooperation between their countries, April 5, 1971.

Congo, Democratic Republic of the

A republic of equatorial Africa, the Congo (Kinshasa), officially renamed Zaire on Oct. 27, 1971, is bounded by the Central African Republic, Sudan, Uganda, Rwanda, Burundi, Tanzania, Zambia, Angola, the Congo (Brazzaville), and the Atlantic Ocean. Area: 905,360 sq.mi. (2,344,885 sq.km.). Pop. (1971 est.): 22,548,830. Cap. and largest city: Kinshasa (pop., 1971 est., 1,463,402). Language: French; Bantu dialects, mainly Swahili and Lingala. Religion: animist approximately 50%; Christian 43%. President in 1971, Joseph Mobutu.

After his uncontested reelection on Oct. 31–Nov. 1, 1970, President Mobutu on December 6 announced amnesty for all rebels who returned to the country by Jan. 31, 1971. A number of former opponents of the state responded, among them Christophe Gbenye, minister of the interior in the governments of Patrice Lumumba and Cyrille Adoula. Gbenye had left Kinshasa in 1963 to become one of the leaders of the pro-Lumumbist uprising against the government of the time and in 1964 proclaimed himself president of the Congolese People's Republic. He subsequently lived in Uganda, Egypt, and Sudan. On his return he announced his support for the policies of Mobutu. Others who took advantage of the president's offer included Michel Mongali, another former minister in Adoula's government, and Nicolas Olenga.

The threat of a scandal involving EEC aid to the Congo made the headlines in January. A West German newspaper published a version of a report prepared by the EEC Commission suggesting that funds granted for the training of between 500 and 600 managerial staff working for the Congolese transportation organization, Otraco, had been misused. The implementation of the plan had been left by the EEC to a West German firm. The aim was to overcome the deficiency in managerial staff suffered after independence and the departure of the Belgians who formerly had occupied the more important posts. The report was said to have alleged that people had been paid without ever going to the Congo, while others had not fulfilled their contracts. The company concerned replied that while there had been difficulties in obtaining documents for some of its personnel, which

resulted in a delay in their arrival in the Congo, and while trainees frequently had been unavailable because of the pressure of their duties, the real origin of the charges lay in the rivalry within the EEC Commission itself over the best means of using funds in emergent territories.

In June the Congolese ambassador to Britain, Gervais Bahizi, and his second in command, Joseph Kalume, were recalled abruptly. It was thought that the reason lay in Mobutu's disappointment over the breakdown of plans for his official visit to Britain, which was to have taken place early in the month.

On October 27 the nation officially changed its name to Zaire. This was the original name of the Congo

CONGO, DEMOCRATIC REPUBLIC OF THE
Education. (1967–68) Primary, pupils 2,338,895, teachers 61,264; secondary, pupils 98,528; vocational, pupils 34,704; teacher training, students 39,892; secondary, vocational, and teacher training, teachers 6,723; higher (including 3 universities), students 5,827, teaching staff 812.
Finance. Monetary unit: zaire, with an official exchange rate of 0.50 zaire to U.S. $1 (1.20 zaires = £1 sterling) and a free market rate (Sept. 27, 1971) of 1.24 zaires to £1 sterling. Gold, SDRs, and foreign exchange, central bank: (March 1971) U.S. $144 million; (March 1970) U.S. $197 million. Budget: revenue (1970 est.) 215 million zaires; expenditure (1971 est.) 285 million zaires. Money supply: (Feb. 1971) 175,630,000 zaires; (Feb. 1970) 153,380,000 zaires. Cost of living (Kinshasa; 1963 = 100): (Jan. 1971) 382; (Jan. 1970) 379.
Foreign Trade. (1969) Imports 205.1 million zaires; exports 322.2 million zaires. Import sources: Belgium-Luxembourg 20%; West Germany 10%; U.S. 9%; France 7%; U.K. 7%. Export destinations: Belgium-Luxembourg 57%; Italy 11%; France 8%; U.K. 8%; West Germany 6%. Main exports: copper 67%; diamonds 5%; coffee 4%.
Transport and Communications. Roads (1970) 140,000 km. Motor vehicles in use (1969): passenger 67,636; commercial 26,412. Railways: (1970) 5,795 km.; traffic (1969) 614 million passenger-km., freight 2,073,000,000 net ton-km. Air traffic (1969): 364,782,000 passenger-km.; freight 12,501,000 net ton-km. Shipping (1970): merchant vessels 100 gross tons and over 6; gross tonnage 28,817. Inland waterways (including Congo River; 1969) c. 13,700 km. Telephones (Dec. 1969) 33,478. Radio receivers (Dec. 1970) c. 65,000. Television receivers (Dec. 1970) c. 7,100.
Agriculture. Production (in 000; metric tons; 1969; 1968 in parentheses): rice 130 (130); corn 350 (250); sweet potatoes and yams 350 (c. 257); cassava 10,000 (c. 8,000); palm oil c. 250 (c. 223); palm kernels c. 110 (c. 100); rubber (exports; 1970) c. 42, (1969) 41; cotton, lint 20 (12); coffee (1970) c. 72, (1969) c. 66; peanuts 200 (c. 200). Livestock (in 000; Dec. 1969): cattle c. 900; sheep c. 570; goats (Dec. 1968) 1,545; pigs c. 442.
Industry. Production (in 000; metric tons; 1969): coal 65; copper 236; zinc 64; tin 1.8; cobalt ore (metal content) 10; manganese ore (metal content) 165; gold (troy oz.) 176; diamonds (metric carats) 13,423; electricity (kw-hr.) 2,912,000.

Confederation of Arab Republics: see Libya; Syria; United Arab Republic

River, which would also be renamed the Zaire River.

After demonstrations at the University of Lovanium at Kinshasa in June, almost the whole student body of 3,074 men and women was conscripted into the Army for two years. Students of Lubumbashi University who, in sympathy, volunteered to undergo the same training were drafted for seven years. Lovanium was temporarily closed and renamed the University of Kinshasa. In July about 20–30 Eastern European diplomats, said to have instigated the troubles, were given 48 hours to leave the country. Relations with Portugal had so improved toward the end of the year that some guerrillas based in Kinshasa, notably the Communist-backed Movement for the Liberation of Angola, moved their headquarters to Zambia. In August several opposition members were tried. (*See* CONGO, PEOPLE'S REPUBLIC OF THE.)

Under consideration on the economic front were various large-scale projects with foreign participants, notably the U.S. and Japan. These included the mining of copper deposits in east Congo, exploitation of petroleum found off the coast, and construction of an iron smelter in Maluku. (K. I.)

Congo, People's Republic of the

A people's republic of equatorial Africa, the Congo (Brazzaville) is bounded by Gabon, Cameroon, the Central African Republic, the Congo (Kinshasa), Angola, and the Atlantic Ocean. Area: 132,000 sq.mi. (342,000 sq.km.). Pop. (1970): 1,089,300, mainly Bantu. Cap. and largest city: Brazzaville (pop., 1970, 175,000). Language: French (official) and Bantu dialects. Religion: mainly animist, with a strong Christian minority. President in 1971, Maj. Marien Ngouabi.

Political developments in the Congo in 1971 revolved around two central themes: unconditional adherence to the revolutionary line laid down by the leadership in Brazzaville, and the strengthening of ties with China.

In February and in June, there were Cabinet re-

CONGO, PEOPLE'S REPUBLIC OF THE
Education. (1968–69) Primary, pupils 212,259, teachers 3,676; secondary, pupils 21,901, teachers 657; vocational, pupils 2,607, teachers 274; teacher training, students 604, teachers 35; higher, students 1,485, teaching staff 116.
Finance. Monetary unit: CFA franc, with a parity of CFA Fr. 50 to the French franc (CFA Fr. 277.71 = U.S. $1; CFA Fr. 666.50 = £1 sterling) and a free rate (Sept. 27, 1971) of CFA Fr. 276.50 to U.S. $1 (CFA Fr. 685.75 = £1 sterling). Budget (1970 est.) balanced at CFA Fr. 18.1 billion.
Foreign Trade. (1970) Imports CFA Fr. 16,640,-000,000; exports CFA Fr. 8,560,000,000. Import sources (1968): France 58%; West Germany 10%; U.S. 5%. Export destinations (1968): West Germany 25%; Netherlands 19%; Belgium-Luxembourg 14%; France 12%; Israel 6%; South Africa 6%. Main exports: timber 53%; diamonds 9%.
Transport and Communications. Roads (1970) *c.* 11,000 km. (including 243 km. with improved surface). Motor vehicles in use (1968): passenger 7,235; commercial 5,585. Railways: (1968) 797 km.; traffic (1970) 144 million passenger-km., freight 516 million net ton-km. Air traffic (1969): 67,657,000 passenger-km.; freight 6,187,000 net ton-km. Telephones (Dec. 1969) 9,812. Radio receivers (Dec. 1969) 62,000. Television receivers (Dec. 1969) 500.
Agriculture. Production (in 000; metric tons; 1969; 1968 in parentheses): cassava 450 (400); coffee 1.8 (1.8); peanuts 20 (17); palm kernels (exports) 2.8 (4); palm oil 5.7 (5.7). Livestock (in 000; 1969–70): sheep *c.* 58; cattle *c.* 37; pigs 17.

shuffles that might fairly be interpreted as purges in the leadership. In March several members of a "gang of counterrevolutionaries" were arrested, accused of having prepared leaflets inciting civil war. They were later tried and sentenced by a military court in Brazzaville. For alleged "subjectivist and tribalist attitudes," Capt. Kibouala Kaya was relieved in April of his position as political commissar for the Army and head of the armoured corps. In May, disquieted by the attitude of the police force, the government merged it with the Army. The Brazzaville authorities closed down the office of the French news agency, Agence France-Presse, in June, accusing its representative of seeking to set the two Congolese republics against one another.

Emulation of China proceeded apace. From May 1, all Congolese workers were obliged to wear a uniform. Moreover, the uniform was to be made from fabrics manufactured at a textile factory set up by the Chinese. Sino-Congolese connections continued to multiply in every sphere. In May the leaders in Peking promised to build a hydroelectric dam on the Bouenza River 250 mi. W of Brazzaville. Also in the spring, 55 Congolese soldiers visited China to undergo a specialized training course there, and in September an agreement on military cooperation with China was signed.

Relations with the neighbouring Democratic Republic of the Congo remained poor, despite various attempts at normalization. In the Democratic Republic, several members of the opposition were tried and sentenced in Kinshasa in August. They were accused, as members of a "Lumumbist" organization, of having plotted with the leadership in Brazzaville to overthrow Gen. Joseph Mobutu, president of the Democratic Republic. At the end of the month, each government proceeded to expel the diplomats of its "sister state." (PH. D.)

Consumer Affairs

The development of consumer affairs in 1971 was characterized by three main trends: widening recognition of consumer interest as a distinct factor in society; continuing growth of the consumer movement, as represented by consumer organizations at the international, national, and local levels; and expansion of the movement's traditional activities—product evaluation, information and education, and pressure for legislation—into new and broader fields of consumer interest. Outside the U.S. there was little evidence in 1971 of the emergence in the consumer sphere of "public interest" groups, of which the Center for Study of Responsive Law and other Ralph Nader (*see* BIOGRAPHY) activities were best known. One possible explanation was that in other countries, notably in Europe, there already existed adequate machinery for surveillance and control of state and other public activities. But in September the U.K.-based representative of Nader's organization told a London newspaper of his plans, after a two-month survey of the problem, to force the British government to reveal the U.K.'s pollution secrets.

The increasing impact of consumerism on public affairs was reflected in the growing incidence of consumer-oriented legislation in many countries, and in the deepening involvement of governments, both nationally and internationally, in consumer affairs. At the national and local levels, consumer legislation

Congregational Churches:
see Religion

Conservation:
see Environment

Construction Industry:
see Engineering Projects; Housing; Industrial Review

and recommendations for new legislation covered a wide field. Examples were reforms of New Zealand laws relating to credit transactions to provide protection for the debtor; the Food Act passed in Sweden in June introducing new regulations covering food standards, additives, labeling, and handling, and the appointment of a consumer ombudsman; a comprehensive government statement in West Germany on federal consumer policy; and the introduction in Norway of regulations making consumer education compulsory from 1972 in all schools for children aged 7–15.

In the U.K. the Crowther Committee Report on Consumer Credit was published in 1971, the Unsolicited Goods and Services Act went into effect on August 13, and the government announced its intention to introduce further safety regulations under the Consumer Protection Act to cover a range of product groups involving electrical safety, flammability, and lead or other toxic contents. The Consumer Council was abolished in 1970 and its Teltag labeling scheme ceased to operate. Teltags, which gave shoppers independent and test facts on labels attached to the product, were being used on a number of electrical appliances, soft furnishings, and floor coverings. Shortly before it went out of existence the Consumer Council advocated the introduction of a special court to deal with small claims. Such a court, to provide a cheap and simple method of resolving contractual disputes for claims of up to £150, was opened in Manchester in June on an experimental basis.

International Activities. At the international level, the United Nations and its specialized agencies took account of the consumer interests inherent in so many of their activities. These interests were represented for the most part by the International Organization of Consumers Unions (IOCU), which was in consultative or liaison status with the Economic and Social Council (ECOSOC), UNICEF, UNESCO, the Food and Agriculture Organization (FAO), and the Codex Alimentarius Commission of the FAO and the World Health Organization (WHO). In 1971, IOCU also entered into consultative status with the UN Industrial Development Organization (UNIDO), whose primary sphere of interest was in the less developed countries.

Environmental pollution continued to attract increasing public attention as preparations built up for the UN Conference on Human Environment—the Stockholm Conference—scheduled for June 1972. Consumer organizations firmly aligned themselves with the objectives of this project and the consumer press gave the subject continuous coverage. One example was the report in April by the Belgian organization Association des Consommateurs linking the incidence of various diseases among bathers using beaches that the same organization had identified the previous summer as being seriously polluted. In May, IOCU submitted a declaration and a dossier of reports on environmental pollution to the Stockholm Conference, pledging its support, stating how consumer organizations could help achieve the objectives of the conference, and detailing the consumer interests involved in such aspects of the problem as air pollution, marine pollution, and noise control.

Consumer organizations in the Western world have long aligned themselves with the interests of their counterparts in less developed countries, and on their behalf IOCU had earlier submitted a number of statements to ECOSOC and its commissions on human

Mayor John Lindsay accompanies Bess Myerson, New York City's commissioner of consumer affairs, on one of her inspection tours of a supermarket to check advertising and sales procedures.
THE "NEW YORK TIMES"

rights and the consumer component in social and economic planning. These submissions led to the incorporation, in the formative Declaration on Social Progress and Development adopted by the UN General Assembly at the end of 1969, of consumer protection and consumer education as factors in social progress and development. In 1971 IOCU followed this up with a further submission, giving its views on the International Development Strategy and expressing the aspirations of consumers for the Second United Nations Development Decade. The submission stressed above all the importance of incorporating from the outset the means of consumer protection and consumer education in the plans to raise living standards in less developed countries.

The formulation of international technical standards was important to the consumer interest, and in 1971 IOCU continued to represent consumers in the FAO/WHO Codex Alimentarius Commission, concerned with standards in food processing, packaging, labeling, and distribution, and in the International Organization for Standardization (ISO), the principal general standards-making body. IOCU was also a member of the International Steering Committee for Consumer Affairs (ISCA), whose main objective was to initiate, within the programs of the ISO and the International Electrotechnical Commission (IEC), items of direct interest to consumers. The ISCA list in 1971 included some 30 such items and subjects— from slide projectors to the sizing of shoes, and from carpets to ceramic ware.

An IOCU member organization, the Bureau Européen des Unions de Consommateurs (BEUC), had special responsibility for consumer groups in the six EEC countries, and represented their interests in the EEC through the Comité de Contact des Consommateurs. In May the BEUC invited consumer organizations in countries that had applied for membership in the EEC to participate in its activities.

In addition to the growth in recognition of con-

Officials of the Grocery
Products Manufacturers
of Canada argue against
the government's proposed
packaging and labeling
bill during hearings
by the House of Commons
Health Committee in
Ottawa in January 1971.

CHARLES MITCHELL—CANADIAN
PRESS

sumerism by national and international governments, there was a widening of the attention paid to it by business at every level in 1971. Thus, the Direct Selling Association, representing many well-known corporations whose products were marketed directly into the home, announced in July that its first World Congress, to be held in May 1972, would consider "the impact of consumerism, and the importance of a code of ethics" that took it into account.

Europe. Directives issued in the EEC in the year covered textile labeling and motor-vehicle braking systems. In February the Economic Commission for Europe (ECE) agreed on two separate lists of governmental standardization activities, one concerned with international trade and the other relating to public safety, health, and "consumer welfare." In May the EFTA convention providing for the mutual recognition by national health authorities of inspections of pharmaceutical manufacturing plants and products went into effect.

The Consultative Assembly of the Council of Europe adopted in January a recommendation on the legal protection of consumers designed to broaden the Council's activities in the consumer field and to introduce greater harmonization of existing legislation in member states. Later in the year a working group of the Council's Consumer Protection Committee completed its draft resolution on misleading advertising; this followed the report of an earlier working group on consumer education in schools. Another draft convention covered social security arrangements for migrant workers. At its April meeting, the Consumer Protection Committee considered the setting up of a consumer education documentation centre, and in the autumn the committee began a study of national facilities for representation of consumers.

One measure of the growth of the consumer movement was the increase in the number and size of consumer organizations. Their formation followed the pattern of industrialization, having originated in the

U.S. in the mid 1930s, spread to Europe in the 1950s and 1960s and more recently to the less developed countries, including Guyana, India, and Malaysia in 1971. According to the *Consumers Directory* published by IOCU, the number of national organizations in existence had risen to 122 by mid-1971. They covered 44 countries and were made up of independent organizations, partly or wholly government-financed organizations, or federations embodying a number of individual unions.

Membership of the established organizations continued to expand and the circulation of their publications in almost every case set new records. Among the monthlies with the largest circulations in 1971 were *Consumentengids* (310,000), published by the Dutch Consumer Council; *Forbruker-Rapporten* (200,000), from Norway's Consumer Council; and *Test* (150,-000), published by the West German Stiftung Warentest. In the U.K., *Which?*, published by Consumers' Association, and its quarterly stablemates *Money Which?* and *Motoring Which?* had circulations of 610,000, 385,000, and 240,000, respectively.

The readership of consumer publications was drawn largely from the middle and upper-middle classes, and a common problem for most organizations was how to reach the less-well-off consumer with the information he needed. One promising method was the "consumer clinic," or advisory centre, where the public could come in to obtain expert and impartial advice on consumer products and a wide range of other problems. Pioneered in Austria by the Verein für Konsumenteninformation, this system was being successfully introduced in countries as diverse as Sweden, Jamaica, and the U.K.

A further innovation tried out with promising results was the legal service initiated by Consumentenbond, which was a development of the complaints and advisory services already operated by a number of organizations, notably in Austria and the Scandinavian countries. In the Netherlands, Consumentenbond not only provided legal advice but, where appropriate, acted on behalf of the member and took the case to court. This enabled the individual consumer to obtain redress and also helped to create a body of jurisprudence in the field of consumer protection and legislation. The U.K.'s Consumers' Association undertook its first test case on behalf of a private individual in a matter of trade misrepresentation.

Another way in which consumer organizations tried to reach a wider public was through consumer education. A few organizations had specialized staff members who were responsible for writing instruction books and for contacts with educational authorities in their country. The best examples of organizations with this kind of educational program outside North America were in England and Sweden. The Dutch Consumers Union decided to appoint an educationalist to its senior staff and a Danish organization called a meeting between teachers' associations and consumer leaders. The main message of these groups was that formal consumer education is an interdisciplinary subject and not an extra subject to be added to the curriculum. Consumer education officers tried to develop new textbooks and visual aids to integrate consumer education with such subjects as languages, mathematics, biography, and the sciences. They recommended that consumer education should start as early as possible.

The testing and evaluation of consumer products and services continued to be the staple task of most consumer organizations, and 1971 saw important advances in the development of cooperative or joint testing. International collaboration was possible where the countries concerned had on their markets a sufficiently high proportion of product brands in common. The joint test had important advantages, particularly the reduction of costs and the pooling of technical skill and know-how.

In January the first reports were published of the initial series of joint tests on cars, carried out in the U.K. by Consumers' Association for a consortium of Belgian, Dutch, and West German organizations. Two more groups of cars were tested in this way during the year and there was also a marked expansion in the joint testing programs of organizations in Belgium, the Netherlands, France, and West Germany. Some 20 joint tests were carried out by this grouping, with the addition of the U.K. in four cases. Links between the EEC countries and Scandinavia also began to be formed, and regular consultations between Sweden, Norway, and Denmark began on cooperative testing between these countries following a comprehensive report on the subject by the InterScandinavian Committee on Consumer Affairs.

Asia and Oceania. A joint testing program was initiated by the Consumers Association of New Zealand in cooperation with Pacific and Southeast Asian organizations. Organizations in these regions also participated in a major international consumer seminar organized by IOCU in Bombay at the end of the year, which brought together delegates from some 20 consumer organizations in 16 countries, including India, Ceylon, South Korea, South Vietnam, Japan, Singapore, and the Philippines, as well as Australia and New Zealand. In addition to holding discussions and working groups on a number of consumer problems, the seminar paved the way for the setting up of a regional organization to act as a clearinghouse for consumer associations in the area along lines similar to the one formed in the Caribbean following an earlier IOCU international seminar in Jamaica. IOCU's Development Committee also planned to hold similar seminars in Africa and in Latin America. One instance of the growing impact of consumer organizations on the retail market came from Japan, where in April the list prices of television sets were reduced sharply after a boycott by the members of five of Japan's largest consumer organizations. (J. H. v. V.)

United States. Although consumer protection activities in the U.S. were directed toward the same ends as in other countries, they took on a different flavour, since much of the initiative came from private sources. Consumer organizations concentrated heavily in 1971 on improving enforcement of laws already on the books and on pressing hard for new legislation designed to improve the administration of regulatory agencies, give the consumer a better chance in court, and plug loopholes in existing laws. Public interest groups were spectacularly successful in focusing attention on government inefficiencies and the continuation of threats to life, health, and pocketbook from business practices the public thought had been outlawed.

Individual consumers showed their frustration by sales resistance. The billings for advertising retail goods and services rose from $2 billion in 1936 to $20 billion in 1970, much of it spent on creating fanciful illusions and all of it added to retail prices. Growing numbers, especially among the young, noisily rebelled against what they called "the junk culture," and more

"And by the time we get there, prices will have shot up again."—Waite, London "Daily Mirror."

BEN ROTH AGENCY

consumers than ever protested their right to rational choice by consulting the reports of independent testing and evaluating organizations: the circulation of *Consumer Reports,* for example, reached two million in 1971, double its 1965 circulation.

Consumer protest groups at every level grew and multiplied. By the end of 1971 the Consumer Federation of America (CFA), the umbrella organization founded in late 1968 whose member groups included 196 area, state, and regional consumer organizations, cooperatives, and labour unions, could speak for an estimated 30 million individual consumers. At its two-day national assembly in Washington in January, the CFA adopted as its top national priorities: an independent consumer advocate in the government, congressional sanction of consumer class actions, and reforms in auto insurance. Other priorities were lower prices and interest rates, more economical health care services, and opposition to high tariffs.

Consumers won a victory at the polls in Virginia when Henry E. Howell, Jr., who based his entire political career as well as his campaign on consumer advocacy, decisively defeated opponents of his own party and the opposition party to become lieutenant governor of the state. Ronald Ostrander, an engineer who had developed Tide laundry detergent for Procter & Gamble, handed a bonus to consumers (and a major tool to environmentalists) when he testified before a congressional committee in October that about a tenth of the recommended amount of laundry detergent would clean the wash even better than the full amount. But the consumer hero of 1971 was Ralph Nader, who continued to shatter the belief that an individual does not stand a chance against big business and big government. Nader's efforts had been organized into the Center for Study of Responsive Law in Washington, D.C., in June 1969 and in 1971 Nader went to the public for financing, asking by direct mail and in newspaper ads for donations of $15 or more, and hoping to get back more than $100,000.

The Nader organization included the Center for Auto Safety, Consumer Action for Improved Foods, the Aviation Consumer Action Project, public interest research groups in Washington, Connecticut, and Ohio, a Corporate Accountability Research Group with a clearinghouse where people working for corporations and government agencies could "blow the whistle" on employers' wrongdoings in confidence, and student groups in seven states (Oregon, Minnesota, Ohio, Connecticut, Hawaii, Iowa, and Indiana). Nader also traveled to Japan and the U.K. in 1971 to help set up similar groups there. By the end of 1971 the centre had published major reports covering auto safety, the Federal Trade Commission (FTC), the U.S. Food and Drug Administration (FDA), the Interstate Commerce Commission, the U.S. Department of Agriculture, air pollution, water pollution, defective automobiles, self-regulation in the medical profes-

Consumer Affairs

Jack Yohe, director of the U.S. Civil Aeronautics Board's Office of Consumer Affairs, recovered almost $100,000 in refunds and penalty payments during a six-month period in 1971.

sion, antitrust enforcement, and occupational safety. Nader and his task forces also charged that the state of Delaware was controlled by the E. I. du Pont de Nemours chemical empire and that land and water resources in California were being endangered by the land use laws and practices in that state. The organization also streamlined its staff to make it less dependent on students and volunteers, and to direct its main thrust away from study and research toward political action. A major undertaking planned for 1972 was a one-year study of Congress.

Industry responded to the barrage of criticism in a variety of ways. The Better Business Bureaus announced a major overhaul. Some grocery chains started dating some perishable items so that customers could tell how fresh they were, and some food processors began experimenting with nutritional labeling. The appliance manufacturers set up the Major Appliance Consumer Action Panel. The advertising industry formed the National Advertising Review Board to undertake self-policing of ad content. In November companies representing 95% of the nation's bottled-water industry voted to establish the industry's first mandatory quality standards. Chrysler Corp. created an Office of Public Responsibility headed by a vice-chairman of the board, and appointed the auto industry's first official ombudsman, "Your Man in Detroit," to deal directly with buyer complaints. Whirlpool Corp., which had started a "Cool-Line" in 1967 for toll-free calls at any hour from purchasers of its products, logged about 20,000 such calls in 1971; other appliance manufacturers inaugurated similar services. The general manager for consumer products at Motorola, which had been routinely contacting buyers of its television sets to make sure they were satisfied, began calling on customers personally.

A 1970 FTC analysis of consumer complaints in five major cities placed new- and used-car dealers at the head of the list of villains, followed by real estate agents, mail-order houses, radio and television repair shops, direct-selling organizations, and furniture stores. The principal complaint was failure to deliver goods, followed by truth-in-lending violations, complaints of defective work or service, inferior merchandise, false advertising, and refusal of refunds without prior notice of a "no refund" policy.

The federal government responded to consumer dissatisfaction in many ways. On February 24, Pres.

Richard M. Nixon upgraded the President's Committee on Consumer Interests, created by Pres. Lyndon B. Johnson in 1964, into the Office of Consumer Affairs. The new office was charged with analyzing and coordinating the consumer activities of all federal agencies and departments, advising the administration on consumer policy, and handling consumer complaints. Instead of referring complainers to the appropriate target, the new office began handling complaints directly and, by the end of 1971, was disposing of some 3,000 a month, more than 80% in favour of the complainer.

Also in February, Nixon sent a special message to Congress outlining his consumer program. The message restated the "Buyer's Bill of Rights" formulated by Pres. John F. Kennedy in 1962—the rights to choose, to be informed, to be protected, and to have complaints heard. To implement these rights, Nixon proposed empowering the FTC to represent consumers as their advocate in court and before other federal agencies and to seek preliminary injunctions to stop apparently unfair practices until a decision could be reached. A Bureau of Product Safety was to be established in the Department of Health, Education, and Welfare with power to establish and enforce safety standards for consumer goods. The message also called for higher penalties for fraud and deception; access to federal courts for consumers suing for damages; identification coding of all drug tablets and capsules to cut down errors; more explicit guarantees and warranties couched in simpler language; and a study of ways to improve the handling of small claims and voluntary settlements.

Since 1971 was the first year of the 92nd Congress, little legislation was enacted. The only new consumer law of note that was signed provided for a nationally coordinated boating safety program. But Congress, under pressure from consumer lobbies, appeared ready to go even further than the president asked. On October 14 the House of Representatives overwhelmingly approved a bill to create an independent agency to represent consumers as their advocate. In the Senate there was considerable support for a drastic measure concentrating responsibility for protecting consumers against unsafe products in an independent agency and abolishing the FDA. The bill would repeal safety laws directed at particular products and specific hazards, replacing them with an omnibus product safety law making manufacturers fully liable for faulty or unsafe goods. A startling and unique feature of the Senate bill would make members of the new agency's staff liable to fines and imprisonment for failure to perform their duties.

In November the Senate passed a bill for federal regulation of the cost of auto repairs. The measure would also give the Department of Transportation power to regulate the strength of steel used in cars in order to reduce damage from collisions. Both houses were working on bills to tighten up guarantees and warranties and to make them comprehensible. On the other hand, consumer "class action" legislation, which would permit individuals who have been damaged in an identical way to join together in a single lawsuit instead of having to take legal action separately, remained bogged down in Congress.

Auto insurance and auto safety were hotly debated in Congress during 1971. No-fault insurance, which required insurance companies to pay damages for auto accidents without regard to which driver or vehicle was at fault, was adopted by Massachusetts in 1970 and by several other states in 1971. After an extensive study, the Nixon administration endorsed the no-fault principle in March and a number of bills to apply the concept nationally were put into the congressional hopper.

The federal regulatory agencies made strenuous efforts to refute accusations that they represented the industries they were supposed to regulate rather than the public. The FTC sought to broaden its rules so that they would cover entire industries. It ruled, for example, that any retail food store advertising a food "special" must have the featured items for sale at all, not just some, of its outlets and in reasonable quantities. Other rules in preparation at year's end would require that the octane rating of a gasoline be posted on every commercial gas pump, and that purchasers from door-to-door salesmen be allowed a "cooling off" period in which to cancel their orders without penalty.

The FTC undertook a major study of advertising, and at midyear began asking some manufacturers to produce proof of their advertising claims. By tackling such giants as the auto industry and the makers of electric razors, the FTC hoped to pressure all advertisers into making only accurate claims without being challenged. The FTC added bite to its advertisers' substantiation program by insisting that some major advertisers whose ads had created a false impression on the public devote a percentage of future advertising space to correcting misrepresentations.

The FDA completed its reexamination of all drugs on the market prior to 1962, when legislation required that their effectiveness as well as their safety be established, and published a list of those that were ineffective or probably ineffective. It also completed a review and revision of the list of food additives "generally regarded as safe" that had been issued in 1958 and that had included food additives such as cyclamates, in use at the time and since regarded as suspect.

The FDA's new Bureau of Product Safety began efforts to reduce the 30,000 deaths and 20 million injuries ascribed annually to accidents involving consumer products. It identified more than 150 defective toys and banned them from the market, and seized several tons of defective fireworks. It also prepared regulations requiring "child-proof" closures on bottles and other containers of such dangerous household items as liquid drain cleaners and furniture oil. Late in the year, the bureau began hooking up 600 poison-control centres by computer to make identification and treatment information available for poison victims throughout the country.

The Federal Communications Commission (FCC) got 60,000 replies, the most it had ever received on one issue, after it invited public comment on proposed rules to limit commercial advertising on children's television programs. Many of the letters protested exploitative and deceptive advertising techniques directed at children and the violence in the programs themselves. Broadcasters hastily undertook long-promised reforms in the hope of staving off tighter government regulation. The FCC continued its leisurely examination (begun in 1963) of whether cable television should be allowed to bring distant new stations into a marketing area and debated whether a single ownership of more than one communications medium in a market area should continue to be allowed. It also prepared recommendations for revising its policy of broadcast license renewal, and tried to deal with almost 100 petitions from groups protesting the renewal of licenses of poorly performing stations.

The Department of Transportation set two new auto safety standards during 1971. One required passive restraints to protect passengers in a crash in all seating positions beginning with 1976 model cars. Air bags, which seemed to offer the best approach to meeting this standard, promptly became the subject of public controversy. The other standard required that, beginning with 1974 models, front and rear bumpers be able to withstand collision at speeds up to five miles an hour. (*See* INDUSTRIAL REVIEW: *Special Report.*)

The Department of Commerce set a new strict flammability standard for children's sleepwear. By July 30, 1973, pajamas, nightgowns, bathrobes, and other sleepwear in sizes through 6X had to be flame resistant. And finally, after long prodding by consumer groups, the General Services Administration, the federal government's civilian purchasing agent, published its first list of the brand names of the products it buys. The list was to be updated quarterly as a service to consumers. (PA. T.)

See also Advertising; Merchandising.

Contract Bridge

The question of whether professionalism would ruin competitiveness in contract bridge was raised for the second time in 1971 when the Dallas Aces, the all-professional team created by Dallas, Tex., industrialist Ira G. Corn, Jr., retained the world championship they had won initially in 1970. The world championship for the Bermuda Bowl was staged for the first time in the Far East, hosted by Taiwan in Taipei in May. Six teams competed: the Dallas Aces, who qualified as defending champions; France, the European champions; Taiwan, Brazil, and Aus-

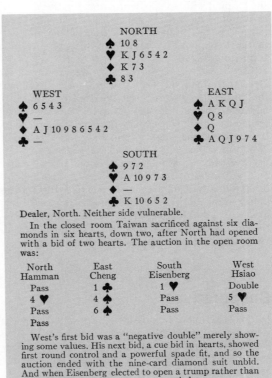

Dealer, North. Neither side vulnerable.

In the closed room Taiwan sacrificed against six diamonds in six hearts, down two, after North had opened with a bid of two hearts. The auction in the open room was:

North Hamman	East Cheng	South Eisenberg	West Hsiao
Pass	1 ♣	1 ♥	Double
4 ♥	4 ♠	Pass	5 ♥
Pass	6 ♠	Pass	Pass
Pass			

West's first bid was a "negative double" merely showing some values. His next bid, a cue bid in hearts, showed first round control and a powerful spade fit, and so the auction ended with the nine-card diamond suit unbid. And when Eisenberg elected to open a trump rather than the ace of hearts the contract succeeded.

tralia, representing respectively the Far East, South America, and Oceania; and a second U.S. team representing North America and referred to as North America 2, the defending champions being styled North America 1.

After an exhausting qualifying competition of 15 rounds the Aces and France proved a cut above the field and qualified for what resulted in a high-quality final. The Aces showed themselves to be good champions and were easy winners of a match that was in close contention until the halfway stage. France was ranked second, Australia third, Taiwan fourth, Brazil fifth, and North America 2 sixth.

The Aces were unchanged from the team that won the title in Stockholm in 1970: Robert Wolff, James Jacoby, Bill Eisenberg, Bob Hamman, Bobby Goldman, and Mike Lawrence, with Oswald Jacoby again as nonplaying captain. Two months after retaining the championship the team, which had worked together for three years, lost one of its members when Bill Eisenberg resigned after personality differences.

The Aces lost heavily to Taiwan in the most spectacular hand of the championship (*see* box).

Shortly after their return to the United States the champions were again defeated by the young U.S. team playing the Chinese Precision Club system; the Precision team went on to win the Spingold Trophy, the major U.S. team championship, for the second successive year. In October, however, the Aces won overwhelmingly the right to represent the U.S. in the next Olympiad, in June 1972, at Miami Beach, Fla.

In November 1971 the European Championships staged in Athens attracted a record entry of 22 countries in the open series and 16 in the women's series. Italy emerged as the victor, with 379 points against 314 for the strong runner-up British team. The Italians routed the British in the final round, despite the absence of Giuseppe Messina, who had been taken to the hospital with an apparent coronary attack. Switzerland finished third. Egypt and Lebanon, both members of the European Bridge League, did not take part in the championships because of the presence of a team from Israel.

The bridge event of the year was reserved for December when the Dallas Aces, world champions for the past two years, met the Italian Blue team, undefeated world champions for 13 years until they retired in 1969. The match, justifiably described as the match of the century, was played in Las Vegas, Nev., for a purse of $15,000. The Italians scored a decisive victory, winning by 84 international match points. The teams seemed to be evenly balanced during the first half of the match, but then the Italians pulled away and were never headed. It appeared that bridge as a spectator game had arrived, and the authorities would inevitably have to consider their as yet unresolved position vis-à-vis professionalism.

(HA. FR.)

Cooperatives

During 1971 new proposals for structural changes were put forward in the consumer movements of some European countries, while in others such reforms were implemented. In West Germany the congress held in Wiesbaden in June authorized reorganization on a threefold basis of 20 regional retail distributive societies, integration of the movement's central func-

tions, and the formation of a limited company to promote and assist the execution of the plan. A plan to amalgamate the Danish cooperative wholesale and retail societies into one national society was approved in May. In the Netherlands the process of integrating 8 of the 17 regional societies into COOP Nederland was completed by the end of 1971. It was decided to speed up amalgamation of the 276 individual societies in Switzerland into 30 large societies.

Cooperative organizations catering for vacation and leisure activities in Italy, Belgium, the Netherlands, and Czechoslovakia completed construction of a holiday village providing accommodation for 2,000 near Palermo, Sicily. The third International Conference on Aid for Cooperatives in Developing Countries, sponsored by the British government, was held at the International Cooperative Training Centre at Loughborough, Leicestershire, in April. The UN signed a Memorandum of Understanding with the International Cooperative Housing Development Association at the end of 1970 designed to stimulate widespread development of low-cost housing in less developed countries.

The International Cooperative Alliance. A message was received from UN Secretary-General U Thant congratulating the ICA on its initiative in designating the 1970s the "Cooperative Development Decade." Thant stated that by promoting cooperative movements in less developed countries, the ICA would be making a greatly needed contribution to the implementation of the goals of the second UN Development Decade. A progress report on the program of the Cooperative Development Decade was presented to the meeting of the ICA Central Committee held in Bucharest, Rom., in October. The meeting also discussed papers dealing with the role of women in the cooperative movement and the financial problems facing cooperative movements in some advanced countries.

The 40th International Cooperative Seminar, held in Moscow in September, discussed cooperative education as a factor enhancing the role of cooperatives in the economic sphere and in public life. The meeting of the ICA research officers held in Trondheim, Nor., in September dealt with distribution costs and dividends.

Under a contract between the ICA and the UN Industrial Development Organization (UNIDO), signed in July, the ICA undertook to provide an expert to advise the El Salvador Institute of Industrial Development on a program for promoting industrial cooperatives. The contract was the first of its kind between the two organizations.

To celebrate the tenth anniversary of the founding of the ICA Regional Office for South East Asia, the February 1971 meeting of the ICA Executive was held in New Delhi, India. The government of India offered to provide training facilities for 50 cooperators from less developed countries in each year of the Cooperative Development Decade.

The Latin American Technical Institute for Cooperative Integration assisted in the establishment of cooperative consumer stores in Antigua, El Salvador, and Pôrto Alegre, Braz. The ICA Insurance Committee promoted new insurance cooperatives in Ecuador, Guatemala, and Singapore during 1971. At its meeting in Bucharest in October, the ICA Housing Committee discussed a document dealing with the contribution of housing cooperatives toward the solution of the housing problem in European countries. The International Cooperative Housing Development Association, at a meeting in Stockholm in June, discussed plans for establishing a technical service organization for housing cooperatives in India INTER-COOP, the ICA committee representing wholesale and retail interests, established a group of experts for food shops and another group for department stores and shopping centres.

Membership and Trade. At the end of 1971, the number of cooperative federations in membership with the ICA totaled 148 in 60 countries. The latest available statistics showed an increase in the number of cooperative societies in membership with the ICA from 533,467 in 1968 to 560,532 in 1969. Membership within these societies rose from 255 million to 268 million during the same period. For the first time, the largest membership was reported from India (59.5 million), followed by the U.S.S.R. (58.5 million) and the U.S. (45 million). Of the total membership, the greatest proportion was in consumer societies (42.82%), followed by credit societies (30.60%), agricultural societies (14.82%), miscellaneous societies (6.43%), building and housing societies (2.40%), workers' productive and artisanal societies (2.36%), and fisheries societies (0.57%).

A further step in the development of joint production in the Nordic countries was taken on Jan. 1, 1971, when a factory producing chemicals for industry in Stavanger, Nor., came under joint ownership of cooperative organizations in Denmark, Finland, Iceland, Norway, and Sweden.

Agreement was reached between the Prince Rupert Fishermen's Cooperative Association of British Columbia and the Japan Cooperative Trading Co. to increase trade in frozen salmon and salmon roe. Centrosoyus, U.S.S.R., and cooperative organizations in Czechoslovakia, Hungary, Poland, Romania, and Yugoslavia signed agreements for the expansion of trade during 1971–75.   (L. Ke.)

Costa Rica

A Central American republic, Costa Rica lies between Nicaragua and Panama and has coastlines on the Caribbean Sea and the Pacific Ocean. Area: 19,650 sq.mi. (50,900 sq.km.). Pop. (1970 est.): 1,710,083, including white and mestizo 97.6%. Cap. and largest city: San José (pop., 1970 est., 205,650). Language: Spanish. Religion: predominantly Roman Catholic. President in 1971, José Figueres Ferrer.

In 1971 Costa Rica's trading relations with Central America and with the rest of the world became the subject of vigorous debate, owing to adverse developments in the nation's balance of payments. There was an overall deficit of $9.6 million in 1970, compared with a previous surplus of $18 million. Gold and foreign exchange reserves had fallen sharply, and although approximately $4 million was repaid to the International Monetary Fund, other international liabilities had risen considerably. The country's trade deficit with other Central American Common Market (CACM) countries had also increased, and the Honduran decision of December 1970 to reestablish tariffs on imports from fellow CACM members further exacerbated the situation. Honduras was Costa Rica's second most important export market in the associa-

tion and the only Central American country with which it had a trade surplus. Moreover, the repeated failure to promote a reconciliation between El Salvador and Honduras led to increasing domestic pressure for a change in Costa Rica's trading relations with the area.

With a large coffee surplus and no immediate prospect of increasing sales to Western countries, attention focused upon relations with Eastern Europe, particularly the U.S.S.R. The possible establishment of a Soviet embassy in Costa Rica became a major political issue. President Figueres favoured the idea, believing that it would strengthen the Costa Rican export drive to the U.S.S.R. Others believed that this could be achieved without the establishment of an embassy and the consequent risk of subversion, while a third body of opinion regarded all relations with the Soviet Union as undesirable.

Meanwhile, immediate action was needed to prevent any further decline in the official gold and foreign exchange reserves. Thus, on June 19 the dual rate of exchange, suspended in January 1970, was reintroduced, with an official rate of 6.62–6.65 colones to the dollar and a free rate of 7.50–7.53. At the same time, restrictions in the form of customs guarantees in the amount of normal import duties were introduced on certain imports from other CACM countries.

These policy changes threatened to cause the complete breakdown of the CACM, already in a critical condition following the Honduran withdrawal during the previous December. After representations from other Central American governments, the customs guarantee restrictions were dropped and a series of meetings held in an attempt to save the association. As a result, the Comisión Normalizadora del Mercado Común was set up to regulate relations between Costa

COSTA RICA
Education. (1968–69) Primary, pupils 322,683, teachers 11,287; secondary, pupils 55,732, teachers 2,404; vocational, pupils 6,524, teachers 315; teacher training, students 1,759, teaching staff (universities only) 678.
Finance. Monetary unit: colón, with a par value of 6.62 colones to U.S. $1 (15.90 colones = £1 sterling) and a free rate (Sept. 27, 1971) of c. 16.40 colones = £1 sterling. Gold, SDRs, and foreign exchange, central bank: (June 1971) U.S. $8,470,000; (June 1970) U.S. $30,360,000. Budget (1970 est.) balanced at 1,263,000,000 colones. Gross national product: (1969) 5,461,000,000 colones; (1968) 4,935,000,000 colones. Money supply: (Jan. 1971) 1,074,600,000 colones; (Jan. 1970) 1,002,300,000 colones. Cost of living (San José; 1963 = 100): (May 1971) 119; (May 1970) 116.
Foreign Trade. (1970) Imports 2,098,100,000 colones; exports 1,517,200,000 colones. Import sources (1969): U.S. 35%; Japan 9%; West Germany 8%; Guatemala 7%; U.K. 6%; El Salvador 6%. Export destinations (1969): U.S. 48%; West Germany 7%; Nicaragua 6%; Guatemala 5%. Main exports: coffee 34%; bananas 29%.
Transport and Communications. Roads (1970) c. 10,000 km. (including 3,250 km. all-weather and 660 km. of Pan-American Highway). Motor vehicles in use (1969): passenger 36,100; commercial (including buses) 20,600. Railways: (1970) 735 km.; traffic (1968) 71 million passenger-km., freight (1967) 56 million net ton-km. Air traffic (1970): 165.8 million passenger-km.; freight 12,344,000 net ton-km. Telephones (Jan. 1970) 56,261. Radio receivers (Dec. 1969) c. 106,000. Television receivers (Dec. 1969) 100,000.
Agriculture. Production (in 000; metric tons; 1970; 1969 in parentheses): coffee 97 (91); bananas (1969) 967, (1968) 703; sugar, raw value (1970–71) 182, (1969–70) 167; dry beans 8 (7); cocoa (1969–70) 8, (1968–69) 8.9. Livestock (in 000; 1969–70): cattle 1,574; horses c. 109; pigs 250.
Industry. Electricity production (1969) 901 million kw-hr. (90% hydroelectric).

Copper:
see Mining

Corn:
see Agriculture

Cosmetics:
see Fashion and Dress

Rica, Nicaragua, El Salvador, and Guatemala, and shortly afterward a system of multiple exchange rates was established.

This eased the situation and attention reverted to the Soviet issue. The government finally decided to suspend the establishment of formal diplomatic relations but to continue fostering trade exchanges. On December 13 President Figueres took the limelight when, armed with a submachine gun, he helped prevent the hijacking of a Nicaraguan airliner from San José airport to Cuba. (Ro. E. S.)

Cricket

The confrontations among the major cricketing countries resulted in an English victory in Australia (2–0), and India's first win ever in the West Indies (1–0). Later England at home beat Pakistan 1–0 but was defeated 1–0 by India, which thus completed a memorable six months.

Australia v. England. England, captained by R. Illingworth, had an exhausting tour of Australia which included, for the first time, six test matches. This became officially seven after the third at Melbourne was washed out by rain without a ball bowled, but as the captains had tossed, it counted in the records, and an extra final test was arranged.

The features of the series between two below-average sides were the batting of England's top three —G. Boycott, J. H. Edrich, and B. W. Luckhurst— the fast bowling of J. A. Snow, the immaculate wicket keeping of A. P. E. Knott, and the determined team spirit inculcated by Illingworth, a hard captain who, though severely criticized for his tactics, achieved his objective. Boycott and Edrich each made more than 600 runs, and Snow took 31 wickets. England made few friends through its stubborn and often slow batting and the bad manners of its three leading players, Illingworth, Boycott, and Snow, who had numerous brushes with umpires. Boycott threw his bat away in anger when given run out; Snow was frequently warned for bowling bumpers; and Illingworth took his team off the field in the final test at Sydney after an altercation with the umpire which caused the crowd to throw cans and bottles onto the field.

For Australia, K. R. Stackpole had a successful series (627 runs), and others who played at least one good innings were I. R. Redpath, W. M. Lawry, I. M. and G. S. Chappell, and K. D. Walters. The selectors made frequent changes in an effort to strengthen their weak bowling, and J. W. Gleeson with 14 wickets was

the most successful bowler. For the final test, Lawry was deposed from the captaincy and dropped; he was replaced by I. M. Chappell.

The first test at Brisbane was drawn. Australia 433 (Stackpole 207, Walters 112, Snow 6 for 114) and 214 (Lawry 84, K. Shuttleworth 5 for 47); England 464 (Edrich 79, Luckhurst 74, Knott 73, B. L. D'Oliveira 57) and 39 for 1. The second test at Perth was drawn. England 397 (Luckhurst 131, Boycott 70) and 287 for 6 declared (Edrich not out 115, Boycott 50); Australia 440 (Redpath 171, G. Chappell 108, I. Chappell 50) and 100 for 3. England won the fourth test at Sydney by 299 runs. England 332 (Boycott 77, Edrich 55) and 319 for 5 declared (Boycott not out 142, D'Oliveira 56, Illingworth 53); Australia 236 (Redpath 64, Walters 55) and 116 (Lawry not out 60, Snow 7 for 40). The fifth test at Melbourne was drawn. Australia 493 for 9 declared (I. Chappell 111, R. W. Marsh not out 92, Lawry 56, Walters 55) and 169 for 4 declared; England 392 (D'Oliveira 117, Luckhurst 109) and 161 for 0 (Boycott 76, Edrich 74). The sixth test at Adelaide was drawn. England 470 (Edrich 130, K. W. R. Fletcher 80, Boycott 58, J. H. Hampshire 55, D. Lillee 5 for 84) and 233 for 4 declared (Boycott not out 119); Australia 235 (Stackpole 87) and 328 for 3 (Stackpole 136, I. Chappell 104). England won the seventh test at Sydney by 62 runs. England 184 and 302 (Luckhurst 59, Edrich 57); Australia 264 (G. Chappell 65, Redpath 59) and 160 (Stackpole 67).

New Zealand v. England. England went on to New Zealand and won a two-match series 1–0. It won the first test at Christchurch by 8 wickets. New Zealand 65 (D. L. Underwood 6 for 12) and 254 (G. M. Turner 76, B. E. Congdon 55, Underwood 6 for 85); England 231 (D'Oliveira 100) and 89 for 2 (Hampshire not out 51). The second test at Auckland was drawn. England 321 (Knott 101, P. Lever 64, D'Oliveira 58, M. C. Cowdrey 54, R. S. Cunis 6 for 76) and 237 (Knott 96); New Zealand 313 for 7 declared (M. G. Burgess 104, Turner 65, G. T. Dowling 53, Underwood 5 for 108) and 40 for no wicket.

West Indies v. India. India, captained by A. L. Wadekar, owed its success in the West Indies to superb batting by S. M. Gavaskar and D. N. Sardesai and accurate spin bowling by S. Venkataraghavan, E. A. S. Prasanna, and B. S. Bedi. Gavaskar made four centuries, two in one match including one double, and Sardesai three centuries, including one double. Off-spinner Venkataraghavan was the best bowler of the series, taking 22 wickets. G. S. Sobers, captain again, was once more the West Indies mainstay, making 594 runs, including three centuries, and taking 11 wickets. C. A. Davis made 531 including two centuries and three 50s, and R. B. Kanhai played one fine century innings. Off-spinner J. Noreiga (17 wickets) shared the bowling honours with Sobers.

The first test at Kingston was drawn. India 387 (Sardesai 212, E. D. Solkar 61); West Indies 217 (Kanhai 56) and 384 for 5 (Kanhai 158 not out, Sobers 93, C. H. Lloyd 57). India won the second test at Port of Spain by seven wickets. West Indies 214 (Davis 71 not out) and 261 (R. C. Fredericks 80, Davis not out 74, Venkataraghavan 5 for 95); India 352 (Sardesai 112, Gavaskar 65, Solkar 55, Noreiga 9 for 95) and 125 for 3 (Gavaskar not out 67). The third test at Georgetown was drawn. West Indies 363 (D. Lewis not out 81, Lloyd 60) and 307 for 3 declared (Davis not out 125, Sobers not out 108); India 376 (Gavaskar 116, G. R. Viswanath 50, S. Abid Ali

A good catch by R. Hutton off N. Gifford for 7 puts out S. Venkataraghavan of India on the final day of the England v. India match at Lord's on July 27, 1971.

50 not out) and 123 for no wicket (Gavaskar 64, A. V. Mankad 53). The fourth test at Bridgetown was drawn. West Indies 501 for 5 declared (Sobers not out 178, Lewis 88, Kanhai 85) and 180 for 6 declared; India 347 (Sardesai 150, Solkar 65) and 221 for 5 (Gavaskar 117 not out). The fifth test at Port of Spain was also drawn. India 360 (Gavaskar 124, Sardesai 75, Venkataraghavan 51) and 427 (Gavaskar 220, Wadekar 54, Noreiga 5 for 129); West Indies 526 (Sobers 132, Davis 105, M. L. C. Foster 99, Lewis 72) and 165 for 8 (Lloyd 64).

England v. Pakistan. Pakistan played a three-test rubber against England, captained again by Illingworth. For England, Boycott, Luckhurst, and D'Oliveira were the most successful batsmen, and bowling honours were shared among D'Oliveira, N. Gifford, R. A. Hutton, Illingworth, and Lever. Snow, suffering from reaction after his efforts in Australia, was not picked. For Pakistan, captained by Intikhab Alam, Zahir Abbas won fame with an innings of 274, and Asif Iqbal and Mushtaq Muḥammad also scored centuries. Asif Masood, fast medium, was their leading bowler.

The first test at Edgbaston, Birmingham, was drawn. Pakistan 608 for 7 declared (Zahir 274, Iqbal not out 104, Mushtaq 100); England 352 (Knott 116, D'Oliveira 73, Masood 5 for 111) and 229 for 5 (Luckhurst not out 108). The second test at Lord's, London, was also drawn. England 241 for 2 declared (Boycott not out 121) and 117 for no wicket (Hutton 58, Luckhurst 53); Pakistan 148. England won the third test at Headingley, Leeds, by 25 runs. England 316 (Boycott 112, D'Oliveira 74) and 264 (D'Oliveira 72, D. L. Amiss 56); Pakistan 350 (Zahir 72, Mushtaq 57, Wasim Bari 63) and 205 (Sadiq Muhammad 91).

England v. India. India, captained again by Wadekar, beat England in a three-match series for the first time in England. Its spin bowlers, Venkataraghavan, B. S. Chandrasekhar, and Bedi, were the decisive factor, as no English batsman made a century, though six made at least one score of over 50. With Boycott able to play in only one test, England's leading batsmen were Knott, Luckhurst, and Illingworth; five bowlers shared the honours—Gifford, Lever, Snow, Illingworth, and J. S. E. Price.

The first test at Lord's was drawn. England 304 (Knott 67, Snow 73) and 191 (Edrich 62); India 313 (Wadekar 85, Vishwanath 68, Solkar 67) and 145 for 8 (Gavaskar 53). The second test at Old Trafford, Manchester, was also drawn. England 386 (Illingworth 107, Lever not out 88, Luckhurst 78) and 245 for 3 declared (Luckhurst 101, Edrich 59); India 212 (Gavaskar 57, Solkar 50, Lever 5 for 70) and 65 for 3. India won the third test at the Oval, London, by 4 wickets. England 355 (Knott 90, J. A. Jameson 82, Hutton 81) and 101 (Chandrasekhar 6 for 38); India 284 (F. M. Engineer 59, Sardesai 54, Illingworth for 70) and 174 for 6.

County and National Cricket. Surrey won the English county championship for the 18th time and the first since 1958, a fitting reward for the nine years' captaincy of M. J. Stewart. It finished even with Warwickshire on points, but won more matches. Lancashire placed third and Kent, the reigning champions, fourth. In a splendid Gillette Cup final, Lancashire retained its title, beating Kent by 24 runs, but failed to hold the John Player Sunday League title, finishing third behind Worcestershire, which won by beating Essex on a fractionally faster run rate.

The individual success of the season was Boycott

(Yorkshire), who became the first man ever to finish with an average of 100.12. Though twice absent because of injuries, he scored 2,503 runs in only 30 innings. M. J. Harris (Nottinghamshire) and Edrich (Surrey) also scored more than 2,000 runs. Six bowlers took more than 100 wickets each, the West Indian L. R. Gibbs (Warwickshire) being the most successful with 131. Others to reach three figures were P. J. Sainsbury (Hampshire), T. W. Cartwright (Somerset), Underwood (Kent), Intikhab (Surrey), and F. J. Titmus (Middlesex). The leading all-rounders were Sainsbury, 959 runs and 107 wickets, and Hutton (Yorkshire), 1,009 runs and 80 wickets.

In Australia, South Australia won the Sheffield Shield; in New Zealand, Central Districts won the Plunket Shield; in South Africa, Transvaal won the Currie Cup; and in the West Indies, Trinidad won the Shell Shield. In India, South Zone won the Duleep Trophy, Bombay the Ranji Trophy, and State Bank of India the Moin-ud-Dowlah Trophy. In Pakistan, Karachi Blues won the Qaid-i-Azam Trophy, and Pakistan International Airlines won the Ayub Trophy, which for political reasons was renamed the BCCP Trophy.   (A. R. A.)

Crime

The disproportionate involvement of young people in crime gave governments in many parts of the world particular cause for concern in 1971. In the U.S.S.R. the justice minister declared that law enforcement agencies should give special priority to the eradication of juvenile crime; youths were said to be responsible for frequent acts of vandalism, street fights, and petty larceny. The U.S. attorney general claimed that "the problem of juvenile crime is a threat to our national well-being." While constituting only 16% of the U.S. population, youths aged 10–17 were involved in 29% of all major index offenses cleared up by police in 1970. Criminal statistics in the U.S. and other highly developed nations also revealed increasing involvement of women in crime; during 1960–70 arrests of men for serious crimes in the U.S. rose by 73% while arrests of women increased by more than 200%.

There was substantial evidence in 1971 that many facets of crime, particularly of aircraft hijacking and drug smuggling, had both national and international implications. The use of specially trained air marshals on certain international flights, together with airport screening devices to detect weapons and potential hijackers, seemed to result in a diminution in the number of successful hijackings. U.S. airlines, however, still experienced periodic seizures of aircraft by persons usually seeking to be flown to Cuba. More troublesome for the airlines in 1971 were bomb hoaxes and alarms. In May an airline company in Sydney, Austr., payed more than U.S. $500,000 to persons who claimed they had hidden an altitude pressure bomb aboard one of the company's aircraft. The claim proved to be false and the extortionists subsequently were apprehended without the money.

International trade in illegal drugs continued to flourish and was bolstered by the lucrative narcotics market among U.S. troops in South Vietnam. The U.S. initiative in seeking agreements to cut off the supply of raw materials for narcotics production from opium-growing countries like Turkey and Thailand appeared to meet with only limited success. (See DRUGS AND NARCOTICS; INTELLIGENCE OPERATIONS.)

Above, deputies search for bodies of 25 murdered farm workers in an orchard near Yuba City, Calif., in May 1971. Below, a trench where some of the bodies were found is shown.

UPI COMPIX

U.S. Senate hearings continued to probe the role of organized crime in gambling, in drug trafficking, in the theft and manipulation of securities, and in cargo theft and hijacking from docks and airports. In Italy the isolation by police of a number of alleged Mafiosi on several islands attracted international attention. So too did the attempted assassination, during an Italian-American Civil Rights League rally in New York City, of Joseph Colombo (*see* BIOGRAPHY), reputed underworld leader. Another suspected underworld figure, Meyer Lansky, experienced difficulties in Israel where the government sought his expulsion from the country.

Politically motivated crimes appeared on the increase during 1971. Latin-American nations, like Uruguay and Brazil, were plagued by kidnappings of officials and foreign diplomats. These kidnappings usually were accompanied by demands for the release of imprisoned terrorists in exchange for the lives of those seized (*see* articles on individual countries). Seeking to curb this practice, Uruguay's representative on the Legal Committee of the UN General Assembly asked for the drafting of a convention that would treat all personal offenses against diplomats and officials as common crimes, putting aside the Latin-American tradition of granting asylum to political offenders. Diplomatic safety also was a point at issue in North America. Following the firing of a number of rifle shots into a room occupied by members of its delegation to the UN, the Soviet government expressed concern and doubt about the ability of U.S. authorities to provide adequate protection to foreign diplomats. The shooting incident allegedly was perpetrated by the militant Jewish Defense League, a group protesting the restrictions placed by the Soviet authorities on Jews emigrating from the U.S.S.R.

In Northern Ireland a group of militants, led by members of the Irish Republican Army, stepped up acts of terrorism following the detention of many of their suspected colleagues.

"Politics, Crime, and the International Scene" was the major theme of an Inter-American Conference on Criminology held in San Juan, P.R., in November. Papers presented included several analyzing the 1970 Quebec political crisis, the kidnapping of officials and diplomats, hijacking and piracy, and political prison-

ers. The topic of political prisoners took on special relevance because of the tragedy at Attica, N.Y., in which 43 persons died in what was by far the most bloody riot in U.S. prison history. The events at Attica raised in dramatic form the plight of inmates who were, by and large, members of minority groups and had come to believe that they were political prisoners of the white majority. (*See* PRISONS AND PENOLOGY.)

Many countries reported public alarm caused by waves of violent bank robberies, holdups, and burglaries. In Italy, for instance, police in the Milan-Turin area had to deal with numbers of raids by gangs on weapon and ammunition stores. The arms stolen by these gangs were believed to have been used in a wave of attacks on local banks and stores. In West Germany police shot dead a hostage taken by robbers during the course of one highly publicized bank holdup in Munich. Victims of crime were also the subject of attention and assistance. The U.S. Congress passed legislation permitting the federal government to underwrite property insurance for those who were unable to secure it through commercial organizations. Crime victim compensation programs, pioneered in New Zealand and the U.K. in the early 1960s, were set up in South Australia and New Jersey in 1971.

Official protection of the public against pornography moved ahead in several countries. Particular attention was focused on the English Old Bailey trial and conviction of the publishers of the magazine *Oz* on charges of obscenity; the prison sentences imposed on the defendants, though later quashed, aroused international controversy. A hardening of official attitudes toward pornography appeared to be taking place in the U.S. following the public stance of Pres. Richard Nixon on the subject. (Du. C.)

Major Crimes. Bombings and threats of bombings continued to present a serious crime problem in the U.S. in 1971. On January 12, six persons, including the Rev. Philip F. Berrigan (*see* BIOGRAPHY), were indicted on federal charges of plotting to blow up heating systems of U.S. government buildings in Washington, D.C., and kidnap presidential adviser Henry A. Kissinger. On September 9, six men, including the reported leader of the Michigan Ku Klux Klan, Robert Edward Miles, were charged with conspiracy in the bombing of buses to be used in carrying out school desegregation in Pontiac, Mich. On January 7 a fire bomb caused damages of $50,000 to the Camp Fire Girls headquarters in Pomona, Calif.; on January 8 a small bomb exploded outside the U.S.S.R. cultural building in Washington, D.C.; and on March 1 a bomb exploded in the United States Capitol.

On April 27, a 19-year-old girl, Leslie Bacon of Atherton, Calif., was arrested as a material witness in the bombing of the Capitol. The arrest was later called illegal because Miss Bacon had not been given an opportunity to appear voluntarily before the grand jury in Seattle, Wash., that was investigating the bombing. A federal grand jury in New York City on June 24 returned an indictment charging Miss Bacon with having conspired to fire-bomb a Manhattan bank. Six other persons were named in the indictment as co-conspirators but they previously had pleaded guilty to charges of conspiracy to dynamite or fire-bomb several New York City buildings.

The first fatal shooting of an airline hijacker in the U.S. occurred on July 23, 1971, when Richard A. Obergfell of Passaic, N.J., hijacked a Trans World Airlines (TWA) jet bound from New York's La Guardia Airport for Chicago and asked to be flown to Milan, Italy. Upon being informed that the plane was not equipped for such a flight, the hijacker agreed to transfer to a plane at Kennedy International Airport, where he was killed by an FBI agent using a rifle with a telescopic sight. The first passenger death during the hijacking of a U.S. plane occurred at Chicago's O'Hare International Airport on June 11, 1971. A TWA jetliner was taking on passengers when a stewardess turned away Gregory White of Harvey, Ill., because he did not have a boarding pass. White had pulled a revolver and demanded to be flown to North Vietnam when a passenger, Howard L. Franks of Darien, Conn., moved and the hijacker fired two shots, killing him. Shots were exchanged between the hijacker and a U.S. deputy marshal while the plane was en route to New York, and again upon landing at Kennedy between an FBI agent and White before he was wounded and captured. On Nov. 25, 1971, a man giving his name as "D. B. Cooper" threatened to blow up a Northwest Airlines jetliner flying between Portland, Ore., and Seattle, Wash., unless he was given $200,000 and four parachutes. When his demands were met, the passengers were permitted to debark at Seattle, the plane was ordered to take off, and the man parachuted from it with the money, probably over a wilderness area northeast of Portland.

The International Air Transport Association estimated that growing traffic in stolen airline tickets was causing airline losses of at least $6 million a year in revenues. In Los Angeles, more than 5,000 fraudulent tickets were used in 1970. When airlines there began checking serial numbers of tickets presented against a computer-stored list in January 1971 there was an upsurge in the number of persons presenting purloined tickets to airlines in Las Vegas, Honolulu, San Francisco, Chicago, Miami, and New York City.

College campuses, once relatively free of crime, were experiencing grand larceny, armed robbery, assault, murder, and rape. Dormitory thefts at Princeton University were reported in February 1971 to be up 52% from the fall of 1970. University of Texas police reported that petty thefts at the Austin campus totaled 691 by mid-fall 1970, compared with 416 for the entire year of 1969. Burglaries on the campus of Stanford University, which had about 11,000 students, increased 228% over a three-year period, compared with an 11% increase in adjacent Palo Alto, with a population of 56,000.

In a limited survey Pinkerton's, Inc., found that 29.2% of retail stores were able to reduce losses from shoplifting and internal dishonesty during 1970; 37.4% suffered higher losses; and 33.4% reported losses at the same level as before. The survey attributed 45.9% of store losses to shoplifting, 27.3% to internal thievery, and 26.8% to other causes. However, Delbert L. Wood of Carson Pirie Scott & Co. of Chicago attributed 40% of all inventory shortages to dishonest employees and 20% to shoplifters.

There were several instances of multiple killings in the U.S. in 1971. In Cleveland, O., on the night of March 6, five persons were killed and 20 injured when a long-smoldering grudge between two motorcycle gangs, the Breed and the Violators, resulted in a ten-minute battle with knives, chains, and clubs at the fourth annual Motorcycle Custom and Trade Show. In California during May and June the bodies of 25 transient farm workers were found buried in peach orchards along the Feather River just outside the Sacramento Valley farming centre. On July 12, Juan V.

Corona, a Mexican-American farm labour contractor, was indicted in Yuba City and charged with the murders. On June 14 in Detroit, a city that had had 316 homicides, 25–50 of which were linked to drug traffic, police received a call from a woman reporting "a bloodbath." Seven persons, three young men and four young women, were found to have been shot to death in a house that also contained a number of weapons and instruments used by heroin addicts. In Phoenix, Ariz., on September 3, Mrs. Novella Bentley, her five children and son-in-law were shot and killed. Police said that Mrs. Bentley's husband and the wife and two children of their suspect, John Freeman, had disappeared in February. In Sheboygan, Wis., on July 19, Mrs. Hildegarde A. Dean was found shot to death in bed. Police making a routine canvass of the neighbourhood also found that Mrs. Naomi Rammer and her three sons had been killed. Murder charges were filed against Mrs. Dean's son Douglas, 19, who had dated Mrs. Rammer's daughter.

The longest criminal trial in California history ended in Los Angeles on Jan. 25, 1971, when hippie cult leader Charles M. Manson and three young women were found guilty and later sentenced to death in connection with the murders of five persons at actress Sharon Tate's home and of Mr. and Mrs. Leno LaBianca in August 1969. At a separate trial in October, Charles ("Tex") Watson, the "robot killer" of the cult, was also found guilty of the Tate-LaBianca murders and sentenced to death.

In New Jersey during 1971 a federal jury found Mayor Thomas J. Whelan of Jersey City and seven of his associates guilty in July of conspiracy to collect kickbacks from contractors; on September 7 Mayor John DeRose of Gloucester Township pleaded guilty to conspiracy and bribery charges and then resigned from office; and on April 23 former Mayor John R. Armellino of West New York and reputed Mafia figure Joseph Zicarelli were sentenced for conspiracy to protect gambling operations. Former West Virginia Gov. William Wallace Barron pleaded guilty in U.S. District Court in Charleston on March 29, 1971, to charges of having bribed the foreman of a federal jury that acquitted him in 1968 of wide-ranging corruption during his administration. San Francisco Mayor Joseph L. Alioto was indicted in March on a federal charge of interstate racketeering while

Barber shop in basement of U.S. Capitol is littered with debris after a bomb blast during the early morning hours of March 1, 1971, extensively damaged several rooms.

he was a private lawyer. On June 30 New Orleans District Attorney Jim Garrison, who had failed in various attempts to prove a conspiracy in the assassination of Pres. John F. Kennedy, was indicted on charges of accepting bribes to protect gambling operations.

In Chicago on August 24, State's Attorney Edward V. Hanrahan was named with 13 others in a long-suppressed indictment charging them with conspiracy to prevent the prosecution of policemen who raided an apartment in December 1969 and killed two occupants, both Black Panther leaders. Black militant leader H. Rap Brown, a fugitive since April 1970, was captured following a robbery at a New York City bar on October 16. On December 15, a federal grand jury indicted Otto Kerner, a former Illinois governor, and four others on various charges in connection with a racetrack stock scandal.

In 1970 the Royal Canadian Mounted Police made arrests at the rate of 1,000 a month in cases involving marijuana and other soft drugs. This was double the arrest rate in 1969. Four men took $1,129,000 in racetrack receipts from a Windsor, Ont., branch of the Bank of Canada in an early morning robbery on December 18. On April 27, in a lightning-fast raid on the Bank of Montreal branch at the Vancouver (B.C.) General Hospital, two masked bandits, armed with pistols, escaped with $327,000 that had been delivered only moments before. During the year Quebec separatists Paul Rose and Francis Simard were sentenced in Montreal to life imprisonment for their roles in the kidnap-slaying of Pierre Laporte, Quebec's minister of labour and immigration, in October 1970.

In the U.K., Scotland Yard announced that serious crimes in London increased 6% in the first half of 1971. There were 54 homicides in London, compared with 51 for all of 1970, and 258 cases of robbery with violence, an increase of 11.3% over the same period in 1970. A husband and wife, Ghulam and Salamante Mohamed, were sentenced to life imprisonment in January for the murder of Mrs. Joan McLean, whose dismembered body was found in a chimney in a house in Cardiff, and her daughter, whose body was found partly encased in concrete in a shallow grave in Glamorgan. A young French teacher, her sister, and her sister's boyfriend were all shot dead while on vacation in Cheshire in July. The case was closed when Michael Bassett, 24, later committed suicide, leaving several notes indicating that he was the murderer.

In March one of the largest police operations ever mounted took place around London after a gang had stolen £32,000 in a Kent bank raid. They escaped in a van, shot and wounded a policeman, kidnapped a passing motorist, stole another vehicle, and finally crashed into a wall, after a 100-mph chase by police. Three of the gang were seriously hurt and two others were captured, but the money was not recovered. The largest robbery in Britain since the £2.5 million great train robbery of 1963 took place in March. Ten raiders wearing stocking masks and carrying shotguns and coshes snatched 28 bags of bank notes worth £456,490 from an eight-ton armoured van which had stopped on its route from Brighton to London to allow one of its guards to use a nearby lavatory. In a weekend raid on the Baker Street branch of Lloyds Bank in London, early in September, a gang escaped with safe deposit items having an estimated value of up to £1 million. The gang tunneled its way under a restaurant and through the vault floor using thermal lances. A radio ham living in the area had accidentally tuned in to the thieves' conversation over two-way radios and

seemingly made several attempts to contact a senior police officer before he was taken seriously. An unofficial police inquiry was held. On August 23 Supt. Gerald Richardson, head of Blackpool, Eng., subdivision of the Lancashire Constabulary, was shot after a struggle with one of the gang that had raided a jewelry shop. Richardson, who died in the hospital, was the highest ranking police officer to be killed on duty in the U.K. A nationwide hunt for his killer ended in London on October 7 with the arrest of Frederick Sewell.

In May two City businessmen, one French, the other Iranian, were accused of fraudulently obtaining more than £11,750,000 from the Standard Bank, the Co-operative Bank, and other sources for the supposed refining and sale of quinine. Another fraud involved the Bank of Sark, registered in the Channel Islands, which was supposed to have had $72,500,001.39 on January 9 but was found in March to have no assets whatsoever, having taken in victims all over the world. The mastermind behind the scheme was unknown.

In Copenhagen in August an armed man kidnapped Viggo Rasmussen, managing director of Tuborg Breweries, and held him prisoner until a ransom of $240,-000 had been paid. The kidnapper claimed that he was working for Al Fatah, the Palestinian guerrilla organization. Frank Mouritzen, a riding instructor, and his wife were arrested on September 27. The largest ransom on record, $2.1 million, was paid in December for the release of West German merchant Theo Albrecht. A Mycenaean city and thousands of tombs on the island of Cyprus were destroyed by peasants and others who realized the prices that artifacts were fetching from dealers acting as middlemen for European and U.S. museums and private collectors. Retired Swedish farmer Karl Gunnar Bengtsson, who lost a court case in February and was ordered to pay damages to his estranged mistress, drew a gun in court and killed her, the judge, and two lawyers. He was later apprehended on his way to a police station to surrender. The largest robbery ever to take place in France occurred in Strasbourg on June 30 when several gunmen disguised as workers attacked postal employees and escaped with more than Fr. 11 million.

Eight Roman thieves held up a bus company cashier in April and escaped with $240,000. Also in Rome Judge Ezio Diez, president of the Labour Tribunal, was charged with manslaughter after a tin filled with dynamite had exploded under the car of one of his women servants. Judge Liberato Graziano of the Genoa Appeal Court was accused of possessing pornographic films and photographs for sales purposes.

A 300-page report by the Italian Parliament's anti-Mafia commission revealed that Sicily's Mafia bosses, described as ruthless killers, continually evaded conviction through the connivance of the authorities. By July more than 40 suspected Mafia bosses were serving long-term exile sentences on small Mediterranean islands after the most determined anticrime drive in years. The campaign began after the daylight assassination of Pietro Scaglione, the chief public prosecutor of Palermo, on May 5. Among other activities the Mafia were accused of destroying the pines around Rome by spraying them with gasoline. Land thus freed for building purposes greatly increased in value.

In Turkey on March 4, four U.S. servicemen were kidnapped in Ankara, allegedly by members of the militant Turkish People's Liberation Army, and later released unharmed. In Istanbul on May 17, Israeli Consul General Efraim Elrom was kidnapped and slain five days later when the government refused to

Seventeen-year-old psychiatric patient holds a gun to the head of an intern during an attempted escape from a St. Paul, Minn., hospital. Earlier, a deputy sheriff was shot and killed in a scuffle with the patient.

UPI COMPIX

meet the demand of the Turkish People's Liberation Army, which claimed responsibility for the abduction, that all revolutionaries jailed in Turkey be released. On May 30 the daughter of Turkish Army Maj. Dincer Erkan was kidnapped in Istanbul and held hostage in the apartment where she resided. On June 1 police stormed the apartment and rescued the girl after a gunfight in which one guerrilla was killed.

In Australia in September police charged Clifford Bartholomew with the slaying of his wife and seven children as well as his sister-in-law and her baby on a small farm 34 mi. S of Adelaide. An argument appeared to have led to what police termed the worst mass killing in Australian history.

It was reported from Nairobi in July that 23 daylight bank robberies had occurred in Kenya since Jan. 1, 1970. The government announced in June that it would introduce legislation to authorize capital punishment for the crime of robbery with violence. In Uganda, the government of Idi Amin, which came to power in January 1971, made the stamping out of *kondos,* or gangsters, a major program. A 36-year-old Nigerian, Busari Adio, was sentenced to jail for three years for unlawful possession of human skulls; he told magistrates, "It's a business I inherited from my father."   (V. W. P.)

See also Law; Police.

Cuba

The socialist republic of Cuba occupies the largest island in the Greater Antilles of the West Indies. Area: 42,827 sq.mi. (110,922 sq.km.), including several thousand small islands and cays. Pop. (1970): 8,553,395, including (1953) white 72.8%; mestizo 14.5%; Negro 12.4%. Cap. and largest city: Havana (pop., 1967 est., 1,008,500). Language: Spanish. Religion: predominantly Roman Catholic. President in 1971, Osvaldo Dorticós Torrado; prime minister, Fidel Castro.

During 1971 Cuba continued to enjoy political stability, but little economic progress was made. A major government preoccupation was relations with the Soviet Union. There were rumours in August that Moscow was seeking to displace Fidel Castro as prime minister by Carlos Rafael Rodríguez, an influential member of the Cabinet and a lifelong Communist, although Castro would remain as commander in chief of the armed forces and secretary-general of the Communist Party. Late in October Soviet Premier Aleksei N. Kosygin visited Havana.

Economic relations between the two countries were difficult, with the Soviet Union seeking a more direct role in Cuban economic policy. A request by Cuba for a long list of capital equipment for factories was refused, as Moscow was dissatisfied with the use made of previously supplied goods. The director of the Soviet State Planning Commission (Gosplan), Nikolai Babakov, visited Havana in April and May to investigate ways of increasing control. Nevertheless, on February 22 a four-year trade agreement had been signed by which Cuba would sell increased amounts of sugar, nickel, and other primary products to the Soviet Union in return for industrial goods and petroleum. At the same time the agreement signed in January 1964, by which the U.S.S.R. paid low prices for Cuban sugar, was renewed for an additional six years. Soviet economic aid to Cuba was estimated at $500 million a year and the total Cuban debt at $5.7 billion.

There were continuing fears in the United States of a Soviet military buildup in Cuba, and the U.S. continued to seek assurances that the Soviet Union still adhered to the secret agreement of 1962 forbidding the installation of offensive weapons systems in the Caribbean area. It was estimated that there were at least 7,000 Soviet technicians in Cuba, and it was reported that a major military base was under construction at Lacubilla.

The economic situation continued to deteriorate. The 1971 sugar crop amounted to 5.9 million metric tons, against a target of 7 million; the 1970 figure was 8.5 million tons. This was the sixth year in succession that the official target had not been met. The coffee, citrus fruit, and tobacco crops were lower than in 1970, mainly due to a severe drought. A serious outbreak of swine fever affected meat production. Consequently, rations of foodstuffs and tobacco were reduced, causing some popular discontent. Moreover, a shortage of petroleum resulted from a cutback in shipments by the Soviet Union. On the other hand, the government claimed that industrial production in the first half of 1971 was up 15–20%.

In the early part of the year an intensive official program was undertaken to try to secure all-round improvement in the economy. Large numbers of people were conscripted to assist harvesting, particularly the sugar crop, and plans were being worked out for future harvests. A decree ending refugee flights from Havana to Miami was seen as a move to prevent the loss of skilled personnel. In February it was decided that durable consumer goods would be distributed to workers who conspicuously raised their productivity. The government aimed to increase production by enforcing greater discipline and at the same time gradually to abolish taxes and the use of money.

There were growing indications that many Latin-

Prime Minister Fidel Castro's government negotiated extensive economic aid agreements with the Soviet Union early in 1971.

CUBA
Education. (1968–69) Primary, pupils 1,332,659, teachers 45,125; secondary, pupils 186,985, teachers 10,799; vocational, pupils 46,962, teachers 3,909; teacher training, students 27,651, teachers 1,504; higher (including 3 universities), students 30,311, teaching staff 4,641.
Finance. Monetary unit: peso, officially at par with the U.S. dollar (2.40 pesos = £1 sterling) and with a free rate (Sept. 27, 1971) of 2.48 pesos to £1 sterling. Budget (1966) balanced at 2,718,000,000 pesos.
Foreign Trade. (1967) Imports 1,001,000,000 pesos; exports 717 million pesos. Import sources (1968 est.): U.S.S.R. 61%; China 7%; France 6%. Export destinations (1968 est.): U.S.S.R. 44%; China 9%; Spain 6%; Czechoslovakia 6%; East Germany 5%. Main export (1966) sugar products 85%.
Transport and Communications. Roads (1970) *c.* 13,000 km. (including *c.* 1,200 km. of the Central Highway). Motor vehicles in use (1965): passenger 162,000; commercial (including buses) 103,700. Railways (1970): 14,444 km. (including 9,441 km. plantation). Shipping (1970): merchant vessels 100 gross tons and over 236; gross tonnage 332,906. Telephones (Dec. 1969) 263,000. Radio receivers (Dec. 1970) *c.* 1,325,000. Television receivers (Dec. 1968) *c.* 575,-000.
Agriculture. Production (in 000; metric tons; 1969; 1968 in parentheses): rice 177 (293); corn *c.* 115 (*c.* 115); cassava *c.* 220 (*c.* 210); sweet potatoes *c.* 240 (*c.* 233); sugar, raw value (1970–71) *c.* 6,000, (1969–70) *c.* 8,533; coffee (1970) *c.* 33, (1969) *c.* 30; oranges *c.* 140 (139); tobacco *c.* 45 (46). Livestock (in 000; 1969–70): cattle *c.* 7,100; pigs *c.* 1,490; sheep *c.* 280; goats *c.* 84.
Industry. Production (in 000; metric tons; 1969): crude oil 91; petroleum products *c.* 5,300; electricity (kw-hr.; 1968) 4,700,000; manganese ore (metal content; 1968) 20; nickel ore (metal content; 1968) 37.

Crops: *see* Agriculture

American countries wished to end the diplomatic and commercial isolation imposed upon Cuba by the Organization of American States (OAS). Relations with Chile became close, diplomatic ties having been restored in November 1970. The foreign ministers of the two countries exchanged official visits in July and August, and a technical and scientific cooperation agreement was signed in August. In November and December Castro spent 25 days in Chile, the longest official visit in Chilean history and Castro's first trip to a South American country since the Cuban revolution. Some of his public statements were believed to have contributed to the disorders that rocked Santiago in early December, although the root causes lay in the Chilean economic situation.

En route home, Castro made brief stops in Peru and Ecuador. Peru was among the countries considering the establishment of diplomatic relations, and in July signed an agreement to sell 105,000 tons of fish meal to Cuba. At the OAS meeting held in San José, Costa Rica, in April there was considerable pressure on the U.S. to end the economic blockade. Moreover, the U.S. position was becoming increasingly difficult to defend in view of Pres. Richard M. Nixon's moves toward a rapprochement with China. In October, 22 Cubans arrived in New Orleans, La., without visas, saying that they had come to take part in a sugarcane conference. They were detained at a U.S. naval air station and returned after the conference—which they never attended—was over.

It became clear that Cuban support for guerrilla movements in Latin America had become rather lukewarm, despite a speech by Castro in July maintaining that it never had wavered. Official policy appeared to be directed toward assisting the overthrow of Latin-American governments by constitutional means to repeat the Chilean success. There were signs that Sweden was to grant substantial amounts of foreign aid to Cuba. A new trade agreement was signed with Spain in September, thus ensuring the maintenance of one of Cuba's best trade outlets in Western Europe.

(RN. C.)

Cycling

Although Europe remained the stronghold of competitive cycling, renewed interest in the bicycle as a health medium continued in the Americas, where supply was unable to keep pace with the demand for high-class lightweight machines. American customers crossed the Atlantic to buy such bicycles and enjoy touring holidays over European roads on them before flying home with their ten-speed prizes. One South American visitor to Europe in August brought his bicycle with him, and on it won the world amateur pursuit title in Italy. He was Martín Rodriguez of Colombia, the first male world champion from the Western Hemisphere since 1912. A month earlier Rodriguez got in valuable training for the world series by winning the individual pursuit title in the Pan-American Games at Cali, Colombia (July 30–August 13) and leading his country to victory in the team pursuit event. Other Pan-American titles went to: Jocelyn Lovell (Can.), 1,000-m. time trial; Leslie King (Trinidad and Tobago), 1,000-m. sprint; and John Howard (U.S.), 110-mi. road race.

Apart from Rodriguez' victory, however, the 1971 world titles all were won by riders from the accepted cycling nations. Officially, Switzerland was the host country, but a suitable stadium not being available,

the track events were held over the frontier at Varese, Italy (August 25–31). The road races took place at Mendrisio, Switz. (September 2, 4, and 5). Results: *Track.* Men, amateur: 1,000-m. time trial, Eduard Rapp (U.S.S.R.); 4,000-m. individual pursuit, Rodriguez; 1,000-m. sprint, Daniel Morelon (France); 4,000-m. team pursuit, Italy; tandem sprint, Werner Otto and Jurgen Geschke (E.Ger.); one-hour motor-paced, Horst Gnas (W.Ger.). Men, professional: sprint, Leijn Loeveseijn (Neth.); 4,000-m. individual pursuit, Dirk Baert (Belg.); 100-km. motor-paced, Theo Verschueren (Belg.). Women: sprint, Galina Tsareva (U.S.S.R.); 3,000-m. pursuit, Tamara Garkushina (U.S.S.R.). *Road:* Men, amateur: 105 mi., Regis Ovion (France); 100-km. team time trial, Belgium. Men, professional: 167 mi., Eddy Merckx (Belg.). Women: 31¼ mi., Anna Konkina (U.S.S.R.).

Since the world road championships are decided on a "one-race" formula, there is often a surprise winner whose name is missing from the results of classic one-day and stage races. Such was not the case with the two 1971 men champions. Regis Ovion won many continental amateur races during the year, including the seven-day Route de France and the ten-day amateur Tour de France.

As for Eddy Merckx, the world championship was the climax of his greatest season. Ignoring the old adage "early ripe, early rotten," the 26-year-old Belgian was soon in form, winning both the Tour of Sardinia (February 27–March 3) and Paris–Nice (March 11–17) stage races. He then triumphed for the fourth time in the opening Italian classic, the 180-mi. Milan–San Remo (March 19). The one big race in which Merckx had difficulties was the Tour de France (June 26–July 18), in which Luís Ocana of Spain took the lead in the Alps. With eight days of racing still ahead, Ocana seemed a certain winner. But 48 hours later he was in the hospital and out of the race, the victim of a fall on the descent of a mountain pass during a violent thunderstorm. Merckx then went on to win.

Other important multistage professional race winners were: Tour of Spain, Ferdinand Bracke (Belg.); Tour of Switzerland, G. Pintens (Belg.); Tour of Italy, Gösta Petterssen (Swed.). One-day races and their winners included Tour of Flanders, Evert Dolman (Neth.); Paris–Roubaix, Roger Rosiers (Belg.);

Cyclists struggle for the lead of La Tour de la Nouvelle France, held in Montreal in September 1971. Guido Reybroek of Belgium won the five-day event, the first of its kind in North America.

"MONTREAL GAZETTE"

Currency:
see Money and Banking

Cybernetics:
see Computers

Amstel Gold Race, Frans Verbeecke (Belg.); Flèche Wallonne, Roger De Vlaeminck (Belg.); Liège–Bastogne–Liège, Merckx; Paris–Tours, Rik Van Linden (Belg.); Tour of Lombardy, Merckx; Grand Prix des Nations time trial, Ocana.

The amateur cycling season began in Algeria. In the Tour of Algeria (March 16–28), which included roads through the semidesert, Soviet and Polish riders were at grips, individual honours going to Zbigniew Krzeszowiec (Pol.) with 34 seconds to spare from Ivan Skossyrev who, however, led the U.S.S.R. to team victory. Well beaten in that race but in top form two months later was another Pole, Ryszard Szurkowski, who achieved the notable feat of winning the "Peace Race" (Warsaw–Berlin–Prague) for the second year in succession.

In the United Kingdom in the mountainous 113½-mi. Manx International, Bernard Bourreau (France) took the trophy. A few weeks earlier a French "double" had seemed likely in the 1,500-mi. Tour of Britain (May 30–June 12) with Marcel Duchemin leading comfortably two days from the finish, only to succumb to a well-timed attack by Fedor Den Hertog (Neth.).   (Jo. B. W.)

Cyprus

An island republic and a member of the Commonwealth of Nations, Cyprus is in the eastern Mediterranean. Area: 3,572 sq.mi. (9,251 sq.km.). Pop. (1971 est.): 634,000, including Greeks 77%; Turks 18%. Cap. and largest city: Nicosia (pop., 1970 est., 115,000). Language: Greek and Turkish. Religion: Greek Orthodox 77%; Muslim 18.3%. President in 1971, Archbishop Makarios III.

Intercommunal talks continued between the Greek and Turkish Cypriots in 1971, but there was little progress toward a final solution. The main source of disagreement was the degree of autonomous control to be accorded to the Turkish community in matters of local government. As the talks between the two communities followed their inconclusive and halting course, a de facto situation existed that amounted almost to partition. The Turkish community controlled a number of enclaves, the most important being located on the west coast at Famagusta in the port area, and in the region between Nicosia and Kyrenia. The failure to resolve the difficulties separating the two communities led to the growth of renewed tension in the summer of 1971—for example, at the villages of Marathovouno and Chatos near Nicosia.

In June, the Greek government communicated to President Makarios proposals that envisaged the inclusion in the Cyprus Cabinet of a Turkish Cypriot minister with a large measure of administrative control over the Turkish community. These proposals also had the approval of the Turkish government in Ankara. It was intimated that if President Makarios rejected this new initiative, in the event of a further crisis he might find himself without support from a Greek government unwilling to risk a major confrontation with Turkey over the Cyprus problem. In spite of this possibility Makarios felt obliged to reject the proposals, declaring that to accept them would mean the creation of a state within a state.

Reports circulating at that time suggested that if the intercommunal talks remained unproductive one possible line of advance might be promotion of a conference, to include Great Britain, Greece, and Turkey as well as representatives of the Greek and Turkish communities in Cyprus. Meanwhile, also in June, Makarios visited Moscow and was able to secure from the Soviet government a statement of support for the maintenance of a united and independent Cyprus. In August, UN Secretary-General U Thant was reported to have informed Makarios that he would be prepared to offer assistance if requested to do so. However, he stressed that the time for mediation was past and that he would only be able to act as an arbitrator whose recommendations would be binding upon all parties.

A further complication arose at the end of August. Gen. Georgios Grivas, leader of the EOKA resistance movement against British rule during the years 1955–59, was reported to have returned secretly to Cyprus. An ardent advocate of *enosis*, the union of Cyprus with Greece, General Grivas had commanded the Greek Cypriot National Guard from 1964 to 1967. The general was known to be strongly opposed to the policies of the Cyprus government, calling for the end of the Makarios regime and for the establishment of an administration dedicated to the achievement of *enosis*.

Early in September, Makarios visited Greece for talks with the Greek prime minister, Georgios Papadopoulos, in order to try to ease the somewhat strained relations that had existed between the two countries during the preceding months and also to discuss the renewal of tension in Cyprus arising from the virtual failure of the intercommunal negotiations. A report emanating from Nicosia in October indicated that Makarios would be prepared to meet Grivas and to examine with him matters of mutual concern. It was even suggested that the president might be willing to consider offering Grivas a ministerial appointment, provided that the general declared his readiness to accept the prospect of a united and independent Cyprus and abandon efforts to bring about *enosis*.   (V. J. P.)

CYPRUS
Education. (1968–69) Primary, pupils 71,745, teachers 2,239; secondary, pupils 33,134, teachers 1,412; vocational, pupils 4,355, teachers 272; higher, students 446, teaching staff 34.
  Finance. Monetary unit: pound, at par with the pound sterling (C£1 = U.S. $2.40) and with a free rate (Sept. 27, 1971) of C£1 = U.S. $2.48. Budget (1969 est.): revenue C£27,390,000; expenditure C£24.6 million. Gold, SDRs, and foreign exchange, monetary authorities: (June 1971) U.S. $228.7 million; (June 1970) U.S. $180 million.
  Foreign Trade. (1970) Imports C£99,370,000; exports C£45,190,000. Import sources: U.K. 29%; Italy 10%; West Germany 7%; U.S. 7%; Greece 5%. Export destinations: U.K. 39%; West Germany 17%; Italy 6%; U.S.S.R. 5%. Main exports: copper 21%; citrus fruit 16%; potatoes 14%; iron pyrites 6%.
  Transport and Communications. Roads (1969) 8,539 km. Motor vehicles in use (1969): passenger 48,849; commercial 11,880. Air traffic (1970): 126,-950,000 passenger-km.; freight 2,642,000 net ton-km. Shipping (1970): merchant vessels 100 gross tons and over 207; gross tonnage 1,138,229. Telephones (Dec. 1969) 42,000.
  Agriculture. Production (in 000; metric tons; 1969; 1968 in parentheses): wheat 81 (66); potatoes 163 (176); oranges 107 (102); grapefruit c. 65 (58); olives 19 (15); grapes 203 (169). Livestock (in 000; 1969–70): sheep c. 410; cattle c. 40; pigs c. 86.
  Industry. Production (in 000; metric tons; 1969): asbestos 22; copper ore (exports; metal content) 19; chromium ore (oxide content) 11; cement (1970) 271; electricity (excluding most industrial production; kw-hr.; 1970) 560,000.

Czechoslovakia

A federal socialist republic of central Europe, Czechoslovakia lies between Poland, the U.S.S.R., Hungary, Austria, and Germany. Area: 49,371 sq.mi. (127,870 sq.km.), including Slovakia 18,922 sq.mi. Pop. (1970 est.): 14,484,620 (Slovakia 4,560,000), including (1968 est.) Czech 65%; Slovak 29%. Cap. and largest city: Prague (pop., 1970 est., 1,103,350). Language: Czech and Slovak (official). General secretary of the Communist Party of Czechoslovakia in 1971, Gustav Husak; president, Ludvik Svoboda; premier, Lubomir Strougal.

Czechoslovakia's situation remained fundamentally unchanged throughout 1971; Gustav Husak consolidated his personal position, and Soviet troops continued to garrison the country, as they had since the August 1968 invasion. The resultant political apathy among the people contributed greatly to the country's economic stagnation. At the beginning of the year the federalization program, designed to create Czech and Slovak states within the republic, became a meaningless formal arrangement when the federal government was given powers to override decisions of the separate Czech and Slovak governments.

The Central Committee of the Czechoslovak Communist Party, meeting at the end of 1970, had explained the 1968 crisis as an imperialist-Zionist-Vatican conspiracy, which more than justified the U.S.S.R.'s military action. The congress of the Slovak Communist Party, which met in May 1971, heard that 40,000 (17.5%) of the party membership in Slovakia had been purged as "right-wing opportunists." The total expelled from the party throughout Czechoslovakia was given as over 300,000 (21.6%). Nevertheless, the Czechoslovak Communist Party retained a membership of 1.2 million (8% of the total population). Its 14th congress, held in Prague, May 25–29, was officially the first party congress since 1966, the dramatic "14th congress" organized the day after the Soviet invasion having been stigmatized as illegal.

The congress seemed to complete the transmutation of Pres. Ludvik Svoboda, one of the heroes of 1968; in his opening speech, with Soviet party chief Leonid I. Brezhnev in the audience, he thanked the U.S.S.R. for its "assistance" in 1968. Husak again spoke of the inevitability of the Soviet intervention and assured the U.S.S.R. of Czechoslovakia's loyalty, an assurance underlined by his attack on the policies of the Chinese Communist Party.

Gen. Vaclav Prchlik, who had dared to criticize the U.S.S.R.'s preponderance within the Warsaw Pact, was sentenced to three years' imprisonment in March (the sentence was later reduced to 22 months by the Czechoslovak Supreme Court). But the wrath of the diehards in the Czechoslovak party leadership was mainly directed against the intellectuals, who were blamed for the ideological infection that had caused the 1968 crisis. The year began with the trial of a group of left-wing "revolutionary" students, who stood united in their rejection of Western capitalism, Soviet Communism, and what they regarded as Dubcek's surrender to the technocrats.

Expulsions from the journalists' union were reported with depressing regularity. The Historical Institute of the Czechoslovak Academy of Sciences had virtually ceased to exist, and more than 230 historians were either driving trucks or working in factories or

on the railways. In the summer the historian Jaroslav Sedivy and the former head of the Czechoslovak film industry, Alois Polednak, joined others on trial for subversion. The remarkable reputation of the Czechoslovak cinema disintegrated, and censorship in the theatre was used to mutilate not only Molière's *Dom Juan* and Shakespeare's *Henry V* but also the writings of the Marxist Bertolt Brecht. A play on the French Commune was banned entirely. A new and more amenable Union of Czech Journalists was set up in May, and a committee was later established to prepare the formation of a new Actors' Union. The chess champion Ludek Pachman was the subject of government persecution, and the journalist Vladimir Skutina, sentenced in February to two years' imprisonment for criticizing policy, was brought back in July to receive an additional 26 months for similar offenses.

The state of the Czechoslovak economy reflected the country's general condition. The 7.5% increase in industrial production reported in 1970 meant very little when adjusted to rising prices. There were serious deficiencies in the power industry and also in housing construction. In the agricultural sector, shortfalls in the production of beef made meat imports necessary. Nominal wages rose by 3.6% in 1970, and the cost of living went up by 1.4%. Husak's need to win the workers' support made it difficult to adopt policies aimed at containing wage inflation. The first general election since the 1968 invasion was held in November, with the unopposed official candidates receiving predictably heavy votes.

CZECHOSLOVAKIA

Education. (1968–69) Primary, pupils 2,052,526, teachers 98,399; secondary, pupils 107,978, teachers 7,121; vocational, pupils 270,208, teachers 14,164; teacher training, students 8,477, teachers 439; higher (including 14 universities), students 137,654, teaching staff 20,146.

Finance. Monetary unit: koruna, with an official exchange rate of 7.20 koruny to U.S. $1 (17.28 koruny = £1 sterling) and a tourist rate of 16.20 koruny to U.S. $1 (38.74 koruny = £1 sterling). Budget (1969 est.) balanced at 156.2 billion koruny.

Foreign Trade. (1969) Imports 23,718,000,000 koruny; exports 23.9 billion koruny. Import sources: U.S.S.R. 34%; East Germany 13%; Poland 8%; Hungary 6%. Export destinations: U.S.S.R. 34%; East Germany 11%; Poland 7%; West Germany 5%. Main exports: machinery 51%; metals, minerals, and fuels 19%; manufactured goods 16%.

Transport and Communications. Roads (1969) 145,919 km. (including 73,220 km. main roads). Motor vehicles in use (1969): passenger 651,625; commercial 173,999. Railways (1969): 13,315 km. (including 2,511 km. electrified); traffic: 20,155,000,000 passenger-km., freight 56,670,000,000 net ton-km. Air traffic (1970): 899 million passenger-km.; freight 18,-230,000 net ton-km. Shipping (1970): merchant vessels 100 gross tons and over 12; gross tonnage 88,868. Telephones (Dec. 1969) 1,895,229. Radio receivers (Dec. 1968) 3,967,000. Television receivers (Dec. 1969) 2,996,000.

Agriculture. Production (in 000; metric tons; 1970; 1969 in parentheses): wheat c. 3,050 (3,257); barley c. 2,400 (2,499); oats 943 (969); rye 575 (687); corn c. 520 (495); potatoes c. 5,500 (5,180); sugar, raw value (1970–71) c. 763, (1969–70) c. 716; beef and veal c. 400 (361); pork c. 600 (558). Livestock (in 000; Jan. 1970): cattle 4,223; pigs 5,037; sheep 977; chickens 33,392.

Industry. Index of industrial production (1963 = 100): (1970) 154; (1969) 144. Production (in 000; metric tons; 1970): coal 28,192; brown coal 81,162; electricity (kw.-hr.) 44,925,000; iron ore (30% metal content) 1,607; pig iron 7,621; steel 11,480; cement 7,401; sulfuric acid 1,110; nitrogenous fertilizers (N content; 1969) 336; superphosphates (1969) 289; cotton yarn 113; cotton fabrics (m.) 533,000; woolen fabrics (m.) 51,000; rayon and acetate yarn and fibres 69; passenger cars (units) 143; commercial vehicles (units) 48. Dwellings completed (1970) 108,000.

Pressures from the U.S.S.R. seemed directed toward a return to old priorities in economic management, and the Czechoslovak development plan for 1971–75, made public in April, forecast an expansion of heavy engineering and a doubling of machine tool production. Overall industrial production was to increase by 34–36%, and Czechoslovakia's trade with its Comecon partners to go up by 45%, while the overall growth target for foreign trade was 35%. Some effort was made to improve the supply of consumer goods.

In foreign policy the government cautiously followed the Soviet lead. It was thought that Husak's visit to Moscow in January included some discussion of the consequences of the 1970 treaties concluded by West Germany with the U.S.S.R. and Poland. In 1968 there had been some fear in Moscow, Warsaw, and East Germany that the reformers in Prague might be too eager to develop economic and political contacts with West Germany. However, the Bonn government chose to pursue its *Ostpolitik* by first establishing some degree of understanding with the U.S.S.R. before deploying initiatives toward the other member states of the Warsaw Pact. In the case of Czechoslovakia, negotiations on the normalization of relations proceeded slowly and without much effect.   (Oт. P.)

Dahomey

A republic of West Africa, Dahomey is located north of the Gulf of Guinea and is bounded by Togo, Upper Volta, Niger, and Nigeria. Area: 43,483 sq.mi. (112,-620 sq.km.). Pop. (1970 est.): 2,718,000, mainly Dahomean and allied tribes. Cap.: Porto-Novo (pop., 1970 est., 87,000). Largest city: Cotonou (pop., 1970 est., 139,000). Language: French and local dialects. Religion: animist, with Christian and Muslim minorities. Chairman of the Presidential Council in 1971, Hubert Maga.

In striking contrast with the permanent atmosphere of political unrest and the military coups and attempted coups that had disrupted Dahomey's internal affairs in previous years, 1971 was a year of calm throughout the country. The only significant politi-

cal event was a Cabinet reshuffle in August. Daouda Badarou, foreign minister, and Michel Ahouanmenou, ambassador in Paris, exchanged posts, while Mama Arouna, high commissioner for the interior, was appointed minister to the presidency, in charge of home affairs and security.

Dahomey's 1971 budget estimated expenditures of CFA Fr. 10.6 billion, compared with 9.8 billion in 1970 Revenue was estimated at CFA Fr. 9.3 billion, compared with the 1970 figure of CFA Fr. 8.3 billion. The budget deficit was thus estimated at CFA Fr. 1.3 billion, slightly lower than in 1970. The minister of finance stated that the budgeted growth in expenditure was largely attributable to increased recurrent costs arising out of the implementation of various educational and social projects. These included the establishment of the University of Dahomey. The increased revenue was expected to arise mainly from economic growth, since the 20% income tax rate had been abolished in August 1970 and no new major taxation measures introduced.

On May 4 a nine-year agreement was concluded between the Dahomean government and the Shell Oil Company for oil prospecting in an area of about 1,500 sq.mi. Shell undertook to invest about CFA Fr. 3.4 billion during the first three years—CFA Fr. 420 million in the first year and CFA Fr. 1.5 billion in each of the two succeeding years. The area involved included an offshore zone. Although offshore petroleum exploration had begun in 1965, and despite indications that new oil deposits had been discovered by Union Oil of California, by the end of 1971 no actual exploitation had taken place.   (Ph. D.; X.)

Dance

A single birthday had special significance for dance in 1971, the 80th of Ted Shawn on October 21, which was marked by a party given by the Dance Collection of the New York Public Library at the Library and Museum of Performing Arts at Lincoln Center. Shawn had made his debut as a dancer in 1911, and was probably the first U.S. male dancer outside of show business to have an international reputation. Shawn had also choreographed and produced the first all-male group dance in modern times, created in the 1920s a dance-drama on a Toltec theme, *Xochitl,* for one of his most promising dancers, Martha Graham, and presided in 1941 over the building of the first theatre built for dance, the Ted Shawn Theater at Lee, Mass., the site of his internationally famous Jacob's Pillow Dance Festival. His marriage in 1914 to Ruth St. Denis, already an established star, led to the founding of the Denishawn schools and companies, the biggest and most influential dance organization in the U.S. from 1915 to 1931. Products of Denishawn included Doris Humphrey, Charles Weidman, and other dancers who made their marks in concert, vaudeville, and cinema.

The 39th year of the Jacob's Pillow Dance Festival opened with performances by the Northeast Regional Ballet Festival, which held its annual series at the Pillow rather than at one of its member cities (there were four regional ballet associations in the U.S. with a membership of about 180 amateur companies). The American Dance Festival, presented by Connecticut College School of the Dance at New London, continued to feature modern dance, including the first East Coast appearances by one of Califor-

DAHOMEY
Education. (1967–68) Primary, pupils 139,734, teachers 3,445; secondary, pupils 13,354, teachers 470; vocational, pupils 727, teachers (public only) 69; teacher training, students 129, teachers 18; higher, students 115, teaching staff (1965–66) 5.
Finance. Monetary unit: CFA franc, with a parity of CFA Fr. 50 to the French franc (CFA Fr. 277.71 = U.S. $1; CFA Fr. 666.50 = £ sterling) and a free rate (Sept. 27, 1971) of CFA Fr. 276.50 to U.S. $1 (CFA Fr. 685.75 = £1 sterling). Budget (1970 est.): receipts CFA Fr. 8,349,000,000; expenditure CFA Fr. 9,836,000,000.
Foreign Trade. (1969) Imports CFA Fr. 14,130,-000,000; exports CFA Fr. 6,690,000,000. Import sources: France 39%; Netherlands 7%; U.S. 6%; West Germany 5%. Export destinations: France 36%; Nigeria 13%; Netherlands 13%; U.S. 10%; West Germany 8%. Main exports: palm products 39%; coffee 5%.
Agriculture. Production (in 000; metric tons; 1969; 1968 in parentheses): cassava c. 1,140 (1,142); sweet potatoes c. 580 (c. 560); corn 205 (222); millet and sorghum c. 75 (c. 50); peanuts c. 30 (c. 25); cotton, lint 9 (9); palm oil c. 40 (c. 35); palm kernels 65 (57); coffee c. 0.9 (c. 0.9). Livestock (in 000; 1969–70): cattle c. 570; sheep c. 570; pigs c. 360.

Kenneth MacMillan's "Anastasia" is premiered by the Royal Ballet at the Royal Opera House in London, July 22, 1971.
STUART ROBINSON

nia's leading dancers, Bella Lewitzky, with her company. The New York Dance Festival, held annually in the open-air Delacorte Theater in New York City's Central Park, was produced for the second year by Donald Saddler.

In Washington, D.C., the John F. Kennedy Center for the Performing Arts opened with Leonard Bernstein's *Mass,* for which Alvin Ailey provided the choreography and dancers. The American Ballet Theatre, the centre's official dance troupe, played an inaugural season and was followed by other dance companies—Ailey's own company, Washington's National Ballet, an Afro-Asian Dance Festival, and others.

The American Ballet Theatre added two modern dance works to its repertory, José Limón's *The Moor's Pavane,* and *The Traitor,* plus Rudolf Nureyev's staging of excerpts from Petipa's *Paquita* and such new works as Agnes de Mille's *A Rose for Miss Emily,* Michael Smuin's *Schubertiade,* and Dennis Nahat's *Mendelssohn Symphony.* Eliot Feld returned to the American Ballet Theatre as a choreographer following the disbanding of his own group, the short-lived American Ballet Company, which could not survive financial difficulties. Bruce Marks, a principal dancer with the American Ballet Theatre, was also appointed principal dancer with the Royal Danish Ballet.

The New York City Ballet, in residence at the State

Laura Connor and Graham Fletcher appear in "St. Thomas' Wake," choreographed by David Drew. Premier performance was June 7, 1971, at the Sadler's Wells Theatre, London.

LESLIE E. SPATT

Theater at Lincoln Center, offered its repertory seasons as well as its annual *The Nutcracker* (Tchaikovsky). The major addition to the repertory was Jerome Robbins' *Goldberg Variations* (Bach), which had been seen incomplete in open rehearsals in 1970 at the company's summer engagement at Saratoga Springs. George Balanchine, the City Ballet's artistic director and chief choreographer, was represented by a novelty, *PAMTGG,* a lighthearted salute to the frequently heard commercial "PanAm Makes the Going Great." There were other new works by junior choreographers, among them Lorca Massine (son of Leonide Massine) and John Clifford.

The Brooklyn Academy of Music not only presided over the final New York season of the American Ballet Company, which featured premieres of Feld's *Romance, Theatre,* and *The Gods Amused,* but it also offered an Afro-Asian Dance Festival featuring national groups from Senegal, Cambodia, Iran, Morocco, India, and Sierra Leone. An American Dance Season featuring Ailey's American Dance Theater, the Dance Theater of Harlem, and Pearl Lang, Louis Falco, Paul Taylor, Alwin Nikolais, Eleo Pomare, Erick Hawkins, Don Redlich, Paul Sanasardo and their companies, played the ANTA Theater. Later in the year, the Ailey troupe, after extensive tours, gave a late fall season at the New York City Center.

The City Center Joffrey Ballet increased its repertory by eight ballets. Revivals were George Balanchine's *Square Dance,* Ailey's *Feast of Ashes,* and Stuart Hodes's *Abyss;* novelties were *Reflections, Valentine,* and *Kettentanz* by Gerald Arpino (the company's principal choreographer), Ailey's *Mingus Dances,* and Margo Sappington's *Weewis.* Joffrey II, the organization's junior group, appeared on tour and for invited audiences in New York City.

The Australian Ballet, co-directed by Dame Peggy van Praagh and Sir Robert Helpmann and with Rudolf Nureyev as guest star, made its first U.S. tour. Other visitors from abroad—and there were many—included Bayanihan from the Philippines, Mazowsze from Poland, Inbal from Israel, the Siberian Dancers and Singers of Omsk, and Maurice Béjart's Ballet of the 20th Century from Brussels.

Other dance highlights in the U.S. in a variety of fields included a new production of *The Sleeping Beauty* (Tchaikovsky) by Ben Stevenson for the National Ballet with Margot Fonteyn as guest star; a new, full-length *Romeo and Juliet* (Prokofiev) by Nicolas Petrov for the Pittsburgh Ballet; appearances in Canada by the Ballet Nacional de Cuba starring Alicia Alonso; performances by the Juilliard Dance Ensemble in new pieces by Limón (*The Unsung* and *Revel*) and Anna Sokolow (*Scenes from the Music of Charles Ives*); the winning of the Antoinette Perry Award (the Tony) for choreography by Donald Saddler for his dances in *No, No Nanette,* the Broadway musical starring Ruby Keeler (*see* BIOGRAPHY); the Royal Winnipeg Ballet's American Indian production, *The Ecstasy of Rita Joe,* commissioned by the Manitoba Indian Brotherhood; and the doubling of federal funds for the National Arts and Humanities Endowment programs to more than $61 million.

(W. Te.)

In the early part of the season at Covent Garden, Jerome Robbins mounted his enormously successful *Dances at a Gathering* (to Chopin music played on a piano). Other works added to the regular Royal Ballet repertory included the successful revival of Sir Frederick Ashton's *Creatures of Prometheus,* a revival of

Tchaikovsky's *Swan Lake* (an amalgamation of previous productions), and Kenneth MacMillan's *Anastasia*.

The new touring Royal Ballet took out to the provinces such works as Ninette de Valois' *The Rake's Progress,* Ashton's *Symphonic Variations,* and Balanchine's *Apollo.* New works added to this repertory included Glen Tetley's *Field Figures* (Stockhausen score), MacMillan's *Checkpoint* (Roberto Gerhard score), Joe Layton's *The Grand Tour* (Hershy Kay's arrangement of Noël Coward music), Geoffrey Cauley's *Ante Room* (Bernard Hermann score), David Drew's *St. Thomas' Wake* (Peter Maxwell Davies score), and MacMillan's revival of *Las Hermanas* (Frank Martin score).

London's Festival Ballet, in its 21st anniversary year, mounted a new production by Mary Skeaping of *Giselle* with most of the Adam music, missing in so many productions. Other revivals included Massine's *Le Beau Danube* (Strauss music) and a collection of pieces from various Bournonville ballets under the title *Bournonville Divertissements,* revived by Mona Vangsaa. The Festival Ballet gave several European and provincial tours and four seasons in London.

Ballet Rambert enlarged its repertory as well as its activities. Norman Morrice, the company's director, created two works, *The Empty Suit* (Salzedo music) and *That Is the Show* (Berio music). Works were also created by dancers in the company. These included Jonathan Taylor's *'Tis Goodly Sport* (to 16th-century court music), Christopher Bruce's *Wings* (Bob Downes score), and Joseph Scoglio's *Metaflow* (to music by Rudnik, Malovec, and Smirley). Several pieces were added to Ballet Rambert's highly successful children's show, Bertram Batell's *Sideshow.*

London Contemporary Dance Theatre, Britain's first company based on the Martha Graham School, became even more firmly established and its repertory was greatly enlarged. The two most important works from Robert Cohan, the artistic director, were *Consolation of the Rising Moon* (to guitar music arranged and played by John Williams) and a full-length mixed-media work, *Stages.* The first part of this effective work had an electronic score by Arne Nordheim, the second a live jazz score by Bob Downes. Among the many other works created during the year, the most notable were Noemi Lapzeson's *Cantabile* (Michael Finnissy music), Richard Alston's *Nowhere Slowly* (Stockhausen score), and a fine revival of Talley Beatty's *The Road of the Phoebe Snow* (to jazz of Duke Ellington and Billy Strayhorn).

Britain's two regionally based companies—Scottish Theatre Ballet and Northern Dance Theatre—gave seasons in their own areas as well as touring other regions. Scottish Theatre Ballet (formerly Western Theatre Ballet), now well established in Scotland, added its first full-length classic to the repertory. As the company was not large, Peter Darrell's production of *Giselle* brought out the dramatic qualities of the work to a greater extent than in any previous production. For this company, Walter Gore revived his *Street Games* from the old Western Theatre Ballet repertory as well as his *Peepshow.* Another part of the company's activity was a series of workshop experimental programs, *Ploys,* first given in London at The Place and later taken on tour to various universities. For Northern Dance Theatre, centred in Manchester, 1971 was a year of touring to other parts of Britain. The most notable works added to the repertory were: John Chesworth's *Games for Five Players*

(Toru Takemitsu score), Laverne Meyer's *Introduction Piece* (Poulenc score), and Walter Gore's *Dance Pictures* (Rudolf Maros score).

In the busiest dance year ever, London's most important visitors were the Kirov Ballet, the Netherlands Dance Theater, Ailey's American Dance Theater, the City Center Joffrey Ballet, and Béjart's Ballet of the 20th Century. There were innumerable other groups—from India, Ceylon, Burma, Korea, and Spain—as well as a great number of modern dance recitals.

In Europe, the Netherlands was once again the focus of creative work. Major works in the Netherlands Dance Theatre repertory were the Tetley-van Manen *Mutations,* which was a big hit during the company's London season, together with other van Manen works—*Grosse Fuge* (Beethoven music) and *Keep Going* (to a Berio score). Jaap Flier, the company's artistic director, created *Hi-kyo* (Fukushima music). Other works included James Waring's *Variations on a Landscape* (Schoenberg music) and Charles Czarny's *Concerto Grosso* (Handel music). The most important new work for the Dutch National Ballet was Rudi van Dantzig's *On the Way* (Isang Yun score).

In France there was little activity as the Paris Opéra Ballet, homeless until the reopening of the Opera House, was in a state of partial disbandment. Béjart's Ballet of the 20th Century had a tumultuous success everywhere, particularly in New York (in spite of adverse criticism) and in London (where notices were mainly favourable). Recent creations by Béjart were *The Firebird* (Stravinsky) and *Choreographic Offering* (Bach).

The Württemberg State Ballet of Stuttgart made two very successful tours of the U.S., and John Cranko, its director, created a new version of *Carmen* (to a collage of Bizet music by Wolfgang Fortner). Former Royal Ballet dancer Ronald Hynd became co-director of the Munich Ballet and added a number of his own works to the repertory, including his version of Stravinsky's *Le Baiser de la Fée;* also for this company, Ashton revived his *La Fille Mal Gardée.* The Royal Danish Ballet continued to be the most accomplished guardian of 19th-century ballet, and Bournonville's *The Life Guards of Amager* was revived to coincide with its centenary.   (P. Wɪ.)

See also Music; Theatre.

Daniel Lommel and Maina Gielgud are featured in "Bhakti" by Maurice Béjart, whose "Ballet of the 20th Century" made its first U.S. appearance in 1971.

MARTHA SWOPE

Defense

The major strategic development of 1971 was the Soviet Union's replacement of the U.S. as the global superpower self-confidently increasing its military strength and political influence throughout the world. Though America's belief in its need or ability to fulfill a global military role had been declining since it first realized that it was unlikely to win the Vietnam war, the cumulative effects, combined with continuing domestic problems, had created a snowballing loss of willpower. This was symbolized by the U.S. Senate's October rejection of the 25-year-old foreign aid program, later restored in a truncated form pending House and Senate agreement on a regular authorization bill.

As the U.S. retreated, the Soviet Union sought to replace American with Soviet influence. The historic treaties signed with Egypt and India represented the first pledge of Soviet military support to major regional powers outside the Soviet sphere of control in Europe, Cuba being a special case. Unlike the U.S. in the early 1950s, the U.S.S.R.'s expansion remained cautious, confined to those areas of fairly well defined Soviet interest: the Middle East, Cuba, and India. As in Europe, the Soviets seemed to follow a stepping-stone strategy, securing one country before moving on to the next and concentrating on diplomatic alignment rather than internal control while acquiescing in their allies' suppression of local Communist parties.

In the Middle East a growing number of Soviet instructors and advisers were evident: 15,000–20,000 in Egypt, 1,500 in Algeria, 1,000 in Syria, and, until the failed coup, in the Sudan. These were supported by the Soviet Navy, whose helicopter cruisers "Moskva" and "Leningrad" could act as commando carriers in conjunction with the 15,000-strong naval infantry, the Soviet equivalent of the Marines. The Navy had secured bases at Latakia and Tartus in Syria; Port Said, Alexandria, and Mersa Matruh, plus an anchorage at Salum, in Egypt, three anchorages in Tunisian waters, and bases at Algiers and Mers-el-Kebir (Oran) in Algeria. If complemented by facilities in Malta, this would give the U.S.S.R. virtually all the old British and French bases, together with the political influence they represented.

This, rather than the Soviet Navy's military capability, was the real significance of Soviet naval expansion. Contrary to the popular impression, the NATO navies continued to outbuild the Warsaw Pact countries quantitatively and qualitatively. The rough balance, excluding the French Navy (superior to the Soviet Mediterranean squadron), was 10 attack and 4 antisubmarine warfare (ASW) carriers in NATO against 2 Soviet ASW carrier cruisers; 6 NATO surface attack cruisers and destroyers to 15 for the Soviets; 276 NATO ASW vessels to 150 for the Soviets; plus 33 NATO nuclear and 90 diesel submarines to the Pact's 20 and 160, respectively. The Western advantage in attack carriers was partly offset in the Mediterranean by the shore-based Soviet naval air arm, with 300 Tu-16 bombers equipped with Kipper or Kelt air-to-surface missiles, some elements being based in Egypt.

The greatest Western weakness was the lack of reliable ship-to-ship missiles, although some progress had been made in short-range missiles comparable to the Soviet Styx. The Soviet ship-to-ship cruise missile Shaddock seemed to be less effective than its 300-mi. range suggested, since it required mid-course guidance and was vulnerable to antiaircraft missiles. New horizon-range systems mounted in the two Kresta II-class cruisers constituted a more serious threat. Even so, the central problem posed by the Soviet Navy remained political. The U.S.S.R., like the U.S. in the 1962 Cuban missile crisis, could now deter outside intervention in its new areas of interest by putting in naval units, forcing its opponent to retreat or risk escalating the conflict. Soviet-U.S. talks in Moscow on new rules of the road for their warships when in contact only served to underline Soviet achievement of naval parity.

This expansion outside Europe, including the establishment of a base for Polaris-type submarines at Cienfuegos in Cuba, was possible because a series of agreements in Europe had provided an effective sub-

KEYSTONE

Above left, Soviet, Hungarian, and Czechoslovak troops participate in "Opal '71," a series of maneuvers to develop tactical cooperation among Warsaw Pact members.
Left, Soviet crews prepare missiles for launching from mobile launchers.

Deaths:
see Vital Statistics; *see also biographies of prominent persons who died in 1971, listed under* Obituaries

Debts, National: *see* Government Finance

LONDON "DAILY EXPRESS"—PICTORIAL PARADE

stitute for a formal European peace settlement. The *Ostpolitik* for which West German Chancellor Willy Brandt received the Nobel Peace Prize aimed at normalizing relations with Eastern Europe and comprised a package deal. The 1970 treaties with Poland and the U.S.S.R. (to be followed by similar ones with other Eastern European states) accepted the Oder-Neisse Line as the eastern border of Germany and renounced the use of force to alter it, while the four-power Berlin agreement signed in September 1971 involved Soviet confirmation of established Western rights. East Germany delayed until December agreement with West Berlin allowing easier access to East Berlin. Following this, however, the four-power agreement seemed likely to be ratified, with the U.S.S.R. accepting the start of the Bundestag procedure for ratifying the 1970 treaties between West Germany and Poland and the U.S.S.R. in lieu of their actual ratification. Even with the delay in the Berlin arrangements, Brandt's Crimea summit with Soviet party chief Leonid I. Brezhnev in October suggested the Soviets felt they had dealt with the West German problem as they had known it since 1949.

This explained the new confidence and energy behind Brezhnev's drive for a multilateral conference including all NATO and Warsaw Pact members, confirming a European settlement that, in recognizing the status quo, would accept existing Soviet influence and provide a basis for its expansion. From 1967 to Brezhnev's May 1971 Tiflis speech, the Soviets had emphasized a European security conference as the appropriate modality, but they now switched to the alternative of discussing mutual and balanced force reductions (MBFR). It was thought that this would be harder for the West to resist in the climate of

détente. The Soviets seemed relatively uninterested in the more sophisticated Western approaches to the problem of balancing reductions, and instead envisaged a largely symbolic and probably very limited withdrawal on a man-for-man basis. This would increase a military balance that already favoured the U.S.S.R. while consolidating the division of political influence. It probably would be done in such a way as to facilitate Soviet intervention, overt or covert, in Yugoslavia after President Tito died.

Moreover, although the Soviet economy continued to grow relatively slowly, it seemed increasingly clear that it could meet the demands of a steady and balanced expansion and modernization of all arms of the forces. The 1971 defense budget was officially 17.8 billion rubles, virtually the same as in the previous year, but total military expenditure was estimated at $55 billion, an increase of $3.3 billion. More significantly, defense expenditure as a percentage of gross national product (GNP) had remained at about 11 since 1967, while in the U.S. it had fallen from 9.5 to 7.8.

Within the Soviet forces, only the Air Force increased numerically—by 70,000 men to 550,000. This reflected the continued introduction of new aircraft: the Yak-28P, Tu-28, Su-11, and MiG-23 interceptors in the Air Defense Command and, in the Tactical Air Force, the MiG-21J and Yak-28P fighters, Su-7 ground attack aircraft, Yak-28 supersonic light bomber, and the Flogger variable geometry fighter, comparable to the U.S. F-111. Army dispositions, including those against China, were virtually unchanged, with no diminution of forces in Europe. Of the 102 rifle, 51 tank, and 7 airborne divisions, 31 were maintained at combat strength in Eastern Europe with 20

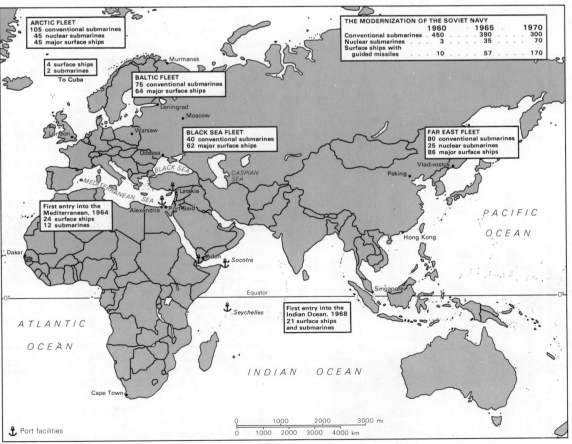

Worldwide expansion of Soviet naval power, 1960–70.

(including 10 tank) divisions in East Germany, 2 tank divisions in Poland, 2 in Hungary (plus 2 infantry), and 5 divisions in Czechoslovakia. On the Sino-Soviet border, 15 of the 33 divisions (including 10 tank) were combat ready. Most remaining combat-ready divisions were among the 60 in Soviet Europe; the 8 divisions in the central U.S.S.R. would require major reinforcements, as would 10 of the 28 in the southern U.S.S.R. The standard tank remained the 36-ton T-54/55 with a 100-mm. gun, introduced in 1954, but it was being replaced by the 37-ton T-62 with a 115-mm. gun. Tactical nuclear weapons and delivery systems were widely available, having been integrated into particular units. Overall, therefore, the Soviet Union was well placed to follow Clausewitz' dictum that force was an extension of diplomacy.

DISARMAMENT

The fourth and fifth sessions of the strategic arms limitation talks (SALT) between the U.S. and the U.S.S.R., held March 15 to May 28 and July 8 to September 23, produced an agreement announced on May 20 to concentrate on limiting antiballistic missiles (ABMs), with some restriction on offensive missiles, and an agreement in September to improve the hotline between Moscow and Washington. When the sixth session adjourned for Christmas, no further progress had been announced.

The maximum probable agreement seemed likely to be a limitation of ABMs to 100 around Moscow and 300 around U.S. Minuteman sites, plus some gross numerical limitations on intercontinental ballistic missiles (ICBMs) and submarine-launched ballistic missiles (SLBMs) without restraint on particular types, chiefly the Soviet SS-9, or on the development of new systems like the underwater long-range ballistic missile system (ULMS). This was allegedly part of a U.S. package put forward in July, which suggested December 1971 as the cutoff date for all new construction of missile silos and submarines and a halt on all partially built systems unacceptable to the U.S.S.R.

U.S. Deputy Secretary of Defense David Packard announced limitations on improvements in the accuracy of U.S. multiple independently targeted reentry vehicle (MIRV) systems, limiting these to penetration aids rather than counterforce weapons able to knock out Soviet silos. In terms of city destruction, the Minuteman III MIRV gave a 70% increase over

previous systems and the submarine-based Poseidon MIRV, 106%; hence suggestions for an extended Poseidon program as a practical substitute for ULMS. The Soviets showed no signs of response, but continued to insist, as they had done since SALT began in 1970, that forward based systems (FBS) be included in any agreement. U.S. Pres. Richard Nixon rejected this, as well as an uninspected MIRV moratorium and an agreement to limit ABMs to deployment around capital cities.

Some analysts detected signs of tacit Soviet arms limitation in their halt in deployment of the SS-9. In the 21 months from August 1969, the U.S.S.R. had begun only 50 new launching sites, thereby delaying until 1974–75 replacement of the 420 missiles that U.S. Secretary of Defense Melvin Laird regarded as a first-strike capability. Other indications, however, were that the halt resulted from a retroactive decision to harden the SS-9 silos to a level comparable to the Minuteman silos.

Clearly, the Soviet Union had consolidated its strategic parity, though the value of this was uncertain. Its 280 SS-9s balanced 55 Titan IIs, the only comparable U.S. missiles, and 100 Minuteman IIIs with MIRV. Against 980 Minuteman Is and IIs with one-megaton warheads, the U.S.S.R. had 950 SS-11s, using less reliable storable liquid fuel, and 60 SS-13s virtually identical to the Minuteman I and II, plus 500 older SS-7s and SS-8s with five-megaton warheads in service since 1961–63. In SLBMs, the U.S. had 160 Polaris A2 and 432 Polaris A3 missiles with multiple reentry vehicle (MRV) warheads against 320 SS-N-6s (the Soviet equivalent of the Polaris A2, 16 of which were mounted in each Yankee-class submarine). The Poseidon missile with ten 50-kiloton warheads entered service in four submarines and four more were converting, leaving the U.S. with 37 submarines carrying Polaris against 20 Soviet equivalents. At the current rate of production, the U.S.S.R. would have parity in Polaris-type SLBMs within two years.

Although the meaning of strategic parity continued to be debated, both superpowers seemed to be exercising prudence in their strategic relations. Their residual ability to destroy each other appeared likely to remain, while the strategic balance was complicated by growing signs of Franco-British nuclear cooperation and China's acquisition of a modest capability. The U.S. and the U.S.S.R. seemed anxious to make sure they could defend themselves against an attack by any third state, or against a possible accidental missile launch; hence their September agreement to upgrade the hotline. Installed in 1963 after the Cuban crisis and later extended to Paris and London, the original telephone and teletype link was relatively vulnerable to disruption. The new link would utilize multiple satellite links and would be based in each state's national command system, designed to function even after a nuclear attack had destroyed both capitals. There also appeared to be provision for joint investigation of any nuclear incident, with an automatic delay in retaliation until the facts had been established.

Lacking any more substantial agreement, the U.S. proceeded with its ABM deployment. On Dec. 23, 1970, the first successful Sprint short-range interception of an ICBM fired over 4,000 mi. had taken place at the Kwajalein test site in the Pacific, and on January 9 two Spartan long-range missiles intercepted separate targets outside the atmosphere. On November 6 a five-megaton Spartan warhead was tested

Soviet Union's secret super destroyer patrols the Baltic. The vessel is equipped to deliver either conventional or nuclear missiles.

underground at Amchitka Island in the Aleutians, despite international protests. The question therefore seemed less whether ABM would work or not than how it could be improved and deployed without jeopardizing SALT. The Defense Department wanted one site protecting Washington and four around Air Force and bomber bases to keep up the momentum of the projected 12-site program, now estimated to cost $13 billion–$15 billion, against the original $9 billion. The House Armed Services Committee approved $1 billion for a third ABM, located in Missouri, plus preparatory work on a fourth. The first, at Grand Forks (N.D.) Air Force Base, was half completed and the second, at Malmstrom (Mont.) Air Force Base, was in the early stages of construction.

The conference of the UN Committee on Disarmament at Geneva became increasingly critical of the lack of progress at SALT, reflecting the inability of smaller states to influence the U.S.-U.S.S.R. arms race. The seabed treaty, opened for signature on February 11, symbolized these grievances since, as amended by the superpowers, it prohibited only the emplacement of (nuclear) weapons of mass destruction on the ocean floor, something only the U.S. and U.S.S.R. could do but had rejected as impractical. Under extreme pressure from Canada and the smaller states, they had accepted an undertaking to assist in verifying observance of the treaty in the waters of third parties who could not do so themselves. Canada, along with Sweden, also renewed pressure for a comprehensive test ban treaty, possibly by stages based on the considerable improvements in unilateral verification techniques. The U.S. and the U.S.S.R. (which had conducted a six-megaton underground test) clearly preferred the status quo that enabled them to test, and regarded a comprehensive test ban as impossible outside the context of a comprehensive SALT agreement limiting the deployment of new weapons requiring new warheads.

The separate consideration of chemical and biological warfare, contrary to the previous Soviet position, was the only bright spot in an otherwise unproductive year. In August the U.S. and the U.S.S.R. agreed on a draft treaty for the prohibition of biological warfare, and this, with amendments, was approved by the UN General Assembly. The convention codified a move started by President Nixon's decision to destroy all U.S. facilities for manufacturing and storing chemical and biological agents over three years. Meanwhile, U.S. ratification of the 1925 Geneva Protocol on Chemical Warfare depended on a compromise between the Pentagon's desire that this should not include nonlethal CS gas and herbicides and the Senate Foreign Relations Committee's belief that such agents should be covered. Suspension of the use of herbicides and a sharp drop in CS use in Vietnam suggested that the Senate's view would prevail. In any case, the protocol's age and ambiguity made the drafting of a new convention on chemical warfare a major priority.

UNITED STATES

Although Secretary Laird's March posture statement described the new U.S. strategy as one of realistic deterrence, it seemed in practice to be nearer the previous Republican administration's policy of massive retaliation. Commonly misinterpreted as a threat to unleash strategic nuclear war in the event of even minor Communist attacks, the Eisenhower-Dulles (and Nixon-Laird) position was that the U.S. could

not financially afford forces able to do more than fight a major conventional war in Europe for a matter of days or a small limited war for clearly defined objectives elsewhere. The first line of defense therefore would be local troops, with U.S. equipment and training. Only in areas of exceptional value to the U.S. would combat units be stationed, mostly aircraft with tactical nuclear weapons able to delay an enemy attack long enough for a decision on intervention. The introduction of ICBMs and the projected ULMS meant that overseas bases no longer were required for the strategic striking force. They would, therefore, be confined to a few major storage depots for heavy equipment and to refueling points facilitating the air and sea transport of the U.S.-based Strategic Reserve.

With the military draft scheduled to end in June 1973 (after almost being killed by the Senate in 1971) and a fiscal 1973 budget of $80 billion that would buy less than the budget for 1964, U.S. forces were to be reduced to 2.5 million or less. The Army's total of 12 divisions (3 armoured, 1 air cavalry, 4 mechanized infantry, 2 infantry, and 2 airborne), plus 1 air cavalry, 1 airborne, and 3 independent infantry brigades, with 5 armoured cavalry regiments, would be reduced to about 11 divisions. Of these a nominal 4 (2 armoured and 2 infantry) would remain in West Germany, and about half an infantry division would remain in South Korea. A mixed force totaling about one division (16,000 men) would replace the current two divisions and two brigades in South Vietnam. The 72,000 men in Japan and Okinawa were being reduced, probably to about one division. Similarly, the 18,400 men in the Philippines would drop, giving a maximum deployment of two divisions in Southeast Asia once the division in South Vietnam was withdrawn. The remaining six–eight divisions would be based in the U.S. with the two from West Germany, like the one in the Strategic Reserve, being dual-based, with heavy equipment in Europe. This might enable the continental reserve to remain at one armoured, one cavalry, one airborne, and one mechanized infantry division, partly under training.

To utilize its helicopter experience against tanks, the Army was experimenting with a new Tri-cap (triple-capable) divisional formation, using 330 helicopters for troop transport and gunfire support. Combined with one tank, one helicopter, and one infantry brigade, these would have a divisional strength of 12,000–13,000 instead of the standard 16,000. Recruitment clearly would be the greatest problem, especially given Senate resistance to raising pay scales, although it finally increased these by $25 million, with 75% going to men in their first 12 years of service. Army morale continued to be a major problem; there were reports of officers being attacked with fragmentation grenades (fragged) by their own men and of increasing use of drugs. Capt. Ernest Medina's acquittal on charges of complicity in the 1968 My Lai massacre, the reduction to 20 years of the sentence meted out to Lieut. William Calley (see BIOGRAPHY), and the acquittal of Col. Oren Henderson on charges of having failed to investigate the massacre did little to dispel the Army's feeling that these men were scapegoats or the public's concern that standards of military conduct were declining.

Under Chief of Naval Operations Elmo Zumwalt (see BIOGRAPHY), Navy morale seemed to be improving, although the number and capabilities of its ships declined. Partly, this reflected the retirement of World

War II vessels and their replacement by fewer, more powerful ships, resulting in a drop from 900 to 600 ships and from 770,000 to 623,000 men between mid-1969 and mid-1971. The Knox DE 1052- and 1078-class destroyer escorts, forming a major part of the rebuilding program, were heavily criticized for being overly geared to antisubmarine warfare. Aircraft carriers, long the symbol of U.S. naval supremacy, also were suffering from age. The planned attack carrier force for June 1972 was 13, instead of the usual 15. By the mid-1970s two additional nuclear carriers ("Nimitz" and "Eisenhower") would provide a force of 11 postwar carriers plus 3 of the Midway class commissioned in 1945–47. Decision on a fourth nuclear-powered carrier, the CVAN 70, was postponed.

As the organization most suited to the Nixon-Laird strategy, the Marine Corps would remain at about the current level of three large divisions (19,000 men apiece), each with one tank and one surface-to-air missile battalion with 24 Hawk missiles. Integral artillery and air support was supplied by three air wings of 540 combat aircraft, chiefly 14 squadrons of F-4 Phantoms, 12 attack squadrons with A-6A and A-4 planes, 1 squadron with U.K. AV-8A Harrier vertical/short-takeoff-and-landing (V/STOL) close-support aircraft, 45 AH-1 Cobra gunship helicopters, and 15 squadrons of helicopters.

The Air Force shared the Navy's problem of obsolescence. Over half its 6,000 planes were more than ten years old. Its major requirement was for a new manned bomber, the B-1, especially since only 70 FB-111s were being added to the Strategic Air Command (SAC) instead of 82. Orders for F-111Ds, with the expensive Mk II avionics system, were held to 96, giving a total F-111 procurement of 519 instead of the 2,400 originally planned. SAC was reduced to 150 B-52C/Fs (two squadrons being based in Southeast Asia) and 210 B-52G/Hs, with 90 in storage. The Air Defense Forces had been reduced to 80,000 men and the Nike-Hercules surface-to-air missile batteries to 27, but the Air National Guard was re-equipping with F-101, F-102, and F-104 fighters in place of the obsolete F-84s and RF-84Fs.

Development of the airborne warning and control system (AWACS) was progressing, complementing the over-the-horizon (OTH) radar able to detect ICBMs regardless of direction or trajectory of launch. The F-15 was the first fighter designed for the Air Force rather than the Navy in 20 years, but was criticized for being unmaneuverable and overly reliant on vulnerable electronics systems. The Air Force received development funds for a new close-support

fighter (the AX). Two major improvements were the increasing standardization around variants of the Phantom and production of the new short-range attack missile (SRAM) with a range of 75 mi. Each B-52 could carry up to 24 SRAMs and the B-1 would carry 32.

Politically, the two most significant developments reflected disenchantment with America's global role and the consequent military involvement. The June publication of the Pentagon papers, despite administration attempts to halt it, produced a sense of betrayal among Army men. Commissioned by Robert McNamara in 1967 to trace the history of the Vietnam war, the study, leaked by one of its authors, Daniel Ellsberg (*see* BIOGRAPHY), was based only on Department of Defense files and revealed little new information. Its impact came from the confirmation that neither John Kennedy nor Lyndon Johnson had properly determined the objectives of the Vietnam war, and that both were served poorly by their military advisers and had misled the public on the nature and scope of the war. Ironically CIA Director John A. McCone was one of the few who had consistently questioned the assumption that increasing applications of U.S. airpower and men would win a war of attrition (*see* PUBLISHING). In the climate created by these disclosures, Sen. Mike Mansfield's resolution seeking to limit the U.S. troops in Europe to 150,000 (about half the existing level), though defeated, suggested a possible reversion to the isolationism of the '20s and '30s. (See *South and Southeast Asia,* below.)

NATO

NATO faced the prospect of MBFR against a worsening military balance vis-à-vis the Warsaw Pact. U.S. forces in Europe had fallen to 300,000, compared with 434,000 in 1962, while the number of Soviet divisions had risen from 26 to 31. Since U.S. divisions contained 16,000 men against the Soviet's 10,000, a more accurate assessment was in terms of division equivalents. In northern and central Europe there were 8 armoured and 16 infantry, mechanized, and airborne NATO divisions to 28 armoured and 37 infantry Warsaw Pact divisions, of which 19 and 22, respectively, were Soviet. These figures concealed a major NATO weakness in northern Norway and the concentration of the strong U.S. forces in the easily defended southern part of Germany rather than the vulnerable North German plain. Mobilization would favour the U.S.S.R., which could increase its divisions in central Europe by 70 within a month.

NATO was outnumbered by three to one in tanks, with 5,500 to the Pact's 16,000, of which 10,000 were Soviet, including the modern T-62. NATO's superiority in antitank weapons offset this disparity to some extent, but inferiority in aircraft tended to tilt the balance in the U.S.S.R.'s favour. The Pact had 4,180 light fighter-bombers, ground-attack, interceptor, and reconnaissance planes (over half Soviet) to NATO's 2,000, a superiority of two to one. In tactical nuclear weapons, this ratio was reversed, with 7,000 nuclear warheads for NATO and 3,500 for the Pact, some delivery vehicles—though not the warheads—being owned by non-Soviet forces. Only in naval forces did NATO enjoy a clear supremacy.

Against this background, it was difficult for NATO to envisage MBFR that would not increase their disadvantages, since any Soviet withdrawal would be only 300–500 mi. to the frontier, while U.S. forces

"Do me a favor—
help me drop it!"
—Pat Oliphant,
"The Denver Post."

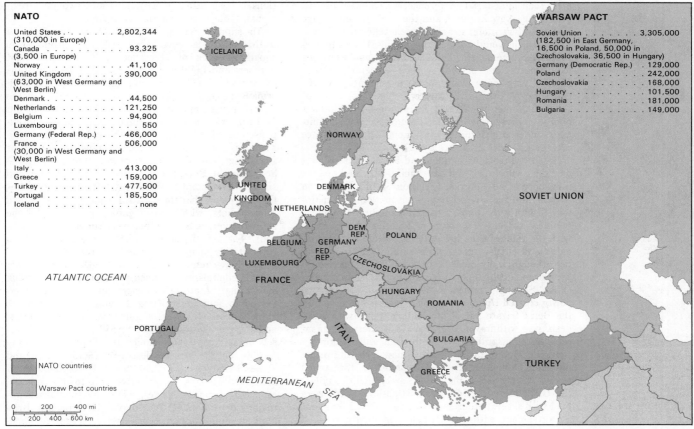

Military forces of NATO and Warsaw Pact nations. NATO has 1,105,000 troops in Western Europe; Warsaw Pact has 1,235,000 stationed in Eastern Europe.

would be 3,500 mi. away. Even if the C-5A Galaxy transports became fully operational by 1973, they would take about a week to airlift an army division and six fighter squadrons to Europe. On the other hand, the prevalent mood of defense and pressures in the U.S. for a reduction in forces made it politically difficult for NATO to appear opposed to force reductions. Hence Brezhnev's Tiflis speech of May 14, inviting NATO to taste the wine of talks on such reductions.

Paradoxically, many Europeans favoured MBFR as the least disadvantageous alternative to a probable outcome of SALT giving the U.S. a near freeze on ABMs in exchange for U.S. reduction of its forward based systems for delivering tactical nuclear weapons. If coupled with a partial withdrawal of superpower forces, this would leave Western Europe much more exposed to Soviet pressure. Instead, MBFR could delay the almost inevitable U.S. reduction to about two divisions while giving them the right to reinforce up to four full divisions. Similarly, the European powers could formalize their cutbacks in defense forces, provide for reinforcement, and trade this for a lesser Soviet presence in Eastern Europe. Nevertheless, the difficulties of deciding such questions as the level of forces to be retained and the allowable size of reinforcements made it unlikely that MBFR talks, if they occurred, would produce rapid results. NATO's secretary-general, Manlio Brosio, resigned to conduct exploratory talks on MBFR, and was succeeded by Joseph Luns of the Netherlands (*see* BIOGRAPHY). The December NATO ministerial meeting regretted the Warsaw Treaty Organization's failure to take up this offer of negotiations.

The major NATO Defense Improvement Program submitted by the Eurogroup (Belgium, Britain, Denmark, West Germany, Greece, Italy, Luxembourg, the Netherlands, Norway, and Turkey) to the defense Planning Committee of the North Atlantic Council in December 1970 recommended additional contributions of $420 million over five years to improve communications systems and aircraft shelters, plus additions to national forces costing $500 million over five years and an additional $79 million in 1971–72. These measures reflected greater consensus than existed on MBFR, as did the Nuclear Planning Group meetings which agreed on initial political guidelines for the use of nuclear land mines and the initial defensive use of tactical nuclear weapons. The Canadian Defence White Paper of August emphasized that their 5,000-man air-portable force would remain committed to NATO, with an additional two squadrons of F-5 fighters being flown over in an emergency.

UNITED KINGDOM

Following an extensive defense policy review, the Conservative government confirmed its Labour predecessor's decision that 1971 would be the last year in which British forces would be deployed in more than token strength outside the U.K. and West Germany. Britain's successful application to join the EEC meant acceptance of a role as a European rather than a global power, with the British Army of the Rhine (BAOR) becoming the focus of its defense effort. Tacit cooperation with France in the development of nuclear weapons was aimed at upgrading each country's independent deterrent, which could be held in trust for the rest of Europe and backstop the U.S. nuclear guarantee. Tragically, the British Army, having largely completed its withdrawal from overseas, found itself repeating in Northern Ireland the internal police function it had sought to avoid east of Suez.

The February Defence White Paper indicated that,

Homebound U.S. soldiers
file into the checkout
building at Bien Hoa
Air Base in South Vietnam
before boarding a charter
flight for Oakland, Calif.

after their ministerial conference, Australia, Malaysia, Singapore, New Zealand, and the U.K. would engage in a five-power defense arrangement, effective Nov. 1, 1971, which would replace the Anglo-Malaysian Defence Agreement. The British contribution would be five frigates, one battalion group, a detachment of Nimrod long-range maritime reconnaissance aircraft, and some Whirlwind helicopters. The total force of some 5,000 men would cost £5 million–10 million annually, representing the maximum British commitment under any circumstances, including a resurgence of guerrilla activity in Malaysia.

Existing Lightning fighters and Hercules transports would be withdrawn and base facilities turned over to Singapore. One Ghurka battalion would remain in Brunei, and the Hong Kong garrison would be maintained with five infantry battalions and one artillery regiment for internal security. Treaties of protection with the rulers in the lower Persian Gulf were terminated and British forces were withdrawn by December, though individual British soldiers remained to serve the local rulers, notably in the Trucial and Oman Scouts, retained as a defense force for the newly created Union of Arab Emirates. Farther south, the Beira frigate patrol blockading traffic with Rhodesia was withdrawn after the November agreement settling the dispute between Rhodesia and Britain.

In the Mediterranean Malta's new left-wing prime minister, Dom Mintoff (see BIOGRAPHY), threatened to end NATO use of the island's port facilities unless the U.K. offered better terms. High-level talks were held with several other countries, including Libya, but an agreement with the British was finally reached in September. Britain raised its level of payment, but in December, when Malta demanded a still bigger increase, decided to withdraw all its personnel stationed there. The NATO Mediterranean naval headquarters previously had been transferred from Malta to Naples, Italy. In addition to the infantry battalion stationed on Malta, British forces in the Mediterranean included two infantry battalions on Cyprus, one of which was part of the UN peacekeeping force, and one in Gibraltar.

With the retreat from empire virtually completed, the all-volunteer Army of 185,300 encountered considerable recruiting problems, although enlistments rose with the prospect of action in Ireland. Theoretically, the BAOR's four divisions would remain at the treaty figure of 55,000 men and the strategic reserve at one division of three air-portable brigades and two parachute battalions, constituting the U.K. Mobile Force. With the Special Air Service Regiment, these would be available for NATO's mobile force. The remaining forces would be training, with armoured forces using Canadian facilities for lack of space in Europe.

The decline in the numbers, efficiency, and morale of the U.S. 7th Army left the BAOR as the most professional force in NATO and the key to what little remained of the flexible response strategy. Its five armoured brigades had 900 Centurion Mk 10–13 and Chieftain tanks, the latter mounting the exceptionally powerful 120-mm. gun. The two artillery brigades had 105-mm. Abbot and M-107 175-mm. self-propelled guns and M-109 155-mm. howitzers, plus Honest John short-range missiles able to use nuclear or conventional warheads. The mechanized brigade's armoured personnel carriers and two armoured-car regiments mounted Vigilant and Swingfire antitank missiles. These units were being regrouped in squared forma-

tions of two infantry battalions and two tank regiments, thought to give greater flexibility.

Air support was provided by four squadrons of F-4M attack-reconnaissance-strike Phantoms, two squadrons each of Buccaneer and Canberra light bombers and Lightning fighters, and three squadrons of Harrier V/STOL ground-attack planes. The RAF remained overdependent on obsolete aircraft, but the situation was improving slowly with the introduction of Phantoms, despite the unnecessary delay and expense caused by fitting them with British engines and avionics. Air defense rested on nine squadrons of Lightnings, one of F-4K Phantoms, four of Harriers, and three of Buccaneers, with only one Hunter and six Canberra bomber squadrons left from the 1950s. Of the eight maritime patrol squadrons, two had Nimrod jets, with Martel guided missiles, and the six with overage Shackletons were converting to Nimrods. The remaining V-bombers were assigned to a support role or used as refueling aircraft.

The Navy remained the third largest in the world; ships in commission included 4 nuclear-powered attack submarines, 2 aircraft carriers plus one being converted to join the existing 2 commando carriers, 1 guided missile cruiser, 8 guided missile destroyers, and 31 general purpose and 22 ASW frigates. New vessels being completed included the Type 82 destroyer (5,600 tons), Type 42 destroyer (3,500 tons), and Type 21 ASW frigate (2,500 tons). Unfortunately, all continued to lack an effective ship-to-ship missile, especially for long ranges, while the submarines remained dependent on World War II torpedoes. Britain's shrinking responsibilities were recognized when, on May 1, all ships were placed under the Western Fleet and the Eastern Fleet was abolished.

Under a new five-year agreement on support costs concluded on March 19, West Germany agreed to pay DM. 160 million per year, provided there were no permanent and substantial changes in the current level of U.K. forces on West German soil. Germany would keep its military purchases to £25 million per year, offsetting British foreign exchange costs by 25%.

The 13,000 U.K. troops in Northern Ireland represented about 20 out of the maximum of 25 battalions available without calling up some of the 49,000 volunteer reserves. It was estimated that 20,000 troops were needed merely to control Belfast, let alone patrol the border, making it virtually certain that part of the Ulster Defence Regiment would have to be mobilized and the police rearmed.

FRANCE

The significant decline in the French defense budget, from $5,982,000,000 to $5,202,000,000 for 1971–72, continued the trend that had brought it down from 5% of GNP in 1967 to less than 4% in 1971. This demonstrated that, despite its internal problems, the nuclear weapons program was by no means as expensive as was commonly supposed. French plans called for a one-megaton warhead to be operational by 1975, with MIRV postponed to form part of a ten-year program starting in that year. The first nine intermediate range ballistic missiles (IRBMs) became operational in the Albion Plateau near Toulon on August 2, with the second group of nine scheduled to follow in a year, each missile having a 150-kiloton warhead and a range of 1,865 mi. Of the missile-carrying submarines, "Le Redoutable" became operational in October, "Le Terrible" was to follow a year later, "Le Foudroyant" in 1974, and "Indomptable" in 1977.

The aging Mirage IV-As were to remain operational until 1980, giving an estimated total striking power of 40,000 kilotons for all the strategic forces by 1976.

Continuing problems with warhead design made exchange of nuclear information with the U.K. exceptionally valuable. Thermonuclear warheads could increase the striking power of the *force de frappe* by a factor of ten, but the 1971 series of tests in French Polynesia had to be cut short in the face of diplomatic protests and in September Minister of Defense Michel Debré visited the U.K. to discuss cooperation. One French weapon under development for which Britain possessed no equivalent was the Pluton tactical nuclear missile system, fired from an AMX-30 tank chassis, with a ten-kiloton warhead and a range of 62 mi. It was due to enter service in 1973, but the program suffered a severe setback in January when an air crash killed Jacques Mabile, head of production of the French Atomic Energy Commissariat.

On the civil-military front, it was decided to build one more nuclear reactor per year, and a proposal was made for a European uranium enhancement plant. Aimed in the first instance at the successful U.K.-West German-Netherlands gas centrifuge project, this nevertheless reflected a growing European reluctance to remain dependent on the U.S. for enriched uranium.

To demonstrate France's conventional as well as its nuclear strength, 40 French warships, 400 aircraft, and 12,000 troops, together with Spanish and NATO forces, participated in June maneuvers based on a scenario involving an international crisis in the Mediterranean. Despite reductions, the Navy remained formidable, with 19 diesel-powered attack submarines, 2 aircraft carriers, 2 helicopter carriers, 2 assault ships, 18 destroyers (4 with Tartar surface-to-air missiles), 3 guided missile frigates with Malafon ASW missiles and Masurca surface-to-air missiles, and 27 frigates. Naval air forces included three fighter-bomber and three reconnaissance squadrons, 2 interceptor squadrons, and 2 helicopter squadrons.

These, combined with the renamed *force d'intervention,* give France a significant overseas presence. The guerrilla war in Chad continued at a low level, with some 1,300 French troops stationed in that country. The Malagasy Republic accounted for 2,500, which appeared to be preventing a guerrilla war rather than fighting one, and the same was true of the 2,000 men in Senegal. Minor forces were also stationed in Gabon, Ivory Coast, and Niger. The Army in France comprised five mechanized divisions with about 600 36-ton AMX-30 tanks with 105-mm. guns and some older M-47s. The AMX-13 light 15-ton tanks were being refitted with 90-mm. guns. A parachute division of two brigades and an air-portable motorized brigade formed the Strategic Reserve. The local defense forces could be increased from 25 to 80 infantry battalions by mobilizing reserves, increasingly trained for an antitank role. In peacetime, the forces in France, 61,500 men, were slightly outnumbered by those in West Germany. France remained technically a member of NATO, but its attitude toward that organization was as ambiguous as ever.

French arms sales continued to be based on the principle of cash on the barrelhead and no questions asked. The value of major sales was not always ascertainable, but these included 300 Exocet ship-to-ship naval missiles to the U.K. ($54 million); 20 La Combattante II patrol boats to West Germany ($240

million); 50 AMX-30 tanks to Greece ($33 million); 19 AMX-30s to Spain; 6 Mirage III-Ds to Australia ($12.4 million); 1 squadron of Mirage 5s to Malaysia; 30 SA-330 Puma helicopters to Congo (Kinshasa); and 4 Noratlas transports to Niger. In an exception to its usual practice, France banned deliveries to Pakistan of 30 Mirage III-E/Vs and 24 Alouette III helicopters, presumably for fear of offending the numerous customers for French arms in the third world.

WEST GERMANY

The Bundeswehr continued to suffer from the contradiction between the political desirability of a conscript army, without selective service, and the military unsuitability of such a force. To accommodate the increased number of men of draftable age, the term of military service was reduced from 18 to 15 months, giving insufficient time for training. This would provide a force of 485,000, of which 45.5% would consist of regular forces, with a shortage of 26,000 NCOs and 2,600 officers.

The problems of creating an army of citizens in uniform, including the issue of permitting hairnets so that conscripts could continue to wear long hair, produced the so-called revolt of the captains, far more significant than the generals' protest four years earlier. It was instigated by the "Thirty of Unna," officers in the 7th Armoured Division who complained in March that the inspector-general of the Army was incapable of fulfilling his role while political leaders were failing to give the armed forces the leadership they needed. The captains were supported by their commanding officer, Maj. Gen. Eike Middeldorf, and by April had over a thousand supporters in the officer corps. A series of visits by Defense Minister Helmut Schmidt did little to alleviate the unrest, which was fanned when the inspector-general's annual report stated that discipline and morale were weak. The number of conscientious objectors had risen again to 15,500 and could reach 40,000 in 1971–72.

In matériel, the successful introduction of the first Phantoms and a new mechanized infantry combat vehicle was offset by the bunching together of requests for equipment to replace that acquired when the

Lieut. Col. Anthony B. Herbert told reporters on June 2, 1971, that he had been threatened by a military investigator who tried to stop him from filing charges of Vietnam war crimes Herbert said he had witnessed.

U.S. Secretary of Defense Melvin Laird (left) tours a South Vietnamese ordnance depot on Nov. 6, 1971. His visit preceded an announcement by Pres. Richard Nixon on November 12 that U.S. troop withdrawals would be accelerated.

CENTRAL PRESS—PICTORIAL PARADE

Vertical takeoff Harrier ground-attack aircraft hovers above the British carrier "Ark Royal" during trials to evaluate the plane under operational conditions.

Bundeswehr was being built up. Eight Starfighter crashes in March brought the total losses of that plane to an incredible 137, more than one-seventh of the original force. As a replacement, an additional 175 F-4E(F) simplified single-seater Phantoms were ordered at $3.2 million each. These were in addition to the 88 RF-4E reconnaissance Phantom IIs, which were finally approved by the Bundestag's Defense Committee. As an economy measure, the government halved its order for the NATO multirole combat aircraft to 420 and threatened to cancel even this if unit costs rose above $4 million. As the Phantoms came into service they replaced the various marks of Starfighter in the ten fighter-bomber, four interceptor, and four heavy reconnaissance squadrons. Eight squadrons of light strike and reconnaissance G-91s continued in service, although they were nearly obsolete.

The Army received the first of 1,900 Madder light fighting vehicles ordered by 1974. Weighing 20 tons and using an eight-wheel drive, they mounted the Swedish Carl Gustav antitank missile. Deliveries of the Leopard 40-ton medium tank with a 105-mm. gun, comparable to the Soviet T-54/55, continued to replace the elderly U.S. M-48A2 Pattons. Some progress was made toward achieving the force structure recommended by the 1970 Defense White Paper. The armoured brigades were increased to 12, against the target of 13½, and the armoured infantry brigades rose to 13, against the needed 16. The three airborne and two mountain brigades were retained as anticipated, while the six reconnaissance brigades were reformed as three rifle brigades and one armoured regiment. Total Army strength remained at 327,000, including the 25,000-man Territorial Force, with 540,000 reserves on immediate recall.

Naval forces continued to be increased to counter the Soviet buildup in the Baltic. The Navy included 3 guided missile destroyers, 9 destroyers, 6 fast frigates, and 40 fast patrol boats, but it still lacked missile gunboats and its four fighter-bomber reconnaissance squadrons used F-104G Starfighters.

CHINA

The Sino-Soviet border remained relatively quiet in 1971, and the internal situation was calm, despite rumours of a behind-the-scenes power struggle. President Nixon's historic July 15 announcement that he would visit Peking to seek the normalization of relations with China meant it had at last been accepted as a major strategic factor, and the Chinese nuclear weapons program seemed designed to underline this fact. No nuclear tests had taken place between the three-megaton air-dropped shot of Oct. 14, 1970, and Nov. 18, 1971. The 1971 test brought the cumulative total to 12, with one failure, including 5 in the 20-kiloton Hiroshima-type range, 2 in the 200–500-kiloton group, and 4 of 3-megaton thermonuclear hydrogen bombs. The long interval suggested that the major problems of producing a usable warhead for missiles and aircraft had been overcome, and that emphasis had shifted to delivery systems.

Production of copies of the Soviet Tu-16 Badger medium bomber began at the rate of 4 to 6 per month with a stockpile of 30. Although it had entered service in 1955 and was regarded as obsolete, it could carry 20,000 lb. of bombs some 1,500 mi. on a return mission, and even the sophisticated Soviet air defense system in Mongolia could not be certain of preventing some planes from getting to their targets. These were plentiful, since Soviet efforts to develop Siberia had resulted in the creation of major industrial and scientific centres that became Chinese hostages. Japan performed a similar function vis-à-vis the U.S., though improved Sino-U.S. relations lessened Japan's importance in this context while increasing Chinese fears of Japanese militarism.

To supplement the interim Tu-16s, China was developing an IRBM. Its satellite booster resembled the Soviet SS-4 and the early U.S. Thor IRBMs with ranges of 1,200–1,700 mi. Westward firings of up to 2,000 mi. into the Sinkiang desert were prepared, while some effort was devoted to producing seagoing tracking ships. Some 20 operational IRBMs were deployed in northwestern and northeastern China, and an ICBM equipped for limited penetration was expected to follow in 1975. Ironically for the Soviet Union, China appeared to be following the late Premier Nikita Khrushchev's gamble in limiting deployment of early delivery systems while accelerating the introduction of sophisticated solid-fuel launchers.

The January 1971 establishment of new provincial party committees in preparation for the National People's Congress confirmed that the ninth congress of the Communist Party in April 1969 had established the People's Liberation Army as the only effective political organization. In 1971 the provincial party committees of four major areas—Kiangsi, Kwangtung, Kiangsu, and Hunan—all had first secretaries who were officers, and by August some 26 provincial committees were dominated by the military.

Although the Army spent 30% of its time on indoctrination and 20% on agriculture, increased attention was being given to major exercises at the divisional and corps level, involving up to 50,000 men. The bulk of the manpower remained concentrated in the 110 infantry divisions of 13,000 men, still lightly equipped but beginning to receive the Chinese T-62 light tank and armoured personnel carriers. The five armoured divisions were starting to reequip with the Chinese T-59 medium tank, an adaptation of the T-54.

Deployment seemed to have altered little. China was divided into 11 military regions subdivided into two or three military districts, each assigned an army of three infantry divisions and three artillery regiments with three armoured regiments sometimes added. Two or three armoured divisions were kept in the Peking and Shen-yang region. This gave a geographic distribution of 33 divisions in north and northeast China (Shen-yang and Peking military regions), 25 divisions in east and southeast China (Tsinan, Nanking, and Foochow military regions), 31 divisions in south-central China (Canton and Wushan military regions), 11 divisions in midwest China (Lanchow military region), and 20 divisions in west and southwest China (Sinkiang, Ch'eng-tu, and K'un-ming military regions), plus 1 military engineer division and construction troops, totaling 15,000–20,000 men, in North Vietnam and Laos.

One of the PLA's least recognized features remained its small size in relation to the population: 3 million out of 827 million.

INDIA AND PAKISTAN

The Pakistan government's decision to dissolve the Constituent Assembly, in which the East Pakistan-based Awami League had won a majority in the December 1970 elections, led in 1971 to guerrilla warfare and a massive influx of refugees into India. (*See* PAKISTAN.) The second Indo-Pakistan war of December was inevitable since Indian support for the League's force, the Mukti Bahini, offered its only hope of resettling the ten million refugees who were costing India $2.5 million per day and upsetting the existing delicate balance of language, religion, and ethnic groups in West Bengal. Only about one million of the refugees were Muslim while the rest were Hindu, suggesting that primarily Muslim Pakistan was using the opportunity to eliminate its Hindu minority.

Pakistani Pres. Agha Muhammad Yahya Khan's expectations that the elections would produce a fragmented assembly he could dominate were disappointed by the overwhelming victory of the Awami League, and while constitutional talks proceeded, Pakistan International Airways doubled the troop strength in the east wing to 60,000 men, using the southern route around India and the northern route, which involved refueling on Chinese bases. A major attack on Bengali nationalists was mounted in March under Gen. Tikka Khan, but it failed despite the heavy casualties inflicted. The Mukti Bahini guerrillas, with Indian aid, succeeded in cutting the rail and road links between Dacca, the capital, and the port of Chittagong, which accounted for over half the interior's food supplies. West Pakistan responded by raising two new divisions, bringing the number of regular troops in East Pakistan to 80,000, supported by 100,000 paramilitary forces. These forces seemed to be experiencing the customary difficulties in suppressing guerrillas with secure external bases, and by August repeated clashes with Indian border forces were taking place.

Before the war started, Pakistan's 1971–72 defense budget had risen by $109 million to $714 million, or some 3.8% of GNP. It provided for two armoured divisions with 600 medium and 200 light tanks and 12 infantry divisions (to be increased to 14) with 300 armoured personnel carriers, about 900 25-pounders and 105-mm. and 155-mm. howitzers, plus 200 130-mm. guns. Paramilitary forces included the 30,000-man frontier corps and 250,000 militia, plus the new East Pakistan Civil Armed Force. The Air Force

had received 32 new Mirage III-E fighter-bombers, but it still had too many types of plane; the main force consisted of 112 F-86 Sabre fighter-bomber/interceptors and 80 MiG-19 interceptors, both relatively obsolete, and 16 Il-12 and 32 B-57B light bombers. The 40 helicopters included Sioux, Huskies, Alouette IIIs, and Mi-8s. The small Navy had four submarines, two destroyers, and three destroyer escorts.

Against this, the Indians' defense plans gave them a considerable advantage. The Army had been stabilized at 860,000 men with a 100,000-strong Frontier Guard, but it had been reequipped and the ratio of combat to support troops had been improved. The one armoured division and two independent armoured brigades had 850 medium tanks plus 300 Vijayanta tanks, an Indian-produced version of a Vickers model, and 250 light tanks. Besides the 10 mountain divisions, reckoned as capable of containing any but an all-out Chinese attack, there were 13 infantry divisions with 3,000 artillery pieces, mostly 25-pounders but including some 350 100-mm. and 140 130-mm. guns being introduced as replacements.

The Air Force had been largely modernized, with 120 modified MiG-21 interceptors produced under license, 80 to 100 Su-7 fighter-bombers of 140 ordered, and 32 HF-24 Marut 1As—the Indian-designed fighter whose engines continued to give trouble, although reheat raised its speed over Mach 1, making it a good ground-attack fighter. Following their success in the 1965 war with Pakistan, production under license of Gnat light fighters had been increased, and there were 130 in service. About 90 of the aging Hunter F-56 fighter-bombers and 50 Canberra B(1)s remained. An air defense network including 50 SAM-2 complexes had been completed, though it was pierced in July when two Pakistan Mirages swept Sungar airfield near West Pakistan. The Navy, which had the task of blockading Pakistan, had two cruisers, three destroyers, nine destroyer escorts (including five of the unsatisfactory ex-Soviet Petya classes), and one Leander-class frigate, with three more building. Four more Soviet F-class submarines had been ordered, plus six missile gunboats. These programs had raised

French destroyers arrive at Valletta, Malta, on Feb. 8, 1971, prior to naval exercises in the Mediterranean. Both vessels were armed with homing torpedoes, automatic guns, and guided missiles.

UPI COMPIX

the defense budget to $1,656,000,000 or 3.41% of GNP.

India's status as a regional great power was confirmed by the Indo-Soviet treaty committing the parties not to enter into military alliances directed against each other or to assist any third party in armed conflict with the other party to the treaty. Apparently under discussion for two years, the treaty had been concluded for three reasons: India's desire to have a secure ally in the event of war; fears occasioned by presidential aide Henry Kissinger's trip to Peking to arrange President Nixon's visit, which was made via Pakistan and included suggestions that India would not receive U.S. aid in a war against China;

and U.S. arms shipments to Pakistan. Although an arms embargo was imposed by the U.S. after guerrilla fighting began in East Pakistan, and economic aid for 1972 was held in abeyance, some $4 million of arms already purchased were being shipped while the U.S. government exerted only mild diplomatic pressure on Pakistan. Above all, the Soviet alliance guaranteed India rapid replacement of combat losses, particularly in aircraft and armour. The short operational life of modern equipment between major refits could have posed a major problem in even a relatively short conflict. But with Soviet aid, Prime Minister Indira Gandhi could be confident of success when she ordered preparations for war before her November world tour,

Approximate Strengths of Regular Armed Forces of the World

Country	Military personnel in 000s Army	Navy	Air force	Aircraft carriers	Warships Submarines*	Cruisers	Destroyers/ frigates	Total ships	Aircraft Bombers†	Fighters	Defense expenditure as % of GNP
I. NATO											
Belgium	71.5	5.0	20.5	—	—	—	—	—	80 FB	40	2.8
Canada	33.0	15.0	37.0	—	4	—	20	24	30 FB	105	2.5
Denmark	24.0	6.5	10.5	—	6	—	6	12	48 FB	48	2.3
France‡	329.0	68.5	104.0	4	19 + 1 SSBN (FBMS)	1	56	96	210 FB, 36 SB	150	4.0
Germany, West	327.0	36.0	104.0	—	11	—	20	31	360 FB	80	3.3
Greece	118.0	18.0	23.0	—	2	—	12	14	75 FB	60	4.9
Italy	295.0	45.0	74.0	—	9	3	21	33	135 FB	75	2.8
Netherlands	76.0	19.0	21.5	—	7	2	18	27	72 FB	36	3.5
Norway	18.0	8.6	9.4	—	15	—	5	20	80 FB	20	2.9
Portugal	179.0	18.0	21.0	—	4	—	11	15	40 FB	20	6.5
Turkey	420.0	38.5	50.0	—	12	—	10	22	200 FB	120	3.7
United Kingdom§	185.3	84.6	111.0	4	26, 5 N 4 FBMS	1	79	115	150 FB, 130 B	150	4.9
United States§	1,319.0	623.0	657.0	18	46, 53 N 42 FBMS	9	218	342	1,500 FB, 520 SB	1,546	7.8
II. OTHER EUROPEAN											
Albania	35.0	3.0	4.0	—	4	—	—	4	—	72 F	...
Austria	44.0	—	4.3	—	—	—	—	—	23 FB	—	1.2
Finland	34.0	2.5	3.0	—	—	—	3	3	—	30 F	1.4
Spain§	220.0	47.5	33.5	1	3	1	27	32	120 FB	70	2.0
Sweden	49.0	12.1	12.2	—	23	—	15	38	150 FB	420	3.7
Switzerland	19.5	—	10.0	—	—	—	—	—	195 FB	100	2.1
Yugoslavia	195.0	18.0	20.0	—	5	—	1	6	150 FB	160	5.4
III. WARSAW PACT											
Bulgaria	117.0	9.0	22.0	—	2	—	—	2	72 FB	144	3.1
Czechoslovakia	145.0	—	40.0	—	—	—	—	—	168 FB	252	5.8
Germany, East	90.0	16.0	20.0	—	—	—	4	4	—	188	5.9
Hungary	90.0	—	12.5	—	—	—	—	—	10 FB	120	3.5
Poland	190.0	20.0	55.0	—	5	—	2	7	144 FB, 72 B	480	5.2
Romania	130.0	9.0	21.0	—	—	—	—	—	—	230	3.5
U.S.S.R.	2,000.0‖	475.0	550.0	2	290, 60 N 20 FBMS 38 BMS	26	208	587	2,000 FB, 1,200 B‖ 140 SB	5,300‖	11.0
IV. FAR EAST AND OCEANIA											
Australia	47.7	17.8	22.6	1	4	—	14	19	48 FB, 12 B	24	3.6
Burma	130.5	7.0	6.5	—	—	—	1	1	18 FB	—	3.3
Cambodia	175.0	1.5	2.3	—	—	—	—	—	7 FB	—	5.9‖
China‖	2,550.0	150.0	180.0	—	33	—	8	41	1,700 FB, 180 B	1,000	10.0‖
India	860.0	40.0	80.0	1	4	2	21	28	225 FB, 45 B	226	3.4
Indonesia§	250.0	34.0	35.0	—	12	1	30	43	10 FB, 32 B	95	2.3
Japan	179.0	38.3	41.7	—	11	—	40	51	140 FB	140 F	0.8
Korea, North	360.0	11.0	30.0	—	3	—	—	3	380 FB, 70 B	110	25.0‖
Korea, South§	593.0	16.7	24.5	—	—	—	10	10	128 FB	95	4.0
Laos	52.6	0.4	2.0	—	—	—	—	—	75 FB	—	11.0‖
Malaysia	43.0	3.0	4.0	—	—	—	2	2	30 FB	—	4.6
New Zealand	5.6	2.9	4.2	—	—	—	4	4	27 FB	—	2.0
Pakistan	365.0	10.0	17.0	—	4	1	7	12	160 FB, 48 B	80	3.8
Philippines	17.6	8.0	9.0	—	—	—	1	1	20 FB	26	1.9
Taiwan	425.0	35.0	80.0	—	—	—	28	28	80 FB	265	8.8
Vietnam, North	480.0	3.0	9.0	—	—	—	—	—	10 B	155	21.3‖
Vietnam, South§	429.0	31.0	40.0	—	—	—	4	4	100 FB	20	...
V. MIDDLE EAST, AFRICA, AND LATIN AMERICA¶											
Algeria	53.0	3.2	4.0	—	—	—	—	—	24 B	30 F	4.0
Argentina	85.0	35.0§	17.0	1	2	3	14	20	25 FB	45 F	2.6
Brazil	120.0	44.3§	30.0	1	4	2	18	25	18 FB	16 F	2.6
Chile	38.0	15.0	8.0	—	2	2	5	9	—	25 F	1.7
Colombia	50.0	8.0	6.0	—	—	—	10	10	—	6 F	2.0
Congo (Kinshasa)	45.0	0.1	0.9	—	—	—	—	—	—	—	2.0
Cuba	90.0	7.5	12.0	—	—	—	2	2	20 FB	165 F	6.1
Egypt	275.0	14.0	25.0	—	12	—	5	17	310 FB, 43 B	200 F	19.6
Ethiopia	39.0	1.5	2.2	—	—	—	—	—	32 FB, 4 B	10 F	2.1
Iran	150.0	9.0	22.0	—	—	—	6	6	112 FB	20 F	7.1
Iraq	85.0	2.0	8.2	—	—	—	—	—	99 FB, 18 B	100 F	9.4
Israel♀	61.5/275.0	4.5/8.0	9.0/17.0	—	3	—	1	4	278 FB, 10 B	9 F	26.5
Jordan	58.0	0.2	2.0	—	—	—	—	—	18 FB	15 F	16.4
Mexico	54.0	7.6	6.0	—	—	—	5	5	15 FB	—	...
Nigeria	240.0	5.0	7.0	—	—	—	1	1	8 FB, 6 B	—	5.6
Peru	35.5	10.1	9.0	—	4	2	11	11	10 FB, 20 B	60 F	3.2
S. Africa	32.3	4.2	8.0	—	1	—	8	9	70 FB, 30 B	16 F	2.6
Syria	100.0	1.7	10.0	—	—	—	—	—	110 FB	100 F	12.1

Note: Data exclude paramilitary, security, and irregular forces. Naval data exclude vessels of less than 100 tons standard displacement.
*Nuclear hunter-killers (N), fleet ballistic missile submarines (FBMS), ballistic missile submarines, short-range (BMS).
†Medium and heavy bombers (B), fighter-bombers (FB), and strategic bombers (SB).
‡French forces were withdrawn from NATO in 1966, but France remains a member of NATO.
§Includes Marine Corps.
‖Approximate.
¶Latin-American data is for 1970; defense expenditure as % of GNP for 1969; there are no significant changes.
♀Second figure is fully mobilized strength.
Sources: International Institute for Strategic Studies, 18 Adam Street, London, *The Military Balance, 1970–71, Strategic Survey 1969–70.*

designed to ensure a favourable reception for Indian action. Pakistan received no outside military aid. China could not provide it with the main mountain passes blocked by snow.

Although the details, especially the losses, remained uncertain, the general course of the war was clear. India followed the obvious strategy of concentrating on destroying East Pakistan first, deploying an estimated nine infantry divisions plus supporting armour and 50,000 Mukti Bahini against Pakistan's four divisions. These faced all-round attack while the Indian Air Force interdicted the supply routes used in March, destroyed the Pakistani planes in the East, and then took out any strongpoints at leisure. The East Pakistani troops fought bravely but were totally defeated, Dacca, the capital, falling on December 16. East Pakistan was recognized by India as the independent country of Bangla Desh.

In the west, India's remaining six regular divisions, reinforced by the call-up of 700,000 reservists (producing about 50,000 combat troops, the manpower for three–four divisions), faced eight–ten Pakistani infantry divisions plus two armoured to the Indians' one armoured division. This advantage was largely a paper one; Pakistan had a total of 800 tanks against India's 1,500, so India could afford to split its forces. Indeed, with air supremacy gained, India launched diversionary attacks against the Lahore, Rawalpindi, and Peshawar supply line. West Pakistan, therefore, was unable to gain sufficiently in Kashmir to offset the loss of East Pakistan. On December 16, after the fall of Dacca and the surrender of the Pakistani forces in the east, India ordered a complete cease-fire. This was accepted by the government of Pakistan the following day.

India's realization that its inherent power and position made the late Prime Minister Jawaharlal Nehru's policy of nonalignment and low defense spending impracticable found further expression in its pursuit of a nuclear weapons option. This was publicly advocated in January by Gen. J. N. Chaudhuri, former chief of the General Staff, reflecting the increasingly powerful pro-bomb lobby within the government and military circles. Supporters of an Indian nuclear capability could point to the establishment of a largely Indian-designed and built plutonium separation plant, enabling it to convert plutonium into weapons-grade fissionable material, while the Kalapakkam reactor currently under construction would be free of even bilateral safeguards against military use. Existing facilities were capable of producing about 100 bombs per year. A five-year weapons program would cost $11 billion. This explained India's continued refusal to sign the nonproliferation treaty, although it agreed to accept trilateral safeguards, with International Atomic Energy Agency supervision, on supplies of nuclear fuel and equipment.

In April, Ceylon experienced an attempted coup by the Maoist Peoples Liberation Movement. The prime minister, Mme Sirimavo Bandaranaike, who had asked India to send a division of regular troops, found herself in the unique position of heading a left-wing government that suppressed a Maoist revolution with aid from the major powers. The U.K. sent small arms and six helicopters, India supplied helicopters and established a naval patrol of five frigates that arrested North Korean gunrunners on May 11, and the U.S.S.R. offered 500-lb. bombs for Ceylon's 4 MiG-17s, some pilots, and 20 armoured cars. By May government control had been reestablished.

The cease-fire along the Suez Canal continued, reflecting the inability of Israel and Egypt to agree on minimum terms for a peace settlement. Intensive U.S. efforts to bring the two sides together proved as unsuccessful as those of UN mediator Gunnar Jarring, which were terminated. Egypt insisted on the ultimate withdrawal of Israeli forces from all territory gained in the 1967 Six-Day War as a precondition for any partial measures such as reopening of the canal, while Israel insisted on retaining at least Sharm el-Sheik, the Golan Heights, and East Jerusalem.

Arab politics continued to be dominated by internal dissent, with unsuccessful coups in Morocco in July and Sudan in August. In May Egyptian Pres. Anwar as-Sadat purged his government of high-ranking officials who had favoured a hard line against Israel. Sadat, preoccupied with domestic problems, seemed disposed to accept something like a de facto settlement, though he was threatening war by the end of the year if Israel did not withdraw. In June he was able to secure a 15-year treaty of friendship and cooperation with the U.S.S.R., formalizing an alliance in which the U.S.S.R. had invested about $5 billion in arms and $800 million in economic aid. Egypt, Syria, and Libya established the Confederation of Arab Republics on September 2, but it seemed uncertain whether it would be any more successful than its predecessor, the short-lived United Arab Republic formed by Egypt and Syria.

The collapse of the Palestinian guerrillas who had dominated events in 1970 underlined the uncertainties of Middle Eastern politics. The lightly armed guerrilla forces were no match for the ruthless Bedouin troops of Jordan's King Husain I, armed with tanks and artillery, including some equipment flown in by the U.S. The king used the September 1970 cease-fire agreements with the guerrillas to push the remaining 4,000 into the hills around Jerash-Ajloun, where the Army could destroy them at leisure. Full-scale fighting broke out between July 3 and July 18 in which King Husain's forces killed several hundred guerrillas and captured 2,300, with a further 100 seeking sanctuary in Israel. Halfhearted Syrian attempts to intervene petered out in a small tank battle. (*See* Jordan.)

Jordan's defense budget was set at $90 million; at 16.4% of GNP, it was proportionately the second highest in the world, though it was $15 million lower than in the previous year. The 58,000-man Army included one armoured division, one mechanized division, and one infantry division, plus three artillery regiments with the ubiquitous British 25-pounder gun and 30 105-mm. and 155-mm. howitzers. These were chiefly responsible for defeating the guerrillas, who lacked antitank and antiaircraft weapons and had no artillery. Jordan's Air Force had received the last of its 15 F-104A Starfighters from the U.S., supplementing its 18 elderly ground-attack Hunters and 7 Alouette III helicopters, all of which were used against the guerrillas. Jordan had countered the British withdrawal from Aden by cooperating with Ethiopia against the Eastern Liberation Front to keep the eastern side of the Strait of Bab el Mandeb in friendly hands, showing how widespread the effects of the Arab-Israeli conflict were.

The central struggle remained that between Israel and Egypt, but in 1971 it was largely confined to the arms race. Egypt drew ahead as unprecedented quantities of Soviet equipment and personnel arrived.

Along the canal, the air defense system was completed in violation of the cease-fire. It included 63 Soviet-controlled sites, each with four SA-3 (and possibly SA-4) short-range missiles for use against low-level aircraft; these, in turn, were deployed in a checkerboard pattern to cover the 70 sites for SA-2 long-range, high-altitude missiles. Coordinated with these were 150 MiG-21J interceptors, flown and controlled by the Soviets. The Soviets also introduced the MiG-23 Foxbat, a stripped-down antibomber version of the standard model that was faster than Israel's Phantoms and had a 10,000-ft. higher ceiling and a greater combat radius of 400–700 mi., although it was less effective at low levels. Against Israel's canal defenses, the Soviets supplied 40 203-mm. siege howitzers, 150 self-propelled guns, and short-range surface-to-surface missiles including 24 FROG-3s and 25 Samlets. Soviet personnel, including the six fighter squadrons and air defense personnel, totaled about 15,000–20,000; in addition, 1,500 were stationed in Algeria and 1,000 in Syria.

The Egyptian Army increased by only one infantry division, presumably to allow time for training a highly mechanized force patterned on Soviet lines. The three armoured divisions had 1,200 medium tanks, while four mechanized divisions had 850 armoured personnel carriers plus 150 light tanks. Sixteen artillery brigades (one more than in the previous year) had 1,500 122-mm., 130-mm., and 152-mm. guns and howitzers. The Air Force was 25% larger, reflecting the increased numbers of MiG-21 interceptors (200) and SU-7 fighter-bombers (110); together with 200 MiG-17 fighter-bombers and assorted older aircraft, they brought the combat force to 523. These increases raised defense spending to $1,495,000,000, $233 million above the 1970 figure. The available amphibious forces, including 50 tanks with 20 landing craft and 18 missile gunboats, remained insufficient for a major attack across the canal.

The Confederation of Arab Republics would add to the Egyptian forces Syria's 100,000-man Army with one armoured division and 750 tanks, two mechanized divisions with 500 armoured personnel carriers, and seven artillery regiments with 800 Soviet guns. The Air Force had added ten MiG-21s, bringing the total to 100, but had lost some ten SU-7 fighter-bombers; 30 SU-7s were left, together with 80 MiG-15 and MiG-17 fighter-bombers. Revised estimates of 1970 defense spending put it at $176 million. Libya's contribution would be its large oil revenues and the French Mirage III fighters, still being delivered despite a theoretical commitment that they were not to be used against Israel; 18 had arrived and 30 of the total order of 100 were scheduled for delivery in 1972, together with eight F-5s to add to the seven in service. Britain had placed Libya's order for 188 Chieftain tanks in abeyance, leaving the 20,000-strong Army dependent on 100 T54/55 medium tanks. Libya's 1971–72 defense budget was unchanged at $84 million.

Israeli strategy was to hold the territory gained in the Six-Day War with minimum casualties, while persuading the U.S. that its peace initiatives were frustrated by Soviet support of Egyptian intransigence, and that this could be offset only by increased U.S. aid. In the year since the August 1970 cease-fire U.S. aid had totaled $500 million, including Shrike air-to-surface missiles, 180 medium tanks, and electronic countermeasures equipment. The sale of 17 more Phantoms brought the total to over 75 F-4E

fighter-bomber/interceptors and 6 RF-4E reconnaissance planes, plus 72 A-4E/H Skyhawk fighter-bombers, with 18 more due for delivery. Israel appeared to be building, from stolen plans, a domestic version of the Mirage V fighter-bomber/interceptor, 50 of which had been purchased from France but placed under embargo, but these seemed unlikely to offset the Soviet-Egyptian buildup. Israel therefore requested more Phantoms and Skyhawks, together with the Lance surface-to-surface missile. The Lance, which had not yet been supplied to the U.S. Army, could neutralize most SAM sites with its multiple high-explosive warhead, while its 50-mi. range would put it beyond the range of Egyptian artillery.

Defense of the Canal Zone depended on the Bar Lev Line, really a series of self-contained strongpoints or hedgehogs covering possible crossing zones, with the main mobile forces held in reserve for a counterattack. Whether these would suffice seemed uncertain. Although qualitatively superior, the forces available on total mobilization amounted to only 275,000, with ten armoured brigades fielding 950 M-48, Ben Gurion (converted Centurions), Isherman, and Tl-67 tanks with 105-mm. guns, plus 200 Centurions. The nine infantry and four parachute brigades relied for transport on 1,000 obsolete M-2 and M-3 half-tanks. Considerable hopes were placed on the new MD-660 surface-to-surface missile, with a range of 280 mi. The Navy's 12 missile gunboats mounting Gabriel surface-to-surface missiles provided some balance to Egypt's theoretical naval supremacy. The 1971–72 defense budget of $1,484,000,000, or 26.5% of GNP, was proportionately the highest in the world.

Despite the uncertainties of the military situation, Israel was able to consolidate its hold on the occupied territories. The elimination of the guerrillas from Jordan was complemented by a drive to resettle the 250,000 Palestinian refugees in the Gaza Strip. By August over 100 persons, mostly Arabs, had been killed within this 25-mi.-long, 8-mi.-wide area. Under Maj. Gen. Uriel Sharon, Israeli forces moved 6,000 refugees from the guerrilla centre of Jehalya to other areas and instituted strict security measures that drastically reduced the incidence of terrorism. But the shooting down of an elderly Israeli Stratocruiser well within the Israeli side of the canal in September emphasized how fragile the cease-fire was. The action was a carefully planned retaliation for the loss of an Egyptian photoreconnaissance plane over Israeli positions.

Farther south, Britain's confirmation of its withdrawal from the Persian Gulf by the end of 1971 focused attention on the local military balance. Britain and the U.S. had decided to support Iran as the dominant local power, able, with Saudi Arabia, to safeguard the flow of oil to the West against possible interference from Iraq. The military balance seemed favourable to the conservative forces; the Iranian Army of 150,000 had three armoured divisions with 860 M-47 and M-60A-1 medium tanks and 800 Chieftain tanks ordered. The three infantry divisions had 870 armoured personnel carriers, 75-mm., 105-mm., and 155-mm. howitzers, and 18 Hughie and Super Frelon helicopters delivered plus more on order. Saudi Arabia's 35,000-strong Army, with 1,000 men in Jordan and 2,000 in Egypt, was negligible compared with the Air Force. Its 20 Lightning interceptors were integrated in an air defense system that included 36 Thunderbird surface-to-air missiles, while 15 F-86 Sabre fighter-bombers and 20 BAC-167 ground-attack aircraft gave a limited interdiction capability. Iran's

Air Force was being modernized; two fighter-bomber squadrons of F-4D Phantoms carrying Sidewinder and Sparrow air-to-air missiles were in service, 32 F-4Es were on order, and a further 109 were being negotiated. Five fighter-bomber squadrons with F-5s were being retained. Air defense was based on Tigercat surface-to-air missiles, with low-level Rapiers on order. This preponderance served to explain Iran's seizure of the three islands (Greater and Lesser Tumbs and Abu Musa) at the mouth of the Persian Gulf on November 31.

Against these forces Iraq could muster an army of 85,000 men, divided into two armoured divisions with 800 T-54/55 tanks and four infantry divisions with 45 PT-76 light tanks, 115 AML armoured cars, and 300 Soviet 120- and 130-mm. guns. The Air Force, with 220 combat aircraft, was numerically superior to Iran's but qualitatively about equal. Its core consisted of 85 MiG-21 interceptors and 48 SU-7 fighter-bombers, with a multiplicity of older types. The major uncertainty was the stability of the Iranian government and its ability to protect the Gulf's oil states from guerrilla infiltration. The Iranian Navy was expanding, with four frigates with Seacat missiles being delivered and ten Hovercraft in service.

SOUTHEAST AND EAST ASIA

The U.S. withdrawal from South Vietnam proceeded rapidly, and by November President Nixon was able to announce that the offensive combat role of U.S. troops had ended. At the same time, he set a target figure of 139,000 U.S. troops in South Vietnam by Feb. 1, 1972, half of this further reduction of 45,000 to be accomplished by Christmas. The withdrawal was covered by the spoiling action against the North Vietnamese in Laos in the spring, when the poor performance of the South Vietnamese Army (ARVN) suggested that the U.S. strategy of vietnamization was unlikely to succeed. Nevertheless, the Nixon administration completed Phase I, transferring combat responsibility to South Vietnam by mid-1971. Air and artillery support were to be handed over in Phase II, leaving a residual force of 30,000–70,000 U.S. troops in South Vietnam by July 1, 1972. Withdrawals were averaging 15,000 men per month, leaving 158,300 troops by Christmas, so by the end of December there had been 24,000 more withdrawals than originally scheduled.

The Pentagon had been pressing for a faster withdrawal because the troops left would be extremely vulnerable—a fear that presumably explained the five days of intensified bombing of North Vietnam late in December. The remaining troops were falling back on the enclave strategy, using bases on the coast and near Saigon for small, quick-reaction forces using helicopters, artillery, and about ten fighter-bomber squadrons. The Marines and the controversial Green Berets were withdrawn from combat by July, while U.S. forces in Thailand were reduced by 10,000 to 32,000 by agreement with the Thai government. A residual U.S. force of 8,000 men was in Taiwan.

The abandonment of the Khe Sanh base symbolized U.S. disentanglement from the Indochina war. The siege of Khe Sanh in 1968 had been compared to that of Dien Bien Phu, which preceded France's defeat in 1954; the Americans had saved themselves from a similar debacle only by a massive application of air power. The base was reactivated in January 1971 for the attack on Laos and evacuated on April 6 following President Nixon's declaration that after May 1, U.S. troops would cease to occupy forward bases. The

ARVN lost Fire Base Fuller in the Northern Defense Line below the demilitarized zone (DMZ) on June 24. Despite Fuller's eventual recapture, two North Vietnamese regiments crossed the DMZ for the first time in three years, bringing their strength in the South to 10,000, with 16,000 just north of the DMZ. The North Vietnamese and Viet Cong were regaining control in Military Regions I and II as the U.S. pulled out, while in the Delta region, 32,000 North Vietnamese and Viet Cong opposed 20,000 U.S. support forces, including 6,000 helicopters but no combat troops.

Viet Cong hit-and-run raids continued to kill administrators and destroy U.S. supply dumps, including that for the Central Region at Qui Nhon, with 10,000 tons of ammunition, on July 1. Cam Ranh Bay lost 1.5 million gal. of aviation fuel on May 14 and half the ammunition dump on August 27. U.S. casualties dropped drastically; as of June 1, 1971, 44,876 had been killed in battle and 9,408 had died from nonhostile causes, giving a total of 54,941 killed, 293,592 wounded, and 1,431 missing or captured in the decade since U.S. involvement started in 1961. Over the same period, North Vietnamese and Viet Cong losses were estimated at 992,000 killed, but they were still able to deploy 40,000 men in Cambodia, 75,000 in Laos, and 90,000 in South Vietnam, plus 150,000 Viet Cong.

South Vietnam nominally deployed a 414,000-man army of ten infantry divisions, although these were considerably understrength and no division could move far away from its home area without suffering heavy desertions. The 40,000-man Air Force had about 100 fighter-bombers, half of them piston-engined, and 275 helicopters, mostly UH-1 Hughies. It seemed unlikely that it would be able to meet the U.S. target of a 50% expansion by 1973–74. Other allied forces comprised 50,000 Koreans, 6,000 Australians, and 320 New Zealanders, all of which were being reduced. Of the 12,000 Thais, the Black Panther Division left by July. The North Vietnamese Air Defense Force comprised 40 MiG-21 F/PF interceptors with Atoll antiaircraft missiles, 25 MiG-19s, 70 MiG-17s, and 20 MiG-15 interceptors, plus 35 surface-to-air missile batteries with 6 SA-2 launchers, each able to inflict significant casualties on the U.S. (*See* VIETNAM.)

Fighting in Cambodia flared up around the capital of Phnom Penh in January, when some 8,000 North Vietnamese attacked the U.S. defenders. A July counterattack by about 12,000 South Vietnamese succeeded, but the Cambodians apparently feared South

New German eight-axled armoured scout car crosses a water ditch during tests after being presented to the Federal Defense Assembly in March 1971.

D.P.A.—PICTORIAL PARADE

Vietnamese domination, since they started negotiating, on September 5, for withdrawal of the 100,000 ARVN in Cambodia. These troops were needed to offset the losses from the operation in Laos. Modeled on the 1970 spoiling attack on Communist supply dumps in Cambodia, operation Lam Son 719 had started on February 8, but it soon encountered obstacles that had been absent from Cambodia. By the end of February the North Vietnamese had reinforced their original 70,000 troops by 20,000–30,000, while ARVN's original 16,000-man force had penetrated only 16 km. inside the border on what seemed to be a premature commitment to a major set-piece operation. On March 3 an airborne brigade was lost trying to hold Hill 37 in one of the few tank engagements of the war.

Reinforcements bringing ARVN strength to 40,000 and that of the U.S. to 10,000 failed to counter North Vietnam's superior bombers and their tactic of using artillery to offset U.S. air power, which was also handicapped by bad weather and unfavourable terrain. The Tchepone valley proved a graveyard for U.S. helicopters, with eight being lost in one day. By April 9, when the operation ended in a retreat that was nearly a rout, ARVN had lost 6,000 killed or wounded and its best soldier, Lieut. Gen. Do Cao Tri, had been killed in a helicopter crash. North Vietnamese supplies had been reduced to one-sixth of their requirement, but by May, North Vietnam had gained control of the Bolovens Plateau, doubling the width of the Ho Chi Minh Trail at its junction with Cambodia. In December joint Lao, Thai, and U.S. forces were driven from the Plaine des Jarres, and Pak Song was taken by the North Vietnamese.

South Korean withdrawal from Vietnam was inevitable as the U.S. implemented its decision to remove 20,000 men from South Korea. The 40,000 remaining comprised one infantry division and elements of the 5th Air Force, which were regarded as implementing the U.S. guarantee under the implicit new doctrine that commitment would be valid only if supported by a physical presence. Against North Korea's two armoured and 20 infantry divisions, South Korea could muster only 2 armoured brigades and 29 infantry divisions. The new local defense militia of one or two million would counter a similar North Korean force. U.S. dependence on tactical nuclear weapons to halt any invasion was clear.

Japan continued to expand its armed forces slowly to compensate for reduction of the 72,000 U.S. forces in Japan and Okinawa. Quantitatively, the Japanese Self-Defense Forces (JSDF) remained smaller than the forces of South Korea, Indonesia, or Taiwan, and Japan's 1971–72 defense budget of $1,864,000,000 represented the smallest percentage (0.81) of GNP devoted to defense in Southeast or East Asia. On the other hand, actual spending was the highest, and qualitatively the Air Force and Navy soon would be the most powerful in the area.

The Defense Agency's hopes of increasing its share of GNP to 1.5% received a temporary setback in July, when the collision of an airliner with a JSDF fighter killed 171 persons and provoked a strong public reaction. Keikichi Masuhara, who had succeeded Yasuhiro Nakasone as director-general in July, resigned and was replaced by Naomi Nishimura. However, the changes in U.S. relations with China and Japan were inevitably forcing Japan to assume greater responsibility for its own defense. The fourth defense plan for 1972–75 envisaged bringing Army strength

to 179,000 and reequipping it with modern weapons systems, including the domestically produced M 61 tanks for the one mechanized division. The ten infantry divisions were to be supplemented by a 40,000-strong National Guard with light arms, forming a second-line reserve. Protection of Okinawa would be taken over by 6,000 men, three Nike surface-to-air missile batteries, and 25 F-104s. The Air Force expected to receive sufficient F-4-E-Js to bring the total to 130, and 360 XT-2 supersonic trainers (prototype to the SF-X light strike fighter) were ordered. The Navy would receive a new 8,000-ton helicopter-carrying destroyer and missile gunboats, though it was estimated that the available forces were still far short of those needed for effective defense. Nevertheless, Japan's military capabilities would be considerable by 1975.

SOUTH OF THE SAHARA

South Africa, Portugal, and Rhodesia seemed increasingly successful in operations against their guerrilla opponents. The guerrillas lacked secure bases and suffered from internal dissension in the face of attacks that combined traditional colonial policing measures with the mobility and firepower of modern military technology. South Africa's defense budget of $442 million, still only 2.61% of GNP, reflected its self-confidence and the absence of a major conventional military threat. Nigeria had the only comparable African force, but its 240,000-strong Army lacked mobility or armour, while the Air Force had only 32 combat aircraft. From a white population of 3.9 million (compared with Israel's 3 million), South Africa produced a small army of 32,000, plus 23,000 trained reserves; it was light in armour, with 240 medium tanks, 500 French AML-60 and AML-90 armoured cars, and 200 Ferret scout cars. Complementing this antiterrorist force were 3,000 paramilitary police with 80 Saracen armoured personnel carriers and a second-line reserve of 75,000 commandos.

The Air Force clearly was designed to secure air supremacy and execute ground attack and transport missions in support of antiguerrilla operations. New fighter-bombers continued to account for most of the expenditure on equipment, with 20 Mirage III-EZ fighter-bombers, carrying AS-20 and AS-30 air-to-surface missiles, and 16 Mirage III-CZ interceptors with R-530 air-to-surface missiles entering service. Arrangements were made for Mirage aircraft to be built under license; also being built under license were the Impala light-strike aircraft, 50 of which were in service with the Citizen Force reserves, surface-to-surface missiles, tanks, and ammunition. Helicopters, which had proved decisive against guerrillas, were being developed as the main form of troop transport. Installation of the Cactus air defense system began, but delivery of the Crotale surface-to-air missile was still awaited. This might be supplemented by the British Aircraft Corp.'s Country 102 system using Rapier and Thunderbird surface-to-air missiles in a package similar to that sold to Saudi Arabia for £100 million.

Much depended on a change in Britain's attitude toward arms sales to South Africa. Although Prime Minister Heath's government continued to refuse to sell arms that could be used for internal suppression, it clearly felt that South Africa had become a more important ally in view of the continued closure of the Suez Canal and the consequent increase in the use of the Cape route for oil shipments to Europe. Under the 1955 agreement allowing the Royal Navy to use the Simonstown naval base, the U.K. was obliged to supply the South African Navy with antisubmarine weapons. The South African government had turned this issue into one of principle, as had the U.K. government, which felt it must be free to take any decision it felt was right after consultation with the Commonwealth heads of government at their January conference. The African and Asian Commonwealth members opposed the sale, and a major split was averted only through a Canadian compromise whereby an eight-nation study group was established to look into security problems in the Indian Ocean. The group, composed of Australia, Canada, India, Jamaica, Kenya, Malaysia, Nigeria, and the U.K., broke up without meeting after Britain announced in March that it would grant licenses for the sale of seven Wasp antisubmarine helicopters to South Africa. The overthrow of one of the U.K.'s most vociferous critics, Milton Obote of Uganda, during the conference cast doubts on the diplomatic importance of opposition to Britain, however. South Africa also suggested it might purchase four to six of the 2,500-ton general-purpose Type 21 frigates at £7 million–£8 million each, for delivery by 1974–75. Whether this would come to anything more than previous expressions of interest remained doubtful.

South Africa had nevertheless scored a major victory, using its new strategy of offering cooperation with NATO members against Soviet naval forces in the Indian Ocean while using the economic carrot and military stick to secure a bloc of friendly African neighbours to the north. These included Botswana, Lesotho, Swaziland, Malagasy, Mauritius, and Malawi, whose president, H. Kamuzu Banda, became the first African head of state to be received in South Africa. South Africa obtained considerable benefit from this cooperation, including the sealing of Malawi's borders against guerrillas and the right to build and use the air base at Lilongwe.

South Africa claimed to have developed a new process for producing cheap weapons-grade uranium, using the jet-nozzle system instead of the established, expensive, diffusion process of the gas centrifuge. In April the chairman of South Africa's Atomic Energy Board claimed, perhaps prematurely, that it could have a nuclear weapons option. The power for this would have to come from Portuguese Africa, since South Africa had committed itself to energy from Portuguese sources and, therefore, to Portugal's victory against the guerrillas in its territories. Cabinda supplied nearly enough oil for South Africa's needs and, of the 15,000 Mw. of electric power needed by 1978, 4,000 Mw. would come from the Cabora Bassa hydroelectric project in northwest Mozambique, which South Africa was helping to finance. South Africa was also involved in the Kurene River scheme in southern Angola and in shipping natural gas from Mozambique.

In light of its closer ties with South Africa, Portugal felt able to reduce its defense expenditure to an estimated $398.1 million in 1970, only 6.51% of GNP, compared with 7.21% in 1969. The Army of 179,000 had only two half-strength divisions in Portugal; 25 regiments were deployed overseas where, supported by locally enlisted troops, they provided 60,000 men in Angola, 45,000 in Mozambique, and 25,000 in Guinea. The Air Force had 150 miscellaneous combat aircraft, mostly light-strike fighters, and 85 helicopters.

Israeli Army Centurion tanks participate in maneuvers conducted on the Golan Heights in the occupied sector of Syria in the summer of 1971.
WIDE WORLD

In June PAIGC guerrillas with Cuban advisers, based in Guinea and Senegal, attacked Bissau, the capital of Portuguese Guinea. The chief of staff of the Portuguese Army, Gen. Deslandes, visited the province and decided against hot pursuit which might expand the conflict. In Mozambique, Tete District, site of the Cabora Bassa project, was put under military rule, and 20,000 troops were stationed there to ensure its completion. Helicopter-supported operations against the guerrillas in January resulted in 650 killed and 1,800 captured as against 130 Portuguese casualties. Operation Whirlwind in the May dry season produced comparable results, but intensified guerrilla attacks along the Malawi border were reported in December.

Divisions within the guerrilla movements were accentuated. COREMO and FRELIMO remained opposed, leading to the formation in June of a splinter group of FRELIMO called FUMO (Mozambique United Front). Increased pressure was put on their host state, Zambia, in March when five Portuguese officials were kidnapped, taken over the border, and murdered. Zambian dependence on the Portuguese port of Beira was underlined by large-scale holdups in shipments. The May disappearance of the crew of the cargo ship "Angoche," apparently taken over by guerrillas in the crew and sailed to Tanzania, brought threats of a retaliatory strike. In Angola, whose £20 million trade surplus made up for Portugal's trade deficit, the guerrillas' 1970–71 offensives cost them 16 camps, 650 killed, and 1,000 captured, leaving about 1,000 operating out of the Congo (Kinshasa).

Rhodesia continued to hold its section of the Zambezi Line, the key to Angola and Mozambique, with South African assistance along 50 mi. of the border. As of March, Rhodesia had lost only 17 soldiers while killing 200 guerrillas. A projected merger of the two principal guerrilla groups failed in January, and the 600 guerrillas involved became preoccupied with tribal feuds. Their funds were frozen, Organization of African Unity aid was suspended, and 129 were deported from Zambia for plotting against Pres. Kenneth Kaunda. The Rhodesian defense budget remained virtually constant at $25 million. Forces included a 3,400-man Army and 6,400 paramilitary British South African Police, with reserves of 8,000 and 28,500, respectively. The small Air Force had 55 obsolete ground-attack aircraft and 8 Alouette III helicopters. (R. J. RA.)

See also Astronautics.

Denmark

A constitutional monarchy of north central Europe lying between the North and Baltic seas, Denmark includes the Jutland Peninsula and 100 inhabited islands in the Kattegat and Skagerrak straits. Area (excluding Faeroe Islands): 16,629 sq.mi. (43,069 sq.km.). Pop. (1971 est.): 4,950,598. Cap. and largest city: Copenhagen (pop., 1971 est., 805,331). Language: Danish. Religion: predominantly Lutheran. King, Frederik IX; prime ministers in 1971, Hilmar Baunsgaard and, from October 11, Jens Otto Krag.

Despite strict financial controls and increased taxation, inflation in Denmark, which had averaged about 6% over the last two years, was running around 8% by mid-1971, and there had been no great improvement in the balance of payments situation. The economic situation thus continued to be a major topic of public debate in Denmark, and many people were dissatisfied with the three-party, right-centre coalition government in spite of some economic improvement during the summer months. Currency reserves were maintained at their normal level, but most of the reserves were loans and credits, many of them short-term. Nevertheless, incomes rose at the "usual" rate of about 10%. Only 5% of this was covered by increased productivity, increased taxation and inflation taking care of the rest.

On September 21 a general election was held, resulting in the defeat of Hilmar Baunsgaard's "bourgeois" coalition and the accession of a Social Democrat minority government under Jens Otto Krag, supported by the leftist Socialist People's Party. The final tabulation gave 89 seats to the Social Democratic and Socialist People's parties and 88 to the outgoing Conservative, Agrarian Liberal, and Radical Liberal parties, the two remaining seats in the 179-seat Folketing (parliament) being taken up by independents from the Faeroe Islands and Greenland. This gave the new government effectively a majority of one. Suggestions that a broad coalition government be formed to carry through the process of Danish entry into the EEC were rejected.

Taking up office after an interval of three and a half years (he had been prime minister from 1962 to 1968), Krag declared that his government would be judged on economic results. The Social Democrats had fought the election on a program directed toward a guided economy, including the establishment of a council to direct capital into industries that were primarily engaged in export or were in competition with imported goods in an attempt to tackle the balance of payments problem.

With the Social Democrats favouring broad economic guidance and the Socialist People's Party favouring the nationalization of certain sectors of the economy, there was considerable speculation as to whether Denmark was about to experience the "mixed economy" favoured in Sweden, where the state was a partner in various industries.

The country's economic problems had been vividly illustrated by a government planning report published in March. The report predicted that, if current trends continued, public authorities would be taking up 60% of the gross national product by 1980 and would swallow up the entire growth in manpower over the intervening period. There was heated controversy on how best to avoid this state of affairs, and advance planning remained a major subject of Danish politico-economic debates.

One of the most important weapons in the fight against the balance of payments deficit was seen as the control of public expenditure. The outgoing government had instituted a ban on the employment of additional personnel in the civil service, controls on municipal expenditure, and other fairly tough measures.

At the first session of the new Folketing, the government announced a 10% import surcharge on almost all goods with the exception of raw materials, medical goods, and unprocessed foods. The surcharge was to remain in effect until March 1973, but would be reduced by 3% in June 1972 and by a further 3% in January 1973. In view of considerable opposition pressure, Finance Minister Henry Gruenbaum conceded further exemptions, raising the proportion of total imports exempted from some 35% to about 42%.

Few obstacles remained in Denmark's negotiations for entry into the EEC. The only major condition of the Danish application had been the wish to join in company with the U.K. and, following the positive decision of the British Parliament on October 28, it only remained for the Folketing to make its official

---

DENMARK

Education. (1968–69) Primary, pupils 506,131; secondary, pupils 194,829; primary and secondary, teachers 43,537; vocational, pupils 133,552; higher (including 4 universities with 35,428 students in 1969–70), students 69,425, teaching staff 8,956.

Finance. Monetary unit: Danish krone, with a par value of 7.50 kroner to U.S. $1 (18 kroner = £1 sterling) and a free rate (Sept. 27, 1971) of 7.30 kroner to U.S. $1. Gold, SDRs, and foreign exchange, central bank: (June 1971) U.S. $398.1 million; (June 1970) U.S. $341.1 million. Budget (1969–70 rev. est.): revenue 29.5 billion kroner; expenditure 28 billion kroner. Gross national product: (1969) 104,920,000,-000 kroner; (1968) 92.2 billion kroner. Money supply: (April 1971) 28,650,000,000 kroner; (April 1970) 29,760,000,000 kroner. Cost of living (1964 = 100): (May 1971) 154; (May 1970) 144.

Foreign Trade. (1970) Imports 33,031,000,000 kroner; exports 25,171,000,000 kroner. Import sources: EEC 33% (West Germany 19%); Sweden 16%; U.K. 14%; U.S. 7%. Export destinations: EEC 23% (West Germany 13%); U.K. 19%; Sweden 17%; U.S. 8%; Norway 7%. Main exports: machinery 21%; meat and meat preparations 18% (including bacon 7%); chemicals 7%; dairy products 6%.

Transport and Communications. Roads (1967) 62,093 km. (184 km. expressways in 1970). Motor vehicles in use (1970): passenger 1,076,900; commercial 247,100. Railways: state (1969) 2,352 km.; private (1968) 846 km.; traffic (1969–70) 3,330,000,000 passenger-km., freight 1,571,000,000 net ton-km. Air traffic (including Danish part of international operations of Scandinavian Airlines System; 1970): 1,696,-000,000 passenger-km.; freight 69,250,000 net ton-km. Shipping (1970): merchant vessels 100 gross tons and over 1,210; gross tonnage 3,314,320; goods loaded 6,774,000 metric tons, unloaded 31,522,000 metric tons. Telephones (including Faeroe Islands and Greenland; Dec. 1969) 1,602,898. Radio licenses (Dec. 1968) 1,566,000. Television licenses (Dec. 1969) 1,228,000.

Agriculture. Production (in 000; metric tons; 1970; 1969 in parentheses): wheat 512 (428); barley 4,813 (5,255); oats 631 (765); rye c. 120 (126); potatoes 1,033 (663); sugar, raw value (1970–71) 291, (1969–70) 304; apples c. 120 (126); butter 131 (144); cheese 110 (109); pork c. 750 (710); beef and veal c. 260 (240); fish catch (1969) 1,275, (1968) 1,467. Livestock (in 000; July 1970): pigs 8,350; cattle 2,835; sheep c. 87; horses c. 40; chickens c. 18,500.

Industry. Production (in 000; metric tons; 1970): pig iron 205; crude steel 473; cement (1969) 2,607; superphosphates (1968) 778; nitrogenous fertilizers (1969–70) 70; manufactured gas (cu.m.) 404,000; electricity (net; excluding most industrial production; kw-hr.) 18,509,000. Merchant vessels launched (100 gross tons and over; 1970) 519,000 gross tons.

decision on the matter. According to the Danish constitution, a decision involving surrender of sovereignty must be supported by a majority of five-sixths of the Folketing. However, it had been agreed that, whether or not such a majority was achieved, the matter would be the subject of a referendum. In order to nullify a positive decision by the Folketing, a majority of at least 30% of the electors would have to vote against the decision. It was expected that the Folketing would vote early in 1972 and the referendum would take place early in the summer.

Debate continued on the subject of economic democracy—the right of workers to a share in profits and in management decisions. There were heated discussions as to how this could be established, whether by law or on a voluntary basis, and there was speculation that it might be introduced as a feature of the guided economy to which the Social Democratic government was committed. (S. Aa.)

Dependent States

The emirate of Bahrain in the Persian Gulf became fully independent on Aug. 15, 1971, following Iran's renunciation of its claim the previous year and the failure of Britain to secure a federation linking Bahrain with Qatar and the seven Trucial States. Qatar, in turn, became independent on September 3. Both states were admitted to the UN and on September 11 became members of the Arab League. Early in December the Trucial States joined together to form the Union of Arab Emirates. The federation was later admitted to the Arab League. The Himalayan kingdom of Bhutan, although still under Indian guidance in foreign affairs, defense, and communications, became a member of the UN in September and exchanged ambassadors with India for the first time, putting its relations with that country on a new basis. (*See* Bahrain; Bhutan; Federation of Arab Emirates; Qatar.)

In January Britain and the U.S. withdrew from the UN Committee of 24 on decolonization following the General Assembly resolutions adopted in 1970, which described any form of colonialism as a "crime" and urged all UN members to work with peoples "struggling for independence" and against the economic and military activities of administering powers. The resolution was rejected by Britain as outside and alien to the UN Charter provisions. It was pointed out that Britain had led the way in granting freedom to its dependent territories and in preparing them for it, contrary to the "irresponsible" demands of committee-sponsored resolutions. The policy of the U.K. was "not to delay independence for those who want it or to impose it on those who do not; the wishes of the people must be the guiding concern"; nor would Britain "reject people who see nothing abhorrent in the continuation of a modern relationship which falls short of total independence."

Britain retained varying measures of responsibility for 16 colonies (excluding Rhodesia); the protectorates of Brunei and the Solomon Islands; three crown dependencies and possessions; the Central and Southern Line Islands dependency; the Anglo-French condominium of New Hebrides; and the six associated states of Antigua, St. Kitts-Nevis-Anguilla (see *Caribbean,* below), Dominica, Grenada, St. Lucia, and St. Vincent, these latter having the right to proceed unilaterally to independence. The territories con-

tained approximately six million people, about four million of them in Hong Kong.

A new department of the British Foreign and Colonial Office was established in 1971 to deal with the problems of the territories. Emphasis was laid on the increasing technical participation of dependencies in inter-Commonwealth conferences; on the value of Part IV of the Treaty of Rome, giving free access to EEC markets and aid; and on the British contribution (£130 million in 1971) to the International Development Association (IDA) and to other multinational channels of assistance contributing to the Second UN Development Decade (1970s). In contrast to the British acceptance of the UN Development Strategy, by which the rich nations would invest 1% of their gross national product (GNP) in the less fortunate, the U.S.S.R. proclaimed that since all the ills of the less developed world were "due to colonialism and capitalism" the socialist countries were under no obligation to contribute 1% of their GNP to assist them.

Talks between Britain and Spain failed to end the Spanish blockade of Gibraltar (ceded to England under the Treaty of Utrecht on July 13, 1713, for use as a fortress). Spain continued to refuse to accept the Gibraltarians' right to settle their own future but was willing to safeguard their rights in all but the question of nominal Spanish sovereignty. The colony's economy continued to weather the closing of its border with Spain by replacing Spanish labour and using British aid for development and defense. The chief minister, Maj. Robert J. Peliza, continued pressure for integration with Britain.

In Buenos Aires on July 1 Argentine and British representatives signed an agreement to reestablish air and sea links between Argentina and the Falkland Islands, broken by the long dispute over their sovereignty. Britain agreed to respect the wishes of the Falklanders and was to finance by loan the building of an airport at Port Stanley. The agreement in no way altered either government's juridical claim.

Africa. *French Africa.* For the French Territory of the Afars and Issas 1971 was a period of political détente, but the continued closure of the Suez Canal caused economic strain. The legislative elections of March resulted in victory for the government party and strengthened the personal position of the prime minister, Ali Aref Bourhan. The French government studied plans for the development of the port and for exploitation of the geothermal resources around Djibouti. Neighbouring Somalia continued to press its claim to the territory.

Pedestrians cross the new Weira Bridge linking Wabag and Wapenamunda in the Western Highlands district of New Guinea.
AUTHENTICATED NEWS INTERNATIONAL

Dentistry:
see Medicine

ARGE guerrillas in Angola attack a Portuguese military convoy in April 1971. The revolutionary group, headed by Holden Roberto, observed its tenth anniversary in 1971.

South Africa. International political pressure on South Africa to terminate its jurisdiction over South West Africa (Namibia) increased following an advisory opinion delivered by the International Court of Justice on June 21 concerning South Africa's continued presence in this territory under a mandate originally granted by the Allies after World War I, and purported to have been revoked by a UN General Assembly resolution in 1966. The court decided (13–2) that in view of the illegality of South Africa's presence it should withdraw immediately. South Africa held that under the UN Charter the General Assembly had no right unilaterally to revoke the mandate or take binding action, but Willem Riphagen, legal adviser to the Dutch Foreign Ministry, argued that the mandate did not give South Africa the right to annex the territory, which still had international status. South Africa countered that to give the assembly virtually unlimited power by implication meant that in future it could bind nonconsenting powers.

Portuguese Africa. On Dec. 14, 1970, the UN General Assembly reaffirmed by 94 votes to 6 the inalienable right of the peoples of Angola, Mozambique, Portuguese Guinea, and the other territories under Portuguese domination to self-determination and independence. The Portuguese government countered in May 1971 by inviting the UN Committee of 24 to see for itself conditions in Angola and Mozambique, offering to conduct members to any part of those territories they might wish to visit. At the same time Portugal refused to continue its participation in the work of UNESCO because of the organization's political involvement in Portuguese affairs as evinced by its demand to send delegates to investigate the educational situation in Portuguese Africa.

Early in the year the Portuguese government displayed some satisfaction with the progress of the campaign against guerrillas in the various African dependencies. In January it was claimed that during 1970 about one-third of the guerrilla forces operating in Portuguese Guinea had been put out of action. This was stated to include at least 895 killed, 740 wounded, and 86 taken prisoner. Portugal continued to maintain about 30,000 troops in Guinea to safeguard its control of the Cape Verde Islands, a key communications centre for Atlantic strategy. Attacks on Portuguese Guinea by the African Party for the Independence of Guinea and Cape Verde (PAIGC), based

in Senegal, and also by the Republic of Guinea, continued. In October PAIGC's leader, Amilcar Cabral, claimed that his forces controlled 75% of Portuguese Guinea. Although the fight for total liberation would continue, the insurgents were willing to negotiate, he said. In Angola a government communiqué in February said that guerrillas were avoiding direct conflict with the Army and concentrating on murder and torture, much of it directed against Africans. In Mozambique, too, it was claimed that during the last six months of 1970, 651 guerrillas had been killed and 1,804 captured. The government also announced the surrender of two guerrilla leaders, Manuel Katur and Miguel Artur Murupa. In April and May, however, a number of European organizations, including the Joseph Rowntree Social Service Trust, the Lutheran World Federation, and the East German Afro-Asian Solidarity Committee, announced substantial recent or forthcoming gifts to the Mozambique liberation movement, FRELIMO, for the purchase of medical supplies, tents, and blankets, and for other welfare and educational purposes.

In Mozambique in January floods devastated huge areas in the wake of Cyclone Felicity. Rice, sugar, and tea crops were destroyed or seriously damaged, communications were cut, and tens of thousands of people rendered homeless when the Lualua River burst its banks. In Angola, too, flooding on a smaller scale occurred in March in Lobito, while in the same month stringent precautions became necessary to control an outbreak of yellow fever.

The Cabora Bassa Dam in Mozambique remained a subject of controversy. In spite of opposition from the Organization of African Unity and the condemnation of the scheme by the UN General Assembly on Dec. 14, 1970, the governments of France and West Germany continued to support companies taking part in the construction of the dam. Though indisputably of great economic value to Africa, the dam was seen by left-wing world opinion as a symbol of white supremacy. The ZAMCO consortium estimated that building would be completed by 1973, with the aid of heavy vehicles supplied by Eastern bloc countries; while the August visit of Malawi's president, H. Kamuzu Banda, and statements by ex-FRELIMO leader Miguel Murupa indicated support by African moderates.

In Angola an economic boom, stimulated by the $960 million second development plan, brought benefits to the 90% agricultural population, with a GNP increase of 9% and industrial expansion of more than 15% in 1970. Though coffee remained Angola's chief export in 1970 at $136,800,000, oil and iron ore exports increased by 50%, and diamond exports doubled to $84 million.

Members of the church also came into conflict with the Portuguese authorities. An Angolan priest, Father Joaquim Pinto de Andrade, was sentenced in Lisbon in March to three years' imprisonment and 15 years' loss of political rights on charges of helping the Angolan liberation movement. This was followed in May by an announcement from leaders of the White Fathers Mission in Mozambique that the society would withdraw from the country by July 1 in protest against the restrictions imposed on its work by the Portuguese authorities. A week later, on May 25, the government issued an order expelling the mission.

Caribbean. The Commonwealth Caribbean countries, still heavily dependent on agriculture for economic survival, were understandably concerned about

Britain's proposed entry into the European Economic Community (EEC). In the dependent territories, sugar remained the largest single employer of labour in Antigua, St. Kitts, and British Honduras, while bananas dominated the economies of the Windward Islands.

Caribbean interests maintained a strong lobby in Britain, pressing Geoffrey Rippon, Britain's negotiator in Brussels, for "bankable assurances" over the future of sugar, particularly after the expiration of the Commonwealth Sugar Agreement in 1974. The new formula took the form of a less concrete assurance that EEC members would "take to heart the interests of all the countries whose primary exports depend on the United Kingdom market." The British government's White Paper, *The United Kingdom and the European Communities,* noted an offer of association under Part IV of the Treaty of Rome for the dependent territories (Bahamas, Bermuda, Belize [British Honduras], British Virgin Islands, Montserrat, Turks and Caicos, and the West Indian Associated States). The secretary-general of the Commonwealth Caribbean Secretariat, William Demas, advised all members of the Caribbean Free Trade Area (CARIFTA) to seek a common link with the EEC in order not to weaken the regional integration movement.

General elections were held in late 1970 and 1971 in several territories: in Dominica, where the outgoing premier, Edward LeBlanc, was returned to power with 8 seats out of 11 for his new LeBlanc Labour Party; Montserrat, where the 18-month-old Progressive Democratic Party under Austin Bramble won all seven elected seats in the Legislative Council from his father's party, the Montserrat Labour Party, which had been in power for 18 years; Antigua, where Vere Bird and his Antigua Labour Party, in power since 1946, were defeated by the Progressive Labour Movement, which won 13 out of 17 seats. This ousting of the old-guard political leaders did not, however, extend to St. Kitts-Nevis, where Robert Bradshaw's Labour Party was returned overwhelmingly in May.

Anguilla refused to participate in the St. Kitts-Nevis elections, and in June accepted new British proposals under which it would be retained as a British colony. As the Anguilla Act went through the British Parliament in July, the minister of state, Joseph Godber, said that the Caribbean governments had been informed that the British government would not be prepared to intervene in this way in the future. Nonetheless, the Anguilla Act was rejected by Bradshaw, while some East Caribbean governments, notably that of Guyana, expressed concern over the "continuing metropolitan presence" permitted by associated status and the legalization of secession from existing regional groupings.

Following developments over Anguilla, a special meeting of Commonwealth Caribbean heads of government met in late July in Grenada, attended by Guyana, Trinidad and Tobago, and the six associated states, but not by Jamaica and Barbados. The conference issued a communiqué stressing the desirability of political unity among the Commonwealth Caribbean nations.

Compared with 1970, there was less overt left-wing and Black Power activity in the Commonwealth Caribbean. In the French overseas *départements* of Martinique and Guadeloupe, however, active agitation for autonomy or independence continued among leftists and militant youth, influenced by black politics in

the U.S. and the student riots and workers' revolts of May 1968 in Paris. An increasing number of natives of Martinique (pop. 339,900) and Guadeloupe (pop. 327,000), estimated variously at between 50,000 and 200,000, were resident in France.

In 1970 Surinam and the Netherlands Antilles moved further toward constitutional independence. Surinam also signed an important agreement with the Reynolds Metals Co. of the U.S. to develop an aluminum complex in West Surinam (Surinam was the world's second leading bauxite producer).

Persian Gulf. Soviet preparations to replace British influence in the Gulf were watched by a wary Iran, which itself made a show of both military strength and historic splendour with the 2,500th anniversary celebration in October. Iran made it clear that it would occupy the two Tumb islands and Abu Musa at the mouth of the Gulf whether or not agreement was reached with the other claimants, the Gulf states of Ras al Khaimah and Sharjah, and would use force if necessary. On November 30 Iranian troops occupied the three islands. Sharjah welcomed them onto Abu Musa, but three soldiers were killed during the landings on the Tumbs, claimed by Ras al Khaimah. Iran agreed to occupy only a designated area on Abu Musa. In July six of the seven Trucial States (with the exception of Ras al Khaimah) agreed to federate. In the new Arab federation the British-officered Trucial Oman Scouts would continue an unofficial presence and would form the nucleus of a federal army. The federation was formally instituted as the Union of Arab Emirates on December 2. Ras al Khaimah joined several days later.

Indian Ocean. *French Dependencies.* In the Comoro Islands the president of the governing council, Prince Said Ibrahim, continued his efforts to reconcile varying political opinions and increase economic development in order to neutralize the influence of the national liberation movement, MOLINACO, based in Tanzania. In January a new government was formed that included two ministers formerly in the opposition Rassemblement Démocratique du Peuple Comorien (RDPC). The Chamber of Deputies was dissolved in March, and the June elections resulted in the RDPC gaining 17 out of 31 seats in the new assembly. The French minister for overseas *départements* and territories, Pierre Messmer, visited Réunion in September.

British Dependencies. The Seychelles received their first investment from the Commonwealth Development Corporation (CDC) in 1971. The CDC was to provide half the financing for a new hotel and for work on Mahé airport. The Aldabra atoll in the Seychelles was leased to the Royal Society until 1985 with an option for an additional 20 years. The islands are the home of the giant tortoise, one of the few breeding grounds of the green turtle, and one of the largest breeding grounds of the frigate bird. The Royal Society planned a research station on the atoll for a small permanent staff and visiting expeditions.

Pacific. *British Pacific Territories.* The demand for secession continued among minority groups of the British Pacific, where, following the independence of Fiji and Tonga, the Solomon and Gilbert Islands achieved elected majorities in their legislative councils and increased internal self-government.

French Pacific Territories. Polynesian nationalists gained important victories in the municipal elections in May and the French senatorial elections in September, and intensified their campaign against continuing

French nuclear tests in the Pacific. New Caledonia, with the world's richest and largest nickel deposits, had a majority of autonomists in its Territorial Assembly—those who demanded greater local control over and expansion of the nickel industry.

Australian External Territories. The UN Visiting Mission to Papua New Guinea, consisting of the U.K., France, Iraq, and Sierra Leone, demanded independence before 1980 by increased localization and the creation of "national feeling and parties." The Australian government, mindful of its 60% contribution to a record 1971 budget of A$242 million, agreed that self-government for the two million inhabitants was within the compass of the territory's House of Assembly, to be elected in 1972.

U.S. Territories. The U.S. Special Trust Territory took a further step toward choosing its future following its Political Status Report. Although the Mariana Islands wanted secession from the Territory and U.S. commonwealth status, the Congress of Micronesia opted for free association on the British model with the right of secession but with economic aid.

Indian-Protected States. India's relations with Bhutan entered a new phase in 1971, when the two countries exchanged ambassadors for the first time. Bhutan's admission to the UN later in the year implied that it now had the standing of a fully independent state. (*See* BHUTAN.)

Sikkim's fourth five-year plan was worked out in detail during a visit to New Delhi by the chogyal (king) in April. It provided for a total expenditure of Rs. 200 million, entirely financed by India, for the development of communications and minor industries.

The Sikkim State Congress, third largest faction in the State Council, held its annual session in January attended by nearly 1,000 delegates from various parts of the state. The session unanimously approved a resolution upholding current treaty relations with India. Other resolutions passed called for the formation of a responsible government in Sikkim with the chogyal as constitutional head and replacement of the existing state and executive councils by a full-fledged ministry.

Economic Aid. Alarmed by the deteriorating economic position of St. Kitts-Nevis, Britain prepared to offer an interest-free loan of £800,000 for airport work at Golden Rock and for tourist facilities. Elsewhere in the Caribbean, British aid varied from a tourist survey in St. Vincent to the payment of £2.5 million to buy out leasehold development in the Virgin Islands. Total British development aid to the Caribbean associated states and dependencies had tripled since 1966. In 1970–71 it rose by £2 million from the previous year to more than £10 million, or £16 per head in a total population of 630,000 (1970 census).

The Commonwealth Development Corporation devoted a majority of its new projects in dependent territories in the Pacific and Caribbean; private investment was aiding the Solomon Islands, especially in timber, mining, and the oil palm industry; while British aid in developing the international airport at Mahé, together with increasing tourism, was revolutionizing the Seychelles economy.

(PH. D.; K. I.; M. MR.; SH. P.; G. U.; X.)

See also Africa; Portugal; South Africa; United Nations.

ANTARCTIC, THE

Claims on the continent of Antarctica and all islands south of 60° S remain in status quo according to the Antarctic Treaty, to which 16 nations are signatory. Formal claims within the treaty area include the following: Australian Antarctic Territory, the mainland portion of French Southern and Antarctic Lands (Terre Adélie), Ross Dependency claimed by New Zealand, Queen Maud Land and Peter I Island claimed by Norway, and British Antarctic Territory, of which some parts are claimed by Argentina and Chile. No claims have been recognized as final under international law.

AUSTRALIA

CHRISTMAS ISLAND

Christmas Island, an external territory, is situated in the Indian Ocean 875 mi. NW of Australia. Area: 52 sq.mi. (135 sq.km.). Pop. (1970 est.): 3,361. Cap.: The Settlement (pop., 1968 est., 1,500).

COCOS (KEELING) ISLANDS

Cocos (Keeling) Islands is an external territory located in the Indian Ocean 2,290 mi. W of Darwin, Austr. Area: 5.5 sq.mi. (14 sq.km.). Pop. (1970 est.): 611.

NEW GUINEA

New Guinea, a trust territory administered with the Territory of Papua, consists of the northeastern part of the island of New Guinea, the Bismarck Archipelago, and several other nearby islands. Area: 92,160 sq.mi. (238,693 sq.km.). Pop. (1970 est.): 1,772,744. Cap.: Port Moresby, Papua (pop., 1970 est., 56,206).

Education. (1968) Primary, pupils 144,572, teachers 4,009; secondary, pupils 9,181, teachers 408; vocational, pupils 2,165, teachers 131; teacher training, students 959, teachers 107.

Finance and Trade. Monetary unit: Australian dollar, with a par value of A$0.89 to U.S. $1 (A$2.14 = £1 sterling) and a free rate (Sept. 27, 1971) of A$0.87 to U.S. $1. Budget (1969–70) balanced at A$135,891,000 (including A$71,-420,000 grant by Australian government). Foreign trade (1968–69): imports A$93,921,000; exports A$64,296,000. Import sources: Australia

53%; Japan 13%; U.S. 6%; U.K. 6%. Export destinations: Australia 33%; U.K. 28%; West Germany 13%; U.S. 8%; Netherlands 6%. Main exports: cocoa 25%; coffee beans 24%; copra 19%; coconut oil 9%.

Transport. Shipping (1970): merchant vessels 100 gross tons and over 47; gross tonnage 24,295.

Agriculture. Production (in 000; metric tons; 1969; 1968 in parentheses): copra 120 (119); cocoa (1969–70) 25, (1968–69) 26; coffee 25 (21); timber (including Papua; cu.m.) 4,100 (4,000). Livestock (in 000; March 1970): cattle *c.* 36; pigs *c.* 5; horses *c.* 1.

Industry. Production (in 000; troy oz.; 1969): gold 26; silver 17.

NORFOLK ISLAND

Norfolk Island, an external territory, is located in the Pacific Ocean 1,035 mi. NE of Sydney, Austr. Area: 14 sq.mi. (36 sq.km.). Pop. (1970 est.): 1,380. Cap. (de facto): Kingston.

PAPUA

Consisting of the southeastern part of the island of New Guinea and several offshore island groups, Papua, an external territory, is governed in an administrative union with the Trust Territory of New Guinea. Area: 86,103 sq.mi. (223,006 sq. km.). Pop. (1970 est.): 668,964. Cap.: Port Moresby (pop., 1970 est., 56,206).

Education. (1968) Primary, pupils 65,035, teachers 1,733; secondary, pupils 5,140, teachers 213; vocational, pupils 1,160, teachers 88; teacher training, students 533, teachers 48; higher (University of Papua and New Guinea), students 595, teaching staff 92.

Finance and Trade. Monetary unit: Australian dollar. Budget (1968–69): revenue A$51,-627,000 (including A$23,001,787 grant by Australian government); expenditure A$51,470,000. Foreign trade (1968–69): imports A$56,534,000; exports A$10,949,000. Import sources: Australia 58%; U.S. 10%; Japan 9%; U.K. 6%. Export destinations: Australia 79%; U.K. 5%. Main exports: copra 24%; rubber 21%.

Agriculture. Production (in 000; metric tons): copra (1969) *c.* 18, (1968) 18; rubber (exports; 1970) *c.* 6.3, (1969) 6.

DENMARK

FAEROE ISLANDS

The Faeroes, an integral part of the Danish realm, are a self-governing group of islands in the North Atlantic about 360 mi. W of Norway. Area: 540 sq.mi. (1,399 sq.km.). Pop. (1970 est.): 38,681. Cap.: Thorshavn (pop., 1969 est., 10,188).

Education. (1968–69) Primary, pupils 5,377; secondary, pupils 1,279; primary and secondary, teachers (1966–67) 299; vocational, pupils 1,162, teachers (1966–67) 88; teacher training, students 77, teachers (1966–67) 12; higher, students 5.

Finance and Trade. Monetary unit: Danish krone, with a par value of 7.50 kroner to U.S. $1 (18 kroner = £1 sterling) and a free rate (Sept. 27, 1971) of 7.30 kroner to U.S. $1. Foreign trade (1969): imports 243,791,000 kroner; exports 182,153,000 kroner. Import sources: Denmark 61%; Norway 21%; U.K. 6%. Export destinations: U.S. 19%; Italy 16%; Denmark 16%; Portugal 14%; U.K. 10%; Spain 6%; Greece 5%. Main exports fish and products 95% (including fish meal 9%).

Transport. Shipping (1970): merchant vessels 100 gross tons and over 120; gross tonnage 38,-990.

Agriculture and Industry. Fish catch (metric tons: 1969) 176,000, (1968) 166,000. Livestock (in 000; Dec. 1969): sheep 69; cattle 3. Electricity production (1969–70): 67 million kw-hr. (84% hydroelectric).

GREENLAND

An integral part of the Danish realm, Greenland, the largest island in the world, lies mostly within the Arctic Circle. Area: 840,000 sq.mi. (2,175,600 sq.km.), 84% of which is covered by icecap. Pop. (1970 est.): 46,331. Cap.: Godthaab (pop., 1968 est., 6,104).

Education. (1967–68) Primary and secondary, pupils 8,618, teachers 501; vocational, pupils 152, teachers 16; teacher training, students 30, teachers 3.

Finance and Trade. Monetary unit: Danish krone. Foreign trade (1969): imports 376,923,-000 kroner (91% from Denmark, 6% from

U.K.); exports 87,774,000 kroner (73% to Denmark, 21% to U.S.). Main exports: fish and products 73%; fur skins 6%; cryolite 5%.

Agriculture. Fish catch (metric tons; 1969) 39,000, (1968) 34,000. Livestock (in 000; Nov. 1969): sheep 32; reindeer 4.

Industry. Production (in 000; metric tons; 1969): coal 21; cryolite (1968) 67; electricity (kw–hr.) 69,200.

FRANCE

AFARS AND ISSAS
The self-governing overseas territory of Afars and Issas is located on the Gulf of Aden between Ethiopia and Somalia. Area: 8,900 sq.mi. (23,000 sq.km.). Pop. (1970 est.): 95,000. Cap. Djibouti.

Education. (1968–69) Primary, pupils 6,932, teachers 224; secondary, pupils 611, teachers 30; vocational, pupils 315, teachers 23; teacher training, students 7, teachers 1.

Finance. Monetary unit: Djibouti franc, with a par value of DjFr. 214.39 to U.S. $1 (DjFr. 38.60 = 1 French franc; DjFr. 514 = £1 sterling) and a free rate (Sept. 27, 1971) of DjFr. 211 to U.S. $1 (DjFr. 523 = £1 sterling). Budget (1970 est.) balanced at DjFr. 2,414,000,000.

Foreign Trade. (1968) Imports DjFr. 8,195,-000,000; exports DjFr. 817 million. Import sources (1967): Iran 24%; France 18%; U.K. 12%; Ethiopia 7%. Export destinations (1966): France 66%; Yemen (Aden) 5%. There is a transit trade through Djibouti for Ethiopia, which fell following the closure of the Suez Canal. Main exports: hides, cattle, coffee.

Transport. Ships entered (1969) vessels totaling 5,142,000 net registered tons; goods loaded (1969) 113,000 metric tons, unloaded (1968) 722,000 metric tons.

COMORO ISLANDS
The self-governing overseas territory of the Comoro Islands is in the Indian Ocean approximately midway between the northern tip of Madagascar and the mainland of Africa. Area: 863 sq.mi. (2,235 sq.km.). Pop. (1970 est.): 267,-000. Cap.: Moroni, Grande Comore (pop., 1970 est., 14,000).

Education. (1968–69) Primary, pupils 13,046, teachers 298; secondary, pupils 1,007, teachers 52.

Finance and Trade. Monetary unit: CFA franc, with a parity of CFA Fr. 50 to the French franc (CFA Fr. 277.71 = U.S. $1; CFA Fr. 666.50 = £1 sterling) and a free rate (Sept. 27, 1971) of CFA Fr. 276.50 to U.S. $1 (CFA Fr. 685.75 = £1 sterling). Budget (1970 est.) balanced at CFA Fr. 1,349,000,000. Foreign trade (1968): imports CFA Fr. 1,763,000,000; exports CFA Fr. 1,008,200,000. Import sources (1965): France 47%; Malagasy Republic 17%; Cambodia 10%; Thailand 7%; Argentina 6%. Export destinations (1965): France 47%; U.S. 26%; Malagasy Republic 6%. Main exports: essential oils 42%; vanilla 35%; copra 17%.

FRENCH GUIANA
French Guiana is an overseas *département* situated between Brazil and Surinam on the northeast coast of South America. Area: 34,750 sq.mi. (90,-000 sq.km.). Pop. (1970 est.): 51,000. Cap.: Cayenne (pop., 1967, 19,668).

Education. (1968–69) Primary, pupils 7,718, teachers (including preprimary) 286; secondary, pupils 1,677; vocational, pupils 886; secondary and vocational, teachers 151.

Finance and Trade. Monetary unit: local franc, at par with the French (metropolitan) franc (Fr. 5.55 = U.S. $1; Fr. 13.33 = £1 sterling). (*See* FRANCE.) Budget (1970 est.) balanced at Fr. 118,580,000. Foreign trade (1969): imports Fr. 259 million (74% from France, 10% from U.S.); exports Fr. 28 million (74% to U.S., 15% to France, 6% to Martinique). Main exports: shrimps 68%; timber 12%.

FRENCH POLYNESIA
An overseas territory, the islands of French Polynesia are scattered over a large area of the south central Pacific Ocean. Area: 1,261 sq.mi. (3,265 sq.km.). Pop. (1971 est.): 114,000. Cap.: Papeete, Tahiti (pop., 1971 est., 24,000).

Education. (1968–69) Primary, pupils 27,-957, teachers 1,010; secondary, pupils 4,266, teachers 219; vocational, pupils 880, teachers 58; teacher training, students 44, teachers 4.

Finance. Monetary unit: CFP franc, with a parity of CFP Fr. 18.18 to the French franc

(CFP Fr. 100.99 = U.S. $1; CFP Fr. 242.36 = £1 sterling) and a free rate (Sept. 27, 1971) of CFP Fr. 100.55 to U.S. $1 (CFP Fr. 249.36 = £1 sterling). Budget (1968) balanced at CFP Fr. 3,072,000,000.

Foreign Trade. (1969) Imports CFP Fr 10,-368,000,000 (56% from France, 18% from U.S.); exports CFP Fr. 1,303,000,000 (81% to France, 7% to Italy). Main exports: coconut oil 19%; vanilla 5%. Tourism (1969): visitors 37,-600; gross receipts (1967) U.S. $4.7 million.

GUADELOUPE
The overseas *département* of Guadeloupe, together with its dependencies, is in the eastern Caribbean between Antigua to the north and Dominica to the south. Area: 683 sq.mi. (1,769 sq.km.). Pop. (1970 est.): 327,000. Cap.: Basse-Terre (pop., 1967, 15,458).

Education. (1968–69) Primary, pupils 69,-762, teachers (including preprimary) 2,026; secondary, pupils 16,583; vocational, pupils 4,129; secondary and vocational, teachers 944; teacher training, students 176, teachers 11; higher (1966–67), students 174, teaching staff 8.

Finance and Trade. Monetary unit: local franc, at par with the French (metropolitan) franc. Budget (1969 est.) balanced at Fr. 362,-849,695. Foreign trade (1969): imports Fr. 523 million (70% from France, 6% from U.S.); exports Fr. 172 million (71% to France, 26% to U.S.). Main exports: sugar 55%; bananas 33%; rum 8%.

MARTINIQUE
The Caribbean island of Martinique, an overseas *département*, lies 24 mi. N of St. Lucia and about 30 mi. SE of Dominica. Area: 431 sq.mi. (1,116 sq.km.). Pop. (1971 est.): 339,900. Cap.: Fort-de-France (pop., 1967, 99,051).

Education. (1968–69) Primary, pupils 70,-170, teachers (including preprimary) 2,704; secondary, pupils 25,483; vocational, pupils 1,994; secondary and vocational, teachers 1,395; teacher training, students 265, teaching staff 11; higher (1966–67), students 1,325, teaching staff 21.

Finance and Trade. Monetary unit: local franc, at par with the French (metropolitan) franc. Budget (1970 est.) balanced at Fr. 328 million. Foreign trade (1969): imports Fr. 538,-169,000 (71% from France, 6% from U.S.); exports Fr. 196,949,000 (89% to France, 5% to Italy). Main exports: bananas 54%; rum 14%; canned fruit 13%; sugar 11%.

NEW CALEDONIA
The overseas territory of New Caledonia, together with its dependencies, is in the South Pacific 750 mi. E of Australia. Area: 7,358 sq.mi. (19,058 sq.km.). Pop. (1971 est.): 113,680. Cap.: Nouméa (pop., 1971 est., 49,315).

Education. (1969) Primary, pupils 23,458, teachers 962; secondary, pupils 3,448, teachers 223; vocational, pupils 1,136, teachers 116; teacher training, students 44, teachers 26; higher (1968), students 63, teaching staff 10.

Finance. Monetary unit: CFP franc. Budget (1970 est.) balanced at CFP Fr. 4,750,000,000.

Foreign Trade. (1969) Imports CFP Fr. 12,-098,000,000; exports CFP Fr. 12,733,000,000. Import sources (1968): France 45%; Australia 17%; West Germany 5%. Export destinations (1968): Japan 44%; France 32%; West Germany 6%. Main exports: nickel castings 41%; nickel 36%; nickel matte 22%.

Industry. Production (in 000; metric tons; 1968): iron ore (metal content) 103; nickel ore (metal content; 1969) 117; electricity (kw–hr.) 663,000.

RÉUNION
The overseas *département* of Réunion is located in the Indian Ocean about 450 mi. E of Madagascar and 110 mi. SW of Mauritius. Area: 970 sq.mi. (2,512 sq.km.). Pop. (1971 est.): 455,-200. Cap.: Saint-Denis (pop., 1971 est., 85,444).

Education. (1968–69) Primary, pupils 92,-919, teachers (including preprimary) 3,114; secondary, pupils 24,262; vocational, pupils 1,956; secondary and vocational, teachers 1,086; teacher training, students 282, teachers 18; higher (1966–67), students 365, teaching staff 26.

Finance and Trade. Monetary unit: CFA franc. Budget (1970) balanced at CFA Fr. 11,-448,000,000 (including French aid of CFA Fr. 1,889,000,000). Foreign trade (1969): imports CFA Fr. 38 billion (65% from France, 10% from Malagasy Republic); exports CFA Fr. 11.8 bil-

lion (74% to France). Main exports: sugar 83%; essential oils 10%.

SAINT PIERRE AND MIQUELON
The self-governing overseas territory of Saint Pierre and Miquelon is located about 15 mi. off the south coast of Newfoundland. Area: 93 sq.mi. (242 sq.km.). Pop. (1971 est.): 5,600. Cap.: Saint Pierre, Saint Pierre (pop, 1967, about 4,000).

Education. (1968–69) Primary, pupils 880, teachers 41; secondary, pupils 264, teachers 25; vocational, pupils 69, teachers 10.

Finance. Monetary unit: CFA franc. Budget (1969 rev. est.) balanced at CFA Fr. 659 million.

Foreign Trade. (1970) Imports CFA Fr. 3,-258,000,000; exports CFA Fr. 1,541,000,000 (including ship's stores CFA Fr. 791 million). Import sources: Canada 50%; France 42%. Export destinations: Canada 62%; U.S. 30%. Main export (excluding ship's stores) fresh fish 29%.

WALLIS AND FUTUNA
Wallis and Futuna, an overseas territory, lies in the South Pacific west of Western Samoa. Area: 98 sq.mi. (255 sq.km.). Pop. (1969): 8,546. Cap.: Matautu, Uvea (pop., 1969, 566).

INDIA

SIKKIM
This protected kingdom is bordered by China, Bhutan, India, and Nepal. Area: 2,744 sq.mi. (7,107 sq.km.). Pop. (1971 est.): 196,852. Cap.: Gangtok (pop., 1968 est., 9,000).

Education. (1963) Primary and secondary, pupils 11,620.

Finance and Trade. Monetary unit: Indian rupee, with a par value of Rs. 7.50 to U.S. $1 (Rs. 18 = £1 sterling) and a free rate (Sept. 27, 1971) of Rs. 7.43 to U.S. $1 (Rs. 18.42 = £1 sterling). Budget (1970 est.) revenue c. Rs. 20 million. Third five-year development plan (1967–72) Rs. 90 million, all financed by India; development aid from India (including aid to Bhutan; 1968–69) Rs. 50 million. Foreign trade mainly with India. Main exports (1960): cardamom, oranges, potatoes, apples.

NETHERLANDS

NETHERLANDS ANTILLES
The Netherlands Antilles, a self-governing integral part of the Netherlands realm, consists of an island group near the Venezuelan coast and another group to the north near St. Kitts-Nevis-Anguilla. Area: 385 sq.mi. (996 sq.km.). Pop. (1970 est.): 223,819. Cap.: Willemstad, Curaçao (pop., 1960, 43,547).

Education. (1967–68) Primary, pupils 44,238, teachers 1,270; secondary, pupils 10,294, teachers 412; vocational, pupils 2,810, teachers 153; teacher training (1966–67), students 311.

Finance. Monetary unit: Netherlands Antilles guilder or florin, with a parity of 0.52 Netherlands Antilles guilder to the Netherlands guilder and a free rate (Sept. 27, 1971) of 1.85 Netherlands Antilles guilders to U.S. $1 (4.60 Netherlands Antilles guilders = £1 sterling). Budget (central; 1968 est.): revenue 69,252,294 Netherlands Antilles guilders; expenditure 69,206,226 Netherlands Antilles guilders. Cost of living (Curaçao; 1963 = 100): (Jan. 1971) 113; (Jan. 1970) 109.

Foreign Trade. (1969) Imports 1,302,773,000 Netherlands Antilles guilders; exports 1,177,-811,000 Netherlands Antilles guilders. Import sources: Venezuela 60%; U.S. 10%; Guadeloupe 7%. Export destinations: U.S. 55%; Canada 7%. Main exports: petroleum products 93% (from crude oil imports, accounting for 70% of imports).

Transport and Communications. Roads (1968) 1,183 km. (Curaçao 541 km.; Aruba 380 km.; Bonaire 209 km.; St. Maarten 53 km.). Motor vehicles in use: passenger (1969) 33,400; commercial (1968) 3,800. Shipping traffic (1969) goods loaded c. 38,450,000 metric tons, unloaded c. 44,930,000 metric tons. Telephones (Dec. 1969) 26,000. Radio receivers (Dec. 1969) 112,-000. Television receivers (Dec. 1969) 30,000.

Dependent States

Industry. Production (in 000; metric tons; 1969): petroleum products 38,170; phosphate rock (exports; 1968) 93; electricity (kw-hr.) 1,256,000.

SURINAM

A self-governing integral part of the Netherlands realm, Surinam is on the northern coast of South America bounded by French Guiana, Brazil, and Guyana. Area: 70,060 sq.mi. (181,455 sq.km.). Pop. (1970 est.): 393,000. Cap.: Paramaribo (pop., 1964, 110,867).

Education. (1964–65) Primary, pupils 71,-397, teachers 2,052; secondary, pupils 10,252, teachers 463; vocational, pupils 1,430, teachers 78; teacher training, students 1,583, teachers 150; higher, students 667, teaching staff 74.

Finance. Monetary unit: Surinam guilder or florin, with a parity of 0.52 Surinam guilder to the Netherlands guilder and a free rate (Sept. 27, 1971) of 1.85 Surinam guilders to U.S. $1 (4.60 Surinam guilders = £1 sterling). Budget (1969 est.): revenue 164.2 million Surinam guilders; expenditure 167.2 million Surinam guilders.

Foreign Trade. (1968) Imports 188.9 million Surinam guilders; exports 218.5 million Surinam guilders. Import sources: U.S. 36%; Netherlands 16%; U.K. 7%; West Germany 6%; Japan 6%. Export destinations: U.S. 50%; Netherlands 10%; West Germany 9%; Norway 8%; Canada 5%. Main exports: bauxite and alumina 70%; aluminum 16%; rice 5%.

Transport and Communications. Roads (1970) c. 1,560 km. Motor vehicles in use: passenger (1969) 11,000; commercial (1968) 3,000. Railways (1970) 86 km. Shipping traffic (1968) goods loaded c. 4.6 million metric tons, unloaded c. 800,000 metric tons. Telephones (Dec. 1969) 9,900. Radio receivers (Dec. 1969) 90,000. Television receivers (Dec. 1969) c. 25,000.

Agriculture. Production (in 000; metric tons; 1969; 1968 in parentheses): rice c. 120 (120); oranges 12 (11); grapefruit c. 6 (6); sugar, raw value (1968–69) c. 15, (1967–68) 17; coffee c. 0.4 (c. 0.4); bananas c. 25 (c. 25). Livestock (in 000; January 1969): cattle c. 49; goats c. 7; sheep c. 5; pigs c. 13.

Industry. Production (in 000; metric tons; 1969): bauxite 6,236; aluminum 53; gold (troy oz.) 2.4; electricity (kw-hr.; 1968) 1,076,000 (72% hydroelectric).

NEW ZEALAND

COOK ISLANDS

The self-governing territory of the Cook Islands consists of several islands in the southern Pacific Ocean scattered over an area of about 850,000 sq.mi. Area: 93 sq.mi. (241 sq.km.). Pop. (1970 est.): 22,000. Seat of government: Rarotonga Island (pop., 1968 est., 10,853).

Education. (1968) Primary, pupils 5,653, teachers 303; secondary, pupils 825, teachers 50; teacher training, students 20, teachers 6.

Finance and Trade. Monetary unit: New Zealand dollar, with a par value of NZ$0.89 to U.S. $1 (NZ$2.14 = £1 sterling) and a free rate (Sept. 27, 1971) of NZ$0.86 to U.S. $1. Budget (1968–69 actual): revenue NZ$559,000 (excluding grant-in-aid NZ$2,062,000); expenditure NZ$619,000. Foreign trade (1967): imports NZ$2,991,307; exports NZ$1,777,369. Main exports: fruit juice 51%; clothing 22%; citrus fruit 9%; copra 6%.

NIUE ISLAND

The territory of Niue Island is situated in the Pacific Ocean about 1,500 mi. NE of New Zealand. Area: 100 sq.mi. (259 sq.km.). Pop. (1970 est.): 5,184.

Education. (1969) Primary, pupils 1,308, teachers 69; secondary, pupils 525, teachers 29; vocational, pupils 19, teachers 5; teacher training, students 5.

Finance and Trade. Monetary unit: New Zealand dollar. Budget (1969–70): revenue NZ$835,000 (excluding grant-in-aid NZ$941,-000); expenditure NZ$1,870,000. Foreign trade (1969): imports NZ$771,044; exports NZ$69,-988. Main exports: copra, bananas, sweet potatoes.

TOKELAU ISLANDS

The territory of Tokelau Islands lies in the South Pacific about 700 mi. N of Niue Island and 2,100 mi. NE of New Zealand. Area: 4 sq.mi. (10 sq. km.). Pop. (1970 est.): 1,687.

NORWAY

JAN MAYEN

The island of Jan Mayen, a Norwegian dependency, lies within the Arctic Circle between Greenland and northern Norway. Area: 144 sq.mi. (373 sq.km.). Pop. (1970 est.): 36.

SVALBARD

A group of islands and a Norwegian dependency, Svalbard is located within the Arctic Circle to the north of Norway. Area: 23,957 sq.mi. (62,050 sq.km.). Pop. (1970 est.): 2,900.

PORTUGAL

ANGOLA

The overseas province of Angola is located on the southwestern coast of Africa, bordered by the Congo (Kinshasa), Zambia, and South West Africa. Area: 481,350 sq.mi. (1,246,700 sq.km.). Pop. (1970 est.): 5,466,600. Cap.: Luanda (pop., 1969 est., 339,938).

Education. (1967) Primary, pupils 296,269, teachers 6,587; secondary, pupils 21,412, teachers 920; vocational, pupils 18,797, teachers 1,063; teacher training, students 1,083, teachers 100; higher, students 989, teaching staff 129.

Finance and Trade. Monetary unit: Angola escudo, at par with the Portuguese escudo (28.75 escudos = U.S. $1; 69 escudos = £1 sterling) and with a free rate (Sept. 27, 1971) of 27.42 escudos to U.S. $1 (68 escudos = £1 sterling). Budget (1970 est.) balanced at 6,836,000,000 escudos. Foreign trade (1970): imports 10,595,-000,000 escudos; exports 12,158,000,000 escudos. Import sources: Portugal 35%; West Germany 11%; U.S. 11%; U.K. 9%; France 5%. Export destinations: Portugal 34%; U.S. 16%; Netherlands 11%; Japan 7%; West Germany 6%. Main exports: coffee 32%; diamonds 19%; iron ore 12%; crude oil 11%.

Transport and Communications. Roads (1969) 72,291 km. Motor vehicles in use (1969): passenger 74,500; commercial (including buses) 26,800. Railways: (1969) 3,159 km.; traffic (1970) 203.6 million passenger-km., freight 5,-189,000,000 net ton-km. Ships entered (1969) vessels totaling 7,105,000 net registered tons; goods loaded (1970) 12,192,000 metric tons, unloaded 1,483,000 metric tons. Telephones (Dec. 1969) 25,315. Radio receivers (Dec. 1968) 90,-000.

Agriculture. Production (in 000; metric tons; 1969; 1968 in parentheses): dry beans c. 64 (c. 64); sugar, raw value (1970–71) c. 70, (1969–70) 63; coffee (1970) c. 215, (1969) 215; cotton, lint 20 (14); sisal c. 67 (66); palm oil c. 31 (c. 32); palm kernels (exports) 12 (12); fish catch 417 (293). Livestock (in 000; Dec. 1969): sheep 191; goats 769; cattle 2,171; pigs 319.

Industry. Production (in 000; metric tons; 1970): crude oil 5,056; cement (1969) 383; iron ore (60–65% metal content) 6,192; diamonds (metric carats; 1969) 2,022; salt (1969) 80; fish meal (1969) 99; electricity (kw-hr.) 542,-000.

CAPE VERDE ISLANDS

The Cape Verde Islands, an overseas province, form an archipelago in the eastern Atlantic Ocean about 380 mi. off the coast of Senegal. Area: 1,557 sq.mi. (4,033 sq.km.). Pop. (1970 est.): 246,000. Cap.: Praia, São Tigao (pop., 1960, 13,142).

Education. (1967–68) Primary, pupils 19,680, teachers 381; secondary, pupils 2,134, teachers 91; vocational, pupils 564, teachers 34.

Finance and Trade. Monetary unit: Cape Verde escudo, at par with the Portuguese escudo. Budget (1968 est.) balanced at 118,952,000 escudos. Foreign trade (1969): imports 418,801,-000 escudos (49% from Portugal, 22% from Angola); exports 44,606,000 escudos (66% to Portugal, 12% to U.S., 5% to Portuguese Guinea). Main exports: bananas 23%; fish products 17%; fish 13%.

Transport. Ships entered (1968) vessels totaling 6,637,000 net registered tons; goods loaded (1968) c. 47,000 metric tons, unloaded c. 511,000 metric tons.

MACAU

The overseas province of Macau is situated on the mainland coast of China 40 mi. W of Hong Kong. Area: 6 sq.mi. (16 sq.km.). Pop. (1970 est.): 314,000.

Education. (1966–67) Primary, pupils 35,520, teachers 916; secondary, pupils 9,177, teachers 562; vocational, pupils 2,276, teachers 123; teacher training, students 114, teachers 26.

Finance and Trade. Monetary unit: patacá, with a par value of 1 patacá to 4.75 escudos (6.05 patacás = U.S. $1; 14.53 patacás = £1 sterling) and a free rate (Sept. 27, 1971) of 5.77 patacás to U.S. $1. Budget (1969 est.) balanced at 49,103,000 patacás. Foreign trade (1970): imports 393,164,000 patacás; exports 257,479,-000 patacás. Import sources: Hong Kong 66%; China 27%. Export destinations: Hong Kong 18%; West Germany 15%; France 14%; Portugal 11%; U.S. 9%; Angola 8%; Mozambique 6%. Main exports: textiles 59%; chemicals 9%; animal products 7%.

Transport. Shipping traffic (1969) goods loaded 56,000 metric tons, unloaded 270,000 metric tons.

MOZAMBIQUE

Mozambique, on the southeastern African coast, is an overseas province bounded by Tanzania, Malawi, Zambia, Rhodesia, South Africa, and Swaziland. Area: 303,073 sq.mi. (784,961 sq. km.). Pop. (1970): 8,233,034. Cap.: Lourenço Marques (pop., 1970, 383,775).

Education. (1967) Primary, pupils 485,045, teachers 6,274; secondary (1966), pupils 10,092, teachers 697; vocational, pupils 15,346, teachers 836; teacher training, students 1,061, teachers 104; higher, students 904, teaching staff 192.

Finance and Trade. Monetary unit: Mozambique escudo, at par with the Portuguese escudo. Budget (1970 est.): revenue 6,452,000,000 escudos; expenditure 6,451,000,000 escudos. Foreign trade (1970): imports 9,363,000,000 escudos; exports 4,497,000,000 escudos. Import sources: Portugal 27%; South Africa 15%; U.S. 10%; U.K. 8%; West Germany 8%; Japan 6%. Export destinations: Portugal 38%; South Africa 10%; U.S. 9%; U.K. 5%; Angola 5%. Main exports: textiles 21%; cashew nuts 19%; sugar 12%; copra 5%; tea 5%.

Transport and Communications. Roads (1969) 37,085 km. Motor vehicles in use (1967): passenger 58,900; commercial (including buses) 13,900. Railways (1968): 3,876 km.; traffic 256 million passenger-km., freight 2,676,000,000 net ton-km. Ships entered (1968) vessels totaling 16,-131,000 net registered tons; goods loaded (1969) 8,588,000 metric tons, unloaded 3,808,000 metric tons. Telephones (Dec. 1969) 24,408. Radio receivers (Dec. 1969) 85,000.

Agriculture. Production (in 000; metric tons; 1970; 1969 in parentheses): cotton, lint c. 43 (41); sisal c. 30 (28); sugar, raw value (1970–71) c. 260, (1969–70) c. 230; copra (exports) c. 60 (c. 60); bananas (1969) c. 25, (1968) c. 25; tea 17 (16). Livestock (in 000; Dec. 1969): cattle c. 2,050; sheep c. 210; goats c. 850; pigs c. 230.

Industry. Production (in 000; metric tons; 1969): petroleum products 753; cement (1970) 362; electricity (kw-hr.) 503,000.

PORTUGUESE GUINEA

The African overseas province of Portuguese Guinea has an Atlantic coastline on the west and borders Senegal on the north and Guinea on the east and south. Area: 13,948 sq.mi. (36,125 sq.km.). Pop. (1970): 487,448. Cap.: Bissau (pop., 1970, 62,101).

Education. (1966–67) Primary, pupils 17,-805, teachers 497; secondary, pupils 446, teachers 21; vocational, pupils 652, teachers 34.

Finance and Trade. Monetary unit: Guinea escudo, at par with the Portuguese escudo. Budget (1968 est.): revenue 333,131,000 escudos; expenditure 305,555,000 escudos. Foreign trade (1968): imports 506,657,000 escudos (64% from Portugal, 5% from U.K.); exports 87,474,000 escudos (75% to Portugal, 16% to West Germany, 5% to Netherlands). Main exports: peanuts 47%; coconuts 23%.

Agriculture. Production (in 000; metric tons; 1970; 1969 in parentheses): peanuts c. 65 (c. 65); coffee c. 16 (12); palm kernels (exports) c. 12 (c. 12); palm oil c. 8 (c. 8). Livestock (in 000; 1969–70): cattle c. 260; pigs c. 113; sheep c. 64; goats c. 174.

PORTUGUESE TIMOR

Portuguese Timor, an overseas province consisting of the eastern portion of the island of Timor, is located about 300 mi. N of Australia. Area: 5,763 sq.mi. (14,925 sq.km.). Pop. (1970): 610,541. Cap.: Dili (pop., 1970, 29,312).

Education. (1966–67) Primary, pupils 20,534, teachers 385; secondary, pupils 879, teachers 64; vocational, pupils 14, teachers 3; teacher training, students 83, teachers 8.

Finance and Trade. Monetary unit: Timor escudo, at par with the Portuguese escudo. Budget (1968 est.): revenue 134,169,000 escudos; expenditure 148,561,000 escudos. Foreign trade (1969): imports 183,504,000 escudos (34% from Portugal, 15% from Macau, 12% from Mozambique, 11% from Singapore, 8% from Australia, 7% from Japan, 6% from U.K.); exports 61,518,000 escudos (28% to Netherlands, 26% to Denmark, 15% to Singapore, 11% to Norway, 11% to Portugal). Main exports: coffee 8%; copra 12%.

Agriculture. Production (in 000; metric tons; 1969; 1968 in parentheses): corn 16 (13); rice 13 (22); sweet potatoes c. 7 (3); copra 2.5 (0.9); coffee 5 (1). Livestock (in 000; 1969): cattle 67; sheep 39; goats 204; pigs 203; buffalo 124; horses 107.

SÃO TOMÉ AND PRÍNCIPE

The overseas province of São Tomé and Príncipe Islands lies in the Gulf of Guinea off the west coast of Africa. Area: 372 sq.mi. (964 sq.km.). Pop. (1970 est.): 61,000. Cap.: São Tomé (pop., 1960, 5,714).

Education. (1967–68) Primary, pupils 7,525, teachers 237; secondary, pupils 643, teachers 39; vocational, pupils 177, teachers 11.

Finance and Trade. Monetary unit: Guinea escudo. Budget (1968, est.): revenue 156,973,000 escudos; expenditure 134,175,000 escudos. Foreign trade (1970): imports 260,522,000 escudos (51% from Portugal, 23% from Angola, 5% from Netherlands, 5% from West Germany); exports 237,460,000 escudos (34% to Portugal, 32% to Netherlands, 12% to West Germany, 7% to Denmark, 5% to U.S.). Main exports: cocoa 80%; copra 11%.

Agriculture. Production (in 000; metric tons; 1969; 1968 in parentheses): copra 5.2 (4.7); bananas 2 (3); cocoa (1969–70) 9.9, (1968–69) 10.4; palm kernels (exports) 2.6 (2.7); palm oil 0.9 (1). Livestock (in 000; Dec. 1969): cattle 3; sheep 2; pigs 3; goats 1.

SOUTH WEST AFRICA (NAMIBIA)

South West Africa has been a UN territory since 1966, when the General Assembly terminated South Africa's mandate over the country, renamed Namibia by the UN. South Africa considers the UN resolution illegal and has stated that it is determined to continue its jurisdiction over the area. Area: 318,261 sq.mi. (824,296 sq.km.). Pop. (1970 est.): 632,000. National cap.: Windhoek (pop., 1967 est., 66,810). Summer cap.: Swakopmund (pop., 1960, 4,701).

Education. (1970) Primary and secondary, pupils 129,927, teachers 3,790.

Finance and Trade. Monetary unit: South African rand, with a par value of R 0.71 to U.S. $1 (R 1.71 = £1 sterling) and a free rate (Sept. 27, 1971) of R 1.77 to £1 sterling. Budget (1968–69): revenue R 88,948,000; expenditure R 85,825,000. Foreign trade included in the South African customs union. Main exports: diamonds and other minerals (1966) R 128 million; karakul pelts (1967) R 14.5 million.

Agriculture. Production (in 000; metric tons; 1970; 1969 in parentheses): corn c. 12 (c. 12); millet c. 13 (c. 13); butter c. 2 (c. 2); beef and veal c. 62 (c. 60); fish catch (1969) 956, (1968) 983. Livestock (in 000; 1969–70): cattle c. 2,500; sheep c. 4,000; goats c. 1,800; horses c. 36; asses c. 56.

Industry. Production (in 000; metric tons; 1969): lead ore (metal content) 76; zinc ore (metal content) c. 70; copper ore (1966) 37; tin concentrates (metal content) 0.7; silver (1968) 0.042; diamonds (metric carats) 1,790; electricity (kw-hr.; 1963) 188,000.

SPAIN

SPANISH SAHARA

Spanish Sahara is a province in northwest Africa, bordered by Morocco, Algeria, Mauritania, and

---

the Atlantic Ocean. Area: 102,703 sq.mi. (266,000 sq.km.). Pop. (1970): 76,425. Cap.: El Aaiún (pop., 1970, 24,519).

Education. (1968–69) Primary, pupils 2,399, teachers 67; secondary, pupils 1,095, teachers 60.

Finance and Trade. Monetary unit: Spanish peseta, with a par value of 70 pesetas to U.S. $1 (168 pesetas = £1 sterling) and a free rate (Sept. 27, 1971) of 69 pesetas to U.S. $1 (172 pesetas = £1 sterling). Budget (1969 est.) balanced at 250 million pesetas. Foreign trade (1968): imports 210,350,000 pesetas; exports negligible.

Agriculture and Industry. Livestock (in 000; 1968): camels 56; goats 141; sheep 18. Electricity production (1969) 5,120,000 kw-hr. Phosphate mining is being developed.

UNITED KINGDOM

ANTIGUA

The associated state of Antigua, with its dependencies Barbuda and Redonda, lies in the eastern Caribbean approximately 40 mi. N of Guadeloupe. Area: 171 sq.mi. (442 sq.km.). Pop. (1970 est.): 60,000. Cap.: Saint John's (pop., 1960, 21,396).

Education. (1966–67) Primary and secondary, pupils 17,027, teachers (1963–64) 470; higher (1963–64), students 50, teachers 3.

Finance and Trade. Monetary unit: East Caribbean dollar (ECar$2 = U.S. $1; ECar $4.80 = £1 sterling), with a free rate (Sept. 27, 1971) of ECar$1.94 = U.S. $1. Budget (1967 est.): revenue ECar$13,759,496; expenditure ECar$12,632,803. Foreign trade (1967): imports ECar$39,094,190 (29% from U.S., 23% from U.K., 10% from Trinidad and Tobago); exports ECar$4,968,599 (21% to Canada, 9% to U.S., 5% to U.K., 5% to Puerto Rico). Main export petroleum products 85%. Tourism (1970) 65,369 visitors.

BAHAMAS

The self-governing colony of the Bahamas comprises a 90,000-sq.mi. archipelago that extends for over 600 mi. ESE of Florida. Area: 5,380 sq.mi. (13,934 sq.km.). Pop (1970): 168,812. Cap.: Nassau, New Providence (pop., 1970, 3,233).

Education. (1968–69) Primary, pupils 32,876, teachers 1,154; secondary, pupils 15,116, teachers 654; vocational, pupils 307, teachers 36; teacher training, students 66, teachers 8; higher, students 234, teaching staff 37.

Finance and Trade. Monetary unit: Bahamian dollar, with a par value equal to the U.S. dollar (B$2.40 = £1 sterling) and a free rate (Sept. 27, 1971) of B$2.48 to £1 sterling. Budget (1970 est.): revenue B$97.6 million; expenditure B$97,050,000. Foreign trade (1970): imports B$343,206,000 (55% from U.S., 13% from U.K., 7% from Italy); exports B$87,021,000 (68% to U.S., 7% to U.K., 6% to Canada). Main exports: petroleum products 34%; cement 13%; chemicals and liqueurs 5%. Tourism (1969) 1,332,400 visitors.

Transport and Communications. Shipping (1970): merchant vessels 100 gross tons and over 144; gross tonnage 276,097. Telephones (Jan. 1970) 53,880. Radio receivers (Dec. 1969) 125,000. Television receivers (Dec. 1964) c. 4,500.

BERMUDA

The colony of Bermuda lies in the western Atlantic about 570 mi. E of Cape Hatteras, North Carolina. Area: 20 sq.mi. (53 sq.km.). Pop. (1970): 53,000. Cap.: Hamilton, Great Bermuda (pop., 1970, 2,127).

Education. (1966–67) Primary, pupils 9,067, teachers 384; secondary, pupils 3,460, teachers 223; vocational, pupils 454, teachers 52.

Finance and Trade. Monetary unit: Bermuda dollar, with a par value equal to the U.S. dollar (Ber$2.40 = £1 sterling) and a free rate (Sept. 27, 1971) of Ber$0.97 to U.S. $1. Budget (1970–71 est.): revenue Ber$35,511,000; expenditure Ber$35,753,000. Foreign trade (1969): imports Ber$149,051,000 (including Ber$63,548,000 for free-port area); exports Ber$78,834,000. Import sources: U.S. 43%; U.K. 23%; Canada 10%. Export destinations (1967): U.K. 22%; Australia 13%; U.S. 12%; Netherlands 11%; France 8%; Japan 7%. Main exports: drugs and medicines 75%; currency 8%. Tourism (1968): visitors 331,400; gross receipts U.S. $63 million.

Transport and Communications. Shipping (1970): merchant vessels 100 gross tons and over 48; gross tonnage 683,529. Telephones (Dec.

1969) 28,094. Radio receivers (Dec. 1969) 29,000. Television receivers (Dec. 1969) 16,000.

BRITISH HONDURAS

British Honduras, a self-governing colony, is situated on the Caribbean coast of Central America, bounded on the north and northwest by Mexico and by Guatemala on the remainder of the west and south. Area: 8,866 sq.mi. (22,963 sq.km.). Pop. (1970): 119,645. Cap.: Belmopan (pop., 1970 est., 1,000).

Education. (1968–69) Primary, pupils 28,910, teachers 1,193; secondary, pupils 3,147, teachers 228; vocational pupils 44; teacher training, students 80, teachers 3; higher, students 94, teaching staff 17.

Finance and Trade. Monetary unit: British Honduras dollar, with a par value of BH$1.67 = U.S. $1 (BH$4 = £1 sterling) and a free rate (Sept. 27, 1971) of BH$1.61 to U.S. $1. Budget (1970 est.): revenue BH$26,460,000 (including U.K. development grants BH$9.9 million); expenditure BH$26,483,000. Foreign trade (1968): imports BH$44,200,780; exports BH$25,194,350. Import sources: U.S. 33%; U.K. 29%; Jamaica 7%; Netherlands 6%. Export destinations: U.K. 32%; U.S. 29%; Mexico 16%; Canada 15%. Main exports: sugar 39%; oranges and products 10%; grapefruit and products 6%.

BRITISH INDIAN OCEAN TERRITORY

Located in the western Indian Ocean, this colony consists of the Chagos Archipelago and the islands of Aldabra, Desroches, and Farquhar. Area: 85 sq.mi. (221 sq.km.). Pop. (1971 est.): 560. Administrative headquarters: Victoria, Seychelles.

BRITISH SOLOMON ISLANDS

British Solomon Islands is a protectorate in the southwestern Pacific east of the island of New Guinea. Area: 10,983 sq.mi. (28,446 sq.km.). Pop. (1971 est.): 166,280. Cap.: Honiara, Guadalcanal (pop., 1971 est., 13,350).

Education. (1969) Primary, pupils 21,635, teachers 1,268; secondary, pupils 897, teachers 53; vocational, pupils 299, teachers 25; teacher training students 116, teachers 12.

Finance and Trade. Monetary unit: Australian dollar. Budget (1970 est.) balanced at A$9,693,000 (including U.K. grant-in-aid $A2,315,000). Foreign trade (1970): imports A$10,020,000 (45% from Australia, 16% from U.K., 10% from U.S., 7% from Japan); exports A$7,047,000 (53% to Japan, 14% to Australia, 11% to Norway, 10% to Netherlands, 8% to West Germany). Main exports: copra 53%; timber 40%.

BRITISH VIRGIN ISLANDS

The colony of the British Virgin Islands is located in the Caribbean to the east of the U.S. Virgin Islands. Area: 59 sq.mi. (153 sq.km.). Pop. (1970): 10,484. Cap.: Road Town, Tortola (pop., 1970, 2,183).

Education. (1968–69) Primary, pupils 1,856; secondary, pupils 860; primary and secondary, teachers (1967–68) 128.

Finance and Trade. Monetary unit: U.S. dollar (par value of U.S. $2.40 = £1 sterling) and a free rate (Sept. 27, 1971) of U.S. $2.48 to £1 sterling. Budget (1969 est.): revenue U.S. $2,960,334 (including U.K. financial aid U.S. $864,259); expenditure U.S. $3,672,000. Foreign trade (1969): imports U.S. $8,099,000; exports U.S. $49,754. Main exports (1968): fish 54%; livestock 32%; fruit 6%.

BRUNEI

Brunei, a protected sultanate, is located on the north coast of the island of Borneo, surrounded on its landward side by the Malaysian state of Sarawak. Area: 2,226 sq.mi. (5,765 sq.km.). Pop. (1971): 135,665. Cap.: Bandar Seri Begawan (pop., 1971, 36,574).

Education. (1968–69) Primary, pupils 26,706, teachers 1,143; secondary, pupils 7,969, teachers 405; vocational, pupils 72, teachers 7; teacher training, students 540, teachers 22.

Finance and Trade. Monetary unit: Brunei dollar, with a par value of Br$3.06 to U.S. $1 (Br$7.35 = £1 sterling) and a free rate (Sept.

Dependent States

27, 1971) of Br$2.97 to U.S. $1. Budget (1969 rev. est.): revenue Br$236,194,000; expenditure Br$214 million. Foreign trade (1969): imports Br$222,035,000; exports Br$270,140,000. Import sources: U.K. 24%; Singapore 15%; U.S. 14%; Japan 13%; Malaysia 5%; Australia 5%. Export destination Sarawak 97%. Main export crude oil 94%.

Agriculture. Production (in 000; metric tons; 1970; 1969 in parentheses): rice *c.* 8 (*c.* 8); rubber (exports) 0.4 (0.3). Livestock (in 000; Dec. 1969): cattle 3; pigs 12; goats 1.

Industry. Production (1969): crude oil 6,107,-000 metric tons; natural gas 191 million cu.m.

CAYMAN ISLANDS

The colony of the Cayman Islands lies in the Caribbean about 170 mi. NW of Jamaica. Area: 100 sq.mi. (259 sq.km.). Pop. (1970): 10,652. Cap.: George Town, Grand Cayman (pop., 1970, 3,975).

Education. (Public only; 1967–68) Primary, pupils 1,185, teachers 39; secondary, pupils 366, teachers 23.

Finance and Trade. Monetary unit: Jamaican dollar, with a par value of Jam$0.83 to U.S. $1 (Jam$2 = £1 sterling) and a free rate (Sept. 27, 1971) of Jam$0.81 to U.S. $1. Budget (1970 est.): revenue Jam$2,345,000; expenditure Jam$2,313,000. Foreign trade (1969): imports Jam$5,847,000; exports Jam$8,754. Main exports (1967): rope 22%; turtle shell 14%. Tourism: visitors (1970) *c.* 25,000; gross receipts (1969) *c.* Jam$2.4 million.

Transport. Shipping (1970): merchant vessels 100 gross tons and over 36; gross tonnage 22,-371. About 950 persons were employed as seamen in 1969.

DOMINICA

The associated state of Dominica lies in the Caribbean between Guadeloupe to the north and Martinique to the south. Area: 289 sq.mi. (749 sq.km.). Pop. (1970): 70,302. Cap.: Roseau (pop., 1970, 10,157).

Education. Primary, pupils (1968–69) 19,-224, teachers (1963–64) 459; secondary, pupils (1965–66) 1,452, teachers (1963–64) 83; vocational (1963–64), pupils 350, teachers 16.

Finance and Trade. Monetary unit: East Caribbean dollar. Budget (1970 est.): revenue ECar$14,002,000; expenditure ECar$13,609,000. Foreign trade (1969): imports ECar$24,712,700 (33% from U.K., 15% from U.S., 11% from Trinidad and Tobago, 10% from Canada, 6% from Netherlands, 5% from West Germany); exports ECar$14,147,700 (84% to U.K.). Main exports: bananas 73%; essential oils 6%; fruit juices 5%.

FALKLAND ISLANDS

The colony of the Falkland Islands and Dependencies is situated in the South Atlantic about 500 mi. NE of Cape Horn. Area: 6,200 sq.mi. (16,058 sq.km.). Pop. (1970 est.): 2,045. Cap.: Stanley (pop., 1970 est., 1,080).

Education. (1969) Primary and secondary, pupils 372, teachers 41.

Finance and Trade. Monetary unit: Falkland pound, at par with the pound sterling (FI£1 = U.S. $2.40) and a free rate (Sept. 27, 1971) of FI£1 = U.S. $2.48. Budgets: (colony; 1969–70 est.) revenue FI£426,559, expenditure FI£480,393; (dependencies; 1969–70 est.) revenue FI£23,000 (including U.K. grant FI£11,-000), expenditure FI£23,000. Foreign trade: (colony; 1968) imports FI£599,000, exports FI£873,000 (mainly wool); (dependencies) imports (1967) FI£12,491, exports (1966) FI£1,-368,361 (mainly whale and seal oil).

GIBRALTAR

Gibraltar, a self-governing colony, is a small peninsula that juts into the Mediterranean from southwestern Spain. Area: 2.25 sq.mi. (5.83 sq.km.). Pop. (1970): 26,833.

Education. (1968–69) Primary, pupils 3,268, teachers 132; secondary, pupils 1,758, teachers 105; vocational (1967–68), pupils 74, teachers 12.

Finance and Trade. Monetary unit: Gibraltar pound, at par with the pound sterling. Budget (1969 est.): revenue Gib£2,396,930; expenditure Gib£2,410,762. Foreign trade (1970): imports

Gib£8.6 million (50% from U.K., 19% from EEC); exports Gib£1.3 million (31% to EEC, 15% to U.K.). Tourism (1968) 306,010 arrivals.

Transport. Shipping (1970): merchant vessels 100 gross tons and over 17; gross tonnage 54,-075. Ships entered (1968) vessels totaling 12,-175,000 net registered tons; goods loaded (1968) 4,000 metric tons, unloaded 237,000 metric tons.

GILBERT AND ELLICE ISLANDS

The Gilbert and Ellice Islands colony is scattered over an area of more than two million sq.mi. in the western Pacific Ocean. Area: 283 sq.mi. (734 sq.km.). Pop. (1970 est.): 56,400. Seat of government: Tarawa Atoll (pop., 1968, 12,642).

Education. (1969) Primary, pupils 13,865, teachers 481; secondary, pupils 872, teachers 44; vocational, pupils 124, teachers 13; teacher training, students 99, teachers 14.

Finance and Trade. Monetary unit: Australian dollar. Budget (1969 est.): revenue A$4,-689,000; expenditure A$4,237,000. Foreign trade (1969): imports A$2,770,000 (60% from Australia, 11% from U.K. in 1968); exports A$7,-306,000 (63% to Australia, 24% to New Zealand, 12% to U.K. in 1968). Main exports (1968): phosphates 84%; copra 14%.

GRENADA

Grenada, a West Indian associated state, includes the island of Grenada and its dependency, the southern Grenadines. Area: 133 sq.mi. (344 sq.km.). Pop. (1970): 94,500. Cap.: Saint George's (pop., 1969 est., 8,644).

Education. (1966–67) Primary, pupils 28,-402, teachers 690; secondary, pupils 2,770, teachers 119; vocational, pupils 432, teachers 9; teacher training, students 77, teachers 11.

Finance and Trade. Monetary unit: East Caribbean dollar. Budget (1971 est.) balanced at ECar$35,613,426. Foreign trade (1968): imports ECar$26,346,000; exports ECar$9,962,000. Import sources: U.K. 33%; U.S. 10%; Canada 10%; Netherlands 5%. Export destinations: U.K. 64%; West Germany 10%; Netherlands 9%; U.S. 5%. Main exports: bananas 40%; cocoa 21%; nutmeg 25%; mace 7%.

GUERNSEY

Located 30 mi. W of Normandy, France, Guernsey, together with its small island dependencies, is a crown dependency. Area: 30 sq.mi. (76 sq.km.). Pop. (1971): 53,734. Cap.: St. Peter Port (pop., 1971, 16,303).

Education. (1969) Primary and secondary, pupils 8,772.

Finance and Trade. Monetary unit: pound sterling. Budget (1969): revenue £6,113,148 (including £160,574 for Alderney); expenditure £7,-649,193 (including £198,492 for Alderney). Foreign trade included with United Kingdom. Main exports: tomatoes; flowers; stone. Tourism (1969) passengers arrived 245,000.

HONG KONG

The colony of Hong Kong lies on the southeastern coast of China about 40 mi. E of Macau and 80 mi. SE of Canton. Area: 400 sq.mi. (1,036 sq.km.). Pop. (1971): 3,950,802. Cap.: Victoria (pop., 1971, 521,612).

Education. (1968–69) Primary, pupils 725,-672, teachers 22,370; secondary, pupils 236,054; vocational, pupils 12,623; secondary and vocational, teachers 8,451; higher, students 14,164, teaching staff 1,737.

Finance and Trade. Monetary unit: Hong Kong dollar, with a par value of HK$6.06 = U.S. $1 (HK$14.55 = £1 sterling) and a free rate (Sept. 27, 1971) of HK$5.88 to U.S. $1. Budget (1970–71 est.): revenue HK$2,584,000,-000; expenditure HK$2,393,000,000. Foreign trade (1970): imports HK$17,607,000,000 (24% from Japan, 16% from China, 13% from U.S., 9% from U.K., 5% from Taiwan); exports HK$15,238,000,000 (36% to U.S., 10% to U.K., 7% to Japan, 7% to West Germany). Main exports: clothing 28%; textile yarns and fabrics 7%; toys and games 7%; electrical equipment 7%. Tourism (1969): visitors arrived 765,200; gross receipts U.S. $216 million.

Transport and Communications. Roads (1969) 955 km. Motor vehicles in use (1969): passenger 82,389; commercial 18,017. Railways (1968) 35 km. Shipping (1970): merchant vessels 100 gross tons and over 116; gross tonnage 670,980. Ships entered (1969) vessels totaling 26,616,000 net registered tons; goods loaded

(1970) 3,012,000 metric tons, unloaded 10,627,-000 metric tons. Telephones (Dec. 1969) 502,-374. Radio licenses (Dec. 1969) 675,000. Television licenses (Dec. 1969) 158,000.

ISLE OF MAN

The Isle of Man, a crown dependency, lies in the Irish Sea approximately 35 mi. from both Northern Ireland and the coast of northwestern England. Area: 221 sq.mi. (572 sq.km.). Pop. (1971): 56,248. Cap.: Douglas (pop., 1971, 20,-385).

Education. (1969–70) Primary, pupils 4,300; secondary, pupils 2,787; vocational, pupils 1,-871.

Finance and Trade. Monetary unit: pound sterling. Budget (1970–71 est.) revenue £10.2 million; expenditure £11.6 million. Foreign trade included with United Kingdom. Main exports: metal ores, tweeds, fish products. Tourism (1969) 532,808 passengers arrived.

JERSEY

The island of Jersey, a crown dependency, is located about 20 mi. W of Normandy, France. Area: 45 sq.mi. (117 sq.km.). Pop. (1971): 72,-629. Cap.: St. Helier (pop., 1971, 28,135).

Education. (1969) Primary and secondary, pupils 10,220.

Finance and Trade. Monetary unit: Jersey pound, at par with the pound sterling. Budget (1969): revenue £13,071,992; expenditure £10,-143,901. Foreign trade included with United Kingdom. Main exports: potatoes, tomatoes. Tourism (1969) passengers arrived by sea 238,-711, by air 543,745.

MONTSERRAT

The colony of Montserrat is located in the Caribbean between Antigua, 27 mi. NE, and Guadeloupe, 40 mi. SE. Area: 40 sq.mi. (102 sq.km.). Pop. (1970): 12,302. Cap.: Plymouth (pop., 1968 est., 3,500).

Education. (1968–69) Primary, pupils 2,743, teachers 112; secondary, pupils 214, teachers 18; vocational, pupils 12, teachers 1; teacher training, students 12, teachers 1.

Finance and Trade. Monetary unit: East Caribbean dollar. Budget (1969 est.) balanced at ECar$4,037,180. Foreign trade (1967): imports ECar$6,923,000; exports ECar$320,239. Main exports fruit and vegetables 14%.

PITCAIRN ISLAND

The colony of Pitcairn Island is in the central South Pacific, 3,200 mi. NE of New Zealand and 1,350 mi. SE of Tahiti. Area: 1.75 sq.mi. (4.53 sq.km.). Pop. (1970): 93. Cap. (de facto): Adamstown.

ST. HELENA

The colony of St. Helena, including its dependencies of Ascension and Tristan de Cunha islands, is located in the Atlantic off the southwestern coast of Africa. Area: 119 sq.mi. (308 sq.km.). Pop. (1969 est.): 6,356. Cap.: Jamestown (pop., 1969 est., 1,600).

Education. (1966–67) Primary, pupils 753, teachers 39; secondary, pupils 416, teachers 26; teacher training, students 7.

Finance and Trade. Monetary unit: pound sterling. Budget (1970 est.): revenue £471,537; expenditure £519,392. Foreign trade (1969): imports £461,000 (61% from U.K., 28% from South Africa in 1968); exports £7,500 (73% to U.K., 20% to South Africa in 1968).

ST. KITTS-NEVIS-ANGUILLA

This associated state consists of the islands of St. Kitts, Nevis, and Anguilla (under direct British administration). Area: 136 sq.mi. (352 sq. km.). Pop. (1970 est.): 62,000. Cap.: Basseterre, St. Kitts (pop., 1970, 13,055).

Education. (Including Anguilla; 1968–69) Primary, pupils 12,986, teachers 367; secondary, pupils 3,313, teachers 108; vocational, pupils 560, teachers 6. (Anguilla only; 1969–70) Primary, pupils 1,351, teachers 67; secondary, pupils 486, teachers 10.

Finance and Trade. Monetary unit: East Caribbean dollar. Budgets (including Anguilla; 1969 est.) balanced at ECar$20.4 million; (Anguilla only; 1967 est.) balanced at ECar$600,000, U.K. development aid (1970) £50,000. Foreign trade (including Anguilla; 1967): imports ECar$16,-241,972 (30% from U.K., 16% from Canada, 13% from U.S., 9% from Trinidad and Tobago,

5% from Barbados); exports ECar$9,047,411 (86% to U.K.). Main exports (Anguilla only): postage stamps, salt.

ST. LUCIA

The Caribbean island of St. Lucia, an associated state, lies 24 mi. S of Martinique and 21 mi. NE of St. Vincent. Area: 238 sq.mi. (616 sq.km.). Pop. (1970): 101,100. Cap.: Castries (pop., 1964 est., 5,100).

Education. (1968–69) Primary, pupils 21,130, teachers 600; secondary, pupils 5,185, teachers 233; teacher training, students 57, teachers 4; higher, students 71, teaching staff 14.

Finance and Trade. Monetary unit: East Caribbean dollar. Budget (1971 est.): revenue ECar $18,344,628; expenditure ECar$18,546,284. Foreign trade (1968): imports ECar$29,452,000 (31% from U.K., 14% from U.S., 12% from Trinidad and Tobago, 11% from Canada, 6% from Netherlands Antilles, 5% from Barbados); exports ECar$12,553,000 (82% to U.K., 7% to Barbados). Main exports: bananas 82%; copra 11%; coconut oil 5%. Tourism (1969): visitors 25,382; gross receipts ECar$7.2 million.

ST. VINCENT

St. Vincent, including the northern Grenadines, is an associated state in the eastern Caribbean about 100 mi. W of Barbados. Area: 150 sq.mi. (389 sq.km.). Pop. (1970): 89,129. Cap.: Kingstown (pop., 1969 est., 4,994).

Education. (1968–69) Primary, pupils 27,209, teachers 763; secondary, pupils 2,584, teachers 92; teacher training, students 295, teachers 25.

Finance and Trade. Monetary unit: East Caribbean dollar. Budget (1970 est.) balanced at ECar$18,517,000. Foreign trade (1967): imports ECar$15,808,000 (31% from U.K., 16% from Trinidad and Tobago, 12% from Canada, 11% from U.S.); exports ECar$6,320,000 (57% to U.K., 14% to Trinidad and Tobago, 9% to U.S.). Main exports: bananas 49%; arrowroot 16%; copra 14%.

SEYCHELLES

The colony of Seychelles consists of a group of about 80 islands scattered over 400,000 sq.mi. in the western Indian Ocean northeast of Madagascar. Area: 107 sq.mi. (278 sq.km.). Pop. (1971): 52,437. Cap.: Victoria, Mahé (pop., 1971, 13,622).

Education. (1968) Primary, pupils 8,531, teachers 362; secondary, pupils 2,024, teachers 96; vocational, pupils 247, teachers 12; higher, students 46, teaching staff 3.

Finance and Trade. Monetary unit: Seychelles rupee, with a par value of SRs. 5.56 to U.S. $1 (SRs. 13.33 = £1 sterling) and a free rate (Sept. 27, 1971) of SRs. 5.37 to U.S. $1. Budget (1969 est.): revenue SRs. 16,326,832 (excluding grant-in-aid, valued at SRs. 1,693,334); expenditure SRs. 19,375,034. Foreign trade (1968): imports SRs. 33,875,000; exports SRs. 16,308,000. Import sources: U.K. 28%; Iran 13%; Kenya 9%; Hong Kong 9%; South Africa 6%; Burma 6%; India 6%; Netherlands 5%. Export destinations: India 36%; U.S. 34%; Israel 8%; U.K. 7%. Main exports: cinnamon bark 46%; copra 44%.

TRUCIAL STATES

The Trucial States, on the eastern Arabian Peninsula, formerly a protected state consisting of a loose federation of seven sheikhdoms, became an independent country in 1971. (*See* FEDERATION OF ARAB EMIRATES.)

Education. Primary and secondary (1968), pupils *c.* 11,500.

Finance and Trade. Monetary units: (Abu Dhabi) Bahrain dinar, with a par value of 0.48 dinars to U.S. $1 (1.14 dinars = £1 sterling) and a free rate (Sept. 27, 1971) of 0.46 dinars to U.S. $1; (other states) Qatar/Dubai riyal, with a par value of 4.76 riyals to U.S. $1 (11.43 riyals = £1 sterling) and a free rate (Sept. 27, 1971) of 4.61 riyals to U.S. $1. Budgets: (Abu Dhabi; 1969 est.) oil revenue *c.* 85 million dinars; (Dubai; 1970 est.) *c.* 4 million dinars. Foreign trade: (Abu Dhabi; 1969) imports 59.3 million dinars (32% from U.K., 18% from U.S., 7% from Dubai), main export crude oil; (Dubai; 1969) imports 921,947,000 riyals (19% from Japan, 17% from U.K., 11% from Switzerland, 8% from U.S., 5% from India); exports 93,075,- 000 riyals (50% to Persian Gulf states, 15% transit via Khorfacan, 9% to Oman), main export dry fish 5%, reexports (entrepôt trade) account

for 93% of total, oil export began September 1969.

Industry. Crude oil production (metric tons; 1970) Abu Dhabi 33,718,000; Dubai 4,306,000.

TURKS AND CAICOS ISLANDS

The colony of the Turks and Caicos Islands is situated in the Atlantic southeast of the Bahamas. Area: 166 sq.mi. (430 sq.km.). Pop. (1970): 5,675. Seat of government: Grand Turk Island (pop., 1970, 2,330).

Education. (1968) Primary, pupils 1,527, teachers 82; secondary, pupils 165, teachers 10.

Finance and Trade. Monetary unit: Jamaican dollar. Ordinary budget (1969 actual): revenue Jam$1,363,000; expenditure Jam$1,367,000. Foreign trade (1969): imports Jam$993,000; exports Jam$216,000. Main exports: crayfish 96%; salt 4%.

UNITED KINGDOM and FRANCE

NEW HEBRIDES

The British-French condominium of the New Hebrides is located in the southwestern Pacific about 500 mi. W of Fiji and 250 mi. NE of New Caledonia. Area: 5,700 sq.mi. (14,800 sq.km.). Pop. (1971 est.): 86,000. Cap.: Vila (pop., 1971 est., 5,000).

Education. (1968) Primary, pupils 15,329, teachers 673; secondary, pupils 459, teachers 39; vocational, pupils 45, teachers 4; teacher training, students 69, teachers 7.

Finance. Monetary unit: Australian dollar and New Hebrides franc (NHFr. 89.76 = U.S. $1; NHFr. 215.44 = £1 sterling; NHFr. 100.54 = A$1) with a free rate (Sept. 27, 1971) of NHFr. 221.66 to £1 sterling (NHFr. 103.23 = A$1). Condominium budget (1969 est.) balanced at A$2,850,000. British administration budget (1969–70 est.) balanced at A$2,266,788. French administration budget (1969 est.) balanced at A$3,442,314.

Foreign Trade. Imports (1969) A$10,571,- 950; exports (1968) A$10,432,050. Import sources: Australia 43%; France 15%; Japan 9%; Hong Kong 5%. Export destinations: France 47%; Japan 23%; U.S. 16%; Venezuela 6%. Main exports: copra 53%; fish 23%; manganese ore 14%.

Agriculture. Copra production (metric tons; 1970) *c.* 42,000, (1969) *c.* 42,000.

UNITED STATES

AMERICAN SAMOA

Located to the east of Western Samoa in the South Pacific, the unincorporated territory of American Samoa is approximately 1,600 mi. NE of the northern tip of New Zealand. Area: 76 sq.mi. (198 sq.km.). Pop. (1970): 27,769. Cap.: Pago Pago (pop., 1970, 2,491).

Education. (1968–69) Primary, pupils 7,018, teachers 323; secondary, pupils 2,305, teachers 105.

Finance and Trade. Monetary unit: U.S. dollar. Budget (1970 est.) revenue $14,446,000 (including U.S. grant $9,423,000). Foreign trade (1970): imports $15,713,000; exports $36,735,- 000. Main exports (1968): canned tuna 89%; pet food 6%; frozen fish 5%.

CANAL ZONE

The Canal Zone is administered by the U.S. under treaty with Panama, and consists of a 10-mi.-wide strip on the Isthmus of Panama through which the Panama Canal runs. Area (land only): 372 sq.mi. (964 sq.km.). Pop. (1970): 44,650. Administrative headquarters: Balboa Heights (pop., 1969 est., 190).

Education. (1968–69) Primary, pupils 8,693, teachers 358; secondary and vocational, pupils 5,709, teachers 265; higher, students 1,190, teaching staff 70.

Finance. Monetary unit: U.S. dollar. Budgets (1970): (Canal Zone government) revenue $43,- 695,000, expenditure $43,768,000; (Panama Canal Company) revenue $175,096,000, expenditure $173,989,000.

Traffic. (1969–70) Total number of ocean-going vessels passing through the canal 13,658; total cargo tonnage 114,257,260; tolls collected U.S. $94,654,468. Nationality and number of commercial vessels using the canal: Liberian 1,- 601; British 1,591; U.S. 1,520; Norwegian 1,- 323; Japanese 1,178; West German 1,108; Panamanian 799; Greek 568; Netherlands 493; Swedish 462; Danish 434.

GUAM

Guam, an organized unincorporated territory, is located in the Pacific Ocean about 6,000 mi. SW of San Francisco and 1,500 mi. E of Manila. Area: 209 sq.mi. (541 sq.km.). Pop. (1970): 86,- 926. Cap.: Agana (pop., 1966 est., 2,036).

Education. (1967) Primary (including pre-primary), pupils 16,182, teachers 564; secondary, pupils 9,535, teachers 451; higher, students 2,- 012, teaching staff 120.

Finance and Trade. Monetary unit: U.S. dollar. Budget (1968 est.): revenue $36,240,734 (including U.S. grants $3,988,825); expenditure $38,983,569. Foreign trade (with U.S. only; 1969): imports $45,539,000; exports $4,146,000. Main exports: transshipped foodstuffs and scrap metal.

Agriculture and Industry. Main crops: corn, sweet potatoes, lemons, cassava. Industrial production (1969): stone 593,000 metric tons; electricity 698 million kw-hr.

PUERTO RICO

Puerto Rico, a self-governing associated commonwealth, lies about 885 mi. SE of the Florida coast. Area: 3,421 sq.mi. (8,860 sq.km.). Pop. (1970): 2,712,033. Cap.: San Juan (pop., 1970, 463,242).

Education. (1968–69) Primary, pupils 479,- 040, teachers 13,910; secondary and vocational, pupils 249,880, teachers 8,870; higher (including 3 universities), students 54,138, teaching staff 3,500.

Finance. Monetary unit: U.S. dollar. Budget (1969): revenue $892,788,000; expenditure $799,122,000. Gross national product: (1969– 7Q) $4,579,300,000; (1968–69) $4,095,000,000. Cost of living (1963 = 100): (May 1971) 127; (May 1970) 122.

Foreign Trade. (1968–69) Imports $2,337,- 517,000 (78% from U.S.); exports $1,535,473,- 000 (87% to U.S.). Main exports (1965–66): clothing 23%; sugar 9%; tobacco 8%; chemicals 7%; petroleum products 6%; electrical machinery and equipment 5%. Tourism (1968–69): visitors 1,067,500; gross receipts U.S. $229 million.

Transport and Communications. Roads (1969) 9,750 km. Motor vehicles in use (1969): passenger 437,000; commercial (including buses) 90,500. Telephones (Dec. 1969) 28,459. Radio receivers (Dec. 1969) 1,625,000. Television receivers (Dec. 1969) 410,000.

Agriculture. Production (in 000; metric tons; 1969; 1968 in parentheses): bananas *c.* 110 (112); sweet potatoes *c.* 25 (24); coffee (1970) *c.* 12, (1969) 12; sugar, raw value (1970–71) *c.* 418, (1969–70) *c.* 418; tobacco 3.6 (5.1); pineapples 49 (59); oranges 33 (31); grapefruit 11 (11); milk 310 (300); beef and veal *c.* 18 (17). Livestock (in 000; Jan. 1970): cattle *c.* 510; pigs *c.* 200; chickens (Jan. 1969) 3,909.

Industry. Production (in 000; metric tons; 1970): cement 1,569; sand and gravel (1969) 8,557; stone (1969) 6,337; electricity (kw-hr.) 8,027,000.

RYUKYU ISLANDS, SOUTHERN

The Southern Ryukyu Islands, under U.S. civil administration, extend northeast to southwest between southern Japan and Taiwan in the Pacific Ocean. Area: 848 sq.mi. (2,195 sq.km.); area of Okinawa, largest island in the group, 454 sq.mi. Pop. (1970): 945,111. Cap.: Naha, Okinawa (pop., 1970, 276,380).

Education. (1968–69) Primary, pupils 139,- 010, teachers 4,816; secondary, pupils 116,309, teachers 5,070; vocational, pupils 15,075, teachers 933; higher (including 3 universities), students 9,647, teaching staff 590.

Finance and Trade. Monetary unit: U.S. dollar. Budget (1970): revenue $170,786,000 (including U.S. grant $20,350,000 and Japanese grant $47,222,000); expenditure $158,797,000. Foreign trade (1970): imports $477,268,000; exports $103,825,000. Import sources (1967): Japan 78%; U.S. 15%. Export destinations (1967): Japan 76%; U.S. 8%. Main exports: sugar 44%; canned pineapple 17%; scrap metal 5%.

Agriculture. Production (in 000; metric tons; 1969; 1968 in parentheses): rice 14 (14); sweet potatoes 115 (119); pineapple 101 (75); sugar, raw value (1970–71) *c.* 210, (1969–70) 209; fish catch 30 (35). Livestock (in 000; Dec. 1969): cattle 26; pigs 228; goats 31; chickens 1,627.

TRUST TERRITORY OF THE PACIFIC ISLANDS

The Trust Territory islands, numbering more than 2,000, are scattered over 3 million sq.mi. in the Pacific Ocean from 450 mi. E of the Philippines to just west of the International Date Line. Area: 700 sq.mi. (1,800 sq.km.). Pop. (1970): 102,-250. Seat of government: Saipan Island (pop., 1970, 10,034).

Education. (1968–69) Primary, pupils 28,-078, teachers 1,066; secondary, pupils 4,630,

teachers 235; vocational, pupils 39, teachers 7; teacher training, students 971, teachers 55.

Finance and Trade. Monetary unit: U.S. dollar. Budget (1968 est.) balanced at $24,680,000 (including U.S. grant $24 million). Foreign trade (1969): imports $13.9 million (50% from U.S., 28% from Japan in 1968); exports $2.8 million (27% to Japan in 1968). Main exports: copra 83%; scrap metal 10%.

Agriculture. Production (in 000; metric tons; 1969; 1968 in parentheses): copra 13 (9); bananas *c.* 2 (*c.* 2). Livestock (in 000; June 1969): cattle *c.* 7; pigs *c.* 24; goats *c.* 4; chickens *c.* 125.

VIRGIN ISLANDS

The Virgin Islands of the United States is an organized unincorporated territory located about 40

mi. E of Puerto Rico. Area: 133 sq.mi. (344 sq.km.). Pop. (1970): 63,200. Cap.: Charlotte Amalie, St. Thomas (pop., 1970, 12,372).

Education. (1968–69) Primary (including preprimary), pupils 11,400, teachers 430; secondary and vocational, pupils 3,700, teachers 250; higher, students 1,205, teaching staff (1967–68) 40.

Finance and Trade. Monetary unit: U.S. dollar. Budget (1968–69 est.): revenue (including grant-in-aid) $70,492,569; expenditure $59,576,-266. Foreign trade (1969): imports $327,193,000 (49% from U.S.); exports $199,951,000 (87% to U.S.). Tourism (1968): visitors *c.* 800,000; gross receipts *c.* $100 million.

Industry. Production (1969): stone 373,000 metric tons; electricity 387.5 million kw-hr.

Development, Economic

It could be said that in 1970–71 the world moved away from a single-focus attention to growth targets in the less developed countries and toward a deeper concern with the underlying realities affecting all human beings. Increasingly the international development effort merged with efforts to prevent the planet from becoming intolerable and to make it a more attractive place for the human race. At the same time, the continuous and frequently unsuccessful efforts to focus adequate attention on the problems of economic and social development were further handicapped in 1971 by mounting economic and social problems in the developed countries, serious difficulties in the functioning of the international monetary system, and what appeared to be a critical reappraisal of foreign aid in the U.S., which had been the principal donor country since World War II.

The best single indicator of progress in economic development remained the changes in gross domestic product (GDP), although, by itself, GDP does not measure changes in productive capacity or potential, nor does it reflect transformations in the economic and social structures of nations that are vital parts of the development process. With these important qualifications, it was still notable that in 1970, the latest year for which figures were available, the combined GDP of the less developed countries grew at

a rate of 5.9%, substantially higher than the average for the decade of the 1960s, though below the rates reached in 1968 and 1969. "Less developed countries" in general refers to all Asian countries except Japan and the Sino-Soviet countries, all African countries except South Africa, all Latin-American countries, and Cyprus, Greece, Malta, Portugal, Spain, Turkey, and Yugoslavia. The group includes about 1,750,000,000 persons, more than 70% of the world's population outside the Sino-Soviet countries. The figures in this article differ from previously published data since they are based on the latest available data, including corrections of earlier figures; 1970 data are preliminary.

The per capita growth rate of the less developed countries paralleled the relatively favourable performance of GDP, amounting to about 3.3%, again well above the 2.7% average for 1960–69. Indeed, it was one of the ironies of the international development scene that at the very time when past efforts had begun to reflect themselves in higher growth rates, attention tended to focus on social and political disturbances in the lower-income countries, thus obscuring the real gains.

However, the average figures, as usual, concealed wide regional variations. For example, it was estimated that increases in gross domestic product in the Middle East countries, taken as a group, declined from 11.3% in 1968 to 8.2% in 1969 and 5.1% in 1970, and substantial declines were also experienced in southern Europe and east Asia. (*See* Table I.) On the other hand, south Asia and the Western Hemisphere countries gained in 1970.

Foreign Trade. Exports of the less developed countries rose again in 1970, reaching nearly $60 billion, or about $6 billion more than in 1969. (*See* Table II.) Even excluding southern Europe and the major petroleum exporters, exports registered a substantial increase, from about $37 billion in 1969 to $41 billion. Imports, as would be expected in the less developed countries, increased correspondingly, resulting in a total negative trade balance or deficit of $6.4 billion. As in the case of GDP, the lower-income countries ended the 1960s at a higher level of exports than at the beginning, and all regions experienced larger increases in exports in 1970 than the average for 1961–69.

Export performance is of particular importance for successful development. Export increases not only provide the bulk of the foreign exchange needed to pay for imports (exports equaled nearly 90% of imports in 1970) and make possible the servicing of external borrowing and other forms of foreign investment, but also act as a major spur to higher levels of output and investment. An even more rapid increase in export earnings, especially in semimanu-

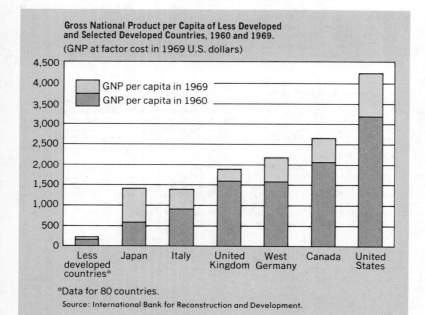

Gross National Product per Capita of Less Developed and Selected Developed Countries, 1960 and 1969.

(GNP at factor cost in 1969 U.S. dollars)

☐ GNP per capita in 1969
▨ GNP per capita in 1960

Less developed countries* / Japan / Italy / United Kingdom / West Germany / Canada / United States

*Data for 80 countries.

Source: International Bank for Reconstruction and Development.

factures and manufactures, was needed to improve the outlook for the lower-income countries. (*See* TRADE, INTERNATIONAL.)

Domestic Savings. The largest source of financing for private and public investment in the less developed countries is domestic savings, despite the low levels of income (about $100 per capita for the most populous lower-income countries like India, Indonesia, and Pakistan, and below $300 per capita even in such relatively "more advanced" countries as Brazil). Within these countries, a very small proportion of the population obtains much higher incomes, but this group forms at best a relatively narrow base for mobilization of the savings needed for investment.

In the 1960s domestic savings financed about 87% of total investment. This meant that, on average, over 16% of the gross national product (GNP equals GDP plus net factor payments on foreign investments) was saved for capital formation. Again, there were significant country and regional variations, from 13.4% in east Asia, 13.6% in south Asia, 14.1% in Africa, and 14.4% in the Middle East to 17.9% and 20.9% in Latin America and southern Europe, respectively. Of considerable significance was the general upward trend in saving during the 1960s (*i.e.*, a rising marginal savings ratio), keeping in mind that even a one or two percentage gain in savings as a proportion of GNP reflects a major effort and achievement. The average for industrial countries in the same period was 22.1%, a key explanation for the widening gap between the lower-income and higher-income countries.

However, helped by the inflow of foreign resources, gross investment in most of the less developed countries was higher than domestic savings. Expressed as a percentage of GNP for the period of 1961–69, the average for all less developed countries was 18.8%, a figure that again conceals wide regional variations (for example, 24.2% in southern Europe, as compared with 16.5% in Africa and 16% in south Asia).

External Sources of Finances. In 1970 it was estimated that the net total flows of long-term financial resources to the less developed countries and the multilateral agencies from the member countries of the Development Assistance Committee (DAC) of the Organization for Economic Cooperation and Development (OECD) amounted to over $14.7 billion, or about $1 billion more than in 1969. (*See* Table III.) The $14.7 billion represented about 0.74% of the GNP of the industrialized DAC countries.

The U.S. continued to be the largest single source, providing nearly $5.4 billion, or nearly 40% of the total. France, Germany, Japan, and the U.K. were also substantial sources of funds, each accounting for well over $1 billion, with France and Japan closer to $2 billion. Most spectacular was the rise in the Japanese figures: the 1970 figure was more than six times that for 1964. Other countries like Australia and Canada were also on a clearly rising trend.

Official Flows. Within this overall picture, official flows continued to be larger than private flows, amounting to nearly $8 billion in 1970 compared with $7.2 billion in 1969. The increase was due to larger contributions from the relatively newer sources of official assistance, such as Canada, West Germany, and Japan. The U.S. declined somewhat. The total official flows represented 0.40% of the GNP of the countries providing these resources.

Of the total official flows, what was regarded as "official development" assistance increased less than

Table I. Selected Economic Indicators for Less Developed and Industrialized Countries, Regional Summary

Region	Average annual real rates of growth (%), 1961–70						Shares in GNP (%)	
	Total GDP	Agricultural production	Manufacturing production	Population	GDP per capita	Total gross investment	Gross investment	Savings
Less developed countries*								
1961–65	5.1	2.4	8.7	2.6	2.5	7.3	18.5	16.1
1969	6.3	4.0	9.8	2.6	3.6	10.8	19.9	17.3
1970†	5.9	1.9	...	2.6	3.3	...	...	...
Africa								
1961–65	4.4	2.4	11.2	2.4	1.9	5.3	15.7	12.6
1969	5.4	4.2	10.0	2.6	2.8	12.5	18.1	16.4
1970†	5.1	0.8	...	2.6	2.4	...	...	...
Southern Europe								
1961–65	7.3	2.9	11.4	1.4	5.8	11.3	24.4	21.1
1969	7.7	2.1	12.4	1.5	6.1	11.7	24.6	20.9
1970†	5.9	−0.5	...	1.5	4.3	...	...	...
East Asia								
1961–65	5.5	3.1	8.5	2.8	2.6	11.3	15.1	11.5
1969	9.1	7.1	14.0	2.8	6.1	14.5	20.6	17.1
1970†	7.1	2.7	...	2.8	3.2	...	...	...
Middle East								
1961–65	7.5	5.6	10.6	2.9	4.4	9.2	19.0	14.3
1969	8.2	−2.5	17.5	3.1	5.0	11.0	20.8	15.0
1970†	5.1	−1.1	...	3.1	2.0	...	...	...
South Asia								
1961–65	3.4	0.8	9.7	2.5	0.8	6.3	16.3	14.1
1969	4.5	3.6	7.6	2.4	2.1	11.0	16.3	14.4
1970†	4.8	3.3	...	2.4	2.3	...	...	...
Western Hemisphere								
1961–65	4.9	4.0	6.0	3.0	1.9	4.6	19.3	18.2
1969	6.3	4.9	8.8	3.1	3.2	8.1	19.7	17.9
1970†	6.6	1.5	...	3.1	3.4	...	...	...
Industrialized countries‡								
1961–65	5.2	1.8	6.1	1.2	3.9	6.7	21.4	21.9
1969	4.8	0.2	7.2	1.0	3.7	7.9	22.3	22.8
1970†	3.4	−1.5	...	1.0	2.4	...	...	...

*Less developed countries (74 countries and territories covering approximately 96% of GDP of all less developed areas with market economies): Africa—Algeria, Angola, Cameroon, Congo (Kinshasa), Egypt, Ethiopia, Gabon, Ghana, Ivory Coast, Kenya, Libya, Malagasy Republic, Malawi, Mali, Mauritius, Morocco, Niger, Nigeria, Rhodesia, Senegal, Sudan, Tanzania, Togo, Tunisia, Uganda, Upper Volta, and Zambia (coverage 91%); south Asia—Burma, Ceylon, India, and Pakistan (coverage 100%); east Asia—Cambodia, Hong Kong, Indonesia, Korea, Malaysia, Philippines, Singapore, Taiwan, Thailand, and Vietnam (coverage 100%); southern Europe—Cyprus, Greece, Portugal, Spain, Turkey, and Yugoslavia (coverage 100%); Western Hemisphere—Argentina, Bolivia, Brazil, Chile, Colombia, Costa Rica, Dominican Republic, Ecuador, El Salvador, Guatemala, Guyana, Honduras, Jamaica, Mexico, Nicaragua, Panama, Paraguay, Peru, Trinidad and Tobago, Uruguay, and Venezuela (coverage 99%); Middle East—Iran, Iraq, Israel, Jordan, Lebanon, and Syria (coverage 78%).
†Preliminary.
‡Industrialized countries: Australia, Austria, Belgium, Canada, Denmark, Finland, France, Germany, Iceland, Italy, Japan, Luxembourg, Netherlands, New Zealand, Norway, South Africa, Sweden, Switzerland, United Kingdom, and United States.
Source: World Bank.

Table II. Trade Balance of Less Developed Countries

Item	In U.S. $000,000,000					
	1965	1966	1967	1968	1969	1970*
Less developed countries						
Exports (f.o.b.)	39.0	42.1	43.7	47.6	53.5	59.6
Imports (c.i.f.)	44.1	48.3	49.7	54.0	59.3	66.0
Trade balance	−5.1	−6.2	−6.0	−6.4	−5.8	−6.4
Excluding less developed countries of southern Europe†						
Exports (f.o.b.)	35.6	38.1	39.3	43.0	48.2	53.4
Imports (c.i.f.)	37.2	40.2	41.6	45.4	49.3	54.0
Trade balance	−1.6	−2.1	−2.3	−2.4	−1.1	−0.6
Excluding southern Europe and major petroleum exporters‡§						
Exports (f.o.b.)	27.5	29.5	29.7	32.3	36.9	41.0(est.)
Imports (c.i.f.)	33.2	35.9	36.9	39.9	43.5	48.0(est.)
Trade balance	−5.7	−6.4	−7.2	−7.6	−6.6	−7.0

*Preliminary.
†Greece, Portugal, Spain, Turkey, Yugoslavia.
‡Iran, Iraq, Kuwait, Libya, Saudi Arabia, Venezuela.
§Estimate for Saudi Arabia derived from growth of 1st and 2nd quarter.
Source: International Monetary Fund, *International Financial Statistics*.

Table III. Total Official and Private Flows of Long-Term Financial Resources (Net)* from DAC Countries to Less Developed Countries and Multilateral Agencies by Country

Country	In U.S. $000,000											
	Official flows				Private flows				Total flows			
	1967	1968	1969	1970†	1967	1968	1969	1970†	1967	1968	1969	1970†
Australia	168	157	175	209	26	49	58	159	194	206	232	368
Austria	27	22	17	20	21	52	64	73	48	74	81	93
Belgium	98	106	119	121	66	137	139	173	164	243	258	294
Canada	213	214	295	402	59	94	69	176	272	308	364	578
Denmark	28	29	55	56	−3	54	96	38	25	83	151	94
France	825	874	959	978	516	846	751	827	1,341	1,720	1,710	1,805
Germany, West	547	596	544	731	594	1,068	1,502	678	1,141	1,664	2,046	1,409
Italy	156	149	137	171	131	401	(710)	553	287	550	848	724
Japan	584	659	811	1,152	214	390	452	669	798	1,049	1,263	1,821
Netherlands	113	135	150	199	115	141	219	241	228	276	369	440
Norway	15	24	38	37	15	35	37	26	30	59	75	63
Portugal	46	35	80	57	32	13	18	7	78	48	98	64
Sweden	60	72	120	117	61	57	86	87	121	129	206	204
Switzerland	5	18	24	26	131	223	95	99	136	241	119	125
United Kingdom	477	429	429	454	326	331	717	784	803	760	1,146	1,238
United States	3,652	3,532	3,257	3,218	1,922	2,116	1,459	2,175	5,574	5,648	4,716	5,393
Total	7,014	7,051	7,210	7,948	4,226	6,007	6,472	6,765	11,240	13,058	13,682	14,713

*Net of loan repayments and private capital repatriation.
†Preliminary.
Source: OECD, *Development Assistance 1970 and Recent Trends*.

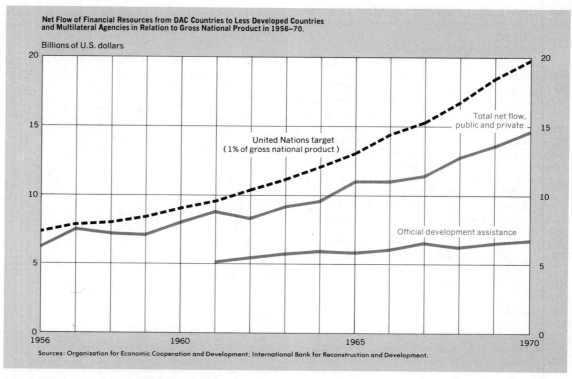

Net Flow of Financial Resources from DAC Countries to Less Developed Countries and Multilateral Agencies in Relation to Gross National Product in 1956–70.

Billions of U.S. dollars

Total net flow, public and private

United Nations target (1% of gross national product)

Official development assistance

Sources: Organization for Economic Cooperation and Development; International Bank for Reconstruction and Development.

the total, amounting to $6.81 billion in 1970, as compared with $6.62 billion in 1969. Grants increased slightly in absolute terms, but remained at about 65% of the total, as compared with almost 90% at the beginning of the 1960s. The increase in the total official flows resulted from a sharp increase in "other official flows," primarily officially financed export credits at rather hard terms. Thus, while the average terms of official development assistance loans tended to improve slightly in 1970 as compared with 1969 (average maturity years lengthened from 28.1 years to 29.7 years while average interest rates declined from 2.9 to 2.7%), the average financial terms of all official loans probably became harder. (*See* Table V.)

Private Capital. The net flow of private capital from DAC countries increased further in 1970 to $6.8 billion, compared with $6.5 billion in 1969. This was more than double the 1964 figure of $3.2 billion and continued an upward trend that began in 1962–63. The U.S. was the single most important source of private capital for the less developed countries, though it provided a somewhat smaller proportion of private capital than of official assistance. Since 1965, there had been rapid and substantial increases in the private capital flows of Australia, Canada, Italy, Japan, and the Netherlands.

The most important changes in private capital had been the large increases in private export credits to the less developed countries and in direct private bilateral lending, consisting for the most part of loans from banks and other financial institutions. These changes paralleled similar developments in official lending and helped explain the seriousness of the growing external debt problem of the less developed countries. By the end of 1969 the total outstanding debt of 81 less developed countries for which data were available had reached $59.3 billion, an increase of 9.3% over the end of 1968. Countries in all regions had assumed large external debts. (*See* Table IV.) Fifteen countries (Argentina, Brazil, Chile, Colombia, India, Indonesia, Iran, Israel, Korea, Mexico, Paki-

Table IV. External Public Debt Outstanding and Debt Service Payments of Less Developed Countries*

In U.S. $000,000

Year	Total	Africa	East Asia†	Middle East‡	South Asia§	Southern Europe‖	Western Hemisphere¶
Debt outstanding Dec. 31							
1966	42,727	7,322	4,306	3,005	10,699	4,346	13,049
1967	48,441	8,231	5,252	3,742	11,489	5,082	14,646
1968	54,258	8,803	6,309	4,355	12,837	5,595	16,359
1969—Total	59,331	9,184	7,609	4,883	13,809	6,228	17,618
—Disbursed	45,741	7,010	5,549	3,883	11,113	4,620	13,567
—Undisbursed	13,590	2,173	2,061	1,001	2,696	1,608	4,051
Service payments during							
1966	3,787	480	226	278	428	442	1,934
1967	3,978	476	260	241	511	440	2,050
1968	4,527	601	284	364	542	497	2,240
1969	4,968	725	436	475	618	532	2,183

Note: Items may not add to totals due to rounding.
*Includes the following countries: Africa—Botswana, Burundi, Cameroon, Central African Republic, Chad, Congo (Kinshasa), Dahomey, Egypt, Ethiopia, Gabon, Ghana, Guinea, Ivory Coast, Kenya, Lesotho, Liberia, Malagasy Republic, Malawi, Mali, Mauritania, Mauritius, Morocco, Niger, Nigeria, Rhodesia, Rwanda, Senegal, Sierra Leone, Somalia, Sudan, Swaziland, Tanzania, Togo, Tunisia, Uganda, Upper Volta, and Zambia, plus the East African Community; east Asia—Indonesia, Korea, Malaysia, Philippines, Singapore, Taiwan, and Thailand; Middle East—Iran, Iraq, Israel, Jordan, and Syria; south Asia—Afghanistan, Ceylon, India, and Pakistan; southern Europe: Cyprus, Greece, Malta, Spain, Turkey, Yugoslavia. Western Hemisphere—Argentina, Bolivia, Brazil, Chile, Colombia, Costa Rica, Dominican Republic, Ecuador, El Salvador, Guatemala, Guyana, Honduras, Jamaica, Mexico, Nicaragua, Panama, Paraguay, Peru, Trinidad and Tobago, Uruguay, and Venezuela.
†Does not include publicly guaranteed private debt of Philippines estimated at $600 million in 1969.
‡Does not include undisbursed portion of the debt of Israel.
§Includes some nonguaranteed debt of the private sector of India.
‖Does not include nonguaranteed debt of the "social sector" of Yugoslavia contracted after March 31, 1966, amounting to $960 million in 1969.
¶Debt outstanding of Brazil includes some nonguaranteed debt of the private sector to suppliers and excludes the undisbursed portion of suppliers' credits and of bilateral official loans except for those owed to the U.S. government.
Source: World Bank.

Table V. Average Terms of Official Development Assistance Loan Commitments

Country	Maturity (years) 1969	1970	Average interest rate (%) 1969	1970
Total DAC countries	28.1	29.7	2.9	2.7
United States	37.1	37.4	3.0	2.6
United Kingdom	24.1	28.6	1.2	1.7
France	17.0	16.2	3.7	3.7
Germany, West	26.0	27.6	3.2	2.9
Italy	10.2	13.1	5.3	4.9
Japan	19.5	21.4	3.7	3.7

Source: OECD, Development Assistance Committee.

stan, Peru, Spain, Turkey, Yugoslavia) had debts of over $1 billion each, with India's external public debt totaling nearly $9 billion. Service payments during 1969 reached nearly $5 billion, about 40% of which was accounted for by the Western Hemisphere since these countries received relatively less "official development" assistance.

The external debt problem gave heightened importance to the consideration being given the third replenishment of the resources of the International Development Association, an affiliate of the World Bank Group providing development finance on highly concessional terms. By June 1971 all of IDA's available funds had been committed for specific projects. Negotiations for the replenishment of IDA's resources at a level of $813 million a year for three years beginning July 1971 had been completed, but the agreement could not become effective without the adherence of the U.S. and 11 other countries. While awaiting U.S. congressional action, a number of countries made advance contributions to enable IDA to continue its operations.

New Developments. On April 21, 1971, U.S. Pres. Richard Nixon submitted to Congress his legislative proposals for a reorganization of the U.S. foreign assistance program. These involved the replacement of the existing Agency for International Development (AID) by two new institutions, an International Development Corporation, which would administer long-term loans to less developed countries while functioning as fully as possible within the framework set by the international financial institutions, and an International Development Institute, which would administer a reformed technical assistance program.

Before action could be taken on these matters, however, the entire concept of a U.S. foreign assistance program was brought into question. In the wake of the anti-U.S. sentiment displayed during the UN debate on seating Communist China, the Senate in a surprise vote on October 29 killed the entire $2.9 billion foreign aid appropriation for fiscal 1972. The administration came vigorously to the program's support; the House repassed its original bill and the Senate passed two bills dividing aid into its economic and military components. When the two houses were unable to compromise their differences, a continuing resolution was passed maintaining the program at its current level until early 1972. It seemed unlikely that foreign aid would be killed entirely, but clearly the subject had ceased to be sacrosanct and the future was unclear.

A more encouraging example of action in the field of international development was the decision reached in September 1970 by DAC regarding the "untying" of bilateral aid, *i.e.,* relating the provision of aid to procurement in the donor country. There was almost unanimous agreement in principle that the 16 member countries would "untie" their bilateral development aid loans.

In July 1971 the UN Development Program (UNDP) and the UN Research Institute for Social Development (UNRISD) announced that they were jointly sponsoring a project to identify all of the major social and economic implications of the Green Revolution, the widespread introduction of new varieties of high-yielding food grains. A number of published reports and studies had claimed that the Green Revolution was giving rise to social and economic problems; for example, small and tenant farmers frequently lack the financial resources needed to

take advantage of the new opportunities, while the mechanization adopted by larger farmers might nullify the hoped-for increases in employment and wages.

A similar sense of urgency permeated the international development strategy for the Second United Nations Development Decade, which had been adopted by the UN General Assembly on Oct. 24, 1970. Among its goals and objectives, the strategy proposed that the average annual growth rate in the gross product of the less developed countries be at least 6%. The growth of the per capita gross product of the less developed countries as a whole "should be about 3.5%," but this was calculated on the assumption that population increases would, on average, be no more than 2.5% annually—or less than current projected forecasts.

The social objectives of the strategy reflected not only the older concerns such as education, nutrition, and housing, but also the more recent concerns with unemployment and the need for the fullest participation of youth and women in the development effort. The strategy also set forth the role the developed countries should play in achieving its objectives, but in this respect it did not go significantly beyond previous statements. (I. S. F.)

See also Agriculture; Commodities, Primary; Industrial Review; Inter-American Affairs; Investment, International; Payments and Reserves, International.

Disasters

The loss of life and property in disasters during 1971 included the following. (*See also* METEOROLOGY.)

AVIATION
Jan. 18 Zürich, Switz. Bulgarian Ilyushin-18 turboprop passenger plane crashed and burned in attempting an instrument landing at the fog-bound Zürich airport; 35 of the 37 persons aboard were killed.
Jan. 20 Near Lima, Peru. Peruvian Air Force transport plane crashed into a mountain; all 31 persons aboard were presumed dead.
Jan. 21 Near Privas, France. French Air Force Nord 262 turboprop transport went down in the mountainous Massif Central region; all 21 persons aboard died, including the crewmen and several high-ranking members of the French armed forces and of the French Atomic Energy Commission.
Jan. 25 Mérida, Venez. Venezuelan Viscount turboprop en route from Mérida to Caracas developed engine trouble and crashed in the Andes Mountains; at least 36 persons were killed.
April 15 Near Manila, Phil. Philippine Air Force plane faltered at takeoff from Basa Air Field, hit a creek embankment and split apart; 39 persons died, a small child survived.
May 23 Rijeka, Yugos. Yugoslav Tu-134 twin-jet charter plane carrying British tourists from London crashed and burned at the airport killing 78.
June 6 Near Azusa, Calif. U.S. Marine Phantom F-4 fighter jet collided with a DC-9 commercial airliner 12,000 ft. above the San Gabriel Mountains; both planes plunged into a mountain ravine killing 50 persons—49 aboard the liner and the F-4 pilot.
June 7 New Haven, Conn. U.S. Convair 580 propjet attempting to land in low visibility at Tweed-New Haven Airport crashed through three empty beach cottages, caught fire, and fell into a swamp; 28 of the 31 persons aboard the plane died.
July 3 Hakodate, Jap. Japanese YS-11 turboprop airliner approaching Hakodate airport in fog and rain struck a mountainside, broke up, and killed all 68 persons aboard.
July 30 Morioka, Honshu, Jap. The world's worst air disaster to date occurred when a Japanese Air Force F-86 jet fighter smashed into a Japanese Boeing 727 passenger plane 26,000 ft. over Morioka; all 162 persons aboard the airliner died, the student pilot of the F-86 parachuted to safety.
July 30 Pau, France. French military transport on a paratrooper training flight over the air base fell to the ground when an engine caught fire; 34 paratroopers and 3 aircrewmen were killed.
Aug. 11(?) Irkutsk, U.S.S.R. Soviet Tu-104 twin-jet commercial airliner en route from Odessa to Vladivostok crashed and exploded on takeoff from Irkutsk airport, killing all 97 persons aboard.
Aug. 18 Pegnitz, W.Ger. U.S. Army CH-47 Chinook twin-engine helicopter exploded in midair, plunged into a hayfield, and killed all 37 U.S. servicemen aboard.

Diamonds: *see* Mining

Disasters

D.P.A.—PICTORIAL PARADE

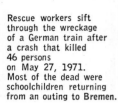

Rescue workers sift
through the wreckage
of a German train after
a crash that killed
46 persons
on May 27, 1971.
Most of the dead were
schoolchildren returning
from an outing to Bremen.

Sept. 4 Juneau, Alaska. U.S. 727 commercial jetliner beginning an approach into Juneau Airport slammed into a bare mountainside, broke into small pieces, and slipped into a deep gorge; all 111 persons died in the worst single-plane accident in U.S. air history.

Sept. 6 Hamburg, W.Ger. West German BAC 111 charter plane flying vacationers to Spain developed engine trouble at takeoff and in attempting an emergency landing on a superhighway struck an overpass bridge; 22 of the 120 persons aboard died, 42 others were hospitalized.

Sept. 16(?) Kiev, U.S.S.R. Hungarian Tu-134 airliner on a scheduled flight from Budapest to Kiev crashed near the Kiev Airport killing all 49 persons aboard.

Oct. 2 Ghent, Belg. British Vanguard turboprop airliner en route from London to Salzburg, Aus., went out of control when an engine exploded and fell in flames to the ground; all 63 persons aboard died.

Nov. 29 Near Phu Bai, S.Viet. U.S. Army CH-47 Chinook helicopter disappeared along the storm-swept north coast of South Vietnam; all 34 crewmen and military passengers were killed.

Dec. 24 Near Pucallpa, Peru. Peruvian Lockheed Electra turboprop passenger plane flying from Lima to Iquitos went down in a mountainous jungle area; all 92 persons aboard were believed dead.

FIRES AND EXPLOSIONS

Jan. 4 Auch, France. An explosion caused by accumulated gas shattered a concrete building and damaged a home; 14 persons died, 12 others were injured.

Feb. 3 Rolde, Neth. Fire sweeping through the wards of a home for the mentally retarded brought death to at least 13 patients.

Feb. 3 Brunswick, Ga. A Camden County munitions manufacturing complex was rocked by a blast thought to have been caused by magnesium trip flares; 25 persons were killed, and more than 100 others injured.

Feb. 16 Bangkok, Thai. Explosion and fire wrecked one wing of the Imperial Hotel and caused the deaths of at least 25 persons.

April 25 Seattle, Wash. Careless smoking was the apparent cause of a fire that raged through a three-story apartment building; 14 persons perished, 9 others were injured.

June 27 Czechowice, Pol. An explosion of unknown cause blew up a number of oil refinery tanks and killed 14 persons; 56 others were injured.

June 28 Near Mexico City, Mex. Fireworks explosion wrecked a building, killing at least 13 persons and injuring 6 others.

Oct. 19 Honesdale, Pa. Leaking gas was believed to have caused a blaze that swept a nursing home; 15 of the elderly residents perished, mostly from smoke inhalation.

Oct. 21 Glasgow, Scot. A busy shopping centre was severely damaged by a gas explosion that blasted 15 newly built stores, killed 13 persons, and injured at least 100 others.

Dec. 2 Hammond, Ont. A farmhouse was set afire when an oil furnace overheated in sub-zero temperature; 12 members of the family perished, 2 others were severely burned.

Dec. 14 Mufulira, Zambia. Nine freight cars being loaded with explosives as they stood at the siding of an explosives factory blew up and killed 29 persons.

Dec. 25 Seoul, S.Kor. The worst hotel fire in history was believed to have started in a second-story coffee shop of the plush 22-story Taeyonkak Hotel; the 12-hour holocaust took the lives of at least 157 persons and injured more than 100 others.

MARINE

Jan. 5 South Korea. Stormy weather in the eastern and southern coastal waters claimed 16 fishing boats; 28 sailors were missing and presumed dead.

Jan. 12 English Channel. West German freighter, the 2,695-ton "Brandenburg," hit the submerged bow of an oil freighter, the 20,545-ton "Texaco Caribbean" (which had gone to the bottom two days before), and sank within two minutes, taking 21 persons to their deaths.

Jan. 22 Off Cagliari, Sardinia. Explosions and fire struck the empty U.S.-owned oil tanker "Universe Patriot," killing 16 crewmen.

March 6 Off Folkestone, Eng. The 2,000-ton Greek freighter "Niki" foundered after striking wreckage in the English Channel and sank with a probable 23 persons aboard.

March 27 Off Cape Hatteras, N.C. The 661-ft. "Texaco Oklahoma," on a run from Port Arthur, Tex., to Boston with a cargo of 220,000 bbl. of heavy sulfur fuel oil, encountered heavy seas and snapped in two; 28 of the 44-man crew were missing and presumed dead.

Automobiles and homes
perch precariously
on the edge
of a 100-ft.-deep crater
left by a landslide
that buried 35 homes
and killed 31 persons
on May 4, 1971,
at St. Jean de Vianney,
Que.

"TORONTO STAR"

May 22 Off Vancouver, B.C. Norwegian cruise ship "Meteor" was severely damaged by an explosion and fire in the Strait of Georgia; all passengers were successfully evacuated but 32 seamen were lost.

June 12 Manila Bay, Phil. An excursion boat carrying factory workers on a trip around Corregidor Island capsized in stormy weather; 54 of the 120 excursionists drowned or were missing and presumed dead.

July 27 Near Palashipara, India. A Kharia river-crossing boat sank in midstream and at least 40 West Bengalis drowned.

Aug. 6 Persian Gulf. An Iranian boat transporting Iranian labourers headed for illegal entry into Kuwait struck a submerged rocky shelf and sank; an estimated 300 passengers drowned.

Aug. 28 Off Brindisi, Italy. Overcrowded Greek ferryboat, the 11,674-ton "Heleanna," caught fire during an overnight trip from Pátrai, Greece, to Ancona, Italy; 25 of the 1,127 persons aboard perished.

Nov. 9 Atlantic Ocean. Encountering a severe storm about 600 mi. off the French coast, the 9,400-ton French freighter "Maori" broke up and sank; most of the 39 crewmen were presumed lost.

Nov. 21 Central Philippines. A 30-ton wooden cargo vessel ferrying passengers between Leyte Island and Cebu ran into turbulent waters and went to the bottom; about 100 of the 200 persons aboard drowned or were missing and presumed dead.

MINING AND TUNNELING

May 16 Near Quetta, W.Pak. An explosion killed 32 workmen in a coal mine at Sinjabi.

June 24 Near Los Angeles, Calif. Natural gas exploded and triggered a 14-hour fire in a 5½-mi. water tunnel being drilled beneath the suburb of Sylmar; 17 workmen lost their lives.

Oct. 30 Hunedoara, Rom. The collapse of a settling tank caused a landslide that trapped a crew of miners working underground; 51 persons died and 88 others were injured.

Dec. 1 Near Keelung, Taiwan. An explosion 7,260 ft. underground in the Seven Star mine killed 41 miners; 7 others were missing and 4 seriously injured.

Dec. 11 Port Huron, Mich. Deadly methane gas exploded and ripped through a 6-mi. water tunnel being drilled 250 ft. under the surface of Lake Huron; 22 of the approximately 40 workers inside the tunnel died and 9 others were injured.

MISCELLANEOUS

Jan. 2 Glasgow, Scot. The end of a closely contested soccer game brought the fans hurtling out of their seats and through a steel crowd barrier; in the ensuing pileup 66 persons were trampled or crushed to death; at least another 100 were injured.

May 15 Sallen, France. Floorboards of a rented hall gave way at the close of a wedding reception and plunged the guests into a well beneath the floor; 13 persons perished.

Nov. 10 Koblenz, W.Ger. Collapse of a bridge under construction across the Rhine River killed 10 workmen; 12 others were missing, and 10 were injured.

Nov. 11 Kawasaki, Jap. A geological experiment to determine how heavy rainfall could trigger a landslide ended in the unexpected crumbling of a nearby cliff; 15 persons died in the roaring mud and dirt slide and 8 others were injured.

NATURAL

Jan. 4 Midwestern United States. Huge storm piled snow into 12-ft. drifts stranding thousands of motorists along a 1,000-mi. belt through Iowa, Illinois, Nebraska, Wisconsin, Kansas, Minnesota, and Michigan; 37 deaths were attributed to the storm.

Jan. 7 Temerloh region, Malaysia. Nine days of rain and flooding brought isolation to some 150,000 victims who perched on rooftops and roads awaiting relief; at least 60 persons were believed dead.

Jan. 29 Zambézia region, Mozambique. Torrential rains accompanying a cyclone inundated lowland areas and threatened 500,000 trapped residents with starvation; estimates of the death toll ranged from 500 to 1,000 persons.

Feb. 6 Toscana, Italy. Twin earthquakes struck within hours to destroy the ancient city of Tuscania; the city and 23 surrounding small towns suffered at least 22 fatalities; 120 other persons were injured, the homeless numbered 4,000, and property damage in Tuscania alone was estimated at $41.6 million.

Feb. 9 Eastern Australia. More than a week of heavy rains and flooding caused by Cyclone Sheila swamped New South Wales, Queensland, and Victoria; at least 27 persons died and damage amounted to about U.S. $20 million.

Feb. 9 San Fernando Valley, Calif. An earthquake of moderate intensity struck the Los Angeles area bringing death to 65 persons and injuring about 1,000 others; the quake proved to be the nation's most costly disaster with damages estimated at up to $1 billion.

Feb. 21 Louisiana and Mississippi. Twisters ripped through the ill-famed "Dixie Tornado Alley," hitting Mississippi with violent fury; 115 persons died (mostly in the Delta area) and 500 others were injured; property damage amounted to more than $7.5 million.

March 9 Near Quito, Ecuador. Tons of earth tumbled off a mountainside, blocking a major road and killing 20 to 30 persons; 6 others were injured.

March 18 Near Canta, Peru. Apparently triggered by a light earthquake, an avalanche of water, mud, and rocks roared down a slope of the Andes, overran the remote mining camp of Chungar, and buried as many as 600 persons.

March 21 Telefomin, New Guinea. A landslide in the Telefomin area buried about 100 villagers.

April 26 Central Philippines. In the wake of off-season Tropical Storm Wanda, heavy rains and violent winds brought death to at least 25 persons; more than 100 others were missing.

April 28 Central United States. Tornadoes slashed Kentucky, touched on Illinois and Tennessee, and killed at least 11 persons; more than 100 others were injured.

April 29 Salvador, Braz. Three days of heavy rain, floods, and landslides left more than 150 persons dead, 10,000 others homeless, and damages amounting to around $6 million.

May 4 St. Jean de Vianney, Que. Excessive rains led to an earth cave-in that dumped 35 homes, several cars, and a bus into a crater 70 ft. wide and 100 ft. deep; 31 persons perished.

May 12 Burdur, Turk. Severe earthquake shook the Burdur area in southwest Turkey, killing 57 persons.

May 22 Bingöl, Turk. Turkey's second quake within ten days centred in the eastern province of Bingöl, destroying 90% of the capital city of Bingöl and wreaking havoc on more than 300 mountain villages and hamlets; the official death toll stood at 1,000 persons.

June 16 Acapulco, Mex. Tropical Storm Brigitte with 95-mph winds and torrential rains struck the west coast resort area, leaving a reported 17 persons dead or missing.

June 26 Salgar, Colombia. Bursting its banks, a swollen mountain stream swept through dozens of village homes, claiming the lives of at least 15 persons; another 36 were missing.

July 8 Central Chile. A major earthquake caused heavy damage to the oil and copper refineries of the central coastal area; at least 82 persons died and about 450 others were injured.

July 20 Seoul, S.Kor. A cloudburst dumped seven inches of rain on the city and caused 45 deaths.

July 27 South Korea. Torrential rains brought on floods and landslides throughout the central and southwestern regions, killing at least 64 persons; 5 others were missing and about 45 injured.

July 28 Khinjan Pass, Afg. A landslide occurring near the pass in the Hindu Kush mountains opened a natural reservoir, allowing floodwaters to sweep through a village below, killing 100 persons.

Aug. 3 Baltimore County, Md. Several days of heavy rain and swollen rivers caused 13 deaths.

Aug. 5 Western Japan. Spawned in the Pacific, Typhoon Olive moved northward across the western part of Kyushu Island, leaving at least 135 persons dead or missing and presumed dead.

Aug. 17 Hong Kong. Typhoon Rose, with 130-mph winds, drenched Hong Kong and the harbour areas with 12 in. of rain, capsized about 40 fishing boats and a ferry (drowning 88 persons), and grounded another 26 oceangoing vessels; official death toll stood at about 90 persons; another 200 were injured.

Sept. 9 Uttar Pradesh, India. The worst floods in 11 years forced the evacuation of 35,000 persons from Lucknow, the capital city; officials stated that 300 persons died.

Sept. 9 Central America. Hurricane Edith came out of the Caribbean Sea with up to 175-mph winds, slammed into the coast of the Nicaragua-Honduras border and eastern areas of British Honduras, killing at least 23 persons.

Sept. 14 Southeastern Pennsylvania. Four-day downpour caused deep flooding and left 13 persons dead or missing; damages in Chester, Delaware, and Montgomery counties were estimated at $14 million.

Oct. 23 South Vietnam. Typhoon Hester tore into five northern provinces, flattening 17,000 homes and damaging another 40,-000 buildings with its 140-mph winds; 89 persons perished.

Oct. 29–30 Eastern India. Preceded by a cyclone, a 15-ft. tidal wave devastated a wide river-laced area of eastern Orissa State; officials estimated that possibly 10,000 to 25,000 persons died, with tens of thousands homeless, isolated, and facing starvation.

Veterans Administration Hospital in San Fernando, Calif., was heavily damaged and 47 patients were killed during an earthquake on Feb. 9, 1971.

UPI COMPIX

Unidentified guest leaps from an upper floor of the burning Taeyonkak Hotel in Seoul, South Korea, on Dec. 25, 1971. At least 157 persons were killed in the blaze.

WIDE WORLD

RAILROAD

Feb. 9 Aitrang, W.Ger. Trans-Europe Bavarian Express jumped the tracks and killed 28 persons; 35 others were injured.

Feb. 14 Near Zenica, Yugos. The engine of a local passenger train caught fire as the train was passing through the Vranduk tunnel; ensuing flames and gas fumes killed at least 34 persons and injured 113 others.

May 27 Near Wuppertal, W.Ger. A two-coach train returning a senior class group from an outing was rammed head-on by a freight as it rounded a blind curve between Oberbarmen and Radevormwald; of the 46 persons killed, 41 were students.

June 10 Tonti, Ill. Amtrak southbound streamliner traveling up to 95 mph tore up 1,200 ft. of track as it derailed into a twisted mass of flame and metal; 11 persons were killed, 164 others injured.

July 6 Mograhat, India. Collision of two trains resulting from the theft of electrical wires from the interstation communications system brought death to at least 16 persons and injured 50 others.

July 21 Near Karlsruhe, W.Ger. Switzerland Express with 300 to 400 passengers aboard derailed on a curve and killed at least 25 persons; about 100 others were injured.

Aug. 4 Belgrade, Yugos. Six-car passenger train collided with a freight, possibly due to poor visibility after a heavy rainstorm, about 16 mi. S of the city; at least 40 persons perished in the wreckage and 100 others were injured.

Oct. 25 Near Tsu, Jap. Two electric-powered passenger trains collided in a single-track tunnel, killing at least 23 persons; 9 others were missing, and at least 214 received injuries.

TRAFFIC

Feb. 5 Near Ibjar, Iran. A bus careened into a deep gorge, killing 30 persons.

March 25 Near Davao, Phil. A bus plunged into a river and brought death to 12 persons; 38 others were injured.

May 10 Near Chongpyong, S.Kor. Trapped in a bus that settled into a reservoir after falling off the roadway, at least 60 persons drowned; 14 others survived.

May 11 Lashkargah, Afg. Careless driving put a bus into an irrigation ditch and killed 21 persons; 6 others were injured.

June 20 Near Afyion, Turk. A collision between a truck and a bus resulted in 33 deaths; 24 persons were injured.

June 21 Cairo, Egy. Jammed with 17 festival-going persons, a taxicab plunged into a lake and sank, drowning 16 of the occupants.

June 27 Cairo, Egy. Swerving to avoid another vehicle, a truck veered into a canal, killing 15 persons and injuring 17 others.

July 11 Nainital Hill district, India. A bus fell into a lake, bringing death to 21 persons.

July 12 Roi-Et Province, Thailand. A bus ran head-on into a truck and killed 12 persons.

July 26 Simla, India. Dropping into a 100-ft. gorge, a bus caused the deaths of 14 persons and injured 45 others.

Aug. 7 Central Ghana. A truck slammed head-on into a bus on the Accra-Cape Coast road and killed 16 persons; 18 others received injuries.

Aug. 18 Near Casablanca, Mor. Plunging into a deep gorge, a rural bus brought death to 45 persons and injured 30 others.

Sept. 11 Bronkhorstspruit, S.Af. Collision between a truck and a school bus resulted in the deaths of 19 children.

Sept. 13 Thelwall, Eng. A patch of fog on M-6 major superhighway caused a massive pileup of 200 cars and trucks; at least 10 persons died and 61 others were hospitalized.

Sept. 17 Near Valdepeñas, Spain. A tourist bus traveling the main road to Andalusia collided with a brick-loaded truck, killing the truck driver and 17 Canadian women tourists.

Oct. 24 Walla Walla, Wash. Two-car collision caused 11 deaths; 1 other person was seriously injured.

Dec. 19 Aswan, Egy. An accident was reported to have occurred involving an overturned trailer that landed in an irrigation ditch and drowned 50 labourers.

Dominican Republic

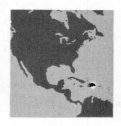

Covering the eastern two-thirds of the Caribbean island of Hispaniola, the Dominican Republic is separated from Haiti, which occupies the western third, by a rugged mountain range. Area: 18,658 sq.mi. (48,323 sq.km.). Pop. (1970): 4,011,589, including (1960) mulatto 73%; white 16%; Negro 11%. Cap. and largest city: Santo Domingo (pop., 1970, 671,402). Language: Spanish. Religion: Roman Catholic. President in 1971, Joaquín Balaguer.

President Balaguer began 1971 by announcing that social service programs would receive 41%, or $106,-659,815, of a total $264,312,333 governmental budget. Education's $53,561,988 allocation indicated the emphasis the government was placing on development of the country's human resources. Approximately 4,000 new teachers were needed to handle the 20% of the total Dominican population that was within elementary school age. Soaring enrollments also at-

---

DOMINICAN REPUBLIC

Education. (1968–69) Primary, pupils 685,562, teachers (including preprimary) 12,239; secondary, pupils 87,752, teachers 3,648; vocational, pupils *c.* 2,098; teacher training, students, 550, teachers 46; higher, students 15,757, teaching staff (1967–68) 918.

Finance. Monetary unit: peso, at parity with the U.S. dollar (2.40 pesos = £1 sterling), with a free rate (Sept. 27, 1971) of 2.48 pesos to £1 sterling. Gold, SDRs, and foreign exchange, central bank: (June 1971) U.S. $38.3 million; (June 1970) U.S. $34 million. Budget (1969 est.): revenue 186.7 million pesos; expenditure 230.3 million pesos. Gross national product: (1968) 1,169,200,000 pesos; (1967) 1,084,400,-000 pesos. Money supply: (March 1971) 161.9 million pesos; (March 1970) 149.4 million pesos. Cost of living (Santo Domingo; 1963 = 100): (March 1971) 105; (March 1970) 102.

Foreign Trade. (1970) Imports 266.8 million pesos; exports 213.6 million pesos. Import sources (1968): U.S. 55%; West Germany 7%; Japan 6%; Netherlands Antilles 5%. Export destination (1969): U.S. 90%. Main exports: sugar 52%; coffee 14%; cocoa 9%; bauxite 7%; tobacco 7%.

Transport and Communications. Roads (1969) *c.* 6,000 km. (including *c.* 2,500 km. main roads). Motor vehicles (1969): passenger 32,900; commercial (including buses) 17,700. Railways (1969) 220 km. (excluding *c.* 1,600 km. on sugar estates). Telephones (Jan. 1970) 40,174. Radio receivers (Dec. 1969) 160,000. Television receivers (Dec. 1969) 100,000.

Agriculture. Production (in 000; metric tons; 1969; 1968 in parentheses): rice 195 (181); corn 43 (40); cassava 170 (155), dry beans *c.* 34 (27); peanuts 70 (47); sweet potatoes 86 (100); sugar, raw value (1970–71) *c.* 1,000, (1969–70) *c.* 1,043; oranges *c.* 58 (58); bananas *c.* 50 (56); coffee 43 (44); tobacco (1970) *c.* 22, (1969) 21. Livestock (in 000; June 1970): cattle *c.* 1,100; sheep *c.* 84; pigs *c.* 1,330; horses *c.* 180; chickens *c.* 7,200.

Industry. Production (in 000; metric tons; 1969): bauxite 1,103; cement 390; electricity (kw-hr.) 855,-000.

tracted massive foreign assistance. At midyear, the U.S. Agency for International Development announced a $10.9 million loan for teacher training and for improving primary-school curricula. Higher education received a boost with the $3.4 million loan from the Inter-American Development Bank (IADB) to Santiago's Catholic University.

The 1971 housing appropriation, $4,135,442, reflected the country's rapid urban development and the need for building low-cost, multifamily units for the low-income group. A 2,000 multifamily unit National Housing Institute urban project, valued from $5 million to $6 million, was expected to provide dwellings for more than 2,000 low-salaried public employees (approximately 12,000 persons) in the Santo Domingo metropolitan region by February 1972. Another 3,000-unit project directed to private sector employees was being planned for Santo Domingo, Santiago, and 18 sugar mill towns throughout the countryside.

The serious water supply shortages that plagued the republic were reflected in a report showing that the national water supply system served only 30% of the population. To correct this imbalance, the government began the year with a $3.9 million water supply appropriation and started construction of approximately 70 rural aqueducts to serve an additional 79,000 Dominicans. IADB provided an additional $4.1 million loan to construct water supply systems for 180 rural communities.

Throughout the year, emphasis was placed on accelerating the timetable of multipurpose regional development projects slated for completion under the government's National Development Plan for the 1971–74 period. The first phase of the Tavera project in the northwest, scheduled to be completed by the end of 1972, included two 40,000-kw. power plants and a feasibility report on the irrigation and agricultural diversification of approximately 40,000 hectares in the project's downstream area. In the south, a $20 million integrated hydroelectric network was being established on the Nizao River.

Industrial production continued its upward trend due in large measure to a favourable investment climate, special provisions offered under the Industrial Incentives Act, and the efforts by the Investment Fund for Economic Development. In May, the UN announced progress made to date on developing an industrial centre near Santiago. Sixty sites were surveyed for small-scale food processing industries, and provision was being made to include an Industrial Free Zone, which would house a number of exporting industries.

On June 30 an attempted right-wing coup against the government was crushed. Its leader, retired Air Force Gen. Elías Wessin y Wessin, was arrested and later exiled.   (G. A. A.)

Drugs and Narcotics

In its report for 1970 to the Economic and Social Council of the United Nations, the International Narcotics Control Board again drew attention to the existence of a vast reservoir of raw materials—opium, coca, and *Cannabis*—from which the illicit traffic drew its supplies. Total seizures of all controlled drugs, whether in the form of raw material or of manufactured products, amounted to 624 tons in 1969. This included 40 tons of raw opium, 5 tons more than in 1968. In addition some 1,105 tons of *Cannabis* plants, in the form of both growing and dried plants (which included the dried flowering or fruiting tops), were seized in South Africa.

The board expressed concern at the apparently increasing volume of drugs finding its way into the illicit market and recorded its conviction that a global approach was essential for the ultimate elimination of illicit and uncontrolled production of narcotic raw materials. It looked forward to the possible formulation of an overall plan in light of the UN General Assembly resolution adopted in December 1968 which invited specialist agencies to cooperate with the other bodies concerned in discovering ways and means to eliminate this production.

The latest available figures furnished by countries that report to the board showed that in 1969 world production of opium rose to 1,219 tons (815 tons in 1968), a figure that had been exceeded only once since the end of World War II—in 1960, when production reached 1,261 tons. The foremost producing countries, India, Turkey, and the U.S.S.R., all increased their output. India produced 868 tons, which alone was more than the world total for each of the previous five years; Turkey's crop of 117 tons was slightly larger than in the two previous years; and the U.S.S.R. obtained 217 tons, its largest crop since it began furnishing statistics. Some 1,083 tons of opium went into the manufacture of 163 tons of morphine, 11 tons more than in 1968. The bulk of the morphine was converted into other narcotic drugs, especially codeine, which accounted for 89.5% of the total.

The total production of 14,603 tons of coca leaves in 1969 was the highest reported since the end of World War II. Of this, 4,860 tons were produced in Bolivia and the rest in Peru. Most of the leaves were used for chewing. Peru continued to be the main supplier of coca leaf for the manufacture of cocaine; in 1969 it exported 318 tons, almost all to the U.S.
                                                    (Pe. B.)

By 1971 reaction to drug use, drug abuse, and the illicit traffic in drugs in the U.S. had progressed from mythology and hysteria, through concern about the problem and an increasing awareness of its roots and scope, to a national involvement in the search for

Saigon police burn opium and marijuana seized in raids on drug dealers in June 1971. U.S. Ambassador to Vietnam Ellsworth Bunker met with Pres. Richard Nixon to discuss growing drug use among U.S. troops in Vietnam.

UPI COMPIX

practical solutions. There was also a growing realization that the problem did not exist in isolation. Curtailment of the opium poppy in Turkey as a cash crop had adverse effects on the Turkish national economy; the smuggling and illicit sale of heroin, hashish, and marijuana throughout Southeast Asia corrupted individuals and governments while addicting U.S. servicemen; the processing of narcotics in southern France for shipment to the U.S. brought with it international discord and distrust, as did the bulk shipment of amphetamines and other dangerous drugs from U.S. pharmaceutical firms to Mexico, for packaged reentry into the U.S. These factors, with others, were current items for debate and negotiation within the UN and among other international groups.

Within the U.S., there was as yet no unanimity of attitude that could be expressed as a national point of view on drug abuse. In some states punitive laws still equated the offense of the first-time experimenter in marijuana with the heroin "pusher," although the trend in attitude toward the drug abuser was veering toward help rather than harassment. At the base of the nationwide involvement, however, was the evolving realization that goals in prevention, treatment, and rehabilitation and goals in law enforcement would have to be reconciled if any national program to combat drug abuse was to be effective. This hypothesis stemmed from one hard fact: in 1971—using any of the measures available—drug use and abuse continued to increase and to increase within an ever widening age group. Heroin use, once contained within the ghetto, was in vogue in the barracks and the well-to-do suburbs. The use of marijuana was so widespread that it was no longer considered a symbol of dissent and rebellion by young people.

Faced with the spread of heroin use and the disdain for legal penalties evidenced by millions of marijuana users, a growing number of governmental and judicial officials at all levels agreed that curtailment of drug abuse could not be achieved solely through statutes and the procedures of "criminal justice." Pres. Richard Nixon signaled this change in official thinking in a statement on Sept. 17, 1971, when he signed Proclamation 4080 designating the week beginning October 3 as Drug Abuse Prevention Week. The president said, in part:

> Not so long ago it was easy enough to regard the tragedy of drug abuse as "someone else's problem." But recent years have brought that tragedy home—often very literally—to all Americans. We have learned that "drug abuse" refers not only to the crime-prone heroin addict that is the disease at its deadliest, with over 1,000 heroin fatalities annually in New York City. The term also refers to the suburban housewife dependent on tranquilizers and diet pills; to the student leaning on amphetamines to help him cram for exams; even to pre-teens sniffing glue.
> It has become a problem that touches each of us. Its manifestations are many and varied, but all grow from a common root—psychological and physical needs unmet through legitimate social channels—and all feed on common ignorance of the profound harm the drug abuser does to himself and society. Drug abuse is nothing less than a life and death matter for countless Americans, and for the moral fiber of this Nation. The drive to meet this threat must command from us our very best—our attention, our energies, our resources and our prayers.

The Federal Role. Acceptance by the federal government of the responsibility for developing a national program to combat the drug problem had been gradual. For many years, the government had operated treatment facilities for narcotic addicts at Lexington, Ky., and Fort Worth, Tex., but, for the most part, federal involvement in drug abuse centred in the Department of Justice and was primarily concerned with law enforcement. The first significant change in this

posture occurred in 1966 with the passage of the Narcotic Addict Rehabilitation Act; under terms of this statute, the federal government received a mandate to provide treatment and rehabilitation for those narcotic addicts who elected to accept civil commitment in lieu of standing trial for federal offenses, as well as volunteers for civil commitment. Development of the NARA program, however, would undoubtedly have proceeded at a deliberate pace had it not been for the sudden spread of the use of LSD and marijuana among young people. The public, which had largely ignored the abuse of narcotics as long as that abuse did not affect it directly, was suddenly confronted with a drug problem of unknown and frightening dimensions.

By 1968 congressional committees were packed with expert witnesses discussing the root causes of LSD and marijuana use. In 1970 Congress adopted the Comprehensive Drug Abuse Prevention and Control Act, which authorized support of a more comprehensive treatment program; grants for development of materials and curricula dealing with drug education; grants for training of professionals in treatment, rehabilitation, and education; and a special project grants program for detoxification and other special services.

As agencies within the federal government jockeyed for position in controlling administration of the program, they assembled data that the drug scene was evidencing marked changes. The "flower children" and "teenie-boppers" had dispersed. Some characteristics of the hippie culture, such as dress and language, had become the life-style of millions of young people, thereby dissipating the impact on the public. Simultaneously, the use of LSD was decreasing among students, the use of marijuana was increasing throughout the population, experimentation with multiple drug use was producing an alarming rise in the consumption of amphetamines and barbiturates, and—of greatest concern—heroin had escaped from the slums into the schools, the colleges, and the armed forces.

The Navy already had indicated public concern over use of LSD and other hallucinogenic drugs aboard ship (especially submarines) where, according to one congressional witness, "because of the possibility of relapse, a man is a constant danger to himself and his shipmates." In late 1970 another witness had testified that the drug picture among GIs in South Vietnam was "almost exclusively one of marijuana," but by mid-1971 evidence of heroin addiction among servicemen returning from Vietnam and stories of heroin peddling and smuggling throughout Southeast Asia were building to a crisis point.

Throughout the first half of 1971, numerous federal agencies prepared proposals recommending a variety of ways in which the federal government might mount a national drug abuse program. This traditional approach was terminated by the "heroin in Vietnam" crisis. By executive order in June 1971, President Nixon assigned central and overriding authority for federal efforts in solving the narcotic and drug abuse problem to the Executive Office of the President. He created the Special Action Office for Drug Abuse Prevention to direct and coordinate all federal programs relating to drug abuse; appointed Jerome H. Jaffe, who had headed a widely acclaimed drug project in Illinois, as the federal drug abuse "czar"; and submitted legislation to establish and fund such an office.

Jaffe's first efforts were directed toward the armed

forces in Vietnam. A poll taken in the spring of 1971 purported to show a 16.15% drug use rate among servicemen in Vietnam. By October, Jaffe reported to the Congress that the rate of drug dependency among servicemen in Vietnam "seems to have reached a plateau" at 5.1%. This conclusion, he said, was drawn from a three-month test of 103,279 men, in which—while the overall percentage was 5.1, or 5,214 men whose urinalysis showed positive for opiates—the Navy scored only 1.7% and the Air Force 1.3%, compared with 6.4% for the Army.

One of the announced objectives of the newly created White House office was to mount a crash program to find a blocking agent that would effectively help addicts to "kick the narcotic habit." This effort was hampered by delay—reportedly within the White House and the Office of Management and Budget—in releasing the funds needed to expand clinical testing of such blocking agents as cyclazocine, naloxone, and other new chemical compounds. The delay continued in the face of the president's June 17 special message to Congress, in which he said, "The deliberate procedures embodied in present efforts to control drug abuse are not sufficient. . . . The problem has assumed the dimensions of a national emergency." As that time, the president amended his fiscal 1972 budget, asking Congress for a government-wide total of $371 million for drug abuse programs, including the testing of antiaddiction compounds.

While waiting for legislative authority for its centralized drug abuse program, the administration was also requesting authority for the Department of Defense to: (1) order an individual to take an examination for the express purpose of determining drug dependency; (2) retain an individual on active duty for 30 days to commence treatment even though his service commitment was expiring. Additionally, the pending legislation would entitle an individual to be treated in a Veterans Administration hospital even if he had a dishonourable discharge.

Extent and Scope of the Problem. The only sources of information on nationwide illicit drug use were the results of polls. Other sources were mainly one-time studies of high school and college students conducted in scattered locations, during a period in which sampling techniques and survey methods varied in quality. Estimates of narcotic addiction in the U.S. are reported annually by the Bureau of Narcotics and Dangerous Drugs. Estimates of the size of the actual addict population in the U.S. can be approached by comparing the BNDD figures with those from the New York City Health Department's *National Register,* as well as through extrapolations of the number of heroin-related deaths in New York. These data indicated that in 1969 there were approximately 104,000 heroin addicts in New York City alone. Thus, the number of addicts throughout the U.S. might have been as high as 250,000.

For 1969, the number of users, categorized by the drug used, was estimated as follows: heroin 250,000; LSD, 1 million; amphetamines, taken orally, 4 million; marijuana, anywhere from 10 to 20 million; barbiturates, 2 million. The number of persons who injected amphetamines (mainlining), mixed barbiturates with other drugs (smorgasbord), or used inhalants (except glue sniffing) could not be estimated, except to assume from observation and anecdotal evidence that their numbers were small in comparison with the above estimates.

The scope of the drug problem had been variously and too often emotionally defined. However, from any point of view, its effects—direct and indirect—were causing national scrutiny of the nation's entire educational system, its legal and judicial procedures, the relevant roles of the medical and other health professions, child-parent relationships, and the availability of resources for drug-related research, treatment, and rehabilitation and for community ability to supply psychological and social support in providing satisfactory living experiences to the population, especially the young.

Treatment and the Methadone Controversy. Throughout the year, experiments in the treatment of heroin addiction under methadone maintenance programs became a nationwide controversy. A chemical blocking agent, methadone blocks the euphoric effects of heroin, but is itself an addictive drug. Taken orally in daily doses, methadone had helped sizable numbers of addicts to resume a more normal life. However, it is a short-acting drug; the long-term effects of widespread usage of an addicting drug to block another addiction had yet to be experienced; and, as methadone became more easily available, it too entered the illicit street market.

Because of the explosion of small methadone programs, regulations to control its use were finally evolved within the federal government and were printed in 1971 in the *Federal Register*. Methadone had become the treatment of choice for many addicts. However, the subject remained highly controversial, and experts in the field agreed that the search for a better way to block the effects of heroin must have the highest priority.

The entire subject of treatment of drug. abusers came under review in 1971, following passage of the Comprehensive Drug Abuse Prevention and Control Act. Because the statute provided for funding mechanisms available to states and communities, local government officials, physicians and other health professionals, and educators were working to assemble treatment components that could operate in a realistic climate of expectations and results.

In summary, professionals were arriving at the belief that prevention of drug abuse in the immediate future was an unattainable goal and that, rather, there must be a "sorting out" of drug abusers, so that treatment would be relevant to the needs of each individual. Increasing numbers of groups within communities were sponsoring "hot lines," which drug abusers could use in securing emergency help and counseling with an assurance of confidentiality. Crisis-intervention centres were also being developed as were detoxification centres.

One need was to provide appropriate services for "soft drug" users without equating them with criminal standards related to heroin users. In this regard, general hospitals, though somewhat reluctantly, had begun to assume responsibility for treatment of acute drug cases, as well as for rehabilitation. Among most physicians, involvement in treatment of drug abuse had been traditionally distasteful. The year 1971, however, saw the development of continuing education programs, through which doctors could learn treatment techniques, and a simultaneous push toward the establishment of new treatment training programs for allied health personnel.

Of importance to future treatment success was the tentative beginning of a search for methods by which organized, traditional medicine and the free clinic movement could collaborate to minimize the adverse

German shepherd trained to detect marijuana sniffs packages at the U.S. Customs Bureau in Oakland, Calif. Despite intensified enforcement procedures and education programs, drug use continued to grow during 1971.

effects of drug abuse. In 1971 approximately 150 "free clinics" existed throughout the U.S. Physicians and other helpers who had associated themselves with these free clinics found that in treating drug abuse, they were called upon to give advice and treatment relating to many other prevalent conditions.

Of equal importance was the need of the medical profession to intensify its review of accepted practice in prescribing drugs with potential for dependency and addiction. Although no study had produced specific evidence of a causal effect between the prescription of drugs and abuse of illicit drugs, common sense said that such a relationship must exist. In isolated instances, groups of physicians took the lead in, for example, ceasing to prescribe amphetamines for weight reduction. These concerns had already set up a chain reaction that also involved public discussion of the dissemination of drug advertising in all media.

Research. Because the "great marijuana debate" continued to develop more on the basis of fable than of fact, the National Institute of Mental Health was assigned responsibility within the federal government in 1969 to provide for a high-priority research effort concerned with all aspects of *Cannabis* (marijuana), ranging from its basic chemistry to the psychosocial correlates of its use. By 1971 the NIMH program, which included some 66 projects costing nearly $3 million a year, had achieved several major objectives:

It had made *Cannabis* research "respectable," so that highly competent researchers were no longer averse to entering the field for fear of adverse publicity and colleague disapproval.

It had made available in standard-dosage forms of known potency a wide variety of natural and synthetic materials basic to continued research.

Investigations had shown that not only is delta-9-THC (the most active ingredient of marijuana) rapidly broken down in the body, but that some metabolites can be found up to six to eight days after a single administration. This suggested a long duration of action and possible interference with other drugs.

Toxicity studies performed during the year clearly showed a very large safety index between the behaviourally active and toxic doses.

Both subjective and objective effects of single-dose, acute administration of *Cannabis* and its active components had been largely elucidated.

Overseas research efforts concerned with the chronic effects of *Cannabis* were to be expanded. Studies of actual users in the U.S. continued to be complicated by the fact that marijuana use was illegal and frequently involved the threat of severe penalties. As a result, it was difficult to obtain accurate information on the extent and changing patterns of use. Development of coding methods to protect the anonymity of

an individual had already been helpful, however, and could be expected to make possible the derivation of increasingly satisfactory data on the long-term career of the drug user.

The marijuana commission funded by Congress completed the first year of its two-year study in 1971. Its findings had not been announced, but their effect had already been limited by statements of the president and the attorney general that no matter what the findings of the commission, they would not favour legalization of the use of marijuana.

Research on other "soft drugs" was also accelerated. Current findings related to the effects of amphetamines, for example, indicated that these drugs have potential for serious dependency, addiction, and even death. The emergence during the preceding year or so of the youthful "polydrug" user heightened the need for additional research on the interrelationship of the effects of all drugs.

Research related to the opiates, as previously indicated, was concentrated on the search for more effective, long-lasting blocking agents. Studies of the heroin user were being conducted simultaneously with treatment of the known addict. However, psychosocial studies of heroin users who had escaped detection by law enforcement officers and the courts were limited to clandestine surveys within the heroin culture. Not until the user was assured of anonymity could this research provide definitive data.

The Search for Alternatives. Among the earliest federal efforts to combat drug abuse was the support, through the National Institute of Mental Health and the Department of Health, Education, and Welfare, of the dissemination of factual information about drugs through the mass media. To emphasize the need to get this information to the public, President Nixon invited TV executives, radio executives, and members of the clergy to successive meetings at the White House where informational materials were presented.

Simultaneously, support was provided to train teachers, so that they could, themselves, understand the drug abuse phenomenon among their students, recognize its symptoms, and provide information and counseling acceptable to young people. This effort continued. Additionally, however, during 1971 countless individuals and groups were involved in a spontaneous search for alternatives to drug abuse that could be provided to young people in their communities. In an effort to channel these efforts into effective action, the NIMH was developing a program of support for such efforts.

The necessity for such action could not be ignored, in light of preliminary results of 1971 surveys of drug use in the junior and senior high schools. According to data assembled by the NIMH, in 1970, at the junior and senior high school level, almost every rate of usage for all drugs surveyed (including alcohol and tobacco) was generally less than during 1969. While marijuana use rates rose in the school year ending in 1970, the rise was much less than between 1968 and 1969. However, preliminary results for the 1971 school year showed a marked increase in the use of all of the drugs with the exception of tobacco. And although the data were incomplete and could not as yet be attributed to their source, alcohol use, which some had suggested might be replaced by marijuana, showed the largest apparent increase. Clearly, much more needed to be learned about the careers of drug users and the factors influencing their behaviour.   (S. F. Y.)

Economics

Inflation and unemployment in theory and practice dominated the literature in economics during 1971. Success in the use of macroeconomic fiscal and monetary policies during the Kennedy-Johnson administrations in the U.S. had led to the optimistic view that economists had at last learned how to stimulate continuous economic expansion with reasonable price stability. As inflation accelerated and unemployment simultaneously worsened, however, more and more economists began to question the basic adequacy of fiscal and monetary policies as the key to noninflationary prosperity.

Robert Eisner of Northwestern University asked a question that was on the minds of many economists: What went wrong? (*Journal of Political Economy,* May/June 1971). His question referred to the failure of restrictive fiscal and monetary measures to retard the war-induced price inflation of the late 1960s and early 1970s. The temporary surtax on personal incomes imposed during the Johnson administration was not likely to be effective because current consumer spending is related to permanent rather than temporary income. Likewise, temporary corporate income surtaxes are not likely to deter business investment. Even the length and variability of time lags elapsing between the inauguration and the effect of fiscal and monetary changes may render them irrelevant in terms of policy. Eisner found monetary policy even less potent than fiscal policy. If his findings were valid, fiscal and monetary policies should not be expected to prevent war-induced inflation, and the way to avoid war inflation, he concluded, was to avoid war.

Throughout the 1960s the predominant Keynesian economics was under challenge from the monetarist school, for whom money was the strategic factor determining prosperity and price stability. The monetarist challenge probably crested and began to recede during 1971. Monetarist influence was strong among some leading economic advisers in Pres. Richard Nixon's administration, but during 1971 Nixon was reported to have said he had become a Keynesian. Certainly the price-wage freeze of 1971, while not a Keynesian measure, was a blow to monetarism.

Harry Johnson of the London School of Economics and the University of Chicago appraised the relative strengths of the Keynesian and monetarist schools of thought in the Ely lecture ("The Keynesian Revolution and the Monetarist Counter-Revolution," *American Economic Review,* May 1971). He concluded that the monetarist counterrevolution would peter out because its appeal rested on the social importance of inflation, which is, according to Johnson, a less serious social problem than mass unemployment, the basis of the Keynesian position.

Inflation is undesirable because it results in an arbitrary and often inequitable redistribution of income and wealth, but unemployment, if it leads to price deflation, may also have this effect, as well as resulting in the loss of real income and wealth. Andrew Brimmer, examining the effect of inflation on income distribution in the U.S. during the 1960s (*Review of Economics and Statistics,* February 1971), found a marked shift in the relative distribution of personal income in favour of the lower two quintiles and away from the top quintile of income recipients.

He also found that nonwhite families gained relative to white families. As W. C. Fields might have said, a phenomenon that redistributes income from the rich to the poor cannot be all bad. Clearly a family with fixed money income is harmed by a fall in the value of a unit of money, but an unsophisticated observer tends to see only one side of the inflationary process. He sees his level of living undermined by a rise in the cost of living (retail price inflation); if he also receives an increase in wages or salary (in excess of any increase in his productivity), he probably will not see that he is helping to cause the inflation he decries. Higher wages mean higher costs, and higher costs lead to higher prices. Cost-push inflation was characteristic of 1970 and 1971, in contrast with the demand-pull inflation of the late 1960s when the Vietnam war added heavy government expenditures to an already full-employment economy.

Among American economists, a longtime advocate of price and wage controls was J. K. Galbraith, who was president-elect of the American Economic Association during 1971. The 1971 price-wage freeze occurred despite the fact that Nixon and his close economic advisers had long opposed direct controls over prices and wages, so that Galbraith characterized the freeze as a "triumph of circumstance over ideology" (*Business Week,* Oct. 16, 1971, p. 74). Galbraith envisioned price and wage restraints as a permanent part of the U.S. economic policy, but he believed that the controls could be largely confined to big corporations and big unions. (D. D.)

See also **Nobel Prizes.**

Economy, World

The world economy in 1971 remained in the phase of lessened growth in which it had found itself in the previous year. The volume of total output of goods and services in the world outside the U.S.S.R., China, and the countries in their spheres of influence increased during 1971 by only 3.3%—somewhat more than in 1970 but markedly below the average annual growth rate of 5.5% during the decade of the 1960s.

The United States, which still accounts for nearly one half of the world's output, experienced a moderate recovery but the pace of economic activity in other countries slowed down. As in the U.S. in 1970, recessionary tendencies in Western Europe and Japan during 1971 were mild by historic standards. But the turmoil in exchange markets stemming from the suspension on August 15 of what remained of the convertibility of the U.S. dollar into gold, and from the imposition of a surcharge on imports of manufactures into the U.S., brought dark clouds to the economic horizons of Western Europe, Japan, and less developed parts of the world. Apprehension about the sluggish recovery of the U.S. economy, evidenced strikingly in the pronounced stock market decline during October and much of November, was widespread among Americans. To dissipate the depressive effects of these uncertainties—and also to alleviate the monetary and commercial tensions and frictions within the capitalist world—the administration in mid-December accepted, subject to congressional approval, devaluation of the dollar in terms of gold as part of the currency realignments and lifted the import surcharge. These steps produced a sense of relief; but the formidable difficulties encountered in international trade and payments remained untouched.

Pres. Richard Nixon,
flanked by the United
Kingdom's Chancellor
of the Exchequer Anthony
Barber (left)
and West Germany's
Finance Minister Karl
Schiller (right), announces
the devaluation
of the dollar at a news
conference in Washington,
D.C., on Dec. 18, 1971.

The Sluggish Pace. The U.S. achieved in 1971 an annual rate of real growth of about 2.7%—an improvement from a decline of 0.7% in 1970, but well below the 4.5% annual average during the decade ended 1969 (*see* Table I). Industrial production posted a rise of only 3.1%, but it picked up more vigorously toward the year-end (*see* Chart 1). The U.S. economy thus managed to show an advance from the depressed level to which it had been reduced in 1970 by the General Motors strike and the underlying recession; but the upturn lacked real bounce—in marked contrast with the recoveries from earlier recessions (*see* Table II).

Like the 1969–70 recession, which had begun in the consumer sector, the recovery in 1971 was sparked by a rise in consumer spending—spending, however, that was more spectacular on automobiles than on other retail goods. Auto sales were stimulated by the promise made in mid-August by U.S. Pres. Richard Nixon to repeal and refund the federal excise tax on autos; the buyers received this "found" money on Christmas Eve. Expectations among consumers that the price freeze imposed in mid-August for three months inevitably would be followed by increases in prices of all manufactured goods also were a factor.

Canada, which entered 1971 with a considerable economic slack, experienced a notable rise in output during the year. In Japan and Western Europe, output slowed. Japan, the most rapidly growing industrial economy and, after the U.S., the second industrial power (not counting the U.S.S.R.), saw its output rise by a mere 4.75%, against 10.7% in 1970—a condition characterized as a mini-recession. West Germany, the third industrial power, began to feel the recessionary tendencies after its longest and strongest boom of the postwar period. For the U.K., the real growth of output was, at 1.5%, even slower than in previous years but, toward the year-end, it began to move upward. France, with a 5.5% advance in real output, was second only to Canada in economic performance; but it slowed down toward the year-end. Italy's production declined markedly, in part because of social unrest. Output also leveled off in Austria, the Netherlands, and Switzerland and turned downward in Belgium and Sweden.

Stagnating or declining industrial output increased unemployment—in several countries to the highest levels since the 1930s. Unemployment in excess of one million in the U.K. was at year-end somewhat over 4% of the labour force. In Italy the number of registered unemployed was more than one million, one-fifth higher than at the beginning of 1971. In West Germany, unemployment late in the year was less than 1% of the labour force, a low figure but more than 50% above the level of 1970.

In the U.S. unemployment reached 6.1% of the labour force in December, a level distinctly higher than a year earlier; technical and professional unemployment created a unique social problem. But civilian employment increased during the year by 1.7 million to 80,133,000. The unemployment rate among white workers in December was 5.4%; nonwhite unemployment was 10.3%, almost double the white rate. If statistics can be trusted, it would appear that

Table I. Growth of Real Gross National Product

Country	Annual percent changes		
	1958–69	1970	1971
Canada	4.8	3.3	5.8
France	5.7	5.9	5.5
Japan	11.2	10.7	4.8
Germany, West	5.1	5.4	3.5
United States	4.5	−0.7	2.7
United Kingdom	3.1	2.2	1.5
Italy	5.7	5.2	0.5
Major countries*	5.4	2.4	3.2
Other industrial countries	5.2	5.4	4.0
Overall increase	5.4	2.7	3.5

*Excluding the U.S.S.R., Eastern European countries, China, etc.
Source: Adapted from OECD, *Economic Outlook* (December 1971).

Table II. Upturn in the U.S. Economy Compared with Earlier Recovery Periods

Item	Percent increase				
	1949–50	1954–55	1958–59	1961–69	1970–71
Real GNP*	12.2	6.9	6.6	6.0	4.1
Industrial production†	27.7	14.8	20.9	13.4	4.3
Unemployment rate:					
At turning point	7.9	6.0	7.4	6.9	5.9
After 12 mos.	4.2	4.2	5.2	5.5	6.0
Real consumer spending*	8.7	6.3	5.1	4.2	4.7
Corporate profits*	52.5	26.8	38.6	23.4	16.8

*Percentage change in three quarters past the business cycle turning point.
†Percentage change in 12 months past the turning point.
Source: Adapted from U.S. Department of Commerce, *Business Conditions Digest.*

Canada, despite its record as the country furthest along on the business cycle upswing, had the highest unemployment—6.2% of the labour force reported for December.

The primary-producing nations of Latin America, Asia, and Africa were affected adversely by the less buoyant demand in the industrial world for metals, rubber, wool, and other commodities, with the main exception of oil; prices of many raw materials slithered to the lowest levels in recent years. This drop occurred at the same time that prices continued to rise on manufactures that the primary-producing countries import. The exchange rates of the less developed countries generally remained unchanged in terms of the U.S. dollar and some of them even were devalued against it—moves that meant lower earnings from exports of the primary-producing nations to Europe and Japan and higher costs of imports from them. The terms of trade thus turned against the less developed countries just as government assistance and private investment slowed down, in part because of balance of payments difficulties and in part because of the less hospitable climate for investment in several countries of Latin America, Africa, and Asia.

Like output, the volume of world trade increased less than in 1970—by some 7%, compared with 8.5% in the previous year. Initially this slowdown in the volume of world trade and world shipping had reflected recessionary conditions in the U.S. in 1970. Despite the renewed growth in the U.S. economy in 1971, however, sluggishness in Europe and Japan held down world trade as a whole.

Factors Behind the Slowdown. Demand pressures eased considerably in Japan and most Western European countries during 1971, as they had in 1970 in the U.S. In the second half of 1971 there was no evidence of overheating in most of the industrial countries of Europe or in Japan, and there existed a significant margin of spare capacity. In the U.S., output was estimated at about 6% below the level compatible with an unemployment rate of 4.5%. In the rest of the industrial world, underutilization of capacity was probably around 3.5%, with particularly large margins in the U.K. and Canada, and more recently in Japan and Italy, but not in France or West Germany. In West Germany, the last economy that cooled off, capacity utilization declined to more normal levels.

As in the U.S. in 1970, output in Western Europe and Japan was being held back by inflation to a decisive extent during 1971. Inflation cuts the buying power of both consumers and businesses, including new outlays for plant and equipment. It cuts the buying power through the rise in prices of goods and services, through declines in the value of assets—equities, bonds, and tangible properties—and through the drying up of access to liquidity. Retrenchment thus becomes a necessity. As one nation after another was compelled to combat inflation, monetary and fiscal restraints also slowed down total demand.

The general price level in industrial countries rose in 1971 by 5.3%, a slight improvement from the 6% increase in 1970 but a disappointing result if compared with the 2.9% annual average increase during the decade ended in 1969 (see Table III). In the U.S., where the annual rate of inflation was 2.2% during the 1960s, the inflation rate was 4.6% in 1971, but the performance was better than the 5.5% rate of 1970, in part perhaps because of the price freeze. Among other major industrial countries, West Germany and the U.K. had substantially higher rates than the U.S., and somewhat higher rates than France and Italy. Only Japan and Canada did marginally better than the U.S. The same was true of consumer prices (see Chart 2).

Table III. Price Trends in Industrial Countries*

Country	Annual percent increases 1958–69	1970	1971
United Kingdom	3.3	7.7	8.5
Germany, West	2.9	7.3	6.8
Italy	3.8	6.3	5.8
France	4.1	5.7	5.5
United States	2.2	5.5	4.6
Japan	4.6	6.7	4.0
Canada	2.6	4.1	3.8
Major countries	2.9	6.0	5.3

*As measured by deflators of gross national product.
Source: Adapted from OECD, *Economic Outlook* (December 1971).

CHART 1.

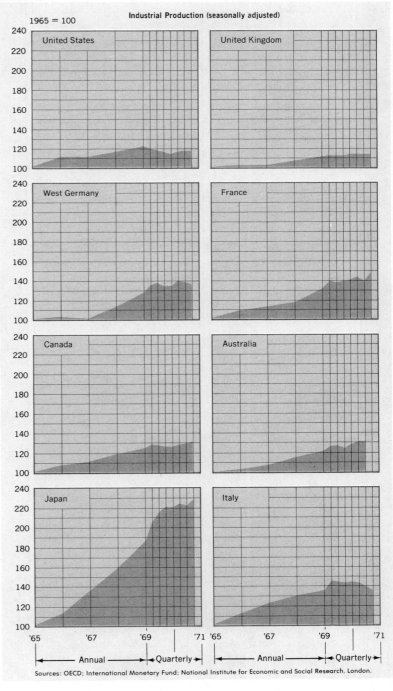

Sources: OECD; International Monetary Fund; National Institute for Economic and Social Research, London.

Money thus depreciated still further (*see* Table IV). In the U.S. during 1971, the average rate of depreciation of the dollar slowed down to a 4.1% pace—an improvement from the 1969–70 rate of over 5% but still uncomfortable. In other industrial countries, rates of depreciation of buying power outstripped the already high pace of 1970.

In the U.S., as well as in the rest of the industrial world, labour costs continued to rise (*see* Chart 2). Increases in labour costs were larger than improvements in productivity. As a result unit labour costs continued to creep upward (*see* Table V). In the U.S., however, the rise was down to about 2% from the 6%

increase in 1970. Outside the U.S. the persistence of wage increases was striking for a period when real resources were not overstrained. Cost-push inflation—in which wage pressures persist even though excess demand is slackening, unemployment is growing, and national output is stationary or even declining—remained widespread throughout the industrial world.

The steep rise in wage costs squeezed corporate profits. In competitive markets it was practically impossible to pass along all increased costs into higher prices. Furthermore, several countries, above all the U.S., established wage-price controls that had an impact on profits. Corporate profits in the U.S. staged a recovery from the depressed level of 1970—the result partly of the renewed growth in output and partly of increased productivity. But even at the $45 billion annual rate during the third quarter of 1971, after-tax corporate profits hardly regained the level of 1967. In real terms, after adjustment for the loss of the buying power of the dollar, they were still 24% below 1966. Profit margins of U.S. corporations in aggregate fell

CHART 2.

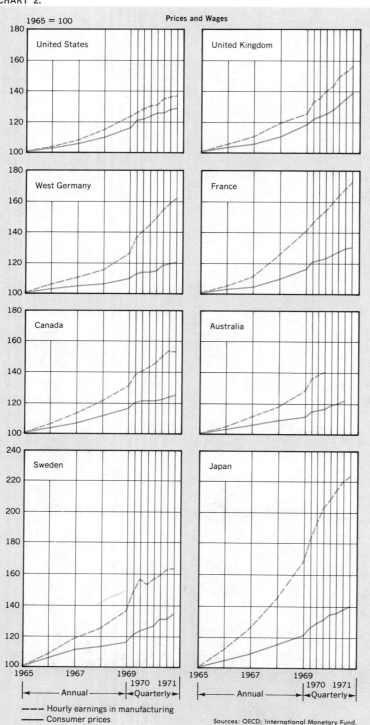

--- Hourly earnings in manufacturing
— Consumer prices

Sources: OECD; International Monetary Fund.

	Indexes of value of money (1960=100)		Annual rates of depreciation (percent)		
Country	1965	1970	'60–'70*	'69–'70	'70–'71†
Industrial countries					
Canada	92	76	2.6	3.3	2.3
Greece	92	81	2.1	3.1	3.1
Belgium	88	74	2.9	3.8	3.9
Luxembourg	90	78	2.5	4.4	4.2
United States	94	76	2.6	5.6	4.2
Austria	83	70	3.5	4.2	4.4
Germany, West	87	76	2.6	3.8	4.7
France	83	67	3.8	4.9	4.9
Italy	79	68	3.8	4.8	5.0
Australia	91	78	2.4	3.7	5.3
Denmark	77	56	5.7	6.4	5.3
South Africa	90	76	2.6	4.9	5.4
Finland	78	62	4.8	2.7	5.4
Switzerland	85	72	3.2	3.5	6.2
Norway	82	64	4.3	9.7	6.2
Japan	75	57	5.4	7.1	6.4
Netherlands	84	66	4.0	4.2	6.8
Sweden	84	67	3.8	6.6	7.0
Spain	71	56	5.7	5.4	7.5
Iceland	59	33	10.6	11.3	7.8
Ireland	81	63	4.5	7.6	8.3
United Kingdom	84	67	3.9	6.0	8.7
Portugal	88	65	4.3	6.0	9.2
New Zealand	88	69	3.7	6.2	9.8
Turkey	84	57	5.5	7.3	11.7
Less developed countries					
Guatemala	99	92	0.8	2.3	0.8
El Salvador	99	94	0.7	2.8	1.1
Thailand	93	82	2.0	2.3	1.3
India	74	54	5.9	4.9	2.2
Venezuela	99	92	0.9	2.1	2.8
Bolivia	78	58	5.2	3.8	2.9
Taiwan	89	72	3.3	3.5	2.9
Costa Rica	89	79	2.3	4.5	3.2
Mexico	91	77	2.6	4.9	3.4
Iran	91	84	1.7	2.1	3.7
Morocco	82	80	2.2	1.3	4.0
Pakistan	88	71	3.4	5.1	4.2
Indonesia	2	‡	57.6	11.0	4.4
Peru	64	40	8.8	4.9	6.3
Colombia	56	35	10.1	6.4	6.6
Jamaica	87	67	3.9	8.9	6.7
Ecuador	82	65	4.2	4.9	9.0
Israel	71	58	5.3	5.7	10.7
Yugoslavia	53	31	10.9	11.3	12.5
Korea	49	27	12.1	13.8	13.3
Philippines	78	58	5.2	14.7	16.2
Chile	30	9	21.0	24.5	16.9
Brazil	9	3	30.6	16.0	17.8
Vietnam	71	14	17.6	26.9	18.7
Argentina	35	15	17.5	12.0	24.1

Note: Depreciation of money is measured by rates of decline in the domestic purchasing power of national currencies (as computed from reciprocals of official cost-of-living or consumer price indexes), not by rates of price inflation. For example, a rate of inflation of 100% is equivalent to a 50% rate of depreciation of buying power of money.
*Compounded annually.
†Based on average monthly data available for 1971 compared with corresponding period of 1970.
‡Less than one.
Source: First National City Bank, New York, N.Y.

to 7.6% in 1970, the lowest level of the entire postwar period; they were only marginally higher in 1971.

In Europe and Japan, with stagnant or even declining output, corporate profits fell markedly. For export-oriented businesses in West Germany, the Netherlands, Switzerland, and, beginning with late August, Japan, the pressures on profits were compounded by the decline of export earnings consequent upon the appreciation of their currencies relative to the U.S. dollar and other currencies.

Although the domestic price level in the U.S. rose in 1971 less than in any other major country except Canada, the U.S. continued to experience a persistent rise in the prices of manufactured products it was exporting. However, the revaluations of the German mark, Japanese yen, and other currencies against the U.S. dollar—upward valuations that took place in the circumstances and in magnitudes reviewed in the article PAYMENTS AND RESERVES, INTERNATIONAL—had the effect of increasing the upvaluing countries' export prices when converted into U.S. dollars. The U.S. competitive power in the world market thus showed an appreciable improvement. Many other factors lie behind the competitive power of nations in world trade, including the impact of trade policies, tax and export credit arrangements, and above all structural changes in the economies of the U.S. and its main competitors.

The profit squeeze that had plagued European businesses for many years led to a growing number of business failures, especially in the U.K. It also depressed the stock markets, particularly in continental Europe. Furthermore, in the U.S. as well as in other countries, the profit squeeze slowed or even halted business investment in plant and equipment. In the U.K. capital expenditures in industry dropped, in real terms, from the previous year. Cuts in business investment reduced the pressure on economic resources and were a stabilizing influence in the short run; but for the longer run they created a self-aggravating condition in the economy, inimical to productivity and efficiency, and hence to the growth of employment and real income—all of which required a revival of corporate profit margins.

At the end of 1971 there were marked divergences between the U.S. and other industrial countries in both the business cycle and the inflation cycle. The U.S. was on the upswing. Abroad, key industrial countries still were experiencing a slowdown; such strength as was discernible came mainly from France and the U.K. While inflation in the U.S. was edging lower, the rate of cost-price increases remained uncomfortable in the rest of the industrialized world despite considerable unutilized capacity. With regard to industrial profits, which are the lifeblood of the economic system and, in the economies of individualistic capitalism, help more than anything else to strengthen business confidence, the U.S. was clearly ahead of Europe and Japan. But even in the U.S. there was apprehension that too tight a rein on profits might hamper increases in business capital spending and employment.

In Search of Reexpansion. Against the background of sluggish business, all industrial countries embarked during 1971 upon monetary and fiscal stimulation aimed at faster growth. While different countries were at varying stages in this process, all geared their policies toward encouraging personal consumption, government expenditure, and, to a lesser degree, private investment in plant and equipment. But because of the persistent inflationary strains and stresses, the moves in an expansionary direction either were ac-

companied by controls on prices and wages, as in the U.S., or were rather cautious, as in Europe or Japan.

Although the U.S. economy began to recover late in 1970, the year 1971 was not, as President Nixon had forecast, shaping up to be a "good year" and there were few signs that 1972 would turn out to be a "very good year" as promised. While the need to pursue still more expansionary financial policies seemed clear enough, the ability to do so was limited severely by two major constraints: the flight of dollars into other currencies, which in midsummer reached crisis proportions, and the still too rapid rise in the price level. These two dangerous "leakages" had to be plugged—the first by suspension on August 15 of what remained of gold convertibility of the dollar and by imposition of the temporary surcharge on imports of manufactures, and the second by a 90-day freeze on prices, wages, rents, and dividends.

The freeze—Phase One of the president's program—stopped the earlier escalation of costs and prices. Beginning with mid-November the freeze was followed by what could be, at best, only a gradual thaw—Phase Two of a transitional but open-ended resort to government-controlled economy. Under the controls prices could not be increased unless the rise was justified by an increase in costs that was not offset by improvements in productivity; that is, if costs per unit of output rose. But if unit costs did increase, they could be fully covered by higher prices unless one of two exceptions held. The first was that price increases could not push the margin of before-tax profits to sales above the average of the best two of the three fiscal years that ended before August 15, 1971. For most corporations, the ceiling on profit margins would not become an effective restriction for some time since average profit margins were running substantially below the base-period level. Second, prices might not be allowed to fully reflect wage increases resulting from above-guideline increases if they were considered inflationary. This limitation was applied sparingly for it created concern over a possible profit squeeze.

Clearly, prices were restrained more than wages, mainly because of concern that labour would not otherwise cooperate—an attitude that has wrecked many an incomes policy in other industrial countries. As the findings of the various boards and commissions were issued, it appeared that the nation was getting not edicts but case-by-case rules with ample leeway for equity considerations—an approach more apt to secure the broad popular support that incomes policy needed in order to succeed. Reassuringly controls were imposed at a point when the U.S. was coming out of the Vietnam war rather than entering a war, and when inflation had begun to edge lower rather than higher. The economy was not saddled with a demand-pull inflation and had considerable unused capacity. The effectiveness of price and wage controls thus appeared to depend less on the administration's machinery and more on the fundamental condition of the U.S. economy.

Whether Phase Two would be followed by a return to a much smaller government role in the area of prices and wages or by a Phase Three—freer than Phase Two but nevertheless a set of controls to which the nation was not accustomed—was a matter of deep concern. On absolute grounds, many Americans questioned the wisdom of government intervention in a free economy. On pragmatic grounds, many pointed out that there was little freedom left in the pre-freeze

continued on page 264

HOW GOOD IS
THE DOLLAR NOW?

By Miroslav A. Kriz

In August 1971, in the midst of a severe foreign exchange crisis, the U.S. dollar lost what had formally remained of its convertibility into gold for foreign governments and central banks, declined in value against other key currencies, and thus abdicated—at least temporarily—its role as the foremost currency in which monetary authorities of nations outside the U.S. were holding a substantial part of their monetary reserves. In mid-December, the Nixon administration announced that it would propose to Congress a devaluation of the dollar in terms of gold through an increase of the official price to $38 per ounce "as soon as the related set of short-term measures [with regard to trade with the European Common Market, Canada, and Japan] is available for Congressional scrutiny." In effect, the new gold price immediately became the nucleus for currency realignments.

Along with the convertibility suspension in August, the administration froze prices and wages for 90 days in order to hold down inflation while providing more leeway for financial stimulation of the economy. In November, it subjected the economy to controls monitoring almost everything and everyone in the country.

The future of the dollar depends critically on the outcome of Pres. Richard Nixon's historic volte-face. This Special Report accordingly seeks to provide answers to the anxious questions about where the dollar stands and where it is heading.

The Dollar Abroad. The depreciation of the dollar against the currencies of most Western European countries and Japan and its devaluation in terms of gold failed to induce any feeling among the great majority of Americans that they had been touched by what had happened. But the world's monetary structure lay in ruin because its cornerstone was the universal acceptability of the dollar and its convertibility into gold. There was much talk about phasing out the dollar as an international currency. But did what Washington Irving observed a century before in *The Creole Village*, namely that "the almighty dollar, that great object of universal devotion throughout our land, seems to have no genuine devotees in these peculiar villages," become really true of today's Frankfurt, Zürich, and London?

It is difficult to visualize a world in which the dollar would cease to be used outside the U.S. in private transactions. It is true that exports of goods and services are invoiced and paid for in many currencies and that private capital investment also takes place in nondollar currencies. But the dollar is used in private international transactions much more than any other currency. Furthermore, corporations and individuals are borrowing dollars from the vast pool deposited with banks in London and other centres outside the U.S.—the Eurodollar market—and then frequently converting them into the particular currency they need. The dollar will, of course, be used in private transactions throughout the world only so long as there is confidence that it will remain dependable, universally acceptable, and convertible into other currencies.

Governments and central banks use the dollar to intervene in exchange markets in order to control—either to support or hold down—the price of their own currency against others. This "intervention" role of the dollar has continued despite the dollar crisis,

---

Miroslav A. Kriz is vice-president of the First National City Bank, New York City.

since the key exchange rates have remained those between the dollar and each of the other currencies. No substitute for this use of the dollar is in sight. Clearly, the role of the dollar as international "intervention" currency is conditioned by the confidence of each government that dollars will be accepted by others in final settlements.

While the "trading" and "intervention" roles of the dollar undoubtedly will continue, there is a possibility—but not more than a possibility—that the dollar also may remain the currency in which governments and central banks outside the U.S. willingly continue to keep part of their international reserves in addition to the amounts they need for normal working balances.

To be preserved, this "reserve" role of the dollar requires that a workable order be reestablished in the international monetary system. There must be some evidence of improvement in the U.S. balance of payments. The excessive overhang of dollars held by governments and central banks of Western European countries and Japan—dollars that fled into other currencies during the crisis—was expected to be, in part, worked down as dollars would return to private hands; but the rest might have to be consolidated. There would have to be reasonable expectation that the dollar would not depreciate. Finally, after a return to stable parities, the dollar would have to be convertible once again.

Convertible into what? Into gold? The suspension of dollar convertibility into gold in August was described officially as temporary and permitting exceptions to such an extent and under such conditions as were "determined to be in the interest of monetary stability and in the best interests of the United States." In the U.S., however, the view often is held that the role of gold in any new monetary system should be reduced, if not eliminated. The financial powers outside the U.S., on the other hand, are determined to retain gold in the international monetary system. These varying standpoints about the future of gold undoubtedly have their roots in the past. Since September 1949, Western European countries and Japan have built up their reserves to more than $20 billion, or almost one half of the world monetary gold stock; at the same time, the U.S. has seen its stock decline from $25 billion to $10 billion, or from 71 to 25% of the world total.

Would the dollar be again convertible into Special Drawing Rights? The SDRs are a collectively managed asset of the International Monetary Fund—"paper gold"—which, in 1972, would be starting the third year of its existence. Its future is viewed by the major governments along sharply divergent lines. The U.S. sees it as progress along the path of "degolding" and hopes to build SDRs into the principal international reserve asset. Most of the other key countries see SDRs as remaining linked to gold and supplementing, not supplanting, gold. In the view of influential governments, the principal attraction of SDRs is that the governments themselves have a decisive influence in SDR creation while they obviously cannot have any voice in the creation of U.S. dollars. The shift from dollars to SDRs as the principal source of international reserves would mean that the U.S. could no longer finance its balance of payments deficit with dollars accumulated by countries with a surplus in their monetary reserves. On the contrary, the U.S., like any other country, could run out of international reserves.

A dollar convertible neither into gold nor into SDRs, as in late 1971, necessarily would lose much of its allure for foreign holders, private as well as official. The major nations do not want to be forced to accept and hold inconvertible dollars, at least in amounts that they do not really want. They refuse to place their currencies on an inconvertible dollar standard.

Surely, with the increased mobility of short-term funds and the expansion of world trade and investment, monetary authorities of foreign countries will need growing amounts of working balances in dollars to intervene in exchange markets. There are also countries that, because of their trade relationships with the U.S., will want to hold dollars in official reserves even if the dollar is not convertible into gold or SDRs. It is thus unlikely that the dollar may be phased out entirely as an international reserve currency. But its future undoubtedly will depend on the restoration of convertibility—not into gold alone but into all international assets. This will depend in turn on intergovernmental negotiations about future international monetary arrangements and, specifically, on how the necessary balance of payments adjustments will work out now that a new exchange rate pattern has been established.

Restoration of dollar convertibility would impose on the United States obligations and responsibilities, particularly with regard to the maintenance of orderly monetary, fiscal, and wage conditions and a steady course in domestic policy making. But the United States needs financial order at home not just to make the dollar an acceptable currency to governments and private traders and investors abroad, but primarily to preserve the efficiency and productivity of its economy and its political and social values.

In a convertible world, governments of many countries may well prefer a living currency to SDRs—a living currency uniquely strong because of the size, resources, and productivity of the U.S. economy, its capability for generating profits, its savings and capital markets, and its record of less inflation than in practically any other country. The future of the dollar as a reliable currency, one that is readily usable throughout the world in private trade as well as for official purposes and that commands universal confidence and respect, is, therefore, intimately linked with its position at home.

The Dollar at Home. The people of the U.S., like the rest of the world, live in a regime of paper money. Unlike 40 years ago when the dollar was redeemable in gold, today's paper dollar has no intrinsic value. U.S. Federal Reserve notes carry the inscription "In God We Trust," but the ordinary citizen knows that he has no choice but to trust the Federal Reserve and, ultimately, the president and Congress. Although far from being perfect, the dollar has lost less of its domestic buying power than practically any other currency.

Yet, even with its relatively good record, the dollar has depreciated too much for the comfort of the American people. The last time the dollar suffered no erosion from one year to the next was in the mid-1950s. The record in 1971 was somewhat better than in 1970, but unless improvement becomes more marked, the outlook will remain, to say the least, doubtful. Human behaviour is naturally deeply affected by the realization that a 4.5% rate of annual depreciation, as in 1971, cuts the buying power of the dollar by one-half in only 16 years. Even at a 3% rate of annual depreciation—now regarded as practically unattainable—the buying power of the dollar would be halved in 23 years. Americans have thus become uneasily aware that the longer they hold money, the less they will get for it.

At year's end the outlook was full of uncertainty. The U.S. economy managed to show an advance, but the pace of expansion was listless. Inflation slowed down, but it remained, politically as well as economically, explosive. The best that could be hoped for was that the administration's new economic policy had a fighting chance and that, at the time the controls could be lifted, natural forces in the economy would work toward more employment with less inflation. The worst that was to be feared was that renewed inflation—stemming from excessive monetary and fiscal stimulation and from persistent wage increases that ran well ahead of productivity increments—would explode at the very moment controls collapsed.

Therefore, unless the recent lessening in the rate of dollar depreciation becomes more marked and convincing, the people of the U.S. may have no choice but to learn to live with inflation. The art of living with inflation already has begun to be practiced in the U.S. on a big scale with regard to wages and pensions. Given the political realities, it is, of course, difficult to deny workers and pensioners compensation for cost-of-living increases. This compensation is assured by linking wages and pensions to the cost of living through escalator clauses.

Savers and lenders of money also seek to protect interest income or principal against depreciation of the dollar. They seek protection by raising interest rates—a phenomenon that is evidenced by the fact that the real level of interest rates, after subtracting inflation and inflationary expectations, does not vary a great deal over the years. But there are narrow limits to compensating in this way for the loss of the buying power of money.

To the surprise of many people, inflation in 1969 and 1970 and its aftermath in 1971 hit not only those who held their savings in fixed-interest securities or savings deposits, but also those who held common stocks. At the end of December 1971, the Dow Jones industrial stock average was 13% higher, on paper, than five years earlier, before the present wave of inflationary pressures had begun; but, in the real sense—after correction for the loss of buying power of the dollar—it was 9% lower. The obvious lesson is that common stocks as a whole do not provide protection against inflation—not too surprising an observation since profits of U.S. corporations, after allowing for price inflation, have declined in recent years. Furthermore, investments in stocks also have been eroded as a result of taxation of fictitious capital gains—fictitious because they are nothing more than a reflection of the depreciation of money. But, even then, the holder of common stocks may fare better than the holder of fixed-income securities—so long at least as taxation does not become wholly confiscatory.

The search for other forms of a suitable hedge against inflation also takes the form of equity "kickers," such as convertible bonds. Variable annuities—with assets invested in common stocks and payments reflecting the result of such investments—also have become popular. Agricultural land, forests, diamonds, stamps, coins, antiques, works of art, vintage cars, and even the bank notes that flooded Germany or Hungary during hyper-inflations after the two World Wars remain steadily in demand on the strength of expectations that they will beat the depreciation of money. Basically, of course, all this is speculation and not particularly helpful to a man of modest means without specialized knowledge.

Americans continue to live with the depreciating dollar without buying gold. They are allowed to use gold only for licensed purposes and must not hold any monetary gold except coins of recognized numismatic value minted before April 5, 1933. This continued prohibition of private gold ownership contradicts the stated official position that, internationally, the role of gold has diminished and, with the passage of time, will be reduced still further. Evidently, if gold were on its way out as a monetary instrument there would be no need for the Treasury to regulate it as a commodity.

People's ingenuity in inventing new devices and gimmicks to try to safeguard the buying power of incomes and savings must not be underestimated. But experience shows that while some individuals can protect themselves up to a point, most people do not have equal ability, bargaining power, or luck at passing on to others the burden of the depreciation of money.

Savings are eroded by inflation directly as well as indirectly in that the government frequently taxes capital gains that may be nothing more than the result of the depreciation of money. Sooner or later, therefore, the government will have to decide whether to make people save voluntarily, which requires appropriate rewards and safeguards, or to extract the badly needed capital through still higher taxation or enforced saving. At stake is the preservation of the fabric of the free economy and free society and, with it, the basic political freedoms of every citizen.

Needless to say, by far the best way out of the present inflationary malaise is to return to reasonable monetary stability. But the malaise can be overcome only if people, in the U.S. system of competing political parties, realize that the only protection against an unacceptable loss of the purchasing power of the dollar is through responsible government at all levels. .

© 1971 UNITED FEATURES SYNDICATE

270 DAYS

180 DAYS

90 DAYS FREEZE

"Let's see how well it floats"—Lurie.

LURIE

continued from page 261

practices of wage bargaining and wage formation and the resulting impact on prices. The cost-price level, if entirely free, would tend to rise at a faster rate than was acceptable to the nation as a whole. The real issue—particularly with an election approaching—was the distribution of income.

To stimulate more rapid expansion in production and employment, President Nixon recommended that Congress cut taxes. These recommendations included the repeal of the 7% excise tax on automobiles retroactive to mid-August; the granting, also retroactively, of a job development tax credit on business purchases of new machinery and equipment (at 7% as Congress approved it), and cuts in personal income taxation (as finally approved, a $25 increase in personal exemption to $675 for 1971 and an increase to $750 for 1972, which, together with higher standard deductions, was scheduled originally to take place in 1973).

In an economy operating considerably below capacity, the tax cuts resulted in a shortfall of revenues and with some sizable further increases in expenditures, the federal deficit for the fiscal year ending June 1972 rose to over $39 billion from $23 billion in fiscal 1970–71. The extent to which fiscal policy became stimulative was visible from the shift in the "full-employment budget," which gauges what the budget would look like if the economy were operating at capacity, to a deficit of about $8 billion for 1971–72 from an earlier "full-employment surplus" of $5 billion.

Monetary policy was highly stimulative during the first half of the year; and although it became somewhat more restrained during the second half, the direction was toward assured ease—an understandable posture for an economy that, having reached the bottom of the recession in late 1970, had a slower recovery than had been expected.

On the eve of 1972, there thus appeared a light at the end of the tunnel through which the U.S. economy was passing. Price inflation had slowed down; the rise in labour costs per unit of output had declined; and the economy had improved, with promising prospects for output and employment. At the same time, however, it was by no means certain that this was the last tunnel on the road toward vigorous growth with a tolerable degree of inflation. Among the dangers was the very circumstance that price and wage controls for which no terminal date was set could encourage an unsustainable monetary and fiscal stimulation.

Many European countries that had maintained standing machinery for price and incomes policy, or both, accentuated its use during 1971. Thus, in Denmark, Norway, and Sweden, prices were frozen in periods preceding major wage negotiations. In France, *contrat anti-hausse*, based on a frame agreement between the government and the employers' federation concluded on behalf of member companies, limited price increases to an average 1.5% over the six months to mid-March 1972; within this framework subsidiary contracts were negotiated with individual branches of industry for separate subtargets (for instance chemicals 1.75%, electrical appliances 0.7%). On its part, the French government undertook that there would be no price rises in the nationalized industries over the same period. Ireland established a new framework of wage-price controls. Italy tightened price controls on foodstuffs and blocked price rises by nationalized industries.

In the U.K. in July, at the same time that the government took expansionary steps (mentioned below), the Confederation of British Industry called upon the 200 largest member companies to undertake "to do their utmost not to raise their prices in the 12 months ending July 31, 1972, and to limit any unavoidable increases in their prices to 5%." The government made it known that it insisted that the nationalized industries also hold back their price increases. Simultaneously, it appealed to the Trades Union Congress to make "a positive contribution to curb inflation."

The results of the freeze and control steps in 1971 in much of the industrial world outside the U.S. confirmed the earlier experience that, even at a time when there were no excess demand pressures, price rises could be halted or restrained for periods of three to six months, and sometimes for up to a year, but rarely longer. In the Netherlands, where intermittent price freezes were resorted to beginning with the spring

continued on page 266

Table V. Productivity and Unit Labour Costs in Manufacturing

Country	Annual percent changes 1969	1970	1971*
Output per man-hour			
Germany, West	5.1	1.4	9.3
United Kingdom	3.2	1.6	6.8
Canada	3.3	2.4	6.0
Japan	15.3	13.8	5.3
United States	−0.1	0.7	3.9
France	13.5	5.3	0.9
Italy	3.4	6.0	−3.8
Unit labour costs			
Italy†	4.2	13.6	24.3
France‡	1.5	4.4	6.2
Germany, West§	2.2	13.1	5.9
Japan§	2.8	4.3	5.1
Canada§	4.6	6.0	3.8
United Kingdom§	5.6	10.8	3.3
United States†	3.6	6.0	1.1

*In descending order of percentage change in most recent 1971 data expressed at an annual rate.
†Labour costs, including fringe benefits and social security.
‡Wage costs, excluding fringe benefits and social security.
§Wage and salary costs, excluding fringe benefits and social security.
Sources: Adapted from data published by the OECD, National Institute for Economic and Social Research (London) and U.S. Department of Commerce.

The United States Poised for Controls

(After the expiration of the price-wage freeze
on Nov. 13, 1971)

The Structure

A Price Commission of seven private citizens; a
Pay Board of five management, five labour, and five
public members; and a Cost of Living Council, made
up of government officials under the secretary of the
treasury, to oversee the two boards.

Also, a Committee on Interest and Dividends; committees on medical costs and state-local government
costs; and a Productivity Commission.

Prices

Target: An average rise in prices of no more than
2.5% per year.

General rules: For manufacturing and service industries: prices to go up only if costs rise.
For manufacturing: profit margins before taxes as a percentage of the best
two of the last three fiscal years that
ended before Aug. 15, 1971. For
services, margins to be no higher than
in the base period (July 16–Aug.
14, 1971). Increases in costs to be reduced by gains in productivity; *i.e.,*
costs to be calculated on a per unit
basis.
For retailers and wholesalers: prices
to reflect higher purchase prices but
the percentage markup not to exceed
the average for the best two of the
past three years. Retailers to post
the maximum prices permitted during
the freeze period before raising prices.
For public utilities with sales of over
$100 million a year: requests for rate
hikes to be submitted to the Price
Commission as well as the usual regulatory bodies.

Exempt: Raw foodstuffs and seafood; financial securities; art objects and antiques; used
products; import and export prices.

Rents in residential properties: Base rent to be raised
by up to 2.5% to cover operating costs
and by amounts necessary to cover increases in property taxes, charges for
municipal services, etc.

Wages

Guideline: Raises not more than 5.5%, including
fringe benefits.

Exceptions:

Future increases—greater than 5.5% allowed if justified by "equity," "catch-up"
for prior inflation, "parallel relationships"
with other groups of workers, etc.

Retroactive increases—allowed if prices
were raised in anticipation of the freeze;
retroactivity established practice; needed
to remedy "severe inequities," etc.

Deferred increases—existing contracts allowed to take effect unless challenged by
interested parties or five members of the
Pay Board.

Note: Wages paid by, and controlled by, the federal
government and those so low as to be under
the statutory minimum wage are not covered
by the 5.5% guideline.

Productivity Assumption

The difference between the 2.5% price target and the
5.5% wage guideline based on the assumption that
output per man-hour would rise to 3%—a productivity assumption that depended on a relatively rapid
rate of output expansion.

Legal Authority

The legal authority for controls to expire April 30,
1973.

Reporting and Surveillance

Categories	Prices	Pay
	Firms with sales of:	Increases affecting:
Required to ask permission in advance to raise prices and wages	$100 million and over (1,300 firms, 45% of total U.S. sales)	5,000 workers or more (500 units, 10% of total U.S. employees)
Required to report promptly as soon as price or wage action is taken	$50 to $100 million (1,100 firms, 5% of total U.S. sales)	1,000 to 5,000 workers (4,000 units, 7% of total U.S. employees)
Subjected to spot checks at any time on prices and wages	Less than $50 million (10 million firms, 50% of total U.S. sales)	Less than 1,000 workers (10 million units, 83% of total U.S. employees)

continued from page 264

of 1969, the institutional machinery of price-incomes policies collapsed in July 1971. In Canada, the Canadian Price and Incomes Commission's one-year price voluntary restraint operation in 1970 was discontinued in 1971.

The problem of wage-price inflation thus remained unsolved in the industrial world outside the U.S., although it was perhaps becoming less acute. But a new problem emerged—how to stimulate demand, which was weakening almost everywhere. The room for maneuver indicated by the slack in the economy was more limited than in the U.S. The moves in an expansionary direction were, therefore, cautious. The last country to embark upon this path was West Germany. Almost everywhere, monetary conditions eased significantly. During 1971 there were 29 cuts in central bank discount rates in 11 countries outside the U.S. Earlier the cuts had been motivated more by the need to narrow short-term interest rate differentials with the U.S. or Eurodollar markets than by domestic considerations. Later in the year, however, the discount-rate reductions and other measures increasingly sought to stimulate business, as evidenced in particular by the steps taken after mid-October in West Germany, Italy, Sweden, Canada, and Japan.

Among specific monetary measures, the most noteworthy were the lifting of all direct controls on credit in the U.K. effective in October and the elimination of consumer credit restrictions in July. In France, consumer credit controls were relaxed. Italy provided special credits for industries. Japan, Canada, and West Germany experienced particularly rapid rates of monetary expansion, mainly because of capital inflows. France and the U.K., on the other hand, had relatively small increases in money supply.

More active use also was made of fiscal stimulation which was quite substantial in some countries. In Canada, Japan, and more moderately in France, government expenditures were stepped up as a countercyclical measure. In Canada personal and corporate income taxes were reduced retroactive to July. Italy had a large budget deficit, partly because of the weak trend in the economy; social reforms in the fields of health, housing, and development of the south and encouragement of investment by small firms and public corporations boosted demand. The West German government announced its readiness to increase public investment financed out of funds accumulated by the central government during the boom; the repayable 10% income tax surcharge imposed in 1970 was allowed to expire in July 1971, as originally intended.

In the U.K. the strong emphasis was on cutting taxes. The mini-budget of October 1970 as well as the budget for 1971–72 as announced in April 1971 provided tax relief to individuals as well as businesses. A bold move was made in July—substantial reductions in indirect taxes, and the provision of investment incentives to business. These moves, together with the lifting of all consumer credit controls, brought about a notable rise in retail sales, especially of durables. But even in Britain, as in other countries including the U.S., consumers held back, despite inflation, as they remained doubtful about the employment outlook.

To conclude, the industrial nations in 1972 entered uncharted waters. The governments, having swung from fighting inflation to reducing unemployment, were trying to push pieces of string to stimulate the economies but these simply refused to respond to budgetary or monetary measures in the normal way.

"Confidence" and "psychology" became crucially important in determining the course of business. There were uncontrollable or disobedient forces at work; and for governments and central banks, the economies were as difficult to steer between recession and inflation as vast ocean liners whose course always lags the helmsman. (M. A. K.)

See also Economics; Employment, Wages, and Hours; Income, National; Industrial Review; Labour Unions; Merchandising; Prices; Profits; Savings and Investments; Trade, International.

Ecuador

A republic on the west coast of South America, Ecuador is bounded by Colombia, Peru, and the Pacific Ocean. Area: 109,483 sq.mi. (283,561 sq. km.), including the Galapagos Islands (3,075 sq.mi.). Pop. (1970 est.): 6,177,127. Cap.: Quito (pop., 1970 est., 528,094). Largest city: Guayaquil (pop., 1970 est., 794,301). Language: Spanish, but Indians speak Quechuan and Jíbaro. Religion: mainly Roman Catholic. President in 1971, José María Velasco Ibarra.

After President Velasco assumed supreme powers in mid-1970, bold government decisions brought about a spectacular improvement in the economy in the latter half of that year. In 1971, however, budgetary and other difficulties reemerged. Provisional estimates put the deficit for 1970 at 29 million sucres, compared with 2,538,000,000 sucres originally estimated; the reduction was achieved by increases in

---

ECUADOR

Education. (1968–69) Primary, pupils 928,687, teachers 24,426; secondary, pupils 105,362, teachers 8,147; vocational, pupils 50,998, teachers 3,300; teacher training, students 17,254, teachers 987; higher (including 7 universities), students 22,637, teaching staff 2,256.

Finance. Monetary unit: sucre, with a par value of 25 sucres to U.S. \$1 (60 sucres = £1 sterling) and a free rate (Sept. 27, 1971) of c. 62 sucres to £1 sterling. Gold, SDRs, and foreign exchange, central bank: (June 1971) U.S. \$64.8 million; (June 1970) U.S. \$64 million. Budget (excluding development budget; 1969 est.) balanced at 2,001,000,000 sucres. Gross national product: (1969) 29,580,000,000 sucres; (1968) 26,710,-000,000 sucres. Money supply: (May 1971) 5,351,-000,000 sucres; (May 1970) 4,072,000,000 sucres. Cost of living (Quito; 1963 = 100): (May 1971) 144; (May 1970) 130.

Foreign Trade. (1970) Imports U.S. \$246.9 million; exports U.S. \$218.2 million. Import sources (1969): U.S. 32%; West Germany 13%; Japan 9%; Colombia 6%; Italy 5%. Export destinations (1969): U.S. 41%; West Germany 12%; Japan 11%. Main exports: bananas 51%; coffee 23%; cocoa 10%.

Transport and Communications: Roads (1966) 18,435 km. Motor vehicles in use (1969): passenger c. 25,500; commercial (including buses) c. 34,000. Railways (1969): 1,041 km.; traffic 86 million passenger-km., freight 61 million net ton-km. Air traffic (1969): 243,903,000 passenger-km.; freight 6,594,000 net ton-km. Telephones (Jan. 1970) 94,300. Radio receivers (Dec. 1969) 1.2 million. Television receivers (Dec. 1967) 71,000.

Agriculture. Production (in 000; metric tons; 1969; 1968 in parentheses): bananas c. 2,700 (2,693); corn c. 210 (177); barley 62 (62); potatoes c. 370 (363); dry beans c. 32 (28); coffee 72 (53); cocoa (1970–71) 65, (1969–70) 60; rice 161 (288); cassava c. 400 (c. 370); oranges c. 195 (196); sugar, raw value (1970–71) c. 293, (1969–70) c. 264. Livestock (in 000; 1969–70): cattle c. 2,440; sheep c. 1,860; pigs c. 1,330; horses c. 240; chickens c. 5,400.

Industry. Production (in 000; metric tons; 1969): petroleum products 1,032; crude oil (1970) 191; electricity (kw-hr.) 858,000; cement 456; gold (troy oz.) 7.4; silver (troy oz.) 125.

revenue resulting mainly from four executive decrees of May 1970 and by reduced expenditure. Revenue collected in the first half of 1971 rose by 434 million sucres (30%) over that obtained in the corresponding period of 1970. This was offset, however, by payments relating to 1970, calculated at 343 million sucres, that had to be met from 1971 revenue. The minister of finance warned that the expenditure budgeted for 1971 did not cover additional requirements totaling some 900 million sucres and that any additional revenue must be used to finance these.

International monetary reserves rose from $17 million just before the devaluation of Aug. 16, 1970, to $49 million at the end of that year, but fell by $15.4 million in the first seven months of 1971 to $33.6 million on July 31. The cost of living, which in Guayaquil had risen by 12.5% in 1970 compared with 5.4% in 1969, continued to rise sharply, due to new taxes and the effects of devaluation. However, the government succeeded in limiting the expansion of the monetary supply to 3.6% in the first seven months of 1971 as against 19.1% in the comparable period of 1970. The trade situation was unfavourable in the first seven months of 1971, with export registrations valued at $123.9 million and import registrations at $146.8 million.

The main political events of the year were a short-lived revolt by the head of the military academy, Gen. Luis Jácome Chávez, a renewal of the so-called "tuna war" with the U.S., and the secret return from exile of Assad Bucaram, the president's main political opponent. The unsuccessful revolt led to preventive detention for General Jácome, and prompted the dismissal of the minister of defense, Acosta Velasco; the president received expressions of support from all the principal military garrisons in Ecuador. In January Ecuador seized 25 U.S. tuna fishing boats that were more than 12 mi. from the country's coast but well within the 200-mi. limit claimed by Ecuador. The U.S. retaliated on January 18 by suspending military sales to Ecuador, which countered by expelling the U.S. military mission on February 1. Some 25 more U.S. vessels had been seized by year's end.

President Velasco repeatedly announced plans for a plebiscite to reinstate constitutional rule, but owing to failure to arrange talks between the minister of the interior and leaders of other political parties, plans for elections in 1971 were abandoned. On June 25 it was announced that presidential and congressional elections would be held on June 4, 1972; the electorate also would be asked either to approve proposed reforms to the 1946 constitution or to delegate the matter to Congress to be resolved at its first session beginning on Aug. 10, 1972. The June 1972 elections would give immediate effect to constitutional order, but the Supreme Court would replace Congress until Aug. 10, 1972. On August 31 Velasco would hand over the presidency to the Ecuadorean citizen elected. According to the 1946 constitution, both president and vice-president must be Ecuadorean by birth; Velasco stated emphatically that the exiled Assad Bucaram could not return until he fully recognized that he could not become president because of his doubtful nationality, or until a constitutional government was in force. Earlier Bucaram had declared himself the presidential candidate of the Concentración de Fuerzas Populares. One of the most influential of the probable candidates was Camilo Ponce Enríquez, head of the Movimiento Social Cristiano. Other possible candidates included Carlos

Arizaga (Conservative), Otto Arosemena Gómez (Coalición Institucionalista Democrática), and former president Carlos Julio Arosemena Monroy (Partido Nacionalista Revolucionario).

The political situation remained complex and uncertain as the various parties began to prepare for the elections against a background of popular unrest due to the sharp rise in living costs, increasing unemployment, and economic stagnation. Many people, however, remained confident that conditions would improve when the rich oil deposits in the northeast began to flow through the trans-Andean pipeline expected to be completed in August 1972.   (R. B. Le.)

Education

A new concern for the rights of children, exemplified in a call for a children's ombudsman from a committee of Britain's National Council for Civil Liberties, was forcing reconsideration of the whole concept of formal schooling in 1971. The year was remarkable for the number of books published on both sides of the Atlantic arguing against compulsory education as it was normally practiced. Advocates of "deschooling," among the most widely known of whom was Ivan Illich (see BIOGRAPHY), declared that, far from encouraging the slum child to escape from his environment, compulsory education merely prepared him to conform to the existing society. Necessary skills, they thought, might be better acquired outside the school than in it.

Even among those who stopped short of deschooling, there was no lack of radical criticism of traditional school practices. In the U.S., especially, accountability was the theme, as educators sought to establish objectives and assign responsibility for the purpose of getting provable results in the learning process. One aspect of this trend was performance contracting, through which business firms or universities took over a particular teaching function and "guaranteed" results, or received no remuneration for students who did not learn up to or beyond an agreed performance standard.

The number of such contracts in effect during 1971 was estimated to be between 50 and 100. The largest, in terms of pupils, covered 15,000 Philadelphia elementary students engaged in a reading program. It was too soon to evaluate the results. There were early indications that the test scores of children in contract schools did, indeed, show improvement. On the other hand, critics (among them many professional teachers) questioned whether the improvement might not be simply a result of the additional attention the children were receiving. There also were objections to the system of rewards used by many contractors on the ground that it encouraged rote performance rather than self-motivated learning.

Self-motivation was the object of the "open classroom" method whereby children were encouraged to proceed at their own pace and to learn through their own interests. Enthusiastic books and articles on the method as practiced in England continued to appear in the U.S., and the influence of such thinking could be seen in the growing trend toward less structured schools. A similar philosophy was behind many of the experiments with storefront schools designed to attract dropouts and potential dropouts.

Administration. While the fundamentals of education came under scrutiny, there was continuing debate

Ecumenical Movement:
see Religion

An instant friendship was formed between Robin Brosset (left) and Paula Moyer upon Robin's arrival by bus at Bagley School in Pontiac, Mich., on Sept. 8, 1971. Court-ordered busing to achieve racial balance in the schools brought protests from some parents.

about administrative arrangements. Margaret Thatcher, secretary of state for education and science in Britain's Conservative government, had softened the insistence of the previous government on comprehensive, nonselective secondary schools; in 1971 she came under fire in some quarters for allowing local plans for school reorganization to be upset. Nevertheless, the movement toward comprehensive secondary schools continued. A feature of the reorganization was the emergence of the so-called middle school, taking pupils from age 9 to 12 or 13. This was dictated partly by educational arguments about the best age of transfer from one school to another and partly by the pressure on existing secondary schools that was expected to follow the raising of the school-leaving age from 15 to 16 in September 1972.

The independent schools, although less fearful for their future under a Conservative government than with the egalitarian policies of the Labour Party, still were alert to the current distrust of selective schooling. The Headmasters' Conference, representative body of these schools, reiterated its eagerness to have close links with the state system, while Eton College, most famous of the independent schools, came out with a plan to offer places to a certain number of working-class children.

The change in the school-leaving age was expected to raise the school roll in England and Wales alone by 233,130 students, and local authorities were asked to prepare detailed plans to meet the increase. Not everyone was in favour of the move. Fears were expressed at educational conferences that the continued presence in school of pupils who wanted to leave would increase the difficulties of discipline, which already were serious in some quarters. Some 80% of Scotland's secondary-school teachers signed a petition to the government urging postponement of the plan. There were doubts, too, that sufficient thought had been given to how the pupils were to be occupied in the extra year.

Another administrative matter gaining attention in 1971 was the arrangement of the school year. In Britain proposals were revived for a four-term year to replace the existing three-term year, and support was being sought, especially among members of the Assistant Masters' Association. In the U.S., where the school year traditionally ran from late summer or early fall until late spring, various schemes for a

12-month year were being proposed and a few were being tried experimentally, mostly in smaller systems. The principal argument used in their favour was economic, since they would permit year-round utilization of expensive plant, but it was also claimed that poor students would be helped because the shorter terms involved would be easier to make up. Since in most cases the actual number of days a given child would attend school was not to be increased, the scheduling under many of these proposals was quite complicated. Among the arguments against it were the difficulty of transferring from one system to another and the problems a large family might have in arranging a family vacation. Interestingly enough, one of the arguments for the four-term year in Britain was that it would allow parents and teachers to avoid the peak holiday season in August.

Another remnant of the past disappeared in November, when the Inner London Education Authority banned caning in the more than 880 primary schools under its jurisdiction. The order, which would go into effect Jan. 1, 1973, was strongly opposed by the headmasters, and caning continued to be permitted in most other parts of Britain.

In Ireland the government was cautiously pursuing reforms under which the existing, mostly church-run, grammar schools and the nondenominational trade schools that were generally their only alternative would be replaced by a comprehensive system of community schools. The government was confident that the reform would be successful in time, but the project was being vigorously contested by vested interests. Other countries also were engaged in ambitious plans for reform. Education headed government spending in Brazil. West Germany intended to establish, by 1980, an integrated system from nursery school to university. Initially nursery education was to have priority, and by 1980 attendance at primary school was to become compulsory at the age of five instead of six. Portugal announced reforms under which the school-leaving age was to be raised from 12 to 14. A chain of polytechnics was to be set up, university entrance examinations were to be abolished, and university education was to be made available to all classes of society.

Free and compulsory education was introduced in Hong Kong in 1971. Secondary education was not yet free, but a five-year government plan was expected to provide 97,000 more state-aided places at this level. In Africa, Nigeria was reestablishing its school system after the civil war, and Magnus Adiele, commissioner for education, reported a "student explosion," with two million pupils enrolled for primary and secondary education. On the other side of the coin, Robert Gardiner, executive secretary of the UN Economic Commission for Africa, declared in a lecture in June at Strathclyde University, Scotland, that while Algeria had decided to build up its educational system at all costs, other African countries seemed to have resigned themselves to only a gradual expansion of their systems.

Finances. All this was going on in the context of the ever increasing costs of education. In Britain Eton College found it necessary to increase its fees from £765 to £861 a year, while Merchant Taylors' raised its fees for day boys from £360 to £450 and for boarders from £550 to £670. In the public sector two economy measures caused an outcry. In April the government raised the price of school meals from 9 to 12 pence. While there was an immediate decrease in the number of children taking meals and opponents of the measure predicted that children would go hungry, the government, calling on past experience, expressed confidence that figures would recover. Mrs. Thatcher in particular maintained that the price of meals in relation to average earnings was much as it had been 16 years earlier. The government's second measure was the Education (Milk) Act, under which free milk at school was withdrawn from the 7 to 11 age group except where it had been recommended for a pupil on medical grounds. This measure was resented bitterly by some local education authorities. As the school year 1971–72 began, some of them were seeking ways of evading it while others were openly defying the new law.

U.S. public schools found themselves in a financial bind from which they seemed unable to extricate themselves. In referendum after referendum, local taxpayers turned down propositions for increased school taxes or bond issues. Some districts tried to pinch pennies by cutting back on so-called frills such as art and music. Philadelphia abolished intermural football for a short time. It was restored with a grant from the Philadelphia Eagles professional football team, but not before the school board had been accused of attempting blackmail by doing away with the program that was most popular with the general public. The schoolmen retorted that this only demonstrated the public's warped sense of educational values. A few districts even found it necessary to close the schools for short periods. Chicago avoided closing the schools for an extra 12 days at Christmas only by borrowing against the next year's budget.

With little hope for increased support from depleted local sources, school officials turned to their state legislatures for assistance while the states, themselves in financial crisis, turned to Washington. As many saw it, the need was for a greater federal commitment to local education. It was argued that the federal government should assume responsibility for upward of one-third of each education dollar. The Nixon administration, hard put to keep expenditures in line during a period of serious inflation, did not accept any such obligation for local schooling. Congress passed, and the president accepted, a $5.1 billion appropriation for education, including $1.3 billion for higher education.

New on the fiscal scene was Pres. Richard Nixon's revenue-sharing proposal relative to education. Part of a broader plan to turn back funds to the states, the education portion of the package would have combined 30 categories of federal aid already available for elementary and secondary education. Proposed funding was $3 billion, of which $200 million would be "new" money. These funds would be allocated to the states on a formula basis, and the states in turn would distribute 57% of the money to local agencies and use the rest for statewide programs. Some big-city superintendents questioned how much would actually filter down to urban districts, where the needs seemed greatest. They preferred direct grants from Washington. In any case, the debate was postponed when Nixon put off consideration of the entire revenue-sharing proposal for a year in order to concentrate on his new economic policy.

Three court decisions striking at use of the local property tax for school support were handed down during the year, with important implications for school financing. Although the ratio of state to local spending varied widely from state to state, the local property tax remained the backbone of America's decentralized public schools. Under these circumstances, a district with a strong tax base and comparatively few children could afford a far higher per-pupil expenditure than a district with a weak tax base and many children. Always present to some extent, these discrepancies had grown more apparent with the flight of affluent citizens to the suburbs and the growth of the typical suburban pattern of small, independent municipalities.

The California Supreme Court found that this arrangement denied equal protection of the laws since it made the quality of a child's education dependent on where he happened to live. A federal judge made a similar ruling regarding the Minnesota schools and, late in the year, a federal court in Texas found the reliance of that state's schools on the local property tax to be unconstitutional, thereby opening the way for eventual appeal to the U.S. Supreme Court. The decisions served to spur the search for alternatives, such as statewide levies on property, income, or sales. Beyond that, they raised the question of whether, if the local tax base was removed, the cherished American system of local control of schools could long survive.

Of more immediate practical effect was a U.S. Supreme Court decision that touched the raw nerve where financial expediency impinged on separation of church and state. In recent years the parochial school system of the Roman Catholic Church had been beset by all the financial problems afflicting the public-school system. In addition, the supply of nuns and brothers who once had manned the parochial schools at very little cost had become insufficient, and their places were being taken by lay teachers who demanded competitive salaries. The situation was underlined in November, when the lay teachers in New York City's Roman Catholic schools struck for higher pay.

The constitutional ban on the establishment of religion had long been interpreted to mean that no public money could go for the support of church schools. However, as the finances of parochial schools worsened and a few closed, it became apparent that it would be cheaper to keep them open than to provide for their pupils in the already overcrowded public schools. In a series of earlier decisions, the Supreme Court had ruled that certain services, such as bus transportation, could be given to parochial school pupils, since in these cases the state was providing for the welfare of the individual child. As the situation grew more critical, some states attempted to expand assistance to parochial schools under a variety of formulas known popularly as parochiaid.

In 1971 the Supreme Court found two of these formulas unconstitutional: a Pennsylvania statute that provided "payment of services" to parochial schools for children educated there, and a Rhode Island law by which the state paid teachers in church-run schools a portion of their salaries. The vote was a decisive 8 to 1. The majority opinion found state aid to parochial schools to be in violation of both the First Amendment to the Constitution (separation of church and state) and the Fourteenth Amendment (equal protection of the laws). Further, the justices specified that the government supervision involved in checking to make sure that state funds were not diverted to religious purposes would constitute "excessive entanglement between government and religion."

World Education

Most recent official data

Country	1st level (primary) Students (full-time)	1st level Teachers (full-time)	1st level Total schools	General 2nd level (secondary) Students (full-time)	General 2nd level Teachers (full-time)	General 2nd level Total schools	Vocational 2nd level Students (full-time)	Vocational 2nd level Teachers (full-time)	Vocational 2nd level Total schools	3rd level (higher) Students (full-time)	3rd level Teachers (full-time)	3rd level Total schools	Literacy % of population	Literacy Over age
Afghanistan	540,685	13,017	3,048	107,609	4,248	542	11,841	773	40	7,400	910	6	20.	7–12
Algeria	1,739,033	44,797	5,559	155,608	6,540	384	45,468	2,483	222	20,243*	1,269*	41*	25.4	10
American Samoa	6,755	291	30	2,545	137	7	27	2	1	650	14	1	100.	...
Angola	333,767	7,434	3,576	28,916	1,779	160	14,693	1,227	69	1,074	123	1	...	...
Argentina	3,632,050	193,213	25,793	403,848	56,434	1,739	570,978	76,287	2,412	274,634	22,477	495	91.	14
Australia	1,795,116	63,400	8,528†	924,615	49,400	2,570†	180,000‡	...	230§	208,700‡	...	269	...	...
Austria	599,954	24,656	4,018	475,314	26,999	2,055	224,698	12,177	1,052	59,990	6,734	66	100.	...
Bahamas	36,642	1,542	208	18,321	1,150	159	650	53	2	379	34	2	59.7	—
Bahrain	38,111	1,561	106	12,657	745	3	1,138	116	5	378	43	3	47.08	10
Barbados	44,630	1,725	131	21,315	925	35	80	19	2	472	62	3	96.0	...
Brazil	12,294,343	435,881	145,479	3,053,255	208,312	8,707	1,030,331	100,240	6,072	425,478	42,968	586	67.95	10
British Honduras	32,610	1,228	179	3,529	225	18	312	25	2	110	13	1	89.5	10
Brunei	27,941	1,190	125	10,421	532	21	553	33	2	—	—	—	65.96	10
Bulgaria	1,070,551	49,953	4,049	100,949	6,270	264	283,210	17,499	574	99,596	7,680	46	91.4	8
Burma	3,328,000	65,326	16,599	692,290	21,814	1,673	7,611	783	32	78,245	4,912	25	68.3	8
Burundi	182,664	4,892	970	3,969	397	18	4,200	457	30	470	67	2	...	...
Cambodia	989,464	22,465	5,699	119,988	3,990	172	5,798	510	107	10,198	1,299	10	54.1	10
Canada	4,056,948	...	...	1,640,330	260,908	17,047	181,511	13,226	381	345,966	24,537	232	98.37	20
Ceylon	2,411,239	57,935	8,105	399,642	36,648	1,539	9,329	708	35	11,725	719	4	71.9	...
Chad	178,894	2,596	877	8,724	186	33	383	52	2	758*	43*	3*	14.	...
Chile	1,980,906	...	7,302	178,887	...	461	85,987	...	257	58,964*	...	27*	83.6	15
Colombia	3,237,182	81,552	30,265	522,074	20,883	2,859	211,183	8,445	1,249	82,615	8,918	41	77.8	15
Congo (Brazzaville)	228,578	3,712	883	25,428	672	54	2,594	315	32	2,369*	155*	7*	30.	...
Congo (Kinshasa)	2,822,908	63,551	4,259	175,603	5,804	521	27,191	2,320	220	48,855*	4,224*	335*	...	...
Costa Rica	345,146	11,656	2,346	64,252	2,888	105	5,757	355	15	13,528*	954*	6*	55.79	...
Cyprus‖	69,160	2,270	565	37,866	1,605	73	4,439	300	11	798	69	7	81.8	7
Denmark	535,063	41,461	2,460	221,629	3,663	209	94,411	...	193	58,272*	7,901*	49*	100.	8
Dominica	20,458	521	58	1,787	89	4	84	2	1	20	2	1	58.5	...
Ecuador	866,539	23,647	7,002	101,568	8,164	359	49,634	3,269	237	19,600	1,969	14	69.4	10
Egypt	3,740,595	96,693	8,418	1,146,474	41,038	1,705	300,213	15,689	317	192,605	9,886	106	26.7	14
El Salvador	562,354	14,203	2,934	74,533	...	497	25,005	...	364	841	...	4	50.8	10
Ethiopia	513,981	10,403	1,844	88,861	3,399	84	7,204	508	74	6,225*§	533*§	24*§	...	...
Fiji	121,374	3,717	616	15,965	598	62	1,233	146	25	425	61	1	81.0	14
Finland	474,299	23,731	5,221	315,710	16,872	661	101,468‡	6,156	786	58,444‡	5,603‡	20	100.	7
France	5,147,282	220,180	64,935	3,032,904	194,107	9,256	825,214	39,722	2,076	728,295	35,000	111	100.	7
French Guiana	10,816	343	55	2,146	128	6	907	63	4	—	—	—	72.	15
French Polynesia	30,660	1,178	157	5,457	318	15	876	70	3	—	—	—	94.5	15
Gambia	17,140	623	95	5,178	225	21	181	18	2	149	12	1	...	...
Germany, West	6,414,161	198,325	26,116	2,212,936	98,667	4,465	1,911,354	35,071	5,793	647,343	44,633	3,676	99.9	6
Greece	919,067	29,011	9,097	458,771	14,277	900	85,322	450	348	97,130	3,458	49	82.	10
Guatemala	326,843	14,593	5,276	79,926	4,580	412	797	216	3	16,572	1,069	4	39.8	7
Honduras	376,966	10,437	4,143	33,392	2,516	110	1,202	140	9	2,883	...	5	47.3	10
Hong Kong	739,619	21,619	1,385	216,775	8,487¶	293	14,104	—	30	14,204	1,073	16	74.6	10
Iceland	27,300	1,067	187	18,116	873	145	10,505	305	99	1,699	134	1	100.	...
India	37,650,549	978,811	395,724	30,892,031	1,079,525	109,393	244,292	16,841	2,757	786,158	70,464	2,787	29.35	...
Iran	3,415,650	107,705	25,758	1,012,920	28,244	2,509	43,867	2,642	279	76,044	2,880	102	29.4	7
Iraq	1,015,942	73,316	5,172	302,611	10,114	863	3,932	391	17	40,288	1,850	64	...	...
Ireland	520,129	15,640	4,284	192,442	11,223	893	4,700	...	100	24,496	...	64	100.	...
Italy	4,891,454	228,998	38,083	2,840,087	247,521	11,068	983,302	84,860	4,162	686,557	10,970	121	91.6	6
Ivory Coast	507,514	11,273	2,367	66,133	2,990	115	4,288	448	24	5,621	189	15	...	...
Japan	9,403,193	361,149	25,013	9,244,605	431,292	16,155	1,414,324	48,916	8,024	1,618,189	90,151	852	98.5	...
Jordan♀	277,619	7,150	865	94,654	4,092	597	2,958	165	13	4,557	208	12	46.	15
Kenya	1,427,589	41,479	6,123	126,855	5,881	783	9,958	622	36	6,398	690	4	60.	16
Korea, South	5,807,448	103,756	6,085	1,958,249	50,279	2,653	362,361	14,908	734	181,453	9,296	179	95.3	11
Kuwait	115,683	6,337	235	13,773	1,215	22	3,558	397	18	4,260*	722*	5*	48.	10
Laos	246,400	6,845	3,281	9,519	410	32	4,686	380	33	1,131	87	4	34.28	15
Lebanon	528,488	429,124	1,881	130,210	2,479	911	...	...	238	35,152*	1,921*	22*	88.	14
Lesotho	180,903	3,583	1,304	5,011	224	29	511	44	21	1,359	...	8	58.6	15
Liberia	120,245	3,384	889	15,494	918	195	1,277	66	5	1,109	164	3	23.6	5
Malagasy Rep.	939,021	14,415	5,858	101,412	4,757	513	11,343	867	114	5,293	307	10	...	...
Malaysia	1,732,230	54,332	6,328	607,693	23,453	1,104	14,851	600	69	21,559	1,390	12	...	...
Mauritius	150,402	4,731	347	43,969	1,747	139	1,160	64	12	375	40	1	62.6	5
Mexico	8,947,555	191,091	44,610	1,502,087¶	107,881‡¶	5,388¶	—	—	—	194,090	20,582‡	105	66.6	10
Netherlands	1,522,957	53,704	8,958	561,657	36,912	1,621	399,946	36,000	1,972	162,184	17,500	350	100.	...
Netherlands Antilles	43,628	1,215	121	11,090	454	38	5,317	268	28	—	—	—	...	...
New Caledonia	24,676	1,015	253	3,745	251	16	1,387	131	7	—	—	—	80.2	15
New Zealand	517,537	18,791	2,593	186,743	9,932	386	1,882	859	8	31,231	2,642	20	100.	...
Nicaragua	278,752	7,540	2,114	41,958	1,733	173	3,666	217	35	7,682	487	6	58.4	...
Norway	537,172	27,893	4,029	90,524	5,132	350	73,017	6,139	711	27,080	2,317	10	88.1	6
Pakistan	10,115,116	219,442	70,082	3,436,879	112,184	11,382	48,185	3,988	319	375,695	13,788	389	15.9	...
Panama	255,287	8,448	1,784	54,040	2,458	71	24,667	1,282	120	8,947	592	2	78.3	10
Peru	2,338,506	65,623	19,837	594,876	24,798	1,255	84,863	7,632	417	112,087	11,977	121	61.1	15
Philippines	6,193,128	208,587	36,679	1,284,306	39,173	2,570	77,890	1,916	781	551,750*	19,463*	555*	72.	...
Poland	5,257,000	211,500	26,126	401,300	17,500	858	1,710,700	63,600	9,726	209,800	31,900	85	95.7	7
Portugal	989,676	29,753	17,190	258,937	16,382	1,602	134,122	8,231	277	46,019	2,285	69	59.	...
Qatar	15,068	767	85	3,448	230	5	446	73	4	—	—	—	...	...
Réunion	114,508	4,697	403	28,548	1,265	60	1,982	174	8	975	112	2	33.	15
Rhodesia	697,107	18,364	3,712	52,685	2,823	193	2,718	271	19	1,799	287	5	30.	16
Romania	2,886,855	133,842	14,928	261,749	13,679	572	344,141	18,721	904	128,796	14,337	94	89.5	10
Ryukyu Islands	210,541	8,301	401	54,653	2,726	57	17,695	1,102	31	7,165	310	4	97.9	15
Saudi Arabia	406,399	17,048	1,859	67,817	4,332	387	12,475	891	60	6,942	573	9	...	...
Sierra Leone	154,898	5,011	1,023	29,058	1,364	81	1,739	189	13	1,116	384	2	...	...
Singapore	363,518	12,248	427	145,740	6,550	123	4,727	440	8	527,668	1,157	5	70.	10
Somalia	61,384	1,665	294	5,947	286	21	736	63	5	964	58	3	...	...
South Africaδ	3,779,864	85,096	13,324	258,442	20,919	1,324	60,760	2,532	203	84,388	12,138	67	...	...
Spain	4,828,600	138,257	137,287	1,396,505	38,869	3,402	361,079	26,582	924	194,464	15,171	58	74.9	10
Sudan	610,798	12,986	3,352	190,749	9,020	1,210	2,983	251	23	11,833	1,002	12	17.1	10
Swaziland	69,055	1,706	351	8,027	432	54	566	56	3	79	18	1	29.2	14
Sweden	622,000	27,700	4,500	379,326	32,600	300	167,980	15,300	800	114,848	4,909	36	...	...
Taiwan	2,445,405	59,489	2,319	977,760	36,777	738	176,829	7,506	147	203,473	10,377	92	85.3	6
Thailand	5,748,534	179,119	29,399	507,368	22,911	1,608	92,502	7,229	220	105,475	9,035	50	...	...
Togo	228,505	3,909	916	19,742	663	64	2,514	185	17	926	59	2	20.	15
Turkey	4,908,743	126,106	37,200	965,697	24,146	2,057	222,507	9,268	1,098	222,503	11,001	203	48.72	6
Uganda	709,708	21,074	2,720	46,483	2,067	118	2,784	245	22	7,711	757	28	...	...
U.S.S.R.	39,746,000	1,758,000□	184,500□	4,401,000	251,000	...	4,166,600◇	134,000	...	4,310,900	201,000	...	...	...
United Kingdom	5,960,129	222,411	28,650	3,406,787	213,464	6,817	311,252	52,183	933	357,207	45,564	250	...	...
United States	36,800,000	1,261,000‡	85,779	14,800,000¶	1,014,000‡¶	31,411¶	...	...	...	7,600,000	593,000‡	2,525	97.6	14
Venezuela	1,818,815	52,350	10,504	321,124	13,640	670	163,874	7,683	420	86,463	8,967	55	55.3	...
Vietnam, South	2,718,056	52,194	7,984	710,541	21,225	886	20,207	1,563	57	57,927	1,662	15	60.	...
Western Samoa	29,419	869	140	9,619	408	63	95	11	1	319	29	2	97.5	10
Yemen, Aden	135,523	4,344	866	17,061	1,469	82	1,043	115	12	439	13	1	...	...

Note: Third level may include individual faculties within a university. *Includes teacher training at both 2nd and 3rd levels.
†Includes 1,316 combined primary-secondary schools. ‡Includes part-time. §Public only. ‖Schools managed by the Turkish communities are excluded.
¶General and vocational combined. ♀Data, except literacy, refer to East Bank of Jordan only. δIncludes some double counting.
□Includes general education at the secondary level. ◇Includes teacher training.

The ruling did not affect indirect aid based on the "child welfare" principle. It also appeared to leave the door open to released time for public-school students to attend religious instruction, shared time between parochial and public schools, and other forms of cooperation.

But direct financial assistance was what church-school officials wanted. They claimed the rate of parochial school closings would accelerate sharply unless government money was received in large amounts (although some sources maintained that the closings would continue, though more gradually, even with government funding since other factors were in part responsible for declining enrollment in church-run schools).

Roman Catholic schoolmen and many state legislators refused to accept the Supreme Court decision as the great barrier to parochiaid that some observers interpreted it to be. Several legislatures enacted laws that appeared to be in direct conflict with the court's ruling. Other states continued to search for ways of circumventing the verdict. These consisted principally of tuition refunds, tax credits, and the "voucher plan." In all of these approaches funds would go to the parents and not directly to the school.

On the national level the alternative receiving the most attention was the voucher plan, which would permit parents to decide whether they wanted to send a child to the public schools or to some private or church school. A local authority would supply a voucher, which the parent would then take to the school of his choice in payment of tuition. The school would redeem the voucher for cash. The U.S. Office of Economic Opportunity had begun espousing the voucher plan in 1970. Feasibility studies were carried out in three cities during the 1970–71 academic year, and planning grants were made available for the next school year. The original intent was to provide alternative means of instruction to the public schools, on the theory that competition would force the established system to improve. Just what effects a voucher plan would have in this or other directions was not clear. Certainly, parochiaid advocates viewed vouchers as a means to their end, as did Southern segregationists who foresaw a possible means of support for all-white private academies.

Although government aid for parochial schools was an established fact in Canada, the issue surfaced in the fall elections in Ontario. Roman Catholic schools received tax support through the tenth grade under terms of the British North America Act, which paved the way for an independent Canadian government. Parochial-school supporters pressed for full provincial aid, through grade 13.

Teachers. The school financial squeeze inevitably led in places to personnel cutbacks. In the U.S. salaries accounted for about 80% of the fiscal outlay of schools, and teachers were not exempt from budget cutting. For the first time in years, education majors and school of education graduates could not count on getting positions immediately. At least one leading university advised education students to consider remedial work or some other specialty rather than aiming toward a general classroom assignment. The tighter teacher job situation was broadly viewed as artificial, resulting from lack of funds rather than lack of need. Openings for teachers dealing with the special problems of the poor and handicapped went unfilled in many districts—either from a scarcity of dollars or of qualified personnel. Still, the number

of teachers increased (though at a reduced rate) at the start of the 1971–72 school year. One reason was that the number of students had risen again, to approximately 60.2 million at all levels, both public and private. This included 36.7 million in grades one through eight and 15.1 million in grades 9 through 12. While these figures reflected an increase at the secondary level, elementary enrollment declined slightly for the second consecutive year.

Applicants for teaching positions in Canada also found jobs scarcer. Efforts continued in several provinces to upgrade teacher preparation by requiring longer study to qualify. Ontario was a case in point. Until recently, an aspiring teacher could be certified on the basis of a one-year college program after 13 years of public schooling; by September 1973 a four-year degree would be required. Meanwhile, efforts moved ahead to transfer teacher training from separate institutions into schools of education at the provincial universities.

Pay disputes still occupied British teachers in 1971. A deadlock over salary negotiations in the spring led to arbitration and a 10% increase in salaries. The 260,000-strong National Union of Teachers and the 70,000-strong National Association of Schoolmasters were at loggerheads, however, the NAS maintaining that the interests of career teachers, as against new entrants, were insufficiently considered in the salary scales. To make its point the NAS staged a one-day nationwide strike on June 30. Schools in Sweden were also disrupted by staff strikes, while in France teachers were withdrawing at intervals during the year over pay and working conditions, as well as over controversial government plans for changes in state aid to private schools.

Some newly trained teachers were finding it hard to get jobs in Britain. At the same time, there were reports that because of the job shortage in the U.S., many American academics were seeking appointments in Britain while some work permits previously issued to teachers from Britain in the U.S. were being canceled. Elsewhere the picture was different. In Australia, New South Wales put its shortage of teachers for 1972 at over 1,000 and sent a recruiting mission to London in July. Australian authorities also were hoping to recruit 100 British teachers for Papua. Hamburg, W.Ger., hired 25 Britons for English teaching at its grammar schools and 76 Americans to relieve its acute shortage of science teachers.

Another aspect of the teaching profession came to public attention when Christopher Searle, a probationary master at Sir John Cass's Foundation and Red Coat School, London, was discharged after he published a book of poems by some of his pupils contrary to the wishes of the school governors. Searle received support from Trevor Huddleston, bishop of Stepney, and others, while groups of pupils staged strikes on his behalf and went on a protest march to Trafalgar Square. The Association of Education Committees defended the governors, however, finding the real issue to be not the publication of the poems but Searle's defiance of the governors.

Curriculum. Besides complaints that not enough money was spent on the salaries of teachers in Britain, there were scathing comments on the allocations for textbooks and other teaching aids. There were also complaints of indifference to the new media. In its evidence to the James Committee (on the training of teachers), the Independent Television Authority maintained that most colleges of education (teacher-

U.S. Education Commissioner Sidney P. Marland, Jr., said after taking office early in 1971 that he would give vocational education top priority.
WIDE WORLD

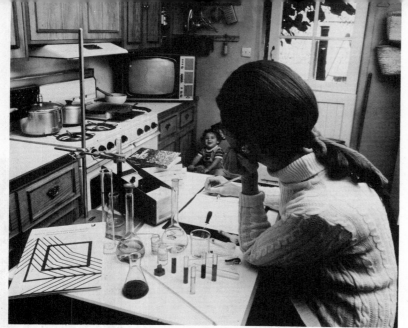

A student of Britain's Open University studies chemistry at home. The new university conducts home study courses through radio and television so that men and women may work toward an academic degree on their own time.

training colleges) either did not see or failed to exploit the educational merits of television. The National Council for Educational Technology proposed a five-year project to improve the use of mixed media in the colleges themselves as a step toward improving the use of educational technology in schools. Meanwhile, in India plans went forward for a satellite-based educational television system to be set up in cooperation with the U.S. National Aeronautics and Space Administration. By 1974 rural communities would receive educational television by direct broadcast from a communications satellite with signals powerful enough to be received by inexpensive equipment on the ground.

Innovative efforts continued during the year, with particular emphasis on environmental studies and—in the U.S.—courses emphasizing the dangers of drug abuse. At Leeds (Eng.) University the first master of science degree course in the control of pollution of the environment was instituted.

In a project for the Open University, Britain's new academic institution conducted by broadcasting, correspondence courses, and associated media, some 4,000 students were assigned to map noise levels throughout the country. Also in Britain, proposals were formulated for an advanced-level secondary-school course in environmental studies for the General Certificate of Education. The new course was expected to include such subjects as spoliation of the countryside, soil erosion, deforestation, and noise and pollution in towns.

Another discernible movement was increased emphasis on vocational training. In his first public address after taking office early in the year, the U.S. commissioner of education, Sidney P. Marland, Jr., announced that he planned to give vocational or "career education" top priority. In Britain the year brought much anxiety over jobs for those out of school. Unemployment or dead-end jobs for teenagers increased the threat of delinquency, and violence in schools was becoming a matter of urgent concern.

Sex education in the schools continued to be a centre of controversy. In Birmingham, Eng., a woman teacher was at first suspended but later reinstated for having taken part in a sex film, privately produced for educational purposes. The film, entitled *Growing*

Up, showed the sex act and some sequences on masturbation. Mrs. Thatcher took the unusual course of announcing in the House of Commons that, although she had no direct powers in the matter, she hoped the local authorities would consider with utmost caution any suggestion that the film should be shown in their schools. There was controversy, too, over the *Little Red Schoolbook,* which included a section on intercourse and petting, and a schoolchildren's issue of the underground newspaper *Oz*. Both publications were the subject of court proceedings under the Obscene Publications Act. (*See* PUBLISHING.)

Among more traditional subjects, Latin received a severe blow in Britain when it was dropped by Oxford University as an entrance requirement for arts undergraduates. At the same time, an institute of modern English studies was set up at Leeds University in Britain to study English as it was spoken in the former British colonies. Britain's entry into the EEC brought fresh attention to the subject of modern languages. Mrs. Thatcher had predicted to the Association of Education Committees that joining the EEC would widen educational horizons and increase the opportunities of Britain's children. The West London College, a general and commercial college run by the Inner London Education Authority, announced plans for courses leading to the new international baccalaureate, recognized by Britain and 19 other countries as a university entrance qualification. The more progressive of the local education authorities were hoping to establish links between their own schools and colleges and similar institutions in France and West Germany, while bilingual secretarial courses increasingly appeared in the colleges of further education.

Minorities. Racial desegregation in the U.S. public schools continued to be a principal concern in both the North and the South. The position of the Nixon administration was clearly one of moderation rather than aggressive pressure on often reluctant school authorities. The president's open opposition to massive busing to achieve desegregation and his preference for neighbourhood schools were critical factors in administration policy, although not all executive-department officials concurred.

The Supreme Court's decisions in *Swann* v. *Charlotte-Mecklenburg Board of Education* and four companion cases in April appeared to undermine the administration's position. The court found that there was a "presumption against schools that are substantially disproportionate in their racial composition" and that the neighbourhood school is not immune from desegregation. The ruling declared that desegregation must be achieved, even by arrangements that are "administratively awkward, inconvenient and even bizarre," and that busing is an acceptable means to the desired end. Many Southern schoolmen accepted the Swann decision as the law of the land, and through the summer officials of the Department of Health, Education, and Welfare worked with them in drawing up desegregation plans and making funds available to cover the purchase of buses and other expenses.

Early in August, however, President Nixon threw the matter into confusion by his comments on the "Austin case." In Austin, Tex., HEW had submitted one desegregation plan to a federal court and the local school board another. The court rejected the HEW proposal in favour of the less extensive board plan, which called for transporting pupils from 40 elementary schools to educational centres for part of each day during one week out of every four. After the decision, the president publicly denounced the HEW proposal and reiterated his opposition to busing, although Atty. Gen. John Mitchell announced at the same time that his department would appeal the Austin ruling in support of still a third plan to be prepared by the board. A week later the president issued an unequivocal warning to federal officials: stop pressing for desegregation of Southern schools through forced busing or find another job. Many Southern school boards and administrators, who had been prepared to move ahead with busing, felt they had been undercut. Not only were they likely to lose federal funds to pay for buses already purchased, but they were exposed to the criticism of fellow citizens who had opposed desegregation all along.

The president's comments were widely interpreted as politically motivated, reflecting in large measure his efforts to undercut Gov. George Wallace of Alabama. Meanwhile, the long-standing Southern complaint that Southern schools were being subjected to a double standard in desegregation matters was losing force as cities all across the North and West faced desegregation orders of one kind or another. Philadelphia, Pittsburgh, Detroit, Los Angeles, San Francisco, and Denver were among the cities affected. San Francisco began large-scale busing to correct the black-white imbalance in the schools and found that the most vehement opposition came from another minority group—the Chinese of Chinatown, who boycotted the program on the ground that integration would destroy their tightly knit culture. In Pontiac, Mich., several buses were blown up a few days before the opening of school, allegedly by persons affiliated with the Ku Klux Klan, but the city's busing program proceeded on schedule. About a month later, a federal court in Michigan handed down a decision stating that Detroit area schools were segregated as a result of the official policies not only of local boards of education but of state and federal agencies as well, and ordering the state to provide a plan for a metropolitan school district. The implication was that all-white suburbs might no longer provide a refuge for parents seeking to escape busing or other forms of integration.

Boston schools were charged late in 1971 with officially maintaining segregation, a violation of the 1964 Civil Rights Act. The charges came after an 18-month study by the Department of Health, Education, and Welfare. The first city in the North to be so accused, Boston was threatened with losing up to $10 million a year in federal aid unless it designed an acceptable plan for desegregation. Earlier in the year the Massachusetts Committee Against Discrimination had charged the Boston School Committee with violation of the state's racial imbalance act. This law, the first of its type in the U.S., required that nonwhites not exceed 50% of a school's enrollment. As a result, the state withheld $14 million in general aid funds and froze construction funds.

In Britain reports from both the Department of Education and Science and the National Foundation for Educational Research pointed to inadequacies in the methods used to test coloured immigrants for educational potential and attainment, and the danger of underestimating the ability of such pupils as a result of language difficulties was stressed repeatedly. Similar problems surfaced in the U.S., where the press carried sensational reports of Spanish-speaking children who had spent years in classes for the retarded because of their low scores on intelligence tests given in English. Education for the Spanish-speaking was a growing problem in such cities as New York and Chicago with large populations of Latin-American immigrants, many of them American citizens from Puerto Rico.

One difficulty was that many of the Latins wished to retain Spanish as the language of instruction. This was new in the U.S. schools, which had americanized generations of immigrants through compulsory use of English, though it was an old story in bilingual countries such as Belgium and in the French-speaking areas of Canada. Welsh, the object of nationalist demonstrations among adults in Wales, led to difficulties in Welsh infant schools, with some parents objecting to projects by which children were taught in English in the morning and in Welsh in the afternoon.

Higher Education. Isolated instances of student unrest continued to occur, although they were far less sensational than had been the case in previous years. In Britain the focus of student unrest seemed to have shifted from the universities to the new polytechnics, and the year was marked by protests from them over such varied matters as the scarcity of lodgings and the appointment of staff to whom the students had political objections. In West Germany students protested at the election of Nikolaus Lobkowicz as rector of Munich University on the ground that he was not sufficiently progressive. Other institutions of higher education where student unrest led to disruption of lectures and temporary closures included the University of Zürich, Switz., the Lisbon (Port.) Technical University, and, in India, the Benares Hindu University, the Sanskrit University, and Kalyani University.

Turkish authorities, exasperated at the continued disruption of higher education by militant students, introduced a series of bills aimed at controlling demonstrations and increasing government powers over the universities, and many academics thought to be sympathetic to the revolutionary movement were subsequently arrested. University finance and the cost of textbooks were the subjects of protest in Ghana. In Rhodesia government grants were withdrawn from a number of African university students who had demonstrated in Salisbury against racial discrimination and other grievances. In July militant students at Zambia University barricaded the campus against reprisals after ten of their number had signed a letter alleging that Pres. Kenneth Kaunda's policy toward South Africa was inconsistent. Subsequently, the university was closed by the Army and police.

Australian universities also experienced trouble with students protesting the visit of a South African rugby team or resisting call-up for national service. In Britain students at Manchester University supporting the antiapartheid movement persuaded the university to withdraw its investments in two South African companies. On the credit side, Pres. H. Kamuzu Banda of Malawi, an advocate of the coexistence of blacks and whites, received an enthusiastic welcome when he visited the Afrikaans University of Stellenbosch, S.Af., in August.

In stark contrast to the previous year's turmoil and disruption, the U.S. campus scene was relatively quiet in 1971. The few protests, sit-ins, and incidents of violence that did occur stood out boldly as exceptions to the general calm. Indicative of the changed mood was the limited response to a nationwide stu-

Mrs. Richard Nixon (right) presents the 1971 National Teacher of the Year award to Mrs. Martha Marian Stringfellow, an elementary schoolteacher in South Carolina, at the White House on April 19, 1971. The 1972 competition will be sponsored by Encyclopædia Britannica, "Ladies' Home Journal," and the Council of Chief State School Officers.

dent strike called for May 5. The spotlight fell briefly on Kent State University in Ohio as demonstrations were held commemorating the May 1970 tragedy, when four students were killed by national guardsmen during an antiwar protest. There were no incidents on the university grounds, although six nights of disturbances in the town led to 87 arrests. Attorney General Mitchell announced that there would be no federal investigation of the 1970 shootings, and the special grand jury report, which had placed the blame on students and other agitators, was burned by federal court order. Of those indicted, one was found guilty of obstructing firemen, two pleaded guilty to first degree riot charges, and indictments against the remaining 22 were dismissed for lack of evidence.

Although the reasons behind the calmer campus mood were not clear, they were eagerly sought and heatedly discussed. Some students pointed to "repression"—a firmer hand by college and police authorities. Observers emphasized the winding down of the unpopular war in Vietnam, student disillusion over the limited achievements of violent protest, and a recoiling from the possibly disastrous effects of turmoil. Some administrators noted a more serious attitude toward study, perhaps attributable to the tightening of the job market. The principal source of town and gown controversy during the year centred around the newly ratified Twenty-sixth Amendment to the Constitution, giving 18-year-olds the right to vote. There were fears of a student take-over of local government in towns where students equaled or outnumbered the resident population, and numerous complaints were made of the difficulties encountered by students attempting to register.

Despite decreased disruption, the effects of the previous year's violence lingered on in state legislatures. Lawmakers seemed determined to bring campuses under stricter control, particularly state colleges and universities. This showed up most noticeably in making these institutions more accountable for dollars spent and in cutting back on appropriation requests. This touched a vulnerable spot since campus administrators were already beginning to feel the financial pinch. Many state institutions as well as heavily endowed independent universities started sending out distress signals during the 1970–71 academic year.

In 1971 more than half of U.S. public universities

participating in a survey conducted by the National Association of State Universities and Land-Grant Colleges reported "standstill" budgets for the current year, though a 10% increase was believed necessary to keep pace with inflation; an additional ten of these institutions said they were operating at a deficit. Harvard, where Derek Bok (see BIOGRAPHY) began his first year as president, announced a budget cut of $1 million for the 1971–72 academic year. Princeton made a similar trim. Columbia's new president, William J. McGill, promised economies that would bring his institution out of the red in five years, and Milton Eisenhower, returning to Johns Hopkins as interim president, ordered a doubling of teaching assignments for faculty members.

There was an evident disenchantment with college, or at least a lessening sense of haste to get there. Many young people were taking a year off to work or travel between high school and college; others were not sure that four years on campus provided the advertised passport to success or happiness in life. Even so, the total number of U.S. students in higher education jumped from 7.9 million to an estimated 8.4 million. Increases were noted especially in state colleges and universities—some 70% of U.S. college students were registered in state institutions—and in low-tuition community colleges, designed for commuting students. Black enrollment was up significantly, and other minority groups also showed noteworthy gains.

To hold their own, private colleges and universities were looking for ways to ease the financial pressure on students. At the start of the academic year, Yale contracted with 1,257 of its students to spread tuition payments over a number of years after graduation. The cost of education was not a fixed dollar amount, but a percentage of students' earnings during the payment period. No more than $800 of an individual's cost per year could be deferred. The next month Duke offered certain students a similar option. Another straw in the wind was the announcement by Beloit (Wis.) College that, beginning in 1972, it would charge students on the basis of ability to pay, computed on family income and assets.

Costs of higher education could also be reduced by cutting the length of programs and by letting students work at home. Glenn S. Dumke, chancellor of California State Colleges, recommended a flexible approach that would allow a student to complete his studies in as little as two and a half years. California was also involved in an "external degree" program that offered full- or part-time students of any age the opportunity to begin or resume their studies without living on campus. New York put a similar plan into effect in two branches of its new Empire State College that opened in the fall of 1971, and Massachusetts planned an "open university" that would offer external degrees based on correspondence study, television courses, and equivalency examinations. These projects resembled Britain's Open University or "university of the air," which received a grant of £15,000 from the Social Science Research Council to monitor the progress of its students over five years. Similarly, in Japan, a broadcast university was launched on commercial radio.

Provincial support of public universities in Canada held firm, though some private universities found themselves in trouble. McGill University, faced with the prospect of an $8.3 million deficit in 1971–72 and an even greater shortage the following year, announced plans for a $3.5 million slash in its budget. Included were a sizable cut in faculty expenditure and the elimination of funds for intercollegiate athletics.

(K. G.; L. R. Bu.)

See also Libraries; Medicine; Motion Pictures; Museums and Galleries; Police; Race Relations.

El Salvador

A republic on the Pacific coast of Central America and the smallest country on the isthmus, El Salvador is bounded on the west by Guatemala and on the north and east by Honduras. Area: 8,098 sq.mi. (21,975 sq.km.). Pop. (1971 est.): 3,564,656. Cap. and largest city: San Salvador (pop., 1971 est., 368,711). Language: Spanish. Religion: Roman Catholic. President in 1971, Col. Fidel Sánchez Hernández.

The brief but bitter hostilities that erupted between El Salvador and Honduras in July 1969 continued to make their effects felt. Of greatest concern was the fate of the five-member Central American Common Market (CACM)—El Salvador, Honduras, Guatemala, Nicaragua, and Costa Rica—which had been jeopardized by the conflict. Maintenance of this regional economic union was of particular concern to El Salvador, the most industrialized and densely populated of the member countries. After the war and the subsequent border closing with Honduras, El Salvador was fortunate in establishing alternate trade routes to its markets in Nicaragua and Costa Rica. Continuing favourable agricultural and marketing conditions combined with vigorous public and private efforts in the wake of the war did much to reduce if not eliminate all of the adversities stemming from the conflict.

By the end of 1971 telephone, telegraph, and postal links had been reestablished between El Salvador and Honduras, and all traffic was moving across the border except that which originated in either of the two nations. In several efforts to further reduce the remaining border barriers and strengthen the CACM, the foreign minister of El Salvador joined representatives from the other CACM countries, except Honduras, at several meetings in 1971. At a January gathering in Antigua, Guatemala, the four ministers agreed to maintain the CACM, with or without Honduras. Another meeting of CACM representatives, again without Honduras, was hosted by El Salvador in July for the purpose of creating a "normalization commission," whose function it would be to resolve differences in the common market and to secure the participation of Honduras.

In September the two principal political parties in El Salvador selected their candidates for the presidential election to be held in February 1972. The incumbent and moderate National Conciliation Party selected Col. Arturo Armando Molina, the private secretary of President Sánchez. The principal opposition party, a coalition of two left-of-centre parties called the Christian Democrats, chose the former mayor of San Salvador, José Napoleon Duarte, as their candidate. The present government's recent reforms on education, social development, and land redistribution were expected to elicit growing opposition from the wealthy families as election time approached.

(A. D. Bu.)

Angry unemployed Canadians picket outside the Royal York Hotel in Toronto March 3, 1971, while Prime Minister Pierre Trudeau attends a Liberal fund-raising banquet.
BLAISE EDWARDS—
CANADIAN PRESS

EL SALVADOR

Education. (1968–69) Primary, pupils 471,622, teachers 13,406; secondary, pupils 53,673, teachers 2,484; vocational, pupils 22,681, teachers 1,033; teacher training (1967–68), students 3,210, teachers 295; higher (including 2 universities; 1967–68), students 6,748, teaching staff 1,017.

Finance. Monetary unit: colón, with a par value of 2.50 colones to U.S. $1 (6 colones = £1 sterling) and a free rate (Sept. 27, 1971) of 6.20 colones to £1 sterling. Gold, SDRs, and foreign exchange, central bank: (June 1971) U.S. $79.2 million; (June 1970) U.S. $77.4 million. Budget (1969 rev. est.): revenue 279,266,000 colones; expenditure 255,831,000 colones. Gross national product: (1969) 2,362,000,000 colones; (1968) 2,265,000,000 colones. Money supply: (June 1971) 308.2 million colones; (June 1970) 285.5 million colones. Cost of living (1963 = 100): (April 1971) 108; (April 1970) 107.

Foreign Trade. (1970) Imports 535.9 million colones; exports 573.4 million colones. Import sources (1969): U.S. 29%; Guatemala 18%; Japan 9%; West Germany 7%. Export destinations (1969): West Germany 22%; U.S. 21%; Guatemala 18%; Japan 10%; Costa Rica 8%; Honduras 6%; Nicaragua 5%. Main exports: coffee 50%; cotton 10%.

Transport and Communications. Roads (1968) 8,527 km. (including 625 km. of Pan-American Highway). Motor vehicles in use (1969): passenger 34,-100; commercial (including buses) 16,400. Railways (1969) *c.* 740 km. Telephones (Jan. 1970) 35,495. Radio receivers (Dec. 1969) 400,000. Television receivers (Dec. 1969) 75,000.

Agriculture. Production (in 000; metric tons; 1970; 1969 in parentheses): rice *c.* 90 (83); corn *c.* 310 (279); sorghum *c.* 115 (107); coffee *c.* 114 (*c.* 150); cotton, lint *c.* 49 (46); sugar, raw value (1970–71) 149, (1969–70) 117. Livestock (in 000; 1969–70): cattle *c.* 1,350; pigs *c.* 418; horses *c.* 67; chickens *c.* 2,200.

Industry. Production (1970): cement 167,000 metric tons; electricity 674 million kw-hr.

Employment, Wages, and Hours

During 1971 rising prices and industrial disputes continued to be the dominating issues in many labour markets. Table I shows two indexes of industrial disputes for 1969 compared with the annual average for the previous nine years. In only 2 of the 14 countries do both indexes fall; in all others one or both indexes show increases: the number of working days lost was more than three times the average in Canada and Italy, and more than two times the average in Australia, Ireland, Sweden, and the United Kingdom. The figures for France exclude the strikes of 1968, and, perhaps in reaction to the 1968 situation, there was only a slight increase in 1969 in the number of strikes, and the number of working days lost was below average.

It was, of course, not possible to give a single explanation of this general rise in industrial disputes, but as a matter of economics, strikes are about real wages and there are two factors that should be taken into account when considering them. As shown in Table II, after the worldwide price inflation during the Korean War, rates of price inflation for the next decade remained at around $2\frac{1}{2}$% per annum. But in the later 1960s this rate accelerated to between $3\frac{1}{2}$ and 4% per annum. This tended to reduce the rate of growth of real wages, and trade unions generally demanded higher rates of increase in money wages.

There was a second, hidden factor that was important for earnings. Fundamentally, a worker's concern was with the real value of his take-home pay; that is, with what he actually had after allowing for price rises and for increased income tax payments and social security contributions. As wages rose to counteract price increases, some workers rose above

Unemployed steelworkers, hit hard by a U.S. Steel announcement that only 30% of its work force would be recalled, wait their turn to sign up for benefits at the Indiana Employment Security Division in Gary, Aug. 5, 1971.

the tax exemption limit and started paying taxes for the first time and those already paying taxes paid progressively larger proportions of their income as tax. Thus, it became increasingly difficult for workers to obtain what they considered satisfactory increases in take-home pay, although this was not the concern of the employer whose labour costs came out of pre-tax income.

A study of the U.K. showed that from 1959 to 1964, the real take-home pay of the median wage earner rose by nearly 2% per annum, but that from 1964 to 1969 the rise had been at only 1% per annum. The reduction was entirely caused by increased taxes and other deductions from income. In two cases where workers went on strike, the average local-government manual worker had absolutely no increase in real take-home pay between 1965 and 1969 and electricity workers suffered an annual decrease in real take-home pay of 0.6%.

Employment and Unemployment. In 1969 the general growth of employment, particularly in manufacturing industries, was rapid, and the average decline in unemployment in industrial market economies was 10% (*see* Table III). In a sample of third world countries, average population growth remained more than double that for industrial countries and the flow of young people into the labour market continued to exacerbate problems of structural unemployment.

Third World Economies. Employment growth in manufacturing was reasonable with two countries, Taiwan and Tanzania, recording spectacular increases as industrialization progressed (*see* Table III). In Taiwan industrial production rose by 7.3% in 1969 and in Tanzania cement production rose by 7% and textile production by 60%. Several countries recorded decreased unemployment in 1969 and 1970 (*see* Table IV). The unusual rise in unemployment in Taiwan in 1969 was largely caused by a fall in farm output as a result of bad weather.

In Zambia, employment rose by 5% between June 1969 and June 1970, and this contributed to the large decline in recorded unemployment; despite economic growth inflation continued to be a problem and between the fourth quarters of 1969 and 1970 the consumer price index for lower income groups rose by 5%.

In Ceylon, unemployment continued to rise at an accelerating rate. In 1970, before the election of a left-wing government, there was a considerable increase in the number of strikes and after the election industrial production was stagnant, with price controls being imposed in a vain attempt to control

inflation. Civil unrest in April 1971 could, in large measure, be ascribed to the failure to relieve unemployment, which stood at over half a million, including over 12,000 university graduates. A new five-year plan was aimed to give an increased emphasis to the creation of jobs.

India's unemployment situation continued to worsen despite a fairly rapid growth in industrial production of about 7% in 1969 and about 5% in 1970, and in food grain output of 4.3% in 1970. In 1971, the economy had to cope with the influx of refugees from East Pakistan and with the brief but heavily fought Indo-Pakistani war.

In Singapore the rapid industrialization necessitated by withdrawal of British military expenditures continued: between 1968 and 1969, industrial employment expanded by 20% and the value of both output and industrial exports by around 27%. An important part of the government's policy was to hold the cost of living stable and thus to moderate wage increases so that the growth of employment would not be discouraged by rapidly rising labour costs. This policy entailed judicial restraint on the activity of trade unions since, with the growing scarcities of skilled labour, the unions were becoming more militant.

Industrial Market Economies. In the more developed economies there was little increase in manufacturing employment in 1970, and an actual stagnation in 1971, as shown in Table V. To deal with rising prices many countries operated policies of economic restraint, and there was an increase of nearly 17% in unemployment in 1971 over the 1970 figures. The countries most severely affected by this downturn were the U.S. and Canada, France, West Germany, Sweden, and the U.K.

The worsening unemployment situation in the U.S. was the result of the combined effects of anti-inflation policies, a cyclical fall in investment, and a major strike in the automobile industry from September to November 1970. Public policies involved a considerable cut in federal expenditures, chiefly on defense, and unemployment among highly skilled labour became common. By mid-1971 there were signs that the peak of unemployment had been reached, and economic policies were being changed so as to hasten recovery. Proportionately more people, however, were entering the labour market, chiefly women, teen-agers, and those discharged from the armed services. Unemployment rates were particularly high among young unskilled workers, and the government was attempting to mitigate this with special manpower programs.

In France the measures taken to restrain consumption and prices after the 1969 currency devaluation

Table I. Index of Industrial Disputes: 1969
Annual average 1960–68=100

Country	Number of disputes	Total working days lost
Australia	159	265
Canada	142	309
Belgium	166	58
Finland	247	62
France	117	82
Iceland	319	136
Ireland	158	258
Italy	117	333
New Zealand	174	185
Netherlands	57	30
Norway	44	26
Sweden	213	229
United Kingdom	131	215
United States	145	166
Average	156	168

Source: International Labour Office, *Year Book of Labour Statistics* (1970).

continued to have effect and unemployment increased considerably, particularly in 1971. But the size of the increase in recorded unemployment was caused partly by regional imbalances in the supply and demand for labour, and partly by improved coverage of those unemployed. In West Germany the ending of the prolonged investment boom that had persisted since 1967 brought a sudden turnaround in economic activity and by mid-1971 unemployment had increased sharply. The revaluation of the mark contributed to this by reducing profits and the demand for exports.

In Sweden the decrease in manufacturing employment was particularly sharp as public and private investment was reduced in an effort to contain inflation and improve a critical balance of payments situation. The economy was running below capacity: in the first quarter of 1970 there were 2.5 vacancies for every unemployed person; by December this ratio was down to 1.5 and unemployment began rising. The situation, however, may have been improved by the reduction in the working week from 42.5 to 40 hours beginning the second half of 1971.

In the U.K., the squeeze on profits (resulting in several notable bankruptcies), the decline in investment, and rises in wages led to a considerable "shake-out" in the labour force, including the likelihood of more than a million unemployed during the winter of 1971–72. In July 1971 measures were taken to stimulate consumption, but excess capacity in manufacturing was so considerable that it would be a long time before investment itself could provide the necessary expansionary expenditure.

The growth of industrial output in Italy was slowing down steadily, as seen in the rise of unemployment in 1971. There was growing industrial unrest, with more and more strikes over issues other than wages. These, together with the large increases in wages, led to bankruptcies and to further losses of jobs. A slight slackening of growth in the Netherlands combined with a rapid rise in labour costs, which reduced the growth in vacancies, led to a rise in unemployment in 1971. But the demand for women workers rose strongly and the recruitment of foreign workers for heavy manual labour was not reduced. In Ireland industrial growth declined in 1970 partly because of the six-month bank strike. Recovery brought a reduction in unemployment in the first half of 1971.

Industrial investment in Japan slowed down during 1970 and although real gross national product (GNP) expanded by 11%, industrial production expanded by only 1.4% between the second quarter of 1970 and the second quarter of 1971. Accordingly, unemployment rose in 1971 for the first time in many years. The causes of this were not clear: to some extent it may have been due to the fact that previous investment overshot the mark and created excess capacity.

Centrally Planned Economies. On average, output growth in the centrally planned economies increased in 1970 because of higher productivity growth as the increase in manufacturing employment fell slightly (*see* Table VI). The U.S.S.R. enjoyed a record grain harvest in 1970, nearly 9% above the previous record, and production of consumer durables, particularly of cars, was expanded in line with the new five-year plan's aim of a "substantial raising of the well-being of the workers."

In Czechoslovakia output growth improved in 1970 because of higher productivity. The rate of price inflation fell by half, following a direct price freeze imposed at the beginning of the year and a restraint on investment and the money supply. Efforts were being made to reduce the high rate of turnover of workers in industry and the high rate of absenteeism caused by workers being engaged on second jobs.

In Hungary productivity increases permitted a considerable increase in industrial output but agricultural production fell because of bad weather. Tight labour markets caused a great turnover of labour and the trade unions were taking a greater interest in management decisions and in price-fixing. Poland suffered a severe social shock late in 1970 as workers struck to protest increases in food prices, partly caused by poor agricultural performance. In February 1971 food prices were restored and the wages of the lowest paid workers were raised. The rapid growth in manufacturing employment in Romania and the outflow of labour from agriculture continued. Bulgaria's agricultural reform was providing a better utilization of labour in large scale units linked to crop-processing industries so that labour could be released for manufacturing industries.

Wages. *Industrial Market Economies.* The movements of wages and prices are shown in Table VII.

Table II. Annual Average Rates of Price Inflation (%)

Countries	1948–52	1953–57	1958–62	1963–68
18 Industrial market economies	5.5	2.6	2.5	4.0
7 Centrally planned economies*	...	–1.0	1.2	2.9
17 African economies	8.8	2.8	2.3	3.7
12 Asian economies	4.6	2.6	2.4	3.8
14 South and Central American economies†	5.0	2.8	2.5	3.5
All countries	6.1	2.3	2.3	3.7

*Official price indexes, which may not be reliable.
†Excluding six countries with an annual average rate of inflation over 20%.

Table III. Employment, Unemployment, and Population

Changes for 1969 over 1968 (%)

Country	Employment General	Employment Manufacturing	Numbers unemployed	Population
Third world				
Cyprus	1.3	—	–14.8	1.6
India	2.4*	2.6	10.4	2.5
Korea, South	0.9	2.2	–5.0	2.2
Philippines	–2.4	1.4	–17.0	3.6
Puerto Rico	3.4	2.9	–8.6	1.1
Sierra Leone	2.9*	1.7	5.6	1.2
Taiwan	6.6	22.5	15.1	2.5
Tanzania	4.4	13.5	—	—
Turkey	4.6*	1.6	4.4	2.5
Average	2.7	6.1	–1.5	2.2
Industrial market				
Australia	0.9	2.6	2.8	2.2
Austria	0.8	3.1	–5.2	0.3
Belgium	1.9	3.6	–16.9	0.3
Canada	3.2	2.5	0	1.5
France	1.2	1.9	–12.1	0.8
Germany, West	1.8	4.2	–44.8	1.2
Italy	–1.0	3.4	–4.5	0.8
Japan	0.7	2.3	–3.4	1.2
Netherlands	1.5	1.0	–26.4	1.2
Norway	1.9	1.1	–5.5	0.8
Sweden	1.3	0.2	–14.1	0.8
United Kingdom	–0.2	1.4	–0.9	0.5
United States	2.7	2.0	0.5	1.0
Average	1.3	2.3	–10.0	1.0
Centrally planned				
Bulgaria	2.2	2.1	—	0.7
Czechoslovakia	1.5	0.6	—	0.4
Germany, East	0.9	0	—	–0.1
Hungary	1.8	7.3	—	0.4
Poland	3.3	3.7	—	0.8
Romania	3.6	5.6	—	1.5
Yugoslavia	3.9	3.6	—	1.0
U.S.S.R.	2.1	2.9	—	1.0
Average	2.4	3.2	—	0.7

*Nonagricultural sector.
Sources: International Labour Office, *Year Book of Labour Statistics* (1970); United Nations, *Monthly Bulletin of Statistics* (September 1971).

The average rate of increase in money wages was very slightly lower in 1971 compared with 1970. But the average rate of price increase rose slightly, so that there was a general tendency for the rate of increase of real wages to decline. The persistence of price inflation alongside increasing unemployment (*see* Table V) stimulated the search for new policy measures that would simultaneously permit economic expansion and reduce the rate of price inflation: in general these policies concentrated on the direct control of wages and/or prices in the U.S., Belgium, Denmark, Finland, Iceland, Ireland, the Netherlands, Norway, and Sweden.

In the U.S., the rate of increase of money wages accelerated from 5.4% in 1970 to 6.6% in 1971, although the rate of price inflation moderated slightly. But the high level of unemployment, together with the growing militancy of the trade unions and a worsening balance of payments situation, made for a gloomy economic outlook. In August 1971 Pres. Richard M. Nixon announced a 90-day wage-price freeze and a 10% surcharge on imports, the former to provide stability, the latter to increase domestic output and employment without further endangering the balance of trade. This was followed by a program of continuing but less rigid controls and, in December, by devaluation of the dollar and revocation of the surcharge as part of a realignment of international currencies.

In Canada the policies of the federal government in requesting price restraint appeared to be having some effect. Wages, however, continued to rise rapidly.

In Japan the rise in money wages continued to be high, and there was a steady tendency toward more uniform increases in all branches of industry, with the pace being set by the branch with the highest productivity growth. Cost-push inflation might thus become a more important problem for Japan and the government proposed to increase competition and to halt the rise in land prices and rents. The recent decline in business activity had a slight moderating effect on price increases.

Very unusually, both wage and price inflation continued to accelerate in West Germany, despite the rise in unemployment. By 1969 the high pressure of demand had led to a shift in the distribution of income in favour of profits, and the trade unions reacted with a series of strikes; negotiated wage increases were substantial, and the employees' share in national income was restored. Trade unions, however, were increasingly being "led from behind" and, to counteract this, the government attempted to persuade unions to moderate their wage demands. Although employers and unions ostensibly complied with

Table VI. Output, Employment, Wages, and Prices: Centrally Planned Economies

Change in 1970 over 1969 (%)

Country	Industrial production	Manufacturing employment	Average earnings	Consumer prices
Bulgaria	9.4	1.7	5.8	—
Czechoslovakia	8.6	—	4.7	1.6
Hungary	7.1	0.4	5.4	1.7
Poland	8.2	2.2	3.0	1.2
Romania	12.3	4.3	—	—
U.S.S.R.*	8.0	1.0†	4.4	—
Yugoslavia	9.6	4.1	16.8	9.7

*Provisional figures announced at December 1970 session of Supreme Soviet.
†Estimated by applying reported productivity growth rate of 7% to output growth.
Sources: *Economist* Intelligence Unit *Reports* and *Annual Supplements* on individual countries; United Nations, *Monthly Bulletin of Statistics* (September 1971).

Table IV. Unemployment: Third World

Changes over previous year (%)

Country	1969	1970
Burma	3.9	5.0
Ceylon	15.0	24.5
Chile	7.2	—
Cyprus	−14.8	4.1
Ghana	−14.8	10.0
Greece	−9.8	−26.8
Guyana	−16.3	−19.1
India	10.4	16.3
Korea, South	−5.0	−5.3
Malaysia	10.0	20.6
Pakistan	19.3	6.0
Puerto Rico	−8.6	10.6
Sierra Leone	5.6	4.4
Singapore	−9.5	−14.7
Taiwan	15.1	−6.0
Zambia	18.6	−33.3
Average	1.6	−0.3

Source: United Nations, *Monthly Bulletin of Statistics* (September 1971).

Table V. Employment in Manufacturing in Industrial Market Economies

Changes over previous year (%)

Country	Employment 1970	Employment 1971*	Unemployment 1970	Unemployment 1971*
Canada	−2.0	−2.7†	29.6	10.4
United States	−3.8	−4.7	44.5	25.6
Japan	3.2	0.1	3.5	10.7
Austria	3.4	6.5†	−11.8	−4.4
Belgium	0	1.1†	−16.5	−5.8
France	1.5	0.4	17.5	28.1
Germany, West	3.8	−0.4	−17.3	37.7
Ireland	2.1	1.0†	16.7	−8.9
Italy	2.5	2.3	−7.1	5.2
Netherlands	−0.9	—	−11.3	21.6
Norway	3.3	—	−19.9	1.1
Sweden	−7.4	0.2	−1.3	66.8
United Kingdom	−0.2	−3.9	7.2	28.7
Average	0.4	0	2.6	16.7

*Second quarter 1971 over second quarter 1970.
†First quarter 1971 over first quarter 1970.
Source: Organization for Economic Cooperation and Development, *Main Economic Indicators* (September 1971).

Table VII. Money and Real Wages in Manufacturing and Consumer Prices: Industrial Market Economies

Changes over previous year (%)

Country	Money wages 1970	Money wages 1971*	Real wages 1970	Real wages 1971*	Prices 1970	Prices 1971*
Canada	8.4	8.6†	4.9	6.8†	3.4	1.7†
United States	5.4	6.6	−0.5	2.1	5.9	4.4
Japan	17.6	16.9†	9.3	9.6†	7.7	6.7†
Austria	10.1	11.3	5.8	6.3	4.1	4.7
Belgium	8.2	9.6†	4.2	5.9†	3.9	3.5†
Denmark	10.8	—	4.9	—	5.6	6.7
France	10.5	11.2	5.0	5.7	5.2	5.2
Germany, West	12.8	13.0	8.6	7.7	3.9	4.9
Ireland	16.1	19.4†	7.3	8.6†	8.2	10.0†
Italy	21.7	13.6	15.8	8.5	5.0	4.7
Netherlands	10.7	7.2	6.0	−0.4	4.4	7.6
Norway	12.0	16.0	1.6	8.1	10.2	7.3
Sweden	13.1	3.8	5.7	−3.0	7.1	6.9
Switzerland	6.7	10.0†	3.0	3.6†	3.6	6.2†
United Kingdom	12.7	13.6	5.9	4.6	6.4	8.6
Average	11.8	11.5	5.8	5.3	5.6	5.9

*Second quarter 1971 over second quarter 1970.
†First quarter 1971 over first quarter 1970.
Source: Organization for Economic Cooperation and Development, *Main Economic Indicators* (September 1971).

Table VIII. Money and Real Wages in Manufacturing and Consumer Prices: Third World

Changes over previous year (%)

Country	Money wages 1969	Money wages 1970	Real wages 1969	Real wages 1970	Prices 1969	Prices 1970
Ceylon	3.7	8.3	−3.4	2.3	7.3	5.9
Colombia	9.5	0	−0.6	−6.6	10.2	7.1
Greece	10.2	5.2*	7.6	1.3	2.4	3.8*
Guatemala	4.9	0	2.7	−2.3	2.2	2.4
Korea, South	34.2	29.6	19.4	8.3	12.4	16.0
Mexico	5.0	5.1	2.0	0	2.9	5.1
Philippines	4.4	9.5†	1.2	4.3	3.2	5.0†
Puerto Rico	6.5	6.7	3.2	3.2	3.2	3.4
Taiwan	2.7	—	−2.2	—	5.0	3.5
Average	9.0	8.1	3.3	1.3	5.4	5.8

*August 1969 to August 1970.
†June 1969 to June 1970.
Source: United Nations, *Monthly Bulletin of Statistics* (October 1970 and September 1971).

official targets, other elements of the wage packet, such as bonuses and holiday allowances, were increased substantially.

In France the rate of wage inflation remained high, especially as the workers sought protection against the rising cost of living: food prices rose by 5.8% in 1970 and at a slightly higher rate in 1971. Wage settlements in the public sector were beginning to contain automatic cost-of-living allowances. The spread of this practice to private industry would institutionalize wage-price inflation in a dangerous way.

The price freeze imposed in the Netherlands in 1969 had some effect in reducing price inflation in 1970. However, wage increases accelerated, partly owing to increased use of automatic cost-of-living allowances. In December 1970 the government decreed a six-month wage freeze. At the end of this period the trade unions succeeded in getting fairly generous wage settlements, with a rash of strikes in the building industry. The new government, formed after the elections in April 1971, abandoned wage and price restrictions in return for promises of voluntary restraint.

The price freeze imposed by Norway in December 1970 appeared to be reducing the rate of price inflation somewhat, but the pace of wage settlements increased from 12% to 16%. Negotiated wage increases in 1970 were about 9%, but, with the tight labour market, extra payments raised this by another 7%.

In Sweden the price freeze of 1970 seemed to have had only a limited effect. The slow growth in money wages and the fall in real wages led to a greater show of militancy among trade unions, and even the army officers threatened to strike. In June 1971 a general wage agreement was signed providing for increases of 9% in 1971 (retroactive), 10% in 1972, and 8% in 1973, with an extra boost for lower paid workers.

In the United Kingdom, the increase in money wages rose to nearly 14% in 1971 and price inflation rose from just under 6½% to just over 8½%. The share of employment income in total domestic income rose from about 67½% in 1965 to 70½% in 1970, while the share of company profits fell from just over 15% to just under 12%, leading to a severe squeeze on profits. The increase in real wages, which was quite marked in 1970, had little effect on consumer spending partly because of the rise in unemployment and partly because of a considerable rise in personal savings. Unofficial attempts to reduce the rate of price inflation were under way.

Third World Economies. Increasingly the economies of the third world were trying to reduce the rate at which wages were rising in their manufacturing industries. One country whose wage restraint policies were successful was India. Compensations for rises in food prices established during World War II pro-

vided for increases that were just sufficient to maintain the standard of living of the lowest income group; since the lowest wage is about 50 rupees a month, compared with an average wage of about 200 rupees, average wages rise by only about 2½% for every 10% rise in prices. An inflationary spiral is thereby avoided, and those with very low pay are protected.

The Greek government seemed to succeed in keeping wage increases level with productivity increases; an 8% increase in the minimum wage at the beginning of 1969 accounted for much of the wage increase in that year. After the International Labour Office declared its disapproval of existing labour laws, the government slightly relaxed its control of unions, but this was unlikely to affect wage movements. Reported shortages of skilled labour for new factories might make it more difficult to hold wage increases down.

In the Philippines prices rose sharply after the devaluation in February 1970, and although a Price Control Council was established, prices rose at an accelerating rate during the year. In response, money wages rose quite sharply.

In Mexico in 1970 the first signs of price inflation, something new to that country, reduced the rate of increase of real wages to zero, and there were experiments to improve marketing and so reduce the rise in the cost of living.

Continued inflation in South Korea was aggravated by devaluation in 1969. The government was trying to ensure that a fall in the rate of growth of money wages would work its way through to price inflation.

Hours. Because of the depression in economic activity in many industrial countries, weekly hours of work tended to decline by an average of about 1½% in 1970. In some cases, this was due to negotiated reductions in the working week. In Austria the agreed weekly hours for weekly-paid workers were cut from 45 to 43 at the beginning of 1970, with the fall in actual hours worked by all workers being slightly less due to a rise in overtime working. In France the hours of work also fell as collective agreements were implemented. The working week was longest in the U.K., at just under 45 hours, and shortest in Norway, at just over 35 hours. (D. A. S. J.)

See also Economics; Economy, World; Income, National; Industrial Review; Prices.

ENCYCLOPÆDIA BRITANNICA FILMS. *The Industrial Revolution—Beginning in the United States* (1968); *The Rise of Labor* (1968); *The Industrial Worker* (1969); *The Rise of Big Business* (1970); *The Progressive Era* (1971).

Engineering Projects

Major engineering developments in 1971 included the inauguration of the Aswan High Dam on the Nile in Egypt, an investigation of the safety of box girder bridges, and considerable progress on the transcontinental network of expressways in Europe.

BRIDGES

The merits of the box girder method of bridge construction continued to be debated during 1971. The technique was questioned when portions of the Cleddau Bridge, Milford Haven, Wales, and of the West Gate Bridge over the Yarra River, Melbourne, Austr., collapsed in October and November 1970. In the United Kingdom, the government restricted traffic on 46 bridges of this kind. The royal commission on the West Gate Bridge collapse criticized the U.K. consulting engineers, but they upheld the method and one of their spokesmen

Table IX. Weekly Hours of Work in Manufacturing			
Country	1969	1970	Absolute change
Austria	38.6	37.4	—1.2
Canada	40.0	39.7	—.3
France	45.4	44.8	—.6
Germany, West	43.8	43.8	0
Japan	43.9	43.3	—.6
New Zealand	40.5	40.4	—.1
Norway	35.6	35.3	—.3
Switzerland	44.7	44.7	0
United Kingdom*	45.7	44.9	—.8
United States	40.6	39.8	—.8
Average	41.9	41.4	—.5

*October of each year.
Source: United Nations, *Monthly Bulletin of Statistics* (September 1971).

Endocrinology:
see Medicine

attributed any failure in such bridges to human error rather than a faulty design concept. In September the U.K. Department of the Environment announced that it accepted, and would implement at once on all current and future trunk road and express highway contracts, recommendations for tightening safety rules in the construction of box girder bridges. The recommendations were made in the interim report of a committee under the chairmanship of A. W. Merrison, vice-chancellor of Bristol University, set up by the government after the Melbourne and Milford Haven collapses. Instructions on procedure were sent by the department to engineering design offices, and adoption of the recommendations was urged on local and other authorities concerned. Peter Walker, U.K. minister for the environment, stated, however, that the committee did not doubt the general soundness of steel box girder bridges, provided they conformed with the rules formulated. The adoption of adequate safety rules was given added urgency by the collapse on November 10 of a box girder bridge being constructed over the Rhine at Coblenz (*see* DISASTERS).

Cable-Stayed Bridges. In 1971, the Zarate and Brazo Largo viaducts, each three miles long, were begun on two branches of the Paraná River north of Buenos Aires. The main features were identical, the viaducts being carried by two groups of lateral cables. This freed a central span of 1,116 ft. and thereby provided two traffic levels, a four-lane highway at the upper and a railway at the lower. Each pylon, in prestressed concrete, consisted of two trapezoidal members 317 ft. high.

In West Germany, a viaduct being built over the Köhlbrand at Hamburg had three spans of 320 ft., 1,066 ft., and 320 ft., carried on two groups of cables inclined from the vertical, with two lozenge-shaped metal pylons. The caisson girder, 11.3 ft. high, carried an orthotropic deck 58 ft. wide, leaving room for two 23-ft. highways.

The Bratislava (Czech.) Bridge was of more original design. It crossed the Danube in three spans of 245 ft., 994 ft., and 177 ft. The A-shaped pylon, inclined toward the nearest bank, was surmounted by a restaurant; despite the angle of the pylon, the pile supporting it was not subject to any horizontal stress since it also carried the fixed stress of the deck, and the cables, at the extremity of the 245-ft. span, were anchored vertically into the buttress after crossing an inflecting device inside the deck.

Work was beginning in France on a viaduct about two miles in length on the Loire estuary between Saint-Nazaire and Mindin, the main part of which would be a cable-stayed bridge with a central span of 1,312 ft. There were also projects for bridging the Little Belt Channel, Denmark, and the Burrard Inlet, Vancouver, which provided for cable-stayed spans of, respectively, 1,970 and 2,500 ft.

Other Metal Bridges. Three wide-span girder bridges were in progress in West Germany. One was the South-Bonn bridge over the Rhine (410 ft., 755. ft., and 410 ft.) with an orthotropic deck 128 ft. wide carried by two caisson girders at a distance of 71 ft. from axis to axis, 22 ft. wide, and with a height varying between 31 ft. on the pier and 14 ft. at the arch. Another was the Rader Insel viaduct on the Kiel Canal, 4,910 ft. long

with a main span of 727 ft. and of similar design to the South-Bonn structure. The third was the A14 motorway viaduct across the Moselle. Resting on piers of varying heights (between 223 and 400 ft.) the deck, consisting of a caisson girder 35 ft. wide and of constant height of 28 ft., carried an orthotropic plate 100 ft. wide. The total length was 3,068 ft.

In the United States an unusual-looking bridge crossed the Houston Ship Channel: it was supported by a 128-ft. strut and a 170-ft. counterstrut that formed an inverted, asymmetrical V resting on piers bordering the navigable channel.

Although virtually abandoned in Europe for aesthetic reasons, large bridges with triangulated girders were still fairly popular in the U.S. Among those currently under construction were the four-mile-long Chesapeake Bay Bridge and the Foresthill Bridge over the reservoir to be formed by the Auburn Dam, north of Sacramento, Calif.

Prestressed Concrete Bridges. The longest viaduct in Europe (19,909 ft.) was under construction in Sweden between Kalmar and the island of Öland. The main structure was of eight spans (213 ft., 6 spans of 426 ft., and 213 ft.). The deck was composed of a single caisson, 26 ft. wide, with a height varying between 28 ft. on the piers and 6 ft. at the span centres, and supporting a 43-ft.-wide platform.

Other structures of outstanding length came into service in various parts of the world. Noteworthy among them were: in the Netherlands, the bridges at Katerveer (main span 494 ft.), Deventer (centre span also 494 ft., total length 3,572 ft.), and Heteren (15 spans with lengths varying between 157 and 396 ft.); in Japan, the Nagoya-Ohashi Bridge, the main span of which was 577 ft., the Amakusa Bridge (main span 525 ft.), and the Yamato-Gawa Bridge (277 ft., 374 ft., 361 ft., 289 ft., 394 ft., and 248 ft.).

For crossing distances of between 80 and 160 ft. the simplest, most economical, and, therefore, preferred method was still that of independent spans with prefabricated girders. This was the method chosen for a structure 7,100 ft. long linking the islands of Makung and Yuweng in the Taiwan archipelago. In Europe, however, more sophisticated construction techniques were sometimes employed for similar spans. One of these was self-launching centring, employed in several structures being built on the A16 motorway between the Ruhr and Kassel in West Germany. These included the bridge over the Frieden Valley (123 ft., 7 spans of 148 ft., and 123 ft., with caisson section); and that over the Otten Valley (93 ft., 12 spans of 114 ft., and 93 ft., in section two T-shaped girders). This method, however, had the disadvantage of requiring expensive equipment. Another technique, developed in West Germany, seemed to have a promising future, since it required only a limited amount of equipment. The deck was prefabricated in successive sections on one bank of the space to be crossed, and then jacked progressively into its final position.   (Ro. Ch.)

BUILDINGS

In 1971, there was considerable evidence that the design and location of buildings was entering into efforts to deal with social and environmental problems. These problems ranged from those of the inner city to those involving health care and education. There was evidence, also, that new applications of technology would influence the design of buildings as well as the design process. In the September 1971 issue of *The Architectural Forum* there was a report on a study that had been made of the central business district of Chicago. According to this report the erection of 150-story towers in selected locations would do much to solve the problems of congestion in Chicago, which were being created by the location of tall office buildings.

Tall structures had come into use as office buildings in the latter part of the 19th century because the communications system then available demanded the concentration of business activities within comparatively small areas. With improvements in communications much of this need to concentrate in small areas no longer existed. In many cities the improvement in communications had resulted in the location or relocation of many office buildings in suburban areas outside the central city. However, the Chicago study looked at the problem not in terms of abandonment of the central city but as the reshaping of all areas of the city by redistributing office space in the towers. As noted, these towers would be distributed throughout the central city and suburbs rather than being

Construction of a second bridge connecting the industrial cities Mannheim and Ludwigshafen was under way in West Germany in 1971.

KEYSTONE

placed in just one location. Some of the towers were to be located in residential areas so that workers could walk to their offices and some located adjacent to major traffic arteries with accompanying ample parking space. In those towers that would be located in the central city, part of the transportation problem would be dealt with by providing living accommodations in the upper stories.

Thus, planning on the drawing boards in 1971 envisioned the use of tall buildings to eliminate many of the problems that had been created by the tall building. As described and pictured in *The Architectural Forum,* the 150-story tower was to be 1,656 ft. high with each floor containing 40,000 sq.ft. The major structural problem of such a building would be to resist wind efficiently and economically. This was to be accomplished by placing as much load as possible at the building's perimeter to resist overturning, and also by placing as much structural material as possible at the perimeter to resist deflection at the top. In order to bring 100% of the load and 65% of the structural steel to the building's perimeter, a superframe structure was to be utilized. It consisted of a large-scale steel skeleton that contained smaller suspended subframes. Various technical features of the prototype included fireproofing by circulating water through the superframe and sheathing of the building with tinted mirrored glass to reduce the load placed on the cooling system.

In 1971 the use of computers to convert basic design and structural information into completed design calculations emerged as a significant development in the structural design process. It was reported that complete structural design calculations were being produced by a computer at a cost of as little as $300 to $400 based on the actual computing time. A firm moving successfully in this direction was Omnidata, Inc. of New York City.

The interrelationship of design and technology to attain objectives of an educational program was illustrated by the evolving Health Sciences Centre at McMaster University in Canada. The design was clearly influenced by the teaching program for medical students at McMaster. The objective of the program was to expose the medical student, starting with the first day of training, to actual health care functions, including all those associated with the operation of a health facility. For example, the same floors were being utilized for patient care and research, and in every area of the centre space was provided for students. The glass-enclosed towers of the centre provided the sole support of its long-span structural system and also served as the mechanical shafts and emergency stairways.

A highly functional approach to design was evident in the Coliseum and Convention Center in New Haven, Conn. A four-level steel superstructure was to provide a parking garage to accommodate 2,400 cars. The 4½-ac. area beneath was to contain a 9,000-seat sports arena. One level of parking was on the exposed roof deck, and three levels fitted into the depth of the transverse trusses that spanned 184 ft. between concrete piers. The strange reversal of placing the garage on top instead of below occurred because underground water conditions and the desire not to raise the sports arena above the street level ruled out an underground facility.

A central feature of the student union on the New York State University campus at Stony Brook, L.I., was that one could walk through it and never enter. Completed in 1971, it was designed as an integral part of the master plan for the campus. The architects were reported to have designed the centre so that a person walking through would want to slow down to hear a student speech in the courtyard below, or to participate in other activities that are a part of the ongoing campus scene.

(C. C. O.)

DAMS

Europe. The Austrian Schlegeis arch-gravity dam (height 426 ft., crest length 2,378 ft., volume 1,255,680 cu.yd., storage 102,870 ac-ft.) was completed during 1971, and construction of the Zillergründl arch dam (height 574 ft., crest length 1,706 ft., volume 1.4 million cu.yd., storage 71,500 ac-ft.) was begun. In Spain construction of the Montanejos concrete gravity dam on the Mijares River (height 492 ft.) and the Atazar arch dam on the Lozoya River (height 443 ft., volume 915,000 cu.yd., storage 370,000 ac-ft.) was well advanced in 1971. Foun-

Major World Dams Under Construction in 1971*

Name of dam	River	Country	Type†	Height (ft.)	Length of crest (ft.)	Volume content (000 cu.yd.)	Gross capacity of reservoir (000 ac-ft.)
Auburn	N.F. American	U.S.	A	685	4,000	6,000	2,300
Ayvacik	Yesil	Turkey	A	551	1,715	1,464	689
Balimela	Sileru	India	E	230	15,200	29,627	3,097
Beas	Beas-Indus	India	E	440	6,400	44,200	6,600
Cabora Bassa	Zambezi	Mozambique	A	550	994	589	129,389
Castaic	Castaic	U.S.	E	340	5,200	44,000	183
Charvakskaya	Chirchik	U.S.S.R.	ER	551	2,499	24,975	1,620
Chirkeyskaya	Sulak	U.S.S.R.	A	764	1,109	1,602	2,252
Cochiti	Rio Grande	U.S.	E	251	28,200	41,100	513
Dworshak	N.F. Clearwater	U.S.	G	717	3,287	6,500	3,453
Emosson	Barberine	Switzerland	A	590	1,821	1,400	182
Gokcekaya	Sakarya	Turkey	A	518	1,529	850	737
Gran Suarna	Navia	Spain	A	499	1,150	882	567
Idikki	Periyar	India	MA	561	1,201	609	1,182
Ilha Solteira	Paraná	Brazil	EG	262	20,300	32,838	17,172
Inguri	Inguri	U.S.S.R.	A	892	2,198	4,967	891
Jayakwadi	Godavari	India	E	120	32,493	15,409	2,110
Kanev	Dnepr	U.S.S.R.	E	82	52,950	49,520	2,125
Kapchagay	Ili	U.S.S.R.	E	164	7,741	10,338	22,761
Keban	Euphrates	Turkey	RG	679	3,598	19,600	25,110
Khantayka	Khantayka	U.S.S.R.	RE	213	21,058	2,452	16,743
Kölnbrein	Malta	Austria	A	607	1,814	1,804	130
Krasnoyarsk	Yenisei	U.S.S.R.	G	407	3,493	5,685	59,425
Las Portas	Camba	Spain	G	498	1,587	977	609
Marimbondo	Grande	Brazil	EG	295	11,970	24,328	5,184
Melones, New	Stanislaus	U.S.	ER	625	1,600	15,970	2,400
Mica	Columbia	Canada	R	800	2,600	42,000	20,000
Missi Falls, Control, South	Churchill	Canada	ER	90	6,500	1,400	30,000
Mratinje	Piva	Yugoslavia	A	722	853	1,019	689
Nurek	Vakhsh	U.S.S.R.	E	1,017	2,390	70,806	8,424
Reza Shah Kabir	Karun	Iran	A	656	1,247	1,600	n.a.
Saratov	Volga	U.S.S.R.	E	131	4,130	19,034	10,854
Sayano-Shuskenskaya	Yenisei	U.S.S.R.	A	774	3,503	11,916	25,353
Tachien	Tachia	Taiwan	A	591	853	562	188
Tarbela	Indus	Pakistan	ER	470	9,000	186,000	11,100
Toktogul	Naryn	U.S.S.R.	A	705	1,352	3,480	15,800
Ust-Ilim	Angara	U.S.S.R.	EG	344	11,695	17,090	48,100
Zeyskaya	Zeya	U.S.S.R.	G	371	2,312	10,456	55,080

MAJOR WORLD DAMS COMPLETED IN 1970 AND 1971*

Name of dam	River	Country	Type†	Height (ft.)	Length of crest (ft.)	Volume content (000 cu.yd.)	Gross capacity of reservoir (000 ac-ft.)
Almendra	Tormes	Spain	AG	649	1,860	2,844	2,147
Aswan, High (Sadd el Aali)	Nile	Egypt	ER	364	12,565	55,809	133,000
Don Pedro, New	Tuolumne	U.S.	ER	585	1,900	16,760	2,030
Talbingo	Tumut	Australia	R	530	2,300	18,500	747

*Having a height exceeding 492 ft. (150 m.); or having a total volume content exceeding 20 million cu.yd. (15 million cu.m.); or forming a reservoir exceeding 12 million ac-ft. capacity.

†Type of dam: E=earth; R=rockfill; A=arch; G=gravity; MA=multiple arch.   n.a.=data not available.

(T. W. Me.)

STEWART BALE LTD.

Tunnel relief flyovers
were built to speed
the flow of automotive
traffic in Liverpool,
Eng. Designers
of the overhead roads won
the 1971 Concrete
Society Award.

dation rock of the Atazar dam consisted of slate, with numerous cracks and fissures requiring extensive grouting works. In Switzerland the Emosson arch dam on the Barberine River was in progress. This dam would have a height of 590 ft., with crest length 1,821 ft., a volume of 1.4 million cu.yd., and storage of 182,000 ac-ft.

Asia. At Hong Kong, work began on the High Island reservoir formed by two 200-ft.-high rockfill dams across the narrow sea passage separating High Island from the Sai Kung Peninsula. One dam was to be 1,500 ft. and the other 1,000 ft. long. Construction involved digging 75-ft.-deep trenches underwater. The foundation of the dam was to be 82 ft. below mean water level.

Indian dams under construction were the Beas earth-core dam on the Beas River at Pong (height 440 ft.), to be completed in 1973, the Idikki double-curvature thin-arch dam on the Periyar River (height 561 ft., width at crest 25 ft. and at foundation 65 ft., volume 609,000 cu.yd.), and the Kulamavu masonry gravity dam on the Killvallithodu River (height 328 ft., volume 592,626 cu. yd.).

Early in 1970, construction of the Nagawado arch dam in Japan (height 508 ft., volume 927,000 cu.yd.) was completed. Elsewhere in Japan construction continued on the Koshibu arch dam (height 344 ft., volume 351,000 cu.yd., storage 47,000 ac-ft.) and the Misakubo rockfill dam (height 344 ft., volume 3,140,000 cu.yd., storage 24,-300 ac-ft.).

The Tsengwen earthfill dam was being built on the Tsengwen River in Taiwan; it would have a height of 427 ft., a volume of 12,570,000 cu.yd., and storage of 574,000 ac-ft. The dam was near an active earthquake zone and was being constructed with an impervious rolled earth core and zones of pervious material and shells composed of cobble and gravel. It was to be completed in 1973.

Construction of two dams began in Turkey. These were the Karakaya arch-gravity dam (height 590 ft., volume 1.8 million cu.yd.) and the Karababa straight concrete buttress dam (height 394 ft., crest length 4,100 ft., volume 4.8 million cu.yd.). Both were on the Euphrates River. The two together were to form the Lower Euphrates multipurpose project. At the end of 1970 construction started on the Oymapinor double-curvature arch dam on the Manavgat River (height 604 ft.), to supply an underground power station housing four 135-Mw. units.

In the U.S.S.R. construction continued on the Sayano-Shushenskaya arch dam on the Yenisei River (height 774 ft., crest length 3,503 ft., volume 11,916,000 cu.yd.); on the Ust-Ilim concrete gravity dam on the Angara River in the Middle-Siberian Plateau (height 344 ft., crest length 11,695 ft., volume 17,090,000 cu.yd., storage 48.1 million ac-ft.); and on the Zeyskaya concrete gravity dam on the Zeya River (height 371 ft., volume 10,456,-

000 cu.yd., storage 55,080,000 ac-ft.). Difficulties with construction, changes in the schedule, and priority delayed until 1976 the completion of the 892-ft.-high Inguri River arch dam.

North and South America. The Libby concrete gravity dam on the Kootenay River in Montana (height 420 ft., crest length 2,900 ft., volume 3,750,000 cu.yd., storage 5.8 million ac-ft.) was under construction; its 90-mi.-long reservoir would extend 42 mi. into British Columbia along the Kootenay lakes. On Nov. 1, 1970, 80% of the concrete was placed by means of six revolving cranes, four on 100-ft. and two on 110-ft.-high gantries. Completion was due in 1972. Also under construction was the Dworshak concrete gravity dam on the Clearwater River in Idaho (height 717 ft., volume 6.5 million cu.yd., storage 3,453,000 ac-ft.).

Construction began on the Pyramid earthfill dam (height 381 ft., storage 183,000 ac-ft.) and the Cascadia rockfill dam (height 225 ft., volume 25 million cu.yd., storage 160,000 ac-ft.) on the South Santiam River, Ore. Work began also on the Gate Creek earthfill dam (height 270 ft., volume 5.7 million cu.yd.).

In Canada the first generator went into operation in September 1970 at Manic 5 (Daniel Johnson) dam, the world's highest multiple-arch dam (703 ft.) with a 115-million ac-ft. reservoir. A special bentonite curtain wall was built to seal the pervious river gravel at the Bighorn earthfill dam (height 300 ft.), also in Canada.

In South America the Tablachaca arch-gravity dam (height 269 ft., volume 196,200 cu.yd.) was completed in Peru in 1970; it was built on subvertical metamorphic schist layers. In Argentina construction started on the Futaleufu earthfill dam (height 394 ft.).

Australia and Africa. The Talbingo earth and rockfill dam on the Tumut River in Australia was completed as part of the Snowy Mountains Tumut III Scheme (height 530 ft., crest length 2,300 ft., crest width 30 ft., volume 18.5 million cu.yd., storage 747,000 ac-ft.) with an earth-fill core sloping upstream.

On Jan. 15, 1971, the Aswan High Dam in Egypt was officially inaugurated by the chiefs of state of Egypt and the U.S.S.R. The construction of the 364-ft.-high dam took 11 years. Its dimensions were 16 times those of the biggest pyramid built in Egypt, and the cost was approximately $994 million.

In South Africa the Hendrik Verwoerd arch dam on the Orange River (height 280 ft.) was completed in July 1971. Building of the Koudiat-El-Rhorfa earth and rockfill dam (height 230 ft.) on the Loukkos River began in Morocco.

Construction started in Tanzania on the Great Ruaha River earth and rockfill dam (height 131 ft.). Four 492-ft.-long vertical steel penstocks embedded in concrete would carry water to four Francis-type turbines vertically coupled to generators. Completion was scheduled for 1975. In Mozambique, progress was made on the Cabora Bassa double-curvature arch dam on the Zambezi River (height 550 ft., crest length 994 ft., volume 589,-000 cu.yd., storage 129,389,000 ac-ft.), due to be finished in 1975. (AL. MA.)

ROADS

Highway engineering projects proliferated in 1971. The transcontinental network of European high-speed roads was being extended, and, as before, the less developed countries continued to build routes running from areas of production to centres of distribution.

Europe. Most European countries completed important parts of their motorway programs, thus extending the complex network of high-speed roads that had been spreading over the continent since the end of World War II. France brought into use in October 1970 the last stretch of its 626-mi.-long motorway linking Lille, near the Belgian border about 150 mi. to the north of Paris, with Marseilles, the country's major port, on the Mediterranean coast. During the year West Germany also completed the last few miles of its Ruhr expressway, an important route through the heavily populated and industrialized Ruhr basin.

Late in 1970 the first major section of the Italian motorway that would ultimately run from the Tyrrhenian coast to the Adriatic Sea was opened to traffic. The completed section, extending from Rome to L'Aquila, rose in several places to more than 3,000 ft. above sea level. The Brescia-Piacenza motorway in northern Italy was completed during the summer of 1971. Eight miles of this 56-mi. express highway were built of concrete as a test for future motorway construction. This was the first time that Italian highway engineers had used concrete for motorways.

In June 1971 the 14-mi.-long Prague-Mirosovice section of Czechoslovakia's Prague-Brno-Bratislava motorway was opened. The expressway eventually would link up with another highway which, in turn, would run to the Austrian border.

In the United Kingdom several new sections were added to existing motorways. These included 28 mi. of the London-Basingstoke motorway (M3), an additional 10 mi. of the London-South Wales motorway (M4), 36 mi. of the M6 section of the Midland Links Motorway project, 3 mi. of the North Cheshire motorway (M56), and the 13.2-mi.-long trans-Pennine section of the Lancashire-Yorkshire motorway (M62).

North and South America. In September 1970 a new 1½-mi. section of the Shirley Highway, part of Interstate Route 95, was opened to traffic in the United States. This section, running through the Virginia suburbs of Washington, D.C., would be used exclusively for buses and emergency vehicles. In Pennsylvania the Keystone Shortway, Interstate Route 80, also came into use in September.

The U.S. Department of Transportation announced in November 1971 that it had designated 34 towns and cities in 16 states as economic growth centres. These urban areas thus became eligible for increased federal funding for the improvement of roads.

In Peru, Tupac Amaru Avenue, leading from Lima, the capital, into the Canta Valley, was replaced by a four-lane express highway. A major road-widening project took place in Brazil along more than 3 mi. of the famous Copacabana Beach in Rio de Janeiro. Traffic along the new six-lane highway was to be computer-controlled. This project was part of an extensive urban-renewal program.

In El Salvador, an important highway project, La Cuchilla-Km 35, was completed. The 8-mi.-long highway formed part of the Central American Highway System. In September 1970 the Lo Prado Tunnel was opened to traffic. The tunnel, 1.7 mi. long, formed part of Chile's Santiago-Valparaiso highway project and was the longest underground road in South America.

Africa. The 70-mi.-long Waza-Maltam road in Cameroon was opened. In South West Africa an additional 9 mi. of tarred road was incorporated in the 1,300-mi. stretch running from the coastal towns of Swakopmund and Walvis Bay through Windhoek to Cape Town. During 1971, part of the six-lane urban autoroute through Las Palmas in the Canary Islands came into service. In 1971 it was also announced that work on the all-weather Nairobi-Addis Ababa highway section extending through Kenya had reached Marsabit. Kenya still had about 100 mi. of its section of the highway to complete.

Asia and Oceania. Among several important projects completed was the first part of an express highway that would ultimately run from Karachi, the chief seaport and industrial centre of West Pakistan, to Lahore, the capital. The completed section, which was opened to traffic, linked Karachi and Hyderabad. The Karakoram Road from Pakistan to Sinkiang in China also was completed. The road, almost 200 mi. long, crossed the Karakoram and Pamir mountains, rising in several places to some 9,000 ft.

Ten miles of the Chugoko expressway, Japan, came into use in June 1970. The new section ran between Suita and Takarazuka. In 1971, the government of Malaysia announced the completion of major reconstruction along the West Coast Highway (Route I), the Cross-Country Highway (Route II), and the East Coast Highway (Route III). In Kuala Lumpur, the capital, the northern section of a new through road was completed.

(R. S. Mi.)

TUNNELS

Projects for tunneling flourished with undiminished vigour in 1971. Eighty countries or states were considering underground transport systems, of which 22 were in Europe and 8 in America. The demand for tunnels required for water supplies and drainage systems continued to increase.

Europe. In Brussels six contractors and 500 men were employed in the construction of 10.4 km. of tunnels for the new subway. By late 1971 approximately 6 km. of a twin-track tunnel section 7.3 m. by 4.5 m. were completed. Work began in Amsterdam on the new sub-

way there. A West German firm headed the consortium constructing the East section, of which 3 km. would be in tunnel.

In Italy work continued on the $40 million Gran Sasso d'Italia tunnel forming part of the four-lane expressway linking Rome and the Adriatic. Each tunnel would provide twin 7.6-m.-wide roadways. Two special boom-type tunneling machines were in use, each costing $1 million.

Two of the largest tunnels in Europe were in construction 1,200 m. level on the expressway between Venice in Italy and Munich in West Germany. The Tauern tunnel was to be 7 km. long and the Katschberg 5 km. Cross sections were 92 and 105 sq.m., respectively, with a maximum width of 11.6 m. A consortium of six companies was carrying out the contract. The estimated cost per metre of the Tauern tunnel was $5,500.

At Lucerne, Switz., Swiss engineers employed a novel method for boring twin tunnels on the route of National Highway 2. Twin 4.5-m.-diameter pilot tunnels were driven with a conventional mole, the tunnel being enlarged to a full diameter of 10 m. by using a West German tunneling machine equipped with two cutting units that enlarged the pilot first to 7.3-m. diameter and then to full size. The cutting heads exerted a force of almost 2,000 tons.

On the Franco-Swiss border, construction was to begin early in 1972 on a tunnel required for the installation of a 300-GeV particle accelerator. The client was the European Organization for Nuclear Research (CERN). The tunnel would form a circle of 2.2-km. diameter and would be 6,900 m. long, bored through sandstone and marl 30 m. below the surface.

In the United Kingdom, work continued on a 3.6-km.-long, 3-m.-diameter cable tunnel under the Severn River, using two hard-rock tunneling machines. Considered one of the most difficult tunneling projects of the century, the tunnel was planned to be complete at the end of 1972. Water inflows of up to 9,000 litres a minute were experienced. Average progress of the machines was only 25 m. a week due to the difficult conditions.

Another tunnel under the Mersey River, to make three in all, was under construction. The estimated cost was approximately $21 million. Driving the pilot tunnel by using a small mole was abandoned in favour of conventional methods because of handling problems caused by wet ground. Of great interest on this project was the precast concrete lining which incorporated a steel outer skin. After erection, steel cover plates were welded to complete a 100% watertight lining, which was then ready for final painting.

South Africa. The Orp Keg tunnel, forming part of the Orange River project, was being driven for 13 km. through the Bosberg range. A U.S. tunneling machine was being used to drive the 5-m.-diameter tunnel.

North America. In the Continental Divide at an altitude of 3,352 m. above sea level in Colorado, work begun in 1967 continued on the tunnel drive at Straight Creek. The tunnel cross-section was 12.8 m. by 13.7 m. Immensely difficult ground conditions slowed down the work. Progress was only maintained through a zone of squeezing ground by abandoning a shield method and driving multiple drifts around the perimeter. The drifts were filled with concrete to form a protective lining while the main core of the tunnel was excavated.

In New York City, despite strong river currents, work continued on the construction of a four-bore section of subway tunnel under the East River. The 954-m.-long tunnel was to connect Queens with Manhattan. The subway and stations were more than 30 m. below the surface, and an interesting feature was the construction of a station under Welfare Island. Completion was expected in 1973.

In the Federal District of Mexico construction began on the main outfall tunnel to form part of a new main drainage system. The tunnel was to be 52 km. long and of 6.5-m. diameter. It was being driven from 17 shafts using conventional drill and blast methods, but a tunneling machine was being used in the last section where the tunnel passes through a bentonitic type of clay. In Mexico City itself, work started on 5-m.-diameter deep interceptors using a British-made slurry digging shield.

(D. A. Ha.)

Encyclopædia Britannica Films. *Holland: Hold Back the Sea* (1967); *The Mississippi System: Waterway of Commerce* (1970).

Environment

In 1971, worldwide interest in environmental problems was showing signs of maturity. The claims and campaigns of those who first drew attention to developing problems of resource exploitation, pollution, and urban congestion had been either modified or reinforced by the studies and deliberations of technical experts, government officials, politicians, and the public taking stock of the situation from a less emotional standpoint. In the U.S., the president's Council on Environmental Quality had published its second report, and the British Royal Commission on Environmental Pollution published its first findings in February. The UN was preparing for a major conference on the environment to be held in Stockholm in June 1972.

The conferences and debates of the year confirmed even more clearly the major origins and general character of the environmental problem. Population growth, economic development, and technological change bring, in turn, the depletion of natural resources, pollution of air and water, visual squalor, rising noise levels, loss of wildlife, and many other effects. While the most dramatic crises tended to occur in the richest countries (the U.S. and Japan were among the hardest hit), other countries showed the same formidable symptoms.

Studies from the Massachusetts Institute of Technology further indicated that the problems of depleted resources and pollution of the environment were equally important and could not be considered in isolation. Research workers at the Victoria University of Manchester, Eng., also showed that threats to clean air, clean water, and other environmental damage could not be dealt with separately—it was seldom helpful to clean air by washing the pollutants into the water; neither should commercial and social costs be considered separately when manufacturers' packaging policies, for example, are devised.

STUDIES AND RESEARCH

There was still a poverty of research on environmental questions, and many of the recommendations and resolutions of the year's conferences were concerned with this need. At the environmental conference convened by the UN Economic Commission for Europe (ECE) at Prague, Czech., in May, the Swedish government called upon the ECE to concentrate its resources on research into the economic aspects of damage to the environment, taking into account the social and political recommendations of the British royal commission. The commission had concluded that a study of the costs of pollution should be mounted and that in general, while some scientific and technical data were readily available, economic information about pollution was inadequate to aid decision makers.

The most well-established research on environmental problems was the study of the scientific and technological aspects of pollution, typically at national research institutes specifically set up for the purpose. In France, for example, a program of research involving many specialist institutes was coordinated by the Délégation Générale à la Recherche Scientifique et Technique (DGRST), and there were plans for a central Environmental Research Institute.

The U.S., Britain, and the Netherlands were among those countries fostering environmental research not only in institutes financed by the government, such as the Warren Spring Laboratory in England, investigating air pollution, but also in independent establishments, such as the National Institute for Public Health in the Netherlands, and in universities.

In Sweden over half the state grants for environmental research were administered by the Environment Protection Board. Most of the projects were scientific investigations financed over several years, with a third of the funds going for water protection studies, a third for the study of particular pollutants (especially mercury and chlorinated hydrocarbons), and 10% for landscape and nature conservation research. In contrast to this scientific work was the preliminary work of the small Pollution Research Unit at the Victoria University of Manchester, headed by an economist. The unit's interim report indicated a main interest in the economic, social, political, legal, and administrative aspects of environmental control.

The work of many research sponsors revealed an increasing concern for environmental problems. The Ford Foundation, for example, sponsored new research and educational work in the U.S. and elsewhere, concentrating especially on problems of urban and regional planning and on environmental pollution. A grant of $180,000 to the Tanzania National Parks was announced in March. The money, together with assistance from other American and European foundations, would support the Serengeti Research Institute, established in 1966 to provide basic knowledge about the preservation of East African wildlife.

The Ford Foundation was also assisting the work of a new international organization for scientific research known as the Scientific Committee on Problems of the Environment (SCOPE), set up by the International Council of Scientific Unions, a confederation of 16 nongovernmental scientific institutes. One of the functions of SCOPE would be to offer independent advice to the UN, especially through international conferences such as that planned for Stockholm in 1972. For this conference it was preparing a design for a global environmental monitoring network based on stations that would measure the occurrence of certain pollutants.

THE URBAN ENVIRONMENT

The automobile was becoming an increasingly important determinant of the quality and form of urban environment. It was already a principal source of atmospheric pollution, urban noise, and accidents, and the cause of growing problems of traffic congestion. In the long term, provision for the automobile in cities (expressways, garages, parking lots) and the flexibility of travel it offers its users were expected to lead to lower densities in urban redevelopment and an accelerated spreading out of towns.

While legislation and technological developments could reduce noise and exhaust levels, problems of traffic congestion could not be solved without drastic capital expenditure (or unpalatable political action). Nor were congestion problems confined to the wealthiest nations. Some citizens of São Paulo, Braz., were reported to be spending up to three or four hours a day traveling to and from their places of work. Mexico, Argentina, and Singapore had rates of vehicle ownership comparable to those of the wealthiest European countries. Although 70% of all journeys (other than walking) were made by bus and train in some big cities (Hamburg, W.Ger., 81%; New

York 73%; Paris 70%), public transport was becoming increasingly uneconomic. Traffic jams held up bus services, rail fares continued to rise, and more and more people chose to travel by car.

As employment centres decentralized, out-of-town shopping centres were constructed alongside new expressways, and old areas were rebuilt, cities tended to lose activities and population beyond their boundaries to surrounding suburban districts.

An increasingly popular solution to the problem of the ever growing suburbs was the construction of new towns—traditionally the method followed in Britain, where 30 had so far been established under the New Towns Act of 1946. In France a National Commission on New Towns had been set up, and official study groups were planning for nine new towns, five in the Paris region and four in the provinces. In March the first residents moved into the Japanese new town of Tama, under construction since 1967. The town, on the southwestern outskirts of Tokyo, would eventually consist of 23 residential districts, each comprising 4,000–5,000 dwelling units. It was planned to become a self-contained community rather than a dormitory town. This was also the objective for a satellite town for Barcelona, Spain, to house 150,000 people with industry, commerce, and entertainment facilities. Work also started in 1971 on the first phase of Sha Tin new town on reclaimed land in Hong Kong.

October 1970 marked the beginning of intensive public interest in long-term plans for several major cities. A mammoth public inquiry was initiated to examine the proposals of the Greater London Development Plan. The most contentious part of the plan was the expressway network, which could cost around £2,000 million and would consume 1,000 ac. in inner London alone. At the same time, Moscow's chief architect gave details of plans for the city to the year 2000. A stable population level of eight million was an important prerequisite.

In December 1970 a world committee of architects, town planners, and art experts considered Israel's master plan for Jerusalem. The meeting roundly condemned the plan on aesthetic grounds, complaining in particular that the city's unique character would be lost amid anonymous modern developments. The plan, which seemed likely to be abandoned, provided for an area eight times that of the existing municipality and included part of the city formerly belonging to Jordan.

Plans also received severe criticism in Edinburgh, Scot., London, and Paris, and a small but significant campaign was waged in Stockholm. A proposal for a 23-story office block in Edinburgh attracted the attention of national and local pressure groups. The opponents of the plan claimed the building would ruin the city's famous skyline and dwarf the historic Castle Rock.

A conservation battle was lost in Paris, where 2 of the 12 iron and glass pavilions of Les Halles, the central Paris markets, were demolished in August, with 4 more to follow. (*See* HISTORIC BUILDINGS.) In London, where the Covent Garden fruit and vegetable market was also due to be moved from its traditional site, a group known as the Covent Garden Community claimed that the extensive redevelopment planned for the area would lead to the collapse of community life. In Stockholm a much publicized protest took place in May concerning the preservation of just three trees, eventually cut down to make way for a

UPI COMPIX

Four-year-old Kathy Schneider wears an air pollution mask and holds a flower to dramatize Survival Associates' drive for cleaner air in New York City, May 19, 1971.

third entrance to a subway station. Such was the indignation that police had to hold back an angry crowd of more than 2,000 conservationists who threw stones and bottles at the helmeted workmen.

Tokyo had a particularly bad year of atmospheric pollution. One cloudy day in May, the Tokyo metropolitan government flashed a photochemical smog warning for the entire city; a total of 1,481 people in 19 different parts of the city reported to health officers with complaints of eye irritation. In London further encouraging progress was reported in the fight against smoke emissions in the city. It was announced in May that a 4% reduction in the smoke content of London's air had been achieved over the preceding 12 months, and the capital's air was cleaner than the average for the whole of Great Britain. Cleaner air was probably a contributory factor in the reported return of several species of birds.   (DA. L. S.)

NATURAL ENVIRONMENT

The deaths of three Soviet cosmonauts as they returned to earth after successfully orbiting it for 24 days in their spaceship Soyuz 11 underlined man's complete dependence on the oxygen available for only a few miles above the world's surface. Yet the extravagant or reckless use of this and other irreplaceable resources continued to increase the pollution of air, water, and even land surfaces near all industrial centres.

Philip Abelson, director of the Carnegie Institution's Geophysical Laboratory in Washington, D.C., and editor of *Science*, put man's role into perspective when he delivered a paper to the American Geophysical Union's national meeting in December 1970. Despite public enthusiasm for a completely pollution-free environment, Abelson declared that pure air, pure rain, pure rivers, and pure oceans were no more than a myth. A single volcanic eruption, that of Krakatau in Indonesia in 1883, put more dust into the air than mankind had done throughout recorded history. Volcanoes and the natural processes of decay contributed volumes of carbon dioxide, sulfur dioxide, and nitrogenous gases to the atmosphere that were greater than any produced by industry. The Mississippi alone carried two million tons of sediments to the ocean each day. Worldwide, pollution by human activity was not yet serious, but its concentration in densely peopled regions raised immediate problems.

Industrial wastes are emitted from an industrial complex in Düsseldorf, W.Ger. Experts estimated that two million tons of dust, four million tons of sulfur dioxide, and six million tons of carbon monoxide are passed into the air annually in Germany.

CAMERA PRESS— PICTORIAL PARADE

Moreover, man was able to produce compounds, such as DDT, whose ultimate rate and course of breakdown had not been investigated.

Monitoring of pollution had become a major weapon for national and, indeed, international control. False-colour photography was proving an invaluable technique for quick detection of individual pollutants. An oilslick, for example, could be made to stand out in vivid green against a blue sea. Abelson reported a new tunable solid-state infrared laser technique that would reveal most common pollutants by sharp and deep absorption lines that could be used for both identification and measurement. The proper role of the scientist, he maintained, was not to cry "Woe! Woe!" whenever a fresh threat was discovered, but rather to assess it, to find the cause, and to promote politically acceptable remedies.

Predictably, the seas proved the most sensitive area of international friction where pollution was concerned. In July 1971 the 700-ton Dutch tanker "Stella Maris," carrying 600 tons of poisonous chemical waste for dumping in the North Atlantic, was refused refueling facilities by harbour authorities at Thorshavn in the Faeroe Islands. After Britain, Ireland, and the Scandinavian countries had joined in protests against the threat to their fishing industries, the vessel returned to the Netherlands so that its deadly cargo could be destroyed by controlled incineration on land.

The critical state of the waters of the Mediterranean was highlighted by the second Pacem in Maribus (Peace in the Seas) convocation held in Malta in July. Pollution problems arose from two sources— the densely peopled lands that discharged sewage into their rivers and thence into this almost enclosed sea, and the growing oil industry with associated industrial effluents. Waste oil, being lighter than water, remains on the surface until it is broken down, but in this process one litre of oil removes all free oxygen from 400,000 litres of seawater. With an estimated 100,000 tons of oily waste added to the Mediterranean annually, marine life was suffering and bathing beaches, particularly in Italy, were being fouled. No less than 20 nations had a stake in the coastline of the Medi-

terranean, but only ten states suggested joint action to remedy matters.

Land Conservation. The Council of Europe, meeting at Strasbourg, France, in February 1970, passed a Declaration on the Management of the Natural Environment of Europe that stressed the interdependence of continental land-use systems, regardless of national frontiers. This theme was expressed again at a UN conference on pollution control, held near Helsinki, Fin., in July 1971, and attended by leading conservationists from all major countries.

As an example of the global approach, Brazil was criticized for failing to conserve the vast rain forest of the Amazon basin, believed to play a key role in carbon dioxide fixation and the renewal of atmospheric oxygen. Lester Muchta, of Air Resources Laboratory, maintained that the oxygen content of the world's atmosphere, overall, had remained the same for the past 60 years, but clearly this only holds good as long as forests renew the quantities removed by combustion.

As a contribution to European Conservation Year, in 1970, the West German government opened its Bavarian Forest National Park, covering 30,000 ac. along the frontier with Czechoslovakia. Comprising mountainous country, dominated by the 4,500-ft. peaks of Rachel and Lusen, the new park was to be managed by the Bavarian State Forest Service to meet the needs of recreation and scientific research and to provide a refuge for the rarer kinds of wildlife.

The national parks in England and Wales, administered by the Countryside Commission but holding land still in private ownership, came under a major threat in July 1971 when Sir John Eden, minister for industry, announced a £50 million grant scheme to encourage mineral exploitation in the British Isles. All ten of the national parks were in regions of highly mineralized rock beds. Each had been exploited locally for high-grade ores in the past, but when they were dedicated as parks around 1950 it was believed that all their worthwhile ores had been exhausted. However, modern mining technology, combined with rising world prices, made it worthwhile to mine or quarry lower-grade ores at greater depths. Although Britain's economic circumstances were such that it could scarcely afford to let valuable resources lie unused, a strong conservation movement opposed all such development.

The International Union for the Conservation of Nature and Natural Resources (IUCN) published a list, called its *Red Data Book*, of 68 species of plants in imminent danger of extinction, based on researches by Ronald Melville of the Royal Botanic Gardens at Kew, Eng. The most serious known threats were to island species with restricted natural spread, which could easily be wiped out when settlers introduced new domestic or feral animals. At St. Helena in the South Atlantic, for example, goats had wiped out 11 of the 33 plants peculiar to the island when it was first discovered in 1502. Extinction could remove many potentially valuable sources of food and drugs. Only the formation of soundly managed reserves could safeguard these threatened plants, many of which would not accept cultivation.

The new developments in aerial photography using false colour, infrared, and heat-sensitive films enabled rapid advances to be made by farmers, foresters, and geographers. A typical application used a photographic emulsion sensitive to chlorophyll, the colouring matter found only in healthy green plants. This technique would at once reveal camouflaged structures that had simply been painted green. It would also isolate areas of diseased vegetation, patches of crops suffering from severe insect attack, and even areas stunted by nutrient deficiencies. Other methods made streams and ponds stand out boldly, and could distinguish, by clear colour differences, fresh water from salt water. Heat-sensitive emulsions had been used in the U.S. to plot a new "hot spot" on the 14,410-ft. Mt. Rainier, a "sleeping volcano" in the Cascade range of Washington state, which had not erupted for 100 years. The increase in temperature, which might presage a new eruption, was not discernible by ground survey. In Canada, forest service fire-spotting planes were using similar methods to chart fires at an early stage.

Water Conservation. In January 1971 Pres. Anwar as-Sadat of Egypt and Pres. N. V. Podgorny of the U.S.S.R. officially opened the Aswan High Dam, designed to hold 163 million cu.m. of Nile water in Lake Nasser as a perpetual safeguard against drought and flood throughout Egypt. Unfortunately, many unexpected and harmful side effects had already become apparent in the Nile basin, which extends for 650 mi. below it. Having no sluices at its base, the dam inevitably trapped all the fertile silt that the river formerly brought down from the Abyssinian highlands, so that a priceless source of nutrients was being wholly lost to the peasant farmers of the Nile Delta. In the absence of silt reinforcement, the coastline was receding through erosion. Coastal fishing was declining because, without the nutrients once carried by the silt, salinity was increasing. Clear Nile water now flowed so rapidly that bridges and embankments, as well as irrigation canals, were endangered, and the clear water appeared less effective than silt-laden floodwaters in countering the salinity that threatened all irrigated fields. At Lake Nasser itself, evaporation losses proved far higher than first estimated, amounting to 15 million cu.m. a year. Seepage losses into permeable rock beds were also suspected, and so far the useful yield of water had been less than the pre-dam average. Only in the production of hydroelectric power did the Aswan High Dam seem wholly successful.

In Ghana the waters held up by the Akosombo Dam, completed in 1965, virtually completed their expansion to the planned 8,000 sq.km. of surface. Lake Volta, formed from the waters of six major rivers—the Black and White Volta, Oti, Sene, Afram, and Pawmpawm—thus became the largest man-made lake in the world. Tomislav Petr, a zoologist from Makerere University at Kampala, Uganda, reported the successful establishment of a major fishery but expressed doubts as to its continuance. Since the nutrients arose largely from the unique submergence of a great tropical forest, they might diminish as time went on.

In the U.S.S.R. the Ministry of Melioration and Water Conservancy announced further studies on the feasibility of diverting Siberian river waters for 3,000 mi. southwest to the Aral and Caspian seas. The rivers considered were the Yenisei, the Ob, and the Irtysh, at present running northwest to the Arctic Ocean. The proposed diversion would involve pumping 50 cu.km. annually into canals that would flow to the Aral Sea basin, in Turkmenia, where 34 million ac. of food crops and cotton could be cultivated on irrigated land in a favourable sunny climate. An extension to the Caspian Sea, lying well below normal sea level, would help to stop the current slow "death" of that body of water.

In northwest England there appeared little hope for the Mersey estuary, polluted by vast volumes of untreated domestic sewage from Liverpool and neighbouring towns, along with industrial effluents from oil refineries, alkali works, and food factories. By contrast, the Thames, in the less industrialized southeast, became noticeably cleaner, as shipping and industry migrated downstream or northward away from London. The Greater London Council finally approved a scheme for a barrage, to be built near Woolwich, to hold back polluted estuarial waters.

In a remarkable paper presented to a symposium at Knoxville, Tenn., W. V. Mickey, seismologist with the National Ocean Survey of the U.S. Department of Commerce, showed that large reservoirs may either increase or lessen earthquake risk. At Lake Mead, impounded by the great Hoover Dam, the addition of an enormous weight of water to an unstable rock crust was shown to increase earthquakes, but at the Grand Canyon of Arizona and at Flaming Gorge in Utah, the creation of huge reservoirs had been followed by a dramatic lessening of seismic shocks.

(H. L. EN.)

Wildlife. In January 1971 delegates from European, Asian, and African countries met at Ramsar, Iran, to consider conservation of wetlands and waterfowl. The Iranian government set an important precedent by its decision to place one of its wetland ecosystems of special international importance in joint trust with a suitable international agency.

R. B. Clark of the Research Unit for the Rehabilitation of Oiled Seabirds at the University of Newcastle upon Tyne, Eng., and K. G. Gregory reported that one technical difficulty had been overcome. Previously, although the oil could be removed from the birds' feathers, the problem of leaving the feathers waterproof had proved intractable. Under laboratory conditions, oiled plumage could now be made clean and waterproof by immersing the bird in a low-toxicity solvent known as Arklone, and then drying it in warm air.

In February Tom Harrison, visiting Easter Island, advised that, during current touristic developments, attention should be given to the importance of the island for its breeding colonies of seabirds and of

Derelict small boats rest near piles of refuse at a neglected beach near Genoa, Italy. Italians fear their tourist business may be affected by growing quantities of refuse and waste left on their beaches.

UPI COMPIX

perhaps four species of marine turtles. The Marine Turtle Group of the Survival Service Commission of the IUCN reported that all marine turtles were in danger of extinction, chiefly through uncontrolled taking of their eggs. On Fripp Island, off the South Carolina coast, the developers established a conservation centre for the Atlantic loggerhead turtle, protecting nests and tagging adults. On both east and west coasts of North America, turtles faced a new danger, through eating plastic bags thrown overboard by ships. In March the Crocodilian Group of the SSC reported that all crocodiles, gavials, and alligators faced extinction except the American alligator, which was recovering under careful management.

In March, following the ban on the export of tiger and leopard skins imposed by most Indian states, the government of Nepal forbade all tiger shooting. Recent estimates of tigers surviving in India, Pakistan, Burma, and Nepal put the total at 3,000, a catastrophic decline from the 40,000 estimated in 1930. By the middle of 1971, ten Western states of the U.S. had classified the cougar (mountain lion or puma) as a game animal, thus giving it some protection. Often considered as vermin, the cougar, according to a six-year study by Maurice Hornocker, in fact had a beneficial influence on the population of its prey species.

On March 31 the first pygmy hog (*Sus salvanius*) to be identified for many years was found in the Assam Valley of India; further specimens followed, confirming the continued existence of this tiny pig. In April, in the same area of Assam, a hispid hare was caught—an animal not recorded for more than ten years. Strenuous efforts were made in the Philippines to preserve the monkey-eating eagle and the tamarau, a small endemic wild ox. After two visits to Ethiopia to report upon the situation of the Somali wild ass, Hans Kingel recommended that two sanctuaries on the Awash River be established immediately and guarded. Tourists who chased the asses to exhaustion, seeking photographs, were believed to be a major cause of mortality.   (C. L. BE.)

NATIONAL POLICIES

Indications of both future problems and future solutions were to be found in the wealthiest countries,

where the pressure was greatest. The toughest new national policies for pollution control came from the U.S., Sweden, and Japan.

During the first celebration of Earth Day, in April 1970, U.S. students, citizen activists, scientists, industry representatives, and government officials appeared at demonstrations throughout the nation to express concern over degradation of the environment. A year later the mood was quite different. There was no mass indignation. Neither was there a celebration. The environment issue was well established, and participants in the movement had become steeped in the complexities of a wide range of problems.

By April 1971 a framework for action had been established in the U.S. At the federal level, the Council on Environmental Quality made important recommendations to the president and commented on the environmental ramifications of federal programs and all government-aided activities. The Federal Water Quality Administration, the National Air Pollution Control Administration, and bureaus that previously dealt with pesticide regulations, radiation safety standards, and solid waste management were reorganized by executive order into a single department called the Environmental Protection Agency. Many states similarly reorganized their executive structures and in some cases passed laws that went beyond the federal establishment. Finally, at the grass-roots level, new attitudes and new life-styles began to take root. Thus, alerted to the dangers of air pollution from automobiles, Americans were creating an unprecedented boom in the bicycle business.

Two events in early 1971 signaled that the time had come for a deep reevaluation of all the traditional definitions of progress and the long-standing assumptions of U.S. technological supremacy. The president ordered a halt to the Cross-Florida Barge Canal, a massive public works project on which some $50 million in federal funds had been committed. Then the U.S. Congress cut off further appropriations toward the construction of a supersonic transport plane, although two presidents had thought it was essential to the maintenance of U.S. prestige and to the balance of payments.

The canal had been a long-time target of conservation groups who claimed it would have destroyed the scenic beauty of the semitropical Oklawaha River, upset the delicate hydrologic equilibrium of two watersheds, and triggered probable ecological consequences by abruptly connecting the Atlantic Ocean with the Gulf of Mexico. The president's action came in response to advice from his Council on Environmental Quality and, more significantly, after a preliminary court injunction obtained by the Environmental Defense Fund and allied groups had halted work on the project, at least temporarily.

The most important new legislation at the national level was the Clean Air Act of 1970, which called for national emission standards for all "significant new pollution sources" and, most importantly, for stringent controls on automobile emissions. William Ruckelshaus (*see* BIOGRAPHY), administrator for the Environmental Protection Agency, issued an enforcement plan for automobiles in June 1971. The EPA set standards for hydrocarbons, carbon monoxide, and nitrogen oxides that would in effect reduce the total volume of automobile pollutants 90% by 1976. The automakers were not certain that they could meet this deadline by modifying the conventional internal-combustion engine. Government-aided and pri-

A mobile laser system, mounted on a truck, sends out powerful beams of light to measure pollution from factory chimneys. Developed by Laser Associates in 1971, it was to be used by Central Electricity Research Laboratories in England to study atmospheric pollution.

vate research programs that might lead to an alternative "clean" car were accelerated—which was, of course, the purpose of the law. (*See* INDUSTRIAL REVIEW: *Special Report.*)

For the moment, it was not thought necessary to set standards on emissions of lead particles that spew in large amounts from cars and cause a real health hazard in cities. Lead additives have been needed in gasoline to prevent engine knocking. However, to the consternation of the automakers, lead has been found to retard significantly the performance of emission-control devices. Under increasing pressure from environmentalists and the federal government, the automakers and oil refiners for the first time worked together to help the situation. The Detroit engineers developed engines that would run efficiently on lower-octane fuel and would thus require less lead, while refiners put out fuels with a far lower lead content. It was estimated that by 1973 nearly 70% of the cars manufactured would be able to use a 91-octane gas containing an average of 0.5 g. of lead, compared with the 1970 average of 2.7 g.

The 1970 act also authorized the EPA to regulate airplane emissions and to set standards for all significant new facilities and for all sources of what the agency considers to be "hazardous substances." Asbestos, mercury, and beryllium were the first in the hazardous category. Initially, five types of stationary facilities were made subject to the national emission standards: nitric acid plants, contact sulfuric acid plants, portland cement plants, large incinerators, and fossil fuel steam generators.

In the field of enforcement, the EPA acted vigorously. Ruckelshaus recognized that the 1899 Refuse Act was still the most stringent antipollution law on the federal books and, throughout 1971, the EPA moved against polluters of navigable waterways under the old statute. In the first 11 months of fiscal 1971, some 159 criminal actions were initiated. The Refuse Act was also cited to obtain injunctions to stop discharges of harmful wastes.

While environmentalists turned to the Congress and the federal government for leadership, developments in the states could not be overlooked. Probably the most drastic move was made by Delaware's Gov. Russell Peterson, a Republican and former du Pont executive, who signed into law a ban on all heavy industry along the entire state coastline. By so acting, the governor turned down an estimated $750 million in new developments that would have meant increased employment and more tax dollars for Delaware. The new law also banned tanker-loading operations in Delaware Bay and severely restricted other new industries within a one- to six-mile strip along the shore.

In Maine an Environmental Improvement Commission, empowered to review all proposals for recreational, residential, commercial, or industrial development involving 20 ac. or more, rejected an application to build a large oil refinery at Searsport, on Penobscot Bay. Wisconsin, California, Florida, Maryland, and New York adopted tough regulations on pesticides, particularly DDT. Indiana was the first of six states to enact a law to restrict the phosphate content of detergents. New Jersey and Maryland took action to cope with the solid waste disposal problem. New Jersey passed a law stating that sewage sludge and industrial wastes could not be dumped within 100 mi. of its coastline. New York and Pennsylvania immediately challenged this action, however, and it was questionable whether the law could ever be enforced.

On the legal front, conservationists for years had been plagued by their lack of standing to sue in the courts. Time and time again, it was held that citizens or conservation organizations could not bring legal action unless they had personally suffered damages or injuries. In the late 1960s and in 1970, however, the courts handed down decisions that finally established the right to sue for relief against air and water pollution or aesthetic degradation.

During 1971, dramatic progress was made under the provision of the National Environmental Protection

A small band of wild mustangs, barely reminiscent of the large herds that once roamed the West, runs free in Nevada. On Dec. 17, 1971, Pres. Richard Nixon signed a law making it a crime to kill or harass wild horses or burros on federal lands.

HOPE RYDEN—ANIMALS ANIMALS

A scuba diver, draped
with algae, emerges
from the bottom
of the Manatawney Creek
in Pottstown, Pa.
Once a sparkling stream,
the creek now is polluted
with chemicals and filled
with stagnant growth.

Appealing to ecological
interests, a sign
at the Kent (O.) State
University campus warns
students of the newly
sodded grass.

IF ALLOWED TO SURVIVE
THIS GRASS WILL PRODUCE
ENOUGH OXYGEN FOR TWO
STUDENTS TO BREATHE
FOR ONE SEMESTER

UPI COMPIX

Act (NEPA) requiring that environmental impact
statements be provided by federal authorities connected in the slightest degree with a project that might
harm the environment. Several groups filed a petition claiming that the Atomic Energy Commission
(AEC) had failed to consider environmental factors
other than radiation hazards when it had granted a
license for construction of a huge nuclear power plant
at Calvert Cliffs on Chesapeake Bay. In September 1971, the 5th Circuit Court of Appeals ruled
against the AEC. Moreover, the court decision meant
that 91 nuclear power plants, either planned or under
construction, would have to be reviewed as to their
total environmental effect.

Other federal laws were the basis for decisive court
action. The U.S. Supreme Court ruled that the Department of Transportation Act of 1966 had been
violated by federal backing of an interstate highway
through Overton Park, a 342-ac. tract in Memphis,
Tenn. The Fish and Wildlife Coordination Act, the
Wilderness Act, the Federal Park Act, the National
Park Service Act, the National Historic Preservation
Act of 1966, and various highway amendments were
among the federal statutes that were being examined
for provisions under which environmentalists could
obtain legal support and relief.

Court action was sought in an effort to prevent
Cannikin, the test detonation of a five-megaton nuclear device under Amchitka Island, Aleutian Islands,
Alaska. An imposing array of opponents, including the
governor of Alaska, the governments of Canada and
Japan, and several scientific and conservation organizations, feared that the test could do incalculable environmental damage and might even trigger an earthquake or a seismic sea wave. The AEC admitted that
such effects were possible, but insisted that the possibility was remote and that the need to test the device
—a warhead for an antiballistic missile—was overriding. Hours before the test was scheduled, the Supreme Court refused a plea by several conservation
and antiwar groups that it be postponed until a secret
government report on its possible consequences, which
allegedly had not been included in the AEC's environ-

mental impact statement, could be considered. The
device was detonated at 5 P.M. EST and, according
to the AEC, there were no untoward effects.

No final decision was taken during the year on what
might be the most far-reaching project of all—the 800-
mi. trans-Alaska pipeline, which would bring oil from
Alaska's North Slope to the ice-free port of Valdez.
After a suit was brought based on NEPA, the Department of the Interior was ordered to submit a more
comprehensive impact statement.

Among long-range environmental problems in the
U.S., most experts tended to regard the energy crisis
as the most critical. Conventional sources of power
were being depleted while demands for power rose.
Moreover, the environmental liabilities of conventional methods of generating power were recognized
by growing numbers of citizens. In May 1971 the
Senate passed a resolution authorizing the Committee
on Interior and Insular Affairs to conduct a national
fuels and energy policy study. A month later, President Nixon, as part of a proposed Cabinet reorganization, asked for a single energy authority at the federal level. Nixon also called for accelerated research
and development to find new ways to generate electricity at less expense to the environment. Some observers felt that the president committed the U.S. too
heavily to nuclear power, and were disappointed that
greater emphasis had not been given to such long-term
possibilities as solar energy. Finally, many experts la-
mented that far too little attention was paid to the
short-term benefits of energy austerity.

Another major dilemma continued to exist in transportation. Urban traffic congestion got worse and
worse. Jet plane travel was efficient in the air, but on
the ground airports were increasingly unable to handle
traffic coming at them from above and from the cities
they served. The federal government began to support
the operation of passenger railroads between the largest cities, but the advocates of rail service noted with
despair that federal subsidies amounted to about one
quarter of the cost of a single shot to the moon. (See
The Urban Environment, above; *see also* TRANSPOR-
TATION.)

If the public expected that environmental imperatives would be formulated in a clear and forthright
manner, they were disappointed by developments in
two controversies, over phosphate detergents and
pesticides. In 1970 the Federal Water Quality Administration issued warnings saying that phosphate-based
detergents were the main contributors to the suffo-
cation and decay of lakes and fresh waterways. The
public was urged to use soaps containing low percentages of phosphates or to try detergents with a substitute water softener. Then in the fall of 1971, the
surgeon general announced that the phosphate substitutes were hazardous to the consumer—one was
found to induce cancer in test animals while others
could burn the skin and eyes and in some cases were
extremely poisonous if accidentally swallowed. The
citizen was left to fend for himself.

The conscientious gardener and farmer also had
good reason to be confused. EPA issued cancellation
notices for all uses of DDT, but that did not mean
that DDT or other persistent pesticides went off the
market. Under the cancellation process, these pesticides could continue in use until hearings had been
completed and all sides of the question judged by the
EPA. While the use of DDT dropped dramatically
anyway, other persistent or toxic chemicals raised
troublesome questions. Moreover, short-lived sub-

stitutes for DDT, organophosphates like Parathion, were extremely harmful if mishandled during application. (R. SA.)

In Japan, as a result of tighter clean-air policies, investment in antipollution by major Japanese manufacturing firms was increasing sharply compared with other business investments. According to a survey of 587 firms released by the Japan Development Bank in September, spending on antipollution equipment during the first part of the new financial year showed an 86% increase over 1970 figures. This form of investment increased from 4.1 to 6.2% of all industrial investments by the firms surveyed.

In May the Japanese government announced national standards for acceptable levels of noise recommended by the Living Environment Council. The standards differed according to time of day and type of area: areas where strict quietness was required (*e.g.*, in the vicinity of hospitals); mainly residential areas; and residential areas that also included industry and commerce. Since traffic was currently a major source of noise, the deadlines for enforcing the standards distinguished between areas that faced main roads and those that did not. In the former the standards were to be achieved within five years; in the latter they should be met as soon as they had been confirmed.

One of the most promising indications that high-level government decisions were being influenced by environmental considerations was the British government's choice of a Thames estuary site for the third London airport. An inland site in the Buckinghamshire countryside, proposed primarily on cost grounds by a special commission, was rejected in favour of a site at Foulness, 50 mi. from the capital and estimated to cost £100 million more than the alternative. The government's choice followed the advice of a minority report by one member of the commission who described the inland proposal as "an environmental disaster." However, even the Foulness site presented problems, since the wintering grounds of certain rare species of birds would be threatened. (DA. L. S.)

See also Cities and Urban Affairs; Life Sciences.

ENCYCLOPÆDIA BRITANNICA FILMS. *Water for Living Things* (1967); *The Everglades: Conserving a Balanced Community* (1968); *Problems of Conservation—Air* (1968); *The House of Man, Part II—Our Crowded Environment* (1969); *Problems of Conservation—Forest and Range* (1969); *Problems of Conservation—Minerals* (1969); *Problems of Conservation—Water* (1969); *The Garbage Explosion* (1970); *Problems of Conservation—Our Natural Resources* (1970); *Problems of Conservation—Soil* (1970); *Problems of Conservation—Wildlife* (1970); *A Field Becomes a Town* (1970); *The Aging of Lakes* (1971); *Noise—Polluting the Environment* (1971); *Turn off Pollution* (1971).

Equatorial Guinea

The African republic of Equatorial Guinea consists of Río Muni, which is bordered by Cameroon on the north, Gabon on the east and south, and the Atlantic Ocean on the west; and the offshore islands of Fernando Po and Annobón. Area: 10,830 sq.mi. (28,050 sq.km.). Pop. (1970 est.): 290,000. Cap. and largest city: Santa Isabel, on Fernando Po (pop., 1965 est., 37,152). Language: Spanish. President in 1971, Francisco Macías Nguema.

Equatorial Guinea's healthy growth rate of the 1960s collapsed after a reign of terror against Span-

---

EQUATORIAL GUINEA
Education. (1966–67) Primary, pupils 38,395, teachers 504; secondary, pupils 2,343, teachers 40; teacher training, students 130, teachers 28.
Finance and Trade. Monetary unit: peseta Guineana, at par with the Spanish peseta, with a par value of 70 pesetas to U.S. $1 (168 pesetas = £1 sterling) and a free rate (Sept. 27, 1971) of 69.25 pesetas = U.S. $1 (171.75 pesetas = £1 sterling). Budget (1969–70 est.): revenue 712.5 million pesetas; expenditure 1,139,000,000 pesetas. Foreign trade (1966): imports 1,278,000,000 pesetas (58% from Spain in 1965); exports 1,817,000,000 pesetas (97% to Spain in 1965). Main exports (1965): cocoa 44%; coffee 21%; timber 19%.
Agriculture. Production (in 000; metric tons; 1970; 1969 in parentheses): coffee *c.* 7.2 (*c.* 7.2); cocoa (1970–71) 35, (1969–70) 30; palm kernels (exports) *c.* 2 (*c.* 2); palm oil *c.* 4 (*c.* 4). Livestock (in 000; 1969–70): sheep *c.* 28; cattle *c.* 3; pigs *c.* 6; goats *c.* 6; chickens *c.* 75.

---

ish and Portuguese settlers. It was touched off by President Macías' attacks on Portugal for allegedly organizing an invasion of the Republic of Guinea. Of the 7,000 Europeans in the country in 1968 only a few hundred remained by 1971. Commercial and agricultural activity was reduced. Many cocoa plantations were neglected, in part as a result of the return of thousands of Nigerian labourers to their homeland after the end of the civil war there and despite an increase in wages to about $22 per month.

The diplomatic rupture with Spain after the occupation of the Spanish embassy and subsequent recall of the Spanish ambassador was ended early in 1971, and a new ambassador was appointed. Apart from $1 million from Libya in January and some help from the Organization of African Unity, Spain remained the country's only source of aid. Western diplomatic representation dwindled as a result of the increasingly authoritarian nature of the regime. A U.S. official died in mysterious circumstances in August. Soviet, North Korean, and Chinese embassies maintained their strength, and on April 14 President Macías recognized East Germany. (K. I.)

Ethiopia

A constitutional monarchy of northeastern Africa, Ethiopia is bordered by Somalia, Afars and Issas, Kenya, Sudan, and the Red Sea. Area: 471,800 sq.mi. (1,221,900 sq.km.). Pop. (1970 est.): 24,319,000. Cap. and largest city: Addis Ababa (pop., 1970 est., 795,900). Language: Amharic (official) and English. Religion: mainly Ethiopian Orthodox (Coptic), with Muslim and animist minorities. Emperor, Haile Selassie I; prime minister in 1971, Akililu Habte Wold.

Martial law was declared in Ethiopia's northern province of Eritrea in December 1970 after the assassination of Maj. Gen. Teshome Erghetu, commander of the 2nd Infantry Division, by Eritrean Liberation Front forces. Foreign Minister Ketema Yifru accused the governments of Syria, Iraq, and Yemen (Aden) of attempting to undermine Ethiopia's territorial integrity. The emperor's cousin, Ras Azrate Kassa, resigned the governor-generalship of Eritrea and in February 1971 was replaced by the commander of Ethiopian ground forces.

Disturbances in May, largely centred in Addis Ababa, took place when secondary-school students protested increases in bus fares and food prices. Schools in the capital were closed until September.

Epidemics:
see Medicine

Episcopal Church:
see Religion

Espionage:
see Intelligence Operations

There were over 800,000 enrolled students, and the figure was expected to top one million by the end of 1975. The U.S. Agency for International Development provided Eth$9,250,000 for expansion of university facilities, and a second loan agreement of Eth$23,750,000 for secondary-school development was signed with the World Bank in January. The year marked the 20th anniversary of Ethiopian higher education.

On the economic front difficulties included significant increases in external freight charges (arising partly from the continued closure of the Suez Canal) and a fall in coffee prices. The country also had to cope with outbreaks of cholera in several lowland areas. Favourable developments included the launching of an assistance program to small farmers in which they were given credit to buy fertilizers and improved seeds. The scheme was designed to reach an estimated one million farmers in 13 years.

On the industrial scene a new Eth$14.5 million tire plant was due to open in December, and a cement plant was planned for construction at Derba, 31 mi. N of Addis Ababa, that would more than double existing production capacity. The new Eth$75 million hydroelectric power investment at Finchaa, 124 mi. W of the capital, due for completion at the end of 1971, was designed to add 100 Mw. to the existing grid system. Also expected to become operational by 1972 was the Awash III plant in the Awash River Valley near Nazareth, with a capacity of 32,000 kw.

At the opening of the eighth summit conference of the Organization of African Unity at Addis Ababa on June 21, Haile Selassie's keynote speech underlined the refusal of a dialogue with South Africa. Official visitors to the capital included Pres. Léopold Sédar Senghor of Senegal, Maj. Gen. Yakubu Gowon of Nigeria, Vice-Pres. Spiro Agnew and Gen. William C. Westmoreland of the U.S., and the Greek deputy prime minister, Stylianos Pattakos. The emperor visited Spain, Burundi, Rwanda, China, and Iran during the year. (G. C. L.)

European Unity

For those who had been faithful in their support of European integration, and optimistic in the face of the many crises this concept had weathered over the years, 1971 was a year of rewards. For this was the year in which negotiators of the six EEC states and Britain, meeting chiefly in Luxembourg, got down to the serious business of determining under what conditions Britain might become a member of the European Economic Community. It was, moreover, a business conducted with dispatch, in an atmosphere of goodwill on the part of all the participants, and it culminated, in June, in a settlement acceptable to all negotiators.

This favourable outcome had been foreshadowed in May when, after intensive conversations in Paris between Prime Minister Edward Heath of Britain and Pres. Georges Pompidou of France, the latter, in contrast to the hostile views invariably expressed by his predecessor, Charles de Gaulle, declared that it would be unreasonable to think that an eventual accord between the Community and Britain would not be reached. Students of integration theory, fond of identifying solid signs of unity as opposed to mere declarations of intent, will be interested in what happened at Luxembourg; for history affords few other examples of great nations deliberately compromising major national interests to further their common welfare through cooperative and unified efforts.

EEC and the U.K. Probably the most expeditiously achieved agreement at Luxembourg was that dealing with Britain's future institutional position in the Community. In such bodies as the Executive Commission and the European Parliament, Britain would be on a footing of equality with France, Germany, and Italy, and English would become one of the official languages. Britain's involvement in the Court of Justice was to be worked out on a mutually satisfactory basis. Equitable arrangements were also spelled out for British participation in the two lesser Communities, that is, the European Atomic Energy Community and the European Coal and Steel Community.

Among the more difficult issues on which agreement was achieved were those arising out of Britain's international trading and fiscal position and its senior membership in the Commonwealth. Less developed Commonwealth countries in Africa, the Caribbean, and the Indian and Pacific Oceans were assured preferential markets in the Community and some might become formally "associated" with the Community. Fifteen Commonwealth sugar producing countries were promised continuance of their preferential market position under an existing convention with Britain that was to expire in 1974 and a benevolent Community policy thereafter. New Zealand, which was particularly concerned about its dairy products market in Britain, was to enjoy a preferential guaranteed market for almost three-fourths of its present exports until 1977, also with assurance of a benevolent review by the Community at the end of this transition period.

ETHIOPIA

Education. (1967–68) Primary, pupils 452,457, teachers 9,525; secondary, pupils 71,467, teachers 3,062; vocational, pupils 6,251, teachers 533; teacher training, students 1,816, teachers 115; higher (at 2 universities; 1968–69), students 3,870, teaching staff 469.

Finance. Monetary unit: Ethiopian dollar, with a par value of Eth$2.50 to U.S. $1 (Eth$6 = £1 sterling) and a free rate (Oct. 11, 1971) of Eth$2.38 to U.S. $1 (Eth$5.90 = £1 sterling). Gold, SDRs, and foreign exchange, central bank: (June 1971) U.S. $68.8 million; (June 1970) U.S. $80.3 million. Budget (1969–70 est.): revenue Eth$602 million; expenditure Eth$631 million. Money supply: (June 1971) Eth$423.1 million; (June 1970) Eth$450.4 million. Cost of living (Addis Ababa; 1963 = 100): (June 1971) 149; (June 1970) 141.

Foreign Trade. (1970) Imports Eth$429.1 million; exports Eth$305 million. Import sources (1969): Italy 15%; West Germany 14%; Japan 11%; U.S. 10%; U.K. 10%; Iran 5%. Export destinations (1969): U.S. 42%; West Germany 10%; Italy 7%; the Afars and Issas 6%; Yemen (Aden) 6%. Main exports: coffee 59%; oilseeds 9%; hides and skins 8%; cereals 6%.

Transport and Communications. Roads (1968) *c.* 23,000 km. (including 7,304 km. all-weather). Motor vehicles in use (1969): passenger 33,000; commercial 10,800. Railways (1969) 1,088 km. Air traffic (1970): 314.4 million passenger-km.; freight 16,-755,000 net ton-km. Telephones (Dec. 1969) 41,106. Radio receivers (Dec. 1969) 155,000. Television receivers (Dec. 1969) 8,000.

Agriculture. Production (in 000; metric tons; 1970; 1969 in parentheses): millet, sorghum, and teff *c.* 2,700 (2,628); barley *c.* 1,540 (1,517); wheat *c.* 780 (764); corn *c.* 895 (860); linseed *c.* 60 (*c.* 60); sunflower seed *c.* 34 (*c.* 34); sugar, raw value (1970–71) *c.* 120, (1969–70) *c.* 107. Livestock (in 000; 1969–70): cattle *c.* 26,000; sheep *c.* 12,700; goats *c.* 12,200; horses *c.* 1,400; mules *c.* 1,400; asses *c.* 3,900; camels *c.* 190; poultry *c.* 46,500.

Industry. Production (in 000; metric tons; 1968–69): cement 166; cotton yarn 5; cotton fabrics (sq.m.; 1966–67) 58,000; electricity (kw-hr.; 1967–68) 361,000.

Britain itself offered guarantees concerning the position of sterling as a reserve currency for sterling area countries. These countries' sterling balances in London would gradually be reduced, the position of sterling as a reserve currency would eventually be liquidated, and, as the Community moved toward an increasing degree of monetary union, Britain's currency would be brought into line with this policy. Britain actually made an initial 10% cut in its sterling balances in September.

The two most difficult issues on which agreement was reached concerned Britain's assimilation into the Community's industrial tariff and agricultural systems, and the level of payments that Britain would be called upon to make to the Community budget, which would soon be nearing $4 billion. The budget consisted of the proceeds of the Community tariff, the agricultural levies, and some direct national payments; and much of the total was used to defray subsidies paid to Community farmers, among whom French farmers had a favoured position. Since it was a large importer of food, Britain feared that, without some maximum figure, it might be called upon to provide a sum that would strain its international payments position.

On the tariff question the agreement provided that duties between Britain and the Community would be reduced by 20% annually over a period of five years with virtually duty-free British access to the Common Market within three years. As for the common external tariff of the Community, Britain would apply it according to a somewhat similar schedule although a dozen raw materials, important to British industry, and also tea, would continue to be imported duty free. British assimilation to the Community farm price system would be achieved by six steps over the five-year transition period; consumer prices would thus go up gradually. Finally, as respects the Community budget, the ceiling on Britain's payments would rise gradually over a seven-year period according to a schedule based on Britain's estimated proportion of the Community's total gross national product (GNP), and the contribution would level off thereafter at close to a half-billion dollars annually.

Even this superficial recital of the principal features of the Luxembourg agreements suggests that they were relatively favourable to Britain. Indeed the chief British negotiator and Prime Minister Heath formally declared them to be so. Nevertheless, that fact did not seem to inspire much enthusiasm on the part of the British public about going into the Community now that there existed a realistic possibility of doing so. Since de Gaulle's second veto of British EEC membership in November 1967, that public had cooled perceptibly toward such a possibility. Thus, though opinion polls taken in June 1966 indicated that 68% of the British electorate would support membership, in May 1971 support had dropped to 20%. Quarter-page advertisements by the European Movement in *The Sunday Times,* extolling compensatory benefits of increased wages and greater prosperity that would come from unimpeded access to the Community market, and other efforts to "sell" membership apparently had little effect on a public that knew food prices would rise because of the high Community farm subsidies and high tariffs against the rest of the world, and that feared British social services, especially the health service, would not be maintained at present levels when placed in direct competition with allegedly lower standards on the Continent.

Public opposition was quickly reflected in Parliament when the Luxembourg agreements were presented. The leader of the opposition Labour Party, former Prime Minister Harold Wilson, who had himself tried to lead Britain into the Community in 1967, now said he opposed entry and made opposition to membership a matter of party policy. In July, the Labour Party's National Executive Committee voted against British membership 16–6. The committee was subsequently joined in its opposition by its ally, the influential general council of the Trades Union Congress, which voted 15–11 against membership.

Whether Wilson would succeed in the long run in playing the role of a British de Gaulle in this third effort to bring Britain into the EEC, and whether the hostile public climate would jeopardize the prospect of entry, remained to be seen. In the White Paper on the subject, Heath insisted that there was no alternative to membership, that if membership were rejected now, in the light of the favourable terms being offered, Britain might never be given another chance. "In a single generation," he said, "we should have renounced an imperial past and rejected a European future. Our friends everywhere would be dismayed. They would rightly be as uncertain as ourselves about our future role and place in the world."

The decisive parliamentary vote on the principle of EEC membership was held on October 28. Although Heath had freed his party's members to vote as they chose while Labour tried to enforce party discipline, the measure was approved 356–244, an unexpectedly high margin of 112 votes. This action was to be followed by detailed legislation on a number of matters necessary to take Britain legally into the EEC and these would consume another year. The actual target date for British membership was Jan. 1, 1973. Thus, if parliamentary approval continued, on that date, Britain would become a formal member of EEC and, after the five-year transition period, a full member.

An interesting sidelight on possible membership for Britain in the EEC was offered by the steps Britain had already taken, deliberately or by chance, that had the effect of aligning it with the Six. These included the transition to the decimal coinage system; the allied step to apply the metric system generally within a few years; and the first efforts to transform the farm price support system into one resembling that of the EEC. Membership would also entail the introduction of VAT (value-added tax), the tax system that the Six had agreed to adopt.

In the wings at Luxembourg and Brussels, while Britain and the Six were coming to terms, were the other three announced candidates for EEC membership, Ireland, Denmark, and Norway. The prevailing opinion in knowledgeable circles was that, once the British case was settled favourably, these three states would have no trouble in making satisfactory arrangements for membership.

Nevertheless there were obstacles, as in Britain, that might be interposed internally in these states. Norway, for example, had even higher farm price supports than the Community, and its leaders in the Storting were having difficulty bringing the farm constituency around. Norway's fishermen were also loath to accept the principle of open fishing rights for all Community citizens; the Norwegians preferred to reserve their fjords to themselves. Irish subsistence farmers also worried about their future and were quite willing to let their government know of their worries. They feared the EEC's Mansholt policy on agriculture, which opposed high prices for subsistence farm-

Demonstrators gather in Trafalgar Square, London, to hear speeches opposing Britain's entry into the European Economic Community.

ers and would retire their farms from production.

The challenges of the Community to existing life styles and traditional values might yet produce more than pro forma opposition to the integrative trend in Europe. On the other hand, each of these three states was so dependent upon Community, and especially British, markets that they probably had no satisfactory alternative to membership. At any rate, there was no reason to suppose that opposition of the nature described would seriously impede their efforts to follow Britain into the EEC.

Other European Regional Organizations. As the EEC expanded its membership and augmented its influence, it overshadowed and even removed the raison d'être of the other instrumentalities of regional integration in Western Europe. Expansion of EEC in the direction of a broad economic union tended to make increasingly superfluous the two other Communities with administrative headquarters in Brussels, the European Atomic Energy Community and the European Coal and Steel Community. For the same reason there was a decline in the significance of the Western European Union, a union of the U.K. and the Six in what was basically a European security organization; Nordek, the proposed Organization for Nordic Economic Cooperation; and the European Free Trade Association (EFTA).

EFTA, which consisted of nine states, was established in 1959 as a less ambitious alternative to the EEC. Now that Britain, the leader of this grouping, was defecting to the EEC, and probably carrying with it two other EFTA members, Norway and Denmark, EFTA would probably disappear. A kind of three-tier arrangement might come into being vis-à-vis the EEC for the nine EFTA states: some would become outright members of the Brussels organization; some, such as Sweden, Switzerland, and Austria, who felt that membership could damage their traditional neutralism, would become "associated" with it; and some would seek special treaty arrangements with it.

Council of Europe. Apparently exempt from this relative decline of other European organizations was one of the oldest, the Council of Europe at Strasbourg, France. Having indicted the present Greek regime in 1969 for its antidemocratic tendencies, and

having thus brought about the resignation of Greece from membership, the Council then consisted of 17 members. Practically every non-Communist European state other than Greece was a member including, of course, the present six EEC members and the four that may join the EEC.

The Council's principal concerns continued to be of a cultural and technical nature and included the special protective apparatus that had been established in Europe for safeguarding the rights of the individual. The range and variety of its cultural activities were underscored during the summer when a committee of artists, who had been operating under the Council's auspices, made the rather unique recommendation to member governments that, in the future, the universal tuning pitch for orchestras and musicians be the treble A with a frequency of 440 vibrations per second. The committee also recommended that this tone be used where convenient in opening and closing radio and television programs and for the telephone dial tone to accustom the public to its sound.

The Council's primary concerns did not, however, exclude a major interest in other spheres. In the political sphere especially, the Council offered frequent reminders that it was a forum for a greater Europe than that of the Six. These reminders were especially emphatic during the occasional joint sessions of the European Parliament of EEC and the Council's Consultative Assembly at Strasbourg (in the case of the Six, members were often the same in both assemblies). In such sessions, debate and discussion might include current major issues between Eastern and Western Europe, such as the proposed European security conference; appropriate future relations between an expanding EEC and those states of Europe that, for any reason, do not feel free to join EEC; and the proper role of Western Europe, and of the EEC particularly, toward the less developed world, including whether trade preferences ought not to be generalized.

That "outside" nations valued this Council forum was at least tacitly indicated during 1971 by New Zealand and the United States. The former, fearful of the potentially detrimental impact upon its European markets of Britain's upcoming membership in the EEC, used the forum to explain its position. The U.S. chose to use the Council forum to explain its position toward Europe as a whole. A State Department representative was sent to Strasbourg to describe current aspects of trade and monetary policy and even to explain why the U.S. was continuing to arm Greece.

(A. J. Z.)

See also Commercial Policies; Defense; Payments and Reserves, International; Trade, International; United Kingdom.

Fairs and Shows

The multibillion-dollar fairs and shows industry continued to flourish in 1971. Over 75% of the estimated 14,000 fairs around the world reported generally favourable results. Revenues were up 10–14% over 1970 on entertainment features; food and beverage grosses rose over 8%; and attendance was up 1.5–5%. Some fairs reported higher gross revenues despite attendance losses attributed to increased admission prices. Steady gains were noted at most Western European commercial trade fairs, while others showed fractionally slower growth margins over the previous year. Seventy-seven countries played host to over 940 trade fairs at which over 42.5 million trade buyers were registered, an increase of 11% over 1970. Some West German trade fairs scored gains as high as 22% in attendance.

Mass entertainment facilities in the U.S. and Canada attracted over 1,100,000,000 persons to over 7,600 arenas, stadiums, and parks. An additional 2,200,000,000 persons worldwide jammed an estimated 17,000 amusement parks, kiddielands, theme parks, zoos, aquariums, and roadside tourist attractions.

The U.S. Congress passed legislation requiring promoters of world's fairs in the U.S. to have approval of the Bureau of International Expositions (BIE), Paris, before any appropriation of federal funds would be made. Among the several applicants for BIE approval were the proposed Expo 74 in Spokane, Wash., which applied for "special category" classification for a fair with an environment and outdoor recreation theme, and the 1976 Bicentennial of Independence Exposition. In September 1970 a presidential commission had recommended that Philadelphia be the principal site for international participation in the bicentennial celebrations.

International Trade Fairs. Most of the world's 940 commercial trade fairs in 77 countries experienced peak capacity attendance. Business results were considered the best in years. Marked gains of 15–20% were seen in buyer and exhibitor interest.

Concern over environmental problems spawned a number of new trade shows during the year including the International Filtration & Separation Exhibition in London; Virology '71 in Moscow; Pro Aqua-Pro Vita Exhibition in Basel, Switz.; and Project 2000, Water Protection-Air Purification & Environment Conservation Show in Graz, Aus. Other major trade fairs of 1971 were the 35th International Levante Trade Fair, Bari, Italy; the Vienna International Trade Fair; and the Hanover (W.Ger.) Fair. The U.S. Department of Commerce sponsored over 250 fairs during the year.

Fairs. Revenue grosses eclipsed previous records at over 60% of the world's annual public fairs; at least 55% reported higher attendance figures. Spending continued at high levels despite increased admission prices, with midway rides and food and beverage stands showing appreciable revenue gains over 1970. Over 115 million persons attended some 4,000 fairs in North America and another 850 million visited over 10,000 fairs elsewhere. The leading fairs in North America were the Canadian National Exhibition at Toronto, which recorded 3,210,000 persons in 1971, and the State Fair of Texas at Dallas, with 3,134,646 visitors.

An estimated 450,000 district and regional retail and wholesale shows were presented in 1971 in exposition buildings and hotel and motel exhibition halls throughout the world. Many were held in conjunction with conferences or conventions that a reported 140 million trade visitors attended.

Amusement Parks. Approximately 2,000,000,000 persons visited an estimated 17,000 amusement facilities in 1971, spending more than $4 billion. Nearly 25% of the attendance and gross business was accounted for by over 2,000 amusement and fun parks in North America. The "super amusement parks" at HemisFair Plaza in Houston, Tex., and Man and His World in Montreal were facing bankruptcy. In October, Walt Disney World opened its 100-ac. amusement park in Lake Buena Vista, Fla. The park was only one part of a $400-million development that was

to include a 150-ac. parking area, hotels, and ancillary recreation facilities.

Carnivals, Rodeos, and Circuses. Approximately 200 midway carnival operators appeared at U.S. and Canadian fairs in 1971, with nearly 600 more at European, Asian, and Latin-American events. The larger carnival units introduced new equipment in an effort to capture a greater share of midway revenues; smaller units and independent operators offered free attractions. An estimated 1,910 mobile carnivals and 970 independent operators around the world reported the best season records in their history. Gross income for 1971 rose to $960 million, an increase of 4.6% over the previous year for an average 229-day season. The highest grossing midway operation was Toronto's Canadian National Exhibition, which grossed over $1.7 million in 19 days.

Rodeos were popular in North, Central, and South America and were featured in increasing numbers at

Selected Major National and International Fairs, 1971		
Country and date	Event and place	Attendance
Algeria		
Aug. 27–Sept. 12	International Trade Fair, Algiers	1,600,000
Australia		
April 2–13	Royal Easter Show, Sydney	1,080,000
Austria		
Sept. 5–12	International Autumn Trade Fair, Vienna	600,000
Belgium		
April 21–May 2	International Trade Fair, Brussels	680,000
Bulgaria		
Sept. 19–28	International Trade Fair, Plovdiv	500,000
Canada		
Aug. 21–Sept. 6	Pacific National Exhibition, Vancouver, B.C.	1,104,513
Aug. 20–29	Central Canada Exhibition, Ottawa	565,243
Aug. 19–Sept. 6	Canadian National Exhibition, Toronto	3,210,000
Chile		
Oct. 9–30	International Trade Fair, Santiago	1,000,000
Cyprus		
Sept. 3–26	17th International Cyprus Fair, Nicosia	2,060,000
Czechoslovakia		
Sept. 11–20	International Trade Fair, Brno	550,000
France		
May 15–24	International Fair, Bordeaux	500,000
Sept. 2–13	European Samples Fair, Strasbourg	678,000
Sept. 23–Oct. 4	International Trade Fair, Marseilles	1,500,000
Germany, East		
Sept. 5–12	International Trade Fair, Leipzig	800,000
Germany, West		
April 22–30	Hanover Fair, Hanover	600,000
Greece		
Aug. 29–Sept. 19	International Trade Fair, Thessaloniki	1,500,000
Hungary		
May 21–31	International Trade Fair, Budapest	1,000,000
Iraq		
Oct. 1–21	International Fair, Baghdad	500,000
Italy		
May 29–June 13	Fair of Rome, Rome	1,320,000
May 27–June 6	International Trade Fair, Padua	1,000,000
Aug. 6–22	International Trade Fair, Messina, Sicily	600,000
Japan		
April 16–May 6	International Trade Fair, Tokyo	2,800,000
Libya		
Feb. 28–March 20	International Fair, Tripoli	500,000
Peru		
Nov. 12–18	Pacific International Trade Fair, Lima	600,000
Poland		
June 13–22	40th International Trade Fair, Poznan	750,000
South Africa		
March 30–April 12	Rand Easter Show, Johannesburg	1,000,000
Spain		
July 1–12	International Trade Fair, Bilbao	700,000
April 15–20	Ibero-American Samples Fair, Seville	558,000
Switzerland		
March 11–21	International Motor Show, Geneva	550,000
Sept. 11–26	Comptoir-Suisse National Fair, Lausanne	1,000,000
April 17–27	Swiss Industries Fair, Basel	1,000,000
Syria		
Aug. 20–Sept. 20	International Fair, Damascus	1,300,000
Tunisia		
May 21–June 6	International Trade Fair, Tunis	800,000
U.S.S.R.		
July–Aug.	Modern Attractions, Park & Theatre Exhibition, Moscow	185,000
United Kingdom		
Oct. 20–30	International Motor Exhibition, London	560,000
United States		
Aug. 19–28	Kentucky State Fair, Louisville	549,938
Aug. 20–Sept. 6	California State Fair, Sacramento	950,000
Aug. 20–28	Erie County Fair, Hamburg, N.Y.	572,598
Aug. 20–29	Iowa State Fair, Des Moines	644,000
Aug. 27–Sept. 6	Michigan State Fair, Detroit	893,405
Aug. 28–Sept. 6	Minnesota State Fair, St. Paul	1,370,000
Sept. 2–6	Allegheny County Fair, Pittsburgh, Pa.	800,000
Yugoslavia		
April 19–25	International Spring Fair, Zagreb	2,000,000
May 14–23	International Technical Fair, Belgrade	800,000

Source: Frederick P. Pittera, *Fairs of the World* (1971).

A new fairground with 120,000 sq.yd. of hall space, built between the Rhine River and the Düsseldorf, W.Ger., airport, was opened in August 1971. The facilities were initiated by the International Plastic Fair in September.

KEYSTONE

fairs, agricultural, and livestock expositions. Efforts to promote rodeos in Europe were, for the most part, dismal failures. Efforts of humane societies to wipe out rodeos and the embargo on horse movements imposed in July by the U.S. Department of Agriculture following an outbreak of Venezuelan equine encephalomyelitis (VEE) forced the cancellation of many shows (*see* VETERINARY MEDICINE). An estimated 3,200 shows were held in 47 states of the U.S. and five Canadian provinces in 1971, which was about 5% below the number held in 1970.

Most of the world's 665 circuses closed their seasons with better-than-average returns; indoor events were more successful than outdoor and tented shows. Independent circus acts played more single dates than ever before. Virtually all of North America's 55 circuses were presented under the auspices of charitable organizations. In the U.S.S.R., where the circus is considered an art form, the Russian State Circus toured some 50 permanent circus buildings and had over 25 other troupes performing abroad.

Livestock and Horse Shows. Almost every agricultural region of the world held livestock shows during 1971 with millions of breed and market animals entered at more than 24,000 different events. Some of the oldest established shows, such as the Royal Smithfield Show at London, the International Livestock Exposition at Chicago, and the Palermo Show at Buenos Aires, paid the highest prize money awards in their history and had over 10,000 animal entries. Market sales were up 12% over 1970.

The VEE epidemic caused a number of horse shows to be canceled and many other events were presented with stock only. Over 4,500 horse shows were held in North America, over 897 of which were sanctioned by the American Horse Shows Association; and over 13,000 other horse shows were held.   (F. P. P.)

Fashion and Dress

In the fashion world, 1971 might go down as the year of contrasts. Never before had fashion moved so swiftly or been subject to so many contradictions. Gabrielle ("Coco") Chanel, the famous designer who had stamped her image on one of the longest periods in fashion history, died in January (*see* OBITUARIES). The world of high fashion encountered growing competition from the ready-to-wear market, whose biannual showings attracted more and more international buyers. Moreover, it got out of its depth by offering

the same type of fun clothes at couture prices. Finally, it was rocked by the sudden deviation of one of the most influential couturiers, Yves St. Laurent (*see* BIOGRAPHY), who declared in August that he had shown the last of his couture collections and would henceforth devote his creative efforts to designing ready-to-wear clothes for his own boutiques. A similar decision was taken by the London couturier Clive and, before that, by Michael; all were influenced by pressure from soaring overheads and the scarcity of customers with time and money.

Influenced by the prevailing permissive atmosphere, the uniform for early 1971 became the shortest of shorts, known as "hot pants," half concealed under a shaggy, midi-length fur coat that covered the top of the inevitable high boots—a fashion essential but higher heeled than in the previous year. From London's King's Road, where they soared to thigh top, hot pants reached Paris' St. Germain des Prés sidewalks, where they modestly descended to mid-thigh. In New York, where long skirts never had been popular and were worn only by a small set, shorts were quickly adopted as an antidote, and there they often cleared the knee in a manner reminiscent of bermuda shorts. Hot pants could be in anything from sleek leather to glistening satin, or sprinkled with rhinestones for evening. Sheer tights to be worn with hot pants were specially produced without a thigh demarcation, and were usually selected in black or earthen shades. Hot pants lived through spring and summer. They could hardly be said to have been a success with haute couture clients, but boutiques did a roaring business at all prices and in all types of material.

Even when they were not skipping about in shorts, trendy young women kept up the anti-Establishment mood, developing whims and picking up inspiration right and left. They floated in Far Eastern robes, swathed themselves in long-fringed wool shawls, or dressed like one of the Three Musketeers, complete with plumed hat. They created a casual, fluid, and often humorous fashion of their own. In the meantime, a large number of women, caught between the eccentricities of the youth styles and the dowdiness of the midi, took refuge in the ever-safe pant suit.

By spring the couturiers had left their ivory towers and sharpened their scissors, the better to cut off hems. The outcome of the spring showings was that hem lengths fluctuated from mid-calf to knee level and ceased to be a point of controversy. But the new collections provided fresh subjects of contention as couturiers produced their version of shorts, more or less concealed under side-slit or front-buttoned skirts, and freely indulged in the charade and folklore look. On the last day of the showings St. Laurent threw his personal bomb, reviving the 1940s look with all the vulgarity of heavily padded shoulder lines, dagger-pointed lapels, long piped jackets over shortened, low-pleated skirts, artificial flowers at tightly draped hiplines, puffed sleeves, silver fox stoles, boxy coats, ankle straps, and even the clumsy wedge soles. When the smoke cleared, faces were puzzled when not indignant, and Yves was roundly criticized for reviving such an abhorred period.

His defense was that his fashion corresponded to the mood of the current period, which was brutal, vulgar, and aggressive. But the press scorned his collection to the point where many journalists, both French and foreign, were not invited to see his collection in August, which purported to be his last. Nevertheless, shorn of St. Laurent's extremes, the tailored style was indeed back, with a slightly lifted shoulder line and wider, more pointed lapels, typified by the blazer and box-pleated skirt. Cardin showed a modernized version of the broader shoulder line by adding a squared-off wing effect over the arm top. At Dior it was the prewar sophisticated Deauville look, often in white. But the suit that scored highest in the Paris haute couture was the perennial Chanel suit in her well-known, beautifully hued tweeds. Whether as a tribute to "Mademoiselle" or to find refuge from the current uncertainty of the fashion world, the result was a deluge of orders that tied up the workrooms for months.

The move toward a more tailored style meant a change in materials. They became more crisp, though retaining their suppleness; wool crepe was important, and flannel and serge were revived. Plain, closely ribbed woolens appeared in the more fitted coats, while tweeds with small discreet patterns were just right for the new suits. An important trend in the way of dressing, launched by Ungaro and developed by the top ready-to-wear firms, was the layered look of garment over garment—waistcoat over blouse, shirt over pullover. The sleeveless, deep-armholed, deep-necked T-shirt was a particular favourite.

Layered dressing became a way of life for the young. Besides adding garment to garment, the new fad was to coordinate and combine patterns and prints: stripes for the skirt, flowers for the blouse, and perhaps dots for the waistcoat. Everything was permissible if the result was easy, natural, and unrestrained—an ideal formula for the younger set, encouraging them to think out their total look for themselves. This they often did with great success, and the result was an ever more definite rejection of dictated fashion. Whether because of the confusion in high fashion circles or as yet another form of the anti-Establishment campaign, the custom of "making your own fashion" appeared well rooted and likely to remain. The ideal material for the layered look turned out to be wool voile, either plain or printed. For all the evening fancy-dress charade outfits, chiffon, printed or woven with metal threads, and organza produced the desired gaudy and festive look.

In the summer strong colours were adopted: Matisse blue, sunflower yellow, lettuce green, and vermilion red, with apricot heralding various shades of rust for the fall. Throughout the spring and summer the blazer eclipsed the pant suit. The success of the blazer was responsible for a further development of the unisex look, with men and women displaying the same cut, the same material, and the same accent on colour. This look went a step further when, in cities and on the beaches, boys and girls put on GI fatigues and battle dress—often the genuine article obtained from surplus stores. Next came work clothes, such as butchers' smocks in pinchecks, a trend manufacturers hoped to exploit in the summer of 1972.

Faced with the dismaying sales figures that resulted from their efforts to outdo the boutiques, the top designers presented fall clothes far more related to life and to haute couture. The hemline was stabilized at knee level. The basic suit was reinstalled. After the squared-off, military-style shoulder line came fuller coats flaring out at the back and with deeper armholes. Sleeves became important, full and cuffed, and for evening St. Laurent revived the leg-of-mutton sleeve on tight-bodiced, frilled taffeta dresses. On the London streets boxy-shouldered jack-

Fashions in 1971 combined tradition and innovation. Top, left, for winter a traditional mohair coat was offered by Renbrook. Top, right, the Mary Quant collection created a wrestler's vest and shorts, draped with a caftan. Above, left, Dior's longer evening shorts were shown with a see-through blouse. Above, right, a tweed suit by Yves St. Laurent revived the 1940s.

ets, often in fake fur, were everywhere, as was the St. Laurent smock jacket. Shorts were replaced by bermudas with above-the-knee knitted socks instead of boots. In Paris there were gay plaids and tartans for coats, duffle coats, trouser suits, and skirts. Coats flared out at the back or were belted with detachable shoulder capelets. In the fall, inspired by the revived interest in China that followed U.S. Pres. Richard Nixon's announcement of his Peking visit, the Chinese influence became pervasive, finding expression in costumes that ranged from the Chinese worker's blue cotton uniform to the most elegant of silks.

The fall evening scene was very feminine and romantic. Again from St. Laurent came tiered frills, flounces and even bustles, tight bodices, and a generally *fin de siècle* atmosphere. There was also a return to hats. Pull-on felts and velours trimmed with long ostrich feathers in London and, in Paris, the soft artist's velvet beret from *La Vie de Bohème*, updated with a star-shaped rhinestone pin.

With couture designers seeking the ready-to-wear pot of gold, the ready-to-wear firms faced a considerable challenge. According to the SAMIA trade fair in Turin, Italy, and the Paris October showings, their 1972 spring clothes would be wearable and easy, with a nautical touch and a reminder of the mini and with small puffed sleeves to satisfy nostalgia for the little-girl look.

Cosmetics and Hair Styles. In the spring and summer an all-over suntan was safe enough, but in the fall complexions were still required to reflect the healthy, outdoor look. Pomades and fingertips took over from powder and brush as implements of cosmetics. Colour was dabbed on cheekbones, the general effect being glazed rather than mat, somewhat like a Russian doll. After the long ascendancy of subdued beige and light apricot, lipstick became brilliantly coloured by autumn, but by remaining fluid and transparent it avoided the harsh look of the 1930s. Some girls chose clear, see-through reds: Mary Quant's "Hot Stuff," Dior's "Happy Tones," or Orlane's "Étincelant"—a shade to make a cardinal's hat turn pale. Others appeared to have been munching strawberries or bilberries (Guerlain's new "Hydra-Rouges" range), sipping brandy (Charles of the Ritz "Brandy Wine" lip pomade), or tasting ripe plums (one of the latest Estée Lauder "Glossamers").

Never before had cosmetics been so tuned to fashion. Matched to the new bright blue, green, and violet, or to the deep rich tones of plum, copper, and burgundy, they were applied simultaneously to cheeks, eyes, lips, and nails. A new idea from Biba was to apply these colours on a yellow "Gloss Foundation" to counteract the natural pink of the skin. Lip colour was intended to complement or match eye shadow. Amber was the new shade chosen in the Helena Rubinstein "Broadway Lights" range, while Elizabeth Arden's "Autumn Lights" range stressed "Bronzetto" and "Purple Smoke." Eyebrows were plucked once more and drawn into a curve; lashes were shaggy or spider-like and well brushed.

There were great changes in hair styles as well. For a brief period curls and waves followed the St. Laurent 1940 revival, giving way in the autumn to a healthy natural look with well-brushed, well-cared-for, lustrous hair, cut medium long and often parted in the middle. Alexandre called his line "Elf" and explained that you could "comb it with your fingers, then add an outsize comb or fancy slide to hold it." Carita, also following the closer-to-nature trend, cut

hair to frame the face, turning the ends inward, and caught it to one side "like an English schoolgirl's." Backcombing finally disappeared, and wigs were worn with discrimination. (T. Sw.)

Men's Fashion. The key word in men's fashion in 1971 was elegance. Signs of a return to elegance on an international scale first became apparent in Britain at IMBEX '71, the International Men's and Boys' Exhibition held in London in March, at which 14 countries were represented. The overall pattern of elegance—economical rather than extravagant in style and shape, though not always in colour—also dominated the International Men's Fashion Week in Cologne, W.Ger., in August and the SAMIA fair in September.

Throughout the year and almost throughout the world, the feeling for elegance emerged slowly and imperceptibly—an evolution rather than a revolution, following the usual mode of change in men's fashion. Frills and frippery began to disappear from both day shirts and evening dress shirts. Shorter, classic sweaters were favoured, body-fitting and ending at the waist. Sports jackets returned with more style and in lighter-weight fabrics such as linen and cotton. Blazers, never unfashionable, were given new interest by both woven and knitted fabrics. Lightweight blazers in check cottons became almost a weekend uniform in Europe as they had been for some time in the U.S.

In suits, the single-breasted, two-button jacket, with slightly wider lapels, deeper flaps to the pockets, and deeper side or centre vents based on the hacking jacket, emerged as the universally accepted style for business. Pure wool worsted remained the most popular choice, but blended materials, usually a worsted with one of the many man-made fibres, made inroads into the world suit market. The decline of the traditional suit continued, however, especially in the U.S., where knitted fabrics, easy-care jackets, and slacks were more commonly worn for business and leisure than in Britain.

In conventional suit patterns, the elegant classics enjoyed a revival: pick-and-picks, chalk stripes (with more colour and wider spacing), pinstripes, neater herringbones, and bird's-eye weaves. The big, bold geometric patterns favoured by the Italians had gained some acceptance in the U.S. but little or none elsewhere. However, the aubergine shade, also emanating from Italy, enjoyed wide success in both suits and knitwear. In lighter shades and in mixtures with black, it added another colour to men's suits. Nevertheless, no appreciable change took place in the top four suit colours—gray, blue, brown, and green, usually in that order. The acceptance of coloured shirts for business wear continued, with a move away from self-colours toward multicoloured patterns and coloured motifs and more discreet stripes on contrasting colour grounds. Cotton shirts made a comeback.

The boom in ties surprised most people, not least the manufacturers. In Britain tie sales rose 20% above the previous year, and the tie buyer for one major retail organization reported an increase of 100%. Walter Koby, chairman of the Tie Manufacturers Association, commented during a BBC radio interview: "Ties are to a man what hot pants are to a woman."

Market research by fibre producers and hosiery manufacturers in Britain and the U.S. confirmed that men still wore more black, dark gray, and dark blue socks than any other colours, despite the wide variety available. In shoes, the rounded toe and slightly lower heel superseded the pointed toe and high heel. Some high boots were worn by younger men, but this type of footwear was of limited appeal. The lace-up shoe made a reappearance. The decline of the hat continued unabated. (S. H. Co.)

See also Furs.

Federation of Arab Emirates

Consisting of six emirates, the Federation (later Union) of Arab Emirates is located on the eastern Arabian Peninsula. Area: 31,650 sq.mi. (81,970 sq.km.). Pop. (1968): 155,756. Cap.: Abu Dhabi town (pop., 1968, 22,023). Language: Arabic. Religion: Muslim. President in 1971, Emir Zaid ibn Sultan an-Nahayan.

Following persistent efforts by Britain to create a federation of Bahrain, Qatar, and the seven Trucial States to preserve its interests in the Persian Gulf after its withdrawal at the end of 1971, on December 2 six of the Trucial States (Abu Dhabi, Dubai, Sharjah, Ajman, Fujairah, and Umm al-Qaiwain) formed the Union of Arab Emirates. The ruler of Abu Dhabi, Emir Zaid ibn Sultan an-Nahayan, became its first president. The seventh Trucial State, Ras al Khaimah, did not join the union immediately. In December the union became the 18th member of the Arab League, and a member of the UN.

Fiji

An independent parliamentary state and member of the Commonwealth of Nations, Fiji is an island group in the South Pacific Ocean, about 2,000 mi. E of Australia and 3,200 mi. S of Hawaii. Area: 7,071 sq.mi. (18,314 sq.km.), with two major islands, Viti Levu (4,010 sq.mi.) and Vanua Levu (2,137 sq.mi.), and several hundred smaller islands. Pop. (1970 est.): 524,457. Cap. and largest city: Suva (pop., 1971 est., 63,200).

FIJI
Education. (1968) Primary, pupils 110,912; secondary, pupils 11,995; higher (University of the South Pacific; 1969), students 430, teaching staff 52.
Finance. Monetary unit: Fiji dollar, with a par value of F$0.87 to U.S. $1 (F$2.09 = £1 sterling) and a free rate (Sept. 27, 1971) of F$0.85 to U.S. $1. Budget (1970 est.): revenue F$36,843,000; expenditure F$35,667,000.
Foreign Trade. (1969) Imports F$77,888,000; exports F$53,227,000. Import sources: Australia 25%; U.K. 20%; Japan 14%; New Zealand 9%; U.S. 5%. Export destinations: U.K. 35%; U.S. 16%; Australia 10%; Canada 9%. Main exports: sugar 66%; coconut products 10%; gold 8%. Tourism (1969): visitors 85,200; gross receipts U.S. $26 million.
Transport and Communications. Roads (1968) 2,316 km. Shipping (1970): merchant vessels 100 gross tons and over 20; gross tonnage 6,277. Telephones (Dec. 1969) 16,021. Radio receivers (Dec. 1969) 45,000.
Agriculture. Production (in 000; metric tons; 1969; 1968 in parentheses): sweet potatoes c. 15 (c. 10); sugar, raw value (1970–71) c. 375, (1969–70) 304. Livestock (in 000; Sept. 1970): cattle c. 133; pigs c. 23.

Language: English, Fijian, and Hindi. Religion: Christian and Hindu. Queen, Elizabeth II; governor-general in 1971, Sir Robert Foster; prime minister, Ratu Sir Kamisese Mara.

Fiji's sixth development plan (1971–75) aspired to an annual growth rate of 6.5%. Maximum stress was placed on agriculture, forestry, and rural development to narrow the income gap between the urban and rural populations. Tourism also was to be encouraged.

Following the decision of the Colonial Sugar Refining Co. of Australia to withdraw on March 31, 1972, the government agreed to purchase its 98% holding in South Pacific Sugar Mills Ltd. and its 77,000 ac. of freehold land. A continuing market and satisfactory prices for sugar in Britain until 1974 were assured after talks held in London between the U.K. and Commonwealth sugar-producing countries.

Admission to the South Pacific Commission and participation in the South Pacific Forum and the South Pacific Conference demonstrated Fiji's determination to play a positive role in the region. Diplomatic missions were established in London, Canberra, and New York; and the high commissioner in London was to be accredited to EEC countries. (My. B. B.)

Finland

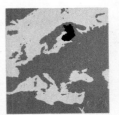

The republic of Finland is bordered on the north by Norway, on the west by Sweden and the Gulf of Bothnia, on the south by the Gulf of Finland, and on the east by the U.S.S.R. Area: 130,128 sq.mi. (337,032 sq.km.). Pop. (1970): 4,602,254. Cap. and largest city: Helsinki (pop., 1970, 517,000). Language: Finnish, Swedish. Religion: Lutheran 91.7%; Orthodox 1.6%. President in 1971, Urho Kaleva Kekkonen; prime ministers, Ahti Karjalainen and, from October 29, Teuvo Aura.

An impasse in important wage talks at the end of 1970 led to President Kekkonen's intervention with a plan for a wage and price policy in 1971. The Confederation of Finnish Trade Unions (SAK) approved the program, but the proposals were rejected by the Communists, whose influence was strong in some of the most important unions. The metalworkers' strike (February 8–March 26) hit heavy industries of great importance to the nation's exports, among them shipbuilding and paper machinery. Some 20,000 building construction workers also went on strike.

The five-party coalition Cabinet's economic policy program was debated in Parliament where, on March 17, the Communists rejected it. As a result, Prime Minister Karjalainen (Centre Party) reorganized the Cabinet, leaving the three Communist ministers outside. It was the Stalinist wing of the Communist Party that had been largely responsible for sabotaging cooperation within the coalition, demanding wage increases and urging unified workers' action on the shop floor. Karjalainen's new coalition included Social Democrats and members of the Centre Party, Swedish Party, and Liberal Party. It had a nonsocialist majority of 9–8 and the support of 108 of Parliament's 200 members. On October 29 the coalition government resigned after it was unable to settle a dispute over agricultural prices. Kekkonen dissolved the Parliament and set elections for January 2 and 3. Teuvo Aura, mayor of Helsinki, was named prime minister to replace Karjalainen.

The situation within the Communist Party, with

the minority Stalinist leader, Taisto Sinisalo, fighting the more moderate chairman, Aarne Saarinen, had been closely followed by Moscow, and obvious Soviet support of Sinisalo resulted in high-level talks on Finnish-Soviet relations. The Soviet deputy foreign minister, Vasili Kuznetsov, had paid a secret visit to Helsinki in December 1970, and the matter was also discussed by President Kekkonen during an unofficial visit to the Soviet Union in February 1971.

President Kekkonen's economic program included a 10% wage increase during the 15 months up to March 1972. A selective bank credit policy was introduced, and measures were taken to decrease imports of luxury and consumer goods. Nonetheless, a slow increase in prices was noticeable throughout 1971. Meanwhile, the foreign trade deficit continued to rise, and had reached $310 million at the end of October. In November, some customs duties were increased by 2 to 5%.

In the international field, Finland continued to seek commercial arrangements with the EEC compatible with its policy of neutrality. Although most Finnish trade was with EFTA and the EEC, important agreements were reached in 1971 with the U.S.S.R., and in the summer Finland announced its willingness to come to some form of special agreement with Comecon. Agreements were signed on April 20 for the delivery of Soviet natural gas to Finland and for a second Soviet nuclear power station.

European security dominated talks at the presidential and ministerial levels, both in Helsinki and during visits abroad by President Kekkonen and members of the Cabinet. The president paid official visits to Italy (January 27–29), the Vatican (February 1–2), and Turkey (June 7–12), and also visited Iran (October 13–17). Romania's head of state, Nicolae Ceausescu, visited Finland (June 29–July 3), as did Hungary's president, Pal Losonczi (August 23–26).

Finland showed readiness to arrange multilateral talks at the ambassadorial level in preparation for a European security conference, and the improved atmosphere following the four-power draft agreement on Berlin gave the Finns new hope that the conference might become an actuality. On September 11 Finland proposed negotiations with the two Germanys on a "package deal," including the establishment of diplomatic relations, recognition of Finland's neutrality, renunciation of the use or threat of force, and a settlement with regard to the destruction caused by German troops in Finnish Lapland in 1944–45. East Germany promised to study the matter carefully, implying that negotiations might follow a final solution on Berlin. (C. F. SA.)

Fisheries

The world fish catch fell in 1969, according to the Food and Agriculture Organization's *Yearbook of Fishery Statistics*. However, the decline was mainly confined to the more technically advanced countries, while in the less developed nations the catch rose noticeably. This trend, which continued into 1971 and

---

FINLAND

Education. (1968–69) Primary, pupils 407,245, teachers (full-time) 18,057; secondary, pupils 387,717, teachers 20,494; vocational, pupils 99,313, teachers 9,164; teacher training, students 1,840, teachers 265; higher (including 8 universities), students 54,886, teaching staff 5,257.

Finance. Monetary unit: markka, with a par value of 4.20 markkaa to U.S. $1 (10.08 markkaa = £1 sterling) and a free rate (Sept. 27, 1971) of 4.16 markkaa to U.S. $1 (10.32 markkaa = £1 sterling). Gold, SDRs, and foreign exchange, central bank: (June 1971) U.S. $462.3 million; (June 1970) U.S. $359.6 million. Budget (1971 est.): revenue 10,957,000,000 markkaa; expenditure 10,956,000,000 markkaa. Gross national product: (1969) 38,380,000,000 markkaa; (1968) 33,870,000,000 markkaa. Cost of living (1963 = 100): (June 1971) 154; (June 1970) 144.

Foreign Trade. (1970) Imports 11,077,000,000 markkaa; exports 9,688,000,000 markkaa. Import sources: West Germany 16%; Sweden 16%; U.K. 13%; U.S.S.R. 13%; U.S. 5%. Export destinations: U.K. 17%; Sweden 15%; U.S.S.R. 12%; West Germany 11%; U.S. 5%; Netherlands 5%. Main exports: paper 27%; timber 16%; wood pulp 13%.

Transport and Communications. Roads (1970) 72,421 km. (including 108 km. expressways). Motor vehicles in use (1970): passenger 711,968; commercial 107,926. Railways (1969): 5,751 km.; traffic 2,154,000,000 passenger-km., freight (1970) 6,270,000,000 net ton-km. Air traffic (1970): 772.8 million passenger-km.; freight 23,672,000 net ton-km. Navigable inland waterways (1969) 6,674 km. Shipping (1970): merchant vessels 100 gross tons and over 388; gross tonnage 1,397,232. Telephones (Dec. 1969) 1,089,700. Radio licenses (Dec. 1969) 1,717,000. Television licenses (Dec. 1969) 987,000.

Agriculture. Production (in 000; metric tons; 1970; 1969 in parentheses): wheat 409 (540); rye 131 (134); barley 933 (906); oats 1,330 (1,235); potatoes 1,139 (891); sugar, raw value (1970–71) 60, (1969–70) c. 55; butter 86 (101); timber (cu.m.; 1969) 43,200, (1968) 40,900; fish catch (1969) 87, (1968) 93. Livestock (in 000; June 1970): cattle 1,873; sheep 189; pigs 1,002.

Industry. Production (in 000; metric tons; 1970): iron ore (66% metal content) 605; pig iron 1,223; crude steel 1,186; copper 34; cement 1,850; plywood (cu.m.; 1969) 681; cellulose (1969) 4,138; mechanical wood pulp (1969) 1,834; chemical wood pulp (1969) 4,463; newsprint 1,362; other paper and board (1969) 2,820; electricity (kw.-hr.) 22,562,000; manufactured gas (cu.m.) 59,000.

Table I. World Fisheries, 1969*

Country	Catch in 000 metric tons	Value in U.S. $000
Peru	9,223.5	117,432
Japan	8,623.5	2,068,735†
U.S.S.R.	6,498.4	...
United States	2,495.4	471,500†
Norway	2,481.0	151,376
South Africa	2,130.0	...
India	1,605.0	275,310
Spain	1,486.2	326,829
Canada	1,408.4	164,700
Denmark	1,275.4	99,558
Thailand	1,269.6	193,722†
Indonesia	1,209.0	...
United Kingdom	1,083.1	165,864
Chile	1,076.9	27,386‡
Philippines	978.1	332,482
Korea, South	852.1	171,853
France	746.3	227,449
Iceland	689.4	...
Germany, West	651.6	99,873
Taiwan	560.9	145,997
Brazil†	495.2	87,561
Vietnam, South	463.8	122,238§
Portugal	457.0	74,107
Pakistan	455.9	191,767
Angola	417.5	8,774
Burma	413.9	82,315
Poland	408.1	...
Malaysia†	406.5	93,234
Mexico	353.6	75,264
Italy	353.1	196,558
Netherlands	323.1	66,938
Germany, East	295.0†	...
Sweden	265.7	39,150
Morocco	226.2	14,425
Argentina	202.8	15,486
Senegal	182.1	23,450
Faeroe Islands	176.3	...
Cambodia	171.1	43,985†
Ghana	162.8	34,984
Ceylon†	143.7	64,269
Turkey	135.4†	...
Venezuela	134.1	30,624

Some double counting may occur.
China, North Korea, and North Vietnam are all estimated to have a catch of more than 300,000 tons a year.
*Excludes whaling.
†1968. ‡1967. §1966.
Source: United Nations Food and Agriculture Organization, *Yearbook of Fishery Statistics*, vol. 28.

Fires:
see Disasters; Insurance

might be expected for many years to come, was indicative of two factors that continued to influence world fisheries development.

First, with traditional fishing grounds liable to closure by unilateral action and many popular species showing signs of maximum exploitation, there was reluctance on the part of established fishing nations to undertake the heavy capital investment necessary for large modern vessels. Typical of the uncertainty among the North Atlantic nations was that arising from Iceland's threat to extend its coastal fishing limits to 50 mi.

Second, the many technical aid programs operated by the FAO, together with nationally sponsored aid-plus-credit schemes, were beginning to show results in less developed nations. At the same time, a number of such nations were undertaking their own development plans, often with foreign advisers or as joint venture schemes with overseas countries. For example, India, during 1971, initiated a joint venture with Union Carbide Corp. to catch and process shrimp with two 86-ft. trawlers.

High prices and returning profits had resulted in new building programs in West Germany and the U.K., but it remained to be seen whether they would be fulfilled. The Soviet bloc countries continued to build steadily, both for themselves and for others. Lithuania was, perhaps unexpectedly, a major customer for these yards; its fleet numbered 350 ships and its annual catch had risen to 400,000 tons.

The EEC fisheries policy, which was announced as a fait accompli during 1971, came in for much criticism. There were objections to the marketing and price regulation clauses, but the major bone of contention was the clause that gave member nations common access to each other's territorial waters, with some safeguards to protect coastal communities dependent on fisheries and endangered fish stocks. None of the existing six EEC members possessed rich coastal grounds, but Britain, Ireland, and Norway—all prospective members—foresaw a massive invasion of their carefully conserved coastal fish stocks.

Increased protection of coastal fish stocks prompted New Zealand to extend its limits to 12 mi., pushing out

Tuna fishermen prepare to leave San Diego, Calif., for the 1971 season off the Ecuadorian coast. Despite disputes over the 200-mi. limit, the tuna fleet made its richest haul in years.

THE "NEW YORK TIMES"

Table II. Whaling: 1969–70 Season
Number of whales caught

Area and country	Fin whale	Humpback whale	Sei whale	Sperm whale	Others	Percentage assigned under quota agreement*
Antarctic: pelagic (open sea)						
Japan	1,821	...	3,495	18	...	47
Norway	4	...	22	6	3	23
U.S.S.R.	1,177	...	2,340	3,066	39	30
Total	3,002	...	5,857	3,090	42	...
Outside the Antarctic†	2,300	5	6,204	21,460	288	...

*Antarctic only.
†1968–69.
Source: Committee for Whaling Statistics, International Whaling Statistics.

a considerable fleet of Japanese vessels. Since much of the fish they caught was of no interest to New Zealand buyers, this was seen as a device to force the Japanese to buy what they could not catch, although the New Zealand fleet lacked the capacity to catch it.

The U.S. continued to buy much of its fish products abroad; imports rose by 26% to 84,000 tons while the home catch fell. The U.S. still led the world in tuna purse seining, and during the year the biggest tuna boat ever built, the 259-ft.-long "Apollo," was commissioned. Meanwhile, the U.S. Bureau of Commercial Fisheries (renamed the National Marine Fisheries Service) continued to explore the use of space hardware and satellites to seek out fish shoals.

Alarm mounted early in the year over the discovery of a dangerous level of mercurial contamination in tuna caught in certain U.S. waters. After withdrawal of suspected cans, the public was reassured, but later the U.S. Food and Drug Administration warned against consumption of swordfish. All this was indicative of the new awareness of ocean pollution, which was the subject of an FAO conference in December 1970 and continued to receive publicity in 1971.

(H. S. N.)

Food

Supply. Agricultural production, by the end of the third quarter of 1971, continued to display most of the perversities that have come to be recognized, if not fully accepted, as features of the world food situation. While officials and traders in the Northern Hemisphere worried that bumper cereal crops from the Ukraine to Kansas would drive down grain prices and increase government costs of maintaining acceptable levels of farm income, the news media periodically reminded well-fed populations of starving East Bengalis and East Africans, suffering equally the effects of political disruption and the vagaries of weather.

Production. By mid-1971 unmistakable signs of record grain crops in Europe indicated a cereal harvest on the order of 174 million tons, exceeding the region's highest previous total, posing grave concern for Common Market officials about the integrity of their farm programs and for U.S. feed-grain producers, whose prospects for exporting the surplus from bountiful grain harvests might be jeopardized. In the Far East encouraging prospects for a fourth consecutive record rice harvest relieved pressures on governments to import cereals, but forced Australian grain traders to seek new markets for surplus grain.

Whatever the outcome of the 1971 harvests, available food supplies were in large measure determined by production a year earlier. The Food and Agriculture Organization of the UN reported in August that

Floods:
see Disasters;
Engineering
Projects

world food production in 1970 rose to an index of 154 (1952–56 = 100), about 2.5% above a year earlier, barely keeping pace with population growth, which was expressed by the FAO as an index of 137, or 2.2% above 1969. But reliance on these gross estimates obscured indications of possible gains in the food-population balance implicit in the wide variation of both agricultural production and population growth throughout the world. Among the less developed regions only the Far East produced enough food to effect a gain in per capita food supply; in Latin America gains were largely the effect of the increase in Cuba's sugar harvest. Among the more developed regions, food production in 1970 and population rose at about the same rate, with the result that per capita food production remained at an index of 125. The standstill was attributed to policies aimed at reducing surpluses. An increase in cereal production in 1970 was largely accounted for by better harvests in Latin America, the Far East, Eastern Europe, and the U.S.S.R. that offset reduced production in North America, Western Europe, and Oceania. Total world production of 316 million tons of wheat was slightly more than in 1969; production gains in the Far East, Eastern Europe, and the U.S.S.R. offset reduced crops in North America and Oceania. Among all the cereals, production of rice in 1970 showed the most gain. Total output of an estimated 307.9 million tons was 4.4% more than in 1969, reflecting a nearly 4% increase in the Far East and a 13% increase in Latin America. World production of an estimated 258.4 million tons of corn in 1970 was 3% less than a year earlier; North American production was 10% less and an even sharper decline suffered among Eastern European countries and the U.S.S.R. was offset by a gain of 14% in Latin America.

Production of root crops (potatoes, cassava, and yams) in 1970 rose to an estimated 542.7 million tons, 5% more than a year earlier. Production of sugar in 1970 was estimated at 74.7 million tons, an increase of more than 10% above a year earlier, with production in Latin America more than 25% above 1969.

World production of meat in 1970 was estimated at 97.1 million tons, a 3% increase over a year earlier; production among the more developed nations accounted for about two-thirds of the total. Production of oilseeds was 5% more than a year earlier; gains were registered in nearly all regions except Western Europe, the Near East, and Africa. World milk production, estimated by the FAO at 399.8 million tons, was less than 1% above a year earlier; gains were registered throughout the less developed regions except Africa, where production was unchanged. The FAO cautioned that an increase twice that shown in 1970 was needed to keep pace with population increases. It also noted in a report released in early May that although good progress was anticipated in overcoming caloric food deficiencies in the less developed world in the 1970s, the problem of protein deficiencies was one for which no near-term solution was evident.

Trade. International trade in food commodities reached high levels in 1970–71. Trade (excluding intra-EEC trade) in wheat was estimated at some 55.9 million tons, 10% above a year earlier, caused mainly by exceptionally high imports by Western European countries. Most of the wheat-exporting countries increased shipments in 1970–71. Canadian exports of 11.4 million tons in 1969–70 were 25% more than a year earlier and Australia's shipments of 9.5 million tons marked a 30% rise. Exports of wheat by Argentina declined about 10% in 1970–71. By late 1971 in-

creased supplies in Europe were a depressing factor in wheat trade in the 1971–72 trading year.

Exports of feed grains in 1970–71 were expected to rise to as much as 44.1 million tons, an increase of 12% over the 39.3 million tons exported in 1969–70. Domestic grain supplies in Europe were low, demand was strong in Eastern Europe, and Japan was expected to continue to increase imports. Even so, U.S. exports of feed grains, reflecting the corn blight of 1970, were expected to decline slightly from the 19.5 million tons shipped in 1969–70. The slack was expected to be taken up in part by increased shipments from Argentina and South Africa. Continued expansion of rice reduced import demand by 1970–71 to around 6.5 million tons. The higher degree of self-sufficiency among traditional rice-deficit areas resulted in stock-building on the order of 12.5 million tons by 1970, some 20% more than a year earlier.

U.S. farm exports in 1970–71 rose to a record level of $7.8 billion, more than 50% above ten years earlier. Overseas commercial sales of U.S. farm products accounted for all of the gain and totaled some $6.8 billion; exports assisted by government programs remained at about the same level as a year earlier. It was estimated that the production of one out of every five acres harvested by U.S. farmers was exported in 1970; in the mid-1960s, it was one out of four. On the basis of crop values, more than half the wheat and soybeans grown in the U.S. were exported. Overseas sales of U.S. farm products to Japan in 1970 reached $1.2 billion, a new record. Announcement of the purchase by Japan in April of more than 100 million bu. of wheat raised the U.S. share of that country's food purchases to 60% in 1970–71. Food imports by West Germany reached a record $5,750,000,000 in 1970, an increase of 8.2% over 1969. Wheat and flour exports to China in 1969–70 were estimated to have been 209 million bu., an increase of nearly 50% over a year earlier; major suppliers were Canada and Australia.

Several events in 1971 indicated changes in the pattern of world food trade. The movement of the U.K. toward full membership in the EEC was of prime concern to traditional suppliers of the U.K. and portended changes both in preferential status of Commonwealth partners and in the outlook for grain sales by U.S. exporters. The resumption of trade between China and the U.S., after more than 20 years, was marked in late June by the delivery of 166 cartons of foodstuffs to San Francisco. At midyear U.S. and EEC negotiations appeared to be moving toward the resolution of some differences raised by the bloc's preferential treatment of some of its overseas suppliers. The EEC agreed to reduce tariffs on U.S. oranges from 15% to 8%, and both agreed to abolish subsidies on exports of poultry products, thus presumably ending the "chicken war" that began in 1963. U.S. Pres. Richard Nixon's "new economic policy" included an immediate additional tax of 10% on goods not under quota imported into the U.S., or 27% of total agricultural imports. The surcharge was removed on December 20.

Efforts continued to extend or establish a variety of international arrangements to stabilize trade in agricultural products. The International Wheat Agreement extended the International Grains Arrangement for three years but did not contain a range of prices at which signatories agreed to trade wheat, or supply and purchase commitments among trading nations. It did contain a proviso calling for further negotiations to establish the missing elements when trading conditions were such that agreement would be likely.

The House of Representatives approved legislation enabling the U.S. to carry out its obligations under the International Coffee Agreement in November. International Cocoa Agreement negotiators were unable to reach agreement. An international arrangement of an informal nature continued among traders in hard fibres, and the International Sugar Agreement was also continued. Negotiators were unable to conclude an extension of an arrangement between Greece, Turkey, and Australia applying to trade in raisins.

Consumption, Expenditures, and Prices. An increase of more than 1% in U.S. per capita food consumption over a year earlier was expected in 1971. Per capita consumption of meat (carcass weight basis) was expected to be 3% more than the 186.3 lb. reported for 1970; consumption of 113.7 lb. of beef in 1970 was expected to rise 1%, and of 66.4 lb. of pork by 9%. Per capita consumption of eggs, which was 319 in 1970, was expected to increase by 1%, and a 2% increase in consumption of turkey over the 8.1 lb. of 1970 was forecast. Among dairy products only the per capita consumption of cheese was expected to exceed 1970 levels, which averaged 11.5 lb. Consumption of fluid milk and cream, which averaged 264 lb. per capita in 1970, was expected to decline by 3%. No change was indicated in per capita use of fats and oils, fresh and processed fruits, canned and frozen vegetables, or cereal grains. Consumption of 102.5 lb. of refined sugar and 99 lb. of fresh vegetables was expected to decline about 1%. Per capita consumption of fresh potatoes, reported at 118.6 lb. in 1970, was expected to increase 3%.

Total expenditures by U.S. consumers for food in 1970 were reported at $119.7 billion; by the end of the second quarter of 1971, outlays for food had advanced 5.3% above the same period a year earlier. Even so, only about 16.2% of disposable income was spent on food, as compared with 16.6% in 1970, 18.1% in 1965, and 20% in 1960.

A report by the U.S. Department of Agriculture (USDA) on food expenditures in selected foreign countries in 1968 indicated that in Western Europe such expenditures ranged from 22.3% of total private consumption expenditures for Denmark to 37.8% for Greece. Food expenditures in Eastern Europe were reported at 40.9% for Yugoslavia, 47.6% for Poland, and 54.4% for Bulgaria; in Africa, at 26.8% for South Africa, 45.6% for Sierra Leone, and 60% for Ghana; in Asia, at 35.4% for Japan (including beverages and tobacco), 47.1% for Korea, and 41.6% for Taiwan. Expenditures for food in Australia were reported at 20.8%.

Retail food prices in the United States at midyear 1971 were reported at an index of 118.4 (1967 = 100), or 3% more than a year earlier. This was a smaller increase than the 4.8% reported for all items in the Consumer Price Index, excluding food, for the same period. Wholesale prices for all food at midyear 1971 were reported at an index of 115.9, or 2.2% more than a year earlier; wholesale prices of farm products increased 2.5%, and processed food 1.8%. By midyear 1971, the USDA Economic Research Service reported that the retail cost of U.S. farm foods had increased 1.6% over a year earlier; at the same time, the "farm-retail spread" had risen 3.6%, while the farm value of foods in a representative market basket had declined 1.5%. The earlier prospect of continued increase in retail food prices may have been dampened by the freeze on wages and prices imposed by executive order on August 15. Retail food prices for Sep-

A young girl suffering from malnutrition feeds her baby brother at the Okporo Hospital in Nigeria. Although conditions improved in the former secessionist state of Biafra, hunger was still a major problem in 1971.
WIDE WORLD

tember 1971 were reported at an index of 119.1, a 2.9% increase over September 1970, but 0.8% less than prices reported for August 1971; September's food price drop represented the largest decrease in four and a half years.

In the U.K., it was reported at mid-July that outlays for food were 8.5% more than a year earlier; this included a 2% increase in volume of foods purchased. Expenditure for food was reported in 1970 to account for 25.7% of average weekly family expenditures. Retail food prices at the end of the 11-month period that ended May 18 showed a 10.4% increase, compared with a 9.5% increase in all retail prices.

Assistance. A wide variety of aid programs continued to account for distribution of large amounts of food in 1971. Participation in the U.S. Food Stamp Program was reported at about 10.5 million persons in June 1971, an increase of about 4 million over a year earlier. The total value of stamps issued for May 1971 was reported at $250.7 million, as compared with $144.6 million a year earlier; the bonus value of these stamps was $137.8 million. Legislation extending the Food Stamp Program for three years was approved by Congress in December 1970. New features in the program included a national uniform income eligibility requirement; free food stamps for families with less than $30 monthly income; and a provision permitting the operation of both the Food Stamp Program and the Commodity Distribution Program in the same county or other jurisdiction. Even though the new program would permit the eligibility of an estimated 6 million more Americans than the one it replaced at midsummer, U.S. Sen. George McGovern (Dem., S.D.), chairman of the Senate Select Committee on Nutrition, estimated that 12 million to 13 million eligible poor people were still without federal food assistance.

New food stamp rules promulgated by the USDA would add an estimated 1.7 million persons to the program, and enable an estimated 900,000 to receive free stamps for the first time. The new regulations

British women, carrying placards, visit Boulogne, France, to check food prices. The British housewives were worried about the possibility of drastic rises in food prices as a result of Britain's entry into the Common Market.

would also remove the eligibility of some 65,000 persons and deny food stamps to "hippie-type" communes and some college students. Congressional pressure, however, turned back an administration proposal to cut an estimated 275,000 welfare recipients from the program. Under the U.S. government's program of direct distribution of food, some 3.7 million people received food valued at $24.5 million in May 1971; this was 300,000 less and $400,000 less, respectively, than a year earlier.

An estimated 8,693,151 schoolchildren participated in the national School Lunch Program in June 1971, as compared with 7,462,509 a year earlier. Congress, in late October, approved legislation that assured a minimum government subsidy of 46 cents per school lunch for the 7.3 million children participating in the program. This action followed a heated controversy generated by the August 13 issuance of regulations by the USDA that would have limited the amount of subsidy for needy children in the program. The new legislation also forbade the administration to carry out proposed changes that would reduce the number of children participating in the program in 1971–72. The administration estimated that the new congressional mandate would cost $525 million, compared with the 1970–71 cost of $390 million. In February President Nixon approved legislation authorizing additional funds to operate expanded summer feeding programs in day care and recreation centres.

The extent of hunger and malnutrition in the U.S. was still unknown in 1971, and at a "second White House conference on hunger," held in February at Williamsburg, Va., the administration, while being credited with efforts to expand food assistance programs, nevertheless was criticized severely for failure to treat hunger with the seriousness delegates felt it deserved. In December 1970, Jean Mayer, former special presidential assistant on nutrition, publicly called on the president to endorse stronger legislation than that being considered by the House Agriculture Committee. In February the Senate Select Committee on Nutrition was told that serious malnutrition—sometimes as severe as that seen in Biafra (Nigeria)—was exhibited in children of migrant workers at a rate ten times greater than among children generally. Early in May, Senator McGovern charged that an administration report to the Congress on the National Nutrition Survey understated the extent of hunger and malnutrition in the U.S. and that data accumulated in a ten-state survey beginning in April 1968 had been tailored for political purposes.

On a global scale, the extent of hunger was as unknown as ever; an FAO senior economist estimated that as much as one-fifth of the world's population had at one time or another suffered malnourishment. More dramatic confrontations with hunger and starvation were demonstrated in 1971 by the flood of refugees into India from East Pakistan. The U.S. Department of State indicated that more than 500,000 tons of food were being delivered to East Pakistan. Famine conditions were reported to exist in Kenya and other areas in East Africa, resulting from drought.

Food relief measures continued under a wide variety of unilateral and multilateral arrangements. Agreements authorized in 1970 under Title I of the Agricultural Trade Development and Assistance Act of 1954 allocated $7.9 million in foreign currencies for economic development loans, most of which went for continued aid to Pakistan's rural public works program in East Pakistan. Under Title II, commodity

donations were made to 79 million people in 100 countries in 1970, under a variety of programs. The U.S. shipped nearly $32 million in food to meet emergency needs of people in 25 countries struck by various natural disasters.

Under the International Wheat Agreement, signatory nations agreed to continue contributions of food grains for relief of less developed countries; nearly 4 million tons were pledged under the new Food Aid Convention, of which the commitments of 1,890,000 tons by the U.S., 1,035,000 tons by the EEC, and 495,000 tons by Canada were the largest. The World Food Program, a joint undertaking of the UN and the FAO, set a goal of $300 million for its operations in the 1971–72 biennium. The U.S. pledged to contribute up to $125 million to the WFP, including up to $85 million in commodities, plus $37 million in ocean freight.

Agricultural Development. Prospects for improving food supplies among the major portion of the world population living in less developed regions continued to rely on—and in some respects, to compete with—the overall economic development objectives of emerging nations. January 1 marked the beginning of the Second UN Development Decade. In the earlier Development Decade a target of 5% overall annual growth had been the goal; new objectives sought to achieve a balanced growth between agriculture, manufacturing, domestic savings, foreign trade, and population. The Second Decade's target of an average annual growth rate of at least 6% for the less developed countries implied a 4% yearly increase in agricultural output; this compared with average annual growth in agricultural output in the 1960–68 period of 2% for Africa, 2.75% for the Far East, 3.2% for the Near East, and 2.38% for Latin America.

· For the years 1969 and 1970 it was believed that growth attributed to the Green Revolution may have added significant momentum to agricultural development. Even so, the UN Development Program (UNDP) reported that 37 out of 71 less developed countries had inadequate food supplies to meet the minimum daily caloric needs of their populations, and that only 4 out of 65 could provide the people with 40% or more of their daily animal protein needs. Under the new program, more developed countries were to try to transfer to less developed countries the equivalent of 1% of the donor nation's gross national product by 1972, or by 1975 at the latest. Steps to expand trade, including provisions for measures in favour of the least developed countries, were included.

A U.S. pledge of $86,268,000 to the UNDP for 1971 brought total contributions, as of April, 'to a record $240,112,365 from 128 governments. In 1970 the UNDP carried out a record volume of development assistance: 3,500 projects in 130 countries. Total cost of the 1971 program included $232 million in aid from UNDP and $275 million in investments by the governments of assisted countries. The Inter-American Development Bank reported that loans for agricultural development made to Latin-American nations in the 1960–70 period totaled $1,066,300,000, and that an additional $1.7 billion in loans went for infrastructure services basic to economic growth. Total loans and credits for agriculture, forestry, and fishing made by the World Bank for the period 1948–70 reached $1,919,000,000. The Asian Development Bank's loans for agriculture in the 1966–70 period totaled the equivalent of $52,320,000.

Much of the hope for agricultural improvement in

the less developed world centred on the continued use of high-yield cereal grains—the so-called Green Revolution. In the 1969–70 crop year, it was estimated that some 43,914,000 ac. were devoted to high-yield wheat and rice. Of this total, 24,664,000 ac. were planted to the new wheats; this was more than twice the acreage devoted to such wheats in 1967–68 and more than a thousand times that of 1965–66. Land devoted to high-yield rice totaled 19,250,000 ac. in 1969–70. (H. R. Sh.)

Processing and Technology. Various environmental problems noted in the past became matters of public and governmental concern requiring international action in 1971. Pollution of lakes and oceans with mercurial compounds from industrial waste and the widespread use of mercurial fungicides caused the U.S. Food and Drug Administration (FDA) to condemn certain consignments of tuna and to warn the public against eating swordfish. Programs were established in the U.S., the U.K., Japan, and some other countries to monitor regularly all foodstuffs for mercury and other contaminants. Excessive nitrate in certain vegetable crops and its entry into water supplies received further attention and a number of countries introduced legislation restricting the nitrate and nitrite content of certain foods. When the nitrate content of a local water supply in Britain reached an undesirable level for use in reconstitution of infant foods, bottled water was issued by the authorities. Heavy damages were awarded against a Japanese company for causing death and injury to consumers through disposing of waste mercurial compounds in a manner that allowed them to enter the food chain.

Authorities in the U.S. and Britain expressed concern at the content of polychlorinated biphenyls in many foodstuffs. This was attributed to the recycling of paper waste for food packaging purposes since these compounds are constituents of printing inks. The extensive use of plastic film for food packaging and the switch of many food processors from glass to plastic containers created serious disposal problems necessitating official warnings and restrictive measures in a number of countries; in Japan the distribution of certain products in plastic containers had to be curtailed. In the U.S., the U.K., and Japan, research projects were established to investigate the feasibility of biodegradable plastics.

The development of unconventional proteins and their conversion to acceptable food products received much attention. A British company produced a protein isolate from the broad bean; this was successfully spun and converted to meat analogues by another British company. There was further development of the fungal protein and preparations were made for commercial production. From many countries came reports of progress in the production of single-cell proteins from carbohydrate-rich wastes. The prospect of using petroleum-derived protein for human food receded after discovery of traces of carcinogens in these products.

Continued growth in the convenience-foods market was seen in most European countries and in the U.S. Dutch, British, and U.S. workers observed that increased use of such foods had resulted in certain compositional changes in the diet. Especially noted was some reduction in the carbohydrate content with a corresponding increase in fat. Attention was also drawn to reduction in roughage.

Production Technology. There was much work on the genetic improvement of cereals to achieve higher yield and protein content and improved nutritive value. Much effort was also devoted to development of new fruit and vegetable varieties suitable for canning, deep-freezing, or mechanical harvesting. There was extensive screening of fruit and vegetable cultivars in the U.S. and the U.K. for susceptibility to agricultural chemicals and taint. It also was reported that some new varieties did not attract bees or other insects needed for cross-pollination. Japanese scientists reported on developments in the breeding of high-quality cattle by causing good strains to produce multiple ova that were fertilized by insemination and subsequently implanted in other cows.

Fisheries. The total world fish catch, which had more than trebled since 1945, registered a 2% decrease, the first in the postwar period. Overfishing and pollution of inshore waters were blamed. A serious shortage of eels in Japan was attributed to pollution of inland waterways; the successful rearing of eels was reported from Ireland. Japanese experts announced the commissioning of a fish farm for the raising of scarce fish, especially sea bream and flatfish; the anticipated yield was 3.5 million fish per year. A three-year program for the breeding of tuna also was commissioned. The U.S.S.R. reported on the successful harvesting of krill and its processing for food. It also reported that the exploitation of ocean fishing resources had been improved by the use of survey satellites.

An experimental turtle farm was opened on Grand Cayman Island. The Norwegian Ocean Research Institute reported the location of large new prawn fields in the Barents Sea near Spitsbergen. A large-scale salmon farm was established in Norway to produce about 1,500 tons a year. Marine research workers in Scotland began investigations into the intensive rearing of herring in enclosed sea lochs. Investigations were started upon the raising of herring larvae and into the high natural rate of wastage since only one egg in about 100,000 survives to maturity. It was considered that battery production of sea fish within inland waters would make an important contribution after Britain's entry into the EEC. The British White Fish Authority sponsored a program for cultivation of large Japanese oysters.

Irradiation. There was new interest in the applications of irradiation caused by increased emphasis on the retardation of microbiological spoilage rather than sterilization, the control of infestation, and the arrest of biological changes such as sprouting. Some 19 countries reached agreement on a project sponsored by the International Atomic Energy Agency, FAO, and the European Nuclear Energy Agency of the Organization for Economic Cooperation and Development. These countries agreed to contribute $225,000 annually to support research into the wholesomeness of irradiated foods. Canadian authorities reported that in a three-year investigation into the safety of irradiation-pasteurized poultry and haddock no detrimental effects were found in respect to growth performance, mortality, or incidence of tumours in mice receiving these diets. A report was issued on the efficacy of irradiation in eliminating pathogenic microorganisms and in prolonging the shelf life of fresh fish, eviscerated poultry, meat products, frozen eggs, and milk powder. An application was made to the Canadian Food and Drug Directorate for the clearance of irradiated mushrooms and strawberries. A chain of supermarkets in the Netherlands was authorized to test-market irradiated mushrooms.

Deterioration of mandarin oranges was retarded by electron bombardment and the sprouting of potatoes was effectively inhibited without significant physical or organoleptic change. Elimination of the rice weevil was achieved by irradiation with 10 Krad whereas the threshold dose affecting quality was found to be 40 to 50 Krad. In spite of these developments there were no international legislative changes.

Automation. The rapid extension of supermarkets and international distribution, and the multiplication of convenience foods, accelerated developments in food preservation techniques, especially aseptic processing and automation, and, with the concentration of manufacturing units, improved designs of paper and foil laminates for aseptic packaging were introduced. In France an aseptic packaging machine was developed in which plastic containers were formed, filled and capped aseptically, and lithoprinted in one sequence. The "clean room" concept of the U.S. space program was adapted to the aseptic packaging of certain convenience foods and yogurts.

The principle of laminar flow of sterilized air was also adapted to certain localized packaging operations. A new method of friction heating was developed in France for the sterilization of milk and other liquids. A notable advance was made in Switzerland in the aseptic processing of yogurt, giving the product much extended keeping quality.

The need to conserve water resources and to purify industrial wastes intensified research on recovery and utilization of wastes by ultrafiltration and reverse osmosis. The USDA and the Federal Water Agency sponsored investigations into the treatment of cheese whey and the wastes from soy protein manufacture. The successful recovery of whey protein by reverse osmosis made commercially available protein concentrates of high nutritive value in the U.S. and New Zealand. In Sweden whey protein was recovered successfully by a process of gel filtration. A fermentation procedure developed in Switzerland enabled a Swedish company to produce food protein from whey and an innocuous effluent.

The widespread use of automation in food manufacture gave rise to the need for automated methods of monitoring the quality of incoming raw materials and outgoing manufactured products. One large U.S. food and feed manufacturer that carried out 800 tests on some 275 raw materials daily introduced new equipment. The sophisticated laboratory instruments fed data on protein, amino acid, and mineral content directly to a computer which assigned priorities to samples. Another U.S. company introduced automated analysis and computerized control throughout manufacture. It was claimed that this system maintained extremely consistent high quality with mass production efficiency. A vegetable processing factory was commissioned in France for the canning and deep-freezing of vegetables to spread manufacture throughout the year. A catering facility was established in a French municipality to provide 20,000 meals which were distributed daily to some 200 terminals in isothermal containers. A Dutch company completed a cane sugar factory in Iran. A U.S. company introduced a new machine for the production of 400 pizzas per minute. Another machine was developed to fill 300 clamshells per minute with a metered amount of mix. The production of 800 onion rings per minute was achieved by making a pumpable mix that was molded into perfectly shaped rings.

Japanese workers announced discovery of an artificial sweetener derived from pine tree rosin that was said to be 1,000 to 2,000 times sweeter than sucrose; an institute in East Germany announced development of an artificial sweetener derived from a substituted triazole; and a British company was awarded a patent for an artificial sweetener claimed to be 500 times sweeter than sucrose and similar in structure to the dipeptide sweeteners under toxicological investigation in the U.S. and Japan.

Governmental Action. The FDA announced its intention to review the status of all additives on the GRAS (generally recognized as safe) list. In view of the proliferation of new protein products, the British Food Standards Committee announced a review of unconventional proteins. A joint FAO/WHO committee recommended that baby foods be manufactured without additives while those containing additives should be properly labeled to ensure that they were not normally consumed by infants under 12 weeks of age.

New Foods. A U.K. company introduced a range of ready-made canned meat meals in which simulated meat made from textured soy protein was used to supplement the protein content. These products were launched especially for older people who lived alone. A schnitzel made entirely from textured vegetable protein was developed in Israel. Danish meat research workers reported on the supplementation of salamis and sausage with textured vegetable protein.

Portion-controlled foods with weight, calorie, and nutritional contents listed on their labels were introduced in the U.S.; a range of low-fat foods including cheese and whipped dessert toppings were developed for the dieter. A new product prepared by the processing of an admixture of seaweed, sesame seed, and cheddar cheese was introduced successfully in Japan. Attention was directed in Britain to the value of the mushroom as a far more economical source of protein than beef or fish. (HE. B. H.)

See also Agriculture; Commodities, Primary; Fisheries; Prices.

ENCYCLOPÆDIA BRITANNICA FILMS. *Produce—From Farm to Market* (1968).

Football

Association Football (Soccer). The year after the World Cup finals is sometimes considered an anticlimax, but nevertheless 1971 had plenty to offer. During the year outbreaks of violence seemed to lessen slightly, probably because of better crowd control rather than any change in spectators' outlook. But there were days of tragedy. At Ibrox Park, Glasgow, Scot., 66 people were killed in January when barriers collapsed under the surge of fans near the end of the local derby game with Celtic. A riot in Haifa, Israel, later in the year when a Jewish team was playing one made up of Israeli Arabs led to a wave of arrests and to about 20 injured; and in Buenos Aires, Arg., when the local Boca Juniors met Sporting Crystal of Peru, 19 players were sent off after a brawl that followed the roughing up of Boca's captain Ruben Zune. In England the Football Association barred Leeds and Manchester United from using their grounds for the opening matches of the 1971–72 season because of misbehaviour by their supporters, and the European Union of Football Associations (EUFA) barred PSV Eindhoven from using their grounds for three matches in European competitions following the hurling of cans and other missiles onto the field causing the injury of Irish linesman David Barrett during the club's Cup-Winners' Cup semifinal with Real Madrid.

In West Germany a bribery scandal case reverberated through the game: Manfred Manglitz, Cologne's international goalkeeper, was suspended for life for accepting a bribe from an Offenbach Kickers official "for making no mistakes" in a match against Rotweiss Essen, one of Kickers' relegation rivals; Horst Canellas, an official of the Kickers, was also banned from holding office for life.

British Isles Championship. England again won the British Isles tournament, played over eight days in May, but although the team's final performance in beating Scotland at Wembley was convincing enough they were far from impressive in their other two games. In the opening matches on May 15, England beat Northern Ireland at Belfast with a goal by Allan Clarke of Leeds. It was fiercely disputed because Francis Lee, the Manchester City forward, appeared to handle the ball before moving on and slipping the ball to Clarke to lob it past Pat Jennings in the Irish goal. And, as if that were not enough, referee Alastair Mackenzie disallowed an earlier effort by George Best, the Manchester United forward, who skillfully flicked the ball from England's goalkeeper Gordon Banks as he was about to clear, and lifted it into the net. Meanwhile, Wales and Scotland were slogging out a goalless draw at Cardiff. Wales too had a "goal" disallowed, for being offside.

In the next round of matches, beginning May 18, the Irish beat Scotland 1–0 at Hampden Park, Glasgow. Twenty-four hours later England, looking far from polished, was forced to settle for a goalless draw against Wales at Wembley. On May 22 England beat Scotland at Wembley as decisively as the 3–1 score suggested, to clinch the title and leave the Scots with the wooden spoon (last place). Martin Chivers (2) and Martin Peters scored England's goals, with Hugh Curran tallying for the Scots.

Meanwhile, Wales traveled to Belfast and fell to a goal for Ireland by Bryan Hamilton. Again the Irish were the dominant side, inspired by the experienced Derek Dougan and by flashes of excellence from Best.

European Cup. Ajax of Amsterdam followed Feyenoord to become the second Dutch team in a row to take the premier European Cup competition trophy back to the Netherlands, defeating the Greek team Panathinaikos 2–0 at Wembley. The game, before 90,000 people, was not one of the more memorable finals, the Greeks, coached by Ferenc Puskas of Hungarian and Real Madrid fame, falling short of their best. They had no one of the stature of Johan Cruyff, the Dutch international centre-forward, although the Panathinaikos captain, Mimis Domazos, strove hard to prompt his players into swift counters. But the finish was not there. It was A. Haan, brought on as a substitute, who scored the second goal off the legs of A. Kapsis, in the dying minutes of a game that Ajax seemed to have won long before the final whistle.

European Cup-Winners' Cup. For the second year running this trophy went to an English club when Chelsea of London beat Real Madrid in a replayed game in Athens on May 21. The two teams had tied in a 120-min. game in the Greek capital two days earlier. Both games contained a tremendous amount of good football, although in the first game it was only in the last seconds that the Spanish club's dynamic forward Ignacio Zoco dashed forward and

Rennes and Lyons compete for the 54th French football cup on June 20, 1971. Rennes scored the only point in the game.
A.F.P.—PICTORIAL PARADE

forced the ball past Peter Bonetti to send the game into extra time. Before that Peter Osgood had put Chelsea ahead in the 56th min. Real Madrid then launched raid after raid in a blistering onslaught during the final 15 min. of normal time, which culminated in the tying goal. Then came a grueling 30 min. in extra time during which neither side scored. In the replay 48 hours later Chelsea produced the same brand of spirited, efficient football that had brought it thus far in the competition and again put the emphasis on going into the lead. This pattern established, Chelsea duly set about winning the battle in midfield. It went ahead following a corner kick, when John Dempsey crashed the ball from a clearance back into the net. Before the Spaniards could recover from this blow, Chelsea, its confidence brimming, swept forward again. And as in the first game it was Osgood who scored. The centre-forward dummied his way through and thumped the ball just inside the post. In the second half Real Madrid followed the pattern of the first clash by mounting an all-out assault. The English side in turn tried to keep the pressure on Real as much as possible. The Spaniards struck back, when Sebastian Fleitas cracked the ball into the Chelsea goal a quarter of an hour before the end of the game. But Chelsea held out, and followed Manchester City in bringing the trophy back to England for the fourth time since its institution in 1960.

European Fairs' Cup. Leeds United became the fourth English club in succession to win this trophy—the last under its title of Fairs' Cup—when it beat Juventus of Turin over two legs on the somewhat dissatisfying away-goals rule, under which a side's goals scored on its opponents' field count double in the event of the teams' finishing even on aggregate. The first time the two teams met was on May 26 in Turin on a wet night, and neither side had scored when six minutes after the interval the referee called a halt to the play because of the waterlogged conditions.

The two teams lined up again 48 hours later in the same stadium, and this time there were goals, four to be precise, and they were to prove vital to Leeds. The Italians were dangerous in the first half, and took the lead through Roberto Bettega. Leeds gradually came more into the game, but it was not until 3 min. into the second half that they tied the score with a goal by Paul Madeley. Within 8 min. Juventus again took the lead when Fabio Capello fastened onto a poor clearance from the Leeds defense and sent a looping drive into the net. Leeds surged forward again, but it was not rewarded until 13 min. from the game's end when goalkeeper Massimo Piloni missed a cross and Mike Bates (substitute for injured Mick Jones) slotted the ball home with his left foot. The game thus ended in a 2–2 draw.

In the return match at Leeds it was Leeds that

slipped into a quick lead when Allan Clarke snapped up a chance with a low, right-foot shot after 11 min. Juventus moved forward at once with Franco Causio, Pietro Anastasi, and Bettega pressing the Leeds defense, and it was Anastasi who tied the score. Though Leeds lost Madeley for the last 35 min. after he was knocked out in a collision, their defense withstood cascading attacks with Sprake making some fine saves. So Leeds, which had scored 2 goals away from home to its opponent's 1, took the trophy, while Juventus lost it without being beaten.

Since the tournament was replaced by the EUFA Cup at the end of the 1970–71 season, Leeds, the last winners, and the Spanish club Barcelona, the first winners, played for the right to retain the trophy in September 1971. Barcelona won the play-off by beating injury-hit Leeds 2–1 in Barcelona.

Inter-Continental Club Championship. The unofficial world club championship maintained its reputation of violent encounters when Feyenoord, the European Cup holders, tangled with their South American counterparts, Estudiantes, from Argentina. The first leg of this two-match contest was played in Buenos Aires in August 1970, and, contrary to the expectations of many observers, was a mild affair. The Dutch players were shaky at the beginning and defensive errors led to the South Americans' jumping into a two-goal lead with scores by J. Echecopar and J. Veron. But Feyenoord fought back, and after a series of incisive raids Swedish World Cup player Ove Kindvall headed a goal and then W. Van Hanegem put the Dutch side level.

In the return match in Rotterdam the next month the South Americans employed the type of tactics that had done much to give this competition a bad name. As it transpired, their "strong-arm" play led to their undoing as Feyenoord replaced their talented forward Colin Moulijn, who was being repeatedly fouled, with Joop Van Deale who wore glasses while playing. Van Deale then scored the only goal of the game with a fierce left-foot shot. His glasses were smashed during the second half, and for the last 20 min. he was almost unable to see. Feyenoord officials revealed afterward that if a replay had been necessary they were going to decline as they were fearful of the probable cost in the injuries to key men.

European Championship. The European championship followed its usual format of being organized in eight groups of four nations each and run over two years. For the upcoming event the four British national teams did not use the home countries tournament as their qualifying group, thereby allowing all to have a chance of reaching the quarterfinals. However, Scotland, in Group 5, lost its chance of qualifying by losing to Denmark, Portugal, and Belgium who headed the standings at the halfway stage. Other group leaders at that juncture were Czechoslovakia, Bulgaria, Switzerland, U.S.S.R., Italy, Yugoslavia, and West Germany.

Administration. In England an experiment was tried in which the offside law operated only in the penalty area, on the ground that it would produce more goals and attacking football. It was tried, however, in a competition between the highest-scoring teams and thus was difficult to evaluate.

During the year Pelé, the great Brazilian forward, bowed out of international soccer amid fantastic scenes of adulation from the 200,000 fans in the Maracanã stadium in Rio de Janeiro on July 18, when Brazil drew 2–2 with Yugoslavia. Pelé had made 110 appearances and scored 95 goals in international matches; his goals in all matches totaled 1,086. Jimmy Greaves (West Ham), one of England's most prolific scorers, retired at the end of the season, and players from throughout the world turned out for a final testimonial for Lev Yashin, the legendary Moscow Dynamo goalkeeper, who played for 50 min. for the Moscow Select XI on May 27. Francisco Gento, the famed Real Madrid winger, retired after 18 years at the top. (T. W.)

Rugby. *Rugby Union.* The outstanding events of the 1970–71 period were the first victory ever by a British Isles team (Lions) in a series in New Zealand and the celebrations concerning the centenary of the Rugby Football Union of England. In addition, the International Board decided to make an experiment by which, for two seasons in the Northern Hemisphere and for one season in the Southern Hemisphere, the value of a try was raised from 3 to 4 points.

The first item of England's centenary celebrations was a congress at Cambridge University in September 1970 at which 98 delegates from 44 countries of the world were present. A special centenary match at Twickenham between England and Wales combined and Scotland and Ireland combined, refereed by a Frenchman, resulted in a draw, 14–14. It was closely followed by a 13-match celebratory tour of England by a representative team from Fiji. This was the first time a team of Fijians had played in England, and they proved popular visitors. When at their best, as when they beat the Barbarians 29–9 at Gosforth, the Fijians played brilliantly spectacular and unorthodox attacking Rugby, but they were beaten 15–11 by an England Under-25 team, and they won only six of their games. In addition to their 13 matches in England the Fijians also played a game against Wales Under-25 in which they were defeated 8–6.

On March 27 England played a special match against Scotland at Murrayfield to mark the exact centenary of the first match between the two countries, which was also the first international Rugby match ever played. The 1971 game ended in a 26–6 victory for Scotland.

This contest was followed in April by four matches played in different parts of England by a team more or less representative of the rest of the world. This

Rod Garcia kicks a 31-yd. field goal with 12 seconds remaining in the game to give Stanford a 13–12 victory over Michigan in the Rose Bowl on Jan. 1, 1972.

UPI COMPIX

party from overseas included seven New Zealanders, five South Africans, five Australians, five Frenchmen, and two Fijians. They were captained by Brian Lochore of New Zealand. The visitors played much fluent attacking Rugby and won all four games, beating Midland, London, and Home Counties 18–13 at Leicester, the North of England 26–12 at Birkenhead, South and Western Counties 28–13 at Bristol, and England 28–11 at Twickenham.

The England team, in its country's centenary season, could not rise to the occasion. It managed to win only one match, against Ireland, in the home international championship. The championship was won emphatically by Wales, which beat all the other four countries. It thus gained the Triple Crown and the Grand Slam. It showed the power of its forwards in the first match, beating England 22–6. In the second game Wales was given a much closer contest by Scotland before it just managed to win 19–18. In the third game Wales got the better of Ireland 23–9, but in the last it had to produce a magnificent defense to keep out the French, who played outstanding attacking Rugby but were eventually defeated 9–5.

France finished second in the championship by beating Scotland 13–8 and drawing with Ireland 9–9 and with England 14–14. The French achieved much spectacular approach work, but their finishing disappointed. Ireland's only victory was over Scotland, 17–5. Scotland managed to beat England 16–15 in their championship encounter, its first victory at Twickenham since 1938, but as it lost its other three matches, it finished last in the standings. Among the individual performances in the championship Barry John, the Welsh standoff half, scored 31 of Wales's 73 points, thus equaling the Welsh scoring record of Keith Jarrett set in 1969.

Barry John's kicking was largely responsible for the Lions' success on their subsequent tour of New Zealand, which took place in May, June, July, and August 1971. He scored 180 points, leaving far behind the tourist record in New Zealand of Gerry Brand, South African fullback, who in 1937 scored 100 points. Another 1971 Lion, Bob Hiller, scored 102 points. The Lions won all their ordinary matches in New Zealand, and also won the four-match test series 2–1 with one match drawn. The only previous team to have won a major test series in New Zealand was the 1937 South Africans.

The Lions won the first test, at Dunedin, 9–3, a victory that owed a great deal to their defense and to the kicking of Barry John. In the second test, at Christchurch, the Lions played with less conviction, and New Zealand, complementing its rugged forward work with thrustful moves by the inside backs, evened the series by winning 22–12. The Lions attacked single-mindedly at the start of the third test, at Wellington, and were worthy winners, 13–3, thus putting themselves in an unbeatable position. The last test, at Auckland, was drawn, 14–14, neither team showing its true form. The Lions, managed by Doug Smith of Scotland, were expertly coached by Carwyn James of Wales and intelligently led by John Dawes, the Welsh centre and captain. Their final record in New Zealand was: played 24, won 22, drawn 1, lost 1, points for 555, points against 204. On their way to New Zealand the Lions played two games in Australia, losing to Queensland 11–15 and defeating New South Wales 14–12. Their defeat by Queensland was generally ascribed to the fact that they played on a

Wednesday, having arrived by air from the other side of the world only on the previous Monday.

Two other, but shorter, international tours took place during the Southern Hemisphere winter. France played nine matches in South Africa in May and June 1971, and South Africa played 13 matches in Australia in June, July, and August. The French won all their provincial games but were beaten in the brief test series. They played only two tests, losing the first 9–22 at Bloemfontein and drawing the second 8–8 at Durban. In Australia the South Africans, although political demonstrators tried to upset their tour, achieved the rare feat of winning every match, including the three tests. They won these by scores of 19–11 at Sydney, 14–6 at Brisbane, and 18–6 again at Sydney.

Rugby League. The World Cup competition was played in England in the fall of 1970, the participants being Great Britain, Australia, France, and New Zealand. After each of these four countries had met the others, Great Britain came out on top of the points table, having won all three of their matches. They then had to play against Australia, the second in the standings, in the final. Great Britain had already beaten Australia 11–4 in their routine match, but in the final, played at Headingley (Leeds), Australia won 12–7.

The season's regular home and away matches between Great Britain and France resulted in a win for each country on its own ground. France won 16–8 at Toulouse, and Great Britain won 24–2 at St. Helens. Because of the World Cup matches, the previous season's triangular tournament between England, France, and Wales was not repeated. During the subsequent season in the Southern Hemisphere New Zealand caused a stir by defeating Australia 24–3 in a test match at Auckland.   (D. B. J. F.)

U.S. Football. Supremacy in U.S. professional football in 1971 was achieved by the Dallas Cowboys when they defeated the Miami Dolphins by a score of 24–3 in the Super Bowl on Jan. 16, 1972. In college competition, the top-ranked team for the second consecutive year was Nebraska.

College. Seldom has there been a more clear-cut winner of the nation's collegiate football championship than Nebraska's Cornhuskers in 1971. With two weeks remaining in the regular season, there were six undefeated teams among the top ten in the wire service polls. But at the finish—after the postseason bowl games—only Nebraska remained undefeated and untied.

The Cornhuskers, moreover, knocked off two of those previously unbeaten teams. On Thanksgiving Day, Nebraska protected its No. 1 rating by defeating second-ranked Oklahoma 35–31 in a game that was nationally televised and billed as "This Year's Game of the Decade." Five weeks later Nebraska finished its season by whipping second-ranked Alabama 38–6 in the Orange Bowl and was the unanimous winner of the national championship. Playing from a power I formation, Nebraska featured a balanced attack and also had an outstanding defense.

Nebraska's triumph enabled the Big Eight Conference to score a rare grand slam. Fellow conference members Oklahoma and Colorado were ranked second and third in the nation. Though records were incomplete, no one could recall the last time, if ever, that all three top teams in the final Associated Press poll belonged to the same conference.

Alabama of the Southeastern Conference, undefeated prior to its Orange Bowl loss to Nebraska, was

NFL Final Standings and Play-offs, 1971

AMERICAN CONFERENCE
Eastern Division

	W	L	T
Miami	10	3	1
*Baltimore	10	4	0
New England	6	8	0
New York Jets	6	8	0
Buffalo	1	13	0

Central Division

	W	L	T
Cleveland	9	5	0
Pittsburgh	6	8	0
Houston	4	9	1
Cincinnati	4	10	0

Western Division

	W	L	T
Kansas City	10	3	1
Oakland	8	4	2
San Diego	6	8	0
Denver	4	9	1

NATIONAL CONFERENCE
Eastern Division

	W	L	T
Dallas	11	3	0
*Washington	9	4	1
Philadelphia	6	7	1
St. Louis	4	9	1
New York Giants	4	10	0

Central Division

	W	L	T
Minnesota	11	3	0
Detroit	7	6	1
Chicago	6	8	0
Green Bay	4	8	2

Western Division

	W	L	T
San Francisco	9	5	0
Los Angeles	8	5	1
Atlanta	7	6	1
New Orleans	4	8	2

*Fourth qualifier for play-offs.

Play-offs

American semifinals
Baltimore 20, Cleveland 3
Miami 27, Kansas City 24

National semifinals
San Francisco 24, Washington 20
Dallas 20, Minnesota 12

American finals
Miami 21, Baltimore 0

National finals
Dallas 14, San Francisco 3

Super Bowl
Dallas 24, Miami 3

Dallas Cowboys'
quarterback
Roger Staubach scrambles
for a first down against
the San Francisco 49ers
in the National Football
Conference championship
game, Jan. 2, 1972.
The Cowboys
defeated the 49ers 14–3
and went on to defeat
the AFC champion Miami
Dolphins in the Super Bowl.

ranked fourth and Penn State fifth. Others in the Associated Press's final top ten were Michigan, Georgia, Arizona State, Tennessee, and Stanford.

Aside from Nebraska the only undefeated team in the Associated Press's top 20 was Toledo, ranked no. 14. Toledo finished with a flawless 12–0 record and with a whopping 28–3 victory over Richmond in the Tangerine Bowl. It was Toledo's 35th successive triumph, the longest winning streak in college football.

It was the year of the runner and of the virtual total success of the wishbone formation, a triple option attack originally popularized by Texas. Oklahoma, which used the wishbone and had a superior running quarterback in Jack Mildren, set National Collegiate Athletic Association (NCAA) team rushing and total offense records. The Sooners had a total offense game average of 565.5 yd. and gained an average of 472.4 yd. rushing, almost 100 yd. more than the previous mark. Mildren set a rushing record for quarterbacks with a 103.6-yd. average.

The trend, clearly, was to running the ball, and records were set in almost all rushing categories. A total of 26 rushers gained more than 1,000 yd. in 1971 against the previous one-season high of 19 in 1970. Ed Marinaro, a Cornell University tailback, was the individual rushing leader with a record 209-yd. game average. Marinaro also set one-season NCAA records for yards gained rushing, 1,881; average number of rushes per game, 39.5; average of touchdowns per game, 2.7; and career records for yards rushing, 4,715; number of rushes, 918; and average points scored per game, 11.8.

Attendance reached the 30 million mark for the first time. A survey by the National Collegiate Sports Services showed that 30,455,442 spectators attended regular-season games at the nation's 618 football-playing four-year colleges and universities.

In the East, Dartmouth and Cornell were the co-champions in the Ivy League, both with 6–1 conference records. Harvard defeated Yale 35–16 in their traditional game, the 88th in the series. It was Harvard's second win in a row.

Penn State, an independent, won the Lambert Trophy, symbolic of Eastern supremacy. The Nittany Lions captured their first 10 games, stretching their

winning streak to 15 before losing to Tennessee. Lydell Mitchell, a running back, was the Penn State star and scored 29 touchdowns, an NCAA record. Penn State climaxed its season with a 30–6 victory over Texas in the Cotton Bowl.

Army beat Navy in a 24–23 thriller, the first contest in the 72-game series to be decided by one point. Massachusetts and Connecticut were the co-winners in the Yankee Conference, both with three wins, one loss, and one tie. Delaware, the nation's No. 1 small-college team, played four major-school opponents, losing only to Temple.

In the South, Alabama, which went through its regular season undefeated, won the Southeastern Conference title for a record tenth time. The Crimson Tide had a 7–0 conference record and were led by Johnny Musso, a running back who set a school and conference record by scoring 100 points. Auburn and Georgia tied for second with 5–1 records. The decisive game in the conference was Alabama v. Auburn, played the last week of the regular season. Auburn went into the game undefeated but was whipped soundly, 31–7. Pat Sullivan, Auburn's star quarterback and the Heisman Trophy winner, was harassed by a four-man Alabama rush led by tackle Terry Rowell.

North Carolina's Tar Heels won the title in the Atlantic Coast Conference with a 6–0 league record and 10–2 overall, its best record since 1963. Richmond won top honours in the Southern Conference, and Western Kentucky triumphed in the Ohio Valley Conference.

In Midwest competition, Michigan won the Big Ten title with a flawless 8–0 conference record, swept through its regular 11-game schedule undefeated, but lost to Stanford in the Rose Bowl. Michigan set seven school offensive records and had a superior defense, especially against the rush. The Wolverines were led by running back Billy Taylor, who became Michigan's all-time leading ground gainer, breaking records previously set by Tom Harmon and Ron Johnson. Taylor finished his collegiate career with 3,079 yd. rushing.

Northwestern finished second in the Big Ten with a 6–3 record, with Ohio State, Illinois, and Michigan State tying for third at 5–3. Michigan State's Eric Allen, who set a single-game NCAA record by rushing for 350 yd. against Purdue, also set three one-season Big Ten records: most yards rushing, 1,283; most points scored, 110; and most touchdowns, 18.

Nebraska, which finished with a 13–0 record, won the championship in the rugged Big Eight Conference. The Cornhuskers were followed by Oklahoma and Colorado. The outstanding game in the Big Eight was the Thanksgiving Day contest between Nebraska and Oklahoma, both undefeated and, at the time, ranked first and second nationally. Nebraska, led by running back Jeff Kinney, who scored four touchdowns, won in a 35–31 thriller. Oklahoma came back in post-season competition to win the Sugar Bowl with a 40–22 triumph over Auburn. Mildren led the team with three touchdowns.

Texas won a record-breaking fourth consecutive championship in the Southwest Conference, barely edging Arkansas. Arkansas defeated Texas 31–7 midway in the season but then slumped and was unable to win its next two games, losing to Texas A & M and tying Rice. Texas had a strong finish, winning the title with a 34–14 triumph over Texas A & M in the final conference game for both teams. Houston, still playing an independent schedule, made a strong showing and finished with a 9–3 record, while Memphis State won the title in the Missouri Valley Conference.

In the Far West, Stanford's Indians, led by quarterback Don Bunce, won the Pacific Eight championship with a 5–1 conference record. The Indians, 9–3 overall, opened their season with victories over Washington, Southern California, and Oregon—the teams that figured to be the most likely contenders for the conference title. Stanford climaxed its season with a 13–12 upset victory over Michigan in the Rose Bowl.

Arizona State, led by sophomores Woodrow Green and Dan White, won its third successive title in the Western Athletic Conference with a 7–0 record. White, a quarterback, threw six touchdown passes in his first college game. Idaho, with a 4–1 record, won the title in the Big Sky Conference.

Professional. The biggest story in the National Football League (NFL) during the regular 14-week season was the sensational rise of the Washington Redskins. George Allen, a veteran coach fired after the 1970 season by the Los Angeles Rams, was brought in to take over the moribund Redskins and given the dual position of general manager and head coach. As he had done in Los Angeles, where he had also built winning teams, Allen immediately started trading future draft choices for established players, forsaking tomorrow in an effort for success today. Allen engineered a series of 19 separate transactions, giving up 24 draft choices and 12 players in exchange for 21 new faces. His strategy was an unqualified success as the Redskins qualified for the NFL play-offs for the first time since 1945.

Dallas, which advanced to the Super Bowl for the second successive season, was led by quarterback Roger Staubach who was not installed as a regular until midseason. The Cowboys closed their regular Eastern Division season with a string of seven consecutive victories and once again had a powerful defense keyed by Bob Lilly, a mammoth tackle who earned all-pro honours for the seventh year.

Defense was also emphasized by the Minnesota Vikings, who had an 11–3 record and retained their title in the National's Central Division. The Vikings ranked only 17th in the league in scoring but were the toughest team to score against, yielding only 139 points, second lowest total ever given up by one team during a 14-game season. Alan Page, a tackle, was the Vikings' defensive star and was chosen in an Associated Press poll as the NFL's most valuable player, the first defensive player to win this honour.

San Francisco's 49ers had to struggle to win the National's Western Division championship, barely finishing ahead of the Los Angeles Rams. Miami's Dolphins, an expansion team born only six years earlier, were surprise winners in the American's Eastern Division. They were 10–3–1 and won the divisional title with an assist from the New England Patriots, who upset Baltimore on the last Sunday of regular-season play.

Cleveland captured the title in the American's Central Division, the weakest of the NFL's six groupings. The Browns finished with a 9–5–0 record, followed by Pittsburgh with a 6–8–0 mark.

The Kansas City Chiefs, a perennial power, repeated as champions in the American's Western Division and had an outstanding passing combination in quarterback Len Dawson to Otis Taylor, a wide receiver who led the American Conference in yardage gained by receptions. Oakland, with an 8–4–2 record, finished second to Kansas City.

In the first round of the play-offs on December 25, Dallas intercepted four passes to defeat Minnesota 20–12, and Miami eliminated Kansas City 27–24. The Miami-Kansas City struggle went into a second overtime and was the longest game in professional football history, lasting 82 minutes and 40 seconds. Miami broke the 24–24 tie on the strength of a 37-yd. field goal by Garo Yepremian.

The next day San Francisco and Baltimore won their first-round matches. San Francisco eliminated Washington 24–20, scoring the decisive touchdown when tackle Bob Hoskins recovered a fumble, on a punt attempt, in the end zone. The Colts defeated Cleveland 20–3 and were led by their defensive unit which intercepted three passes, recovered two fumbles, and blocked two field-goal attempts.

A week later, Miami and Dallas qualified for the Super Bowl. Miami defeated Baltimore's defending NFL champions 21–0 to win the American Conference title, and Dallas defeated San Francisco 14–3

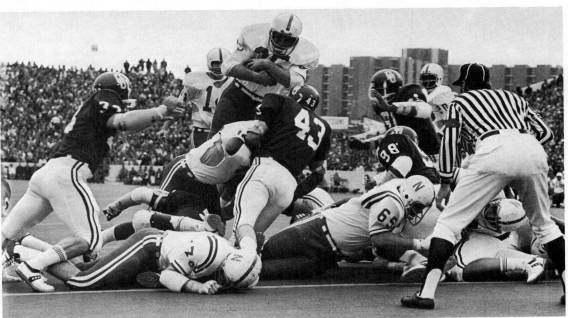

Nebraska running back Jeff Kinney plunges over the line to score a touchdown against Oklahoma on Nov. 25, 1971. Nebraska's 35–31 victory maintained its unbeaten record and number one national ranking.

WIDE WORLD

for top honours in the National Conference. Both Miami and Dallas led all the way and had strong performances from their defensive units.

Led by quarterback Roger Staubach, Dallas dominated Miami to win the Super Bowl 24–3 in New Orleans. The Cowboys scored on passes from Staubach to Lance Alworth and Mike Ditka, a 3-yd. run by Duane Thomas, and a 9-yd. field goal by Mike Clark. The outmanned Dolphins were held to a 31-yd. field goal by Garo Yepremian. Dallas' team rushing total of 252 yd. set a Super Bowl record.

In the NFL Pro Bowl game at Los Angeles on January 23, the American Conference all-stars defeated the National Conference team 26–13. Jan Stenerud of the Kansas City Chiefs led the winners by kicking four field goals.

Kicking specialists dominated the season and were the only players to score more than 100 points. The leaders were Yepremian, Miami, who was first in the American Conference with 117 points, and Curt Knight of Washington, who led in the National Conference with 114. The NFL total attendance, for the regular 182-game schedule, was 10,362,448, bettering the record of 9,884,580 which had been set the previous year for the same number of games.

Canadian Football. The Calgary Stampeders won their first Grey Cup, emblematic of the Canadian Football League championship, since 1948 by defeating the Toronto Argonauts 14–11 in a fierce defensive struggle. The Calgary front four of John Helton, Dick Suderman, Fred James, and Craig Koinzan continually put the pressure on Argo quarterback Joe Theismann, who suffered a broken nose during the second quarter.

Don Jonas of Winnipeg was voted the league's outstanding player. Jonas led the league in scoring with 121 points and was also first in passing with 253 completions in 485 attempts for 4,036 yd. and 27 touchdowns. At the season's end, there was considerable speculation that the league would expand and possibly put a team in New York City, but no action was taken.

(JE. HO.)

France

A republic of western Europe and head of the French Community, France is bounded by the English Channel, Belgium, Luxembourg, West Germany, Switzerland, Italy, the Mediterranean Sea, Monaco, Spain, Andorra, and the Atlantic Ocean. Area: 210,038 sq.mi. (543,998 sq.km.), including Corsica. Pop. (1971 est.): 51,027,000. Cap. and largest city: Paris (pop., 1968, 2,590,771). Language: French. President in 1971, Georges Pompidou; premier, Jacques Chaban-Delmas.

During 1971 Georges Pompidou (*see* BIOGRAPHY) consolidated his authority as president, as was clearly shown in his press conferences held in January and September. The latter, in particular, confirmed that his special interest, like that of his predecessor, Charles de Gaulle, was in foreign affairs.

Foreign Affairs. In the wake of the world monetary crisis and the financial measures announced by U.S. Pres. Richard M. Nixon on August 15, President Pompidou made a historic speech outlining and justifying French policy decisions in the matter. The president referred more specifically than in the past to the link between special drawing rights and gold and suggested a common European defense against speculative inflows. He endorsed the establishment of an

executive organ of the council of governors of Common Market central banks to ensure planned management of reserves. He also declared himself in favour of regulating the draft budget for 1972 in order to achieve a better distribution of the increase in income tax that the French would have to pay.

While only a small part of his comments were devoted to domestic and electoral issues, the president issued a warning to anyone seeking premature elections (legislative elections normally would not take place before the spring of 1973). He also stressed the distinction between the presidential majority and the legislative majority, which were "not necessarily parallel or in agreement." He vigorously rebutted imputations against him in connection with the Garantie Foncière financial scandal (*see* below) and spoke of his "inexhaustible reserve of contempt for slander and slanderers."

Above all, Pompidou brought significant precision to the subject of Franco-German relations, against the background of West German Chancellor Willy Brandt's *Ostpolitik* and the détente in Europe. He issued a timely reminder that Paris and Bonn were in no way engaged in a "race," with Moscow as both umpire and goal. Such a contest, he pointed out, would be not merely absurd but positively disastrous. He also noted with satisfaction that West Germany now wished to be a free agent.

During his press conferences Pompidou also showed himself a convinced European. "Once the international system has recovered, Europe must play the card of economic and monetary union," he declared in September. He had stated in January that he favoured a Europe comprising "a confederation of states committed to political harmony and economic integration." It was in the light of this statement that his talks in Paris on May 20 and 21 with U.K. Prime Minister Edward Heath took place. Despite the delays and breakdowns that had characterized negotiations at this level for many years past, the meeting between Pompidou and Heath finally paved the way for the U.K.'s entry into the European Communities.

France's dramatic change of heart in Luxembourg in June in coming to agreement on the question of the status of sterling, thus removing a major obstacle to Britain's entry into Europe, was a direct consequence of the Paris talks. The meeting in Luxembourg on June 23 merely confirmed an agreement that, with the approval of the British Parliament, would allow Great Britain to enter the European Communities. On this occasion, Pompidou's attitude diverged significantly from that of de Gaulle. Moreover, the agreement between Britain and the Six marked not merely a decisive stage in the concept of European unity but also, ultimately, the emergence of a new power bloc that, while its precise form and direction remained unclear, would nevertheless play an increasingly important role in international affairs. Pompidou's subsequent highly successful visit to Belgium gave him the opportunity not only to reaffirm the traditionally cordial links between the two countries but also to continue the debate on Europe in greater depth and detail.

In February, Pompidou made a ten-day grand tour of French-speaking black Africa, visiting five capitals: Nouakchott (Mauritania), Dakar (Senegal), Abidjan (Ivory Coast), Yaoundé (Cameroon), and Libreville (Gabon). On each occasion he reaffirmed the close ties of friendship that linked France with its former African territories.

In July 1970 André Bettencourt, minister of planning and development, had visited China, and in July 1971 Alain Peyrefitte headed a parliamentary mission to Peking. In return, on September 29 a nine-member Chinese government delegation arrived in Paris for a 12-day visit. Headed by the minister for foreign trade, Pai Hsiang-kuo, the delegation was received by Pompidou, Premier Chaban-Delmas, Foreign Minister Maurice Schumann, and Finance Minister Valéry Giscard d'Estaing. The delegation also visited various provincial towns including Toulouse, Marseilles, and Lyons. This was the first visit by a member of the Chinese government to any Western European country since Mao Tse-tung's government took over in 1948, with the exception of the Geneva conferences on Indochina in 1954 and 1962. It reflected the satisfactory relations maintained between the two countries since France's diplomatic recognition of China in 1964, the result of de Gaulle's personal initiative. Pai Hsiang-kuo's visit, less than a month before that of Soviet party leader Leonid I. Brezhnev (*see* BIOGRAPHY), confirmed the French government's commitment to the independent line established by de Gaulle.

During his tour of Europe, Emperor Hirohito of Japan visited Paris from October 2 to 4. At a time of tension in relations between Japan and the U.S., the emperor's European tour was regarded as having a certain symbolic value, illustrating in some degree the Tokyo government's desire for independence in relation to the U.S. during the international monetary crisis.

Brezhnev's five-day visit at the end of October was the occasion of lengthy discussions between the French and Soviet leaders. A ten-year economic, technical, and industrial agreement was signed, designed to facilitate industrial cooperation between the two countries and the conclusion of important long-term contracts. In the political sphere, Pompidou emphasized that France must still be regarded as a member of the Western bloc, but he reaffirmed his support for the European security conference proposed by the U.S.S.R. with considerably more enthusiasm and emphasis than many of his Western allies. While no major political agreement or treaty of friendship emerged from the discussions, the French and Soviet

leaders signed a document listing the basic principles that would guide future cooperation. These included the inviolability of present European frontiers, noninterference in the internal affairs of other states, equality, independence, and the renunciation of force or the threat of force.

Both sides attached great importance to the normalization of the Berlin problem as an essential step toward the convocation of a European security conference. Pompidou's action in delaying his reply to Willy Brandt's proposals for an unofficial Franco-German "summit" meeting until the end of the Soviet visit suggested that the German question figured prominently in discussions between the French and Soviet leaders. The meeting with Brandt took place in Paris on December 3–4. Later in the month Pompidou completed his year of intense diplomatic activity by flying—in the French Concorde SST prototype—to the Azores for meetings with President Nixon (December 13–14), during which they agreed on a basis for a settlement of the international monetary crisis.

France's efforts in the sphere of international friendship also were pursued by Chaban-Delmas and Schumann in a number of visits abroad. Chaban-

Police battle to restore order between extremist organizations in Paris on March 9, 1971. The confrontation occurred after leftist groups disrupted a political meeting held by the rightist organization Ordre Nouveau.

FRANCE

Education. (1968–69) Primary, pupils 5,163,575, teachers (public only) 182,779; secondary, pupils 2,879,264; vocational, pupils 962,670; secondary and vocational, teachers 229,930; teacher training, students 28,399, teachers 2,116; higher (including 24 universities), students 622,405, teaching staff (universities only; 1964–65) 16,904.

Finance. Monetary unit: franc, with a par value of Fr. 5.55 to U.S. $1 (Fr. 13.33 = £1 sterling) and free rates (Oct. 11, 1971) for the "commercial" franc of Fr. 5.53 to U.S. $1 (Fr. 13.78 = £1 sterling) and for the "financial" franc of Fr. 5.20 to U.S. $1 (Fr. 13 = £1 sterling). Gold, SDRs, and foreign exchange, official: (June 1971) U.S. $5,655,000,000; (June 1970) U.S. $4,447,000,000. Budget (1970 actual): revenue Fr. 169,940,000,000; expenditure Fr. 178,170,000,000. Gross national product: (1969) Fr. 725.6 billion; (1968) Fr. 628.5 billion. Money supply: (May 1971) Fr. 234,370,000,000; (May 1970) Fr. 210,330,000,000. Cost of living (1963 = 100): (June 1971) 138; (June 1970) 131.

Foreign Trade. (1970) Imports Fr. 106,190,000,000; exports Fr. 99,640,000,000. Import sources: EEC 48% (West Germany 22%, Belgium-Luxembourg 11%, Italy 9%, Netherlands 6%); U.S. 10%; U.K. 5%. Export destinations: EEC 48% (West Germany 21%, Italy 11%, Belgium-Luxembourg 11%, Netherlands 6%); U.S. 5%; Switzerland 5%. Main exports: machinery 19%; motor vehicles 11%; chemicals 9%; iron and steel 9%; textile yarns and fabrics 5%; cereals 5%. Tourism (1969): visitors 12.1 million; gross receipts U.S. $1,223,000,000.

Transport and Communications. Roads (1970) 785,171 km. (including 1,553 km. expressways). Motor vehicles in use (1970): passenger 12,470,000; commercial 1,810,000. Railways: (1969) 36,502 km.; traffic (state only; 1970) 41,080,000,000 passenger-km., freight 70,403,000,000 net ton-km. Air traffic (1969): 11,716,539,000 passenger-km.; freight 518,624,000 net ton-km. Navigable inland waterways in regular use (1969): 7,526 km.; freight traffic 14,601,000,000 ton-km. Shipping (1970): merchant vessels 100 gross tons and over 1,420; gross tonnage 6,457,900. Telephones (Dec. 1969) 8,114,041. Radio licenses (Dec. 1969) 15,796,000. Television licenses (Dec. 1969) 10,121,000.

Agriculture. Production (in 000; metric tons; 1970; 1969 in parentheses): wheat 12,922 (14,459); rye 302 (309); barley 8,009 (9,452); oats 2,070 (2,309); corn 7,431 (5,734); potatoes 9,034 (8,962); rice 101 (95); rapeseed 567 (506); tomatoes (1969) 506, (1968) 549; onions (1969) 197, (1968) 208; apples 4,236

(3,751); pears 509 (452); flax fibre 39 (57); sugar, raw value (1970–71) c. 2,696, (1969–70) 2,672; wine 6,988 (5,129); tobacco 46 (43); beef and veal c. 1,570 (1,600); pork c. 1,250 (1,212); milk 30,413 (31,010); butter (1969) c. 540, (1968) 575; cheese (1969) c. 730, (1968) 715; fish catch (1969) 746, (1968) 794. Livestock (in 000; Oct. 1969): cattle 21,886; sheep 10,037; pigs 10,622; horses 730; poultry c. 210,000.

Industry. Index of production (1963 = 100): (1970) 152; (1969) 142. Fuel and power (in 000; 1970): coal (metric tons) 37,351; electricity (kw.-hr.) 139,910,000; natural gas (cu.m.) 6,880,000; manufactured gas (cu.m.; 1969) 7,059,000. Production (in 000; metric tons; 1970): iron ore (32% metal content) 56,746; bauxite 2,993; pig iron 19,220; crude steel 23,765; aluminum 469; lead 144; zinc 223; cement 29,010; cotton yarn 260; cotton fabrics 202; wool yarn 143; wool fabrics 60; rayon filament yarn 52; rayon staple fibre 79; nylon filament yarn 82; nylon staple fibre 93; sulfuric acid 3,684; petroleum products (1968) 71,273; nitrogenous fertilizers (1969–70) 1,313; passenger cars (units) 2,458; commercial vehicles (units) 292. Merchant shipping launched (100 gross tons and over; 1970) 986,000 gross tons.

During the October strike of the Métro, the public transit in Paris, Parisians line up at the Charenton Bridge and await their turn to take a boat ride to the centre of the capital.
KEYSTONE

Delmas visited Yugoslavia in March and Poland later in the year. In October he represented France at the ceremonies held in Iran to mark the 2,500th anniversary of the Persian monarchy. Schumann visited several Eastern European countries, including Romania and Bulgaria in September. He also visited Switzerland, and early in October he returned to Paris after a ten-day trip that had taken him successively to Ottawa and New York, where he attended the UN General Assembly, and finally to Quebec, where he had talks with Robert Bourassa, premier of the province. The Canadian talks were concerned mainly with economic cooperation and served to reaffirm the normalization of relations between the two countries. Schumann had also visited Scandinavia in July, and trips to Ireland and London later in the year completed a circle of visits to all countries seeking admission to the EEC.

Domestic Affairs. The new parliamentary session began on October 2. Alain Poher was reelected president of the Senate, while the presidency of the Chamber of Deputies, an appointment lasting for the duration of the government, was retained by Achille Peretti. Meanwhile, conferences organized at Toulon by certain leftist Gaullist groups and at Paris by the Centre Démocratie et Progrès (CDP) indicated a desire on the part of various elements in the majority to renovate their image.

There was, in fact, immense activity on the part of the majority. Each of the various forces composing it proclaimed a desire for autonomy, renewal, originality, and imagination. This was clear from the Union des Démocrates pour la République (UDR) conference at Hyères in September, and again in Toulouse at the beginning of October during the first national congress of the Independent Republicans. Michel Poniatowski, secretary-general of this group, did not renew earlier attacks on Chaban-Delmas, but he nevertheless continued to look toward the centre. However, Giscard d'Estaing, president of the Federation of Independent Republicans, made a speech that was interpreted by some as a proclamation of candidacy for the presidency of the republic. He too had made advances toward the centrists. In view of this race for the centre, the renewed optimism of Jean Lecanuet, president of the Centre Démocrate, was not surprising.

While there was certainly dissent in the ranks of the majority, there was no less disarray on the opposition side. The tactics and strategy of the Communists and Socialists would doubtless depend to a large extent on the outcome of talks between the new Socialist leader, François Mitterrand, and his colleagues and Georges Marchais, deputy secretary-general of the French Communist Party, and his colleagues. However, Mitterrand and his party seemed unwilling to enter negotiations before the spring of 1972. The Socialists, at their congress at Épinay in June, announced their support for "a break with capitalism," but it was clear that the Communists were not to be satisfied that easily. In his "program for a democratic government of popular union," published at the beginning of October, Georges Marchais showed little affection for the Socialist leaders, whom he accused of sweeping under the carpet the declaration made by the two formations in December 1970. The Radical Party congress in mid-October was dominated by a personal battle between Maurice Faure and Jean-Jacques Servan-Schreiber. The latter was finally elected president of the party.

The social situation in 1971 was characterized by a new wave of strikes affecting Air France, the national railway system, the Renault factories (for almost a month), and finally the Paris Métro, where a conflict between drivers and unions deprived Parisians of their principal mode of transport for ten days.

The Garantie Foncière property fund scandal, involving the arrest of its chairman, Robert Frenkel, and his wife and charges against former chairman André Rives-Henrys, UDR deputy for Paris (19th arrondissement), led Chaban-Delmas to promise a full investigation into the affair. Some Fr. 2 billion in private savings were believed to be involved.

On December 17 the National Assembly approved the 1972 budget proposals, the draft finance bill having been adopted by the Council of Ministers on September 15. The Fr. 192,730,000,000 budget anticipated 9.74% (Fr. 17 billion) in additional expenditure. A surplus of Fr. 110 million was to derive from a 9.8% increase in revenue and a saving of Fr. 200 million to be effected by March 1. Development credits would rise by 17% in the next year to guarantee a 5.2% expansion, while running expenses would rise by only 9.8%. "This budget must be an instrument of economic progress," declared Giscard d'Estaing, pointing out the need for stability and declaring that the budget avoided both monetary upheavals and acceleration of price increases.

On October 6 the Council of Ministers approved the draft regionalization bill presented by Roger Frey, minister of state responsible for administrative reforms. The text submitted for the approval of the Council of State was definitively adopted by the Council of Ministers at the end of October. Submitted to the National Assembly in November, the draft bill was to be examined by parliamentary committees and it seemed unlikely that a vote could be taken by the whole house before the spring 1972 parliamentary session. The reform would thus not come into effect until after the legislative elections of 1973 and the renewal of half the general councils scheduled to take place at the same time.

The proposed regional reform bore scant resemblance to the one that de Gaulle had unsuccessfully submitted to popular referendum two and a half years previously. The text of Frey's bill was inspired by the principles laid down by Pompidou at Lyons on Oct. 30, 1970, and at Saint-Flour on June 26, 1971, and by the premier in his statement to the National Assembly on April 20, 1971. The bill outlined the basic principle of the reform, by which the regions were to be organized into "associations of *départements*." It created two regional assemblies, one composed of members elected by the regional communities involved, the other comprising representatives of the various social-professional groups. It also specified what powers would be transferred from the state to the regions.

In a television interview on September 9, Chaban-Delmas stressed that the aim of French domestic policy was to protect production, and hence employment, from the consequences of decisions taken by the U.S. In the meantime he rejected the idea of a price freeze. He believed that this could be envisaged only in the case of failure of the contracts to be proposed to management, whereby firms would undertake not to increase prices during a six-month period. During the debate on a motion of censure put forward by the Socialists in April, Chaban-Delmas made a general policy statement in which he gave a broad outline of government action. The premier stressed that he had not abandoned the construction of the "new society." Some weeks later, by 351 votes to 99 with 22 abstentions, the National Assembly approved the draft bill on the merging and regrouping of communes. The assembly also voted on four draft bills dealing with professional training.

As a result of the deaths of Edmond Michelet on Oct. 9, 1970, and of Raymond Mondon on December 31, respectively ministers of cultural affairs and of transport, together with the poor health of Jacques Duhamel (agriculture), a reshuffle of the government was announced on Jan. 7, 1971. Its most notable feature was the creation of a new Ministry of the Environment. The new portfolio was assigned to Robert Poujade, who was succeeded as secretary-general of the UDR by René Tomasini, deputy for the Eure. Jacques Duhamel succeeded Edmond Michelet as minister of cultural affairs and was replaced at the Ministry of Agriculture by Michel Cointat. Jean Chamant succeeded Raymond Mondon as minister of transport.

Municipal elections took place on March 14 and 21. In the 95 metropolitan *départements* and four overseas *départements*, 29,204,296 electors from 37,713 communes had to appoint 468,000 municipal councillors. The presence among the candidates of 36 ministers, 379 of the 487 deputies, 191 of the 283 senators, and many other persons of note sufficed to show that the running of town councils, great or small, was an essential basis for many political careers. The result was satisfying to the parliamentary majority in Paris, where they took 46 of the 90 seats. It was much less so for the UDR in the provinces, where the Communists, the only real victors among the opposition parties, gained six seats. In Bordeaux, Chaban-Delmas was reelected easily.

Senate elections took place on September 26 in 37 metropolitan *départements,* one overseas *département,* and two overseas territories. With a fairly large number of changes (40 new senators in metropolitan France and three overseas), these partial elections generally profited the majority. Parliamentary by-elections held on December 5 in Hautes-Alpes, Aveyron, and Drôme had no appreciable effect on the party balance in the National Assembly.

Council of Paris. At the beginning of April the 90 councillors elected 43-year-old Jean Cherioux (UDR), councillor for the 15th arrondissement, as president by 46 votes to 31 for the Communist candidate, Maurice Berlemont. In June the administrative council of the Parisian region elected as its president Robert Wagner, UDR deputy for Yvelines. (J. Kn.)

Fuel and Power

Compared with 1970, when there was an interruption in the international oil supply and a supply crisis in the U.S. that involved all of the fuels and electric power, 1971 was relatively calm. The Trans-Arabian Pipeline (Tapline) carrying oil from Saudi Arabia to the Mediterranean, which had been shut down by Syria since May 1970 when it was accidentally damaged by a bulldozer, was reopened on January 29. Tanker rates receded from their high levels of 1970 as the need subsided for emergency movement of Persian Gulf oil around Africa to Europe. Nor were there any serious voltage cutbacks or power supply difficulties in the electric utility industry caused by heat waves.

International oil markets were, nevertheless, subjected to a series of severe shocks during the year as the result of a series of new price agreements between oil-exporting countries and the companies producing oil in those countries. The agreements were the result of the countries' determination to increase their share of the revenues from the oil, and they climaxed a series of moves in that direction that had begun in 1970. In February, after a month's negotiation under a threat of embargoing oil exports, the Persian Gulf members of the Organization of Petroleum Exporting Countries (OPEC) signed an agreement with the oil companies increasing the total taxes imposed by the countries on Persian Gulf crude oil. In March negotiations with Libya, under a similar embargo threat, led to an agreement raising the total oil taxes in that country. Both agreements also contained provisions for further escalation through 1975. Similar tax increases were imposed by Nigeria, Algeria, Venezuela, and Indonesia in separate negotiations between each of those countries and the companies producing oil within their territories.

Libya in December nationalized the properties of the British Petroleum Co. in retaliation for Britain's support of Iran when that nation seized three islands in the Persian Gulf. Britain responded by expelling Libya from the sterling area.

Because of the complexity of the specific tax provisions and their application to different grades of oil, their effect on the price of crude oil varied widely, ranging from a few cents to as much as 90 cents per barrel. The impact of these increases on the prices of refined products in different parts of the world also varied, but consumers quickly felt the effect. Prices of a wide variety of petroleum products increased in Europe and the Far East.

These events demonstrated two things: that the oil-exporting countries, having proved their ability to impose heavy new tax burdens on their oil exports, were well on the way toward their announced goal of cartelizing the international oil market; and that Europe and Japan, because they were heavily dependent on oil from the exporting countries, were politically and strategically in a highly vulnerable position. The U.S. was also not without its degree of vulnerability due to its reliance on foreign sources for heavy fuel oil, the major use of which was for electric power generation.

Europe was able to take some consolation in favourable developments at home. In June production began at the giant Ekofisk oil field discovered the previous year in the Norwegian portion of the North Sea. Other discoveries were made during 1971 in the Danish and British portions. The British discoveries were especially encouraging to that country, for they represented the first indications of significant oil occurrences in the British North Sea territories, all previous discoveries having been natural gas. An encouraging oil discovery (again the first of its kind) was also made in the territorial waters of Spain in the Mediterranean Sea.

These discoveries plus further finds in Norwegian waters indicated that there was a far larger oil potential in the offshore waters of Western Europe than had previously been thought. It was suggested that production might eventually reach 8 million bbl. per day, which would satisfy a large portion of current European demand. As yet, however, there was no indication that over the long term Europe could be relieved of its fundamental reliance on the oil of North Africa and the Middle East.

A highly significant natural gas discovery was made in the Canadian Arctic. In late 1970 a well drilled on King Christian Island blew out and caught fire. The wild well burned until it was capped in January 1971, and the size of the gas flow indicated that it was a large find. A second well confirmed this and, together with the discovery in December of a field on Ellef Ringnes Island, was sufficient to cause four U.S. gas companies to advance $75 million for further exploration and development of gas from the Arctic to be marketed in the U.S.

Another significant gas discovery was indicated by initial results of a well drilled on Sable Island, a sandbar 20 mi. long located in the Atlantic Ocean 175 mi. E of Halifax, Nova Scotia. The well yielded the first commercial test of petroleum hydrocarbons off the east coast of Canada.

In April the last of a group of 12 burning wells in the Gulf of Mexico south of Louisiana was brought under control, having been burning out of control for 133 days. The final control valve on the 22 wells at the platform was not installed until a month later. It was estimated that the total cost of extinguishing the fire and bringing all wells back under control was $26 million, making it the most expensive fire in the history of offshore operations.

Several administrative actions and pronouncements by the federal government during 1971 were of significance for the fuel and power industries of the U.S. In June, U.S. Pres. Richard Nixon sent a "clean energy message" to the Congress based on the findings of a committee formed in 1970 to study the energy situation. Among the items included in the program proposed by the president were: increased funding of research and development in sulfur dioxide control technology; a commitment to demonstrate a successful liquid-metal, fast-breeder nuclear reactor by 1980; an expanded pilot plant program in cooperation with industry to develop commercial coal gasification; accelerated oil and gas leasing on the federal lands of the outer continental shelf; development of

leasing programs for oil shale and geothermal lands; increased imports from Canada through agreement with that country; modernization and expansion of capacity at the uranium enrichment plants; and centralization of all energy resource development programs within the proposed Department of Natural Resources.

In the field of air pollution the Environmental Protection Agency issued national air quality standards for sulfur oxides, particulates, carbon monoxide, photochemical oxidants, nitrogen oxides, and hydrocarbons, and announced that it intended to abolish the use of lead additives in gasoline for 1975 model light-duty vehicles. This intensified the pressure on all fuel users—especially the electric utilities—to use low-sulfur fuels, on oil refiners to produce lead-free gasoline, and on car manufacturers to produce engines that would perform satisfactorily on such gasoline.

In May the U.S. secretary of the interior declared a moratorium on construction of new power plants or additions to existing plants in the Four Corners area of Utah, Colorado, Arizona, and New Mexico, pending completion of a departmental study of the environmental aspects of such plants. The five plants already in operation were not affected, but construction of a sixth (and largest) plant was halted by the order. The action reflected the mounting concern with the environmental effects of installing large power plants in the area to use the coal mined locally in very large strip-mining operations. Opposition to the plants was based on the polluting effects of their stack emissions and the adverse scenic effects of large-scale strip mining. The electric utilities involved argued, on the other hand, that use of the area's coal resources was essential if the power needs of the Southwest were to be met.

A similar problem of reconciling environmental goals with power needs was brought into sharp focus in a federal court decision in July requiring the U.S. Atomic Energy Commission (AEC) to give more weight than in the past to environmental factors in granting construction and operating licenses for nuclear power plants. The AEC complied with the court ruling by issuing new regulations in September requiring all utilities that had received construction permits or operating licenses for nuclear plants since 1969 to file an environmental justification of those plants. Approximately 90 nuclear plants were affected by these developments and the industry feared that the additional delay they introduced into the timetable for bringing the plants into operation would lead to severe local power shortages during 1972. (See Special Report.)

The world's first fuel cell for home use was installed in a house in Farmington, Conn., marking the halfway point in a nine-year program to develop a commercial unit. The fuel cell in this application supplied all heating and electricity needs in the house, using natural gas as a fuel. If successful, the home fuel cell would drastically change the structure of the electric power industry by replacing central station generation with generation at the point of use.

A technological development of great potential significance was marked by the installation by some utilities of combined-cycle generating units using a gas turbine in combination with the conventional steam turbine to generate electricity. The combined cycle had the advantage of offering significant fuel savings because of its potentially higher efficiency than the conventional power plant.   (B. C. N.)

COAL

World coal production in 1971 was expected to show a modest increase; in 1970 demand exceeded production in many countries, thus reducing stockpiles, but this seemed unlikely in 1971. A notable feature was the increase in Canada's exports, almost exclusively to supply the Japanese steel industry, and giving Canada a significant percentage of the Japanese market at the expense of other exporting countries.

Hard coal production in 1970 was an estimated 2,177,000,000 metric tons, a significant increase of 67 million metric tons over the 1969 level. Most of the increased output came from the United States, the U.S.S.R., Poland, Australia, Canada, and China. The biggest gain shown in the 1970 estimates was for China, with an increase of 35 million tons to a level of 360 million metric tons.

U.S.S.R. A total of 615.4 million metric tons was produced in 1970 from the industry's deep and surface mines, an increase of 2.7% over the 1969 production figures. Of this 468.2 million tons were hard coal (an increase of 2%) and 147.2 million tons lignite (an increase of 5.2%). In addition, 8.6 million tons were produced, presumably as a by-product, from mines not included in the coal industry.

The Soviet government estimated during the year that by 1980 production of coal and lignite would reach 1,200,000,000 metric tons, of which 625 million tons would be strip mined; 26.7% of the total coal produced in 1970 was obtained from strip operations.

United States. The coal industry in 1971 was expected to exceed its 1970 sales, themselves the highest since 1947. This rise was due to a 5.5% increase in demand from the electric power industry, which consumed a record 322 million short tons in 1970.

The expected 1971 consumption of bituminous coal was 598 million short tons, an increase over 1970 of 1.7%. In the first half of 1971, total output was up by 6.2% over the corresponding period in 1970. Bituminous coal production in 1970 was 587 million short tons, an increase of 5% over 1969. Anthracite production continued to fall, with a 9.5% reduction in output to 9,481,000 short tons in 1970. Exports in the first half of 1971 ran at a lower level than for the same period in 1970, with 42% going to Japan.

European Economic Community (*EEC*). Output for the five EEC coal-producing nations was again reduced in 1970, but only 4 mines, with a total capacity of just over 1 million metric tons, were closed, compared with 12, having a capacity of 3.7 million tons, in 1969. There was an overall drop of 3.9% in production with a total output of 164.7 million metric tons. Belgium lost 13.6%, with an output of 11,360,000 metric tons. An estimated 1,035,000 tons were lost through a strike in early 1970. France, with an output of 37,353,000 metric tons, declined 7.9%. West Germany, the largest producer, remained stable with 111,270,000 tons, a drop of only 0.32%. Italy lost 1.32%, but with an output of only 299,000 metric tons this did not affect EEC totals. The Netherlands reported the greatest loss—22% —with a total output of 4,334,000 tons.

The EEC underground labour force was reduced by 7.3% in 1970. Output per manshift, however, increased by February 1971 to 3.602 metric tons, compared with 3.445 tons a year before. Once again, hard coal production was expected to fall in 1971.

United Kingdom. During the financial year ended March 1971, the total output was 142.4 million long tons, a reduction of 5.2 million tons from the previous year.

This was mainly attributable to colliery closings, a strike in the fall of 1970 that caused the loss of 3.3 million tons, and a smaller increase in productivity than forecast. Output per manshift was a record 2.21 tons, a modest 1.7% increase compared with the previous year. This was due to the declining benefits gained from closing uneconomic pits and the completion of mechanization programs. Only six National Coal Board (NCB) collieries were closed, compared with 19 closings in the previous financial year.

Prospects for the industry looked promising; although prices rose steeply, competitive fuels underwent higher increases. Sales amounted to 150.7 million long tons, and for the second successive year demand exceeded supply. As a consequence, stockpiles were reduced to 6.2 million tons, the lowest in 12 years.

Poland. In 1970, Poland produced a total of 173.9 million metric tons, of which 141.1 million were hard coal, an increase of 4.5% over 1969. The production of lignite for the year was 32.8 million metric tons.

Since the end of World War II, 14 new mines had been opened and mechanization programs implemented to increase productivity. By 1970, 83.2% of the total output was achieved by mechanized cutting, and output per manshift for underground workers had risen to 2.55 metric tons.

India. Output in 1970, at 74 million metric tons, was only 1.2% higher than in the previous year. Although India had estimated reserves of about 96,300,000,000 tons, only 20% of this was coking coal needed by the expanding Indian steel industry. In 1970 16.3 million tons of coking coal were produced. Lignite production was 3.7 million metric tons, all from Neyveli in Tamil Nadu. It was expected to rise to 6 million tons in 1971.

Japan. Output in 1970 fell by 5 million to 39.9 million metric tons. The industry was beset with geographic and geologic difficulties, making it cheaper to import than to use the limited indigenous resources. Imports reached a record 50,172,265 metric tons, a 24% increase over 1969. The U.S. contributed 50.3% and Australia 32.8% of the total imports. With slackening world demand for steel, it was thought that Japanese importers would have to cut the contracted volume from the U.S. for the fiscal

A third power plant was being added to the Grand Coulee Dam on the Columbia River in Washington during 1971. The new plant was designed to increase the dam's output by over 100%.
UPI COMPIX

year 1971–72 from 38 million metric tons to an estimated 20 million.

Australia. The Australian coal-mining industry had expanded considerably in the 1960s due partly to the demands of the expanding Japanese steel industry but also to increased domestic demand. During this period, exports rose from 1.1 million to 17.7 million long tons. Australia's nearby geographic position, relative to Japan's other suppliers, and low operating costs assured a growing percentage of the Japanese market. In 1971 Japan imported 34% of its coking coal from Australia, and some believed that this figure would rise to 40% by 1975.

A gain of 4.6 million metric tons of black coal (bituminous and anthracite) in 1970 represented an increase of 10% over 1969. The output of black coal was 50.7 million metric tons, with an additional 23 million metric tons of lignite.

South America. Coal production in 1970 was 8.3 million metric tons, a gain of 100,000 tons over 1969. Colombia (where investigation began into the possibility of exports to Japan) was the largest producer, with 3.3 million, while Brazil produced 2.6 million and Chile 1.7 million metric tons. Argentina's Rio Turbio mines reported an 18% increase in production to 615,500 metric tons, and by 1975 production was planned to increase to 1.5 million tons to meet the rising demand for electricity generation.

Canada. An increase of 55.6% in production was recorded for 1970, due mainly to the growth of two relatively new markets: prime coking coal exports to supply the Japanese steel industry, and the domestic consumption of lignite and subbituminous coal by the electricity industry. A total of 16.6 million short tons was produced in 1970, only 1 million short tons less than the 1952 record.

Canada's coal exports reached a record 4.4 million short tons in 1970, compared with 1.4 million for the preceding year. Exports to Japan accounted for 4,120,000 short tons; by the mid-1970s these were expected to reach 14 million short tons a year.

(R. J. Fo.)

| colspan table |

Installed Capacity and Production of Electric Power in Selected Countries, Jan. 1, 1970

Political division	Hydroelectric power – Operating plants – Installed capacity (000 kw.)	Production (000,000 kw.-hr.)	Total electric power – Installed capacity (000 kw.)	Production (000,000 kw.-hr.)
World	...	...	...	4,567,900
Afghanistan	212	306	230	325
Algeria	340*	361*	639*	1,434*
Angola	211	386†	296	542
Argentina	609	1,341	6,318	19,879
Australia	3,592*	8,339*	12,263*	48,787*
Austria	5,176	16,718	7,469	26,346
Belgium	66†	230†	6,730†‡	29,127§
Bolivia	171	601	252	731
Brazil	7,858	32,692	10,263	41,648
Bulgaria	810	1,839	4,019	17,230
Burma	103	371	258	572
Cambodia*‖	—	—	63	128
Cameroon	152	1,025	179	1,046
Canada	26,979	147,924	39,469‡	190,320§
Central African Republic*	7¶	40	10¶	41
Ceylon	195	549	282	752
Chile	997	7,134	1,901	4,024
Colombia	1,164†	4,080¶	2,250	7,345*
Congo (Kinshasa)		2,847	237	2,912
Costa Rica	179	808	237	766
Cuba	...	81*†	1,400†	4,700†
Czechoslovakia	1,519	2,494	10,162	43,017
Denmark	...	22*	4,195	16,573
Ecuador	95	356	272	858
El Salvador	109*†	486*†	188	619
Ethiopia	92*†	233*†	292¶	361†
Finland	2,093	8,745	4,683	19,979
France	14,740	52,888	36,326‡	131,516§
Germany, East	690†	1,243	11,970‡	65,463§
Germany, West	4,728	14,590	48,812‡	221,199§
Ghana	512*†	2,728*	631†	2,772
Greece	1,249	2,031*	1,897†	8,422
Guatemala	43*†	160*	144†	589†
Honduras	31*†	164*†	91†	268†
Hungary	20*	95*	2,537	14,069
Iceland	244*	860*	354	913
India	6,130	22,846	15,493	56,190
Indonesia*	310†	1,113†	652†	1,756†
Iran	309*†	855*†	1,089*†	5,862
Ireland*	219†	770†	1,290†	5,124
Israel‖	—	—	1,012*	6,079
Italy	14,775	42,001	31,034‡δ	110,447§□
Jamaica	16*	113*	257†	1,275
Japan	19,309	76,860	59,482‡δ	316,084§□
Kenya*	66	287	153	459
Korea, South	327†	1,427*	1,636*	7,980
Lebanon*	246	901	426	1,139
Liberia	38	221	259	632
Libya*‖	—	—	166	351
Luxembourg	932*°	847*†	1,157	2,202
Malagasy Rep.	29*°	110*	82*	150*
Malaysia:				
Malaya	...	1,014	293†	3,068
Sabah‖	—	—	32*	78*
Sarawak‖	—	—	40	96
Mauritius	16	27*	101†	130
Mexico	3,333	13,406	6,987	25,554
Morocco*	300	1,417	546	1,912
Mozambique	66*†	251*	274†	502
Netherlands‖	—	—	9,645‡	37,144§
New Zealand*	2,791	10,203	3,568δ	12,942□
Nicaragua	57†	253*	157†	484†
Nigeria	29*†	899*	804	1,248
Norway	12,352	56,803	12,492	57,021
Pakistan	629*†		2,062	4,991ϙ
Panama	15*†	70*†	124*†	670†
Peru	934†	3,160ϙ	1,672†	5,107
Philippines*	547	1,763	1,490	6,312
Poland	508*	908*	12,861	60,053
Portugal	1,246	6,326	2,033	6,838
Rhodesia	705*¶	5,253*	1,191†	6,002
Romania	850	2,217	6,432	31,509
Singapore*	—	—	584	1,876
South Africa	...	...	...	44,233
Spain	8,534†	30,670	15,660‡	52,090§
Sweden	10,529	41,844	14,797‡	58,065§
Switzerland	9,120†	28,145	9,880‡	29,666§
Syria	—	—	294	1,023
Taiwan	721*	3,052*	2,375	11,369
Tanzania*	41¶		72‡	360
Thailand	451*†	1,046*	1,044	3,728
Tunisia	28*	39*	259	732
Turkey	723	3,456	1,982	7,830
Uganda*	150	727	157	731
U.S.S.R.	29,645	115,181	153,790‡	689,050§
U.A.R. (Egypt)	1,051*†	2,951*†	2,725*	7,316
United Kingdom	2,160	4,384	61,372‡	238,256§
United States	53,375	253,361	331,905‡δ	1,552,298§□
Uruguay	225*†	1,141*†	470ϙ	2,026*
Venezuela	...	2,748†	2,448†	11,000
Vietnam, South*	163ϙ		513	1,042
Yugoslavia	3,277	14,305	5,541	22,947
Zambia	96ϙ	...	256ϙ	693

*Public sector only. †1968. ‡Includes nuclear in 000 kw.: Belgium 11; Canada 240; France 1,771; Germany, East 75; Germany, West 933; Italy 642; Japan 510; Netherlands 54; Spain 153; Sweden 10; Switzerland 350; U.S.S.R. (1968 est.) 1,150; U.K. 4,647; U.S. 3,980. §Includes nuclear in 000,000 kw-hr.: Belgium 22; Canada 494; France 4,465; Germany, East 425; Germany, West 4,937; India 1,330; Italy 1,679; Japan 1,082; Netherlands 315; Spain 829; Sweden 523; Switzerland 523; U.S.S.R. (1968) 2,500; U.K. 28,582; U.S. 13,897. ‖Thermal only. ¶1966. ϙ1967. δIncludes geothermal in 000 kw.: Italy 395; Japan (1968) 31; New Zealand 192; U.S. 84. □Includes geothermal in 000,000 kw-hr.: Italy 2,765; Japan (1968) 276; New Zealand (1968) 1,206; U.S. 615. °Sales. (F.H.SK.)

ELECTRICITY

Total electric power supplies in the main industrial countries increased at a slower rate in 1971. There was a continued revival in orders for nuclear power stations. In conventional electricity production, coal firing declined and oil increased, despite the rise in oil prices.

Production growth in individual countries during 1969–70 was: Japan +11.3%; France +8.2%; U.S.S.R. +7.4%; West Germany +7.3%; Canada +7.0%; U.S. +5.5%; and U.K. +0.3%.

Nuclear Electric Power. At the beginning of 1971, there were 32 magnox-type reactors (using natural uranium that is graphite-moderated and gas-cooled) in service in the world; they had produced a cumulative total of 170 billion kw-hr. Nonetheless, they were less economical than enriched-uranium reactors. In 1971, therefore, light-water-cooled, enriched-uranium reactors of the PWR (pressurized water reactor) or BWR (boiling water reactor) type developed in the U.S. were in greatest demand except in the U.K., which remained faithful to the AGR (advanced gas-cooled reactor); this also used slightly enriched uranium but was cooled by carbon dioxide.

The U.K. led among countries taking a positive interest in the development of breeder reactors. Studies had begun in 1950, and the 250-Mw. prototype at Dounreay was scheduled to reach full capacity in 1972 (an experimental 14-Mw. fast breeder having been in operation there since 1962). Following Britain was France, which, after perfecting its Rapsodie mini-reactor, was building the prototype 250-Mw. Phénix. In West Germany construction of the 300-Mw. SNR (Schnell Natrium Reaktor) was delayed because of site difficulties. The Soviet Union announced the start of work on BER-60 (60 Mw.) at Melekess and of BN-350 (350 Mw.) at Shevchenko, as well as its plans for a 600-Mw. breeder at Beloyarsk. Although the U.S. had no significant project under way in the breeder field, the budget of the Atomic Energy Commission (AEC) approved by Congress in August 1971 included $110 million for the construction of a breeder before 1980.

The need for enriched uranium grew constantly, and with the U.S. virtually the sole source of supply, a world shortage threatened when the U.S. plants become saturated, probably by 1980. Three possible solutions for Europe were: (1) the joint construction of a European plant for enriching natural uranium by gas diffusion, a method already in use in Britain and France in relatively small plants; (2) adoption of the ultracentrifuge process, if current joint British, West German, and Dutch work gave positive results; and (3) use of enriched uranium supplied by the U.S.S.R. The Soviet Union began negotiations on these lines with West Germany, and signed an agreement with France for the manufacture of a first consignment for the Fessenheim station, 80 metric tons with a rate of enrichment slightly above 3%, to be obtained by processing 400–450 tons of French natural uranium. In July the U.S. offered EEC countries and the U.K. a technique for uranium enrichment by gas diffusion, together with joint examination of the possibility of building a multinational enrichment plant.

In the U.S. the revival in orders for nuclear power stations, already evident in 1970, speeded up. In the first half of 1971, total capacity ordered was 12,820 Mw., compared with 7,600 Mw. in the corresponding period in 1970. The number of reactors in service, under construction, or on order reached 119, with a total capacity of 99,730 Mw.

In the U.K. the Wylfa station, ninth and last of the magnox type, began to supply electricity in January 1971. It consisted of two reactors with a capacity of 590 Mw. each. In addition, the Central Electricity Generating Board signed a contract for the construction of Sizewell B, in Suffolk, to consist of four AGR reactors with a capacity of 2,640 Mw.

The capacity of stations in service in West Germany in 1971 did not exceed 845 Mw., but ten were under construction or on order representing a capacity of 9,440 Mw. In France the second group of 515-Mw. reactors at Saint-Laurent-des-Eaux on the Loire River was completed in August 1971, bringing the capacity of the station, which used natural uranium, to more than 1,000 Mw.

The Soviet Union in 1971 had an available nuclear power station capacity of approximately 1,500 Mw. This was expected to increase by 6,000 Mw. during the ninth five-year plan (1971–75). Premier Aleksei N. Kosygin announced an additional nuclear program aimed at an ultimate capacity of about 30,000 Mw. to be achieved in the next 10 to 12 years.

In Canada production began at the Gentilly (Quebec) station (capacity 250 Mw.). This was equipped with the first reactor in the world using natural uranium as fuel, heavy water as a moderator, and light water as a cooler.

There were 17 nuclear stations in service or under construction in Japan in October 1971, with a total capacity of 10,736 Mw. Japan thus ranked third in the world after the U.S. and U.K.

Thermoelectricity. In most industrial countries the cost of fossil fuels rose sharply, with coal prices showing a greater proportional increase than those for oil. At Fawley, near Southampton, U.K., oil was used as fuel for a station brought into service in May. This 2,000-Mw. plant was the first British station that could be brought back to full production automatically after an overnight halt. Oil would also be used in the Isle of Grain, Kent, station, construction of which began in 1971. Another new station ordered was Inverkip on the Renfrewshire coast of Scotland. These projects marked the transition in Britain from the 500-Mw. to the 660-Mw. scale as the standard for high-capacity power-generating groups.

France also decided to raise the norm for conventional thermoelectric groups. Thus, the 600-Mw. group opened in the Cormetais station near Nantes was to be the last of the series, the next being in the 700-Mw. region. The same tendency toward raising unit capacity appeared in West Germany, where orders were announced for groups of 600 Mw. or more.

In East Germany work began on what was to be the most powerful thermoelectric station in Europe, with an ultimate capacity of 3,860 Mw. It was situated at Kottbus, about 40 mi. S of Berlin, and would be coal-fired.

Australia's largest station was opened at Hazlewood in the Latrobe Valley, and was designed to provide 60% of the requirements of the state of Victoria. It had a capacity of 1,200 Mw. in six groups and was coal-fired.

In nonconventional electricity generation, at the fifth International Conference on Magnetohydrodynamic Production of Electricity, in Munich, W.Ger., the Soviet Union announced the establishment of a 25-Mw. plant using magnetohydrodynamic conversion, to which might be added 50 Mw. from recuperation of heat in the exhaust gases. (Magnetohydrodynamics involves heating a gas until it becomes ionized and then passing it through a magnetic field.)

Hydroelectricity. France and Italy opened, in June 1971, their joint undertaking harnessing water from Mont Cenis in the Alps. It comprised a dam creating a reservoir of 321 million cu.m. The accumulated water fed two hydroelectric stations, one in France and the other in Italy.

In August, Austria completed the Zemm station in the Ziller Valley, with a productive capacity of about 700 million kw-hr., and was also to build the Malta station in Carinthia, which would have a capacity of 630 Mw. and supply 683 million kw-hr. annually.

The Aswan High Dam on the Nile, brought into service in 1970, was officially inaugurated on Jan. 15, 1971, by the Egyptian and Soviet chiefs of state. The station, equipped with 12 power-generating groups having a total capacity of 2,100 Mw., would have an annual mean output of nearly 10,-000,000,000 kw-hr.

In 1971 the Philippines began the construction of the Patabangan hydroelectric station, with a planned capacity of 120 Mw. It formed part of the project to harness the Upper Pampanga River in central Luzon.

Following satisfactory results from a small experimental plant at Murmansk, the Soviet Union decided to build two tidal stations on the shores of the Black Sea with a capacity of approximately 1,500 Mw. each. It was thought that if this area were completely equipped, it could yield an output of 36,000,000,000 kw-hr. a year.

(L. Ch.)

GAS

Natural gas reserves in the U.S. continued to decline. New production failed to keep up with increased demand. Producers complained of a lack of monetary incentive to add to the gas supply; users argued that producers were attempting to force the price of gas upward by withholding still-untapped supplies in the face of increasing demand. The federal government, which regulated the industry, still had to rely on industry production figures in its assessment of the situation. Prominent members of Congress and others, however, began exploring the possibility of making their own independent surveys.

Amid the uncertainty as to whether increases in the price of gas would assure exploration to meet future demand, President Nixon imposed ceilings on prices and wages and moved to stem imports. His action, taken on most commodities, further clouded the picture in regard to natural gas. Questions of ecology delayed efforts to tap gas in Alaska.

The data showed a 17.8 trillion cubic foot (Tcf) decrease in reserves of 66 major interstate pipeline companies during 1970, the third consecutive year of declining reserves; in 1969, a reserves drop of 7.3 Tcf was reported. Production rose in 1970 by 4.8%, compared with 6.5% in 1969.

Marketed natural gas production was 21.92 Tcf in 1970, up 5.9% over 1969. Texas and Louisiana accounted for 16.15 Tcf, or 73.7% of the total, while Oklahoma accounted for 7.3% and New Mexico 5.2%. Gas consumed in the U.S. totaled 22.05 Tcf, up 5.4% over 1969. Residential consumption was 4.84 Tcf, up 2.3% over 1969, while commercial use was 2.06 Tcf, compared with 2 Tcf in 1969. Electric utilities consumed 3.90 Tcf in 1970; industrial use was 7.89 Tcf.

Imports in 1970 totaled 0.82 Tcf, up 12.9% over 1969, of which 0.78 Tcf were imported from Canada. Exports were 0.07 Tcf, compared with 0.05 Tcf in 1969. The volume of gas put in storage in 1970 exceeded withdrawals by 0.4 Tcf, compared with 0.12 Tcf in 1969. The value of natural gas at the wellhead totaled $3.75 billion or about 17.1 cents per million cubic feet (Mcf).

The potential supply of natural gas in the continental and contiguous U.S. was estimated at 851 Tcf, of which 218 Tcf were probable, 326 Tcf possible, and 307 Tcf speculative. In Alaska the potential supply was estimated at 327 Tcf, of which 39 Tcf were probable, 61 Tcf possible, and 227 Tcf speculative.

In 1971 about 96% of the demand for gas was expected to be met. But by 1975 only 86% of the total requirements, exclusive of field use, was expected to be met. In addition, because gas is a clean-burning fuel, demands for a pure environment may add to consumption of gas. Four solutions to meet the demand for gas were under consideration: higher rates for gas in the hope that discovery and production would be induced; new methods of tapping gas and new discoveries; substitutes for natural gas and the manufacturing of gas; and increased imports.

On higher rates, the FPC set a ceiling price of 24 cents per Mcf for gas produced in the Texas Gulf Coast area under contracts dated after Oct. 1, 1968. Gas produced in the area under contracts after 1961 sold in the 18–19 cents per Mcf range. The FPC moved to raise the price of southern Louisiana's newest gas to 26 cents per Mcf, boosted pre-1968 gas by two cents, and ordered further increases in the years to come. It raised 1970 Rocky Mountain gas to the 22.5–24 cent per Mcf price range in contrast to earlier contracts that ranged from 13 cents to 17.5 cents per Mcf. The FPC also freed small producers from price regulations and directed some sales from the industrial to the residential market. It agreed to update its 1970 investigation into prices.

In seeking new methods of tapping gas, a "pure" nuclear explosion was triggered near Mercury, Nev., in the hope of freeing from fractured sandstone gas that would not be contaminated by radioactivity. The industry also made a commitment to efforts to gain usable gas from coal.

Canada proposed a solution for U.S. problems in Alaska—its own pipeline through the Northwest Territories and the Prairie Provinces, paralleling the Mackenzie River. The route was said to be cheaper than an Alaskan one and safer for the environment. Canada expected to increase exports of natural gas to the U.S. tenfold by 1990.

(J. J. Ac.)

The main feature of the year in the United Kingdom was again the conversion of appliances to burn natural instead of manufactured gas. In contrast to the previous year, however, there was less criticism of the program, although there was adverse publicity over conversion mishaps. The program reached its peak in 1971 with more than 40,000 conversions weekly. By the end of the year over five million domestic customers were using direct supplies of natural gas. Conversion would continue in 1972, after which the numbers would fall until completion of the program in about 1977. Conversion of appliances would cost the industry more than £500 million over a ten-year period—the customer paying nothing for the service.

Large sums were required also for pipelining. At the end of 1971 the national natural gas transmission system in the U.K. totaled more than 2,000 mi. All but 350 mi.,

laid in the early 1960s to handle imported Algerian natural gas, had been constructed since 1966. The system chiefly comprised 36-in.-, 30-in.-, and 24-in.-diameter pipeline. It was designed to work at between 550 and 1,000 lb. per sq.in., feeding bulk quantities of natural gas into the distribution systems of the area gas boards, which supplied all the country's domestic and commercial gas consumers and all but the biggest of the industrial users.

The U.K. transmission system was being built so that additional discoveries of gas off the east coast could readily be integrated. Control would eventually be entirely automatic, with a complex system of microwave radio and telephone cables providing communications for telemetry equipment. A computerized operational control centre was nearing completion at Hinckley, Leicestershire, which was geographically at the centre of the system.

Britain's only onshore gas field—Lockton, on the Yorkshire moors—came into service in the fall. Supplying only a small proportion of the country's gas requirements, up to 75 Mcf a day, it might become the country's first underground store of natural gas. After a proportion of gas had been taken from it, plans were to pump gas back into the reservoir at times of low demand and draw it out as required. Further storage of this seasonal kind would be provided by the liquid natural gas stores being built at the extremities of the pipeline system.

All this development could be justified only if demand could be expanded at a high enough rate. In the financial year 1970–71, sales grew by the record amount of 17.1% to 6,167,000,000 therms. Sales were on their way to the objective of doubling the 1965 (pre-North Sea gas) level of demand (3.5 billion therms) by 1971–72 and quadrupling it by 1974–75.

North Sea reserves of natural gas, according to the latest available estimate, amounted to 30 Tcf. Further finds were made in 1971, mostly associated with the oil discoveries in the north of the area. Prospecting continued onshore, and preparations were made for further drilling in the Irish Sea, and for work in the Bristol and English channels.

The U.K.'s reserves accounted for some 2% of the world total, estimated at 45 trillion cu.m. The largest reserves of natural gas were in the U.S.S.R., which was estimated to have 27% of the world supply. The U.S. was second with 17%, followed by Iran (13%), Algeria (9%), the Netherlands (5%), Canada (4%), Saudi Arabia (3%), Kuwait (2%), and Libya (2%); the remainder was distributed among 45 other countries.

The rapid rise in oil prices during 1970 and 1971 aroused increased interest in the international trade in liquefied natural gas (LNG). The first commercial LNG scheme was one between Algeria and the U.K. that began in 1964. In 1970–71 the equivalent of 100 Mcf a day was shipped from Algeria to Britain. This was almost one-sixth of total world trade in LNG, which, by the end of the 1970s, was expected to rise to approximately 6.5 billion cubic feet (Bcf) a day.

In West Germany, gas output in 1970 rose 45% to 1.14 Bcf a day following 6 gas discoveries among 41 exploratory wells. Proved and probable reserves increased to 12.7 Tcf. Italy produced 434 Bcf in 1970, up from 395 Bcf the previous year. Italy had contracts with the Soviet Union and the Netherlands to receive 210 Bcf a year from each, and also for 105 Bcf from Libya. French natural gas output rose 5% to 987.7 Mcf a day. Total Dutch production in 1970 was 3.6 Bcf a day. About one-third of Dutch gas was exported. Austrian production was 67 Mcf a day in 1970, against 52 Mcf in 1969; imports from the Soviet Union and Czechoslovakia totaled 31 Mcf a day.

The U.S.S.R.'s gas output in 1970 rose to 19.4 Bcf a day. Total proved gas reserves in mid-1971 were officially estimated to be 547 Tcf.

Reserves of natural gas in Australia were estimated at 12 Tcf. Approximately 750,000 customers were using the fuel by the spring of 1971, after two years of rapid development. By 1973-74 another 500,000 consumers were expected to have natural gas supplies, leaving only a small percentage using other gases. (X.)

PETROLEUM

The most important development affecting the international oil industry during 1971

A Soviet oil rig began drilling operations near Glinyany Island in the Caspian Sea during 1971. The oil rig, called the "Khazar," weighs 12,000 tons and can probe to depths of 3.75 mi.

CAMERA PRESS—PIX

was the series of meetings between the principal oil companies and members of the Organization of Petroleum Exporting Countries (OPEC) from January to June. Arising from Resolution 120 passed at the OPEC meeting in Caracas, Venez., in December 1970, negotiations took place that resulted in the signature of new agreements in Teheran, Tripoli, and Baghdad.' These, among other terms, greatly increased posted prices annually over five years in return for a guaranteed five-year period of price stability by the producing countries. Over these five years the total revenues payable to the countries of the Middle East and Libya were estimated to reach $15.6 million in 1975, almost triple those of 1970.

Major differences arose between France and Algeria, when, after protracted negotiations, the Algerians took over 51% of the French oil industry in their country, offering unacceptable terms of compensation. By the end of the year the French oil interests had reached agreement with the Algerians on compensation and the other issues raised by the Algerian take-over. In Venezuela the government passed in mid-year three measures enabling it to exercise increased control over the operations, assets, and investment of the oil companies there. It also instituted a new form of service contract for the new concessions offered, the first of which was signed by an oil company on July 29. At the 24th OPEC Conference at Vienna in July, which formally proposed the participation of the producing countries in the oil companies operating on their territory, Nigeria became the 11th member of the organization.

In the U.S. the oil industry and the public were preoccupied with the problems of national energy supply. The National Petroleum Council drew attention to the growing overdependence of the U.S. on the importation of crude oil and the reduced development of domestic sources of oil and gas. The secretary of the interior acknowledged the need for an energy policy, but controversy raged on its possible scope, the relevance of a multienergy approach, and the role of nuclear energy. Meanwhile, the issues of pollution and conservation remained paramount.

The confirmation of large reserves of oil in the North Sea, estimated at more than 2,250,000 bbl., which began with the discovery of the Ekofisk field toward the end of 1970, was of great importance for Europe, and limited production began in June. The largest field discovered in the Bass Strait, Austr., Kingfish, came into production in April. These discoveries showed the way in which offshore technology was extending areas for exploration and production, and equipment orders rapidly increased. In contrast to the unsatisfactory results of 1970, oil industry earnings as a whole rose in the first half of 1971 as a result of the higher volume of product sales and lower freight costs, but demand seemed likely to fall below the 8.7% growth rate of 1970. In 1970 Western Europe imported half the Middle East production and most of the North African, while Japan took more than 85% of its supplies from the Middle East. The Soviet Union hosted the eighth World Petroleum Congress in June 1971.

Reserves. At the beginning of 1971 the total world proved and probable oil reserves increased to 620,700,000,000 bbl., compared with 540,600,000,000 bbl. for the previous year, enough for 33 years at current rates of consumption and discovery. The Western Hemisphere share was 83,300,-000,000 bbl., a slight drop to 13.4% of the total, and that of the Eastern Hemisphere,

537,000,000,000 bbl., an increase to 86.6%. The Middle East accounted for the largest share of the world reserves at 55%, while the U.S.S.R., Eastern Europe, and China totaled 16.1%, and the U.S. 7.5%.

Production. During 1970 world crude oil production increased by 9.6% to 47,875,000 bbl. a day. The Middle East dominated production with a share of 29.3%, 13,855,000 bbl. a day, with a marked recovery by Saudi Arabia to 3,550,000 bbl. a day. The U.S. produced 9,630,000 bbl. a day, 21% of the world total, an increase of 4.3% over 1969. Venezuelan production was 3,740,000 bbl. a day in 1970, 8% of the total and a 3% increase over 1969. During 1970 Nigeria made a spectacular recovery to double production to 1,085,000 bbl. a day.

World crude oil production totaled 48,-608,000 bbl. a day during January–June 1971, an increase of 8.7% over the corresponding period of 1970. Middle East production, reduced by restrictions in Libya and embargoes on Algerian production and in spite of the Nigerian increase, registered no percentage increase, and stood at 6,157,-000 bbl. a day. Soviet production was estimated at 7,945,000 bbl. a day, an increase of 6.5%.

Consumption. World consumption of petroleum in 1970 was 46,560,000 bbl. a day, an increase of 8.7% over 1969. Japanese demand again increased 17.7% to 4,030,000 bbl. a day, 9% of the world total. The U.S. remained the largest single consuming nation, 14,370,000 bbl. a day in 1970, a 4% increase over 1969 and 31% of the world total. Japan consumed only slightly less fuel oil than the U.S., 1,780,000 bbl. a day against 1,925,000, but only 725,000 of gasoline against 6,340,000 bbl. a day in the U.S. Western European consumption in 1970 was 12,710,000 bbl. a day, an increase of 11.4% over 1969, 28% of the world total. In the first half of 1971 world consumption ran at approximately the same level as current production. Japanese consumption during that period was 4.5 million bbl. a day, an increase of 11.5%, and Western European consumption was 13.5 billion bbl., an increase of 4.5%.

Refining. World refining capacity in 1970 was 50,260,000 bbl. a day, an increase of 7.3% over 1969. The capacity of the Western Hemisphere was 19,560,000, Western Europe 14,410,000, the Middle East 2,290,-000, and U.S.S.R., Eastern Europe, and China 7,350,000 bbl. a day. The U.S. accounted for 25.3% of the world total and Japan for 6.6%. In Western Europe, Italy had the largest share at 5.8%, while the region as a whole had 28.7%. Western European refiners planned to add half again as much to the area's capacity within five years.

Petrochemicals. The 1970–71 period was difficult for the petrochemical industry. After years of accelerating expansion, which averaged a growth of 15% annually from 1950 to 1970, a number of problems arose. Lower profits, rising costs, and slackening economic activity caused companies everywhere to adopt a more cautious approach to capital expenditure. Economies of scale helped to stabilize prices, but inflation and the complexity of modern technology tended to push some plants to the limits of economic risk. The industrial concentration characteristic of petrochemicals also led to pollution difficulties, and permission for plants was refused in 1971 in South Carolina, Scotland, and Amsterdam, among other places. Polyethylene plants continued to be the most numerous.

(R. W. Fe.)

See also Engineering Projects; Industrial Review; Mining; Transportation.

NUCLEAR POWER— PROMISE OR PERIL?

By Laurie John

We are convinced, on the basis of our research, that radiation to be expected from the rapidly-burgeoning atomic energy programs is a far more serious hazard than previously thought possible. We also estimate that the danger of cancer and leukemia as a result of atomic radiation is twenty-fold higher than the experts thought less than ten years ago. And we believe that the public is being deceived by a clever, well-financed propaganda campaign of delusion about 'clean, cheap, safe nuclear power.' There is no such thing."

Strong words. They were written by two U.S. Atomic Energy Commission (AEC) scientists, J. W. Gofman and A. R. Tamplin, and epitomized the virulent attack that has set the U.S. nuclear power industry reeling since early 1970. Caught in the ground swell of a public revolt against environmental pollution, the industry has witnessed the growth of a series of legislative obstacles in the way of its natural development, culminating in the Calvert Cliffs case in which a nuclear power station was planned, approved, and partly built in Maryland only to be denied a permit to operate. There it languished—surely one of the most expensive monuments to the power of public opinion. Whatever happened to the dream of clean, cheap, limitless power from the atom? Is the present state of affairs a pronounced case of overreaction, or is the American public waking up just in time?

Energy Crisis. Whatever answer is attempted to this highly charged question must be seen against the rapidly developing energy crisis in the United States. Between 1971 and 2001 the U.S. is expected to consume more energy than it has in its entire history. By the year 2001 the annual U.S. demand for energy is expected to double, while the annual worldwide demand will probably triple.

Meanwhile, ecologists have been using the mass media extensively to deliver an undeniable message: In pursuing the dream of improving his standard of living, man usually has plunged toward an immediate objective with too little care and planning for the by-products of his progress. As Chauncey Starr, dean of the School of Engineering and Applied Sciences at UCLA wrote: "These projected increases [in energy demand] will tax man's ability to discover, extract and refine fuels in the huge volumes necessary, to ship them safely, to find suitable locations for several hundred new electric-power stations in the U.S. (thousands worldwide) and to dispose of effluents and waste products with minimum harm to himself and his environment." Note the use of the word "minimum"; it implies that if man demands energy on this scale he will have to accept some sacrifices. It is impossible even now to extract coal without jeopardizing lives or scarring the surface of the earth, to find acceptable sites for power plants, or to control the effluents of our present fuel-burning machines so that nothing harmful emerges. Whether or not the power industry likes it, environmental considerations will loom ever larger in the design, siting, and operation of its production facilities. What worries those in the industry, though, is the climate of opinion that has allowed an environmental lobby to delay construction of a pumped-storage scheme to supply New York

City (arguably the cleanest way of all to supply power) so that the city now has to be fed from gas turbine generators floated on barges in the Hudson River—a costly and fume-producing process.

According to an AEC report to the 1971 UN international conference on the peaceful uses of atomic energy, held in Geneva, the dates by which time it will become uneconomic to produce fossil fuels are the year 2000 for oil, 2015 for natural gas, and 2400 for coal. Thus, if ever an energy source could be said to have arrived in the nick of time, it was nuclear energy. Although a 1,-000-Mw. nuclear power plant costs about 10% more than a fossil-fueled plant of the same capacity ($280 million as against $250 million), nuclear fuel was by 1971 cheaper than coal at the mouth of the mine. And the future economics favour the atom. New U.S. safety regulations have reduced the number of tons of coal produced per man-day from the 20 achieved in 1969 to fewer than 15 with the result, according to some estimates, that coal may double in price between 1971 and 1980. Any hope that the situation might be improved by automation was dealt a severe blow by the British Coal Board's experiences with the highly automated colliery at Bevercotes. So ultimately the public appears to be faced with a stark choice: get the oil lamps down from the attic and throw away your air conditioning, or accept nuclear power.

Shift to Nuclear Power. The history of mankind's changes from one predominant energy source to another suggests that roughly 50 years are needed for the energy economy to shift substantially to a new fuel. This is determined primarily by the long operating life of power-generating machinery and secondarily by the time needed to redirect the efforts of the manufacturers of this machinery. In the early 1970s the rapidly expanding demand for electricity was calling for power stations to be built faster than was possible for the relatively infant nuclear power industry. Consequently, fossil-fueled power stations would continue to be built for at least a decade. And because those stations generally had an economic life of about 30 years it was obvious that they would be playing a useful role even half a century after the swing to nuclear power.

But even with the slow phasing out of fossil-fueled plants, there was truth to the words of the president of the UN atomic energy conference, Glenn Seaborg: "Nuclear power is no longer around the corner but here." By 1971 the stage had been reached where nuclear power could compete with conventional means for generating electricity, and although the nuclear proportion of installed capacity was only 2%, by 1980 it was expected to be 13%. By 2000 nuclear power will probably account for 50% of the world's generating plant. Nuclear power obviously is going to be very big business indeed, and with the Americans, the Europeans, and the Japanese all eager to carve out their share of the business, the competition is certain to be intense. This is hardly the best climate in which to expect the nuclear power industries to concern themselves with environmental considerations for purely altruistic reasons.

There always will be those who point out that the increase in world energy consumption could be reduced if we all exercised restraint. But even if we do, the increase will still occur. Of the increase in demand by 2000, half will be due to the increase in population and half to the increase in per capita consumption. Assuming a total world demand for electricity of about 10 million Mw., the annual rate of installation of new generating capacity will be approximately 500,000 Mw. With nuclear power supplying half this electricity, it seems probable that one 1,000-Mw. nuclear power station will be brought into operation somewhere in the world every day.

Not that the geographic distribution of these reactors will be even. Far from it. Experience in the developed countries shows that nuclear reactors for public utilities are economic only in sizes of 500 Mw. and above. In such countries as Chile, Greece, and Israel the total consumption of electricity is only about 2,000 Mw., and so they cannot install nuclear stations large enough to

Laurie John is producer for the Science Unit of the British Broadcasting Corporation.

compete with fossil-fueled ones, even though the fossil fuels may be difficult to obtain.

As a result, the lion's share of the nuclear stations is sure to go to the developed countries. In the U.S. the number of nuclear plants operating in 1971 was 22. Another 55 plants were under construction, and more than 40 were on order. Westinghouse Electric Corp. estimated that U.S. utilities must build more than 1 million Mw. of new capacity between 1970 and 1990, or more than three times the present capacity. Of this 35% will be nuclear.

Pollution and Safety. The one nagging doubt is that the public may decide otherwise. "Strong and sometimes strident voices have been raised against the use of nuclear power on environmental grounds in a number of countries," said Seaborg. The irony was, he added, that "no field of science and technology —perhaps of all human endeavor—has applied such intensive voluntary restraints to ensure the safety of its activities as has nuclear energy . . . nuclear activities have achieved safety records at the very top of all industrial activities. Viewed objectively, nuclear power offers an unparalleled opportunity to reverse the trend towards greater and greater environmental pollution from conventional fuels and combustion products, with all their known and unknown hazards."

While this carries the ring of truth, it should be noted that Seaborg is retiring chairman of the AEC and, although a Nobel prizewinner for chemistry, is not thereby automatically free from bias. Perhaps one would do better to refer to another Nobel laureate, Hannes Alfvén, 1970 Nobel prizewinner for physics. In a memorandum to Sen. Mike Gravel of Alaska in April he wrote:

> In the long run fossil fuels cannot satisfy the rising energy demand in the world. There are only three sources of energy known which are sufficiently powerful: (a) solar energy, (b) fusion energy, and (c) fission energy. The first one is completely pollution-free, the second one almost pollution-free. The third one is necessarily combined with production of large quantities of radioactive poisonous elements. . . . In my opinion, the dangers associated with fission energy have not received necessary attention. Whether the pollution caused by fission reactors in normal operation is below a safe level or not is a controversial matter. If a reactor goes out of control, the consequences may be terrible. Even if extreme safety precautions are taken, the large quantities of radioactive material in them constitute a permanent danger. For example, in periods of political or social unrest, sabotage against reactors may cause catastrophes. Furthermore, in a full-scale fission program, the radioactive waste will soon become so enormous that a total poisoning of our planet is possible.

Alfvén went on to say that under such conditions, safety margins that might be quite acceptable in other fields were inadequate. Moreover, it was not clear whether there was any satisfactory solution to the problem of radioactive waste.

Gordon Rattray Taylor referred to this nuclear waste disposal problem in his *The Doomsday Book.* No one yet has contradicted his statement that in the Colorado River basin there are approximately 12 million tons of radioactive sand lying in uncovered heaps, being washed by the rain into a water system that provides drinking water to parts of California, Nevada, Utah, Wyoming, Colorado, New Mexico, and Arizona. When the AEC cut back its demand for uranium in the 1960s, he says, many mines closed, simply abandoning about 3 million tons of radioactive tailings, some directly on the riverbank. Attempts to cover them with gravel and establish vegetation were being made at the instigation of the Water Pollution Control Administration, but nothing could be found to grow on them. "Altogether there are now 30 million tons of this stuff in the U.S.," Taylor says, "and the amount increases daily."

As to the question of what to do with the radioactive waste from the reactors themselves, at present they travel to their final resting place in 70-ton containers that have been described as "the most hazardous objects, short of an atom bomb, known to man." They contain enough radioactivity, Taylor says, to poison whole cities. Radioactive materials also are transported by air. So undesirable are these wastes that they are buried deep in the earth, but only recently have we awakened to the fact that the earth's tremors might dislodge them. Rolf Eliassen of the

Wylfa nuclear power station on the island of Anglesey in Wales was completed early in 1971. The station has a generating capacity of 1,180 Mw., and was operated by the Central Electricity Generating Board.

AEC's General Advisory Committee posed a solution by describing processes for the separation and concentration of fission products from reactors in stable, solid materials like glass, to be stored in deep, geologically stable salt mines, but how near this was to being adopted was not made clear.

Public Relations. It is in this area that the nuclear power industry seems to be making a massive public relations miscalculation. While the opponents of nuclear power are, for the most part, articulate, to the point, and clear in their arguments, the defense is verbose and jargon-ridden to the point of apparent deviousness. Thus, if in its reports the AEC wishes to refer to the possibility of a reactor running away and the whole plant exploding, it does not use such direct language as that but says instead that there is a prospect of the core going "prompt critical" following which the plant will "disassemble." Addressing the UN conference on the peaceful uses of atomic energy, C. E. Larson, a commissioner of the AEC, said that the agency had a credibility problem: "No matter how factually correct the information and technically responsive the action, the public must believe that the information is factual and that the action is responsive."

Nuclear industry leaders have maintained that believability is a matter of trust and depends on candour in dealing with the public and affording the public a "timely and effective voice." Candour? Where in the multiplicity of literature from the nuclear power industry comparing the radiation from a nuclear power station to that from natural sources (brickwork and the granite in buildings in Aberdeen is the favourite example) has it been candidly explained that the nuclear radiation is *in addition to* natural sources and, since radiation effects are cumulative, that this increases the risk? And what is true for the AEC also applies to the United Kingdom Atomic Energy Authority (AEA). The AEA is justly proud of its safety record. The first and second generation of thermal nuclear power stations operated around the coast of Britain have proven amply their safety performances and have become acceptable urban neighbours. The next generation, fast-breeder reactors, is expected to be adopted as a standard for a series of reactors to be built in Britain. But where will they be built?

The prototype, built at Dounreay on the northernmost tip of Scotland, is as far away from any of Britain's population centres as is geographically possible. Why such extreme caution? There is no candid explanation in the literature that the AEA directs at the public. If the public forms the opinion that in the event of a serious accident the fast-breeder reactor could go off like a bomb, can they be blamed? So far the environment lobby in Britain has not developed the strength of its U.S. counterpart, but this is probably only a question of time.

The tragedy is that, properly and clearly stated, nuclear power would have an open and shut case. The increase in prosperity that cheap electricity from nuclear power could bring to India, for example, is unimaginable. The poorly irrigated Ganges Plain is riddled with wells that could be used if only cheap power were available to operate individual farm pumps. Nuclear-based energy centres producing electricity, water, and fertilizers could revolutionize the domestic economies of Chile, Peru, Mexico, many of the Mediterranean countries, Pakistan, and northern Australia. In the developed countries, too, dual-purpose nuclear plants could be attractive. Apparent drawbacks such as the outflow of warm cooling-water could be turned to advantage in such applications as heating enclosed spaces and boosting the action of sewerage works, while difficulties of siting could be overcome by floating the whole plant out to sea.

The reason for the present credibility gap, which is at the heart of all the opposition to nuclear power in the U.S., is not hard to guess. As far as the public is concerned, the bomb came first. Fission became subliminally synonymous with Hiroshima and Nagasaki, and fission power carried the same overtones. In vain did the industry start its whitewashing campaign by semantic juggling: "nuclear power" for "atomic power." (Nuclear was somehow more neutral.) So it overcorrected, oversold, and underplayed the dangers. Eventually, though, it was found out, and a reaction set in.

What the nuclear power industry now needs to do is to stop acting as if it has something to hide. The chances of dying as a result of the proximity of a nuclear power station compared with the chances of being killed on the roads are infinitesimal, and this comparison should be stressed. Alfvén may well be right when he claims that when we achieve power from fusion "the fission reactor, especially the breeder, will be of interest only as a danger which must be eliminated as soon as possible." But fusion is a long way off. Meanwhile, unless we can put a brake on our own breeding, and on the expectations of more and more people for a more comfortable life, we must make do with fission.

First section of Europe's largest nuclear power station is under construction near Biblis, W.Ger., in April 1971. When completed the station's reactor would produce 1,150 Mw. of electric current.

KEYSTONE

Furs

The U.S. fur industry turned in one of its poorest years ever in 1971, with business across the board falling further below the severely depressed levels of 1970. Economic difficulties, employment problems, and uncertainties arising from Pres. Richard Nixon's economic measures combined with a concentrated antifur campaign mounted by conservationist and humane societies to hand the industry a severe setback. Prices for nearly all types of furs either remained at the low 1970 levels or declined still further. Only a few managed to advance: certain longhairs, wild furs, and some scarce types of mutation mink.

In sharp contrast, the European fur industry remained prosperous, especially in West Germany, Switzerland, and Italy. Economic stability in these countries was credited for their better showing, together with the strength of their currencies in relation to the American dollar.

Furthermore, Paris and the other fashion centres strongly endorsed furs as part of the fashion world's return to elegance after several seasons of novelties and "costumes." Even this failed to lift the U.S. business out of the doldrums, although it did lead to greater use of fur as trimming on cloth coats and in small scarfs and boas.

The poor U.S. business brought further depletion in the ranks of mink ranchers in most producing countries. Probably the only exception was the Soviet Union, where economic factors seldom affect state-operated industries. There was about a 20% decline in the number of ranchers in the U.S. and Canada—where mink originated—and in the four Scandinavian countries, which produce at least half the world's supply. The U.S. Department of Agriculture reported that there were 2,227 ranches in all states producing mink in 1970, a drop of 20% from the previous year. By the end of the year, unofficial estimates were that 1971 would show a similar decline. On the basis of female mink held for breeding purposes, production of pelts in 1971 was estimated at approximately 3.2 million, compared with 4.5 million in 1970.

Other segments of the industry also continued to shrink. In New York, where the industry had once been concentrated in ten square blocks, the fur market area was down to about four square blocks and other businesses had begun to appear in the furriers' midst. The number of independent fur retailers also decreased, as furriers whose families had been in the craft for generations retired or went out of business and the retailing of furs shifted to larger department and specialty stores.

For the marketing year 1971–72, the world supply of mink was expected to be between 16 million and 17 million pelts, a decline of as much as 5 million. Production of other ranched furs, such as karakul lamb and fox, remained relatively stable. The supply of wild furs continued to decline as lower prices discouraged professional and amateur trappers.

Another factor was conservation. Newly enacted laws now controlled the killing of those species believed to be threatened with extinction. For fur purposes, these were mainly spotted types, such as leopard, tiger, cheetah, and jaguar, which had never constituted more than 1% of the overall fur business. However, some wide-ranging conservationist groups

Hunter kills baby harp seals during the annual hunt in the Gulf of St. Lawrence in March 1971. Canadian law requires hunters to kill seals with a blow to the skull, a method considered less cruel than others.

THE "NEW YORK TIMES"

were demanding that no animal be killed for its fur—even those raised on ranches specifically for the purpose. The antifur campaign was joined by one producer of fake furs although, ironically, the U.S. Environmental Protection Agency listed the producers of the synthetic fibres from which fake furs are made high among the major contributors to pollution.

One continuing target of conservation groups was the seal industry, despite praise for the U.S. government's Alaska seal program by, among others, the National Audubon Society (*Audubon Magazine*, March 1970). The strong anti-seal-fur campaign severely affected retail sales of this item, and prices at both semiannual sealskin auctions fell appreciably. Moreover, about 90% of the skins sold were taken by European buyers.

At year's end, representatives of the mink-ranching industries of the U.S., Canada, and Scandinavia were meeting in an attempt to submerge their traditional rivalries and rebuild their industry on an international level. Joint promotion programs, exchange of statistics and other information, and a more orderly marketing program were being negotiated.   (S. Pa.)

See also Fashion and Dress.

Gabon

A republic of western equatorial Africa and a member of the French Community, Gabon is bounded by Río Muni, Cameroon, the Congo (Brazzaville), and the Atlantic Ocean. Area: 103,100 sq.mi. (267,000 sq.km.). Pop. (1970 est.): 500,000. Cap. and largest city: Libreville (pop., 1969, 73,000). Language: French and Bantu dialects. Religion: traditional tribal beliefs; Christian minority. President in 1971, Albert Bernard Bongo.

Germain M'ba, an influential former member of the Gabonese opposition, was assassinated in September in Libreville under mysterious circumstances. He

had roundly condemned the intervention of French paratroops in Gabon after the coup of February 1964 but had been officially reconciled with the government for some years.

In February President Bongo received an official visit from Pres. Georges Pompidou of France in Libreville, during the latter's tour of five black African capitals. In December, Bongo visited Paris. In June the Gabonese ambassador to Paris, Georges Rawiri, was appointed minister of state for foreign affairs and cooperation. He replaced Jean-Rémy Ayouné, who was named minister of justice.

The 1971 budget set total expenditures at CFA Fr. 24.5 billion, an increase of about 24% over the original budget estimates in 1970. Ordinary expenditure was budgeted at CFA Fr. 16.7 billion, an increase of about 17% over 1970. More than CFA Fr. 3 million was allocated for educational purposes. Government revenue was expected to increase by about 8%.
(Ph. D.; X.)

Gambia, The

A small republic and member of the Commonwealth of Nations, The Gambia extends from the Atlantic Ocean along the lower Gambia River in West Africa, and is surrounded by Senegal. Area: 4,467 sq.mi. (11,569 sq.km.). Pop. (1971 est.): 374,770, including (1963) Mandingo 40.8%; Fula 13.5%; Wolof 12.9%; Jola 6.9%; Serahuli 6.8%; non-Africans 1.9%. Cap. and largest city: Bathurst (pop., 1971 est., 36,570). Language: English (official). Religion: predominantly Muslim. President in 1971, Sir Dauda Jawara.

A treaty of friendship with Nigeria was signed in February 1971, and relations between The Gambia and Senegal improved with the signing of a joint defense and security agreement in March. President Jawara in July visited Egypt, Sudan, and France. France agreed to extend cultural aid and promised Fr. 40 million toward the Gambia Bridge project.

In his New Year's message President Jawara pointed out that the budget had been balanced without outside aid for the fifth year; he summarized the diversity of developments, especially noting the proposed Gambia River basin project aimed at integrating agricultural development with Senegal. Good prices were obtained for the peanut and rice crops, and the 1967–71 development plan seemed likely to achieve its objectives, in particular the expansion of Bathurst Port and Tundum Airport, with £3 million of British aid.   (M. Mr.)

Gardening

Trees and shrubs properly placed can significantly reduce distracting noise caused by trucks, automobiles, and motorcycles, according to a three-year study completed in 1971 by the University of Nebraska with the cooperation of the Rocky Mountain Forest and Range Experiment Station of the U.S. Forest Service. Evergreen trees were found to be best for year-round noise screening. A belt located close to the noise source was more effective than one close to the protected area, and a belt midway between source and receiver was the least efficient. Best noise abatement was achieved by using trees and shrubs in conjunction with a soft surface such as tall grass or a plowed field. The best way to reduce noise from trucks starting up from toll booths on expressways was found to be a narrow band of soft ground very near the source, while dense foliage was effective in reducing noise of high-speed traffic.

A new insecticide, Zectran, was found to be effective against spruce budworm and jack pine budworm, which have caused extensive damage to forests and gardens in North America, particularly in Montana, Idaho, and Maine. Unlike DDT, Zectran was said to be nonpersistent, generally breaking down into harmless elements less than two days after exposure. It was being tested for use against other serious tree defoliators, including the gypsy moth, which was reaching epidemic proportions in the northeastern U.S.

In Britain, the Royal National Rose Society awarded its President's International Trophy for best seedling rose of the year and a gold medal to Fountain, a blood-red, moderately full rose raised by M. Tantau of Germany. The Henry Edland Memorial Medal for most fragrant rose went to the coral salmon and orange Truly Yours, raised by H. Robinson, and to a cherry-pink rose raised at the Melle, Belg., experimental station.

At Courtrai, Belg., Liverpool Echo won the Golden Rose award for the best rose of 1971. Scented Air (Dicksons) won the Golden Rose of The Hague at the international trials at The Hague, Neth.; two McGredy roses, John Waterer and Sant Catalina, were named most fragrant rose of the year and best climber, respectively. These and other awards in 1971 indicated a trend away from the bright orange colouring so popular in recent years and toward more delicate shades. The Gold Medallion of Baden was won jointly by Mullard Jubilee and Satchmo (both McGredy). Pania (McGredy) was judged the best hybrid tea at the first international rose trials to be held in New Zealand.

Apollo, a sunrise-yellow hybrid tea, and Portrait, a deep-pink hybrid tea, were All-America rose selections for 1972. Apollo is the result of a cross between High Time and Imperial Gold by David L. Armstrong. Portrait was hybridized by Carl Meyer, an amateur, from near Cincinnati, O. Two F_1 hybrid dwarf double zinnias, Peter Pan Plum and Peter Pan Pink, won gold medal awards as All-America selections for 1971. Both scored higher than any other entry in the almost 40 years of competition. Other All-America selections for 1971 included Queen of Hearts, an F_1 hybrid *Dianthus chinensis* with scarlet red single flowers; Southern Belle, an F_1 *Hibiscus moscheutos* in various shades of red, pink, and white; Little Darling, an F_1 hybrid snapdragon in mixed colours; Silver Puffs, a dwarf double pink hollyhock; and Early Xtra Sweet, an F_1 hybrid sweet corn.

A new evergreen magnolia, Majestic Beauty, able to withstand temperatures as low as five degrees below zero F, was introduced by a Pacific Coast nursery. The leaves are up to 15 in. long and the blooms 12 in. across.

Cheyenne, an extra cold-hardy, free-flowering lilac with highly fragrant, light-blue flowers, was released to nurserymen by the U.S. Department of Agriculture Plant Introductions Station. Grown from seed collected in northern China in 1930 by USDA plant explorers, Cheyenne does best in northern states where some lilacs are damaged by severe cold.

A new race of red, pink, purple, and white flowering streptocarpus was bred at the John Innes Institute in Britain; it has the same characteristics as the institute's successful but sterile blue-flowered Constant Nymph. Meanwhile, the Dutch experimental station at Aalsmeer produced five new mutations from Constant Nymph, using a combination of radiation and colchicine treatments. All are free-flowering and stand up well under normal home conditions.

Gerberas continued to increase in popularity in Europe. *Phytophthora* root rot had been the main obstacle to rapid expansion, but resistant strains— *e.g.,* Sympathy—were being bred in the Netherlands. At the Fünfhausen Experimental Station near Hamburg, W.Ger., plants that had been grown (isolated) in black polythene bags using a peat compost were still disease-free after four years.

Ornamentals bearing pure white blooms appeared possible with the discovery that an experimental compound, designated 6706 by its commercial developer, prevents colouring in flowers and plant foliage. Research with the compound was in progress at the USDA's Agricultural Research Center, Beltsville, Md. Chrysanthemum, marigold, and poinsettia plants produced pure white flowers after treatment with no sign of damage.

Plum rootstock clones selected for resistance to bacterial canker, good anchorage, compatibility with

Summer Carnival hollyhock was one of the All-America Selections award winners for 1972.

a full range of scion varieties, and ease of propagation from hardwood cuttings were shown by the East Malling Research Station in Britain. Sharka disease (plum pox) was identified on a small number of plum trees in Kent. Apart from an isolated case in 1966, this disease had not been recorded previously in England, but it had caused substantial losses in some countries of Europe.

Green Ball, a cross between cauliflower and broccoli, was introduced by Michigan State University. The head resembles cauliflower but is chartreuse green in colour rather than the customary white. It cooks rapidly and does not show a tendency to brown. In Britain mini-cauliflower or "minicolis" were developed at the National Vegetable Research Station, Wellesbourne. A big potential market was thought to exist for freezing, processing, and prepacking the cauliflowers, which range from $1\frac{1}{4}$ to 4 in. in diameter.

Dry summers and wet winters were being blamed for an epidemic of Dutch elm disease that was sweeping Britain. Biological methods of controlling the beetles (*Scolytus*) that spread the disease were being attempted, using a parasitic wasp called *Dendrosoter protuberans* obtainable from the Commonwealth Institute of Biologic Control, Geneva.

(J. G. S. M.; Tm. S.)

See also Agriculture; Life Sciences.

Encyclopædia Britannica Films. *Gardens for Everyone* (1967).

Geography

In his presidential address to the Association of American Geographers in 1969, Clyde F. Kohn characterized the 1960s as a decade during which geographic theory, modeling, and formal verification techniques grew in both utility and priority. The 1970s appeared to be marked not by a shift away from these techniques but by a decided emphasis on applying them to problems of the environment. John R. Borchert's AAG presidential address in 1970, "The Dust Bowl in the 1970's," and J. Ross Mackay's presidential address in 1971, "The World of Underground Ice," reflected this increasing attention to man's spatial activities and their interaction with the physical environment. This was coupled with expanded research, teaching, and planning in areas relevant to contemporary social problems.

The theme of social awareness was stressed by AAG president Norton S. Ginsburg in his remarks on "The Mission of a Scholarly Society" at the AAG annual meeting in Boston in April 1971. The immediate background to Ginsburg's address lay in the formation by the AAG council in 1970 of an ad hoc Committee on Development and Planning, charged with exploring how the association might respond to society's needs by mobilizing its membership toward significant, large-scale research efforts. The committee identified seven problem areas: urban problems, environmental quality, international development, minority groups in America, poverty, graduate education, and marine resources. Panels were appointed which met and prepared statements identifying long- and short-range goals in geographic research and training with particular reference to these concerns. A number of research and training proposals were prepared and various sources of financial support were being sought.

Meanwhile, similar research and training efforts were going forward under federal sponsorship and in university and private research programs. There was further planning for analysis of data to be derived from the projected Earth Resources Technical Satellite, and analysis techniques for processing and mapping data gained from a variety of remote sensing receptors were being refined. Federal research continued on geographic aspects of the law of the sea, specifically on problems of maritime jurisdiction, uses of the sea, and ultimate uses of the seabed. This work included cartographic inquiries on boundary problems of the continental shelf and on national claims to territorial seas.

In September 1971 a number of outstanding geographers presented a symposium on Geographical Perspectives and Urban Problems in Washington, D.C., sponsored by the Committee on Geography of the National Academy of Sciences. Throughout there was an appeal for a stronger emphasis on spatial perspectives in urban planning and development. Similarly, the annual meeting of the National Council for Geographic Education, held in Atlanta, Ga., in November, emphasized the quest for societal relevance. Topics included transportation, economic development, migration, social conflict and resolution, environmental quality, and responsive government.

Internationally, final planning for the 22nd International Geographical Congress, to be held in Montreal, Aug. 10–17, 1972, was virtually completed. Over 2,000 geographers from practically every nation in the world were expected to attend. Joint international conferences, seminars, and exchanges among geographers, especially among the Communist and non-Communist countries, were increasing. During the summer of 1971, 19 American and 10 Yugoslav graduate students in geography participated in a 12-week seminar in Yugoslavia.

Corresponding to the growth of geographic research was a proliferation of periodicals in geography and peripheral fields. The *Geographical Review* reported the inception of 135 geographic and 84 peripheral periodicals from 1961 through 1970, and new periodicals appearing in 1971 exceeded the number of those appearing in 1969 and 1970.

Geographers, while experiencing somewhat limited

Scientist inspects the canister used to orbit the PAGEOS satellite, a ten-story balloon orbited at 2,500 mi. and used as an aerial reference point in a program to survey the shape and dimensions of the earth.

UPI COMPIX

employment opportunities and alternatives, were not plagued with the underemployment or unemployment facing many in other natural and social sciences. Graduate and undergraduate enrollments in geography in the U.S. and Canada continued to grow, but at a decreasing rate.   (S. J. N.)

See also **Antarctica; Oceanography.**

Encyclopædia Britannica Films. *If You Could See the Earth* (1967); *Earth: Man's Home* (1970).

Geology

The growing acceptance of the theory of plate tectonics caused a revolution in geologic thought during recent years. According to this theory the earth's surface consists of a small number of rigid plates in motion relative to one another. Increasingly, the theory was providing a unifying framework that linked widely separated fields in the earth sciences, from volcanology and seismology to sedimentary geology and paleontology.

Until recently, the science of petrology, the study of rocks, had seemed unchanged by this general conceptual revolution. Petrology made enormous advances in the 1960s, particularly in the application of chemical experiments to minerals and rocks. These experiments had become increasingly sophisticated and were conducted over wide ranges of such physical conditions as temperature, pressure, and water-vapour pressure. Thus, a petrogenic grid, which relates a given mineral assemblage in a rock to those physical conditions under which it was formed, had been painstakingly erected. Then, with the acceptance of plate tectonics, the relevance of the petrogenic grid for the various rock types to the overall functioning of the lithosphere (solid part of the earth) was becoming apparent.

During 1971 several symposia and reviews dealt with petrologic aspects of plate tectonics, and a new concept, that of "petrotectonic assemblages," began to emerge. A petrotectonic assemblage is an association of rocks characteristic of a specific plate tectonic regime.

Divergent plate boundaries are characterized by mid-ocean ridge environments, where low-potassium basalt lavas overlie partly metamorphosed basalt, dolerite, and gabbro. In the oceanic abyssal plains thin marine argillite sediments, containing chert, overlie submarine basalts and then metamorphosed basalts, serpentinites, and peridotites. These so-called "ophiolite" sequences appear on land only when they have been subsequently uplifted at convergent plate boundaries where multiple thrusting commonly creates a mixture of sheared and thrust ophiolites.

At convergent plate boundaries, associated with ocean trench-island arc systems, one plate plunges beneath the other forming a "subduction zone." Beneath the trench, low temperature and high pressure form blueschists, whereas high temperature and low pressure beneath the island arc form a complementary belt of amphibolites or greenschists. The resulting paired metamorphic belts can be used to indicate the direction of plate motions in an ancient subduction zone. Characteristic igneous rocks of the arc are andesitic volcanics and granitic intrusives. The amount of potassium contained in the igneous rocks always increases away from the trench in the direction of increasing depth of the seismic activity of the subduction zone.

The above examples indicate that petrologists can make significant contributions to the plate tectonic concept. This approach to interpreting geologic history is expected to be particularly valuable in recognizing old plate boundaries in the Paleozoic regions and the Precambrian shields.

Lunar Geology. A new phase in lunar exploration began in August when the Apollo 15 astronauts greatly increased their surface mobility by using a lunar roving vehicle. The astronauts landed in the Hadley Rille area at the edge of the Mare Imbrium (Sea of Rains) and near the lunar Apennine Mountains. The results of the three-day mission tended to confirm the previously held theory that the Mare Imbrium, one of the moon's many large, dark-coloured, circular basins called "maria," probably was caused by the impact of a giant meteorite. This cataclysm created a large depression bordered by uplifted and tilted blocks of rock, forming the 15,000-ft. Apennine Mountains.

A major objective of Apollo 15 was to sample the rocks of the Apennine highlands in the hope that they might be part of the moon's original crust. Apollo 11, Apollo 12, and the Soviet Union's Luna 16 each returned rocks from mare sites that consisted essentially of younger lava flows extensively fragmented by meteorite impacts over a long period of time. Apollo 14 landed on the Fra Mauro formation, believed to be a blanket of material thrown out by the giant meteorite that excavated the 600-mi.-wide basin of the Mare Imbrium.

A second major objective was to study and sample Hadley Rille, a 1,200-ft.-deep gorge that winds across the floor of the Mare Imbrium. The origin of such sinuous rilles, which superficially resemble a meandering river valley on the earth, remained undetermined. Some observers attributed them to erosion by fluids, such as water, flowing over the lunar surface. Others suggested that they are lava channels or collapse features formed over lava tunnels from which the lava had drained out.

Perhaps the most surprising observation made by astronauts David Scott and James Irwin was that both the lower slopes of the Apennine Mountains and the upper part of the Hadley Rille show evidence of

A huge dome of lava boils upward to a height of 50 ft. during an eruption of the Kilauea volcano in Hawaii in May 1971. The eruptions had continued for more than two years and added over 100 ac. to the island of Hawaii.

well-defined rock layering. The discovery of up to ten layers in the wall of the rille was particularly significant. It would seem to create problems for the lava channel hypothesis of rille formation, as there is no obvious way in which molten lava can erode through earlier, solidified flows. The rock layering further suggests that the flooding of the mare basin involved a series of flows rather than being a single event. A team of seismologists announced in December that analysis of the tremors induced by space vehicle impacts led them to the conclusion that the moon is layered.

A preliminary determination of the age of a basalt from the rim of the rille gave 3,360,000,000 years. This contrasted with an Apollo 14 basalt sample from Fra Mauro that was 500 million years older. It previously had been thought that the violence of the impact that formed the Mare Imbrium caused melting, which generated basaltic lavas that then flooded the excavated basin. However, the wide range of observed ages suggested that the basalts of the Mare Imbrium are not simply impact melts but must reflect some other kind of volcanic activity.

Detailed measurements being carried out on photographs of the layering observed in the Apennine Mountains were expected to help decide if the layering predates the formation of the mare, or if it too was caused by the cataclysmic impact that formed the basin itself. Analysis of the rock and soil samples brought back by the astronauts and of the thousands of photographs, the moonquakes, and the data from various other geophysical experiments was expected to take many months or even years.

Drilling Technology. It is technologically easier to sample the surface of the moon than to sample the deep interior of our planet. The deepest holes in the earth drilled by man through 1971 penetrated less than 5 mi., only a meagre $\frac{1}{800}$ of the earth's radius. The past year, however, brought a number of new developments that may overcome the depth limitations that the high pressures and temperatures found at great depths impose on conventional drilling equipment.

The Moscow Institute of Drilling Engineering designed and was building equipment capable of boring to a depth of 9.5 mi. It was to use a turbine drilling system and drill pipes made of aluminum alloys instead of steel. An even more revolutionary concept was proposed by a group at the Los Alamos (N.M.) Scientific Laboratory. Their report suggested that a deep-drilling technique using rock melting is within the grasp of present technology. An operational laboratory-scale device melted rocks by using electrical heating. The major limitation of this system is the difficulty of delivering sufficient heat to the melting face of the penetrator. An initial design for a field-test unit proposed to overcome this problem by using heat pipes between the heat source and the rock face.

In the future, more ambitious plans call for using a nuclear reactor to melt its way through the rock. This device, called a "Nuclear Subterrene" by its designers, would be a self-contained tunneling probe that would require no drill-rotation system. The Los Alamos group suggested that ultimately a rock-melting Subterrene should be capable of probing deeply into the earth's crust, even perhaps as deep as 18 mi.

(W. A. E.)

See also Antarctica; Mining; Oceanography; Seismology; Speleology.

ENCYCLOPÆDIA BRITANNICA FILMS. *How Solid Is Rock?* (1968); *Reflections on Time* (1969); *Heartbeat of a Volcano* (1970); *How Level Is Sea Level?* (1970); *Controversy over the Moon* (1971); *Earthquakes—Lesson of a Disaster* (1971).

German Literature: *see* Literature

Germany

A country of central Europe, Germany was partitioned after World War II into the Federal Republic of Germany (Bundesrepublik Deutschland; West Germany) and the German Democratic Republic (Deutsche Demokratische Republik; East Germany), with a special provisional regime for Berlin. Germany is bordered by Denmark, the Netherlands, Belgium, Luxembourg, France, Switzerland, Austria, Czechoslovakia, and Poland and the North and Baltic seas.

Federal Republic of Germany. Area: 95,934 sq.mi. (248,469 sq.km.). Pop. (1970 est.): 61,846,400. Provisional cap.: Bonn (pop., 1970 est., 299,400). Largest city: Hamburg (pop., 1970 est., 1,817,100). (West Berlin, which is an enclave within East Germany, had a population of 2,134,300 in 1970.) Language: German. Religion (1966): Protestant 47.8%; Roman Catholic 47.8%; Jewish 0.04%. President in 1971, Gustav Heinemann; chancellor, Willy Brandt.

The most important event of 1971 was the signing on September 3 of the first major four-power agreement on Berlin since World War II. It provided for unimpeded transit between West Germany and West Berlin and for visits by West Berliners to East Berlin and East Germany. The federal government allowed the mark to float, or find its own parity in the currency markets, from May until the settlement of international monetary problems in December.

On October 20 the federal chancellor, Willy Brandt, was awarded the 1971 Nobel Peace Prize in recognition of the peace-promoting effect of his *Ostpolitik* and of his efforts toward Western European integration. (*See* NOBEL PRIZES.)

Domestic Affairs. The results of the several Länder elections did not show a clear political trend nationally, although it was obvious that the extreme rightist National Demokratische Partei (National Democratic Party, or NPD) had become a spent force. In November 1970 it had been eliminated altogether from the parliaments of Hesse and Bavaria, and suffered a similar fate in 1971 in Rhineland-Palatinate, Schleswig-Holstein, and Bremen. The Freie Demokratische Partei (Free Democratic Party, or FDP) lost five seats in Rhineland-Palatinate, and its representation in the Schleswig-Holstein Parliament. The Christlich-Demokratische Union (Christian Democratic Union, or CDU) increased its poll by 3.3% in Rhineland-Palatinate, and the Sozialdemokratische Partei Deutschlands (Social Democratic Party, or SPD) polled 3.7% more than at the previous election in 1967. The CDU won an absolute majority in Schleswig-Holstein, while the SPD polled just under 42%, a gain on its 1967 performance but two points down from its poll in Schleswig-Holstein in the federal election of September 1969. The SPD won an absolute majority in Bremen, increasing its vote by 5%, while the CDU poll went up about 20%.

At the CDU conference in Saarbrücken in October Rainer Barzel (*see* BIOGRAPHY), the party's parliamentary floor leader since 1963, was elected chairman with 344 votes. This was an important preliminary step toward his being chosen chancellor candidate for the next federal election in 1973. He was assured of the support of the CDU's Bavarian sister party, the

Christlich-Soziale Union (Christian Social Union, or CSU).

In his first policy statement to the Bundestag in 1969 Brandt had emphasized the need for electoral reform. By 1971 a great deal of legislation to this end had been prepared, although the chancellor's objectives were far from being realized. Educational reform was still very much in the planning stage. The aim was the creation of a democratic, adaptable educational system, offering equality of opportunity and attention to the special needs of individuals. This was to be attained by the introduction of comprehensive education—there were already experimental comprehensive schools in various parts of the country—by extending compulsory education to age 16, and by improving vocational training. At a cost of about DM. 28 billion, it was planned to create 200,000 new student places in the next four years, so that by 1975 a total of 665,000 places would be available. Within this period the capacity of the universities would thus be doubled.

In May the federal government approved a divorce law reform bill that based the grounds for divorce on the evidence of a broken marriage. After the divorce each partner was to be put on the same legal footing and the husband would not have to support his wife financially if she could adequately provide for herself. The bill was expected to become law by the summer of 1973. The government was also planning to reform the law on abortion to give three main grounds for legal abortion: ill health or poor social circumstances of the mother; pregnancy brought about as the result of rape; and a strong likelihood that the child would be born abnormal.

The Economy. By midyear the economic boom clearly had passed its peak, with real growth in the gross national product representing a 4% increase over the first half of 1970. Economic difficulties were blamed to a large extent on the import surcharge imposed by the U.S. government in August. In the fall there were reports of shortened workweeks and layoffs in certain industries, particularly steel. Increased militancy among workers, countered by a growing conviction in industry that the country was facing a serious recession, led to a strike by some 55,-000 metalworkers on November 22–23 against Audi,

Demonstrators burn East German and Communist red flags during a rally in West Berlin in August 1971 protesting the wall dividing the city.

Daimler-Benz, and 75 smaller concerns. The workers demanded 11% wage increases and rejected employers' offers of 4.5%. Before the strike was settled on December 10, according to a formula proposed by a state mediation commission that provided for 7.5% increases, more than 600,000 workers nationwide were out of work because of lockouts or layoffs caused by parts shortages.

The May floating of the mark, mainly in order to stem the inflow of dollars, had the effect of an upward revaluation of 13.57%, which was institutionalized by the December 18 agreement ending the international monetary crisis. The agreement provided for a smaller revaluation than had been expected with respect to the average of other Western currencies, but export capacities were weakened and were expected ultimately to reduce employment. Although Foreign Minister Walter Scheel noted that "we have, especially with our European neighbours, a new currency relationship that will also bring relief for our economy," the Cabinet promptly opened discussions on moves to stimulate the economy.

The resignation of the finance minister, Alex Möller, in May was not connected with the decision

---

GERMANY: Federal Republic

Education. (1968–69) Primary, pupils 5,877,-384, teachers 215,110; secondary, pupils 2,038,-948, teachers 129,121; vocational, pupils 2,185,-789, teachers 107,021; higher (including 39 universities), students 430,904, teaching staff 36,-438.

Finance. Monetary unit: Deutsche Mark, with a par value of DM. 3.66 to U.S. $1 (DM. 8.78 = £1 sterling) and, following the floating of the Deutsche Mark, from May 9, 1971, a free rate (Sept. 27, 1971) of DM. 3.31 to U.S. $1 (DM. 8.22 = £1 sterling). Gold, SDRs, and foreign exchange, central bank: (June 1971) U.S. $15,698,-000,000; (June 1970) U.S. $8,443,000,000. Budget (federal; 1970 est.): revenue DM. 90,459,-000,000; expenditure DM. 89,316,000,000. Gross national product: (1970) DM. 677.7 billion; (1969) DM. 602.8 billion. Money supply: (May 1971) DM. 104.2 billion; (May 1970) DM. 92.4 billion. Cost of living (1963 = 100): (June 1971) 127; (June 1970) 121.

Foreign Trade. (1970) Imports DM. 109,140,-000,000; exports DM. 125,160,000,000. Import sources: EEC 44% (France 13%, Netherlands 12%, Italy 10%, Belgium-Luxembourg 10%); U.S. 11%. Export destinations: EEC 40% (France 12%, Netherlands 11%, Italy 9%, Belgium-Luxembourg 8%); U.S. 9%; Switzerland

6%; Austria 5%. Main exports: machinery 29%; motor vehicles 15%; chemicals 10%; iron and steel 9%; textile yarns and fabrics 6%.

Transport and Communications. Roads (1970) 416,000 km. (including 4,461 km. autobahns). Motor vehicles in use (1970): passenger 14,376,484; commercial 1,143,565. Railways (1969): federal 29,574 km. (including 8,165 km. electrified), private 4,199 km.; traffic (1970) 38,-960,000,000 passenger-km., freight 71,996,000,-000 net ton-km. Air traffic (1970): 8,254,000,000 passenger-km.; freight 529,802,000 net ton-km. Navigable inland waterways in regular use (1969) 4,415 km.; freight 47,650,000,000 ton-km. Shipping (1970): merchant vessels 100 gross tons and over 2,868; gross tonnage 7,881,000. Telephones (Dec. 1969) 12,456,268. Radio receivers (Dec. 1969) 28.5 million. Television receivers (Dec. 1969) 15,970,000.

Agriculture. Production (in 000; metric tons; 1970; 1969 in parentheses): wheat 5,662 (6,-000); rye 2,663 (2,886); barley 4,754 (5,130); oats 2,484 (2,976); potatoes 16,250 (15,985); apples 1,745 (2,552); sugar, raw value (1970–71) 2,060, (1969–70) 2,019; wine (1969) 547, (1968) 556; milk c. 22,545 (22,262); butter (1969) 522, (1968) 537; cheese (1969) 470,

(1968) 537; beef and veal 1,271 (1,187); pork 2,163 (2,141); fish catch (1969) 652, (1968) 682. Livestock (in 000; Dec. 1969): cattle 14,-286; pigs 19,323; sheep 841; horses used in agriculture 255; chickens 96,153.

Industry. Index of production (1963 = 100): (1970) 153; (1969) 144. Unemployment: (1970) 0.7%; (1969) 0.8%. Fuel and power (in 000; metric tons; 1970): coal 111,272; lignite 107,767; crude oil 7,536; coke (1969) 39,010; electricity (kw-hr.) 242,610,000; natural gas (cu.m.) 25,400,000; manufactured gas (cu.m.) 20,122,000. Production (in 000; metric tons; 1970): iron ore (32% metal content) 5,531; pig iron 33,896; crude steel 45,041; aluminum 568; copper 40; lead 306; zinc 319; cement 37,-944; sulfuric acid 4,436; cotton yarn 239; woven cotton fabrics 182; wool yarn 79; rayon, etc., filament yarn 78; rayon, etc., staple fibre 149; nylon, etc., filament yarn 277; nylon, etc., fibre 294; nitrogenous fertilizers (1969–70) 1,574; potash (oxide content; 1969) 2,626; synthetic rubber 320; plastics and resins 4,297; passenger cars (units) 3,525; commercial vehicles (units) 307. Merchant vessels launched (100 gross tons and over; 1970) 1,693,000 gross tons. New dwelling units completed (1970) 478,000.

Wearing gas masks and carrying a poster that reads "Save our city," German adults and children march down streets in Bonn in March 1971 to protest improper traffic planning.
KEYSTONE

to float the mark. He felt that he could not summon the necessary strength to persuade some of his Cabinet colleagues to trim their budget estimates. His post was taken over by the economics minister, Karl Schiller (*see* BIOGRAPHY), who combined the two ministries and thus became economics "overlord."

Foreign Affairs. The four-power agreement on Berlin meant that the Soviet Union had accepted the reality of the close economic and political ties between West Berlin and West Germany, but it also underlined that West Berlin was not part of the Federal Republic. The first part of the agreement was signed in West Berlin in September; the second part, implementing the principles laid down by the four powers, was initialed, after several setbacks in negotiations, by representatives of the two German governments and of the West Berlin Senate on December 11. The third part, consisting of a final protocol, remained to be signed by the four powers. This was expected to be delayed at least six months because the Soviet government had made its approval contingent upon the Bundestag's ratification of the treaties concluded in 1970 by the West German government with the Soviet Union and Poland, which Brandt submitted only after the Berlin package had been initialed.

Some two weeks after the first part of the agreement had been signed, Brandt went to the Crimea to meet the leader of the Soviet Communist Party, Leonid I. Brezhnev, at the invitation of the U.S.S.R. The most important topics of the talks were mutual and balanced force reductions and a European security conference. The chancellor gained the impression that Brezhnev agreed that troop reductions were not a prerogative of the superpowers, and that not only troops stationed on foreign soil but national forces also should be reduced. It was agreed that a normalization of relations between the two German states on the basis of equality and respect for each other's sovereignty "seems today possible" and that an important step in this direction would be the entry of both states into the United Nations. Hitherto Bonn had insisted that this would come at the end of the process of normalization.

There was some criticism at home and abroad of the chancellor's visit, and when he returned he took pains to emphasize his loyalty to the Atlantic Alliance. On December 28–29 he journeyed to the United States for talks with Pres. Richard Nixon at Key Biscayne, Fla. (N. CR.)

Trucks wait at checkpoint Marienborn after East Germany blocked traffic to West Berlin for six hours during a conference of West German leaders in March 1971.

West Berlin. Ten years after the building of the Berlin wall, after 33 sessions over 17 months, the ambassadors of Britain, France, the United States, and the U.S.S.R., meeting in the U.S. sector of the city, signed the first stage of a Quadripartite Agreement on Berlin. In it the four powers declared that "there shall be no use or threat of force in the area and that disputes shall be settled solely by peaceful means." This was the first written agreement on Berlin reached by the four powers since 1949. It brought to an end a period that reached acute crises in 1948 with the blockade, in 1958 with the Khrushchev ultimatum, and on Aug. 13, 1961, with the construction of the wall.

On the all-important question of access to Berlin, the U.S.S.R. abandoned the position of a decade and a half that civilian transit traffic was the responsibility of East Germany and accepted again its postwar obligation of combined responsibility with the three Western powers. Civilian passenger traffic by road, rail, and water between the Western sector of Berlin and West Germany across East German territory would be "simplified and unhindered." A lump sum to be paid by the West German government was to replace individual fees for the use of the autobahn and for East German visas.

Existing West German government offices were to remain in West Berlin, but the federal president and members of the government, while continuing to visit the city, would no longer be permitted to carry out "acts of sovereignty" there. The West German president would no longer be elected in Berlin, nor would plenary sessions of the two houses of the Bundestag be held in West Berlin. But the established procedures regarding the application of federal legislation in West Berlin would remain unchanged.

West Berliners visiting the Soviet Union and other Eastern European countries would be entitled to the consular protection of West Germany and West German passports used by West Berliners would be recognized, provided they contained a stamp showing that they had been issued on behalf of the three Western powers in West Berlin. West Germany was to represent West Berlin in international organizations.

The Western powers in their turn agreed to the establishment of a Soviet consulate general in West Berlin whose activities would be purely consular in character and would not encroach on the political functions or any other aspect of four-power rights. The consul general was to be accredited "to the appropriate authorities of the three [Western] governments."

The agreement entitled citizens of West Berlin to visit East Berlin and East Germany under conditions comparable to those applying to other persons entering these areas. Negotiations on the administrative details bogged down twice over East Germany's insistence that some limits be placed on the flow of West Berliners into East Berlin. This prevented the initialing of the two other aspects of the negotiations, which were concluded on December 4, regulating the transit of goods and West Germans across East Germany to West Berlin and the exchange of small parcels of land between West Berlin and East Germany. Under a compromise reached on December 10, West Berliners would be able to pay periodic visits of up to 30 days a year to East Berlin, but would have to obtain entry permits—to be issued on demand but only during designated hours—and could not use their own transportation except under certain conditions.

D.P.A.—PICTORIAL PARADE

In the elections for West Berlin's Parliament the Social Democratic Party retained its majority, receiving 50.4% of the votes cast, although this represented a decline of 6.5% from the results of the previous election. The Christian Democratic Union, on the other hand, gained 5.3% to give it 38.2% of the total vote. The Free Democratic Party, the SPD's coalition partner, increased its share slightly to 8.5%. In contrast, the West Berlin branch of the East German Socialist Unity Party received only 2.3% of total votes cast. Klaus Schütz, the governing mayor, was reelected for a further four years. (S. E. S.)

German Democratic Republic. Area: 41,768 sq.mi. (108,178 sq.km.). Pop. (1971): 17,040,926. Cap. and largest city: East Berlin (pop., 1971, 1,084,-866). Language: German. Religion (1950): Protestant 81.3%; Roman Catholic 11%. First secretaries of the Socialist Unity (Communist) Party (SED) in 1971, Walter Ulbricht and, from May 3, Erich Honecker; chief of state, Ulbricht; minister president (premier), Willi Stoph.

The resignation of 77-year-old Walter Ulbricht from the post of first secretary of the SED was announced on May 3, 1971, and marked the beginning of a period of collective leadership. When *Neues Deutschland,* the party organ, published the photos of the members of the new SED Politburo elected after the eighth party congress on June 19, that of Erich Honecker (*see* BIOGRAPHY), the new first secretary, was the same size as those of other members. This was in striking contrast to past occasions when Ulbricht's picture had been larger than the others. Members were now listed in alphabetical order rather than by seniority.

Ulbricht had been the longest surviving Communist Party leader in Eastern Europe; he had become the SED's secretary-general in 1950. He was to remain chief of state as chairman of the State Council, and the title of party chairman was revived for him. When the congress opened on June 15, Ulbricht, who was due to welcome the 90 delegations from 79 countries, was absent and remained so for its duration. His address was read by Hermann Axen, a member of the Politburo, who announced that Ulbricht could not attend because of illness. On June 24 Ulbricht was relieved of a further function, that of chairman of the National Defense Council; the People's Chamber elected Erich Honecker in his place. On November 14, 99.8% of the votes cast for the 434 members of the People's Chamber went to the official slate. On November 26 the new Chamber reelected Honecker, Ulbricht, and Willi Stoph, the premier, to their posts.

Erich Honecker joins delegates at the ninth Congress of Free German Youth. Honecker succeeded Walter Ulbricht in May 1971 as first secretary of the East German Socialist Unity (Communist) Party.

SED party membership, according to the Central Committee report, was 1,909,859, compared with 1,769,912 at the time of the seventh congress in 1967. The Politburo had 16 full members including Ulbricht, against 15 after the seventh congress, and seven candidate members (formerly six); for the first time since 1953 the state security chief had a seat in the Politburo, as a candidate member. The new appointments to the Politburo and Secretariat and the accompanying changes in the Central Committee strengthened the representation of party officials at the expense of economists and technocrats.

Commenting on the four-power agreement on Berlin, Honecker said on September 5 that it had further strengthened the international standing of East Germany because for the first time the three Western powers had made declarations about East Germany as a sovereign state that had the binding character of international law. The same point was made in a resolution issued by the Central Committee, which also added that a policy of peaceful coexistence was not tantamount to ideological coexistence. The first positive result of the talks between the two Germanys was a postal agreement reached on September 30, which provided for considerable improvements in post, telegraph, and telephone services between the two countries and between West and East Berlin.

The directives for the 1971–75 five-year-plan, published ahead of the party congress on May 5, envisaged slightly lower targets for productivity, national income, and industrial production than in the previous plan. Emphasis was to be on proportional develop-

---

GERMANY: Democratic Republic

Education. (1968–69) Primary, pupils 2,378,-257; secondary, pupils 109,382; vocational, pupils 580,580; teacher training, students 24,556; primary, secondary, vocational, and teacher training, teachers 131,000; higher (including 7 universities), students 78,308, teaching staff (1966–67) 14,200.

Finance. Monetary unit: "Mark of the German Bank of Issue" (MDN. or Ostmark), with (Sept. 27, 1971) an official exchange rate of MDN.(O.) 2.22 to U.S. $1 (MDN.[O.] 5.33 = £1 sterling) and a general rate (valuta Mark) of MDN.(O.) 4.20 to U.S. $1 (MDN.[O.] 10 = £1 sterling). Budget (1969): revenue MDN.(O.) 65,761,000,000; expenditure MDN.(O.) 65,004,-000,000. Gross material product: (1968) MDN.(O.) 108.1 billion; (1967) MDN.(O.) 102.6 billion.

Foreign Trade. (1970) Imports MDN.(O.) 20,357,000,000; exports MDN.(O.) 19,240,000,-000. Import sources: U.S.S.R. 40%; Czechoslo-

vakia 9%; West Germany 9%; Poland 6%. Export destinations: U.S.S.R. 38%; Czechoslovakia 10%; Poland 9%; West Germany 8%; Hungary 6%. Main exports (1969): machinery 38%; transport equipment 10%; chemicals; lignite.

Transport and Communications. Roads (1970) c. 160,000 km. (including 45,729 km. main roads and 1,413 km. autobahns). Motor vehicles in use (1969): passenger 1,039,200; commercial 171;675. Railways (1970): 14,658 km. (including 1,357 km. electrified); traffic 17,667,-000,000 passenger-km., freight 41,514,000,000 net ton-km. Air traffic (1969): 842.7 million passenger-km.; freight 23,319,000 net ton-km. Navigable inland waterways in regular use (1970) 2,519 km.; freight (1969) 2,143,000,000 ton-km. Shipping (1970): merchant vessels 100 gross tons and over 423; gross tonnage 988,640. Telephones (Dec. 1969) 1,986,190. Radio receivers (Dec. 1969) 5,983,000. Television receivers (Dec. 1969) 4,337,000.

Agriculture. Production (in 000; metric tons; 1970; 1969 in parentheses): potatoes c. 10,500 (8,832); wheat c. 2,012 (1,987); rye c. 1,474 (1,544); barley c. 2,048 (2,067); oats c. 780 (841); sugar, raw value (1970–71) c. 489, (1969–70) c. 440; rapeseed c. 220 (165). Livestock (in 000; Dec. 1969): cattle 5,171; sheep 1,696; pigs 9,273; horses used in agriculture 148; poultry c. 38,900.

Industry. Index of production (1963 = 100): (1970) 153; (1969) 144. Production (in 000; metric tons; 1970): lignite 260,600; coal (1969) 1,334; petroleum products (1969) 9,903; manufactured gas (cu. m.; 1969) 4,066,000; electricity (kw-hr.) 67,650,000; iron ore (25% metal content) 900; pig iron 1,996; crude steel 5,053; potash (oxide content; 1969) c. 2,300; cement (1969) 7,410; sulfuric acid 1,100; synthetic rubber (1969) 114; cotton yarn (1969) 69; rayon filaments and fibres (1969) 160; passenger cars (units) 121; commercial vehicles (units) 27.

ment and on the introduction of more modern technology in an attempt to reduce costs. This appeared to indicate criticism of the previous investment policy. At the second plenary session of the Central Committee on September 15, Honecker said that despite an increase in output of about 6.1% in the first eight months of 1971, there were still "anomalies" and "a number of negative factors" in the economy.

Diplomatic relations were established with Chile on March 16, Equatorial Guinea on April 14, and Chad on July 6. Only 16 months after recognizing East Germany, the Central African Republic broke off relations with it; Pres. Jean-Bédel Bokassa made it clear on August 13 that the main reason for his move was his dissatisfaction with the implementation of agreements on development aid.

On May 28 two West German businessmen who earlier in the year had been sentenced to long-term imprisonment for economic sabotage were released. Six young U.S. citizens who had been sentenced to prison terms of from 6 to 22 months were unexpectedly freed on July 17.   (S. E. S.)

Ghana

A republic of West Africa and member of the Commonwealth of Nations, Ghana is on the Gulf of Guinea and is bordered by Ivory Coast, Upper Volta, and Togo. Area: 92,100 sq.mi. (238,500 sq.km.). Pop. (1970): 8,545,561. Cap. and largest city: Accra (pop., 1970, 562,220). Language: English (official); local Sudanic dialects. Religion (1960): Christian 43%; Muslim 12%; animist 38%. President in 1971, Edward Akufo-Addo; prime minister, Kofi Busia.

GHANA

Education. (1967–68) Primary, pupils 1,288,383; secondary, pupils 179,044; primary and secondary, teachers 52,097; vocational (1966–67), pupils 17,587, teachers 775; teacher training, students 16,782, teachers 1,200; higher, students 4,768, teaching staff 672.

Finance. Monetary unit: new cedi, with a par value of 1.02 cedi to U.S. $1 (2.45 cedis = £1 sterling) and a free rate (Sept. 27, 1971) of 0.99 cedi to U.S. $1. Gold, SDRs, and foreign exchange, official: (June 1971) U.S. $67 million; (June 1970) U.S. $70.6 million. Budget (1970–71 est.): revenue 426.7 million cedis; ordinary expenditure 324.4 million cedis; development expenditure 137.5 million cedis. Gross domestic product: (1969) 2,328,000,000 cedis; (1968) 2,067,-000,000 cedis. Money supply: (April 1971) 276 million cedis; (April 1970) 287.7 million cedis.

Foreign Trade. (1970) Imports 419,047,000 cedis; exports 467,378,000 cedis. Import sources: U.K. 24%; U.S. 18%; West Germany 11%; Japan 6%. Export destinations: U.K. 23%; U.S. 18%; West Germany 10%; Netherlands 9%; U.S.S.R. 9%. Main exports: cocoa 64%; timber 8%; gold 7%; cocoa butter 6%.

Transport and Communications. Roads (1969) c. 31,000 km. Motor vehicles in use (1969): passenger 29,400; commercial 17,400. Railways: (1969) 953 km; traffic (1970) 536 million passenger-km., freight 311 million net ton-km. Air traffic (1970): 135.2 million passenger-km.; freight 3,490,000 net ton-km. Shipping (1970): merchant vessels 100 gross tons and over 73; gross tonnage 166,465. Telephones (Dec. 1969) 43,863. Radio receivers (Dec. 1969) 700,000. Television receivers (Dec. 1969) 12,000.

Agriculture. Production (in 000; metric tons; 1970; 1969 in parentheses): corn c. 290 (305); cassava (1969) c. 1,400, (1968) 1,446; sweet potatoes (1969) c. 1,400, (1968) 1,351; millet and sorghum c. 150 (189); cocoa (exports; 1970–71) 385, (1969–70) 415. Livestock (in 000; 1969–70): cattle c. 630; sheep c. 650; pigs c. 330; goats c. 770.

Industry. Production (in 000; 1969): gold (troy oz.) 708; diamonds (metric carats) 2,391; manganese ore (metal content; metric tons) 160; bauxite (metric tons; 1970) 341; electricity (kw-hr.; 1970) 2,920,000.

Prime Minister Busia's major policy statement at the conference of Commonwealth heads of government in Singapore in January 1971 enhanced his stature as a leading moderate. Though condemning the sale of British arms to South Africa, he upheld the Ivory Coast's proposals for a continued dialogue on the issue, subject to a joint African approach.

Ghana was quick to recognize Idi Amin's Uganda coup of January 25, a decision based on the principle of noninterference in the domestic affairs of other states as expressed in the charter of the Organization of African Unity. The April demand by the National Union of Ghana Students for return and amnesty for ex-president Kwame Nkrumah was officially denounced, and in August it was made a crime to display his picture.

Support for Israel's right to a secure existence was expressed during Foreign Minister Abba Eban's visit to Ghana in June; on May 28 a general agreement on a Joint Commission on Cooperation in cultural and technical affairs, trade, and communications was signed with the Ivory Coast. Good relations with other African states suffered with the effecting in July of the second phase of the Control of Aliens Act, involving deportation, limitation of residence, and the take-over of certain categories of alien-owned business.

In a Cabinet reshuffle in January, Busia took over the ministries of Information and Economic Planning and transferred the minister of foreign affairs, Victor Owusu, to the Justice Department. Other government reforms included the July Civil Service Code, banning public servants from political activities and enforcing an oath of secrecy, and the 1971 Local Administration bill, which established local, district, and regional councils. Members of the local councils were scheduled to be elected in April 1972, while the chairmen of the others were to be chosen by the prime minister. The 1971 auditor-general's report expressed the hope that the bill would end the "chaotic finances" of local government.

Political stability continued to depend on economic recovery from the extravagances of the Nkrumah regime. Ghana's economy remained geared to cocoa with its notoriously volatile world prices. Not only did these prices fall during 1970–71, but Ghana's share in the world production total had declined from 35 to 27% since 1964. A World Bank loan, announced in June, established a 15 million cedi, five-year cocoa rehabilitation project. Aid was also provided to improve conditions for peasant farmers, who provided 75% of Ghana's exports.

Despite the second International Fair, held in February, the 25% bonus offered to Ghanaian exporters, and brighter prospects for mineral exploitation, an acute shortage of foreign exchange remained Ghana's chief problem. High unemployment figures and increasing political frustration also became evident during the year. In his speech opening the third session of Parliament in July, President Akufo-Addo spoke of unemployment of the expanding labour force as a major national problem. He condemned strikers and deteriorating labour relations and saw the solution in terms of labour-intensive agriculture and the development of local production to ease the pressure on foreign exchange. In August the finance minister, J. H. Mensah, introduced an austerity budget that banned a number of imports. The Trades Union Congress was abolished in September and its assets were frozen. In December the cedi was devalued by 44%.

(M. Mr.)

Gibraltar:
see Dependent States

Glass Manufacture:
see Industrial Review

Gold:
see Mining; Payments and Reserves, International

Golf

When Lee Trevino (*see* BIOGRAPHY) rapped home his final putt in the British Open at Birkdale, he completed an achievement without parallel in the history of championship golf. Nineteen days earlier he had beaten Jack Nicklaus in a play-off for the U.S. Open at the Merion Golf Club, Ardmore, Pa., and in between had won the Canadian Open as well. Only Bobby Jones (1926, 1930), Gene Sarazen (1932), and Ben Hogan (1953) previously had won the British and U.S. opens in the same year, and none of them faced as severe competition as Trevino did in both events. Week after week during the early summer Trevino was in the championship reckoning, and he came to Merion almost exploding with confidence. After three rounds he was four strokes behind a young amateur, Jim Simons, who stayed within a stroke of the pace until the 72nd hole. Trevino's final round of 69 put him out of reach of all but Nicklaus, who needed a four to tie on one of the world's most demanding final holes. Just as Hogan had done 21 years earlier, when faced with a similar crisis, Nicklaus played it superbly and almost made a winning birdie. In the play-off round next day, however, Nicklaus made three costly mistakes, twice taking two shots to escape from a bunker, and Trevino's ruthless steadiness gained him the title by three strokes. The championship was a triumph for the quality of Merion, one of the shortest courses used for the U.S. Open in modern times. Only Trevino and Nicklaus could match par for the 72 holes.

The magic was still upon Trevino at Birkdale. His first round might have cost him many more than 69, but seven times in the first nine holes he holed out in a single putt. He finished his second round with an eagle and afterward was never caught: yet just when he seemed to have the championship won easily his drive to the 71st landed in a sand trap and he took a seven. His partner and closest rival, Liang Huan Lu of Taiwan, whose courtly manners and beautiful straight golf had made him a hero with the crowds, also had a dramatic finish. His second shot on the last hole was violently hooked but bounced from a woman's head back to the fairway, from where he was down in two more strokes. This meant that Trevino had to finish with a four to win. He did so, and Liang Huan Lu was second. Tony Jacklin, who had lost his U.S. title at Merion and had been out of form for some time, gave a courageous performance to finish third, two strokes behind Trevino. Nicklaus shared fifth place with Charles Coody, who had earlier won the Masters at Augusta, Ga. This was the surprise of the professional year. Coody had not been outstandingly successful on the tour, but he opened the Masters with a 66. With a round to go he was even with Nicklaus who, having won the U.S. Professional Golfers' Association (PGA) championship at Palm Beach Gardens, Fla., in February, was bent upon the professional "grand slam." But it was Coody, not Nicklaus, who finished solidly under great pressure similar to that which had destroyed him two years earlier. He was 70; Nicklaus at 72 tied for second with John Miller, one of the brightest young lights to arrive on the scene in many years. Later Coody again beat Nicklaus in the World Series of Golf at Akron, O., winning the first prize of $50,000.

The established champions did well on the tour during the year. For months the money list was headed by Trevino, Nicklaus, and Arnold Palmer, each of whom had won four events by September, with Gary Player and Miller Barber not far behind. Nicklaus and Palmer teamed as the most formidable combination in the world in foursome competition. Palmer came surging back to his old form with a commanding victory in the Westchester Open at Harrison, N.Y., but could not revive it in the major championships. Nicklaus emerged as the season's leading money winner with a record $244,490.

On the international front, teams from the British Isles had one of their most successful years for a generation and more. In the Walker Cup match at St. Andrews, Scot., Michael Bonallack led the British magnificently to a memorable victory (13–11) over a powerful U.S. team that included several outstanding young players, of whom Steve Melnyk, Lanny Wadkins, and Allen Miller turned professional later in the year. For the first time in history the British won all foursome matches on the opening morning, but the Americans retaliated by winning six of the singles and led by a point going into the final day. They increased this lead to two after the foursomes, and seemed destined for an easy victory when Wadkins shot away from Bonallack in the first single. The British had to win five and tie one of the remaining seven matches, and in an unforgettable counterattack actually won six in succession. Hugh Stuart made the first thrust by beating Marvin Giles, but the great inspiration came from the youngest player, Warren Humphreys, who overcame the powerful Melnyk. Finally, David Marsh hit a superb number three iron to the heart of the 17th green, the menacing Road Hole, making sure of at least a tie with Bill Hyndman, and in fact winning by halving the 18th; and so Britain won for the first time since 1938. The Americans plainly were troubled on occasion by the type of strokes demanded on certain holes, and this failure to read the course, more than anything else, cost them the match. They had some consolation the following week at Carnoustie, Scot., when Melnyk beat a fellow American, James Simons, 3 and 2 in the final of the British Amateur championship. In the U.S. Amateur championship Gary Cowan of Canada, winner in 1966, finished in spectacular fashion by holing a number nine iron shot out of trees to the last green for an eagle when needing a par four to beat Eddie Pearce.

Proof that British golfers had lost their fear of

Lee Trevino sinks a birdie putt on the first sudden-death hole to win the Canadian Open in Montreal on July 4, 1971.

UPI COMPIX

Tom Weiskopf leaps
into the air to shake
hands with his caddy
after winning the Kemper
Open in Charlotte, N.C.,
on June 13, 1971.

Americans came in the Ryder Cup matches in St. Louis, Mo. One of the strongest teams ever to represent the United States, including, for the first time, Palmer, Nicklaus, and Trevino, won 18½–13½, by far the best British showing in the U.S. The British led by a point after the eight foursomes matches, but the Americans won six of the foursomes the following day. When Trevino, morning and afternoon in the singles, gave his side a great lead by beating Jacklin and Brian Huggett, a U.S. victory was almost assured, but the British made a match of it. Peter Oosterhuis, their outstanding golfer, beat Gene Littler and Palmer.

Nicklaus and Trevino represented the United States in the World Cup tournament at Palm Beach Gardens and won comfortably with a combined score of 555. Nicklaus also won the Qantas Australian Open and the Dunlop Masters by overwhelming margins.

In women's golf JoAnne Gunderson Carner, who had won the U.S. Amateur title five times before turning professional, had a great triumph in the U.S. Women's Open. Laura Baugh, aged 16, became the youngest winner of the U.S. Amateur championship, and Hollis Stacy won the U.S. Girls' Junior championship for a record third successive year, beating Miss Baugh in the quarterfinals.   (P. A. W.-T.)

Government Finance

Financing activities present national governments with some important and difficult problems not encountered by state or local governments or by the private sector. Financing state and local governments, as well as private households and companies, is primarily a matter of arranging revenues and borrowing required to cover the costs of current and long-term expenditure commitments. National governments, however, have the additional requirement of arranging taxes, borrowing, and expenditures in such a way as to promote high employment, stable prices, and long-term growth in the overall national economy. Attention to these economic stabilization and growth requirements was featured prominently in the financing activities and fiscal policies of a number of national governments in 1971.

United States. U.S. authorities in 1971, as in 1970, had the difficult problem of designing fiscal and monetary policies appropriate for an economy in which both unemployment and the rate of inflation were at excessively high levels. Unemployment equal to 4% of the civilian labour force was commonly assumed to represent reasonably full employment in the U.S. But actual unemployment was about 6% at the beginning of 1971, and remained there most of the year. Price inflation in the first half of 1971 was proceeding at a rate of 4 or 5% a year (depending on what index of prices was used), a clearly excessive rate that threatened erosion of living standards of individuals on fixed incomes and deterioration of the international competitiveness of U.S. exports.

In the past in most countries, a rapid rate of price inflation was a reflection of excess business and personal demand for goods and services relative to an economy's overall productive capacity. In this standard type of inflation, featuring low unemployment, prudent government financial policy called for a restrictive fiscal policy. In the current U.S. situation, however, a restrictive fiscal policy would only exacerbate the unemployment problem. Conversely, a stimulatory fiscal policy (one aimed at stimulating aggregate demand through tax cuts or federal expenditure increases), while it might have reduced unemployment, might also touch off a new round of price and wage inflation. Confronted with this dilemma, the administration recommended an essentially "neutral" fiscal policy in the official budget transmitted to the Congress in January 1971 for the fiscal year scheduled to start the following July 1 (*see* Table).

The extent to which the federal budget was stimulatory, restrictive, or neutral in its economic impact could be judged with reference to the "full employment budget," an accounting convention developed in recent years to help distinguish between deliberate, or active, changes in fiscal policy and induced, or passive, changes. Although attention to this concept had been recommended in 1967 by the President's Commission on Budget Concepts, it received prominent attention in the official budget for the first time in 1971. In the full employment budget, the income side represents the hypothetical revenues that would be collected at assumed high employment levels of taxable income rather than at actual levels; if the economy was at or near full employment, there would be little difference between the actual budget and the full employment budget.

In 1971, and in the projections made for the fiscal 1972 budget, the U.S. economy was some distance from full employment. Thus, a more rapid growth of receipts than of expenditures was expected, yielding a forecast decline in budget deficit from $18.6 billion in fiscal 1971 to $11.6 billion in fiscal 1972. This forecast, however, included the effects of cyclical recovery of the economy on federal revenues. An alternative revenue calculation based on assumed full employment in both years would indicate a budget showing little change in surplus or deficit ($100 million in fiscal 1972, compared with $1.4 billion in fiscal 1971). This modest change might properly be interpreted to indicate an approximately neutral fiscal policy in the official January budget recommendations.

On Aug. 15, 1971, Pres. Richard M. Nixon announced one of the most dramatic packages of economic stabilization measures ever undertaken by U.S. authorities. The immediately precipitating cause was an acute wave of speculation against the U.S. dollar in European currency markets, following massive deficits in the U.S. balance of international payments in the first and second quarters of the year. A more fundamental cause was the persistence of price and wage inflation in the U.S. in the face of several years of highly restrictive fiscal and monetary policies. Although the important parts of the package, the suspension of U.S. gold payments and the institution of a temporary three-month freeze on price and wage increases, were aimed at the immediate threats, several tax and budget actions were either announced for immediate implementation or requested of the Congress.

These measures included a temporary across-the-board import duty surcharge (rescinded in December as part of the agreement realigning the currencies of the major trading nations); repeal of the 7% automobile excise tax, institution of a 10% tax credit for the purchase of new machinery and equipment (subsequently reduced in congressional action to 7%), and acceleration of previously scheduled increases in personal exemptions under the individual income tax. Other major tax actions recommended earlier by the administration that received renewed attention after August 15 included acceleration of depreciation allowances for tax purposes on a wide range of investment goods and deferral of income tax on export income earned by Domestic International Sales Corporations (DISCs).

Partly to offset the revenue loss from these changes and partly to accommodate changes Congress appeared likely to make to his January budget requests anyway, President Nixon's message also included several recommended expenditure cutbacks. These included deferred implementation of the administration's recommendations for federal revenue sharing and welfare reform (which were having slow going in Congress), reductions in federal employment, and a freeze on federal pay increases.

Under the combined impact of the tax and expenditure actions, a slower growth in the national economy and in federal revenues than projected in the January budget, and the enactment of new legislation not foreseen in January (such as the Emergency Employment Act approved in July), the fiscal 1972 federal budget appeared headed, as 1971 drew to a close, toward a deficit well in excess of $20 billion, compared with the January estimate of $11.6 billion, although no revised official estimates had been made public. Since a major portion of this change was caused by more sluggish growth of the economy, and only partly by new tax or expenditure actions, the full employment deficit had undergone less massive change. Thus, the emerging federal budget for fiscal 1972 was moderately more stimulating to the economy than that recommended in January, but a return to full employment of the national economy appeared unlikely until sometime after 1972.

State legislatures were distinctly more active in levying new taxes and increasing rates on existing taxes in 1971 than they had been in 1970. New personal income taxes were levied in two states, Pennsylvania and Rhode Island; the Ohio legislature also was considering similar action. Nine other states—Arkansas, Delaware, Iowa, Massachusetts, Michigan, Missouri, Montana, North Dakota, and Oklahoma—enacted significant tax rate increases under already existing personal income taxes.

Federal revenue sharing, a controversial proposal to return some portion of federal income tax collections to the states to help finance the rapidly growing costs of state and local government services, seemed no closer to enactment in 1971, although Nixon renewed his support for it in his January budget.

United Kingdom. Fiscal policy in the U.K. during 1971 was directed increasingly toward reducing unemployment. Inflation, as in other industrial countries, remained a major problem but the low rate of industrial capacity utilization convinced the authorities that reflationary measures, by increasing productivity, might diminish rather than increase price and wage pressures. The reflationary actions chosen reflected by and large the Conservative government's conviction that longer-term fiscal strategy should aim at reducing public sector claims on resources so as to provide more elbow room for private initiative.

This philosophy was reflected in the first package of fiscal measures announced when the Conservative government came to power in October 1970: income tax cuts were offset by reductions in public expenditures; the system by which cash grants were provided for investment purposes was replaced by depreciation allowances; and agricultural support payments were shifted from budget subsidies to import levies. The net effect of all these measures was intended to be neutral. However, as demand continued to lag and unemployment to rise, the need for reflationary action became increasingly clear. Accordingly, measures in the 1971–72 budget presented on March 30, 1971, included further income tax cuts, a 50% cut in the selective employment tax (SET), and increases in child allowances and in social insurance benefits, which were partly offset by a rise in contributions. The revenue losses from these actions were estimated to amount to £670 million (or just over 2% of the GNP) on a full year basis.

Tax reform proposals were aimed at simplifying a cumbersome tax system, which, according to the chancellor of the Exchequer, had played a significant role in the disappointing longer-run performance of the British economy. By April 1973 a single graduated income tax was to replace the current two-tier income tax and surtax system, and the purchase tax and the SET would make way for a value-added tax; in 1972 the corporation tax would be altered to reduce fiscal discrimination against distributed as compared with retained earnings; and a simplification of capital gains tax rules was made effective immediately.

During the course of the year, it became evident that the budgetary measures taken in March were insufficient to achieve economic policy goals. Accordingly, on July 19 first-year depreciation allowances were increased, controls on installment credit removed, and purchase-tax rates cut. This package was followed by further measures on November 23, when planned capital expenditures by the nationalized industries were speeded up and public works expenditures increased. In addition, budget payments still

Summary of the U.S. Federal Budget

Actuals and estimates as of Jan. 29, 1971
in $000,000,000

| Item | Fiscal year ending June 30 | | |
	1970 actual	1971 estimate	1972 estimate
Budget receipts	193.7	194.2	217.6
Budget outlays	196.6	212.8	229.2
Actual deficit (−)	−2.8	−18.6	−11.6
Full employment surplus	2.6	1.4	0.1

Source: *The Budget of the United States Government, Fiscal Year 1972* (U.S. Government Printing Office, Washington: 1971).

outstanding on the now abolished cash investment grant program were to be prepaid.

West Germany. Public policy in West Germany in 1971 attempted to achieve a balance between the desire to dampen continuing inflationary pressures and the fear of sliding into a recession in the process of doing so. The restrictive fiscal policy measures taken, somewhat belatedly, in 1970 included a temporary 10% repayable surtax on personal and corporate incomes, temporary suspension of accelerated depreciation allowances, and freezing of a portion of federal and state revenues in a "countercyclical" fund to be held in a special account at the central bank. In addition, tight expenditure ceilings were set. Corporate profit tax receipts were lower than expected and expenditures, partly because of price and wage increases in the public sector, were higher. Nevertheless, the overall financial surplus was a shade higher than in the previous year because of the pro-cyclical nature of the social security system.

By the end of 1970 the economy showed definite signs of cooling off and it was thought that the time for a mildly expansionary fiscal policy stance had come. A number of expansionary measures had already been scheduled: the investment tax was to be reduced from 6 to 4% on Jan. 1, 1971; accelerated depreciation allowances were to be reinstated on February 1; and the surcharge on income taxes was to expire on June 30. In addition, the Business Cycle and Financial Planning Councils recommended a rather higher rate of growth in public expenditures for 1971 than for 1970. Early in 1971, however, there was a temporary spurt of economic activity, which led the authorities to believe that the boom was still very much alive, and strict expenditure ceilings were reintroduced. In early May, after the decision to float the mark, these expenditure ceilings were reconfirmed: planned expenditures on federal and state levels were to be reduced by DM. 1.5 billion; new orders involving final expenditures of DM. 4 billion–5 billion over a number of years were to be postponed; borrowing authority of the public sector was reduced; and contributions by the federal and state governments to the frozen anticyclical fund were increased. On balance, however, these restrictive actions no more than offset the easing earlier in the year.

Toward mid-1971 it became abundantly clear that the long-lived boom had tailed off and that the continued high rates of inflation were attributable to cost rather than to demand pressures. Nevertheless, the government was reluctant to shift its policy stance because of fears that this might rekindle inflationary expectations. Accordingly, the budget proposals for 1972 published in September attempted to show as low an increase as possible in expenditures: the 8.4% growth over 1971 was reckoned from budgeted 1971 levels; the actual outturn was expected to be lower, so that the actual expenditure growth rate was likely to be about 9.5% higher. Certain unusual financial transactions also tended to hold down the expenditure level. Thus, the optically moderate growth in federal expenditures might turn out to be appreciably higher in effect. This probably was appropriate in the context of the slowing economic trends.

In recognition of these probable needs, a contingency budget was prepared that provided for DM. 2.5 billion in additional expenditures to be financed from the countercyclical funds accumulated during 1970–71. Furthermore, the government had the option to begin to repay the income tax surcharge at any time

before the legally required date of March 1973. Finally, two further steps were taken to broaden the revenue base of state and local governments: state governments were to receive 33%, rather than the current 30%, of the revenues accruing under the value-added tax. The loss in federal revenues was to be covered by an increase in tax rates on alcohol and tobacco. Local authorities were to receive 75% of the revenues accruing from an increase in the petroleum tax.

Canada. Canadian budgetary policy, which in previous years was aimed at containing inflationary pressures, shifted toward increasing ease in the course of fiscal 1970–71. The Economic Council estimated that the high employment surplus of the public sector declined from about 3% of the potential GNP in 1969 to about 2.25% by the end of 1970, and probably further during 1971.

Budgetary actions during 1970–71 reflected the change toward greater flexibility in fiscal policy adopted a few years earlier; fiscal changes were more frequent and the official budget was supplemented by mini-budgets as economic requirements changed. Thus, the 1970–71 budget was followed by fiscal packages in June and December 1970 that were designed to impart additional stimulus to economic activity. Most of the measures taken were aimed at increasing capital expenditures at both private and public levels.

The 1971–72 budget, presented with a three-month delay in June 1971, contained measures mainly related to tax reform designed to redistribute the tax burden, but its overall effect was likely to stimulate private consumption. The major demand-management measure was the removal of the 3% surtax on personal and corporate incomes, in effect since 1968.

Unemployment, despite the fact that production had begun to expand at about trend rates, continued to increase through the third quarter of 1971. The supplementary budget introduced in mid-October, therefore, concentrated on measures designed to expand employment: federal expenditures for job-creating and manpower-training programs were increased, spending programs on residential construction were accelerated, and federal tax rates on personal and corporate incomes were reduced.

Japan. Demand management policies in Japan had been restrictive until the autumn of 1970, when the rate of inflation began to decline and recessionary tendencies became apparent. Toward the end of 1970 fiscal policy became stimulative and was progressively expansionary thereafter. In December the Fiscal Investment and Loan Program (FILP) was increased by 7% over the budgeted amounts. For fiscal 1971 expenditure increases budgeted for programs with high multiplier effects (mainly fixed investments) exceeded the 1970 rates of growth appreciably. Because of smaller increases in transfer payments, total expenditures were programmed to rise at a somewhat slower rate than in the preceding year. But in June and July expenditure totals were increased considerably when infrastructure programs through FILP were expanded to counter the persistent economic slowdown. In order to help offset the retarding effects of the U.S. balance of payments measures, in October personal income tax rates were cut and exemptions raised, government expenditures from the general account were increased, and the FILP loan and investment program was further expanded.

The effect of the various budget measures was to increase the importance of government investment

Great Britain:
see United Kingdom

outlays. This was consistent with the 1970–75 Development Plan's aim to shift resources from the private to the public sector, but it still fell far short of the 1975 target of bringing the share of such investments to 10.1% of the GNP.

France. Demand management policies in France were significantly eased during the second half of 1970. During 1971, authorities were faced with the policy dilemma of persistent inflation accompanied by relatively high rates of unemployment, despite a rate of economic expansion that was about in line with trend rates. The dilemma was resolved in favour of expansion of demand by fiscal means while monetary policy aimed at containing the growth of liquidity.

The 1971 budget outturn probably was somewhat more expansionary than had been intended. The consolidated general government account probably would be a net borrower in 1971 rather than a net lender, as had been estimated. The 1972 budget was intended to be in balance in order to avoid inflationary financing. However, the structure of budget expenditures, which was heavily weighted toward investment in equipment, was likely to have an expansionary impact on economic activity, albeit somewhat smaller than that provided in 1971. In addition, the official statement that expansionary measures would be taken if economic activity were to slow down implied that the authorities were prepared to move to a planned budget deficit if necessary. (H. B. J.; W. Le.)

See also Economics; Economy, World; Payments and Reserves, International.

Greece

A constitutional monarchy of Europe, Greece occupies the southern part of the Balkan Peninsula. Area: 50,944 sq.mi. (131,944 sq.km.), of which the mainland accounts for 41,-277 sq.mi. Pop. (1971): 8,745,084. Cap. and largest city: Athens (pop., 1971, 862,133). Language: Greek. Religion: Orthodox. King, Constantine II, in exile since Dec. 14, 1967; regent in 1971, Lieut. Gen. Georgios Zoitakis; prime minister, Georgios Papadopoulos.

Domestic Affairs. The political and constitutional moratorium proclaimed for 1971 by Prime Minister Papadopoulos was observed faithfully. In fact, he took advantage of the lull to consolidate his personal position while, for the sake of the U.S., enunciating "liberalization" measures, the merits of which usually were minimized by legal fine print. This policy featured a Christmas amnesty that culminated in April 1971, when two political prison camps for Communist exiles were shut down and all but 70 political prisoners who had been banished in villages were released. Although there were still about 400 Greeks serving prison sentences for antiregime activities, the regime called off the arrangements that had given the International Committee of the Red Cross free access to all prisoners.

That the presence of the Red Cross delegates was needed became quite evident after the major wave of security arrests in late 1970, in the course of which the authorities paid little heed to constitutional safeguards that had been restored earlier that year. Over 100 persons were arrested and detained and several were charged with sedition (later adjusted to "con-spiracy" to commit sedition). It was on a similar "conspiracy" charge that Lady Fleming, the Greek-born widow of Sir Alexander Fleming, the discoverer of penicillin, was sentenced by an Athens court-martial to 16 months' imprisonment on September 28. She was accused of trying to help in the abortive escape from prison of Alexandros Panaghoulis, a soldier sentenced in connection with an assassination attempt against the Greek prime minister in August 1968. Temporarily released from prison because of ill health, she subsequently was deprived of her Greek citizenship and deported.

The prime minister reformed his Cabinet on August 26. The main innovation was a division of the country into seven major districts under the control of governor-undersecretaries—most of them the former colonels who had staged the 1967 coup and who since then had been secretaries-general in ministries. By dispatching these revolutionaries to the provinces and stripping his two principal associates, Stylianos Patakos and Nikolaos Makarezos, of their executive powers as ministers of interior and economic coordination, respectively (they were made deputy premiers), Papadopoulos was believed to have eliminated the main sources of antagonism within his administration.

While the Papadopoulos regime thus was becoming more personalized and certainly more confident, its opponents at home and abroad continued to react with halfhearted amateurism. On March 23 the principal opposition groups issued a joint declaration calling for the restoration of democracy and an end to martial law. Militant opposition was limited to a score or so plastic bomb explosions. A National Resistance Council (EAS) had been formed in London in December 1970, but the Pan-Hellenic Liberation Movement (PAK) led by Andreas Papandreou refused to participate.

GREECE

Education. (1967–68) Primary, pupils 973,912, teachers 27,963; secondary, pupils 405,947, teachers 12,469; vocational, pupils 94,995; higher (including 5 universities), students 73,438, teaching staff 2,327.

Finance. Monetary unit: drachma, with a par value of 30 drachmas to U.S. $1 (72 drachmas = £1 sterling) and a free rate (Sept. 27, 1971) of 74.30 drachmas to £1 sterling. Gold, SDRs, and foreign exchange, central bank: (June 1971) U.S. $296 million; (June 1970) U.S. $253 million. Budget (1970 rev. est.): revenue 57.8 billion drachmas; expenditure 55,302,000,000 drachmas. Gross national product: (1969) 252.2 billion drachmas; (1968) 227.8 billion drachmas. Money supply: (April 1971) 52,290,000,000 drachmas; (April 1970) 47,130,000,000 drachmas. Cost of living (1963 = 100): (June 1971) 122; (June 1970) 118.

Foreign Trade. (1970) Imports 58,750,000,000 drachmas; exports 19,276,000,-000 drachmas. Import sources: EEC 40% (West Germany 19%, Italy 8%, France 7%); Japan 13%; U.K. 9%; U.S. 6%. Export destinations: EEC 46% (West Germany 20%, Italy 10%, Netherlands 6%, France 6%); U.S. 8%; Yugoslavia 7%; U.K. 6%; U.S.S.R. 5%. Main exports: tobacco 14%; iron and steel 8%; chemicals 7%; fresh fruit 6%; cotton 6%; dried fruit 6%; aluminum 6%. Tourism (1969): visitors 1,139,400; gross receipts U.S. $150 million.

Transport and Communications. Roads (1970) 35,064 km. (including 11 km. expressways). Motor vehicles in use (1970): passenger 226,499; commercial 106,729. Railways: (1969) 2,571 km.; traffic (1970) 1,531,000,000 passenger-km., freight 688 million net ton-km. Air traffic (1970): 2,126,300,000 passenger-km.; freight 35,602,000 net ton-km. Shipping (1970): merchant vessels 100 gross tons and over 1,850; gross tonnage 10,951,993. Telephones (Dec. 1969) 881,-003. Radio receivers (Dec. 1969) 1,184,000. Television receivers (Dec. 1969) 86,000.

Agriculture. Production (in 000; metric tons; 1970; 1969 in parentheses): wheat c. 2,000 (1,701); barley c. 630 (447); oats c. 105 (101); corn c. 527 (400); potatoes c. 590 (559); rice c. 79 (99); tomatoes (1969) 822, (1968) 634; tobacco c. 92 (79); oranges c. 510 (502); lemons 120 (118); sugar, raw value (1970–71) c. 188, (1969–70) c. 146; cotton, lint c. 105 (111); olive oil c. 180 (173); wine c. 516 (516); raisins c. 188 (188); currants and sultanas (1968) 142, (1968) 149; figs (1969) c. 130, (1968) 128. Livestock (in 000; Dec. 1969): sheep c. 7,700; cattle 1,050; goats c. 4,000; pigs c. 440; horses c. 260; asses c. 396; chickens c. 25,500.

Industry. Production (in 000; metric tons; 1970): lignite 7,681; electricity (excluding most industrial production; kw-hr.) 8,977,000; petroleum products (1969) 4,430; bauxite 2,281; magnesite (1969) 580; cement 4,846; cotton yarn 41.

The regime reacted against the activities of expatriate Greeks with a series of decrees depriving many of them of their Greek nationality. Among them were Papandreou; Helen Vlachos, the conservative publisher; Georgios Plytas, former mayor of Athens; and two senior army officers. It was natural for the regime to resent these activities, especially in Washington where one direct result was the dispatch to Greece of two investigators of the Senate Foreign Relations Committee. In their published report, the investigators were critical of the U.S. embassy's lack of contacts with opponents of the regime and cast doubt on the Greek rulers' promises to restore democracy at an early date.

The inquiry was the first success of the Greek expatriate lobby in Washington, led by a former Greek journalist, Elias Demetracopoulos. Their second was the August vote in the House of Representatives approving an amendment to the U.S. foreign aid authorization bill suspending all aid to Greece until the restoration of constitutional rule in that country. There was, however, an escape clause authorizing the aid if the president certified in writing that this was in the interests of U.S. security. The U.S. government reassured Athens that the escape clause would permit the granting of military aid as before, but at the same time ordered its Athens ambassador, Henry J. Tasca, to resume contacts with the exiled monarch, King Constantine. The ambassador, who had had talks with most deposed political leaders in Athens, also flew to Paris on September 30 to see former Prime Minister Konstantinos Karamanlis. Washington tried further to keep the regime happy by sending Vice-Pres. Spiro T. Agnew, himself of Greek descent, on a visit to Greece in October.

Foreign Affairs. The regime tried to make up for Western disdain by cultivating relations in all directions, with the result that the main feature of foreign affairs was the exchange of visits with Arab and African leaders and officials of Communist neighbours in the Balkans. On May 6 it was agreed with Albania to resume diplomatic relations and exchange ambassadors for the first time in 31 years. Other official visitors to Athens were Pres. Demetrio Lakas Bahas of Panama and the foreign minister of Spain.

There was a broadening of the rift between Archbishop Makarios III, president of Cyprus, who remained adamant on preserving the unitary nature of the independent state, and Papadopoulos, who believed that some substantial concessions should be made to the Turkish-Cypriot demand for self-government. The outlook was aggravated by the disappearance from his Athens apartment of Gen. Georgios Grivas, the former guerrilla leader. It was assumed that he was in Cyprus, possibly plotting to overthrow President Makarios, whom he often accused of betraying *enosis* (union of Cyprus with Greece). During October 1–5 the Greek and Turkish governments were in consultation in an effort to avoid any incident on the island that could force them into conflict.

The Economy. The Greek economy continued to make impressive strides and the growth of the gross national product in 1971, as in the two previous years, was expected to exceed 7% in conditions of relative monetary stability. The spectacular increase in revenue from tourism, probably in the range of 50% over 1970, combined with the fact that Greece let its currency devalue by adhering to its dollar parity, offset losses from declining exports after a slump in the nickel market. Due to the revaluation of gold,

official reserves increased by nearly 50% to $450 million within the first nine months of the year. A major setback to long-term economic prospects was shipping magnate Aristotle Onassis' decision to call off his $600 million investment package. (Mo. M.)

Greek Prime Minister Georgios Papadopoulos reorganized the Cabinet in August 1971 to eliminate opposition within his administration.

POPPERFOTO—PICTORIAL PARADE

Guatemala

A republic of Central America, Guatemala is bounded by Mexico, British Honduras, Honduras, El Salvador, the Caribbean Sea, and the Pacific Ocean. Area: 42,042 sq.mi. (108,889 sq.km.). Pop. (1971 est.): 5,347,787. Cap. and largest city: Guatemala City (metro. area pop., 1971 est., 730,991). Language: Spanish, with some Indian dialects. Religion: predominantly Roman Catholic. President in 1971, Carlos Manuel Arana Osorio.

On Sept. 15, 1971, Guatemala celebrated the 150th anniversary of its independence. The date was marked by a continuation of the political strife that had characterized the nation from its beginning. On the brighter side, President Arana initiated the first phase of his widely heralded five-year plan, and the national economy continued to demonstrate a favourable rate of growth.

The relative peace that followed Arana's inauguration in July 1970 had been broken by a resurgence of terrorism, reportedly the work of leftist elements, that led to a declaration of a state of siege on Nov. 13, 1970. In the ensuing months, it was reported that the government made over 1,600 arrests and that there were between 700 and 1,000 deaths attributable to the

GUATEMALA

Education. (1968–69) Primary, pupils 493,241, teachers 13,009; secondary, pupils 37,278; vocational, pupils 12,994; teacher training, students 7,573; secondary, vocational, and teacher training, teachers 5,122; higher (including 4 universities), students 11,935, teaching staff 707.

Finance. Monetary unit: quetzal, at par with the U.S. dollar (2.40 quetzales = £1 sterling) and with a free rate (Sept. 27, 1971) of 2.48 quetzales to U.S. $1. Gold, SDRs, and foreign exchange, central bank: (June 1971) U.S. $95.3 million; (June 1970) U.S. $90.5 million. Budget (1971 est.) balanced at 221.4 million quetzales. Gross national product: (1969) 1,645,000,-000 quetzales; (1968) 1,533,000,000 quetzales. Money supply: (March 1971) 178.2 million quetzales; (March 1970) 173.6 million quetzales. Cost of living (Guatemala City; 1963 = 100): (May 1971) 106; (May 1970) 106.

Foreign Trade. (1970) Imports 284.3 million quetzales; exports 298.3 million quetzales. Import sources (1969): U.S. 34%; El Salvador 13%; West Germany 10%; Japan 10%. Export destinations (1969): U.S. 28%; El Salvador 14%; West Germany 10%; Japan 8%; Costa Rica 7%; Honduras 7%; Nicaragua 5%; Italy 5%. Main exports: coffee 34%; cotton 9%; bananas 7%.

Transport and Communications. Roads (1969) *c.* 12,000 km. (including 830 km. of Pan-American Highway). Motor vehicles in use (1969): passenger 39,900; commercial (including buses) 22,600. Railways (1969): 826 km.; freight traffic 106 million net ton-km. Air traffic (1970): *c.* 104 million passenger-km.; freight *c.* 6,820,000 net ton-km. Telephones (Jan. 1970) 38,489. Radio receivers (Dec. 1969) 219,000. Television receivers (Dec. 1969) 72,000.

Agriculture. Production (in 000; metric tons; 1970; 1969 in parentheses): corn *c.* 720 (709); cotton, lint *c.* 52 (54); cane sugar, raw value (1970–71) *c.* 207, (1969–70) 180; coffee *c.* 108 (*c.* 105); bananas (1969) *c.* 80, (1968) *c.* 76.

Industry. Production (in 000; metric tons; 1969): cement 224; petroleum products 719.

action of the military, the police, and vigilante groups. Among those assassinated or missing were many criminals with long records of arrest, rebel leaders, student leaders, and prominent moderate-leftist politicians. Among the latter were two members of the national Congress, several prominent labour leaders, and professors from the University of San Carlos in Guatemala City.

An additional 25 to 30 assassinations were said to be the work of urban guerrillas with Castroite or Maoist sympathies, who appeared to have given up kidnapping for ransom in favour of murder. Killings attributable to rightist elements reached new heights in April and May, when several rebel strongholds were uncovered and three top leaders killed. Assassinations by urban guerrillas declined thereafter, but renewed terrorism by rightist elements in the fall led to agitation against the continued use of repressive action by the government. The assassination of yet another professor from the University of San Carlos in mid-September resulted in vigorous student protests and a call by Roman Catholic and Protestant clergymen for the cessation of the systematic extermination of Guatemalan citizens. Two clergymen were deported on charges of interfering with national politics.

The expansion of the Guatemalan economy during 1970 carried over into 1971, and it was estimated that the rate of economic growth for the year would approximate 6%. Across-the-board increases in the export of a variety of products provided a favourable trade balance of $5 million for the first five months of the year and contributed significantly to increasing foreign currency reserves to $80 million.

Under the National Development Plan for 1971–75, the government placed particular emphasis on the agricultural sector of the economy. To that end, an investment of $132 million was projected, and a new development bank to provide financial and technical assistance to agriculture was established. Another $11.2 million was to be invested in tourism, with priority being given to the development of facilities to serve the principal Maya sites in the Petén region of the Yucatán Peninsula. Of major significance to both the nation and the Petén region was the successful conclusion of long-dragged-out negotiations with the International Nickel Co. of Canada. The company agreed to provide for the investment of $250 million over 40 years for the exploitation of nickel deposits in northeastern Guatemala. (O. H. H.)

Guinea

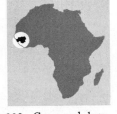

A republic on the west coast of Africa, Guinea is bounded by Portuguese Guinea, Senegal, Mali, Ivory Coast, Liberia, and Sierra Leone. Area: 94,925 sq.mi. (245,856 sq. km.). Pop. (1970 est.): 3,921,000. Cap. and largest city: Conakry (pop., 1967 est., 197,267). Language: French (official). Religion: mostly Muslim. President in 1971, Sékou Touré.

In 1971 Guinea's domestic affairs were dominated increasingly by President Touré's suspicious attitude toward the outside world, a result of the attempted invasion of his country in November 1970, for which Portugal was held responsible by the UN Security Council despite that country's protestations to the

GUINEA
Education. (1968–69) Primary, pupils 167,340, teachers (1965–66) 3,990; secondary, pupils 33,448, teachers (1965–66) 567; vocational, pupils 5,334, teachers (1965–66) 261; teacher training, students 2,954, teachers (1965–66) 52; higher, students 942, teachers (1965–66) 95.
Finance. Monetary unit: Guinea franc, with a nominal par value (Sept. 27, 1971) of GFr. 246.85 to U.S. $1 (GFr. 592.45 = £1 sterling). Budget (1969–70 est.) balanced at GFr. 24,386,000,000.
Foreign Trade. (1964) Imports GFr. 11,201,000,-000; exports GFr. 16.1 billion. Import sources: U.S. 22%; U.S.S.R. 12%; China 10%. Export destinations: France 16%; U.S. 11%; Cameroon 10%; Poland 8%. Main exports (1962): aluminum 60%; bananas 10%; palm products 7%; coffee 6%; iron ore 6%.

contrary. The unsuccessful invasion was followed by a wave of arbitrary and hasty trials in Conakry. In January 92 people were sentenced to death for conspiracy. Many others, including the archbishop of Conakry, were sentenced to life imprisonment.

However, these macabre episodes did little to dispel the president's fears, and in April he declared that he had escaped an attempt on his life. The government and military high command were reorganized in February, and the military again in July. In September, a UN commission of inquiry, dispatched at the urgent request of President Touré, concluded that Guinea was indeed in danger of aggression.

Touré accused several nations of having aggressive intentions toward his country and of being involved in plots to overthrow his government. They included Portugal, West Germany, the Vatican, Senegal, and France. It was announced that a large number of alleged conspirators were to stand trial by giving evidence on Guinea radio. Judgment would be passed by the people of Guinea after hearing the broadcasts. The trial by radio opened at the end of July and ended in October, with approximately 15 ex-ministers, as many ex-officers, some 30 senior civil servants, and a large number of priests and foreign nationals being tried in this way.

In March Guinean troops went to the assistance of Prime Minister Siaka Stevens of Sierra Leone when his political opponents attempted to seize power in Freetown. (Ph. D.)

Guyana

A republic and member of the Commonwealth of Nations, Guyana is situated between Venezuela, Brazil, and Surinam on the Atlantic Ocean. Area: 83,000 sq.mi. (215,000 sq.km.). Pop. (1970): 714,233, including (1964) East Indian 50.2%; Negro 31.3%; mestizo and mulatto 11.9%; Amerindian 4.6%. Cap. and largest city: Georgetown (pop., 1970, 66,070). Language: English (official). Religion: Protestant, Hindu, Roman Catholic. President in 1971, Arthur Chung; prime minister, Forbes Burnham.

Prime Minister Burnham pursued policies during the year that brought Guyana closer to the Soviet Union and China. He paid a cash contribution to African freedom fighters and called for the withdrawal of Israel from "conquered territories" and of "all foreign troops" from Southeast Asia. Early in the year he established diplomatic relations with the U.S.S.R. and entertained a trade mission from China. He later voted to seat mainland China in the UN.

Within its home Caribbean area Burnham's govern-

Guiana:
see Dependent States; Guyana

Guided Missiles:
see Defense

Guinea, Portuguese:
see Dependent States

GUYANA

Education. (1967–68) Primary, pupils 138,672, teachers 4,383; secondary, pupils 49,163, teachers 1,741; vocational, pupils 1,717, teachers 115; teacher training, students 561, teachers 39; higher, students 597, teaching staff 63.

Finance. Monetary unit: Guyanan dollar, with a par value of Guy$2 to U.S. $1 (Guy$4.80 = £1 sterling) and a free rate (Sept. 27, 1971) of Guy$1.94 to U.S. $1. Budget (1970 est.): revenue Guy$121 million; expenditure Guy$116.4 million.

Foreign Trade. (1970) Imports Guy$268,240,000; exports Guy$267,976,000. Import sources: U.K. 31%; U.S. 23%; Trinidad and Tobago 12%; Canada 9%. Export destinations: U.S. 29%; U.K. 19%; Canada 18%; Trinidad and Tobago 8%; Norway 8%. Main exports: bauxite 34%; sugar 27%; alumina 17%; rice 7%.

Agriculture. Production (in 000; metric tons; 1970; 1969 in parentheses): rice c. 238 (171); sugar, raw value (1970–71) 396, (1969–70) 310; cassava (1969) c. 12, (1968) c. 10; oranges c. 10 (10). Livestock (in 000; 1969–70): cattle 257; sheep 99; pigs 81.

Industry. Production (in 000; 1969): bauxite (metric tons) 4,306; diamonds (metric carats) 49; electricity (kw-hr.) 292,000.

ment remained the most loyal advocate of economic and political integration by strengthening the operations of the Caribbean Free Trade Area (CARIFTA), urging the harmonizing of fiscal incentives and the establishment of a common external tariff (major steps toward the creation of a common market), and by drafting plans for a constituent assembly that would consider some form of political association. Jamaica, Barbados, and Trinidad and Tobago were cool toward the idea, and they abstained from the Grenada Declaration of November 1, in which Guyana, Dominica, Grenada, St. Kitts-Nevis, St. Lucia, and St. Vincent declared their intention to form a new state by 1973.

In July 1971 the government nationalized the Canadian-owned Demerara Bauxite Co., which represented a major source of export earnings. Compensation was computed on the basis of the company's book assets, plus interest, minus local tax. The much smaller U.S.-owned Reynolds Metals was left untouched, as was the British-owned sugar industry, the second mainstay of the economy. On the other hand, the Guyana Cooperative Bank, in which the government held 90% of the equity, was to be the launching pad for a wholly indigenous banking system; the foreign-owned banks were to be "miniaturized."   (Ra. R.)

Haiti

The Republic of Haiti occupies the western one-third of the Caribbean island of Hispaniola, which it shares with the Dominican Republic. Area: 10,714 sq.mi. (27,750 sq.km.). Pop. (1971 est.): 4,969,113, of whom 95% are Negro. Cap. and largest city: Port-au-Prince (pop., 1970 est., 386,250). Language: French and Creole. Religion: Roman Catholic; Voodooism practiced in rural areas. Presidents in 1971, François Duvalier and, from April 22, Jean-Claude Duvalier.

The problems caused by the death on April 21 of Pres. François Duvalier (*see* OBITUARIES) dominated political and economic events in Haiti during 1971. Duvalier, who had ruled the country for nearly 14 years, was succeeded as president-for-life by his 19-year-old son, Jean-Claude (*see* BIOGRAPHY), whose chief lieutenants were his sister, Marie Denise; her husband, Col. Max Dominique; Gen. Claude-Louis Raymond, the army chief of staff; his brother, Adrien Raymond, foreign minister; Luckner Cambronne, the

Gynecology and Obstetrics:
see Medicine

minister of the interior, national defense, and police; together with the commanders of the Bataillon Desallines and the Presidential Guard, Col. Breton Claude and Col. Gracia Jacques, respectively. The new president's main civilian arm was the Conseil Privé, or Cabinet, to which several distinguished civilians were appointed, including Antonio André, president of the national bank.

In August a dispute between Marie Denise Dominique and Cambronne provided the new president with his first serious political problem. Duvalier sided with Cambronne, who had angered Mrs. Dominique by jailing her husband's cousin on charges of forging passports.

The new government's immediate task was to consolidate the support of the armed services. To this end, the powers of the former president's unofficial militia, the Tontons Macoutes, were curbed. Three of the force's regional commanders were dismissed in May, and in December it was transferred to agricultural and other development work under Army supervision. A new, smaller U.S.-trained force called the "Leopards" took over the Tontons Macoutes' former role of an internal security force to combat "guerrillas, invaders, and Communist subversion."

Steps were also taken to promote political liberalization and to ensure economic growth. A total of 38 political prisoners, including 27 soldiers, sentenced to death or imprisonment by the former president, were reprieved, and several prominent exiles allowed to return. A five-year development plan was announced in May, which concentrated on the undertaking of public works projects and on expanding farm production, particularly coffee, the country's principal export. A program was announced to overhaul the road network, almost entirely neglected since 1934. The legal minimum wage was raised by 40%, the first increase in 20 years, and the pay of the lower ranks of the armed forces by 20%. The Péligré hydroelectric plant, the country's most important infrastructure project, was inaugurated in July. An official program began in the same month to curb corruption,

HAITI

Education. (1966–67) Primary, pupils 280,187, teachers 6,460; secondary, pupils 21,010, teachers 1,289; vocational, pupils 6,211, teachers 359; teacher training, students c. 210, teachers 83; higher (at University of Haiti), students 1,527, teaching staff 209.

Finance. Monetary unit: gourde, with a par value of 5 gourdes to U.S. $1 (12 gourdes = £1 sterling) and a free rate (Sept. 27, 1971) of 12.40 gourdes to £1 sterling. Gold, SDRs, and foreign exchange, central bank: (June 1971) U.S. $7.8 million; (June 1970) U.S. $5.7 million. Budget (1967–68 est.) balanced at 140.2 million gourdes. Cost of living (Port-au-Prince; 1963 = 100): (June 1971) 137; (June 1970) 122.

Foreign Trade. Imports (1968) 187.9 million gourdes; exports (1969) 185.8 million gourdes. Import sources: U.S. 61%; Japan 7%; France 6%; Canada 5%. Export destinations (1968): U.S. 61%; France 11%; Italy 7%; Belgium-Luxembourg 5%. Main exports: coffee 38%; bauxite 17%; sisal 6%; sugar 6%.

Transport and Communications. Roads (1969) c. 3,000 km. (including c. 350 km. with improved surface). Motor vehicles in use (1969): passenger 14,700; commercial 1,300. Railways (1970) 301 km. Telephones (Jan. 1969) c. 4,450. Radio receivers (Dec. 1969) 81,000. Television receivers (Dec. 1969) 11,000.

Agriculture. Production (in 000; metric tons; 1970; 1969 in parentheses): coffee c. 29 (c. 26); sugar, raw value (1970–71) c. 68, (1969–70) c. 65; bananas (1969) 212, (1968) 212; sisal c. 25 (27). Livestock (in 000; 1969–70): pigs c. 1,750; cattle c. 940; goats c. 1,340; sheep c. 79.

Industry. Production (in 000; metric tons; 1969): cement 55; bauxite (exports) 748; electricity (kw-hr.) 1967) 115,000.

and many privileges of senior government officials were abolished.

There were indications in August and September that the U.S. was preparing to resume financial aid to Haiti, suspended since 1962. It was reported that the government would be allowed to buy enough U.S. matériel to equip the two battalions of the "leopards," and U.S. officials came to Haiti to help reorganize the customs and postal services. The minister of finance visited Washington in August to discuss the granting of credits for development purposes with representatives of the Inter-American Development Bank and other international financial institutions. A large delegation from these institutions subsequently visited Port-au-Prince in September for the same purpose.

There were signs of economic progress during the year. The tourist boom continued, and a considerable increase in U.S. visitors to Port-au-Prince was reported. Industrial production showed a small rise, reflecting the results of the setting up of approximately 50 processing installations by U.S. companies over the previous two years. These investments had created more than 8,000 new jobs.   (Rn. C.)

Historic Buildings

The 16th session of the General Conference of UNESCO in November 1970 resulted in the drawing up of a recommendation and an international convention on the protection of monuments, groups, and sites of universal value (including natural sites and landscapes). Drafts were to be submitted to the General Conference for adoption at its 17th session in 1972.

World campaigns for the preservation and restoration of the temples of Philae (Egypt) and of Venice continued. The island of Philae, in the Nile near the First Cataract, had been partially submerged after the original Aswan Dam was built. Following construction of the High Dam farther upstream, the lake that formed behind it submerged the island completely. The Egyptian government decided to dismantle all the temples and to reassemble them on a neighbouring island that would be landscaped to resemble the original. UNESCO was to assist in raising the U.S. $13.3 million required. Work began during 1971 and was to last for approximately four years.

During the second session of the Advisory Committee for Venice, held in September 1970, the Italian government had declared its intention to implement a comprehensive plan for the preservation and development of the city. However, a bill authorizing appropriations still awaited approval a year later. On Oct. 24, 1971, Premier Emilio Colombo announced details of the $384 million plan for saving the city. These included the introduction of new aqueduct and sewerage systems, the closing of two arms of the lagoon to keep out high seas, and measures against pollution. The U.S. government placed at the disposal of the Italian authorities an obsolescent antimissile radar unit for use in connection with an aerial survey of the lagoon. Funds to adapt and transport the unit to Venice were provided by UNESCO.

In January 1971 Indonesia convoked a meeting of international experts to examine a plan to stabilize the 9th-century Buddhist monument of Borobudur, near Jogjakarta. Essentially the plan called for dismantling of the lower squared terraces bearing sculptured panels and the construction of massive reinforced-

Construction crews raised two of Manchester's ancient inns, the Wellington and Sinclair's Oyster Bar, five feet to fit in with a £10 million redevelopment scheme in the marketplace where the city had its origins.

"THE TIMES," LONDON— PICTORIAL PARADE

concrete shelving on which the terraces would be reassembled. The shelving would "float," cushioning any seismic shocks. A new drainage system would be introduced, and an anticorrosive consolidant was to be employed. The total cost was estimated at $5.5 million.

A report of extensive damage to Angkor Wat in Cambodia by bombardment during February 1971 aroused widespread dismay, but the first accounts were later believed to have been exaggerated. The great site, built during the 12th century by one of the Khmer kings, was under the control of North Vietnamese troops. The École Française d'Extrême Orient maintained a small staff there working on consolidation and repairs. Most of the important movable works of art had been carefully packed, transported, and stored in the national museum under the supervision of UNESCO experts. As a result of the scare, the Cambodian government proposed that Angkor Wat be administered under international control and be made a neutral zone.

A preliminary report by three UNESCO experts found that the marble of the Parthenon was seriously imperiled by atmospheric corrosion. More damage had been caused in the past 40 years by industrial pollution carried from the plain of Athens than in all the previous 2,350! Sculptures were affected by carbon and sulfur carried in raindrops, and marble had cracked as iron clamps used by modern restorers had rusted.

In the Netherlands work began on the reconstruction of the 2,000-year-old Temple of Taffeh, one of the temples rescued from inundation following the building of the Aswan High Dam. Once a shrine to the goddess Isis, it was presented to the Netherlands by the Egyptian government in appreciation of Dutch contributions to the campaign to preserve the Nubian monuments. Other temples were presented to the U.S., Italy, and Spain.

In his environmental message to the U.S. Congress on Feb. 8, 1971, Pres. Richard M. Nixon called for preservation of the nation's natural and cultural heritage. On an international level, he proposed creation of a "World Heritage Trust" to provide protection for and international recognition of objects of unique natural, historic, and cultural value to mankind. Nationally, almost $6 million was appropriated by Congress for preservation grants during fiscal 1971. Abraham Lincoln's home in Springfield, Ill., was designated as a national historic site.

The most shocking U.S. experience was the damage suffered by the Capitol building in Washington, D.C., when a bomb, believed to have been planted by political activists, exploded within the remaining visible section of the original building. The site of the blast was beneath the main Senate and House chambers, and over $300,000 worth of damage was caused.

In the U.K. the 17th annual report of the Historic Buildings Council, published in June, appealed to Peter Walker, secretary of state for the environment, for an increase in annual government aid to owners of historic buildings. Subsequently, it was announced that the government's grant to the council was being stepped up from £700,000 to £1 million for 1971, the largest such increase ever made. Among 46 buildings of historic interest to receive grants were the defensive Redoubt at Harwich, built under threat of Napoleonic invasion; the Great Hospital at Norwich, an outstanding example of a medieval hospital; and a National Trust property, Compton Castle in Devon, a fine example of a fortified castle of 14th-century origin.

The Chapel Royal of St. Peter ad Vincula at the Tower in London was restored by the Department of the Environment at a cost of £20,000. It was the oldest chapel royal in the kingdom, dating from 1105. Goodwood House near Chichester, built between 1780 and 1800 by the 3rd duke of Richmond and Gordon, was opened to the public in May after three years of restoration. A Palladian mansion, Clandon, near Guildford, became the home of £1 million worth of art treasures which were opened to public view in the spring. Built by the Venetian architect Giacomo Leoni (1686–1746), Clandon had been given to the National Trust in 1956.

In France considerable debate was provoked by plans to raze the 19th-century cast-iron framed buildings that made up the old central food market, Les Halles, in Paris. The 12 shelters were among the first large cast-iron structures ever built (*c.* 1855). After the transfer of wholesale food distributors to Rungis, south of Paris, in 1969, many of the old pavilions had been taken over spontaneously for shows, discussion groups, exhibitions, and similar uses. Following the

order for their demolition, a mass campaign was begun to preserve some of the Baltard pavilions (designed by Napoleon III's architect Victor Baltard). Pres. Georges Pompidou finally decided to save one or more of the pavilions, which were to be transferred to another site for museum purposes.

The introduction of natural gas, installation of new telephone exchanges, and expansion of the Metro (subway) tore up the streets of Paris. Work on the new Metro stations at the Place Charles de Gaulle (formerly Place de l'Étoile) had been completed in the fall of 1970, and work was begun on restoring the pink, greenish, and gray cobblestones that form rays surrounding the Arc de Triomphe.

In Rome the government purchased and opened to the public the Villa Doria Pamphili. The Princess Doria Pamphili, a descendant of the admiral and statesman Andrea Doria (1466–1560), sold the park to the city for the equivalent of U.S. $3.2 million. The 230 ac. included pastures, woods, and gardens with many rare trees, Roman statuary, and a building encrusted with sculpture and reliefs. The acquisition tripled the amount of parkland in Rome.

The Belgian government sponsored a "Year of the Chateaux." Many historic homes and castles were opened to the paying public for the first time. In some cases the owners prepared special exhibitions; for example, at Corroy-le-Chateau, a turreted feudal castle with a drawbridge, the Marquise de Traziegnies placed her collection of antique puppets on display.

Following the 1944 Warsaw uprising, the Germans began methodical destruction of the city, including the medieval section (the Stare Miasto, since painstakingly restored) and the ancient royal palace. Rebuilding of the palace had been deferred because of the expense involved, but in 1971 the decision was made to begin the work and to open a campaign to raise the required $10 million. An exhibition of the project was organized in the National Museum, where architectural samples of building details such as cornices, photographs, and original architectural plans were shown.

The U.S. government joined the International Centre for the Study of the Preservation and the Restoration of Cultural Property, located in Rome. In the 12 years of its existence, the centre, which began with five member states, had grown to a membership of 50. It had established a library on conservation and was one of the most important centres for the training of specialists in the field.

The International Council of Monuments and Sites (ICOMOS) continued to expand its activities in close collaboration with UNESCO. A number of meetings of experts were organized, among them several aimed at defining a program for the UNESCO/ICOMOS documentation centre. Other meetings of considerable significance included one on the preservation of historic quarters and the quality of the urban environment, held in Bruges, Belg., and another on historic gardens, held in cooperation with the International Federation of Landscape Architects.   (H. Du.)

See also Museums and Galleries.

London's Trinity Church, built in 1820 to celebrate the Battle of Waterloo, had become derelict by 1971. Permission was granted to convert the church into seven flats and preserve the building's exterior.

Hockey

Field Hockey. The first World Cup competition in field hockey, which was to have been held in Lahore, W.Pak., in February 1971, had to be postponed for political reasons until October, when it was held in Barcelona, Spain. The Cup was won by Pakistan, which defeated India in the semifinal (2–1) and Spain in the final (1–0). India beat Kenya 2–1 for third place.

In England the growth of competition at the club level continued to be largely uncoordinated. The county championship was won for the first time by a Midlands entry, Staffordshire. At the international level England was undefeated in six matches, winning four, drawing two, and scoring 5 goals to none. In the three matches forming its part in the Home Countries' Championship program, England won the triple crown with an aggregate score of 4 goals to none.

England's performance against continental countries indicated appreciable improvement over previous form. In the European Cup at Brussels, Belg., in September 1970, England had placed sixth behind West Germany, Netherlands, Spain, France, and Belgium. Yet six months later, at Nottingham in April 1971, England defeated the West Germans and played a goalless draw with the Netherlands. Undoubtedly the coaching and training of W. Vans Agnew, a former Scottish international player, had given the team a much more scientific capability.

Vans Agnew handed over his duties as England team manager shortly after the cup competition in September 1970 to Stuart Mayes, an English international, but this was a change with no great difference in style and method. In England's first international match of 1971 the team had to be content with a goalless draw against France at Lord's ground, London. But victories over Wales (1–0) and Ireland (2–0) were some compensation, and the season ended on a high note at Nottingham with the victories over West Germany and Scotland and the goalless draw with the Netherlands.

In the U.K. emphasis then shifted from the separate countries, England, Scotland, and Wales, to preparation of a combined Great Britain team for the Olympic Games at Munich in 1972. On relinquishing his responsibility for the England team, Vans Agnew took over the Great Britain commitment and put his players through a series of training exercises. Progress was put to the test of match practice in May when Great Britain defeated Poland 2–1 at Bushey, Herts. Then in September and October Britain played against two powerful opponents, West Germany and Australia, with mixed results. At Frankfurt am Main, the West Germans were at concert pitch on the eve of the World Cup competition, whereas Great Britain was in need of a match, not having faced international competition for four months, and the result was a 3–0 win for West Germany. Stung by this defeat, Great Britain gave a more lively and determined display against Australia at Bristol and drew 1–1.

In February, the Hockey Association announced that it had accepted a sponsorship of £5,000 from Benson and Hedges, a member of the Gallaher group of tobacco companies. Under this agreement, the county championship was renamed the Benson and Hedges county hockey championship, and the national club knockout competition, which the Hockey Association introduced in the 1971–72 season, was christened the Benson and Hedges national club knockout. Subsequently the firm agreed to donate a further sum of £1,000 toward the cost of preparing the Great Britain team for the 1972 Olympics.

County and divisional associations affiliated with the Hockey Association were all asked to hold eliminating competitions to find their champion clubs, and the Hockey Association nominated March 5, March 26, and April 16, 1972, as the dates for the preliminary, semifinal, and final rounds of the Benson and Hedges national club knockout competition.

The International Hockey Rules Board held its last meeting in May 1971. The board had won widespread respect for its rulings and universal recognition as the rule-making body for all countries affiliated with the International Federation. Nevertheless, beginning in 1972 responsibility for the rules of the game would pass to the International Hockey Federation. Fundamentally, this change resulted from dissatisfaction among some countries that the rules of the now-worldwide game should remain in the hands of a body on which England, Ireland, Scotland, and Wales had always enjoyed a privileged position.

In women's hockey the big event of 1971 was the international tournament at Auckland, N.Z. England was unbeaten in the tournament until losing its last match 1–3 to West Germany. In the unofficial ranking list the Netherlands was placed first, New Zealand second, and England third. In the women's home internationals, England played a goalless draw with Wales and defeated Scotland and Ireland to share first place with Wales, also unbeaten. (R. L. Hs.)

Amateur Ice Hockey. Although the Soviet Union became world champions in 1971 for the ninth successive year, the concurrently decided European title went to Czechoslovakia. Six nations contested the Group A matches, each playing the other twice, at Bern and Geneva, Switz., on March 19–April 3. All the teams except the United States were from Europe —U.S.S.R., Czechoslovakia, Sweden, Finland, and West Germany. For the European championship, matches involving the U.S. were disregarded.

Crucial games of the series were the first, when the U.S. beat Czechoslovakia 5–1, and the last, when the Soviet Union defeated Sweden 6–3. But the highlights were the two matches between the Soviet and Czechoslovakian teams, the first a 3–3 draw and the second a 5–2 triumph for the Czechoslovakians, who estab-

Montreal's Henri Richard cracks a drive past Chicago Black Hawks goalie Tony Esposito during Stanley Cup play-off, May 18, 1971. Richard's goal gave the Canadiens a 3–2 lead, which they kept to win the cup.
UPI COMPIX

NHL Final Standings

	Won	Lost	Tied	Goals	Goals against	Pts.
EAST DIVISION						
Boston Bruins	57	14	7	399	207	121
New York Rangers	49	18	11	259	177	109
Montreal Canadiens	42	23	13	291	216	97
Toronto Maple Leafs	37	33	8	248	211	82
Buffalo Sabres	24	39	15	217	291	63
Vancouver Canucks	24	46	8	229	296	56
Detroit Red Wings	22	45	11	209	308	55
WEST DIVISION						
Chicago Black Hawks	49	20	9	277	184	107
St. Louis Blues	34	25	19	223	208	87
Philadelphia Flyers	28	33	17	207	225	73
Minnesota North Stars	28	34	16	191	223	72
Los Angeles Kings	25	40	13	239	303	63
Pittsburgh Penguins	21	37	20	221	240	62
California Seals	20	53	5	199	320	45

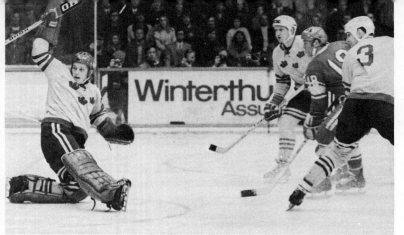

Starshinov of the Soviet Union scores a goal against Sweden at the world ice hockey championship in Geneva, April 3, 1971. The Soviet Union won the championship for the ninth consecutive time.

KEYSTONE

lished their superiority in the third period and knew then that their earlier defeat by the U.S. had cost them the world title. Outstanding on the Soviet team were two forwards, Aleksandr Maltsev, at centre, and the leading scorer, Anatoli Firsov, on the left wing. The most successful goalkeeper was Czechoslovakia's Jiri Holecek. The games between the Soviets and Americans provided a striking contrast in styles. The U.S. players hustled the Soviet team, causing it to lose its normal smooth rhythm through constant body-checking, but the Soviets' fitness and stamina proved decisive. As in the previous year, Canada did not enter a team because of difficulties involved with the laws of amateurism.

In the Group B tournament, at Bern on March 5–14, Switzerland took first place to gain promotion to Group A in the next series at the expense of West Germany. The runner-up was Poland, followed by East Germany, Norway, Yugoslavia, Japan, Austria, and Italy, the last two to be relegated to Group C.

The International Ice Hockey Federation decided to organize a separate world championship series for 1972 instead of incorporating it with the Winter Olympic Games, as in previous Olympic seasons. (H. B.)

Professional Ice Hockey. The Montreal Canadiens, unable even to qualify for the play-off tournament the season before, rebounded in 1971 to win their third Stanley Cup in four years. The comeback was accomplished mainly because of the startling acrobatics provided by goalkeeper Ken Dryden, a freshman professional and former star at Cornell University. As the replacement for Montreal goalies Rogatien Vachon and Phil Myre, Dryden won the Conn Smythe Trophy as the outstanding player in the Stanley Cup play-offs (see BIOGRAPHY).

Montreal had finished third in the East Division, behind the Boston Bruins and the New York Rangers. In the first round of the play-offs, the Canadiens defeated the favoured Bruins in seven games. Montreal then beat the Minnesota North Stars in six games in the semifinals and won the Cup in a seven-game final series against the Chicago Black Hawks. Chicago, runaway winner of the West Division in its first season in that section, qualified for the finals by eliminating the Philadelphia Flyers and the New York Rangers.

Boston finished first in the East Division by 12 points over New York and reaped most of the individual awards. Phil Esposito, the Bruins' rangy centre from Sault Ste. Marie, Ont., won the Art Ross Trophy as the game's leading producer of points—a record-setting 76 goals and 76 assists. Bobby Orr, also of Boston, finished second to Esposito in the points race, won the James Norris Memorial Trophy as the best defenseman in the National Hockey League (NHL),

and was awarded the Hart Memorial Trophy as the most valuable player in the sport. John Bucyk, Boston's veteran left wing, was third in the scoring competition and winner of the Lady Byng Memorial Trophy as the player best combining skill with sportsmanship.

Ed Giacomin and Gilles Villemure shared goalkeeping duties for New York and received the Vezina Trophy as representatives of the team allowing the fewest number of goals, 177. Gilbert Perreault, centre for the Buffalo Sabres, won the Calder Memorial Trophy for distinguished play among rookies.

The first-team all-stars, picked by writers and broadcasters covering NHL teams, were: goalkeeper, Giacomin; defense, Orr and J. C. Tremblay (Montreal); centre, Esposito; right wing, Ken Hodge (Boston); left wing, Bucyk. The second-string stars included goalkeeper, Jacques Plante (Toronto); defense, Brad Park (New York) and Pat Stapleton (Chicago); centre, Dave Keon (Toronto); right wing, Yvan Cournoyer (Montreal); left wing, Bobby Hull (Chicago).

The Springfield Kings won the play-off championship of the American Hockey League, and the Portland Buckaroos clinched the title in the Western League. Other minor league champions were the Charlotte Checkers in the Eastern League, the Port Huron Flags in the International League, and the Omaha Knights in the Central League. (R. H. BE.)

Honduras

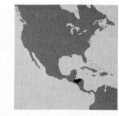

A republic of Central America, Honduras is bounded by Nicaragua, El Salvador, Guatemala, the Caribbean Sea, and the Pacific Ocean. Area: 43,277 sq.mi. (112,088 sq. km.). Pop. (1971 est.): 2,669,100, including 90% mestizo. Cap. and largest city: Tegucigalpa (pop., 1971 est., 316,414). Language: Spanish; some Indian dialects. Religion: Roman Catholic. Presidents in 1971, Osvaldo López Arellano and, from June 6, Ramón Ernesto Cruz.

Presidential elections were held on March 28. Ramón Ernesto Cruz (see BIOGRAPHY), a lawyer and diplomat and leader of the National Party, narrowly won over his Liberal Party opponent, Jorge Bueso Arias. Only about half of the 900,000 eligible voters went to the polls. This was the highest proportion of voter abstention ever recorded in a Honduran general election, and also the first direct election of a president the nation had seen since 1932.

Earlier, in January, both major parties agreed to a national unity plan whereby representation of all elective parties would be divided equally to give 32 deputies each to the National and Liberal parties in a 64-member National Assembly. Both party nominees for the presidency joined incumbent Pres. Osvaldo López Arellano in announcing the plan. The post of president of the National Assembly went to the National Party, as the victor in the March elections; the Liberal Party was allowed to select the president of the Supreme Court. The plan also stipulated equal party representation on the Supreme Court and in the Cabinet.

As a presidential contender, Cruz spoke in support of the actions of the Honduran Congress of Dec. 30, 1970, which gave approval to a presidential request for emergency legislation to withdraw from the Central American Common Market (CACM) agreements on free trade and taxes. He blamed his opponent, Bueso Arias, for allowing Honduras to join the CACM under terms not advantageous to the country. As president-elect, Cruz pledged that he would seek a peaceful solution to Honduras' border dispute with El Salvador. Cruz began his six-year term as president on June 6, replacing Osvaldo López Arellano who had held the office since 1965. However, López, a former army general, retained the key post of armed forces chief and was expected to exercise considerable power in the government.

Efforts to repair the rift in relations between Honduras and El Salvador, resulting from the armed conflict in July 1969, continued. Some minor border flare-ups were reported in 1971. The border observer force of the Organization of American States, made up of personnel from 11 Latin-American countries, remained, though in smaller numbers than previously. Their supervisory efforts led to a reestablishment of telephone, telegraph, and postal communications between the two countries, and the reopening of the border to all traffic except that originating in either of the two nations.

The more serious problem of bolstering the CACM, which was faltering as a result of the Honduras-El Salvador conflict, remained unresolved. Honduras continued to be a member of the regional economic body, but in little more than name only.

In November the U.S. agreed to cede the Swan Islands to Honduras. The three tiny Caribbean islands, long claimed by Honduras, had been under U.S. sovereignty since 1863. (A. D. Bu.)

HONDURAS
Education. (1967–68) Primary, pupils 366,907, teachers 10,322; secondary, pupils 22,711; vocational, pupils 3,828; teacher training, students 4,606; secondary, vocational, and teacher training, teachers 2,311; higher, students 3,459.
Finance. Monetary unit: lempira, with a par value of 2 lempiras to U.S. $1 (4.80 lempiras = £1 sterling) and a free rate (Sept. 27, 1971) of 4.96 lempiras to £1 sterling. Gold, SDRs, and foreign exchange, central bank: (June 1971) U.S. $26.3 million; (June 1970) U.S. $28,950,000. Budget (1970 est.) balanced at 225.2 million lempiras. Gross national product: (1969) 1,293,000,000 lempiras; (1968) 1,238,000,000 lempiras. Money supply: (April 1971) 172,310,000 lempiras; (April 1970) 167,280,000 lempiras. Cost of living (Tegucigalpa; 1963 = 100): (June 1971) 120; (June 1970) 125.
Foreign Trade. (1970) Imports 444.1 million lempiras; exports 341.5 million lempiras. Import sources (1969): U.S. 43%; Guatemala 10%; El Salvador 7%; Japan 6%; West Germany 6%. Export destinations (1969): U.S. 47%; West Germany 12%; Japan 6%; Italy 5%. Main exports: bananas 42%; coffee 15%; timber 9%.
Transport and Communications. Roads (1969) 5,185 km. (including c. 500 km. paved). Motor vehicles in use (1969): passenger 13,500; commercial (including buses) 16,700. Railways (1969) 1,028 km. Air traffic (1970): 131,160,000 passenger-km.; freight 12,310,000 net ton-km. Shipping (1970): merchant vessels 100 gross tons and over 52; gross tonnage 60,216. Telephones (Jan. 1970) 12,511. Radio receivers (Dec. 1968) 140,000. Television receivers (Dec. 1969) 17,000.
Agriculture. Production (in 000; metric tons; 1970; 1969 in parentheses): corn c. 390 (c. 380); coffee c. 33 (c. 33); sorghum c. 69 (c. 69); sugar, raw value (1970–71) c. 85, (1969–70) 81; dry beans c. 60 (c. 60); bananas (1969) c. 1,350, (1968) c. 1,255; cotton, lint c. 4 (c. 8); beef and veal c. 23 (c. 22). Livestock (in 000; 1969–70): cattle c. 1,830; pigs c. 980; chickens c. 6,350.
Industry. Production (in 000; metric tons; 1969): silver 0.11; gold (troy oz.) 3.8; lead ore (metal content; exports) 6.7; zinc ore (metal content; exports) 8.4; electricity (kw-hr.; 1968) 268,000.

Horse Racing

Thoroughbred Racing. *U.S.* Not in many years was Thoroughbred racing in America as stirred as it was in 1971 by the early-season exploits of Canonero II. Kentucky-bred and Venezuelan-owned, the three-year-old son of Pretendre won the Kentucky Derby and Preakness Stakes. He then finished fourth in the Belmont Stakes when he was not at his best physically, thus failing to become the first winner of horse racing's Triple Crown since Citation in 1948.

Canonero II was purchased for $1,200 by Luis Navas at the 1969 fall yearling sales at Keeneland, Ky., and then taken to Venezuela and resold to Pedro Baptista, a Caracas furniture manufacturer. The large bay annexed the 1¼-mi. Derby at Louisville, Ky., by almost four lengths in the slow time of 2 min. 3⅕ sec. after coming from far behind. So lightly regarded was he in the 20-horse lineup that he was coupled in the mutuel field with several other long shots. In the shorter Preakness at Baltimore, Md., in which Canonero II was co-favourite with Jim French, jockey Gustavo Avila changed tactics completely. He took Canonero II to the lead immediately and raced head and head with Eastern Fleet to the eighth pole, at which point Canonero II drew away to win by 1¼ lengths in the track record time of 1 min. 54 sec. for 1³⁄₁₆ mi.

Before a crowd of 82,694 at Belmont Park on Long Island, the most people ever to attend a U.S. race track, Canonero II led for one mile in the Belmont Stakes. He then yielded to the successful Pass Catcher in the 1½-mi. classic, which was broadcast worldwide and brought everything virtually to a standstill in Venezuela.

Shortly after the Belmont Canonero II came down with a severe hock infection that put him out of action for the balance of the season. He also acquired a new owner, Robert J. Kleberg of the King Ranch in Texas, who paid a reported $1 million for him.

Other early-season stars of the three-year-old division, besides Canonero II, were Hoist the Flag, the 1970 two-year-old champion who was barely saved for stud duty after suffering a severe leg injury; Executioner; Eastern Fleet; Good Behaving; Jim French; and Bold Reasoning. They tired or went out of action later in the year and were replaced by

Pass Catcher (left), with Walter Blum up, charges across the finish line to win the Belmont Stakes in New York, June 5, 1971. Jim French (right), ridden by Angel Cordero, Jr., was second.

WIDE WORLD

Rokeby Stable's Run the Gantlet, William A. Levin's Bold Reason, Raphael Escudero's Tinajero, and Oxford Stable's West Coast Scout.

Run the Gantlet won five consecutive turf (on grass) stakes against older horses, including the United Nations, Man o'War, and the Washington (D.C.) International. Bold Reason captured four stakes, including the Travers on dirt and the American Derby on turf. Tinajero, bred in Kentucky, won several stakes in the U.S. after arriving in midyear from Puerto Rico, where he had been practically unbeaten.

Forked Lightning Ranch's Ack Ack, racing exclusively in California, was by far the most consistent handicap performer. After finishing second in his season's debut, he won seven stakes at various distances on dirt and turf, while carrying high weight. He later was retired to stud.

Ogden Phipps' Numbered Account dominated the two-year-old filly division, and Meadow Stable's Riva Ridge was supreme in the two-year-old male ranks. Numbered Account, trained by Roger Laurin, challenged Riva Ridge, trained by Roger's father, Lucien Laurin, in the Garden State Stakes in the final race of the season for both. The first filly ever to compete in America's richest race, Numbered Account finished fourth while Riva Ridge won. Riva Ridge previously had triumphed in the Flash Stakes, Belmont Futurity, Champagne Stakes, and the Pimlico-Laurel Futurity to account for earnings of $503,303. This came close to the record of $568,096 for a two-year-old, established by Buckpasser in 1965.

Best of the older mares were Mrs. Whitney Stone's Shuvee, by Nashua, and James Drymon's and Vance Greenslit's Double Delta, by Delta Judge, on dirt courses; and James Moseley's and Mrs. Alice Bell's Drumtop on turf. Drumtop won five grass stakes, all against males. Double Delta finished first in the Beldame Stakes, and the Maskette, Susquehanna, Molly Pitcher, Whitemarsh, Distaff, and Bayou Handicaps. Shuvee took the Top Flight and Diana Handicaps and dramatically ended her career by routing males for the second consecutive year in the two-mile Jockey Club Gold Cup. Shuvee was then retired for breeding purposes with earnings of $890,445 in a four-year career to replace Cicada ($783,674) as the greatest money-winning mare of all time.

Canonero II's heroics earned for him the three-year-old colt divisional championship in the major poll at year's end. It was conducted, for the first time, by members of the National Turf Writers Association; editors and writers on the *Morning Telegraph* and *Daily Racing Form;* and racing secretaries at tracks belonging to the Thoroughbred Racing Associations of the United States. Ack Ack was voted Horse of the Year after being acclaimed best handicap horse and best sprinter. Other champions included: three-year-old filly, Turkish Trousers; two-year-old colt, Riva Ridge; two-year-old filly, Numbered Account; older filly or mare, Shuvee; turf horse, Run the Gantlet; steeplechaser, Shadow Brook.

The major yearling sales established all-time highs in average price despite the business recession. At Keeneland 333 yearlings fetched $10,581,000 for an average price of $31,775. The sale of 224 yearlings at Saratoga grossed $6,841,100 for an average of $30,-541.   (J. AG.)

Canada. Highlighting Canada's 1971 Thoroughbred season was the unfolding of an amazing success story in the prestigious three-year-old division. In 1970,

in their first serious venture as breeders and owners of race horses, Mr. and Mrs. Arthur Stollery had brought a crop of just three two-year-olds to the races. In 1971, one of the trio captured Canada's most-coveted classic prize, the Queen's Plate, while another won top honours in the three-year-old filly division by taking the Canadian Oaks. The Plate winner was Kennedy Road, who had been named the country's top two-year-old the previous year. The Stollerys' Oaks winner was Lauries Dancer, a daughter of 1964 Kentucky Derby winner Northern Dancer. The Oaks proved to be just a beginning for Lauries Dancer. Later in the year she defeated the United States' best three-year-old fillies in the Alabama Stakes and Delaware Oaks, staking a strong claim to North American championship honours for her division.

Several other three-year-olds performed with distinction in 1971. At Fort Erie, Ernie Lieberman's New Pro Escar beat Kennedy Road in the Prince of Wales Stakes, the second leg, after the Queen's Plate, of the Canadian Triple Crown. The third leg, the Breeders Stakes on the grass at Woodbine, went to Mrs. W. D. Latimer's Belle Geste, who captured stakes prizes in two other turf events during the year. Another three-year-old grass specialist, Charles Rathgeb's Speedy Zephyr, set two track records and won stakes at Woodbine and at Assiniboia Downs (the Manitoba Derby).

For the better part of the season, the Canadian two-year-old division was dominated by Willow Downs Farm's Gentleman Conn, a half-brother to 1970 two-year-old filly of the year, Queen Louie. Gentleman Conn won more than $100,000 in 1971, including the rich Coronation Futurity. In the autumn, however, a late-developing colt named Presidial, bred and owned by E. P. Taylor's Windfield's Farm, climaxed a rapid rise through the ranks by winning over the best of the division (including Gentleman Conn) in the Cup and Saucer Stakes.

Although still bothered by infirmities that had plagued him throughout his career, Green Hills Farm's Dance Act was the outstanding older horse for the second consecutive year. Sandy Hawley, a native of Oshawa, Ont., easily won the Canadian riding championship for a third straight year, although the youthful reinsman did not maintain his pace of 1970, when he led all North American jockeys in number of wins.   (ER. AS.)

Europe and Australia. The 1970–71 season brought no new steeplechasing champion to capture the public's imagination, and the great hurdler Persian War showed that his star had waned when at the end of a difficult season he could not win his fourth consecutive Champion Hurdle, the race going to Bula. The Cheltenham Gold Cup Steeplechase was won by the Irish horse L'Escargot, for the second year running, followed home by Leap Frog and The Dikler. The Mackeson Gold Cup was won by Chatham, the Black and White Gold Cup by Into View, and the Hennessy Gold Cup by Border Mask. The King George VI Steeplechase had to be called off because of frost and snow. The Schweppes Gold Trophy hurdle was won by Cala Mesquida, with Volunteer second, both horses being trained by J. S. Sutcliffe. Under a big weight, Titus Oates won the Whitbread Gold Cup Steeplechase. In a thrilling Grand National Steeplechase Specify, ridden by J. Cook, got the better of Black Secret by a neck. Graham Thorner was champion National Hunt jockey.

In flat racing two horses stood out as undisputed champions. U.S.-bred Mill Reef (owned by Paul Mellon, trained by Ian Balding, and ridden by G. Lewis) won the Derby from Linden Tree, the Eclipse Stakes (from Caro), the King George VI and Queen Elizabeth Stakes, and, perhaps his greatest feat of all, the Prix de l'Arc de Triomphe from the fillies Pistol Packer and Cambrizzia in Paris in record time over fast going: he captured public imagination only a little less than Nijinsky had done the previous season as the best colt over $1\frac{1}{2}$ mi. in Europe. His only defeat was at the hands of Brigadier Gerard (owned by John Hislop, trained by Major R. Hern, and ridden by J. Mercer) in the Two Thousand Guineas. Brigadier Gerard then proceeded to win the St. James's Palace Stakes at Royal Ascot, the Sussex Stakes at Goodwood, the Queen Elizabeth Stakes at Ascot, and the Champion Stakes at Newmarket and was considered to be incomparably the best miler in Britain and probably Europe. The St. Leger was won by Athens Wood, who led the whole way. Altesse Royale was the year's outstanding filly, taking the One Thousand Guineas, the Oaks, and the Irish Oaks.

Of the older horses Rock Roi proved himself a better stayer than any other horse. He won the Ascot Gold Cup (only to be disqualified later because he was found to have been administered an unpermitted drug to cure an ailment), the Goodwood Cup, and the Doncaster Cup. Of the sprinters, Swing Easy won the Nunthorpe Stakes, and Realm and Green God also won major races. Royben triumphed in two big sprint handicaps in September, the Portland Handicap and the Ayr Gold Cup.

Among the two-year-olds Yaroslav, who took the Royal Lodge Stakes; High Top, who won the Observer Gold Cup; Roberto in Ireland; Sharpen Up; Philip of Spain; and Wishing Star performed well. Greatest interest was perhaps shown in Crowned Prince, who had cost the world record figure of the equivalent of £212,000 at the 1970 Keeneland sales in the U.S.; he flopped in his first race but made no mistake about the Champagne Stakes at Doncaster and the Dewhurst Stakes at Newmarket. Among the two-year-old fillies Rose Dubarry and Waterloo stood out. Lester Piggott was Britain's champion jockey for the ninth time.

In other countries the Irish Two Thousand Guineas went to King's Company and the One Thousand to Favoletta. Irish Ball from France took the Irish Derby. In France, the equivalents of the Two and the One Thousand Guineas were won by Zug and Bold Fascinator, respectively. The Prix du Jockey Club (Derby) was won by Rheffic, ridden by W. Pyers, from Nymbio and Tarbes. The Prix Royal Oak (St. Leger) went to Bourbon. Rheffic added the Grand Prix de Paris to his laurels, and Bourbon had won the Prix Hocquart earlier in the season. The brilliant Pistol Packer took the Prix de Diane (Oaks) from Cambrizzia. Ramsin won the Prix du Cadran (Ascot Gold Cup equivalent) from Rock Roi and Hallez. The Prix Morny at Deauville went to Daring Display, while the Grand Criterium was won by Hard to Beat. The Italian Derby was won by Carlo Vittadini's Ardale from Camigliatello and Trattegio. The Deutscher Derby at Hamburg, W.Ger., was won by Lauscher.

In Australia the $A102,000 Melbourne Cup was won by the New Zealand four-year-old Silver Knight. The winner was owned by Sir Walter and Lady Norwood, was trained by Eric Templeton and ridden by Bruce Marshall. (R. M. Gn.)

Harness Racing. An outstanding harness racing year in the U.S. saw the fastest mile in history, the two fastest race miles ever contested, and unprecedented accomplishments by its world-record-holding driver. The record speed performers were the three-year-old pacer Albatross, named harness horse of the year, and the four-year-old pacer Steady Star, whose 1 min. 52 sec. mile lowered by $1\frac{3}{5}$ sec. the fastest previous mile in the history of the sport. The man who rewrote the record book among drivers was Hervé Filion.

Albatross, a colt offered for sale at $7,000 as a yearling in 1969 with no takers, was syndicated for $1,250,000 in the spring of 1971 by owner Bert James of Pittsburgh, Pa. The spectacular bay son of Meadow Skipper–Voodoo Hanover paced the two fastest race miles in the history of the sport—identical efforts of 1 min. 54$\frac{4}{5}$ sec.—in the $52,865 Tattersalls pace at the Red Mile in Lexington, Ky., October 2 for trainer-driver Stanley Dancer. No harness horse had ever covered a mile that fast in a race, but Steady Star had preceded the performance with his 1 min. 52 sec. time trial one day earlier.

These superb performances were preceded and followed throughout the year by the driving heroics of Hervé Filion of Angers, Que., who surpassed his own world record of 486 victories in a single season, set in 1970, by winning more than 540 races in 1971. He also broke the sport's single season earning record for a driver, set by William Haughton in 1968 at $1,654,-172, by driving the winners of over $1.7 million in purses. In passing the 500-victory milestone, Filion earned his fourth consecutive North American race-winning championship. He had become the first driver ever to win 400 races in a single season in 1968, when he won 407.

While Filion was winning both race- and money-winning championships among drivers, Albatross was setting a new all-time high in money earnings for a single season by a harness horse. His $558,009 in 1971 purses not only was a harness racing record but also was high for the year in world racing of any breed. Albatross amassed his earnings while winning 25 of 28 races during the season. He finished twice second and once third in the three he did not win, and his two-season total at the end of 1971 showed 39 victories, 4 seconds, and 2 thirds in 45 starts, with earnings of $741,549.

Two American harness horses passed the $1 million mark in earnings during the 1971 season, bringing the roster of millionaire harness horses to four. The U.S.-bred, Canadian-owned trotter Fresh Yankee and the pacer Rum Customer joined the French trotting queen Une de Mai and the New Zealand-bred, American-raced pacing gelding Cardigan Bay in the exclusive million-dollar club. Rum Customer's $1,001,448 made him the biggest money-winning pacer ever.

Fresh Yankee, perhaps the most consistent trotter in the history of the sport, entered 1971 with a string of firsts and seconds extending back to 1969, and before that streak was broken at Goshen, N.Y., in July she had trotted 56 consecutive races in which she finished either first or second against major competition. But as superb as Fresh Yankee was, she was denied Trotter of the Year honours by members of the U.S. Harness Writers' Association in year-end balloting. The scribes voted that honour to Speedy Crown, winner of the $129,770 Hambletonian, who also was the fastest trotter of 1971 with a race mile victory in 1 min. 57$\frac{1}{5}$ sec. at Lexington, Ky., in early October.

Savoir, winner of the $103,120 Colonial at Liberty Bell Park in Philadelphia and the historic $63,415 Kentucky Futurity in Lexington, Ky., was Speedy Crown's foremost rival for three-year-old trotting honours. Albatross dominated the three-year-old pacers, but was upset by the colt Nansemond, driven by Hervé Filion, in the most traditional classic for that age and gait, the $102,964 Little Brown Jug at Delaware, O., in September.

In the juvenile ranks, the colts Super Bowl and Strike Out emerged as champion trotter and pacer, but not without strong challenge. Super Bowl, a trotter colt trained and driven by Stanley Dancer, was upstaged early in the season by his stablemate Star's Chip, and outtrotted in midseason by Songcan. Super Bowl was clearly the best at season's end, however, and won the divisional balloting in a landslide.

Strike Out, a son of the former world champion Bret Hanover, won most of the major stakes for juvenile pacers but was beaten twice in three encounters with Silent Majority. The latter colt, like Strike Out, was U.S.-bred but Canadian-owned.

The five-year-old pacer Super Wave was named the best aged pacing performer in North America and was voted harness horse of the year in Canada. Owned by George K. Boyce of London, Ont., and trained and driven by Jack Kopas, Super Wave won 12 of 26 races against the best older pacers in the world in 1971 and earned $214,018 while doing it. (St. F. B.)

The $25,000 New Zealand Cup (November 1970) was won by the pacer James. Find of the New Zealand season was the supremely fast Australian-owned but New Zealand-bred Mount Eden. After failing in the Inter-Dominion Championship, he went on to win the Miracle Mile in Sydney in 1 min. 58⅘ sec. and to pace miles of less than 2 min. in Melbourne and Perth before being sold for more than $200,000 to U.S. interests. In the Inter-Dominion championships West Australian pacer Junior's Image won from the mare Stella Frost. A swab taken from the winner proved positive to caffeine and he was disqualified, the race then going to Stella Frost, who also took the $26,500 Auckland Cup. The $10,000 trotters' section of the Inter-Dominion was won by Geffin.

Australia produced the Southern Hemisphere's fastest two-year-old pacer of all time when Nicotine Prince won the Challenge Stakes in Sydney in 2 min. ⅖ sec. An International Drivers Race held in Sydney in January was won by Hervé Filion, driving Sydney pacer Bay Foyle.

In January the French trotting mare Une de Mai became the first millionaire trotter and the biggest money winner in harness racing history. She added further to her illustrious record in August when she journeyed to the U.S. and won the $125,000 Roosevelt International Trot, a race she had won two years earlier. Tidalium Pelo won the $142,000 Prix d'Amérique at Vincennes near Paris for the second time, with Vanina B second, and Une de Mai third. During March the Gran Premio dell'Europa of $50,000 at Milan, for four-year-old European-bred trotters, was won by Italian-bred Tedo. Heat winners of the $96,-000 Premio Lotteria at Naples were Une de Mai, Barbablu, and Smokey Morn. The final went to Une de Mai for the third straight year. The $56,000 Gran Premio della Fiera went to the Italian-bred four-year-old trotter Akabo, which also won the $67,000 Premio Triossi at Rome, while the Gran Premio Nazionale three-year-old trot of $52,800 was won by Uriele.

In England a new track opened at Chasewater in

the Midlands, where the National Pacing Derby was won by Russian Patrol from Turn of the Tide. Scottish-bred Red Sails campaigned in the U.S. during the year, winning several races in fast times. (N. St.)

Housing

During 1971 housing construction stagnated in most of the less developed and many developed countries. Exceptions were Ireland, Italy, and South Korea, all of which attained an increase of more than 10% in housing construction over 1970.

A comparative study was made for 1970 and 1971 housing activities based on the UN *Monthly Bulletin of Statistics,* November 1971. This is based on monthly averages of housing construction activities during the first three to six months of 1971 and those during the full year of 1970. The number of new dwelling units completed, started, or for which building permits were issued increased greatly in Italy (15%, 29,198 to 33,692 units), followed by Ireland (15%, 1,093 to 1,255 units), South Korea (12%, 6,009 to 6,741 units), Japan (8.7%, 123,713 to 133,528 units), and South Africa (7.5%, 1,144 to 1,230 units), and decreased considerably in Czechoslovakia (−43%, 9,619 to 5,461 units), Chile (−31%, 1,482 to 1,018 units), Turkey (−16%, 12,905 to 10,857 units), and Brazil (−15%, 15,708 to 13,319 units). Some decrease was observed in Greece (−8.4%, 9,558 to 8,755 units), Switzerland (−8%, 1,858 to 1,710 units), New Zealand (−6.3%, 1,972 to 1,847 units), and the U.K. (−5%, 30,303 to 28,799 units). There was a slight change of housing

A squatter sits on the steps of a condemned building in New York, passively resisting removal from his home. Attempts to relocate persons evicted from their homes have largely failed due to the severe housing shortage in New York.

production in the following countries: Morocco (3.5%, 1,178 to 1,219 units), Netherlands (2.3%, 9,774 to 9,996 units), France (0.5%, 49,830 to 50,100 units), and Sweden (−4%, 9,154 to 8,790 units).

During the first UN Development Decade (the 1960s), only a few countries in Africa, Asia, and Latin America could produce sufficient numbers of dwelling units for needy families. In most less developed countries housing production was far below the target: less than two units per 1,000 inhabitants as compared with the goal of seven to ten.

In almost all less developed countries, squatter and uncontrolled settlements spread at an enormous pace. In Ankara and Izmir in Turkey about 60% of the population lived in such settlements; in Recife, Guayaquil, Mexico City, and Maracaibo, 46–50%; in Colombo, 44%; in Calcutta, Karachi, and Manila, 35%; and in Dakar and Lusaka, 30%. The development of squatter or uncontrolled settlements can be checked effectively by positive policies and measures concerning land use and tenure. At the Interregional Seminar on Improvement of Slums and Uncontrolled Settlements, held in Medellín, Colombia, in February–March 1970, problems of urban land reform were discussed and the following recommendations were made: (1) the elaboration of master plans for land use; (2) the establishment of property taxation; (3) the regulation of private property rights; (4) the acquisition of land by the public authorities; and (5) the acquisition of land for future urban expansion.

The big metropolitan areas in the world continued to face a great housing shortage. In London a shortage of at least 100,000 dwelling units was forecast for 1974 with an additional 230,000 unsatisfactory dwelling units, while in Tokyo the number of households suffering from overcrowding had reached more than 175,000 by 1968. In the U.S., authorities estimated that 24 million people still lived in substandard housing in 1971.

The situation was the same in the less developed countries, with the population of the large cities increasing rapidly through in-migration. It was estimated in Nigeria that the minimum requirement to meet the most urgent housing shortage was about 47,-000 dwelling units per year, but the public authorities were able to produce less than 500 units per annum.

One bright spot in the less developed countries was Singapore, where the Housing and Development Board (HDB) made a considerable effort to solve housing problems in middle- and low-income groups. One-third of the total population in Singapore lived in public housing, and it was expected that by 1975 not less than 45% of the population would be accommodated in dwelling units built by the HDB.

In Western Europe the importance of public housing was being recognized by the governments. In Italy the housing shortage reached three million, roughly 17% of all the nation's families, and was concentrated mostly in the industrial cities of the northern regions. To encourage the construction of public housing, Italy's Instituto Case per Lavoratori was expected to receive 1,500,000,000,000 lire out of 1,800,000,-000 of public funds, a considerably greater amount than in previous years. In West Germany the federal government was considering whether to provide loans to families with five or more children for the acquisition of suitable existing accommodations on the condition that the head of the household was a qualified recipient of public funds under the Second Housing Act.

Two large cranes move a concrete floor plank in the Westinghouse Electric Corp.'s housing system plant, which opened April 12, 1971. This was the first major U.S. factory to mass-produce precast floors and walls for high-rise buildings.
COURTESY, WESTINGHOUSE

One of the major obstacles to providing adequate housing throughout the world was land. The price of land suitable for residential construction was so high that most developers could not afford it. Furthermore, antiquated legislative procedures hindered speedy acquisition of land through expropriation, and the outdated taxation system for real estate widened the gap between official evaluation and the market price of land, thus accelerating land speculation. A partial solution was attempted in Italy where, to accelerate working-class subsidized housing, municipalities were guaranteed special powers of intervention in expropriation and development of real estate. In West Germany the municipal government of Cologne submitted to the city council a proposal for making urban land available on a leasehold basis only.

The improvement and development of rural housing was seen as a way to stop the huge population flow into the big cities. Attempts to provide such housing in Burma, Ceylon, India, and the Philippines showed that there was a great need for a comprehensive and long-term program. It was expected to take about 10 to 15 years to coordinate various facets of rural development, such as providing job opportunities, installing necessary health and sanitary facilities, and training for technical professions and management.

In the U.K. the government in July published its housing proposals in a White Paper. Three basic principles were put forward: ". . . a decent home for every family at a price within their means, a fairer choice between owning a home and renting one, and fairness between one citizen and another in giving and receiving help toward housing costs." The keynote of the reforms was to fight poverty and squalor by channeling public funds to people in need through means testing. To replace the current control of rents in the unfurnished private sector—the controlled rents often barely covering the costs of maintenance and insurance for the landlords who were often poorer than their tenants—rent allowances would be made to enable the needy to pay a fair rent.

One effect of controlling rents was to cause the supply of rented accommodations to run out or be replaced by uncontrolled furnished tenancies. In London this resulted in there being 348,000 more families than homes, the number of homeless having doubled in ten years. But neither the government nor the Francis Committee, set up to look at this problem, could agree on how to extend the rent allowance system to the furnished sector where the tenant has no security. And the White Paper seemed far from fair in allowing the other great political vested-interest group in housing, the owner-occupiers, to continue to receive a minimum of £300 a year tax relief on mortgage interest payments; the more expensive the house, the greater the tax relief, and people earning large incomes thus found buying expensive property a profitable investment. There were increasing demands that home ownership be extended to those with little job security or with little capital for the down payment.

In the U.S. major issues being examined by Congress included the government's proposal for consolidation and simplification of Department of Housing and Urban Development programs, bloc grants as housing subsidies, mandatory metropolitan-area-wide housing programs, and special revenue sharing for urban community development. Especially noteworthy were the proposals made by the House Banking and Currency Subcommittee. These included bloc grants to communities for housing and urban development that would reinforce national goals of decent housing and economic opportunity for working people and low-income families.

Most of the special revenue sharing fund (80%) was planned for use in metropolitan areas. In selecting an area or a city the following factors were taken into account: the number of residents, the degree of overcrowding, the condition of existing housing, and the proportion of very-low-income families in the total population. According to the government's proposal, the cities would administer the funds virtually free of federal control.

The government proposed more than $2.5 billion in grants for programs for urban renewal, Model Cities, water and sewer provision, and the rehabilitation of existing structures. The Senate Appropriations Committee, however, recommended more than $3.5 billion to be spent on urban renewal ($1.5 billion), Model Cities ($150 million), rehabilitation loan fund ($90 million), rent supplements ($91.3 million), home ownership assistance ($299 million), rental housing ($149 million), open space acquisition ($100 million), and neighbourhood facilities ($40 million). The committee also recommended programs for low-rent public housing ($24.5 million) and college housing ($10 million). (HI. S.; L. C. BR.)

See also Architecture; Cities and Urban Affairs; Economy, World; Industrial Review; Money and Banking.

ENCYCLOPÆDIA BRITANNICA FILMS. *Equality Under Law— The California Fair Housing Cases* (1969); *The House of Man, Part II—Our Crowded Environment* (1969).

Hungary

A people's republic of central Europe, Hungary is bordered by Czechoslovakia, the U.S.S.R., Romania, Yugoslavia, and Austria. Area: 35,919 sq.mi. (93,030 sq.km.). Pop. (1970): 10,314,152, including (1970) Hungarian 95.8%; German 2.1%. Cap. and largest city: Budapest (pop., 1970, 1,939,522). Language (1970): Magyar 95.8%. Religion (1956): Roman Catholic 67%; Protestant 27.3%; Orthodox 2.5%; Jewish 1.5%. First secretary of the Hungarian Socialist Workers' (Communist) Party in 1971, Janos Kadar; president of the Presidential Council (head of state), Pal Losonczi; president of the Council of Ministers (premier), Jeno Fock.

The Hungarian people elected a new National Assembly on April 25, 1971. It was officially announced that 98.7% of the electorate of 7,334,918 went to the polls and that 98.9% of voters cast valid votes. According to the electoral law of Oct. 3, 1970, there were 352 single-seat constituencies and voters could choose between two or even three candidates, provided every candidate was nominated by a special meeting of electors in the respective constituency, and that he accepted the program of the Patriotic People's Front. In 48 constituencies there were two candidates, and in one there were three. In three constituencies no candidate received an absolute majority and by-elections had to be held on May 9; this time a relative majority was sufficient for election. A quarter of the seats in the National Assembly went to nonparty members.

The new Parliament assembled on May 13. Antal Apro, former deputy premier, was elected speaker to succeed Gyula Kallai. Jeno Fock was reelected premier, and the new government included three new ministers: Lajos Faluvegi (finance), Gyula Szeker (heavy industry), and Mrs. Janos Keserue (light industry). Peter Valyi, former minister of finance, became one of the four deputy premiers and succeeded Apro as Hungarian member of the Executive Committee of the CMEA (Comecon).

On June 23 the premier presented the new government's program to Parliament, indicating its intention to raise family allowances and pensions. In 1951 one in 17 Hungarian citizens was a pensioner; in 1970 that proportion was one in seven. Between 1960 and 1970 expenditure on pensions rose from 4,427,000,000 forints to 13 billion forints. Total expenditure in 1970 was 175.7 billion forints, while revenue totaled 171.9 billion forints.

On September 25, returning from his talks with Yugoslav President Tito, Leonid Brezhnev stopped in Budapest and probably repeated to Janos Kadar what he had said publicly in Belgrade, that the so-called

Workman at the Bayer Leverkusen Co. in West Germany "builds" a dome-shaped dwelling by spraying plastic compounds on a revolving balloon skin. Completion time for the basic structure is approximately one hour. The house was shown in Essen in 1971.

Hovercraft:
see Transportation

D.P.A.—PICTORIAL PARADE

"Brezhnev Doctrine" (of limited sovereignty) was nothing but a "slanderous concoction." Having examined the current international scene, the two leaders confirmed their "complete identity of views on all questions under discussion." Kadar was determined to show that Hungary was a faithful ally of the Warsaw Treaty Organization and a loyal member of Comecon (more than one-third of Hungary's foreign trade was with the U.S.S.R. and another third was with other Comecon members). Within that framework, however, Kadar wanted to continue experimenting with his New Economic Mechanism (*see* SOVIET BLOC ECONOMIES), and to ensure to the Hungarian people a measure of relaxed political life.

The annual average natural increase of Hungary's population in 1960–70 was 0.35%. The 1970 census revealed that 15% of all men and 18% of all women were aged 60 or more. This demographic stagnation helped the Hungarian leadership to alleviate some social problems, especially housing. During the second five-year plan (1961–65) 282,000 dwellings had been built, during 1966–70 another 327,000 were erected, and 400,000 were expected to be built during 1971–75, making a total of more than a million apartments or detached family houses in 15 years. By 1971 about two-thirds of all Hungarian families lived in their own apartments or houses and the rest in state-owned dwellings, paying rents costing from 6 to 8% of average family earnings. But in Budapest, where 20% of the population was concentrated, the housing problem was still serious; the waiting list

exceeded the 91,000 apartments scheduled for 1975.

Jozsef Cardinal Mindszenty (*see* BIOGRAPHY), the 79-year-old Roman Catholic archbishop of Esztergom and primate of Hungary, arrived in Rome on September 28, ending, on the Vatican's order, his self-imposed exile in the U.S. embassy in Budapest after 15 years. (K. SM.)

Iceland

Iceland is an island republic in the North Atlantic Ocean. Area: 39,768 sq.mi. (103,000 sq.km.). Pop. (1970 est.): 204,578. Cap. and largest city: Reykjavik (pop., 1970 est., 81,684). Language: Icelandic. Religion: 98% Lutheran. President in 1971, Kristjan Eldjarn; prime ministers, Johann Hafstein and, from July 14, Olafur Johannesson.

A swing to the left in the general election of June 13, 1971, resulted in the defeat of the socialist-conservative coalition after 12 years in power. The Independence Party lost one seat in the Althing, retaining 22; the Social Democrats retained 6 of their 9 seats; the Progressive Party lost one seat, retaining 17; the People's Union kept its 10 seats; and the Liberal Left coalition, founded in 1970 by Hannibal Valdimarsson, leader of the Confederation of Trade Unions, won 5 seats. On July 14 a new coalition of Progressives, People's Union, and Liberal Left was formed with the principal aim of extending the Icelandic fisheries limit from 12 to 50 mi. (the claim, to be effective Sept. 1, 1972, was announced in November). At the same time the new administration called for the closure of the NATO base at Keflavik within four years, a request that met with disquiet in Washington and Brussels.

HUNGARY
Education. (1968–69) Primary, pupils 1,254,745, teachers 62,523; secondary, pupils 125,616, teachers 8,086; vocational, pupils 102,613, teachers 4,862; higher (including 15 universities), students 52,061, teaching staff 9,230.
Finance. Monetary unit: forint, with (Sept. 27, 1971) an official exchange rate of 11.74 forints to U.S. $1 (28.18 forints = £1 sterling) and a tourist rate of 30 forints to U.S. $1 (72 forints = £1 sterling). Budget (1971 est.): revenue 193,061,000,000 forints; expenditure 195,226,000,000 forints. National income (net material product): (1969) 243.7 billion forints; (1968) 221.2 billion forints.
Foreign Trade. (1970) Imports 24,410,000,000 forints; exports 27,197,000,000 forints. Import sources (1969): U.S.S.R. 37%; East Germany 10%; Czechoslovakia 7%; Poland 6%. Export destinations (1969): U.S.S.R. 35%; East Germany 11%; Czechoslovakia 9%; Poland 6%; West Germany 6%; Italy 5%. Main exports: machinery 26%; chemicals; iron and steel; fruit and vegetables; textiles.
Transport and Communications. Roads (1970) 109,159 km. (including 85 km. expressways). Passenger vehicles in use (1970) 240,265. Railways: (1969) 8,768 km.; traffic (1970) 13,932,000,000 passenger km., freight 19,142,000,000 net ton-km. Air traffic (1969): 290,223,000 passenger-km.; freight 6,150,000 net ton-km. Telephones (Dec. 1969) 777,739. Radio licenses (Dec. 1969) 2,531,000. Television licenses (Dec. 1969) 1,596,000.
Agriculture. Production (in 000; metric tons; 1970; 1969 in parentheses): corn 4,072 (4,820); wheat 2,723 (3,585); rye c. 160 (239); barley 553 (909); potatoes 1,430 (1,590); sugar, raw value (1970–71) 252, (1969–70) 449; tobacco c. 27 (27); tomatoes (1969) 400, (1968) 434; sunflower seed c. 105 (119); dry peas 105 (119); apples c. 700 (819); wine c. 570 (561); beef and veal c. 178 (198); pork c. 290 (305). Livestock (in 000; March 1970): cattle 1,933; pigs 5,970; sheep 3,024; horses 231; chickens 58,121.
Industry. Index of production (1963 = 100): (1970) 144; (1969) 135. Production (in 000; metric tons; 1970): coal 4,152; lignite 23,679; crude oil 1,937; natural gas (cu.m.) 3,469,000; electricity (kw-hr.) 14,536,000; iron ore (25% metal content) 629; pig iron 1,838; crude steel 3,116; bauxite 2,022; cement 2,769; sulfuric acid (1969) 478; nitrogenous fertilizers (nitrogen content; 1969) 300; cotton yarn 57; wool yarn 14; commercial vehicles (units) 9.7.

ICELAND
Education. (1968–69) Primary, pupils 27,356, teachers 1,319; secondary, pupils 15,675, teachers 1,229; vocational, pupils c. 5,000, teachers 548; teacher training, students 909, teachers c. 100; higher (at Reykjavik University), students 1,302, teaching staff 150.
Finance. Monetary unit: króna, with a par value of 88 krónur to U.S. $1 (211.20 krónur = £1 sterling) and a free rate (Sept. 27, 1971) of 86 krónur to U.S. $1 (213 krónur = £1 sterling). Gold, SDRs, and foreign exchange, central bank: (June 1971) U.S. $61.2 million; (June 1970) U.S. $52 million. Budget (1970 est.): revenue 8,397,000,000 krónur; expenditure 8,187,000,000 krónur. Gross national product: (1970) 42,160,000,000 krónur; (1969) 33.7 billion krónur. Money supply: (May 1971) 5,828,000,000 krónur; (May 1970) 5,081,000,000 krónur. Cost of living (Reykjavik; 1963 = 100): (May, 1971) 249; (May 1970) 227.
Foreign Trade. (1970) Imports 13,860,000,000 krónur; exports 12.9 billion krónur. Import sources: West Germany 15%; U.K. 14%; Denmark 13%; U.S. 8%; U.S.S.R. 7%; Netherlands 6%; Norway 6%; Sweden 5%. Export destinations: U.S. 30%; U.K. 13%; West Germany 11%; Denmark 8%; U.S.S.R. 7%; Sweden 7%. Main exports: fish and products 78%; aluminum 13%.
Transport and Communications. Roads (1970) 10,993 km. Motor vehicles in use (1970): passenger 40,786; commercial 5,589. There are no railways. Air traffic (1970): 1,781,000,000 passenger-km; freight 12,970,000 net ton-km. Shipping (1970): merchant vessels 100 gross tons and over 279; gross tonnage 119,305. Telephones (Dec. 1969) 67,973. Radio licenses (Dec. 1969) 62,000. Television licenses (Dec. 1969) 31,000.
Agriculture. Production (in 000; metric tons; 1969; 1968 in parentheses): potatoes 4 (6); hay (1968) 371, (1967) 344; mutton and lamb 13 (13); fish catch 689 (601). Livestock (in 000; 1969–70): cattle 53; sheep 780; horses 34; chickens c. 140.
Industry. Electricity (public supply only; 1970) 1,458,000,000 kw-hr.

Hurricanes:
see Disasters; Meteorology

Hydroelectric Power:
see Engineering Projects; Fuel and Power

Ice Hockey:
see Hockey

The most important cultural event of the year was the return by Denmark after a long dispute of several manuscripts of the Icelandic Sagas, brought to Copenhagen early in the 18th century, when Iceland was under Danish suzerainty. The *Flatoe Book* and *Codex Regius* were sent to Reykjavik in April.

The 1971 fish harvest was good and sales of frozen fish increased because U.S. prices were very high. As pollution took its toll in other European fresh waters, sport fishing for salmon in Iceland's rivers increased and by 1971 was costing U.S. $100 per day per person, with accommodations, in the most popular areas. In May British European Airways began regular flights to Iceland. (VA. K.)

Ice Skating

Skaters from 16 nations took part in the 1971 world ice figure and dance skating championships at Lyons, France, on February 22–27. There were 119 contestants. Ondrej Nepela of Czechoslovakia became the new men's champion after an enthralling freestyle duel with Patrick Péra, eventually decided by the Frenchman's injured toes. Nepela, a student from Bratislava, was the first Czechoslovakian to win the title since it was inaugurated in 1896. His jumping highlights were a triple Salchow, a triple toe-loop, and an exceptionally high double axel. The judges divided 7–2 in Nepela's favour and eight gave him 5.9 (maximum is 6) for technical merit. Péra was born in Lyons, but a storybook ending of local boy making good was thwarted by the injury that interrupted his training and interfered with his jumps. Third place went to Sergei Chetverukhin of the Soviet Union.

Beatrix Schuba gained the women's title because her exceptional superiority in figures offset her relatively average freestyle performance. She was the first Austrian to succeed in 45 years, having been runner-up in the two previous seasons. There were several better free-skaters on view, but the tall Viennese shop accountant deserved the prize because of her earlier dominance. Bolstered by her substantial

halfway lead, she jumped with greater confidence than previously. Julie Holmes of California fractionally took second place from a Canadian, Karen Magnussen, but the outstanding freestyle performer, though overall fourth, was another U.S. skater, Janet Lynn of Illinois. Miss Lynn's near-faultless display earned two sixes for artistic impression and was notable for original jump-spin combinations.

Both the pairs and ice dance titles were retained by Soviet skaters, but each by slender margins. Aleksei Ulanov and Irina Rodnina scored their third successive pairs win after the closest possible challenge from their compatriots, Andrei Suraikin and Ludmila Smirnova, with the third-place Americans, Ken Shelley and Jo Jo Starbuck, also close behind.

Husband and wife Aleksandr Gorshkov and Ludmila Pakhomova gained their second ice dance victory by a hairline 5–4 verdict over the West German brother and sister, Erich and Angelika Buck, in another exciting triple finish that also involved Americans, James Sladky and Judy Schwomeyer, who finished third.

Dutch racers were again prominent in the year's speed skating. Ard Schenk retained his overall title in the world men's championship, at Göteborg, Swed., on February 13–14. Schenk was first in three of the four distances, setting a new world record of 15 min. 1.6 sec. for the 10,000 m. Göran Claesson, of Sweden, was overall runner-up and Schenk's Dutch compatriot, Kees Verkerk, third. The 500-m. sprint was won by a Norwegian, Dag Fornaess.

Though winning only one event, the 1,500 m., Nina Statkevich (U.S.S.R.) became the new world women's champion at Helsinki, Fin., on February 6–7. Stien Kaiser (Neth.), winner of the 3,000 m., was overall runner-up with Ludmila Titova (U.S.S.R.) third. The two shorter distances, 500 m. and 1,000 m., were won by Americans, Anne Henning and Dianne Holum, respectively.

Separate new International Skating Union (ISU) sprint championships, held at Inzell, W.Ger., on February 20–21, proved a popular venture. Decided by four races, two each of 500 m. and 1,000 m., the combined men's winner was Erhard Keller (W.Ger.) and the women's victor, Ruth Schleiermacher (E. Ger.). Two new world records were established at this tournament, Schenk lowering the men's 1,000 m. to 1 min. 18.8 sec. and Miss Henning twice reducing the women's 500-m. time, the faster being 42.75 sec.

The ISU's 34th biennial congress, in Venice, Italy, on June 1–4, agreed on some important changes in ice skating championships, to come into force on Sept. 1, 1972. The award of separate medals for figures, a move widely sought for years, finally was approved, the idea being to encourage specialization. Previously, titles had been recognized only for the best overall performances in figures and freestyle. Separate medals also were approved for each of the distances covered in speed skating, distinct from the combined titles awarded to date. But by far the most revolutionary alteration was one to abolish the traditional six figures and free-skating on a 50–50 marking ratio. It was agreed to divide all senior figure skating championships and competitions into three parts: (1) three compulsory figures (reduced from six), to receive 40% of the total marks; (2) a new short program of compulsory moves with prescribed free-skating elements, to receive 20%; (3) free-skating, to receive the remaining 40%. Luxembourg swelled the ISU membership to 31 nations. (H. B.)

Erhard Keller of West Germany breaks the world's record in the 500-m. sprint at speed skating competition at Inzell, W.Ger., March 14, 1971. Keller's time was 38.42 sec.

Immunology:
see Medicine

WIDE WORLD

Income, National

The world economy went into recession in 1970, as demonstrated by the statistics presented in Table III, which show real increases in production for 56 countries. The recession was led by the United States, where gross national product (GNP) fell below its 1969 level. Overall, the rate of growth of the 15 industrial countries fell from 4.7% in 1969 to 2.5% in 1970, compared with their long-term average yearly growth of 5.1% from 1960 to 1968. In Europe the countries of the EEC grew on average by 5.4% in 1970, compared with 7.1% a year earlier, but this was still above their average growth rate of 5% between 1960 and 1968. The countries of the European Free Trade Area (EFTA) grew more slowly—by 3.4% in both 1970 and 1969—but at about their average growth rate of 3.6% from 1960 to 1968. This group was heavily influenced by the slow growth of the United Kingdom.

Estimates of the growth of some major countries for the year 1971, included in Table III, are taken from the Organization for Economic Cooperation and Development publication *Economic Outlook* and based on the latest available information, but they should be regarded as provisional. According to these figures, growth picked up in 1971. For the 15 industrial countries as a whole the growth rate in 1971 was $3\frac{1}{4}\%$ and for the EEC, $3\frac{3}{4}\%$. However, in EFTA the growth rate fell to about $2\frac{1}{4}$–$2\frac{1}{2}\%$, largely as a result of the U.K.'s performance. The year was also notable for the improvement in the U.S. economy and the sharp decline in Japan's previously sustained rapid growth.

In the group of other developed areas, most countries experienced a fall in their growth rate in 1970, but in Portugal growth picked up and Iceland emerged from its recession. In 1971 Finland entered a recession and Ireland improved.

Experience was varied in the less developed countries, but the general position worsened. There were some sharp declines in growth rate (Argentina, Cyprus, Israel, South Korea, Syria, Thailand, and Uganda). Venezuela experienced an improvement on previous performance.

Comparisons between Eastern European and other countries are difficult because the former excludes from national income accounts certain "unproductive services" such as public administration and personal and professional services. If such items were included, the growth rates in those countries would probably be somewhat lower than the ones recorded. A comparison of the section of Table III summarizing their recent record with the growth targets set in the five-year plans that ended in 1970 shows that the targets appear to have been achieved. In Czechoslovakia and Hungary, recorded growth was substantially above the rate called for in the plan.

Recent trends in expenditure of GNP are analyzed for a large number of countries in Table II. The figures are not always completely comparable because of differences in national accounting practices,

Table I. National Income and Income per Capita

Country	National income in U.S. $000,000,000 1970	National income per capita in U.S. $ 1958	1963	1970	Country	National income in U.S. $000,000,000 1970	National income per capita in U.S. $ 1958	1963	1970
Industrial countries					**Caribbean and**				
Austria	10.7	590	830	1,450	**Latin America**				
Belgium	20.4	935	1,190	2,105	Argentina	16.8*	490	485	735*
Canada	55.2	1,505	1,600	2,580	Brazil	24.0*	140	225	260*
Denmark	10.7*	890	1,335	2,175*	Chile	5.0*	330*	260	520*
France	110.3	855	1,320	2,175	Colombia	5.0*	190	225	245*
Germany, West	143.7	790	1,255	2,335	Costa Rica	0.8	295	315	440
Italy	75.5	495	795	1,405	Ecuador	1.2	155	160	195
Japan	156.8	290	575	1,515	El Salvador	0.9	205	215	250
Luxembourg	0.6*	1,075†	1,340	1,970*	Guatemala	1.3	235	265	275
Netherlands	25.3	695	995	1,945	Honduras	0.6	175	185	225
Norway	8.4	870	1,205	2,165	Jamaica	0.9	315	375	445
Sweden	23.2‡	1,180‡	1,700‡	2,890‡	Mexico	24.2‖	270	350	510‖
Switzerland	16.7	1,195	1,675	2,655	Nicaragua	0.7	225	265	375
United Kingdom	92.9	1,015	1,305	1,665	Peru	3.1‖	165	200	245‖
United States	801.0	2,115	2,560	3,910	Puerto Rico§	3.8*	540	830	1,390*
Other developed areas					Uruguay	1.6‖	540	535	550‖
Australia§	26.4*	1,125	1,470	2,150*	Venezuela	7.8‖	630*	605	805‖
Finland	8.0	725	1,130	1,705					
Greece	6.6*	325	455	750*	**Asia, East and Southeast**				
Iceland	0.2‖	965	1,270	1,095‖	Burma▲	1.8‖	55	60	65‖
Ireland	2.7*	465	655	935*	Ceylon	1.7*	120†	130	135*
New Zealand¶	5.2‡	1,170	1,505	1,840‡	Hong Kong	1.3⬚	245	381	...
Portugal	4.8*	215	300	505*	India¶	41.6*	65†	80	75*
South Africa♀	13.2‖	315	400	675‖	Indonesia	9.7‖	80	75	85‖
Spain	27.4	305	450	815	Iran¶	7.8*	145	185	275*
Turkey	10.8§	180	225	320§	Korea, South	6.9	125	130	215
Less developed areas					Malaysia	2.5◇	195	225	255◇
Africa					Pakistan§	14.7*	60	80	130*
Algeria	2.2⬚	235	195	...	Philippines	6.8*	195	220	180*
Congo (Kinshasa)	0.9‖	70†	120†	50‖	Singapore	1.3‖	420	480	650‖
Egypt§	4.8⬚	110†	140	156⬚	Taiwan	4.3	90	150	305
Ghana	1.6‖	140	190	200‖	Thailand	4.4*	80	100	125*
Kenya	1.1*	70	85	105*	Vietnam, South	3.0‖	90	80	170‖
Libya	2.2§	110	360	1,240‖					
Morocco	2.8*	160	165	185*	**Middle East**				
Nigeria¶	4.1◇	50	65	70◇	Iraq	2.3*	160	190	255*
Rhodesia	1.2	175	185	235	Israel	4.3	630	840	1,470
Sudan§	1.4⬚	80	90	95⬚	Jordan	0.5‖	140	190	225‖
Tanzania	0.8‖	50†	60	60‖	Kuwait¶	2.2*	1,825†	3,430†	3,335*
Tunisia	0.9*	160	195	180*	Lebanon	1.2‖	210	380	465‖
Uganda	0.7‖	60	65	80‖	Saudi Arabia§	2.2⬚	125†	225	310⬚
Zambia	1.0‖	110	135	235‖	Syria	1.3‖	155	165	215‖

*1969.
†Data not strictly comparable with later years.
‡Unofficial estimate.
§Financial year beginning July 1.
‖1968.
¶Financial year beginning April 1 (for Iran, March 21).
♀Including Botswana, Lesotho, Swaziland, and South West Africa (Namibia).

⬚1963.
⬚1967.
◇1966.
▲Financial year ending September 30.
Sources: Publications of United Nations, Organization for Economic Cooperation and Development, and International Monetary Fund; official national sources and research institute estimates.

but they do serve to show major differences. In some cases the original national accounts include a statistical discrepancy between the total and the sum of its components, so that the items shown do not add up to 100%.

In virtually all countries the share of private consumption expenditure fell after the late 1950s. This was also generally true for 1970 in relation to 1969, except in the U.S., Italy, New Zealand, the Netherlands, South Korea, Malawi, and some Latin-American countries. In some countries, government current expenditure took a higher share in 1970 than in 1969 (Canada, the Netherlands, and the U.K.), but in others the share declined (Austria, Italy, and Norway). During the 1960s the general tendency was for this category to rise faster than total expenditure in nearly every country.

During 1970 the share of fixed investment rose in many industrial countries (quite markedly in West Germany and Norway). Among the less developed countries, as well as in most of the advanced ones, investment's share in GNP had generally risen during the 1960s, but there were several declines in 1970. Inventory building was modest in most of the advanced countries, although in Japan this item accounted for nearly 5% of total production.

The international surplus as shown in Table II includes all transactions in goods and services, and the net effect of factor incomes (payments such as dividends and interest arising in one country, which are paid to residents of another). Thus, the figures are comparable to the current account of the balance of international payments, excluding the effect of current international transfer payments. The largest relative surpluses were recorded in Belgium, West Germany, Switzerland, and the U.K.; the largest deficits by Ireland, Israel, New Zealand, South Korea, Malawi, and by several of the Latin-American countries.

Table I shows the latest available figures for levels of national income, considered on both a total and a per capita basis, in more than 70 countries. The concept of national income is designed to measure the output of the national economy at the cost of producing that output, less the value of the depreciation of the capital stock for that year. The table includes all countries for which 1970 data were available or that had a national income of $1 billion or more in 1963. The national figures at current prices have been converted to U.S. dollars at current exchange rates. Thus, the figures are affected by changes in the price level and do not indicate the growth of real per capita income.

Two important qualifications have to be made about the use of this procedure. First, the use of current exchange rates determined for foreign trade and pay-

Table II. Disposal of Gross National Product (%)

Country	Year	Private con-sumption	Public con-sumption	Gross fixed capital formation	Change in inven-tory	Inter-national surplus	Country	Year	Private con-sumption	Public con-sumption	Gross fixed capital formation	Change in inven-tory	Inter-national surplus
Industrial countries							Ireland	1968	68.4	12.5	19.0	1.3	1.2
Austria	1968	58.9	14.6	26.1	1.2	−0.9		1969	68.2	13.0	22.2	1.3	−4.7
	1969	57.1	14.7	25.5	2.0	0.8		1970	67.4	13.9	21.5	1.1	−3.8
	1970	56.1	14.4	26.8	2.5	0.2							
Belgium	1968	63.7	13.9	21.0	1.1	0.3	New Zealand	1968–69	61.3	14.9	21.1	1.5	1.2
	1969	62.5	13.9	20.9	1.9	0.8		1969–70	60.6	15.3	21.1	2.5	0.5
	1970	59.9	13.9	21.9	1.3	3.1		1970–71†	61.7	16.2	22.0	3.8	−3.7
Canada	1968	59.3	17.0	22.1	1.0	−0.4	Spain	1968	69.3	10.4	20.9	2.1	−2.6
	1969	59.2	17.4	21.9	1.3	−1.2		1969	68.6	10.7	21.9	2.0	−3.2
	1970	58.0	18.7	21.3	0.1	1.3		1970	67.8	11.1	21.2	1.7	−1.7
Germany, West	1968	55.9	15.7	23.2	2.0	3.3	**Less developed areas**						
	1969	55.3	15.6	24.3	2.3	2.5	Costa Rica	1968	70.5	13.8	20.5	2.6	−7.3
	1970	54.7	15.7	26.5	1.4	1.7		1969	66.7	13.8	20.8	6.0	−7.4
Italy	1968	63.6	13.5	19.7	0.2	3.0		1970	68.3	14.0	23.1	6.1	−11.5
	1969	63.1	13.3	20.5	0.8	2.3	El Salvador	1968	80.4	9.5	10.9	0.3	−2.6
	1970	63.9	12.7	21.1	1.6	0.7		1969	78.8	10.5	11.6	1.3	−3.4
Japan	1968	52.1	8.4	33.9	4.8	0.9		1970	79.6	10.2	11.4	0.6	−1.3
	1969	51.2	8.3	35.2	3.9	1.4	Guatemala	1968	81.7	7.5	14.4	0.2	−3.9
	1970	50.3	8.1	35.6	4.9	1.1		1969	80.0	7.9	14.6	−0.3	−2.2
Netherlands	1968	56.7	15.7	26.3	0.7	0.6		1970	79.3	8.1	14.5	0.4	−2.3
	1969	56.2	15.7	25.2	2.5	0.4	Israel	1968	65.9	29.6	20.5	2.4	−18.3
	1970	56.7	16.1	26.3	2.1	−1.2		1969	66.8	31.2	23.8	0.7	−22.6
Norway	1968	53.8	17.6	27.2	−0.2	1.6		1970	63.3	36.8	25.4		−25.5
	1969	55.0	18.1	24.8	0.7	1.5	Korea, South	1968	75.6	11.1	25.5	1.2	−11.7
	1970	53.2	17.7	27.4	3.2	−1.5		1969	71.9	10.9	26.7	3.3	−11.2
Switzerland	1968	57.9	11.8	25.0	0.7	4.7		1970	72.5	11.0	25.6	2.4	−9.8
	1969	57.4	11.9	25.6	0.6	4.5	Malawi	1968	85.5	17.2	17.3	−1.1	−19.0
	1970	57.3	12.0	29.1		1.6		1969	82.5	16.4	17.8	1.1	−17.8
United Kingdom	1968	63.3	18.0	18.3	0.5	−0.1		1970	82.8	16.3	16.5	0.4	−16.0
	1969	62.5	17.6	17.6	0.8	1.5	Nicaragua	1968	77.3	11.2	15.8	2.3	−6.6
	1970	61.9	18.0	17.6	0.9	1.6		1969	75.0	11.5	17.0	2.1	−5.5
United States*	1968	62.0	23.0*	13.8*	0.8*	0.3		1970	76.7	10.9	17.7		−5.3
	1969	62.4	22.6*	14.0*	0.8*	0.2	Paraguay	1968	82.4	8.5	14.8	0.5	−6.1
	1970	63.2	22.5*	13.6*	0.3*	0.4		1969	80.0	9.2	15.8	0.6	−5.5
Other developed areas								1970	79.4	9.2	14.9	0.2	−3.7
Australia	1967–68	63.3	13.1	27.4	0.6	−4.4	Taiwan	1968	59.5	17.8	22.1	3.6	−3.0
	1968–69	60.7	12.8	27.1	2.6	−3.5		1969	57.7	18.3	22.6	2.7	−1.0
	1969–70	60.2	12.7	26.9	1.6	−2.4		1970	56.0	18.2	24.1	2.2	−0.6
Finland	1968	55.1	16.8	23.0	4.2	0.8							
	1969	54.7	16.2	23.9	5.3	0.0							
	1970	53.5	16.2	26.0	6.6	−2.3							

*Fixed capital formation and inventory-building figures are for the private sector only. Public sector fixed investment and inventory building are included in public consumption.
†Unofficial estimate.
Sources: UN, OECD, and IMF publications; official national sources and research institute estimates.

ments purposes may not adequately reflect differences in the purchasing power of the various national currencies. Furthermore, devaluations and revaluations will distort the figures as between different years. Second, the figures in national currencies are themselves estimated in a variety of ways, and there are differences in the definitions used among various countries. For these reasons, small differences in per capita national income are insignificant.

Bearing these difficulties in mind, one may draw some tentative conclusions from the data presented. About four-fifths of the aggregate income of the listed countries is accounted for by the 15 industrial countries, while the 51 less developed countries represent 10–15% of the total. The dominating size of the U.S. economy in relation to all other non-Communist countries is shown in the table; it is roughly five times the size of the next largest, Japan, and five to six times the size of West Germany. It is likely, however, that a more sophisticated analysis allowing for differences in the internal purchasing power of national currencies would show a somewhat different picture. The available evidence suggests that, in comparison with the U.S., real output in several Western European countries was relatively higher than suggested by the 1970 figures, particularly in West Germany and Italy.   (M. F. F.)

See also Economy, World.

India

A federal republic of southern Asia and a member of the Commonwealth of Nations, India is situated on a peninsula extending into the Indian Ocean with the Arabian Sea to the west and the Bay of Bengal to the east. Area: 1,229,424 sq.mi. (3,184,212 sq.km.). Pop. (1971): 546,955,945; Indo-Aryans and Dravidians are dominant, with Mongoloid, Negroid, and Australoid admixtures. Cap.: New Delhi (pop., 1971, 292,857). Largest city: Bombay (pop., 1970 est., 5,700,358). Language: Hindi and English (official). Religion (1961): Hindu 83.5%; Muslim 10.7%; Christian 2.4%; Sikh 1.8%; Buddhist 0.7%; others 0.9%. President in 1971, Varahagiri Venkata Giri; prime minister, Mrs. Indira Gandhi.

Domestic Affairs. By the end of 1971, following India's swift and decisive victory over Pakistan and the resultant "liberation" of East Bengal, or Bangla Desh (*see* below), Prime Minister Indira Gandhi's prestige, reinforced earlier in the year by a sweeping electoral success, rose to new heights, and her position seemed unassailable.

India was in the grip of election fever as the year began. The president had dissolved the Lok Sabha (House of the People) on Dec. 27, 1970. Conscious that her popularity was at a high level, Mrs. Gandhi (*see* BIOGRAPHY) sought to increase her parliamentary majority by going to the polls a year earlier than necessary. She also sought to separate central and state elections, so that the focus would not be on local problems but on the need to provide a government at the centre stable and strong enough to introduce rapid social change. She herself became the main issue of the elections. The Jan Sangh, the Swatantra Party, and the Opposition Congress formed

Table III. Growth of Real Gross National Product, 1960–71				
		Percentage real increase		
Country	Average 1960–68	1969 over 1968	1970 over 1969	1971* over 1970
Industrial countries				
Austria	4.3	6.4	7.1	5½
Belgium	4.5	6.5	6.1	3¾
Canada	5.2	5.0	3.3	5¾
Denmark	4.4	7.7	3.2	2
France	5.5	7.9	5.9	5½
Germany, West	4.3	7.9	5.4	3½
Italy	5.7	5.0	5.2	½
Japan	10.9	12.5	10.7	4¾
Luxembourg	2.9	7.0	2.9	...
Netherlands	5.0	5.1	6.0	5
Norway	5.1	4.7	3.5	5¼
Sweden	4.5	5.8	4.8	½
Switzerland	4.4	5.4	5.0	4½
United Kingdom	3.0	1.3	2.2	1½
United States	4.8	2.8	−0.7	3
Other developed areas				
Australia†	4.6	8.6	5.7	...
Finland	4.1	9.3	7.4	1½
Greece	7.4	7.8	8.1	...
Iceland	4.3	0.0	7.9	...
Ireland	4.3	4.3	1.5	3
New Zealand‡	3.7	5½§	4§	...
Portugal	6.5	4.4	6.4	...
South Africa‖	6.0	7.0	5.1	...
Spain	7.6	7.7	5.5	4½
Turkey	5.5	6.2	4.8	...
Centrally planned economies¶				
Albania	8.0	11.0	6.0	...
Bulgaria	7.5	9.9	7.0	...
Czechoslovakia	4.0	6.5	5.0	...
Germany, East	4.1	5.1	5.2	...
Hungary	5.3	7.2	5.0	...
Mongolia	2.0	8.5	...	...
Poland	6.6	2.9	6.0	...
Romania	8.6	7.9	6.6	...
U.S.S.R.	7.2	4.8	8½	...
Yugoslavia	6.5	9.8	5.5	...
Less developed areas				
Argentina	3.7	7.9	4.8	...
Brazil	5.2	9.0	9.4	...
Burma	3.2ᵠ	...	3.9	...
Ceylon	4.5	5.7	5.5	...
Cyprus	6.1	9.6	3.3	...
Ghana	2.3	3.6	3¾	...
India‡	3.3	5.5	...	...
Indonesia	2.6	6.3	...	...
Iran‡	8.7	11.4	...	...
Israel	8.6	9.3	6.9	...
Kenya	6.5	6.7	6.3	...
Korea, South	8.4	16.1	10.1	...
Malaysia, West	6.0	9.0	...	...
Mexico	6.6	7.2	6.0	...
Pakistan†	5.5	5.8	5.8	...
Philippines	4.6	7.7	5.0	...
Puerto Rico†	9.2	6.7	7.0	...
Syria	5.7ᵠ	15.5	4.6	...
Thailand	7.3	9.4	5.4	...
Uganda	3.9	10.0	3.2	...
Venezuela	4.6	3.5	6.1	...

*OECD estimates, based on incomplete data.
†Financial year ending June 30.
‡Financial year beginning April 1 (for Iran, March 21).
§Unofficial estimate.
‖Including Botswana, Lesotho, Swaziland, and South West Africa (Namibia).
¶Growth of material product. See text for discussion of comparability with other figures.
ᵠBurma 1960 to 1969; Kenya 1964 to 1968 only; Syria 1961 to 1968 only.
Sources: Publications of UN, OECD, and IMF publications; official national sources; research institute estimates.

Anti-American demonstrators greet Henry Kissinger, adviser to Pres. Richard Nixon, as he arrives in New Delhi for talks with Indian leaders on the East Pakistan issue.

UPI COMPIX

An elderly woman casts her vote in the state of Uttar Pradesh during national parliamentary elections held March 1–10, 1971.
RAVI BEDI—CAMERA PRESS FROM PIX

Socialist Party 3 (0); Kerala Congress 3 (0); Praja Socialist Party 2 (15); Bharatiya Kranti Dal 1 (10); smaller parties and unattached members 23 (43); nominated 2; vacant 5; total 521. The "grand alliance" parties were practically wiped out in the Lok Sabha. Among important candidates who were defeated were S. K. Patil, Atulya Ghosh, Sanjiva Reddy, M. R. Masani, N. G. Ranga, Madhu Limaye, S. N. Dwivedi, George Fernandes, and Balraj Madhok.

Simultaneously, elections were held for three state assemblies, those of West Bengal, Orissa, and Tamil Nadu. In West Bengal there was a keen fight between a Ruling Congress-led front and an alliance led by the Communist Party (Marxist). The former gained support of a few smaller parties, claimed 141 out of the 277 assembly seats, and formed the government under Ajoy Mukherji. In Orissa, a coalition of Swatantra, Utkal Congress, and Jharkhand formed the government, Ruling Congress securing only 51 out of 139 seats. In Tamil Nadu, Ruling Congress left the field open to the Dravida Munnetra Kazhagam (DMK), in return for the party's support of Congress in the national election. DMK secured 184 out of the 234 assembly seats.

Mrs. Gandhi was formally reelected leader of the Ruling Congress Parliamentary Party and was sworn in as prime minister for a third time on March 18. In her Cabinet of 14, 7 were newcomers—C. Subramaniam, Moinul Haq Chaudhury, U. S. Dikshit, Raj Bahadur, S. S. Ray, Mohan Kumaramangalam, and H. R. Gokhale, the last three of them lawyers with a reputation for radicalism.

The new government moved expeditiously on some of its election promises. Management of general insurance was taken over in May. The 24th Constitution Amendment Bill was introduced in July to restore to Parliament the right to amend the constitution, even including the chapter on fundamental rights. The bill was passed early in August by the Lok Sabha by 384 votes to 23 and by the Rajya Sabha (Council of States) by 177 votes to 3. The 25th Constitution Amendment Bill also was introduced in Parliament with the object of keeping out of the courts' jurisdiction payments made for acquisition of property.

Meanwhile, events further afield began to threaten. Within a week of the new Parliament's meeting in Delhi, negotiations broke down in Pakistan between Pres. Agha Muhammad Yahya Khan and Sheikh Mujibur Rahman, who had won a sweeping victory

a "grand alliance" to oust her, with help from the Samyukta Socialist Party.

Polling was spread between March 1 and March 10. Of an electorate of 273.8 million, 151.5 million exercised their franchise. Suspense was heightened because counting began only after polling had been completed throughout the country. Even as first results came in it was apparent that Mrs. Gandhi had won a landslide victory. Her Ruling Congress Party secured more than two-thirds of the seats in the Lok Sabha although it had contested only 441. The party position on May 15 (with the strength in the previous House shown in parentheses) was Ruling Congress 349 (223); Communist Party of India (Marxist) 25 (19); Communist Party of India 24 (24); Dravida Munnetra Kazhagam 23 (25); Jan Sangh 22 (33); Opposition Congress 16 (63); Telengana Praja Samiti 10 (0); Swatantra Party 7 (35); Muslim League 3 (0); Samyukta Socialist Party 3 (17); Revolutionary

INDIA

Education. (1965–66) Primary, pupils 49,499,-000, teachers 1,393,930; secondary, pupils 7,022,-394, teachers 342,350; vocational, pupils 450,101, teachers 31,220; teacher training, students 177,-607, teachers 13,460; higher (including 62 universities), students 1,054,273, teaching staff (1963–64) 80,247.

Finance. Monetary unit: rupee, with a par value of Rs. 7.50 to U.S. $1 (Rs. 18 = £1 sterling) and a free rate (Sept. 27, 1971) of Rs. 7.43 to U.S. $1 (Rs. 18.42 = £1 sterling). Gold, SDRs, and foreign exchange, official: (April 1971) U.S. $1,032,000,000; (April 1970) U.S. $1,095,000,000. Budget (1970–71 est.): revenue Rs. 40,367,000,000; expenditure Rs. 31,522,000,-000. National income: (1969–70) Rs. 308 billion; (1968–69) Rs. 286 billion. Money supply: (April 1971) Rs. 72,950,000,000; (April 1970) Rs. 65,520,000,000. Cost of living (1963 = 100): (May 1971) 169; (May 1970) 166.

Foreign Trade. (1970–71) Imports Rs. 16,-250,000,000; exports Rs. 15,350,000,000. Import sources: U.S. 27%; U.K. 8%; Canada 7%; West Germany 7%; U.S.S.R. 6%; Iran 6%; Japan 5%. Export destinations: U.S. 16%; Japan 12%; U.S.S.R. 11%; U.K. 11%. Main exports: jute manufactures 13%; tea 8%; iron ore 6%; iron and steel 6%; cotton fabrics 6%; leather 5%; fruit and vegetables 5%.

Transport and Communications. Roads (1970) 1,009,515 km. (including 24,000 km. main roads). Motor vehicles in use (1970): passenger 588,837; commercial 318,915. Railways: (1968) 59,401 km.; traffic (1969–70) 111,054,-000,000 passenger-km., freight 119,668,000,000 net ton-km. Air traffic (1970): 3,740,000,000 passenger-km.; freight 118,940,000 net ton-km. Shipping (1970): merchant vessels 100 gross tons and over 399; gross tonnage 2,401,656. Telephones (Dec. 1969) 1,120,357. Radio receivers (Dec. 1969) 10,035,000. Television receivers (Dec. 1969) 12,000.

Agriculture. Production (in 000; metric tons; 1970; 1969 in parentheses): wheat 20,093 (18,-652); rice c. 64,500 (60,645); barley 2,716 (2,-424); corn c. 6,500 (5,674); millet c. 9,400 (9,176); sorghum c. 10,000 (9,721); potatoes 4,093 (4,726); cassava (1969) 4,636, (1968) 4,644; tea 420 (396); chick-peas 5,546 (4,310); bananas (1969) c. 3,100, (1968) 3,007; sugar, raw value (1970–71) c. 4,326, (1969–70) c. 4,620; tobacco 338 (361); rapeseed and mustard seed 1,507 (1,347); linseed 415 (329); peanuts 6,065 (5,143); cotton, lint 1,106 (1,052); jute 883 (1,018). Livestock (in 000; 1969–70): cattle c. 176,450; sheep c. 42,600; pigs c. 4,800; buffaloes 54,200; goats c. 67,500; poultry c. 116,500.

Industry. Production (in 000; metric tons; 1970): coal 71,942; iron ore (61% metal content) 30,781; pig iron 7,051; crude steel 6,069; electricity (excluding most industrial production; kw-hr.) 54,953,000; aluminum 161; cement 13,-986; cotton yarn 965; woven cotton fabrics (m.; 1969) 7,706,000; petroleum products (1969) 15,610; sulfuric acid 1,050; caustic soda 376; gold (troy oz.; 1969) 109; manganese ore (metal content; 1969) 575.

in the elections held in 1970. His Awami League was outlawed, and the West Pakistani-dominated regime took action to suppress the East. This resulted in a massive migration of refugees from East Pakistan into adjacent parts of India. By October 10, official figures placed the number of East Pakistan refugees at 9.3 million, of whom more than 7 million were said to have sought shelter in West Bengal.

Large amounts of money and energy had to be spent to provide food, shelter, and medical aid to the refugees. Late in October the Cabinet voted to levy new taxes and duties to help finance refugee relief. The relief expenditures as well as the general political uncertainty led to a rise in prices. In West Bengal, the strain on the state administration, combined with interparty confrontation, led to political deadlock. President's rule was proclaimed in the state on June 29. The massive popular vote in favour of Mrs. Gandhi caused a split in the Opposition Congress in many states. As a result, the Opposition Congress governments fell in Mysore and Gujarat, and those states also came under president's rule in March and May, respectively. Punjab followed suit in June. In Uttar Pradesh, the chief minister, T. N. Singh, was defeated in a by-election, leading to the fall of his coalition ministry. This paved the way for a Ruling Congress government to be sworn in under Kamalapati Tripathi. In Kerala the Ruling Congress, which had supported a ministry led by the Communist Party of India, joined the government formally in September. In Rajasthan, Mohanlal Sukhadia stepped down from the chief ministership for unstated reasons, and Barkatullah Khan took over. K. Brahmananda Reddy made way for P. V. Narasimha Rao in Andhra Pradesh to help the Telengana Praja Samiti to merge in the Ruling Congress and give up its demand for separate statehood.

The decennial census placed the population of India on April 1 at 546,955,945 (males 283,055,987; females 263,899,958), an increase of 24.57% over the 1961 figure. The density of population was 445 per square mile, the sex ratio 932 females per 1,000 males, and the literacy rate (including the age group 0–4) 29.35%. The urban population totaled 19.87%; the percentage of workers to total population was 33.54%, being composed of cultivators (42.9%), agricultural labourers (25.7%), and other workers (31.4%). There were 142 cities with populations above 100,000. The nine largest metropolitan areas were Calcutta (7,040,345), Bombay (5,931,989), Delhi (3,629,842), Madras (2,470,288), Hyderabad (1,798,910), Ahmedabad (1,746,111), Bangalore (1,648,232), Kanpur (1,273,042), and Poona (1,123,399).

Parliament adopted a medical termination of pregnancy bill by which abortion was made legal if a doctor certified that pregnancy would cause mental or physical damage or was due to failure of family planning methods.

Winds of 100 mph and a 16-ft. tidal wave struck the coast of Orissa state on the Bay of Bengal on October 29. Thousands of people, mostly inhabitants of low-lying coastal villages, were killed.

Foreign Affairs. Soon after the crisis in East Pakistan (or Bangla Desh as it subsequently called itself), Parliament adopted a resolution recording "profound conviction that the historic upsurge of the 75 million people of East Bengal [a common Indian designation for East Pakistan referring to its one-time status as the eastern part of Bengal] will triumph," and assuring them that their struggle had the wholehearted sympathy and support of the people of India. Mrs. Gandhi took the position that the Pakistani government should reach a political solution with the leaders who had won the election in East Pakistan, and thus create conditions by which the refugees could return to their homes. She wrote to numerous heads of government (including Premier Chou En-lai of China) explaining India's point of view and also sent emissaries to several countries. But the effort to mobilize international pressure on Pakistan yielded no conclusive result.

On August 9, after a visit by the Soviet foreign minister, Andrei Gromyko, to New Delhi, a 20-year treaty of peace, friendship, and cooperation was signed with the Soviet Union. Its operative clause called for consultations between the two countries in the event of an attack or threat of attack on either. Later in the year Mrs. Gandhi visited Moscow, the United States,

Prime Minister Indira Gandhi campaigns for reelection to a third term in 1971.

UPI COMPIX

and capitals of Western Europe. The announcement of U.S. Pres. Richard M. Nixon's plans to visit Peking caused popular consternation, but the government welcomed the decision as being in line with the policy adopted by India for two decades.

By mid-October Indian sources reported a buildup of Pakistani troops adjoining the Indian provinces of Rajasthan and Punjab. Military activity also was reported near the Rann of Kutch. Both armed forces canceled all leaves; they had been building up oil and gasoline reserves for several months and were poised on both sides of the eastern and western fronts.

On November 22 Pakistan accused India of having launched all-out war in East Pakistan. Both countries declared states of emergency and called up their reserves. Fighting spread to Kashmir, and by December 3 a state of open warfare existed on both fronts. Indian forces heavily outmatched in manpower and equipment those of Pakistan, whose 90,000 troops in the East fell back on Dacca, which surrendered on December 16. With the East under Indian control and an arranged cease-fire in the West, the brief war ended. (*See* DEFENSE.)

The Indian government recognized the provisional government of Bangla Desh, sought to return the refugees to that country, and to restore a peaceful situation. The Indian Army, however, was in the difficult position of having to restrain excesses by the Bengali Mukti Bahini ("Liberation Army") guerrillas against "collaborators" without alienating the local population of Bangla Desh. After the fall of Dacca evidence was found that pointed to an organized massacre by Pakistani paramilitary forces of large numbers of leading Bengali intellectuals and other prominent citizens who might have been expected to play a leading part in the emergence of independent Bangla Desh. Their bodies were found in disused clay pits, where they had apparently been shot or bayoneted shortly before the city was taken. Because of the intense feeling among the local population against the Pakistani troops, the Indian commander allowed them to retain their weapons for the first 12 hours after their surrender.

The U.S. administration's unequivocal support for Pakistan throughout the confrontation was deeply resented in India, where the movement of the U.S. 7th Fleet into the Bay of Bengal was interpreted as an open threat. Mrs. Gandhi rejected suggestions that the cease-fire had been hastened as a result of U.S. Pres. Richard Nixon's urging the Soviet Union to exert its influence with India. Feelings against China, which had vied with the U.S. in supporting Pakistan, also ran high, and the previous moves toward a normalization of relations with Peking seemed unlikely to develop.

The Economy. For the fourth successive year food production increased. The 1970–71 grain harvest was estimated to be 107.8 million metric tons, 8% higher than the previous year. National income at constant prices was estimated to have increased by 5 to 5.5% and employment in the organized sector by 2.7%. But the rate of growth of industrial production was slowing down: the increases had been 7.1% in 1969 and 4.5% in 1970 but only 1.5% in the first quarter of 1971. Although a survey of the Reserve Bank of India stated that the economy was in a better position than ever before to attain a high and sustained rate of growth, there was disquiet because of a sharp rise in prices.

The annual budget of the union government, presented on May 28, placed revenue receipts at Rs. 36,970,000,000 (including Rs. 1,770,000,000 as the central government's share of new taxation) and revenue disbursements of Rs. 35,870,000,000. Along with capital receipts of Rs. 20,240,000,000 (including Rs. 4,370,000,000 from foreign aid) and outgoings of Rs. 23,960,000,000, the deficit was estimated at Rs. 2.2 billion. However, it became clear toward the end of the year that higher expenditure on the refugees from East Pakistan would vastly increase the deficit. With an additional expected increase in defense spending, this burden threatened to cause a serious recession unless enormous amounts of foreign aid were forthcoming. A preliminary survey by the Ministry of Finance put the total cost of supporting the refugees at approximately $840 million. Of further concern was the strain on the road and rail system caused by the movement of large stocks of supplies to refugee camps. By late 1971 depletion of food supplies and other essential commodities had increased the rate of inflation from 5 to 7% and sent prices spiraling beyond the means of ordinary Indians. Disruption of the supply of raw materials and steel to key industries was an additional hazard. On October 16 the Indian government nationalized 214 coking coal mines.

(H. Y. S. P.)

See also **Pakistan.**

Indonesia

A republic of Southeast Asia, Indonesia consists of the major islands of Sumatra, Java, Kalimantan (Indonesian Borneo), Celebes, and Irian Barat (West New Guinea) and approximately 3,000 smaller islands and islets. Area: 779,675 sq.mi. (2,019,360 sq.km.). Pop. (1971 est.): 122,663,000. Cap. and largest city: Jakarta (pop.,

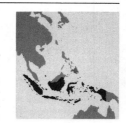

INDONESIA

Education. Primary (1968–69), pupils 12,234,-824, teachers 319,976; secondary (1967–68), pupils 1,148,502, teachers 64,576; vocational (1967–68), pupils 325,235, teachers 24,512; higher (1967–68), students 192,416, teaching staff 21,309.

Finance. Monetary unit: rupiah, with an official rate (following devaluation of Aug. 23, 1971) of 415 rupiah to U.S. $1 (996 rupiah = £1 sterling) and a free rate (Sept. 27, 1971) of 1,029 rupiah to £1 sterling. Budget (total; 1970–71 est.) balanced at 444,899,000,000 rupiah. Gross national product: (1968) 1,973,900,000,000 rupiah; (1967) 838.2 billion rupiah.

Foreign Trade. (1970) Imports U.S. $1,137,-900,000; exports U.S. $810.6 million. Import sources (1969): Japan 29%; U.S. 20%; West Germany 8%; China 5%; Singapore 5%; Netherlands 5%. Export destinations: Japan 33%; Singapore 18%; U.S. 14%; Australia 8%. Main exports: petroleum and products 35%; rubber 26%; coffee 8%.

Transport and Communications. Roads (1970) 84,292 km. Motor vehicles in use (1970): passenger 235,816; commercial 99,814. Railways: (1969) 7,282 km.; traffic (1968) 3,884,000,000 passenger-km., freight 655 million net ton-km. Air traffic (1970): 708 million passenger-km.; freight 20.3 million net ton-km. Shipping (1970): merchant vessels 100 gross tons and over 489;

gross tonnage 642,530. Telephones (Dec. 1969) 182,319.

Agriculture. Production (in 000; metric tons; 1970; 1969 in parentheses): rice 18,090 (15,-782); corn 2,433 (2,271); cassava (1969) 10,-845, (1968) 11,356; sweet potatoes (1969) 1,904, (1968) 2,364; sugar, raw value (1970–71) 624, (1969–70) 731; copra *c.* 660 (660); soybeans 420 (416); peanuts 520 (428); coffee *c.* 167 (157); rubber *c.* 770 (766). Livestock (in 000; Dec. 1969): cattle *c.* 7,000; pigs *c.* 2,650; sheep *c.* 3,740; buffaloes *c.* 2,735; goats *c.* 7,030.

Industry. Production (in 000; metric tons; 1970): crude oil 41,086; coal (1969) 192; bauxite 1,229.

1971 est., 4,542,146). Language: Bahasa Indonesian (official); Javanese; Sundanese; Madurese. Religion: mainly Muslim; some Christian, Buddhist, and Hindu. President and prime minister in 1971, General Suharto.

For Indonesia, 1971 was a watershed year in domestic and foreign affairs. Domestically, for the second time since the proclamation of independence in 1945 and for the first time since 1955, the country elected a parliament. In foreign affairs, perhaps the most important long-term development centred on Indonesia's quiet movement toward a closer relationship with Japan.

Domestic Affairs. In the first test of public support for President Suharto, who assumed power from the late President Sukarno in the aftermath of an abortive Communist coup in 1965, the country went to the polls July 3 to elect a Council of People's Representatives. Of the Council's 460 seats, 360 were up for election by secret ballot and the remainder were to be filled by government appointees with 75 of those reserved for the armed forces and 25 for "functional groups," such as physicians, lawyers, and students. Those elected by ballot were evenly divided between Java, where two-thirds of the country's population lived, and the non-Javanese islands. This was done chiefly to allay fears of Javanese domination, a smoldering regional issue since independence.

The shape of the electoral struggle was dictated by the Army's decision not to align itself with any of the existing political parties in the race but to throw its weight behind a government-created "nonparty" organization, the Joint Secretariat of Functional Groups (Sekber Golkar). A loose coalition of civil servants ranging from village headmen to Suharto, Golkar became the dominant political machine virtually overnight. Opposition parties accused the government of intimidating villagers into joining Golkar, and some critics charged that the balloting was not a general election but an election of generals.

The outcome of the election was a foregone conclusion, but even the government was surprised by the extent of Golkar's victory. It captured more than 65% of the popular vote (35 million votes) and 261 seats in the Council. With the addition of government appointees, Golkar emerged with an absolute majority in the legislative body. Since the Council takes part in the election of a head of state, this clearly ensured General Suharto's reelection to a new five-year presidential term in 1973. For all practical purposes, the election wiped out political parties. The four Muslim parties garnered 94 seats, and Sukarno's old Nationalist Party gained only 20.

Foreign Affairs. On August 26 Queen Juliana of the Netherlands became the first ruling sovereign of the House of Orange to set foot in Indonesia. As the Dutch East Indies, the archipelago had been the crown jewel of the Dutch Empire for almost 350 years until 1945 when it declared itself independent. In the course of Juliana's ten-day visit, in the company of her consort, Prince Bernhard, the 62-year-old queen was accorded a tumultuous welcome.

The highlight of the year in foreign relations was the agreement reached between Japan and Indonesia to "exchange military experiences," following a visit to Japan by the Indonesian Army chief of staff, Gen. Umar Wirahadikusumah, at the invitation of the chief of staff of Japan's Ground Self-Defense Force, Gen. Hazao Kuningasawa. Under the terms of the Indo-Japanese understanding, Japan expressed its willingness to dispatch military instructors to Indonesia at Jakarta's request. In addition, Japan agreed to permit Indonesian Army officers to attend the Ground Self-Defense Force Staff College.

During the year, while moving closer to Japan, Indonesia made repeated efforts at restoring a dialogue with China and normalizing diplomatic relations, which had been frozen in 1966 after Jakarta accused Peking of playing a hand in the abortive Indonesian Communist coup of 1965. Indonesia made it plain that although it sought a revival of Sino-Indonesian relations, it did not intend to do so at the expense of its integrity and self-respect. Before relations could be normalized the Chinese regime was told that it must halt its subversion against Indonesia, which ranged from propaganda attacks to financing Indonesian Communist exiles in Peking. China not only rebuffed Jakarta's overtures but also during the year was accused of meddling in rebel movements in Sumatra and Borneo. China also responded by inviting the leader of the outlawed Indonesian Communist Party, Jusuf Adjitorop, to share the reviewing platform with Mao Tse-tung during the May 1 celebrations in Peking.

Later in the year, Peking circulated a map, which for the first time showed as Chinese islands and reefs in the South China Sea that had been internationally recognized as Indonesian territory since independence. The Indonesians rejected China's territorial claim out of hand. Then, at the UN, in the debate over Peking's admission, Indonesia voted in favour of declaring the expulsion of Nationalist China (Taiwan) an "important matter" which would require a two-thirds vote rather than a simple majority. The resolution was defeated, and in the aftermath the Nationalists were expelled and the Peking regime seated. By its voting, despite its protestations to the contrary, Indonesia endorsed a "two China" policy within the United Nations. This was underlined by the acceptance address of Indonesia's Foreign Minister Adam Malik (*see* BIOGRAPHY) after the 26th General Assembly elected him its president.

The Economy. The economy continued its recovery from the devastating Sukarno years. Prices remained remarkably stable in 1971; the country's balance of payments showed an almost 20% improvement in exports; and the government continued to welcome private foreign investment, which had increased to more than $1.5 billion since the Suharto government announced an open-door policy in 1967. U.S. and Japanese private capital maintained the lead as the heaviest investors in Indonesia's economic recovery. Nonetheless, there were signs that the government was becoming more selective in approving foreign investment projects, and nearly 40 light industries dominated by Indonesian firms were closed to new investment from abroad. In midyear, Indonesia devalued its currency by about 10%, from 378 to 414 rupiahs to $1.

In outlining a 25-year development plan for Indonesia, President Suharto, for the first time, put unusual stress on the need for a vigorous birth-control program. He expressed fear that population growth would wipe out the country's economic gains. However, the paramount economic development of the year was the beginning of offshore oil production. During 1971 Indonesia produced about one million barrels of onshore crude oil daily. With the introduction of offshore crude, the figure was expected to double by the end of 1972. (AR. C. B.)

Industrial Review

Whereas in 1968–69 industrial activity grew vigorously and the world index increased 7% per annum, during 1970 this rapid progress was rudely interrupted. The aggregate world index reflecting manufacturing activity in the market economies (Table I) stopped rising about the middle of the year and fell until the end; its annual average was only about 2% higher than that of 1969.

This deceleration was almost entirely due to a slowdown in the industrialized countries; their aggregate output grew by only 2%, after an advance of $6\frac{1}{2}$% a year earlier. Manufacturing activity in other countries increased faster, but the growth rate there also declined from $9\frac{1}{2}$% in 1969 to $6\frac{1}{2}$% in 1970.

The change in the industrial countries was caused by a serious recession in North America, especially in the United States; the output of North American manufacturing, currently accounting for 43% of world manufacturing activity (if the Soviet bloc and China are excluded), rose more than $4\frac{1}{2}$% from 1968 to 1969, but fell back to almost the 1968 level during 1970. In Western Europe the progress continued, but its speed was significantly reduced from $9\frac{1}{2}$% in 1969 to 5% in 1970. In the Soviet Union and Eastern Europe, on the other hand, manufacturing activity continued to increase, and the rise during 1970 was somewhat faster than in the previous year.

In the first half of 1971 the situation changed considerably; the stimulus given to the various sectors of demand in the U.S. sparked an expansion in North America, where output started rising, although only

moderately. By contrast, in Western Europe, and to some extent in Japan, the earlier upswing came to a halt, and until about the end of the summer output fluctuated around the level already reached at the beginning of the year. Thus, whereas in the U.S. and Canada progress in manufacturing during 1971 was considerably more favourable than in 1970, the rate of increase in practically all industrial countries of Western Europe, and in Japan, lagged behind that achieved a year earlier.

The setback in industrial output in the U.S. was the natural outcome of the general economic recession, which was the not unexpected result of monetary and other restrictive measures implemented in 1969 that were aimed principally at restraining price inflation. The recession had already begun in the second half of 1969, and it continued until the early months of 1971. The trough was reached at the end of 1970 when the level of industrial activity was approximately 7% below the point where it first turned down. The general decline in all sectors of demand was aggravated by cuts in defense spending and by a strike at General Motors Corp. that lasted from mid-September to late November 1970. The expansionary measures introduced by the administration had a delayed and modest effect and, despite the upturn, output at mid-1971 was still well below the peak reached two years earlier. The development of Canadian industry, to a large extent dependent on the U.S. economy, followed a similar pattern, although the recession was milder and of shorter duration.

Industrial production in the United Kingdom was stagnant through 1970 and fell early in 1971. Earlier, strong deflationary measures braked both investment and private consumption; output was further hit by a wave of strikes, and the number of working days lost by industrial disputes in 1970 was the highest since 1926. The moderate relaxation of the budget presented in the spring of 1971 somewhat improved the economic climate but was insufficient to halt rising unemployment; this led to further expansionary steps in July, which showed signs of stimulating industrial activity toward the end of 1971.

West German industry increased its output by 6% in 1970, following a record rise of 14% in 1969; this annual increase, however, concealed the fact that output, although at a high level, had declined in the second half of 1970. At its peak in mid-1970, the nationwide utilization of physical capacity was as high as 96%. This caused such heavy pressure on resources that the economy became overheated, but demand later weakened and the rate of growth slowed down, leading to a slight decline in output. The mild winter enabled West German industry to reach yet another peak early in 1971, but output fell to a somewhat lower level toward the middle of the year (when the utilization of industrial capacity fell below 90%).

In France there was a rapid rise in output in the

Table I. Index Numbers of World Production, Employment, and Productivity in Manufacturing Industries
1963 = 100

Area	Relative importance 1963	1970	Production 1968	1969	1970	Employment 1968	1969	1970	Productivity* 1968	1969	1970
World†	1,000	1,000	136	146	149	...	...	...	...	...	...
Industrial countries	876	867	135	145	148	...	...	...	...	...	...
Less industrialized countries	124	133	138	151	161	...	...	...	...	...	...
North America‡	480	429	133	139	135	...	...	...	...	...	...
Canada	28	26	137	144	147	115	118	116	119	122	127
United States	452	403	133	139	135	116	118	114	115	118	119
Latin America§	49	52	139	150	160	...	...	...	...	...	...
Mexico	8	...	159	175	...	...	...	...	...	...	...
Asia‖	88	132	173	199	225	...	...	...	...	...	...
India	16	...	121	129	135	...	...	...	...	...	...
Japan	55	97	193	227	264	111	114	117	174	199	226
Pakistan	3	...	156	168	...	...	...	...	...	...	...
Europe¶	350	343	128	140	147	...	...	...	...	...	...
Austria	7	7	127	142	154	95	97	101	134	146	152
Belgium	11	11	124	137	144	99	...	...	125	...	...
Finland	4	4	132	148	161	102	107	...	129	138	...
France	51	52	128	143	154	96	98	100	133	146	154
Germany, West	89	93	129	147	156	98	102	108	132	144	144
Greece	2	2	151	168	152	108	112	117	140	150	130
Ireland	1	1	139	147	152	106	114	116	131	129	131
Italy	36	36	136	140	151	100	104	107	136	135	141
Netherlands	12	14	138	152	169	97	98	...	142	155	...
Norway	4	4	129	136	143	105	107	110	123	127	130
Portugal	2	...	148	164	173	...	...	...	...	...	...
Sweden	14	15	135	146	158	97	97	99	139	151	160
United Kingdom	73	62	121	126	127	99	100	100	122	126	127
Yugoslavia	13	15	142	159	174	110	114	119	129	139	146
Rest of the world◊	33	...	...	...	...	...	...	...	...	...	...
Australia	14	13	129	136	138	114	117	119	113	116	116
South Africa	5	5	137	151	159	138	146	155	99	103	103
Centrally planned economies δ	...	...	153	164	179	...	...	...	...	...	...

*This is 100 times the production index divided by the employment index, giving a rough indication of changes in output per person employed.
†Excluding Albania, Bulgaria, China, Czechoslovakia, East Germany, Hungary, Mongolia, North Korea, North Vietnam, Poland, Romania, and the U.S.S.R.
‡Canada and the United States.
§South and Central America (including Mexico) and the Caribbean islands.
‖Asian Middle East and East and Southeast Asia, including Japan.

¶Excluding Albania, Bulgaria, Czechoslovakia, East Germany, Hungary, Poland, Romania, and the U.S.S.R.
◊Africa, the Middle East, and Oceania.
δThese are not included in the above world total and consist of Albania, Bulgaria, Czechoslovakia, East Germany, Hungary, Poland, Romania, and the U.S.S.R.
Sources: UN *Monthly Bulletin of Statistics;* U.K. National Institute of Economic and Social Research, *Economic Review.*

Table II. Industrial Production in the U.S.S.R. and Eastern Europe
1963 = 100

Country	1968	1969	1970
Bulgaria	181	199	218
Czechoslovakia	136	144	154
Germany, East	134	144	153
Hungary	132	135	144
Poland	151	163	178
Romania	182	201	229
U.S.S.R.	151	162	175

Source: UN *Monthly Bulletin of Statistics.*

361

Industrial Review

First Lockheed TriStar airbus nears completion in 1971. Progress on the airbus project was threatened by the bankruptcy of Rolls-Royce, builder of the engines.
KEYSTONE

early months of 1970; during the remainder of the year industry stagnated because of the successful deflationary measures that followed the earlier devaluation of the franc. Activity increased again early in 1971, but the rise was halted in the spring by strikes. The revival, however, seemed likely to continue after midyear; the consumer goods industries operated in 1971 under especially booming conditions.

Italian manufacturing was seriously hampered by strikes (partly of a political nature). These, accompanied by weaker demand, resulted in no upward movement during 1970 and a recession in 1971. Output at the end of 1970 was on the same level as at the beginning of the year, and in May 1971 was 4% lower than in January.

The smaller industrial countries in Europe, on the whole, experienced a year of rapid growth in 1970. In many of them the advance achieved was extremely high by postwar standards (for example, in Austria, Netherlands, Spain, Sweden, Yugoslavia). The pressure on resources was heavy; restrictive measures for countering inflation and weaker demand in the larger countries reduced the rate of growth in almost all the smaller countries during 1971.

In both 1969 and 1970 Japanese manufacturing output rose by more than 10%; before the end of 1970, however, this long-lived and fast advance came to a halt. Demand weakened considerably, and during the first six months of 1971 industrial activity fluctuated around the level that had been reached at the turn of the year.

Outside the industrial belt of Western Europe-North America-Japan, output rose generally rather rapidly in many of the less industrialized countries but relatively slowly in the more developed areas. Thus, in Australia, manufacturing output rose hardly 2% in 1970, following a growth of 5½% a year earlier, and there was a minor setback in South Africa, where the 10% growth rate of 1969 was halved in 1970.

Productivity, as measured by output per hour worked in manufacturing, continued to increase but at varying rates; its growth was the highest in Japan (14%), somewhat lower (4–5%) in France and in

Italy, mediocre (3%) in the U.S., and low (about 1½%) in West Germany and the U.K.

Industrial output in the U.S.S.R. rose at the rate of 8% in 1970, fractionally faster than in the previous year; this was about the same as the average medium-term growth rate of Soviet industry since 1963. In all Eastern European countries the growth of industrial output was faster in 1970 than a year earlier, with the exception of East Germany, where the rate of increase declined from 7 to 6%. Hungarian industry recovered from the temporary halt in 1969, and Czechoslovakian output rose faster; in both these countries the recorded rise was 7%. This was exceeded by Poland (9%) and Romania (14%). (G. F. R.)

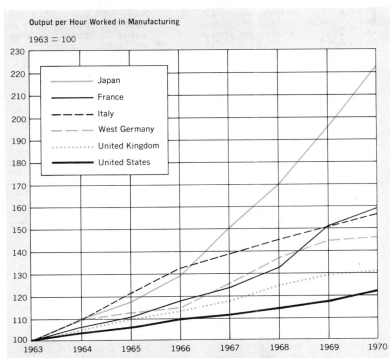

Output per Hour Worked in Manufacturing
1963 = 100

Source: National Institute of Economic and Social Research, *Economic Review*.

AEROSPACE

The general recession in the West, which reached its trough toward the end of 1970, left its mark on the aerospace industry in 1971, particularly in the U.S. and U.K. Work on U.S. space programs declined as the Apollo series of flights neared an end; defense programs continued to consolidate rather than expand; and the civil aircraft market continued to suffer from lack of investment by airline operators, although this situation was showing signs of improving at the end of the year.

The two major events affecting civil aviation were the discontinuance of the U.S. supersonic transport (SST) aircraft program, in which the Boeing Co. had been involved with the B-2707, and the collapse of Rolls-Royce, the aircraft engine company that was previously regarded as the unassailable bastion of British aerospace technology. The Rolls-Royce liquidation was also felt in the defense field, but its main repercussion centred on the contract for RB.211 engines that were to be supplied to the Lockheed Aircraft Corp. for the TriStar wide-bodied jet. Both these events had effects on a much wider sector of the aerospace industry than might at first be apparent. Apart from the airframe and engine manufacturers, thousands of subcontractors and suppliers were affected. In some cases the lost orders meant the collapse of companies. Such was the diversity of skills required in aerospace technology that any major change meant cutbacks throughout the entire industry—in some cases affecting companies overseas.

Although Rolls-Royce went into liquidation in early February, it was not until September that the situation in regard to Lockheed was clarified. The British government, inevitably politically committed to supporting the country's only aerospace engine firm, financially supported the RB.211 engine program, on condition that the U.S. government guarantee a loan of $250 million to Lockheed to finance production of the TriStar. This loan was approved on September 9.

The U.S. Senate voted 51 to 46 on March 24 to cancel the U.S. SST aircraft program. Attempts to find private funding for the program proved fruitless, and both Boeing and the engine manufacturer, General Electric, were forced to lay off thousands of workers.

Employment in U.S. aerospace continued to decline. The factors involved in the fall-off included the shutdown of the SST program, but the reduction in size of the space industry and the drastic cutting back of defense production as the Vietnam war wound down were mainly to blame. For comparison, the figures for 30 aerospace companies across the industry spectrum showed a peak employment total in 1967 of 942,000 workers. This figure had declined by December 1970 to 606,000, to 552,000 by mid-1971, and to 529,000 by December 1971. In the U.K. there were also reductions in staffs during 1971, although not as drastic. In the rest of the world aerospace activity was growing, slowly but steadily, as specific programs were begun and expanded.

European collaboration continued to flourish, with test flying of the two preproduction prototypes of the Concorde SST (made by the British Aircraft Corp. and Aérospatiale, France) going along on schedule. The European airbus program was also

Full-sized mock-up of the B-1 strategic bomber expected to make its first flight in 1974. The four-engine swing-wing craft was designed to fly at twice the speed of sound.
WIDE WORLD

progressing, along with military collaborative efforts on such aircraft as the Jaguar strike-trainer, MRCA (multirole combat aircraft), and the Lynx and Gazelle helicopters. The decision by the U.K. government in October to join the European Economic Community was expected to provide further stimulus to the growing collaborative trend.

In the U.S. military field, despite the diminution of effort in the Vietnam war, approximately $30 billion was spent during fiscal 1971 on aerospace defense programs, with Lockheed Aircraft heading the list of contractors for the third successive year. Next was General Dynamics, followed by American Telephone & Telegraph, Grumman, and General Electric. Each of these companies received more than $1 billion of contracts.

Interest in V/STOL (vertical and short takeoff and landing) aircraft continued to develop, although many of the civil applications were back at the design stage after prototype trials with early models. The military field continued to be dominated by the Hawker Siddeley Harrier, already in service with the U.S. Marines and the Royal Air Force.

The business aircraft market continued to be depressed, reflecting the general economic situation. The number of units sold in 1970 fell by 50%, and there were few signs of any real leveling off in 1971. One British manufacturer went into liquidation, mainly because of an apparent lack of working capital. This was Britten-Norman, whose sales of their Islander had been going well. There was a strong possibility that the company would be taken over by another before finally being dispersed. This, in fact, happened to aircraft of another British company which had gone into liquidation in 1970; although Handley Page did not itself survive, its product, the successful business turboprop, the Jetstream, was put into production by another U.K. firm, and relaunched into the difficult market.

(J. B. BE.)

AUTOMOBILES

Few entirely new models or mechanical novelties were introduced during 1971, a situation due in part to the continuing concentration of engineering personnel and resources upon design changes demanded by proliferating legal standards with regard to safety and exhaust emissions. In a broad social context, it clearly was more constructive to devote research and development skills to such problems rather than to matters of performance, style, and fashion, but there was a sharp division of opinion between automobile engineers and legislators regarding the validity of some standards. An outstanding example of this controversy in the United States stemmed from passage of the 1970 Clean Air Act by Congress, which called for a further and drastic reduction in exhaust pollutants by 1975 in terms that car manufacturers considered unachievable by any foreseeable changes in the piston engine. This was believed to be one of the reasons

that prompted General Motors Corp. to recruit a strong research team to work on the Wankel rotary engine after acquiring a license at the end of 1970. In November 1971 Ford's German subsidiary, Ford Werke A.G., also acquired a Wankel license.

In Europe, after some years of negotiation, agreement was reached on a standard for exhaust emissions that became mandatory in most EEC countries in October and seemed likely to become accepted by the others before long. In the practical terms of engine design, this standard called for measures similar in scope and cost to those needed to meet the U.S. federal standard of 1972. However, the state of California announced unilateral requirements for 1972 that included a restriction on the emission of oxides of nitrogen that was absent from the U.S. and EEC standards; in consequence, many U.S. car manufacturers found themselves unable to modify some of their engine options for sale in that state.

Comparatively few new safety regulations became mandatory in the U.S. during 1971, and in the fall the Department of Transportation changed its attitude toward the controversial air-bag system of "passive restraint" by announcing that the deadline for its introduction into automobiles was postponed from August 1973 to 1975. Tests had shown that the system presented many difficulties, and a redrafting of the relevant Standard 208 gave scope for alternative methods of protecting drivers and passengers from their persistent disinclination to safeguard themselves by wearing seat belts.

International cooperation in the development of "safety cars" embodying new design concepts was stimulated by agreements concluded among the U.S., U.K., West Germany, Italy, and Japan for the free exchange of knowledge and practical experience.

Car production figures available for the first half of 1971 showed a small but general upward trend in Europe (compared with the same period in 1970), with bigger gains reported from the U.S. and Japan. Manufacturers in the United States produced more than 8.5 million automobiles in 1971, the third highest total in their history. A reduction in the purchase tax in July and the concurrent removal of restrictions on installment buying gave a big stimulus to car sales in Britain later in the year, but this did not extend to the truck market owing to a continued reluctance to invest in plant or equipment. Another special factor was a nine-week strike that closed all Ford Motor Co. plants in the U.K. early in the year and left dealers without stocks in subsequent months. FIAT and Renault also suffered from various kinds of industrial unrest. The prolonged General Motors strike in the U.S. at the end of 1970, which was a major cause for the big decline in total American car and truck production in that year, was followed by a major resurgence of GM output and profits in 1971; during the first eight months GM built 3,282,585 cars and trucks, compared with 2,558,094 in the same period of 1970. Although both the Chevrolet Vega and

Table III. Production and Exports of Motor Vehicles by the Principal Producing Countries
In 000 units

Country	1968 Passenger cars	1968 Commercial vehicles	1969 Passenger cars	1969 Commercial vehicles	1970 Passenger cars	1970 Commercial vehicles
Production						
United States	8,848.6	1,971.8	8,224.3	1,980.7	6,550.2	1,733.4
Japan	2,055.8	2,030.0	2,611.5	2,062.8	3,178.7	2,110.4
Germany, West	2,862.2	244.8	3,312.5	292.0	3,527.9	314.4
France	1,833.0	242.6	2,168.5	290.6	2,458.0	292.0
United Kingdom	1,815.9	409.3	1,717.0	465.7	1,641.0	457.5
Italy	1,544.9	118.7	1,477.4	185.6	1,719.7	134.5
Canada	900.9	279.1	1,035.4	314.4	937.2	250.2
Australia	345.0	73.4	371.1	80.7	391.9	81.8
Sweden	223.3	21.4	242.9	27.8	279.0	31.2
U.S.S.R.*		801.0	293.6	550.7	344.0	572.0
Other countries*		1,529.3		1,830.0	1,412.3	520.7
World total		28,151.0		29,351.2	22,439.9	6,498.1
Exports						
Germany, West	1,801.6	145.6	1,875.1	164.3	1,934.5	177.7
United Kingdom	676.6	142.0	771.6	181.2	690.3	172.3
France	628.6	47.5	787.5	56.6	1,061.3	65.9
Italy	557.7	29.5	594.6	35.5	632.1	38.9
United States	330.5	92.2	333.4	103.5	285.0	92.7
Sweden	138.8	15.4	141.8	18.8	186.5	24.0
Japan	406.3	206.2	560.4	297.6	788.9	306.1
Canada	522.1	155.0	714.5	409.7	733.2	430.9

*A reliable breakdown between cars and commercial vehicles was not available for the U.S.S.R. until 1969, or for "Other countries" until 1970.
Source: British Society of Motor Manufacturers and Traders, *The Motor Industry of Great Britain.*

the Ford Pinto were successfully sold in large numbers, their impact on the U.S. market did not reverse the increasing share taken by imported cars, which had risen to a level of about 16% when U.S. Pres. Richard Nixon announced his 10% surcharge on imports in August. An increasing sales ratio of imported cars in the U.K., due in part to successive reductions in import duty under international agreements, also troubled British manufacturers; it reached a total of 20% for the first eight months of 1971. However, in the same period, British exports of cars, trucks, and agricultural tractors attained a record total value of £500 million. The Rolls-Royce automotive division, which exported about half of its production, was re-formed as a separate company following bankruptcy of the parent organization.

The upward trend in motor vehicle prices continued unabated during 1971, the rising costs of labour and materials being augmented by the design changes and extra equipment needed to meet new legal requirements. This situation applied (though in varying degrees) to all the vehicle-manufacturing countries. In general, industrial strife was a somewhat less disruptive factor than in 1970. International trading was hampered by floating rates of exchange, the U.S. surcharge, and the U.S. dock strikes.

The long-awaited decision by the Japanese government to liberalize participation in the domestic motor industry was announced in April; it permitted a foreign firm to found a new company in equal partnership with Japanese capital. Foreign investment in existing Japanese companies was also allowed, conditional upon screening and approval by the Ministry of International Trade and Industry. The first of the three big American motor manufacturers to file an application was the Chrysler Corp., which secured a share in the Mitsubishi Motors Corp. The Japanese company announced plans to sell Colt Galant sedans through Chrysler dealerships in North America and to market Australian-built Chrysler Valiant models in Japan. Ford announced a future investment of 20% in Toyo Kogyo, Japan's third largest car maker, and this was quickly followed by the unexpected news that General Motors had concluded an agreement with the small Isuzu company.

Of the comparatively few entirely new models that were announced during the year,

the Morris Marina had a special commercial significance because it expressed the intention of British Leyland Motor Corp. to market a conventional front-engine, rear-wheel-drive car in competition with its highly successful Austin 1100/1300 front-drive models. Announced in May, the Marina competed in size and price with the well-established Vauxhall Viva, Ford Escort, Renault 12, Opel Kadett, FIAT 128, Simca 1000, Citroën GS, and Volkswagen 1300. Another important new model, competing at the lower end of the same price class, was the FIAT 127, announced in April. This provided exceptional passenger space within an overall length of 142 in. by the ingenious packaging of the transverse engine and front-drive transmission.

The popularity of the two-door coupe in Europe was emphasized by the introduction during the year of examples as dissimilar in size and price as the Rolls-Royce Corniche, the Mercedes-Benz 350 SL and 350 SLC,

FIAT 130, Peugeot 504, Renault 15 and 17, and Vauxhall Firenza. Jaguar announced its long-awaited V-12 engine in March in which light aluminum alloys were widely used.

The crop of model changes, which had been an annual event for so many years in the U.S., was reduced to a very low level in 1971 for reasons already explained. Many of the 1972 cars were outwardly almost indistinguishable from their counterparts of a year earlier. GM and Ford made good their promises to avoid early styling changes on the Vega and Pinto but improved the mechanical specifications of the cars to some degree. For example, the Vega automatic transmission option provided three speeds, while disc front brakes became standard equipment on Pintos sold with the 2,000-cc. engine.

Some of the engineering changes forced on the industry by legislation added cost and complication in ways that did not seem easy to justify, but others had practical merit—such as the new "long-life" ignition systems developed by General Motors and Chrysler. The new energy-absorbing bumpers on General Motors' big cars were another example.

The main Japanese car manufacturers, Toyota and Nissan, with outputs comparable with Volkswagen and a vital export market in North America, were deeply concerned with meeting U.S. federal standards and also undertook to design and develop experimental safety cars by government appointment. Nissan announced a new "U-series" ("user-oriented") Datsun 610 in September with major mechanical units inherited from the 1600 model but with a larger, restyled body. Earlier in the year, Toyota's Corolla became a size larger with a new body and engine options. The little two-cylinder Honda "Life" was a more refined version of the "N" series, with a water-cooled engine in place of air cooling. Toyo Kogyo launched its new Savanna models in the fall; in common with the existing Mazda models, they could be equipped with either a two-rotor Wankel or a four-cylinder piston engine. (M. PL.)

COURTESY, FORD MOTOR CO.

LONDON "DAILY EXPRESS"—PICTORIAL PARADE

New automobiles introduced in 1971 included the Lincoln Continental Mark IV (above), the Ford GT 70 competition car (above, right), and the Dodge Monaco (right).

COURTESY, CHRYSLER CORP.

BUILDING AND CONSTRUCTION

According to the midyear report of the U.S. Department of Commerce, the value of all new construction put in place in 1971 in the U.S. was expected to be $106 billion, compared with $91 billion in 1970. This 16% rise was the largest annual increase in total dollar outlay for construction since 1950, but more than half of it was due to inflation. The high rate of inflation in the construction industry from 1965 to 1971 posed serious threats not only to long-term goals in housing and other construction but to the economy generally. In an effort to cope with this threat, President Nixon issued an executive order in March establishing the Construction Industry Stabilization Committee to deal with wages and the Interagency Committee on Construction to deal with the prices of materials and certain other matters.

The inflationary trend throughout the economy led the president to stronger action in August 1971, when he instituted an overall wage-price freeze. Nixon's "new economic program," which brought about a wage-price freeze in Phase One and restraints in Phase Two, produced much uncertainty about the possible effects on the construction industry. The Department of Commerce predicted, however, that in 1972 the value of new construction put in place would rise to $117 billion.

The housing sector continued to give strong support to the national economy. It appeared that private housing starts in 1971 would exceed two million units, and the prediction was that the 1972 figure would be slightly higher. The adverse effect of inflation on construction was revealed in the nonresidential sector. Because the dollar outlays for new nonresidential construction in 1971 were expected to be equal to or slightly above those of 1970, it was reasonable to assume that the physical volume of production would be lower.

In July 1971, the Department of Commerce construction composite cost index stood at 166 (1957–59 = 100). The rate of inflation in 1971 was much greater than it had been in 1970. The increase was the result of substantial increases in the price of both labour and materials. In July 1971, the construction materials index stood at 120.9 (1967 = 100), compared with 113.4 in January. The index of union hourly wage rates stood at 143.8 (1967 = 100) in July 1971, compared to 133.2 in January.

In Canada, the outlook for economic activity for 1971 was good at midyear as a result of an increase in government spending and consumer expenditures on durable goods and housing. The growth rate in real output in 1970 was approximately 4%, and it appeared that in 1971 this would exceed 4½%. Government reports indicated that gross fixed investments in 1971 should increase by 10%, compared with a 4% increase in 1970. The combined industrial growth in Western Europe in 1971 was expected to be about 4% according to the *National Institute Economic Review*. In Great Britain in 1970 gross fixed investments were at about the same level as in 1969, and the estimate for 1971 was only slightly higher than in 1970. The overall economy was in a state of stagnation, and it appeared that the gross national product would be lower in 1971 than in the preceding year. The forecast was that the investments in dwellings in 1971

would be at about the same level as in 1970. In France the 6% rise in the gross national product in 1970 was a result of the rapid growth in 1969 and the first part of 1970. It reflected heavy investments in private industries and exports. It was anticipated that in 1971 the increase in the gross national product would be lower than in 1970. In West Germany the gross national product in 1970 increased at a slower rate than in 1969. In Italy the economy, suffering from inflation, was not expanding.

In most of the smaller industrial countries it appeared that the increase in the gross national product in 1971 would be about 4%. A general slowing down of economic growth was evident in Denmark, the Netherlands, Sweden, Belgium, Switzerland, and Austria.

(C. C. O.)

CHEMICALS

In industrialized countries throughout the world, chemical industries were trying to make headway against generally unfavourable economic conditions in 1970 and 1971. In that respect, they were coping with problems similar to those of other industries. In addition, however, they had some problems peculiar to their own operations, resulting from legislation and pressures to provide a cleaner, safer environment.

In the U.S., shipments of chemicals and allied products in 1970 were $49,611,000,000, according to the Office of Business Economics of the U.S. Department of Commerce. This was only 2% higher than the $48,698,-000,000 of chemicals shipped in 1969. Sales of companies making chemicals and allied products, tabulated by the Securities and Exchange Commission (SEC) and the Federal Trade Commission, rose 5% in 1970 to $58,054,000,000 from $55,508,000,000 in 1969. Profits declined, however, by 4% to $3,434,000,000 in 1970.

Recovery in 1971 got under way but at a slower rate than had been anticipated. Sales of chemicals and allied products companies climbed to $30,541,000,000 for the first half of 1971; profits were $1,922,000,000. Production of chemicals was up approximately 3% during the first eight months of 1971, and the sales figures indicated an increase of 6% for the first half. Buoyed by the new government economic policies introduced on August 15, chemical companies in the fourth quarter of 1971 were expecting that sales for the full year would show a 7% rise and that production would be up by 5%.

Investment in new plant and equipment continued at a high level. A survey taken by the U.S. Office of Business Economics and the SEC in late January and early February 1971 showed that the chemical industry had spent $3.1 billion in 1969, $3,440,-000,000 in 1970, and was expected to spend $3,620,000,000 in 1971.

The U.S. chemical industry continued to make an important contribution to the national balance of trade. In 1970 chemical exports came to $3,826,000,000, while imports were $1,450,000,000, giving a favourable trade balance for chemicals of $2,376,-000,000. For the first seven months of 1971 the U.S. chemical trade surplus was $1,510,-000,000, approximately $12 million lower than the same period in 1970. The surtax on imports and the healthier economy, however, were expected to lead to a fourth quarter that would offset the difference.

A number of products of the chemical industry felt the impact of increased concern over the environment. Because the antiknock agents used in gasoline (tetraethyl [and tetramethyl] lead) would hamper the efficiency of some advanced emission-control devices for automobiles, considerable pressure had mounted to restrict or eliminate the

use of lead in gasoline. Although no irrevocable decisions had been reached, petroleum companies started marketing both lead-free and low-lead gasoline and the use of lead for gasoline declined 13.8% for the first seven months of 1971 from the same period in 1970. New York City introduced a tax of two cents on plastic containers because they were said to magnify solid-waste disposal problems. The Society of the Plastics Industry filed suit to have the tax declared illegal, maintaining that the tax was discriminatory and would encourage the use of competitive materials.

The Japanese chemical industry in 1968 had sales of $9,605,000,000 according to figures tabulated by the Organization for Economic Cooperation and Development (OECD). This made it the second largest chemical industry in the non-Communist world, although size comparisons could not be precise because of the varying definitions of "chemicals" in the different countries. Indications were that sales levels in Japan increased 15% a year in both 1969 and 1970. New investment in chemicals in Japan was at a high level. The OECD reported an expansion of $1,331,000,000 in 1968. Unofficial figures pointed to further large increases in 1970.

In 1971 the pace of the Japanese industry began to slacken somewhat. Higher construction costs, wage increases, and overcapacity in some lines contributed to a slowdown in the rate of growth. Domestic demand for chemical products was leveling off, and the resistance to imports in the U.S. was causing the industry to look increasingly to Europe, particularly to the Eastern bloc, and to Latin America as export targets.

The West German chemical industry, according to the OECD, had sales of $9,440,-000,000 in 1968. Although this was lower than Japanese chemical sales, West Germany maintained a comfortable margin in the important category, value added by chemical production: $5,430,000,000 to Japan's $3,-945,000,000 in 1968. West German chemical sales increased substantially in 1969 and 1970, an estimated 12% and 7%.

International monetary developments were particularly painful to West Germany's chemical industry, which counted on exporting almost 40% of production. The West German government's decision to let the mark "float" raised the price of West German exports in world markets, and the year-end agreement to revalue the mark promised little immediate relief. In addition, the U.S. 10% surcharge on imports, in effect during the latter part of the year, boosted even more the price of imports into the U.S. Higher wage rates also were taking a toll on profits.

United Kingdom chemical sales in 1968 were placed by the OECD at $6,985,000,000. Increases were also registered in 1969 and 1970, with the total reaching an estimated $9.4 billion in the latter year. Reduced consumer spending and a generally sluggish economy dimmed prospects for chemical producers early in 1971. However, government policies introduced in July to bolster the economy brought a change for the better. Concerted cost reduction programs undertaken by the chemical industry also appeared to be yielding results. Chemical production increased 4–5% during the first half of 1971, and it was expected that the increase for the full year would be about 6%. A stronger economy, better control of costs, and rising production indicated better prospects for the British chemical industry.

French chemical sales in 1968, according to the OECD, were $6,940,000,000, only slightly behind those of the United Kingdom. Indications were that sales increased 20%

in 1969 and 10% in 1970 to surpass $9 billion. The industry was facing the same problem as was West Germany although in a less severe form. Government planners were anticipating an annual growth rate of 12–13% in the early 1970s, a sharper rate increase than the 10%-a-year average for the 1960s. Labour unions, however, were seeking wage boosts and fringe benefits that would add more than 10% to the labour costs. The possibility of labour-management disputes, it was believed, could dampen growth prospects.

The Italian chemical industry, which had had a spectacular growth rate in the past, had sales of $5.6 billion in 1968, according to the OECD. A series of strikes hit the industry in 1969 and sales dropped, perhaps by as much as 7%. (D. P. B.)

ELECTRICAL

Growth of world trade in electrical machinery and apparatus slowed considerably during the latter half of 1970 and further eased in 1971. This trend was borne out by the decline in commodity prices. For example, one of the most important raw materials in the electrical industry, copper, stood at $1,700 a ton at the beginning of 1970; by the fall of 1971 that figure had been almost halved. Trade prospects for 1972 as viewed in the summer of 1971 looked somewhat brighter in spite of the difficulties confronting the U.S. economy, but the measures taken by President Nixon on August 15 upset all short-term forecasts. The chief worry for British and European electrical manufacturers was the 10% import surcharge imposed by the U.S. government. In addition the Liaison Group for the European Engineering Industries (ORGALIME) and the British Electrical and Allied Manufacturers' Association (BEAMA) regarded the U.S. government's proposal to give job development tax credits to American purchasers of U.S.-made equipment, as unfair. These credits, together with the surcharge, were said to give U.S. manufacturers an advantage of up to 20% over foreign competitors.

Heavy electrical equipment, such as power station generators, transformers, and switchgear, could be produced successfully only by a limited number of very large companies because of the physical size of the equipment and the advanced technology needed to build it. The cost of developing that kind of equipment had risen to such an extent that international cooperation between large companies was becoming imperative in order that both the development costs and markets could be shared. In a report published in May 1971, *Politics of Trade in Power Plant*, the Trade Policy Research Centre, London, stated that the ideal worldwide structure for the heavy electrical industry under conditions of free trade would comprise six or seven multinational companies. Earlier, the EEC recommended that its heavy electrical industry should be restructured in two or three multinational companies out of the existing ten. Some moves in that direction were made, but progress was slow because of two factors: first, each government tended to protect its own national manufacturers because electricity generation and supply is vital, and, second, a degree of caution was imposed by the prospect of eventual enlargement of the EEC.

The main conclusion of many surveys undertaken in 1971 in attempts to quantify the effect on trade in electrical equipment of the enlargement of the EEC was the need to make the industry more efficient by mergers of even the small single-product companies. One survey, covering medium-sized manufacturers of motor control gear and electrical accessories, suggested that the only practical way in which those companies could maintain their vital market share was through mergers, which would reduce their number in Europe by 85%.

Merger and take-over activity in 1971, however, was well below the 1969 peak. Rockwell Parsons Corp., the jointly owned company formed in 1970 by Reyrolle Parsons (U.K.) and North American Rockwell (U.S.) to exploit the U.S. turbogenerator market, was dissolved in August 1971. The main reasons were failure of the company to win a single order in the first year of its existence and higher than anticipated costs for building a factory in the U.S. to manufacture Parsons-designed turbogenerators. Compared with the Kraftwerk Union (West Germany) and Allis-Chalmers (U.S.) agreement, the Rockwell-Parsons venture had little significance in the restructuring of the world heavy electrical industry, since Rockwell was a newcomer to the market.

During the year many countries announced price increases in electrical equipment averaging about 6%, but in July General Electric (U.S.) reduced small AC motor prices by 3%. This was in response to "competitive price actions in the market place" and was needed to "retain customer confidence" and preserve the company's market participation. General Electric admitted, however, that the changes were not economically sound in view of labour, material, and other costs, and in the long term the provision of products and services in the best interests of the customer could be maintained only on a realistic economic basis.

In the domestic appliance market, consumer rights became national political issues, particularly in the U.S., where manufacturers were forced to offer stronger guarantees and better customer services. Standardization of components and the provision of a comprehensive after-sales service were the main reasons for the predominance of large companies in this market. The French domestic appliance manufacturers, for example, suffered from considerable intrusion into their home markets by West German and Italian makers. The reason, according to one French manufacturer at the 1971 Arts Ménagers exhibition in Paris, was that the domestic industry had not combined quickly enough, after the implementation of EEC tariff policies, to fight on equal terms with the German and Italian giants.

Recent innovations in electrical equipment generally resulted from the development of new materials. For example, one of the more advanced designs of extra-high-voltage cable in 1971 was based on the development of polymeric paper insulation by the 3M Co. in the U.S. This material had man-made fibres instead of cellulose, and the "paper" could be easily graded to suit the operating voltage. Another cable material development was for polyvinyl chloride (PVC) cables by Felten and Guilleaume in West Germany, where several cases of extensive damage had occurred in factories due to the formation of hydrochloric acid from PVC cables involved in small fires. The new coating produced a microporous foam when heated and, by excluding air from the PVC, effectively overcame the fire hazard. (T. C. J. C.)

GLASS

Sales increased in 1971 despite competition from alternative materials. Environmental questions affected the glass container industry. Criticism of the use of "no deposit, no return" bottles linked them with pollution, and in the United States bills prohibiting them were under consideration by state and federal authorities; Denmark had similar moves in view. Most glass container industries in Europe and the U.S. were studying active recycling of used glass, either within their batch of raw materials or for use in other fields, for example, as aggregate for road making.

Glass container manufacturers actively sought to develop lighter and stronger bottles. Following the glass composite package, Owens-Illinois, Inc., announced testing of lightweight glass containers in an expanded polystyrene jacket. In the United Kingdom one company, United Glass Ltd., introduced additional coatings to give improved abrasion resistance and lubricity. The West German company H. Heye Glasfabrik developed machinery for lightweight bottle production and reached an agreement with the Lynch Corp. of the U.S. for manufacturing and marketing them.

The U.S. Glass Container Manufacturers Institute announced development of a fast-filling line for soft drinks and beer rated at 2,000 bottles a minute, twice as fast as any line currently available. An interesting U.S. development was the production of multicoloured opal glass giving a greater variety of colour.

In the U.K., Pilkington Brothers Ltd., the technological leader in the world flat glass industry, went public. Licenses for its float process were held by 18 manufacturers in 11 countries. A merger between Pilkington, the Société Européenne d'Isolateurs en Verre, and the Compagnie Générale d'Électro-Céramique, in France, created one of the largest electrical insulator companies, with one-quarter of the world market.

The development of thinner float glass foreshadowed, within the foreseeable future, the replacement of sheet. Libbey-Owens-Ford Co. reported the development of double-glazed mirror glass units for building, claimed to be warmer in winter and cooler in summer.

In Eastern Europe, automation in the Polish industry increased from 11% in 1950 to 85%. Czechoslovakia reported a 200% increase in production in the past 15 years. Hungary reported entry into the electrothermic refractories market for high-temperature glass furnaces.

Research into damage to domestic glassware in dishwashing machines was intensified. A Swedish research institute reported development of a glass composition extremely resistant to such damage. Many glass-makers, however, had developed glasses for their intrinsic value and did not wish to forfeit goodwill to manufacture special kinds for dishwashing machines. The industry felt that manufacturers of machines and detergents should produce equipment and materials that would not damage glass.

In the U.S., Corning Glass Works reported an order for a 101-in. fused mirror for a new telescope in Chile. Two U.K. developments were new glass developed as a cover for solar cells, giving them longer life in space through increased protection from radiation, and heat-shield visors for the Concorde SST, to protect the windshields from high temperature and, at the same time, to streamline the nose. (Cy. W.)

IRON AND STEEL

World crude steel production was estimated to have fallen in 1971 to 591 million metric tons. Although this was only slightly less than in 1970, it was the first time since 1958 that world output did not increase compared with the previous year.

Industrial Review

World trade in steel during 1971 was affected by the buying of imported steel in the United States during the first half of the year to hedge against possible strike losses, and later by the imposition of the U.S. 10% surcharge on imports. The year's final trade figure could be estimated to have slightly exceeded the 1970 level of approximately 60 million net product tons.

The year opened in an aura of uncertainty for world steel industries in general. In most of the major producing countries outside the Communist bloc, demand, which had declined during the latter part of 1970 under the influence of various deflationary policies, continued to weaken. In many countries the consuming industries depleted their stocks, and order books were shortened. In the U.S. the steelmakers fared better, since demand was boosted by the precautionary purchasing of steel by consumers in the expectation of a strike.

Price levels in international trade continued to weaken, and steel producers increasingly suffered from the pressures that lower prices exercised on domestic price levels. The underlying upward movement in costs continued. The result of declining or stagnant steel production, rising costs, and unsatisfactory price levels was a sharp decline in profitability in the steel industries of a number of major producing countries. In these circumstances many firms sought to make their operations more efficient through mergers and shutting down old facilities, and there were some postponements of future investment decisions.

There were important international trade policy developments with implications for steel. While the general movement toward trade liberalization continued in the form of further Kennedy Round tariff reductions and the granting by some industrially advanced countries of nonreciprocal tariff preferences for less developed countries, there was a sudden check to this liberalization in the series of economic measures introduced by the U.S. in August, including the 10% surcharge on imports. The ending of the surcharge, agreed to by the U.S. as part of the December international monetary accord, allayed immediate fears of a worldwide swing toward protectionism, although the precise effect of the agreement on trade patterns remained in doubt.

Steel output in the U.S. in 1971 was estimated at 120 million tons, only slightly above production in the previous year. Output was at a high level during the first half year as consumers increased their stocks, but in the second half production slumped badly, causing many workers to be laid off. Costs continued to rise, but in order to avoid the further severe financial losses attributable to a threatened walkout the industry conceded a 31% pay increase for the three-year period beginning August 1971. This in turn led to the announcement of an across-the-board increase in steel prices of 8%, but the August package of economic measures included a three-month freeze on prices and wages. The increase was finally approved by the U.S. Price Commission on December 16.

Capital expenditure in investment projects by the U.S. steel industry was expected to be about 10% lower in 1971 than in the previous year. Imports of steel into the U.S. in 1971 were at a high level. In the first seven months a total of 11 million tons was imported, compared with 6.6 million tons in the same period of 1970.

Japanese steel output declined in 1971 to approximately 88 million tons. This was about 6% less than in the previous year. The decline resulted from a recession in home demand and the cutback in production introduced in November 1970, which was carried through and intensified in 1971. On the other hand, Japanese steel exports rose sharply during the first half of 1971, particularly to the U.S. In the second half, uncertainties in export prospects developed because of the 10% surcharge and the floating of the yen. The profitability of the Japanese steel industry declined sharply during 1970–71, and Japanese projections of future demand and capacity tended to become more cautious. Nevertheless, the rate of capital expenditure remained high.

Steel production in the European Coal and Steel Community (ECSC) declined in 1971 to 105 million tons. This was nearly 4% below the level of output in the previous year. Part of the decline in the ECSC output was attributable to the running down of domestic consumers' stocks during the first half of the year, but by the year's end it appeared that the process had been completed and steel production was again in line with the level of steel consumption. Increased export orders helped to support the level of steel output in certain ECSC countries. Actual capital expenditure on new plant was at a record level in 1971, although there was a sharp fall in investment during the year.

In the United Kingdom steel production declined to less than 25 million tons. Home demand, which began to level out in the latter part of 1970, continued to weaken during the first part of 1971. By the middle of the year, however, it appeared that the reduction in consumers' stocks that had contributed to the decline had run its course.

Production in the U.S.S.R. and Eastern Europe again rose. In the Soviet Union output reached 120 million tons, 3½% more than in 1970. In Poland, Czechoslovakia, East Germany, and Bulgaria there were increases in output compared with the previous year. Output in China was estimated to have increased in 1971 by 1 million tons.

Elsewhere in the world there were important increases in output. For example, in Canada steel production rose to 14,250,000 tons, some 30% above output in the previous year. In South Africa production increased to 5,250,000 tons, 12% above 1970.

(L. C. BA.)

MACHINERY AND MACHINE TOOLS

The economic uncertainty in 1971 directly affected the sale of machinery and machine tools in the U.S. The small amount of optimism that prevailed at the start of the year was offset by the failure of Congress to enact President Nixon's proposed 10% investment tax credit, by the drop in aerospace orders, and by the depressed state of the economy that found many companies operating at about 75% of plant utilization. Another fac-

Table IV. World Production of Pig Iron and Blast Furnace Ferroalloys
In 000 metric tons

Country	1966	1967	1968	1969	1970
World	335,200	351,630	376,320	407,420	426,030
U.S.	83,010	78,910	80,540	86,620	83,320
U.S.S.R.	70,260	74,810	78,790	81,630	85,930
Japan	32,020	40,090	46,400	58,150	68,050
Germany, West	25,410	27,270	30,310	33,760	33,630
United Kingdom	15,960	15,400	16,700	16,650	17,670
France	15,590	15,710	16,450	18,210	19,220
China*	14,000	15,000	15,500	16,000	16,000
Belgium	8,230	8,900	10,370	11,210	10,840
Italy	6,270	7,310	7,840	7,780	8,330
Canada	6,550	6,310	7,600	6,770	8,280
India	7,040	6,890	7,290	7,190†	6,900
Czechoslovakia	6,270	6,820	6,920	7,040	7,620
Poland	5,610	6,330	6,640	7,030	7,300
Australia†	4,450	4,970	5,290	5,800	6,150
Luxembourg†	3,960	3,960	4,310	4,870	4,810
South Africa	3,460	3,470	3,830	3,930	3,930
Brazil†	2,890	2,960	3,350	3,700	4,200
Romania	2,200	2,460	2,990	3,490	4,210
Netherlands†	2,210	2,590	2,820	3,460	3,590
Spain†	2,100	2,680	2,780	3,330	4,160
Sweden	2,230	2,360	2,490	2,500	2,610
Austria†	2,190	2,140	2,470	2,820	2,960
Germany, East	2,450	2,530	2,330	2,100	2,000
Korea, North*	1,800	1,800	1,800	1,800	2,200
Hungary	1,640	1,670	1,650	1,760	1,840
Mexico†	1,140	1,290	1,600	1,700	1,660
Yugoslavia†	1,140	1,180	1,200	1,200	1,270
Bulgaria	870	1,240	1,080	1,120	1,200
Finland	980	1,040	1,140	1,230	1,210
Norway	630	640	670	680	680

*Estimated.
†Pig iron only.
Source: British Steel Corporation.

Table V. World Production of Crude Steel
In 000 metric tons

Country	1966	1967	1968	1969	1970	1971 Year to date	1971 No. of months	1971 Annual rate	Percent change 1971–70
World	473,110	496,010	528,440	571,620	593,610	...	...	591,240	...
U.S.*	121,660	115,410	119,260	127,980	119,140	74,210	7	120,000†	+ 0.7
U.S.S.R.	96,910	102,240	106,530	110,290	115,820	59,870	6	119,740	+ 3.4
Japan	47,780	62,150	66,890	82,170	93,320	29,320	4	87,950	− 5.8
Germany, West	35,320	36,740	41,160	45,320	45,040	28,220	8	42,330	− 6.0
U.K.	24,710	24,280	26,280	26,850	28,320	18,630	9	24,840	−12.3
France	19,590	19,660	20,410	22,510	23,770	11,750	6	23,500	− 1.1
Italy	13,640	15,890	16,960	16,430	17,260	7,110	5	17,060	− 1.2
China‡	13,000	14,000	15,000	16,000	18,000	...	...	19,000	...
Belgium	8,910	9,710	11,570	12,840	12,610	2,190	2	13,130	+ 4.1
Poland	9,850	10,410	11,010	11,290	11,790	5,170	5	12,410	+ 5.3
Czechoslovakia	9,130	10,000	10,560	10,820	11,480	5,100	5	12,240	+ 6.6
Canada	9,090	8,800	10,210	9,350	11,200	6,120	5	14,680	+31.1
India	6,610	6,330	6,510	6,500	6,230	1,610	3	6,440	+ 3.4
Australia	5,720	6,290	6,470	6,690	6,820	1,600	3	6,390	− 6.3
Sweden	4,760	4,770	5,090	5,330	5,480	3,350	8	5,030	− 8.2
Spain	3,850	4,510	4,920	5,990	7,390	630	1	7,620	+ 3.1
Luxembourg	4,390	4,480	4,830	5,520	5,460	3,550	8	5,320	− 2.6
Romania	3,670	4,090	4,750	5,540	6,520	2,610	5	6,260	− 4.0
Brazil	3,710	3,670	4,440	4,900	5,390	...	...	5,700	+ 5.7
Germany, East	4,540	4,650	4,700	5,140	5,050	1,310	3	5,220	+ 3.4
South Africa	3,290	3,700	4,050	4,620	4,750	1,330	3	5,320	+12.0
Netherlands	3,260	3,400	3,710	4,710	5,030	1,970	5	4,740	− 5.8
Austria	3,190	3,020	3,470	3,930	4,080	2,010	6	4,020	− 1.5
Mexico	2,790	3,040	3,260	3,420	3,830	930	3	3,710	− 2.9
Hungary	2,650	2,740	2,900	3,030	3,120	1,310	5	3,140	+ 0.6
Yugoslavia	1,860	1,830	2,000	2,220	2,230	610	3	2,480	+11.2
Argentina	1,270	1,330	1,550	1,650	1,830	770	5	1,840	+ 0.5
Bulgaria	700	1,240	1,460	1,510	1,800	810	5	1,940	+ 7.8

*Excludes production of independent foundries.
†Adjusted.
‡Estimated.
Sources: British Steel Corporation; International Iron and Steel Institute.

tor was the loss of foreign orders, which were about 35% below 1970 levels.

The European Machine Tool Show, held in Milan, Italy, October 2–10, indicated that buyers were looking for simpler machines and were shifting away from the complex computer-based control systems. There were 1,112 exhibitors from 12 countries. They displayed 4,500 machines, of which 200 were of the numerical-controlled (NC) variety, and these manufacturers displayed a number of new machines with low-cost controls. Interest at the show ran above expectations, and there were about 100 observers from the Soviet Union who were seeking information on all types of machine tools built in Western Europe.

Orders for textile machinery were encouraging, ending a decline that started in 1969. U.S. companies that produced this specialized equipment were able to make gains in the export market even though they were at a price disadvantage. Many U.S. textile manufacturers expanded their plants, leading to expectations of increased orders for machinery.

Assembly machines were another area of increased sales activity in 1971. Manufacturers of these machines found an increasing market as many assembly plants tried to cut the man-hours involved in assembly-line activity. Automotive-related industries contributed the greater share of the activity in 1971 as they replaced conventional machines with NC assembly machines. Many companies that were not purchasing other machine tools bought assembly units to increase productivity while reducing employees and the use of hand tools.

The outlook for mining machinery producers was encouraging in 1971 even though the mining industry continued to be depressed. These manufacturers found that their business was stimulated by the new technologies for crushing rock, which, in turn, required new machines. Among the new methods being employed were ultrasonics, powerful water jets, lasers, and super-pressure hydraulic power.

Fifteen U.S. machine-tool companies sent representatives to Moscow in the spring of 1971. They found much interest there, and hopes ran high that the U.S. government would grant them export licenses to sell machines that they had not been able to market in the U.S.S.R. since 1947. The Soviets were seeking to learn about production systems engineering and, in turn, were looking for market possibilities in the U.S.

Japanese machine-tool builders were retooling their plants by installing conveyerized assembly lines. Milling machines, lathes, and grinders were the types of machines most frequently assembled on such lines. The Japanese plants that were equipped with these lines produced high-quality machines that competed successfully in the world markets.

The West German manufacturers of machine tools were seriously affected by a cancellation of major tool orders by Volkswagenwerk AG in October. The orders amounted to $135 million and were expected to wipe out the order backlog in many medium-sized firms. (O. K.)

NUCLEAR INDUSTRY

The bearing of environmental issues on the United States nuclear industry was the subject of much debate in 1971. Discussion centred on public hearings for site licensing and operation permits. Delays to the utilities caused by groups and individuals taking part in public hearing proceedings cost them millions of dollars, and in almost all cases they finally agreed to install additional safety and environmental components. The U.S. Atomic

Energy Commission (AEC) was criticized as both the regulator and the promoter of nuclear power. The AEC also was shocked by a court ruling that it was not adequately fulfilling the provisions of the National Environmental Policy Act of 1969. Although disagreeing, the AEC did not appeal the decision, and subsequently issued stricter regulations.

By late 1971 there were more than 100 nuclear power stations in operation throughout the world, many more under construction, and others on order. Many new countries became interested in nuclear power. U.S. firms were poised to make profits after many years of pioneering and experimentation. New developments included Westinghouse's plans to build floating platform power plants. Gulf General Atomic Co., a division of the Gulf Oil Corp., won an order for two 1,115-Mw. high-temperature reactor systems. Straightforward fuel leasing began in the U.S.

Toward the end of 1970 and continuing into 1971 there was an upsurge in nuclear plant ordering in the U.S. The original breakthrough for the industry had come in 1965 and culminated in 1967, when 31 nuclear reactors were ordered. Since then evidence indicated that costs would be much higher, due to the growing pains of a new industry as well as inflation, licensing fee increases, and variable safety and environmental requirements. The added costs, plus longer construction times, forced utilities to start buying fossil fuels again. But the shortage of such fuels, particularly environmentally clean ones, and rising oil prices made nuclear power look attractive. By September 1971 there were already orders for more than 20 power reactors with a total generating capacity of over 20,000 Mw.

A noticeable trend was the development of transnational alliances of nuclear plant suppliers, enabling the associates to meet third-market competition, particularly from U.S. firms with large capital backing and a strong home market. General Electric strengthened its European base by joining with the Rijn-Schelde group of the Netherlands and Comprimo of Switzerland to offer systems in both countries. Westinghouse established Westinghouse Electric Nuclear Energy Systems Europe (WENESE) in Belgium, which offered medium-sized plants worldwide and seemed well placed to obtain orders from developing countries. Babcock and Wilcox (U.S.), in association with Deutsche Babcock and Wilcox and Brown Boveri of Switzerland, planned to challenge the Kraftwerk Union (KWU) monopoly in West Germany. To combat the Americans, KWU (a joint AEG-Telefunken-Siemens nuclear company) joined with The Nuclear Power Group (TNPG), one of Great Britain's two nuclear consortia for third-country export sales. In the first four months of 1971, KWU received five plant orders, including the first Austrian plant.

Under the tripartite agreement signed in 1970 by the United Kingdom, West Germany, and the Netherlands, pilot plants for the production of enriched uranium by the gas centrifuge process (also called the ultracentrifuge process) were being built at Almelo, Neth., and at Capenhurst in Cheshire, Eng. Two companies were formed, Urenco and Centec, to handle marketing, construction, and operation of ultracentrifuges and plants.

The U.S., partly due to the possible commercial success of ultracentrifuges, allowed American industry access to gas diffusion technology. The government also sought other countries that might wish to cooperate in building a gas diffusion plant. U.S. industry was hesitant because of the vast capital

needed for a diffusion project and because Europe might be too far ahead. France, Canada, Australia, and Japan were other countries that showed interest in gas diffusion.

South Africa announced new enrichment techniques said to be cheaper than gas diffusion. No information was available about the method, but it appeared that facilities were being provided for development. The U.S.S.R. offered enriching service at competitive prices, and signed a contract with France to supply fuel for the Fesshenheim station.

The French and U.K. liquid metal fast-breeder reactor (LMFBR) demonstration plants made good progress. The U.K. expected a commercial prototype station on line by 1975, and the French and West Germans were each to build commercial breeder plants with capacities of more than 1,000 Mw. early in the 1980s. The LMFBR program in the U.S. began to move with the announcement by President Nixon of increased financial support of $27 million in addition to the $103 million budgeted for fiscal 1972.

Following Soviet success with the Tokamak fusion device, world fusion programs increased, and it was expected the true feasibility of a fusion reactor would be demonstrated by the end of the decade.

(R. W. Ko.)

See also FUEL AND POWER: *Special Report.*

PAINTS AND VARNISHES

Figures for 1970 showed that paint production increased substantially in value compared with 1969, the United States value of $2,738,000,000 comparing with a total of $2,159,000,000 for Western Europe. The largest producers in Europe were West Germany with $667 million (31%), Britain with $418 million (19%), and France with $336 million (16%). Although production rose in the less developed countries, surprising increases in exports from Western countries were recorded. Exports from West Germany, for example, increased by 17% and from France by 22%.

In general, the growth in tonnage produced did not match the growth in value, which was in part due to higher prices. The industry had achieved more realistic profit margins, and over 18 months prices in the U.K., for example, rose by 12 to 14%. As in other sectors of the chemical industry, the entire question of profitability was examined closely. Important factors that were discussed included bigger batches, streamlined deliveries, and matching small accounts to small producers.

Emulsion-based paints further increased their share of the market at the expense of conventional solvent-based types; their simplicity in application, the easier cleaning of equipment that they permit, and their non-flammability appealed to the do-it-yourself decorator. Emulsion primers for woodwork largely replaced alkyd-based primers and undercoats. Building paints constituted more than half the industry's output, and the intense competition between basically similar brands was essentially a promotional contest.

In the field of industrial paints, *i.e.,* those for use on mass-produced articles, the output of cellulose lacquers continued to expand, large users being car refinishers and furniture manufacturers. The electrocoat system, by which metal surfaces in a tank are "plated" with priming paint, continued to make progress. Such paints were used on over half the automobiles produced in the U.K.

Coil coating lines provided ready-painted metal sheets for the manufacture of a variety of articles. After early difficulties with lack of exterior durability, cladding panels for buildings were increasingly produced in this way, excellent weather resistance being obtained with polyvinylidene fluoride.

Electron beam curing, another attempt to speed up industrial painting processes, made little progress; high cost and possible health hazard were barriers to wider adoption. Paint curing by ultraviolet light, although more economical, aroused little interest. On the other hand, powder coatings, as opposed to liquid paint dispersions, continued to forge ahead. The powders, 20–30 microns in particle size, were originally epoxy resins with pigment and a solid curing agent such as dicyandiamide. They were applied to hot metal surfaces by electrostatic spray or by fluidized bed, and then heat-cured. The epoxy types were especially suitable when outstanding resistance to chemicals and corrosion was required, but alkyd-amine and acrylic coatings currently being developed were preferable in some respects.

(R. J. Le.)

PAPER AND PULP

World production of paper and paperboard increased slightly in 1970, to 143 million short tons from 140 million in 1969. A slowing of economic activity in some principal industrial countries, especially the United States, held the increase to a considerably smaller figure than had been recorded in most recent years.

Besides this slower growth in demand, paper manufacturers in many countries were faced with lower levels of operation, reflecting the completion of large additions to productive capacity in North America and Europe. At the same time, their costs increased considerably. Thus papermaking in 1970 in the major producing countries was not as profitable as in earlier years, and in some areas earnings declined to well below the levels necessary to attract new investment.

These various trends—slow growth, high costs, and low profits—continued through the first half of 1971. However, because the use of paper and paperboard parallels very closely the level of economic activity, some improvement in demand was expected from renewed growth of the U.S. economy. On the other hand, the course of economic activity in Western Europe and Japan, the other two largest paper-using areas, was uncertain.

North America continued as the largest pulp and paper producing region in 1970, accounting for 64.2 million short tons, slightly less than the 66.1 million of 1969. By contrast, most other areas showed a modest increase, production in Europe rising to 49.8 million tons from 47.7 million in the previous year, in Asia to 22.6 million from 20.2 million, in Latin America to 4 million from 3.7 million, and in Africa to 1 million from 950,-000.

Building a paper mill to use local raw materials and conserve foreign exchange ranked high in the priorities of many less developed countries. Numerous new plants or expansions of existing ones were under construction in 1970 in Latin America, Asia, and Africa. The plants would use a variety of materials in addition to softwoods, such as bagasse, straw, bamboo, flax, and grasses.

More study was being given in many countries to the possibilities of recycling larger quantities of paper and paperboard, and thus using them a second time. In a few countries where other sources of fibre were small in relation to needs, as much as 40% of the paper and board used already was being recycled. In countries having large forest resources, the proportion was generally much smaller, but was expected to increase during the next decade.

World trade in pulp and paper amounted to some 35 million short tons in 1970, or about one-quarter of the total production. It consisted mostly of newsprint and pulp, which were duty-free in most countries, with smaller quantities of paperboard, book and writing papers, and other grades, which generally encountered tariffs. The largest pulp and paper exporting country in 1970 was Canada, accounting for 14.7 million tons, and the largest international movement of pulp and paper in its various forms was from Canada to the U.S.   (Go. M.)

PETROLEUM PRODUCTS

Petroleum in 1971 felt the sharp focus of public attention as several unrelated events made oil and gas newsworthy throughout the world. Some of the news was good, and some was bad. The net effect was a growing alertness on the part of the petroleum industry that it must meet increasing demands for energy and that it must do so without damaging the environment. This was matched by the beginnings of an awareness, especially in the U.S., that the vast amounts of energy so lavishly consumed in the past might not always be available in unlimited quantities at bargain prices.

Politics played a strong role early in the year. Suddenly, in concerted action, the principal petroleum-exporting nations confronted world consumers with new demands for their oil and gas. Protracted negotiations with major and independent oil companies resulted in sharply higher prices for crude oil, worldwide. This, modified to some extent by an easing in world tanker rates, caused net consumers of energy to be confronted with new cost factors and with a growing consciousness of the risks of overdependence on foreign sources for energy.

Environmental concerns continued to influence both the demand for oil and gas and ways and means to meet that demand. The petroleum industry recognized in 1971 as never before its need to consider the environment. Although government agencies dealing with oil and energy gave the industry reasonably good marks in this regard, both industry and government came under intensified fire during the year from environmentalists. Ironically, the best prospects for relatively low-cost new energy in the U.S. lay offshore and that, because of spills and fires, was where the resistance to new exploration was the greatest. Despite exoneration for the Santa Barbara (Calif.) spill of 1969, the industry was all but stopped from further exploring and developing the costly leases it bought there from the U.S. government.

Reflecting these outside factors, petroleum technology took some new directions in 1971. Much effort went into the efficient manufacture of substitute natural gas. A mounting need for cleaner air stimulated the search for better methods of taking the sulfur out of stack gases at major power plants. The ongoing program to phase lead out of gasoline gained relatively less attention as the petroleum industry awaited the next move of the automobile companies.

Throughout the year, alarms were raised in the U.S. about the "energy crisis." The fact that the nation was running out of cheap energy gained credibility with more and more consumers, legislators, and administrators. But the corollary fact emerged that energy in oil and gas form could be made available if its price would cover the added costs of political, environmental, and technical levies being laid on it.

The gas shortage in the U.S., which became believable to some consumers facing reduced supply, sustained the demand for distillate heating oils during 1971. And oil companies, with higher import quotas in prospect, geared themselves to meet severe winter demand.

With added supply from conventional domestic sources practically nonexistent, gas distributors moved rapidly to augment available gas from alternate sources. As the year progressed and the shortage became more evident, this effort rose almost to panic proportions. The new sources, whatever their origin, would enter the gas system at measurably higher prices. In contrast to domestic natural gas, which is moved in long-distance transmission lines from the southwest to New York City at a price to distributors averaging 42 cents per thousand cubic feet, the new supplies would demand at least one dollar.

Liquefied natural gas (LNG) gained much added attention in 1971. Already in use to augment short peak demands on winter nights, it was being sought in increased quantities. But no substantial new supplies were committed during the year. In addition to cost, the issue of security and dependability emerged to delay at least one major program based on Algerian LNG sources. With most of the U.S. East Coast dependent on imported fuel oil for industrial and electric power, consumers and even some government circles were questioning the extent to which the U.S. should commit its energy requirements to sources beyond direct control. Even so, new LNG supplies from Nigeria, Trinidad, Algeria, Malaysia, Indonesia, Papua, and the Canadian Arctic were being considered for possible future shipment to the U.S.

So-called SNG, which stands for supplemental, or synthetic, natural gas, also gained much attention during the year. Several feasibility studies and a few plants were announced. Some were based on naphtha and others on natural gas liquids from Canada, but most utilized coal. None, however, seemed to promise high-heating-value gas at any delivered price under $1 per thousand cubic feet. Some SNG projects could be built quickly, because they used processes proved in use in Europe and elsewhere. But most of them, primarily those based on coal, were still under development.

Meanwhile, new exploration for natural gas turned slightly upward at the close of 1971. The promise of higher prices provided some incentive.   (Ge. We.)

PLASTICS

It was possible that 1971 might prove to be a watershed year in the philosophy if not the performance of the plastics industry. The history of plastics, just over a century old, was one of seemingly endless expansion, especially in the last 25 years. Although expansion during 1970–71 was a little slower, it doubtless would continue for many years to come. Nevertheless, recent difficulties, of a commercial rather than a technical nature, forced the industry to recognize that its astronomical performance could not be sustained forever.

The manufacture of plastics involves huge investments by the oil and chemical companies, which, to gain as great a share as possible of a rapidly growing world market, vied with each other in the size of their plants. Overcapacity had therefore become common in recent years, and intense price competition already had reduced profit margins sharply when the industry was caught up in the rapid inflation of 1970–71 combined with reduced economic activity in Europe and the U.S. The inevitable result was that nearly every major chemical concern returned extremely poor financial results in 1971. Not only were plastics prices on a strongly rising trend after a long decline but many plans had to be modified, and it was evident that in the future investment would be much more selective. Toward the end of the year there were indications that the worst was over.

World output of plastics materials in 1970 was about 30 million metric tons, and final figures were expected to show that a further 10% expansion to approximately 33 million tons took place in 1971 (compared with an average annual growth of 16% over the preceding 20 years). Of this estimated 1971 total, about 9,250,000 tons were made in the U.S., 6 million tons in Japan (which remained comparatively immune to the troubles experienced elsewhere and again had the highest growth rate), and perhaps 3.5 million tons in the Eastern bloc (with the U.S.S.R. approaching the 2 million-ton mark). Western Europe accounted for just under 12 million tons, with West Germany producing 4.7 million tons in another disappointing year. France, which was third in the European league, after Italy, managed a little better than the other major producers in the area, with output increasing more than 10% to 1.7 million tons. The U.K. remained decidedly stagnant, and production was thought not to have exceeded 1.6 million tons, a 6% expansion.

The commercial setbacks summarized above did not inhibit the pace of technical development. The bulk of output continued to consist of the three major groups of "commodity" thermoplastics—PVC (polyvinyl

Klepper Trainer, 14.3 ft. long, is the largest boat produced from Cycolac ABS thermoplastic by Klepper-Werke of Germany.

chloride), polyolefins, and styrene plastics—which between them accounted for nearly two-thirds of the world's total production. No other materials were even remotely likely to challenge their predominance in tonnage terms. Nevertheless, there were many potentially profitable fields of application for the higher priced, specialized "engineering" plastics, and, with greater selectivity, much interest centred on these.

The research laboratories continued fundamental work on new polymers in 1971. One that became commercially available was Eastman Chemical's polytetramethylene terephthalate—an engineering thermoplastic that was said to have extreme resistance to abrasion and chemical attack. But most development continued to centre on the modification of known materials, with the object of enhancing processing capabilities or of altering properties to widen opportunities for applications. This was emphasized at the Kunststoffe exhibition—the largest ever held in the field—at Düsseldorf, W.Ger., in September. There, Badische Anilin und Soda Fabrik (BASF) introduced styrene polymers with improved self-extinguishing and heat-resistant properties, and also new grades of expanded polythene—as did Bayer—with packaging and insulation potential. Among the engineering plastics, both Bayer and General Electric demonstrated new polycarbonate ranges, while interest attached to an Imperial Chemical Industries (ICI) display of solid urethane components, many of massive section. Polyvinylidene fluoride in film or dispersion form, for which a high degree of chemical inertness and weathering resistance was claimed, was shown by the German firm Süddeutsche Kalkstickstoff-Werk.

Structural foams for applications such as furniture generated much interest in 1971, considerable attention being paid to special machinery to handle them. A significant processing development introduced by Aquitaine-Organico (France) was a new method for producing complex thermoplastic components of thick section. The increasing availability of wide (more than 3 m.) extruded sheet in engineering materials, together with big thermoforming machines capable of dealing with it, resulted in increased use of this economical process for producing large structural parts like boat hulls and car panels.

Plastics materials manufacture, in common with other branches of the chemical industry, had problems in connection with environmental questions. So far as plastics usage was concerned the debate centred on litter. It appeared generally accepted that plastics waste could be dealt with without great problems once it was collected, and that its indestructibility, particularly in the form of disposable packaging, was what lay at the core of the problems. It might be that in the end the only real answer lay in the public's sense of responsibility, but further research took place into the possibility of making plastic degradable by the action of bacteria or light. (R. C. PE.)

PRINTING

Printing and its allied industries suffered some contraction in 1971, especially in the U.S., U.K., and Italy. West Germany, a major supplier of printing equipment, experienced a decline in exports after the 1969 mark revaluation, and the nation's printing industry suffered accelerating labour costs following substantial wage increases and the introduction of a new union-administered investment fund to which employers were obliged to contribute.

In the U.K. several well-known printing companies closed down, but others expanded, such as the "world's largest non-heatset-web

offset installation" of Papers & Publications Ltd., at Banbury, Oxfordshire, where heatsetting to dry printed paper webs was introduced at the same time as a new compact phototypesetting system. Phototypesetting continued to make the headlines. In the U.S., Photon, Inc., introduced no less than 26 new models of compact machines and additional high-speed cathode-ray-tube (CRT) photosetters and computer-printout photosetters. Much new development came from Britain, with the multipurpose Crosfield Magnaset machine introducing a combination of video and CRT techniques to permit unusual flexibility and range in highest quality type production. In West Germany Linotype GmbH followed the previous year's introduction of the Europa photosetter with a tape-operated model.

Editing terminals—permitting direct editing of material displayed on a cathode-ray tube—were entering phototypesetting and computer-assisted composition methods in Europe and the U.S. Among them were the Cossor, Harris 1100, and Mergenthaler Linotype Co. terminals.

In Finland a project started by the Technical University, Helsinki, in cooperation with major newspapers, aimed at bringing about an economical method of electronic page makeup, and at Time-Life Books in the U.S. a complete page makeup system using computer generation and page display and printout was introduced.

Electronic colour scanners to produce direct enlargement or reduction became generally accessible. Best seller was the Crosfield Magnascan 450. In West Germany the digital Chromagraph DC 300 was developed. The PDI electronic colour scanner was further enhanced by the addition of CRT display and layout facilities, making it the first truly universal machine to accomplish not only colour separation and size change, but also page makeup and variable size change.

Little change occurred in printing processes. Major manufacturers introduced new faster machines or larger formats. Planeta unitized offset machines scored some sales successes after a comparatively long absence from major markets. Komori in Japan and Kovo in Czechoslovakia introduced new compact two-colour machines for small offset formats that offered large-press technical features. Extreme flexibility and unitization to provide for modular interchangeability of units was introduced in rotogravure presses made by such firms as Tecmo of Italy, Masson-Scott-Thrissell of Britain, and Chambon of France. Dual-purpose rotary presses to produce both newspaper and commercial colour work aroused renewed interest, and major press makers showed plans for such machines. Press costs had risen to such an extent that multipurpose utilization of machines was becoming important to increasingly large printing groups. A curious aspect of the dropping of sheet-fed letterpress machines from many manufacturers' production was the relatively strong sales position of the remaining makers of such equipment, especially in the less developed countries. Automatic offset plate processors became available from most plate manufacturers.

A new plate for direct production of offset plates, bypassing the intermediate film state, was shown in New York. Itek and 3M direct plates became available in larger formats, and Itek plate production was started in Britain by Howson-Algraphy Ltd. The West German BASF Nyloprint letterpress photopolymer printing plate was gaining ground in both job printing and the newspaper field. New automatic gravure cylinder etching machines were introduced by the Swiss Graphicart, and by Daetwyler and the West German Walter companies. Burda in West Germany introduced a colour control system for the pressroom using Gretag colour densitometry linked to scanning heads for checking print colour accuracy. IDAB in Sweden installed a Tele-Ekonomi newspaper production system at the *Arbetet* newspaper for production control over all technical stages from composing room to pressroom and to allow greater press scheduling flexibility. Harris-Marinoni in Paris introduced the Tele-Color remote control system with display screen for the setting of rotary press ink ducts. MGD Graphic Systems put into operation their PCS press control system, starting with ink duct control from remote position and designed eventually to cover all aspects of rotary press operation.

Completely automatic bindery and warehouse operations were introduced by several leading printers in Europe. Book sewing machines, such as Hepp-Brehmer or Smyth-Europa, dispensed with much labour. In Edinburgh packaging printers William Thyne devised a method of laser-cutting of dies for boxmaking. Programmed die cutting was made possible by means of new systems from Schoen in West Germany and Notting in Britain.   (W. P. Ja.)

SHIPBUILDING

In the latter half of 1970 cargo freight rates started to fall in all sections of the market, but this had only a minor effect on the rate of ordering new vessels. Existing orders with delivery in 1971 already had reached a record level.

Toward the end of 1971 the total deadweight (dw.) tonnage on order in the world's shipyards had reached 162,160,425 tons dw. represented by 3,241 vessels. The largest share of the order book was held by Liberian flag ships, of which more than 373 were on order, totaling 33,294,503 tons. Close behind came Great Britain, with 351, for an aggregate of 21,097,403 tons, and third was Japan with 251 ships totaling 19,463,520 tons dw.

Many shipyards tried to renegotiate existing contracts with owners because of unprecedented rises in the cost of building, but with only moderate success. Some yards in Sweden, West Germany, and the U.K. were faced with financial difficulty as a result of inadequate productivity.

Among the shipbuilding countries Japan led the field by a wide margin. By the end of 1971 Japanese shipyards held orders for 1,060 vessels totaling 32.8 million gross registered tons (grt), representing more than 40% of the total order book.

Considered by geographic groups, the world order book comprised 22.6% Liberian flag, 17.6% Scandinavian flags, 13% British, 12% Japanese, and 11.1% European Economic Community (EEC). The remainder was split among the United States, West European countries outside the EEC, the Middle East, Far East (excluding Japan), and the Communist bloc.

During the last two quarters of 1970 and the first two of 1971 there was a decline in the rate of ordering, but the figures still constituted an impressive total. For the four quarters involved, the increases were 10, 15.1, 13.9, and 9.5 million tons, respectively. From May to July 1971, nearly 16 million tons dw. were ordered, but this high figure was sustained by the call for large tankers and bulk carriers, with dry-cargo vessels and special-purpose tankers losing ground. Small but relatively steady ordering of the not-so-large tankers in the 100,000- to 150,000-ton-dw. range was backed by more orders for specialized carriers.

The only group to show an order increase toward the end of 1971 was the container section, which was up 40% compared with a year earlier. More than 215 container ships were on order representing nearly 4.3 million tons dw. The average size and speed of new container ships continued to rise, with the result that many smaller shipyards were no longer able to build them. This continued scaling-up in size slowed down in the tanker section, where only one vessel of 400,000 tons dw. was on order; however, there were 306 tankers of over 150,000 tons dw. on order.

Shipbuilders had to accept an increase in the size of the bulk carrier, and, whereas in 1970 the average was about 30,000 tons dw., it had now increased to 40,000. There were 693 bulk carriers on order with an aggregate deadweight tonnage of 28,630,000.

The trend to very large vessels proved expensive for many, and U.K. shipbuilders were not alone in losing a considerable amount of money. Yards in Sweden and West Germany also suffered, and the fall 1971 price of about $36 million for a 250,000-ton-dw. tanker was more realistic than the figure of $20 million quoted two years earlier.

Japan increased its lead in ships under construction, with more than 400 totaling 6.6 million grt under way. This compared with a world total of 1,950 ships with an aggregate of 22.2 million grt.

British shipyards held their share of the world market in 1971, and by midyear more than 307 vessels were on order, totaling 5.5 million grt, compared with just over 5 million grt a year earlier.

In the U.K. the future of the Clydeside yards became a major political and social issue following the government's refusal in June of further support to the Upper Clyde Shipbuilders consortium created by the previous government (*see* UNITED KINGDOM).   (W. D. E.)

TEXTILES AND FIBRES

Textile Industry. In general, the world textile situation in 1971 was anything but satisfactory. Despite strenuous efforts to avert it, most countries showed reduced consumption and production of fibres, yarns, and fabrics. Paradoxically, the need for textiles for apparel and household purposes was never greater, but international uncertainty gave rise to escalating costs in raw materials, labour, production, and transport charges.

In the fall fears were expressed during an international textile seminar at The Hague, Neth., that there was overcapacity in the EEC, and that the Lancashire cotton industry's experience might have to be faced by textile manufacturers in EEC countries.

In Tokyo and in Washington there were efforts at the government level to reach a Japanese-U.S. agreement on the prolonged controversy over fixing a ceiling for Japanese man-made fibre and woolen textile exports to the U.S., which totaled more than $550 million in 1970. These moves took place in the face of strong opposition from the Japanese textile federation, but on October 15 the U.S. administration was able to announce that Japan, Taiwan, Hong Kong, and South Korea had agreed to limit exports to the U.S. and that in return the U.S. would lift its 10% import surcharge on all categories of textiles covered by the agreement. In the U.K. more Lancashire and Yorkshire mills either were absorbed by mergers or closed down and dismantled. In many cases excellent machinery was ruthlessly scrapped because it had become a "drug on the market." Platt International Ltd. made substantial reductions in its machinery manufacturing operations at Keighley, Yorkshire. Changes inevitable with the adoption of the metric system resulted in a study group proposing Dec. 31, 1973, as a suitable date for complete metrication throughout the industry. A step-by-step program covering conversion procedures was circulated to all mills.

At no time in the past was textile research and machinery development more intensive. The Wool Industry Research Association set up technical advisory panels to guide some of these projects. The same institute also developed a new treatment to remove all grease and suspended solids from industrial effluent and substantially reduce the biochemical oxygen demand. During the year, a new textile engineering facility was opened at Leeds University to concentrate on new methods for increasing productivity and quality of textile processes, including automatic control of yarn weight, and solvent degreasing.

Among machinery developments, a Scottish firm introduced a new wet-winding, semiautomatic winding frame. Another announced an automated system for cutting and packing carpeting. Intended mainly for spinning carpet yarns from man-made fibres and blends, a new open-end spinner was claimed to have five times the productive capacity of conventional systems. Du Pont introduced a new yarn for tire reinforcement. A new tufted carpet machine incorporated mechanisms for making both loop and cut-pile faces. Another new process for making high-speed patterned carpets was designed to do the work of 10 to 15 conventional looms.

At the International Textile Machinery Exhibition in Paris, more than 1,000 exhibitors from every machinery-making country were represented. British exhibits included high-efficiency opening and cleaning systems; carding, combing, drawing, and doubling equipment; the Repco spinner—employing a self-twist technique to produce a two-ply yarn—and tow-cutting and texturizing machines. High-speed winding, warping, and weaving machinery was designed for every type of yarn (natural or man-made) and for cloth in dobby or jacquard constructions. On the finishing side, new machinery was shown for yarn or cloth scouring, raw stock, and sliver or fabric dyeing. A range of solid-state dye-cycle controllers attracted much attention, as did a wide variety of testing, counting, and electronic control systems.   (A. Dr.)

Natural Fibres. *Cotton.* Further substantial tightening of supplies, and upward price movements marked the 1970–71 raw cotton season. While producers secured welcome relief from the squeeze that had resulted in planting alternative crops, spinners faced limited availability of certain varieties and rising costs at a time when yarn and cloth markets lacked buoyancy.

Cotton's competitive position against the man-made fibres became more difficult; carry-over stocks at the season's end represented little more than four months of consumption, the lowest average over 25 years.

Disappointing financial returns from cotton growing in the previous season brought sharp declines in acreage in several countries, the world harvest bringing only 51.3 million bales against 51,850,000 in the previous year. Adverse conditions in the U.S. kept yields low, production rising only marginally to 10.2 million bales. In contrast, ideal harvesting in the U.S.S.R. was reflected in a record output of about 10.8 million bales, compared with 8.8 million in 1969–70. Elsewhere, production declined more than 2 million bales to about 26 million, with reductions in Mexico, South America, India, Nigeria, and Egypt.

As a result of substantial expansion in manufacturing facilities in many Asian and Eastern European countries, world consumption of raw cotton continued at record levels, being estimated at more than 54 million bales against 53.5 million in the previous season. The deficit in production had a pronounced impact on prices, and the Liverpool index covering better qualities reached unprecedented heights. The average quotation at the beginning of 1971 was 30.75 cents per pound, and by the end of May it had risen to more than 33 cents. The firm undertone persisted, with 34 cents quoted in July followed by a renewed advance when early reports of the 1971–72 U.S. crop came in. By the end of September average prices exceeded 36 cents per pound.

Mill managements faced a difficult position; they needed supplies urgently but often were unable to cover the cost of the raw material in their yarn quotations. Permanent closings and short-time working were forced on many firms in the United Kingdom, where the trend toward wider use of man-made fibres persisted. Early estimates of conditions in 1971–72 suggested that higher prices would encourage cotton production but, with continuing greater consumption, observers still forecast an output deficit of up to one million bales.   (A. TL.)

Silk. The silk industry assumed a new aspect in 1970–71. The 10% price hike imposed by China in January 1970 was seen, as time went by, to have affected demand more adversely than was immediately apparent. At the Canton Trade Fair in April 1970, buyers, conscious through hard experience of the difficulty of ensuring continuity of supplies due to nonavailability and late shipments over past years, more than covered their requirements at the new price level.

Some months elapsed before consumer resistance to the higher price plateau began to show itself. This snowballed over the months with the result that both merchants and manufacturers in the Western world found themselves overstocked by the end of the year, as silk bought at the fair began to arrive in abundance and strictly in accordance with schedules. Purchases made to cover needs up to the end of 1970 lasted over the first six months of 1971 and beyond, with consequent loss of financial liquidity to many. Purchases at the 1971 autumn fair were consequently minimal.

Conscious of what amounted to almost a cessation of demand for raw silk, China in February 1971 reduced prices by 5% in the hope of reviving interest, but the result was contrary to that expected. Stocks had to be written down, with considerable loss to the industry, but the real damage done by this, the first price reduction for many years, was to undermine confidence.

Meanwhile, the Japanese market showed signs that the exuberance of recent years was on the wane. Prices fell between December 1970 and April 1971 by approximately 20%. There was a recovery in May, when it became clear that China would not further reduce prices at the spring fair, but the market again sagged, and a limitation of raw silk imports to maintain prices was widely advocated in June; at that time, however, pressure was being brought to bear upon Japan to liberalize rather than further restrict imports, if a revaluation of the yen were to be averted. Some stabilization was established on June 24 by the Raw Silk Corporation's announcement that it would start buying up to 30,000 bales at 6,800 yen per kilo.

In recent years silkmen had asked what would happen if the Japanese prosperity bubble burst. Who else could consume the world's production? Would Japan reappear as a potential exporter in competition with China or would its own production shrink? It was thought that President Nixon's determination to curb imports from Japan and the revaluation of the yen late in the year might bring the answer nearer. In the fall of 1971 there were reports of diminishing kimono sales. Among the consuming public, interest in silk goods remained high, but upheavals in market conditions were inhibiting manufacturers, who could turn to other fibres rather than run the risk of what was again becoming a speculative market.
                              (P. W. GA.)

Wool. Consumption of wool in the nine leading consuming countries of the West in 1970 was 1,853,600,000 lb. (clean basis), compared with 1,998,600,000 lb. in 1969. World consumption in 1970 was estimated at 3,465,000,000 lb. (clean basis), compared with 3,537,000,000 lb. in 1969. The decline of 2% overall covered varying changes in individual countries, many in the Western world being larger in extent than elsewhere. Consumption in the U.K., for example, was 12% lower, in the United States 23% lower, and in Italy 13% lower. However, consumption in Japan, the largest consuming country, was nearly 2% higher than in 1969, and in France there was an increase of nearly 3%.

In the first half of 1971 consumption in nine leading countries as a group, including those listed above, was 8% lower than in the corresponding period of 1970. In these countries there was no clear sign of a general trend toward recovery in the later months of 1971.

This downward trend continued at a time when wool prices already were extremely low, whether measured historically or in relation to other commodities. The downward trend in 1970 caused Australia to introduce a system of price supports, involving direct purchase of wool offered at auction at rigid prices and thus the accumulation of a stockpile.

Modest recovery in demand during the second quarter of 1971 was followed by a deterioration in the situation in the third quarter, and the opening of the new selling season was generally described as "disastrous," involving very heavy purchases at the supported price. The situation in the other principal growing countries was little different, and governments felt compelled to support the wool growing industry in one way or another.

The severity of the problem facing wool as a fibre, and thus wool growers, could scarcely be exaggerated. Basically it related to world oversupply and the difficulty of reducing production rapidly and painlessly in an industry with a fragmented and worldwide structure. There was also a long-term uncertainty concerning the likely future level of demand for wool in consuming countries. This related partly to competition from man-made fibres, partly to rapidly changing fashions, and partly to the world economic situation.

Toward the end of the year, the International Wool Secretariat introduced a scheme to extend the principle of the well-established "Woolmark," familiar globally as a sign of goods made in pure new wool. The Woolmark was given a partner, the "Woolblendmark," to identify 11 categories of textiles containing IWS-approved blends of wool and other fibres, whether natural or man-made.   (H. M. F. M.)

Man-Made Fibres. In 1971 the man-made fibres industry was still suffering from a textile recession in most countries. This appeared to have more effect on the profitability of the major fibre-producing companies than on overall consumption, and certainly affected some groups of fibres far more severely than others.

In the latter part of the year the European industry was disturbed by the prospect of curtailment of the vast U.S. market as a result of the 10% import surcharge. President Nixon lifted the import surcharge late in December but, even so, it appeared that some of the livelier outlets for European man-made fibres in the United States were likely to contract. For example, a substantial business in textured polyester yarns for jersey fabric, and in the fabric itself, was certain to be affected by large-scale installations of both texturing equipment and jersey fabric knitting machines that were being set up in the U.S.

The future of texturing also seemed in the balance as a result of the availability of machines that combined the traditional drawing process for man-made fibre filament yarns and the texturing process. Combined drawing and texturing, up to 1971, had only been on a limited scale and largely confined to heavy denier specialized yarns for the tufted carpet trade. There could be no short-term swing to draw-texturing, particularly as a vast amount of capital had been sunk in high-speed, false-twist texturing equipment, but the evolution of the shorter process immediately raised the question whether future texturing would be done by the fibre producers themselves or whether they would be prepared to supply undrawn yarns to outside processors. In the United Kingdom, ICI Fibres, by buying a substantial interest in existing texturing companies, pointed to a likely swing away from outside processing.

Overproduction of nylon in several countries meant uneconomic selling, and doubtless influenced the tendency for leading fibre producers to cut down on nylon and concentrate on polyester fibres, although a similar position could arise with polyesters if the trend continued. More appealing qualities of nylon, not based on new polymers but on additives that inhibited static electricity and improved moisture absorption, gradually became available in both nylon 6.6 and nylon 6.

The outlook for the cellulosic fibres, particularly the high-wet-modulus types of viscose, appeared extremely favourable, with a general return to more normal buying conditions, as they offered both technical and price advantages over cotton, the full benefits of which had yet to be reaped. A large-scale swing to blends of high-wet-modulus rayon and cotton, or the 100% use of this advanced type of rayon, seemed inevitable.

Unconventional methods of fabric production and the rapid growth of both warp and weft knitting increasingly reacted against traditional woven fabrics. Considerable commercial progress was made with self-welding nylon fibres, based on a low melting point outer skin with a core of normal nylon.
                              (P. M. RE.)

See also Advertising; Alcoholic Beverages; Cooperatives; Economy, World; Employment, Wages, and Hours; Fisheries; Food; Fuel and Power; Housing; Labour Unions; Merchandising; Metallurgy; Mining; Prices; Rubber; Television and Radio; Timber; Tobacco; Tourism; Toys and Games; Trade, International.

AUTOMOBILES OF THE FUTURE

By Jerry M. Flint

The era in automobiles of longer, lower, wider—of designers vying for the most massive grille or the wildest tailfins—ended formally in 1971 with the introduction of the 1972 models. Style was no longer the most important feature. Practically every model was a ringer for its 1971 predecessor; even those that were changed beneath the sheet metal looked much the same on the outside. For the time being, the Volkswagen concept—no change without reason—had defeated "planned obsolescence," the policy of redesigning each year to keep the buyers coming back.

But, in spite of the freeze on styling, the ferment in the American automobile industry was greater in 1971 than at any time since World War II. The federal government with its demands for safer, damage-resistant, and pollution-free cars, and the public with its demand for fewer defects became the main forces in product planning. Indeed, it was the costs posed by their demands that made the expense of restyling intolerable, even for the largest companies. Thus, the engineers were initiating the changes, while the stylists had to content themselves with trying to make the safer cars reasonably attractive; the engine specialists were too busy de-polluting the engine to spend time developing more powerful motors for the horsepower race.

The potential for engineering changes in the automobile is dramatic. For the first time a substitute for today's gasoline engine appeared available, and thousands of engineers were at work on it. The bump was being put back into bumpers, and the day was in sight when a parking lot scrape would not mean several hundred dollars in repair costs. And the shape of the car of the future, of 1975 and 1980, was beginning to emerge—more smaller cars and bigger cars, with the sizes in the middle and the specialty models, such as convertibles, squeezed out.

Engines. The most exciting development was the prospect of a new type of car engine, the Wankel or rotary engine, invented by Felix Wankel in West Germany in the early 1950s. The first versions of this engine, built for German cars, broke down. Then

---

Jerry M. Flint is Detroit correspondent for the New York Times.

a Japanese manufacturer improved the design and began turning out Wankel-powered cars in volume, shipping some to the U.S. in 1971. The Wankel future brightened considerably in the fall of 1970, when General Motors Corp., the world's largest car maker, agreed to pay $50 million for the patent rights. A year later GM's engineering force went to work to ready the Wankel for production, and engineers within the company were predicting it would be on small GM cars by the mid-1970s.

The Wankel is a simple, small, lightweight engine. Engineers expected it to be cheaper to build than the motor in today's cars, easier to service, quieter, and with less vibration. But the feature attracting the most attention was its potential in the fight for cleaner air. The present internal-combustion engine emits carbon monoxide, unburned hydrocarbons, and oxides of nitrogen. The Wankel engine does this too, but because it is smaller there is more room under the hood for antiemission devices, and the Wankel venting system makes emissions easier to handle.

In the car engine of today gasoline and air are mixed in a carburetor. The resulting fumes are then pumped into a combustion chamber where they are compressed by pistons and ignited by an electric spark. The gaseous mixture then explodes, forcing the four or six or eight pistons to keep pumping up and down and thereby supplying the power that eventually turns the wheels.

In the Wankel the air-fuel mixture is compressed and ignited as in the piston engine, and expansion from the burning fuel provides the force that eventually turns the wheels. But there are no pistons moving up and down. Instead, a triangular-shaped rotor revolves around a shaft in an eccentric path within the working chamber, and the spinning shaft sends power to the wheels. The tips of the triangular rotor continually touch the chamber surface as it spins, forming continually changing pockets of fuel. Fuel enters an intake port and is compressed as the rotor swings around, squeezed in the narrowing space between the chamber wall and the rotor face. A sparkplug ignites the fuel, and the gases expanding against the rotor face drive it around and thus turn the shaft. As the cycle continues, the rotor swings past an open exhaust port and the spent gases leave the chamber. A Wankel may have fewer than half the moving parts of a V-8 engine and take up less than one fourth the space.

One other engine has a future in the automotive industry: the turbine. In a turbine, air is compressed and heated in a combustion chamber and then forced through a turbine wheel, which spins and creates power for the wheels. The turbine can use a variety of fuels, has few moving parts, is quiet, and has little vibration. But it appears to be difficult and expensive to mass-produce, and, more important, is not at its best when pulling a light load through stop-and-go traffic. Instead, the

Left, experimental General Motors vehicles include (left to right) the hybrid gasoline-electric, the electric and the gasoline in the 512 series, and the 511 commuter. Above, the canopy is raised on the hybrid to permit entry.

turbine engine seems likely to be used in heavy trucks and buses rather than in automobiles.

There are other engines—some built and tested, others just fantasied. A variety of battery-powered electric cars have been built, but engineers have so far been unable to find a relatively inexpensive power source that will give a car the speed and range needed. Another drawback is that the power plants needed to recharge the engines of 100 million electric cars might cause more pollution than would be removed by withdrawal of the gasoline engine.

The steam-powered vehicle has been hailed by William Lear, the inventor of a number of electronic aircraft devices and developer of the Lear Jet, as a cure for automobile pollution. Lear spent several million dollars attempting to develop a steam car and a steam bus. The car makers of Detroit have noted that there are some steam cars around—relics of the 1920s and a few they themselves have built recently—but they have continued to insist that the steam engine is too bulky and complicated to be a practical automobile power plant.

Natural gas can be used in an automobile engine, but this clean-burning fuel already is in short supply. And most of the other engines considered do not seem practical. Thus, despite a $50 million effort by the U.S. government to research new engines, only the old internal-combustion engine, the Wankel, and, for trucks and buses, the turbine seem likely to power the nation's vehicles over the next decade.

Antipollution Devices. But even the internal-combustion engine will be cleaner burning, and the heart of the antiemission effort is the development of devices to eliminate the auto pollutants. By 1975 it is likely that all cars built in the United States will carry a catalytic converter, a mufflerlike device laced with a catalyst such as platinum to help burn the fumes escaping through the exhaust system. In addition, cars may need a small reactor, a furnacelike device near the engine to burn fumes. Such systems along with air pumps and fuel injection to feed gasoline to the engine accurately will remove the bulk of the carbon monoxide and unburned hydrocarbons. The automobile makers do not believe that their systems will meet the government's standards for clean-burning engines by 1975, but they are certain they can come so close that the car will no longer be an important source of air pollution.

The U.S. Environmental Protection Agency announced in September that the Ford Motor Co. had developed a clean-burning engine that incorporated many of the above-mentioned design features. When tested on an army jeep with a manual transmission, the four-cylinder internal-combustion engine consistently performed better than required by the government's 1976 antiemission standards. Ford, however, warned that "because of its highly experimental nature, there is virtually no chance that the engine could be mass-produced and certified" in time to meet the 1976 deadline.

Safety Equipment. For those worried about how easily cars can be damaged the changes are coming faster. For years the massive steel bumpers gracing the front and rear ends of American cars were decorations, designed by stylists uninterested in protecting the car. They were pressed against the sheet metal of the body so that when they received even the lightest knock, at speeds of only two or three miles per hour, some sheet metal would be crumpled.

This, in turn, helped boost insurance rates. When the insurance companies complained about the car designs to Congress, showing tests proving that low-speed bumps caused hundreds of dollars in damage, the government and the auto industry decided to create a better bumper. Many of the 1972 cars claim front ends that are safe in a 5-mph crash into a parked car—the equivalent of a 2.5-mph ride into a concrete wall. But the 1973 cars are to have double this protection, 10 mph into a parked car without serious front-end damage. In 1974 rear ends are to be strengthened. Some car makers planned to toughen bumpers by making them out of stronger steel, placing more

The Japanese rotary or Wankel engine produces about twice as much horsepower as the piston engine. Dual ignition in each rotor chamber provides cleaner combustion and smoother operation.
COURTESY, KENNETT PR ASSOCIATES

reinforcements behind them, pushing them out a few inches in front of the car grille and sheet metal, and providing them with bigger rubber bumper guards. But others are introducing energy-absorbing systems—bumpers backed by shock absorbers that accept a hard knock, are pressed in, and then bounce back without damage and without much shock to the riders.

More controversial than the bumper is the next step to make cars safer. Collapsible steering columns, shatterproof glass, padded instrument panels, seat belts, and doors reinforced with steel rails have been added to cars, and the number of traffic deaths in the U.S. actually has begun to decline, despite the increasing number of cars on the road. Still, 55,000 Americans die each year in traffic accidents. If all car riders wore seat and shoulder belts this number could drop dramatically, but only a fraction wear them. Thus, the goal of safety research is to develop a system that works as well as the belts without requiring any action by the rider.

The government, which has the power to order safety devices on cars, believes that the air bag is the best such system. It is a balloonlike device that in an accident pops up from the steering wheel or glove compartment area, fills with gas, braces against the rider as he pitches forward, and then deflates, all within a fraction of a second. It thus protects the driver from his impact against the car interior, the "second collision" that causes most accident deaths and injuries. Engineers believe that an air bag can protect a rider in a 30-mph crash into a concrete wall (60 mph into a parked car), and probably can also be effective at higher speeds.

The auto makers also liked the idea of the air bag, but they said they would not be ready with a foolproof device by the 1974 deadline set by the government and thus gained a postponement until 1976. For an air bag must be foolproof: its trigger mechanism must be able to ride unused for years, then sense a crash and activate the bag. If the trigger does not set off the bag, the rider would have little protection because he probably would not be wearing his seat belts. If the bag should be inflated inadvertently—when the car hits a deep chuckhole, for instance—a driver might well have an accident because the bag goes off with the sound of a shotgun blast and hits the driver hard in the face or chest. There are also the problems of deactivating the system when the car is junked, and repairing it when the car is damaged.

But there is another way that cars might be made safer if the air bags are not ready by the mid-1970s. Already, the auto makers are beginning to install buzzer systems that warn riders in the front seat to fasten their seat belts. The U.S. government has ordered these buzzers to be installed on all cars built after Jan. 1, 1972. The next step could be a seat belt, connected to the door, that automatically snaps around a rider when he enters the car. Such systems are relatively easy to build and less costly than air bags. The government also proposed a system in which seat belts must be buckled before ignitions would work.

Computers. Another major change coming in cars of the 1970s will be the increasing use of computers. In 1971 only a few thousand cars carried computers, which were used to control an antiskid braking system. By 1980, however, Detroit's auto executives predict that uses for the computer will have increased so much that it could be the heart of the automobile. Among its functions would be braking the car in emergency situations; keeping the antipollution system working, and controlling the injection of fuel into the engine; monitoring the engine and electrical systems and diagnosing any troubles; and controlling the lock system to reduce car theft. Computers also are likely to have a more important place in manufacturing. The first production line of its type, with computer-controlled robots handling much of the welding, is operating at the General Motors Vega car plant at Lordstown, O.

Styling. What, then, will the cars look like? Over the next few years they will look much like the cars of today. Pressed by climbing costs of labour, material, and tooling, and by government requirements for safety and pollution control, the industry is cutting costs by simplifying production and eliminating models. For 1972, for example, 296 models have been counted from the four U.S. manufacturers, down from 375 in 1970. The styling cycle, which used to include a major change every three years, now spans six years between major changes.

More specifically, production of convertibles has almost stopped, with Chrysler and American Motors already abandoning them and Ford likely to do so soon. Hardtops will fade away because they lack the pillar at the end of the front door that gives added roof support if a car should roll over. The full-sized rear side windows on two-door models will disappear, to be replaced by small fixed windows. This will be a prelude to the elimination of all roll-down windows, but that will not happen until all cars are air conditioned. There will be more small cars, and more big cars. The small cars—imports and U.S. minicars and compacts—were taking more than a third of the market in 1971, and U.S. manufacturers were working on designs for still smaller models, the so-called commuter cars, that might be introduced by 1975. But the big cars, the full-size Fords and Chevrolets, Chryslers and Cadillacs, also seemed to have a secure place in the American market. It is the in-between sizes—the sporty cars such as the Ford Mustang and intermediate-size models such as the Chevrolet Chevelle—that could be squeezed out by the end of the decade.

Best System. What seems certain is that there will be cars. They will survive in spite of such criticisms as: they cause 55,000 deaths a year and billions of dollars of damage; they dirty the air and are wasteful of the nation's resources; they have created such eyesores as block after block of garish drive-ins, auto junkyards, and billboards; they have led to the chewing up of the cities and countryside for concrete expressways; and they have contributed importantly to urban sprawl and the social ills of the cities, since the whites and the middle class used the car to escape to the suburbs, leaving the poor and black in the city. Despite all these charges, there is no other transportation system in sight that appears able to service suburban America.

Some cities have banned automobiles from a few downtown streets, and more may do the same. In some cities there has been a general revolt against freeway building, and in some cities new mass transit systems are being built or planned, and, again, there may be more.

But as long as Americans move from city cores to the suburbs or even farther out the automobile will remain the key to the nation's transportation system. Today, instead of having one downtown for shopping, each urban area has dozens of major shopping centres. Instead of one dirty factory area, there are new plants and offices spread out along the freeways. The colleges, the doctors' offices, the supermarkets are all scattered about the countryside, as is the housing, and the only transportation system able to handle such a pattern is the combination of freeway and automobile.

Insurance

Insurance sales by private insurers throughout the world exceeded $100 billion in 1971, maintaining an average annual growth rate of approximately 9% for the past decade. Premium volume was unevenly distributed, however, with the United States accounting for more than 60% of the total, Japan and West Germany for 7% each, Great Britain 5%, France 4%, and Canada 3.5%. North American insurers sold two-thirds of the global insurance, and Western Europe one-fourth. Substantial progress occurred in Asia, which rose from less than 3% of world premium volume ten years before to 8% in 1971. In Japan sales had expanded by more than 20% for each of the past ten years. Growth rates in nine countries of Western Europe, as well as in Argentina and Australia, were between 9 and 16% a year, while in the U.S. insurance grew at an approximate annual rate of 8%. Mounting concern for rapidly rising health care costs and pressure for national health insurance systems to lighten and control the financial burden were common to many countries (see MEDICINE: *Special Report*).

Life Insurance. The Western and industrialized nations continued to lead in the use of insurance for protection and savings. Eight countries had more life insurance in force than annual national income: Canada (with a ratio of 2:1), New Zealand, U.S. (1.7:1), Japan, Sweden, Netherlands, Australia, and the U.K. In the U.S. total life insurance in force exceeded $1,500 billion, and purchased amounts during 1971 passed the $200 billion mark for the first time. Assets held by U.S. life insurance companies were almost $215 billion at midyear 1971. Investment of this capital was 41% in bonds, 35% in mortgages, nearly 9% in stocks, 8% in policy loans, 3% in real estate, and 4% miscellaneous.

Total income of life insurers, of which three-fourths was from premium receipts and one-fifth from investment earnings, was more than $50 billion in 1971. Of total premiums, 60% were for life insurance, 30% for health insurance, and 10% for annuities. The $2 billion pledged in 1967–69 by life insurers for loans to improve housing, create jobs, and promote community services in the core areas of U.S. cities neared completion in 1971.

The three British life associations reported new ordinary and industrial (home service) business was £10,900 million in 1970, compared with £9,401 million in 1969, an increase of 16% in 1970 against a 13% increase in 1969. Of the new business £10,082 million was written in the ordinary branch and £818 million in the industrial branch. New premiums and considerations to secure the new benefits were £436 million. A gross investment yield of around 7.5% was general among offices, and bonus distributions to participating policyholders were again at or above previous levels. The total sum in force at the end of 1970, including accrued additions, amounted to £51,-900 million, plus £1,820 million a year in annuities.

Property and Liability Insurance. In 1971 U.S. property-liability insurance avoided the losses of catastrophic proportions that floods and Hurricane Celia had caused in 1970. The U.S. did, however, suffer a major earthquake in the Los Angeles area involving $50 million, the largest insured earthquake loss since San Francisco in 1906.

The year-end effects of Pres. Richard M. Nixon's

August price freeze made annual sales and underwriting results difficult to assess. Total premiums were expected to rise above the $35 billion mark. There were some early reports by individual companies that statutory underwriting profits would be attained in 1971 and overall economic losses from automobile accidents were reported to have decreased (by 1.8%) in 1970 for the first time in 25 years. Most insurers, however, hoped for slight improvement over the break-even underwriting results of 1970. "No fault" systems for automobile insurance, under which most claims would be paid by the policyholder's own insurance company, were adopted in Delaware, Florida, and Illinois.

With Federal Bureau of Investigation reports again showing a more than 10% annual increase in crimes against property, the new federal insurance administrator, George Bernstein, announced that after August 1 the U.S. Department of Housing and Urban Development would write crime insurance in urban areas where such insurance was not readily available at reasonable rates. HUD also was underwriting flood insurance in a combined government-private program available in many areas, but the public was slow in making use of it. The merger trend in the insurance business appeared slowed in 1971. Nonetheless, the major purchase of Hartford Fire Insurance Co. by International Telephone and Telegraph Corp. was approved by the Justice Department with guidelines approved by the Connecticut insurance department. A report by the House Subcommittee on Antitrust warned of the problems of economic concentration in the insurance business in acquisitions proposed by Leasco Corp., Gulf and Western, Litton Industries, and others.

Worldwide premium income of British Insurance Association (BIA) members in 1970 reached a total of £3,702 million. Of this, general (nonlife) insurance accounted for £2,084 million, an increase over 1969 of 11.6%. Fire and accident business accounted for £1,176 million, automobile insurance for £683 million, and marine, aviation, and transport for £225 million. Of the combined fire, automobile, and miscellaneous accident premium income, £655 million (35.2%) was written in the U.K., £522 million (28%) in the U.S., and £682 million (36.7%) in other markets. Underwriting results worldwide showed a loss of £51.5 million on automobile business against a profit of £21 million on fire and miscellaneous for an overall loss of £30.5 million.

The impact of inflation, both in the U.K. and overseas, where British insurers transact two-thirds of their short-term business, was the major factor affecting underwriting profitability in 1970. The loss of £31.3 million on automobile underwriting in the U.K. in 1970 was the worst ever recorded, both absolutely and as a percentage of premiums. Insured crime losses met by BIA members in 1970 rose 6% to a record £21 million. Losses under "all risks" and household policies were up 20% but losses from commercial and industrial premises were 3% below the £6 million peak recorded in 1969. In contrast, 1970 U.K. fire damage was down 8% to £110.9 million, against £120.4 million in 1969, and, with no major weather disasters, the home fire departments had a better year than for some time.

Premiums written by British companies in the U.S. market consisted of £325 million in fire and miscellaneous accident business, against £290 million in 1969, and £197 million, against £179 million, in

automobile insurance. Hurricane Celia in 1970 was estimated to cost British insurers upward of £8 million, the costliest disaster since Hurricane Betsy in 1965. In Canada, an improving overall market trend was retarded somewhat by the effects of inflation. There was serious damage to property and automobiles, totaling about $10 million, when the area of Sudbury, Ontario, experienced an 80-mph windstorm. British insurers were withdrawing from direct operations in Uganda, Zambia, Sudan, Ethiopia, Morocco, and Guyana, either as the result of outright nationalization or the imposition of unacceptable conditions.

Substantially higher fire losses in France were caused by two major industrial fires costing over £4 million, serious forest fires on the Côte d'Azur, and the dance-hall fire that killed 146 persons at Saint-Laurent-du-Pont. West Germany's industrial fire insurance was even more unprofitable than the markedly bad year of 1969; Hamburg harbour suffered its worst fire loss since World War II.

Continuing inflation and its effect on the cost of repairs forced marine insurance underwriters to increase their rates and this, coupled with substantial increases in the insured values of both ships and cargoes, contributed to a marked rise in marine premiums. The number of vessels totally lost rose to 151 with an aggregate gross tonnage of 708,855. In the aviation market, the advent of the wide-bodied jets and expansion of airline fleets contributed to a rise in premium income. Some 20 or more jet airliners were lost. The combined premiums from marine, aviation, and transport insurance increased by 24% to £225 million, the largest percentage rise of any sector.   (D. L. Bi.; P. Ss.)

See also Cooperatives; Disasters; Industrial Review; Social Services.

Intelligence Operations

On Sept. 24, 1971, after Britain's foreign secretary, Sir Alec Douglas-Home, had twice written to his Soviet counterpart, Andrei A. Gromyko, complaining of Soviet spying activities in the U.K. and had received no reply, the British government announced the expulsion of 90 Soviet officials and the barring from reentry of 15 others, for a total of 105, including all 12 counselors and 7 out of the 12 first secretaries of the Soviet embassy. It also was stated that the number of Soviet officials in various categories (embassy,

Soviet agent collects material left by a scientist with the knowledge of British security forces, who filmed the incident. The film was shown by the BBC to explain the expulsion of 105 Soviet diplomats.
CENTRAL PRESS—
PICTORIAL PARADE

Information Science and Technology: *see* Computers

WIDE WORLD

The Sun Defector puts finger on Russia's secret army

BRITAIN KICKS OUT 105 SPIES

HEATH BEATS 'SABOTAGE

London morning newspapers on Sept. 25, 1971, reported the expulsion of 105 Soviet espionage agents from Great Britain. A high-ranking Soviet defector exposed the spy network.

trade delegation, and other organizations) would in the future be limited to the level after the expulsion, and that if in the future a Soviet official was required to leave the country for spying, the ceiling in his category would be reduced by one. Soviet representation in Britain had surpassed 550 by 1971, and included 83 accredited diplomats (compared with 40 in the British embassy in Moscow), plus 120 trade delegation officials and 70 contract inspectors, all for a relatively modest amount of trade (in 1970 the U.S.S.R. had sold Britain £220 million worth of goods, compared with British exports to the U.S.S.R. of only £102 million).

As expected, the U.S.S.R. rejected the British allegations, which it regarded as part of an overall policy of obstructing European détente and the Communist

Lily Selmair, known as "Red Lily," leaves a psychiatric hospital to attend court for her trial in Zürich, Switz., in 1971. Miss Selmair allegedly gave information and official documents to a Romanian and a Soviet diplomat.

LONDON "DAILY EXPRESS"—PICTORIAL PARADE

desire for a European security conference. In October, British official strength in the U.S.S.R. was reduced by the expulsion of four diplomats and one businessman and the barring from reentry of 13 other Britons.

In connection with the British expulsion of Soviet officials, the Foreign and Commonwealth Office confirmed on September 30 that Oleg Lyalin, ostensibly an employee of a London-Moscow import and export company but in fact an agent of the Soviet State Security Committee (KGB) attached to the sabotage and assassination department, had sought and been granted asylum and had "brought with him certain information and documents including plans for the infiltration of agents for the purpose of sabotage." Lyalin's secretary, Mrs. Irina Teplyakova, was also granted asylum.

It was revealed in early October that a reputed friend of Lyalin, Anatoli Chebotarev, a member of the Soviet Trade Mission in Brussels, had also defected to the West. According to press reports he, too, had supplied NATO with valuable information about agents of the KGB and the military Principal Intelligence Board (GRU), whose director was Col. Gen. P. I. Ivashutin. The Belgian prime minister, Gaston Eyskens, denied on October 21 that 15 Soviet officials had fled to Moscow as a result of Chebotarev's denunciation, but confirmed that they had left Brussels after the scandal had broken. On November 4 it was admitted that the Belgian government had sent home "more than 30 Soviet citizens suspected of spying." Belgium chose to expel the officials with the minimum of fuss in order not to harm moves toward détente. On December 26 Chebotarev returned to the U.S.S.R. at his own request after receiving letters from his family through the Soviet embassy in Washington.

Francis Roussilhe, a NATO archivist, was sentenced to 20 years' "criminal detention" by the French State Security Court in Paris on January 20. He had been charged in August 1969 with treason and espionage for a foreign power. Constantin Melnik, former director of intelligence in France under Michel Debré during the latter's premiership (1959–62), wrote in *L'Express* (October 4) that the various Warsaw Pact missions in France comprised about a thousand members, of whom 60% were considered to be agents, half of them dealing with logistics and the rest being masters who recruited and controlled spies in France: "This means that there are in France more East European spies than the entire staffs of the SDECE [External Documentation and Counter-Espionage Service] and the DST [Internal Security Service] put together."

In November it was alleged that a former SDECE agent, Roger Delouette, and a senior SDECE officer, Col. Paul Fournier (possibly a cover name), had been members of a drug-smuggling ring. Delouette was arrested at Port Elizabeth, N.J., in April, and in mid-November both he and Fournier were indicted by a federal grand jury in Newark, N.J.

On May 26 a high-ranking member of the Soviet delegation to the Paris Air Show disappeared; he later turned up in Britain and was granted asylum. The official, Anatoli Fedoseyev (real name I. A. Nikitrin), was thought to have been involved in the Luna and Soyuz space programs.

In June, Nicholas Anthony Prager, a former Royal Air Force sergeant who had been engaged in highly secret electronic work in the late 1950s and early 1960s, was sentenced in Leeds to 12 years' imprisonment for selling to Czechoslovakia secrets relating to

Britain's Blue Diver radar jamming device fitted to V bombers.

An unnamed KGB colonel masquerading as a commercial counselor was expelled from Italy in September for receiving NATO material from Franco Silvestri, a petty officer in the Italian Navy. In October, Leonard Michael Hinchliffe, a British Foreign and Commonwealth Office official, was charged with passing on a document of possible use to a foreign enemy sometime between 1968 and 1971 in Khartoum, Sudan.

A Czechoslovak journalist was sentenced to ten years' imprisonment in Prague in October for espionage and currency speculation. Arnost Vrajik, it was alleged, had had close contacts with U.S. embassy officials. He had access to coded messages from the Ministry of Defense, data on Soviet troop movements in Czechoslovakia, on confidential negotiations, and on Czechoslovak Army maneuvers.

Col. Rudolf Abel (real name unknown), Soviet master spy and a leader of the Soviet intelligence network in the U.S. in the 1950s, died at the age of 68 in Moscow in November (*see* OBITUARIES).

(K. SM.)

Inter-American Affairs

It became apparent during 1971 that there was increasing frustration among Latin-American governments caused by the "low profile" policy toward the region adopted by Pres. Richard M. Nixon's administration in the U.S. At the majority of meetings of official hemispheric organizations, delegates pressed for greater U.S. interest in the region and easier access for their products to the U.S. market. Some governments, particularly those of Peru and Chile, sought development aid from sources other than the U.S. The Soviet Union and China showed increased interest in expanding their influence in Latin America. There also were signs that Japan was intensifying efforts to expand trade and investments there; this was demonstrated by the announcement in April of a program involving investments to the value of $300 million for petroleum prospecting in Colombia, Peru, and Ecuador.

The sense of frustration was reflected in the increasingly left-wing course pursued by Chile and Peru (and by Bolivia prior to the overthrow of Pres. Juan José Torres Gonzales in August), and also in the nationalistic foreign policies adopted by some governments, even by those friendly toward the U.S., such as that of Brazil. Indeed, Brazil appeared to be determined to press its leadership among Latin-American countries, as shown by the succession of visits by foreign ministers of neighbouring countries between July and September, and the granting of development loans to Uruguay, Bolivia, and Ecuador.

The greatest imponderable in inter-American relationships in 1971 was the effect of policies pursued by the government of Pres. Salvador Allende Gossens in Chile. The U.S. government was already seriously aggrieved by the prompt resumption of diplomatic relations with Cuba and the nationalization of the copper industry that occurred soon after Allende took office in November 1970. The Chilean government intensified its nationalization program, and in August the U.S. suspended financial aid following the failure to compensate the Cerro Corp. for the take-over of its installations, and the presentation of a bill for

compensation to replace profits unjustifiably taken out of the country. The Soviet Union appeared ready to give Chile the technical and financial aid withdrawn by the U.S.; Soviet missions advised on the restructuring of the copper industry and offered a loan for the purchase of Ilyushin aircraft after the U.S. Export-Import Bank withdrew a previous credit offer for the purchase of Boeing jet airliners. Neighbouring governments became increasingly nervous as to Chilean intentions. However, in July and August Allende visited Argentina, Colombia, Peru, and Ecuador, and official communiqués published during the visits stressed his government's support for Latin-American economic integration, noninterference in other countries' internal affairs, and friendship toward nations in the hemisphere. At year's end Chile's attention turned inward as disturbances in Santiago led to the declaration of a state of emergency.

Organization of American States. The General Assembly of the Organization of American States (OAS) met in San José, Costa Rica, in April. During its sessions, motions were submitted calling for an end to trade barriers and restrictions throughout the world, a huge increase in development aid to Latin-American countries, and the introduction of preferential arrangements for imports from less developed countries to the rest of the world. The governments of Brazil and Paraguay pressed for a declaration outlining coordination in antiterrorist measures, but failed to achieve the necessary two-thirds majority.

Many countries complained of unfavourable trading conditions with the U.S.; the Brazilian representatives stressed that Latin-American exports were not increasing in line with world trade; and many governments were concerned about the falloff in U.S. development aid in recent years. The U.S. secretary of state, William Rogers, said that he understood these problems and that Congress would be asked to adopt some preferences for imports from Latin America. The presence at the assembly of UN Secretary-General U Thant led to considerable speculation that it would in time become similar to the UN General Assembly—a body that could not impose binding policy resolutions on its members but a forum offering opportunities for unofficial bilateral meetings.

The attack on U.S. protectionist policies was renewed at the meeting in Buenos Aires in September of the Special Latin-American Coordinating Committee (CECLA) after the U.S. dollar crisis in August. The delegates agreed to adopt a common front against the suspension of the convertibility of the U.S. dollar into gold, and to demand the immediate withdrawal of the 10% surcharge imposed by the U.S. on all imports except for raw materials as part of a package of measures to stabilize the U.S. economy. These motions were submitted to the Inter-American Economic and Social Council meeting held in Panama City in the same month. The U.S. refused to comply with them, but made it clear that Latin-American countries would be exempted from the 10% cut in development aid included in President Nixon's August measures. Notably, when the surcharge was removed in late December it was done not in response to the representations of less developed countries, but as part of an international monetary settlement among the principal industrialized nations. Further, the devaluation of the dollar, which formed the basis of the settlement, promised to make all U.S. imports more expensive and, in consequence, entry into the U.S. market even more difficult. Another source of worry was the uncertain future of the U.S. foreign aid program, which was killed by the Senate and revived only tenuously toward the close of the year.

The problem of Cuba also was considered at San José. Chile and Bolivia advocated the lifting of the quarantine imposed by the OAS in 1964 at the behest of the Venezuelan government, although Cuban Prime Minister Fidel Castro stated that his government was not prepared to join the organization. Meanwhile, there were growing signs that Cuba's long isolation from the Latin-American fold was ending. Although it was increasingly difficult for the U.S. to maintain its economic blockade, it still appeared to be determinedly resisting Cuba's admission to the OAS. Relations between Cuba and Chile grew closer during the year; the foreign ministers of the two countries exchanged visits in July and regular scheduled flights between Havana and Santiago began in June. Castro paid an official visit to Santiago in November, with a stopover in Peru. Peru was considering the reopening of diplomatic relations with Cuba and in July signed an agreement to sell large quantities of fish meal to Cuba. Trinidad and Tobago, Guyana, Panama, and Barbados were also reported to be ready to establish diplomatic and commercial links if Venezuela took a favourable attitude; it was also believed that Colombia, Costa Rica, and the Dominican Republic might do so. The Cuban government stated in July that it might participate in a conference of foreign ministers although it was not interested at present in formal affiliation with Latin-American organizations. The increasing acceptance of Havana was partly explained by the decline in Cuban support for guerrilla movements in Latin America during the past two years.

Regional and Subregional Integration. Little progress was made during the year toward achieving the ultimate objective of the Montevideo Treaty of 1960, which set up the Latin American Free Trade Association (LAFTA), of complete free trade within the region by 1980. At the tenth ordinary annual conference of the association, held in Montevideo in November and December 1970, only 31 tariff cuts were negotiated, compared with 989 reductions in 1968.

Four industrial agreements, however, were signed. The most important of these were on photographic equipment, involving Argentina, Brazil, Uruguay, Mexico, and Venezuela, and on petrochemical projects, to which all these countries were signatories with the exception of Uruguay. The United Nations Economic Commission for Latin America (ECLA) reported that the many problems faced by LAFTA prevented its achieving its aims; this set a formal seal on the general feeling of many observers.

On the other hand, the Andean group, comprising Bolivia, Chile, Colombia, Ecuador, and Peru, which was set up by the Cartagena Agreement of 1969, made a fair measure of progress. The grouping, so far the most successful of the regional integration projects, was established after the failure of initiatives by Pres. Eduardo Frei Montalva of Chile and Pres. Carlos Lleras Restrepo of Colombia in 1965 and 1966 to revitalize LAFTA. Considerable progress was made in 1969 and 1970 toward a common external tariff, to become operative in Colombia, Chile, and Peru in 1980 and in Bolivia and Ecuador in 1985. It became increasingly unlikely in 1971 that Venezuela would join the group, although in April it submitted proposals for constitutional membership. Meanwhile, the Peruvian foreign minister, Gen. Edgardo Mercado Jarrín, visited Brussels in September to discuss the possibility of increased technical and economic cooperation with the European Economic Community, and a delegation from the Andean Development Corporation, established by the group in 1970, visited London in October to discuss European financing of industrial projects.

The most significant development was the working out by the group of a common foreign investment policy. After much negotiation and discussion in 1970, agreement was finally reached on this early in 1971 in a document limiting foreign investment in the countries served by the group. This stated that foreign investment would only be authorized when considered to be advantageous to the country's development; direct investment would not be permitted in activities where local firms were already operating satisfac-

Anti-U.S. graffiti are coupled with slogans of support for Pres. Salvador Allende on a wall in Santiago, Chile.

FRED OHRINGER—NANCY PALMER AGENCY

torily, and it would be forbidden in the mass-media, banking, insurance, and certain other basic industries. Foreign companies already operating in the Andean region would be forced to sell a majority shareholding to the state within a stipulated period in Chile, Colombia, and Peru, and within a longer period in Ecuador and Bolivia; however, with the exception of Ecuador, all the member countries were prepared to relax this stipulation.

Further restrictions were decided upon in February by the Andean Group Commission, the group's administrative organization; these included restrictions on the use of local credit, to be reserved for domestically owned firms, and a ruling that new foreign companies wishing to invest in the area must sign an undertaking that in order to obtain access to the larger market represented by the five member countries they would within three years enter into partnership with a local firm. If they were unable to agree to this, they would be required to hand over control to the state within a stipulated period. No new ventures in mining, petroleum, and forestry would be permitted prior to 1980, and a ceiling would be imposed on all remittances abroad of profits or repatriations of capital; fair compensation would be given to all expropriated companies. Finally, it was agreed that member countries should be allowed to pursue a different policy from the group as a whole in certain circumstances if they were in severe economic difficulties.

The document was ratified by the five member countries on July 1, but with a few modifications to ease its provisions: it was agreed that some short-term credit should be made available to foreign-owned concerns; a rule applying to resale to local interests of shares acquired by foreign concerns in near-bankrupt local concerns was to be relaxed; a requirement that foreign concerns selling shares to local interests must give first option to the state was virtually eliminated; and the definition of existing foreign companies was changed to those legally constituted on June 30, 1971, rather than on Dec. 30, 1970.

There were growing signs during the year of an easing in the crisis brought upon the Central American Common Market (CACM; El Salvador, Honduras, Nicaragua, Guatemala, and Costa Rica) by the aftermath of the war in July 1969 between Honduras and El Salvador. The year began badly when in January Honduras imposed tariff barriers on imports from other member countries. In March the Guatemalan government partially withdrew its cooperation from the CACM's institutions unless a way to ensure smooth operation of the organization could be arrived at. At the end of April, however, Honduras and El Salvador seemed to have reached agreement on establishing diplomatic and commercial relations.

There were other favourable developments between July and September. A meeting of heads of state of the CACM countries was scheduled for September; a series of meetings by the economic ministers of the five was held in Managua, Nic., San Salvador, El Salvador, and Tegucigalpa, Hon.; and Costa Rica, Nicaragua, El Salvador, and Guatemala agreed to set up a joint committee to regulate their relations. Honduras agreed to further talks on the refurbishing of the market. This agreement followed the cancellation by Costa Rica in mid-June of a decision taken in May to impose controls on imports by its CACM partners. There was growing concern, however, as to the future attitude of Nicaragua toward the market; the

PRENSA LATINA—KEYSTONE

Chilean demonstrators in Santiago protest on March 25, 1971, the death sentence given a Brazilian student, Teodomiro Dos Santos, by the Brazilian government.

Somoza government had never been enthusiastic toward it. Costa Rica was also uneasy about the trade imbalance with the other four member countries in intra-CACM trade.

Some progress was made during the year toward fostering cooperation in the joint development of the resources of the Río de la Plata basin. Argentina, Bolivia, Brazil, Paraguay, and Uruguay agreed early in June to establish a common fund for this purpose. A series of presidential meetings during the year all stressed the need to develop the basin's water resources and transport and communications.

Territorial Waters. The claims of some Latin-American countries to territorial waters up to 200 mi. offshore were maintained during the year. On June 1, Brazil began to enforce a decree issued in March 1970 increasing the limit of its waters. U.S. fishing vessels were ordered to ignore the ruling, but after an exchange of protests the U.S. appeared to accept the Brazilian demands. Ecuador also made a strong protest over Californian tuna boats fishing in its waters. (Rn. C.)

ENCYCLOPÆDIA BRITANNICA FILMS. *Siqueiros: "El Maestro" (March of Humanity in Latin America)* (1969).

International Organizations

The following table shows the membership of the world's sovereign states in various international organizations in 1971. The growing realization that political and economic problems transcended international boundaries led to a proliferation of international organizations after World War II. Of these, the UN and its specialized agencies (some of which, such as the ILO and the UPU, antedated the war) aimed at least theoretically at universality. The World Bank, originally established to provide help to war-devastated nations, turned more and more in succeeding years toward concentration on the problems of economic development. Organizations with more restricted membership included regional political groupings (OAS, OAU), military alliances (NATO, the Warsaw Pact), and organizations with a primarily economic orientation (EEC, Comecon). Such groupings as the Colombo Plan were chiefly vehicles for channeling aid from the developed to the less developed countries.

International Bank for Reconstruction and Development: *see* Development, Economic

International Criminal Police Organization: *see* Police

International Labour Organization: *see* Labour Unions

International Law: *see* Law

International Monetary Fund: *see* Payments and Reserves, International

Membership in International Organizations, 1971

Country	UN 1	FAO 2	IMCO 3	IAEA 4	ICAO 5	ILO 6	IBRD 7	IDA 8	IFC 9	IMF 10	ITU 11	UNESCO 12	UPU 13	WHO 14	WMO 15	GATT 16	CE 17	AL 18	OAS 19	WEU 20	OCAS 21	C-Plan 22	Comecon 23	Euratom 24	ECSC 25	EEC 26	EFTA 27	IDB 28	LAFTA 29	OECD 30	ANZUS 31	CENTO 32	NATO 33	SEATO 34	WTO 35	Antarctic treaty 36	OAU 37	SPC 38
Afghanistan	•	•		•	•	•	•	•	•	•	•	•	•	•	•							•														•		
Albania	•										•	•	•	•	•			•																			•	
Algeria	•	•	•	•	•	•	•	•		•	•	•	•	•	•			•																			•	
Argentina	•	•	•	•	•	•	•	•	•	•	•	•	•	•	•	•			•									•	•									
Australia	•	•	•	•	•	•	•	•	•	•	•	•	•	•	•	•						•								•	•			•		•		•
Austria	•	•	•	•	•	•	•	•	•	•	•	•	•	•	•	•	•	•									•			•								
Bahrain	•		•			•					•	•		•				•																				
Barbados	•	•	•		•	•			•	•	•	•	•	•					•																			
Belgium	•	•	•	•	•	•	•	•	•	•	•	•	•	•	•	•	•		•	•				•	•	•		•		•			•					
Belorussia	•										•	•	•	•	•																				•			
Bhutan	•																																					
Bolivia	•	•		•	•	•	•	•	•	•	•	•	•	•	•				•									•	•									
Botswana	•	•			•	•	•			•	•	•	•	•	•				•																		•	
Brazil	•	•	•	•	•	•	•	•	•	•	•	•	•	•	•				•									•	•							•	•	
Bulgaria	•	•	•	•	•	•					•	•	•	•	•								•												•			
Burma	•	•	•	•	•	•	•	•		•	•	•	•	•	•							•																
Burundi	•	•		•	•	•	•	•		•	•	•	•	•	•																						•	
Cambodia	•	•		•	•	•	•	•		•	•	•	•	•	•							•																
Cameroon	•	•		•	•	•	•	•	•	•	•	•	•	•	•																						•	
Canada	•	•	•	•	•	•	•	•	•	•	•	•	•	•	•	•						•						•		•			•					
Central African Rep.	•	•		•	•	•	•	•	•	•	•	•	•	•	•							•															•	
Ceylon	•	•		•	•	•	•	•		•	•	•	•	•	•							•																
Chad	•	•			•	•	•	•	•	•	•	•	•	•	•																						•	
Chile	•	•	•	•	•	•	•	•	•	•	•	•	•	•	•				•									•	•									
China	•																																					
Colombia	•	•		•	•	•	•	•	•	•	•	•	•	•	•				•									•	•									
Congo (Brazzaville)	•	•				•	•	•		•	•	•	•	•	•																						•	
Congo (Kinshasa)	•	•		•	•	•	•	•		•	•	•	•	•	•																						•	
Costa Rica	•	•	•		•	•	•	•	•	•	•	•	•	•	•				•		•							•										
Cuba	•	•	•	•	•	•					•	•	•	•	•				•																			
Cyprus	•	•	•		•	•	•	•	•	•	•	•	•	•	•							•																
Czechoslovakia	•	•	•	•	•	•					•	•	•	•	•								•												•			
Dahomey	•	•		•	•	•	•	•	•	•	•	•	•	•	•																						•	
Denmark	•	•	•	•	•	•	•	•	•	•	•	•	•	•	•	•						•					•	•		•			•					
Dominican Rep.	•	•	•		•	•	•	•	•	•	•	•	•	•	•				•									•										
Ecuador	•	•	•		•	•	•	•	•	•	•	•	•	•	•				•									•	•									
Egypt	•	•	•	•	•	•	•	•	•	•	•	•	•	•	•			•										•									•	
El Salvador	•	•		•	•	•	•	•		•	•	•	•	•					•		•							•										
Equatorial Guinea	•											•		•																							•	
Ethiopia	•	•		•	•	•	•	•		•	•	•	•	•	•																						•	
Fiji	•					•					•			•																								
Finland	•	•	•	•	•	•	•	•	•	•	•	•	•	•	•							•					•			•								
France	•	•	•	•	•	•	•	•	•	•	•	•	•	•	•	•	•		•	•				•	•	•				•			•	•	•	•		•
Gabon	•	•		•							•	•	•	•	•							•															•	
Gambia, The	•	•				•	•			•	•			•								•															•	
Germany, East											•												•												•		•	
Germany, West	•	•	•	•	•	•	•	•	•	•	•	•	•	•	•	•	•			•				•	•	•				•			•					
Ghana	•	•	•	•	•	•	•	•		•	•	•	•	•	•							•															•	
Greece	•	•	•	•	•	•	•	•	•	•	•	•	•	•	•	•														•			•					
Guatemala	•	•		•	•	•	•	•	•	•	•	•	•	•	•				•		•							•	•									
Guinea	•	•			•	•	•	•		•	•	•	•	•	•																						•	
Guyana	•	•			•	•	•	•	•	•	•	•	•	•								•																
Haiti	•	•		•	•	•	•	•	•	•	•	•	•	•					•									•										
Honduras	•	•		•	•	•	•	•		•	•	•	•	•					•		•							•										
Hungary	•	•		•	•	•					•	•	•	•	•								•												•			
Iceland	•	•	•		•	•	•	•	•	•	•	•	•	•	•	•											•			•			•					
India	•	•	•	•	•	•	•	•	•	•	•	•	•	•	•	•						•																
Indonesia	•	•	•	•	•	•	•	•	•	•	•	•	•	•	•							•																
Iran	•	•	•	•	•	•	•	•	•	•	•	•	•	•	•																	•						
Iraq	•	•		•	•	•	•	•		•	•	•	•	•	•			•																				
Ireland	•	•	•	•	•	•	•	•	•	•	•	•	•	•	•	•														•								
Israel	•	•	•	•	•	•	•	•	•	•	•	•	•	•	•	•														•								
Italy	•	•	•	•	•	•	•	•	•	•	•	•	•	•	•	•	•			•				•	•	•				•			•					
Ivory Coast	•	•		•	•	•	•	•	•	•	•	•	•	•	•				•																		•	
Jamaica	•	•	•		•	•	•	•	•	•	•	•	•	•					•			•						•										
Japan	•	•	•	•	•	•	•	•	•	•	•	•	•	•	•	•						•						•		•								
Jordan	•	•		•	•	•	•	•		•	•	•	•	•	•			•																				
Kenya	•	•		•	•	•	•	•	•	•	•	•	•	•								•															•	
Korea, South	•	•	•	•	•	•	•	•	•	•	•	•	•	•	•							•																
Kuwait	•	•	•	•	•	•	•	•		•	•	•	•	•	•			•				•																
Laos	•	•			•	•	•	•		•	•	•	•	•	•							•																
Lebanon	•	•		•	•	•	•	•	•	•	•	•	•	•	•			•																				
Lesotho	•	•				•	•	•		•	•	•	•	•																							•	
Liberia	•	•	•	•	•	•	•	•		•	•	•	•	•	•																						•	
Libya	•	•	•		•	•	•			•	•	•	•	•	•			•																			•	
Liechtenstein											•																											
Luxembourg	•	•		•	•	•	•	•	•	•	•	•	•	•	•	•	•			•				•	•	•				•			•					
Malagasy Rep.	•	•	•	•	•	•	•	•	•	•	•	•	•	•	•																						•	
Malawi	•	•			•	•	•	•		•	•	•	•	•																							•	
Malaysia	•	•	•		•	•	•	•	•	•	•	•	•	•	•							•																

Membership in International Organizations, 1971

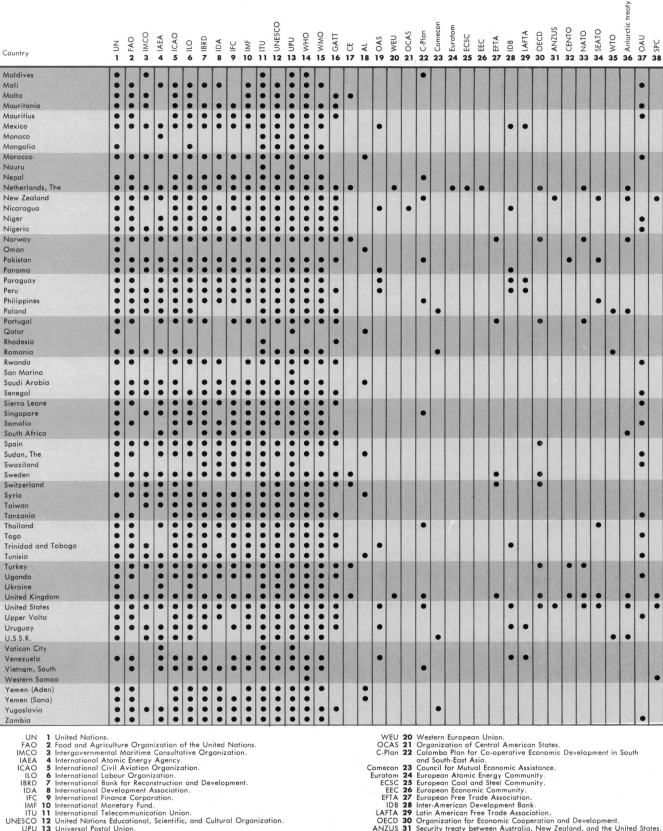

UN **1** United Nations.
FAO **2** Food and Agriculture Organization of the United Nations.
IMCO **3** Intergovernmental Maritime Consultative Organization.
IAEA **4** International Atomic Energy Agency.
ICAO **5** International Civil Aviation Organization.
ILO **6** International Labour Organization.
IBRD **7** International Bank for Reconstruction and Development.
IDA **8** International Development Association.
IFC **9** International Finance Corporation.
IMF **10** International Monetary Fund.
ITU **11** International Telecommunication Union.
UNESCO **12** United Nations Educational, Scientific, and Cultural Organization.
UPU **13** Universal Postal Union.
WHO **14** World Health Organization.
WMO **15** World Meteorological Organization.
GATT **16** General Agreement on Tariffs and Trade.
CE **17** Council of Europe.
AL **18** Arab League.
OAS **19** Organization of American States.

WEU **20** Western European Union.
OCAS **21** Organization of Central American States.
C-Plan **22** Colombo Plan for Co-operative Economic Development in South and South-East Asia.
Comecon **23** Council for Mutual Economic Assistance.
Euratom **24** European Atomic Energy Community.
ECSC **25** European Coal and Steel Community.
EEC **26** European Economic Community.
EFTA **27** European Free Trade Association.
IDB **28** Inter-American Development Bank.
LAFTA **29** Latin American Free Trade Association.
OECD **30** Organization for Economic Cooperation and Development.
ANZUS **31** Security treaty between Australia, New Zealand, and the United States.
CENTO **32** Central Treaty Organization.
NATO **33** North Atlantic Treaty Organization.
SEATO **34** Southeast Asia Treaty Organization.
WTO **35** Warsaw Treaty Organization.
36 Antarctic Treaty.
OAU **37** Organization of African Unity.
SPC **38** South Pacific Commission.

Investment, International

The value of international investment by the principal investing countries (U.S., U.K., Canada, Japan, and the EEC) amounted to about $14.5 billion in 1970, compared with $15 billion in 1969. Of this total, direct investment accounted for $9.6 billion and portfolio investment (the purchase of foreign bonds and securities) for about $5 billion. The main feature in 1970 was the sharp reduction in the net outflow of capital from every country of Western Europe except Belgium, due to relatively tight credit in several countries. The net outflow from West Germany fell by $2.3 billion. The U.S. net outflow increased by $1.7 billion, with U.S. investment increasing by $900 million and foreign investment in the U.S. falling by $800 million. There was also a substantial increase in the net outflow of Japanese international investment.

United States. International investment by the U.S. amounted to about $9 billion in 1971. Although direct investment was at a very high rate in the first half of the year, it was expected to slow down later because most of the year's allowance under the Foreign Direct Investment Program was used in the first half. This investment brought the total value of U.S. foreign assets to about $114 billion at the end of 1971, double their value eight years earlier. The book value of direct investment assets was approximately $86 billion, while portfolio investments amounted to $28 billion. The rate of investment in 1970 was at the record level of $8.2 billion, which was $1 billion higher than in 1969 (see Table I). Portfolio investment fell by $500 million, but direct investment registered a record 25% increase to $7.3 billion.

A great part of the increase in direct investment in 1970 was accounted for by a large gain in the outflow of new funds. This was a marked change from previous years, when reinvested profits rather than new capital had been financing an increasing proportion of the total investment. The change was largely due to the fact that reinvested earnings in manufacturing industries were held down by the slower than normal increase in earnings.

The regional breakdown of U.S. direct investments is shown in Table II. Investment in the U.K. and the EEC was at a high level in 1970, being, respectively, $440 million and $315 million higher than in 1969. At the end of 1970 U.S. assets in Europe amounted to almost one-third of the total, compared with only 25% in 1963. The major part of the increase in the rate of investment in Europe in 1970 was due to the expansion of petroleum investment in connec-

tion with North Sea gas and oil fields, although manufacturing investment in the U.K. also increased. Substantial increases were recorded in U.S. direct investment in 1970 in the Caribbean and Africa. The overall pattern of U.S. investment in 1970 was dominated by petroleum investment, which more than doubled to $1,960,000,000. Manufacturing investment fell by $300 million, with declines of $200 million being recorded in both Canada and the EEC.

U.S. portfolio investment declined sharply in 1970 from its very high level of 1969. U.S. purchases of newly issued foreign securities fell by $200 million, although purchases of stock issued by international organizations increased by a similar amount. The narrowing of the difference between U.S. and Canadian interest rates caused a reduction in the sales of Canadian securities in the U.S. by $500 million; these sales were also reduced as a result of the Canadian government's efforts to encourage Canadian borrowers to use domestic markets. U.S. purchases of outstanding foreign securities had amounted to $300 million in 1969, but in 1970 U.S. investors sold $200 million of foreign securities. Purchases of Japanese stocks had amounted to $300 million in 1969, but fell to almost nothing in 1970. In the first half of 1971 U.S. portfolio investment recovered to an annual rate equal to 1969. Purchases of Japanese securities in the first half of 1971 were $220 million more than in the corresponding six months in 1970.

The earnings on U.S. foreign assets rose by 11% in 1970, a smaller increase than in the previous two years (see Table III). Figures for the first half of 1971 suggested a similar increase for the year as a whole, with a larger increase in direct investment earnings offsetting the more slowly growing portfolio earnings. The largest increase in direct investment earnings in 1970 came from the petroleum industry. Manufacturing industry earnings rose little as a whole in 1970, but increased by $100 million in the EEC. There was a decline of $170 million in earnings in Latin America, due largely to mining activities in Chile and Venezuela.

Foreign investment in the U.S., which had reached exceptionally high levels in 1968 and 1969, fell considerably in 1970 and continued to decline in the first half of 1971 (see Table IV). Foreign direct investment in 1969 and 1970 included some major foreign acquisitions of U.S. companies (amounting to $800 million in 1970). There were no such activities in the first half of 1971, and foreign direct investment was at a very low level. Similarly, foreign portfolio investment continued to decline from its high levels of 1968 and 1969 to more "normal" values in 1971.

United Kingdom. Investment abroad by the U.K. recovered in 1970 almost up to the record level reached in 1968. Provisional figures based on the first half of the year indicated that in 1971 investment at over £800 million was £100 million higher than in 1970 (see Table V). In 1970 direct investment fell by more than 10%, but portfolio investment recovered and the oil and miscellaneous category recorded a substantial increase. Much of the increase in 1971 was due to the large expansion in direct investment.

About one-third of U.K. direct investment in 1970 represented the outflow of new funds, the remainder being financed from reinvested profits. This meant that new funds were relatively somewhat less important than in 1969, but the proportions were similar to the years before that. It can be seen from Table

Table I. U.S. Investment Abroad
In $000,000

Item	1966	1967	1968	1969	1970	1st half 1971*
Direct investment						
New funds	3,661	3,137	3,209	3,254	4,403	5,370
Reinvested profits	1,739	1,598	2,175	2,604	2,885	...
Total	5,400	4,735	5,384	5,858	7,288	...
Portfolio investment	261	1,292	1,133	1,484	943	1,498
Total	5,661	6,027	6,517	7,342	8,231	...

*Seasonally adjusted; at annual rate.
Source: U.S. Department of Commerce, *Survey of Current Business*.

VI that there was a sharp decline in U.K. investment in the sterling area in 1970. Investment in nonsterling area countries continued to expand and accounted for almost 60% of U.K. direct investment in 1970, with investment in EEC countries continuing at a high level.

Earnings on U.K. foreign investments increased only slowly in 1970 and 1971 (Table VIII). This was in contrast to the large increases in the previous two years. Earnings on direct investments grew quite rapidly in the first half of 1970 but failed to show any growth after the middle of the year, and the total for 1971 was provisionally estimated at a level similar to that of 1970. The growth in earnings in 1970 was evenly shared between sterling area and nonsterling area countries; earnings on investments in the EEC and in Australia led this growth, reflecting the benefits of the high level of recent investment in those areas (see Table VI). Earnings on portfolio investments, which had shown a substantial increase in 1968 following devaluation, continued at much the same level in 1970 and 1971.

Foreign investment in the U.K. continued to increase and in 1970 reached a level double that of 1967 (see Table IX). A further substantial increase was recorded in 1971. Historically a net exporter of investment capital, the U.K. in the first half of the 1960s had a net outflow that averaged more than £100 million. In 1969 and 1970, however, there was a very small net inflow of capital, which was increased in 1971. Foreign direct investment in the U.K. was relatively stable at about £320 million in 1969-71, but the petroleum and miscellaneous category of investment increased strongly over this period, as foreign oil companies explored and developed the North Sea gas and oil fields for the U.K. market. Portfolio investment recovered sharply in 1971 from its decline in 1970.

Other Industrial Nations. *Belgium.* In contrast to most European countries, the Belgian balance on capital flows shifted from a net inflow of $95 million in 1969 to a net outflow of $190 million in 1970. Belgian direct investment abroad, which had been negligible in 1969, rose to $130 million in 1970; portfolio investment also increased sharply, and total international investment in Belgium doubled to $515 million. There was a substantial increase in direct investment by other countries within Belgium, but this was matched by an equally large decline in portfolio investment caused by the halting of the inflow of flight capital from France.

Canada. The outflow of capital from Canada continued in 1970 at much the same rate as in the previous year. Canadian direct investment declined slightly, but this was offset by a similar rise in portfolio investment. Foreign direct investment in Canada rose by $100 million to $760 million, but by far the most important feature was the reduced inflow of portfolio investment—from $1,730,000,000 in 1969 to only $600 million in 1970. The higher level of interest rates in Europe and the U.S. reduced the attractiveness of Canadian bonds, and the reduced investment was particularly noticeable among European buyers.

France. International investment by French residents increased from $260 million in 1969 to $440 million in 1970, helped by the relaxation of exchange controls imposed during 1969. The higher level of direct investment accounted for $100 million of the increase. The major change in the French international investment scene in 1970 was the inflow of foreign capital, which more than doubled from its 1969 level to a record level of $1.4 billion. Encouraged by the more stable economic conditions, foreigners increased their direct investment by more than $300 million. There were similarly large increases in foreign portfolio investment.

West Germany. The pattern of West German international investment returned to a more normal flow from the exceptionally high level of portfolio investment in 1969, which, coupled with disinvestment by foreigners, had given the nation a net outflow of international investment of $2,630,000,000; this figure was higher than that of the U.S. in 1969. In 1970 West German investors purchased $700 million of foreign bonds and securities, compared with $2.1 billion in 1969; their purchases of foreign bond issues denominated in marks fell from $1.9 billion to $700 million,

Table II. U.S. Direct Investment and Earnings by Region, 1970
In $000,000

Area	Total value of assets at end of year	Net investment Reinvested profits	New funds	Total	Earnings Repatriated profits	Total
Canada	22,801	791	915	1,706	972	1,622
Latin America	12,201	319	307	626	899	1,236
Other Western Hemisphere	2,483	83	252	335	182	252
EEC	11,695	448	971	1,419	774	1,245
United Kingdom	8,015	236	642	878	375	592
Other European countries	4,761	270	291	561	229	486
Africa	3,476	157	363	520	680	845
Asia	5,613	187	210	397	1,526	1,714
Australia and New Zealand	3,485	143	226	369	215	325
International (unallocated)	3,563	251	226	477	174	416
Total	78,090	2,885	4,403	7,288	6,026	8,733

Source: U.S. Department of Commerce, *Survey of Current Business.*

Table III. U.S. Investment Earnings
In $000,000

Item	1966	1967	1968	1969	1970	1st half 1971*
Direct investment						
Repatriated profits	4,045	4,517	4,973	5,658	6,026	6,868
Reinvested profits†	1,657	1,516	2,049	2,316	2,707	...
Total	5,702	6,033	7,022	7,974	8,733	...
Portfolio investment						
Total income	1,605	1,717	1,949	2,267	2,597	2,506
Total earnings	7,307	7,750	8,971	10,241	11,330	...

*Seasonally adjusted; at annual rate.
†Excluding interest but before deducting foreign withholding taxes.
Source: U.S. Department of Commerce, *Survey of Current Business.*

Table IV. Foreign Investment in U.S.
In $000,000

Inflow of funds	1966	1967	1968	1969	1970	1971*
Direct investment	86	258	319	832	969	136
Portfolio investment	909	1,016	4,389	3,112	2,190	1,530
Total	995	1,274	4,708	3,944	3,159	1,666
Total earnings†	1,593	1,764	2,231	3,686	4,032	2,914

*First half of year, seasonally adjusted; at annual rate.
†Excluding undistributed profits, which amounted to $431 and $434 million in 1969 and 1970, respectively.
Source: U.S. Department of Commerce, *Survey of Current Business.*

Table V. U.K. Investment Abroad
In £000,000

Item	1960	1967	1968	1969	1970	1971*
Direct investment†						
New funds	165	91	133	226	177	...
Reinvested profits	85	190	277	321	309	...
Total	250	281	410	547	486	620
Portfolio investment‡	−37	59	236	34	79	30
Oil and miscellaneous	109	116	81	86	149	165
Total	322	456	727	667	714	815

*Estimate based on first half of year.
†Excluding oil and, in 1960, insurance.
‡Net disinvestment in 1960.
Sources: U.K. Balance of Payments 1971; Economic Trends.

Table VI. U.K. Direct Investment and Earnings: by Region*

In £000,000

Area	Investment				Earnings			
	1967	1968	1969	1970	1967	1968	1969	1970
U.S.	52	84	53	...	73	86	94	...
EEC	30	73	104	...	25	65	83	...
EFTA	-8	19	14	...	11	13	17	...
Others	65	57	65	...	92	118	112	...
Total nonsterling area	139	233	236	277	201	282	306	333
Australia	54	80	116	...	62	76	99	...
South Africa	47	43	70	...	65	76	86	...
India	11	9	9	...	18	20	21	...
Others	30	45	116	...	92	114	138	...
Total sterling area	142	177	311	209	237	286	344	368
Total	281	410	547	486	438	568	650	701
Of which less developed countries (included above)	63	66	115	...	136	170	193	...

*Excluding oil companies.
Souces: *U.K. Board of Trade Journal; U.K. Balance of Payments, 1971.*

Table VIII. U.K. Investment Earnings

In £000,000

Item	1960	1967	1968	1969	1970	1971*
Direct investment†						
Repatriated profits	173	248	291	329	392	...
Reinvested profits	85	190	277	321	309	...
Total	258	438	568	650	701	695
Portfolio investment	125	145	164	161	171	162
Oil and miscellaneous	286	401	383	530	509	580
Total	669	984	1,115	1,341	1,381	1,437

*Estimate based on first half of year.
†Excluding oil and, in 1960, insurance.
Sources: *U.K. Balance of Payments, 1971; Economic Trends.*

Table IX. Foreign Investment in U.K.

In £000,000

Item	1960	1967	1968	1969	1970	1971*
Direct investment†						
New funds	68	73	98	187	151	...
Reinvested profits	67	97	176	132	166	...
Total	135	170	274	319	317	325
Portfolio investment‡	63	-21	34	136	74	180
Oil and miscellaneous	55	211	259	218	326	360
Total	253	360	567	673	727	865

*Estimate based on first half of year.
†Excluding oil and, in 1960, insurance.
‡Net disinvestment in 1967.
Sources: *U.K. Balance of Payments, 1971; Economic Trends.*

and purchases of foreign investment fund units fell from $500 million to almost nothing in 1970. On the other hand, foreign investors, who had sold West German bonds and securities to the value of $330 million in 1969 (largely due to profit-taking after revaluation), purchased West German stock again in 1970, particularly toward the end of the year.

West German direct investment abroad increased to a record level of $650 million in 1970, while foreign direct investment fell to $230 million. This net outflow of direct investment in 1970 of $420 million was a big change from previous years when West Germany had been a net receiver of direct investment funds. A balance was reached in 1968 and a small net outflow first recorded in 1969. The reduced flow of U.S. direct investment contributed considerably to this changed pattern.

Italy. The outflow of capital from Italy during 1970 was more than $100 million lower than in the previous year, while the inflow of foreign capital increased by $165 million. The net outflow, which had been $300 million in 1969, was thus negligible in 1970. The main changes were in direct investment, where Italian investment fell sharply to $110 million with reduced investment in oil prospecting a contributing

factor. On the other hand, foreign direct investment in the Italian manufacturing, oil, and construction industries helped to increase the inflow from $420 million to $605 million.

Japan. International investment by Japan increased somewhat in 1970, mainly because of the higher rate of direct investment by Japanese companies. The principal change was the sharp reduction in the inflow of foreign portfolio investment, from $930 million in 1969 to $235 million in 1970. Foreign purchases of Japanese securities fell by more than $500 million to $190 million, and foreign issues of Japanese bonds denominated in foreign currencies declined from $200 million to $50 million. Foreign direct investment in Japan increased in 1970 but continued to be a relatively insignificant amount. (A. G. A.)

See also Development, Economic; Payments and Reserves, International; Trade, International.

Table VII. Other OECD Countries' International Investment, 1969-70

In $000,000

Country	1969			1970		
	Direct	Portfolio	Total	Direct	Portfolio	Total
Belgium						
Outflow	20	245	265	130	385	515
Inflow	70	290	360	335	-10	325
Net	-50	-45	-95	-205	395	190
Canada						
Outflow	255	-105	150	215	-60	155
Inflow	655	1,730	2,385	760	600	1,360
Net	-400	-1,835	-2,235	-545	-660	-1,205
France						
Outflow	...	...	260	...	...	440
Inflow	...	...	660	...	...	1,410
Net	-110	-290	-400	...	...	-970
West Germany						
Outflow	565	2,100	2,665	650	680	1,330
Inflow	365	-330	35	230	365	595
Net	200	2,430	2,630	420	315	735
Italy						
Outflow	285	460	745	110	520	630
Inflow	420	25	445	605	5	610
Net	-135	435	300	-495	515	20
Japan						
Outflow	...	...	1,235	...	...	1,375
Inflow	55	930	985	90	235	325
Net	...	...	250	...	...	1,050
Netherlands						
Outflow	...	240	...	...	250	...
Inflow	...	375	...	...	665	...
Net	145	-135	10	-35	-415	-450

Sources: Annual Reports of International Monetary Fund, Bank for International Settlements, and national banks.

Iran

A constitutional monarchy of western Asia, Iran is bounded by the U.S.S.R., Afghanistan, Pakistan, Iraq, and Turkey and the Caspian Sea, the Arabian Sea, and the Persian Gulf. Area: 635,932 sq.mi. (1,647,064 sq.km.). Pop. (1971 est.): 30,159,000. Cap. and largest city: Teheran (pop., 1970 est., 3,378,000). Language: Farsi (Persian). Religion: (1966) Muslim 96%; Christian, Jewish, and Zoroastrian minorities. Shah-in-shah, Mohammed Reza Pahlavi Aryamehr; prime minister in 1971, Emir Abbas Hoveida.

Early in 1971 the continuing student agitation in Teheran, which had been treated tolerantly by the government, met with angry reaction from workers' and peasants' organizations, who claimed that much of the agitation was encouraged and inspired from foreign sources, and demanded that the government take firmer measures. Before long, discipline was restored without drastic action, and agitation died down. What particularly exasperated public opinion were the attacks on the monarchy, which in Iran was regarded not so much as an accepted institution as the embodiment of all that was best in the country's

The ruins of Persepolis
provide the setting
for the celebration
of the 2,500th anniversary
of the founding
of the Persian Empire.
The camp of Persepolis,
located in a conifer
forest behind the ruins,
was built to house
the royalty and heads
of state for the occasion.

cultural and political tradition. This feeling was exemplified in the strongest manner in 1971, when two
anniversaries connected with the monarchy were
celebrated throughout the country. The first, on
August 5, was the 65th anniversary of the original
step toward democratic institutions on which Iran's
parliamentary regime was founded. The second, held
in October, was the celebration of the 2,500th anniversary of the Persian monarchy, held at the ancient

capital of Persepolis. A great city of tents was erected
near the remains of the palace; many heads of state
and representatives of foreign governments attended.

Domestically, the anniversary of the monarchy was
marked by the launching of a number of appeals designed to help provide increased social services, particularly in the field of education. The Central Centenary Committee asked for money to build 2,500
new schools and teachers' quarters in villages which
were without such amenities; the response from the
public was so enthusiastic that funds for more than
4,000 such projects were quickly subscribed. National
pride was further gratified by the gathering of many
well-known specialists in Iranian history and culture
at the Pahlavi University of Shiraz to pay tribute to
the contributions that Persian philosophers, savants,
and men of letters had made to the world's cultural
heritage.

The pattern of external relations showed no great
change; but Iran's relations with Lebanon, broken off
in 1969 because of Lebanon's refusal to extradite an
Iranian general faced with criminal charges in Teheran, were resumed in July 1971. Relations with Turkey and Pakistan, the country's two partners in the
flourishing Regional Cooperation for Development
(RCD), continued close. Meetings of the RCD committees on trade, communications, banking, and
other cooperative enterprises were held regularly;
and progress was made in arrangements to implement the recommendations of the UN Conference on
Trade and Development regarding mutual tariff reductions. On September 27 Pres. Cevdet Sunay of
Turkey and the shah took part in ceremonies at the
lake town of Van in eastern Turkey to inaugurate
the Turkish-Iranian railway, a 215-mi. line through
mountainous terrain. The project, which cost $81.6
million and took six years to complete, was sponsored
by the Central Treaty Organization, which also
planned a 500-mi. rail link between Iran and Pakistan.

Iran's friendship with Pakistan was the means of
promoting closer diplomatic relations between Iran
and China. The Iranian and Chinese ambassadors to
Pakistan signed an agreement in Islamabad in August
by which the Iranian government recognized the
Peking regime as the sole legal government of China.

A few days earlier, the Turkish and Chinese ambassadors to France signed a similar agreement in Paris; thus Iran, like its two RCD partners, was aligned in friendship with Peking.

The situation in the Persian Gulf had eased somewhat after the renunciation of Iranian claims to sovereignty over Bahrain in 1970. But on Nov. 30, 1971, as British withdrawal from the area neared, Iran occupied three small islands at the mouth of the Persian Gulf, the British protectorates of Greater and Lesser Tumbs and Abu Musa, which was taken over by agreement with the local ruler. Iraq immediately broke relations with Iran, which retaliated on December 4.

(L. F. R. W.)

Iraq

A republic of western Asia, Iraq is bounded by Turkey, Iran, Kuwait, Saudi Arabia, Jordan, Syria, and the Persian Gulf. Area: 169,284 sq.mi. (438,446 sq.km.). Pop. (1970 est.): 9,465,800, including Arabs, Kurds, Turks, Assyrians, Iranians, and others. Cap. and largest city: Baghdad (pop., 1970 est., 2,183,-760). Language: Arabic. Religion: mainly Muslim, some Christian. President in 1971, Gen. Ahmad Hassan al-Bakr.

In 1971 Iraq's Baathist regime maintained its hold over the country despite acute unpopularity in some quarters at home and general isolation in the Arab world. A serious problem for the government was implementation of the March 1970 agreement with the Kurdish minority. In January a Kurdish governor was appointed to the predominantly Kurdish district of Sulaymaniyah, and in February new powers were given to a ministerial committee to carry out the settlement, which also involved heavy expenditure on the reconstruction of northern Iraq through the building of roads, power stations, and new factories. The Kurdish leadership of Mustafa al-Barzani and his Kurdish Democratic Party was strengthened by the decision of the smaller Kurdish Revolutionary Party to merge with the KDP. In May there were signs that Barzani was becoming restive over delays in implementing the March 1970 agreement. He accused the government of postponing the holding of a census to establish the extent of Kurdish majority areas (which were to have a Kurdish administration) in order to dilute the population with non-Kurdish elements.

The withdrawal of about 18,000 troops previously stationed in Syria and Jordan strengthened the government's hand in its active foreign policy in the Persian Gulf area. When the British government announced in March its final decision to withdraw from the Gulf, the Iraqi Baathists concentrated on the need

to maintain the "Arabism" of the area and on the rejection of Iran's claim to three small islands controlling the Gulf entrance, two of which were protected by the British under treaty with the sheikh of Ras al Khaimah, one of the Trucial States. Following Iran's occupation of the islands on November 30, one day before Britain's treaty with Ras al Khaimah expired, Iraq broke relations with Iran and with Britain for having failed to prevent the take-over. Relations were bad with the Syrian Baathist regime, and Baghdad denounced the trials of former Syrian Baathist politicians supported by Iraq. Communist sources accused Iraq of persecuting its Communists. Relations with the Soviet Union were also troubled by Iraq's continued refusal to accept UN Security Council Resolution 242, which called for a peaceful settlement as a basis for ending the conflict in the Middle East. However, the Iraqis acknowledged the U.S.S.R.'s role as the Arabs' principal ally, and in April a 200 million ruble loan was announced for the construction of power stations, factories, and oil pipelines.

During the year the Iraq government attempted to repair the damage to its claim to Arab leadership caused by its failure to assist the Palestinian guerrillas in the September 1970 civil war in Jordan. It continued to denounce the nonmilitary solutions to the Arab-Israeli problem adopted by other Arab states (notably Egypt and Jordan) and to criticize the Palestinian guerrillas for "hesitation and vacillation." In March a meeting of the left-wing Democratic Front for Palestine Liberation was held in Baghdad, and shortly afterward a delegation of the Palestine Liberation Organization also visited Baghdad following Cairo reports that it had cut off aid to the PLO. Iraq's outspoken criticism of other Arab states— especially the signatories of the Tripoli Charter (Egypt, Syria, Libya, and Sudan)—increased its own isolation. In a bid to remedy the situation, in early July President al-Bakr sent seven of his ministers on missions to other Arab heads of state, claiming to have detected a growing realization by Arab governments that political solutions to the Arab-Israeli struggle would not work. Following moves by the Jordanian Army against the Palestinian guerrillas in July, Iraq closed its borders with Jordan.

Relations with Sudan were strained by Iraqi support for the briefly successful pro-Communist coup in Khartoum in July. Senior members of the Baathist hierarchy were killed in an air crash near Jidda on their way to Khartoum to congratulate the coup leaders. On July 24, after Pres. Gaafar Nimeiry had been restored to power, Sudan broke relations with Iraq despite the latter's denial that it had had any hand in the coup. Hardan Takriti, a former Iraqi vice-president and air marshal, who had been working

---

IRAQ

Education. (1968–69) Primary, pupils 1,017,-050, teachers 46,958; secondary, pupils 285,721, teachers 9,428; vocational, students 10,596, teachers 986; teacher training, students 10,861, teachers 442; higher (including 6 universities), students 41,189, teaching staff 1,879.

Finance. Monetary unit: Iraqi dinar, with a par value of 0.357 dinars to U.S. $1 (0.857 dinars to £1 sterling) and a free rate (Sept. 27, 1971) of 0.346 dinars to U.S. $1. Gold, SDRs, and foreign exchange, central bank: (June 1971) U.S. $605.1 million; (June 1970) U.S. $413.9 million. Budget (1969–70 est.) balanced at 379 million dinars. Money supply: (April 1971) 217.2 million dinars; (April 1970) 213.6 million dinars.

Cost of living (Baghdad; 1963 = 100): (June 1971) 125; (June 1970) 115.

Foreign Trade. (1970) Imports 181,651,000 dinars; exports 392.4 million dinars. Import sources: U.K. 12%; U.S.S.R. 11%; France 6%; Belgium-Luxembourg 5%. Export destinations: Italy 29%; France 15%; Netherlands 7%; Greece 5%. Main export crude oil 94%.

Transport and Communications. Roads (1968) 17,893 km. Motor vehicles in use (1969): passenger 64,200; commercial (including buses) 41,700. Railways: (1968) 2,352 km.; traffic (1968–69) 367 million passenger-km., freight 1,032,000,000 net ton-km. Air traffic (1970): 202,280,000 passenger-km.; freight 2,273,000 net

ton-km. Telephones (Jan. 1970) 119,650. Radio receivers (Dec. 1969) c. 1 million. Television receivers (Dec. 1969) 220,000.

Agriculture. Production (in 000; metric tons; 1970; 1969 in parentheses): wheat 1,059 (1,-189); barley 691 (1,250); rice 203 (293); dry broad beans c. 18 (18); dates c. 330 (c. 330); sesame c. 12 (12); linseed 14 (12); cotton, lint c. 17 (14); tobacco c. 16 (15). Livestock (in 000; 1969–70): sheep c. 11,600; cattle c. 1,700; goats c. 1,780; buffalo c. 200; camels c. 200.

Industry. Production (in 000; metric tons): crude oil (1970) 76,445; cement (1969) 1,399; electricity (excluding most industrial production; kw-hr.; 1969) 1,914,000.

against the Baathist regime since his dismissal in 1970, was assassinated in Kuwait on March 30.

In January the government announced a ten-year campaign against illiteracy, which it estimated at 70% of the population. As a result of increases in crude-oil posted prices arising from the Organization of Petroleum Exporting Countries (OPEC) agreements in Teheran, Iraq's oil revenues were expected to increase from 156 million dinars in 1970 to 284 million dinars in 1971.   (P. Mp.)

Ireland

Separated from Great Britain by the North Channel, the Irish Sea, and St. George's Channel, the Republic of Ireland shares its island with Northern Ireland to the northeast. Area: 27,136 sq.mi. (70,282 sq.km.), or 83% of the island. Pop. (1971): 2,971,230. Cap. and largest city: Dublin (pop., 1971, 566,034). Language: English (80%) and Gaelic. Religion: predominantly Roman Catholic (95%). President in 1971, Eamon de Valera; prime minister, John Lynch.

The steadily worsening situation in Northern Ireland created grave problems throughout 1971 for John Lynch and his government. Tied to a policy of uniting Ireland by peaceful means, Lynch was continually under pressure from the opposition parties, Fine Gael and Labour, to show results in the various negotiations

IRELAND

Education. (1967–68) Primary, pupils 502,840, teachers 15,941; secondary, pupils 125,374, teachers 8,592; vocational, pupils 83,206, teachers 5,595; higher, students c. 23,160, teaching staff c. 1,370.

Finance. Monetary unit: Irish pound, at par with the pound sterling (U.S. $2.40 = £1) and with a free rate (Sept. 27, 1971) of U.S. $2.48 = £1. Gold, SDRs, and foreign exchange, official: (June 1971) U.S. $770 million; (June 1970) U.S. $670 million. Budget (1970–71 est.) balanced at £474.9 million. Gross national product: (1969) £1,460 million; (1968) 1,298 million. Money supply: (June 1971) £454.8 million; (Feb. 1970) £365.6 million. Cost of living (1963 = 100): (May 1971) 157; (May 1970) 144.

Foreign Trade. (1970) Imports £675.7 million; exports £466.8 million. Import sources: U.K. 53%; West Germany 7%; U.S. 7%. Export destinations: U.K. 66%; U.S. 10%. Main exports: meat 17%; livestock 13% (cattle 10%); textiles and clothing 11%; dairy produce 6%; machinery 5%. Tourism: visitors (1968) 1,917,000; gross receipts (1969) U.S. $188 million.

Transport and Communications. Roads (1968) 86,427 km. Motor vehicles in use (1969): passenger 353,961; commercial 46,970. Railways: (1969) 2,145 km.; traffic (1970) 582 million passenger-km., freight 475 million net ton-km. Air traffic (1970): 1,776,500,-000 passenger-km.; freight 59,693,000 net ton-km. Shipping (1970): merchant vessels 100 gross tons and over 86; gross tonnage 174,977. Telephones (Dec. 1969) 287,108. Radio receivers (Dec. 1968) 860,000. Television receivers (Dec. 1969) 446,000.

Agriculture. Production (in 000; metric tons; 1970; 1969 in parentheses): potatoes c. 1,550 (1,453); oats c. 210 (251); barley c. 800 (788); wheat c. 380 (363); sugar, raw value (1970–71) c. 150, (1969–70) 149; milk c. 3,700 (3,678); butter c. 75 (78); cheese (1969) c. 29, (1968) c. 29; meat 508 (510); fish catch (1969) 68, (1968) 53. Livestock (in 000; June 1970): cattle 5,842; sheep 3,975; pigs 1,155; horses c. 110; chickens c. 9,700.

Industry. Index of production (1963 = 100): (1970) 152; (1969) 152. Production (in 000; metric tons; 1970): coal 152; cement 857; electricity (excluding most industrial production; kw-hr.) 5,653,000; manufactured gas (cu.m.) 214,000; beer (hl.; 1968–69) 3,692; wool fabrics (sq.m.) 7,600; rayon, etc., fabrics (sq.m.) 9,960.

with U.K. Prime Minister Edward Heath, Northern Ireland Prime Minister Brian Faulkner (see BIOGRAPHY), the Northern Ireland opposition, and in the UN. At the same time, the rift within his own party between militants, who advocated a tougher line toward the North, and those who supported Lynch's leadership refused to heal. One of the dissidents, Kevin Boland, who resigned in May 1970 when two ministers were dismissed, formed a new Republican Unity Party with the support of many grass-roots defectors from Fianna Fail as well as one deputy in the Dail. The major state inquiry into the expenditure of Northern Ireland distress funds came to grief when the Supreme Court, in a judgment on Padraig Haughey, the brother of a former minister, ruled that the inquiry had no powers to demand evidence. Criticism of Lynch's Northern Ireland policy continued among his parliamentary supporters.

It was against this background that Lynch and his foreign minister, P. J. Hillery, carried out a series of meetings with British government officials, culminating in the tripartite talks between Lynch, Faulkner, and Heath on September 27–28. In these talks Lynch condemned the introduction of internment in Northern Ireland and pressed for an early political solution that would give full participation in Northern Ireland affairs to the Roman Catholic minority. He gained no concessions, and clearly weakened his position within his own party. To some extent Lynch prejudiced the talks by calling for the abolition of the Northern Ireland government a month before his meeting with Heath on September 6–7. At the tripartite talks, the statement by the three leaders was fundamentally an agreement to differ.

Lynch also held meetings during the year with the leaders of the combined Northern Ireland opposition parties, and backed them in their withdrawal from the Northern Ireland Parliament and in their campaign of civil disobedience. The worsening situation that followed the introduction of internment in Northern Ireland on August 9 led to tighter border security, and this in turn led to several incidents in which British troops confronted police and soldiers of the republic. Lynch condemned the many intrusions by British troops into the republic, and firmly asserted that control within the republic over the movement of gelignite and Irish Republican Army (IRA) men across the border was adequate. In December, Ireland formally asked the European Commission on Human Rights in Strasbourg to investigate charges of mistreatment of internees in Northern Ireland by British troops.

The difficult negotiations for Ireland's entry into the EEC were carried out by Foreign Minister Hillery, who won important concessions for Ireland, including special terms for Irish industry. Entry did not depend, as in Britain, on a parliamentary decision, but required a referendum, and plans were made during the year for this to be held in mid-1972.

Following the disruptions in 1970 and early 1971 caused by strikes, which placed Ireland third in the world for days lost through industrial disputes, the economy settled down to a much quieter year. There was a modest growth rate of just under 3%, good observance of the national wages agreement of the fall of 1970, which had placed a 7% ceiling on wage increases, and a fairly widespread avoidance of strikes. On the debit side, there was a rise in unemployment during the year, an increase in the number of layoffs caused by factory closings, and a worsening in the balance of payments. Tourism, a major money earner for the republic, was hit by both inflation and the troubles in the North, and it was reliably reported that at the end of the summer season almost 100 hotels throughout the country were up for sale because their owners were losing money and saw no early improvement in their hazardous situation.

There was also trouble with the farmers, again over the question of income. Because of increased costs that were not being met by higher farm prices, the farmers staged a boycott of farm machinery purchases and held demonstrations. In April the minister for labour and social welfare, Joseph Brennan, cut off unemployment assistance for unmarried men—12,000 of them—and caused an outcry that resulted in the resignation from the government party of a west of Ireland rural deputy, Joe Leneghan. This further weakened the strength of the government.

On May 11, Sean Lemass, prime minister from 1959 to 1966, died in Dublin (*see* OBITUARIES). President de Valera, in his 89th year, made one of his rare trips abroad when he went to Lourdes in April. John Lynch also traveled abroad, visiting the U.S. as the guest of Pres. Richard M. Nixon.

The issue of contraception was raised by women's liberation groups, who organized a much-publicized visit to Belfast for the purpose of illegally importing banned contraceptive devices into the Republic. At a more serious level, an attempt to introduce legislation in the Senate aimed at legalizing contraception was defeated.

Ireland was the scene of a major international art exhibition, Rosc '71, during the fall, and this was accompanied by a large number of smaller but well-organized regional exhibitions—an attempt, partially successful, to demonstrate that Irish culture was not entirely verbal.　　　　　　　　　　　　(B. AR.)

See also United Kingdom.

Israel

A republic of the Middle East, Israel is bounded by Lebanon, Syria, Jordan, Egypt, and the Mediterranean Sea. Area (not including territory occupied in the June 1967 war): 7,992 sq.mi. (20,700 sq.km.). Pop. (1971 est.): 3,066,000. Cap.: Jerusalem (pop., 1970 est., 291,700). Largest city: Tel Aviv-Yafo (pop., 1970 est., 384,000). Language: Hebrew and Arabic. Religion: predominantly Jewish. President in 1971, Schneor Zalman Shazar; prime minister, Mrs. Golda Meir.

Israel began 1971 in a strangely ambivalent mood. The sudden alarm about a possible outbreak of fighting on Dec. 30, 1970, was symptomatic of the general uneasiness concerning the intentions and capabilities of Pres. Anwar as-Sadat of Egypt. On the one hand, Prime Minister Golda Meir (*see* BIOGRAPHY) had told the Knesset on December 29 that there was a broad basis of understanding between Israel and the United States on most outstanding issues, and that Israel had agreed to resume talks through UN special representative Gunnar Jarring, which had been broken off on Sept. 6, 1970. On the other hand, the Israeli defense forces were placed on alert that day in view of evidence of a possible Egyptian attempt to cross the Suez Canal.

At the same time, the country appeared unusually relaxed, confident, and accustomed to the quasi-peace that had existed since August. This confidence was

reinforced by the report that the defense minister, Moshe Dayan, had brought back from Washington, where he had talked with Pres. Richard M. Nixon and the secretaries of state and defense in mid-December. The U.S., in Dayan's opinion, still treated the Suez Canal as part of the front line of the cold war.

This confident assessment was qualified by the increasing effect of Israel's domestic politics on foreign policy discussions. Dayan's proposed Suez Canal peace initiative, linked to a limited Israeli withdrawal from the canal, received no support from the Cabinet or the Israeli press. Moreover, during Dayan's Washington talks the Americans studiously avoided the subject, so that Dayan returned home convinced that the U.S. was not really interested in a limited solution of the Egyptian-Israeli conflict. With the issue of the succession to Golda Meir beginning to intrude into domestic politics, the powerful anti-Dayan lobby in the Israeli press helped to write off the Dayan initiative.

The government sent a formal reply to a series of questions put to it by Jarring early in the year. The 14 answers largely restated the familiar Israeli position but did not insist on direct negotiations and did not negate the general principle of an ultimate withdrawal from occupied territories. This was over-shadowed, however, by the events that followed. On Feb. 4, 1971, President Sadat announced a 30-day extension of the cease-fire and his preparedness to negotiate the opening of the canal in return for a substantial Israeli withdrawal. The offer took Israeli officials by surprise, and Israeli public opinion saw it as an Egyptian seizure of the political initiative. Before the Cabinet had recovered fully from this shock, it received a further unpleasant surprise in the form of a letter from Jarring saying, in effect, that the time had come, if he was to make headway, when he himself had to formulate the steps to be taken by Egypt and Israel.

This angered the Israeli government, and it refused to answer Jarring's new questions except in the form of a reply addressed directly to the Egyptian government—which the Egyptian authorities, for their part, refused to accept. On February 9, Mrs. Meir told the Knesset that Israel was not prepared to consider the canal opening "on Sadat's terms." Cairo immediately pronounced that this was tantamount to a rejection of the Egyptian offer. When the actual Egyptian and Israeli answers to the Jarring questions were published much later, it became evident that neither had dealt with the main issue on which Jarring had sought clarification.

Public opinion in Israel seemed to become restless over the lack of initiative shown by the Israeli government, and this was reflected in the public opinion poll at the end of February, which showed a more than 50% vote for Dayan as Mrs. Meir's successor—more than three times the votes cast for his nearest rival. But once again—as in the previous year—Israeli attention suddenly became focused on a largely artificial and imaginary "crisis" in Israel's relations with the U.S. Reports in the press and radio spoke of the "erosion" of U.S. support for Israel. In vain Defense Minister Dayan pointed out on March 16 that Israel's military position was "stronger than it had ever been" and that Israel was receiving U.S. military supplies on a level never before achieved.

At the beginning of April attention was preempted by the convention of the Israel Labour Party in Jerusalem, attended by over 3,000 delegates. The convention was more concerned with social realities at home than with the somewhat spurious "crisis" in Washington. It wanted to know government intentions concerning the 500,000 underprivileged in the country. It considered the underrepresentation of Oriental Jews in the higher grades of the civil service and the growing conflict between organized religious interests and the state. These questions were driven home by the discontent of organized labour and by such new expressions of unrest as the demonstrations of the Black Panthers, a group of militant young Oriental Jews.

In May attention switched once more to relations with Washington. On May 6, U.S. Secretary of State William P. Rogers arrived in Israel, together with Assistant Secretary Joseph J. Sisco. The first round of their talks with Mrs. Meir ended in deadlock, but in a private session between Dayan and Sisco, a formula was agreed upon that was acceptable to Mrs. Meir and Rogers. Sisco then submitted this to President Sadat in Cairo. Meanwhile, however, the situation in Cairo had undergone drastic change. Leading members of the Cabinet, the armed forces, and the president's office had been arrested and charged with treason, and it became evident that no real advance in a settlement between Egypt and Israel would be possible until the Egyptian president had consolidated his internal position.

Meanwhile, figures released in Jerusalem showed that in the four years since June 10, 1967, 125,000 new immigrants had arrived in Israel, 45,000 from Europe, 35,000 from the Western Hemisphere, 41,000 from Asia and Africa, and 3,500 from Oceania. It was a substantial number, although not quite as large as had been anticipated or publicized; 80% of the immigrants were under 50 years of age and a very high proportion were highly skilled. Included in this total was an unpublicized but considerable number of Soviet Jews who had been allowed to leave the U.S.S.R. They represented only a small proportion of the 2,150,000 Jews whose condition as a national minority within the Soviet Union had become a major issue in Israeli politics. But even as a worldwide campaign in support of Soviet Jewry received active support and encouragement from the Israeli government, there were indications of moves by both sides to resume diplomatic relations, which had been broken off in June 1967. These moves made some progress during the summer but seemed to have lost momentum by the fall.

Much the same happened to the U.S. peace initiative. Assistant Secretary Sisco returned to Israel (July 28–August 6) and proposed a Suez disengagement not unlike that advocated by Dayan, but both the official Israeli and Egyptian positions had hardened. The Egyptians insisted on a military presence on the Sinai side of the canal in the wake of an Israeli withdrawal. Added to these differences came the Israeli rejection of the Security Council resolution of September 26 calling on Israel not to change the character of Jerusalem and to rescind all steps already taken in that direction.

Following Rogers' speech to the UN General Assembly on October 14, the previous scenario of Israeli criticism of the "erosion" of U.S. support was repeated, only to be corrected by Mrs. Meir's informal journey to Washington for talks with President Nixon on December 2. In these talks, held in the shadow of the assassination of Jordan's Prime Minister Wasfi at-Tal in Cairo on November 28, Mrs. Meir again conceded much that the U.S. had asked for and Israel received assurances of the kind of military aid Dayan had requested. Once more the largely artificial crisis in Israel-U.S. relations had been resolved.

The tone of Arab pronouncements became more belligerent toward year's end, but other matters remained foremost in Israeli consciousness. For the first time since the establishment of the state, internal differences and divisions caused the government the greatest concern. Nor was the government itself im-

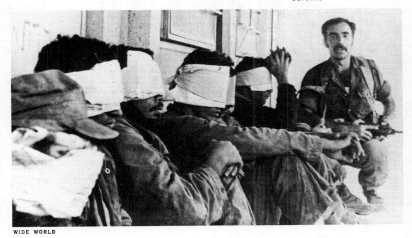

An Israeli soldier guards blindfolded Arab guerrillas, captured after crossing the border into Israel on July 19, 1971. The guerrillas were fleeing from a military offensive launched by King Husain against Palestinian nationalists in northern Jordan.

WIDE WORLD

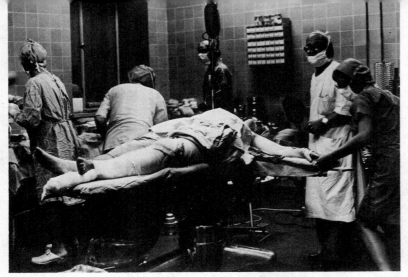

A surgery team prepares to operate on a patient injured when a rocket hit Rivka Hospital in Petah Tiqva. Two people were killed in the attack on the hospital.

KEYSTONE

mune. Both the minister of justice, Ya'acov Shimshon Shapiro, and the deputy finance minister, Zevi Dinstein, were involved in a public inquiry into the practices of a government-sponsored oil corporation in occupied Sinai. On a wide front, the impression was growing that Golda Meir's administration had failed to consider the home front adequately in its concentration on defense and foreign policy. The unrest and criticism were unmistakable, and for the first time the question was asked whether, under these conditions, Mrs. Meir would remain in office, as had been expected, until 1973.

(J. K.)

Italy

A republic of southern Europe, Italy occupies the Apennine Peninsula, Sicily, Sardinia, and a number of smaller islands. On the north it borders France, Switzerland, Austria, and Yugoslavia. Area: 116,313 sq.mi. (301,250 sq.km.). Pop. (1970 est.): 54,683,136. Cap. and largest city: Rome (pop., 1970 est., 2,778,-872). Language: Italian. Religion: predominantly Roman Catholic. Presidents in 1971, Giuseppe Saragat and, from December 29, Giovanni Leone; premier, Emilio Colombo.

Domestic Affairs. An atmosphere of political uncertainty, intensified by social unrest and economic decline, turned 1971 into one of the most critical years for the republic. In February and March violent riots broke out in the cities of Catanzaro and Reggio di Calabria, and numerous bombings took place. As in the previous October, the reason was the dispute over which of the two cities should be the capital of the new Calabria region. A compromise was reached with the choice of Catanzaro as the capital and Reggio as the regional assembly's permanent seat. There were riots in the city of L'Aquila, in the province of Abruzzi, and more riots were sparked in September during a memorial demonstration commemorating the first anniversary of the death of a Reggio riot victim.

Common to all the riots were clashes between members of extreme right-wing and left-wing organizations. Urgent questions were tabled in Parliament, especially after the police uncovered a right-wing plot in March reportedly aimed at overthrowing the Italian government. Leader of this "National Front" movement, of fascist inspiration, was Prince Junio Valerio Borghese, who escaped arrest, although many of his followers were apprehended. A few weeks later 15 people belonging to "New Order," another neofascist organization, were also arrested. In this climate even the final result of the inquiry into the "deplorable initiatives and inadmissible preparations by General Giovanni De Lorenzo," which in the summer of 1964 had led to rumours and disclosures about the preparation of a coup, passed almost unobserved.

Provincial, regional, and local elections on June 13 were expected to indicate how the country had reacted to the handling of riots and unrest by Premier Colombo's centre-left coalition. This government, which had led the country since Aug. 6, 1970, had been disappointed in the early part of the year by the growing unwillingness of minority coalition parties to cooperate fully with the majority Christian Democrats. First the Socialists, who in 1969 had broken their alliance with the Social Democrats, gave signs of dissatisfaction, and it was even rumoured that they might join forces with the Communist Party. Later the Republican Party withdrew its representatives from the government, although it announced at its conference that it would continue to support the centre-left political formula. The party justified its decision by pointing to differences with coalition part-

---

ITALY

Education. (1968–69) Primary, pupils 4,706,-180, teachers 218,922; secondary, pupils 2,365,-059, teachers 188,955; vocational, pupils 874,401, teachers 71,487; teacher training, students 250,-155, teachers 18,242; higher (including 36 universities), students 420,417, teaching staff 31,908.

Finance. Monetary unit: lira, with a par value of 625 lire to U.S. $1 (1,500 lire = £1 sterling) and a free rate (Sept. 27, 1971) of 612 lire to U.S. $1 (1,518 lire = £1 sterling). Gold, SDRs, and foreign exchange, official: (June 1971) U.S. $5,783,000,000; (June 1970) U.S. $3,934,000,-000. Budget (1970 est.): revenue 12,152,000,-000,000 lire; expenditure 14,019,000,000,000 lire. Gross national product: (1969) 51,456,000,000,-000 lire; (1968) 47,134,000,000,000 lire. Money supply: (May 1971) 31,647,000,000,000 lire; (May 1970) 25,535,000,000,000 lire. Cost of living (1963 = 100): (June 1971) 134; (June 1970) 128.

Foreign Trade. (1970) Imports 9,340,000,-000,000 lire; exports 8,256,000,000,000 lire. Import sources: EEC 41% (West Germany 20%, France 13%); U.S. 10%. Export destinations: EEC 43% (West Germany 22%, France 13%, Netherlands 5%); U.S. 10%; Switzerland 5%. Main exports: machinery 25%; textiles 11%;

clothing 8%; chemicals 7%; motor vehicles 6%; petroleum products 5%. Tourism (1969): visitors 12,086,800; gross receipts U.S. $1,632,000,000.

Transport and Communications. Roads (1970) 284,988 km. (including 3,907 km. expressways). Motor vehicles in use (1970): passenger c. 10.2 million; commercial 914,000. Railways: state (1969) 16,014 km.; private (1968) 4,211 km.; traffic (1970) 32,357,000,000 passenger-km., freight 18,070,000,000 net ton-km. Air traffic (1970): 8,420,000,000 passenger-km.; freight 300.1 million net ton-km. Shipping (1970): merchant vessels 100 gross tons and over 1,639; gross tonnage 7,447,610. Telephones (Dec. 1969) 8,528,354. Radio licenses (Dec. 1969) 11,333,000. Television licenses (Dec. 1969) 9,016,000.

Agriculture. Production (in 000; metric tons; 1970; 1969 in parentheses): wheat 9,630 (9,-585); corn 4,729 (4,519); barley 315 (292); oats 486 (491); potatoes 3,668 (3,970); rice 819 (862); dry broad beans 369 (402); onions (1969) 468, (1968) 464; sugar, raw value (1970–71) c. 1,198, (1969–70) 1,406; tomatoes (1969) 3,670, (1968) 3,258; tobacco 74 (79); wine 6,500 (7,147); olives 2,100 (2,405); oranges 1,737 (1,707); lemons 806 (822); apples

1,831 (2,009); pears 1,721 (1,634); peaches (1969) 887, (1968) 1,280; figs 198 (222); cheese (1969) 464, (1968) 469; beef and veal c. 590 (563); pork c. 370 (387). Livestock (in 000; Jan. 1970): cattle 9,563; sheep 8,138; pigs 9,224; goats 1,031; horses, mules, and asses 777; poultry 112,000.

Industry. Index of production (1963 = 100): (1970) 150; (1969) 140. Unemployment: (1970) 3.1%; (1969) 3.4%. Fuel and power (in 000; metric tons; 1970): lignite 1,393; coal 295; crude oil 1,408; natural gas (cu.m.) 13,172,000; manufactured gas (cu.m.) 2,968,000; electricity (kw-hr.) c. 117,500,000. Production (in 000; metric tons; 1970): iron ore (50% metal content) 757; pig iron 8,527; crude steel 17,236; aluminum 147; zinc 142; lead 54; cement 33,127; cotton yarn 176; rayon, etc., filament yarn 85; rayon, etc., staple fibre 98; nylon, etc., filament yarn 99; nylon, etc., fibres 142; nitrogenous fertilizers (1969–70) 960; sulfuric acid 3,315; petroleum products (1969) 98,397; passenger cars (units) 1,720; commercial vehicles (units) 135. Merchant vessels launched (100 gross tons and over; 1970) 597,000 gross tons. New dwelling units completed (1970) 350,000.

ners over tax and university reform bills then under discussion by Parliament.

The election results confirmed a growing dissatisfaction among voters. Regional elections in Sicily and local ones in Rome gave an overall boost to right-wing parties, particularly the militant neofascist Italian Social Movement (MSI). The Christian Democrats obtained 31% of the votes, against 35.2% in the regional and provincial elections held in 1970. The Socialist vote increased from 10.3 to 11%, that of the Social Democrats from 6.7 to 7.8%, and that of the Republicans from 4 to 4.2%. The Communist Party lost ground (21.1% against the previous 25%), but the neofascists surged ahead, from the previous level of 8.2% to 13.9%. Their progress was particularly clear in Sicily, where they collected 16.3% of the votes and the Christian Democrats fell from 40.3 to 33.7%. Many observers felt that the Sicilian results were attributable partly to the apparently inefficient way in which the government dealt with the problem of the Mafia on the island.

Giovanni Leone, a Christian Democrat, was elected as Italy's sixth president on December 24. His election came on the 23rd ballot in a parliamentary voting battle that lasted 16 days.

The year saw the first divorces following the introduction of the divorce law in December 1970. Measures introduced by the government opened new possibilities in the way of birth control, which had been severely handicapped by laws governing the sale and public display of contraceptives.

Natural disasters hit various areas of Italy. The town of Tuscania and many of its artistic treasures were destroyed by earthquakes in February, and an eruption of Etna, the Sicilian volcano, from April until June burned villages and vineyards. Venice continued to sink, and an international operation was mounted to save it. On October 24 Premier Colombo gave details of a special bill for Venice (ratified in Parliament on December 3); the plan specified responsibilities of the state, the regional authority, and the Venice municipality in spending the $384 million international loan for the city's revitalization. Most of the money would be spent on large-scale state-run public works projects, including devices for closing two of the lagoon's mouths in the face of high seas. Aqueduct and sewerage systems would be introduced and measures taken against atmospheric and water pollution. The municipality would be responsible for restoration of historic buildings.

Foreign Affairs. In a year when four applicant countries, including Britain, stood on the threshold of an enlarged EEC, most diplomatic activities were to be seen against this background. Premier Colombo met British Prime Minister Edward Heath, French Pres. Georges Pompidou, and U.S. Pres. Richard M. Nixon. Other important meetings were with West German Chancellor Willy Brandt and New Zealand Prime Minister Keith Holyoake, while President Saragat had a series of meetings with, among others, Finland's Pres. Urho Kekkonen, Yugoslavia's President Tito, and U.S. Secretary of State William Rogers. Foreign Minister Aldo Moro had a full schedule, visiting his counterparts in many European and African countries.

Following Italy's recognition of China in November 1970, ambassadors were exchanged between the two countries. In May, Foreign Trade Minister Mario Zagari led an economic mission to Peking. During his visit he arranged a series of trade agreements with

UPI COMPIX

Police retaliate as fire bombs, tossed by demonstrators, burn in Reggio di Calabria on Feb. 16, 1971. The outbreak of violence was precipitated by the decision of the Calabria regional council to make Catanzaro the regional capital.

the Chinese government, which were later approved by other EEC countries. Italy's major firms, including FIAT, Olivetti, and Pirelli, were deeply involved in this initiative, which was designed to increase exchanges between the two countries.

The Economy. "We have now succeeded in strengthening the lira, in neutralizing inflation and in laying the ghost of devaluation. Productivity has increased, and 1971 will be a year of economic, social and civic development": too soon these words, pronounced by Premier Colombo in his New Year's speech, proved to be overoptimistic. In June the governor of the Bank of Italy, Guido Carli, stressed the need "to balance advantages gained by trade unions against increases in productivity," and the following month Colombo announced a series of measures aimed at injecting new vigour into the Italian economy. The main measures were credit and tax relief for medium and small industries, a partial tax reimbursement to exporting industries, credit relief for agriculture, and greater financing for industrial research projects.

In August Colombo again stressed the need for more fruitful cooperation between industry and the unions, and in September he admitted: "We are faced by a situation of stagnation." During the first seven months of 1971, industrial production had dropped by 3.6% as compared with the same period in 1970. Employment had not risen, domestic demand was failing to stimulate production, and foreign trade was failing to make up for the weak demand at home. Investment had not revived, and there was low utilization of industrial plant. A further threat to the economy was the 10% import surcharge announced in August by President Nixon as part of his program to defend the dollar, but this was rescinded in December after the international monetary settlement agreed to by the Group of Ten. Following U.S. devaluation of the dollar, it was announced in Rome that the lira would fluctuate within a range of between 569.40 and 594.60 to the dollar, with a median point of 581.50.

A long-awaited tax reform bill was finally presented by the Socialist finance minister, Luigi Preti, and passed in October 1971 after stormy parliamentary debates. The bill, aimed at adjusting the Italian tax system to the requirements of the EEC, was intended to cancel at a stroke all possibilities of tax evasion. (F. G.)

Italian Literature: see Literature

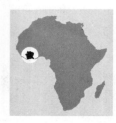

Ivory Coast

A republic on the Gulf of Guinea, West Africa, the Ivory Coast is bounded by Liberia, Guinea, Mali, Upper Volta, and Ghana. Area: 123,485 sq.mi. (319,-822 sq.km.). Pop. (1970 est.): 4,310,000, including about 15,000 Europeans. Cap. and largest city: Abidjan (pop., 1963 est., 285,000). Language: French and local dialects. Religion: animist 65%; Muslim 23%; Christian 12%. President and premier in 1971, Félix Houphouët-Boigny.

President Houphouët-Boigny's offer to open a dialogue with the white-dominated South African government kept the Ivory Coast in the forefront of African affairs throughout 1971. In April the president held a major press conference at which he renewed the proposals outlined the previous year and explained his intentions in greater detail. The conference was attended by resident diplomats and almost every prominent figure in Ivory Coast affairs.

The issue of dialogue with South Africa was one on which black African states were deeply divided, the majority remaining steadfastly opposed to any rapprochement with Pretoria. However, President Houphouët-Boigny was not to be deterred. An official delegation visited South Africa in October, and a visit by the president himself was considered likely.

In February Pres. Georges Pompidou of France was given an exceptionally warm welcome on his visit to the Ivory Coast in the course of his African tour. During the spring antigovernment agitation developed at the University of Abidjan, and in April the president ordered the university closed. It was reopened in May.

Economic expansion continued at the same exceptional rate as in previous years. The Ivory Coast Tobacco Company (SITAB), formed in May, was the first concern to be financed solely by private interests within the republic. On December 7, during an official visit to Ivory Coast, Pres. Léopold Senghor of Senegal announced the imminent formation of an Economic Community of West Africa, consisting of Ivory Coast, Senegal, Mauritania, Mali, Upper Volta, Niger, Dahomey, and Togo.   (Ph. D.)

Pres. Georges Pompidou of France and Pres. Félix Houphouët-Boigny of the Ivory Coast travel from Abidjan airport to the presidential palace during the official French visit to the Ivory Coast in February 1971.

A.F.P.—PICTORIAL PARADE

IVORY COAST

Education. (1968–69) Primary, pupils 427,029, teachers 9,640; secondary, pupils 44,851, teachers 1,476; vocational, pupils 4,020, teachers 337; teacher training, pupils 1,217, teachers 75; higher, students 2,943.

Finance. Monetary unit: CFA franc, with a parity of CFA Fr. 50 to the French franc (CFA Fr. 277.71 = U.S. $1; CFA Fr. 666.50 = £1 sterling) and a free rate (Sept. 27, 1971) of CFA Fr. 276.50 to U.S. $1 (CFA Fr. 685.75 = £1 sterling). Gold, SDRs, and foreign exchange, central bank: (June 1971) U.S. $88 million; (June 1970) U.S. $87.2 million. Budget (1971 est.) balanced at CFA Fr. 62.7 billion. Money supply: (March 1971) CFA Fr. 89,840,000,000; (March 1970) CFA Fr. 81,010,000,000.

Foreign Trade. (1970) Imports CFA Fr. 107.7 billion (46% from France, 9% from West Germany, 8% from U.S., 6% from Italy, 5% from Netherlands); exports CFA Fr. 130,190,000,000 (33% to France, 19% to U.S., 10% to West Germany, 9% to Netherlands, 9% to Italy). Main exports: coffee 33%; cocoa 21%: timber 18%.

Agriculture. Production (in 000; metric tons; 1969; 1968 in parentheses): corn 260 (206); sweet potatoes 1,541 (1,409); cassava 532 (530); coffee (1970) c. 240, (1969) 270; cocoa (1969–70) 180, (1968–69) 144; bananas 172 (172); peanuts 43 (32); cotton, lint 14 (18); timber (cu.m.) 9,000 (8,900). Livestock (in 000; 1969–70): cattle c. 400; pigs c. 180; sheep c. 820; goats c. 810; poultry c. 7,900.

Jamaica

A parliamentary state within the Commonwealth of Nations, Jamaica is an island in the Caribbean Sea about 90 mi. S of Cuba. Area: 4,244 sq.mi. (10,991 sq.km.). Pop. (1970): 1,861,300, predominantly Negro, but including Europeans, Chinese, Indians, and persons of mixed race. Cap. and largest city: Kingston (pop., 1970, 117,400). Language: English. Religion: Christian, with Anglicans and Baptists in the majority. Queen, Elizabeth II; governor-general in 1971, Sir Clifford Campbell; prime minister, Hugh Lawson Shearer.

The long-threatening crisis in the banana industry once again was postponed in 1971 as both the representatives of the industry and their marketing agents, Fyffes, agreed to make new attempts to solve their difficulties. Local sugar production was noticeably affected by the uncertainty arising from Britain's entry into the EEC. Some of the smaller can factories experienced considerable losses.

There was vigorous government support of public and private building, geared largely toward improvement and diversification of tourist accommodations. But the state of the utilities upon which the resorts depended for their efficient operation caused great public concern. Electrical, water, transport, and telephone services could not be expanded rapidly enough to meet existing needs. Long negotiations over rates, franchises, and financing slowed down plant modernization and necessary expansion.

An election was widely predicted for early 1972 as the government neared the end of its five-year term. Both major parties, the Jamaica Labour Party, which formed the government, and the People's National Party, in opposition since independence, clearly regarded the election as crucial, and there was a noticeable heightening of political activity.

As a result of the dollar crisis and the consequent upheaval in the world monetary situation, the government severed the legal tie of Jamaican currency to sterling.   (G. C. Cu.)

JAMAICA

Education. (1965–66) Primary, pupils 323,816, teachers 5,743; secondary, pupils 34,594, teachers 1,429; vocational, pupils 3,524, teachers 218; teacher training, students 212, teachers 10; higher (at University in Mona; 1967–68), students 2,234.

Finance. Monetary unit: Jamaican dollar, with a par value of Jam$0.83 to U.S. $1 (Jam$2 = £1 sterling) and a free rate (Sept. 27, 1971) of Jam$0.81 to U.S. $1. Budget (1970 actual): revenue Jam$204 million; expenditure Jam$245.6 million.

Foreign Trade. (1970) Imports Jam$435,226,000; exports Jam$283,090,000. Import sources (1969): U.S. 42%: U.K. 21%; Canada 9%; Venezuela 5%. Export destinations (1969): U.S. 34%; U.K. 16%; Canada 15%; Norway 9%. Main exports: alumina 39%; bauxite 27%; sugar 11%.

Agriculture. Production (in 000; metric tons; 1969; 1968 in parentheses): sweet potatoes c. 210 (c. 207); cassava c. 10 (c. 10); sugar, raw value (1970–71) 438, (1969–70) 376; bananas c. 210 (c. 210); oranges c. 71 (62); grapefruit c. 21 (21); copra 16 (17). Livestock (in 000; 1969–70): cattle c. 250; goats c. 360; pigs c. 180; sheep c. 13.

Industry. Production (in 000; metric tons; 1969): bauxite 10,319; cement 414; gypsum (exports; 1968) 253; petroleum products c. 1,440; electricity (kw-hr.) 1,275,000.

Japan

A constitutional monarchy in the northwestern Pacific Ocean, Japan is an archipelago composed of four major islands (Hokkaido, Honshu, Kyushu, and Shikoku) and minor adjacent islands. Area: 142,885 sq.mi. (370,-073 sq.km.). Pop. (1971 est.): 104,116,120. Cap. and largest city: Tokyo (pop., 1971 est., 8,787,249). Language: Japanese. Religion: primarily Shinto and Buddhist; Christian 0.5%. Emperor, Hirohito; prime minister in 1971, Eisaku Sato.

Domestic Affairs. Analysis of data from the October 1970 census showed clearly that the Japanese population had over the past five years continued its massive migration to the city. Urban population accounted for 72% and rural 28% of the total (in 1920 urban made up only 24%; rural, 76%). Japan's population, ranking seventh in the world, had a density of 725 per sq.mi. (280 per sq.km.). Under the Local Autonomy Law six cities (in addition to Tokyo) had been known as "designated municipalities": Osaka (pop., 1970, 2,980,487), Yokohama (2,238,264), Nagoya (2,036,053), Kyoto (1,419,165), Kobe (1,-288,937), and Kitakyushu (1,042,321). Effective April 1972, three cities were to be added: Sapporo (1,010,-123), Kawasaki (973,486), and Fukuoka (853,270). Attendant problems such as the impact of inflation on city dwellers, traffic hazards, and damage to the environment were increasingly discussed.

On Dec. 26, 1970, the 65th session of the Diet had been organized, only to enter the normal year-end recess and to be reconvened on January 22 for its 150-day deliberations. Party representation was as follows: House of Representatives (lower): Liberal-Democrats (LDP) 303, Japan Socialists (JSP) 91, Komeito (KMT) 47, Democratic Socialists (DSP) 32, Japan Communists (JCP) 14, independents 3, vacancies 1 (total, 491); House of Councillors (upper): LDP 137, JSP 63, KMT 24, DSP 9, JCP 7, Niin Club 5, independents 1, vacancies 6 (total, 252).

Opposition parties, sometimes in alliance, steadily chipped away at the governing majority of the LDP in one national and a series of local elections. On April 12 the incumbent governor of Tokyo, Ryokichi Minobe, won a landslide victory with the largest collection of votes cast for any single candidate in any election ever held in Japan. Backed by an alliance of JSP, JCP, and independent supporters, Minobe garnered 3,615,299 votes while his LDP-backed rival, Akira Hatano, received 1,935,694. Similarly, in Osaka opposition-backed Kyoichi Kuroda defeated the incumbent conservative governor. The dominant role of the LDP in local politics, however, remained intact with conservative candidates winning gubernatorial posts in 16 of the 18 prefectures at stake. Also in April in elections in 161 other cities, LDP-supported candidates won 114 mayoralties.

On June 4 the five major parties began the campaign for half of the seats in the House of Councillors. Major issues were revaluation of the yen, high prices, urban life (including pollution), and the agreement on reversion of Okinawa to Japan. In the election held on June 27, the ruling LDP barely held its own in number of seats; its share of the vote in local districts dipped to 44%. The opposition JSP made impressive gains and at the local level attracted 30% of the vote. The vote for the JCP exceeded 10% for the first time. Post-election party standings in the House of Councillors were: LDP 136, JSP 66, KMT 23, DSP 13, JCP 10, independents (including Niin Club) 4.

Thereafter, LDP leadership "reflected" on the "defeat," and on July 5 in the first such reshuffling in 18 months Prime Minister Sato formed a new Cabinet. Preparing toward the day of his own retirement (after the longest tenure as prime minister in Japan's history), he balanced LDP factional strength by naming two likely successors: Takeo Fukuda (foreign affairs) and Kakuei Tanaka (international trade and industry). A younger member of the Sato faction, Noboru Takeshita, became chief Cabinet secretary. Former defense chief (potentially a future prime minister) Yasuhiro Nakasone became chairman of the LDP executive council. State Minister Buichi Oishi headed the newly established Environment Agency, and Mikio Mizuta (finance) also joined the Cabinet. The prime minister stated that his new administration would give priority to price stabilization, pollution control, medical reform, reorganization of education, housing, and welfare measures. Foreign Minister Fukuda announced that he would concentrate on improvement of economic relationships with the U.S.

Despite strong opposition from within his own government, Prime Minister Eisaku Sato agreed to co-sponsor the U.S. resolution opposing Taiwan's expulsion from the UN.

continued on page 397

JAPAN
Education. (1968–69) Primary, pupils 9,383,-182, teachers 358,080; secondary, pupils 7,700,-622; vocational, pupils 1,892,481, secondary and vocational, teachers 474,330; higher (including 138 universities), students 1,526,764, teaching staff 140,527.

Finance. Monetary unit: yen, with a par value of 360 yen to U.S. $1 (864 yen = £1 sterling) and a free rate (Sept. 27, 1971) of 335 yen to U.S. $1 (832 yen = £1 sterling). Gold, SDRs, and foreign exchange, official: (June 1971) U.S. $7,156,000,000; (June 1970) U.S. $3,250,000,-000. Budget (1971 est.) balanced at 9,414,000,-000,000 yen. Gross national product: (1970) 70,-618,000,000,000 yen; (1969) 59,704,000,000,000 yen. Money supply: (June 1971) 23,252,000,-000,000 yen; (June 1970) 18,577,000,000,000 yen. Cost of living (1963 = 100): (June 1971) 154; (June 1970) 142.

Foreign Trade. (1970) Imports 6,797,300,-000,000 yen; exports 6,954,300,000,000 yen. Import sources: U.S. 29%; Australia 8%; Iran 5%; Canada 5%. Export destinations: U.S. 31%; South Korea 4%. Main exports: machinery 23% (telecommunications 7%); iron and steel 15%; motor vehicles 10%; textile yarns and fabrics 9%; ships 7%; chemicals 6%.

Transport and Communications. Roads (1970) 1,013,558 km. (including 1,035 km. expressways). Motor vehicles in use (1970): passenger 8,778,975; commercial 8,850,439. Railways: (1968) 28,022 km.; traffic (1970) 286,833,000,000 passenger-km., freight 62,610,-000,000 net ton-km. Air traffic (1970): 14,280,-000,000 passenger-km.; freight 427,020,000 net ton-km. Shipping (1970): merchant vessels 100 gross tons and over 8,402; gross tonnage 27,003,-704. Telephones (Dec. 1969) 19,898,988. Radio receivers (Dec. 1968) 25,742,000. Television receivers (Dec. 1969) 21,879,000.

Agriculture. Production (in 000; metric tons; 1970; 1969 in parentheses): rice 16,479 (18,-186); wheat 474 (758); barley c. 573 (812); sweet potatoes (1969) 2,855, (1968) 3,594; potatoes c. 3,730 (3,575); tea 91 (90); onions (1969) 1,723, (1968) 1,668; apples c. 1,050 (1,085); oranges c. 3,000 (2,392); tobacco c. 150 (174); timber (cu.m.; 1969) 51,600, (1968) 54,700; fish catch (1969) 8,623, (1968) 8,670; whale and sperm oil (1968–69) 73, (1967–68) 80. Livestock (in 000; Feb. 1970): cattle 3,593; sheep c. 62; pigs 6,335; chickens 169,277.

Industry. Index of production (1963 = 100): (1970) 258; (1969) 222. Fuel and power (in 000; metric tons; 1970): coal 39,693; crude oil 808; natural gas (cu.m.) 2,629,000; manufactured gas (cu.m.) 11,607,000; electricity (kw-hr.) 350,590,000. Production (in 000; metric tons; 1970): iron ore (55% metal content) 1,-573; pig iron 69,712; crude steel 93,324; petroleum products (1969) 140,625; cement 57,-189; cotton yarn 526; woven cotton fabrics (sq.m.) 2,617,000; rayon, etc., filament yarn 136; rayon, etc., staple fibres 377; nylon, etc., filament yarn 457; nylon, etc., fibres 559; sulfuric acid 6,932; cameras (units) 5,813; radio receivers (units) 32,618; television receivers (units) 13,-782; passenger cars (units) 3,179; commercial vehicles (units) 2,124; motorcycles (units) 2,948. Merchant vessels launched (100 gross tons and over; 1970) 10,477,000 gross tons. New dwelling units started (1970) 1,485,000.

JAPAN: ECONOMIC GIANT

By Gregory Clark

In 1971 Japan emerged as the country holding the key to the world currency crisis. Its rapid economic growth and the competitiveness of its exports made it perhaps the most dynamically influential element in the world economy.

Earlier, in 1968, Japan had overtaken West Germany in size of gross national product (GNP) to become the world's third richest country after the United States and the Soviet Union. By the late 1970s it was expected to overtake the U.S.S.R. And if growth rates over recent years are extrapolated directly, Japan could overtake even the U.S. before the end of this century.

For a country that in the late 1940s had been close to bankruptcy and starvation, this is a remarkable record. Since the end of World War II, Japan has maintained a real average growth rate of 10% annually, twice the average for the advanced Western countries. Over the five years to the end of 1970, its real growth averaged an amazing 12%. In per capita production of many important commodities, it outstripped the European countries and even the U.S. Over the past five years, Japan's trade with the rest of the world increased annually at 16.5% in real terms, or twice the rate at which total world trade has increased.

Comparison of international income levels has become difficult, possibly meaningless, since the U.S. dollar has lost its status as undisputed world currency. But even at the previous 360 yen/$1 fixed rate of exchange, Japan's gross national product of 73 thousand billion yen in fiscal 1970 (ending March 31, 1971) meant an average income of $1,580 for each of Japan's 103.7 million citizens—equal to the average per capita income in the United Kingdom. If the subsequent appreciation in the value of the yen is taken into account, Japan's average income level in 1971 was close to the highest European levels. Ten years ago, average per capita income was only $600.

Piano manufacturers in Japan produced about 100,000 instruments in 1971.

Almost equally important for a trading nation such as Japan, the balance of trade moved to a favourable $3,963,000,000 in 1970, while the overall surplus in the balance of payments reached an all-time high of $2 billion. Until 1967 Japan's growth had suffered from the constant need to restrain deficits in its balance of payments.

The record of Japanese economic success is not entirely without blemish, however. The rapid growth in income outstripped the growth of public utilities and the formation of capital for purposes of human welfare. Comparison with Western countries showed that Japan was still well behind many of them in its existing stock of roads, parks, educational facilities, sewerage and drainage facilities, and housing, and also in its spending on them.

There was also a growing awareness of negative economic factors, in particular the problems of urban overcrowding and pollution. This gave rise to the concept of net national welfare (NNW) to supplement GNP as an indicator of economic prosperity. According to Japan's Economic Planning Agency, the new indicator will reflect negative changes in the quality of life that do not show up in the figures for gross national product.

However, and this is a point rarely made in judging the success of Japan's growth, the negative factor of overcrowding has generated positive economic effects that are not included in any estimate of national welfare. The efficiency with which the labour force has been employed is one example. In particular, and as will be argued in more detail later, overcrowding has led to the formation of a sophisticated, well-informed, urbanized, industrial society, and this may have been the crucial factor in Japan's unusual growth.

Historical Factors. Finding the explanation of this growth, concentrated as it is in several small islands devoid of natural resources, has rapidly become one of the major, and perhaps the most fascinating, riddles in the theory of economic development. The historical factors assisting Japan's growth are well known. To sustain its early industrial expansion it was endowed with a hard-working peasantry that provided a surplus of, first, capital (through taxes and rents) and, later, labour (through rising agricultural productivity). This supply of labour allowed the continued and very necessary expansion of the work force, despite a slowing birthrate.

The energy and purposefulness of Japan's leaders during the Meiji period (1868–1912) was another factor in the nation's development. Seeing as their goal the attainment and even surpassing of Western economic standards, they worked singlemindedly to introduce Western industrial techniques into Japan. This tradition of enlightened government leadership continues and has allowed the planned transformation of Japan's economy, first to labour-intensive, light industry, and more recently to the capital-intensive heavy and chemical industries. In particular, it has allowed the mobilization of resources needed to develop efficient, competitive export industries—machinery, electrical and electronic appliances, automobiles—which many regard as a major stimulus and guarantee for Japan's future economic progress.

Another factor is the very high rate of personal savings in Japan, channeled smoothly into industrial investment with the help of an efficient financial system. The Japanese traditionally have saved a high proportion of their personal income. Between 1960 and 1971 this proportion rose from 14 to 18%, the latter figure being more than twice the rate found in many Western countries. These savings have contributed to a high rate of formation of fixed domestic capital.

Another major reason for Japan's rapid growth has been its success in turning its natural disadvantages into positive advantages. Deficient in land and natural resources, it was forced to make the most of its one major asset—labour. Universal education was introduced as early as 1872; industrial and technical

Gregory Clark is Tokyo correspondent for the Australian.

training became highly developed. Japan's literacy rate—close to 100%—is one of the highest in the world.

Japan succeeded in dealing with its lack of natural resources by locating factories close to the sea where, because of the development of bulk carriers, they could be supplied with raw materials very cheaply. In the ten years to 1970, the cost of importing a ton of iron ore to Japan fell 34% to $3.65. Oil freight declined 50% to $2.93 a ton. In addition, the seaboard location of Japan's factories means that finished goods can be transported to markets cheaply. Other countries better endowed with natural resources have insisted on using their own resources, regardless of transport costs. They are now high-cost producers vulnerable even in domestic markets to Japanese competition.

The problem with most explanations of Japan's economic success, however, is that they tend to describe the effects of that success rather than the causes. And even if they do touch on causes, they may be only secondary causes. For example, in many less developed countries modern factories, no matter where they were built, would quickly go bankrupt. In Japan, they can compete with rival firms in the world's most advanced industrial countries. Similarly, high savings are of little use in themselves. The crucial question is why in Japan the investment based on these savings is so highly productive.

The leaders of many less developed countries have wanted economic growth just as strongly as has Japan. In most cases they too realize what is needed for this growth—improved education, technology, a sound financial system; in many cases they are actively helped with outside capital and technical assistance. And in some cases, such as Communist countries, they can enforce a high rate of personal saving. Yet none of these countries has approached Japan in terms of economic growth. Why?

Racial Explanation. Realizing the circularity of standard economic explanations for Japan's growth, some observers have turned to the unique characteristics of the Japanese as a race: their diligence, their group-consciousness and consensus decision-making, the hierarchical structure of their society, and their craving for education. Others have stressed the close links between industry and government—"Japan Incorporated," as some have called it.

The problem with the "racial" arguments, however, is that they are often neither unique to the Japanese nor clearly related to economic growth. The Japanese do have a strong group-consciousness, it is true, and it helps some aspects of their economic activities. Herman Kahn, the prophet of Japanese growth, rates it as a major factor behind Japan's success. But to the extent that this consciousness also stifles individualism it can be as much an obstacle as an aid to growth. In his study of the reasons for U.S. economic success, the French writer and politician Jean-Jacques Servan-Schreiber states approvingly: "Each individual, whoever he may be, possesses the degree of intelligence necessary to manage those affairs which concern him exclusively. . . . From this comes the belief that the individual is the best judge of his own particular interests."

Thus, one is confronted with two contradictory explanations for progress.

Again, the Chinese are diligent and hardworking, but they have yet to find the key to economic growth: work must be productive as well as difficult if it is to assist growth. A hierarchical society exists in India, but it has hindered rather than helped growth there. The Indonesians also have consensus decision-making, but they remain one of the most economically underdeveloped nations in Asia.

The educational system has given a good basic training to wide sectors of the Japanese population, but it is widely recognized as weak at the college level and has done little to stimulate creative thinking. Measured in terms of patent royalties paid and received in 1970, Japan imports much more technology than it exports—$413 million to $55 million.

The Japanese system of lifelong service to a single employer often is identified as important to productivity, but this clearly

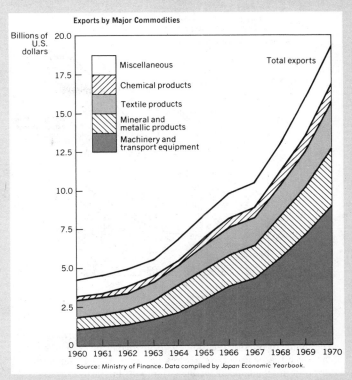

Exports by Major Commodities

Billions of U.S. dollars

Miscellaneous
Chemical products
Textile products
Mineral and metallic products
Machinery and transport equipment

Total exports

Source: Ministry of Finance. Data compiled by *Japan Economic Yearbook*.

negates mobility, which in the West is seen as crucial to optimum use of labour resources. Neither view, in fact, may be entirely correct, but if Japanese business management techniques are clearly superior, why are so many progressive Japanese firms moving to introduce Western techniques based on efficiency rather than seniority? Why are Japanese firms so concerned about the entry of Western firms into Japan? The success in Japan of 100% foreign-owned firms such as Coca-Cola Japan and IBM Japan is ascribed largely to their use of Western management techniques.

Similarly, close links between government and industry sometimes can be a negative factor in economic growth. In Japan, the fastest-growing firms usually have been those which lie outside the cloying web of government connections.

Why Others Fail. Thus, it seems that instead of asking why the Japanese have been able to catch up with the West, a better question would be why other peoples have not succeeded. In other words, one should take the "nonracial" approach of assuming that it is natural for the Japanese to be able to emulate Westerners and that if other races fail to do the same it is because of some objective obstacle rather than racial inferiority.

Within any economically advanced Western nation it is assumed there will be no great regional differences in wealth. If one area is relatively depressed, for example southern Italy or the southern U.S., skills and capital flow in to maintain some balance with the rest of the country.

If skills, and the capital needed to make them productive, can flow freely within a society, why then do they not flow freely beyond the society? There is one obvious answer—the bureaucratic obstacles imposed by national frontiers. But this has become less important as nations have come to accept the need for international flows of skills and capital. By far the greater obstacles are the psychological barriers within societies to the free absorption of foreign skills.

In Japan these barriers have been as great as elsewhere. Indeed, to the extent that the Japanese believe themselves to be unique, they have suffered even more than others from self-imposed isolation. The 215 years of the Tokugawa era before 1853, when all intercourse with the outside world was forbidden, was a classic example of such an attitude. China and, to a greater or lesser extent, the other Communist countries provide contemporary examples.

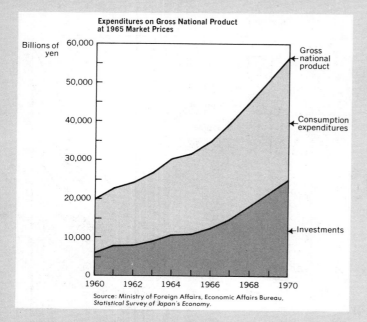

Expenditures on Gross National Product at 1965 Market Prices

Billions of yen

Source: Ministry of Foreign Affairs, Economic Affairs Bureau, Statistical Survey of Japan's Economy.

Internal Information Flow. But while barriers were imposed to the inflow of outside technology (or information, which is what technology really is), there always has been a high demand for and rapid movement of information within Japanese society. The uniformity and compactness of the Japanese nation—the relative absence of barriers due to language, geography, or customs—make it perhaps the largest homogeneous nation in the world. This, plus its cultural unity under a tradition of emperor worship and paternalistic government, combine to create a society in which communication is regarded as a common right and information as a common good. The proliferation of published material and the emphasis on literacy in Japan is one result of this attitude. This in turn has a direct relation to economic growth.

Each year, for example, the government publishes more than 30 white papers covering every topic from trade to pollution. Within every trade or industry a full range of services and publications exists to provide firms with the information they need. And as the need for more and more sophisticated information has grown, Japan inevitably has begun to look overseas. Through the direct purchase of foreign technology, the sending of personnel overseas, and the massive importation and translation of foreign publications, the Japanese gradually have broken down the psychological barriers that separated them from the outside world.

The value of this information (technology) to Japan cannot be overemphasized. The Japanese industrialist has access to the latest machinery and techniques; he is able at any moment to know exactly the supply situation of his materials and the demand for his product. He can estimate his likely future market, and because he knows almost exactly the likely labour situation for several years in the future, he can plan his machinery and plant to the highest possible degree of economy. The trader with full information of supply and demand can calculate stocks with a minimum of waste. The Japanese exporter knows quickly and accurately the market situation in a full range of overseas countries.

The gains and savings produced by this access to needed information, multiplied many times throughout the economy, help to explain the high productivity of investment in Japan. For investment to be productive, more than capital is required; there must also be an input of know-how and technology. The amount of new and productive technology available in a society over a fixed investment period is usually limited, and this is the major factor restricting growth in an already developed economy. In Japan, a large supply of needed information is available to the

capitalist, and this both encourages his investment and guarantees its profitability.

The theory that the "informationalization" of Japanese society, or *johoka* as it is called in the Japanese language, underlies Japan's growth is necessarily speculative. Few observers—Japanese or foreign—give much weight to this fact. However, there is some evidence that the Japanese themselves instinctively recognize the importance of information to their society; the fact that they alone have a word to describe the concept is indicative. One example of this recognition is the rapid introduction of computers and other data-processing techniques into Japan. Almost all major industrial groups have set up "think tanks" to coordinate information needed for future planning.

The need for information processing is also spreading into ordinary life. In May 1971 the Japanese Diet passed legislation allowing government-operated telecommunications circuits to be used by private interests for home facsimile devices and data transmission terminal telephone systems. As one Japanese observer described it, this was intended to "accelerate the development of the information-oriented society. Information and data as a commodity now available in computer and other electronic industrial systems will come into the household field as a vital part of daily life."

Another sign of the unique importance attached to information in Japanese society is the existence of the *sogo shosha*, or general trading company. Five major trading companies and a host of smaller specialized firms handle most of Japan's external trade and a large proportion of its internal trade. These companies rely for their existence—and no other country in the world provides an equivalent—on their ability to collect and process the information needed for successful trading.

Japan's economic planners frequently mention *johoka* as an element in future Japanese society. They express the same concept when they speak of Japanese industry as moving from labour-intensive, and even capital-intensive, to knowledge-intensive. In this way, as they see it, Japan will be able to continue its rapid growth even after it has caught up with Western levels.

Identifying the free flow of information as a key factor in Japan's economic growth helps to explain one puzzling aspect of this growth. Simply outlined it is this: Both Japan and Germany suffered severe economic setbacks in the late years of World War II and the early postwar era. Recovery from these setbacks, when it finally began, was naturally rapid. Both countries retained their reservoir of economic skills; once economic order was restored the investment of capital was highly productive because unused skills were readily available.

Eventually, however, this reservoir should be exhausted and growth should return to its prewar level. In other words, the growth rate should fall to the level at which skills and know-how accumulate in the society under normal peacetime conditions. In the case of Germany, such a slowdown has occurred. But in the case of Japan, the postwar rate of growth has, if anything, accelerated with time. And if information is seen as the key to growth, then the reason for this acceleration can be suggested, namely Japan's postwar democratization and forced contact with the West. This broke down most of the remaining barriers to information flow in Japanese society, providing new reservoirs of technology to be exploited and leading to accelerated growth.

To the extent that much of this new technology has come from abroad, a limit is placed on Japan's future growth. Already, the technical levels in many Japanese industries have caught up with, and in a few cases (steel manufacture, shipbuilding, appliance making) have surpassed, the West. Japan will in the future have to develop more of its own technology to sustain its rapid growth rate. But to the extent that Japan keeps open the channels for domestic information, it will continue to enjoy a natural economic advantage over the more conservative, less dynamic societies of the Western and Communist worlds.

continued from page 393

Japan's gross national product (GNP) in fiscal 1970 (April 1, 1970–March 31, 1971) totaled 72,717,700,-000,000 yen ($202 billion). This represented a GNP growth rate in real terms of 9.8%, the lowest in five years. Per capita national income reached $1,580, surpassing that of Israel or of Italy but leaving Japan 15th in the world. Moreover, the GNP during the second quarter (April–June) of 1971 showed a nominal gain of only 1.4%; the annual real growth then was believed to be somewhere between 4 and 5%, a sharp drop from 1970. (*See* Special Report.)

Foreign Affairs. On June 17 Japan and the U.S. signed the historic agreement whereby Okinawa would revert to Japan in 1972 after 27 years of American occupation. The Japan-U.S. security treaty, with related understandings including the status-of-forces agreement, would be extended to post-reversion Okinawa without modification. Thus, the U.S. military presence might continue but subject (for the first time in Okinawa) to restrictions and negotiation. Major deployment of U.S. forces would occur only after "prior consultation." Most significant, in view of Japanese sensitivity on the issue, was the oblique statement that reversion would be effected with due regard for Japan's nonnuclear policy. During debate on the agreement in the Diet, JSP deputy Yanosuke Narazaki created a furor by producing what he claimed was proof that the U.S. had stored nuclear weapons in southern Japan. Nevertheless, the agreement was approved by the lower house on November 25, thus assuring ratification.

To Prime Minister Sato, the majority LDP, and many Japanese, Okinawa reversion represented a triumph, a major milestone on the road away from defeat in 1945, and a justification for reliance on the U.S. as a postwar ally. The agreement seemed appropriate in light of Japan's growing economic strength. In April, the Foreign Ministry announced that Japan's overall balance of payments for fiscal 1970 registered an all-time high surplus of $2 billion, more than double the government's earlier estimate. Gold and foreign exchange reserves at the end of March amounted to $5.5 billion. This very strength, however, also produced increasing friction in the realm of monetary and trade relations, particularly with the U.S. Japanese Foreign Ministry officials openly expressed concern over the demand at home and abroad for a revaluation of the yen. There was also the long-smoldering problem of textile exports to the U.S.

In July the Japan Textile Federation began a three-year program of voluntary controls on textile shipments to the U.S. The U.S. government and the American textile industry, however, remained strongly opposed to a unilateral limitation without official agreement. At a conference for Japanese-American financial leaders in Washington July 17–18, Shigeo Nagano of Nippon Steel and Yoshizane Iwasa of Fuji Bank warned Prime Minister Sato of the need for drastic Japanese action in the international economic field. The government responded by promising to implement its eight-point program announced in June: (1) promotion of import liberalization; (2) early application of preferential tariffs on products from less developed nations; (3) reduction of import tariffs; (4) liberalization of capital investments; (5) elimination of nontariff barriers; (6) promotion of overseas economic cooperation; (7) abolition of aggressive export promotion; and (8) flexible manipulation of fiscal and monetary policies.

Protesting students hurl Molotov cocktails at riot police during a violent demonstration near Tokyo on Sept. 16, 1971. The students were attempting to prevent the government from converting 2,663 ac. of farmland into Tokyo's second international airport.
WIDE WORLD

Meanwhile, deteriorating Japanese-American economic relations were greatly complicated by the first tremor from "Nixon shock," the abrupt announcement on July 15 that the U.S. president would visit Peking before May 1972. In fact, many Japanese, including Prime Minister Sato, long had argued for a rapprochement with mainland China. The China issue, however, had always been not simply a matter of diplomatic recognition but one of the most sensitive issues in domestic Japanese politics.

On July 21 Prime Minister Sato told the Diet that he was prepared to visit Peking to attempt to normalize relations with China. In reference to Taiwan, however, he repeated, "Japan has to live up to its international commitments. This means not only keeping its peace treaty [with Taiwan] but also maintaining friendly relations." Not until September 16 did he receive an explicit reply from China. In Peking Premier Chou En-lai said that China would welcome the visit of a *new* Japanese prime minister, if he came with due respect for "Chinese principles."

Under severe pressure from the opposition, the government tried valiantly to project an image of smooth coalition diplomacy with the U.S. The U.S. announcement on August 2, favouring admission of the People's Republic to the UN and opposing Taiwan's expulsion, was officially greeted in Tokyo as little different from Japan's basic posture. American strategy, the Sato government stated, was in line with agreements reached in consultations on China policy between the two countries. Meanwhile, Japan felt the second tremor of the "Nixon shock."

Refuse and waste, washed ashore at Mabori, 25 mi. S of Yokohama, indicate pollution found in Tokyo Bay. Mercury, cadmium, and hydrocyanic acid also are present in the water, rapidly killing sea life. Of 160 species of fish found in Tokyo Bay in 1957, only ten remained in 1971.
KEYSTONE

Japanese recruiting
posters were part
of a massive campaign
to encourage young men
and women to enlist
in Japan's Self-Defense
Forces.
KEYSTONE

President Nixon's announcement August 15 of a
dollar defense plan, including a 10% surcharge on imports, dismayed government leaders, plunged foreign
exchange transactions into utter confusion, and sent
Tokyo stock market prices into a tailspin. At first,
the Japanese government affirmed a policy of keeping
the yen-dollar parity unchanged, but Japan stood to
suffer a huge loss (more than $1.2 billion in exports
annually) as a result of the import surcharge. Minister
Tanaka reported that in fiscal 1970 Japan's exports to
the U.S. had totaled $6 billion (more than 30% of
total exports).

The Tokyo Stock Exchange was thrown into confusion on August 19 when massive sell orders flooded the
chamber following rumours of an imminent revaluation of the yen. The day's decrease in average stock
price was the third largest in the history of the market. Two days later in Honolulu Japanese and American businessmen agreed that revaluation of the yen
should be studied as part of a comprehensive plan to
deal with the chaotic monetary situation. After a one-
day record $1.2 billion purchase of dollars (to protect
yen parity) by the Bank of Japan on August 27, the
Foreign Ministry decided to float the yen temporarily,
effective August 28. On September 1, according to International Monetary Fund (IMF) calculations, the
value of the yen shot up 6.44%. (By early December,
it had climbed to more than 10%.)

Japan and the U.S. ended a two-day Cabinet-level
discussion in Washington on September 10, leaving
major differences unresolved. The Japanese delegation
stressed that the surcharge, if prolonged, would encourage protectionism throughout the world and
threaten the free trade system, which had been crucial
to postwar expansion of commerce. On September 13
in Ottawa Foreign Minister Fukuda urged that Canada
and Japan, America's no. 1 and no. 2 trading partners,
should ally in the face of the U.S. measures.

The stridency in Japan-U.S. relations fell off slightly
when Finance Minister Mizuta returned to Tokyo
from Washington, where he had attended a Group of
Ten ministers' meeting September 26 and the annual
meeting of the IMF September 27–October 1. The
path had been cleared, Mizuta reported, for an eventual multilateral realignment of currency parities. In
Mizuta's absence from Tokyo, however, U.S. special
envoy Anthony Jurich on September 30 had given Ja-

pan what amounted to an ultimatum: either Tokyo
would replace voluntary restraints on textile exports
with a government-level agreement, or strict import
quotas would be imposed by the U.S. on October 15.
Finally, on October 15 Japan (together with Taiwan, South Korea, and Hong Kong) agreed to limit
for three years exports of man-made fibres (to an increase of 5% per year) and woolen goods (1% per
year) over a period of three years. The U.S. in turn
agreed to remove the 10% import surcharge on textiles, retroactive to October 1.

A final shock was reserved for December, when the
Group of Ten reached accord on a settlement of the
monetary crisis. While the U.S. agreed to remove the
10% surcharge entirely, the sharp upward revaluation
of the yen (to 308 = $1) was greater than that of any
other currency and much more than had been expected. It was feared that this could have a considerable adverse effect on Japanese trade with the U.S.
Prime Minister Sato called the settlement "not unreasonable," although Foreign Minister Fukuda considered it the "greatest economic shock" for Japan
since World War II.

Meanwhile, the intricate Japan-China-U.S. relationship—specifically, the China representation issue at
the UN General Assembly—further complicated Japan's external relations. In August, after the announcement of the U.S. official posture, Japan began
intensive consultations with other countries to decide
its position on the representation issue. In principle,
Japan had agreed with the new assumption of the U.S.
(shared by many UN members) that Communist
China no longer could be prevented from entering the
General Assembly. Nor was Japan willing to argue the
assumption that a majority of the UN would probably
also assign China's permanent Security Council seat
to the mainland regime.

For quite different reasons, Japan shared the public
U.S. view that expulsion of Nationalist China (Taiwan) should be designated an "important question,"
therefore requiring a two-thirds majority in the General Assembly. Many older Japanese carried sympathetic feelings toward the Nationalists in Taiwan, who
had at the end of the Pacific war treated Japanese
prisoners of war gently. Furthermore, Japan had in
1952 signed a treaty with "China," in that case the
regime in Taiwan. On the other hand, Japanese leaders
realistically feared that the ill-disguised "two-China"
strategy (embodied in two U.S. resolutions) might fail
in the forthcoming General Assembly, thus further
alienating the mainland regime.

On September 6 in Tokyo, Deputy Foreign Minister
Haruki Mori informed U.S. representative Richard
Sneider that Japan would support the two American
resolutions in the UN. With unusual candour, Mori
admitted that Japan had not yet decided whether to
co-sponsor the resolutions, because opinion on the
issue within the LDP remained deeply divided. By late
September, three major factions within the majority
LDP had announced their firm opposition to Japan's
co-sponsorship of the resolution designating Taiwan's
expulsion from the UN as an "important question."
Nonetheless, on September 22 Prime Minister Sato
announced that Japan would co-sponsor the two
American resolutions, one admitting Communist
China to the UN and the other designed to preserve
membership for Taiwan.

On October 25 in the UN General Assembly the two
resolutions co-sponsored by Japan and the U.S., as
well as by other nations, went down to defeat. The

designation of Taiwan's expulsion as an "important question" lost by a 59–55 margin, following which the Albanian resolution admitting mainland China and expelling Taiwan won by a vote of 76–35.

Meanwhile, there were signs of improvement in economic relationships with Japan's other major Communist neighbour, the Soviet Union. In September, the two countries signed a five-year payments agreement as well as letters of intent on coastal trade. Officials predicted that two-way trade in the 1971–75 period would reach $5.2 billion, an increase of 70% over the previous five-year term.

Symptomatic of the ambivalence inherent in Japan's status as a revived world power was the unprecedented tour by the Emperor Hirohito (*see* BIOGRAPHY) and his wife, Empress Nagako, in the autumn. The mixed reception to them abroad was compounded of 30-year-old but persistent images of Japanese aggression and contemporary fears of Japan's overwhelming economic strength. On September 26 Emperor Hirohito, Empress Nagako, Foreign Minister Fukuda, and their entourage descended on U.S. soil in Alaska during a brief refueling stop on their Tokyo–Copenhagen flight. For the first time in Japanese history a reigning emperor had left his nation, and for the first time a U.S. president met a Japanese ruler. Hirohito later visited Denmark, Belgium, France, Britain, the Netherlands, Switzerland, and West Germany. (A. W. Bs.)

Jordan

A constitutional monarchy in southwest Asia, Jordan is bounded north by Syria, northeast by Iraq, east and south by Saudi Arabia, and west by Israel. Area (including territory occupied by Israel in the June 1967 war): 37,737 sq.mi. (97,740 sq.km.). Pop. (1970 est.): 2,348,000. Cap. and largest city: Amman (pop., 1970 est., 570,000). Language: Arabic. Religion (1961) Muslim 94%; Christian 6%. King, Husain I; prime ministers in 1971, Wasfi at-Tal and, from November 29, Ahmed al-Lawzi.

In 1971 the Jordanian government and Army established full control over the areas of the country not under Israeli occupation and crushed the Palestinian guerrilla movement at the cost of Jordan's virtual isolation within the Arab world. Fighting between the Army and guerrillas flared up in Amman on January 12 and was followed by a 13-point agreement between the two sides that temporarily restored calm, although the left-wing Popular Democratic Front for the Liberation of Palestine (PDFLP) expressed strong reservations about the agreement. Fighting resumed between February 11 and 16 and again on March 26, when it started in Irbid and spread to Amman. On March 28 the chairman of the Supreme Follow-up Committee for the 1970 Cairo and Amman agreements between Jordan and the guerrillas accused Jordan of violating these agreements "in a clear and decisive manner" and resigned on April 13. Egypt, and later Sudan, withdrew their officers from the Arab Ceasefire Committee in April. On March 30 King Husain called for an Arab summit meeting but without success, while the Libyan head of state, Col. Muammar al-Qaddafi, demanded his overthrow.

A planned visit of King Husain to Cairo in February was canceled because Egypt objected to his being accompanied by the prime minister, Wasfi at-Tal, regarded as anti-Egyptian and anti-Palestinian. In April King Husain rejected an Egyptian invitation to Cairo to discuss the situation in Jordan but agreed to a Moroccan proposal for an Arab summit meeting in Algiers. On April 4 the Palestine Liberation Organization agreed to move its heavy arms out of Amman. The situation worsened during June, and on July 13 the Jordanian Army launched a major operation against the remaining guerrilla strongholds in the Jarash-Ajlun area. The government announced that the Cairo and Amman agreements no longer applied and claimed that 2,300 out of 2,500 guerrillas had been taken prisoner.

About 70 guerrillas surrendered to the Israelis rather than to the Jordanian Army. A new Syrian mission came to Amman in an unsuccessful attempt to mediate, but after border clashes between Syrian and Jordanian forces Syria closed its borders with Jordan on July 25. The result was a serious economic crisis for Jordan as all its trade had to be diverted through Aqaba instead of Beirut.

Most Arab states were openly critical of Jordan. Libya and Kuwait cut off their subsidies, and Jordan was forced to rely on the Saudi subsidy and U.S. aid. On November 28, Wasfi at-Tal, in Cairo to attend a meeting of the Arab League's Joint Defense Council, was shot and killed on the street in front of the Sheraton Hotel. The assassins were said to have been connected with a militant Palestinian organization called Black September—a reference to King Husain's attack on the Palestinians in September 1970—and to have entered Egypt with Syrian passports. The following day Husain named Ahmed al-Lawzi, who had been finance minister in Tal's Cabinet, as the new prime minister. (P. MD.)

JORDAN

Education. (1968–69) Primary, pupils 229,691, teachers 5,662; secondary, pupils 75,139, teachers 3,252; vocational, pupils 2,491, teachers 107; higher (including University of Jordan), students 4,077, teaching staff 329.

Finance. Monetary unit: Jordanian dinar, with a par value of 0.357 dinars to U.S. $1 (0.857 dinars = £1 sterling) and a free rate (Sept. 27, 1971) of 0.346 dinars to U.S. $1. Gold, SDRs, and foreign exchange, central bank: (June 1971) U.S. $225.4 million; (June 1970) U.S. $248.7 million. Budget (1971 est.): revenue 95.4 million dinars; expenditure 106.6 million dinars. Gross national product: (1968) 197.3 million dinars; (1967) 206 million dinars. Money supply: (March 1971) 108,560,000 dinars; (March 1970) 96,130,000 dinars. Cost of living (Amman; 1967 = 100): (June 1971) 120; (June 1970) 114.

Foreign Trade. (1970) Imports 65,830,000 dinars; exports 12,170,000 dinars. Import sources (1969): U.K. 14%; U.S. 8%; Japan 8%; West Germany 8%; Syria 7%; Lebanon 7%. Export destinations (1969): Kuwait 14%; Iraq 12%; Lebanon 11%; Saudi Arabia 11%; India 10%; Syria 9%; Yugoslavia 7%. Main exports: phosphates 18%; tomatoes 12%; oranges 7%.

Transport and Communications. Roads (1970) 5,634 km. Motor vehicles in use (1970): passenger 15,411; commercial 6,129. Railways (1968) 366 km. Air traffic (1970): 168,480,000 passenger-km.; freight 1,540,000 net ton-km. Telephones (Dec. 1969) 29,864. Radio receivers (Dec. 1968) 250,000. Television receivers (Dec. 1969) 25,000.

Agriculture. Production (in 000; metric tons; 1969; 1968 in parentheses): wheat 159 (111); barley 53 (29); lentils 20 (16); onions c. 20 (7); tomatoes 195 (258); olives c. 35 (13); oranges 27 (17); lemons c. 10 (8); figs 6 (8); grapes 14 (31); bananas 19 (18). Livestock (in 000; 1969–70): cattle 49; goats 468; sheep 854; camels 13; asses 53; chickens c. 2,320.

Industry. Production (in 000; metric tons): phosphate (1969) 1,089; cement (1970) 378; electricity (kw-hr.; 1968) 156,000.

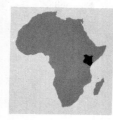

Kenya

A republic and a member of the Commonwealth of Nations, Kenya is bordered on the north by Sudan and Ethiopia, east by Somalia, south by Tanzania, and west by Uganda. Area: 224,960 sq.mi. (582,647 sq.km.), including 5,172 sq.mi. of inland water. Pop. (1971 est.): 11,694,000, including (1969 est.) African and Somali 97.5%; Asian 1.7%. Cap. and largest city: Nairobi (pop., 1969 est., 509,000). Language: English and Swahili (official). Religion (1962): Christian 57.8%; Muslim 3.8%. President in 1971, Jomo Kenyatta.

The worst drought in more than 50 years brought famine to the North Eastern Province early in 1971, and it was estimated that as many as 250,000 people were affected. In spite of transport difficulties the government, assisted by a number of voluntary organizations, channeled large quantities of food into the area. Help also came from an unexpected quarter: China, with whom diplomatic relations were cool, offered cash and supplies worth nearly $394,000.

On the diplomatic front, the main fear concerned the possibly adverse impact upon the East African Community of the military coup in Uganda in January. While Tanzania was openly hostile to the new regime, Kenya adopted a more moderate attitude. But concerning relations with South Africa the government took an overtly critical line. In January Vice-Pres. Daniel Arap Moi rejected Britain's at-

Chief Justice Maluki Kitili Mwendwa resigned when his loyalty was questioned publicly in the aftermath of a plot to overthrow the government. He was Kenya's first African chief justice.
MARION KAPLAN

KENYA

Education. (1968–69) Primary, pupils 1,209,680, teachers 37,923; secondary, pupils 101,361, teachers 4,644; vocational, pupils 1,872, teachers 161; teacher training, students 6,634, teachers 468; higher (at Nairobi University College), students 4,967, teaching staff 395.

Finance. Monetary unit: Kenyan shilling, with a par value of KShs. 7.14 to U.S. $1 (KShs. 17.14 = £1 sterling) and a free rate (Oct. 11, 1971) of KShs. 17.71 to £1 sterling. Gold, SDRs, and foreign exchange: (June 1971) U.S. $189 million; (June 1970) U.S. $188.4 million. Budget (1970–71 est.): revenue KShs. 1,874,500,000; expenditure KShs. 1,625,800,000. Gross national product: (1969) KShs. 10,228,000,000; (1968) KShs. 9,456,000,000. Cost of living (Nairobi; 1963 = 100): (June 1971) 115; (June 1970) 112.

Foreign Trade. (Excluding trade with Tanzania and Uganda; 1970) Imports KShs. 2,841,000,000; exports KShs. 1,549,000,000. Import sources: U.K. 29%; Japan 11%; U.S. 8%; West Germany 8%; Iran 6%. Export destinations: U.K. 21%; West Germany 10%; U.S. 9%; Netherlands 5%; Sweden 5%. Main exports: coffee 29%; tea 16%; petroleum products 12%.

Transport and Communications. Roads (1970) 41,467 km. Motor vehicles in use (1970): passenger 61,152; commercial 55,509. Railways: (1968) 2,069 km. (operated under East African Railways Corp., serving Kenya, mainland Tanzania, and Uganda with a total of 5,906 km.); traffic (total East African; 1966) 4,529,000,000 passenger-km., freight (1969) 3,888,-000,000 net ton-km. Air traffic (East African Airways Corp., including Tanzania and Uganda; 1970): 805 million passenger-km.; freight 33.7 million ton-km. Telephones (Dec. 1969) 72,456. Radio receivers (Dec. 1969) 500,000. Television receivers (Dec. 1969) 16,-000.

Agriculture. Production (in 000; metric tons; 1970; 1969 in parentheses): corn c. 1,350 (c. 1,400); wheat c. 220 (210); coffee 48 (50); tea 41 (36); sugar, raw value (1970–71) c. 147, (1969–70) c. 132; sisal c. 41 (46); cotton, lint 5 (4); fish catch (1969) 32, (1968) 28. Livestock (in 000; 1969–70): cattle c. 7,850; sheep c. 7,500; pigs 27; goats c. 6,800; camels c. 184; poultry c. 11,200.

Industry. Production (in 000; metric tons; 1969): salt 42; magnesite 0.5; soda ash 103; gold (troy oz.) 18; cement (1970) 792; electricity (excluding most industrial production; kw-hr.; 1970) 515,000.

tempted justification for supplying arms to South Africa, maintaining that Britain could not ensure their use solely for maritime defense and questioning the existence of any threat to the security of the trading route around the Cape of Good Hope. With similar conviction President Kenyatta joined with his guest, Maj. Gen. Yakubu Gowon of Nigeria, in May to issue a joint statement condemning the proposal made by a number of other African states to hold a dialogue with South Africa.

The question of British Asians who left Kenya for Britain also remained contentious, and in February Arap Moi announced that any such people refused entry to Britain would not be readmitted to Kenya. However, Kenyatta was at pains to reassure foreign nationals that these decisions did not indicate any general censure of Britain or the Western world. At the state opening of Parliament in February, he said that overseas investors would be encouraged to prospect for and develop the country's mineral resources, and two months later he publicly emphasized that Kenya needed skilled expatriates and that they, and tourists too, would be welcomed as long as they kept the law. The same note of reassurance was echoed in the president's announcement on June 1 that a new bank was to be formed in October involving a partnership between the government and local offices of the Standard Bank Ltd. and Barclays Bank D.C.O. The government would hold 50% of the shares, leaving an incentive to foreign investment and a continuing attraction to overseas resources and skills. Kenyatta said that while the government might take similar action in any of the country's key development industries, any such step would be taken with caution and there would be no wholesale adoption of a policy of interference in private enterprise.

An attempt at reconciliation was made in the political field in March when Oginga Odinga, former vice-president of Kenya and later leader of the opposition, was released after 18 months' detention. In September Odinga was readmitted to the Kenya African National Union, which had been split by his resignation five years previously. He said he hoped to run for political office in the elections planned for March 1972.

In contrast to the Odinga case was the trial and conviction in June of 12 Kenyans on charges of conspiring to overthrow the government. It was claimed that the accused had approached Pres. Julius Nyerere of Tanzania with a request for arms and money but that he had refused. Subsequently, Maj. Gen. Joe Ndolo, chief of Kenya's defense staff, and Chief Justice Maluki Kitili Mwendwa resigned after their loyalty had been publicly questioned.   (K. I.)

Encyclopædia Britannica Films. *Youth Builds a Nation in Tanzania* (1970).

Korea

A country of eastern Asia, Korea is bounded by China, the Sea of Japan, the Straits of Korea, and the Yellow Sea. It is divided into two parts at the 38th parallel.

Republic of Korea (South Korea). Area: 38,022 sq.mi. (98,477 sq.km.). Pop. (1970): 31,469,132. Cap. and largest city: Seoul (pop., 1970, 5,536,337). Language: Korean. Religion: Buddhist; Confucian;

Tonghak (Chondokyo). President in 1971, Gen. Park Chung Hee; prime ministers, Paik Too Chin and, from June 3, Kim Chong Pil.

On Jan. 23, 1971, the third anniversary of North Korea's seizure of the U.S. intelligence ship "Pueblo," a young South Korean made an abortive attempt to hijack a Korean Air Lines plane to the north. The KAL pilot crash-landed on a beach barely ten miles south of the border. The hijacker was killed along with the copilot in a grenade explosion. Reports that some of the 65 passengers on board were killed were not confirmed.

On August 23, 23 men escaped from the Air Force prison on Silmi Island off Inchon, west of Seoul, killing at least 12 prison guards in the process. They reached the mainland, seized a bus, and drove to the capital, firing at police checkpoints on the way. Fifteen of them then blew themselves up in the bus, while four were wounded and later captured. The breakout was first reported as a raid by North Korean infiltrators but later the minister of defense, Jung Nae Hiuk, corrected the original announcement and offered his resignation.

President Park was busy during the early months of the year making careful preparations for his third-term election on April 27. In January he announced a major purge in the party, dropping 40 senior members from the list of candidates who would represent his ruling Democratic Republican Party in the National Assembly elections to take place a month after the presidential poll. He also pledged he would not run for a fourth term but would groom a capable successor. The main opposition candidate, Kim Dae Jung, was quick to point out that Park had made similar promises during his previous campaign, only to disregard them when the next election came.

A week before the presidential election, the Army security command announced what it called the biggest crackdown on Communist agents in South Korea. Critics saw it as another election maneuver. The Army claimed it had broken up four spy rings and arrested 51 persons including students who had been operating for four years with instructions to assassinate political leaders and incite student riots.

Election day was peaceful and Park won his expected victory with a majority of almost one million

South Korean soldiers stand by bus in which 15 military prisoners killed themselves on Aug. 23, 1971, when faced with a massive blockade during an attempted escape. The prisoners, after staging a bloody mutiny in an island prison off the western coast, sought to raid Seoul in a seized bus.
UPI COMPIX

votes. On May 25 voters again turned out in large numbers to elect a new 204-member single-chamber National Assembly. With 51 seats distributed among the parties under a system of proportional representation, Park's party obtained 113 seats and the main opposition New Democratic Party, 89.

His power consolidated and party position secured for another four years, Park took his oath of office on July 1 and said he would make South Korea strong enough by the middle of the decade to achieve peaceful reunification of the country. Earlier, on June 3, he had appointed retired Brig. Gen. Kim Chong Pil, his principal aide in the military coup of 1961, prime minister in place of Paik Too Chin.

Relations with the U.S. were a major problem for the new government. As scheduled, Washington had cut its troop strength in South Korea from 63,000 to 43,000 by June. U.S. Vice-Pres. Spiro T. Agnew reiterated plans to withdraw all U.S. troops by 1975, although Secretary of Defense Melvin R. Laird pro-

KOREA: Republic

Education. (1968–69) Primary, pupils 5,548,-577, teachers 92,530; secondary, pupils 1,287,106, teachers 32,951; vocational, students 232,237, teachers 9,489; higher (including 27 universities), students 172,410, teaching staff (full-time) 8,706.

Finance. Monetary unit: won, with a free rate (Sept. 27, 1971) of 371 won to U.S. $1 (921 won = £1 sterling). Gold, SDRs, and foreign exchange, central bank: (June 1971) U.S. $568.9 million; (June 1970) U.S. $591.3 million. Budget (1971 est.): revenue 510.7 billion won; expenditure 523.2 billion won. Gross national expenditure: (1969) 2,047,100,000,000 won; (1968) 1,575,700,000,000 won. Money supply: (May 1971) 315.7 billion won; (May 1970) 268.6 billion won. Cost of living (1963 = 100): (June 1971) 280; (June 1970) 245.

Foreign Trade. (1970) Imports 570,820,000,-000 won; exports 259,370,000,000 won. Import sources (1969): Japan 40%; U.S. 29%. Export destinations (1969): U.S. 50%; Japan 21%. Main exports: clothing 26%; plywood 13%; textile yarns and fabrics 11%; electrical machinery and equipment 6%; fish and products 5%.

Transport and Communications. Roads (1970) c. 34,000 km. (including 428 km. express-

ways). Motor vehicles in use (1969): passenger 50,300; commercial (including buses) 39,800. Railways: (1969) 5,080 km.; traffic (1970) 9,-624,000,000 passenger-km., freight 7,958,000,000 net ton-km. Air traffic (1969): 138,430,000 passenger-km.; freight 2,310,000 net ton-km. Shipping (1970): merchant vessels 100 gross tons and over 329; gross tonnage 849,457. Telephones (Jan. 1970) 562,111. Radio receivers (Dec. 1969) 3,242,000. Television receivers (Dec. 1969) 246,000.

Agriculture. Production (in 000; metric tons; 1970; 1969 in parentheses): rice 5,515 (5,528); wheat c. 360 (366); potatoes c. 600 (599); barley c. 2,200 (2,066); sweet potatoes 2,136 (2,-123); soybeans c. 229 (229); tobacco c. 76 (59); fish catch (1969) 852, (1968) 841. Livestock (in 000; Dec. 1969): cattle 1,225; pigs 1,-338; goats 99; chickens 22,651.

Industry. Production (in 000; metric tons; 1970): coal 12,384; iron ore (c. 50% metal content) 600; steel 480; cement 5,827; tungsten concentrate (oxide content; 1969) 2.5; kaolin (1969) 136; fluorspar (1969) 39; limestone (1969) 7,415; gold (troy oz.; 1969) 46; silver (troy oz.; 1969) 630; electricity (excluding most industrial production; kw-hr.) 9,198,000.

KOREA: Democratic People's Republic

Education. (1964–65) Primary, pupils 1,113,-000, teachers 25,221; secondary, pupils 704,000, teachers 27,162; vocational, pupils 441,000, teachers 17,176; higher, students 186,000, teaching staff 9,013.

Finance and Trade. Monetary unit: won, with (Sept. 27, 1971) an official exchange rate of 2.57 won to U.S. $1 (6.17 won = £1 sterling). Budget (1970 est.) balanced at 6.2 billion won. Foreign trade (excluding trade with China; 1966): imports c. U.S. $126.5 million (68% from U.S.S.R., 6% from France); exports c. U.S. $148,742,000 (62% to U.S.S.R., 15% to Japan, 7% to Czechoslovakia). Main exports (1964): metals 50%; minerals 12%; farm produce 11%.

Agriculture. Production (in 000; metric tons; 1970; 1969 in parentheses): rice c. 2,500 (c. 2,500); corn c. 1,800 (c. 1,800); barley c. 275 (c. 275); potatoes c. 1,000 (c. 1,000); fish catch (1964) 770, (1963) 640. Livestock (in 000; Dec. 1969): cattle c. 730; pigs c. 1,330.

Industry. Production (in 000; metric tons; 1969): coal c. 20,100; iron ore (metal content; 1968) c. 3,500; pig iron (1968) c. 2,000; steel (1968) c. 1,750; lead c. 55; zinc c. 60; magnesite c. 1,000; cement c. 2,798; electricity (kw-hr.; 1965) 13,300,000.

vided some relief by announcing that there would be no withdrawals during 1972. In March the U.S. transferred 54 Phantom fighters from Japan to South Korea in a move to reassure Seoul of a continuing U.S. commitment. The withdrawal of South Korean troops from South Vietnam began in November.

However, the changing pattern of the world's power structure in the wake of China's return to active diplomacy evidently was making an impact on Seoul. The government revised the trade law to distinguish between "hostile" and "nonhostile" Communist countries. On December 6 President Park declared a state of national emergency "to make the Korean people look at the rapid changes in the international situation." A six-point national emergency program was established, which curtailed certain forms of opposition and "irresponsible arguments."

In June the Korean won was devalued by about 13%, bringing it down to slightly more than 370 to the U.S. dollar. The government also announced details of the third five-year development plan which was to take effect from April 1972. It envisaged a growth rate of 8.5%, self-sufficiency in rice, and a decrease in the proportion of foreign capital investment from 36.4% in the second plan to 18.7%.

Democratic People's Republic of Korea (North Korea). Area: 46,800 sq.mi. (121,200 sq.km.). Pop. (1970 est.): 14 million. Cap.: Pyongyang (pop., 1960 est., 653,100). Language: Korean. Religion: Buddhist; Confucian; Tonghak (Chondokyo). Secretary-general of the Korean Workers' (Communist) Party and chairman of the Council of Ministers (premier) in 1971, Marshal Kim Il Sung; president, Choi Yong Kun.

North Korea moved closer to China during 1971. At a banquet in honour of a North Korean delegation visiting Peking in July, the chief of the Chinese People's Liberation Army's general staff, Gen. Huang Yung-sheng, spoke plainly of China's fears: "Historical experience has proved that when an enemy invades China it invariably invades Korea first and that when it invades Korea it invariably further invades China." In September a highly publicized tour of China by a North Korean military delegation culminated in a formal treaty under which China was to give North Korea free military aid for the first time since the end of the Korean War.

Relations with South Korea entered an unprecedented phase following North Korean agreement to participate in Red Cross talks over the problem of separated Korean families. Red Cross delegations from the two halves of the country met at Panmunjom in August and again in September, and a full-fledged conference was scheduled for a future date. The Red Cross initiative was understood to have been a cautious attempt to produce a thaw between the two Koreas. In Seoul, President Park welcomed the talks although he cautioned his people that the North was not to be trusted. Significantly, the first telephone link between the two countries in 23 years was opened in September.

In April the foreign minister made an eight-point proposal for the reunification of the two Koreas. As on previous occasions the South rejected it as propaganda. In an interview with visiting Japanese correspondents in September, Premier Kim Il Sung said that his government would abrogate its military treaty with the Soviet Union if the South would similarly break off its alliances with the U.S. and Japan with a view to bringing about reunification. A spokesman of

the South Korean Foreign Ministry dismissed the proposal as "sheer nonsense."

The party congress, the first in nine years, had reelected Kim as secretary-general. Kim said in his report that "had even a part of the nation's defense spending been diverted to economic construction, our national economy would have developed more rapidly." Nevertheless, he called for increased defense preparedness.

After the congress 7 members of the all-important 11-member Politburo of the party were dropped. Their replacements were believed to be men who owed their political careers to Kim Il Sung.   (T. J. S. G.)

Kuwait

An independent emirate, Kuwait is on the northwestern coast of the Persian Gulf between Iraq and Saudi Arabia. Area: 6,880 sq.mi. (17,818 sq.km.). Pop. (1970): 738,-663. Cap.: Kuwait (pop., 1970, 80,008). Largest city: Hawalli (pop., 1970, 106,507). Language: Arabic. Religion: (1970) Muslim 94.7%; Christian 4.6%. Emir in 1970, Sheikh Sabah as-Salim as-Sabah; prime minister, Crown Prince Sheikh Jabir al-Ahmad al-Jabir as-Sabah.

In 1971 the balance of political forces in Kuwait was reflected in the results of the country's third general election, held on January 23, which was widely accepted as having been free from government interference. Ten members of the radical Arab Nationalist Movement were elected and, with six independents, formed an opposition bloc within the 50-member National Assembly. The prime minister, Crown Prince Jabir al-Ahmad, resigned after the election and then formed a new 12-man government which included two elected members of the Assembly.

In its foreign relations Kuwait's principal concern was with developments in the Persian Gulf following Britain's final withdrawal at the end of the year. In January the foreign ministers jointly led a Kuwaiti-Saudi delegation to the Persian Gulf sheikhdoms to urge them to form a federation.

In the rest of the Arab world Kuwait repeatedly emphasized its good relations with Egypt and declared its support for the new Syrian-Libyan-Egyptian federation.   (P. Md.)

KUWAIT

Education. (1968–69) Primary, pupils 54,377, teachers 2,577; secondary, pupils 49,559, teachers 3,352; vocational, pupils 1,550, teachers 269; teacher training, students 2,477, teachers 379; higher, students 1,320, teaching staff 119.

Finance. Monetary unit: Kuwaiti dinar, with a par value of 0.357 dinars to U.S. $1 (0.857 dinars = £1 sterling) and a free rate (Sept. 27, 1971) of 0.346 dinars to U.S. $1. Gold and foreign exchange, official: (June 1971) U.S. $196.5 million; (June 1970) U.S. $191.8 million. Budget (1970–71 est.) balanced at 319.4 million dinars. Money supply: (June 1971) 106.6 million dinars; (June 1970) 107.8 million dinars.

Foreign Trade. (1970) Imports 223.3 million dinars; exports 564.6 million dinars. Import sources (1969): U.S. 15%; Japan 13%; U.K. 13%; West Germany 10%; Italy 5%; India 5%. Export destinations (1969): U.K. 25%; Italy 18%; Japan 16%; Netherlands 10%; France 8%. Main exports petroleum and products 95%.

Industry. Crude oil production (1970) 137,441,000 metric tons.

Labour Unions

The characteristic features of labour relations in 1971 were the intensified intervention of governments in order to contain wage demands, reduce strikes, and increase productivity, and the growing concern of unions with this intervention and with the power of the multinational companies, whose activities as mass employers rivaled those of governments.

Industrialized Countries. Union-government relations dominated the year in the U.S., where the giant AFL-CIO headed by George Meany (*see* BIOGRAPHY) opposed the 90-day wage-price freeze announced by Pres. Richard Nixon on August 15, especially insofar as it affected pay raises due under existing contracts. Eventually labour agreed to participate in the Pay Board (five representatives each of labour, management, and the public), set up to pass on the permissibility of pay raises during Phase Two of the president's program, following expiration of the freeze period. Labour's cooperation remained tenuous, however. The tension was clearly apparent during the president's appearance before the AFL-CIO convention in Miami, Fla., on November 19, when Nixon's angry speech and his cool reception by the delegates amounted almost to mutual insult.

A particularly touchy problem involved retroactivity of pay raises that had come due during the freeze. Over labour opposition, the Pay Board decided against granting retroactivity except in certain special cases. However, Congress, in passing legislation extending the president's power to regulate wages and prices, added an amendment specifying that most such raises should be paid retroactively. Another source of difficulty appeared when the Pay Board approved the 15% raise embodied in a contract ending a 45-day strike among soft-coal miners—far in excess of the president's 5.5% guideline. Subsequently, the Price Commission, another part of the Phase Two machinery, permitted a soft coal company to raise prices by only 6% and served notice that management could not expect to pass increased wage costs on to the consumer automatically—a decision that might presage a harder management line at the bargaining table.

Government intervention in labour disputes was also apparent in other areas. A two-day nationwide strike by railway signalmen was ended May 18 when Congress passed special legislation granting an interim pay raise of $13\frac{1}{2}$% and providing for a cooling-off period until October 1. To avoid congressional intervention, the United Transportation Union in July adopted a strategy of selective railway strikes; by August 2, when a contract was signed granting a 42% raise over 42 months, ten railroads, including five major carriers, had been shut down. Contracts between the railroads and most operating and shop-craft unions were signed during the year; the signalmen's dispute was finally settled in December.

President Nixon's first use of the injunctive procedure provided by the Taft-Hartley Act came as a result of dock strikes that tied up both East and West Coast ports and threatened to frustrate the administration's efforts to improve the sagging U.S. balance of trade. The International Longshoremen's and Warehousemen's Union closed 24 West Coast ports on July 1, and the president invoked the Taft-Hartley Act to end the strike on October 9. By that time the

Drawbridges providing access to Manhattan are locked open, causing massive traffic jams, during a municipal employees' strike in New York City on June 7, 1971. Only a rail bridge spanning the Harlem River remained closed.
WIDE WORLD

International Longshoremen's Association had struck most ports on the East and Gulf coasts, but the president delayed use of Taft-Hartley in that dispute until early December. Under Taft-Hartley, strikes endangering the national health or safety can be enjoined for 80 days.

The predicted steel strike failed to materialize when a contract, providing for a 31% pay increase over three years, was signed before the old contract expired on August 1. However, buyers had stockpiled steel in expectation of a strike, and the settlement was followed by widespread layoffs. The contract followed the pattern set by the United Steelworkers and major can companies after a strike in the spring. A copper strike that had idled some 39,000 workers in five Western states ended when a new three-year agreement was signed with the Anaconda Co. in September. Essentially completing the round of negotiations between major automobile companies and the United Auto Workers that had begun with the 1970 strike against General Motors, Chrysler and the UAW signed an agreement for production workers in January. A 19-day UAW strike against International Harvester ended January 31.

Strikes and other forms of job action by public employees continued to be an unsolved problem. The most spectacular such strike occurred on June 7, when New York municipal employees, striking over a pension plan, caused massive traffic jams by leaving the city's drawbridges open.

James Hoffa, who for several years had continued in office as president of the teamsters' union while serving a prison sentence for jury tampering, announced that he would not seek reelection. He was succeeded by Frank E. Fitzsimmons (*see* BIOGRAPHY). Just before Christmas, President Nixon commuted Hoffa's prison sentence, freeing him on condition that he refrain from engaging in the management of labour unions until 1980.

In the U.K. the Conservative government had introduced its Industrial Relations Bill in the House of Commons on Dec. 3, 1970. The General Council of the British Trades Union Congress arranged for a mass demonstration against the bill on Jan. 12, 1971,

continued on page 405

THE FOUR-DAY WORKWEEK

By Riva Poor

By mid-1971, some 600 employers in the U.S., primarily manufacturers in the northeast and municipal governments in the southwest, were offering their employees a workweek of 40 hours spread over four or even three days. About 75,000 persons were working the shorter week and although they represented only one in every 1,000 workers in the U.S., they were also the vanguard of a movement that had captured the public imagination. While the standard workweek remained approximately 40 hours in five days, the feasibility of a four-day week for all workers was discussed in articles in most major publications. It was subjected to opinion polls of the general public, union memberships, and corporate executives, and was denounced as a regression to sweatshop hours just as frequently as it was touted as the solution to problems of absenteeism, tardiness, turnover, and low productivity.

Experience with the four-day workweek was hardly extensive enough for anyone to predict whether it was a wave of the future. The manufacturing concerns that had adopted it generally were small, employing fewer than 500 persons and averaging 190 persons. They were usually nonunion or had contracts with small unions or locals of national unions; few were capital-intensive; and virtually none competed in world markets. Most were firms whose units of work could not be completed conveniently within an eight-hour schedule (such as paint manufacturing), whose equipment had to be used for long periods to justify its expense (computer processing), or whose plant conditions were by necessity so unattractive or inconveniently located that good help could not be attracted or kept without an incentive other local industry did not provide.

One area in which the four-day week was being adopted to greatest advantage was in police departments in small communities, where neither profits nor collective bargaining were involved. Putting the policeman on a ten-hour day permitted a more effective use of limited manpower and an ability to overlap schedules without extending the policeman's day. Greater manpower was available during the peak crime hours and for emergencies. The fact that the policeman had three days off in every seven was a secondary consideration in these cases, where the primary concerns were to get "30 hours of police work in a 24-hour period," increase the number of arrests, and boost morale and recruiting.

Other businesses being attracted to the four-day workweek were banks, hospitals, municipal offices, and other organizations where an extension of the working day meant that services could be provided at hours and on days not previously possible. Employees' work schedules varied in these situations but generally were arranged so that the employee had a three-day weekend every fourth or fifth week.

Toward the Three-Day Weekend. The principal attraction of the four-day week for the employee most often was found to be the chance for a three-day weekend. But it remained to be seen which of two trends in labour in the U.S. would be the most dominant in deciding the ultimate fate of the four-day week.

Riva Poor is president of Bursk and Poor Publishing of Cambridge (Mass.) and editor of 4 Days, 40 Hours, *from which parts of this article have been adapted.*

Would the American labourer continue to want more income and income-related benefits for the same number of hours of work, as unions generally maintained he did? Or would he become more interested in increased blocks of leisure time, as might be indicated by the extension of the number of paid vacation days granted in union contracts during the 1960s? The history of the labour movement might well indicate that what the labourer wanted would be what would come about. Despite a few spectacular developments in legislation and union activity, the major force behind the downward trend in hours of labour always had been the prolonged growth of real income per capita.

In 1850, the average workweek in the U.S. was 69.8 hours. As long as labour remained cheap and output per worker relatively unchanged, the number of hours worked per week was fairly constant, falling only to 60.2 hours in 1900, despite the demand of most labour unions for an eight-hour day. By 1900, however, labour was becoming more expensive and efforts to use it more efficiently were under way. Studies established that by improving surroundings and decreasing the number of hours worked per day to ten, or even eight, a worker's hourly production, and usually his daily output, would increase. This concept of "scientific management" of work gained such wide acceptance that by 1930 the average workweek was 45.9 hours. At this point unions and economists were arguing that even shorter hours would spread available employment opportunities among a larger number of workers and could thereby reduce unemployment. The Depression gave this idea widespread acceptance and although employment opportunities improved with the start of World War II, the average five-day workweek of 40 hours in 1950 remained the standard.

Fear that technological progress would create job shortages prompted some unions to call for four-day, 35-hour workweeks in the mid-1950s, but most workers appeared to be more interested in increased wages than in shortened hours, and productivity was not increasing enough to make a shorter workweek economically feasible.

More recently, however, gains in productivity actually lagged, with output per man-hour increasing only 2.1% per year in 1966–70, compared with 3% per year over the previous 20 years. By 1971 the possibility of stimulating productivity by changing the structure of the workweek was becoming increasingly attractive. If a work schedule could be keyed to the time required to complete the operation rather than to the standard workweek, if higher output could be gained by reducing the number of times production is started up and closed down, and if a shorter week would improve morale and reduce absenteeism, tardiness, and turnover, a workweek of even less than 40 hours could be made profitable.

Labour and the Law. The key to the success of such a scheme, however, was the workers' interest in more leisure time. And this seemed quite assured. The average number of hours worked weekly was decreasing steadily year by year from 40 in 1948 to 37.1 in 1970, and the total number of hours worked per person per year was estimated to have decreased by a record 50 hours during the 1960s. Two-fifths of this reduction was in the form of paid vacations and holidays. In addition, beginning in 1971, in response to public demand, national holidays were being rearranged by law to provide more three-day weekends. Workers might well be willing in the 1970s to trade longer daily hours for longer blocks of leisure. A three-day weekend also might be sufficient rest to help avoid the health and safety hazards that the physical, mental, or emotional strain a 10- or 12-hour day might produce.

Ironically, efforts to guard against these hazards, in the form of legislation restricting work hours and clauses in collective bargaining agreements calling for premium pay for work over eight hours a day, now stood as major obstacles to any significant spread of the four-day week. Under federal law, all workers employed directly by the federal government received premium pay for work in excess of eight hours in a day and an additional 3.7 million persons employed by firms doing $10,000 or more business with the federal government received the same compensation under the Walsh-Healey Public Contracts Act. State laws focused on the number of hours and types of work women can do. Many of these statutes, however, had become unenforceable, particularly since the adoption of the Civil Rights Act of 1964. A California law limiting women's working hours was ruled discriminatory in June 1971, and in other states, notably Massachusetts and Wisconsin, labour statutes were being abrogated or changed for firms on four-day, 40-hour work schedules.

While state statutes could be and were being changed with some ease, opposition of organized labour to any extension of the working day beyond eight hours remained solid. AFL-CIO Pres. George Meany announced his personal opposition to the four-day, 40-hour week and I. W. Abel of the United Steel Workers called it "a step backward." Although the United Automobile Workers and Chrysler Corp. had established a committee to explore the feasibility of the four-day week, the aim in doing so was to determine if it would curb absenteeism, which was running as high as 12% on Mondays and Fridays. In September 1971 the U.S. Department of Labor held public hearings to examine whether changes in federal overtime legislation would be in the public interest. Union spokesmen cited possible exploitation of the worker under a four-day system in which a workday could stretch beyond ten hours without premium pay. The goal of labour remained, according to one witness, "to gradually reduce the working hours per week while maintaining the eight-hour day overtime standard for which we traditionally fought."

A Matter of Personal Preference. Since the unions had accomplished a reduction of 1.5 hours in the workweek of the typical production worker in the 1960s, it was entirely likely that they would achieve further reductions in the 1970s, if not the goal of a 4-day, 32-hour week by 1980. (Abel already had declared this to be his union's goal in 1974 bargaining.) For the average worker, however, the basic needs for goods and time for rest were being met. What interested him increasingly was the possibility that they could be met in a way suited to his life-style. For some this was being realized with more vacation days and occasional longer weekends. Others found it in the variety of working hours they could have with firms whose operating schedules fell outside the five-day, 40-hour mold. Still others found it in the availability of part-time schedules, a trend that had been growing since its introduction more than 50 years before and that was permitting many to select their arrival and departure times as long as they maintained a required number of weekly hours or accomplished the work assigned. The appearance of the four-day, 40-hour workweek was likely to reinforce this trend, since its great advantage to the employer and employee alike was the ability to select the most comfortable of an almost unlimited variety of workweek-weekend schedules.

Variety of choice was perhaps the most attractive aspect of the four-day, 40-hour week and the one that stimulated the most interest in it for the average worker. While considerably more experience was required to determine whether rearrangement of the workweek would answer any problems in employment in the U.S., the hint that it might provide more agreeable blocks of leisure time could easily stimulate even greater variety in work scheduling.

Interest in a work schedule more suited to an individual's life-style was hardly limited to the worker bound to an eight-hour-a-day routine or the employer struggling to increase productivity. Nobel Prize-winning economist Paul A. Samuelson noted that what interested him in the four-day work pattern was "the fact that it offers new variety of choice in an area where modern man has had the fewest personal options. . . . In contrast with freedom in the spending of the money we earn, the modern industrial regime denies us a similar freedom in choosing the work routine by which we earn those dollars."

continued from page 403

but the unofficial Liaison Committee for the Defence of Trade Unions called for mass strike action. About 350,000 workers went on strike against the bill on Dec. 8, 1970. This was followed by a series of demonstrations and strikes culminating in a special TUC meeting on March 18 and a one-day strike by about three million workers on the same day. Meanwhile the Commons continued to debate the bill and the numerous amendments to it submitted by the Labour opposition. Despite this opposition the bill became law on August 5. On September 7 the TUC decided to instruct its members not to register under the act, which took effect in stages, beginning on October 1.

On Jan. 14, 1971, talks between the Union of Post Office Workers and the Post Office broke down and the union called the first national strike in its history (January 20–March 8). No strike pay was provided, but a hardship fund was set up for special cases. The strike (the longest national strike in the U.K. since 1945) ended when the government established a three-man committee of inquiry into the 15% wage claim. The majority finding of the committee was that the postal workers should receive a 9% increase, 1% higher than the initial Post Office offer.

On June 14 the government decided not to prevent the Upper Clyde Shipbuilders consortium from going into liquidation. Over 100,000 workers throughout the West of Scotland struck for a day on June 23 against the closures. On August 9 the 8,000 workers in the four yards returned from their annual vacations and immediately occupied them. Workers who had been laid off remained at work and were financed by their unions or by donations. Despite negotiations involving leading government ministers, the issue dragged into the winter months without a settlement.

A pay dispute stopped work in Britain's Ford Motor Co. plants for more than nine weeks. On January 31 the Ford management offered an additional £2 a week in reply to a union claim for parity with similar plants in the Midlands. Almost immediately an unofficial strike began which became official on February 2. On November 24, 85,000 workers were involved in stoppages throughout the U.K. and 20,000 clashed with police outside the House of Commons in a demonstration against the rise in unemployment, which had surpassed 970,000.

In France the year began with a union protest over government interference in wage negotiations. The Confédération Générale du Travail refused to sign an agreement with the management of French Railways which, in accordance with the government's incomes policy, stipulated the percentage by which wages could be increased. The offending clause was dropped from the agreement. At the beginning of February, a widespread miners' strike began against a government-supported plan to cut coal production by half in 1973. The state-owned Renault automobile concern was seriously disrupted by strikes that began in April. At the end of the month workers at the Le Mans factory decided to occupy it over a wage demand. The dispute spread to other Renault plants, and by May 6 production at the main Renault assembly plants was virtually paralyzed. An agreement was reached on May 24 involving a reorganization of the wage structure.

In West Germany the IG Chemie trade union presented its employers with a demand for a 12% increase in March and was offered 5%. The government had stated that wage demands of more than 8% would

A British motorcycle gang
delivers mail
to the Greater London
area on Jan. 21, 1971,
during the British
postal workers' strike.
"THE TIMES," (LONDON)—
PICTORIAL PARADE

A mass rally demonstrating
support for the ailing
Upper Clyde shipyards
was held in Dumbarton,
Scot., on June 18, 1971.
UPI COMPIX

endanger the economy. Arbitration talks broke down early in June, and the union organized a series of sporadic strikes, on some days involving up to 10,000 workers. After four weeks an agreement was reached giving a pay increase of just over 7%. A similar situation arose in the metal industry in November. Western Europe's largest trade union, IG Metall, submitted a wage demand of 11% for 550,000 workers in the Nordbaden-Nordwürttemberg region, which was countered by an offer of 4.5%. The union voted to support a strike, and the prospect arose of the worst series of strikes in West Germany in 20 years. A nine-day, nationwide strike by the metalworkers that effectively shut down West Germany's automobile industry ended December 10, when the union, which had originally asked for an 11% raise over one year, settled for 7.5%.

About 1.5 million Italian workers organized by the three leading trade-union federations went on strike January 26, not only to improve pay and working conditions but to force the Italian government to apply far-reaching social reforms. FIAT, which employed 185,000 workers, experienced nine weeks of strike-troubled negotiations before an agreement giving unions greater shop-floor control was reached on June 20. A 24-hour general strike, involving a large range of workers, was called on April 7. On April 13 strikes paralyzed postal and telephone services, shipping, tourism, law courts, and freight transport. Even doctors from Milan joined in. One in every four doctors in Italy struck for 24 hours on April 26.

Spain continued to be troubled with labour unrest, much of it arising from the 1970 military trial of 16 Basque nationalists. Widespread strikes in support of the Basques were called by illicit trade unions, and trade-union organizations all over the world protested against the sentences after the Basques had been found guilty. Under this pressure the government revised the labour law in March, although more in terminology than in content. Elections to the state-run unions were held on May 17. The industrial situation deteriorated further in the fall. Sit-in protests by auto workers in Barcelona on October 18 led to a retaliatory lockout. Workers and police clashed and a worker was shot. A strike in Spain's main coal-mining region in Oviedo in October seriously depleted the country's coal reserves.

Evidence was given to the International Labour Organization (ILO) in Geneva concerning the violation of trade-union rights in Portugal. Three union leaders of the Lisbon branch of the metalworkers' union were suspended in November 1970 by a labour court for failing to sign an agreement with the Portuguese Air Transport Company, for addressing workers in "terms of class mentality," and for attacking the principles of the corporative state. The three officials had been elected in June 1970 by an overwhelming majority in opposition to government-sponsored candidates. The government banned all meetings of metalworkers and forbade the union to hold its general assembly.

Sweden, which had experienced a rash of unofficial strikes in 1970, faced new industrial troubles early in 1971 when about 10,000 civil servants went on strike over pay on January 30. By February 23, 47,-000 railway officials, teachers, administrators, and professional people were involved, through either strikes or lockouts. On March 10 the government introduced emergency legislation banning strikes and lockouts for six weeks. This legislation was supported by the Trade Union Confederation (LO), which represented about 90% of Sweden's industrial workers. A marked division of interest existed between the relatively highly paid white-collar workers and the manual workers. LO, however, was involved in its own negotiations with the Swedish Employers' Confederation (SAF) for pay increases of 30% spread over three years. On June 16 the president of LO, Arne Geijer, threatened a "massive conflict," which was averted by government mediators a few days later. (See SWEDEN.)

Eastern Europe proved no exception to the widespread pattern of industrial unrest. Following the governmental changes in Poland resulting from strikes against increased food prices in Gdansk, Gdynia, and Szczecin in December 1970, renewed strike action in January 1971 was settled by direct negotiations between strike representatives and the new political leaders. The price increases that had led to the troubles were canceled on February 15. (See POLAND: Special Report.)

In February the Australian Council of Trade Unions refused to allow the export of merino stud rams because it believed that the government decision to lift the 40-year embargo was unwise and should have been debated in Parliament. Two months later the ACTU organized a successful total union ban against Dunlop Australia Ltd. and its 125 subsidiaries in order to force it to remove resale price conditions.

Less Developed Countries. Miners at the Luanshya Mine in Zambia's Copper Belt contravened a statutory order by Pres. Kenneth Kaunda in May declaring the mining industry an essential service and were promptly arrested. Fifteen out of the 100 miners arrested received orders confining them to their homes; the remainder were released on police bonds. In the early months of the year Nigeria experienced strikes or slowdowns among doctors, teachers, clerks, and technicians, aimed at forcing the government and private employers to carry out a pay award. On August 16 the Nigerian police detained seven trade unionists for allegedly staging an illegal strike. The Nigerian TUC renewed its appeals to secure the release from prison of its president and general secretary, who were arrested in January. On September 10 the Ghana National Assembly passed a bill abolishing the Ghana TUC in its existing form with the intention of bringing trade-union legislation into line with democratic procedures. At the same time, however, trade-union offices and the homes of union leaders were searched by police, documents were seized, and the TUC funds were frozen.

In January the Malaysian government introduced amendments to the labour legislation of 1969 restricting the choice by unions of their leaders and the ability of unions to deal with individual cases of dismissals, transfers, and promotions. A series of strikes disrupted the economic and social life of Israel during the summer to such an extent that the Israeli government drafted antistrike legislation in September. A general strike was called in West Bengal on February 22 as a political protest, while in Pakistan the Awami League called a general strike on March 3 in the initial stages of the struggle for the political independence of East Pakistan.

Interunion Relations. The most significant factor in unions' attempts to achieve greater unity in 1971 was their common interest in the activities of multinational companies. The Metal Trades Committee of the ILO, at a 27-nation conference in Geneva in February, urged the organization to undertake a full-scale study of the effect of multinational firms on the lives of workers. Also in February, the Caribbean Bauxite Mine and Metalworkers' Federation called for coordinated trade-union action and establishment of a Bauxite Producers' Council to confront the area's giant multinational aluminum companies.

Representatives of workers in the automobile industry throughout the world met at the conference of the International Metalworkers' Federation in London in March and condemned the multinational corporations for neglecting their social responsibilities and for their "divide and rule" tactics against trade unions. The conference demanded a rapid harmonization of wages and working conditions, and contracts with common termination dates in order to prevent the corporations from playing off unions in one country against those in another.

The matter was taken up again at a World Trade Union Economic Conference in Geneva in June, when unions were urged to strengthen cooperation on the international level through research into the activities and organization of multinational companies. In particular, the conference wanted the UN agencies, GATT, the ILO, and the Organization for Economic Cooperation and Development to secure the adoption of an international agreement laying down a code of conduct for multinational companies. In July the International Federation of Chemical and General Workers' Unions initiated a campaign to secure a decisive voice in the investment programs of 40 multinational companies, including Michelin, du Pont, ICI, and CIBA-Geigy.

A European Committee for workers employed on the Concorde SST and the European airbus projects was set up in January at a meeting in Bremen, W.Ger. The meeting brought together delegates from the U.K., France, Italy, West Germany, and the Netherlands. The first meeting of the committee was held on April 28, when demands were made for direct discussions with the employers' organizations and governments responsible for the multinational production of the two aircraft.

An internal restructuring of unions occurred in a number of countries. Early in the year a committee of the Federation of Danish Trade Unions suggested that nine industrial unions should take the place of the existing 60 unions. If implemented, this would eliminate Denmark's biggest union, the General Workers' Union with 50,000 members.

The metalworkers' trade unions in Denmark, Norway, Sweden, and Finland, with a total membership of nearly 700,000, decided to establish a joint secretariat in Stockholm to deal with Nordic and international questions. Two large unions in the U.S., the United Automobile Workers of America and the International Association of Machinists & Aerospace Workers (AFL-CIO), agreed in March not to raid each other's membership, to cooperate in organizing nonunionists, and to set up a joint bargaining committee for the 1971 negotiations in the aviation industry. Also in March, the leaders of the five U.S. postal unions agreed to a merger, subject to membership ratification. It was announced in Italy in November that an agreement had been reached to merge the three main national trade-union federations within the next 15 months. The agreement concerned the Italian General Confederation of Labour, comprising Communists and Socialists; the Italian Confederation of Labour Syndicates, comprising mainly Roman Catholics; and the Italian Union of Labour, a moderate centre organization.   (V. L. A.)

See also Employment, Wages, and Hours; Race Relations.

Encyclopædia Britannica Films. *The Rise of Labor* (1968); *The Industrial Worker* (1969); *The Rise of Big Business* (1970); *The Progressive Era* (1971).

Laos

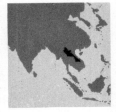

A constitutional monarchy of Southeast Asia, Laos is bounded by China, North and South Vietnam, Cambodia, Thailand, and Burma. Area: 91,400 sq.mi. (236,800 sq.km.). Pop. (1971 est.): 3,033,000. Administrative cap. and largest city: Vientiane (pop., 1968 est., 140,000). Royal cap.: Luang Prabang (pop., 1968 est., 25,000). Language: Lao (official); French and English. Religion: Buddhist; tribal. King, Savang Vatthana; premier in 1971, Prince Souvanna Phouma.

The most important event of 1971 was the Lam Son 719 operation in February and March when 20,000 South Vietnamese troops, with massive U.S. air support, attempted to cut the Ho Chi Minh Trail, the complex communications and supply network running through Laos and linking North Vietnam with Communist forces in South Vietnam, southern Laos, and Cambodia. The operation demonstrated how closely the fate of Laos depended on that of its neighbours and greatly lessened the impact of negotiations aimed at a separate settlement of the Laotian problem. Negotiations, nevertheless, continued between Prince Souvanna Phouma, head of the Vientiane government, and his half brother Prince Souphanouvong, president of the pro-Communist Neo Lao Hak Sat (Laotian Patriotic Front—the political wing of Pathet Lao).

The deteriorating military situation throughout the country, together with the difficulties of recruiting locally, led to the recruitment, at first secret but later officially admitted in the U.S., of Thai reinforcements estimated toward the end of the year at about 8,000 men. Military setbacks, together with uncertainty as to future U.S. involvement in Indochina, produced growing uneasiness in government circles and increasing optimism in the Neo Lao Hak Sat. The trend was reinforced by grave economic difficulties, which finally led to the devaluation of the kip in November.

Launched on February 8, the Lam Son 719 operation led initially to increased extreme right-wing pressure on Prince Souvanna Phouma to abandon official

South Vietnamese troops
land inside Laos
on Feb. 9, 1971,
during Operation Lam
Son 719. The campaign,
designed as a major
assault on the Ho Chi
Minh Trail, received
U.S. air support.
WIDE WORLD

neutrality in favour of open alignment with the anti-Communist regimes of South Vietnam, Cambodia, and Thailand. However, after a month the campaign came to grief at the strategic intersection of Tchepone without the Ho Chi Minh Trail having been completely cut at any point. This development strengthened Souvanna Phouma's position in stressing the need for continuing official contact with North Vietnam, China, the U.S.S.R., and the Neo Lao Hak Sat.

The military respite that had begun in mid-1970 proved short-lived. Early in 1971 North Vietnamese forces began to harass the Long Cheng base, headquarters of Gen. Vang Pao's force of hillmen supported by the U.S. Central Intelligence Agency (CIA), and the base was only saved by the urgent dispatch of several battalions of Thai reinforcements. By March the outskirts of the royal capital, Luang Prabang, were seriously threatened and the airport was temporarily put out of action.

At this delicate juncture for the anti-Communist forces, Souphanouvong on May 8 dispatched his special envoy to the Vientiane government, Prince Souk Vongsak, with a message proposing an immediate general cease-fire, to include the cessation of U.S. bombing throughout the country and the reopening of talks between the two main political groups. There was no immediate reply from the government, and the proposals were renewed in a further message on June 25.

Meanwhile, the North Vietnamese and Pathet Lao had increased their military pressure by taking the Dong Hene area of mid-Laos and, more importantly, almost the entire Boloven Plateau, including the town of Paksong in the south. However, the dry season was drawing to a close, and, as in previous years, the military initiative returned to the anti-Communist forces supported by the U.S. Air Force, since the rains hampered the mobility of the Communists, who had no air support.

Royalist troops encountered little resistance in driving the North Vietnamese back from the immediate outskirts of Luang Prabang. In June–July Gen. Vang Pao's Special Forces, airlifted by U.S. helicopters, took control of the Plaine des Jarres, and four artillery bases manned by Thai forces were established there. Dong Hene was recaptured and government forces advanced to the outskirts of Muong Phalane, which they had lost in January.

At this point, Souvanna Phouma replied to the cease-fire proposals, suggesting neutralization of the Plaine des Jarres with talks to be held alternately there

and at Vientiane. The counterproposals implicitly rejected the idea of an immediate general cease-fire, in accordance with the wishes of the Americans, who sought to obtain a limited cease-fire in the north while retaining the possibility of daily bombing of the Ho Chi Minh Trail in the south. They accordingly were rejected by the Communists, who sought principally a cessation of U.S. bombing of the trail.

Meanwhile, in Vientiane, the government was preoccupied with two unrelated but equally worrysome issues: U.S. pressure on the Laotian government to clamp down on the widespread production of prohibited drugs, which supplied a large proportion of the U.S. black market, and the Sino-U.S. rapprochement. A law prohibiting the production, possession, transport, and sale of opium and its derivatives was reluctantly passed in September. The Sino-U.S. rapprochement was generally better received. Even before U.S. Pres. Richard M. Nixon's projected visit to Peking was announced in July, Souvanna Phouma had proposed the appointment of an ambassador in Peking, where for several years Laos had been represented by a chargé d'affaires.

The government's most permanent worries, nevertheless, continued to be military ones. On September 16 government forces succeeded in recapturing Pak Song, but at the cost of a six-week campaign with a total of 1,200 dead, wounded, or missing; ten days later, in a final rainy season operation, they recaptured the former base of Muong Soui to the east of the Plaine des Jarres. However, with the approach of the dry season the initiative returned to the other side. A Communist attack in late December recaptured the Plaine des Jarres and drove the Thais out of their artillery bases, and in the same month North Vietnamese forces once again took Pak Song. In another development North Vietnamese MiG-21s shot down four U.S. fighter-bombers over northern Laos in December.

In August and September Souvanna Phouma had talks with leaders in Washington, London, and Paris, but despite wide-ranging efforts to strengthen contacts with friendly Western powers he was unable to prevent a 20% devaluation of the kip on November 7.

(M. Cт.)

LAOS
Education. (1968–69) Primary, pupils 205,268, teachers 5,737; secondary, pupils 7,245, teachers 318; vocational, pupils 1,629, teachers 183; teacher training, students 2,443, teachers 190; higher, students 542, teaching staff 27.
Finance. Monetary unit: kip, with an official exchange rate of 240 kips to U.S. $1 (576 kips = £1 sterling) and a free rate (Sept. 27, 1971) of *c.* 500 kips to U.S. $1 (*c.* 1,250 kips = £1 sterling). Budget (1970–71 est.): revenue (excluding foreign aid) 9,048,000,000 kips; expenditure 18,248,000,000 kips (including military expenditure 8,869,000,000 kips).
Foreign Trade. (1969) Imports 19,855,000,000 kips (26% from Thailand, 18% from U.S., 8% from France, 6% from Singapore); exports 1,033,000,000 kips (49% to Malaysia, 37% to Thailand, 7% to South Vietnam). Main exports: tin 54%; timber 36%.
Transport. Roads (1969) 6,275 km. (including 2,156 km. all-weather). Motor vehicles in use (1969): passenger 11,400; commercial (including buses) 2,900. Air traffic (1969): 22,810,000 passenger-km.; freight 734,000 net ton-km. Telephones (Dec. 1969) 1,813. Radio receivers (Dec. 1970) *c.* 200,000.
Agriculture. Production (in 000; metric tons; 1970; 1969 in parentheses): rice 813 (805); coffee *c.* 3.5 (3.5); corn *c.* 25 (25); tobacco *c.* 4 (4). Livestock (in 000; 1969–70): cattle *c.* 420; buffalo *c.* 935; pigs *c.* 1,100; chickens *c.* 11,500.
Industry. Production (in 000): tin concentrates (metric tons; 1969) 1.1; electricity (excluding most industrial production; kw-hr.; 1970) 12,200.

Law

Court Decisions and Related Developments.

Courts of the world were heavily engaged in 1971 in trying cases involving women's rights, the news media, and the environment. Some of these court decisions undoubtedly influenced, or were influenced by, legislative and executive resolutions on these fronts.

Women's Rights. The women's liberation movement was undoubtedly stronger in the United States than in any other country and sparked a number of judicial, legislative, and executive actions. On the judicial level, four cases reached the U.S. Supreme Court, but most of the really significant gains by women were achieved in the lower courts, by out-of-court settlements, and by legislative or executive responses to court decisions.

A good illustration of this point was the unsuccessful legal action that a women's liberation group brought in 1970 in New York City against McSorley's Old Ale House to compel it to discontinue its policy of denying women entry to its taproom. The decision of the court upholding McSorley's right to make this sex discrimination was largely responsible, in the view of many observers, for a strong executive reaction that had far-ranging implications in New York City and New York State. The New York City Council enacted a bill barring sex discrimination in public places. This bill, enthusiastically signed into law by Mayor John V. Lindsay, in effect overturned the McSorley Ale House case, and thereafter women were permitted to enter those premises, though few availed themselves of the opportunity, according to the press. Shortly thereafter, Lindsay signed an executive order barring discrimination on the basis of sex or age in New York City employment and in the execution of contract work for the city. Subsequently the New York State Human Rights Commission started an investigation of sex discrimination. This investigation was not completed by the end of the year, but without doubt the fact that it was being conducted had the immediate effect of removing many obstacles that New York women contended stood in their path to full equality with men.

Some New York men, on the other hand, were now making claims based on sex discrimination that might have been regarded as bizarre a few years before. For example, a male public school teacher in New York City made application to the school board for a "maternity leave," contending that those words include both maternity and child-care leaves and that the board's policy of granting them only to women violated his right to be treated equally. The teacher threatened a lawsuit if his application was denied. In a development that was perhaps parallel, a suit was brought challenging the constitutionality of the U.S. draft law, claiming that it discriminated against men by exempting women.

In California and New Jersey, the highest courts of these states held that women have the right to work as bartenders. In Pennsylvania a woman launched a successful attack in federal court against a state statute that limited the number of hours that women could work. An Ohio statute similarly designed to "protect" women was challenged by the U.S. Justice Department when it brought an action against Libbey-Owens-Ford and the United Glass and Ceramic Workers of North America and its Local 9, contending that the company and union had discriminated against women by agreeing to treat them differently from men with regard to training, promotion, and pay. This action, the first brought by the Justice Department, was defended by Libbey-Owens-Ford on the ground that an Ohio statute required its conduct through provisions protecting women. The lawsuit finally was settled by an agreement on the part of the company and union to give women the same rights that men enjoy.

The U.S. Supreme Court decided two cases involving women's rights. In *Phillips* v. *Martin Marietta* (91 S.Ct. 496) it ruled unanimously that employers could not deny jobs to women on the sole ground that they had small children, unless this ground also was used to deny employment to males. In *Reed* v. *Reed* (91 S.Ct. 917) it held that an Idaho law was unconstitutional because it preferred men to women as administrators of decedents' estates. The court agreed to hear two other important "women's lib" cases. In one

William Frazee, press chief for the "Washington Post," signals victory after the Supreme Court gave its approval for the resumption of publication of the Pentagon papers in the Thursday, July 1, 1971, edition.

WIDE WORLD

case, *Stanley* v. *Illinois* (91 S.Ct. 584), the court agreed to hear arguments as to whether or not an unwed father can be deprived of his child under a law that permits the unwed mother to keep it. In the other case, *Alexander* v. *Louisiana* (91 S.Ct. 946), the court agreed to hear a case in which unconstitutional sex discrimination was alleged because a woman was refused the right to sit on a jury.

In spite of these important developments, the main focus of the women's liberation movement in the U.S. was on reforming the laws concerning abortion. Attacks on these laws were made on the judicial, legislative, and executive levels. On the judicial front, the U.S. Supreme Court considered three cases dealing with the problem of abortion and handed down one decision in 1971 that legal scholars predicted would have great significance. This case, *United States* v. *Vuitch* (91 S.Ct. 1294), dealt with the abortion law of the District of Columbia. Vuitch, a licensed physician, was indicted for performing abortions in violation of a law of the District of Columbia that permits physicians to perform abortions only when they are necessary to preserve the mother's life or health. The indictment was quashed by the trial court on the ground that the statute was too vague to meet con-

French judges silently protest derogatory remarks made by René Tomasini, secretary-general of the Gaullist movement, who called judges "cowards" for being lenient with young agitators.

stitutional requirements. This ruling was appealed to the Supreme Court, where Justice Hugo L. Black (*see* OBITUARIES), writing for a 5–2 majority in one of his last opinions, held that the law met constitutional muster.

Although the opinion was careful to state that no implications or conclusions were to be drawn from it concerning the constitutionality of laws of the states that prohibit abortions or permit them under limited circumstances, many legal scholars proclaimed it as a landmark portending the court's acceptance of many of these laws. The matter probably would be decided in the next term because the court had decided to hear a case challenging the abortion law of Georgia by a pregnant woman who contended that she had a constitutionally protected right to decide whether or not she should have children. The Georgia law under attack provided that an abortion could be performed legally only where there was a danger to the life or health of the mother, where the woman had been raped, or where the child might be defective.

On the state and lower federal court levels beginning in 1970 a number of interesting abortion cases reached diverse results. For example, a federal court held the Texas abortion law unconstitutional because it infringed on the woman's right to decide whether or not she wanted to be a mother. On the other hand, a federal court in Louisiana held constitutional a century-old law that permitted abortion only when two doctors agreed that continued pregnancy would cause the mother's death. A dramatic trial took place in Minnesota as a result of a doctor's decision to perform an abortion on a woman who had contracted German measles, possibly endangering the mental or physical health of the unborn child. The U.S. Supreme Court refused to prohibit the trial and the doctor was convicted and given a suspended sentence. In convicting the doctor the federal trial court held the Minnesota abortion law constitutional. In Pennsylvania, on the contrary, a county court judge held the state abortion law unconstitutional. In Illinois a panel of three federal judges ruled that that state's abortion law was unconstitutional, but the decision was stayed until the Supreme Court could hear the case.

On the executive scene, Pres. Richard M. Nixon directed the Pentagon to make its policy on abortions conform with the laws of the states in which the military personnel involved were situated. In most situations this was an advance for those who desired a more liberal abortion law, but in any case it prevented the conflict of state and federal policy where those policies were different.

Other countries than the U.S. also were concerned with questions of women's rights and particularly with abortion. Results that seemed curious to some observers occurred. Pres. Salvador Allende Gossens of Chile, for example, while praising the rights of women, seemed to be against legalizing abortion, claiming that it, like prostitution, was the result of the failure of the capitalistic system. By the same token, the Communist Party of France rejected the request of women's groups to support their efforts to pass legislation that would permit abortions to be performed where pregnancy resulted from incest or rape or where the mother's life was endangered by it. But the World Council of Churches, conferring in Geneva, Switz., recommended worldwide population control and suggested that discussions begin to determine how this control could be accomplished, including the possibility of abortion. Predictably, Pope Paul VI reiterated his opposition to abortion, and Roman Catholic bishops renewed their fight against attempts to legalize abortion in Italy and Scotland.

In Britain, Sweden, and the Netherlands the women's liberation movement was greatly aided by official support from trade unions. This support may have grown out of the fact that in these countries, as well as others in Europe, the most active members of the movement were women from the working classes, and their goals seemed to be more closely aligned to those of the trade unions than to those having unique significance to women. Thus, although advocating standard "women's lib" claims, such as equal pay for equal jobs, European women, far more than their U.S. counterparts, seemed more concerned with redefining the role of men and women in the family, stressing the need for both men and women to liberate themselves from the traditional roles in which society had cast them to the end of being able to function more effectively as individuals and family members.

News Media. The U.S. Supreme Court handed down an important decision dealing with the matters of "the right to know" and "prior restraint" on the dissemination of information in the celebrated case *New York Times* v. *United States* (91 S.Ct. 2140). The case involved the right of the *New York Times* and *Washington Post* to publish the contents of a classified study, "History of the U.S. Decision-Making Process on Vietnam Policy," which was purloined from the government. The government sought to enjoin the publication of the stolen report. The lower federal courts denied the injunction and with great speed an appeal was taken to the U.S. Supreme Court. The court affirmed the lower courts' decisions, holding that the publication of the study could not be suppressed. Each justice filed a separate opinion, and the decision was based on the philosophy that: "Any system of prior restraints of expression comes to this court bearing a heavy presumption against its constitutional validity. . . . The government thus carries a heavy burden of showing justification for the enforcement of such a restraint." It found that the government had not met that burden.

A concurring opinion by Justice William O. Douglas attracted much attention because of its breadth and vigour. Under his view the government has no right, short of its war powers (which he said can be invoked only if war is officially declared, and that declaration had not been made in the case of the Vietnam conflict), to restrain the press. The public has a right to know. "Secrecy in government is fundamentally anti-democratic, perpetuating bureaucratic errors. Open debate and discussion of public issues are vital to our national health."

Dissenting opinions by Chief Justice Warren E. Burger and Justices John M. Harlan (see OBITUARIES) and Harry A. Blackmun stressed the fact that the case had been rushed through the lower courts and was not ready for rational resolution. "We do not know the facts of the case," said Burger. "No district judge knew all the facts. No court of appeals judge knew all the facts. No member of this court knows all the facts." He opined, therefore, that the case should be remanded for further hearings. In response to the criticism that such a remand would deny the public its right to know immediately facts of great importance, the chief justice stated that the *New York Times* had had unauthorized possession of the stolen documents for three or four months during which it had its experts analyzing them and preparing them for publication. "No doubt this was for a good reason . . . the writing of good news stories takes time. But why should the U.S. government, from whom this information was illegally acquired by someone, along with all the counsel, trial judges, and appellate judges be placed under needless pressure? After these months of deferral, the alleged right-to-know has somehow and suddenly become a right that must be vindicated instanter." (*See* PUBLISHING.)

In France the minister of the interior started 20 libel actions against young revolutionaries of the New Left on account of statements published by them in their newspapers and journals. These actions were thought by some to be designed to appease police, who had come under increasingly sharp public attack for their repeated seizure of these publications and arrest of those selling them.

In Athens the owner of a newspaper was convicted in a criminal trial for printing a misleading headline involving U.S. Vice-Pres. Spiro Agnew, but in other cases courts acquitted a publisher, an editor, and a letter-writing reader of charges that their published statements were likely to harm public confidence in the state.

In South Africa, an English-language newspaper and its informants were convicted in a criminal case because of statements they published on prison conditions in the country. The case caused many people to worry that censorship might be imposed on the English-language press, widely regarded by many as an important moderating force in that country.

Environment. In the U.S. a great number of cases were brought by the Justice Department and by state environmental protection agencies to recover damages or to enjoin various companies and others from polluting air or water. The U.S. Supreme Court, in an 8–1 decision, declined to take original jurisdiction of a case brought by the state of Ohio against three chemical companies for allegedly polluting Lake Erie. The Supreme Court said that it did not have the expertise to hear the case on the trial level, and it stated that it would not hear pollution cases that had not first been tried in the lower courts.

In West Germany a shipowner and some of his employees were tried for dumping pollutants in the Rhine River. In Italy a magistrate filed charges against 449 companies in Milan, accusing them of polluting three rivers. (W. D. HD.)

International Law. *The Sea.* There were three major areas of concern in 1971: pollution, to be discussed at the Stockholm Conference on Protection of the Environment in 1972, and rights to the sea floor and exclusive fishery rights, both to be discussed at the United Nations Conference on the Law of the Sea to be held in Geneva in 1973. Preparatory work for both conferences resulted in many meetings, working papers, and drafts. There were also many treaties, national laws, and arrangements on particular aspects of marine law.

The main sources of pollution were (from the land) sewage and industrial waste and (from the sea) oil spillage and dumping of waste. Little international action had been taken so far on outflow damage, although countries were becoming aware of its dangers and the need to enact legislation providing indirect control through river pollution regulation. But only Norway, in legislation passed during the year, appeared to have taken specific account of outflow into coastal waters. The emphasis had been rather on control of offshore pollution. The draft Oslo agreement to ban dumping of industrial waste in the North Atlantic and discussions on a similar ban for the North Sea and the Mediterranean marked a new subject of public concern, sparked off by the U.S. proposal to dump unwanted stocks of poison gas into the west Atlantic, together with the discovery by Scandinavian fishermen of mustard gas that had leaked from crumbling concrete containers in the Baltic.

Most activity was centred on oil pollution from ships at sea, whether from the cleaning of tanks or spillage after collision. Apart from certain measures taken by the Inter-Governmental Maritime Consultative Organization (IMCO), amending the 1954 and 1962 conventions on Prevention of Pollution of the Sea by Oil, the pioneering work here was the U.K. Oil in Navigable Waters (Amending) Act, which gave the government wide powers to reduce danger from oil pollution after collisions and even authorized action against foreign ships in international waters. An Italian bill, introduced in August, was less bold and related only to acts within Italian territorial waters, while the Australian government was preparing to follow the British example. The preparatory committee for the Stockholm conference was also working on a draft treaty to forbid various forms of marine pollution.

Pollution danger also led to the institution of navigation control to avoid collision hazards. Navigation lanes had for some time been in voluntary operation in the Øresund (Sound) and the English Channel. During 1971, as a result of further disasters, the U.K., France, Belgium, and the Netherlands took a further step toward enforcement by agreeing to the establishment of a radar surveillance station to survey all shipping using the Dover Strait and a systematic identification of vessels traveling the wrong way in traffic lanes. IMCO had also recommended that member governments make it an offense for vessels flying their flags to go against the approved traffic flow when using any of the 60–70 traffic separation programs so far approved.

There was little action with regard to the seabed during the year, as the UN continued its discussions, particularly on the U.S. and U.K. proposals for exercise of jurisdiction over the seabed beyond the outer limits of the continental shelf. The General Assembly adopted a declaration in December 1970 affirming the nonexclusive nature of such areas and the need for them to be exploited "for the benefit of mankind as a whole." In February, the treaty prohibiting emplacement of nuclear weapons on the seabed and ocean floor was signed by 63 nations. Other significant events were the conclusion of treaties between West Germany on the one hand and the Netherlands and Denmark on the other delimiting their respective continental shelf boundaries. These came about after two years of negotiation following the judgment of the International Court of Justice in the North Sea Continental Shelf cases. In addition, the Commission of the European Communities issued a memorandum claiming jurisdiction of the Treaty of Rome over all economic activities pursued under the authority of the member states in or upon their respective continental shelves.

Iceland's intention to extend its fishery limits to coincide with its continental shelf was put into effect after a general election in which it was an important platform issue, but in the slightly altered form of 50 mi. Negotiations had begun with the U.K. to denounce the existing U.K.-Iceland treaty as from the fall of 1972. As with the Canadian Arctic waters legislation of June 1970, Iceland was unwilling to allow the issue to go to the International Court of Justice, despite the provision to that effect in the Anglo-Icelandic treaty. The Canadian "fisheries closing lines" under the 1970 act had been promulgated across the Gulf of St. Lawrence, Bay of Fundy, Queen Charlotte Sound, and Dixon Strait. The French government introduced a bill to extend its territorial waters to 12 miles, specifically to give it powers to control shipping hazards in the English Channel.

Finally, the EEC adopted a common fisheries policy providing for free access to each other's maritime waters by fishermen of all member states. This was strongly resisted by the four applicant countries, who were unwilling to surrender control over their inshore fishery grounds.

Hijacking and Kidnapping. At Guatemala a protocol was concluded to the Warsaw Convention, after many years of agitation, raising the maximum compensation for death or injury to air passengers to $100,000 per passenger. Otherwise, the main emphasis was on hijacking. Many countries introduced domestic legislation to impose penalties for the hijacking of aircraft, such as the U.K. Hijacking Act. This was passed in implementation of the Hague Convention for the Suppression of Unlawful Seizure of Aircraft (International Civil Aviation Organization [ICAO], December 1970), which made hijacking an extraditable offense even when carried out for political reasons; the convention came into force in October 1971. A number of extradition treaties concluded during the year, for example that between the U.S. and New Zealand, included a similar provision. Later in 1971 an ICAO-sponsored conference in Montreal resulted in a Convention for the Suppression of Unlawful Acts Against the Safety of Civil Aviation.

Closely linked with some cases of hijacking were the kidnappings of diplomats, mainly in Latin America although also in Canada and Europe, for political ends. The Organization of American States adopted a Convention to Prevent and Punish the Act of Terrorism Taking the Form of Crimes Against Persons and Related Extortion That Are of International Significance (Washington, February). This also made the offenses extraditable in spite of their political nature. The protection of journalists in theatres of war was the subject of a new UN convention.

Economic Relations. International economic relations underwent a serious crisis when the Bretton Woods formula broke down under U.S. Pres. Richard M. Nixon's measures to protect the dollar, and the EEC suffered severe disruption of its common agricultural policy and a setback in its plans for a single currency when the West German mark and the Netherlands guilder were floated. The General Agreement on Tariffs and Trade (GATT) principles came under strain following adoption of an import surcharge by the U.S. (later rescinded) and Denmark; protests concerning a breach of GATT rules continued to be made also against the EEC preferential trade agreements with Mediterranean countries and the proposed adoption of an industrial free trade arrangement between the Community and Western European countries not joining the EEC. Against this, GATT agreed in June to waive its Article I for ten years as far as was necessary to allow more developed countries to grant preferential tariff treatment to products originating in less developed countries, without having to apply most-favoured-nation treatment to other developed member countries. The EEC was the first to implement these generalized preferences.

More detailed economic legislation included a Comecon system of standardized bills of lading and, in 1970, a Council of Europe convention on stops on bearer securities in international circulation. In the field of industrial property the important World Patent Cooperation Agreement, signed in Washington, established a central filing system and the use of standardized international patent applications. The Council of Europe adopted an Agreement on the Classification of Patents and Investors' Certificates, and the Benelux Uniform Trade Mark Law, signed in 1962, at last came into force.

International Organizations. Membership in international organizations aroused particular attention in two cases. The United Nations voted heavily in favour of admitting representatives of mainland China to the Chinese seat in the Security Council

Below, Capt. Ernest Medina awaits a verdict after his court-martial at Ft. McPherson, Ga. Charged with premeditated murder of Vietnamese civilians at My Lai in 1968, he was acquitted Sept. 22, 1971. Bottom, Lieut. William Calley leaves court-martial building at Ft. McPherson after he was granted permission not to testify at Medina's trial. Calley previously had been convicted of murder at My Lai.
WIDE WORLD

WIDE WORLD

and General Assembly. The existing representatives were expressly expelled, and no decision was taken as to the position of Taiwan, claimed by both rivals as an integral part of China.

The other membership drama centred upon the European Communities. Negotiations with the four applicant countries (U.K., Ireland, Denmark, and Norway) were concluded in midsummer, subject to settlement of a few outstanding issues. The U.K. Parliament voted in October in favour of signing the Treaty of Accession and the government gave notice of its intention to withdraw from EFTA from Jan. 1, 1973. The other three applicants were to hold referenda during 1972. In the spring, Sweden, which had been sitting on the fence, firmly declared its unwillingness to join.

The European Court of Human Rights issued two judgments. In *Ringeisen* v. *Austria* the court upheld the applicant's complaint of excessive pretrial detention under Art. 5(3) of the convention. In the *Belgian Vagrancy* cases the court first held that it had jurisdiction to determine whether an application was admissible even though the Commission had already done so; it then went on to hold that there had been a violation by Belgium of Art. 5(4) in that the applicants, who had been imprisoned under the vagrancy laws, were denied any judicial appellate remedy.

The International Court of Justice issued its advisory opinion on South West Africa (Namibia) in which it supported the UN Security Council and General Assembly in their purported termination of South Africa's mandate over South West Africa. Later in the year the court was asked to decide whether the ICAO Council was entitled to deal with a complaint by Pakistan against India's refusal to allow overflying rights to Pakistani aircraft moving from the western to the eastern segment of the country.

Two further significant events were the signing in August of a permanent charter for Intelsat in Washington, which also involved a relaxation of the monopoly position maintained until then in its control by the U.S.; and the creation by the Nordic countries of a Council of Ministers, the first permanent institutional arrangement to be made between the Nordic nations.

Family Law. In the first six months after the Italian divorce act came into force, 40,382 petitions were filed and 4,732 divorces granted. The Constitutional Court held that the act was constitutional and not in breach of the Concordat with the Vatican. However, over 350,000 signatures were deposited in request for a referendum on continuance of the act. Referendum procedures were set in motion by the Court of Cassation during the year and a referendum was expected to be held in the spring of 1972. The Constitutional Court also held that the ban on the promotion and sale of contraceptive materials was unconstitutional and that the provisions in the inheritance laws discriminating against illegitimate children, whether or not recognized, were also unconstitutional.

In West Germany the divorce bill came before the Bundestag and a family courts bill was introduced to provide for special courts to grant divorce decrees and to settle questions of custody and maintenance of children. The Dutch lower house passed a divorce bill providing for breakdown of marriage as a ground for divorce.

Censorship. In Britain the unprecedented sentences of imprisonment given the three editors of the under-

PETER L. GOULD

William Baird (right) displays birth-control devices at lecture in Huntington, N.Y. Police arrested Baird and Mrs. Nancy Manfredonia (standing), who took her 14-month-old daughter to the lecture, for impairing the morals of a minor.

ground paper *Oz* for obscenity were quashed by the Court of Appeal but accompanied by some disturbing statements of the law by the lord chief justice. The conviction of the publisher of *The Little Red School Book* for obscenity in advocating unorthodox views on sexual conduct was, however, upheld. The mailing of nonobscene advertising matter relating to publications describing the techniques of sexual intercourse was made an offense under the Unsolicited Goods and Services Act.

In France the Lindon Commission recommended the adoption of a press council similar to the British one. The West German bill to decriminalize pornography met with considerable opposition and was likely to be passed in a diluted form. The Norwegian Storting rejected a government bill to criminalize war propaganda, thus preventing the government's ratifying the UN Civil and Political Rights Convention without a reservation. An unsuccessful prosecution under the Official Secrets Acts of the U.K. *Sunday Telegraph* and others for publication of an official report on Biafra during the Nigerian civil war led to pressure for reform of the legislation and the setting up of the Franks Committee to study the matter. The Younger Committee on Privacy completed its work.

Bills introduced in Canada and West Germany gave protection against eavesdropping and telephone tapping—in the latter case to remedy a Constitutional Court decision of December 1970, which held that a person upon whom the police were eavesdropping was entitled to be told so. In Sweden, telephone tapping by the police in cases of suspected drug offenses was permitted for a further year. The Danish Criminal Law Committee's report on privacy recommended protection against bugging and spying in the home. The Council of Europe reportedly was considering alternative drafts for a European Convention on Protection of Privacy. (N. M. H.)

See also Crime; Defense; Police; Race Relations.

ENCYCLOPÆDIA BRITANNICA FILMS. *Equality Under Law—The Lost Generation of Prince Edward County* (1967); *Freedom to Speak* (*N.Y.* v. *Feiner*) (1967); *Equality Under Law—California Fair Housing Cases* (1969); *Free Press vs. Fair Trial by Jury—The Sheppard Case* (1969); *The Schempp Case—Bible Reading in Public Schools* (1969).

Lebanon

A republic of the Middle East, Lebanon is bounded by Syria, Israel, and the Mediterranean Sea. Area: 3,950 sq.mi. (10,230 sq.km.). Pop. (1969 est.): 2,645,000. Cap. and largest city: Beirut (pop., 1964 est., 131,-500). Language: Arabic. Religion: Christian majority with strong Muslim minority. President in 1971, Suleiman Franjieh; prime minister, Saeb Salam.

Lebanon's internal problems in 1971 were alleviated by two major factors: the weakening of the Palestinian guerrillas resulting from the Jordanian civil war, and the marked improvement in relations with Syria. The guerrillas continued their actions against Israel in Lebanon's southern border areas, provoking occasional reprisal raids by Israeli forces into Lebanese territory. These emphasized Lebanon's military weakness but did not cause as much public alarm as before. During the year the minister of defense toured Italy, Spain, France, Britain, and the U.S.S.R. looking for arms supplies as part of a plan to spend $70 million on modernizing the armed forces. A $15 million deal for the purchase of arms from the Soviet Union was concluded in November.

The improvement in internal security due to the inability of the Palestinian guerrillas to act any longer as an independent power centre was partly offset by other disorders. The legalizing of the Parti Populaire Syrienne and the release of its leaders led to a revival of the party's long-standing rivalry with the right-wing Christian Katayib Party, and several armed clashes occurred. A series of strikes and disturbances in the north organized by the left-wing Democratic Socialist Movement in alliance with radical peasant groups in the Akkar and Hermel regions led to a security sweep through the north by government forces in early June. In March and in May there were strikes by university students demanding reforms in the educational system. There also were strikes by bakers, taxicab drivers, government schoolteachers, and bank employees, but a general strike of all unions was narrowly avoided in May by means of a general 5% increase in wages and an increase in the minimum wage.

The extraparliamentary government led by the veteran politician Saeb Salam was fairly successful in maintaining its reformist image in the country, but it faced a severe test in its efforts to raise new revenues to meet the demands of essential economic development and increased defense costs. The economy benefited from a sharp upswing in agricultural and industrial exports and tourism, and Beirut's transit trade continued to enjoy a special advantage from the closing of the Suez Canal.

The improvement in relations with Syria, which began with the change in the Syrian regime in November 1970, was confirmed by President Franjieh's visit to Damascus in March—the first by a Lebanese head of state since either country's independence. A joint Syrian-Lebanese commission was set up to settle outstanding problems concerning Lebanese export and transit trade. Relations with Saudi Arabia (Lebanon's principal foreign market) also improved as a result of the Lebanese government's decision to license the construction of the nation's third oil refinery, in which the Saudis would hold a 50% interest.

(P. MD.)

LEBANON

Education. (1968–69) Primary, pupils 425,840; secondary, pupils 129,960; primary and secondary, teachers 29,974; vocational, pupils 2,103; teacher training, students 2,661, teachers 416; higher (including 4 universities), students, 33,587, teaching staff 1,697.

Finance. Monetary unit: Lebanese pound, with a free rate (Sept. 27, 1971) of L£3.15 to U.S. $1 (L£7.81 = £1 sterling). Gold, SDRs, and foreign exchange, central bank: (June 1971) U.S. $420.9 million; (June 1970) U.S. $348.1 million. Budget (1970 est.) balanced at L£736.6 million. Gross national expenditure: (1968) L£4,428 million; (1967) L£3,961 million. Money supply: (June 1971) L£1,831 million; (June 1970) L£1,647 million.

Foreign Trade. (1970) Imports L£1,886 million; exports L£563 million; transit trade L£1,532,938,000. Import sources: Switzerland 12%; U.K. 11%; U.S. 10%; France 9%; West Germany 9%; Italy 7%; Iraq 5%. Export destinations: Saudi Arabia 16%; Kuwait 10%; Syria 6%; Jordan 5%; Iraq 5%; Libya 5%. Main exports: fruit and vegetables 13%; precious stones and metals 10%; machinery 10%; textiles and clothing 8%; transport equipment 7%; chemicals 6%; livestock and meat 5%. Tourism (1969): visitors 777,-100; gross receipts U.S. $103 million.

Transport and Communications. Roads (1970) 7,350 km. Motor vehicles in use (1970): passenger 136,016; commercial 14,795. Railways: (1969) 335 km.; traffic (1970) 7.4 million passenger-km., freight 19.9 million net ton-km. Air traffic (1970): 830 million passenger-km.; freight 137,570,000 net ton-km. Shipping (1970): vessels 100 gross tons and over 79; gross tonnage 181,790. Telephones (Jan. 1969) 150,370. Radio receivers (Dec. 1969) 590,000. Television receivers (Dec. 1968) 375,000.

Agriculture. Production (in 000; metric tons; 1969; 1968 in parentheses): grapes 77 (84); wheat 33 (48); tomatoes 70 (60); dry beans 30 (38); olives 46 (32); figs 13 (13); bananas 29 (30); oranges 162 (175); lemons 65 (63); apples c. 70 (163); tobacco 6.7 (6.6). Livestock (in 000; 1969–70): cattle c. 85; goats c. 330; sheep c. 214; poultry 17,463.

Industry. Production (in 000; metric tons; 1970): cement 1,339; petroleum products (1969) 1,779; electricity (excluding most industrial production; kw-hr.) 1,229,000.

Lesotho

A constitutional monarchy of southern Africa, Lesotho is completely surrounded by South Africa. Area: 11,720 sq.mi. (30,355 sq.km.). Pop. (1971 est.): 1,060,000. Cap. and largest city: Maseru (pop., 1971 est., 16,250). Language: English and Sesotho (official). Religion: about 80% Christian. Chief of state in 1971, Paramount Chief Moshoeshoe II; prime minister, Chief Leabua Jonathan.

LESOTHO

Education. (1968) Primary, pupils 179,386, teachers (1967) 3,065; secondary, pupils 4,141, teachers (1967) 152; vocational, pupils 511, teachers (1967) 44; teacher training, students 675, teachers (1967) 47; higher (University of Botswana, Lesotho, and Swaziland), students (1969) 388, teaching staff (1967) 60.

Finance and Trade. Monetary unit: South African rand, with a par value of R 0.71 to U.S. $1 (R 1.71 = £1 sterling) and a free rate (Sept. 27, 1971) of R 1.77 to £1 sterling. Budget (1970–71 rev. est.): revenue R 11,704,510; expenditure R 11,041,000. Foreign trade (1969): imports R 23,907,000; exports R 4,069,000. Main exports: diamonds 29%; wool 21%; cattle 14%; mohair 12%; wheat 10%; peas and beans 5%. Most trade is with South Africa.

Agriculture. Production (in 000; metric tons; 1969; 1968 in parentheses): corn c. 70 (c. 112); wheat c. 40 (c. 60); wool c. 2.2 (2.3); meat 22 (22). Livestock (in 000; Feb. 1970): cattle c. 400; goats c. 930; sheep (Sept.) c. 1,700.

A return to political calm was evident during 1971, with Chief Jonathan successfully defusing a tense situation. Opposition Congress Party leader Ntsu Mokhehle was released on June 8 after more than a year in prison, and Chief Jonathan's confidence was further exemplified by subsequent tours through ten African countries to explain Lesotho's policies, and by attendance at the Organization of African Unity, the UN, and the Commonwealth conference at Singapore. The British Conservative government's restoration of aid in mid-1970 helped to revitalize the regime after four months on the defensive, and to alleviate distress caused by the serious 1970 drought, estimated by the minister of agriculture to have cost more than R10 million.

Despite rapid development of the diamond industry (and record exports), giving more home employment, Lesotho remained bound economically to South Africa. Much of its large trade deficit was met by remittances from the 62,500 workers employed in South Africa in 1970 and from vastly increased receipts following the revised Customs Union Agreement (R 4.7 million for 1970–71). The largest single investment in the country was the R 1.6 million Holiday Inn, one of a worldwide chain of U.S.-owned hotels. (M. Mr.)

Liberia

A republic on the west coast of Africa, Liberia is bordered by Sierra Leone, Guinea, and Ivory Coast. Area: 43,000 sq.mi. (111,400 sq.km.). Pop. (1970 est.): 1,171,000. Cap. and largest city: Monrovia (pop., 1970, 100,000). Language: English (official) and tribal dialects. Religion: mainly animist. Presidents in 1971, William V. S. Tubman and, from July 23, William R. Tolbert, Jr.

LIBERIA
Education. (1968–69) Primary, pupils 120,101, teachers 3,211; secondary, pupils 12,866, teachers 669; vocational, pupils 913, teachers 81; teacher training, pupils 348, teachers 34; higher, students 1,282, teaching staff 163.
Finance. Monetary unit: Liberian dollar, at par with the U.S. dollar (L$2.40 = £1 sterling) and with a free rate (Sept. 27, 1971) of L£2.48 to £1 sterling. Budget (total; 1969 est.): revenue L$58 million; expenditure L$60.1 million.
Foreign Trade. (1969) Imports L$114.6 million; exports L$195.9 million. Import sources: U.S. 34%; West Germany 14%; U.K. 8%; Japan 9%; Sweden 5%. Export destinations: U.S. 28%; West Germany 23%; Netherlands 10%; Italy 9%; Belgium-Luxembourg 7%; Japan 6%; France 6%; U.K. 6%. Main exports: iron ore 70%; rubber 16%; diamonds 5%.
Transport and Communications. Roads (1969) c. 3,700 km. Motor vehicles in use (1969): passenger 14,700; commercial (including buses) 8,700. Railways (1969) 493 km. Shipping (1970): merchant vessels 100 gross tons and over 1,869 (mostly owned by U.S. and other foreign interests); gross tonnage 33,296,644. Telephones (Jan. 1970) 6,051. Radio receivers (Dec. 1969) 152,000. Television receivers (Dec. 1969) 6,000.
Agriculture. Production (in 000; metric tons; 1969; 1968 in parentheses): rice c. 152 (152); cassava c. 370 (c. 372); rubber (exports) 67 (64); palm kernels (exports) 12 (12); cocoa (1970–71) 1.9, (1969–70) 1.8; coffee c. 4.5 (c. 3.9). Livestock (in 000; Aug. 1970): cattle c. 28; pigs c. 82; sheep c. 150; goats c. 139.
Industry. Production (in 000; 1969): iron ore (metal content; metric tons) 14,786; diamonds (exports; metric carats) 836; electricity (kw-hr.) 632,000.

William V. S. Tubman, president of Liberia since 1944, died in London after surgery on July 23. Tubman, 75, had been elected to a seventh term as president in May. William R. Tolbert, 58, vice-president for 19 years, was sworn in as president the same day that Tubman died.

In his long tenure as chief executive, Tubman had increased the national budget from less than $1 million to more than $60 million a year; pacified some 28 indigenous tribal groups and integrated them into the country's political life; extended suffrage to women; and established freedom of religion as a national policy. He also opened Liberia's vast iron and rubber resources to foreign investment and encouraged the construction of schools, hospitals, seaports, railroads, hydroelectric dams, television and radio stations, roads, and a new business centre in Monrovia.

Thousands of Liberians poured into Monrovia to mourn the death of their "chief of chiefs." From the United States came a delegation headed by presidential counselor Robert H. Finch. Heading the list of foreign dignitaries were nine African heads of state, including Emperor Haile Selassie of Ethiopia.

Tolbert's reserved manner stood in sharp contrast to the ebullient, easygoing personality of his predecessor. Nevertheless, Tubman had made it clear in May 1971 that he regarded Tolbert as a worthy successor. Tolbert indicated that, in order to progress, Liberians must "work harder and sacrifice everything for the benefit of the country." He regarded keeping the people of Liberia united as the most urgent task facing his administration but also said that, "as a developing country, we have many problems—we need more roads throughout the country; we need more schools, and we need a higher standard of living for our people." A World Bank loan of $4.7 million, announced June 24, was expected to help to achieve these goals. (Ri. W.)

Libraries

In the field of international librarianship, the climax of 1971 was the annual session of the International Federation of Library Associations (IFLA), held at Liverpool City libraries by invitation of the British Library Association. Some 750 participants from 60 different countries were in attendance, and the session was preceded by a UNESCO seminar on advanced librarianship for less developed countries. The main theme of the IFLA session was "The International Organization of the Library Profession."

The UNESCO Department of Documentation, Libraries and Archives completed a number of research studies, including *A Handbook on Library Statistics; Public Library Legislation; The Role of Libraries and Documentation Services in Economic and Social Development;* and *The Application of Mechanized Methods for the Dissemination of UNESCO Reports and Documents.* UNESCO's Computerized Documentation Service (CDS) became operational in 1971. A master negative microfiche would be made for all documents, so that any document could be distributed on demand, either on positive microfiche or in enlarged form. UNESCO continued to operate pilot projects for the development of services, including one on public and school library development in Ceylon and one in Honduras on school libraries for Central America.

UNESCO also continued to send library experts to various countries under its participation program, and the UNESCO microfilm unit completed its work of microfilming important books and documents in Algeria, Nepal, Sierra Leone, and Sudan. Studies began on the international bibliographical control of publications, to be based on computerized national bibliographies. Following the computerization of its West German counterpart some years earlier, from the beginning of 1971 the British National Bibliography was prepared from the MARC (machine-readable cataloging) service, in collaboration with the Library of Congress, Washington, D.C. Finally, in collaboration with the International Council of Scientific Unions (ICSU), UNESCO's science section completed its feasibility study on UNISIST, the proposed world system of scientific and technical information.

Preparations were well under way in 1971 for UNESCO's 1972 International Book Year, in which all organizations in the book field would take part.

In Finland a new library for Helsinki Technical University, designed by Alvar Aalto, and the large new Töölö branch of Helsinki public libraries were opened, continuing the fine tradition of Finnish library architecture. Finnish library development was strengthened in 1971 by coordination of research in a Joint Committee for Library Research, and by the establishment of the first chair in library and information science at Tampere University.

The monthly issues of the *Bulletin des bibliothèques de France* revealed steady progress in improving library services, the biggest achievements of 1970–71 being the opening of the new building for the university library at Rennes, the university library at Nanterre (Paris), and of the public library at Massy, near Paris. The list of 57 functioning central libraries in the May issue of the *Bulletin des bibliothèques de France* indicated the degree to which the French departmental library network had developed, while the newly designed "bibliobuses" (bookmobiles) at Brest and Nice were symbolic of the efforts being made to bring new services to many districts.

The most important news in the United Kingdom was the publication of the White Paper on *The British Library,* providing the machinery for bringing the British Museum Library, the National Central Library, and the National Lending Library for Science and Technology (NLLST) into one unified national framework, which would also include the British National Bibliography. The paper gave authority to the

As a deterrent to rising book thefts, Pace College in New York City installed an electronic Checkpoint system during 1971. Two sensing screens detect laminated plates pasted inside books.
THE "NEW YORK TIMES"

plan to build a new national library opposite the British Museum in London. There were 18,285 members in the Library Association in 1970, and 2,575 full-time students at schools of librarianship. The annual amount spent on the public library service rose by 15% to over £60 million.

On July 1 the U.S. Library of Congress started its experimental "Cataloging in Publication" program, under which cataloging information was provided for publication in the books themselves. Each library receiving these books could catalog them for use more quickly; it would also be a great help to very small libraries without catalogers. The information included classification numbers and the International Standard Book Number (ISBN). The promotion and defense of intellectual freedom had been a task of the American Library Association (ALA) since it established its Office for Intellectual Freedom in 1967; at the end of 1969 the Freedom to Read Foundation was formed, to support and defend librarians whose jobs were endangered when they challenged violations of such freedom. At the ALA conference at Dallas, Tex., in June 1971, an advisory statement was made by the Office for Intellectual Freedom interpreting the "Library Bill of Rights." The ALA also established an Office for Library Service to the Disadvantaged and Unserved. The Lyndon Baines Johnson Library complex on the University of Texas campus at Austin was dedicated May 22. The library contained over 31 million pages of documents and some 500,000 photographs pertaining to the Johnson presidency.

A large new building in Moscow was nearing completion for the Fundamental Library of the Social Sciences of the U.S.S.R. Academy of Sciences, designed largely under the guidance of the architect F. N. Pascenko, a specialist in library planning. In the Ukraine the 1965–70 five-year plan added 3,905 new libraries, making a total of over 69,000 libraries in the republic. (A. TH.)

ENCYCLOPÆDIA BRITANNICA FILMS. *Library of Congress* (1969).

The LBJ Presidential Library, dedicated on May 22, 1971, in Austin, Tex., contains more than 31 million pages of documents from the Johnson administration.

COURTESY, LYNDON BAINES JOHNSON LIBRARY

Libya

A socialist republic on the north coast of Africa, Libya is bounded by Egypt, Sudan, Tunisia, Algeria, Niger, and Chad. Area: 680,000 sq.mi. (1,760,000 sq.km.). Pop. (1971 est.): 2,010,000. Co-capitals and largest cities: Tripoli (pop., 1970 est., 264,000) and Benghazi (pop., 1970 est., 170,000); federal administrative centre: al-Bayda (pop., 1968 est., 15,000). Language: Arabic. Religion: predominantly Muslim. Leader of the Revolutionary Command Council and prime minister in 1971, Col. Muammar al-Qaddafi.

Few changes were made in the 17-man Cabinet (12 of whom were members of the Revolutionary Command Council) in 1971, and the population as a whole seemed to adjust to the military regime. Trials of political and other figures charged with corruption during the previous regime began in August. Considering the charges, the trials concluded with comparatively light sentences, generally four years of imprisonment.

Colonel al-Qaddafi (*see* BIOGRAPHY) seemed to press a claim to Gamal Abd-an-Nasser's mantle in the Middle East. He was the most vigorous of leaders in pursuing Arab unity and in speaking out for the Palestinian cause. A "summit meeting" in Damascus August 18–20 was followed on September 1 by a referendum of the 42 million people of Libya, Syria, and Egypt, in which federation was approved unanimously.

That the Sudan was not associated in the federation was a disappointment to the Libyan leader, especially after the cooperation evident in 1970. The accord of the Sudanese and Libyan leaders was confirmed, however, after the failure of a supposed "Communist coup" against Sudan's President Gaafar Nimeiry (*see* BIOGRAPHY) in July. Qaddafi accomplished this by forcing down a British airliner at Benghazi in mid-flight from London to Khartoum, and detaining Col. Babakr an-Nur Osman, a leader of the coup who was to have been the Sudan's new president. He later was executed by a Sudanese firing squad.

Another Tripoli summit meeting in July criticized King Husain of Jordan for his treatment of the Palestinian guerrillas. Relations were also strained with Morocco following the premature support given by Qaddafi to the abortive coup there in July.

In April, Western oil companies agreed to a 90-cent price increase to $3.45 a barrel. In December Libya nationalized the British Petroleum Co. and withdrew its funds from British banks in retaliation for Britain's failure to stop Iran from seizing three small Persian Gulf islands.

(Jo. A. A.)

Liechtenstein

A constitutional monarchy between Switzerland and Austria, Liechtenstein is united with Switzerland by a customs and monetary union. Area: 62 sq.mi. (160 sq.km.). Pop. (1970): 21,078. Cap.: Vaduz (pop., 1970, 3,790). Largest city: Schaan (pop., 1970, 3,878). Language: German. Religion: Roman Catholic 92.3%. Sovereign prince, Francis Joseph II; chief of government in 1971, Alfred Hilbe.

A referendum of the all-male electorate on Feb. 28, 1971, defeated by 1,897 to 1,817 a constitutional amendment to grant women's suffrage. The amendment had passed Parliament by a decisive vote on Dec. 18, 1970. Liechtenstein thus remained the only Western European state to deny women the right to vote, Switzerland having approved female suffrage on the federal level on February 7.

The defeat engendered great surprise in the principality. Both major political parties, leaders of the Roman Catholic Church, and virtually all of the young had actively supported the measure.

Many said the referendum came too soon after the Swiss vote and that Liechtensteiners did not want to appear to be meekly following the Swiss example. Others blamed the peasant mentality of the older inhabitants. Finally, it was pointed out that only one-third of the inhabitants had full citizenship rights and that many feared domination by foreigners.

(R. D. Ho.)

LIBYA

Education. (1966–67) Primary, pupils 215,841, teachers 7,278; secondary, pupils 26,846, teachers 1,807; vocational, pupils 1,064, teachers 121, teacher training, students 4,681, teachers 405; higher (at University of Libya), students 2,215, teaching staff 252.

Finance. Monetary unit: Libyan dinar (replacing the Libyan pound at par from Sept. 1, 1971), with a par value of 0.357 dinars to U.S. $1 (0.857 dinars = £1 sterling) and a free rate (Sept. 27, 1971) of 0.342 dinars to U.S. $1 (0.848 dinars = £1 sterling). Gold and foreign exchange, central bank: (June 1971) U.S. $2,324,400,000; (June 1970) U.S. $1,468,500,000. Budget (total; 1970–71 est.) balanced at 382.7 million dinars. Gross national product: (1968) 908.7 million dinars; (1967) 664.1 million dinars. Money supply: (March 1971) 280,470,000 dinars; (March 1970) 209,460,000 dinars. Cost of living (Tripoli; 1964 = 100): (Dec. 1970) 137; (Dec. 1969) 137.

Foreign Trade. (1970) Imports 198 million dinars; exports 844,960,000 dinars. Import sources (1969): Italy 23%; U.S. 19%; U.K. 12%; West Germany 9%; France 5%; Japan 5%. Export destinations (1969): Italy 23%; West Germany 22%; U.K. 14%; France 12%; Netherlands 10%; U.S. 5%; Spain 5%. Main export crude oil 99.5%.

Transport and Communications. Roads (with improved surface; 1969) *c.* 5,200 km. (including 1,822 km. of coast road). Motor vehicles in use (1969): passenger 90,700; commercial (including buses) 40,700. Railways (1969) 165 km. Air traffic (1969): 191,503,000 passenger-km.; freight 1,864,000 net ton-km. Ships entered (1969) vessels totaling 4,908,000 net registered tons; goods loaded (1969) 148,061,000 metric tons, unloaded (1969) 3,099,000 metric tons. Telephones (Dec. 1969) 34,790. Radio receivers (Dec. 1969) 77,000.

Agriculture. Production (in 000; metric tons; 1970; 1969 in parentheses): wheat 21 (78); barley 53 (124); olives (1969) 33, (1968) 140; dates 49 (55). Livestock (in 000; 1969–70): goats 1,234; sheep 2,163; cattle 108; camels 163; asses 98.

Industry. Production (in 000; metric tons; 1969): salt 9; crude oil (1970) 162,692; electricity (Tripolitania; excluding most industrial production; kw-hr.) 351,000.

LIECHTENSTEIN

Education. Primary (1967–68), pupils 2,295, teachers 77; secondary (1968–69), pupils 938, teachers 76.

Finance and Trade. Monetary unit: Swiss franc, with a par value of SFr. 4.08 to U.S. $1 (SFr. 9.80 = £1 sterling) and a free rate (Sept. 27, 1971) of SFr. 3.97 to U.S. $1. Budget (1971 est.): revenue SFr. 54,091,000; expenditure SFr. 43,227,000. Exports (home produce; 1969) SFr. 280,270,000. Main export destination Switzerland 35%. Main exports: light manufactures; corn, vegetables, fruit, wine, livestock products. Tourism (1969): visitors 66,109; gross receipts *c.* SFr. 16 million.

Agriculture. Livestock (in 000; April 1970): cattle *c.* 7; sheep *c.* 1; pigs *c.* 7; chickens *c.* 41.

Life Insurance: *see* Insurance

Life Sciences

The life sciences cover a wide spectrum, and, as for several years past, the main points of interest in 1971 were near the two ends of the series, namely in conservation and molecular biology. Problems of conservation spread their influence on the one hand into politics, economics, and social planning, and on the other into almost every aspect of plant and animal life (*see* ENVIRONMENT). Likewise, while molecular biology continued to make spectacular advances within its conventional limits, the widened interest in it came from its association with problems and techniques of a wide range of subjects such as cell surgery, immunology, general physiology, embryology, and phylogeny. The most immediate prospects of practical applications came in botany, where extensions of the uses of such techniques as cell fusion, haploid cell cultivation, and introduction into cells of foreign genes or nucleic acids brought nearer prospects not only of the quicker and more economic production of conventional hybrids but of entirely new types of hybrid (between unrelated species) that cannot be produced by the normal process of pollination. The similar production of new types of microorganism offered exciting prospects in many fields.

For animals, despite sensational press stories about genetic engineering (especially following suggestions by J. F. Danielli early in the year), practical applications seemed more remote although potentially no less important. Most promising were those relating to cancer, especially the role of viruses, both direct and in relation to other carcinogens. A team of California scientists tentatively announced isolation of a virus that might be implicated in human cancer. U.S. Pres. Richard M. Nixon's guarantee of funds for an all-out attack on cancer promised a rapid extension of such work and, through it, of the life sciences in general. The discovery that, in multicellular organisms, RNA, but not DNA, can be readily transferred between cells and, in green plants, between nucleus and chloroplast, would have widespread effects on all problems involving cell communication.

Philosophically, the great interest in these investigations lay in their progress from analysis to synthesis, from the study of processes to that of organization, which was leading toward a bridging of the gap between chemistry and life. This gap was still unbridged in discussions on the origin of life and was commonly ignored by the romantic school of exobiologists who assumed that life is a normal product of stellar evolution. Evidence continued to accumulate of chemical evolution in the universe leading to the presence of organic molecules, including hydrocarbons (both straight-chained and aromatic) and amino acids, and the conditions for the nonbiological production from these of proteins and amino acids were discussed, notably by Manfred Eigen. But no evidence or plausible hypothesis for the transition from molecule to organism was yet presented.

These considerations gave especial significance to the publication by the Nobel laureate molecular biologist Jacques Monod (*see* BIOGRAPHY) of his book *Le hasard et la nécessité* (*Chance and Necessity*) in which he developed in modern terms the basic Darwinian principle that evolution is not a teleological or purposeful process leading inevitably toward some preordained idea but a continuous series of chance re-

actions to temporary combinations of circumstances. The violence of much of the public reaction to this book indicated how imperfectly the fundamental ideas of biology had been assimilated into our supposedly scientific culture.   (H. SA.)

BOTANY

Recognition that relatively minor increases in the cold resistance of many crop plants could be of great economic importance led several laboratories to focus their attention on the mechanisms whereby plants become acclimated. It had been shown that woody acclimated plants that could withstand cooling to $-196°$ C ($-320°$ F) in winter were killed by a slight frost (from ice-crystal damage) during the spring and summer growing season. Several environmental factors, including day length, temperature, and nutritional status, were found to influence cold acclimation, suggesting a variety of receptors within the plant, probably including phytochrome and abscisic acid. Following a slowing of metabolism, involving regulation of many gene products, the final phase of acclimation was the loss of water from the cell protoplasm to extracellular ice crystals, a process requiring a high permeability of the cell membrane. One hypothesis of the cause of death at very low temperatures was that water loss from the cell is restricted, causing ice crystals to form within the protoplasm. Another theory was that a stage of dehydration is reached when further loss of water causes denaturation of normally hydrated macromolecules.

Taxonomists and evolutionary botanists continued to explore the biochemical traits of plant species to aid identification and affinity studies. A relatively new technique, polyacrylamide gel electrophoresis of soluble proteins, was found to be of value in assessing the degree of similarity between species of the fungus *Aspergillus*. These relationships closely adhered to those previously suggested on morphological and genetic grounds. The differences in protein pattern between strains of the same species made it impracticable to use the method for species identification. In *Phlox*, it was recognized that a stable source of protein that would be little affected by local changes in nutritional conditions was needed. Consequently, the storage proteins from seeds were analyzed. It was possible to trace a reticulate pattern of evolution in the genus, and, again, this agreed with data from morphological, cytological, and chromatographic studies. Similar experiments on species of *Gossypium* (cotton) enabled the genus to be divided into six genomic groups.

The fate of photosynthetically fixed carbon within plant leaves was shown to be largely controlled by a few key enzymes, which, in turn, are regulated by a variety of internal and external factors. Important enzyme regulation factors were: feedback control in which a component of the reaction combines with and either activates or deactivates the enzyme; the energy balance of the cell as the ratio of adenosine triphosphate (ATP) to adenosine diphosphate; and the pH of the cell, which could be affected by ion concentration. Once incorporated into an organic molecule, the fixed carbon could enter a carbohydrate biosynthetic pathway leading to sucrose or starch, or could be converted via amino acids to proteins or via fatty acids and glycerol to fats. A fuller understanding of these pathways might enable them to be manipulated from outside so that, for example, leaves with increased protein content could be produced.

In an experiment at the University of Lancaster, Eng., a scientist applies hormones in a dilute solution to a coffee plant leaf. The new technique was designed to enable plants to survive longer under drought conditions.

An important contribution was made to knowledge of the internal structure of chloroplast photosynthetic membranes. It was known that during the preparative procedure called freeze fracturing, the membranes tended to split in half, revealing complementary inner surfaces. Particles of various sizes, often thought to represent some photosynthetic unit, had been seen on these inner surfaces. A reinvestigation of the distribution of these particles in normal and mutant cells of *Chlamydomonas reinhardi* showed that the larger ones, of mean diameter 160 Å, were located only where the chloroplast membranes were closely adpressed, or stacked. Under certain conditions, however, unstacked membranes could be stacked in vitro, and the large particles could be found. It was clear that the appearance of particles in freeze-fractured membranes did not indicate the presence of fixed intramembranous units.

Improvements were reported in the nutritional value and growing properties of basic food plants using both conventional breeding methods and induced mutations. A strain of *Zea mays* (corn) with increased amounts of the amino acids lysine and tryptophan (normally so low in corn protein as to constitute a serious nutritional deficiency) was developed by repeated backcrossing of a mutant to a normal strain. The less conventional method of inducing random mutations in seeds with various types of radiation produced a number of mutants with favourable characteristics. In some cases, the irradiation technique was successful where crossbreeding methods failed to produce strains with a particular combination of traits. Among the reported achievements were increased resistance to disease, increased and redistributed protein content, and better cooking quality of cereal crops.   (C. L. F. W.)

See also Gardening.

MARINE BIOLOGY

Two innovations during 1971 improved man's ability to study marine animals in near natural conditions. One was an automatically closing pressurized vessel attached to a net, permitting the recovery of plankton from considerable depths. The animals could then be studied in a pressurized system aboard ship. Another development was an ultrasonic tag attached to a free-swimming fish. The device transmitted information such as the position of the fish and its tail-beat frequency to hydrophones on shore or aboard ship.

Corals have been shown to benefit from their associated zooxanthellae not only because the latter photosynthesize but also because they convert inorganic nitrogenous substances from the coral, and from the sea, into amino acids. This may help to explain the success of corals in seas poor in nutrients. New information about the growth of corals showed that on Aldabra atoll most active growth occurred on the western, more sheltered part of the reefs, contrary to current theory that best growth is usually toward the prevailing winds.

In the controversy over the depredations of coral reefs by the crown of thorns starfish *Acanthaster planci*, the view was put forward that the apparent starfish "plagues" were perhaps no more than normal and local increases in numbers which had occurred before but had been somewhat overemphasized recently by heightened public attention and increased activity by divers. Related studies confirmed that the scallop (*Pecten maximus*) could distinguish between predatory and nonpredatory starfish, tending to move away from the former and remain stationary in the presence of the latter. The chemically active fraction inducing the responses appeared to be a steroid glucoside exuded from the body surface of the predator starfish.

A striking development in marine fisheries was the closure of the North Sea to herring fishing in 1971 in an attempt to resuscitate this dying fishery. Some fish farming work reached the stage where plaice were reared to the third generation in the laboratory. The second generation were big enough to eat after 18 months and some spawned after only two years. Wild plaice, in contrast, needed at least three or four years to reach marketable size and three to five years to mature.

An entirely synthetic mixture of chemicals was shown to be attractive to crabs. The mixture, based on the composition of the short-necked clam *Tapes japonica,* opened up the possible economic use of artificial baits. Related laboratory studies described a unique row of short, squat, chemosensitive hairs on the cutting edge of a lobster chela which erected when stimulated by extracts of crushed mussels. Histochemical work with the euphausid *Thysanoessa raschi* showed increased subcuticular acid phosphatase activity during the 24 hours of ecdysis. Use of this technique should permit quick assessments of the numbers of molting individuals in a sample.

The slipper limpet (*Crepidula fornicata*), a pest of oysters in the U.S. and U.K., was accidentally introduced into Tokyo Bay, and was recorded on a variety of mollusks in Japan, but so far not on oysters; the Japanese material may belong to a new physiological race. Morphological differentiation between eastern and western populations of Atlantic gastropods was found to be inversely related to the density of their veligers in open sea plankton. This supported the view that pelagic larvae are important in maintaining genetic continuity.

Observations on the responses of air-breathing animals to the combined effects of gases and pressure offered hope for deeper-diving achievements for man. Narcotic gases mixed with helium were proposed to overcome the excitability produced by hydrostatic pressure at depth. Other work on pressure proposed modification of a current view of pressure perception in marine invertebrates which postulates a thin but compressible layer of gas produced electrolytically on the body surface. The copepod *Calanus* retained sensitivity to small pressure increments even at high ambient pressures, which made it necessary to postulate that any gas layer is prevented from passing into solution under pressure or is produced at a rate proportional to the increased pressure. New research on the buoyancy mechanisms of cephalopods gave the clearest account yet of the processes involved in the formation of new buoyancy chambers in *Spirula*. The animal initially secretes the rigid walls of the chamber which at first contains seawater. Later the salts and then the water are pumped out to create a gas-filled chamber capable of withstanding the hydrostatic pressures exerted at depth in the sea.

In shore barnacles at copulation, sperm from the active male are transferred as a compact, inactive mass which is stimulated to activity only by a fluid secreted from the oviducal glands of the active female. Transfer of sperm in an inactive state ensures that they are not accidentally lost from the mantle cavity before the eggs are also shed into the mantle cavity for external fertilization. Adult barnacles detached from the substratum were shown to produce a secondary cement and reattach. The primary cement ducts appear to be used for new secretion, apparently having been kept open by a unique mechanism whereby a nonhardening flushing fluid prevents blockage by the original cement.

In the shore gastropods *Littorina littorea* and *Monodonta lineata*, acclimation to temperatures of 5°–16° C (41°–60° F), but not higher, enhanced survival at high temperatures. Evidently summer elevation of sea temperatures is sufficient to enable the animals to tolerate unusually high air temperatures at low tide in summer.

Recent interest in patterned activity in invertebrate nerve ganglia was extended to show that the isolated

buccal mass of the gastropod *Archidoris* produces normal-patterned sequences of nerve activity in response to pieces of sponge. The sequence relates to normal radula movements made by the intact animal when it feeds on the sponge.

Octopus learning experiments were extended to studies of "single session learning." It became possible to detect long-term consequences of a small number of trials in which octopuses were trained to recognize objects by touch. Development of such techniques was desirable in the strategy of the study of learning mechanisms.

Pollution of the marine environment came under extensive discussion during the year. Much information was of necessity acquired retrospectively, and notable recurring themes emphasized a need for more predictive studies and more information on overall ecological effects.   (E. Na.)

See also Oceanography.

MOLECULAR BIOLOGY

The staggering complexity of life was more apparent than ever before in the developments in molecular biology in 1971. Studies of protein architecture produced as many questions as answers (biochemistry), and intensive investigation of replication was stimulated by the two major findings of 1970: that ribonucleic acid, or RNA, can serve as a template for the synthesis of deoxyribonucleic acid, or DNA (biophysics), and that DNA polymerase serves to repair DNA rather than to replicate it (genetics).

Biochemistry. Enzymes were probed fruitfully in 1971 by new methods, including X-ray crystallographic analysis of three-dimensional structure and solid phase synthesis. Among the proteins whose structures were reported at a symposium at Cold Spring Harbor, N.Y., were the enzymes trypsin, subtilisin novo, malic dehydrogenase, lactic dehydrogenase, carboxypeptidase, and carbonic anhydrase; the hormone insulin; and the electron-transferring proteins flavodoxin, rubredoxin, and cytochrome *c*. Active sites readily were identified and their structures studied in proteins that contained a prosthetic group, which had previously been shown to be intimately associated with catalytic function. This was the case with the NAD^+-containing malic and lactic dehydrogenases, the FMN-containing flavodoxin, the iron-containing rubredoxin, and the zinc-containing carboxypeptidase and carbonic anhydrase. In the case of those proteolytic enzymes that lacked identifiable prosthetic groups, active sites were labeled by covalent attachment of active site-directed, irreversible inhibitors.

An extracellular nucleic acid hydrolase (nuclease), which accumulates in cultures of *Staphylococcus aureus*, was studied thoroughly by C. B. Anfinsen and his associates at the U.S. National Institutes of Health. Its complete amino acid sequence and three-dimensional structure were elucidated. It was also cleaved into two large fragments by the action of trypsin in the presence of calcium, which is essential for nuclease activity, and of deoxythymidine 3′,5′-diphosphate, which is a competitive inhibitor of the nuclease. These fragments associated to regenerate a structure similar to that of the native enzyme and retained about 10% of its activity. The smaller of the polypeptide fragments was completely synthesized by the solid phase procedure and found to associate with the large fragment to generate enzymatic activity. It was, therefore, possible to explore the importance

Giant African snails, found in the Miami area, were being exterminated by the U.S. Department of Agriculture in 1971. Ecologists feared the snails would upset the balance of Florida's plant life.

UPI COMPIX

of specific amino acid residues in the small fragment by synthesizing analogues bearing known substitutions and then testing their ability to generate nuclease activity when mixed with the natural large fragment. Four residues (asp$_{21}$, arg$_{35}$, asp$_{40}$, glu$_{43}$) were found to be essential; even conservative, charge-retaining substitutions of these residues caused loss of nuclease activity.

The biosynthesis of insulin, which is composed of two polypeptide chains covalently cross-linked by disulfide bridges, had long posed a problem: if its chains were synthesized separately within a cell how could they be expected to co-associate and establish the correct disulfide bridges with high efficiency? This problem was solved by the discovery of proinsulin, a single polypeptide chain that has two segments, which correspond with the two chains of insulin, connected by a 30-residue segment. The connecting segment is removed by the action of intracellular proteinases after it has served to facilitate correct folding and cross-linking of an active insulin molecule.

The actions of a number of hormones on a diversity of target tissues were shown to be mediated and amplified by 3',5' cyclic adenylic acid (cyclic AMP). The role of cyclic AMP was uncovered in the laboratory of E. W. Sutherland (see NOBEL PRIZES) during attempts to explain the hyperglycemic action of epinephrine and of glucagon. The sequence of events brought to light thus far was certainly more involved than might have been anticipated. Thus, in the liver, epinephrine activates adenyl cyclase, which is the source of cyclic AMP. The resultant increase in cyclic AMP stimulates phosphorylase kinase kinase, which catalyzes the phosphorylation and consequent activation of phosphorylase kinase. The latter enzyme, in its turn, catalyzes the phosphorylation and consequent activation of phosphorylase b, which then acts directly upon glycogen and leads to the production of glucose. It was suggested that such arrays of sequential activations interposed between a hormone and its final effect provide for cascaded amplification of the original signal. The actions of a variety of drugs were being explained in terms of their effects on levels of cyclic AMP. It was also not unreasonable to anticipate that other small molecules serve as "second messengers."

R. L. Perlman and I. Pastan showed that cyclic AMP also exerts stringent controls on the metabolism of bacteria. A number of enzymes whose synthesis is inhibited by glucose cannot be synthesized in the absence of either cyclic AMP or a specific cyclic AMP-receptor protein. Mutants of *Escherichia coli* unable to produce cyclic AMP or the cyclic AMP-receptor protein were unable to synthesize the glucose-repressible enzymes and were, therefore, unable to grow on a variety of substrates. This mechanism of action of cyclic AMP in bacteria was distinct from that previously found in mammalian cells.   (I. FR.)

Biophysics. Observations reported in 1971 demonstrated that DNA replication occurs in a variety of ways and that more than one enzyme may be involved. Most of the evidence for replication variability came from studies of viruses or bacteriophages. The single-stranded DNA phage ϕX 174 was an outstanding example since its maturation involves three distinct and separate phases of DNA synthesis. First, after attachment of the phage to a host bacterium and injection of the phage DNA, this DNA is found in the form of a single-stranded ring that directs the synthesis of a complementary copy of itself to form a double-

stranded circle called the replicative form (RF). The RF then attaches to a site, thought to be on the membrane of the host cell, and proceeds to replicate semiconservatively, giving rise to a series of daughter molecules, all double stranded. In the third phase, RF synthesis ceases and the double-stranded daughter molecules synthesize single-stranded progeny, which are packaged into protein coats and released later with the rupture of the cell.

Another type of DNA synthesis that appeared to be different from each of the three types found in ϕX 174 was found by J. Vinograd and his associates at the California Institute of Technology in their examination of mitochondrial DNA from mouse cells. From their electronmicrographs they concluded that replication of this circular DNA proceeds through the formation of D-shaped loops composed of three strands. The Watson-Crick model would have predicted the appearance of four strands.

Replication of DNA was also found to vary in the degree to which Okazaki fragments are formed. Several years before, R. Okazaki (now at Nagoya [Jap.] University) showed that much of the newly synthesized DNA is found in relatively short pieces of about 1,000 nucleotides each, and that these are incorporated quickly into the macromolecular DNA of the genome. Since then investigators had found different amounts of Okazaki fragments in newly synthesized DNA and, as a result, several different models of DNA replication were proposed, suggesting either that these fragments were precursors to only one of the newly forming daughter strands of DNA or to both.

During 1971 Okazaki found that these fragments may account for only 50% of the newly synthesized DNA in some organisms but up to 80% in others. He suggested that these fragments may be replicative intermediates for both newly forming strands of DNA and that the apparent variability is due to different degrees of efficiency in joining the ends of these fragments in the formation of the macromolecular polymer.

Recent autoradiographs obtained by R. G. Wake (Sydney) supported the finding that at least some DNA replication is bidirectional (see *Genetics*, below). Wake's autoradiographs were obtained from cells of the bacterium *Bacillus subtilis* that had been exposed to radioactive thymidine for a large part of the cell cycle. In one case he observed labeled material in a large loop in which two smaller loops were inserted near the top and the bottom of the circle. Wake's interpretation was that the parent loop was generated by bidirectional replication at an initiation site located at 6 and 12 o'clock on the circular DNA, and that the smaller loops were generated in a second round of initiation from the same points.

Proteins with a very high affinity for single-stranded DNA were found by Y. Hotta and H. Stern (University of California at San Diego) in meiotic cells of the lily, as well as in spermatocytes of rats, bulls, and humans. This protein, which does not stimulate DNA replication or denature double-stranded DNA, appears only during meiotic prophase and seems to have an essential function in the pairing of chromosomes and upon chromatid exchanges following pairing. Another class of DNA-associated proteins recently discovered by M. Oishi (Public Health Research Institute, New York City) were enzymes that degrade adenosine triphosphate (ATP) residues in macromolecular DNA. Oishi found three such enzymes, with molecular weights from 30,000 to 300,000. These enzymes attacked single- and double-stranded DNA to different degrees, but none of them showed RNA activity.

Many observations suggested that the elongation phase of DNA replication may occur by different mechanisms in different organisms, but new evidence indicated that an even greater degree of complexity may be found in the initiation phase. It had been known for some time that protein synthesis must take place before certain viruses can begin replication, especially for those that must produce their own DNA polymerase. Synthesis of a "nicking" enzyme also seemed to be required to break one of the double strands of circular DNA in mitochondria and in the RF form of bacteriophages before these could initiate DNA replication. K. G. Lark (University of Utah) extended these findings to bacteria and observed that RNA synthesis also seems to be required to initiate DNA replication. This was bolstered by D. Brutlag's (Stanford [Calif.] University) observation that replication of the DNA phage M13 is initiated only if the host cell produces RNA polymerase. If production of RNA polymerase of the host cell is blocked by addition of rifampicin, then the single-stranded, circular DNA injected by the bacteriophage cannot replicate to the double-stranded RF. Further complexities of initiation were revealed by Y. Hirota (Pasteur Institute, Paris), who showed that mutant bacteria blocked in initiation may escape from this condition when foreign genetic material in the form of a transmissible plasmid is incorporated into the host chromosome near or at the point of initiation.   (H. E. Ku.)

Genetics. Increasing evidence supported the view that the first DNA polymerase discovered, now called polymerase I, functions as a DNA repair enzyme rather than as a replicating enzyme. This enzyme makes DNA slowly compared with the rates at which it is synthesized inside cells. Also, it can synthesize DNA in only one direction, from 5′ to 3′, and has exonuclease activity.

The turning point for work in this area was the finding by P. DeLucia and J. Cairns from Cold Spring Harbor Laboratory of a mutant in the bacterium *E. coli* that is deficient in this enzyme yet grows normally. These mutants were also unusually sensitive to damage produced by ultraviolet radiation. Different repair systems were known to exist that repair the damage to DNA caused by ultraviolet radiation. The DNA polymerase I mutant was found to be deficient in one type of this repair. An independent mutation known to affect this mode of repair when combined with the polymerase I mutation did not make it any less efficient, further indicating that the polymerase I enzyme belongs to the same repair system as the enzyme determined by this other mutated gene.

Other work showed that combination of the polymerase I mutation with a mutation in a second repair system, which is also required for recombination, makes these cells inviable. This observation suggested that during normal cell growth damage to DNA continually being produced in the form of single-strand gaps is continually being repaired. The gaps may be the result of gene readout or transcription or of DNA duplication. Apparently either repair system can function to repair these gaps, but a cell that is defective in both repair systems remains unrepaired and dies.

The availability of the polymerase I-deficient mutant led to the discovery of another distinct enzyme, DNA polymerase II, by Thomas Kornberg (the son of Arthur Kornberg who discovered polymerase I) and Malcolm Getter of Columbia University. In fact, a third DNA polymerase may be distinguishable from the other two. Although polymerase II has a number of characteristics that distinguish it from polymerase I, it synthesizes DNA only in the same 5′,3′ direction and has an associate nuclease activity. This, of course, suggested that it, like polymerase I, functions as a repair, rather than a replicating, enzyme.

A number of cell-free systems held out promise of being able to isolate and characterize the enzyme or enzyme system responsible for replicating DNA. Work done with the organism *B. subtilis* by A. T. Ganesan (Stanford University) and N. Sueoka (Princeton University) allowed the DNA synthesized to be further characterized for its biological activity by genetic transformation. These methods involve treating cells with a detergent or with toluene, which disrupts the cellular membrane but retains gross cellular structure. These disrupted cells supported DNA synthesis if they were supplied with the four deoxynucleotide triphosphate precursors and ATP, a molecule that provides energy to drive many chemical reactions in the cell. If ATP was not supplied, DNA synthesis was of the repair type. When it was supplied, the DNA synthesized semiconservatively as in normal replication.

An interesting class of proteins was discovered by B. Alberts (Princeton) and called unwinding proteins. They were first found in the bacteriophage T4 and later isolated from *E. coli*, another bacteriophage, and from calf thymus, which illustrates their general occurrence. These proteins serve to denature or unwind the double-stranded DNA molecule. In the T4 they play an essential role in the replication process. These proteins bind very tightly to single-stranded DNA but not to double-stranded DNA. In effect, they facilitate the DNA's unwinding, a process that must precede DNA replication.

Still another protein, found in *E. coli* cells by J. C. Wang (University of California), acts to untwist supercoiled DNA. This protein, called omega protein, apparently introduces a transitory nick into the supercoiled DNA molecule allowing it to untwist.

Synthesis of the human growth hormone at the University of California Medical Center was announced on Jan. 6, 1971. Choh Hao Li (left), head of the research team, describes the equipment involved in the synthesis; Donald H. Yamashiro (right) also took part in the experiment.

When it comes off the DNA molecule the nick is closed and the DNA is left unchanged but less twisted. DNA inside bacterial cells was known to exist in a twisted compact form; omega protein was thought to allow it to untwist prior to its replication.

Two independent reports, by M. Masters (University of Edinburgh) and by R. E. Bird and L. Caro (University of Geneva), provided evidence that the *E. coli* chromosome replicates bidirectionally, that is, replication proceeds in two directions from a particular point. This kind of replication had been reported for DNA in Chinese hamster cells and bacteriophage lambda. Previously it was thought that the *E. coli* chromosome replicated unidirectionally.

The configuration of replicating molecules was also elucidated in a report by D. Dressler (Harvard University) that the bacteriophage T7 DNA molecule replicates in a linear form. Until this finding, replicating DNA molecules were observed to take on a circular configuration. The T7 molecule begins replication at a point about one-third from an end and proceeds bidirectionally. The short arm of the molecule is completed first, resulting in a Y-shaped molecule.

Work with reverse transcriptase, first reported in 1970, continued at a rapid pace. To measure the activity of this enzyme, it was found that synthetic RNA, DNA, and RNA/DNA hybrid molecules are far more efficient templates than the RNA tumour virus genome. These synthetic templates were used to detect reverse transcriptase activity in human and animal cancer cells. It was also found, however, that the same enzymatic activity was present in normal cells and that normal cells could utilize the synthetic molecules as templates but not the RNA tumour virus molecules. It remained to be determined whether the enzymes causing this in normal cells were true reverse transcriptase. (JA. C. C.)

See also Chemistry; Medicine.

ZOOLOGY

The search for the underlying mechanisms of certain animal behavioural patterns continued to provoke many interesting findings. For example, it was found that the production of light by the light organs of certain luminescent fishes is caused by luminous bacteria. Y. Haneda and F. I. Tsuji studied two rare species of bioluminescent fish, *Photoblepharon palpebratus* and *Anomalops katoptron*, from the Banda Sea, at the eastern end of the Indonesian Archipelago. Light is emitted from a pair of large elliptical organs, each lying in a depression below the eye. In *Photoblepharon* the light is extinguished when a black fold is drawn up over the organ, and in *Anomalops* the luminous face of the organ is rotated downward. Electron microscopy of the light organs showed large numbers of bacteria to be present in them. Furthermore, luminous emulsions prepared from the light organs quickly became dark upon standing, except for a layer at the top. Shaking in air restored the luminescence of the whole emulsion, showing that the loss upon standing was due to the absence of oxygen. Luminescence was optimum between 23°–26° C (73°–79° F), but it decreased as the temperature of the emulsion was increased, and disappeared irreversibly at 50° C (122° F) because of the death of the bacteria.

Another example of the control of a behavioural pattern was found in the triggering of the feeding response in a sea anemone, *Anthopleura elegantissima*. Feeding behaviour in most coelenterates is under the control of one chemical compound, such as the tripeptide reduced glutathione (GSH) or the amino acid proline. Some, however, respond to two different compounds, although there do not appear to be differences in the behavioural responses to the two compounds. *Anthopleura* is unique in that for complete feeding to occur two substances must be present. Experiments were conducted by K. J. Lindstedt using pieces of filter paper. These were eaten when impregnated with extracts of the larvae of brine shrimp (*Artemia*). However, when they were impregnated with reduced GSH, only the first phase of the feeding response, ingestion, occurred. Other agents were ineffective. The anemones would ingest pieces of clean filter paper if GSH was present in the medium. A complete feeding response of both ingestion and swallowing could be obtained by placing a piece of filter paper treated with asparagine on the tentacles of anemones that had been bathed with GSH solutions, which clearly showed the importance of reduced GSH in inducing ingestion and of asparagine in inducing swallowing.

Another behavioural pattern turned out to be of probable significance to environmental adaptation. Roadrunners (*Geococcyx californianus*) spread their feathers to reveal a large amount of dark pigmentation when they sun themselves. R. D. Ohmart and R. C. Lasiewski studied the effect of artificial solar radiation on the oxygen consumption of roadrunners. They found that during sunning oxygen consumption decreased and there was a reduction in the amount of energy expended to maintain a constant body temperature. They concluded that the reduced energy expenditure may result from increased absorption of sunlight by the pigmented body surface. This work extended earlier studies with less natural situations and indicated that although bird pigmentation probably serves mainly for protective coloration and communication, it may also permit energy conservation during sunning.

In one case, a behavioural pattern turned out to be of poor adaptive value for the survival of the animal. In Antarctica, crabeater seals (*Lobodon carcinophagus*) are normally resident in the pack ice but annually visit McMurdo Sound, usually in the late summer. During winter, they may share a breathing hole through the ice with a Weddell seal (*Leptonychotes weddellii*), which is a striking case of interspecific tolerance. Mummified carcasses of crabeater seals found deep inland were a source of puzzlement until I. Stirling and G. L. Kooyman concluded from their observations that the trips inland occur because the seals go in the wrong direction when they become trapped in McMurdo Sound by the freezing sea ice. Thus, instead of heading out to sea and survival, they head inland toward destruction. Even when a seal heading inland was turned around, it reversed its direction and continued to go inland.

Until recently, it was accepted that bare zones adjacent to shrubs are a result of the toxic action of volatile inhibitors from the plants. In 1970 J. Rood showed that grazing by a hystricomorph rodent, *Microcavia australis,* is also responsible for the presence of a bare zone in Argentina. B. Bartholomew reported evidence that animal grazing is the major factor in the production of the bare zone adjacent to shrubs of the chaparral in coastal California. There was a concentration of feeding activity in the bare zone by rodents, rabbits, and birds. The most convincing evidence came from the use of exclosures de-

X-ray studies in West Germany revealed the soft parts of Paleozoic fossils. This radiograph provided the first indication of the soft structure of the Lobobactrites.

signed to prevent access of any vertebrates to small areas during a period of one year. In the absence of vertebrates, an impressive growth of shrubs was reported.

R. M. Mengel, who studied two generations arising out of the mating of a male coyote and a female dog, produced perhaps the most extensive study ever published of coydogs in captivity. He found that the pups were more aggressive than dog pups, that individuals looking most like coyotes behaved more like coyotes, and that coydogs howl like coyotes but are somewhat less versatile in the higher ranges. From observations on breeding, Mengel found that whereas coyotes mate in January–March, with young being born in April or May, coydogs mate about three months earlier, with young being born in February or March. He concluded that there is probably very little introduction of dog genes into wild coyote populations through hybridization because coydogs would not be able to find coyotes to mate with when they came into breeding condition and because any second generation coydogs born in the winter would stand a small chance of surviving the weather. Coydogs would also be less able to survive because of the relative absence of coyote characteristics. The same reasons might also explain the absence of swarms of wolf-dog hybrids, in spite of the existence of occasional hybrids under domestic conditions in the hands of Eskimos or Indians. (R. R. No.)

Entomology. A major legal battle over the use of insecticides in the U.S. began in August, when chemical manufacturers and the Department of Agriculture appealed a "cancellation order" on the use of DDT imposed in January by the Environmental Protection Agency. The contest was likely to continue into 1972.

DDT not only was persistent but had by 1971 become widely dispersed to all parts of the world. The appearance of the insecticide even in Antarctic penguins had hitherto seemed puzzling, but C. P. Lloyd-Jones of Long Ashton Research Station, U.K., found one possible explanation when he discovered that up to half the total amount of DDT distributed on fields evaporated and was carried away in the atmosphere. It also was found that sublethal residues of persistent insecticides sometimes had effects precisely the opposite of those originally intended by the users. T. F. Walker of the London School of Hygiene and Tropical Medicine found that houseflies laid more eggs after treatment with low doses of DDT; and Hodjat S. Hossein of the Imperial College of Science and Technology, London, found that both DDT and dieldrin increased the fertility of the cotton stainer bug, *Dysdercus*.

Despite accumulating evidence of the deleterious effects of the persistent insecticides, the fact remained that the world's food economy and, over large areas, its public health depended on the continued use of the relatively cheap and effective DDT. Means of replacing it were under active investigation. G. Holan of the Commonwealth Scientific and Industrial Research Organization in Australia calculated the formulas of compounds that ought to have insecticidal properties on theoretical grounds but that would be short-lived because inherently unstable. Most insecticides seem to work against the nervous system. Because of their shape and the distribution of electrical charges on their molecules, such insecticides were believed to "wedge" permanently open the channel that allows momentary flows of sodium ions during the normal transmission of neural impulses. Holan

was particularly successful in devising insecticidally active but short-lived compounds that had a low toxicity to mammals because of a greatly reduced effectiveness at the high body temperatures maintained by warm-blooded animals.

Pheromones—compounds that act externally and determine major aspects of the behaviour of insects—were further investigated. William Bowers and William Bodenstein of the U.S. Department of Agriculture (USDA) discovered that bornyl acetate from the needle and cone oil of spruce and fir caused sexual excitement in the male cockroach. They showed that this compound was not present in the natural hormone produced by the female; moreover, 18 out of 100 common plants were found to produce structurally diverse compounds that excited sexual activity in the male cockroach, although the significance of findings such as these remained obscure.

The "monogamy" pheromone that male houseflies impart to females when mating, causing them to become unattractive to other males, had only a temporary effect according to R. A. Leopold and his research associates at USDA. Further, the males, which could mate several times, did not entirely replace their supply of the pheromone, and thus the greater their sexual experience, the less they reduced the desirability of their mating partners to other male houseflies.

It had long been suspected that some insects, especially the plant-sucking bugs, carry out their own form of conservation. This was confirmed dramatically by D. R. Scott of the University of Idaho, who demonstrated that despite their notoriety for causing damage, *Lygus* bugs actually increased the growth and yield of carrot and bean plants that germinated from seeds on which insects had fed, even when up to 30% of the contents of the seeds had been removed by the insects. Scott called attention to recent reports that the plant growth hormone indoleacetic acid may be a regular constituent of the saliva that plant bugs leave behind in their food materials.

The sounds produced and detected by insects also received attention. W. B. Broughton of the City of London Polytechnic and K. M. Harris of the Royal Horticultural Society found that colonies of the black citrus aphid made a sound audible within 18 in. by rhythmically rubbing the hind legs against the abdomen in unison. The hind legs bore rows of minute, toothlike hairs. The significance of such sound production remained uncertain, but Broughton and Harris thought it might be involved in warding off enemies, such as parasitic wasps. Meanwhile, Lee A. Miller at the University of Kentucky discovered that lacewings were sensitive to ultrasound and that, similarly to noctuid moths, they could "hear" the sonar waves emitted by bats and take reflex evasive action.

Larry E. Milliger of the Southwest Missouri State College and his colleagues at North Texas State University discovered that beetles carried out a considerable air passenger traffic. The 23 species of aquatic beetles investigated carried an average of six genera of algae and protozoa per individual, and even the 16 terrestrial species averaged half this figure. Altogether, their passengers included over 100 species of algae, over 20 of protozoa, and also rotifers, nematodes, and fungi, which the beetles were capable of carrying live over several miles at a time. (P. W. Mi.)

Ornithology. In a remarkable paper L. Brown and A. Root described for the first time the detailed breeding biology of the lesser flamingo (*Phoeniconaias* *minor*), one of two flamingo species found in Africa. The bird's only known regular nesting ground is on the inaccessible soda-mud flats of Lake Natron in Tanzania. Due to exceptional rains one year, this site was denied to them and they chose to nidificate instead at Lake Magadi in Kenya where observations were much more easily undertaken. The total world population of this species is 3 million–4 million birds. Not all breed at once; the Magadi colony comprised about 1.1 million pairs. In nuptial display lesser flamingos congregate in a tightly packed flock that moves rapidly in a kind of communal stomp in which various ritual movements are performed. They build mud-mound nests; the huge Magadi colony excavated a total of 20,000 metric tons of soda mud! One egg is laid, incubated for a month, and stands an 85% chance of hatching successfully. Fledging takes 10–13 weeks. Only about 40% of eggs laid result in flying young. One cause of mortality is predation by large mammals (from lions to jackals) and by vultures, particularly Egyptian vultures.

Two French ornithologists reported the rediscovery of a little-known bird, Prince Ruspoli's touraco. It was previously known only from the original specimen collected in southern Ethiopia in 1893, and from five more specimens from the same locality obtained in 1941. In 1971 it was revealed that two more had been shot and killed at a locality about 60 mi. from the original one.

In Israel the social behaviour of wintering white wagtails that had previously bred farther north in Eurasia was studied. A. Zahavi showed that in searching for food wagtails may show flocking behaviour in one situation and defend individual territories in another situation. The way the food is distributed over the habitat seems to determine the choice. Once the wagtails have to fight one another in order to acquire food, territorial behaviour develops. If, on the other hand, there is enough food in one area to satisfy the flock, the birds remain social. The ability to adopt alternative arrangements according to the distribution of the food supply must mean that more wagtails can survive in a given area in winter.

David Lack's *Ecological Isolation in Birds* (1971), though including a critical review of later research on the subject, was primarily a new assessment. Ecologists studying other kinds of animals might be specially interested in the theories and general comparisons, and ornithologists in the examples, which included both familiar European and North American birds and the nuthatches of the world, tropical fruit-eaters, white-eyes, vultures, the land birds of the West Indies, and seabirds. The main means of isolation differ in different types of birds, and in migrants may even differ in their two homes. These and other differences were interpreted in terms of competition and natural selection, and the importance of ecological isolation in evolution and ecology was indicated in the final chapter.

South America has more avian families and more species than any other continent—2,926 out of a world total of about 8,600. R. Meyer de Schauensee's *Guide to the Birds of South America* (1971) provided in a single, if abbreviated, volume a review of all the living species.

An ornithological biography was *An Eye for a Bird* (1970), the life story of Eric Hosking, probably the world's finest bird photographer.

The dark-bellied brent goose nests in the U.S.S.R. but winters mainly in British estuaries. The avail-

Lesser and greater flamingos lived in a mixed colony at Lake Magadi, Kenya, in 1971. Observations of the lesser flamingo indicated that the eggs laid in mud-mound nests are incubated for a month and stand an 85% chance of hatching.

ability of suitable habitat and food appeared to be the main factors limiting its numbers. Two British wildfowl specialists, M. A. Ogilvie and G. V. T. Matthews, stated vehemently that the present tiny world population of only 25,000–30,000 was not likely to increase as the destruction of habitat continued and, indeed, was likely to decrease dramatically following the planned construction of London's third airport off Foulness in Essex.

H. N. Southern of Oxford published his long-term study on a tawny owl population and two of its rodent prey species in a deciduous woodland. The number of fledged chicks produced each season depends on the availability of rodents. In one year when rodents were exceptionally scarce, the owls did not even attempt to breed. Variable food supply was shown to be of fundamental importance in the population dynamics of the red grouse in Scotland.

Reviewing another long-term investigation, D. Jenkins and A. Watson showed that fluctuations in grouse numbers were correlated with variable breeding success and that this in turn was related to variations in the food supply. Red grouse feed on heather shoots. These vegetational differences changed from place to place according to the chemical content of the underlying rocks and man's heather-burning activities.

An exceptional ringing recovery was that of a tufted duck caught, marked, and released in Essex, Eng., in May 1969 and shot on May 14, 1971, near Rawalpindi in West Pakistan. It was the first recovery of a British-marked bird anywhere on the Indian subcontinent.

A British veterinary surgeon, George A. Smith, drew attention to some noteworthy tool-using behaviour by captive members of the parrot family. Parrotlike birds of these species, including the well-known African gray, would scratch themselves with, for example, a matchstick. Tool-using in birds is extremely rare, being known from less than ten species.

(J. H. Bo.)

ENCYCLOPÆDIA BRITANNICA FILMS. *Chromosomes of Man* (1967); *Life Story of a Social Insect: The Ant* (1967); *Looking at Mammals* (1967); *Monarch Butterfly Story* (2nd ed., 1967); *Photosynthesis* (2nd ed., 1967); *Water for Living Things* (1967); *Insect Parasitism—The Alder Woodwasp and Its Enemies* (1968); *The Ears and Hearing* (2nd ed., 1969); *Muscle: Chemistry of Contraction* (1969); *Muscle: Dynamics of Contraction* (1969); *Muscle: Electrical Activity of Contraction* (1969); *The Origin of Life—Chemical Evolution* (1969); *Radioisotopes: Tools of Discovery* (1969); *Theories on the Origin of Life* (1969); *Succession on Lava* (1970); *The Nerve Impulse* (1971); *Seed Dispersal* (3rd ed., 1971).

Liquors, Alcoholic: *see* Alcoholic Beverages

Literature

The 1971 Nobel Prize for Literature went to a candidate who reportedly had been under consideration for a number of years, Chilean poet Pablo Neruda. (*See* NOBEL PRIZES.)

AMERICAN

Fiction. Following the rather lean year of 1970, American fiction in 1971 seemed as profuse and abundant as an orchard after a wet summer—not only in the number of books published, but in their inventiveness, their range of subjects and interests, and their imaginative quality. Because of the bumper crop of good novels, it was difficult to arrive at any general statement about the fiction of the year. The best novel, the most substantial in matter and manner, was a poetic evocation of the last two days of the life of Sir Walter Ralegh, but the most common subject proved to be a concern about the seeming inability of the young and their elders to understand each other.

George Garrett's fourth novel, *Death of the Fox,* was a book of epic proportions, poetic in its richness of language and the intensity of its imagination, historical in its genre but fully modern in its approach to its subject. The novel is an account of the last days of Sir Walter Ralegh and of the impact of those days and his approaching execution on those around him. In a style that is a remarkable fusion of contemporary clarity and Elizabethan manner and elegance, Garrett shapes the Elizabethan world into a living place, colourful, detailed, and exact. Ralegh takes, as he should, much of his life from that world, for with his death, that world and time died too, or at least changed into something akin to itself but forever different.

But Ralegh in the novel is something more than the last Elizabethan, more even than the great courtier, sailor, soldier, explorer, and historian. He is a poet, and it is as a poet, a man of the imagination, that Garrett is able to come fully to terms with him. During his last days in the Tower and in London, Ralegh imagines the life that moves around him by fusing what he is able to see with what he remembers and what he knows; he moves from fact to the possibilities of fact, and he is able to see in his imagining a much truer world than any of the free men outside the Tower. The prisoner Ralegh can see the limits of freedom and its true sources, while his enemies are able to see only the schemes of the day and feel the fears of the night. Ralegh chooses his death on the scaffold with the same care and imaginative concern that any artist chooses the close of his poem or the last chords of his symphony. And the end he chooses is right for himself and for his time, as right as the couplet full of faith and hope that he wrote as the new ending for an old poem the night before his death.

Death of the Fox is more, too, than an account of Ralegh's proper finish to his life, for it is also the story of a modern artist's imaginative communion with another artist, long dead but needing only to be dreamed anew to come alive again. For as much as Ralegh imagines his world and day, so Garrett brings all of his memory and seeing into Ralegh's story. When Ralegh writes a last letter to his son, his letter concludes with the language of Garrett's poem "For My Sons." The quotation is no act of literary cuteness or arrogance on Garrett's part, but rather a recognition that he and his Ralegh are one on the page, sharing each with the other a wisdom that is separately beyond them both. *Death of the Fox* is, then, the story of the imagination's fierce love for the living moment and its power to make that moment live again and again with each new contact with a vital mind.

If Garrett's Ralegh finds a present moment secure in its relation to eternity by an act of artistic control, none of Robert Penn Warren's characters in *Meet Me in the Green Glen* has that kind of control, for they are victims of the past because of their own inability to imagine or see a real world beyond themselves. One of them, Cy Grinder, thinks "how his whole damned life had been working to bring him here to stand shivering, locked in a can like he was afraid, saying, *now, now,* for if you could just live *now,* no backwards and no forwards, you could live through anything." But, of course, he learns that "a man can't." Warren's people in this novel cannot live in the now because they are all blinded to it by the hurt and failure, by the loss of their dreams of the past. They invent rituals to protect them from having to open their eyes, but the rituals fail. And even the saving power of love is warped by the illusions of lust into as deadly a weapon as hate and fear.

Two other novels published in 1971 were concerned primarily with the relationship of the past, that of fact and of imagination, to the present. Herman Wouk's large novel *The Winds of War* is an attempt to recreate the time of Hitler in order to see more clearly the time after him when he is the ghost that haunts and possibly blinds both the U.S. and the U.S.S.R. And Evangeline Walton's *The Children of Llyr,* a modern evocation of much of the mystery and magical value of the second branch of the Welsh *Mabinogion,* is the second volume of a proposed tetralogy (the first of which, *The Virgin and the Swine,* was published in 1936), and it has the "deep emotional sympathy for the old mythology" that John Cowper Powys praised in its predecessor.

A number of novels dealt with the relationship of past and present in the more direct terms of the generation gap. Among them were Mary McCarthy's *Birds of America,* the complex account of a boy's relationship to his mother; William Harrison's *Lessons in Paradise,* a darker account of a child prodigy's re-

Robert Penn Warren's novel "Meet Me in the Green Glen" was published in 1971.

MICHAEL V. CARLISLE

lationship with his mother and with the demands of a world painfully post-Edenic; Ross Macdonald's *The Underground Man* in which Lew Archer struggles to uncover, often literally, the dead past to offer at least the possibility of free life to the young present; and James A. Michener's *The Drifters,* an almost reportorial account of the youthful American drifters in Europe and Africa.

The two best novels based on the generation gap were James Jones's *The Merry Month of May* and Wright Morris' *Fire Sermon.* Jones's novel is the most powerful and controlled book he had done since *From Here to Eternity.* It uses the events of the French student revolution of 1968 to explore the shams and failures of a group of Americans living in Paris. The story is solid, the characters are thoroughly imagined, and the narrator has sufficient moral complexity to tell the story and to act in it. It has weight and substance and a sense of the dark hurt at the centre of modern consciousness. Wright Morris' *Fire Sermon* is a very different sort of book—a small fable, like his earlier *In Orbit,* in which the details are sketched in quickly and vividly to give colour to its parabolic form. Its account of the journey of a small boy and his ancient next-of-kin across the U.S. to the old man's lost past and the boy's unrevealed future is a masterpiece of liveliness and compression. The fire sermon is one of the necessity of creation and destruction to the process of life, and in it Morris is able to preach another sermon of the value of love in the face of fire and of understanding that crosses all gaps of age and misunderstanding. Both Jones and Morris feel the pains of the passing day, and both are able to sense the living form that gives value even to the days of fire.

The approaches of three other novelists to these same harsh days are more comical and satirical, if just as serious. Walker Percy's third novel, *Love in the Ruins,* is a comic version of America's approach to the year 2000 and its promised apocalypse, but his unorthodox Christian vision allows him to end his tale with no Second Coming, but rather with a family at home, holy in spirit with no need for an end. Charles Newman's *The Promise-keeper* is an equally lively view of a future America, as unfamiliar as any science fiction vision and as familiar as vice and folly will ever be. Possessed of a wildly comic vision, Newman is a young writer who sees things with remarkable clarity. And Richard Condon's *The Vertical Smile* is the satirical novel that, as readers of his other novels might expect, goes for broke, taking on everything in sight with great gusto and satirizing even itself as it goes along.

There were numerous other fine novels as well: David Slavitt's *Anagrams,* a novel about the maintenance of artistic vision in the midst of the "LitBiz" game; Shirley Ann Grau's *The Condor Passes;* John Hawkes's *The Blood Oranges,* a darkly comic continuation of his imaginative passage through the heart; J. P. Donleavy's *The Onion Eaters,* his most vital novel since *The Ginger Man;* Bernard Malamud's *The Tenants;* Joyce Carol Oates's *Wonderland;* and John Updike's sequel to *Rabbit Run, Rabbit Redux.* There were also two first novels that were superior works: poet James Whitehead's *Joiner,* a strong novel about professional football, and Mark Steadman's *McAfee County,* a Georgia comic novel with much of the vigour and value of early Erskine Caldwell. All in all, it was a good year and one that boded well for the future of American fiction.   (R. H. W. D.)

Germaine Greer, spokeswoman for women's lib, wrote the controversial book "The Female Eunuch," which was published in 1971.

Poetry. John Ciardi's poetry remained unmistakably Ciardi, and he showed the kind of growth from book to book that proves a man a true poet. Yet his poems were not as frequently anthologized or as publicly praised as others of his generation. If his new book of autobiographical poetry at its most narrative, *Lives of X,* did not receive its due, the fault remained with his contemporaries, not with Ciardi.

Galway Kinnell's *The Book of Nightmares* fulfilled and expanded the style that emerged in *Body Rags.* These are harrowing poems in the old sense of that flinty word: poems about travel and arrest, a son and his future, war and memory, a wife and poetry. Not one of these subjects is shortchanged, but none is exploited for its own sake either.

If an increasing social awareness is a sign of poetic growth, Adrienne Rich had grown. The real question was whether her new poems were better or merely different. She had never written a bad book, and her new one, *The Will to Change,* did not invalidate that assertion. Yet the poems to Daniel Berrigan and Godard seemed limited rather than ransomed by the person they praise.

Stanley Kunitz' *The Testing Tree* was his first book in a decade, and if the only poem in it were "Journal for My Daughter" it would have justified its appearance. Of course, there are more poems, including the beautiful title poem of reminiscence—a song of innocence in 20th-century terms.

The books by New Directions that deserved particular notice were Robert Fitzgerald's *Spring Shade,* an erudite but somewhat level culling of poems and translations from 1931 to 1970; Lawrence Ferlinghetti's *Back Roads to Far Places,* which is Ferlinghetti with a Japanese accent, and Cid Corman's *Sun Rock Man,* a gathering of impressionistic poems carefully wrought and memorable as inscriptions glimpsed in passing. Another omnibus of consequence was James Wright's *Collected Poems,* which contains the poet's own picks from earlier works, numerous translations, and over 30 new poems. There is undoubted skill in Wright's poems, but there is an awkwardness of feeling—as if the poems are attempts at trying to feel and not the all-of-a-sudden moment that is a real poem's alpha and omega.

Charles Simic's *Dismantling the Silence* was the

Dee Brown's book "Bury My Heart at Wounded Knee: An Indian History of the American West" was published in 1971.

first of George Braziller Inc.'s poetry series under the general editorship of Richard Howard, and it was a good way to start. Simic's virtue is leanness, the sketchiness of line that implies whole portraits while eschewing prolixity. There is an echo or two of Mark Strand and W. S. Merwin, both of whom, not coincidentally, wrote blurbs for the book, but Simic's real voice and talent will outlive the indebtednesses.

Nothing but good can be said about Richard Shelton's *The Tattooed Desert,* winner of the International Poetry Forum's 1970 U.S. award. The real and surreal world change places in Shelton's poetry with ease and brilliance. Also published during the year was Richard Wilbur's verse translation of Molière's *The School for Wives,* which completed the trilogy that began with *Tartuffe* and *The Misanthrope.*

History, Biography, and Essays. Arthur Krock supplemented his *Memoirs* with a book of additional reminiscences called *The Consent of the Governed and Other Deceits.* Call it anecdotal history, if you like, but it is of a rare order. Here are "inside" facts that only one like Krock would know; facts that he obviously felt some impulse to keep secret before he retired but that now seem (to him at least) a matter for the public domain. Why else would he now say that Jacqueline, then Kennedy, would privately request him to criticize her and not the president? His ratification of Nixon is quite apparent, and he says that Johnson's frequent and frequently televised visits to the healthy or ailing Dwight Eisenhower were what most people thought they were—snow jobs in the Pedernales manner. This book is in the tradition of editorial journalism that Theodore White and Norman Mailer perfected in the 1960s, but Krock's advantage, if any, is that his inside information predates both.

Willie Morris' *Yazoo* can be considered an outgrowth of rather than a sequel to his autobiographical *North Toward Home.* It abandons the theme of a native Mississippian's discovery in Manhattan of the unsheddable Mississippi in himself. But it maintains the viewpoint of a native son in its reportage of Yazoo City's ordeal of compliance with the Supreme Court's order for school desegregation. That Yazoo came through the ordeal without violence or the presence of the National Guard is a tribute to the leadership of both races and to the kind of bedrock fairness that Morris himself so eminently personifies.

The Many Americas Shall Be One is Harrison E. Salisbury's analysis of and anodyne for contemporary ills. The book's good points, however, are often diluted by a tendency toward unjustified generalization. Sentences like: "We have killed one president, compelled a second to retire from office, and the fate of a third is in doubt" ring with editorial pontification, but Salisbury's arguments for participatory democracy are irrefutable and his chapter on revolutionary morals says more on the subject than the brevity of it would suggest.

B. H. Liddell Hart's essentially military and long-awaited *History of the Second World War* is an important book. It is important not just because Hart can lay claim to having been one of the greatest military thinkers of the 20th century, was one of the few, along with Charles de Gaulle, who foresaw the impact of mechanization on warfare (prophesying accordingly and accurately), and was one of the very few specializing in military thought who could write English well. It is also important because it is essentially a work of scholarship—a historical work

rather than the memoirs or apologetics of a retired general or politician. Thus Hart's controlling aim is to understand what happened instead of justifying a course of action, and his conclusions flow largely from the free and disinterested play of his consciousness.

Hart's basic judgment on World War II is, unhappily, that an enormous and needless price was paid for a phantom victory. He agrees with Churchill that it was an unnecessary war. He believes that the British were able to survive prior to Pearl Harbor more because of Hitler's folly than because of their efforts, however heroic. He also makes clear that the Allied policy of revenge was self-defeating since "the ultimate peace merely produced a fresh menace and the looming fear of another war. For the unnecessary prolongation of the Second World War, in pursuit of the opponents' 'unconditional surrender,' proved of profit only to Stalin—by opening the way for Communist domination of central Europe."

John Is Easy to Please by Ved Mehta is a collection of six pieces originally published in *The New Yorker.* Each is an account of impressions and conversations with what the cover flap calls "literary personages" (George Sherry of the UN, Sir William Haley formerly of the BBC and *The Times* [London], the Oxford bookman Sir Basil Blackwell, the Urdu critic Ram Babu Saksena, the Indian novelist R. K. Narayan, and the American linguist Noam Chomsky). Mehta's interviews are truly in depth and go so far beyond reporting that they constitute authentic miniature biographies, beautifully crafted cameo portraits of lives. Further, his range is astonishing. The manner and the matter of communication about Ram Babu Saksena are quite different from those about Sir Basil Blackwell, but both profiles have the ring of authenticity.

Eric Hoffer is not a genius, but he surely is one of the few interesting, provocative, and imaginative social critics around. His *First Things, Last Things* is not quite as impressive as *The True Believer* (largely because it repeats many of the insights of the latter work), but it again displays his mastery of the aphorism, his philosophical daring, the breadth of his interests, and the freshness of imagination that brought him to prominence. His views cover a number of matters. Some of them are simply fanciful, such as the notion that the time is not far off when U.S. business tycoons, bedecked with beads and medallions, will feel at home in literary-intellectual salons and will be devoted primarily to public service. Some are obvious (though they need to be stressed and repeated), such as the position that most of the activist young are basically brazen, callow, and pretentious and that a national sin has been the deference of adults to this aggressive ignorance. Some views are puzzling, such as the insistence on the absolute uniqueness of the American social and political experience. And some are irritating, especially Hoffer's uncompromising antielitism. What he seemingly is unwilling to see, or perhaps admit, is that the distinction between the few and the many can be perverted and corrupted but it cannot be eliminated.

The Memoirs of Chief Red Fox is a basic American document. The author, now 101, has written of the Indian past from the perspective of his youth, the decades of the decisive Indian wars, and, finally, the tragedy of the post-reservation era. One overlooks the occasionally rhapsodic prose for the true and forlorn melody of the account: the broken treaties, the

E. L. Doctorow published "The Book of Daniel" in 1971.

Gay Talese, whose narrative "Honor Thy Father" was published in 1971, lived and traveled with the crime syndicate in order to write his account of the rise and decline of a Mafia family.

Wounded Knee (S.D.) massacre, the Christianizing of the Indian by force, and the cartoon carnival of Buffalo Bill. Reading the narrative is like listening to the guilty conscience of the U.S. (SA. H.)

CANADIAN

English Language. The settings of *St. Urbain's Horseman* by Mordecai Richler include hilarious aspects of the London film and theatrical world and Richler's ghetto childhood on Montreal's St. Urbain Street. In his latest novel, Richler reveals himself as still dominated by his background but capable of providing wildly amusing character portrayal and descriptions of great feeling and intensity. Brilliant and quietly shattering, *Lives of Girls and Women* by Alice Munro is a beautiful work and an intimate portrayal of the drives, moods, and longings of the female spirit. The insular life of a small Canadian town is witnessed and experienced by the complex girl-woman, Del Jordan.

Ikhnaton—pharaoh of Egypt, visionary and heretic, is the subject of *King of Egypt, King of Dreams*, a striking historical novel by Gwendolyn MacEwen. The author makes imaginative use of the riches of Egyptian mythology and symbolism in this recreation of the spirit of a remote civilization. James Houston's *The White Dawn* is a haunting evocation of the Eskimo culture before the coming of the white man—in this case, three lost whalers. Tragedy and corruption result when the sudden intrusion of new customs and foreign ways changes the lives of the Eskimo people. Moving from his native Toronto to Montreal and rural Ontario, Hugh Hood, in *The Fruit Man, the Meat Man, and the Manager,* explores aspects of contemporary life in backstreet communities. *Come a Long Journey,* by Alan Fry, traces the slow growth of friendship and understanding between two men of different backgrounds, a white man and an Indian, as they travel together down the treacherous Yukon River.

Johnny Crackle Sings, by Matt Cohen, depicts in an uncompromisingly honest fashion the successes and failures of a young rock singer. A striking physical format, as well as a fragmented and experimental prose-style narrative, newspaper accounts, and flashbacks make for much originality. This book provides insights into the attitudes, motivations, and even the quiet desperation of today's youth counterculture. Norman Levine, in *I Don't Want to Know Anyone Too Well,* presents a wistful and varied collection of short stories that illustrate the author's credo: "When you go to a writer's work, it is his personal world that you enter."

Few established Canadian poets produced new work in 1971; those who published were represented mainly by retrospective collections. Phyllis Webb's *Selected Poems 1954–65,* George Bowering's *Touch: Selected Poems 1960–1970,* and Raymond Souster's *The Years* brought together from magazines, broadsheets, and earlier works selections from these writers' best works that they wished to see preserved. Louis Dudek and Irving Layton both brought out collections of their complete works to date. Alden Nowlan's collection, *Between Tears and Laughter,* was chiefly new work. His poetry continued to be distinguished by an affirmation of life that infuses all his work, whether he is writing about the minutiae of daily life or the death of Martin Luther King.

Among the younger poets there was a ferment of activity. Their writing appeared mainly in poetry magazines and in chapbooks and broadsheets published by the small presses. For the most part, there was no innovation in established attitudes but a greater concern for wider issues was notable. Also, a new and broader kind of regionalism was apparent in a sense of the vastness of the land and a rejoicing in the idea of great spaces. Dale Zieroth, one of the four poets represented in *Mindscapes,* skillfully evokes the landscape and people of Manitoba in coming to terms with his own past. Bill Howell, in *The Red Fox,* celebrates the Maritimes in poems distinguished by their warmth and concern for people. Andreas Schroeder was represented by a chapbook, *File of Uncertainties,* one of a set of ten published by Sono Nis Press.

An interesting work was the collection of poems by Eskimos, *I Breathe a New Song,* selected by Richard Lewis and introduced by Edward Carpenter. Many of these are simple and direct, describing the activities of daily life, others are magical and incantatory. In her *Power Politics,* Margaret Atwood, a disciplined writer using traditional forms, explores with superb mastery and sometimes frightening cruelty the lacerating and abrading possibilities inherent in close personal relationships. In *Nobody Owns the Earth,* Bill Bissett brings an ecstatic vision to his treatment of a wide range of subjects and expresses concern and compassion in terms either damning or celebrating.

The second half of Pierre Berton's history of the construction of the Canadian Pacific Railway, *The Last Spike,* covers the period 1881–85, and describes the building of the railway, which accompanied the development of continent-wide confederation. Ramsay Cook, in *The Maple Leaf Forever,* examines Canadian writings on nationalism, contrasting the viewpoints of French and English writers and presenting his own condemnation of nationalism as dangerous and harmful. Glen Frankfurter's *Baneful Domination* is a Toronto businessman's history of Canada that deplores the fact that Canada has always existed under and against foreign influences, English and U.S., and proposes an attitude of strong Canadian independence. The government and personality of Pierre Elliott Trudeau are raked over the coals by Walter Stewart in his frankly opinionated *Shrug: Trudeau in Power.* The author's initial uneasiness about Trudeau, "the de Gaulle fist in the Kennedy glove," crystallized into a wide-ranging critique of every aspect of his performance.

The events of October 1970, which included the murder of a Quebec Cabinet minister and the invocation of the War Measures Act, continued to reverberate. The need to understand the significance of those harrowing days was partially satisfied by two very different books: *The October Crisis,* by Gerard Pelletier, which presented the case for the firm line taken by the Trudeau government, and, considerably more impassioned in tone, *White Niggers of America,* by Pierre Vallières. Vallières was convicted for terrorist activities in 1967 and was detained in Quebec under the War Measures Act. His autobiography gives insight into the thoughts and philosophy of a man who finds violence a justifiable answer to what he conceives to be a deliberate conspiracy to degrade and exploit the Quebec working class.

Voyage into Danger: Adventure in the Queen Charlotte Islands, by Ted Ashlee, is a fast-paced adventure mystery for young people that takes place in the islands off the British Columbia coast. James Houston's *Wolf Run: A Caribou Eskimo Tale* is an exciting story with dramatic pictures illustrating the efforts of a young Eskimo boy to keep his family from starving. Shizuye Takashima, in *A Child in Prison Camp,* depicts life in a prison camp as experienced by a young Japanese girl and her family in British Columbia in 1942–45. (H. C. Cl.)

French Language. Poets made the major contribution to French-Canadian literature in 1971. Editions de l'Hexagone published the complete works of Paul-Marie Lapointe (*Le Réel absolu*), considered by many the best contemporary French-Canadian poet, and of Olivier Marchand (*Par Détresse et tendresse*). Many well-known poets added to their work: Rina Lasnier, whose poetry was getting better and better, published *La Salle des rêves;* Jacques Brault published *La Poésie ce matin* in Paris; Juan Garcia, a young poet, received the review *Études françaises* prize for his *Corps de gloire;* Gilbert Langevin added two titles, *Ouvrir le feu* and *Stress.* Two important names among the avant-garde also published: Raoul Duguay (*L'Apokalypso*) and Claude Péloquin (*Pour la Grandeur de l'Homme*). In all, more than 60 books of poetry were published.

About 50 novels were published in 1971, compared with 65 in 1970, and only a few were good. Those expected to draw attention included *Le Cycle,* Gérard Bessette's first novel since *L'Incubation,* and a short novel by Jacques Ferron, *Les Roses sauvages,* which proved that Ferron can be a novelist and not just a "storyteller." Ferron's sister Madeleine published her second novel, *Le Baron écarlate,* which was less well-organized and well-written than her first. Among the newcomers, Gilbert La Rocque, with his second novel, *Corridors,* seemed on the way to becoming a really good writer, and Pierre Gravel, with *À perte de temps,* showed much talent. Another young man rapidly becoming a major French-Canadian novelist was Victor-Lévy Beaulieu, who proved his worth in *Jos Connaissant.*

In history, Jean-Paul Bernard's *Les Rouges, libéralisme, nationalisme et ultramontanisme au dix-neuvième siècle* covered the political, sociological, and religious history of 1835–70. Other historical works were *Histoire économique et unité canadienne* by Albert Faucher and *Histoire économique du Québec 1851–1901* by Jean Hamelin and Yves Roby. The publication of the *Journal d'Henriette Dessaules 1874–1880* appeared to be a major contribution to the literary heritage. Playwright Michael Tremblay had two works published, *Les Belles Soeurs* and *À toi pour toujours, ta Marie-Lou.*

The crisis of October 1970 was recalled in one way or another in all literary forms. There were at least five novels with revolutionary plots, six books of poetry recreating the revolutionary symbol, and a good dozen essays trying to analyze the crisis.

(Ad. T.)

DANISH

An implied reappraisal of life in modern Denmark was common to much prose in 1970 and 1971. In *Døden i skoven* (1970) Frank Jaeger centred his themes on people out of their normal surroundings, notably an actor reassessing his life and attitudes in a lonely forest. Tage Skou-Hansen's *Tredje halvleg* showed a bachelor looking critically at modern society but finally starting a relationship with a young unmarried mother, and on her terms. A more humorous view characterized Leif Panduro's *Daniels anden verden,* which took the traditional course of rejecting middle-class respectability and finding a meaning in some

sort of commitment. Equally humorous, though more disturbing, was Christian Kampmann's *Nok til hele ugen,* in which the unnamed main character arranges her life and thoughts in accordance with the ideals put forth in the popular press and women's magazines.

Pride of place for innovation, however, went to Anders Bodelsen's *Straus,* in which, in diary form, a fictitious author, Bang, comments on his life and outlines a new novel. Bang gradually merges with his principal character and murders Straus, the slickest novelist in Denmark, to whom Bang has always had to take second place. Obsession and loneliness were also studied in Bodelsen's short stories in *Hjælp.* In 1970, in a very different novel called *Ferie,* Bodelsen portrayed early adolescence with great insight and delicacy. Late adolescence was the subject of Klaus Rifbjerg's less delicate *Leif den lykkelige Jr.*

An outstanding nonfiction work was Tove Ditlevsen's *Gift* (the Danish word "gift" denoting both "marriage" and "poison"), in which the author describes her marriage to a mentally unstable doctor under whose guidance she became a helpless drug addict. In contrast, Grethe Heltberg's *Vi* was a beautiful description of a supremely happy marriage.

Lyric poets produced a number of volumes of "pure" poetry. Regin Dahl's *Ærinde uden betydning* (1970) was a middle-aged poet's look at the past coupled with forebodings for the future. Jørgen Gustava Brandt's *Vendinger* revealed a lyric poet of some standing who was not seeking to put something across, while Jørgen Leth's *Eventyret om den sædvanlige udsigt* was concerned with happiness found in everyday life. In Klaus Rifbjerg's *Mytologi* ancient and modern myths were demolished.

The Nordic Council's literature prize for 1971 was awarded to Thorkild Hansen for his trilogy on the Danish slave trade between Africa and the West Indies. (W. G. J.)

ENGLISH

Prose. "We are in metamorphosis": once more it was George Steiner, that most European of English critics, who went to the heart of the matter in 1971, as Britain teetered on the brink of Europe. Indeed, the enthusiastic pessimism of his T. S. Eliot Memorial Lectures coloured the literary pages for months, being briefly reported as he gave them at the University of Kent, then broadcast, printed serially in the *Listener* in April, and finally published together in the autumn with the formidable title *In Bluebeard's Castle: Some Notes Towards the Re-definition of Culture.*

As usual, reviewers were cool about Steiner's style and hectic polymathy, but many of his arguments seemed to gain ground; it was less easy to ignore his thesis about the observable collapse of confidence in the values of European culture, or to refute such assertions as: "Expanding areas of fact and sensibility . . . are out of reach of verbal account or paraphrase." Stuart Hampshire, in the *Observer,* provided the most interesting review: "This imaginative history, or sociology, does not amount to real history or sociology; it is rather a new, licensed genre of literary criticism, which finally allows the critic himself to be an imaginative author of interesting fictions." Hampshire acknowledged that "the questions raised, even in these very general terms, are not to be avoided."

Fiction. V. S. Naipaul, the champion prizewinner among British novelists, this time won the most valuable English fiction prize, the £5,000 Booker award,

REDMAN AND HIGGS

Gérard Bessette, French-Canadian author, published his novel "Le Cycle" in 1971.

COURTESY, GYLDENDAL FORLAG

Christian Kampmann's novel "Nok til hele ugen" was published in 1971.

with something that was neither simply a novel nor a collection of stories but a "sequence," part fiction, part reportage, called *In a Free State,* the title of the novella that was its centrepiece. This part of the book, a powerful narrative of an auto trip through an African country tense with crisis, was widely admired, chiefly for its account of postcolonial Africa and for its acute insight into the condition of the European remnant there, as indeed were the other sections, although opinions diverged on the question of the book's coherence and structural integrity.

David Caute's more ambitious response to present existential pressures on literature, *The Confrontation,* took the form of a trilogy: a play (*The Demonstration*), a novel (*The Occupation*), and a long critical essay (*The Illusion*), each involving a middle-aged, ex-academic writer, Stephen Bright, whose career bore a marked (and intentionally recognizable) resemblance to Caute's own. In the novel and the play, Bright, a radical of Suez vintage, is caught up in fascinated conflict with students from the newer left, respectively in the U.S. and in England. Bright is presented as the author of the critical essay, giving a fictional dimension to its arguments against both Marxist realism and the thin neo-aestheticism of some U.S. and French theorists and practitioners of the novel. The whole project bristled with problems, but the ferment of intellectual energy and creative will that it represented was something rare and fine on the English scene.

Another novelist reluctantly compelled to abandon the realism of her former work was Doris Lessing, whose *Briefing for a Descent into Hell* recounts a spiritual odyssey that was at once the case history of a particular psychotic and an allegorical history of the whole human case. Even those who jibbed at the verbal strain set up by the constant allegorizing were impressed by the force of the novel's exploratory impulse. With Iris Murdoch, the strain complained of by reviewers was, as usual, that of trying to synopsize the fantastic patterns of the plot. *An Accidental Man* resumed the author's masque of mind, its airy, dazzling figures now strangely familiar to constant readers, like the moods of a recurring dream. The more substantial pageant of Anthony Powell's "A Dance to the Music of Time" sequence reached its tenth scene with *Books Do Furnish a Room,* Widmerpool having gained a parliamentary seat in the Labour interest and lost his dangerous wife, Pamela, to a mere scribbler.

The year that saw the 90th birthday of P. G. Wodehouse brought also the last novel of an even more formidable English comic writer, Ivy Compton-Burnett. *The Last and the First,* presenting another version of the eternal family power struggle, was unrevised when she died and was neither the best nor the worst of her work. But, as Norman Shrapnel reminded us, "there is no talk in our literature like this," and one was grateful for the chance to overhear these final bars.

There was notably less gratitude for a posthumous work by E. M. Forster—the famous homosexual novel *Maurice,* written before World War I and revised on and off until 1960, when it was left with a final note: "Publishable—but worth it?" "I fear," wrote Philip Toynbee in his *Observer* review, "that Forster's literary executors have given the wrong answer to that question." V. S. Pritchett was kinder, but many critics shared Toynbee's view. What embarrassed them was not the subject but the shadow that the novel's intrinsic weakness cast back over its author's reputation as a middling English classic and liberal "touchstone." Julian Mitchell was not alone in foreseeing that "the academics who depend so much on Forster for 'value' would have a terrible time trying to justify the feebly sentimental ending." No doubt some embarrassment was also caused by T. C. Worsley's *Fellow Travellers,* a thinly fictionalized memoir of the sexual and political exploits of some of the author's eminent friends of the "Pink Decade."

Kingsley Amis' *Girl, 20* was an amusing bout of huffing and puffing at current forms of fashionable daftness, particularly daft speech forms. William Trevor and Melvyn Bragg each advanced their reputations with good new novels. Auberon Waugh thought *Miss Gomez and the Brethren,* Trevor's odd, sad comedy of the disruption of life in a slum-clearance area, "as good as *The Old Boys* and better than anything he has written since," while Bragg with *The Nerve* broke away from his well-observed Cumberland landscapes into more dangerous country—Hampstead and a nervous breakdown, and the narrator's attempt to decide who he is and where he belongs by writing out the story of his crisis. Nicholas Mosley's reputation may have slipped a notch or two under the portentous weight of *Natalie/Natalia,* while the monstrous riddling in Anthony Burgess' *MF* must have baffled many fans of his Enderby novels (perhaps even those who tried to take Frank Kermode's advice and read it with Lévi-Strauss in one hand and Edmund Leach in the other). John Le Carré's *The Naïve and Sentimental Lover* was an ambitious attempt (not noticeably more successful than *A Small Town in Germany*) to live morally on the earnings of his thrillers, and Allan Sillitoe's *Travels in Nihilon* was an engaging, energetic, but muddleheaded attempt at inverting and updating *Erewhon.* Thomas Kilroy's *The Big Chapel* was a striking first novel, bringing back to fierce life the protagonists in a notorious clerical scandal in Kilkenny a century ago.

Nonfiction. In a year not especially notable for English literary criticism, John Bayley's *Pushkin: A Comparative Commentary* was something of a landmark—a perceptive reading of the Great Untranslatable and a copious offering of more interesting analogues than the traditional "Russia's Byron" to help English readers understand him. Tony Tanner's *City of Words* provided a useful, if indulgent, guide to the hectic output of American fiction in the years 1950–70. It said something slightly depressing for the state of criticism of English literature that, after George Steiner's book, one of the most lengthily reviewed was Roy Fuller's collection of his Oxford lectures on poetry, *Owls and Artificers,* with its sensible, modest, and mildly amusing objections to the current thin diet of superficially rebelly verse, which, he says, may come to be seen as "the poetry of a society moving towards the reactionary and authoritarian." There were two good collections of essays by Frank Kermode and some late, and more eccentric, essays on 19th- and 20th-century writers, *Neglected Powers,* by George Wilson Knight.

It was a more rewarding year for native biography. The richest and strangest work here was Christopher Isherwood's memoir of his parents, *Kathleen and Frank,* quarried largely, but with great shaping tact and skill, from the diaries that his mother kept for nearly 70 years and from the lesser but still substantial store of letters from his father, who disappeared at Ypres when Christopher was a child. It is rare for a

Yoko Ono and husband John Lennon sign autographs in a London department store to promote her book "Grapefruit."

Doris Lessing's book "Briefing for a Descent into Hell" was published in 1971.

son to have such materials through which to rediscover and comprehend his parents, rarer still that the son should be able to respond so fully and seriously to the opportunity. Roy Fuller found an almost Proustian fullness in recalling these past lives, and thought this "a far more profound book than any he has written since the war," whetting the appetite sharply for the eventual publication of his own diaries. Isherwood's old friend and literary collaborator, W. H. Auden, gave us the nearest we are likely to have in the way of autobiography from him in *A Certain World: A Commonplace Book,* a record, salted with anagrams, riddles, and jokes, of the poet's reading, but since, as Frank Kermode remarked, "what Mr. Auden reads turns into Mr. Auden," there were teasing hints for the seriously curious reader.

Graham Greene, in his very different way, was almost as drily reticent in his autobiography, *A Sort of Life:* so much of his world is reinvented and mythologized—one more aspect of his war (to the death) with boredom—and there is plenty of the familiar Greene bile that stains the novels, even to the point of self-parody. (John Bayley reminded us that the winners of a *New Statesman* competition for a parody of his style were: (1) G. Greene; and (2) the author's younger brother, Hugh.)

The second volume of V. S. Pritchett's autobiography, *Midnight Oil,* showed the author emerging from (but not rejecting) the rich, post-Dickensian seediness of his lower-middle-class, suburban family life into the Life of Letters (under Clifford Sharp at the *New Statesman*) after an apprenticeship served in Paris and Ireland. Another memorable life was that of the poet, ex-boxer, ex-soldier, deserter, and poet again Vernon Scannell. *The Tiger and the Rose* was a gentle, modest, and uncomplaining account of one man's work in a demanding calling, as well made and decently feeling as the best of his poems.

There was a particularly heavy crop of politicians' memoirs, that usually unlovely genre the compiling and reviewing of which sometimes seems, neverthe-

less, to be the most favoured mode of writing about politics in Britain. Inevitably the most fiercely worked over was Harold Wilson's personal apologia for *The Labour Government 1964–1970,* instant history that was hardly literature, except perhaps in a vivid and detailed account of his meetings with Charles de Gaulle in 1967. George Brown's *In My Way* was generally thought to be embarrassing, and the fourth volume of Harold Macmillan's memoirs, to be too much after nearly 3,000 pages. Lord Butler's *The Art of the Possible,* however, was a delight—short, tightly but elegantly written, and full of those sidelong glances at contemporaries that, during his active career, made him the most collectable speaker in British postwar politics. Lord Robbins called his memoirs simply *Autobiography of an Economist,* which seemed like quite Butlerian modesty in a man who, as John Vaizey pointed out, ran or had run practically every national institution on London's axial number 11 bus route except St. Paul's Cathedral. In fact, it did deal primarily with his apprenticeship and career as an economist and only peripherally with his other roles as a man of influence and affairs on a scale beyond the wildest dreams of C. P. Snow's meritocrats.

Two eminent historians, one of them also a considerable political figure, were the subjects of memoirs by their widows. Julia Namier's *Lewis Namier: A Biography* was, wrote Arnold Toynbee in *The Guardian,* "a book by one very notable person about another, and . . . worthy of them both." The same might have been said, with even more justice, about Margaret Cole's *The Life of G. D. H. Cole.* "In terms of their contribution to the Labour movement and the common good, the Coles rank with the Webbs," wrote Laurence Thompson in the *Listener,* "and in the long run I do not think they will be seen as lesser figures." Thompson was himself the author of *The Enthusiasts,* an admired study of an earlier pair of disciples of William Morris and makers of the English Labour movement, John and Katherine Bruce Glasier, of whom a wealthy American admirer said despairingly, "These people are early Christians."

Smartly on the heels of the Conservative Restoration there appeared two considerable assaults on Labour's record and political theory by leading Tory ideologues: *The Impact of Labour 1920–1924* by the Cambridge historian Maurice Cowling, and Peregrine Worsthorne's *The Socialist Myth,* which centred on the thesis that social democracy's egalitarianism prevented it from producing a new governing class to run the country with the firmness demanded by its residually collectivist economic policies.

Alasdair MacIntyre produced a ground-clearing volume of essays in ideology and philosophy, *Against the Self-Images of the Age,* with more meat in one of them, "The End of Ideology and the End of the End of Ideology," than in many another dozen volumes of routine academic philosophy or political theory. MacIntyre suggests that what is most needed now is not a "value-free" science of politics but a humane and intelligent ideology whose political and philosophical contents, disciplined by human needs and limitations, are clearly stated. Gilbert Ryle's two volumes of *Collected Papers,* covering 40 years of work in philosophy, formed a rich summation of a brilliant career.

The most substantial work by an English historian was Keith Thomas' large and long-awaited *Religion and the Decline of Magic: Studies in Popular Beliefs in Sixteenth- and Seventeenth-Century England.*

Hugh Thomas' historical and political study of *Cuba* was even longer and would have been better shorter, most reviewers felt. F. S. L. Lyons produced a useful account of *Ireland Since the Famine,* which weakened as its author became bogged down in the mire of more recent Irish history. More light was thrown on those dark and troubled places by the third volume of Thomas Jones's *Whitehall Diary,* in which Keith Middlemas brought together the Irish papers of Lloyd George's confidant.

Several unusually interesting "house" histories appeared, with a good deal of social and cultural history in them. To mark the 150th anniversary of his old paper, David Ayerst wrote *Guardian: Biography of a Newspaper,* a feeling and well-documented history of a great British liberal institution; Donald McLachlan's *In the Chair: Barrington-Ward of The Times 1927–1948* dealt competently with an important shorter phase in the history of *The Guardian*'s chief competitor. Michael S. Howard's *Jonathan Cape, Publisher* was a careful explanation of how one of the finest of modern publishers' lists was built.

There was a welcome revival of interest in the character and mechanisms of British society, with several humane, literate, and nonacademic studies. Three of the best were Ursula Sharma's *Rampal and His Family,* the story of a Punjabi immigrant; Robert Roberts' *The Classic Slum,* a carefully observed account of Salford in the early years of the century; and *City Close-Up,* Jeremy Seabrook's anatomy of present-day life in another northern industrial town.

(W. L. WE.)

Poetry. Variety in style, form, and attitudes was the main feature of publications in 1971. Once again a considerable number of new poets were brought to the notice of the public, and if none could accurately be described as outstanding, most displayed real competence—perhaps they were a little too competent in the sense that they appeared to be more concerned with methods of presentation than with having something to present.

In *Voices Round a Star,* for instance, Michael Ffinch exhibited a high degree of intelligence, but his elliptical use of language tended to obscure what he was trying to say; *Language-Games,* by Veronica Forrest-Thomson (winner of the second annual New Poets Award), was appropriately titled, although the author's sense of humour managed to break through her intricate patterns; *The Flying Men,* by Patricia Whittaker, tended at times to be brought suddenly down to earth by the sheer weight of its imagery. John Cotton seemed more relaxed in *Old Movies,* an unpretentious collection that displayed both wit and intellect without taking the various situations featured in the volume out of the reach of the ordinary reader, while Elaine Feinstein produced some very effective personal poems in *The Magic Apple Tree.* The most unusual of the new poets undoubtedly was Donald Ward who, having worked as a postman for most of his life, published his first collection, *The Dead Snake,* at the age of 61—a surprisingly modern collection containing some well-drawn character sketches and pleasing lyrics.

Several of the established poets turned their attention to history and mythology. Geoffrey Hill's *Mercian Hymns* was focused upon Offa, the 8th-century king of Mercia, but throughout the volume the poet manipulated his central figure, "the presiding genius of the West Midlands," so as to be able to deal with man's use of power in any given circumstances and at the same time to contemplate his own childhood experiences in the Midlands (Offa's memories often being confused with those of the poet himself). Nevertheless, this impressive volume added substantially to Hill's growing reputation. George Mackay Brown, on the other hand, attempted to trace the development of a Norwegian settlement in the Orkneys over a period of several centuries in his rhetorically inclined *Fishermen with Ploughs.*

Thom Gunn's title for *Moly* was taken from the *Odyssey,* "moly" being the herb that Hermes gave to Odysseus to protect him against the enchantments of Circe. Some of the poems in Gunn's collection were written under the influence of LSD; others described the actual experience of "taking a trip," and the poet seemed to be suggesting that LSD, for him, was the modern equivalent to moly, enabling him to sharpen his perceptions and attain a new sense of unity with the external world. In "From the Waves," a more lucid and better constructed poem about surf-riders, Gunn effectively illustrated what he was awkwardly trying to say in other poems—that man achieves balance with the external world when he cooperates with, and makes use of, natural forces.

Since her suicide in 1963 Sylvia Plath had become something of a cult symbol, assuming almost mythic proportions. When her second volume, *Ariel,* appeared two years after her death, it took critics off guard by the sheer force of its impact and was immediately proclaimed the work of an accomplished poet, largely because it was impossible to trace any kind of development from her first volume, published in 1960. *Crossing the Water,* published in 1971 but containing poems written in 1960 and 1961, provided the necessary link and made it possible to see how Sylvia Plath had developed the command of language and the complicated metaphorical devices she was to employ with such devastating effect in *Ariel.*

Other volumes deserving consideration were *In the Happy Valley* by Tony Connor, *Poems of Places and People* by George Barker, *High Tide in the Garden* by Fleur Adcock, *Amana Grass* by Jon Silkin, the selected poems of Frances Bellerby, Vernon Scannell, and George Mackay Brown, and *The Young British Poets,* an anthology edited by Jeremy Robson.

(Ho. S.)

Thom Gunn's collection of poems, "Moly," dealing with the relationship of man's inner self to the external world, was published in 1971.

ANDER GUNN, COURTESY, FABER & FABER LTD.

FRENCH

Fiction. In the space of a few weeks in 1971 French presses turned out a number of works of monumental richness and complexity. *Les Bêtises,* which gained the 1971 Prix Goncourt for Jacques Laurent (better known under the name of Cécil St. Laurent), was comprised of four overlapping novels in one, a "murmur of intelligence" impregnated with eroticism. The hero engages in every possible escapade during the World War II occupation of France; ten years later he is found in a Saigon hospital and then followed across the world, in 600 closely packed pages teeming with disordered reflections and brilliant "imaginary memories." The Prix Renaudot went to Pierre-Jean Rémy (the pseudonym of a young diplomat) whose *Le Sac du palais d'été* presented a multiplicity of characters and scenes from past and present China through which moved the shade of the novelist-poet Victor Ségalen; the movement back and forth in time of this bewitching fresco demonstrated a major talent.

The bearer of a famous name, Jean d'Ormesson carried off the French Academy's Grand Prix for fiction with a historico-fictional spoof, *La Gloire de l'Empire.* The setting was an imaginary Greco-Roman empire; fictional, fabulous, and sometimes real characters bore witness to a vast erudition put at the service of the unbridled imagination of a philosopher-historian. Angelo Rinaldi, in *La Maison des Atlantes* (Prix Fémina), his second novel, dealt once more with the Corsican bourgeoisie that he sought to renounce. His hero, arriving like himself in Paris from Corsica, marries a young socialite and becomes a famous barrister; his social life is a success and his private life a failure. He tells his story for his son whom he despises as he does his nymphomaniac wife. Pascal Laîné, a young philosophy teacher, won the Prix Médicis with *L'Irrévolution,* which drew its inspiration from the events of May 1968 and reflected a crisis both public and private. The hoped-for insurrection remained verbal and sombre with resignation.

In Jean Bloch-Michel's *Daniel et Noémie* a man looks back on his happy adolescence rudely interrupted by war and by Nazi persecution; this was not, however, a racial novel, but a psychological quest that radiated warm affection and almost mystical love. *L'Enclave* by C. Charrière was concerned with the fate of a French contingent in the Far East which, forgotten by the home country, struggles under atrocious conditions while disintegrating both materially and morally. Didier Decoin, who received votes from all the literary juries, was again preoccupied with mysticism and allegory in *Abraham de Brooklyn,* his setting on this occasion being the construction of the Brooklyn Bridge in 19th-century New York.

G. Rosset's *La Chair à vif* was a sprightly piece of libertinage on the affair of a 40-year-old man with a very young girl, a rather less perverse Lolita. Similarly libertine was Geneviève Dormann's cheeky *Je t'apporterai des orages,* but here the woman was in control. *Un Soir à Pise* by P. Rossi was a long and sophisticated novella, involving both love and cruelty, that some writers thought bore comparison with Stendhal and Mérimée. Cruelty again, tinged with sadism, was found in P. Jeancard's powerful first novel, *La Cravache.* In *Le Chantier* A. Deza chose a dormitory town as the arena for the adulterous affair of a woman as monstrous physically as she is morally. In *Le Passé composé* F.-M. Banier brought his insolent, Cocteau-like talent to bear on an incestuous love between brother and sister. J. Lanzmann's *Mémoires*

d'un amnésique, the story of a modern Don Juan, would be of little account were it not for the passion and suffering that accompany the hero's affairs and the sense of humour that spices them. *Fiesta* by J. L. de Vilallonga presented a gripping portrayal of a young aristocrat during the course of the Spanish civil war.

There was a crop of well-made and well-intentioned novels. M. Larneuil's *Le Vautour et l'enfant,* soaked in human goodness and mysticism, was played out in the India of 1950; *L'Héritage de violence* by J. Laborde depicted a father who gets himself accused of murder to protect his son from suspicion. The journalist Pierre Rouanet received the Prix Interallié from a jury composed of eminent journalists for *Castell,* the clinical and psychological study of a woman who, after being horribly mutilated in a car accident, makes heroic efforts, supported by her faith in life, toward physical and mental recovery—a carefully written and moving book.

Most of the year's novels from older writers and members of the Academy seemed to be set in the provinces. R. Grenier's *Avant une guerre* presented the downfall of a petit-bourgeois family as told by the youngest son: the father's suicide and the mother's bewitchment by an impostor told with "the pulse of life maintained by the art of the writer." *Le Voisinage des cavernes* by Jean Cassou, recipient of the Prix National des Lettres, was a traditional novel, a family saga, nicely arranged and with convincingly well-drawn characters. Pierre-Henri Simon's *La Sagesse du soir* was in a similar vein; a retired teacher brings together his children and grandchildren in his country house. The contrast of the generations and the serenity of the aging man were presented in a subdued style.

Jean-Louis Curtis shifted the scene back to Paris; his *Le Roseau pensant,* under the guise of a very successful *roman bourgeois,* satirized snobbish avant-garde society. A. Chamson, in a long historical novel, *La Tour de Constance,* painted an accurate and moving picture of a distressing episode in the struggle between Catholics and Protestants. *L'Autre* by Julien Green (*see* BIOGRAPHY), a new member of the Academy, was a strange story of love, hate, and struggle for salvation set in Denmark before and after World War II—not one of this great writer's best works. The same could be said of *Un Assassin est mon maître* by Henry de Montherlant, whose style lacked its customary grandeur in this depressing tale of an obsessive intellectual failure. After ten years of silence Antoine Blondin made a brilliant reappearance with *Monsieur Jadis,* an amusing and poignant book whose hero, very sympathetically portrayed, wanders from bar to bar and from one fantastic adventure to another.

Among the representatives of the *nouveau roman,* Suzanne Prou confirmed her reputation with *Méchamment les oiseaux;* the central figure, a victim of nervous depression, becomes monstrous in his obsessions. Claude Simon's *Les Corps conducteurs* was a static work feeding on the images arising in the mind of a man suddenly stricken with illness in an American street. Pierre Silvain's four men abandoned on a desert island in *Les Éoliennes* were easier to follow with interest and enjoyment. P. Bouissac's *Les Demoiselles* were two mysterious provincial ladies. These works, while engaging the attention of the critics, found few readers. Others, however, written with perfect clarity, were highly successful: Georges Simenon's *Le riche homme,* Paul Vialar's *Mon seul amour,* Guy des Cars' *Une certaine dame* (on those who undergo a change of sex), and Edmonde Charles-Roux's *Elle, Adrienne* (based on the life of Coco Chanel).

Nonfiction. Historical surveys and popularizations such as André Castelot's *Le Calendrier de l'histoire* or Alain Decaux's *Grands secrets, grandes énigmes* enjoyed a growing success. *L'Histoire de France* by the duc de Castries presented the synoptic view of a philosophical mind that was nevertheless readily accessible. G. Bordonove's *La Guerre de six cents ans* depicted the six centuries of rivalry between the English and French that had once divided Europe and now seemed gone forever. *Le Palais du Luxembourg* by Bernard Morice traced the various transformations undergone by Marie de Médicis' palace. F. Vaux de Foletier's *Mille ans d'histoire des Tsiganes* was an absorbing and well-documented study of gypsies in Europe from the 15th century.

Among the many books about Charles de Gaulle, André Malraux's *Les Chênes qu'on abat* was the spiritual testament of the statesman presented by a great writer; *Un autre de Gaulle* by Claude Mauriac, who was the general's private secretary from August 1944 onward, revealed his day-to-day moods. J.-R. Tournoux' *Jamais dit* contained sensational revelations and secret documents from adolescence down to de Gaulle's resignation in 1969. Pierre Viansson-Ponté's *L'Histoire de la république gaullienne* and P.-O. Lapie's *De Blum à de Gaulle* were also successful.

Henri Troyat produced an exhaustive biography of Gogol. Based principally on Russian sources, the book perfectly recreated the climate of the age. Chapters on the works were inserted between those on the life of this poor student, unbalanced from childhood, a liar, impostor, and parasite in and out of Russia. The 2,200 pages of *L'Idiot de la famille* by Jean-Paul Sartre (*see* BIOGRAPHY), which formed only the beginning of his study of Flaubert, were a historical and biographical essay in reaction against structuralist criticism. With *Marcel Proust romancier,* one of the many books marking the centenary of Proust's birth, Maurice Bardèche became G. D. Painter's most serious competitor. Maurice Toesca's *Alfred de Musset* and Gabriel d'Aubarède's *André Chénier* were written with both fervour and erudition. J. Paris devoted two studies to Rabelais: *Rabelais au futur* established parallels between the questions raised by Rabelais and those of our own time; *Hamlet et Panurge* was an essay in comparative literature followed by a searching discussion between the author and other adherents of the New Criticism. V. del Litto's edition of Stendhal's *Journal Littéraire* brought to light hitherto unpublished texts. This was a wild chase after ideas composed of notes, sketches, and projected works in outline.

Michel Butor, "a cultural commercial traveller between divers continents," alternated in *Ou* sections of clear and resonant prose with others devoid of syntax or sense and embellished with typographical whimsies. René Huyghe, regarded by many as the greatest art critic alive, in his authoritative *Formes et forces* followed the transformation of humanity through art, passing from psychology to philosophy "with both precision and broad compass." Autobiographical reflections and memoirs of importance included Paul Morand's *Venises,* Emmanuel Berl's *À contretemps,* and Jacques de Bourbon-Busset's *Comme le diamant.*

Jean Cau, a pamphleteer with a sharp-edged pen, berated in *Le Temps des esclaves* an age that, in its

French poet and novelist Georges-Emmanuel Clancier was awarded the Grand Prix de Littérature in 1971.

hyperegalitarianism, destroys culture to produce slaves. In a lighter, delicately barbed style, Pascal Jardin's *La Guerre a neuf ans* described life in Vichy under Marshal Pétain. Louis Pauwels' *Lettre ouverte aux gens heureux* was a merciless attack on intellectuals and others intent on the destruction of contemporary society and civilization. He faced counterattacks from many quarters while heading the list of best sellers with this reaction against "the church of pessimism." D. Lapierre and L. Collins were similarly successful with *O Jérusalem.* On the basis of countless interviews and secret documents they brought to life those who fought in the Holy City in 1947–48, depicting scenes of horror, heroism, and cruelty with exemplary objectivity. On the same subject, Joseph Kessel in *Les Fils de l'impossible* espoused the cause of those Israelis who came from the four corners of the earth to defend "an impossible future among barren rocks."

Poetry. Some first-rate anthologies appeared to reawaken the public taste for poetry. In *La Poésie Surréaliste* J. L. Bédouin studied the movement whose exponents included Louis Aragon and Paul Éluard. A novelist-poet, Pierre Seghers, produced *La Poésie symboliste,* in which the names of Baudelaire, Mallarmé, and Verlaine—poets whose influence on American writers remained strong right down to the beat generation—figured prominently.

In such company the contemporary poets did not come off badly. *L'Évidence même,* by L. Bérimont, portrayed the enchantment and ferocity of love, while René Char's *L'Honneur devant Dieu* was an encounter with death. *L'Expérience magique* by P. Damarix was a work rich in rhyme and rhythm "wrought from irresistible flights of the soul." M. Bataille's *Le Cri dans le mur* revealed the poet in a celebrated novelist. R. Lorho, who had begun with successful emulation of Guillaume Apollinaire, suddenly, under the name of L. Ray, went in search of "a poetic state . . . through the complete dislocation of diction." Alain Bosquet produced a study on Roger Caillois, the eminent essayist and poet who had recently been elected to the French Academy.

French poetry suffered sad losses during the year. A few days after the publication of *Éspaces d'instants,* "the condensation of a whole work dedicated to giving place and eternity to the most fugitive moments of the inner life," Jean Follain was killed in an accident. Not long afterward came the deaths of the journalist and scholarly critic André Billy, and then of the poet and playwright Charles Vildrac.   (Ae. B.)

GERMAN

The continuing crisis in contemporary German literature featured little as a subject for comment in West Germany in 1971. While the people were aware that all was far from well with their literature, they increasingly were disinclined to read the all too familiar diagnoses of its ills, since nobody seemed able to suggest any suitable course of treatment.

As usual, serious fiction was being crowded out by documentary works of all kinds, together with numerous books of popularized science. The number of new writers publishing in 1971 was reduced considerably and poetry had vanished almost completely from the scene. Moreover, works by prominent writers, announced with excessive displays of publicity and hence awaited with considerable excitement, more often than not put reviewers in an extremely embarrassing position when they finally appeared.

Thus, the Austrian lyric poet Ingeborg Bachmann disappointed admirers of her verse when, after a decade of silence, she published her novel, *Malina.* The book told the story of a writer in love with one man but living with another who finally turns out to be but a figment of the imagination, the alter ego of the heroine. What promised to be a tale of passionate love proved to be an extremely confused and muddled book.

Admirers of Swiss dramatist Friedrich Dürrenmatt fared no better: his latest tale, *Der Sturz,* was an anti-Soviet satire that used such a facile and senseless means to achieve its ends that most critics felt the only decent thing to do was to ignore the book altogether. Peter Weiss's play *Hölderlin,* however, was not to be ignored; it was staged by several German playhouses and was a failure on every occasion. After several mainly documentary plays, Weiss had returned to the dramatic style of his famous *Marat/ Sade,* but effects that once had a direct and original impact now seemed clumsy and naïve. The dramatic sequence illustrating the struggle and defeat of the German poet Friedrich Hölderlin, who died mad, was supposed to show the tragedy of the isolated intellectual broken against the attitudes of his age. It constituted a misuse of the stage for simple pictorial instruction of a political nature.

More original, if likewise somewhat questionable, was *Der Ritt über den Bodensee,* a play by the young but already famous Austrian Peter Handke. Consisting of a series of separate studies, the play illustrates and dissects social chitchat and everyday speech in an attempt to show the emptiness of the words we use. On this occasion man was to be seen as the victim of his language. Amusing stylistic tricks and decorative lyricism, however, failed to save the play, which suffered from intellectual poverty and that very linguistic bankruptcy that it sought to point out.

Hubert Fichte's novel *Detlevs Imitationen "Grünspan"* was also a disappointment. The experiences of a child in Hamburg toward the end of World War II and in the years immediately afterward were related in what amounted to little more than a hotchpotch of reminiscences and impressions, facts and details. The device of seeing events through the eyes of a child proved particularly unfortunate, leading to a general infantilization of the world.

Against this dismal backdrop, a patchy work that was nevertheless interesting in parts acquired considerable importance. Heinrich Böll's novel *Gruppenbild mit Dame* presented a cross section of society ranging from the multimillionaire to the garbageman and embraced a period of time extending from the end of Kaiser Wilhelm II's reign to the present day. The central figure, Leni, is the embodiment of an old German sentimental ideal of feminine perfection: she is blond, natural, and unsophisticated, true-hearted and eager to serve. Her tender love affair with a young Russian prisoner of war in the middle of World War II is to be seen as a protest against the injustice and cruelty of the world. The book, however, suffered from its composition, whose form seemed to have no guiding principle at all. Allowing himself to be carried along by his own fancy, Böll did not hesitate to set a variety of separate pieces side by side: stories and sketches, comic interludes and scenes from everyday life, gossip and anecdote. While the fragments that went to make it up were variable in quality, the book as a whole provided many illustrations of Böll's ability, above all other German writers, to observe and pinpoint nuances and details, atmospheres and turns of phrase that give immediate and palpable life to the spirit of the age. Whatever faults could be imputed to it, the novel provided a considerable number of quite splendid portraits and impressions, close-ups and episodes. Most masterly of all were those miniatures where the horror and the humour of Böll's vision of the world were present side by side.

Erich Maria Remarque's posthumous novel, *Schatten im Paradies,* achieved considerable success, if not with the critics at least with the less exacting public. Set among German immigrants who had fled from Hitler to the United States, the novel demonstrated yet again that if Remarque was no great artist, he was certainly a first-rate craftsman who could tell highly dramatic stories in an exciting way.

Walter Kempowski's "bourgeois novel," *Tadellöser & Wolff,* was also set in the years of the Third Reich. The novel was broken up into very short, very precise scenes and anecdotes that together succeeded in throwing into extraordinarily sharp relief the day-to-day life of a middle-class family during that period.

Mario Szenessy, a Hungarian writer living in West Germany and writing in German, showed himself to be a storyteller of great humour, although admittedly restraining his ambition somewhat on this occasion by taking up the old form of the picaresque novel with *Lauter falsche Pässe.* Fantasy and simplicity were triumphant in *Der Bahnwärter Sandomir,* an amusing volume of stories by Günter Bruno Fuchs, while Austrian H. C. Artmann's tales in *How much, Schatzi?* offered comical flights of fancy and linguistic acrobatics quite out of the ordinary.

Max Frisch was very successful once again, this time with a little volume in a peripheral field. *Wilhelm Tell für die Schule,* as might be expected, retells the traditional story in a completely different way from the familiar version and consistently and amusingly debunks a national myth.

First and foremost in the sphere of poetic prose pieces was the slim but significant little volume *Steht noch dahin,* by Marie Luise Kaschnitz. The lyrical diary jottings that went to make up the book took their life from bald comments and announcements, direct statement, and simple enumeration. The apocalyptic form, which dominated the work, remained consistently subdued and for that reason had a startling and gripping effect.

Works that attracted particular attention in the marginal area between literature and documentary writing were Horst Krüger's travel book, *Fremde Vaterländer*, Wolfgang Hildesheimer's reminiscences, *Zeiten in Cornwall*, and above all Golo Mann's comprehensive biography of Wallenstein, which was both a historical work and a novel.   (M. R.-R.)

ITALIAN

It seems to be now generally accepted that literature is related to the society that produces and consumes it. This does not mean, of course, as naïve determinists would have it, that precise inferences can be drawn from one to the other. One might otherwise be forgiven for supposing that obscure literary works such as Germano Lombardi's *Il confine* or Gianni Toti's *L'altra fame*, comprehensible only to a few friendly critics, could not appear in print in a country where over half of the population still uses dialects rather than standard Italian, where few families regularly buy books, and where even a best seller rarely prints more than 50,000 copies. The fact that they do appear must be viewed in a social context where the cultural and literary industry is geared largely to the modes of consumption of an educated minority.

Obscurity is not objectionable in itself. It may indeed be a sign of the writer's struggle to raise his language to the intensity and sharpness of his vision of reality, which is what really matters. This seemed true of Lucio Mastronardi's *A casa tua ridono*, a complex work whose avant-garde style results from the combination of several narrative levels in cyclical time with perceptive social commentary. All too often, however, reality does not seem to matter at all, and is used by writers merely as a pretext for experimenting with unusual (but not new) techniques. Life is turned into a metaphor for art where art should be held as a mirror to life.

This was basically the difference between *Io e lui*, by A. Moravia, in which the warped sex life of the protagonist becomes a symbol of the artist's intellectual frustration and creative sterility, and *Una città in amore*, by Alberto Bevilacqua, in which the consciously literary themes of sexual passion and repressed love point to class violence and political repression in the world outside. It was also the difference between several novels (*Conspiratio oppositorum* by Mario Spinella, *La torre capovolta* by Mario Tomizza, *La spiaggia d'oro* by Raffaello Brignetti) where facts, images, memories appear as the tokens of a literary game, and *Le masche*, by Franco Cordero, or *La paura*, by Piero Gadda-Conti, where, through the well-worn devices of the fictional autobiography and the historical novel, contemporary facts and situations are dealt with effectively. To consider the characters and plot of *Ligabue come un cavallo* by Giuseppe Raimondi, *I cieli della sera* by Michele Prisco, or *Il gioco sul ponte* by Sergio Ferrero, was like remembering a dream the following morning: coherent and logical while it lasted, it later lacks consistency and credibility. On the other hand, to read Carlo Sgorlon's *La notte del ragno mannaro* was to be caught in the grip of a powerful and absorbing dream whose emotional intensity is so great that credibility and logic cease to be of any consequence.

For more restful and less adventurous reading, one might turn to several books halfway between fiction and autobiography. Gianna Manzini's *Ritratto in piedi* contained a very moving portrait of her anarchist father. Sergio Antonielli also remembered a father figure in *Oppure niente*, but the memory is of no help to the protagonist in trying to make sense of his present life. Felice Chilanti's interesting journey through Fascism and Communism, *La paura entusiasmante*, was unfortunately marred by a self-consciously arty style, seemingly unrelated to the needs of the narrative process. Luca Asprea's unusual documentary novel, *Il previtoccolo*, which might have been entitled "The Sex Life of a Peasant's Son," had a preface by Franco Cordero so full and detailed as to make the reading of the book almost unnecessary. The subject of *Il ritorno* by Manlio Cancogni was a potentially thrilling war story; its treatment, however, did not live up to the initial promises. Enrico Raffi's *Sposa mia* was a witty and caustic satire of the Catholic idea of marriage. One knew what to expect from Natalia Ginzburg (*Mai devi domandarmi*, a collection of urbane essays) and Carlo Cassola (*Paura e tristezza*).

The only book to come out in 1971 whose survival beyond the end of the century one could already confidently predict was *Satura*. The book was probably the best so far by Eugenio Montale and a remarkable collection of poems by any standard. Satisfying poems were also to be found in *Di brace in brace*, by Libero de Libero, and *Su fondamenti invisibili*, by Mario Luzi. *Metropolis*, by Antonio Porta, was a sort of modern "dictionary of commonplaces"; the mere enunciation and juxtaposition of a few hundred gems of traditional wisdom suffices to bring out their inherent inanity and falsity.

There was also a good crop of essays on Marxism: *Sul materialismo*, written by Sebastiano Timpanaro with his usual immense erudition and persuasion; *Teoria della crisi sociale in Marx*, by Umberto Cerroni; and a useful *Il pensiero di Gramsci*, by Giorgio Nardone. A most interesting survey of Italian women's opinions on maternity, divorce, and abortion was *La sfida femminile* by Elvira Banotti, and more material for women's liberation was provided by Chiara Saraceno in *La parte della donna*. In the field of literary criticism, Davide Lajolo returned to his favourite authors (*Pavese e Fenoglio*); Giorgio Petrocchi's *Manzoni: letteratura e vita* was a collection of previously published and unpublished essays. Alberto Arbasino's essays in *Sessanta posizioni* were like chocolates: wrapped in a tinselly style, unsuitable as a meal, but pleasant and with some food value. *Che cos'è la tradizione*, by Elémire Zolla, was an extremely erudite rehearsal of already discredited arguments in favour of intellectual repression, conservatism, and reaction.   (G. C.)

JAPANESE

The suicide of Yukio Mishima on Nov. 25, 1970, gave a profound shock to Japanese society in general, and especially to literary circles, where his demise marked the end of a literary epoch. Together with Nobel prizewinner Kawabata and a handful of others, Mishima had belonged to a group that sought to capture and express a beauty that was uniquely Japanese, in form and spirit. Among these only Tatsuzo Ishikawa continued to publish, but his writing had always had more social than literary significance. Creations in the traditional forms—tanka and haiku—no longer commanded wide popularity, but precisely because of that, perhaps, their literary values were being appreciated even more deeply.

Most of the competent authors were being influenced by Western ideologies, and some by a fin-de-siècle nihilism. The prevailing mood was perhaps summed up by Katsumi Takahashi, a novelist and essayist popular among college students: "It is as if one has seen, in one's youth, a ruin of a great city, and observed at the same time the desolation within the hearts of a people—and because of this one continues to see the desolate ruin behind the brilliant facade of a newly decorated city."

Belonging to a somewhat different school was Shusaku Endo, a Catholic writer who frequently found his material in the history of Christianity in Japan (*One Who Is Mother*). Morio Kita, son of Mokichi Saito, one of the last great poets in the Japanese tradition (tanka), wrote light and whimsical tales and essays. His irony seemed to appeal to a wide variety of readers, though his current book amounted to nothing more than a humorous report on a drab trip to see a rocket taking off for the moon.

Of the women writers, Ayako Sono, Sawako Ariyoshi, and Yumiko Kurashashi were considered outstanding. Sono's *For Whom Must We Love*—a series of essays of a timeless and somewhat banal variety—broke the best-seller record. Ariyoshi continued to show her skill as a raconteuse in two books of fiction, *Shinnyo* (*Seamstress*), a love story set during the years of World War II and its aftermath, and *House No. 3, Yuhiga-oka*, an exposé of the life in corporate housing areas. Kurashashi came out with *Anti-Tragedy*, a collection of novelettes based on the tragedies of Sophocles and Aeschylus.

In the meanwhile, a crop of young writers was emerging, many of them appearing to belong to the antiliterature school. Tatsuzo Ishikawa, who had served on the selection committee for the Akutagawa literary prize for the past several decades, resigned in August, saying he "no longer could understand what is being written." There was also a mass movement to create a new "children's literature." Several series in this genre, penned by known authors, were being prepared for publication.   (R. H.)

JEWISH

Hebrew. The unsettled political conditions in Israel did not deter Hebrew literature there from producing some valuable works in various categories. The outstanding event was the posthumous publication of S. Y. Agnon's *Shira*, a richly textured novel by the Nobel laureate. A. Kahana-Karmon's *ve-Yareah be Emek Ayalon* attracted considerable attention. In *Adnai ha-Nahar*, A. Appelfeld again proved impressive, as did D. Shahar in *Moto shel ha-Elohim ha-Katan* and A. B. Yehoshua in *9 Sippurim*. An anthology of new Israeli short stories was *ha-Sippur ha-Yisraeli be-Mivhar Hadash*, edited by Y. Haezrahi. Related to this was G. Shaked's *Gal Hadash ba-Sipporet ha-Ivrit*, on the "new wave" in Hebrew fiction. Publications of importance were the three-volume collection of S. Halkin's critical essays, *Derakhim ve-Tsidai Derakhim ba-Sifrut*, B. Y. Michaly's incisive evaluations in *Demuyot Uzdudiot*, and *Avnai Gader*, D. Sdan's erudite disquisitions.

Noteworthy as histories were the volume *Michtvai Avraham Mapu*, the letters of the first modern Hebrew novelist, and *Ketavim Genuzim*, the early writings of the national Hebrew poet H. N. Bialik. M. Benayahu gave a fascinating account of the history

of Hebrew printing in *ha-Defus ha-Ivri be-Cremona*. Going back in time was M. Merhavia's comprehensive work *ha-Talmud bi-Rei ha-Natzrut*. M. Namir's *Shelihut be-Moskvah* was politically instructive; *ha-Kibbutz ke-Maarehet Hevratit Petuha* by N. Golub and D. Katz had sociological interest.

Many volumes of poetry appeared. Leah Goldberg's *Shearit ha-Chaim*, the last book by a distinguished and beloved poet, was published posthumously. *Shirim*, the collected poems of I. Efros, an older poet, frequently bespoke the new. In an extremely modern vein was D. Avidan's *Shirim Hitzoniim*, while *Al Menat Lo Lizkor* was Y. Amichai's sharp contemporary statement. Far removed from these were the nostalgic poems of N. Yonatan, *Shirim ba-Arov ha-Yam*. D. Pagis struck a forceful note in the volume *Gilgul*. Noteworthy also were R. Adi's *Mishaa le-Shaa*, A. Eldon's *Levado ba-Zerem ha-Koved*, and R. Shani's *Shalom la-Adoni ha-Melech*. Collections by such promising poets as M. Meir (*ha-Aretz Hahi Mitahat la-Mayim*) and M. Oren (*Adam Muad*) also appeared. A much needed work was M. Megged's anthology of modern Hebrew poetry, *Shirim Lyriim*.

In the U.S. the hiatus of Hebrew literature continued. Nevertheless, new books by U.S. writers included a socio-historical study by M. Davis, *Bait Yisrael be-Amerika;* a volume of aphoristic yet lyrically felt poems, *Igrotai le-Dorot Aherim*, by E. Silberschlag; and two collections of verse, *be-Misholai* by R. Avinoam and *El Parvarai ha-Shemesh* by R. Lee.   (G. P.)

Yiddish. The eminent American Yiddish poet and essayist Jacob Glatstein died in November 1971, a few weeks after Yiddish cultural circles the world over had marked his 75th birthday. Two new books had been published for the occasion: a collection of verse entitled *Songs from Right to Left* and essays entitled *In the World with Yiddish*.

U.S. and Canadian contributions to Yiddish poetry in 1971 included *Not on Bread Alone*, by Brakha Coodley; Leo Kussman's *Ballads of a Generation; Poems for Children*, by Berl Siegal; the second volume of Meir Shtiker's *Jewish Landscape;* M. M. Saffir's *Creator of Various Dreams; Songs at Midnight*, by Menakhem Stern; Rochelle Weprinski's *The Only Star;* and the second volume of *Poems of Destruction and Faith*, by Aaron Zeitlin. Collections by poets in other lands included *Song Between Teeth*, by Joseph Kerler, formerly of Moscow, now living in Tel Aviv, Israel, and *In the Circle of Years*, by Jacob Sternberg, Romania's eminent Yiddish poet.

In fiction the appearance of Isaac Bashevis Singer's *Tales from Behind the Stove* was an important event. The third volume of Mendel Tabachnik's trilogy *Kalman Bulan* depicted the life of Jews in South Africa, while *The Uhamas*, by Fajwel Zygielbaum, portrayed the life of the Zulus. Jewish life in England was presented in the collection of short stories *In the Past and in the Present*, by Moshe Beckerman. France was represented by Menukha Ram's *Around the Willow Tree* and Joseph Schein's *Comedian on the Rock*. Of special significance was L. Treister's *Vision at the Vistula*, on Jewish life in Poland immediately after World War I.

New accomplishments in literary criticism and in the general essay were found in *Writers and Works*, by Hayman Bass; *To the Summits of the Jewish Spirit*, by Abraham Golomb; Isaak Turkow-Grudberg's *On My Way;* Isaac Kahan's *On the Crossroad;*

Between Sadness and Joy, by Mordecai Kaufman of Buenos Aires, Arg.; *Figures of My Generation,* by the late Canadian editor and critic Gershon Pomerantz; *Figures and Profiles,* by Israeli novelist Isaiah Spiegel; *Intimately with the World,* by the late Eliezer Steinman; S. Tenebaum's *Hunger for the Word;* and Itzchak Goldkorn's *Singers and Sayers. My Summation* included Aaron Karlin's reminiscences of an editor-pioneer of modern Yiddish literature in the U.S. An outstanding contribution to the field of literary criticism was Chone Shmeruk's *Peretz's Vision of Despair.* A biography worthy of special mention was *In Struggle,* the life and deeds of writer and labour leader Jacob Patt by his son Emanuel. (M. SN.)

LATIN-AMERICAN

While the 1960s had been a "boom" period for the novel in Latin America, it appeared the 1970s might be an era of poetry, which had a firm tradition on the continent. An indication of this was seen in the fact that the second Nobel Prize for Literature to be awarded in Latin America in five years went not to a novelist but to a poet, Pablo Neruda, who continued to maintain his artistic excellence in *Más piedras del cielo,* published in 1971.

The authors of the *nueva novela,* who had constituted a close group and had received innumerable eulogies, found themselves subjected to literary and political attacks in their own countries and divided in their attitudes on the matter of Cuban poet Heberto Padilla. Padilla had been arrested in Havana in March and was released after signing a confession in which he called himself a "vicious character" who had taken part in counterrevolutionary activities. In a letter to Prime Minister Fidel Castro made public May 20 in Paris, 60 leftist intellectuals, all defenders of the Cuban revolution, expressed their disillusionment at the treatment of Padilla, accusing Castro of imposing Stalinism. Castro countered by expressing "repugnance" toward those who suggested the confession had been obtained by torture. Among those signing the letter were Jean-Paul Sartre, Simone de Beauvoir, Susan Sontag, Alberto Moravia, and a number of Latin-American writers, including Mexican novelist Carlos Fuentes and Peruvian novelist Mario Vargas Llosa. The latter, however, maintained his support of the revolution. In contrast, Julio Cortázar of Argentina reaffirmed his support for Castro in a sort of verse manifesto, *Policrítica en la hora de los chacales,* which led its readers to fear that his best creative period was past.

None of the new-wave novelists published another book of fiction. Some, like the Mexicans Fuentes and Vicente Leñero, tried drama—Fuentes in *Los reinos originarios* (*El tuerto es rey* and *Todos los gatos son pardos*); Leñero in *La carpa* and *El juicio.*

In Argentina, Jorge Luis Borges (*see* BIOGRAPHY) continued his trilingual interviews with the world press and published a story in booklet form, *El congreso. El laberinto de Sion,* the most interesting novel of the year, was written by 25-year-old Marcos Ricardo Barnatán; *Gabriel Andaral* did not add much to Eduardo Mallea's reputation as a novelist, nor did *Caína muerte* enhance that of H. A. Murena. The fantastic tales of Silvina Ocampo (*Los días de la noche*) and, above all, those of Enrique Anderson Imbert, who contributed his best book to date (*La locura juega al ajedrez*), were more fortunate. In poetry greater quantity meant poorer quality; the

austere density of Alberto Girri in *Valores diarios* occupied a place apart. Noteworthy among the overwhelming yield of critiques and essays were the eighth series (1968–70) of *Testimonios* by Victoria Ocampo; the *Enciclopedia* of national authors compiled by Pedro Orgambide and Roberto Yahni; the Marxist analysis of David Viñas in *Literatura argentina y realidad política: de Sarmiento a Cortázar;* and *Fundadores de la nueva poesía latinoamericana* in which Saúl Yurkievich studied Vallejo, Neruda, Borges, Huidobro, and Paz.

The masters of Brazilian poetry were very active. Joaquim Cardozo (*De uma noite de festa*), Murilo Mendes (*Convergência*), and Henriqueta Lisboa (*Nova lírica*) all published new books; Manuel Bandeira compiled a selection (*Meus poemas perferidos*) and, among the younger generation, Foed Castro Chamma (*O andarilho e a aurora*) and Anderson Braga Horta (*Altiplano*) called for attention. In fiction the best books came from two new authors, Autran Dourado (*O risco do bordado*) and Antônio Calado (*Bar Don Juan*), while the famous Erico Veríssimo was also present, with *O arquipélago.* Antônio Cândido dominated the essay field once more with *Literatura e cultura, Varios escritos.* Other critics examined the Brazilian and Portuguese classics: *Os romances de Machado de Assis* (A. Draemer); *Graça Aranha, o dotrinador* (J. A. Almeida); *Estética das escolas literarias do Brazil* (L. Marobin); and *Crítica social de Eça de Queiroz* (D. Menezes).

Once again the poetry of Nicaragua was the exception in the desolate scene of Central American literature, and outstanding among this poetry was *Estelas/homenajes* of Ernesto Mejía Sánchez. In *Las celdas,* the Guatemalan Carlos Solórzano dealt with the famous case of the priest Lemercier and his rebellious monastery in Cuernavaca. Five authors published jointly *Poesía joven de Panamá;* of the five Agustín del Rosario stood out.

Before his arrest and self-accusation made him, briefly, a world figure, Heberto Padilla published *Por el momento,* which presented him as a minor poet well versed in North American poetry. The best of his generation in Cuba was Roberto Fernández Retamar, as evidenced by *A quien pueda interesar.* But the best Cuban book was the dazzling *Poesía completa* of José Lezama Lima in which the most extraordinary baroque figures become natural and unaffected forms.

In Colombia the pros and cons of a guerrilla utopia appeared to be the sole theme: *La guerrilla por dentro* (Jaime Arenas), *Usheda, violencia en llamas* (Alvaro Valencia), and *Diario de un guerrillero* (Arturo Alape). Out of step with the times, Germán Espinosa, in *Los cortejos del diablo,* recounted tales of witchcraft in colonial Cartagena.

Under the leadership of Salvador Allende, Chile seemed to capture the attention that had earlier gone to Cuba, Brazil, or Mexico. Not only did Chile get the Nobel Prize, it contributed the most important political book, *Conversaciones con Allende* by Régis Debray, and the best Latin-American novel of the year, *El obsceno pájaro de la noche.* José Donoso created two characters worthy of Beckett or Buñuel— "Boy," the child-monster, and "El Mudito"—in this phantasmagoria that presents the sordidness of old age and deformity as a metaphor of man's unforgivable transgression, having been born. Compared with such a book, novels as worthwhile as *Zoom* by Hernán Valdés, *Las noches y un día* by Mercedes

Pablo Neruda, poet and Chilean ambassador to France, received the Nobel Prize for Literature in 1971.

Valdivieso, or *Palomita blanca*, in which a former "angry young man," Enrique Lafourcade, casts his sour middle-aged gaze on the Chilean youth of today, might be said to be of minor import. As to the rest, the surrealist poet Braulio Arenas tried drama (*Samuel*) and narrative (*El laberinto de Creta*); Fernando Alegría combined studies of poets and novelists in *Literatura y revolución;* and Humberto Díaz Casanueva appeared a little behind the times in *Sol de lenguas.*

Mexican literature revolved around the student rebellion of 1968 and the slaughter of Tlatelolco in Mexico City on Oct. 2, 1968. There were documentaries gathered from eyewitnesses (*La noche de Tlatelolco* by Elena Poniatowska, which was reprinted 14 times within eight months), lyrical impressions (*Con él, conmigo, con nosotros tres* by M. L. Mendoza), and intensely virulent satires (*El gran solitario de Palacio* by R. Avilés Favila). None of these, however, reached the clarity and sincerity of *Los días y los años,* a nonfiction novel written in prison by a student leader, Luis González de Alba. Starting with Tlatelolco and moving on to a general analysis of Mexico's problems, Carlos Fuentes demonstrated his acuity as a political essayist in *Tiempo mexicano;* Carlos Monsiváis presented accounts worthy of Norman Mailer in *Días de guardar.* Another example of journalism as art was the third volume of *Los indios de México,* in which Fernando Benítez denounced the exploitation of the Cora and Mazatec peoples. Political literature experienced a revival in the editorial pages of *Excélsior,* especially in articles by Gastón García Cantú, who also demonstrated his ability as a historian in *Las invasiones norteamericanas a México.* The master of style Juan José Arreola published his first book in eight years, *Palindroma.* A 26-year-old, Jorge Aguilar Mora, attracted attention with his novel *Cadáver lleno de mundo.* Marco Antonio Montes de Oca rewrote his 12 books as a collection, *Poesía reunida,* a testimony of an astonishing poetic imagination.

Peru experienced a great literary year with the publication of an excellent antinovel, *El cuerpo de Giulia-no* by the poet Jorge Eduardo Eielson; a psychological novel, *Un mundo para Julius* by Alfredo Bryce; and a posthumous novel by José María Arguedas, *El zorro de arriba y el zorro de abajo. Contranatura* by Rodolfo Hinostroza was an enterprising adaptation of the babelizing poetic method of Ezra Pound. The best books, however, were literary criticisms. In *Figuración de la persona,* Julio Ortega analyzed the state of Peruvian and Latin-American poetry; José Miguel Oviedo wrote what would be the classical text on the life and work of novelist Mario Vargas Llosa, *La invención de una realidad;* and Vargas Llosa himself did a study of the author of *Cien años de soledad,* called *García Márquez, historia de un deicidio.*

Montevideo, Uruguay, tried to become the world capital of the urban guerrilla and the bibliography on this theme extended from documentaries like *Los tupamaros* by Omar Costa to an attempt to unite the artistic and political vanguards in the novel in verse by Mario Benedetti, *El cumpleaños de Juan.* By comparison, novels like *Los escándalos* (Ariel Méndez) or *Los maniáticos* (Julio Ricci) appeared excessively timid and conventional. The state of emergency that the country experienced inflamed its poetry as well, as demonstrated by Milton Schinca in *Cambiá, Uruguay.*

(S. Bs.)

NORWEGIAN

Two novels by Terje Stigen confirmed his position as a leading writer of Norwegian prose. *Besettelse* was an intense account of a country schoolmaster's uncontrolled passion for one of his girl pupils, and *Kains merke* dealt with the internal and external conflicts of a former Nazi torturer living under an assumed identity. A headstrong woman's ruthless efforts to get the man she wanted was at the centre of Sigbjørn Hølmebakk's Strindbergian *Jentespranget.* A pessimistic view of modern man in a sterile suburban atmosphere was elegantly presented by Odd Winger in *Supermarked.* Kåre Holt based his *Oppstandelsen* on irrefutable but fictitious evidence that Christ never rose from the dead.

Gunnar Bull Gundersen, in *Min reise til Egypt,* obtained fascinating effects from a juxtaposition of momentous international events and private experiences. Bjørg Berg, in *Jeg er så ensom, frøken,* showed a sure hand at presenting the frustrated atmosphere of a provincial hotel. In Karin Bang's *Soria Moria,* the heroine from *Blues* (1968) was groping her way back from the twilight world of drugs and promiscuity.

The dramatic clash between heathen and Christian modes of life in 11th-century Norway was colourfully portrayed in Felix Thoresen's *Brødrene på Harm,* the last volume of a trilogy. The clash between Roman Catholic belief and Lutheran teaching in 16th-century Norway formed the background to Vera Henriksen's *Trollsteinen,* which was continued in *Pilegrimsferd.* Bergljot Hobæk Haff took up this theme in a modern setting in *Sønnen,* the story of the heir of a wealthy industrialist wanting to become a monk.

"Indianeren," in Espen Haavardsholm's *Den avskyelige snømannen,* was outstanding among short stories. Through a collage of clippings from local newspapers, Rolf Sagen, in *Kvengedal,* drew a touching, sad, and very amusing picture of life in a small community in western Norway. Finn Carling's *Gjesten* was a concentrated observation on extralingual communication and family tensions. Finn Havrevold's *En benk i parken* contained four plays for radio. Helmer Grundt Spang's *Den hemmelige kampen* caused a sensation with its frank antiheroic presentation of Norwegian pilots in the RAF during World War II.

Among a cornucopia of poetry, Sigmund Skard's *Popel ved flyplass* was important for its treatment of the theme of approaching death, and Alfred Hauge's *Det evige sekund* for its religious atmosphere and wealth of perspectives. Modernistic tendencies were reflected in Peter R. Holm's *Synslinjer,* and nostalgia, irony, and despair in Hans Borli's *Isfuglen.*

Main contributions to Norwegian scholarship were Owe Apeland's *Alexander L. Kiellands romaner* and Rolf N. Nettum's *Konflikt og visjon,* a close reading of early novels by Knut Hamsun. Fascinating inside information concerning several leading Norwegian writers was contained in an enlarged edition of publisher Harald Grieg's monumental memoirs, *En forleggers erindringer.* Alf Prøysen's *Det var da det og itte nå,* based on autobiographical broadcasts, appeared posthumously.

(To. S.)

SOVIET

Once again in 1971 there was a wide divergence of opinion about the merits and achievements of Soviet literature. Even within the Soviet Union the official view was opposed by some whose literary judgment had not become wholly subservient to a political ideology. In the West, where writers praised by conformist Soviet critics were almost unknown, Soviet literature continued to be represented by writers such as Aleksandr Solzhenitsyn, whose works were banned in the U.S.S.R.

The speeches at the fifth congress of the Soviet Writers' Union (Moscow, June 29–July 2) were of particular interest in showing how the "establishment" assessed achievement since the fourth congress in 1967. Progress was measured mainly in terms of adherence to accepted political tenets and of the growth in variety of linguistic output in the various republics of the U.S.S.R. Nikolai Tikhonov, "elder statesman" of Soviet poetry, opening the first session, stated that "the principles of the Communist Party have been and will remain the cornerstones of Soviet literature." Novelist Georgi Markov (appointed first secretary to the Writers' Union during the congress) said in his report that "in its development our literature is indissolubly linked with the future consolidation of our society . . . its strength depends on its awareness of its duty to the workers and its assertion of Communist ideals." A resolution passed by the congress stated definitively that for Soviet writers the "first duty is to show the strength and beauty of a socialist society, the greatness of its aims, the nobility of its aspirations."

The congress also provided opportunity for official condemnation of those "inveterate idlers" and "parasites" who criticized the regime or wrote about their own experience. No names were mentioned, but everyone knew the greatest "offender" was Solzhenitsyn. Another "parasite" was Andrei Amalrik, the brilliant young author of two penetrating indictments of the Soviet political system published in the West in 1970, who in April 1971 was sent to Siberia.

Some cautiously worded criticisms showed that even within the official ranks there was dissatisfaction. The poet Nikolai Gribachov called for more exact and more objective literary criticism; critic and poet Aleksandr Chakovski responded with a strong complaint at the growing numbers of boring books of no literary merit. In a challenging speech, poet Evgeni Yevtushenko demanded an end to neo-Stalinist repression, and to a policy that treated writers as children, not to be trusted with the management of their own affairs.

Most writers, however, seemed all too ready to, in Tikhonov's words, "take courage for the future in remembering with pride our heroic past." For "consensus" writers the "heroic past" began with Lenin, and leftovers of the 1970 centenary celebrations of his birth included *The Ulyanovs*, a weighty novel crammed with historical characters drawn from life, and based on 20 years' research on Lenin and his family. Its author, Vladimir Kanivets, won the Shevchenko Prize of the Ukrainian S.S.R. Three shorter novels—V. Dmitrievski's *Comrade Friday*, Vasilii Aksonov's *Love of Fire*, and *To Each His Own Happiness* by Latvian writer Janis Niedra—took as their theme the loyalty to Lenin of those Bolsheviks who fought at his side in the revolutionary struggles of 1905–17. Mikhail Sholokhov continued his painstaking study of Lenin's influence in the fourth volume of his novel *Sparks* (begun in 1969); and Gennadi Fish, in the short *After July 1917*, produced a fictional flashback of Lenin at the height of his achievement.

Several novelists sought inspiration in the heroic efforts of the peoples of the outlying provinces to share in the November Revolution. Among them were Georgi Markov, with volume two of his grandiose epic *Siberia;* Aibek of Uzbekistan, whose *The Great Road* described the struggles of the scattered Uzbeks to become a nation; Myhalo Stelmakh's *Thinking of You,* a vigorous account of the long struggle of Lithuania to achieve independence; and Sergei Sartakov, winner of a 1970 State (formerly Stalin) Prize for his trilogy *Barbin Stories,* with the second volume of his cycle *The Philosopher's Stone.*

As elsewhere, writers continued to find an escape route from present tensions and stresses in recalling the unity of purpose of the "Great Patriotic War." Konstantin Simonov's two-part *The Last Summer* (1970–71), reintroducing characters from earlier novels, recaptured the sense of national achievement of the summer of 1944. In the first volume of *War,* Ivan Stadniuk evoked the false calm of the days immediately preceding the German attack in June 1941. The hero of *Kio-ku-mitsu! Top Secret,* a real-life spy story by Y. Koroltkov, was Richard Sorge, the famous Soviet intelligence officer.

Peacetime heroism was not neglected. L. Obukhova dedicated her novel *In the Beginning Was the Earth* to Yuri Gagarin, the first astronaut, on whose exploits it was based; and, in *My Brother Yuri,* Valentin Gagarin told the story of his brother's life. Novels of working-class life included M. Kolesnov's *The Right to Choose,* a sensitive study of the close bond between father and son; Viktor Likhonosov's *Autumn in Taman;* and *The Seventh Western,* by the Estonian writer Boris Kaugver. Anatoli Kalinin's *Ring Out, Bells!* told a love story of ordinary life with humour and delicacy.

Among autobiographies of interest were *A Worker's Destiny,* the reminiscences of I. Gudin, who took part in the Stakhanovite movement; *Man and Time,* by Marietta Shaginian, famous for her detailed researches on Lenin; playwright Vera Panova's *From the Storehouse of Memory;* and poet Aleksandr Voronski's *Quest for the Waters of Life and Death.*

The event of the year, although few in the Soviet Union would acknowledge it, was the publication in Paris in June of the Russian-language edition of Solzhenitsyn's new novel, *August 1914: Part One.* The first of his works not based on his own experience, it covered the days August 10–21, 1914, providing a vast panorama of Russia and a gripping account of the 2nd Russian Army's offensive and defeat. Written in a prose of great strength and suppleness, it combined fictional narrative, fact, battle scenes depicted in Goyaesque style, and profound philosophical and religious reflection.

Solzhenitsyn was harassed during the year (*see* POLICE) and denied the right to receive his Nobel Prize, but suffered less than many other "dissidents." Yuli Daniel's *Prison Poems,* published in the West, were a stark reminder of the agony inflicted on one who stated, "It was not to win but to fight/That I came into the ring." Andrei Voznesenski, the most widely read of the new "metaphysical" Soviet poets, had been forced in February 1970 to withdraw a play put on at the Taganka, Moscow's avant-garde theatre, and was under close surveillance during 1971, although, like Solzhenitsyn, he declared that he was not a politically engaged writer. Vladimir Bukovski, a literary radical of an older generation, was charged in April with publishing "anti-Soviet propaganda," and in October, declared insane, was detained in a mental hospital.

Swedish poet Lars Norén
published the first part
of his autobiographical
novel "Biskotärna"
in 1971.

One liberal intellectual who commanded official respect up to the time of his death in December was Aleksandr Tvardovski (*see* OBITUARIES). Although in February 1970 he had been dismissed from the editorial chair of *Novy Mir,* which under him had become the journal of literary dissent, in June 1971 he received a State Prize for his contribution to literature. (X.)

SPANISH

Of the plethora of books that burdened the bookshops, most were useless, and the majority faddish. Still, the mere sight and feel of so many books in Spain, unbookish since the expulsion of the Jews in 1492, furnished a certain delight. The Spanish novel remained dormant in the hands of the Spanish-born but the void was filled by Latin-American writers, many of them living and writing in Spain. New editions of works, both early and late, by Jorge Luis Borges were to be seen everywhere and essays and papers on Borges burgeoned: typical of them was "El otro Borges," in the notable book of essays and impressions, *Las palabras de la tribu,* by the poet José Angel Valente. Everything ever written by two Latin-American novelists residing in Spain, Mario Vargas Llosa and Gabriel García Márquez, was resuscitated. Miguel Angel Asturias, the Guatemalan Nobel prizewinner, took up more or less permanent residence in Majorca, contributed to the Spanish press, and finished a new novel, *Viernes de Dolores.* Barral Editores issued José Lezama Lima's *Introducción a los vasos órficos.*

There were two editions of the long-suppressed (for family reasons) *Diario íntimo* of Miguel de Unamuno, one prepared by Félix García, the other by Elaine Kerrigan; neither placed this spiritual record in its context. (Some chronological explanation was furnished in English in the fourth volume of *The Selected Works of Miguel de Unamuno.*) The *Diario* seemed a sketchbook for Unamuno's masterpiece, *Del sentimiento trágico de la vida* (*The Tragic Sense of Life*). Another literary event was the appearance of the second volume of the *Diccionario secreto* of Camilo José Cela, its 680 pages dedicated entirely to a historical study of the variants and literary usage of the one word: *pene.* A notable double number of Cela's journal, *Papeles de Son Armadáns,* was dedicated to Asturias.

A sensational publication was the first appearance in Spain of the definitively authoritative book on the assassination in Mexico of Leon Trotsky. In *El asesinato de Trotsky,* Julián Gorkin, co-founder of the POUM party in Barcelona and former editor of *Cuadernos* (Paris), made use of the vast collection of documents to lay the crime at the door of named Stalinist and post-Stalinist agents, some of them still active.

Two important collections of verse were: *Poesía superrealista,* with ancient—and new—surprises from the mind of 74-year-old Vicente Aleixandre; and *Enseñanzas de la edad, 1945–70,* by José María Valverde, a poet whose sensibility was constantly marred by an overanxious "message." (AY. K.)

SWEDISH

That part of Sweden known as Norrland, which includes Lapland and is larger than the rest of the country put together, was gradually being depopulated and "closed down," with population and industries struggling to survive the southward pull. The negative

consequences of this development inspired 20 writers to contribute their views to the anthology *Detta djävla Norrland.* Margareta Sarri continued the theme in her amusing first novel, *Då Simon Fjällborg med flera kom till insikt,* describing the meagre living eked out by tourist-dependent Lapps. In *Sekonden* (belonging to the genre of technically impressive documentary fiction) Per Olof Enquist examined the political and moral aspects of organized sport.

Per Gunnar Evander published two novels: *Sista dagen i Valle Hedmans liv,* an effectively laconic account of the struggles of labour and private enterprise in the lives of three men, and *En kärleksroman,* with amusingly well-informed interiors from the Swedish Radio Corporation, but, on a deeper level, an exploration of the relationship of two brothers. Reidar Jönsson's *En borgares död* was overtly and passionately political, concerning the moment of (left-wing) truth of a worker who had been laid off. Sven Delblanc's novel *Åminne,* published in 1970, consolidated this university don's status as one of Sweden's leading novelists.

The young poet Lars Norén published the first part of his autobiographical novel *Biskotärna.* His marvelous prose style transformed an account of life among drug addicts and prostitutes into a literary masterpiece. Lars Gyllensten, medical scientist, thinker, and novelist, published meditations and essays in *Mänskan djuren all naturén.* It was a good year for religious poetry with 20-year-old Ylva Eggehorn's joyfully Christian *Ska vi dela* and Bo Setterlind's lyrical affirmations of faith in *Himlen har landat.* Poet Karl Vennberg had no comparable faith, but in *Sju ord pa tunnelbanan,* his first collection in 11 years, he lost none of his dialectical brilliance or astringency, being as at home with the medieval mystic Meister Eckhart as with Marx.

Lars Forssell, poet, playwright, and member of the Swedish Academy, proclaimed his preoccupation with revolution and Lenin in the title of *Oktober dikter* (October poems). Göran Palm's exciting short prose poems and aphorisms *Varför har nätterna inga namn?* recorded his experience that theoretical Marxism is not enough; the subconscious, irrational element in life cannot be hidden. In *Följetong i skärt och svart* Kerstin Thorvall's poetry was colloquial yet stylish as she described the blossoming and withering of a love affair between a middle-aged woman and a young man. (K. R. P.)

See also Libraries; Philosophy; Theatre.

ENCYCLOPÆDIA BRITANNICA FILMS. *Bartleby by Herman Melville* (1969); *Dr. Heidegger's Experiment by Nathaniel Hawthorne* (1969); *The Lady, or the Tiger? by Frank Stockton* (1969); *The Lottery by Shirley Jackson* (1969); *Magic Prison* (1969); *My Old Man by Ernest Hemingway* (1969); *James Dickey: Poet* (1970); *The Deserted Village* (1971); *The Lady of Shalott* (1971); *The Prisoner of Chillon* (1971); *Shaw vs. Shakespeare—Part I: The Character of Caesar; Part II: The Tragedy of Julius Caesar; Part III: Caesar and Cleopatra* (1971).

Luxembourg

A constitutional monarchy, the Benelux country of Luxembourg is bounded on the east by West Germany, on the south by France, and on the west and north by Belgium. Area: 999 sq.mi. (2,587 sq.km.). Pop. (1970): 339,-848. Cap. and largest city: Luxembourg (pop., 1970,

Livestock and Animal Products:
see Agriculture

Lumber:
see Timber

Lutherans:
see Religion

76,143). Language: French, German, Luxembourgian. Religion: Roman Catholic 97%. Grand duke, Jean; prime minister in 1971, Pierre Werner.

On March 31, 1971, a moderate splinter group of the Socialist Party of Luxembourg broke away to form the new Social Democratic Party. Henri Cravatte, former president of the Socialist Party and a former Cabinet minister, was selected as leader. The Socialist split began in late January, when five deputies resigned from the party in opposition to the party committee's decision to cooperate with Communist candidates at the communal level. A sixth deputy eventually joined the new faction. As a result of the split, the composition of the Chamber of Deputies was: Christian Social 21, Socialist 12, Democratic (Liberal) 11, Social Democrat 6, and Communist 6. The government was a coalition of the Christian Social and Democratic parties.

(R. D. Ho.)

Malagasy Republic

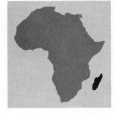

The Malagasy Republic occupies the island of Madagascar and minor adjacent islands in the Indian Ocean off the southeast coast of Africa. Area: 226,660 sq.mi. (587,050 sq.km.). Pop. (1970 est.): 7,423,864. Cap. and largest city: Tananarive (pop., 1970 est., 343,670). Language: French and Malagasy. Religion: Christian (approximately 50%) and traditional tribal beliefs. President in 1971, Philibert Tsiranana.

A profound political malaise developed during 1971, culminating with the arrest on June 1 of André Resampa, long considered the ailing president's heir-apparent. In January there was a bomb attack on the home of the minister of public works; in March the university at Tananarive was closed after disturbances there; and in October Tsiranana announced the discovery of a "Maoist" plot allegedly involving European elements.

The gradual ousting of Resampa was of major political significance and was designed to ensure that the succession would pass to a leader committed to the continuity of the regime. Over a period of several months Resampa was replaced by Calvin Tsiebo as first vice-president, dismissed from his post as secretary of the government Social Democratic Party, and finally arrested, accused of high treason and collaboration with a foreign power.

In April, Malagasy political life was disrupted by an uprising in the south under popular leader Monja Jaona. Administrative centres were under attack for several days, and the National Guard moved in to quell the uprising. A number of rebels were killed, Monja Jaona was arrested, and more than 500 persons were placed under house arrest, most of them being released some two months later.

In foreign affairs, the rapprochement with South Africa progressed with the exchange of commercial missions and the establishment in August of a joint committee representing both countries. (PH. D.)

Malawi

A republic and member of the Commonwealth of Nations in east central Africa, Malawi is bounded by Tanzania, Mozambique, and Zambia. Area: 45,747 sq.mi. (118,484 sq.km.). Pop. (1971 est.): 4,552,000, nearly all of whom are Africans. Cap.: Zomba (pop., 1971 est., 20,000). Largest city: Blantyre (pop., 1971 est., 169,000). Language: English and Nyanja. Religion: predominantly traditional beliefs. President in 1971, Hastings Kamuzu Banda.

In November 1970 Malawi's constitution was amended to enable President Banda (see BIOGRAPHY) to become president for life, and on July 6, 1971, the fifth anniversary of the republic, he took his oath of

AGIP—PICTORIAL PARADE

Pres. Philibert Tsiranana of the Malagasy Republic made an appeal to the public on April 3, 1971, after violence erupted in the south of Madagascar, killing 30 people.

Machinery and Machine Tools: see Industrial Review
Madagascar: see Malagasy Republic
Magazines: see Publishing

The site of a former village is being transformed into the new capital city of Malawi. Construction of the ministry buildings in the new city, named Lilongwe, began during 1971.

office. In the general election on April 17 all the candidates were voted in unopposed. Each of the 58 constituencies had proposed five names, and Banda had then selected one of the five to be the candidate.

The main feature of the year was President Banda's continuing attempt to find a solution to Africa's racial problems by friendly contacts with white-dominated southern Africa. During the Commonwealth conference in Singapore in January, he defended British arms sales to South Africa, arguing that they could not affect the balance of military strength in Africa, already heavily weighted in South Africa's favour, and that blocking them would alienate liberal white elements.

MALAWI
Education. (1968) Primary, pupils 333,876, teachers 8,564; secondary, pupils 9,283, teachers 508; vocational, pupils 536, teachers 53; teacher training, students 1,085, teachers 119; higher, students 788, teaching staff 129.
Finance. Monetary unit: kwacha (replacing the Malawi pound from Feb. 15, 1971, at 2 kwachas = Mal£1), with a par value of 0.83 kwacha to U.S. $1 (2 kwachas = £1 sterling) and a free rate (Sept. 27, 1971) of 0.81 kwacha to U.S. $1. Gold, SDRs, and foreign exchange, official: (June 1971) U.S. $28.4 million; (June 1970) U.S. $23,970,000. Budget (1970–71 est.) balanced at 45.4 million kwachas.
Foreign Trade. (1970) Imports 82,478,000 kwachas; exports 49,291,000 kwachas. Import sources (1969): U.K. 30%; Rhodesia 17%; South Africa 14%; Japan 5%. Export destinations (1969): U.K. 45%; Zambia 11%; Rhodesia 7%; U.S. 5%. Main exports: tobacco 34%; tea 22%; peanuts 9%; cotton 6%.
Transport and Communications. Roads (1970) 10,721 km. Motor vehicles in use (1969): passenger 9,857; commercial 6,700. Railways: (1969) 491 km.; traffic (1970) 58.4 million passenger-km., freight 190.3 million net ton-km. Air traffic (1969): 20,555,000 passenger-km.; freight 396,000 net ton-km. Telephones (Dec. 1969) 11,437. Radio receivers (Dec. 1969) 105,000.
Agriculture. Production (in 000; metric tons; 1970; 1969 in parentheses): corn c. 900 (1,153); cassava (1969) c. 123, (1968) c. 117; sweet potatoes (1969) c. 43, (1968) c. 40; tobacco 19 (13); cotton, lint 7 (6); peanuts c. 141 (171); tea 19 (17). Livestock (in 000; 1969–70): sheep 82; cattle 493; goats 599; pigs 142; poultry c. 8,500.
Industry. Production (1970): electricity (public supply) 122 million kw-hr.; cement 69,000 metric tons.

In July, Joe Kachingwe became the first black ambassador to South Africa, and the next month President Banda became the first black head of state to pay an official visit to South Africa. He was guest of the South African president at a state banquet and was host at a multiracial banquet in Johannesburg. He met the leaders of the Bantustans (black African reserves within South Africa) and visited Stellenbosch University and Simonstown naval base. During his visit he stressed that he disliked apartheid but preferred to talk with its supporters rather than break off relations with them and thus with the black population of South Africa. On his return to Malawi it was believed that Banda had agreed to convene a conference of countries wishing to enter into a dialogue over the issues dividing black and white Africa. In September he followed his visit to South Africa with an official visit to Mozambique which coincided with the opening of a new rail link between Malawi and the Mozambique port of Nacala.   (K. I.)

Malaysia

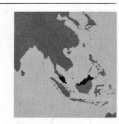

A federation within the Commonwealth of Nations comprising the 11 states of the former Federation of Malaya, Sabah, and Sarawak, Malaysia is a federal constitutional monarchy situated in Southeast Asia at the southern end of the Malay Peninsula (excluding Singapore) and on the northern part of the island of Borneo. Area: 128,727 sq.mi. (333,401 sq.km.). Pop. (1970): 10,434,034. Cap. and largest city: Kuala Lumpur (pop., 1970, 451,728). Official language: Malay. Religion: Malays are Muslim; Indians mainly Hindu; Chinese mainly Buddhist, Confucian, and Taoist. Supreme head of state in 1971, with the title of *yang di-pertuan agong,* Tuanku Abdul Halim Mu'azzam Shah ibni al-Marhum Sultan Badlishah; prime minister, Tun Abdul Razak bin Hussein.

On Feb. 20, 1971, Parliament went into session and Malaysia thus returned to parliamentary democracy after 21 months of emergency rule (imposed after the racial disturbances of May 13, 1969). In March Parliament approved the Constitutional (Amendment) Bill, which placed beyond challenge citizenship, national language and the use of other languages, the special position of the Malays, the legitimate interests of the non-Malays, and sovereignty of the rulers. With the dissolution of the National Operations Council, a National Unity Council was set up to discuss problems of national unity and foster racial harmony.

The Anglo-Malaysian defense agreement, under which Britain was automatically committed to the defense of Malaysia, terminated at midnight on October 31, and the new five-power defense arrangements —involving Britain, Australia, New Zealand, Malaysia, and Singapore as equal partners—came into force. The new arrangements provided for the physical presence of British, Australian, and New Zealand forces —ground and naval in Singapore and air defense in Butterworth, northern Malaya—with an Australian as supreme commander. An integrated air defense system for Malaysia and Singapore came into operation in September.

Communist subversion in East and West Malaysia, though well under control, continued to pose a threat;

government countermeasures included setting up combined Army, police, and civilian committees at federal, state, and district levels. The government in October published a White Paper outlining a Communist plan that called for the Communist Party of Malaya to establish a military presence on Malaysian soil.

Relations with China took a new turn in 1971. Nineteen prominent Malaysian businessmen and officials paid an unofficial visit to Peking in May. A one-week visit to Malaysia by a Chinese delegation followed, and agreement was reached for direct trade between China and Malaysia, with the government-owned National Trading Corp. acting as sole agent for Malaysia. Until then, two-thirds of Malaysia's trade with China was handled by intermediaries in Hong Kong and Singapore. During January there were the worst floods in the history of the nation. At least 60 people lost their lives, and more than 200,000 had to be evacuated.

The second five-year plan (1971–75) provided for a total expenditure of M$14,350,000,000 on development, of which the government contribution was to be M$7,250,000,000 with the private sector expected to invest M$7.1 billion. The plan emphasized the government's aim of eradicating poverty among all races and the vital program of "restructuring Malaysian society to reduce and eventually eliminate the identification of race with economic function." Nearly 600,000 new jobs were to be created, enough to contain unemployment at just over 7.3% of the labour force. Despite a moderately high rate of economic growth, unemployment continued to be serious, reaching 9% in 1971, the highest in 25 years.

The 1971 budget, presented under emergency regulations and passed without debate on Dec. 22, 1970, provided for M$2,463,000,000 in ordinary expenditure and M$847 million in development expenditure. Revenue, including an additional M$18 million from new taxes, would give a surplus of M$38 million over ordinary expenditure. Defense and internal security, second on the list of priorities, received M$813 million.

The Malaysian economy expanded at a slower rate in 1970 than in the previous year. GNP rose by 6.3% to M$11,821,000,000, compared with an increase of 9.8% in 1969, and per capita income rose from M$1,060 in 1969 to M$1,080, the main impetus to growth coming from domestic demand. (M. S. R.)

Maldives

Maldives, a republic in the Indian Ocean consisting of about one thousand small islands, lies southwest of the southern tip of India. Area: 115 sq.mi. (298 sq.km.). Pop. (1970): 114,469. Cap.: Male (pop., 1970, 13,610). Language: Divehi. Religion: Muslim. Sultan, Emir Muhammad Farid Didi; president in 1971, Ibrahim Nasir.

Maldives continued to pursue a nonaligned policy, although this proved difficult with unrest in nearby Ceylon and with international interest focused on the strategic significance of the Indian Ocean. Aid from Britain included the support of students overseas and the grant of £214,000 for a 5,440-ton ship for use in the tramping service between the republic and Ceylon, India, Pakistan, the Persian Gulf, and the Red Sea. This operation provided essential foreign exchange and employment for several hundred Maldivians.

Britain's Royal Air Force staging post on Gan (leased until 1986) continued its pivotal work in the Commonwealth defense agreement, its importance increasing as Britain began to pull out of the Persian Gulf. The RAF unit of about 600 continued to provide a 24-hour service to aircraft and ships as well as maintaining an extensive air-sea search unit. (M. MR.)

MALAYSIA
Education. *West Malaysia.* (1968) Primary, pupils 1,338,454, teachers 44,353; secondary, pupils 484,737, teachers 17,764; vocational, pupils 17,251, teachers 443; higher (including 2 universities), students 13,045, teaching staff 1,160. *East Malaysia:* Sabah. (1968) Primary, pupils 95,979, teachers 3,382; secondary, pupils 21,921, teachers 892; vocational, pupils 188, teachers 9; teacher training, students 509, teachers 40. *East Malaysia:* Sarawak. (1969) Primary, pupils 145,379, teachers 4,536; secondary, pupils 35,240, teachers 1,410; vocational, pupils 460, teachers 30; teacher training, students 348, teachers 55; higher, students 367.
Finance. Monetary unit: Malaysian dollar, with a par value of M$3.06 to U.S. $1 (M$7.35 = £1 sterling) and a free rate (Sept. 27, 1971) of M$2.97 to U.S. $1. Gold, SDRs, and foreign exchange, official: (June 1971) U.S. $787 million; (June 1970) U.S. $652 million. Budget (1970 est.): revenue M$2,263,000,000; expenditure M$2,282,000,000. Gross national product: (1969) M$11,377,000,000; (1968) M$10,325,000,000. Money supply: (May 1971) M$1,986,000,000; (May 1970) M$1,897,000,000. Cost of living (West Malaysia; 1963 = 100): (June 1971) 106; (June 1970) 105.
Foreign Trade. (1970) Imports M$4,252,000,000; exports M$5,142,000,000. Import sources (West Malaysia only): Japan 19%; U.K. 14%; U.S. 8%; Singapore 6%; Australia 6%; West Germany 6%; China 5%. Export destinations (West Malaysia only): Singapore 20%; U.S. 15%; Japan 13%; U.K. 7%; U.S.S.R. 5%. Main exports: rubber 34%; tin 20%; timber 16%.
Transport and Communications. Roads (1969) 23,080 km. Motor vehicles in use (1969): passenger 254,600; commercial (including buses) 66,200. Railways (1970): 1,822 km.; traffic (including Singapore) 622 million passenger-km., freight 1,201,000,000 net ton-km. Air traffic (Malaysia-Singapore Airlines; 1970): 1,327,200,000 passenger-km.; freight 22,411,000 net ton-km. Shipping (1970): merchant vessels 100 gross tons and over 89; gross tonnage 48,148; vessels entered (excluding Sabah; 1969) 26,709,000 net registered tons; goods loaded (1969) 21,785,000 metric tons, unloaded 9,230,000 metric tons. Telephones (Jan. 1970) 168,826. Radio licenses (Dec. 1968) 423,000. Television receivers (Dec. 1969) 130,000.
Agriculture. Production (in 000; metric tons; 1970; 1969 in parentheses): rice 1,488 (1,605); rubber 1,373 (1,290); copra *c.* 188 (*c.* 179); palm oil (excluding Sarawak) *c.* 426 (352); tea (West Malaysia only) *c.* 3.4 (3.5); bananas (excluding Sarawak; 1969) *c.* 339, (1968) *c.* 339; pineapples (West Malaysia only; 1969) 329, (1968) 324; pepper (Sarawak only; 1969) 29, (1968) 26; timber (cu.m.; 1969) 16,500, (1968) 16,000; fish catch (excluding Sarawak; 1968) 406, (1967) 367. Livestock (in 000; July 1970): cattle 321; pigs 1,024; goats 345; sheep (West Malaysia only) 39; buffalo (Dec. 1969) 328; poultry *c.* 28,500.
Industry. Production (in 000; metric tons; 1970): tin concentrates (metal content) 74; bauxite 1,139; cement (West Malaysia only) 1,030; iron ore (West Malaysia only; 60% metal content) 4,490; crude oil (Sarawak only) 859; gold (troy oz.; 1968) 5.1; electricity (kw-hr.; 1968) 3,076,000.

MALDIVES
Education. (1969–70) Primary, pupils 799, teachers 29; secondary, pupils 258, teachers 22.
Finance and Trade. Monetary unit: Maldivian rupee, with a par value of MRs. 4.76 to U.S. $1 (MRs. 11.43 = £1 sterling; 1 Maldivian rupee = 1.25 Ceylonese rupees) and a free rate (Sept. 27, 1971) of *c.* MRs. 4.59 to U.S. $1. Budget (1969) expenditure MRs. 17,532,000. Foreign trade mainly with Ceylon. Main exports (metric tons; 1969): fish 3,680; copra 46; shells 31.

A man repairs his roof in a Dogon village at the foot of Sanga Cliff near the bend of the Niger River in Mali. The Dogon existence has remained unchanged since the 12th century.

PIERRE PITTET, COURTESY, WHO

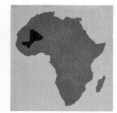

Mali

A republic of West Africa, Mali is bordered by Algeria, Niger, Upper Volta, Ivory Coast, Guinea, Senegal, and Mauritania. Area: 478,819 sq.mi. (1,-240,142 sq.km.). Pop. (1970 est.): 5,031,500. Cap. and largest city: Bamako (pop., 1968 est., 182,000). Language: French (official); Hamito-Semitic and various tribal dialects. Religion: Muslim 63%; animist 36%. Head of military government in 1971, Col. Moussa Traoré.

The major trends in Mali's political life during 1971 were a move toward greater liberalization in domestic affairs and, in foreign affairs, greater efforts toward bringing about better relations with France.

In March approximately 30 political prisoners were released after two months' detention, and in August labour union activities, which had been suspended when union leaders had come into conflict with official government policy, once again were permitted. But in spite of these liberalization measures the authorities in Bamako announced in April that a conspiracy against the government had been discovered.

MALI
Education. (1968–69) Primary, pupils 196,078, teachers 5,583; secondary, pupils 2,512, teachers 184; vocational, pupils 2,809, teachers 302; teacher training, students 1,409, teachers 86; higher, students 420, teaching staff 112.
Finance. Monetary unit: Mali franc, with a par value of MFr. 555.42 to U.S. $1 (MFr. 1,333 = £1 sterling) and a free rate (Sept. 27, 1971) of MFr. 553 to U.S. $1 (MFr. 1,371 = £1 sterling). Budget (1970 est.) balanced at MFr. 22,651,000,000. Money supply: (March 1971) MFr. 30,210,000,000; (March 1970) MFr. 26,960,000,000.
Foreign Trade. (1970) Imports MFr. 21,660,000,-000; exports MFr. 13,560,000,000. Import sources (1968): France 32%; U.S.S.R. 19%; China 13%; Ivory Coast 9%; Senegal 7%. Export destinations (1968): Ivory Coast 25%; France 17%; Senegal 16%; Ghana 9%. Main exports: cotton 12%; peanuts 11%; fish 10%.
Agriculture. Production (in 000; metric tons; 1969; 1968 in parentheses): millet and sorghum 852 (757); rice 99 (94); corn 76 (72); peanuts (1970) *c.* 100, (1969) *c.* 120; sweet potatoes *c.* 67 (*c.* 65); cassava *c.* 220 (*c.* 220); cotton, lint *c.* 15 (*c.* 15). Livestock (in 000; 1969–70): cattle *c.* 5,000; sheep *c.* 5,900; horses 170; asses *c.* 540.

The plot was said to involve two members of the ruling Military Committee of National Liberation (CMLN): its vice-president, Capt. Yoro Diakité, who had been dismissed from his post as minister of defense in the fall of 1970, and the minister of information, Capt. Malik Diallo. Both men were expelled from the CMLN and the Army.

The Mali government's desire for better relations with France was evident throughout the year. In January new agreements were signed for cooperation between the two countries.   (PH. D.)

Malta

An island in the Mediterranean Sea, between Sicily and Tunisia, Malta is a parliamentary state and a member of the Commonwealth of Nations. Area: 122 sq.mi. (316 sq. km.), including Malta, Gozo, and Comino. Pop. (1970 est.): 326,000. Cap.: Valletta (pop., 1970 est., 15,-547). Largest city: Sliema (pop., 1970 est., 21,983). Language: Maltese and English. Religion: mainly Roman Catholic. Queen, Elizabeth II; governors-general in 1971, Sir Maurice Dorman and, from June 21, Sir Anthony Mamo; prime ministers, Giorgio Borg Olivier and, from June 17, Dom Mintoff.

After nine years in power, G. Borg Olivier's Nationalist Party lost the June 1971 general election by a narrow margin. Under a new law, 55 as against the previous 50 members of Parliament were elected; the Labour Party, led by Dom Mintoff (*see* BIOGRAPHY), won 28 seats and the Nationalists, 27.

The new Maltese government informed the U.K. government that defense and financial arrangements would have to be renegotiated. After protracted discussions, it appeared that an understanding had been reached in September. Malta would receive an annual rental for the use of the bases of slightly less than $26 million, half of which (covering the next six months) was paid by Britain on September 30. Restrictions placed on the British forces in Malta were removed, and negotiations were to continue on a new long-term treaty. In December, however, Mintoff demanded the immediate payment of a further $11 million, and on December 29 Britain ordered the with-

MALTA

Education. (1967–68) Primary, pupils, 52,585, teachers 2,494; secondary, pupils 9,946, teachers 791; vocational, pupils 2,359, teachers 215; higher (including Royal University of Malta), students 1,449, teaching staff (1966–67) 172.

Finance. Monetary unit: Maltese pound, at par with the pound sterling (M£1 = U.S. $2.40) and with a free rate (Sept. 27, 1971) of M£0.98 to £1 (M£1 = U.S. $2.42). Gold, SDRs, and foreign exchange, official: (June 1971) U.S. $186.3 million; (June 1970) U.S. $130.2 million. Budget (1970–71): revenue M£41,893,000; expenditure M£43,343,000.

Foreign Trade. (1970) Imports M£67,121,000 (42% from U.K., 17% from Italy, 5% from West Germany); exports M£16,065,000 (38% to U.K., 11% to Italy, 6% to West Germany, 5% to Netherlands, 13% as ship's stores). Main exports: clothing 24%; textile yarns and fabrics 12%; rubber products 10%; petroleum products 10%; textiles and fibres 6%. Tourism (1969): visitors 186,100; gross receipts U.S. $26 million.

Transport and Communications. Roads (1968) 1,175 km. Motor vehicles in use (1969): passenger 37,200; commercial (including buses) 10,500. There are no railways. Air traffic (1970): 202,460,000 passenger-km.; freight 2.7 million net ton-km. Shipping (1970): merchant vessels 100 gross tons and over 23; gross tonnage 35,393; ships entered (1969) vessels totaling 1,722,000 net registered tons; goods loaded (1969) 65,000 metric tons, unloaded 1,004,000 metric tons. Telephones (June 1970) 32,839. Radio licenses (Dec. 1968) 89,000. Television licenses (Dec. 1969) 44,000.

drawal of its forces from the island. During the summer, Malta received financial aid from Libya, and NATO announced the withdrawal of its Mediterranean naval headquarters from Malta to Naples in accordance with the wishes of the Maltese government. After a stoppage of six months, work at the dry docks returned to normal; the administration would henceforth be shared by the government and the General Workers Union.

Measures were taken to introduce decimalized currency by May 1972. (A. G.)

Mathematics

There were a number of notable advances in the theory of numbers in 1971. Partly with the aid of computers, problems that had been previously inaccessible to investigation were being mastered.

The Fermat numbers $F_n = 2^{2^n} + 1$ are named for Pierre de Fermat, who in 1640 asserted that he thought they were prime, but admitted he could not prove it. The first five ($F_0 = 3$, $F_1 = 5$, $F_2 = 17$, $F_3 = 257$, $F_4 = 65537$) are in fact prime. But in 1739, Leonhard Euler found that Fermat was wrong by factoring F_5 into 641×6700417. Since then, F_n has been shown to be composite for many larger values of n, but no prime F_n with n greater than 4 is known. So Fermat's belief has turned out to be very wrong indeed. In 1880 F. Landry factored F_6:

$$F_6 = 2^{64} + 1 = 274177 \times 67280421310721$$

In 1905 J. C. Morehead and A. E. Western independently proved that F_7 is composite, by a method that did not find the factors. It took 66 years until 1971 when John Billhart and Michael Morrison accomplished the factorization:

$$F_7 = 2^{128} + 1 =$$
$$59649589127497217 \times 5704689200685129054721$$

They combined theory with a computation performed on a calculator (IBM model 360/91) at the University of California at Los Angeles. For F_8, the next number,

the same challenge remains; Morehead and Western (jointly) proved F_8 to be composite in 1909, but its factors are not yet known. The lowest Fermat number whose status as a prime is uncertain is F_{17}. The largest proved to be composite is F_{1945}, the factor $5 \times 2^{1947} + 1$ having been found by R. M. Robinson in 1957. In the journal *Mathematics of Computation* of 1964, Claude P. Wrathall gave a thoroughgoing summary of information about the Fermat numbers, but this needs updating by the 1971 factorization of F_7.

In 1971 more was learned about the class numbers of imaginary quadratic fields. Such a field is obtained by adjoining $\sqrt{-m}$ to the rational numbers, where m is a positive integer that can be taken to be square-free. The class number may be described as a measure of the departure from unique factorization. Thus, class number one signifies unique factorization, and after that, class number two is the closest approach to unique factorization. In 1967 H. M. Stark found that the class number is one precisely for $m = 1, 2, 3, 7, 11, 19, 43, 67,$ and 163. In 1971 he and A. Baker found that there were just 18 cases of class number two: $m = 5, 6, 10, 13, 15, 22, 35, 37, 51, 58, 91, 115, 123, 187, 235, 267, 403,$ and 427.

In 1770 E. Waring conjectured that any positive integer can be written as a sum of nineteen 4th powers (with a similar conjecture on nth powers for any n). Nineteen may actually be needed; for instance, the best we can do with 79 is write it as a sum of four 16s and fifteen 1s. Joseph Liouville (1859) was the first to show that some number of 4th powers are enough; he found 53 to suffice. This was slowly lowered through the years till L. E. Dickson achieved 35 in 1933. It took 38 years for this record to be improved. In 1971 François Dress proved that 30 will do. He used a combination of mathematical reasoning and high-speed computing. Mathematicians still believed that 19 was the right answer, but the goal of proving this still seemed distant.

An entertaining new puzzle that passed around in mathematical circles in 1971 illustrated how a simply stated problem in number theory might be surprisingly difficult. Start with any odd number. Multiply it by 3, add 1, and then divide by the appropriate power of 2 so as to get an odd number again. Then repeat the procedure. For instance, starting with 29 we get in succession $(3 \times 29 + 1) \div 8 = 11$, then 17, 13, 5, 1. The question is: do we eventually reach 1, starting from any odd number? There appeared to be no way of attacking this problem by known methods.

Specialists in the field of Banach spaces were gratified by the solution of one of the oldest problems in the subject. These spaces had been invented by the Polish mathematician S. Banach as a vehicle for the study of functional analysis. A special kind of Banach space called Hilbert space had the property that numerous splittings of a desirable kind existed. The question arose: was a Banach space that possessed such splittings necessarily Hilbert space? J. Lindenstrauss and L. Tzafriri, by a brief ingenious argument, showed that the answer was yes.

The ratio of the mass of a proton to the mass of an electron has been found by experiment to be between 1836.1 and 1836.12. By an approach to the subject that remained controversial, Armand Wyler was led to the formula $6\pi^5 = 1836.118 \ldots$ for this physical constant. Possibly more refined experiments in the future will cast additional light on the matter.

An important award in mathematics is the Salem

Prize, given annually to a young mathematician in recognition of the most outstanding work in the field of Fourier series. It was awarded first in 1968 to Nicholas Varopoulos. Subsequent awards went to Richard Hunt (1969), Yves Meyer (1970), and Charles Fefferman (1971). At the age of 22, Fefferman was appointed to a full professorship at the University of Chicago, the youngest person to hold such a rank in the university's history. (I. KA.)

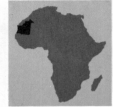

Mauritania

The Islamic Republic of Mauritania is on the Atlantic coast of West Africa, adjoining Spanish Sahara, Algeria, Mali, and Senegal. Area: 398,000 sq.mi. (1,030,700 sq.km.). Pop. (1970 est.): 1,171,000. Cap.: Nouakchott (pop., 1969 est., 20,000). Language: Arabic, French. Religion: Muslim. President in 1971, Mokhtar Ould Daddah.

As sole candidate of the Mauritanian People's Party, the nation's only legal political party, Mokhtar Ould Daddah was reelected president in August 1971 with 510,000 out of 511,280 votes cast.

A Cabinet reshuffle in August allowed several young "technocrats" to join the government, which had been weakened by several resignations and dismissals, including that of the finance minister, who later was arrested for embezzlement.

As chairman of the Organization of African Unity (OAU), President Ould Daddah sought to act as a mediator in disputes arising from the Arab-Israeli situation and in connection with the policy of "dialogue" with South Africa proposed by some OAU

members. In January he received Pres. Léopold S. Senghor of Senegal and in March, Maj. Gen. Yakubu Gowon of Nigeria. Ould Daddah visited Saudi Arabia and Tunisia in October.

In pursuance of the government's policy of rapprochement with China, a new agreement was signed in April for economic and technical cooperation between the two countries. (PH. D.)

MAURITANIA
Education. (1969–70) Primary, pupils 28,500, teachers (1965–66) 1,025; secondary, pupils 3,012, teachers (1963–64) 61; vocational (1964–65), pupils 197; teacher training (1964–65), students 107.
Finance. Monetary unit: CFA franc, with a parity of CFA Fr. 50 to the French franc (CFA Fr. 277.71 = U.S. $1; CFA Fr. 666.50 = £1 sterling) and a free rate (Sept. 27, 1971) of CFA Fr. 276.50 to U.S. $1 (CFA Fr. 685.75 = £1 sterling). Gold, SDRs, and foreign exchange, central bank: (June 1971) U.S. $4.8 million; (June 1970) U.S. $2.2 million. Budget (1970 est.) balanced at CFA Fr. 8,257,000,000.
Foreign Trade. (1969) Imports CFA Fr. 10,963,000,000; exports CFA Fr. 19,562,000,000. Import sources (1968): France 51%; U.S. 16%; Netherlands 11%; Senegal 5%. Export destinations: U.K. 25%; West Germany 17%; France 17%; Belgium-Luxembourg 14%; Italy 11%; Japan 9%. Main export iron ore 87%.

Pres. Mokhtar Ould Daddah welcomes the visiting French Pres. and Mrs. Georges Pompidou in a ceremonial tent in Nouakchott on Feb. 3, 1971.

A.F.P.—PICTORIAL PARADE

Mauritius

The parliamentary state of Mauritius, a member of the Commonwealth of Nations, lies about 500 mi. E of the Malagasy Republic in the Indian Ocean. Area: 720 sq.mi. (1,865 sq.km.). Pop. (1970 est.): 844,000, including Indian and Pakistani 67%; Creole (mixed French and African) 29%; others 4%. Cap. and largest city: Port Louis (pop., 1970 est., 140,640). Language: English (official). Religion (1962): Hindu 49%; Roman Catholic 32%; Muslim 16%. Queen, Elizabeth II; governor-general in 1971, Sir Leonard Williams; prime minister, Sir Seewoosagur Ramgoolam.

During 1970–71 Mauritius extended diplomatic relations to Egypt, Yugoslavia, and the Vatican, and continued active membership in the Organization of African Unity and the African, Malagasy, and Mauritian Common Organization. External policies reflected the island's vulnerability in the Indian Ocean; internal affairs, a divisive racial composition. A supporter of dialogue with South Africa, Foreign Minister Gaëtan Duval held that Mauritius could not ask Britain to defend it while denying the means of defense by opposing arms sales to South Africa. At the same time, the prime minister, on a state visit to Zambia, pledged uncompromising support for the fight against apartheid. Differences within the coalition had already led to Duval's temporary resignation in November 1970. Reinstated as minister for foreign affairs, tourism, and emigration on Dec. 26, 1970, he visited South Africa in May 1971 and predicted that diplomatic relations between the two countries would be established.

The state of emergency declared in 1968 was lifted in December 1970. A Public Order Act was then introduced, and after disturbances in April public meetings were banned. (M. MR.)

MAURITIUS
Education. (1968–69) Primary, pupils 142,959, teachers 4,253; secondary, pupils 39,703, teachers 1,706; vocational, pupils 603, teachers 34; teacher training, students 642, teachers 25; higher, students 178, teaching staff 41.
Finance and Trade. Monetary unit: Mauritian rupee, with a par value of MauRs. 5.55 to U.S. $1 (MauRs. 13.33 = £1 sterling) and a free rate (Oct. 11, 1971) of MauRs. 5.37 to U.S. $1. Budget (1969–70 est.): revenue MauRs. 228,020,000; expenditure MauRs. 227,340,000. Foreign trade (1969): imports MauRs. 376 million (15% from U.K., 12% from Thailand, 8% from South Africa, 7% from Australia, 7% from France, 5% from Iran, 5% from West Germany); exports MauRs. 371 million (59% to U.K., 17% to Canada, 5% to U.S.). Main export sugar 89%. Tourism: visitors (1968) 15,600; gross receipts (1969) U.S. $3 million.
Agriculture. Production (in 000; metric tons): sugar (1970–71) 585, (1969–70) 669; tea (1970) c. 3.2, (1969) c. 3.2; tobacco (1970) 0.5, (1969) 0.5. Livestock (in 000; April 1970): cattle c. 48; pigs c. 3; sheep c. 3; goats c. 67; chickens c. 390.

Medicine

The 50th anniversary of the isolation of insulin and its use in diabetes was celebrated in 1971 and the only surviving member of the team that made the discovery, Charles H. Best, a medical student at the time, was honoured throughout the world. No similar epoch-making event was reported during the year but progress continued to be made on many medical fronts: research proceeded in the fight against cancer, new forms of treatment were devised for some common diseases, old scourges caused new problems, and there was continuing concern about the effects of man's actions on his health.

Announcements of blood tests for the detection of cancer always had been viewed with skepticism in the past but it looked as though two types of tests had been discovered that might furnish a means of diagnosing certain types of cancer. Further insight was gained into the part played by hormones in certain types of cancer, especially in women, and it was suggested that hormone estimation might be used as a screening test. In the U.S., Pres. Richard M. Nixon signed into law a bill earmarking $1.6 billion for cancer research over a three-year period.

Hay fever sufferers either were treated with a series of desensitizing injections, with varying relief, or suffered discomfort until the pollen season ended. Disodium chromoglycate, already successful in a proportion of patients with asthma, was said to improve about half of hay fever subjects when sprayed into the nose. Approaches to the treatment of obesity by radical new intestinal bypass operations were reported. The danger of operating on grossly overweight subjects was stressed, and it was not known whether there would be long-term complications since the small intestine was the site of absorption of minerals and vitamins as well as of food.

A hormone, medrogestone, was found to be capable of reducing the size of the prostate gland, which frequently enlarges in elderly men, causing difficulty in passing urine. Hitherto, surgery was the only treatment.

Exactly ten years after its appearance in Indonesia the El Tor variety of cholera reached Western Europe and was reported in the Saragossa area of Spain in July. Mass inoculation was known to give only partial protection. Past experience and the extent of the tourist industry suggested that other European countries would soon be affected, and isolated cases occurred in other countries during the summer as a result of vacationers returning from Spain.

The occurrence of rabies in dogs in Britain after an absence of more than 50 years led to a committee of inquiry, which recommended continued stringent quarantine of imported animals and inoculation of all pets with killed vaccine. There was thought to be an added risk from the large reservoir of infection among urban foxes on the continent of Europe. The advisability of routine vaccination of babies against smallpox was questioned in Britain. One hundred deaths occurred as a result of vaccination between 1951 and 1970, compared with 103 cases of smallpox with 37 deaths. The incidence of smallpox was falling throughout the world. An outbreak of malaria among heroin addicts in California was traced to an infected serviceman who had returned from Southeast Asia, while a death in New York from a rare neurological disease, botulism, prompted several food processors to warn that some of their products might be unsafe.

Environmental hazards caused concern during the year. A committee of the American Academy of Allergy, set up at the request of the U.S. Food and Drug Administration (FDA), reported that enzyme detergents caused respiratory symptoms in workers engaged in the manufacture of the product and occasionally in housewives, as well as skin sensitization in a few users. But tests on 7,000 housewives, divided into two groups and given either enzyme or nonenzyme washing powders in identical packets, failed to reveal any difference in harmful effects. Nevertheless, Procter & Gamble Co., makers of the largest-selling enzyme detergents, announced that they were removing the enzyme because of public fears. Meanwhile, legislation was being passed in the U.S. reducing the amount of phosphates (salts used to soften water and disperse dirt) in washing powders from the present 12.5 to 8.7% because of their action in promoting the growth of algae in water, which leads to death of fish and other larger organisms. One substitute for phosphates was nitrilotriacetic acid, but this also was considered a possible health hazard since it caused birth defects in experimental animals. Methyl (organic) mercury was detected in canned tuna fish, although the levels were not thought to be dangerous. Lakes in Sweden, North America, and Japan, however, were already contaminated with inorganic mercury as a result of industrial effluent, and it was probable that fish were able to synthesize the methyl compound, which is much more toxic to man than inorganic mercury itself.

A second report on the effect of smoking on health was produced by the Royal College of Physicians, in London, eight years after the first. Reemphasizing the dangers of cigarette smoking, it confirmed the connection between smoking and lung cancer, chronic bronchitis, coronary thrombosis, hypertension, gastric ulcer, and carcinomas of the mouth, esophagus, and bladder; it reaffirmed the deleterious effect on the fetus of smoking during pregnancy. The main impact of the report lay in its call for effective measures to reduce cigarette smoking, and the British government agreed to the labeling of cigarette packets with a warning notice similar to that required in the U.S. Other suggestions included a complete ban on smoking in public transport and places of entertainment, differential taxation of tobacco products according to harmfulness, and increasing the premiums on life insurance for heavy smokers. Latest figures issued by the U.S. National Clearing House for Smoking and Health revealed that one in four smokers had given up smoking in the last four years, though, disappointingly, tobacco consumption began rising again in 1970 and continued to rise in 1971.

Abortion on demand, introduced in New York State on July 1, 1970, appeared to be generally accepted by the public and medical profession, with an estimated 120,000 operations a year reported. In Britain, on the other hand, there was continued debate over interpretation of the social clauses in the 1967 Abortion Act, and a government committee of inquiry was asked to look into its working. It seemed probable that in the private sector abortions could be obtained "on demand," while under the National Health Service differing interpretations of the act by gynecologists, and a shortage of beds and staff, resulted in considerable variation in practice throughout the country.

A can of soup is tested for traces of botulin after the death of a man who ate some Bon Vivant vichyssoise contaminated with the deadly poison. All products processed by the company were promptly recalled, and FDA spokesmen later indicated that improper sterilization procedures were responsible for the tragedy.

THE "NEW YORK TIMES"

The more frequent use of vacuum extraction as a means of abortion was recommended since it could be performed safely on outpatients provided the pregnancy was not advanced more than 12 weeks.

The first experiment on "genetic engineering" was undertaken at Cologne, W.Ger., in two young girls with congenital deficiency of the enzyme arginase, and resulting excessive production of the amino acid arginine. They were injected with the harmless Shope papilloma virus, which had been shown to reduce levels of amino acids, including arginine, in animals by altering a portion of the DNA that makes up the host's genes. A 29-year-old woman in Sydney, Austr., who had been treated with gonadotropins to stimulate fertility, gave birth to 9 premature infants, all of whom subsequently died. Doctors in Rome removed 15 fetuses from a 35-year-old woman after a four-month pregnancy. From Sussex, Eng., came a report of a pregnancy lasting 381 days, with the birth of a normal infant weighing 7½ lb.

Much interest was aroused by the demonstration that pheromones, external chemical stimuli comparable to hormones and acting as sex attractants among insects, were also present in primates. Pheromones are detected through the sense of smell, and if, as seemed likely, they were present in man, the widespread use of deodorants and cosmetics might be expected to reduce rather than enhance sexual attraction. It was even suggested that it might be possible to produce an "olfactory contraceptive."

(AL. PA.)

Since December 1967, when the first human heart transplant in medical history was performed, 174 operations have been done on 171 patients, with a high of 77 cases in 1968. From December 1970 to May 1971 only 6 such operations were performed. Caution took the place of blind optimism. Many transplantees died from overwhelming rejection assaults. The longest survivor was a man operated on at the Medical College of Virginia in August 1968 and still living in 1971. Seven patients had lived for more than 2½ years and 12 over 2 years.

Sickle-cell anemia, a hereditary condition affecting about 10% of the world's blacks, shortened life expectancy. In December, the U.S. Congress passed a bill authorizing the expenditure of $142 million in 1973–75 for programs to combat sickle-cell disease. A sickle-cell detection package was devised, as well as an automatic laboratory technique that could test 120 samples in an hour, at a cost of 2 cents per test.

Inflammation of the liver called hepatitis was increasingly frequent. In the most severe cases, only 10 to 20% of patients survive. The disease apparently is related to the presence in the blood of a substance called the Australia antigen, for which a vaccine was being developed. Many other treatments had been tried, including exchange transfusion of the blood. While most cases of hepatitis were presumed to be transmitted in the blood, it was suggested that the virus can be transmitted also on eating utensils, in water, and perhaps via sexual intercourse.

Prostaglandins are hormones that influence many functions of the body. Among the prostaglandins is a group that causes contractions of the uterus and is therefore of consideration as an inducement to abortion. Research in the Institute of Basic Medical Sciences of the Royal College of Surgeons of England, in London, showed that two antiarthritis drugs—indomethacin and aspirin—block the formation in the body of two prostaglandins. Among the widely noted effects of prostaglandins are "morning-after" contraception and also decrease of acidity in instances of peptic ulcer. Prostaglandins can also induce fever and inflammation.

During 1971 reported cases of syphilis and gonorrhea increased in the United States over the number in 1970. A national campaign was being developed, directed particularly at adolescents. Some interest developed during 1971 in the study of venereal diseases among soldiers returning from Vietnam. The suggestion was made that a new type of gonorrheal organism had been seen that seemed to have exceptional virulence and required far greater doses of antibiotics in treatment.

It was discovered in Austria that migraine headaches are not caused solely by dilation of the blood vessels; overexcitability of deep brain centres may also be involved. Migraine seems to be inherited. During the migraine attack, some of the brain cells may be changed in their character.

In Great Britain, "do-it-yourself" pregnancy tests were widely advertised. A new test developed in the Netherlands could be made nine days after a missed menstrual period. In about two hours the test can be read as either positive or negative; other tests can be read in as short a span as 20 seconds. Most of the tests are based on measuring the level of a hormone that circulates in the blood during the development of pregnancy. They are most effective in the first three months of pregnancy, and have replaced the former rabbit and frog tests. Thus far the tests have not come under government regulation.

In the attempt to control addiction to heroin, treat-

Current Status of Some Common Vaccines

I. Vaccines generally regarded as satisfactory

Diphtheria
Measles
Mumps
Poliomyelitis
Rocky Mountain spotted fever
Rubella
Tetanus

II. Licensed vaccines currently under improvement

Cholera
Influenza
Smallpox
Tuberculosis
Yellow fever

III. Improvement desirable but little or no work is being done

Pertussis

IV. New vaccines in the course of development

Meningococcal meningitis
Mycoplasma pneumonia
Pneumococcal pneumonia
Rabies
Respiratory syncytial virus disease
Shigellosis
Streptococcal infections

V. Diseases against which it would be desirable to have a vaccine

Chicken pox
Cytomegalovirus infection
Gonorrhea
Hepatitis
Para-influenza

Source: *Medical World News.*

ment centres were established that depend on substitution of methadone. Some 275 centres, established by the FDA, with the cooperation of the Bureau of Narcotics and Dangerous Drugs, were treating nearly 30,000 addicts. Thirteen of the centres were sponsored by the National Institute of Mental Health and nine by the Veterans Administration.

Soviet scientists developed an electrical device that can disintegrate bladder stones. The urologist injects an irrigating fluid into the patient's bladder, then pushes a probe through the urethra, watching its progress with a cystoscope, and puts the tip next to the stone. The probe then generates a shock wave that breaks up the stone.

Through the development of the flexible fibre-optic endoscope, physicians were able to see inside the human body as far as 185 cm. upward from the rectum and 125 cm. downward from the mouth. These devices can also be inserted into the uterus. A new device called a pyelourethroscope has enabled physicians to see and photograph the interior of the kidney. Under investigation, and already tested in animals, are devices that can reveal the interior of the heart and certain blood vessels.

During 1971 genetic services continued to be developed with a view to detecting birth defects at the earliest possible moment. Amniocentesis, the investigation of fetal cells from uterine fluid, was being performed in many places. Laboratory and counseling services dealing with inherited disorders had increased almost 75% in less than four years. There were 680 genetic service units in the U.S. providing genetic counseling; about 5 of these services were able to offer amniocentesis, which can uncover certain congenital disabilities in the fetal stage.

In the Royal Dental College in Aarhus, Den., investigators found that a solution of chlorhexidine gluconate used as a mouth rinse twice daily would prevent the formation of inflammation of the gums and plaque on the teeth.

Psoriasis, a skin disorder that afflicts about six million people in the U.S., varies from a mere annoyance to an incapacitating disease. It is believed to be the result of a combination of genetic and environmental factors. Several anticellular drugs and other cancer drugs were tested against psoriasis. The disease has not been found among South American Indians, and it is more common among Caucasians and Japanese than among blacks.

Rabies continued to be a threat in 1971. An Ohio boy, bitten by a rabid bat, became one of the few cases in history of recovery from rabies. His treatment included the rabies vaccine. He developed paralysis and lapsed into coma. Spinal fluid was drained off to decrease pressure on the brain, and the drug dilantin was used to control convulsions.

Medical writings have concentrated for some years on the appearance of chromosomes taken from the body as an indicator of whether or not any drug or hormone might be a source of harm or perhaps be in some way related to cancer. It was reported that chromosome breaks can be caused by a variety of drugs, including oral contraceptive pills, by infections, and even by coffee. Examinations of over 10,000 blood cells disclosed that more breaks occurred in spring and summer than in fall and winter. The studies were being continued.

Vaccines are now available against many diseases but many more can be developed. The accompanying table shows the current status of common vaccines.

Neighbourhood storefront clinics in some large U.S. cities provide free or low-cost medical service for the poor. Blackman's Free Clinic is located in a poverty-stricken area of San Francisco.

Following the knowledge that some instances of paralysis agitans would yield to L-dopa, penicillamine was found useful in treating Wilson's disease, in which there is degeneration of certain cells in the brain and an increase in the glial cells of the nervous system. An important discovery was the isolation in pure form of erythropoietin, a hormone derived from the kidney. The blood of 150 anemic sheep produces only 0.000002 g. of erythropoietin. If this drug is found useful in treating the severe anemia of kidney disease, the cost at present would be about $15,000 a person.

It was shown that urokinase can dissolve blood clots in the lung or elsewhere. More successful than heparin, another anticoagulant drug, in such treatments, urokinase is being verified in a half dozen clinics around the world.

A new anti-inflammatory drug, used especially in treating rheumatoid arthritis, is benzothiazine carboxamide, which in animal experiments has proved to be more effective than some drugs now used. It is not yet available for prescription by physicians.

Trobicin, scientifically spectinomycin, is a new antibiotic demonstrated to be especially effective in the treatment of gonorrhea. The drug was given in a single injection into the muscles of the buttock. It is not effective against syphilis.

The combination of the drugs rifampin and isoniazid, which can be taken by mouth and which is relatively nontoxic, eliminated the germs of tuberculosis from the sputum of 95% of patients with far advanced tuberculosis in 16 to 20 weeks. The investigators are convinced that such treatment will provide shorter hospitalization and is definitely an advance over current treatment of tuberculosis. Patients who are taking isoniazid for the prevention of tuberculosis should be monitored monthly by appropriate methods for signs or symptoms of liver disease, which has developed in a few patients taking the drug.

(M. Fi.; X.)

ALCOHOLISM

The first major national commitment to the prevention and treatment of alcoholism in the United States became law in 1971. Called the Comprehensive Alcohol Abuse and Alcoholism Prevention, Treatment, and Rehabilitation Act of 1970, it established a National Institute on Alcohol Abuse and Alcoholism within the National Institute of Mental Health, and authorized appropriations of $100 million during fiscal 1972 for grants to agencies for prevention, treatment and rehabilitation programs, and demonstration projects.

The law also called for the development of alcoholism programs for federal civilian employees. The guidelines provide that alcoholism shall be considered a treatable illness, that no employee shall have his job threatened because he seeks assistance, that confidentiality shall be assured, and that sick leave for treatment shall be granted on the same basis as for any other illness.

Meeting in Vail, Colo., in August 1971, the National Conference of Commissioners on State Laws adopted a Uniform Alcoholism and Intoxication Treatment Act that will enable states that pass it to take optimal advantage of the provisions of the new federal law. It provides for creation of a division of alcoholism in the state government, with authority to prepare and administer plans for alcoholism programs that the state submits for federal funding. The uniform act declares as a matter of policy that alcoholics and intoxicated persons shall not be treated as criminals but rather shall be given opportunities for treatment.

The alcoholism program that claims one of the highest recovery rates—about 60% of its members achieve abstinence—lost one of its co-founders. Wil-

Volunteers try to persuade a skid row derelict to participate in the Manhattan Bowery Project, a new program providing five days of detoxification and rehabilitation free of charge to alcoholics on New York City's Bowery.

WARREN JORGENSEN FROM "MEDICAL WORLD NEWS"

liam G. Wilson, who helped start Alcoholics Anonymous in 1935, died at the age of 75. At the time of his death early in 1971, AA's international membership was estimated to be 475,000.

Whereas AA's goal is total abstinence, investigators at Patton State Hospital in San Bernardino, Calif., were trying to discover if they could convert alcoholics into moderate social drinkers. This novel experiment was based on the hypothesis that alcoholism is largely learned behaviour and therefore can be unlearned. It was too early to tell whether the method would work, but at least half of the patients were either "drinking socially" or abstaining after six months of participation in the program.

The attempts to find treatment methods that have a clear superiority over others continued. In one state hospital two methods of treatment—detoxification only and milieu (or social) therapy—showed no significant difference when judged by readmittance rates. Neither, for that matter, did intensive aftercare as opposed to standard aftercare. These results seemed consistent with an earlier study at the same institution, which assessed the efficacy of LSD in alcoholism treatment; about three-fourths of the patients showed significant improvement regardless of whether LSD was part of their therapy. A third method of treatment at the hospital, in which the patient learned to adopt behaviour other than drinking to relieve anxiety, was only half as successful as either detoxification alone or detoxification with milieu therapy.

Milieu therapy continued to be tested in a pilot treatment program in Albuquerque, N.M., where four federal agencies, the state division of vocational rehabilitation, and the county alcoholism treatment authority were pooling resources and funds to establish a model that could be followed elsewhere. Patients were hospitalized for a four-week period beyond detoxification, during which time they received psychotherapy and vocational counseling. Beyond that, social workers and volunteers made home visits to bolster the patient's self-confidence and to help with adjustment problems.

Elsewhere on the research front, these results were reported during 1971:

1. Chronic drinking of alcohol accelerates the metabolism of sedative drugs in humans, while a sudden large consumption of alcohol impedes drug metabolism. This may explain why sober alcoholics (the chronic drinkers) often show high tolerance to barbiturates, whereas inebriates display an increased sensitivity to such drugs.

2. The intravenous administration of the sugar fructose is superior to either a salt solution or the sugar glucose in slowing the rise of blood alcohol and reducing the peak level of alcohol in the blood.

3. After treatment with vitamins and balanced diet, alcoholics no longer exhibit defects in red-green colour vision. Previously it had been thought that such defects might be related to genetic factors that also could be predisposing to alcoholism.   (E. M. ST.)

ALLIED HEALTH PROFESSIONS

Many of the allied health professions, or paramedical professions, individually date back several decades, and some to the beginning of this century, but for the most part today's professionals in allied health have arisen as a result of recent scientific and technological advances. More than 200 separate allied health professions exist, representing a huge manpower source (in the U.S. alone about 2 million out of the national total of 3.5 million persons active in providing health services). Many of these professions are well known, such as the medical technologist, physical therapist, and dental hygienist; others are not so well known, such as the electroencephalographer, respiratory and inhalation therapists, and physician assistant. Although some of these workers deal directly in caring for the patient and others play an indirect role, they all work together as a coordinated team, usually under the direct supervision of either a physician or a dentist.

In 1900 there was an average of one allied health professional for each physician. In 1971 that figure had grown to more than 13 such professionals for each physician, and by 1975 it was expected to exceed 20. Historically, many of the allied-health-professions personnel have been trained in hospitals or have learned their skills from doctors. With the extension of education beyond high school for a larger number of students, it has become essential to prepare more of the health personnel in colleges and universities. Allied-health-profession educational programs were being offered in increasing numbers of academic institutions and clinical facilities throughout the world, offering programs from those leading to advanced graduate degrees to those recognizing competence by certification. (W. M. Sa.)

CANCER

Studies in Boston revealed an association between adenosis or adenocarcinoma of the vagina in young women and a history of treatment of their mothers with diethylstilbestrol, a synthetic female hormone, during pregnancy. The hormone was given to the mothers because of abnormal bleeding during pregnancy or because previous pregnancies had aborted. This observation suggested that hormones may act not only to regulate function in the adult, but also to organize structural development in the embryo.

An important book by Israel Penn was concerned with the high risk of cancer among human kidney-graft recipients who are treated with immunosuppressive drugs over prolonged periods to retain the grafts. Penn's survey indicated that there was an increased risk of a wide variety of cancer types; the increase may exceed one hundredfold the incidence in the normal population. This finding provided further evidence for the view that an immunological surveillance system is an important defense against the development of cancer, and that the seeds of cancers are probably present in the bodies of many normal individuals but cannot grow so long as immunological defenses are intact.

An earlier discovery, in 1965, that certain tumours of the intestinal tract released a substance termed carcinoembryonic antigen (CEA), was applied to detection of cancer in 1971. A medical team at Columbia University developed a sensitive radioimmunoassay method for detecting CEA in serum. They detected the antigen in patients with a variety of cancers unconnected with the intestinal tract. Raised levels of CEA were also found in patients with ulcerative colitis, who are recognized to bear an increased risk of developing bowel cancer. Other workers, using a different assay method, found CEA in the serum of noncancer patients with chronic liver disease or chronic kidney failure. Although CEA in serum could no longer be regarded as a specific test for cancer, many hospital laboratories were planning to test for

A chain smoker lights another cigarette as a cash register in the background rings up the cost of potential lung cancer in a scene from a 1971 antismoking commercial commissioned for British television by the Health Education Council.

it on a routine basis, on the ground that its detection does have some diagnostic value.

The exciting discovery, reported independently by three researchers in June 1970, of the enzyme reverse transcriptase continued to revolutionize the concept of how certain viruses can give rise to cancer. The biological effects of a synthetic form of the enzyme were studied in many laboratories. The results were somewhat puzzling, however, since under some conditions the enzyme appeared to enhance the risk of tumour development in experimental animals, whereas under other conditions it exhibited anti-tumour activity.

Particles similar to type B mouse mammary tumour virus have been observed in human milk and in human mammary cancers for several years. It was reported that these particles contained reverse transcriptase activity (however, milks lacking the particles also lacked this enzymic activity). It was suggested that it would soon be possible to resolve, by molecular hybridization experiments, the relationship between the human type B particles and the similar agents associated with mammary tumours in mice and monkeys. It should also be possible to resolve many questions concerning the relevance of the particles to the development of breast cancer in humans.

In December 1971 a team of scientists in Los Angeles announced the isolation of a virus that might be implicated in human cancer. If the identification was substantiated by later work, this could prove to be of great importance in cancer research.

Workers in Italy reported the development of tumours of the skin, lungs, and bones in rats exposed for a year to vinyl chloride vapours. Also, certain ethers were found to be highly potent initiators of cancers in the nasal cavity and lungs of rats. The discovery of the potent carcinogenic activity of these widely used industrial agents will have important consequences in the field of occupational medicine.

Using new assay methods, several groups of workers found volatile nitrogen compounds (nitrosamines) in nitrite-preserved meats. It was not known whether the minute concentrations of nitrosamine found have significance in relation to any human cancer, but as with many food additives it must be held suspect. Other workers showed that nitrosamine may be formed in the stomach by the interaction of secondary amines, ingested as drugs or as food constituents, with nitrites added to foodstuffs as preservatives.

(F. J. C. R.)

CARDIOLOGY

The performance of the heart as a pump continued to be studied in laboratory animals and in man. The range of investigations included observations on individual heart muscle fibres, experiments on the isolated heart, measurements of pressures and flows, determination of rates of change of heart contraction in human subjects under a variety of conditions, special studies using X-ray techniques to visualize changes in heart size and shape, and techniques for monitoring the heart by "reading" the peripheral pulse. A new area of interest requiring more attention was concerned with the peripheral circulation of blood through the various vessels after it leaves the heart. A clinical team demonstrated that an increase in pressure in the carotid arteries, carrying blood to the brain, produces a decline in the contractile force of the heart muscle. Another group studied the action of blood components called catechol amines on cardiac and circulatory functions.

With the continued decline in rheumatic fever in most parts of the world, fewer new cases of rheumatic heart disease were recorded; however, heart conditions as a result of rheumatic fever contracted 20 and more years ago were still appearing for medical attention. Some patients were left with damaged heart valves following the infection that initiates rheumatic fever. Other patients exhibited weakness of the heart related to heart muscle strain and developed in an attempt to compensate for defective heart valves. The replacement of diseased valves continued to be widely employed in such situations and with notable success. Of particular interest in 1971 was a report from New Zealand on a follow-up of 584 operations in which a diseased valve had been replaced not by an artificial valve but by a healthy human valve taken from a recently deceased person. Despite earlier fears by many surgeons that such human valves would not prove durable, this report of cases—some as old as seven years—indicated a remarkable degree of success, with an early hospital mortality of 8.8% and a subsequent mortality of 13.5%.

The shift from emphasis on research to better application of existing knowledge continued in 1971. Nowhere was this better demonstrated than in the

field of high blood pressure (hypertension). The principal effort was in doing a better job of identifying and treating the large number of hypertensive persons. Studies in the U.S. disclosed that adequate treatment of mild and moderate hypertension lessened the incidence of strokes and heart failure; there was reason to believe that prolonged treatment trials would help also to reduce the number of heart attacks. Unfortunately, other studies showed that the majority of hypertensive persons are not diagnosed, and those that are, do not receive adequate treatment. It was suggested that an intensive educational campaign be mounted to inform the public and the medical profession of the hazards of high blood pressure, and that community screening and treatment clinics be made available for diagnosis and long-term management of hypertensive patients. It was apparent that the dimensions and implications of this vast health problem were just being realized.

Reports from many parts of the world continued to emphasize the frequency of heart muscle disease of unknown origin (cardiomyopathy). It appeared highly likely that this problem represented not one but a number of disorders in which serious and indeed fatal heart disease might result from infections of unknown origin: deficiency states, exposure to toxic substances, and inherited susceptibility. It was especially for these patients—for whom medical treatment consisted of little more than prolonged rest—that heart transplantation had been suggested and attempted. In 1971, however, the enthusiasm for such operations was minuscule, as the result of their enormous cost, transient benefit, and untoward side effects.

Hardening of the coronary arteries, which supply blood to the heart, and its consequences (coronary or ischemic heart disease) are known to have their origins years before their effects are obvious. The year 1971 saw the beginnings of efforts to interest pediatricians in the earliest predisposing factors of this disease. It appeared likely that blood fat and cholesterol levels, blood pressure levels, and smoking determined a person's susceptibility to coronary heart disease later in life. The implications for the nutrition of young people, for weight control, and for an exercise routine were just beginning to be assessed, and there was no unanimity as to a total program. In general, physicians in the U.S. were more receptive than their foreign colleagues to a major attempt to convince the public to reduce their intake of saturated fats.

Much investigative effort was aimed toward the problem of sudden death caused by coronary heart attacks, or the failure of the coronary arteries to supply blood to the heart. A report from Denmark disclosed that approximately 70% of the deaths from this condition in Copenhagen occurred in the first hour following the onset of symptoms. This and other reports stressed the necessity for an individual experiencing an unusual chest discomfort (or signs similar to a prior heart attack) to seek immediate help at an emergency station rather than waste precious moments trying to reach his own physician.

Surgery to correct faulty coronary arteries was undertaken in large numbers in some centres in the United States. The indications for such operations were becoming extended to include not only persons suffering from repeated severe chest discomfort (angina) but also those with milder symptoms and even individuals without symptoms but considered to be

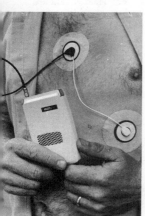

Pocket alarm system (above) alerts wearer to heart irregularities. Attached to paste-on electrodes, the system can also relay electrocardiogram signals to the doctor's office via telephone (below). The Ventricular Impulse Detector and Alarm was undergoing field trials at numerous medical centres in 1971.

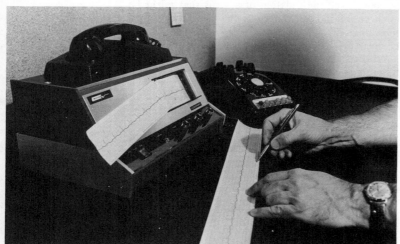

DENNIS GALLOWAY FROM "MEDICAL WORLD NEWS"

high risks as a result of family history, blood fat levels, and X-ray findings. Many physicians criticized the use of such surgery as a preventive or in mild coronary cases, suggesting that there was not enough evidence that it modified the development of the disease.

There was increasing utilization of procedures to determine blood levels of various drugs employed to treat the heart. Whereas in the past the physician often administered a drug solely on the basis of an estimated correct dose, it was now possible to obtain exact blood levels of a drug as a guide to more precise therapy. This development will certainly help to avoid drug intoxications as well as failures due to under-treatment. (O. PL.)

CHILD ABUSE

Children occupy a favoured position in our current society and are usually well cared for, often pampered. History relates that this has not always been the case. Historical records are filled with accounts of infanticide and of maiming, crippling, and other acts of excessive punishment of children. A disturbing regression in solicitude for children, and resultant child abuse, has been noticeable during the past ten years, however. The trend continued in 1971, reaching alarming proportions in large, densely populated urban centres. Such children were commonly referred to under the catch phrase "the battered baby." Accurate statistics concerning the prevalence of this condition are not yet ascertainable, but estimates in excess of 500,000 incidents annually have been quoted for the U.S. Increasing instances of abused children also were being reported in many other countries.

The battered baby is usually (66%) under three years of age, and unable to escape his abuser or to tell others how he was injured. Records show that more boys than girls are victims of abuse. Injuries inflicted include: bruises, lacerations, broken bones, burns, and ruptured internal organs from abdominal beating. Malnutrition, human bites, multiple scars, missing teeth, and stab and gunshot wounds are also encountered. Children have been confined and even chained to restrict them; some have been buried alive. Approximately 10% of the hospitalized abused children die; a comparable percentage are left physically or mentally handicapped, or both.

Mothers have been among the worst offenders, but others entrusted with the care of a child are often guilty. The abusers may be from any level of society and, as a rule, are apparently normal. Only a few are overtly psychotic, or have acted under the influence of alcohol or other drugs. Many of them are persons whose lives are filled with frustrations. Often they themselves were abused when young. For a variety of reasons they may temporarily break down under stress and lash out at their children. Ordinarily, one child in a family is the target for the abuse. The child is abused repeatedly, and with each new instance of trauma, the possibility of fatal injury is increased.

The medical, legal, and social-service professions, supported by law enforcement agencies, continued to cooperate to stem the rising tide of child abuse. In the U.S., for example, laws were enacted that required a report of any suspected or confirmed case of such abuse. If investigation revealed a clear possibility of danger to the child, immediate steps could be taken to remove the child from the threatening situation. An effort was then made to help the family solve its problems, and prepare it to accept the youngster into its proper place in the home. If attempts at rehabilitation failed, the child could be cared for temporarily in a foster home until a resolution of the problem could be effected.

Many difficulties surround the determination of child abuse. A definite diagnosis should first be established by a doctor, who is required to report the case to a welfare or social agency, or to the police department, according to local law. If the case requires a court hearing, the fate of the child may still be in jeopardy because the judge will require proof, often "beyond a reasonable doubt," that the accused was in fact the actual offender. Such proof is difficult to obtain since the abuse usually occurs within the privacy of the home. It is either unobserved or seen only by a spouse, who cannot be compelled legally to testify against the accused. Without such proof, the case is dismissed, and the child returned home, where it often suffers subsequent abuse, as records indicate.

In 1971 all involved disciplines continued in attempts to eradicate the causes of child abuse. The communications media did much to bring the sad story of the battered child to the public. Corrective measures began to lay less stress on punishment and more emphasis on constructive assistance to the troubled offender. Demands for relief were made to those dedicated to public service to spur economic and social reforms that—it is hoped—will decrease the stresses that underlie child abuse. (R. H. B.)

DENTISTRY

In a 1971 report titled "Oral Disease, Target for the '70s," the U.S. National Institute of Dental Research outlined a five-year plan for improvement in dental research. Areas of proposed study include the control of anxiety and pain associated with dental procedures; the continued exploration of methods of combating caries (tooth decay), periodontal disease, and oral ulcerations (cold sores) and the feasibility of immunization against these disorders; and further development of techniques for handling oro-facial deformities (disfigurement involving the mouth, such as cleft palate and malocclusion).

Experiments performed at the Royal Dental College in Aarhus, Denmark, held promise of helping reduce the development of such mouth disorders as bacterial plaque formation and gum infections (gingivitis). A 0.2% solution of chlorhexidine gluconate used as a mouth rinse by a group of male students confirmed previous observations that two daily mouth rinses with this solution effectively prevent plaque formation and gingivitis if properly administered. The investigation made it clear that chlorhexidine is only moderately effective in reducing the number of bacteria in saliva and that its inhibitory effect on plaque formation is due primarily to an interaction with the tooth surface to form a resistant chemical barrier.

A report in the *International Journal of Dental Research* on 500 patients, referred over the past 14 years to the National Institute of Dental Health for a study of their severe caries problem, suggested that one or more of the following factors was implicated: (1) frequent or prolonged ingestion of sugar-containing foods, between meals and at bedtimes; (2) xerostomia, or lack of saliva as a result of X-ray therapy for tumours of the head and neck, or prolonged medication with salivary depressant drugs; and (3) poor oral hygiene, especially during prolonged illnesses. (D. L. McE.)

DERMATOLOGY

Immunological aspects of skin diseases were the focus of research in 1971. Migration inhibitory factor, a substance produced by lymphocytes of patients with delayed-type (cellular) hypersensitivity, inhibits the migration of certain blood cells (macrophages) of guinea pigs. First developed into a test for cellular hypersensitivity in man, it has now been applied to the study of skin diseases, such as leprosy and chronic fungous infections.

Complement, a system of nine protein factors occurring in normal blood serum, was found to be involved in a number of biological phenomena. A normal inhibitor of one component of complement, and also of the enzyme kallikrein, is either absent or nonfunctional in patients with hereditary angioedema, a disease characterized by swelling of the skin, gastrointestinal tract, and upper respiratory tract. It was shown that in this disease the activation of plasma kallikrein leads to the formation of peptides that enlarge the blood vessels. Another component of complement is elevated in some patients with pemphigus vulgaris, a chronic disease characterized by serum-filled blisters on the skin. Still another component of complement is low in the cerebrospinal fluid of patients suffering from systemic lupus erythematosus (SLE) with involvement of the central nervous system.

Immunoglobulins (antibodies), divided into five classes—IgG, IgM, IgA, IgD, and IgE—were linked to several types of skin diseases. Patients with dermatitis herpetiformis (oozing blisters of the skin) cause a deposition of IgA in portions of clinically normal skin. Using antibodies tagged with radioactive material, ultrastructural studies detect labeled material along the basal layers in pemphigoid and SLE, and in the intercellular spaces of the epidermis in pemphigus vulgaris, sites that are known to be affected by the disease. IgE is elevated in the serum of patients with atopic dermatitis and in patients with Wiskott-Aldrich syndrome, in which there is also an increased prevalence of eczematous dermatitis. Deficiencies of IgA and IgE are found in patients with a muscular-vascular disorder called ataxia-telangiectasia.

Prostaglandins were found to be capable of producing prolonged dilation of cutaneous blood vessels.

The disposition of pigment cells in packages called melanosomes was found to correspond to human races. In Caucasoids and Mongoloids the melanosomes are incorporated into groups, whereas in Negroids and Australian Aborigines, the melanosomes are dispersed individually.

Evaluation of topical sunscreens (tanning lotions) showed that one of the most effective agents available to protect against the injurious effects of prolonged exposure to the sun is a solution containing 5% para-aminobenzoic acid in 50–70% ethyl alcohol. A single application was effective in screening out damaging ultraviolet light for the entire day.

Another class of sunscreens, benzophenones, was found effective in preventing untoward skin reactions as a result of the application of psoralens used to treat vitiligo, a disease characterized by white spots on the skin. The benzophenones also may be used to protect operating-room personnel from mercury-arc lamps, which are used for their bactericidal effect.

Primary cutaneous melanomas, malignant tumours arising from pigment cells in the skin, were classified into three forms. Each of these melanomas has a characteristic development and a distinctive appearance that can be related to the prospect for patient survival. The clinical signs of utmost importance are irregularities of surface, outline, and especially colour, with variations in shades of blue being especially significant.

There was clarification of a disease entity, or syndrome, designated by the coined word "LEOPARD"; it is a dominantly inherited disease characterized by *L*entigines (freckle-like spots all over the body), defects on an *E*lectrocardiogram, *O*cular defects (hyperteleorism), *P*ulmonary malfunction (infundibular stenosis), *A*bnormal genitalia, mental and physical *R*etardation, and *D*eafness.

The year saw an increasing emphasis on the fact that impetigo, a skin infection caused by group A of the β-hemolytic streptococci, is associated with the later development of glomerulonephritis, a kidney disorder. Therapeutic regimens were reevaluated, and it appears that benzathine penicillin administered intramuscularly is the treatment of choice for impetigo.

A new aid in the diagnosis of viral skin disorders was described. Bits of skin or ooze, or even old stained slides of tissue, can be examined under the electron microscope and the viral agent rapidly detected and classified. Using such a technique, it was confirmed that there are two distinct types of herpes simplex virus: type I causes lesions about the mouth, and type II causes lesions on the genitalia.

A strain of newborn mice was developed in which an eruption similar to toxic epidermal necrolysis (scalded-skin syndrome) in children was reproduced with a specific type of staphylococcus bacterium. These developments are expected to provide an experimental system for further study.

It was noted that the use of barbiturates may produce characteristic large blisters of the skin; such signs may provide a life-saving clue to the condition of an unconscious patient.

The hazards of using the drug methotrexate in treating patients with psoriasis were underscored again. Both hypersensitivity pneumonitis and a relationship to cancer were suggested as possible dangerous side effects. Vitamin A preparations applied to the skin appeared to be of value in treating the comedo (blackhead) type of acne.   (N. A. So.; T. B. F.)

EDUCATION

Medical education continued in a state of transition during 1971, with changes related to both its quantity and quality. New medical schools opened and planning of others began, in both the more and the less developed countries. Rising costs and the need, created by specialization in science and medicine, to provide an increasingly wider range of teachers forced many medical schools to take on more students. On the other hand, countries traditionally accustomed to admitting very large numbers of students to their medical schools, with subsequent rejection of a high proportion of them during the early years of the program, began to reconsider the wisdom of this procedure, in the light of the waste in both funds and educational efficiency. Everywhere the need for training auxiliary medical workers in the allied health professions was clearly recognized.

Changes related to improving the quality of medical education continued to follow earlier trends. Despite much talk of relating the basic medical courses to local health needs, the majority of the world's new medical graduates proceeded to postgraduate training. Only in the Soviet Union and Eastern Europe was such training required of all graduates; elsewhere it continued to be required only of those desiring to become specialists. In most countries serious efforts were made to improve the quality of postgraduate study. In Britain, particularly, progress was made in reorganizing, along lines recommended by the royal commission of 1968, the lengthy and rather haphazard postgraduate training that had evolved in postwar years. Similar programs took place in Scandinavia, while in North America study of the educational processes involved in postgraduate training continued.

In many countries attempts were made to provide appropriate postgraduate or postdiploma professional training for general practitioners (as opposed to internists), but only in Eastern Europe was such training compulsory. Perhaps partly in consequence, the majority of the world's new medical graduates continued to train in medical specialties rather than becoming involved as general practitioners in service to the community. Only in countries with a trend toward the grouping of general practitioners into central premises equipped for current practice was there any tendency for this field of medicine to become more popular. In countries such as India, where the number of undergraduate medical schools has been increased without any provision for postgraduate training, the majority of graduates continued to migrate to foreign lands where such training was available; many became specialists and returned to their homeland but, unfortunately, a significant number remained in their adopted countries and thereby deprived their own people of adequate medical services.

In countries in which postgraduate training improved, the basic undergraduate course became less centred on the traditional, but hopeless, task of introducing the student to a little of every aspect of medicine. The trend was toward a core curriculum containing the minimum essential knowledge, together with opportunities for the student to delve deeper into areas of his choice. All curricula came increasingly to resemble each other through their more flexible nature and by the increasingly systematized and interdepartmentally integrated core.

The study of the educational process in medical education was intensified in some countries and taken up in many others, assisted by the increasing number of national associations for the advancement of medical education. Some of this effort continued to be devoted to the continuing education by which doctors keep abreast of advances in their own fields and of new developments in other fields. Educational technology continued to offer new means of self-learning, and more objective types of assessment were increasingly applied almost everywhere.

Every country continued to find more applicants for medical schools than it could accommodate. There was, however, evidence that recruits included a greater variety of young people than in the past, with differing ambitions as to the means whereby they wished to help the sick or prevent disease, and with differing capabilities in relation to the many different elements of the long medical preparation.

(J. R. EL.)

ENDOCRINOLOGY

An important development in endocrinology was the confirmation that cyclic AMP (adenosine monophosphate) was a "second endocrine messenger." The hormone is regarded as the prime messenger, which activates the formation of cyclic AMP within the target cell.

Prolactin, the pituitary hormone responsible for mammary growth and lactation, became the subject of renewed interest. For some time growth hormone and prolactin were considered the same hormone in the human. Researchers in New York determined, after a series of experimental observations, that the two hormones are indeed separate substances.

For several decades many investigators contended that the female hormones called estrogens induced mammary cancer. Prolactin, another hormone, is now suspect, not estrogens. The estrogens stimulate prolactin secretion and mammary development only in the presence of the pituitary gland. In rats with breast tumours, injections of prolactin contributed to the rate of tumour growth. Further evidence absolving the estrogens is that they failed to maintain tumour growth after hypophysectomy (removal of the pituitary). On the basis of such data the temporary regressions observed in human breast malignancies after hypophysectomy can be explained as resulting from lack of prolactin. That large doses of estrogens produce comparable benefits in controlling mammary cancer is attributed to interference with the tumour-stimulating potential of prolactin at the level of the target organ.

The simultaneous involvement of more than one gland of internal secretion was being recognized with greater frequency. A report in 1971, from Edinburgh, Scot., disclosed that 44 of 105 patients with Addison's disease also displayed other endocrine disorders. The association of medullary carcinoma of the thyroid with Sipple's syndrome, or pheochromocytoma (a dysfunction of the adrenal glands), was frequent enough to warrant special efforts to rule out one in the presence of the other.

It was estimated that 20–25% of hypertensive persons exhibit suppressed plasma renin activity (PRA). It was suspected that abnormally high production of a newly recognized adrenal hormone, 18-hydroxydesoxycorticosterone (18-OH-DOC), was responsible. In some patients with essential hypertension, suppressed PRA, and hypersecretion of 18-OH-DOC, the administration of a glucocorticoid (dexamethasone), an antagonist of 18-OH-DOC, resulted in significant reduction in blood pressure associated with a fall in the urinary excretion of the hormone. Hypertension due to primary aldosteronism (Conn's disease) differs from this disorder in that it does not respond to glucocorticoid therapy.

The year 1971 was noteworthy in that the chemical synthesis of two polypeptide hormones was accomplished. The biologically active portion of parathyroid hormone—the first 34 amino acids in the 84 amino acid chain that makes up the entire molecule—was assembled in a collaborative effort by teams in Bethesda, Md., and in Boston. Workers in New Orleans, La., announced the synthesis of luteinizing releasing hormone which, it is believed, could eliminate the problem of multiple births so common following medical treatments to stimulate fertility.

Oral contraceptives were shown to induce hypertension in susceptible women by causing a sodium loss, which in turn induces renin release, thus stimulating aldosterone secretion. Which of the two hormones in the classical birth control pill—the estrogen or the progestogen—triggers such hypertensive episodes remains the subject of much controversy.

It was found that low hormone levels may signal an impending abortion. In an Australian study of 33 women who aborted, estrogen excretion was abnormally low in 22, progesterone production was poor in 20.

A French report disclosed that high levels of testosterone-estrogen binding globulin (TEBG) in the bloodstream, as occurs naturally in women, are associated with scant body hair. The TEBG inactivates the hormones responsible for stimulating hair follicles. The observation that large doses of estrogens slow sexual hair growth in many hairy women can now be viewed as the result of a concomitant increase in TEBG.   (R. B. Gt.)

EPIDEMICS

Cerebrospinal meningitis continued to be a serious problem in Africa, and nearly all of its countries recorded sporadic cases in 1970 (the latest year for which epidemic figures were available). An epidemic, with some 7,000 cases and a fatality rate of about 10%, occurred in Niger in the first part of the year, the causative organism being *Neisseria meningitidis* group A. Smaller outbreaks occurred in Northern Nigeria and Upper Volta. In Mali, where there had been a large outbreak in 1969, cases were relatively few in 1970.

During 1970, 46,469 cases of cholera were reported: 33,570 from Asia; 10,988 from Africa; and 1,911 from Europe. Cholera, which had long been endemic in Southeast Asia, showed a gradual spread to many areas in Africa and Europe. Cases were reported from the following countries: India (13,675 cases), East Pakistan (5,969), Indonesia (4,778), Mali (2,603), Guinea (2,000), Ethiopia (850), Ivory Coast (828), Ghana (213), Turkey (1,185), and the Soviet Union (720). *Vibrio cholerae,* biotype El Tor, prevailed in all countries (except East Pakistan where the classical strain predominated) as the causative organism.

Severe epidemics of influenza, generally due to virus A2/Hong Kong/68, hit several European countries as well as Canada, India, Israel, and Mexico from December 1969 to March 1970. In the Southern Hemisphere widespread epidemics were reported from Australia, Argentina, the Canal Zone (Panama), Papua New Guinea, New Zealand, and South Africa. Minor outbreaks from areas in these countries and in Chile were reported as well. No unusual increase in the incidence of influenza in the fall of 1970 was reported in any country of the Northern Hemisphere. The only outbreaks of influenza-like illness reported

were in Puerto Rico, Thailand, and Indonesia (virus A2/Hong Kong/68) and in Fiji (virus B). In the winter of 1970, Romania and Bulgaria both reported epidemics due to virus B; a small rise in the incidence of influenza B cases was reported in other European countries, often at the decline of the A2/Hong Kong/ 68 wave.

Relapsing fever was reported in 1970 from the same three countries that reported it in 1969: the Congo (Kinshasa; 47 cases), Ethiopia (2,336, during the first nine months of the year), and Sudan (242).

Louse-borne typhus was reported from Burundi (16,055 cases), Ethiopia (2,841, during the first eight months), Congo (Kinshasa; 6), South Africa (26), Bolivia (3), Ecuador (56), Peru (23), Yugoslavia (14), and France (2). The world total was 19,026 cases in 1970, a decrease from the 22,107 cases recorded in 1969.

During the last half century, malaria was endemic in areas inhabited by over two-thirds of the world's population. Due to the global malaria eradication campaign undertaken with assistance from the World Health Organization (WHO) since 1957, many of the less developed countries throughout the world had, in 1970, either controlled or eradicated the disease. Of the 145 malarious countries in 1940, 37 had claimed eradication of the disease by 1970, 48 had begun eradication programs, and 44 had control programs in progress. In the remaining 16 countries, mainly in tropical Africa, where the disease was still highly endemic, large-scale antimalaria activities had not yet been implemented.

In 1970 mosquito-borne hemorrhagic fever, or dengue, was reported from 56 provinces of Thailand (2,757 cases and 46 deaths). The mosquito *Aedes aegypti* was implicated as the main carrier of the causative viruses. A severe outbreak was reported from Rangoon, Burma, in 1970, where milder dengue virus infections had become common in recent years; a total of 323 cases and 29 deaths were reported within a period of four months. *Aedes aegypti* and *A. albopictus* are both vectors of dengue virus infections in Burma.

Hemorrhagic fever in South America is different from dengue. There is no proof of arthropod transmission; wild and domestic rodents are vertebrate hosts of the Junin (Argentina) and Machup (Bolivia) viruses, which cause the disease. In 1970, Argentina reported 1,541 cases of hemorrhagic fever.

In Africa, 20 out of 36 countries have reported an increase in poliomyelitis cases since 1951, before the use of vaccines. In 1969 more than half the reported

Waste and old clothes are burned to maintain hygiene at a field hospital at Bigberia camp, India, where a team of British doctors and volunteers were helping Pakistani refugees in their fight against disease and starvation in 1971.

KEYSTONE

cases for that year (4,800) occurred in five countries (Congo [Kinshasa], Congo [Brazzaville], Kenya, South Africa, and Mali). The total number of cases for 1970 (1,835) is unusually low, but this is due partly to incomplete reporting by nearly half the countries. North and South America, with the exclusion of the United States, reported 3,998 cases in 1970, against 2,582 cases in 1969. Outbreaks were reported from Bolivia (99 cases), Paraguay (122), Colombia (788), and Argentina (242). Mexico reported the greatest number of cases of any country in the Western Hemisphere (1,848). In Asia, 13 countries reported 1,551 cases. The overall situation was obscured, however, by the absence of data from such populous countries as China, India, and Indonesia.

No extensive outbreaks of plague occurred in 1970. A total of 807 cases and 47 deaths were recorded, a slight decrease when compared with the 1969 data of 1,166 cases and 98 deaths. South Vietnam had the highest number of cases in 1970 (616 cases and 27 deaths). Burma and Indonesia reported a total of 60 cases and 5 deaths. In the Americas, Brazil, Bolivia, the United States, and Peru altogether recorded 273 cases in 1970, against 401 cases in 1969. In Africa during 1970, 16 cases were reported from the Congo (Kinshasa) and 12 cases from the Malagasy Republic. One imported case of plague was reported in France in 1970.

The global program of smallpox eradication completed its fourth year in 1970, a period during which the world incidence of the disease declined by 75%. About 31,500 cases were reported in 1970. Brazil, the only country in South America with an endemic situation, recorded 1,759 cases. Eleven African countries reported 3,566 cases, nearly all in East and South Africa. In Asia, 26,327 cases were reported from eight countries, a decline from 1969. As in 1969, the greatest incidence of the disease occurred in India and Indonesia. In Europe, where no cases were reported in 1969, 24 cases were reported in 1970: 22 from West Germany and one each from Denmark and Norway.

During 1970 a total of 75 cases of yellow fever with 57 deaths were recorded. Bolivia, Brazil, Colombia, and Peru altogether reported 86 cases and 64 deaths (75 cases and 57 deaths from Peru alone). In 1969, 48 cases and 36 deaths were reported from these countries and Surinam. From Africa only a few sporadic cases were reported during the year, in contrast to the series of outbreaks that simultaneously struck Ghana, Mali, Nigeria, Togo, and Upper Volta in 1969 (322 cases and 119 deaths). In 1970 a total of 21 cases and 11 deaths were reported from the Cameroon, Equatorial Guinea, Ghana, Nigeria, and Togo.   (M. Ta.)

GASTROENTEROLOGY

The devising of improved instruments in 1971 extended the range of gastrointestinal diagnostic examinations to include not only the esophagus and stomach but also the duodenum, the portion of the small intestine just beyond the stomach. Direct visualization of the duodenum permitted more accurate diagnosis of duodenal ulcer and the detection of diverticula and tumours. New instruments also facilitated more complete examination of the pancreas, detection of overlooked stones in the bile ducts, and more extensive inspection of the colon beyond the usual range of the proctoscope, making possible the diagnosis of polyps and cancers not seen by conventional diagnostic methods.

The diagnosis and management of gastrointestinal hemorrhage remained a major problem. The recommended approach in 1971 included: treating the resultant shock, with restoration and maintenance of normal blood volume; locating the source and the underlying cause of the bleeding; and establishing specific treatment appropriate to the individual diagnosis.

The inability to absorb milk sugar, lactose, properly was found to be responsible for a variety of symptoms including diarrhea, flatulence, and bloating. It is due to a deficiency of the enzyme lactase. Occasionally, the accompanying abdominal pain suggested more serious abdominal disease, and led to unnecessary surgery. Lactose malabsorption also was associated with other diseases causing digestive symptoms, such as peptic ulcer, Crohn's disease, and ulcerative colitis. Populations in which the majority of adults were found to be lactase deficient included African Negroes, Australian aborigines, Chinese, Europeans (Caucasoid), Indians of North and South America, New Guineans, Filipinos, and Thais. The trait appeared to be largely under genetic control. Exclusion of lactose from the diets of patients with lactose malabsorption rapidly relieved the digestive symptoms.

Unusually severe cases of infantile gastroenteritis, or intestinal inflammation, were traced to the bacterium *Escherichia coli* 0014. The disease, characterized by severe vomiting and mucus-like, watery stools with a distinctive odour, occasionally resulted in death. Sugar intolerance was prominent, and there was difficulty in returning the infants to their routine formulas. Intravenous feeding was therefore required for long periods. Two other strains of *E. coli*, isolated from diarrhetic American soldiers in Vietnam, produced a toxin that caused a diarrheal syndrome resembling cholera in adult volunteers. Two nontoxigenic *E. coli* strains caused a Shigella-like (dysentery) illness in man, characterized by bloody diarrhea and extreme rectal discomfort. These observations indicated that *E. coli* should be considered the possible disease agent in those patients with acute diarrhea and from whom a recognized pathogen cannot be isolated. The widespread incidence and the associated high mortality rate of enteropathogenic *E. coli* (EPEC) disease stimulated interest in the possible development of a safely administered vaccine as a preventive. A human vaccine trial was initiated in West Germany, with a vaccine consisting of a cell-free extract of an EPEC strain.

Good results were reported with a modified intestinal bypass operation for the management of extremely obese patients. It consisted of bypassing 90% of the small intestine in such a way that backup of intestinal contents—an unfortunate result of earlier bypass techniques—was prevented.

It was estimated that in 1971, 75,000 new cases of cancer of the colon appeared in the U.S. population, approximately 46,000 of which were fatal; a five-year survival rate was predicted for about 40% of all cases of cancer of the colon and rectum.

In most of the Western world the large bowel, after the bronchial tubes, is the most common site of cancer in man. Current evidence suggests that the high incidence of bowel cancer is a relatively recent development, probably related to alterations in dietary habits as a result of improved socioeconomic status. The incidence of large bowel cancer was highest in the United States, Canada, and Europe, and lowest in rural African communities. The close relationship between bowel cancer and other noninfective diseases of the bowel, such as benign tumours and diverticular disease, indicated that these conditions may have a common related cause. These diseases were found to be rarest in communities that exist on a high fibre, or residue, diet, and highest in countries where a low residue diet is common. Dietary fibre is known to regulate the speed of transit, bulk, and consistency of stools and, together with other dietary factors, probably is responsible also for the type of bacterial flora of the feces. It seemed likely that a carcinogen produced by the action of an abnormal bacterial flora, when held for a prolonged period in concentrated form in contact with the sensitive bowel lining, might account for the high incidence of bowel cancer in economically developed countries.

Chronic liver disease (hepatitis) continued to be a common problem among narcotic addicts. In the majority of cases, the hepatitis reached a certain limited level of severity, but persisted for extremely long periods, probably because of repeated exposure to the hepatitis virus. Evidence from cases of drug abuse supported the hypothesis that the so-called Australia antigen caused viral hepatitis. The hepatitis was frequently contracted through the use of contaminated "community" hypodermic needles. It was emphasized that a dangerous—almost epidemic—situation could occur in view of the known tendency of drug users to become professional blood donors to support their habit. An increased risk of post-transfusion hepatitis was documented following transfusions of blood obtained from commercial sources supplied by such blood donors.

Evaluation of the status of liver transplantation during the past decade indicated that it was rapidly becoming a feasible and legitimate, albeit imperfect, surgical procedure. Patients who have undergone such treatment have survived for periods only up to $2\frac{1}{2}$ years. With more experience, and with improvements in the special postoperative supportive treatments required, the record will improve. Patients with non-malignant terminal liver disease, and no other hope

for recovery, are becoming willing candidates for liver transplantation. (J. B. KR.)

GYNECOLOGY AND OBSTETRICS

The Karolinska Institutet, Stockholm, described a new method of staining the male Y chromosome and identifying it under the fluorescence microscope. It thus became possible to diagnose the sex of any human cell quickly and accurately. The sex of the fetus was accurately diagnosed by examining cells sloughed off the uterine wall of the mother at a sufficiently early stage of pregnancy for termination to be undertaken if the mother was known to carry a sex-linked disease manifested only by males, such as hemophilia. Since the dyes were toxic to the sex cells but were preferentially taken up by the Y chromosome, it was suggested that it might be possible to predetermine the sex of offspring. Very small doses could be incubated with the sperm and might kill the Y-bearing sperm, leaving the X-bearing sperm unharmed, thus ensuring the production of a female fetus on insemination.

Regarding the predetermination of the sex of the unborn child, data from a number of studies indicated that insemination early in the menstrual cycle was more likely to result in the formation of males. It followed therefore that couples who had intercourse frequently were more likely to produce sons. This might explain the observed facts that among first births there was an excess of male children born to women under the age of 25 and a deficit to women over the age of 35, and that a higher proportion of males were born to women who conceived within 18 months of marriage than to those who conceived later.

In Boston, a team of doctors reported that an extremely rare form of adenocarcinoma of the vagina in young women was related to the administration to their mothers of large daily doses of the synthetic hormone diethylstilbestrol, then in vogue for the treatment of previous fetal loss or bleeding in early pregnancy. Attention was subsequently drawn to the possible harmful effects of using stilbestrol to fatten cattle and poultry, particularly common in North America, although it was conceded that the slow-release preparations usually injected in those animals probably did not enter human food in dangerous amounts.

In the United States the law relating to abortion changed rapidly in all but four states. During the year the ratio of legal abortions to live births exceeded 15 to 100, the ratio for the United Kingdom and Scandinavia. Concern was expressed in England and Wales over the increased mortality rate for abortion with sterilization, 108 deaths per 100,000 abortions. Statistics from Eastern Europe showed mortality rates for termination of pregnancy before 12 weeks at least ten times lower than those in Britain and Scandinavia; in Czechoslovakia and Hungary the rates were lower than the mortality rates for full-term pregnancy in any other country in the world. Pregnancies up to ten weeks along were terminated in California, New York, Novi Sad (Yugoslavia), and London by means of vacuum aspiration (suction) through a flexible tube only 4 or 6 mm. (about .16 or .24 in.) in diameter. No enlargement of the cervix was required and a local anesthetic was adequate. This technique could be used in the outpatient department and the patient allowed home two or three hours later.

A report from Denmark described the use of a sterile disposable suction curette for abortion in outpatients. The endometrial lining of the uterus was

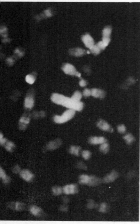

A bright fluorescent dot identifies the presence of a Y chromosome in white blood cells stained with quinacrine mustard. The technique may be applied to cells taken from the amniotic fluid surrounding the fetus in a pregnant woman to determine the sex of her child.

Women picket Chicago's Grant Hospital in February 1971 to protest a legal abortion performed during the 12 days between a federal court decision voiding the Illinois abortion law and an order staying that decision until the case could be heard by the U.S. Supreme Court.

STEVE MURATA FROM "MEDICAL WORLD NEWS"

sucked out through a stainless steel tube 3 mm. (about .12 in.) in diameter attached to an electric suction pump. No anesthetic was needed, and hospital beds were left free for other patients.

A research chemist in Ottawa developed a simple paper-strip test for indicating the onset of ovulation in women. The test reveals an increase in the enzyme alkaline phosphatase in a woman's saliva during the days immediately preceding ovulation. The enzyme is detected by means of a chemical colour change in a paper strip held in the mouth for a short while. Thus coitus could be planned either to coincide with, or to avoid, the time of ovulation in order to increase or diminish the likelihood of conception. (T. L. T. L.)

HEMATOLOGY

Despite the high costs involved, some large organizations were able to apply blood-separation machines, working on the differential centrifugation principle, to practical therapeutic uses in 1971. One use was in separating red blood cells of rare groups from other blood cells. The separated cells could then be frozen in a glycerol mixture and kept almost indefinitely. Another use was in separating abnormal white cells from leukemic blood, returning the rest of the blood to the patient. In addition to the immediate benefits to the patient, the procedure provided leukemic cells that were used in a form of immunotherapy. The cells were killed by irradiation and then injected into a patient suffering from the same form of leukemia in the hope that the cells would evoke an immune response that would be effective against the patient's own leukemic cells as well. This type of immunotherapy was used only after a remission of the disease had been induced by chemical treatment. Soviet and French hematologists claimed good results, but experience elsewhere was less encouraging.

The method of combined drug treatment for leukemia and conditions such as Hodgkin's disease continued to gain popularity, although much closer control of dosage and effects on the blood was needed. In Hodgkin's disease, where survival is normally measured in years, clear results could not be expected for some time. Since most of the drugs used were very toxic, some unpleasant side effects were reported. Efforts were being made to find less toxic drugs; bis-chloroethyl-nitrosourea, among a few other drugs, appeared a promising candidate. Workers in several centres reported on treatment of myeloma, a condition allied to leukemia, and the biochemical abnormalities present. In myeloma, plasma cells normally concerned with the production of immunoglobulins grow excessively; in addition, they produce an abnormal globulin. The excessive growth is mostly in bone marrow, producing localized areas of thinning of bone that can cause fractures, and often causes much pain even without fracture. Two drugs, cyclophosphamide and melphalan, were found to be equally effective in managing myeloma; they relieved the pain and appeared to slow the progress of plasmacell proliferation. Unfortunately, some patients who were on these drugs developed an acute leukemia that rapidly proved fatal; as a rule, the complication did not appear for some years and affected only a few patients. Nevertheless, this episode underlined the reality that combined drug treatment exposes some patients to combined toxic risks as well.

Advances continued to be made in the treatment of myocardial infarction (coronary thrombosis) with anticoagulants, although the popular quick-acting in-

danedione drugs were abandoned because of their unpleasant side effects. In the first 48 hours of treatment it had been customary to give heparin, a simple anticoagulant, but a new drug, streptokinase, was becoming more popular; as an enzyme it actively digests the clot blocking an artery. A European team reported significantly better results with streptokinase than with heparin.

Significant advances were made in the prevention of hemolytic disease in Rhesus-positive infants born to Rhesus-negative mothers. With each birth the level of anti-Rhesus antibodies in the mother's blood is raised, increasing the risk to the next child. It was discovered in 1971 that major sensitization of the mother occurred only during birth, which led to the development of a serum to neutralize the anti-Rhesus antibody. Such a serum, given soon after labour, prevented the development of antibodies. Six months after delivery only one out of 173 treated mothers was shown to have the unwanted anti-Rhesus antibody in the bloodstream, whereas out of 176 untreated mothers 38 had the antibody. The crucial test of this preventive therapy was the presence of antibodies at the end of the next pregnancy; of 86 mothers treated only 2 had antibodies at this time, compared with 20 out of 65 untreated mothers. A limiting factor was the availability of serum material, which had to be human. (M. C. G. I.)

The year saw an increase in many areas of blood banking, with development of greater exchange facility of rare blood. At the urging of the American Association of Blood Banks, the largest organization in the world specifically concerned with collecting and supplying blood, several states passed laws regulating the collection, storage, and transfusion of blood. Tests for the detection of hepatitis virus in donated blood were being developed because of the increased incidence of that virus among the population, and therefore among blood donors. (X.)

HOSPITALS AND CLINICS

During 1971 worldwide attention was focused on the worsening problems of cost, availability, and accessibility of health care. In the United States alone more than a dozen proposals for some form of national health insurance were introduced during the year.

Hospital costs continued to climb during the year in the U.S., to the projected figure of $93.26 a day for each patient. The increasing cost of general labour continued to be a major factor behind rising hospital expenses, but other contributory factors included the increase in the number of skilled employees required to care for patients and the increase in cost of medical supplies and equipment.

In the U.S. during 1970 (the most recent year for which data were available), 5,859 community hospitals employed 292 workers per 100 patients. This figure represented a new high in hospital manpower. Ten years earlier, community hospitals employed only 226 personnel per 100 patients. Following President Nixon's 90-day wage-price freeze in August 1971, hospitals and other health care institutions—constituting the nation's third largest industry—were asked to hold the line in wages and prices.

The average occupancy rate for U.S. community hospitals showed a small drop, from 78.8% in 1969 to 78% in 1970, and average length of stay decreased slightly, from 8.3 days to 8.2 days. Ambulatory, or

Pathologist Robert Nalbandian shows evidence of how intravenous infusions of urea convert abnormal sickled red cells into essentially normal disk shapes. Urea could join dozens of other agents as "possible" solutions to sickle-cell anemia.

RON UNTERNAHRER FROM "MEDICAL WORLD NEWS"

continued on page 465

THE RISING COST OF MEDICAL CARE

By David Mazie

A man or woman hospitalized in the U.S. in 1960 expected to pay about $35 a day for hospital care. In 1971, the charge for one day's hospital care was $90–$100 and was expected to climb to over $150 by 1975. This increase represented only one aspect of the cost of medical care in only one nation; rising health-care costs elsewhere in the world were equally staggering. In Sweden, France, West Germany, as well as in the U.S., health service expenditures rose in the 1960s three times faster than the national consumer price indexes. In the U.K., Canada, Israel, and dozens of other nations the proportion of the gross national product (GNP) devoted to health care increased substantially. As the cost of medical care rose so did public concern. By 1971 health service was a major issue producing political battles, strikes, spates of legislation, and program reexaminations in many countries.

A look at health-cost statistics indicates the extent of the problem. Total expenditures on health care in the U.S. rose from $26.4 billion (5.3% of the GNP) in 1960 to $67.2 billion (6.9%) in 1970, an outlay greater than that for education or Social Security. By 1974, according to estimates of the U.S. Department of Health, Education, and Welfare, health costs were expected to exceed $100 billion a year. On the cost-of-living index, medical costs already held the dubious distinction of being the fastest rising commodity, having jumped over 50% in a decade when the index as a whole rose 31%. In Canada and West Germany, the portion of GNP devoted to health services rose 25% in six years. Great Britain's health budget tripled between 1950 and 1965. A Swedish citizen was paying 20% of his taxes for health care. In six European nations, health expenditures grew much more rapidly in the 1960s than in the 1950s and at rates well above consumer price indexes.

Although rising medical costs are common to almost every country, the manner in which those costs are met and the medical care they purchase is not the same. National health service systems have developed in varying forms, influenced by such factors as a nation's social and political background, its economic conditions, the historic attitude of its government toward social security, and the role of private charities and medical associations. Every major industrialized nation except the U.S. has some kind of national program to provide or subsidize comprehensive health care. The U.S. still relies on private enterprise and private health insurance, but the day of greater federal involvement appears near.

The U.S. Experience. The approach to health care in the U.S. is based on the general philosophy that those who provide medical care should be able to choose their own patients, and patients should be responsible for paying their own bills. Government has stepped in with direct help only in extreme situations. The result is a conglomeration of public and private programs that has resisted change and economies. This health care system—or "nonsystem" in the eyes of its critics—has come under searching examination in recent years. Pres. Richard M. Nixon warned that the entire nation faces a "massive crisis" in health

---

David Mazie is an associate of syndicated columnist Carl T. Rowan and a free-lance writer contributing regularly to Reader's Digest.

care unless something is done immediately. Others, from politicians to physicians to patients, have described the present setup as "outworn," "outrageously inefficient," "a mess," "chaotic," "a disaster."

The difficulty lies primarily in the delivery of services and the expenses involved. One delivery problem is the shortage of primary care physicians (general practitioners, pediatricians, and internists), dentists, and nurses. This is exacerbated by an uneven distribution of medical facilities and manpower in which millions, primarily the urban poor and rural populations, are without adequate care and sometimes without any care. Other trouble spots in the delivery of health care are the training of medical personnel, organization and management of hospitals, and coordination of private and public services.

But despite all the sources of discontent within health care delivery, it is financing, and its several ramifications, that is the most disturbing aspect of medical care. It is estimated that $75 billion a year, or more than $350 a person, is being spent on all aspects of health service in the U.S. Of each $100 spent, roughly $40 goes for hospital care, $20 for physicians' services, $10 for drugs, $6 for dental care, $4 for nursing homes, and the rest for research, construction, and administration. Private sources provide about 62% of this money either through insurance plans (22%) or directly from the patients' pockets (40%). The remaining 38% comes from federal, state, or local governments, which traditionally provide some forms of direct service, support for research, funds for construction of medical facilities, and care for specified groups of patients, such as seamen, tuberculars, veterans, and the mentally ill.

A major expansion of government responsibility for health costs occurred with the passage in 1965 of legislation establishing the federal Medicare and Medicaid programs. Medicare offers limited hospital care and medical insurance coverage to persons over 65, most of whom would be unable to get insurance otherwise. Under Medicaid, federal and state governments share part of the medical bills for the poor. The two programs have more than doubled the public contribution to health-care costs but neither meets the full needs of the groups served. Medicare pays less than 50% of the personal health-care bills of the aged it insures; moreover, premiums have been going up. Medicaid recipients are subject to the whims of states. Some states refuse to tax heavily enough to match federal contributions; some exclude the working poor and adults in families headed by a male. Although Medicare and Medicaid were not meant to revamp the system of health care in the U.S., they were bound to affect aspects of the system. In fact, by increasing the demand

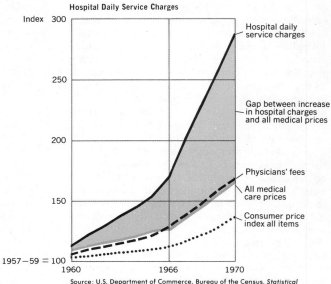

Hospital Daily Service Charges

Index 300

Hospital daily service charges

Gap between increase in hospital charges and all medical prices

Physicians' fees

All medical care prices

Consumer price index all items

1957–59 = 100

1960　　　1966　　　1970

Source: U.S. Department of Commerce, Bureau of the Census, *Statistical Abstract of the United States.* Data compiled by the U.S. Department of Labor, Bureau of Labor Statistics.

for medical services without providing for an increase in services, and by paying generous fees, they have contributed to the rise in medical costs.

Private health insurance has expanded greatly in the U.S. since World War II. An estimated four out of five persons under 65 have some kind of coverage. But premiums are rising rapidly, and large gaps exist in coverage. At the end of 1969, according to government reports, 34 million persons, a disproportionate number of them children and the poor, were wholly unprotected. About half of the population could not file claims for X rays, laboratory service, or doctors' care outside of a hospital; 96% had no dental insurance; 55% were not covered for prescription drugs. Many health insurance policies did not cover preventive services, excluded or limited maternity care, and put maximum limits on catastrophic incidents.

Overall, less than 40% of private spending on health care in the U.S. is paid by insurance; the consumer is expected to pay the rest. As a result, vast numbers of Americans, whatever their finances, face crushing if not ruinous medical bills when serious or prolonged illness strikes. A New York insurance salesman, for example, owned the best health insurance policy his firm offered, paying benefits up to $40,000. When his son was paralyzed by a football injury, the bills came to $6,000 a month. In seven months the family had exceeded the policy's maximum benefits. In Cleveland, O., a man whose wife almost died in childbirth owed nearly $20,000 for medical services; his health insurance maternity benefits provided only $350 and he had to declare bankruptcy.

National Health Systems. Financial tragedies like these would be rare, if not impossible, in countries with national health insurance programs. A stark illustration of the contrast was cited by Edwin P. Hoyt in *Your Health Insurance: A Story of Failure*. A man from the Netherlands was earning $12,000 a year as an accountant in Arcadia, Calif., and carrying health insurance that he thought adequate until he developed a serious kidney ailment. The $20,000 limit on his benefits was not nearly enough to cover the costly treatment. Eventually, he lost his job and was faced with financial ruin when he learned that if he returned to the Netherlands, the national program would pay his medical expenses and the city where he settled would take care of his rent and the special facilities required by his kidney machine.

Government involvement in medical care has been part of European welfare states since 1883 when Otto von Bismarck's Germany adopted a compulsory health insurance program as the first part of social reform legislation. The concept spread quickly throughout Europe and eventually well beyond to industrialized countries like Canada, Israel, and Japan and to many less developed nations. The national systems may differ in scope, coverage, methods of financing, and the role of physicians, their relationship to hospitals, and the way in which they are paid, but two broad patterns of organization are distinguishable. Under one, doctors and facilities remain professionally independent and contract to serve patients under specified conditions. In the other method, services are provided directly by the personnel and facilities of the social security system. Financing of health care also is handled in one of two ways—either out of general tax revenues, as in the U.K. and the countries of Eastern Europe, or out of employer-employee contributions, as in most other European nations.

The best known and one of the most highly structured government programs is the National Health Service of the United Kingdom. Adopted in 1948, it offers universal coverage with wide benefits. Each family can choose its own doctor and can change doctors, but only those who buy private health insurance (4% of the population) can choose their specialists. Each physician can accept up to 3,500 patients and is paid according to the number of patients enrolled, with some special allowances and incentives. The program is financed about 75% through general income taxes and the rest through property tax, payroll

taxes, and partial payments by patients for drugs and other items. It must compete for money with other demands on government— education, defense, housing—and the payments to doctors and hospitals each year depend on the state of the national budget.

Sweden's national health program, which began in 1955, lies somewhere between the U.K. and U.S. systems. It provides free hospitalization, including food, treatment, nursing, and medicines, for all. A patient who wants a private room must pay the difference between its cost and that of a bed in a ward. Patients may choose their own physicians and three-fourths of their bills for doctors in the public health service will be paid, based on a standard fee schedule. Private practitioners and specialists may charge more than the standard rates.

The trend in countries with national health insurance has been toward broader coverage and increasing benefits. Critics, however, cite problems, many of which sound like those encountered in the U.S.: hospitals are inefficient, poorly managed, and suffer medical and staff personnel shortages; patients tend to abuse and overuse services when they are free; overburdened doctors lack the time to practice good, personal medicine and must turn away some patients; doctors receive insufficient pay and incentives. (Attempts to force doctors and hospitals to reduce demands for higher prices have led to confrontations in France, Belgium, Israel, Canada, the U.K., and elsewhere.) Despite these criticisms, and despite rising costs, there appears to be little sentiment for abandoning national health insurance.

Diagnosis. Several factors lie behind the precipitous rise in personal and national health expenditures in all countries. These include higher expectations for health care on the part of a better educated public; broadened scope of services through improved techniques, drugs, and treatment; and increased use of these services, especially as populations grow and heavy medical consumers (women, children, and the elderly) join the ranks of the insured. Since 60% of the U.S. medical dollar goes to hospitals and doctors, these factors are critical in rising costs.

Several things have contributed to the inflation of hospital costs. Large salary increases have been granted in recent years to nurses, janitors, and other hospital workers, who previously had been notoriously underpaid. The sophisticated new techniques, which have been introduced to prolong and save lives, are very expensive. (A heart-lung machine, for example, costs $17,000 initially, plus $50,000 a year for maintenance. A bed in the intensive care unit for respiratory diseases at one Boston hospital runs $425 a day.) The lack of planning and cooperation in and among hospitals has resulted in duplication of expensive equipment and special services. (Three Boston-area hospitals within a mile of each other do open heart surgery and kidney transplants.) Demand for hospital care is artificially stimulated in the U.S. because health insurance policies are more likely to cover hospitalization than office services. Patients ask to be hospitalized to save money; doctors are willing to oblige, since this reduces their risk of malpractice charges. As a result, the entire pattern of medical care is tipped toward providing treatment in hospitals and 16% of U.S. hospital beds are estimated to be occupied by people who don't need hospital care.

Rising hospital costs are not strictly a U.S. phenomenon, however. A comparison of health systems in England, Sweden, and the U.S. published by the University of Chicago Center for Health Administration Studies found that hospitals in all three countries were experiencing the same dramatic increases in spending, apparently for the same basic reasons. The authors concluded that these rising costs were inherent in any modern health care system.

Next to hospital costs, the biggest chunk of the personal medical-care dollar goes to physicians. Over the past decade, fees have increased twice as fast as other items on the U.S. cost-of-living index.

Part of the blame for the higher fees has been laid to Medicare and Medicaid. Physicians' charges, which had been going up an average of 3% a year, have doubled since the programs

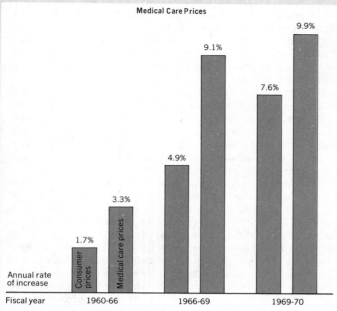

Medical Care Prices

Annual rate of increase

Fiscal year	1960-66	1966-69	1969-70
Consumer prices	1.7%		
Medical care prices	3.3%		
		4.9%	7.6%
		9.1%	9.9%

Source: U.S. Department of Commerce, Bureau of the Census, *Statistical Abstract of the United States.* Data compiled by the U.S. Department of Labor, Bureau of Labor Statistics.

began. Physicians are free to charge their "customary fees" to persons covered by Medicare or Medicaid and, as Harvard economist Rashi Fein has noted, physicians can more readily raise fees that will be paid by an "impersonal" third party like the government or an insurance company rather than by individual patients. Physicians offer another explanation for rising charges, an even faster rise in the cost of malpractice insurance, which for some surgeons is as much as 16 times higher than it was 25 years ago.

Other factors pushing up medical costs in the U.S. include overspending on drugs, many of which are prohibitively expensive, legal barriers in several states to the formation of group medical practices and to the delegation of responsibilities to medical assistants, two steps that could cut expenses and the prolonged training required of medical and paramedical personnel.

Remedies. Many of the suggestions being made to curb inflation in health care costs would also improve its delivery. In some cities, improved management of hospitals and increased cooperation already have resulted in joint use of laundry or computer facilities or arrangements to purchase drugs and insurance. Clusters of hospitals could also be formed in which each unit assumed a specialized task. Greater use could be made of paramedical personnel for routine tasks; loans and grants to medical schools and students could promote innovations in medical education and help train practitioners for specialties where there is the greatest need; and incentives could induce more medical manpower to go into underserved areas. One important way to cut costs would be to keep people out of hospitals by caring for them in less expensive outpatient facilities, changing insurance coverage to include out-of-hospital care, and convincing physicians to reduce hospitalization.

Still another way to cut the load on hospitals and reduce overall health-care costs would be increased emphasis on preventive medicine. One of the most hopeful and closely watched developments along this line is the prepaid group plan or health maintenance organization (HMO) in which an individual or family pays a fixed yearly fee covering virtually all health costs from a routine checkup to a $5,000 operation. Doctors who work for the plan are paid a fixed salary and the organization usually operates its own clinics and hospitals, or both. Limited experience indicates that HMOs reduce patient time in hospitals, lower the total health-care costs of consumers, and deliver high-quality service. Critics of these plans claim they are impersonal

and inconvenient and limit an individual's choice in selecting a doctor.

Any or all of these suggestions would relieve some of the inflationary strain on a national health care system. The situation in the U.S., however, has become so critical that everyone with any reason to be involved in health care, the administration, Congress, medical and hospital associations, and health insurance organizations, agrees that reform of the entire health care system involving the federal government is a necessity. In 1971 the movement for change was taken to Congress where a dozen health care bills were introduced.

These bills differ considerably in approach, costs, and the extent to which they would change the system. The two-part, administration-sponsored National Health Insurance Partnership Act would cover most of the population under 65 through the existing private health insurance industry. Employers would be required to provide private health insurance for all workers and their families. The consumer would pay up to $100 of the doctors' bills and the first two days of hospital costs; insurance would cover most additional medical bills up to $50,000. Insurance costs would eventually be financed 75% by employers and 25% by employees. Federally operated health insurance, not as complete as the private coverage, would be provided for low-income families. The government would pay the entire cost for families of four with incomes below $3,000 a year, part of the cost for those earning under $5,000, and an increased portion of the bills of Medicare recipients.

In contrast, the Health Security Act, proposed by Sen. Edward M. Kennedy (Dem., Mass.) and Rep. Martha W. Griffiths (Dem., Mich.) offers far-reaching coverage through a government-run health insurance program. All major health care costs (including preventive care), except some dental and psychiatric services and some drugs and medical appliances, would be covered. The federal government would administer the plan, with private practitioners and institutions continuing to provide the health services. Patients could go to the same doctors or hospitals as before, but they would no longer pay directly or buy private insurance. A national health budget established by Congress each year would pay hospitals according to a negotiated annual schedule. Doctors and dentists could choose to receive per capita compensation for the number of patients they treat, a full- or part-time salary, or fees for services based on a schedule. The plan would be financed 50% from general federal revenues, the rest from payroll and self-employed taxes. Both of these plans call for reforms and innovations in health care delivery. They encourage greater use of prepaid group practice and provide additional funds for medical education. While the Kennedy-Griffiths bill is more far-reaching in this aspect, as well as in its insurance coverage, it is also considerably more expensive. Other programs before Congress would provide relief from medical costs through insurance packages but would have little impact on the delivery system. Under the Medicredit Plan, sponsored by the American Medical Association, people would continue to buy their own health insurance from private companies and, if the policy met standards set by law, would get income tax credits for all or part of the insurance costs. The amount of credit would depend on the tax liability of the individual, with those in higher tax brackets receiving smaller credits. The federal government would pay the entire cost of insurance for persons whose income tax was $300 or less. Other plans would supplement private insurance coverage with protection against "catastrophic" illness financed through payroll taxes.

This plethora of proposals testifies that few issues are more important to a people at this time than the quality, delivery, and cost of its medical service. Unless reforms and efficiencies are adopted, the cost of medical care will continue to soar. Yet reality must be faced; the growing demand for quality medical care and the constant improvement of techniques for providing it offer scant hope that health care will ever again be inexpensive.

outpatient, care continued to be the fastest growing service of hospitals. For every patient admitted for a stay in a hospital in 1970, there were 5.7 outpatient visits. As almost all legislative proposals dealing with health placed more emphasis on ambulatory care, this trend was almost certain to intensify in the future.

The year 1971 marked the 25th anniversary of the passage in the U.S. of the Hill-Burton program. As of April 1971, a total of 10,663 projects, providing 466,053 beds in voluntary nonprofit and public hospitals and nursing homes, had been approved since the beginning of the program. Of the total number of grants, nearly 30%, or 3,045 projects, were for outpatient and other health care facilities, such as public health centres, rehabilitation facilities, and state health laboratories. The projects approved were built at a total cost of $12.5 billion, of which Hill-Burton funds provided $3.7 billion.

Another noteworthy occurrence during 1971 was that consumers and their advocates became quite vocal concerning the shortcomings of the health care system and the insurers of health care. As 1971 drew to a close, it became clear that the U.S. presidential election year of 1972 would bring the health care controversy into sharper focus. It was almost certain to be one of the key domestic issues.   (E. L. Cy.)

IMMUNOLOGY

One of the major tasks that concerned immunologists during 1971 was to prove the existence of the so-called receptor sites on cell surfaces. Such sites long have been postulated as playing a key role in providing an immune response to foreign material that enters the body. Studies were devised, which, while they were not intended to prove any immunological function for such sites, strongly suggested such a function. Experiments were aimed at determining whether immunoglobulins, which are associated with the cell surface, are simply incidental surface components or are significantly involved in immune responses as a part of the receptor site. Increasing evidence indicated that the immunoglobulins on the surface of lymphoid cells of the mouse, rabbit, and man appear to be essential elements in the immune reaction.

It became clearer that antibody production involves the collaborative efforts of two kinds of lymphoid cells and most likely an accessory cell. The two lymphoid cells are thymus derived (T cells) and bone marrow derived (B cells); some fundamental differences exist between these cells regarding their putative receptor sites. The T cell has 0.1 to 1% of the number of surface immunoglobulin molecules that the B cell has. Since B cells are the progenitors of antibody-producing cells, the markedly larger number of surface immunoglobulins suggests that they constitute the antigen recognition unit for the primary response, which then stimulates the production of antibody.

In contrast to the B cells, whose specificity is presumed to exist prior to the introduction of antigen, the preexistence of specificity in T cells has not been proven. The function of the T cells in antibody production remains to be clarified. The suggestion was offered that activated T cells elaborate an important nonspecific factor that supports the performance of antigen-activated B cells, most likely in the regulation of proliferation. Experiments showed that lymphocytes—even dead ones—assist their function, which may be attributable to a substance elaborated in life or released upon death. While these elaborated substances have not been identified, analogous materials have been investigated. The activation of immune responsive cells most likely involves steps that are similar to those now known to occur in the activation of hormone-dependent cells by a relevant hormone.   (A. S. M.)

MENTAL HEALTH

Community mental health centres remained the topic of major interest in 1971, as reflected in many scientific and public programs and publications. Skepticism appeared more widespread regarding the meaning of "community psychiatry" for patient care and the role of the psychiatrist in such programs.

A shift in emphasis for schizophrenia and the neuroses continued during the year. The mental problem of adolescent and geriatric patients and the personality disorders associated with drug addiction came more into focus.

The chemistry of disordered mental functions and the growing prospects of specific drug therapy for altering the chemical balance continued to spur interest in finding the "disordered molecule" associated with "disordered thought." The clinical syndrome of depression had thus far come closest to fulfilling the dream of specific drug therapy in the mental disorders. The use of tranquilizers and antidepressant drugs continued to be a major treatment emphasis.

Lab technician checks unharvested measles vaccine, one of three viral agents in a new combination vaccine developed at Merck Institute for Therapeutic Research in West Point, Pa.

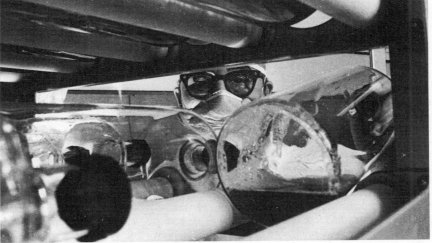

Successes with lithium treatment for mania were somewhat tempered by reports of thyroid disorders following such treatment.

Psychotherapy, with emphasis on the most efficacious program with regard to number of visits, duration of visits, and total period of treatment, was a topic of continued interest, appeal, and research. Brief psychotherapy, with a therapeutic focus and with interventions that provide an element of confrontation, has become the most generally used method of treatment.

In the United States threatened loss of federal support for residency programs was the basis for considerable discussion, group resolutions, and attempts to convince legislative bodies of the serious impact such a move would have on future mental health care. The tendency to shorten the curriculum for medical students and remove internship requirements required a shift in thinking about the standard type of residency training. Interest in psychoanalytic training continued to wane as brief psychotherapy methods expanded.

Publications continued to reflect a broadening of the scope of psychiatry considerably beyond its classical description as that branch of medicine that deals with diagnosis, treatment, and prevention of mental disease. Broad social issues, such as the "treatment" of a community, the violence of society, and drug abuse as a social concern, appeared increasingly as topics dealt with in the journals and featured in programs of major mental health organizations.

(H. H. G.)

NUTRITION

Consumers were more concerned in 1971 about the foods they purchased than ever before. Their concern not only encompassed price but was expressed in questions about the safety, quality, and nutritional value of foods. Public reaction toward the use of chemicals in the production and processing of food continued to grow. The minute traces of chemical residues that can be detected by new analytical techniques were assumed to be biologically meaningless, but much public apprehension was aroused by their presence in any quantity.

The trend toward belief in the virtues of "organic foods" continued. It was difficult to convince adherents of such a belief that vegetables and fruits produced by either "chemical" or "natural" fertilizers have the same protein, carbohydrate, vitamin, and mineral content and in the same quality and quantity. An important and significant difference is that organically grown vegetables are more likely to carry *Salmonella* organisms, which can cause a common form of food poisoning.

Previous reports of inadequate nutrition in the U.S. population triggered a reassessment of the FDA's program of food standards and labeling.

The FDA contracted with the National Academy of Sciences to obtain recommendations as to which classes of foods should have nutritional guidelines and what the values should be for various nutrients. The guidelines were to be aimed at reaching specified nutritional levels with natural foods; and also at supplementation with specific nutrients to reach desired nutrient levels. Emphasis was to be given to nutritive value of the food as consumed. New foods created through technology would be given guidelines depending on their use as meal replacements or as fabricated foods. Initially, the FDA would seek to establish guidelines for such products as frozen dinners, meat replacements, cereals, breakfast drinks, and probably certain foods consumed extensively by low-income groups.

Good nutrition is obviously an important part of maintaining public health, and it is an equally important aspect of preventive medicine. At the present time, however, it is extremely difficult for the consumer, impressed with the tremendous variety of food items available, to know what constitutes good nutrition. Manufactured and processed foods, consumed so widely now, cannot be easily assessed as to nutritional value by the average shopper.

The FDA began a program to investigate the possibilities of using food labels as part of a program to help consumers select a nutritious diet.

Three nutrient labeling methods were to be tested. The first describes the nutrients in food by percentage of the recommended dietary allowances, the second lists the nutrients by symbol, and the third uses positive adjectives to indicate nutrients.

(JE. WI.; F. J. SE.)

OCCUPATIONAL MEDICINE

Although toxicologic problems continued to be of immediate concern, the long-term effects of industrial exposure on mortality and morbidity came increasingly under study. The behavioural patterns of working groups and socioeconomic problems such as absences also were studied.

A study of hematite miners in Britain showed that lung cancer mortality among underground workers was about 70% above the average death rate for the rest of the population. Whether the cancer risk was due to radioactivity in the air of the mine or to a carcinogenic effect of iron oxide was undetermined. The mortality of steel workers in the U.S. also was examined; workers employed in areas above coke ovens and exposed to their fumes had a markedly high rate of death from respiratory cancers.

Evidence on the carcinogenic effects of asbestos, particularly crocidolite asbestos, continued to accumulate. The shipbuilding industry in Hamburg, W. Ger., the Netherlands, and Northern Ireland was studied extensively. A very high proportion of men dying from mesothelial tumours of the pleura (the membrane surrounding the lungs) either had worked in the shipyards or lived close to a source of asbestos dust; of 12 women dying from mesothelial tumour in the Liverpool (Eng.) area during the past 15 years, 6 had been employed in the repair of sacks used in the transport of asbestos. A common feature of deaths from mesothelial tumours and other industrial cancers was that first exposure usually occurred 25 to 30 years before the onset of the symptoms.

Industrial exposure to carbon disulfide among workers in the rayon industry also was characterized by mortality after a latent period of many years. A significant number of deaths from coronary heart disease occurred among men under the age of 65 who had been exposed to carbon disulfide for five years or longer. Rayon workers currently employed, who had been exposed to carbon disulfide for at least five years, showed higher blood pressure than a comparable but unexposed group and were more apt to suffer from angina pectoris.

Vibration syndrome, an occupational disease in users of vibrating tools, received attention during 1971. The syndrome consists essentially of blanching of the fingers (Raynaud's phenomenon), often ac-

After working all summer at the altitude of 14,110 ft. in Colorado, a university coed participates in a medical study to determine the effects of working at high altitudes for prolonged periods.

companied by pain in the wrist, elbow, or shoulder. The chief predisposing factor was cold, particularly on the journey to work and during rest periods. Symptoms were also more common in smokers than in nonsmokers. Although they could be severe enough to affect outdoor leisure activities, the symptoms did not usually precipitate a change of employment. In some countries vibration syndrome was compensatable.

Occupational ecoosteolysis is also characterized by Raynaud's phenomenon, with fragility of the bones of the fingertips being a prominent feature. The condition, which was associated with the cleaning of polymerizers, appeared to be systemic (affecting the entire body) rather than local, but neither the causative agent nor the portal of entry was identified.

In a one-day symposium on sickness absence in industry, held in London, it was reported that there was less absenteeism among shift workers than among day workers, both for sickness and for other causes. An examination of sickness absence rates over the previous two decades in nine countries showed substantial rises in certified sickness absence in several countries of Western Europe and in the U.S., and to a lesser extent in Eastern Europe. The decrease in time lost through tuberculosis, skin, and urinary diseases was more than matched by rises in ill-defined conditions, cardiovascular and psychological diseases, and nonoccupational injuries. It was speculated on another occasion that frustration due to the extreme tediousness of some jobs might be behind much sickness absence and strike behaviour in industry.

In the U.S., a year after passage of the Occupational Health and Safety Act, which imposed strict requirements upon employers and permitted government inspection of premises without notice, a national Institute of Occupational Safety and Health was created. (M. L. N.)

OPHTHALMOLOGY

In an attempt to reduce eye injury from shattered eyeglasses, the FDA ordered that sunglasses and corrective glasses dispensed after Jan. 1, 1972, must be resistant to breakage, unless an eye specialist designates that such lenses are not required by individual patients. It was emphasized that the special lenses are impact resistant only and should not be expected to protect the eye from all potential breakage hazards. Unfortunately, lenses made impact resistant by heat-tempering—heating in oil followed by rapid cooling—are more likely to shatter when scratched than are ordinary lenses. During 1971 it was discovered, in experimental animals, that protecting the eye from light prevented the normal deterioration of the eye. This knowledge awakened interest in the study of hereditary disorders of the retina related to pigmentary degeneration (such as retinitis pigmentosa), in which protection from light delays the development of the degeneration. These findings were an apparent contradiction of earlier observations that failure to stimulate the eye with light (visual deprivation) results in failure of visual cells to develop and leads to blindness.

A variety of soft, or flexible, contact lenses became available. They could be used for the improvement of vision; for the delivery of medication to the eye, as in the treatment of glaucoma; or for the protection of the cornea. Although the soft contact lenses are more or less similar chemically, subtle differences make some more suitable for one purpose than another.

A variety of biochemical disorders of the body are associated with blindness and often mental retardation. By means of new chemical tests it became possible to detect individuals who have such biochemical abnormalities so subtle as to cause no observable physical infirmity. If two individuals with mild disorders mate, however, there is a one in four chance that their offspring will be afflicted with severe manifestations of the disease. During 1971, mass chemical tests began for the detection of one such disease, Tay-Sachs disease (amaurotic familial idiocy), which occurs with particularly high incidence among Jews originating in eastern Europe. A simple blood test can indicate to prospective parents whether they are carriers of the disease. During pregnancy, study of the fluid in which the child is bathed in the uterus (the amniotic fluid) will indicate whether or not the infant is afflicted.

Studies continued on the development of a man-made device to assist the sightless to "see," perhaps an electronic prosthesis that will render patterns and spots of light detectable. Considerable progress had been made in this area, and while there appeared to be no conceptual obstacle to its development, there were enormous engineering problems. (F. W. N.)

ORTHOPEDICS

Success was reported with the cast-brace method for treating fractures of the thighbone (femur) and upper end of the lower leg bone (tibia). The method permitted early walking and allowed movement of the knee joint through a hinge connecting plaster casts applied closely to the thigh and leg. There was also

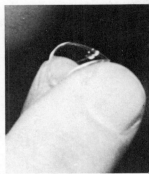

Using the new plastic polymacon, Bausch and Lomb in 1971 developed the Soflens contact lens, which will return to its original form after being bent.
AUTHENTICATED NEWS INTERNATIONAL

extensive experience in the U.S. of early walking in patients with femoral fractures, in some cases within four days of the injury.

Advances were made in prostheses, the replacement of limbs with artificial devices. In Sweden, a ten-year-old boy received intensive treatment after accidental amputation of a lower limb and half-pelvis; 18 months later he was walking on his artificial limb with the aid of crutches. From Jaipur came a report of the use of a rubber foot in rural India. The amputee fitted with this prosthesis did not normally wear shoes and required the extra range of movement provided by the rubber footpiece to enable him to sit crosslegged on the floor, as his social custom dictated.

Beneficial effects were reported in treating curvature of the spine in children through the use of a Milwaukee spinal brace throughout growth; the brace was modified by using throat molds rather than chin pieces, to avoid pressure on the jaws and possible orthodontic problems, and a thermoplastic material replaced leather for the pelvic girdle. Another device to correct spinal curvature used special plates applied to the convex side of the spinal curve with an internal cable to lessen the curvature.

Severe deformities of the spine, resulting from scoliosis, tuberculosis, and poliomyelitis, were treated by a head to pelvic traction. Perthes' disease, a deterioration of the growing tip of the head of the femur in boys aged five to ten, was shown to be associated with congenital anomalies of the groin and the urinary tract.

Total hip replacements in Britain continued to be successful. New developments in total knee-joint replacement included a metallic prosthesis on the femur and a plastic component attached to the tibia. As an alternative to self-curing acrylic cement in bonding total joint replacements to bone, a group of Chicago orthopedists found that a fibre-metal composite provided an excellent medium for mechanical interlocking with bone. The use of cartilage grafts obtained from cadavers to resurface arthritic hip and knee joints was reported independently from Czechoslovakia and from West Germany.

Osteoporosis, the loss of bone tissue with advancing age, was found to have multiple causes. It was discovered that post-menopausal women, who are more prone to osteoporosis than men of the same age, showed a noticeable loss of calcium during fasting, and suggested that calcium loss to the urine during sleep might be an important contributory factor.

(R. G. Bu.)

PEDIATRICS

A continuing concern of pediatricians in 1971 was excessive weight gain in young infants, attributed in the past decade to feeding infants whenever they cry and to the decline in breast feeding. In a survey conducted at the University of Sheffield, Eng., about 60% of formula-fed infants gained excessive weight, while only 19% of breast-fed infants showed such gains. It was also determined that an obese infant is likely to remain obese throughout later childhood. Other studies, conducted at Northampton, Eng., demonstrated an increased incidence of respiratory infections in overweight infants between the ages of 3 and 24 months, compared with babies of the same ages but of normal weight. It was surmised that obesity leads to poor ventilation of the lungs, with consequent damage from coughing, and a tendency for minor

respiratory infections to become more serious. Obese infants also were found to have been introduced early to solids in the diet. A report from Washington University, St. Louis, Mo., indicated that overweight children generally tend to have higher blood pressure than children of normal weight. Such obese children were felt to be likely candidates for hypertension in adult life.

Researchers at Harvard University pointed out that the incidence of syphilis in newborn infants had been increasing since 1959, attributed to a general rise in sexual promiscuity. The infection is transmitted from the mother to her fetus during the last three to four months of pregnancy. Prompt treatment during pregnancy can bring the mother's infection under control and prevent transmission to the unborn child. The widespread use of penicillin for mild respiratory infections in the newborn resulted in suppressing symptoms of syphilis and thereby obscuring the more serious disease. As a result the clinical picture of syphilis in the newborn had changed considerably and made diagnosis more difficult. The tendency of pregnant adolescents to avoid medical attention also hampered early diagnosis and treatment of syphilis. Studies at the University of Miami (Fla.) were concerned with an outbreak of a respiratory disease in young infants due to one of the groups of viruses known as adenovirus. The children, under three years of age, all had the classical symptoms of whooping cough. There was evidence, however, that this disease is more damaging to the lungs than whooping cough, and results in lung scarring. Several centres were actively engaged in producing a vaccine against this particular adenovirus.

Controversy continued regarding the German measles vaccine. As of 1971 several million children in the U.S. were vaccinated, but in England only preadolescent females were vaccinated, the assumption being that potential mothers should be protected

An air mattress that sounds an alarm should a premature baby stop breathing is a new addition to detection devices used in monitoring infants at West Suburban Hospital, Oak Park, Ill.

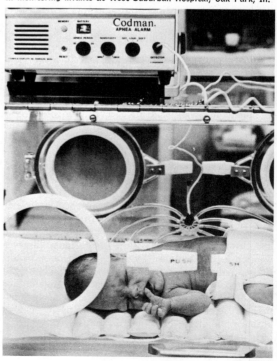

against this dangerous viral disease, which often causes severe damage to the developing fetus. Immediately after vaccination, antibodies are produced against the virus, but begin to decline in production very rapidly. Subsequent exposure to the natural disease, however, induces a very mild infection that causes antibody production to rise sharply. Unfortunately, it is felt that during a subsequent exposure viruses may be released into the bloodstream and, in the case of a pregnant female, may invade the developing fetus. There is no clear evidence as yet of such invasion.

Sudden unexpected death in apparently normal infants was estimated to affect between 15,000 and 20,000 babies a year in the U.S. alone. This mysterious affliction occurred most frequently in infants of about three months of age, who appeared quite healthy, or at most showed signs of only a mild respiratory infection. The latest of many theories to account for this early infant mortality was proposed in 1971 by a California pediatrician. It rests on the observation that a large number of newborn infants do not breathe reflexively through the mouth when their nostrils are obstructed as a result of very mild respiratory infections. The study suggested that it may be possible to "train" an infant to breathe through its mouth at an age earlier than it might normally do so. Whether this newest theory to account for sudden infant deaths is tenable remains to be determined.

(S. S. G.)

REHABILITATION

A record 291,272 disabled persons were rehabilitated under U.S. government programs during fiscal 1971, an increase of 9% over 1970, and the highest yearly total since the state-federal vocational rehabilitation program began in 1920.

Research activities in rehabilitation in the U.S. were curtailed severely as research and demonstration grants to universities, research institutes, and private agencies were postponed awaiting the adoption by the Department of Health, Education, and Welfare of a new priority system designed to focus research on the problems of disability among public welfare clients, minority groups, and the poor. Training activities for the academic year 1971–72 also were reduced.

Mary E. Switzer, who had directed the state-federal vocational rehabilitation program from 1950 to 1970, died on Oct. 16, 1971. At the time of her retirement, Miss Switzer was the highest ranking woman in the federal government. After her retirement, Miss Switzer was vice-president of the World Rehabilitation Fund.

UN Secretary-General U Thant announced on October 20 a new program of coordination and cooperation between the UN and its specialized agencies and the World Rehabilitation Fund. The new program was aimed at doubling expenditures for international rehabilitation projects in 1972 and a fivefold increase in such activities by 1976.

The U.S. Committee of the International Society for Rehabilitation of the Disabled was reconstructed and became Rehabilitation International USA, and the affiliate for the U.S. in the International Society for Rehabilitation of the Disabled. Mrs. Helen Wilshire Walsh, of Connecticut, was elected president of the new organization.

Major international activities included two international conferences on vocational rehabilitation of the physically handicapped and the mentally retarded,

held in the U.S. in May and June; a Pan Pacific Conference on Mental Retardation, held in Honolulu in October; and a Pan Pacific Conference on Vocational Rehabilitation, held in Tokyo in November.

(H. A. Ru.)

RESPIRATORY DISEASES

The United States was the only major advanced country in the world in which vaccination against tuberculosis was rare in 1971. The reasons were the continuing decline in occurrence and severity of the disease, which was no longer one of the leading causes of illness and death; the efficacy of the currently available medicines; and the possibility of mishaps (reports of tuberculosis being induced by the vaccination under certain conditions). The vaccine, known as BCG, or Bacillus Calmette-Guérin, is a live, but weakened, strain of a tubercle bacillus of cows. It produces sensitization of the tissues, as evidenced by a positive tuberculin test. This, though not preventing infection by newly acquired virulent organisms, tends to limit their spread so that the organisms stay at the original site (the lung, if they are inhaled), and does not produce extensive local and serious disseminated disease. In unvaccinated persons a positive tuberculin test is evidence of active infection. The protective action of the vaccine has not been clearly demonstrated by all investigators. A recent experimental study on guinea pigs at the University of Wisconsin, however, clearly confirmed the restraining effect of BCG vaccination on tuberculosis infection.

In the treatment of tuberculosis, evidence continued to be accumulated for the efficacy of rifampin, one of a series of chemicals that has a wide range of activity against bacteria, certain viruses, and apparently some forms of malignancy.

A cooperative study done under the auspices of the U.S. Public Health Service found the combination of rifampin and isoniazid to be the most effective of three combinations of drugs in eliminating tubercle bacilli from sputum.

A report from Belgium suggested the frequent occurrence of sensitization to rifampin, particularly when the drug is given intermittently. The patients developed fever, chills, and joint pains.

The Tuberculosis Division of the U.S. Public Health Service in Atlanta, Ga., reported that the number of beds required for treatment of tuberculosis in different states dropped in five years from 23,000 to 15,000; this was accompanied by a drop of 12 million hospital-bed-days, and a saving of $431 million. The cost of treatment for one patient over one year was about $500 for rifampin and only $2.50 for isoniazid.

From Copenhagen there was a report on the risk of tuberculosis in relation to marital status. A study of cases reported in Denmark from 1960 to 1968 revealed that in males the incidence of tuberculosis was lowest at all ages among married men; it was twice as high among single and widowed men, and four times as high among divorced men.

Tuberculosis involving the glands of the neck was found to persist after apparently successful treatment of the infection in the lungs.

(M. Fd.)

SURGERY

Although the condition known as hyperidrosis, or pathologically excessive sweating, had been recognized for a long time, and was well described by Charles Dickens in the character of Uriah Heep, sur-

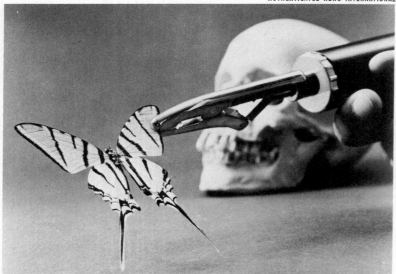

The Ronjair air-powered bone cutter, a surgical instrument produced by Hall International Inc., is able to slice through bone with a pressure of 300 lb. per sq.in., and yet its blades do not mar the delicate wing of a butterfly.

gical treatment was a fairly recent development. While some cases of sweating result from systemic disorders such as overactivity of the thyroid, anxiety states, and so on, and examples of localized sweating are due to damage to the central nervous system, the great majority of cases are of completely unknown cause. In 1971 a number of London surgeons published the results of two operations designed specifically to control excessive sweating by removal of parts of the sympathetic nervous system that influence certain sweat glands. Hyperidrosis of the feet can be effectively treated by removing the lumbar sympathetic chain through a short abdominal incision; excessive sweating of the hands and armpits can be abolished either through an incision in the neck or a short incision in the upper chest wall in the armpit region.

Another anathema of modern Western society is obesity. While the great majority of overweight patients can be treated adequately by means of a low calorie diet, a small number seemed resistant to all known forms of conservative treatment. In a number of centres, such patients were treated by extensive by-pass operations of the small intestine, which shunt food away from the main absorptive surface of the small intestine, and thereby reduce uptake of nutriment. (See *Gastroenterology,* above.)

In Western communities, the commonest pathological condition affecting the large bowel is diverticula of the colon, a series of out-pouchings of mucosa measuring up to $\frac{1}{2}$ in. in diameter projecting through the muscle wall of the colon, especially in its terminal (sigmoid) portion. This condition, almost unknown before the 20th century, was becoming increasingly common in the developed countries, remaining extremely rare in Africa and Asia. Studies from the U.S., the U.K., Australia, and France indicated a dramatic rise in the incidence of diverticulosis, affecting 30 to 50% of the population over the age of 40. Diverticula were common in the American Negro but almost unknown in black Africa, and incidence of diverticulosis in Japanese who had migrated to Hawaii was higher than in those remaining in Japan. Researchers suggested an association between this condition and food refining, which removes vegetable fibre from the diet. The same geographic distribution was found for acute appendicitis, common in communities prone to diverticula of the colon and appearing shortly after traditional high-bulk diets were abandoned in favour of refined Western foods.

Surgeons continued in their efforts to make surgery safer. For some 20 years cornstarch powder had been used to lubricate surgical gloves, on the assumption that any starch finding its way into the abdominal cavity during an operation would be rapidly absorbed. An Australian report, however, warned of the dangers of this practice. Cases of inflammatory nodules, termed granuloma, induced by starch deposits, occurred in the peritoneal cavity of one patient and in surgical wounds of two other patients. Increasing numbers of such cases were being reported. If the abdomen is reopened, the starch granulomata, which may be confused with tuberculosis or even with disseminated malignant disease, when viewed under the polarized microscope clearly show the optical properties of starch granules. (HA. E.)

VENEREAL DISEASE

The incidence of syphilis continued to rise alarmingly in 1971. In the U.S. alone 23,336 cases of primary and secondary syphilis were reported, which represents an increase of more than 15% over 1970. This is the second consecutive year of increase in reported infectious syphilis, following a four-year period of decline from 1965 to 1969. Reported congenital syphilis among infants under one year of age also rose from 300 cases in 1970 to 397 cases in 1971. Total syphilis cases in all stages numbered 94,255 in 1971, compared with 87,934 in 1970.

Gonorrhea, which ranks first of all nationally reported communicable diseases, has been increasing at an alarming rate since 1962. The rate of increase during 1971, however, was somewhat lower than in recent years. Even so, the total of 624,017 cases reported was almost 10% greater than that for 1970. Increases were reported in all races, both sexes, all age groups, all locales (urban and rural), and among patients in both public and private treatment facilities. The large reservoir of females that carry gonorrhea bacteria but do not exhibit symptoms continued to pose a perplexing problem.

The syphilis surveillance program in the U.S. involved an extensive serologic testing program among such diverse groups as applicants for marriage licenses, pregnant females, blood donors, hospital admissions, persons examined for or discharged from the military service, alleged contacts to known infectious cases, persons undergoing employment and preemployment examinations, and persons undergoing examinations in physicians' offices.

Of the 38 million blood specimens examined annually in the U.S., about 1.1 million tests were reactive for syphilis. Of this total number reactive, 800,000, or 73%, were reported to health departments. Follow-up of these reactors results in approximately 10,000 case reports of infectious syphilis and 62,000 reports of syphilis in other stages.

Infectious syphilis patients were interviewed and their sex contacts were vigorously pursued in order to bring to medical examination and treatment as many as possible of the source cases. During 1971, 98% of public cases and 90% of private cases of early syphilis were interviewed by specially trained public-health personnel. From these interviews, contact tracing activities resulted in an additional 4,500 cases of primary and secondary syphilis being brought to diagnosis and treatment. Also, approximately 18,300 sex contacts exposed to infectious syphilis, who were clinically and serologically negative at initial examination, were given preventive treatment. Syphilis research activities concentrated on the continuing search for a vaccine and on improvement of blood tests.

Pinta treponemes—organisms related to the syphilis organism (*Treponema pallidum*)—were successfully transferred from humans to chimpanzees. The pinta-infected animals were undergoing experiments with virulent *Treponema pallidum* to determine if infection with the mild treponeme conferred immunity to the more virulent organism.

A new blood test for incubating syphilis appeared imminent, and a new congenital syphilis test was developed to distinguish between infants merely carrying antibodies passively transferred from the mother and infants actively infected with syphilis.

Efforts to control gonorrhea have been intensified during the past two years. Patient interviewing and contact investigation activities designed to detect untreated cases have been carried out in many areas. In addition, in an attempt to solve the asymptomatic female problem, screening programs have been started that involve culture tests for gonorrhea being performed on females having a pelvic examination for any reason.

In gonorrhea research, a recently developed medium, "Transgrow," showed hope of solving the problems inherent in routine transportation of fragile culture specimens from doctors' offices to laboratories. A successful blood test for gonorrhea is expected in the near future.

A program of venereal-disease education aimed at the general public was being pursued throughout the United States. All forms of mass media were utilized, including radio, television, films, newspapers, magazines, billboards, and car cards. Programmed instruction books for teachers and students in elementary and high schools were developed. (W. J. Bn.)

WORLD HEALTH ORGANIZATION

The 24th World Health Assembly, held in Geneva in May 1971, endorsed a program emphasizing the need to improve environmental health and sanitation in all, especially less developed, countries; to establish international agreement on codes of practice with respect to known environmental influences on health; to stimulate the development of epidemiological health surveillance; and to extend knowledge of the effects of environmental factors on health by collecting and disseminating information, stimulating research, and assisting in personnel training.

The assembly stressed that cholera, which continued as a scourge in tropical Africa and in Asia, was a long-term socioeconomic as well as public-health problem and that its only lasting solution was to make countries "cholera proof" by means of improved water supplies, sanitation, and hygiene. WHO supplied cholera vaccine, rehydration fluid, antibiotics, and other items to affected or threatened countries.

An effective working budget of $82,023,000 was adopted to finance WHO's work in 1972. The number of member states was 132 at the end of the year.

(WHO)

See also Drugs and Narcotics; Insurance; Life Sciences; Psychology; Social Services; Vital Statistics.

Encyclopædia Britannica Films. *Chromosomes of Man* (1967); *The Eyes and Seeing* (1968); *The Work of the Heart* (1968); *Ears and Hearing* (1969); *Muscle: Chemistry of Contraction* (1969); *Muscle: Dynamics of Contraction* (1969); *Radioisotopes: Tools of Discovery* (1969); *Respiration in Man* (1969); *The Nerve Impulse* (1971).

Merchandising

Currency problems, credit restrictions, and antitrust legislation in West Germany, stringent proposals for price controls in Belgium, and the uncertain economic climate in Italy were some of the difficulties that posed marketing problems in 1971. In Britain the seven-week postal strike adversely affected trading conditions early in the year. Unemployment reached its highest level in 31 years and the general index of retail prices was up 10¼%. A survey showed that in the second quarter of 1971 there was a check in the sales of relatively expensive convenience foods. On the brighter side, the change to decimal currency on February 15 proceeded smoothly with no more than the expected changes in prices.

The retail sales picture appeared to be improving in the U.S. Despite an increase in personal income of 7% over 1969, consumers had banked a higher percentage of their money and spent less in 1970. Consumer installment credit, used mainly to purchase durables, rose $2 billion, compared with $8 billion in 1969, while retail sales totaled $364.6 billion, a gain of only 4%. There were encouraging signs toward the end of the year, however, and in the first six months of 1971, retail sales totaled about $182.5 billion, more than 6% above the same period a year earlier. Department store sales were 10% higher and automobile sales advanced 9%. In contrast, restaurant sales rose only 3%, apparel sales 4%, and furniture and appliances a negligible 1%.

On August 15, Pres. Richard Nixon announced a 90-day price-wage-rent freeze, to be followed by a period of continued, though less stringent, controls. A study of 52 large retailing companies published by a national business magazine showed an average sales increase of 9% over 1970 during the third quarter of 1971. It appeared that the freeze had produced no identifiable change in the pattern of sales. However, most of the companies under study reported profit gains. For example, Marshall Field & Co. of Chicago reported a 21% gain in profit, while Sears, Roebuck's earnings were up 18%. The 10% surcharge on most dutiable imports, in effect from mid-August to late December, appeared to have had no adverse effect on the sale of imported goods. There were few substantial reductions of orders, despite the tax and the uncertain international monetary situation.

The trend toward polarization of retail trade in the U.S. continued, with mass-merchandising operations at one extreme and highly specialized boutique-type stores at the other. The development of discount commodity-line stores as major mass-merchandising operations was expected to be of great importance in the 1970s. Examples were Wickes Lumber and Home-Improvement Centers, Handyman, and Gold Triangle Stores, and, in another line of trade, Children's Palace, Children's World, and Lionel.

The most spectacular growth was in warehouse-showroom outlets in the furniture industry, such as those of the Levitz Furniture Co. All Levitz units consisted of a 100,000-sq.ft., specially designed warehouse combined with a 55,000-sq.ft. area containing 200–300 "room displays" of furniture, bedding, lamps, and accessories (floor coverings and appliances were not carried). The emphasis was on national brand merchandise. To enter the showroom sections, customers had to walk through the warehouse, where

Mental Health: *see* Medicine

Salesgirls in a Tokyo department store greet customers dressed in the traditional Japanese kimono. Downtown stores developed the hotpants uniform to attract younger customers in 1971.

the merchandise was stored 30 ft. high. The merchandise was picked from the warehouse by specially designed trucks and delivered to the customer's vehicle in the original carton. Home delivery and set-up were available, but at a higher price. Levitz units were generally located near expressway systems. Their overhead cost was 25–26% of sales, compared with the industry average of 37–38% for conventional furniture stores.

In addition to Levitz, several other firms had entered this field, among them Wickes, Crossroads, and Mangurians. Federated Department Stores announced plans to open several similar outlets. In Canada, Consumer Distributing Company Ltd. operated with the same techniques. On the average, each outlet was staffed by four persons and carried around 5,000 items, including housewares, jewelry, appliances, sporting goods, lawn and garden products, toys, and home-entertainment items.

Mass-merchandising establishments continued to make gains in Europe, but their progress in Britain was slow, mainly because of planning restrictions. Among others, a Proba 2000 store was opened near Antwerp, Belg., while a second was being built at Liège; both had some 9,000 sq.m. of sales area. A Superbazars centre on the outskirts of Louvain included a restaurant, parking facilities, and a garden centre. It was estimated that there were about 500 such "hypermarkets" in Europe, the largest ones with some 200,000 sq.m. of space. Claims were made that they permitted price savings of from 8 to 12%.

A survey by R. K. Schiller of Reading (Eng.) University indicated that a new pattern was emerging whereby specialist traders such as antique shops and high-class fashion boutiques were moving out of the shopping centres of large cities to intrinsically attractive rural retreats and historic town centres. He suggested that the old idea of shops servicing a geographic hinterland needed to be rethought, at least for those trades that relied on the affluent and mobile. A decline in chemists' (pharmacists') shops in England was forecast as general practitioners increasingly grouped together in health centres that managed their own dispensing. Over 130 of these centres already existed and 900 more were planned. Tate and Lyle, a British sugar firm, joined the coupon gift craze. All

their sugars would carry gift coupons redeemable for a wide range of goods at discount prices. The most exotic premium offer was a reading from an astrologer.

In West Germany the British International Distillers and Vintners group acquired the August Hartmann shops and apparently intended to form a chain of wine merchant outlets similar to their Peter Dominic shops in the U.K. The West German subsidiary of the British-American Tobacco Company of London and Hamburg also announced plans to open a chain of at least 100 wine stores by 1975; their first, at Freiburg, also offered hot and cold foods.

An event of some importance was the setting up by the European VeGe Union and its associate U.K. VG organization of a new distributive network called Interdis. VeGe operated in West Germany, the Netherlands, Belgium, France, Switzerland, Italy, and Spain. Its operations covered cash and carry, giant shops and warehouses, discount and supermarket stores, catering, distribution, and trading. The new organization was likely to cause a radical rethinking among the 186 wholesale members.

In West Germany the Karstadt group of department stores announced a long-term plan whereby their stores would be divided into five grades. Düsseldorf, Hamburg, Cologne, Hanover, Bremen, Dortmund, and Munich were to have the largest type of department store, with 16,000–24,000 sq.m. of floor space including specialized fashion shops. Stores of 7,000–15,000 sq.m. were planned for other sizable towns. Urban areas where the potential was around 35,000 customers would have stores of 4,000–6,000 sq.m., carrying a reduced range of stock grouped into 16 departments with the emphasis on rapid turnover and complete self-service. Smaller self-service stores of some 3,000 sq.m. were planned for the secondary areas of large towns or the centres of small towns. Finally, there would be "satellite" stores attached to larger stores.

A furnishings centre was opened at Karlsruhe, W.Ger., by Mann-Mobilia, with further centres planned at Wiesbaden, Stuttgart, and Mannheim. The centre had a new-style structure reminiscent of a theatre. Contemporary-style rooms and backgrounds lined the walls of the building encircling an open central well, so that customers were aware of the goods on other floors. Modern living themes were reinforced by a cinema in which films and lectures were to be presented continuously.

In Paris, Printemps opened what they described as "the most important men's store in Europe." A sales area of 6,400 sq.m. was spread over six floors, with the basement specializing in unisex clothes and clothes for the younger customer. The leading French companies in the maternity and infants' wear field, Prénatal and Materna, were reported to be discussing collaboration. Boussois-Souchon-Neuvesel (BSN) and Perrier-Sapiem engaged in negotiations on a joint distributive network for their drink products. The two companies already monopolized over 70% of the French mineral-water market, about 40% of the beer market, and a quarter of the soft-drink market.

The Standa group of variety stores and supermarkets in Italy was proposing a type of voluntary retail chain. Independent shopkeepers could become members and would be able to sell Standa goods at the same price as Standa stores. They would have access to advice from Standa, as well as benefiting from the large-scale buying power of the group. AGIP, the marketing subsidiary of the Italian state-owned Ente Nazionale Idrocarburi (ENI) group, was cooperating with Neckermann, the leading West German mail-order house, to open 30 filling-station outlets in West Germany and about 700 in Italy. Called "Big Bon," they would offer 500 lines, as well as facilities for customers wishing to order from the mail-order catalog.

Significant modifications were taking place in the design of regional shopping centres in the U.S. The new trend was toward multilevel, climate-controlled malls with between one and two million square feet of sales area. The key word was not so much giantism as completeness, with the integration of retail and commercial operations and such other activities as entertainment, recreation, health, eating, and education. Galleria in Houston, Tex., and Woodfield near Chicago, both opened in 1971, were excellent examples. Woodfield featured 2 million sq.ft. of space and 215 shops and services, including the largest Sears and J. C. Penney branch stores ever built and Marshall Field's largest suburban branch store. Galleria, although not as large as Woodfield, had three floors overlooking an ice-skating rink. The first and second levels were for shopping, while the third level provided leasable office space.

Many retailers had remained skeptical about the benefits of automated sales operations, since human errors could not be avoided when the checker had to punch in the code information by hand. In 1971, however, an electronic register was introduced in the U.S. that might eliminate the problem. It was equipped with a hand-carried optical scanner that could read a colour code on a product label electronically and relay the information to a central computer. This new point-of-sale technology was being utilized in some Montgomery Ward stores. A similar electronic register system, tested during 1971 by Migros Stores in Switzerland, featured a laser scanner that read the information as the merchandise passed on the checkout conveyor belt.

Shoplifting continued to be a major problem. According to a recent study in New York City, one out of every 12 customers walked out with merchandise not paid for. It was estimated that retail inventory losses had increased 150% since 1960, and many retail stores reported losses of 4 to 5% of sales volume. In an effort to cut down on thefts, retailers were using uniformed guards, plainclothes security detectives, warning signs, television cameras, and two-way mirrors. A few had begun to use sensitized tags that, unless removed or neutralized by a sales clerk, activated an alarm when the merchandise was carried out of the store.   (A. F. D.; G. C. Ho.)

See also Advertising; Consumer Affairs; Cooperatives; Industrial Review; Prices.

Metallurgy

As with many industries, metallurgy in 1971 was concerned mainly with problems of environment and economics. Cutbacks, particularly in the space programs and defense, reduced the demand for exotic and special advanced materials.

The nonferrous smelters continued to be among the manufacturers most concerned about air pollution. They still treated most sulfide ores by pyrometallurgical methods, which produced sulfur dioxide, one of the most strictly watched pollutants. The greatest amount of pollution was produced during roasting,

when much of the sulfur was burned out of the ore, but this was being overcome by an improved roaster design that prevented the escape of untreated gas and produced a higher concentration of sulfur dioxide in the gas for more efficient recovery as sulfuric acid. A new copper plant in Arizona treated copper oxide ore by leaching, purifying the solution, and electrowinning (*i.e.,* using electrolysis to recover from a solution) pure copper. In this process the leaching solution was regenerated, and there was no discharge of pollutants. An aluminum smelter in Britain used specially treated filters to eliminate fluoride emission, the most harmful pollutant, and also dust.

In the iron and steel industry removing dust from enormous quantities of gas was a major pollution-control problem that was being fairly well solved with conventional dust-removal equipment of unusual size. To meet federal water standards a large U.S. gold producer eliminated all use of mercury, but the effect on the rate of gold recovery from their ore was not reported. About 15% of the cost of a new Canadian plant producing nickel addition agents for alloy manufacture, a fairly clean process, was for dust- and fume-control equipment.

Increased productivity was being attempted by many means. In the expectation of increasing output by about 50%, a West German blast furnace was equipped with sophisticated instrumentation to supply information to a computer, which had full control of the operation. To gain the advantages of a continuous process, a new proposal for steelmaking was being investigated. A flowing layer of slag carried the charge of iron ore, coal, and flux through the reduction furnace and into the refining zone where most of the slag was removed, oxygen lances burned out the excess carbon and other impurities, and alloy additions were made. The use of continuous casting in steel expanded again in 1971, with development aimed at improved deoxidation, protecting the metal from the air during pouring, and improving the as-cast steel surface. The aluminum industry was also seriously looking at continuous casting as a possible replacement for the widely used semicontinuous ingot process. The use of oxygen instead of air for combustion in fuel-heated melting furnaces was expanded rapidly as a means of increasing production with minimum capital expense.

The new alloys being introduced were mostly modifications of standard grades for improvement of some particular property. Special attention was given to resistance to fatigue and corrosion since these conditions were closely related to reliability. A new 5% nickel alloy was shown to have sufficiently good low-temperature impact strength along with other properties to replace the more expensive 9% nickel in such applications as the increasingly important storage and shipping of liquefied natural gas. Tool steel bar stock of exceptional quality and uniformity was produced by powder metallurgy techniques. A combination of silver with 10% mica being produced in the Soviet Union combined wear and corrosion resistance with good electrical conductivity for sliding contacts, such as slip rings in electrical devices. In probably the first industrial application to metal refining of contamination-free electron beam heating, high-purity stainless steel of superior corrosion resistance was being produced.

Rapid development continued in surface treatments, ranging from cladding to ion bombardment. The purpose of such treatments was to achieve economy or

Merchant Marine:
see Transportation

special combinations of properties. Researchers found that structural steel could be clad with a strong, corrosion-resistant aluminum alloy by explosive bonding if a layer of pure aluminum was put between the steel and the alloy so that differences in properties of the two would not cause eventual separation. An unusually hard and adherent layer was produced on steel by bombarding it with high-energy carbon ions, apparently an adaptation of transistor technology. Nitriding, which gives a hard surface layer and improves resistance to fatigue, received much attention, particularly the gas processes that used nontoxic, nonpolluting gases in small quantities instead of the cyanide-containing salt baths. When titanium is nitrided, its surface is hardened and it does not cohere to lightweight bearings. Also developed was an electroplating process that could deposit any of several metals on titanium to eliminate galling or to make brazing or soldering practical.

A promising nontoxic replacement for cadmium plating was aluminum containing 10–30% manganese electrodeposited from a low-temperature salt bath. It was easily applied to complex shapes and did not introduce hydrogen into steel parts. Hydrogen, easily introduced into steel, makes it brittle and reduces fatigue strength; therefore, much effort was being made to develop processes ranging from melting to heat treating and electroplating that either did not introduce hydrogen or aided in its removal.

(D. F. C.)

See also Industrial Review; Mining; Physics.

ENCYCLOPÆDIA BRITANNICA FILMS. *The Miner* (1967); *Problems of Conservation—Minerals* (1969).

Meteorology

For many of man's purposes the weather is a local matter; he is concerned primarily with atmospheric conditions occurring here and now. But the key to local weather is to be found in the behaviour of the atmosphere over a large area, and for many years research meteorologists have realized that a complete global approach is needed to understand and predict the weather locally as well as worldwide.

The 1950s and 1960s produced several highly sophisticated "ten-year programs" for obtaining basic data required for hemispheric and global analysis of the atmosphere's mechanics. Some of these programs evolved into projects that were either in operation during 1971, undergoing analysis of data, or still in the planning stages. Among them were BOMEX (Barbados Oceanographic and Meteorological Experiment), whose on-location operating phase was completed in the summer of 1969, and GARP (Global Atmospheric Research Program), whose operational stage would not reach its maximum until 1974–76. A recently organized component of GARP was designated GATE (GARP Atlantic Tropical Experiment), designed to supplement and extend the data obtained from BOMEX. It was hoped that GATE could be in operation on location by 1974.

A broad progress report and prospectus, *The Atmospheric Sciences and Man's Needs,* was published by the Committee on Atmospheric Sciences through the (U.S.) National Research Council. Typical of the theoretical approach and the practical thinking of leading meteorologists in many countries, the committee's work reviewed the purpose and progress of atmospheric research during the 1960s, examined the broad features of weather prediction, and emphasized the urgency of further studies into air quality and environment, possibilities of weather and climate modification, and the dangers and disasters resulting from anomalous and violent weather disturbances.

International coordination for global atmospheric research efforts came mostly through the World Meteorological Organization (WMO) and its affiliates under the UN and the International Council of Scientific Unions (ICSU). The World Weather Watch (WWW), augmented and formalized about 1962 as an outgrowth of the 19th-century international synoptic weather network, extended and improved its weather-observing grid and communications during 1971. The WMO, at its sixth quadrennial congress in Geneva during April, authorized a budget of $17 million for the period 1971–75. Delegates from 123 member countries attended the congress. Muhammad Fathi Taha, director general of the Egyptian Meteorological Department, was elected president for a four-year term.

Many research reports bearing on air pollution were published during 1971. Experts agreed that the exponential increases in the contaminants poured into the air in recent years must cease, and that corrective measures must be adopted, but there were differences of opinion as to the danger of catastrophic climatic change. Warnings that the quantities of particulate matter, carbon dioxide, and other atmospheric contaminants were already near disastrous levels con-

A resident of Inverness, Miss., scavenges through massive debris after a rash of tornadoes hit the area Feb. 21, 1971, causing severe damage and killing 115 persons.
WIDE WORLD

trasted with such reports as that by the U.S. National Oceanic and Atmospheric Administration (NOAA) stating that no appreciable change could be found in the turbidity of the high atmosphere over Hawaii during the years 1957–70. Any great increase in turbidity would modify the total energy from the sun's radiation retained by the earth and atmosphere and would therefore change the earth's heat balance and the climate.

Another prominent subject was CAT (clear air turbulence). After the advent of high-altitude jet aircraft in the 1950s, CAT became a critical problem for high-speed aircraft designers and operators, as well as an occasional worry to air passengers. In a few instances, severe turbulence in clear air without visible warning had shattered airplane structures and resulted in the loss of all on board. For more than a decade researchers had sought desperately for the causes of CAT and for means of identifying and avoiding the localities where it might occur.

After years of intensive studies using ultrahigh-resolution radar and other advanced technology, it was discovered that CAT seemed to result from relatively tight vortices incident to the creating and breaking of horizontal waves on the boundary surface of contrasting air masses in the upper atmosphere. The general synoptic weather situations conducive to the formation of such waves could often be identified by use of the daily weather map, although the exact place where CAT-producing factors would be generated was still impossible to foresee. As of 1971, it was expected that several years of experimentation would be required before CAT-forecasting would become a standard feature of primary aviation meteorology analysis.

Air turbulence in the form of violent thunderstorms, gusty gale winds, and horizontal (gravity) waves accompanied by clouds had been well known since the beginnings of aircraft but were not yet fully understood. In its *Quarterly* for February 1971, the National Center for Atmospheric Research, Boulder, Colo., reported the results of recent research in the dynamics of convection in the free air and also described mathematical models for moist convection relating in some respects to hail production. Comparable research projects were in progress in Europe, notably the U.S.S.R.

Cloud seeding and other attempts to modify weather made headline news at various times and in various places during 1971. The U.S.S.R. continued to report remarkable success in suppressing hailstorms by selective seeding of threatening cumulonimbus clouds, using artillery shells to inject the seeding agent into the critical locus of the cloud. A few reports of success in hail suppression also came from western Canada, Brazil, the U.S. Midwest, and other widely separated localities.

After all-time records for rainfall deficiencies had been broken in certain localities in southern Florida during March–May 1971, authorities requested the federal government to try cloud seeding to induce rain. Seeding operations again demonstrated that no methods were successful in ending drought artificially as long as the general synoptic weather situation was unfavourable. Reports indicated that small but usually insignificant increases in precipitation were induced in some instances, but the general drought did not end until mid-May when the weather map showed changes in the hemispheric circulation of the atmosphere.

Another attempt to modify weather occurred in September when Project Stormfury, an experimentation facility of NOAA, performed a series of seedings on Hurricane Ginger. The task force that attacked the storm was larger and better equipped than in any previous attempt at hurricane "control." The theory underlying the attack rested essentially on seeding to intensify shower activity in critical sectors of the cyclone, thus reducing atmospheric pressure in that area, modifying the isobaric configuration, and possibly altering the course and intensity of the storm. Although the experiment succeeded in modifying shower clouds, no practical success in suppressing the storm was observed. After milling around a few hundred miles east of the Carolina-Georgia coast for about 25 days, Ginger eventually moved westward and inland, bringing heavy rains to eastern North Carolina and Virginia. However, scientists reported that some evidence was found to support the underlying theory and to justify further studies and experimentation.

The daily nephograms or worldwide cloud maps made possible through orbiting weather satellites had become commonplace by 1971, and the new epoch that began with the launching of the Tiros 1 satellite on April 1, 1960, no longer seemed fabulous. In major cities the public could view the largest cloud systems over their hemisphere on the current day on television, and thereby visualize the location and extent of important storm developments. The growing sophistication in weather satellite design and the extension of coverage through international cooperation had made possible gigantic steps forward in worldwide mapping of meteorological conditions.

Nephograms now gave early evidence of tropical cyclones in the process of formation far out at sea, and showed pilots of hurricane-reconnaissance planes where to gather the data needed by forecasters to warn the public when evacuation of exposed coastal zones was advisable. Warning systems based on these facilities were credited with reducing loss of life from

Killer Storms

Date	Place	Kind of storm	Casualties
October 1971	NE coast of India	Cyclone and tidal wave (similar to West Indies hurricane)	At least 10,000 and possibly 20,000 dead
October 1971	Vietnam and Far East	Typhoon Hester (similar to hurricane)	Winds exceeded 130 mph; 89 lives lost; thousands homeless
February 1971	Louisiana, Mississippi, and Tennessee	Several interrelated tornadoes	Heavy damage in Louisiana, Mississippi, and Tennessee; 113 fatalities
November 1970	Manila	Typhoon	Storm surge drowned 120 or more; "worst" typhoon in many years in Manila
November 1970	East Pakistan	Cyclone	Greatest loss of life ever recorded in one natural disaster; estimated 600,000 dead
August 1969	Coasts of Texas and Louisiana	Hurricane Camille (one of most severe)	Estimated 400 drowned in storm surge; hundreds of thousands evacuated
June 1957	Louisiana	Hurricane Audrey	Approximately 200 drowned; storm surge 12 ft. deep on coast reached 25 mi. inland
November 1950	Midwest U.S.	Winter storm, "blizzard"	Heavy snow and unexpected freezing temperatures resulted in 150 lives lost
September 1938	New England	Hurricane	Storm during weekend; warnings not heeded; heavy destruction; 600 fatalities
September 1928	Florida	Hurricane	Indefinite forecasts and warnings; approximately 1,800 drowned
March 1925	Missouri area	Tornadoes	Swarm of tornadoes cut through three states; nearly 700 deaths
September 1900	Galveston, Tex.	Hurricane	Before adequate warning system was established; 6,000 drowned in storm surge
March 1888	Eastern U.S.	Winter storm, "blizzard"	Before warning system; Boston, New York, Washington "paralyzed"; 400 deaths
Unverified report for year 1737	Ganges delta, India	Cyclone	Reports regarded as authentic but not certain allege 300,000 persons drowned in hurricanelike storm surge

drownings in storm surges. Without these warning services, tens of thousands probably would have drowned. The most disastrous storm of 1970–71, the East Pakistan cyclone of November 1970, in which untold thousands were killed, tragically demonstrated the value of a modern early warning and evacuation emergency plan. The nephogram service from weather satellites had provided an early warning of the cyclone, but no facilities were available to warn or evacuate the populace.

Newly designed ocean weather buoys were launched in 1971 to assist in closing the gaps in weather data from remote areas at sea. Studies continued using data of air/sea interactions and their relationships with the earth's heat budget and storm development, much of the data having been collected from the BOMEX and Line Island Experiment (Pacific). The "Flip" upending survey vessel of the U.S. Navy also obtained some of these data. One of several important international scientific gatherings at which results of such studies were reported was the 15th general assembly of the International Union of Geodesy and Geophysics in Moscow, August 1971. This assembly also keynoted the overriding importance of environmental problems.   (F. W. Rr.)

See also Astronautics; Disasters; Oceanography.
Encyclopædia Britannica Films. *Whatever the Weather* (1967); *Reflections on Time* (1969).

Mexico

A federal republic of Middle America, Mexico is bounded by the U.S., British Honduras, and Guatemala. Area: 761,600 sq.mi. (1,972,547 sq.km.). Pop. (1971 est.): 50,829,474, including about 55% mestizo and 29% Indian. Cap. and largest city: Mexico City (pop., 1970, 2,902,969). Language: Spanish. Religion: predominantly Roman Catholic. President in 1971, Luis Echeverría Álvarez.

Domestic Affairs. Mexico's political and economic stability, although not seriously or permanently impaired, suffered some important setbacks in 1971. The steady development of the economy over the last three decades had created changes in the fabric of Mexican society for which no political outlets had been devised so far. In addition, the economy had reached a stage where future growth would depend to a large extent on a widening of the internal market, at a time when continued expansion of international

trade was in question as a result of unresolved world monetary problems. It was propitious for Mexico to have found in President Echeverría a dynamic leader committed to reform, whose performance during his first year in office—fighting corruption, releasing political prisoners, and opening a dialogue with those in the nation expressing independent opinion—endeared him to the public and the press, and gained the respect of all but the most extreme political opponents. The latter included influential right-wing groups who seemed to believe that no corrective action was needed to maintain Mexico's political and economic status quo indefinitely.

It was to these groups, upset by Echeverría's reforming zeal, that the serious political disturbances of June 10 were widely attributed. Student unrest at the University of Nuevo León in Monterrey the previous month forced the federal government to intervene by requesting the governor of Nuevo León to resign because of alleged interference in university affairs. Although the incident was by then closed, the university students of Mexico City, stirred by agents provocateurs, decided to carry out a demonstration of solidarity with Monterrey on June 10, Corpus Christi Day. The peaceful demonstration was broken up by a paramilitary organization, identified as the Halcones, who killed several students and wounded or manhandled many others while police stood passively by. As an attempt to discredit Echeverría by association, the disruption of public order failed, due to his prompt reaction and obvious anger at the Halcones. The attorney general was instructed to conduct an investigation, which was followed by the immediate resignation of the mayor and the chief of police of Mexico City. Two months later the attorney general was replaced, having failed to bring to justice any persons responsible for the incidents.

With some exceptions—such as the well-known painter David Alfaro Siqueiros, who requested other Communists to cooperate with the new administration—the extreme left also created problems. On September 27, Julio Hirschfeld Almada, head of airports and auxiliary services, was kidnapped in Mexico City in broad daylight; he was released, unharmed, only three days later for a ransom of 3 million pesos. The coup was credited to the Movement for Revolutionary Action. This group had been uncovered in March when its leaders and ten members were arrested and charged with subversion; the incident was followed by the expulsion of five Soviet diplomats.

MEXICO
Education. (1968–69) Primary, pupils 8,539,462, teachers 182,851; secondary, pupils 1,085,829; teachers 79,752; vocational, pupils 170,768, teachers 13,133; teacher training, students 58,751, teachers 5,753; higher (including 38 universities), students 192,472, teaching staff 21,087.
Finance. Monetary unit: peso, with a par value of 12.50 pesos to U.S. $1 (30 pesos = £1 sterling) and a free rate (Sept. 27, 1971) of 30.85 pesos to £1 sterling. Gold, SDRs, and foreign exchange, central bank: (April 1971) U.S. $738 million; (April 1970) U.S. $640 million. Budget (1971) balanced at 79,656,000,000 pesos. Gross national product: (1968) 334.3 billion pesos; (1967) 301.4 billion pesos. Money supply: (Sept. 1970) 44,610,000,000 pesos; (Sept. 1969) 40.2 billion pesos. Cost of living (Mexico City; 1963 = 100): (June 1971) 129; (June 1970) 124.
Foreign Trade. (1970) Imports 30,760,000,000 pesos; exports 17,526,000,000 pesos. Import sources (1969): U.S. 62%; West Germany 8%;

Japan 5%. Export destinations (1969): U.S. 56%; Japan 7%. Main exports: cotton 9%; sugar 7%; coffee 6%; shrimps 5%. Tourism (1969): visitors 1,817,800; gross receipts U.S. $1,224,000,000.
Transport and Communications. Roads (1970) 71,520 km. (including 1,002 km. expressways). Motor vehicles in use (1970): passenger 1,242,845; commercial (including buses) 581,814. Railways: (1968) 19,749 km.; traffic (1969) 4,620,000,000 passenger-km., freight 20,996,000,000 net ton-km. Air traffic (1970): 2.9 million passenger-km.; freight 41,260,000 net ton-km. Shipping (1970): merchant vessels 100 gross tons and over 132; gross tonnage 381,096. Telephones (Dec. 1969) 1,326,670. Radio receivers (Dec. 1969) 12,990,000. Television receivers (Dec. 1969) 2,553,000.
Agriculture. Production (in 000; metric tons; 1970; 1969 in parentheses): corn *c.* 9,100 (8,496); wheat *c.* 2,100 (2,200); sorghum *c.* 2,350 (2,405); rice 383 (397); potatoes *c.* 540 (576);

coffee *c.* 182 (184); cotton, lint *c.* 360 (514); dry beans *c.* 1,300 (1,200); bananas (1969) 1,025, (1968) 1,040; oranges 1,020 (937); lemons 171 (186); sugar, raw value (1970–71) *c.* 2,383, (1969–70) *c.* 2,365; tobacco 78 (62); sisal *c.* 140 (150); fish catch (1969) 354, (1968) 366. Livestock (in 000; Dec. 1969): cattle 24,876; sheep 5,580; pigs 10,298; horses 5,034; mules 2,716; asses 3,295; chickens *c.* 141,000.
Industry. Production (in 000; metric tons; 1970): cement 7,423; crude oil (1969) 21,415; coal (1969) 1,500; natural gas (cu.m.) 18,838; electricity (kw-hr.) 28,592,000; iron ore (metal content) 2,614; pig iron 1,657; steel 3,823; sulfur (1969) 1,716; sulfuric acid 1,235; nitrogenous fertilizers (1969–70) 359; lead 150; zinc 81; copper, smelter 60; aluminum 34; manganese ore (metal content; 1969) 60; antimony ore (metal content; 1969) 3.2; silver (1969) 1.3; gold (troy oz.; 1969) 181; cotton yarn (1969) 145; woven cotton fabrics (1969) 128.

The controversial Halcones ("Falcons") battle with university students in Mexico City on June 10, 1971, during a street fight in which several persons were killed. Unofficial sources claim the Halcones are detectives, but the mayor and the police department denied any official connection with the group.

UPI COMPIX

The Economy. The year 1970 as a whole had shown a very high rate of economic growth, the gross domestic product increasing by 7.5% in real terms. This result, however, concealed a decline in activity over the second half of the year due partly to investment restraint by the public sector in order to counteract inflation and partly to caution by private investors in view of the imminent change of government. Foreign trade showed considerable deterioration in 1970, yielding a deficit of $1,088,000,000 ($395 million larger than the 1969 deficit), imports having risen by 18.2% while exports fell by 1.2%. All these trends persisted throughout the first half of 1971. In the second half of the year, however, a decline in internal demand combined with monetary and tax measures brought the rise in prices to more acceptable levels; foreign trade also showed signs of recovery, and business began to accelerate. It was nevertheless predicted that for the whole of 1971 there would be a slower rate of growth than in the preceding years (probably 6%) and that rapid growth would not be resumed before 1973.

In a country where economic activity was closely related to import levels, rapid development had led to a growing trade deficit that put considerable strain on the balance of payments. Income from tourism and border transactions was increasing, but more slowly than the trade gap, while receipts from new foreign capital already were exceeded by remittances of profits and royalties outside the country. To maintain its holdings of international reserves, successive Mexican governments had resorted to borrowing abroad. Because of its good record, Mexico had experienced no difficulty in obtaining funds, but the overall amount of the debt and the sizable sums required every year to settle interest and amortization (23.5% of foreign exchange earnings in 1970) were causing some concern. Faced with these difficulties, Echeverría did not hesitate to slow down development, however unpopular and at variance with his own long-term goals such a step might be.

Foreign Relations. In any case, much of the initiative was taken out of his hands when on August 15 U.S. Pres. Richard M. Nixon announced a range of economic measures, including a 10% import sur-

charge, intended to correct the United States' own balance of payment difficulties. Since more than 80% of Mexico's foreign debt was negotiated in U.S. dollars, and the U.S. accounted for two-thirds of all Mexico's foreign trade as well as nine-tenths of its tourist income, the Mexican government had no choice but to retain the parity of 12.50 pesos to the dollar in force since April 1954. Although sugar and later textile quotas were excluded, and the surcharge was subsequently rescinded as part of the December international monetary agreement, the entire affair reinforced one of the stated aims of the new administration, namely to work for a greater degree of economic independence from the U.S. Accordingly, a series of Mexican trade missions was sent overseas, particularly to Western Europe and the Far East, where it was believed that because of the peso tie to the dollar Mexican exports might offer marginal price advantages.

U.S.-Mexican relations remained otherwise friendly and cooperative throughout the year. Toward the end of 1970, a treaty had been signed embodying the verbal agreements reached by Pres. Gustavo Díaz Ordaz and President Nixon. The treaty provided for the return to Mexico of 1,600 ac. of land of the Ojinaga-Presidio area and the handing over to the U.S. of 500 ac. of the Horcon and Morteritos islands; it also laid down a formula for any future disputes, and fixed permanent boundaries in offshore waters between Tijuana and San Diego, Calif., and between Matamoros and Brownsville, Tex.   (M. Pu.)

Middle East

In 1971 the Middle East was relatively peaceful in terms of military action. Arab-Israeli tension remained high and there was no visible progress toward a political settlement, but there was no fighting except for minor incidents. The suppression of the Palestinian guerrillas in Jordan by the Jordanian Army confined them to limited activities near the Lebanese border, but they struck back in November when members of a guerrilla organization assassinated Jordan's prime minister, Wasfi at-Tal (*see* OBITUARIES). There

Methodists:
see Religion

Microbiology:
see Life Sciences

were no violent changes of regime in any Middle East state except for the briefly successful pro-Communist coup in Sudan in July, which was followed by executions of the coup's leaders. An agreement between oil companies and members of the Organization of Petroleum Exporting Countries in Teheran in February brought substantially increased oil revenues to all Middle East oil-producing states, but economic development continued to be handicapped by the high arms expenditures of most countries in the area.

Arab-Israeli Conflict. During the year Western, and especially United States, diplomacy concentrated on trying to achieve a partial Arab-Israeli settlement based on the reopening of the Suez Canal. The Soviet attitude was that only the U.S. could persuade Israel to make concessions and that the lack of progress toward a settlement was due to Israel's obstructionism and U.S. support for Israel. It was assumed by most members of the UN that no Middle East settlement was possible without some form of U.S.-Soviet understanding.

The indirect Arab-Israeli peace talks that had begun in August 1970 were resumed on January 5, when UN special envoy Gunnar Jarring met separately with representatives of Israel, Jordan, and Egypt in New York. The talks continued later in the month after Jarring had visited Israel. Although some progress was reported, the fundamental difference between the two sides remained—Israel insisted on direct peace talks leading to the signing of a peace treaty, while the Arabs demanded that an Israeli withdrawal from occupied territories should precede any discus-

sion of a peace treaty. Egypt proposed that Jarring be issued a precise set of instructions for the implementation of UN Security Council Resolution 242 of Nov. 22, 1967, which called for Israeli withdrawal from all territory gained from the 1967 Arab-Israeli war. Israel specifically rejected another Egyptian proposal that an international peace force be stationed in the area on the ground that the Arab-Israeli conflict was a regional problem. In February it was reported that Jarring had submitted specific proposals to both Israel and Egypt concerning the future status of Gaza and Sharm el-Sheikh. An Israeli statement issued after a Cabinet meeting on February 14 said that Israel was continuing the moves it had initiated in January and was still awaiting Egypt's response to proposals it had submitted to Jarring.

Representatives of the U.S., the Soviet Union, the U.K., and France met in New York on February 4 and 12 to discuss guarantees and possible peacekeeping arrangements once a settlement had been reached. The U.S. had previously refused to discuss guarantees on the ground that it did not wish to establish a link between them and the Jarring mission. Its change of mind was regarded as a response to agreement by Egypt's Pres. Anwar as-Sadat (*see* BIOGRAPHY) to extend the cease-fire for 30 days from February 5.

In an interview published in the February 22 issue of *Newsweek* magazine, Sadat described the 1967 UN resolution as "an embryonic peace treaty." He said that if Israel returned the occupied territories its integrity would be guaranteed by the four powers and it would have freedom of navigation in the Suez Canal and the Strait of Tiran. But all this was conditioned on a just solution of the Palestinian problem. In an interview with the London *Observer* on February 28, King Husain of Jordan said that his country's views on a peace treaty were identical with those of Egypt. On February 16 the Israeli defense minister, Moshe Dayan, said he would prefer Sharm el-Sheikh without peace to peace without Sharm el-Sheikh. On February 25 U.S. Pres. Richard Nixon said that no Middle East settlement would be permanent unless it provided for the recovery of Arab territories lost in war, that Israel must have confidence that it would not be attacked, that supplementary guarantees by the four powers would be needed, and that any settlement must meet the legitimate interests of the Palestinian people. On the following day Israeli Prime Minister Golda Meir (*see* BIOGRAPHY) said that the U.S. was well aware that Israel could not concede the Golan Heights, occupied Jerusalem, or Sharm el-Sheikh. She repeated this position more specifically in an interview with *The Times* (London) published March 13, while at the same time rejecting the idea of a Palestinian state on the West Bank of the Jordan River. There were increasing signs of strain in U.S.-Israeli relations, with the U.S. Department of State giving the impression that Israel was being more inflexible than the Arabs and withholding further supplies of Phantom jets to Israel. British Foreign Minister Sir Alec Douglas-Home said on March 2 that Israel should make a matching commitment on withdrawal in response to Egypt's "clear, unequivocal, and specific commitment" on the nature of peace. On March 16, U.S. Secretary of State William Rogers said that Israel's security did not necessarily require the acquisition of territory. Egypt's attitude continued to be that it had made as many concessions as it could and that it was now up to the U.S. to put pressure on Israel.

Withdrawal from the Sinai Peninsula is a basic issue in Middle East peace efforts. Box indicates possible Israeli negotiating points.

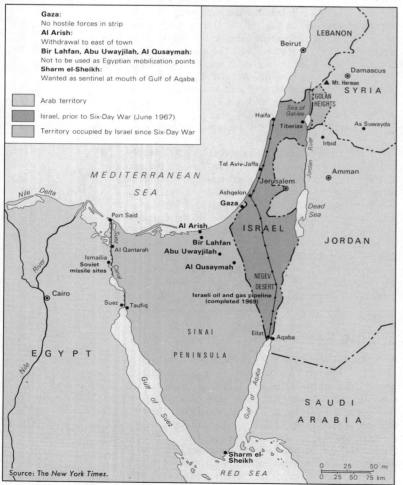

Gaza:
No hostile forces in strip
Al Arish:
Withdrawal to east of town
Bir Lahfan, Abu Uwayjilah, Al Qusaymah:
Not to be used as Egyptian mobilization points
Sharm el-Sheikh:
Wanted as sentinel at mouth of Gulf of Aqaba

Arab territory

Israel, prior to Six-Day War (June 1967)

Territory occupied by Israel since Six-Day War

Source: *The New York Times.*

Rogers toured Jordan, Saudi Arabia, Lebanon, Egypt, and Israel in early May in an effort to promote U.S. proposals for a settlement and specifically to try to arrange an interim agreement involving a pullback of Israeli forces from the Suez Canal to allow its reopening. At this stage Israel reported that Rogers had agreed that for the interim settlement no Egyptian or Soviet troops should be allowed to cross the canal but that the U.S. government confirmed its support for a near-total Israeli withdrawal in any final settlement. The U.S.S.R. was critical of U.S. efforts to reopen the canal, and Egypt insisted that its forces must cross the canal if it was to be reopened.

On May 21 it was announced that Jarring was returning to his post as Swedish ambassador in Moscow. A stalemate ensued that lasted throughout the summer, although the U.S. tried to keep its latest diplomatic initiative alive. On June 30 it was reported that the U.S. had modified its proposals for an interim settlement to allow a token Egyptian force to cross the Suez Canal. Much of the Arab criticism of Israel was directed against judaization of Jerusalem and the alteration of the Arab character of the Old City.

In July several Israeli ministers publicly complained that the U.S. had suspended arms shipments and protested that, in view of the Soviet-Egyptian treaty and new Soviet arms shipments to Egypt, this was holding up negotiations. Sadat said on July 23 that he would not allow 1971 to pass without the battle being resolved "either by war or peace." In August it was reported that Israel had rejected several different proposals for a phased withdrawal in Sinai as part of an interim settlement. The diplomatic battle moved to the UN in September with the opening of a new session of the General Assembly. On October 4 Rogers presented a six-point proposal for an interim settlement to the General Assembly. This was strongly criticized by the Israeli government because it allowed Egyptian forces to cross the canal and linked an interim settlement with a final settlement. Following Soviet promises to increase military aid to Egypt during Sadat's Moscow visit (October 11–13), Rogers said that the U.S. might have to review the Middle East arms situation and 78 U.S. senators called for the supply of Phantoms to Israel. Golda Meir visited the United States in December and met with President Nixon. Later in the month the U.S. announced that it was resuming the sale of Phantoms to Israel. Also in December the UN General Assembly voted that Israel and Egypt resume their indirect peace talks through Jarring.

Despite the new arms shipments to Egypt it was generally considered that the balance of military power remained favourable to Israel, at least for the time being, although Egypt's defensive capacity had been substantially improved. The acquisition by Egypt of at least 25 Soviet Tu-16 bombers, equipped with Kelt and Kennel air-to-ship standoff missiles, meant that for the first time Egypt had lent itself to furthering the attack capacity of the U.S.S.R. against the U.S. 6th Fleet.

Israel's security position was improved by the virtual elimination of the Palestinian guerrillas' military effort in Jordan during July. This meant that all Israel's borders were relatively quiet except those with Lebanon, where sporadic guerrilla action provoked Israeli retaliatory raids. There was also a revival of guerrilla activity on a small scale in the Golan Heights in July. Apart from a handful of bomb-throwing incidents, Jerusalem and the West Bank

"We're much stronger now"—Lurie.

were quieter than they had been for some time. The Arab inhabitants of the West Bank generally were resigned to the prolongation of Israel's military occupation and, after the Jordanian Army's suppression of the guerrillas, they showed little desire for a return to Jordanian rule. Although there were some among them who favoured the establishment of an autonomous Palestinian state on the West Bank, they received no encouragement from the Israelis, Jordanians, or the Palestinian guerrilla leadership. A new Israeli policy allowed more than 100,000 Arabs from outside Israel and the occupied territories to visit the country during the summer.

Israel's most serious security problem was among the 360,000 inhabitants of the Gaza Strip, where there was a series of strikes and bomb incidents. Additional security forces had to be moved there in January. The Israelis dismissed the Arab mayor of Gaza and disbanded the Municipal Council. In February Defense Minister Dayan said that there had been 1,300 acts of sabotage in Gaza since the 1967 war, causing 1,600 casualties including 250 deaths. Most of these were Arabs. Incidents continued at a high level throughout the summer with many of the attacks being made against Arabs who continued to work in Israel. In June the Israelis announced that they were building a security fence around Gaza similar to the one along the Jordan River. Accordingly, the Israeli military authorities began resettling refugees from the Gaza camps in new accommodations in the area. This provoked a strike by shopkeepers and merchants in the Gaza Strip but, by the end of August, Israel said that 13,000 had been resettled. The policy continued, and Israel planned various steps to improve economic conditions in Gaza in the hope of alleviating the security situation. In November Zaid el-Husseini, commander of the Arab liberation forces in the Gaza Strip, committed suicide in the basement of the mayor's house.

The 115-member Palestine National Council met in Cairo (February 28–March 5) and adopted the Arafat Plan for the unification of guerrilla activities. However, the left-wing extremist Popular Democratic Front for the Liberation of Palestine and the Popular Front for the Liberation of Palestine of George

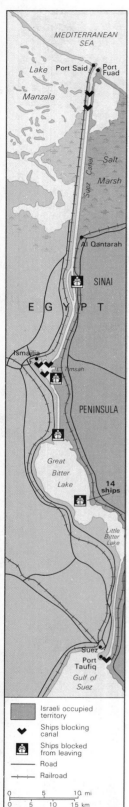

MEDITERRANEAN
SEA

Lake Port Said Port
Manzala   Fuad

Salt
Marsh

Al Qantarah

SINAI

E G Y P T

Ismailia

L. Timsah

PENINSULA

Great
Bitter
Lake

14
ships

Little
Bitter
Lake

Suez
Port
Taufiq
Gulf of
Suez

Israeli occupied
territory

Ships blocking
canal

Ships blocked
from leaving

Road

Railroad

0   5   10 mi
0   5   10   15 km

Symbols indicate sunken
vessels blocking the Suez
Canal and areas where
ships are blocked.
Officials have estimated
that if a political
agreement could
be concluded the canal
could be reopened in two
to three months.

Habash described the meeting as a failure and demanded the immediate overthrow of the Jordanian regime. Guerrilla disunity contributed to the liquidation of their military effort in Jordan in July. The majority, under the leadership of Yasir Arafat, were prepared to consider settling their differences with the Jordanian government, and in November Saudi and Egyptian mediation efforts were successful in arranging a meeting between the two sides.

Efforts to achieve reconciliation received a serious setback on November 28 when Jordan's prime minister, Wasfi at-Tal, was assassinated by guerrillas while attending an Arab League meeting in Cairo. The four men arrested for the shooting were described as members of a Palestinian organization known as the Black September.

Inter-Arab Relations. The year saw creation of the new Arab federation of Egypt, Libya, and Syria. Sudan, which had been closely associated with the idea from the start, did not join but the way was open for it to do so in the future. The People's Democratic Republic of Yemen made approaches to the three federating states but was reported to have been told by the others to settle its internal unity problems first. The rest of the Arab world was in a state of disunity. In particular the so-called Arab "eastern front" with Israel was in disarray. The rival Baathist regimes in Syria and Iraq were in continuous dispute—united only in their hostility to King Husain of Jordan. In July they both closed their borders with Jordan, and there were serious clashes between Syrian and Jordanian forces. Iraq continued to bid for Arab leadership through a uniquely intransigent attitude to political settlement with Israel but was fairly effectively isolated by the other Arab states. On the other hand, the old division between the conservative and radical camps in the Arab world was alleviated by the rapprochement between Egypt and Saudi Arabia that resulted from the visit of King Faisal to Cairo in June. A Moroccan proposal for an Arab summit in Rabat came to nothing although a majority of members of the Arab League favoured it.

Leaders of the Tripoli Charter states—Sudan, Syria, Egypt, and Libya—met in Cairo (January 20–22) and discussed means of strengthening the eastern front. The Syrian president said on March 16 that the Syrian and Egyptian war fronts had been put under a joint command and that a complete military union between the two countries had been achieved. Another meeting was held in Cairo (April 13–14), but on the second day Sudanese Pres. Gaafar Nimeiry (*see* BIOGRAPHY) flew off to Moscow. The other three leaders continued their talks in Bengasi, Libya, and on April 17 announced that a Confederation of Arab Republics comprising their three states would be formed following referendums in all three on September 1. The first announcement stated that decisions in the federation's Presidential Council could be made by a majority vote, but this was later changed to a requirement for a unanimous vote at Sadat's request. Sudan was reported to have remained outside the federation for the time being because of Nimeiry's domestic preoccupations with Communists and because of Libyan objections to the continued presence of Marxists in the Sudanese regime. An important provision of the agreement stated that "if disturbances occur in one of the republics, from within or without, the government of the republic will notify the federation government so that the latter can take

necessary measures to maintain law and order." It added that if appropriate notification could not be made the federal authorities could intervene to restore order without being asked. In July Egypt and Libya acted to help Nimeiry against his opponents although the agreement had not been ratified and Sudan was not yet a member of the federation. On July 25 Nimeiry said Sudan would join as soon as a national political party was established.

After the suppression of the Palestinian guerrillas in Jordan, King Husain invited Arab heads of state who had doubts about the normality of the situation in Jordan to come to see for themselves. The offer was not accepted, and instead the heads of state of Libya, Syria, Egypt, Yemen (Aden), Yemen (San'a'), and a delegation of the Palestine Liberation Organization met in Tripoli, Libya, on July 30 to discuss the crisis. The meeting condemned Jordan for refusing to implement the 1970 Cairo and Amman agreements that provided for the withdrawal of all Jordanian Army and guerrilla forces from every city in Jordan under the supervision of a three-man inter-Arab committee. Following the visit of King Faisal of Saudi Arabia to Egypt in June, a joint Saudi-Egyptian team visited Jordan and Syria in order to mediate between the Jordanian government and the guerrillas. It proposed complete adherence by both sides to the Cairo and Amman agreements and the release by the Jordanian authorities of all Palestinian guerrillas held hostage in return for the abolition of all underground Palestinian organizations in Jordan.

The draft constitution of the Arab federation was approved by the heads of state of Libya, Syria, and Egypt at a series of meetings in Damascus which ended on August 20. In an accompanying declaration they said there would be no reconciliation or negotiation with Israel and no surrender of Israeli-occupied territory. The federation was endorsed by overwhelming majorities in referendums held in the three countries on September 1. Observers noted that it provided for a looser federal structure than previous attempts at Arab union, which might give it greater durability. It had the advantage of combining Libya's oil wealth with the greater political experience of Egypt and Syria. On the other hand, it deepened some of the divisions in the Arab world. Jordan was excluded, Iraq was neutral, and Saudi Arabia unenthusiastic.

The Persian Gulf. The British government's confirmation on March 1 that it would be withdrawing its forces from the Persian Gulf by the end of 1971 and that its defense treaties with the Arab sheikhdoms would consequently terminate gave added impetus to the discussions of federation between the small Arab states of the area. Bahrain and Qatar were unable to agree on terms for entering the proposed federation and chose complete independence. Six of the seven Trucial States—Abu Dhabi, Ajman, Dubai, Fujairah, Sharjah, and Umm al-Qaiwain—joined together to form the Union of Arab Emirates on December 2, and Ras al Khaimah joined a few days later. On November 30 Iran occupied three small islands at the mouth of the Persian Gulf to which it had long laid claim: Greater and Lesser Tumbs, protected by Britain under a treaty with Ras al Khaimah that expired December 1, and Abu Musa, hitherto regarded as belonging to Sharjah.   (P. Mn.)

See also **Defense;** also articles on the various political units.

Migration, International

During 1971 there was a continuation of the situation noted in late 1969 by the Population Division of the UN Secretariat—namely, that intercontinental migration had ceased to play an important part in population growth, except in a few areas (notably Australia and New Zealand). Intracontinental movements had become increasingly important, but the shorter distances and easier communications involved made it less likely that immigrants would settle permanently in the receiving countries.

Europe, for generations a reservoir of emigrants to other continents, was increasingly characterized by large-scale intracontinental labour migration, mainly from south to north, from rural to urban areas, and from the less developed Mediterranean countries to the highly industrialized societies of Northern and Western Europe. The 19th-century flow from Eastern to Western Europe was not repeated, except in the case of Yugoslavia, because of the restrictive policies of the Soviet bloc states.

By 1971 there were at least eight million foreigners, mostly from Italy or non-EEC Mediterranean countries, living in the five EEC labour-importing countries and in Switzerland, Sweden, and Austria. Apart from Luxembourg, Switzerland had the largest number of alien residents (nearly one million out of a total population of six million, and over 25% of the labour force). This large inflow threatened the country's delicate linguistic and religious equilibrium, and produced a sequence of xenophobic reactions that continued into 1971. Xenophobic reactions were also reported for Sweden, but these were attributable to the sudden impact of an alien culture on a homogeneous and conservative society.

West Germany's foreign-born population totaled about 3,750,000 in 1971, 2,250,000 of them workers. France, the Netherlands, and Britain were the only countries in which former colonial links were reflected in immigration patterns. The great majority of Britain's postwar immigrants had come on free entry from Ireland or from the new Commonwealth countries (mainly the West Indies, India, and Pakistan), but the latter flow had been cut to a trickle by increasingly restrictive legislation from 1962 onward. As Britain prepared to enter the EEC, a new Immigration Act was passed in 1971 that did away with free entry for any but those in the "patrial" category.

By 1968 the EEC had fully implemented its policy of free movement of labour for workers who were citizens of member countries and their dependents. The EEC Commission also declared its intention of extending the privileged arrangements for Community workers by stages to the large numbers of workers from associated and other nonmember countries. In practice, however, there were signs of a growing economic, social, and legal gap between first-class "Community workers" and second-class "non-Community" workers, with little more than lip service being paid to the needs of the latter.

The patterns of migration to some traditional overseas countries of settlement continued to change. In Canada, where a new "points" system for immigrants had been introduced in 1966, there was a decrease in the overall total of immigrants (from 161,531 in 1969 to 147,713 in 1970), as well as a decline in the proportion of immigrants from Europe (from 75% in

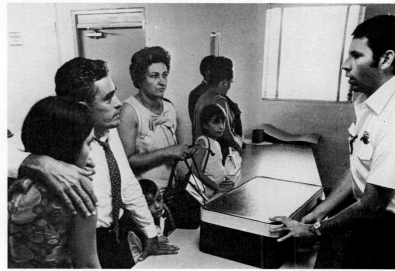

A Cuban family passes through customs and immigration clearance in Miami, Fla., on Aug. 31, 1971, the day Prime Minister Fidel Castro announced his intention to end the refugee flights. Since the airlift began in December 1965, more than 245,000 Cubans had flown to the U.S.

1966 to just over 50% in 1970) and an increase in the proportion from Asia and the Caribbean (from 10% in 1965 to 23% in 1969). Changes in Canadian and U.S. immigration laws afforded some relief to the overpopulated societies of the Commonwealth Caribbean, whose entry to Britain had become increasingly blocked since 1962. Another outlet had opened up in the underdeveloped back country of Guyana, but only a relatively few pioneers from Barbados and the East Caribbean had taken advantage of it.

The flow of European emigration to Argentina, another traditional country of immigration from Europe, had diminished considerably in the last decade or so, but increasing influxes were noted of legal and illegal immigrants from neighbouring countries. Australia's immigration total for 1969–70 was 160,000. The former "white Australia" policy had been slightly dented to include 6,000 people of mixed European and non-European descent and some 3,300 non-Europeans; about 1,400 of these were admitted on the basis of professional qualifications. New Zealand's intake of "preferred" immigrants from Britain continued to decline (only one-third of the total of 39,380 in 1970–71), and the government was reported to be considering the extension of assisted immigrant subsidies to the Netherlands, Belgium, France, Switzerland, West Germany, and the U.S.

Israel remained a country of permanent immigration with an estimated intake of 50,000 in 1971. Stresses and tensions showed up in the ethnic mosaic, notably in divisions between European and Asian Jews. In Africa there was no cessation of voluntary economic migration, mainly seasonal or transitory, between poorer, less urbanized countries and their richer, more labour-hungry neighbours. This often reflected traditional nomadic movements and tribal customs. One such traditional migration flow, increasingly characterized by controls, recruitment, and work contracts, was from Malawi to Rhodesia and South Africa. African workers from former French West African territories, prevented since independence from crossing into other African countries for seasonal work, continued to emigrate to France under bilateral agreements with the French government. Xenophobic restrictionism was shown by some independent African countries. (SH. P.)

Immigration policies involving the Western Hemisphere captured considerable attention in the U.S. in

A young Tibetan is among 16 refugees arriving in Montreal on March 25, 1971. Tibetan spiritual leader, the Dalai Lama, arranged with Prime Minister Pierre Trudeau to allow entry into Canada for 200 Tibetans who had been living in refugee camps in India since 1959, when the Chinese Communists took over their country.

1971. The six-year-old airlift of Cuban refugees to Miami, Fla., had been under increasing criticism because of its cost and because it was straining welfare, health, educational, and other services in areas where the Cubans settled, particularly around Miami. A Senate attempt to cut off funding was unsuccessful, but on August 31 it was announced that the Cuban government wished to terminate the program. This turnabout in Cuban policy was attributed in some Washington circles to growing manpower shortages in Cuba. Also cited was the possible embarrassment caused by the steady exodus.

A related problem, which could become moot following the termination of the Cuban airlift, concerned the question of whether the approximately 40,000 Cuban refugees arriving in the U.S. annually should be counted under the Western Hemisphere ceiling of 120,000 immigrants per year. It was argued that the Cubans amounted to about one-third of the allowable number of immigrants and delayed other hemisphere residents in their effort to migrate to the U.S. The whole question of the hemispheric ceiling also came under review in 1971. Supporters of relaxation argued that countries of the hemisphere always had enjoyed a special relationship with the U.S., whereas opponents contended that such special treatment discriminated against the rest of the world.

During 1971 the U.S. Immigration and Naturalization Service and Congress began paying closer attention to the problem of illegal entries into the U.S. Throughout the year the Immigration Service's border patrol and other officers captured aliens trying to cross the Mexican border and staged raids to apprehend groups of illegal aliens; the most widely publicized raid involved a firm belonging to Pres. Richard Nixon's nominee for treasurer of the United States. Some 420,000 illegal immigrants were apprehended in fiscal 1971, a substantial increase over earlier years.

The House of Representatives Judiciary Subcommittee on Immigration held hearings on the problem. It found that, in addition to seeking out the traditional sources of agricultural employment, illegal aliens were congregating in most major urban areas. These persons were entering the U.S. through a variety of means. Some merely crossed the Mexican-American border. Others traveled first to Puerto Rico, where they acquired Puerto Rican identification documents. Some residents of the Caribbean and other parts of the hemisphere went directly to the U.S. Virgin Islands or Puerto Rico, where wage rates were

higher than in their homelands. In addition, some simply did not return home from a visit or vacation or following completion of their studies. As a result of these disclosures, the subcommittee considered legislation making willful employment of illegal aliens a criminal offense. On October 14 a House committee approved a provision prohibiting employment of illegal aliens. Similar prohibitions had been proposed unsuccessfully in the California legislature. (D. Fo.)

See also Refugees.

Mining

Economic and political uncertainties that confronted the mineral industries in 1970 worsened in 1971. A decline in aerospace and military expenditures reduced the demand for metals in particular. Despite general inflation, prices weakened for many minerals and metals, and corporate profits declined. The market for energy minerals continued strong, however, though the outlook there was clouded by debate over environmental issues.

The minerals and metals market in 1971 was irregular and unstable. U.S. Pres. Richard Nixon's new economic policy, announced in August and extended in November, was a stabilizing influence, partly because it gave a temporary halt to speculation and had a generally sobering effect on commerce. While the initial reaction was to defer business decisions, the plan enhanced the long-term confidence that was essential to mineral resource development decisions. Nevertheless, many mineral prices were still at depressed levels late in the year, though hopes of higher demand and prices rose because of expected manufacturing growth in 1972. The favourable impact of the new economic policies on residential construction and automobile manufacturing particularly strengthened the mineral market prospects, both for metals and for nonmetallic construction materials.

A labour strike in the U.S. copper industry resulted in a loss of about 250,000 tons of copper supply, as well as by-product gold, silver, and molybdenum. There was little commercial disruption, however, because of the oversupply of copper. A coal miners' walkout on October 1 raised the possibility of an energy shortage, but there were large industry stocks on hand and the strike was settled before any shortages developed.

Uranium exploration was a notable exception to the

decline in general mining activity. Fossil fuels were affected by rising costs and growing environmental concern. Thus, expectations were revived for a rapid growth of generating power by nuclear energy, supplied at its outset by uranium.

Gold and silver continued to make international news headlines because of their irregular market behaviour. Gold lost a bit more of its once preeminent position as the linchpin of the international monetary system when President Nixon first suspended the convertibility of dollars into gold and then, as part of the international monetary agreement of December, devalued the dollar by raising the price of monetary gold from $35 an ounce to $38 without restoring convertibility. It seemed likely that, whatever monetary arrangements emerged to succeed the Bretton Woods agreement of 1944, they would be less dependent on gold. (*See* PAYMENTS AND RESERVES, INTERNATIONAL.) As a result of the uncertain monetary situation, the world price of gold fluctuated widely, primarily reflecting speculative trading. World demand for industrial use, including jewelry, was strong, however, and helped to sustain the price level.

The long-awaited bull market in silver again failed to develop, and instead of testing the $3 per ounce price expected by many the price dropped in September to a low of about $1.31. Thereafter, the market fluctuated in a narrow range, closing for the year at $1.38.

Markets for other metals also confounded analysts. There were sharp declines in the prices of cadmium, mercury, antimony, and platinum. Aluminum sold under its quoted price throughout the year, and while copper, lead, and zinc markets held relatively steady they were without any upward strength. Both copper and lead were in potential oversupply because of large world production capacity, but political impediments in the less developed countries held copper supply down and lead producers used restraint in bringing new capacity to production. The low lead price also resulted in reduced production or shutdowns at some mines. U.S. zinc output was curtailed by the closing of three smelters and an electrolytic refinery, and by the combined effect of stringent air pollution requirements and economic difficulties. About 250,000 tons per year of capacity was lost.

Industry Developments. The decade-long intensive search for minerals and metals slowed perceptibly in 1971. Knowledge gained during the 1960s had revealed mineral resources adequate to meet the foreseeable demand for the short-term commercial future, until about 1985. Thus, in 1971 industry was faced with the difficult evaluation of many mineral resource exploitation opportunities. Political, technological, economic, and geologic factors had to be assessed and compared in order to assign corporate priorities for capital investments. An added dimension was introduced late in the 1960s when environmental and ecological factors gained in significance.

There was a sharp drop in exploration for new ore deposits in Canada, but activity on committed mining projects continued at a high level. In British Columbia and the Yukon alone approximately $500 million in capital expenditures were planned in order to almost double ore output to 270,000 tons per day. In Quebec plans were made to triple ore output at the Gaspé Copper Mines, Ltd. Additional smelting capacity using newly developed technology was to be added at Noranda. The two major Canadian nickel producers, International Nickel Co. of Canada, Ltd.

(Inco) and Falconbridge Nickel Mines, Ltd., were developing new capacity, but slowed their expansion plans when the world nickel shortage was overcome and a surplus accompanied by price weakness seemed inevitable. There was renewed interest in uranium in Canada in 1971, in anticipation of rising requirements for nuclear energy. A proposal was made to build a $1 billion uranium enrichment plant in Labrador. Low-cost hydroelectric power and abundant cooling water favoured a site on the Churchill River.

Mexico became the leading world fluorspar producer. In 1971 plans were made to build four processing plants to convert the fluorspar to hydrofluoric acid and other fluorine chemicals, largely for export to the U.S.

Southeast Asia and Australia were the scenes of major mining developments, but for the most part these were continuing projects based on earlier discoveries. The nickel search by Inco on Sulawesi (Celebes) Island in Indonesia disclosed large commercially attractive deposits. A $200 million project to produce 50,000 tons of nickel per year was contemplated. Development of the Ertsberg copper mine in Indonesia moved ahead. Facilities were being built at the Bougainville copper-gold project to mine on an open-pit basis the billion-ton deposit at a rate of 90,000 tons per day starting in 1972. In Australia further delineation of nickel sulfide ores and the discovery of major high-grade uranium deposits highlighted 1971. Development of iron, aluminum, base metal, coal, and manganese deposits gave promise of increasing Australian mineral output by 50% by 1976.

Continuing nationalization actions, primarily affecting copper mines in Chile and Peru, dominated the South American news in 1971. On the other side of the continent, in Brazil, more favourable government policies sparked a mining boom and attracted capital from major industrial countries. New nickel mine facilities were being installed in the Dominican Republic and Guatemala. Exploration for copper and nickel was pursued throughout Central America and the Caribbean. The development of copper mines in Puerto Rico was delayed by environmental disputes. A world surplus of aluminum and bauxite adversely affected the huge Caribbean bauxite operations.

The diverse mineral industries in Africa had less than normal change. Expansion plans for platinum in South Africa and phosphate rock in the north were deferred. The relatively new Sherbro Minerals Ltd. rutile dredge operation in Sierra Leone was closed, as was offshore dredging for diamonds in South West Africa. In Zambia a cleanup of the 1970 cave-in at the Mufulira mine was still under way and full production was not expected to be restored until 1972. Zambia completed negotiations with Roan Consolidated Mines to develop the Baluba concession. South African gold output appeared likely to reach a new high, but many observers believed that uncertainty about the monetary role of gold might soon lead to a leveling off or decline.

The soft market for minerals and metals combined with environmental concern slowed down mineral activity in the U.S. The large copper expansion projects under way in the Southwest continued, but there was a controversy about air pollution from conventional copper smelters. The large lead deposits of southeast Missouri were not mined at capacity, and developed zinc reserves in Tennessee were idle. The Selby, Calif., lead smelter was closed after 85 years of operation. Three zinc smelters and one electrolytic zinc refinery also were closed. In aerospace metals two sponge titanium plants were closed; beryllium demand was down; and aluminum was sold at significant discounts. An oversupply of molybdenum led to the closing of the Questa mine in New Mexico in July.

The Soviet Union continued its intensive state-operated exploration program for minerals. It appeared that mineral production was rising steadily and that the Soviet Union had achieved a high degree of mineral self-sufficiency. Discovery of huge copper deposits in the Udokan Mountains, Siberia, was noteworthy because the Soviets invited Western European countries to join a multinational consortium to finance the venture. Daily output of 90,000 tons of ore was contemplated.

Technological Developments. The technology of mineral production to supply raw mineral materials at the low constant dollar prices prevailing in 1971 was severely tested. Declining ore grade, new health and safety requirements, rising wages, and added costs to prevent environmental damage combined to force intensive research efforts to maintain profitability. Mining methods, land reclamation, and mineral processing technologies all were given attention. Incremental advances in rock breaking were made chiefly through improved equipment design. Rock drills mounted on jumbos monopolized hard-rock drilling, but continuous miners and large-diameter rotary drill rigs were able to handle increasingly tough and abrasive ground. Research was done on such potential rock-drilling mechanisms as laser beams, water jets, chemical methods, and electronic beams. Kerf cutting machines were used experimentally on hard quartzite in South Africa. None of the advanced research showed promise of early success.

Large-diameter rotary drill technology showed impressive advances. A 16½-ft.-diameter shaft was drilled to a depth of 784 ft. at a New Mexico uranium mine, the largest vertical opening ever drilled in the U.S. At Canadian hard-rock mines it was reported that 200-ft. raises could be bored in two weeks, compared with two months using drilling and blasting.

The most promising ground control technology continued to be rotary drilling to avoid the overbreakage caused by blasting, and improved rock bolt anchorage and placement. Rock bolts anchored with resin were particularly effective in stabilizing openings reliably. Their performance was expected to lead to better design of rock control systems. The control of rock bursts in deep mines was aided by a computerized monitoring system to measure ground stresses. The system used geophones (instruments designed to detect vibrations passing through rocks) connected to a computer to record shifts in stress patterns. High stress areas were relieved by controlled blasting.

Metallurgical research focused a major effort on sulfide mineral treatment to avoid or control sulfur dioxide emissions from smelters. New air pollution requirements could not be met with existing technology. As an immediate response to the problem, Inco built a 1,250-ft. smelter stack at its Copper Cliff, Ont., plant. The $5.5 million chimney thus became the world's tallest structure.

Looking further ahead there were research efforts of three principal types. The most practical short-term approach was the conversion of sulfur oxide stack gases to sulfur, sulfuric acid, or a solid waste sulfate material. While some conversion was technically feasible, it proved unusually difficult to remove the last vestiges of sulfur oxides, particularly when the stack gas fluctuated in its composition. Another approach was to develop hydrometallurgical techniques for copper extraction. Already in use for some types of ores, copper extraction by solution was expected to improve and be more widely applied. The third research alternative was to modify and improve the conventional roast-smelt-refine process. The use of flash smelters and electric furnaces was proposed.

The recent stricter U.S. mine safety laws induced a shift in research efforts to health and safety problems. In 1971 the emphasis was largely on improving the ability to determine and measure health and safety hazards. Considerable research was being planned, however, to attack with greater intensity the principal causes of injuries in mines.   (P. F. Y.)

Production. The worldwide economic slowdown that began in 1970 and continued through 1971 affected the mineral industries first as a reduction in demand for minerals and mineral commodities and second, as would be expected, as weakening prices. Because there is always a time lag before actual mineral production begins to decline, overall world mineral production continued to rise in 1970, the latest year for which reasonably complete data were available. Output of 53 minerals was reported higher by an average of 8.38%, while 17 were lower by an average of 3.82%, compared with 1969. Nevertheless, in most cases the rate of increase was less than the average annual rate of growth observed over most of the preceding decade. Mineral prices were affected in 1970 and began a slide, in many cases from record or near-record highs established in 1969, that continued downward throughout 1971.

On 70 mineral commodities examined, the U.S. led the world in production of 28; the Soviet Union in 15; Australia in 4; Canada, South Africa, and Zaire, formerly Congo (Kinshasa), in 3; Brazil, Japan, Malaysia, and Mexico in 2; and six other countries in one each.

Despite nearly two years of an unfavourable economic climate, the long-term trend in world demand for ever increasing quantities of a growing variety of minerals was clear, and exploration for new deposits therefore continued. More countries were formulating national policies designed to foster domestic mineral development both as a means of earning foreign exchange and as a basis for national economic development.

Canada and Australia were the major sites of new mineral developments in the late 1960s and early

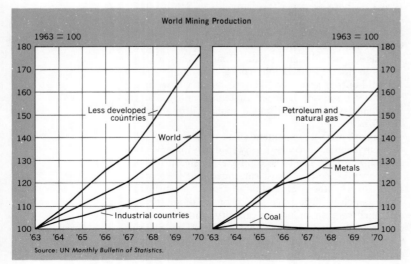

World Mining Production

1963 = 100

1963 = 100

Less developed countries
World
Industrial countries

Petroleum and natural gas
Metals
Coal

Source: UN *Monthly Bulletin of Statistics.*

1970s, but probably the most important impact of the new technology was to be found in Europe. There, new deposits of many minerals were being discovered and developed not only in old mining areas long since virtually abandoned as exhausted, but also in new regions previously believed to be lacking in minerals. Examples ranged from the resurgence of the Cornish tin industry in England to gas in the North Sea, sulfur in Poland, an apparent copper belt running through most of central Europe, bauxite in Greece, and base metals in Ireland.

The revitalization of mining in Europe and the intense concentration of mining activity in Canada and Australia contrasted strongly with the virtual absence of new mineral development and the waning of extant mining activity in a number of places in the world well known for their mineral potential. The primary consideration underlying both those situations was the strong wave of economic nationalism spreading through many less developed nations, which during 1970–71 reached new heights in relation to minerals. Unhappily, the methods chosen by the developing countries to control their mineral industries were too often inappropriate to the international markets in which the majority of the minerals are traded. These developments accounted in large measure for the concentration of mining activity in the more stable nations and for the renewed concern of the industrialized countries with developing their own mineral resources to the fullest extent practicable.

Aluminum. Although world aluminum production (8.7 million metric tons) rose by 7.2% in 1970, consumption in the non-Communist countries increased barely 2%. The trend continued throughout 1971 as major new producing facilities, many years in planning and construction, came into service during a period of declining demand. At 29 cents per pound, aluminum ingot prices reached their highest point in several decades by mid-1970, but almost immediately began to decline to the 22–23 cent level prevalent at the end of 1971. At that time inventory in the non-Communist nations was estimated at about 640,000 tons more than normal. U.S. and Canadian primary producers were operating at about 70–75% of capacity, and cutbacks and closings in aluminum facilities were reported from Europe and Japan. By late 1971 the effects of weakened demand, falling prices, and production cutbacks were beginning to affect the mining of bauxite, the ore from which aluminum is made.

Antimony. World antimony production (65,367 metric tons) increased only 1.4% in 1971 in comparison with the gain of 7% in 1970. The 1969 withdrawal of China from the market as a supplier fostered a strong rise in prices to a record high of $1.78 per pound (domestic U.S.) and $4 per pound (imported) by April 1970. Weakening demand arising from the general world economy and surplus productive capacity brought into being by the abnormally high 1969 prices caused a downward trend to 57–60 cents per pound by the end of 1971. During 1970, antimony output fell or made only slight gains in most producing countries except Thailand where production rose from 750 metric tons in 1969 to 2,357 metric tons in 1970, making that country the world's seventh largest producer.

Asbestos. World asbestos output at 3.5 million metric tons rose 5.1% in 1970 with little change among the relative ranks of the larger producers except for Italy supplanting the U.S. in fifth place. Among the seven largest suppliers in 1970, U.S. output showed the only decline, but a number of large new projects were under development in several different countries and the industry was becoming more internationalized.

Cement. World cement output increased 5.4% in 1970 to 571,373,936 metric tons. There was no change in rank among the leading producers whose respective shares of world output were: Soviet Union 16.7%, U.S. 12.1%, Japan 10%, and West Germany 6.7%. The domestic U.S. industry continued to suffer from the overcapacity created in the late 1950s, although the situation was improving. Prices were recovering from the disastrous levels of the early 1960s, and plant utilization was about 80% of capacity, highest in a decade or more. Capacity itself had remained more or less stable since about 1967.

Chromium. At 5,921,100 metric tons, world chromite production in 1970 was 10.7% above that of the previous year. The continuing UN boycott of Rhodesian chromite sustained the artificial shortage of metallurgical chromite and permitted prices for Turkish, Soviet, and South African chromite to reach very high levels. At the end of 1971, they stood at

$38–$40 per ton for South African, $58 per ton for Turkish, and $58–$63 per ton or $62–$67 per ton for varying grades of the Soviet material. As a result of the Rhodesian boycott, the U.S. became largely dependent upon the Soviet Union for supplies of metallurgical-grade chromite, a situation that late in 1971 led the U.S. Congress to initiate legislation permitting resumption of purchases from Rhodesia despite the boycott.

Cobalt. World mine production of cobalt (23,610 metric tons) increased 20.1% in 1970, but demand began to weaken early in the year, particularly in contrast to the abnormally high demand of 1969 for cobalt as a substitute for nickel. Demand continued weak through 1971, largely because of the lowered consumption of steel, but prices remained relatively steady, possibly a result of apprehension concerning continued availability of supplies, a significant portion of which originated from politically unstable areas (about 65% from Zaire and 11% from Zambia).

Copper. World mine and smelter output of copper rose 4% and 3.9%, respectively, in 1970 to 5.8 and 6.2 million metric tons. Like the aluminum industry, however, copper producers were faced with surplus productive mine capacity in 1970 and 1971 as a number of large new projects, under development for several years, began to come into service at a time when demand was declining. Prices declined from a mid-1970 high of 60 cents or more per pound to about 48–50 cents per pound by the end of 1971. A copper strike in the U.S. mines, which began at the end of June and was settled on a piecemeal basis until fall 1971, helped reduce output. Likewise, the inability of expropriated and nationalized Chilean mines to fulfill sales contracts, strikes in Peru, and continued reduced production from Zambia arising from the 1970 cave-in at the large Mufulira mine helped reduce 1971 output, thereby lessening the potential surplus. As noted above, antipollution legislation also had considerable impact upon copper smelters and refineries in several countries, causing cutbacks in production and outright closings.

Diamonds. Total world diamond production reached 42.4 million carats in 1970, an increase of 3.7% over the previous year. The rise was due to gem diamonds, up 16.5% to 13.7 million carats. Industrial diamond output declined for the third consecutive year to 28.6 million carats, 1.5% below 1969 levels. Industrial diamond output was affected by weak prices, lagging demand, ready availability of synthetic stones, and illicit mining activity which continued to seriously curtail production from Bakwanga in Zaire, the world's largest diamond mine. The generally sluggish world economy of 1970–71 reduced demand for both types of stone, and the Central Selling Organization, which accounted for about 80% of world diamond sales, retained a large proportion of the stones produced in those years. In Botswana during 1971, De Beers Consolidated Mines Limited brought the new Orapa mine, discovered in 1967 after 12 years of exploration, into production at a rated capacity of 2 million carats per year.

Gold. World gold output rose 1.8% in 1970 to 47.4 million troy ounces. There were no changes in the relative ranking of major producers: South Africa 67.9%, Soviet Union 13.7%, Canada 4.9%, and U.S. 3.7%. Throughout 1970 the price remained close to the $35 per troy ounce monetary level save for a brief lift to about $39 in October. In 1971, however, monetary speculation pushed the price up to about $41 per troy ounce by May, its highest level since August 1969, and the imposition of wage/price controls in the U.S. lifted it still further to more than $43 per troy ounce. The price remained high throughout the remainder of the year. During September in South Africa the rich No. 4 shaft area of the West Driefontein Mine, which had undergone disastrous flooding in October 1968, was brought into condition that permitted the work of dewatering and repair to begin, leading to resumed production by April 1972.

Iron. In 1970 world output of iron ore (766.4 million metric tons) increased 6.7%, while pig iron (434.7 million metric tons) rose 4.9% and steel (593.7 million metric tons) 3.5%. The extraordinary iron-ore developments in Australia continued, encouraged by further long-term contractual agreements with Japanese steel producers. Announcements of large new iron-ore mining projects were made from several parts of the world. Supply and demand for iron were more or less in balance for the first time in nearly a decade, and prices for ore and pellets strengthened somewhat. The general decline in the world economy that began in 1970, however, together with the protracted General Motors Corp. strike in the U.S., began to affect the demand for steel. As a result, steel output in the U.S. fell almost 6% in 1970, and continuing economic stagnation caused steel production to decline throughout the world in 1971. During 1970 there was no change in rank among the leading iron-ore producers except that Australia rose from sixth to fourth place.

Lead. World lead mine production in 1970 rose 5.1% to 3.4 million metric tons but smelter output, at 3.3 million metric tons, increased only 2%. Since secondary lead output also rose, it was not surprising in view of the slowing of world economic activity beginning in the latter half of 1970 and extending into 1971 that a surplus developed. Lead prices, reasonably strong at 16.5 cents per pound through the first half of 1970, began to weaken in response to the general economic situation to 13.5 cents by the end of the year. Prices increased somewhat in 1971 to 14 cents, but uncertainty struck the market in June when U.S. producers split at 14 and 14.5 cents per pound, a condition that continued throughout the year; the London Metal Exchange price fell to below £100 per metric ton in the latter part of the year, its lowest level since 1968.

Manganese. World production of manganese during 1960 increased 6.2%, reaching 18.5 million metric tons. The condition of overcapacity that had been plaguing the industry for several years continued into 1970 despite a slight increase in prices toward the end of the year (caused by increased transportation costs rather than better returns to producers). There were no changes in relative position among the leading producing countries. The decline in general economic activity that began in 1970 and continued through 1971 was reflected in the steel industry and consequently in the demand for manganese. Prices declined slightly in 1971.

Mercury. World mercury output registered a 1.9% decline in 1971 to about 285,000 flasks, of which the Soviet Union (16.9%) was the leading producer followed by Spain (16.8%), Italy (15.6%), and Mexico (10.6%). Demand for mercury fell 20% or more in the U.S., partially as a result of the general business decline but more importantly as a consequence of the antipollution movement. Worldwide, the situation appeared to be one of some change in the areas of production as old mines in Spain and Italy declined and newer properties such as the Pinchi Mine in Canada were developed. Mercury prices fell steadily from $490 per flask in January 1970 to about $260–$270 per flask at the end of 1971. A number of U.S. producers closed, and even large new mines such as Pinchi were cutting back output in 1971.

Molybdenum. World molybdenum output rose to 82,695 metric tons in 1970, a 12.6% increase with no change in the relative rank of major producing countries. The economic downturn that began in 1970 reduced steel consumption and, therefore, the demand for molybdenum, something of a relief after the tight supply situation that had prevailed. Prices remained virtually unaffected throughout the year. However, continued decline in demand during 1971 led to considerable curtailment of output.

Nickel. World output of nickel, 620,000 metric tons, increased 28.7% in 1970. Canada (44.6%), the Soviet Union (17.7%), New Caledonia (17%), and Cuba (5.7%) maintained their respective positions as the four largest producers, followed by two newcomers, Australia and Indonesia. During 1970, nickel production rebounded from the 1969 Canadian strike that had resulted in a shortage that pushed dealer prices to over $7 per pound. Supply and demand were more or less balanced in 1970 despite an estimated 13% gain in consumption, and producer prices were stabilized at $1.27 per pound most of the year. Toward the end of 1970, however, the first effects of economic weakness, especially lessened demand from the steel industry, were felt. U.S. demand was estimated to have dropped 15% during the first five months of 1971, and the oversupply position that quickly developed was exacerbated by the coming into production of a number of large new mines in several countries. As a result, although the producers' price was maintained at $1.33 per pound and the nominal dealer price fell just below it to $1.30, by the end of the year nearly 25% of Inco's Canadian productive facilities were closed and placed on standby while similar cutbacks were taking place in other parts of the world.

Phosphate. World production of phosphate rock increased 4.2% to 85.1 million metric tons in 1970, largely due to increased Moroccan output. The general condition of overcapacity and weak demand, which had been prevalent for several years, continued throughout 1970 and 1971. Prices were weak and a number of producers reduced their output. U.S. exports of phosphate continued to decline, while those from Morocco and Mexico, a newcomer to the industry, began to increase.

Platinum Group Metals. Output of the platinum group metals increased 22.9% to 4.2 million troy ounces in 1970 as a result of major expansion programs undertaken by producers in response to several previous years of shortages. The sluggish world economy could not absorb the new output, however, and prices began to weaken, dealer prices falling from $177–$179 per troy ounce at the beginning of 1970 to $122–$125 at the year's end. In early 1971, the producer price, $130–$135 per troy ounce through most of 1969 and all of 1970, was lowered to $120–$125 and the dealer price to about $5–$10 less than that by the end of the year. Rustenberg, the largest producer, reported 1971 production cutbacks of 50% and other producers also reduced output.

Potash. Despite a continuing oversupply, world potash production rose 8.7% in 1970 to 18.5 million metric tons. In January 1970, the Saskatchewan provincial government imposed production controls upon producers which, by the year's end, held output to about 45% of capacity; the province also imposed price controls in June 1970. The controls continued through 1971, resulting in some firming of prices. Meanwhile, the centre of world potash production appeared to be shifting from Canada (16.7% of world total in 1970) to Europe, as new or enlarged facilities were brought into service in the U.K. and West Germany.

Silver. At 304.5 million troy ounces, world silver production in 1970 was 4.1% greater than in 1969. Annual consumption continued to outstrip mine production, by about 120 million troy ounces in 1970. Prices were somewhat erratic during 1970, falling from their first quarter high of about $1.93 per troy ounce to $1.57 in May but rising again later in the year, in anticipation of the termination of U.S. Treasury sales, to hover above the $1.70–$1.80 mark. The price began to fall at the year's end and continued downward to a 1971 year-end figure of $1.38 per troy ounce.

Sulfur. World sulfur output, 22.1 million metric tons in 1970, was 4.7% higher than in 1969. Prices continued very low throughout 1970 and 1971 as surplus capacity and weak demand continued to rack the industry. Effective control of international sulfur prices passed from the U.S. Gulf Coast Frasch producers to the Canadian recovered-sulfur producers, who in 1970–71 were offering elemental sulfur at $8–$9 per long ton f.o.b. plant in contrast to U.S. list prices of $35–$40 f.o.b. Gulf ports. A number of U.S. and Mexican sulfur mines closed during the period, and the Alberta provincial government announced its intention of instituting production and price controls on sulfur similar to those on potash in Saskatchewan. The industry was further disturbed by the potentially very large quantities of sulfur that might be dumped into the market as a result of antipollution controls.

Tin. World production of mine tin rose 1.4% to 227,000 long tons in 1970, while smelter output declined 1% to 221,000 long tons. A weakening economy and major gains in the canning industry by tin-free steel (TFS) depressed 1970 demand for tin. Prices were extremely erratic, but their overall trend for the year was down. These conditions essentially continued through 1971.

Titanium. Aggregate output of titanium minerals, ilmenite and rutile, increased 10.6% in 1970 to about 3,990,000 metric tons; ilmenite was up 11.3% to 3.6 million metric tons, and rutile increased 5.3% to 400,000 metric tons. Australia remained the largest producer of both minerals, providing 31.1% of the world's ilmenite and 88.2% of the rutile. Demand for titanium weakened along with the general economic slowdown of 1970 and 1971, but severe aerospace program reductions in the U.S. and elsewhere, particularly termination of the U.S. supersonic transport program, caused prices to fall and a number of titanium plants to close.

Tungsten. World output of tungsten rose 4.6% to 1.2 million metric tons in 1970. From a high of about $75–$76 per short-ton unit in early 1970, tungsten prices declined, erratically, to about $55 toward the end of the year and, continuing the slide, to $40 or less by late in 1971. The fall in price was a reflection of general economic conditions. In the U.S., the Tungsten Queen Mine near Henderson, N.C., was closed and placed on standby, having been reopened barely one year after a five-year closure.

Uranium. Production of uranium oxide in the non-Communist world in 1970 increased 4.1% to 21,770 metric tons. Demand continued uncertain and there was a mild condition of oversupply through 1970–71, due in considerable part to slowdowns in the expected rate of nuclear power plant development. These delays arose from opposition by environmentalists and others to building nuclear power plants and also from technical construction difficulties. Several spectacular new discoveries of uranium ore deposits were made in Australia; one of the discoveries was believed to contain 50,000 tons of uranium oxide at an incredible grade of 25% U_3O_8, in contrast to the more usual grade of 0.3–0.5%.

Zinc. World mine output of zinc rose 2.9% to 5.5 million metric tons, while smelter production declined 1.1% to 4.9 million tons. Depressed U.S. demand, followed later in 1970 by similar effects in Europe, caused first U.S. and then other smelters to cut back production. Prices declined somewhat but held reasonably steady through 1970 and rose slowly by 2 cents per pound during 1971. Environmentalist pressures, together with a continuing situation of oversupply, caused at least four U.S. smelters to close during 1971.   (F. H. Sk.)

See also Fuel and Power; Geology; Industrial Review; Metallurgy.

Westinghouse technicians test new equipment 740 ft. below ground level in Gary, W.Va. The new communications system, utilizing radio and seismic sensors, was devised to enable rescuers on the surface to pinpoint the location of trapped miners.

Monaco

A constitutional monarchy on the northern Mediterranean coast, Monaco is bounded on all land sides by the French *département* of Alpes-Maritimes. Area: 0.65 sq.mi. (1.68 sq.km.). Pop. (1971 est.): 24,200. Language: French. Religion: Roman Catholic. Prince, Rainier III; minister of state in 1971, François-Didier Gregh.

The gross national product (GNP) of Monaco remained heavily dependent on tourism. According to the most recent estimates, tourism directly contributed 55% of the GNP while small, tourist-oriented industries added between 25 and 30%. An additional 4% stemmed from the Monte Carlo Casino.

The principality continued to develop cultural and recreational programs to attract additional foreign tourists. On May 1–2, 1971, Princess Grace, the former movie star Grace Kelly, sponsored the fourth International Flower Show of Monaco. The International Festival of the Arts, held from July 2 through September 29, featured the London Festival Ballet, the Netherlands Dance Theatre, La Comédie Française, and the Vienna Symphony.

After vacationing in New Hampshire for a month during the summer, Prince Rainier and Princess Grace returned to the United States in mid-September to attend the Texas "Fête des Fleurs." The central theme of the fair, sponsored by the Nieman-Marcus department store, was based upon the prince's cactus garden. In October the royal couple flew to Teheran to attend the 2,500th anniversary celebrations of the founding of the Persian monarchy.   (R. D. Ho.)

MONACO

Education. (1967–68) Primary, pupils 1,162, teachers 51; secondary, pupils 1,424, teachers 86; vocational, pupils 204, teachers 7.

Finance. Monetary unit: French franc, with a par value of Fr. 5.55 to U.S. $1 (Fr. 13.13 = £1 sterling) and free rates (Oct. 11, 1971) for the "commercial" franc of Fr. 5.53 to U.S. $1 (Fr. 13.78 = £1 sterling) and for the "financial" franc of Fr. 5.20 to U.S. $1 (Fr. 13 = £1 sterling). Budget (1969 est.): revenue Fr. 161,804,000; expenditure Fr. 160,664,000. Tourism: visitors (1969) 85,600; gross receipts (1966) U.S. $6.1 million.

Money and Banking

In 1971 the long-persisting disequilibrium in the international monetary system, focusing on the relation between gold and the dollar, reached a dramatic turning point. Early in the year divergent monetary conditions led to heavy flows of funds, partly through the Eurocurrency markets, from the U.S. and into Western Europe, particularly West Germany. These movements reached crisis proportions in early May, whereupon the mark was set free to float upward accompanied by the Dutch guilder, and the Swiss franc and Austrian schilling were revalued outright by 7.07 and 5.05%, respectively.

A second massive capital flow gathered force in early August, this time reflecting a more general flight from the dollar itself. Rejecting a devaluation in terms of gold, U.S. authorities suspended the dollar's convertibility into gold and other reserve currencies,

imposed a 10% surcharge on imports, and took additional measures to restore external and domestic equilibrium. The other principal countries, no longer feeling committed to support the dollar, allowed their exchange rates to float upward, though to an extent this was limited by various forms of intervention. Thus, the formal severance of the gold-dollar link, long foreshadowed by chronic U.S. payments deficits, marked a major breakdown, if not the end, of the Bretton Woods "par value" system as conceived in 1944.

Monetary authorities, besides having to cope with external disturbances, were faced in 1971 with a sharpening dilemma between sluggish or declining production and continuing cost inflation. In the U.S., Canada, the U.K., and Japan, monetary policy was kept relatively easy in order to promote renewed expansion. But, while output was slow to respond and unemployment remained considerable (except in Japan), wages went on rising at nearly the same high rates as before.

In Western Europe most countries were in a phase of incipient economic decline rather than of recovery. Compared with year-earlier levels, industrial output by the early autumn of 1971 was significantly lower in Italy and Sweden, slightly down in West Germany, and about even in Switzerland. The pace of advance continued to be fairly satisfactory in France, Belgium, and the Netherlands, though some signs of a slowing down had become evident. After having in varying degrees resisted the earlier decline in interest rates abroad, monetary authorities turned during 1971 to policies of more active ease.

Caught between market softness and intense wage pressures, the industrial sector in practically all Western countries was faced with a severe profit squeeze. In these circumstances, the U.S. measures of mid-August, together with the exchange-rate adjustments from May onward, subjected the international monetary system to a wrenching shock. Outside the U.S., business expectations were dealt a blow of uncertain proportions, while within the U.S. a newfound confidence quickly waned as efforts to launch an incomes

Country		1969 June	1970 June	1970 Sept	1970 Dec	1971 March	1971 June	1971 Sept
Belgium	A	6.00	7.50	7.50	6.50	6.00	6.00	5.50
	B1	4.28	6.34	5.30	5.55	2.66	2.34	3.88
	C	7.19	7.77	8.01	7.72	7.42	7.35	7.15
France	A	7.00	8.00	7.50	7.00	6.50	6.75	6.75
	B1	9.46	9.35	8.13	7.46	5.77	6.45	5.98
	C	8.01	8.47	8.42	8.12	8.04	8.12	8.13
Germany, West	A	5.00	7.50	7.00	6.00	6.00	5.00	5.00
	B2	4.75	7.00	6.75	5.75	5.75	4.25	4.25
	C	6.70	8.70	8.50	8.20	7.90	8.20	8.10
Italy	A	3.50	5.50	5.50	5.50	5.00	5.00	5.00
	B	4.44	6.95	6.95	6.95	5.82	5.54	5.70
	C	5.65	7.95	8.10	7.94	6.95	7.11	7.14
Netherlands	A	5.50	6.00	6.00	6.00	6.00	5.50	5.00
	B2	5.66	6.18	6.18	6.08	4.60	4.51	4.49
	C	7.53	8.52	8.08	7.68	7.29	7.22	7.58
Switzerland	A	3.00	3.75	3.75	3.75	3.75	3.75	3.75
	B1	3.25	2.38	2.00	4.25	2.00	1.88	0.50
	C	4.69	5.87	5.74	5.70	5.44	5.38	5.10
United Kingdom	A	8.00	7.00	7.00	7.00	7.00	6.00	5.00
	B2	7.90	6.87	6.82	6.82	6.66	5.60	4.83
	C	9.38	9.40	9.30	9.70	9.00	9.30	8.49
United States	A	6.00	6.00	6.00	5.50	4.75	4.75	5.00
	B2	6.49	6.74	6.24	4.86	3.32	4.70	4.67
	C	6.06	6.99	6.63	6.00	5.71	5.94	5.56
Canada	A	7.50	7.00	6.50	6.00	5.25	5.25	5.25
	B2	7.03	5.90	5.44	4.47	3.30	3.15	3.93
	C	7.54	8.03	7.88	6.99	6.76	7.30	6.97
Japan	A	5.84	6.25	6.25	6.00	5.75	5.50	5.25
	B1	6.57	8.00	8.25	7.75	7.00	6.25	5.75
	C	8.80	9.38	9.15	9.20	8.42	7.95	7.44

A = Central bank's discount rate.
B = Money-market rate.
B1 = Day-to-day money.
B2 = 90-day Treasury bills; one-year bills in the case of Italy.
C = Long-term government bond yield.

Missiles:
see Defense

Molecular Biology:
see Life Sciences

policy, with effective controls over prices and wages, dragged on indecisively.

Representatives of the Group of Ten countries and Switzerland, meeting in Washington, acted on Dec. 18, 1971, to resolve the crisis. The United States agreed to devalue the dollar relative to gold by 7.89%, while the other countries undertook either to revalue or to keep at or near to their existing gold parities. In addition, the U.S. import surcharge was to be lifted immediately, and the permissible margin of exchange fluctuation on either side of the new parities, or so-called central rates, was for the time being to be increased from 1 to $2\frac{1}{4}$%. Significantly, the United States made no commitment with regard to the restoration of the dollar's convertibility into gold.

The growth of money and quasi-money (mainly time and savings deposits) accelerated in most countries, in some cases quite sharply. Several factors contributed to this development, though in varying degrees in different countries. First, domestic credit policies, and often public-sector financing requirements, were generally more expansive than in 1970. Second, a complex of uncertainties led business firms and consumers to build up their liquidity positions. Third, large inflows of funds, particularly into West Germany, Japan, the Netherlands, Switzerland, and the U.K., added to domestic liquidity creation.

The easing of monetary conditions was evidenced clearly in the behaviour of short-term interest rates. Among the Organization for Economic Cooperation and Development (OECD) countries, there were 35 reductions—and only 4 increases—in official discount rates in the 12 months to October 1971, against 10 reductions and 7 increases in the previous year. Long-term bond yields were slow to come down, however, because inflationary expectations continued to influence the attitudes of borrowers and lenders alike. Both short- and long-term rates registered fairly sharp declines in late 1970 and early 1971, though more in North America than elsewhere. From the early spring up to August, market rates tended to stiffen, but a general decline was resumed following the introduction of the U.S. program.

Eurocurrency and Eurobond Markets. The steep slide in Eurodollar rates that had characterized 1970 continued in early 1971. In March the three-month deposit rate reached a low of 5%—a full six percentage points below its late-1969 peak. Nonetheless, the market continued to expand. There was further demand from nonbank firms, particularly in West Germany, while large repayments by U.S. banks to their branches abroad were partly offset by U.S. official borrowing.

Currency uncertainties took hold of the market from April onward. The demand for Eurodollar funds for conversion into other currencies—notably marks, Swiss francs, and yen—pushed rates up again to peaks of over 8% in early June and 10% around mid-August. At the height of the crisis, call-money rates at times exceeded 50%. Although uncertainties persisted, a decline in U.S. interest rates, together with the defensive measures taken elsewhere against capital inflows, contributed to an easing of quotations in September and October, with the three-month rate falling back to 6%.

On the Eurobond market, new-issues activity strengthened further in late 1970 and early 1971 as monetary conditions eased. Subsequently, it fell back, owing to exchange disturbances and rising interest rates, but by the autumn it showed signs of renewed

recovery. In the period January–November "international" (Eurobond) issues with maturities of five years or more, after falling from $2.9 billion in 1969 to $2.5 billion in 1970, went up in 1971 to $3.4 billion.

International issues denominated in U.S. dollars had regained favour by the first quarter of 1971, when they accounted for 68% of the total, but by the third quarter this proportion was down to 44%. Investor interest had turned increasingly to issues denominated in strong currencies and in units of account or European monetary units. After declining from mid-1970, yields on straight dollar bonds rose from a level of $8\frac{1}{4}$% in January 1971 to $9\frac{1}{2}$% in September, while those on bonds denominated in marks fluctuated narrowly around 8%.

United States. By late 1970 a policy of monetary ease had been in effect for the better part of a year. To help stimulate economic recovery, the Federal Reserve authorities sought to keep the money supply growing at an annual rate of close to 6%. In the autumn, however, a strike at General Motors, with its widespread repercussions, had frustrated these efforts. For this reason the authorities, continuing their emphasis on the "monetary aggregates," tried to put monetary expansion back on course. Reserve funds were supplied generously through open-market operations, and the official discount rate was reduced in five stages from 6 to $4\frac{3}{4}$% between November and February. By March 1971 the rate on federal funds had declined to 3.71%, while the member banks' net borrowed reserves had fallen to almost nil.

In these circumstances, credit in all forms expanded vigorously from the end of 1970 to September 1971. The growth of total net credit, which on an adjusted annual basis had already risen from $93 billion in the first half of 1970 to $103 billion in the second half, leaped to $150 billion in the first nine months of 1971. Borrowing by the federal government, related to deficit-financing requirements, went up from an annual rate of $16 billion in July–December 1970 to one of $22 billion in January–September 1971. Funds raised by all other sectors, earlier slow to increase, advanced sharply from $87 billion to $128 billion. The demand for funds concentrated mainly on the capital market, where there were large issues of corporate and state and local government securities and of mortgages. The growth of bank loans and consumer credit, though considerable, was not high by past standards.

On the lending side, the first three quarters of 1971 saw a continued large volume of lending by the banking system and a further acceleration in credit granting by other financial institutions, particularly the savings institutions. Another notable feature was the large volume of "lending" by foreigners ($32 billion at an annual rate), representing mainly increased holdings of U.S. securities by foreign central banks.

The strength of long-term credit demand derived largely from the need to consolidate short-term debt and rebuild liquidity. In the first half of 1971 the monetary aggregates expanded at an unusually high rate. The money supply rose at an annual rate of nearly 10%, while money plus time deposits grew at a rate of more than 15%. Taking these developments to reflect persisting inflationary expectations, the authorities aimed to moderate monetary expansion in the late spring and summer. Market interest rates tightened further, and in mid-July the discount rate was raised to 5%. By August the banks' net borrowed reserves were over $600 million, while the federal funds rate reached an average of 5.57%.

Democrat John B. Connally, secretary of the treasury, was chief economic spokesman for the Nixon administration during the economic stabilization program introduced in August 1971.

WIDE WORLD

The atmosphere was quickly transformed following the president's announcement in mid-August of a broad stabilization program. Initially, this had a euphoric effect on the domestic outlook, but optimism gradually eroded as new uncertainties multiplied at home and abroad. On the other hand, the new policy did contribute toward reducing inflationary psychology. The money supply grew much more slowly in July and August and, paralleling an easing of interest rates, actually declined in the six weeks to mid-October. In these circumstances, with external constraints now less severe and the domestic economy still sluggish, monetary policy resumed a stance of relative ease. The money supply began to expand again, interest rates moved lower, and in November and December the discount rate was reduced in two stages to $4\frac{1}{2}\%$. The prime lending rate came down to $5\frac{1}{4}\%$; meanwhile, some banks had introduced a flexible prime rate linked to that on prime commercial paper.

The year was featured by a vigorous increase in the availability of funds for building purposes. In January–September mortgages rose at an annual rate of $43 billion, compared with only $22 billion in the same period of 1970, and new housing lent considerable support to the economy. Consumption also benefited from easier credit terms. Another sustaining element was the federal government's large budget deficit, which rose to an annual rate of over $20 billion.

United Kingdom. The balance of payments showed renewed signs of strength from late 1970 onward, and the current-account surplus rose in 1971 to an unprecedented level of around £900 million. This achievement, however, was largely ascribable to domestic slack and unemployment, which was expected to exceed one million workers in the winter of 1971–72. In 1970 business firms had been caught in a severe liquidity squeeze, owing both to a two-year stint of tight fiscal and monetary policies and to particularly large wage increases. With personal savings high, consumption grew slowly over most of 1971 and industrial investment remained in a slump.

The worst of the liquidity squeeze was over by late 1970. The money supply increased over the financial year 1970–71 (April–March) by £2,045 million or nearly 13% following a rise of only 2% the year before. The acceleration was attributable partly to the larger external surplus and partly to a turnaround in "domestic credit expansion" via the banking system.

Largely because of economic slack, the public sector shifted from a surplus of £540 million in 1969–70 to a borrowing requirement of £835 million in 1970–71. The monetary effect of this change was kept in check, however, by substantial sales of government debt to the nonbank private sector, particularly in early 1971 as interest rates fell. During 1970–71 the expansion of bank lending in sterling to the private sector was subject to a general guideline of 5%. In practice, bank lending to companies, including exempted forms of credit and approved borrowing in foreign currencies for domestic use, rose by nearly 14%. Altogether, bank lending to the private sector went up by £1,070 million, compared with a rise of £575 million the previous year. With effect from January 1971, exchange control approval was given only for credits with terms of five years or more. Partly for external reasons, the bank rate was lowered to 6% on April 1.

In October 1970 significant fiscal changes had been made, but the aim was to encourage private initiative rather than aggregate demand. The new budget of April 1971 was clearly expansionary, however, providing for higher income-tax allowances, a further cut in the corporate tax, and a halving of the selective employment tax. Simultaneously, bank credit guidelines were relaxed so as to permit sterling advances to increase for the time being by $2\frac{1}{2}\%$ a quarter.

In May the authorities outlined proposals for new monetary control techniques that would entail a shift away from quantitative credit ceilings in favour of interest rates as a means of allocating bank credit. The cash and liquidity ratios applying to the London clearing and Scottish banks were to be replaced by a single reserve ratio valid for the banking system as a whole. In addition, special deposits could be called, and debt-management policy would be used to influence the structure of interest rates. The new reserve ratio would be fixed in relation to sterling deposits and other "eligible" liabilities. Furthermore, the London clearing banks were to abandon their collective agreements concerning interest rates other than those on savings deposits. Finally, but with immediate effect, the Bank of England declared itself no longer obliged to provide support for gilt-edged government securities having a maturity of over one year.

A continuation of weak demand combined with cost inflation prompted a new policy package on July 19. It was preceded by a new initiative on the part of private firms and nationalized industries to keep price increases to within 5% over the coming year. On this basis, the government reduced all categories of purchase tax by 18.2%, removed controls over installment credit terms altogether, and increased depreciation allowances.

Following the U.S. measures in August, sterling was permitted to float upward on a limited scale. On September 2 the bank rate was reduced further on external and domestic grounds to 5%. Subsequently, on September 16, the new credit-control arrangements were introduced along the lines proposed in May, with the uniform reserve ratio being established at $12\frac{1}{2}\%$. Concurrently, outstanding special deposits were repaid and funding arrangements were undertaken to absorb excess liquidity.

In the autumn expenditure on durable consumer goods and housing was fairly strong, but aggregate demand still lacked buoyancy. In particular, industrial investment in fixed capital and inventories remained weak, and companies borrowed relatively little from either banks or the capital market. On the other hand, by the autumn annual gains provided for in newly negotiated wage settlements had dropped to 10% from about 14% a year earlier. It was expected, moreover, that the expansionary measures already taken would soon work themselves through to final demand.

EEC Countries. In West Germany, despite earlier restraint measures, the economy in early 1971 showed renewed buoyancy. On April 1, purely as an attempt to curb capital inflows, the discount rate was reduced from 6 to 5%. Simultaneously, the Bundesbank reduced the banks' rediscount quotas by 10% and made known its intention to step up its open-market operations. However, the effort to keep monetary conditions comparatively tight was undermined by West German business firms' continued heavy borrowing abroad. The policy conflict came to a head in early May, when speculative funds poured in on a huge scale. Rather than impose exchange controls or relax their monetary restraint efforts, the authorities opted in favour of a free upward float for the mark. Altogether, the banks' net foreign exchange purchases in January–May increased their liquidity by over DM. 20 billion, one-quarter of which was absorbed by open-market operations, reserve requirements, and cuts in rediscount quotas.

Soon after the mark began to float, some funds moved out again, thus helping to reduce liquidity. This effect was reinforced by new restrictive policy measures. In mid-May the public-sector authorities decided to cut back their expenditure and to sterilize funds with the central bank. Shortly afterward, the informal capital issues committee called for a temporary halt on all capital issues. In early June the Bundesbank raised the minimum reserve ratios for domestic liabilities by 15% and that for foreign liabilities to twice the new domestic ratios. On the other hand, a refundable 10% surcharge on income and corporate taxes expired at the end of June, but repayment terms were not to be fixed until later.

The upward float of the mark, which after mid-August at times exceeded 10%, proved to be a mixed blessing. On the one hand, official reserves tended to level off, the trade account held up well, and industry started to repay funds taken up from abroad. The money supply, which had risen at an annual rate of 16% in the period October–May, grew at a rate of about 6% in June–September. On the other hand, the export outlook became bleak, the profit squeeze intensified, and investment turned downward. Against this background, an expansionary budget for 1972 was presented in September, and in mid-October the Bundesbank reduced its discount rate to 4½% while lowering reserve requirements against domestic liabilities by 10%.

In France, against the background of an external surplus together with some weakness in domestic demand, interest rates were adapted in late 1970 and early 1971 closely in line with the declines on international markets. From a high of 8% in August 1970, the discount rate was reduced to 6½% by January 1971, and money-market rates were brought down even more. To broaden the scope of monetary policy,

a new type of reserve requirement, applicable to all credits granted to the economy by banks and other financial institutions, was introduced on a limited basis in April.

In May, to counter inflationary influences from abroad, the discount rate was raised to 6¾%, and reserve requirements were changed twice. Two further increases in July and August brought reserve requirements against sight deposits, for example, to 12¼%, compared with 7¼% in early May, and in the meantime the same rate had come to be applied to non-resident banks' franc deposits. The requirement against credits granted was also progressively raised, to 3% by early August. After the U.S. measures, the authorities adopted a two-tier exchange system—the official rate remaining at the old parity—and tightened direct controls against the inflows of funds while easing them in respect of outflows. Through these insulating techniques, France withstood the crisis well. At the end of October, the discount rate was reduced again, to 6½%.

Italy, after experiencing a stagnating trend of production over most of 1970, slipped into recession from early 1971, with industrial output falling by 8% over the first nine months. The root of the difficulty lay largely in a further weakening of business firms' propensity to invest in the face of rising wage costs, persisting labour unrest, and political uncertainties. Monetary policy had become easier from August 1970 onward, and bond yields came down considerably by March 1971, thereafter keeping to about the same level. In May the introduction of a new cartel agreement facilitated a reduction in bank lending rates. Nonetheless, the private sector's demand for credit remained weak, and the banks, after repaying indebtedness to the central bank, began again to invest in securities.

Recessionary influences contributed to a sharp increase in the budget deficit, which was financed largely by the banking system. In July, in order to give the economy a more positive stimulus, new budget measures were introduced, consisting of additional funds for interest subsidies and grants, a "budgetization" of social insurance charges for smaller firms, and an acceleration of tax rebates. Moreover, efforts continued to be aimed at fostering public investment, including public housing. In mid-October the discount rate was reduced, on external and domestic grounds, to 4½%.

In Belgium the economy had to adjust in early 1971 to the value-added tax system introduced at the beginning of the year. In late March, as a safeguard against inflationary strains, it was decided to prolong the existing credit ceiling until September. At the same time, in view of declining interest rates abroad, the discount rate was reduced to 6%, and the banks were asked not to increase their net foreign liability positions. Nevertheless, funds continued to move in, and after the May exchange crisis the authorities acted to separate more strictly their dual exchange markets, official and financial, and to erect new barriers against foreign inflows. Following the August crisis, the commercial franc was floated against all currencies except, by special arrangement, the Dutch guilder.

Meanwhile, a weakening in exports, consumption, and investment had caused output to grow more slowly from the spring of 1971 onward. However, the private sector's demand for bank credit had strengthened, and the external surplus also contributed to

An American youth reads a newspaper outside the American Express office in London in August 1971 for news of the dollar crisis at home and how it would affect his vacation plans.

KEYSTONE

monetary expansion. The government, though having a larger budget deficit, borrowed domestically in excess of its needs and reduced its indebtedness abroad. In the year to August 1971 the money supply expanded by 11½%, against 5% in the previous 12 months. In mid-September, after the franc had floated upward, the National Bank lifted restrictions that recently had been placed on inflows via the banks. One week later, with demand conditions much easier, it reduced its discount rate to 5½% and decided not to extend the credit ceilings further.

In the Netherlands the main preoccupation in 1971 was again the combination of severe inflation, a large current-account deficit, and excessive capital inflows. Though exchange controls limited other movements, large capital inflows entered by way of the securities markets, thus tending to nullify monetary restraint. To discourage these movements, the discount rate was lowered in April, and in May the guilder followed the mark in going on a floating basis. Domestically, trade-union recalcitrance led the government in August to abandon direct controls over wages and prices and to seek voluntary cooperation instead. Labour markets had eased somewhat by then, but wages went on rising rapidly and consumer prices in October were 7½% higher than a year earlier. In September a separate market was established for nonresident transactions in Dutch securities, and the discount rate was reduced further.

Canada. A turnaround in economic activity in late 1970 was given reinforcement by a supplementary budget in December and a further easing of monetary conditions in early 1971. Although the Canadian dollar had been floating since June 1970, the basic surplus was still fairly large in the first half of 1971 and more than offset short-term capital outflows. After strengthening over the winter months, the Canadian dollar weakened for a time in the late spring and again after the August crisis, but by early October it was close to parity with the U.S. dollar.

Over the first nine months of 1971 the money supply grew at an annual rate of nearly 18%, against about 11% in January–September 1970, and was accompanied by a sharp rise in the banks' general loans, mortgages, and government bond holdings. In view of Canada's heavy dependence on trade, the U.S. measures in August gave a severe shock to Canadian business expectations, and by early autumn unemployment had risen to over 7%. This situation prompted new tax and expenditure measures in mid-October designed to raise the budget deficit for 1971–72 to Can$1 billion. Shortly afterward, the discount rate was cut to 4¾%.

Japan. After five years of strong expansion, industrial production leveled off from the late summer of 1970. In consequence, the discount rate was reduced in four steps from 6¼% in October to 5¼% in July 1971. Moreover, the system of target limits for increases in city-bank credit was abolished as from January 1971. These relaxations, together with the continuing large external surplus, contributed to a rapid acceleration in the money supply, which increased in January–September at an annual rate of nearly 32%. In order to reduce the external surplus, the authorities took measures to encourage a shift to yen financing, to eliminate preferential treatment for export-related lending, and to relax exchange controls on outflows of funds. In June an eight-point balance of payments program was outlined but, overwhelmed by huge inflows following the U.S. measures,

the authorities were impelled to let the yen float upward from late August. On the domestic front, stimulatory budget measures were taken in early July and again in October. (W. D. McC.)

See also Cooperatives; Economics; Economy, World; Government Finance; Housing; Investment, International; Merchandising; Payments and Reserves, International; Stock Exchanges.

Mongolia

A people's republic of Asia lying between the U.S.S.R. and China, Mongolia occupies the geographic area known as Outer Mongolia. Area: 604,000 sq.mi. (1,565,000 sq.km.). Pop. (1970 est.): 1,285,000. Cap. and largest city: Ulan Bator (pop., 1969 est., 262,-600). Language: Mongolian. Religion: Lamaistic Buddhism. First secretary of the Mongolian People's Revolutionary (Communist) Party and chairman of the Council of Ministers (premier) in 1971, Yumzhagiyen Tsedenbal; chairman of the Presidium of the Great People's Hural, Zhamsarangibin Sambuu.

The 16th congress of the Mongolian People's Revolutionary Party, held in Ulan Bator, June 7–11, adopted its fifth five-year development plan (1971–75). The main aims were to continue toward reasonable industrialization and to increase livestock to more than 25 million head by 1975, although the total number of cattle, sheep, horses, and camels rarely surpassed 22 million. Tsedenbal told the congress that shortcomings in livestock herding were slowing down industrialization and holding back export earnings. The U.S.S.R. depended on Mongolia for meat imports to eastern Siberia.

In his report Tsedenbal criticized China for its attempts to disrupt the socialist world. He revealed that for the first time since 1943 the Mongolian party lists had been scrutinized and "unworthy" members excluded. By April 1 the party had 58,048 members and candidates. The congress elected a new Central Committee, which reappointed the old seven-member Politburo. In late August, after several years during which Chinese-Mongolian relations had been at a low ebb, Hsu Wen-i, a new Chinese ambassador, presented his credentials to Chairman Sambuu. (K. Sм.)

MONGOLIA

Education. (1968–69) Primary and secondary, pupils 213,590, teachers 7,500; teacher training, pupils 9,-700; higher (including University of Ulan Bator), students 9,000, teaching staff 700.

Finance. Monetary unit: tugrik, with (Sept. 27, 1971) an official exchange rate 4 tugriks to U.S. $1 (9.60 tugriks = £1 sterling) and tourist rate of 6 tugriks to U.S. $1 (14.40 tugriks = £1 sterling). Budget (1970 est.): revenue 1,920,000,000 tugriks; expenditure 1,913,000,000 tugriks.

Foreign Trade. (1962) Imports U.S. $102.6 million; exports U.S. $68.5 million. Import sources (1960): U.S.S.R. 62%; China 23%; Czechoslovakia 5%. Export destinations (1960): U.S.S.R. 75%; Czechoslovakia 8%; China 5%. Main exports (1960): wool 44%; cattle 34%; butter and meat 8%; hides 6%.

Transport and Communications. Roads (1969) c. 75,000 km. (including c. 8,600 km. main roads). Railways (1969) c. 1,462 km. Telephones (Jan. 1970) 17,830. Radio receivers (Dec. 1969) 108,000. Television receivers (Dec. 1969) 7,000.

Agriculture. Production (in 000; metric tons; 1970; 1969 in parentheses): wheat c. 330 (c. 330); barley c. 15 (c. 16); potatoes c. 27 (c. 27). Livestock (in 000; Dec. 1969): cattle c. 2,030; sheep c. 12,800; goats c. 4,270; horses c. 2,250; camels c. 630.

Industry. Production (in 000; metric tons; 1969): coal 80; crude oil 4; electricity (kw-hr.) 388,000.

Mormons:
see Religion

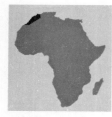

Morocco

A constitutional monarchy of northwestern Africa, on the Atlantic Ocean and the Mediterranean Sea, Morocco is bordered by Algeria and Spanish Sahara. Area: 174,471 sq.mi. (451,880 sq.km.). Pop. (1970 est.): 15,579,000. Cap.: Rabat (pop., 1970, 325,000). Largest city: Casablanca (pop., 1970, 1,395,000). Language: Arabic; Berber. Religion: Muslim. King, Hassan II; prime ministers in 1971, Ahmed Laraki and, from August 6, Muhammad Karim Lamrani.

In 1971 the Moroccan monarchy suffered—but survived—the only serious threat to its existence since full independence in 1956. King Hassan's (see BIOGRAPHY) seemingly assured control of the country was threatened when a group of army generals, using trainee NCOs as their dupes, attempted a coup d'etat on July 10, aimed at eliminating corruption and, it appeared, deposing the king. The prime movers in the attempted coup were of right-wing complexion, although the crowds in Rabat—and, further afield, the Libyan revolutionary regime—quickly welcomed it as a potential move to the left.

The attempted coup was staged during a royal birthday party at the seaside palace of Skhirat. Train-

King Hassan II
during a press conference
in Rabat, July 11, 1971,
comments
on the attempted
military coup that took
place the night before
at his summer palace.

WIDE WORLD

MOROCCO

Education. (1968–69) Primary, pupils 1,124,333, teachers (including preprimary) 32,729; secondary, pupils 271,895, teachers 12,199; vocational, pupils 13,772, teachers 911; teacher training, students 10,-908, teaching staff 512.

Finance. Monetary unit: dirham, with a par value of 5.06 dirhams to U.S. $1 (12.15 dirhams = £1 sterling) and a free rate (Sept. 27, 1971) of 4.96 dirhams to U.S. $1 (12.29 dirhams = £1 sterling). Gold, SDRs, and foreign exchange, central bank: (June 1971) U.S. $180 million; (June 1970) U.S. $131 million. Budget (1971 est.): revenue 3,125,000,000 dirhams; expenditure 3,124,000,000 dirhams. Gross national product: (1969) 16,110,000,000 dirhams; (1968) 15,360,000,000 dirhams. Money supply: (April 1971) 5,625,000,000 dirhams; (April 1970) 5,185,000,000 dirhams. Cost of living (Casablanca; 1963 = 100): (June 1971) 114; (June 1970) 108.

Foreign Trade. (1970) Imports 3,471,000,000 dirhams; exports 2,470,000,000 dirhams. Main import sources: France 31%; U.S. 11%; West Germany 9%; Italy 5%; U.S.S.R. 5%; U.K. 5%. Main export destinations: France 37%; West Germany 9%; Italy 7%; U.K. 6%; Netherlands 5%. Main exports: phosphates 23%; citrus fruit 14%; tomatoes 7%; fish 5%. Tourism (1969): visitors 606,600; gross receipts U.S. $121 million.

Transport and Communications. Roads (1970) 24,775 (including 14 km. expressways). Motor vehicles in use (1970): passenger 220,808; commercial (including buses) 83,449. Railways: (1968) 1,778 km.; traffic (1970) 522 million passenger-km., freight 2,635,000,000 net ton-km. Air traffic (1970): 383.6 million passenger-km.; freight 5,470,000 net ton-km. Shipping (1970): merchant vessels 100 gross tons and over 31; gross tonnage 54,725. Telephones (Dec. 1969) 165,019. Radio receivers (Dec. 1969) 884,000. Television receivers (Dec. 1969) 145,000.

Agriculture. Production (in 000; metric tons; 1970; 1969 in parentheses): wheat c. 1,700 (1,469); barley 2,032 (2,044); corn 456 (414); potatoes c. 300 (300); oranges c. 816 (729); dry peas c. 38 (33); dry broad beans 160 (155); chick-peas c. 59 (73); wine c. 75 (70); olive oil c. 34 (22); figs (1969) c. 65, (1968) c. 65; dates c. 90 (c. 90); tomatoes (1969) c. 250, (1968) 245; fish catch (1969) 226, (1968) 219. Livestock (in 000; 1969–70): cattle c. 3,600; sheep c. 17,000; goats c. 7,850; poultry c. 15,600.

Industry. Production (in 000; metric tons; 1970): coal 433; crude oil 46; cement 1,421; iron ore (55–60% metal content) 872; phosphate rock (1969) 10,-662; manganese ore (metal content; 1969) 69; lead concentrates (metal content) 80; zinc concentrates (metal content; 1969) 32; electricity (excluding most industrial production; kw.-hr.) 1,829,000.

ees from the Ahermoumou military training school fired wildly at the royal guests, killing several ministers, army generals, civilian officials, and one foreign diplomat. Public buildings in Rabat were temporarily occupied, but order soon was restored once King Hassan, briefly detained in a room at the seaside palace, was released and had given full powers to his minister of the interior, Gen. Muhammad Oufkir. The ostensible leader of the coup, Gen. Muhammad Madbouh, the king's personal military adviser and close companion, was killed in the shooting at Skhirat. Four other generals and six junior officers were executed later after summary investigation. The trainee NCOs were held in detention pending a decision on whether to bring them to trial.

In his annual policy review in March, the king had mentioned official speculation as one of his main preoccupations, and a Cabinet reshuffle in April was accompanied by rumours of a financial scandal linked to prospective U.S. investment in tourism projects. After the attempted coup, the king embarked on a long-term plan to improve the administration. The new government formed in August under former finance minister Muhammad Karim Lamrani, a successful businessman, was pledged by the king to change a system that "makes the rich richer and the poor poorer." Heavy penalties for corruption were promised, and there was a general reshuffle in top administrative posts. In November some evidence that corruption was being seriously tackled was provided by the arrest of a former minister of finance and a former minister of works. The military threat to the monarchy was met by the appointment of General Oufkir to the Ministry of Defense and a revision of the system of semiautonomous regional military commands to provide more direct central control over individual units.

In January the king had announced the uncovering of a plot by quite another group, the leftist National Union of Popular Forces (NUPF) and its sympathizers; 193 alleged conspirators were brought to trial at Marrakesh in June, and in September five were sentenced to death for treason.

The presence of a U.S. communications base at Kenitra, near Rabat—officially admitted during congressional hearings in Washington late in 1970—provoked some minor agitation by Moroccan opposition groups early in 1971, but Morocco's close relations with the U.S. were not seriously impaired. Although the October visit of Soviet Prime Minister Aleksei N. Kosygin included some talk of increased aid, there was no suggestion of any alteration in Morocco's firm pro-Western stance. (PR. K.)

Motion Pictures

There was little apparent change in the general economic patterns and drift of the motion-picture industry during 1971. In most of the nonsocialist countries the progressive decline of the mass audience continued to make commercial film production an ever more hazardous venture. There was an apparent acceleration in the seemingly inevitable spiral that had marked most of the cinema's history: commercial caution leading to conservative production policies; conservatism in an industry that is also an art tending to kill the innovation, experiment, and excitement that alone can maintain audience enthusiasm; consequently, audience and economy still further depressed. The impasse was easier to understand than to cure.

Increasingly, the most militant efforts to discover new language and new ideas seemed to be outside the commercial cinema. The "underground" continued to flourish and expand, generally rejecting the conventional technical and narrative standards of commercial movies, and addressing a minority, converted, essentially youthful audience. At the same time there was evidence—for instance in the films of Rainer Werner Fassbinder in West Germany and Barney Platts-Mills in Britain—of attempts to make films independently and cheaply but still designed to attract the larger regular cinema audience. For the most part such experiments were severely restricted, the means of distribution normally being inseparably linked with the more organized old-style methods of commercial production.

The English-Speaking Cinema. *United States.* Confirming the principle that there is no means of predicting what will attract cinema audiences, the year's outstanding box-office success throughout the English-speaking world was *Love Story,* directed by Arthur Hiller. This related the love affair and marriage of a couple of college students, concluding with mawkish scenes of the girl's death from a lingering unidentified disease and the too-late repentance of the boy's rich father who had opposed the socioeconomically unequal match. Inevitably the entire film industry puzzled to identify the formula that had worked such magic: were the viewers drawn by some nostalgia for their own college days or attracted by a simple story of sentimental love at a time when films were becoming ever more explicit in their depiction and discussion of physical love?

Other films also hinted at nostalgia for some past age of innocence when the campus was associated with clumsy experimental sexual discovery rather than revolution and dissent. Robert Mulligan's *Summer of '42* was a more romantic treatment of the theme of first love than Mike Nichols' caustic *Carnal Knowledge,* which subjected American sexual mores to harsh

Ali MacGraw and Ryan O'Neal play a young couple in "Love Story," a box-office hit in 1971 adapted from Erich Segal's poignant best-selling book.

Gian Maria Volonte (left) as Bartolomeo Vanzetti and Riccardo Cucciolla as Nicola Sacco relive the notorious Sacco and Vanzetti trial in the film "Sacco & Vanzetti," released in 1971.

satirical examination through a story of the adventures of two men (Arthur Garfunkel and Jack Nicholson) from college days to maturity in years, if not in emotional control.

Following *Tora! Tora! Tora!,* the costly re-creation of the attack on Pearl Harbor released at the end of 1970, massive spectacular films were perhaps less in evidence in 1971 than in previous years. Among the handful of large-scale musicals were Norman Jewison's disappointingly unimaginative transfer to the screen of *Fiddler on the Roof,* the enormously successful stage production based on Sholem Aleichem tales of Russian Jewry in the days of the pogroms; Blake Edwards' *Darling Lili,* with Julie Andrews in an uneasy role as a beautiful World War I spy; and Vincente Minnelli's *On a Clear Day You Can See Forever,* again based on a stage musical, and starring Barbra Streisand in a complicated tale involving reincarnation and hypnosis.

There was also marginally less evidence of the compulsion to explore every channel afforded by the new permissive censorship in many parts of the Western world. Twentieth Century-Fox sought to exploit the sex market by engaging Russ Meyer, an experienced producer of "sexploitation" movies, to direct *Beyond the Valley of the Dolls.* This purported to be a sequel to their earlier success, *Valley of the Dolls,* but proved instead to be a lurid sexual extravaganza. Gore Vidal's sensational best-selling comic novel *Myra Breckinridge* was filmed by English director Michael Sarne; the film's principal interest was the return to the screen of the legendary Mae West, her extreme age seeming only to underline the wit and comedy of her characteristic parody of styles in female sexuality. Another subject only possible in the new climate of permissiveness was William Friedkin's film version of Mart Crowley's play *The Boys in the Band,* which related the tensions among a group of homosexuals assembled for the birthday of one of their number.

The continuing appeal of science fiction was reflected in the surprising box-office success of a low-budget film, *Willard,* a horror story about an army of trained rats that get out of their owner's control. Walon Green's *The Hellstrom Chronicle* used documentary nature photography in a similarly horrendous demonstration of the possibility of insects taking control of the world. Robert Wise's *The Andromeda*

Strain employed a reportage style and convincing scientific exposition in an intelligent allegory about a noxious organism brought to earth from outer space.

Other directors dealt with present-day realities rather than the projection of a fictional future. Two especially vivid reflections of contemporary American society were outsiders' views. Czechoslovak director Milos Forman turned his shrewd and comic powers of observation to the American bourgeoisie in *Taking Off,* a merciless satire on the generation gap. Within the framework of a lightweight thriller, French director Roger Vadim's *Pretty Maids All in a Row* delivered some no less accurate blows at some of the conventional values—ambition, virility, aggression—maintained in various guises in high school society.

Race issues inevitably continued to loom large. The veteran William Wyler made *The Liberation of L. B. Jones,* from a highly melodramatic scenario by Stirling Silliphant about the persecution of a black businessman by corrupt white police in a Southern community. Ralph Nelson's *. . . Tick . . . Tick . . . Tick* told of the trials and triumph of a Negro who accepts appointment as sheriff of a racist community. Other films approached the theme less directly, through historical or symbolic stories. Ralph Nelson also directed *Soldier Blue,* a film of unsparing violence whose story of a massacre of Indians by U.S. cavalry seemed to be a commentary on the My Lai events as well as on more domestic race issues. In an adaptation of Thomas Berger's *Little Big Man,* Arthur Penn brought a lighter touch and more sophisticated approach than Nelson's to the question of interracial relationships. An allegorical *Candide* of the old West, its picturesque tale was seen through the eyes and flashback memories of a 121-year-old hero, played by Dustin Hoffman.

Films released near the end of the year that received critical acclaim included Stanley Kubrick's *A Clockwork Orange,* an adaptation of Anthony Burgess' chilling 1962 novel about London in the "near future"; Peter Bogdanovich's *The Last Picture Show,* from the Larry McMurtry novel dealing with a small Texas town in the early 1950s; and William Friedkin's detective thriller, *The French Connection.*

Underground preoccupations became appreciably more politically militant in 1971: Robert Kramer's *Ice* supposed the possibilities of an American radical

revolution; other films effectively discussed race conflicts (Yolande DuLuart's *Angela: Portrait of a Revolutionary,* Mike Gray's *The Murder of Fred Hampton*); women's liberation (Julia Reichert and James Klein's *Growing Up Female,* New York Newsreel's *Janie's Jane,* San Francisco Newsreel's *The Woman's Film*); and Vietnam (Alan Levin's *Who Invited Us?*). Perhaps the year's most distinguished underground film was Paul Morrissey's *Trash,* produced in the Andy Warhol "factory," a strange, funny, and sad *Lower Depths* of contemporary New York, with a hero rendered impotent by hard drugs.

The U.S. Academy of Motion Picture Arts and Sciences presented its annual Academy Awards in April. *Patton* took seven Oscars, including awards for best movie, best director (Franklin J. Schaffner), best original screenplay (Francis Ford Coppola and Edmund North), and best actor (George C. Scott, who declined the award on the principle that art should not be made competitive; *see* BIOGRAPHY). The best actress award went to Glenda Jackson (*see* BIOGRAPHY) for her role in *Women in Love;* the best supporting actor and actress were John Mills (*Ryan's Daughter*) and Helen Hayes (*Airport*).

Britain. Despite continuing economic difficulties, the year brought a number of distinguished new films. *The Go-Between,* directed by Joseph Losey (*see* BIOGRAPHY), deservedly carried off the Palme d'Or at the Cannes Film Festival in May, against stiff competition that included Luchino Visconti's *Death in Venice.* Adapted from L. P. Hartley's novel about the lasting effects upon a small boy of his involuntary involvement in the subterfuges of a clandestine love affair, the film sensitively evoked the atmosphere of a far-off summer in rural, class-ridden England.

After *Midnight Cowboy* John Schlesinger returned to Britain to make *Sunday, Bloody Sunday,* from a script by Penelope Gilliatt. The film marked a new stage of maturity in which he succeeded in casting off an earlier tendency to irrelevant effect. The story told of an unconventional triangle in which an egotistical young artist shares his sexual favours between a middle-aged man and a divorced woman.

Several of the most important middle- and younger-generation British directors—Lindsay Anderson, Karel Reisz, John Boorman—produced no new work. However, Ken Loach followed *Kes* with *Family Life* —an adaptation of David Mercer's television play *In Two Minds*—the tragic story of a young girl driven into madness by her family and others who seek to "cure" her. Ken Russell seemed wholly preoccupied with a desire to shock. *The Music Lovers* was a vulgar extravaganza loosely based upon the life of Tchaikovsky, with crude crosscutting of scenes and a use of the composer's music as a background for luridly literal sexual fantasies. *The Devils* was a no less hysterical and ludicrous version of the history of the nuns of Loudon.

Although made two years earlier, *Performance*—an allegory of the encounter between a gangster and the hippie world—did not appear in Britain until 1971, and was a singularly auspicious directorial debut for former cameraman Nicholas Roeg. His second feature film, *Walkabout,* based on an Australian children's classic, also related the meeting of two worlds: two schoolchildren stranded in the desert are befriended by an aborigine boy on his initiation "walkabout." Roeg showed himself a director of substantial gifts, able to translate stimulating and intelligent ideas into coherent and often dazzling images. Other 1971

Ann-Margret and Jack Nicholson portray jaded lovers in Mike Nichols' film "Carnal Knowledge," released in 1971.

COURTESY, AVCO EMBASSY PICTURES CORP.

debuts included Stephen Frears with a tribute to Bogart gangster movies, *Gumshoe*, starring Albert Finney; actor Lionel Jeffries with an elegant and lively adaptation of Edith Nesbit's children's classic *The Railway Children;* and editor Reginald Mills with a charming film-ballet, *Peter Rabbit and Tales of Beatrix Potter.* Barney Platts-Mills's *Private Road* showed the same sympathy for ordinary, baffled young people as his first feature, *Bronco Bullfrog.*

While the young were operating on small budgets and dealing with intimate themes, the older generation of British directors were taken up with spectacular productions. David Lean's *Ryan's Daughter* was a showy melodrama set in the revolutionary Ireland of 1916, scripted by Robert Bolt; Ronald Neame's *Scrooge* was a lively musical version of *A Christmas Carol,* with a notable acting ensemble led by Albert Finney and Sir Alec Guinness.

Canada. Harvey Hart directed a vivid and effective adaptation, scripted by the playwright, of John Herbert's successful stage play, *Fortune and Men's Eyes,* about homosexuality in prisons.

Western Europe. *France.* From the most senior surviving French generation, Marcel Carné returned to direction with *Les Assassins de l'ordre,* an efficient adaptation of Jean Laborde's novel about a magistrate's fight to expose police corruption. Robert Bresson and Jacques Tati represented the generation that came to the fore during and immediately following World War II. In *Quatre Nuits d'un rêveur,* Bresson again adapted Dostoevski, who had provided the theme of his 1970 film *Une Femme douce,* transforming the story and characters of *White Nights* into something authentically and unmistakably Bressonian, with the characteristic calm, understated intensity. In *Traffic,* Tati recorded a further encounter between his determinedly human everyman, Monsieur Hulot, and a cold, mechanized world.

The generation that constituted the "new wave" of the previous decade remained active. In *Domicile conjugale,* François Truffaut made the touching fourth (and, he asserted, the last) film on the life and adventures of Antoine Doinel, first seen as the unhappy boy hero of *Les 400 Coups* (1959). Claude Chabrol continued his series of stylish, Hitchcock-influenced thrillers with *La Rupture.* In *Je t'aime, je t'aime* Alain Resnais' fascination with space and time found expression in a science-fiction story about a young man chosen for an experiment involving a time machine. Jacques Demy's delight in the decorative and pretty also found an ideal outlet in his adaptation of Charles Perrault's *Peau d'Âne,* a fairy tale about the fragility of human happiness. Eric Rohmer's *Le Genou de Claire,* the fifth in his series of so-called *contes moraux* (moral tales), was a minute analysis of the behaviour of a mature man temporarily separated from his loved one and thus vulnerable to competing sexual interests. One of the year's most notable French films was Louis Malle's *Le Souffle au coeur,* in which without any sense of pastiche he adopted the style of the French cinema of the early 1950s to underline the period feeling of his story, set in 1954. With faultless taste and discretion, he related the problems of the boy-hero's coming of age, culminating in the fulfillment of a frequent Freudian wish-dream of sleeping with his young mother. Despite the impeccable handling, the incest element caused considerable censorship difficulties.

Polish director Walerian Borowczyk, whose work had been confined to animated films until his first feature, *Goto, Île de l'amour,* made a bizarre and exquisite second feature, *Blanche,* a medieval tale of passion and horror. Among the year's most interesting debuts were Spanish writer Fernando Arrabal's *Viva la Muerte!,* a paroxysmic and sadistic view of the Spanish Civil War seen through the eyes of a maturing 12-year-old boy, and Joël Séria's *Mais ne nous délivrez pas du Mal,* an anarchic tale of two small girls determinedly pursuing their hobby of evil-doing.

One of the most publicized films of the year, Marcel Ophuls' documentary *Le Chagrin et la pitié,* presented an unflattering account of the French under Nazi occupation, at marathon length and with conscientious documentation. The film enjoyed great success in the cinema after French television, co-producers with Swiss and German television, declined to show it.

Italy. An interesting aspect of Italian production was the growing patronage of feature films by the radio and television organization, Radiotelevisione Italiana. Major productions financed by television included: Bernardo Bertolucci's *The Spider's Strategy* (in 1970); Federico Fellini's poetic documentary *The Clowns;* Roberto Rossellini's re-creation of the last days of Socrates, *Socrate;* and Nelo Risi's *Diary of a Schizophrenic.*

The year's big film was clearly Luchino Visconti's adaptation of Thomas Mann's *Death in Venice,* at its elegant, evocative best when most faithful to Mann, at its uneasy worst when interpolating the director's own gloss on the narrative and his (not very firmly based) theory that Mann's hero was inspired by the composer Gustav Mahler. Another veteran, Vittorio de Sica, after years dedicated to lightweight comedy and sentiment, returned to a serious subject with *I giardini di Finzi Contini.* The film traced the history of a Jewish family in Fascist Italy, and took the major prize at the Berlin Film Festival.

Ermanno Olmi's two latest releases were in markedly different styles. *Un certo giorno* told a strictly realistic story about the crisis in a successful executive's life when he is charged with culpability in a road death. *Durante l'estate,* on the other hand, was on the surface pure whimsy, although closer examination revealed that it too had comments to make on contemporary society's forgetfulness of the individual. In startling contrast was Pier Paolo Pasolini's earthy *The Decameron,* visually inspired by Giotto (whom the director himself portrays in the film).

Among the newer Italian directors, Liliana Cavani made *L'ospite,* the story of a no longer young woman (Lucia Bose) released from a mental hospital to the care of a family whose indifference and distaste finally drive her back to permanent asylum. In *Nel nome del Padre,* Marco Bellocchio seemed to be using his picture of life in a third-rate boys' school as a symbol of an oppressive closed society.

West Germany. The very least that could be claimed for the new generation of German film makers, many of them still in their 20s, was that even when their work was at its worst they remained individualists. Werner Herzog's *Fata Morgana* was completely successful on its own terms: superficially a documentary on the Sahara, it provided a neo-biblical parable of man's life on earth. Rainer Werner Fassbinder exceeded his past prolific record by having a different new film at each of the major festivals, at Cannes, Berlin, and Venice, and one to spare. At Cannes, *Recruits at Ingolstadt* was an updated ver-

Annual Cinema Attendance		
Country	Total in 000	Per capita
Algeria	28,700	2.3
Andorra	200	11
Angola	2,800	0.5
Argentina	98,000	4
Australia	37,500	3
Austria	50,600	7
Bahrain	1,000	5
Barbados	1,200	5
Belgium	39,500	4
Bhutan	500	0.6
Brazil	234,700	3
British Honduras	2,000	18
Brunei	2,300	21
Bulgaria	114,000	14
Burma	218,000	8
Burundi	500	0.2
Canada	97,600	5
Canal Zone	500	9
Cape Verde Is.	300	1.3
Cayman Islands	60	7
Ceylon	41,300	4
Chad	1,300	0.4
Chile	75,000	8
Colombia	85,400	4
Comoro Islands	20	0.1
Congo (Brazzaville)	1,700	2
Cook Islands	300	13
Cyprus	6,700	11
Czechoslovakia	118,700	8
Denmark	31,100	6
Ecuador	15,100	3
Egypt	65,800	2.1
Equatorial Guinea	480	1.7
Faeroe Islands	200	6
Falkland Islands	20	10
France	215,700	4
French Guiana	700	14
Germany, East	100,600	6
Germany, West	192,000	3
Ghana	11,800	1.5
Greenland	400	11
Guam	500	6
Guatemala	9,000	2
Hong Kong	88,600	23
Hungary	84,500	8
Iceland	2,300	1.2
India	1,825,000	4
Iran	15,400	0.6
Iraq	8,300	1
Israel	57,500	22
Italy	567,000	11
Jamaica	3,600	2
Japan	313,400	3
Jordan	6,100	3
Korea, South	173,200	6
Laos	1,100	0.4
Liberia	900	0.8
Luxembourg	1,900	6
Maldives	100	1.3
Mali	2,500	0.5
Malta	3,800	12
Martinique	2,100	6
Mauritius	7,400	9
Mexico	358,800	8
Monaco	100	6
Montserrat	10	0.7
Morocco	18,200	1.3
Netherlands	34,300	3
New Caledonia	1,000	11
New Hebrides	250	3
New Zealand	26,000	10
Pakistan	276,600	3
Panama	5,000	4
Poland	153,500	5
Portugal	29,700	3
Portuguese Guinea	200	0.4
Réunion	800	2
Romania	203,700	10
Ryukyu Islands	3,200	3
St. Kitts-Nevis-Anguilla	70	1
St. Lucia	500	5
San Marino	200	11
Senegal	5,200	1.5
Singapore	25,900	14
Spain	357,800	11
Spanish Sahara	400	8
Swaziland	100	0.3
Sweden	30,400	4
Switzerland	35,000	6
Taiwan	868,100	66
Tunisia	8,300	1.8
U.S.S.R.	4,715,000	20
United Kingdom	237,000	4
United States	1,300,000	7
U.S. Virgin Islands	400	6
Upper Volta	600	0.1
Venezuela	37,500	4
Western Samoa	400	3
Yugoslavia	100,200	5

Note: Figures given are most recent available.
Source: *UNESCO Statistical Yearbook* (1969).

COURTESY, WARNER BROS.

Dorothy, played by Jennifer O'Neill, offers to help Hermie, played by Gary Grimes, with the groceries he is carrying for her in the 1971 motion picture "Summer of '42," the story of a boy's loss of innocence.

sion of a play by Marieluise Fleisser, for whose story of maidservants and military in a provincial garrison town Fassbinder devised a successful pseudo-theatrical style. At Berlin he showed an (apparently) unintended parody of American deep South melodrama—an extravagant tale about a decadent white family and their Negro servant, ending in a final holocaust. At Venice, *Warnung vor einer heiligen Nutte* was a claustrophobic study of a penniless film unit holed up in a Spanish hotel.

Sweden. Sweden's two major international directors both made English-language co-productions in 1971. Ingmar Bergman's *The Touch* recounted the breakdown of a middle-class marriage, with Bibi Andersson as the model wife who allows herself to be seduced by a rootless foreigner, played by Elliott Gould, the husband in this tormented triangle being played by Max von Sydow. In *The Ballad of Joe Hill* Bo Widerberg created a highly pictorial biography of the Swedish-American folk-hero of the labour movement.

Denmark. A notable debut was Christian Braad Thomsen's *Kære Irene,* a witty account of the political and sexual adventures of a young girl activist that received critical acclaim both at Cannes and at Venice.

Eastern Europe. *U.S.S.R.* The year's biggest prestige production was *King Lear,* directed by Grigori Kozintsev, one of the great veterans of the "heroic" 1920s. Perhaps less successful and dramatically gripping than his famous *Hamlet,* Kozintsev's *Lear* remained a supremely intelligent grappling with the play's dramatic and psychological problems. The Soviet cinema still seemed under the spell of the big superproduction, such as Alov and Naumov's *The Flight,* which was largely interesting for its subject matter—the fortunes of Russian exiles in the years following the Revolution. Rather more modest new productions of quality were: Andrei Konchalovski's adaptation of *Uncle Vanya;* Yuli Karasik's more pedestrian adaptation of *The Seagull;* Angrei Smirnov's *Belorussian Station,* examining the individual problems of four war veterans 25 years later; Otar Yoseliani's *Day After Day,* an intimate Georgian comedy; and Leonid Gaidai's adaptation of the classic Ilf and Petrov comedy, *The Twelve Chairs.*

Hungary. Despite major reorganizations in the film industry, Hungary still boasted one of the liveliest cinemas of Eastern Europe. The year's biggest success abroad was *Love,* adapted from two stories by Tibor Déry and marking a significant comeback by Karoly Makk, a notable director of the 1950s. Set in the oppressive days of the Rakosi regime, the film is concerned with a single family and the agonizing fantasies that the wife feeds her ailing mother-in-law to prevent the old lady's knowing that her son is a political prisoner. In *Agnus Dei* Miklos Jancso, Hungary's most individual and internationally celebrated director, treated the era of Admiral Horthy's overthrow of the Hungarian Republic of Councils (1919) rather in the style of a medieval pageant or mystery. A film of more conventional form but justly admired for the truthfulness and sincerity of its treatment of disaffected youth was Pal Gabor's second feature, *Horizon.*

Yugoslavia. The various Yugoslav nationalities seemed to be competing in a cinema of rapidly growing artistic vitality and politico-philosophical intelligence. Yugoslavia, it was frequently said, had a truly Marxist cinema in taking account of *both* Marxes—Karl and Groucho. Typical of the new cinema was the Croatian Bata Cengic's *My Family's Role in the World Revolution,* in which, among other absurdist incidents, Stalin's head is eaten in the form of a cake.

The most remarkable Yugoslav film to emerge to international celebrity was Dusan Makavejev's *WR—Mysteries of the Organism.* Starting out from a documentary study of Wilhelm Reich's work and theory, the film broadens into a wide-ranging collage in which the values of both East and West are submitted to the test of Makavejev's fine philosophical intelligence and rich and scabrous sense of comedy.

Poland. The most striking Polish feature film in the year's international festivals was Krzysztof Zanussi's *Family Life,* a brilliant, almost Chekhovian study of a young man's return from the socialist present to the claustrophobic past of his family home.

Czechoslovakia. Along with the other arts, the cinema had remained stifled since the 1968 invasion. While only anodyne comedies and thrillers reached the international festivals, there were reports of the suppression of numerous films for seeking to express ideas or new artistic approaches. Occasionally, however, films banned at home were briefly seen abroad, among them Juraj Jakubisko's fantastic comedy-allegory *Birds, Orphans, and Fools.*

Asia. *Iran.* The first film of international stature to emerge from Iran was Daryush Mehrjui's *The Cow,* shown at the Venice festival. A naïve tale of a man whose grief at the loss of his cow—the only beast possessed by his village—is such that he is metamorphosed and takes the animal's place is brilliantly used as a shrewd allegory of the third world's perils of introspection and isolationism.

Japan. The most remarkable of Japan's contemporary film makers, Nagisa Oshima, continued to apply a highly intellectual and critical vision to the modern Japanese character. In *The Ceremony* a series of ceremonies is described: the marriages, funerals, and other reunions that reveal the history of a Japanese family and of Japanese society as a whole over the past 30 years.

India. The great Bengali director Satyajit Ray made a very uncharacteristic and on the whole not very successful film *Pratidwandi (The Adversary).* It was uncharacteristic in its use of flamboyant technical effects, although its best moments were in the familiar Ray style, with sensitive observation of the problems, doubts, and optimism of a young man seeking his first job.

Latin America. *Brazil.* In 1971 Nelson Pereira Dos Santos emerged as the most prolific as well as one of the most remarkable directors of the *cinema nôvo. Lust for Love,* while superficially a conventional exercise in sexual permutations, served as a bitter allegory on political attitudes; *A Very Lunatic Asylum,* in which the local priest sets up a madhouse to cure the discontent of the rich and the dissent of the poor, was described as "a kind of Brazilian *Marat/Sade";* and *How Tasty Was My Little Frenchman* was a strange, blackly comic morality play about a 16th-century French adventurer who becomes the friend and later the hors d'oeuvre of a tribe of cannibal Indians.

Cuba. Indicating that the remarkable progress of the Cuban revolutionary cinema was being maintained, a striking new film by Manuel Octavio Gomez was shown at the Moscow and London Film festivals. *Los Dias del Agua* reconstructed a true incident in the 1930s in which the miraculous healing powers of a Bernadette-like peasant woman in a remote part of the island were exploited for political ends.

(DA. J. R.)

Nontheatrical. An event of unusual interest to film makers and producers of related audio-visual materials was the opening in April in Nürnberg, W.Ger., of a yearlong exhibit celebrating the 500th anniversary of the birthday of Albrecht Dürer. The presentation, entitled "Noricama: Nuremberg in Multi-vision, The Symphony of a City in Picture, Sound, and Movement," was the creation of the noted Czechoslovak scenographer Joseph Svoboda, whose radical innovations in the use of film, still pictures, and sound, sometimes combined with live action, attracted wide attention in recent years. The main feature of the show was a ten-minute documentary of Nürnberg's history in which nine kinetic projection screens carried a complex flow of images from ten synchronized projectors with a cluster of mobile speakers providing narration and sound effects.

The use in schools of multimedia systems of teaching was featured at the seventh International Education Film Week held at Brussels in March by the International Council for Educational Media. The meeting of representatives of 17 nations saw demonstrations of multimedia "packs" combining 8-mm. films with tapes and printed materials. Also viewed were 94 conventional films in 16 mm. and 8 mm., selected from among 157 films submitted by member countries. The 12th International Industrial Film Festival was staged at Barcelona, Spain, in November. The Grand Prize was won by a U.S. entry, *The Real World,* produced for IBM.

Trends in U.S. nontheatrical films showed a continuing slump in investment and production of films for use in major markets. According to industry-wide reports for 1970, there was a 2% decline in spending for motion pictures, from $488.2 million in 1969 to $480.6 million in 1970. Spending for all audio-visual products, including motion pictures, equipment, and services, showed an increase of 3% overall, but this was the smallest gain in several years.

The slump in spending for films had a depressing effect on the number of films produced. According to estimates for 1970, there were 14,175 regular nontheatrical motion pictures produced in the U.S., a decline of 7% from the previous year. Films produced for use in elementary and secondary schools declined

to 1,310, a drop of 20%. Films produced for business and industry leveled off at 9,000, a decline of 4%. On the other hand, production was up by 12% in films for medicine and health, and by 9% in films for use in universities.   (J. T. B.)

See also Photography; Television and Radio.
ENCYCLOPÆDIA BRITANNICA FILMS. *Let Them Learn* (1967); *Growing* (1969)—a computer-animated film.

Motor Sports

Automobiles. Formula One racing continued under the ruling that specified three litres as the maximum engine size. Before the end of the season Jackie Stewart (*see* BIOGRAPHY) had taken the 1971 world drivers' championship on points, driving a Tyrrell powered by the well-established Cosworth-designed Ford V-8 power unit. Ken Tyrrell, Stewart's race manager, had decided to race with cars of his own make, and the first of these was designed and built in approximately nine months in 1970 by Derek Gardner, working in secret with very few facilities. For the 1971 season it had been expected that the Ford V-8 engine, after performing unreliably in 1970, would be outclassed by the Ferrari and other 12-cylinder power units. This proved not to be the case. Stewart started the new season testing tires at Kyalami in South Africa but crashed because the throttle stuck open. His Tyrrell was rebuilt in time for the Grand Prix at that circuit and a longer Tyrrell was available for François Cevert. Stewart's car finished second in the race, behind Mario Andretti's Ferrari 312, which won at 112.36 mph after setting the fastest lap at 114.31 mph. That this was no flash in the pan by the Italian builder was shown by Clay Regazzoni's taking third place in another Ferrari 312. Cevert crashed the second Tyrrell when he was momentarily blinded.

Grand Prix racing was regarded as hazardous enough by Stewart for him not to accept lightly what he regarded as ineffective safety arrangements. He caused some race promoters to alter barriers and remove banks, trees, and other obstacles he regarded as dangerous. In the Spanish Grand Prix at Barcelona, Stewart won for Tyrrell in the rain at a speed of 97.19 mph, driving the third car from the Tyrrell factory. Jackie Ickx was in great form in this event, driving the fastest lap at 99.64 mph, a circuit record, in a flat-12 Ferrari 312B. This gave him second place, third being taken by Chris Amon (N.Z.) in a Matra-Simca MS.

In the "round-the-houses" Grand Prix at Monaco, Stewart dominated the race, winning at 83.49 mph in the new Tyrrell. A new star, Ronnie Peterson of Sweden, placed second in a March 711, while Ickx was third in a Ferrari. The Belgian Grand Prix, which should have been run over the very fast Spa circuit, was canceled because certain members of the Grand Prix Drivers Association decided it was not a safe course, especially in the rain. For the Dutch Grand Prix at Zandvoort the Tyrrells had the new Girling double-disc brakes, but Stewart spun at a corner and failed to finish higher than 11th, and Cevert crashed. The race was dominated by the 12-cylinder cars, Ickx's Ferrari 312B winning at nearly 94 mph and recording the fastest lap, with second place occupied by Pedro Rodriguez in a V-12 BRM P160. However, in the Grand Prix of France, held at the Castellet circuit, the Tyrrells were right back on form. Indeed, in a race of 23 starters and 14 finishers, after Stewart had

Motorboating: *see* Motor Sports

Motor Industry: *see* Industrial Review

driven the fastest lap at 113.9 mph, he won the event at 111.6 mph from his teammate Cevert. A Lotus 72D driven by Emerson Fittipaldi came in third in a season of poor showing by the once-invincible cars from Norfolk.

The British Grand Prix, this time sponsored by Woolmark to the extent of being named the Woolmark Grand Prix, saw Stewart again master of the situation with a winning time of 130.48 mph on the fast Silverstone circuit. Peterson's March 711 was second, and the Lotus of Fittipaldi secured another third place. In the German Grand Prix at the Nürburgring, Stewart and Cevert finished first and second in that order, Stewart averaging 114.4 mph and Cevert driving the fastest lap at 116.1 mph, a new record. It was British Racing Motors' (BRM's) turn at Zeltweg in the Austrian Grand Prix, with Jo Siffert first past the checkered flag, with a race speed of 150.9 mph. Fittipaldi managed second place in a Lotus 72D, ahead of Tim Schenken's Brabham BT33, Brabham cars continuing to be raced in spite of the retirement of their instigator, Jack Brabham. The Tyrrells that Stewart and Cevert were driving broke down in this race.

The Italian Grand Prix at Monza, another fast track, had an extremely close and unexpected finish when four drivers, Peterson (March 711), Cevert (Tyrrell), Mike Hailwood (Surtees TS9), and Peter Gethin (BRM P160) raced for the finish in a bunch. Gethin, a newcomer to Grand Prix racing, just made it, followed by Peterson, Cevert, and Hailwood. The race was a triumph for the Yardley-sponsored British Racing Motors team, their winning car averaging just over 150 mph.

Unruly spectators had killed off the Mexican Grand Prix, but the U.S. and Canadian events were held as usual. The American race at Watkins Glen, N.Y., went to Tyrrell, Cevert winning at more than 115 mph from Siffert's BRM, while Stewart won a foggy Canadian race, at Mosport, at nearly 82 mph. The superiority of the Tyrrell-Elf petroleum-Cosworth combination was thus thoroughly demonstrated, with Stewart winning the world drivers' championship and Tyrrell winning the builders' world championship for the car.

Apart from the classic races, there were other Formula One contests, notably the Jochen Rindt Me-

morial Race at Hockenheim in West Germany, won by Ickx's Ferrari, and the Daily Express International Trophy Race at Silverstone, which gave veteran Graham Hill a victory in a Brabham-Cosworth after faster cars had developed troubles.

The major European sports car races continued much as in previous seasons, but the impending three-litre formula of 1972 damped some of the enthusiasm. The Le Mans 24-hour race in France, now divorced from its traditional start with the drivers sprinting to their cars, was voted of waning appeal, despite the large number of spectators who watched it and the high speed at which it was run. Most of the sports car contests were raced by cars of the 1,000-kg. formula. Of these, the BOAC race at Brands Hatch, Kent, was won by an Alfa Romeo T33/3 with three-litre V-8 engine; the Monza race by the Rodriguez/Jack Oliver Porsche 917 with a five-litre flat-12 power unit; and the Francorchamps race at Spa, Belg., by the same combination. The event at Nürburgring went to a three-litre flat-8 Porsche 908, and the Austrian edition, at Österreichring, was another Porsche 917 victory. Le Mans was won for the second time by a Porsche 917, driven by the team of Helmut Marko of Austria and Gijs van Lennep of the Netherlands, and the age-old Targa Florio road race by an Alfa Romeo T33/3, Porsche running into dire troubles.

A full season of Formula Two and Formula Three racing backed up these events, and there were some important additional fixtures, such as the Brands Hatch Race of Champions where Regazzoni (Ferrari 312B) scored and the Rothmans Gold Cup at Oulton Park, won by John Surtees in a Surtees-Cosworth. Ignazio Giunti died when his Ferrari crashed into the rear of another car which had run out of gas during the 1,000-km. race in Buenos Aires, Arg. Pedro Rodriguez lost his life at the Norisring, and Jo Siffert was killed during a Formula One race at Brands Hatch in October.

International rallies remained an important part of the motor sports scene in 1971. The customary European rally championships, for drivers and manufacturers, were maintained, and in Britain there was the usual Royal Auto Club Rally Championship, which went to Stig Blomquist and Arne Hertz and a championship for club rally drivers sponsored by *Motoring News,* which was won by George Hill and Keith Wood. The winter Monte Carlo Rally was a walkover for Alpine-Renault. The small French cars took the first two places and tied for third, with Ove Andersson and David Stone driving the leading one.

Buoyed by large amounts of cigarette sponsorship money available because of the television ban on that kind of advertising, U.S. automobile racing survived the national recession with few cash inflow difficulties. All of the groups making up the Automobile Competition Committee for the United States—the Sports Car Club of America (SCCA), the National Association for Stock Car Racing (NASCAR), the National Hot Rod Association, and the United States Auto Club (USAC)—had reason for joy.

In USAC racing the new Triple Crown of 500-mi. races for single-seat cars was well received. Defending champion Al Unser repeated at Indianapolis; versatile Mark Donohue won the first Schaefer 500 at Long Pond, Pa.; and Unser's teammate on the Parnelli Jones-Vel Miletich racing team, Joe Leonard, won the second California 500 at Ontario and a month later, at Trenton, N.J., earned enough points to clinch the 1971 USAC championship. The first at Ontario

Jackie Stewart crosses the finish line to become winner of the German Grand Prix on Aug. 1, 1971. Stewart later won the world drivers' championship competition on points.

D.P.A.—PICTORIAL PARADE

was the steady 37-year-old Leonard's only victory of the year on the Marlboro Championship Trail, but he was a consistent finisher.

The Indianapolis 500 began disastrously when the pace car, driven by an automobile dealer, went out of control on leaving the track and hit a movable cameramen's bleacher, injuring at least 20. The McLarens had come to Indianapolis with a vengeance, and in the qualifying time trials Peter Revson set a new mark, gaining the pole from Donohue at 178.696 mph to 177.087. The old pole record, by Leonard, had been 171.559. Donohue led the first 50 laps easily but eventually succumbed to gearbox trouble 16 laps later. Leonard and Bobby Unser led briefly before Al Unser in a PJ Colt-Ford took command for the second half of the race. Only 12 of 33 cars finished, Revson finishing second, 22.8 sec. behind Unser.

Donohue, however, did not let the first Schaefer 500 slip through his driving gloves. The triangle track not far from his Pennsylvania home saw him lead 126 laps at an average speed of 138.649 mph. Second place went to Leonard.

But Donohue did let the California 500 at Ontario slip away after qualifying for the pole position at 185.004. He ran out of fuel on the 52nd lap while leading and lost time. Strain to his engine finally sidelined him on the 123rd lap. Al Unser then seemed a shoo-in until he had gearbox trouble. Leonard in a PJ Colt-Ford charged into the lead on the 161st lap and won easily. His average speed was over 152 mph.

USAC was much less successful in splitting its championship single-seater division into three parts. George Snider won the first national dirt track title, but the races generally suffered for lack of USAC accepted stars; the road racing division virtually died aborning with only one race being held. That race, supported by a heavy entry of Formula A (Formula 5000) machinery from the rival SCCA, was won by Jim Dittemore of California making his first Formula 5000 ride. The third part, the USAC stock car crown, was won by a relative newcomer, 31-year-old Butch Hartman. Hartman's major triumph was the Pocono 500 in a 1969 Dodge.

SCCA also experienced a year of mixed notices. The Continental, buoyed by an infusion of money from L&M cigarettes, attracted enough automobiles and overseas driving talent to continue its steady improvement in quality. David Hobbs, of the U.K., won rather handily from budding U.S. Grand Prix driver Sam Posey in this single-seater road course series.

Only one factory team competed in the Trans-American sedan series, Javelin of the American Motors Corp. led by team manager Roger Penske and Mark Donohue. Javelin triumphed in the series. Donohue won seven times after some early competition from George Follmer of the Bud Moore Mustangs.

SCCA's newest national championship for professionals and semiprofessionals, contested in Super-Vee formula cars based on Volkswagen parts, was considered a success as nine events for a minimum race purse of $10,000 were staged. Not until the final event in the series at Monterey, Calif., did Bill Scott of McLean, Va., narrowly beat out Tom Reddy of Bronxville, N.Y., for the title.

The Canadian-American Challenge Cup for Group Seven automobiles again was the property of Team McLaren. Peter Revson of New York, second man on the team to defending champion Denis Hulme, became the first American to win the Can-Am title. He won at Road Atlanta in Georgia, Watkins Glen,

Road America in Wisconsin, and Donnybrooke in Minnesota. Hulme was victorious at Riverside, Calif., and at Mosport and Edmonton in Canada.

Two of the three manufacturers' championships held in the United States were won by Porsche. The team of Pedro Rodriguez and Jackie Oliver won the 24 Hours of Daytona, going 2,621 mi. after the Ferrari of Tony Adamowicz and Ronnie Bucknum fell from the lead. Donohue and Hobbs in another Ferrari finished third. Sebring's 12-hour race saw Vic Elford and Gerard Larousse in an independent car save the day for Porsche as they covered 1,352 mi. Second and third were Alfa Romeos. In the Watkins Glen six-hour race, the final manufacturers' event of the season, the Porsche string was broken. Andrea de Adamich and Ronnie Peterson covered 677.4 mi. for Alfa Romeo.

Among NASCAR racers in 1971 there were two superstars—Richard Petty and Bobby Allison. Petty became the first NASCAR driver to have career winnings of more than $1 million as he rolled to 21 Grand National victories, including the prestige-laden Daytona 500. But Allison and his Holman & Moody 1969 Mercury won an unprecedented seven races of 400 miles or more, including the Southern 500 and 500s at Talladega, Ala., Charlotte, N.C., and Byron, Ga. Petty became the only three-time winner of the Daytona 500 with a 144.456 mph average speed.

A. J. Foyt triumphed in NASCAR's Miller 500 at Ontario, Calif., and the Atlanta 500 but later vacated his Wood Bros. Mercury to campaign in USAC events. Petty's other major victories included the Dixie 500 at Atlanta, Ga., and the Rockingham 500. Both Allison and Petty seemed certain to approach $300,000 in gross winnings.   (W. C. Bo.; R. J. Fe.)

Motorcycles. In spite of indications that the MV Agusta motorcycles did not possess the clear-cut speed superiority they had earlier enjoyed, Giacomo Agostini drove them to both the 350- and 500-cc. world road race championships in 1971. He ended the season well ahead of the 500-cc. runner-up, K. Turner of New Zealand (Suzuki), and of the Finn J. Saarinen (Yamaha) in the 350-cc. class. P. W. Read was the only Englishman to win a world title; he took the 250-cc. class, riding a privately entered Yamaha. A. de Nieto of Spain (Derbi) was the 125-cc. class winner, and Jan de Vries of the Netherlands (Kreidler) won the 50-cc. class. H. Owesle and P. Rutterford, with the West German four-cylinder Münch machine, won the sidecar class.

Results of the Isle of Man Tourist Trophy races were: 500-cc. senior, Agostini (MV Agusta), 102.59 mph; 350-cc. junior, A. Jefferies (Yamsel), 89.98 mph; 250-cc. lightweight, P. W. Read (Yamaha), 98.02 mph; 125-cc. lightweight, C. Mortimer (Yamaha), 83.96 mph; 750-cc. sidecar, G. Auerbacher (BMW), 86.86 mph; 500-cc. sidecar, S. S. Schauzu (BMW), 86.21 mph. In the new Formula 750-cc. class the winner was A. Jefferies, riding a Triumph Trident, at 102.85 mph. The production race 750-cc. class was won by R. Pickrell (Triumph), 100.07 mph; the 500-cc. class by J. Williams (Honda), 91.04 mph; and the 250-cc. class by W. A. Smith (Honda), 84.14 mph. Winners of the British road race championships were: 125 cc., B. Sheene (Suzuki); 250 cc., S. Machin (Yamaha); 350 cc., A. Rutter (Yamaha); 500 cc., P. May (Norton); 750 cc., P. Tait (Triumph); sidecar, C. Vincent (CVS).

In world moto cross the Japanese firm of Suzuki scored a notable success, taking all four main titles— the 250- and 500-cc. manufacturers' and individual

Motor Vehicles:
see Disasters;
Industrial Review;
Motor Sports;
Transportation

awards. In the 250-cc. class Joel Robert of Belgium carried all before him, and his countryman, Roger de Coster, won the 500 cc. (C. J. Ay.)

Motorboats. An American won the world offshore powerboat racing championship in 1971, after getting off to a slow start in South American waters and buying a new boat midway through the campaign. Bill Wishnick of New York raced in the oceans bordering three continents in his quest for one of the few genuinely international motorboating titles. His leading competitor was the 1970 world titleholder, Italian industrialist Vincenzo Balestrieri.

Seeking to win the championship again, Balestrieri began the 1971 season with a pair of victories in offshore races approved by the Union of International Motorboating in Argentina and Uruguay. Wishnick placed second in both events. Aware that he was outclassed in equipment, Wishnick then bought a new boat. It was a Cigarette, designed by former world titlist Don Aronow and built in Miami. Twin MerCruisers were used for power. Wishnick's riding mechanic, Bobby Moore, completed the boat and installed the engines and the fuel and electrical systems. Wishnick made a dramatic comeback in the Griffith Memorial Race, at Fort Lauderdale, Fla., finishing two minutes ahead of Balestrieri.

Moore took the boat to Europe for the summer, and Wishnick began an exhausting campaign there. He won in Italy at Naples and Viareggio, and also triumphed in Yugoslavia and Sweden. Balestrieri added a victory in France to his early-year wins in South America, but fared badly for the rest of the season. It gave Wishnick, who was the American national offshore champion in the inboard division for 1970, a chance to wrap up the world title.

On the American scene, Bob Magoon of Miami Beach replaced Wishnick as national inboard offshore titlist, moving up from his spot as 1970 outboard champion. Driving inboards for the first time, Magoon scored a series of steady victories that began with the Hennessy Key West Race in November 1970 (the American racing year officially begins November 1). Magoon also finished first in a short-course race off Miami Beach, in the California and New Jersey Hennessy Cup races, and in the Catalina Challenge and Bushmills-KBIG races on the West Coast.

Willie Meyers of Nassau, in the Bahamas, ultimately emerged as winner of the American offshore outboard championship. He was locked in a year-long duel for the title with Steve Shere of Miami, Fla., and won only after finishing fourth in the Miami–Nassau race on October 15, the final event of the racing year.

America's thunderboats completed their 1971 season at Dallas, Tex., with driver Dean Chenoweth and his "Miss Budweiser" again emerging as national unlimited champions. It was the third consecutive year the speedy hydroplane won the national crown, and Chenoweth's second year. (JA. E. M.)

Mountaineering

New routes were climbed in the Alps in the late summer of 1970, including ones on the west faces of the Aiguille de Saussure and the Évêque. New routes also were climbed on the Civetta north wall, on the southwest face of the Piz di Ciavazes in the Sella group, and up the north face gully of the Piccolo Margartdi, an outstanding problem in the Julian Alps.

In the winter of 1970–71 in the Alps there were a great number of winter first ascents, especially of solo winter ascents, particularly in the Mont Blanc group. Among these were ascents of Mont Blanc itself. Other routes in the area were the Cordier Couloir and the Arête sans Nom of the Aiguille Verte, the Cornuau-Davaille route on the north face of the Droites, and the Crétier-Ollietti route on the southeast face of the Aiguille Noire de Peuterey (solo), the north face of the Aiguille du Midi, the northeast couloir of Mont Blanc de Tacul, the Ségogne route on the northeast face of the Aiguille du Chardonnet, and the northwest face (by the west arête) of the Aiguille de la Lex Blanche (Trélatête). An attempt on a new route left of the Walker Buttress of the Grandes Jorasses ended in the death of one of the party and the rescue of the other by teams landed by helicopter. In Switzerland the northeast face of the Finsteraarhorn, the north face of the Morgenhorn, the south face of the Pointe de Mourty, the Grande Gendarme on the Jägigrat, and the Hiebeler route on the north face of the Lyskamm were climbed. In the summer of 1971, on Mont Blanc, a direct route on the Pilastro Rossi of the Brouillard face and a new route up the east flank of the Eckpfeiler were made.

New routes in the Caucasus in 1970 were on the north face of Pik Shchurovsky by a British party, on the south face of Shkhara west peak by a Georgian party, and on the north face (central part) of Chatyn Tau and the north face of Chanchakhi Khokh by Soviets. In the Pamirs 60 people reached the summit of Pik Communism, which had new routes on the southeast ridge and southwest face. In the Tian Shan, Pik Pobeda was climbed several times in 1970, 63 people reaching the summit, and new routes were made on the north ridge and north flank (the latter combined with a traverse of all the peaks of the mountain). In the Koshaal Tau, nearby, a traverse of 7.8 km. was made over Chontura, Pik Dankov, and Pik Goelro.

In the Himalayas most expeditions in 1970–71 were in Nepal. In late 1970 the major event was the ascent of Dhaulagiri I, by a Japanese expedition, by a new route (the southeast ridge). Other new ascents in this area were Dhaulagiri VI, Churen, Dakura (the successful party here being killed on the descent), Junction Peak, and Kanjiroba I by Japanese parties, and Modi Peak (second ascent, by a new route) by a party of guides from Chamonix in the French Alps.

In 1971 the most striking features of climbing in the Himalayas were the number of Japanese expeditions in the field, many from universities, and the number of fatalities. The year's major event was the international expedition to Everest, which was marred by the publicity given to differences of opinion within the party, in part with an element of nationalistic feeling. The attempt on the west ridge was abandoned on the death of the Indian member, after which the French, Swiss, and Italian members left the expedition. The attempt on the southwest face failed. An Argentine expedition to the mountain was abandoned after its sick leader had been evacuated by King Mahendra's personal helicopter. A South Korean attempt on Lhotse Shar failed, as did a Japanese attempt on Pumo Ri. Makalu was climbed by the French. The Japanese failed on Makalu II, one member dying. An Austrian expedition made the first ascent of Dhaulagiri II. The Japanese failed on Dhaulagiri IV (because of a strike of Sherpas) and Dhaulagiri V (three dying on this peak). The South Koreans failed on the northeast peak of Manaslu, losing one member.

A Czechoslovak party climbed Nanga Parbat by the Rakhiot route, this being the second ascent by this route and the fourth (or possibly fifth) of the mountain. A British expedition made the first ascent of Indrasan by the west ridge.

In the Karakorum in 1971 Japanese, West German, and British expeditions failed on Malubiting, Rakaposhi by the north flank, and the Ogre, respectively, but an Austrian party succeeded on Malubiting West. A Polish expedition made the first ascent of Khinyang Chhish. In the Hindu Kush in late 1970 a British party failed on Koh-i-Bandaka Sakhi. In 1971 a Yugoslav expedition made the first ascent of the south face direct of Istor o Nal, and another Eastern European party climbed Khyang Kish.

The "last great problem" of the Southern Alps of New Zealand fell in the 1970–71 summer: the Caroline face of Mount Cook.   (Jo. N.)

Museums and Galleries

Museums, once singularly free from labour disputes, had become increasingly prone to strike action. Museums in France and Italy had been affected in 1970, and in the spring of 1971 museums in Italy remained shut for four weeks. Although wages were not the only issue, museum attendants, especially those employed by the state or public bodies, were particularly low paid, and recommendations on the subject made at the seventh General Conference of the International Council of Museums (ICOM), though reasonable, had not so far been put into practice. In the U.S., too, staff members were talking of unionization. Some 200 professional and other employees of the Museum of Modern Art in New York, members of the Professional and Administrative Staff Association, struck in August after 51 staff members were fired as part of an economy move. The 51 were not rehired, but the strikers won some concessions, including a pay increase.

The strikes highlighted the growing budgetary problems that had been part of the museum profession for several years, especially as demands grew for increased public services. In the U.S. the National Museums Association was trying to persuade federal and local authorities to devote a progressively larger por-

tion of their budgets to cultural policy. A bill was introduced in Congress that would appropriate $40 million on a matching basis for museum services and renovation, while the National Endowment for the Arts announced its first museum assistance program with $1 million in grants. At the state level, St. Louis County, Mo., voted a tax assessment of 9 cents per $100 assessed valuation to support three museums in the county. The New York State Council on the Arts also recognized current museum problems with its $4 million museum aid program.

In Britain there were strong protests both from museum staff and from the general public against proposals for the introduction of admission charges to British museums, where for two centuries admission always had been free. The only known portrait from life of Nelson was offered a home on board HMS "Victory" if its owner, Hugh Leggatt, withdrew it from the National Portrait Gallery as a protest. A petition had been signed by 200,000 individuals, and the National Union of Teachers, with 318,000 members, had officially joined the protest campaign.

Following similar developments in the U.S., firms were being set up in a number of Western European countries with the avowed aim of "investing in art." Noting the incredible extent to which "works of art" had increased in value over the past ten years, groups of businessmen, financiers, and collector-dealers set up joint-stock companies whose official activity was the purchase and sale of such works. Profits were used partly for reinvestment and partly to pay dividends on capital. In this connection ICOM advised its members to refuse to exhibit works of art, objects, or collections belonging to such firms; to break off all contacts with private collectors or pseudo-museums known to have dealings with them; to support any and every national or international initiative to institute legal regulations governing the material and moral rights of the artist; and to refuse to act as expert advisers in any capacity in any case where speculation was involved.

Underscoring the continuing search for new modes of operation was the merger of the California Palace of the Legion of Honor with the De Young Memorial Museum. Both of these San Francisco museums would continue to operate from their present buildings, but with a joint staff. The relative ease of travel and close

Children from the summer
program in the arts
for inner-city children
exhibit examples
of their work
at the Guggenheim Museum
in New York City
in September 1971.
The program, providing
instruction for 200
children aged 10 to 12,
included courses
in painting, film, puppetry,
dance, and arts
of the American Indian.

AUTHENTICATED NEWS INTERNATIONAL

A coral reef exhibit in John G. Shedd Aquarium in Chicago was opened to the public on June 13, 1971. The $1.2 million exhibit contains about 1,000 fish, including such species as the French angelfish, green moray eels, yellowtail damselfish, and Atlantic stingrays.

proximity of museums along the East Coast led to the establishment of a cooperative museum membership among the Philadelphia Museum of Art, the Boston Museum of Fine Arts, the Corcoran Gallery in Washington, D.C., and the Metropolitan Museum of Art in New York City. Several important New York museums went further in the establishment of branch or neighbourhood museums. The Whitney Museum opened a branch in a new office building in the Wall Street area of lower Manhattan, where space was given rent-free by the developer. The Metropolitan Museum converted the rotunda of the Bronx County Courthouse into a semipermanent museum space, with a major loan exhibition of 28 paintings.

New Museums. Out of 682 architectural projects entered for the Centre Beaubourg competition in Paris, the international jury selected a project submitted by a British-Italian team of Piano, Rogers, Franchini and the civil engineers Ove Arup and Partners. Located on the Plateau Beaubourg next to the site of the old Halles, the centre's facilities would include an art documentation centre with full computer and audiovisual facilities.

The Denver (Colo.) Art Museum was the largest structure added to the ranks of U.S. museums during the year. In Minneapolis, Minn., the 45-year-old Walker Art Center opened in a new building, and the new University of California Art Museum, designed by Mario Ciampi and his associates, was opened in Berkeley. The new education wing of the Cleveland Museum of Art was one of the finest examples of contemporary architecture in the U.S. The Salvador Dalí Museum, the first U.S. museum devoted to the permanent exhibition of works by a single living artist, was opened in Beachwood, O., by Mr. and Mrs. A. Reynolds Morse, who had amassed the world's largest collection of Dali's works. The Detroit Institute of Arts opened a large north wing, a companion to the five-year-old south wing. The Metropolitan Museum of Art opened its new permanent American galleries and Costume Institute and announced plans for an $8 million structure, the Lehman Pavilion, to house the vast Lehman collection given to the museum two years earlier. The Houston (Tex.) Museum of Fine Arts inaugurated a multimillion-dollar fund campaign to finish its Mies van der Rohe wing. In Washington, D.C., the National Gallery of Art presented I. M. Pei's widely acclaimed plans for that museum's $50

million new East Building; half of the funds were given by the Mellon Foundation.

In the U.S.S.R. a new art museum was opened in one of Moscow's old private residences, presented to the city by the collector Felix Vichnevski, together with his 200 paintings and objets d'art. Vichnevski was appointed curator of the museum, to be run in conjunction with the museum housing the works of the Ostankino serfs. The Fundación John Boulton museum, in the harbour town of La Guaira, Venez., was opened officially. The museum, giving a picture in miniature of the life of the country's chief port, was housed in a fine residence of the colonial period. In Belgium a new museum in Courtrai, housed in an ancient tower of Broel, displayed prehistoric and Gallo-Roman discoveries in Flanders. Lisores in northern France, where Fernand Léger did much of his work, finally had a museum devoted to that artist. The Cesena Museum of Ancient History in Italy was designed on boldly modern lines and gave a comprehensive picture of economic, social, administrative, and cultural history. The museum was housed in a crypt underneath the Biblioteca Malatestiana, the oldest of all Italian public libraries and a masterpiece of Renaissance architecture.

There were important museum developments in many Asian and African countries. Much modernization and new building had already taken place in Japan, and ambitious current projects included the creation of a Museum of Man in Tokyo, the renovation of the National Science Museum, and the rebuilding of the Osaka Natural History Museum. Three new museums were opened in Ceylon, and in Thailand the Kamphaeng Phet National Museum was officially opened on March 19. One of the most important projects in West Africa was the Cape Coast Castle Historical Museum in Ghana. Adaptation of the ancient Portuguese castle would not be an easy task, but both the University College of Cape Coast and the Ghana Museums and Monuments Board offered the closest cooperation. Also in Africa, the Lake Malawi Museum was opened on April 24 at Mangochi Township near Lake Malawi.

In Egypt a new Science Museum was opened in Damietta, and three new wings were opened in the Museum of Science and Technology, Cairo. The Iraq Museum, Baghdad, was enlarged by Abdullah al-Sarraf Hall, named for a donor of the most rare and precious numismatic collections in the country. In Israel the new building for Tel Aviv's art museum opened in the spring, set in extensive gardens to be used partly as an open-air museum of modern sculpture. The architects were I. Yashar and D. Eitan.

Acquisitions. The Louvre's most important acquisition was undoubtedly "The Crucifixion" by Giovanni Bellini (from the Contini Bonacossi Collection). Other important acquisitions were "The Buddha" by Odilon Redon and a 13th-century collection of Limoges enamels. The National Gallery in Prague acquired Picasso's "Rape of the Sabines" and Léger's "Two Lovers in the Campaign."

The Whitney Museum announced the receipt of the entire remaining estate of the painter Edward Hopper, including more than 2,000 works. The Museum of Modern Art announced that Picasso had donated what it had long sought as a purchase: "Guitar," one of the most valued sculptures of the Cubist period. Other important acquisitions included Velázquez' "Portrait of Juan de Pareja" for the Metropolitan Museum of Art; Ingres' "Portrait of the Marquis de Pastoret" for the Art Institute of Chicago; Correggio's "Cardinal Bibiena" for the Minneapolis Institute of Arts; Bierstadt's "Rainbow over Valley" for the California Palace of the Legion of Honor; and Botticelli's "Madonna, Child, and St. John" for the Cleveland Museum of Art. J. Paul Getty purchased Titian's "The Death of Actaeon" for about $4.2 million for the Getty Museum, under construction in Malibu, Calif., but its release was delayed for a year while the U.K. government sought funds to keep the work in Britain. Later in the year, the Boston Museum of Fine Arts returned a Raphael portrait to Italy after claims that the work had been exported illegally were substantiated.

The National Gallery, London, whose grant for purchases was increased as of April 1, 1970, from £230,000 to £480,000, acquired "Le déjeuner à Villeneuve-sur-Yonne" (Vuillard), "Salome Receives the Head of St. John the Baptist" (ascribed to Caravaggio), "Landscape in the Roman Campagna with a Man Scooping Water" (Nicolas Poussin), "The Adoration of the Magi" (Bartholomäus Spranger), "Portrait of Ludovicus Nonnius" (Rubens), and the Rogier van der Weyden masterpiece "Portrait of St. Ivo."

It was found that a small Renaissance bronze statue entitled "Boy with a Ball" in the National Gallery, Washington, and a larger statue in the Louvre known as "Hercules" or "Atlas" were both misnamed. After a study carried out by Bertrand Jestaz of the Louvre, they were rejoined as a single work, entitled "St. Christopher Carrying the Christ Child" and attributed to Bartolomeo Bellano. Separated parts of the famous cross of Bury St. Edmunds, one of the most important medieval ivory masterpieces in the Metropolitan Museum of Art, were also brought together at least temporarily. The missing figure of Christ was found in Scandinavia, and the owner, the Oslo Museum of Applied Art, agreed to its exhibition for two years at the Cloisters' "The Year 1200" exhibition, replaced in its original position on the cross.

The British Museum, the Metropolitan Museum of Art, the Ashmolean in Oxford, the Ankara (Turk.) Museum, the Louvre, and the Museum of Primitive Art, New York City, all discovered that their neolithic Anatolian pottery collections contained a very high percentage of forgeries. The discovery was made by three Oxford professors using a thermoluminescence method of dating.

International Cooperation. An international convention "Prohibiting and Preventing the Illicit Import, Export, and Transfer of Ownership of Cultural Property" was adopted by UNESCO. Article 6 instituted a form of "passport" for legally exported cultural property, making it illegal for museums and institutions to acquire it without this document.

The third International Congress of Agricultural Museums, which took place in Budapest, Hung., in April, attracted 213 experts from 24 countries. The ICOM International Committee for Museums of Applied Art held a joint seminar at the Ghana National Museum, Accra, with the Museums Association of Tropical Africa. The seminar included visits to museums and craft centres as well as working sessions.

The three UNESCO regional training centres in Jos (Nigeria), Mexico City, and New Delhi offered courses in 1971 for over 40 students in the conservation, restoration, and preservation of cultural property.　　　　　　　　　　　　　　(A. S.; J. Kɪ.)

See also Architecture; Art Exhibitions; Art Sales.

Music

On Oct. 8, 1970, Leonard Bernstein and the New York Philharmonic Orchestra gave the American premiere of Luciano Berio's *Sinfonia* in Philharmonic Hall. On October 21, with the same orchestra and conductor, Gregor Piatigorsky celebrated his 40th anniversary of concert-giving in the U.S. by playing Richard Strauss's *Don Quixote*. In London's Festival Hall on October 14, Mstislav Rostropovich gave the first performance of Witold Lutoslawski's cello concerto at a Royal Philharmonic Society concert. On October 21, in the same hall, Pierre Boulez directed the premiere of the revised version of his *Éclat/Multiples* with the BBC Symphony Orchestra. The 25th anniversary of the United Nations was celebrated in Carnegie Hall, New York, on October 6, with the premiere of Gian Carlo Menotti's *Triplo Concerto à tre*, given by the American Symphony Orchestra conducted by Leopold Stokowski. The premiere of György Ligeti's *Lontano* was given by the Los Angeles Philharmonic Orchestra under Zubin Mehta on October 31. On October 29 Aaron Copland's 70th birthday was celebrated in New York with a concert of five of his works given by the New York Philharmonic Orchestra, the composer conducting.

On November 20, the Bournemouth (Eng.) Symphony Orchestra gave the first performance outside Finland of Sibelius' *Kullervo* symphony. During that month the Music Weeks in Budapest, Hung., presented a wide conspectus of modern works. A similar survey took place in December at the fourth Brussels Reconnaissance des Musiques Modernes, which included the presentation of two pages of Karlheinz Stockhausen's *Aus den sieben Tagen* on each morning of the week-long festival. Boulez' *Domaines* was another major piece given. On December 3, the first performance of Ned Rorem's piano concerto was given in Pittsburgh, Pa., by Jerome Lowenthal and the Pittsburgh Symphony Orchestra under William Steinberg. On December 7, Georg Solti and the Chicago Symphony Orchestra presented the premiere of Martin David Levy's First Piano Concerto, with Earl Wild as soloist. In London on the 200th anniversary of Beethoven's birth (December 16) Carlo Maria Giulini conducted the *Missa Solemnis* in Festival Hall with the New Philharmonia Chorus and Orchestra. In New York, Daniel Barenboim and Rudolf Serkin each celebrated the bicentenary with a series of Beethoven sonatas late in the year. During December, the Musica Viva Society of Australia celebrated its 25th anniversary with a season of new music.

The first performance of Ingolf Dahl's saxophone concerto was given in New York on Jan. 13, 1971, by the Boston Symphony Orchestra with Harvey Pittel as alto saxophone soloist. The conductor, Michael Tilson Thomas, had been taught by Dahl and dedicated the concert to the composer's memory. On January 5, Eugene Ormandy gave the U.S. premiere of Shostakovich's 14th Symphony in New York with the Philadelphia Orchestra. On January 22, the Los Angeles Philharmonic Orchestra, conducted by Mehta, gave the premiere of Lalo Schifrin's *Pulsations* for electronic keyboard (controlled by the composer), jazz band, and orchestra. Edmund Rubbra's Eighth Symphony was given its premiere in Liverpool, Eng., by the Liverpool Philharmonic Orchestra (January 5), conducted by Charles Groves.

Above, "Mass" is performed to celebrate the opening of the John F. Kennedy Center for the Performing Arts in Washington, D.C., on Sept. 8, 1971. Above, right, the composer, Leonard Bernstein, appears on stage for a curtain call at the end of the performance.

FRED FIGALL—FLETCHER DRAKE

Lukas Foss conducted the first performance of his *Baroque Variations* with the Los Angeles Philharmonic (February 4), and the New York Philharmonic invited Stockhausen to conduct the first New York performances of his *Hymnen, Regions I, II,* and *IV* and the world premiere of *Region III* on February 25. The same orchestra presented an all-Schoenberg concert (February 28), conducted by Seiji Ozawa, at which Peter Serkin played the piano concerto. Haruma Miyake-Shibata's *Six Voices in June* had its premiere at Alice Tully Hall on February 21. In London's Queen Elizabeth Hall on February 26, the London Sinfonietta, which over the past few years had brought a breath of fresh air to London's musical life, gave the first performances of Iain Hamilton's *Voyage* and Harrison Birtwistle's *Meridian*. On February 16, a new quintet for clarinet, horn, violin, cello, and piano by Alan Rawsthorne (who died later in the year) was given in the same hall by the Music Group of London.

In Philadelphia on March 5 Vincent Persichetti's *Sinfonia: "Janiculum"* had its first performance by the Philadelphia Orchestra under Ormandy. On the 12th, Berio's *Memory,* for electronic piano and electronic harpsichord, had its premiere at New York's Alice Tully Hall by the Chamber Music Society of Lincoln Center. Other "firsts" during the month in New York were William Mayer's *Octagon* for piano and orchestra (March 21) with William Masselos as soloist supported by the American Symphony Orchestra under Stokowski, and Peter Mennin's *Sinfonia for Orchestra* (March 25) by the New York Philharmonic under Stanislaw Skrowaczewski. A retrospective concert of music by Morton Feldman was given at the New York Cultural Center on March 26.

In London, John Joubert's Second Symphony had its premiere at a concert of the Royal Philharmonic Society in Festival Hall given by Sir Adrian Boult and the London Philharmonic Orchestra (March 24). During the month the Cardiff (Wales) Festival of Twentieth-Century Music gave the first performances of Benjamin Britten's song cycle *Who are These Children?* (only partly finished; it was given complete later in the year at Edinburgh, Scot.), and of Martin Dalby's *Cancionero para una mariposa*. In Leningrad, Sergei Slonimsky's *Concerto Buffo* received its first performance. On March 30 the Royal Albert Hall in London celebrated its centenary with a concert attended by Queen Elizabeth II; the concert included a piece by her great-great-grandfather Prince Albert, his setting of the *Jubilate*.

On April 1, Stephen Douglas Burton's *Symphony for Large Orchestra* had its premiere in Chicago with the Chicago Symphony Orchestra conducted by Solti, who took his orchestra on an extensive tour of Europe from August to October, sharing the programs with the orchestra's principal guest conductor, Giulini. On April 4, the Juilliard Quartet gave the first of a series of all of Bartók's quartets at Alice Tully Hall. On April 5, at the same venue, the season's series entitled "New and Newer Music" included new works by Berio and Gheorghe Costinescu. During the month "Days of English Music in the U.S.S.R." took place in Leningrad and included programs by the London Symphony Orchestra conducted by Britten. At the Moscow Conservatory during April, Rodin Shchedrin played his own 24 Preludes and Fugues for piano.

The Royan (France) Festival of New Music had as its theme *"Musique des Pays de l'Est,"* and the usual piano competition took place there. One novelty of this festival was a mystery tour organized by Greek composer Iannis Xenakis that lasted from seven o'clock one evening until four the next morning. There was also an important concert by the Paris group Domaine Musical. This was conducted by composer Gilbert Amy and included music by Stockhausen.

From May 18 to May 29, the fifth Inter-American Music Festival in Washington, D.C., included 12 world and seven U.S. first performances; sonic collage was much in evidence. The Vienna Festival took place from May 22 to June 20 and included an extensive survey of Franz Schubert's works. The English Bach Festival in London and Oxford during April and May honoured Greek composers to celebrate the 150th anniversary of Greek independence; among those represented were Yassis Ionanddis, Nikos Skalkottas, and Jani Christou. The London wing of the festival also featured Stockhausen's music and the composer was on hand to supervise performances of his *Stimmung, Mantra,* and *Prozession*. The Bergen (Nor.) Festival from May 25 to June 9 included the first performance of Sven-Erik Back's *Transfjädrarna*. The Granada (Spain) Festival from June 21 to July 11 included concerts in the palace of Charles V. The year's International Society for Contemporary Music Festival was held in London. By and large, the new music proved disappointing; it featured Swedish, Austrian, and British evenings. Among the more interesting works was Nicolaus Hüber's *Versuch über Sprache.* At the Lincoln Center, New York, from June 21 to 25 the first Josquin Festival-Conference was held.

The Cheltenham (Eng.) Festival (July 2–11) introduced three interesting works: Reginald Smith Brindle's *Apocalypse,* Dalby's *Concerto Martin Pescatore,* and Peter Racine Fricker's *Nocturne.* The festival at Tours, France, beginning on July 4, was once again graced by a visit from Sviatoslav Richter; Pierre Boulez conducted concerts given by the London Sinfonietta. During the month the Temple University Music Festival in the U.S. gave Andrew Lloyd Webber's pop opera *Jesus Christ Superstar.* At the Tanglewood Festival (July 2–August 22) Leonard Bernstein conducted the *Missa Solemnis,* a performance in memory of conductor Serge Koussevitzky. Bernstein's new multimedia *Mass* opened the new John F. Kennedy Center for the Performing Arts in Washington in September.

The 77th season of Henry Wood Promenade Concerts opened in London on July 23 with a magnificent performance of Mahler's Eighth Symphony—the "Symphony of a Thousand"—conducted by Colin Davis (*see* BIOGRAPHY). The same symphony was recorded by no less than three conductors during the year—Bernard Haitink with the Concertgebouw in Amsterdam, Rafael Kubelik with Bavarian Radio in Munich, W.Ger., and Solti with the Chicago Symphony and a Vienna chorus in Vienna. The Proms at the Albert Hall included an 80th birthday tribute to Sir Arthur Bliss, master of the Queen's Musick; for the first time in its history the series went to other venues—Westminster Cathedral, the Round House, and the Royal Opera House, Covent Garden, for a performance of *Boris Godunov* with Boris Christoff in the title role. The South Bank Festival in London's Elizabeth Hall featured song programs organized by Gerald Moore, who gave master classes during the day. The Edinburgh Festival (August 22–September 11) celebrated its 25th anniversary with a typically wide-ranging, internationally flavoured program. The Birmingham (Eng.) Triennial Festival (September 20–October 2) included the first performances of John McCabe's Second Symphony and John Joubert's *The Raising of Lazarus.* Graz, Aus., held its usual Autumn Festival of New Music (October 8–26) and the Warsaw Autumn Festival took place during September and October.

During October the appointment of Lorin Maazel as chief conductor of the Cleveland (O.) Orchestra was announced, to take effect from the beginning of the 1972–73 season. Maazel took up his appointment as associate principal conductor with the New Philharmonia Orchestra in January 1971, and conducted the orchestra on a tour of the U.S. in November. The London Philharmonic Orchestra appeared during British Week at San Francisco at the end of September. Pierre Boulez became chief conductor of the BBC Symphony Orchestra in September.

Opera. *United States.* At the beginning of the 1970–71 season, the New York City Opera gave a new production of Donizetti's *Roberto Devereux* (Oct. 15, 1970) with Beverly Sills as Queen Elizabeth I. *The Makropoulos Affair* followed on November 3. On March 7, 1971, the company presented the premiere of Gian Carlo Menotti's *The Most Important Man.* The main events at the Metropolitan at the end of 1970 were *Fidelio,* conducted by Karl Böhm with Leonie Rysanek as Leonore in December, and *Parsifal*

with Cesare Siepi singing his first Gurnemanz on November 14. On February 18 the company gave a new production of Massenet's *Werther* with Franco Corelli in the title role and Christa Ludwig as Charlotte. Later, Régine Crespin took over the latter role with great success. The first new production of the 1971–72 season was *Der Freischütz* on September 28; *Tristan und Isolde,* conducted by Erich Leinsdorf (returning to the Met after a long absence), followed on November 18.

Otello (November 7) and *The Rake's Progress* (November 14) were the last productions at the San Francisco Opera in the autumn of 1970. The 1971 season opened with *Manon,* with Sills in the title part. The end of the Chicago Lyric Opera's 1970 season saw Benjamin Britten's *Billy Budd* (November 6) and a double bill of Bartok's *Bluebeard's Castle* and Puccini's *Gianni Schicchi* (November 27), with Tito Gobbi in the title role, entering the repertory. The 1971 season opened on September 24 with *Semiramide,* featuring Joan Sutherland and Marilyn Horne. *Werther,* with Tatiana Troyanos as Charlotte, followed on October 23. In November, Georg Solti and the Chicago Symphony Chorus and Orchestra gave the Chicago and New York premieres of Schoenberg's *Moses and Aaron.*

During the year, the appointment of Göran Gentele, of the Royal Swedish Opera, as general manager of the Metropolitan beginning with the 1972–73 season was announced. Rafael Kubelik was appointed musical director at the same time.

United Kingdom. The first new production of the year at the Royal Opera, Covent Garden, was *Eugene Onegin* (February 10), staged by Peter Hall and conducted by Georg Solti. The same team was responsible for a new *Tristan und Isolde* on June 14. On July 3, Solti conducted this work at his farewell appearance, with Birgit Nilsson as Isolde. Important revivals during the year included *Così fan tutte* and *Peter Grimes,* both conducted by Colin Davis, who took over as musical director from the beginning of the 1971–72 season, conducting *Fidelio* on October 15, his first assignment in his new job. In June, Peter Hall resigned as artistic director and was not replaced. The first new production of the season was *Le nozze di Figaro,* conducted by Davis and produced by John Copley at the beginning of December.

New productions of the Sadler's Wells Opera Company at the Coliseum were *The Twilight of the Gods* (January 29), conducted by Reginald Goodall, and *The Seraglio* (March 13). The 1971–72 season opened in July with a new production of *Lohengrin,* conducted by Charles Mackerras. *Cavalleria Rusticana* and *I Pagliacci,* in modern dress, followed on September 29, and *The Coronation of Poppea,* with Janet Baker in the title role, on November 24. The year's major production of the Welsh National Opera was *Lulu* in September at Cardiff. Scottish Opera produced *Der Rosenkavalier* in the spring, and Britten's television opera *Owen Wingrave* was given for the first time, on BBC 2 on May 16. The Glyndebourne Festival gave new productions of *The Queen of Spades* (in Russian) and *Ariadne auf Naxos* in May and June. There was an exhibition from August to October at the Victoria and Albert Museum in London to celebrate 25 years of post–World War II performances at Covent Garden.

West Germany. In West Berlin at the end of 1970, the premiere of Kessler's *Nationale Feiertage* was given on October 2. On Jan. 16, 1971, the original

Mussorgsky version of *Boris Godunov,* with Martti Talvela in the title role, was given in West Berlin by the Deutsche Oper, which later in the year gave the premiere of Aribert Reimann's *Melusine* at the Schwetzingen, Edinburgh, and Berlin festivals. At the Berlin Festival, the company also gave the premiere of Hans Werner Henze's *Der langwierige Weg in die Wohnung der Natascha Ungeheuer.* The work, however, was poorly received. The first performance of Günter Kochan's *Karin Lenz* was given on October 2.

Frankfurt presented a new production of Cherubini's *Medée,* with Anja Silja in the title role (March 17). At Hamburg at the end of 1970, Karl Böhm conducted a new production of *Salome* with Gwyneth Jones. On April 25 Mauricio Kagel's new opera *Staatstheater* provoked interruptions and disturbances. The same composer's *Antithese* was given at Munich together with *Sümtome,* a group work. Also at Munich there was a new production of *Lohengrin* produced by Rudolf Hartmann and conducted by Wolfgang Sawallisch, who also conducted a new production of Richard Strauss's rarely heard *Die schweigsame Frau,* produced by Gunther Rennert, at the Munich Festival during July. The festival included a new production of Mozart's *La clemenza di Tito,* produced by Jean-Pierre Ponnelle, who also staged a new *Don Giovanni* at Cologne in September that was notable for Margaret Price's brilliant singing as Donna Anna. There were no new productions at the Bayreuth Festival in July and August. At the Göttingen Festival, Johann Adolf Hasse's *Attilio Regolo* was revived in July.

Austria. Richard Strauss's rarely heard *Die ägyptische Helena* was revived at the Vienna State Opera on Dec. 5, 1970. The season continued with a new production of Mozart's *Idomeneo* on March 13. The premiere of Gottfried von Einem's *Der Besuch der alten Dame,* with Christa Ludwig in the title role, was given at the Vienna Festival (May 23) and much praised. At the Salzburg Easter Festival, Herbert von Karajan conducted and produced *Fidelio.* At the summer festival there, new productions of *Wozzeck,* with Geraint Evans, and of *Don Pasquale* were given. The Bolshoi company from Moscow visited Vienna beginning on October 5.

Italy. The 1970–71 season at La Scala, Milan, opened on Dec. 7, 1970, with Verdi's *I Vespri Siciliani* with Renata Scotto as Elena. *Wozzeck,* conducted by

Claudio Abbado, was given a new production on March 25, and the following month Montserrat Caballe and Shirley Verrett sang in a memorable revival of Donizetti's *Maria Stuarda.* At the Teatro dell'Opera, Rome, *Khovanshchina* was revived on January 28 and Rossini's *Mosè* on March 19, both with Boris Christoff in the cast. At the Florence Festival, Meyerbeer's *L'Africaine* had a notable revival on April 29 with Jessye Norman in the title role. Venice produced Saverio Mercadante's *Le due illustri Rivali* to celebrate the centenary of the composer's death. Also in Venice, Verdi's rarely performed *Il Corsaro* was produced on March 29. Naples also noted the Mercadante centenary with a revival of his *Elisa e Claudio* on January 24, and also revived Carlos Gomes' *Il Guarany* (April 2). The Verona Festival in July and August gave Verdi's *Macbeth* for the first time in the Arena.

France. The Paris Opéra announced the appointment of Rolf Liebermann as administrator and Georg Solti as musical director from the beginning of the 1972–73 season. Meanwhile, the refurbished opera house was reopened in September with a revival of Wieland Wagner's old production of *Die Walküre.* The Opéra-Comique also reopened after a long break. At Lyons, Christiane Eda-Pierre appeared in the Brecht-Weill *Mahagonny.* At the Aix Festival in July the premiere of J. Charpentier's *Beatris* was given.

Other Countries. The Prague (Czech.) Spring Festival featured a new production of Smetana's *Libuše.* At the Budapest Opera, Gyorgi Ranki's *Az Ember Tragédiája* was given its premiere on Dec. 4, 1970. At the Royal Opera, Stockholm, *The Opera* of Bengt Ernryd and Gunnar Valkare had its first performance on Nov. 5, 1970. At the Teatro Colon, Buenos Aires, Arg., on April 7, the season opened with a new production of Berlioz' *La Damnation de Faust* with Nicolai Gedda in the title role. At Brno, Czech., the first performance of Bohuslav Martinu's opera-film *The Three Wishes* was given on June 16. In Ireland, at the Wexford Festival, at the end of October 1970, *Lakmé* was revived with Eda-Pierre in the title role. She also appeared in Bizet's *Les Pêcheurs des Perles* in the 1971 festival.   (A. G. BL.)

Jazz. It was perhaps symptomatic of the creative blight in the contemporary jazz world that by far the most outstanding event of 1971 was a negative one, the death in July, a few days after his 71st birthday, of its most revered and renowned figure, Louis Armstrong (*see* OBITUARIES). The worldwide celebrations that had marked his 70th birthday had been informed perhaps by a touch of hysterical apprehension that even Armstrong must die some day, and that when he did jazz would finally have lost its innocence forever. Indeed, his death finally invalidated the old claim that jazz was the one art form whose entire evolution was encompassed within the professional life-span of a still living person. Although Armstrong had long since forfeited his full instrumental effectiveness, his death was nonetheless the most traumatic event that jazz historians ever had been obliged to record.

A native of New Orleans, La., Armstrong was an archetype in the sense that his migration north conveniently symbolized the spread of jazz throughout the world. Leaving his hometown for Chicago in 1922, he reached New York two years later, and by 1928 had completed his Hot Five and Hot Seven recordings, those remarkable series in which unwittingly he codified the vocabulary of the jazz soloist and destroyed forever the validity of the old New Orleans tradition that subordinated the individual voice to the require-

Jeff Fenholt plays Christ in the 1971 Broadway version of the rock opera "Jesus Christ Superstar," produced by Robert Stigwood.

ZODIAC

ments of the ensemble. Although his stylistic evolution had remained static since 1930, Armstrong remained a colossus in the jazz world who, after enjoying and occasionally transforming the fleshpots of Hollywood and Broadway, vaudeville and variety, returned in the last 25 years of his life to the small-group formula with which he had begun. While posterity would have to decide his place in 20th-century music at large, it would be extremely surprising if, when the passage of time had rendered irrelevant the social context of his work, Louis Armstrong were not eventually acknowledged as one of its most extraordinary geniuses.

Worlds removed from the intuitive candour of Armstrong's art were the machinations of the younger players who continued to deny, vociferously in words if less convincingly in sound, the tradition of improvisation on a harmonic base that had endured in an unbroken line from Armstrong's boyhood down to the modern era. One innovation of the 1960s that looked as if it was becoming standard practice for the 1970s was the reliance by the avant-garde on electronic gadgetry for new tonal effects. Electrification, for some years confined in jazz to the guitar and vibraphone, spread quite suddenly, so that by 1971 neologisms such as "electric piano" and "electric saxophone" had become commonplace in jazz recordings. But paucity of inspiration remains paucity of inspiration whatever instrument is used to express it, an inconvenient truth that appeared so far to have escaped the notice of the players themselves and their admirers. These, like an earlier generation of saxophonists who transferred their platitudes to the flute to win a new but spurious lease on life, seemed to have forgotten that the act of improvisation is justified only when the soloist improves on the given theme.

With Armstrong gone, the Grand Old Man of jazz was now clearly Edward Kennedy "Duke" Ellington, although it was perhaps misleading to apply such a title to one so obviously bursting with life. In 1971 Ellington was more active than ever, surviving with apparent nonchalance the depletions in his ranks caused by the death of saxophonist Johnny Hodges and the departure of key brassmen Lawrence Brown and William "Cat" Anderson. Ellington continued to stress the importance to him of his sacred concerts, in which his musical expression of a homespun Christian faith was interpreted by his orchestra in a succession of churches and cathedrals, revealing an unexpected obverse side to the bon viveur image he had striven so sedulously to create over the last 30 or 40 years. September 1971 brought one of his most prestigious triumphs, when his tour of the Soviet Union drew full houses and ecstatic praise, marking the biggest step yet by the aesthetic dialecticians of the Kremlin in their retreat from the "decadent bourgeois music" platform of Stalinist days.

Surviving veterans huddled closer together as the obituary lists lengthened. The year was the worst yet for the disappearance of important musicians. Apart from Armstrong, the saddest losses were probably those of the brilliant modern pianist Wynton Kelly and the spectacular trumpeter Charlie Shavers. Connoisseurs also were especially grieved to hear of the death of ex-Count Basie saxophonist Talmadge "Tab" Smith, one of the tiny elite of players who had managed to master the soprano saxophone. Other outstanding jazz and fringe-jazz deaths were those of saxophonists Ernie Caceres, Derek Humble, and Harold McNair, pianists Joe Sullivan, Sonny White, Len-

nie Hayton, and Lilian Hardin Armstrong, drummers Ben Pollack and Morey Feld, trombonist Lou McGarity, and bandleader Ted Lewis. In the midst of this glum picture of an art form apparently at the moment of dissolution, at least two active musicians, Oscar Peterson and Buddy Rich, both products of an earlier age, were at the very summit of their powers, Peterson as a solo pianist of prolific technique and great depth of melodic resource, Rich as a barnstorming showband-drummer whose pyrotechnical displays inspired almost as much awe as delight.   (B. Gr.)

Popular. The year saw an ironic decline in the popularity of "popular" music; it was no longer the music of the masses, but of a definite group of young people every bit as specialistic as classical musicians. They took their music very seriously, listening rather than dancing to it.

The heroes of this group were the composer-performers, who could, on their own, hold an audience of several hundred for an hour or more. The most popular were James Taylor, from a talented East Coast family, and Neil Young, one of the Laurel Canyon "aristocracy" which also included Graham Nash and David Crosby. Many of the musicians were women, and the male dominance of pop was being challenged by such fine singer-writers as Joni Mitchell, Melanie, Laura Nyro, and, above all, Carole King. Having started out as a songwriter in the early 1960s, Carole King had emerged by 1971 as a performer in her own right. In contrast with the more introverted writing of Taylor and Young, the simplicity and directness of Carole King's songs, rooted in teen-beat pop rather than folk, made her deservedly popular. Notable British artists of this kind were Elton John, who achieved superstar status in 1971, the highly individual Gilbert O'Sullivan, and former session singer Lesley Duncan.

Most of these "new" stars had several years' experience behind them, and technically the standard of pop music had never been so high. The musicians who had started in the '60s were still active, and groups formed, split, and re-formed with great frequency. One of the more enduring partnerships was that of Keith Emerson, virtuoso keyboard player and former leader of The Nice, with the brilliant young drummer Carl Palmer and King Crimson's ex-bassist and songwriter Greg Lake.

With so many experienced musicians around and performing venues decreasing in number, new talent had a hard time emerging. Rock promoter Bill Graham closed his Fillmore East in New York and Fillmore West in San Francisco, citing the increasingly high costs of rock groups and the difficulty of booking top talent in his small theatres. Probably the greatest impact made by new talent was that by Grand Funk Railroad, an American trio who drew record-breaking crowds wherever they appeared. Due to the overcrowding of the pop business at home, many British artists sought—and found—appreciation abroad; Humble Pie and The Faces made successful U.S. tours, and the Scottish quartet Middle of the Road, whose single "Chirpy Chirpy Cheep Cheep" was one of the biggest commercial successes of the year, made their name in Italy before they were even known in Britain.

The year saw the official dissolution of the Beatles, in a lawsuit brought by Paul McCartney against the other three members of the group. However, their solo activities continued to flourish. It was a particularly good year for George Harrison, whose triple album drew high praise from the critics; one of the

Alone onstage in Los Angeles during a benefit for the Motion Picture and Television Relief Fund, Frank Sinatra sings his last farewell with the song "Angel Eyes." During his long career, Sinatra filmed 58 movies and recorded 100 albums and nearly 2,000 individual records.

FRANK LEONARDO—KEYSTONE

Former Beatle George
Harrison sings
at a benefit rock concert
at Madison Square Garden
in New York City
to raise funds
for Pakistani refugees
in 1971.

tracks, "My Sweet Lord," was voted the year's best single by readers of *Melody Maker* magazine. He also managed to organize a concert in New York, in aid of Pakistani refugees, at which Bob Dylan appeared alongside George, Ringo Starr, and many others.

From the point of view of record sales, the Beatles had less pulling power individually than as a group, and the loss of their sales was keenly felt. Generally, however, business flourished despite high prices, and prerecorded tapes and cassettes became increasingly popular. In Britain there was a huge nostalgia market, and many record companies made special reissues of old hits, recoupled and at bargain prices. Some of these records became hits all over again, including Elvis Presley's "Heartbreak Hotel." Also on the increase was the number of illegal recordings. Most of these were made in very bad conditions, but despite poor sound quality the records still sold. In answer to companies and artists angered at the loss of royalties, the "bootleggers" replied that they were simply meeting a demand for material that the companies were not supplying.

Pop lost one of its more controversial figures in July when Jim Morrison (*see* OBITUARIES), lead singer with The Doors, died in Paris at the age of 27, and of course the death of Louis Armstrong was a loss to popular music as well as to jazz.

Compared with the previous year, 1971 was almost void of pop festivals. Of those that were scheduled, Louisiana's "Celebration of Life" closed early, following three deaths related to drug abuse and financial troubles, and the Newport (R.I.) Festival's last two days were canceled after thousands of young people crashed the gates, destroying property and injuring some 300 persons. Festival promoters were unwilling to run financial risks, and suitable sites were hard to find. The pop festival had become less of an entertainment than an endurance test for all concerned; groups might have to play at two in the morning, having waited for several hours, to an audience half-asleep and camping in primitive conditions. Yet people still flocked to festivals—a sign of the great seriousness with which pop was taken; the music was to be considered and analyzed rather than enjoyed. Its aficiona-

dos eschewed commercialism: if any artist suddenly had a hit single, then he had surely "sold out." Groups thus accused included Free, who split up, and Deep Purple, who ignored the criticism and stormed ahead with great success.

The type of music in favour varied, but the general trend was away from heavy percussion and electric guitars and toward softer sounds. This, plus the new passion for old pop, indicated a desire to return to the roots. There was considerable interest in the "Afro-rock" of such groups as Osibisa, and soul music and reggae kept their devotees. Tamla Motown had another very successful year, developing both its business and its music; Diana Ross launched out on a brilliant solo career, and her former group, The Supremes, scored their own successes both "live" and on record.

Pop music had never been so sophisticated and varied as it was by the fall of 1971; within its framework lay a multiplicity of sounds and styles. But while it was musically mature, commercially it lacked fire, and hopes of a "new Beatles" to rekindle public interest remained unfulfilled.   (H. R. Mo.)

Folk Music. Throughout the world, in towns and villages alike, folk song and folk dance attracted an ever increasing number of participants. Numerous national and international festivals were held. Some were of long standing, such as the Llangollen annual International Musical Eisteddfod in North Wales and the big national festivals of Romania and Bulgaria, but there were also a number of festivals of more recent growth. It was, however, in the countless local gatherings where neighbours met for the enjoyment of singing and dancing together that the continuing popularity of folk music was most clearly seen. The English Folk Dance Society, which was founded by Cecil Sharp in 1911 and had amalgamated with the Folk-Song Society in 1932 to become the English Folk Dance and Song Society, had its 60th birthday in 1971. The diamond jubilee was marked by festivities in all parts of the country.

A flood of folk-song records was issued during the year, particularly in England and the U.S. However, a large proportion of these were folk songs in name only, being contemporary songs composed in a "folk" style. Unfortunately, this type of song had to a great extent become confused in the public mind with the traditional folk song, orally transmitted and evolved by generations of singers. However, there were signs of a growing appreciation of the distinctive qualities of real folk song.

The extent to which the arts of folk song and dance were still practiced by traditional exponents varied considerably from country to country. In some countries, the tradition had persisted with but little interruption. In others, particularly in the industrialized nations of Western Europe, it had tended to wane with the impact of modern civilization. During the year there was a welcome renewal of confidence among folk singers and dancers in the value of their art, which in turn led to a strengthening of the tradition.

The existing archives of traditional music were greatly enlarged by recordings made in the field, and several new archives were formed. Among these was the Archive of Maori and Pacific Music established by the University of Auckland, N.Z., where an ambitious program was envisaged for the future. A number of new societies and organizations concerned with folk music were formed, including the Irish Folk Music Society and the Institute of Traditional Arts, which was located at Dartington Hall, Devonshire.

The International Folk Music Council (IFMC), which had its headquarters in Kingston, Ont., although it had in fact been founded in London in 1947, held its 21st conference in Jamaica. Among the subjects that were discussed were folk music in education, the acculturation of folk music, and the impact of electronic technology on the practice and study of folk music. The delegates who attended the conference represented 30 countries and were drawn from the five continents. One of the most important roles the IFMC had fulfilled was that of a permanent centre for information and coordination. (MA. KA.)

See also Dance; Motion Pictures; Television and Radio; Theatre.

Nauru

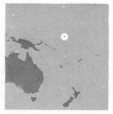

An island republic in the Pacific Ocean, Nauru lies about 1,200 mi. E of New Guinea. Area: 8.2 sq.mi. (21 sq.km.). Pop. (1970 est.): 6,603. Seat of government: Uaboe District. Language: English and Nauruan. Religion: Christian. President in 1971, Hammer de Roburt.

On Jan. 23, 1971, the first elections were held in the republic since independence: 48 candidates contested 18 available seats in the Nauruan Parliament. Pres. Hammer de Roburt, running unopposed, was reelected by Parliament for a term of three years. De Roburt raised the possibility that Nauruans might in the future have to pay taxes. He predicted that the supply of phosphate, on which the national wealth was founded, would run out in about 20 years.

During 1971 the Nauruans planned closer diplomatic ties with Japan, and the republic decided to open a consulate in Tokyo. (A. R. G. G.)

NAURU
Education. (1968) Primary, pupils 1,396, teachers (1966) 79; secondary, pupils 339, teachers (1966) 19; teacher training, students 18, teachers 1.
Finance and Trade. Monetary unit: Australian dollar (A$0.89 = U.S. $1; A$2.14 = £1 sterling), with a free rate (Sept. 27, 1971) of A$0.87 to U.S. $1. Budget (1969–70): revenue A$7,640,000; expenditure A$6,311,000. Foreign trade (1968–69): imports A$5,225,000 (72% from Australia, 7% from New Zealand); exports (phosphates) A$24,046,000 (65% to Australia, 24% to New Zealand, 7% to Japan by tonnage).
Industry. Production: phosphate rock (1968–69) 2,198,000 metric tons; electricity (1968) 19.3 million kw-hr.

Nepal

A constitutional monarchy of Asia, Nepal is in the Himalayas between India and Tibet. Area: 54,362 sq.mi. (140,797 sq.km.). Pop. (1971): 11,289,968. Cap. and largest city: Kathmandu (pop., 1971, 153,405). Language: Nepali (official); also Newari and Bhutia. Religion: Hindu 85%; Buddhist 8%; Muslim 2%. King and (to April 1971) chairman of the Council of Ministers (prime minister), Mahendra Bir Bikram Shah Deva; prime minister from April, Kirti Nidhi Bista.

The appointment of a new Cabinet headed by former prime minister Kirti Nidhi Bista in April 1971, after a year of direct rule by King Mahendra, and the resumption of normal legislative powers by the national Panchayat (parliament) were generally welcomed in Nepal. The king kept tight control over the administration and intervened directly to reinstate Panchayat member Ramraja Prasad Singh, who had been prosecuted by the government on sedition charges. Differences between the king and some members of the Cabinet led to the resignation of the Bista ministry in August. But the crisis was short-lived and Bista was brought back as head of the new government from which three of his senior colleagues, including Foreign Minister G. B. Rajbhandary, were dropped.

Relations with India were normalized with the signing of a new five-year trade and transit treaty in August, providing preferential treatment for goods of either country. It was of special significance for Nepal as its implementation would help diversify Nepalese trade. Nepal's industrial development was to be boosted through unrestricted flow of goods to India and Indian investment in joint ventures. A Sino-Nepalese agreement for Chinese experts to make a feasibility survey for cotton cultivation and erection of a textile plant in the Terai region, close to the Indian border, was shelved temporarily because of Indian sensitivity over the presence of Chinese in the border area. (G. U.)

NEPAL
Education. (1969–70) Primary, pupils 448,754, teachers 17,563; secondary and vocational, pupils 94,731, teachers 4,145; teacher training (1966–67), students 217, teachers 19; higher (including University at Kathmandu; 1966–67), students 10,235, teaching staff 751.
Finance. Monetary unit: Nepalese rupee, with a par value of NRs. 10.12 to U.S. $1 (NRs. 24.30 = £1 sterling; NRs. 1.35 = 1 Indian rupee) and a free rate (Sept. 27, 1971) of c. NRs. 10.03 to U.S. $1 (c. NRs. 24.87 = £1 sterling). Gold, SDRs, and foreign exchange, central bank: (June 1971) U.S. $99.6 million; (June 1970) U.S. $89.3 million. Budget (1970–71): revenue NRs. 973 million (including foreign aid NRs. 333 million); expenditure NRs. 973 million (including development expenditure NRs. 633 million).
Foreign Trade. (1967–68) Imports NRs. 444,754,000 (98% from India in 1964–65); exports NRs. 395,121,000 (99% to India in 1964–65). Main exports: food and livestock 52%; crude materials (including timber and jute) 28%; manufactures 18%.
Agriculture. Production (in 000; metric tons; 1970; 1969 in parentheses): rice 2,500 (2,410); jute c. 35 (c. 35). Livestock (in 000; 1969–70): cattle c. 6,300; pigs c. 310; sheep c. 2,180; goats c. 2,260.

Netherlands

A kingdom of northwest Europe on the North Sea, the Netherlands, a Benelux country, is bounded by Belgium on the south and West Germany on the east. Area: 15,770 sq.mi. (40,844 sq.km.). Pop. (1971 est.): 13,119,430. Cap. and largest city: Amsterdam (pop., 1970 est., 820,406). Seat of government: The Hague (pop., 1970 est., 679,032). Language: Dutch. Religion (1960): Roman Catholic 40.4%; Dutch Reformed 28.3%; Reformed Churches 9.3%. Queen, Juliana; prime ministers in 1971, Piet J. S. de Jong and, from July 6, Barend W. Biesheuvel.

On April 28, 1971, 6,316,114 voters (78.6% of the electorate) chose their representatives in the lower house of the Netherlands Parliament. In all, 28 politi-

Damage to the Soviet trade delegation's building in Amsterdam was extensive after a bomb exploded on April 15, 1971, injuring ten persons.
ANEFO—PIX

cal parties took part, and 14 were successful in gaining seats. (For the distribution of seats *see* POLITICAL PARTIES.) The most significant features of the election were the continued decline in support for the religious parties—the Catholic People's Party (KVP; down 7 seats to 35) and the two major Protestant parties, the Christian Historical Union (CHU; down 2 seats to 10) and the Antirevolutionary Party (ARP, down 2 seats to 13)—growing discontent with government policies, support of the main opposition, and the success of the Democratic Socialists-70 (DS-70; 8 seats), a breakaway group from the Labour Party.

After the election, the Cabinet of Piet J. S. de Jong remained in office for over two months in a caretaker capacity while efforts were made to form a new majority administration. In mid-May Queen Juliana asked Pieter A. J. M. Steenkamp, a leading member of the KVP, to undertake exploratory talks with other party leaders to this end, and on June 22 it was announced that the queen had charged Barend Biesheuvel (*see* BIOGRAPHY), leader of the ARP, with the formation of a new coalition government. Biesheuvel succeeded in forming a five-party coalition consisting of the four

former coalition partners—the ARP, the KVP, the CHU, and the Liberals (down 1 seat to 16)—plus the DS-70. This gave the new government 82 out of the 150 seats in the lower house. The right-of-centre Cabinet comprised six members of the KVP, three from the Liberals, three from the ARP, two from the CHU, and two from the DS-70.

Joseph M. A. H. Luns (*see* BIOGRAPHY), who had held uninterrupted office as Cabinet minister for a record 19 years, left the government after his appointment as secretary-general of the North Atlantic Treaty Organization (NATO), a post that he assumed officially on October 1.

On September 21 Queen Juliana opened the new session of Parliament. Her speech, prepared by the government, underlined the general alarm felt at the deterioration of the economy, the chief causes of which were wage and price inflation and continuing overexpenditure. The budget for 1972, presented by Finance Minister Roelof J. Nelissen, forecast revenue of 35,429,000,000 guilders against expenditure of 37,-741,000,000 guilders, the deficit to be made up by tax increases. A survey by the Central Planning Bureau was pessimistic about attempts to control inflation in 1972 and predicted 80,000 unemployed. Prices were expected to increase by 12% during 1971 and wages by 6.5%, according to Jelle Zijlstra, president of the Netherlands Bank. One of the new government's first actions was to suspend, from August 4, wage and price controls that had been in effect since late 1970. This reflected the government's intention to reestablish good relations with employers and unions in the hope of controlling inflation.

On May 1 the last of 12 caissons was successfully sunk in the northern channel of the Brouwershavense Gat, and by the end of the month the southern channel was also closed. This represented an important phase in the execution of the Delta Project for land reclamation in the southwest. On June 11 Queen Juliana opened the entrance to Europoort, giving Rotterdam a new 7½-mi.-long channel suitable for tankers with a 64-ft. draft.

On Dec. 28, 1970, Foreign Minister Luns signed an agreement with the French and West German ambassadors whereby the Netherlands allocated 100 million guilders (about $30 million) for its part in the joint A-300B airbus project.

NETHERLANDS

Education. (1967–68) Primary, pupils 1,427,-966, teachers 46,008; secondary, pupils 552,087, teachers 29,788; vocational, pupils 559,343; teacher training, students 13,121, teachers 1,149; higher (including 9 universities), students 182,-044.

Finance. Monetary unit: guilder or florin, with a "pivot" rate of 0.0724 guilders to 1 Belgian franc, a par value of 3.62 guilders to U.S. $1 (8.69 guilders = £1 sterling), and a free rate (Sept. 27, 1971) of 3.36 guilders to U.S. $1 (8.34 guilders = £1 sterling). Gold, SDRs, and foreign exchange, central bank: (June 1971) U.S. $2,-980,000,000; (June 1970) U.S. $2,150,000,000. Budget (1971 est.): revenue 35,319,000,000 guilders; expenditure 37,381,000,000 guilders. Gross national product: (1969) 102,340,000,000 guilders; (1968) 91,870,000,000 guilders. Money supply: (May 1971) 30.4 billion guilders; (May 1970) 25,330,000,000 guilders. Cost of living (1963 = 100): (June 1971) 150; (June 1970) 140.

Foreign Trade. (1970) Imports 48,482,000,-000 guilders; exports 42,597,000,000 guilders. Import sources: EEC 56% (West Germany 27%, Belgium-Luxembourg 17%, France 8%); U.S. 10%; U.K. 6%. Export destinations: EEC 62%

(West Germany 33%, Belgium-Luxembourg 14%, France 10%, Italy 5%); U.K. 7%. Main exports: chemicals 14%; petroleum products 11%; textile yarns and fabrics 8%; electrical machinery and equipment 7%; machinery (non-electrical) 7%; iron and steel 6%; meat products 5%; dairy products 5%.

Transport and Communications. Roads (1970) 78,551 km. (including 500 km. expressways). Motor vehicles in use (1970): passenger 2,591,607; commercial 349,355. Railways: (1969) 3,147 km. (including 1,645 km. electrified); traffic (1970) 8,023,000,000 passenger-km., freight 3,532,000,000 net ton-km. Air traffic (1970): 6,020,000,000 passenger-km.; freight 392.3 million net ton-km. Navigable inland waterways (1969): 5,707 km. (including 2,434 km. for ships of 1,000 tons and over); freight traffic 30,077,000,000 ton-km. Shipping (1970): merchant vessels 100 gross tons and over 1,598; gross tonnage 5,206,663. Ships entered (1969) vessels totaling 113,610,000 net registered tons; goods loaded (1970) 64,206,000 metric tons, unloaded 206,183,000 metric tons. Telephones (Dec. 1969) 3,120,168. Radio receivers (Dec. 1968) 3,174,000. Television receivers (Dec. 1969) 2,-869,000.

Agriculture. Production (in 000; metric tons; 1970; 1969 in parentheses): wheat 634 (677); rye 172 (207); barley 350 (389); oats 201 (322); potatoes 5,648 (4,704); tomatoes (1969) 356, (1968) 344; apples 440 (475); pears 150 (100); sugar, raw value (1970–71) *c.* 699, (1969–70) 764; dry peas 37 (40); rapeseed 22 (12); linseed *c.* 5 (12); flax fibres 5 (11); beef and veal *c.* 308 (273); pork *c.* 640 (614); milk 8,150 (7,922); butter 121 (112); cheese 276 (268); eggs 271 (258); fish catch (1969) 323, (1968) 323. Livestock (in 000; May 1970): cattle 4,366; pigs 5,650; sheep 610; horses used in agriculture 99; chickens 56,209.

Industry. Index of production (1963 = 100): (1970) 175; (1969) 160. Production (in 000; metric tons; 1970): coal 4,322; crude oil 1,918; natural gas (cu.m.) 31,667,000; manufactured gas (cu.m.) 945,000; electricity (kw-hr.) 40,-818,000; pig iron 3,594; crude steel 5,041; zinc 46; cement 3,830; cotton yarn 52; wool yarn 17; rayon, etc., filament yarn 36; nylon, etc., filament yarn (1969) 58; nylon, etc., staple fibres (1969) 33. Merchant vessels launched (100 gross tons and over; 1970) 471,000 gross tons. New dwelling units completed (1970) 117,000.

Queen Juliana and Prince Bernhard paid the first official visit of a ruling monarch of the Netherlands to Indonesia, Aug. 26–Sept. 5, 1971. The new Dutch foreign minister, Norbert Schmelzer, held talks with his Indonesian counterpart, Adam Malik, on economic aid to Indonesia, the position of exiles from Amboina (who wanted independence from Indonesia), and the question of political prisoners in Indonesia. On October 26 Queen Juliana and Prince Bernhard paid an official visit to West Germany for the first time since World War II.

A visit by Japan's Emperor Hirohito and his wife to the Netherlands in October was met with public hostility, although there were no serious incidents. Many thousands of Dutch colonials had perished in prisoner-of-war camps in Japanese-occupied territory during World War II.

Disputes regarding the delimitation of the North Sea continental shelf were ended by a treaty signed between the Netherlands and West Germany in The Hague on January 28, whereby the Netherlands ceded 5,000 sq.km. to West Germany. The treaty was subject to ratification.   (D. Bo.)

See also Dependent States.

New Zealand

New Zealand, a parliamentary state and member of the Commonwealth of Nations, is in the South Pacific Ocean, separated from southeastern Australia by the Tasman Sea. The country consists of North and South islands and Stewart, Chatham, and other minor islands. Area: 103,736 sq.mi. (268,675 sq.km.). Pop. (1971): 2,860,-475. Cap.: Wellington (pop., 1971, 135,242). Largest city: Christchurch (pop., 1971, 165,086). Largest urban area: Auckland (pop., 1971, 649,458). Language: English, Maori. Religion (1966): Church of England 33.7%; Presbyterian 21.8%; Roman Catholic 15.9%. Queen, Elizabeth II; governor-general in 1971, Sir Arthur Porritt; prime minister, Sir Keith J. Holyoake.

On June 23, 1971, the New Zealand government announced to Parliament its provisional agreement to the terms under which Britain would enter the European Economic Community. It was the most important and controversial agreement a New Zealand government had been required to negotiate in decades. New Zealand never had contested that it was in Britain's interests to join the EEC, but it fought for provisions that would permit its own dairy and meat products to continue to sell inside the new trading area or be phased out gradually.

In Luxembourg, with New Zealand Trade Minister John Marshall looking over his shoulder, Britain's Geoffrey Rippon and the members of the EEC finally agreed that New Zealand butter and cheese exports to Britain would gradually decrease over a five-year period, so that in 1977 they would be 71% of current quotas, with cheese decreasing the faster. At the end of the period there would be no continued guarantee for cheese trading. A review formula for butter was agreed on (the meaning of which became a point of controversy inside New Zealand), and the Community undertook to conduct its butter-trading policies in such a way as not to interfere with New Zealand's efforts to diversify its exports. Price would

be averaged on the four years 1969–72, which included two years of low prices.

It was because of "gray areas" in this pricing formula that New Zealand qualified its acceptance as only "provisional." The spirit of the butter agreement implied that continued accommodation for the commodity would be based on evidence, reviewed from time to time, of the reality of New Zealand's efforts to sell elsewhere, and the Community promised not to compete unfairly in the new market areas. On lamb, which was hit by a 20% tariff imposed by Britain's Conservative government, New Zealand accepted an assurance from Britain that there would be adequate and remunerative access, and that an acceptable volume of trade would flow over the tariff. Prime Minister Holyoake assured Parliament that New Zealand's interests could be safeguarded within the framework of the broad agreement reached; though some details were less attractive than others, the package represented substantial concessions toward New Zealand's request for special arrangements.

The working of New Zealand's first container ships was marred by industrial disputes, and a settlement still had not been worked out by the end of the year. The main factor in other industrial unrest was the enactment of legislation to submit wage agreements in excess of 7% to a stabilization tribunal, which operated through much of the year. Shipping holdups, it

NEW ZEALAND
Education. (1968) Primary, pupils 509,841, teachers 18,555; secondary and vocational, pupils 179,922, teachers 8,788; teacher training (1969), students 8,-471, teachers 512; higher (including 6 universities), students 50,433, teaching staff 2,887.
Finance. Monetary unit: New Zealand dollar, with a par value of NZ$0.89 to U.S. $1 (NZ$2.14 = £1 sterling) and a free rate (Sept. 27, 1971) of NZ$0.86 to U.S. $1. Gold, SDRs, and foreign exchange, central bank: (June 1971) U.S. $210 million; (June 1970) U.S. $170 million. Budget (1969–70 est.): revenue NZ$1,265,400,000; expenditure NZ$1,275,100,000. Gross national product: (1969–70) NZ$4,756,000,-000; (1968–69) NS$4,353,000,000. Money supply: (May 1971) NZ$849.5 million; (May 1970) NZ$802 million. Cost of living (1963 = 100): (2nd quarter 1971) 149; (2nd quarter 1970) 134.
Foreign Trade. (1970) Imports NZ$1,111,800,000; exports NZ$1,093,800,000. Import sources: U.K. 27%; Australia 20%; U.S. 13%; Japan 10%. Export destinations: U.K. 35%; U.S. 17%; Japan 10%; Australia 8%. Main exports: wool 17%; lamb and mutton 15%; butter 9%. Tourism (1969): visitors 148,100; gross receipts U.S. $27 million.
Transport and Communications. Roads (1970) 93,763 km. Motor vehicles in use (1970): passenger 899,623; commercial 177,435. Railways: (1969) 4,959 km.; traffic (1969–70) 511 million passenger-km., freight 2,760,000,000 net ton-km. Air traffic (1970): 1,578,000,000 passenger-km.; freight 40,-610,000 net ton-km. Shipping (1970): merchant vessels 100 gross tons and over 122; gross tonnage 185,-836. Telephones (Dec. 1969) 1,202,590. Radio licenses (Dec. 1969) 665,000. Television licenses (Dec. 1969) 617,000.
Agriculture. Production (in 000; metric tons; 1970; 1969 in parentheses): wheat 278 (457); barley 165 (233); oats 55 (52); potatoes 250 (258); dry peas 46 (57); apples 130 (115); mutton and lamb 575 (563); beef and veal 398 (377); milk 6,400 (6,479); butter 223 (276); cheese 102 (98); wool c. 238 (234); timber (cu.m.; 1969) 8,300, (1968) 7,400; fish catch (1969) 49, (1968) 59. Livestock (in 000; Jan. 1970): cattle 8,839; sheep (June) 60,-276; horses c. 82; pigs 584; chickens (April) c. 5,300.
Industry. Fuel and power (in 000; metric tons; 1970): coal 460; lignite 1,915; manufactured gas (cu.m.) 180,000; electricity (excluding most industrial production; kw-hr.) 14,151,000. Production (in 000; metric tons; 1970): cement 829; chemical fertilizers (1969) 1,968; mechanical wood pulp (1969–70) 245; chemical wood pulp (1969–70) 317; newsprint 213; other paper (1969–70) 239.

was hoped, would be fewer with the sale of the P. and O. subsidiary Union Steamship Company, the main coastal trader, in half portions to New Zealand investors and Thomas Nationwide Transport of Australia in a NZ$24 million transaction. Efforts during the year to appoint an industrial chief mediator broke down in personality clashes with the government after employers and unions had reached some agreement. Shipping freight rates continued to rise.

In his budget, introduced on June 10, Finance Minister Robert Muldoon revoked a 10% income-tax surcharge, liberalized some social security benefits, increased home building loan limits, abolished a scheme by which New Zealanders could import cars with no-remittance funds, and allocated another NZ$5 million for unassembled car imports and licenses for 10,000 additional built-up cars.

The Railways Department introduced new trains in both islands (Southerner in South, Silver Star in North). A new receiving station enabled satellite television transmissions to be received from August, when New Zealanders saw the Apollo 15 astronauts take their historic moon-buggy ride on a live broadcast.

The government announced in August that the last company of New Zealand combat troops in Vietnam would be withdrawn to Singapore by the end of the year. In October, South Africa's team withdrew from a Commonwealth golf tournament at Auckland in the face of threats that the tournament would be disrupted. In an equivocal reaction to opposition to the proposed raising of Lake Manapouri to provide power for an aluminum smelter, the government promised that the matter would be referred to Parliament if it was raised again but provided that, in the meantime, some preparatory work would be undertaken. Princess Alexandra toured New Zealand in April. The first Pacific Forum meeting of island leaders was held at Wellington in August.　　　　　　(Jo. A. K.)

See also Dependent States.

Nicaragua

The largest country of Central America, Nicaragua is a republic bounded by Honduras, Costa Rica, the Caribbean Sea, and the Pacific Ocean. Area: 49,173 sq.mi. (127,358 sq.km.). Pop. (1968 est.): 1,809,477, including mestizo 70%; white 17%; Negro 9%; Indian 4%. Cap. and largest city: Managua (pop., 1968 est., 380,966). Language: Spanish. Religion: Roman Catholic. President in 1971, Brig. Gen. Anastasio Somoza Debayle.

Speculation as to presidential succession after the expiration of President Somoza's term in May 1972 was ended early in the year when Somoza, the powerful, firmly entrenched leader of the Liberal Party but constitutionally unable to succeed himself, announced that he would step down. The succession, however, was not to be decided by the usual two-party election. Instead, the president would be succeeded by a three-man junta which would govern during a 2½-year period designated as a period of constitutional reform.

Such an action was made possible by an agreement between the leaders of the two major parties, the Liberals and the Conservatives, which would allow the Liberals to continue as the major party of the nation but at the same time would give the Conservatives their strongest voice in the government in several decades. By this arrangement, rather than by the regular election of a new president and Congress,

a 100-man Constitutional Assembly was to be elected early in 1972. The majority party, expected to be the Liberals, was to get 60% of the seats and the minority party 40%. This division would give the Conservatives far more voice in the government than they had had in many years. They would also get to appoint 6 of the 16 major department heads and would be represented by one man elected to the three-man executive. This Constitutional Assembly was to revise the constitution and serve as the legislative body for 2½ years. At the end of that time regular elections would be held, probably under supervision of the Organization of American States.

Machinery to implement this plan was set in motion September 1 when Congress met and dissolved itself, leaving the nation to be governed by executive decree until the Constitutional Assembly was elected in the spring of 1972. The arrangement was not popular with all of the Conservatives, especially as it permitted President Somoza to run for reelection in 1974. Fernando Agüero Rocha, leader of the Conservative Party and one of the architects of the plan, was denounced by Pedro Joaquín Chamorro, publisher of the newspaper *La Prensa,* as having sold out to the Somozas. Some observers speculated that there would arise on the political scene a third force made up of dissident Conservatives and various splinter and special interest groups.

Economically, there was a reversal of the recession that had plagued the nation the last few years. Governmental belt-tightening and additional revenues gained from a sales tax probably contributed to this reversal, but seemingly more important was the fact that there was a good cotton crop.　　　　(A. W. O.)

NICARAGUA

Education. (1967–68) Primary, pupils 247,065, teachers (including preprimary) 7,437; secondary, pupils 28,637, teachers 1,397; vocational, pupils 2,851, teachers 194; teacher training, students 2,733, teachers 260; higher (including 2 universities), students 5,144, teaching staff 592.

Finance. Monetary unit: córdoba, with a par value of 7 córdobas to U.S. $1 (16.80 córdobas = £1 sterling) and a free rate (Sept. 27, 1971) of 17.40 córdobas to £1 sterling. Gold, SDRs, and convertible currency, central bank: (June 1971) U.S. $60,980,000; (June 1970) U.S. $58,330,000. Budget (1970 est.) balanced at 686 million córdobas. Gross national product: (1970) 5,823,000,000 córdobas; (1969) 5,307,-000,000 córdobas. Money supply: (June 1971) 618.6 million córdobas; (June 1970) 583.5 million córdobas. Cost of living (Managua; 1963 = 100): (1969) 117; (1968) 117.

Foreign Trade. (1969) Imports 1,239,200,000 córdobas; exports 1,082,600,000 córdobas. Import sources: U.S. 38%; Guatemala 7%; Costa Rica 7%; Japan 7%; El Salvador 7%; West Germany 7%. Export destinations: U.S. 33%; Japan 18%; West Germany 11%; Costa Rica 9%. Main exports: cotton 29%; meat 13%; coffee 13%; sugar 5%.

Transport and Communications. Roads (1970) 6,124 km. (including 368 km. of Pan-American Highway). Motor vehicles in use (1969): passenger 24,-400; commercial (including buses) 8,700. Railways: (1969) 348 km.; traffic (1968) 35 million passenger-km., freight 13 million net ton-km. Air traffic (1970): 77 million passenger-km.; freight 1.1 million net ton-km. Telephones (Dec. 1969) 25,634. Radio receivers (Dec. 1969) 107,000. Television receivers (Dec. 1969) 45,000.

Agriculture. Production (in 000; metric tons; 1970; 1969 in parentheses): corn c. 190 (c. 182); rice c. 70 (c. 60); sorghum c. 60 (c. 60); dry beans c. 43 (c. 45); cotton, lint c. 60 (69); coffee c. 36 (c. 34); sugar, raw value (1970–71) c. 150, (1969–70) c. 141. Livestock (in 000; 1969–70): cattle c. 1,700; pigs c. 570; chickens c. 2,600.

Industry. Production (in 000; 1969): cement (metric tons) 109; gold (exports; troy oz.) 107; electricity (kw-hr.; 1968) 484,000.

Niger

A republic of north central Africa, Niger is bounded by Algeria, Libya, Chad, Nigeria, Dahomey, Upper Volta, and Mali. Area: 458,993 sq.mi. (1,188,794 sq.km.). Pop. (1970 est.): 4,016,000, including (1962) Hausa 49%; Zerma and Songhai 22%; Fulani 11%; Tuareg 6%. Cap. and largest city: Niamey (pop., 1969 est., 78,-991). Language: French and Sudanic dialects. Religion: Muslim, animist, Christian. President in 1971, Hamani Diori.

For Niger 1971 was a year of calm and stability. In February President Diori pardoned a number of political prisoners who had been involved in an attempted coup in December 1963 and in various other subversive activities.

Uranium mining operations at Arlit continued to prosper. Mining was expected within five years at the Akokan site about 12 mi. S of Arlit, and other potential sites had been identified. A number of international oil companies had concessions in Niger, and although no commercially exploitable deposits had been found by the end of 1971, the government remained hopeful.

President Diori also was anxious to diversify the sources of foreign aid to Niger, the bulk of which still came from France. Canada had provided a grant for road building, and the Libyan government had promised credits for projects being worked out by a joint committee. The possibility of developing a trade in refrigerated meat from Niger to Libya was also being considered. Diori made use of his country's friendly relations with Libya in seeking to promote a reconciliation between Libya and Chad, diplomatic relations having been broken off when Libya was accused by Pres. François Tombalbaye of Chad of assisting rebels attempting to overthrow his government. Niger was one of the countries mentioned by Pres. Léopold Sédar Senghor of Senegal on December 7 as a participant in the prospective Economic Community of West Africa, the others being Ivory Coast, Senegal, Mauritania, Mali, Upper Volta, Dahomey, and Togo.   (Ph. D.)

NIGER
Education. (1968–69) Primary, pupils 81,954, teachers 2,176; secondary, pupils 4,213, teachers 219; vocational, pupils 137, teachers 21; teacher training, students 621, teachers 40.
Finance. Monetary unit: CFA franc, with a parity of CFA Fr. 50 to the French franc (CFA Fr. 277.71 = U.S. $1; CFA Fr. 666.50 = £1 sterling) and a free rate (Sept. 27, 1971) of CFA Fr. 276.50 to U.S. $1 (CFA Fr. 685.75 = £1 sterling). Budget (1970–71 est.) balanced at CFA Fr. 10,903,000,000.
Foreign Trade. (1969) Imports CFA Fr. 12,570,-000,000; exports CFA Fr. 6,250,000,000. Import sources: France 49%; West Germany 6%; U.S. 5%. Export destinations: France 63%; Nigeria 16%. Main exports: peanuts 60%; livestock 14%.
Transport and Communications. Roads (1970) 6,943 km. Motor vehicles in use (1970): passenger 4,337; commercial 1,878. Telephones (Dec. 1969) 3,298. Radio receivers (Dec. 1969) 100,000.
Agriculture. Production (in 000; metric tons; 1970; 1969 in parentheses): millet 800 (1,095); sorghum 200 (289); cassava (1969) 199, (1968) 197; peanuts c. 190 (207); rice c. 30 (c. 35); dates c. 5 (c. 5). Livestock (in 000; 1969–70): cattle c. 4,300; sheep c. 2,750; goats c. 6,000.

Nigeria

A federal republic and a member of the Commonwealth of Nations, Nigeria is located in Africa on the north coast of the Gulf of Guinea, bounded by Dahomey, Niger, Chad, and Cameroon. Area: 356,-669 sq.mi. (923,768 sq.km.). Pop. (1970 est.): 55,-074,000, including (1963 est.): Hausa 18%; Ibo 16%; Yoruba 14%; Fulani 10%. Cap. and largest city: Lagos (pop., 1971 est., 900,969). Language: English (official). Religion: Muslim 48%; Christian 23%. Head of provisional military government in 1971, Maj. Gen. Yakubu Gowon.

In 1971 the Nigerian military government faced the long-term problem of reestablishing unity and peace among a vast association of diverse peoples. Demands increased for a return to civilian rule before 1976, but without open debate, a free press, or party politics their strength was not known. Although the 200,000-strong Army was costing N£90 million annually, it was impossible to contemplate its reduction in the face of high unemployment, an increase in armed robbery, and accusations of police corruption; the Army also was useful in public works and was considered a possible nucleus for an African High Command.

Nonetheless, Nigeria's administration was already part civilian: the Supreme Military·Council included the East-Central State administrator; the Federal Executive Council included 12 civilian commissioners; and within each state civilian commissioners worked with the administrator (although all were appointed rather than elected, and were accountable to governors and not to an electorate). The chief problem in the return to civilian rule was to achieve a national consensus on fair boundaries for viable state units. The shortage of trained personnel to run the states was still a difficulty, as was the strength of tribal affiliations cutting across states which themselves lacked separate identity.

Particularly troublesome was the relationship of the central government with the East-Central State (Iboland), and that of Iboland with the new South-Eastern and Rivers states carved out of the Eastern Region. General Gowon's first visit to the East-Central State since the end of the war, in January, played a successful part in the work of reconciliation, rehabilitation, and reintegration of eight million Ibos But he was made aware of their grievances—vast amounts of property and land lying waste in the Rivers State, the barring of Ibos from employment there, and discrimination against their reemployment in the public services.

Reconciliation with the Ibos, if not as magnanimous as claimed by the government, was enough to strengthen Nigeria abroad during 1971 and bring reconciliation with those countries that had recognized Biafra. Nigeria took a lead in the Organization of African Unity as a neutral in relation to the Middle East and Communist bloc and expressed strong views against dialogue with South Africa. In March it was host to the International Year against Racism meeting in Lagos.

Nigeria's economic recovery had been based on post-civil war oil expansion. By April, there was a 60% increase in production over 1970, at 1.5 million bbl. a day. A National Oil Corp. was established in April. Forty-four fields developed by five com-

Nickel:
see Mining

Education. (1966–67) Primary, pupils 3,025,-981, teachers 91,049; secondary, pupils 202,638, teachers 11,055; vocational, pupils 26,092, teachers 1,378; teacher training, students 28,673, teaching staff 1,738; higher (universities only; 1967–68), students 7,058.

Finance. Monetary unit: Nigerian pound, with a par value of N£0.36 to U.S. $1 (N£0.86 = £1 sterling) and a free rate (Sept. 27, 1971) of N£0.35 to U.S. $1. Gold, SDRs, and foreign exchange, official: (June 1971) U.S. $334 million; (June 1970) U.S. $141 million. Federal budget (1970–71 est.): revenue N£278 million; expenditure N£268 million. Money supply: (April 1971) N£330.3 million; (April 1970) N£259.9 million. Cost of living (Lagos; 1963 = 100): (June 1971) 166; (June 1970) 140.

Foreign Trade. (1970) Imports N£376.2 million; exports N£443.6 million. Import sources: U.K. 31%; U.S. 14%; West Germany 13%; Japan 6%; Italy 5%. Export destinations: U.K. 28%; Netherlands 17%; U.S. 12%; France 8%; West Germany 7%. Main exports: crude oil 58%; cocoa 15%; peanuts and oil 7%.

Transport and Communications. Roads (1969) c. 90,000 km. (including c. 21,000 km. with improved surface). Motor vehicles in use (1968): passenger 63,000; commercial (including buses) 30,000. Railways: (1968) 3,505 km.; traffic (1969–70) 728 million passenger-km., freight 1,615,000,000 net ton-km. Air traffic (1970): 210 million passenger-km.; freight 7,310,000 net ton-km. Shipping (1970): merchant vessels 100 gross tons and over 49; gross tonnage 98,634. Telephones (Jan. 1970) 81,440.

Radio licenses (Dec. 1969) 1,265,000. Television licenses (Dec. 1969) 53,000.

Agriculture. Production (in 000; metric tons; 1970; 1969 in parentheses): millet c. 2,800 (c. 2,800); sorghum c. 3,500 (c. 3,500); corn c. 1,220 (c. 1,219); sweet potatoes (1969) c. 12,-500, (1968) c. 12,500; cassava (1969) c. 6,800, (1968) c. 6,800; peanuts c. 1,175 (c. 1,360); palm oil c. 480 (c. 425); cocoa (1970–71) 218, (1969–70) 210; cotton, lint c. 87 (55); rubber (exports) c. 70 (57). Livestock (in 000; 1969–70): cattle c. 11,550; sheep c. 8,000; goats c. 23,400; pigs c. 820; horses (Northern Region only) c. 335.

Industry. Production (in 000; metric tons; 1970): crude oil 53,500; cement (1969) 566; tin 8.1; electricity (kw.-hr.) 1,532,000.

panies, led by Shell-BP, provided over half the central government revenue. In July, Nigeria joined the Organization of Petroleum Exporting Countries (OPEC) and indicated that greater government control was to be expected, in particular over the French company SAFRAP, whose resumption of activities the government had delayed until April.

The 1971 budget was tailored for the needs of the 1970–74 second national development plan, estimated at N£1,595,000,000, of which it was hoped 80% could be raised internally. Britain's contribution was increased by £13 million to £39 million in June, apart from its £5 million in rehabilitation aid, and the Nigerian government took steps to bolster foreign reserves by limiting foreign travel and modifying company tax regulations. Nigerianization of new categories of retail and small-scale enterprises increased. In July complaints were made against Equatorial Guinea for ill-treatment of and discrimination against Nigerian workers there.

Industrial unrest increased during the year, especially in the shipyard and dock industries of Lagos, where charges of corruption and sabotage led to a delegation of foreign shipowners visiting the port. Subsequently wide authority was given to the port manager to discipline the staff. Provided the development plan could siphon off enough oil revenue to combat unemployment, which was the government's stated aim in launching the plan in November 1970, by devoting 60% of resources to economic development Nigeria showed every sign of surmounting its postwar turmoil. (M. Mr.)

Nobel Prizes

For the first time in half a century, the Nobel Peace Prize was awarded in 1971 to an active head of government—West German Chancellor Willy Brandt. The year also saw an easing of the recent practice of dividing prizes in specific disciplines among two or more recipients; each prize went to a single man. The other laureates to receive the honoraria, each amounting to more than $87,000, were: Pablo Neruda for literature, Dennis Gabor for physics, Gerhard Herzberg for chemistry, Earl W. Sutherland, Jr., for medicine, and Simon S. Kuznets for economics.

The annual designation of the persons who "have conferred the greatest benefit on mankind" was first made in 1901. Alfred B. Nobel, the Swedish inventor of dynamite who bequeathed his fortune to establish the prestige-laden prizes, stipulated in his will that a committee named by the Norwegian Storting (parliament) should select the peace laureate and that three Swedish academies should select prizewinners for physics, chemistry, literature, and medicine or physiology. In 1968, to commemorate its 300th anniversary, the Bank of Sweden set up a fund to endow the economics award, which is administered under the Nobel establishment.

BRANDT, WILLY

Willy Brandt's *Ostpolitik* or "eastern policy" earned him new friends among West Germany's foreign adversaries, renewed opposition from conservative forces at home, and the 1971 Nobel Peace Prize. The chancellor of West Germany was chosen unanimously over 40 other nominees because he had "stretched out his hand to reconciliation between countries that have long been enemies." His citation declared: "Preconditions for peaceful development are a political and military relaxation of tension between East and West Europe. The committee attaches importance to the fact that Willy Brandt, both as foreign secretary of the Federal Republic of Germany in 1966 and as federal chancellor since 1969, has taken concrete initiatives leading to such relaxation of tension."

Brandt's selection was heavy with political ramifications, not the least being the implicit strengthening of the liberal Social Democrat's position in Bonn. As one Christian Democrat complained, "How can you campaign against a man who is billed as 'the Peace Chancellor'?" Nonetheless, since 1969 most West German voters seemingly approved his *Ostpolitik* (if not his economic policies). The keystone of his administration, it had resulted in friendship treaties with the Soviet Union and Poland and new conversations with East Germany.

When Brandt was asked how he would like to be viewed by historians, he said, "I would be happy if they found that I had done something to make my country a good neighbour in Europe." On another occasion he explained, "It is not only a question of moral responsibility because of recent German history, but also the fact that peace in Europe is not possible without specific German contributions." The last of his countrymen to make a contribution that won a Nobel Peace Prize was pacifist Carl von Ossietzky in 1935.

That was two years after Brandt had left the country as a youthful political exile. Born Herbert Ernst Karl Frahm on Dec. 18, 1913, the illegitimate son of a shopgirl in Lübeck, he was deeply influenced by his grandfather, an ardent Social Democrat. He became a protégé of Julius Leber, a Social Democratic editor, who encouraged him to write newspaper articles under the pen name he later formalized. By 1931 he had joined a left-wing splinter group that, like many others, was anathema to the Nazis who took over in 1933.

Brandt fled to Scandinavia, covered the Spanish Civil War briefly as a journalist, and was imprisoned for several months in Norway after invading Nazis captured him, disguised as a local soldier. Escaping to Sweden, he worked as a journalist and resistance supporter and earned Norwegian citizenship. After World War II he returned to Germany as a press attaché at the Norwegian military mission in Berlin. In 1947 he resumed his German citizenship and rejoined the Social Democrats. Brandt served under the first two mayors of West Berlin, an office he was elected to fill in 1957. He became vice-chancellor and foreign minister in Kurt Kiesinger's coalition government in 1966 and chancellor in 1969.

GABOR, DENNIS

A Hungarian-born, self-styled scientific outsider, Dennis Gabor won the Nobel Prize for Physics in 1971 for "an invention"—a process of lensless three-dimensional photography. Called holography (from the Greek words for "whole" and "writing"), it was referred to by the *New York Times* as "one of the most exciting developments in modern optical science."

The process employs coherent light, a beam in which all the light waves are of the same frequency and oscillation phase, such as that produced by a laser. The beam is split by a mirror, with half aimed directly at a photographic plate and half bounced off the subject before it. This results in an unintelligible pattern of spots on the film, caused by waves from the two beams reinforcing or nearly canceling each other as they reach the film. When similar coherent light is beamed through the developed film, the effect is reversed and the image of the object is projected in air as if magically; a viewer can see hidden sides of it by changing his vantage point. The process has myriad practical applications wherever true dimensional depth is required, as in topographic mapmaking, medicine, communications, or computer technology. *Fortune* magazine reported that holography was a worldwide industry grossing several hundred million dollars annually.

Gabor hit on the idea in 1947 while waiting his turn for a tennis court in Rugby, Eng. At the time he was working for a British company exploring ways to improve electron microscopes. He was struck with the related problem of seeing the unseeable, in this case all sides of a tennis ball at once. Working with filtered conventional light sources, he developed the basic technique, but he was unable to get a commercially practical holograph because his light was either too feeble or too incoherent. Charles Townes' invention of the laser, for which he shared a Nobel Prize in Physics, provided the missing ingredient.

Gabor was born in Budapest, June 5, 1900, and attended the technical university there. "Like most Hungarians," he recalled, he did graduate work abroad, earning a doctorate in electrical engineering at the Technische Hochschule, Berlin. His research assistant there was Peter Goldmark, who became president of Columbia Broadcasting System Laboratories in Stamford, Conn., where Gabor spent about half his working time. He devoted the balance to the Imperial College of Science and Technology in London, where he was professor emeritus of applied electronic physics. Before World War II he worked for a company in Germany until, like chemistry laureate Gerhard Herzberg, he fled Nazism.

"Every Nobel winner is lucky, but I'm extra lucky," he told interviewers. "Most people get the prize for one thing they spend a long life in science to accomplish. I'm an outsider. I've worked in industrial laboratories most of my life. . . . What I did was not pure science. I consider it an invention."

HERZBERG, GERHARD

A German-born physicist whose work was too basic to conform to taxonomic niceties, Gerhard Herzberg won the Nobel Prize for Chemistry in 1971. The Swedish Academy of Sciences conferred the honour on the naturalized Canadian "for his contributions to the knowledge of electronic structures and geometry of molecules, particularly free radicals." The latter are minute fragments of molecules that are critical to the reactions the molecule can undergo. Understanding their physical characteristics is crucial to the study of basic chemistry and has immense implications for both the immediate advancement of theoretical science and the ultimate development of technology.

Herzberg's work involved the molecular application of spectroscopy, the science of the visible light emitted or absorbed by irradiated materials. Under laboratory conditions, every material gives off a characteristic light pattern that is the chemical and physical "fingerprint" of the substance. He studied the changes in spectra given off by certain molecules when their energy states are altered. His investigations, the academy said, "provide extremely precise information on molecular energies, rotation, vibrations and electronic structures which, in turn, yield data on molecular geometries"—the infinitesimal geographies of elemental building blocks.

His citation declared that his research had "many results of fundamental importance for chemical physics and

quantum mechanics. . . . This work has already led to a revitalization of studies of chemical reaction in gases. However, Herzberg's influence in chemistry is far wider, as his ideas and discoveries have stimulated the whole modern development from chemical kinetics—dealing with forces that influence the motion of bodies and with gases used as refrigerants—to cosmic chemistry." Indeed, his work led to the identification of free-floating molecules in outer space. It, in turn, built on the discoveries of other scientists, including the 1967 Nobel Chemistry Prize winners, Britons Ronald Norrish and George Porter.

The author of 200 published works, including the colossal *Molecular Spectra and Molecular Structure,* Herzberg made Ottawa "a Mecca of electronic spectroscopy." He joined the National Research Council of Canada there in 1948. A refugee from Hitler's Germany, he left Europe with his late wife, also a physicist, for the University of Saskatchewan in 1935. He was born Dec. 25, 1904, in Hamburg, trained at Darmstadt Institute of Technology, the University of Göttingen, and at Britain's University of Bristol.

KUZNETS, SIMON S.

The winner of the 1971 Nobel Prize for Economics, Simon S. Kuznets, was no idle theoretician. The Royal Swedish Academy of Sciences cited him for his ". . . empirically founded interpretation of economic growth which has led to new and deepened insight into the economic and social structure and process of development." Before World War II, Kuznets pioneered in developing the conceptual basis for national income accounts in the U.S., and after World War II he helped set up national income accounting systems in other countries. As a consequence of this work, quantitative studies of the comparative economic growth of nations became possible. A 1971 book by Kuznets, *Economic Growth of Nations,* was the most recent in a series of wide-ranging studies.

Kuznets' approach to economics contrasted sharply with that of the 1970 prizewinner, Paul A. Samuelson. Kuznets' approach was that of a genetic economist interested in describing what actually happens in the process of growth of an economic system. Samuelson's work was in the tradition of economic theory as a kit of tools of analysis, applicable to all kinds of problems, including the solution of policy issues. In Samuelson's economics the

Nobel Prize winners in 1971 included Earl Sutherland, Jr. (top, left), recipient of the prize for medicine, and Harvard economist Simon Kuznets (top, right), winner of the prize for economics. Dennis Gabor (above, left) was awarded the prize for physics, and West German Chancellor Willy Brandt (above, right) received the 1971 Nobel Peace Prize.

central concept was equilibrium, which played no role in Kuznets' economics. With respect to method, Samuelson was in the orthodox tradition of classical, neoclassical, and Keynesian economists. Kuznets' work was a successful attempt to wrestle with what Samuelson referred to in the closing sentence of his *Foundations of Economic Analysis* as ". . . the majestic problems of economic development."

The laureate himself recalled that as a youth "I started out with the general notion that economics is the basis of all social problems." Born in Kharkov in the Ukraine, April 30, 1901, he emigrated to the U.S. in 1922 after the upheavals of World War I and the Russian Revolution. His decision to join his father, who had emigrated 15 years earlier, was prompted by "the usual economic problems" of sociopolitical chaos.

Kuznets' father had translated the family name to Smith. Within a year, the son had readopted his patronym, entered Columbia University, and received a bachelor's degree. After being awarded his doctorate in 1926, he joined the Social Science Research Council as a fellow, then worked on the staff of the National Bureau of Economics studying business cycles. During World War II he was associate director of the War Production Board's Bureau of Planning and Statistics. Meanwhile, he had been a professor of economic statistics at the University of Pennsylvania. In 1954 he moved to Johns Hopkins University and six years later became George F. Baker professor of economics at Harvard, a chair he held until the end of the 1971 academic year. He remained active as a professor emeritus.

NERUDA, PABLO

The Nobel laureate for literature in 1971 was Pablo Neruda, a Chilean by birth, a Communist by inclination, a diplomat by sinecure, and the preeminent lyricist of Latin America by vocation. A popular poet for half a century, he long enjoyed national patronage in the traditional form of a diplomatic career marked by assignments to lesser foreign service posts around the world. Having served as consul in Rangoon, Colombo, Buenos Aires, Madrid, and Barcelona, and as ambassador to Mexico (1940–42), Neruda was named ambassador to France after the election of his friend and fellow Marxist, Pres. Salvador Allende Gossens.

The poet was born July 12, 1904, in the southern frontier town of Parral, and christened Neftalí Ricardo Reyes Basoalto. At 17 he published his first poems under the pen name that he borrowed from a 19th-century Czech writer because he feared sneering relatives. Though he had been a Nobel Prize candidate for 20 years, it was not until 50 years after his debut that he won the award.

One cause for the delay might have been his political identification. He had been a Communist Party member since 1945 and a Marxist since the Spanish Civil War, which he witnessed. During that war he became a friend of Federico García Lorca, the dramatically tragic antifascist poet who called Neruda "a poet nearer death than philosophy, nearer pain than intelligence, which he fortunately cannot interpret, a real man who knows that the reed and the swallow are more immortal than the hard cheek of a statue."

Other honours did not elude him. The author of nearly 20 books of verse, he saw his work translated into 81 languages. He won a Stalin Peace Prize in 1953 and was elected an honorary member of the American Academy of Arts and Letters and the National Institute of Arts and Letters in 1968 (he refused the diplomas to protest the Vietnam war). He was also successful in politics, serving in the Chilean Senate and on the Communist Party Central Committee.

His work has been compared to that of the Western Hemisphere's other lyric celebrant of the common man, Walt Whitman. "With such men [as Whitman and Neruda]," wrote one of his American translators, "the reign of the small, the cultured, the domesticated, and their celebration of tight little lyrics comes to an end."

Neruda's poetry consciously champions the exploited Indians of Latin America, and he reportedly tried to articulate a voice for the continent and its indigenous people. "A poet who does not keep in step with the struggles against offenses to humanity is not a poet—he is only a showcase puppet for slick magazines," he told an interviewer. He built his often fanciful, sometimes surrealistic images out of the whole clay of the harsh Andean landscape. At the same time, he was a lyricist of many keys, a composer of love poems and erotic lyrics.

Among his most significant works were *Twenty Poems of Love, Canto General, Memorial to Isla Negra,* and *The Heights of Macchu Picchu.*

SUTHERLAND, EARL W., JR.

Earl W. Sutherland, Jr., of Vanderbilt University won the 1971 Nobel Prize for Medicine or Physiology for discovering the chemical that makes hormones perform their vital function of carrying messages via the bloodstream. "Very seldom can a discovery today be credited to a single person," said a spokesman for Stockholm's Karolinska Institutet; the matter of cyclic adenosine 3',5'-monophosphate was exceptional.

In the late 1950s, when he identified the substance, Sutherland was almost alone in the field, and other scientists dismissed his preoccupation if they thought much about him at all. But he demonstrated that cyclic AMP, as it is called for convenience, was the missing link in a multitude of biological reactions. Contrary to then-accepted belief, he showed that hormones themselves do not directly activate their target organs; rather, the hormones increase or decrease the organ's cellular level of cyclic AMP, which triggers or inhibits the cellular activity.

The implications of his chain of discoveries were beyond cataloging, since cyclic AMP is found in every animal cell and affects "everything from your memory to your toes," in his words. In 1971 some 2,000 scientists were studying cyclic AMP, and this aspect of hormonal study had become one of the most popular medical research fields. The substance was found to inhibit the characteristic pathology of some kinds of cancer cells. Its importance to metabolic disorders was becoming clear; investigations in Britain demonstrated a direct relationship between the symptomatic states of manic-depressive psychotics and cyclic AMP levels.

A Kansan, Sutherland was born in Burlingame, Nov. 19, 1915, and decided on a medical career when he was a high school student and read about Louis Pasteur. The depression of the '30s erased the family's prosperity, and he had to work his way through Washburn College in Topeka and Washington University Medical School in St. Louis, Mo. After service as an army doctor in World War II, he returned to Washington University to begin his hormonal research under Carl and Gerty Cori, who won the 1947 Nobel Prize for Medicine for their work on glycogen conversion. He was a lecturing professor in pharmacology at Case Western Reserve University in Cleveland when he identified cyclic AMP in 1956. He moved to Vanderbilt in 1963 to devote his 6½-day work week exclusively to research. In 1970 he won the Lasker Award.

Sutherland's selection came as no surprise to him; he said he had heard reports for several years that his work was under consideration. As his citation said, "The mechanism by which various hormones exert their important functions has until recently been a complete enigma. Because of the work of Dr. Sutherland we can today understand the general mode of action of many of them."

(PH. K.)

Norway

A constitutional monarchy of northern Europe, Norway is bordered by Sweden, Finland, and the U.S.S.R.; its coastlines are on the North Sea, the Norwegian Sea, and the Arctic Ocean. Area: 125,049 sq.mi. (323,878 sq.km.), excluding the Svalbard Archipelago, 23,957 sq.mi., and Jan Mayen Island, 144 sq.mi. Pop. (1971 est.): 3,891,739. Cap. and largest city: Oslo (pop., 1971 est., 481,204). Language: Norwegian. Religion: Lutheran (96.2%). King, Olav V; prime ministers in 1971, Per Borten and, from March 17, Trygve Bratteli.

After more than five years of uneasy alliance, the coalition of the four nonsocialist parties finally foundered in March 1971. The immediate cause was an indiscretion by Prime Minister Per Borten, who first denied and then admitted having leaked confidential documents on negotiations with the European Economic Community to the leader of the People's Movement against Norwegian Membership of the EEC. Borten's own Centre Party declared for continuing the coalition under his leadership, but the Conservative, Liberal, and Christian People's Party members of the Cabinet demanded his resignation. Accordingly, Borten resigned his office on March 2.

On March 17 the Labour Party, with 74 of the 150 seats in the Storting (parliament), formed a minority administration under its leader Trygve Bratteli (*see* BIOGRAPHY). Bratteli declared that his government would work for a European security conference, increased support for less developed countries, and mutual diplomatic relations with North Vietnam. The government would complete negotiations with the EEC, but only on satisfactory terms, particularly for farmers and fishermen, and would do its best to combat inflation.

In the course of the Brussels negotiations for EEC membership, Norway insisted on retaining its 12-mi. fishing limit and proposed that EEC fishermen should be allowed access only insofar as they established themselves in Norway in accordance with EEC rules. The government confirmed that a Storting vote on joining the EEC would be preceded by a consultative referendum, probably early in 1972.

The September municipal elections, with a voter participation of 71% as against 76% in 1967, showed a small gain for the anti-EEC Centre Party, which won 11.6% of the votes, compared with 9.3% in 1967. Both the Labour Party, with 41.9% of the votes, and the Conservative Party, with 17.8%, lost slightly. In contrast to party disappointments, Norway's women carried out a successful coup in the elections by—quite legally—altering party lists to replace males with female representatives. In this way, an unprecedented number of women were assured office in local councils throughout the county.

The new government's budget for 1972 provided fresh grounds for discontent with the announcement of an almost 15% increase in state expenditure, to be financed in part by new taxes (including a 50% tax on profits from the sale of stocks, retroactive from Jan. 1, 1971) and increased social insurance premiums. The steeply rising cost of social security, particularly the retirement pension scheme, was a matter of mounting concern in national budgeting. Pensions were based on income earned during the pensioner's working life automatically adjusted to the cost-of-living index. In spite of the increasing burden that the scheme imposed on the working population, the government put forward proposals for lowering the retirement age from 70 to 67 beginning in January 1973.

The balance of trade deteriorated. Market demand for certain important products, particularly aluminum and ferroalloys, weakened, although full employment was successfully maintained. In spite of a depression in freight rates, net currency earnings of the merchant fleet were forecast at a record high of almost 8 billion kroner. On the other hand, there was also an exceptionally heavy import bill for new ships delivered from foreign yards. The balance of payments deficit was forecast at 2,550,000,000 kroner, an increase of 1,250,000,000 kroner compared with 1970.

The brightest feature of the economic scene was the start of oil production on a trial basis by Phillips Petroleum at the Ekofisk field in the Norwegian sector

of the North Sea. In full production, Ekofisk was expected to yield at least 15 million tons of oil a year, compared with Norway's total current annual oil consumption of 8 million tons.

A daughter was born to Crown Princess Sonja on September 22. Christened Märtha Louise, the princess was the first-born child of Sonja and Crown Prince Harald, married in 1968. According to the constitution, only male heirs could succeed to the throne, but sentiment increasingly favoured an amendment whereby females could also succeed.   (O. F. K.)

Oil drilling is under way at Ekofisk, an oil field lying inside the Norwegian sector of the North Sea. Operated by the Phillips Petroleum Co. and two European partners, Ekofisk promised to be a prodigious oil resource for Norway.
PHILLIPS PETROLEUM COMPANY

NORWAY
Education. (1968–69) Primary, pupils 387,042, teachers 19,468; secondary, pupils 232,323, teachers 18,106; vocational, pupils 64,436, teachers 9,733; higher (including 3 universities), students 41,790, teaching staff 4,629.

Finance. Monetary unit: Norwegian krone, with a par value of 7.14 kroner to U.S. $1 (17.14 kroner = £1 sterling) and a free rate (Sept. 27, 1971) of 6.86 kroner to U.S. $1. Gold, SDRs, and foreign exchange, central bank: (June 1971) U.S. $814.5 million; (June 1970) U.S. $572.5 million. Budget (1971 est.): revenue 20.7 billion kroner; expenditure 23.7 billion kroner. Gross national product: (1969) 69,532,000,000 kroner; (1968) 64.6 billion kroner. Money supply: (May 1971) 16,220,000,000 kroner; (May 1970) 14,230,000,000 kroner. Cost of living (1963 = 100): (June 1971) 148; (June 1970) 139.

Foreign Trade. (1970) Imports 26,410,000,000 kroner; exports 17,537,000,-000 kroner. Import sources: Sweden 20%; West Germany 14%; U.K. 12%; U.S. 7%; Denmark 6%; Canada 5%. Export destinations: U.K. 18%; West Germany 18%; Sweden 16%; Denmark 7%; U.S. 6%. Main exports: ships 12%; aluminum 11%; machinery 9%; fish 8%; chemicals 8%; paper 8%; iron and steel 7%.

Transport and Communications. Roads (1970) 72,261 km. Motor vehicles in use (1970): passenger 747,237; commercial 147,118. Railways: (state only; 1969) 4,242 km. (including 2,269 km. electrified); traffic (state only; 1970) 1,570,000,000 passenger-km., freight 2,840,000,000 net ton-km. Air traffic (including Norwegian apportionment of international operations of Scandinavian Airlines System; 1970): 1,954,100,000 passenger-km.; freight 73,211,000 net ton-km. Shipping (1970): merchant vessels 100 gross tons and over; 2,808; gross tonnage 19,346,911. Ships entered (1969) vessels totaling 14,889,000 net registered tons; goods loaded (1970) 35,323,000 metric tons, unloaded 19,079,000 metric tons. Telephones (Dec. 1969) 1,090,662. Radio licenses (Dec. 1969) 1,171,000. Television licenses (Dec. 1969) 796,000.

Agriculture. Production (in 000; metric tons; 1970; 1969 in parentheses): barley 581 (486); oats *c.* 153 (140); potatoes 857 (763); apples *c.* 57 (66); milk *c.* 1,763 (1,771); butter 18 (18); cheese 53 (49); beef and veal *c.* 60 (59); pork *c.* 68 (65); timber (cu.m.; 1969) 7,100, (1968) 6,700; fish catch (1969) 2,481, (1968) 2,804. Livestock (in 000; June 1970): cattle *c.* 980; sheep 1,754; pigs 642; goats *c.* 85; chickens *c.* 5,500.

Industry. Fuel and power (in 000; 1970): coal (Svalbard mines; Norwegian operated only) 466 metric tons, (U.S.S.R. operated; exports; 1969) 449 metric tons; manufactured gas 32,500 cu.m.; electricity 57,201,000 kw-hr. Production (in 000; metric tons; 1970): iron ore (65% metal content) 4,007; pig iron 1,230; crude steel 870; aluminum 530; zinc 61; copper 26; cement 2,634; sulfur (1969) 352; nitrogenous fertilizers (N content; 1969–70) 371; mechanical wood pulp (1969) 1,195; chemical wood pulp (1969) 893; newsprint 584; other paper (1969) 852. Merchant vessels launched (100 gross tons and over; 1970) 637,000 gross tons. New dwelling units completed (1970) 36,500.

Obituaries 1971

The following is a selected list of prominent men and women who died during 1971.

ABEL, RUDOLF IVANOVICH, Soviet intelligence agent (b. 1903—d. Moscow, U.S.S.R., Nov. 15, 1971), was convicted of conspiring to obtain and transmit defense information from the U.S. to the Soviet Union, sentenced to 30 years' imprisonment in 1957, and exchanged for U-2 pilot Francis Gary Powers in 1962. Abel used at least five aliases during his nine years in the U.S. and his real name was never known, nor was the information that he passed on ever disclosed. Abel apparently had been a member of Soviet intelligence since 1927.

ACHESON, DEAN, U.S. government official (b. Middletown, Conn., April 11, 1893—d. Sandy Spring, Md., Oct. 12, 1971), secretary of state under Pres. Harry S. Truman from 1949 until 1953, was considered to have been the principal architect of U.S. "cold war" strategy. His State Department services embraced the Bretton Woods agreement that led to the establishment of the World Bank; the Truman Doctrine of aid to Greece and Turkey; preliminary work on the Marshall Plan for bolstering the European countries; defining of an atomic policy; agreement on the North Atlantic Treaty Organization; the Korean War; nonrecognition of Communist Chinese and support of Gen. Chiang Kai-shek. Acheson was instrumental in creating and rearming West Germany, and in establishing bipartisanship in foreign policy. During the latter part of his term Acheson frequently came under attack by Sen. Joseph R. McCarthy.

ADAMS, SIR GRANTLEY HERBERT, Barbadian statesman (b. Barbados, April 28, 1898—d. Bridgetown, Barbados, Nov. 28, 1971), was prime minister of the former West Indies Federation (1958–62). For many years an advocate of federation, Adams had drawn up a draft constitution as early as 1938. The federation was dissolved in 1962. First elected to the Barbados House of Assembly in 1934, Adams became a member of the executive committee in 1941 and in 1954 was appointed Barbados' first premier. He initiated many reforms including the introduction of adult suffrage, workmen's compensation, and a peasant loan system. He was knighted in 1957.

AGAGIANIAN, GREGORY PETER XV CARDINAL, Armenian patriarch of the Roman Catholic Church (b. Akhaltsikhe, Russia, Sept. 15, 1895—d. Rome, Italy, May 16, 1971), was head of the Sacred Congregation for the Propagation of the Faith (1958–70). In 1935 he was appointed papal emissary to Lebanon. In 1946 Pope Pius XII created him cardinal, and in the conclave of 1958 he was among those considered eligible for the papacy. Pope John XXIII appointed him chairman of the preparatory commission for the missions before the second Vatican Council.

ALBRIGHT, WILLIAM FOXWELL, U.S. biblical archaeologist (b. Coquimbo, Chile, May 24, 1891—d. Baltimore, Md., Sept. 19, 1971), was the first world-renowned scholar to authenticate the Dead Sea Scrolls after their discovery in 1947. Albright, who had been emeritus professor of Semitic languages at Johns Hopkins University since 1958, was the author of a number of books, including *From the Stone Age to Christianity* (1940–46).

ALLEN, JAMES E., JR., U.S. educator and public official (b. Elkins, W.Va., April 25, 1911—d. Grand Canyon, Ariz., Oct. 16, 1971), was U.S. commissioner of education during 1969–70 but was dismissed from office after a disagreement with the Nixon administration over school desegregation and Vietnam war policy. Earlier he had been New York State commissioner of education for 14 years.

ANDERSON, EDWARD BERTRAM, British horticulturist (b. 1886—d. Redhill, Eng., July 29, 1971), an authority on alpine plants and wild bulbs, received the Veitch Medal in 1952, the Victoria Medal in 1960, the Cory Cup in 1967, and the Lyttel Cup in 1971.

ANDRADE, EDWARD NEVILLE DA COSTA, British physicist (b. London, Eng., Dec. 27, 1887—d. London, June 6, 1971), best known for his research on the physics of metals, was professor of physics at the Artillery College, Woolwich (1920–28), and later at London University. During World War II he was scientific adviser at the Ministry of Supply. He was president of the Physical Society (1943–45) and director of the Royal Institution (1950–52), and was the physics editor of the 14th edition of the *Encyclopædia Britannica*. He received the Royal Society's Hughes Medal in 1958.

ANDREWS, GEORGE WILLIAM, U.S. congressman (from 1944) from Alabama (b. Clayton, Ala., Dec. 12, 1906—d. Birmingham, Ala., Dec. 25, 1971), a Democrat and third ranking member of the House Appropriations Committee, was elected to the House in 1944 and won each succeeding election thereafter.

ANGELI, PIER (Anna Maria Pierangeli), U.S. film actress (b. Sardinia, 1932—d. Beverly Hills, Calif., Sept. 10, 1971), appeared in movies during the 1950s and '60s, including *The Moon and Sixpence* and *Somebody Up There Likes Me.*

ARBENZ GUZMÁN, JACOBO, Guatemalan army officer and political leader (b. Quezaltenango, Guat., Sept. 14, 1913—d. Mexico City, Mex., Jan. 27, 1971), served as president of his country from 1951 until 1954, when he was ousted by a right-wing military coup. An army colonel, he appeared on the political scene in 1944 as a member of the revolutionary junta that overthrew the dictator Jorge Ubico. Arbenz was minister of defense in the new government of Juan José Arévalo, then became president himself in 1951. Known as the "Red Colonel," he was opposed to foreign economic interests and clashed with the U.S. over his expropriation of the United Fruit Co. He extended relations with the Communist countries and, on domestic affairs, upheld his predecessor's land reform program.

ARMAND, LOUIS, French engineer (b. Cruseilles, France, Jan. 17, 1905—d. Villers-sur-Mer, France, Aug. 30, 1971), who played a leading part in France's industrial reconstruction after World War II and in European technological cooperation, was chairman of the European Atomic Agency (1958–59) and president of the Société Nationale de Chemins de Fer Français (SNCF, or French State Railways). Under his administration French railways became the most technically advanced in the world, and the system of 25-kv., 50-cycle electrification subsequently adopted by other countries was introduced. He was a member of the French Academy from 1963.

ASTOR OF HEVER, JOHN JACOB ASTOR, 1st Baron, British philanthropist (b. New York, N.Y., May 20, 1886—d. Cannes, France, July 19, 1971), was chief proprietor of *The Times* newspaper (1922–66) and chairman of The Times Publishing Co. (1922–59). In 1911 Astor was appointed aide-de-camp to the viceroy of India; he served in France during World War I. He was MP for the Dover division of Kent (1922–45), chairman and director of numerous companies, a BBC adviser, president of the Press Club and Commonwealth Press Union, and vice-president of the Royal College of Music (1934–62). He was a benefactor of many causes and contributed over £750,000 for improvements to the Middlesex Hospital. He was made a baron in 1956.

BACCI, ANTONIO CARDINAL, Italian prelate of the Roman Catholic Church (b. Giugnola-Castel Del Rio, Italy, Sept. 5, 1885—d. Vatican City, Jan. 20, 1971), who was the church's ranking Latinist, wrote the Latin versions of the encyclicals of four popes—Pius XI, Pius XII, John XXIII, and Paul VI. He was ordained to the priesthood in 1909 and elevated to cardinal by Pope John in 1960.

BALLARD, EDNA (Mrs. Guy Ballard), U.S. religious leader (b. 1890[?]—d. Chicago, Ill., Feb. 10, 1971), was titular head of the "I Am" religious movement, established by her husband (d. 1936) on Mt. Shasta in California in 1930.

BARABASHOV, NIKOLAI P., Soviet astronomer (b. Ukraine, March 29, 1894—d. Kharkov, U.S.S.R., April 29, 1971), noted for his studies of the moon and planets, graduated from Kharkov University in 1919. He remained at Kharkov and was associated with the university throughout his career, serving as director of the astronomical observatory and chairman of the astronomy department as well as rector (president) of the university from 1943 to 1945. Many of his findings concerning the surface of the moon were confirmed in the subsequent moon landings. Barabashov was the recipient of four Orders of Lenin.

Louis Armstrong   WIDE WORLD

ARMSTRONG, LOUIS DANIEL ("Satchmo"), U.S. jazz musician (b. New Orleans, La., July 4, 1900—d. New York, N.Y., July 6, 1971), trumpeter and singer, made his way from a waif's home in New Orleans to the great concert stages of five continents. He played with pickup bands in his native city until, at 22, he joined Joe "King" Oliver and his Creole Jazz Band in Chicago. Armstrong next played with Fletcher Henderson's band in New York but returned to Chicago to lead his own small groups, the Hot Five and the Hot Seven, at the Dreamland Cafe. It was during these halcyon days of jazz in the 1920s that Armstrong attained his finest performances and produced the recordings that were to become classics: "My Heart," "Cornet Chop Suey," "Potato Head Blues," "West End Blues."

Armstrong's popularity had spread to Europe by the 1930s and he made his first trip abroad in 1932. Following that were appearances in the Middle East, the Orient, Africa, South America, and the U.S.S.R., many sponsored by the U.S. State Department. Armstrong knew his public and always included in his programs such all-time favourites as "Ain't Misbehavin'," "Muskrat Ramble," "When the Saints Go Marchin' In," and his great "Sleepy Time Down South." (*See* Music: *Jazz.*)

BARNARD, CHARLES DOUGLAS, British aviator (b. 1895—d. Brighton, Eng., Aug. 7, 1971), who made the first London-to-Malta flight (1923), a 5,000-mi. tour of Europe and North Africa (1927), a trip to India and back in under eight days (1929), and the flight from London to Cape Town and back in 20 days (1930).

BARROS CAMARA, JAIME CARDINAL DE, Brazilian prelate of the Roman Catholic Church (b. São José, Braz., July 3, 1894—d. São Paulo, Braz., Feb. 18, 1971), archbishop of Rio de Janeiro, was ordained in 1920, became a bishop in 1935, and in 1941 was named archbishop of Belém, Pará state. He was elevated to cardinal on Feb. 18, 1946.

BASHEV, IVAN KHRISTO, Bulgarian politician (b. Feb. 11, 1916—d. near Sofia, Bulg., Dec. 12, 1971), was Bulgaria's foreign minister from 1962.

BEAGLEHOLE, JOHN CAWTE, New Zealand historian (b. Wellington, N.Z., June 13, 1901—d. Wellington, Oct. 10, 1971), was professor of British Commonwealth history, Victoria University of Wellington (1963–66), and the leading authority on the life and voyages of Capt. James Cook. He received the Royal Geographical Society's Gill Memorial Award in 1957. His books include *The Exploration of the Pacific* (1934), *The Discovery of New Zealand* (1939), and *New Zealand and the Statute of Westminster* (1944). He was awarded the Order of Merit in 1970.

BEATON, DONALD LEONARD, Canadian-British journalist (b. Montreal, Que., June 20, 1912—d. Venice, Italy, June 9, 1971), was an important contributor to the international debate on arms control in the 1960s while on the staff of the Institute for Strategic Studies, of which he became director in 1963. In 1957 he joined *The Guardian* as defense correspondent, and from 1965 to 1970 he edited *The Round Table*. Among his writings were *The Spread of Nuclear Weapons* (1962) and the script for a TV series, *The Struggle for Peace*.

BEBERMAN, MAX, U.S. mathematician (b. New York, N.Y., Aug. 20, 1925—d. London, Eng., Jan. 24, 1971), one of the creators of the "new math," was educational director of the Computer-Based Education Research Laboratory at the University of Illinois from 1966. He graduated from City College of New York in 1944 with a bachelor of arts degree in mathematics, received his master's degree in 1949 from Teachers College of Columbia University, and his doctorate in education from Columbia University in 1953. Joining the faculty of the University of Illinois in 1950, he became involved in what was to be known as new math, which sought to develop the reasoning powers of children rather than stressing rules and formulas. Beberman, having become a full professor in 1958, was named director of the university's Curriculum Laboratory in 1965.

BEN-MEIR, RABBI ISRAEL S., Israeli leader of the National Religious Party (b. Warsaw, Pol., 1911—d. Jerusalem, Israel, April 4, 1971), who emigrated from the U.S. in 1950 and became a member of the Knesset (parliament) that same year, served as deputy minister of welfare (1953–58) and deputy minister of the interior (1963–69).

BENTLEY, WALTER OWEN, British automobile designer (b. London, Eng., Sept. 16, 1888—d. Woking, Surrey, Eng., Aug. 13, 1971), who gave his name to the famous Bentley marque. After training on locomotives, Bentley became interested in the internal-combustion engine and took up motor racing. In 1910 he joined the National Motor Cab Company and two years later took over the London agency of three French cars. During World War I he designed his own Bentley rotary aeroengine. The first car of his design was delivered for sale in September 1921, and three years later Bentley cars became firmly established when one of them won the Le Mans 24-hour race. The company was acquired by Rolls-Royce in 1931.

BENTWICH, NORMAN DE MATTOS, British Zionist (b. London, Eng., Feb. 28, 1883—d. London, April 8, 1971), was attorney general in mandated Palestine (1920–31). After an attempt on his life by Arab extremists, the Colonial Office decided that he should be transferred. He therefore resigned, and was appointed professor of international relations at the Hebrew University of Jerusalem (1932–51). He was director of the League of Nations High Commission for Refugees (1933–36) and adviser to Emperor Haile Selassie of Ethiopia during his exile. Among his many publications were *Philo Judaeus* (1910), *Josephus* (1914), *Hellenism* (1919), *The Jews* (1934), *Israel* (1952), and *The Jews in Our Time* (1960).

BERNAL, JOHN DESMOND, British physicist (b. Nenagh, Ire., May 10, 1901—d. London, Eng., Sept. 15, 1971), was professor of physics at Birkbeck College, London University (1937–63), and its first professor of crystallography (1963–68). While a Cambridge undergraduate Bernal wrote a paper that gained him a research post at the Royal Institution to study crystal chemistry. Back at Cambridge from 1927 he turned his attention to a range of studies. He took the first X-ray photograph of a single protein crystal (pepsin) in 1933. Bernal was a fellow of the Royal Society. His books include *The Social Function of Science* (1939), *The Freedom of Necessity* (1949), *Science in History* (1954), *World Without War* (1958), and *Origin of Life* (1967).

BILLY, ANDRÉ, French writer (b. Saint-Quentin, France, Dec. 13, 1882—d. Fontainebleau, France, April 10, 1971), was awarded the French Academy's Grand Prix in 1944 and the Grand Prix National des Lettres in 1954. He produced a number of novels including *Benoni* (1907), *La Dérive* (1909), *L'Ange qui pleure* (1925), and *Quel homme es-tu?* (1936).

BLACK, HUGO LAFAYETTE, U.S. jurist (b. near Ashland, Ala., Feb. 27, 1886—d. Bethesda, Md., Sept. 25, 1971), member of the U.S. Supreme Court, was sworn into office by Pres. Franklin D. Roosevelt in 1937 and served until his retirement on Sept. 17, 1971. Prior to his appointment to the court he had held a seat in the U.S.

Senate for 11 years after winning his first election as a Democrat in 1926.

Pres. Richard M. Nixon said of the jurist's philosophy: "Justice Black believed that the primary responsibility of the judiciary was that of giving force and effect to constitutional liberties. . . . His faith in the United States Constitution was absolute, and so his convictions were rooted absolutely." Some of Black's important decisions included his dissent (in 1947) in *Adamson* v. *California*, a case in which he held that the Fifth Amendment's privilege against self-incrimination forbade a prosecutor to comment on a defendant's failure to take the witness stand. Probably Black's most criticized opinion was given in the 1944 case of *Korematsu* v. *United States* in which he upheld the right of the military to evacuate Japanese-American citizens from the West Coast after the 1941 Japanese attack on Pearl Harbor.

BLANCHFIELD, FLORENCE A., colonel (ret.), U.S. Army Nurse Corps (b. Shepherdstown, W.Va., April 1, 1884—d. Washington, D.C., May 12, 1971), the first U.S. woman to receive (1947) a commission in the regular Army, entered the Army Nurse Corps in 1917. She served in China, the Philippines, and Europe, as well as in the U.S., during her more than 30 years as an army nurse.

BLEGEN, CARL W., U.S. archaeologist (b. Minneapolis, Minn., Jan. 27, 1887—d. Athens, Greece, Aug. 24, 1971), professor of classical archaeology (1927–57, emeritus from 1957) and head of the classics department (1950–57) at the University of Cincinnati, was the leader of many expeditions to Greece in search of the site of ancient Troy. In 1939 he discovered the palace of Nestor, king of Pylos, and turned up several tablet fragments in Linear B (Mycenaean) script. Blegen was the author of a number of books including six volumes on Troy and Nestor's palace.

BLESSING, KARL, West German banking executive (b. Enzweihingen, Ger., Feb. 15, 1900—d. Orange, France, April 25, 1971), president of the Central Bank (Bundesbank) from 1958 until 1969, was a resolute defender of the stability of the mark and an opponent of inflationary policies. From 1920 to 1939 he worked for the Reichsbank and was closely involved in the Hague reparations conferences. In 1939 he joined a Unilever affiliate but two years later was forced out by Nazi pressure. He spent the war years in the petroleum industry, returning to Unilever in Hamburg after the war.

BOURKE-WHITE, MARGARET ("MAGGIE"), U.S. photographer (b. New York, N.Y., June 14, 1904—d. Stamford, Conn., Aug. 27, 1971), a pioneer in photojournalism, first worked for *Fortune* magazine, photographing factory workers, dams, sharecroppers, and the dust bowl of the early 1930s. In 1936 she joined the staff of the newly established *Life* magazine, remaining with the publication until 1969 when ill health

Rudolf Abel

Dean Acheson

Hugo Black

forced her to retire. For *Life* she covered World War II and the Korean War. She interviewed and photographed most of the notables of the era— Pres. Franklin D. Roosevelt, Winston Churchill, Mohandas K. Gandhi, Emperor Haile Selassie, Pope Pius XII, and Stalin (in the Kremlin, 1941). After World War II she covered the disorders in India and in South Africa.

BOYD-ORR, JOHN BOYD ORR, 1ST BARON, Scottish scientist and nutritionist (b. Kilmaurs, Scot., Sept. 23, 1880—d. Edzell, Scot., June 25, 1971), world authority on nutrition and food-supply problems, a founder (1945) and first director (1945–48) of the United Nations Food and Agriculture Organization, was awarded the 1949 Nobel Peace Prize for his tireless work with the FAO. Boyd-Orr received a degree in medicine from Glasgow University and in 1914 became director of the Institute of Animal Nutrition at Aberdeen University; in 1929 he founded the Imperial Bureau of Animal Nutrition at Rowett. His 1936 report, *Food, Health, and Income,* formed the basis for the British system of food rationing during World War II. After that war Boyd-Orr was invited by the British Labour government to attend the conference in Quebec that established the FAO. In 1945 he was appointed rector of Glasgow University.

BRAGG, SIR WILLIAM LAWRENCE, British physicist (b. Adelaide, Austr., March 31, 1890— d. London, Eng., July 1, 1971), joint holder of the 1915 Nobel Prize for Physics, was Fullerian professor of chemistry at the Royal Institution (1953–66) and its director (1964–66). In 1914 he became a fellow of Trinity College, Cambridge, having already produced original work on the structure of crystals. From 1919 to 1937 he was Langworthy professor of physics at Victoria University of Manchester, then director of the National Physical Laboratory for a year, and Cavendish professor of experimental physics at Cambridge (1938–53). He did fundamental work on the structures of metals and minerals and developed new techniques for the study of X-ray diffraction. From 1954 he worked on the structure of proteins. He became a fellow of the Royal Society in 1921.

BRANDON, THE REV. SAMUEL GEORGE FREDERICK, British scholar and theologian (b. Devon, Eng., Oct. 2, 1907—d. Oct. 29, 1971), was professor of comparative religion at Manchester University from 1951 and pro-vice-chancellor (1967–70). In his *Time and Mankind* (1951) Brandon first put forward his thesis that religion originates in man's awareness of and reaction to the passage of time. Other works include *The Fall of Jerusalem and the Christian Church* (1951), *Jesus and the Zealots* (1967), and *The Trial of Jesus of Nazareth* (1968). He was a contributor to *Encyclopædia Britannica.*

BROWNE, MICHAEL CARDINAL, Irish prelate of the Roman Catholic Church (b. Grangemockler, County Tipperary, Ire., May 6, 1887—d.

Rome, Italy, March 31, 1971), was chief theologian (1951–55) of the Vatican, and master general (superior) of the Dominican Order (1955–63). He was ordained in 1910 and in 1919 began teaching philosophy at the Angelicum, Rome's Dominican university. He was elevated to cardinal in 1963 by Pope John XXIII.

BUNCHE, RALPH JOHNSON, U.S. diplomat (b. Detroit, Mich., Aug. 7, 1904—d. New York, N.Y., Oct. 11, 1971), recipient of the 1950 Nobel Peace Prize, was the highest ranking U.S. official of the United Nations, serving as undersecretary-general for special political affairs from 1957 until his retirement Oct. 1, 1971. After serving with the OSS during World War II, Bunche joined the State Department in 1944 and participated in the UN planning sessions at Dumbarton Oaks and in the San Francisco Conference of 1945. First on loan to the UN (1946), he joined the permanent staff in 1947 and shortly thereafter was called upon to mediate the partition of Palestine. Bunche presented the plan for indirect negotiations that led to the Arab-Israeli agreement of 1948–49. For this work he received the Nobel Peace Prize in 1950. In 1956 he planned for the UN Emergency Force that succeeded in keeping the peace in the Middle East for more than ten years. Other peace missions involved the organization of the UN effort in containing the civil war in the Congo (1960) and the establishment of the UN force on Cyprus (1964). He received many honours including the Medal of Freedom presented by Pres. John Kennedy in 1963.

BURNETT, LEO, U.S. advertising executive (b. St. Johns, Mich., 1892—d. Lake Zurich, Ill., June 7, 1971), was founder (1935) and chairman of the board (until 1967) of the Leo Burnett Company, Inc. advertising agency. His Chicago-based company was fifth largest in the world.

BURROWS, LARRY, British press photographer (b. London, Eng., May 29, 1926—d. Laos [missing, presumed dead], Feb. 10, 1971), won international repute for his photography in *Life* magazine of the world's trouble spots over more than two decades. Among his assignments were the Suez crisis, the U.S. landing in Lebanon, the Congo, the Mosul uprising in Iraq, and in particular the war in Vietnam. He won the Robert Capa Award in 1964 and 1966, on both occasions for "superlative photography requiring exceptional courage and enterprise."

BURT, SIR CYRIL LODOWIC, British psychologist (b. near Stratford-upon-Avon, Eng., March 30, 1883—d. London, Eng., Oct. 10, 1971), professor of psychology at University College, London (1931–50) and for more than 40 years a leading exponent of applied psychology in education, pioneered in intelligence tests for grammar school applicants. His writings include *The Young Delinquent* (1925), *The Backward Child* (1937), and *The Causes and Treatment of Backwardness* (1952). Burt was knighted in 1946. He was an adviser to the editors of *Encyclopædia Britannica.*

BYINGTON, SPRING, U.S. actress (b. Colorado Springs, Colo., Oct. 17, 1893—d. Hollywood, Calif., Sept. 7, 1971), who appeared in more than 30 stage plays and 75 films, portrayed the mother-

in-law in *December Bride,* popular radio and television series of the 1950s.

CALLORI DI VIGNALE, FEDERICO CARDINAL, Italian prelate of the Roman Catholic Church (b. Vignale Monferrato, Italy, Jan. 15, 1890—d. Vatican City, Aug. 10, 1971), served as steward to Pope John XXIII, and was elevated to cardinal by Pope Paul VI in February 1965.

CANNON, CHARLES ALBERT, U.S. industrialist (b. Concord, N.C., Nov. 29, 1892—d. Kannapolis, N.C., April 2, 1971), president (from 1921) and chairman of the board (from 1962) of Cannon Mills, one of the largest U.S. textile manufacturing companies.

CERF, BENNETT, U.S. book publisher and TV performer (b. New York, N.Y., May 25, 1898— d. Mount Kisco, N.Y., Aug. 27, 1971), was head of Random House from 1927 until 1970, and for 16 years a weekly panelist on the TV parlor-game show "What's My Line?" He was the publisher of *Ulysses* by James Joyce, and of Marcel Proust, William Faulkner, Franz Kafka, Eugene O'Neill, and of Plato. In the early 1920s Cerf redesigned the Modern Library, a series of reprinted classics, and turned it into the successful forerunner of the paperback books. One of Cerf's greatest projects was *The Random House Dictionary of the English Language,* a 2,059-page volume started in the late 1950s and issued in 1966.

CHANEL, GABRIELLE BONHEUR ("Coco"), French couturière (b. Saumur, France, Aug. 19, 1883—d. Paris, France, Jan. 10, 1971), founded one of the most illustrious haute couture houses of the century in the rue Cambon in Paris in 1914. With her introduction of jersey, tweed, and pearls, "Coco" Chanel revolutionized the fashion scene, proving that the casual could also be elegant. In 1920 she made the first chemise dress and in 1925 introduced the collarless, braid-trimmed cardigan jacket. At the height of her career she controlled a $15 million fashion empire of a couture house, textile and costume jewelry factories, and perfume laboratories for the famous Chanel No. 5 scent. In 1938 she retired from the fashion scene, eclipsed by Schiaparelli, but in 1954 made a remarkable comeback starting where she had left off—with cardigan suits, lace and chiffon dresses and blouses, pleated skirts, and masses of "junk" jewelry. In 1957 she won the Neiman-Marcus Award. *Coco,* a musical based on her career and starring Katharine Hepburn, was produced on Broadway in 1969.

CHAPMAN, FREDERICK SPENCER, British explorer and author (b. May 10, 1907—d. Reading, Eng., Aug. 8, 1971), was warden of Wantage Hall, University of Reading, from 1966. After participating in several expeditions to Greenland, Chapman joined a Himalayan expedition in 1935 and while in Sikkim was persuaded to join the British diplomatic mission in Lhasa, Tibet. In 1937 he climbed Chomolhari (24,000 ft.). Among his books were *Northern Lights* (1932), *Watkins' Last Expedition* (1934), *Lhasa: The Holy City* (1938), and *The Jungle Is Neutral* (1948).

CHISHOLM, BROCK, Canadian psychiatrist (b. Oakville, Ont., May 18, 1896—d. Victoria, B.C., Feb. 2, 1971), was director general of the World Health Organization from 1948 until 1953.

Lord Boyd-Orr

Ralph Bunche

Spring Byington

CLARK, J(OSEPH) J(AMES) ("JOCKO"), admiral (ret.), U.S. Navy (b. 1894—d. New York, N.Y., July 13, 1971), was commander of the 7th Fleet in 1952, during the conflict with North Korea. His career in the Pacific during World War II and the Korean War was recounted in his autobiography, *Carrier Admiral* (1967).

CLARK, WALTER VAN TILBURG, U.S. author (b. East Orland, Me., Aug. 3, 1909—d. Reno, Nev., Nov. 10, 1971), wrote *The Ox-Bow Incident* (1940), a classic in the literature of the Old West; it was adapted for the screen in 1943.

CLUNE, FRANK (FRANCIS PATRICK), Australian author (b. Sydney, Austr., Nov. 27, 1893—d. Sydney, March 11, 1971), published his first book, *Try Anything Once,* an autobiography, in 1932. Many of his 67 books were best sellers, including *Wild Colonial Boys* about the early settlement of Australia.

COLLIER, MARIE, Australian soprano opera singer (b. Ballarat, Austr., April 16, 1927—d. London, Eng., Dec. 8, 1971), was acclaimed in 1965 when at short notice she took over from Maria Callas in the Zeffirelli production of *Tosca* at Covent Garden. After beginning her career in musicals she went to England and signed a contract with Covent Garden in 1956. Among her roles were Musetta in *La Bohème,* the title role in Janacek's *Kata Kabanova,* Santuzza in *Cavalleria Rusticana,* and Elizabeth in *Don Carlos.* She created the role of Hecuba in Michael Tippett's *King Priam* in 1962 and played the title role in the first British performance of *Katerina Ismailova* and Emilia Marty in Janacek's *The Makropulos Case* at Sadler's Wells.

CONNIFF, FRANK, U.S. journalist and editor (b. Danbury, Conn., April 24, 1914—d. New York, N.Y., May 25, 1971), once national editor of Hearst Newspapers, was editor of the *World Journal Tribune* (New York) from 1966 until the paper ceased publication in 1967. Conniff interviewed Premier Nikita S. Khrushchev in Moscow in 1955 and was awarded a Pulitzer Prize in that year for his report of the meeting.

CONSTANTINE, LEARIE NICHOLAS CONSTANTINE, BARON, West Indian cricketer (b. Diego Martin, Trinidad, Sept. 21, 1901—d. London, Eng., July 1, 1971), was high commissioner in London for Trinidad and Tobago (1962–64) and a lifelong campaigner against racial prejudice. On tour in England in 1928 he became the first West Indian to gain the "double" of 1,000 runs and 100 wickets in one season. But it was his brilliant play against Middlesex in June of that year at Lord's that established him and West Indian cricket in the English public eye. In 1954 he qualified as a barrister, and practiced in the English courts, wrote and broadcast on cricket, and in 1966 became a member of the Race Relations Board. He was rector of St. Andrews University and a governor of the BBC. Knighted in 1962, he was made a life peer in 1969.

COOPER, DAME GLADYS, British actress (b. Lewisham, Eng., Dec. 18, 1888—d. Henley-on-Thames, Eng., Nov. 17, 1971), began her career with a touring company in Seymour Hicks's *Bluebell in Fairyland* in 1905. In 1908 came her first serious role as Cecily in Wilde's *The Importance of Being Earnest;* in 1913 she played the lead in Sardou's *Diplomacy,* and in 1922 the lead in *The Second Mrs. Tanqueray.* In 1934 she made her American debut in Keith Winter's *The Shining Hour.* Her film career in Hollywood began with *Rebecca,* and was followed by *Now, Voyager, The Song of Bernadette,* and *Mrs. Parkinton.* She appeared on the stage in *A Passage to India* (1962), *The Sacred Flame* (1967), *His, Hers and Theirs* (1969), and *The Chalk Garden* (1971).

COPLAND, SIR DOUGLAS BERRY, Australian economist (b. Timaru, N.Z., Feb. 24, 1894—d. Melbourne, Austr., Sept. 27, 1971), became first principal of the Australian Administrative Staff College in 1956 and in 1960 founded the Committee for the Economic Development of Australia. He was knighted in 1950.

DANIELS, BEBE (MRS. BEN LYON), U.S. screen star and radio entertainer (b. Dallas, Tex., Jan. 14, 1901—d. London, Eng., March 16, 1971), was known to the British public for her role in the 1950s radio show "Life with the Lyons." She was active in all forms of light comedy, playing in many of the top U.S. movies of the 1920s and '30s: *Rio Rita, 42nd Street, Counselor at Law.* In 1933 she went to England to star in films and later, with her husband Ben Lyon, appeared at the Palladium and on British television. For her work during World War II she was awarded the highest U.S. civilian award, the Medal of Freedom.

DAY, EDITH, British actress (b. Minneapolis, Minn., April 10, 1896—d. London, Eng., May 1971), was a leading figure in musical comedy on the London stage in the 1920s. Her first success, *Going Up,* in 1917, was followed by *Irene,* which ran for 670 performances in the U.S. and for more than 300 in London. She played lead roles in *Rose Marie, The Desert Song,* and *Showboat* from 1925 to 1930. In 1960 she appeared in Noel Coward's *Waiting in the Wings.*

DAY, EDWARD GATELY, JR. ("NED"), U.S. bowler (b. 1911—d. Milwaukee, Wis., Nov. 26, 1971), held many world records, including the world's tournament record of 834 (300-276-258) set in Los Angeles in 1939. Day was elected to the American Bowling Hall of Fame in 1952, the same year he won the American Bowling Congress all-title event.

de KRUIF, PAUL HENRY, U.S. bacteriologist and author (b. Zeeland, Mich., March 2, 1890—d. Holland, Mich., Feb. 28, 1971), was best known as a writer on medical and other scientific topics. Of his more than a dozen books, his best sellers included *Microbe Hunters* (1926), *Hunger Fighters* (1928), and *Men Against Death* (1932). He was co-author (with Sidney Howard) of *Yellow Jack!,* a Broadway play that depicted Walter Reed's fight against yellow fever. De Kruif's own investigations in the field of bacteriology were carried out at the Rockefeller Institute in New York City (1920–22) and at the Pasteur Institute in Paris. In his book *Health Is Wealth,* published in 1940, de Kruif proposed that preventive medical care be guaranteed all Americans through public health facilities.

de VAUX, ROLAND, French archaeologist (b. 1903—d. Jerusalem, Israel, Sept. 10, 1971), head of the French École Biblique, was a leader of the international team of scholars who edited the Dead Sea Scrolls, which he had aided in excavating from the Qumran caves in 1947.

DEWEY, THOMAS EDMUND, U.S. lawyer and political figure (b. Owosso, Mich., March 24, 1902—d. Bal Harbour, Fla., March 16, 1971), was defeated twice in his bid for the U.S. presidency. Dewey, who received his law degree from Columbia University Law School in 1925, was elected district attorney of New York County in 1937 after having gained a reputation as a "racket buster" during a two-year stint as special rackets prosecutor for the city. In 1942 he was elected governor of New York, and won a second term in 1946. He ran for president on the Republican ticket in 1944, against Franklin Delano Roosevelt, and again in 1948 against Harry S. Truman, who narrowly won an upset victory. In 1950 Dewey was voted a third term as governor. He retired from public office and returned to his private law practice in 1955.

DOBROVOLSKY, GEORGI T., Soviet cosmonaut (b. Odessa, U.S.S.R., June 1, 1928—d. in space, June 30, 1971), commander of the Soyuz 11 spacecraft, died with his two fellow crewmen at the controls of the craft near the time of its reentry into earth's atmosphere. He was with the Soviet space program eight years before making his first flight with the Soyuz 11. (See *Patsayev, Viktor I.,* and *Volkov, Vladislav N.,* below.)

DODD, THOMAS JOSEPH, U.S. senator (1959–71) from Connecticut (b. Norwich, Conn., May 15, 1907—d. Old Lyme, Conn., May 24, 1971), executive trial counsel at the 1946 Nürnberg war crimes trials, was elected to the U.S. House of Representatives in 1952. Defeated once in seeking election to the Senate, Dodd was voted a seat in 1958 and reelected in 1964. In 1967 he was censured by his colleagues for alleged financial misconduct in converting a $116,000 campaign fund to his personal use. Dodd lost his bid for a third term in the Senate in 1970.

DONOVAN, TERENCE NORBERT DONOVAN, BARON, British jurist (b. June 13, 1898—d. London, Eng., Dec. 12, 1971), was a judge of the High Court (1950–60), a lord justice of appeal (1960–63), and a lord of appeal in ordinary from 1963. He presided over a Royal Commission on Trades Unions and Employers' Associations from 1965 until 1968. He was Labour MP for East Leicester (1945–50) and for North-East Leicester (1950).

DUN, THE RIGHT REV. ANGUS, U.S. clergyman (b. New York, N.Y., May 4, 1892—d. Washington, D.C., Aug. 12, 1971), Episcopal bishop of Washington from 1944 until 1962, served as dean of the Episcopal Theological School at Cambridge, Mass., from 1940 until 1944.

Bennett Cerf

WIDE WORLD

Thomas E. Dewey

WIDE WORLD

Georgi T. Dobrovolsky

TASS—SOVFOTO

DUNHILL, ALFRED, British company director (b. London, Eng., March 26, 1896—d. Hove, Eng., July 8, 1971), was president of Alfred Dunhill Ltd. and a distinguished figure in the tobacco industry. He succeeded his father (who had founded the business in 1907) as chairman in 1928. Dunhill was master of the Worshipful Company of Tobacco Pipe Makers and Tobacco Blenders (1955–56).

DUVALIER, FRANÇOIS ("PAPA DOC"), president of Haiti (b. Port-au-Prince, Haiti, April 14, 1907—d. Port-au-Prince, April 21, 1971), dictator of his country from 1957, named himself president for life in 1964. Duvalier received a medical degree from the University of Haiti Medical School in 1934 and served on various hospital staffs. Under a U.S.-financed program against yaws (a tropical skin disease), he traveled through much of the back country searching out cases and inoculating against the disease. During this time he built up a large following of peasants. In 1948 he became secretary of labour, but in 1950 a coup deposed the government of Paul Magloire and Duvalier was forced to postpone his political career. In 1956–57 one coup followed another until finally, on Sept. 22, 1957, Duvalier was elected president, with the support of the Army. He acted swiftly to dispose of "troublemakers" and was soon in complete control of the government. Having formed his private armed force, the Tontons Macoutes, Duvalier easily survived a long series of rebellions and attempted coups, becoming stronger with each disorder. In 1970 Duvalier rewrote the Haitian constitution to pave the way for his son, Jean-Claude, to succeed him as president for life.

ECKERT, WILLIAM DOLE, lieutenant general (ret.), U.S. Air Force (b. Freeport, Ill., Jan. 20, 1908—d. Freeport, Bahamas, April 16, 1971), served as U.S. commissioner of baseball from 1965 until 1968.

EDWARDS, CLIFF ("UKELELE IKE"), U.S. singer and stage and screen star (b. Hannibal, Mo., 1895—d. Hollywood, Calif., July 17, 1971), appeared in more than 100 movies and sold at least 74 million records. He gave the squeaky tenor voice to Jiminy Cricket in Walt Disney's 1940 production of *Pinocchio,* and sang the song "When You Wish upon a Star," which won an Academy Award.

EMERY, WALTER BRYAN, British Egyptologist (b. New Brighton, Cheshire, Eng., July 2, 1903—d. Cairo, Egypt, March 12, 1971), was Edwards professor of Egyptology at London University from 1951 to 1970. His association with the Saqqarah excavations spanned more than 40 years, and he was responsible for the discovery of the tombs of the Buchis bulls at ancient Hermonthis, and the tombs of the pagan kings of Lower Nubia.

ERVINE, ST. JOHN GREER, British playwright and author (b. Belfast, Ire., Dec. 28, 1883—d. London, Eng., Jan. 24, 1971), manager of Dublin's Abbey Theatre (1915–16), was for many years dramatic critic of *The Observer.* His most notable works included the plays *Mixed Marriage, John Ferguson,* and *The First Mrs. Fraser* (1928), the novels *Mrs. Martin's Man* and *The Wayward Man,* and a number of biographies.

EVANS, HERBERT McLEAN, U.S. anatomist (b. Modesto, Calif., 1882—d. Berkeley, Calif., March 6, 1971), was the discoverer of vitamin E and its function in reproduction, which he demonstrated in 1922. Evans received his medical degree from Johns Hopkins University in 1908 and taught there until 1915, when he joined the faculty of the University of California at Berkeley as professor of anatomy. After retiring from that institution in 1952, he continued his research until 1966. Through his study of the pituitary gland, Evans was able to isolate the growth-promoting factor of the gland (1939) and in 1944, with C. H. Li, achieved purification of the hormone.

FAIRCHILD, SHERMAN MILLS, U.S. inventor and industrialist (b. Oneonta, N.Y., April 7, 1896—d. New York, N.Y., March 28, 1971), who numbered among his major inventions the Fairchild aerial camera, attended Harvard University and studied engineering at Columbia University. He started work on his camera, used in mapmaking and aerial surveying, for the U.S. War Department in 1918, and by 1920 had established his own company, Fairchild Camera and Equipment Co. Fairchild shortly went into aircraft manufacturing, with the aim of making planes better suited for mapping and surveying. His first technical changes (in 1926) were the enclosed cabin and folding wings; the next year he introduced hydraulic brakes and landing gear. Fairchild was board chairman of his company and a director of International Business Machines Corp.

FALLS, CYRIL BENTHAM, British military historian (b. Dublin, Ire., March 2, 1888—d. London, Eng., April 23, 1971), was military correspondent of *The Times* (1939–53) and Chichele professor of the history of war at Oxford (1946–53). He wrote regularly for the *Illustrated London News,* and was a contributor to *Encyclopædia Britannica.*

FANNING, LAWRENCE F., U.S. newspaperman (b. Minneapolis, Minn., April 14, 1914—d. Anchorage, Alaska, Feb. 3, 1971), was publisher and editor of the *Anchorage Daily News* from 1967. Previously he had been managing editor of the *San Francisco Chronicle* (1943–55); assistant executive editor (1957–59) and executive editor (1959–62) of the *Chicago Sun-Times;* executive editor (1962–65) and editor (1965–66) of the *Chicago Daily News;* and editorial director of Publishers Newspaper Syndicate (1966–67).

FARNSWORTH, PHILO TAYLOR, U.S. pioneer in electronics (b. Beaver, Utah, Aug. 19, 1906—d. Salt Lake City, Utah, March 11, 1971), who developed the techniques that made television possible, worked out the basic features of his system as a high school student in 1921. Six years later his first patented television film was filed, and by 1935 he was ready to give a ten-day demonstration of his new entertainment device, on which he held more than 165 patents. He founded the Farnsworth Radio and Television Corp. and served as its president, and as president of subsequent companies formed by mergers, until 1967.

FARRELL, GLENDA (MRS. HENRY ROSS), U.S. film, stage, and TV star (b. Enid, Okla., June 30, 1904—d. New York, N.Y., May 1, 1971), appeared in about 120 movies, chiefly in the 1930s, including *Little Caesar,* and *The Gold Diggers* and *Torchy Blane* series. Long a Broadway favourite, her roles included those in *Separate Rooms* and *Forty Carats.* In 1963 she won an Emmy as best supporting actress in a TV show.

FERNANDEL (FERNAND CONTANDIN), French comedian (b. Marseilles, France, May 8, 1903—d. Paris, France, Feb. 26, 1971), who appeared in about 150 motion pictures, was best remembered for his portrayal of Don Camillo, an Italian village priest, in films based on the stories of Giovanni Guareschi. Fernandel first played Don Camillo in 1951 and continued the characterization through 1970, when illness forced him to leave the last film uncompleted.

FILDES, SIR PAUL, British bacteriologist (b. London, Eng., Feb. 10, 1882—d. London, Feb. 5, 1971), was director of chemical bacteriology at Britain's Medical Research Council, and during World War II a leading worker on bacteriological warfare. His early researches concentrated on treatments of syphilis and dysentery; later he studied bacterial nutrition, provided a classic proof that tetanus bacilli are inhibited by the oxidizing power of normal tissue, and determined the sequence of enzyme reaction by which a microbe synthesizes a complex substance from simpler chemicals. He was elected to the Royal Society in 1934, received its Royal Medal in 1953, and its highest honour, the Copley Medal, at the age of 81.

FIO RITO, TED, U.S. orchestra leader (b. Newark, N.J., Dec. 20, 1900—d. Scottsdale, Ariz., July 22, 1971), whose big bands were popular during the 1930s, was featured on "The Hollywood Hotel" radio program. Also a composer, he wrote a number of hit songs, including "Toot Toot Tootsie," "Charlie My Boy," and "Now that You're Gone."

FLEMING, (ROBERT) PETER, British author and explorer (b. Oxfordshire, Eng., May 31, 1907—d. Black Mount, Argyllshire, Scot., Aug. 18, 1971), made his name with the publication in 1933 of *Brazilian Adventure,* a hilarious parody of a fashionable style of contemporary travelogue. Based on a journey of his own, this book was followed by *One's Company* and *News from Tartary,* the results of further travel. From the late 1940s he contributed regularly to *The Times* and to the *Spectator.* Other of his writings include *Invasion, 1940, The Siege at Peking, Bayonets to Lhasa,* and *The Fate of Admiral Kolchak.*

FOLLAIN, JEAN, French poet (b. Canisy, France, Aug. 29, 1903—d. Paris, France, March 9, 1971), holder of the French Academy's 1970 poetry prize, whose first collection, *La Main chaude,* appeared in 1937. Two years later he was awarded the Prix Mallarmé and in 1941 the Prix Blumenthal. Other works were *Usage du*

François Duvalier

Fernandel

Lord Goddard

Temps (1943), *Territoires* (1953), *Tout instant* (1957), *Des Heures* (1960), and *D'après tout* (1967).

FOYLE, GILBERT, British bookseller (b. London, Eng., March 9, 1886—d. Eastbourne, Eng., Oct. 28, 1971), with his brother William built up the largest bookselling business in Britain, and possibly in the world. In 1951 Gilbert Foyle lodged £20,000 with the London County Council to form the Gilbert Foyle Educational Trust for needy students.

FULTON, JAMES G., U.S. congressman (from 1944) from Pennsylvania (b. Allegheny County, Pa., March 1, 1903—d. Washington, D.C., Oct. 6, 1971), was ranking Republican on the House Science and Astronautics Committee and member of the Foreign Affairs Committee.

GALE, SIR HUMFREY MYDDELTON, British Army officer (b. Liphook, Eng., Oct. 4, 1890—d. La Tour-de-Peilz, Switz., April 8, 1971), was chief administrative officer and deputy chief of staff to Gen. Dwight D. Eisenhower during the World War II campaigns in North Africa and Western Europe. At the start of World War II he was assistant director of supplies and transport at the War Office. In 1941 he transferred to the Scottish Command and a year later became chief administrative officer for General Headquarters, Home Forces.

GARCÍA, CARLOS P., Filipino statesman (b. Talibon, Phil., Nov. 4, 1896—d. Quezon City, Phil., June 14, 1971), president of the Philippines from 1957 until 1961, lost only one election in his 46-year political career. García served three terms as a member of the House of Representatives, was three times governor of Bohol, his native province, and had just been elected to the Senate at the time of Japan's attack on the Philippines in World War II. At war's end, after three years of guerrilla fighting, he returned to the Senate. He was elected vice-president in 1953, as the Nationalist Party candidate; the following year he was appointed minister of foreign affairs. Upon the death of Pres. Ramón Magsaysay in a plane crash on March 17, 1957, García became president, and he was elected to his own four-year term the following November. In 1962 he was defeated in his bid for reelection. In June 1971 he was elected president of the Philippine constitutional convention, which was to study proposals for restructuring the political and social systems of the country.

GODDARD, RAYNER GODDARD, Baron, British jurist (b. London, Eng., April 10, 1877—d. London, May 29, 1971), lord chief justice of England (1946–58), was a controversial supporter of corporal and capital punishment. He was called to the bar at the Inner Temple in 1899 and held high judicial office for more than 25 years. He became successively recorder of Poole, Bath, and Plymouth before being appointed a judge of the King's Bench Division in 1932. He went to the House of Lords in 1944 and served as lord of appeal until 1946 when he became lord chief justice.

GOSLIN, LEON ALLEN ("Goose"), U.S. baseball player (b. Salem, N.J., Oct. 16, 1900—d.

Bridgeton, N.J., May 15, 1971), an American League outfielder, was elected to baseball's Hall of Fame in 1968. During his 18-year career (1921–38), Goslin played left field with the Washington Senators, the St. Louis Browns, and the Detroit Tigers. His lifetime batting average was .316.

GROMAIRE, MARCEL, French painter and engraver (b. Noyelles-sur-Sambre, France, July 24, 1892—d. Paris, France, April 11, 1971), first exhibited his work in 1911 at the Paris Salon des Independents. He received the Carnegie Prize in 1952, the Guggenheim Prize in 1956, and the Prix National des Arts in 1959. He was given a retrospective exhibition at the Musée d'Art Moderne in Paris in 1963.

GUGGENHEIM, HARRY F., U.S. publisher, philanthropist, and horseman (b. West End, N.J., Aug. 23, 1890—d. Sands Point, L.I., Jan. 22, 1971), was co-founder (1941) with his wife, Alicia Patterson, of *Newsday*, the Long Island daily that was to become the country's largest suburban paper. By 1963 Guggenheim was editor, publisher, and president of *Newsday*. He was long interested in his family's many philanthropic enterprises and was instrumental in expanding these endeavours, especially in the areas of aeronautics and art. Owner of racing stables at his Cain Hoy plantations in South Carolina, and at Lexington, Ky., Guggenheim numbered among his Thoroughbreds Dark Star, winner of the 1953 Kentucky Derby.

GUTHRIE, SIR (WILLIAM) TYRONE, British director, author, and producer (b. Tunbridge Wells, Eng., July 2, 1900—d. Newbliss, Ire., May 15, 1971), was administrator at the Old Vic and Sadler's Wells (1939–45), and director of the Old Vic (1951–52). He founded the Tyrone Guthrie Theatre at Minneapolis in 1963 and produced numerous plays and operas in London, New York, Canada, Australia, Finland and Israel. He published several plays and nonfiction works, was knighted in 1961, and became chancellor of Queen's University, Belfast, in 1963.

GUTT, CAMILLE, Belgian economist, journalist, and lawyer (b. Brussels, Belg., Nov. 14, 1884—d. Brussels, June 7, 1971), was managing director of the International Monetary Fund (1946–51). With Johannes van den Broeck he established the customs union with the Netherlands and Luxembourg known as Benelux.

HARLAN, JOHN MARSHALL, U.S. jurist (b. Chicago, Ill., May 20, 1899—d. Washington, D.C., Dec. 29, 1971), 89th justice of the U.S. Supreme Court, was sworn into office on March 28, 1955, following an appointment by Pres. Dwight D. Eisenhower, and served until his retirement on Sept. 23, 1971. Harlan, a conservative, believed in a sharp dividing line between federal and state authority and felt the court made a mistake in a 1962 Tennessee decision that opened the federal courts to voter complaints regarding apportionment of seats in state legislatures. Harlan then dissented in 1964 when the court issued its "one man, one vote" ruling as applied to both houses of state legislatures. He approved several important civil rights decisions, including *Cohen* v. *California* (June 1971) for

which he wrote the majority opinion finding that wearing a jacket emblazoned with an obscene reference to the draft into a courthouse was constitutionally protected free speech.

HART, THOMAS CHARLES, admiral (ret.), U.S. Navy (b. Davidson, Mich., June 12, 1877—d. Sharon, Conn., July 4, 1971), was commander in chief of the U.S. Asiatic Fleet at the time of Japan's 1941 attack on Pearl Harbor. He retired from the service in 1945 to accept an appointment as U.S. senator from Connecticut.

HASE, ANNEMARIE, German actress (b. Berlin, Ger., June 14, 1900—d. West Berlin, Feb. 22, 1971), performed in the top German cabarets of the 1920s.

HAYNES, HENRY D., U.S. entertainer (b. Knoxville, Tenn., 1920—d. Hammond, Ind., Aug. 7, 1971), was Homer of the Homer and Jethro (Kenneth Burns) country music team. First appearing in 1939, at the Renfo Valley Square Dance in Tennessee, Homer and Jethro went on to national fame on radio and TV, cutting more than 50 record albums and numerous single hits. The first of the team's million-copy sellers, "Battle of Kukamonga," was recorded in the 1950s; other hits included "Hound Dog in the Window," "Daddy Sang Bass," and "Let Me Go Lover."

HEFLIN, VAN (Emmet Evan Heflin, Jr.), U.S. actor (b. Walters, Okla., Dec. 13, 1910—d. Hollywood, Calif., July 23, 1971), who achieved his first success in the Broadway production *Philadelphia Story* (1939), began his Hollywood film career in 1940 in *Santa Fe Trail*. He won an Oscar in 1942 as best supporting actor for his role in *Johnny Eager*. He starred in many more films, including *Shane* (1953), *A Case of Libel* (1964), and *Airport* (1970). On Broadway he played Eddie in *View from the Bridge* (1955); television successes included *Certain Honorable Men* in 1968.

HERBERT, SIR ALAN PATRICK, British author (b. Elstead, Eng., Sept. 24, 1890—d. London, Eng., Nov. 11, 1971), writer of more than 50 books, musical plays, revues, light verses, articles, and letters to *The Times* on innumerable causes, was Independent member of Parliament for Oxford University (1935–50). He wrote his first of many contributions to *Punch* while still at school, and his first literary success was *The Secret Battle* (1919), a story of front-line warfare; another novel, *The Water Gipsies* (1930), described Thames riverside life. Herbert wrote many successful comic operas and musicals, among which were *Riverside Nights, La Vie Parisienne, Tantivy Towers, Helen, Derby Day, Paganini, Big Ben, Bless the Bride, The Water Gipsies* (from his novel), and *Home and Beauty.* His *Misleading Cases* was adapted as a television series. He was knighted in 1945 and was made a Companion of Honour in 1970. At 80, he published *A.P.H. His Life and Times.*

John Marshall Harlan

Thomas C. Hart

Henry D. Haynes

HICKENLOOPER, BOURKE BLAKEMORE, U.S. senator (1944–69) from Iowa (b. Blockton, Ia., July 21, 1896—d. Shelter I., L.I., Sept. 4, 1971), co-sponsor (with Rep. W. Sterling Cole) of the Atomic Energy Act of 1954, was head of the Joint Congressional Committee on Atomic Energy from 1949.

HOLMAN, LIBBY (ELIZABETH HOLMAN REYNOLDS HOLMES SCHANKER), U.S. entertainer (b. Cincinnati, O., May 23, 1906—d. Stamford, Conn., June 18, 1971), torch singer of the 1920s, was famous for her renditions of "Moanin' Low," "Something to Remember You By," and "Body and Soul." In 1932 Libby Holman was charged in the murder of her husband, wealthy young Zachary Smith Reynolds, but for lack of evidence was exonerated after a highly publicized trial. She never regained her earlier fame but did continue to appear in nightclubs and in the recording studios. Her last public appearance was in 1968.

HOUGH, THE REV. LYNN HAROLD, U.S. clergyman (b. Cadiz, O., Sept. 10, 1877—d. New York, N.Y., July 14, 1971), prominent Methodist educator, was professor (from 1930) and dean (1934–47) of Drew University in Madison, N.J. Hough served as a member of the executive committee of the National Council of Churches of Christ in America (1936–48) and was the author of several books, including *The Dignity of Man.*

HOUSSAY, BERNARDO ALBERTO, Argentine physiologist (b. Buenos Aires, Arg., April 10, 1887—d. Buenos Aires, Sept. 21, 1971), recipient of a Nobel Prize for Physiology or Medicine (1947), was professor and director of the Physiological Institute of the University of Buenos Aires school of medicine at various times from 1929 through the 1950s, having several times been ousted from the post for opposing Juan Perón's education policies. Houssay shared (with Carl and Gerty T. Cori) the 1947 Nobel Prize for Physiology or Medicine for his discovery of the role of the pituitary hormones in sugar metabolism.

HUGHES, CHARLES F. ("CHUCK"), U.S. pro football player (b. Philadelphia, Pa., March 23, 1943—d. Detroit, Mich., Oct. 24, 1971), wide receiver for the Detroit Lions, collapsed and died of a heart attack while participating in an NFL game against the Chicago Bears.

HUTCHINSON, A(RTHUR) S(TUART) M(ENTETH), British novelist (b. Goralpur, India, June 2, 1879—d. Crowborough, Eng., March 14, 1971), author of the best seller *If Winter Comes* (1921), which sold 750,000 copies in the U.S. and Britain, was editor of the *Daily Graphic* from 1912 to 1916. He early abandoned a medical career to take up writing and his first novel, *Once Aboard the Lugger* (1908), was followed by 16 other books including the novels *The Happy Warrior* (1912), *The Clean Heart* (1914), and his last, *It Happened Like This* (1942).

ISAYEV, ALEKSEI, Soviet rocket designer (b. St. Petersburg, Russia, Oct. 24, 1908—d. Moscow, U.S.S.R., June 25, 1971), was the U.S.S.R.'s chief designer of space propulsion engines, including units for the rockets that launched the Vostok, Voskhod, and Soyuz manned spacecraft. He also engineered the units for the Soviet Soyuz-Salyut space laboratory and the two Mars deep-space-probe rockets of 1971.

ISELIN, COLUMBUS O'DONNELL, U.S. oceanographer (b. New Rochelle, N.Y., Sept. 25, 1904—d. Vineyard Haven, Mass., Jan. 5, 1971), was administrator of the Woods Hole Oceanographic Institution from the early 1940s until 1950, and in 1956–57 was director of the institution. He resigned to become the first Henry Bryant Bigelow oceanographer and devoted his full time to research.

JACOBSEN, ARNE, Danish architect (b. Copenhagen, Den., Feb. 11, 1902—d. Copenhagen, March 24, 1971), received acclaim for his revolutionary Bellavista housing estate (near Copenhagen) and for the Bellevue Theatre, with its sliding roof, opening the auditorium to the night sky. Other notable buildings were the Rødovre town hall (1955), the SAS building in Copenhagen (1959), a factory at Ålborg, and the controversial St. Catherine's College, Oxford.

JAHN, GUNNAR, Norwegian economist (b. Trondheim, Nor., Jan. 10, 1883—d. Oslo, Nor., Jan. 31, 1971), was chairman of the Nobel Peace Prize committee from 1942 until 1969.

JOHNSON, ALVIN, U.S. educator (b. near Homer, Neb., Dec. 18, 1874—d. Upper Nyack, N.Y., June 7, 1971), was a founder (1919) of the New School for Social Research in New York City and president emeritus from 1945.

JONES, BOBBY (ROBERT TYRE JONES, JR.), U.S. champion golfer (b. Atlanta, Ga., March 17, 1902—d. Atlanta, Dec. 18, 1971), was the only man ever to win golf's grand slam, the U.S. Open, the British Open, and the U.S. Amateur tournaments—a feat he accomplished in 1930. His major championships included the U.S. Open four times, the British Open three times, and the U.S. Amateur five times.

KABIS, DOROTHY ANDREWS, U.S. government official (b. Wilkes-Barre, Pa., March 1917—d. Sheffield, Mass., July 3, 1971), served as treasurer of the United States from March 1969.

KARRER, PAUL, Swiss chemist (b. Moscow, Russia, April 21, 1889—d. Zürich, Switz., June 18, 1971), a pioneer in vitamin research, was awarded the 1937 Nobel Prize for Chemistry (with W. N. Haworth) for his studies of plant pigments, chiefly those constituting the carotenoids, flavins, and vitamins A and B_2. Karrer received his doctorate from the University of Zürich in 1911 and was professor of chemistry there from 1919 until 1959; he also served as director of the Chemical Institute during the same period. As early as 1930 Karrer set the correct constitutional formula for beta carotene, the precursor of vitamin A, and the following year he elucidated the chemical structure of vitamin A. Subsequently he turned his attention to vitamins C and B_2. Karrer's several books include a textbook of organic chemistry, *Lehrbuch der organischen Chemie* (1930).

KENT, ROCKWELL, U.S. artist (b. Tarrytown Heights, N.Y., June 21, 1882—d. Plattsburgh, N.Y., March 13, 1971), landscape painter, cartoonist, architect, illustrator of books, and controversial supporter of left-wing causes, exhibited his realist oils in the leading galleries of the United States and in the Soviet Union. In his youth he attended the Columbia School of Architecture and practiced that profession for a number of years. He received recognition as a serious painter while in his early 20s, and his works of that period later were acquired by the Frick Collection. He illustrated special editions of Shakespeare, *Leaves of Grass, Moby Dick, Candide,* and others, as well as books of his own writing—*Voyaging Southward from the Strait of Magellan* (1924), *N. by E.* (1930), *Greenland Journal* (1962), and his autobiography, *It's Me O Lord* (1955). A consistent supporter of the U.S.S.R., Kent presented a number of his drawings and landscape paintings to Soviet museums, and in 1967 received a Lenin Peace Prize.

KING, DENNIS, U.S. actor (b. Coventry, Eng., Nov. 2, 1897—d. New York, N.Y., May 21, 1971), matinee idol of the 1920s and '30s, made his London stage debut in 1919. In 1921 he first appeared in the United States in the Broadway show *Claire de Lune.* Other popular musicals, in which he was the star, followed: *Rose Marie* (1924), *The Vagabond King* (1925; also the screen version in 1930), *The Three Musketeers* (1928), *Show Boat* (1932), and *I Married an Angel* (1938).

KNATCHBULL-HUGESSEN, SIR HUGHE, British diplomat (b. London, Eng., March 26, 1886—d. Barham, Kent, Eng., March 22, 1971), was ambassador to Turkey during World War II. While he was serving at Ankara his Albanian valet (Elyesa Bazna or "Cicero") gained access to top secret documents, photographed their contents, and passed them on to the German ambassador, Franz von Papen, being paid £300,000 for the job (much of it counterfeit). With the liberation of Belgium in 1944 Hugessen was transferred to Brussels, where he remained as ambassador until his retirement in 1947.

KNOX, E(DMUND) V(ALPY), British humorous writer (b. Oxford, Eng., May 10, 1881—d. London, Eng., Jan. 2, 1971), was editor of *Punch* from 1932 until 1949, and a regular contributor (under the penname "Evoe") for more than 50 years.

KHRUSHCHEV, NIKITA SERGEEVICH, Soviet statesman (b. Kalinovka, Kursk Province, Russia, April 17, 1894—d. Moscow, U.S.S.R., Sept. 11, 1971), was responsible, as first secretary of the Communist Party of the Soviet Union (1953–64) and head of government (1958–64), for attempting to bring his country out of the shadow cast by his predecessor, Stalin, and for initiating a policy of coexistence with the capitalist world. He was also the first Soviet leader to make his mark in the West as a distinct and colourful personality. Beginning his career as a shepherd boy and then a metalworker in the Ukraine, Khrushchev joined the Bolsheviks in 1918 and fought against the Germans and the White Army of Gen. A. I. Denikin. After demobilization he was sent to a party technical college, emerging in 1925 as a full-time political leader. In 1934 he became second secretary of the Moscow Regional Party Committee and a member of the Central Committee of the Soviet Communist Party. In 1938 he was transferred to the Ukraine as first secretary and in 1939 became a full member of the Politburo.

He spent the World War II years directing guerrilla activities behind German lines and on the Stalingrad front. He returned to the Ukraine in 1944 as party first secretary and chairman of the Council of Ministers, and with merciless zeal conducted a ruthless purge of collaborators and enemies of Stalin. In 1949 he became again first secretary of the Moscow Region.

Six months after Stalin's death in 1953 Khrushchev was appointed first secretary of the Communist Party of the Soviet Union. He urged greater incentives for collective farmers and began a massive campaign to settle the virgin lands of Central Asia. His involvement in foreign affairs began with visits to Poland and China in 1954, then on to Belgrade in 1955, and to the Geneva talks of that year, ending with a tour of India and Burma.

The 20th party congress of 1956 marked Khrushchev's final break with Stalin, against whom he delivered a bitter attack. This denunciation encouraged the Polish and Hungarian uprisings of 1956, resulting in Poland in the reinstatement of the moderate Wladyslav Gomulka, and in Hungary in the defeat of the insurrectionists by the Soviet Army.

In 1957 central ministries dealing with industry were abolished and replaced by more than 100 regional economic committees, against strong opposition from within the Presidium. The next year Khrushchev became chairman of the Council of Ministers following N. A. Bulganin's resignation.

Khrushchev's chief interest now lay in foreign affairs. Failing to obtain a "Big Four" summit, he made a hasty visit to China and on returning challenged Western rights in Berlin and threatened to sign a separate treaty with the East Germans. Following a subsequent foreign ministers' meeting in Geneva to discuss Berlin, Khrushchev visited the U.S. at the invitation of Pres. Dwight D. Eisenhower. Soviet-U.S. relations deteriorated after the shooting down of a U.S. U-2 spy plane over Soviet territory on May 1, 1960, and an invitation to President Eisenhower to visit the U.S.S.R. was withdrawn.

Becoming increasingly worried by the drain of East German labour into West Berlin, in 1961 Khrushchev sanctioned the building of the Berlin Wall which effectively plugged the gap. His attempts to install missiles in Cuba in the following year were met by a U.S. blockade that forced their removal, narrowly avoiding a nuclear catastrophe. Relations with the U.S. under Pres. John F. Kennedy thereafter improved and in 1963 the nuclear test ban treaty was signed.

Khrushchev's final year in office was spent mostly outside Moscow. He visited the U.A.R., Czechoslovakia, and East Germany and then journeyed across the Asian farmlands. A brief announcement by Tass on Oct. 15, 1964, stated that he had been forced to resign by ill health. In the West it was thought that more likely reasons for his deposition were the failure of his domestic policies, his excessive anti-China zeal, and his moves toward rapprochement with West Germany. He spent his retirement quietly in a country house outside Moscow, emerging to public view only at elections. When *Khrushchev Remembers,* purporting to be his memoirs, was published in the West in 1970 he issued a statement denying authorship. His death received little publicity in the U.S.S.R.

Nikita S. Khrushchev. Below, walking with Soviet troops during the defense of Stalingrad in 1942. Left, meeting with Cuban Prime Minister Fidel Castro. Above, delivering a speech before the General Assembly of the United Nations. Below left, with U.S. Pres. John F. Kennedy in Vienna.

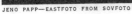

KSCHESSINSKA-NECHNI, MATHILDA-MARIA, Russian prima ballerina (b. Ligovo, Russia, Sept. 1, 1872—d. Paris, France, Dec. 7, 1971), was one of the finest ballerinas of Imperial Russia. Her most famous roles were in the classic ballets; in 1911 she danced *Swan Lake* with the Diaghilev Ballet in London, and her last appearance was in a Russian dance at a Covent Garden gala in 1936. She had opened a ballet school in Paris in 1929 and taught there until 1964. Her memoirs, *Dancing in St. Petersburg,* were published in 1960.

KYROLLOS VI, 116th patriarch of the Coptic Orthodox Church (b. 1902—d. Cairo, Egy., March 9, 1971), head of the church in Egypt, Africa, and the Near East, was chosen for the post by lot on April 17, 1959. He instigated extensive church reforms and modernized theological studies. He tried to activate means to end the long estrangement of all the Christian churches, and was successful in obtaining the return of the relics of St. Mark the Apostle (the first Coptic patriarch) from Venice to Egypt in 1968.

LAMMERDING, HEINZ BERNHARD, German Army officer (b. 1905—d. Bad-Tölz, W.Ger., Jan. 13, 1971), was judged responsible for the massacre of 741 French men, women, and children at Tulle and Oradour, France, in June 1944. French courts three times sentenced him to death, but he escaped justice through a loophole in the West German constitution and settled openly in Düsseldorf, where he founded a construction company.

LANDER, HARALD, Danish choreographer (b. Copenhagen, Den., Feb. 25, 1905—d. Copenhagen, Sept. 14, 1971), ballet master of the Royal Danish Ballet (1932–51), created about 36 ballets and was responsible for preserving many of August Bournonville's 19th-century classics.

LAWLESS, THEODORE K., U.S. dermatologist (b. Thibodaux, La., Dec. 6, 1892—d. Chicago, Ill., May 1, 1971), faculty member of the Medical School of Northwestern University from 1924 until 1941, was a leader in the use of radium for treating cancer. He received the Harmon Award for outstanding work in medicine (1929) and the Spingarn Medal (1954), given by the National Association for the Advancement of Colored People for "distinguished merit and achievement among American Negroes."

LEE, SIR FRANK GODBOULD, British administrator (b. Essex, Eng., Aug. 26, 1903—d. Cambridge, Eng., April 28, 1971), was permanent secretary at the Ministry of Food (1949–51) and at the Board of Trade (1951–59), and joint permanent secretary of the Treasury (1960–62). He became master of Corpus Christi College, Cambridge, in 1962.

LEMASS, SEAN FRANCIS, Irish politician (b. Dublin, Ire., July 15, 1899—d. Dublin, May 11, 1971), was prime minister of the Irish Republic (1959–66). Lemass was several times imprisoned for his active participation in the Irish republican movement before serving as minister for industry and commerce in successive Fianna Fail governments from 1932. He was minister for supplies during World War II, and deputy prime minister on three occasions from 1945 until 1959 when he became prime minister. He was the initiator on the Irish side of the Free Trade Area with Britain and sought dialogue with Northern Ireland for better relations, traveling to Belfast in 1965 to meet Capt. Terence O'Neill, the Ulster premier.

LEOPOLD, NATHAN F., U.S. convicted slayer (b. Chicago, Ill., 1905—d. San Juan, P.R., Aug. 29, 1971), a participant, with Richard Loeb, in the infamous 1924 kidnapping and murder of 14-year-old Bobbie Franks, served 34 years of a life sentence before being paroled in 1958. In prison Leopold helped in setting up a prison library and joined in a number of medical testing projects. With a chance for further rehabilitation and paroled in the custody of the Church of the Brethren, Leopold took up residence in Puerto Rico, serving as a church medical mission assistant while he earned a master's degree at the University of Puerto Rico. He later taught mathematics as well as continuing his activities in the work of the church.

LEWIS, JOE E., U.S. nightclub entertainer (b. New York, N.Y., Jan. 12, 1902—d. New York, June 4, 1971), whose comic routine depended on a microphone to bring out his foghorn voice. Lewis played the Copacabana in New York for 26 consecutive years and appeared in most other top U.S. nightclubs.

LEWIS, TED (THEODORE LEOPOLD FRIEDMAN), U.S. entertainer (b. Circleville, O., June 6, 1891—d. New York, N.Y., Aug. 25, 1971), who opened his shows with the greeting "Is Everybody Happy?," gained his first success, as a jazz clarinetist, in 1911. For more than 50 years Lewis appeared on the stages of Europe and the United States, in nightclubs and motion pictures, and on radio and TV. Many of his recordings sold in the millions and included "Me and My Shadow," "When My Baby Smiles at Me," "On the Sunny Side of the Street," "St. Louis Blues," and "Tiger Rag."

LLOYD, HAROLD CLAYTON, U.S. film comic (b. Burchard, Neb., April 20, 1893—d. Beverly Hills, Calif., March 8, 1971), wore glassless horn-rimmed spectacles as his trademark. Portraying a shy, bumbling youth, Lloyd performed many dangerous stunts in his hair-raising movies, which included the classics *Grandma's Boy, A Sailor Made Man, Girl Shy, Safety Last,* and *The Freshman,* all in the 1920s. With the coming of sound, he made a number of equally successful films before retiring in 1938.

LONSDALE, DAME KATHLEEN, British scientist (b. Newbridge, County Kildare, Ire., Jan. 28, 1903—d. London, Eng., April 1, 1971), the first woman president of the British Association for the Advancement of Science, was professor of chemistry and head of the department of Crystallography at University College, London, from 1949 to 1968. Her discovery of the structure of the hexamethylbenzene molecule led to theoretical work on the nature of aromatic compounds. She also investigated the structure of diamond and did fundamental work on the magnetic susceptibilities of crystals. Her many honours included fellowship of the Royal Society in 1945, and its Davy Medal in 1957. A pacifist and a Quaker, she spent a short time in prison for refusing to register for service as a firewatcher in World War II. She was created Dame of the British Empire in 1956.

LOWE, EDMUND DANTES, U.S. actor (b. San Jose, Calif., March 3, 1892—d. Hollywood, Calif., April 21, 1971), who played in more than 100 movies, was best remembered for his role as Sergeant Quirt in the silent classic *What Price Glory?* (1926). In the 1950s Lowe starred in the television series "Front Page Detective."

LUKACS, GYORGY, Hungarian philosopher and critic (b. Budapest, Hung., April 13, 1885—d. Budapest, June 4, 1971), a leading figure in the history of Marxism, was commissar for education in Bela Kun's short-lived Communist regime of 1919 and minister for culture in Imre Nagy's government in 1956. During the Nazi era Lukacs lived in the U.S.S.R., returning to Hungary in 1944 to be made professor of aesthetics at Budapest University. After the revolt of 1956 he was deported to Romania but soon allowed to return, although he lost his post and membership in the Communist Party. He was readmitted to the party in 1967. His chief works include *The Soul and Its Forms* (1911), *The Theory of the Novel* (1916), *History and Class-Consciousness* (1923), *The Young Hegel* (1938), *The Destruction of Reason* (1954), and *The Specific Nature of the Aesthetic* (1963).

LUKAS, PAUL, U.S. actor (b. Budapest, Hung., May 26, 1895—d. Tangier, Mor., Aug. 15, 1971), who appeared in many motion pictures of the 1930s and '40s, won an Academy Award as best actor in 1943 for his portrayal of Kurt Mueller in the film *Watch on the Rhine,* a part he had created in the Broadway production of the play (1941).

LYNN, DIANA (DOLLY LOEHR), U.S. actress (b. Los Angeles, Calif., Oct. 7, 1926—d. Los Angeles, Dec. 18, 1971), who played in light comedy films during the 1940s, was also a concert pianist, having recorded several albums. She appeared on the New York stage in the 1950s, and in the Broadway hit *Mary, Mary* in 1963.

McAVOY, JOCK (JOSEPH BAMFORD), British boxer (b. Nov. 20, 1908—d. Cheshire, Eng., Nov. 20, 1971), an outstanding boxer of the 1930s who held both British middleweight and light-heavyweight professional titles, took the middleweight title from Len Harvey in 1933 and successfully defended it four times before moving up to light-heavyweight, the championship of which he won in 1935.

McDONALD, MAURICE JAMES, U.S. franchise executive (b. Manchester, N.H., 1902—d. Palm Springs, Calif., Dec. 11, 1971), co-founder (with his brother Richard) of McDonald's Hamburgers, a huge chain of roadside eateries stretching across the U.S. The enterprise started in 1948 with one quick-order hamburger stand in San Bernardino, Calif., and by 1970 had grown to 2,000 outlets with sales for that year amounting

Ted Lewis

WIDE WORLD

Harold Lloyd

WIDE WORLD

Gyorgy Lukacs

CAMERA PRESS—PICTORIAL PARADE

to $587 million. In 1961 the McDonald brothers sold all rights in the company to an associate, Ray Kroc, for $2.7 million.

McGREGOR, GORDON ROY, Canadian airline executive (b. Montreal, Que., Sept. 1, 1901—d. Montreal, March 8, 1971), president (1948–68) of Air Canada, which he had established and developed, almost single-handedly, as the Trans-Canada Air Lines.

McLACHLAN, DONALD HARVEY, British journalist and author (b. London, Eng., Sept. 25, 1908—d. Moray, Scot., Jan. 10, 1971), was the first editor of *The Sunday Telegraph* (1961–66).

MACPHERSON, SIR JOHN STUART, British civil servant (b. Edinburgh, Scot., Aug. 25, 1898—d. Nov. 5, 1971), was governor of Nigeria (1948–54), governor-general of the Federation of Nigeria (1954–55), and permanent undersecretary of state for the colonies (1956–59).

MAGNELLI, ALBERTO, Italian artist (b. Florence, Italy, July 1, 1888—d. Meudon, France, April 21, 1971), a pioneer of abstract art, first painted under the influence of classical masters but later developed toward Fauvism. After visiting Paris in 1914 and meeting Pablo Picasso, Max Jacob, and Juan Gris, Magnelli devoted himself to abstract art. In 1968 a retrospective exhibition of his work was held at the Musée d'Art Moderne.

MAIER, REINHOLD, West German politician (b. Schorndorf, Ger., Oct. 16, 1889—d. Stuttgart, W.Ger., Aug. 18, 1971), was president of the Free Democratic Party and prime minister (1945–53) of the newly formed postwar state in southwest Germany which became Baden-Württemberg. From 1953 to 1963, as the "grand old man" of German liberalism, he served variously as deputy in the state Assembly in Stuttgart and in the Bundestag in Bonn.

MAKITA, YOICHIRO, Japanese industrialist (b. Shizuoka, Jap., Jan. 15, 1903—d. Tokyo, Jap., Dec. 7, 1971), was president of Mitsubishi, Japan's largest industrial company, from 1969.

MALVERN, GODFREY MARTIN HUGGINS, 1st Viscount, Rhodesian governmental administrator (b. Bexley, Eng., July 6, 1883—d. Salisbury, Rhod., May 8, 1971), prime minister of the short-lived Federation of Rhodesia and Nyasaland (1953–56), was for 20 years prime minister of Southern Rhodesia. He was elected to represent Salisbury North in 1923, reelected in 1928, and led the new United Party to victory in 1934, remaining in office until 1956—the longest period of service of any Commonwealth prime minister. He publicly opposed Rhodesia's unilateral declaration of independence in 1965.

MANRY, ROBERT, U.S. newspaper editor and adventurer (b. Landour, India, June 2, 1918—d. Union City, Pa., Feb. 21, 1971), was skipper of the "Tinkerbelle," thought to be the smallest craft ever to cross the Atlantic Ocean. From the harbour at Falmouth, Mass., Manry put to sea alone in his 13½-ft. sailboat on June 1, 1965, and landed at Falmouth, Eng., 78 days later, on August 17. He recounted his 3,200-mi. voyage in the book *Tinkerbelle* (1966).

MASSINGHAM, HUGH, British journalist (b. London, Eng., 1905—d. London, Dec. 26, 1971), political correspondent on *The Observer* (London) until 1961 and, since 1962, literary adviser to *The Sunday Telegraph*. His books include *I Took Off My Tie, The Best Days, Ripe for Shaking,* and *The Wandering Eye.*

MIKKELSEN, EINAR, Danish Arctic explorer (b. Copenhagen, Den., Dec. 23, 1880—d. Copenhagen, May 3, 1971), inspector general of East Greenland (1933–51), devoted his life to the exploration of Greenland and the Arctic and to describing his adventures. Marooned in East Greenland for two years, he told of this experience in his *Lost in the Arctic* (1913). He held the British Royal Geographical Society's Patron's Gold Medal and the Livingstone Gold Medal of the Royal Scottish Geographical Society.

MONCRIEFF, SIR ALAN AIRD, British pediatrician (b. Bournemouth, Eng., Oct. 9, 1901—d. Waterford, Eng., July 24, 1971), physician at the Hospital for Sick Children, Great Ormond Street, London (1934–64), became the first recipient of the James Spence Medal of the British Paediatric Association. He was knighted in 1964. Moncrieff was active in the administration of the International Children's Centre in Paris. He was an adviser to the editors of *Encyclopædia Britannica.*

MONDADORI, ARNOLDO, Italian publisher (b. near Poggio Rusco, Italy, Nov. 2, 1889—d. Milan, Italy, June 8, 1971), creator of a vast publishing empire, was apprenticed to a printer in 1906 and several years later bought the enterprise and began publishing socialist journals. After he bought another printing works in Verona he started publishing literature, including the complete works of Pirandello and Gabriele d'Annunzio. Successful projects of his own included the *Mondadori Encyclopædia.*

MOREAU, ÉMILIENNE, French resistance heroine (b. Wingles, France, June 4, 1898—d. Lens, France, Jan. 5, 1971), was the last survivor among eight women members of Gen. Charles de Gaulle's Order of the Liberation. For her part in the battle of Loos-en-Gohelle in 1914 she won both the British Military Cross and the Croix de Guerre. During World War II she helped to organize the network through which allied agents were smuggled into Switzerland.

MORRISON, HARRY W., U.S. construction executive (b. Kenney, Ill., Feb. 23, 1885—d. Boise, Ida., July 19, 1971), co-founder (1912), president (1943–60), and chairman (1960–68) of the Morrison-Knudsen Co., Inc., one of the world's largest contracting firms. Under his direction the company built the giant Hoover Dam on the Colorado River, major parts of the Grand Coulee Dam on the Columbia, and the St. Lawrence Seaway.

MORRISON, JIM (James Douglas), U.S. rock musician (b. Melbourne, Fla., 1945—d. Paris, France, July 3, 1971), was lead singer of The Doors, a widely acclaimed rock group he formed in 1965. Morrison wrote most of the group's songs, which included "Break on Through (to the Other Side)," "The End," and "Light My Fire."

MOSSMAN, JAMES, British television commentator (b. London, Eng., Sept. 10, 1926—d. Gissing, Norfolk, Eng., April 5, 1971), was known as a humane critic of human folly on the BBC current affairs program "Panorama" and on the arts program "Review," which he edited and presented. He was the author of *Beggars on Horseback, The Thing Itself,* and *Rebels in Paradise.*

MOTTRAM, RALPH HALE, British writer (b. Norwich, Eng., Oct. 30, 1883—d. King's Lynn, Eng., April 15, 1971), was the author of *The Spanish Farm,* a best-selling novel about World War I. Mottram served in France during that war, and in 1919 returned to his civilian position of bank clerk. In 1924 *The Spanish Farm* was published; it won the Hawthornden Prize and thereafter achieved wide public recognition. With its successors, *Sixty-four, Ninety-four* (1925) and *The Crime at Vanderlynden* (1926), it was reissued as *The Spanish Farm Trilogy* in 1967. Mottram wrote more than 60 other works but none was as successful as the war books.

MULCAHY, RICHARD, Irish patriot (b. County Waterford, Ire., May 10, 1886—d. Dublin, Ire., Dec. 16, 1971), one of the last surviving figures of the Anglo-Irish struggle, was chief of staff of the Irish Republican Army during the war of Irish independence (1919–21). After participating in the 1916 insurrection, he became commanding officer of the second battalion of the Dublin brigade of the IRA and in 1918 chief of staff. After the creation of republican Ireland he became minister of defense and commander in chief of the Army under Pres. W. T. Cosgrave. He later held the portfolio of local government and public health until Eamon de Valera came to power in 1932. He served as president of Fine Gael until 1960 and retired from active politics in 1961.

MUNSHI, KANIALAL MANEKLAL, Indian politician (b. India, Dec. 30, 1887—d. Bombay, India, Feb. 8, 1971), was a member of the Assembly that framed India's republican constitution. He was also founder president of India's largest educational and cultural organization, Bharatiya Vidya Bhavan, a notable author in his native Gujarati and in English, and an active opponent of British colonial rule (for which he served several prison sentences). He was minister of food and agriculture in Jawaharlal Nehru's government and in 1952 became governor of Uttar Pradesh.

MURPHY, AUDIE, U.S. war hero (b. near Kingston, Tex., June 20, 1924—d. near Roanoke, Va., May 28, 1971), was the nation's most decorated World War II soldier. Murphy was awarded the Medal of Honor for heroism displayed during an encounter with the Germans in the Colmar pocket in eastern France on Jan. 26, 1945. He received 27 other decorations, including the Distinguished Service Cross, the Legion of Merit, the Silver Star (with Oak Leaf cluster), and the Croix de Guerre (with palm), for his participation in the action at Casablanca (1943), in the landing in

Robert Manry

Jim Morrison

Audie Murphy

WIDE WORLD   WIDE WORLD   WIDE WORLD

Sicily, and at Anzio. After the war Murphy wrote his autobiography, *To Hell and Back*, and, having taken up an acting career, played himself in the film version (released in 1955) of the book. Murphy appeared in about 40 movies made in the 1950s and '60s.

NASH, OGDEN, U.S. poet (b. Rye, N.Y., Aug. 19, 1902—d. Baltimore, Md., May 19, 1971), was the nation's best-known writer of humorous poetry. After a year at Harvard he worked briefly as a bond salesman and as an ad writer before launching into a career as a poet with the sale of his first verse (1930) to *The New Yorker* magazine. In 1931 he published his first collection, *Hard Lines*. After a short time as an editor on *The New Yorker*, Nash turned to free-lance work and began a 40-year career during which he produced 20 volumes of verse with such titles as *You Can't Get There from Here*, *I'm a Stranger Here Myself*, and *Bed Riddance*. Nash collaborated with S. J. Perelman (the book) and Kurt Weill (the music) to write the lyrics for *One Touch of Venus*, the Broadway hit of 1943. In later years Nash frequently participated in TV panel shows.

NEVINS, ALLAN, U.S. historian (b. near Camp Point, Ill., May 20, 1890—d. Menlo Park, Calif., March 5, 1971), was DeWitt Clinton professor of history at Columbia University (1931–58) where he established (1948) the successful oral history program, a collection of tapes and typescripts covering the opinions and recollections of hundreds of contemporary figures. His numerous historical writings brought Nevins many high honours, including two Pulitzer Prizes, one in 1933 for his biography *Grover Cleveland: A Study in Courage*, and the other in 1937 for *Hamilton Fish: The Inner Story of the Grant Administration*. He also received the $10,000 Scribner's Centenary Prize and the Bancroft Prize for the first two volumes (1947) of his eight-volume history of the U.S. from 1850 through the Civil War, *Ordeal of the Union*, the last two volumes of which were published in 1971.

NEWSOM, SIR JOHN HUBERT, British educator (b. Glasgow, Scot., June 8, 1910—d. Sawbridgeworth, Eng., May 23, 1971), was chairman of a commission on the education of average and below-average children (1963), and of another on the public schools (1965). He was appointed to the Central Advisory Council of the then Ministry of Education in 1961. He was knighted in 1964.

NIEBUHR, THE REV. REINHOLD, U.S. Protestant theologian (b. Wright City, Mo., June 21, 1892—d. Stockbridge, Mass., June 1, 1971), who was a pioneer in the post-World War II Neoorthodox movement, which sought to relate the traditional orthodox teachings of biblical Christianity to contemporary events and culture. Ordained by the Evangelical Synod of North America, Niebuhr held a long-time association with Union Theological Seminary in New York

City, serving first as associate professor of the philosophy of religion (1928–30), then as William E. Dodge, Jr., professor of applied Christianity (1930–55), and as Charles A. Briggs graduate professor of ethics and theology and vice-president of the seminary (both positions from 1955). Niebuhr was also active in politics as a member of the Socialist Party in the 1920s and '30s, later as chairman of the Liberal Party in New York, and as an officer in the Americans for Democratic Action. The author of almost 50 books, Niebuhr published his last major work, *Man's Nature and His Communities*, in 1965.

NIEMEYER, SIR OTTO ERNST, British financier (b. Streatham, Eng., Nov. 23, 1883—d. Lindfield, Sussex, Eng., Feb. 6, 1971), appointed controller of finance at the Treasury in 1922, became chairman of the Financial Committee of the League of Nations in 1927, then left the Treasury to become a governor of the Bank of England. He was chairman of the board of the Bank for International Settlements (1937–40), retiring as a director in 1965.

NOGUÈS, CHARLES ALBERT AUGUSTE PAUL, French army officer (b. Monléon Magnoac, France, Aug. 13, 1876—d. Paris, France, April 20, 1971), was resident-general in Morocco (1936–43), when with the outbreak of World War II he was named commander in chief of all French forces in North Africa. Siding with the Vichy government in 1940, General Noguès hunted down Free French partisans and enforced the Nazis' anti-Semitic laws. After Gen. Charles de Gaulle's seizure of power in North Africa in 1943, Noguès went into hiding in North Africa. In 1947 he was tried (in absentia) for his alleged traitorous activities and sentenced to 20 years at hard labour. He returned to France in 1956, was arrested but later released.

OGUNDIPE, BABAFEMI OLATUNDE, brigadier general, Nigerian Army (b. Nigeria, Sept. 6, 1924—d. London, Eng., Nov. 27, 1971), was Nigeria's high commissioner to Britain (1966–70) at the time of the Nigerian civil war. He served in India and Burma during World War II and with the UN in the Congo (Zaire) from 1960 to 1963. In 1966 he was for a short time chief of staff at the Nigerian Supreme Headquarters.

O'HANLON (DOUGLAS), VIRGINIA, U.S. teacher (b. New York, N.Y., 1890—d. Valatie, N.Y., May 13, 1971), the little girl who wrote a letter to the *New York Sun* that brought the editorial reply, "Yes, Virginia, there is a Santa Claus." The editorial, written by Francis Pharcellus Church (d. 1906) and published in the *Sun* on Sept. 21, 1897, was reprinted annually before Christmas through 1949. Mrs. Douglas was a teacher in the New York City school system from 1912 until retiring in 1959.

PARKER, CECIL, British stage and film actor (b. Hastings, Eng., Sept. 3, 1897—d. Brighton, Eng., April 20, 1971), well known for roles that demanded a combination of gentlemanly pomposity and bewildered obtuseness, made his stage debut in 1922. He appeared in London in *The Inheritors* (1925), toured South Africa in *The Matriarch*, and returned to London in a revival of *Lady Windermere's Fan*. His role of Charles Con-

damine in Noel Coward's *Blithe Spirit* (1941) established his reputation as a leading comedy actor. He appeared on the New York stage in 1950 in *Daphne Laureola*. His films included *Caesar and Cleopatra* and *The Detective*.

PATSAYEV, VIKTOR I., Soviet cosmonaut (b. Kazakhstan, U.S.S.R., June 19, 1933—d. in space, June 30, 1971), civilian engineer aboard the Soyuz 11 spacecraft, died with his two companions at the controls of the craft as it neared earth for a soft landing. Patsayev graduated from the Industrial Institute in Penza and worked as a design engineer in precision instruments before joining the Soviet space program in 1968. He received posthumously the U.S.S.R.'s highest title, Hero of the Soviet Union. (See *Dobrovolsky, Georgi T.*, above, and *Volkov, Vladislav N.*, below.)

PAUMGARTNER, BERNHARD, Austrian musicologist (b. Vienna, Aus., Nov. 14, 1887—d. Salzburg, Aus., July 27, 1971), director of the Salzburg Mozarteum (1917–38 and 1945–71), had been conductor of the Vienna Tonkünstler Orchestra (which later became the Vienna Symphony Orchestra). He founded the Mozarteum orchestra, collaborated on a film of Mozart's life (*Whom the Gods Love*), and produced standard biographies of Mozart (1927) and Shubert (1945). In 1945 he was one of the founders of the Salzburg Festival.

PENNEY, J(AMES) C(ASH), U.S. merchant (b. Hamilton, Mo., Sept. 16, 1875—d. New York, N.Y., Feb. 12, 1971), founder (1902) and honorary chairman (after 1958) of the J. C. Penney department store chain, who believed in conducting his business on the basis of the Golden Rule. He opened his first Golden Rule store in Kemmerer, Wyo., in 1902 and by 1971 his chain numbered 1,660 outlets with sales of $4.1 billion.

PENNINGTON, ANN, U.S. dancer (b. Camden, N.J., Dec. 23, 1894—d. New York, N.Y., Nov. 4, 1971), star of several George White's Scandals musical revues of the 1920s, introduced the "Black Bottom" in 1926.

PEW, J. HOWARD, U.S. oil tycoon (b. Bradford, Pa., Jan. 27, 1882—d. Ardmore, Pa., Nov. 27, 1971), was president (1912–47) of the Sun Oil Company and chairman of the board from 1963 until 1970.

POPOVIC, MILENTIJE, Yugoslav politician (b. Crna Trava, Serbia, July 7, 1913—d. Belgrade, Yugos., May 8, 1971), a veteran Communist official, was elected president of the Yugoslav Parliament in 1967. He became a member of the then-outlawed Communist Party in 1939 and in 1941 joined Tito's partisans fighting against the German occupation. His government posts after World War II included those of foreign trade minister and finance minister. In 1969 Popovic became a member of the party Presidium.

PORTAL OF HUNGERFORD, CHARLES FREDERICK ALGERNON PORTAL, 1ST VISCOUNT, marshal of the RAF (b. Hungerford, Eng., May 21, 1893—d. Chichester, Sussex, Eng., April 22, 1971), was largely responsible for shaping and directing the RAF from October 1940 to January 1946. After winning a famous motorcycle race in

Ogden Nash

UPI COMPIX

Viktor I. Patsayev

TASS—SOVFOTO

Matyas Rakosi

CAMERA PRESS—PICTORIAL PARADE

1914, he enlisted in World War I as a dispatch rider in the Royal Engineers. In 1915 he joined the RFC and by 1918 had won the MC and DSO (with bar). In 1934 he became commanding officer at Aden and two years later was appointed RAF instructor at the Imperial Defence College. He became a marshal of the RAF in 1944, was created baron in 1945 and viscount in 1946. From 1946 to 1951 he was controller of atomic energy at the Ministry of Supply and in 1960 became chairman of the British Aircraft Corporation.

PROUTY, WINSTON L., U.S. senator (from 1959) from Vermont (b. Newport, Vt., Sept. 1, 1906—d. Boston, Mass., Sept. 10, 1971), a Republican and junior senator from his state, served as a member of the House of Representatives from 1951 until 1959 when he took his seat in the Senate.

PULLER, LEWIS BURWELL ("Chesty"), lieutenant general (ret.), U.S. Marine Corps (b. West Point, Va., June 26, 1898—d. Hampton, Va., Oct. 11, 1971), most decorated Marine in the Corps, served in World War I, World War II, and the Korean War.

RAFFERTY, CHIPS (John William Goffage), Australian actor (b. Broken Hill, Austr., March 26, 1909—d. Sydney, Austr., May 27, 1971), his country's best-known film actor, who typified the rugged, good-humoured adventurer. His first film was *Ants in His Pants* (1938), followed by *The Fighting Rats of Tobruk* (1942). He played the lead in *The Overlanders* in 1946, and in *Eureka Stockade* in 1947. He had a role in the remake of *Mutiny on the Bounty* in 1962.

RAKOSI, MATYAS, Hungarian Communist Party leader (b. Ada, Yugos., March 14, 1892—d. Gorky, U.S.S.R., Feb. 5, 1971), premier of Hungary (1952–56), was responsible for establishing the country's Stalinist-type dictatorship. Commissioned in the Hungarian Army in World War I, Rakosi was captured by the Russians and interned in the Far East. At the outbreak of the Russian Revolution he made his way to St. Petersburg, where he met Lenin. In 1918, returning to Hungary, he became a minister in the short-lived Communist regime of Bela Kun. He was in Hungary again in 1924 as a Comintern representative, but in 1926 was arrested and imprisoned until 1940. He became a Soviet citizen, but returned to Hungary with the victorious Soviet Army in 1944; in 1948 he took the post of deputy premier and became the leading executor of Soviet policy in Hungary. He became premier in August 1952 and remained the dominant influence until the revolt of 1956, when he was exiled to the Soviet Union.

RAYNAL, PAUL, French playwright (b. Narbonne, France, July 25, 1885—d. Paris, France, Aug. 19, 1971), became famous through his play *Le Maître de son coeur* (1920). Other plays included *Tombeau sous l'arc de triomphe* (1924), *Au soleil de l'instinct* (1932), *Napoléon unique* (1937), and *A souffert sous Ponce Pilate* (1939).

REEVES, DANIEL F. ("Dan"), U.S. sports executive (b. New York, N.Y., 1913—d. New York, April 15, 1971), owner of the Los Angeles Rams football team, who took the club's franchise from Cleveland to Los Angeles in 1946.

REITH, JOHN CHARLES WALSHAM REITH, 1st Baron, British administrator (b. Stonehaven, Scot., July 20, 1889—d. Edinburgh, Scot., June 16, 1971), first director general of the British Broadcasting Corporation, who shaped the development of public broadcasting in Britain from its inception, was appointed general manager of the newly formed British Broadcasting Company in 1922. On Jan. 1, 1927, the British Broadcasting Corporation was established with Reith as director general. In 1938 he resigned to become chairman of Imperial Airways. In the early 1940s he headed the ministries of information, transport, and works and buildings. He resigned the latter to join the Navy, becoming in 1943 director of the Combined Operations Materials Department. Later posts included chairmanship of the Commonwealth Telecommunications Board (1946–50), Hemel Hempstead Development Corp. (1947–50), National Film Finance Corp. (1948–51), and Colonial Development Corp. (1950–59). In 1967 he was appointed lord high commissioner to the General Assembly of the Church of Scotland. Knighted in 1927, he was raised to the peerage in 1940.

RENNIE, MICHAEL, U.S. screen and television actor (b. Bradford, Eng., Aug. 25, 1909—d. Harrogate, Eng., June 10, 1971), was the star of "The Third Man" television series (1959 through the early 1960s). He made his stage debut in *Pygmalion* in 1938 and his first film, *Dangerous Moonlight*, in 1940. In the late 1940s, he went to Hollywood where he played in more than 50 films. In 1961 Rennie co-starred in the Broadway comedy *Mary, Mary* and later appeared in the screen version. In television he had parts in "Playhouse 90," "Climax," and "Wagon Train."

RICHARDS, CERI GIRALDUS, British artist (b. Dynfant, Wales, June 6, 1903—d. London, Eng., Nov. 9, 1971), was one of the foremost British painters of the past 50 years, whose collages represent a significant contribution to the European art of the 1930s. He was one of the five British artists exhibited at the São Paulo II Bienal (1953–54), and at the Venice Biennale in 1962 he won the Einaudi Prize. His most recent major commissions included an altarpiece for St. Edmund Hall, Oxford, and two windows for Derby Cathedral.

RICHARDSON, THOMAS DOW, British sportsman (b. Yorkshire, Eng., 1887—d. Jan. 7, 1971), was founder (1958) of the first Commonwealth Winter Games. An authority on ice skating, he was the author of several books, including *Modern Figure Skating* (1930). He contributed to many journals and newspapers and to the *Encyclopædia Britannica*.

ROMANOFF, MICHAEL (Harry Gerguson), U.S. restaurateur (b. Vilna, Lith., 1892—d. Los Angeles, Calif., Sept. 1, 1971), who, posing as his imperial highness, the Prince Michael Alexandrovitch Dmitry Obolensky Romanoff, parlayed a pleasing personality and noble bearing to the height of a bon vivant's career as restaurateur and confidant to Hollywood's brightest stars. He assumed the title of a Russian prince in the late 1930s and opened his restaurant, Romanoff's, in Beverly Hills. The "prince" closed his business and retired in 1962.

ROPER, ELMO BURNS, JR., U.S. pollster (b. Hebron, Neb., July 31, 1900—d. West Reading, Pa., April 30, 1971), the first to develop the scientific poll for political forecasting, three times predicted the reelection of Franklin D. Roosevelt (1936, 1940, 1944) within 1%.

ROSMER, MILTON, British actor (b. Southport, Eng., Nov. 4, 1882—d. Chesham, Eng., Dec. 7, 1971), played leading parts in Shaw, Galsworthy, and Ibsen as well as Shakespeare. His first stage appearance was in a burlesque, *Don Quixote*, in 1899. He toured the U.S. in *Everyman* and Shakespeare and for four years was at the Gaiety Theatre, Manchester. He directed the Stratford-on-Avon Memorial Theatre company during the 1943 season. He appeared in many films including the silent version of *Lorna Doone*, and as Heathcliff in a silent *Wuthering Heights*.

ROTH, ERNST, British music publisher (b. Prague, Bohemia, June 1, 1896—d. Middlesex, Eng., July 17, 1971), took a doctorate in law in Prague in 1921, continued music studies in Vienna, and in 1922 commenced his career in music publishing with the Wiener Philharmonischer Verlag. In 1928 he joined Universal Edition in Vienna and sometime later was invited to join the publishing firm of Boosey and Hawkes in London, of which he later became chairman. His own books included *The Business of Music* (1969) and *A Tale of Three Cities* (1971).

ROY, HARRY, British bandleader (b. London, Eng., 1902—d. London, Feb. 1, 1971), a popular bandleader of the 1930s, was a member of his brother Sid Roy's Lyricals at the Café de Paris before setting up on his own at the Bat Club.

RUSSELL, RICHARD BREVARD, U.S. senator (from 1933) from Georgia (b. Winder, Ga., Nov. 2, 1897—d. Washington, D.C., Jan. 21, 1971), a Democrat and chief strategist of the Southern senators in their fight against civil rights legislation, was first elected to the Senate in 1932 and subsequently returned to his seat each time he sought re-election. Russell was chosen president pro tem of the Senate on Jan. 3, 1969; he served as chairman of the Appropriations Committee (from 1969), and as chairman (1951–69) and member of the Armed Services Committee.

SACHER, HARRY, British journalist, philanthropist, and Zionist (b. London, Eng., Sept. 3, 1881—d. London, May 10, 1971), was the founder and leading spirit of the "Manchester Group" of Zionism that secured for Chaim Weizmann leadership of the International Zionist movement. From 1920 to 1930 he lived in Palestine, establishing himself as its leading lawyer. He endowed numerous causes, including the Weizmann Institute in Israel and the Sacher building at New College, Oxford. He wrote *Israel: The Establishment of a State* (1952) and *Zionist Portraits and Other Essays* (1959).

Michael Rennie

Michael Romanoff

Elmo Roper

WIDE WORLD

WIDE WORLD

WIDE WORLD

SADIQ, GHULAM MOHAMMED, Indian politician (b. 1921—d. Chandigarh, India, Dec. 12, 1971), first ruled Kashmir as prime minister (1964–67), then as chief minister. He was a member of the Congress Party.

SAMPSONOV, NIKOLAI NIKOLAYEVICH, Soviet geophysicist (b. St. Petersburg, Russia, 1906 —d. U.S.S.R., 1971), whose death was reported in the 18th issue of the Soviet clandestine journal *Chronicle of Current Events,* was an outspoken critic of Stalinist bureaucracy. In the 1930s he worked for the Directorate of the Northern Sea Routes and was in charge of prospecting for valuable Arctic minerals. In 1956 he published *Thinking Aloud,* an attack on Stalin and a call for a return to Leninist democracy. He was arrested and placed in a special psychiatric hospital. For eight years he refused to plead insane, but after threats to his health, finally gave in. He was discharged with a pension in 1964. In 1950 he and S. A. Poddubny were awarded the Stalin Prize for designing a new type of gravimeter.

SARNOFF, DAVID, U.S. executive (b. Uzlian, Minsk, Russia, Feb. 27, 1891—d. New York, N.Y., Dec. 12, 1971), called the "father of American television," was president of the Radio Corporation of America (RCA) from 1930 until 1947 when he became chairman of the board, a position he held until retiring in 1970. General Sarnoff (a World War II communications officer) brought TV to America for the first time when he appeared before the cameras at the New York World's Fair in 1939.

SEFERIS, GEORGE (Georgios Seferiadis), Greek poet and diplomat (b. Smyrna [Izmir], Turk., Feb. 29 [or March 1], 1900—d. Athens, Greece, Sept. 20, 1971), was the recipient of the 1963 Nobel Prize for Literature. Feeling oppressed under the Greek military who had assumed rule in 1967, Seferis refused to publish any of his poetry during this period which he considered an era of censorship. His final poem, "The Cats of St. Nicholas," was published in an anthology of antidictatorial prose and verse. Seferis was awarded the Kostis Palamas Prize in 1947 for his outstanding contribution to Greek poetry, and in 1963 he received the Nobel Prize. Much of his work was gathered into *The Collected Poems of George Seferis, 1924–55* (1967); *Three Secret Poems* was published in 1966.

SIFFERT, JO, Swiss racing driver (b. Fribourg, Switz., July 7, 1936—d. Brands Hatch, Eng., Oct. 24, 1971), who had given Porsche a string of victories since 1968, began as a motorcycle racer, becoming Swiss 350-cc. champion in 1959. He made his world championship debut in Formula 1 motor racing in 1962 when he came in tenth in the Belgian Grand Prix. In 1968, driving a Lotus 49 B, he won the British Grand Prix. In 1969 he was placed ninth in the drivers' championship table. During this period he won the Daytona 24 Hours; the Sebring 12 Hours; the Monza 1,000, and the Austrian Grand Prix (twice). In 1971 he won the Buenos Aires 1,000 km. and the Austrian Grand Prix again. Siffert was the British BRM team's chief driver at the time of his death in an accident while practicing on the Brands Hatch circuit.

SILVER, ANNON LEE, British opera singer (b. Nova Scotia, Canada, November 1938—d. London, Eng., July 28, 1971), appeared at Glyndebourne on several occasions from 1963 and in 1970 created the role of Atalanta in Nicholas Maw's *The Rising of the Moon.* In 1966 she won the first Dame Maggie Teyte Prize. She joined the Frankfurt (W.Ger.) Opera in 1969.

SIMONDS, GAVIN TURNBULL SIMONDS, 1st Viscount, British lawyer (b. Basingstoke, Eng., Nov. 28, 1881—d. London, Eng., June 28, 1971), lord chancellor from 1951 to 1954, was chairman of the National Arbitration Tribunal (1940–44), a lord of appeal in ordinary (1944–51; 1954–62), and became high steward of Oxford University in 1954.

SIROKY, VILEM, Czechoslovak politician (b. Slovakia, May 31, 1902—d. Czechoslovakia, Oct. 6, 1971), premier of Czechoslovakia (1953–63), was chairman of the Czechoslovak Communist Party from 1945 to 1954, and played a prominent part in the purges of 1952–54, for which, in addition to economic mismanagement, he was later to lose the premiership.

SKEFFINGTON, ARTHUR MASSEY, British politician (b. London, Eng., Sept. 4, 1909—d. Feb. 18, 1971), Labour MP for Hayes and Harlington from 1953, was chairman of the Labour Party 1969–70. After World War II he became MP for Lewisham West but lost his seat in 1950. In 1951 he was called to the bar. From 1967 until 1970 he was parliamentary secretary to the Ministry of Housing and Local Government.

SKOURAS, SPYROS P., U.S. movie magnate (b. Skourahorian, Greece, March 28, 1893—d. Mamaroneck, N.Y., Aug. 16, 1971), was president of 20th Century-Fox from 1942 until 1969.

SMITH, STEVIE (Florence Margaret Smith), British poet (b. Hull, Eng., 1903—d. London, Eng., March 7, 1971), won the Queen's Gold Medal for Poetry in 1969. She expressed an original and visionary personality in her poems, novels, and comic drawings. Her work combined the ludicrous and pathetic with an absence of sentiment, as expressed in the title of one of her collections, *Not Waving But Drowning* (1957). Other publications included *Novel on Yellow Paper* (1936), *Over the Frontier* (1938), *The Holiday* (1950), and a book of drawings entitled *Some Are More Human than Others* (1958). In the 1960s she had considerable success with readings of her verse.

SOONG, T. V., Nationalist Chinese government official (b. Shanghai, China, 1894—d. San Francisco, Calif., April 25, 1971), who in the 1930s served as minister of communications and minister of finance, and from 1945 until 1947 as prime minister under his brother-in-law, Pres. Chiang Kai-shek. After the Nationalist government fled to Taiwan Soong dominated its financial affairs.

SORENSEN, REGINALD WILLIAM SORENSEN, Baron, British politician (b. London, Eng., June 19, 1891—d. London, Oct. 8, 1971), was MP for West Leyton (1929–31; 1935–50) and for Leyton (1950–64).

SPINGARN, ARTHUR B., U.S. attorney (b. New York, N.Y., March 28, 1878—d. New York, Dec. 1, 1971), long-time leader in the struggle for equal rights for the American Negro, was a founder (1909), vice-president (1911–40), and president (1940–65) of the National Association for the Advancement of Colored People (NAACP).

STANGL, FRANZ, Austrian war criminal (b. Altmünster, Aus., March 26, 1908—d. Düsseldorf, W.Ger., June 28, 1971), was commandant of the Nazi extermination camp at Treblinka from 1942 until a prisoners' uprising in 1943. He was transferred to Italy at that time, to organize a campaign against the partisans. In 1945 U.S. troops captured him in Austria, but he escaped before he could be brought to trial. In 1951 he went to São Paulo, Braz., where he worked at the Volkswagen auto plant. Traced by Simon Wiesenthal, the Austrian Nazi hunter, Stangl was arrested in February 1967 and extradited to West Germany. He was tried for the murder of 400,000 Jews and condemned to life imprisonment by a Düsseldorf court in 1970.

STANLEY, WENDELL MEREDITH, U.S. virologist (b. Ridgeville, Ind., Aug. 16, 1904—d. Salamanca, Spain, June 15, 1971), recipient of the 1946 Nobel Prize for Chemistry, whose pioneering work into the nature of viruses laid the foundation for many later medical advances, was professor of molecular biology and biochemistry at the University of California at Berkeley. In 1946 Stanley shared one-half the Nobel Prize for Chemistry with John H. Northrop, also a virologist, for their preparation of enzymes and virus proteins in a pure form. (The other half went to James B. Sumner, researcher in enzymes and viruses.) Stanley's work was on the tobacco mosaic virus.

STENHOUSE, HUGH COWAN, Scottish executive (b. Kilsyth, Scot., 1915—d. Leicester, Eng., Nov. 25, 1971), was head of Govan Shipbuilders, a company set up at government request to examine the potential for a reorganization of the Upper Clyde shipyards. Stenhouse began his career in insurance in 1932 and in 1938 joined his father's insurance-broking company. He became chairman of Stenhouse holdings in 1957 and by 1970 had increased its profits from £35,-000 to more than £2 million.

STONHAM, VICTOR JOHN COLLINS, 1st Baron, British industrialist and civil servant (b. London, Eng., July 1, 1903—d. Enfield, Eng., Dec. 22, 1971), was minister of state at the Home Office (1967–69) and made significant contributions toward prison reform. He held special responsibilities for Northern Ireland during 1969 and handled important Home Office and Ministry of Power legislation in the House of Lords. He joined the Labour Party in 1942 and sat for Taunton (1945–50) and Shoreditch and Finsbury (1954–58). He became a life peer in 1958.

David Sarnoff

Stevie Smith

Franz Stangl

UPI COMPIX

Igor Stravinsky

STOPFORD, SIR MONTAGU GEORGE NORTH, general (ret.), British Army (b. Nov. 16, 1892—d. Chipping Norton, Eng., March 10, 1971), was commander in chief of Allied Land Forces South East Asia during 1946–47. Stopford was chief instructor at the Camberley Staff College at the outbreak of World War II, when he took command of the 17th Infantry Brigade, which later covered the retreat of the British Expeditionary Force from Dunkerque. In 1943 he was appointed commander of the 33rd Indian Corps in Burma.

SVEDBERG, THEODOR H. E., Swedish nuclear scientist (b. Fleräng, Swed., Aug. 30, 1884—d. Stockholm, Swed., Feb. 26, 1971), was awarded the Nobel Prize for Chemistry in 1926. After graduation from Uppsala University in 1907 he developed a method for studying the movements of very small particles, and introduced techniques for solving difficult experimental problems. One such achievement was the development of the ultracentrifuge by which he could accurately measure the size of very large molecules, such as the proteins found in living cells.

TAL, WASFI AT-, Jordanian politician (b. Irbid, Jordan, 1920—d. Cairo, Egypt, Nov. 28, 1971), prime minister of his country, was shot dead by Palestinian guerrillas while leading Jordan's delegation to the Arab Defense Council in Cairo. Tal served in the British Army (1946–48) while simultaneously putting the Arab case for Palestine at the Arab Office in London. After partition he returned to Jordan and in 1955 became director of the Press Bureau. In 1957, after a period as counselor in Bonn, W.Ger., he returned to Amman as director of ceremonies at the royal palace. He was chief of national guidance (1959–61) and director general of Jordan radio before serving as prime minister during 1962–63, 1965–67, and from 1970. Already unpopular with the left over his pro-Western attitude, his support for the Yemeni royalists, and his hostility to the Palestinian guerrillas, Tal gave his enemies further reason for hatred by his destruction of guerrilla bases in Jordan in the 1970 civil war.

TAMM, IGOR EVGENYEVICH, Soviet physicist (b. Vladivostok, Russia, July 8, 1895—d. Moscow, U.S.S.R., April 12, 1971), shared the 1958 Nobel Prize for Physics with two other Soviet scientists, P. A. Cerenkov and I. M. Frank. The award was in recognition of their discovery and interpretation of the Cerenkov effect in nuclear physics (the emission of light waves by electrons or other electrically charged atomic particles moving in a medium at any speed greater than the velocity of light in that medium). Tamm produced a quantum theory of acoustical vibrations and scattering of light in solid bodies, and developed a theory of the interaction of light with electrons. In 1950 he suggested that in attempts to control thermonuclear reactions a magnetic field might be used to insulate extra-high-temperature hydrogen plasma from its container, which would otherwise not withstand such extreme heat. Subsequent efforts were based on this idea. Tamm was made a Hero of Socialist Labour.

TERRISS, ELLALINE (LADY HICKS), British musical comedy star (b. Stanley, Falkland Islands, April 13, 1871—d. London, Eng., June 16, 1971), popular in theatre and music hall from the 1890s to the 1920s, whose early successes included *Two Roses, David Garrick, Betsy,* and *Cinderella,* in which she toured the U.S. Returning to the Gaiety Theatre in 1895, she was seen in *The Shop Girl, My Girl, The Circus Girl,* and *A Runaway Girl.* She appeared in two hits of the 1920s, *Sleeping Partners* and *The Man in Dress Clothes.*

THATCHER, W. ROSS, Canadian politician (b. Neville, Sask., May 24, 1917—d. Regina, Sask., July 23, 1971), member of the Liberal Party, was premier of Saskatchewan from 1964 until his defeat for reelection in April 1971.

TIGER, DICK (DICK ITEHU), Nigerian boxer (b. Amaigbo, Nigeria, Aug. 14, 1929—d. Aba, Nigeria, Dec. 14, 1971), middleweight and light-heavyweight fighter, won the Nigerian middleweight title before going to Britain in 1955. In 1958 he won the Empire middleweight title from Pat McAteer, lost it to W. Greaves of Canada two years later but won it back shortly after. In 1962 he won the World Boxing Association version of the world middleweight title. He lost it in 1963, won it back two years later, and then took the light-heavyweight title in 1966. He lost the middleweight title in 1966 and the light-heavyweight in 1968. During the Nigerian civil war Tiger served in the Biafran Army.

TISELIUS, ARNE WILHELM KAURIN, Swedish chemist (b. Stockholm, Swed., Aug. 10, 1902—d. Uppsala, Swed., Oct. 29, 1971), was awarded the 1948 Nobel Prize for Chemistry for his work on electrophoresis and absorption analysis. He was assistant to T. Svedberg at the Institute of Physical Chemistry at Uppsala University (1925–32) and lecturer in chemistry (1930–38). In 1934 he went to Princeton University, returning to Uppsala to become professor of biochemistry (1938–68). He was chairman of the Swedish State Council for Research in Natural Science (1946–50) and president of the Nobel Foundation (1960–64).

TOVEY, JOHN CRONYN TOVEY, 1ST BARON, British admiral of the fleet (b. March 7, 1885—d. Madeira, Spain, Jan. 12, 1971), served as a destroyer captain in World War I. At the outbreak of World War II he commanded the Mediterranean Fleet's destroyer flotillas; in July 1940 he became second in command, Mediterranean, and the following autumn took command of the Home Fleet and was responsible for sinking the German battleship "Bismarck" in May 1941. In July 1943 Tovey was promoted to admiral of the fleet and appointed commander in chief of "The Nore," a command that contributed greatly to the success of the Normandy landings.

TREVETHIN (3RD BARON) **AND OAKSEY** (1ST BARON), **GEOFFREY LAWRENCE,** British jurist (b. Wiltshire, Eng., Dec. 2, 1880—d. Aug. 28, 1971), was president of the Nürnberg Tribunal in 1945. In 1924 he became recorder of Oxford and was elected to the High Court in 1932, being

STRAVINSKY, IGOR FEODOROVICH, U.S. composer (b. Oranienbaum, Russia, June 17, 1882—d. New York, N.Y., April 6, 1971), considered the most influential composer of the 20th century, was recognized by the musical world in 1910 in Paris with the performance of *The Firebird* (written in 1909). In 1911 he wrote the score for Sergei Diaghilev's ballet *Petrouchka;* two years later Stravinsky wrote the score for *The Rite of Spring,* with its intricate rhythmic innovations and explosive dissonances, which touched off a near riot at its premiere in Paris. Later major works included *Symphony of Psalms,* for orchestra (1930), *Symphony in C* and *Symphony in Three Movements* (in the 1940s), and *The Rake's Progress,* an opera (1951); in the 1960s he wrote *Abraham and Isaac,* a sacred ballet, and *Retrospections and Conclusions.*

Wendell M. Stanley

WIDE WORLD

Dick Tiger

WIDE WORLD

promoted to the Court of Appeal in 1944, and in 1947 he was appointed a law lord, with the title of Baron Oaksey.

TUBMAN, WILLIAM VACANARARAT SHAD-RACH, Liberian statesman (b. Harper, Liberia, Nov. 29, 1895—d. London, Eng., July 23, 1971), was president of Liberia from 1944 until his death. After beginning his career in teaching and law Tubman at 23 became the youngest Liberian ever elected to the ten-man Senate. In 1937 he became a judge and in 1943 president-elect. His administration, the longest in Liberian history, coincided with the discovery of huge deposits of high-grade iron ore, with the growth of "aid" from the rich nations, and with the development of an independent African voice in world affairs. He did much to lessen the traditional conflict between "Americo-Liberians" and "tribesmen" and to weaken the U.S. economic monopoly by encouraging other countries to share in Liberia's development.

TURLEIGH, VERONICA, British actress (b. County Donegal, Ire., Jan. 14, 1903—d. London, Eng., Sept. 3, 1971), was well known on the English stage for 40 years. She was first engaged at the Oxford Playhouse in the 1920s and gave impressive performances in Synge's *Deirdre of the Sorrows,* Ibsen's *Hedda Gabler,* and as Rosalind in *Love's Labour's Lost.* She appeared in the first joint production of W. H. Auden and Christopher Isherwood, *The Dog Beneath the Skin* (1936). She was frequently seen at the Old Vic and at Stratford-upon-Avon.

TVARDOVSKI, ALEKSANDR TRIFONOVICH, Soviet poet (b. Zagorye, Russia, June 21, 1910—d. Moscow, U.S.S.R., Dec. 18, 1971), was editor of the leading Soviet literary journal *Novy Mir* ("New World") from 1950 to 1954 and from 1958 to 1970. Tvardovski fought hard to maintain *Novy Mir's* traditional independence, often in the face of official disapproval. Under his guidance the magazine was responsible for publishing such works as Ilya Ehrenburg's *Thaw* (1954), Aleksandr Yashin's *The Vologda Wedding* (1962), and Aleksandr I. Solzhenitsyn's *One Day in the Life of Ivan Denisovich* (1962). Tvardovski joined the Communist Party in 1940 and during World War II served as a war correspondent. His own war verses won him popularity before his appointment to *Novy Mir.* Although forced to resign by conservative pressures in 1970, Tvardovski was awarded the Order of the Red Banner "for services in the development of Soviet poetry" in that year, and in 1971 he received the State Prize for Literature.

VILAR, JEAN, French actor and director (b. Sète, France, March 25, 1912—d. Sète, May 28, 1971), was director (1951–63) of the state-owned Théâtre National Populaire in Paris. In 1945 he won the Prix du Théâtre for his productions of Strindberg's *Dance of Death* and T. S. Eliot's *Murder in the Cathedral.* In 1947 he

founded the Avignon Festival, the first drama festival in France.

VILDRAC, CHARLES (CHARLES MESSAGER), French poet and dramatist (b. Paris, France, Nov. 22, 1882—d. Saint-Tropez, France, June 25, 1971), won the French Academy's Grand Prix for literature in 1963. His first poems were written in the 1890s and in 1901 he published *Le Verlibrisme,* a defense of traditional verse. A collection of prose poems followed in 1912. He later took to drama with *Paquebot Tenacity* (1920), *La Brouille* (1930), *Poucette* (1936), and other plays. Further poetry collections include *Chants du désespéré* (1920), *Poèmes de l'Abbaye* (1925), and *Prolongements* (1927).

VOLKOV, VLADISLAV N., Soviet cosmonaut (b. Moscow, U.S.S.R., Nov. 23, 1933—d. in space, June 30, 1971), civilian engineer of the Soyuz 11 spacecraft, died with his two companions at the controls of the craft as it was about to land. The three cosmonauts had completed a record of 24 days in earth orbit. Volkov graduated from the Moscow Institute of Aviation in 1959 and in 1966 joined the Soviet space program as an aeronautical engineer. He made his first space flight with the three-man crew of the Soyuz 7 in 1969. He was awarded posthumously his country's second highest medal, the Gold Star, having already been made a Hero of the Soviet Union. (See *Dobrovolsky, Georgi T.,* and *Patsayev, Viktor I.,* above.)

WEBSTER, SIR DAVID LUMSDEN, British opera administrator (b. Dundee, Scot., July 3, 1903—d. London, Eng., May 11, 1971), was responsible for establishing Covent Garden as one of the world's greatest centres of opera and ballet. In 1944 he became chairman of the preliminary committee set up to plan the future of the Royal Opera House. He was appointed administrator of the newly formed company in 1946, and retired in 1970.

WEIR, SIR JOHN, British physician (b. Glasgow, Scot., October 1879—d. London, Eng., April 17, 1971), was personal physician to Queen Elizabeth II (1952–68), to Queen Mary (1936–53), to King George VI (1937–52), to the queen of Norway (1928–38), and to the prince of Wales (1923–36). He was president of the British Homeopathic Society.

WIATA, INIA TE, Maori bass singer (b. Otaki, New Zealand, 1916 [?]—d. London, Eng., June 26, 1971), member of the Royal Opera House, Covent Garden (1950–54), whose operatic roles included Pimen in *Boris Godounov,* Ramphis in *Aida,* and Bartolo in *The Marriage of Figaro.*

WISEMAN, STEPHEN, British educator (b. Haswell, County Durham, Eng., Sept. 1, 1907—d. Windsor, Eng., July 24, 1971), was director of the National Foundation for Educational Research (1968–71).

WISKEMANN, ELIZABETH, British historian (b. Sidcup, Kent, Eng., 1899—d. London, Eng., July 5, 1971), was Montague Burton professor of international relations at Edinburgh University (1958–61) and tutor in modern European history at Sussex University (1961–64). Her books include *Undeclared War* (1939), *The*

Rome-Berlin Axis (1949), *Europe of the Dictators* (1966), and *Fascism in Italy* (1969). She was a contributor to *Encyclopædia Britannica.*

WITTKOWER, RUDOLF, German-born art historian (b. Berlin, Ger., June 22, 1901—d. U.S., Oct. 11, 1971), was professor of fine arts, Columbia University (1956–69), and Slade professor of fine art, Cambridge University (1970–71). In 1932 he became a lecturer in art history at Cologne, Ger., but left for England following Hitler's accession. At the Warburg Institute in London he worked for more than 20 years and in 1956 was offered a chair at Columbia, where he rapidly built up a great school of art history. He was the first writer to chart systematically the history of Baroque architecture. His writings include a Michelangelo bibliography (with E. Steinmann; 1927), a catalog of Bernini's drawings (1931), *British Art and the Mediterranean* (1948), and *Architectural Principles in the Age of Humanism* (1949).

WOOD, BARRY, U.S. bacteriologist (b. Milton, Mass., May 4, 1910—d. Boston, Mass., March 9, 1971), collegiate star in football, hockey, and baseball at Harvard University (B.A., 1932), and preeminent in the field of bacteriology, held the chairmanship of the Washington University school of medicine in St. Louis, Mo., from 1942 until 1955 when he assumed the post of vice-president at Johns Hopkins University. He became head of the department of microbiology in 1959. Author of a number of textbooks, Wood was to have received the Kober Award, highest honour bestowed by the American Academy of Physicians, in May 1971.

WOOD, GARFIELD ARTHUR ("GAR"), U.S. boat racer and industrialist (b. Mapleton, Ia., Dec. 4, 1880—d. Miami, Fla., June 19, 1971), won the first Harmsworth Trophy for the U.S. in the early 1930s and successfully defended it seven times, racing one of his long line of "Miss America" motorboats. Wood backed the Chris-Craft boat manufacturing company in the 1930s and early '40s.

WYLIE, PHILIP, U.S. writer (b. Beverly, Mass., May 12, 1902—d. Miami, Fla., Oct. 25, 1971), prolific author of books, including the controversial *Generation of Vipers* (1942), also wrote many stories and articles for the *Saturday Evening Post, Reader's Digest,* and *Look* magazines.

YOUNG, WHITNEY M., JR., U.S. champion of civil rights (b. Lincoln Ridge, Ky., July 31, 1921—d. Lagos, Nigeria, March 11, 1971), executive director of the National Urban League since 1961, was dean of the School of Social Work at Atlanta University from 1954 until 1961. Young had at various times served on seven presidential commissions, was president of the National Association of Social Workers, and the author of *To Be Equal* and *Beyond Racism.* Young was the recipient of a Medal of Freedom, highest U.S. civilian award.

ZUBERIA, ALBERT F., Uruguayan statesman (b. 1902—d. Montevideo, Urug., Oct. 4, 1971), was president of the nine-man National Council (equivalent to being president of the nation) during 1956–57.

William V. S. Tubman

Garfield ("Gar") Wood

Whitney Young

Oceanography

The U.S. National Science Foundation's Deep Sea Drilling Project aboard the vessel "Glomar Challenger" continued to provide researchers with new data on the age and structure of the earth. Drilling and coring in the North Atlantic in latitudes up to 60° N were interrupted by only half a day of inclement weather during the 52-day operation in the summer of 1971. At the nine sites drilled in depths of water ranging from 3,500 to 16,000 ft., 3,000 ft. of core were recovered representing layers of sediment as old as 100 million years. The evidence indicated that glaciers began to cover the continents about three million years ago; a warm branch of the Gulf Stream flowed into the Labrador Sea before that time; fragments of the continents sank into the Atlantic Ocean after Canada, Greenland, and Europe broke apart over 100 million years ago; and a high rate of sedimentation in the Bay of Biscay is related to phases of active building of the Alps Mountains.

Work done in the Atlantic west of Portugal resulted in recovery of the oldest sediments yet from the eastern North Atlantic. The discovery of sediment of this age confirmed that the Iberian block and Africa broke away from Europe prior to 130 million years ago. Other work indicated that the floor of the Mediterranean has been affected continually by the drift of Europe and Africa. The narrowing of the Mediterranean region, caused by compression between Europe and Africa, resulted in the isolation of the basin. From ten to five million years ago, the sea apparently became desiccated; no organisms could survive in the concentrated salt brines, and sterile muds were formed. Approximately five million years ago the stagnation came to an abrupt halt, and normal marine life has flourished fairly constantly ever since.

Deep Sea Drilling Project scientists found that the Caribbean Sea is not so old as was previously believed. Samples of sediments and rock taken from the sea bottom under two to three miles of water were identified as being from 75 to 85 million years old. In comparison, the oldest part of the North Atlantic is about 180 million years old, and the age of the continents is about 3,500,000,000 years. Scientists explain this curious age relationship by using the presently popular theory of continental drift. According to this theory, the continents of North and South America at one time were attached to Europe and Africa; about 170 million years ago, they pulled apart and drifted westward, leaving behind a young ocean crust. When the continents are "fitted" together, South America overlaps where the Caribbean should be. Due to the youthful nature of the Caribbean crust, scientists envisage South America tearing apart from the Greater Antilles and a new crust slowly developing.

The work also provided data to back up a recently developed hypothesis about the formation of the Isthmus of Panama. The theory suggests that 10 to 15 million years ago an ocean ridge extended eastward from the present position of the Galápagos Islands (in the Pacific). The ridge split lengthwise, as a rift formed at the eastern end, and the northern half of this ridge began to break up and drift northward. Successive pieces of the ridge were pulled down into a deep-sea trench, off the coast of present-day Panama and Costa Rica, eventually sealing it up from east to west. The sea floor on the west side of the trench rose in compensation, forming the Isthmus of Panama and, slightly later, the southeastern part of Costa Rica.

Drilling and sampling of the ocean bottom along the western continental margin of North America from Oregon to Alaska turned up evidence of activity caused by the action of the ocean floor sliding underneath the continental mass at the rate of two inches per year. The underthrust by the sea floor causes sediment to be scraped off and crumpled

Current production of major ocean resources with areas of petroleum and gas exploration.

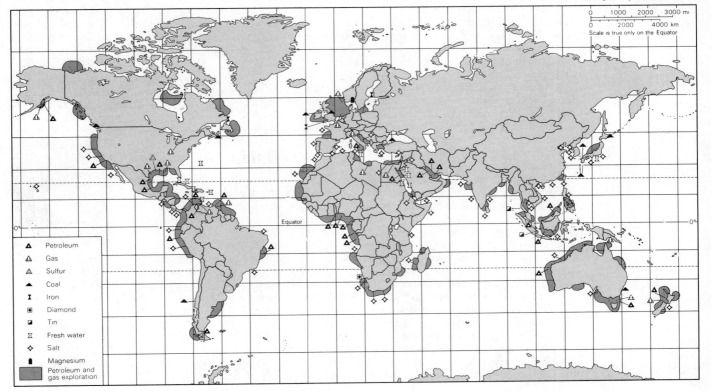

Legend:
- △ Petroleum
- ⬚ Gas
- ⬚ Sulfur
- ▲ Coal
- Ⅰ Iron
- ⊕ Diamond
- ⬚ Tin
- Ⅱ Fresh water
- ◇ Salt
- ⬛ Magnesium
- ▨ Petroleum and gas exploration

against the continent. For the first time, scientists had a chance to examine the various crumpled layers of sediment. Complete records of marine organic productivity could be seen in the core samples. These records also showed the climatic oscillation characteristic of the Ice Ages.

Increasing concern over the effects of pollution in the ocean led to a systematic series of measurements of the concentrations of various pollutants and their effects upon the plants and animals. This initial series, financed by the National Science Foundation, was part of a general baseline study of conditions as they are now, against which future changes can be measured. The initial sampling program aimed at measuring the present levels of suspected contaminants as a guide for selecting groups of marine organisms and critical locations in the ocean for more detailed studies. Measurements were to be made of lead, radioactive contaminants, arsenic, mercury and other metals, petroleum, chlorinated hydrocarbons, and DDT. Samples collected more than 20 years ago also would be examined, so that the rates of increase of pollutants could be estimated.

The SS "Hudson" of the Canadian Department of Energy, Mines, and Resources became the first vessel ever to have circumnavigated the American continents. Beginning in Nova Scotia, she traveled southward around South America, northward in the Pacific, through the Bering Sea, and eastward north of Canada to the Atlantic. Her mission was a general study of the ocean, including measurements of the water characteristics, the organisms within the water, the depth of the bottom along the 35,000-mi. track, and variations in the earth's gravity field.

Recent trends in biological oceanography indicated a growing interest in the ways in which marine food chains operate. Some of the interest arose from the question of how much food man can obtain from the sea, and some of it from questions about the uptake and concentration of pollutants by organisms. For example, it is generally accepted that inorganic phosphorus in the ocean seldom falls to levels that limit biological production, although nitrogen frequently does. Thus, the increasing introduction of waste phosphorus would not be likely to cause the excessive growth of organisms that could lead to undesirable eutrophication (and, hence, oxygen depletion) of ocean waters, although it would do so in certain inland waters where phosphorus is sometimes limiting. The exact extent to which nitrogen is limiting is complicated by the various combinations in which the microscopic plants or phytoplankton can utilize it. They can utilize it as ammonia and urea as well as nitrate.

Interest in the micronekton, active pelagic animals intermediate in size between zooplankton and the kinds generally harvested by man, was increasing for several reasons. One was the possibility, which was being considered seriously, of their being used as human food. Soviet vessels were engaged in experimental fishing for the Antarctic krill, *Euphausia superba.*

Current meters placed 200 m. (656 ft.) above the bottom beneath the Gulf Stream (near 37° N 70° W) at a depth of 4,226 m. (13,866 ft.) for a period of 60 days revealed a high variability in the flow. Averaged over the entire period, the flow was toward the north at about $\frac{1}{4}$ mph, but the range of variation was about 1 mph. For example, during the first nine days the net drift was toward the south at about $\frac{3}{4}$ mph; dur-

ing the remainder of the time the net drift was northward at about $\frac{4}{10}$ mph. The fluctuations might be related to fluctuations in the path of the Gulf Stream at the surface.

Investigations in the Indian Ocean revealed what might be the ocean's thickest layer of sediment. Seismic refraction studies indicated that some areas of the Bay of Bengal deep-sea fan of sediments, extending southward from the Ganges River, are as much as 54,000 ft. thick; the fan covers an area about 2,000 mi. long and 1,000 mi. wide. The material of this layer is mud and sand that has been eroded from the Himalayas.

The deeper layers of the world ocean are filled with colder waters that have sunk from the surface in high latitudes in winter, yet the details of this overturn have never been measured, partly because work in these areas in winter is almost impossible to conduct. The Mediterranean Sea is cut off by a shallow sill from the deeper waters of the Atlantic and forms its own deep and bottom water by a similar process of sinking and overturn in winter. At these more temperate latitudes, studies were carried out south of France by scientists and ships from the U.S., the U.K., France, and Italy. Although overturn may take place in several areas of the northern Mediterranean, the results from south of France may indicate the general nature of the phenomenon.

The preliminary results of this study showed a general cooling of the surface (less dense) waters in early winter, and an increase in their salinity from the evaporation. The cold mistral winds from the north set up a cyclonic (counterclockwise) circulation. An increase in the winds to about 40 mph, with air temperature about 3° C (37.4° F), caused further cooling and evaporation; the surface waters were made more dense and, in the centre of the cyclonic spiral, overturned within about six days' time to about 1,400 m. (4,593 ft.) depth. After 30 days more, the effect of the penetration could be seen at depths of 2,430 m. (7,972 ft.). During this time the water was observed to be spreading outward from the source as well as vertically downward. The more detailed analyses to follow may allow an estimate of the total amount of deep water reformed or renewed annually. (J. L. Re.)

See also Antarctica; Geology; Law; Life Sciences; Meteorology; Seismology.

ENCYCLOPÆDIA BRITANNICA FILMS. *How Level Is Sea Level?* (1970).

The stonefish (Synanceja verrucosa) is displayed at the Vaughan Aquarium-Museum, Scripps Institution of Oceanography in San Diego, Calif. The stonefish, a master at camouflage, generally is considered the most dangerous of all stinging fishes.

COURTESY, SCRIPPS INSTITUTION OF OCEANOGRAPHY, UNIVERSITY OF CALIFORNIA, SAN DIEGO

Oil:
see Fuel and Power; Industrial Review

Oman

An independent sultanate, Oman occupies the southeastern part of the Arabian Peninsula and is bounded by the Union of Arab Emirates, Saudi Arabia, the Gulf of Oman, and the Arabian Sea. A small part of the country lies to the north of the rest of Oman and is separated from it by the Union of Arab Emirates. Area: 82,000 sq.mi. (212,000 sq.km.). Pop. (1970 est.): 750,000. Cap.: Muscat (pop., 1969, 9,973). Largest city: Matrah (pop., 1960, 14,119). Language: Arabic. Religion: Muslim. Sultan in 1971, Qabus ibn Sa'id.

In 1971 a series of Omani goodwill missions on behalf of the new sultan toured the Arab states in an effort to gain membership in the Arab League, regarded as a necessary prelude to admission to the United Nations (for which formal application was made on May 24). Opposition to Oman's admission to the Arab League was met from Yemen (Aden), which claimed that Oman was still a British colony, from Imam Ghaleb who claimed to be the real ruler of Oman and had previously been recognized as such by the league, and, at first, from Saudi Arabia. However, on September 29 the league accepted Oman's application, and it became the 17th member state. Following this, on October 7 the UN General Assembly approved Oman's membership in the UN by 117 votes to 1 (Yemen).

Although some former rebels had pledged loyalty to the young sultan, the Chinese-directed Popular Front for the Liberation of the Occupied Arabian Gulf continued operations in Dhofar and threatened Salalah. In February a major military offensive was launched against these guerrillas by Oman's British-officered forces. In March a big new offshore oil concession was granted to the Wendell Phillips Oil Co. of the U.S., but it was canceled in September. Oman's oil revenues, which had risen from $3,120,000 in 1967 to $105.6 million in 1970, were expected to exceed $144 million in 1971.   (P. Md.)

Pakistan

A federal republic and member of the Commonwealth of Nations, Pakistan is divided into two parts, separated by India. West Pakistan, the larger part of the country, is bordered on the south by the Arabian Sea and on the west by Afghanistan and Iran; East Pakistan lies on the Bay of Bengal. Total area: 366,041 sq.mi. (948,042 sq.km.), excluding the Pakistani-controlled section of Kashmir. Pop. (1971 est.): 116,598,000. Cap.: Islamabad (pop., 1967 est., 226,000). Largest city: Karachi (pop., 1970 est., 2,340,042). Language: Urdu, Bengali, English. Religion (1961): Muslim 88.1%; Hindu 10.7%; Christian and Buddhist minorities. Presidents in 1971, Lieut. Gen. Agha Muhammad Yahya Khan and, from December 20, Zulfikar Ali Bhutto.

For Pakistan 1971 was a year of unrelieved disaster, ending with resounding defeat in a brief war with its subcontinental neighbour India, the loss of East Pakistan and more than half its total population, and economic bankruptcy. These misfortunes were the legacy of the military regime headed by President Yahya Khan, who resigned on December 20.

The year had opened in the shadow of the cyclone disaster of November 1970, which had aggravated the situation caused by flood devastation of great areas of East Pakistan during the preceding monsoon. Despite relief efforts by the Pakistan armed forces and civil authorities, the difficulties of restoring communications and supplying aid to the stricken districts were enormous. These difficulties were nonetheless gradually overcome; generous assistance poured in from the Red Cross, from charitable organizations, and from many governments, and after the initial loss of life, estimated at 300,000, the threats of starvation and disease were averted.

The cyclone did not merely strike a blow at Pakistan's economy; it had serious repercussions on an already uneasy political situation. In the general elections of December 1970 and January 1971, the East Pakistan Awami ("People's") League, led by Sheikh Mujibur Rahman (see BIOGRAPHY), had won 167 of East Pakistan's 169 seats out of a National Assembly total of 313, and 288 out of the 300 seats in the Provincial Assembly. Thus, the league was in a strong position to realize its program for a reduction in centralized power and for maximum local autonomy for East Pakistan despite its having support from only 41% of the fully enfranchised adult electorate. Long-held grievances concerning West Pakistan's alleged exploitation of the more populous and, in earlier years, more productive East seemed at last on the point of answer. On Feb. 13, 1971, President Yahya Khan announced that the National Assembly would meet on March 3. Two days later former foreign minister Zulfikar Ali Bhutto, leader of the West Pakistan majority Pakistan People's Party, declared that he would boycott the National Assembly unless there was prior agreement between East and West on a constitutional

Sheikh Mujibur Rahman, leader of East Pakistan's Awami League, addresses a mass meeting in Dacca, E.Pak., on March 7, 1971. Sheikh Mujibur and his followers sought to establish an independent state of Bangla Desh.
WIDE WORLD

A small Bengali unit
trains to fight
the government of Agha
Muhammad Yahya Khan
in East Pakistan. Reports
indicated the formation
of a number of guerrilla
training camps
inside India.

G. SIPAHIOGLU—
JOCELYNE BENZAKIN

formula. In the East propaganda against the central government intensified.

It had been generally assumed that Sheikh Mujibur Rahman would become prime minister of Pakistan, and would institute a constitution granting East Pakistan regional autonomy and control over its foreign trade, foreign exchange, and foreign aid. On March 1, Yahya Khan postponed the National Assembly meeting, which would have resulted in a political confrontation between East and West. On March 6 he set a new date of March 25, and warned Mujibur that he would use the Army to prevent the country's disintegration. In reply the sheikh demanded immediate transfer of power to the elected representatives of the people, withdrawal of martial law, return of troops to their barracks, and an inquiry into alleged massacres in the East. By March 10, the populace in East Pakistan had accepted the Awami League leadership as its government.

In a desperate effort to avert disaster, Yahya Khan arrived in Dacca on March 15 for talks with Mujibur. He offered a commission "to inquire into the circumstances which led to the calling out of the Army in aid of civil powers in East Pakistan." This Sheikh Mujibur rejected. The National Assembly was postponed indefinitely, Yahya Khan flew back to West Pakistan on March 25, and the following day full-scale war erupted in the East and a clandestine radio announced the "sovereign independent people's republic of Bangla Desh." Yahya Khan on the same day announced the outlawing of the Awami League, a total ban on political activity in both wings of the country, and complete press censorship. The Awami League was denounced as a treasonable movement aiming for secession. Sheikh Mujibur and many of those who had been elected to represent the Awami League were arrested and charged with treason.

Thereafter, the situation became extremely confused, with conflicting reports coming from the military authorities, the clandestine radio, and the foreign press. Communications were disrupted, and food-deficit areas accustomed to receiving supplies from outside faced starvation. The Indian government announced that by April 21 a total of 258,734 Hindu and Muslim refugees had fled across the border of East Pakistan into India. By August 10 the number was put at 7.5 million and by late in the year some estimates were as high as 12 million; the Pakistani authorities stated that the maximum number was 2 million.

Broadly speaking, the Muslim world supported the view that the East Pakistan tragedy was a domestic matter. Of the major powers, China and the U.S. took the same view, while the U.S.S.R., anxious for good relations with both Pakistan and India, tried to hold a balance but sided with India in its demand for return of the refugees to East Pakistan.

As tension with India neared open hostilities, Yahya Khan on October 21 urged UN Secretary-General U Thant to visit both countries to discuss troop withdrawals from border areas. Pakistan complained that Indian border activities were hindering the return of the refugees in spite of an amnesty; India maintained that East Pakistan was not safe for the refugees, unless it became independent.

Meanwhile the Soviet Union, which had signed a 20-year treaty of friendship with India on August 9,

continued on page 538

Victims of a major
Pakistani Air Force
offensive are piled
into pedicabs
in the town of Dinajpur,
E.Pak., in April 1971.

AMIYA TARAFDAR

PAKISTAN: A NATION DIVIDED

By J. D. F. Jones

In retrospect, nothing in 1971 seems so certain and inevitable as the climaxing of the year with the two-week India-Pakistan war. But, of course, the progress from Awami League electoral victory in East Pakistan in December 1970 through the bloody military repression of March, the flight of more than nine million refugees into India, the buildup of guerrilla activities, and, finally, the full-scale confrontation in December could probably have been halted on a hundred occasions by a fractional shift of policy in various high places. It could have been averted by a little flexibility in the Pakistani government, for instance, or by a faltering of resolution in India, by a dash of moderation from Sheikh Mujibur Rahman (*see* BIOGRAPHY) of the Awami League, or even, conceivably, by some determination or agreement on the part of the major powers. Yet, in the end, all that was surprising about the war was the speed and efficiency of the Indian victory.

The Indian subcontinent is too complex for there to be any simple cause—or, for that matter, any straightforward responsibility—for the war. At one level, the Indians were compelled to fight the war in order to secure the return of the refugees who had fled into India from the military repression in East Pakistan. At the other extreme, the war may be seen as one significant stage in the breakup of the system that had been set up by the British Empire—itself merely the latest of the attempts of successive empires to order and govern the subcontinent. But whether the Indian government of Mrs. Indira Gandhi sought and welcomed the conflict, or merely accepted and acknowledged it, will be a matter of controversy for a long time to come.

Certainly, there could have been no war without Pakistani Pres. Agha Muhammad Yahya Khan's decision in March to end his efforts to transfer political power from the Army to a government arising out of the December elections. The military government, bedeviled by the antagonism between the electoral winners in East and West Pakistan—the Awami League of Sheikh Mujib and the Pakistan People's Party of Zulfikar Ali Bhutto, respectively—decided that the Awami League was planning secession. The subsequent military crackdown on East Pakistan was brutal, and the bloodshed was maximized by the eruption of intercommunal strife in the East, both before and after the military operation. The Awami League was proscribed, the sheikh was taken to the West and put on trial for treason, and refugees poured across the Indian frontier, creating an economic burden that India insisted was intolerable.

The question at this point is, why should what had so far been a domestic dispute between the two wings of Pakistan proceed, apparently inexorably, to become war with India? Was it simply because of the refugees? The answer to the latter question surely must be no, despite the fact that Yahya Khan at no stage then or later seemed prepared to accept the result of the elections he had called, and despite the fact that at no time were the major powers prepared either to apply pressure to Yahya to force him to do so or to contribute adequately to the support of the refugees.

Therefore, before the middle of the year, there were two

J. D. F. Jones is foreign editor of the Financial Times, *London.*

elements playing upon the traditional Indo-Pakistani enmity: the revolt of the East Pakistani Bengalis against the Punjab-dominated Pakistani government, and the Indian determination to have the refugees go home. Yet neither element was as simple as it appeared. The precise truth about the Awami League "secession," for example, remains obscure. The "six points" of Sheikh Mujib went so far toward autonomy for the Eastern wing that the alarm of the military government was understandable. But was there, as the government claimed, a plot to secede?

As for the Indian determination not to accept the refugees, the precise conclusions the Indian government then adopted also are a matter of controversy. Mukti Bahini liberation forces speedily emerged from out of the refugees' ranks and soon were having remarkable success against Pakistani forces. Yet the successes of the Mukti Bahini were almost too good to be true, and slowly it became clear that the Indian Army was playing a very important role in assisting the guerrillas.

The true extent of that assistance is important because it would be the best clue in gauging the degree to which the Indians carried their commitment to return the refugees to East Pakistan (Bangla Desh). The prowar "hawks" in Delhi were alleged to have decided that India must seize its great chance to strike against Pakistan at the moment of maximum advantage. In effect, of course, this is what the Indian Army eventually did, and the nature of the December victory was confirmation of the arguments of the hawks earlier in the year. But the role of the Mukti Bahini, especially at a time when the autumn monsoon prevented the two armies from moving, was to be vital as a preliminary to the full-scale conflict—as a softening up of the Pakistani troops stranded in the hostile East, as a daily reminder to international opinion of the Bengali revolt, and, perhaps, as a cover for the steady buildup of Indian Army activity to the point of open warfare.

What is beyond controversy is that there had for years been a range of powerful arguments available to Indians who favoured some eventual resumption of the 1965 war. There was the enmity naturally engendered by the 1947 distinction between India, self-styled representative of secular, socialist, and democratic ideals, and Pakistan's authoritarian and military regime that united Punjabis, Bengalis, Sindis, Baluchis, and Pathans in the one common allegiance of Islam. In the simplest terms, this enmity in turn arises out of the age-old Hindu-Muslim hatreds.

In addition, both countries knew that they were menaced by various forms of disintegration: why else should the Indians so cling to Kashmir, with its population mainly consisting of hostile Muslims, if not because the secession or loss of one state could be the signal to other states, and so threaten the whole fragile edifice of union? A similar concern preoccupied Pakistan: if the East should go, what would prevent separatism among the peoples of the West?

Sometimes the argument for war became more humanitarian: how else—it was said in Delhi in 1971—can we hope to cut back the nation's immense defense budget in the future? Let Pakistan be defeated and turned in on itself and the funds that ever since partition have had to be devoted to defense can be directed to economic development where they are so desperately needed.

Finally, the Indians could not escape their concern for, and fear of, their great Asian rival, China. The Sino-Pakistani alliance, incongruous though it always has appeared, has been the central strategic preoccupation of the Indians. Then, as 1971 neared its end, everything might have seemed to conspire against the alliance: the Indians' treaty of friendship with the Soviet Union had been signed; China was preoccupied with a domestic crisis; the embarrassment for China of being associated with Yahya Khan's policies appeared to be growing to a point where Chou En-lai seemed to be making friendly noises to India; and the Indian Army in the north was confident of its ability to forestall any repetition of the Chinese advance in 1962. For India, if war there had to be, the time was ripe.

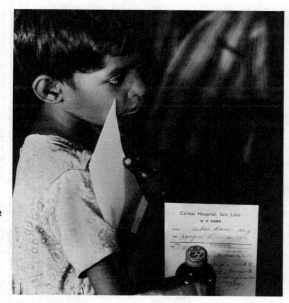

A Pakistani child patiently waits to receive medical treatment in a refugee centre. The refugee problem became more acute as war and natural disasters plagued East Pakistan.
COURTESY, CARITAS

continued from page 536

stepped up its verbal attacks on Pakistan. On November 22 Pakistan accused India of having launched all-out war in the East; clashes between Indian and Pakistani troops spread to Kashmir; China began to speak up in defense of Pakistan; and by December 3 India and Pakistan were at war.

Heavily outnumbered in equipment and manpower, especially in the East where the Mukti Bahini guerrillas were an added hindrance, Pakistani forces in East Pakistan were routed and surrendered with the fall of Dacca on December 16; shortly afterward India announced a unilateral end to the fighting. India recognized the provisional government of Bangla Desh and claimed that it had no desire for territorial gain but only to see a return of the refugees to a truly representative system of government.

With half his country lost and at least 60,000 men captured, Yahya Khan became the inevitable scapegoat for Pakistan's humiliation and defeat. He resigned the presidency on December 20 and was replaced by Zulfikar Ali Bhutto, who immediately retired him from the Army and had Sheikh Mujibur released from prison and placed under house arrest. Bhutto, the first civilian president Pakistan had had for 13 years, promised to restore democracy and to take revenge on India, but with a country in debt to the extent of $3 billion, reduced from one-fifth to one-tenth the size of India and with a 54% reduction in population, the immediate future looked bleak.   (X.)

Panama

A republic of Central America, bisected by the Canal Zone, Panama is bounded by the Caribbean Sea, Colombia, the Pacific Ocean, and Costa Rica. Area: 29,208 sq.mi. (75,650 sq.km.). Pop. (1971 est.): 1,474,910. Cap. and largest city: Panama City (pop., 1971 est., 372,375). Language: Spanish. Religion (1967 est.): Roman Catholic 87%. Provisional president of the civilian-military government in 1971, Demetrio Lakas Bahas.

The strong man of Panama, Gen. Omar Torrijos, maintained his grip over the political and economic forces of his country and also his considerable popularity. Enemies of his regime charged him, however,

Palestine:
see Israel; Jordan

with such acts of oppression and intimidation as wiretapping, threats of injury and confiscation, arbitrary arrest, illegal detention, and torture.

The government also was believed to be involved in the strange disappearance of Father Héctor Gallego, a priest of Santa Fe. His preachments of social justice and his practice of promoting a rural cooperative movement were said to have offended the authorities. Gallego was supported by Archbishop Marcos McGrath, who appealed to the Vatican in his behalf, and his fate stirred the Colombian government and press, for he was a Colombian citizen. The Panamanian rulers denied involvement in the case.

Conscious of the necessity of an acceptable image, despite his measures of force, Torrijos shuffled the personnel of his Cabinet in April 1971, restoring to his official family two leftist leaders whom he had removed a year earlier. A few weeks later, President Lakas indicated Panama's willingness to restore relations with the Communist nations, including Cuba.

A revival of the plan to build a sea-level transoceanic canal was under way. In November 1970, the Atlantic-Pacific Interoceanic Canal Study Commission reported its findings to U.S. Pres. Richard M. Nixon. In asserting the feasibility of such construction it discarded the fears of some marine biologists that crown-of-thorns starfish, sea-going cobras, or other ocean creatures might migrate from the Pacific to the Atlantic, and it rejected the method of excavating the canal with nuclear explosives as dangerous and contrary to treaty commitments. The commission envisioned a new channel some 36 mi. long that would have the capacity to handle twice as many ships at one time as the present canal; the ships could

PANAMA

Education. (1968–69) Primary, pupils 222,513, teachers 9,887; secondary, pupils 44,179, teachers 2,252; vocational, pupils 22,829, teachers 1,066; teacher training, students 1,310, teachers 72; higher (including 2 universities), students 10,063, teaching staff (1967–68) 417.

Finance. Monetary unit: balboa, at par with the U.S. dollar (2.40 balboas = £1 sterling) and with a free rate (Sept. 27, 1971) of 2.48 balboas to £1 sterling. Gold, SDRs, and foreign exchange: (Dec. 1970) U.S. $302.8 million; (Dec. 1969) U.S. $182.3 million. Budget (1970 est.) balanced at 162.7 million balboas. Gross national product: (1969) 971.2 million balboas; (1968) 836.1 million balboas. Money supply (deposits only): (Dec. 1970) 112.6 million balboas; (Dec. 1969) 92.7 million balboas. Cost of living (Panama City; 1963 = 100): (2nd quarter 1971) 113; (2nd quarter 1970) 111.

Foreign Trade. (1970) Imports 352,680,000 balboas; exports 114,350,000 balboas. Net service receipts from Canal Zone (1970) 130.2 million balboas. Main import sources (1969): U.S. 36%; Venezuela 22%; Panama Canal Zone 12%. Main export destinations (1969): U.S. 65%; West Germany 14%; Canada 5%. Main exports: bananas 57%; refined petroleum 19%; shrimps 9%.

Transport and Communications. Roads (1968) 6,720 km. Motor vehicles in use (1969): passenger 42,100; commercial (including buses) 13,000. Railways (1969) 671 km. Shipping (1970): merchant vessels 100 gross tons and over 886 (mostly owned by U.S. and other foreign interests); gross tonnage 5,645,-877. Telephones (Dec. 1969) 62,092. Radio receivers (Dec. 1969) c. 230,000. Television receivers (Dec. 1969) 125,000.

Agriculture. Production (in 000; metric tons; 1970; 1969 in parentheses): rice c. 167 (168); sugar, raw value (1970–71) c. 80, (1969–70) 76; bananas (1969) c. 900, (1968) 949; oranges c. 40 (c. 40); coffee 5.2 (5.5); cocoa (1970–71) 0.5, (1969–70) 0.5. Livestock (in 000; 1969–70): cattle c. 1,297; pigs c. 203; horses c. 158.

Industry. Production (in 000; 1969): cement (metric tons) 174; manufactured gas (cu.m.) 20,000; electricity (kw-hr.; 1968) 670,000.

be up to double the size of the largest permitted in 1971. Their passage would proceed along the single lane in convoys of 40 to 50 so timed as to match the opening and closing of tidal gates at either end of the canal.

The commission recommended a route roughly parallel to and some ten miles to the west of the present channel, estimated the cost of building at somewhat less than $3 billion, and suggested that construction begin 15 years before the present canal reached its capacity. Effective control of the operation and defense of the canal system, in the view of the commission, should reside in the U.S. under the terms of a new treaty between Panama and the U.S. In April both countries named representatives to begin negotiations, and they began their conversations in June. Early in October Panama delivered a report of the negotiations to UN Secretary-General U Thant.

Panama on October 11 celebrated the third anniversary of the military coup that brought the present regime to power. At a mass rally in Panama City General Torrijos told a crowd of about 200,000 that the time might soon come "for one generation to offer its lives" to regain Panamanian sovereignty over the Canal Zone. Authorities expected anti-U.S. demonstrations during the celebration, but they did not occur.   (A. R. W.)

Paraguay

A landlocked republic of South America, Paraguay is bounded by Brazil, Argentina, and Bolivia. Area: 157,047 sq.mi. (406,752 sq.km.). Pop. (1970 est.): 2,386,000. Cap. and largest city: Asunción (pop., 1970 est., 437,136). Language: Spanish (official), though Guaraní is the language of the majority of the people. Religion: Roman Catholic. President in 1971, Gen. Alfredo Stroessner.

President Stroessner, who first took office in 1954, continued to govern Paraguay firmly with the backing of the Colorado Party, the small oligarchy of business leaders, and the Army. There were no further disturbances by priests and students as had occurred in late 1969, and the clash between the church and the state over the quelling of those disturbances had subsided. In any event the government continued to renew regularly the "state of siege" measures, and in late 1970 an even stricter set of national security measures was introduced.

The tensions existing within the population arose mainly from the low increase in gross domestic product achieved in recent years. Efforts to correct this were made in early 1971 when Paraguay's first five-year development plan was published. It placed greater emphasis on boosting the rate of economic growth with a planned annual growth rate of 6%. The official trade forecast for 1971 was for a deficit of $7 million (exports $64 million; imports $71 million), compared with an actual deficit in 1970 of $12 million (exports $64 million; imports $76 million). However, the increased capital goods imports associated with the development plan made it likely that the 1971 trade deficit would turn out to be larger than anticipated. Paraguay continued to attract loans at favourable terms from the international lending agencies (the largest during 1971 being $29 million from the

Inter-American Development Bank, for electrical energy development), and thus in 1970 the overall balance of payments showed a surplus of $3 million.

The long-standing policy of maintaining price stability was not so successful in 1971, and the government was obliged to grant a general 10% increase in minimum wages (the first since 1964). This increase, combined with higher fuel costs and the effect on industry of the introduction of income tax legislation, led to a quickening in the rate of inflation.

The taxation of both personal and company income was finally introduced in March 1971, after Congress had exhibited one of its rare shows of resistance to Stroessner's wishes. Later, however, due to the pressures exerted by the business oligarchy, its implementation was postponed until the beginning of 1972.

(J. J. SM.)

PARAGUAY

Education. (1968) Primary, pupils 399,591, teachers (including preprimary) 12,722; secondary, pupils 40,795, teachers 3,596; vocational, pupils 2,507, teachers 621; teacher training, students 4,024, teachers 1,021; higher (including 2 universities), students 7,134, teaching staff (1965) 780.

Finance. Monetary unit: guaraní, with a free rate (Sept. 27, 1971) of 123 guaraníes to U.S. $1 (305 guaraníes = £1 sterling). Gold, SDRs, and foreign exchange, central bank: (June 1971) U.S. $14,750,-000; (June 1970) U.S. $12,070,000. Budget (total 1970 est.) balanced at 9,878,000,000 guaraníes. Gross national product: (1969) 68,360,000,000 guaraníes; (1968) 64,160,000,000 guaraníes. Money supply: (March 1971) 6,584,000,000 guaraníes; (March 1970) 5,729,000,000 guaraníes. Cost of living (Asunción; 1964 = 100): (June 1971) 116; (June 1970) 111.

Foreign Trade. (1970) Imports 8,019,600,000 guaraníes; exports 7,933,600,000 guaraníes. Import sources: U.S. 23%; Argentina 19%; West Germany 14%; U.K. 9%; Japan 7%; Algeria 6%. Export destinations: Argentina 27%; U.S. 14%; Netherlands 9%; U.K. 7%; Spain 6%; West Germany 5%; France 5%. Main exports: meat 24%; timber 20%; oilseeds 10%; tobacco 9%; cotton 6%.

Transport and Communications. Roads (1970) 11,225 km. Motor vehicles in use (1970): passenger 7,369; commercial (including buses) 10,084. Railways (1968): 1,220 km.; traffic 28 million passenger-km., freight 22 million net ton-km. Navigable inland waterways (including Paraguay-Paraná river system; 1966) c. 3,000 km. Telephones (Dec. 1969) 21,225. Radio receivers (Dec. 1969) 169,000. Television receivers (Dec. 1969) 17,000.

Agriculture. Production (in 000; metric tons; 1970; 1969 in parentheses): corn c. 200 (153); cassava (1969) 1,549, (1968) 1,504; sweet potatoes (1969) 94, (1968) 85; peanuts c. 16 (16); dry beans c. 18 (17); sugar, raw value (1970–71) c. 48, (1969–70) 46; oranges c. 225 (221); bananas (1969) c. 250, (1968) c. 250; tobacco 24 (21); cotton, lint c. 13 (13). Livestock (in 000; 1969–70): cattle c. 5,800; sheep c. 470; pigs c. 980; horses c. 730; chickens c. 6,600.

Industry. Production (in 000; 1969): cement (metric tons) 37; electricity (kw.-hr.) 203,000.

Payments and Reserves, International

When U.S. Pres. Richard M. Nixon dramatically coupled fresh efforts to stimulate spending in the economy with a price-wage freeze in mid-August 1971, he confronted the American people with new approaches to old problems. But by simultaneously severing the remaining tenuous link of the dollar to gold, he made world monetary history. The dollar crisis in mid-August arrived like a thunderbolt; but the thunder did not come out of a clear blue sky. It had been preceded by six currency crises between November

Panama Canal Zone:
see Dependent States;
Panama

Paper Industry:
see Industrial Review;
Timber

Papua New Guinea:
see Dependent States

1967 and May 1971, as evidenced in the accompanying panel.

The Monetary Crisis. The exchange crisis from April through August 1971, which centred around the dollar, was by no means only a dollar crisis. It began to be sensed in early 1971. Even though the world grew accustomed to U.S. payments deficits, which lasted for 20 years, attention was focused on the persistence of the imbalance in the "basic" international payments (all identified current and long-term capital transactions), and even more on the superimposition upon them of huge outflows of short-term funds out

---

International Currency Crises, 1967–71
November 1967
The pound sterling was devalued on November 18 by 14.3% and followed by 13 other currencies, including those of Denmark, Ireland, New Zealand, and Spain.

March 1968
Support by U.S. and six other monetary authorities of the gold price in the London market was suspended on March 17 after a $3 billion loss of gold to private and corporate buyers. A "two-tier" gold price system was established. On March 18, following a decline of the ratio of gold to U.S. Federal Reserve notes close to the minimum of 25%, the gold cover requirement on domestic currency was eliminated by the U.S. Congress.

August 1969
The French franc was devalued by 11.1% on August 10.

September 1969
Under the impact of heavy short-term capital inflows, the West German mark was allowed to float upward on September 29, but was legally stabilized on October 24 at a level 9.3% above its earlier parity.

May 1970
The Canadian dollar was allowed to float beginning June 1 to counter inflows of unwanted U.S. dollars.

May 1971
The West German mark, under the avalanche of U.S. dollars, was allowed to float upward on May 9. To counter the backwash of the West German move, the Dutch guilder was also allowed to float while the Swiss franc and the Austrian schilling were upvalued legally.

August 1971
Convertibility into gold of U.S. dollars held by governments and central banks abroad was suspended formally on August 15 and a 10% import surcharge was introduced—moves that brought about the most widespread float of currencies since the 1930s and a relapse into restrictive trade and payments practices. Currencies were realigned and devaluation of the dollar was announced on December 18; the import surcharge was lifted.

Note: The changes in exchange rates during 1971 are set forth in Table II. For a discussion of the currency turmoil during the preceding years, reference should be made to the earlier editions of the *Book of the Year*.

---

of U.S. dollars into West German marks, Swiss francs, and other currencies (*see* Table I.)

Early in 1971, funds had flown out of U.S. dollars largely because interest rates were much lower in U.S. markets than in those of Europe and Japan. These disparities were the natural result of the differences in business and inflationary conditions and, therefore, in monetary and fiscal postures and policies of central banks and governments—stimulative in the U.S. and restrictive in Europe, particularly in West Germany, and in Japan. However, beginning with April, when armchair monetary strategists and certain high-ranking government officials in West Germany and the U.S. recommended the floating of currencies as a therapy for the world's monetary ills, funds moved out of U.S. dollars in enormous amounts because of expectations that the German mark, the Swiss franc, and other currencies might increase in value relative to the dollar. Corporate treasurers and others responsible for protection of funds in their care thus sold dollars even when their need for marks and other currencies was well in the future or postponed sales of such currencies for dollars that they otherwise would have made. By early May, these "leads and lags" had reached truly colossal proportions. Blaming international speculation, as the governments did, touched only part of the truth.

Three other factors contributed to the dollar crisis: the U.S. merchandise trade deficit; continued large flows of U.S. private funds for long-term investments, mostly in Europe and Canada, and the sharp dwindling of foreign fund inflows for purchases of U.S. corporate securities; and the Vietnam war.

The Currency Float. To defend itself against the veritable avalanche of dollars that descended into their official reserves—and thus to counter an unwanted expansion of domestic money supply and help to cool off an overheated economy—West Germany on May 5 stopped buying dollars at a fixed price and, as a result, allowed the mark to float (or the dollar to float against the mark, for everything depends on the vantage point). The Netherlands followed suit. Switzerland and Austria upvalued their currencies to new fixed parities; for the Swiss franc, the parity was legally fixed again in terms of gold.

As the German mark and the Dutch guilder floated upward, they tended to become barometers of weakening confidence in the dollar. In July and early August, events moved inexorably toward a climax as trade and investment decisions throughout the world were influenced by anticipations of a depreciation of the dollar in terms of other currencies. When the U.S. gold stock was about to fall below $10 billion—the level that had for long been regarded as the safety minimum—President Nixon, on Sunday, August 15, formally suspended what remained of the U.S. commitment made in 1934 to convert dollars into gold at the request of foreign governments and central banks. For the U.S. Treasury policy of redeeming dollars in gold had for many years been like the applause in the fairy tale about the Emperor's new clothes: everybody saw, but pretended not to see, that the Emperor was naked.

The suspension of convertibility of the dollar into gold and other reserve assets—Special Drawing Rights (SDRs) and the reserve positions in the International Monetary Fund (IMF)—marked the end of an era. Foreign governments found themselves compelled to choose between keeping their currencies pegged to an inconvertible dollar, or defending themselves against unwanted dollars by allowing their currencies to float or by imposing controls on dollar inflows. The U.S. action thus removed the linchpin of the post-World War II international monetary system of fixed, although by no means immutable, parities of currencies, based on a U.S. dollar of fixed gold content and supported by arrangements under the International Monetary Fund to provide international liquidity and preserve convertibility among currencies in an environment of basically multilateral and nondiscriminatory international trade and payments. Along with the suspension of convertibility, President Nixon imposed, effective August 16, a temporary 10% surcharge on dutiable imported goods not covered by quotas (primarily manufactures, representing about half of total U.S. imports).

The following week, the principal European governments kept the foreign exchange markets closed while seeking to develop some joint policy response to the U.S. steps. These efforts failed and on Monday, August 23, the markets were reopened on an uncoordinated basis. Each government maintained the pre-August 15 parity for its currency, but all except the French government suspended their commitment under the IMF to defend the previous upper limits set for permissible fluctuation of their exchange rates. France established a dual exchange market—with the "commercial" franc unchanged vis-à-vis the dollar and, therefore, reduced in value in terms of currencies like the German mark; only the "financial" franc was allowed to float. The last currency to float was the Japanese yen. The Canadian dollar had begun to float in June 1970. The world had never before experienced a situation in which as many exchange rates were floating as in 1971; but marked differences appeared in the degree of appreciation of nondollar currencies against the dollar and, as a result, intra-European exchange rates were deeply disrupted.

Because of floating, the dollar became convertible only through the exchange markets and entirely at the risk of the holders. By mid-December, it had, in effect, depreciated by about 8% against the currencies of industrial countries abroad. The import surcharge was equivalent to an additional effective dollar depreciation of 3–4%. This direct and indirect depreciation was sought by the U.S. as a way of remedying the overvaluation of the dollar, as evidenced by the U.S. balance of payments deficit. President Nixon's action was thus tantamount to asking other industrial nations that had progressed so rapidly in recent years in terms of output, productivity, and market potentials to upvalue their currencies in order to make room for a swing in the U.S. basic balance of payments from a large deficit to a small surplus—a turnaround estimated by U.S. authorities at $13 billion. In the U.S. view, most of the turnaround would occur in the merchandise trade account and not in the long-term capital account. The U.S. also was pressing for trade liberalization and for the sharing of worldwide defense commitments.

The principal industrial countries abroad declined to accept a reshuffling of their trade and payments to bring about a U.S. surplus even for a few years. They rested content with an overall equilibrium or even a U.S. deficit matched by a demand for dollars by private traders and investors. At the same time, they felt that the U.S. should reduce those direct investments in Europe that were not accompanied by contributions to technology, management, and markets.

Not too surprisingly, therefore, all the industrial powers outside the U.S. resisted an unwanted appreciation of their currencies. They resisted principally through direct controls or through official intervention in exchange markets—steps that, in a regime of floating exchange rates, were political decisions, not technical operations. The actual experience with the "dirty" float thus differed greatly from the theoretical model of exchange rates floating freely in response to market forces that monetary theoreticians had visualized earlier in the year.

There were several reasons for the resistance to upward floating. The governments could not allow the currencies to be influenced decisively by short-term capital flows, which were the biggest single factor in the international imbalance. Under the circumstances of 1971, floating exchange rates could not indicate reliably where realistic and commercially bearable rates would finally settle. Furthermore, governments were deeply concerned about the consequences—for the profitability of their export industries and, therefore, for domestic output, employment, and votes—of the appreciation of their nations' currencies and of the U.S. import surcharge.

On a broader level, the floating of currencies and the relapse into restrictions on trade and payments threatened to destroy the standards of economic behaviour embodied in the international rule book elaborated under the auspices of the IMF and the GATT (General Agreement on Tariffs and Trade). Whatever

Table I. Main Components of the U.S. Balance of Payments

In $000,000,000

Item	1969	1970	January–September 1971
Exports: Commercial	33.4	38.9	30.7
Financed by govt. aid	3.1	3.1	2.5
Total	36.5	42.0	33.2
Imports	−35.8	−39.9	−34.5
Balance on merchandise trade	0.7	2.1	−1.3
Income on investments	5.8	6.4	6.2
Other services	−1.8	−2.0	−1.5
Balance on "civilian" goods and services	4.7	6.5	3.4
Military expenditures	−3.3	−3.4	−2.0
U.S. govt. grants and transfers	−2.2	−2.7	−2.7
Balance on current account	−0.9	0.4	−1.3
U.S. govt. capital	−1.9	−2.0	−1.8
Long-term private capital	−0.1	−1.5	−4.4
Of which:			
U.S. investments abroad	−4.0	−4.6	−5.5
Foreign investments in U.S.	3.9	3.1	1.1
Balance on current and long-term capital account	−2.9	−3.0	−7.6
Short-term loans and borrowings by U.S. banks and businesses	−0.6	−0.5	−1.9
Errors and omissions	−2.6	−1.1	−8.6
Allocations of SDRs	—	0.9	0.5
Balance on net liquidity basis	−6.1	−3.8	−17.6
Flows of private capital into deposits and money-market investments	8.8	−6.0	−5.8
Of which:			
U.S. claims abroad	0.1	0.2	−0.7
U.S. liabilities abroad	8.7	−6.2	−5.1
Balance on official settlements basis	2.7	−9.8	−23.4

Note: There are three official measurements of the U.S. balance of payments. The first—balance on current and long-term capital account—may be regarded as a rough indicator of "basic" long-term trends. This balance plus the flows of short-term "nonliquid" private capital, "errors and omissions" (believed to reflect mainly capital outflows), and allocations of SDRs add up to the balance on net liquidity basis, which is a broad indicator of potential pressures on the dollar resulting from changes in the U.S. liquidity position. This net liquidity balance plus flows of U.S. and foreign private "liquid" capital sum up to the balance on official settlements basis. This balance is measured by changes in U.S. official reserve assets—gold, reserve positions in the IMF, SDRs, and foreign exchange—plus changes in liabilities to foreign governments and central banks, and international monetary institutions. This third balance is intended to indicate net exchange market pressure, either favourable or adverse, on the dollar resulting from international transactions of the U.S.
Source: Adapted from U.S. Department of Commerce, Survey of Current Business.

the drawbacks of the fixed exchange-rate system might have been in the past 20 years, the industrial nations by and large observed the code. Even when one or another country "misbehaved," it recognized the infraction and, sooner or later, returned to the right path. If allowed to drag on for too long, therefore, the regime of floating currencies threatened to escalate exchange-rate manipulation, including multiple currency practices, and restrictions on trade and payments.

The Currency Realignments. For these reasons, the governments of the key countries endeavoured, by political negotiation, to restore a satisfactory pattern of exchange rates. Since each country's decision on its exchange rate was dependent on what every other major country did, negotiation had to take place multilaterally—a display of cooperation never before tried, since each country faced very real domestic economic and political pressures. It was a genuinely collective victory and, although some were perhaps more victorious than others, the end result brought relief to the whole Western world.

The key to the understanding, made public on December 18, was the announcement that the Nixon administration would propose to Congress a devaluation of the dollar in terms of gold through a rise in the official price from $35 to $38 per fine ounce "as soon as the related set of short-term measures [with regard to trade with the EEC, Canada, and Japan] is available for Congressional scrutiny." The U.S. acceptance of dollar devaluation emerged from the meeting in the Azores, in mid-December, between President Nixon and President Pompidou of France. Earlier, the U.S. position had been that the role of gold in the international monetary system should gradually be reduced, if not eliminated, and that nothing should be done to enhance its position. Subsequently, it was said that no importance could be seen in an increase in a gold price at which the U.S. was not selling or would not sell. This interpretation, however, missed the significance of a move that might not only become a precedent but actually reaffirmed the position of gold as the anchor in the international monetary system.

While formally postponed until 1972, the 7.89% devaluation, entailing an 8.57% increase in the U.S. monetary gold price, immediately became the nucleus of currency realignments. Among the major currencies, the pound sterling and the French franc remained unchanged relative to gold; the South African rand was devalued against gold by more than the U.S. dollar; the Japanese yen, the German mark, the Dutch guilder, and the Belgian franc were, in effect, up-

Table II. How Currencies Fared in 1971

Country	In terms of gold % of devaluation(−) or upvaluation(+)	In terms of the U.S. dollar Currency units per U.S. dollar May 1	Dec. 31	% change
I. IMF members				
Unchanged against gold*				
France†	—	5.55419	5.11570	7.89
United Kingdom	—	0.416667	0.383772	7.89
Ireland	—	0.416667	0.383772	7.89
Spain	—	70.0000	64.4737	7.89
New Zealand	—	0.892857	0.822370	7.89
Australia	—	0.892857	0.822370	7.89
Devalued against gold‡				
South Africa	−14.00	0.714286	0.750000	−5.00
United States§	−8.57	1.0000	0.921052	−7.89
"Central" rate established‖				
Japan	+7.12	360.0	308.0	14.44
West Germany	+4.41	3.66	3.2225	11.95
Austria	+2.70	26.0	23.3	10.38
Belgium	+2.69	50.0000	44.8159	10.37
Luxembourg	+2.69	50.0000	44.8159	10.37
Netherlands	+2.68	3.6200	3.2447	10.37
Sweden	−1.01	5.17321	4.8129	6.96
Norway	−1.01	7.14286	6.64539	6.96
Italy	−1.01	625.0	581.5	6.96
Denmark	−1.04	7.50	6.98	6.93
Turkey	−1.33	15.0	14.0	6.67
Portugal	−2.91	28.75	27.25	5.22
Finland	−5.99	4.19997	4.10	2.38
Greece	−8.57	30.0	30.0	—
Mexico	−8.57	12.5	12.5	—
Kept unchanged against dollar or floating¶				
Canada	—	1.009082	1.002406	0.66
Brazil	—	5.11000	5.52486	−8.12
Argentina	—	4.056351	5.016278	−23.7
II. Other countries				
Switzerland♀	—	4.37282	3.84000	12.18
U.S.S.R.♂	—	0.900	0.829	7.89
China	—	2.000	1.8422	7.89

*Also: Barbados, Cyprus, Ethiopia, Gambia, Hong Kong, Iraq, Jamaica, Kuwait, Libya, Malawi, Malaysia, Morocco, Nigeria, Ruanda, Saudi Arabia, Sierra Leone, Singapore, Somalia, and Tunisia.
†Rates for franc zone countries, which maintained their value in terms of the French franc, are not shown separately.
‡Also: Bahamas, Botswana, Ghana, Kenya, Lesotho, Surinam, Swaziland, Tanzania, Uganda, Yugoslavia, and Zambia.
§Subject to congressional approval (see text).
‖Also: Burma, Dominican Republic, Guyana, Haiti, Honduras, Iceland, India, Israel, Jordan, Malta, Netherlands Antilles, Nicaragua, Panama, and Zaire.
¶Also: Chile, Costa Rica, Ecuador, Egypt, El Salvador, Indonesia, Iran, Korea, Lebanon, Liberia, Nepal, Pakistan, Paraguay, Peru, Philippines, Sudan, Syria, Thailand, and Yemen.
♀Switzerland, on May 10, raised the gold parity of the franc from 142.944 to 153.049 francs per fine ounce—equivalent to an upvaluation by 6.60%. In December 1971, it left the franc's gold parity unchanged but gave the franc a new middle rate of 3.84 francs per dollar, compared with 4.0841 francs per dollar on May 10.
♂Other Eastern European countries—Albania, Bulgaria, Czechoslovakia, East Germany, Hungary, Poland, and Romania—presumably followed the U.S.S.R. and left the nominal gold content of their currencies unchanged.

valued against gold; and the Italian lira and the Danish, Norwegian, and Swedish crowns were devalued slightly in terms of gold. The net result was that, relative to the dollar, the pound sterling and the French franc rose in value while other currencies were upvalued or devalued in varying degrees (*see* Table II).

The significance of these changes in the gold values of currencies was circumscribed in two ways. For one thing, the new monetary value of gold made no contact with the hard facts of gold supply-demand conditions and the price in the international market, which reached at year-end $43.63 per ounce. The discrepancy between the new $38 official price and the market price threatened to accentuate expectations of a further and more substantial rise in the official price in order to underpin fixed exchange rates, or else increased belief that a relapse into floating exchange rates was unavoidable. And, for another thing, the U.S. gave no indication that it would convert dollars into gold at the new price. In this sense, the meaning attached to the gold price rise was more limited than in the

"Take it off! Take it all off!"—Oliphant.

THE "DENVER POST" 1971 © THE LOS ANGELES TIMES SYNDICATE

1930s when the devalued dollar was made convertible into gold.

At the same time, however, the rise in the official dollar price of gold came to be regarded as the explicit abandonment of the thought to demonetize gold. Gold was retained as the measuring rod of currencies—a common yardstick and a common denominator. Other results were the rise in the dollar value of monetary gold stocks; an increase in the value of SDRs, which are defined in gold; and, for the upvaluing countries that keep gold in reserves, a reduction in the bookkeeping losses on dollar holdings.

The countries that did not upvalue or devalue their currencies against gold established new middle—or "central"—rates in terms of the dollar; these could be changed without formal permission from the IMF. The Canadian dollar continued to float, as did the currencies of Argentina, Brazil, and several other countries. The establishment of the central rates and the continued acceptance of a floating rate for the Canadian dollar were motivated by the need for more exchange-rate flexibility at a time of great uncertainty about the shape of international monetary relationships. For this reason, too, the permissible margins of fluctuation for exchange rates around the new central rates were widened to 2.25% on each side—a total spread of 4.5% against the dollar and possibly as much as 9% for any pair of nondollar currencies; the previous margin prescribed by the IMF was 1% on each side of the par value. The widening was expected to help counter unwanted flows of short-term funds; but it was circumscribed to prevent self-serving manipulation of exchange rates to improve the relative competitive positions among countries.

Greater flexibility in exchange rates among the key currencies than had, at times, been the case over the past quarter century became a practical necessity because of the immense difficulties for governments to make reliable judgments about the suitability, for trade and basic balance of payments positions, of exchange rates decisively influenced by short-term capital flows. For the longer run, greater flexibility was also required because of the differences in inflationary pressures, in the relative tolerance to inflation, and in the political and social conditions among the major countries. There was, however, greater awareness outside the U.S. than in the U.S. of the universal drawback of floating exchange rates: they weaken one of the last obstacles to continuing inflation.

Following the currency realignment the U.S. import surcharge was eliminated on December 20. The whole package was welcomed as a working compromise on bothersome issues that, it was widely feared, could have led to monetary disorder, protectionism, and recession. The U.S. came off with an effective devaluation of the dollar, variously estimated at 9–12% against the world mix of other currencies.

A realignment of exchange rates was only one element in dealing with international imbalance. It was not sufficient in itself. Its usefulness depended upon domestic economic and financial conditions and policies. It also depended on steps taken to avoid the disturbing effects of short-term capital movements. Furthermore, exchange-rate readjustments could have no direct influence on such noneconomic factors as the U.S. balance of payments like the military expenditures in West Germany and Japan. Last but not least, the U.S. pressed for removal of obstacles to trade, above all, the EEC barriers against U.S. farm products and Japanese restrictions against U.S. industrial

goods. It also was placed at a disadvantage by practices abroad like indirect tax refunds on exports and a maze of regulations on imports.

Perspectives on the Future of Gold. The dollar crisis also forced an unprepared world into a hurried examination of international monetary reforms. As evidenced in the Special Report *How Good Is the Dollar Now?* (*see* ECONOMY, WORLD: *Special Report*), the future of gold, SDRs, and the dollar as an international currency was envisaged by governments of the key industrial countries along sharply divergent lines (not to mention the less developed countries that sought to use SDRs as a vehicle for development assistance).

The varying perspectives from which the future was approached and the degree of heat that the debate generated seemed to have reflected changes in the recent past. The U.S. gold stock was eroded sharply while U.S. liabilities to governments and central banks abroad increased substantially. Conversely, the gold and dollar reserves of the rest of the world experienced a spectacular rise, especially those of West Germany and Japan.

A distinctive feature of gold developments in 1971 was the careful management of monetary gold stocks. No new gold was, in the aggregate, added during 1971 to official stocks, which remained at $41 billion. But, at the same time, gold moved in substantial amounts from South Africa, the U.K., and other countries to the IMF, and from the IMF and the U.S. to Japan and Western Europe (*see* Table III).

The international monetary institutions, which in

Exchange Rates

U.S. cents per unit of foreign currency

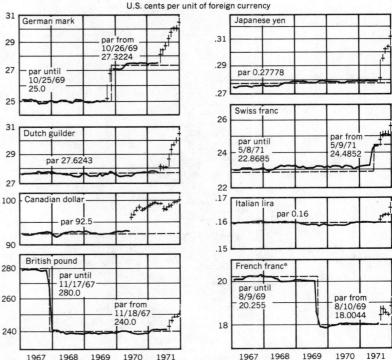

Note: Par values are shown by dashed lines. Exchange rates (monthly averages of daily rates) are shown by solid lines for periods when the central banks were intervening within the foreign exchange markets to hold fluctuations within prescribed limits; for the periods of floating, the rates are shown each month as:

High
Average
Low

*The rate shown from August 1971 is that for the "financial" franc.

Source: Board of Governors, U.S. Federal Reserve System.

1970 added $2.2 billion to their already large reserves, increased their stocks by $900 million during January–November 1971. Most of this gold came to the IMF from repayments by the U.K. and France on their drawings; repayments could not have been made in dollars because the IMF had reached the statutory limit for its dollar holdings. The U.K. used gold from its stock to repay the IMF, while France repaid with gold bought from the U.S. The U.S. Treasury also sold gold to Switzerland, Belgium, the Netherlands, and several other countries. But all gold acquired by Japan and West Germany and some of that added to reserves by other continental countries came from the IMF, which sold it against currencies required for its own operations.

Two conclusions emerged from the experience of 1971. For the most part, governments bought gold from the IMF rather than from the U.S. Treasury. At the same time, gold stocks increasingly acquired the character of a heavily defended "last ditch" reserve. In 1968 and 1969, France and West Germany managed to pass through periods of substantial drawings on their reserve assets while selling gold only as a very last resort. In mid-August 1971, the U.S. Treasury closed the gold window as its stock fell below $10 billion. For, on August 31, the U.S. had, against its stock of $10,209,000,000, gold liabilities totaling $544 million, of which $400 million represented gold sales by the IMF to the U.S. Treasury under a repurchase agreement and $144 million, gold deposited by the IMF with the Treasury to lessen the strain occasioned

in 1965 by Treasury sales to enable certain countries to pay gold subscriptions required by the increase in the Fund's quota for member countries.

The use of gold as the pivot for currency realignments and the efforts of governments to augment or protect gold stocks strongly suggested that phasing gold out of international monetary arrangements would be, at the very least, a delicate, difficult, and time-consuming process.

The varying perspectives from which the future of gold was approached and the degree of heat that the debate generated seemed to reflect changes in the recent past. In the U.S.—which in 1971 had 25% of the world's monetary gold stock, as compared with 71% in September 1949—it was frequently said that the role of gold should be reduced, if not eliminated, in any new monetary system. In Europe—as Karl Klasen, president of the Bundesbank, remarked in November 1971—in practice the monetary authorities were as attached to gold as ever.

The financial powers outside the U.S. saw decisive advantages in the continued use of gold. Gold—as distributed among the key countries in 1971 (see Table IV)—is an international monetary instrument independent of the financial conditions and policies, and the domestic politics, of any single nation. Furthermore, gold has an intrinsic value. Every convertible currency has a gold content, directly or indirectly. The IMF system is based on gold and the SDRs are linked to it. Moreover, gold remains unique in that it is universally acceptable at all times and under all circumstances as a means of payment of last resort.

It is true that gold could be replaced by SDRs if the major countries agreed upon it. But the SDR, which on Jan. 1, 1972, entered its third year of life, was still a tender plant. And behind SDRs is the IMF. "We have just experienced a worldwide flouting of its rules," noted West Germany's Klasen. "Can we be sure that the same thing will not happen some day to the code of good conduct which would have to be devised on the adoption of Special Drawing Rights as a general reserve medium?"

Governments in 1971 thus were not ready to strip gold of its monetary role. It remained by far the largest component of reserves in the principal countries of continental Europe, countries that tripled their stocks over the past 15 years to about $20 billion. SDRs fulfilled only a marginal role. Furthermore, many of the dollars on the books of foreign central banks would—once upvaluation had run its course—be reconverted into nondollar currencies or returned for placement in the Eurodollar market. The talk about the "overhang" of dollars in official hands all too often disregarded the fact that they were, in large part, dollars borrowed by private businesses and individuals and would have to be repaid.

Gold thus emerged from the 1971 monetary crisis with its position in the international monetary system challenged but not weakened. The question remained whether, at its new monetary price, gold could fulfill the function that was expected of it as still the most important single component of international monetary reserves of governments and central banks.

Thus, on the eve of 1972, the reordering of international monetary relationships seemed to depend largely on how the necessary balance of payments adjustments would work out after the new exchange-rate pattern had been established.   (M. A. K.)

See also Commercial Policies; Commodities, Primary; Investment, International; Prices; Trade, International.

Table III. Changes in Monetary Gold Stocks
In U.S. $000,000

Country	1969	1970	January–November 1971
United States	967	−787	−866
United Kingdom	−3	−122	−572*
South Africa	−128	−449	−223
France	−330	−15	−9
Italy	33	−69	−3
Switzerland	18	−90	177
Japan	57	119	147
Netherlands	23	67	102
West Germany	−460	−99	97
Belgium	−4	−50	94
Continental Europe and Japan	−688	−318	622*
All countries	185	−1,940	−955*
International institutions†	−85	2,220	880*
Total	100	280	−75*

*January-September 1971.
†International Monetary Fund, Bank for International Settlements, etc.

Table IV. Distribution of Monetary Gold Stocks

Country	September 1949 $000,000,000	September 1949 % of total	September 1971 $000,000,000	September 1971 % of total
United States	24.7*	70.9	10.2	24.8
United Kingdom	1.4*	4.1	0.8	1.9
West Germany	—	—	4.1	9.9
France	0.5	1.5	3.5	8.5
Switzerland	1.5	4.3	2.9	7.1
Italy	0.3	0.7	2.9	7.0
Netherlands	0.2	0.5	1.9	4.6
Belgium	0.7	2.1	1.6	3.8
Japan	—	—	0.7	1.6
Continental Europe and Japan	3.8	9.6	20.4	49.6
All countries	33.4	95.7	36.2	87.9
International institutions†	1.5	4.3	5.0	12.1
Total	34.9	100.0	41.2	100.0

*Includes a small amount of U.S. and Canadian dollars held in exchange equalization account.
†International Monetary Fund, Bank for International Settlements, etc.

Peace Movements

Both successes and failures marked 1971 for the various strands of the peace movement. While the number of U.S. soldiers directly engaged on the ground in Indochina decreased, peace leaders stressed that the geographic scope of the struggle had enlarged. They also asserted that the Nixon administration's vietnamization effort basically implied a continuation of the conflict and a "change in the colour of the corpses" from American to Asian. The U.S. Congress seemed more than ever responsive to arguments for military deescalation, but it was proving difficult to translate these sentiments into forceful legislative form.

While peace leaders welcomed Pres. Richard Nixon's plans to visit Peking and Moscow, they pointed to the relative absence of major agreements in international trade policies or in the strategic arms limitation talks (SALT). Further, the peace movement itself was only partially successful in seeking means to change its episodic influence upon public policies into more sustained, long-range influence and power. The public exposure given to the secret Pentagon papers (an extensive Defense Department account of the war in Vietnam) suggested to many that government policymakers had engaged in tacit and overt deception of the public in their prosecution of that conflict. The continued revelations of the My Lai trials and Pres. Nguyen Van Thieu's victory in a one-man election in South Vietnam were seen as mocking U.S. efforts to support self-determination and free, contested elections in that nation.

As a result of these and related developments, peace leaders witnessed the addition of new elements into the antiwar coalition. In particular, groups such as the activist Vietnam Veterans Against the War, business executives, and segments of the labour movement publicly joined with the traditional peace groups. Nevertheless, many members of the peace movement were badly divided over strategies; much of the working force remained relatively untouched; and the black population was still largely preoccupied with problems related to minority status and economic deprivation. Finally, the U.S. antiwar movement remained split between those who simply protested U.S. participation in Vietnam and mainline peace organizations, which were more inclusively pacifist in strategy and tactics.

In a notable display of unity, two major peace coalitions, the National Peace Action Coalition (NPAC) and the People's Coalition for Peace and Justice, organized a major series of antiwar activities during April and May, and again in the fall. Shifting from concentrated, one-day protests, leaders of the coalition sponsored two weeks of multitactical action after April 24, when mass marches protesting the war and conscription were held in Washington, D.C., and San Francisco. In the vanguard of these demonstrations, about a thousand Vietnam veterans set up an encampment on the Mall in Washington and for several days lobbied intensively for an immediate end to the war. Their spokesman, former Navy Lieut. (jg) John Kerry, testified forcefully before the Senate Foreign Relations Committee, and some of the veterans threw away their medals in an emotional ceremony at the Capitol.

The April 24 rally was held on the Capitol grounds before a crowd that authorities estimated at 200,000.

A demonstrator displays an antidraft sign during a march for peace in Washington, D.C., on April 24, 1971. An estimated 200,000 people participated in the Washington antiwar protests; another 156,000 demonstrators gathered in San Francisco.

Subsequently, the tactics switched to civil disobedience. On May 3, when the Mayday Tribe attempted to disrupt Washington traffic, police arrested an estimated 7,000 persons, many of whom were placed in temporary detention centres (including the Washington Redskins' practice field). Because usual arrest procedures had been suspended, charges against most of those arrested eventually were dismissed for lack of evidence. This raised civil rights questions that were still matters of controversy at year's end. The fall series of demonstrations began October 26 with a rally in Washington. Coalition leaders said it was the beginning of a year-long campaign, partially aimed at the defeat of President Nixon in 1972.

During the spring protests, a people's lobby met with congressmen and government officials to demand support for the People's Peace Treaty, an effort to end the war by negotiating a people-to-people settlement that would bypass formal governments. The treaty called on the U.S. to fix a definite date for the withdrawal of all military personnel from Vietnam, stipulated the abolition of the Thieu-Ky government of South Vietnam, urged a provisional coalition government to organize democratic elections, and provided for the release of all political prisoners.

Advocates of the People's Peace Treaty gained significant support, although some leaders of the peace movement viewed it as calling for settlement essentially on the terms of the National Liberation Front and thereby simply sustaining that organization's war goals. These spokesmen urged, instead, a peace without victory for either side.

After the series of mass demonstrations and protests peaked in the spring, peace leaders attempted with mixed success to devise additional tactics to dramatize the continuation of the war. One of their more successful efforts involved a four-day referendum in San Diego, Calif. Nearly 55,000 persons, including 10,-000 in the military, voted on whether or not the attack carrier "Constellation" should return to Vietnam duty. Over 45,000 voters, including about 38,000 civilians and over 7,000 military personnel, registered their opinions that the carrier should stay home.

Related efforts sought to tie in the war-peace issue with ecological perspectives. The Federation of American Scientists and environmentalists protested the "Cannikin" underground nuclear explosion on Amchitka Island, Alaska, designed to test an antiballistic missile warhead. The Dai Dong The Gioi (Community of Man) transnational project of the Fellowship of Reconciliation sponsored the signing of the Menton Statement by over 2,100 biologists from 23 countries, including Nobel laureates George Wald (U.S.) and Jacques Monod (France). The declaration demonstrated the relationships between environmental problems and the classic problems of war, poverty, and injustice. In the economic area, a diversified mutual fund, Pax World Fund, Inc., was founded to give investors the opportunity to support such socially useful, nonwar activities as housing, pollution control, education, and international development.

In a much-discussed episode, Daniel Ellsberg (*see* BIOGRAPHY) admitted giving copies of a 47-volume secret Pentagon study of the Vietnam conflict—which he had helped compile some years earlier—to the press for national exposure. After litigation, the Supreme Court denied a government attempt to stay publication of sections of the study. Ellsberg himself entered a plea of "not guilty" to federal charges of illegally possessing and copying the papers, and planned a broadly formulated political defense suggesting that the study revealed "high crimes by officials of our government." Pretrial hearings were scheduled to begin in early 1972. (*See* PUBLISHING.)

Perhaps the most significant development in 1971 was the marked growth of Common Cause, headed by former Cabinet member John W. Gardner. Attaining a membership of about 200,000 in its initial year, Common Cause utilized sophisticated lobbying techniques in seeking legislative majorities for its proposal for U.S. withdrawal from Vietnam on a scheduled timetable. In a significant turnabout from past voting patterns, 198 representatives (20 less than a majority) were recorded as favouring total U.S. withdrawal from Vietnam by June 1972, providing U.S. prisoners of war were released. In related issues, Common Cause could claim credit for accelerating the move to ratify the constitutional amendment giving 18-year-olds the

John Kerry, a spokesman for the Vietnam Veterans Against the War, testifies before the Senate Foreign Relations Committee in April 1971. Kerry made a moving plea to end the war in Southeast Asia.

Demonstrators, wearing hoods to symbolize the blindness of man in the face of the nuclear threat, participate in the Campaign for Nuclear Disarmament's 13th Easter Monday Rally in Trafalgar Square, London.

vote and the defeat of government support for the supersonic transport (SST).

SANE, representative of the moderate peace-oriented organizations, initiated a five-year program stressing education and organization aimed at the reordering of national priorities. It stressed the building of coalitions at the local level, and focused upon the cutting of excess fat from an allegedly swollen military establishment.

One of the more ambitious citizens' initiatives to stimulate negotiations to end the war involved a citizens' conference of 171 members which convened in Paris in March. Planned jointly by the Fellowship of Reconciliation, the American Friends Service Committee, and Clergy and Laymen Concerned About Vietnam, the group secured first-hand information concerning obstacles to agreement among the Paris peace negotiators. After discussions with each of the four delegations in Paris, the citizens' conference urged that the U.S. set a date for withdrawal, and declared that the Nixon administration's vietnamization program was not the primary road to peace.

The first instance of a Senate majority voting for withdrawal from Vietnam by a specified date occurred in June, when the Senate passed (61–38) the Mansfield amendment to a bill renewing the military draft. The amendment declared that it would be U.S. policy to withdraw all U.S. forces within nine months of enactment, and requested the president to announce such a date, contingent upon the release of prisoners. These provisions subsequently were watered down, but the controversy over the amendment delayed passage of the bill until after the old Selective Service Act had expired, so that for some weeks the country was actually without the draft. Subsequent attempts to effectively legislate withdrawal from Vietnam also failed, but Senator Mansfield announced that he would continue the effort in the 1972 session of Congress. Another Mansfield-sponsored measure calling for a reduction of U.S. forces in Europe met a similar fate. The defeat of the Proxmire-Mathias amendment, which envisaged a moderate cut in the defense budget, suggested the difficulty of embodying sentiments against excessive defense spending in concrete legislation.

The peace effort varied in its response to the emergency in East Pakistan following the outbreak of violent conflict and the outpouring of many millions of refugees from Bangla Desh into India. Some organizations stressed humanitarian relief and nonviolence while others underlined U.S. complicity in the situation through the supplying of arms. Many critics of administration policy called for strict U.S. neutrality during the Indo-Pakistani war in December, and condemned the administration's apparent favouritism toward Pakistan as evidenced in a statement accusing India of aggression. (*See* INDIA; PAKISTAN.)

Cautiously encouraged by indications of a strengthened détente in central Europe, peace spokesmen also attempted to formulate realistic proposals for a peaceful resolution of conflict in the Middle East. But the year also witnessed the virtual end of the Prague-based Christian Peace Conference as an effective instrument of East-West church interaction. Formed in 1958 by the late Josef L. Hromadka, a noted Czech churchman, the Conference had fallen increasingly under the domination of Orthodox members from the Soviet Union, especially after the Soviet military intervention in Prague in 1968.

In Japan many opposed efforts to stimulate the re-

'They are weapons of total war designed for mass destruction, and we must banish total war from the world, if civilisation is to...

armament of that nation by strengthening its Self-Defense Forces, protested increased Japanese corporate investment in Southeast Asia, and warned against the potential dangers of neocolonialist expansionism. In June over 10,000 young workers and students rallied in Tokyo to protest the plan whereby Okinawa would "revert" from the U.S. to Japan on the ground that it could allow U.S. troops, munitions, and nuclear bases to remain on the island. Chiefly, however, opposition to remilitarization seemed to be expressed more in local movements and groups than through the structures of the basic parties. (R. Hy.)

Peru

A republic on the west coast of South America, Peru is bounded by Ecuador, Colombia, Brazil, Bolivia, Chile, and the Pacific Ocean. Area: 496,-222 sq.mi. (1,285,215 sq.km.). Pop. (1971 est.): 14,014,600, including approximately 52% whites and mestizos and 46% Indians. Cap. and largest city: Lima (pop., 1971 est., 2,673,400). Language: Spanish; Indians speak Quechuan or Aymaran. Religion: Roman Catholic.

PERU

Education. (1968) Primary, pupils 2,334,982, teachers (including preprimary) 68,089; secondary, pupils 470,664, teachers 26,915; vocational, pupils 93,034, teachers 8,439; higher (1967), students 101,099, teaching staff 11,649.

Finance. Monetary unit: sol, with a free exchange rate (Sept. 27, 1971) of 62.50 soles to U.S. $1 (155 soles = £1 sterling). Gold, SDRs, and foreign exchange, central bank: (June 1971) U.S. $261.3 million; (June 1970) U.S. $339.5 million. Budget (1970 est.): revenue 42,715,000,000 soles; expenditure 44,-877,000,000 soles. Gross national product: (1969) 198,320,000,000 soles; (1968) 181,240,000,000 soles. Money supply: (June 1970) 31,090,000,000 soles; (June 1969) 21,180,000,000 soles. Cost of living (Lima and Callao; 1963 = 100): (April 1971) 217; (April 1970) 204.

Foreign Trade. (1970) Imports 23,323,000,000 soles; exports 40,389,000,000 soles. Import sources (1969): U.S. 31%; West Germany 11%; Argentina 10%; Japan 7%. Export destinations (1969): U.S. 35%; Japan 16%; West Germany 12%; Netherlands 8%; Belgium-Luxembourg 5%. Main exports: fish meal 28%; copper 25%; sugar 6%; iron ore 6%; silver 6%; cotton 5%.

Transport and Communications. Roads (1966) 45,549 km. Motor vehicles in use (1968): passenger c. 201,500; commercial (including buses) c. 122,500. Railways: (1967) 2,880 km.; traffic (1968) 249 million passenger-km., freight 591 million net ton-km. Air traffic (1969): 752,401,000 passenger-km.; freight 20,673,000 net ton-km. Shipping (1970): merchant vessels 100 gross tons and over 494; gross tonnage 377,812. Telephones (Jan. 1970) 192,604. Radio receivers (Dec. 1969) 1,815,000. Television receivers (Dec. 1969) 390,000.

Agriculture. Production (in 000; metric tons; 1970; 1969 in parentheses): rice 607 (444); corn c. 630 (580); wheat c. 150 (149); barley c. 180 (174); potatoes c. 1,900 (1,856); cassava (1969) 502, (1968) 399; dry beans c. 70 (c. 70); sugar, raw value (1970–71) c. 790, (1969–70) c. 792; citrus fruit c. 272 (358); coffee c. 57 (53); cotton lint c. 91 (88); fish catch (1969) 9,223, (1968) 10,520. Livestock (in 000; 1969–70): cattle c. 3,750; sheep c. 14,500; pigs c. 2,000; goats c. 3,860; horses c. 610; poultry c. 21,500.

Industry. Fuel and power (in 000; metric tons; 1969): coal c. 162; crude oil 3,555; electricity (kwhr.) 5,107,000. Production (in 000; metric tons; 1969): cement 1,132; iron ore (metal content) 5,477; pig iron 176; steel (1968) 84; lead 78; zinc 62; copper 34; tungsten concentrates (oxide content) 0.8; silver 1.07; gold (troy oz.) 92; fish meal 1,611.

President of the military government in 1971, Maj. Gen. Juan Velasco Alvarado.

In April 1971, after two and a half years in office, Peru's revolutionary military regime handed in its collective resignation to President Velasco to allow him a free hand in carrying out a Cabinet reshuffle. Up to this time the regime had maintained a cohesive policy, both in ministerial statements and in actual reforms introduced, with a marked tendency toward centralized control over the economy plus a significant social contribution. In the event, the reshuffle affected only three ministries: Industry and Commerce, Education, and Agriculture. The most significant change was the ousting of Jorge Dellepiane Ocampo, who had been responsible for the industrial law of July 1970.

The reshuffle did not seem to herald any major change in policy, since further reforms in the fishing, mining, and financial sectors were forthcoming afterward. More probable was a slowing down of the rate of change and consolidation of reforms already introduced. Thus, proposed changes in education and in commerce had yet to be released. Foreign participation in the petroleum sector was sanctioned, beginning in June when the government signed a 35-year contract authorizing the U.S. firm Occidental Petroleum to begin an oil exploration and operation program in the northeast jungle region. If commercial quantities of oil were discovered, total investment, including the laying of a pipeline, would be some $500 million. The contract assigned 50% of the oil produced to Petroperú (the state agency set up to operate the expropriated installations of the International Petroleum Co.) in lieu of royalty and tax payments, and guaranteed the availability of foreign exchange for the remittance of profits.

In the internal economy, the cost of living increase was once more held to about 8% per year, but there had been a change in budget policy away from tight controls after the 1969 and 1970 budget deficits were reduced to manageable proportions. To this end a biennial budget was introduced in 1971, to be closely linked to development projects and also to reduce administrative costs.

A medium-term development plan for the period 1971–75, published later in the year, included a basic industrialization program. One of the largest individual projects envisaged was the strengthening of the steel industry. The refineries of Petroperú were also to be expanded. Large investments were to be made to promote an increase in the supply of fish for human consumption, and specific benefits were granted under the general fishery law to encourage enterprises in this field.

During the period of the plan an annual increase in the gross domestic product of 7.5% was foreseen, and prices and productivity were expected to rise by 7.2% and 3.5% per year, respectively. Some 1.2 million new jobs were to be created, bringing total employment up to 4.2 million persons by 1975. Internal investment in industry and agriculture was set at 270 billion soles, and it was expected that external financing of some $1,816,000,000 would also be required.

In March a new state finance and development company, the Corporación Financiera de Desarrollo (Cofide), was set up to channel both public and private investment into development. Cofide would act as a holding company for the state in publicly owned enterprises and in private firms in which the state was involved; it would also engage in the setting up

Peruvian families wait to obtain land in the "new city" to be built south of Lima.

Pediatrics:
see Medicine

Penology:
see Prisons and Penology

of new companies and would place shares in public entities on the local and foreign securities markets. An initial capital of 15 billion soles was to be subscribed.

In the external sector, trade performance during 1971 fell below 1970, when a record export level of $1,048,000,000 was achieved. During the year production of minerals was hit by numerous mining strikes, and export revenues were also affected by declining commodity prices, especially for fish meal and copper. Furthermore, with imports increasing and with continued heavy servicing of foreign debt despite the rescheduling of recent years, Peru's balance of payments position deteriorated. In June an official mission led by the minister of economy and finance, Gen. Francisco Morales Bermúdez, visited Paris to discuss Peru's foreign debt with creditors comprising the six EEC countries, Spain, Finland, Japan, and the U.K. Peru had hoped to refinance the foreign debt falling due in 1972, 1973, and 1974, involving total repayments of $205 million, $223 million, and $183 million, respectively, but the request was turned down by the conference.   (J. J. SM.)

Philately and Numismatics

Philately. During 1971 the United Kingdom stamp market showed a marked slump in the prices of British commemorative issues for the years 1965–70 as a result of the unloading of speculative stocks in view of the imminent demonetization of all predecimal stamps. But the market in good classic issues stayed strong and prices advanced considerably, as indicated by the £58,034 realized by the London auction of the Joseph Silkin collection of British stamps. The only unsold lot in the auction was the specialized study of the Victorian £5 orange, which proved too big for sale in one lot. In New York, H. R. Harmer, Inc., completed the dispersal of the Dale-Lichtenstein collections, bringing the three-year series of auctions to an end with sales totaling just over $3 million. The same auctioneers handled the airmail collection of the late Henry M. Goodkind of New York, when a record realization of $31,000 was established for a mint copy of the U.S. 1918 24-cent air stamp with inverted centre.

Bangla Desh (East Pakistan) declared its inde-

pendence and in July issued a set of definitive stamps. Doubt existed as to the international status of the stamps in the absence of membership in the Universal Postal Union (UPU) on the part of Bangla Desh. However, India accepted the stamps as proper franking and passed letters into the international mail.

There were three major exhibitions in 1971. In May Japanese philatelists staged in Toyko their first international stamp exhibition, to mark the centenary of the first Japanese stamp. The open Grand Trophy was won by Tatsonosuke Koizumi and the Class of Honour Grand Trophy by Hiroyuki Kanai. An international exhibition was held in Cape Town, also in May, as part of the celebrations connected with the 10th anniversary of the Republic of South Africa. The International Grand Prix winner exhibited a Swiss collection under the nom de plume of "Helvetia." H. E. Levitt (U.S.) won the National Grand Prix for the best exhibit of South African stamps with his Cape of Good Hope collection. The third, and largest, exhibition took place in Budapest in September to mark the centenary of Hungary's first stamps. This time the Grand Prix International went to Rolf Rothmayr (Switzerland) for a Swiss collection. The Grand Prix National, awarded for the best exhibit of Hungarian stamps, was won by Gyula Madarasz of Hungary, and the Grand Prix d'Honneur for the best collection submitted by a previous Gold Medal winner (and, therefore, not eligible for the open class) was won by Michel Liphschutz (France) for his outstanding collection of Russian stamps. In the *hors concours* Court of Honour, the British Museum, for the first time, allowed a portion of the Tapling Collection (the early Hungarian issues) to be shown outside the museum.

At the meeting of the Fédération Internationale de Philatélie in Budapest, Lucien Berthelot (France), president of the FIP for 16 years, retired and was succeeded (unopposed) by the senior vice-president, Léon Putz (Luxembourg). In the ballot to fill the vice-presidential vacancy, Ladislav Dvoracek (Czechoslovakia) was the successful candidate.

The 1971 elections to the Roll of Distinguished Philatelists at the Norwich meetings of the Philatelic Congress of Great Britain were: John H. E. Gilbert (U.K.), Marcel C. Stanley (N.Z.), Jean J. Winkler (Switzerland), and Soichi Ichida (Japan), the last

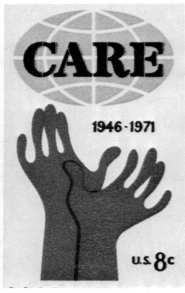

Left, U.S. stamp issued in 1971 recognizes the national problem of drug abuse. Centre, left, U.S. stamp marks the 25th anniversary of CARE. Centre, right, first stamp honouring the establishment of the U.S. Postal Service. Right, Leonardo da Vinci's "Madonna Litta" is represented on the Soviet 50-kopeck stamp.

KEYSTONE

Top, Portuguese coin honours navigator Vasco da Gama, discoverer of the sea route to India. Above, Egyptian coin commemorates Pres. Gamal Abd-an-Nasser.
A.N.A.

named being the first Japanese national to sign the Roll since 1921 when the late Umejiro Kimura was one of the inaugural signatories. The Philatelic Congress Medal for 1971 was awarded to Valmar McFarlane (N.Z.), the first non-U.K. resident to receive the award since its inception in 1959.

On August 2, the Apollo 15 astronauts, using an improvised post office established at Hadley Rille on the lunar rover, canceled a one-of-a-kind cover of the first day of issue of the United States "decade of space achievements" 8-cent twin stamps. The U.S. Postal Service entered the merchandising field, selling, among various items, starter kits for beginning stamp collectors. Post office lobbies began to display for sale full-coloured 30- by 40-in. stamp posters which portrayed enlargements of 35 historic stamps of the United States.

Major U.S. exhibitions included the National Postage Stamp Show in November in New York City and ANPHILEX '71 from November 26 to December 1, also in New York. The former featured displays by more than 100 dealers, who offered stamps and other philatelic equipment for sale. ANPHILEX '71 was an unusual invitation-only exhibit that displayed some of the world's rarest stamps, including the British Guiana one-penny magenta of 1856 that sold for $280,000 in 1970.   (K. F. C.; R. F. Mi.)

Numismatics. The major event of the year for coin collectors in the United States, and in many other countries, was the release of the Eisenhower-Apollo 11 dollar. This coin, the first metallic dollar issued by the U.S. since 1935, was made available in three forms: 0.400 fine silver clad proofs at $10; 0.400 fine silver clad regular strikes at $3; and copper-nickel clad (no silver) for circulation. The two premium-priced coins were available only from the U.S. Mint during 1971 but would be struck again with 1972 dates, as would those for regular circulation.

After having produced only 2,150,000 Kennedy half dollars in 1970, all for use in special "mint sets" for collectors, the Mint began striking them for circulation in 1971. However, those dated 1971 did not contain any silver, being composed of copper-nickel outer layers bonded to pure copper cores.

Other countries issued commemorative coins, including Austria (three: Chancellors Karl Renner and Julius Raab, and the 200th anniversary of the Vienna

stock exchange); Canada (silver and nickel dollars for the centennial of British Columbia's entry into the Confederation); Czechoslovakia (centennial birth of Lenin); East Germany (Wilhelm Conrad Röntgen, discoverer of X rays); Egypt (Gamal Abd-an-Nasser); Haiti (discovery by Columbus); Isle of Man (its first coinage since 1839 depicts a Manx cat); Israel (atomic theme for 23rd anniversary of independence); Italy (centennial of Rome as capital); Malaysia (dedication of Bank Negara Malaysia); Philippines (visit of Pope Paul VI); Portugal (500th anniversary of the birth of explorer Vasco da Gama); Ras al Khaimah (Dwight Eisenhower); Vatican City (eight coins, eighth year of reign of Pope Paul VI); West Germany (Konrad Adenauer); and Western Samoa (two: Capt. James Cook and the visit of Pope Paul VI).

Various organizations, most of them commercial, continued to issue medals in commemoration or observance of events and persons. Among the noteworthy subjects were Ludwig van Beethoven (two), Charles Dickens, Albert Einstein, Booker T. Washington, John Wesley, and the start of a series depicting scenes from Shakespeare's works. While these art works were offered mainly to numismatists, they also were available to the public.

Numismatic books, especially rare out-of-print works, were in strong demand. A dealer who specialized in numismatic book auctions listed a small 1809 edition of a book on Massachusetts paper money, and a 1962 reprint of it. The original realized $320 while the reprint brought only $3.75. Possibly the purchaser of the 1809 edition was more of a bibliophile than a numismatist.   (G. B. Sm.)

See also Postal Services.

Philippines

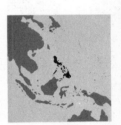

Situated in the western Pacific Ocean off the southeast coast of Asia, the Republic of the Philippines consists of an archipelago of about 7,100 islands. Area: 115,800 sq.mi. (300,000 sq.km.). Pop. (1970): 36,684,486. Capital: Quezon City (pop., 1970, 754,-452). Largest city: Manila (pop., 1970, 1,330,788). Language: Pilipino (based on Tagalog), English, Spanish, and many dialects. Religion (1960): Roman Catholic 84%; Aglipayan 5%; Muslim 5%; Protestant 3%. President in 1971, Ferdinand E. Marcos.

The knowledge that, in the midst of considerable unemployment and poverty, half the nation's wealth remained in the hands of 5% of the population served as a source of great irritation to young leftist intellectuals of the country in 1971. The prevailing belief that most politicians in the government were corrupt and were partly responsible for the imbalance of wealth led to a series of demonstrations by radical students and other dissenters.

A strike by Manila bus drivers in the early part of the year, protesting a price increase by the oil companies, was supported by university students, who gave vent to their antigovernment feelings. In the demonstrations, which lasted several days, students barricaded roads and fought police with homemade bombs. A note found near a U.S.-owned oil company office read, "This is the anger of the Filipino people against American imperialism."

A grenade attack on a political rally in Manila on August 21 killed 10 persons and wounded almost 100, including the 8 opposition Liberal Party senatorial

Petroleum Industry: *see* Fuel and Power; Industrial Review

Top, a wounded man lies amid debris shattered by terrorist grenades during a political rally of the opposition Liberal Party in Manila, Aug. 21, 1971. Above, Ramon D. Bagatsing, recuperating from wounds suffered at the August 21 rally, was elected mayor of Manila in November 1971.

candidates. President Marcos blamed the violence on Communists, saying it was part of a plan to mount an insurrection. He thereupon suspended the right of habeas corpus "for persons presently detained or those who might be detained for the crimes of insurrection or rebellion." On August 24 Marcos vowed to "impose martial law if necessary" to "liquidate the Communist apparatus." He accused Sen. Benigno Aquino, Jr., secretary-general of the Liberal Party and a possible contender for the presidency in the 1973 elections, of aiding the Communist subversives by providing them with guns and ammunition and other support. He said that Aquino had been linked with Communist groups since 1965. The senator, denying the statement, challenged the government to file specific charges against him and try him in court.

On September 13 about 15,000 demonstrators marched through Manila demanding the immediate restoration of the right of habeas corpus and the release of political prisoners, who included a college president, a political commentator, and several youth leaders. Marcos restored the right of habeas corpus in some areas of the country on September 19, saying that "the condition of Communist insurgency and subversion has now substantially eased" in those areas. It remained suspended in the Manila area, the centre of political and social dissent, and also in parts of Luzon and Mindanao islands.

Mindanao was the scene during the year of bitter fighting between armed bands of Christians and Muslims. The hostilities originated from land disputes that had arisen more than 50 years earlier as a result of resentment and resistance by the Muslims to the influx of Christian settlers from the north. Besides land disputes, the situation was complicated by a Muslim secessionist movement, spearheaded by a militant armed group rumoured to have 300 members. An intensification of the violence in mid-1971, particularly in Lanao Province, could be attributed partly to the approach of the November 8 elections, in which a Muslim and a Roman Catholic were campaigning against each other for governor.

In a September 25 meeting with President Marcos, after witnessing two months of fighting in the province during which 200 people lost their lives, both candidates agreed to withdraw from the race. Throughout

the island, more than 100,000 people lost their homes and over 1,000 were killed during the year as a result of the feuds.

The elections were bloody throughout the nation. On election day, 51 persons were killed. The balloting for the Senate, through which President Marcos called on Filipinos to give his six-year-old government a vote of confidence, gave the opposition Liberal Party six of the eight contested seats. In local elections for provincial and city offices, the administration's Nacionalista Party won two-thirds of the posts, but the senatorial race appeared to be the key indicator of the people's feelings toward Marcos. Immediately after the election, the president invited opposition leaders to participate in the policy- and decision-making arms of the government. He asked critics of his policies to join him in discarding the "feeling of arrogance of infallibility."

The Tasaday, a tribe living in a Stone Age culture and isolated from the rest of the world for at least 400 and possibly 2,000 years, was discovered in June. The members of the tribe, who numbered about 100, lived in a rain forest in Mindanao. They claimed to have no single leader, and matters of mutual concern were discussed in open meeting. They had never heard of fighting and had known no unfriendly people. The Philippine government was asked to set aside the Tasaday's forest as a preserve, out-of-bounds to interlopers. (RA. PA.)

PHILIPPINES

Education. (1967–68) Primary, pupils 6,407,268, teachers 210,450; secondary and vocational, pupils 1,365,889, teachers 40,995; higher (including 34 universities), students 599,658, teaching staff 21,740.

Finance. Monetary unit: peso, with an official rate of 3.90 pesos to U.S. $1 (9.36 pesos = £1 sterling) and a free rate (Sept. 27, 1971) of 6.54 pesos to U.S. $1 (16.22 pesos = £1 sterling). Gold, SDRs, and foreign exchange, central bank: (June 1971) U.S. $299 million; (June 1970) U.S. $196 million. Budget (1969–70 est.): revenue 3,502,000,000 pesos; expenditure 3,197,-000,000 pesos. Gross national product: (1969) 32,-044,000,000 pesos; (1968) 29,459,000,000 pesos. Money supply: (May 1971) 4,826,000,000 pesos; (May 1970) 4,087,000,000 pesos. Cost of living (Manila; 1963 = 100): (June 1971) 171; (June 1970) 146.

Foreign Trade. (1970) Imports 9,078,000,000 pesos; exports 6,233,000,000 pesos. Import sources (1969): Japan 29%; U.S. 29%; West Germany 7%; Australia 5%. Export destinations (1969): Japan 41%; U.S. 39%. Main exports: timber 24%; coconut products 20%; sugar 17%; hemp 6%.

Transport and Communications. Roads (1970) 75,714 km. Motor vehicles in use (1969): passenger 272,200; commercial (including buses) 207,600. Railways (1969): 1,144 km.; traffic 584 million passenger-km., freight 115 million net ton-km. Air traffic (1970): 1,769,000,000 passenger-km.; freight 33,290,000 net ton-km. Shipping (1970): merchant vessels 100 gross tons and over 313; gross tonnage 946,400. Telephones (Jan. 1970) 293,543. Radio receivers (Dec. 1968) 1,633,000. Television receivers (Dec. 1969) c. 350,000.

Agriculture. Production (in 000; metric tons; 1970; 1969 in parentheses): rice 5,343 (5,233); corn 2,005 (2,008); sweet potatoes (1969) 706, (1968) 706; cassava (1969) 506, (1968) 487; copra c. 1,350 (1,255); sugar, raw value (1970–71) 2,268, (1969–70) 1,926; coffee 49 (44); bananas (1969) c. 760, (1968) 747; abaca (1969) 65, (1968) 67; tobacco 61 (57); rubber 20 (18); pork c. 200 (c. 200); timber (cu.m.; 1969) 12,000, (1968) 11,400; fish catch (1969) 978, (1968) 945. Livestock (in 000; March 1970): cattle c. 1,650; buffalo c. 4,430; pigs 6,446; goats c. 700; horses 295; chickens c. 65,000.

Industry. Production (in 000; metric tons; 1969): coal 59; iron ore (metal content) 991; chrome ore (oxide content) 168; manganese ore (metal content) 6.4; copper concentrates (metal content) 131; gold (troy oz.) 571; silver (troy oz.) 1,562; cement (1970) 2,445; electricity (excluding most industrial production; kw-hr.) 6,312,000.

Philosophy

The philosophical works published in 1971 did not indicate new trends or new interests. They gave evidence of the extension of international communication among philosophers and a growing ecumenism in philosophy.

An important movement of recent years in religious thought, the growing acceptance of the metaphysics of "becoming," was recorded in essays by Protestant, Jewish, and Catholic philosophers and theologians in *Process Philosophy and Christian Thought,* edited by Delwin Brown, Ralph James, Jr., and Gene Reeves. *Mysticism,* a volume based on papers read at the Abo Symposium on Mysticism, was edited in Stockholm by S. S. Hartman and Carl-Martin Edsman.

Essays setting forth the evolutionary naturalism and critical realism of U.S. realist Roy Wood Sellars were edited by W. Preston Warren in *Principles of Emergent Realism.* In a small volume, *Problems of Mind,* Norman Malcolm critically analyzed typical concepts of the mind as an introduction to the study of Ludwig Wittgenstein's views on the nature of mind. *Materialism and Sensations* by James Cornman concluded that it is plausible that sensations are reducible to brain processes only when they are regarded as having no objective or phenomenal properties.

The distinguished U.S. philosopher Horace M. Kallen presented a volume of intimate essays entitled *What I Believe and Why—Maybe.* In *Freedom of Mind and Other Essays,* Oxford philosopher Stuart Hampshire dealt with the confusion of reconciling explanations of our own mental states with our explanations of the mental states of others. *Logic and Art,* edited by Richard Rudner and Israel Scheffler, honoured U.S. philosopher Nelson Goodman.

Die Philosophie Carnaps by Lothar Krauth, published in Vienna, was one of the first treatments of Rudolf Carnap's work since his death in 1970. *Studies in Inductive Logic and Probability,* vol. i, edited by Carnap and Richard C. Jeffrey, included Carnap's last projected work. Gottlob Frege's influential treatises *On the Foundations of Geometry* and *Formal Theories of Arithmetic* were published in an English translation by Eike-Henner W. Kluge. Georg Henrik von Wright, treating the problem of explanation both historically and analytically in *Explanation and Understanding,* held that it cannot be reduced to simple causality. Bernhard Bolzano's *Logic and Scientific Method* was published in English for the first time in a translation by Rolf A. George. *Criticism and the Growth of Knowledge,* edited by Imre Lakatos and Alan Musgrave, was a series of essays debating the views of Thomas S. Kuhn of Princeton and Karl Popper of London with a concern for the fundamental values of science. *Problems of the Logic of Scientific Knowledge,* edited by P. V. Tavanec, was the first English translation of major Russian studies in the philosophy of science. Essays read at the Salzburg Colloquium on the Philosophy of Science were edited by Paul Weingartner and Gerhard Zecha as *Induction, Physics and Ethics.*

Of special interest among scholarly works was the publication in facsimile, with English translation, of an early version of Wittgenstein's *Tractatus Logico-Philosophicus,* a manuscript discovered in 1965 in Vienna by G. H. von Wright. English translations of the second and third volumes of Karl Jaspers' *Philos-*

ophy by E. B. Ashton, Jaspers' *Philosophy of Existence* by Richard F. Grabau, and Gregor Malantschuk's *Kierkegaard's Thought* by Howard W. Hong and Edna H. Hong were published. The Deutsche Akademie der Wissenschaften of Berlin brought out the eighth volume of the *Complete Writings and Letters* of G. W. Leibniz.

In *History, Man, and Reason,* Maurice Mandelbaum traced mainstreams in the development of 19th-century thought. *Selected Writings of Hermann von Helmholtz,* edited by Russell Kahl, exhibited the large influence of Helmholtz on 19th-century scientific thought. *Hegel and the Philosophy of Religion,* edited by Darrell E. Christensen, comprised papers written in celebration of the bicentennial of Hegel's birth; *New Studies in Hegel's Philosophy* was a collection of papers edited by Warren E. Steinkraus.

(S. M. Mc.)

ENCYCLOPÆDIA BRITANNICA FILMS. *The Medieval Mind* (1969); *Spirit of the Renaissance* (1971).

Photography

Despite worldwide trade difficulties, Germany and Japan, the two leading countries in the production of photographic goods, reported favourable results in 1971.

The Japanese domestic market remained strong, although the export situation did not satisfy manufacturers. Japan reported a 25.4% increase in the value of overall camera production to a total $359 million—a growth of $73 million over the previous year. Unit production of still cameras increased 20.5% (up one million), while value increased by 24.7% to $248 million, or 41.6% of the total value of production of still and movie equipment ($596 million). The camera type showing the highest growth rate was the 35 mm. with interlens shutter, unit production of which increased 39.4% over 1970 to 2,639,031. This was almost one

This profile of a steelworker is one of the studies of man presented by W. Eugene Smith in his photographic essay "Let Truth Be the Prejudice," exhibited by the Jewish Museum in New York City from Feb. 3 to April 4, 1971.

W. EUGENE SMITH FROM AUTHENTICATED NEWS INTERNATIONAL

million more than that of its nearest rival, the 35-mm. single-lens reflex (SLR) with focal-plane shutter.

The next highest growth sector was in 126 cartridge-loading cameras, with unit production up 34.1%. Somewhat unexpectedly, unit production of the 16-mm. subminiature camera also rose, and its value increase of 59.7% was the largest of any camera sector. Unit production of the twin-lens reflex camera increased 22.4%, although the total of 131,799 was small in comparison with other types. The total number of cameras of all types manufactured in Japan was 5,-824,253. Of these, 2,845,755, valued at $129 million, were exported, representing a 9.9% growth in export value over 1970. The strongest export items in value were the 35-mm. camera with interlens shutter, accounting for $34,221,200, and the 35-mm. SLR with focal-plane shutter, accounting for $76,436,500.

Unit production of motion-picture cameras decreased to 91% of the previous year's figure, although a small value increase of 2.1% was achieved in exports. In the 8-mm. field, where unit production rose a modest 3.1%, a 12% increase in value reflected the trend toward production of high-priced cameras of the Super 8 type. Production of 8-mm. projectors, however, rose by 23% in volume and 32.4% in value, with exports keeping pace. Unit production of lenses for motion-picture cameras rose 40% and value increased 71%, explained by the incorporation of Japanese lenses in U.S. and European equipment. The export of motion-picture lenses virtually doubled in both volume and value, with the latter exceeding $1 million.

Another growth sector was in lenses for still projectors and interchangeable lenses for still cameras: 1,326,266 units of the former were valued at $3.7 million and 2,002,752 of the latter at $36.9 million. The Japanese had achieved a virtual monopoly of lenses with interchangeable adapters to fit various camera bodies; no other nation was able to produce them at comparably low prices. Also of interest was the $10 million export value of electronic flash equipment.

In West Germany international exchange problems and the tighter money situation in the U.S. (Germany's biggest export market for photographic goods) caused difficulties. Overall turnover of the photographic industry was DM. 2,136,000,000, with exports accounting for DM. 1,215,000,000, or 57%.

Carl Zeiss reported an overall increase in turnover of 14% to a value of DM. 293 million. Domestic sales grew more strongly (18%) than exports (11%). Despite rising costs, orders for 1972 were reported to be running 15% higher than a year earlier. However, Zeiss Ikon AG reported a loss of DM. 9.9 million at its annual general meeting in June. This resulted in a change of production policy; photographic products were to be restricted eventually to the higher-priced lines, thus providing spare manufacturing capacity for nonphotographic products.

This decision by Zeiss Ikon made an interesting comparison with Rollei, whose 1971 turnover was expected to be approximately DM. 100 million. Capital investment was increased from DM. 12 million to DM. 18 million as a result of investment by the Norddeutsche Landesbank, which held 63% of the stock, and co-managing director Horst Franke, who held 31%. The previous year's investment in manufacturing plant in Singapore, aimed at lowering labour costs, had allowed an over-the-counter price decrease of 15% for many items.

Agfa-Gevaert reported an overall growth rate of 16.1%; exports, up 17.5%, accounted for 67.1% of total sales. Gross profits were listed at DM. 746.8 million and net profits at DM. 46.6 million.

The biggest international exhibition of the year was the Photo Expo 71 held in Chicago, which attracted 79,500 visitors. The Inter-camera exhibition in Prague, Czech., provided a useful shopwindow for Eastern European countries. A few novelties were shown at both fairs, particularly the former, but the great majority of exhibits had already appeared at the 1970 Photokina in Cologne, W.Ger. Other fairs were the Kinophototechnik at Moscow, Photoexpo Zürich, and the (West) German Industrial Exposition at São Paulo, Braz.

Processes and Equipment. Kodak introduced a new Super 8 film with a speed of ASA 160. This type A film (balanced for artificial light) allowed motion-picture photography at light levels as low as seven footcandles. This was a considerable speed increase compared with previous ASA 40 or 25 types. Agfa introduced a completely new type of material in Agfacontour, a film that produced a line along areas of strong tone change. Repeated copying onto this material could result in a multiplicity of lines that could be used for pictorial effect. Indeed, Agfacontour was able to produce abstract-type results previously obtainable only with the so-called solarization process (more ac-

This photograph by Euan Duff appears in "How We Are," a book of photographs published by Penguin Press in 1971. The photograph was exhibited in the Institute of Contemporary Arts in London during October 1971.

curately, utilization of the Sabatier effect to achieve Mackie lines). The great advantage of the new material was the repeatability of the process. However, its chief value lay in technical and scientific fields, and it was for this that Agfa received the International Interkamera Medal for Technical Progress.

The 3M Co., which had recently absorbed Ferrania, introduced an excellent masked negative film that provided far better results in practice than the company's previous material; however, this development passed almost unnoticed because of the company's policy of selling film mainly to other distributors who then marketed it under their own brand names. Kodak tidied its range of photographic printing paper by more equal contrast spacing between grades at the lower contrast end. The company also made some improvements toward more uniform emulsion speeds over various grades. The latest Agfa colour printing paper, MCN 111, for use with masked colour negatives, was capable of producing prints of high quality.

Edith Weyde, whose early work on diffusion transfer led to the Agfa-Gevaert Copyrapid system, revealed at Photo Expo 71 a new form of "vesicular" or bubble-generating image formation incorporating silver halides. Minute quantities of developed silver acted as an image-intensifying catalyst, thus providing a high emulsion speed with minimum silver content. For example, sufficient silver to produce an emulsion speed of ASA 4 with conventional chemistry was said to provide ASA 40 with the new process. The economy achieved was obvious, especially in view of continually rising silver prices. Claims of quick processing, obviating fixation and washing stages, also were made.

The introduction in 1970 of the Magicube, a flashcube fired mechanically instead of by electricity, had resulted in widespread manufacturing plans for 126-type cameras, especially in Japan. Minolta, Ricoh, Konishiroku, Fuji, and Sedic all were negotiating terms with Kodak, and some cameras had been produced. The 126 with conventional flashcube was to be generally discontinued in favour of the X-type. Meanwhile, General Electric's Hi-Power Cube (a development of the electrically ignited cube, giving twice the normal output) was receiving comparatively little attention, although a new range of Polaroid cameras, the 400 series, incorporated them. An unusual system of flash control was used, in which the flashgun had adjustable louvres in a shield that altered transmitted light to suit the distance.

Multicoated lenses were beginning to appear on the market. The latest range from Asahi had seven coatings, and high claims were made for the reduction in internal reflection. Nippon Kogako, in conjunction with the Japanese National Geography Department, produced a marine camera capable of working at a depth of 200 m. The camera body was separate from the control unit and was housed in the columnar pressure-resistant cover. The lens was designed to compensate for the difference in the refractive index between water and air.

Tungsten halogen lamps were introduced, especially for enlarger illumination. In ordinary incandescent lamps, tungsten evaporates from the filament and is deposited on the glass, causing blackening, which reduces light emission, and increasing the filament resistance, which also reduces light and causes a drop in colour temperature. In halogen lamps the evaporated tungsten combines with iodine to form a compound that does not deposit on the hot lamp envelope and is decomposed by the filament, redepositing tungsten and

An exhibit dealing with "The Concerns of Roman Vishniac: Man, Nature and Science" included Vishniac's depiction of life in the Jewish ghettos of Eastern Europe before World War II. The exhibit was displayed in the Jewish Museum from Oct. 20, 1971, through Jan. 2, 1972.

releasing the iodine for recycling. The constant light output and lack of colour change made these lamps particularly valuable for colour printing work.

An electrostatic colour processor, the 3M Color-in-Color, was capable of making colour separations, prints, and transparencies with correct or substituted colours. Also, colour could be applied to transfer paper for subsequent application to such surfaces as leather, plastic, or wood. The machine was operated in a fashion similar to a conventional copier, with the original face down. On pressing a button, the machine took three exposures, one for each primary colour, via optical filters, and in each case a monochrome print was produced. These prints were on yellow-, cyan-, and magenta-backed material. The colour side transferred a dry powder to the final print, the result being a three-colour print that emerged from the machine in the same way that a normal black-and-white print was produced from an ordinary copier. The three monochrome prints could be used as offset separations by colour printers, with the colour print serving as a proof. Colours could be changed or altered at will, derivative prints could be obtained directly, and the results could be observed without delay. Copies were made precisely 1:1, and the machine accepted sizes up to $11 \times 8\frac{1}{2}$ in.; larger originals had to be copied in sections.

Scientific Developments. Photography was being used to an increasing extent as a scientific and industrial tool. Interference holography was demonstrated in 1971 by Britain's National Physical Laboratory as a tool for nondestructive testing. For example, a metal object was recorded as a hologram and, after processing, the plate was replaced so that the object coincided with its holographic image. Any distortion of the object, such as might be caused by temperature rise, produced a pattern of interference fringes, and analysis of these fringes could disclose structural flaws. Contour intervals were about one half the wavelength of light, or about 0.32 μm. An allied technique used two beams of coherent light intersecting at an angle to form a fringe pattern. A single exposure could record time-averaged fringes or patterns produced by vibration of the object. It was frequently convenient to attach the photosensitive material onto the object, or even to coat the object with suitable emulsion.

Interesting work carried out under the aegis of the National Physical Laboratory in the assessment of photographic image quality confirmed that Weber's law for psychophysical quality judgments could be applied in this context to subjective interpretation. In other words, the scale of perceived response was in logarithmic proportion to the stimulus scale.

Exhibitions and Competitions. A definite trend toward the reportage style was noticeable in the major exhibitions of the year, such as that of the London Salon and the Autumn Pictorial of the Royal Photographic Society. While traditional pictorial work, with a full tone gradation and pleasantly placed subject matter, was still strongly represented, there was a drift toward the "slice of life" type of photo in which a scene was supposedly recorded without any attempt at selective bias or interpretation by the photographer. Frequently, high contrast and deliberately contrived grains were used to enhance the quality.

The prophecy that in the 1970s colour would become more popular than monochrome in photographic exhibition work had not yet been fulfilled, and while the ordinary amateur photographer took more colour print snaps than in any previous year, the dedicated exhibitor still worked mainly in monochrome. In photographic competitions, where the rules allowed, colour transparencies outnumbered colour prints by several hundred to one, while the high-quality self-processed colour print was extremely rare. Despite the wide popularity of photographic contests, the vast majority of entries were photographs taken for other reasons, not specifically made for the competition. Technical quality in colour pictures continued to rise, however, while monochrome appeared to have reached a plateau where little change seemed likely. (N. MA.)

See also Motion Pictures.

The National Accelerator Laboratory near Batavia, Ill., was placed in operation in June 1971. Below, the main accelerator is 4 mi: in circumference and 1.24 mi. in diameter. Below, right, the linear accelerator, stretching approximately 500 ft., was designed to accelerate protons received from the Cockcroft-Walton preaccelerator to an energy level of 200 MeV.

Physics

High-Energy Physics. Many theoretical physicists in the last few years have predicted the stability of elements with an atomic number Z of 114 or thereabouts (*Phys. Lett.*, 21:688, 1966; 22:500, 1966; 26:184, 1968). The heaviest known element that is not man-made is uranium with $Z = 92$; nuclear physicists have manufactured heavier elements with atomic numbers up to 105 by high-energy bombardment from linear accelerators. Further progress with this conventional technique is much hindered by the very small half-lives of the resulting atomic nuclei with Z just greater than 105. In this connection, much controversy was generated by the claim of a British team of investigators (*Nature*, 229:464, 1971) that they had produced a superheavy element with atomic number 112 by a different technique.

The British workers bombarded a tungsten target with very high-energy protons, imparting to some tungsten nuclei sufficient energy to overcome the coulomb repulsion of neighbouring tungsten nuclei and to coalesce with them. The investigators claimed that the resulting nucleus then decays to a more stable man-made element 112, producing some other much smaller atomic fragments as well. Chemical separation of the treated target indicates that the resulting element is a homologue of mercury, and observation of both its alpha-particle emission and its spontaneous fission indicates a Z greater than 92; these conditions would be satisfied if the element indeed had an atomic number of 112.

Many theorists argued against the interpretation of the British experimenters, some critics (*Nature-Physical Science*, 232:77, 1971), for example, holding that the effects reported could not have arisen from recoil tungsten nuclei irradiated by high-energy protons because the collision cross-sections involved are too small. The latter theoretical objections were countered (*Nature-Physical Science*, 232:78, 1971) by the observation that they are in conflict with other experimental evidence and thus should be treated with caution.

Investigators planned to use more recently available heavy-ion linear accelerations in an attempt to produce a man-made element with $Z = 114$ by the older, more conventional technique. Theoretically, the stability of this element should ease the problems of chemical and physical analysis.

Gravity Waves. Einstein's theory predicting the existence of waves in gravitational fields was both contested and supported by work reported during the year. Following the reported detection of gravity waves (*Phys. Rev. Lett.*, 22:1320, 1969), workers in Dublin, Ire., and Cambridge, Eng., searched for the radio pulses from deep space that should be produced

COURTESY, NATIONAL ACCELERATOR LABORATORY

simultaneously with the units of gravitational energy (gravitons). Their searches had been unsuccessful so far (*Nature, 228:346, 1970*); however, very close observations with the Mariner 6 and Mariner 7 spacecraft indicate fluctuations in radio-wave motion of the order of a few centimetres that could be attributed to gravitons (*Nature, 229:547, 1971*).

Lasers. Recent laser developments have consisted of small advances and of a search for applications rather than the emergence of any major innovations. Research continued into producing a continuous wave (CW) laser tunable over the visible region of the spectrum. A CW laser using the dye rhodamine 6G mixed with soapy water was reported (*Appl. Phys. Lett., 17:245, 1970*); the same investigators succeeded in making the dye laser tunable over a band of wavelengths of light ranging from 5500 to 6500 Å (*Physics Today*, January 1971). Applications in high-sensitivity spectroscopy abound; for example, a tunable semiconductor laser was used for detecting atmospheric pollutants (*Science, 171:635, 1971*) by measuring the selective absorption of infrared radiation.

Work on hydrogen lasers brought the realization of an X-ray laser a little nearer. Eighteen spectral lines were reported between 1520 and 1615 Å from a hydrogen laser (*Phys. Rev. Lett., 25:494, 1970*); this was the shortest wavelength of laser light so far reported and indeed begins to approach the soft X-ray region of the electromagnetic spectrum.

Isotope separation, normally achieved by electric or magnetic techniques for charged ions or by diffusion for uncharged atoms, is another possible laser application. It has been hypothesized that the force imposed on an atom by light waves reaches a peak at a characteristic resonance wavelength for each element or isotope (*Phys. Rev. Lett., 25:1321, 1970*). If this is so, tuning the wavelength of laser light impinging on a stream of different kinds of atoms should result in sorting the atoms of each isotope into their own unique trajectories, thus separating one kind from another. Although this hypothesis remained to be tested, experimental success was achieved by chemical separation from selective laser excitation (*Appl. Phys. Lett., 17:516, 1970*). A mixture of equal parts of methanol (H_3COH) and deuteromethanol (D_3COH) was exposed to a high-power hydrogen fluoride laser. The methanol was selectively excited to react with bromine, probably forming hydrogen bromide and formaldehyde. The deuteromethanol was unaffected and hence could be separated; less than 5% methanol was found in the final product.

Amorphous Water ("Polywater"). Much doubt was cast during the year on the announcement (*Proc. Acad. Sci. U.S.S.R. Phys. Chem., 165:807, 1965*) of the discovery of so-called anomalous water. Some reports (*Nature, 226:1033, 1970*, and *Nature-Physical Science, 229:21, 1971*) indicated that it is a gel or solution of silicates that appears in fine glass tubes as the result of chemical contamination from the capillary walls. Electron spectroscopy measurements (*Science, 171:167, 1971*) show that the "polywater" contains high concentrations of sodium, potassium, sulfate, chloride, nitrate, borate, silicate, and carbon-oxygen compounds, but has very little actual water. Infrared measurements (*Science, 171:170, 1971*) are even more definite, showing that "polywater" has a spectrum reasonably similar to that of sodium lactate, or human sweat, suggesting that the substance is a case

of contamination on a grand scale. Some of these findings were challenged by Soviet investigators (*Nature-Physical Science, 232:131, 1971*), who suggested that evidence of contamination results from faulty preparation technique; they pointed out that "polywater" can be prepared only by condensation of the vapour and can be distilled only up to 500° C. The general consensus, however, seemed to be that "polywater" indeed is nothing but the result of minute samples of water becoming contaminated during condensation within capillary tubes.

General. A most surprising speculative hypothesis was the suggestion that Planck's constant (h), the basic scaling factor in quantum theory, may not be so constant, but will vary throughout the universe (*Nature, 228:845, 1970*). If this were so, photons (quanta of light) from a galaxy other than earth's (with a different and unknown value of h) would mislead astronomers about the nature of the space through which they had traveled.

The idea that the proton is one of the fundamental building blocks of matter seems untenable since inelastic scattering of high-energy electrons from them indicates that protons are made up of point constituents. Theoretical arguments have been raging about these constituents; *e.g.*, as to whether they are partons, stratons, or quarks (*Physics Today*, February 1971).

Thus far only liquid helium 4 has been found to show the property of superfluidity, a manifestation of quantum effects in bulk material. It was proposed (*Phys. Rev. Lett., 25:1543, 1970*) that some solid insulating substances will show similar properties, although on a much smaller scale. The prediction should stimulate efforts to update theories of superfluidity and to improve the sensitivity of experiments designed to observe the phenomenon.

(S. B. P.)

See also **Astronautics; Astronomy; Chemistry.**

Poland

A people's republic of Eastern Europe, Poland is bordered by the Baltic Sea, the U.S.S.R., Czechoslovakia, and East Germany. Area: 120,725 sq.mi. (312,677 sq.km.). Pop. (1970): 32,589,000. Cap. and largest city: Warsaw (pop., 1970, 1,308,000). Language: Polish. Religion: predominantly Roman Catholic. First secretary of the Polish United Workers' (Communist) Party in 1971, Edward Gierek; chairman of the Council of State, Jozef Cyrankiewicz; chairman of the Council of Ministers (premier), Piotr Jaroszewicz.

Throughout 1971 Edward Gierek (*see* BIOGRAPHY) consolidated his position in both the party hierarchy and the country at large. He traveled extensively and addressed 187 public meetings, explaining the events of December 1970, when a workers' revolt brought him to power (*see* Special Report), and his answers to them.

Although highly critical of Wladyslaw Gomulka's ruthless and repressive methods, Gierek had not plotted against him, and when elected first secretary had no ready list of his "shadow cabinet" in his pocket. Mieczyslaw Moczar had such a list, but the Central Committee did not consider him suitable for the post. A compromise was reached, with Gierek succeeding Gomulka while Moczar was elected a full member of the Politburo, of which he had been a candidate member since 1968 as well as a secretary in charge of

Pipelines:
see Fuel and Power; Transportation
Plastics Industry:
see Industrial Review
Poetry:
see Literature

Citizens of Warsaw attend the May Day parade on May 1, 1971, to celebrate socialism in Poland.

national defense and security. In addition, four of Gomulka's friends were ejected from the Politburo and replaced by Piotr Jaroszewicz, the new premier, Stefan Olszowski, in charge of the press, culture, and youth affairs, and two of Gierek's Silesian friends, Edward Babiuch and Jan Szydlak.

On Jan. 5, 1971, Gierek and Jaroszewicz visited Moscow for talks with Leonid I. Brezhnev and Aleksei N. Kosygin. They thanked the Soviet leaders for providing Poland with two million tons of grain, one million tons of cement, and $100 million in hard currency, enabling the government to cancel Gomulka's December price increases and raise the lowest wages and pensions. Together with other measures, the total increase in income in 1971 over 1970 amounted to 56 billion zlotys. Wages rose by an average of 5%.

In Moscow Gierek was advised that Moczar, as leader of the "nationalist deviationist" trend within the Polish party, was not trusted by the Soviets. By mid-April Moczar's job in the Secretariat was transferred to Stanislaw Kania and in June Moczar ceased to be a secretary of the Central Committee and was appointed chairman of the Supreme Audit Office.

There were no further changes in the membership of the Politburo until the sixth congress of the Polish United Workers' Party. Held in Warsaw on December 6–11, 1971, only three years after the fifth congress, it assembled 1,815 delegates representing 2,270,000 members and candidates, 165,000 more than in November 1968 (although during 1971 about 100,000 members were asked to resign and 10,500 were expelled). More than 70% of the delegates participated in the party congress for the first time. A new Central Committee of 115 members was elected, and appointed a new Politburo. Jozef Cyrankiewicz, a veteran statesman who had been in office since 1947, Stefan Jedrychowski, minister of foreign affairs since December 1969, and Moczar were dropped from this key body and replaced by Henryk Jablonski, minister of education, Mieczyslaw Jagielski, deputy premier, and army Gen. Wojciech Jaruzelski, minister of defense. Another new member was Franciszek Szlachcic, minister of the interior since February 1971, former security head in Katowice and a friend of Gierek. Only three of the Politburo's 11 members had presided on it prior to December 1970. On December 22, 1971, Gierek's position was strengthened further when Stefan Olszowski was appointed minister of foreign affairs, while Jedrychowski became minister of finance

and Wieslaw Ociepka, a member of the Central Committee, succeeded Szlachcic, who was promoted to secretary of the Politburo.

In his opening speech at the congress Gierek formulated four "lessons brought to light by the December events." These were that the building of socialism had to result in a steady and sensible increase in the material and cultural standard of living of the masses; that the working class was the main force of socialism; that the building of socialism demanded a constant refinement of the party's leading role; and that party discords, retarding social progress, produced opportunities for the enemies of socialism.

Outlining the guidelines of the 1971–75 development plan in the wake of the December riots and further strikes in January, Gierek announced that national income would rise by 39% (as compared with 34% during the 1966–70 period), industrial production of consumer goods would increase by 42% (38%), while the target for producer goods remained at 52%. Total investments in the national economy would amount to 1,430,000 million zlotys, and real wages were to increase by 18%. Housing remained a problem, mainly because of the shortage of building materials, but the 1,075,000 apartments to be built during 1971–75 would alleviate this situation. Chief industrial targets for 1975 were high indeed (actual 1970 figures in parentheses): hard coal, 167 (140) million tons; electric power, 96,000 (64,500) million kw-hr.; crude steel, 15 (11.8) million tons; cement, 18 (12.2) million tons. The Central Committee was to adopt a new system of planning and management of the national economy. The principle of central planning would be retained, but industrial enterprises, freed from punctilious production norms, would begin to apply market economy principles. In elections for a new Sejm, to be held in 1972, one year ahead of schedule, the new system of planning would form part of the platform of the Front of National Unity.

In his first speech as premier, Jaroszewicz had announced that the government would do its utmost to normalize relations with the Roman Catholic Church. On March 3 he had a three-hour interview with Stefan Cardinal Wyszynski, the primate of Poland. At the end of April Aleksander Skarzynski, director of the Office for Religious Affairs, visited the Vatican for talks with Archbishop Agostino Casaroli, the church's secretary for public affairs. On June 23 the Sejm trans-

continued on page 559

POLAND

Education. (1968–69) Primary, pupils 5,603,-955, teachers 255,142; secondary, pupils 311,153, teachers 18,804; vocational, pupils 846,802, teachers (full time; 1967–68) 53,637; teacher training, pupils 50,630, teachers 6,195; higher (including 10 universities), students 305,561, teaching staff 37,402.

Finance. Monetary unit: zloty, with (Sept. 27, 1971) an official exchange rate of 4 zlotys to U.S. $1 (9.60 zlotys = £1 sterling) and a tourist rate of 24 zlotys to U.S. $1 (57.60 zlotys = £1 sterling). Budget (1969 est.): revenue 357.6 billion zlotys; expenditure 351 billion zlotys. National income (net material product): (1969) 696.1 billion zlotys; (1968) 668.8 billion zlotys.

Foreign Trade. (1970) Imports 14,430,000,-000 zlotys; exports 14,191,000,000 zlotys. Import sources: U.S.S.R. 38%; East Germany 11%; Czechoslovakia 9%; U.K. 5%. Export destinations: U.S.S.R. 35%; East Germany 9%; Czechoslovakia 7%; West Germany 5%. Main exports (1969): machinery 30%; coal and coke 11%; transport equipment 7%; iron and steel 7%; textiles and clothing 6%; meat and products 5%.

Transport and Communications. Roads (1970) 307,810 km. (including 139 km. expressways). Motor vehicles in use (1970): passenger 479,354; commercial 263,004. Railways: (1969) 23,196 km. (including 3,477 km. electrified); traffic (1970) 36,892,000,000 passenger-km., freight 99,326,000,000 net ton-km. Air traffic (1970): 550 million passenger-km.; freight 8,-830,000 net ton-km. Shipping (1970): merchant vessels 100 gross tons and over 516; gross tonnage 1,580,298. Telephones (Dec. 1969) 1,756,-248. Radio licenses (Dec. 1969) 5,649,000. Television licenses (1969) 3,828,000.

Agriculture. Production (in 000; metric tons; 1970; 1969 in parentheses): wheat 4,616 (4,-710), rye 5,455 (8,166), barley 2,148 (1,948); oats 3,205 (3,063), potatoes 50,270 (44,935); sugar, raw value (1970–71) c. 1,649, (1969–70) 1,527; rapeseed 580 (204); linseed c. 60 (57); dry peas c. 65 (c. 64); apples c. 730 (654); onions (1969) 315, (1968) 347; tobacco c. 91 (91); flax fibre c. 55 (53); hemp fibre c. 20 (c. 17); butter 200 (192); cheese c. 230 (224); beef and veal c. 590 (570); pork c. 1,300 (1,-

312); timber (cu.m.; 1969) 18,100, (1968) 18,-100; fish catch (1969) 408, (1968) 407. Livestock (in 000; June 1970): cattle 10,844; horses 2,585; pigs 13,446; sheep 3,199; chickens c. 150,000.

Industry. Index of industrial production (1963 = 100): (1970) 178; (1969) 163. Fuel and power (in 000; metric tons; 1970): coal 140,-101; brown coal 32,766; coke (1969) 14,820; crude oil 425; natural gas (cu.m.) 5,183,000; manufactured gas (cu.m.; 1969) 6,686,000; electricity (kw-hr.) 64,526,000; Production (in 000; metric tons; 1970): cement 12,181; iron ore (30% metal content) 2,556; pig iron 7,299; crude steel 11,794; aluminum (1969) 97; zinc (1969) 208; copper (1969) 55; lead (1969) 51; sulfuric acid 1,917; nitrogenous fertilizers (N content; 1969) 938; superphosphates (1969) 1,713; cotton fabrics (m.) 880,000; woolen fabrics (m.) 99,000; rayon and synthetic fabrics (m.) 118,000; passenger cars (units) 64; commercial vehicles (units) 55. Merchant vessels launched (100 gross tons and over; 1970) 412,-000 gross tons.

THE WORKERS' REVOLT

By Nicholas Bethell

A country erupts into violence and into the headlines of the world's press. Then, with the blood spilled and the passion apparently spent, it slips back into quiet obscurity. For so many years this had been the fate of Poland, a country of some 30 million people, but sandwiched between two giants, Germany and Russia, who for two centuries have taken turns stealing its territory and independence. In recent history Poland has been a boiling saucepan with the lid held down. Every few decades it contrives a little explosion, such as the events of December 1970.

The Trouble Begins. The spark was the sudden announcement on December 13 of massive increases in food, fuel, and clothing prices, including 16% on flour, 14% on sugar, 18% on meat, 37% on jam, 92% on coffee, 20% on coke. To do this a few days before Christmas was to turn the knife in the wound; the fact that the prices of some durable consumer goods—television sets, household appliances—were simultaneously lowered was merely an added twist, for such goods were in any case not widely available. A letter announcing the changes was read at local Communist Party meetings, and soon the news was being widely circulated and the people, especially the poor, were plunged into despondency. This was no wonder when one considers that the minimum monthly wage was only 850 zlotys, the equivalent in purchasing power of about U.S. $25. This had been fixed in July 1966 and had been diminished by inflation for more than four years.

There were deeper underlying causes of the explosion. The ruler of Poland, Wladyslaw Gomulka, first secretary of the Polish United Workers' (Communist) Party, had been in power since October 1956, when he was elected in a wave of popular enthusiasm seldom encountered in any country, let alone a Communist one. Imprisoned for three years under Stalin, he had become a symbol of resistance to the terror and blatant oppression of the post-World War II years, and Poles as a whole accepted his promise that he would lead them out of the wilderness into a freer and more prosperous land. But as the years passed it became clear that they had been deceived. Gomulka was allowing Poland to slip into economic, political, and cultural stagnation. In March 1968 there were riots involving the students and liberal intelligentsia, but since they were not supported by the workers they failed to achieve any significant objective. After it was over a writer in the French newspaper *Le Monde* summed up the position well: "The Polish October has turned into an endless winter. It is a little less harsh than previous winters, but just as gray."

On Dec. 14, 1970, a crowd of about 3,000 workers collected in front of the main administration building of the shipyard in Gdansk, the former Danzig. According to the local party newspaper, "leaders emerged spontaneously," and when a local official tried to address them he was booed and shouted down. The strikers were treated like mutineers. "Go back to work and behave yourselves," they were told, "and then we will consider discussing your grievances." Infuriated, they dispersed and some of them went on a rampage. They set fire to part of the party

Lord Bethell, a writer on Eastern European affairs, is the author of Gomulka: His Poland and His Communism. *He is the translator of Aleksandr I. Solzhenitsyn's* Cancer Ward.

headquarters, cars and buses were overturned, and there was some looting.

Gomulka's reaction to the news was one of fury. It was pure counterrevolution, he said, and he compared the strikers to the mutineers of Kronstadt whom Lenin had to crush in 1921. As a good Marxist, Gomulka knew that there was only one way of dealing with counterrevolution—by force ruthlessly applied—so he had no hesitation in dispatching his right-hand man, Zenon Kliszko, to the north to deal with the crisis and in authorizing the use of firearms by militia and army units. It was a mark of the rigidity that had begun to dominate his thought processes that he should turn to dogma at such a time.

Besides his Marxist theory, he had a strange historical justification for his decision to crush the strikers by brute force. Again and again, he told his Politburo colleagues, Poland had been let down and led to disaster by its ruling class. As a result of the anarchy and indecision of the 18th-century nobility, Poland was conquered and partitioned. As a result of the blind hatred of the Soviet Union by the bourgeoisie, which ruled Poland between the wars, the country again fell under foreign control in 1939. And now here was the working class (which in a socialist country like Poland, according to Marxist theory, must also be the ruling class) once again behaving in an irresponsible way, putting the country's interest and very existence in jeopardy.

The Attempt at Repression. On December 15 the Army was brought into Gdansk and the first deaths occurred. By now the whole city was on strike, and crowds numbering more than 10,000 were milling about the streets. Their main targets were the party headquarters and the prison, where some workers arrested the previous day were being held. Military helicopters were hovering over the city, radioing reports on crowd movement to the armed men on the ground. Official casualty figures for that day show that six were killed and about 300 injured.

Meanwhile, in Gdynia, a few miles to the north of Gdansk, strikes and rioting broke out on December 15, and two days later the most horrible event of all occurred. The management of the Gdynia shipyards had received reports that rioters were planning to sabotage machinery. They decided to close for the day, but they were not able to inform all their workers of this decision, so on the morning of December 17 people began arriving at the docks by train from the dormitory suburbs. As they left the station they found themselves surrounded by militiamen and tanks. The workers were ordered to disperse, but they could not do so at once because of the crush. Suddenly they were fired upon in cold blood. Bullets ricocheted off the paving stones into the crowd, while tear-gas grenades rained down from helicopters overhead. Officially it was announced that 13 people were killed that day in Gdynia, but many eyewitnesses put the figure much higher.

It quickly became apparent that certain groups and forces were defying Gomulka's will and that not everyone was obeying his and Kliszko's orders. Their position at the head of the Communist Party had never been quite secure since they were nearly overthrown in 1968 by the group loyal to Mieczyslaw Moczar, who controlled the internal security forces. As soon as the riots started, it was clear that Gomulka might not be able to survive politically. The question was, what attitude would the various forces take? Which side would Moczar back? What about Edward Gierek (*see* BIOGRAPHY), the practical economist? The Army? The Soviet Union? It was a crisis point for many political careers, and not a few must have asked themselves at what point they should shift horses. If Gomulka was going to regain control quite easily, they would do well to remain loyal to him. But if the situation got out of hand, Gomulka would go down, dragging his supporters with him.

There are those who think that the massacre at Gdynia was deliberately provoked by forces connected with the security service, to demonstrate that the situation was out of control and that Gomulka had failed. Eyewitnesses have testified that the crowd in Gdynia that morning was in no way aggressive and that it was quite unnecessary to open fire on them. For anyone to have deliberately caused violence and death in order to achieve an internal political end would, of course, be an act of extreme brutality and cynicism, but such is Poland's recent history that the possibility cannot be ruled out.

On the evening of December 17 a state of emergency was declared, and Premier Jozef Cyrankiewicz addressed the nation on television. It was an unwise speech, clinging closely to the Gomulka line that there were no legitimate grievances and that the striking workers were behaving disgracefully. "By your action," said Cyrankiewicz, "you encouraged the social scum, the hooligans and enemies of socialism to vandalism, looting, and murder." He went on to repeat Gomulka's strange historical theory that the working class was now leading Poland to perdition. His tone was one of panic, and the broadcast only served to irritate the strikers still more. That same day the violence had spread to Szczecin, Poland's third big port on the Baltic. The local newspaper blamed it on "hooligans, anarchists, and longhaired young louts." The party headquarters was burned down, and the official count of the dead was 14.

Warsaw was now full of rumours that L. I. Brezhnev and the other Soviet leaders were about to descend upon it—shades of October 1956 when N. S. Khrushchev, A. I. Mikoyan, L. M. Kaganovich, I. S. Koniev, and others arrived unannounced to try to forestall Gomulka's election. In fact Brezhnev was not on his way, but he had sent a letter to the Polish Central Committee advising that "the problem must be solved by political and economic means," that is, not by military or violent means, whether Soviet or Polish. Gomulka was later accused of concealing this letter from his colleagues. There is no doubt that it was a blow to him, for it ran contrary to his thesis that the strikes were "counterrevolutionary" and was an implied criticism of the methods of repression he had already authorized. It was probably not tenderheartedness toward the Poles that motivated Brezhnev to write the letter, but disillusionment with Gomulka and a desire to see him replaced.

Gomulka's Downfall. It was all too much for Gomulka, and during the afternoon of December 18 he was taken to the government clinic in Emilia Plater Street suffering from blurred vision, high blood pressure, and what a panel of physicians called "a feeling of general exhaustion." It was clear now that his political end was at hand, and the kingmakers, Polish and Soviet, made contact with Edward Gierek, who was the obvious choice to replace him. Gierek had been playing no part in suppressing the violence and was staying in Katowice in the south of Poland, which remained quiet. It was in this rich mining area that Gierek had made his name, turning the workers there into the most prosperous in the country. The area was popularly known as Poland's "Katanga," after the copper-rich Congolese secessionist province. In 1956 the mood of Poland had required a martyr to Stalinism, and it got one in Gomulka. Now in 1970 it needed a man with a record of economic success, who could be presented to the Poles with plausibility as the one likely to improve their material lot. Gierek was the man.

At 9 A.M. on December 20 the Politburo met to conclude matters, but news of what was happening had reached Gomulka in his sickroom. He was still first secretary and he still had the trappings of office about him, his official car and escort. Gomulka announced that he was leaving the hospital. The doctors advised against it, but they could not prevent him, so as he got into his car and drove to the Central Committee building, they followed him. Gomulka burst into the room where the Politburo was meeting in a highly nervous state. He shouted at the members, accusing them of condoning counterrevolution and plotting behind his back. A few minutes later the doctors arrived and told the Politburo members that unless their patient returned to the clinic they could take no responsibility either for his health or for his actions. He was persuaded to go with them.

Kliszko and Cyrankiewicz were then sent to the clinic to obtain Gomulka's resignation in writing. They got it, but meanwhile it was decided that Gomulka's removal was not enough, that Kliszko, Ryszard Strzelecki, Boleslaw Jaszczuk, and Marshal Marian Spychalski (the nominal head of state, replaced by Cyrankiewicz on December 23) would also have to resign their posts in the Politburo and Secretariat. The problem was that for such major changes it would be necessary to summon a full meeting of the Central Committee, about 90 people. Telegrams were sent ordering them to make for the nearest airport, from which the Air Force flew them to Warsaw. By 4 P.M. most of the members were there, and two hours later business was completed in time for Gierek to address the nation on television as the new first secretary. He spoke of the strikers in terms quite different from those used by Cyrankiewicz three days earlier. Their action had put Poland in danger, he said, but "the motives for it were mostly honest." He promised "a full reply" to the question of why the tragedy had been allowed to happen. It would be "a difficult reply and a self-critical one, but it will be clear and true." He ended by appealing to the workers to return to work. Almost all of them were impressed by Gierek's sincerity and went back to their jobs.

A New Page. And so the leadership was overthrown and the new first secretary made, hardly by democratic process but at least, on this occasion, in response to a genuine popular demand. Very seldom do workers' demonstrations bring down governments, and it is doubly interesting that this should happen in 1970 for the first time in a Communist country. Of course the form of government was not changed, only the few people at the top, but at least that was a start. It showed that there is a limit to what a Communist government can foist upon its people. It will make present and future leaders a little more cautious and amenable to public opinion.

It is, of course, too early to judge what the new regime will mean for Poland. For several years the country has been going rapidly downhill economically and culturally, so rapidly that the reaction of many Poles to the events was that any change must be a change for the better. But their memories were still full of the "palace revolution" of 1956 that brought Gomulka to power. They had believed the extravagant promises he made, which is why they came to dislike him all the more when it became clear that he had deceived them. Gierek made no such promises and wisely so, for they would never be believed by the once-bitten-twice-shy Poles.

Another point is that after the Soviet invasion of Czechoslovakia in 1968 the people of Eastern Europe have come to appreciate that their own governments have very little room for maneuver. Their countries' ideology, economy, and military and foreign policy are tied closely to those of the Soviet Union, which has set strict limits on local leaders' independence. Even if Gierek were a Daniel come to judgment, he would not be able to make radical improvements. The difference from the 1956 situation is that the Poles have come to appreciate this sad fact. They will be less likely to blame Gierek for the shortcomings of the men in the Kremlin who guide him, so long as he seems to be trying his best.

But to keep Poland's politics in a state of equilibrium and its people tolerably happy, Gierek will have to do something. He may, for instance, succeed in launching a less centralized and more consumer-oriented economic policy. The Poles may then feel that there is some point in their working harder, and the result could be an improvement in the country's very slow rate of growth. He may succeed in tapping Poland's administrative talent by promoting not only those few Poles who are convinced Marxists but also those others who, while not Communists, are loyal to "People's Poland." He may succeed in restoring Poland's position in European culture; in the late 1950s this stood very high, but by the late 1960s it had all but collapsed. Gierek has made a start along such lines. If he does succeed, it will only be in making the best of a bad job, but as a politician he has to concentrate on the art of the possible. There is some small room for improvement, even within the framework of the Brezhnev Doctrine.

continued from page 556

ferred to the church, without payment and tax-free, the property of all churches and chapels in the new western and northern territories. In October Skarzynski was back in Rome to attend the beatification of Maximilian Kolbe, a Polish Franciscan priest who in 1941 chose to die in Auschwitz to save the life of another prisoner, a Polish soldier. On that occasion Skarzynski met Pope Paul VI.   (K. Sm.)

Police

The General Assembly session of the International Criminal Police Organization (Interpol), to which 107 countries were affiliated in 1971, was held in Ottawa, September 6–11. Topics of reports submitted included international illicit drug traffic and currency counterfeiting in 1970, the use of dogs to detect drugs, technical assistance in police operations, and cooperation between police and customs authorities.

A drugs symposium, held at the Interpol headquarters at Saint-Cloud, France, Oct. 14–16, 1970, was attended by 123 participants from 57 countries. A symposium for heads of police colleges was held in November 1970 and attended by 72 experts from 43 countries. Studies were made concerning the laws on counterfeiting, drugs, and theft and fraudulent negotiation of travelers' checks. A conference on burglaries of jewelers' shops was held for European member countries.

There was a marked increase in the work of most National Central bureaus: collaboration among NCBs led to 2,197 arrests and the exchange of 191,840 items of information. Between June 1970 and June 1971 the General Secretariat studied 10,875 cases, resulting in 554 arrests. NCBs received 8,964 items of information and 451 persons were the subject of international notices.

Europe. *United Kingdom.* In an unusually outspoken interview published in *The Times* of London, two unnamed senior Metropolitan Police officers were highly critical of what they regarded as the undue leniency of Parliament, the Home Office, the courts, and penal institutions. They were greatly concerned at the inducements to violent crime offered by the abolition of corporal and capital punishment and at the isolation of the police from public sympathy. Suspended sentences, parole, radio and television in prisons, a choice of food, and weekend leave seemed to them no deterrent to the increase in violent crime.

In England and Wales in 1970, 88 police officers were convicted of criminal offenses and 32 were sent to prison. During 1971 at least 75 policemen were involved in allegations of corruption. The Metropolitan Police Commission warned London's 3,000 detectives that they should avoid undue involvement with the criminal community. A study of the special problems of the police, particularly of the need to reduce turnover and improve recruitment, was undertaken as part of the 1970 biennial pay review. The result, effective from Sept. 1, 1970, was a general increase in wages of about 11% plus improvements in the pay structure and an additional increment for higher ranks. Following extensive advertising for recruits, the number of police at the end of 1971 was about 96,500. The number of civilians employed in supporting roles increased, as did that of traffic wardens, whose functions were extended. The number of indictable offenses known to the police during 1970

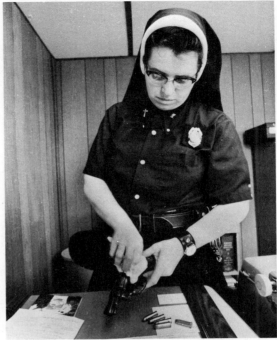

Sister Mary Cornelia, a Roman Catholic nun, joined the police department as a special officer in Pontoon Beach, Ill., to work with young drug offenders.

was 1,555,995. Inquiries dealt with by the City of London Fraud Squad alone involved more than £30 million.

In September a £10,000 "stop autocrime" campaign was launched after thefts of and from cars in 1970 had amounted to 25% of London's recorded crimes. In June the Police Federation asked the government to drop proposals that would have involved police in the compulsory registration of "nonpatrial" Commonwealth citizens. Friction between the force and the nonwhite community was considered bad enough without this added imposition. In St. Ives, the police department lost a court effort to change the name of the street on which its new headquarters would be located to something other than Pig Lane.

In May members of the Royal Ulster Constabulary met to demand greater protection for their mobile patrols in Belfast, N.Ire., and urged the issue of submachine guns to officers involved in police car duties.

In Scotland in 1970, for the second year in succession, there was a slight reduction in the number of crimes against the person, although total crimes of all kinds increased by about 7%. Scottish police numbered approximately 10,500, and total manpower was increased by the appointment of over 200 additional civilians as traffic wardens and clerical and technical staff. In 1971 the central government, in conjunction with individual police forces, started a major review of the approved size and structure of police forces in order to promote the most efficient use of manpower.

France. Disaffection within the police force continued in 1971 and the Federation of Police Unions complained of shortage of personnel, lack of equipment, low wages, and unrewarding conditions of work, in addition to a lack of public sympathy. Public feeling was considerably aggravated by the case of Alain Jaubert, a journalist on the *Nouvel Observateur*, who on May 29 voluntarily entered a police van to accompany a wounded demonstrator. On arrival at the hospital Jaubert himself was found to be suffering from a damaged skull and severe bruising and was later charged with having assaulted three policemen in the police van. Jaubert charged the police with

PETER L. GOULD

A New York Police
Department captain
testifies before
the Knapp Commission
on Oct. 29, 1971,
in hearings concerning
police department
corruption.

grievous bodily harm and his case became a cause célèbre of the French press. Further hostility was caused by government proposals for reform of the Prefecture, involving decentralization of duties within the Greater Paris area and the transference of responsibility for suburban Paris to overworked and understaffed local police forces. In September union threats to occupy government buildings led to the dismissal of officials of the National Union of Uniformed Policemen, and to a reminder from the minister of the interior, Raymond Marcellin, that under a law of 1948 the police had no right to strike. To forestall discontent Marcellin had announced on September 6 measures that included an increase in police strength, improvement of working conditions, modernization of technical equipment, improvement in promotion and status, and a return of the title of *inspecteur* to chief police officers.

A protocol was signed with the U.S. on Feb. 26, 1971, calling for close cooperation in the struggle against the narcotics trade. The strength of the Marseilles drug squad (whose lack of success in detecting clandestine narcotics laboratories was criticized by the U.S.) was increased from 9 to 63 men.

West Germany. Although the number of public demonstrations decreased in 1971, the 8.8% increase in indictable offenses in 1970 over 1969 was a cause for concern. Crimes involving narcotics increased in the same period by no less than 238%. About 95% of known murders and frauds were solved, but the figure for thefts, by far the largest constituent of offenses, was much lower. To meet the increases in crime the Bundeskriminalamt was to be considerably reinforced and provision was made for salary increases.

Scandinavia. Total strength of the Danish police on Jan. 1, 1971, was 7,986 (excluding civilian staff). The number of offenses reported through the decade increased from 132,000 in 1960 to 263,000 in 1970, a growth of 99%. In February 1971 a Ministry of Justice report on the reorganization of Danish police districts recommended their reduction from 72 to 48. A report issued in March forecast a modest 3% annual increase in the crime rate. To meet this challenge the police force would require 12,600 men.

A Norwegian government-appointed committee recommended the setting up of a directorate to take over from the Ministry of Justice the central direction of the police force. The 53 police districts were to be reorganized within five new regions. Attempts by members of the public to set up vigilante committees to overcome police shortages were quickly stopped.

U.S.S.R. On July 12, 1970, a law was adopted under which a first offender committing a minor crime could be given a suspended sentence of one to three years and sent to do compulsory work at an industrial enterprise instead of a labour camp.

In March 1971 Soviet archaeologists called for legal measures to protect coin collectors from police harassment and criminal prosecution. The collectors had inadvertently been violating the law against "speculation"; the sale of valuables for profit. On August 12, Aleksandr Gorlov was beaten when he found several men in the summer cottage of his friend, Nobel prizewinning novelist Aleksandr I. Solzhenitsyn. Solzhenitsyn protested to the State Security Committee (KGB) and to Premier Aleksei N. Kosygin and received official notification that the assault was the "mistake" of local policemen.

Oceania. *Australia.* The results of two government-sponsored inquiries into police affairs tended to dominate law enforcement news during 1971. In Victoria, Sir Eric St. Johnston, former chief inspector of constabulary for England and Wales, recommended abolition of the seniority rule for police promotions; radical reappraisal of police salaries; major upgrading of police communications equipment; expansion of foot patrols in urban areas; and the ending of police responsibility for duties such as service of civil process and registration of motor vehicles. In South Australia, a royal commission report on police handling of antiwar demonstrations in Adelaide in September 1970 was mildly critical of the police decision to disperse demonstrators forcibly. The report recommended clarification of laws affecting demonstrations, and of the status of the chief of police.

Confrontations between police and demonstrators were common throughout Australia in a year of continuing social unrest. The tour of Australia by the South African Rugby team provoked particularly violent demonstrations (*see* AUSTRALIA).

In 1971 the New South Wales force became the first to computerize many of its crime records. Initial results were somewhat embarrassing; official crime clear-up rates fell dramatically from levels formerly calculated by manual techniques. The cost of law enforcement continued to rise as police in several states were awarded substantial pay increases. Training procedures were revamped in a number of forces, particularly in Queensland and Tasmania.   (X.)

North and South America. *United States.* Federal Bureau of Investigation (FBI) Uniform Crime Reports revealed that as of Dec. 31, 1970, U.S. cities had an average of 2.3 police employees per 1,000 inhabitants, an increase of 5% over the 1969 rate of 2.2. On the average, 13.2% of all city police personnel were civilian employees, up from 12.5% in 1969. State police and highway patrol organizations had a total personnel of 54,754, an increase of 4%. Of these, 74% were sworn personnel and 26% civilian employees. During the decade 1960–70, police arrests for all criminal acts, excluding traffic offenses, increased 31%. In 1970, law enforcement agencies made an estimated 8 million arrests for all criminal acts, excluding traffic offenses, an increase of 5% over 1969. There were 43 arrests for each 1,000 persons in the U.S. In 1970, only 19% of burglaries, 17% of auto thefts, 18% of larcenies, and 29% of robberies were solved by law enforcement agencies through arrests. However, 86% of murder offenses, 56% of forcible rapes, and 65% of aggravated assaults were solved through arrests.

A variety of new police techniques and devices were credited with reducing crime in some cities. In Reading, Pa., during 1970, a special police platoon patrolled high crime areas from 7 P.M. to 3 A.M. An intensified community relations program was designed to keep the police in constant touch with neighbourhood groups. In addition, a telephone police watch, a device that fits on the cradle of the phone of a person away from home, could carry any noise in the house to the police bureau, which dispatched officers to investigate. Reductions in robberies, assaults, burglaries, auto thefts, rapes, and murders were reported in Reading in 1970.

Louisville, Ky., which also experienced a decrease in crime in 1970, had a "rooftop detail" patrol the roofs of downtown buildings to watch the streets below. About 3,000 lights were installed in high crime sections and policemen resumed patrolling the neighbourhoods on foot. In April the Mount Vernon, N.Y.,

Police Department became the first department to place in operation two remote-control television cameras for surveillance of the city's main business district, where street crimes were frequent.

On Aug. 23, 1971, the New York City Police Department began 30 days of test runs in Staten Island of helicopter patrols similar to those employed in Los Angeles, Kansas City, Kan., and Memphis, Tenn., against car thieves, car strippers, and housebreakers. Several smaller police departments initiated a four-day, 40-hour workweek for patrolmen. The schedule permitted improved law enforcement during peak crime times and boosted officer morale. (*See* LABOUR UNIONS: *Special Report*.)

According to the second annual report filed with the U.S. Congress, 597 court orders granted in 1970 authorized the installation of electronic listening devices by state and federal officers throughout the U.S., compared with 302 the previous year. Of these, 215 were obtained in New York, 132 in New Jersey, and 183 by the U.S. Department of Justice. In 1970, 1,874 arrests resulted from eavesdropping.

The recruitment of black police officers had been a failure in most cities, according to the results of a survey announced in January 1971. In Philadelphia, blacks on the force had actually decreased from 20.8% in 1967 to 18.6% in 1970. Stepped-up recruitment drives, however, had been most successful in Washington, D.C., whose police force was 35.9% black in August 1970, Chicago (16.5% black), and Atlanta, Ga. (28%). Although a state-financed training program had tutored minority group members in New York City to help them pass police entrance exams, the percentage of blacks on the force increased only from 5 to 7.5% during the 1960s. In Detroit, the percentage of blacks on the police force jumped from 2 in 1960 to about 12 in 1970, most of the increase having occurred after the 1967 riots. Plans were under way to increase the number of blacks on the Detroit force to 45% by 1980.

The upward trend of assaults on police continued in 1970, when there were 18.7 assaults for every 100 officers. One hundred law enforcement officers, including ten in Chicago, were killed by felonious criminal action, an increase of 16% over 1969. Violent attacks on police continued to present a major problem in 1971.

The International Association of Chiefs of Police reported that during May 1971, 11 U.S. policemen were killed and 17 injured. Handguns were involved in nine of the deaths. In the first five months of 1971, seven policemen had been killed in New York City, the same number killed in all of 1970. Pres. Richard Nixon held a meeting in Washington, D.C., with police chiefs and sheriffs to examine the crises arising from criminal attacks on law enforcement officers. Senators James O. Eastland (Dem., Miss.) and Richard S. Schweiker (Rep., Pa.) both called for legislation making assaults on policemen and firemen a federal crime.

For the first time the New York City Police Department made a study on the use of firearms by its officers. There were 634 incidents in 1970 in which a policeman reported firing his pistol or being attacked with a deadly device. Officers fired a total of 1,643 shots, including 183 warning shots fired during 81 incidents that led to 63 arrests. Fifty-four persons were killed and 238 injured by policemen. Members of the force were involved in 75 gunfights and 23 sniper attacks. Of the city's 30,000 policemen, only

1,053 were initially involved in the incidents, about 60% of which took place in 23 of the city's 76 precincts.

On July 1, 1971, the Commission to Investigate Alleged Police Corruption in New York City, headed by Whitman Knapp, made public an interim report on its 11-month inquiry. The report revealed widespread corruption in the New York Police Department that extended beyond narcotics, gambling, and prostitution. It was asserted that an atmosphere of corruption made it easier for a rookie policeman to become corrupt than to remain honest; that many policemen were venal; and that only a few actively opposed corruption within the force. The Knapp Commission was created by Mayor John Lindsay in May 1970, following public charges of widespread police corruption and allegations that high officials in the Lindsay administration had not acted when informed of specific acts of venality.

In early November, after the Knapp Commission had completed two weeks of public hearings, a federal grand jury indicted 12 New York City policemen, including two lieutenants, on charges ranging from selling narcotics to committing perjury in testimony before the commission. Several of the charges grew out of the testimony of a patrolman working as an undercover agent for the commission. Further indictments based on information collected by the commission were expected.

In September New York Police Commissioner Patrick V. Murphy, who had just staged a shake-up of his high-ranking officers in order to stiffen command, urged his fellow chiefs of police to stand together in establishing a "zero level" of tolerance for corruption. He said that chiefs in some cities were hampered by civil service procedures in trying to dismiss corrupt policemen and other chiefs asserted that policemen's associations failed to support efforts to combat corruption.

Canada. For the first time in its 98-year history the Royal Canadian Mounted Police came under public fire in May 1971 when charges were made in the House of Commons that surveillances had been conducted not only of Marxists, Maoists, drug addicts, and U.S. military deserters, but of members of Parliament. To overcome some of the public anxieties over surveillance and "bugging," the government prom-

Policeman talks to masked demonstrators on March 4, 1971, a day set aside by Paris police to try to improve their image. Students, protesting a recent incident in which a youth lost an eye in a tear-gas attack, pasted an advertisement for an outlawed Maoist paper on the policeman's back.

POPPERFOTO—PICTORIAL PARADE

ised legislation to prescribe bounds for wiretapping and computerized data banks and dossiers.

Mexico. In Mexico City on June 10, 1971, about 1,000 right-wing youths armed with submachine guns, pistols, and long bamboo sticks were permitted to pass through a police cordon to attack student demonstrators who were protesting against the government of Pres. Luis Echeverría Álvarez. At least ten students were killed and 160 wounded in the fighting.

Guatemala. It was announced in April 1971 that six U.S. law enforcement experts were training police in Guatemala in techniques aimed at building a reliable force and stemming the violence that had plagued the country for 20 years. Guatemala's police had been recruited largely from unemployed migrants to the cities. Pay had been low and complaints of corruption were frequent.

Brazil. Practically unrestricted police powers had remained in force in Brazil since 1968. Despite government denials, reliable reports indicated that some prisoners had been tortured while they were interrogated.

In February 1971 Roman Catholic Archbishop Paulo Evaristo Arns of São Paulo charged that political police had tortured "in an ignominious manner" a young Italian priest and a woman Brazilian social worker who had been arrested on suspicion of antigovernment subversion. In January Rubens Paiva, a former member of the Chamber of Deputies, was led from home by unidentified security agents. On August 2, 1971, Hélio P. Bicudo, a prosecutor-at-large in São Paulo state, was removed from the investigation he had initiated in 1970 into charges of summary executions by policemen of petty criminals. Brazilian police death squads had been linked to more than 1,000 killings since 1964. (V. W. P.)

See also Crime; Law; Prisons and Penology; Race Relations.

Encyclopædia Britannica Films. *Our Community Services* (1969).

Political Parties

The following table is a general world guide to political parties. All countries that were independent on Dec. 1, 1971, are included; there are a number for which no analysis of political activities is given.

Parties are included in most instances only if represented in parliaments (in the lower house in bicameral legislatures), but the figures in the last column of the table do not necessarily add up to the total number of seats in parliament because independents and certain small political groupings are sometimes omitted. The date of the most recent general election follows the name of the country.

The code letters in the affiliation column show the relative political position of the parties within each country; there is, therefore, no entry in this column for single-party states. There are obvious difficulties involved in labeling parties within the political spectrum of a given country. The key chosen is as follows: F—fascist; ER—extreme right; R—right; CR—centre right; C—centre; L—non-Marxist left; SD—social-democratic; S—socialist; EL—extreme left; and K—communist.

The percentages in the column "Voting strength" indicate proportions of the valid votes cast for the respective parties, or the number of registered voters who went to the polls in single-party states.

COUNTRY AND NAME OF PARTY	Affiliation	Voting strength	Parliamentary representation
Afghanistan (1969)			
Royal government with an elected House of the People (Wolesi Jirga)	—	—	216
Albania (1970)			
Albanian Labour (Communist)	—	100%	214
Algeria			
Military government since June 19, 1965	—	—	—
Andorra (1969)			
No parties	—	—	24
Argentina			
Military government since June 28, 1966	—	—	—
Australia (1969)			
Country (Conservative)	R	...	20
Liberal	CR	...	46
Democratic Labor (DLP)	C	...	—
Australian Labor (ALP)	L	...	59
Austria (1971)			
Freiheitliche Partei Osterreichs	R	5.4%	10
Osterreichische Volkspartei	C	43.0%	80
Sozialistische Partei Osterreichs	SD	50.0%	93
Kommunistische Partei Osterreichs	K	1.4%	0
Bahrain			
Emirate	—	—	—
Barbados (1971)			
Democratic Labour Party	C	...	18
Barbados Labour Party	L	...	6
Belgium (1971)			
Volksunie (Flemish)	R	11.0%	21
Front Démocratique des Bruxellois Francophones } Rassemblement Wallon	R	11.4%	24
Parti pour la Liberté et le Progrès	CR	16.7%	34
Parti Social-Chrétien } Christelijk Volks-Partij	C	30.0%	67
Parti Socialiste Belge	SD	27.2%	61
Parti Communiste Belge	K	3.2%	5
Bhutan			
No parties	—	—	130
Bolivia			
Military government since Sept. 26, 1969	—	—	—
Botswana (1969)			
Botswana Democratic Party	C	...	24
Botswana People's Party	L	...	3
Botswana National Front	EL	...	3
Botswana Independent Party	L	...	1
Brazil (1970)			
Aliança Renovadora Nacional	CR	...	223
Movimento Democratico Brasileiro	L	...	87
Bulgaria (1971)			
Bulgarian Communist 266 } Agrarian Union 100 } Fatherland Front Nonparty 34 }	—	99.9%	400
Burma			
Military government since March 2, 1962	—	—	—
Burundi			
Military government since Nov. 28, 1966	—	—	—
Cambodia			
Military government since Nov. 1, 1970	—	—	—
Cameroon (1969)			
Union Nationale Camérounaise	—	...	50
Canada (1968)			
Social Credit	R	0.7%	—
Progressive Conservative	CR	31.4%	73
Liberal	C	45.5%	154
Rassemblement des Créditistes	C	4.8%	14
New Democratic	L	16.7%	22
Central African Republic			
Military government since Jan. 1, 1966	—	—	—
Ceylon (1970)			
United National	R	34.2%	17
Sri Lanka Freedom	CR	33.0%	91
Federal (Tamil)	C	4.4%	13
Lanka Sama Samaja (Trotskyist)	S	7.9%	19
Communist	K	3.0%	6
Others		...	5
Chad (1969)			
Union pour le Progrès du Tchad	—	...	75
Chile (1969)			
Partido Nacional	R	20.9%	34
Partido Radical	C	13.4%	24
Partido Demócrata-Cristiano	C	31.1%	55
Partido Socialista Chileno	S	12.8%	15
Partido Comunista de Chile	K	16.6%	22
China, People's Republic of			
Communist (Kungchan-tang)			
Colombia (1970)			
Alianza Nacional Popular	R	...	72
Partido Conservador } Partido Liberal	R } C }	...	{ 90
Congo (Kinshasa; Zaire, 1970)			
Mouvement Populaire de la Révolution	—	98.3%	420
Congo (Brazzaville)			
Military government since September 1968	—	—	—
Costa Rica (1970)			
Partido de Liberación Nacional	R	...	32
Partido de Unificación Nacional	C	...	22
Acción Socialista	L	...	2

COUNTRY AND NAME OF PARTY	Affiliation	Voting strength	Parliamentary representation
Cuba			
Partido Comunista de Cuba	—		
Cyprus (1970)			
Greek-Cypriot			
Progressive Front	R	...	7
Unified Party	C	...	15
Democratic Centre Union	L	...	2
Independents	—	...	2
Progressive Party of Working People	K	...	9
Turkish-Cypriot			
National Solidarity	—	...	15
Czechoslovakia (1971)			
National Front	—	99.8%	350
Dahomey			
Civilian Presidential Council replaced military government on May 1, 1970	—	—	—
Denmark (1971)			
Conservative	R	16.7%	31
Liberal Democratic (Venstre)	C	15.6%	30
Radical-Liberal	C	14.3%	27
Social Democratic	SD	37.3%	70
Socialist People's	S	9.1%	19
Communist	K	1.4%	0
Faeroe Islands and Greenland		...	2
Dominican Republic (1966)			
Partido Reformista	R	...	48
Partido Revolucionario Dominicano	C	...	26
Ecuador (1968)			
Alianza Popular	R	...	...
Izquierda Democrática	L	...	...
Egypt (United Arab Republic; 1971)			
Arab Socialist Union	—	...	338
El Salvador (1970)			
Partido de Conciliación Nacional	R	60.0%	34
Partido Demócrata Cristiano	C	28.8%	16
Partido Popular Salvadoreño	L	1.8%	1
Equatorial Guinea (1968)			
Movimiento por Unión Nacional de Guiné Ecuadorial (MUNGE)			
Idea Popular de Guiné Ecuadorial (IPGE)	—	...	35
Movimiento Nacional por Liberación de Guiné Ecuadorial (MONALIGE)			
Ethiopia (1965)			
Imperial government with an elected Yeheg Memria (lower chamber)	—	—	250
Fiji (1966)			
Alliance Party (mainly Fijian)	—	...	22
National Federation Party (mainly Indian)	—	...	9
Independents (mainly Chinese)		...	3
Finland (1970)			
Kansallinen Kokoomus Poulue (Cons.)	R	18.2%	37
Svenskapartiet (Swedish Party)	R	5.4%	12
Keskusliitto (Centre, ex-Agrarian)	C	18.2%	37
Christian League	C		1
Kansan Poulue (Liberal)	C	5.4%	8
Rural Party	L	10.5%	18
Sosialidemokraatinen Poulue	SD	23.8%	51
People's Democratic League	K	18.1%	36
France (1968)			
Extreme right	ER	0.2%	—
Union des Démocrates pour la République (Gaullists)	CR	38.1%	292
Independent Republicans	CR	5.1%	61
Centre Démocrate	C	10.8%	33
Fédération de la Gauche Démocrate et Socialiste	L	18.0%	57
Parti Socialiste Unifié	EL	4.1%	10
Parti Communiste Français	K	22.1%	34
Gabon (1969)			
Parti Démocratique Gabonais	—	—	—
Gambia, The (1966)			
People's Progressive Party	C	...	24
United Party	L	...	8
German Democratic Republic (1971)			
National Front	—	99.9%	434
Germany, Federal Republic of (1969)			
Christlich-Demokratische Union	R	46.1%	242
Freie Demokratische Partei	C	5.8%	30
Sozialdemokratische Partei Deutschlands	SD	42.7%	224
Ghana (1969)			
People's Action Party	R	...	2
National Alliance of Liberals	CR	...	29
Progress Party (Busia)	C	...	105
United Nationalist Party	...	...	2
Greece			
Military government since April 21, 1967	—	—	—
Guatemala (1970)			
Movimiento de Liberación Nacional	R	...	31
Partido Institucional Democrático	CR	42.9%	19
Democracia Cristiana Guatemalteca	C	21.5%	5
Partido Revolucionario	L	35.6%	...
Guinea (1968)			
Parti Démocratique de Guinée	—		75
Guyana (1968)			
People's National Congress	C	...	30
United Force	L	...	4
People's Progressive Party	EL	...	19
Haiti			
Presidential dictatorship since 1957	—	—	—

COUNTRY AND NAME OF PARTY	Affiliation	Voting strength	Parliamentary representation
Honduras (1971)			
Partido Nacional	R	...	33
Partido Liberal	C	...	32
Hungary (1971)			
Patriotic People's Front	—	98.9%	352
Iceland (1971)			
Independence (Conservative)	R	36.2%	22
Progressive	C	25.2%	17
Liberal Left	L	8.9%	5
Social Democratic	SD	10.4%	6
People's Union	EL	17.1%	10
India (1971)			
Jan Sangh (Hindu Nationalist)	ER	...	22
Swatantra (Freedom)	R	...	7
Dravida Munnetra Kazhagam	R	...	23
Ruling Congress	C	...	349
Opposition Congress	C	...	16
Praja Socialist	SD	...	2
Samyukta Socialist	S	...	3
Communist (pro-Soviet)	K	...	24
Communist (pro-Chinese)	K	...	25
Independents and others	—	...	43
Indonesia (1971)			
Sekber Golkar (Functional Groups)	—	...	261
Partai Nasional Indonesia	R	...	20
Nahdatul Ulama (Muslim Teachers)	R	...	58
Partai Sarikat Islam Indonesia (United Muslims)	C	...	10
Perti (Islamic Party)	C	...	2
Parmusi (Liberal Muslims)	C	...	24
Partai Keristen Indonesia (Protestants)	C	...	7
Partai Katholik	C	...	3
Partai Murba (Party of the Masses)	EL	...	0
West Irian	—	...	9
Iran (1971)			
Iran Novin (New Iran)	R	...	226
Mardom (People's) Party	C	...	36
Pan-Iranian Party	C	...	1
Religious groups	—	...	5
Iraq			
Military governments since 1958	—	—	—
Ireland (1969)			
Fianna Fail (Sons of Destiny)	C	...	75
Fine Gael (United Ireland)	C	...	50
Labour	L	...	18
Israel (1969)			
Free Centre	ER	1.2%	2
Gahal (Herut-Liberal Alignment)	R	21.7%	26
National Religious	C	9.7%	12
Agudat Israel	C	3.2%	4
Poalei Agudat Israel	C	1.8%	2
Independent Liberal	C	3.2%	4
State List (Ben-Gurion)	L	3.1%	4
Maarakh (Labour Alignment)	L	46.2%	56
Two Arab lists	L		4
Haolam Hazé (Avnery)	L	1.2%	2
Communist (Maki or pro-Israel)	K	1.2%	1
Communist (Rakah or pro-Arab)	K	2.8%	3
Italy (1968)			
Movimento Sociale Italiano	F	4.5%	24
Partito Democratico Italiano di Unità Monarchica	R	1.3%	6
Partito Liberale Italiano	CR	5.8%	31
Partito Democrazia Cristiana	C	39.1%	266
Partito Socialista Italiano	SD	14.5%	91
Partito Socialista Italiano di Unità Proletaria	EL	4.5%	23
Partito Comunista Italiano	K	26.9%	177
Südtiroler Volkspartei		...	3
Ivory Coast (1970)			
Parti Démocratique de la Côte d'Ivoire	—	...	100
Jamaica (1967)			
Jamaica Labour Party	L	...	33
People's National Party	L	...	20
Japan (1969)			
Komeito	CR	10.91%	47
Liberal-Democratic	CR	47.63%	300
Democratic Socialist	SD	7.74%	32
Socialist	S	21.44%	90
Communist	K	6.81%	14
Jordan			
Royal government, no parties	—	—	60
Kenya (1969)			
Kenya African National Union	—	—	171
Korea, North (1967)			
Korean Workers' (Communist) Party	...	100%	300
Korea, South (1971)			
Democratic Republican Party	R	...	113
New Democratic Party	C	...	89
Taejung Dang (Party of the Masses)	EL	...	2
Kuwait			
Princely government	—	—	30
Laos			
Royal government; pro-Communist Neo Lao Hak Sat party controls area bordering North Vietnam	—	—	—

COUNTRY AND NAME OF PARTY	Affiliation	Voting strength	Parliamentary representation
Lebanon (1969)			
Chamber of Deputies elected by universal suffrage according to the proportional division between Christians and Muslims	—	—	99
Lesotho (1970)			
Constitution suspended Jan. 30, 1970, following the apparent defeat of the ruling National Party in the Jan. 27 general election.	—	—	—
Liberia (1968)			
True Whig Party	—	...	41
Libya			
Military government since Sept. 1, 1969	—	—	—
Liechtenstein (1970)			
Vaterlandische Union	CR	...	8
Fortschrittliche Burgerpartei	C	...	7
Christlich-Soziale Partei	C	...	—
Luxembourg (1968)			
Parti Chrétien-Social	CR	35.3%	21
Parti Libéral	C	16.6%	11
Parti Ouvrier Socialiste	SD	32.3%	18
Parti Communiste	K	15.5%	6
Malagasy Republic (1970)			
Parti Social-Démocrate	C	...	104
Parti du Congrès de l'Indépendance de Madagascar (AKFM)	L	...	3
Malawi (1971)			
Malawi Congress Party	CR	...	58
Malaysia			
Malaya (1969)			
Federal Alliance Party	R	...	66
Panmalayan Islamic Party	R	...	12
Gerakan Rakyat Malaysia	C	...	8
Democratic Action (Chinese)	L	...	13
People's Progressive Party	K	...	4
Sarawak (1970)			
Federal Alliance Party	R	...	10
Opposition groups	L	...	14
Sabah (1970)			
Federal Alliance Party	R	...	6
Opposition groups	L	...	10
Maldives (1965)			
Government by the Didi family	—	...	54
Mali			
Military government since Nov. 19, 1968	—	—	—
Malta (1971)			
Nationalist Party	R	48.1%	27
Malta Labour Party	SD	50.8%	28
Mauritania (1965)			
Parti du Peuple Mauritanien	—	92%	40
Mauritius (1967)			
Independence Party (Indian-dominated)	C	...	39
Parti Mauricien Social-Démocrate	L	...	23
Mexico (1970)			
Partido Acción Nacional	CR	13.8%	20
Partido Revolucionario Institucional	C	84.4%	178
Partido Auténtico de la Revolución Mexicana	L	0.9%	5
Partido Popular Socialista	S	0.5%	10
Monaco (1968)			
Union Nationale et Démocratique	—	...	18
Mongolia (1967)			
Mongolian People's Revolutionary Party	—	99%	295
Morocco (1970)			
Independents (pro-government)	CR	...	159
Popular Movement	C	...	60
Istiqlal	C	...	8
National Union of Popular Forces	L	...	1
Others	—	...	12
Nauru (1971)			
No political parties	—	...	18
Nepal			
Royal government since December 1960	—	—	—
Netherlands (1971)			
Statkundig Gereformeerde Partij	R	2.4%	3
Boerenpartij (Farmer's Party)	R	1.1%	1
Anti-Revolutionaire Partij (Calvinist)	CR	8.6%	13
Christelijk Historische Unie (Protestant)	CR	6.3%	10
Katholieke Volkspartij	C	21.9%	35
Volkspartij voor Vrijheid en Democratie	C	10.3%	16
"Democraten '66" (Nonconformist)	C	6.8%	11
Democraten-Socialisten 70	L	5.3%	8
Partij van de Arbeid	SD	24.6%	39
Pacifistisch Socialistische Partij	S	1.4%	2
Communistische Partij	K	3.9%	6
Three other parties	—	4.9%	6
New Zealand (1969)			
National (Conservative)	CR	...	44
Labour Party	L	...	40
Nicaragua (1967)			
Partido Liberal Nacionalista (Somoza)	R	...	36
Partido Conservador Tradicionalista	R	...	15
Partido Demócrata Cristiano	C	...	2
Partido Liberal Independenta	C	...	1
Niger (1970)			
Parti Progressiste Nigérien	—	...	50
Nigeria			
Military governments since Jan. 15, 1966	—	—	—
Norway (1969)			
Høyre (Conservative)	R	19.4%	29
Kristelig Folkeparti	CR	9.4%	14
Senterpartiet (ex-Agrarian)	C	10.6%	20
Venstre (Liberal)	C	9.3%	13
Arbeiderpartiet (Labour)	SD	46.7%	74
Sosialistisk Folkeparti	S	3.5%	—
Norges Kommunistiske Parti	K	1.0%	—
Oman			
Sultanate	—	—	—
Pakistan (1970, 1971)			
People's Party of West Pakistan	C	...	86
Awami League of East Pakistan	L	...	167
Panama			
Civilian-military government since Oct. 11, 1968	—	—	—
Paraguay (1967)			
Partido Colorado (Stroessner)	R	69.4%	80
Partido Liberal Radical	C	21.5%	29
Partido Liberal	C	6.2%	8
Partido Revolucionario (Febrerista)	SD	2.8%	3
Peru			
Military government since Oct. 3, 1968	—	—	—
Philippines (1969)			
Partido Nacionalista	R	...	...
Partido Liberal	CR	...	...
Poland (1969)			
Polska Zjednoczona Partia Robotnicza | Front of National Unity	—	97.6%	255
Zjednoczone Stronnictwo Ludowe			117
Stronnictwo Demokratyczne			39
Nonparty			49
Portugal (1969)			
Acção Nacional Popular	—	...	130
Qatar			
Emirate	—	—	—
Rhodesia (1970)			
Rhodesian Front (European)	R	70%	50
Centre Party (mainly African)	C	10%	7
National People's Union (African)	L	...	1
Others (elected by councils of chiefs)	—	...	8
Romania (1969)			
Partidul Comunist Romîn | People's Front	—	99.75%	465
Nonparty			
Rwanda (1965)			
Parmehutu Party	—	...	47
San Marino (1969)			
Partito Democratico-Cristiano	CR	...	27
Partito Social-Democratico	SD	...	11
Partito Socialista	S	...	7
Partito Communista (pro-Soviet)	K	...	14
Partito Communista (pro-Chinese)	K	...	1
Saudi Arabia			
Royal government	—	—	—
Senegal (1968)			
Union Progressiste Sénégalaise	—	...	80
Sierra Leone (1967)			
All People's Congress	—	...	48
Sierra Leone People's Party	—	...	12
Singapore (1968)			
People's Action Party	C	...	58
United People's Party	EL	...	—
Somalia			
Military government since Oct. 21, 1969	—	—	—
South Africa (1970)			
Nationalist Party	R	...	117
United Party	C	...	47
Progressive Party	L	...	1
Spain (1971)			
Movimiento Nacional	—	...	558
Sudan			
Military government since May 25, 1969	—	—	—
Swaziland (1968)			
Imbokodvo Party	...	...	...
Sweden (1970)			
Moderata Samlingspartiet (ex-Höger)	R	11.5%	41
Centerpartiet (ex-Agrarian)	CR	19.9%	71
Folkpartiet (Liberal)	C	16.2%	58
Socialdemokratiska Arbetarepartiet	SD	45.3%	163
Vänsterpartiet Kommunisterna	K	4.8%	17
Switzerland (1971)			
National Action	R	...	4
Republican Movement	R	...	7
Conservative Christian Social People's	R	20.4%	44
Evangelical People's	R	1.9%	3
Swiss People's (formerly Farmers and Artisans)	CR	11.4%	23
Radical Democratic (Freisinnig)	C	21.3%	49
League of Independents	C	7.6%	13
Liberal Democratic	L	2.3%	6
Social Democratic	SD	23.1%	46
Communist (Partei der Arbeit)	K	2.7%	5
Syria			
Baath and military government	—	—	—
Taiwan (Republic of China)			
Nationalist (Kuomintang)	—	—	773

COUNTRY AND NAME OF PARTY	Affiliation	Voting strength	Parliamentary representation
Tanzania (1970)			
Tanganyika African National Union (elected)	C	...	120
Zanzibar Afro-Shirazi Party (nominated)	L	—	52
Thailand			
Royal and military government	—	—	—
Togo			
Military government since Jan. 13, 1967	—	—	—
Tonga (1969)			
Legislative Assembly of seven nobles, seven ministers, and seven elected delegates	—	—	21
Trinidad and Tobago (1971)			
People's National Movement	C	...	36
Action Committee for Dedicated Citizens	L	—	—
Tunisia (1969)			
Destourian Socialist Party	—	—	101
Turkey (1969)			
Turkish Justice	R	56.9%	257
Republican Nation's	R	1.3%	6
Republican People's	C	31.8%	144
Reliance (breakaway from RPP)	C	3.3%	15
Union	C	1.8%	8
New Turkey	C	1.3%	6
Nationalist Action (Peasants)	L	0.2%	1
Turkish Workers'	EL	0.4%	2
Uganda			
Uganda People's Congress	—	...	...
Union of Soviet Socialist Republics (1970)			
Communist Party of the Soviet Union	—	99.74%	767
United Kingdom (1970)			
Conservative and Unionist	R	46.4%	330
Liberal	C	7.4%	6
Labour	L	43.0%	287
Others	—	...	7
United States (1970)			
Republican	CR	...	180
Democratic	C	...	255
Upper Volta (1970)			
Union Démocratique Voltaïque	CR	...	37
Parti du Regroupement Africain	C	...	12
Mouvement de Libération Nationale	L	...	6
Uruguay (1971)			
Partido Nacional (Blanco)	R	40.3%	...
Partido Colorado (Liberal)	C	41.0%	...
Frente Amplio	EL	18.7%	...
Venezuela (1968)			
Cruzada Cívica Nacional	ER	11.4%	21
Unión Republicana Democrática	R	9.6%	17
Frente Nacional Democrático	R	2.6%	5
Fuerza Democrática Popular	C	5.5%	10
Comitado Organización Política Electoral Independiente (COPEI; Social Christians)	C	25.4%	57
Acción Democrática	C	28.0%	68
Movimiento Electoral del Pueblo	L	14.5%	27
Unión para Avanzar (Communist)	K	2.8%	5
Vietnam, North (1971)			
Lao Dong (Communist Party)	—	...	420
Vietnam, South (1971)			
National coalition	—	...	152
Western Samoa (1970)			
No political parties	—	...	45
Yemen (Aden)			
National Liberation Front	—	—	—
Yemen (San'a')			
Republican regime since November 1967	—	—	—
Yugoslavia (1969)			
League of Communists of Yugoslavia / Socialist Alliance of the Working People	—	...	670
Zambia (1968)			
United National Independence Party	—	...	81
African National Congress	—	...	23
Independents	—	...	1

(K. Sm.)

Political Science

No single spectacular event marked the work and thinking of political scientists in 1971, but there seemed to be an increasing awareness of recent and important changes in many countries and on the international scene. Several political systems that had been considered stable had experienced great unrest and severe disruptions in recent years. The consensual basis of democratic politics could no longer be taken for granted; neither could the strength of authoritarian regimes. The emergence of China as a potential superpower made obsolete much of the previous theorizing on the international system.

New challenges to political science thus appeared, and the responses were becoming clear. Only a minority of political scientists believed that the discipline was worthless, harmful, or, at best, irrelevant. Few were willing to turn away from the theoretical and methodological advances achieved since 1945, or to confuse the desire for scientific relevance with the urge to political militancy. Most believed that they had tools, still crude and greatly in need of improvement, that could contribute to an understanding of domestic and international politics. They realized, however, that much of their knowledge applied only to the historical situation in which it was obtained, and that much greater caution had to be used before timeless generalizations could be made.

In the U.S. the climate of political science continued to be affected by the war in Vietnam. The circumstances of the My Lai massacre, the publication of the Pentagon papers by the *New York Times* and the administration's failure to prevent it, and the September presidential elections in South Vietnam again led many political scientists to intervene in public affairs. A major survey of college and university professors, analyzed by E. C. Ladd and S. M. Lipset in *PS* (spring 1971), made it clear that political science was among the most liberal of disciplines. Only when the politics of political scientists was set against that of sociologists did the former appear as relatively "conservative." But "liberal" did not mean "radical" and, as in 1969, the "caucus for a new political science" failed to gain control of the American Political Science Association (APSA): its candidate for the presidency of APSA for 1971–72, Hans Morgenthau of the University of Chicago, obtained 3,563 votes in the mail ballot conducted in November 1970, as against 4,711 for Heinz Eulau of Stanford University, presented by the APSA nominating committee.

The European Consortium for Political Research, set up in 1970 by eight universities and research institutions, held its first Summer School in Quantitative Techniques, set up a Data Information Service, and made plans for a *European Journal of Political Research.* Its success was apparent from its increase in membership to 30 institutions. The creation in France of an *agrégation de science politique,* through which political science professors were to be recruited starting in 1973, pointed up the diminishing hold of the legal approach throughout Europe.

The International Political Science Association announced the program of the ninth World Congress of Political Science, to be held during Aug. 19–25, 1973, in Montreal. Its two major themes were to be "politics between economy and culture" and "key issues in international conflict and peace research," in addition to a large number of special topics.

There was a striking increase in political science publications. Among recent additions were: *Affari Esteri* (Rome); *African Review* (Nairobi); *Annals of International Studies* (Geneva); *British Journal of Political Science* (Cambridge, U.K.); *Études internationales* (Quebec City); *Foreign Policy* (New York City); *Japan Institute of International Affairs Annual Review* (Tokyo); *Journal of Comparative Administration* (Beverly Hills, Calif.); *Pacific Community* (Tokyo); *Political Science Annual* (New York City); *Politics* (Kensington, Austr.); *Politics and Society* (Los Altos, Calif.); *Polity* (Amherst, Mass.); *Public Choice* (Blacksburg, Va.); *Revista latinoamericana de Ciencia política* (Santiago, Chile); *Revue libanaise des Sciences politiques* (Beirut); *Rivista italiana di Scienza politica* (Bologna); *Sozialwissen-schaftliches Jahrbuch für Politik* (Munich); *L'Univers politique* (Paris); and *Verfassung und Recht in Übersee* (Hamburg). (Se. H.)

Encyclopædia Britannica Films. *The Presidency—Search for a Candidate* (1970); *The Progressive Era* (1971); *The Modern Presidency and the Limits of Power* (1971).

Populations and Areas

The population of the earth passed the 3.7 billion mark by mid-1971, and was continuing an annual gain of approximately 2%, according to United Nations estimates. The world gained a total of 74 million persons, which was the difference between 126 million births and 52 million deaths. Although absolute population figures were sketchy for large areas of the world, and major nations like the United States had shown definite signs of a growth slowdown, it was still a pretty good guess that the world would have to house, clothe, and feed an additional 3.7 billion people within the next 35 years. With increasing tensions, environmental pollution, diminishing natural resources, and conditions of abject poverty for more than half the world's people, the addition of more billions of inhabitants was increasingly being viewed with alarm. What was more, the fastest growth records were being set in the impoverished, less developed nations in Africa, Latin America, and Asia. In beleaguered Pakistan, for example, 600,000 people died in a disastrous cyclone and its aftermath in 1970, but within 60 days the country had 600,000 new mouths to feed.

It had become a rule of thumb that the rich nations of the world were those where growth continued at a rate below 2% a year and the poor ones were those in which growth exceeded 2%. Generally, the richest nations were also those with growth rates of 1% a year or lower and per capita annual incomes exceeding $1,000. In effect, a high birthrate combined with a low death rate produces a high rate of growth. For example, the African nation of Zambia, whose birthrate was estimated at 50 live births per 1,000 population, had a relatively high death rate of 30 per 1,000 population. The difference between these rates produced a high growth of 3% a year. This meant that this poor country, with a per capita gross national product (GNP) of $220, would double its 4.4 million population in only 24 years. The slower growing industrially developed countries had relatively low birthrates and death rates. The U.S.S.R., for example, was increasing its population by 1% each year, which suggested that it would double its current population of 242 million people in 70 years.

Centre of population for conterminous U.S. moved steadily westward from 1790 to 1970.

World records were being set in a number of small countries. The fastest growing nation on earth continued to be Kuwait on the Arabian Peninsula, which was an exception to the rule that the poor nations are the fastest growing. Kuwait, an emirate enriched with working oil fields, grew 8.2% in 1971 because of continued immigration and a birthrate of 43 and a low death rate of 7. Should that rate of growth continue, Kuwait would add another 800,000 persons to its population in only nine years.

Costa Rica in Central America continued to set a high growth record without the benefit of immigration. Because of its annual growth rate of 3.8%, which stemmed from a high birthrate of 45 and a low death rate of 8, Costa Rica could double its 1.7 million population in 19 years. Costa Rica typified the Latin-American growth pattern in which birthrates were high and death rates were brought under control by disease-destroying drugs. Annual income in Latin America hovered between $70 and $950, with the average around $350. The population was also young; close to half the people were under 15 years of age, in contrast to the U.S., with 30% under 15, and to Europe, where less than 25% were that young.

The nations of Europe remained at the slow end of the growth scale. Malta, with 300,000 persons, was experiencing a decline in population of 0.8% annually because of emigration. In East Germany the low birthrate of 14 was exceeded by a death rate of 14.3, but the country grew by 0.1% annually because of immigration. At the present rate, it would require 700 years for East Germany to double its 17 million population. Slow growth, in fact, characterized all of Europe, where birthrates tended to fall below 18 per 1,000 and the average death rate was 10 per 1,000. The continent as a whole grew by 0.8% in 1970 for a total of 466 million. By maintaining this slow growth rate, Europe could be expected to double its population in 88 years.

By contrast, Latin America, as the world's fastest growing region, would experience a jump from its present 291 million population to 435 million by 1985 if the present trend of 2.9% annual growth continued. Its population would exceed 600 million by the year 2000. Although population control programs were at work throughout these predominantly Roman Catholic nations, birthrates there continued to average 38 per 1,000.

Africa, with the world's highest birthrates, had the potential for exceeding Latin-American growth rates. These rates were slowed, however, by high death rates attributed to poor medical facilities in Africa. Even so, Africa was expected to grow from 354 million persons in 1971 to 530 million by 1985. The current 2.7% growth rate meant that the continent would double its

continued on page 569

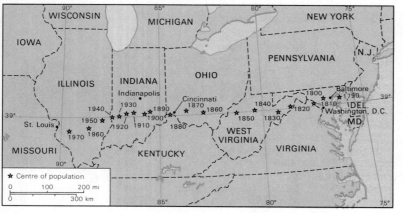

POPULATION GROWTH AND AMERICA'S FUTURE

By John D. Rockefeller III

In March 1972 the Commission on Population Growth and the American Future will issue its final report to the president, the Congress, and the people of the United States. The report will urge the creation of an explicit national population policy. No other nation has yet moved decisively in this direction but the commission is persuaded that if we hope to alleviate our society's present problems, as well as head off greater crises in the future, we must act now. In its interim report, issued on March 16, 1971, the commission stated that "continued population growth serves as an intensifier or multiplier of many problems impairing the quality of life in the United States." In our final report we will examine trends that eventually may bring the birthrate of this country down to a level consistent with a zero rate of population growth.

On a personal basis, I believe that beyond welcoming this development if it occurs, we ought to take steps to encourage it. Zero population growth is not guaranteed and if it comes it may not last. Many features in our society stand in its way.

The Expansion Ethic. In the brief history of the United States its people have evolved an ethic of expansion, conquest, progress, accumulation, innovation, untrammeled growth—not growth of human numbers alone, but growth in every material facet of our existence. We have evolved institutions, laws, political ideologies, and social norms that take this perpetual growth as their unexamined primary axiom. Industrial man too often has acted as if he is seized by a demon that directs him to plunder the earth in his quest of means for increasing his satisfactions,

but denies him the true enjoyment of these means for fear that the rate of increase may diminish tomorrow.

At the root of the explosion of numbers, despoliation of the environment, the threat of military catastrophe, the breakdown of our sense of community and belonging is the extraordinary increase in man's power to manipulate the external, material world. We characteristically have reacted to the growth of technology as though it were a free gift of the gods, to be employed according to the whim and fancy of the instant without regard to consequences. Much that we have done with technology—to improve health, which lengthens life, to spread knowledge, and to increase the security of daily existence—can be applauded. But we have failed to see that with the new "goods" we have acquired hosts of new "bads" and, more important, that in accepting new powers we must accept new responsibilities.

It is not easy to question the assumptions on which we have all erected our lives—particularly if those assumptions seem so natural that we hardly are aware of them. But we have learned of late to question much of what we had formerly taken for granted, for example, the air that we breathe. Here and there thoughtful persons are raising questions about our way of life that did not come to mind a few decades ago. One of those questions is how well served are we by continuing population growth.

The Cost of Continued Growth. In its interim report the Commission on Population Growth and the American Future plotted some of the effects that small changes in family size would have on total population size and the quality of life in the United States in the years to come:

> If families in the United States have only two children on the average and immigration continues at current levels, our population would still grow to 266 million by the end of the century; if they have three children, the population would reach 321 million. One hundred years from now the two-child family would result in a population of 340 million persons; the three-child average would produce nearly a billion....
>   Small differences in family size will make big differences in the demands placed on our society.... If families average three children, in the year 2000 elementary school enrollment will be 50% above what it would be if families average only two children. Similarly, secondary school enrollment will be 43% higher and college enrollment 34% higher.... This would mean a 30% higher level of educational expenditures per working member of society.... In the health field, the three-child family implies an annual cost of $14 billion more in the year 2000 than the two-child family just to maintain present standards.... If the three-child family is the norm in the year 2000, the economy will have to produce 20% more than would be necessary to provide the two-child family with the same standard of living.

Many people believe that the world already faces a scarcity of vital natural resources. As our numbers increase, so do our demands upon those resources. We will not survive as a society in the long haul without resolving the issue of balance between numbers of people and the life-support system of our finite planet. But neither will we survive the stresses that our ethic of perpetual expansion puts on our social fabric as well as on our external environment. Naturally, those institutions that weave our social fabric—our health, legal, educational, and welfare systems, for instance—clearly have to find new ways of meeting society's needs. But I strongly believe that the resistance to change within most of our people-serving institutions is partly traceable to our demand that they devise new methods to serve us even as they must reach ever increasing numbers. My point is quite simple. What I am trying to convey is the notion that in many parts of the world potential gains in the quality of life are offset by the demand to meet the basic needs of ever increasing quantities of people.

We Cannot Grow Forever. However desirable it may be for us to stop—or slow—our growth, let me refer to the many basic features of our society that stand in the way of reaching, and maintaining, population replacement over the long run:

1. As a nation we have an ideological addiction to growth, for reasons which, as I suggested earlier, no longer apply.

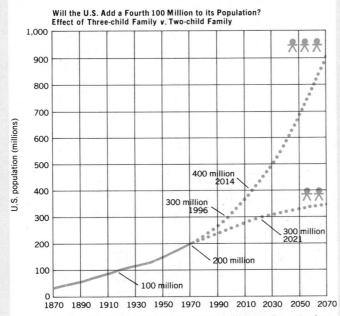

Will the U.S. Add a Fourth 100 Million to its Population?
Effect of Three-child Family v. Two-child Family

U.S. population (millions)

400 million 2014

300 million 1996

300 million 2021

200 million

100 million

1870 1890 1910 1930 1950 1970 1990 2010 2030 2050 2070

Sources: U.S. Department of Commerce, Bureau of the Census, *Current Population Reports*; Commission on Population Growth and the American Future, *Population Growth and America's Future.*

John D. Rockefeller III is chairman of the Commission on Population Growth and the American Future, established by the U.S. Congress, and chairman of the Population Council, Inc.

2. Our social institutions, including many of our laws, are basically pronatalist in their effect. This includes the images of family life and women's roles as they are projected in television programs, the child-saves-marriage theme that permeates women's magazines, legal restrictions on contraception, sex education, and abortion, tax disabilities imposed on single people and working wives, and many others.

3. Many witnesses appearing before the Commission on Population Growth and the American Future provided evidence indicating that throughout all segments of our society there is a totally unsatisfactory level of understanding of the role of sex in human life and of the reproductive process and its control.

4. Although statistics prove that the birthrate maintained by the white middle-class majority is the factor most responsible for population growth, we must recognize that the failure to bring racial minorities and the poor into the mainstream of American life has prevented the development in these people of a stake in slower population growth and impaired their ability to implement low family size goals.

5. If it should happen that in the next few years the birthrate falls to replacement levels or below, we are likely to observe a strong counterreaction. In the United States in the 1930s, and in several other countries at various times, the response to a leveling in the birthrate has been a cry of anxiety over national virility, spirit, and health.

In spite of these factors that favour continued population growth, I believe our population cannot grow forever. Any growth rate, even our current rate of 1% per year, would lead to physical absurdity if continued indefinitely. Simple arithmetic shows that continuation of current U.S. population growth rates for 1,300 years would result in one person per each square foot of the entire land area of the United States. Obviously we shall stop short of this. But where? One person per square yard? If that is too many people, where short of that shall we stop? It is clear that we *shall* stop; the question is how and when.

The Chances for Zero Growth. I am not trying to suggest that our population is going to stop growing immediately. Our past high birthrates produced a record 31 million babies in the 1950s who have grown up and are now beginning to enter their childbearing years. The baby boom that produced them is bound to be echoed in rising numbers of births in the 1970s and beyond. What I do want to urge is that we can move toward reproductive habits that eventually will be consistent with a balance of births and deaths. I say "eventually" because it will take time for the high proportion of our current population that is in its childbearing years to decline.

In preindustrial times, an average of zero growth in population was achieved over the long term because the rapid growth experienced in good times was offset by rapid declines in times of famine, disease, or war. In modern times, we have reduced the death rate and kept it under control. Last year's high school graduates were born in a period when the expectation of life was 70 years; their parents were born with an expectation of life of 60 years, and their grandparents with an expectation of 50 years. Much of this improvement was achieved through control of infant and child death rates. Although important groups are still disadvantaged relative to the national average, we have achieved a good thing—more babies living to maturity and a

U.S. Population Trends

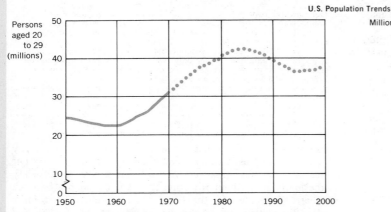

An average of 2 children per family would slow population growth, but would not stop it soon because the number of people of childbearing age is increasing . . .

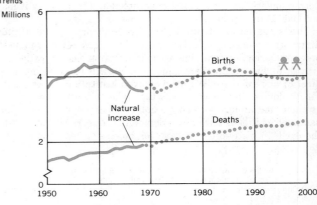

. . . the resulting births will continue to exceed deaths for the rest of this century . . .

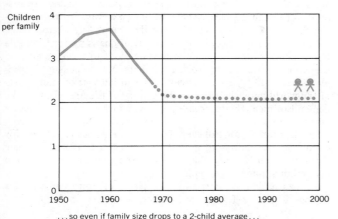

. . . so even if family size drops to a 2-child average . . .

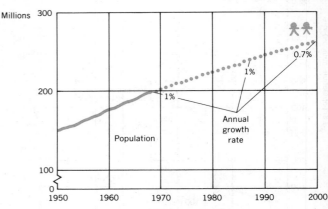

. . . the population will still be growing in the year 2000, but at a decreasing rate.

Sources: U.S. Department of Commerce, Bureau of the Census, *Current Population Reports*; Commission on Population Growth and the American Future, *Population Growth and America's Future*.

longer, healthier, and more productive life for the average person. A consequence of this has been a larger and larger population. The birthrate has fallen in recent years, but it is still twice the death rate.

I began by suggesting that our "growth ethic" no longer serves us well. Let me outline a number of other developments—some of ancient and some of recent origin—that further enhance the likelihood of achieving a level of fertility ultimately commensurate with zero growth.

1. The trend of the average family size has been downward, from 8 children per family in colonial times to 2.5 children in recent years—interrupted, however, by the baby boom, when fertility rates were at a level that, if continued, would have produced 3.7 children per family.

2. The increasing employment of women, and the movement to liberalize women's options as to occupational and family roles, promises to continue to expand alternatives to the conventional role of wife-homemaker-mother.

3. Concern over the effects of population growth has been mounting. Two-thirds of the general public interviewed in the survey conducted in 1971 by the Commission on Population Growth and the American Future felt that the growth of U.S. population was a serious problem. Half or more expressed concern over the impact of population growth on the use of natural resources, on air and water pollution, and on social unrest and dissatisfaction.

4. The family-size preferences of young people entering the childbearing ages are significantly lower than the preferences given by their elders at the same stage in life.

5. The technical quality of contraceptives has increased tremendously in the past ten years; their effectiveness in use, however, is still so low that many unwanted births result.

6. The legalization of abortion in a few states has resulted in major increases in the number of reported abortions. The evidence so far indicates that legalized abortion is being used by many women who would otherwise have sought illegal and unsafe abortions. The probable effect of easier access to abortion on the birthrate is not yet clear.

The Need for a Change of Values. As my initial statements indicate, many of us who are students of the population problem find it is so closely entwined with the other major issues facing our society that we find it difficult to narrow our discussions on the topic. I have tried to suggest that dealing with population growth is only one element, albeit an underlying one, in finding solutions to our nation's tough problems.

As I pointed out earlier, Americans are living in a way that is inconsistent with our finite environment and fragile ecological structure. Rapid population growth, high levels of income, poor choices of technology, and a failure to ration the use of our commonly held resources, such as air and water, have combined to cause far-reaching damage to our environment. It is my view that we must act on each of the causes. We must reproduce at a responsible rate, use our comparatively high level of income in ways that do not exacerbate environmental problems, develop technologies that do not damage ecological systems, and, finally, make the purity of our air and water everyone's responsibility.

In the short run, slowing population growth may not be the most effective way of fighting pollution and preserving resources. Indeed, it is almost always true that population size and composition change slowly. However, a population that has increased by 50% in 30 years is clearly an important factor in determining the nation's use of resources and its environment.

While I believe that any effort made to alleviate our resource and environmental problems should include an effort to limit population size, I emphasize, at the same time, that slowing population growth is no substitute for changes in the way we chose to use our great wealth. A change of values is necessary—a change of values to those more consistent with our environment and with our human nature; a change that may move us to make good on our promise of "unalienable rights" to all segments of our society.

continued from page 566

population in 26 years, if no change in present conditions occurred. Three African nations tied for first place among nations with high birthrates: Mauritania, Rwanda, and Swaziland each recorded 52 births per 1,000. In each country, the death rate ranged between 22 and 23 per 1,000. The highest death rate, 30, was recorded in Portuguese-controlled Angola. Zambia reported an infant mortality rate of 259, which meant that more than one-fourth of all infants that were born died before their first birthday. Death among infants was common in most African countries; about one in eight did not survive more than one year.

Despite this high incidence of infant mortality, African populations tended to be young, with 44% of the total under the age of 15. The introduction of modern medical facilities in Africa would bring death rates down, but the steady addition of millions of mouths to feed would make it difficult for these nations, with per capita GNPs of between $50 and $250 a year, to improve the quality of life for their citizens.

Asia, with 57% of the world's population, was not only the largest and most populous continent but also contained five of the seven most populous nations in the world. (The U.S.S.R. and the U.S. ranked third and fourth, respectively, in population.) According to conservative estimates, Asia had 2.1 billion people, an average birthrate of 38, and a death rate of 15. This meant that by 1985 the continent would add another 770 million to its present population, a figure equal to some estimates of the present population of China, the world's most populous nation. There was some feeling, however, that China might have as many as 900 million persons and that if it were growing at the rate of 1.8% a year, its population would double in 39 years.

India, the world's second most populous nation, grew by more than 30 million persons in one year, for a total population of 546.9 million in 1971. The country's 2.6% annual growth rate consisted of a high birthrate of 42 and a death rate of 17. India's per capita GNP was $100 and fully 41% of the people were under 15. The nation ranking fifth in population was Indonesia, with 122.6 million persons, an annual growth rate of 2.9%, and a per capita GNP of $100. Pakistan, with 116.5 million persons, was the sixth most populous nation. East Pakistan, which broke away in December 1971 to become Bangla Desh, had a 1969 population of almost 60 million. Japan with 104.1 million persons, ranked seventh. Unlike these other Asian nations, however, Japan had a birthrate of 18 and a death rate of 7, was increasing by only 1.1% annually, and had a per capita GNP of $1,190, which was the highest in East Asia.

The population of the U.S. was estimated to have reached 207 million by mid-1971. Although the country had shown enormous gains in population growth for the last three decades, signs of a slowdown in this growth were increasing. The birthrate had dropped steadily for the last few years, reaching levels recorded previously only during the depression years of the 1930s. The rate recorded for the year ending August 1971 was 17.7 per 1,000, a drop from 18.1 per 1,000 for the previous year. The death rate declined slightly from 9.4 to 9.3. In effect, the growth of the U.S. had slowed from 1.1% annually to about 1%. This meant it would take 70 years for the population to double.

What seemed to be affecting the birthrate in the U.S. was a new trend toward smaller family size, which was considered to be brought on by a combination of

continued on page 573

Table II. World Census Data

POLITICAL UNIT	Year of census	ENUMERATED POPULATION Total	Male	Percent urban*	AGE DISTRIBUTION 0 to 15	16 to 45	46 and over	ECONOMICALLY ACTIVE Total	Agriculture	Mining and manufacturing
Afars & Issas	1964	82,100	...	57.4	...	...	...	...	...	...
Albania	1960	1,626,315	834,384	30.9	...	...	...	730,800	...	...
Algeria	1966	11,833,126	6,079,900	...	5,947,800	4,387,700	1,744,800	2,335,200	1,300,000	183,500
American Samoa	1970	27,769†	14,450	28.0	13,145‡	10,865‡	2,980‡	14,195	1,218	3,674
Angola	1960	4,830,449†	2,459,015	10.6	2,011,378‡	2,177,631‡	641,440‡	1,421,966	944,716	26,508
Antigua	1960	54,060†	25,230	60.1	23,154	20,964	9,942	16,873	12,564	4,084
Argentina	1960	20,008,945	10,034,544	...	5,772,043§	10,486,674§	3,663,094§	7,599,071	1,460,541	1,959,041
Australia	1966	11,550,462	5,816,359	83.2	3,392,488	4,873,899	3,284,073	4,856,455	...	1,368,468
Austria	1961	7,073,807	3,296,400	50.1	1,660,615	2,729,599	2,683,593	3,369,815	767,604	1,093,046
Bahamas	1970	168,812†	83,661	...	73,601‡	69,316‡	25,895‡	69,791	4,791	3,902
Bahrain	1971	216,078	116,314	...	95,640‡	90,994‡	29,444‡	60,301	3,990	8,464
Barbados	1960	232,327	105,519	40.3	88,882‡	88,636‡	54,809‡	85,040	22,440	13,468
Belgium	1961	9,189,741	4,496,860	66.4	2,333,846	3,543,729	3,312,166	3,512,463	253,922	1,326,732
Bermuda	1960	42,640	21,233	9.6	14,199	18,179	9,470	19,498	309	322
Botswana	1964	543,105	264,535	...	242,424	204,797	80,198	250,678	227,009	1,800‖
Brazil	1970	93,204,379†	46,330,629	55.9	38,865,773¶	44,048,881¶	10,289,725¶	29,545,293	13,071,385	5,263,8059
British Honduras	1960	90,505	44,659	53.7	40,369	34,615	15,521	26,029	8,833	3,329
British Solomon Islands	1970	160,998	85,179	...	71,761‡	66,326‡	22,911‡	13,690‖	3,182‖	960‖
British Virgin Islands	1960	7,338	3,930	12.1	3,793	2,737	808	2,128	629	107
Brunei	1960	83,877	43,676	43.6	39,109‡	33,059‡	11,709‡	24,830	8,317	5,171
Bulgaria	1965	8,227,866	4,114,167	46.4	2,112,364	3,789,130	2,326,372	4,267,793	1,891,398	1,124,885
Cambodia (Khmer Rep.)	1962	5,740,115	2,880,780	16.0	2,513,300‡	2,381,215‡	845,600‡	...	...	...
Canada	1966	20,014,880	10,054,344	73.6	6,591,757‡	8,325,686‡	5,097,437‡	6,458,156	648,910	1,101,553
Canal Zone	1960	42,122†	23,278	31.9	15,204¶	19,888¶	7,030¶	17,085	336	...
Cape Verde Islands	1960	199,661	94,027	23.2	99,0236	69,8166	29,3586	105,570	42,387	1,294
Cayman Islands	1960	8,511†	3,974	41.4	3,020	3,515	1,976	3,132	...	...
Ceylon	1963	10,624,507	5,503,000	18.8	4,616,920	4,408,550	1,564,590	2,542,920	1,272,800	258,170
Channel Islands Guernsey	1961	47,099	22,718	33.3	11,262‡	17,410‡	18,427‡	...	...	...
Jersey	1961	63,550	30,715	...	12,534	25,643	25,373	30,696	3,259	2,028
Chile	1970	8,853,140	4,321,500	76.0	3,456,700‡	3,729,320‡	1,547,300‡	2,607,360	552,340	490,740
Christmas Island (Australian)	1966	3,381	2,151	...	...	...	...	...	...	...
Colombia	1964	17,484,508	8,614,652	52.8	8,155,529▫	7,022,627▫	2,306,508▫	5,134,059	2,427,059	81,279
Comoro Islands	1966	244,905†	120,385	13.9	109,364‡	95,358‡	42,183‡	82,090	52,415	11,035
Cook Islands	1966	19,247	9,749	...	9,983‡	6,693‡	2,571‡	5,426	2,146	619
Costa Rica	1963	1,336,274†	668,957	34.5	636,665‡	516,395‡	183,214‡	395,273	194,309	46,459
Cyprus	1960	573,566†	281,983	35.9	221,656‡	226,612‡	125,298‡	241,823	93,287	37,718
Czechoslovakia	1961	13,745,577†	6,704,674	47.6	3,960,752	5,370,682	4,414,143	...	...	...
Denmark	1965	4,767,597	2,362,000‖	77.1	1,215,000‖	1,957,000‖	1,596,000‖	2,251,000‖	608,000‖	1,282,000‖
Dominica	1960	59,916	28,167	25.6	26,802‡	21,599‡	11,515‡	22,477	11,693	2,553
Dominican Republic	1960	3,047,070	1,535,820	30.1	1,440,900‡	1,218,440‡	387,730‡	820,710	504,820	58,890
Ecuador	1962	4,476,007	2,236,476	36.0	2,014,505	1,838,160	623,342	1,442,591	800,390	215,617
El Salvador	1961	2,510,984	1,236,728	38.5	1,176,744	1,011,819	322,421	807,092	486,213	104,227
Equatorial Guinea	1960	245,989	132,293	...	...	...	...	...	...	...
Faeroe Islands	1966	37,122	...	...	...	...	...	...	...	...
Falkland Islands	1962	2,172	1,195	49.4	568°	1,134°	470°	930	359	...
Fiji	1966	476,727	242,747	33.4	232,826	190,543	53,112	125,809	656,921	10,451
Finland	1960	4,446,222†	2,142,263	38.4	1,338,991	1,831,849	1,275,382	2,033,268	720,817	444,516
France	1968	49,654,556†	24,196,528	70.0	11,790,960‡	20,655,544‡	17,208,052‡	19,961,852	3,131,320	7,903,324
French Guiana	1961	33,295†	16,288	75.1	12,127¶	14,296¶	6,872¶	11,981	3,273	...
French Polynesia	1962	84,550	43,106	...	45,232	34,591	3,643	25,593	9,484	5,715
Gabon	1960–61	444,264†	204,698	16.7	135,574	210,611	98,079	311,959	153,414	21,512
Gambia, The	1963	315,486	160,849	8.8	118,586‡	155,834‡	41,066‡	160,000‖	135,000‖	2,500‖
Germany, East	1964	17,011,931†	7,751,862	72.9	4,262,941	6,338,075	6,410,915	7,657,786	1,267,257	3,140,721
Germany, West	1961	56,174,826†	26,413,362	77.8	12,184,784	22,935,570	21,054,478	26,527,328	3,587,000	12,908,000
Ghana	1960	6,726,815	3,400,270	23.1	2,996,506‡	2,894,238‡	836,071‡	2,723,026	1,581,331	282,168
Gibraltar	1970	26,833	12,914	...	2,865‡	6,333‡	3,716‡	11,748	...	258
Gilbert and Ellice Islands	1968	53,517	26,404	14.9	20,323‡	17,130‡	7,187‡	13,121	8,601	496
Greece	1961	8,388,553	4,091,894	43.3	2,392,514	3,710,437	2,285,602	3,638,601	1,960,446	510,087
Greenland	1965	39,600	20,354	...	19,091	15,752	4,757	13,248	3,651	300
Grenada	1960	88,677	40,660	8.2	42,268‡	30,472‡	15,937‡	15,219	10,895	2,657
Guadeloupe	1967	312,724†	159,760	45.8	139,346‡	126,281‡	59,412‡	...	...	...
Guam	1960	67,044	39,211	...	28,014	31,709	7,321	26,304	411	535
Guatemala	1964	4,287,997	2,172,456	33.6	1,949,395‡	1,786,505‡	551,519‡	1,362,669	...	...
Guyana	1960	560,330	279,128	15.5	259,228‡	215,228‡	85,874‡	174,730	59,790	32,371
Honduras	1961	1,884,765	939,029	23.2	940,827	730,153	213,785	567,988	379,125	45,779
Hong Kong	1966	3,716,400	1,880,870	86.9	1,571,440	1,493,630	643,850	1,454,730	27,970	557,300
Hungary	1961	9,961,044	4,804,043	39.7	2,691,036	4,096,392	3,173,616	5,312,831	1,872,730	1,378,987
Iceland	1966	196,933	...	...	...	...	...	...	...	...
India	1961	439,234,771†	226,293,201	18.0	188,500,020	192,142,333	58,294,565	188,675,500	131,142,816	18,561,671
Indonesia	1961	96,318,829	47,493,854	14.8	40,544,678	42,458,049	13,316,102	34,578,234	23,516,197	1,943,546
Iran	1966	25,078,923	12,981,665	38.1	11,639,200	9,861,700	3,642,800	7,584,085	3,168,515	1,293,912
Iraq	1965	8,261,527	4,205,201	44.1	...	...	...	...	...	...
Ireland	1966	2,884,002	1,449,032	49.2	...	...	...	1,106,000	330,000	277,000
Isle of Man	1966	50,423	23,226	56.0	10,385	16,450	23,588	13,837	1,829	...
Israel	1961	2,179,491†	1,106,069	77.9	786,196‡	869,045‡	524,250‡	751,230	96,420	168,895
Italy	1961	50,623,569†	24,791,683	47.7	11,549,620▫	22,903,305▫	16,170,638▫	20,096,693	5,657,446	7,886,1819
Jamaica	1960	1,609,814†	773,439	32.0	662,508‡	646,281‡	301,025‡	677,003	229,718	94,172
Japan	1965	98,274,961†	48,244,445	68.9	27,390,062	48,894,840	21,990,059	48,268,767	10,866,693	12,018,479
Jordan	1961	1,706,226	867,597	47.4	815,910▲	638,732▲	251,584▲	389,978	137,757	41,932
Kenya	1969	10,943,000	5,482,000	10.1	5,293,000‡	4,237,000‡	1,413,000‡	...	...	...
Korea, South	1966	29,207,856	14,700,966	33.5	12,851,456‡	11,975,220‡	4,381,178‡	9,325,000	4,826,000	940,000
Kuwait	1970	738,662	419,886	...	319,299‡	353,210‡	66,154‡	233,534	4,060	39,263
Lesotho	1966	969,634	465,784	...	370,390‡	306,208‡	172,756‡	...	...	...
Liberia	1962	1,016,443	503,588	19.7	394,509	471,553	150,381	411,794	298,404	22,913
Libya	1964	1,564,369†	813,386	...	683,431‡	630,379‡	249,160‡	405,258	146,709	43,636
Liechtenstein	1960	16,628	8,130	...	4,792	6,267	5,569	7,575	962	3,273
Luxembourg	1966	334,790	164,575	...	75,450‡	138,781‡	120,559‡	164,575	14,554	45,864
Macau	1960	169,299†	83,897	95.2	68,556	60,472	40,271	37,905	1,717	22,000†
Malawi	1966	4,039,583	1,913,262	5.0	1,774,766‡	1,645,740‡	619,077‡	...	...	...
Malaysia West Malaysia	1957	6,278,758	3,237,579	26.5	2,752,208‡	2,576,252‡	950,298‡	2,164,861	468,317	58,499
East Malaysia	1960	1,198,950	612,462	15.0‖	197,826‡	199,091‡	57,504‡	470,911	381,941	7,451
Maldives	1967	103,801†	55,346	...	46,086‡	45,422‡	12,293‡	...	...	...
Malta	1967	314,216†	150,598	...	93,759‡	136,884‡	83,573‡	94,367	7,109	22,893

Table II. World Census Data (Continued)

POLITICAL UNIT	Year of census	ENUMERATED POPULATION Total	Male	Percent urban*	AGE DISTRIBUTION 0 to 15	16 to 45	46 and over	ECONOMICALLY ACTIVE Total	Agriculture	Mining and manufacturing
Martinique	1967	320,030	155,212	45.8	139,262‡	120,406‡	60,211‡	89,464	22,746	8,091
Mauritius	1962	681,619	342,306	34.2	323,007	258,285	100,327	187,401	70,866	27,560
Mexico	1970	48,377,363†	24,140,309	58.6	22,359,416‡	19,446,516‡	6,571,029‡	12,994,395	5,131,666	2,353,814
Monaco	1968	23,035†	10,424	100.0	2,979‡	8,273‡	11,783‡	10,093	11	2,170
Mongolia	1963	1,018,800†	508,800	39.5	411,300	378,100	227,700	483,400	279,200	41,900
Montserrat	1960	12,167†	5,407	16.0	5,198	3,946	3,023	4,282	1,881	...
Morocco	1960	11,626,232†	5,809,172	29.3	5,307,824	4,738,350	1,580,058	3,290,950	1,721,000‖	...
Mozambique	1960	6,578,604†	3,149,270	...	...	...	...	...	...	...
Nauru	1966	6,048	3,696	...	...	...	...	...	...	...
Nepal	1961	9,387,661	4,619,973	2.8	3,684,000‖	4,258,000‖	1,445,000‖	...	...	...
Netherlands	1960	11,461,964†	5,706,874	55.4	3,516,623**	6,952,166**	993,175**	4,168,626	446,695	1,306,480
Netherlands Antilles	1960	192,538†	94,811	...	79,683‡	77,069‡	35,786‡	59,806	1,029	16,059
New Caledonia	1969	100,579†	52,591	41.6	34,964‡	46,028‡	19,587‡	39,185	13,357	7,152
New Guinea, Territory of	1966	1,578,650	821,899	47.3	694,633	700,669	183,348	889,287	818,739	9,023
New Zealand	1966	2,676,919	1,343,858	62.4	...	...	...	...	...	...
Nicaragua	1963	1,535,588	757,922	40.9	740,729	603,072	191,787	474,960	283,106	59,644
Nigeria	1963	55,670,046	28,112,118	16.1	25,514,354	25,980,055	4,175,637	18,267,669	10,209,122	2,205,476
Norway	1960	3,591,234†	1,789,406	32.1	989,927	1,396,484	1,204,823	1,406,358	188,431	367,296
Pakistan	1961	93,831,982†	49,308,645	13.1	40,178,518	36,322,838	13,781,318	30,205,981	22,441,788	...
Panama	1960	1,075,541	545,774	41.5	491,102	435,207	149,232	336,969	155,690	25,964
Papua	1966	606,336	318,460	87.7	274,873	270,698	60,765	312,748	269,076	4,375
Paraguay	1962	1,816,890	895,551	36.1	866,052	684,563	266,275	596,555	312,647	91,077
Peru	1961	10,420,351††	4,925,518	47.4	4,290,084¶	4,143,473¶	1,468,200¶	3,124,579	1,555,560	477,393
Philippines	1970	36,684,486†	18,250,351	...	17,858‡	15,422‡	4,679‡	...	...	...
Poland	1970	32,589,000	15,834,000	52.2	8,605,000‡	14,965,000‡	9,019,000‡	16,442,100	5,999,600	...
Portugal	1960	8,889,392†	4,254,373	22.6	2,757,895	3,792,171	2,339,326	3,316,472	1,393,624	717,117
Portuguese Guinea	1960	521,336	260,650	...	...	...	...	...	...	...
Portuguese Timor	1960	517,079	267,783	...	...	...	...	...	...	...
Puerto Rico	1970	2,712,033†	1,329,949	58.1	990,920‡	1,138,462‡	582,551‡	...	...	...
Réunion	1967	416,525	203,497	42.8	189,997‡	163,253‡	62,166‡	94,334	27,845	6,910
Rhodesia	1961–62	3,857,470	1,984,050	21.6	1,866,850	1,990,620		713,640	247,030	147,710
Romania	1966	19,103,163†	9,351,075	38.2	4,968,524‡	8,864,512‡	5,253,555‡	10,362,300	5,889,591	2,013,525
Rwanda	1965	3,744,723†	1,493,963	...	1,397,928□	1,235,648□	487,147□	1,136,378	...	...
Ryukyu Islands	1965	934,176†	447,693	...	363,048‖	393,001‖	178,077‡	357,801	108,937	34,934
St. Helena	1966	4,649	2,233	...	1,944¶	1,501¶	1,204¶	1,562	...	...
St. Kitts-Nevis and Anguilla	1960	56,693†	26,149	32.9	25,920	19,378	11,395	32,023	8,565	2,078
St. Lucia	1960	86,108	40,693	24.9	38,109	33,122	14,877	28,544	15,144	3,485
St. Pierre and Miquelon	1967	5,186	2,593	...	1,676‡	2,216‡	1,294‡	1,876	...	374
St. Vincent	1960	79,948	37,561	...	39,305‡	28,267‡	12,376‡	23,310	9,954	2,868
São Tomé and Príncipe	1960	63,485†	35,259	...	...	...	...	...	...	2,151
Seychelles	1960	41,425	20,289	25.4	15,934	16,491	9,000	17,665	5,910	...
Sierra Leone	1963	2,180,355	1,081,123	...	800,404‡	1,016,240‡	363,711‡	...	682,588	88,846
Sikkim	1961	162,189	85,285	4.2	68,019	73,748	20,422	2,728	249	64
Singapore	1970	2,074,500	1,062,100	...	804,800‡	933,100‡	336,600‡	...	...	...
South Africa	1960	16,002,797	8,043,493	46.7	6,418,492‡	6,945,380‡	2,638,925‡	5,696,060	1,700,958	1,285,113
South West Africa (Namibia)	1960	526,004	265,312	21.9	217,541	227,238	81,225	203,271	118,996	18,647
Spain	1960	30,430,698	14,763,388	42.5	8,365,000	13,506,800	8,652,900	11,634,214	4,803,316	2,749,419
Spanish Sahara	1960	23,793	13,070	...	...	...	...	...	...	...
Surinam	1964	324,211	161,855	40.1	147,927‡	122,897‡	46,668‡	80,199††	19,922††	12,713††
Swaziland	1966	374,571	178,795	12.5	174,455	145,618	54,498	121,063	85,103	23,480
Sweden	1965	7,765,981†	3,879,772	77.4	1,608,528‡	3,158,391‡	2,999,062‡	3,449,897	407,560	1,122,294
Switzerland	1960	5,429,061†	2,663,432	42.0	1,361,210	2,302,312	1,765,539	2,512,411	280,191	1,006,038
Syria	1960	4,565,121	2,344,224	41.9	2,014,509	1,656,452	680,094	1,016,347	518,933	128,954
Taiwan	1966	13,348,096†	7,031,644	59.2	5,775,194‡	5,622,590‡	1,950,312‡	8,619,952	1,437,944	592,082
Tanzania	1967	12,313,469	6,005,894	...	5,398,445‡	4,932,236‡	1,960,130‡	5,577,567	5,078,038	96,502
Thailand	1960	26,257,916	13,154,149	12.5	11,823,535	10,949,932	3,484,393	13,836,984	11,334,382	500,595
Togo	1958–60	1,439,772	689,556	9.6	695,411	558,839	185,550	566,868	452,889	...
Tonga	1966	77,429	39,157	...	...	...	...	...	...	...
Trinidad and Tobago	1960	827,957	411,580	17.0	351,050‡	336,730‡	140,177‡	262,570	52,528	53,617
Trust Territory of the Pacific Islands	1960	75,836†	38,721	...	33,332	27,139	15,092	...	...	...
Tunisia	1966	4,533,351	2,314,419	40.1	2,191,088	1,678,465	663,798	1,093,735	448,296	103,582
Turkey	1965	31,391,207	15,945,768	...	13,844,128	12,775,996	4,771,083	13,591,822	9,764,652	1,025,022
Turks and Caicos Islands	1960	5,668†	2,667	...	2,557	1,975	1,136	2,034	393	...
Uganda	1969	9,548,847	4,818,449	7.7	4,404,291‡	3,781,156‡	1,350,865‡	...	...	...
Union of Soviet Socialist Republics	1970	241,720,000	111,399,000	56.0	74,710,000▲	104,880,000▲	61,861,000▲	...	...	...
United Arab Republic	1966	30,053,861	15,168,000	40.5	...	...	...	...	...	...
United Kingdom	1961	52,708,934	25,480,791	79.0	12,335,703‡	20,784,033‡	19,589,198‡	23,616,620	865,129	6,975,166
United States	1970‡‡	203,165,699	98,881,820	...	31,553,078▲	79,392,198▲	61,834,725▲	...	181,800	213,600
Uruguay	1963	2,592,563	1,289,454	...	721,500‖	1,143,600‖	727,500‖	1,015,500	773,650	1,633,075
Venezuela	1961	7,523,999††	3,823,569	62.5	3,538,949	3,022,725	962,325	2,406,725	6,377,024	537,761
Vietnam, North	1960	15,916,955	7,687,814	9.5	7,055,544§§	7,556,129§§	1,305,282§§	8,119,286		
Virgin Islands of the United States	1960	32,099	15,930	57.9	12,768‡	12,510‡	6,821‡	10,845	610	...
Western Samoa	1966	131,379	67,809	19.2	...	...	...	...	...	...
Yugoslavia	1961	18,549,291†	9,043,424	28.8	5,770,817‡	8,168,259‡	4,610,215‡	8,340,400	4,674,856	1,137,848
Zambia	1961–63	3,493,590	1,734,860	21.3	1,492,150	3,092,400	401,190	693,000	220,000	72,000

DEMOGRAPHIC AND/OR SAMPLE SURVEYS

POLITICAL UNIT	Year of census	Total	Male	Percent urban*	0 to 15	16 to 45	46 and over	Total	Agriculture	Mining and manufacturing
Burundi	1962	2,319,540	1,104,266	...	...	...	...	...	...	...
Central African Republic	1959–60	1,177,000	577,000	6.8	429,000‡	661,000‡	81,000‡	610,000	461,000	52,000
Chad	1964	3,254,000	1,567,000	7.8	...	...	...	950,000	600,000	60,000
Congo (Brazzaville)	1960–61	794,400†	...	...	...	...	...	...	...	...
Cuba	1965	7,630,700	2,895,155	53.0	2,808,190‖‖	4,009,110‖‖	813,400‖‖	2,546,000	838,000	390,000
Dahomey	1961	2,106,000	...	...	...	...	...	...	...	...
Malagasy Republic	1966	6,200,000	3,049,000	...	2,882,000‡	2,326,000‡	992,000‡	2,733,000	2,396,000	337,000
Mali	1960–61	4,100,000	...	...	1,763,000	2,127,900	209,100	...	...	...
Niger	1959–60	2,556,211	...	...	...	...	...	1,506,490	703,610	4,510
Senegal	1960–61	3,109,840†	1,531,760	23.7	1,320,680	1,641,420	147,720	1,317,580	1,087,020	73,800
Upper Volta	1960–61	4,400,000	2,208,800	4.6	1,830,400	1,892,000	677,600	2,627,000	1,300,000	...

Note: Data reflect results of enumerations conducted 1957 to 1971, as available. Age groups may not add to country total due to ages not specified in census.

*That population defined as urban by the political unit.

†De jure population.
‡0–14, 15–44, 45 and over.
§0–13, 15–49, 50 and over.
‖Estimate.
¶0–14, 15–49, 50 and over.
♀Includes public utilities and construction.

□0–19, 20–49, 50 and over.
□0–14, 15–45, 46 and over.
◇0–14, 15–49, 50 and over.
▲0–15, 16–44, 45 and over.
†Includes transportation.
●0–19, 20–64, 65 and over.
**0–14, 15–64, 65 and over.

††Excludes Amerindian.
‡‡1970 final; subject to revision.
§§0–15, 16–55, 56 and over.
‖‖0–14, 15–54, 55 and over.

Table III. Populations and Areas of the Countries of the World

Continent and state	Area in sq.mi.	Population in 000	Persons per sq.mi.
World total	57,864,610	3,681,389	70.3*
AFRICA	11,637,931	352,841	30.3
Algeria	896,588	13,547	15.1
Botswana	220,000	667	3.0
Bouvet Island (Norwegian)	23	—	—
British dependencies	311	59	—
Burundi	10,759	3,600	334.6
Cameroon	179,557	5,836	32.5
Central African Republic	240,377	1,522	6.3
Chad	495,750	3,706	7.5
Congo, Brazzaville	132,000	1,089	8.3
Congo, Kinshasa (Zaire)	905,360	22,549	24.9
Dahomey	43,483	2,718	62.5
Egypt	386,900	34,000	87.9
Equatorial Guinea	10,830	290	26.8
Ethiopia	471,800	24,319	51.5
French dependencies	10,733	817	—
Gabon	103,100	500	4.8
Gambia, The	4,467	375	83.9
Ghana	92,100	8,546	92.8
Guinea	94,925	3,921	41.3
Ivory Coast	123,485	4,310	34.9
Kenya	224,960	11,694	52.0
Lesotho	11,720	1,060	90.4
Liberia	43,000	1,171	27.2
Libya	680,000	2,010	3.0
Malagasy Republic	226,660	7,424	32.8
Malawi	45,747	4,552	99.5
Mali	478,819	5,031	10.5
Mauritania	398,000	1,171	2.9
Mauritius	720	844	1,172.2
Morocco	174,471	15,579	89.3
Niger	458,993	4,016	8.7
Nigeria	356,669	55,074	154.4
Portuguese dependencies	800,300	14,494	—
Rhodesia	150,820	5,400	35.8
Rwanda	10,169	3,736	367.4
Senegal	76,124	3,925	51.6
Sierra Leone	27,699	2,550	92.1
Somalia	246,155	3,000	12.2
South Africa	471,445	21,448	45.5
South West Africa (Namibia)	318,261	632	2.0
Spanish Sahara (Spanish)	102,703	76	0.7
Sudan	967,494	15,695	16.2
Swaziland	6,704	433	64.6
Tanzania	364,943	13,273	36.4
Togo	21,900	1,956	89.3
Tunisia	63,378	5,137	81.1
Uganda	91,073	9,549	104.8
Upper Volta	105,870	5,486	51.8
Zambia	290,586	4,054	14.0
ANTARCTICA	5,500,000†	‡	—
Australian Antarctic Territory	2,472,000	—	—
British Antarctic Territory§	650,000	—	—
French Southern and Antarctic Lands	202,916	—	—
Norwegian dependencies	96‖	—	—
Ross Dependency (New Zealand)	160,000	—	—
ASIA (exclusive of U.S.S.R.)	10,683,921	2,093,984	196.0
Afghanistan	250,775	17,480	69.7
Australian dependencies	58	4	—
Bahrain	256	216	843.8
Bhutan	18,000	836	46.4
Brunei (British protected state)	2,226	136	61.1
Burma	261,789	27,600	105.4
Cambodia (Khmer Republic)	69,898	6,818	97.5
Ceylon	25,332	12,514	494.0
China	3,691,500	827,000	224.0
Cyprus	3,572	634	177.5
Federation of Arab Emirates	32,300	180	5.6
Hong Kong (British)	400	3,951	9,877.5
India (incl. Kashmir)	1,229,424	546,956	444.9
Indonesia	779,675	122,663	157.3
Iran	635,932	30,159	47.4
Iraq¶	169,284	9,466	55.9
Israel	7,992	3,066	383.6
Japan	142,885	104,116	728.7
Jordan	37,737	2,348	62.2
Korea, North	46,800	14,000	299.1
Korea, South	38,022	31,469	827.7
Kuwait	6,880	739	107.4
Laos	91,400	3,033	33.2
Lebanon	3,950	2,645	669.6
Malaysia	128,727	10,434	81.1
Maldives	115	114	991.3
Mongolia	604,000	1,285	2.1
Nepal	54,362	11,290	207.7
Neutral Zone	7,000	...	—
Oman	82,000	750	9.1
Pakistan	366,041	116,598	318.5
Philippines	115,800	36,684	316.8
Portuguese dependencies	5,769	925	—
Qatar	4,400	160	36.4
Ryukyu Islands (United States)	848	945	1,114.4
Saudi Arabia¶	865,000	7,740	8.9
Sikkim (Indian protected state)	2,744	197	71.8
Singapore	226	2,075	9,181.4
Syria	71,498	6,292	88.0
Taiwan	13,892	14,811	1,066.2
Thailand	198,500	34,152	172.1
Turkey	301,380	35,667	118.3
Vietnam, North	63,360	19,900	314.1
Vietnam, South	67,108	18,000	268.2
Yemen (Aden)	112,000	1,436	12.8
Yemen (San'a')	75,290	6,500	86.3
EUROPE (exclusive of U.S.S.R.)	1,904,603	462,224	242.7
Albania	11,100	2,168	195.3
Andorra	180	21	116.7
Austria	32,374	7,444	230.0
Belgium	11,781	9,691	822.6
British dependencies	298	209	—
Bulgaria	42,823	8,490	198.3
Czechoslovakia	49,371	14,485	293.4
Denmark (incl. Faeroe Islands)	17,169	4,989	—
Finland	130,128	4,602	35.4
France	210,038	51,027	242.9
Germany, East	41,768	17,041	408.0
Germany, West (incl. W. Berlin)	95,934	61,846	644.7
Greece	50,944	8,745	171.7
Hungary	35,919	10,314	287.1
Iceland	39,768	205	5.2
Ireland	27,136	2,971	109.5
Italy	116,313	54,683	470.1
Liechtenstein	62	21	338.7
Luxembourg	999	340	340.3
Malta	122	326	2,672.1
Monaco	0.6	24	40,000.0
Netherlands	15,770	13,119	831.9
Norway (incl. Svalbard and Jan Mayen)	149,150	3,895	—
Poland	120,725	32,589	269.9
Portugal	35,553	8,668	243.8
Romania	91,700	20,253	220.9
San Marino	25	19	760.0
Spain	194,881	33,824	173.6
Sweden	173,648	8,092	46.6
Switzerland	15,941	6,270	393.3
United Kingdom	94,216	55,347	587.4
Vatican City	0.2	0.6	3,000.0
Yugoslavia	98,766	20,505	207.6
NORTH AMERICA	9,360,023	321,638	34.4
Barbados	166	238	1,433.7
British dependencies	15,749	858	—
Canada	3,851,809	21,688	5.6
Costa Rica	19,650	1,710	87.0
Cuba	42,827	8,553	199.7
Dominican Republic	18,658	4,012	215.0
El Salvador	8,098	3,565	440.2
French dependencies	1,207	673	—
Greenland (Danish)	840,000	46	0.5
Guatemala	42,042	5,348	127.2
Haiti	10,714	4,969	463.8
Honduras	43,277	2,669	61.7
Jamaica	4,244	1,861	438.5
Mexico	761,600	50,829	66.7
Netherlands Antilles (Dutch)	385	224	581.8
Nicaragua	49,173	1,975	40.2
Panama (excl. Canal Zone)	29,208	1,475	50.5
Trinidad and Tobago	1,980	945	477.3
United States	3,615,122	207,180	57.3
United States dependencies	4,114	2,820	—
OCEANIA	3,285,561	19,655	6.0
Australia	2,967,909	12,794	4.3
Australian dependencies	178,467	2,442	—
British dependencies	11,326	223	—
Canton and Enderbury Islands (U.K.-U.S.)	27	—	—
Fiji	7,071	524	74.1
French dependencies	8,717	236	—
Nauru	8	7	875.0
New Hebrides (Fr.-U.K.)	5,700	86	15.1
New Zealand	103,736	2,860	27.6
New Zealand dependencies	197	29	—
Tonga	269	86	319.7
United States dependencies	998	219	—
Western Samoa	1,136	149	131.2
SOUTH AMERICA	6,892,221	189,327	27.5
Argentina	1,072,157	23,364	21.8
Bolivia	424,162	5,062	11.9
Brazil	3,286,470	93,204	28.4
Chile	292,256	8,853	30.3
Colombia	439,735	21,786	49.5
Ecuador	109,483	6,177	56.4
Falkland Islands (British)	6,200	2	0.3
French Guiana (French)	34,750	51	1.5
Guyana	83,000	714	8.6
Paraguay	157,047	2,386	15.2
Peru	496,222	14,015	28.2
Surinam (Dutch)	70,060	393	5.6
Uruguay	68,536	2,921	42.6
Venezuela	352,143	10,399	29.5
U.S.S.R.	8,600,350	241,720	28.1

Note: A dash (—) in the population column indicates none or negligible; a dash in the density column indicates figure not relevant; three dots (...) indicate not available.
*In computing the world density the area of Antarctica is omitted.
†Estimated area, including some unclaimed territory.
‡Less than 1,000 persons.
§Includes some territory claimed by Argentina and Chile.
‖Insular dependencies only. Norwegian claims to continental Antarctica are undefined.
¶Excluding Iraq-Saudi Arabia neutral zone of 7,000 sq.mi.

continued from page 569

higher levels of education, pressures of urbanization, and higher living costs. Demographers noted that polls indicated that women wanted an average of 2.5 children in 1971, compared with 3.03 children in 1965, and the actual number of births in the U.S. declined sharply despite the fact that the number of possible mothers in the country was at an all-time high. There was also a noticeable increase in the number of young women remaining single. According to a U.S. Census Bureau survey, one-half of the women who were 21 in 1970 were single, compared with one-third in 1960.

Family size and actual number of births in a country like the U.S. were related as much to economic conditions as they were to individual family decisions. Economist Joseph Spengler estimated that the U.S. was being forced to spend 4% of its total national income, or $30 billion, to increase the investment in plant facilities, public services, housing, and consumer goods that were needed to meet the economic demands of a 1% annual gain in population. However, if a substantial upswing in economic conditions were to occur, the present downward trend in the birthrate might also suddenly be reversed. (W. EI.)

Portugal

A unitary corporative republic of southwestern Europe, Portugal shares the Iberian Peninsula with Spain. Area: 35,553 sq.mi. (92,082 sq.km.), including the Azores (905 sq.mi.) and Madeira (308 sq.mi.). Pop. (1970): 8,-668,267. Cap. and largest city: Lisbon (pop., 1970, 782,266). Language: Portuguese. Religion: Roman Catholic. President in 1971, Rear Adm. Américo de Deus Rodrigues Tomás; premier, Marcello José das Neves Alves Caetano.

Portugal enjoyed political stability during 1971, but made little economic progress. Premier Caetano emerged as undisputed national leader, and the movement toward political liberalization gathered speed.

In July the National Assembly approved constitutional reforms granting the overseas territories greater autonomy in financial and administrative matters, and in August it passed laws easing press censorship, except for the reporting of military matters, and granting freedom of religious worship. After years of dormancy, the National Assembly showed signs of becoming a lively forum for debates, with the supporters of the government constantly coming under attack from advocates of *salazarista* conservative policies.

The activities of urban guerrilla groups, Armed Revolutionary Action (ARA) and the League of Union and Revolutionary Action (LUAR), caused increasing concern. Their most spectacular exploit was a bomb explosion that disrupted communications from Lisbon on the eve of an important NATO meeting in June; several kidnappings and bank robberies were also carried out. The security forces launched a determined drive to eradicate the groups and, in October, 31 persons accused of membership in LUAR were sent for trial. Meanwhile, it became increasingly apparent that the government enjoyed the support of the majority of the public. Opposition was limited to a small cadre of extremists, a few dissidents among the military, and a nucleus of liberal and socialist elements. Nevertheless, when Parliament reopened on November 16, Caetano asked it to consider whether subversion was sufficiently grave to warrant repressive measures.

The dynamic foreign policy pursued since September 1968 was showing concrete results, the most notable of which was the achievement of closer relations with Brazil. The Brazilian finance minister, Antônio Delfim Neto, visited Lisbon in June, and the communiqué published afterward stressed the need for increased trade and joint industrial and commercial ventures. In September the foreign ministers of the two countries exchanged official visits, and during that month a double-tax treaty and an agreement providing for the reciprocal granting of full civil rights were signed. It was announced that President Tomás was to visit Brasília in 1972. British Foreign Secretary Sir Alec Douglas-Home and U.S. Vice-Pres.

The Portuguese continue construction on the Cabora Bassa Dam on the Zambezi River in Africa.
CAMERA PRESS—PIX

Spiro T. Agnew visited Portugal during the summer. In December the U.S. and Portugal negotiated a five-year extension of the agreement giving the U.S. use of air and naval bases in the Azores; in return, the U.S. would provide $435 million in aid. The Azores were the scene of Pres. Richard Nixon's December summit meeting with French Premier Georges Pompidou.

A formal announcement had been made in November 1970 of Portugal's intention to seek a form of association with the EEC. At the same time, the government wished to negotiate separate arrangements for the Portuguese overseas territories and to ensure that Portugal would continue to receive the special concessions that it enjoyed as a member of the European Free Trade Association. However, observers believed that the EEC would only be prepared to enter into a commercial agreement similar to the arrangements with Greece and Spain.

A further indication of official long-term economic planning was the submission early in the year of an industrial reform bill to the Corporative Chamber.

PORTUGAL

Education. (1967–68) Primary, pupils 904,120, teachers 28,434; secondary, pupils 166,925, teachers 8,027; vocational, pupils 169,666, teachers 9,318; teacher training, students 2,555, teachers 298; higher (including 5 universities), students 39,209, teaching staff 2,293.

Finance. Monetary unit: escudo, with a par value of 28.75 escudos to U.S. $1 (69 escudos = £1 sterling) and a free rate (Sept. 27, 1971) of 27.42 escudos to U.S. $1 (68 escudos = £1 sterling). Gold, SDRs, and foreign exchange, official: (June 1971) U.S. $1,527,-000,000; (June 1970) U.S. $1,352,000,000. Budget (1970 est.): revenue 22,033,000,000 escudos; expenditure 17,847,000,000 escudos. Gross national product: (1969) 162.2 billion escudos; (1968) 146.9 billion escudos. Money supply: (April 1971) 92,820,000,000 escudos; (April 1970) 91,070,000,000 escudos. Cost of living (Lisbon; 1963 = 100): (June 1971) 161; (June 1970) 143.

Foreign Trade. (1970) Imports 44,725,000,000 escudos; exports 27,191,000,000 escudos. Import sources: West Germany 15%; U.K. 14%; Angola 10%; France 7%; U.S. 7%; Italy 5%. Export destinations: U.K. 20%; Angola 15%; Mozambique 9%; U.S. 9%; West Germany 6%; Sweden 5%; France 5%. Main exports: textile yarns and fabrics 24%; machinery 10%; chemicals 9%; wine 7%; cork 6%. Tourism (1969): visitors 2,785,400; gross receipts U.S. $180 million.

Transport and Communications. Roads (continent; 1969) 29,932 km. (including 77 km. expressways). Motor vehicles in use (1969): passenger 454,-178; commercial 24,561. Railways: (continent; 1969) 3,592 km.; traffic (1970) 3,550,000,000 passenger-km., freight 776 million net ton-km. Air traffic (1970): 2,268,000,000 passenger-km.; freight 42,220,000 net ton-km. Shipping (1970): merchant vessels 100 gross tons and over 376; gross tonnage 870,008. Telephones (Dec. 1969) 698,075. Radio licenses (Dec. 1969) 1,406,000. Television licenses (Dec. 1969) 352,000.

Agriculture. Production (in 000; metric tons; 1970; 1969 in parentheses): wheat 516 (452); barley c. 63 (54); oats 76 (79); rye 150 (167); corn 586 (553); rice 198 (176); potatoes 1,207 (1,126); dry broad beans 24 (28); other dry beans c. 55 (51); chick-peas 21 (21); wine 913 (808); olive oil 69 (72); figs (1969) 221, (1968) c. 219; oranges 126 (124); apples 55 (62); pears 54 (55); meat 198 (208); timber (cu.m.; 1969) 5,900, (1968) 5,900; fish catch (1969) 457, (1968) 506. Livestock (in 000; 1969–70): sheep c. 6,170; cattle c. 1,070; pigs c. 1,380; goats c. 551; horses 79; mules c. 139; asses c. 200; chickens c. 8,200.

Industry. Fuel and power (in 000; metric tons; 1970): coal 271; lignite (1969) .7; electricity (kw-hr.) 7,203,000; manufactured gas (Lisbon only; cu.m.) 118,000. Production (in 000; metric tons; 1970): iron ore (50% metal content) 126; sulfur (1969) 235; cement 2,332; tin 0.4; manganese ore (metal content; 1969) 3; tungsten concentrates (oxide content; 1969) 1.7; gold (troy oz.; 1969) 18; cotton yarn 81; woven cotton fabrics 45; preserved sardines (1969) 23; cork products (1969) 304.

This measure provided for the ending of controls over the establishment of new plants and the expansion of existing ones and the establishment of a fund to finance industrial development. The bill was not expected to become law before the end of 1972.

Economic performance was poor during 1971. Inflationary pressures intensified (during the first six months of the year the cost of living in Lisbon had risen by 12.2%) and there was no sign of a reduction in the traditional trade deficit ($24.2 million in the first half of 1971). Agricultural production was in a state of stagnation, and industrial output, though showing a moderate increase, was far from satisfactory. There was also growing official concern about the high rate of emigration. Preliminary results of the latest census indicated that the population of metropolitan Portugal had declined by 2% during 1961–71. However, the economies of Portugal's African territories prospered. A start was made on the vast Cabora Bassa hydroelectric plant and dam project in Mozambique, and guerrilla attacks aimed at disrupting the work were contained.   (RN. C.)

See also Dependent States.

Postal Services

The number of member states of the Universal Postal Union (UPU) rose to 145 with the admission of Fiji (June 18, 1971) and Oman (August 17). The acts of the UPU revised at the 16th Universal Postal Congress in Tokyo in 1969 came into force on July 1, 1971. At the meeting of the Consultative Council for Postal Studies (CCEP) in Bern, Switz., during September–October, interest centred on furthering financial and technical aid to less developed countries through both the UN Development Program and the UPU Special Fund. The total cost of 39 Development Program projects in 1970 amounted to $550,280.

In the U.K. a strike for higher pay, called by the Union of Post Office Workers, affected postal services from Jan. 20 to March 7, 1971. Most main post offices were closed, but all the agency offices remained open. Mail services were suspended nationally except for isolated local deliveries, but were restored on a phased basis and were fully operational by March 11. The immense, challenging, and complex task of converting the postal business to decimal currency was successfully accomplished, even though the postal strike was in effect on February 15, when decimal currency officially came into use.

By international agreement, the number of classifications in the U.K. overseas letter post was reduced to seven on July 1 (1, 2, 4, and 8 oz. and 1, 2, and 4 lb.); previously there had been 64 steps at the 1- and 2-oz. levels. Surface postage rates were increased to meet rising costs throughout the world, but airmail letter rates held steady because of a reduction in air conveyance costs. The Datapost service, providing highly reliable overnight postal transmission for computer data and similar material, was extended to the U.S. Mechanization of both parcel and letter handling continued, and more parcel concentration offices were to be opened in 1972. It was hoped that the entire U.K. would be postal-coded by the end of 1972.

The strike had an adverse effect on productivity, but some progress was achieved. The policy of taking a more commercial approach toward the postal services was given fresh impetus by the creation of a postal marketing department, and studies of existing

Portuguese Overseas Provinces:
see Dependent States

and potential services with a view to meeting customer demand and improving profitability were in progress. In October proposals for reshaping the postal service were announced. These included the abolition of second deliveries and Saturday parcel deliveries to residential and rural areas, fewer weekend and evening collections, and a 5% increase in the charges on heavy letters and parcels, beginning in February 1972. About 25,000 post office jobs would be eliminated.

In 1965, as a first stage in the introduction of a new postal code system in France, the public had been asked to begin completing the addresses on correspondence with the identification of the *département* and that of the sorting office. A five-character alphabetical and numerical code was originally considered, consisting of two figures indicating the registration numbers of the *département* and the first three letters of the sorting office. A comprehensive experiment using an automatic Hotchkiss-Brandt sorting machine for 50 to 100 locations failed to provide efficient service because of the complexity of the system of interpreting the codes, however. After careful study, it was decided to use a numerical code, the existing two-number departmental code being extended by adding three numbers identifying the sorting office. This code would constitute the keystone of the proposed automatic sorting system.

Several steps remained to be taken. Large organizations that used computers for addressing their mail, such as government departments and public and quasi-public institutions, were to be provided with magnetic tape devised by the operational research section of the Post Office, carrying the names of distribution centres and their postal codes. The public at large was to be informed by a major publicity campaign, combined with the distribution to all homes of code lists in the form of directories.

In Italy a pilot automatic sorting installation came into use in Florence on June 18. The installation, which represented a major step in the complete automation of the Italian postal service, was capable of handling up to 60,000 letters and postcards hourly, sorting them into as many as 720 different destinations. Several others of a similar type were under contract, and when completed would be coordinated to constitute an up-to-date, country-wide network.

In West Germany, where plans were being made for the reorganization of the Federal Ministry of Transport, Post, and Telecommunications, the federal postal services continued to expand. The rate of increase in traffic for posts and telecommunications together reached 9.1% in 1970, the slight decline of the growth rate in telecommunications (12.6%, compared with 13.5% in 1969) being almost counterbalanced by the gain for the postal services (4.4%, compared with 3.7%). Postal revenue rose by 9.9% to DM. 14.5 billion, but the financial position of the Federal Post Office continued to be strained. Personnel expenditure rose by 14.8%, interest expenditure by 21.3%, and expenditure on operations and the maintenance of fixed tangible assets also increased, resulting in a net loss during 1970 of DM. 531 million. Expenditure on supplies and services rose to DM. 6,094,000,000, compared with DM. 1.3 billion in 1969.

As part of the effort to improve working conditions, consideration was given to restricting weekend services. Investment activity was again concentrated on telecommunications; telecommunications plant alone (excluding real estate, buildings, and vehicles) ac-

Postmaster General Winton Blount announces inauguration of the U.S. Postal Service to replace the Post Office Department on July 1, 1971. The agency assumed a semi-independent status; the change was designed to end political patronage and improve service.

counted for nearly DM. 4 billion. In view of the increasing international traffic, the Post Office established a third antenna at its satellite tracking station at Raisting, which was also to be used for television transmissions and telecommunications traffic during the 1972 Olympic Games. Subscriber trunk dialing with the U.S. was begun. An agreement was concluded between the Federal Ministry of Transport, Post, and Telecommunications and the East German Ministry of Postal Services and Telecommunications providing for the establishment of additional telephone and telex circuits between the two parts of Germany, as well as for the annual payment of DM. 30 million to the East German postal administration.

With depopulation of Sweden's rural areas continuing, in 1971 a number of rural postmen in some western parts of the country began delivery of food and other goods to private households along their routes. In addition, they began to act as social workers, visiting old people in isolated areas. The experiment was being carried out under the combined supervision of the Post Office and social welfare authorities. As a possible step toward the "cashless" society, the Post Office Bank of Sweden and a group representing a major part of Sweden's banking system collaborated in developing an integrated on-line payments system based on the electronic transmission of data.

For the first time in four years the New Zealand Post Office showed a loss—NZ$13.7 million for 1970–71, with salary increases of NZ$18 million being a major factor. To meet the rapid increases in costs, postal charges were raised as of Feb. 15, 1971. The postal staff on March 31, 1971 totaled 31,373, compared with 30,270 a year earlier. As one of its anti-inflationary measures, the Cabinet issued a directive at the end of January 1971 that no additional staff beyond the actual figure then employed would be authorized without its approval.

The number of articles posted rose 3.3% to 614

million, and airmail dispatched overseas increased 8.8% to 1,156,300 lb. Telephone subscribers in 1970–71 totaled 835,328, a gain of 4.05%, and outward international telephone calls increased by nearly one-quarter. To meet the growth in long-haul toll traffic, the government approved the installation of a NZ$3 million microwave radio telecommunications system between Auckland and Wellington. New Zealand's first satellite-tracking station, costing approximately NZ$5 million, was opened near Warkworth on July 17, 1971. It would communicate with other countries in the Pacific basin, first via Intelsat III and later via its successor, Intelsat IV.

Between 1966 and 1970 the Soviet postal system had built 42 post offices in cities, near railway stations, and at airports, as well as 25 centres for the decentralized printing of newspapers and periodicals (the centres relayed type pages to 16 different points in the U.S.S.R. over communication channels). Mail-handling operations had been mechanized at 52 large postal enterprises and in 750 shops, and by 1971 the number of mail-handling machines totaled nearly 100,-000. The Soviet postal system included over 80,000 regular post offices and over 1,000 mobile offices. In 1970 it handled some 8,000,000,000 letters and postcards, 74 million registered-mail and printed-matter units, over 650 million money orders and pension drafts, 176 million parcels, and over 33,000,000,-000 newspapers and magazines; 320,000 tons of mail were carried by air. (X.)

Major changes in postal activities in the U.S. were launched in 1971, as the semi-independent United States Postal Service took over direct responsibility for operations from the old Post Office Department on July 1. Postmaster General Winton M. Blount, who became chief executive officer of the newly created USPS, announced his resignation late in the year. Key features of the new system included authority for the USPS to engage in direct collective bargaining with labour unions, to set its own budget, and to develop rate schedules on a businesslike basis. A Postal Rate Commission was to recommend rates.

Newspaper delivery boys and girls sort mail in a shop in Epsom, Surrey, during the British postal strike.
POPPERFOTO—PICTORIAL PARADE

Numerous precedent-setting actions had taken place by the end of 1971, including the signing of the first collective bargaining agreement in postal service history between the USPS and officials of seven major labour unions representing 650,000 of the system's 750,000 employees. The two-year contract called for raises totaling $1 billion, guaranteed that no employee would be laid off because of technological changes during the life of the pact, and permitted the USPS to begin implementing plans to intensify the introduction and use of automated classifying and sorting equipment. Meanwhile, officials of the predominantly black National Alliance of Postal and Federal Employees accused the service of practising discrimination by locating new automated processing facilities in white areas that offered little or no low-income housing, and of bypassing blacks for promotion.

With a deficit that had reached $2,593,728,000 by June 30, 1971, the USPS raised postal rates as of May 16. The cost of a first-class letter rose from 6 to 8 cents an ounce, and the cost of airmail went from 10 to 11 cents an ounce. However, proposals to increase rates for other classes of mail were being challenged in the courts. Revenues for the year ending June 30, 1971, totaled $6,998,589,000, up 2.3% from the previous year. The postal system processed 87,000,000,000 pieces of mail. Officials projected a flow of 88,100,-000,000 pieces for fiscal 1972. It was expected that the flow would reach 124 billion within ten years.

In a major realignment of the service's internal management structure, the 15 postal regions were merged into 5, each headed by a regional postmaster general. At the same time, three operating staffs were created to cover the major areas of mail processing, customer service, and specialized support for postal activities. A formally designated Office of Consumer Affairs was organized in an effort to deal more adequately with individual complaints about service and delivery. New services included a "facsimile mail" project between Washington, D.C., and New York City involving electronic transmission of written material over telephone lines.

New service standards were announced that were designed to provide 95% overnight delivery of airmail to cities within a 600-mi. radius of the point of origin, and next-day delivery of 95% of local first-class mail deposited before 5 P.M. Officials claimed success for both programs, despite criticism that the USPS was "fudging" by stamping all mail received after 5 P.M. with the next day's date. Another announced innovation was the "Bulk Mail Network," consisting of 21 highly mechanized centres designed to handle parcels with a minimum of damage. Scheduled for completion by the end of 1975, the network was expected to cut processing costs by $300 million annually, apart from other costs incurred through claims lodged against parcels said to have been damaged in transit.

Officials also turned to new ways to produce revenues, such as offering for sale enlarged poster versions of historic stamps and promoting stamp collecting among schoolchildren. Despite these efforts, officials conceded that it would be a number of years before the Postal Service was self-supporting. A massive $1.5 billion program to modernize postal facilities was announced, including 30 new major centres to be constructed as part of a $700 million capital investment program. (Jy. L.)

See also Philately and Numismatics; Telecommunications.

Prices

For almost 20 years—until 1969—annual increases in the cost of living of 5% or more were quite unusual among developed market economies. By the summer of 1971, however, the experience had become fairly common. There was growing internal pressure on governments, therefore, to deal with a rapidly deteriorating situation. Consequently, the authorities almost everywhere employed a wide range of policies, often including direct controls of incomes and prices. In less developed countries recent trends were not so uniform, though the rate of inflation did accelerate dramatically in a number of cases. However, the situation was generally much more encouraging at the wholesale level. The average annual increase for developed market economies, for instance, was only 3.2% in 1971.

Consumer Prices. Nine of the 17 industrial countries included in Table I had increases in the cost of

living of less than 4% in 1969. Two years later similar price rises were recorded in only two of them. The worst rates of inflation in 1971 were experienced by New Zealand and the U.K. The New Zealand government introduced a number of measures to stabilize money incomes and prices. A limit was imposed on wage and salary increases, though some rates of pay that had not reached the national average were to be raised and both wages and salaries were to be adjusted every six months for cost-of-living increases. The U.K. economy continued to stagnate and unemployment rose to record postwar levels despite a series of reflationary measures, but there was little sign of any noticeable reduction in the rate of inflation. In August the Confederation of British Industry called for voluntary restraint in price increases by member firms during the following 12 months.

Sweden, the Netherlands, and Switzerland also had rates of inflation well above the average. The Swedish government announced in June that the price freeze imposed in the autumn of 1970 would continue until the end of 1971. The freeze covered some 60% of all goods and services. In the Netherlands the attempt to impose a freeze on wages and prices early in the year had little effect. The authorities decided, therefore, to abandon direct controls and rely mainly on fiscal and monetary policies to deal with the problem of "stagflation." It was surprising to find Switzerland, traditionally an example of price stability, among the countries suffering from an exceptionally high rate of inflation, but the economy had enjoyed full employment for some time. The decision to limit the number of foreign workers added, therefore, to the difficulty of maintaining price stability.

Of the four industrial countries with increases in consumer prices fairly close to the average, Norway had pursued a comprehensive incomes and prices strategy since World War II: commodities were subsidized, prices controlled, and income determination coordinated. At the end of 1970 the government announced a series of stabilization measures that included a temporary freeze on prices of goods and services. In Japan the underlying problem of prices and costs continued to be structural. This was also one of the problems in Denmark, where the authorities had to deal with stagnation, inflation, and serious balance of payments difficulties. After trying, without much success, to freeze prices early in the year, the outgoing government replaced the freeze with new rules that made it an offense for companies to pass on wage drift in the form of higher prices. The overall situation was much better in France where the government, nevertheless, undertook to control prices of certain foodstuffs. It also signed contracts with several industrial associations specifying that price increases for a number of industrial products were to be restricted to 1.5% until the middle of March 1972. Wages were tied to the cost-of-living index in order to achieve a guaranteed increase of 2% in real incomes.

The cost of living went up at almost identical rates in several countries. In Australia incomes and prices increased very rapidly early in 1971, while the rate of unemployment was only about 1.2% of the labour force. In Finland a large number of items in the cost-of-living index were still under various controls. However, it was in the U.S. that some of the biggest policy changes were made. Confronted with a serious and deteriorating economic situation, Pres. Richard M. Nixon in August announced a comprehensive set of measures, perhaps the most surprising of which was a

George Boldt (top) and C. Jackson Grayson (above), chairmen of the U.S. Pay Board and the Price Commission, were appointed by Pres. Richard Nixon in the fall of 1971.
WIDE WORLD

90-day freeze on prices, wages, and dividends. The intention was that the program of wage and price restraint would continue at the end of the freeze. Accordingly, the president appointed a Price Commission to "hold down" prices; a Pay Board "to stop inflationary wage and salary increases"; and a Government Committee on Interest and Dividends to watch over developments in these two forms of income. All were expected to rest on voluntary cooperation. At the same time, the first two, at least, would have full legal powers to enforce their decisions. If necessary, a Cost of Living Council was to back them with government sanctions. Nothing so dramatic was attempted in Austria, where the exceptionally strong pressure on resources that developed during 1970 continued into 1971. In spite of this, as well as increases in certain import prices, the price level remained reasonably stable. In Italy substantial increases in unemployment and prices, especially those of food and other essentials, contributed to already serious industrial unrest.

The smallest increases in consumer prices among industrial countries took place in West Germany (4.2%), Belgium (3.1%), and Canada (2.4%). West Germany, despite its favourable position vis-à-vis other industrial nations, experienced between 1970 and 1971 some of the biggest price rises in more than

20 years. The government relied on the usual deflationary measures to deal with the problem, but the stabilization program also attempted to check the inflow of dollars in order to reduce the enormous growth in liquidity of the banking system. The Belgian government first imposed and then tightened price controls to neutralize the effects of the introduction of the value-added tax. In Canada the Prices and Incomes Commission abandoned its voluntary program of price restraint and wage guidelines at the beginning of 1971 because of lack of cooperation from both sides of industry.

The experience was much more mixed in the case of less developed economies, though some of them were rapidly approaching the exceptionally high rates of inflation normally associated only with a few countries. The situation improved noticeably in Chile, but it deteriorated sharply in Argentina where, in September, the government announced a series of short-term measures and called for a "social truce" so that it could deal with the crisis. The rate of inflation in South Vietnam was only to be expected in an economy disrupted by war, but the war had an even more disastrous effect on the price level in Cambodia. The rate of inflation appeared to be accelerating rather dangerously in the Philippines, Turkey, Israel, Tunisia, Ecuador, and Yugoslavia.

A particularly serious aspect of inflation in less developed countries is the extent to which it is reflected in food prices. Food normally accounts for a very high proportion of total expenditure in these countries and, as Table II shows, in most of them food prices increased relatively faster over the period than total consumer prices. (The indices in Table II are calcu-

Table II. Indices of Food Prices in Relation to Cost-of-Living Index
(1963 = 100)

Country	1968	1969	1970	1971*
Developed market economies				
Denmark	100	102	104	107
Japan	103	103	105	104
Norway	100	101	103	103
Sweden	100	101	102	103
Finland	104	105	103	102†
Australia	103	101	101	100
New Zealand	101	101	101	100
U.K.	97	98	99	100
Belgium	101	102	101	99†
Austria	99	100	100	99†
U.S.	100	100	99	98†
France	98	98	98	98
Canada	100	99	98	96
Italy	97	97	96	96‡
Netherlands	98	98	98	94
Germany, West	96	96	95	94†
Less developed countries				
Vietnam, South	135	135	134	124
Nigeria	94	103	113	121‡
Cambodia	91	94	98	112
Taiwan	110	110	109	109
Ethiopia	103	104	109	109†
Thailand	109	111	110	108‡
Costa Rica	103	105	108	108
Puerto Rico	104	105	106	107‡
Tunisia	102	103	103	107
Korea, South	94	97	102	107
Pakistan	104	104	106	106
Yugoslavia	99	99	100	105
Ceylon	105	104	104	103†
Greece	101	102	102	103†
Chile	99	99	101	103
India	106	108	109	102
Kenya	104	103	103	102†
Malta	102	103	103	102
Cyprus	102	103	102	102†
Argentina	98	96	99	102
South Africa§	104	103	102	101
Mexico	101	101	102	101
Guatemala	101	100	101	101‡
Morocco	99	100	99	101
Zambia	101	99	100	100
Iraq	101	99	99	100‡
Singapore	101	99	98	99†
Paraguay	97	97	96	99†
Venezuela	96	97	96	96‡
Israel	96	96	94	96
Portugal	100	99	98	95†
Colombia	98	98	97	95‡
Ireland	98	97	96	95‡
Spain	96	96	94	93‡
Brazil	91	92	91	92

*January–June (average) except where stated otherwise.
†January–July (average).
‡January–May (average).
§White population only.
Sources: United Nations, *Monthly Bulletin of Statistics*; International Labour Office, *Bulletin of Labour Statistics*.

Table III. Wholesale Prices for Selected Countries

Country	Index (1963 = 100) 1969	1970	1971*	Annual % change 1963–68 (Average)	Annual % changes over preceding year 1969	1970	1971†
Developed market economies							
Finland	136	142	147	5.6	3.8	4.4	4.2
U.K.‡	120	128	136	2.8	4.3	6.7	8.9
New Zealand	121	127	134	2.8	5.2	5.0	8.1
Denmark	117	127	130	2.7	2.6	8.5	3.2
Sweden	118	126	128	2.5	4.4	6.8	3.2
Austria	117	122	128	2.7	2.6	4.3	4.9
Norway	115	123	127	2.3	3.6	6.0	5.0
France§	116	124	126	1.0	10.5	6.9	0.8
Netherlands	117	124	125	3.0	0.9	6.0	0.8
Italy	111	119	122	1.4	3.7	7.2	3.4
U.S.	113	117	120	1.6	4.6	3.5	3.4
Belgium	113	118	117	1.4	5.6	4.4	−0.8
Canada	116	117	117	1.9	5.4	0.9	−0.8
Switzerland	107	112	114	0.8	2.9	4.7	1.8
Japan	108	112	112	1.2	1.9	3.7	0.0
Germany, West	101	107	111	−0.2	2.0	5.9	4.7
Less developed countries							
Brazil	739	902	1,037	43.8	20.2	22.1	20.7
Chile	489	665	752	29.1	36.6	36.0	19.2
Argentina	274	313	391	20.9	6.2	14.2	33.9
Vietnam, South	251	312	349	16.0	19.5	24.3	17.1
Korea, South	198	216	231	13.3	6.4	9.1	8.4
Colombia	181	195	208	11.3	6.5	7.7	8.3
Yugoslavia§	142	156	171	6.3	4.4	9.8	12.5
India	156	166	169	8.9	2.0	6.4	3.0
Philippines	121	145	162	3.7	0.8	19.8	16.5
Turkey	137	144	162	5.2	6.2	5.1	12.5
Tunisia	133	138	145	5.6	1.5	3.8	6.6
Spain	122	124	132	3.7	1.7	1.6	5.6
Portugal	120	125	126	3.2	2.6	4.2	0.0
South Africa	116	120	124	2.7	1.8	3.4	5.1
Costa Rica	109	118	122	2.3	−2.7	8.2	7.0
Morocco	108	116	121	1.2	1.9	7.4	6.1
Iran	109	113	120	1.4	1.9	3.7	6.2
Greece	114	115	117	2.1	2.7	0.9	1.7
Thailand	117	117	116	2.7	1.8	0.0	0.0
Dominican Republic	109	109	109	2.7	−4.4	0.0	0.0
Taiwan	104	107	107	1.0	−1.0	2.9	0.0

*January–June (average).
†First half 1971 over first half 1970.
‡Prices of finished goods only.
§Prices of industrial products.
Sources: International Monetary Fund, *International Financial Statistics*; United Nations, *Monthly Bulletin of Statistics*.

lated by dividing the index of food prices by the total cost-of-living index, which includes food. The numbers greater than 100 show, therefore, that food prices went up faster than those for all goods and services, while those below 100 indicate the opposite.)

The problem was not serious in industrial countries, although, in recent years, food prices increased at relatively higher rates in several of them, *e.g.*, Denmark, Norway, Sweden, and the U.K. On the other hand, in many less developed countries where the rate of inflation was very rapid, the effect on real incomes of even faster increases in the price of foodstuffs was extremely serious. For instance, in Cambodia the war caused a serious fall in the production of rice, the staple food, and a tremendous increase in its price. On the more favourable side, India's record output of many food grains, together with various controls, helped to keep food prices relatively stable.

Wholesale Prices. Table III shows that, unlike the cost of living, wholesale prices increased at a lower rate in 1971 than in 1970 in all but three developed market economies. Even in the U.K., where the index rose at almost three times the average for industrial countries, there were signs in the latter part of 1971 that wholesale prices were becoming more stable. Undoubtedly, the favourable trend was helped by the fall in prices of primary products, especially those of certain industrial materials.

The situation was not so encouraging in less developed countries. There was a substantial improvement in Chile. At the same time, the rate of inflation at the wholesale level was becoming dangerously high in Argentina and the Philippines and rather serious in Yugoslavia and Turkey. (M. PAN.)

See also Commodities, Primary; Economy, World; Employment, Wages, and Hours; Income, National; Industrial Review; Investment, International; Merchandising; Money and Banking; Payments and Reserves, International; Stock Exchanges; Trade, International.

Prisons and Penology

The worst prison disaster in recent U.S. history occurred in September 1971, when 43 persons died in a riot at the Attica (N.Y.) state prison. Together with the death of George Jackson, one of the so-called Soledad Brothers, at San Quentin prison in California, Attica served to focus public attention on problems of the U.S. correctional system. It also pointed up the elements of racial antagonism that, to an increasing degree, were being superimposed on the overcrowded and poor conditions endemic in many American penal institutions.

The disturbance at Attica began on September 9, when a strike by members of a work detail erupted into violence that spread rapidly throughout the prison. The rioters eventually were confined to one cellblock and a yard, where they held more than 30 guards and civilian employees as hostages. The prisoners were armed with homemade clubs and knives, but neither they nor the guards they had captured possessed firearms.

In the subsequent negotiations, the prisoners made 30 demands, 28 of which concerned such improvements in the prison regime as an end to mail censorship. These were accepted by Russell Oswald, the state commissioner of corrections. Oswald refused to remove the warden, however, and Gov. Nelson Rockefeller said that, since a guard had been fatally injured in the initial fighting and murder charges were

involved, he lacked constitutional authority to promise complete amnesty. A committee of some 24 outside negotiators, many of them prominent figures, was unable to resolve the deadlock. On September 13 the authorities, convinced that the situation was deteriorating, ordered over a thousand state troopers, sheriff's deputies, and guards to storm the cellblock.

Thirty-eight men, including nine hostages, died in the fighting (five died later of injuries). At first it was announced that the prisoners had cut the throats of their hostages. The next day, however, the county medical examiner reported that all the dead, including the hostages, had been killed by gunshots, and his findings later were confirmed by two pathologists. Since the prisoners had no guns, it was apparent that the hostages had been killed by their would-be rescuers.

The Attica riot almost overshadowed Jackson's death a few weeks earlier. Jackson was one of three black inmates charged with murdering a white guard at the Soledad (Calif.) correctional facility in 1970. While in prison, he had espoused revolutionary views and had gained considerable prominence outside through his best-selling book, *Soledad Brother*. The cause of the "Soledad Brothers" had been adopted by many California radicals, the most prominent of whom, Angela Davis, was in prison awaiting trial for conspiracy.

According to official sources, Jackson, while being returned to San Quentin's Adjustment Center following a visit from a lawyer on August 21, produced a gun and ordered a number of inmates released from their cells. Three guards, two white prisoners, and Jackson died in the ensuing melee. As at Attica, reports of what had happened were confused. Prison officials initially claimed that Jackson had been killed by a guard in a tower as he ran across the prison yard. Autopsy, however, revealed he had been shot in the back from a low angle, and the authorities later said that a guard moving between gun stations had fired the fatal shot from a prone position. Others, including Jackson's mother, insisted he had been murdered.

Much of the resulting public controversy centred around the details of the two incidents: the exact circumstances of Jackson's death; whether excessive force had been used at Attica; why officials at both institutions had issued such erroneous reports. There were also claims that Attica inmates had been maltreated after the riot ended, and several groups, including a U.S. congressional committee, began investigations.

Penal officials feared that Attica would set off a chain reaction of prison riots. A number of disturbances did occur in the following weeks, though none approached Attica's dimensions. In one of the most serious, at the Rahway (N.J.) state prison, the superintendent and five guards were held hostage for 24 hours, but the uprising was ended without bloodshed.

Beyond these immediate crises lay the continuing problems of the entire U.S. penal system. Despite reform efforts of recent years, critics from Chief Justice Warren Burger to the New Left had warned that prison neither rehabilitated the criminal nor protected society, since most inmates were released eventually and many went on to commit further crimes. Furthermore, racial difficulties were becoming increasingly intractable. Nearly half the prisoners in California were nonwhites. Blacks and Spanish-speaking Americans made up about 85% of the prison population at Attica while the guards,

Printing:
see Industrial Review

Far left, hundreds of prisoners huddle in a courtyard at Attica during riot that began on Sept. 9, 1971. Above, prisoners raise clenched fists during a negotiating session with New York State Commissioner of Corrections Russell Oswald (left). The prison disturbance ended tragically on September 13 when troops stormed the prison, leaving 43 persons dead.

drawn principally from the surrounding semirural area, were white. These situations were not uncommon. Meanwhile, like Jackson, many black inmates began to claim they were "political prisoners," deprived by society and punished not so much for their crimes as for their revolutionary ideas.

If racial overtones were most noticeable in the U.S., the overall problems of prison reform were common to all industrialized nations. Attica and San Quentin were the year's most shocking incidents, but riots elsewhere, for example in Kingston, Ont., and Turin, Italy, further emphasized the discrepancy between the growing daily average prison population in many countries and the lack of suitable staff, accommodation, and treatment for them.

In an attempt to cope with the situation, many new prisons were being built and many old ones were having new additions made. In the U.K. a report by the Home Office estimated that up to 20 more penal institutions would be needed to house the expected increase in adult and young offenders in the 1970s. Scotland, which had its own, separate penal system, was building a new block in the Old Saughton prison in Edinburgh in which prisoners were to have the keys to their own cells. In Belgium there was already a wing of an old prison without any prison staff. (In both cases the prisoners concerned were in somewhat special categories.)

In Sweden, Österåker prison was planned on the lines of the maximum security Kumla but, as a result of public criticism, it was not completed as a maximum security institution. At the same time, disputes had arisen between prisoners and staff. This led to negotiations and eventually to sweeping reforms, including establishment of a special committee of prisoners allowed to communicate freely with the mass media. The difficulty with such hopeful measures was that their rapid introduction could lead not only to fresh security problems but to staff demoralization. For example, at Albany prison on the Isle

of Wight, Eng., high-risk prisoners were dispersed among other inmates instead of being held separately in high security wings. Allegedly these conditions caused the more dangerous prisoners to tyrannize the rest, and in May and September warders were attacked and beaten, fires were started, and prison staff expressed fears that the situation was becoming uncontrollable.

Perhaps ironically, Japan with its overcrowded cities proved an exception to the general pattern of bursting prisons. Although the total population of Japan had more than doubled since the beginning of the century, and the number of suspected persons investigated by the police had increased fivefold, the prison population was only 46% of what it had been in 1905.

The 120-year-old Holloway prison for women in London was being rebuilt as a psychiatric prison hospital. In general, women offenders show more psychiatric abnormalities than men offenders, and although feminine criminality is quantitatively a far smaller problem than masculine crime, it is often much more complex psychologically. Personality disorders, depression, lesbianism, alcoholism (in the older age groups), and drug addiction (in the younger ones) are common.

The new Holloway was planned to contain small units for 32 women and girls, split into subunits of 16 each, and accommodating about 500 inmates in all. Each unit was to be a small therapeutic community. There was to be an outpatient department that would reduce the need to remand in custody for medical and psychiatric reports. Also planned were a gynecological surgical unit and a plastic surgery unit, the latter because a better physical self-image can lead to improved self-esteem.

Many female offenders feel inadequate and find it difficult to cope with the demands of everyday life. The therapeutic communities in the new Holloway were to have facilities for intensive individual psychotherapy and for group therapy. Instead of the usual prison atmosphere where few decisions can be made and little responsibility accepted, there was to be a good deal of self-administration. This would help to produce situations in which inmates would need to make choices and accept the consequences of their own actions.

By and large, the pressure on prisons could probably be eased only through development of effective alternative means of dealing with large categories of offenders in the community. The most important of these were probation and parole. In Western Europe generally the judiciary was strikingly more involved in these matters than in Britain or the U.S., as was clearly demonstrated during a two-day conference on probation held at the Institut des Hautes Études de Belgique in Brussels in April 1971. Certainly the detail into which European judges go as probation takes its course enables them to have considerable understanding of how this method operates. A further advantage is flexibility in that all sorts of conditions can be attached to a probation order—for example, enforced attendance at a psychiatric outpatient clinic.

In England, with its fast-growing prison population, it was realized that treatment-intensive alternatives to imprisonment were badly needed. During the year proposals were made to establish community training centres. As a condition of a probation order, those not at work could attend such centres during the day, while those who had work could attend in the evenings or on weekends. The hope was that this would help to keep out of prison the many thousands of relatively minor offenders who needed a good deal of help to deal with their problems. Ordinary probation was too little for them. They needed something more intensive—education, if they had missed out on it, good industrial training, or, if there were personal problems, group therapy.

The use of volunteers in rehabilitation was undergoing an interesting reversal of policy. In many countries, help for discharged prisoners used to consist of a little charitable money collected by volunteers. The next step was the employment of professional social workers. Later, trained volunteers were associated with probation and aftercare; for example, volunteers in England managed special hostels for alcoholic or epileptic former prisoners. The most sophisticated use of volunteers was often to group them around a professional social worker whose task was to guide and support them.

But the most recent development—and the next logical step—was the use of former offenders in the treatment of offenders, an approach that was pioneered in the U.S. In Chicago, for example, selected former offenders proved effective as probation officer aides. The Hawaii Corrections Division employed former offenders on its staff. In England, former offenders served successfully as detached social workers in high delinquency areas.

The rationale behind this was that former offenders understand the problems of offenders and also that it demonstrates to those who are still in trouble that helpful and acceptable roles for former offenders are possible. This idea had worked well in the treatment of drug addicts (Synanon) and alcoholics (Alcoholics Anonymous).

But there were also many difficulties in the way. Offenders could be suspicious of those who seemed to them to have "sold out" to straight society, and cor-

rectional personnel could feel very threatened in their professional status if many former offenders were to join their ranks. Clearly much depended on careful selection and good training. (H. J. KL.)

See also Crime.

Profits

In broad profile, 1971 was a year of cyclical expansion in North America—fairly robust in Canada and moderate in the U.S.—and of slowdown in Europe and Japan. Available data, although incomplete, generally confirmed that profits, as would be expected, moved with the business cycle. The trend of profits was up in the U.S. and Canada and down in Japan and West Germany. Of the five countries for which current data were available only the U.K. experienced a movement of profits counter to general economic conditions, at least in the first half of the year when profits rose while the British economy slumped.

United States. In the U.S. recovery from the 1969–70 recession proceeded at a disappointingly slow pace. A moderate revival of consumption was the economy's chief propellant, although low consumer confidence in the face of high unemployment and inflation limited the vigour of the rebound. While the recession deepened until November 1970, corporate profits before taxes reached their low point in the first quarter of that year and began a mild uptrend thereafter, interrupted only by the strike against General Motors in the fourth quarter. However, at $83.6 billion in the third quarter of 1971 (seasonally adjusted annual rate), pretax profits were still 6% below the peak reached in the final quarter of 1968, while gross national product (GNP) was up 19% over the same period (*see* Table I).

The increase in the rate of pretax profits from the second to the third quarter of 1971 was small—only $300 million (seasonally adjusted)—and this gain was entirely attributable to an increase of $1.3 billion in the rate of inventory profits stemming from inflation. Without such inventory gains, profits before taxes would have declined $1.1 billion in the third quarter, to $77.2 billion (seasonally adjusted). Principal reasons for the third quarter weakness were depressed conditions in the steel industry and a somewhat lower rate of profit remittances from U.S. foreign investments.

In the face of sluggish recovery, continuing high rates of cost and price inflation, and flagging confidence in the economy, Pres. Richard Nixon on August 15 declared a wage-price freeze, suspended the con-

Table I. United States Corporate Profits and Related Indicators

Period	Profits (in $000,000,000) Before taxes	Less inventory profits	After taxes	Profits per dollar of sales (cents)*	Ratio of profits to income originating in corporations (%)†	Ratio of price to unit labour cost index‡
1969: First quarter	88.7	82.7	46.9	5.0	10.2	99.7
Second quarter	86.9	80.7	45.9	4.9	9.8	99.3
Third quarter	81.2	78.0	43.0	4.8	8.9	99.5
Fourth quarter	80.0	73.3	42.3	4.5	8.7	98.2
1970: First quarter	75.6	69.8	41.5	4.1	8.5	96.7
Second quarter	75.8	71.5	41.3	4.3	8.5	97.7
Third quarter	78.5	73.0	42.9	4.0	8.7	97.6
Fourth quarter	71.6	69.0	39.2	3.6	7.9	96.0
1971: First quarter	79.1	75.5	42.9	4.0	8.4	96.1
Second quarter	83.3	78.3	46.0	4.4	8.6	97.4
Third quarter	83.6	77.2	45.8	—	8.6	96.8

*After taxes, all manufacturing.
†All industries.
‡Manufacturing; 1957–59 = 100.
Sources: *Survey of Current Business* (July and November 1971); *Business Conditions Digest* (November 1971).

vertibility of the dollar, and imposed new import restrictions. The freeze was followed on November 14 by "Phase Two." Preliminary indications were that the rules and procedures of Phase Two were somewhat unfavourable to profits. In general, wage increases were to be held to a guideline of 5.5% and prices to 2.5%. However, sellers would be permitted to increase prices only if costs rose more than the improvement in productivity. Profit margins could increase in response to higher volume, but price increases toward that end were precluded if the effect would be to raise margins above the average of the best two of the last three years. The regulations also required windfall profits to be "converted into price reductions." The profit margin rule was perhaps less severe than it appeared because the base period average was higher than current performance for most firms. Pitfalls remained, but, all things considered, the outlook for profits in the U.S. as 1971 drew to a close was for further expansion.

Canada. Unlike the U.S., Canada experienced only a slowdown, not a recession, in 1969–70. Nevertheless, profits declined sharply from a peak of Can$8.2 billion (seasonally adjusted) in the first quarter of 1969 to a trough of Can$6.7 billion in the final quarter of 1970. In 1971, however, the acceleration of the economy carried profits along. Real GNP rose at a seasonally adjusted annual rate of 6.1% in the first half of the year, aided by resurgent cyclical forces and stimulative monetary and fiscal policies.

Fiscal policy was progressively eased in 1971, while monetary policy was aggressively expansionary as the authorities endeavoured to lower Canada's interest rates relative to those in the U.S. with a view to moderating the upward pressures on Canada's exchange rate. The upward float impinged severely on the labour-intensive secondary industries, thereby adding to the problem of unemployment. At the same time, it blunted the cyclical recovery of profits, especially in numerous industries whose export prices were quoted in U.S. dollars. Still, corporate profits before taxes rebounded smartly in 1971, reaching Can$7.8 billion (seasonally adjusted) in the second quarter, higher than at any time since the second quarter of 1969 (*see* Table II).

West Germany. West Germany's economy gave the appearance of considerable strength in the first

half of 1971, but the underlying reality was less impressive. Monthly industrial production figures showed that activity topped out in February and then began a declining trend that, together with rising unemployment, gave rise to fears of a serious recession in the making.

Profits were caught in an ever tightening squeeze. In the economy at large, wages and salaries (including fringe benefits) were around 15% higher in the first half of 1971 than in the year earlier period. In the face of this wage inflation and increases in other costs, only a 4% year-over-year gain in real GNP limited the growth of costs per unit of real GNP to around 10% in the first half of 1971.

The profit squeeze was particularly marked in manufacturing, where productivity gains virtually ceased during the first seven months of 1971 while wages and salaries regained upward momentum at the end of the second quarter. As a result, unit labour costs reached unprecedented heights in the third quarter. During the first half of 1971, the share of profits in national income fell to the lowest level since World War II (*see* Table III). Since West Germany's official data on profits include not only company profits but also interest and rental income, as well as the earnings of doctors, lawyers, farmers, and other self-employed, the entire series shows an upward trend that conceals the deterioration in the company sector. Moreover, no seasonal adjustment is provided for the official data, with the result that large interest payments at year's end seriously impede the analysis of trends. Even so, before- and after-tax incomes in the first half of 1971 were only 1.9 and 0.3% higher than a year earlier, respectively.

United Kingdom. With the exception of an unusually strong balance of payments, there was little that was encouraging in the British economy of 1971. In the face of the economy's continuing sluggishness, public policy became increasingly expansionary. Monetary policy, too, was expansive, but the economy's response was disappointing.

In the circumstances, a profits recovery seemed more than could have been expected. Yet such a recovery actually occurred, as is shown in Table IV. Total company income, seasonally adjusted before taxes, rose 14.5% between the second quarters of 1970 and 1971, with all three components of the total —gross trading profits, rent and nontrading income, and income from abroad—participating in the increase. The explanation lay partly in higher productivity; a 1% gain in industrial production between September 1970 and 1971 was achieved with 4.5%

Table II. Canada: Corporation Profits Before Taxes, Seasonally Adjusted Annual Rates

In Can$000,000

Period	1969	1970	1971
First quarter	8,160	7,740	7,216
Second quarter	8,084	7,412	7,800
Third quarter	7,576	7,596	
Fourth quarter	7,588	6,708	

Source: *Canadian Statistical Review* (October 1971).

Table III. West Germany: Profit and Income Developments

In DM. 000,000; without adjustment for seasonal variation

Income from entrepreneurial activity and property

Period	Before income taxes	Share of national income (%)	After income taxes	Change from previous corresponding period (%) Before income taxes	After income taxes
1969: First half	74,130	34.5	56,880	9.0	8.9
Second half	84,840	34.7	66,030	2.8	0.2
1970: First half	81,050	32.8	64,390	9.3	13.2
Second half	92,280	33.0	74,050	8.8	12.1
1971: First half	82,560	30.2	64,570	1.9	0.3

Source: *Wirtschaft und Statistik* no. 9 (1971).

Table IV. United Kingdom: Company Income, Seasonally Adjusted

In £000,000

Period	Total	Income arising in the United Kingdom		Income from abroad
		Gross trading profits*	Rent and nontrading income	
1969: First quarter	2,163	1,217	451	495
Second quarter	2,209	1,246	472	491
Third quarter	2,252	1,258	484	510
Fourth quarter	2,255	1,240	503	512
1970: First quarter	2,285	1,247	513	525
Second quarter	2,275	1,243	517	515
Third quarter	2,301	1,240	534	527
Fourth quarter	2,432	1,298	564	570
1971: First quarter	2,517	1,375	573	569
Second quarter	2,634	1,424	582	628

*Before providing for depreciation and stock appreciation.
Source: *Financial Statistics* (October 1971).

fewer workers. The further recovery of profits in the third quarter may have been blunted, however, by the commitment in July of Britain's leading companies to hold price increases to 5% during the next year.

Japan. Japan shared in the worldwide inflationary trend of the late 1960s and its authorities, like those in other countries, adopted restrictive policies to hold price increases within acceptable limits. Economic growth declined in 1970 and 1971 under the combined pressure of monetary restraint and falling business investment spending. Real growth fell from 12% in 1969 to around 6% (seasonally adjusted) in the first half of 1971, while inflation continued at a high rate. Still, the government gradually relaxed its restraints, beginning in the final quarter of 1970, to avert an unduly severe slowdown. By mid-1971, the economy seemed poised for an acceleration, but recovery was set back by the upward float of the yen after the August 15 currency crisis and by the new U.S. import restrictions.

Corporate profits reflected the underlying trend of the economy. Surveys of earnings reports by corporations listed on the Tokyo Stock Exchange for successive six-month reporting periods showed that, as the economy slowed in 1970, profit growth slumped sharply. While both sales and after-tax profits were up around 13% in the six months between October 1969 and March 1970, their growth declined in the following period to approximately 8 and 2%, respectively. In 1971 profit growth turned into sharp decline. A sample of 549 companies listed in the first and second sections of the Tokyo Stock Exchange showed after-tax profits down 5.8% in the October 1970–March 1971 period and down 16.2% in April–September. Not since the 1964–65 recession had profits dropped so severely. Moreover, the decline was broadly based. Two-thirds of the companies listed in the first and second sections of the Exchange reported lower profits, and virtually all lines of business suffered declines. As 1971 drew to a close the devaluation of the dollar held out the prospect of a further rise in the cost of Japanese exports, despite the revocation of the U.S. import surcharge. (G. A. Po.)

See also Stock Exchanges.

Propaganda

The traveling statesman was the leading performer on the international propaganda scene during 1971. Prompted by U.S. Pres. Richard Nixon's planned visit to Peking, the Soviet Union initiated a diplomatic offensive featuring trips by its top leaders on a scale not seen since 1955. Even Emperor Hirohito broke 2,600 years of Japanese tradition by meeting with President Nixon in Alaska and visiting seven Western European countries. The shifting but uncertain play of relationships between the U.S., U.S.S.R., and China intensified Sino-Soviet propaganda warfare. With U.S. soldiers less active in combat in South Vietnam, propagandists emphasized political events, such as the unopposed election of Pres. Nguyen Van Thieu, more than actual fighting.

Egypt's Pres. Anwar as-Sadat, calling 1971 the "year of decision," threatened war against Israel as the precarious cease-fire along the Suez Canal was broken in the early fall, apparently by both sides. Soviet propagandists showed some irritation over the persecution of Communists in the Sudan and the inability of the Arab nations to develop a united front

and were critical of U.S. diplomatic efforts toward reaching a Middle Eastern settlement. Sudanese Pres. Gaafar Nimeiry accused the U.S.S.R. of planning a coup against him in July.

The war that broke out between India and Pakistan in December was preceded and accompanied by bitter propaganda exchanges. Pakistan accused India of unprovoked attack, while India found the root causes of war in Karachi's repression of East Pakistan.

In late September the U.K. government announced the expulsion of 105 Soviet nationals whom they accused of spying. Soviet and Eastern European media first ignored the charges by the British government, then spelled them out and denied them, and finally counterattacked by saying that Great Britain, the U.S., and NATO made false accusations in order to whip up anti-Soviet hysteria designed to restore "the stone-age of anti-Communism," impede the convoking of a conference on European security, and torpedo West German Chancellor Willy Brandt's *Ostpolitik.* (*See* INTELLIGENCE OPERATIONS.)

The major propaganda coup of 1971 was President Nixon's announcement of his planned trip to Peking and the reorientation of U.S. policy toward China. Nixon's mid-October announcement of plans to visit Moscow came as a decided anticlimax. The new U.S. economic policies, however, eroded the U.S. image overseas. Chinese and Soviet propagandists for once were in agreement, both predicting the end of the monetary system of the capitalist world, and saying that Nixon's unpopular measures reflected the seriousness of the U.S. economic crisis and the decay of the entire capitalist system. The *New York Times*'s publication of the Pentagon papers on U.S. involvement in Southeast Asia gave Communist media another field day. (*See* PUBLISHING.)

The report by Leonid I. Brezhnev, general secretary of the Soviet Communist Party, to the 24th party congress in March 1971 showed clearly that Soviet propaganda would support the first goal of Soviet foreign policy, to develop further the friendship and cooperation of the socialist countries. Unmistakably, however, greater emphasis would be given to increased political and economic cooperation with less developed countries liberated from colonial rule and to the new prospects opening up in Europe as a result "of a substantial shift in our relations with the Federal Republic of Germany."

Following President Nixon's announcement that he would visit Peking, Soviet propaganda directed to the Western industrial nations increased its emphasis on reducing tensions and improving relations. Several Soviet concessions, such as the signing of the Four Power agreement on Berlin and indications of readiness to consider a reduction of armed forces and armaments in Central Europe, were exploited. An earlier apparent propaganda attempt to intimidate Albania, Yugoslavia, and Romania was offset by Brezhnev's visit to Belgrade where he and Yugoslav President Tito signed a new declaration. The Kremlin clearly wanted to lessen tensions that had been building up in the Balkans.

Soviet propaganda toward China moderated somewhat in early 1971, but after ten days of cautious assessment of the Nixon China trip, it reached peaks of polemics. The Soviets charged China with nuclear hypocrisy, trampling on its non-Chinese minorities, inviting Nixon and thus dealing a blow to the peoples of Indochina, rejecting constructive proposals made by Moscow to settle disputed border questions, and

Soviet Premier Aleksei N. Kosygin wears an Indian headdress after receiving the honorary title of Chief Golden Eagle in Edmonton, Alta., during his tour of Canada in October 1971.

Queen Elizabeth
accompanies Emperor
Hirohito on the way
to Buckingham Palace
during his state visit
to Great Britain
on Oct. 5, 1971.
By leaving Japanese soil
to visit Alaska and seven
Western European
countries,
Emperor Hirohito broke
2,600 years of tradition.
KEYSTONE

trying to push the U.S. and the U.S.S.R. into a nuclear war. Moscow warned the U.S. that collusion with China could become a political boomerang, forecast failure of any effort by Washington and Peking to squeeze the U.S.S.R., took concrete steps to improve relations with the U.S., and initiated a diplomatic campaign of remarkably broad dimensions, including the signing of a defense treaty with India. China intensified its propaganda against the Soviet Union; attacked its economic policies and accused the leadership of selling the Soviet people for a handful of U.S. dollars; and revived Chairman Mao Tsetung's thesis of dual policy, which argues that the imperialist enemy of yesterday can become a temporary ally of today.

Communist countries continued to expand international radio propaganda faster than the rest of the world. The U.S.S.R. increased its international radio services by over 14% during the past four years. Its Asian service became 25% larger than its European, and it allocated more radio time to Africa than any other broadcaster and built up programs to European Communist countries. Communist Chinese foreign broadcasts had increased 27% since 1967, with Asia the principal target, but Albania's Radio Tirana, the European voice of Peking, added significantly to dissemination of Chinese views, especially to European Communist countries. The most recent study by Radio Free Europe showed official Communist foreign radio programming at over 900 hours daily in 79 languages with over 100 of these hours devoted to broadcasts by Albania, China, and the U.S.S.R.   (H. H. SA.)

Psychology

In 1971 there was a continuation and extension of both practice and research in such behavioural therapies as systematic desensitization and reconditioning. These procedures are based on findings and principles drawn from learning theory and are aimed toward alleviating disorders such as excessive anxiety, or toward altering maladaptive behaviours such as the use of children as sex objects, or peeping tom activity. In the case of systematic desensitization (usually of a phobia) the individual is taught a technique of relaxation using suggestion, muscle exercises, or hypnosis. The fear-arousing situation is presented in a step-by-step fashion, gradually increasing the total number of anxiety-arousing cues until the person learns to deal with the once-feared object or activity in comfort. The fear-arousing cues can be presented in fantasy, in real life, or both, and the individual's level of anxiety indicates the degree of progress at any point in the procedure. Behaviour therapy continues to draw growing attention as an alternative to or addition to the more traditional forms of talking-out (insight) therapy such as psychoanalysis.

Laboratory animals have been conditioned to control their skeletal muscle responses and glandular and visceral activity by rewarding them appropriately with pleasurable electrical stimulation to the brain. A team of researchers reporting to the 79th (1971) annual convention of the American Psychological Association described studies on humans in which hypnosis was used as an aid in training for voluntary control of visceral and other bodily functions. Subjects were placed in hypnotic trances and told to make one hand hotter and the other hand colder by imagining, for example, that one was in ice water and the other was under an electric blanket. While all hypnotized subjects were able to do this, effecting average changes of 7° C colder in one hand to 2° C warmer in the other, no nonhypnotized control subject could match such results. While the underlying mechanisms are not clearly understood, these results indicate that similar bodily functions found in psychosomatic illnesses such as ulcers, rapid heart rate, and some forms of high blood pressure may be cured through combinations of suggestion and reconditioning (American Psychological Association, *Annual Proceedings,* p. 778, 1971).

In seeking to discover relationships between brain function and behaviour, investigators report (*Science,* vol. 172, pp. 599–601, May 7, 1971) that verbal stimuli (such as spoken words) evoke greater brain-wave responses in the left half of the brain and nonverbal stimuli (such as simple clicking sounds) are processed by the right side. The data add support to the idea of functional asymmetry in the two hemispheres of the brain. Other investigators further localized specific speech functions in the brain. Part of the left hemisphere (called Broca's area) long has been associated with speech function. It now has been found that, when people utter polysyllabic words, greater brain-wave changes (larger negative potentials) appear on the left side than on the right. On the other hand, when people make nonverbal spitting or coughing movements, larger potentials are recorded from the right side. This may be the first direct physiological evidence of localization of speech-related function within the left hemisphere (*Science,* vol. 172, pp. 499–502, April 30, 1971).

New light has been thrown on the problem of overweight by examining the cues that lead people to eat. Surprisingly, the felt sense of hunger, the cue most people rely on, was not among them. In a series of studies reported in *Psychology Today* (April 1971), external stimuli such as taste, smell, and awareness of the time of day are more important than are internal cues such as stomach contractions. Indeed, fat people are relatively insensitive to internal cues as compared with people of normal weight. When external cues were reduced or eliminated, and fat subjects were fed a bland, low-calorie diet, they lost weight easily; but they regained the lost poundage when reexposed to food-relevant external stimuli. Another report (*American Psychologist,* vol. 26, pp. 129–144, February 1971) drew striking parallels between the eating behaviour of obese humans and of rats that had undergone brain surgery (bilateral lesions in the ventromedial nuclei of the hypothalamus). In rats, these brain lesions produce voracious eating and rapid weight gain, and it may be that hypothalamic activity also plays an important regulatory role in human eating behaviour. (J. T. G.)

See also **Biography:** Skinner, B(urrhus) F(rederic); **Medicine.**

Publishing

Newspapers. A sombre review of the state of the world's press at the beginning of 1971 came from Ernest Meyer, director of the International Press Institute (IPI). He saw no sign of any easing of the rigid controls in the totalitarian countries. Throughout Latin America press freedom was under attack from extremists of both right and left, with journalists murdered, imprisoned, or assaulted. In Western countries publishers were less and less disposed to adopt editorial policies that might risk loss of either readers or advertisers and the trend toward concentration of ownership was causing a single editorial viewpoint to be disseminated through a publishing chain.

In mid-1971, however, these concerns appeared to be secondary in comparison to the threats inherent in the Pentagon papers controversy in the U.S. At issue was the freedom of the press to report the conduct of government versus the power of that government to prevent publication of any information it opted to conceal in the name of national security. The cause célèbre was the first instance in U.S. history in which the federal government forcibly imposed judicial bans on political reporting. The U.S. Supreme Court ultimately resolved the question in favour of the press, but the guarantee of press freedom contained in the First Amendment to the U.S. Constitution seemed less immutable as a result.

The matter began quietly enough one Sunday in June when the *New York Times* carried a page one article by Neil Sheehan modestly headlined "Vietnam Archive: Pentagon Study Traces 3 Decades of Growing U.S. Involvement." It was the first of a projected series of articles based on a purloined, supersecret, 7,000-page study formally entitled "History of the United States Decision-Making Process on Vietnam Policy" initiated in 1967 by the then Secretary of Defense Robert S. McNamara. McNamara hoped to compile for future study a factual record of the chain of decisions that finally dictated no alternative to periodic military escalation of the Vietnam conflict.

Reviewing the actions of the administrations of Presidents Harry S. Truman, Dwight D. Eisenhower, John F. Kennedy, and Lyndon B. Johnson, the study recorded frequently hasty acts by often shortsighted or self-serving officials and documented some startling deceptions of the public. Among the report's conclusions were: The Truman administration's decision to give France military aid in Indochina established the course of U.S. policy. The Eisenhower administration prevented the otherwise-inevitable establishment of a pro-Communist South Vietnamese government, thereby contributing to the breakdown of the 1954 Geneva settlement. The Kennedy administration expanded a "limited risk gamble" into a "broad commitment" that left Johnson with the choice between withdrawal and escalation. When Johnson chose the

The first of the series of articles based on the Pentagon papers appeared in the "New York Times" on June 13, 1971. Three installments were published before the Justice Department obtained a federal court order temporarily banning further disclosures until the case could be tested in court.

latter, his decision was kept secret for a year and was implemented through a consciously deceptive scenario.

The *New York Times* published three installments of the series before the Justice Department, arguing that publication of classified documents endangered the national security, won a New York federal court order temporarily banning further disclosures. Meanwhile, the *Washington Post* had acquired the Pentagon report and was publishing its own interpretive series by veteran foreign affairs experts Chalmers Roberts and Murrey Marder. *Times* attorneys argued that this fact rendered moot the government's case against their paper, especially since more than 300 newspapers subscribing to the Los Angeles Times-Washington Post News Service were receiving and publishing the *Post*'s dispatches. The Justice Department hastily sought to enjoin the *Post*. In the next five days, as federal courts in New York and Washington issued four sets of contradictory rulings each, other papers across the country, including the *Boston Globe,* the *St. Louis Post-Dispatch,* and the 11-paper Knight group, published stories faster than the Justice Department could file new injunctions.

While there was a common denominator to all the accounts, there was no apparent journalistic collusion; all the papers based their reports on portions of the same documents, apparently photocopies of a set Daniel Ellsberg (*see* BIOGRAPHY) admitted smuggling from the archives of the Rand Corporation. It appeared that Ellsberg had underground assistance from antiwar activists in distributing the documents.

The Supreme Court swiftly agreed to hear oral arguments in an unusual Saturday session after the adjournment of its normal term. Its 6–3 decision, announced on June 30, freed the newspapers to publish but turned on an unusually narrow definition of the legal question—and was all the more exceptional in that all nine justices filed separate opinions and no single opinion had the concurrence of more than two other justices. (*See* LAW.)

The *New York Times*'s operation, dubbed Project X, was unique in the annals of modern journalism. First, it was not the normal investigative reporting job that bore fruit after tireless digging. Work began only after Ellsberg, impressed with Neil Sheehan's skills and the views he expressed in reviewing recent books on the war, supplied Sheehan with the raw material, apparently the entire 47-volume Pentagon study excluding only those sections Ellsberg considered to be legitimately "top secret."

After the *Times*'s top editorial echelon approved the

Public Utilities:
see Cooperatives;
Fuel and Power;
Industrial Review;
Transportation

World Daily Newspapers and Circulations, 1970–71*

Country	Daily newspapers	Circulation per 1,000 of population
AFRICA		
Algeria	4	14
Angola	5	10
Cameroon	1	2
Central African Republic	2	0.6
Ceuta	1	58
Chad	2	0.4
Congo (Brazzaville)	3	1.3
Congo (Kinshasa)	7	1
Dahomey	1	0.4
Egypt	8	28
Ethiopia	8	2
Gabon	1	1
Ghana	6	34
Guinea	1	†
Ivory Coast	3	...
Kenya	4	15
Liberia	1	3
Libya	7	20
Malagasy Republic	10	9
Mali	3	0.6
Mauritius	9	28
Melilla	1	60
Morocco	6	14
Mozambique	5	7
Niger	1	0.4
Nigeria	11	7
Portuguese Guinea	1	4
Réunion	2	64
Rhodesia	3	14
Senegal	1	5
Seychelles	2	45
Sierra Leone	6	16
Somalia	2	2
South Africa	21	40
South West Africa	2	12
Sudan	13	5
Tanzania	4	5
Togo	2	6
Tunisia	4	16
Uganda	5	5
Upper Volta	2	†
Zambia	2	9
Total	**183**	
NORTH AMERICA		
Bahama Islands	3	142
Barbados	2	115
Bermuda	1	223
British Honduras	2	49
Canada	118	206
Costa Rica	5	60
Cuba	9	88
Dominican Republic	6	32
El Salvador	8	51
Guadeloupe	1	9
Guatemala	9	27
Haiti	6	5
Honduras	7	17
Jamaica	2	66
Leeward Islands	3	33
Martinique	1	136
Mexico	157	116
Netherlands Antilles	6	153
Nicaragua	7	51
Panama (incl. Canal Zone)	12	81
Puerto Rico	4	95
Trinidad and Tobago	3	119
United States	1,748	305
Virgin Islands (U.S.)	3	153
Total	**2,123**	
SOUTH AMERICA		
Argentina	89	128
Bolivia	17	34
Brazil	282	37
Chile	122	86
Colombia	51	53
Ecuador	27	42
French Guiana	1	31
Guyana	3	54
Paraguay	9	40
Peru	93	47
Surinam	5	41
Uruguay	31	400
Venezuela	38	71
Total	**768**	
ASIA		
Afghanistan	20	7
Burma	43	9
Cambodia	26	22
Ceylon	17	58
China	392	19
Cyprus	10	92
Hong Kong	74	485
India	636	13
Indonesia	73	7
Iran	26	...
Iraq	5	...
Israel	24	205
Japan	169	503
Jordan	2	12
Korea, North	7	...
Korea, South	42	76
Kuwait	5	52
Laos	7	3
Lebanon	33	97
Macao	6	114
Malaysia	37	74
Mongolia	3	16
Nepal	16	3
Pakistan	139	6
Philippines	16	27
Ryukyu Islands	10	271
Saudi Arabia	6	8
Singapore	11	154
Syria	4	15
Taiwan	32	64
Thailand	24	21
Turkey	400	41
Vietnam, North	7	...
Vietnam, South	38	70
Yemen	5	18
Total	**2,365**	
EUROPE		
Albania	2	51
Austria	33	268
Belgium	33	260
Bulgaria	12	189
Czechoslovakia	27	283
Denmark	59	363
Finland	68	358
France	109	243
Germany, East	17	445
Germany, West	398	331
Gibraltar	2	254
Greece	110	85
Hungary	27	212
Iceland	5	379
Ireland	7	240
Italy	70	127
Luxembourg	7	368
Malta	6	...
Netherlands	94	307
Norway	82	388
Poland	43	204
Portugal	20	71
Romania	51	166
Spain	116	105
Sweden	115	528
Switzerland	121	368
U.S.S.R.	628	320
United Kingdom	122	488
Vatican City (Holy See)	1	‡
Yugoslavia	23	79
Total	**2,408**	
OCEANIA		
American Samoa	1	65
Australia	61	363
Cook Islands	1	38
Fiji	1	26
French Polynesia	3	78
Guam	1	127
New Caledonia	1	52
New Zealand	41	377
Niue	1	60
Tonga	2	16
Total	**113**	
Grand Total	**7,960**	

*Only newspapers issued four or more times weekly are included. Areas not listed had no known daily newspapers. †Total circulation less than 1 per 1,000 population. ‡Circulation largely outside territory.
Sources: UN Statistical Yearbook 1970 (1971); Editor & Publisher International Yearbook 1971; Newspaper Press Directory 1970; other secondary sources.

(W. A. Ha.)

project in principle, Sheehan disappeared from his Washington beat into a New York hotel suite where he was joined by three other top reporters, E. W. Kenworthy, who was said to be on vacation, Hedrick Smith, soon to man the *Times*'s Moscow bureau and supposedly off studying Russian somewhere, and Fox Butterfield, pulled in from a suburban assignment. Typesetting was done by a special crew of trusted compositors working under guard in an isolated composing room. Justifiably the *Times* was proud of its journalistic coup. Less heralded was the *Post*'s accomplishment of getting an almost equally valuable appraisal of the report into print without the six weeks of preparation time. (PH. K.)

The episode of the Pentagon papers was not the only clash between the press and the administration. In February newsmen complained that the Defense Department was placing undue restrictions on their reporting of the war in Laos. In September the Justice Department filed a friend-of-the-court brief with the Supreme Court that, in essence, sought to have the court declare in certain cases under its consideration that newsmen had no constitutional right to withhold their confidential sources of information. During the fall U.S. Sen. Sam J. Ervin, Jr. (Dem., N.C.), conducted hearings into the increasing antagonism between government and the press before his subcommittee on constitutional rights.

Total daily circulation of newspapers in the U.S. as of Sept. 30, 1970, was 62,107,527, according to *Editor & Publisher Year Book*. The small gain of 47,938 over the previous year was absorbed by the 334 morning dailies, which also picked up the 73,782 in circulation lost by the 1,429 evening papers. An indication that circulation figures at the end of 1971 might not be encouraging was the report that U.S. newsprint consumption in the first half of the year was about 2% below the all-time high recorded in 1970. Newsprint prices rose twice during the year, bringing the New York base price to $168 a ton. Many papers increased their prices, with about 200 dailies charging 15 cents an issue.

At the beginning of 1971 half of the dailies in the U.S. were owned by 157 newspaper chains, which controlled a record 63% of total circulation. During the year, Gannett Newspapers made several acquisitions, including a merger with Federated Publications, Inc., and purchase of the newspaper interests of the Honolulu Star-Bulletin, Inc., to bring its list of dailies to 52, the largest number ever owned by a U.S. company. Pulitzer Publishing Co. purchased the *Arizona Daily Star*, one of two jointly operated papers involved in a lengthy antitrust suit that had led to the passage of the Newspaper Preservation Act in 1970. Also under pressure of U.S. Justice Department antitrust action, the E. W. Scripps Co. sold controlling interest in one of its two Cincinnati, O., papers, the *Cincinnati Enquirer*.

Severe losses of advertising revenue increased postal rates, and rising production costs led to personnel cutbacks on many papers. The *New York Times*, which reported a 7% decline in advertising linage in the first half of the year, eliminated some 300 jobs. In two cities newspapers beset with heavy financial losses suffered long shutdowns. Pittsburgh's *Press* and *Post-Gazette* were closed for 129 days because of a strike by the International Typographical Union. The New Jersey Newspaper Guild struck Newark papers on May 26 and before the strike was settled 112 days later, the *Evening News* had agreed to sell its Sunday edition and much of its physical assets to its competitor, the *Newark Star-Ledger*.

Tabloids appeared to be thriving. In New York City, two new tabloids appeared, the *Daily Mirror* and the *American*. In Canada, the *Sun*, a tabloid published five days a week, appeared in Toronto on November 1, the day following the close of the 95-year-old *Toronto Telegram*. *Newsday,* the Long Island, N.Y., tabloid, announced it would launch a Sunday edition in 1972.

The Pulitzer Prize for national reporting was awarded in 1971 to Lucinda Franks and Thomas Powers of United Press International for their coverage of the explosion of an underground bomb factory in New York's Greenwich Village. Horance Davis, Jr., won the Pulitzer editorial award for a series supporting school desegregation in the *Gainesville* (Fla.) *Sun*. Jim Hoagland of the *Washington Post* won the international reporting prize for a series on South Africa.

Awareness of the responsibilities of newsmen took a variety of forms. Minnesota became the first state in which a press council was established to hear complaints against the press and to defend and explain the role of the press. In Chicago, about 140 editorial employees of the *Chicago Sun-Times* and *Chicago Daily News* were refused their request for editorial space to oppose publisher Marshall Field's endorsement of Mayor Richard J. Daley (*see* BIOGRAPHY). The employees ran ads explaining their stand. In Canada journalists on many papers were pressing for a greater voice in editorial policies and a press council was established in Quebec.   (X.)

In the U.K., the circulation of the popular national dailies continued to decline, with one notable exception—the *Sun*. Since its take-over in 1969 by Rupert Murdoch (*see* BIOGRAPHY), the *Sun*'s circulation had risen from under one million to well over two million, proving that Murdoch's policy of running it on brash tabloid lines had paid dividends. The quality national papers, with about one-eighth of the market, advanced slowly. *The Guardian,* which celebrated its 150th anniversary in May, averaged 328,000 circulation, the highest in its history.

Profit on turnover was reckoned at less than 1%, and some papers were known to be running at substantial losses, among them *The Times* and *The Guardian*. One loss-maker disappeared in May, when the *Daily Sketch,* a tabloid with an average circulation of 750,000, was merged with the *Daily Mail*. The *Daily Mail* adopted a tabloid format but proved unable to hold the combined circulations of the two papers. The *Sketch*'s closure, with severe cuts on other papers and magazines of Harmsworth Publications, contributed to the labour troubles that aggravated the newspaper industry's other difficulties. Losses were increased by endemic short-term disputes, by two one-day strikes in March against the Industrial Relations Bill, and by a four-day stoppage in September—and this in an industry that until 1970 had prided itself on a strike-free record. To offset rising costs, all national papers substantially increased their prices during the year, the popular dailies to 3 pence, the popular Sundays to 5 pence, and the quality papers to even higher figures. The regional press, mainly operating in monopoly situations, was less seriously disturbed by economic problems.

On two occasions in 1970 printing unions had refused to print matter to which they objected in *The Observer;* the London *Evening Standard* and the Glasgow *Evening Citizen* had both been involved in attempts by printing workers to censor cartoons; and regional dailies at Bristol and Southend were stopped by unions because of the reports they contained of industrial disputes. In January 1971 the Press Council condemned such attempts to censor the contents of newspapers. Censorship was also at issue in a case in which the editor of *The Sunday Telegraph,* a free-lance journalist, and an army officer were tried and acquitted under the Official Secrets Act for publication in January 1970 of a confidential report on the military situation in Nigeria during the Biafran war.

In France, pressure by journalists for a greater say in the control of the papers on which they worked continued. At *Le Figaro* an agreement was reached at last setting up an editorial directorate. At *L'Express,* Jean-Jacques Servan Schreiber finally gave up his position as chairman in response to objections that his political activities endangered the editorial freedom of the paper. At *Le Nouvel Observateur,* the left-wing weekly, there were staff protests against police brutality to a journalist (*see* POLICE). Marseilles journalists went on strike over the proposed merger of the right-wing *Le Méridional* and the Socialist *Le Provençal*. Daily newspaper circulation in France was stagnating at around 12 million, with a continuing decline in the number of papers. Rising costs had forced *Le Monde* to increase its price by 40% in October 1970. The English-language weekly edition of *Le Monde,* begun in 1969, was discontinued in June, but reappeared in August on an experimental basis as a supplement to *The Guardian Weekly*.

In Sweden the government intervened in July to try to check the trend toward monopoly ownership and the decline of weaker papers. A levy of 6% for newspapers and 10% for magazines on advertising above a total of 3 million kronor was expected to raise 48 million kronor in 1971–72. This was to be distributed to weaker papers at a rate of 3,000 kronor per ton of newsprint, less newsprint used for advertising. In the Netherlands a committee set up by the Ministry of Culture recommended creation of a special fund to help finance new plants and to reorganize ailing papers, with a general subsidy on the cost of newsprint. In August, the government announced that an initial sum of 10 million guilders would be available for distribution in 1971 and 1972.

In West Germany, where the Axel Springer Group controlled nearly 40% of newspaper circulation, as well as other mass media, both the number of papers published and their total sales were falling sharply. The regional press, however, remained strong. The total number of papers fell during 1971 from 1,065 to 998. Fear of a Springer-dominated press was highlighted by the war waged by his papers on Chancellor Willy Brandt's *Ostpolitik,* which caused Brandt to accuse the press in general of misusing its freedom. Italy, with the lowest newspaper sales per capita of any EEC country (total circulation was at about five million) saw a continuing decline in papers published. The Cabinet announced in August its intention to grant a subsidy of $8 million to aid the weaker dailies and weeklies. Switzerland, with 110 dailies and another 57 papers published between three and five times a week, continued to enjoy a flourishing regional and local press.

In June Amnesty International listed 48 journalists imprisoned by the Greek regime. A press law and

The nostalgia boom brought revival of two magazines during 1971. Left, "The Saturday Evening Post" returned as a quarterly. Right, the new "Liberty" magazine reprinted stories from the old magazine, using the original photographic plates.

COURTESY, LEFT, "THE SATURDAY EVENING POST"; RIGHT, "LIBERTY" MAGAZINE

code of ethics promulgated in August required both Greek and foreign journalists working in Greece "to serve the interests of the people and of the nation, being inspired in this by the Hellenic-Christian tradition." A government-nominated press council was to determine what was and was not in the public interest. Objections by the Greek and foreign press quickly led to amendment of the code. In Portugal, where a press law was introduced in August, ostensibly to replace political censorship, attempts by liberal deputies to draft a code that would define and respect both the responsibilities and the rights of the press were defeated. Turkey had established something of a reputation for maintaining a free press, but during a political crisis in April two left-wing Istanbul papers were closed for ten days and three right-wing dailies were suspended for a week for criticizing the regime.

The most widely publicized instance of suppression of a newspaper was the closure of the English-language *Singapore Herald* because of undisclosed (supposedly U.S.) ownership. Prime Minister Lee Kuan Yew found himself defending his action before the IPI annual assembly in Helsinki, Fin., in June. Freedom, he argued, came second to state security. The government had also detained four members of the staff of the Chinese-language *Nanyang Siang Pau* on a charge of glamourizing Communism and stirring up chauvinistic sentiment for Chinese culture and language. Censorship was also imposed during the year in Pakistan and Ceylon. In India, a draft bill designed to diversify ownership was challenged as a threat to press freedom.

In Japan three big national papers accounted for half the total of 52 million copies sold daily. With circulation reaching saturation point, and advertising providing 60% of revenue, the Japanese press, like the Western press, was increasingly sensitive to setbacks in the economy. Australia acquired two new quality Sunday papers in February, the *National Times* (Canberra) and the *Sunday Australian* (Melbourne). The first was a sober, high-priced tabloid; the second, owned by Rupert Murdoch, was bigger, cheaper, and edited on somewhat English lines by a former Fleet Street journalist.   (W. H. Ts.)

Magazines. The trends of the past few years continued to modify and govern the magazine industry. Self-criticism, generated as much by economic loss and recession as by editorial concern, resulted in internal shakeups and mergers; women seeking equal rights managed several victories; and there were

the usual number of new periodicals and failures.

Except for increased cigarette advertising, now banned on television, the economic health of magazines in the U.S. appeared no better than in 1970. Even where advertising pages were up, rising labour costs and postal rates cut deeply into profits. Countering the expenses, publishers raised subscription and newsstand prices. In 1971 the price index for periodicals was 237 (1957–59 = 100). Significantly enough, the magazine *Hard Times* virtually called it quits and became part of *Ramparts* magazine. Caught in a $5 million yearly loss pattern, owner Gardner Cowles closed down *Look,* ending once and for all the notion that financial success was equated with a large number of subscribers. After 34 years, *Look* had over 7 million readers, but could not lure advertisers to make up the difference between low subscription rates and skyrocketing costs. The only mass magazine still being published more than once a month was *Life,* which announced two circulation cuts during the year, slashing its 8.5 million circulation to 5.5 million. One healthy publication, *I. F. Stone's Bi-Weekly,* ceased to exist at the end of the year—because Stone wanted time to write books. The liberal newsletter's list of 70,000 subscribers was sold to *The New York Review of Books.*

Despite hard times, 82 new magazines were started in the U.S. in 1970 and about an equal number in 1971. Although 50–60% of them would fail, those that succeeded would do so by reversing the time-honoured formula of being all things to all men. Ecology, environment, health, liberation, consumer news, and hobbies were among the specialized interests served by new ventures. Among the more interesting new titles was only one general magazine, *Companion* (no relation to the defunct *Women's Home Companion*), which stressed current interest topics. Specialized publications included: *Audience,* a bimonthly hard-cover magazine of the arts; *New Woman; Vintage Magazine,* given over entirely to wine; *Kids,* which limited contributors to its audience, children 15 years old and younger; *Imani,* one of a number by and for blacks; *Travel and Leisure,* for cardholders of American Express; and *Sexual Behavior.* Betting on the current love affair with nostalgia, the *Saturday Evening Post* reappeared as a quarterly directed to middle America and the quarterly *Liberty* reprinted previous published work from photographic plates of the original magazine pages.

During the year Cowles Communications gave up *Family Circle* and *Modern Medicine,* among others, to the New York Times Co. and *The New York Review of Books* acquired *Kirkus,* a 35-year-old review favoured by librarians and bookstores. In July the *Saturday Review* came under the new leadership of John Veronis and Nick Charney. Editor Norman Cousins resigned after 31 years in a dispute over plans to make the cultural weekly more topical. The highly profitable *New York* saw the departure of publisher George Hirsch and writer Jimmy Breslin.

Economic pressures forced U.K. magazines to make substantial price increases and, as a result, many suffered considerable loss of sales. Hardest hit were mass circulation women's magazines, with circulations already down to around two million from the four million to five million and more of the mid-1960s. Nevertheless, Britain's popular magazine invasion of the U.S. continued. *Penthouse,* the challenge to *Playboy,* became an accepted part of U.S. newsstand trade and was joined by *Forum,* a four-year-old digest-sized magazine offering serious articles on sex.

The growing demand that staffs have as much—if not more—to say about editorial policy as owners received a crucial test in 1971 at *Harper's Magazine* when editor Willie Morris walked out, taking with him virtually the entire staff. Board chairman John Cowles, Jr., wanted the contents of the lively magazine to be guided more by reader surveys—an idea Morris refused to consider. Four months after the fight, Cowles hired a new editor, Robert B. Shnayerson of *Time*. Speculation, in terms of both the specific case and its wider ramifications for editorial freedom from owners, surfaced in many magazines, notably Stuart Little's piece "What Happened at Harper's?" in *Saturday Review*. Internal press criticism was responsible for a new breed of magazine analyzing how news is, or is not, reported. The latest to join the ranks was *AP Review*, issued by employees of Associated Press; and [*More*], which scrutinized the New York press. Older members of this genre were the *Columbia Journalism Review*, the *Chicago Journalism Review*, and the weekly *Media Industry Newsletter*.

Women continued to harass the heretofore male-dominated magazine world. Women employees of Time, Inc., reached agreement on equal salaries and working conditions with men. *Newsweek* followed, and the seven slick women's magazines began in earnest to introduce innovations appropriate to the new role of women.

Following a feature story on college humour magazines, the *New York Times* bemoaned in an editorial "the dreary lack of humour all over the world." But if the *Harvard Lampoon* and the *Princeton Tiger,* among other college humour magazines, suffered from lack of satire and parody, part of the slack was taken up by the *Antioch Review*, which incorporated the defunct *Monocle*, a national humour magazine, into its pages. An example of their efforts that resulted in national publicity was a survey of prominent persons asked to answer the question, "Why did you (or did you not) sell out?" The editors dutifully reported "that 27.6% have not sold out; 12.1% don't say. The largest number, 32.8%, won't say." The only national humour magazine to survive in its own right was *The National Lampoon*, which noted circulation, if not profits, rising in 1971. The British satirical review *Private Eye*, which completed ten years of publication in October, had established itself with a circulation of 58,000.

The principal death among the more broad muck-raking journals was that of *Scanlan's*. The monthly magazine of investigative reporting lasted a little more than one year, built a circulation of over 100,000, but went down over a controversial issue on guerrilla war in the U.S. Finding U.S. printers unwilling to work on the issue, the publisher moved to Canada and shortly after the issue appeared the firm declared bankruptcy. Another magazine of this same type beat the odds and won the coveted George Polk award in 1971. *Washington Monthly* built an influential circulation on such stories as its award-winning one revealing Army intelligence surveillance of U.S. civilians involved in protests and political activity.

Protest of another sort erupted in the U.K. when *Oz*, an underground magazine with 500,000 readers, became the object of the longest obscenity trial in British legal history. Jail sentences for its three editors, called "severe" even by the Law Society, set off bitter arguments and resulted in 13 members of Parliament condemning the verdict "as discrediting the British system of justice." The sentences were later quashed; predictably, the circulation of *Oz* increased.

Despite both legal and economic setbacks, the basically youth-oriented underground press and "hip" publications continued to grow. By mid-1971 there were some 700 such newspapers and magazines from *Rags* to *Rolling Stone* and the *East Village Other*. Robert J. Glessing's *The Underground Press in America*, released in October 1970, was the first concerted effort to evaluate in book form the contributions and history of this highly personalized form of journalism. It came out as many saw the underground movement giving way to other, more traditional types of magazines—and as the general magazines were putting new emphasis on the personal touch. Signed columns and sections of issues from *Life* and *Time* to *Newsweek* and the *National Review* analyzed and attacked everything from student protest to economics. Hard news items were increasingly played down in favour of so-called personalized journalism and current trend articles. No one symbolized this movement better than Norman Mailer, who began it several years back and whose 1971 contribution was "The Prisoner of Sex," a controversial attack on Kate Millett's *Sexual Politics*, in *Harper's Magazine*.

William Buckley's *National Review* published what he first claimed to be secret U.S. government documents dealing with Vietnam that proved the CIA and the Pentagon were not composed of incompetents. After wide publicity, Buckley admitted the documents were "in fact composed ex nihilo" (out of nothing), and spent a good deal more space trying to explain away what many did not think a joke at all.

(W. A. Ka.; W. H. Ts.)

Books. Although world book production continued to rise in 1970–71, for most publishers it was a year of problems. Spiraling costs cut profit margins to the danger point, but when prices were raised, sales fell. The success of the paperback increased sales resistance to the higher-priced hardback, and fiction, the breadwinner of general book publishing, was hardest hit. As profits fell need for capital became increasingly urgent to enable publishers to reap the full benefits of the technological revolution in printing, costing, marketing, and distribution methods. Savings in manpower were swallowed up by rising wage rates, and the economic recession discouraged investment and forced education authorities and libraries to cut spending on books.

At the same time, new media were challenging the preeminence of print. During 1971 the audiovisual cassette became a marketable reality. Publishers began to specify terms in their contracts for use of material from books in cassette programs. In Europe a Publishers' Consortium recommended that publishers should be ready to link up with television programmers and electronics firms to initiate audiovisual programs and to promote, market, and rent cassettes. In the U.K. in December 1970 Oxford Visual Productions, the first company formed for integrated book-and-cassette production, was founded by the Oxford University Press and the Prestel Group of television professionals. The first "volume" of its 20-cassette, 12-book *Oxford Visual History of the Twentieth Century* came out in December 1971. Two events in 1971 showed the potential magnitude of the problem posed by the rapid increase in the use of copying machines: the production and sale by Rank Xerox Ltd. of ma-

Three editors
of the underground
magazine ''Oz''
(from left to right),
James Anderson, Felix
Dennis, and Richard
Neville, were convicted
on obscenity charges
during a controversial
trial in London.

chines for facsimile transmission, and the promise in the White Paper on the new British national library that it would provide a copying service to other U.K. libraries. It was proposed that the U.K. Copyright Act, 1956, be amended to ensure payment to publishers and authors for material copied by machine.

The Copyright Act was up for review as a result of the long agitation for Public Lending Right (PLR) to compensate authors for books borrowed from public libraries. In West Germany an amendment to the copyright law to provide payment to authors whose books were stocked by public libraries came into effect during the year; and in Denmark, where a PLR system had been in force for 25 years, the Authors' Union was agitating for a higher subsidy. The U.S. copyright law, passed in 1909 and "silly and anachronistic," remained unchanged. A revision bill had been passed by the House of Representatives in 1967 but continued to fail to win approval in the Senate.

The problem of international copyright was at last resolved in July, when the Bern Union and Universal Copyright conventions, meeting simultaneously in Paris, confirmed revisions proposed in September 1970. The "Paris Act" replaced the controversial Stockholm Protocol of 1967, which had attempted to make it easier for less developed countries to acquire books.

The rapid growth of publishing in the less developed countries was shown by the fact that in 1970 and 1971 newcomers to West Germany's Frankfurt International Book Fair (the main meeting place of the world's publishers) included Afghanistan, Ethiopia, Indonesia, the Malagasy Republic, Tanzania, and Zambia. Attendance at Frankfurt in October 1971 once again broke all records, with 3,581 publishers present, 482 more than in 1970, 75% from abroad. Economic pressures prevented the spectacular take-over bids of some previous years, but political incident was provided by the withdrawal of Romania, in protest against publication by the Frankfurt Suhrkamp Verlag of a novel by Paul Goma banned in Romania. A notable addition to the world's book fairs was the first Singapore fair, held in April.

Censorship continued to harass authors and publishers. In Greece 18 writers challenged the press and publication law of 1969 by publishing in 1970 *Eighteen Texts* to comment on the political situation. They avoided prosecution by sharing legal responsibility and their success encouraged them to attack the regime more openly in 1971 with *New Texts*, contain-

ing contributions from 21 writers. In the U.K. several prosecutions of authors and publishers under the Obscene Publications Act culminated in the case of *The Little Red School Book,* the English edition of a Danish handbook for boys and girls that had sold 500,000 copies on the Continent. The core of the case against its publisher was the chapter on sex, containing advice on masturbation, sexual intercourse, and contraception. The publisher lost the case and the appeal and was forced to publish an expurgated edition. In West Germany a draft bill to liberalize the pornography law came under fire from both Catholics and Lutherans and was strongly attacked in the Bundestag.

Large-scale take-overs seemed to have been replaced by regroupings of publishers to share installation and distribution costs. The only big take-over of the year was in Scandinavia, where in August Swedish publisher Albert Bonnier, already owner of companies in Norway and Finland, acquired control of the Danish Palle Fogtdal, publisher of popular scientific books and of four pictorial magazines. The popularity of the paperback encouraged formation of paperback subsidiaries and linkups between hardback and paperback companies. Penguin Books, the pioneer of paperback publishing, was reconstituted as the Penguin Publishing Co. Ltd. after its take-over by Pearson Longman, completed in 1971. Pan Books, a popular paperback imprint jointly owned by Collins, Macmillan, and Heinemann, linked up in 1970 with David and Charles, an independent publisher, and later signed an exchange agreement with Ballantine Books of New York.

Although book production in the U.K. rose in 1970 to a record total of 33,489 titles, 1,096 more than in 1969, output was declining from the 1966 peak. Fiction remained the largest category, but figures for January–June 1971 showed a drop in fiction titles of 631 compared with the first half of 1970. Total turnover, at some £155 million, had risen by about £13 million, but only £70 million was in foreign exchange, an £11 million drop from 1969, and for the first time since 1967 imports exceeded exports. These figures took no account of rising prices: the average price of a hardback book had risen from under £1 in 1960 to about £3 in 1970, with rises of some 10% planned by most publishers. Returns on sales were little more than 3 or 4% for many publishers.

In West Germany paperback production rose 8.4% in 1970 for a total output of 47,096 titles, 1,519 more than in 1969. Turnover was up 14%, much of which was accounted for by higher book prices. Exports rose by DM. 17.3 million to DM. 314.7 million, and imports by DM. 4.2 million to DM. 145.9 million. In June a new company was formed by Cornelsen Velhagen and Klasing and the Oxford University Press, called Cornelsen Oxford University Press, to develop language-teaching materials.

In France, where production fell yet again, by some 500 titles, to 21,371, total turnover rose by 10%, and exports, as a result of efforts to encourage overseas trade, rose by a record 16%. For the first time, however, imports exceeded exports by more than Fr. 5 million. French publishers, determined to resist U.S. infiltration and to preserve the national character of their industry, continued to form larger groups and to concentrate production.

With production up by 6.8% to 6,436 titles, exports up by 18%, and imports up by only 13.8%, Swiss publishing continued its healthy expansion. An encouraging development was expansion of exports to

Australia, which had tripled since 1967, and to New Zealand. Danish book production, after a near-stagnant year, was moving again in 1970, with 5,032 titles, 174 more than in 1969. In the Soviet Union, too, a decline in output in 1969 was followed by a recovery, with a record 78,800 books and pamphlets in 1970. Of 4,608 fiction titles, 30% were translations. Under the 1971–75 economic development plan, publishing was to be expanded and improved.

Angus and Robertson Ltd., Australia's largest publishing house, was acquired in November 1970 by a firm with interests in insurance whose policies alienated staff and customers. F. W. Cheshire Pty. and Australia's only paperback firm, Sun Books, both partly owned by the International Publishing Corporation (IPC), were sold respectively to the U.S. Xerox Corp. and to the U.K. Macmillan and Co. Ltd. Distribution of books was hampered by the sorry state of bookselling; only 5% of all bookshops were reported to have made a profit in 1970. Nevertheless, the trade in books continued to expand, with total turnover up from A$11,866,595 in 1969 to A$13,-967,226 in 1970. Production rose from 1,881 titles in 1969 to 2,100 in 1970. Despite this, almost all publishers found their profits declining steeply.

The number of titles issued in the U.S. in 1970 jumped to 36,071 from 29,579 in 1969. Although the increase indicated a strong growth in new editions and reprints in both hard-cover and paperback from 26% of total titles in 1969 to about 33% in 1970, it also reflected the improved listing procedures of *Publishers' Weekly*, which reported the figures. New titles and new editions published in 1971 were expected to exceed 36,000. Total publishers' receipts were estimated at $2,933,000,000 for 1970 and, despite continuing economic uncertainties, were expected to top $3 billion in 1971. Book prices continued to rise. The average price of $11.66 for a hard-cover book in 1970 represented a 22.7% increase over the 1969 figure. The median price for a novel in 1971 appeared to be $6.95, compared with $5.95 in 1970. The popularity of paperbacks continued, with titles issued jumping from 7,097 in 1969 to 9,279 in 1970 and sales increasing as much as 27% in some bookstores.

The flurry of corporate mergers and acquisitions of the late 1960s was over by 1971. Farrar, Straus & Giroux, Inc., however, acquired Hill and Wang, and the Henry Regnery Co. purchased the book publishing subsidiary of Cowles Communications, Inc. Donald W. Brown, founder-publisher of Pegasus, which was sold by Western Publishing to Bobbs-Merrill late in 1970, established his own trade-book house. Other new houses included a number of black, Chicano, and American Indian publishers.

In an effort to bolster the fiction market, two publishers, Alfred A. Knopf and Liveright, began issuing first novels in low-cost, hard-cover series. Bantam Books gave purchasers of the paperback edition of *Future Shock* six choices of cover colour to support author Alvin Toffler's contention that technology multiplies rather than restricts man's choices. The New American Library had the distinction of having its paperback *Boss*, Mike Royko's uncomplimentary book on Chicago's Mayor Richard J. Daley, "banned in Bosstown," according to a *Chicago Sun-Times* headline. A supermarket chain in Chicago removed the book from its shelves, reportedly at the urging of the mayor's wife.

A Gallup Poll reported in February that 26% of all adults surveyed had read a complete book in the pre-

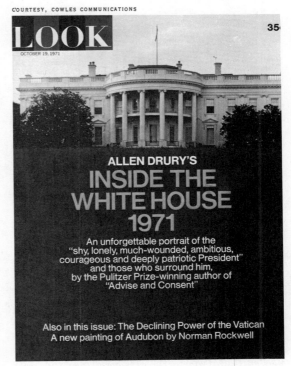

COURTESY, COWLES COMMUNICATIONS

LOOK

OCTOBER 19, 1971

35¢

ALLEN DRURY'S
INSIDE THE WHITE HOUSE 1971

An unforgettable portrait of the
"shy, lonely, much-wounded, ambitious, courageous and deeply patriotic President" and those who surround him, by the Pulitzer Prize-winning author of "Advise and Consent"

Also in this issue: The Declining Power of the Vatican
A new painting of Audubon by Norman Rockwell

"Look" magazine ceased publication with the Oct. 19, 1971, issue. Gardner Cowles, chairman of the board of Cowles Communications, the publisher of the magazine, blamed mounting costs and declining advertising revenue for the death of the magazine.

ceding month, the highest percentage reported since the poll had begun in 1958. Judging by the themes represented in books released in 1971, these readers were interested in economic analyses, biographies and current affairs, and social concerns, notably consumer protection and environmental controls. Books by or about American Indians appeared to be replacing the earlier profusion of black power publications, while interest in Jewish themes persisted and books on all aspects of life in China, Japan, Germany, and Latin America received increasing attention. Interest in sex books appeared to be diminishing.   (X.)

Books topping out as best sellers in late 1971 made up a fiction list dominated by works of well-established novelists and a nonfiction list representing a wide range of interests:

Fiction: *The Day of the Jackal* by Frederick Forsyth; *Wheels* by Arthur Hailey; *The Drifters* by James A. Michener; *The Exorcist* by William Peter Blatty; *Message from Malaga* by Helen MacInnes; *The Other* by Thomas Tryon; *The Bell Jar* by Sylvia Plath; *The Passions of the Mind* by Irving Stone; *The Winds of War* by Herman Wouk; and *Rabbit Redux* by John Updike.

Nonfiction: *Bury My Heart at Wounded Knee* by Dee Brown; *The Female Eunuch* by Germaine Greer; *Stilwell and the American Experience in China* by Barbara Tuchman; *The Sensuous Man* by "M"; *Honor Thy Father* by Gay Talese; *The Gift Horse* by Hildegarde Knef; *The Last Whole Earth Catalog* from Portola Institute; *Beyond Freedom and Dignity* by B. F. Skinner; *The Ra Expeditions* by Thor Heyerdahl; and *The Pentagon Papers* by the *New York Times* staff.

Figures released in February indicated that the top ten nonfiction best sellers for 1970 outsold the best-selling fiction list almost four to one despite the lack of "how to" books on the nonfiction list for the second straight year. The top-selling nonfiction title, David Reuben's *Everything You Always Wanted to Know About Sex but Were Afraid to Ask*, outsold Erich Segal's *Love Story* (906,484 copies to 405,044). The Bible returned to the nonfiction list in second place in the form of *The New English Bible* (730,520 copies), and the two top sellers of 1969, *American Heritage Dictionary of the English Language* and *In Someone's Shadow* by Rod McKuen, remained on the list in 1970. Other best sellers in 1970 were:

Hard-cover fiction: *The French Lieutenant's Woman* by John Fowles; *Islands in the Stream* by Ernest Hemingway; *The Crystal Cave* by Mary Stewart; *Great Lion of God* by Taylor Caldwell; *QB VII* by Leon Uris; *The Gang That Couldn't Shoot Straight* by Jimmy Breslin; *The Secret Woman* by Victoria Holt; *Travels with My Aunt* by Graham Greene; and *Rich Man, Poor Man* by Irwin Shaw.

Hard-cover nonfiction: *The Sensuous Woman* by "J"; *Better Homes and Gardens Fondue and Tabletop Cooking; Up the Organization* by Robert Townsend; *Ball Four* by Jim Bouton; *Body Language* by Julius Fast; and *Caught in the Quiet* by Rod McKuen.

The National Book Awards for works of 1970 were announced in March 1971 amid controversy stemming from a new procedure for selecting half of the list of nominees by national poll. The fiction jury threatened to resign if *Love Story* remained on the list, finally giving its award to Saul Bellow (*see* BIOGRAPHY) for *Mr. Sammler's Planet.* The poetry jury rejected every title on the polled list and was the subject of further controversy when a jurist, poet Allen Ginsberg, denounced the panel's choice of Mona Van Duyn.   (PH. K.)

See also Literature.

Qatar

An independent emirate on the west coast of the Persian Gulf, Qatar occupies a desert peninsula east of Bahrain, with Saudi Arabia and the Trucial States bordering on the south. Area: 4,400 sq.mi. (11,300 sq.km.). Pop. (1971 est.): 160,000. Capital: Doha (pop., 1971 est., 95,000). Language: Arabic. Religion: Muslim. Emir in 1971, Ahmad ibn Ali ibn Abdullah ath-Thani; prime minister, Sheikh Khalifa ibn Hamad ath-Thani.

On Sept. 3, 1971, Emir Ahmad, while on vacation in Geneva, Switz., signed a new treaty of friendship with Britain, ending all former treaty obligations (dating back to the 19th century) and establishing Qatar's full independence. Qatar's application for membership in the United Nations was approved by the UN General Assembly, and the country was also admitted to the Arab League. During the year work progressed on a $45.6 million fertilizer plant, one of several projects aimed at diversifying Qatar's petroleum-dependent economy.   (X.)

QATAR
Education. (1968–69) Primary, pupils 13,000, teachers 679; secondary, pupils 2,636, teachers 163.
Finance and Trade. Monetary unit: Qatar/Dubai riyal, with a par value of 4.76 riyals to U.S. $1 (11.43 riyals = £1 sterling) and a free rate (Sept. 27, 1971) of 4.61 riyals to U.S. $1. Oil revenues (1968) 521 million riyals.
Industry. Crude oil production (1970) 17,257,000 metric tons.

Race Relations

Black-white confrontations were less violent in 1971, but there was a resurgence of populism, ethnocentrism, or nationalism in countries as different as Switzerland, Zambia, and Pakistan. Long-smoldering religious and ethnic divisions lay at the root of the violence in East Pakistan and the subsequent outbreak of war between Pakistan and India.

The emergence of an outward-looking China had its bearing on race relations in the widest sense. Al-

Puerto Rico:
see Dependent States

Quakers:
see Religion

ready the biggest Communist donor of aid to the third world (surpassing Soviet credit offers by more than $400 million in 1970), China accompanied its aid with a renewed diplomatic offensive to back its entry into the UN. (*See* UNITED NATIONS.) For years Taiwan had held 14 African votes by diplomatic skill and offers of agricultural expertise, increasing this to 21 during the 1960s. In 1971, however, Ethiopia and Nigeria, among others, transferred support to Communist China. China's main beneficiaries were Tanzania and Zambia in Africa and Pakistan in Asia. In Africa, where the liberation and guerrilla movements had long been dominated by the U.S.S.R., the Chinese presented themselves not only as a more flexible, spontaneous, and practical alternative, but also as the major representatives of the world's coloured majority.

Africa also became increasingly an area of Arab-Israeli diplomatic competition, with technical and military aid as the counters. Israel was at some disadvantage because of its seeming affinity with South Africa, but it established particularly good relations with Ethiopia and Uganda, both countries traditionally at odds with their Arab neighbours over minority problems. In November, following Arab pressure on the Organization of African Unity, a peace mission consisting of Pres. Joseph Mobutu of Zaire (formerly Congo [Kinshasa]), Pres. Léopold S. Senghor of Senegal, Pres. Ahmadou Ahidjo of Cameroon, and Maj. Gen. Yakubu Gowon of Nigeria visited Israel and Egypt.

South Africa. In 1971 the increasingly firm demands of Bantustan leaders for greater autonomy and better treatment for Africans by whites went side by side with a growing separatism among black Africans. While Chiefs Matanzima (Transkei), Mangope (Tswana Assembly), and Buthelezi (Zulu Territory) extended their dialogue overseas as guests of the British government in October, the South African government pursued its outward-looking policy by entertaining for the first time a black head of state, Pres. H. Kamuzu Banda of Malawi (*see* BIOGRAPHY). Banda's frequently reiterated aim was to kill apartheid with kindness, and his enthusiastic reception by whites and blacks alike certainly dented the institutions and attitudes of apartheid, if only temporarily. Another African leader who expressed his interest in a dialogue with South Africa was Pres. Félix Houphouët-Boigny of the Ivory Coast, while Prime Minister Kofi Busia of Ghana said during a visit to Canada that he did not believe black Africa would ever overthrow the South African government by military means.

The demands of the Bantustan leaders underlined the basic inconsistencies in the program of "separate development" for ten "Bantu ethnic groups," totaling nearly 15 million persons. Of these, 8 million lived outside the reserves, nearly 4.5 million of them in urban areas. The reserves themselves were a patchwork of overgrazed rural areas representing less than 14% of South Africa's total area, with a population density of about 117.7 per sq.mi., compared with 34.8 in the rest of the country.

The contradictions between the theory and reality of apartheid emerged even more clearly in the case of the two million Cape Coloured, who had and could have no true homeland or distinct culture separate from the whites. These peoples experienced increasing bitterness over the continued operation of negative apartheid, particularly the resettlement taking place under the Group Areas Act. In Port Elizabeth a riot broke out in March over a rise in bus fares. The

Coloured Persons' Representative Council, an apartheid institution intended as compensation for the loss of Coloured rights in Parliament and the provincial councils (completed in November 1971 with the removal of Coloured workers from the Cape Province municipal rolls), was being turned into a base for "brown power" by the opposition Labour Party. Many Coloured people were reported to be opting out altogether by emigrating to Canada or Australia.

The contradictions inherent in pursuing separate policies of economic development in a centralized economy were evident in the country's growing economic difficulties, which took the form of continuing inflation and an artificial but critical shortage of skilled and semiskilled labour resulting from the colour bar. The rise in the cost of living hit hardest at the lowest paid and most insecure urban Africans, some 75% of whom were estimated to be below the poverty line in certain areas. Coloured and Indian workers were moving into a wide range of jobs formerly held by whites, and their average earnings were rising. Nevertheless, over 50% of the Coloured population of the Western Cape was still reported to be below the poverty line.

The effect of differential and restrictive legislation showed most strongly in the sphere of movement control, and of law and order in general. For the year ended June 1970, there were 932,127 prosecutions for "technical offenses" by Africans under the pass laws. There were 1,363,528 criminal cases in magistrates' courts, 3,935 of which (mostly concerning Africans) were on charges that could have ended in the death sentence. Of the total charged, 2,715 were found guilty of capital and other offenses, including 2,154 Africans, 437 Coloureds, 15 Asians, and 109 whites; 89 of these (60 Africans, 28 Coloureds, and 1 white) were sentenced to death during the year. Charges brought under the Immorality Act totaled 617 men (591 of them white) and 567 women (234 Coloured and 300 Africans). Of these, 351 men (336 whites) and 328 women (121 Coloured and 188 Africans) were convicted.

The application of the security laws and the powers they conferred on the police were criticized increasingly after the 17th death of a detainee in police hands in eight years, and the sentencing of the dean of the Anglican cathedral in Johannesburg, the Very Rev. Gonville A. ffrench-Beytagh, to five years in prison for "terrorism." After years of evading outright protest, the opposition United Party came out uncompromisingly against indefinite detention, incommunicado and without trial.

The trial of the dean and the harassment, banning, or deportation of an active minority of white Anglican, Catholic, and other ministers of religion marked an intensification of government action against dissident churchmen. In August the minister of the interior, Theo Gerdener, advised the churches to refuse to allow themselves to be influenced by overseas forces hoping to cause a revolution (a clear reference to the decision by the World Council of Churches in September 1970 to contribute to organizations combating racism and the Anglican Communion's subsequent decision, by 140 votes to 6, to remain a member of the WCC). Other attempts to influence the situation from outside included protest demonstrations during the tour of the Springbok Rugby team in Australia and criticism of vested business interests, not only from the left wing but, as in the case of Wates Ltd. of the U.K., from within business itself. Wates, a large building and construction firm, decided not to extend operations to South Africa because "we should . . . profit from . . . exploitation and ultimately end up with a vested interest in its maintenance." (*See* South Africa.)

United Kingdom. Immigration and race relations continued to fade as major political issues in Britain, as xenophobia tended to focus more on the alleged threat to national identity posed by entry into the EEC. Escalating violence in Northern Ireland provided yet another distraction.

Reassurances to the British population that there would be no further large-scale immigration, and to the immigrants already in Britain that they would suffer no loss of civic status, were the main objectives put forward by Home Secretary Reginald Maudling when he introduced the 1971 Immigration Bill in March. The bill basically brought future Commonwealth immigrants under the same restrictive system that had operated for aliens since World War I. An exception was made for a new class of "patrials," who would have a "right of abode" in Britain and be exempt from controls (12-month work permits for a specific job in a specific place and registration at employment exchanges). The bill was received apprehensively or resentfully by coloured immigrants. Its restrictive provisions, contrasted with the free entry that would be available to all EEC workers and their families, marked the reversal of the former two-tier system giving preference to Commonwealth immigrants. As several trade unions pointed out, the nonpatrial worker would be dependent on his employer and might even become part of a low-wage, low-status, potentially strikebreaking work force.

Belying continued attempts by Enoch Powell and others to play upon local fears of mass coloured immigration and high birthrates, "new Commonwealth" immigration figures continued to decline. The total admitted for settlement in 1970 was 26,362 (22% below the 1969 figure), of whom 21,337 were dependents, while admissions in the first half of 1971, at 11,264, were 12% fewer than in the first half of 1970. Excluded from the foregoing figures were U.K. passport holders from East Africa, of whom 6,839 (4,466 of them dependents) were admitted in 1970 and 3,354 in the first half of 1971, increases of 9.4 and 11.6%, respectively, over 1969 and the first half of 1970.

In May 1971 the home secretary announced that the special voucher quota for U.K. passport holders from East Africa would be increased as of June 1 from 1,500 to 3,000 per annum. In addition, a further 1,500 vouchers were made available on a "once only" basis for the last six months of 1971 to dispose of the "backlog of urgent cases." The government was also to cut the maximum issue of A (unskilled and semiskilled) and B category employment vouchers to the rest of the Commonwealth from 8,500 to 2,700 per annum. Special arrangements were being introduced for doctors and dentists.

In the 1971 U.K. population census, some immigrant bodies objected to two new questions (parents' birthplace and date of entry to the U.K.) on the ground that these could be exploited by a future government bent on a policy of immigrant repatriation. The registrar-general's *Quarterly Return* for the third quarter of 1970 estimated the population of "new Commonwealth" origin, including children born in Britain and those of mixed marriages, at between 500,000 and 1,370,000 in mid-1970. Figures published in the Department of Education *Gazette* of July 1971 showed a total of 11,323 unemployed coloured adults

A night hood ceremony
is held in front
of Whitehall, London,
March 7, 1971.
Young Liberals
protested what
they claimed
were disturbing aspects
of the government's
Immigration Bill.
KEYSTONE

in August 1970 (2.1% of the total unemployed) and 15,643 in May 1971 (2.2% of the total). Employment prospects for coloured school-leavers in 1970 were not seen as unduly difficult by most career officers, but other inquiries contradicted this. A *Business Management* survey showed that unemployment among coloured male workers aged 16–24 years was four times higher than the national average.

The Industrial Relations Act, 1971, aimed at creating a set of legal rules for labour relations, seemed likely to affect immigrant workers' interests in several ways. Its thrust against "unofficial" and "unconstitutional" strikes could lead to legal action against ethnic work groups striking without official union support. On the other hand, it established certain new rights for individual workers, including provisions for compensation in respect of unfair dismissal or treatment by workers' organizations.

Only employees with at least two years' continuous service could lodge a complaint of dismissal on grounds of race, colour, or ethnic or national origin under the new act. This applied to only about 20% of the dismissal complaints received by the Race Relations Board. In its annual report for 1970–71, the board reported a decrease in the number of complaints, from 1,549 the previous year to 1,024. Half of this drop was due to the fact that the number of complaints about discriminatory advertisements fell from 181 to 48, while complaints against the police, which were found to be outside the act's scope, were no longer registered. Over half of the 1,110 complaints disposed of by the board during the year were concerned with employment. An opinion of discrimination was formed in 172 cases, and of no discrimination in 696, while 242 complaints fell outside the scope of the act. The board reported that the act had been successful in the insurance industry, especially automobile insurance, and in the virtual elimination of discriminatory notices and advertisements from shopwindows and newspapers, but it had substantially failed to reduce discrimination in employment agencies, accommodation agencies, and workingmen's clubs. Among other urgent problems were housing and alienation among coloured youth, who were described as "living in two worlds" between a rigid family base and a new and strange permissive environment. (SH. P.)

United States. Confrontations and violence subsided in 1971 as other issues from war to economics crowded racial conflict off the front pages of newspapers. Yet race relations during the year presented a complex pattern of both gains and retrogression. Momentum from the civil rights era of the 1960s con-

tinued in such realms as the occupational upgrading and greater political participation of black Americans. But 1971 also witnessed such trends as growing unemployment among racial minorities and an administration that did not appear to place a high priority on civil rights.

Each realm of American life revealed these crosscurrents. In employment, for example, the Census Bureau announced that nonwhites had made significant advances during the 1960s. While only 16% of the nonwhite labour force had white-collar employment in 1960, 28% had by 1970. There was also upgrading in blue-collar employment. The portion of the nonwhite labour force in service occupations declined during the decade from 32 to 26%, but it climbed from 26 to 32% among craftsmen, foremen, and operatives. These trends continued, albeit at a slower pace, into the 1970s.

On the other hand, by 1970 only 3.5% of the nonwhite labour force were managers and proprietors and only 2.1% were sales workers. Blacks were still rare among such professional groups as medical doctors; the nation boasted over 300,000 physicians in 1971, but less than 3% were black. Moreover, nonwhites continued to register unemployment rates approximately double those of whites. The nation experienced serious unemployment in many sectors throughout 1971, but workers from racial minorities suffered extreme rates. Thus, Labor Department statistics in November estimated the total unemployment percentage at 6% and the black percentage at 9.3%. Even these figures did not record the underemployed or those who needed but no longer sought work, categories in which blacks were disproportionately numerous. If they were included, the rates of black underemployment and unemployment would probably range from 25 to 50% in some ghettos.

Many factors contributed to these racial disparities, but the major cause was still discrimination. Little improvement in eradicating discrimination was recorded during the year. In March the U.S. Supreme Court ruled unanimously against the use of job tests that discriminated against blacks and "cannot be shown to be related to job performance." In October, Spanish-speaking leaders filed suit against four federal agencies for allegedly discriminatory employment practices; they claimed Latins comprised 7% of the nation but only 2.9% of its federal employees. The administration's principal initiative involved extending the "Philadelphia Plan" to five other major cities. Upheld as legal by the 3rd Circuit Court of Appeals, this plan fixed quotas of minority employment on federal construction projects. It had scant effect, however, since minority workers could be shifted from other projects to federal work. Symbolic of the apparent progress and continuing problems was the election to the board of General Motors in January of its first black, the Rev. Leon Sullivan, founder of a well-known job-training program for blacks. Yet only about a dozen of the firm's 1,300 automobile dealerships were black-owned.

Not surprisingly, then, black income continued to lag far behind that of whites. While the median black family income went from $4,000 to $6,191 between 1960 and 1970, the racial differential expanded as the median white family income climbed from $7,252 to $9,794. By 1971 roughly a quarter of black families received over $10,000 in annual income, but a fifth still received less than $3,000. Defining poverty as a family of four with less than $3,968 in 1970, the Census Bureau reported that 25.5 million Americans were living in poverty, including one in every three blacks (7.7 million) but only one in ten whites (17.5 million).

The Black Caucus, composed of the 13 black members of the U.S. House of Representatives, proposed a manpower program to create 600,000 new jobs and a guaranteed minimum annual income of $6,500 for a family of four. The administration, however, preferred "welfare reform" with a federal floor beneath that already provided by most states. More encouraging were the preliminary results of a major study of a federal income-assistance plan involving direct payments to 700 poor families in five eastern cities. The findings, which indicated that extra funds did not cause the working poor to quit their jobs, might become an important consideration for the eventual federal enactment of comprehensive income assistance.

One increasingly important factor in minority unemployment was the inability of minority group members to follow the movement of industry to the outer rings of metropolitan areas. Thus, racial problems of employment were intertwined with demographic trends and housing discrimination. The census revealed that the black movement out of the South and to cities had continued during the 1960s at almost the pace of the previous two decades. By 1970, 10.6 million, or 47%, of the black population lived outside the South; one half of all blacks resided in just 50 cities; and 6 cities had black majorities (Washington, D.C.; Compton, Calif.; East St. Louis, Ill.; Newark, N.J.; Gary, Ind.; and Atlanta, Ga.).

The most critical demographic statistics, however, concerned the racial separation between suburbs and central cities. Only 15% of blacks lived in suburbia in 1970, compared with 40% of whites. During the 1960s, central cities lost 2.5 million whites and gained 3 million blacks, while suburbs remained about 95% white. In January, Pres. Richard Nixon opposed any efforts of the federal government "to force integration in the suburbs" as "counterproductive, and not in the interest of better race relations." In June he drew a distinction between racial and economic integration and promised not "to impose economic integration upon an existing local jurisdiction." He also rejected the Black Caucus's proposal to open more sites for low-income housing.

Nevertheless, the Justice Department brought suits in scattered cities against racial discrimination by developers, apartment owners, and real estate dealers. The Department of Housing and Urban Development (HUD) offered guidelines to prevent racial and religious designations in newspaper advertisements for housing and to limit development grants to communities that agreed to plan for low- and medium-income housing. The administration's ambivalence was dramatized by the case of Blackjack, Mo. This white community had incorporated itself in order to establish zoning regulations that blocked construction of a federal housing project for low-income families. Though Secretary George Romney of HUD asked in January that the government sue Blackjack, it took five months of internal debate before the Justice Department agreed.

Private groups also took action against the widespread use of zoning requirements by suburbs to exclude blacks and the poor generally. The American Civil Liberties Union took Blackjack to court. The United Automobile Workers Union filed a state complaint against the one-acre-per-house minimum in Mahwah, N.J., that effectively excluded workers—many of them black—from living near the town's automobile plant. The National Association for the Advancement of Colored People took Oyster Bay, N.Y., to court to oppose its lavish house-lot requirements that the NAACP claimed excluded families with less than a $17,000 annual income. Sen. Abraham Ribicoff (Dem., Conn.) submitted a bill that would require all suburbs maintaining federally aided facilities to have housing for low- and medium-income families. The bill had no chance of passage, but it suggested the shape of future legislation.

The Supreme Court rendered two decisions on the issue in April. It upheld a ruling against the attempt of Lackawanna, N.Y., to block construction of a low-income housing development in a white neighbourhood. But it also upheld, by a 5–3 margin, the constitutionality of a California referendum law allowing a majority of voters to block low-rent public housing in their community. This latter decision could prove to be a major barrier to residential integration in future years.

There were encouraging developments in political rights. The Supreme Court supported a black challenge to an election in Canton, Miss., by ruling that Southern communities covered by the 1965 Voting Rights Act must obtain federal approval before instituting changes that affected the rights of black voters. This act and such decisions had swelled the ranks of black Southern voters; in Mississippi, a record 307,000 blacks were registered.

The effects of this increased black political power were evident throughout the nation. At the national level, the possibility of a black candidate for vice-president was discussed seriously. Although presidential aspirant Sen. Edmund Muskie of Maine publicly doubted that the Democratic Party could win in 1972 if a black joined the ticket, many observers disagreed with him. Rep. Shirley Chisholm of New York, the only black woman in Congress, took the next step and announced her candidacy for president. Other black leaders favoured supporting a single black candidate as a lever to win blacks more federal jobs and high appointments.

The increase in black elected officials also was impressive. By April there were at least 1,860 such officials, compared with approximately 1,500 in 1970 and only 475 in 1967, although this still constituted only about 0.3% of the country's elected officials. Recent gains had been particularly notable in the South, where 711 elected blacks held office in 1971, compared with 563 in 1970. Black mayors won election in Ben-

Fayette, Miss., Mayor Charles Evers' bid for governor of his state in 1971, though unsuccessful, marked the first time a black politician had run for governor of Mississippi.

ton Harbor, Mich.; Berkeley, Calif.; East St. Louis, Ill.; Englewood, N.J.; and Kalamazoo, Mich. The first black commissioner in the history of Chattanooga, Tenn., was elected. The Rev. Walter Fauntroy (*see* BIOGRAPHY) won the first District of Columbia seat in the House of Representatives. Richard Hatcher was easily reelected as mayor of Gary, Ind. However, blacks lost by substantial margins in mayoralty elections in Boston, Baltimore, Cleveland, and Minneapolis, and Charles Evers lost decisively in his gubernatorial bid in Mississippi.

The formation of the Black Caucus was itself symptomatic of growing political strength and sophistication. Though the 13 members ranged from radical to conservative, they initiated united action on racial matters and received considerable attention. In January they boycotted President Nixon's state of the union address because of his "consistent refusal to hear the pleas and concerns of black Americans." Invited to meet with the president in March, the Caucus introduced a 32-page booklet of recommendations concerning race relations. The president later rejected the proposals, and his relations with the Caucus, all of whose members were Democrats, remained strained. The Caucus also opposed, unsuccessfully, a 60,000-ton sugar quota granted to South Africa. Despite these reverses, it emerged by year's end as a new and powerful force in black politics. If demographic trends continued, it could grow to a formidable bloc of more than 25 members.

One Black Caucus concern centred on the continuing tension between largely white police forces and black communities. In February there were four days of racial violence in Wilmington, N.C., that involved 600 National Guardsmen and led to two deaths, including that of a 19-year-old black youth killed by a policeman. In Jacksonville, Fla., in June, ten days of racial unrest, 274 arrests, $250,000 damage, and the call-up of 500 National Guardsmen resulted in part from the fatal shooting of a 15-year-old black youth by policemen. Also in June, three days of violence and the killing of a black youth by a white detective in Columbus, Ga., followed a rally by black policemen protesting alleged discrimination by white offi-

cers. Racial disturbances also erupted in Newburgh, N.Y., and Lubbock, Tex.; and in Chattanooga the disorders included the shooting of a black man by police, the arrests of 400, and a dusk-to-dawn curfew enforced by 2,000 National Guardsmen. Tensions flared, too, between police and Puerto Ricans in Camden and Hoboken, N.J. All told, however, there were fewer mass racial disorders in 1971 than in recent years, and they tended to occur in smaller cities.

In the South an 18-year-old black girl was shot dead from a passing car in Drew, Miss. Three whites were charged with the murder. Another young black girl, in Butler, Ala., was run over by a car driven by a local white man while she took part in a demonstration. The incident followed 14 weeks of organized protests and a black boycott of Butler's white merchants. In Jackson, Miss., 11 members of the militant black Republic of New Africa were charged with killing a policeman in a gunfight that broke out during a police raid of the group's headquarters. And in Darlington County, S.C., an all-white jury found three whites guilty of rioting in connection with the destruction of two school buses in opposition to school desegregation.

Racial tensions combined with the frustrations of incarceration to produce a wave of prison disorders. In August, George Jackson, the best-known of three black convicts calling themselves the Soledad Brothers, was shot dead as he attempted to escape from California's San Quentin Prison. Race was also a factor in the riot at New York state's Attica Correctional Facility, where 43 prisoners and guards died in September. (*See* PRISONS AND PENOLOGY.) Racial tensions also flared in the military. Racial incidents among U.S. servicemen increased in South Vietnam and West Germany. At Travis Air Force Base in Marysville, Calif., black airmen became incensed by the detention of two blacks but no whites following an interracial altercation. In the ensuing riot, 1 fireman died, 10 airmen were hurt, and 97 were arrested.

Black militants were involved in court trials throughout the year. In January seven black gang members were acquitted in the sniper shooting of a Chicago detective. In May four blacks were found guilty and one was acquitted of possession of weapons in a New York City trial involving an alleged plot to kill policemen. Black Panther leader David Hilliard, after being freed of charges of threatening the president in a speech, was sentenced in July to one to ten years in prison on an assault charge growing out of a 1968 police and Panther shoot-out. The Black Panthers continued to receive attention despite dissension within their ranks. In January two Panthers were arrested after an exchange of fire with police in Winston-Salem, N.C., and 13 Panthers were arrested in Memphis, Tenn., after a housing dispute. In May, 13 Panthers were cleared of charges of a New York City bomb plot; in June, 12 Panthers were cleared of charges of murdering a New York City policeman; and in August, 12 more were cleared of charges of attempting to murder New Orleans police. In New Haven, Conn., murder charges against the national chairman of the group, Bobby Seale, and a local Panther leader were dismissed. Finally, two retrials of Huey Newton, a co-founder of the organization, for the killing of an Oakland, Calif., policeman both ended in mistrials with hung juries, and the charges were dismissed.

The repeated acquittals of the Black Panthers during 1971 called into question earlier fears that they would not be able to receive fair trials in the U.S. In

Police break up Operation Breadbasket sit-in at the Atlantic and Pacific Tea Co. headquarters in New York on Jan. 29, 1971. Breadbasket's head, the Rev. Jesse Jackson, was suspended by the parent Southern Christian Leadership Conference in December.

WIDE WORLD

June the Supreme Court furthered this trend by unanimously reversing the draft conviction of Muhammad Ali, the former world heavyweight boxing champion; the high court decided the Selective Service System erred when it refused Ali conscientious objector status. Moreover, in August, 14 law enforcement officials were indicted in Chicago on charges of conspiring to obstruct justice in connection with a 1969 police raid on an apartment in which two Panther leaders were killed.

None of this court action received the publicity accorded the trial of Angela Davis in San Rafael, Calif. Miss Davis was charged with murder, kidnapping, and criminal conspiracy growing out of a courtroom shoot-out in 1970 in which four persons were slain. Though absent from the shooting, she could be charged with the crimes under California law for having allegedly bought the murder weapons. After her capture in New York City, she pleaded innocent at her January arraignment. The proceedings dragged on throughout the year as five judges withdrew or disqualified themselves. The trial was finally set to begin Jan. 31, 1972, in San Jose.

Racial issues in education attracted wide attention. The greatest changes during 1971 occurred at the college level. In 1964, 234,000 black youths attended college, with 51% in predominantly black institutions. Seven years later, almost 400,000 black youths attended college with only about a third in black institutions. This increase was faster than the growth rate of white college enrollment, but blacks still represented only 7% of the nation's undergraduates and 2% of graduate students.

More controversy and less progress were recorded at the elementary and secondary school levels. Desegregation made headway in the South, with the percentage of black children attending mostly white schools reaching 38% in the fall of 1970, compared with 28% in the North. But it was also true that many Southern districts experienced "massive firings" of black teachers and administrators; that white private school enrollment in the South had risen from roughly 300,000 to 500,000 (4% of the region's public school enrollment between 1968 and 1971); that only 23 of these private schools had lost their tax exemption privileges by March; and that, according to both private and official evaluations, much of the $75 million in emergency school aid going to Southern districts in 1970–71 had been misused.

The federal courts retained their central role. Sweeping school desegregation plans were ordered for Richmond, Va., and San Francisco, Calif. In September a federal court judge found Detroit's extensive school segregation to have been deliberate and called for remedial plans that utilized a metropolitan approach. The year's most important school opinion was handed down by the Supreme Court in April in a case involving the schools of Charlotte-Mecklenburg County, N.C. It ruled that busing children as a means of dismantling dual school systems was constitutional, but it limited its ruling to previously de jure segregated systems and did not order precise racial percentages or the elimination of all-black schools. The president supported the court, though he did "not believe that busing to achieve racial balance is in the interest of better education," and in August he disavowed a federal plan of busing to achieve school integration in Austin, Tex. (See EDUCATION.)

The nonpartisan U.S. Commission on Civil Rights reacted sharply and unanimously to the president's position, maintaining that "transportation of students is essential to eliminating segregation" and that busing had long been a feature of U.S. education.

In summary, 1971 would not be remembered as a year of significant progress toward the solution of America's racial problems. The patterns in employment, housing, education, and other areas included both improvement and retardation. The Rev. Theodore Hesburgh, chairman of the U.S. Civil Rights Commission, concluded that there was "a lack of moral commitment both in and out of government." In 1964 and 1968, following the assassinations of Pres. John Kennedy and the Rev. Martin Luther King, Jr., the nation appeared on the brink of making the necessary moral commitment. No such possibility emerged during 1971. (T. F. P.)

See also Cities and Urban Affairs; Police; Religion; United States.

Refugees

The several million refugees from East Pakistan who arrived in India from March 1971 onward overshadowed all other refugee problems during the year. At an early stage the government of India asked the UN secretary-general to appeal to the international community to help. Subsequently, the Office of the UN High Commissioner for Refugees (UNHCR) was designated to act as "focal point" for the coordination of humanitarian assistance to these refugees through or by the UN system. The response of the international community was unprecedented. By the end of November, contributions in cash and in kind amounted to some U.S. $182 million, and a further $100 million was being contributed bilaterally or through voluntary agencies and other sources. Appeals to the international community were based on assessments of need prepared by the government of India. In early October, these showed requirements of an order of $558 million.

With the outbreak of open conflict between India and Pakistan, humanitarian relief action was interrupted briefly, but it was resumed shortly afterward when assurances were received concerning the arrival of relief supplies in the refugee areas. From the beginning, UNHCR had endeavoured to facilitate the early repatriation of the refugees as the only viable long-range solution. After the cease-fire, India held talks on the subject with the leaders of Bangla Desh, the new nation proclaimed by the East Pakistanis. India agreed to underwrite the cost of repatriation, including transportation and rations, and the movement of refugees back across the border began almost at once. (*See* INDIA; PAKISTAN.)

Other than those receiving "focal point" assistance in India, the number of refugees of concern to UNHCR in 1971 was estimated to be in excess of 2.5 million. By far the largest number requiring direct material assistance from UNHCR were the refugees in Africa (more than one million) and Asia (some 216,000). Other refugee groups of concern to UNHCR were the 649,000 living in Europe and the 680,000 in other parts of the world. Except for the refugees in Africa and Asia, however, the great majority had become socially and economically integrated.

Most of the refugees in Africa were located in Botswana (4,000), Burundi (39,000), the Central African Republic (28,500), Ethiopia (20,000), Senegal (82,500), Sudan (61,000), Tanzania (71,500), Uganda

WIDE WORLD

Frank Render was asked to resign as civil rights chief for the Pentagon on Aug. 26, 1971. Render said he was fired because of differences of opinion with his superiors over methods of solving racial problems in the armed forces.

Radio:
see Television and Radio

Railroads:
see Transportation

Recordings:
see Music

(179,000), Zaire (formerly Congo [Kinshasa]; 490,-000), and Zambia (16,500). UNHCR assistance covered the emergency stage following the refugees' arrival, the stage when refugees could be moved to land made available by the country of asylum, and, generally speaking, the various aspects of rural settlement and the promotion of conditions favouring consolidation of new rural communities. Settlement in a rural environment continued to be the main solution in Africa, although a growing number of refugees were attracted to the towns where their presence created new problems.

In Asia (apart from the East Pakistani problem), the High Commissioner was essentially concerned with some 216,000 refugees, among them about 70,000 Chinese in Macao and approximately 64,500 Tibetans located in India (56,500) and Nepal (8,000). Programs undertaken on their behalf were largely geared toward local integration and included rural settlement, vocational training, extension of health facilities, handicrafts, provision of medical equipment, training workshops, and counseling. UNHCR also provided assistance in varying degrees to refugees of diverse origins in the Middle East (5,500), Cambodia (20,000), and South Vietnam (55,000). Resettlement opportunities were being sought for some 1,000 refugees of European origin in China.

Most of the refugees who were the High Commis-

sioner's concern in Europe continued to require protection but were no longer in need of material assistance. For those who were, the accent was on assistance toward local settlement, promotion of resettlement elsewhere, and legal assistance. In Latin America, the High Commissioner was still concerned with 110,000 refugees, but in the main provided assistance to a defined caseload of aged and handicapped who, for a variety of reasons, had not yet become fully integrated.

The UNHCR program is financed exclusively through voluntary contributions, primarily from governments. The target figure for the UNHCR's regular program for 1971 was set at $6.6 million, and, by mid-December 1971, 75 governments had contributed a total of $5,207,060 toward it. The program target for 1972 was $8 million. At the pledging conference held at UN headquarters on November 23, 38 countries announced contributions totaling $4,603,210 and a number of others indicated they would announce contributions later.

Three anniversaries of particular significance to the cause of refugees were observed in 1971: the 50th anniversary of the inception of international assistance to refugees under Fridtjof Nansen of Norway, the League of Nations' first high commissioner for refugees; the 20th anniversary of the signing of the 1951 Convention Relating to the Status of Refugees;

The struggle between the Pakistani government and the Bengali separatist movement left a large portion of the population of East Pakistan homeless. Right, the tragedy of the struggle is visible on the gaunt face of a refugee. Below, refugees seek shelter in drainage pipes in a refugee camp in Calcutta, India. Far right, a woman whose entire family died from cholera trudges down the road.

BELOW AND RIGHT, WIDE WORLD;
FAR RIGHT, POPPERFOTO—
PICTORIAL PARADE

and the 20th anniversary of the beginning of humanitarian activities in the service of refugees by the UNHCR. The UNHCR was originally established for three years, but its lifetime was subsequently extended for several five-year periods. In addressing his Executive Committee, the high commissioner expressed his distress that, over the years, the refugee situation had, if anything, become grimmer and more explosive.

(X.)

See also Migration, International.

Religion

If 1970 carried the label "the year of shock" for the Christian churches throughout the world, 1971 in the world of religion might be marked as the year of the rediscovery of Jesus Christ, particularly in North America and Western Europe. The shock waves of the previous decade still were being felt. Church concerns about poverty, racial oppression, war, and ecumenism remained important agenda items, and denominations and church groups frequently found themselves embroiled in controversies because of their espousal of activist causes. There were also serious quarrels between theological liberals and conservatives in some major denominations.

In a nationwide survey of clergymen in the U.S. released by George Gallup, Jr., and John O. Davies, Jr., the American Institute of Public Opinion cited figures showing that religion in the U.S. had fallen on evil days: 59% of Protestant ministers, 61% of Roman Catholic priests, and 63% of rabbis said that religion as a whole was losing its influence on American life, while 75% of the general public held to that view. Churchgoing, while remaining fairly constant among Protestants and Jews, fell off sharply among Catholics with the largest drop among young Catholics in their 20s. The report also showed that nearly four in ten young Protestant and Roman Catholic clergymen under the age of 40, and six in ten young rabbis, had seriously considered leaving the religious life. The survey indicated a gap between the general public and Protestant and Catholic clergymen in terms of what were considered the most critical problems facing the nation. The public placed the Vietnam war and economics at the top, while clergymen felt the major problems were indifference to spiritual values, sin and immorality, and polarization of attitudes.

There was a positive side on the survey's balance sheet, however. Younger clergymen were more inclined to say that changes now going on would help Christianity. The movement toward Protestant-Catholic unity was backed by solid majorities in all age groups. The survey revealed no evidence that there was a general turning away from basic beliefs, even among those considering leaving professional church life.

Underscoring the revival of interest in the spiritual was the burgeoning of the so-called Jesus movement led by the "Jesus people." This move away from "secular" Christianity was significant because it was led not by conservative churchmen who had in the past been critical of the church's emphasis on social and political issues, but by members of the youth counterculture and those sympathetic with them. While the movement had its start in California, it spread so rapidly that it was difficult to pinpoint one specific cause for it or to single out any one leader. Robert S. Ellwood of the University of Southern California stated that the direction of religion among youth in the late 1960s had been toward Eastern mysticism, accompanied by the use of "mindblowing" drugs. But drugs and meditation "didn't deliver what they promised," according to Ellwood, and youth were now focusing on one man—Jesus. Through him they felt they were reaching infinity without drugs or meditation. Arthur Blessitt, a California evangelist and leader in the Jesus movement, said that youth had become disillusioned with the dreams of a material utopia and were "turning on" with Jesus. Emphasis on the person of Jesus linked together a wide range of manifestations of the movement, from youth groups operating within conventional churches to small cults with highly unorthodox theologies.

Tied in with the Jesus movement was the increasing frequency of religious themes in popular entertainment. The record of the rock opera *Jesus Christ Superstar* became a best seller, and performances attracted overflow crowds to churches and theatres. Although some churchmen criticized the opera as irreverent, the large majority of church youth applauded it as an expression of their faith. The Broadway musical *Godspell*, based on the Gospel of Matthew, was equally popular, despite criticisms from conservative church groups. The rock musical *Hair* celebrated its third anniversary in New York and London with services at the Episcopal Cathedral of St. John the Divine and at St. Paul's Cathedral, respectively. The Jesus movement also spread to Europe and into Asia. In Indonesia, Baptist missionaries reported enthusiastic revival meetings with the Jesus people taking over the leadership. Evangelist Billy Graham welcomed the Jesus people, and many of them were present at his revival meetings in various parts of the world.

In the Middle East, some Christians accused Israel of expelling Christians and Muslims from the former Jordanian sector of Jerusalem under the guise of urban development. Other Christians, together with the Jewish community, defended Israel and commended its policy of maintaining open access to all holy places. Among those supporting Israel were six evangelical leaders who issued a statement while attending the Jerusalem Conference on Biblical Prophecy.

The Soviet Union's 50-year campaign against religion as "the opiate of the people" was revealed during the year as less than successful. In an annotated study, *Religious Minorities in the Soviet Union (1960–1970)*, by the Minority Rights Group, a research unit in London, fresh documentation was offered to show that religious services were going on in virtually every major city of the country and a certain proportion of young people were turning to religion. The main body of Soviet believers were Orthodox, and recent estimates showed about one-quarter of the adult population of the U.S.S.R. to be of the Orthodox faith. According to the report, young newcomers to the Orthodox faith did not understand the liturgy or care for the sermons, but were baptized into the faith nonetheless. Worldwide concern was expressed during the year over the condition of the Jews in the Soviet Union, who—despite the double burden of racial prejudice and antireligious oppression—were becoming increasingly vocal. A significant number were permitted to emigrate to Israel. (See *Judaism,* below.)

Black assertiveness manifested itself to an increasing degree on the U.S. religious scene. There were calls

for a black Roman Catholic archbishop in Washington, D.C., where the population was predominantly black, and there was growing black participation and influence in high-echelon Protestant councils. The rise of black Catholic militancy was accompanied by the charge that the Roman Catholic Church had a "racist history" in America. Similarly, black Protestant church leaders declared that American blacks had been "scarred" by the failure to end discrimination and injustice. At a caucus in Cincinnati, O., black Christians agreed to make every effort to establish black Christian identity. Black voices were being heard in international church circles as well, one indication being the rising criticism of racial policies in southern Africa. The World Council of Churches Program to Combat Racism allocated funds to some groups that the South African government, among others, claimed were fostering guerrilla activities. The council pointed out, however, that none of the money would be spent for military purposes. Meanwhile, a group of Black Israelites, U.S. blacks claiming to be descendants of the 12 tribes of Israel, attempted unsuccessfully to emigrate to Israel.

Separation of church and state remained a sensitive issue in the U.S., where the constitutional ban against the "establishment of religion" had historically been interpreted to mean that no public aid could be provided to church-related schools. With many parochial school systems in financial difficulty, a number of states attempted to assist them, chiefly on the ground that this would be cheaper than caring for an influx of Roman Catholic children into the public schools. In June, however, the Supreme Court struck down "parochiaid" laws passed in Pennsylvania and Rhode Island because they caused "excessive entanglement between government and religion." (*See* EDUCATION.) In a related issue, a proposed constitutional amendment that would permit "nondenominational" prayer in public buildings was introduced in Congress, but was defeated.

Progress on the proposed merger of the nine major Protestant denominations involved in the Consultation on Church Union (COCU) slowed considerably. According to Methodist Bishop Gerald H. Kennedy, the efforts to merge the nine bodies had reached a stalemate. Final decision on the merger talks might not be made until 1975 or later. Meantime, the Presbyterian and Congregational church assemblies of Great Britain voted for the union of the two churches, which had been separated since Cromwellian times. This was the first major church union in Great Britain since the Reformation. The first synod of the Church of North India, organized in 1970 as a merger of Anglican, Presbyterian, and other churches, issued an invitation to the Methodist, Baptist, and Lutheran churches asking them to participate in the new church body.

Doctrinal controversies between conservatives and liberals were the major concerns of several large denominations. Messengers (delegates) to the Southern Baptist Convention's annual meeting fired a British biblical scholar who was the author of a Bible commentary considered too "liberal." Delegates to the General Assembly of the Presbyterian Church in the U.S. (Southern) were almost evenly divided on whether or not the church had abandoned "historic Presbyterianism" for "a modern social gospel," and conservatives predicted an ultimate split in the one million-member body. Doctrinal controversy in the Lutheran Church-Missouri Synod came to a head when delegates refused to endorse a move backed by Pres. J. A. O. Preus to discipline "liberal" ministers and professors. Neither liberals nor conservatives were able to obtain a working majority. (See *Lutherans*, below.)

A significant call to demolish the "Berlin walls" that have divided Christians over the centuries was issued by Léon Josef Cardinal Suenens, archbishop of Malines-Brussels, at a meeting of the Faith and Order Commission of the World Council of Churches at Louvain, Belg., during August. Pope Paul VI expressed his "profound Christian joy" over a United Methodist "Resolution of Intent" to drop all comments derogatory to Roman Catholicism in its Articles of Faith. On the other hand, Lutheran-Roman Catholic dialogue received a setback when the Vatican refused to lift its 450-year-old excommunication of Martin Luther. Continued ferment within the Roman Catholic Church failed to gain concrete expression at the synod of bishops held at the Vatican in the fall. (See *Roman Catholic Church*, below.)

Adherents to new religious cults in the U.S. jumped from 100,000 to 2.5 million during the 1960s, according to a study by Peter Rowley (*New Gods in America*). Largest of the new religions was Scientology with 600,000 members. In second place was Nichiren Shoshu (200,000), known in Japan as Soka Gakkai. Membership in the mainstream churches remained at a virtual standstill, increasing only 0.03% in 1970. According to the 1971 *Yearbook of American Churches*, which covers 230 church bodies, church membership in the U.S. totaled 128,505,084, including 69,740,413 Protestants, 47,872,089 Roman Catholics, 5,780,000 Jews, and 3,745,315 Orthodox. The *Yearbook* placed the number of ordained clergy in all churches at 387,642. (A. P. KL.)

PROTESTANTS

Anglican Communion. The Church of England reached a new landmark late in 1970, when a General Synod of bishops with elected clergy and laity was inaugurated at Westminster in the presence of Queen Elizabeth II. The new body absorbed both the 50-year-old Church Assembly and the ancient clerical convocations that looked back on a history of nearly a millennium. The synod was described by the queen as "full of promise and opportunity" and as a body with "full responsibility for the government of the church." Whether the new General Synod would in fact live up to these high hopes remained a matter of some speculation, since its agenda was grossly overloaded and many doubted whether "full responsibility" could become a reality as long as the historic church-state connection continued.

In the pursuit by Anglicans of reunion between separated Christian brethren, a vital step forward was taken with the announcement on Sept. 7, 1971, of "substantial agreement on the doctrine of the Eucharist" between representatives of the International Commission of the Anglican and Roman Catholic Churches, set up in 1968 by the pope and the archbishop of Canterbury, the Most Rev. Michael Ramsey. In New Zealand the new Anglican cathedral being built at Auckland was designed to serve a united church comprising many denominations. The United Church of Canada and the Anglican Church in that country commended a draft plan of union to their people for study. (See *United Church of Canada,* below.) The Church of England agreed to recognize the new united churches of North India and Pakistan as "true parts of the Church Universal" and approved full intercommunion with them. The official scheme for organic reunion between Anglicans and Methodists in Britain still hung fire, with a definite decision on the Anglican side postponed yet again. (See *Methodists,* below.) Nonetheless, there were signs that Anglicans were moving toward acceptance of all baptized Christians at their central service of Holy Communion.

In the field of inter-Anglican cooperation, the Anglican Council of North America, meeting in Toronto in September, discussed guidelines for more effective aid from the churches of North America to those in the Caribbean area. But the major event in this sphere was the first meeting, in February–March 1971 at Limuru, Kenya, of the Anglican Consultative Council, a body created by the 1968 Lambeth Conference and consisting of episcopal, clerical, and lay representatives from Anglican churches and provinces throughout the world. Though its role was only advisory, the council's conclusions attracted publicity. The archbishop of Canterbury was among those who dissented from the narrow majority vote in favour of ordaining women to the priesthood. Two women were ordained as priests in Hong Kong in November.

The archbishop also dissented from the council's decision, by a larger majority, to "endorse and commend" the action of the World Council of Churches in giving grants of money to "guerrilla" movements in Africa. Two bishops—Paul Burrough of Mashonaland, Rhodesia, and Robert Selby-Taylor of Cape Town, S.Af.—walked out of the meeting in protest. A few months later, in November, the Very Rev. Gonville A. ffrench-Beytagh, dean of the Anglican cathedral in Johannesburg, S.Af., and an opponent of apartheid, was sentenced to five years' imprisonment for channeling funds to persons and organizations banned under South Africa's Terrorism Act of 1967.

Another sign of the mental turmoil afflicting official Anglicanism was the sudden recommendation by a commission appointed by the archbishop of Canterbury that the Church of England abandon its age-old opposition to church remarriage of the divorced, provided that a "moral consensus" in favour of the change (already carried into effect by Anglicans in Canada and New Zealand) was found to exist in England. Early action on the recommendation was not expected.

(R. L. R.)

Baptists. On May 12–16, 1971, some 5,000 delegates of the American (formerly Northern) Baptist Convention met in Minneapolis, Minn. A communion service was held in which the elements were pre-

pared by local Baptists, the grain was grown by a Baptist farmer and milled by a Baptist, and the bread baked by members of local Baptist churches. The delegates, who a year earlier had rejected a resolution calling for a quick end to the Vietnam war, reversed their position and urged the withdrawal of all U.S. forces by the end of 1971, if at all possible. A convention resolution voiced "deep agony" over America's continued involvement in Vietnam, the massive bombing, the devastation of land and commerce, and the continued killing of civilians.

In 1968, Bexley Hall, an Episcopal seminary, had moved from Ohio to affiliate with Colgate-Rochester, a Baptist seminary in Rochester, N.Y., and these two schools, with St. Bernard's Seminary (Roman Catholic), formed the Rochester Center for Theological Studies. In 1969–70 historic Crozer Theological Seminary (American Baptist) moved from Chester, Pa., to join this cluster. Crozer had been founded in 1863 in memory of the Baptist layman and philanthropist John P. Crozer.

Over 13,000 messengers from local churches of the Southern Baptist Convention met in St. Louis, Mo., June 1–3, 1971. In a resolution concerning the Vietnam war, Pres. Richard Nixon was "commended . . . for his part in reducing the number of troops in Vietnam" and was encouraged to continue the U.S. withdrawal in keeping with Americans' desperate concern for the prisoners of war. The original text, not published, referred to the "moral ambiguities of the Vietnam War" and recommended that the president continue to accelerate the withdrawal of troops. In another resolution, the Convention urged the legalization of abortion "in certain cases" such as rape, incest, or evidence of severe fetal deformity.

Meeting in Moose Jaw, Sask., in the summer of 1971, 225 delegates from Baptist churches in western Canada expressed concern about present-day secularism and its effect on Christian values, and proposed a task force on Christian life and work to deal with secular challenges. The conference also expressed concern "about the increasing maltreatment of children by their parents."

World evangelism was the chief topic for the nearly 1,000 delegates at the 28th annual meeting of the Conservative Baptists, held in June 1971 in Wheaton, Ill. Of 39 missionary appointees, 27 were slated for foreign work.

The European Baptist movement, though comprising only a small part of the world total of more than 31 million members in 1971, provided many examples of its vitality. In Hungary reconstruction work was begun on buildings destroyed in the disastrous floods of 1970. There were 11 students preparing for the ministry in the Baptist Theological Seminary, and homes for 60 elderly people were being maintained. A new church and youth centre was under construction in Strasbourg, France, and at Cheb in Czechoslovakia the congregation was building, by its own labour, a church to seat 180. Another Czech congregation, at Jablonec, was also building its own church. In the Czech-speaking regions of Bohemia and Moravia, the 19 Baptist churches reported 92 conversions, almost double the number of the previous year.

Information about the state of the Baptist Church in the Soviet Union was given by the Rev. Michael Zidkov, a minister of the Moscow Baptist Church, in a letter to *The Times* (London) replying to an article that had alleged serious and widespread persecution in the U.S.S.R. He reported that 20,000 copies

Archbishop Frank Woods was elected primate of Australia on April 23, 1971. The election of the Swiss-born archbishop ended speculation that the Anglican Church of Australia might for the first time elect an Australian-born leader.

of the Bible and 30,000 copies of the Psalms had been put into the hands of Baptists. He also reported that the reform movement among Baptists (the "Initiatives") numbered only 5% of the total number of Baptists, and that some were returning to the main Baptist family, though he admitted that some Baptists had been imprisoned for infractions of the law.

William R. Tolbert, Jr., a former president of the Baptist World Alliance, became president of Liberia.

In Britain, the Council of the Baptist Union of Great Britain and Ireland, at its meeting in March, discussed the report *Ministry Tomorrow.* (The report, issued in 1970, envisaged a smaller full-time ministry, more highly trained and better paid, aided by a large number of "supplementary ministers" earning their livings in secular occupations.) Though it caused great controversy, the report was accepted by the council in principle, and committees were established to find ways of implementing its recommendations.

(R. E. E. H.; R. W. T.)

Christian Church (Disciples of Christ). In October 1971 the General Assembly of the Christian Church (Disciples of Christ) elected the church's first black moderator, Walter D. Bingham, a Louisville, Ky., pastor who had served as a vice-moderator and who would hold the Disciples' top elected post until the fall of 1973. The 1.4 million-member church body had an estimated 50,000 Negro communicants. The assembly also adopted the church's first official symbol —a chalice bearing the X-shaped cross of St. Andrew, signifying the Disciples' historical emphasis on the Lord's Supper and their Scots Presbyterian heritage.

Church leaders reported a 2% gain in operational income for the year ended June 1971, after two consecutive years in which the church had registered its first decreases. In addition, giving to the church's special Reconciliation race and poverty program reached a peak, bringing receipts for the first three years of the program to about $1.7 million. A high-level committee, responsible for further steps in the restructuring of the church begun in 1968, proposed fewer regions in place of the existing 38.

Ecumenical officer George G. Beazley, Jr., served as chairman of the Consultation on Church Union during the year. The overseas mission boards of the Disciples and the United Church of Christ met for the first time to explore relationships beyond their already-effected joint administration of work in India and Latin America. In September the World Convention of Churches of Christ (Disciples), the movement's confessional body, named Allan W. Lee of Seattle, Wash., as its new general secretary, succeeding Laurence V. Kirkpatrick. (R. L. F.)

Christian Science. Renewed emphasis was placed during the year on the healing thrust of the movement. A new radio series entitled "The Truth that Heals" was launched in January, in which participants described the relevance of spiritual power to everyday problems. The weekly broadcasts were carried by some 1,000 stations in Africa, Asia, Australia, and Europe, as well as in North and South America.

Individual members of the board of directors of the Mother Church, the First Church of Christ, Scientist, in Boston, Mass., visited 20 cities in the U.S., Canada, England, France, Switzerland, and West Germany, to listen to the representatives of branch churches, hear needs, and exchange views. Two important meetings were held in June: the annual meeting, which had as its theme "But What Can I Do?—A Progress Report," and a special workshop attended

The General Assembly of the Christian Church (Disciples of Christ) adopted an official symbol, a chalice bearing the X-shaped cross of St. Andrew, during its October 1971 meeting.

COURTESY, CHRISTIAN CHURCH (DISCIPLES OF CHRIST)

by Christian Science teachers from many parts of the world. In August more than 5,000 Christian Science college students came to the Mother Church for the 1971 biennial College Organization Meeting, which featured student talks on the healing of racism, drug abuse, and other world problems.

Mrs. Elizabeth Glass Barlow of New York City was named president of the Mother Church for the year. William Milford Correll of Cleveland, O., became the new first reader, and Mrs. Virginia Nichols Chancey of Dallas, Tex., the new second reader. Paul D. Sampson of Wellesley, Mass., was appointed executive manager of the Christian Science Publishing Society. (J. B. St.)

Churches of Christ. A major thrust for the year was the increase in preaching schools, with training concentrated on the Bible and related subjects. The number of such schools grew to 40 in the U.S., and others were begun in India, Africa, Australia, and South America. One survey indicated that 2,300 young men were preparing to preach in the U.S.

The greatest growth in mission work was in India, Australia, and Brazil, while Churches of Christ were the second fastest growing religious movement in Spain. In all, there were an estimated 700 mission workers in foreign fields. A medicine and missions conference was held to exchange information on mission methods for doctors.

A growing trend was for two congregations in an area to merge for strength. Many churches decided to hold two worship services on Sunday morning rather than build enlarged auditoriums. A growing concern for personal, spiritual growth was evidenced by the use of small study and prayer groups, especially for young people. The Madison, Tenn., Church of Christ was selected by *Guideposts* as the church of the year; it was the largest Church of Christ and ranked 11th in Sunday school size among all U.S. churches.

Pepperdine University, the first university related to the Churches of Christ, constructed a new liberal arts college on a 490-ac. campus overlooking the Pacific at Malibu, Calif., at a cost of $30 million. Lubbock (Tex.) Christian College and Freed-Hardeman College, Henderson, Tenn., announced moves from junior to senior college status. The number of student centres offering religion courses at state universities and colleges increased to 150. The flexibility of the church in having no organization beyond the local congregation seemed to appeal to the young, who were reacting against centralized control. (M. N. Y.)

Church of Jesus Christ of Latter-day Saints. A far-reaching program had been established in 1961 to coordinate and systematize church organizations and curricula, with the aim of minimizing repetition and overlapping and assisting the individual member to achieve his fullest potential. As a corollary of this effort, major organizational changes were made in 1971, when the Young Men's Mutual Improvement Association was correlated more closely with the Aaronic Priesthood. Another significant aspect of the correlation program was the publication, beginning in January 1971, of three new church magazines: *The Ensign,* for adult members; *The New Era,* for youth; and *The Friend,* for children.

Russell M. Nelson, Joseph B. Wirthlin, and Richard L. Warner replaced David Lawrence McKay, Lynn S. Richards, and Royden G. Derrick as the Superintendency of the Church Sunday School. Sunday school enrollment was 2,076,687 in May 1971. Stakes and wards throughout the church rescheduled activities to comply with a church-wide program, established in October 1970, setting aside Monday night for family home evenings.

The year 1971 saw church membership exceed three million in the more than 550 stakes and 102 missions throughout the world. The increased growth of the church necessitated the inauguration of regional general conferences, the first of which was held in Manchester, Eng., in August for the benefit of the 70,000 church members there. The completion of two new temples at Provo and Ogden, Utah, brought to 15 the number of these edifices in operation in 1971; in May construction contracts were let for another temple to be built in Washington, D.C. (Jo. A.)

Jehovah's Witnesses. The society of Christian ministers known as Jehovah's Witnesses was active in 207 countries during 1971; 26,800 congregations operated under the direction of 93 branch offices of the Watchtower Bible and Tract Society. During 1971, 148,400 new ministers (members) were baptized, bringing the worldwide total to 1,590,700.

During the summer, Jehovah's Witnesses arranged over 65 "Divine Name" district assemblies in the U.S., Canada, the British Isles, and central Europe. More than 919,000 heard the principal discourse, "When All Nations Collide, Head On, with God." Additional assemblies in this same series were scheduled for Latin America, Africa, Asia, Australia, and elsewhere. At this assembly a new Bible reference book entitled *Aid to Bible Understanding* was released, climaxing seven years of research and writing by biblical scholars. Also released were *Listening to the Great Teacher*, a new publication designed for teaching children the basic precepts of Christianity, and a volume explaining the book of Ezekiel entitled *"The Nations Shall Know that I Am Jehovah"—How?*

Organizational growth of the society was demonstrated by a total attendance of 3,447,500 at the annual celebration of the Lord's Evening Meal, over 200,000 more than in 1970. The Brooklyn headquarters printing plant produced 25,063,395 Bibles and bound books and over 237 million magazines during 1971. Total circulation of *The Watchtower*, the official journal of Jehovah's Witnesses, rose to 7.5 million in 73 languages, while its companion magazine, *Awake!*, attained a circulation of 7,175,000 in 27 different languages. (N. H. K.)

Lutherans. Global membership of Lutheran churches dropped to 73,307,479 in 1971—a loss of 2% or 1,816,736 adherents. The 82 church bodies in the Lutheran World Federation had 53,281,661 members, down slightly from a year earlier. Statistics compiled by the LWF showed a substantial increase of 6% in Africa, plus small gains in Asia and Oceania. European Lutheranism suffered an overall decline of 2% to 58.4 million, with losses of up to 20% in some countries. In the U.S. and Canada membership fell for the second consecutive year, by 0.5% to 9,176,846.

Possibly the year's most significant development occurred in South West Africa, where two black Lutheran churches issued a pastoral letter that sharply assailed the apartheid policies of South Africa. In an open letter to Prime Minister John Vorster of South Africa, they called for an end to control over South West Africa to pave the way for "a self-sufficient and independent state." Both statements were signed by Bishop Leonard Auala of the Evangelical Lutheran Ovambokavange Church and the Rev. Paulus Gowaseb, moderator of the Evangelical Lutheran

Church in South West Africa. Their parishioners comprised 55% of the territory's population.

In a historic confrontation, South Africa's prime minister met with Lutheran church leaders in a four-hour session August 18 that ended in a deadlock. A communiqué issued after the talks said the church leaders had emphasized that the unity proclaimed in the gospel "should be of more consequence than differences of race and colour." Vorster, it was said, "broadly explained" his government's policy of separate development of black and white communities and stressed his intention to carry it out. It was noted that Vorster was "disposed" to keep the door open for further discussion.

At LWF headquarters, General Secretary André Appel said the statements by the two churches were "directly in line with the resolution on human rights" adopted by the LWF's fifth assembly in 1970. In implementation of another assembly resolution, the LWF's Commission on World Service allocated $92,-900, with a pledge of more to come, to aid people in areas liberated from colonial rule, mainly in Mozambique. As in the case of previous grants by the World Council of Churches, it was stressed that the assistance would be for humanitarian, social, and economic—not military—purposes.

Examination of the papacy from historical and theological perspectives marked the seventh year of doctrinal discussions in the U.S. between Lutheran and Roman Catholic theologians. Also in the U.S., Lutheran and Reformed leaders agreed that doctrinal discussions between the two traditions should be resumed. Apostolic succession, a thorny issue between Lutherans and Episcopalians, was explored by American churchmen of the two communions in their fourth meeting in two years. At Logumkloster, Den., Lutheran and Anglican representatives ended the second in a series of official conversations with the statement that there were "considerable areas of agreement and convergence."

A proposal that a "genuinely universal council" be considered as a future major development in the ecumenical movement was endorsed by a joint committee of the LWF and the World Alliance of Reformed Churches. Such a council, it was said, could be a means toward a new realization of the diversity that exists within Christianity but does not necessarily stand in the way of unity.

The 49th General Convention of the Lutheran Church-Missouri Synod focused on issues sharply dividing conservatives and moderates of the second largest Lutheran body in the U.S. Conservatives later organized the Federation for Authentic Lutheranism as a new church body, but comparatively few congregations seemed to be involved in the secessionist movement. The Synod gave conditional approval to continuing fellowship with the American Lutheran Church. Expressing "strong regret" over the ALC's decision to ordain women and urging "serious reconsideration" of the action, delegates deferred new implementations of fellowship until the ALC had had opportunity to respond to "this and other doctrinal differences." Delegates also adopted a resolution asking the Synod's president to assure the Lutheran Church in America, which had also approved the ordination of women, "of our readiness to meet officially with a view toward finding the agreement in doctrine necessary for the establishment of altar and pulpit fellowship."

In response to demands for withdrawal from the

Lutheran Council in the U.S.A., organized in 1967 as the cooperative agency of the ALC, LCA, and LCMS, the Synod voted to conduct a two-pronged study of the council's operations and theological stance. The Synod received but did not adopt a statement on Lutheran unity that raised the possibility of eventual merger of the three major Lutheran bodies. Efforts to make convention interpretations of the Bible binding on the Synod's pastors, teachers, and congregations were defeated.   (E. W. M.)

Methodists. The quinquennial meeting of the World Methodist Council and Conference took place at Denver, Colo., Aug. 18–26, 1971. Several other conferences were held in connection with the main council meeting, representing interests such as the World Federation of Methodist Women, home and family life, youth, theological educators, worship, and liturgy. In the council itself, a purely consultative body, 18 new member churches or regional units were formally received, bringing the total to 55. In order to avoid the predominantly Anglo-American leadership that had characterized the council since its inception in 1881, it was agreed that no two member churches together should have a majority of votes in the executive committee and that no two officers should come from the same member church. The single president was replaced by an eight-man presidium. A black leader of the U.S.-based United Methodist Church, Bishop Price A. Taylor, was appointed chairman of the executive committee. A report from the joint commission between the Roman Catholic Church and the World Methodist Council (1967–70) was described as the most significant document on the subject that had so far appeared. Another highlight of the conference was adoption of a program to emphasize evangelism.

Evangelism was also stressed in two United Methodist meetings. More than 2,400 persons participated in a rally and training program at New Orleans, La., sponsored by the Board of Evangelism and Council on Evangelism, while some 1,600 took part in an unofficial Convocation of United Methodists for Evangelical Christianity at Cincinnati, O. Many activities within the church involved preparations for the quadrennial General Conference at Atlanta, Ga., in 1972. In the election of delegates, the church's annual (regional) conferences increased the number of ethnic minority representatives by nearly 60%. The number of women and young adults elected as delegates was also higher than ever before.

The number of black ministers serving as superintendents of predominantly white districts rose to 23, in 22 of the 75 annual conferences in the U.S. New church-wide staff positions were filled by representatives of black, Indian, and Asian Americans. For the first time, a major gathering of Indian members of United Methodism was held, in Oklahoma, with some 2,800 attending from many states and tribes. Mergers of annual conferences saw the number of all-black units decline to five. Only three years after the two denominations united, the last two of the former Evangelical United Brethren conferences merged with their geographic Methodist counterparts.

Statistically, the picture was mixed. Membership of United Methodism in the U.S. dropped again, to 10,671,774, although giving for all purposes rose to $723,778,211, including $114,243,010 for benevolent causes. Health and welfare agencies related to the church reported caring for 3,203,934 persons, an increase of some 10%. The church's Committee for

Overseas Relief had the highest year's receipts in its 30-year history, $2,364,503. The Fund for Reconciliation reached its halfway point of $10 million by mid-1971. Its income was being used primarily for the aid of minorities and deprived persons, as well as for rehabilitation of persons in Vietnam.

Reports from all over England indicated a new range and depth in ecumenical cooperation, all the more meaningful in contrast to the delay in reaching complete agreement in high official quarters. Anglican and Methodist theological students were training together at Queen's College, Birmingham; several team ministries had started in ecumenical centres; and many churches had taken advantage of the Sharing of Church Buildings Act. On July 6 a joint meeting of the Central Committee of the Methodist Missionary Society and the Council of the United Society for the Propagation of the Gospel (Church of England) decided to undertake new work in Latin America at the invitation of the church there. At the Anglican General Synod meeting in York, 65.3% voted in favour of union with the Methodists. If the scheme was to go ahead, 75% would be required in the Anglican General Synod of 1972. The Methodist Conference had already approved union by more than the required 75%.

Following the death of Bishop Odd Hagen in 1970, Ole E. Borgen was consecrated bishop of the Northern Europe Central Conference of the United Methodist Church. He retained the bishop's seat in Stockholm. Fifty-eight ministers shared in the pastoral exchange program between British and American churches, the largest number since the scheme began in 1947. On April 25, The Gambia celebrated 150 years of Methodist history. At the tenth annual conference of the Methodist Church in Italy in May, the members made clear that their goal was the unity of all Italian Protestants.   (M. W. Wo.; W. H. Ta.)

Presbyterian, Reformed, and Congregational. For the new World Alliance of Reformed Churches (Presbyterian and Congregational), 1971 was a year of consolidation following the 1970 merger of the former WARC and the International Congregational Council (ICC).

The Nairobi (Kenya) Uniting Assembly continued to dominate the programs of the WARC and to contribute to the life of its churches. Three major theological study projects approved by the assembly were undertaken by the member churches. Starter papers for discussion and comment were sent to a representative group of theologians in Alliance churches all over the world: "Theology as a Process of Christian Freedom" was introduced by David Willis (U.S.); "The Theological Basis of Human Rights and a Theology of Liberation" by Jürgen Moltmann (W.Ger.); and "Church, Politics, and Society" by Daniel Jenkins (U.K.).

The first full meeting of the WARC Executive Committee since the Nairobi assembly met in Cartigny near Geneva, Switz., August 25–31. Four new applications for membership from churches in Asia, Africa, and Europe were presented: the Church of North India (600,000 members and 2,000 ordained ministers); the Hong Kong Council of the Church of Christ in China (200,000 members and 33 congregations); Lesotho Evangelical Church (64,500 and 56 congregations); and the Swedish Mission Covenant Church (SMCC; 86,000 and 1,300 congregations). When the merger between the WARC and the ICC took place, the Covenant Church, while not opposing the merger, felt unable to join the new organization. The decision to apply for membership in the Alliance was taken less than a year later by a unanimous vote in the SMCC assembly in June.

The Executive Committee decided that "to strengthen and render more significant" relationships between the member churches, specific priority areas were to be designated over a three-year period. For the period 1971–72 the committee asked that relationships with churches in southern Africa and their Christian witness in a segregated society be a priority concern. Reacting to WARC assembly resolutions on the racist issue, the Synod of the Dutch Reformed Church in South Africa decided to retain its membership in the Alliance for the time being, but with misgivings.

In September discussions took place in Leuenberg, Switz., between Lutheran, Reformed, and United churches in Europe on proposals for full pulpit and altar fellowship between the churches concerned. The reopening of conversations between Lutheran and Reformed churches in North America, first held during 1962–66, was also announced. Joint Lutheran-Reformed dialogue with the Roman Catholic Church on the theology of marriage and the problems of mixed marriages began with a first meeting in Strasbourg, France, November 22–27.

Thirty-eight member churches of the WARC in different parts of the world were engaged in church union negotiations in 1971. At their May assemblies the Congregational Church in England and Wales and the Presbyterian Church of England voted overwhelmingly in favour of a merger plan that would bring into being the United Reformed Church.

In the U.S. children and youth of the United Methodist Church and the United Presbyterian Church in the U.S.A. (UPUSA) began using the same church school publications in September 1971. At its General Synod meeting, the Associate Reformed Presbyterian Church urged its officials to develop closer relationships with other churches, specifying the Cumberland and Orthodox Presbyterian churches, the Reformed Presbyterian Church, Evangelical Synod, the Christian Reformed Church, and the Reformed Church in America.

During the year the joint committee for reunion of the two largest Presbyterian bodies (the Presbyterian Church in the U.S. and the UPUSA) worked on plans for the widest possible study of the proposed union. At the UPUSA General Assembly, a motion to study the draft of a reunion plan for a two-year rather than a one-year period was approved. If the draft was eventually approved by both assemblies, it would be sent to the presbyteries for their action. A favourable vote by the regional bodies of each denomination would be the next to the final step in bringing about a reunion of the two churches, which had separated more than 100 years earlier. Statistics for the two bodies were contrasting. Membership in the Presbyterian Church in the U.S. was slightly higher in 1970 (958,195) than in the preceding year, due in part to the formation of several union presbyteries. A membership loss of 76,969 was reported by the UPUSA, with a net gain of 130 ministers.

A grant of $10,000 to be used for the defense of Angela Davis (*see* RACE RELATIONS) was the subject of extensive debate at the General Assembly meeting of the UPUSA. A considerable volume of mail from congregations, presbyteries, and synods was brought on by this action. (F. H. KA.; W. B. MI.)

Religious Society of Friends. British Friends took steps, in conjunction with the University of Bradford, Yorkshire, to establish a chair of peace studies in that university. They continued an examination of the finances of London Yearly Meeting and decided on a thorough review of the organization's investments to take account of social value as well as financial return.

British Friends continued to cooperate with U.S. and Canadian Friends in rehabilitation work in Nigeria, and sent Friends to East Pakistan to investigate the possibility of starting relief work there. During the disturbances in Northern Ireland, Friends opened a temporary shelter for children in Belfast. Australian Friends condemned Australian participation in military action in Vietnam and urged that conscription be ended.

The Friends United Meeting (Richmond, Ind.) reorganized its structure and staff. California Yearly Meeting of Friends Church created two new yearly meetings in missionary areas: the Central American Yearly Meeting of Evangelical Friends, with headquarters in Chiquimula, Guatemala; and the Alaska Yearly Meeting of Friends Church, Kotzebue.

The American Friends Service Committee spent a total of $8.6 million for programs in the U.S. and 15 other nations. The release of a paper on the need for a new U.S. policy vis-à-vis China was followed by a visit to that nation by two AFSC officials and their wives. (CD. H.; E. B. BR.)

Salvation Army. Leaders of the Salvation Army representing 74 countries met for a two-week International Commissioners' Conference in Ocean City, N.J., in September 1971, the first such conference to be held outside Britain. Top priority was given to evangelism, especially work with young people; the position of women; outreach to the poor and underprivileged; officer recruitment; and the ecumenical movement.

Commissioner Edward Carey was appointed national commander for the U.S., succeeding Commissioner Samuel Hepburn, who retired. Carey had served as national coordinator of the Army's emergency aid to Peru following the disastrous earthquake in the spring of 1970.

The Salvation Army transferred its relief programs in Vietnam to indigenous personnel. In preparation for the change, hundreds of hours of training and fieldwork were given to the Vietnamese personnel who would assume responsibility. During the year the Salvation Army established representation in Portugal, Spain, and the Dominican Republic but withdrew its officers from Algeria after 34 years' work there. To help meet the crisis in East Pakistan, five field dispensaries and a field hospital, staffed by 12 doctors and 15 nurses, were set up in the Barasat subdivision of India, where a refugee population of some 1,020,-000 had gathered. The operation was directed from Calcutta.

Concentration on the welfare of young people during "Children's Year," as the Army had designated 1971, revealed so many needs that the "year" was extended to cover 1972. Gen. Erik Wickberg traveled to Rhodesia and South Africa. Twenty-seven Salvationists from 14 countries attended the International Conference on Social Welfare in Manila, Phil.

(C. E. N.; W. P.)

Seventh-day Adventists. Oct. 1, 1971, marked the beginning of the largest single evangelistic endeavour the Adventist Church had ever attempted through international radiobroadcasting. On that date, 22 broadcasts each week in 16 languages began to be aired over a 250,000-w. shortwave station in Lisbon, Port. The broadcasts reached across all of Western and Eastern Europe, as well as North Africa and the Middle East. This was in addition to the well-established "Voice of Prophecy" broadcast, which was released over 650 stations weekly.

An unprecedented spiritual awakening took place on the campuses of Adventist colleges and secondary schools in North America, and spread to other continents, notably Australia. As a result of this revival, a 30-member team of students from North American Adventist colleges, called the "Gymnaires for Christ," presented 135 programs in the major cities of the U.S. and Canada from June 15 through September 15. Every program included music, personal testimony, gymnastics, and youth witnessing training.

Throughout 1971 the church was engaged in planning Mission 72, a coordinated evangelistic effort scheduled to begin on March 4, 1972, with hundreds of simultaneous evangelistic meetings.

During 1971 church activities were carried on in 187 countries. New hospitals were opened in Hong Kong and Addis Ababa, Eth. Church membership reached a new high of 2,051,864, up 5% from 1969, and tithes and offerings totaled approximately $211 million. (K. H. W.)

Unitarians and Universalists. Reacting positively to the identity crisis besetting most movements today, Unitarian Universalist congregations and organizations in the U.S. launched a 15-month study program. Polarization and the differing expectations of liberal churches and progressive religionists had seriously weakened numerous churches and projects. In practical terms, a statistical compilation for the preceding decade indicated that Unitarian Universalist membership had increased only 5.8% while the U.S. population had risen 13.3% (Canadian membership had increased 36.5%, compared with a population gain of 19.2%). The budgets of 75% of all church societies were below $30,000 annually, and fewer than 10% had memberships exceeding 400 people.

Nevertheless, the tenth General Assembly of the Unitarian Universalist Association, held in Washington, D.C., in June 1971, struggled to be relevant. Debate on funding the nonintegrationist Black Affairs Council program, which its opponents declared would destroy the historic pluralism of the denomination, went into its fourth year. A compromise resolution was passed, 467–404, calling for a joint fund-raising campaign for racial justice, to be carried on in cooperation with UUA groups already functioning in the area. Other resolutions urged a unilateral cease-fire in Vietnam, a federally sponsored national health in-

surance plan, opposition to any kind of surveillance of private citizens or government employees, penal reform and child care centres, amelioration of pollution and population problems, and amnesty and repatriation of war resisters.

The Western Canada (Unitarian) District observed the 70th anniversary of its founding in Gimli, Man., in June 1901. Then known as the Western Icelandic Unitarian Association, it had helped knit together Icelandic Unitarian churches that had been established in the 1890s. The Canadian Unitarian Council held its tenth annual national meeting in Winnipeg, Man. Possible damage to the environment by oil tankers skirting the Canadian coastline from Alaska to the U.S. and the unwise export of Canada's natural resources were subjects urged upon the government for serious examination. As in the U.S., abortion law reform received high endorsement.

The North American chapter of the International Association for Religious Freedom (IARF) held a week-long conference in Emerson's own Concord, Mass., parish. Thirty-two groups in 20 countries on all continents comprised this association. The issues of transcendence in religious experience, contemporary European thought, youth cultural concern with the non-Christian, and the great social-political-military confrontations of the age were discussed.

The British General Assembly of Unitarian and Free Christian Churches met in Birmingham, Eng., April 16–20, 1971. Among resolutions aimed at improving administrative efficiency and the better use of resources, it was agreed to examine the possibility of payment of ministerial stipends from a central fund and the problems involved in the deployment of ministers to the best effect. (B. L. Go.; J. N. B.)

United Church of Canada. Early in 1971 the General Synod of the Anglican Church of Canada and the General Council of the United Church of Canada met in Niagara Falls, Ont., at the same time to consider the *Plan of Union—First Draft*. The movement toward union began in 1943, but it was not until the '60s that a breakthrough was achieved, based on the concept of "a new manifestation of the One Church of God." In 1969 the Christian Church (Disciples of Christ) entered into the discussions. The three churches recommended the *Plan of Union—First Draft* to their ministers and laity for study and comment, on the understanding that the issue of union did not depend on its acceptance. There would almost certainly be other drafts.

The new church, still unnamed, would have an episcopal ministry, but a bishop's appointment would be subject to periodic review. The *Plan of Union* proposed that the ordained ministry of the new church consist of bishops, presbyters, and deacons and be open to both men and women, while the diaconate would be a ministry with specific functions rather than merely a stage in the process of becoming a presbyter. Freedom in the forms and styles of worship would characterize the new church. An important aspect would be a new organization, based on four areas of government from local congregations to the National Assembly, rather than a combination of traditional structures.

In spite of the good work done in the *Plan of Union*, enthusiasm for union appeared to be languishing while ecumenical projects flourished. Shared ministries involving two or more denominations were multiplying, and the number of agencies formed and supported by ecumenical groups was growing rapidly. One of the most important results was the formation of the Atlantic School of Theology in Halifax, N.S. (Anglican, Roman Catholic, and United Church), and the Vancouver (B.C.) School of Theology (Anglican and United Church). These institutions represented a closer form of union than the Toronto School of Theology, Canada's first ecumenical theological school, which was a federation of several autonomous colleges.

During 1971 the United Church issued an important statement on abortion, which was approved by the General Council. In essence the statement insisted that abortion should be a private matter between a woman and her doctor, but also that it is only a last resort and should never be regarded as a means of birth control. (A. G. R.)

United Church of Christ. The membership of the United Church of Christ in 1971 stood at 6,727 congregations and 1,960,608 members. When the church came into being in 1957, it brought together four U.S. churches, the Congregational and Christian churches, which had united in 1931, and the Evangelical Synod of North America and the Reformed Church in the United States, which had merged in 1934.

The eighth General Synod of the United Church held its biennial meeting in Grand Rapids, Mich., in June 1971. Under a new bylaw recommended in 1969, the composition of the delegate body was changed so that at least 20% of the 750 delegates were under the age of 30. This marked a considerable change from the preceding meeting, when less than 2% of the delegates were under 30.

The style of the General Synod also underwent a considerable change with far-reaching implications for the program of the denomination. In prior General Synods, program proposals had originated in the national offices and delegates were asked to assent to them. As the result of the work of a new Council on Mission Priorities, regional consultations were held across the country in the fall of 1970 in order to discover what issues local churches and conferences thought the denomination ought to address itself to during the next several years. The issues that surfaced were presented to the delegates with proposed goals and objectives. The four priorities that were approved were as follows:

1. *The Faith Crisis.* It was recognized that times are changing so radically that late 19th- and early 20th-century expressions of the Christian faith will no longer serve. There is a need to restate the gospel in terms of the issues of the times.

2. *Racial Justice: Liberation, Justice, and Empowerment for the Racially Oppressed.* It was clear from the regional consultations that churches all across the country had had to face this issue. More than this, the United Church Board for World Ministries, particularly, was facing this problem in its relationships with churches in southern Africa. Among other things, the General Synod agreed to embark on a major fund-raising effort to support the six black colleges in the South that were related to the United Church of Christ and to strengthen educational projects overseas where there is racial injustice. It was also agreed to give the highest priority to the areas of judicial and penal reform. In this connection, during 1971 the denomination's Commission for Racial Justice was given a major grant, along with two other organizations in the black community, to work in the field of the rehabilitation of women offenders.

3. *Peace and United States Power: Enabling U.S. Power to Serve Humane Ends and Contribute to World Peace.* Programs were proposed to assist in informing church members of the nature of U.S. power and its implications in a world context, of the nature and scope of military power within the nation, and of the need to reorder national priorities. Strong stands were taken for complete U.S. withdrawal from Vietnam no later than March 31, 1972, and for supporting "those policies of the United States Government which decrease the element of great power rivalry in the Middle East."

4. *Strengthening the Local Church in Mission.* The most important programs proposed under this heading dealt with the empowerment of the black local church within the denomination, the need for a coordinated program of leadership development for clergy and lay people alike, and the need to study the role and status of women in church and society.

Officers of the church for 1971 were Robert V. Moss, president; Joseph H. Evans, secretary; and Charles H. Lockyear, director of finance and treasurer. (See *Presbyterian, Reformed, and Congregational,* above.) (R. V. M.)

ROMAN CATHOLIC CHURCH

The third international Synod of the Roman Catholic Church met in Rome on Sept. 30, 1971, and adjourned on November 6. Its agenda had been published as early as January, and the two themes it proposed to deal with—the ministerial priesthood and justice in the world—became the focus for discussion and dissension throughout the year. The debate on the priesthood was concerned with its relevance to the contemporary world, whether there should be part-time priests having other jobs, and whether a priest could or should engage in political activities. Another topic inevitably raised was the question of celibacy. In this debate, the U.S. seemed to take over the lead from the Netherlands, largely through the activities of the National Federation of Priests' Councils (NFPC). At its annual conference in Baltimore, Md., in March, it voted overwhelmingly in favour of an immediate end to the obligatory link between the priesthood and celibacy. In July, after a discouraging reply from the bishops, the NFPC repeated its plea, and criticized the bishops for being unwilling even to discuss the matter. A sociological survey, prepared by the National Opinion Research Center of Chicago, had discovered that "the majority of priests do not accept the present position on obligatory celibacy, and expect that a change in the law is likely."

At Geneva, in April, a meeting of elected representatives of European priests took place. Their discussions were more wide-ranging than those of the NFPC, but they passed a motion in favour of ordaining to the priesthood men who were already married. Again, surveys had shown a shift of opinion among the clergy. One in Italy in late 1970 had shown that about 40% of priests were in favour of a relaxation of the celibacy ruling, and that 15% might marry if it were abolished. One-third of Spanish priests declared themselves in favour of optional celibacy. In various parts of the world, bishops' conferences had been studying the same problem, and while the Congolese bishops supported the ordination of married men, CELAM, grouping all the bishops' conferences of Latin America, went further and called for optional celibacy. But these surveys and opinions did not appear to have greatly impressed the Roman Curia, to judge by the working document prepared for the synod. For the first time the guidelines for discussion had been published in advance. They revealed a suspicion of sociological methods, vigorously reasserted the appropriateness of celibacy to the priesthood, and cautiously raised the possibility of the ordination of respectable married men of mature age.

The other document prepared for the synod, on justice in the world, received a more general welcome. The ground was prepared by an apostolic letter published on May 14 in which Pope Paul VI (*see* BIOGRAPHY) "drew attention" to a number of pressing problems and saw the task of the church as setting down some of the conditions for a more human future. Thus it dealt with the effects of urbanization and the "new loneliness" that it can bring. It showed itself not unaware of the demands of the women's liberation movement, and spoke of the "new poor," the fringe members of society, the handicapped, and the maladjusted. The synodal document took up these themes and stressed the interdependence of the rich nations and the third world. It also showed itself aware of the development of a theology of revolution and noted that "young people manifest a growing skepticism toward any doctrinal message that turns out to be unable to achieve the liberation of man."

Debate on the celibacy issue occupied much of the synod's time and captured most of the headlines, but in the end the bishops strongly reaffirmed the church's traditional position. The bishops were much more closely divided on the subject of ordaining men of "mature age and upright life," however, and both a conservative and a somewhat more liberal proposal on the subject fell short of the two-thirds needed for acceptance. There was agreement that priests should not accept full-time secular jobs, except in special circumstances, or engage in militant political activity. As finally approved, the document on justice included a recommendation that a commission be established to study whether women were being accorded their proper place in the church and urged recognition of conscientious objection to military service.

The church's practical concern for social justice had been tested throughout the year, especially in Latin America and Africa. Brazil was a flashpoint. The archbishop of São Paulo, Agnelo Cardinal Rossi, was removed from his post by promotion to a Roman curial appointment, and this was widely seen as an implicit rebuke of his strong support for the Brazilian government. The pope had several times spoken out against the use of torture against political prisoners, but without mentioning any country by name. In Paraguay, church-state relations deteriorated still further, culminating in the excommunication of the minister of the interior and the police chief of Asunción. In Chile the situation was slightly more hopeful, and the Marxist president, Salvador Allende, was greeted with cautious approval by the local church. The cardinal archbishop of Santiago became the first cardinal in the history of Chile to take part in a socialist-inspired workers' rally when he joined the

president on the platform for the May Day celebrations.

In Africa the major event of the year was the decision of the White Fathers to leave Mozambique. The superior general of the congregation explained that the colonialist structure of the state militated against the White Fathers' mission to africanize the church in Mozambique. In Rhodesia the bishops found themselves forced to accept the requirements of the Land Tenure Act obliging church schools in European areas to apply for permission before admitting African pupils. Despite a strongly worded protest from the bishops, many judged their reluctant concession as an unworthy compromise.

In the U.S. three priests and a nun were among those named as members of an alleged conspiracy to kidnap a presidential aide. One of the priests, Philip Berrigan, together with his brother Daniel (*see* BIOGRAPHY), was serving a prison sentence for having defaced Selective Service records.

A major theological controversy was sparked off by the publication of *Infallible? An Inquiry,* the English translation of a book by the Swiss theologian Hans Küng. Its author claimed that the promises made by Christ to the church did not entail any doctrine of infallibility as defined by Vatican I and reaffirmed by Vatican II. A more practical controversy arose in the Netherlands over the appointment to the bishopric of Rotterdam of a noted conservative, A. Simonis. What made the appointment even more unwelcome in the Netherlands was the fact that there had been much preliminary consultation among the people. It looked like a straight clash between the claims of the local church and the claims of the central organization. The same conflict was felt in the response to the project for a basic law or constitution for the whole church (*Lex Ecclesiae Fundamentalis*). Drafted by a restricted group of canon lawyers in secret, it aroused critical comment from theologians when it was unofficially published in an Italian magazine. It was unreservedly condemned by 220 theologians from German-speaking lands. Léon Cardinal Suenens of Belgium gave another of his celebrated interviews attacking it, and the Canon Law Society of America added its voice to the chorus. A report on the comments of bishops on the basic law was given to the synod. In the context of this clamour for reform, the pope's decision that cardinals over the age of 80 should not be admitted to the conclave to elect his successor seemed small comfort.

Meanwhile, the year saw increasing diplomatic activity between the Vatican and Eastern Europe. The first visit of a Communist head of state to the Vatican took place in March with the meeting between the pope and President Tito of Yugoslavia. The change of leadership in Poland brought hope for improved church-state relations there, and meetings between Polish and Vatican representatives justified this confidence. The Hungarian foreign minister also visited the pope, and Jozsef Cardinal Mindszenty (*see* BIOGRAPHY) left his long asylum in the U.S. embassy in Budapest. Archbishop Agostino Casaroli and the Jesuit superior general, Father Pedro Arrupe, visited Moscow, and there were talks with the Czechoslovak government on the repressive measures taken against the church. Finally, U.S. Pres. Richard M. Nixon's proposed visit to Communist China aroused the interest and approval of the pope, whose Asian journey in late 1970 had been characterized by wistful glances in the direction of Peking.   (P. A. H.)

The Rev. Victor Salandini, research director for the United Farm Workers Organizing Committee, offers communion with a corn tortilla for Mexican farm workers in San Diego, Calif. His bishop suspended him for the procedure, which does not comply with church canon law, but later reinstated him.

EASTERN CHURCHES

The Orthodox Church. Two Orthodox patriarchal sees were provided with new incumbents during 1971. The first and most important election took place during a provincial council of the Russian Orthodox Church, held at the Monastery of the Holy Trinity at Zagorsk, near Moscow, May 30–June 2. In accordance with the statutes of the patriarchate, the council included bishops, priests, and laymen. The total voting membership was 236. The Patriarchate of Moscow and All Russia had been vacant since April 17, 1970, when Patriarch Alexii died at 92. To succeed him, the council elected Metropolitan Pimen, who had been the late patriarch's vicar. The new patriarch had spent time in exile, but more recently he had shown full conformity to the official government policy. His election was not a surprise, though many were disappointed by the fact that the balloting was oral and open and that Metropolitan Pimen was the only candidate.

The council also approved a new parish statute, which had won the provisional endorsement of the episcopal assembly (1961). The statute, which placed the parish clergy under the economic and administrative control of lay committees, had been widely criticized by both Russian and foreign observers as a state-imposed limitation of the church's freedom. Finally, the council took a measure of internal Russian ecumenical significance: it lifted the anathemas that had been placed in the 17th century upon the Old Believers, a dissident group who had opposed the liturgical reforms of the Patriarch Nikon and still counted numerous adherents.

The second election, held on July 4 in Sofia, Bulg., chose a patriarch of the Bulgarian Church to succeed Kiril, who died on March 7. An electoral college of 101 members, including bishops, clergy, and laymen, elected Maxim, the metropolitan of Lovets, by a large majority. At both elections, in Moscow and in Sofia, representatives of all Orthodox churches, as well as Roman Catholic and Protestant guests, were in attendance.

Four official consultations of a Pan-Orthodox character took place during the summer. The Pre-Conciliar Commission, charged with the preparation of the agenda of a forthcoming Pan-Orthodox Council, met in Chambéry, France (July 11–28). A meeting of the Pro-Synod, an even more representative body, was announced for July 1972. A Pan-Orthodox Commission for the preparation of a dialogue with the Old Catholics met in Bonn, W.Ger. (June 22–30), and a similar commission for a dialogue with the Anglicans held a session in Helsinki, Fin. (July 7–11). The session of the commission for a dialogue with Eastern Non-Chalcedonian churches met in Addis Ababa, Eth. (August 18–29).

These various Pan-Orthodox activities were conducted despite the disagreement between the patriarchates of Constantinople (Istanbul) and Moscow over Moscow's grant of autocephalous (independent) status to the Orthodox Church in America in 1970. Many observers felt that an understanding was likely to be reached soon. Representatives of the Orthodox Church in America were present at the patriarchal elections in Moscow and Sofia and were officially received in Damascus, Athens, Belgrade, Bucharest, and Warsaw.

Increased Turkish pressure against the Ecumenical Patriarchate in Istanbul led to the closing of the historical patriarchal theological school on the island of

Metropolitan Pimen was elected to fill the vacant Patriarchate of Moscow and All Russia during a provincial council of the Russian Orthodox Church held from May 30 to June 2, 1971, at the Monastery of the Holy Trinity in Zagorsk.

Halki. A schism that had divided the bishops of the Orthodox Patriarchate of Antioch and had involved the metropolitan of Toledo, Ohio, ended. Russian émigré parishes in Western Europe, which were unwilling to depend upon Moscow, were reintegrated into the jurisdiction of the Ecumenical Patriarchate, under the Greek metropolitan of France. The Church of Cyprus, under the leadership of Archbishop Makarios, developed a new interest in Orthodox missions in East Africa. The archbishop visited Nairobi, Kenya, in March, where he announced the founding of new seminaries for African students in Kenya and in Cyprus.

Eastern Non-Chalcedonian Churches. The patriarch of the Coptic Church of Egypt, Kyrollos VI, a revered figure with the reputation of a holy ascetic, died on March 9 (*see* OBITUARIES). His successor, chosen on October 31, was Bishop Shenuda, a former army officer who had been in charge of religious education. Numbering several million faithful, the Coptic Church represented an influential though often segregated and repressed minority in Muslim Egypt. Kyrollos had succeeded in establishing an understanding with the government led by Gamal Abd-an-Nasser, but the future role of the Copts, against the explosive background of the Middle East, was not clear.

The Church of Ethiopia, which also had lost its leader, proceeded with the election of Abuna Theophilos as its new patriarch. The election was confirmed by Emperor Haile Selassie, and the enthronement took place on May 9. The new patriarch pronounced a confession of faith, formulating the dogmas of the Ethiopian Church in such a way as to make them acceptable to the Orthodox Chalcedonian churches. A fourth unofficial meeting between theologians of the Orthodox and the Non-Chalcedonians took place on January 22–23. (J. ME.)

JUDAISM

According to an estimate published by the *American Jewish Year Book, 1971*, the world Jewish population at the end of 1970 stood at about 13,951,000 and was distributed as follows: Europe (including Asian territories of the U.S.S.R. and Turkey), 4,046,-150, or 29% of the total; North and South America, 6,962,925 (50%); Asia, 2,668,200 (19%); Africa,

American Jews demonstrate in front of the White House on March 21, 1971, to protest the treatment of Jews in the Soviet Union. Nearly 800 demonstrators were arrested for sitting down and blocking traffic in a busy intersection.

196,600 (1.5%); and Oceania, 77,000 (0.5%). No major changes occurred in the distributional pattern of the Jewish populations in 1971. There was an increased flow of immigration to Israel from the U.S.S.R. (some 8,000 as against 1,000 in 1970), from Western Europe, and from North and Latin America, but the total, reported at about 40,000, did not exceed the figure for the previous year.

The cease-fire in Israel turned attention away from the Israeli-Arab conflict during much of the year, so that the intensification of the fight for Soviet Jewry came at an opportune time. There were two major developments: the growing protest by the Jews of the U.S.S.R. themselves, and the change in the reaction of the Soviet authorities. Soviet Jews became increasingly articulate and bold in defending their constitutional rights, including the right to emigrate, and engaged in many daring acts of defiance unthinkable only a few years earlier. They were supported in this by world Jewry, which in various ways attempted to awaken the conscience of the world at large. Only a small minority followed the extremist tactics of Rabbi Meir Kahane and his largely New York-based Jewish Defense League, but Jews throughout the world engaged in open protests, highlighted by the World Conference of Jewish Communities, held in Brussels in February 1971.

The rather inept conduct of the Soviet authorities in holding a series of political trials in Leningrad, Riga, Kishinev, and elsewhere gave public opinion a specific issue on which to batten. On this issue heads of state, UN Secretary-General U Thant, and the pope were willing to make themselves heard, and thus for the first time world public opinion became acquainted with the seriousness and magnitude of the problem. The Soviet authorities, who for decades had refused their Jewish citizens the right to emigrate, apparently reached the conclusion that attempts to stifle dissident Jews by oppression were self-defeating, and finally decided to allow some of them to depart. This affected not only elderly Jews who were allowed to join their families in Israel but also some of those who were causing trouble.

This policy was consistently maintained throughout the year, though there were no means of knowing what proportion of Soviet Jews wished to leave the country. The 1970 census of population of the U.S.S.R., released in April, revealed a very dubious total of 2,151,000 Jews, as against 2,268,000 shown in the census of 1959—a decrease of 117,000; Soviet

and other analysts tried to explain this as the result of growing assimilation, the desire to hide Jewish identity from the enumerators, and natural decrease.

A recent report reflected fear of imminent total assimilation of the vast majority of Jews in the U.S.S.R. According to Boris Smolar, author of *Soviet Jewry Today and Tomorrow* (1971), the percentage of mixed marriages in the one district of Moscow that he checked was in excess of 60. Children of mixed Jewish and gentile parents were given the option of registering according to the nationality of either parent, and many were discouraged from choosing Jewish nationality by the prevalence of anti-Jewish discrimination. This was especially true in the Ukraine, where the Nazis during their brief occupancy succeeded in combining the appeals of nationalism and anti-Semitism, and where anti-Semitism was most flagrant in the factories and universities. Not all observers concurred in this judgment, however. There had been an amazing resurgence of Jewish loyalty in the U.S.S.R. during the past few years, evidenced in massive demonstrations of young people at the synagogues of big cities on the festival of Simhath Torah (the last day of the Sukkoth holiday), and many of the youths who seized every occasion to show pride in their heritage were children of mixed marriages.

In Poland the anti-Zionist campaign with its strong anti-Semitic undertones faded out, having served its purpose and reshuffled countless jobs. Few Jews remained to be affected by the demotion of the main promoter of this campaign, Gen. Mieczyslaw Moczar, although several hundred exit permits were given by the Polish authorities to those Jews whose previous applications had been rejected. In Czechoslovakia rumours continued about planned trials and other unfavourable measures centred around pro-Dubcek Jews, but the deterioration thus far was less rapid than had been feared. The position of the Jewish communities in Romania (100,000) and Hungary (80,000) continued to be satisfactory.

Another critical area of Jewish collective concern was Latin America, containing some 25 Jewish communities ranging from 500,000 strong in Argentina to a few dozen families in Honduras and Nicaragua (the Jewish population in all Latin-American countries was estimated at about 813,000). These communities feared the prospect of being buffeted between left and right in developing revolutionary situations. In Chile (estimated Jewish population 35,000), following the electoral victory of Salvador Allende Gossens, a number of Jews left the country, prompted not by the fear of potential anti-Semitism but by the effect of socialist reforms on the economic class to which they belonged (as happened in Cuba); as time went on some of them returned. The economic crisis caused serious financial difficulties to the Jewish community in Uruguay, and in Argentina there was growing concern for the increasing number of old people and the inability of the community to care for them.

With the disappearance or spiritual dissipation of the once great centres of Jewish religious learning and secular cultural activity in central and Eastern Europe, the foci of Jewish creativity moved westward toward France, Great Britain, the U.S., and especially Israel. One of the most important achievements of Western and Israeli collective scholarship was the completion in 1971 of a 16-volume *Encyclopaedia Judaica*, edited by Cecil Roth (who died in Jerusalem in 1970) and Geoffrey Wigoder.

In the world of Israeli-Diaspora relations, a significant formal step was the reconstitution of the Jewish Agency and the broadening of its base and interests. In the past the Jewish Agency had acted as the governing body or the world Zionist movement. Henceforth it was to be responsible only for activities within the borders of Israel, dealing with such matters as immigration, agricultural settlements, health and welfare, education and finance. Outside Israel, the World Zionist Organization would head activities connected with Jewish communities, education and culture, and youth movements.

The ecumenical movement within Christendom had had some impact on Judaism. The chief rabbi of the United Hebrew Congregations of the British Commonwealth, Immanuel Jakobovits, pointed out that although some Jewish and Christian interests would remain irreconcilable, few of the revolutionary changes that had reshaped the postwar world could be greeted with greater satisfaction than the dramatic improvement of interreligious relations. The pressure of antireligious forces called for some accommodation in order to strengthen "the ramparts of Judeo-Christian patrimony against the common foe of materialism, secularism, atheism, and sheer paganism sweeping the world."

The rabbinate of Israel continued to grapple with the problem of what procedure to adopt for the conversion of the gentile spouses of Jewish immigrants. Many gentile spouses would gladly accept conversion in order to regularize the Jewish status of their children, but the requirements of the Orthodox rabbinate for a sincere acceptance of the entire Law were frequently incompatible with the conscience of the immigrants. A special rabbinic court had been set up in Vienna to aid refugees who planned to settle in Israel, and the Israeli government enacted a new law, which in effect accepted the conversion of Conservative and Reform rabbis if it was performed in the lands of the Diaspora. The Orthodox rabbis in Israel and America were dissatisfied with this ruling, however.

(J. B. A.; P. GL.)

BUDDHISM

The energetic activities of Buddhists throughout the world in 1970–71 indicated that Buddhism, often regarded as the most otherworldly of religions, was now deeply involved in practical affairs. The World Fellowship of Buddhists (WFB), which started in 1950 with 29 regional centres, boasted 50 scattered over various continents. The WFB, which had its headquarters in Bangkok, Thai., had been recognized as an international nongovernmental organization competent and qualified to assist UNESCO with its activities. In addition to the WFB, there were three other international Buddhist organizations: the World Buddhist Sangha Council with headquarters in Ceylon; the World Buddhist Social Service with headquarters in Vietnam; and the World Buddhist Union in Korea.

A variety of Buddhist arts were introduced to the world in the Buddhist Exhibition at the National Museum in Copenhagen, Den. A repository of Buddhist relics was discovered in southern Uzbekistan, where Soviet archaeologists assumed a large settlement with a Buddhist temple had been situated about 2,000 years ago. In Burma an old marble statue of the Buddha, probably dating from the Pagan era (11th–13th centuries), was unearthed. An eight-nation committee, with the backing of UN Secretary-General U Thant, launched an appeal for $6 million for the development

of Lumbini, Nepal, believed to be the Buddha's birthplace. Meanwhile, an Indian scholar advanced the startling theory that the Buddha was actually born at Kapilesvara, near Bhubaneswar.

In India the so-called New Buddhists continued to grow steadily. They celebrated Maha Mahinda Day in Bombay, commemorating the missionary-son of the 3rd century B.C. Buddhist king Asoka. In New Delhi hundreds of Indian Buddhists held a demonstration protesting alleged U.S. atrocities against Buddhists in Southeast Asia. In Dharamsala, the Dalai Lama's headquarters in India, the cornerstone of the Library of Tibetan Works and Archives was laid and the first meeting of the Tibetan Youth Conference was held.

Prime Minister Sirimavo Bandaranaike of Ceylon continued to work closely with the Sri Lanka Buddhist Congress and other Buddhist organizations (see *Religions of Asia,* below). The Buddhist symbol of the four Bo-tree leaves was to be reintroduced on the Ceylonese national flag, and the Army planned to set up official quarters for the bhikkhus (monks) who acted as chaplains. In Burma the Buddhist Missionary Society reported that it had sent 868 monks to 187 schools in border areas during the preceding ten years. A new pinnacle (*hti*) was to be placed on the Shwe Dagon in Rangoon, Burma's national shrine; it would replace the historic jeweled *hti* given by the pious queen of King Mindon (d. 1878), which had been severely damaged by earthquakes in 1970. Despite pleas from both the Cambodian government and Prince Sihanouk's United National Front to protect Angkor Wat, artillery fire damaged the south side of the historic temple in March 1971. (*See* HISTORIC BUILDINGS.)

Four Buddhist organizations jointly established the Singapore Buddhist Youth Organization with a new journal, *The Young Buddhist.* It was reported that the North Vietnam National Assembly now had three seats for Buddhist representatives—two bhikkhus and one lay leader. In South Vietnam a noted Hungarian scholar, Ernest Hetanyi, was appointed honorary vice-director of the Bo-tat Csoma Institute for Buddhology.

Very little was reported about the current status of Buddhism in China. In Japan, where the Soka Gakkai-based political party, Komeito, continued its active role, another Buddhistic "new religion," Rissokosei-kai, was taking the initiative in an interfaith effort to lobby in the UN for peace, arms control, and human rights.

In the U.S. notable events included the 70th anniversary of the Young Buddhist Association in Honolulu, the appointment of Tatsugami Roshi as abbot of the San Francisco Zen Center, and the establishment of the Tri-State Buddhist Church in Denver. A new Buddha Dhamma (Theravada) Center was organized in Pickering, Ont. In Europe it was reported that a new Buddhist group had been formed in Lausanne, Switz., and that Jonas Statkievicious, the first Lithuanian Buddhist, trained under a Polish bhikkhu, would soon be ordained in Colombo. (J. M. KA.)

ISLAM

For Muslims the most important events of 1971 were the civil war in East Pakistan that began in March and the war between Pakistan and India in December. The effects of these tragedies would be felt for a long time, not only by Pakistanis but by Muslims elsewhere, particularly in India. A number of other essentially political problems continued to be of major concern to Muslims in various countries. In the Middle East the Arab-Israeli situation remained stalemated; relations between Jordan and other Arab countries, especially Syria, continued to be cool; and a coup and countercoup in the Sudan in July had repercussions beyond its borders. Hopes for closer Arab relations were raised in April with the announcement of an agreement on union among Syria, Egypt, and Libya; the constitution of the Confederation of Arab Republics was signed on August 20. (*See* PAKISTAN; MIDDLE EAST.)

More directly religious developments appeared less spectacular, though they were indicative of a number of recent trends. The pilgrimage to Mecca was once again the largest ever: some 430,000 attended the rite in February. As a result of the Islamic Conference attended by the foreign ministers of Islamic countries, held in Karachi, Pak., at the end of 1970, a permanent secretariat was established in January with headquarters in Saudi Arabia. In July, Egypt announced the building of an Islamic centre in Cairo, at a cost of E£1 million, for printing and distributing abroad the Koran and other works including a monthly magazine. The centre would work for the spread of Islam and Islamic culture all over the world. In May, Morocco was host to the second African Women's Conference under the sponsorship of Princess Lalla Fatima Zuhra, president of the National Union of Moroccan Women.

A number of events within individual Muslim countries were directly related to Islamic interests. In November 1970 the Islamic University in Libya was dissolved and its faculty incorporated into the national University of Libya. In February, Libya's Revolutionary Command Council established a general commission for waqfs (charitable or religious trusts) which was to supervise Islamic teaching and to be responsible for the administration of all mosques. In June that country's mufti wrote a letter forbidding the consumption of meat imported from non-Muslim countries because it had not been ritually slaughtered.

Algeria announced in June that 25,000 ha. of land would be cleared of vineyards and turned to the production of meat and dairy products. In July, Algeria's minister of religious affairs made a plea for the use of Arabic instead of foreign languages in science teaching; the previous December students had demonstrated in favour of greater use of Arabic in schools. The Committee for Fatwas in the same ministry declared in August that the drawing of interest on savings accounts and government bonds was acceptable.

One or two other announcements were relevant to religious news in general. In February, Lebanon banned the activities of the Jehovah's Witnesses as disruptive. In June, Egypt forbade women students to wear miniskirts to their university examinations because they were distracting. It was hoped that a report in April that four Iraqi Jews had been appointed members of the government-controlled Iraqi press syndicate signaled some relaxation of internal tensions in that country.   (R. W. SM.)

RELIGIONS OF ASIA

All religions of Asia in 1971 seemed to reflect the inner turmoil of Asians who found it difficult to comprehend the meaning of life in the midst of continued economic insecurity, political instability, wars, insurrections, antigovernment demonstrations, and youth revolts. Religious factors also complicated the foreign relations and domestic politics of Asian nations.

In India conservative Hindus severely criticized Prime Minister Indira Gandhi for collaborating with the Muslim League in the 1970 election in Kerala, calling her a reincarnation of Kali, the goddess of destruction. However, in March 1971, Mrs. Gandhi's Ruling Congress Party won a decisive victory in the parliamentary elections. (*See* INDIA.) A number of Muslim-Hindu riots occurred, including one in Allahabad in February and one in Aligarh in March. For much of the year India's most critical problem was that of the East Pakistani refugees, estimated to total as many as ten million. Many were Hindus, who said they had suffered brutal treatment from the West Pakistani troops attempting to suppress the East Pakistani separatist movement. Following the December Indo-Pakistani war and East Pakistan's declaration of independence as the state of Bangla Desh, efforts were made to repatriate the refugees. Indian troops were welcomed as liberators by the predominantly Muslim Bengalis of Bangla Desh, but it was questionable how long this euphoria would paper over ancient hatreds.

In Ceylon, Mme Sirimavo Bandaranaike's government followed pro-Buddhist and anti-Western policies, but it did not seem able to reconcile the aspirations of the Buddhists and the demands of the extreme Marxists. Relations were established in 1970 with North Korea, North Vietnam, and other Communist nations, and Ceylon welcomed a delegation from the militant Palestinian Al Fatah movement and a visit

Muslim labourers from 31 countries pray before petitioning the Danish government in Copenhagen in April 1971 for land and facilities to form a Muslim community centre. Approximately 12,000 Muslims work in Denmark.

from Mme Nguyen Thi Binh, foreign minister of Vietnam's National Liberation Front. In the spring and summer of 1971, however, the government had to use force to suppress an insurrection of extreme leftists, allegedly instigated by North Korean Communists. Meanwhile, the government continued to suffer from the age-old tensions between Sinhalese Buddhists and the Hindu Tamils. It was particularly nervous about "illicit immigration from India," which strengthened Hindu-Tamil power in northern Ceylon.

In Burma the Defense Ministry acknowledged late in 1970 that Karen rebels were collaborating with Buddhist leader and former prime minister U Nu, although it denied reports from Bangkok that U Nu had actually slipped into Burma in 1970 to set up a United National Liberation Front. In Thailand, where U Nu had been given political asylum, it was reported that a farewell letter from him posted from Vientiane, Laos, had been received by the Thai prime minister.

Many Buddhist leaders in South Vietnam were critical of Pres. Nguyen Van Thieu, a convert to Catholicism, for allegedly favouring Catholic schools and Catholic relief services. Some time prior to the October presidential election, Thich Thien Minh, deputy chairman of the powerful and militant An Quang Buddhists, announced that his group would back any candidate who represented the wishes of the people, regardless of religious affiliation. When it became apparent that Thieu would be unopposed, the An Quang (which had been instrumental in Ngo Dinh Diem's overthrow in 1963) called for a boycott of the election, but Thieu was reelected easily. In Cambodia, Man Pram Moni, a charismatic monk and confidant of Premier Lon Nol, predicted that the war in Southeast Asia would end by Jan. 9, 1972.

A series of conflicts between Muslim inhabitants and Christian settlers on Mindanao in the Philippines cost more than 1,000 lives during the course of the year. In Taiwan, where all religions were rigidly con-

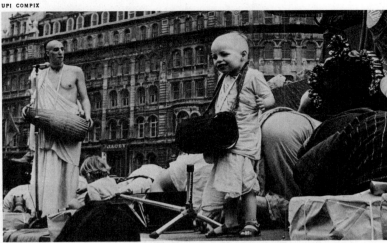

A young follower of the Society of Krishna Consciousness participates in ceremonies in front of the empty throne of the society's founder during the third international Hare Krishna Rathayatra festival in London on July 12, 1971.

trolled by the government, an American Methodist missionary, the Rev. Milo L. Thornberry, Jr., and his wife were deported in March 1971 on the ground that they had supported antigovernment causes. Meanwhile, China seemed to have outgrown the Cultural Revolution. According to some observers, the cult of Mao had become more ritualistic and had lost much of its emotional appeal. (J. M. Ka.)

World Church Membership. With the expansion of the ecumenical movement, scholarly representatives of world religions, confronting each other, in many cases for the first time, often discovered that they lacked a common language. Nowhere was this more evident than in the matter of statistics.

Even in the West there is a wide variety in styles of reckoning. Where religious liberty and voluntary adherence obtain, as in the U.S., the relationship of the religious person to his faith community is termed "membership," comparable to membership in a union or professional association. In European Christen-

Estimated Membership of the Principal Religions of the World*

Religions	North America†	South America	Europe‡	Asia	Africa	Oceania§	World
Total Christian	224,880,000	168,258,000	407,717,700	76,468,000	100,692,600	7,347,100	985,363,400
Roman Catholic	128,705,000	164,527,500	190,488,000	46,106,000	35,178,000	1,767,100	566,771,600
Eastern Orthodox	3,900,000	50,000	92,927,500	1,920,000	25,000,000‖	80,000	123,877,500
Protestant¶	92,275,000	3,680,500	124,302,200	28,442,000	40,514,600⁹	5,500,000	294,714,300
Jewish	6,160,000	784,000	4,390,500	2,766,000	310,000	80,000	14,490,500
Muslimδ	168,000	400,000	24,347,200	331,114,500	114,784,000	525,000	471,338,700
Zoroastrian□	—	—	—	125,000	—	—	125,000
Shinto°	30,000	100,000	—	60,000,000	—	—	60,130,000
Taoist▲	15,000	18,000	—	51,250,000	—	—	51,283,000
Confucian▲	95,000	100,000	50,000	304,300,000	—	50,000	304,595,000
Buddhist⁺	200,000	160,000	18,000	301,058,000	—	—	301,436,000
Hindu⊕	55,000	700,000	180,000	469,988,500	1,060,000	375,000	472,358,500
Totals	231,603,000	170,520,000	436,703,400	1,597,070,000	216,846,600	8,377,100	2,661,120,100
Population**	314,000,000	186,000,000	700,000,000	1,988,000,000	345,000,000	18,900,000	3,552,000,000

*Religious statistics are directly affected by war and persecution. World refugees approximate 27.5 million today, of which the largest blocs are 10 million in India from East Pakistan, 2 million in Hong Kong from China, 550,000 in Congo (Kinshasa) from Angola, 450,000 in the U.S. from Cuba.

†Includes Central America and the West Indies.

‡Includes the U.S.S.R., in which the effect of a half century of official Marxist ideology upon religious adherence is much disputed among specialists. There are 17 officially Marxist governments among nations in the United Nations, and in all cases it is difficult to estimate religious adherence.

§Includes New Zealand and Australia as well as islands of the South Pacific.

‖Including Coptic Christians.

¶Protestant statistics usually include "full members" rather than all baptized persons and are not comparable to those of ethnic religions or churches counting all adherents.

⁹Including many new sects and cults among African Christians.

δThe chief base of Islam is still ethnic, although some missionary work is now carried on in Europe and America (viz. Black Muslims). In countries where Islam is established, minority religions are frequently persecuted and their statistics are difficult to come by.

□Zoroastrians are found in Iran, Pakistan, and India.

°A Japanese ethnic religion, Shinto has declined markedly since the Japanese emperor gave up claim to divinity (1947). Japanese religious statistics are highly problematical because adherents frequently are related to several different religions simultaneously.

▲Figures on China are highly speculative, since the abiding effects of the Cultural Revolution upon Taoism and Confucianism are yet to be measured.

⁺Buddhism has several modern renewal movements which have gained adherents in Europe and America, areas not formerly ethnic-Buddhist. In Asia it has also made rapid gains in recent years.

⊕Hinduism's strength in India has been enhanced by nationalism, and modern Hinduism has also developed renewal movements that have reached into America and Europe for converts.

**Source: United Nations, Population and Vital Statistics Report (Jan. 1, 1971).   (F. H. Li.)

dom, where state churches long dominated the religious scene, those in traditional relationship are termed "communicants" or "constituents."

In the Eastern religions, even these terms are too precise. Hinduism, Buddhism, and Islam have "adherents." In Confucianism, Taoism, and Shinto, philosophy and life-style are so intertwined that no terms implying a separation of the religious relationship from other functional roles can be used accurately. In the mixed religious situation of modern Japan, for example, the total of religious statistics runs to four times the total population. A considerable number of Japanese "belong" to one or more Buddhist sects, observe festivals at Shinto shrines, and are perhaps counted as adherents of one of the unique universal cults that have sprung up in the Orient since World War II.

Clearly the compilation of reliable religious statistics is severely compromised by the different ways of counting. The membership of the Zen Buddhist Society in Boston can be determined exactly; the number of Buddhist adherents in Burma is often based on estimates of population and population growth. The membership of Lutheran churches in Chicago can be totaled quite precisely; in Sweden and Denmark the state churches reckon over 98% of each population as Lutheran, though official studies show only 3.6 and 3.4%, respectively, in active connection. Similar problems exist for such countries as Spain, Greece, West Germany, Italy, Norway, and other lands where some form of religious establishment still prevails. The problem for totaling Christian statistics reaches its ultimate level of speculation in areas where Marxism is the official ideology. Accordingly, readers who use the statistics provided in the table are advised to do so with consciousness that mixed styles of reckoning are incorporated.   (F. H. Li.)

Rhodesia

Though Rhodesia declared itself a republic on March 2, 1970, it remained a British colony in the eyes of many other nations. It is bounded by Zambia, Mozambique, South Africa, and Botswana. Area: 150,820 sq.mi. (390,622 sq.km.). Pop. (1970 est.): 5.4 million, of whom 94% are African and 5% white. Cap. and largest city: Salisbury (pop., 1970 est., 93,000). Language: English (official) and Bantu. Religion: predominantly traditional tribal beliefs; Christian minority. President in 1971, Clifford Dupont; prime minister, Ian D. Smith.

After a year of negotiations initiated through the British ambassador in South Africa, Sir Arthur Snelling, and including several visits to Salisbury by Lord Goodman (*see* BIOGRAPHY), a settlement of the six-year dispute that had separated the U.K. and Rhodesia was reached on Nov. 24, 1971. The following day it was announced in the British Parliament by Foreign Secretary Sir Alec Douglas-Home, who had personally conducted the concluding stages of the negotiations in Salisbury.

The Economic Survey of Rhodesia 1970, published in April 1971, showed once again that sanctions had been having an adverse effect. Although the balance of payments still showed a surplus (of £456,000), this was only 4% of that for 1969. Particularly serious were the continuing shortage of foreign exchange, sharp falls in corn and cotton sales, and an 8% decline in the production of flue-cured tobacco. The growth in

the African population presented further problems as employment opportunities diminished.

For these reasons the settlement was welcomed widely among white Rhodesians. It would end Rhodesia's diplomatic isolation, lift sanctions, revive the economy, and bind Rhodesia more closely to the West via economic aid and political strategy, while deferring proportional representation of the African population for perhaps half a century.

Disregarding the African call for no independence before majority African rule, the five principles accepted by all parties were: a guarantee of unimpeded progress toward majority (black African) rule; guarantees against retrogressive amendment of the constitution; immediate improvement in the political status of the Africans; progress toward an end to racial discrimination; and the acceptability to the Rhodesian population as a whole of any proposed basis for independence.

In the agreement reached between Ian Smith and Douglas-Home the Rhodesian regime did abandon key clauses in the 1969 constitution which had laid down that there would never be African majority rule. Under the proposed settlement progress toward parity of representation between Africans (94% of the population) and whites (5% of the population) was allowed for through British aid of £50 million over 10 years for African education and a proposed "higher African electoral roll," income qualifications for which were far in excess of average African earnings. Once parity had been reached, and no time limit for this was laid down, a complex four-stage program would follow which, though it might result in a slight numerical African majority in the House of Assembly, could not guarantee a political majority.

RHODESIA
Education. (1970) African: primary, pupils 677,415, teachers 16,958; secondary, pupils 24,201, teachers 1,027; vocational and teacher training, students 2,113, teachers 121. Non-African: primary, pupils 39,504, teachers 1,588; secondary, pupils 26,462, teachers 1,539; vocational and teacher training, pupils 2,818, teachers 189. African and non-African: higher (University of Rhodesia), students 867, teaching staff 162.

Finance. Monetary unit: Rhodesian dollar, with a par value of R$0.71 to U.S. $1 (R$1.71 = £1 sterling) and a free rate (Sept. 27, 1971) of R$1.77 to £1 sterling. Budget (1970–71): revenue R$158,280,-000; expenditure R$215,715,000. Gross national product: (1969) R$938.8 million; (1968) R$824.4 million.

Foreign Trade. (1969): Imports R$199.4 million; exports R$226.9 million. Import sources (1965): U.K. 30%; South Africa 23%; U.S. 7%; Japan 6%. Export destinations (1965): Zambia 29%; U.K. 20%; South Africa 11%; West Germany 8%; Malawi 6%; Japan 5%. Main exports (1965): tobacco 51%; asbestos 12%; machinery 9%; clothing 6%; chemicals 5%.

Transport and Communications. Roads (1969) 78,064 km. Motor vehicles in use (1969): passenger 126,600; commercial (including buses) 52,000. Railways: (1968) 3,235 km.; freight traffic (including Botswana; 1969) 6,289,000,000 net ton-km. Telephones (Dec. 1969) 131,281. Radio receivers (Dec. 1969) 135,000. Television receivers (Dec. 1969) 48,-000.

Agriculture. Production (in 000; metric tons; 1970; 1969 in parentheses): corn *c.* 700 (*c.* 1,020); millet *c.* 200 (*c.* 220); peanuts *c.* 122 (*c.* 122); tobacco *c.* 62 (*c.* 62); tea *c.* 2.3 (*c.* 2.3); sugar, raw value (1970–71) *c.* 142, (1969–70) *c.* 127; beef and veal (on farms and estates; 1969–70) *c.* 70, (1968–69) *c.* 68. Livestock (in 000; 1969–70): cattle *c.* 3,900; sheep *c.* 450; goats *c.* 690; pigs *c.* 143.

Industry. Production (in 000; metric tons; 1969): coal 3,332; chrome ore (oxide content; 1965) 281; asbestos (1968) *c.* 86; iron ore (metal content; 1966) *c.* 830; gold (troy oz.; 1967) 500; electricity (kw-hr.) 6,002,000.

The immediate improvement in the Africans' political status offered by the settlement was the addition of two African representatives to the 16 already sitting in the 66-member House of Assembly, to be directly elected by "higher roll" Africans within a year of ratification of the agreement. The following year two additional African MPs would be elected by indirect electoral college votes (regarded by opponents of the settlement as a means of retaining government control over at least half the Africans elected). The sequence would be repeated in relation to subsequent additional African seats up to 34, thus giving a total of 50 and parity.

The proposed agreement contained no commitment to end racial discrimination. Although a commission was to be set up to examine the question, with special regard to the Land Tenure Act, it had no real power to enforce its proposals on any Rhodesian government; approval of its findings by the British government was not required before ratification.

Reactions to the settlement varied widely. Most white Rhodesians were pleased, and few of Smith's right-wing opponents threatened resignation. Most Africans within Rhodesia were critical or noncommittal.   (K. I.)

Romania

A socialist republic on the Balkan Peninsula in southeastern Europe, Romania is bordered by the U.S.S.R., the Black Sea, Bulgaria, Yugoslavia, and Hungary. Area: 91,700 sq.mi. (237,500 sq.km.). Pop. (1970 est.): 20,252,541, including (1968) Romanian 87.8%; Hungarian 8.4%. Cap. and largest city: Bucharest (pop., 1970 est., 1,475,050). Religion: Romanian Orthodox 70%; Greek Orthodox 10%. General secretary of the Romanian Communist Party and president of the State Council in 1971, Nicolae Ceausescu; chairman of the Council of Ministers (premier), Ion Gheorghe Maurer.

During 1971 President Ceausescu was more than usually busy defining the Romanian brand of communism to other countries of the socialist bloc. On April 1, addressing the 24th congress of the Communist Party of the Soviet Union in Moscow, he stressed once more that the Romanian Communist Party was "against any interference in the internal affairs of other parties." Moscow radio commented shortly afterward, in Romanian, that "proletarian internationalism and bourgeois nationalism were irreconcilable." Ceausescu retorted on May 7, in a speech celebrating the 50th anniversary of the Romanian Communist Party, that there was "no contradiction between the concern for the prosperity of a socialist homeland and the principle of internationalism."

From June 1 to 24, Ceausescu paid state visits to China, North Korea, North Vietnam, and Mongolia. In Peking the leaders of the two countries expressed their determination "to further strengthen their revolutionary friendship and fighting unity." In Pyongyang and Hanoi the principles of equal rights, sovereignty, and noninterference were reaffirmed, but Ceausescu's reception in Ulan Bator was frosty. A consequence of Ceausescu's Oriental travels was that he was not invited by Soviet party leader Leonid I.

Brezhnev to the meeting of leaders of Communist states held August 2 in the Crimea.

On June 23, speaking at the Hungarian National Assembly, Zoltan Komocsin, a member of the Hungarian party's Politburo, remarked that cooperation with Romania was difficult because of differences of views on China. He added: "We are fundamentally interested that the inhabitants of both our country and of Romania—including the Hungarian minority living there—should come to understand that the fate of our peoples is inseparable from socialism." Paul Niculescu-Mizil, a member of the Romanian party's Politburo, pointed out in *Scinteia* (July 9) that Komocsin's assertions had caused "amazement" in Bucharest. Alluding to Komocsin's thinly veiled reference to the Transylvanian issue, Niculescu-Mizil replied that "nobody and nothing could weaken the unshakable brotherhood between the Romanian people and the coinhabiting nationalities."

Ceausescu's reaction to his relative isolation within the socialist bloc was the launching of a nationwide campaign to reinstill Communist discipline. On July 7

ROMANIA
Education. (1968–69) Primary, pupils 2,871,816, teachers 131,948; secondary, pupils 261,355, teachers 12,993; vocational, pupils 357,763, teachers 20,245; teacher training, students 17,373, teachers 864; higher (including 11 universities), students 147,637, teaching staff 12,950.

Finance. Monetary unit: leu, with (Sept. 27, 1971) an official exchange rate of 6 lei = U.S. $1 (14.40 lei = £1 sterling) and a tourist rate of 18 lei = U.S. $1 (43.20 lei = £1 sterling). Budget (1969 est.): revenue 146,957,000,000 lei; expenditure 142,805,000,000 lei.

Foreign Trade. (1969) Imports 10,443,000,000 lei; exports 9,799,000,000 lei. Import sources: U.S.S.R. 27%; West Germany 10%; East Germany 7%; Czechoslovakia 6%; U.K. 6%; France 5%; Italy 5%. Export destinations: U.S.S.R. 28%; Czechoslovakia 9%; West Germany 7%; Italy 6%; East Germany 6%. Main exports: machinery 22%; foodstuffs 14%; raw materials (minerals, metals, etc.) 13%; petroleum products 7%; chemicals 7%.

Transport and Communications. Roads (1969) 76,566 km. (including 9,557 km. with improved surface). Motor vehicles in use: passenger (1965) c. 250,000; commercial (1969) 43,900. Railways: (1969) 11,006 km.; traffic (1970) 17,790,000,000 passenger-km., freight 48,050,000,000 net ton-km. Air traffic (1970): 353.5 million passenger-km.; freight 7,060,000 net ton-km. Inland waterways in regular use (1968) 1,115 km. Shipping (1970): merchant vessels 100 gross tons and over 65; gross tonnage 341,161. Telephones (Dec. 1969) 605,983. Radio licenses (Dec. 1969) 3,050,000. Television licenses (Dec. 1969) 1,288,000.

Agriculture. Production (in 000; metric tons; 1970; 1969 in parentheses): wheat 3,351 (4,349); barley 511 (544); oats c. 150 (137); corn 6,395 (7,676); potatoes c. 2,500 (c. 2,150); onions (1969) 208, (1968) 148; tomatoes (1969) 676, (1968) 874; sugar, raw value (1970–71) c. 372, (1969–70) 428; sunflower seed 769 (748); dry beans c. 100 (c. 100); soybeans 82 (51); dry peas c. 150 (c. 145); plums (1969) 962, (1968) 562; apples c. 260 (367); grapes (1969) 1,189, (1968) 1,167; tobacco c. 24 (24); linseed c. 35 (38); hemp fibre c. 20 (c. 21). Livestock (in 000; Jan. 1970): cattle 5,035; sheep 13,836; pigs 5,972; horses 686; poultry 53,894.

Industry. Index of production (1963 = 100): (1970) 229; (1969) 201. Fuel and power (in 000; metric tons; 1970): coal 6,401; lignite 14,130; coke (1969) 939; crude oil 13,377; natural gas (cu.m.) 24,789; manufactured gas (cu.m.) 522,000; electricity (kw-hr.) 35,057,000. Production (in 000; metric tons; 1970): cement 8,127; iron ore (30–35% metal content) 3,206; pig iron 4,210; crude steel 6,517; sulfuric acid 995; nitrogenous fertilizers (nitrogen content; 1969) 494; cotton yarn 109; cotton fabrics (sq.m.) 437,000; wool yarn 36; woolen fabrics (sq.m.) 62,800; newsprint 53; other paper (1969) 450; passenger cars (units) 4.3; commercial vehicles (units) 38. New dwelling units completed (1969) 140,000.

he presented to the party Executive Committee 17 propositions aimed at "improving political and ideological activity in the spirit of Marxism-Leninism." An enlarged meeting of the party Central Committee (November 3–5) discussed and adopted the 17 propositions. It was probably Ceausescu's hope that, after such a drive toward puritanical Marxism-Leninism, it would be difficult for Romania's Warsaw Treaty allies to mount an ideological offensive against it.

On November 23–24 President Tito of Yugoslavia paid a friendly visit to Ceausescu at Timisoara. Though absent from the Bulgarian, Czechoslovak, and East German party congresses during the year, Ceausescu attended the Polish party congress in Warsaw in December. (K. Sм.)

Rowing

The 1971 European rowing championships, held in Copenhagen in August, produced five new European records. East Germany and the U.S.S.R. both qualified for all seven finals. Sixteen other countries also reached the finals, but only eight managed to win medals. East Germany won four gold and three silver medals. The U.S.S.R. collected four bronze medals, and additional Eastern European successes were scored by Czechoslovakia with two silver medals and Poland with a bronze. New Zealand was well rewarded for its long journey with a gold and a bronze medal, after reaching the final in each of the three events it contested. West Germany also won a gold and a bronze medal, while Norway earned distinction with silver medals in both events it entered. The eighth winning country was Argentina.

On the windswept finals day, the biggest surprise was the triumph of the New Zealanders in the eights. They rowed magnificently to gain just enough lead by 1,250 m. to hold off a thunderous finish by East Germany over the remaining 750 m. The winning margin was $\frac{2}{5}$ sec., with the U.S.S.R. finishing 6 sec. behind in third place. In coxed fours West Germany finished 2 sec. ahead of East Germany, which

The Cambridge crew rows toward the finish line leaving the Oxford team far behind during the 117th annual varsity Boat Race on March 27, 1971.

CENTRAL PRESS—
PICTORIAL PARADE

was nearly 3 sec. faster than Norway in the coxless fours. The East German coxed pair narrowly defeated Czechoslovakia by 1.49 sec., while their coxless pair won over the same country by a comfortable 5 sec. World champion A. Demiddi (Arg.) was also a comfortable winner in single sculls, the closest verdict being the triumph in double sculls of H. Schmied and H. Boehamer (E.Ger.) over F. Hansen and S. Thorgersen (Nor.) by 0.38 sec. The winners broke the European record by 11.92 sec., and their fellow countrymen also knocked 11 sec. or more off the European records for coxless fours and coxed pairs. West Germany cut 1.62 sec. from the European coxed fours record, while New Zealand lowered the eights record by 16.68 sec. to a new world best of 5 min. 33.92 sec. for 2,000 m.

The Soviet Union won three events and also collected a silver medal in the Women's European championships held in Copenhagen a week before the men raced. Romania with a gold, a silver, and a bronze medal and East Germany with a gold, two silver, and a bronze were the other outstanding countries. West Germany took the bronze medals in two events, and France a silver and a bronze. The Soviet oarswomen won the coxed fours by 0.68 sec. after being led by Romania at the halfway mark by $4\frac{1}{2}$ sec. They were also nearly 3 sec. behind East Germany at the same stage in double sculls before winning by 2.68 sec. They won the eights by more than 7 sec. and finished second to Romania in quadruple sculls; East Germany scored its only success in single sculls.

Eastern European countries also took most of the honours in the world youth championships in Bled, Yugos., in early August. East Germany's score in the seven events was five gold and two silver medals. Its only defeats, in double sculls and eights, were at the hands of the U.S.S.R., which finished second in coxless pairs and third in coxed fours and pairs.

In the U.K. only three events at Henley Royal Regatta were won by overseas entries. Demiddi won the Diamond Sculls, and Harvard University pulled off a double U.S. triumph in the Thames and Wyfold cups. In the 117th Boat Race, the Cambridge crew stroked to their 65th victory over Oxford, by ten lengths. Then they flew to the United States where they beat Brown University seven days later in the intercollegiate regatta at Miami, Fla., by 2.30 sec., after trailing at the halfway point. (K. L. O.)

Rubber

World production of natural rubber in 1970 was estimated at 2,895,000 metric tons, an increase of 9,000 metric tons over 1969. Production for the first six months of 1971 was estimated at 1,410,000 metric tons, up 62,500 metric tons from the corresponding period in 1970. The management committee of the International Rubber Study Group (IRSG), meeting in Ottawa, Ont., in September 1971, estimated 1971 world production of new rubber as follows: natural rubber supplies, including delivery from government surplus stocks, 3,090,000 metric tons; synthetic rubber, 5,170,000 metric tons. It was estimated that some 3,050,000 metric tons of natural rubber and 5,050,000 metric tons of synthetic rubber would be consumed (*i.e.*, turned into manufactured products) in 1971. (Estimates for synthetic rubber production do not include the U.S.S.R., non-IRSG countries in Eastern Europe, or China.) The New

York spot price for no. 1 ribbed smoked sheets was 18 cents per pound on Oct. 1, 1971, the same as it was at that time in 1970.

West Malaysian production of natural rubber in 1970 totaled 1,222,622 metric tons; the total for all of Malaysia was 1,276,000 metric tons. Yields from rubber trees continued to increase as research on "yield stimulants," such as Ethrel, was carried on at the Rubber Research Institute of Malaya. The latest reports indicated production as high as 6,000 lb. per ac. per year, compared with 500 lb. per ac. per year 40 years earlier.

The U.S. remained the largest single buyer of natural rubber, taking 568,290 metric tons in 1970. World consumption of natural rubber latex (dry basis) was estimated at 256,756 metric tons in 1970. Estimates of world consumption of synthetic latices were unavailable, but the U.S. alone consumed a total of 124,-132 metric tons (dry basis) of the SBR (styrene-butadiene rubber) type. World production of all types of synthetic rubbers in 1970 (excluding countries not reporting) was estimated at 4,985,500 metric tons, of which the U.S. produced 2,232,260 metric tons. In 1970 synthetic rubber accounted for 77% of total rubber consumed in the U.S. and 66% worldwide. World consumption of both natural and synthetic rubbers in 1970 was estimated at 7,798,500 metric tons. Production of all types of reclaimed rubber in 1970 amounted to 297,458 metric tons. The area under cultivation of plantation (natural) rubber was estimated at 5,875,000 ha.

The disposal of tires after they are no longer serviceable was a major ecological problem. Goodyear announced that it had developed an artificial turf made from ground-up scrap tires which was quite resilient and could be dyed green to resemble grass. A related use for old tires was to grind them and then bond the dust into pads to cover the concrete floors of dairy barns to provide greater comfort for the cows. Columbian division of Cities Service Co. announced that a small percentage of finely ground rubber from old tires could be substituted for the oil feedstock in the manufacture of carbon black. Ground-up tires had been thermally treated to produce oils and other usable materials. It had also been proposed that old tires be used to construct artificial reefs for fish breeding.

Three new synthetic rubbers were announced that showed promise of being useful. By the use of suitable catalysts, completely alternating copolymers of butadiene with either acrylonitrile or propylene as the second monomer were made. The butadiene-acrylonitrile copolymer exhibits improved low-temperature properties, while the butadiene-propylene copolymer has excellent rebound or elasticity. The third rubber, available in experimental quantities, was a polypentenamer with excellent low-temperature properties, crystallization on stretching, good green strength in the unvulcanized state, and excellent building tack.

(J. R. By.)

Rwanda

A republic in eastern Africa, Rwanda is bordered by the Congo (Kinshasa), Uganda, Tanzania, and Burundi. Area: 10,169 sq.mi. (26,338 sq.km.). Pop. (1970): 3,735,585, including (1967) Hutu 73%; Tutsi 14.5%; Twa 0.6%; others 1.9%. Cap. and largest city: Kigali (pop., 1970, 59,100). Language (official): French and Kinyarwanda. Religion: animist 45%; Roman Catholic 45%; Protestant 9%; Muslim 1%. President in 1971, Grégoire Kayibanda.

In 1971 diplomatic relations were established with Egypt, and cooperation with Burundi and Congo (Kinshasa) increased. Although Rwanda held to moderate policies, including support for dialogue with South Africa, it was among those states accused by Idi Amin in April of attending a conference in Tanzania to discuss operations against Uganda with the aim of reversing Amin's overthrow of former president Milton Obote in January. In July, Amin accused Rwanda of allowing passage to guerrillas from Tanzania and closed the Uganda-Rwanda common frontier, cutting Rwanda's only reliable trade route to the

Table I. Natural Rubber Production

In 000 metric tons

Country	1966	1967	1968	1969	1970
Malaysia	998	998	1,100	1,268	1,276
Indonesia	716	762*	752*	790	778*
Thailand	207	214	259	282	287
Africa*	177	164	170	181	206
Ceylon	131	143	149	151	159
India	53	63	69	80	90
Vietnam	49	41	29	26	29
Brazil	24	21	23	24	25
Cambodia	51	53	51	52	13
Others*	31	28	31	32	32
Total*	2,437	2,487	2,633	2,886	2,895

*Estimate.

Table II. Synthetic Rubber Production

In 000 metric tons

Country	1966	1967	1968	1969	1970
United States	2,001	1,943	2,165	2,286	2,232
Japan	233	281	381	526	697
France	163	189	223	275	316
United Kingdom	194	204	237	273	306
Germany, West	196	190	238	292	302
Netherlands, The	110	125	163	214	206
Canada	203	200	197	199	205
Italy*	122	118	125	135	155
Germany, East	101	109	102	114	118
Brazil	54	52	59	62	75
Poland	37	40	41	48	62
Romania	35	51	54	55	...
Belgium	20	20	25	35	50
Czechoslovakia*	30	33	35	40	50
Mexico*	1	20	34	36	40
Spain	1	11	26	34	40*
Argentina	10	17	23	38*	39*
Australia	20	26	30	33	33*
India	16	22	25	25	30
South Africa	19	24	25	24	29
Total*	3,566	3,675	4,208	4,744	4,985

*Estimate.
Source: International Rubber Study Group.

RWANDA
Education. (1967–68) Primary, pupils 372,184, teachers 5,921; secondary, pupils 6,466; vocational, pupils 912; teacher training, students 1,464; secondary, vocational, and teacher training, teachers 580; higher, students 253, teaching staff 59.
Finance. Monetary unit: Rwanda franc, with a par value of RwFr. 100 to U.S. $1 (RwFr. 240 = £1 sterling) and a free rate (Sept. 27, 1971) of RwFr. 99 to U.S. $1 (RwFr. 245 = £1 sterling). Gold, SDRs, and foreign exchange, central bank: (June 1971) U.S. $2,950,000; (June 1970) U.S. $4,010,000. Budget (1969 est.): revenue RwFr. 1,636,618,000; expenditure RwFr. 1,664,000,000.
Foreign Trade. (1970) Imports RwFr. 2,909,900,-000; exports RwFr. 2,470,800,000. Import sources (1969): Belgium-Luxembourg 15%; Japan 14%; Uganda 12%; West Germany 11%; Kenya 7%; U.S. 7%; France 5%. Export destinations (1966): U.S. 57%; Belgium-Luxembourg 33%. Main exports: coffee 57%; tin 19%.
Agriculture. Production (in 000; metric tons; 1970; 1969 in parentheses): sorghum c. 130 (126); dry beans c. 95 (c. 96); dry peas c. 40 (c. 40); potatoes c. 129 (129); sweet potatoes (1969) 324, (1968) 368; cassava (1969) 283, (1968) 233; coffee c. 13 (13). Livestock (in 000; July 1970): cattle 676; sheep c. 228; pigs 47.

sea. The border was reopened in August after Rwanda agreed to suppress anti-Amin guerrillas operating in its territory.

Rwanda's trade continued mainly with Belgium, but it was also party to the second Yaoundé Convention, which took effect from January 1971, continuing the association of 18 African states with the EEC. In December 1970 at Bukavu, Congo (Kinshasa), Rwanda agreed to extend the lifetime of the three joint commissions it had established with Burundi and Congo (Kinshasa): law and politics, technology and finance, and cultural cooperation. Further collaboration with the Congo was established in February with joint plans for exploitation of the hydroelectric power potential in the great lakes of their territories. (M. Mʀ.)

Sailing

In 1971 sailing fleets throughout the world increased in size. While the dinghy fleets raced around buoys and ocean racers around lightships, Chay Blyth, single-handed, sailed his "British Steel" the wrong way (east to west) around the world in a very fast time of 292 days, and Nicolette Milnes-Walker, in her 30-ft. sloop "Aziz," became the second woman to sail the Atlantic single-handed.

The Sydney to Hobart race began the ocean racing year, and produced some rough going. The British-built and designed Camper and Nicholson 61-ft. aluminum yacht "Pacha," owned by Australian Bob Crichton-Brown, won the race after a season of racing in British waters where the boat was conspicuous for its absence from the lists of winners.

The Southern Ocean racing circuit, based in Florida and the Caribbean, was once more to be the series to watch for new developments, particularly in U.S. yacht design. Ted Turner, in his ex-12-m. "American Eagle," was favoured to repeat his overall victory of the previous year. He won the rough St. Petersburg–Fort Lauderdale race, but a broken mast cost him the series, won by the Sparkman and Stephens custom-built "Running Tide." Two other boats made their mark—the Gary Mull-designed "Improbable" won the downwind surge to Montego Bay, Jam., in

"American Eagle" of the U.S. won the St. Petersburg to Fort Lauderdale race in 1971.

COURTESY, BAHAMAS NEWS BUREAU

record time, and the tiny ½-ton Scampi "Smuggler" easily won the small class in the series. "Panacea," a 52-ft. yawl owned by Jack Eckerd of the U.S., won the Lipton Cup.

In New Zealand the one-ton cup series was held in March; it was a battle between Sparkman and Stephens and Carter designs. The Carter-designed "Optimist" had won the trophy the previous year, and its owner was depending on a new boat, "Optimist B." As it turned out, the Australian-built Sparkman and Stephens-designed "Stormy Petrel," owned by Syd Fischer, dominated the series. Hans Beilken in "Optimist B" took second place for West Germany, finishing the series strongly. Alan Warwick in "Young Nick," another Sparkman and Stephens design, gave New Zealand third place.

The half-ton cup series was raced in England and resulted in the third successive victory for Peter Norlin in his "Scampi III." Two other Scampis finished second and third, emphasizing the dominance established by this Swedish design in the series.

The quarter-ton cup series went back to La Rochelle in France. Marcel Briand in his lightweight "Tequila" won the series, having been runner-up in 1970. It was a year for light-displacement craft with only the bare essentials in the cabin: the French had many of these boats and therefore won, but the Italians, second in 1971 and third in 1970, were gaining strength.

After the Bermuda race, dominated by U.S. yachts once more, attention turned to the Admiral's Cup series in England. The Australians and Americans both had strong teams, but the British had selected not only three first-class yachts but also their prime minister, Edward Heath, to lead them. The British team spirit proved the dominating factor. After a close series Heath's "Morning Cloud," Arthur Slater's "Prospect of Whitby," and Bob Watson's "Cervantes IV," all Sparkman and Stephens designs, had scored enough points to ensure that the Admiral's Cup returned to the Royal Ocean Racing Club's mantelpiece in London. Individual honours went to Australia in the form of Syd Fischer's "Ragamuffin," which also won the coveted Fastnet Cup.

To end the season, the Middle Sea race, which starts and finishes in Malta, was won by the Italian class-V boat "Comet." The British "Sea Wraith," owned by the Royal Navy, finished second.

The 12-m. scene was quiet on the water but noisy in conference; the Royal Thames Yacht Club took the initiative and announced they would organize an elimination series for the America's Cup challenger off Newport, R.I., if by 1974 there were still enough contenders left to warrant it. The Canadians and Sir Frank Packer from Australia indicated that they were no longer interested. The defending Americans were, in the meantime, sitting back and quietly organizing syndicates and crews.

With the Olympic yachting to take place in Kiel, W.Ger., in 1972, the six Olympic classes were hotly contested in 1971. King of the single-handed Finn class was, for the second year in a row, Jorge Bruder of Brazil. The controversy raging all season over which masts would be used in the Olympics finally was decided in favour of Needlespar's metal ones. In the Flying Dutchman class Britain's Rodney Pattisson still ruled the waves, but narrowly. Still sailing his faithful gold-medal-winning "Superdocius," he soon would have to decide whether or not he would change to the new boat he had bought earlier in 1971. The

Tempest title was won for the U.S. again, this time by Glen Foster, but Ben Staartjes of the Netherlands and Alan Warren of Britain showed promise for 1972. The Solings were dominated in Europe by multi-gold-medalist Paul Elvstrøm of Denmark, but when he went to the U.S. to defend his world title, he looked anything but a champion in the first few races. In the end he came back in customary fashion to finish third overall to Bob Mosbacher and Bruce Goldsmith of the U.S. The Star class, now racing with metal masts, saw James Schoonmaker and Joe Duplin of the U.S. sweep to five victories in a row at the Kiel pre-Olympics, in a new boat. The Dragon-class honours were taken by the Americans at the pre-Olympics by the very fast "Caprice," sailed by owner Don Cohan and on occasion by sailmaker John Marshall, but the East German, Danish and Swedish crews all demonstrated that they would be strong contenders in the 1972 Olympics.

In the International trapezing dinghies British crews showed universal mastery, winning the Flying Dutchman, 5-0-5, and Fireball and Tornado catamaran world titles. In the keelboats, the U.S. sailors led with world titles in the Tempest, Soling, Dragon, and Star classes.

Competitors for the 1972 single-handed transatlantic race were busy building and preparing their yachts. There seemed to be fewer sponsors coming forward, and consequently the vessels so far entered seemed much smaller than in the past. Once more, it was likely to be a multihull versus monohull battle.

In Switzerland the prototype of a new International three-man keelboat was being built to Skip Etchell's (U.S.) design. To be built of fibreglass, the boat aimed to fill an existing gap by providing a modern racing yacht with a high ballast ratio that older yachtsmen could race in international events. It was likely to attract yachtsmen from such classes as the 5.5-m. Dragon, as well as those who had found that the physical effort required to race a Soling was not for them. The boat was 29 ft. long and would weigh approximately 3,000 lb. Of this weight 2,000 lb. represented the lead keel, which was to be detachable; owners would be able to tow the hull alone on a trailer behind a car to international regattas, sending the keel separately or borrowing one in the host country.

(A. J.)

San Marino

A small republic, San Marino is an enclave in northeastern Italy, 14 mi. SW of Rimini. Area: 25 sq.mi. (61 sq.km.). Pop. (1971 est.): 19,000. Cap.: San Marino (metro. pop., 1971 est., 4,400). Language: Italian. Religion: Roman Catholic. San Marino is united with Italy by a customs union. The country is governed by two *capitani reggenti*, or coregents, appointed every six months by a Grand and General Council. Executive power rests with two secretaries of state: foreign affairs and internal affairs. In 1971 the positions were filled, respectively, by Federico Bigi and Gian Luigi Berti.

In a protocol signed in Paris on May 6, 1971, San Marino and the People's Republic of China established diplomatic relations at the consular level. San Marino recognized the Communist government as the

SAN MARINO
Education. (1968–69) Primary, pupils 1,519, teachers 85; secondary, pupils 809, teachers 56.
Finance. Monetary unit: Italian lira, with a par value of 625 lire to U.S. $1 (1,500 lire = £1 sterling) and a free rate (Sept. 27, 1971) of 612 lire to U.S. $1 (1,518 lire = £1 sterling). Budget (1969–70 est.) balanced at 7,391,000,000 lire. Tourism (1968) 2,153,-000 visitors.

legal government of China while the People's Republic agreed to respect "the policy of neutrality pursued by the Republic of San Marino." A *Peking Review* editorial stated that the protocol "opens a new page in the friendly cooperation between the peoples of the two countries." Secretary of State Bigi signed the agreement for San Marino while the Chinese ambassador to France, Huang Chen, signed for the Chinese government. The protocol required ratification by the Grand and General Council before it could enter into force.

The government remained a coalition of Christian Democrats and Socialists. The 60-member council currently contained 25 Communist deputies. The 1971 national budget totaled approximately $12 million, with the sale of postage stamps constituting the major source of government revenue. Substantial payments were also received from Italy in exchange for an Italian monopoly on the sale of tobacco, gasoline, and associated items in the republic. (R. D. Ho.)

Saudi Arabia

A monarchy occupying four-fifths of the Arabian Peninsula, Saudi Arabia has an area of 865,000 sq.mi. (2,240,000 sq.km.). Pop. (1970 est.): 7,740,000. Cap. and largest city: Riyadh (pop., 1965 est., 225,000). Language: Arabic. Religion: Muslim. King and

SAUDI ARABIA
Education. (1968–69) Primary, pupils 363,426, teachers (including preprimary) 16,645; secondary, pupils 58,674, teachers 3,341; vocational, pupils 855, teachers 272; teacher training, students 7,678, teachers 543; higher, students 5,352, teaching staff 410.
Finance. Monetary unit: riyal, with a par value of 4.50 riyals to U.S. $1 (10.80 riyals = £1 sterling) and a free rate (Sept. 27, 1971) of 4.66 riyals to U.S. $1 (11.56 riyals = £1 sterling). Gold, SDRs, and foreign exchange, official: (June 1971) U.S. $912 million; (June 1970) U.S. $664 million. Budget (1970–71 est.) balanced at 6,380,000,000 riyals. Money supply: (March 1971) 2,566,000,000 riyals; (March 1970) 2,410,000,000 riyals.
Foreign Trade. (1968–69) Imports 2,804,000,000 riyals; exports 8,953,000,000 riyals. Import sources: U.S. 20%; Japan 10%; Lebanon 10%; U.K. 8%; West Germany 7%; Italy 5%; Netherlands 5%. Export destinations: Japan 23%; Italy 10%; U.K. 6%; Spain 6%; Netherlands 6%; Bahrain 5%. Main exports: crude oil 79%; petroleum products 14%.
Transport and Communications. Roads (1970) c. 22,000 km. (including 12,360 km. with improved surface). Motor vehicles in use (1970): passenger 42,-161; commercial 30,662. Railways (1968) 606 km. Shipping (1970): merchant vessels 100 gross tons and over 37; gross tonnage 48,543. Telephones (Jan. 1969) 44,250. Radio receivers (Dec. 1969) c. 1 million. Television receivers (Dec. 1969) c. 50,000.
Agriculture. Production (in 000; metric tons; 1970; 1969 in parentheses): wheat c. 150 (c. 150); barley c. 34 (c. 34); millet c. 16 (c. 16); sorghum c. 52 (c. 52); dates c. 220 (c. 220). Livestock (in 000; 1969–70): cattle c. 300; sheep c. 3,200; goats c. 2,000; camels c. 550; asses c. 130.
Industry. Production (in 000; metric tons; 1969): cement 550; crude oil (1970) 176,140; electricity (excluding most industrial production; kw-hr.) 599,-000.

prime minister, Faisal ibn 'Abd al-'Aziz ibn 'Abd ar-Rahman Al Sa'ud.

Saudi diplomacy in 1971 was marked by continued efforts to promote stability in the Persian Gulf area through the formation of a federation of Gulf emirates, by improved relations with the Yemen (San'a'), and by closer ties with Pres. Anwar as-Sadat's regime in Egypt. In January King Faisal's foreign affairs adviser, Prince Nawaf, joined the Kuwaiti foreign minister on a tour of the Gulf emirates to urge them to federate. The king traveled to the Far East in May, stopping in Iran, Taiwan, and Japan and returning, at Pres. Richard M. Nixon's invitation, via Washington, D.C., where he urged the U.S. president to devote attention to "the aggression suffered by certain Arab countries." In July U.S. Vice-Pres. Spiro T. Agnew visited Saudi Arabia.

From June 19–26 King Faisal visited Cairo, where he had wide-ranging discussions with President Sadat. The result was a strong Saudi-Egyptian entente despite the king's pronounced anti-Communism and Egypt's close relations with the U.S.S.R. The two heads of state agreed to try to mediate between the Palestinian guerrillas and the Jordan government, and in this connection King Husain of Jordan visited Faisal in Taif in July. Saudi Arabia continued to pay its $33.6 million share of the annual $96 million subsidy to Jordan, although both Libya and Kuwait had cut off their shares. In August President Sadat paid a brief return visit to Jidda, and on September 30 King Faisal met Yasir Arafat, leader of the Palestine Liberation Organization, in Beirut, Leb.

Following Saudi Arabia's recognition of the Yemen (San'a') in 1970, relations with that nation improved and several economic and cultural agreements were concluded. Relations with Yemen (Aden) remained bad, and the Saudis vigorously denied Aden's accusations that it was promoting antigovernment movements there. On January 29 the flow of Saudi oil to the Mediterranean through the Tapline resumed, after a nine-month interruption during which Syria had refused to allow the repair of minor damage to the pipeline on its territory. The stoppage had been causing Saudi Arabia an estimated loss of $1.5 million a week in royalties and transit fees. Syria's action in allowing the repair led to an improvement in relations with Damascus, and the ban that had been imposed on Syrian imports was lifted. Despite the pipeline stoppage, Saudi oil production had risen 18% in 1970. In January an agreement was reached with the oil companies to increase the Saudi share of the profits from 50 to 55%. (P. Md.)

Savings and Investment

The behaviour of savings and investment in 1971 was markedly different from what it had been in 1970 and 1969. Apart from reflecting basic changes in the economic climate, the new pattern was the result of fundamental changes in official monetary, fiscal, and, above all, exchange-rate policies pursued by the main industrial countries. Their influence became especially pronounced later in the year. On August 15, U.S. Pres. Richard Nixon announced his new economic program, which included suspension of the formal convertibility of dollars into gold, the introduction of a 10% import surcharge, and domestic measures designed to eliminate the balance of payments deficit, reduce inflation, and accelerate economic activity.

Table I. Changes in Gross National Product, Fixed Domestic Investment, Stock Building, and Foreign Balance in Selected Countries
In percent

Country	Year	Increase in GNP	Change in total fixed domestic investment	Change in stock building*	Change in foreign balance*
U.S.	1969	2.8	5.4†	0.0	−0.1
	1970	−0.4	−4.1†	−0.6	0.3
	1971‡	3.0	4.5†	0.0	0.0
Canada	1969	5.1	4.5	0.5	−0.9
	1970	3.3	1.1	−1.4	2.6
	1971‡	5.0	4.75	0.5	−0.5
U.K.	1969	2.3§	0.5	0.25	1.75
	1970	2.0§	−0.5	0.25	−0.5
	1971‡	0.5§	2.0	−0.75	−0.5
West Germany	1969	8.1	12.1	0.5	−0.5
	1970	4.9	10.7	−0.9	−1.5
	1971‡	3.5	2.25	−1.0	−0.25
France	1969	7.7§	11.4	1.0	−0.6
	1970	5.9§	7.4	−0.2	−1.2
	1971‡	5.5§	6.5	−0.25	−0.25
Italy	1969	6.1§	8.0	0.7	−0.7
	1970	5.2§	3.1	0.8	−1.7
	1971‡	3.0§	−0.5	−0.75	0.5
Japan	1969	11.9	17.3	−0.1	0.7
	1970	10.9	14.5	1.6	−0.2
	1971‡	8.0	9.0	−1.5	1.0

*As a percentage of GNP in the previous year.
†Private fixed investment.
‡All 1971 figures are estimates.
§Gross domestic product.
Source: Organization for Economic Cooperation and Development, *Economic Outlook* (July 1971).

This was followed, in December, by an agreement on the realignment of currencies among the principal trading nations: the U.S. devalued the dollar in terms of gold and rescinded the 10% surcharge; the Japanese yen and West German mark were drastically revalued; and various adjustments were made in other currencies. By altering, directly and indirectly, the relative attraction of various ways of financing investment and holding savings, these developments had a considerable effect on the volume and pattern of savings and investment. In addition, they altered the cost of capital, thus affecting the prospective appeal of and willingness to invest in real assets.

The strong cyclical upswing that characterized all the Western industrial countries in 1969 and that was associated with a large increase in fixed domestic investment and inventory buildup came to an end in 1970 and 1971, although the timing differed as between the various countries. The reversal was brought about mainly by strong countercyclical policies designed to contain inflationary pressures and, in some cases, to improve external accounts. By the end of 1971, all the major industrial countries had reversed these policies, with a view toward raising the level of economic activity and, above all, increasing investment.

In the U.S. the gradual shift toward more expansionary fiscal and monetary policies led to a recovery, starting around the turn of the year, that was particularly noticeable in housing. However, expansion in output and a downward movement in interest rates were associated with continuing pressure on costs and a deterioration in external accounts, causing the administration to introduce the drastic measures of August 15.

The stagnation of the U.S. economy in 1970 had been accompanied by a large increase in the financial surplus of the personal sector. The return to monetary ease after the spring of 1970, helped by large and growing government deficits, reversed the process, while also causing the financial institutions to add to their financial assets and liabilities on a greatly increased scale. The corporate nonfinancial sector reduced its additions to financial assets and liabilities, while the foreign sector, influenced by the large volume of repayment of short-term borrowings in the international markets following a fall in U.S. interest rates, played a less important role. These tendencies continued during 1971, except that the foreign sector moved into deficit.

In the EEC the slowdown of the cyclical expansion was gradual and limited, especially as regards the behaviour of investment and its main components, fixed domestic investment in plant and machinery, housing, additions to inventories, and foreign balance. The main elements responsible for the downturn were the weakness of fixed domestic investment, unwillingness to add to inventories, and a reduction in the foreign balance, especially marked in the case of West Germany, France, and Italy.

In West Germany the slowdown in fixed domestic investment was moderate in 1970 but started gaining momentum in the second quarter of 1971. The main elements in this process were much lower additions to inventories and foreign balance, with fixed domestic investment displaying weakness later on. In France the deceleration in investment in 1970 was particularly marked in inventory building and foreign balance. The easing of monetary policy in 1970 moderated the downward trend, but also caused the corporate nonfinancial sector to have greater recourse to external sources of finance. In Italy housing and foreign balance declined in 1970, while expenditure on

plant and equipment and spending on inventories continued to rise. This reflected the increasing degree of self-finance and the ability of industrial and commercial enterprises to raise their financial indebtedness through additional bank credit and stock exchange securities. Both Belgium and the Netherlands raised their total domestic investment in 1970, although their foreign balances came under pressure. However, in 1971 developments increasingly followed those in other European countries.

In the U.K. the tight fiscal and monetary policies followed throughout 1970 resulted in an absolute fall in domestic investment; this was due principally to a sharp decline in private and public house building, with spending on plant and equipment rising fractionally. The restrictive policies led to a large financial surplus in the public sector and a rise in the financial deficit of the corporate nonfinancial sector, causing the latter to increase its fund-raising activities from external sources at home and abroad. A gradual shift in the policies pursued by the authorities after the autumn of 1970 had no significant effect on private investment in plant and machinery in 1971, but did lead to a recovery in private housing.

In Japan the loss of momentum resulting from the restrictive policies adopted in the autumn of 1969 was limited until the spring of 1971, and was characterized by involuntary additions to stocks and a modest fall in foreign balance. The gradual reversal of tight monetary policies after the autumn of 1970

Table II. Savings and Investment in Main Industrial Countries in 1970

Country	House-holds	Enter-prises	Public sector	Financial institutions	Foreign sector	Total
U.S. (in $000,000,000)						
Gross saving	+160.4	+81.7	−19.1	+4.6	−0.7	+226.6*
Gross physical investment	−113.1	−110.0	—	−1.9	—	−226.6*
Capital transfers and adjustments	+1.0	−3.0	+2.6	−0.3	+1.3	—
Net financial saving	+48.2	−31.3	−16.6	+2.3	+0.6	—
Financial assets	−68.3	−23.1	−12.1	−105.3	−5.2	−210.8
Indebtedness	+20.2	+54.4	+28.7	+103.0	+4.6	+210.8
U.K. (in £000,000)						
Gross saving	+2,726	+1,960	+4,954	+335	—	—
Gross physical investment	−1,130	−3,580	−4,034	−596	—	—
Capital transfers and adjustments	+116	+465	−352	−76	—	—
Net financial saving	+1,712	−1,155	+568	−337	−788	+4,365
Financial assets	−3,056	−1,008	−1,618	−7,835	−2,495	−16,012
Indebtedness	+1,344	−2,163	−1,050	+8,172	+3,283	+16,012
West Germany (in DM. 000,000,000)						
Gross saving	+53.27	+61.27	+47.15	+10.32	−2.40	+189.01
Gross physical investment	—	−157.06	−29.09	−3.52	—	−189.01
Capital transfers and adjustments	−6.97	+16.32	−9.37	−0.73	+0.75	17.07
Net financial saving	+46.30	−59.41	+8.69	+6.07	−1.65	+61.75
Financial assets	−50.42	−24.40	−16.83	−111.13	−32.88	−235.01
Indebtedness	+4.12	+83.82	+8.11	+105.05	+34.53	+235.01
Italy (in 000,000,000 lire)						
Gross saving	+6,506	+6,728	−22	+550	−530	+13,222
Gross physical investment	—	−1,347	−1,665	−220	—	−13,232
Capital transfers and adjustments	—	+1,490	−1,734	−156	+21	1,228
Net financial saving	+6,506	−3,129	−3,421	+174	−509	6,836
Financial assets	−6,635	−2,869	−1,145	−12,682	−3,156	−27,487†
Indebtedness	+129	+5,998	+4,566	+12,508	+3,665	+27,487†
France (in Fr. 000,000,000)						
Gross saving	+95.32	+91.52	+16.75	+27.42	}+4.01	—
Gross physical investment	−39.59	−164.92	−20.24	−10.28		—
Capital transfers and adjustments	−24.45	+32.66	−0.11	+1.74	−9.84	—
Net financial saving	+31.28	+40.73	−3.60	+18.88	−5.83	50.16
Financial assets	−48.34	−24.35	−4.57	−109.32	−17.76	−204.33
Indebtedness	+17.07	+65.08	+8.17	+90.45	+23.58	+204.33
Japan (in 000,000,000 yen)						
Gross saving	+12.446	+10,514	+5,722	—	—	—
Gross physical investment	−7,509	−15,255	−5,693	—	—	—
Capital transfers and adjustments	+812	+231	−500	—	—	—
Net financial saving	+5,749	−4,509	−531	—	+709	+6,800
Financial assets	−10,506	−13,987	−1,964	−14,803	−839	−43,891
Indebtedness	+4,757	+18,496	+3,313	+14,803	+1,548	+43,891

Note: For gross saving, gross physical investment, and capital transfers and adjustments, + means receipts and — means expenditure; for financial assets, — means spending on assets; for indebtedness, + means increase in indebtedness.
For the U.S., public sector includes federal, state, and local governments and financial institutions includes monetary authorities, commercial banks, other private financing institutions, and government-sponsored lending agencies; for the U.K., public sector includes central government, local authorities, and public corporations; for West Germany, enterprises includes housing and public sector includes all social security funds; for Italy, public sector includes social security funds and autonomous government agencies; for Japan, public sector includes central government, local authorities, and public corporations.

*The total includes discrepancy of 1.7 in investment and −1.7 in adjustments in 1970.
†The total includes adjustment for discrepancy of −379.

Source: Organization for Economic Cooperation and Development, *Financial Statistics*, vol. 3 and supplements 3A and 3B (1971).

had not had any marked effect on investment, which was also affected adversely by the upward movement of the yen and the U.S. import surcharge, or on total output. The restrictive monetary policies followed by the Japanese authorities till the autumn of 1970 resulted in a considerable slowdown in the rate of creation of additional financial assets and liabilities on the part of financial institutions. It also increased the financial deficit of the corporate nonfinancial sector, causing it to reduce the level of its external borrowings and limiting its ability to invest in real assets.

The recessionary tendencies in the main industrial countries in 1970 and in 1971 influenced the behaviour of investment and total output in the smaller European countries, as well as developed non-European countries and the less developed countries. In Eastern Europe only three countries, the U.S.S.R., Romania, and Hungary, succeeded in raising the rate of domestic investment in 1970 above that achieved in 1969. In the remaining four, Bulgaria, Czechoslovakia, East Germany, and Poland, the rate of expansion in domestic investment slowed down, mainly as the result of policy changes placing a greater emphasis on consumption and living standards. Available evidence suggested that these trends continued during 1971.

(T. M. R.)

See also Money and Banking; Profits; Stock Exchanges.

Seismology

The San Fernando, Calif., earthquake of Feb. 9, 1971, which was of moderate strength, inflicted severe damage along the foothills of the San Gabriel Mountains and the valley floor. Deaths totaled 65, and over 2,500 hospital-treated injuries were reported. Losses to buildings and other structures were estimated at $511 million. Spectacular effects were observed at the complex of buildings at the Veterans Hospital, a nonearthquake-resistant structure constructed about 1920, where 47 lives were lost, and at the recently dedicated Olive View Hospital-Medical Treatment and Care Building, which was designed as earthquake resistive.

Wood-frame houses and light industrial buildings performed very well. High-rise earthquake-resistive buildings, located 15 to 25 mi. from the epicentre, suffered more damage than adjacent low-rise construction. The Pacoima Dam suffered considerable damage and was the site of the largest ground acceleration—approximately one unit of gravity—ever recorded. The 56-year-old Van Norman Dam was severely damaged, necessitating the evacuation of 80,000 residents. The National Research Council, in summarizing the effects of this earthquake and making recommendations to cope with future disasters, gave serious warnings about the effects of severe earthquakes in urban areas. This had been emphasized by an earlier federal report indicating that a major earthquake in a metropolitan area has a loss potential of $20 billion.

Charles A. Whitten, chief geodesist of the National Ocean Survey, U.S. Department of Commerce, found "a definite correlation" between the earth's wobble and earthquakes. The earth wobbles slightly as it spins in space, so that the north-south polar axis on which it rotates shifts. This shift, as measured by astronomers, is such that the axis zigs and zags around the geographic North Pole in a generally circular motion, shifting as much as six inches per day for a maximum of 72 ft. over a 14-month period. The daily shift of the pole reaches its maximum every seven years, with 1971 as a peak year. The earth's wobble is not considered the sole cause of earthquakes, but as working in combination with such forces as the shifting of the earth as strain builds up beneath the surface and the pull exerted by the moon and sun.

In the past, Japanese builders refused to construct very tall buildings in Japan because of the heavy toll in property and lives from earthquakes. Two major advances in design have changed all this. One is a newly developed computer model that allows engineers to see what effect earthquakes will have on their proposed designs. The other is the development of a slitted, reinforced-concrete wall that, in combination with the main structural frame of the building, provides a high degree of stiffness even for normal tremors. Furthermore, if a severe earthquake strikes, these new walls will reduce the rigidity and the forces acting on the building. Two asbestos sheets are used as spacers in the wall to make a slit. Both the concrete and the reinforcing bars are made discontinuous at the slits, so that the wall becomes a series of vertical columns separated at the slits.

Earthquake lightning is a phenomenon associated with great earthquakes in some parts of the world, such as Japan, New Zealand, and India. The only causal connection that seems possible is that the seismic strains of the earthquake somehow cause an electric field in the air, which in turn produces ball lightning. U.S. scientists attempted to explain the mechanism of this seismoelectric effect as the piezoelectric condition of the earth's crust. They have found that the only significant piezoelectric constituent of the crust is quartz. The mere presence of quartz is not sufficient, however; it must be the right kind of long-range crystalline texture, and the range must be about 2 km. (the wavelength of certain seismic waves). Such crystals must exist in a single tectonic unit, and at relevant temperatures a large percentage of the crystals must line up in the prin-

Map shows San Andreas fault and related faults in California. The Feb. 9, 1971, earthquake in San Fernando, which killed 65 persons and caused extensive damage to buildings, dams, and highways, occurred along a fault line near Los Angeles.

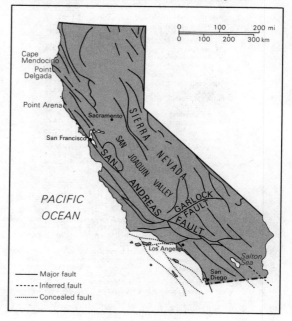

cipal stress direction. Under such conditions the generated voltage may be comparable to that responsible for lightning in storms. The piezoelectric conditions of the quartz in the North Idu Peninsula of Japan are ideally suited for the generation of seismoelectricity, and this was confirmed by over 1,500 sightings of lightning associated with the major North Idu earthquake of Nov. 26, 1930. There is a tradition in Japan of predicting earthquakes from unusual clear-sky lightning.

Plate tectonics, a theory that the earth's surface consists of a small number of rigid plates in motion relative to each other, has gained wide acceptance during the past five years. Plate motions and interactions are thought to be responsible for the present positions of the continents, for the formation of many of the world's mountain ranges, and for all major earthquakes. The driving mechanism for the motion of these plates may have a number of sources. The energy may come from heat released by the radioactive decay of uranium, thorium, and potassium in the mantle. Thermal convection can occur in a fluid heated from below, and over long periods of time the mantle can behave like a fluid. Another mechanism depends on the assumption that the weight of the relatively cold surface plate descending in a trench into the warmer and less dense material of the mantle would help to pull along behind the portion of the plate still in the earth's surface. A third mechanism is based on the assumption that the convection is occurring deep within the lower mantle. The plates may be driven by a small number of hot spots that represent convection plumes rising from the lower mantle. Despite the uncertainties about the driving mechanism, plate tectonics has had a remarkably unifying effect on the earth sciences and has stimulated renewed activity in continental as well as marine geology. (L. M. M.)

See also Disasters.

Senegal

A republic of northwestern Africa, Senegal is bounded by Mauritania, Mali, Guinea, and Portuguese Guinea, and by the Atlantic Ocean. The independent nation of The Gambia forms an enclave within the country. Area: 76,124 sq.mi. (197,161 sq.km.). Pop. (1970 est.): 3,925,000. Cap. and largest city: Dakar (pop., 1970 est., 580,-000). Language: French (official); Wolof; Serer;

SENEGAL
Education. (1966–67) Primary, pupils 231,146, teachers 4,509; secondary, pupils 30,270, teachers 861; vocational, pupils 11,270, teachers 432; teacher training, students 821, teachers (1965–66) 80; higher (including University of Dakar), students 3,338, teaching staff (1965–66) 230.
Finance and Trade. Monetary unit: CFA franc, with a parity of CFA Fr. 50 to the French franc (CFA Fr. 277.71 = U.S. $1; CFA Fr. 666.50 = £1 sterling) and a free rate (Sept. 27, 1971) of CFA Fr. 276.50 to U.S. $1 (CFA Fr. 685.75 = £1 sterling). Budget (1970–71 est.) balanced at CFA Fr. 39 billion. Foreign trade (1970): imports CFA Fr. 53,560,000,000; exports CFA Fr. 42,180,000,000. Import sources (1969): France 40%; West Germany 11%; U.S. 6%; Ivory Coast 5%. Export destinations (1969): France 60%; Netherlands 5%. Main exports: peanuts and peanut oil 48%; phosphates 8%.

other tribal dialects. Religion: Muslim 90%; Christian 6%. President in 1971, Léopold Sédar Senghor; premier, Abdou Diouf.

After a period of domestic tension early in 1971, there was a marked relaxation later in the year. In January several bomb and incendiary attacks were carried out in Dakar by extreme left-wing elements. Dakar University was closed in February after disturbances there, and trouble broke out again in March and April. However, in October several imprisoned labour union leaders were released and there were plans for freeing former president Mamadou Dia, serving a life sentence for conspiracy.

In February and March President Senghor, who planned to be a candidate for chairman of the Organization of African Unity, received visits from the leaders of two of the major black African states: Pres. Joseph Mobutu of the Congo (Kinshasa; later renamed Zaire) and Maj. Gen. Yakubu Gowon of Nigeria. Also in February, Pres. Georges Pompidou of France spent two days in Dakar.

During the year President Senghor made determined efforts to establish closer links with neighbouring states, particularly Mauritania and The Gambia. Relations with Guinea became progressively worse. Guinean Pres. Sékou Touré claimed that Senegalese territory was being used as a base by forces planning aggression against his country. Senegal's refusal to repatriate Guinean insurgents and the arrest of five Guinean spies in Dakar further aggravated the situation. Disputes of this kind had so paralyzed the Organization of Senegal River States (Guinea, Senegal, Mauritania, and Mali) that Senegal contemplated leaving the organization. During an official visit to the Ivory Coast in December, President Senghor announced that an eight-nation Economic Community of West Africa would be formed in the near future. (Ph. D.)

Sierra Leone

A republic within the Commonwealth of Nations, Sierra Leone is a West African nation located between Guinea and Liberia. Area: 27,699 sq.mi. (71,740 sq.km.). Pop. (1970 est.): 2,550,000, including (1963) Mende and Temne tribes 60.7%; other tribes 38.9%; non-African 0.4%. Cap. and largest city: Freetown (pop., 1970 est., 178,600). Language: English (official); tribal dialects. Religion: animist 66%; Muslim 28%; Christian 6%. To April 19, 1971: queen, Elizabeth II; governors-general, to March 31 Justice Banja Tejan-Sie and to April 19 Justice Christopher Okoro Cole; prime minister and, from April 21, president, Siaka Stevens; prime minister from April 21, Sorie Ibrahim Koroma.

Following an abortive army coup and two assassination attempts on Prime Minister Siaka Stevens on March 23, Guinean armed forces entered Sierra Leone at Stevens' request to safeguard the position of the government in accordance with the defense agreement of March 26 by which the armies of the two countries "became one." Although Soviet sources blamed the revolt on imperialist displeasure at the government's take-over of diamond mining, its sources lay in tribal dissension and Army fears of Communist links with Guinea, whose forces were reputed to be in Freetown before the attempted coup. Prime Minister Stevens was believed to be recruiting Limba tribesmen for training in Guinea, while the governor-

SIERRA LEONE
Education. (1968–69) Primary, pupils 139,412, teachers 4,772; secondary, pupils 25,207, teachers 1,202; vocational, pupils 1,732, teachers 97; teacher training, students 901, teachers 101; higher, students 837, teaching staff 192.

Finance and Trade. Monetary unit: leone, with a parity of 0.83 leones to U.S. $1 (2 leones = £1 sterling) and a free rate (Sept. 27, 1971) of 0.81 leones to U.S. $1. Budget (1970–71 est.): revenue 51 million leones; expenditure 46.3 million leones. Foreign trade (1970): imports 96,960,000 leones; exports 85,550,-000 leones. Import sources (1969): U.K. 31%; Japan 10%; U.S. 8%; West Germany 5%. Export destinations (1969): U.K. 71%; Netherlands 8%. Main exports: diamonds 62%; iron ore 12%; palm kernels 8%.

Agriculture. Production (in 000; metric tons; 1970; 1969 in parentheses): rice c. 425 (407); cassava (1969) c. 65, (1968) c. 63; palm oil c. 50 (c. 46); coffee c. 6.3 (c. 4.5). Livestock (in 000; 1969–70): cattle c. 240; sheep c. 57; goats c. 156; chickens c. 2,900.

Industry. Production (in 000; metric tons; 1969): iron ore (metal content) c. 1,800; bauxite 445; diamonds (metric carats) 1,937; electricity (kw-hr.; 1969) 144,400.

SINGAPORE
Education. (1968–69) Primary, pupils 371,970, teachers 12,422; secondary, pupils 127,927, teachers 5,319; vocational, pupils 24,913, teachers 1,509; higher (including 3 universities), students 12,447, teaching staff 982.

Finance and Trade. Monetary unit: Singapore dollar, with a par value of Sing$3.06 to U.S. $1 (Sing$7.35 = £1 sterling) and a free rate (Sept. 27, 1971) of Sing$2.97 to U.S. $1. Budget (1970–71 est.): revenue Sing$1,041,200,000; expenditure Sing$1,040,900,000. Foreign trade (1970): imports Sing$7,533,800,000; exports Sing$4,755,800,000. Import sources (1969): Japan 19%; Malaysia 19%; U.S. 11%; China 5%; Kuwait 5%; Australia 5%. Export destinations (1969): Malaysia 22%; U.S. 11%; Japan 8%; South Vietnam 7%; U.K. 7%. Main exports: rubber 25%; petroleum products 17%; machinery 8%; coffee and spices 5%.

Transport and Communications. Roads (1970) 1,912 km. Motor vehicles in use (1969): passenger 135,600; commercial (including buses) 32,400. Railways (1969) 39 km. Railway and air traffic: see MALAYSIA. Shipping (1970): merchant vessels 100 gross tons and over 153; gross tonnage 424,417; goods loaded 15,794,000 metric tons, unloaded 26,864,000 metric tons. Telephones (Dec. 1969) 136,267. Radio receivers (Dec. 1969) 202,000. Television receivers (Dec. 1969) 131,000.

general, Justice Banja Tejan-Sie, himself a Temne, was relieved of his post for "planning subversion."

On April 19 Sierra Leone, celebrating the tenth anniversary of its independence, declared itself a republic. Constitutional changes approved by Parliament abolished appeal to the Judicial Committee of the Privy Council and converted Stevens into an executive president for a five-year term. Sorie Ibrahim Koroma, appointed vice-president, automatically became prime minister and leader of the House.

Political turmoil together with a decline in diamond prices depressed the economy, while the departure of many senior officials impaired the efficiency of administration. Reassurance for foreign investors, necessary for any diversification of the economy away from dependence on diamonds, was slow and the closing of the rutile mining operations proved a setback for developing other mineral assets.

(M. MR.)

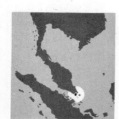

Singapore

Singapore, a republic within the Commonwealth of Nations, occupies a group of islands, the largest of which is Singapore, at the southern extremity of the Malay Peninsula. Area: 226 sq.mi. (584 sq.km.). Pop. (1970): 2,074,507, including 76% Chinese, 15% Malays, and 7% Indians. Language: official languages are English, Malay, Mandarin Chinese, and Tamil. Religion: Malays are Muslim; Chinese, mainly Buddhist; Indians, mainly Hindu. President in 1971, Benjamin Henry Sheares; prime minister, Lee Kuan Yew.

Benjamin Henry Sheares (see BIOGRAPHY), elected by Parliament on Dec. 30, 1970, was installed as president on Jan. 2, 1971, for a four-year term, succeeding Pres. Yusof bin Ishak, who had died on Nov. 23, 1970. During January, Singapore was host to the annual conference of Commonwealth heads of state and of government—the first such conference to be held in an Asian country.

At midnight on October 31, 152 years of British military presence in Singapore came to an end. The 14-year-old Anglo-Malaysian Defence Treaty, which also covered Singapore and which had automatically committed Britain to the defense of the region, terminated, and in its place a five-power defense arrangement involving Britain, Australia, New Zealand,

Malaysia, and Singapore as equal partners came into force. The new arrangement provided for the physical presence in the area of British, Australian, and New Zealand (ANZUK) forces—ground and naval in Singapore and air defense in Butterworth, northern Malaysia—with an Australian in command. There also came into force a five-power integrated air defense system. The closing of the huge British Far East Command bases meant the reversion of nearly one-tenth of Singapore's land area to the Singapore government.

In domestic politics the creation of the People's Front and the National Party of Singapore gave the republic 15 political parties, although only a few were active. In Parliament there was no opposition and the People's Action Party of Prime Minister Lee Kuan Yew occupied all the 58 seats.

Despite the phasing out of the British bases, economic growth of 15% in 1970 maintained the unprecedented rate achieved in 1968 and 1969. The gross national product rose by more than 50% from Sing$3,692,000,000 in 1967 to Sing$5,565,000,000 in 1970, and per capita income rose by 17.6% to Sing$2,620. Official overseas assets increased from Sing$2,278,900,000 to Sing$3,556,400,000 over the same period. The accelerated pace of development caused a shortage of labour and skills. The unemployment figure, at 21,000, was the lowest in years, and 53,000 work permits were issued to outsiders, mainly Malaysians. More than one-third of the growth output in domestic product in 1971 was in manufacturing, and industries were beginning gradually to move from import substitution toward the more promising field of exporting.

(M. S. R.)

Skiing

The continued increase in mechanical means of mountain ascent during 1971 brought a considerably greater acreage of suitable snow terrain within more practicable reach of skiers. Membership in the International Ski Federation (FIS) rose to 50 nations, more than two-thirds possessing their own recognized holiday ski centres. Typical of the expanding worldwide interest was activity in the tiny autonomous principality of Andorra, where new facilities for ski fields on the Pyrenees were likely to give serious competition to neighbouring Spanish and French resorts.

For most of the year a shadow lingered over all Olympic trainees while the FIS tried to reach agreement with the International Olympic Committee (IOC) concerning amateur status for eligibility purposes. The situation grew tense when the IOC declared several prominent Alpine racers to be ineligible after they accepted payment for coaching. This sparked a threat from leading ski nations to boycott the 1972 Winter Olympics at Sapporo, Jap., but, after clarified eligibility rules were agreed upon by the FIS at its 28th congress on May 26–30 at Opatija, Yugos., it seemed likely that the Olympic program would be kept intact.

Alpine Racing. In a season without the biennial world championships, major interest switched to the fifth annual World Alpine Ski Cup series, experiencing its best-supported year to date. After 23 men's and 24 women's events contested in a four-month circuit on two continents, North America and Europe, the overall winners were a 20-year-old Italian, Gustavo Thoeni, and a 17-year-old Austrian, Annemarie Proell. Their successes underlined not just the technical ability but the sustained consistency of form required throughout the season.

Thoeni headed three Frenchmen, Henri Duvillard, Patrick Russel, and Jean-Noël Augert, in the final standings, placing second to Augert in the slalom and second to Russel in the giant slalom. Bernhard Russi (Switz.) was top scorer in the downhill, in which Thoeni finished 13th. Gaining a record number of women's points, Miss Proell proved best in both downhill and giant slalom, withstanding powerful pressures from two French girls, Michèle Jacot and Isabelle Mir, overall second and third respectively. Britt Lafforgue (France) and Betsy Clifford (Can.) tied for first in the slalom.

Racing conditions in the European Alps were seriously affected by an unseasonable scarcity of snow, which caused the cancellation of some senior competitions and the last-minute transferring of others to sites at higher altitudes. Because of the dearth of snow, the downhill races originally scheduled as part of the classic Arlberg-Kandahar meeting, first run in 1928 and now an important part of the World Cup circuit, were held outside Europe for the first time, moving from Mürren, Switz., to the U.S. courses at Sugarloaf Mountain in Maine.

A new Canadian-American Ski Trophy competition series, patterned after the World Cup, had a successful inaugural season. Both the men's and women's victors were U.S. skiers, Lance Poulsen and Karen Budge. From a good start, Poulsen managed to stay ahead of the Norwegian runner-up, Otto Tschudi, one of the few Europeans competing. Miss Budge narrowly defeated Judy Crawford of Canada.

Something of a record was established by an American family, the Cochrans—Bob, 19, and his three sisters, Marilyn, 21, Barbara Ann, 20, and Lindy, 18. Three were on the U.S. national team and the youngest, Lindy, was on the fringe of it in the training squad.

Spider Sabich of Kyburz, Calif., won the world professional championship at Vail, Colo., on March 20–21. He also won the Lange Cup and netted $21,188 prize money during nine meetings, all held in North America after difficulties in the planning of some events for Europe. It was the first really successful professional racing season, following trial-and-error experimentation in previous years.

A feature of professional racing, parallel skiing, was designed with spectator appeal particularly in mind. Slalom and giant slalom events were staged on a knockout principle, one competitor pitted against another, each racing down similar-style and roughly parallel courses. Each match between two racers was determined by an agreed number of runs, opponents swapping courses for each descent.

Nordic Events. In ski jumping probably the season's best criterion for predicting success in the 1972 Winter Olympic Games was the annual Four Hills tournament, during the New Year period at Oberstdorf and Garmisch-Partenkirchen, W.Ger., and Innsbruck and Bischofshofen, Aus. The overall winner was the Czechoslovak 1968 Olympic gold medalist, Jiri Raska, who gained his first victory in this event in nine attempts, with Ingolf Mørk (Nor.) runner-up and Zbynek Hubac (Czech.) third. Jerry Martin, the U.S. national ski jumping champion, extended by five feet the North American distance record for 90-m. hills with a jump of 345 ft. at Iron Mountain, Mich.

King Olav V of Norway was among more than 100,000 spectators at the 79th Holmenkollen meeting, near Oslo, on March 11–14. Gerhard Grimmer (E.Ger.) won the 50-km. cross-country marathon by an impressive margin of nearly seven minutes. Osmo Karjalainen, a Finnish lumberjack, took the 15 km. Another Finn, Rauno Miettinen, won the Nordic combination event, and the 80-m. Holmenkollen jump winner was Mørk, whose consistency throughout the season seemed a good omen for the Olympics. The women's cross-country honours went to Finns, coached by Toini Gustafsson for the events she once dominated. Marjatta Kajosmaa and Helena Takalo finished first and second in the 10 km. and were members of the winning 15-km. relay team.

The 48th annual Vasa 53½-mi. cross-country race, the world's longest, from Salen to Mora, Swed., in March, was won by Ole Ellefsaeter, a Norwegian. Ellefsaeter was only the second non-Swede to win this unique double marathon, in which 15 countries were represented by 611 competitors.   (H. B.)

French skier Jean-Noël Augert won the slalom in the fifth annual World Alpine Ski Cup series in 1971.

A.F.P.—PICTORIAL PARADE

Social Services

The general trend in 1971 was for countries to stabilize and improve their existing social welfare schemes. In the U.K. and Canada new provisions were made, especially for the elderly. Among international conferences, the International Council on Social Welfare (ICSW) held its first Asian conference of ministers of social welfare in Manila in September 1970. It was recommended that social welfare planning should be undertaken alongside economic and physical planning and that, because of the great shortage of trained social manpower, other related professions should undertake social work. To speed up development in member countries, it was agreed that there should be region-wide cooperation in formulating policies. It was suggested that an Asian conference of ministers be held every four years, alternating with the ICSW's biennial international conference.

United Kingdom. The Family Income Supplements Act 1970 introduced a new social security benefit for families with small incomes where the breadwinner worked full-time and there were dependent children. Family benefit was payable if a family with one child had an income of less than £15 a week, and this amount increased by £2 for each additional child. The benefit was one half of the difference between this minimum and actual earnings, subject to a limit of £3. These figures would be increased by ministerial regulations. There was to be a simple test of normal gross income at the time of the claim and, when established, benefit would continue for 26 weeks irrespective of any change in circumstances. It was estimated that nearly 190,000 households with about 500,000 children would be helped at a cost of some £8 million a year. The only previous instance in England of supplementation of wages from public funds for a person in full-time work had been more than a century before when parish relief was available for rural workers with low earnings.

Under the National Insurance Act 1971, benefits, including pensions, were increased from £5 to £6 for a single person and from £8.10 to £9.70 for a married couple. The earnings rule was modified to enable a retirement pensioner to earn £9.50 a week instead of £7.50 before pension was abated by earnings. The increment for deferred retirement was increased from 5 to 6 pence a week for every nine flat-rate contributions paid. An improvement was also made in the pensions of those over 80 who, the previous year, had been granted pensions although they had not contributed under the national insurance scheme. The new attendance allowance for the severely disabled was increased from £4 to £4.80 and was to be tax free. For those who were incapable of work and continuously chronically sick for six months or more, there would be an invalidity pension at the standard national insurance rate, plus an invalidity allowance for those becoming sick more than five years before pension age. Another improvement was the provision of an increase in the retirement pension of anyone over 80 by 25 pence a week, and there was also to be an increase of 25 pence in the long-term addition to supplementary benefit. The cost of implementing the act was estimated at £537 million in the first full year. It was to be financed mainly by increasing the percentage rate of the graduated contributions paid by employers and employees on earnings over £18 a week from 3.25 to 4.35%. There was to be no increase in the flat-rate contributions.

On average, the number of benefits and allowances (including supplementary benefits) being paid in any week in 1970 was about 17 million, somewhat more than half to retirement pensioners. At the end of the year there were about 25 million persons within the scope of the contribution provisions of the national insurance scheme, of whom nearly 15 million were employed men and over 8 million were employed women. Of these about 4.75 million men and nearly one million women were paying graduated contributions. Flat-rate contributions were being paid by employers and insured persons at the rate of about £3,860 million a year. At the end of 1970, 69% of old people, 12% of the sick, and 9% of the unemployed were receiving supplementary benefits. It was estimated that at the end of 1970, 19.5% of beneficiaries were receiving unemployment benefit (compared with 22.5% in 1969), 15% were receiving sickness benefit (14%), 27.5% were receiving retirement pensions (27.7%), and 16.3% were receiving widows' benefits (16.3%).

The proposals in the bill introduced by the former Labour government for general alterations in the social security scheme were not adopted by the new Conservative government. In September 1971 a White Paper was published setting out Conservative proposals for the provision of a pension fund with about 7 million members and assets of about £5,000 million by the end of the century. The Reserve Pension scheme, as it was to be called, was designed to give a form of earnings-related pension to employees who could not join an occupational pension scheme or whose occupational scheme was not considered to be satisfactory. The new fund would start in April 1975. The national insurance scheme would remain largely in its existing form, with improved fringe benefits for people in need. The payment of both flat-rate and graduated contributions would be abolished; instead, there would be a new scheme of wholly graduated contributions collected through the income tax Pay As You Earn (PAYE) machinery. Nonemployed per-

Social worker encourages children to use practical toys at an after-school play centre associated with St. Anns Community Craft Centre, Nottingham, Eng. The community centre, established by a group of young social workers, provides free assistance to needy people.

LONDON "DAILY EXPRESS"—PICTORIAL PARADE

sons would be able to opt out of continued contributions if they so wished, but those who wished to qualify for full state pension would be able to continue payments. The existing graduated pension scheme would be abandoned, but graduated pension rights earned up to 1975 would be preserved and paid with the basic pension on retirement.

Following the practice of other large voluntary organizations, the National Old People's Welfare Council adopted the cover name of Age Concern. The training of voluntary and paid staff employed by old people's welfare committees continued to be a primary activity of the council. A study of voluntary visiting of old people was conducted for Political and Economic Planning (PEP) and sponsored by the council and the Department of Health and Social Security. The need for efficient paid organizers was found to be paramount, so that voluntary helpers could be used to the full.

Norway. The State Insurance Office assumed responsibility for all social security schemes. The single contribution by an insured person amounted to a tax of 4½% on all earnings up to a fixed limit, with 13% paid by the employer. Self-employed persons paid 9.75%. The basic retirement pension was fixed at 7,-200 kroner a year for a single person (about $20 a week) and 10,800 kroner (about $30 a week) for a married couple. The rate was to be increased or reduced according to changes in the cost of living index. Retirement pensioners received certain concessions, including the right to travel at half rates on public transport and reduced fares on inland air services at offpeak and nonholiday periods.　　　(JN. M.)

United States. After a decade of expansion and liberalization of welfare programs, several states moved to reduce benefits and tighten eligibility, and national welfare rolls began to decline. Congressional consideration of Pres. Richard Nixon's controversial welfare reform legislation was delayed. At the same time, the year saw a rise in Social Security benefits, passage by Congress of a comprehensive federal program of subsidized child care (subsequently vetoed by President Nixon), and the start of congressional debate on a national health care program.

A measure setting a $1,600 national income floor for a family of four had been passed by the House of Rep-

Social Security Programs, by Country, 1971*

Type of program available

Country	Old age, invalidity, survivors	Health, sickness, maternity	Work injury	Unemployment	Family allowances
Afghanistan			X		
Albania	X	X	X		X
Algeria	X	X	X		X
Argentina	X	X	X	X	X
Australia	X	X	X	X	X
Austria	X	X	X	X	X
Barbados	X	X	X		
Belgium	X	X	X	X	X
Bolivia	X	X	X		X
Botswana			X		
Brazil	X	X	X	X	X
Bulgaria	X	X	X	X	X
Burma		X	X		
Burundi	X		X		
Cambodia			X		X
Cameroon	X	X	X		X
Canada	X	X	X	X	X
Central African Rep.	X	X	X		X
Ceylon	X	X	X		
Chad			X		X
Chile	X	X	X	X	X
China	X	X	X		
Colombia	X	X	X		X
Congo (Brazzaville)	X	X	X		X
Congo (Kinshasa)	X	X	X		X
Costa Rica	X	X	X		
Cuba	X	X	X		
Cyprus	X	X	X	X	
Czechoslovakia	X	X	X		X
Dahomey	X	X	X		X
Denmark	X	X	X	X	X
Dominican Rep.	X	X	X		
Ecuador	X	X	X	X	
Egypt	X	X	X	X	
El Salvador	X	X	X		
Ethiopia			X		
Finland	X	X	X	X	X
France	X	X	X	X	X
Gabon	X		X		X
Gambia, The			X		
Germany, East	X	X	X	X	X
Germany, West	X	X	X	X	X
Ghana	X		X		
Greece	X	X	X	X	X
Guatemala	X	X	X		
Guinea	X	X	X		X
Guyana	X	X	X		
Haiti	X		X		
Honduras			X		
Hungary	X	X	X	X	X
Iceland	X	X	X	X	X
India	X	X	X		
Indonesia			X		X
Iran	X	X	X		
Iraq	X	X	X		
Ireland	X	X	X	X	X
Israel	X	X	X		X
Italy	X	X	X	X	X
Ivory Coast	X	X	X		X
Jamaica	X		X		
Japan	X	X	X	X	
Jordan			X		
Kenya	X	X	X		
Korea, South					
Lebanon	X	X	X		X
Liberia	X		X		
Libya	X	X	X		
Luxembourg	X	X	X	X	X
Malagasy Rep.	X	X	X		X
Malawi			X		
Malaysia	X	X	X		
Mali	X	X	X		X
Malta	X	X	X	X	
Mauritania	X	X	X		X
Mauritius	X		X		X
Mexico	X	X	X		
Morocco	X	X	X		X
Nauru	X		X		X
Netherlands	X	X	X	X	X
New Zealand	X	X	X	X	X
Nicaragua	X	X	X		
Niger	X		X		X
Nigeria	X	X	X		
Norway	X	X	X	X	X
Pakistan		X	X		
Panama	X	X	X		
Paraguay	X	X	X		
Peru	X	X	X		
Philippines	X	X	X		
Poland	X	X	X		X
Portugal	X	X	X		X
Romania	X	X	X		
Rwanda	X		X		
Saudi Arabia	X		X		
Senegal		X	X		X
Sierra Leone			X		
Singapore	X	X	X		
Somalia			X		
South Africa	X		X	X	X
Spain	X	X	X	X	X
Sudan			X		
Swaziland			X		
Sweden	X	X	X	X	X
Switzerland	X	X	X	X	X
Syria	X		X		
Taiwan	X	X	X		
Tanzania	X		X		
Thailand			X		
Togo	X	X	X		X
Trinidad and Tobago	X		X		X
Tunisia		X	X		X
Turkey	X	X	X		
Uganda	X		X		
U.S.S.R.	X	X	X		X
United Kingdom	X	X	X	X	X
United States	X	X	X	X	
Upper Volta	X	X	X		X
Uruguay	X	X	X	X	X
Venezuela	X	X	X		
Vietnam, North	X		X		X
Vietnam, South		X	X		X
Western Samoa	X		X		
Yugoslavia	X	X	X	X	X
Zambia	X		X		

*Data as of mid-1971.
Source: U.S. Department of Health, Education, and Welfare, Social Security Administration, Office of Research and Statistics, *Social Security Programs Throughout the World.*

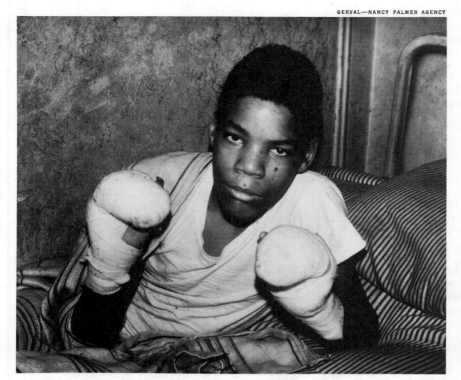

Willie Holland, a member of one of 115 welfare families housed in New York's Kimberly Hotel, displays his bandaged hands after he fell through an apparently faulty elevator door; he was able to grab the cables and slide down 17 floors. Willie's six-year-old brother was killed in a similar fall.

resentatives in 1970, but was blocked in the Senate. On June 22, 1971, the House of Representatives, by 288–132, passed a new welfare reform bill, which had been shaped to a large extent by Rep. Wilbur Mills (Dem., Ark.), but again the legislation received a less enthusiastic reception in the Senate. It suffered a further setback when President Nixon, as part of his new economic policy budget restrictions, called for a one-year postponement in the starting date of the new welfare program—to July 1, 1973. As a result, final action on the measure was put off until 1972.

As passed by the House, the welfare reform bill was in some ways more ambitious than the 1970 version and in other ways more restrictive. Its key section provided for replacing the existing federal-state welfare structure with two programs—the Family Assistance Plan (FAP) and the Opportunities for Families Program (OFP). These would shift the major burden of costs from states to the federal government and would provide a nationally uniform system of minimum cash grants to families who met federal standards of eligibility.

Under FAP, families with no outside income would receive assistance at the rate of $800 for each of their first two members, $400 each for the next three, $300 each for the next two, plus $200 for the next family member. Thus, a family of four would be guaranteed $2,400 a year, and the maximum payment to any family of eight or more would be $3,600. If one or both parents had marginal income, the family would receive decreasing federal assistance, which would vanish when the total earnings reached $4,320 a year for a family of four. Families with an employable adult would be assigned to the Opportunities for Families Program under the Department of Labor. Every employable member of the family would have to register for work or work training, except those who were ill, incapacitated, under 16, or a mother with a child under 6. A variety of supportive programs was authorized to assist employable adults, including child care, public service employment, and manpower training

and placement. The bill also contained changes in Social Security, Medicare, and other programs.

The welfare reform bill came under fire from both conservatives and liberals. The former objected to the basic concept of an income floor and to what they considered the costliness of the proposal. The latter charged that benefit levels were inadequate (the National Welfare Rights Organization lobbied for a $6,500 minimum); that many poor people might actually get less than at present if states reduced their contributions as federal funds increased; and that the work requirements would delay benefits, harass innocent citizens, and destroy family life.

In a surprise move, the "workfare" portion of the administration bill was enacted into law by Congress just before adjournment. Effective July 1, 1972, all recipients of benefits under Aid to Families of Dependent Children would have to register for work or training unless they were under 16, ill or elderly, mothers of children under 6, or required to care for an incapacitated person at home. The federal government would finance 100% of the public service jobs for employable adults in the first year, 75% in the second, and 50% in the third, and would pay 90% of the cost of day care or other baby-sitting services for children of working mothers.

An across-the-board increase in Social Security benefits did go into effect in 1971. In March Congress approved a 10% rise in Old Age, Survivors, and Disability benefits, retroactive to Jan. 1, 1971, for 27.4 million persons. This raised the minimum monthly payment to individuals from $64 to $70.40 and to couples from $96 to $105.60. The measure also provided a 5% increase in special benefits payable to individuals 72 years old and over who were not insured for regular benefits. The increases were to be financed by raising the base wage on which payroll taxes are assessed. That wage was $7,800 in 1971 and would go up to $9,000 in 1972. The tax rate would remain the same —5.2% each for employers and employees and 7.5% for self-employed individuals covered by Social Security. The law set up a table of gradual future rate increases for employers and employees, reaching 6.05% in 1987. The effect of the changes for wage-earners was that the maximum tax in 1972 would be $468, compared with $405.60 in 1971. By 1987 the maximum under the law would be $544.50. All rates were subject to future readjustments to guarantee enough revenue for the Social Security trust fund, and they would go up if Congress approved further benefit increases as part of welfare reform.

While the future federal role in welfare remained uncertain, many states moved in 1971 to cut back public assistance programs. A survey by the *New York Times* indicated that at least 19 states—including California and New York, which had two of the most liberal welfare programs—had acted to tighten relief rolls and cut costs. The steps came as total national spending for welfare reached $16.3 billion in the fiscal year ended June 30, 1971, an increase of 27% over the preceding 12 months and four times the outlay of 1961. A total of 14.3 milllion persons were on welfare at the end of fiscal 1971, 17% more than a year before. It was not known how much of the increase was due to increased unemployment.

Some of the methods employed by states included: a requirement that able-bodied recipients take non-paying public works jobs and pick up their checks in person rather than by mail; stiffer eligibility rules and more rigid investigations to screen out ineligibles; lower grants to families with outside incomes; a requirement that relatives of welfare recipients share support costs when possible. For the first time in three years, the total number of persons on state welfare rolls showed a decrease during the year. According to the latest available figures declines were reported in May, June, and July, after average monthly increases of about 2% earlier in the year.

In a ruling that was interpreted as another setback to liberalized welfare, the U.S. Supreme Court held, 6–3, that welfare caseworkers could insist on going inside recipients' homes to check on their eligibility and could halt payments to persons who refused admission. On the other hand, the court also held that states cannot deny welfare benefits to needy persons solely because they are aliens, to dependent children who are attending college, or to the mother of an illegitimate child because she refuses to divulge the name of the father.

Congress passed a $2.1 billion program of comprehensive, quality child care for millions of preschool children from low- and middle-income families, but the measure was vetoed by President Nixon and Congress upheld the veto. Under the proposal, a variety of services, including educational, nutritional, psychiatric, and health care, would have been provided free to children from very poor families and at graduated costs for families with higher incomes. In vetoing the measure, Nixon said it was administratively unworkable, fiscally irresponsible, and would weaken the family role in child rearing.

In a preview of what was likely to emerge as one of the most hotly contested social welfare and political issues of 1972, Congress began hearings in 1971 on the nation's health care system. At least a dozen bills proposing changes and reforms in health care delivery and financing were introduced in Congress. Behind the increasing demand for action were two major factors: the soaring costs of medical care—the most rapidly rising commodity on the U.S. cost-of-living index —and the feeling that, in spite of the huge outlays, high quality medical care was not available to all Americans. (*See* MEDICINE: *Special Report*.)

The bills that were introduced in Congress varied greatly in their approach to the problem, their price tag, and the degree to which they would change the existing system. Of the three proposals receiving the most attention, the administration bill would require employers to provide private health insurance for all workers and their families and would provide less comprehensive, federally operated health insurance for low-income families out of general tax revenues. The Kennedy-Griffiths Bill, a plan backed by organized labour, would use a combination of general tax revenues and payroll taxes to underwrite almost all major health care costs for all Americans. Medicredit, a measure sponsored by the American Medical Association, would offer income tax credits toward the purchase of health insurance from private companies. The government would pay the entire cost of premiums for the very poor.

The role of social welfare programs in the U.S. was underscored during the year by a report issued by the Census Bureau. According to the bureau, the number of poor persons in the U.S. had increased 5% in 1970, reversing a ten-year downward trend. There were 25.5 million poor persons in the U.S. at the end of the year, an increase of 1.2 million over 1969. A major factor was increased unemployment. Although poor whites outnumbered poor blacks 17.5 million to 7.7 million, one Negro in three lived in poverty, compared with one white in ten. The poverty level was defined as $3,968 for a family of four for 1970.

(D. ME.)

Canada. A White Paper on Unemployment Insurance published in June 1970 put forward major changes, including the extension of coverage to additional workers—totaling up to 96% of the labour force—the addition of sickness and maternity benefits, and substantial improvement of unemployment benefits. Some benefits would be payable after only 8 weeks of employment in the last year, and all benefits were payable after 20 weeks of employment; previously 30 weeks of contributions in the last two years were required. Benefits were to be raised to 66⅔% (75% in exceptional cases) of average earnings up to a maximum of Can$100 a week. There would be five phases of benefits, the maximum duration of which would depend on the length of previous employment, the level of the national average unemployment rate, and the level of the unemployment rate in each region. The benefit cost up to a national level of unemployment of 4%, and the administrative costs, would be shared by employees and employers.

In November 1970 a White Paper on Income Security was published and was agreed upon after amendment, following discussion with the provinces. Substantial increases were proposed for pensioners with low incomes. For the first time, wives with dependent children would be eligible for benefit up to Can$80 a month. New levels of maximum benefit for retirement pensions would be made possible by increasing the maximum annual earnings on which pensions were calculated and pension rates were based. The White Paper also provided for a new Family Income Security plan under which Can$16 per child aged 15 or under would be paid to families with incomes of Can$4,500 or less, with an addition of Can$500 income for each additional child. Smaller amounts would be payable to families with a higher income.

Members of the Social Service Employees Union in New York City picket the Human Resources Administration on Jan. 21, 1971, to protest suspension of three welfare workers. The suspended social workers were accused of placing a welfare family in the Waldorf-Astoria at city expense.

Other Countries. In New Zealand, 61% of the total Social Security Department expenditure on monetary benefits was paid without a means test. The total represented about NZ$102 per capita and about 8% of the national income. Age benefit for an unmarried beneficiary was increased to NZ$767 a year, diminished by NZ$2 for every complete NZ$2 of annual income in excess of NZ$676 a year. Other benefit rates were also increased. For the first time, a child born out of wedlock could be considered for orphan's benefit if both parents were deceased. Under 1971 regulations, payments to a beneficiary in an institution were payable to the institution. In the year to March 1971 the special annuities previously paid from funds appropriated for war pensions were paid out of the social security fund.

In Brazil benefits were extended to agricultural workers for the first time. In Cyprus a more effective system of payments to destitute persons was introduced. Public assistance allowances were increased, and preparatory work was completed for the introduction of a statutory public assistance scheme guaranteeing a minimum level of subsistence. In India there was a phenomenal rise in the number of women engaged in the welfare services. There was controversy about the proper time to introduce a comprehensive social security program, which was to include old-age pensions and a public assistance scheme. The bulk of the population was without any form of regular assistance. (JN. M.)

See also Education; Housing; Insurance; Medicine; Race Relations; Refugees.

Sociology

Sociologists continued during 1971 to focus attention on student unrest, which could no longer be dismissed as a passing fad. J. David Colfax of Washington University noted that one of the thrusts of New Left student activism has been toward the development of "radical scholarship" to serve "anti-Establishment" purposes—a participatory radicalism aimed at the discovery of truths that will be useful as propaganda. This radical style of research brought criticism both from established sociologists, who decried the imprecise research methods employed and the ephemeral character of the results, and from radical philosophers, who complained about the absence of effort devoted to the development of substantive ideas to guide the radical movement.

Solomon Encel, president of the Sociological Association of Australia and New Zealand, took issue with the widespread belief that student movements of protest and revolution are usually led by sociology students and inspired by sociology teachers. This was true of the movement led by Daniel Cohn-Bendit that disrupted the University of Paris in 1968, but the better-known student activists in Australia have emerged from the mathematics and history departments. Looking beyond departments of sociology, Seymour M. Lipset of Harvard stated that the more intellectual fields tend to recruit and produce practitioners who are sympathetic to reform and at times to radicalism, while such fields as engineering, education, business, and agriculture tend to include more conservatives. A survey by Allan Kornberg and Mary Brehm of Duke University disclosed that favourable attitudes toward a particularly controversial "sit-in" predominated among younger students, males, students from large population centres, and students identifying themselves as Jews, agnostics, or unaffiliated. Unfavourable attitudes were most common among older students, females, students from smaller towns and cities, and students identifying themselves as Protestants or Catholics.

Sociologists also pondered the content of the youth revolution. José Leopoldo Decamilli of the University of Berlin expressed puzzlement at the extent to which many seemingly hypercritical young people in Europe and America have quite uncritically enshrined Che Guevara, Ho Chi Minh, and Mao Tse-tung in their pantheon of heroes. Don Ihde of the State University of New York at Stony Brook doubted that the creation of Marxist states, either Soviet or Chinese in style, is actually sought by radical young people. Their quest is for a utopia characterized by meaningful leisure. In contrast, Ivan Kuvacic of the University of Zagreb declared that youthful radicalism is a revolt against the traditional distinction between the sexes. The true folk heroes of the youth revolution are the Beatles, who were not afraid to display emotions and mannerisms that in earlier times would have been labeled as effeminate.

Soviet sociologist V. L. Glazychev concluded that the goal of the government-sponsored drive toward cultural conformity is unattainable. He regarded the passive rebellion of the hippies and the challenge of the New Left—both inside and outside the Soviet bloc—as clear indications of a worldwide revolt against mass culture. Joseph Roucek of the University of Bridgeport, Conn., went much further, describing the situation not as a youthful rejection of mass culture but as an actual uprising of the younger generation against the older.

In his first year as president of the International Sociological Association, Reuben Hill of the University of Minnesota moved rapidly to convert that organization from an assembly of delegates from various associations and institutions to an international fellowship of individual sociologists. It was hoped that he could accomplish this task despite the tensions between Western and Soviet bloc sociologists and between young revolutionaries and established scholars. (J. E. McK.)

See also Psychology; Social Services.

ENCYCLOPÆDIA BRITANNICA FILMS. *Operation Bootstrap* (1968); *Heritage in Black* (1969); *The House of Man, Part II—Our Crowded Environment* (1969); *Manuel from Puerto Rico* (1969); *Chicano from the Southwest* (1970); *Linda and Billy Ray from Appalachia* (1970); *Jesse from Mississippi* (1971); *Johnny from Fort Apache* (1971).

Somalia

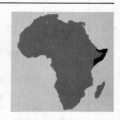

A republic of northeast Africa, the Somali Democratic Republic, or Somalia, is bounded by the Gulf of Aden, the Indian Ocean, Kenya, Ethiopia, and Afars and Issas. Area: 246,155 sq.mi. (637,541 sq.km.). Pop. (1970 est.): 3 million, predominantly Hamitic, with Arabic and other admixtures. Cap. and largest city: Mogadiscio (pop., 1969 est., 200,000). Language: Arabic, English, Italian. Religion: predominantly Muslim. President of the Supreme Revolutionary Council in 1971, Maj. Gen. Muhammad Siyad Barrah.

President Siyad and the Supreme Revolutionary Council (SRC) showed no signs in 1971 of relinquish-

SOMALIA

Education. (1968–69) Primary (public only), pupils 24,697, teachers 792; secondary, pupils 13,116, teachers 537; vocational, pupils 628, teachers 58; teacher training (1966–67), students 476, teachers 61; higher, students 304, teaching staff 47.

Finance. Monetary unit: Somali shilling, with a par value of 7.14 Somali shillings to U.S. $1 (17.14 Somali shillings = £1 sterling) and a free rate (Sept. 27, 1971) of 6.86 Somali shillings to U.S. $1. Gold, SDRs, and foreign exchange, central bank: (March 1971) U.S. $21.7 million; (March 1970) U.S. $15.9 million. Budget (1971 est.): revenue 316.3 million Somali shillings; expenditure 306.3 million Somali shillings. Money supply: (Dec. 1970) 314.2 million Somali shillings; (Dec. 1969) 279.7 million Somali shillings. Cost of living (Mogadiscio; 1963 = 100): (June 1971) 141; (June 1970) 143.

Foreign Trade. (1970) Imports 322.2 million Somali shillings; exports 223.9 million Somali shillings. Import sources: Italy 29%; West Germany 9%; U.S. 8%; Japan 7%; U.S.S.R. 7%; U.K. 6%; Kenya 5%; Singapore 5%. Export destinations: Saudi Arabia 52%; Italy 26%; Yemen (Aden) 10%. Main exports: livestock 53%; bananas 28%; hides and skins 7%.

Transport and Communications. Roads (1969) 13,396 km. Motor vehicles in use (1969): passenger 5,900; commercial 8,000. There are no railways. Shipping (1970): merchant vessels 100 gross tons and over 79; gross tonnage 369,118. Telephones (Jan. 1969) c. 4,800. Radio receivers (Dec. 1969) 45,000.

Agriculture. Production (in 000; metric tons; 1969; 1968 in parentheses): millet and sorghum c. 63 (c. 67); cassava c. 23 (c. 23); bananas c. 190 (c. 190). Livestock (in 000; 1969–70): cattle c. 2,100; sheep c. 4,600; goats c. 4,800; camels c. 2,200.

ing power in what Siyad had formally declared a socialist state on Oct. 21, 1970. A campaign to eliminate "tribalism" began with a law abolishing the traditional payment of blood-money compensation for homicide, and the office of government-salaried chief. Censorship boards were to be set up to cover the news and entertainment media. In May, the vice-president of the SRC, Gen. Muhammad Ainanshe Guleid, was arrested with several associates on charges of treason in what was later announced to have been a plot to assassinate all government leaders and "reinstate capitalism."

In internal affairs the emphasis on national self-reliance continued. Plans were made to expand the educational system and replace foreign teachers with Somalis with the help of a $3.3 million loan from the International Development Association. The interior of the country suffered from a severe drought that lasted until March. Relief was organized with Soviet and Chinese aid. The future of the Italian-owned banana plantations in the south remained uncertain.

The outstanding event of 1971 in Somalia was the conference of East and Central African heads of state, held at Mogadiscio, October 18–20. Elsewhere in foreign affairs, the government continued its policy of cooperation with the surrounding states, and attempting to find by peaceful means a solution to territorial disputes with its neighbours. (V. R. Lu.)

South Africa

A republic occupying the southern tip of Africa, South Africa is bounded by South West Africa, Botswana, Rhodesia, Mozambique, and Swaziland. Lesotho forms an enclave within South African territory. Area: 471,445 sq.mi. (1,221,037 sq.km.), excluding Walvis Bay, 372 sq.mi. Pop. (1970): 21,448,169, including Bantu 70.2%; white 17.5%; Coloured 9.4%; Asian 2.9%. Executive cap.: Pretoria (metro. pop., 1970, 561,-703); judicial cap.: Bloemfontein (pop., 1970, 180,-179); legislative cap.: Cape Town (metro. pop., 1970, 1,096,597). Largest city: Johannesburg (metro. pop., 1970, 1,432,643). Language: Afrikaans and English. Religion: mainly Christian. State president in 1971, Jacobus J. Fouché; prime minister, B. J. Vorster.

Domestic Affairs. Important changes in financial relations between the central government, provinces, and local authorities in 1971 transferred certain powers of direct taxation, notably in respect to income tax, from the provinces to the central government and in lieu of these a system of considerably increased subsidies to the provinces was instituted. Responsibility for various services also was transferred from local authorities to the government.

In April the government announced plans for a television service to be operated by the state-controlled South African Broadcasting Corporation under the minister of national education.

The defense expenditure was increased for 1971–72 by $82.6 million to $442.4 million. The minister of defense, P. W. Botha, declared that South Africa was becoming more and more self-sufficient in armaments production and was on the way to producing certain military equipment for export to friendly countries. A central master plan committee was set up to coordinate development in large urban complexes and growth points throughout the country. Construction began on the new deep-sea harbour at Richard's Bay on the Natal (Zululand) coast at an estimated initial cost of R 100 million and on a new lubricating oil refinery in Durban at a cost of R 19 million.

Legislation was passed for the better control and regulation of stock exchange transactions in the interests of the investing public. The social evils arising from drug addiction were investigated by a commission, whose recommendations formed the basis of legislation providing heavy penalties for drug peddlers.

A bipartisan committee representing the government and the official opposition was appointed to study proposals for amending contentious provisions in the Federal Laws Amendment Act of 1970 relating to the Bureau of State Security (the so-called BOSS law). A confidential report by a one-man judicial commission recommended the establishment of a State Security Board headed by the prime minister.

Race Relations. Further steps were taken to extend self-government in nine Bantu territories (constituting 13.7% of the land and containing about half the African population), which had been promised independence at an unspecified future date. The Bantu Homelands Constitution Act of 1971 empowered the state president to grant to a homeland limited self-rule of the kind granted to the Transkei by proclamation and without previous recourse to Parliament. Another act made it possible to have a Bantu language proclaimed the official language of a territory and to permit its being used as an official language outside the territory. The government announced its intention to hasten the consolidation of the scattered portions of the homelands to form contiguous units.

In the Transkei a Bantu Townships Board was established to administer municipalities and other local government bodies hitherto controlled by whites. A territorial authority was established in Zululand, with Chief Gatsha Buthelezi as the chief executive officer. Provisions were made under the Bantu Homelands Citizenship Act for the issuing of certificates of citizenship in their homelands to Bantu living in areas outside these territories. This would create formal links between the Bantu in the white areas and those in the homelands and would make it possible at some future date for the government to regard South Africa's black labour force as "foreign."

A major change in the handling of Bantu affairs in white urban areas was the provision of government-nominated administration boards (under the control of the new Ministry of Bantu Administration and Development) to take over from local authorities. Several aid centres were established for dealing with Bantu charged with contravening the influx control and pass laws, under which many hundreds of thousands were imprisoned annually.

For the Coloured people the government defined a policy of "parallel development," aimed at their economic and social elevation alongside whites, with separate political institutions at national and local levels. The Coloured were to have no direct representation in Parliament or other legislative bodies except in the Coloured Persons' Representative Council, through which they could have a say in their own affairs. In November the all-white Cape Provincial Council voted 35–16 in favour of removing all Coloured voters from the municipal rolls. The eight Coloured city councillors would inevitably lose their seats.

During the year a number of persons, mostly non-whites, were detained without trial under the security laws. Several trials were held on charges under the Suppression of Communism Act or the Terrorism Act, including those of the dean of Johannesburg's Anglican cathedral, G. A. ffrench-Beytagh (sentenced to five years' imprisonment in October), and of 13 non-whites at Pietermaritzburg, Natal. An Anglican priest, Bernard Wrankmore, fasted in Cape Town for 66 days in protest against the conditions under which detained persons were kept and in a fruitless effort to secure a public inquiry into the 1969 death in detention of the Cape Muslim leader Imam Abdullah Haron. Author Helen Joseph, who had been held for six years under house arrest, was conditionally freed. Robert Sobukwe, former president of the banned Pan-African Congress, who was released from Robben Island after serving six years without trial and placed under house arrest, was refused permission to leave the country to take up an academic post in the United States.

On October 24 police raided 115 homes throughout the country, including those of several bishops and of John Sutherland, editor of the *Port Elizabeth Evening Post,* and Athol Fugard, the country's leading playwright. Of the 19 persons detained after the raid, Ahmed Timol, an Indian teacher, was killed when he was said to have jumped from the tenth floor of Johannesburg's main police station.

Foreign Affairs. At the request of the UN Security Council, the World Court at The Hague in June ruled 13–2 (Britain and France) that South Africa's presence in South West Africa (Namibia) was illegal. South Africa was required to withdraw its administration immediately and to put an end to its occupation. By a vote of 11–4 the court held that member states were obliged to recognize the illegality of South Africa's presence and to refrain from any acts and dealings implying recognition of the legality of its presence or lending support to its administration. The South African government rejected the court's opinion as being politically motivated and contrary to the principles of international law. A South African offer to hold a plebiscite in the territory was rejected. In October the Security Council on a 13–0 vote, with Britain and France abstaining, adopted a resolution accepting the court's advisory opinion and declaring that "any further refusal by the South African government to withdraw from Namibia could create conditions detrimental to the maintenance of peace and security in the region."

After an incident in the Caprivi Strip on the South West Africa border, in which a South African police officer of the border guard was killed and four policemen were wounded by land mines, Zambia accused South Africa of violating its frontiers in pursuit of those responsible. South Africa denied the charge and accused Zambia of harbouring terrorist forces. In a unanimous resolution the Security Council called on South Africa to respect Zambia's sovereignty and territorial integrity.

In February Britain agreed to grant export licenses for the sale of seven helicopters to South Africa for antisubmarine patrol. In October ships of the British and South African navies held joint exercises in South African waters.

Prime Minister B. J. Vorster (*see* BIOGRAPHY) welcomed the offer of "dialogue" proposed by presidents Félix Houphouët-Boigny of the Ivory Coast and Hastings Kamuzu Banda (*see* BIOGRAPHY) of Malawi, and in August Banda paid a five-day state visit to South Africa. Diplomatic relations between the two countries

---

SOUTH AFRICA

Education. (1967) European: primary, secondary, and vocational, pupils 793,189, teachers 33,-235; teacher training, students 9,985, teachers 772; higher (1966), students 44,184, teaching staff 8,013. African: primary, secondary, and vocational, pupils 2,853,837, teachers 59,000; teacher training, students 8,173, teachers c. 4,600; higher (1966), students 4,218, teaching staff 398.

Finance. Monetary unit: rand, with a par value of R 0.71 to U.S. $1 (R 1.71 = £1 sterling) and a free rate (Sept. 27, 1971) of R 1.77 to £1 sterling. Gold, SDRs, and foreign exchange, official: (June 1971) U.S. $804 million; (June 1970) U.S. $1,271,000,000. Budget (1970–71 est.): revenue R 1,992,000,000; expenditure R 1,885,000,000. Gross national product: (1969) R 11,351,000,-000; (1968) R 10,122,000,000. Money supply: (June 1971) R 2,275,000,000; (June 1970) R 2,169,000,000. Cost of living (1963 = 100): (June 1971) 133; (June 1970) 126.

Foreign Trade. (1970) Imports R 2,546,500,-000; exports (excluding gold) R 1,553,300,000

(outflow of gold R 837 million). Import sources: U.K. 22%; U.S. 17%; West Germany 15%; Japan 9%. Export destinations: U.K. 29%; Japan 12%; U.S. 8%; West Germany 7%. Main exports (excluding gold): diamonds 11%; fruit and vegetables 10%; copper 8%; iron and steel 7%; metal ores 6%; wool 5%.

Transport and Communications. Roads (1968) c. 320,000 km. (including c. 30,000 km. with improved surface). Motor vehicles in use (1970): passenger 1,653,000; commercial 428,-000. Railways: (1969) 19,736 km. (excluding Namibia 2,354 km.); freight traffic (including Namibia; 1970) 56,526,000,000 net ton-km. Air traffic (1969): 2,177,000,000 passenger-km.; freight 59,489,000 net ton-km. Shipping (1970): merchant vessels 100 gross tons and over 249; gross tonnage 510,504. Telephones (Dec. 1969) 1,482,299. Radio receivers (Dec. 1967) 2.7 million.

Agriculture. Production (in 000; 1970; 1969 in parentheses): corn 6,133 (5,339); wheat (on farms and estates only) 1,358 (1,328); sorghum

445 (232); oats 122 (110); peanuts 296 (368); sunflower seed 109 (89); potatoes c. 750 (776); sugar, raw value (1970–71) c. 1,399, (1969–70) 1,622; oranges c. 473 (c. 467); apples c. 230 (c. 230); wine c. 548 (c. 482); tobacco 34 (38); wool c. 57 (c. 70); meat c. 605 (c. 590); milk 2,820 (2,850); fish catch (1969) 1,345, (1968) 1,133. Livestock (in 000; June 1970): cattle c. 11,700; sheep c. 39,300; pigs c. 1,230; goats (Aug.) c. 12,251; horses c. 440; chickens (on farms and estates; Aug.) c. 12,300.

Industry. Index of manufacturing production (1963 = 100): (1970) 159; (1969) 151. Fuel and power (in 000; 1970): coal (metric tons) 54,166; electricity (kw-hr.) 48,682,000. Production (in 000; metric tons; 1970): cement 5,752; iron ore (60–65% metal content) 9,272; pig iron 4,344; crude steel 4,651; copper ore (metal content) 149; asbestos (1969) 258; chrome (oxide content; 1969) 539; antimony concentrate (metal content; 1969) 1,044; gold (troy oz.) 32,145; diamonds (metric carats; 1969) 7,863; fish meal (1969) 222.

were raised to ambassadorial level. Joe Kachingwe was appointed as the first Malawian ambassador to South Africa and the first from any black African state.

Agitation against South African participation in international sport continued. Vorster announced a new sports policy permitting racially mixed open international sporting events to be staged in South Africa.

The Economy. In the March budget for 1971–72 the minister of finance, N. J. Diederichs, continued the attempt to curb inflation, which was occasioned mainly by excessive consumer expenditure and low savings. Measures taken to reduce consumption included stringent consumer credit regulations on the purchase of cars, furniture, and electrical goods; higher income tax; increased excise duties; and a heavier sales tax. Government spending on capital works was cut. Demands for higher wages were discouraged, although the government rejected a wage or price freeze. Restraints on bank credit were maintained.

There was little unemployment, especially among the whites. Labour costs ranged high, with a shortage of skilled labour in work reserved for white employees. Job reservation was to some extent eased to permit the employment of nonwhite labour in occupations for which whites were not available. The colour bar in the mining industry was relaxed to enable Bantu workers to be trained for skilled work in mines in the Bantu homelands.

With more imports and no compensating increase in exports, the balance of payments deficit for the first nine months of 1971 stood at R 1,017 million, compared with R 676 million in the same period in 1970. An influx of foreign capital totaling R 725 million in the first half of the year and sales of gold to the International Monetary Fund and on the free market helped to even out the account. Tightened import control was introduced in late November to protect the balance of payments and the declining foreign exchange and gold reserves. In the international crisis that followed the U.S. decision to suspend the convertibility of the dollar South Africa announced that it would maintain the parity value of the rand against the dollar and gold. Following devaluation of the U.S. dollar in December, South Africa devalued the rand by 12.28% in terms of gold.   (L. H.)

Southeast Asia

A watershed in Southeast Asian politics was clearly marked by the actions of Communist China in 1971. The new pragmatic foreign policy inaugurated by Peking sent reverberations through every Asian capital, demolishing some old theories and building up some new ones. A general indication of the region's new attitude was provided by Philippine Pres. Ferdinand E. Marcos when he opened the sixth ministerial conference of the Asian and Pacific Council in Manila in July. He said a rapprochement between the United States and China would have a definite effect on the political climate of Asia and enable countries of the region to concentrate more on solving their economic and development problems.

Relations with China. China's motive might have been, as Marcos said, to shut out the Soviet Union or to check Japan's growing economic hold on the region, or both. China always had considered Southeast Asia its natural sphere of influence. As its new diplomatic policy unfolded, Peking indicated its willingness

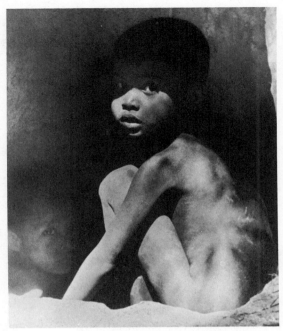

Cambodian children attempt to hide during an operation by South Vietnamese troops in Svay Rieng in eastern Cambodia on Aug. 15, 1971.
WIDE WORLD

to establish relations with Asian nations including those that in the past had considered China a "non-country." Almost all Southeast Asian governments seemed willing and ready to grasp the opportunity.

The necessary climate for such a major change in attitude was provided by the U.S. government's decision to disengage itself from Asia, wind down the Vietnam war, and maintain only a low profile in the region thereafter. Southeast Asian countries that had formerly closely identified themselves with all aspects of U.S. policy in Asia therefore felt obliged to change some of their fundamental assumptions. They were pushed further when Washington began dealing directly with Peking and Pres. Richard M. Nixon announced his intention to visit China.

Thailand, long a bastion of U.S. policy in the region, became one of the first countries publicly to advocate a dialogue with China. The Philippines sent a high-level Chamber of Commerce delegation to China. Malaysia achieved perhaps the most spectacular successes with China, exchanging delegations, receiving a Communist dance troupe from Hong Kong, signing a useful trade agreement, and, above all, practically eliminating Singapore as a middleman in the import of Chinese goods. Curiously enough, Malaysia had an internal Communist insurgency problem to cope with—as had Thailand—and Peking was widely believed to be lending tacit support to the rebels.

Two Southeast Asian countries did not share Malaysia's enthusiasm. Singapore clearly was worried about the prospects of a peaceful and respectable China exercising a gravitational pull on the predominantly Chinese population of the island republic and thereby upsetting government plans to create a "new Singaporean identity." Indonesia, still licking the wounds caused by the Communist-inspired 1965 coup that had led to the suspension of diplomatic relations with Peking, showed little interest in normalizing relations.

There was no doubt, however, that the region as a whole was overhauling its fundamental attitudes. The dominant mood was to see China as a friendly giant with whom it was possible to get along and desirable to trade. This rethinking promised to bring about a

Allied helicopters prepare to land on highway in Cambodia on Jan. 19, 1971, to pick up South Vietnamese troops for a combined Cambodian-South Vietnamese offensive at Pich Nil Pass.

UPI COMPIX

restructuring of the political forces in the region, affecting the shape of things to come for many years.

Soviet and U.S. Roles. In the face of China's new status, the U.S.S.R. was apparently holding its own in Southeast Asia during 1971. The number of Soviet cultural and trade delegations to the region was increasing sharply. Soviet sailors and Aeroflot crews were becoming a familiar sight in more and more Asian cities. Malaysia and Singapore had established diplomatic relations with Moscow, and the Philippines and Thailand were expected to follow suit. An insight into the thinking behind the policies of these governments was provided by Singapore Prime Minister Lee Kuan Yew when he said "the Soviet naval capacity in the Indian Ocean and the South China Sea can be a counterpoise to China's might on the littoral countries of Asia and Southeast Asia."

The Soviets were believed to be maintaining three operations in Asian waters—a fishing fleet, a space-effort-support flotilla, and a potential combat force that usually comprised 20 vessels of all types. In addition to this, the Soviet merchant navy emerged as an important factor in Pacific shipping, offering cut-rate prices.

At the 24th Soviet Communist Party Congress in April, party leader Leonid I. Brezhnev scathingly attacked the West for talking in terms of a "Soviet threat" in the Indian Ocean. Soviet commentators said repeatedly during 1971 that their naval force in the region was there to stay. This Soviet stance and Southeast Asian governments' own political calculations indicated a continuing, and steadily increasing, Soviet influence in the region.

In contrast, there were indications during the year of a diminution of U.S. influence. While U.S. initiative in normalizing relations with China directly affected all Asian governments, it also tended to erode the credibility of U.S. commitments to its old Asian allies. Washington announced that it would break no promises, but that could not prevent old allies from looking for new options.

Two other factors contributed to the devaluation of U.S. prestige in the region—the presidential election in South Vietnam and the UN vote on China's admission, both in October. The South Vietnamese election turned out to be a farcical one-man race. In the UN, the U.S. delegation's apparently emotional attitude isolated it from most Asian countries. The consensus in Southeast Asia was that the UN vote constituted a humiliating defeat for Washington when it need only have been a victory for China.

There was speculation that President Nixon's projected visit to Peking would be preceded by the pullout of all U.S. combat troops from Asia. But at a press conference in April Secretary of Defense Melvin Laird said that the U.S. would maintain a naval and air presence in Southeast Asia after U.S. ground troops had been withdrawn. Such a presence, he said, would be required if the U.S. were to maintain a policy of "realistic diplomacy."

Regional Defense Plans. China's return to normal international diplomacy, together with the de-escalation of the war in Vietnam, helped soften Southeast Asia's preoccupation with security problems and defense preparations. Such activities as took place in this field were more or less confined to the five-power grouping that linked Malaysia and Singapore with Britain, Australia, and New Zealand. When the five countries met in London in April, some contradictory tendencies were in evidence. Britain said that the na-

ture of its commitments required review. Australia was anxious to point out that Britain was seeking no escape clause. Malaysia's concern was to explain that its call for a neutralized Southeast Asia was not incompatible with the five-power defense arrangement. Singapore's prime minister underlined the importance of a relationhip of trust between his country and Malaysia.

The communiqué issued at the end of the London talks reported "full agreement" with the proviso that there would still be bilateral discussions between members. The communiqué made it clear that no country was committed to go to the aid of Malaysia or Singapore. It also declared that any of the participating governments was free to ask at any time for a meeting to review the agreement.

Early in the year there was some vague talk about the possibility of a wider defense arrangement embracing Indonesia, Thailand, and the Philippines as well as Malaysia and Singapore. The deputy commander of the Indonesian armed forces and the chairman of the Philippines Senate referred to members of ASEAN (Association of Southeast Asian Nations) coming together under a joint defense agreement. Eventually Indonesian Foreign Minister Adam Malik said that such a possibility was theoretically under discussion but "it is by no means certain it will be realized."

Another noteworthy plan aired during the year came from the Philippines. In July President Marcos issued an order to his foreign secretary, Carlos P. Romulo, asking him to initiate consultations with Asian foreign ministers to determine if an Asian summit conference was needed in the light of recent international developments. At a meeting of ASEAN foreign ministers held at Kuala Lumpur, Malaysia, in November, it was agreed that a summit meeting of ASEAN countries would be held in Manila early in 1972. The foreign ministers also issued the "Kuala Lumpur Declaration" in which the area was declared to be a "zone of peace, freedom, and neutrality."

ASEAN. Summit consultations by ASEAN foreign ministers, and references earlier in the year to the possibility of a joint defense agreement, underlined the regional organization's continuing difficulty in deciding whether it was an economic or politico-military grouping. Ostensibly it still concentrated on economic issues although tangible results were hard to come by. In March, when leaders of the five member countries (Indonesia, Malaysia, Philippines, Singapore, and Thailand) met in Manila, President Marcos called on them to help organize a regional common market. But, said Singapore's foreign minister, ASEAN's future depended on how successful each of the member countries was in promoting rapid economic growth.

One result of the Manila meeting was the decision to establish formal cooperation between ASEAN and the Southeast Asian Business Council, an association of leading businessmen and industrialists in the area. The only concrete achievement of the meeting was a multilateral air agreement that enabled nonscheduled commercial aircraft of one member country to operate freely in other member countries.

There was recognition in Manila of the value of organizing concerted action among ASEAN countries on international issues and presenting a united stand to advance their common interests. But the China debate in the UN pointed up the problems, Malaysia and Singapore voting for Nationalist China's expulsion, Philippines voting against, and Indonesia and Thailand abstaining.

South Vietnamese troops, part of a task force operating in Cambodia near the South Vietnamese border, move across a wooden bridge in pursuit of the enemy.

WIDE WORLD

SEATO. While ASEAN managed to maintain its status as the most promising regional organization in Southeast Asia, the military-oriented Southeast Asia Treaty Organization (SEATO) continued to be overtaken by events. Its 16th annual ministerial conference in London in April attracted hardly any serious notice in Asia. Its resolutions were seen as largely platitudinous—that South Vietnam had further developed its capability to defend itself effectively, that the Cambodians continued to show a firm determination to resist the North Vietnamese, that the U.S.-Saigon incursion into Laos in February had been justified.

More relevant to Asian reality were the conference's call for external assistance to development programs in member countries and for regional cooperation. But it gave no indication of being able to pursue these objectives. Thai Foreign Minister Thanat Khoman, who had strongly criticized SEATO the previous year, said that the organization might change its structure completely if China showed a new attitude of reconciliation in Asia. U.S. Secretary of State William Rogers lent weight to the idea by saying that U.S. policy was not to deny China's growing role in Asia but to encourage it. Under these circumstances, SEATO's military advisers were hard put to prove that "the military concept of SEATO was even more valid and necessary today than in the past."

ECAFE. The only noteworthy feature of the 27th session of the UN Economic Commission for Asia and the Far East (ECAFE), held in Manila in April, was the participation of a new member—Papua New Guinea. For the rest, the session remained true to pattern and passed seven resolutions, each either elaborating or adding to an already substantial stockpile of paper plans. They included financing an Asian Centre for Development Administration, giving landlocked countries free access to the sea, preparation of an Asian Plan of Action for the application of science and technology to development, convening a special conference to consider plans for the Second UN Development Decade, and changing ECAFE's name to reflect the social aspects of its work. (T. J. S. G.)

Soviet Bloc Economies

In keeping with the guidelines for achieving increased cooperation among the member states of the Council for Mutual Economic Assistance (CMEA, or Comecon), the 25th session of the Council met in Bucharest in July 1971 and endorsed a paper entitled "A Comprehensive Program for the Further Deepening and Perfecting of Cooperation and for Developing Socialist Economic Integration Among the Member Countries of the CMEA." While the 23rd session in 1969 had been attended by first secretaries of the Communist parties of all the eight member states (the U.S.S.R., East Germany, Czechoslovakia, Poland, Hungary, Romania, Bulgaria, and Mongolia), the delegations at the 24th (1970) and 25th sessions were headed by premiers. In addition, delegations from Yugoslavia, an associate member of the CMEA, attended the 1970 and 1971 meetings.

The "Comprehensive Program," a lengthy document taking up more than six pages of *Pravda* and other leading Communist daily newspapers, set out the principles, goals, and methods for achieving economic integration, stage by stage, over a period of 15 to 20 years. The Bucharest communiqué proclaimed that be-

Table I. Growth of National Income in Eastern Europe

Country	1965 actual (1960=100)	1970 actual (1965=100)	1975 plan (1970=100)
U.S.S.R.	137	145	140
Germany, East	118	129	128
Czechoslovakia	110	139	128
Poland	135	134	139
Hungary	122	139	132
Romania	154	145	182
Bulgaria	138	152	150

Table II. Rates of Industrial Growth in Eastern Europe

Country	1961–65 actual	1966–70 actual	1971–75 plan
U.S.S.R.	8.6	8.5	7.9
Germany, East	5.9	6.4	6.3
Czechoslovakia	5.2	6.3	6.3
Poland	8.6	8.3	8.5
Hungary	8.1	6.1	7.3
Romania	13.0	11.8	11.0
Bulgaria	11.7	11.2	9.9

tween 1951 and 1970 industrial production in the CMEA member countries went up 6.8 times, while in the developed capitalist countries it rose during the same period only 2.8 times. Mikhail A. Lesechko, deputy premier and permanent Soviet member of the CMEA Executive Committee, gave the "unprecedented" figure of 8.2% as the annual average rate of growth for the whole CMEA area between 1951 and 1970. Nikolai V. Faddeyev, secretary-general of the CMEA, wrote in *Izvestia* that "none of the economic groupings of capitalist countries ever achieved such rates of industrial growth." (Progress in industrialization of the socialist countries was undeniable, but comparisons between rates of growth of highly developed countries and those of countries in the process of development could be misleading; for example, the fastest rates of growth were achieved in Romania and Bulgaria, where before World War II there was very little industrial plant at all.)

Since 1951 CMEA's share of world industrial production grew in value from one-sixth to one-third, but its share of world trade remained modest. According to data compiled by the International Monetary Fund, world exports in 1970 reached $310.2 billion, including the CMEA countries, whose share amounted to $31.2 billion (10%); the respective figures for imports were $322.5 billion and $30.2 billion (9.4%).

The control panel of the Druzhba oil pipeline is located near the town of Almetyevsk in the U.S.S.R. A second section of the oil pipeline, under construction in 1971 and scheduled for completion in 1975, would greatly increase the shipment of petroleum from the Soviet Volga region to Eastern Europe.

NOVOSTI—SOVFOTO

Textile worker inspects
polyamide fibres
in a chemical plant
in Vidin, Bulg. in 1971.
With the completion of new
plants, the country's
artificial fibre output
was expected to reach
70,000 tons by 1975.

UPI COMPIX

More than three-fifths of the total CMEA foreign trade was interchange of goods among the Eastern European countries, largely on a barter basis. This mutual goods exchange had grown sevenfold in 20 years. During the 1966–70 period the yearly rate of increase of that trade was 8.2%. Under the five-year plan for 1971–75, as a result of coordination of national plans and a series of bilateral long-term trade agreements, it was expected that the annual rate of increase would reach 10.4%. Speaking at Bucharest on July 29, Piotr Jaroszewicz, the premier of Poland, expressed doubt as to whether the new rate of increase would be sufficient "to overcome our lagging behind the developed industrial countries."

The CMEA group of countries was not comparable to the customs union of the European Economic Community. Tariff reductions meant nothing among countries whose external trade was state controlled, with nonconvertible currencies, and with arbitrary pricing systems unrelated to real costs. The socialist countries were interested in developing trade and cooperation with the capitalist world, mainly for two reasons: they were eager buyers of Western machinery, and they were short of hard currency. The difficulty was that the East had few goods of high quality to sell to the West, while the trade in the opposite direction—especially that in highly technical equipment and machinery—remained hampered by political and strategic considerations.

The officials working at the Moscow headquarters of the CMEA were fully aware of all the obstacles impeding the advance toward socialist economic integration. First, there was the apprehension of the smaller states of losing their national identity, especially because of the obvious discrepancy in size and power between them and the U.S.S.R. To appease these fears the "Comprehensive Program" explicitly stated: "Socialist economic integration proceeds on a completely voluntary basis, is not accompanied by the creation of supranational organs; and does not affect questions of domestic planning or financial and cost-accounting activities of national organizations."

Second, the Bucharest program declared that the member countries of the CMEA believed that cooperation in planning, and especially in the coordination of national plans, was the main method of deepening the international "socialist division of labour." A great deal of specialization in engineering had been achieved, but there was still a gap between principle and practice.

Third, the CMEA countries regarded it as necessary to pool their efforts so as to ensure more fully the meeting of their growing requirements in the production of fuel and power and for metallurgical and other raw materials. Even before the endorsement of the Bucharest program, the U.S.S.R. had decided to help Bulgaria, Hungary, and East Germany in building nuclear power stations. The doubling of the 4,800-km. Druzhba ("Friendship") pipeline bringing Soviet crude petroleum from Tatarian oil fields to Poland, East Germany, Hungary, and Czechoslovakia was half completed, while the Mir ("Peace") power grid linking all Eastern European people's democracies with the U.S.S.R. was being extended. It was also decided that by a collective effort a huge iron and steel combine would be built and exploited near Kursk, in south central U.S.S.R., where high-grade ore reserves of approximately 47 billion tons had been discovered in the 1950s.

Fourth, though the 1970 meeting of CMEA created the International Investment Bank with capital of 1 billion rubles—of which 70% was in "convertible" rubles and the rest in hard currency—multilateral trading within the area was still difficult. As O. Bogomolov admitted in his article devoted to CMEA integration (*Kommunist*, November 1971), convertible rubles were not a reserve currency that the partners in integration could accumulate and use at their convenience. Romania, which in 1970 had not participated when the International Investment Bank was formed,

Table III. Growth of Agricultural Production in Eastern Europe

Country	1961–65 actual (1960 = 100)	1966–70 actual (1961–65 = 100)	1971–75 plan (1966–70 = 100)
U.S.S.R.	112	121	122
Germany, East	104	120	...
Czechoslovakia	97	119	114
Poland	115	116	121
Hungary	106	116	116
Romania	113	123	149
Bulgaria	117	126	120

Table IV. Basic Industrial Products in Eastern Europe*

Product	1951	1966	1970
Electric power (000,000 kw-hr.)	143.8	729.9	986.6
Coal† (000,000 metric tons)	444.8	1,152.2	1,243.0
Crude petroleum (000,000 tons)	49.6	280.6	369.4
Natural gas (000,000,000 cu.m.)	...	162.8	230.6
Crude steel (000,000 tons)	41.4	127.0	155.3
Sulfuric acid (000 tons)	3,524	13,684	18,125
Cement (000,000 tons)	21.3	114.0	137.4

*U.S.S.R., East Germany, Czechoslovakia, Poland, Hungary, Romania, and Bulgaria.
†Hard coal, brown coal, and lignite.
  Source: National statistics.

changed its mind a year later and joined the bank's
seven founder members.   (K. Sм.)

See also Communist Movement.

Spain

A nominal monarchy of southwest Europe, Spain is bounded
by Portugal, with which it
shares the Iberian Peninsula,
and by France. Area: 194,881
sq.mi. (504,741 sq.km.), in-
cluding the Balearic and Canary islands. Pop. (1970):
33,823,918, including the Balearics and Canaries. Cap.
and largest city: Madrid (pop., 1970, 3,146,071). Language: Spanish. Religion: Roman Catholic. Prince of
Spain, Don Juan Carlos de Borbón y Borbón; chief
of state and premier in 1971, Gen. Francisco Franco
Bahamonde.

During most of 1971 the position of General Franco
and his government seemed stronger than it had been
for some time. The struggle for power within the
Spanish establishment caused by the Burgos controversy toward the end of 1970, which surrounded the
trial in Burgos and harsh sentences, later commuted,
of a group of Basque guerrillas, had ended in stalemate. The Opus Dei faction of the administration remained in the ascendancy, and the Army, though incensed at having been used as a convenient scapegoat
(it had conducted the Burgos trials), had prudently
withdrawn from open conflict with the government.

The sense of security felt by the administration was
such that the suspension of Article 18 of the Fuero de
los Españoles, imposed for six months on Dec. 14,
1970, to enable police to make arrests without war-
rants, was allowed to expire on June 14. On October 1,
the 35th anniversary of Franco's coming to power, the
government's confidence was further illustrated by
the declaration of an amnesty by Franco, authorizing release of more than 3,000 prisoners from jail.
Some observers noted that because the declaration also
spared high officials involved in the Matesa export-
fraud scandal of 1969 from appearing in court it was
the government that was receiving an amnesty.

Although there was an increase in the number of industrial strikes during the year compared with 1970,

KEYSTONE

Streets remain flooded
in the aftermath
of torrential rains
in September 1971
in Gerona, Spain. Several
persons lost their lives
during the disaster.

a greater measure of freedom was given to workers in
the form of the long-awaited labour organization reform law, which went into effect on March 11. By it,
the "vertical" structure of the *sindicatos* was retained
under the control of a member of the Cabinet, to be
known as the minister for syndical relations, but management, technicians, and workers would be allowed
to set up independent associations within each *sindi-
cato;* workers also would be allowed to hold meetings
in the shop or factory under certain conditions and be
given the right to appeal in courts against certain decisions of the government.

Speculation continued over how long Franco would
continue to retain absolute power. It was rumoured
in the international press that pressure, particularly
from the U.S., was being put on him to at least appoint a premier to take over some of his responsibilities. The speculation was not abated by the increasing importance Franco was giving the prince of Spain,
Don Juan Carlos de Borbón y Borbón. In July it was
decreed that in the event of Franco's absence from

SPAIN
Education. (1968–69) Primary, pupils 3,664,-
823, teachers 108,195; secondary (1967–68), pupils 1,124,947, teachers 34,119; vocational
(1967–68), pupils 326,416, teachers 22,688;
teacher training (1967–68), students 61,927,
teachers 2,648; higher (including 19 universities;
1967–68), students 158,290, teaching staff 10,-
894.
Finance. Monetary unit: peseta, with a par
value of 70 pesetas to U.S. $1 (168 pesetas = £1
sterling) and a free rate (Sept. 27, 1971) of 69.25
pesetas to U.S. $1 (171.75 pesetas = £1 ster-
ling). Gold, SDRs, and convertible currencies,
central bank: (June 1971) U.S. $2,254,000,000;
(June 1970) U.S. $1,386,000,000. Budget (1969)
balanced at 271,795,000,000 pesetas. Gross national product: (1969) 2,011,700,000,000 pesetas; (1968) 1,804,900,000,000 pesetas. Money
supply: (May 1971) 797.9 billion pesetas; (May
1970) 669.4 billion pesetas. Cost of living
(1963 = 100): (June 1971) 167; (June 1970)
152.
Foreign Trade. (1970) Imports 330.1 billion
pesetas; exports 164 billion pesetas. Import
sources: EEC 33% (West Germany 13%, France
10%, Italy 5%); U.S. 19%; U.K. 7%. Export
destinations: EEC 36% (West Germany 12%,

France 10%, Italy 7%, Netherlands 5%); U.S.
14%; U.K. 9%. Main exports: machinery 20%;
fruit 11%; vegetables 7%; vegetable oils 6%;
chemicals 5%; ships and boats 5%. Tourism
(1969): visitors 21,682,100; receipts U.S. $1,-
311,000,000.
Transport and Communications. Roads
(1969) 138,712 km. (including 143 km. expressways). Motor vehicles in use (1969): passenger
1,998,838; commercial 654,088. Railways:
(1969) 16,841 km. (including 3,866 km. electrified); traffic (state system only; 1970) 13,-
294,000,000 passenger-km., freight 9,138,000,000
net ton-km. Air traffic (1970): 5,874,000,000
passenger-km.; freight 111,506,000 net ton-km.
Shipping (1970): merchant vessels 100 gross tons
and over 2,234; gross tonnage 3,440,952. Telephones (Dec. 1969) 4,093,494. Radio receivers
(Dec. 1969) 7,042,000. Television receivers (Dec.
1969) 5.5 million.
Agriculture. Production (in 000; metric tons;
1970; 1969 in parentheses): wheat 4,064 (4,-
626); barley 3,029 (3,969); oats 409 (547); rye
250 (320); corn 1,868 (1,577); potatoes 4,937
(4,789); rice 388 (404); sorghum 192 (157);
chick-peas *c.* 97 (107); dry broad beans *c.* 150
(130); other dry beans *c.* 115 (116); tomatoes

1,560 (1,398); onions 941 (934); apples *c.* 416
(467); pears *c.* 194 (223); oranges 2,150 (2,-
463); lemons *c.* 105 (130); sugar, raw value
(1970–71) *c.* 904, (1969–70) 744; sunflower
seed 153 (55); bananas 330 (432); dates *c.* 17
(16); figs 148 (158); olive oil 427 (368); wine
2,577 (2,451); tobacco 25 (19); cotton, lint 59
(59); meat *c.* 919 (844); fish catch (1969)
1,486, (1968) 1,503. Livestock (in 000; 1970–
70): cattle 4,288; pigs 6,916; sheep 18,729;
goats 2,570; horses 285; chickens 45,197.
Industry. Index of industrial production
(1963 = 100): (1970) 205; (1969) 190. Fuel
and power (in 000; metric tons; 1970): coal 10,-
687; lignite 2,827; crude oil (1969) 190; manufactured gas (cu.m.) 2,143,000; electricity (kw-
hr.) 55,903,000. Production (in 000; metric tons;
1970): cement 16,536; iron ore (50% metal content) 6,955; pig iron 4,291; crude steel 7,388;
aluminum 115; copper 83; zinc 90; lead 69; potash (oxide content; 1969) 636; sulfur (1969)
1,194; cotton yarn 97; cotton fabrics 90; wool
yarn 37; rayon, etc., yarn and fibres 55; nylon,
etc., yarn and fibres 68. Merchant vessels launched
(100 gross tons and over; 1970) 907,000 gross
tons.

Spanish territory or illness, his functions would be entrusted directly to the prince; the rank of captain general was given to Don Juan Carlos in October, bestowing on him a position of great importance within the Army. But Franco gave no positive indication of retiring from the political arena himself and, in fact, during his October 1 speech he announced that he would remain in power "as long as God gives me life and a clear mind."

In the field of foreign affairs, Spain showed a marked interest in Latin America. The foreign minister, Gregorio López Bravo, visited Argentina, Chile, Uruguay, Paraguay, and Brazil in March and April, formulating new policies of economic and cultural cooperation and signing several agreements. In June and July he held talks with leading officials in Colombia, Venezuela, Peru, Bolivia, and Ecuador. After years of strained relations, a movement was begun to improve contacts between Spain and the U.S.S.R. A Spanish government mission led by José·Luis Cerón visited the U.S.S.R. in March to hold exploratory talks on a projected trade agreement and the setting up of consular relations.

Spain's economic progress during the year was particularly frustrating. After experiencing rapid growth up to 1969, the economy was considered overheated and the brakes on expansion were applied toward the end of that year and in early 1970. In 1971 the authorities were struggling to stimulate the economy once more. A condition of "stagflation"—an inflationary price spiral combined with a stagnant rate of growth—seemed to have set in.

Government policy included abolition of the prior import deposit system; lowering of the rediscount rate over the year from $6\frac{1}{2}$ to 5%; establishment of new regulations for credit availabilities. But throughout the year businessmen remained undecided about their future courses of action, and there was only a slight increase in investment activity in the second half of the year.

The recession did not lead to any restraint on price increases. Over the first six months of 1971 the general level of prices increased by 4%, compared with virtual stability in the same period of 1970. The chief element in this increase was the price of food, which rose in the first half of 1971 by 5.3%, compared with a decline of 1% in January–June of the previous year. The level of unemployment rose, from 1.6% in December 1970 to 1.9% in April 1971, largely because of growing unemployment in the manufacturing and construction industries. The figure remained steady throughout the summer.

Imports during the first nine months of the year reached a value of U.S. $3,663,000,000, or 3.7% more than in the same period of 1970, but exports rose by 24.1% to $2,078,000,000. The resulting deficit represented a decline of over 20% from that for the period January–September 1970. Moreover, tourism continued to grow.　　　　　　　　　　　(D. K. Da.)

Speleology

Late in 1970 a Polish expedition in the Ukraine explored the Optimistitscheskaya gypsum cave to a length of 34 mi., making it the longest cave in the U.S.S.R., the third longest in the world, and the largest gypsum cave known. In February 1971 new exploration in the Mammuthöhle (Dachstein, Aus.) brought its total length to 14 mi. With the discovery

John Parker stands atop a stalagmite flow about 500 ft. from the end of the new passage of Wookey Hole, Somerset, Eng., discovered in 1971.

of a new passage, the Tantalhöhle (Austria) became 10.7 mi. long. A new section discovered in the Almberg-Eis- und Tropfsteinhöhle (Austria) made it 4 mi. long.

Work in Tassy Pot, Tasmania, late in 1970 brought its depth to 800 ft., making it the deepest cave in Australia until 1971 when another Tasmanian cave, Khazad-Dum, was descended by explorers first to 860 ft. in January and then in March to 970 ft. without reaching the bottom.

In England, in Somerset, the small Mendip cave known as Rhino Rift was extended by blasting to some 400 ft. deep. It contained successive pitches of 100 ft., 50 ft., and 75 ft. in one rift, which was unusual in that region. In Wookey Hole, Somerset, John Parker dived the 500-ft.-long, 90-ft.-deep sump from Wookey 20 on April 18 and entered 600 ft. of new passage beyond.

At the end of 1970 the British Karst Research Expedition to the Himalayas explored a large river cave at Pokhara in Nepal and studied the karst morphology there and in India. A 12-man British expedition explored the limestone Zagros Mountains in Kurdistan.

Analysis of a stalagmite from the Aven d'Orgnac (France) showed that between 130,000 and 100,000 years ago it grew at the rate of 0.15 in. per 100 years, but between 100,000 and 92,000 years ago the rate was 0.59 in. per 100 years. Research in West Germany used fractures in cave formations as an aid in investigating prehistoric earthquakes. Unusual stalactites made of peat occurring in caves at Ystradfellte, South Wales, were found to consist of redeposited particles of peat that had been carried in suspension through the pores of the rock.

In the Grotte de Niaux, Ariège, France, the passing of an underwater sump led to the discovery of new chambers with Magdalenian wall paintings and the footprints of two prehistoric people. A skull of a pithecanthrope man, found in the Pyrenean cave of Tautavel in August, was the oldest human skull found in Europe that could be dated with certainty.

　　　　　　　　　　　　　　　　　(T. R. Sh.)

Sporting Record

AEROBATICS

Event	Winner	Country
European Cup, open	B. Zegels	Belgium
European Cup, standard	N. Ragot	France

ANGLING

Event	Winner	Country
WORLD CHAMPIONS		
Individual	D. Bassi	Italy
Team	Italy	
WORLD SEA-ANGLING CHAMPIONSHIP		Yugoslavia

ARCHERY

Event	Winner	Country
WORLD CHAMPIONS		
Men's individual	J. Williams	U.S.
Men's team	U.S.	
Women's individual	E. Gapchenko	U.S.S.R.
Women's team	Poland	

BADMINTON

Event	Winner	Country
ALL-ENGLAND OPEN CHAMPIONS		
Men's singles	R. Hartono	Indonesia
Men's doubles	P. Gunalan, Ng Boon Bee	Malaysia
Women's singles	E. Twedberg	Sweden
Women's doubles	N. Takagi, K. Yuki	Japan
Mixed doubles	S. Pri, U. Strand	Denmark

BIATHLON

Event	Winner	Country
WORLD CHAMPIONS		
Individual	D. Speer	East Germany
Team	U.S.S.R.	
Junior individual	J. Tzaurs	U.S.S.R.
Junior team	U.S.S.R.	

BILLIARDS

Event	Winner	Country
World professional championship	R. Williams	U.K.
World amateur championship	N. Dagley	U.K.
European single pocket	L. Dielis	Belgium

BOBSLEDDING

Event	Winner	Country
World two-man champions	M. Armano, G. Gaspari	Italy
World four-man champions	R. Stadler, M. Forster, K. Schaerer, P. Schaerer	Switzerland
European two-man champions	P. Bader, H. Floth	West Germany
European four-man champions	I. Panturu, N. Neagoe, P. Hristovici, G. Maftei	Romania

CANOEING

Event		Winner	Country
WORLD CHAMPIONS—MEN			
Kayak singles	500 m.	N. Kakol	U.S.S.R.
	1,000 m.	H. Sziedzewski	Poland
	10,000 m.	V. Tsarev	U.S.S.R.
Kayak pairs	500 m.	L. Andersson, R. Peterson	Sweden
	1,000 m.	J. Kirt, D. Sienov	East Germany
	10,000 m.	A. Kostyenko, V. Konyonov	U.S.S.R.
Kayak fours	1,000 m.	U.S.S.R.	
	10,000 m.	Romania	
Kayak relay		Hungary	
Canadian singles	500 m.	D. Lewe	West Germany
	1,000 m.	D. Lewe	West Germany
	10,000 m.	T. Wichmann	Hungary
Canadian pairs	500 m.	C. Danilov, K. Simoniov	Romania
	1,000 m.	G. Petrikovics, T. Wichmann	Hungary
	10,000 m.	N. Prokupets, A. Vinogradov	U.S.S.R.
WORLD CHAMPIONS—WOMEN			
Kayak singles	1,000 m.	L. Pinayeva	U.S.S.R.
Kayak pairs	1,000 m.	G. Höllösy, A. Pfeffer	Hungary
Kayak fours	10,000 m.	U.S.S.R.	

Event	Winner	Country
WORLD SLALOM CHAMPIONS—MEN		
Kayak singles	S. Horn	East Germany
Kayak singles team	Austria	
Canadian singles	R. Kaudder	East Germany
Canadian singles team	East Germany	
Canadian pairs	Kretschmer, Trummer	East Germany
Canadian pairs team	East Germany	
WORLD SLALOM CHAMPIONS—WOMEN		
Kayak singles	A. Bahmann	East Germany
Kayak singles team	East Germany	
WORLD SLALOM CHAMPIONS—MIXED		
Canadian pairs	J. Koudela, J. Koudelova	Czechoslovakia
Canadian pairs team	East Germany	
WORLD WILD-WATER CHAMPIONS—MEN		
Kayak singles	B. Kast	West Germany
Kayak singles team	B. Kast, U. Pech, J. Schwarz	West Germany
Canadian singles	P. Sodomka	Czechoslovakia
Canadian singles team	West Germany	
Canadian pairs	G. Lefauconnier, P. Lefauconnier	France
Canadian pairs team	West Germany	
WORLD WILD-WATER CHAMPIONS—WOMEN		
Kayak singles	U. Deppe	West Germany
Kayak singles team	West Germany	
Canadian singles team	West Germany	
Canadian pairs team	West Germany	
WORLD WILD-WATER CHAMPIONS—MIXED		
Canadian pairs	U. Spitz, H. Ramelow	Austria
Canadian pairs team	France	

CROSS-COUNTRY

Event	Winner	Country
INTERNATIONAL CHAMPIONS		
Senior, individual	D. Bedford	U.K.
Senior, team	England	
Junior, individual	N. Rose	U.K.
Junior, team	England	
Women, individual	D. Brown	U.S.
Women, team	England	
NATIONAL CHAMPIONS—MEN		
Belgium	G. Thorley	N.Z.
Canada	R. Finlay	
England	D. Bedford	
France	N. Tijou	
Ireland	P. Coyle	
Scotland	R. Wedlock	
U.S. (AAU)	F. Shorter	
U.S.S.R.	O. Raiko (8 km.)	
	R. Sharafutdinov (12 km.)	
Wales	M. Thomas	
West Germany	H. Norpoth (4.4 km.)	
	L. Philipp (12 km.)	
NATIONAL CHAMPIONS—WOMEN		
Canada	S. Miller	
England	R. Ridley	
Ireland	A. O'Brien	
Scotland	C. Haskett	
U.S.	D. Brown	
U.S.S.R.	L. Bragina (2 km.)	
	N. Gimatova (3 km.)	
West Germany	E. Tittel (1.5 km.)	
	E. Tittel (3.4 km.)	

CURLING

Event	Country
WORLD CHAMPIONS	Canada

CYCLING

Event	Winner	Country
WORLD CHAMPIONS—MEN, AMATEUR		
Sprint	D. Morelon	France
Individual pursuit	M. Rodriguez	Colombia
Team pursuit	Italy	
Time trial	E. Rapp	U.S.S.R.
Tandem sprint	J. Geschke, W. Otto	East Germany
Motor-paced	H. Gnas	West Germany
Team time trial, road	Belgium	
Road	R. Ovion	France
WORLD CHAMPIONS—MEN, PROFESSIONAL		
Sprint	L. Loeveseijn	Netherlands
Individual pursuit	D. Baert	Belgium
Motor-paced	T. Verschueren	Belgium
Road	E. Merckx	Belgium
WORLD CHAMPIONS—WOMEN		
Sprint	G. Tsareva	U.S.S.R.
Individual pursuit	T. Garkushina	U.S.S.R.
Road	A. Konkina	U.S.S.R.
PAN-AMERICAN GAMES CHAMPIONS—MEN		
Sprint	L. King	Trinidad and Tobago
Individual pursuit	M. Rodriguez	Colombia
Team pursuit	Colombia	
Time trial	J. Lovell	Canada
Team time trial, road	Cuba	
Road	J. Howard	U.S.

Event	Winner	Country
MAJOR PROFESSIONAL ROAD-RACE WINNERS		
Circuit "Het Volk"	E. Merckx	Belgium
Dunkirk Four Days	R. de Vlaeminck	Belgium
Tour of Dauphine	E. Merckx	Belgium
Flèche Wallonne	R. de Vlaeminck	Belgium
Frankfurt Grand Prix	E. Merckx	Belgium
Ghent–Wevelghem	G. Pintens	Belgium
Liège–Bastogne–Liège	E. Merckx	Belgium
Midi-Libre	E. Merckx	Belgium
Milan–San Remo	E. Merckx	Belgium
Paris–Nice	E. Merckx	Belgium
Paris–Roubaix	R. Rosiers	Belgium
Tour of the Basque Country	L. Ocana	Spain
Tour of Belgium	E. Merckx	Belgium
Tour of Flanders	E. Dolman	Netherlands
Tour of France	E. Merckx	Belgium
Tour of Italy	G. Pettersson	Sweden
Tour of Lombardy	E. Merckx	Belgium
Tour of Luxembourg	A. Dierickx	Belgium
Tour of Portugal	J. Agostinho	Portugal
Tour of Normandy	G. Motta	Italy
Tour of Spain	F. Bracke	Belgium
Tour of Switzerland	G. Pintens	Belgium
Grand Prix des Nations	L. Ocana	Spain
MAJOR AMATEUR ROAD-RACE WINNERS		
Circuit de la Sarthe	G. Nelyubin	U.S.S.R.
Route de France	R. Ovion	France
Tour of Britain	F. den Hertog	Netherlands
Tour of Italy	C. Moser	Italy
Tour of Morocco	C. Magni	France
Warsaw–Berlin–Prague	R. Szurkowski	Poland
Grand Prix des Nations	G. Bischoff	Switzerland
Tour de l'Avenir	R. Ovion	France
NATIONAL ROAD-RACE CHAMPIONS		
Belgium	H. van Springel	
France	Y. Hezard	
Italy	F. Bitossi	
Luxembourg	E. Schutz	
Netherlands	J. Zoetemelk	
Portugal	J. Agostinho	
Spain	E. Castello	
Switzerland	L. Pfenninger	

EQUESTRIAN SPORTS

Event	Winner	Country
EUROPEAN CHAMPIONS		
Show jumping, men	P. Jonqueres d'Oriola	France
Show jumping, women	A. Moore	U.K.
Show jumping, junior	M. Snoek	West Germany
Dressage, individual	L. Linsenhoff	West Germany
Dressage, team	West Germany	
Three-day event, individual	Princess Anne of England	U.K.
Three-day event, team	U.K.	
Three-day event, junior	C. Brooke	U.K.
PAN-AMERICAN GAMES CHAMPIONS		
Show jumping, men	J. Perez	Mexico
Dressage, team	Canada	
Three-day event, individual	M. Mendevil	Argentina

FENCING

Event	Winner	Country
WORLD CHAMPIONS		
Men's foil	V. Stankovich	U.S.S.R.
Men's épée	G. Kriss	U.S.S.R.
Men's sabre	M. Maffei	Italy
Men's team foil	France	
Men's team épée	Hungary	
Men's team sabre	U.S.S.R.	
Women's foil	M. Demaille	France
Women's team foil	U.S.S.R.	
WORLD JUNIOR CHAMPIONS		
Men's foil	B. Boscherie	France
Men's épée	R. Abuskametov	U.S.S.R.
Men's sabre	V. Komar	U.S.S.R.
Women's foil	I. Schwarzberger	Hungary
PAN-AMERICAN GAMES CHAMPIONS		
Men's foil	E. John	Cuba
Men's épée	S. Netburn	U.S.
Men's sabre	A. Orban	U.S.
Men's team foil	U.S.	
Women's foil	M. Rodriguez	Cuba
Women's team foil	U.S.	

FOOTBALL, ASSOCIATION

Event	Winner	Country
MAJOR INTERNATIONAL TOURNAMENTS (National Teams)		
British Isles international championship	England	
Asian Games	South Korea	
Pan-American Games	Cuba	
MAJOR INTERNATIONAL TOURNAMENTS (Clubs)		
European Champions' Cup	Ajax Amsterdam	Netherlands
European Cup-Winners' Cup	Chelsea	England
European Fairs' Cup	Leeds United	England
South American Champions' Cup	Nacional Montevideo	Uruguay
African Champions' Cup	Asante Kotoko SC	Ghana

NATIONAL CHAMPIONS (National Cup and League Winners)		
Albania	League	Partizan Tirana
Argentina	League (2)	Chacarita Juniors, Rosario Central
Austria	Cup	FK Austria
	League	Wacker Innsbruck
Belgium	Cup	Beerschot AC
	League	Standard Liège
Brazil	League (2)	Fluminense (Rio)
		São Paulo FV (São Paulo)
Bulgaria	Cup	Levski Sofia
	League	CSKA Sofia
Colombia	League	Atletico Nacional
Czechoslovakia	Cup	Spartak Trnava
	League	Spartak Trnava
Denmark	Cup	BK 1909 Odense
East Germany	Cup	Dynamo Dresden
	League	Dynamo Dresden
England	Cup (FA)	Arsenal
	(FL)	Tottenham Hotspur
	League	Arsenal
France	Cup	Rennes
	League	Olympique Marseille
Greece	League	AEK Athens
Hawaii	Cup	University of Hawaii Rainbows
	League	Honolulu International
Hungary	League	Ujpest Dosza
Italy	Cup	Torino
	League	Internazionale Milan
Luxembourg	Cup	Jeunesse Hautcharage
	League	Union Luxembourg
Netherlands	Cup	Ajax Amsterdam
	League	Feyenoord
Poland	Cup	Gornik Zabrze
	League	Gornik Zabrze
Portugal	Cup	Sporting Lisbon
	League	Benfica
Romania	Cup	Steaua Bucharest
	League	Dinamo Bucharest
Scotland	Cup	Glasgow Celtic
	League	Glasgow Celtic
Spain	League	Valencia
Sweden	Cup	Åtvidaberg
Switzerland	Cup	Servette Geneva
	League	Grasshoppers
Turkey	Cup	Eski Sehirspor
	League	Galatasaray Istanbul
U.S.S.R.	Cup	Spartak Moscow
Wales	Cup	Cardiff City
	League	Llanelli
West Germany	Cup	F.C. Bayern Munich
	League	Borussia München-Gladbach
Yugoslavia	Cup	Red Star Belgrade
	League	Hajduk Split

GYMNASTICS

Event	Winner	Country
EUROPEAN CHAMPIONS—MEN		
Combined exercises	V. Klimenko	U.S.S.R.
Floor exercises	R. Khristov	Bulgaria
Pommeled horse	N. Andrianov	U.S.S.R.
Rings	M. Voronin	U.S.S.R.
Long horse vault	N. Andrianov	U.S.S.R.
Parallel bars	G. Carminucci	Italy
Horizontal bars	K. Koste	East Germany
EUROPEAN CHAMPIONS—WOMEN		
Combined exercises	L. Tyurisheva	U.S.S.R.
Floor exercises	L. Tyurisheva	U.S.S.R.
Horse vault	L. Tyurisheva	U.S.S.R.
Asymmetrical bars	N. Lazyikovich	U.S.S.R.
Beam	N. Lazyikovich	U.S.S.R.
PAN-AMERICAN GAMES CHAMPIONS—MEN		
Combined exercises	H. Crosby	U.S.
Pommeled horse	J. Rodriguez	Cuba
Rings	H. Crosby	U.S.
Long horse vault	F. Cuervo	Cuba
Parallel bars	J. Elias	U.S.
Horizontal bars	J. Rodriguez	Cuba
PAN-AMERICAN GAMES CHAMPIONS—WOMEN		
Floor exercises	L. Metheny	U.S.
Horse vault	A. Pierce	U.S.
Asymmetrical bars	A. Pierce	U.S.
Beam	P. Chase	U.S.

HANDBALL

Event	Winner	Country
EUROPEAN CHAMPIONS (INDOOR)		
European Cup, men's team	V. F. L. Gummersbach	West Germany
European Cup, women's team	Spartak Kiev	U.S.S.R.

JUDO

Event	Winner	Country
WORLD CHAMPIONS		
Lightweight	T. Kawaguchi	Japan
Light-middleweight	H. Tsuzawa	Japan
Middleweight	S. Fujii	Japan
Light-heavyweight	F. Sasahara	Japan
Heavyweight	W. Ruska	Netherlands
Unlimited weight	M. Shinomaki	Japan
EUROPEAN CHAMPIONS		
Lightweight	J. Mounier	France
Light-middleweight	R. Hendel	East Germany

Event	Winner	Country
Middleweight	G. Auffray	France
Light-heavyweight	H. Hawiller	East Germany
Heavyweight	W. Ruska	Netherlands
Unlimited weight	Y. Kuznyetsov	U.S.S.R.
Team	U.K.	
BRITISH OPEN CHAMPIONS		
Lightweight	D. Lawrence	U.K.
Welterweight	E. Cassidy	U.K.
Middleweight	P. Aubert	Switzerland
Light-heavyweight	D. Starbrook	U.K.
Heavyweight	A. McConnell	U.K.
Unlimited weight	D. Starbrook	U.K.

KARATE

Event	Winner	Country
EUROPEAN CHAMPIONS		
Individual	D. Valera	France
Team		France

MODERN PENTATHLON

Event	Winner	Country
WORLD CHAMPIONS		
Individual	B. Onischenko	U.S.S.R.
Team	U.S.S.R.	

MOTORCYCLING

Event	Winner	Country
WORLD CHAMPIONS		
50 cc.	J. de Vries	Netherlands
125 cc.	A. Nieto	Spain
250 cc.	P. Read	U.K.
350 cc.	G. Agostini	Italy
500 cc.	G. Agostini	Italy
Sidecar	H. Owesle	West Germany

ROLLER HOCKEY

Event		Country
European champions		Portugal

SAILING

Class	Helmsman	Country
WORLD CHAMPIONS		
Albacore	J. Langmaid	Canada
Canoe	J. Biddle	U.K.
Dragon	P. Sundelin	Sweden
Fireball	J. Caig	U.K.
Flying Dutchman	R. Pattisson	U.K.
G.P. 14	A. Read	U.K.
Hornet	C. McKenzie	U.K.
Moth	J. Fauroux	France
O.K.	T. Jungbluth	West Germany
Star	D. Connor	U.S.
Tempest	G. Foster	U.S.
Tornado, catamaran	I. Fraser	U.K.
4-7-0	Van Essen	Netherlands
5-0-5	R. Dalgleish	Australia
5.5 m.	T. Turner	U.S.
EUROPEAN CHAMPIONS		
Dragon	P. Sundelin	Sweden
Finn	B. Binkhorst	Netherlands
Soling	P. Elvstrøm	Denmark
Hornet	D. Derry	U.K.
4-7-0	J. Follenfant	France
5-0-5	R. Symonette	Bahamas
Star	J. Schoonmaker	U.S.
Admiral's Cup	U.K.	

SPEEDWAY

Event	Winner	Country
World champion, individual	O. Olsen	Denmark
World champion, pairs	J. Szczakiel, A. Wygleda	Poland
World champion, team	U.K.	
European champion, individual	I. Mauger	New Zealand

SQUASH RACKETS

Event	Winner	Country
WORLD CHAMPIONS		
Men's individual	G. Hunt	Australia
Men's team		Australia
OTHER MAJOR TOURNAMENT WINNERS		
Australian amateur, men	G. Hunt	Australia
Australian amateur, women	H. McKay	Australia
British amateur, men	G. Ala-uddin	Pakistan
British open, men	J. Barrington	U.K.
British open, women	H. McKay	Australia

TABLE TENNIS

Event	Winner	Country
WORLD CHAMPIONS		
Men's singles	S. Bengtsson	Sweden
Men's doubles	T. Klampar, I. Jonver	Hungary
Women's singles	Lin Hui-ching	China
Women's doubles	Lin Hui-ching, Cheng Min-chin	China
Mixed doubles	Chang Shin-lin, Lin Hui-ching	China
Men's team	China	
Women's team	Japan	
BRITISH COMMONWEALTH CHAMPIONS		
Men's singles	T. Taylor	U.K.
Men's doubles	A. Hydes, T. Taylor	U.K.
Women's singles	J. Shirley	U.K.
Women's doubles	K. Matthews, P. Piddock	U.K.
Mixed doubles	A. Hydes, P. Piddock	U.K.
ENGLISH OPEN CHAMPIONS		
Men's singles	T. Klampar	Hungary
Men's doubles	S. Bengtsson, B. Persson	Sweden
Women's singles	M. Alexandru	Romania
Women's doubles	M. Alexandru, E. Mihalca	Romania
Mixed doubles	A. Stipancic, M. Alexandru	Yugoslavia, Romania
Men's team	U.K.	
Women's team	West Germany	
SCANDINAVIAN OPEN CHAMPIONS		
Men's singles	H. Alser	Sweden
Men's doubles	Chuang Tse-tung, Li Chang-kuang	China
Women's singles	Cheng Min-chin	China
Women's doubles	Li Li, Liang Lih-chen	China
Mixed doubles	Chuang Tse-tung, Lin Hui-ching	China
Men's team	Hungary	
Women's team	China	
EUROPEAN LEAGUE CHAMPIONSHIP		
	Hungary	

TOBOGGANING

Event	Winner	Country
WORLD CHAMPIONS		
Men	K. Brunner	Italy
Women	E. Demleitner	West Germany

TRACK AND FIELD

Event	Winner and country	Performance
EUROPEAN OUTDOOR CHAMPIONS—MEN		
100 m.	V. Borzov, U.S.S.R.	10.3 sec.
200 m.	V. Borzov, U.S.S.R.	20.3 sec.
400 m.	D. Jenkins, U.K.	45.5 sec.
800 m.	Y. Arzhanov, U.S.S.R.	1 min. 45.6 sec.
1,500 m.	F. Arese, Italy	3 min. 38.4 sec.
5,000 m.	J. Väätäinen, Finland	13 min. 32.6 sec.
10,000 m.	J. Väätäinen, Finland	27 min. 52.8 sec.
Steeplechase	J. Villain, France	8 min. 25.2 sec.
110-m. hurdles	F. Siebeck, East Germany	14.0 sec.
400-m. hurdles	J. Nallet, France	49.2 sec.
400-m. relay	Czechoslovakia	39.3 sec.
1,600-m. relay	West Germany	3 min. 2.9 sec.
High jump	K. Shapka, U.S.S.R.	7 ft. 2½ in.
Pole vault	W. Nordwig, East Germany	17 ft. 6½ in.
Long jump	M. Klauss, East Germany	25 ft. 11¾ in.
Triple jump	J. Drehmel, East Germany	56 ft. 3½ in.
Shot put	H. Briesenick, East Germany	69 ft. 2 in.
Discus	L. Danek, Czechoslovakia	209 ft. 5½ in.
Hammer throw	U. Beyer, West Germany	237 ft. 4½ in.
Javelin	J. Lusis, U.S.S.R.	297 ft. 6 in.
Decathlon	J. Kirst, East Germany	8,196 pt.
Marathon	K. Lismont, Belgium	2 hr. 13 min. 9.0 sec.
20-km. walk	N. Smaga, U.S.S.R.	1 hr. 27 min. 20.2 sec.
50-km. walk	V. Soldatenko, U.S.S.R.	4 hr. 2 min. 22.0 sec.
EUROPEAN OUTDOOR CHAMPIONS—WOMEN		
100 m.	R. Meissner-Stecher, East Germany	11.4 sec.
200 m.	R. Meissner-Stecher, East Germany	22.7 sec.
400 m.	H. Seidler, East Germany	52.1 sec.
800 m.	V. Nikolic, Yugoslavia	2 min.
1,500 m.	K. Burneleit, East Germany	4 min. 9.6 sec.
100-m. hurdles	K. Balzer, East Germany	12.9 sec.
400-m. relay	West Germany	43.3 sec.
1,600-m. relay	East Germany	3 min. 29.3 sec.
High jump	I. Gusenbauer, Austria	6 ft. 1½ in.
Long jump	I. Mickler-Becker, West Germany	22 ft. 2¼ in.
Shot put	N. Chizhova, U.S.S.R.	66 ft. 1¾ in.
Discus	F. Melnik, U.S.S.R.	210 ft. 8½ in.
Javelin	D. Jaworska, Poland	200 ft. 1½ in.
Pentathlon	H. Rosendahl, West Germany	5,299 pt.
PAN-AMERICAN GAMES CHAMPIONS—MEN		
100 m.	D. Quarrie, Jamaica	10.2 sec.
200 m.	D. Quarrie, Jamaica	19.8 sec.
400 m.	J. Smith, U.S.	44.6 sec.
800 m.	K. Swenson, U.S.	1 min. 48.0 sec.
1,500 m.	M. Liquori, U.S.	3 min. 42.1 sec.
5,000 m.	S. Prefontaine, U.S.	13 min. 52.6 sec.
10,000 m.	F. Shorter, U.S.	28 min. 50.8 sec.
Marathon	F. Shorter, U.S.	2 hr. 22 min. 44.0 sec.
Steeplechase	M. Manley, U.S.	8 min. 42.2 sec.
110-m. hurdles	R. Milburn, U.S.	13.4 sec.
400-m. hurdles	R. Mann, U.S.	49.1 sec.
400-m. relay	Jamaica	39.2 sec.
1,600-m. relay	U.S.	3 min. 0.6 sec.
High jump	P. Matzdorf, U.S.	6 ft. 10¾ in.
Pole vault	J. Johnson, U.S.	17 ft. 5¾ in.
Long jump	A. Robinson, U.S.	26 ft. 3¾ in.

Even	Winner and Country	Performance
Triple jump	P. Perez, Cuba	57 ft. 1 in.
Shot put	A. Feuerbach, U.S.	64 ft. 10 in.
Discus	R. Drescher, U.S.	204 ft. 3 in.
Hammer throw	A. Hall, U.S.	216 ft.
Javelin	C. Feldmann, U.S.	267 ft. 5 in.
Decathlon	R. Wanamaker, U.S.	7,648 pt.
20-km. walk	G. Klopfer, U.S.	1 hr. 37 min. 30.0 sec.
50-km. walk	L. Young, U.S.	4 hr. 38 min. 36.0 sec.

PAN-AMERICAN GAMES CHAMPIONS—WOMEN

100 m.	I. Davis, U.S.	11.2 sec.
200 m.	S. Berto, Canada	23.5 sec.
400 m.	M. Neufville, Jamaica	52.3 sec.
800 m.	A. Hoffman, Canada	2 min. 5.5 sec.
100-m. hurdles	P. Johnson, U.S.	13.1 sec.
400-m. relay	U.S.	44.5 sec.
1,600-m. relay	U.S.	3 min. 32.4 sec.
High jump	D. Brill, Canada	6 ft. ¾ in.
Long jump	B. Eisler, Canada	21 ft. 1¼ in.
Shot put	L. Graham, U.S.	51 ft. 8½ in.
Discus	C. Romero, Cuba	187 ft. 8 in.
Javelin	T. Nunez, Cuba	177 ft. 3 in.
Pentathlon	D. Van Kiekebelt, Canada	4,885 pt.

TRAMPOLINE

Event	Winner	Country
EUROPEAN CHAMPIONS		
Men	P. Luxon	U.K.
Women	N. Dull	West Germany

VOLLEYBALL

Event	Winner	Country
MAJOR TOURNAMENT WINNERS		
European Champions' Cup, men	Alma Ata	U.S.S.R.
Pan-American Games, men	Cuba	
Pan-American Games, women	Cuba	
South American championships, men	Brazil	
European Nations' Cup, men	U.S.S.R.	
European Nations' Cup, women	U.S.S.R.	

WATER SKIING

Event	Winner	Country
WORLD CHAMPIONS—MEN		
Slalom	M. Suyderhoud	U.S.
Figures	R. McCormick	U.S.
Jumping	M. Suyderhoud	U.S.
Combined	G. Athans	Canada
WORLD CHAMPIONS—WOMEN		
Slalom	C. Freeman	U.S.
Figures	W. Stahle	Netherlands
Jumping	C. Weir	U.S.
Combined	C. Weir	U.S.
WORLD CHAMPIONS—COMBINED TEAMS		
	U.S.	
WORLD CUP CHAMPIONS—MEN		
Slalom	M. Suyderhoud	U.S.
Figures	B. Cockburn	Australia
Jumping	M. Suyderhoud	U.S.
Combined	B. Cockburn	Australia
Team	Americas (Continent)	
EUROPEAN CUP WINNERS—MEN		
Slalom	R. Zucchi	Italy
Figures	R. Zucchi	Italy
Jumping	H. Klie	West Germany
Combined	R. Zucchi	Italy
Team	Italy	

WEIGHT LIFTING

Event	Competitor, country, date	Performance
WORLD RECORDS SET IN 1971		
Flyweight		
Press	A. Gnatov, U.S.S.R., March 10	253 lb.
	A. Gnatov, U.S.S.R., July 16	254 lb.
Bantamweight		
Press	S. Holzreiter, Hungary, May 16	278 lb.
Total	G. Chetin, U.S.S.R., July 17	827 lb.
Featherweight		
Press	I. Földi, Hungary, July 11	302 lb.
Jerk	D. Chanidze, U.S.S.R., July 11	339 lb.
Lightweight		
Press	J. Mathe, Hungary, May 16	325 lb.
	V. Dreksler, U.S.S.R., May 30	327 lb.
	V. Dreksler, U.S.S.R., July 18	336 lb.
Snatch	W. Baszanowski, Poland, April 23	303 lb.
Jerk	W. Baszanowski, Poland, April 23	380 lb.
Total	W. Baszanowski, Poland, April 23	986 lb.
	W. Baszanowski, Poland, June 22	992 lb.

Stamp Collecting:
see Philately and
Numismatics

Steel Industry:
see Industrial Review

Event	Competitor, country, date	Performance
Light-heavyweight		
Snatch	P. Korol, U.S.S.R., July 13	377 lb.
Middle-heavyweight		
Press	H. Bettembourg, Sweden, April 18	426 lb.
Jerk	D. Rigert, U.S.S.R., July 14	448 lb.
Total	D. Rigert, U.S.S.R., April 25	1,201 lb.
Heavyweight		
Press	J. Talts, U.S.S.R., February 14	449 lb.
	V. Yakubovskiy, U.S.S.R., April 25	449 lb.
	Y. Khozin, U.S.S.R., July 23	450 lb.
	J. Talts, U.S.S.R., August 8	454 lb.
Snatch	K. Utzar, U.S.S.R., July 15	372 lb.
	P. Pervushin, U.S.S.R., July 23	375 lb.
Jerk	J. Talts, U.S.S.R., August 8	479 lb.
Total	V. Yakubovskiy, U.S.S.R., April 25	1,250 lb.
	J. Talts, U.S.S.R., August 8	1,289 lb.
Super-heavyweight		
Press	V. Alekseyev, U.S.S.R., March 28	492 lb.
	V. Alekseyev, U.S.S.R., April 7	493 lb.
	V. Alekseyev, U.S.S.R., April 18	508 lb.
	V. Alekseyev, U.S.S.R., June 23	512 lb.
Snatch	K. Lahdenranta, Finland, June 8	393 lb.
	V. Alekseyev, U.S.S.R., July 25	397 lb.
Jerk	V. Alekseyev, U.S.S.R., July 25	518 lb.
Total	V. Alekseyev, U.S.S.R., June 23	1,389 lb.
	V. Alekseyev, U.S.S.R., July 25	1,411 lb.
WORLD CHAMPIONS		
Flyweight	Z. Smalcerz, Poland	749¼ lb.
Bantamweight	G. Chetin, U.S.S.R.	815¼ lb.
Featherweight	Y. Miyake, Japan	854 lb.
Lightweight	Z. Kaczmarek, Poland	969¾ lb.
Middleweight	Y. Kanygin, U.S.S.R.	1,052¼ lb.
Light-heavyweight	B. Pavlov, U.S.S.R.	1,091 lb.
Middle-heavyweight	D. Rigert, U.S.S.R.	1,195¼ lb.
Heavyweight	Y. Khozin, U.S.S.R.	1,217¼ lb.
Super-heavyweight	V. Alekseyev, U.S.S.R.	1,400¾ lb.
Team	U.S.S.R.	
EUROPEAN CHAMPIONS		
Flyweight	Z. Smalcerz, Poland	732¾ lb.
Bantamweight	I. Földi, Hungary	809¾ lb.
Featherweight	J. Wojnowski, Poland	876 lb.
Lightweight	W. Baszanowski, Poland	991¾ lb.
Middleweight	V. Kurentsov, U.S.S.R.	1,019¼ lb.
Light-heavyweight	G. Ivanchenko, U.S.S.R.	1,102 lb.
Middle-heavyweight	D. Rigert, U.S.S.R.	1,184½ lb.
Heavyweight	V. Yakubovsky, U.S.S.R.	1,234 lb.
Super-heavyweight	V. Alekseyev, U.S.S.R.	1,388¾ lb.
Team	U.S.S.R.	
PAN-AMERICAN GAMES CHAMPIONS		
Flyweight	J. Romero, Cuba	661 lb.
Bantamweight	R. Chang, Cuba	754 lb.
Featherweight	M. Mateos, Mexico	771 lb.
Lightweight	P. Rodriguez, Cuba	865 lb.
Middleweight	R. Knipp, U.S.	992 lb.
Light-heavyweight	P. Kartchut, U.S.	1,041 lb.
Middle-heavyweight	P. Grippaldi, U.S.	1,091 lb.
Heavyweight	G. Deal, U.S.	1,173 lb.
U.S. CHAMPIONS		
Flyweight	P. Moyer	589 lb.
Bantamweight	F. Dominguez	666 lb.
Featherweight	E. Hernandez	765 lb.
Lightweight	J. Benjamin	860 lb.
Middleweight	R. Knipp	1,008 lb.
Light-heavyweight	P. Kartchut	1,008 lb.
Middle-heavyweight	R. Holbrook	1,096 lb.
Heavyweight	G. Deal	1,157 lb.
Super-heavyweight	K. Patera	1,305 lb.

WRESTLING

Event	Winner	Country
WORLD FREESTYLE CHAMPIONS		
Light-flyweight	E. Javadi	Iran
Flyweight	M. Ghorbani	Iran
Bantamweight	H. Yamagida	Japan
Featherweight	A. Abdulbekov	U.S.S.R.
Lightweight	R. Gable	U.S.
Welterweight	G. Gusov	U.S.S.R.
Middleweight	S. Tediashvili	U.S.S.R.
Light-heavyweight	B. Petrov	Bulgaria
Heavyweight	S. Lomidze	U.S.S.R.
Super-heavyweight	A. Medved	U.S.S.R.
WORLD GRECO-ROMAN CHAMPIONS		
Light-flyweight	S. Zubkov	U.S.S.R.
Flyweight	P. Kirov	Bulgaria
Bantamweight	E. Kazakov	U.S.S.R.
Featherweight	M. Markov	Bulgaria
Lightweight	S. Damyanovic	Yugoslavia
Welterweight	V. Igumenov	U.S.S.R.
Middleweight	I. Hegedus	Hungary
Light-heavyweight	V. Rezyanov	U.S.S.R.
Heavyweight	N. Martinescu	Romania
Super-heavyweight	P. Svensson	Sweden

(D.K.R.P.)

See also Baseball; Basketball; Bowling and Lawn Bowls; Boxing; Chess; Contract Bridge; Cricket; Cycling; Football; Golf; Hockey; Horse Racing; Ice Skating; Motor Sports; Rowing; Sailing; Skiing; Swimming; Tennis; Track and Field Sports.

Stock Exchanges

Stock markets throughout the world recorded mixed results in 1971. The threatened collapse of the post-World War II currency exchange system was the principal influence on stock price movements. Other influences were the state of consumer and business confidence, the intensity of wage and price inflation, the direction of corporate profits, and social unrest. Half of the world's 12 major stock price indexes were higher at the end of 1971 than at the end of 1970. (*See* Table I.)

In 1971 there were three separate attempts to resolve the world's currency exchange system for conducting international trade, each of which affected stock price movements to a significant degree. On May 9 the West German government released the mark from a ratio of 3.66 to the dollar, allowing it to float freely for all capital and trade transactions. It was the first European country to permit the value of its currency to be determined by the free-market forces of supply and demand.

The postwar currency exchange and trade system was altered even more radically on August 15 when the United States cut the dollar loose from gold and imposed a 10% surcharge on imports. This action was precipitated by the long-standing deficit in the U.S. balance of international payments, including an apparent foreign trade deficit in 1971, the first such for the nation since 1893.

The convertibility of dollars into gold had been the backbone of the world's monetary system since its adoption at the Bretton Woods Conference in 1944. The Bretton Woods agreement called for the free world's currencies to be pegged to the dollar, with the dollar tied to gold at a fixed rate of $35 to the ounce. Nevertheless, the desire of the U.S. to devalue the dollar without increasing the price of gold could be frustrated if each country maintained the dollar parity of its currency by buying U.S. dollars in the open market to keep the value of its currency from rising above the fixed rate to the dollar. Meanwhile, the added levy of 10% on foreign goods coming into the U.S. meant that some European and Asian countries would be unable to compete against U.S. manufacturers in the richest market of the free world.

The threatened breakdown of the world's monetary exchange and trade relations, however, was averted in December after a series of meetings, in Rome and Washington, among the finance ministers and central bank governors of the United States and nine other industrial countries, formally known as the Group of Ten. These meetings culminated with an agreement on December 18 to establish a new system of monetary exchange rates and to eliminate certain trade barriers. The key features were a dollar devaluation of 7.89% as part of an international realignment of major currencies, and the removal of the U.S. 10% import surcharge.

The general movement of stock prices throughout the world in 1971 tended to follow more or less the same pattern. The early part of the year was characterized by strong stock prices. This was followed by widespread price weakness following the floating of the West German mark. The subsequent decline lasted until the end of June, when a strong rally carried many stock price indexes to their highest levels of the year. After the U.S. announced its new policy on gold and international trade, prices plummeted. As the year came to a close, most stock markets were rallying from their late autumn lows. The mid-December announcement from the Group of Ten meeting that the U.S. was prepared to devalue the dollar sparked the advance. (R. H. TR.)

United States. Securities prices displayed a roller-coaster pattern in 1971 as the recovery from the 1970 mini-recession was stalled at midyear by profound monetary crises and uncertainty about the course of the U.S. economy; this was followed by a vigorous rally in December. Among the consequences of these swift-moving economic changes was a considerable degree of uncertainty about price prospects for securities. The reaction of the stock market to economic uncertainty was more pronounced in 1971 than in any year during the previous decade.

The Dow Jones industrial average reached its 1971 high on April 28 at a level of 950.82, well below the 1,000 mark set on Jan. 18, 1966. The year's low was 797.97, established on November 23. Following Pres. Richard Nixon's announcement of price and wage controls, the Dow Jones went up 33 points and in the next 23 days it rose an additional 32 points to a level of 921 on September 8. A subsequent ten-week decline of 123 points culminated in the November 23 low, the first time since Dec. 1, 1970, that the Dow Jones average had been under 800. With the resolution of the world monetary crisis in December, the averages bounced up by almost 100 points. Another important December development was the reduction of the margin requirement from 65 to 55% by the Federal Reserve Board, which had maintained an easy money policy throughout most of 1971.

Activity in the securities market picked up sharply during the last half of the year as the volume of new issues achieved record highs. In September alone the volume of new issues, at $1.5 billion, was almost four times the amount underwritten in the corresponding month of 1970.

Average stock prices on the New York Stock Exchange (NYSE) were much higher in 1971 than they had been a year earlier. (*See* Table II.) The 500 stocks in the composite index began a recovery in June 1970 that moved ahead month by month in 1971 and peaked in April at a level of 103.04, a gain in one year of 19%. The index dipped in May and moved unevenly within a narrow range to its lowest day at 90.16 in November. At the end of 1971 the index closed at 102.09, an improvement of 9.94% over the 1970 close.

The 425 industrial stocks outperformed their 1970 results every month during 1971. From a low of 82.96 in June 1970, they climbed to 102.22 in January 1971 and then moved smartly up to 113.68 in April before falling back in May and drifting to a November low. A closing rally carried this index from a low of 99.36 to a December 31 figure of 112.72. The year-to-year gain in this index was 11.82%.

Public utilities stock traded within a relatively narrow range and did not do as well as the other groups. While the average price of utilities stock remained above the 1970 levels throughout most of the year, the index closed at 59.83, a loss of 1.88% from Dec. 31, 1970. Railroad stocks in 1971 outperformed 1970 by a comfortable margin as investors moved to take advantage of the radical change in the industry brought about by the removal of most passenger services from the private railroads to Amtrak, a government-sponsored corporation. A brisk movement in the

WIDE WORLD

Paul Kolton was elected president of the American Stock Exchange on May 20, 1971, to replace Ralph S. Saul, who resigned.

first months of 1971 carried the index from January levels of 36.64 to a peak in April of 42.29. Even when the downturn began in May, there was an improvement of 35.2% over the preceding year's figures.

Common stock yields fell from their high level of 4.51 in June 1970 to 3.56 by the end of 1970 and continued downward in 1971 from a high of 3.47 in January to a low of 3.19 in April. This was followed by a slow recovery, but by August yields were falling once more as prices spurted upward.

Government bond prices were much firmer in 1971 than they had been in 1970 as interest rates generally fell throughout most of the year. (*See* Table III.) Prices moved within a narrow range, rising from 66.10 in January to a high of 67.94 in March before dipping back to 67.57 in April, and a low of 65.72 in May. Beginning in June prices rose, as the trend of interest rates was downward. But despite the downward drift of the bond yields, they still remained at abnormally high levels in 1971. A peak of 6.71 was achieved in March and was followed by relatively steady declines during the remainder of the year. In the short-term fixed-income securities field, Treasury bills were sold at an average rate of 4.09% in mid-December, the lowest since May.

Corporate bond prices paralleled the behaviour of government bonds, although their year-to-year differentials were not so pronounced. (*See* Table IV.)

The year's high was attained in February at 66.8, and the low of 63.2 occurred in July. Corporate bond yields were much lower in 1971 than in 1970. Between the June 1970 level and that of June 1971 there was a reduction of more than 10%.

Among the positive factors affecting investors' expectations in 1971 were solid signs of business revival. Consumer spending for goods and services was running about 7.5% ahead of 1970; home building was brisk; automobile sales were running at an annual rate of more than 10 million; corporate profits were up; personal income was rising at an increasing rate; unemployment was slowly declining; consumer prices by November were rising at an annual rate of only 2.4%; and the money supply was increased substantially during the first half of the year.

Among the unfavourable factors in the market were continuing high unemployment rates and a federal budget deficit generally regarded as excessive. There were expectations that under Nixon's wage-price control program there would be a bias toward a tighter rein on prices than on wages, leading to a squeeze on profits. However, by the end of 1971 most of these doubts had been resolved and the market had turned highly bullish.

During 1971 the Securities and Exchange Commission (SEC) continued to tighten up the rules governing broker-customer relations by requiring more effective escrowing and segregation of customer funds; by giving management the burden of issuing bulletins to correct erroneous or exaggerated reports published outside the company's control so that the public might not be misled by the company's silence; and by requiring mutual funds to make capital gain distributions on a less regular basis to correct the impression of a steady earnings flow. The SEC also sought power to approve or disapprove stock exchange rules and the right to enforce those rules directly if deemed necessary. In a forecast of prospective developments in the near future, the SEC staff anticipated a worldwide central marketplace for stocks, a central clearing system, a central quotation service, and fully computerized stock transfers with simultaneous debits and credits of the bank accounts of buyer and seller.

Aggregate volume on the NYSE for the 12 months of 1971 totaled 3,890,000,000 shares, an increase of 953 million over 1970. The number of stock issues traded rose from 1,846 in 1970 to 1,945 in 1971. Bond activity was even more expansive, with 1,791 issues traded in 1971, compared with 1,510 in 1970. Through November, 283 new issues totaling $18.6 billion were listed, compared with 246 issues totaling $17.7 billion in all of 1970.

The NYSE depository grew faster than expected and had holdings of more than 1 billion shares in 1971. More than 60% of all transactions were handled through floor bookkeeping and the depository, instead of through normal transfer agent activity involving traditional certificates. The new method was estimated to have saved an annual sum of $50 million. The NYSE automatic transactions system was prepared to handle all odd lot orders (less than 100 shares) on a ⅛ point spread. Fixed commissions on portions of transactions involving more than $500,000 were removed and made a matter of negotiation between broker and client.

The NYSE tightened its net capital rules in 1971. The ratio of a firm's liquid capital to total debt was increased from 1 to 20 to 1 to 25 during the summer. When the ratio reached 1 to 12, the exchange had to

New York Stock Exchange prices and average daily volume, 1971.

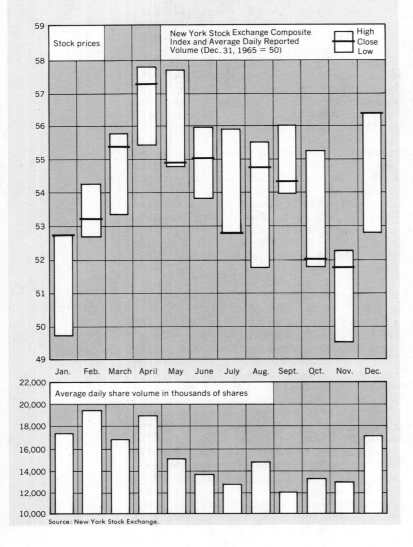

Source: New York Stock Exchange.

be notified immediately and remedial measures taken within 15 business days. When the ratio reached 1 to 10, firms were barred from expanding their businesses.

Volume was up 28% on the American Stock Exchange during 1971 to 1,070,924,002 shares from the 1970 level of 843,116,260, but fell far short of the 1968 record of 1,460,000,000 shares. Stock issues traded rose to 1,309 from 1,234 in 1970, and bond issues traded increased to 175 from 167 a year earlier. Experimental execution of trades by computer was begun in 1971, with full utilization expected in 1972.

In the over-the-counter market, the most significant development was the use of NASDAQ, a reporting service that provided closer price comparisons and caused some shifting of activity from the central exchange markets. In April, 30 listed stocks were included on this automated quotation system, with the result that price spreads dropped about 12% almost immediately on quotations of the stock on the exchanges.

Canada. The Canadian stock market followed the U.S. pattern throughout most of the year, although Canada was affected by a more prolonged recession, higher unemployment, and less stock market bullishness. The U.S. 10% surcharge on imports hit Canada in August and depressed the market severely.

Industrial stocks on the Toronto and Montreal exchanges rose during the first quarter to their 1971 highs, leveled off during the summer months, and dipped in the autumn. December brought a sharp rally coincident with the lifting of the U.S. import surcharge. Gold stocks were erratic, rising irregularly in the first four months, dropping all the gains in the summer, jumping upward in August and September, and declining sharply subsequent to the devaluation of the U.S. dollar. At the year's end the index was at a two-year low. Base metals also fell to a two-year low in the last quarter of 1971.

Interest rates in Canada during 1971 rose during the first half of the year and after August declined irregularly. Long-term Canada bonds began the year at 6.2%, rose to 7.2% by August, and ended the year at 5.9%. Ninety-day Treasury bills, which traded at 4½% in January, were selling to yield slightly more than 3% by December. (I. Pr.)

European Economic Community. Recent stock price information was available for five of the EEC countries. The two most economically powerful members, West Germany and France, experienced contrasting stock markets in 1971. The former posted higher stock prices, while the latter experienced declines. Lower prices were also shown by Italy and the Netherlands. Stock prices in Belgium were able to post a gain over the entire year.

After falling 27% in 1970, the West German stock market reversed its bearish trend in 1971. For the year as a whole, the average rise in stock prices was 4%. The monetary crisis in May and the U.S. dollar crisis in August were major disruptions to a sharper uptrend in equity values.

West German stock prices increased significantly in the early part of the year. The reduction of U.S. and Canadian interest rates in March, coupled with signs of a cooling off in the West German economy, created hopes of an easing of the country's restrictive economic policies. From January 1 to May 7, the West German stock market rose 12%. On May 9 the government announced its intention to permit the West German mark to float freely for both capital and trade transactions. The immediate effect was a de facto revaluation (rise in value) of the mark of roughly 4%. The fact that this action occurred at a time when the West German economy was slowing down created a cautious attitude among investors. Between May 9 and August 13, stock prices increased at the much slower rate of 2%.

A downtrend in West Germany's stock prices developed after the U.S. cut the dollar's tie to gold and slapped an added levy of 10% on imports in mid-August. From August 13 to early November the decline in equity values amounted to 16%. On November 5 stock prices reached a point nearly 22% below the highs of mid-February.

The combined effect of the float and U.S. initiatives on trade and currency exchange resulted in the mark's 13% upward revaluation against the dollar by early

Table I. Selected Major World Stock Market Price Indexes*

Country	1971 range High	1971 range Low	Year-end indexes 1970	Year-end indexes 1971	Percent change
Australia	519	405	516	504	− 2
Austria	2,088	1,977	2,055	1,989†	− 3
Belgium	107	91	92	97	+ 5
France	79	62	75	67	−11
West Germany	113	88	94	98	+ 4
Italy	60	44	57	47	−18
Japan	2,741	1,982	1,987	2,714	+37
Netherlands	128	93	113	106	− 6
South Africa	89	61	79	76	− 4
Sweden	308	246	246	306	+24
Switzerland	357	307	302	343	+14
United Kingdom	477	305	341	477	+40

*Index numbers are rounded, and limited to countries for which full year's data were available.
†As of Dec. 24, 1971.
Sources: Barron's, The Economist, Financial Times, New York Times.

Table II. U.S. Stock Market Prices and Yields

Month	Railroads (20 stocks) 1971	Railroads (20 stocks) 1970	Industrials (425 stocks) 1971	Industrials (425 stocks) 1970	Public utilities (55 stocks) 1971	Public utilities (55 stocks) 1970	Composite (500 stocks) 1971	Composite (500 stocks) 1970	Yield (200 stocks; %) 1971	Yield (200 stocks; %) 1970
January	36.64	37.62	102.22	99.40	63.43	55.72	93.49	90.31	3.47	3.94
February	38.78	36.58	106.62	95.73	62.49	55.24	97.11	87.16	3.41	3.73
March	39.70	37.33	109.59	96.95	62.42	59.04	99.60	88.65	3.29	3.75
April	42.29	36.05	113.68	94.01	62.06	57.19	103.04	85.95	3.19	4.09
May	42.05	31.10	112.41	83.16	59.20	51.15	101.64	76.06	3.35	4.28
June	42.12	28.94	110.26	82.96	57.90	49.22	99.72	75.59	3.38	4.51
July	42.05	26.59	109.09	83.00	60.08	50.91	99.00	75.72	3.51	4.20
August	43.55	26.74	107.26	85.40	57.51	52.62	97.24	77.92	3.34	4.04
September	47.18	29.14	109.85	90.66	56.48	54.44	99.40	82.58	3.35	3.94
October	44.58	31.73	107.28	92.85	57.41	53.37	97.29	84.37	3.48	3.96
November	41.19	30.80	102.22	92.58	55.86	54.86	92.78	84.28	3.47	3.75
December		32.95		98.72		59.96		90.05		3.56

Source: U.S. Department of Commerce, Survey of Current Business. Prices are Standard and Poor's monthly averages of daily closing prices with 1941–43=10. Yield figures are Moody's index of 200 stocks.

Table III. U.S. Government Long-Term Bond Prices and Yields
Average price in dollars per $100 bond

Month	Average 1971	Average 1970	Yield (%) 1971	Yield (%) 1970	Month	Average 1971	Average 1970	Yield (%) 1971	Yield (%) 1970
January	66.10	58.33	5.91	6.86	July	66.16	60.59	5.91	6.57
February	66.78	61.63	5.84	6.44	August	67.33	59.20	5.78	6.75
March	67.94	62.04	6.71	6.39	September	69.35	60.10	5.56	6.63
April	67.57	60.89	5.75	6.53	October	70.33	60.44	5.46	6.59
May	65.72	57.78	5.96	6.94	November	70.47	60.44	5.44	6.24
June	65.84	57.37	5.94	6.99	December		65.63		5.97

Source: U.S. Department of Commerce, Survey of Current Business. Average prices are derived from average yields on the basis of an assumed 3% 20-year taxable U.S. Treasury bond. Yields are for U.S. Treasury bonds that are taxable and due or callable in ten years or more.

Table IV. U.S. Corporate Bond Prices and Yields
Average price in dollars per $100 bond

Month	Average 1971	Average 1970	Yield (%) 1971	Yield (%) 1970	Month	Average 1971	Average 1970	Yield (%) 1971	Yield (%) 1970
January	66.5	62.2	7.36	7.91	July	63.2	59.0	7.64	8.44
February	66.8	62.4	7.08	7.93	August	63.4	60.0	7.59	8.13
March	65.8	62.8	7.21	7.84	September	64.2	60.8	7.44	8.09
April	65.0	62.8	7.25	7.83	October	65.2	61.3	7.29	8.03
May	63.7	61.2	7.53	8.11	November	66.4	61.9	7.26	8.05
June	63.5	59.4	7.64	8.48	December		64.7		7.64

Source: U.S. Department of Commerce, Survey of Current Business. Average prices are based on Standard and Poor's composite index of A1+ issues. Yields are based on Moody's Aaa domestic corporate bond index.

Workers clear debris
from the New York
Stock Exchange
on Aug. 16, 1971, after
a record-breaking
day on Wall Street.
Heavy trading followed
Pres. Richard Nixon's
message on the wage-price
freeze.

WIDE WORLD

December. The government sought to offset the export-damaging effect of the floating mark by lowering the bank rate from 5 to 4½%, effective October 14. Also, announcements of work cutbacks and production stoppages threatened to bring about a general slump in economic activity. Unemployment in November was 1.2% greater than in October and 1.6% higher than the previous year. Nevertheless, the year closed with a flurry of stock buying, fueled by the trade and currency agreement reached at the Group of Ten meeting in Washington. As a result, equity values rose 11% above the November 5 low.

Prices on the Paris Bourse took a beating in 1971, its equity price index dropping 11%. All of the decline came in the second half of the year. Contributing factors included a series of strikes, which had a disrupting effect on industrial activity, and fears that gold would be excluded as the basis for any future multilateral currency realignment.

Stock prices had ended the first half of 1971 about 3% higher than they began the year. Prices also rose in July, at one time showing a 5% gain over the 1970 close. However, the entire rise, and more, was wiped out in the period between mid-August and the end of November (−21%). France had been the chief advocate of gold as a reserve currency, with the nation's gold and currency reserves increasing to $6.3 billion by Aug. 1, 1971, from $1.4 billion the year before. Thus, the decision by the U.S. to cut the dollar loose from gold and to oppose the use of gold as a reserve instrument was disheartening for French investors. The gloom persisted even though the government announced a two-tier exchange system. Under the plan, the French franc would be supported within 1% of its existing parity to the dollar for trade and related transactions, but allowed to float "freely" in speculative transactions.

With the December news that the U.S. was willing to consider an increase in the price of gold as part of a monetary settlement, French stock prices rebounded from their November lows. By the end of December the stock market rally had added 8% to equity values.

The price index of shares traded on the Milan Stock Exchange finished 1971 with the largest average loss (−18%) among the major world stock price indexes, after losing 20% in 1970. In fact, the Solex index of industrial shares ended 1971 at its lowest level since 1959. Declining industrial activity, worker discord over prices and wages, and continuing instability on the domestic political scene were responsible.

In the Netherlands the seesaw movement of stock prices resulted in a moderate net decline in the leading stock averages. From year-end 1970 to year-end 1971 the loss amounted to 6%. The international monetary crisis in mid-August initiated most of the decline. From the August close to the end of November, average stock prices dropped 18%. The rally following the monetary talks in December amounted to 7%.

Belgium experienced higher stock prices in 1971 (+5%). The rise in equity values on the Brussels Bourse began in early January and continued throughout the summer. The May decision of the government not to allow the Belgian franc to float was regarded favourably by investors. The year's high, recorded on July 30, was 16% above the 1970 close.

European Free Trade Association. Current stock market information was available for four of the eight EFTA countries. The stock market performance of the United Kingdom (+40%) was the best in the

Index of industrial
ordinary share prices
on the London Stock
Exchange, 1950–71.

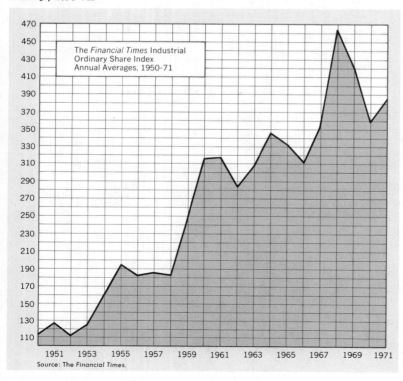

The *Financial Times* Industrial
Ordinary Share Index
Annual Averages, 1950-71

Source: The *Financial Times*.

world. Bull markets were also experienced in Sweden (+24%) and Switzerland (+14%), while Austria's stock market showed a 3% loss.

After a period of hesitation, the British stock market rose throughout most of the year. From the end of 1970 to the end of 1971, the *Financial Times* index of 30 British industrial stocks was up 40%. New tax and investment incentive policies designed to increase economic growth, relatively sharp increases in the country's gold and dollar reserves, and substantial improvement in the nation's balance of trade were the major contributing factors.

U.K. stock prices dropped 9% between the end of 1970 and March 3. The confidence of consumers and businessmen was shaken by the highest unemployment figure since 1963; a series of strikes against the national postal system and British Ford Motor Co.; and the bankruptcies of two major British corporations, Rolls-Royce Ltd., a world-renowned aircraft engine and automobile manufacturer, and Vehicle and General Insurance Co., a leading automobile insurance company. Countering these unfavourable developments was the fact that in 1970 the nation had achieved its first trade surplus since 1958.

Most of the decline was wiped out with the March 30 announcement that the government planned to overhaul the entire tax system, including cuts in corporate and capital gains taxes. The *Financial Times* index jumped almost 21 points to 352, the largest one-day advance in history, and the index ended the first quarter with a gain of nearly 2%.

The third quarter of 1971 also saw a relatively sharp increase in equity values (7.8%). In mid-July the government announced excise tax cuts on virtually all consumer goods and the elimination of all consumer credit controls. At the same time, the government obtained a pledge from the Confederation of British Industry to hold price increases to 5% over the next year. Consumer prices had risen 10% during the most recent 12-month period.

October brought news that British gold and dollar reserves had climbed for the 12th successive month, reaching a new high of $5.2 billion. Also, for the sixth consecutive month the value of the country's exports of goods and services exceeded the cost of imports. These developments were largely responsible for the relative strength of the British pound after the U.S. suspended the convertibility of the dollar. In addition, investors in stocks were hoping that under a new monetary system British sterling would be revalued less than other European currencies.

Stock prices finished the year on a strong upward trend. The ebullient mood of investors was strengthened by Parliament's approval on October 28 of British entry into the EEC and by the settlement of the international monetary crisis. Assuming the treaty of accession was ratified by Britain and each of the existing members of the EEC, Britain would become a member on Jan. 1, 1973.

The Swedish stock market was not only one of the better performing markets but also one of the most volatile. After dropping about 25% in 1970, stock prices on the Stockholm Exchange increased 24% from the end of 1970 to the end of 1971. The rally that got under way in late 1970 accelerated during the first half of 1971. The stock price index moved up almost in a straight line until it reached 293 on June 23, a 19% rise from the 1970 close. The Swedish Central Bank lowered the bank rate by a half a point effective March 19 and again April 23. Equity investors inter-

preted these actions as signs that the government's anti-inflationary program, adopted in mid-1970, would bring about a more orderly pattern of growth.

Stock prices in Switzerland also followed a bullish pattern. From year-end 1970 to year-end 1971, prices on the Zürich Stock Exchange rose 14%. The strength of the Swiss stock markets was evident during the first half of 1971 (+14%). But the dollar crisis of mid-August brought the rally to an end. The 10% import surcharge imposed by the U.S. was expected to have a damaging effect, particularly on watch exports. At the end of October equity values were 12% below the level reached on August 13. However, as 1971 came to a close the possibility that the U.S. and other leading nations would resolve currency and trade issues created an upsurge in investor confidence. Stock prices rose 10% from the October close.

For the first time in three years, the Austrian stock market turned in a poor performance. The price of equities declined an average of 3%. During the first

Stock trading on the New York Stock Exchange: yearly range of prices and number of shares sold, 1950–71.

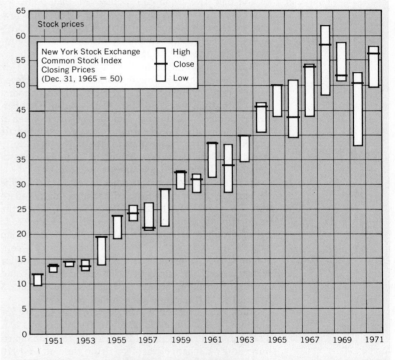

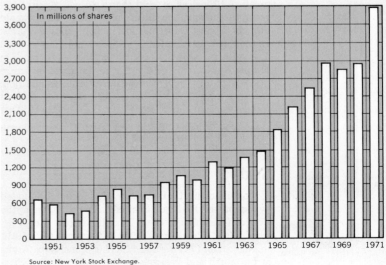

Source: New York Stock Exchange.

half of 1971, prices on the Vienna Stock Exchange were relatively unchanged (+0.4%). However, uncertainties over currency changes and trade liberalization were responsible for the bearish trend that developed during the rest of the year. The market reached its lowest point near the end of November.

Other Countries. The trend of the stock markets in the other countries for which current information was available varied. Japan experienced the second largest increase in equity prices (+37%) among the major world stock market indexes in 1971. On the other hand, lower stock markets prevailed in Australia and South Africa.

Prices on the Tokyo Stock Exchange began 1971 in a bullish atmosphere. To reduce the wide fluctuations in prices and control the volume of trading, the exchange raised margin requirements for all stocks eligible for margin trading from 40 to 50%, effective April 19. Nevertheless, the index of 225 common stocks on the Tokyo exchange continued to rise, reaching an all-time high in early August, just prior to the new U.S. economic policy. At that point the index was approximately 117% above the 1968 low, the year in which the bull market began, and 38% above the 1970 close. The uptrend was reversed, however, after the U.S. August measures.

During the immediate period following the U.S. action, prices on the Tokyo Stock Exchange suffered some of the severest one-day declines in recent memory. From the August 13 close to the end of October, prices plunged on average almost 17%. But when it appeared that the world's finance officials would settle the currency and trade dispute, the subsequent rally was also relatively sharp. From the October close to the end of December, average prices rose 19%.

In Australia stock prices were lower in 1971. The decline on the Sydney Stock Exchange amounted to 2%. Between May 14 and November 23, when the international monetary crisis was at its peak, stock prices dropped 21%. Since about 25% of Australian exports go to Japan and most of the country's contracts with Japanese merchants are arranged in dollar terms, losses from currency value changes alone could reach $100 million. However, from the November 23 low to the 1971 close, equity values rose 24%.

Stock prices in South Africa were also largely influenced by the international monetary events of 1971. The average decline in gold stocks on the Johannesburg Stock Exchange was 4%. From the end of 1970 to April 19, prices of gold shares rose 13%. But uncertainties about the future monetary role of gold brought a very sharp decline in gold mining shares. In the third quarter alone, the drop amounted to 12%. The willingness of the U.S. to consider an increase in the price of gold in return for an adequate exchange rate realignment reversed the downtrend. In addition, the uptrend was fueled by higher prices for gold on foreign exchange markets. (R. H. TR.)

See also Economy, World; Investment, International; Money and Banking; Savings and Investments.

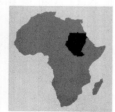

Sudan

A republic of northeast Africa, the Sudan is bounded by Egypt, the Red Sea, Ethiopia, Kenya, Uganda, the Congo (Kinshasa), the Central African Republic, Chad, and Libya. Area: 967,494 sq.mi. (2,505,813 sq.km.). Pop. (1971 est.): 15,695,000, including Arabs in the north and Negroes in the south. Cap.: Khartoum (pop., 1969 est., 230,600). Largest city: Omdurman (pop., 1969 est., 232,200). Language: Arabic; various tribal languages in the south. Religion: Muslim in the north; predominantly animist in the south. Chairman of the Revolutionary Council (later president) and prime minister in 1971, Maj. Gen. Gaafar Nimeiry.

Sudan in 1971 came close to having the Arab world's first Communist-controlled regime. On July 19 a group of army officers, in direct alliance with the Sudan Communist Party (SCP), seized power and arrested President Nimeiry (*see* BIOGRAPHY). Three days later the armoured corps, encouraged by Egypt and Libya, restored Nimeiry to power. During those three days the Marxist revolutionaries had shot 28 officers and men; Nimeiry's revenge was swift. After summary courts-martial 12 officers were executed and 3 prominent civilian SCP leaders hanged.

The coup attempt climaxed eight months of growing tension between Nimeiry and the SCP. In November 1970 he had dismissed three of his colleagues from the Revolutionary Council for leaking Cabinet secrets to the SCP executive and "abroad"; it was those three who led the July coup. In February 1971 Nimeiry—still retaining three Communists in his Cabinet—accused the SCP of sabotaging the country's unity and threatened to "crush and destroy" it.

The SCP, which had only about 7,000 members, fought back, but its power was steadily undermined as Nimeiry successively shut down popular front organizations under its control—the Farmers' Union, the Youth Organization, and the Women's Federation. In the aftermath of the coup, Nimeiry purged the administration of known SCP sympathizers and set up a single political organization, the Sudanese Socialist Union. After a month-long personal campaign

SUDAN
Education. (1967–68) Primary, pupils 496,088, teachers 10,337; secondary, pupils 138,042, teachers 7,296; vocational, pupils 4,880, teachers 385; teacher training, students 1,559, teachers 179; higher (including 2 universities), students 10,404, teaching staff 1,081.
Finance. Monetary unit: Sudanese pound, with a par value of Sud£0.348 to U.S. $1 (Sud£0.836 = £1 sterling) and a free rate (Sept. 27, 1971) of *c.* Sud£0.864 to £1 sterling. Gold, SDRs, and foreign exchange, official: (June 1971) U.S. $27.6 million; (June 1970) U.S. $39.2 million. Budget (1970–71 est.): revenue Sud£158 million; expenditure Sud£113 million. Money supply: (June 1971) Sud£111,660,000; (June 1970) Sud£105.1 million. Cost of living (1963 = 100): (Dec. 1969) 121; (Dec. 1968) 105.
Foreign Trade. (1970) Imports Sud£100,120,000; exports Sud£103,910,000. Import sources: (1969) U.K. 20%; India 10%; Japan 8%; West Germany 7%; China 6%; Italy 5%; U.S.S.R. 5%. Export destinations (1969): Italy 13%; India 13%; West Germany 12%; Japan 9%; China 8%; U.K. 7%; U.S.S.R. 5%. Main exports: cotton 61%; gum arabic 8%; peanuts 5%.
Transport and Communications. Roads (1969) *c.* 50,000 km. (mainly tracks, including 335 km. asphalted). Motor vehicles in use (1969): passenger 30,100; commercial (including buses) 17,700. Railways: (1968) 4,752 km.; freight traffic (1969) 2,398,000,000 net ton-km. Air traffic (1970): 198 million passenger-km.; freight 2,950,000 net ton-km. Navigable waterways (1969) 4,068 km. Telephones (Dec. 1969) 44,508. Radio receivers (Dec. 1968) *c.* 180,000. Television receivers (Dec. 1969) 30,000.
Agriculture. Production (in 000; metric tons; 1970; 1969 in parentheses): millet *c.* 400 (427); sorghum *c.* 1,350 (1,417); dry broad beans *c.* 12 (11); peanuts *c.* 383 (383); durra (1969) 619, (1968) 1,980; sesame *c.* 201 (202); dates *c.* 72 (*c.* 72); bananas *c.* 10 (*c.* 10); cotton, lint 225 (225). Livestock (in 000; 1969–70): cattle *c.* 13,500; sheep *c.* 13,000; goats *c.* 10,050; camels *c.* 3,000; asses *c.* 620.
Industry. Production (in 000; metric tons; 1969): cement 169; salt 51; electricity (kw-hr.) 528,000.

Loyal army troops arrest Sudanese Communists on July 25, 1971, in Khartoum after an abortive Communist-supported coup against the government of Maj. Gen. Gaafar Nimeiry.

throughout the country, Nimeiry was elected president in October by a popular referendum in which he was the sole candidate; the Revolutionary Council was then dissolved.

In forming his new Cabinet, Nimeiry went far toward satisfying the demands of the southern provinces, ravaged by civil war for eight years. To each province he appointed a southerner as ministerial commissioner, and negotiations were entered into with the exiled leaders of the southern secessionist movement.

While no evidence of Soviet involvement in the July plot was made public, Nimeiry in a speech in September accused the European Communist states, except Yugoslavia, of acting on Moscow's orders in fomenting his overthrow. (Pr. K.)

Swaziland

A landlocked constitutional monarchy of southern Africa, Swaziland is bounded by South Africa and Mozambique. Area: 6,704 sq.mi. (17,-364 sq.km.). Pop. (1971 est.):

SWAZILAND
Education. (1969) Primary, pupils 64,411, teachers (1968) 1,627; secondary, pupils 6,762, teachers (1968) 300; vocational, pupils 144, teachers (1968) 10; teacher training, students 296, teachers (1968) 29; higher (1968), students 69, teaching staff 15.
Finance and Trade. Monetary unit: South African rand (R 0.71 = U.S. $1; R 1.71 = £1 sterling), with a free rate (Sept. 27, 1971) of R 1.77 to £1. Budget (1970–71 est.) balanced at R 15,164,000 (including U.K. grant-in-aid of c. R 4.2 million). Foreign trade (1969): imports c. R 38 million; exports c. R 48 million. Main exports: sugar 22%; iron ore 20%; wood pulp 15%; asbestos 13%.
Agriculture. Production (in 000; metric tons; 1969; 1968 in parentheses): corn 58 (52); sorghum c. 22 (c. 22); rice 8 (8); sugar, raw value (1970–71) c. 170, (1969–70) c. 165; cotton, lint 2 (3). Livestock (in 000; 1969–70): cattle c. 540; sheep c. 44; pigs c. 13; goats c. 220; chickens (Sept. 1970) c. 354.
Industry. Production (in 000; metric tons; 1969): coal 110; iron ore (metal content) 1,469; asbestos 36; electricity (kw-hr.) 73,300.

433,000. Cap. and largest city: Mbabane (pop., 1966, 13,803). Language: English and Siswati (official). Religion: Christian 60%. King, Sobhuza II; prime minister in 1971, Prince Makhosini Dlamini.

Swaziland celebrated its third year of independence and the 50th year of King Sobhuza II's reign in an atmosphere of stability, progress, and respect for tribal tradition. Race relations continued to be good, although increased attempts to replace expatriates with natives in business and labour caused some fears of loss of private investment. Swaziland's usual trade surplus, especially with the U.K. and Japan, continued to rise, and foreign exchange was earned in remittances from workers in South Africa, increased revenue from the revised customs union agreement with South Africa, and in U.K. aid for the five-year development plan.

The mining industry, with iron ore and asbestos accounting for 90% of total value, also continued to expand. South Africa's Rand Mines, controlling the coal industry, the third most important mining activity, investigated the possibility of a new mine near Manzini, as progress on the proposed rail link with South Africa continued. Embarrassment was caused in January with the arrival of Leonard Nikane, a South African wanted on charges in the Maritzburg terrorist trial. Refused refugee status and declared a prohibited immigrant, he was held in jail. The government, unable either to return him to South Africa because this would anger other African countries or to send him to an African state because of South Africa's overfly rights, could not free him because of rumours that he had come to assassinate the king.

(M. Mr.)

Sweden

A constitutional monarchy of northern Europe lying on the eastern side of the Scandinavian Peninsula, Sweden has common borders with Finland and Norway. Area: 173,648 sq.mi. (449,750 sq.km.). Pop. (1971 est.): 8,091,782. Cap. and largest city: Stockholm (pop., 1971 est., 740,486). Language: Swedish, with some Finnish and Lapp in the north. Religion: predominantly Lutheran. King, Gustaf VI Adolf; prime minister in 1971, Olof Palme.

In 1971 Sweden's famous "middle way" appeared to be at the crossroads and in need of repair. In March the Social Democratic government declared that full membership in the EEC was not a "realistic possibility" for Sweden. The announcement came at a time when restrictive economic measures were pushing unemployment to its highest level for many years, when the country's renowned labour-market harmony was under heavy pressure, and when three of Sweden's largest trading partners—Britain, Denmark, and Norway—were announcing their hopes of joining the Community.

The national budget for 1971–72 reinforced the restrictive fiscal policies already in operation. Its main goals were outlined as full employment, rapid growth, more uniform distribution of income, better regional balance, stabilization of price levels, and a healthy balance of payments position. Revenue was expected to rise by 10%, considerably less than the 1970–71 figure. A large part of the increase was to come from indirect taxation, especially the value-added tax, which stood at 17.6%. Revenue from income tax was expected to fall as a result of a reform introduced to secure more

Strikes:
see Labour Unions

Sugar:
see Agriculture

Sulfur:
see Mining

Surgery:
see Medicine

Surinam:
see Dependent States

King Gustaf Adolf displays a sculpture of a ram's head dated from 600 B.C., uncovered in 1971 at a site formerly inhabited by Etruscans near Viterbo, Italy. King Gustaf spent his holidays in Italy, participating in the archaeological excavations.

equal distribution of income. The predicted rise in expenditure of 8% denoted a somewhat slower rate of growth than that expected for 1970–71. As usual, the largest allocation went to the Ministry of Social Affairs, followed by education and defense. The budget's "novelty" was a tax on advertisements in newspapers and other publications, which came into force in July after much debate.

The economy was in a depressed state throughout the year, and there was little hope of a quick improvement. The recession derived to some extent from the restrictive economic policies of the previous two years, designed to counteract the effects of the boom of 1969–70: large wage rises, soaring costs and prices, and a record balance of payments deficit. With regard to the latter, the restrictive policies appeared to have succeeded. For the first eight months of 1971, the balance of payments was 1,309,000,000 kronor in Sweden's favour, compared with a deficit of 1,385,000,000 kronor for the corresponding period in 1970. The other side of the coin was darker, however: factory closures increased, unemployment queues lengthened, and there was pressure from both business and labour for strong government action. Employment was threatened not only by the government's own restrictive policies, but also by a listless world trade scene and import charges adopted by two of Sweden's most important export markets, Denmark and the U.S.

Measures already taken to combat unemployment included the allocation of extra funds to the Labour Market Board, three reductions in the bank rate since March (from 7 to $5\frac{1}{2}$%), a softening of credit policies, release of special investment funds, and tax concessions to industry for investments in machinery and stock. When these proved insufficient, the government announced a 2-billion kronor "unemployment package" in October. This included a further softening of credit policies, an extension of the tax allowance for investments in machinery and stock, and state support for work projects, environmental protection projects, and low-income groups. Whether or not the package would be successful was an open question. Critics called for more general measures to stimulate the economy, such as a reduction in the value-added tax or a cut in the income tax.

The situation was aggravated by uncertainty over the outcome of Sweden's negotiations with the EEC. While it considered full membership incompatible with Swedish neutrality, the government had stated its will-

ingness to participate in a customs union comprising both industrial and agricultural goods. It thus appeared that Sweden wanted full customs union, participation in the common agricultural policy and other joint policies, and institutional machinery to give it a say in some Community decisions—in other words, an arrangement going far beyond an industrial free trade area while preserving Sweden's traditional neutrality. It seemed likely that some kind of deal would be worked out eventually, although Sweden received a firm rebuff on the question of influencing Community decisions. The business community was deeply disappointed over the government's decision not to seek, at the least, association with the EEC.

Businessmen also had been uncertain about the result of the spring wage round between the Trade Union Confederation (LO) and the Employers' Confederation (SAF), which dragged on for seven months before agreement was reached in June. The three-year agreement, affecting some 800,000 blue-collar workers, provided a 28% wage rise, to be paid in three installments, and would cost the employers an estimated 6 billion kronor. The agreement narrowly averted a series of strikes that threatened to paralyze certain sectors of the economy.

In February, Sweden experienced its first union-sponsored strike since 1966, when 2,500 members of the Confederation of Professional Associations (SACO) struck following protracted wage talks in which the union was asking for a wage rise of about 22%. Shortly afterward, SACO members were joined by other white-collar workers from the Federation of Civil Servants (SR) and the Central Organization of Salaried Employees (TCO). Eventually more than 50,000 state and municipal employees were on strike or locked out, after the government Board for Collective Bargaining had issued lockout notices. The strike-lockout was particularly disruptive because the union members involved held key positions in local administration and state enterprises. For example, the absence of a small number of SR members in the state railway system paralyzed commuter and truck services throughout the country.

The strike-lockout continued for six weeks, until the government, in an unprecedented move, passed a back-to-work law, valid for six weeks, covering the whole labour market. The government emphasized that this was only a temporary expedient and that it had no desire to alter the traditional labour-market machinery.

SWEDEN

Education. (1968–69) Primary, pupils 597,007, teachers 30,270; secondary, pupils 405,644, teachers 36,701; vocational, pupils 212,022, teachers (1967–68) 16,019; teacher training, students 10,053; higher (including nine universities), students 115,610, teaching staff (1964–65) 2,296.

Finance. Monetary unit: krona, with a par value of 5.17 kronor to U.S. $1 (12.42 kronor = £1 sterling) and a free rate (Sept. 27, 1971) of 5.05 kronor to U.S. $1. Gold, SDRs, and foreign exchange, central bank: (June 1971) U.S. $873 million; (June 1970) U.S. $544 million. Budget (1970–71 est.): revenue 43,949,000,000 kronor; expenditure 40,795,000,000 kronor. Gross national product: (1968) 132,292,000,000 kronor; (1967) 124,884,000,000 kronor. Money supply: (May 1971) 15,640,000,000 kronor; (May 1970) 14,440,000,000 kronor. Cost of living (1963 = 100): (June 1971) 143; (June 1970) 134.

Foreign Trade. (1970) Imports 36,244,000,000 kronor; exports 34,978,000,000 million. Import sources: West Germany 19%; U.K. 14%; U.S. 9%; Denmark 8%; Norway 6%; Finland

5%. Export destinations: U.K. 12%; West Germany 12%; Norway 11%; Denmark 10%; Finland 6%; U.S. 6%; France 5%; Netherlands 5%. Main exports: machinery 25%; paper 9%; iron and steel 9%; motor vehicles 9%; wood pulp 8%; timber 6%; ships and boats 5%.

Transport and Communications. Roads (1970) 173,963 km. (including 403 km. expressways). Motor vehicles in use (1970): passenger 2,287,709; commercial 144,418. Railways: (1969) 12,547 km. (including 7,520 km. electrified); traffic (state system only; 1970) 4,061,000,000 passenger-km., freight 16,085,000,000 net ton-km. Air traffic (including Swedish apportionment of international operations of Scandinavian Airlines System; 1970): 2,451,000,000 passenger-km.; freight 111,887,000 net ton-km. Shipping (1970): merchant vessels 100 gross tons and over 995; gross tonnage 4,920,704. Telephones (Dec. 1969) 4,110,579. Radio licenses (Dec. 1969) 2,833,000. Television licenses (Dec. 1969) 2,420,000.

Agriculture. Production (in 000; metric tons; 1970; 1969 in parentheses): wheat 965 (917);

barley 1,904 (1,575); oats 1,686 (1,129); rye 211 (184); potatoes 1,490 (931); sugar, raw value (1970–71) 218, (1969–70) 185; rapeseed 201 (208); meat c. 408 (400); butter 42 (63); cheese 60 (58); timber (cu.m.; 1969) 53,700, (1968) 50,100; fish catch (1969) 266, (1968) 317. Livestock (in 000; June 1970): cattle c. 2,050; horses c. 66; sheep c. 350; pigs c. 2,100; chickens c. 8,500.

Industry. Index of industrial production (1963 = 100): (1970) 156; (1969) 145. Production (in 000; metric tons; 1970): cement 3,994; coal (1969) 22; electricity (71% hydroelectric in 1969; kw-hr.) 60,610,000; iron ore (60% metal content) 31,815; pig iron 2,600; crude steel 5,480; copper 51; lead (1969) 42; gold (troy oz.; 1969) 42; silver (troy oz.; 1969) 3,684; cotton yarn 13; mechanical wood pulp (1969) 1,412; chemical wood pulp (1969) 6,191; newsprint 1,030; other paper (1969) 3,179. Merchant vessels launched (100 gross tons and over; 1970) 1,731,000 gross tons. New dwelling units completed (1969) 109,000.

There were changes of leadership in two of Sweden's main political parties. In November 1970 the Conservative Party had elected Gösta Bohman to replace Yngve Holmberg, and in June 1971 the Centre Party replaced its retiring leader, Gunnar Hedlund, with Thorbjörn Fälldin. In January, according to a constitutional reform, the Riksdag held its first session as a 350-member unicameral body in the new Riksdagshuset in the centre of Stockholm. In September, Prime Minister Palme visited Zambia and Tanzania, and Rune Johansson, the minister of industry, visited China. In April the Yugoslav ambassador to Sweden, Vladimir Rolovic, was attacked inside his embassy in Stockholm by two Yugoslav citizens. He sustained three bullet wounds and later died.

It was announced in September that two of Sweden's largest banks—Stockholms Enskilda and Skandinaviska—would merge to form a new bank, the Skandinaviska Enskilda Bank, to be operational from January 1972. The new bank would be the largest in Scandinavia, with a share capital of approximately 543 million kronor and total assets of around 22 billion kronor.

The government's concern over environmental protection was reflected in the 1971–72 budget which, despite its restrictive nature, allowed 350 million kronor for spending in this field, an increase of 16% over the previous figure and more than twice the 1968–69 allocation.

(A. D. Wı.)

Swimming

International matches in 1971 provided the last tune-up for the 1972 Olympic Games and, for the first time ever in any sport, a United States team competed in East Germany. The U.S.S.R. also broke precedent by entering the Santa Clara International Meet, marking the initial appearance of a Soviet swim team in the U.S. Australia, always a perennial swim power, sent a strong team to London for the 14-nation Coca-Cola International Meet, where they outscored the U.S. 122–121, and also entered the Santa Clara International. World records were shattered on 25 occasions, 9 achieved in the post-season contests held in East Germany and the U.S.S.R.

U.S. Competition. U.S. male swimmers completely dominated the 1971 Pan-American Games at Cali, Colombia, winning 14 gold medals out of 15 races, plus 9 silver and 2 bronze. The U.S. women, however, were barely able to outscore a strong Canadian team, winning but 8 of 14 races, with 9 silver and 5 bronze medals, to the Canadians' 6 gold, 5 silver, and 3 bronze.

Highlight of the Pan-American Games was the feat of Frank Heckl, a giant 6-ft. 5-in., 195-lb. 20-year-old from Cerritos, Calif., who won six gold medals and one silver, plus anchoring the men's 800-m. freestyle relay that lowered the world mark to 7 min. 45.8 sec.

In 1971, U.S. swimmers broke the world records for individual events on nine occasions and snapped up five world relay marks. The U.S. Amateur Athletic Union (AAU) long course (outdoor) championships in Houston, Tex., August 25–28, produced five world and seven U.S. records.

Mark Spitz established himself as the "world swimmer" of 1971, as he lowered his own 100-m. butterfly world standard to 55 sec. Two days later he regained, for four days, his world mark for the 200-m. butterfly by clocking 2 min. 3.9 sec. in a preliminary

Event	Name	Country	Time
World Records Set in 1971			
MEN			
200-m. freestyle	Mark Spitz	U.S.	1 min. 54.2 sec.
200-m. freestyle	Mark Spitz	U.S.	1 min. 53.5 sec.
400-m. freestyle	Tom McBreen	U.S.	4 min. 2.1 sec.
800-m. freestyle	Graham Windeatt	Australia	8 min. 28.6 sec.
100-m. backstroke	Roland Matthes	East Germany	56.7 sec.
200-m. backstroke	Roland Matthes	East Germany	2 min. 5.6 sec.
100-m. butterfly	Mark Spitz	U.S.	55.0 sec.
200-m. butterfly	Mark Spitz	U.S.	2 min. 3.9 sec.
200-m. butterfly	Hans Fassnacht	West Germany	2 min. 3.3 sec.
800-m. freestyle relay	National team (J. Heidenreich, J. McConica, S. Genter, F. Heckl)	U.S.	7 min. 45.8 sec.
800-m. freestyle relay	National team (M. Spitz, J. Heidenreich, F. Tyler, T. McBreen)	U.S.	7 min. 43.3 sec.
400-m. medley relay	National team (C. Campbell, P. Dahlberg, M. Spitz, J. Heidenreich)	U.S.	3 min. 50.4 sec.
WOMEN			
100-m. freestyle	Shane Gould	Australia	58.9 sec.
200-m. freestyle	Shane Gould	Australia	2 min. 6.5 sec.
200-m. freestyle	Shane Gould	Australia	2 min. 5.8 sec.
400-m. freestyle	Karen Moras	Australia	4 min. 22.6 sec.
400-m. freestyle	Shane Gould	Australia	4 min. 21.2 sec.
800-m. freestyle	Ann Simmons	U.S.	8 min. 59.4 sec.
800-m. freestyle	Shane Gould	Australia	8 min. 58.1 sec.
1,500-m. freestyle	Cathy Calhoun	U.S.	17 min. 19.2 sec.
1,500-m. freestyle	Shane Gould	Australia	17 min. 0.6 sec.
200-m. butterfly	Karen Moe	U.S.	2 min. 18.6 sec.
200-m. butterfly	Ellie Daniel	U.S.	2 min. 18.4 sec.
400-m. freestyle relay	National team (L. Johnson, D. Deardurff, S. Babashoff, K. Peyton)	U.S.	4 min. 0.7 sec.
400-m. medley relay	National team (S. Atwood, C. Clevenger, E. Daniel, L. Johnson)	U.S.	4 min. 27.3 sec.

heat. Tom McBreen swam the 400-m. freestyle in 4 min. 2.1 sec., chipping 0.5 sec. off the record.

In women's competition Ellie Daniel lowered not only the listed world 200-m. butterfly mark of 2 min. 19.3 sec. but also a pending mark of 2 min. 18.6 sec. set at the Los Angeles Invitational three weeks earlier by Karen Moe. Miss Daniel was timed in 2 min. 18.4 sec.

The U.S. unveiled a bright new star at Houston. Cathy Calhoun, 13, an unheralded junior high school student, lowered Olympic champion Debbie Meyer's 1,500-m. freestyle world record by 0.7 sec. to 17 min. 19.2 sec. En route, her 9 min. 9.6 sec. surpassed Miss Meyer's U.S. 800-m. freestyle mark.

European and Commonwealth Competitors. A team from Australia made a spring tour of Europe and achieved its greatest success when it edged the U.S. team at the Coca-Cola International Meet in London April 30–May 1. Shane Gould gave Australia its brightest swimming hours since the 1956 Olympics when she equaled the oldest women's record in the book by swimming the 100-m. freestyle in 58.9 sec., a time first achieved by Dawn Fraser of Australia in 1964. Later in the meet Miss Gould lowered the 200-m. freestyle to 2 min. 6.5 sec., erasing the world record held by Debbie Meyer, and on November 25 she cut it further, to 2 min. 5.8 sec. On December 3 she set a new 800-m. freestyle record of 8 min. 58.1 sec., and on December 12 set a new 1,500-m. freestyle record of 17 min. 0.6 sec.

Another of Australia's outstanding teen-agers, Karen Moras, continued the world record onslaught as she retired the last of Miss Meyer's records, ripping 1.7 sec. from the 1970 400-m. freestyle mark to 4 min. 22.6 sec. Miss Moras' record was to last less than 90 days, for at the Santa Clara International Meet on July 9 Miss Gould lowered the time to 4 min. 21.2 sec.

On August 29–30 the Soviet Union regained European supremacy from East Germany by winning the men's European Cup at Uppsala, Swed., by scoring

Swedish Literature: see Literature

Above, Mark Spitz lowered his own 200-m. butterfly world record to 2 min. 3.9 sec. at the National AAU swimming championships in Houston, Tex., on Aug. 27, 1971. Right, 17-year-old Karen Moras set a world record for the 400-m. freestyle on April 30, 1971, at the Coca-Cola International Meet in London.

121 to the 1970 European champions' 117, with West Germany third at 111. However, the East German girls continued to hold their number one rank when they won the women's European Cup at Bratislava, Czech., 118 to 95 for the U.S.S.R., with the Netherlands scoring 101 for runner-up position.

The final days of the swimming season were highlighted by a series of international matches between the U.S. and the swimming powers of Europe, East Germany and the Soviet Union. The Americans lowered world marks on seven occasions. On September 3–4 at Leipzig, E.Ger., a select U.S. team of 12 men and 12 women swimmers, plus 6 divers, swamped their host. Mark Spitz lowered the 200-m. freestyle record he had shared with Don Schollander as he won the event in 1 min. 54.2 sec. East Germany's Roland Matthes continued on his unbeaten way as he lowered both of his world backstroke records, slashing his 100-m. time to 56.7 sec. and his 200 m. to 2 min. 5.6 sec.

From Leipzig the U.S. swimmers moved on to Minsk where they competed in a triangular meet on September 9–11 against Great Britain and the U.S.S.R. Again the Americans trounced their rivals as they scored 342 points to the Soviet Union's 205.

World records brought an enthusiastic response from the capacity 2,000 spectators. Mark Spitz, by more than $\frac{1}{2}$ second, lowered his pending 200-m. freestyle record set at Leipzig to 1 min. 53.5 sec. An hour later Spitz joined by Jerry Heidenreich, Fred Tyler, and Tom McBreen took more than two seconds off the 4 x 200 m. freestyle relay record set by the U.S. Pan-American team. The quartet was timed in 7 min. 43.3 sec.

What the 4-minute mile meant to the world of track many years ago, the 9-minute barrier is to the women's 800-m. freestyle. It was approached in 1971 by Ann Simmons, 18, from Lakewood, Calif., who set a new record of 8 min. 59.4 sec. at Minsk, and by Miss Gould, who surpassed this by swimming the distance in 8 min. 58.1 sec.

Diving. At the U.S. Nationals in Houston, Cynthia Potter swept all three women's titles, the 1- and 3-m. springboards and the 10-m. platform. Mike Brown and Jim Henry divided the men's 1- and 3-m. springboard championship, while Dick Rydze won the 10-m. platform.

On April 17-18, at Fort Lauderdale, Fla., in a head-on match, teams from North America opposed Europe with the U.S. men scoring 22 points to Europe's 16, and the U.S. women tallying 18 to 12. U.S. divers won

all four events. Mike Finneran and Rick Early won the springboard and the platform, while Micki King and Janet Ely won similar events for the women.

At the European Cup match in London, on August 19–21, East Germany maintained its supremacy by outscoring the Soviet Union 364 to 358, with Italy third at 328. Marina Janicke of East Germany won the springboard event, but Czechoslovakia's Olympic champion, Milena Duchkova, upset East Germany's Sylvia Fiedler in the platform. Italy's 1968 Olympic champion Klaus Dibiasi met the stiffest challenge from Soviet diver Vladimir Strakhov in the springboard, edging the Soviet by less than two points. In the platform event, the Italian champion outpointed his teammate Giorgio Cagnotto to give the Italians a one-two finish.   (A. Sd.)

Switzerland

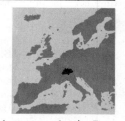

A federal republic in west central Europe consisting of a confederation of 22 cantons, Switzerland is bounded by West Germany, Austria, Liechtenstein, Italy, and France. Area: 15,941 sq.mi. (41,288 sq.km.). Pop. (1970): 6,269,783. Cap.: Bern (pop., 1970, 162,405). Largest city: Zürich (pop., 1970, 422,640). Language: French, German, Italian, Romansh. Religion (1960): Protestant 52.7%; Roman Catholic 45.4%. President in 1971, Rudolf Gnaegi.

In a nationwide plebiscite on Feb. 7, 1971, the male citizenry granted Swiss women the right to vote in federal matters, by a decision of 621,403 (14 cantons and 3 half cantons) to 323,596 (5 cantons and 3 half cantons). Opposition clearly was concentrated in the poorer central and eastern sections of the country. At the same time, several cantons approved the introduction of the women's vote in cantonal matters. The election results left three cantons and two half cantons where women still had no vote in cantonal or local matters (Bern and Thurgau granted women's suffrage in December). Nevertheless, one of the two obstacles to Switzerland's signing of the European Convention on Human Rights was thus eliminated—the remaining one being the constitutional prohibition of Jesuit activity and the founding of new monasteries.

The first federal issue on which women were able to vote was the plebiscite of June 6 on the proposed constitutional amendment concerning the protection of the environment. The result was 1,222,493 to 96,380 in favour of the amendment.

The political event of the year was the parliamentary election of October 31. Since the introduction of proportional representation in 1919, the political composition of Parliament had varied little. This time there were new factors, including the participation of women, the new distribution of seats by cantons according to the results of the 1970 census, and the entry of the right-wing National Action and Republican Action parties into national politics. The results confirmed the established pattern, however, with Social Democrats, Radicals, and Conservatives remaining dominant. Ten women were elected to the National Council (lower chamber) and one to the Council of States (upper chamber). The National Action and Republican Action parties together obtained 11 out of 200 seats in the National Council.

The new Parliament met for the first time on November 29, one of its first agenda items being the confirmation of the seven-member Federal Council. The council already had drafted its program for 1972, which included plebiscites on housing, armaments exportation, the stabilization of the building market, a constitutional amendment for nationwide school co-ordination, and another on old-age insurance.

The economic scene was marked by the continuation of boom conditions. The most important single event was the 7% revaluation of the Swiss franc on May 10 as a measure of protection against "undesirable speculation" and inflation. At the end of June, the government proposed the introduction of a constitutional amendment authorizing control of the business cycle, if necessary, at the expense of free enterprise. In pursuit of this policy, a temporary halt in building was imposed on nine "critical" areas of the country and on certain categories of buildings.

The labour market remained very tight. As a result of measures taken in 1970, the number of foreign workers was stabilized at a little below one million (16% of the total population). The situation remained precarious, however, from both the economic and the political point of view. On the one hand, the labour shortage continued and, on the other, immigration had given rise to xenophobic reactions.

The decision of the British government at the end of October to adhere to the Treaty of Rome was described by the Swiss government as an indispensable prerequisite to Switzerland's negotiations with Brussels on the establishment of the "particular kind of ties" that Switzerland desired to have with the EEC. It expressed the hope that an agreement between the EEC and Switzerland could be obtained by Jan. 1, 1973, the date of British entry. In November the Federal Council decided to set up a consultative commission to elaborate the conditions under which Switzerland might become a member of the United Nations, under safeguard of its neutrality. Meanwhile, the UN Economic and Social Council made Switzerland a member of its Economic Commission for Europe.

Early in the year the federal Parliament, by a vote of 122 to 4, approved the appropriation of a new credit of SFr. 400 million for financial aid to less developed countries for 1971–74. A motion to subject this to a popular referendum was defeated, but the entire issue remained controversial.   (M. F. S.)

SWITZERLAND

Education. (1968–69) Primary, pupils 480,642, teachers (excluding craft teachers; 1961–62) 23,761; secondary, pupils 269,490, teachers (full time; 1961–62) 6,583; vocational, pupils 148,541; teacher training, students 10,994; higher (including 8 universities), students 38,197, teaching staff 3,210.

Finance. Monetary unit: Swiss franc, with a par value (following the devaluation of May 9, 1971) of SFr. 4.81 to U.S. $1 (SFr. 9.80 = £1 sterling) and a free rate (Sept. 27, 1971) of SFr. 3.97 to U.S. $1. Gold, SDRs, and foreign exchange, central bank: (June 1971) U.S. $5,083,000,000; (June 1970) U.S. $4,299,000,-000. Budget (1970 est.): revenue SFr. 7,571,000,000; expenditure SFr. 7,594,000,000. Gross national product: (1970) SFr. 88.1 billion; (1969) SFr. 80.7 billion. Money supply: (May 1971) SFr. 47,140,000,000; (May 1970) SFr. 39,930,000,000. Cost of living (1963 = 100): (June 1971) 134; (June 1970) 126.

Foreign Trade. (1970) Imports SFr. 28,152,000,-000; exports SFr. 22,065,000,000. Import sources: EEC 58% (West Germany 30%, France 12%, Italy 9%); U.S. 9%; U.K. 8%. Export destinations: EEC 37% (West Germany 15%, Italy 9%, France 8%); U.S. 9%; U.K. 7%; Austria 5%. Main exports: machinery 30%; chemicals 21%; watches and clocks 12%; textile yarns and fabrics 7%. Tourism (1969): visitors 6,259,400; gross receipts U.S. $795 million.

Transport and Communications. Roads (1970) 59,233 km. Motor vehicles in use (1970): passenger 1,388,000; commercial 132,500. Railways: federal (1969) 2,913 km. (including 2,897 km. electrified); private (1968) 2,107 (including 2,098 km. electrified); traffic (federal railways; 1970) 7,997,000,000 passenger-km., freight 6,600,000,000 net ton-km.; (private railways; 1968) 1,153,000,000 passenger-km., freight 389 million net ton-km. Air traffic (1970): 4,421,-000,000 passenger-km.; freight 187,613,000 net ton-km. Shipping (1970): merchant vessels 100 gross tons and over 32; gross tonnage 195,880. Telephones (Dec. 1969) 2,846,535. Radio licenses (Dec. 1969) 1.8 million. Television licenses (Dec. 1969) 1,144,000.

Agriculture. Production (in 000; metric tons; 1970; 1969 in parentheses): barley c. 143 (132); wheat (including spelt) 370 (379); oats c. 32 (37); rye c. 40 (43); potatoes 930 (979); apples c. 425 (530); pears c. 185 (180); sugar, raw value (1970–71) 67, (1969–70) 62; wine 118 (74); milk 3,230 (3,214); butter 32 (32); cheese 87 (84); meat 326 (325). Livestock (in 000; April 1970): cattle c. 1,900; horses 54; sheep 291; pigs 1,753; chickens c. 6,500.

Industry. Index of industrial production (1963 = 100): (1970) 138; (1969) 132. Production (in 000; metric tons; 1970): cement 4,800; aluminum 91; rayon, etc., yarn and fibre (1969) 17; nylon, etc., yarn and fibre (1969) 46; cigarettes (pieces; 1969) 24,177,000; watches (units; 1969) 49,951; manufactured gas (gasworks only; cu.m.; 1969) 381,000; electricity (kw-hr.) 34,886,000.

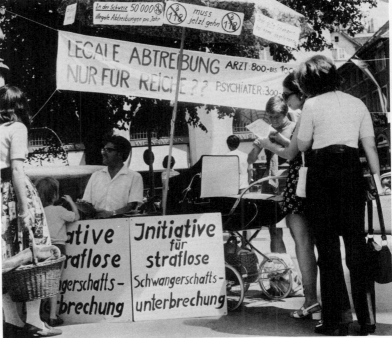

The Committee for Legal Abortion collects signatures on the streets of Zürich on Aug. 3, 1971, in a campaign to make abortion constitutionally legal in Switzerland.

Syria

A republic in southwestern Asia on the Mediterranean Sea, Syria is bordered by Turkey, Iraq, Jordan, Israel, and Lebanon. Area: 71,498 sq.mi. (185,180 sq.km.). Pop. (1970): 6,292,000. Cap. and largest city: Damascus (pop., 1970, 835,000). Language: Arabic (official); also Kurdish, Armenian, Turkish, and Circassian. Religion: predominantly Muslim. Presidents in 1971, Ahmed al-Khatib until February 22 and, from March 14, Gen. Hafez al-Assad; premiers, al-Assad and, from April 3, Abdul Rahman Khleyfawi.

For Syria, 1971 was marked by some relaxation in the internal political atmosphere and an improvement in relations with most other Arab states. Having ousted the civilian wing of the Baath Party in November 1970, Gen. Hafez al-Assad (*see* BIOGRAPHY) brought the as-Saiqa guerrilla organization, which the civilian Baathists had controlled, under Army authority. He released several hundred political prisoners and announced the restoration of public liberties. He broadened the base of the regime to give Communists, Nasserites, and other left-wing Arab nationalist groups a genuine share of power for the first time since 1963. Another consequence of the change of regime was the "personalization" of authority for the first time since Gamal Abd-an-Nasser lost power in Syria with the breakup of the Syrian-Egyptian union in 1961. Amendments to the provisional constitution announced on February 16 gave the president wide powers similar to those of the Egyptian president. He

Gen. Hafez al-Assad was sworn in as president on March 14, 1971, after winning a national referendum with 99.2% of the votes.

UPI COMPIX

SYRIA

Education. (1968–69) Primary, pupils 813,225, teachers 22,249; secondary, pupils 242,917, teachers 11,108; vocational, pupils 9,972, teachers 1,208; teacher training, students 4,856, teachers 514; higher (including 2 universities), students 35,005, teaching staff 1,116.

Finance. Monetary unit: Syrian pound, with an official exchange rate of S£3.81 to U.S. $1 (S£9.14 = £1 sterling) and a free rate (Sept. 27, 1971) of S£4.28 to U.S. $1 (S£10.62 = £1). Gold, SDRs, and foreign exchange, official: (March 1971) U.S. $51 million; (March 1970) U.S. $64 million. Budget (1970) balanced at S£2,780 million. Money supply: (March 1971) S£2,350 million; (March 1970) S£2,067 million. Cost of living (Damascus; 1963 = 100): (April 1971) 131; (April 1970) 119.

Foreign Trade. (1970) Imports S£1,374.6 million; exports S£775.3 million. Import sources: U.S.S.R. 8%; Canada 7%; West Germany 7%; Italy 7%; Iraq 6%; Lebanon 6%; Japan 6%; France 5%. Export destinations: Italy 21%; Lebanon 11%; U.S.S.R. 9%; China 8%; Japan 7%; Turkey 5%; France 5%. Main exports: cotton 40%; crude oil 17%; livestock 9%.

Transport and Communications. Roads (1969) *c.* 15,000 km. (including 10,532 km. with improved surface). Motor vehicles in use (1969): passenger 29,379; commercial 16,012. Railways: (1968) 992 km.; traffic (1969) 96 million passenger-km., freight *c.* 130 million net ton-km. Air traffic (1969): 179,925,000 passenger-km.; freight 1,283,000 net ton-km. Ships entered (1969) vessels totaling 15,457,000 net registered tons; goods loaded (1969) 32,284,000 metric tons, unloaded 1,165,000 metric tons. Telephones (Dec. 1969) 103,687. Radio receivers (Dec. 1969) 1,241,000. Television receivers (Dec. 1969) 130,000.

Agriculture. Production (in 000; metric tons; 1970; 1969 in parentheses): wheat 625 (1,004); barley 235 (627); chick-peas 15 (50); lentils 58 (90); grapes (1969) 248, (1968) 215; raisins *c.* 8 (*c.* 9); figs (1969) 50, (1968) 53; olive oil *c.* 4 (20); tobacco *c.* 9.1 (8.9); cotton, lint 159 (137); wool 7 (8). Livestock (in 000; 1969–70): cattle *c.* 520; sheep *c.* 6,200; horses *c.* 65; asses 245; goats *c.* 770; chickens (Dec. 1969) *c.* 4,500.

Industry. Production (in 000; metric tons; 1969): petroleum products *c.* 1,300; cement (1970) 966; cotton yarn 22; electricity (kw-hr.) 1,023,000.

was commander in chief of the armed forces, could appoint the vice-presidents and prime minister, and also had the power to dissolve the People's Council appointed by the Baathist Regional Command.

The composition of the People's Council—Syria's first legislative assembly since 1966—was announced on February 16. Its 173 members included 87 Baathists, 8 Communists, 36 representatives of the General Union of Farmers, and a variety of Nasserites, ex-Baathists, and similar groups. The head of state, Ahmed al-Khatib, resigned on February 22 and was elected speaker of the People's Council. In the national plebiscite held on March 12 al-Assad, the only presidential candidate, received 99.2% of the votes in a 95.76% turnout. On April 3 the appointment of the former interior minister, Abdul Rahman Khleyfawi, as head of the new government was announced. The Baath Party international conference held in Damascus in August announced the election of a new leadership, which in turn had elected al-Assad secretary-general. Six members of the new leadership were Syrians and ten were representatives of party organizations in a variety of Arab states.

President al-Assad acted in various ways to end Syria's isolation in the Arab world. On Nov. 27, 1970, he had announced Syria's adherence to the union of Libya, Sudan, and Egypt as envisaged in the Declaration of Tripoli. Diplomatic relations with Morocco and Tunisia were restored and relations with Saudi Arabia improved after permission had been given for the repair of the Tapline oil pipeline, closed since May 1970. The most important rapprochement was with Lebanon. When Pres. Suleiman Franjieh came to Damascus on March 16 it was the first official visit of a Lebanese head of state since either country's independence. Relations with Jordan did not improve despite Syrian attempts to mediate between King Husain and the Palestinian guerrillas and, following the suppression of the guerrillas in Jordan in July, Syria closed the border on July 25. Special measures had to be taken to alleviate the effect of this on Lebanon. Relations with the rival Baathist regime in Iraq also were cool, although some new economic links were established and the final section of the Baghdad–Damascus highway was opened in September.

On April 17 al-Assad signed the agreement for the Egyptian-Libyan-Syrian federation in Benghazi and, after a three-day meeting in Damascus, he signed the constitution of the federation with the Egyptian and Libyan heads of state on August 20. A referendum in Syria on September 1 gave a 96.4% majority in favour of federation.

On several occasions in 1971 al-Assad affirmed that Syria did not accept UN Resolution 242 of Nov. 22, 1967, as the basis for a political settlement in the Middle East. But he also said Syria accepted Egypt's right to seek every means to recover its lost territory. Following al-Assad's visit to the U.S.S.R. in February, Soviet sources expressed the view that Syria had withdrawn its opposition to Resolution 242. In October al-Assad said Syria had 250,000 men under arms ready to fight Israel.

Provisional results of the 1970 census showed a 3.3% average annual population growth since 1960. Because this was well above the growth envisaged in the 1970–75 third development plan, increased investment in development was required. However, Syria's economic difficulties were increased by a trade recession caused by the severe drought and bad weather of 1970, which had reduced cotton output.　(P. Mᴅ.)

Taiwan

Taiwan, which consists of the islands of Formosa and Quemoy and other surrounding islands, is the seat of the Republic of China (Nationalist China). It is situated north of the Philippines, southwest of Japan and Okinawa, and east of Hong Kong. The island of Formosa has an area of 13,807 sq.mi.; including its 77 outlying islands (14 in the Taiwan group and 63 in the Pescadores group), the area of Taiwan totals 13,892 sq.mi. (35,980 sq.km.). Pop. (1971 est.): 14,810,929. Cap. and largest city: Taipei (pop., 1971 est., 1,802,756). President in 1971, Chiang Kai-shek; vice-president and premier (president of the Executive Yuan), C. K. Yen.

On October 10 the Republic of China celebrated its 60th anniversary. This national day marked the 22nd year of exile on Taiwan for the Nationalist government, with its claim to be the sole legal government of China and the legitimate Chinese representative in the UN eroded. An increasing number of countries had shifted recognition from the Nationalist to the mainland Communist government. A particular blow to Taiwan was the sudden and drastic policy shift of the United States in seeking normal relations with Communist China.

TAIWAN

Education. (1968–69) Primary, pupils 2,383,204, teachers 56,348; secondary, pupils 770,102, teachers 28,449; vocational, pupils 150,131, teachers 6,556; teacher training, students 933, teachers 44; higher (including 9 universities), students 161,337, teaching staff 17,816.

Finance. Monetary unit: New Taiwan dollar (NT$40 = U.S. $1; NT$96 = £1 sterling), with a free rate (Sept. 27, 1971) of NT$99 to £1. Gold, SDRs, and foreign exchange, official: (June 1971) U.S. $504 million; (June 1970) U.S. $531 million. Budget (1969–70 est.): revenue NT$44,480,000,000; expenditure NT$42,019,000,000. Gross national product: (1969) NT$190.4 billion; (1968) NT$167,980,000,-000. Money supply: (June 1971) NT$40.2 billion; (June 1970) NT$30,850,000,000. Cost of living (1963 = 100): (June 1971) 126; (June 1970) 121.

Foreign Trade. (1970) Imports U.S. $1,524,000,-000; exports U.S. $1,428,300,000. Import sources: Japan 44%; U.S. 24%. Export destinations: U.S. 38%; Japan 15%; Hong Kong 9%; South Vietnam 5%; West Germany 5%. Main exports (1969): fruit and vegetables 16% (bananas 5%); textile yarns and fabrics 13%; clothing 12%; telecommunications equipment 9%; plywood 6%.

Transport and Communications. Roads (1969) 16,933 km. Motor vehicles in use (1969): passenger 39,600; commercial 35,400. Railways: (1969) 4,400 km.; traffic (1970) 6,205,000,000 passenger-km., freight 2,659,000,000 net ton-km. Air traffic (1970): 953.9 million passenger-km.; freight 25,275,000 net ton-km. Shipping (1970): merchant vessels 100 gross tons and over 274; gross tonnage 1,166,230. Telephones (Jan. 1970) 338,803. Radio receivers (Dec. 1969) 1,428,000. Television receivers (Dec. 1968) 193,000.

Agriculture. Production (in 000; metric tons; 1970; 1969 in parentheses): rice 3,226 (3,041); sweet potatoes 3,702 (3,445); cassava (1969) 316, (1968) 342; peanuts 122 (101); oranges c. 150 (146); tea 28 (26); sugar, raw value (1970–71) 875, (1969–70) 673; bananas 462 (586); tobacco 21 (20); sisal 11 (10); jute 14 (13); pork c. 310 (313). Livestock (in 000; Dec. 1969): cattle 103; pigs 3,048; goats 169; chickens 14,435.

Industry. Production (in 000; metric tons; 1970): coal 4,471; crude oil 90; natural gas (cu.m.) 918,000; electricity (excluding most industrial production; kw-hr.) 13,213,000; cement 4,304; pig iron 61; crude steel 294; salt (1969) 383; caustic soda (1969) 107; petroleum products (1969) 4,228; cotton yarn 86; paper (1969) 407.

While the turn of world events greatly dampened spirits at the 1971 anniversary celebration in Taiwan, the Nationalist leaders in their pronouncements still clung to the goal of destroying the Communist regime and recovering the mainland. In his annual anniversary message to the nation, Chiang Kai-shek continued to stress the importance of principle and pride rather than pragmatism in entertaining any compromise with Communism, and urged his countrymen not to lose heart in the face of challenges to the Nationalist international position. However, with the sagging diplomatic status of the Nationalist government, Cabinet officials laid greater stress on the unity and development of Taiwan economically and socially as a model province.

The Nationalist and Communist regimes, while conflicting in ideology and political systems, both regarded Taiwan as an integral part of China with its status long settled by history and international agreements. Nevertheless, the future of Taiwan remained the main obstacle to the normalization of relations between Peking and Washington. Peking was strongly committed to the "liberation of Taiwan," while by treaty the U.S. was obligated to defend the island against any attack. However, Washington in 1971 took the position that it no longer would support the Nationalist claim as the sole government of China, although it would continue to maintain diplomatic relations and provide the Nationalists with other kinds of support.

On July 15 U.S. Pres. Richard Nixon announced that he had accepted an invitation from Chinese Premier Chou En-lai to discuss Sino-American differences in Peking. This heightened the apprehension in Taiwan that Peking and Washington might have reached tentative understanding on such issues as the firm U.S. commitment to defend Taiwan and China's representation in the UN. Nationalist leaders viewed cessation of the patrol of the Formosa Straits by the U.S. 7th Fleet and the reduction of the U.S. military presence in Taiwan as measures to create an atmosphere of confidence in preparation for the Nixon-Chou meeting.

Although Nixon emphasized in his announcement that the U.S. was not seeking a new relationship with the People's Republic of China "at the expense of our old friends," the immediate reactions from the government and people on Taiwan were dismay, disillusionment, hurt, and anger. Ambassador James C. H. Shen denounced Nixon's planned visit as a "shabby deal," and said: "We do not believe this kind of thing should be done to a friend and ally without prior consultation and without sufficient notice."

President Nixon's planned visit to China appeared to have revealed an implicit understanding that the Taiwan question no longer would be an obstacle to the admission of mainland China into the UN. The U.S. formally announced in July its "two-China" policy, supporting admission of the People's Republic into the UN while preserving the Nationalist membership in the General Assembly. This resulted in protests from Taiwan, but there were no threats, as earlier, that the Republic of China would not under any circumstances share a seat with Communist China in the UN. Thus Nationalist China tacitly accepted the U.S. proposal of dual representation for China and launched a diplomatic offensive in July and August by dispatching special missions to Japan, Africa, and Latin America to persuade UN member states to defeat Albania's proposal to unseat the Republic of China in favour of the People's Republic.

Despite efforts by the Nationalist government and the U.S., the General Assembly on October 25 rejected the U.S. "important question" resolution, which would require a two-thirds majority for expelling a member. The vote was 59-55 with 15 abstentions. The Nationalist delegation immediately walked out of the assembly with a statement that it could not participate in further proceedings. The assembly then adopted the Albanian resolution 76–35 with 17 abstentions. Thus, after 26 years of participation, the Republic of China was expelled from the UN. On October 26, in a message to the people of mainland China and Taiwan, President Chiang declared that neither his government nor the Chinese people would ever recognize the validity of the resolution by the General Assembly and considered it "in flagrant violation" of the provisions of the UN Charter.

Despite diplomatic setbacks Taiwan's economic growth continued, with industry expanding to form one-third of the total output. During the 1960s the economy had an average growth rate of 10%. The gross national product reached $5,444,500,000 in 1970 with per capita income at slightly over $292. The Council for International Economic Cooperation and Development predicted that the 1971 GNP would reach $6.2 billion and that in 1972 it would be over $7 billion. (H.-T. Ch.)

See also China.

Tanzania

This republic, an East African member of the Commonwealth of Nations, consists of two parts: Tanganyika, on the Indian Ocean, bordered by Kenya, Uganda, Rwanda, Burundi, the Congo (Kinshasa), Zambia, Malawi, and Mozambique; and Zanzibar, just off the coast, including Zanzibar Island, Pemba Island, and small islets. Total area of the united republic: 364,943 sq.mi. (945,203 sq.km.). Total pop. (1970 est.): 13,273,000, including (1966 est.) 98.9% Africans and 0.7% Indo-Pakistani. Cap. and largest city: Dar es Salaam (pop., 1967, 272,821) in Tanganyika. Language: English and Swahili. Religion: predominantly traditional beliefs; many Muslims in coastal areas and in up-country settlements; Christian minority. President in 1971, Julius Nyerere.

Events in neighbouring Uganda tended to overshadow home affairs in Tanzania throughout 1971. In January Uganda's deposed president, Milton Obote, took refuge in Tanzania and President Nyerere refused to recognize the new government. This led to accusations from Uganda that Tanzania was encouraging guerrilla activities against its neighbour, although observers felt that many of these charges were intended to divert attention from domestic troubles in Uganda. A number of light border skirmishes did take place leading to the closing of the frontiers by Uganda in July, but Tanzania firmly denied that Chinese military advisers had been involved and in October countered with its claim that Ugandan forces were trying to annex Tanzanian territory.

During the conference of Commonwealth heads of government in Singapore in January, Nyerere distributed a document challenging British Prime Minister Edward Heath's insistence on Britain's right to sell arms to South Africa which, Nyerere claimed, implied a compromise with racism and a threat to the Commonwealth concept.

In February four persons accused of plotting to overthrow the government received life sentences, two others, ten years' imprisonment each (later quashed), and one was acquitted. Gray Mattaka (a cousin of Oscar Kambona who, although in exile in London, had been accused of masterminding the plot) was found not guilty on appeal but was immediately detained.

Further trouble for the government broke out at the University of Dar es Salaam in July. Symonds Akivaga, the students' Kenyan president, was arrested after he had signed a protest on behalf of the students against the vice-chancellor's assessment of the university's progress. The protest was deemed libelous and Akivaga was removed by members of a paramilitary force.

Progress on the Tanzam railway to link Tanzania with Zambia maintained a steady rate and it was anticipated that 300 mi. of track would be open to passenger traffic by the beginning of 1972.

Further protests reached the press from families of Asian women forcibly married to leading Africans in Zanzibar. In May, 19 men of Arabian descent, who were accused of plotting against the Zanzibar government, were paraded before a crowd on the island and it was announced they would be shot. Then, in October, Radio Zanzibar issued a government statement requiring all noncitizens who had been refused trading licenses to quit the island. (K. I.)

Encyclopædia Britannica Films. *Youth Builds a Nation in Tanzania* (1970).

TANZANIA

Education. (1967) Primary, pupils 825,000, teachers 15,850; secondary, pupils 27,512, teachers (1966) 1,171; vocational, pupils 2,077, teachers (1968) 68; teacher training, students 2,687, teachers (1966) 230; higher (including University of Dar es Salaam; 1970), students 1,194, teaching staff 123.

Finance. Monetary unit: Tanzanian shilling, with a par value of TShs. 7.14 to U.S. $1 (TShs. 17.14 = £1 sterling) and a free rate (Oct. 11, 1971) of TShs. 17.71 to £1. Gold, SDRs, and foreign exchange: (June 1971) U.S. $65.9 million; (June 1970) U.S. $68.6 million. Budget (1970–71 est.): revenue TShs. 1,654,000,000; expenditure TShs. 1,652,000,000. Money supply: (June 1971) TShs. 1,996,000,000; (June 1970) TShs. 1,461,000,000. Cost of living (Dar es Salaam; 1963 = 100): (May 1971) 129; (May 1970) 124.

Foreign Trade. (Excluding trade with Kenya and Uganda; 1970) Imports TShs. 1,939,000,000; exports TShs. 1,708,000,000. Import sources: U.K. 21%; China 14%; West Germany 9%; U.S. 9%; Japan 7%; Italy 6%; Iran 6%. Export destinations: U.K. 22%; U.S. 10%; Hong Kong 8%; India 7%; Zambia 7%; Singapore 6%; Japan 6%; West Germany 5%. Main exports: coffee 18%; cotton 14%; sisal 10%; diamonds 9%.

Transport and Communications. Roads (1969) 16,743 km. Motor vehicles in use (1968): passenger 36,238; commercial (including buses) 29,788. Railways (1968) 2,612 km. (for traffic *see* Kenya). Construction of a *c.* 1,600-km. railway linking Dar es Salaam and Zambia began in 1970. Air traffic: *see* Kenya. Shipping traffic (mainland only; 1969): goods loaded 1,303,000 metric tons, unloaded 1,988,000 metric tons. Telephones (Dec. 1969) 31,727. Radio licenses (Dec. 1969) 135,000.

Agriculture. Production (in 000; metric tons; 1970; 1969 in parentheses): corn *c.* 650 (*c.* 750); sweet potatoes (1969) *c.* 310, (1968) *c.* 285; millet and sorghum *c.* 1,160 (*c.* 1,155); sugar, raw value (mainland; 1970–71) *c.* 98, (1969–70) *c.* 93; rice 172 (262); cassava (1969) *c.* 1,200, (1968) *c.* 1,200; coffee (mainland) *c.* 54 (46); cotton, lint *c.* 81 (71); sisal 202 (209); timber (cu.m.; 1969) 30,500, (1968) 29,500. Livestock (in 000; 1969–70): cattle *c.* 11,000; sheep *c.* 3,000; pigs *c.* 25; goats *c.* 4,150; asses 160; poultry *c.* 17,800.

Industry. Production (in 000; metric tons; 1969): cement 169; salt 34; tin concentrates (metal content) 0.1; gold (troy oz.) 16; diamonds (metric carats) 777; electricity (excluding most industrial production; kw-hr.) 360,000.

Telecommunications

"Today, my friends, whether you intend to or not, whether you wish to or not, you have just signed far more than yet another intergovernmental agreement. You have just signed the first draft of the articles of Federation of the United States of Earth."

With these words, Arthur C. Clarke startled the representatives of 54 nations who had met at the U.S. Department of State on a historic date: Aug. 20, 1971. The occasion was the signing of a permanent charter for Intelsat, the International Telecommunications Satellite Consortium. As the acknowledged "father" of the telecommunications satellite (he wrote the first reputable paper on the subject in October 1945), science fiction writer Clarke prefaced his views by the observation that the U.S. was created by two inventions. "Without them the United States was impossible; with them it was inevitable. Those inventions, of course, were the railroad and the electric telegraph. Today we are seeing, on a global scale, an almost exact parallel to that situation. What the railroads and the telegraph did here a century ago, the jets and communications satellites are doing now—to all the world."

What differentiated this declaration from mere histrionics was the reaching and passing in 1971 of the economic break-even point of a whole range of far-reaching applications of advanced telecommunications techniques, from pocket-radio links for industry through computer-guided maintenance of telephone exchanges to intercontinental communications via satellites. By 1971 satellites had slashed overseas telephone rates by 25 to 50%. For example, a three-minute call between Madrid and New York cost about $12.75 in 1964. Via satellite, the call in 1971 cost about $6.50. Service was also considerably improved. A call from Washington, D.C., to Santiago, Chile, which once took three days to set up, in 1971 took three minutes. But, possibly of greater social significance, the world had grown accustomed to the instant portrayal of domestic events in the most distant countries. The Olympic Games, the investiture of Prince Charles, table tennis in Peking, and the arrival in Manila of Pope Paul VI were seen worldwide on television, thanks to telecommunications satellites.

Governmental and Research Activities. By far the most important governmental activities concerned the signing by 54 countries of the Intelsat agreement. During the course of 27 months, starting in February 1969, delegations from 98 countries (including observers) convened periodically to hammer out a permanent charter for the organization. The key issues were whether Intelsat, which had been largely under U.S. influence from its inception in 1964, should be internationalized; if so, how, and what would be the future role of the major U.S. entity in the effort; namely, the Communications Satellite Corp. (Comsat). Under the agreement Comsat would manage Intelsat for six years, as it had done since the organization was launched. At the end of that time, the technical operation would be contracted out to anyone who could successfully meet the requirements.

In the 37 years of its existence, the U.S. Federal Communications Commission (FCC) kept an extremely tight rein on the telecommunications and broadcasting industries. But in 1971 the FCC seemed to be edging away from its role as the heavy-handed

COURTESY, BRITISH POST OFFICE

A polythene-covered cable undergoes rigorous tests at the Post Office Research Centre in London. The British Post Office planned to lay a new transatlantic telephone cable during 1973–74.

administrator and in doing so took positions on two vital communications issues that indicated stress would be placed more on competition than it ever had in the past.

The first of the two FCC decisions hastened the hookup of the fairly young computer industry with the century-old communications industry by throwing wide open for competition the specialized microwave transmission field. On May 26 the commission ruled that virtually any company, or common carrier, could enter the microwave transmission field provided it could meet financial and technical specifications and clear a site for its operation so that no harmful radio interference was indicated. Microwave can be used for both voice and data transmission, and it was in the latter field that tremendous growth was expected. By the end of the decade most observers believed that the microwave transmission business would outstrip telephone communications.

The expected growth in demand for telecommunications facilities would of course benefit such established carriers as American Telephone and Telegraph Co. (AT & T) and Western Union, but the new carriers such as Microwave Communications, Inc. (MCI), Data Transmission Corp. (Datran), and Southern Pacific Communications were also expected to play an ever increasing part in handling the nation's burgeoning need for more communications facilities. The commission said that the new microwave firms could enter the market almost at will, while the established carriers such as AT & T, Western Union, and General Telephone and Electronics would be given the freedom to compete with the new firms "fairly and fully"—meaning on a price basis—as long as they did not subsidize their microwave operations with income from other monopoly operations such as toll telephones, wide-area telephone service, and public message telegraph service.

The second of the FCC moves came on August 5 when the commission sent what it called a "letter of intent" to both houses of Congress. The letter outlined the rules the FCC would like to see govern

KEYSTONE

A Japanese girl reads a newspaper page produced by the new AT-4 Telenewspaper machine in 4½ minutes. This home facsimile machine was shown by the Japanese newspaper "Asahi Shimbun" at the 1971 International Trade Fair in Tokyo.

community antenna television, or, as it is more widely known, cable television or CATV. In essence, the FCC wanted the cable television market expanded and would allow cable television firms for the first time to "import" distant signals (pictures) into the nation's larger cities.

Research on new methods of transmission continued. In the U.K. conventional transmission techniques—coaxial cable and microwave radio—were not expected to be able to cope with a demand which, between 1960 and 1970, doubled its entire previous expansion. Advanced trials on a system based on radio waves beamed through hollow copper tubes buried in the ground like conventional cables overcame one of the most difficult problems: how to bend the radio waves around corners in the tubes without distorting the signals. The system, which can accommodate up to 400,000 telephone conversations or 250 simulta-

neous television pictures in a tube not much wider than an automobile exhaust pipe, was being used successfully to carry telephone conversations on part of their journey between the Post Office's new research centre at Martlesham, Suffolk, and the telecommunications headquarters in London.

Satellites. The fourth generation of satellites was begun with the launching in January by the U.S. National Aeronautics and Space Administration (NASA) of the first Intelsat 4 satellite to serve the Atlantic region. This satellite and others to follow it were designed to have a capacity of more than 5,000 telephone circuits plus one for colour television transmission. Eight such satellites were ordered, two for the Atlantic region, two for the Pacific, and a fifth above the Indian Ocean. The remaining three were to be spares. Each satellite was designed to provide service for seven years. A third ground-station aerial at Goonhilly Downs, Cornwall, Eng., was being constructed to begin operation in 1972 for service with the new Atlantic satellite.

In Europe, the European Space Research Organization was studying the possibility of a satellite system for that continent but there remained considerable doubt as to whether satellites were the best way of serving densely populated areas. In comparison with submarine cables, traffic on the transatlantic route in 1971 was divided 5:1 in favour of satellites, but for longer distances satellite-cable linking was preferred because of the time delay introduced by a double-hop satellite link. The most striking rejection of space systems in densely populated areas was by the Japanese who, despite immense practical difficulties, chose a terrestrial system. Rather than use a satellite, they decided on an undersea cable with the huge capacity of 25,000 telephone channels. Coming into operation between 1975 and 1977, it was to be laid 18 mi. offshore between Tokyo and Osaka and would be connected to the mainland by microwave links built on floating platforms.

In the U.S. a White House decision on who would build and operate a domestic communications satellite system was being awaited at the year's end. Applications had been pending for such systems with the FCC since 1965.

Cables. On September 24, AT & T along with Commonwealth of Nations and Japanese companies announced plans for a new era in transpacific communications. The first phase in the plan, scheduled for completion in 1974, called for the installation of an 845-voice grade circuit submarine cable between California and Hawaii, links between Guam and Australia, and extensions from Japan to points in Southeast Asia. The second phase, expected to be completed in 1977, included a 3,500-voice circuit cable between the U.S. mainland and Hawaii, a 1,840-voice circuit cable between Hawaii and Australia, and a 1,600-circuit cable between Hawaii and Japan. It was awaiting approval by the FCC.

A new 640-channel submarine cable between Goonhilly and Bilbao, inaugurated in April, provided the first direct cable communication between the U.K. and Spain. The cable also connected with the transatlantic TAT5 cable, brought into operation in 1970 between Spain and the U.S., and thereby gave Britain more connections with North America. Customers in six British cities could dial directly to all automatic exchanges in the U.S. except those in Alaska or Hawaii.

An example of advances in economy was the

Countries Having More Than 100,000 Telephones
Telephones in service, 1970

Country	Number of telephones	Percentage increase over 1960	Telephones per 100 population	Country	Number of telephones	Percentage increase over 1960	Telephones per 100 population
Algeria	169,188	5.1	1.25	Lebanon*	150,370	232.4	5.76
Argentina	1,668,408	34.1	6.90	Luxembourg	105,531	126.0	31.31
Australia*	3,598,692	69.6	29.27	Malaysia	168,826	140.4	1.58
Austria	1,334,339	104.2	18.07	Mexico	1,327,702	170.0	2.67
Belgium	1,936,814	78.6	20.05	Morocco	153,662	18.3	1.01
Brazil	1,787,000	85.4	1.94	Netherlands	3,120,766	108.0	24.09
Bulgaria	414,113	...	4.89	New Zealand	1,202,590	75.3	42.63
Canada	9,302,828	71.0	43.76	Norway	1,090,662	50.6	28.20
Chile	348,258	89.8	3.60	Pakistan	193,493	178.1	0.17
Colombia	545,851	105.5	2.63	Peru	192,604	88.1	1.44
Cuba	263,166	37.5	3.16	Philippines	293,543	193.6	0.78
Czechoslovakia	1,895,229	102.5	13.12	Poland	1,756,248	116.2	5.38
Denmark	1,599,952	56.9	32.45	Portugal	698,075	91.3	7.27
Egypt*	365,000	66.3	1.14	Puerto Rico	302,214	269.8	10.91
Finland	1,089,700	90.7	23.13	Rhodesia	122,129	55.5	2.36
France	8,114,041	98.6	16.05	Romania*	596,000	...	2.99
Germany, East	1,986,190	60.5	11.61	Singapore	136,267	136.9	6.70
Germany, West	12,456,268	125.8	20.36	South Africa	1,482,299	61.4	7.34
Greece	881,003	362.5	9.96	Soviet Union*	9,900,000	146.1	4.14
Hong Kong	502,374	423.7	12.45	Spain	4,126,363	151.4	12.46
Hungary	777,739	69.4	7.54	Sweden	4,306,905	63.3	53.74
India	1,159,519	173.3	0.21	Switzerland	2,846,535	82.2	45.38
Indonesia	182,319	58.5	0.16	Syria	103,687	112.0	1.74
Iran	286,220	209.1	1.01	Taiwan	338,803	404.8	2.37
Iraq	119,650	157.5	1.25	Thailand	134,663	252.1	0.38
Ireland	287,108	96.8	9.83	Turkey	513,569	97.5	1.48
Israel	457,721	347.5	16.00	United Kingdom	13,947,000	77.7	24.96
Italy	8,528,354	142.4	15.98	United States	115,221,970	62.7	56.70
Japan	23,131,688	375.5	22.41	Uruguay	206,600	50.8	7.18
Korea, South	562,111	507.5	1.80	Venezuela	377,662	109.8	3.70
				Yugoslavia	622,939	163.6	3.05

*1969.
Source: American Telephone and Telegraph Co., The World's Telephones, 1960 and 1970.

CANTAT 2 cable, which was designed to more than double the number of connections across the Atlantic from the U.K. to Canada. Its capacity would be 1,840 circuits and it would cost only £16,500 per circuit, compared with £100,000 a circuit for the first U.K.-Canada cable laid in 1961.

Radio. Britain's trunk telephone and television traffic continued to grow so rapidly that the microwave radio relay systems which carried a good deal of it were becoming congested. As a result, the Post Office was studying the possibility of exploiting frequency bands up to 4,000 MHz. At these high frequencies, however, the weather, especially thunderstorms, tended to affect performance. It was hoped that research into multipath transmissions would provide the answer. Research was also being conducted into the effect of the erection of tall buildings in the path of microwave beams and into the use of high-speed digital transmissions via microwaves.

Mass production of pocket radiotelephones in late 1970 produced a rapid increase in their applications to industry in 1971. The runway staff at all Britain's major airports was being reequipped with them, and safety on a 2,000-ac. industrial complex was enhanced by equipping patrolmen with pocket transmitter-receivers.

Telephones. The FCC, which had been studying complaints about poor telephone service since May 1970, said on Oct. 15, 1971, that there had been service improvement in 1970 and that the improvement was continuing into 1971. The commission said that four cities—New York, Chicago, Boston, and Miami—had demonstrated "aggravated service difficulties" in 1969. The picture improved in 1970 and 1971, but by the year's end New York, Boston, and Miami were still in the "aggravated" condition. Despite the faint praise from the FCC, its survey showed that some services had deteriorated since 1966. About 2% of long-distance calls dialed by an operator could not be completed on the first attempt in 1971, while in 1966 only 1.4% went incomplete. Similarly, in 1966, 2.9% of direct-dialed calls could not be completed immediately, while in 1971 the figure rose to 3.2%. New York City was still plagued with troubles apparently worse than the rest of the nation. From 3 to 6% of New York callers could not receive a dial tone within 10 seconds, while the national average was about 1%.

That apparent contradiction in terms, the telephone for the deaf, received British Post Office approval. Deaf people could now establish their own connections with equipment that changes audible signals into visible lamp signals. An electrowriter that transmits and receives handwritten messages over any distance then permits communication. While not of tremendous significance in itself, this development did illustrate the ability of the telephone network to accept and communicate much more than sound.

Vision by telephone continued to exercise the minds of telecommunications experts. In the U.S., Bell planned to offer Picturephone services in the areas served by its new 6.54 megabit digital carrier system to be installed by late 1972 between Los Angeles and San Francisco, between Houston and Dallas, and among groups of cities in the Midwest and on the East Coast. These isolated systems would probably be linked together in late 1974–75. The West Germans began operating a 240-mi. experimental videophone link between Darmstadt and Munich.

(Do. B.; L. H. Jo.)

International Telecommunication Union. During 1971 membership in the International Telecommunication Union (ITU) increased to 140 with the accession of Fiji to the International Telecommunication Convention. The 26th session of the Administrative Council took place at ITU headquarters in Geneva, May 1–21. The council examined a report on international recruitment procedure and passed a resolution designed to speed recruitment. The council also authorized the signature of an agreement between the Swiss Federal Council and the ITU concerning the latter's juridical status in Switzerland.

The World Administrative Radio Conference for Space Telecommunications (WARC-ST) met in Geneva from June 7 to July 17 to revise parts of the Radio Regulations. One of its main purposes was to redistribute frequencies in the light of the technical developments that had occurred since the last space conference held in 1963. It reexamined existing frequency allocations with respect to the space service and also made frequency allocations in the region between 40 GHz and 275 GHz. In particular, frequency bands were assigned to the broadcasting-satellite service (sound and television), the amateur-satellite service, and to all other space radiocommunications services. (ITU)

See also Industrial Review; Television and Radio.

ENCYCLOPÆDIA BRITANNICA FILMS. *Getting the News* (1967); *What Is a Computer?* (1971).

Television and Radio

Almost every country in the world had some radio service, and all industrial nations except South Africa had television in 1971—and the South African government was considering the introduction of television by 1975. The number of television and radio sets in use throughout the world numbered more than 881 million, according to estimates compiled by *Broadcasting* magazine and *Broadcasting Yearbook*. Television sets totaled about 241,740,000 and radios 640 million. The United States accounted for about 36%, or 87 million, of the world's television sets, followed by Japan with 30 million and the U.S.S.R. with 28 million. Other *Broadcasting* estimates reported the United Kingdom with 20 million television sets, West Germany with 16.2 million, France 10.5 million, Italy 9.7 million, Canada 7 million, Poland 4 million, Spain 3.9 million, Argentina 3.3 million, Australia and Czechoslovakia 3 million each, Sweden 2.5 million, Belgium 2.1 million, Bulgaria 2 million, Hungary and Yugoslavia 1.7 million each, Denmark 1.4 million, and Austria 1,380,000. At the opposite extreme, *Broadcasting* showed Kuwait with 90,000 sets, the Sudan with 50,000, Mauritania 20,000, Uganda 10,000, Ethiopia 8,000, Liberia 6,500, Gibraltar 6,000, and Sierra Leone 3,500.

More than half of the world's radios, or about 336 million, were in use in the U.S. No nation of any size was without some form of radio service, although in a few cases receivers hooked to loudspeakers still were used for community listening. Also, in some countries broadcasts came from booster and relay stations as well as from direct broadcasting facilities.

There were approximately 6,380 television stations, including satellites and repeaters, throughout the world in 1971, according to *Broadcasting*. No area had gained or lost significantly since 1970. About 2,100 were in the Far East, 2,000 in Western Europe,

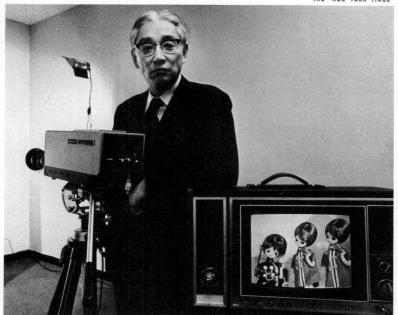

Akio Morita, executive vice-president of Sony Corp., demonstrates a new single-tube colour television camera designed by his Tokyo-based company. The camera weighs only 20 lb., and was expected to cost $500 when perfected for consumer use.

1,013 in the U.S., 905 in Eastern Europe, 175 in South America, 80 in Canada, and 35 in Africa. In many countries, viewers were offered a choice of several programs; in others, only one or two were available. In the U.S., it was estimated that 17% of all households with television could receive 10 or more stations, more than half (57%) could receive 7 or more, 90% could receive 4 or more, and 97% could receive at least three stations. Another analysis, published in *Broadcasting* in February 1971, reported that as many as 26 television stations and 104 radio stations could be received in the New York metropolitan area, and that even in Glendive, Mont., which with 4,600 homes was ranked 204th among U.S. television markets, 8 radio stations and 5 television stations were available, counting radio and TV signals coming in from outside the market area.

Radio stations on the air or under construction throughout the world in 1971 totaled more than 13,100. Most were amplitude modulation (AM) stations, but the proportion of frequency modulation (FM) outlets was increasing. In the U.S., which had about 56%, or 7,341, of the world's radio stations, almost 40% (2,930) were FM stations.

Organization. A major accomplishment in organization occurred in May 1971 when an international conference, first convened in 1969, finally reached agreement on the form of organization for permanent administration of the International Telecommunications Satellite Consortium (Intelsat). (*See* TELECOMMUNICATIONS.)

International broadcasting organization during 1971 was marked by growing cooperation between regional unions. This resulted in part from the challenge presented by rapid progress toward worldwide coverage by satellite communications networks and in part from the need, in a period of financial pressure and high investment in new media, to spread costs and pool resources.

Cooperation was encouraged both by the European Broadcasting Union (EBU), with 92 member organizations in 66 countries by 1971, and by the Organisation Internationale de Radio et Télévision (OIRT), which drew its 25 members mainly from Soviet-bloc

and less developed countries. In July, for the first time since its foundation in 1950, the EBU invited to its general assembly the presidents of the OIRT, the Asian Broadcasting Union (ABU), the Arab States Broadcasting Union (ASBU), and Union de Radiodiffusion-Télévision des Nations d'Afrique (URTNA). Plans were made for an intercontinental committee in Rome in March 1972 to discuss satellite transmission.

One problem hindering intercontinental satellite transmission was the disparity between earth station charges in different areas; the lowness of U.S. rates in comparison with those of Europe, for example, had encouraged a "one-way traffic." In January a step toward equalization was taken by the Spanish, Italian, and French national broadcasting organizations (all EBU members), which persuaded the earth stations at Buitrago (Spain), Fucino (Italy), and Pleumeur-Bodou (France) to reduce their charges. In return EBU undertook to allocate equally among the three stations all transmissions for its Eurovision network. As a first result, in March a daily news exchange was introduced between Eurovision and Latin America, transmitted from and received at Buitrago, and coordinated by Televisión Española (TVE).

The year's big achievement in live intercontinental transmission was "Children of the World," a one-hour program demonstrating the progress of satellite technology since transmission in 1967 of "Our World," and relayed from the opening (Geneva, June 17) of TELECOM 71, the world's first telecommunications exhibition, to 49 organizations in 45 countries. Ten countries contributed.

Two of the year's most extensive satellite arrays were set up for the coverage of the U.S. Apollo 14 moon mission in February and the more extended Apollo 15 mission in late July and early August. Both included colour television pictures from the surface of the moon. For Apollo 15 there was also protracted live coverage of the astronauts at work on the moon and, for the first time, of the blast-off of a space capsule from the lunar surface and its docking with the command ship in orbit. Approximately 20 satellite earth stations in the U.S., Latin America, Europe, the Western Pacific, and the Middle East were employed in transmitting the live pictures to stations around the world.

Work to create domestic satellite systems for the distribution of programs within rather than between countries was in progress but at varying stages of development in several nations. Canada expected to have a six-channel system ready to serve the entire country by about the end of 1972. India hoped to have a long-planned but much-deferred Satellite Instructional Television Experiment (SITE) in operation in 1974–75, using a satellite to be supplied by the U.S. as a one-year experiment in direct satellite broadcasting. Its main use would be to provide television for a massive educational program reaching into remote villages, where special community receivers would be installed. The Soviet Union's Orbita system of satellites continued in operation, relaying programs from Moscow to distant regions. In the U.S., responding to an invitation from the Federal Communications Commission (FCC), eight companies submitted proposals for operating their own complete domestic satellite systems, but as of the end of 1971 the FCC had not yet adopted a basic domestic satellite policy.

Interest was shifting from satellites to a new technological development. The holding in May at Cannes of Videa, the first international market for TV cassettes, gave television-set manufacturers and programmers their first glimpse of the market potential of audiovisual cassettes and playback equipment. The U.S. Videorecord Corp. had formed Canadian and European subsidiaries, and to avoid duplication had planned an international network of TV cassette-program licensees who would share in output through exchange agreements. By 1975, when the boom in sales of colour television sets was expected to have passed its peak, TV cassettes and equipment would be ready to take over.

Despite wide economic recession, colour continued to spread, although Radio Telefís Éireann (RTE; the Irish republic's broadcasting organization), £21,283 in the red for 1969–70, was forced to postpone its introduction indefinitely. In Japan, where spectacular success was being achieved by a colour standard converter installed at the earth station at Yamaguchi, and where Nippon Hoso Kyokai (NHK), the national broadcasting organization, was to go over to all-colour programs on both channels in October, colour set ownership was expected to overtake black-and-white by March 1972.

In the U.K., after tripling during 1970, colour set sales reached boom proportions in the summer of 1971. It was forecast that 20% of all families would have colour by the end of the year. In the Netherlands, where TV set ownership had stabilized at about 3 million, by late 1971, 400,000 colour sets were in use, and sales were expected to overtake those of black-and-white sets early in 1972.

United States. For the first time, estimates indicated that more than half—50.1%—of U.S. television households were equipped with colour television sets as of Oct. 1, 1971. The total was put at 31 million colour-TV homes. All three networks—American Broadcasting Co. (ABC), Columbia Broadcasting System (CBS), and National Broadcasting Co. (NBC)—transmitted virtually all of their programs in colour. So did most of the 1,013 stations, whether affiliated with the networks or not. The 31 million colour-equipped homes in October 1971 represented a gain of 1.3 million since July 1971 and 4.8 million since October 1970.

The question of U.S. domestic-satellite policy was still under debate in November 1971. The major issues were whether the FCC should adopt an "open skies" plan, under which any qualified applicant would be permitted to put up and operate his own system, or whether the number of systems should be limited and, in any case, whether the satellites should be "dedicated" to specific services—that is, one for television, another for cable television (CATV), still another for telephone service, etc.—or whether they should be "multipurpose," required to operate as common carriers and relay all or some combination of communications services at once. The three U.S. television networks told the FCC they had decided not to apply for a separate satellite system of their own, provided that one or more of the ultimate satellite operators could provide, at reasonable cost, the facilities they needed to distribute programs to affiliated stations. (*See* TELECOMMUNICATIONS.)

The pressures upon broadcasters that had been building up over the past several years, including challenges of station license renewals by local minority groups and in an increasing number of instances by groups seeking to take over the licenses and operate the stations themselves, intensified in 1971 to a point where many authorities thought the entire nature of broadcasting might be basically changed. The potential changes stemmed as much from court decisions as from FCC actions. First in 1966 and again in 1969, a federal appeals court had upheld the right of a group of local blacks to challenge the renewal of the license for a television station in Jackson, Miss., on grounds that the station had ignored black interests. From these decisions came a spate of challenges and competing license applications that culminated, in November 1971, in 18 petitions against 17 stations in California alone. Stations in other states whose licenses came up for renewal met similar challenges. The FCC, which had done its part in opening the door to such challenges by awarding the license for station WHDH-TV in Boston, Mass., to a competing applicant in 1969, had sought to shut the door partially by holding that, on license renewals, competing applications for a broadcast station license would not be accepted if the incumbent operator could demonstrate that he had performed "substantial service" in his operation of the station. The U.S. Court of Appeals for the District of Columbia knocked down that ruling in 1971, however, on grounds that it unconstitutionally denied a hearing to qualified applicants, and the incidence of license-renewal challenges spurted.

Even more threatening to the traditional structure of broadcasting, in the opinion of many experienced observers, were two other decisions by the District of Columbia appeals court in 1971. In one the court held that broadcasters who sell time for commercials may not, as a matter of policy, refuse to sell time for the broadcast of opinion on controversial issues. That seemed to broadcasters to open the gates for all sorts of opinion, perhaps more than could be accommodated in available air time, although the court decision called upon the FCC and broadcasters to develop workable guidelines.

In the second crucial decision the court ruled that automobile and gasoline commercials raise a controversial issue of public importance in relation to the environment, just as cigarette commercials were held to do in relation to health in earlier years, and that the fairness doctrine therefore required that reply time, as in the case of cigarette advertising, be made available to those who felt that gasolines and automobiles were polluting the air. To broadcasters, the critical question was how far this sort of reasoning might go, since there were few products or services advertised that did not have critics opposing them on one ground or another.

Pay television remained another source of concern for broadcasters in 1971, but less so than cable television, which finally received tentative clearance to move into big cities and seemed, for the first time, on the verge of a major expansion that could lead eventually to what many broadcasters felt would be a serious erosion of their own audiences. Zenith Radio Corp., whose Phonevision system of pay-TV had won FCC approval in 1970 after 18 years of consideration, acquired two television stations in 1971, KWHY-TV in Los Angeles and WCFL-TV in Chicago. But the purchases, like all station transfers, were subject to approval by the FCC, which had not acted on them as of the end of 1971. Thus, there were still no pay-TV stations in operation.

CATV, on the other hand, had established a firm foothold. *Broadcasting* estimated in mid-1971 that there were 2,500 operating systems in the U.S., serv-

Actor Carroll O'Connor (seated, right) and actress Jean Stapleton (seated, left) were stars of the popular CBS television series "All in the Family," a situation comedy satirizing racism and bigotry.

ing an average of 2,000 homes each, and that another 2,200 systems had been approved but not yet built. In addition, some 1,400 applications for systems were pending before local governments. CATV systems had been authorized in all states and were operating in all but Connecticut.

Although CATV was firmly established, construction of new systems had been increasingly in the doldrums in recent years as the FCC refused to permit the importation of television-station signals into big cities via CATV. New system starts, according to estimates published in *Broadcasting* in November, had dropped from about 260 in 1968 to 185 in 1969, 165 in 1970, and probably fewer than 100 in 1971. In mid-1971, however, the FCC reversed its course and announced a plan that would let CATV into big markets by permitting the importation of distant TV signals to provide, in the 50 largest television markets, the programming of all three networks plus that of three independent stations; in the next 50 markets the importation of the three networks plus two independent stations; and in all smaller markets, three networks plus one independent station. In addition, on all systems built in the top 100 markets in the future the FCC announced it would require an actual or potential capability of delivering programming on at least 20 channels into the home; additional bandwidth for nonbroadcast services—such as electronic burglary alarms, meter-reading, and shopping from the home—equal to the number of channels used for carrying broadcast programs; a free noncommercial "access channel" for use by the public and an additional one later; a channel for educational use; and a channel for state or local government use.

The organizational structure of public broadcasting became the centre of a growing dispute in 1971, its fourth year of "official" operation. Basically, the issue was "localism" versus "centralization" of program authority. Programs were produced by National Educational Television (NET) and six other regional program centres, in addition to those produced by the stations individually, and were distributed by the Public Broadcasting Service (PBS) network. A National Public Affairs Center for Television was added

to the structure in 1971, to provide public-affairs programs, and in radio the National Public Radio (NPR) network came into being in May to both produce and distribute programs to noncommercial radio stations. At the top of the structure was the Corporation for Public Broadcasting (CPB), created by Congress in 1967 as an independent, nonprofit body to promote and finance the development of noncommercial TV and radio. As the financing agency, and itself dependent on Congress for basic funds, the CPB was heavily involved in the mounting controversy. Ranked against it as 1971 progressed was the White House Office of Telecommunications Policy (OTP), whose director, Clay T. Whitehead, told a National Association of Educational Broadcasters conference in October that public broadcasting had ignored the goals of the Public Broadcasting Act, which he saw as providing for a locally based system, and had chosen instead a "centralized national network" concept. CPB officials responded that Whitehead in effect was threatening to oppose permanent financing for the corporation "until public broadcasting shows signs of becoming what this Administration wants it to be."

Europe. Most broadcasting organizations in Western Europe were forced "to keep running to stand still," to quote Lord Hill, chairman of the BBC. Rapidly rising operating costs were combined with the need for higher investment in research and construction of more powerful transmitters to put an improved, multichannel, full-colour television service and a national, regional, and local radio network within reach of the whole population. Higher coverage would result in higher revenues from licenses, but inflation reduced the value of such deferred dividends.

Government insistence that public services must pay their way or earn their keep, and that the fabric of broadcasting organization and finance should be nationalized, conflicted with demands for more colour, more viewing time and round-the-clock listening, more live coverage of sport, and consistent maintenance on all channels of high quality and wide variety. Program directors and producers wanted more money and greater independence; politicians, backed up by public pressure groups, increasingly insisted that broadcasting should present an honest view of events, personalities, and current social behaviour while avoiding bias, incitement, however indirect, to disorderly conduct, and any representation of sexual practices that could possibly be seen as "corruptive."

Commercially financed organizations faced additional problems. Stockholders regarded high dividends as the criterion of success; and advertisers demanded programs designed to attract, at low cost, the largest possible audiences, and to put them in a buoyant, spending-spree frame of mind.

The main aspects of confrontation between broadcasting's claim to autonomy and political demands and necessities were shown most clearly in France, the Netherlands, and the U.K. West Germany's problems were mainly financial as the long postwar boom began to decline; and in Spain and Portugal state control encouraged planned expansion and, with EBU membership, determined policy. The Scandinavian countries, all EBU members with Finland also a member of OIRT, had shown their awareness of the need for forming a separate, closely linked group within the European community by founding late in 1970 Nordvision, an independent organization with its own television network providing most of the programs transmitted in the five countries.

In France, where the state-controlled Office de Radiodiffusion-Télévision Française (ORTF) had been "liberated" from political pressures on its programming policies in 1969, trouble began in January with cancellation of a television debate due to take place in February on the political issues involved in the March municipal elections between Hubert Dubedout, reformist mayor of Grenoble, and the Gaullist deputy Jean Charbonnel, mayor of Brive. Its postponement to April, by order of French Pres. Georges Pompidou, would have robbed the program of its point. Gaullist support for "liberalization" of the ORTF was known to be lukewarm, and in November, when presenting his 1972 budget, the ORTF's director general proposed a bargain. He would reduce his budget in exchange for the government signing a program contract that would ensure for a stated period ORTF's independence of decision and action.

The financial crisis faced by broadcasting in the Netherlands resulted from steeply rising costs and high expenditures on automation, near saturation of the radio- and television-set markets, and government refusal to raise license fees in an election year. Fewer commercials were being offered to television, and although its share of advertising was up by more than 17% (to 25% of all advertising), 5 million guilders from the revenues of commercial broadcasting went in 1971 to help newspapers.

In the U.K. both the BBC and the Independent Television Authority (ITA) were under heavy financial and political pressure. In January Lord Hill asked that license fees, due to go up in April, be raised still further. The April rise had been planned to cover the cost of local radio, but £7 million had already been spent on more than a year's local broadcasting, and to this deficit wage increases amounting to £3.5 million, steeply rising operating costs, and a loss from license-fee evasion of about £6 million had to be added. The ITA, with income from advertising down 3% in 1970, an annual levy costing it some £20 million, and heavy losses by most of its companies, was pressing for a considerable cut in the levy and hoping that introduction of commercial radio would strengthen its position. The BBC feared lack of support from a government pledged to encourage competition; the ITA, still losing the battle with the BBC for sports coverage contracts and for a regular lead in audience ratings, feared that this, along with its financial weakness, the wide publicity given to some of its companies' problems, and the country's economic difficulties, might deny it the chance to become a widely based, financially stable alternative service.

The first engagement in the battle between BBC, ITA, and government was won by the BBC which, backed up by public opinion, succeeded in saving its existing 20 local radio stations and its "pop" radio program (Radio 1) from being eliminated or turned over to commercial ownership. In principle, therefore, it had maintained its right to provide a fully "national" service and to broadcast "pop" as well as quality programs.

The commercial radio battle was thrown open to Parliament and public by the White Paper put forward in March by Christopher Chataway, minister of posts and telecommunications. It proposed the establishment of a network of up to 60 stations licensed by the ITA, to become the Independent Broadcasting Authority (IBA). They would combine popular shows with local news and information programs, while the BBC's local stations were to concentrate on minority

Daniel Ellsberg, who later admitted giving the Pentagon papers to the "New York Times," appeared in a filmed interview on CBS in June 1971.

interest programs. This was a battle with many minor skirmishes: between commercial interests, the press, the churches, and a variety of minority groups for the right to IBA licenses and broadcasting time; and between small local firms and the big battalions of industry and commerce for advertising time. While Parliament, press, and public tore his White Paper to shreds, Chataway was preparing his November Sound Broadcasting Bill. This confirmed the White Paper's main provisions, named the first IBA stations (Glasgow, Birmingham, Manchester, and London, to be on the air by 1973), and repeated soothingly that competition would do the BBC good.

A rise in license fees in July, postponed from April but increased to £7 for black-and-white and £12 for colour, left the BBC still expecting a £27.5 million deficit by 1974. The accompanying £10 million drop in the ITA levy, to be spent on program improvement, was even less helpful to ITA companies which, with rising costs and high rentals, would have little left for programs.

In Eastern Europe organization continued to be dominated by work protocols between OIRT members, encouraged by the establishment in November 1970 of a prize for the best multilateral "OIRT Interradio Program." The Soviet Union was still keeping a watchful eye on Czechoslovakian broadcasting, and the 1971 Soviet-Czechoslovak work protocol stipulated a "Day of Soviet Radio" on all Czechoslovakian stations, organized in person by the All-Union Radio program director.

The Soviet Union had seven radio and six television channels by March 1971, when the Vostok channel was opened to carry Channel 1 programs eastward, to a region with a population of approximately 50 million. With 53 sets per 100 families (to be increased to 73 by 1975), television was available to 165 million, 23.2 million more than in 1970; and in about 50 large cities two or more channels were available. Colour programs could be seen in Moscow, Kiev, and Tbilisi.

Africa. The "continent of contrasts" exemplified contrasting attitudes to broadcasting development in 1971. Zanzibar planned to introduce television by late 1972 as part of its educational program, with sets located in schools and community centres, while South

continued on page 667

THE ASSAULT ON BROADCAST JOURNALISM

By Fred W. Friendly

The congressman looked down at the witness and asked if he considered broadcast journalism to be part of the press.

"We are," said Frank Stanton, president of CBS. The congressman read a definition of the press from *Webster's Collegiate Dictionary:* " 'The publishing establishment and also its personnel; newspapers and periodicals collectively.' . . . You are not an electronic newspaper."

The dictionary was from the early '50s. If the congressman, William L. Springer (Rep., Ill.) of the special House subcommittee investigating the CBS program "The Selling of the Pentagon," had read from the most recent edition of *Webster's,* he would have found that it specifically mentions radio and television.

The congressman's homework was a good deal sloppier than any flaw he or his chairman had detected in "The Selling of the Pentagon." Indeed, the documentary, produced by CBS News and broadcast over the CBS Television Network in February 1971, had charged "that the Pentagon is a runaway bureaucracy that frustrates attempts to control it," but nowhere in the committee hearing was there any real reference to the substance of those charges.

The flaw in the committee debates and, later, those on the House floor was that they turned on a whole series of alleged small errors and never produced a witness who contended that the program had represented him as saying something he did not believe.

The final vote, on July 13, was a squeaker, with the House refusing to cite CBS and Stanton for contempt by only 226 to 181. The tally probably reflected the individual congressman's loyalty to House Speaker Carl Albert, who wished to avoid a confrontation with CBS, more than any clear-cut assertion that the journalist working with camera and/or microphone is entitled to the same protection as a colleague with a typewriter and rotary press. In the end, "The Selling of the Pentagon" proved far more effective in dramatizing the principles of the First Amendment's application to the electronic media than in exposing the excesses of military propaganda, which was its primary intention.

In June the *New York Times* and the *Washington Post* published a secret Pentagon history of the Vietnam war, thereby stimulating a crucial debate over the First Amendment and "prior restraint" before publication. And in deciding for the newspapers, the Supreme Court judged the controversy on the high ground of that crucial issue. The contrast between that debate and the debate over "The Selling of the Pentagon" could not have been greater. The investigation of the documentary irrelevantly bounced back and forth between "payola," the rigged quiz program scandals of 1959, and the quality and motives of producer Peter Davis' editing. The House debate should have

---

Fred W. Friendly is Edward R. Murrow professor of broadcast journalism at Columbia University and television consultant to the Ford Foundation. From 1964 to 1966 he was president of CBS News.

examined the proper relationship between broadcast journalism and the First Amendment dictum that "Congress shall make no law . . . abridging the freedom of speech, or of the press." As Subcommittee Chairman Harley O. Staggers (Dem., W.Va.) said, "A broadcast license is a great and privileged responsibility," but there is a difference between the right of Congress to restrain violence in entertainment or the use of cigarette commercials and its right to restrain in advance the news performance of Walter Cronkite or Peter Davis.

The Siege of the "Pentagon." Few could have predicted the storm that would swirl around "The Selling of the Pentagon" when it was shown on February 23. It did not make a sweeping indictment of the entire defense establishment, as "Harvest of Shame" had indicted the treatment of migrant workers in 1960. Nor did it argue a particularly controversial point of view, as Edward R. Murrow's exposé of Sen. Joseph McCarthy did 17 years earlier. Its field of focus had narrow parameters: "To investigate . . . the range and variety of the Pentagon's public affairs activities." It made no attempt to examine the massive $73 billion defense budget, its effect on the U.S. economy or its ramifications, such as the price America's beleaguered cities pay for this security. In truth, the most damaging indictment in the program came from Pres. Richard Nixon, who in November 1970 had issued a memorandum to executive agencies criticizing what he called "self-serving and wasteful public relations efforts" and directing an end to such "inappropriate promotional activities." Unfortunately, neither the Pentagon nor its protectors chose to address themselves to the major points of the broadcast.

Rep. F. Edward Hébert (Dem., La.), chairman of the House Armed Services Committee, who felt he had been unfairly used on the broadcast, called it "one of the most un-American things I've ever seen . . . on the tube." *Air Force/Space Digest,* a major spokesman for the aerospace industry (from which it derives most of its revenue), called it a contrived product of "scissors, paste and a collection of callous consciences." And the financial weekly *Barron's,* in a bold headline over a full front-page editorial, said, "CBS has forfeited access to the nation's airwaves." Even the Peabody award jurors, before voting the program a special award, were circulated with material such as the *Air Force/Space Digest* critique.

There is no doubt that, in making "The Selling of the Pentagon," CBS was guilty of some marginal errors of fact and oversimplification. Errors of fact are never excusable, but the verdict on a broadcast should turn on such imperfections only if they are massive and/or affect a series of decisive points. The broadcast was subject to some criticism from its detractors for errors of fact, but a veritable outcry arose over the editing techniques that were employed. It is certainly true that broadcast editing *can* be crucial to a program. Editing is vital, not because television techniques entail any more or less staging than any other kind of interview, as some newspapers have suggested, but because of the immediacy and intimacy of the medium. The driving force behind editing is to give the interview pace and to make it interesting while preserving the original meaning and context. "The Selling of the Pentagon" controversy elicited some wild charges about its editing from normally sober sources, but that windmilling ignored the existence of editing standards or insisted that they were violated in the interest of some kind of hanky-panky in an attempt to "get" the military.

Editing other people's words is always a complicated responsibility. The journalistic or poetic license to edit varies with the personality and with the type of broadcast. Generally, the editing of "The Selling of the Pentagon" deserves a clean bill of health, although there probably are several instances where compression of separate sentences coupled with a line recorded earlier make the program vulnerable to those in search of mischief.

But no editing process deserves the overkill reaction that came from the special subcommittee of the House Interstate and

Public relations activities of the U.S. military establishment came under investigation in the news special "The Selling of the Pentagon," presented by CBS on Feb. 23, 1971. Newsman Roger Mudd reported on the military's use of speakers, films, and various media to gain public support.

Foreign Commerce Committee. Ironically, on the very day (April 8) the Pentagon announced that some excesses "The Selling of the Pentagon" had revealed were being eliminated, Frank Stanton, president of CBS, received a subpoena from the House subcommittee chaired by Representative Staggers. In chilling language, CBS was ordered to provide "all work prints, outtakes [unused film], sound tape recordings, written scripts [and] a statement of all disbursements of money made by CBS" in connection with the program. Stanton replied that he would supply what was broadcast and nothing else. He was on solid ground, because film outtakes and unused scripts are analogous to a reporter's notebooks, which the courts have held to be privileged unless they contain evidence pertaining to national security or some high crime, and then only in very extenuating circumstances to be specified and limited by the courts. The final House vote on Staggers' demand that CBS and Stanton be cited for contempt of Congress for their refusal to comply with the subpoena offered precious little reassurance to jittery broadcast news executives.

Besides the Staggers committee subpoena, what differentiated "The Selling of the Pentagon" from virtually all other documentaries was that the assault on it involved such high levels of the executive branch of government—unprecedented since Pres. Dwight Eisenhower criticized a CBS interview with Khrushchev in 1957. Vice-Pres. Spiro Agnew, whose attacks on the media had been comparatively restrained since the November 1970 congressional elections, was one of the first to raise a critical voice. After denouncing CBS in a speech he termed "perhaps the most important I will deliver in my term as Vice President," he charged in later televised comments that the program was a "clever propaganda attempt to discredit the defense establishment" of the U.S. (An aide to the vice-president later admitted that Agnew had not seen the broadcast before he criticized it.) Secretary of Defense Melvin Laird suggested that his department had been helped in Congress "because of the very unprofessional type of work that was done." And Herbert Klein, the White House head of communications, said that while the president had nothing to do with the vice-president's attack on the documentary, there was no reason to believe "the President didn't share his [the vice-president's] views."

Presidents and Press. The attack on "The Selling of the Pentagon" was not an isolated case, however. In 1971 the standards and traditions of broadcast journalism found themselves under a general siege from the executive branch of government. There are those who challenge that assumption. The president of the United States, they argue, believes in a free press and never criticizes the news media. In fact, they point out, Nixon himself said in an interview with ABC's Howard K. Smith on March 22: "I am not complaining about my treatment from

the press . . . I have never taken on a member of the press individually. I have never called a publisher since I have been President. I have never called a television station to complain about anything, and I never shall."

The president's statement was literally true, but it ignored what some of his chief officers were doing at precisely the same time. In April, for example, Vice-President Agnew denounced the news media generally for a wide variety of "masochistic" sins, including "the movement to plead America guilty . . . on the war in Indochina, military surveillance of civilians, J. Edgar Hoover's leadership of the FBI, supersonic transport development and the economy." Herb Klein, who told the convention of the National Association of Broadcasters that the White House believed in strong local stations, was later reported to have told a CBS station owner what he meant: "You fellows do an excellent news job. Why do you rely on CBS News?" And three days after the president's remarks, Ronald Ziegler, the White House press secretary, was asking, on official stationery, for a station manager to outline for him "in the most specific terms, what you consider to be the Nixon administration's embarrassing failures at home and in Indochina." Ziegler's letter was in response to an editorial broadcast on a local station criticizing the Nixon administration.

Other presidents have had their quarrels with the press. Harry Truman was offended when the music critic of the *Washington Post* criticized his daughter's singing. John Kennedy banned the *New York Herald Tribune* from the White House. Richard Nixon, tired and defeated after his unsuccessful bid for the California governorship in 1962, attacked the *Los Angeles Times* and its coverage of his campaign. And Lyndon Johnson often had his hand on the telephone after the evening network news. But these outbursts were isolated and usually made against the advice of staffs and families.

What makes the Nixon administration's attacks unique are their chilling consistency. Led by the second highest officeholder in the land, the executive branch of government seems to be systematically attempting to sow seeds of serious doubt about the news media. The distrust that the executive branch is spreading applies not just to the news media but to a crucial American freedom. The fallout from that distrust can be as damaging as if the chief executive tried to circumvent due process of law.

With all its power to communicate, can the government be so insecure about its policies that it must jam the system of searchlights and beacons that are the very safeguards of public opinion? As Walter Lippmann said 50 years ago, "Communications in a free society should make a picture of reality on which men can act." And as Edward R. Murrow warned in a practically unreported speech ten years ago, "Democracy will not survive . . .

if the efforts to inform people, to enlighten them, to argue with them . . . finally convince them that the nation's problems are beyond their grasp. If the people finally . . . believe either that they cannot . . . cope with America's problems, or that those who inform, those who argue and those who act are inept or malign or both, then distrust, dissatisfaction, fear and laziness can combine to turn them in desperation to that 'strong man' who can take them only to destruction."

It is true that there *is* an abundance of disturbing news on television and in the newspapers today, but, contrary to the opinion of the vice-president, that situation will not be remedied by eliminating or muting protest and confrontation. The way to reduce the budget of discouraging news is with bold, new policies, not by eliminating depressing stories. It is ironic that at a time when journalism has so crucial a role to play, people in high places are critical of it not for doing too little but for attempting to do too much. If "The Selling of the Pentagon" had been as favourable as coverage of the space program had been, CBS News would be accepting plaques of appreciation. When our national leaders indict broadcast journalists for doing their best, while encouraging the amusement and mercantile departments of television to do their worst, they are weakening an essential link in the nervous system by which the republic makes its decisions.

The Public's Duty to Know. The news media are powerful, but as James Madison noted at the creation of the Bill of Rights, "The censorial power is in the people over the government, not in the government over the people." Even if there were the conspiracy among the Eastern news elite that Vice-President Agnew and Gov. George Wallace like to speak of, there is always the strong, clear voice of the president of the United States and his articulate spokesmen to act as counterweight. The only proper antidote for the absolute power of politicians is the press, and the only sure control over the excesses and inadequacies of that power is the discernment exercised by the reading and viewing public.

What makes the continuing climate of distrust of the news media and, in particular, broadcast news so ominous is the imminence of the 1972 presidential election. It does not appear that the news media will be able to perform the vital service required of them during that election unless there is public support for their mission—support not for content or style of coverage but support that reminds politicians of all parties that the First Amendment still means what it says. Indeed, the true purpose of Agnew's oratorical emissions may be to promote the exact opposite of this kind of atmosphere. Convention coverage and elections always have been a challenge to responsible journalists. The delicate balance between fairness and probing analysis during the heat of a campaign always causes tempers to flare. But in the current atmosphere of distrust, the provision of well-rounded and comprehensive coverage will be exceedingly difficult.

We had better all face the fact that the news is going to get worse before it gets better. It is easy to blame it all on the politicians, but what about the voters who gave those politicians their mandate? What about those in journalism who provided both voters and politicians with much of their information? Obviously, something has gone wrong with our "searchlight." But to curse the darkness and single out Johnson, McNamara, and Rusk for Tonkin Gulf, or General Motors or Consolidated Edison for air pollution, or U Thant or the Soviets for the failure of the United Nations is an exercise in futility. Most of the decisions that have brought us to our current confluence of crises were made with general public support. The reluctant conclusion that must be drawn from all of this is that most of the decisions that brought America to its current predicament were based on flawed information and incomplete analysis by the political leadership and by the news media. In fact, it is only when the news media really perceive a problem and do their job of interpretive reporting that decision-making can be improved.

If free government is going to work, all those in communications must work harder at identifying the sources of news reports. At the same time, the people themselves must learn how to properly identify sources of news reports. Every citizen must know the difference between straight reporting, news analysis, and editorials. He should recognize whether an interview or a documentary has been edited and how. He must be aware that news magazines are often written ten days or more before the date on the cover and that the writer of a given story is probably neither the reporter nor the researcher, unless it is a signed article. These are not things to beware of—just aware of.

Broadcast Journalism: A Special Case. There is another problem that an informed citizenry should understand—and that not enough of those in broadcast journalism are aware of—the relationship of broadcast journalism to the First Amendment. Not too many people realize that there is a difference between newspapers and magazines and broadcast stations. Stations are licensed. By prior restraint, this prevents more than one station from occupying the same place on the dial. It is necessary because of the limitations of the electromagnetic spectrum, although in time cable television may overcome these restrictions. The broadcaster feels he is vulnerable to government pressure because of the license. Politicians on the receiving end of documentaries and news analysis feel they are vulnerable because of the power and pervasiveness of television. All truth and wisdom probably do not rest with either of these increasingly polarized positions. The tragedy of the Staggers investigation and Vice-President Agnew's criticisms was one of missed opportunity. They never understood that by concentrating on this issue, rather than on how a certain producer edits his film or gathers information, they might have created a constructive dialogue that could have served broadcasters and politicians as well as the public.

This may well be the time for an independent study of the freedom of broadcast journalism in a licensed industry. The government's implicit need to regulate use of the airwaves certainly does not include the regulation of news content. The broadcaster's responsibility to be independent does not give him immunity from accountability if he fails to fulfill his license requirements to serve the public interest.

Beyond question, much is wrong with the state of journalism. The broadcast industry continues to use the Bill of Rights more as an excuse for its commercial excesses than as an obligation to fulfill its responsibilities. But those who would nullify its strengths because there is not enough "good" news really want a tranquilizer instead of a searchlight on reality. Those in Congress who would investigate reporting and editing are really in search of restraints against penetrating news analysis and investigative reporting. Vigilantism on the part of politicians leads only to sterility and suppression. It will cause fewer penetrating documentaries like "The Selling of the Pentagon," more insufficiently analyzed Tonkin Gulf incidents, more inadequately reported elections. The Spiro Agnews in both political parties seem to understand that. It is to be hoped that an informed and enlightened public does too.

What we now refer to as network television will not always function in its current form. Cable television probably will provide anywhere from 30 to 60 channels for every home, thus ending the present monopoly role of the broadcaster. CATV and public broadcasting—if it ever obtains a long-range, nonpolitical method of financing—could provide the standards for whatever lies in the future. But whatever it is called—television, the wired city, or the electronic village—the journalism it carries will be its essential ingredient. Even if a few congressmen insist on defining it with an antiquated dictionary, the public will more and more continue to depend upon it as a central source of news and information. As they do, its relationship to the First Amendment becomes critical. That relationship must be defined and guaranteed. Otherwise, neither journalism nor the Bill of Rights will be worthy of their traditions.

continued from page 663

Africa, after waiting 23 years for the government to sanction television, was to remain indefinitely the only developed country without it. The reason given in October for postponement of a service outlined in April for introduction by 1975 was inflation, which would be increased by the high initial expenditure on sets and the encouragement of consumer spending caused by commercials.

In Kenya, where most of the 25,000 television sets in use by 1971 were owned by Europeans and Asians, the government introduced a plan to raise local-content transmissions, mainly in Swahili, to 75% of the total output. Such popular imports as "Peyton Place" were to be replaced by African cultural and educational programs, likely to win low ratings with viewers unable to understand them.

Programming. News remained a basic service of television and radio around the world in 1971. Coverage of the U.S. Apollo 14 and 15 moon missions was seen in scores of countries through a network of communications satellites and ground stations, with millions of viewers impressed with what experts called the "extraordinary" quality and "awesome clarity" of colour pictures sent back from the surface of the moon.

In the entertainment field, comedies, Westerns, and mysteries produced in the U.S. remained staple fare in most television countries, while many programs produced abroad, especially in the U.K., continued to find wide audiences in other countries, including the U.S. Network programs from the U.S. such as "Gunsmoke," "Bonanza," "Perry Mason," and "The Carol Burnett Show" were being seen in scores of countries. Even so, overseas sales of U.S. programs in 1971 did not come up to expectations. Estimates published in *Broadcasting* in late November indicated that overseas program sales, after reaching $99 million in 1970, were expected to fall short of the predicted $100 million mark for 1971 by approximately $10 million, due in part to sluggish economic conditions in many world markets and a surge of "localism" in others. In Hong Kong, as a minor instance, a government advisory board held that the two local stations were carrying "too much filmed material of non-British and non-Commonwealth origin." On a large scale, stations in Canada and Latin America in particular curtailed their use of U.S. films.

Improved satellite transmission encouraged cooperation in programming as well as in organization, but programs produced by coordination between regional broadcasting unions were in general more interesting as examples of combined operations than for originality of conception or presentation. Even the viewing of the Apollo moon missions or international sports events depended on the increased skill with which television was being used as a mass communications medium rather than on development of its creative or experimental potentialities.

Cooperation between national broadcasting organizations often attempted little more than the provision of entertainment or information, which paid dividends by sharing resources and costs, and ensured international sales for the programs produced. The 13-installment "Arsène Lupin" detective series, made by seven EBU organizations in 1970, with France providing five installments, West Germany three, and Austria, Belgium, Italy, the Netherlands, and Switzerland one each, seemed likely by mid-1971 to rival the BBC's "The Forsyte Saga" in popularity. Even "The Forsyte Saga"—which gained new viewers in 1971 in the U.S.S.R. (where it was accompanied by a commentary on its ideological implications), Hungary, and Portugal—depended more for its continued success on the appeal of a good story, a photogenic period setting, and superb acting and production than on creative use of television.

"The Forsyte Saga" was not the only British best seller. "The Six Wives of Henry VIII," which broke records by winning the five main awards of the U.K.'s Society of Film and Television Arts in March, had already been sold to 15 countries, and its successor, "Elizabeth R," was in worldwide demand. Granada's "Coronation Street," a long-standing tearjerker in Australia, New Zealand, and the Netherlands, was bought by Sweden in July for showing on the Scandinavian Nordvision network. London Weekend TV had earned £600,000 from export of programs in 1970. The BBC's award-winning program for under-fives, "Play School," already spreading English nursery rhymes and games in Australia, New Zealand, France, West Germany, and in Italy and Switzerland (which began a two-way traffic by providing the U.K. with Italian and Swiss contributions to the series), was off to Israel in 1971. The BBC's zany comedy series "Monty Python's Flying Circus," which had won the 1971 Silver Rose award at Montreux, Switz., was also winning worldwide audiences.

In Australia television continued to pursue a policy of pleasing the majority; and the upsurge of home-produced programs that followed the Australian Broadcasting Control Board's ruling that from September 1970, 45% of all programs shown between 6 P.M. and 10 P.M. should be Australian, if it weakened dependence on British imports, revealed a depressing dependence for ideas on popular British series.

Programming policies in Japan were more ambitious. A documentary series launched by NHK in 1970 made effective use of satellite linkage and international cooperation. Called "Our World 70," it included a program illustrating young people's reactions to their first contacts with the worlds of commerce and industry, in which hippies and leaders of student revolutionary movements in Japan, the U.S., and France expressed their views; a survey of environmental pollution in which the problem was highlighted

Actresses Elsa Wagner (left) and Ursula Jockett appear in a scene from playwright Gerhart Hauptmann's "The Weavers." Produced especially for German TV in 1971, the drama commemorated the 25th anniversary of Hauptmann's death.

D.P.A.—PICTORIAL PARADE

David Burns (centre), as a used-furniture dealer, is caught in a confrontation between two estranged brothers, played by Barry Sullivan (left) and George C. Scott, in the Hallmark Hall of Fame presentation of Arthur Miller's "The Price," on Feb. 3, 1971.

by shots of Fuji City, where a pulp mill's waste drain was causing widespread pollution, followed by discussions between its citizens and those of New York, Stockholm, and London, linked by satellite, on their pollution problems; and a confrontation, also made possible by satellite linkage, between 100 U.S. citizens in NBC studios and 100 Japanese citizens in NHK studios, who simultaneously answered questions about their views on U.S.-Japanese relations.

United States. The most fundamental change in programming in the U.S. in 1971 evolved from the FCC's so-called prime-time access rule, under which TV stations in the top 50 markets were required to give up a half hour of prime-time programming a night on weekdays, and an hour on Sundays, formerly supplied by the networks. FCC's idea was to increase the diversity of sources of programming by making it necessary for stations to program those periods on their own initiative or seek programming from syndicators or other nonnetwork sources. The rule went into effect Oct. 1, 1971, and as a practical matter it affected all network affiliates, not just those in the top 50 markets, because the networks considered it uneconomical to supply programs that would not be seen in the top 50 markets.

In practice, the rule was not considered a success. For the first year, the FCC permitted stations to present old movies and reruns of old network series in the periods turned back by the networks, and this was the sort of programming that most stations used, augmented by some new musical, variety, and games programming and an occasional purely local news or entertainment show. The reaction of audiences was not particularly encouraging. Estimates compiled by *Broadcasting* in November indicated that fewer people were watching the new "local" programs than watched when the same time periods were filled by the networks in 1970.

In network programming, the concern with ecology and minority-group problems that had distinguished the new programming on all three TV networks in 1970 clearly had not been well received, judging by the rating-service measurements. As a result, the networks in 1971 tended to concentrate their efforts on entertainment rather than on series with a "do-good" theme. Westerns, mysteries, and comedy-variety pro-

grams were once more the basic form, with ecological, sociological, and other issues increasingly dealt with, like news and public affairs, in documentaries and "specials." The success of this blend of programming was pointed up by estimates, compiled and published by *Broadcasting* in November, that average family viewing was totaling more than 11 hours a day, which was more than half an hour more per day than in the fall of 1970.

One of the most spectacular program developments of the year centred on "The Selling of the Pentagon," dealing with the public-relations activities of the Department of Defense, which was produced by CBS News and broadcast on CBS-TV early in 1971. Angered supporters of the Defense Department contended that the program made false accusations and distorted the words of Pentagon spokesmen, and a House subcommittee voted to subpoena interoffice papers and other nonbroadcast material related to the program, which CBS consistently refused to supply. The upshot was a protracted debate over broadcast journalists' responsibilities under the First Amendment to the Constitution. In the end, after a dramatic confrontation, the House refused to cite CBS for contempt and instead referred the issue back to the Commerce Committee, whose leaders then declared the issue dead. (*See* Special Report.)

Sports remained a major feature of broadcasting in 1971. Radio and TV networks and stations paid an estimated $40.4 million for rights to cover major league baseball during the year, according to *Broadcasting,* and more than $66.2 million for professional and collegiate football rights. These prices represented a $2.6 million increase for baseball, but—in the first indication that football prices may have peaked —a small decline of about $54,000, all of it in college-game rights, for football. Basketball, ice hockey, golf, and other sports claimed additional thousands from television.

Programming for children came increasingly into the limelight. Action for Children's Television (ACT), one of the most vocal advocates of better programming, continued to insist that commercials be banned from programming directed at children and that, in addition, stations be required to present at least 14 hours a week of programming aimed at different age groups. While that issue was awaiting FCC resolution, all three TV networks introduced new, and for the most part widely acclaimed, programs for children in the fall of 1971.

More than television, radio continued to serve the varying musical goals of the public. Except for a relatively few radio stations devoted to all-news and a somewhat larger number devoted to all-talk (primarily through the device of telephone call-in and answerback programs), the majority dispensed music that they thought their audiences would like best.

In noncommercial broadcasting "Sesame Street," for preschool children, remained one of the most widely talked about programs, and as it opened its third season in the fall of 1971 it had an older-audience counterpart, "The Electric Company," also produced by the Children's Television Workshop but aimed at helping second, third, and fourth graders with reading problems. The Public Broadcasting Service's lineup of adult programming—in which "The Great American Dream Machine" was the standout hit of 1971 but which also included a variety of dramatic presentations, public-affairs offerings, and programs on the arts—appeared to be attracting bigger and bigger audiences, though not on a scale to rival those of the commercial networks.

Europe. Partly because financial pressures and competitive policies encouraged program planners to give priority to high audience ratings, programming in Western Europe continued to lack creative inspiration and imaginative direction. Colour could still be relied on to give a "glossy magazine" appeal to even the most commonplace programs, and few were even trying to explore its creative potentialities.

In France, where the creative potentialities of television had been most fully recognized, administrative changes were discouraging program directors and producers. Pierre Sabbagh, director of the first channel, was to take over the second from Maurice Cazeneuve, who had produced high-quality programs in 1970–71. Roland Dhordain, Sabbagh's successor, announced his intention of maintaining and increasing the first channel's popular character, while Sabbagh had been specifically instructed to broaden the second channel's appeal. Among outstanding documentaries shown on Channel 2 in 1970–71 the most memorable were Maurice Failevic's "De la belle ouvrage"; Gerald Chouchan's "Une fatigue passagère"; "Les Coups," a joint production by Roger Boussinot and Jacques Lefebvre; Dirk Sanders' "La petite auto"; and Jacques Kriers's "L'Homme d'Orlu." Literary adaptations included Claude Santelli's haunting "Lancelot du Lac," based on the Lancelot theme from the Arthurian cycle; "Alice au pays des merveilles," a visualization in "electronic images" by Jean-Christophe Averty of Lewis Carroll's *Alice in Wonderland;* and "Ma femme," based on a short story by Chekhov and imaginatively directed by Françoise Dumayet and Jean L'Hôte. Three notable original dramatic productions were Eric Le Hurg's "La possedée," a skillful historical reconstruction of the character and career of Marcelle Maurette, Jean-Marie Drot's masterly "Un Giovanni Brua," and "Anatomie d'un Laussure," a psychological exploration of motivation by Christian-Daniel Watton and Alain Boudet.

With many good ideas for programs in both West Germany and the Netherlands, sports, especially boxing and football, continued to win the highest ratings. There were record West German audiences for the Muhammad Ali–Oscar Bonavena fight and the Köln-Bayern München Cup final. In the Netherlands more than 30% of all viewers watched the live transmissions at 4 A.M. of the Joe Frazier-Ali world championship fight, while on April 28, when elections of the lower house of Parliament coincided with two European cup finals in which Netherlands teams were playing, the ratio between the two channels was 1:9, with 60% watching the cup finals and 7.3% the elections.

Among West German drama programs, "Chance for a Million," a sly satire on television that won the 1971 Prix Italia for the best television comedy at Venice in September, was outstanding; "Max der Taschendief," a picturesque series about a pickpocket, and "Der Kommissar," a crime series that made dramatic viewing from a police inspector's daily tasks, were widely popular.

Two of the year's most impressive programs in both the Netherlands and West Germany aimed to encourage a more positive attitude toward death. The Netherlands program began with a televised talk by a doctor telling how he prepared patients for death, continued with a conversation (on radio only) between the doctor and a dying patient, and ended with an announcement of the patient's death. The West German

program, made in a charitable foundation in the U.K. by a West German television team led by a Jesuit priest, showed an old man's last moments before death, with his family at his bedside and the priest talking quietly about his life.

The BBC was under fire during the year for bias in reporting industrial disputes, for its coverage of the crisis in Northern Ireland, and for its representation, in the program "Yesterday's Men," of Labour Party leaders. Complaints of "sniping" at British soldiers in Northern Ireland were accompanied by accusations of supporting the Irish Republican Army (IRA). Labour Party complaints gave undeserved publicity to "Yesterday's Men," a program summed up by Anthony Crossland (one of the 12 Labour Party leaders interviewed in it) as "good cheap entertainment." Harold Wilson added fuel to the fire by threatening legal action against the interviewer, David Dimbleby, who had asked him how much he had earned from his memoirs; and refused to broadcast for the BBC until he had received an apology. The BBC refused to apologize, and defended the program and the principle of journalistic independence in a 17-page report. Only after two months of argument were normal relations resumed.

Lack of new ideas for programs caused program directors to fall back on old ones. The BBC attempted to recapture the late-night sparkle of early David Frost with "Parkinson," who used all the Frost formulas without the Frost flair; and replaced "Dr. Finley's Casebook" by "Owen M.D.," which began at the level of banality at which Dr. Finley had wisely decided to retire. Thames Television tried to emulate the success of the BBC's "Civilisation" series with "Treasures of the British Museum," made at a cost of approximately £150,000 with worldwide and TV-cassette markets in mind, but, despite the presence in its team of commentators of Sir John Betjeman and Sir Tyrone Guthrie (recorded before his death in May), the series failed to get off the ground.

It was a good year for drama, with William Trevor's "O Fat White Woman," Rhys Adrian's "Foxtrot," and Jeremy Sandford's semidocumentary study of "Edna, the Inebriate Woman" among BBC 1's avant-garde offerings in "Play for Today." But the dramatic experience of the year was Chekhov's *Platonov,* with Cedric Messina directing a company that brought to the play assurance, pace, and delicacy of touch.

Benjamin Britten's opera *Owen Wingrave,* commissioned by BBC 2, was the year's most impressive musical program. Most of the good ideas for presentation of music were on Radio 3, with "Cross-section," made up of compositions belonging to the same year by composers of different countries, styles, and ages; "The Sincerest Form of Flattery," illustrating the subtle influence of one major work on another; and "Presented Recital," in which distinguished musicians discussed and performed music for which they had a particular affection. Television's best new music program, London Weekend's "Music in the Round," presented musicians of all kinds talking about their instruments and playing or singing to live audiences.

(S. Tf.; R. W. Cr.; M. Ty.; X.)

Amateur Radio. With dramatic impact, radio amateurs demonstrated their value as communicators in time of disaster when on February 9 an earthquake racked the populous San Fernando Valley in California. The disruption of utilities and services resulting from the quake placed a great burden on existing communications channels, causing a communications emergency. Radio amateurs assisted during the disaster in two major ways: communications support for Civil Defense and ambulance services was provided by amateurs located in the disaster area; and amateurs throughout the U.S. organized into an informal network to handle thousands of inquiries from relatives and friends of individuals in the disaster area.

Amateurs regularly test their operating and technical skills in preparation for emergency communications. During 1971 nearly 12,000 U.S. and Canadian amateurs took part in "Field Day" sponsored by the American Radio Relay League, the binational association of radio amateurs. The participants in this event operate amateur stations from field sites, using gasoline-powered electric generators, in order to simulate emergency operating conditions. (WI. D.)

See also Advertising; Astronautics; Motion Pictures; Music; Telecommunications.

ENCYCLOPÆDIA BRITANNICA FILMS. *Getting the News* (1967).

Tennis

The administrative crisis that had arisen from a conflict of interest between the International Lawn Tennis Federation (ILTF), the world's governing body since 1913, and the commercial World Championship Tennis (WCT), controlled by Lamar Hunt, son of a Texas oil millionaire, deepened in 1971. Hunt organized a world championship comprising 20 tournaments in opposition to the Grand Prix series initiated in 1970 by the ILTF. Efforts to create a calendar of events satisfactory to both sides failed. So did efforts to find mutually satisfactory conditions of entry into the traditional ILTF events for the 32 players under contract to WCT. These players comprised many of the most notable men, including Rod Laver (Austr.), John Newcombe (Austr.), Ken Rosewall (Austr.), and Arthur Ashe (U.S.). The upshot was that at its meeting in July the ILTF decreed that from Jan. 1, 1972, all players not accepting the authority of their national associations were barred from ILTF events and clubs were forbidden to allow their courts to be used by such players.

A change was made in the format of the Davis Cup competition. Since its inception in 1900 the winning nation remained out of the next year's competition, defending the trophy in the challenge round at a site of its own choosing. In 1971 the Davis Cup nations, an administrative body distinct from the International Federation, decided to abolish the challenge round beginning in 1972, the defending nation playing through from the start. This meant that the challenge round in which the U.S. defended its crown against Romania at Charlotte, N.C., in October 1971 was the last of its kind.

The pattern of increasing prize money and commercial sponsorship of tournaments was maintained. Among the important events, only the Wimbledon championships remained independent of sponsorship.

As in 1970 the leading prize money earner was Rod Laver. In that year he earned a record $200,000 in prizes. He passed that total after the first six months of 1971 though he was not as successful in winning the events of traditional prestige and importance. In the final round of the world championship series, he lost to Rosewall 6–4, 1–6, 7–6, 7–6.

There was a move among women to bring prize

money earnings nearer to those commanded by the men. Gladys Heldman, owner and editor of the U.S. magazine *World Tennis,* organized a series of sponsored tournaments for women only through the U.S. As a result, Billie Jean King (U.S.) won more than $100,000 in prize money, a record for a woman. Players participating, mainly Americans and some Australians, signed nominal $1 contracts with Mrs. Heldman. It was never made clear whether such contracts took players outside the control of their national associations or not. The first ranking list issued by the U.S. Lawn Tennis Association at the end of 1970 excluded them. An amended list including them was issued a few weeks later, and the definition of the technical status of women players under contract was carefully avoided.

The experimental changes in the scoring system started in 1970 were continued. In various forms the "tie break" method of shortening sets was used. In the United States a slightly amended form of its nine point "sudden death" system was maintained. In this system when a set was tied at 6–6, the issue was decided on the best of the next nine points. At Wimbledon and in British tournaments a different method was used. At 8–8 in all sets except the deciding one the best of 12 points was played, it being mandatory for the winner to be at least two points in front. Notably, the Davis Cup excluded such novelties and continued to require a 2-game margin, as did the deciding set in British tournaments.

Men's Competition. *Singles.* At the end of 1970 the first Grand Prix competition was won by Cliff Richey of the U.S. The subsequent Masters' tournament, held on a round-robin basis in Tokyo, between the six leading players (with Richey not competing because of injury), was won by Stan Smith (U.S.), who beat all his rivals except Arthur Ashe. Laver placed second.

The first of the traditional major championships, the Australian, was won by Ken Rosewall when he beat in the last three rounds Roy Emerson, Tom Okker (Neth.), and Arthur Ashe. Rosewall maintained his success in the South African championships, defeating his fellow Australian Fred Stolle in the final.

The Italian meeting in Rome had an unusual formula in that it was part of the world championship series organized by WCT. Unlike most WCT events, it included players not under contract to WCT and was notable for the success achieved by Jan Kodes of Czechoslovakia, an independent professional. He beat John Newcombe and Tom Okker to reach the final. There Laver triumphed over Kodes to gain his only success in any of the seven major meetings.

The French championships in Paris lacked the entry of some of the world's leading players, WCT members. Kodes was a strong winner, defeating the Romanian Ilie Nastase in the final.

Wimbledon was the only meeting in which the majority of the world's leading players took part. Newcombe won the title for the second year in a row. The only major test of his prowess was in the last two rounds; in the semifinal he beat Rosewall 6–1, 6–1, 6–3 and in the final Smith 6–3, 5–7, 2–6, 6–4, 6–4. The best match of the tournament was in the quarterfinal where Rosewall beat Richey 6–8, 5–7, 6–4, 9–7, 7–5. Tom Gorman of Seattle beat Laver in his quarterfinal but lost his semifinal to Smith.

The U.S. Open championships at Forest Hills, N.Y., had notable absentees in Laver and Rosewall, the latter the titleholder. Smith dominated. He beat

Marty Riessen in the quarterfinal, Okker in the semifinal (the only occasion he was taken to five sets), and Kodes in the final by 3–6, 6–3, 6–2, 7–6. The biggest upset came on the opening day when Newcombe, the number one seed, was beaten by Kodes, who won his semifinal against Ashe before yielding to Smith.

Doubles. Newcombe and Tony Roche (Austr.), the latter unable to play in the last half of the year because of injury, were the most successful pair in winning two of the major titles, the championships of Australia and Italy. Roy Emerson and Laver were the victors at Wimbledon. Newcombe partnered Roger Taylor of Britain to take the U.S. title. Their victory was unorthodox. In the final against Smith and Erik Van Dillen (U.S.) the score was tied at two sets apiece when darkness made conditions impossible. It was ruled that the match finish on the outcome of a tie-break sequence, and accordingly Newcombe and Taylor won their title with the unique score of 6–7, 6–3, 7–6, 4–6, and 5 points to 3 points (tie break). Its strict legality was questionable.

Davis Cup. In the last challenge round ever to be played (*see* above), the U.S. defended its title against the challenge of Romania. With many leading players under contract to WCT and consequently not eligible to represent their countries, a lowering of the standard of the event as compared with some previous years was inevitable. Notably Australia, represented in every challenge round from 1946 to 1968, again failed to get far, India winning the Eastern Zone final 3–2 against Japan. Brazil won the American Zone, defeating Mexico 3–2 in the final. In the European Zone "A" Czechoslovakia won the final 3–2 against Spain. Romania won section "B," beating West Germany in the final, 5–0. In the interzone matches Brazil defeated Czechoslovakia 4–1, and Romania beat India 4–1. Romania qualified to challenge the U.S. with a 3–2 win over Brazil.

In the Davis Cup finals, played at Charlotte, N.C., in October, the U.S. successfully defended its title by defeating Romania 3–2. The contest opened with Smith defeating Nastase 7–5, 6–3, 6–1. Frank Froehling then beat Ion Tiriac 3–6, 1–6, 6–1, 6–3, 8–6 to stretch the U.S. lead to 2–0. Nastase and Tiriac won

the doubles from Smith and Erik Van Dillen 7–5, 6–4 8–6, but Smith then clinched victory for the U.S. by defeating Tiriac 8–6, 6–3, 6–0. In the final contest Nastase beat Froehling 6–3, 6–1, 4–6, 6–4.

Women's Competition. *Singles.* The most successful player of the year was the Australian Evonne Goolagong (*see* BIOGRAPHY). In only her second season in international competition she was runner-up in the Australian and South African championships to Margaret Court. She won the French championship in Paris, where she competed for the first time, and then went on to win at Wimbledon.

Another young player to make her mark was 16-year-old Chris Evert from Fort Lauderdale, Fla. On the merits of a strong defensive game based on beautifully controlled baseline driving, she played a leading part in winning the Wightman Cup for the U.S. against Great Britain at Cleveland, O., in August. She then went on to win the Eastern Grass Court championship at South Orange, N.J., and continued her winning streak until beaten in the semifinal of the U.S. Open.

Mrs. Court, the outstanding player of 1970, won the Australian and South African titles. The Italian title was won from a field less strong than usual by Virginia Wade of the U.K. In the French championships Miss Goolagong won the title, beating Helen Gourlay (Austr.) in the final.

Miss Goolagong triumphed convincingly at Wimbledon. She defeated Nancy Richey Gunter in the quarterfinal, Mrs. King in the semifinal, and Mrs. Court in the final, 6–4, 6–1. Pregnancy caused Mrs. Court's temporary retirement from the game soon afterward. Mrs. King, the winner in 1967, won the U.S. Open for the second time, beating Rosemary Casals 6–4, 7–6.

Doubles. Mrs. King and Miss Casals won the German and Wimbledon titles, defeating Mrs. Court and Miss Goolagong in the Wimbledon final. The latter pair won the Australian and South African championships. Miss Casals paired with Judy Dalton (Austr.) to win the U.S. championship, beating the French champions, G. Chanfreau and Françoise Durr, in the final.

Wightman Cup. The U.S. defeated Great Britain 4–3 to retain the trophy. The American side consisted of Julie Heldman, Chris Evert, Kristy Pigeon, Valerie Ziegenfuss, Mary Ann Eisel, and Carole Graebner. Virginia Wade, Winnie Shaw, Joyce Williams, Christine Janes, and Nell Truman represented Britain.

Federation Cup. The 1971 competition took place in December 1970 in Perth, Austr., and was won by

Left, Billie Jean King competes against 16-year-old Chris Evert during the U.S. Open championships in Forest Hills, N.Y., on Sept. 10, 1971. Mrs. King won the match. Below, Army Pfc. Stan Smith leads the U.S. to victory against Romania's Ion Tiriac at the 1971 Davis Cup challenge round in Charlotte, N.C.

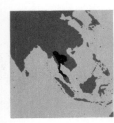

Australia, represented by Mrs. Court and Miss Goolagong. In the semifinals Great Britain beat the U.S. 3–0, and Australia triumphed over France 3–0. In the final Australia defeated Great Britain 3–0.   (L. O. T.)

Thailand

A constitutional monarchy of Southeast Asia, Thailand is bordered by Burma, Laos, Cambodia, and Malaysia. Area: 198,500 sq.mi. (514,000 sq.km.). Pop. (1970): 34,152,000. Cap. and largest city: Bangkok (pop., 1970 est., 2,213,522). Language: Thai. Religion (1964): Buddhist 93.7%; Muslim 3.9%. King, Bhumibol Adulyadej; prime minister in 1971, Field Marshal Thanom Kittikachorn.

Prime Minister Thanom, backed by the Thai Revolutionary Party, overthrew his own government on Nov. 17, 1971. The Revolutionary Council abolished the 1968 constitution, dismissed the Cabinet, dissolved Parliament, and proclaimed martial law. A National Executive Council was established with the prime minister as its chairman; Gen. Prapas Charusathiara, deputy prime minister and chief of the armed forces, became deputy chairman in charge of military affairs and Gen. Prasert Ruchirawongse, the police chief, was appointed to direct civilian affairs. The country's criminal law was to be revised; life sentences would be extended from 20 to 50 years and summary executions were sanctioned for the most serious cases. All but juvenile offenses would be tried by military courts.

In the light of the Nixon doctrine calling for reduced U.S. involvement in Asia, Thailand began a shift in its foreign policy. On Dec. 20, 1970, after long postponement, the government signed for the first time a trade pact with the U.S.S.R. The decision to sign had seemed evidence of Thailand's inclination to bend with the times. Early in 1971 there had been complaints that insufficient U.S. military and economic aid was forthcoming to help the country meet its new responsibilities under the Nixon doctrine. It was also felt that sales of U.S. rice under the Food for Peace program had cut deeply into such traditional Thai rice markets as Indonesia and South Korea. These complaints were followed by U.S. assurances of substantial aid. In April there were reports from Washington that Thailand would be made the centre of U.S. air power in Southeast Asia.

Foreign Minister Thanat Khoman, long considered the architect of Thailand's U.S.-leaning posture, emerged early in 1971 as an articulate proponent of a "dialogue with China"; his policy split the Thai Cabinet into two camps, opponents arguing that it was too early to think of a rapprochement with Peking and discounting prospects of any meaningful trade with China which, they pointed out, was actively supporting Communist insurgents in northern Thailand. Then, on November 3, after the U.S. Senate had voted to cut off all foreign aid, the Thai National Security Council took the historic decision to annul the former prime minister Sarit Thanarat's prohibition on trade with China, to relax anti-Communist laws, and to engage in athletic and cultural exchanges with Peking though not yet to seek or grant diplomatic recognition. The coup that followed hard on these decisions took place amid bitter argument over the policies of Economics Minister Bunchana Atthakor, the prime minister having threatened to resign if proposed defense-spending cuts were not restored.

In defense of the coup Thanom cited left-wing pressure for the pro-Peking policy, the dangers of the spread of Maoism in the large Chinese community within Thailand, the increase in Communist guerrilla activity, and the corruption of self-seeking politicians.

Rumours of major Cabinet changes had persisted for several months before the coup. Thanat Khoman faced a united boycott by the press over the arrest of three journalists; it ended after mediation by the prime minister. Four MPs also publicly shaved their heads as a protest against Thanat's alleged insults in Parliament. On June 5 the Cabinet, presided over by General Prapas, voted to extend for another year Prime Minister Thanom's concurrent post as supreme commander of the armed forces. Local reports indicated that Prapas' initiative in the matter belied rumours of a power struggle between him and Thanom; in August the prime minister announced that he would retire after completing his term of office before the February 1973 elections.

The government announced in July its decision to lower the annual growth rate target from 7.5 to 5% in the third five-year plan, which was to start with the new financial year in October. The change was attributed to the need for increased expenditures on defense and security.   (T. J. S. G.; X.)

THAILAND

Education. (1967–68) Primary, pupils 4,983,113, teachers (including preprimary) 119,250; secondary, pupils 358,221, teachers (state only) 10,285; vocational, pupils 57,751, teachers 5,796; teacher training, students 20,534, teachers 2,098; higher (including 7 universities), students 38,204, teaching staff 3,186.

Finance. Monetary unit: baht, with a par value of 20.80 baht to U.S. $1 (49.92 baht = £1 sterling) and a free rate (Sept. 27, 1971) of 20.95 baht to U.S. $1 (51.95 baht = £1). Gold, SDRs, and foreign exchange, official: (June 1971) U.S. $900 million; (June 1970) U.S. $954 million. Budget (1969–70 est.): revenue 19,020,000,000 baht; expenditure (including capital account) 27,299,000,000 baht. Gross national product: (1969) 115,470,000,000 baht; (1968) 103,250,-000,000 baht. Money supply: (April 1971) 19,750,-000,000 baht; (April 1970) 17.9 billion baht. Cost of living (Bangkok; 1963 = 100): (June 1971) 119; (June 1970) 117.

Foreign Trade. (1970) Imports 26,064,000,000 baht; exports 14,490,000,000 baht. Import sources (1969): Japan 37%; U.S. 15%; West Germany 9%; U.K. 8%. Export destinations (1969): Japan 22%; U.S. 15%; Hong Kong 8%; Singapore 8%; Malaysia 7%; Netherlands 7%. Main exports: rice 17%; rubber 15%; corn 13%; tin 11%; tapioca 8%; kenaf 5%.

Transport and Communications. Roads (1968) 12,671 km. Motor vehicles in use (1968): passenger 125,600; commercial (including buses) 102,400. Railways (1969): 3,765 km.; traffic 3,962,000,000 passenger-km., freight 1,974,000,000 net ton-km. Air traffic (1970): 798 million passenger-km.; freight 8,040,000 net ton-km. Shipping (1970): merchant vessels 100 gross tons and over 60; gross tonnage 82,271. Telephones (Dec. 1969) 120,379. Radio receivers (Dec. 1969) 2,767,000. Television receivers (Dec. 1969) 241,000.

Agriculture. Production (in 000; metric tons; 1970; 1969 in parentheses): rice 13,400 (13,410); corn 1,600 (1,568); peanuts c. 220 (c. 220); sweet potatoes (1969) c. 248, (1968) c. 247; sorghum 120 (c. 70); dry beans c. 130 (c. 130); soybeans c. 60 (c. 60); cassava (1969) 1,932, (1968) 1,896; sugar, raw value (1970–71) c. 460, (1969–70) c. 466; bananas (1969) c. 1,200, (1968) c. 1,200; tobacco 93 (89); rubber c. 287 (c. 282); cotton, lint 25 (23); jute c. 12 (10); kenaf c. 360 (320); timber (cu.m.; 1969) 3,700, (1968) 4,500; fish catch (1969) 1,270, (1968) 1,089. Livestock (in 000; 1969–70): cattle 5,263; buffalo 6,941; pigs c. 4,200; chickens 32,863.

Industry. Production (in 000; metric tons; 1970): cement 2,627; tin concentrates (metal content) 22; tungsten concentrates (oxide content; 1969) 0.8; lead concentrates (metal content; 1969) 1.7; electricity (kw.-hr.; 1969) 3,728,000.

Textiles:
see Industrial Review

Theatre

Great Britain and Ireland. The rivalry between the National Theatre and the Royal Shakespeare Company grew deeper when each rented a second London theatre to meet increased audience demand. The National leased the New Theatre, thus renewing the postwar link between the Old Vic Theatre and the West End. Despite the ambitious choice of plays— Jean Giraudoux's *Amphitryon 38,* Luigi Pirandello's *The Rules of the Game,* Jonathan Miller's new view of *Danton's Death* by Georg Büchner, and *Tyger,* Adrian Mitchell's musical "celebration" of William Blake as a radical poet—attendance fell off; the situation worsened with the departure of several of the National's leading players, until Sir Laurence Olivier, backed by Constance Cummings, revived his theatre's fortunes with Eugene O'Neill's *Long Day's Journey into Night,* movingly staged by Michael Blakemore.

At the National's parent theatre several controversial productions suggested a lack of proper direction, as in Fernando Arrabal's baroque *The Architect and the Emperor of Assyria,* and *Coriolanus,* staged as a facsimile of the Berliner Ensemble's version, resulting in Christopher Plummer's retirement midway in rehearsal. Saving graces were Frank Dunlop's colourful handling of Carl Zuckmayer's *The Captain of Köpenick,* John Dexter's sparkling contributions of Thomas Heywood's *A Woman Killed with Kindness* and Oliver Goldsmith's *The Good-Natured Man,* and, above all, the continuing popularity of the Young Vic, under Frank Dunlop's artistic direction. There the landmarks were *Measure for Measure* and *Romeo and Juliet,* Samuel Beckett's *Endgame,* Vanessa Redgrave in Robert Shaw's *Cato Street,* the world premiere of the New York Shakespeare Festival Theatre's rock version of *Iphigenia,* and the opening of a studio stage with *The Painters* by Heinrich Heinkel.

Other guest performances at the Old Vic included August Strindberg's *The Father,* from Bolton, and two offerings by the National Belgian Theatre. Both were overshadowed by the Paris production of *1789* at the Round House, but once again the World Theatre Season at the Aldwych Theatre, London home of the Royal Shakespeare Company, stole the visiting companies' thunder with the Paris Théâtre Michel in Henry de Montherlant's *La Ville dont le prince est un enfant;* Ingmar Bergman's version of Strindberg's *The Dream Play* from Stockholm; the Berlin Schiller Theatre in Witold Gombrowicz' *Yvonne, Princess of Burgundy* and Samuel Beckett's *Endgame* and *Krapp's Last Tape;* the Genoese Stabile in *The Venetian Twins; A Tale of Istanbul,* a musical by the first Turkish company to play in England; and the Spanish Nuria Espert Company in Jean Genet's *The Maids.*

The Royal Shakespeare Company broke all boxoffice records by exceeding a million visitors a year for the fifth consecutive year at both its houses, and almost selling out nightly at its third studio theatre. The studio theatre offered new chances to young directors, who put on Strindberg's *Miss Julie;* Trevor Griffiths' study of a failed revolution, *Occupations;* and the American Robert Montgomery's *Subject to Fits.* The hits at the Aldwych were Peter Brook's *A Midsummer Night's Dream* and Ronald Eyre's *Much Ado About Nothing,* James Joyce's *Exiles* staged by Harold Pinter, Pinter's latest fantasy-drama,

Old Times, Maksim Gorki's *Enemies,* Sir George Etherege's *The Man of Mode,* and Genet's *The Balcony.*

A new subsidized theatre was the Shaw, home of the National Youth Theatre and its professional offshoot and inaugurator, the Dolphin Theatre company. The Dolphin opened with George Bernard Shaw's *The Devil's Disciple* and two new plays by Peter Terson. Two Shaw revivals at the Mermaid (*John Bull's Other Island* and *Geneva*) confirmed the topicality and the absurdity of each, while other memorable items were Michael Redgrave's return to the stage after nine years' absence, in William Trevor's *The Old Boys,* and an *Othello* that boasted a topless Desdemona. The first West End transfer of a new play staged at the Royal Court's studio stage (the Theatre Upstairs), *The Foursome,* heralded a new talent in E. A. Whitehead, promoted to house dramatist. A singularly effective repertoire at the Theatre Upstairs included *Lay-By,* a critique of the ills of pornography; the West Indian Mustapha Matura's London debut, *As Time Goes By;* the South African Athol Fugard's *Boesman and Lena;* the Belgian Hugo Claus's *Friday;* and Bertolt Brecht's *Man Is Man.* On the large stage below, Peggy Ashcroft illuminated Marguerite Duras' *The Lovers of Viorne,* followed by David Hare's *Slag,* Peter Gill's stylized rendering of John Webster's *The Duchess of Malfi,* John Osborne's *West of Suez* (with Ralph Richardson), Edward Bond's *Lear,* and David Storey's football drama *The Changing Room.*

At the Hampstead Theatre Club, newcomers Peter Ransley and Tom Mallin made their mark with two works, Clifford Odets' *Awake and Sing* and Sandy Wilson's skittish musical version of John Collier's *His Monkey Wife.* At the Greenwich Theatre an ambitious new *Macbeth* was followed by Peter Nichols' *Forget-Me-Not-Lane* and newfangled versions of *Antigone* and *Electra.* At Charles Marowitz' Open Space the best offerings were a centre-stage adaptation of Oscar Wilde's *The Critic as Artist* and an inspired evocation of Pablo Picasso's *The Four Little Girls,* a world premiere. The Round House featured Jean-Louis Barrault's restaging of his own *Rabelais,* in English, and the U.S. musical *Godspell,* acted by an English cast.

The upsurge of outlying studio stages and lunchtime shows gave London such unusual attractions as David Parker's *The Collector* (from John Fowles's novel), Joe Orton's *The Good and Faithful Servant,* and one-acters by, among others, James Saunders, John Grillo, Michael Almaz, David Snodin, Snoo Wilson, Barry Bermange, Henry Livings, Stanley Eveling, Charles Wood, John McGrath, David Mowat, David Halliwell, Tom Mallin, David Mercer, and Olwen Wymark. American authors in the West End provided *1776, Child's Play, The Dirtiest Show in Town, Show Boat,* and a musical adaptation of Henry James's *The Ambassadors* (retitled *Ambassador*). Commercial hits ranged from the serious *Kean* by Jean-Paul Sartre or John Mortimer's *A Voyage Round My Father* to the trivial *Dear Antoine* by Jean Anouilh or the unpretentious comedy of middle age, *Getting On* by Alan Bennett, and also included two Hamlets (Alan Bates and Ian McKellen), Ingrid Bergman in *Captain Brassbound's Conversion* by Shaw, David Mercer's *After Haggerty,* two studies of the homosexual by Simon Gray, *Spoiled* and *Butley,* and the popular farces *Move over Mrs. Markham* by Ray Cooney and John Chapman, *Don't Just Lie There, Say Something!* by Michael Pertwee, *No Sex, Please—We're British*

The Black Light Theatre of Prague began its first U.S. tour on Sept. 27, 1971, at the New York City Center. The theatre, combining Chaplinesque scenes of fantasy and illusion with mime and moving objects, received worldwide acclaim.

by Anthony Marriott and Alistair Foot, and *Charley's Aunt.*

The theatre in Belfast was hit badly by the political unrest, and the Arts Theatre closed its doors "for the duration." By contrast Dublin saw the reopening of a rebuilt Gate Theatre, where the Hilton Edwards-Micheál MacLiammóir regime put on Anouilh's *Ornifle* as *It's Later than You Think,* and the resuscitation of the Festival with such theatrical treats as Conor Cruise O'Brien's *Murderous Angels,* Thomas Murphy's Joycean morality *The Morning of the Optimism,* Hugh Leonard's Irish farce *The Patrick Pearse Motel,* and John Peacock's "Oresteian" thriller *Children of the Wolf.* The Abbey staged *Macbeth,* and both Brian Friel and John B. Keane had new plays at the Olympia.

France. The appointment of Jacques Duhamel as minister of culture resulted in a widening of official policy toward the arts, leading to the official conversion of the Théâtre de l'Est Parisien (TEP) into a "National Theatre" and the opening of the derelict state cartridge factory in Vincennes (the Cartoucherie) to theatrical production. In an open hangar in the latter Ariane Mnouchkine re-created her open-stage production of the French Revolution drama *1789* (after a pre-Paris tryout in Milan). This collectively written multiple-stage play, fully involving the audience that sat or stood around as well as in among the players, became France's most popular theatrical export of the year. Duhamel's other major move was to reentrust the moribund Théâtre des Nations to Jean-Louis Barrault. As forerunners of things to come Barrault presented the New York Manhattan Project's *Alice in Wonderland* and Patrice Chéreau's Milan production of Pierre Carlet de Marivaux's *La Fausse Suivante.*

Pierre Dux's new policies at the Comédie-Française began to take shape: among them was a take-over of the Odéon, renamed the Théâtre National de l'Odéon, for the occasional performance of new one-acters and for alternate programs by visiting companies and a new resident company drawn from the parent group. The inaugural play, an anti-fascist allegory *L'Amorphe d'Ottenburg,* by Jean-Claude Grumberg, was followed by the Brazilian Ariano Suassuna's *Le*

Testament du Chien. At the parent theatre Jacques Charon played the lead in a hilarious new *Le Malade Imaginaire.* The government intervened in the Théâtre National Populaire's (TNP) production of *Murderous Angels,* on the eve of a visit by French Pres. Georges Pompidou to Belgium, but neither author O'Brien nor guest director Joan Littlewood would agree to cut the part of the Belgian king and the effort to censor the play was defeated. Bad business had momentarily threatened Georges Wilson's position as manager of the TNP, but with his contract renewed he recouped losses and reputation with the satirically scurrilous first play of the half-Persian, half-Russian French writer Rezvani, *Captain Shell, Captain Esso,* and the parabolic *Turandot.* Gorki's *Enemies* at the TEP was followed by *The Merchant of Venice* set in the 19th century, while the two best offerings at the Théâtre de la Ville were Giraudoux's *Tiger at the Gates* and a political musical by Dario Fo (first seen at the Avignon Festival).

After staging *Rabelais* in London Barrault revived Jean Vauthier's *Le Personnage Combattant* at the Récamier, where Madeleine Renaud was also seen in Beckett's *Happy Days.* A new talent emerged with Eric Westphal, making his Paris debut with *Toi et Tes Nuages,* and Remo Forlani's *Le Bal des Chiens,* a verse-play about the events of May 1968, fulfilled his earlier promise. Among popular comedy hits were *La Gobedouille,* by several authors, *Vos Gueules les Mouettes!* by Robert Dhéry, Gaby Bruyère's *La Maison de Zaza,* the musical *Monsieur Pompadour* by Françoise Dorin, and a superb revival of Georges Feydeau's *Le Main Passe.* After working for six months in their International Theatre Research Centre in Paris on an experimental ritualistic drama entitled *Orghast* and three more months of rehearsals in Iran, Peter Brook and his players performed it publicly at the Shiraz-Persepolis Arts Festival. Jean Vilar's death was a blow to the Avignon Festival and the French theatre in general.

Switzerland, Germany, Austria, Belgium, Netherlands. The death of veteran actor-director Leonhard Steckel in a train accident was a loss to the German-speaking stage and especially to the Zürich Schauspielhaus, where Harry Buckwitz entered his penultimate year in office before yielding to a triumvirate that was to include the dramatist Friedrich Dürrenmatt. Dürrenmatt exercised his directorial flair once more at Zürich with his own *Portrait of a Planet,* and there, too, guest director Karl Heinz Stroux, from Düsseldorf, put on a version of *Mourning Becomes Electra.* A new management at the small Theater am Neumarkt introduced several new plays, in the wake of the Swiss premiere of *After Haggerty.* The even smaller Theater an der Winkelwiese scored a palpable hit with the dramatic monologue *Jonah,* by the Romanian Marin Sorecu. At the rival City Theatre in Basel, Shakespeare's *Twelfth Night* vied in popularity with Hans Hollmann's extravagant *Le Dame de chez Maxim,* but Heinrich Heinkel's *Games for Money,* which equated society with a gambling casino, was disappointing.

At Basel was staged the second of four premieres of Peter Weiss's allegorical verse-drama, *Hölderlin,* first seen at Stuttgart in a soberly symbolical production by Peter Palitzsch, and then in very different versions by Claus Peymann in Hamburg and by Hollmann in Berlin. *Hölderlin* purported to mirror the German poet Friedrich Hölderlin's dilemma at a time when revolutionary fires were flickering or even doused, but also contained strong autobiographical traits and implied an ambivalent faith in Marxist doctrine. Palitzsch also proved by his new *Waiting for Godot* in Stuttgart that a convinced Marxist could make an adequate interpreter of Beckett; also at Stuttgart Hans Neuenfels breathed new life into Ramón del Valle-Inclán's *Divinas Palabras* and Martin Walser's latest drama, *Child's Play*, had its world premiere.

The appointment of ex-critic Ivan Nagel to the state-owned Hamburg Schauspielhaus deepened the rivalry between it and the city-run Thalia under Boy Gobert, whose successes included the simultaneous world premiere (with Bremen) of Rainer Werner Fassbinder's drama about an 1831 murder, *Freedom of Bremen*, and a near-blasphemous production of Dieter Forte's anti-Luther drama of 1970. Nürnberg staged a new play by Jochen Ziehm and a spectacular production of Brecht's *Galileo* as part of the festivities honouring the 500th anniversary of the birth of the painter Albrecht Dürer; Essen saw the first professional production of Peter Weiss's nearly 20-year-old "drama of cruelty," *The Insurance;* Kassel held the world premiere of Armand Gatti's play about Rosa Luxemburg; and Munich saw the East German poet Wolf Biermann's antitotalitarian satire, *Der Dra-Dra*, banned in the East.

In West Berlin, a poor season in the state theatres (excepting Rudolf Nölte's one-night digest of Strindberg's *The Dance of Death* at the Schiller, *Hanserl*, by the Austrian Franz Buchrieser, and the above-named *Hölderlin*, in Hollmann's production) was compensated for by Peter Stein's inventively spectacular seven-hour-long version of Ibsen's *Peer Gynt*, acted on two consecutive evenings and staged in the arena of the gutted Schaubühne am Halleschen Ufer. This was universally proclaimed the finest production of the year. The summer German theatre review brought to Berlin Hamburg's fine production of Christopher Hampton's *The Philanthropist*, with Helmut Griem, and the autumn Arts Festival brought the Atelje 212 from Belgrade, in a repertory of five plays, all of unusual interest. In East Berlin Ruth Berghaus assumed formal direction of the Berliner Ensemble and staged Brecht's *In the Jungle of Cities*, followed by a revival of the playwright's *Galileo*. The Göteborg City Theatre created a precedent in Ralf Långbacka's brilliantly comic Swedish-language *Puntila*, the first foreign troupe to do Brecht at his former theatre. Benno Besson, at the Volksbühne, restaged Brecht's *The Good Woman of Setzuan* and put on two comic hits, Molière's *Doctor in Spite of Himself* and Carlo Gozzi's *King Stag;* a popular updated version of *The Brigands*, by Johann Schiller, was the work of Manfred Karge and Matthias Langhoff.

The main draws at Vienna's Burgtheater were Gerhard Klingenberg's modern-dress *Julius Caesar*, a revival of Arthur Schnitzler's *Miss Elsa*, and Lotte Ingrisch's *Damenbekanntschaften*. The long-awaited *New Year's Eve, or Mass-Murder at Hotel Sacher*, by Wolfgang Bauer, at the Volkstheater, proved a fiasco, but a new work by Walter Lieblein, based on Fëdor Dostoevski's *The Eternal Husband*, was well received at the Josefstadt.

The Belgian National Theatre's London visit (with Frank Dunlop's guest production of Michel de Ghelderode's *Pantagleize*) was capped by Dunlop's return to Brussels to stage *Antony and Cleopatra*. A novelty was the first professional production outside France of Montherlant's *La Ville dont le prince est un enfant*, staged by Jean Meyer at the Rideau. The Netherlands feted veteran actor Paul Steenbergen in Karl Guttman's sensitive production of David Storey's *Home* in The Hague and mourned the death of Albert van Dalsum.

Italy. After two years' absence, Giorgio Strehler was reported as being willing to return to the Milan Piccolo, where Paolo Grassi had been in sole charge. Grassi also announced his take-over of the empty and newly redecorated Argentina in Rome for the regular presentation of visiting Stabile theatre productions, following the glittering inaugural production of *Julius Caesar*, with an all-star cast. In Milan the Piccolo had Eduardo de Filippo stage his own review of the 1930s, *Ogni Anno Punto e Da Capo*, while Dario Fo's latest political satire with music, *Death and Resurrection of a Puppet*, was put on at the reopened Comune. A new group, the Teatro Insieme, gave *L'Amante Militare* as the opening event of the Venice Festival, while at Spoleto *La Finta Serva* (*La Fausse Suivante* by Marivaux) was directed by Patrice Chéreau. In Turin Franco Enriquez staged *Macbeth*, and Valeria Moriconi appeared there in *Isabella comica gelosa*, by Enriquez and Vito Pandolfi, based on the life of the 16th-century actress Isabella Andreini.

Eastern Europe. Two strikingly different adaptations of Boris Vasilyev's war novel *All Quiet at Dawn* were staged in Moscow, one by Boris Erin at the Central Army Theatre and one by Yuri Liubimov at the Taganka. A highly praised Shakespeare production was *Antony and Cleopatra*, staged by Yevgeni Simonov at the Vakhtangov for its 50th jubilee festivities. The hopes that Oleg Yefremov would rejuvenate the Moscow Art Theatre began to be fulfilled with his striking adaptation of Gorki's *The Last Ones*. Ignaty Dvoritski's *The Country Lad*, staged by Anatoli Efros at the Malaya Bronnaya, was one of several plays dealing realistically with contemporary social and economic problems.

The Warsaw Theatre Festival confirmed the claim that there was no "provincial theatre" in Poland, witness Andrzej Wajda's original treatment of Dostoevski's *The Devils* and Jerzy Jarocki's of Stanislaw Witkiewicz's *The Shoemakers* with the Stary Theatre from Cracow, or Helmut Kajsar's autobiographical *Paternoster* from Wroclaw. Warsaw highlights included condensed versions of Johann Schiller's *Don Carlos*, staged by Macjej Prus at the Ateneum, and Anton Chekhov's *Three Sisters*, staged as an absurdist comedy by Adam Hanuszkiewicz at the National.

Alexis Smith (left) portrays the leading character, Phyllis, in Harold Prince's 1971 musical production, "Follies."

MARTHA SWOPE

Cliff Gorman performs the title role in Broadway's resurrection of comedian Lenny Bruce. The 1971 production, entitled "Lenny," was directed by Tom O'Horgan.

The replacement of Otomar Krejca by Ladislav Bohac as head of the Gate Theatre of Prague could not still international protests when the former was fired and prevented from leaving the country on a Western European tour. Jan Kacer, after *The Lower Depths* at the Cinoherni Klub, mounted a notable *Mother Courage* at the National in Josef Svoboda's symbolic decor, with Dana Medricka. In Romania several leading directors were forced to renounce earlier productions and artistic policies. The two main events in Budapest were the world premiere of Istvan Orkeny's comic dialogue *Cat's Games* at the Pesti Theatre and the opening of the experimental "25th Theatre" in the capital.

Scandinavia. At the Royal Dramatic Theatre in Stockholm pride of place was taken by Ingmar Bergman's eye-catching production, with Gunilla Palmstjerna-Weiss's stunning decor, of Lars Forssell's *Show*, a tragicomedy inspired by the story of Lenny Bruce and starring Allan Edwall. Alf Sjöberg's major offering was Witkiewicz's *The Mother*, while Birger Norman's first play, based on his documentary novel about the Ådalen massacre of 1931 (filmed by Bo Widerberg), was done on the small stage, and Michael Meschke's unorthodox presentation of *Danton's Death* broke all precedent by being performed within the debating room of the Old Parliament House. In the new Parliament House was inaugurated the Klara Theatre, the City Theatre's fourth stage and permanent children's playhouse; the main events at the parent theatre were a drama about John F. Kennedy and Johan Bergenstråhle's production of *The Good Woman of Setzuan*, with Lena Granhagen. Leningrad's Georgi Tovstonogov put on *Three Sisters* at the National in Helsinki, scene of Jack Wittikka's strikingly staged *Endgame*. At the neighbouring Swedish National, Erik Lindström scored incisively in Strindberg's *The Father*. (O. Tr.)

U.S. and Canada. Most observers agreed that the American theatre—the commercial theatre, at least—was in a state of slow, steady decline. Complete and accurate figures were difficult to obtain, but the long-range trend was toward fewer and fewer Broadway and off-Broadway productions, and smaller total audiences. In 1971, some measures were being taken to try to arrest this decline. The standard curtain time for Broadway shows was moved from 8:30 to 7:30

P.M. in an attempt to suit the convenience of theatregoers. A new "limited gross agreement" was introduced, whereby, under certain conditions, Broadway producers willing to keep their ticket prices low could obtain concessions from the theatrical unions, thus reducing expenses and, it was hoped, enabling small-scale productions to survive. "Middle theatres," not large enough for Broadway and not small enough for off-Broadway, became increasingly prominent, widening the range of possible economic arrangements. The Theatre Development Fund, a foundation-supported philanthropy that purchases tickets for resale at low prices to students and others, made its presence felt, and more productions seemed to be offering student discounts than ever before. It remained to be seen how successful these endeavours would be in making the commercial theatre economically viable.

Artistically, 1971 was not a distinguished year for the U.S. theatre. The surprise sensation of the Broadway season was a revival of *No, No, Nanette*, billed as "The New 1925 Musical," starring Ruby Keeler (*see* BIOGRAPHY); it set off a much publicized "nostalgia boom." Late in the year came another sensation: *Jesus Christ Superstar*, a big rock musical version of the gospel story, based on a best-selling record album. In spite of unfavourable reviews, it was a tremendous hit. Other musicals aroused less excitement, including (late in 1970) *Two by Two*, a vehicle for Danny Kaye with a score by Richard Rodgers, based on *The Flowering Peach*, Clifford Odets' play about Noah; and (in April 1971) *Follies*, an innovative experiment in wryly ironic nostalgia, produced and directed by Harold Prince.

Nor was it a good year for straight plays on Broadway. At the end of 1970 Neil Simon, Broadway's most successful comedy writer, offered an uncharacteristically sombre work, entitled *The Gingerbread Lady*, about an alcoholic female nightclub singer; it was not enthusiastically received. *And Miss Reardon Drinks a Little*, Paul Zindel's play about three unhappy sisters, disappointed many who had admired his previously produced play, *The Effect of Gamma Rays on Man-in-the-Moon Marigolds*. *The Philanthropist* by Christopher Hampton, an intelligent English comedy about an overly complaisant English don, was highly praised but sparsely attended. *All Over* by Edward Albee, about a group of friends and relations who are waiting for a famous man to die, generally was found somewhat bloodless, in spite of the fine acting of Colleen Dewhurst and Jessica Tandy as the dying man's mistress and wife, respectively. *Lenny* by Julian Barry, an evocation of the late comedian Lenny Bruce, was admired mostly for Tom O'Horgan's phantasmagoric staging and Cliff Gorman's galvanic performance in the title role. The fall season of 1971 began with *Solitaire/Double Solitaire* by Robert Anderson, a pair of scrupulous but rather subdued one-act plays about marriage. In November Neil Simon returned to comedy with *The Prisoner of Second Avenue*, while *Old Times*, Harold Pinter's enigmatic London success, came to Broadway.

There were two notable classic revivals on Broadway in 1971: Molière's *The School for Wives*, starring Brian Bedford, and the Royal Shakespeare Company's acrobatic and brilliant production of Shakespeare's *A Midsummer Night's Dream*, directed by Peter Brook.

The New York Drama Critics Circle Award for the best play of 1970–71 went to an off-Broadway production, *The House of Blue Leaves* by John Guare;

it was a grim farce, combining high jinks and deep agony, about an amateur songwriter who dreams of Hollywood. Another notable off-Broadway play, *The Trial of the Catonsville Nine* by the Jesuit priest Daniel Berrigan, was an account of the trial of nine antidraft civil-disobedience activists at which Father Berrigan was one of the defendants. A popular off-Broadway musical was *Godspell*, a rock version of the St. Matthew's Gospel with music and lyrics by Stephen Schwartz. There were successful off-Broadway revivals of Beckett's *Waiting for Godot* (directed by Alan Schneider), O'Neill's *Long Day's Journey into Night* (directed by Arvin Brown, with Robert Ryan, Geraldine Fitzgerald, and Stacy Keach), and *One Flew Over the Cuckoo's Nest* by Dale Wasserman. Claire Bloom scored a personal triumph in a repertory of two plays by Henrik Ibsen, *A Doll's House* and *Hedda Gabler*.

On the avant-garde front, the Performance Group, under the direction of Richard Schechner, presented a new environmental/participational work entitled *Commune*, concerned with America, the career of Charles Manson, and other matters. Even more participational was an import from Los Angeles called *The James Joyce Memorial Liquid Theater*, directed by Steven Kent, and presented in New York at the Guggenheim Museum. Billed as "an experiment in making people feel good," it involved games, sensitivity exercises, dancing, and various forms of body contact.

As has been usual in recent years, permanent, nonprofit theatre organizations contributed a great deal to the New York theatre scene. Black theatre in New York, for instance, was largely the product of permanent off-Broadway organizations. Two plays by Ed Bullins were produced: *In New England Winter* at the Henry Street Settlement's New Federal Theatre and *The Fabulous Miss Marie* at the New Lafayette Theatre. The Henry Street Theatre also offered *Black Girl*, a naturalistic first play by J. E. Franklin. The Negro Ensemble Company presented, among other plays, *The Dream on Monkey Mountain*, a dense fantasy on black-white themes by the Trinidadian poet-playwright Derek Walcott. It previously had been done by the Center Theatre Group of Los Angeles.

The Public Theatre of the New York Shakespeare Festival, which comprised several auditoriums of different shapes and sizes under one roof, had a tremendously productive season in 1970–71. It introduced two notable plays by new young U.S. playwrights, *Subject to Fits*, "a response to Dostoevski's *The Idiot*," by Robert Montgomery, and *The Basic Training of Pavlo Hummel*, a play about an American soldier in Vietnam, by David Rabe. Other Public Theatre presentations included a one-man show, *Jack MacGowran in the Works of Beckett*, and a one-woman show, *Here Are Ladies*, in which Siobhan McKenna performed work by Irish writers, including a superb rendition of Molly Bloom's monologue from James Joyce's *Ulysses*. The Public Theatre began its 1971–72 season with *Sticks and Bones*, another play by Rabe. Meanwhile, in its open-air summer home in Central Park, the Shakespeare Festival offered a musical version of Shakespeare's *Two Gentlemen of Verona* adapted by John Guare and Mel Shapiro, with music by Galt MacDermot, the composer of *Hair*. The production was so popular that it was transferred to Broadway.

The 1970–71 season of the Chelsea Theatre Center in Brooklyn featured two new plays by British playwrights. *Saved* by Edward Bond was a grim piece of naturalism; in its most famous scene, a baby was shown being stoned to death onstage. *AC/DC* by Heathcote Williams was a baffling expression of the Electronic Age. The 1971–72 season began with the American premiere of *The Screens* by Jean Genet. The American Place Theatre opened its 1971–72 season in new, custom-built quarters in Manhattan; the first completed result of the New York City Planning Commission's policy of encouraging the building of theatres in new office buildings in the theatre district.

The Repertory Theatre of Lincoln Center aroused little enthusiasm with its main stage productions; the general consensus was that the work done in the Repertory Theatre's second auditorium, the Forum, was far more interesting. The Forum productions included a revival of Harold Pinter's *The Birthday Party*, the American premiere of *Play Strindberg* by Friedrich Dürrenmatt (a parody of Strindberg's *Dance of Death*), and *Scenes from American Life*, a sardonic comedy by A. R. Gurney, Jr., about the decline and fall of Buffalo, N.Y. In the autumn of 1971, a plan was made public for the remodeling of the Vivian Beaumont Theatre, the headquarters of the Repertory Theatre of Lincoln Center. Under this proposal, the Forum would have been demolished and replaced by three film theatres, to be administered by Henri Langlois of the Paris Cinémathèque; a new Forum would have been built in a currently unused scenery storage area elsewhere in the building. The plan evoked furious opposition from many prominent members of the theatrical community who were incensed at the idea of destroying the Forum, and who claimed that the use of the storage area to build a new auditorium would prevent the Repertory Theatre from ever operating in true rotating repertory. The proposal was withdrawn; the result of the controversy was an outpouring of support for the Repertory Theatre.

Outside of New York, the Charles Playhouse in Boston closed its doors late in 1970 after 13 years of existence, and the professional repertory company of Princeton University's McCarter Theatre suspended operations for at least a year in April 1971. But most of the other resident professional theatres appeared to be surviving the economic recession. For its 1970–

Janet Ward (left) enacts the role of a domineering, fiendish nurse in Dale Wasserman's "One Flew over the Cuckoo's Nest," a successful off-Broadway revival depicting the terrifying life in a mental institution.

ZODIAC PHOTOGRAPHERS

71 season the American Conservatory Theatre of San Francisco retrenched somewhat, performing in only one theatre instead of in two simultaneously, but its season was generally a successful one, highlighted by Ellis Rabb's modern-dress staging of *The Merchant of Venice*. The Arena Stage of Washington, D.C., resisted the tendency toward retrenchment by opening a second auditorium with the U.S. premiere of *The Ruling Class*, a savage comedy by the British playwright Peter Barnes. The Arena also offered the U.S. premiere of *Moonchildren* by Michael Weller, a witty, perceptive, and powerful comedy-drama about a group of bright U.S. college students and the mysterious emptiness of their lives, written by a U.S. playwright who lived in England. With two theatres, a high standard of acting and production, and a program almost equally balanced between new plays and revivals, the Arena more and more appeared to be the leader among American resident professional theatres. Also in Washington, the John F. Kennedy Center for the Performing Arts opened in 1971, but this monumental complex of three auditoriums, serving music and dance as well as drama, was to function mainly as a rental facility.

Meanwhile, the Tyrone Guthrie Theatre in Minneapolis, under its new artistic director, Michael Langham, reversed a steep decline in attendance. The Seattle Repertory Theatre had the biggest success in its history, a production of Shakespeare's *Richard II* starring Richard Chamberlain. The Long Wharf Theatre of New Haven, Conn., one of the most enterprising of the resident companies, offered the world premiere of *Solitaire/Double Solitaire* by Robert Anderson; this production subsequently appeared at the Edinburgh Festival, and then was transferred to Broadway. The American Shakespeare Festival in Stratford, Conn., mounted a successful revival of Eugene O'Neill's *Mourning Becomes Electra*, with Jane Alexander and Sada Thompson.

In Canada, the Stratford (Ont.) Festival offered successful productions of Webster's *The Duchess of Malfi*, with Pat Galloway in the title role, and Ben Jonson's *Volpone*, with William Hutt and Douglas Rain as Volpone and Mosca. The St. Lawrence Centre in Toronto had a success with Brecht's *Puntila*, while the Shaw Festival at Niagara-on-the-Lake, Ont., revived Shaw's rarely performed early play, *The Philanderer*. The National Arts Centre in Ottawa adopted a policy of strengthening local professional theatre companies, from Halifax to Vancouver, by booking them into the centre and sponsoring other touring engagements for them.

In the French-speaking Canadian theatre, centred in Montreal, the young French-Canadian playwright Michel Tremblay had two successes: a revival of *Les Belles-Soeurs* (*The Sisters-in-Law*) at the Rideau Vert, and a new play, *A Toi Pour Toujours, Ta Marie-Lou* (*Yours Forever, Your Marie-Lou*) at the Théâtre de Quat' Sous. Another Montreal company, the Théâtre du Nouveau Monde, toured Europe with two productions: a French-Canadian play, *La Guerre, Yes Sir* by Roch Carrier, about the impact of World War II on a Quebec town, and Molière's *Tartuffe*.

(J. No.)

See also Dance; Literature; Music.
ENCYCLOPÆDIA BRITANNICA FILMS. *The Cherry Orchard I—Chekhov: Innovator of Modern Drama* (1967); *The Cherry Orchard II—Comedy or Tragedy?* (1967); *A Doll's House I—The Destruction of Illusion* (1967); *A Doll's House II—Ibsen's Themes* (1967); *Shaw vs. Shakespeare Part I: The Character of Caesar, Part II: The Tragedy of Julius Caesar, Part III: Caesar and Cleopatra* (1970).

Theology:
see Religion

Tibet:
see China

Timber

The world's production of lumber, pulpwood, and other forest products continued its steady rise in both volume and value in 1969, the latest year for which figures were available. Total removals of roundwood from forests were estimated at 2,184,739,000 cu.m., compared with 2,149,775,000 cu.m. in 1968 and 1,908,-872,000 cu.m. in 1960 (1 cu.m. = 35.31 cu.ft.). Of the 1969 total, 1,219,428,000 cu.m. was removed for industrial uses and the remainder for fuelwood, charcoal, and other domestic and nonindustrial purposes. Removals of coniferous (softwood) roundwood and broad-leaved (hardwood) roundwood were about equal in volume, although for industrial uses, coniferous roundwood accounted for about 70% of the total. Total value of the world's production in 1969 was $48.4 billion, compared with $45.5 billion in 1968 and $33.9 billion in 1960.

Of the total, the value of processed wood (sawn wood, railway sleepers, and boxboards) was $16.3 billion; pulp products (paper and paperboard), $20.7 billion; panel products (veneers, plywood, particle board, and fibreboard), $6 billion; and all other wood products, $5.4 billion. Estimates were in terms of U.S. dollars based on constant 1960 prices.

Sawn wood or lumber accounted for about one-third of total removals. According to the UN Food and Agriculture Organization (FAO), the 1969 total of sawn-wood production was 399,835,000 cu.m. (1 cu.m. = 424 bd-ft.).

The U.S.S.R. ranked first in production of sawn wood and sleepers, with a reported total of 116,290,-000 cu.m. This was approximately equal to the combined total of the U.S. and Canada. Western Europe produced 58,087,300 cu.m.; Eastern Europe, 20,396,-400 cu.m.; Latin America, 15,530,700 cu.m.; the Far East, 13,639,500 cu.m.; the Near East, 3,524,400 cu.m.; and Africa, 2,828,900 cu.m.

Preliminary estimates of U.S. lumber production for 1970 placed output at 36,692,000,000 bd-ft., including 28,639,000,000 bd-ft. of softwood lumber and 8,053,000,000 bd-ft. of hardwood lumber, which was below the output of 37,949,000,000 bd-ft. in 1969. U.S. exports of lumber in 1970 totaled 1,290,500,000 bd-ft., including 1,152,400,000 bd-ft. of softwood and 116.2 million bd-ft. of hardwood lumber, 6.2 million ft. of box shooks, and 6.3 million of sawed railroad ties. Imports were 6,116,400,000 bd-ft., including 5,769,200,000 of softwood, 338.7 million of hardwood, and 8.5 million of sawed railroad ties. The wholesale price index of lumber at the end of June 1971 was 99.7, down 3.6 points from June 1970 (1967 = 100).

Total Canadian production of lumber in 1969 was reported at 11,474,000,000 bd-ft., which was slightly above the 1968 figure. About 95% of the total was softwood lumber; about two-thirds was exported.

World production of pulp continued its rapid increase, reaching 98 million metric tons in 1969, compared with 91.4 million metric tons in 1968. Expansion of output in the U.S. accounted for more than a third of the rise. Chemical (including semichemical) pulp represented more than two-thirds of the total output.

A total world output of 122.6 million metric tons of paper and paperboard in 1969 was reported by the FAO. The U.S. led with 46.1 million metric tons, followed by Japan, with 11.3 million metric tons, and

Canada, with 11.1 million metric tons. The 1969 total included 20,540,200 metric tons of newsprint, up about 1.5 million tons from 1968. More than half was produced in North America, with Canada accounting for 7,943,900 metric tons and the U.S. for 2,877,-600 metric tons.

World production of plywood, according to the FAO, showed only a slight increase, from 30,032,300 cu.m. in 1968 to 30,703,800 cu.m. in 1969, indicating a leveling off after a sixfold increase since 1950. Particle board production continued its rapid growth, with world output increasing from 13,690,000 cu.m. in 1968 to 16,089,000 cu.m. in 1969. West Germany led the world in 1969 production, with 3,401,300 cu.m., followed by the U.S., with 3,017,500 cu.m., and the U.S.S.R., with 1,722,800 cu.m. From 1960 to 1968 world exports of particle board rose from 265,-000 cu.m. to 1.5 million cu.m. and total export value increased from $20 million to nearly $90 million. More than 70% of this trade occurred inside Western Europe, with Belgium the largest and fastest growing exporter.

In the U.S., criticism of the practice of clear-cutting in timber stands by the Sierra Club and other groups led to the introduction of legislation to declare a moratorium on clear-cutting on federal lands. Representatives of the U.S. Forest Service and the forest industries explained, however, that certain types of trees, including the Douglas fir, can reproduce themselves only on open ground with full sunlight.

(C. E. R.)

See also Environment; Industrial Review.

ENCYCLOPÆDIA BRITANNICA FILMS. *Trees and Their Importance* (1966); *Science Conserves Forests* (1967); *The Coniferous Forest Biome* (1969); *Problems of Conservation—Forest and Range* (1969); *Problems of Conservation—Our Natural Resources* (1970).

Tobacco

In 1970 larger crops in the less developed countries brought world production of tobacco to 4.6 million tons, a 2% increase over the previous year but more than 3% below the record crop of 1967. The Food and Agriculture Organization (FAO) of the United Nations confirmed Latin America as the leader in increased output for the year, and less developed countries as a whole showed a 5% gain. Tobacco production in the developed countries remained static at the 1969 level despite a 7% increase in Europe. Although output of all types of tobacco increased, the flue-cured and Burley crops did not do as well as other types. A 30% increase in the Greek crop of Oriental tobacco was offset by a further decline in Turkey.

World exports of manufactured tobacco remained relatively stable in 1970, with increases in the less developed countries balancing cutbacks in the U.S. Imports for consumption were up by about 3%. Most traditional leaf-importing countries contributed to this increase, although the takings of the two largest buyers, the U.K. and West Germany, went down considerably.

Cigarette consumption rose in the majority of developed countries, despite increased publicity about smoking and health. Leaf consumption for cigarettes continued to decline in the U.S. and the U.K., however, largely because of the application of leaf-saving techniques and the growing use of filter tips. Cigarette advertising was increasingly restricted in various countries, but the FAO thought it was too early to assess the effect of this and other antismoking moves. World demand for cigars and cigarillos was static, and the waning popularity of smoking (pipe) tobacco continued.

With the 1970 and 1971 crops, the countries of the EEC began to establish a common market for leaf tobacco and to adjust state monopolies where they existed. Fiscal harmonization was to be achieved through regulation of taxes and excise duties on manufactured tobacco. These basically protectionist market regulations would in time affect both production and consumption among EEC members. The EEC was the second largest tobacco market in the world, with an annual leaf consumption in recent years of 800 million–900 million lb., approximately two-thirds of which was imported. Within the EEC, West Germany was the leading consumer of both leaf and tobacco products, followed by France, Italy, and the Benelux countries.

The basic regulations of the market involved a price and subsidy system and intervention and trade arrangements that, in part, reflected various other EEC market organizations. Currently, intra-Community trade in domestically produced leaf accounted for less than 5% of total imports. This proportion might increase if the common agricultural policy in tobacco produced the expected effects. There were signs of discord early in 1971, when Greece complained that it was not consulted in drafting the policy. This was said to be a violation of the agreement under which Greece participated in the Common Market. Greece stated that, despite guarantees in the agreement, it was losing its former competitive advantage in EEC countries.

The 1970 U.S. crop, at 1,873,700,000 lb., was slightly higher than expected and some 67 million lb. more than in the previous year. This reflected an increase in production of flue-cured leaf, resulting chiefly from higher yields. Exports of U.S. unmanufactured tobacco fell during 1970. The total of 577 million lb. was some 10% below 1969. Production of flue-cured tobacco in Canada in 1970 amounted to 214 million lb., exceeding the target for the second successive year.

The area under tobacco in India in the 1970–71 season was estimated to be 5.6% higher than that reported in the first estimate for the previous season. The government was encouraging the cultivation of Virginia flue-cured tobaccos in light soils to meet export demand. At 746 million lb., the 1969–70 Indian crop was 6% below 1968–69, mainly because of a reduction in the area planted in Andhra Pradesh, exacerbated by severe storm damage. Exports of unmanufactured tobacco in 1970 were reported to be down 14%. Provisional data suggested that production of unmanufactured tobacco in Japan declined further to 330.8 million lb. in 1970.

The outlook for Rhodesian exports improved following the November settlement of the dispute with the U.K. The 1971 target was set at 132 million lb. Rhodesia was in the forefront in anticipating the spread of import regulations controlling chemical residues in tobacco. In 1971 Rhodesian growers pressed for local regulations proscribing the use of prohibited substances. Health regulations concerning permitted pesticides were to come into force in West Germany in 1973, and similar moves were expected elsewhere.

Brazil's production was estimated to be up from 409 million lb. in 1969 to 438 million lb. in 1970. Flue-cured leaf constituted about two-fifths of the total and dark air-cured leaf, more than half.   (V. F. RA.)

Tin:
see Mining

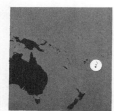

Togo

A West African republic, Togo is bordered by Ghana, Upper Volta, and Dahomey. Area: 21,900 sq.mi. (56,-600 sq.km.). Pop. (1970): 1,955,916. Cap. and largest city: Lomé (pop., 1970, 148,443). Language: French (official). Religion: animist; Muslim and Christian minorities. President in 1971, Gen. Étienne Eyadema.

In September 1971 President Eyadema announced that the Army was ready to relinquish its control and that he had vetoed a recommendation by the country's only political party that he should be the sole presidential candidate in the 1972 election; it later transpired that a referendum was to be held on Jan. 9, 1972, and that he expected to be confirmed in office.

On September 28 a radio broadcast announced that, in reaction to the president's speech, the people had indicated that the Army's mission was far from complete. The president had therefore reconsidered his decision and "in the superior interests of the people" agreed to remain in office.

In March, 27 people had been given prison terms for complicity in a plot to overthrow the president in August 1970.

In September a special meeting of government officials decided to recognize China. A communiqué published after the meeting described the decision as a demonstration of political realism and an important factor in world peace. On October 25, Togo voted in favour of the Albanian resolution in the UN to admit China and to expel Taiwan.

President Eyadema visited France in December and discussed the possibility of increased aid.   (Ph. D.)

TOGO
Education. (1968–69) Primary, pupils 189,391, teachers 3,350; secondary, pupils 14,963, teachers 523; vocational, pupils 1,615, teachers 143; teacher training, students 84, teachers (1966–67) 7; higher, students 321, teaching staff 24.
    Finance. Monetary unit: CFA franc with a parity of CFA Fr. 50 to the French franc (CFA Fr. 277.71 = U.S. $1; CFA Fr. 666.60 = £1 sterling) and a free rate (Sept. 27, 1971) of CFA Fr. 276.50 to U.S. $1 (CFA Fr. 685.75 = £1). Budget (1971 est.) balanced at CFA Fr. 10 billion.
    Foreign Trade. (1970) Imports CFA Fr. 17,928,-000,000; exports CFA Fr. 15,176,000,000. Import sources: France 30%; U.K. 13%; West Germany 8%; Netherlands 7%; Japan 6%; U.S. 6%. Export destinations: France 28%; Netherlands 25%; West Germany 20%; Belgium-Luxembourg 7%; U.S.S.R. 6%. Main exports: cocoa 41%; phosphates 25%; coffee 18%.

Tonga

An independent monarchy and member of the Commonwealth of Nations, Tonga is an island group in the Pacific Ocean east of Fiji. Area: 269 sq.mi. (697 sq.km.). Pop. (1970 est.): 86,005. Cap.: Nukualofa (pop., 1966, 15,685). Language: English and Tongan. Religion: Christian. King, Taufa'ahau Tupou IV; prime minister in 1971, Prince Tu'ipelehake.

With annual population growth of about 3%, Tonga had to provide in 1971 for its increasing proportion of landless unemployed. Because there were limits to the number of bananas and coconuts that could be produced for export, Tonga looked to commercial fishing and the international shipping trade. A record

Tornadoes:
see Disasters;
Meteorology

budget provided for the establishment of small-scale labour-intensive industries. An exploratory oil well was about to be sunk. An official birth control program had only limited success. New Zealand initiated a pilot program providing some temporary factory employment.

The sixth and largest meeting of the Pacific Islands Producers' Association in Nukualofa revealed the poor state of the New Zealand banana market and considered possibilities for a regional copra-crushing mill and shipping line. Participation in the Asian Coconut Community, the South Pacific Forum (a top-level August meeting of South Pacific states in Wellington, N.Z.), and the 11th South Pacific Conference demonstrated Tonga's growing awareness of the benefits of regional cooperation.

New Zealand offered NZ$10,000 a year for three years to equip and train a Tongan defense force. Prince Tu'ipelehake attended the January conference of Commonwealth heads of government in Singapore.
(My. B. B.)

TONGA
Education. (1968) Primary, pupils 16,424, teachers (1967) 692; secondary, pupils 9,421, teachers (1967) 358; teacher training, students 70, teachers 6.
    Finance and Trade. Monetary unit: pa'anga, at par with the Australian dollar (0.89 pa'anga = U.S. $1; 2.14 pa'angas = £1 sterling) and with a free rate (Sept. 27, 1971) of 0.86 pa'anga to U.S. $1. Budget (1969–70 est.): revenue 2,513,000 pa'angas; expenditure 2,725,000 pa'angas. Foreign trade (1969): imports 5,087,529 pa'angas; exports 3,398,684 pa'angas. Import sources: New Zealand 34%; Australia 24%; Fiji 22%; U.K. 10%. Export destinations: Norway 30%; New Zealand 30%; Netherlands 15%; Japan 5%.

Tourism

By mid-1971 some 20 countries had ratified their approval of the new World Tourism Organization (WTO), whose statutes had been adopted at an extraordinary General Assembly of the International Union of Official Travel Organizations (IUOTO) in Mexico City in September 1970. The new body would come into existence 120 days after 51 ratifications had been deposited with the Swiss federal government.

The 50th session of the United Nations Economic and Social Council, meeting in New York in 1971, defined the tasks of the WTO, and four recommendations were put forward as guidelines for its activities: (1) the WTO should have a decisive and central role in world tourism in cooperation with existing agencies of the United Nations; (2) the main function of the WTO should be to develop and promote tourism worldwide, paying particular attention to the interests of less developed countries; (3) the WTO should be duly designated as a participating and executing agency of the United Nations Development Program, in fulfillment of its functions relative to tourism development; and (4) the secretary-general would submit proposals aimed at the effective coordination of activities in tourism undertaken by the WTO.

In preparation for its world role in tourism, IUOTO had agreed in 1969 to open regional offices or secretariats to provide on-the-spot assistance to governments in the development of tourism and to implement decisions taken by the General Assembly and the relative regional commissions of IUOTO. The first of these, for the Americas, opened in December 1970 in Lima, Peru. During 1971 agreement was also reached to open a regional secretariat in Lagos, Nigeria, to serve Africa. Ultimately five regional offices were planned to complement the General Secretariat, which continued to be based in Geneva.

Over the decade 1960–70, world tourist arrivals more than doubled, while world tourist receipts increased two and a half times. This was equal to an average rate of increase of 9% in arrivals and 9.5% in receipts. World tourist arrivals stood at 168 million in 1970, compared with 70 million in 1960, and world tourist receipts were worth $17.4 billion in 1970, compared with $6.8 billion in 1960.

With the need to plan the multimillion dollar world tourist industry being more urgently felt, IUOTO published the results of its first long-term forecasts study on world tourism. This showed that arrivals should reach the 200 million mark in or before 1975, while by 1980 between 250 million and 280 million international arrivals could be expected. The study foresaw an intensification of North Atlantic passenger travel, and, under the influence of the growing migration of Europeans to the coasts of the Mediterranean, a strong increase in the touristic development of the northern coast of Africa. Longer distance travel, cautioned the report, must depend on air-fare policies in the 1970s. Tourists would not automatically travel farther afield unless and until an appropriate price-promotional package was hammered out between tour operators and the airline industry. The U.S. administration took a further step in its recognition of the role of tourism as an important earner of invisible exports. With receipts from foreign tourism reaching an all-time high of $2,318,000,000 in 1970, the appointment of an assistant secretary of commerce responsible for tourism was announced.

Middle East tourism had been severely disturbed in 1970, the effect of continuing political uncertainty and the hijacking tactics adopted by the Palestinian guerrilla movement, in which $52 million worth of aircraft were destroyed and 500 passengers held hostage. Meanwhile, a comprehensive tourism development and marketing study prepared by IUOTO and the World Bank for the governments of seven Arab countries was studied. Implementation, it seemed, had to await the restoration of normal political relations among all countries of the region.

Tourism in 1971. International tourism continued to grow rapidly during 1971 in European countries, as well as in the U.S., although arrivals in Japan were at a level below that of the record-breaking year of Expo 70. Arrivals in Greece in the first half of 1971 were 27% higher than in 1970, while in Spain arrivals were 19% higher. Travel abroad from countries such as West Germany, France, and the United Kingdom grew strongly. A sign that all was not quite back to normal in the U.S. was the decrease in citizen departures in the first half of 1971: these were 7% below 1970 levels. It was clear that some potential travelers were waiting for more positive signs of an upturn in the business cycle before renewing foreign travel plans. In contrast, the sharp rise in unemployment in the United Kingdom through the first three quarters of 1971 appeared not to dampen British enthusiasm for visiting foreign parts.

A report published by the British Tourist Authority in 1971 joined the debate concerning U.K. entry into the European Economic Community, this time from a tourism viewpoint. There were, it concluded, no clear advantages from U.K. entry into the EEC so far as tourism was concerned, largely because free movement of tourists already existed. There was, moreover,

London Bridge at Lake Havasu, Arizona, opens amid elaborate ceremonies on Oct. 10, 1971. U.S. oil tycoon Robert P. McCulloch bought the bridge and reconstructed it in the Arizona desert.

a danger that the tourism balance of payments could move back into deficit if spending by U.K. residents in Europe grew faster than European spending in Britain. In all, it was important that British resorts improve their standards to attract both domestic travelers and European visitors in greater numbers.

In the field of travel facilitation 1971 was a year of little general change. However, in March, the French government announced the raising of the foreign currency allowance from $270 to $360 per person per trip abroad.

By 1971, public opinion had become increasingly sensitive to the effects of environmental pollution on tourism, and in particular the fouling of inland and coastal waters. During the year, IUOTO sent out a call to all sectors to take joint action to protect the well-being of travelers as well as local and regional amenities. Tourism officials were also asked to offer resistance to the impression that tourism was somehow responsible for destroying those features that made up its basic factors of attraction. The menace of pollution, IUOTO recalled, occurred in spite of tourism and not because of it. A tourism industry that was prepared to compromise with pollution would be taking rapid steps toward the destruction of its own livelihood, which was unthinkable. Indeed, it was in full consciousness of the pollution hazard that tourism officials had been among the first to raise a cry of alarm, and there was no doubt that, without the constant antipollution pressure exerted by them, the situation would be grave indeed.

Table I. International Tourist Arrivals and Receipts

Region	Arrivals 1969	Arrivals 1970*	Percent change
Europe	116,260,000	126,700,000	+ 9
Americas	29,390,000	31,150,000	+ 6
Asia/Pacific	4,155,000	5,290,000	+27
Middle East	2,360,000	2,480,000	+ 5
Africa	2,065,000	2,360,000	+14
Total arrivals	154,000,000	168,000,000	+ 9
Total receipts	$15,500,000,000	$17,400,000,000	+12

*Estimated.
Source: International Union of Official Travel Organizations, Geneva.

Cinderella Castle at Disney World, Fla., which opened in October 1971.

Parity adjustments between one international currency and another were identified by economists as alternatively stimulating or dampening travel demand between the countries concerned, as might be expected. A number of exchange rate adjustments in 1971 were not without consequences on international travel and tourism. The devaluation of the Yugoslav dinar was the first, a measure aimed directly at improving the competitive position of the tourist sector after a year (1970) in which total arrivals and nights in accommodation had been virtually unchanged from the previous year.

Subsequent adjustments were made by Austria and Switzerland in May 1971, this time in the direction of revaluation. In this context, both countries, while not making these adjustments for reasons related to tourism, were deeply conscious of possible effects that might be exerted on the tourist sector. In Austria, tourism officials reflected that 75% of their country's travel income came from West Germany, whose floating mark had prompted Austria's own 5.05% revaluation. In Switzerland there was some concern about the effect of the 7% revaluation of the Swiss franc in reinforcing an image, already current in some circles, of Switzerland as a relatively expensive country for travelers, although confidence was also expressed in the adaptive dynamism and quality of the Swiss travel trade.

If these adjustments were seen as, in general, not unfavourable to the expansion of international tourism in Europe, rather different considerations applied to the floating of the U.S. dollar on world money markets, announced by Pres. Richard M. Nixon in August, and to the December realignment of the world's major currencies, which included devaluation of the dollar and the revaluation of various other currencies, most notably the West German mark and Japanese yen. Industry executives were quick to observe that this parity adjustment would help redress price differences on the two sides of the Atlantic—to the benefit of European tourists whose currencies rose in value—without making U.S. tourists overseas feel the pinch to any untoward extent. However, as was underlined pointedly by the British Tourist Authority in advertisements in the national press at the time of President Nixon's August measures, it was of the utmost importance that U.S. visitors to Europe should not feel exploited in the situation in which they now found themselves.

The U.K. tourist industry was not without its own growing pains in 1971. The newly established regional and national tourist boards, set up to promote tourism and help dynamize the tourist sector, soon came into conflict with the "old guard" of British travel. The English Tourist Board's proposals for a compulsory system of hotel classification were greeted as "bureaucratic nonsense" by a former president of the British Travel Association.

One consolation was to be had by the traditional backbone of the U.K. domestic tourist market, the boarding house landladies, and that came from a report prepared at the University of Sussex. This expressed confidence in the future of the small firm in the hotel business, but added that steps needed to be taken to consolidate the position including, among other actions, those aimed at joint promotion. A slightly different viewpoint came from the party of Blackpool landladies invited by a tour operator to visit a Spanish resort, and who conceded that they would be hard put to it to beat the competition.

Air fares continued to preoccupy the world's scheduled airlines in 1971, and there were growing signs that many were unwilling to maintain the high-fare, low-capacity utilization situation that had prevailed in 1970. British European Airways was among the airlines serving Europe that pointed to the need to take swift action about the increasing number of empty seats on scheduled services. In 1970, the airlines serving intra-European routes offered 43.4 million seats, of which 20.3 million, or over half, were empty. The International Air Transport Association, world airlines, and their respective governments struggled to resolve what the BEA chairman described as "the dominating conflict of the world-wide civil aviation today."

Promotion of Tourism. While countries in the Western Hemisphere prepared for the 1972 "Tourism Year of the Americas," and the renewed promotional effort that this would involve, signs pointed to 1971 being a banner year for travel marketing and the promotion of tourism. Global spending on public relations and market research in 1971 was expected to exceed $100 million, and the total budgets of national tourist organizations worldwide were expected to exceed $200 million—a double first.

The travel marketing climate of the 1970s could truly be described as dynamic. Up to 1969, North America had spent most on tourist promotion, but first place had been taken in 1970 by Europe. Advertising took up from one-third to two-thirds of promotional budgets, with periodicals as the favourite medium. Among individual countries of the world, 19 spent more than $2 million on their promotional activities on international tourism in 1970.

(P. Sh.; O. Me.)

See also Transportation.

Toys and Games

The quiet of an uneventful year for world toy manufacturers was ended in September by the collapse and liquidation of the second largest toy company in the world, Lines Bros. This British giant, with such household trade names as Tri-Ang, Dinky, Pedigree, and Meccano, crashed under the weight of a £17.5 million loss revealed when British cigarette manufacturer Gallagher withdrew from a £5 million bid made a few weeks earlier in return for a 51% stake in the ailing company.

Despite the shock, Lines Bros. demise was not wholly unexpected. World sales of £58 million were not consistently matched by significant profits, and the company's operating procedure of continuous extensive manufacture of hundreds of toys, which often duplicated themselves, was unrealistic in a period of economic stagnation.

Although the continued growth of Mattel (whose annual sales exceeded $288 million), the world's leading toy manufacturer, had no bearing on the Lines Bros. collapse, it continued to affect the fortunes of two of the few remaining British companies. Lesney Products' and Mattoy Playcraft's formerly large die-cast toy sales in the United States were curtailed, with a consequent slump in profits, by Mattel's continued success with Hot Wheels.

Total sales of U.S. toy manufacturers were about $2,340,000,000; British manufacturers sold £81 million ($194.4 million) of toys, of which 31% were exported.

The year was not particularly distinguished for innovation, although "clacker balls," "Klik-kers," or "Knock-ers," two glass or plastic balls joined by a cord, which children could swing together with a satisfying clash, swept from the U.S. across the globe, but not without clashes of another kind with consumer and governmental groups who considered the plaything dangerous. The success of this low-cost, relatively unpromoted novelty was an example of the phenomenal way in which children will snap up the simplest ideas if they see a potential for play value, and how in weeks such a toy can be in every playground in the world. In April the U.S. Food and Drug Administration warned consumers that some clacker balls were dangerous because they could be shattered easily.

Board games, many for adults, continued to proliferate, but their very numbers prevented any one from having large sales. In their search for ideas there was no aspect of life that game manufacturers would not consider as a theme, and it was no surprise when up popped "Women's Lib," a game for seven players who assume the roles of male and female moderates, traditionalists, liberationists, and radicals. Action board games where, instead of merely playing with tokens, scoring is achieved by successfully popping, hitting, rolling, or banging an object, increased their sales, undoubtedly because in most of them all the players compete at the same time rather than having to wait their turn.

One of the most colourful ideas of the year came from a U.S. toy company, which obtained permission from food manufacturers to reproduce large plastic versions of their cans and bottles, fit them with wheels and other attachments, and sell them as "sit-'n-ride" toys, the idea being that children would associate the toys with everyday items they see around the home.

Advanced playground structures installed at Margaret Brent School in Baltimore, Md., in 1971 provide unique recreation facilities.

Thus, children were seen riding on Heinz baked beans cans and HP sauce bottles.

Dolls, the staple of so many toy companies, continued to reflect modern fashions, but biggest sellers in the U.S. were "Baby Dolls," whose soft skin was achieved by the use of foam-stuffed vinyl. The doll of 1971 had hair that grew, a voice, her own fashion wardrobe, and a boyfriend.

Bicycles made a strong comeback in the U.S., both the conventional type and those with high-rise handlebars such as the Chopper. Demand was so high for a market that spread beyond children's cycles to a large adult clientele that U.S. manufacturers were unable to supply it, and European exporters shared in the boom. Also enjoying great renewed popularity was the plastic "Frisbee."

The briefer childhood of modern children was responsible for what was probably the most significant change in the nature of toys. Toys lost their importance at an increasingly early age, and the only process that retarded decreasing sales was the correspondingly earlier age at which children became interested in toys more varied than rattles and beads. It thus became embarrassingly difficult for manufacturers to market a toy with any certainty that it would appeal to the age group for which it was intended. Children who a few years before would have still been considered babies were showing a precocious eagerness to learn, and preschool "educational" toys were appearing in far greater numbers and value. Following progressive educational techniques, games were available, often accompanied by music, that enabled children to learn to spell, read, add, and subtract, and appreciate form and colour enjoyably.

It was evident during 1971 that some toy makers appreciated that if they were to continue to grow they would have to engender interest in adult toys or diversify into the leisure market. Although the long-predicted leisure boom was not yet in sight, worldwide sales of craft toys, embroidery, tapestry,

Two English schoolgirls ride the "Pogo-Pony," one of many new toys shown at the 18th British International Toy Fair in Brighton, Sussex, during January 1971.

pottery, enameling kits, and the like enjoyed strong increases.

Strangely, the latest marvels of the technological age had no major influence in toys, as was once predicted. The popularity of "space" toys waned considerably.

For a company contemplating toy manufacturing the message from 1971 seemed to be "keep it basic, keep it inexpensive, and aim it at the very young or at adults."　　　　　　　　　　　　(D. R. J.)

Track and Field Sports

New world records were set in a number of Olympic events in the pre-Olympic season of 1971, and notice was served that nearly every record set in the 1968 Games at Mexico City would be in danger of falling at Munich in 1972—this despite the altitude of the Bavarian capital being 5,700 ft. lower than that of Mexico City.

It was in the long-stagnant quest for "higher" (the Olympian motto is *Citius-Altius-Fortius*, or Further-Higher-Stronger) that both the men's and women's high-jump world records were raised from figures set, respectively, in 1963 and 1961. At Berkeley, Calif., in a U.S. v. U.S.S.R. meeting, Pat Matzdorf cleared 7 ft. 6¼ in. to erase the 7-ft. 5¾-in. mark established by Valery Brumel of the Soviet Union in 1963. The even more venerable woman's record of 6 ft. 3¼ in. by the Romanian Iolanda Balas-Söter, set in Sofia, Bulg., in 1961, fell to Austria's Ilona Gusenbauer in Vienna when she cleared 6 ft. 3½ in. on September 4.

The margins of improvement were in each case a predictable single centimetre (⅜ in.), but what was truly surprising was that both the new marks were achieved not by the new back-bending layout but by the traditional stomach-down straddle style. It seemed, nevertheless, that the two great deeds must represent a swan song for the old style.

In the track events the most significant, if one of the briefest, was the electric high-hurdling run of Rod Milburn (U.S.) over 120 yd. in the Amateur Athletic Union (AAU) semifinals at Eugene, Ore., on June 25.

Milburn, who was led to the first hurdle by Lance Babb, ran away to win by three clear yards in 13 sec.—one-fifth of a second better than the oldest record on the books set when West Germany's Martin Lauer ran a 13.2-sec. race at Zürich, Switz., in 1959. Because the electric timer caught Milburn in 12.94 sec., the claim to the International Amateur Athletic Federation (IAAF) ought to be submitted for 12.9 sec. since, if the hundredths are at 4 or below, the time is by IAAF rule rounded down to the tenth below.

International Tournaments. During 1971 there were four major multinational meetings—the tenth European Championships at Helsinki, Fin. (August 10–15), and the sixth Pan-American Games at Cali, Colombia (July 31–August 13); an inaugural match between Africa and the U.S.; and the tenth edition of the U.S. v. U.S.S.R. dual meet at Berkeley, Calif., on July 2–3, in which a third team of "World All-Stars" also competed.

The greatest of these tournaments was that at Helsinki, which produced records that indicated the 80-year-long dominance of the sport by the U.S. might conceivably end during the 1970s. Indeed, it became predictable that the individual men's gold medals that the U.S. would be favoured to win in the 1972 Olympics would shrink to 5 (400 m., high hurdles, high jump, long jump, and discus throw) out of 22.

The Ukrainian Valery Borzov became the world's leading sprinter by virtue of his wins at Berkeley and at Helsinki. His margin of victory over the rest of Europe was greater than in any major meeting since Bob Hayes in the 1964 Olympics, and his time of 10.27 sec. was against a 2.9 mph wind. His arm and leg coordination gave the appearance of being sufficiently induced rather than involuntary and natural to give cause for wondering whether or not he was the first product of intensive Soviet research into the dynamics of sprinting.

The greatest sensation was the continued emergence of an East German team that had been forged as an instrument of governmental policy. This team, pro-

Table I. World 1971 Outdoor Records—Men

Event	Competitor, country, date	Performance
200 m. (turn)	Donald Quarrie, Jamaica, August 3	19.8 sec.*
440 yd.	John Smith, U.S., June 26	44.5 sec.
2 mi.	Emile Puttemans, Belgium, August 21	8 min. 17.8 sec.
20 mi.	Jack Foster, New Zealand, August 15	1 hr. 39 min. 14.4 sec.
120-yd. hurdles	Rod Milburn, U.S., June 25	13.0 sec.
High jump	Pat Matzdorf, U.S., July 3	7 ft. 6¼ in.
Triple jump	Pedro Perez, Cuba, August 5	57 ft. 1 in.
Discus	Jay Silvester, U.S., May 16	230 ft. 11 in.†
Hammer throw	Uwe Beyer, West Germany, July 9	245 ft. 8¾ in.
	Walter Schmidt, West Germany, September 4	250 ft. 8 in.

*Ties record.
†Pending.

Table II. World 1971 Outdoor Records—Women

Event	Competitor, country, date	Performance
100 m.	Renate Meissner-Stecher, East Germany, July 31	11.0 sec.*
800 mi.	Hildegard Falck, West Germany, July 11	1 min. 58.3 sec.
1,500 m.	Karin Burneleit, East Germany, August 15	4 min. 9.6 sec.
1 mi.	Ellen Tittle, West Germany, August 20	4 min. 35.4 sec.
440-yd. relay	Tennessee State, July 9	44.7 sec.
1,600-m. relay	East Germany, August 15	3 min. 29.3 sec.
1-mi. relay	Atoms Track Club, July 11	3 min. 33.8 sec.
3,200-m. relay	West Germany, July 31	8 min. 16.8 sec.
High jump	Ilona Gusenbauer, Austria, September 4	6 ft. 3½ in.
Discus	Faina Melnik, U.S.S.R., August 12	210 ft. 8½ in.
	Faina Melnik, U.S.S.R., September 3	212 ft. 10 in.

*Ties record.

Table III. NCAA Outdoor Championships
Seattle, Wash., June 17–19, 1971

Event	Competitor, affiliation	Performance
100 yd.	Harrington Jackson, University of Texas, El Paso	9.5 sec.
220 yd.	Larry Black, North Carolina Central	20.5 sec.
440 yd.	John Smith, UCLA	45.3 sec.
880 yd.	Mark Winzenried, Wisconsin	1 min. 48.8 sec.
1 mi.	Marty Liquori, Villanova	3 min. 57.6 sec.
3 mi.	Steve Prefontaine, Oregon	13 min. 20.2 sec.
6 mi.	Garry Bjorklund, Minnesota	27 min. 43.2 sec.
3,000-m. steeplechase	Sid Sink, Bowling Green State	8 min. 30.9 sec.
120-yd. hurdles	Rod Milburn, Southern University	13.6 sec.
440-yd. hurdles	Ralph Mann, Brigham Young	49.6 sec.
440-yd. relay	Southern California	39.5 sec.
1-mi. relay	UCLA	3 min. 4.4 sec.
High jump	Reynaldo Brown, California Polytechnic, San Luis Obispo	7 ft. 3 in.
Pole vault	Dave Roberts, Rice	17 ft. 6½ in.
Long jump	Bouncy Moore, Oregon	25 ft. 9¾ in.
Triple jump	Mohinder Gill, California Polytechnic, San Luis Obispo	54 ft. 8½ in.
Shot put	Karl Salb, Kansas	66 ft. 11½ in.
Discus	Mike Louisiana, Brigham Young	194 ft. 10 in.
Hammer throw	Jacques Accambray, Kent State	227 ft. 10 in.
Javelin	Cary Feldman, Washington	259 ft.
Decathlon	Ray Hupp, Ohio State	7,456 pt.
Team	UCLA	52 pt.

Table IV. NCAA Indoor Championships
Detroit, Mich., March 12–13, 1971

Event	Competitor, affiliation	Performance
60 yd.	Jim Green, Kentucky	6 sec.
440 yd.	Tom Ulan, Rutgers	48.8 sec.
600 yd.	Tommie Turner, Murray State	1 min. 9.6 sec.
880 yd.	Mark Winzenried, Wisconsin	1 min. 50.9 sec.
1,000 yd.	Bob Wheeler, Duke	2 min. 7.4 sec.
1 mi.	Marty Liquori, Villanova	4 min. 4.7 sec.
2 mi.	Marty Liquori, Villanova	8 min. 37.2 sec.
60-yd. hurdles	Marcus Walker, Colorado	7 sec.
1-mi. relay	Adelphi	3 min. 15.5 sec.
2-mi. relay	University of Texas, El Paso	7 min. 37.4 sec.
High jump	Pat Matzdorf, Wisconsin	7 ft. 2 in.
Pole vault	Scott Wallick, Miami (Ohio)	16 ft. 8 in.
Long jump	Henry Hines, Southern California	26 ft. 1¾ in.
Triple jump	Mohinder Gill, California Polytechnic, San Luis Obispo	52 ft. 9¾ in.
Shot put	Karl Salb, Kansas	65 ft. 9 in.
35-lb. weight throw	Al Schoterman, Kent State	68 ft. 10¼ in.
Team	Villanova	22 pt.

Table V. AAU Outdoor Championships
Eugene, Ore., June 25–26, 1971

Event	Competitor, affiliation	Performance
100 yd.	Delano Meriwether, Baltimore Olympic Club	9 sec.
220 yd.	Don Quarrie, Southern California Striders	20.2 sec.
440 yd.	John Smith, S. C. Striders	44.5 sec.
880 yd.	Juris Luzins, U.S. Marine Corps	1 min. 47.1 sec.
1 mi.	Marty Liquori, New York Athletic Club	3 min. 56.5 sec.
3 mi.	Steve Prefontaine, Oregon Track Club	12 min. 58.6 sec.
6 mi.	Frank Shorter, Florida Track Club	27 min. 27.2 sec.
3,000-m. steeplechase	Sid Sink, Bowling Green State	8 min. 26.4 sec.
120-yd. hurdles	Rod Milburn, Southern University	13.0 sec.
440-yd. hurdles	Ralph Mann, S. C. Striders	49.3 sec.
2-mi. walk	Larry Young, Mid-America Track Club	13 min. 49.5 sec.
High jump	Reynaldo Brown, California Track Club	7 ft. 3 in.
Pole vault	Jan Johnson, U. of Chicago Track Club	17 ft.
Long jump	Arnie Robinson, San Diego Track Club	26 ft. 10¾ in.
Triple jump	John Craft, U. of Chicago Track Club	54 ft. 7 in.
Shot put	Karl Salb, Mid-America Track Club	67 ft. 2¾ in.
Discus	Tim Vollmer, U.S. Army	208 ft. 4 in.
Hammer throw	George Frenn, Pacific Coast Club	230 ft. 1 in.
Javelin	Bill Skinner, New York Athletic Club	267 ft. 2 in.

Table VI. AAU Indoor Championships
New York City, Feb. 26, 1971

Event	Competitor, affiliation	Performance
60 yd.	Jean-Louis Ravelomanantsoa, Westmont (Calif.)	6.1 sec.
600 yd.	Andrzej Badenski, Poland	1 min. 10.7 sec.
1,000 yd.	Tom Von Ruden, Pacific Coast Club	2 min. 7.3 sec.
1 mi.	Henryk Szordykowski, Poland	4 min. 6 sec.
3 mi.	Frank Shorter, Florida Track Club	13 min. 10.6 sec.
60-yd. hurdles	Willie Davenport, unaffiliated	7 sec.
1-mi. relay	Villanova	3 min. 16.9 sec.
2-mi. relay	U. of Chicago Track Club	7 min. 28.6 sec.
Sprint medley relay	Pacific Coast Club	1 min. 53.9 sec.
1-mi. walk	Ron Laird, New York Athletic Club	6 min. 24.9 sec.
High jump	Reynaldo Brown, California Track Club	7 ft. 2 in.
Pole vault	Dick Railsback, S. C. Striders	17 ft. 6¾ in.
Long jump	Norm Tate, New York Pioneer Club	26 ft. 4¼ in.
Triple jump	Dave Smith, California Track Club	53 ft. 4¾ in.
Shot put	Al Feuerbach, Pacific Coast Club	66 ft.
35-lb. weight throw	George Frenn, Pacific Coast Club	71 ft. 3½ in.

duced from a population of only 16 million, outshone that of the U.S.S.R. (population 242 million).

In women's events Renate Meissner-Stecher (E.Ger.) won the 100 m. and 200 m. by margins of more than a yard and more than five yards, respectively. Karin Burneleit (E.Ger.) broke the world 1,500-m. record with 4 min. 9.6 sec., and the Soviet discus thrower Faina Melnik unleashed another world record with 210 ft. 8½ in. on August 12, which she later bettered with a throw of 212 ft. 10 in.

One of the most amazing but least publicized events of the year was a run over a full 26-mi. 385-yd. marathon course by a 28-year-old Australian woman, Adrienne Beames, at Werribee, Victoria, on August 31. No woman had ever broken 3 hr. (compared with the male record of 2 hr. 8 min. 33.6 sec.), but she recorded 2 hr. 46 min. 30 sec.—equivalent in degree to slicing 20 sec. off a mile record.   (N. D. McW.)

U.S. and Pan-American Competition. Youth was served in the Americas in 1971 as none of the five world record setters was over 21 years old. Three countries contributed to the record production, unusual in the Western Hemisphere where the U.S. traditionally dominates the sport. Two of the marks broken were among the most durable records.

The U.S. national (AAU) championships, run on a fast synthetic track at the University of Oregon in late June, accounted for the first pair of global bests. Rod Milburn, 21, started it off by whipping over ten high hurdles to cover 120 yd. in 13 sec. (*see above*). The next day, June 26, 20-year-old John Smith of UCLA raced to glory in the 440-yd. dash with a time of 44.5 sec. He was hard-pressed by teammate Wayne Collett, whose 44.7 clocking tied the previous record established by Curtis Mills in 1969. A week later at Berkeley, Calif., the oldest untied individual world record was broken when Pat Matzdorf, 21 and the oldest of the new record setters, pulled off the biggest surprise of the U.S. year when he high-jumped 7 ft. 6¼ in. (*see above*).

Two more record setters won their honours at the quadrennial Pan-American Games in Cali, Colombia. While the U.S. continued to overwhelm the opposition in these hemispheric championships, the records were not set by U.S. athletes. (*See* SPORTING RECORD.) Don Quarrie, a 20-year-old Jamaican, sped around a turn to dash 200 m. in 19.8 sec. He thus equaled the mark established by Tommie Smith of the U.S. in capturing the 1968 Olympic Games title. A surprise at least equal to Matzdorf's came when unsung Pedro Perez of Cuba produced the longest triple jump in

Rod Milburn easily passes Willie Davenport to set a world record in the 120-yd. high hurdles in the national AAU track and field championships in Eugene, Ore.

RICH CLARKSON, SPORTS ILLUSTRATED © TIME INC.

Ilona Gusenbauer of Austria clears the bar at a height of 6 ft. 3½ in., setting a new women's world high-jump record, on Sept. 4, 1971, in Vienna.

Pat Matzdorf of the University of Wisconsin sets a world high-jump record at 7 ft. 6¼ in. during the U.S.-U.S.S.R. meet at Berkeley, Calif., on July 3, 1971.

world history. Only 19, Perez hopped, stepped, and jumped 57 ft. 1 in., adding ¼ in. to the 1968 effort of Viktor Saneev of the Soviet Union.

One other U.S. athlete, at the opposite edge of the age range, twice topped accepted world standards but under conditions that probably would rule out acceptance of his throws. Jay Silvester, 33, bettered his own international discus best of 224 ft. 5 in. with an effort of 230 ft. 11 in. at Lancaster, Calif., in a May 16 meet that lacked official sanction. The same problem clouded his 229-ft. 9½-in. throw at Ystad, Swed., on June 10.

Four U.S. national records also were bettered. Three-time Olympic veteran George Young, 34, ran 5,000 m. in 13 min. 32.2 sec. only to lose the record later in the season to Steve Prefontaine when the 20-year-old from the University of Oregon ran 13 min. 30.4. sec. The other performance at a standard distance was an 8-min. 26.4-sec. effort in the 3,000-m. steeplechase by Sid Sink of Bowling Green State. At less frequently contested distances, Marty Liquori of Villanova University lowered the national 2,000-m.

record to 5 min. 2.2 sec., and Juris Luzins, U.S. Marine Corps, sped 1,000 m. in 2 min. 17.7 sec.

Africa's burgeoning track talent went on display in Durham, N.C., in the first tournament ever between the U.S. and Africa. In a well-received affair that seemed to foster goodwill both on and off the track, African athletes continued to impress in the longer runs.

In domestic team competition, UCLA won the coveted National Collegiate Athletic Association (NCAA) crown at Seattle, Wash. Kentucky State captured the NCAA's college division meet; Eastern Michigan won the National Association of Intercollegiate Athletics title, and the Pacific Coast Club was high scorer in the United States Track and Field Federation (USTFF) championships. The AAU, in a rule change, did not keep team scores.

Indoors, records were more numerous as Villanova won the NCAA title and the University of Wisconsin won at the USTFF meet. World bests (there are no official world records indoors) were set in two field events. Little-known Al Feuerbach of the Pacific Coast Club surprised Olympic champion and outdoor record holder Randy Matson by putting the shot 68 ft. 11 in. and Kjell Isaksson of Sweden leaped 17 ft. 9 in. in the pole vault. On the track, the outstanding performance was by Kerry O'Brien of Australia who recorded 8 min. 19.2 sec. for two miles, 8 sec. under the previous indoor low and 1.4 sec. short of the outdoor record. Kerry Pearce, also of Australia, and Frank Shorter of the U.S. ran 8 min. 20.6 sec. and 8 min. 26.2 sec. in the same race, Shorter's mark becoming a U.S. indoor record. In the same San Diego Invitational meet, Jim Ryun, making a comeback at 23, equaled the best previous indoor mile time of 3 min. 56.4 sec. Later in the year he became an allergy victim and had to withdraw from further competition.

Other indoor bests included: 5.9 sec. for 60 yd. by Mel Pender, Jean-Louis Ravelomanantsoa, Jerry Sims, Willie McGee, and Herb Washington, tying the existing record; 6.8 sec. at 70 yd. by Pender, also equaling the previous mark; 9.3 for 100 yd. by Quarrie and Carl Lawson; 54.4 sec. twice for 500 yd. by Lee Evans; 2 min. 20.4 sec. for 1,000 m. by Tom Von Ruden; 3 min. 9.4 sec. for the mile relay by the Pacific Coast Club; and 9 min. 39.8 sec. by the University of Pittsburgh for the distance medley relay.

Two world records were bettered by U.S. women in relay events only seldom contested outside the U.S. A national team of Esther Stroy, Mavis Laing, Gwen Norman, and Cheryl Toussaint ran 3 min. 38.8 sec. in the mile relay, and Diane Hughes, Debra Wedgeworth, Mattline Render, and Iris Davis sprinted 44.7 sec. in the 440-yd. relay for Tennessee State University. In the Pan American Games medal and unofficial point honours were equally divided among Canada, Cuba, and the U.S. Texas Women's University won the intercollegiate championships. Indoors, Doris Brown set a new record in the 880-yd. run, at 2 min. 7.3 sec., and the Texas Track Club won the USTFF title. (BE. N.)

Trade, International

The value of world trade in 1971 increased by 11–12% over the 1970 level, but because of the general increase in world prices this represented an increase in the volume of trade of only about 7%, somewhat less than in recent years. The growth in world trade, as measured by the total value of individual countries' exports, depends to a large extent on the rate of growth of world industrial production and demand for imports. World industrial production grew quite rapidly during 1969, but there was virtually no growth in 1970 after the first quarter. Expansion was renewed early in 1971. The effect of these fluctuations on the level of trade can be seen from the following figures, which show the increase in the value of trade over the previous half year: 1969 (first half) +5%; 1969 (second half) +8.5%; 1970 (first half) +7.5%; 1970 (second half) +5%; 1971 (first half) +6.5%. The value of world trade had increased by 14.5% in 1969 and at the same rate in 1970. Prices, however, rose more rapidly in 1970; the increase in the volume of trade in 1970 was 8.5%, compared with 10.5% in 1969.

The growth in world trade in 1970 and in 1971 was not shared evenly between the industrial countries and the primary producers. During the boom in trade in 1969 primary producers' exports increased by 12%, almost as fast as those of industrial countries. In 1970, however, the growth rate of their exports fell to 9.5%, compared with 15.5% for industrial countries. Primary producers' exports benefited from the revival of world industrial production and import demand in 1971, and their exports were then growing almost as rapidly as those of industrial countries.

One factor that sustained the growth in the volume of world trade in 1970 was the strength of the U.S. demand for imports, which was somewhat unexpected in view of the recession in U.S. economic activity. Western European demand continued to expand at much the same rate in 1970 as in 1969, although within Europe the import growth rate of the European Free Trade Association (EFTA) countries accelerated from 10 to 16% while that of the EEC countries dropped from 22 to 17%. Another major factor in the growth in world trade in 1970 was the rapid growth of exports by industrial countries to primary producers. Industrial countries' exports to Latin America increased by 17% and to the Sino-Soviet area by 20%. In the first half of 1971 the largest stimulus to world trade came from the increased demand in the EEC and in Japan.

A notable feature of world trade in 1970 and 1971 was the sharp increase in the prices of industrial countries' exports. The average price of exported manufactured goods, which had increased by only 10% in the ten years up to 1968, rose by 3% in 1969 and in the first half of 1971 had reached a level 11% higher than that of two years earlier.

Primary Producing Countries. As the 1969 boom in world trade slackened during 1970, the expansion of exports from primary producing countries slowed down. The value of their exports increased by 10% in 1970, compared with a 13% increase in 1969. Indeed, in the latter half of 1970 there was little growth in their exports, the value in the fourth quarter being only 1.5% higher than in the third quarter. This slackening was due partly to the failure of demand in industrial countries to grow rapidly and partly to the decline in the primary product prices from their peak level in mid-1970. Primary producers' exports expanded more rapidly in 1971 as industrial demand increased, but the growth in export receipts was held back by a further decline in prices.

The average export prices of primary producers were about 5% lower in mid-1971 than in mid-1970. The 12% rise in export prices between 1968 and 1970 was largely the result of much higher prices for metals,

coffee, tea, and cocoa. From about the middle of 1970 many of these trends were reversed. The average price of minerals and metals was 20% lower in mid-1971 than a year earlier, and the prices of coffee and cocoa had fallen by 20 and 15%, respectively.

Table I shows that the balance of trade of the primary producing countries declined by almost $2.8 billion between 1969 and 1970. Most of this decline ($2.3 billion) occurred in the more developed countries. New Zealand exports were hit by lower wool prices and showed very little growth in value, while the nation's imports increased by 24% and its trade balance declined by $230 million. Political pressures prevented any growth in South African exports, but that nation's imports increased by 20%, causing a deterioration in the balance of trade of $660 million. Among the remaining countries in this group (the less industrialized countries in Western Europe), Greece and Yugoslavia both recorded large increases in imports and larger trade deficits in 1970.

Among the less developed primary producers there were no marked changes in the trading balances of the main areas, which all shared fairly evenly in the export expansion. The only exceptions were the Middle Eastern countries, where low prices kept the growth in their exports down to 7% in 1970. In Latin America, within an unchanged overall balance of trade, the main changes occurred in Mexico, Brazil, and Peru. The Mexican trading balance had improved in 1969 but a 19% increase in imports and lower exports brought a $400 million increase in the deficit in 1970. The Brazilian balance worsened by $170 million, while in Peru the surplus increased by a similar amount. The surplus of African countries was largely accounted for by Libya, which recorded a surplus of $1,810,000,-000 in 1970, even larger than the record $1,490,000,-000 in 1969. Strongly growing demand for imports outstripped the 11% growth in exports from Asian countries, and their overall trading deficit consequently increased by $500 million. Much of this deterioration was accounted for by Singapore, whose deficit increased by $400 million as a result of no export growth and a 20% rise in imports.

Industrial Countries. The trade of industrial countries increased by 15.5% in both 1969 and 1970. The rate of expansion, however, slowed down during 1970

Japanese automobiles at pier in Nagoya, Jap., await shipment to the United States. The Toyota Motor Sales company reported an 896% increase in its U.S. sales over a five-year span.

THE "NEW YORK TIMES"

Table I. Primary Producing Countries' Foreign Trade

In $000,000

Area	1969 Exports	1969 Imports*	1969 Balance of trade	1970 Exports	1970 Imports*	1970 Balance of trade
More developed countries†	15,970	22,530	−6,560	18,000	26,860	−8,860
Less developed countries						
Latin America	12,350	12,270	80	13,600	13,500	100
West Indies	2,050	3,050	−1,000	2,200	3,400	−1,200
Middle East	10,100	7,310	2,790	10,800	7,850	2,950
Asia	12,820	17,260	−4,440	14,200	19,160	−4,960
Africa	10,540	8,730	1,810	11,800	10,000	1,800
Total	63,830	71,150	−7,320	70,600	80,770	−10,170

*Imports in most cases include freight and insurance charges.
†Australia, New Zealand, South Africa, and the less industrialized countries of Western Europe.
Source: International Monetary Fund, *International Financial Statistics*.

Table II. World Exports of Manufactured Goods

Year	Total value in $000,000,000*	United States	United Kingdom	West Germany	France	Italy	Japan	Others†
1955	34.0	24.5	19.8	15.5	9.3	3.4	5.1	22.4
1960	52.4	21.6	16.5	19.3	9.6	5.1	6.9	21.0
1965	82.8	20.3	13.9	19.1	8.8	6.7	9.4	21.8
1967	99.2	20.4	12.3	19.5	8.5	7.0	9.8	22.5
1968	114.0	20.1	11.6	19.4	8.2	7.3	10.6	22.8
1969	134.0	19.3	11.3	19.5	8.2	7.3	11.2	23.2
1970‡	154.4	18.5	10.8	19.8	8.7	7.2	11.7	23.3
1971‡	167.8	18.0	10.8	20.0	8.9	7.1	12.8	22.4

Percent of total value

*Excluding arms.
†Belgium, Luxembourg, Canada, Netherlands, Sweden, and Switzerland.
‡First half of year (seasonally adjusted); value at annual rate.
Source: National Institute of Economic and Social Research, London.

Table III. Trade of Industrial Countries

In $000,000,000

Country	1970 Exports	1970 Imports	1970 Balance of trade	1971* Exports	1971* Imports	1971* Balance of trade
United States	43.22	39.96	3.26	45.26	45.31	−0.05
Canada	16.14	13.31	2.83	17.29	14.72	2.57
EEC	88.68	88.62	0.06	96.25	95.63	0.62
Belgium	11.59	11.35	0.24	11.45	11.92	−0.47
France	17.94	19.12	−1.18	19.75	20.17	−0.42
Germany, West	34.18	29.82	4.36	37.48	33.40	4.08
Italy	13.18	14.94	−1.76	14.29	15.63	−1.34
Netherlands	11.77	13.39	−1.62	13.29	14.51	−1.22
EFTA	43.13	51.02	−7.85	46.12	53.71	−7.59
United Kingdom	19.36	21.72	−2.36	20.81	23.31	−2.50
Japan	19.32	18.88	0.44	23.14	19.45	3.69
Total	210.49	211.79	−1.26	228.06	228.82	−0.76

*First half of year (seasonally adjusted) at annual rate.
Source: Organization for Economic Cooperation and Development, *Main Economic Indicators*.

but increased again during 1971 following the revival in world economic activity. The pattern of expansion of individual industrial countries' exports within these three years was similar to the cyclical pattern of total world trade described above. In the first half of 1971 industrial countries' exports were expanding at an annual rate of 11–12%.

There were some changes in 1970 in the direction of expansion of industrial countries' exports. The unusually rapid growth in exports to primary producing countries has already been noted. In previous years the main stimulus to the expansion of industrial countries' exports was the rapid growth of trade among EEC countries. Although this growth slowed down from 26% in 1969 to 18% in 1970, EEC exports to North America and particularly to Japan expanded in 1970 much more rapidly than in 1969. The pattern of EFTA exports was exactly the reverse of EEC exports, with trade among EFTA members increasing by 19% (compared with 17% in 1969 and only 6% in 1968) while EFTA exports to North America, Japan, and primary producing countries grew less rapidly than in the previous year.

A considerable part of the increase in the value of industrial countries' exports in 1970 was accounted for by a 6% increase in prices, the volume of trade increasing by only 8%. In 1969 prices had risen by less than 3% and the same increase in value had represented a 12% increase in volume. Between 1968 and 1970 the prices of exported manufactured goods rose by an average of 10% and by approximately that amount in the U.S., U.K., Japan, and Italy. However, due to changes in the exchange rate the West German price increase was larger, at 15%, and the French was less, at under 3%. The relative movements in national export prices did not seem to have a marked effect on the shares of the world market obtained by the various exporters (*see* Table II).

During 1970 and 1971 the imports of industrial countries grew slightly less rapidly than their exports (*see* Table III). As a result their overall balance of trade deficit was reduced in 1970 and further reduced in the first half of 1971. There were, however, marked differences in the performances of the trade balances among individual industrial countries in the two years. The improvement in the overall picture in 1970 was due to large increases in the U.S. and Canadian trade surpluses, which more than offset the increased EFTA deficit. In 1971 the U.S. surplus was drastically reduced but there was an equally large increase in the Japanese surplus, which, together with improvements in the EEC and EFTA balances, reduced the overall trade deficit of the group to one of the lowest levels in several years.

With the recession in domestic economic activity in 1970 the U.S. balance of trade improved, although the improvement was not as great as had been expected on the basis of improvements during the 1958 and 1964 recessions. There were some disturbing features about the situation in the U.S. Imports actually increased faster in 1970 (11%) than in 1969 (9%); imports of consumer goods (other than food) rose by 14% and of capital goods by 15% despite a lower level of domestic investment expenditure. Much of the improvement in export growth compared with 1969 was due to a more rapid expansion of agricultural exports. The improvement in the trade surplus came abruptly to a halt in the final quarter of 1970. The U.S. recorded a small deficit on visible trade in the first half of 1971, compared with a surplus of almost $2 billion during the corresponding period of 1970. With the recovery in U.S. industrial production in the early months of 1971 the prospect was for a further deterioration in the trade balance during the year as the demand for imports expanded. This deterioration was in large measure responsible for the U.S. economic measures of August, including the imposition of a 10% import surcharge, and the realignment of major currency values in December. Even so, it appeared that the U.S. trade balance would be in deficit for the year as a whole.

Canada in 1970 recorded its largest trade surplus since World War II. Exports increased by 17% and imports by only 2%. These divergent movements partly reflected the strikes in 1969, which caused an increased demand for imports in that year and which delayed the export of some products until 1970. In 1971 exports were growing in line with imports and the surplus was maintained, although at a lower level.

The exports and imports of EEC countries remained in balance in 1969 and 1970; in the first half of 1971 a slightly faster growth of exports compared with imports brought a small surplus. The strength of the West German trading balance remained a dominant factor. Following the revaluation of the mark in 1969, the growth in imports slackened in 1970 to 18%, compared with 25% in 1969. This slowdown applied to most products but was particularly noticeable in semimanufactured goods. There was a small improvement in West Germany's trade surplus.

The French trading deficit had reached a peak annual rate in mid-1969 of almost $3 billion. After that, and following the devaluation of the franc, there was a steady reduction in this deficit to an annual rate of only $400 million in the first half of 1971. Exports in 1970 increased by 20% and imports by only 10%.

The deterioration in the Italian trading balance that began in 1969 continued in 1970, which recorded a deficit $100 million larger than in the previous year. Imports continued to rise by about 20%, while exports increased by no more than 12%. About two-thirds of the deterioration was accounted for by the very rapid growth in imports of semimanufactured goods.

The trading balance of EFTA countries had improved during 1968 and 1969, but there was a sharp increase in the overall deficit in 1970. This deterioration was halted in 1971, and the deficit was somewhat reduced. A large part of the 1970 increase in the deficit was due to the large increase in the Swiss deficit from $600 million in 1969 to more than $1.3 billion in 1970.

The sharp improvement that occurred in the U.K. trading balance during 1969 was not maintained in 1970, and the deficit was only slightly smaller than in 1969. This improvement was only achieved by the continued recession in domestic economic activity. The growth in exports owed much to a 9% increase in the volume of nonmanufactured goods, as the volume of exports of manufactured goods rose by only 1% in 1970. The rise in prices caused an 11% increase in the value of exports in 1970, with exports to EEC and other EFTA countries increasing by 15 and 18%, respectively. In 1971, after a poor first quarter, there was a marked reduction in the U.K. deficit, which was expected to be about $200 million less than in the previous year. (A. G. A.)

See also Commercial Policies; Commodities, Primary; Payments and Reserves, International.

Encyclopædia Britannica Films. *Rotterdam—Europort, Gateway to Europe* (1971).

Transportation

During 1971 there was much consolidation of different forms of transport, a recovery of commercial traffic from the 1970 recession, and advances in technology and its application. Speeds, both air and land, increased. There were further successful tests of the Anglo-French Concorde and Soviet Tupolev Tu-144 supersonic passenger aircraft, advances in railway traction, and successful full-scale testing of tracked Hovercraft. The trend to larger bulk carriers at sea, particularly tankers, continued.

The total movement of persons and goods increased. The railways began to benefit from large capital investment in recent years; although their proportion of total traffic showed no gain, they did do increased business. Despite the elimination of many unprofitable lines more than 1,275,000 km. of railways were in operation in 1971, of which about one-tenth were electrified. New lines were built mainly in less developed countries.

The use of duorail steel wheels on steel was increasing for urban rapid transit systems. In the 1950s there were ten underground railway systems, but by 1971, 38 cities had them and 40 more were considering them. Road passenger systems, faced with private automobile competition, received more assistance from public funds, and many schemes were aimed at inducing preference for public over personal transport. Commercial freight transport grew, especially transit by piggyback and roll-on/roll-off services.

During the year one of the oldest urban transportation systems, the bicycle, made a comeback. On a wet Sunday in May in Washington, D.C., Secretary of Transportation John Volpe, together with 150 others, rode seven miles to Rock Creek Park. They did so to help demonstrate the intended policy to make Washington a model city for bike riders, with reserved lanes along main city streets so as to encour-

Trade of Selected Industrial Countries

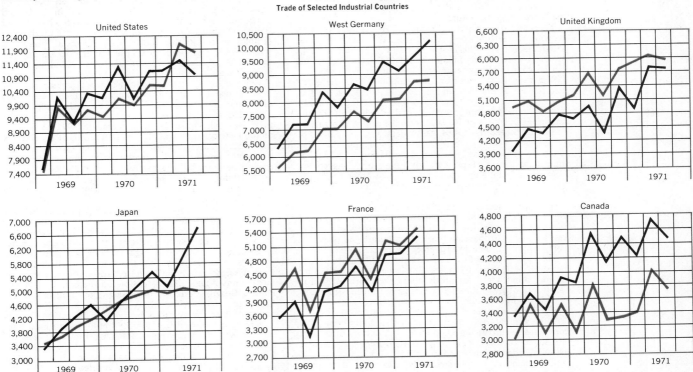

In millions of U.S. dollars   Exports ▬▬▬   Imports ▬▬▬   Source: International Monetary Fund, *International Financial Statistics.*

A laser beam, projected from the new Asahi Tokai building in Tokyo, was designed to aid aircraft. An illuminated signboard between the laser beams gives weather forecasts and air-pollution warnings.
KEYSTONE

age motorists to leave their cars on the edge of the city centre and cycle in to work.　　　(E. A. J. D.)

AVIATION

Profitless growth would be the keynote for the airline industry in 1971, said the director general of the International Air Transport Association (IATA) at the close of 1970. As the year progressed, events tended to prove him correct. The economic depression that hit U.S. airlines hardest in 1970 spread to other areas in 1971, and inflation continued to give all carriers cause for concern. It was not until the fall that a faint sign of recovery appeared in the U.S., with an improvement in the profitability of the major airlines.

It was a difficult year for air transport in other respects. There was an unusual number of international disputes. The U.S. became involved in controversy over traffic rights with Australia and Ireland, and in the process seemed to foreign observers to be moving toward a new protectionist attitude. The U.S.S.R., after several years of consideration, finally joined the International Civil Aviation Organization (ICAO) in November 1970. But ICAO's technical proceedings were marred by the intrusion of political bickering during the organization's summer congress, which provoked a walkout on two separate occasions by the U.S. delegation.

Within the ranks of IATA, representing most of the world's international scheduled airlines, a dispute over fares and tariff policy went unresolved. As a result, an "open-rate" situation or, as some would have it, a price war, seemed certain to develop in 1972, particularly on the North Atlantic routes.

The main preoccupation of all IATA members was the growing strength of competition from the charter airlines. Their resolve to fight it was noticeably greater than in previous years. Widespread abuse of charter regulations caused concern to governments and to the industry.

A significant development in equipment was the entry into service of the McDonnell Douglas DC-10, a trijet in the 300-seat category. The future of its rival, the Lockheed TriStar, was for some months in doubt because of the financial difficulties of Rolls-Royce, the engine contractor, and of Lockheed itself, but the project was saved by U.S. government action in September. Of less immediate interest to the airlines was the cancellation of the U.S. supersonic transport project, confirmed by Congress on May 20. Development continued on two other SSTs, the Anglo-French Concorde and the Soviet Union's Tupolev Tu-144, but airlines still were reluctant to place orders.

Hijackings decreased in 1971. Figures given by IATA officials for the first half year showed that of 34 attempted hijackings 22 were foiled and 12 were successful; in the first half of 1970 there had been 59 attempts, 38 of which were successful. The improvement was attributed to increased security checks by airport authorities and airlines, increased acceptance of international legislation providing for punishment and extradition, and an improved political situation. But sabotage attempts continued, especially against Middle Eastern carriers, while in one of several bomb hoaxes Qantas parted with $560,000 on May 26.

Amid a great deal of international activity aimed at improving security, the U.S. Federal Aviation Authority (FAA) complained in October that airlines were lax in enforcing precautions, and proposed a rule that would require them to have officially approved security programs. Because of the airlines' attitude, the FAA doubted

whether the government expenditure of $37 million on antihijacking measures was being used efficiently. The Air Transport Association of America, on the other hand, said that security measures had proved effective and that in just under a year seven potential hijackers had been prevented from boarding aircraft.

A current feature of the air transport industry was that, notwithstanding economic difficulties, growth of passenger traffic on scheduled services continued at about 12% per year (somewhat less in the U.S.). Figures for 1970 published by the ICAO showed that scheduled passenger traffic of the world's airlines (the principal exclusions being the U.S.S.R. and China) amounted to 387 billion passenger-kilometres. Scheduled cargo traffic amounted to 10,770,000,000 metric ton-kilometres, and total scheduled traffic to 48,090,000,000 ton-kilometres. With the inclusion of the U.S.S.R., these figures increased to 466 billion, 12,425,000,000, and 57,270,000,000, respectively.

Cargo growth was considerably less than that of passenger traffic, and was only 8% in 1970, compared with 21% in 1969. Load factors (the ratio between the passengers or load carried and the seats or capacity made available) were low but more or less stable for scheduled services in general, following declines in preceding years. The average weight load factor in 1970 was 47.4%, the third successive year in which it fell below 50%.

As the load factors showed, excessive capacity, accentuated by the introduction of the Boeing 747 in 1970, continued to cause problems in 1971. More than 140 Boeing 747s were delivered by midyear. Introduction of the DC-10 in August added another large aircraft to the world's fleets. A side effect of the situation was the availability, secondhand at low prices, of a large number of earlier-model jets, in particular Boeing 707-120s.

Together with excess capacity went rising costs. Sharp increases in fuel costs and (in the U.S. in particular) labour expenses were major items. There was an increasing tendency for governments to pass the cost of providing air navigation services on to airlines, and on Nov. 1, 1971, IATA members introduced a ticket surcharge designed to pass these costs on directly to the passenger.

Losses by U.S. carriers in 1970 were heavy; Pan American showed a net loss on its airline activities of $51.4 million, TWA of $72.2 million, and United of $62.4 million. (Merger discussions between Pan American and TWA—not the first in the two airlines' history—were broken off in September 1971.) Only Eastern among the big U.S. carriers showed a profit in 1970 ($6.2 million). Mergers pending in the U.S. industry included those between National Airlines and Northwest Airlines, American Airlines and Western Air Lines, and between Delta Airlines and Northeast Airlines. In August 1971 in the United Kingdom both British European Airways (BEA) and British Overseas Airways Corp. (BOAC) reported sharp declines in profits for the 1970–71 financial year, and doubts were expressed about their ability to break even in 1971–72. Qantas of Australia also reported a decline in profits during the year.

Charter airline traffic continued to grow strongly in 1971. It was estimated that about 1.5 million passengers, or a quarter of the total, crossed the Atlantic on nonscheduled services in 1970, and the charter share of the total was believed to have increased in 1971. A feature of the charter scene was the overt flouting of regulations concerning "affinity-group" charters. The regulations, designed to prevent diversion of traffic from scheduled to charter airlines, laid down that charter flights might be operated for the members of clubs or associations provided that those involved had been members for a certain period in advance, that the club was not constituted for the express purpose of travel, and that membership did not exceed a certain figure.

Evasion of the regulations by travel organizers, by, for example, backdating passengers' membership or inventing phony chartering organizations, gave authorities grounds for concern during the year. In British law at least it seemed that the travel organizers were not committing any offense. The situation led the U.S. Civil Aeronautics Board (CAB) to propose the opening of charter flights to groups without any "affinity" status—a move opposed strongly by the scheduled airlines. The British government removed the "affinity" requirement on a limited scale; following representations from the recently formed flag carrier, British Caledonian Airways, about loss of charter traffic to foreign airlines, an exemption from the affinity regulations was granted for flights between the U.K. and the Far East. A similar exemption

World Transportation

Country	Railways Traffic			Motor transport			Merchant shipping Ships of 100 tons and over		Air traffic		
	Route length in 000 km.	Passenger in 000,000 pass.-km.	Freight in 000,000 net ton-km.	Road length in 000 km.	Vehicles in use Passenger in 000	Commercial in 000	Number of vessels	Gross reg. tons in 000	Total km. flown in 000	Passenger in 000 pass.-km.	Freight in 000 net ton-km.
EUROPE											
Austria	5.9*	6,316*	9,781*	94.8	1,196.6	120.9	3	10	12,945	452,200	8,860
Belgium	4.3*	8,260	7,780	91.8	2,033.9	212.2	230	1,062	46,329	2,449,000	192,100
Bulgaria	4.2	6,223	13,859	36.1	9.3†	20.4†	139	686	7,460	294,620	5,330
Czechoslovakia	13.3	20,155	56,670	145.9	651.6	174.0	12	89	19,567	899,000	18,230
Denmark	2.4*	3,330	1,571	62.1†	1,076.9	247.1	1,210	3,314	30,265‡	1,696,000‡	69,250‡
Finland	5.8	2,154	6,270	72.4	712.0	107.9	388	1,397	17,228	772,800	23,672
France	36.5	41,080*	70,403*	785.2	12,470.0	1,810.0	1,420	6,458	199,031	11,716,539	518,624
Germany, East (excluding Berlin)	14.7	17,667	41,514	c.160.0	1,039.2	171.7	423	989	...	842,700	23,319
Germany, West (excluding Berlin)	33.8	38,960	71,996	416.0	14,376.5§	1,143.6§	2,868	7,881	123,225	8,254,000	529,802
Greece	2.6	1,531	688	35.1	226.5	106.7	1,850	10,952	26,347	2,126,300	35,602
Hungary	8.8	13,932	19,142	109.2	240.3	42.0†	20	31	7,345	290,223	6,150
Ireland	2.1	582	475	86.4†	354.0	47.0	86	175	23,726	1,776,500	59,693
Italy	16.0*	32,357	18,070	285.0	c.10,200.0	914.0	1,639	7,448	128,232	8,420,000	300,100
Netherlands	3.1	8,023	3,532	78.6	2,591.6	349.4	1,598	5,207	82,565	6,020,000	392,300
Norway	4.2*	1,570*	2,840*	72.3	747.2	147.1	2,808	19,347	37,554‡	1,954,100‡	73,211‡
Poland	23.2	36,892	99,326	307.8	479.4	263.0	516	1,580	15,147	550,000	8,830
Portugal	3.6	3,550	776	29.9	454.2	24.6	376	870	34,161	2,268,000	42,220
Romania	11.0	17,790	48,050	76.6	c.250.0†	43.9	65	341	9,453	353,500	7,060
Spain	16.8	13,294*	9,138*	138.7	1,998.8	654.1	2,234	3,441	90,913	5,874,000	111,506
Sweden	12.5	4,061*	16,085*	174.0	2,287.7	144.4	995	4,921	49,049‡	2,451,000‡	111,887‡
Switzerland	2.9*	7,997*	6,600*	59.2	1,388.0	132.5	32	196	67,915	4,421,000	187,613
U.S.S.R.	134.6	261,283	2,480,000	1,368.4†	c.1,100.0†	c.4,500.0†	5,924	14,832	...	71,500,000	1,950,000
United Kingdom	19.5‖	29,612	24,340	354.7	11,516.0‖	1,621.0‖	3,822	25,825	299,873	17,431,000	591,602
Yugoslavia	10.5	10,940	18,741	88.3	562.5	104.8	348	1,516	15,567	757,000	6,760
ASIA											
Burma	3.1	2,016	808	c.25.0	29.4	30.0	35	51	5,180	168,840	3,192
Cambodia	0.7	170	71	10.8†	23.1†	10.7†	3	4	1,730	68,350	810
Ceylon	1.5†	2,867	337	21.3	87.3	33.0	26	10	2,756	109,470	2,461
China	c.35.0	45,670†	265,260†	c.800.0	c.60.0	c.409.0	248	868	...	63,882†	1,967†
India	59.4†	111,054	119,668	1,009.5	588.8	318.9	399	2,402	66,559	3,740,000	118,940
Indonesia	7.3	3,884†	655†	84.3	235.8	99.8	489	643	10,909	708,000	20,300
Iran	3.5	1,595	2,205	39.1	187.5	66.8	56	129	10,657	555,766	6,115
Iraq	2.4†	367	1,032	17.9†	75.8†	46.5†	35	37	4,083	202,280	2,273
Israel	0.8	358	468	9.1†	136.4	57.6	108	714	27,841	2,150,370	89,658
Japan	28.0†	286,833	62,610	1,013.6	8,779.0	8,850.4	8,402	27,004	188,951	14,280,000	427,020
Korea, South	5.1	9,624	7,958	c.34.0	50.3	39.8	329	849	5,320	138,430	2,310
Malaysia	1.8	622¶	1,201¶	23.1	254.6	66.2	89	48	9,873⁹	663,600⁹	11,205⁹
Pakistan	11.2	c.14,000	c.9,000	c.200.0	93.5	32.5	179	566	27,846	1,747,700	79,560
Philippines	1.1	584	115	75.7	272.2	207.6	313	946	40,355	1,769,000	33,290
Syria	1.0†	96	c.130	c.15.0	29.4	16.0	4	1	3,360	179,925	1,283
Taiwan	4.4	6,205	2,659	16.9	39.6	35.4	274	1,166	9,124	953,900	25,275
Thailand	3.8	3,962	1,974	12.7†	125.6†	102.4†	60	82	14,840	798,000	8,040
Turkey	8.0	5,562	5,618	70.0	137.0	122.0	324	697	12,444	640,100	6,390
Vietnam, South	1.3	83	53	21.1	57.1	29.9	31	28	14,462	641,400	5,198
AFRICA											
Algeria	4.0†	1,016*	1,391*	76.0	121.2	70.8	9	29	8,696	417,515	3,548
Central African Republic	—	—	—	21.3	7.3	2.4	...	...	1,688ᵟ	61,867ᵟ	6,017ᵟ
Chad	—	—	—	30.7	4.0	5.3	...	...	2,243ᵟ	73,435ᵟ	6,786ᵟ
Congo (Kinshasa)	5.8	614	2,073	140.0	67.6	26.4	6	29	10,274	364,782	12,501
Dahomey	0.6	65	85	6.9	12.5	7.2	...	...	1,278ᵟ	60,507ᵟ	6,017ᵟ
Egypt	4.9†	5,796	2,670	c.50.0	121.8	28.1	124	238	16,357	1,009,900	17,604
Gabon	0.4	...	...	6.0	7.1	5.8	4	1	2,828ᵟ	80,717ᵟ	6,177ᵟ
Ghana	1.0	536	311	c.31.0	29.4†	17.4†	73	166	1,708ᵟ	65,820ᵟ	6,120ᵟ
Ivory Coast	0.7	522	394	35.0	55.0	29.1	27	26	6,096°	233,428°	9,892°
Kenya	2.1†	4,529†□	3,888†□	41.5	61.2	55.5	23	19	897	20,555	396
Malawi	0.5	58	190	10.7	9.9	6.2†	...	...	2,992	44,324	2,670
Mali	0.6†	66†	110†	12.1	1.7	1.4	...	...	7,576	383,600	5,470
Morocco	1.8†	522	2,635	24.8	220.8	83.4	31	55	5,524	210,000	7,310
Nigeria	3.5†	728	1,615	c.90.0	42.6†	21.5†	49	99	2,834†⁺	72,112†⁺	891†⁺
Rhodesia	3.2†	...	6,289▲	78.1	126.6	52.0	...	...	1,768ᵟ	68,887ᵟ	6,037ᵟ
Senegal	1.0†	264	183	15.4	36.0	16.9	19	9	34,107	2,177,000	59,489
South Africa	19.7	...	56,526⊕	c.320.0†	1,653.0	428.0	249	511	6,096°	233,428°	9,892°
Tanzania	2.6†	4,529†□	3,888†□	16.7	36.2†	29.8†	10	18	6,096°	233,428°	9,892°
Uganda	1.2†	4,529†□	3,888†□	24.2†	32.3	6.0	1	6	3,810	138,140	3,338
Zambia	1.0	...	...	34.7	48.2†	25.8†	1	6			
NORTH AND CENTRAL AMERICA											
Canada	72.9	3,891	140,830	810.1	6,433.3	1,682.5	1,266	2,400	218,476	15,111,000	412,295
Costa Rica	0.7	71†	56†	c.10.0	36.1	20.6	6	3	4,807	165,800	12,344
El Salvador	c.0.7	...	...	8.5†	34.1	16.4	11	2	4,620	c.104,000	c.6,820
Guatemala	0.8	...	106	c.12.0	39.9	22.6	2	4	8,829	131,160	12,310
Honduras	1.0	...	...	5.2	13.5	16.7	52	60	50,808	2,900	41,260
Mexico	19.7†	4,620	20,996	71.5	1,242.8	581.8	132	381	1,980	77,000	1,100
Nicaragua	0.3	35†	13†	6.1	24.4	8.7	7	16			
Panama	0.7	...	...	6.7†	42.1	13.0	886	5,646			
United States	336.4†	17,400	1,117,270	5,971.2	89,861.0	17,871.0	2,983	18,463	3,838,000	211,459,000	7,298,847
SOUTH AMERICA											
Argentina	39.5	14,146	12,949	201.1	1,390.0	722.0	327	1,266	43,196	2,127,600	58,228
Bolivia	3.5	249†	316†	25.0†	17.7	23.7	...	...	3,820	109,000	1,730
Brazil	32.2†	13,338	25,207	1,089.0	c.1,650.0	c.1,100.0	422	1,722	91,914	4,620,000	181,480
Chile	9.0	2,217	2,652	70.5	207.8	59.4	134	308	34,373	842,000	43,832
Colombia	3.5	223	1,180	c.45.0†	c.150.5	123.2†	49	235	46,652	2,030,000	71,008
Ecuador	1.0	86	61	18.3†	c.25.5	c.34.0	18	45	9,782	243,903	6,594
Paraguay	1.2†	28†	22†	11.2	7.4	10.1	26	22	...	...	...
Peru	2.9†	249†	591†	45.5†	c.201.5†	c.122.5†	494	378	18,975	752,401	20,673
Uruguay	3.0	...	...	c.42.0†	195.6	83.0	41	141	2,545	78,200	220
Venezuela	0.5	29	10	39.6	562.4	90.9	96	393	29,366	1,178,000	62,140
OCEANIA											
Australia	40.3	3,504*†**	21,463*	903.1†	3,836.0	963.0	344	1,074	155,995	7,404,000	250,885
New Zealand	5.0	511	2,760	93.8	899.6	177.4	122	186	32,814	1,578,000	40,610

Note: Data are for 1969 or 1970 unless otherwise indicated.

(—)Indicates nil or negligible; (...) indicates not known; (c.) indicates provisional or estimated.

*State system only.
†Data given are the most recent available.
‡Including apportionment of traffic of Scandinavian Airlines System.
§Including West Berlin.
‖Excluding Northern Ireland.
¶Including Singapore.

⁹Apportionment of traffic of Malaysia-Singapore Airlines Ltd.
ᵟIncluding apportionment of traffic of Air Afrique.
□Total for Kenya, Tanzania, and Uganda (East African Railways Corp.).
°Including apportionment of traffic of East African Airways Corp. and Caspair Ltd.
▲Including traffic for Botswana.
⁺Including apportionment of traffic of Central African Airways Corp.
⊕Including South West Africa (Namibia).
**Excluding New South Wales and Queensland.

Sources: UN, *Statistical Yearbook 1970*; *Monthly Bulletin of Statistics*; *Annual Bulletin of Transport Statistics for Europe 1969*; Lloyd's Register of Shipping, *Statistical Tables 1970*; International Road Federation, *World Road Statistics 1971*; *Jahrbuch des Eisenbahnwesens 1970*.

(M. C. MacD.)

was also granted to BOAC, which during the year formed its own charter subsidiary company outside IATA.

At the year's end there was clearly a long way to go before governments rationalized the conflict between charter and scheduled services and evolved a suitable balance. In a June 1970 policy statement, U.S. Pres. Richard Nixon affirmed the right of charter operators to coexist with scheduled airlines. In June 1971 the leading U.S. nonscheduled carriers took the initiative in forming, with their European counterparts, the international Air Carrier Association, an organization designed to protect its members' interests, especially in a political sense.

IATA members' tariff negotiations showed a desire to meet the charter challenge by attracting "leisure" travelers to the empty seats on scheduled services. At a conference on North Atlantic fares in Montreal in July, BOAC and the North American members proposed a new "advance-purchase" fare at 50% of normal fares as a means of increasing load factors without unduly diluting revenue. The requirement for booking and paying three months in advance would, it was argued, deter normal-fare travelers from taking advantage of the new rate, while encouraging new business in the leisure market.

Strong objections to the scheme from Lufthansa prevented the conference from reaching the unanimity required by IATA rules, and it was thought that an "open-rate" situation might result on the North Atlantic in 1972. Another conference at Miami, Fla., in September revealed similar disagreement. The IATA rate-making machinery was placed under considerable stress in the process; it was clear, however, that most governments were anxious to see the system survive and that they would continue to give IATA their moral support.

Scheduled airlines' capacity meant fewer orders to manufacturers in 1971. The DC-10 was certified on July 29 and entered service with American Airlines on August 5. Approximately 200 DC-10s had been ordered by the end of the year. Orders for the Lockheed TriStar, due to enter service in the spring of 1972, stood at about 180 aircraft. After the demise of the project had been staved off by Congress' approval of rescue action (a $250 million loan guarantee) to save Lockheed, the customers for the aircraft reaffirmed their orders. The British government gave an assurance of its support for the engine program, and a new engine contract came into force on September 14. The basic price of the aircraft increased from $15.2 million to $15.8 million, but the project appeared safe.

A notable first flight was that of West Germany's jet feederliner, the VFW 614, in July. News from the Soviet Union indicated that the Ilyushin design bureau was working on an airbus.

Hawker Siddeley on August 24 announced an important sale of six Trident 2s to the national airline of China (CAAC). Although not the first Western aircraft to be bought by China—six Viscounts were bought from Britain in 1966 and four secondhand Trident 1s from Pakistan in 1970—observers believed that the Trident 2 order heralded international operations by CAAC.

The safety record in the first half of the year was generally good, although 78 died when a Tu-134 crashed in Yugoslavia on May 23. There were unfortunately a number of fatal accidents in the latter part of the year. All 162 persons on board a Boeing 727 died in a collision with a military aircraft over Japan on July 30. All 97 aboard were killed when a Soviet Tu-104 exploded in August. In Alaska on September 4 all 111 persons on board a Boeing 727 were killed. A BAC One-Eleven crashed near Hamburg on September 6 with the loss of 22 lives. The Hungarian airline Malev lost two Il-18 turboprops within a space of three weeks, and BEA suffered the loss of a Vanguard turboprop in Belgium on October 2, killing 63. On December 24 a Peruvian Lockheed Electra crashed into the jungles of Peru; 92 persons were believed lost.

Preliminary figures for 1970 issued by ICAO showed that the fatality rate on scheduled services was the lowest since 1950, at 0.29 per 100 million passenger-miles. A total of 700 passengers were killed that year on scheduled services. The rate of fatal accidents per 100,000 aircraft hours flown was 0.23 in 1970. When nonscheduled operations are included, the total number of passengers killed in 1970 was 1,096. (All the above figures exclude the Soviet Union and China.)

The British government announced its decision on April 26 to build a third airport for London at a coastal site 60 mi. NE of the capital, known as Foulness. In doing so, the government overrode the recommendation for an inland site by a special commission of inquiry. The govern-

ment later made clear that its policy was to open the new airport in 1980 and thereafter restrict development at existing London-area airports, so as to alleviate noise and disturbance. There were signs of opposition to the policy from airlines. In France, the first runway of the entirely new Paris airport, known as Paris Nord, was completed during the summer. The airport was expected to open in 1974.

Atmospheric pollution and noise became increasingly controversial issues. New York assemblyman Andrew Stein was one who lobbied against the supersonic transport (SST) because of noise. In April, the manufacturers stated that the production version of the Concorde would be no noisier than the older narrow-bodied jets. Noise-certification regulations for new aircraft types (but not covering SSTs) were introduced in the U.S. and Britain. It became clear that both the new trijets, the DC-10 and the TriStar, should be appreciably quieter than current jets, thus continuing the improving trend set by the Boeing 747.

A new law enacted in Britain during 1971 provided for setting up a Civil Aviation Authority in 1972. It was to be responsible for the economic and safety regulation of British air transport, and for providing air traffic control services. The act also created the British Airways Board, to be responsible for strategic management of the two airline corporations, BEA and BOAC. Some form of merger of the two was considered possible in the future should the board decide that it would be economically desirable. (D. H. Wo.)

COMMERCIAL MOTOR TRANSPORTATION

Carriage of freight by road increased in 1971, and motor transport's share of overall freight movements rose. The trend to through carriage by container and roll-on/roll-off services continued. The European Conference of Ministers of Transport (ECMT), representing the Western European countries, agreed to multilateral quotas for international road freight transport. This involved the allocation of licenses to each country for an experimental three-year period. Each license enabled its holder to undertake freely any international transport of goods between areas within the ECMT's jurisdiction.

West Germany increased by 5% the quotas assigned to long-distance public haulage and extended taxation of road transport to prevent excessive growth. Sweden set up seasonal limits on the number of commercial freight vehicles operating. In the United Kingdom all remaining quantity licensing of freight vehicles was finally abolished, although qualitative licensing to ensure efficient operation remained. Regulations for controlling the operational efficiency of vehicles in regard to overloading, size, effective mechanical control, noise, and pollution were more vigorously enforced.

In Europe generally, the number of trucks increased at rates that varied among different countries from zero to 11%, with an overall increase of about 4%. The total number of trucks and tractors drawing articulated vehicles (semitrailers, etc.) approached seven million, excluding the trailers. Capacity rose by 6%, increasing more rapidly than the vehicles. The total amount of freight carried was about 21.5 million tons, and vehicle ton-mileage increased by something under 4%. Carriage of freight grew on the spreading expressway network and on the improved roads; the number of trucks passing through the Mont Blanc tunnel, for example, rose to 138,000, compared with 45,000 in the first full year after opening in 1966. In the U.K. 85% of inland freight was moved by road and accounted for 60% of the combined ton-mileage. The British nationalized road haulage concern, the National Freight Corporation, operating 28,000 vehicles, increased container carryings by 21%.

Although rail piggyback services (truck trailers riding on railroad flatcars) grew in some countries, the proportion originating and terminating by motor carrier declined. Ship roll-on/roll-off by truck increased, however, and a number of new services between the U.K. and continental Europe began in 1970–71.

In the United States ton-mileage of motor carriers rose, but their proportion of the total carried by all transport fell from second to third place, overtaken by pipeline carryings. Railroads continued to hold first place. Trucks, however, hauled well over 50% of manufacturers' intercity tonnage, although this represented only 31% of the total ton-miles shipped, petroleum and coal products excluded. In the U.S. total operating revenues of motor carriers went on rising, but expenses grew faster still and net revenues declined. In Canada motor carriers transported 12.2 million tons in 1970. In the U.S.S.R. road freight increased, with a rise of 7% in the first half of 1971 over the corresponding period in 1970.

Statistics for passenger road transport were sparse, but the trend was for the number of bus passengers to decrease in urban areas while long-distance traffic increased. Several countries tried to improve mass road transportation by giving priority to public transport services through increased subsidies. The U.K. relaxed bus licensing to give small private operators a better chance of entry into the industry. In the U.S. bus passengers were fewer, but charter or special service operators recorded increases in both passengers and mileage, accounting for about 9% of the total number of bus riders. In Canada passenger intercity and rural bus transport increased from 10,060,000 vehicle-miles in 1969 to 10,280,000 in 1970.

PIPELINES

There was additional installation of pipelines for natural gas and other purposes in 1971, but the major development was in the chemical industry. More producers and consumers integrated their separate ethylene grids and pipelines, and many other chemical feedstocks were being moved by pipeline. The phenomenon was worldwide. In the United States a liquid ammonia pipeline network was being extended to a total length of 3,000 km., while in Texas no fewer than 25 products were carried by long-distance lines totaling 2,000 km. Hungary was constructing a new ethylene plant at Leninvaros, the output of which would be piped to a chemical plant in the Soviet Ukraine.

At the beginning of 1971 natural gas pipelines were estimated to total more than 1.5 million km., and there were several projects for extensions and additions. The biggest was in the U.S.S.R., where the network of trunk gaslines already extended over 65,000 km. The major projects were for the construction of long-distance, large-diameter lines from the Siberian and Soviet Central Asian areas.

In West Germany a 90-cm.-diameter pipeline was in construction from Aachen to Basel, Switz., to bring gas from the Drenthe field in the Netherlands. Denmark planned to import gas from the Norwegian offshore field in the North Sea, east by pipeline to Copenhagen. In the U.K. an additional 533 lines were under construction, and another 330 were planned.

A 700-mi. extension to the Trans-Canada system was under construction, together with an extension to the reserves in the Painted Mountains of the Yukon. In Australia plans were considered with Japanese interests to pipe gas over 600 mi. to a new port on the Gulf of Carpentaria for shipment to Japan.

Oil pipeline projects on which work progressed included 6,000 mi. of a line in the U.S.S.R. to take West Siberian crude oil to the Pacific, with connections as far as Irkutsk and an extension through Chita and Khabarovsk to Nakhodka; this line was to supply the Soviet Far East and exports to Japan. New oil pipeline projects in Western Europe included the duplication of the Northwest line from Wilhelmshaven to the Rhine-Ruhr industrial region. In the U.K. pipelines linking the refineries at Milford Haven to marketing areas in Manchester and the Midlands were being constructed.

Canada embarked on an extensive program to carry gas and oil exports to the U.S. A new 42-in. crude-oil line from Edmonton, Alta., to Superior, Wis., was planned, as was a products line (193 mi.) from Edmonton to Calgary, Alta. In the U.S., the new 1,300-mi. Explorer line from refineries on the Gulf of Mexico to the Chicago market went into operation. At the end of 1971, approval was still being awaited for construction of the 800-mi., 48-in.-diameter crude oil line from the North Slope of Alaska to Valdez on the Gulf of Alaska.

RAILWAYS

Until the end of the 1960s, the railways' share of the transport business declined, but the process stopped in 1969 and there was an upturn in 1970. Heavy capital investment began to pay off, as did technological advances in traction, speeds, freight handling, and improved passenger comfort.

By 1971 railways were restructured to serve high-speed routes connecting major areas of population and industry, with a reduced number of intermediate passenger stations and freight depots and a limited number of freight terminals and transfer points at strategic locations, including ports; these had full facilities for handling block trains of container and wagon-load freight, with fully automated marshaling yards. Conversion to diesel and electric traction continued.

There was a drastic elimination of passenger services in the United States, despite the Interstate Commerce Commission's refusal to grant approval for their withdrawal in a record number of cases. The mileage of U.S. railroads operating with passenger services declined from 58,155 in 1969 to 51,723 mi. by the end of 1970. Early in May 1971 most intercity passenger trains came under the operation of Amtrak, a quasi-governmental organization, and there was a further reduction in mileage.

In Britain a new generation of high-speed trains of a conventional type designed as multiple-unit sets with a power car at each end developing 2,250 hp. was planned

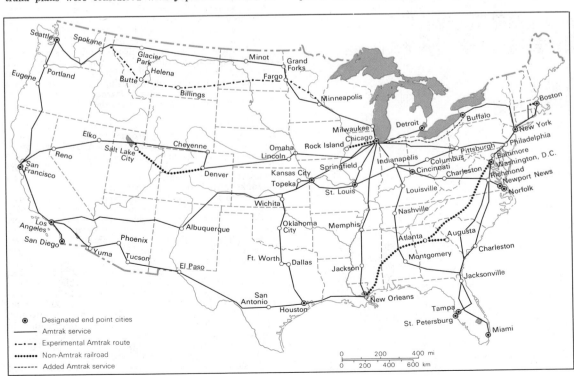

Routes of the National Railroad Passenger Corporation (Amtrak) which operates intercity passenger trains under the terms of the U.S. Rail Passenger Service Act.

Designated end point cities
Amtrak service
Experimental Amtrak route
Non-Amtrak railroad
Added Amtrak service

for introduction in 1974, prior to the coming into service of the advanced passenger train (APT) in 1976. The APT was planned to operate at 125 mph but designed for speeds of 150 mph. Powered by a gas turbine engine and with a new form of suspension based on aerodynamics, it would run on existing tracks.

Two air-cushion aerotrain prototypes were developed in France, and the government authorized a service of 160-mph aerotrains, for commuter services around Paris, to be operational by 1980. In West Germany a magnetic-cushion train, driven by a linear induction motor, with a top speed of 350 mph, was in an advanced stage. The Council of Europe drew up a plan for a high-speed air cushion railway, "Europolis," to connect Strasbourg, France, with Brussels in 72 minutes, and with Basel, Switz., in 19 minutes. In the U.S. the government sponsored research on a 1,000-mph magnetically propelled "train" to run in a vacuum tunnel.

Conversion from steam to diesel and electric traction continued in many parts of the world. In the less developed countries several feasibility studies began on new lines. Elsewhere, the Turkey-Iran link of the Trans-Asian railway was completed, full services starting in 1971 on the 751-km. Teheran–Yazd line, with a branch to Isfahan, Iran. In Japan progress was made on the high-speed 165-mi. extension of the Tokaido line from Osaka to Okayama. An interesting development in rail transport was the establishment of a "land bridge" between Europe and Japan via the Trans-Siberian railway. U.K. Far East freight could be dispatched by container-ship service between London and Leningrad, connecting with an express rail freight service to Nakhodka and thence by ship to Japan.

Higher railway operating revenues were offset by rising costs. In the U.S., whereas total railroad operating revenues rose 5.3% in 1970, the total deficit of Class I railroads was considerably higher than in the previous year. In Europe the recovery begun in 1969 continued with overall increases in the first half of 1970. The Polish railways carried most freight, with the German Federal Railways next and the French third. British Rail increased its ton-miles by 5.3% and passenger-miles by 2.7%, but the operating surplus fell from £14.7 million to £9.6 million.

In the area of urban mass transit the first 75 mi. of the $1.5 billion San Francisco Bay Area Rapid Transit system were scheduled for completion in January 1972.

In London the first new under-Thames subway crossing for 40 years, the extension of the Victoria line to Brixton, was opened in July. Also in the U.K. in August a £35 million government grant was given for the first stage of London's proposed Fleet Line, as well as a grant for a Mersey rail loop under central Liverpool.   (E. A. J. D.)

WATER TRANSPORTATION

Shipping. The shipping industry ran into the doldrums in 1971 after several years of good business. Costs shot up at an unprecedented rate, and the buoyant freight markets of early 1970 collapsed. The massive orders for new ships, stimulated by high freight rates and optimistic assumptions over the past five years, were reduced to a trickle with dawning appreciation that world shipping had once again overreacted to boom conditions.

As a result, retrenchment was the order of the day, with sharply reduced profits and, in some cases, losses and mergers. In the U.K. one of the great names of world shipping, Cunard, succumbed to a take-over bid from a property group, Trafalgar House, with results that were awaited with keen interest toward the end of the year. In the U.S. disenchantment set in over the results of an earlier series of take-overs of shipping groups by non-shipping conglomerates; with substantial overtonnaging and losses in the Atlantic container trade, where much of their activity was concentrated, there were moves toward collaboration between these lines.

Costs rose in practically every department of shipping, with bunkers leading the way. In the spring, bunker prices were more than double the level a year earlier, as oil companies sought to cope with soaring transportation costs and demand. Seafarers and dock workers in various parts of the world were securing wage increases of 20–30%; ship purchase and repair costs were up by about 50% and dock and harbour charges in many places by similar amounts.

Both passenger and cargo lines reacted with price increases of 10–20%. In the case of cargo lines, there was substantial shipper resistance to such high and widespread increases, which in at least one case had startling but perhaps salutary results: the shipping lines planning containerization of the Europe-New Zealand trade decided to cancel it on the ground that the investment would yield an inadequate return. It appeared that shipowners wanted more security and a better return on capital than had been the case generally over the past 50 years if they were to continue with their massive investment in such new methods as containerization.

Concern over water pollution grew. A number of ameliorative measures were formulated by the Inter-Governmental Maritime Consultative Organization (IMCO). The traffic separation project in the Dover Straits, probably the world's busiest international seaway, was to become mandatory, it was decided, and a radar and helicopter watch was instituted by the U.K. for traffic offenders who might cause collisions and, thus, pollution. IMCO also recommended a limitation on internal tank sizes in large tankers to reduce leakage in the event of collision, a move that, by increasing the cost and weight of the vessel, could delay the introduction of the next generation of even larger tankers in the 500,000–1,000,000-ton class.

While car ferries proliferated in an increasingly motorized world, conventional passenger shipping continued to decline. For the first time the North Atlantic was without any regular passenger services at all in the winter of 1970–71, as the remaining liners shifted to the more lucrative winter-cruise market.   (M. By.)

Docks and Harbours. Port facilities were much extended and adapted to new requirements in 1970 and 1971. Container berths and roll-on/roll-off facilities increasingly replaced conventional wharfage. Indeed, an excess of port capacity seemed likely and consolidation appeared inevitable. These possibilities were emphasized because containerization proceeded so quickly and to such an extent that some projected container shipping services were abandoned and a few were withdrawn. At the same time, provisions were made to accommodate ever bigger tankers. Rotterdam, Neth., could take vessels of 250,000 deadweight tons (dwt); Wilhelmshaven, W.Ger., 200,000 tons, with plans to take 250,000-tonners; and Fos-sur-mer, France, could handle 300,000-ton tankers and planned to provide for 500,000-ton vessels.

The Port of London continued to improve the Tilbury Docks container and unit load berths, and to reduce conventional general cargo facilities, which were to be halved

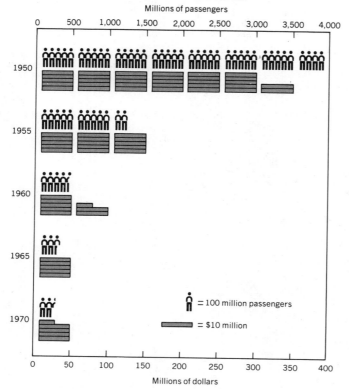

Passengers Carried and Passenger Revenue in U.S. Railroads

Millions of passengers

$$\hat{n} = \text{100 million passengers}$$

▬ = $10 million

Source: American Transit Association, *Transit Fact Book.*

by 1975. The Port of London Authority was associated with the tentative plan for a new deep-sea port at Foulness on the Thames estuary. Work progressed on the £33 million U.K. Seaforth project, the first stage of which, with ten container berths, was opened. Two more berths in the Western Dock of Southampton's container port were scheduled for service in 1972. Another big project was a £4 million marine oil terminal at Milford Haven to accommodate 20,000- to 275,000-dwt tankers.

At Bremerhaven, W.Ger., the first berth of the new container terminal was inaugurated in April 1971. The port would eventually have eight container berths more than 2 km. long.

The U.S.S.R. and Japan cooperated in work on the third stage of the port of Nakhodka, the largest port in the Soviet Far East, southeast of Vladivostok. Modernization of Archangel, on the White Sea, normally icebound from January to April, would enable the port to receive ships throughout the year.

In Taiwan construction proceeded on a second container shipping centre at Kaohsiung, with four deepwater berths, at a cost of $8 million. At Shuwaikh what would be the largest port in the Middle East was under construction in Kuwait at a cost of $27 million. In Iran a major loading terminal (1,800 ft. long) for the export of crude oil was being built at Khark Island off the western shore as part of a $38.4 million project to accommodate the new generation of giant tankers.

In South America improvements were made at Santos Port, Brazil, at a total cost of $78.5 million, with assistance from the World Bank; in Argentina work progressed on making a new channel connecting Buenos Aires to the Río Paraná de las Palmas, serving Bolivia and Paraguay.

In North America there were extensive programs at many major ports. In New Orleans, La., a $37 million new master plan was drawn up, the first stage of which was to be completed by 1972. Additional facilities were to be provided in stages over the next 25 years for competitive handling of an estimated 400% increase in annual tonnage.

The Port of New York Authority pressed on with its construction program. At Port Newark a 40-ac. combination container-break bulk terminal with 2,058 ft. of berths was completed. This ended the development of all berthing areas on the Elizabeth Channel and represented an investment of $125 million. On the Elizabeth side, five-vessel berths at the south end of the Elizabeth Marine Terminal were under way, and the 3,870-ft. wharf was completed during the year. By the end of 1973, the last phases of Elizabeth's development were expected to have been accomplished and there would then be available 16,850 ft. of berthing space, capable of accommodating 25 modern container ships, and over 900 ac. of supporting upland area. The total cost of these facilities was estimated at $170 million.

At Port Kembla, New South Wales, Austr., the harbour was deepened to 50 ft., allowing accommodation of ships of 100,000 dwt; Port Lincoln, South Australia, was to provide new berthing and bulk loading facilities at a cost of A$87.5 million. And at Cape Lambert, Western Australia, an ore-loading port was planned to take ships of up to 100,000 dwt. Work went forward on the first stage of the development of Botany Bay as a major port and industrial complex. Adjacent to Sydney's existing port, Port Jackson, which handled approximately 17 million tons of cargo annually, a new port was being constructed with a total of 11,000 ft. of wharfage. Dredging was being done to a depth of 70 ft.

Auckland and Wellington, N.Z., were to be developed as the country's major container ports. Auckland would have two fully operational container terminals by 1972 and additional roll-on/roll-off facilities.

Seaborne trade improved in 1970, most of the greater ports reporting increased business. London dealt with 59.5 million tons of cargo, an increase of 1.5 million tons over 1969. Petroleum traffic rose by 1.3 million to 28.9 million tons, coal declined, and general cargo increased; 1.5 million tons of unit load traffic were handled in the port—double the 1969 tonnage. The net registered tonnage of ships using the docks totaled 28.5 million, a decrease of 1.6 million tons. Britain's ports as a whole handled 16.6 million tons of unit traffic on both lift-on and roll-on services, including 9.7 million tons of container cargo. This was nearly half that handled by all northwestern European ports together.

There was a marked increase in the freight passing through the Port of New York's six marine terminals.

In 1970, at 12.3 million tons of general cargo, there was an increase of 18.9% over 1969, despite a six-week strike that closed the port. The Elizabeth Marine Terminal recorded a 48% increase in containerized cargo, exceeding the 6-million-ton mark for the first time. Total seaborne freight traffic through the whole port reached about 100 million tons in 1970.

Inland Waterways. During the year carryings by inland waterways in Europe appeared to be leveling off, and indications were that final figures for 1970 would show no increase over 1969. Both inward and outward barge traffic at some European ports also fell in 1970 but rose in 1971.

In the United States intercity ton-miles moved on inland waterways exceeded the previous record of 300 billion ton-miles and represented about 16% of total intercity traffic. The Tennessee Valley Authority waterways carried 22,375,000 tons of commercial freight in 1970, and it was estimated that savings in transportation costs were about $51.5 million in 1970, or more than six times the federal costs of the waterway of $8 million. The St. Lawrence Seaway in 1970 had its best year since the opening in 1959. Traffic increased on both sections and surpassed the 1966 record. Total cargo tonnage moved was 71,113,000 tons in 9,115 ship transits. Oceangoing ships carried 20.1% and lakers 79.9% of total cargoes, compared with 24.2% and 75.8% in 1969. Cargoes on the Montreal-Ontario section increased 24.7% to 51.1 million tons, and on the Welland section they totaled 62.8 million tons, 9.3 million tons more than in 1969.

Traffic through the Panama Canal in the U.S. fiscal year 1970 totaled 116,143,000 metric tons, of which 74,877,000 tons crossed the isthmus from the Atlantic to the Pacific and 41,266,000 tons moved in the opposite direction. The 1970 traffic was 13 million tons higher than in 1969. Kiel (W.Ger.) Canal traffic was 33,697,000 metric tons from the Baltic to the North Sea and 24,425,000 in the reverse direction for a total of 58,122,000 tons, an increase of more than 1.5 million tons over 1969. In the U.S.S.R. during the first six months of 1971 inland navigations carried 140 million tons of freight and recorded a total of 66 billion ton-miles.

In the U.S. President Nixon in January ordered a halt, for environmental reasons, to the construction of a canal across northern Florida that would have linked the Atlantic with the Gulf of Mexico.   (E. A. J. D.)

Hovercraft. It seemed that 1971 might be the turning point for Hovercraft as a transport medium in both civil and military fields. The U.S. Navy program to build two 100-ton craft went ahead, and both began their initial sea trials in the fall. At the same time funding for studies on 2,000-ton craft was made available, and the U.S. Navy was discussing the possibility of using 10,000-tonners before the end of the 1970s. This meant that the costly development phase of a comparatively new mode of transport would be borne by a military program—as had been the case with the aircraft industry.

The scheduled Hovercraft services across the English Channel showed an operating profit during the year for the first time, despite increasing engine maintenance costs resulting from the Rolls-Royce collapse. The British Hovercraft Corp. began to develop an expansion program for smaller craft, "stretching" civil versions so that they would carry more passengers and modifying military craft so that they could carry vehicles and equipment. Even so, in Britain, where the Hovercraft was first developed, the industry was in a state of suspended animation for most of the year, waiting for orders, which, in a less stringent financial climate, would have been forthcoming in 1970.   (J. B. BE.)

See also Cities and Urban Affairs; Engineering Projects; Industrial Review.

ENCYCLOPÆDIA BRITANNICA FILMS. *The Mississippi System: Waterway of Commerce* (1970); *The Great Lakes— North America's Inland Seas* (1971); *Rotterdam—Europort, Gateway to Europe* (1971).

Trinidad and Tobago

A parliamentary state and a member of the Commonwealth of Nations, Trinidad and Tobago consists of two islands off the coast of Venezuela, north of the Orinoco River delta. Area: 1,980 sq.mi. (5,128 sq.km.). Pop. (1970): 945,210, including (1960) Negro 43.3%; East Indian 36.4%; mixed 16.3%.

Cap. and largest city: Port-of-Spain (pop., 1970, 67,-867). Language: English (official); Hindi, French, Spanish. Religion (1960): Christian 66%; Hindu 23%; Muslim 6%. Queen, Elizabeth II; governor-general in 1971, Sir Solomon Hochoy; prime minister, Eric Williams.

In the general elections of May 1971, Prime Minister Williams' People's National Movement won all 36 seats (8 unopposed) on a 32% vote, following a general opposition campaign not to participate unless certain electoral reforms, starting with the scrapping of the voting machines, were enforced. To minimize the effects of a one-party government, several extra-parliamentary bodies and techniques were improvised.

In a major political announcement Williams had declared at his party's convention in September 1970 that the economy would be fashioned into a "nationally oriented private sector," a state-owned "public sector," and a "people's sector" within which cooperatives would be emphasized and all efforts made to bring economic power into the hands of nationals of African and Indian origin. The 1971 budget provided for total expenditure of U.S. $200 million, of which nearly $50 million would go toward development. At the same time a special 5% levy on a certain range of incomes went toward alleviation of unemployment. Economic nationalism was somewhat discouraged by the request from the state-owned sugar company, Caroni (formerly wholly owned by Tate and Lyle), for a $10 million loan.

The year was marked by a wave of strikes, all of which were in violation of the Industrial Stabilization Act, and by slowdowns and sit-ins in almost every sector of the public service. Massive wage increases in the private sector, plus public service settlements costing some $23 million, brought a temporary halt to labour discontent until October, when labour disputes involving oil workers led to the proclamation of a state of emergency.

In March three officers and six soldiers were sentenced to from 2 to 20 years' imprisonment for participating in the April 1970 mutiny. (RA. R.)

Tunisia

A republic of North Africa, lying on the Mediterranean Sea, Tunisia is bounded by Algeria and Libya. Area: 63,-378 sq.mi. (164,150 sq.km.). Pop. (1969 est.): 5,137,000.
Cap. and largest city: Tunis (pop., 1966, 468,997). Language: Arabic (official). Religion: Muslim; Jewish and Christian minorities. President in 1971, Habib Bourguiba; prime minister, Hedi Nouira.

The precarious health of President Bourguiba and the problem of his successor continued to dominate Tunisian political life in 1971. On his triumphant return to Tunisia in June after several months' absence, the president made it clear that he had no intention of "becoming merely a figurehead" or of delegating any of his power. On the republic's 40th anniversary in July he declared: "I still have the strength to lead the country and I am determined to carry on with the job I began 40 years ago."

The president was increasingly concerned over the growing movement in favour of liberalization among some sectors of the government party. These groups advocated such changes as parliamentary direction of political affairs and elections at all political levels. Ahmed Mestiri, leader of the liberal wing of the party, was dismissed from his post as minister of the interior

---

TRINIDAD AND TOBAGO
Education. (1967–68) Primary, pupils 223,164, teachers 6,282; secondary, pupils 47,224, teachers 1,866; higher, students 1,267, teaching staff 200.
Finance and Trade. Monetary unit: Trinidad and Tobago dollar, with an exchange rate of TT$2 to U.S. $1 (TT$4.80 = £1 sterling) and a free rate (Sept. 27, 1971) of TT$1.94 to U.S. $1. Budget (1970 est.): revenue TT$295.2 million; expenditure (recurrent) TT$277.2 million. Foreign trade (1970): imports TT$1,087,000,000; exports TT$964.2 million. Import sources: Venezuela 25%; U.S. 16%; U.K. 13%; Saudi Arabia 9%. Export destinations: U.S. 46%; U.K. 10%; Sweden 6%; ship and aircraft bunkers 6%. Main exports: petroleum products 69%; crude oil 8%; sugar 5%.
Transport and Communications. Roads (motorable; 1969) 4,870 km. Motor vehicles in use (1969): passenger 68,500; commercial (including buses) 18,-500. Air traffic (1970): 506.9 million passenger-km.; freight 10,741,000 net ton-km. Shipping traffic (1969) goods loaded c. 22.6 million metric tons, unloaded c. 15 million metric tons. Telephones (Jan. 1970) 51,570. Radio receivers (Dec. 1969) 293,000. Television receivers (Dec. 1969) 43,000.
Agriculture. Production (in 000; metric tons; 1970; 1969 in parentheses): rice c. 10 (c. 10); sweet potatoes c. 18 (c. 18); oranges c. 11 (c. 11); grapefruit c. 18 (16); sugar, raw value (1970–71) 234, (1969–70) 222; copra c. 13 (c. 13). Livestock (in 000; 1969–70): cattle c. 63; pigs c. 50; goats c. 35; poultry c. 5,130.
Industry. Production (in 000; metric tons; 1970): crude oil 7,223; petroleum products (1969) 20,992; electricity (kw-hr.) 1,202,000.

TUNISIA
Education. (1967–68) Primary, pupils 826,069, teachers (state only) 15,188; secondary, pupils 81,717; vocational, pupils 45,595; secondary and vocational, teachers 5,299; teacher training, students 7,297; higher (at University of Tunis; 1968–69), students 7,668, teaching staff 304.
Finance. Monetary unit: Tunisian dinar, with a par value of 0.52 dinar to U.S. $1 (1.26 dinars = £1 sterling) and a free rate (Sept. 27, 1971) of 0.515 dinar to U.S. $1 (1.277 dinars = £1). Gold, SDRs, and foreign exchange, central bank: (June 1971) U.S. $93.8 million; (June 1970) U.S. $53.3 million. Budget (1971 est.) balanced at 154 million dinars. Gross national product: (1969) 596.9 million dinars; (1968) 558.7 million dinars. Money supply: (May 1971) 212,280,000 dinars; (May 1970) 187,170,000 dinars. Cost of living (Tunis; 1963 = 100): (June 1971) 134; (June 1970) 125.
Foreign Trade. (1970) Imports 160.4 million dinars; exports 95.8 million dinars. Import sources (1969): France 34%; U.S. 19%; Italy 9%; West Germany 8%. Export destinations (1969): France 26%; West Germany 13%; Italy 13%; Libya 7%; Switzerland 6%; Bulgaria 5%. Main exports: crude oil 24%; phosphates 20%; olive oil 9%; wine 5%. Tourism (1969): visitors 373,300; gross receipts U.S. $54 million.
Transport and Communications. Roads (1970) 17,856 km. Motor vehicles in use (1970): passenger 66,382; commercial 35,288. Railways: (1968) 2,298 km.; traffic (1970) 443 million passenger-km., freight 1,328,000,000 net ton-km. Air traffic (1969): 195,120,-000 passenger-km.; freight 2,190,000 net ton-km. Telephones (Dec. 1969) 68,908. Radio receivers (Dec. 1968) 450,000. Television receivers (Dec. 1969) 37,-000.
Agriculture. Production (in 000; metric tons; 1970; 1969 in parentheses): wheat c. 450 (300); barley c. 150 (c. 80); tomatoes (1969) c. 108, (1968) 108; wine c. 60 (c. 85); dates c. 60 (c. 60); figs (1969) c. 30, (1968) 33; olive oil c. 90 (25); oranges c. 75 (c. 67); lemons c. 12 (c. 12). Livestock (in 000; 1969–70): sheep c. 3,200; cattle c. 610; goats c. 460; camels c. 230; poultry c. 8,500.
Industry. Production (in 000; metric tons; 1970): crude oil 4,151; cement 538; iron ore (55% metal content) 774; phosphate rock (1969) 2,599; lead 21; sulfuric acid 422; electricity (excluding most industrial production; kw-hr.) 676,000.

Trucking Industry:
see Transportation

Trust Territories:
see Dependent States

Tunnels:
see Engineering Projects

and during the year was ousted gradually from any position of influence in the country.

The conflict between conservative and liberal elements dominated the eighth congress of the Neo-Destour Socialist Party, the country's only legal political grouping, held at Monastair in October. Shortly before the congress opened, Bourguiba described it as a decisive one in the party's history, likening it to those of March 1934 and November 1955. During the debates, Mestiri advocated liberalization under the guidance of Bourguiba, while others such as Muhammad Masmoudi spoke of the dangers of parliamentarianism. Bahi Ladgham, who had been dismissed as prime minister in 1970 for prematurely assuming the role of successor to Bourguiba, attempted to bring together the two conflicting tendencies. Prime Minister Hedi Nouira, a conservative who had taken over from Bahi Ladgham, was presented to the congress as Bourguiba's successor.

Despite the president's obvious support for the conservatives, and despite his immense popularity and prestige, voting for the party's Central Committee did not entirely follow his views. The greatest number of votes went to Bahi Ladgham, closely followed by Ahmed Mestiri, while Hedi Nouira was in sixth place.

Bourguiba increasingly surrounded himself with known loyalist elements, and by the end of the year Mestiri seemed to have been more or less completely eliminated from public life and indeed threatened with total excommunication. Meanwhile, Hedi Nouira formed a new government at the end of October.

(Ph. D.)

Turkey

A republic of southeastern Europe and Asia Minor, Turkey is bounded by the Aegean Sea, the Black Sea, the U.S.S.R., Iran, Iraq, Syria, the Mediterranean Sea, Greece, and Bulgaria. Area: 301,380 sq.mi. (780,576 sq.km.), including 9,158 sq.mi. in Europe. Pop. (1970): 35,-666,549. Cap.: Ankara (pop., 1970, 1,440,779). Largest city: Istanbul (pop., 1970, 2,312,751). Language: Turkish, Kurdish, Arabic. Religion: predominantly Muslim. President in 1971, Gen. Cevdet Sunay; prime ministers, Suleyman Demirel and, from March 26, Nihat Erim.

In 1971 the Justice Party administration, headed by Suleyman Demirel, survived the defection of its right wing (which had formed a new Democratic Party) but was ousted from power by the armed forces. The two victories won by Prime Minister Demirel in Parliament on Dec. 17, 1970 (when the report clearing him of charges of nepotism was endorsed by 309 votes to 276), and on Feb. 28, 1971 (when the budget was approved by 230 votes to 198), were of no avail in the face of mounting urban terrorism spearheaded by the extreme leftist Turkish People's Liberation Army (TPLA). In December 1970, as bombings and killings increased, Air Force Commander Muhsin Batur proposed sweeping constitutional changes. President Sunay in January 1971 undertook consultations with political leaders and university rectors on reestablishing order, but no agreement emerged. In the meantime riots and kidnappings continued. The demand for a credible government, backed by the threat of a di-

Homeless victims survived a severe earthquake that shattered the town of Bingol in eastern Turkey on May 22, 1971. Only 180 buildings out of 4,000 remained, and the official death toll reached 1,000.

rect military take-over, was put forward in an army memorandum on March 12. Prime Minister Demirel resigned on the same day, protesting that the memorandum was incompatible with the rule of law. Nevertheless, he allowed five members of the Justice Party to serve in a government "above the parties," which was formed on March 26 by Nihat Erim (see BIOGRAPHY), a professor of constitutional law.

The new government's program, which attributed the crisis to a failure to carry out structural reforms, was approved by the National Assembly by 321 votes to 46. However, student militancy and terrorism continued until on April 26 martial law was imposed on

TURKEY

Education. (1968–69) Primary, pupils 4,790,183, teachers 113,211; secondary, pupils 849,533, teachers 28,003; vocational, pupils 153,437, teachers 11,230; teacher training, students 60,576, teachers 2,355; higher (including 8 universities), students 143,279, teaching staff 7,627.

Finance. Monetary unit: Turkish pound or lira, with a par value of 15 lire to U.S. $1 (36 lire = £1 sterling) and a free rate (Sept. 27, 1971) of 14.50 lire to U.S. $1. Gold, SDRs, and foreign exchange, central bank: (June 1971) U.S. $442 million; (June 1970) U.S. $218 million. Budget (1969–70 est.): revenue 24,-497,000,000 lire; expenditure 25,697,000,000 lire. Gross national product: (1969) 127,490,000,000 lire; (1968) 114,750,000,000 lire. Money supply: (Nov. 1970) 17,240,000,000 lire; (Nov. 1969) 14,780,000,000 lire. Cost of living (Istanbul; 1963 = 100): (April 1971) 175; (April 1970) 152.

Foreign Trade. (1970) Imports 9,161,000,000 lire; exports 6,909,000,000 lire. Import sources: U.S. 19%; West Germany 19%; U.K. 10%; Italy 8%; Switzerland 5%. Export destinations: West Germany 20%; U.S. 10%; Switzerland 8%; France 7%; Italy 7%; U.K. 6%; U.S.S.R. 5%; Lebanon 5%. Main exports: edible nuts 21%; cotton 21%; tobacco 15%; dried fruit 6%.

Transport and Communications. Roads (1970) c. 70,000 km. (including 33,855 km. main roads). Motor vehicles in use (1969): passenger 136,965; commercial 122,009. Railways: (1969) 7,985 km.; traffic (1970) 5,562,000,000 passenger-km., freight 5,618,000,000 net ton-km. Air traffic (1970): 640.1 million passenger-km.; freight 6,390,000 net ton-km. Shipping (1970): merchant vessels 100 gross tons and over 324; gross tonnage 696,824. Telephones (Dec. 1969) 513,569. Radio receivers (Dec. 1969) 3,030,000. Television receivers (Dec. 1969) 25,000.

Agriculture. Production (in 000; metric tons; 1970; 1969 in parentheses): corn 1,040 (1,000); rye 630 (817); wheat (including spelt) 10,081 (10,593); barley 3,250 (3,740); oats 400 (468); onions (1969) 585, (1968) 525; potatoes 1,915 (1,936); sunflower seed 380 (310); chick-peas c. 110 (111); dry beans c. 140 (140); lentils 92 (107); oranges 509 (483); apples 700 (620); pears 165 (160); grapes (1969) 3,635, (1968) 3,725; raisins c. 310 (318); figs (1969) 215, (1968) 215; sugar, raw value (1970–71) c. 629, (1969–70) 546; olive oil 125 (54); tobacco 146 (127); cotton, lint 400 (400). Livestock (in 000; Dec. 1969): cattle 13,189; sheep 36,351; horses 1,100; asses 1,938; buffalo 1,178; goats 20,267; chickens (Oct.) c. 32,600.

Industry. Fuel and power (in 000; metric tons; 1970): crude oil 3,461; coal (1969) 4,684; lignite (1969) 4,356; electricity (kw-hr.) 8,617,000. Production (in 000; metric tons; 1970): cement 6,371; iron ore (metal content; 1969) 1,411; pig iron 1,033; crude steel 1,312; sulfur (1969) 86; sulfuric acid (1969) 30; superphosphates (1969) 151; manganese ore (metal content; 1969) 5.2; chrome ore (oxide content; 1969) 259; cotton yarn (1969) 37; wool yarn (1968) 28.

Turkey's 11 most important provinces. While public order and discipline thereafter were ensured, some individual outrages continued to occur, the most notorious being the kidnapping on May 17 and subsequent murder of the Israeli consul general, Ephraim Elrom, in Istanbul. Countermeasures were severe: suspects were hunted down, some being shot while resisting capture; the first trial of TPLA activists, accused of kidnappings and robberies but not of murder, ended with 18 death sentences; almost all the mentors of the Turkish left-wing movement—academics, creative writers, and journalists—were detained at one time or another; newspapers and books were banned; and military men were appointed to key positions. In August and September the two chambers of Parliament approved constitutional amendments subordinating some civil rights to the national interest and limiting the independence of universities and the media. Two university students were sentenced to death for the kidnap-murder of Elrom in December.

While these draconian measures were largely successful in establishing order, the government's management of the economy was less effective. Businessmen were put off by government intervention in foreign trade, farmers by a land reform project of uncertain impact, foreign investors by threats of nationalization, and the public by rising prices.

At the end of September a rift developed between the Justice Party and Erim, who had to accept Demirel's demand that social changes such as land reform be discussed as bills instead of being introduced by decree. A few days later, the ministers of communications and of power (the latter a noted critic of foreign oil corporations) resigned. A statement by the three military commanders that they were determined to see the reforms through was defended by the prime minister against protests that Parliament was being dictated to. On October 5 the Justice Party decided to withdraw its five members from the government. Three weeks later the government resigned, but its resignation was refused by President Sunay. On December 3 Erim resigned again, after half the Cabinet members had quit in a disagreement over the pace of reform. He subsequently formed a new government that included additional members of Parliament.

In foreign affairs, the most notable initiative of the new government was the recognition of China in August. However, Turkey's continued loyalty to the Western alliance was reaffirmed, particularly during the visits in October of U.S. Vice-Pres. Spiro Agnew and of Queen Elizabeth II. Relations with the U.S. were improved by the government's decision to ban the cultivation of the opium poppy from the fall of 1972.   (A. J. A. M.)

See also Cyprus.

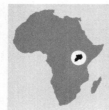

Uganda

A republic and a member of the Commonwealth of Nations, Uganda is bounded by the Sudan, the Congo (Kinshasa), Rwanda, Tanzania, and Kenya. Area: 91,073 sq.mi. (235,880 sq.km.), including 16,363 sq.mi. of inland water. Pop. (1970 est.): 9,831,000, about 99% of whom are African. Cap. and largest city: Kampala (pop., 1969, 330,700). Language: English (official), Bantu, Nilotic, Nilo-Hamitic, and Sudanic. Religion: predominantly traditional beliefs, with Hindu, Muslim, and Christian minorities. President to Jan. 25, 1971, Apollo Milton Obote; chief of state

from January 25 and president from February 20, Gen. Idi Amin.

On Jan. 25, 1971, while President Obote was attending the conference of Commonwealth heads of government in Singapore, a military coup led by Maj. Gen. Idi Amin (*see* BIOGRAPHY), commander of the Army, ousted him. Obote's tribal policy apparently had aroused fear for their lives in officers who were not members of Obote's own Lango tribe; it also was claimed that the government had been guilty of corruption. Amin was assured of the support of the majority of the Baganda, who had remained hostile to Obote since his expulsion of the kabaka of Buganda in 1966. Amin could rely, too, on those areas of the country that had been alienated by Obote's imprisonment of their parliamentary representatives. These leaders were released on Amin's order, and early in April the body of the kabaka, Mutesa II, was flown from England (where he had died in exile in 1969) for reinterment in Buganda.

Immediately on seizing power Amin promised a return to civil government; he soon appointed a Cabinet composed almost entirely of civilians and recruited all the new ministers into the Army. Later in February Amin had himself declared president and promoted to general.

Elements of the Army still loyal to Obote maintained a sporadic opposition, and discipline was weakened by the flight or death of officers who could not accept the coup. This indiscipline hampered the general maintenance of order. (In July two U.S. citizens —a journalist and a lecturer at Makerere University, Kampala—were murdered, allegedly on orders of a senior army officer after it was discovered that they

UGANDA
Education. (1967) Primary, pupils 641,639, teachers 19,257; secondary, pupils 35,617, teachers 1,671; vocational, pupils 3,252, teachers 322; teacher training, students 3,472, teachers 242; higher (at Makerere University), students 2,179, teaching staff (1966) 216.

Finance. Monetary unit: Uganda shilling, with a par value of UShs. 7.14 to U.S. $1 (UShs. 17.14 = £1 sterling) and a free rate (Oct. 11, 1971) of UShs. 17.71 to £1. Gold, SDRs, and foreign exchange: (March 1971) U.S. $52.5 million; (March 1970) U.S. $52.7 million. Budget (1970–71 est.): revenue UShs. 1,142,000,000; expenditure UShs. 1,121,000,000. Cost of living (Kampala; 1963 = 100): (2nd quarter 1971) 185; (2nd quarter 1970) 153.

Foreign Trade. (Excluding trade with Kenya and Tanzania; 1970): Imports UShs. 865 million; exports UShs. 1,775,000,000. Import sources: U.K. 32%; Japan 12%; West Germany 9%; U.S. 6%; Italy 5%. Export destinations: U.S. 21%; U.K. 21%; Japan 11%; West Germany 5%. Main exports: coffee 57%; cotton 20%; copper 9%; tea 5%.

Transport and Communications. Roads (1969) 24,300 km. Motor vehicles in use (1969): passenger 32,300; commercial (including buses) 6,000. Railways (1968) 1,226 km. (for traffic *see* KENYA). Air traffic: *see* KENYA. Telephones (Dec. 1969) 27,802. Radio receivers (Dec. 1967) 509,000. Television receivers (Dec. 1969) 12,000.

Agriculture. Production (in 000; metric tons; 1970; 1969 in parentheses): millet *c.* 630 (630); sorghum *c.* 332 (332); sweet potatoes (1969) *c.* 170, (1968) 666; cassava (1969) 2,321, (1968) 1,945; peanuts *c.* 234 (*c.* 234); dry beans *c.* 260 (*c.* 260); coffee *c.* 240 (225); tea 8 (18); sugar, raw value 152 (163); sesame *c.* 20 (*c.* 20); cotton, lint *c.* 88 (85); timber (cu.m.; 1969) 11,300, (1968) 11,000; fish catch (1969) 124, (1968) 108. Livestock (in 000; Dec. 1969): cattle *c.* 3,900; sheep *c.* 760; goats *c.* 1,680; pigs *c.* 48; chickens *c.* 10,000.

Industry. Production (in 000; metric tons; 1969): copper, smelter 17; tin concentrates (metal content) 0.17; tungsten concentrates (oxide content) 0.11; salt 5; phosphate rock 368; cement (1970) 191; electricity (excluding most industrial production; kw-hr.) 731,000.

knew of a massacre of 160 soldiers of the Acholi tribe by other members of the Army.) To divert attention from these difficulties Amin began accusing Tanzania and the Sudan of encouraging guerrilla movements against his regime. Although relations with Sudan subsequently improved, Tanzania presented a less tractable problem. Obote had taken refuge in Dar es Salaam and Tanzanian Pres. Julius Nyerere firmly maintained that in his view Obote was still president. In May Amin offered a £60,000 reward for the return of Obote to Uganda. A number of minor border skirmishes with Tanzania led Amin to close their common frontiers from July until November.

In spite of the unsettled state of the country Amin visited Israel, Britain, and France during the year. Uganda's African neighbours were wary of committing themselves too openly to Amin. The meeting of the Organization of African Unity, which was to have taken place in Kampala, was transferred to Addis Ababa. Nevertheless, in October delegations from Kenya, Uganda, and Tanzania did meet in Nairobi, Kenya.   (K. I.)

Union of Soviet Socialist Republics

The Union of Soviet Socialist Republics is a federal state covering parts of eastern Europe and northern and central Asia. Area: 8,600,350 sq.mi. (22,274,900 sq.km.). Pop. (1970): 241,720,000, including Russians 53%; Ukrainians 17%; Belorussians 4%; Uzbeks 4%; Tatars 3%. Cap. and largest city: Moscow (pop., 1970, 6,942,000). Language: officially Russian, but many others are spoken. Religion: about 40 religions are represented in the U.S.S.R., the major ones being Christian denominations. General secretary of the Communist Party of the Soviet Union in 1971, Leonid I. Brezhnev; chairman of the Presidium of the Supreme Soviet (president), Nikolai V. Podgorny; chairman of the Council of Ministers (premier), Aleksei N. Kosygin.

Domestic Affairs. The central event of 1971 was the 24th congress of the Soviet Communist Party, which met in Moscow in April. It was a relatively uneventful gathering, and consolidation was its principal theme. The main issues dealt with economic policy, emphasizing centralized control, more efficient labour discipline, and technological progress. The congress also approved the strengthening of party control, through "grass roots" party units, over "institutes engaged in scientific research, educational establishments, and establishments engaged in cultural and enlightenment work and in medical care." This decision occurred against the background of criticisms of the Soviet system made by some scientists, who showed remarkable solidarity on those occasions when the authorities decided to stifle particularly irritating criticism.

The most prominent scientist, Andrei Sakharov, known for the controversial Sakharov Memorandum published in 1968 and for helping to found the Soviet Committee for Human Rights in November 1970, took up the cudgel on behalf of Soviet Jews. At the end of 1970 Sakharov appealed to President Podgorny for clemency on behalf of the two Jews sentenced to death in the Leningrad hijack trial; in March 1971

New Soviet research ship "Academician Sergei Korolev," the largest scientific ship in the Soviet expedition fleet, made its first voyage in 1971. The ship's radar is capable of tracking space satellites.

he wrote to the Ministry of Internal Affairs protesting violations of human rights in the case of several Jews arrested during a demonstration at the office of the chief prosecutor; and in May he joined with other members of the Soviet civil rights movement in addressing an appeal to the Supreme Soviet criticizing the persecution of Soviet Jews and the authorities' reluctance to issue exit permits to those wishing to emigrate to Israel.

The Soviet authorities were well aware that the Jews presented them with a special problem. Many Soviet Jews felt a greater loyalty to Israel than to the U.S.S.R., whose anti-Semitic tendencies they could not forget. For some, emigration to Israel was mainly a means of escaping to the West. The Soviet authorities found it difficult to admit that there were large numbers of people within their system who openly stated their preference for living outside it. The possible effect on Arab opinion of large-scale emigration from the Soviet Union to Israel also had to be considered, yet repression did not seem the answer either, partly because Soviet society had become less tolerant of it since Stalin's death and partly because of Soviet concern for world public opinion, a taste of which Premier Kosygin faced during his visit to Canada in October. He explained there that the Soviet government had to draw the line at allowing Jews who had recently received an expensive education to take their skills to Israel. Nevertheless, the Soviet authorities, from time to time, granted exit permits, usually to the most persistent would-be emigrants, in the hope of defusing the protest movement. Throughout 1971 there was some increase in the number of elderly Jews allowed to leave, notably from the Georgian S.S.R. Yet the problem could not be solved as long as the Soviet state continued to restrict the free movement of its citizens. (See *Foreign Policy*, below.)

In a sense, Soviet scientists occupied a privileged position since the regime could not do without them. Other intellectuals were less fortunate. The fifth Soviet Writers' Congress, which took place in June 1971, illustrated the ascendancy of conformist views in literature. The secretary of the Writers' Union, Georgi Markov, devoted a considerable part of his keynote address to the role of the Russian language in unifying the various nationalities of the U.S.S.R.; he produced all the old slogans about the proper function of literature as serving the aims of the party. Dissenters and critics of the system were dismissed by Markov as "a few dyed-in-the-wool idlers," who would have to face the consequences of "their parasitic way of life." Ironically, the death on December 18 of Aleksandr T. Tvardovski (*see* OBITUARIES), former editor of *Novy Mir,* was the occasion for public grief

Unemployment:
see Employment, Wages, and Hours; Social Services

UNESCO:
see United Nations

WIDE WORLD

Mrs. Nikita Khrushchev pays her last respects to her husband during graveside services in Moscow on Sept. 13, 1971.

Grishin, the secretary of the Moscow city party organization; Dinmukhammed Kunayev, the first secretary of the Communist Party in Kazakhstan; Fyodor Kulakov, the party secretary responsible for agriculture; and Vladimir Shcherbitsky, the chairman of the Ukrainian Council of Ministers. In the powerful Central Committee, which was elected by the congress, 44.5% of the membership (107 out of 241) were party officials; the party retained a firm grip on the direction of affairs and Brezhnev enjoyed its confidence.

The evolution of the power game in the U.S.S.R., from the revolutionary élan of Lenin's day through the crude simplicities of Stalin and the uncertainties of the collective leadership to the current situation, was recalled by the death of Nikita S. Khrushchev in September 1971, which passed almost unnoticed in his own country (*see* OBITUARIES). Khrushchev's very real achievements were obscured by some failures and by his eccentric style of public behaviour. But the collapse of his agricultural reforms, the failure of economic reorganization, and the inglorious outcome of the Cuban missile adventure must be set against the diminution of the Stalinist practice of government by fear. Khrushchev and his successors, who in this respect followed his lead, may have committed blunders and acts of repression in Eastern Europe and in the Soviet Union itself, but under Khrushchev the party did succeed in placing some limits on the powers of the political police.

The Economy. The ninth five-year plan for the period 1971–75 was published in February 1971. It made some concession to the consumer by targeting an increase of 44–48% in the production of consumer goods as against an increase of only 42–46% in gross industrial production overall. The growth rate of heavy industry was slightly reduced, thus giving light industry a somewhat higher priority.

Those economists who had hoped for a complete departure from the old overcentralized pattern of management were disappointed, but some of the ideas advocated by Yevsei G. Liberman of Kharkov University and others since 1965 seemed to have taken root. The main thesis of the reformers was that profit and profitability should be the principal yardstick in stimulating economic performance and determining its efficiency (although in February Liberman felt obliged to publish a paper rejecting the view that his proposals

among the Communist Party leadership. Tvardovski had been a nuisance to the government in sponsoring a number of "liberal" authors, in particular Aleksandr I. Solzhenitsyn (who made a rare public appearance to attend his friend's funeral). Almost the entire Soviet leadership signed a eulogizing obituary in *Pravda,* which, however, neglected to mention Tvardovski's long editorship of *Novy Mir.* On December 10 the Sakharov committee addressed an appeal to the Supreme Soviet to grant the release of the writer Andrei Amalrik, author of *Will the Soviet Union Survive Until 1984?* In 1970 Amalrik had been sentenced to three years' detention in a labour camp in the Soviet far east for having allowed his book to be published outside the U.S.S.R. He was believed to be seriously ill.

The supremacy of the party in the Soviet power structure covered more than control over official literary establishments. At the 24th party congress, Leonid I. Brezhnev (*see* BIOGRAPHY) emerged as the most powerful man in the Soviet Union, thus confirming yet again the importance of the position at the head of the party. Four new members were added to the Politburo—all of them Brezhnev supporters: Viktor

U.S.S.R.

Education. (1968–69) Primary, pupils 40,310,-000; secondary, pupils 4,440,000; primary and secondary, teachers 1,782,000; vocational and teacher training, pupils 4,261,500, teachers (1965–66) 251,000; higher (including 105 universities), students 4,469,700, teaching staff (1965–66) 201,000.

Finance. Monetary unit: ruble, with an official exchange rate of 0.90 ruble to U.S. $1 (at Sept. 27, 1971, 2.20 rubles = £1 sterling). Budget (1970 est.): revenue 153.9 billion rubles; expenditure 152.3 billion rubles.

Foreign Trade. (1969) Imports 9,294,000,000 rubles; exports 10,490,000,000 rubles. Import sources: Sino-Soviet area 65% (East Germany 16%, Poland 11%, Czechoslovakia 11%, Bulgaria 9%, Hungary 7%). Export destinations: Sino-Soviet area 66% (East Germany 15%, Poland 10%, Czechoslovakia 10%, Bulgaria 8%, Hungary 6%, Cuba 5%). Main exports: machinery 23%; iron and steel 10%; crude oil 7%; timber 6%; nonferrous metals 5%.

Transport and Communications. Roads (1967) 1,368,400 km. (including 483,200 km. surfaced roads in 1969). Motor vehicles in use (1965): passenger *c.* 1.1 million; commercial *c.*

4.5 million. Railways (1969): 134,600 km. (including 32,400 km. electrified); traffic 261,283,-000,000 passenger-km., freight (1970) 2,480,-000,000,000 net ton-km. Air traffic (1969): 71,500,000,000 passenger-km.; freight 1,950,-000,000 net ton-km. Navigable inland waterways (1969) 144,800 km.; traffic 160,100,000,000 ton-km. Shipping (1970): merchant vessels 100 gross tons and over 5,924; gross tonnage 14,831,-775. Telephones (Dec. 1969) 12 million. Radio receivers (Dec. 1969) 90.1 million. Television receivers (Dec. 1969) 30,744,000.

Agriculture. Production (in 000; metric tons; 1970; 1969 in parentheses): wheat 99,500 (79,-917); barley 38,100 (32,652); oats 14,100 (13,-090); rye *c.* 13,000 (10,945); corn 9,400 (11,-954); rice 1,280 (1,107); millet 2,090 (3,289); potatoes 96,551 (91,779); sugar, raw value (1970–71) *c.* 9,293, (1969–70) *c.* 8,853; sunflower seed 6,073 (6,358); linseed *c.* 525 (344); dry peas *c.* 4,730 (*c.* 5,130); soybeans *c.* 598 (434); tea 67 (60); wine 2,700 (2,402); cotton, lint *c.* 2,310 (1,915); flax fibre 442 (487); tobacco *c.* 260 (*c.* 250); wool 349 (234); eggs *c.* 2,222 (*c.* 2,038); meat 9,013 (8,550); milk 82,900 (81,500); butter 1,067 (1,065); cheese

c. 530 (*c.* 500); timber (cu.m.; 1968) *c.* 380,000, (1967) *c.* 383,000; fish catch (1969) 6,498, (1968) 6,082. Livestock (in 000; Jan. 1970): cattle 95,000; pigs 56,100; sheep 130,665; goats 5,148; horses 7,522; poultry 565,700.

Industry. Index of production (1963 = 100): (1970) 175; (1969) 162. Fuel and power (in 000; metric tons; 1970): coal and lignite 624,-000; crude oil 352,667; natural gas (cu.m.) 199,485,000; electricity (kw.-hr.) 754,000,000. Production (in 000; metric tons; 1970): cement 95,233; iron ore (60% metal content) 196,000; pig iron 85,925; steel 115,863; aluminum (1969) *c.* 1,100; copper (1969) *c.* 1,020; lead (1969) *c.* 440; zinc (1969) *c.* 610; gold (troy oz.; 1969) 6,250; silver (troy oz.; 1969) *c.* 37,000; manganese ore (metal content; 1969) 2,386; tungsten concentrates (oxide content; 1969) 8.2; magnesite (1968) *c.* 3,000; sulfuric acid 12,055; caustic soda 1,938; plastics and resins 1,672; mineral fertilizers 55,400; newsprint (1969) 1,051; other paper (1969) 5,234; passenger cars (units) 344; commercial vehicles (units) 526; cotton fabrics (sq.m.) 6,148,000; woolen fabrics (sq.m.) 644,000; rayon and synthetic fabrics (sq.m.) 1,146,000.

should ever have been regarded as an attack on the primacy of centralized planning). At the beginning of 1971 more than 44,000 industrial enterprises, accounting for 95% of profits in industry, had gone over to the new method of planning and management based to some extent on Liberman's ideas.

In the agricultural sector, the ninth plan foresaw an annual average grain harvest of 195 million tons as against an annual average of 163 million tons in the period 1966–69. Massive investments in farming were intended to bring about a growth in labour productivity of 21% for state farms and 39% for collective farms, and this was expected to lead to a 12% reduction in the agricultural labour force. (In 1971 about 33% of the total Soviet labour force worked in agriculture, compared with 6% in the U.S.). These trends in agricultural planning were related to the comparatively poor results achieved in the eighth five-year plan, and although the record harvest of 1970 helped to redress the statistical balance, agricultural gross output in the years 1966–70 rose by only 21% instead of the 25% originally laid down.

Despite the difficulties experienced in agriculture, the economic outlook in 1971 did not cause undue concern. The increase in productivity (an annual average of 4.5% in recent years) seemed to be keeping pace with the West, and the forecast that real wages would go up by 31% in the period of the ninth plan appeared to be reasonably realistic. For the immediate future it appeared that steps were being taken to reduce the pressures that defense expenditure had exerted for so long on the Soviet economy. The significance of the strategic arms limitation talks (SALT) in this context was evident. (*See* DEFENSE.)

The draft of the budget for 1972 presented to the Supreme Soviet on November 24 by Finance Minister Vasily Garbuzov stressed that the allocation for defense was the same as in 1971, although as the overall budget was to rise, only 10.3% of all budget appropriations for 1972 were to go for defense, compared with 11.1% in 1971. Garbuzov was reporting only on declared defense expenditure, which did not include items such as space development concealed in the budget appropriations of other sectors. The 1972 budget forecast revenues totaling 173.7 billion rubles and expenditures totaling 173.5 billion rubles. Higher rates of development in the manufacture of consumer goods and of sectors exercising a special impact on the acceleration of technological projects were provided for in the budget. The minimum monthly wage was to be raised to 70 rubles, and additional incentives were to be provided for workers in distant parts of the country—the north, the far east, the Urals, and Siberia. Incomes of teachers and doctors were to be raised, and student and postgraduate grants increased.

The initial stages of the latest plan period had gone well. An increase of 3% in the number of employed was reported for the first half of 1971, bringing the labour force in industry and management to 91.3 million. Some of the wage increases forecast in the plan directives had been partially implemented—from July 1 wages in the railways were raised, and pay for workers in agriculture and the income of collective farmers also had increased. Minimum old-age and disability pensions also were raised. In the first six months of 1971 the turnover of state and cooperative retail trade rose by 7%, but the official report issued by the Central Statistical Board admitted that much remained to be done in order to satisfy consumer demands.

Consumer satisfaction was one of the party's main preoccupations, and a special decree published on October 29 again called for a rapid increase in the output of consumer goods; it promised that, by comparison with 1970, production of goods in "mass demand" would go up by 90% during the ninth plan. On November 24 Premier Kosygin informed the Supreme Soviet that it had been decided to raise the growth rate of consumer goods production in the plan to 49%, compared with the 44–48% of the original directive. Kosygin's claim that by 1975 the Soviet Union's industrial and agricultural output would outstrip 1971 U.S. levels had projected the U.S.S.R. back into the national economic race with the U.S. that had been so close to Khrushchev's heart. The U.S. secretary of commerce was present at the Supreme Soviet session during Kosygin's address, which also included a call for a reduction of U.S. trade barriers to facilitate the extension of U.S.-Soviet trade relations.

The basic difficulties confronting Soviet industry stemmed from lack of technological progress. A government decree issued in June aimed to accelerate such progress by encouraging enterprises that introduced new and better goods by means of new and more flexible bonus schemes. The authorities also had recourse to the "socialist competition" system, which had failed to produce any worthwhile results more than 20 years previously: a decree issued by the Soviet Communist Party's Central Committee on September 4 spoke of the continuation of "material and moral stimuli" provided by socialist competition. The real problem was that material incentives only served to increase consumer demand, and thus added to the problem.

Foreign Policy. Soviet diplomacy was active, particularly in the second half of the year, although most of the activity seemed to have been designed to underpin the precarious stability of the international political system in areas where this would serve the Soviet national interest. The most urgent target remained the convening of a European security conference, which had been high on the Soviet list of priorities since 1966. The environment for such a conference depended on the status of East Germany, the settlement of the Berlin issue, and the ratification of West Germany's treaties with the Soviet Union and Poland, concluded in 1970. With the signature of the first stage of the four-power agreement on Berlin in September 1971, and the subsequent agreement between the East Germans and the West Berlin Senate, the climate became favourable. During Brezhnev's visit to Paris at the end of October, French Pres. Georges Pompidou agreed that a preparatory meeting for a European security conference should be called in Helsinki as soon as possible. At the end of November, Walter Scheel, the West German foreign minister, went to Moscow to discuss the timing of the preparations.

Brezhnev's visit to Paris was perhaps the most interesting of the many diplomatic journeys undertaken by Soviet leaders during 1971, mainly because Pompidou, although ready to support moves for a European security conference, made it quite clear that a formal Franco-Soviet friendship treaty was not under consideration. However, the U.S.S.R. did get an agreement under which the Renault company was to supply machinery and services worth about $230 million for the construction of a large truck plant on the Kama River in the Urals. A more general ten-year agreement on economic and technical cooperation between the U.S.S.R. and France was also signed.

Eduard Kuznetsov was one of two Soviet Jews convicted of treason in a Leningrad hijack trial. His death sentence was reduced to 15 years in a labour camp by the Supreme Court of the U.S.S.R. on Dec. 30, 1970.
WIDE WORLD

continued on page 704

1970 SOVIET CENSUS RESULTS

By Vadim V. Pokshishevski

A general population census was conducted in the U.S.S.R. on Jan. 15, 1970. According to precise data published on April 17, 1971, the number of inhabitants of the Soviet Union at the time of the census was 241,720,134, including approximately 111.4 million men and 130.3 million women. A later assessment of the U.S.S.R. Central Statistical Board on July 1, 1971, was 242.8 million.

Population growth in pre-Revolutionary Russia and the U.S.S.R. is expressed in Table I. These figures reflect the considerable manpower losses suffered in the two world wars. The losses were especially great in World War II. The direct losses alone exceeded 20 million; with the addition of indirect losses—the drop in births during the war years and the increased mortality as a consequence of lower living standards—the overall manpower losses caused by World War II exceeded 50 million (*Nauka i zhizn* ["Science and Life"] no. 3, 1967).

In the five years preceding the 1970 census the natural growth of population in the U.S.S.R. averaged about 1% a year (17.6 births and 7.6 deaths per 1,000 population). As in all highly developed countries, there was a tendency for this growth to decline; in 1969 it was 0.89% with 17 births and 8.1 deaths per 1,000 population. The dynamics of natural growth also must be viewed in relation to the losses of the war years. During the war the birthrate naturally fell, and the generation born in the war years and now of marriageable age is relatively small. As this generation passes into the older age groups, an increase in the birthrate can be expected.

The deformations of the age pyramid and the disproportion in the sex composition of the population are represented in Table II. Among persons 44 years of age and over there are only 547 men for every 1,000 women. The shortfall in births, reducing the size of the generation born in the war years, is seen in the fact that in 1970 the number of children up to four years of age was only 20.5 million, compared with 24.3 million in the previous census of 1959.

The relation between the age groups also shows the manpower potential of the U.S.S.R. According to the 1970 census there were 130.5 million people (54% of the total population) of so-called working age (16–59 years for men and 16–54 years for women; in the U.S.S.R. men are entitled to state pensions at the age of 60 and women at the age of 55). Of these, 120.6 million persons (92.4% of those of working age) were employed or were studying full-time. In addition, of the 40.1 million pensioners in the U.S.S.R. in 1970, 7 million were in fact working.

In 1970 the urban population of the U.S.S.R. totaled 136 million (56%) and the rural population 105.7 million (44%). The urban population surpassed the rural population in 1961. In the latest period between censuses (1959–70), the U.S.S.R.'s urban population grew by 36 million, more than the present population of Poland or Spain. Of this, 14.6 million was accounted for by natural growth, 5 million by granting rural centres of habitation the rights of towns or urban-type settlements, and over 16 million by influx from rural areas. Table III illustrates the distribution of urban population in 1970.

There were ten cities in the U.S.S.R. with a population of more than one million: Moscow (7.1 million); Leningrad (4 million); Kiev (1.6 million); Tashkent (1.4 million); Baku (1.3 million); Kharkov, Gorki, and Novosibirsk (1.2 million); and Kuybyshev and Sverdlovsk (1 million). There were 23 towns with a population of over 500,000. According to the 1959 census there were only three cities with over a million population (Moscow, Leningrad, and Kiev) and 22 cities with a population of over 500,000. In 1970 there were 188 towns with a population of 100,000–500,000 inhabitants, compared with 123 in 1959. The total number of urban settlements (towns and urban-type settlements) rose from 4,619 to 5,504 during 1959–70.

Table I. Selected Population Figures*

1897†	124,600,000	1950	178,500,000
1913	159,200,000	1959†	208,800,000
1940	194,100,000	1970†	241,700,000

*Data adjusted with reference to present U.S.S.R. boundaries.
†Census (other figures are estimates). The 1897 census was the sole general census conducted in the old Russian Empire before the 1917 Revolution. Censuses were also held in 1920 (partial, because of continuing Civil War), 1926, and 1939.

Table II. Age and Sex Breakdown of the 1970 U.S.S.R. Census

Age group	Men In 000	Women In 000	Comment
Total population	111,399	130,321	An "age zone" with a certain preponderance of males. In the U.S.S.R., as in most countries, 106 boys are born for every 100 girls
0–4 years	10,435	10,075	
5–9 years	12,475	12,001	
10–15 years	15,145	14,579	
16–19 years	8,810	8,453	
20–24 years	8,627	8,478	In this "age zone" the numbers of males and females are about equal
25–29 years	6,813	6,957	
30–34 years	10,408	10,737	
35–39 years	8,140	8,454	
40–44 years	8,759	10,244	The disproportion in the sexes is directly linked with losses of men in World War II
45–49 years	4,744	7,512	
50–54 years	3,430	5,648	
55–59 years	4,273	7,740	
60–69 years	5,922	11,673	A powerful factor contributing to these male losses is their higher mortality in older age groups
70 years and over	3,288	7,631	

Table III. Urban Distribution of Population in 1970

Towns with a population of over 1,000,000	20,900,000 (15.3%)
300,000–1,000,000	30,700,000 (22.7%)
100,000–300,000	24,000,000 (17.6%)
50,000–100,000	13,000,000 (9.6%)
Urban settlements (towns and urban-type localities) with a population of 20,000–50,000	18,500,000 (13.6%)
Urban settlements with fewer than 20,000	28,900,000 (21.2%)

Table IV. Ethnic Distribution Within the U.S.S.R.

Nationality	Number in 000	Percentage of total U.S.S.R. population	Percentage within own national republic	Percentage of nationality living in their own national republic*
Russians	129,015	53.4	82.8	83.5
Ukrainians	40,753	16.9	74.9	87
Uzbeks	9,195	3.8	64.7	84.1
Belorussians	9,052	3.7	81	80.5
Kazakhs	5,299	2.2	32.4	78.5
Azerbaijanis	4,380	1.8	73.8	86.2
Armenians	3,559	1.5	88.6	62
Georgians	3,245	1.3	66.8	96.5
Moldavians	2,698	1.1	64.6	85.4
Lithuanians	2,665	1.1	80.1	94.1
Tadzhiks	2,136	0.9	56.2	76.3
Turkmens	1,525	0.6	65.6	92.9
Kirgiz	1,452	0.6	43.8	88.5
Latvians	1,430	0.6	56.8	93.8
Estonians	1,007	0.4	68.2	91.9

*Percentage of the numbers living in the U.S.S.R. This qualification is important for the Tadzhiks, Armenians, Turkmens, and others who have ethnic settlements in other localities.

Vadim V. Pokshishevski is a senior scientific worker of the Institute of Ethnography of the U.S.S.R. Academy of Sciences. He holds the title doctor of geographical sciences and is the author of Population of the U.S.S.R. *and* Geography and Population of Foreign Countries.

The Soviet Union is a multinational state, embracing 15 union republics, 20 autonomous republics, 8 autonomous regions, and 10 national districts. The main nations constituting the union republics comprise nine-tenths of the total population. Table IV illustrates their number, the proportion of each in the country's population, and indices of the compactness of their ethnic areas.

A comparison of columns 4 and 5 is instructive. Column 4 shows that in two instances (the Kazakhs and Kirgiz) the basic nationality of the union republic does not have an absolute majority in it, and in a further seven instances the basic nationality constitutes only 50–70% of the union republic population. In column 5 the figures, as a rule, are much higher; in the case of five nationalities, more than 90% live within the relevant union republic; in the case of seven others, the figure is between 80 and 90%. The Armenians seem to be an exception. The historical destinies of the Armenian people, who were subjected to severe repression by Turkey and Persia, led to the resettlement of considerable masses of Armenian refugees throughout Transcaucasia and even in the Russian Soviet Federated Socialist Republic. The first line of the table shows that 16.5% of the Russian citizens of the U.S.S.R. live outside the R.S.F.S.R. In absolute figures this constitutes 21.3 million people, of whom 9.1 million live in the Ukraine and 5.5 million in Kazakhstan.

There are substantial differences in the natural growth of the population in various parts of the U.S.S.R., reflecting, basically, differences in the birthrate, since the death rate in the U.S.S.R. varies insignificantly from one area to another. These differences show the effect of urbanization, peculiarities of the age structure (rapidly developing regions, which have a considerable influx of population, are on the whole much "younger" than the regions from which the settlers come), and the customs and morals of the different nationalities. While the average growth in 1969 was 0.89%, in Latvia, for instance, it was only 0.29% and in Estonia, 0.42%. In Central Asia, on the other hand, it exceeded 2% (2.86% in Tadzhikistan, 2.73% in Turkmenia). In the R.S.F.S.R. the average growth was 0.57%.

In Table V population changes of 23 nationalities of the U.S.S.R. are shown according to all the censuses. For a portion of them this can be done only according to the two post-World War II censuses; it should also be noted that the census of 1897 is not entirely reliable, as it did not thoroughly examine the question of nationality, which was determined according to a person's mother tongue.

The average growth of the total population in the U.S.S.R. during 1959–70 was 15.8%. In the sixth column of Table V, italic figures indicate those nationalities whose growth during 1959–70 was at least double the average, and boldface figures indicate those whose growth was more than three times the average. Underlined figures indicate nationalities whose numbers fell. The explanation of this comparatively rare occurrence lies in the continuance of assimilation.

One of the signs of this assimilation may be considered to be the loss of the use of the mother tongue. In 1970, 141.8 million people named Russian as their mother tongue. Since the census listed 129 million Russians in the U.S.S.R., presumably Russian has become the mother tongue for about 13 million "non-Russians." Apart from this, almost 42 million more non-Russians named Russian as their second language. Thus Russian is the basis for direct cultural communication among more than 180 million Soviet people, or three-quarters of the country's population.

The percentage who in 1970 named the language of their nationality as their mother tongue is as follows (figures for 1959 in parentheses): Jews 16.3% (17.7%), Morduates 77.8% (78.1%), Poles 32.5% (45.2%). Although the Morduates have their own autonomous Soviet socialist republic, their ethnic area has been eroded to a pronounced degree since 1959, when they constituted only 35.8% of the population of the Mordvinian A.S.S.R., while less than 28% of the total Mordvinian population was concentrated in this autonomous republic. For similar reasons of assimilation the 1970 census showed a reduction in the numbers of Karelians (from 167,000 to 146,000), only 63% of them (as against 71.3% in 1959) considering the language of their nationality to be their mother tongue.

The group of nations with an extremely high level of natural growth includes the peoples of Central Asia and the Azerbaijanis, followed by the Kazakhs and most of the nations of the Northern Caucasus included in the survey. All these nations live predominantly in the southern belt of the U.S.S.R., and most belong to the Turkic language group (an exception are the Tadzhiks, who belong to the Persian language group). Among this whole cultural ring of peoples, early marriages and great love of children are firmly established traditions; in the past these traditions were reinforced by Islam, which dominated in Central Asia, Kazakhstan, and among the greater part of the Caucasian peoples. However, the heightened level of natural growth among these nations is a comparatively recent phenomenon. Mortality here was previously much higher than in the central regions of the country or in the Ukraine, so that, even though the birthrate was also higher, growth was held back.

Table V. Numbers of Nationalities Exceeding One Million in 1970
(in 000)

Nationality	1897*	1926	1939	1959	1970	Comment
Russians	54,564	77,043	100,392	114,114	129,015	
Ukrainians	(Territory not comparable)			37,253	40,753	The 1897 census did not include Khiva and Bukhara.
Uzbeks	—	3,904	4,844	6,015	**9,195**	
Belorussians	3,571	(Territory not comparable)		7,913	9,052	
Tatars	} 3,679	2,916	4,300	4,968	5,931	In 1926 kindred Karakalpaks, Turkmens, and Uzbeks were counted as Kazakhs.
Azerbaijanis		1,706	2,275	2,940	**4,380**	
Kazakhs	} 4,286	3,960	3,099	3,622	5,299	
Kirgiz		769	884	969	1,452	
Armenians	1,065	1,568	2,152	2,787	3,559	Repatriation has added about 200,000 since 1920.
Georgians	1,329	1,821	2,249	2,692	3,245	
Moldavians	(Territory not comparable)			2,214	2,698	
Lithuanians†	—	—	—	2,326	2,665	
Jews‡	(2,436)	(2,673)	(3,020)	2,268	2,151	
Tadzhiks	—	979	1,229	1,397	2,136	The 1897 census did not include the Tadzhiks of Bukhara, i.e., the present territory of Tadzhikistan.
Germans	—	—	—	1,620	1,846	
Chuvash	840	1,117	1,368	1,470	1,694	
Turkmens	—	676	812	1,002	**1,525**	In 1897 the Turkmens living in Khiva were not counted.
Latvians†	—	—	—	1,400	1,430	
Peoples of Dagestan	(Were not brought together in published figures)		857	945	1,365	
Mordvins	1,021	1,340	1,451	1,285	1,263	
Bashkirs	1,492	983	843	989	1,240	
Poles	(Territory not comparable)			1,380	1,167	
Estonians†	—	—	—	989	1,007	

*On the territory within the 1926 borders (adjustments made by the U.S.S.R. Central Statistical Board on publishing the results of the 1926 census).
†Lithuania between 1919 and 1940, and Latvia and Estonia between 1918 and 1940, were independent of the U.S.S.R.
‡Territory not fully comparable (Jews living in lands comprising part of Austria-Hungary and later bourgeois Poland are not included). A further calculation by the U.S.S.R. Central Statistical Board in 1939 (count of the population of western territories that became part of the U.S.S.R. after the census of that year) fixed the number of Jews as 4.6 million.

continued from page 701

From Paris, Brezhnev went to East Berlin, and soon after his visit there was marked progress in the Berlin negotiations between the East Germans and the West Berlin Senate. A visit to Moscow in November of a Polish delegation, led by First Secretary Edward Gierek, produced a communiqué that stressed the great importance of the early ratification of the treaties concluded in 1970 by the U.S.S.R. and Poland with West Germany. Brezhnev repeated this demand in his speech to the Polish party congress in December. Soviet relations with the new Polish leadership, which had taken power at the end of 1970, had developed without difficulties, despite the refurbished economic policies put into effect in Poland; in February 1971 the U.S.S.R. granted the Poles economic aid to the tune of $500 million. An agreement projecting an increase of 12% in trade with Czechoslovakia was concluded in November, and the Soviet leadership appeared to be content with the policies pursued by Gustav Husak in Prague. Brezhnev's journeys in the fall also included a visit to Belgrade, where he was given a cordial reception by President Tito, and there were no signs that the Soviets had tried to exploit the internal differences that were troubling Yugoslavia.

Kosygin's visit to Canada was disturbed by protests against the treatment of Jews in the U.S.S.R. and by a young Hungarian refugee who assaulted him physically in Ottawa. He was less troubled in Cuba and Scandinavia. Great Britain was the least-liked Western country in the U.S.S.R. in 1971, following the expulsion of 105 Soviet officials from Britain. The British government had decided to cut about one-fifth of the total number of accredited Soviet officials in the U.K. to curb the extent and scope of Soviet espionage. (*See* INTELLIGENCE OPERATIONS.)

In the Middle East, the U.S.S.R. continued to give general support to the Arab cause, although some Arab governments, notably Libya, criticized Soviet support for India in its war with Pakistan in December. In May a new treaty between the U.S.S.R. and Egypt was signed, recording Soviet approval of Pres. Anwar as-Sadat's regime almost immediately after the elimination of Ali Sabry, who had been regarded as Moscow's special contact in Cairo. The treaty placed great emphasis on mutual consultation, and this was understandable in the light of Egypt's military dependence on the Soviet Union. Toward the end of the year there were indications that Moscow was seeking to reestablish a diplomatic link with Israel in return for a more liberal policy with regard to Jewish emigration. Relations had been broken off after the Six-Day War in 1967; their renewal would permit the Soviet Union to talk to both sides in the Arab-Israeli dispute and so enhance its influence as a Mediterranean power.

Elsewhere in the Middle East, the U.S.S.R. watched helplessly in July while the Sudanese government carried out the destruction and liquidation of the Communists who had supported an abortive coup against the regime of Gen. Gaafar Nimeiry. *Pravda* and other Soviet newspapers carried reports of worldwide protests against the mass arrests and executions of Communist leaders, but the Soviet government remained relatively cool, obviously pursuing its established policy of ideological flexibility in Arab affairs.

Asia provided Moscow's major foreign policy preoccupations in 1971. The dramatic rapprochement between the U.S. and China created a new dimension to the U.S.S.R.'s role in Asia, and the initial Soviet reaction was almost hysterical, expressing itself in ac-

cusations charging the Romanians with organizing an anti-Soviet bloc under Chinese and U.S. patronage. Romania's rejection of the Soviet note containing these accusations was quite unambiguous and was unanimously endorsed by the Romanian Communist Party's Central Committee when it met in August. The Soviet friendship treaty with India was perhaps a more rational reaction, and when it was signed in August the Bangla Desh crisis and its bellicose solution were still some months away. When the India-Pakistan conflict broke out, the U.S.S.R. found itself aligned with India against Pakistan, while China gave some political backing to the other side. In the UN the U.S.S.R. was able to frustrate all attempts to force a cease-fire resolution through the Security Council, and Indian Prime Minister Indira Gandhi's visit to Moscow at the end of September obviously had been useful in strengthening the relationship between India and the Soviet Union. India's military victory against Pakistan, achieved with Soviet diplomatic support and in the teeth of U.S. and Chinese diplomatic opposition, undoubtedly strengthened the position of the U.S.S.R. in Southeast Asia.

Soviet foreign policy was faced with a new pattern of power relations by the U.S. initiative vis-à-vis China. Although they had not really come to terms with this spectacular development, Brezhnev and his colleagues in the Politburo did pursue fairly consistent policies throughout the world—they moved toward the strengthening of the territorial status quo in Europe; they managed to keep the Eastern European situation in a reasonably stable condition; they maintained the Soviet Union's influence in the Middle East; they became the paramount external influence in the Indian subcontinent; and they asserted the global range of the Soviet Union's interests as a world power by challenging U.S. naval power in the Mediterranean, by deploying Soviet naval capability over a wider area, and by establishing diplomatic contacts with many countries at the highest level. At the same time, they were negotiating for a limitation of the cripplingly expensive and dangerous arsenals of the nuclear superpowers, while maintaining their ability to face any nuclear challenge.

When the Central Committee of the Soviet Communist Party met at the end of November, it devoted a major part of the session to a discussion of foreign affairs. It approved the Politburo's policy "in its entirety and with complete unanimity." The Central Committee's resolution took great pride in the economic, political, and military power of the Soviet Union, and it adopted a hard line in ideological terms by stressing the importance of the "ideological struggle against all the enemies of Marxism-Leninism." The Central Committee approved the "practical and constructive steps taken by the Politburo to liquidate the dangerous imperialist aggressions in Indochina and the Middle East, to assist in the peaceful solution of the conflict in the Indian subcontinent and to strengthen peace and security in Asia." On China the Central Committee showed some reluctance to engage in polemics, but, turning to Europe, the resolution was full of praise for the progress made toward "a solution of the central problem of contemporary international relations—the safeguarding of the relaxation of tension in Europe and the practical application of the principles of peaceful coexistence and . . . cooperation among all European states."   (OT. P.)

See also Communist Movement; Propaganda.

ENCYCLOPÆDIA BRITANNICA FILMS. *The Soviet Union: Epic Land* (1971).

First completed section of the Novovoronezh atomic power station was rated at 575,000 kw. Construction on a second section rated at 880,000 kw. was under way in 1971.
LONDON "DAILY EXPRESS"—PICTORIAL PARADE

Unions:
see Labour Unions
Unitarians:
see Religion

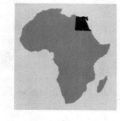

United Arab Republic (Egypt)

A republic of northeast Africa, Egypt is bounded by Israel, Sudan, Libya, the Mediterranean Sea, and the Red Sea. Area: 386,900 sq.mi. (1,002,000 sq.km.). Pop. (1970 est.): 34 million. Cap. and largest city: Cairo (pop., 1970 est., 4,961,000). Language: Arabic 97%. Religion: Muslim 91%; Christian 8%. President in 1971, Anwar as-Sadat; prime minister, Mahmoud Fawzi.

In 1971 the United Arab Republic entered into a federation with Libya and Syria and changed its name to the Arab Republic of Egypt. The government pursued its broad diplomatic offensive with some success, but the stalemate with Israel continued and there was little progress toward a settlement. At home the year was marked by a major upheaval in the regime from which President Sadat (see BIOGRAPHY) emerged in a strengthened position.

On February 4 President Sadat agreed to a 30-day extension of the cease-fire with Israel. He declared his readiness to reopen the Suez Canal if Israeli forces were to pull back. Egyptian sources said that the canal could be cleared of obstructions in four months. On February 17 the authoritative Cairo newspaper *Al Ahram* said that Egypt had told UN envoy Gunnar V. Jarring it would sign a formal peace treaty with Israel once all the provisions of UN Security Council Resolution 242 had been carried out, but Sadat insisted that Egypt would not sign any separate peace with Israel. When the 30-day cease-fire extension ended on March 7 Sadat refused to extend it but added "this does not mean that political action will stop and that guns will start shooting." In April Western sources reported heavy additional Soviet arms deliveries to Egypt, including MiG-23 aircraft and SAM-4 and SAM-6 ground-to-air missiles.

Although Egyptian spokesmen repeatedly accused the U.S. of continued support of Israel, diplomatic contacts between the two countries continued throughout the year and U.S. Secretary of State William Rogers visited Egypt May 4–6. The Egyptian response to U.S. efforts to secure an interim Arab-Israeli settlement through the reopening of the Suez Canal was that it must be a first stage toward a complete Israeli withdrawal and that Egyptian forces

must be allowed to cross the canal. In a speech to front-line troops in November, after a summer of diplomatic deadlock, Sadat expressed total disillusionment with U.S. mediation efforts and told his men "our decision is to fight." At the same time a delegation of the presidents of Senegal, Cameroon, and Congo (Kinshasa) and Maj. Gen. Yakubu Gowon of Nigeria, representing the Organization of African Unity, visited Cairo to try to overcome the deadlock in negotiations with Israel.

On April 17 Sadat agreed in Benghazi to the formation of a Syrian-Libyan-Egyptian federation. Although the form of the projected federation was modified in response to criticisms within the Arab Socialist Union (ASU), Sadat dismissed Vice-Pres. Ali Sabry, who had led the opposition, on May 2. Since Sabry was considered the most pro-Soviet member of the regime, his dismissal was widely regarded as a move against the left. On May 13 it was announced that Sadat had accepted the resignation of a score of ministers and senior officials, including the deputy prime minister and interior minister, Sharawi Gomaa, the minister of war, Gen. Muhammad Fawzi, and the minister for presidential affairs, Sami Sharaf, who had resigned en bloc in a clear challenge to the president's authority. Sadat responded swiftly by forming a new government under Mahmoud Fawzi that included 12 new ministers—mostly young technocrats. He replaced General Fawzi with the former army chief of staff, Gen. Muhammad Sadiq, who had pledged the Army's loyalty to the regime, and dismissed 15 members of the National Assembly and several leading figures in the press and radio who were associated with the resigning ministers. Following an investigation of Sabry and of the resigning ministers and their associates, it was announced that 91 would be put on trial for conspiracy against the state.

Declaring that he would end all previous abuses of police power and introduce "freedom and democracy," Sadat announced on May 20 the reform, although not the abolition, of the ASU from top to bottom. He appointed a 100-member committee to supervise the reforms at all levels and also asked the National Assembly to draft a permanent constitution. Elections to all professional associations were held during the summer, followed on July 1 by elections in 5,720 ASU ten-member basic units throughout the country.

Governorate congresses met on July 17 and the ASU National Congress in Cairo on July 23 to discuss and approve the new permanent constitution drafted by the National Assembly. This defined the state as

After receiving assurance of Soviet support for the Arab cause on a visit to Moscow, Pres. Anwar as-Sadat announced that Egypt would no longer consider itself bound by the Suez Canal cease-fire.
WIDE WORLD

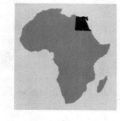

UNITED ARAB REPUBLIC (EGYPT)
Education. (1968–69) Primary, pupils 3,550,-462, teachers 88,237; secondary, pupils 1,051,-850, teachers 41,692; vocational, pupils 202,585, teachers 10,759; teacher training, students 29,-457, teachers 2,921; higher (including 6 universities), 174,614, teaching staff (1964–65) 10,406.
Finance. Monetary unit: Egyptian pound, with a nominal par value of E£0.35 to U.S. $1 (E£0.84 = £1 sterling), an official exchange rate of E£0.43 to U.S. $1 (E£1.04 = £1), and a free rate (Sept. 27, 1971) of c. E£1.08 to £1. Gold, SDRs, and foreign exchange, central bank: (June 1971) U.S. $124 million; (June 1970) U.S. $155 million. Budget (1970–71 est.) balanced at E£1,911 million. Gross national product: (1968–69) E£2,649 million; (1967–68) E£2,510 million. Money supply: (June 1971) E£774.8 million; (June 1970) E£760.9 million. Cost of living (Cairo; 1963 = 100): (Jan. 1971) 149; (Jan. 1970) 143.

Foreign Trade. (1970) Imports E£336.2 million; exports E£331.2 million. Import sources (1969): U.S.S.R. 14%; France 10%; U.S. 7%; West Germany 7%; Italy 6%; India 6%; Spain 5%. Export destinations (1969): U.S.S.R. 33%; India 5%; Czechoslovakia 5%. Main exports (1969): cotton 40%; rice 16%; cotton yarn 11%; cereals 10%; cotton fabrics 5%.
Transport and Communications. Roads (1969) c. 50,000 km. Motor vehicles in use (1969): passenger 121,800; commercial (including buses) 28,100. Railways: (1968) 4,940 km.; traffic (1968–69) 5,796,000,000 passenger-km., freight 2,670,000,000 net ton-km. Air traffic (1970): 1,009,900,000 passenger-km.; freight 17,-604,000 net ton-km. Shipping (1970): merchant vessels 100 gross tons and over 124; gross tonnage 238,282. Telephones (Dec. 1968) 365,000. Radio receivers (Dec. 1968) c. 4,275,000. Television receivers (Dec. 1969) 550,000.

Agriculture. Production (in 000; metric tons; 1970; 1969 in parentheses): corn 2,359 (2,366); wheat 1,516 (1,269); barley 83 (105); sorghum 874 (813); potatoes 522 (487); rice 2,605 (2,557); sugar, raw value (1970–71) c. 515, (1969–70) c. 491; tomatoes (1969) 1,547, (1968) 1,496; onions (1969) 585, (1968) 469; dry broad beans 277 (297); dates c. 355 (355); oranges c. 750 (717); lemons c. 70 (69); bananas (1969) 91, (1968) 86; grapes (1969) 104, (1968) 111; cotton, lint 509 (541); cheese c. 267 (c. 265). Livestock (in 000; 1969–70): cattle 1,760; sheep 1,968; goats c. 820; buffalo c. 1,800; asses 1,306; chickens c. 24,300.
Industry. Production (in 000; metric tons; 1970): crude oil 17,243; iron ore (metal content; 1969) 230; cement 3,686; phosphate rock (1969) 660; salt (1969) 385; asbestos (1968) 2.6; cotton, yarn 163; cotton fabrics (m.) 730,-000; electricity (kw-hr.; 1969) 7,316,000.

"democratic and socialist" with Islam as its religion. It gave strong powers to the president, who had the right to appoint vice-presidents and ministers and to dissolve the National Assembly. His term was for six years, but he could serve a second term. The constitution was approved by a 99.9% affirmative vote in a referendum on September 11 in which 98.3% of the electorate were reported to have voted. Three days before the referendum Sadat dissolved the assembly, and it was announced that elections for a new parliament, to be called the People's Assembly, would be held in October. The election took place on October 26, all candidates being members of the ASU, and the new assembly convened on November 11.

The trial of Ali Sabry and 90 others accused with him opened on August 25 before a special three-man court appointed by Sadat, but it was adjourned until September 4 after the defense lawyers had declared the court unconstitutional. In December Sabry and three others were given the death penalty, but Sadat reduced the sentences to life imprisonment.

The federation of Egypt, Libya, and Syria was formally proclaimed in Damascus on August 20 and approved in Egypt by a 99.9% favourable vote on September 1. On September 2 the country's name was changed from the United Arab Republic to the Arab Republic of Egypt. Libya and Syria agreed that Cairo should be the capital of the federation and Sadat the head of the three-man Presidential Council.

The dismissal of Ali Sabry caused concern to the Soviet Union, and Soviet Pres. Nikolai V. Podgorny visited Egypt at the head of an important delegation shortly afterward. Sadat apparently succeeded in reassuring the Soviet leaders, and on May 27 a 15-year Soviet-Egyptian treaty of friendship and cooperation was concluded. The Soviet government repeated promises to strengthen Egyptian defenses during Sadat's visit to Moscow October 11–14.

During 1971 Egypt improved its formerly strained relations with several countries. In April the Egyptian foreign minister, Mahmoud Riad, visited Iran, and in September the British foreign secretary, Sir Alec Douglas-Home, paid a three-day visit to Cairo. King Faisal of Saudi Arabia visited Egypt June 19–26; a joint communiqué following the visit warmly pledged Saudi-Egyptian cooperation. When the pro-Communist coup in Sudan in July was briefly successful, Egypt facilitated the return to Sudan of Sudanese troops stationed in Egypt who helped restore Gen. Gaafar Nimeiry to power.   (P. Md.)

See also **Middle East.**

Encyclopædia Britannica Films. *The Egyptologists* (1967).

**United Church of
Canada:**
see Religion

**United Church of
Christ:**
see Religion

United Kingdom

A constitutional monarchy in northwestern Europe and member of the Commonwealth of Nations, the United Kingdom comprises the island of Great Britain (England, Scotland, and Wales) and Northern Ireland, together with many small islands. Area: 94,216 sq.mi. (244,018 sq.km.), excluding 1,188 sq.mi. of inland water, and the crown dependencies of the Channel Islands and Isle of Man. Pop. (1971): 55,-521,534. Cap. and largest city: London (pop. [Greater London], 1971, 7,379,014). Language: English; some Welsh and Gaelic also are used. Religion: mainly Protestant. Queen, Elizabeth II; prime minister in 1971, Edward Heath.

The major issues of 1971 were entry into the European Economic Community, inflation, industrial unrest, and a situation approaching civil war in Northern Ireland. To these were added, in November, a settlement of the Rhodesian question by which the former colony's independence, unilaterally declared six years before, was to be recognized.

The decennial census held on April 25, 1971, showed an increase in the population of the United Kingdom (including the Isle of Man and the Channel Islands) of 2,653,818. The first returns, published on August 18, put the total population at 55,521,534. The preponderance of 1,058 females to every 1,000 males was slightly less than in 1961 (1,067 females to 1,000 males). All conurbations except the West Riding of Yorkshire recorded a decline in population, the largest loss, of more than 600,000, being in Greater London. Other cities showing a decline in population were Glasgow, Liverpool, Manchester, Edinburgh, Leicester, Nottingham, Birmingham, Bradford, Leeds, and Sheffield. Rural areas showed an increase in population, reflecting the increasing number of city workers commuting from the suburbs. The areas of fastest growth were found to be in a belt stretching down the middle of England from the North Midlands to the Solent. Only small increases were recorded in Scotland and Wales.

Domestic Affairs. The Conservative government elected in June 1970 persisted in its radical change of approach in economic affairs. In a keynote speech at the Conservative Party conference on October 16 Prime Minister Edward Heath (*see* Biography) argued that a new Britain was seeking to establish a new place for itself in a new world. He foresaw decline in the U.S. commitment in Europe, which made necessary Britain's entry into the European Economic Community (EEC). Negotiations on Britain's application for membership of the EEC, which had opened on June 30, 1970, were completed on all the main issues on June 23, 1971. Subject to the enactment by Parliament of consequential legislation, Britain would become a member of the EEC on Jan. 1, 1973. A running debate among economists on the likely costs and benefits of entry continued throughout the year, with widely differing views being expressed. At one stage during the negotiations there was some anxiety that they might be blocked again by the French, who were raising objections to Britain's request for transitional stages in taking on the full commitment for financial contributions to the Community budget. The breakthrough came following two days of talks between Heath and French President Georges Pompidou held in Paris on May 19 and 20.

Under the terms negotiated Britain would adopt the common external tariff, the common agricultural policy, and the rules of the Community by transitional stages over a period of five years. Britain's contribution to the Community budget would start at 8.64% in the first year, rising to 18.92% in the fifth year. Special arrangements were made for Commonwealth interests. A decision on fisheries policy was held over because the Commission's plans for common access to fishing waters up to the shoreline were resisted strenuously not only by Britain but by the other applicant countries with local fishery interests to protect, notably Norway and Ireland. However, an agreement was reached on December 11 providing six-mile and 12-mile limits in British and Irish coastal waters until 1982.

The question of entry into the EEC split the political parties as well as dividing public opinion. After the conclusion of the main negotiations the government allowed more than three months for a "great debate" before asking Parliament to vote on accepting the terms negotiated. The Commons debated the White Paper setting out entry terms for four days at the end of July, but without taking a vote. The debate then continued in the country and at the autumn conferences of the three parties and of the Trades Union Congress (TUC). The effect was to polarize differences rather than to shift opinion—although Heath secured a more emphatic declaration of support than had been expected from the Conservative Party, which voted 8 to 1 in favour of entry. Encouraged, Heath decided to make the crucial vote in the House of Commons on October 28 a free vote.

The Labour Party, particularly in the trade unions and among the rank and file party workers, had swung heavily against entry into Europe. Recognizing the strength of this feeling, Harold Wilson himself switched to the anti-European wing of the party, arguing that his former revival of the British application had been conditional on satisfactory terms. A number of former Labour ministers, however, remained firmly convinced that the terms for entry were satisfactory and ought to be accepted—among them the deputy leader of the party and former chancellor of the Exchequer, Roy Jenkins, the former foreign minister, Michael Stewart, and the minister formerly in charge of the preliminaries to negotiations, George Thomson.

With majorities against entry in the Labour Party conference, the TUC, the Labour Party executive committee, and the parliamentary Labour Party, Labour imposed a "three-line whip" requiring all Labour MPs to vote against the motion approving the terms, but in the vote on October 28, 69 Labour MPs defied these instructions and voted for entry into Europe. There were 39 anti-Market Conservative MPs voting against entry, but this left the government with an impressive majority of 112 (356 votes to 244) supporting entry. In the aftermath of this vote there was much bitterness on the Labour left against the pro-Market Labour MPs who, it was said, had let slip a chance of overthrowing the government. In the annual elections for parliamentary party leaders this ill-feeling was directed against Roy Jenkins who,

In preparation for the introduction of the decimal currency system in Great Britain on Feb. 15, 1971, children in school in Surrey learn the principle behind changing pounds, shillings, and pence into pounds and new pence.

however, retained his post as Labour's deputy leader by a margin of 14 votes.

A series of bomb and machine gun attacks over a period of several years, including explosions at the homes of Robert Carr, the secretary of state for employment and productivity, in January 1971, and John Davies, secretary of state for trade and industry, in August, culminated in police raids in the north of London in the fall and the trial of two men in November and December. A group calling itself the "Angry Brigade" had claimed responsibility for a number of the incidents and was regarded by the authorities as a dangerous anarchist organization. Jack Prescott, a 27-year-old decorator, was found not guilty of causing bomb explosions, but was sentenced to 15 years' imprisonment for conspiracy to cause explosions. Ian Purdie, a 24-year-old film technician, was acquitted of this charge.

In December Parliament agreed to double the income of the queen to £980,000, in accordance with the recommendation of a select committee under Lord Boyle of Handsworth. The committee also called for increased annuities for other principal members of the royal family, and increased pay and allowances for MPs and ministers.

UNITED KINGDOM

Education. (1968–69) Primary, pupils 6,126,-100, teachers (1967–68) 176,440; secondary and vocational, pupils 3,286,700, teachers 174,808; teacher training, students 123,350; higher (44 universities only), students 240,002, teaching staff 31,499.

Finance. Monetary unit: pound sterling, with a par value of £0.42 to U.S. $1 (U.S. $2.40 = £1 sterling) and a free rate (Sept. 27, 1971) of U.S. $2.48 to £1. Gold, SDRs, and convertible currencies, official: (March 1971) U.S. $3,317,-000,000; (March 1970) U.S. $2,710,000,000. Budget: (1971–72 est.): revenue £16,762 million; expenditure £14,446 million. Gross national product: (1970) £50,340 million; (1969) £45,-930 million. Money supply: (March 1971) £17,-536 million; (March 1970) £15,497 million. Cost of living (1963 = 100): (June 1971) 149; (June 1970) 135.

Foreign Trade. (1970) Imports £9,052 million; exports £8,063 million. Import sources: EEC 20% (West Germany 6%, Netherlands 5%); U.S. 13%; Canada 8%. Export destinations: EEC 22% (West Germany 6%); U.S. 12%; Ireland 5%; Netherlands 5%; Sweden 5%. Main exports: machinery 28%; motor vehicles 10%; chemicals 10%; textile yarns and fabrics 5%. Tourism (1969): visitors 5,821,000; gross receipts U.S. $862 million.

Transport and Communications. Roads (1969) 354,696 km. (including 1,069 km. expressways). Motor vehicles in use (excluding Northern Ireland; 1970): passenger 11,516,000; commercial 1,621,000. Railways (excluding Northern Ireland; 1969): 19,470 km.; traffic 29,612,000,000 passenger-km., freight (1970) 24,340,000,000 net ton-km. Air traffic (1970): 17,431,000,000 passenger-km.; freight 591,602,-000 net ton-km. Shipping (1970): merchant vessels 100 gross tons and over 3,822; gross tonnage 25,824,820. Ships entered (1969) vessels totaling 130,496,000 net registered tons; goods loaded (1969) 44,512,000 metric tons, unloaded 188,554,000 metric tons. Telephones (Dec. 1969) 14,061,209. Radio licenses (Dec. 1970) 18,407,-000. Television licenses (Dec. 1970) 16,333,000.

Agriculture. Production (in 000; metric tons; 1970; 1969 in parentheses): wheat 4,174 (3,364); barley 7,496 (8,664); oats 1,233 (1,308); potatoes 7,482 (6,215); sugar, raw value (1970–71) 984, (1969–70) 937; apples 517 (469); pears c. 81 (65); dry peas c. 66 (66); dry broad beans c. 205 (236); tomatoes (1969) 94, (1968) 84; onions (1969) 117, (1968) 120; eggs 882 (865); beef and veal c. 973 (909); mutton and lamb c. 234 (215); pork c. 885 (903); wool 30 (31); milk 12,675 (12,-709); butter 65 (58); cheese 130 (120); fish catch (1969) 1,083, (1968) 1,040. Livestock (in 000; June 1970): cattle 12,697; sheep 26,374; pigs 8,062; chickens 127,168.

Industry. Index of production (1963 = 100): (1970) 124; (1969) 123. Fuel and power (in 000; 1970): coal (metric tons) 144,560; natural gas (cu.m.) 11,463,000; manufactured gas (cu.m.) 20,697,000; electricity (kw-hr.) 245,-964,000. Production (in 000; metric tons; 1970): cement 17,050; iron ore (25–30% metal content) 12,010; pig iron 17,660; crude steel 28,-320; nitrogenous fertilizers (1969–70) 710; passenger cars (units) 1,640; commercial vehicles (units) 457; cotton fabrics (m.) 628,000; woolen fabrics (sq.m.) 215,000; rayon and other synthetic fabrics (m.) 485,000. Merchant vessels launched (100 gross tons and over; 1970) 1,237,000 gross tons. New dwelling units completed (1970) 364,000.

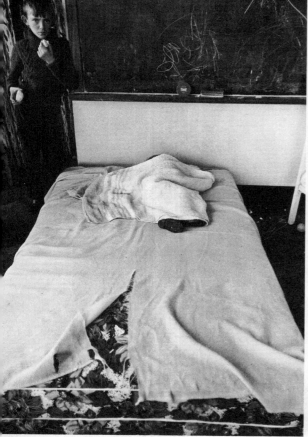

Violence was the way
of life in Northern
Ireland, the British
province torn by civil
strife in 1971.
Above, a Catholic family
continues to live
in a damaged house
in Belfast. Top, right,
a grief-stricken father
carries a coffin bearing
his daughter, who was
killed during fighting
between British troops
and their adversaries
in Belfast. Bottom, right,
Joe Cahill (second from
left), head of the IRA,
discusses the plight
of Northern Ireland
during a press conference.

(TOP, RIGHT) POPPERFOTO—
PICTORIAL PARADE; (OTHERS)
P. MICHAEL O'SULLIVAN

Industrial Relations. Inflation caused considerable labour unrest, as the government and employers sought to reduce the rate of annual wage increases from 15% at the start of the year to below 10%, with an unofficial target of 7%. The strike record calculated on the number of working days lost was the worst since 1926, the year of the general strike, but there was some decline in the number of strikes, and the situation continued to improve into the fall. The two most important and longest stoppages were in the Post Office (47 days) and in the Ford Motor Company (9 weeks). Political objections to the Industrial Relations Bill also provoked a number of one-day protest strikes.

The Industrial Relations Act, which became law on August 5, was the most comprehensive piece of industrial legislation ever passed through the British Parliament and was the centre of political dispute in the 1970–71 session, when it was debated for 56 days. It set up a new machinery of industrial courts and established a framework of rules for management, trade unions, and individuals. It was to be accompanied by an advisory code of practice to be promulgated in 1972, with the object of improving the voluntary system of industrial relations. The act gave statutory effect to the rights of trade union members, with protection against unfair dismissal, and introduced the concept of unfair industrial practices. To benefit from these provisions trade unions had to register with a registrar who was required to see that the union's rules met minimum standards. Because many trade unionists claimed that the act involved objectionable statutory interference in free collective bargaining, the TUC in September voted to instruct unions not to register. The act provided for a "cooling off" period of 60 days where a strike threatened to create an emergency for the community.

The purpose of the legislation was to maintain free collective bargaining within an orderly procedure for settling disputes. The new institutional setup was due to come into being early in 1972. The Industrial Court, with the status of a High Court, would handle the more serious issues arising under the act. The industrial tribunals, already existing in most large towns, had extended powers, including investigation of complaints of unfair dismissal. The Industrial Relations Board would deal with terms and conditions of employment. The Commission on Industrial Relations, already in existence, was to advise and make recommendations on disputes and procedures.

Local Government. On Feb. 15, 1971, the Conservative government published its proposals for the reform of English, Welsh, and Scottish local government. Differing in important respects from the proposals of the previous Labour government, the new plans provided for a two-tier system of county and district (or borough) councils.

England outside Greater London was to be remapped into 44 counties, including six "metropolitan counties"—Merseyside, South-East Lancashire and North-East Cheshire (SELNEC), the West Midlands, West Yorkshire, South Yorkshire, and the Tyne and Wear area. The metropolitan counties were to contain 34 metropolitan districts. In addition there would be 370 district councils alongside the existing parish councils, which were not to be altered.

A Local Government Bill published on November 4 revealed that the government had accepted over 60 changes to its original proposals; these included the loss by Lincolnshire of Grimsby and Scunthorpe to the proposed county of Humberside and of Colchester and Clacton by Essex to Suffolk. Harrogate was to be excluded from West Yorkshire and Ellesmere Port from Merseyside. The government intended to appoint an ombudsman to deal specifically with complaints concerning local government.

Foreign Policy and Defense. On November 24, after a year of negotiations, including several visits by Lord Goodman (*see* BIOGRAPHY), Edward Heath's government reached agreement with Ian Smith's regime in Rhodesia on a basis for the granting of the independence that Smith had seized unilaterally more than six years before. The following day Foreign Secretary Sir Alec Douglas-Home, having conducted the concluding stages of the negotiations himself in Salisbury, flew home to announce the terms of the agreement to a divided Parliament.

Neither the Labour nor Liberal opposition were at all convinced that the terms fell within the five principles previously accepted by all parties as obligatory for an honourable settlement. Points of controversy included the time scale for African majority rule, estimated at between 60 and 100 years by many, the lack of effective external guarantees, and inadequate assurances on an end to racial discrimination. (*See* RHODESIA.)

The government halted its predecessor's policy of withdrawal from "east of Suez." A new five-power defense agreement between the U.K., Australia, New Zealand, Malaysia, and Singapore went into effect on November 1. This included an integrated air defense system for Malaysia and Singapore. The British commitment to stations east of Suez was to be six frigates or destroyers, one submarine, a battalion group, a detachment of Nimrod maritime reconnaissance aircraft, and Whirlwind helicopters. In October the defense minister, Lord Carrington, announced a decision to build two destroyers and four frigates. It earlier had been decided to keep the aircraft carrier "Ark Royal" in service until the late 1970s. Partly because of the demands made on the Army in Northern Ireland, four new battalions were formed. At the meeting of Commonwealth heads of state and of government in Singapore in January the proposed sale of

British arms to South Africa was condemned by nearly all the African members. After the conference the British government obtained a legal opinion that under the Simonstown defense agreement with South Africa it was bound to supply helicopters to equip antisubmarine frigates and replacement equipment and stores for vessels already delivered.

On September 24 the government announced the expulsion of 105 alleged Soviet intelligence agents (*see* INTELLIGENCE OPERATIONS). The U.S.S.R. condemned the move as an attempt to obstruct European détente and the desire of the Kremlin for a European security conference. In retaliation several Britons were expelled from the Soviet Union and cultural visits hampered.

The Economy. Stagflation—the anomalous combination of inflation with industrial stagnation and high unemployment—continued to afflict the Conservative government in 1971. With record exports being reported month after month (reaching £797 million in September) and imports somewhat depressed, a visible trade surplus averaging £20 million a month was recorded during the first nine months of the year, so that with the addition of invisible earnings it seemed possible that the balance of payments surplus for 1971 might come to something like £800 million. But this brought little joy to the public and little credit to the government, for it was offset by continuing inflation, with prices in autumn about 10% up on the previous year. This was largely accounted for by wage inflation, which was slowing down a little from the 15% increase in earnings prevailing at the end of 1970 to $12\frac{1}{2}$% in September, compared with a year previously.

Yet stagnation persisted in industry. In the first half of the year total output was down by 1.75%, and it was up by only 1% by the end of the summer in spite of a substantial stimulus from the easing of taxes

Left, a Catholic rioter, armed with only a stone, retaliates against a British Army officer. Top, soldiers frisk Catholics suspected of using guerrilla tactics against the British Army in the streets of Belfast during August 1971. A British soldier (centre) threatens a potential assailant with a gun in Belfast, and a soldier (above) charges a group of Catholics in Londonderry.

and credit restrictions. Unemployment continued to rise, reaching 970,022 in November, representing 4% of the work force and a worsening of over 45% compared with a year earlier. The worst-hit areas were Scotland and Northern Ireland where the unemployment rate reached 8.6% and 10.2%, respectively.

The economy was proving strangely resistant to the stimulus applied by the chancellor of the Exchequer, Anthony Barber, in his budget of March 30, which reduced revenue from taxation by £546 million. Judging the effects to be inadequate, Barber introduced a "mini-budget" on July 19 with the object of achieving a growth rate of from 4 to 4½% in the first half of 1972, compared with the previous year. The main elements of the new budget were the removal of restrictions on installment buying and a reduction of the sales tax by nearly 20%. The bank rate was lowered twice during the year, to 6% in April and to 5% in September.

The uneasy state of the economy was reflected in the collapse of a number of business enterprises, most spectacularly two in which the government was heavily committed by its Labour predecessors—Rolls-Royce and Upper Clyde Shipbuilders. Rolls-Royce was placed in the hands of a receiver in view of the mounting losses incurred in the development of the RB-211 engine that had been ordered for the U.S. Lockheed TriStar airbus. In February, the financial collapse of the company obliged the government to nationalize those parts of it considered vital to national defense, but the government did not accept liability for the Lockheed contract. Renegotiation of the contract followed and ultimately was backed by a U.S. government loan guarantee.

Upper Clyde Shipbuilders, formed by a merger of five Clydeside shipyards in February 1968, with a 48% government shareholding, had inherited a number of unprofitable fixed-price contracts. By June 1971, some £25 million in grants and loans had been put into the concern, but it was about to run out of cash for wages and materials and forecast a continuing loss amounting to £4–5 million in the following three months. On June 15 the government announced that the group would be declared bankrupt and reorganized. The less efficient yards were to be closed, and the labour force reduced from 8,500 to 2,500. When these plans were announced at the end of July the trade unions took over the yards threatened with closure and continued to operate them. Work continued on 14 ships while negotiations on the future of the yards took place, the trade unions insisting that all should remain open. The financial crisis occurred at a time when the yards had orders worth £90 million.

A revolution in British banking practice was announced in September when government-imposed ceilings on bank lending were removed and the clearing banks abandoned their cartel arrangements whereby they had agreed not to compete on deposit and overdraft rates. The Bank of England would control liquidity by calling for special deposits. The banks now found themselves competing for both deposits and profitable lending. Decimal currency based on 100 new pence to £1 was introduced on February 15.

The effect of the December international monetary agreement was to change the value of the U.S. dollar vis-à-vis the pound to $2.60 = £1.

Northern Ireland. A relative lull in the feud between Ulster Protestants and Catholics in the winter of 1970–71 was the prelude to a succession of planned attacks by the Irish Republican Army and its extrem-

ist Provisional wing against the British Army. As the situation deteriorated into a form of sustained urban guerrilla war in Belfast, Londonderry, and, from time to time, in other towns, the Northern Ireland government, with the approval of the British government in Westminster, resorted on August 9 to the internment of IRA leaders and militants.

This proved the signal for even more violent attacks on troops and police, with the bombing and machine-gunning of police stations, military posts, public houses, shops, hotels, offices, and industrial premises. The IRA, taking the law into its own hands in the Catholic areas, was said to have shot or maimed alleged collaborators. Young women had their hair cut off and were tarred and feathered for associating with British troops. Statistics released by the Army on November 9 stated that 36 British soldiers, 2 members of the Ulster Defence Regiment, and 9 police had been killed, and 171 soldiers injured. The Army reported that at least 76 civilians had died, of whom 33 had been shot by soldiers. On December 12, a Protestant senator, John Barnhill, became the first member of the Northern Ireland Parliament to be killed in the violence. By the fall the number of British troops in Northern Ireland had risen to 13,600. British Home Secretary Reginald Maudling saw the IRA as aiming to induce weariness in Britain that would lead to the withdrawal of British forces and the abandonment of British responsibility for Northern Ireland.

Political pressure for more rigorous action against the IRA led to the resignation of Maj. James Chichester-Clark as prime minister on March 20. Brian Faulkner (*see* BIOGRAPHY) was elected leader of the Unionist parliamentary party on March 23, and took over as prime minister, declaring that his main task was to restore law and order. He broke with tradition in appointing a Labour Party man, David Bleakley, to his Cabinet as minister for community relations. In an attempt to broaden the political base of government, Faulkner announced on June 22 the formation of parliamentary committees on social, environmental, and industrial services on which opposition members would serve. This initiative was frustrated when the Social Democratic and Labour Party members withdrew from Stormont in protest against the refusal of a public inquiry into the shooting of two civilians by troops in Londonderry. Meanwhile the government persisted with a reform program that included introducing one-man one-vote suffrage in local elections, the appointment of parliamentary and local ombudsmen, housing allocation on a points system, special grants for socially deprived areas, a declaration of equality of opportunity in employment, steps to avoid sectarian discrimination in official contracts, and penalties under the Incitement to Hatred Act.

The reform program, however, was overshadowed by the intensification of the drive against the IRA, culminating in internment. A committee under Sir Edmund Compton, formerly the U.K. parliamentary commissioner for administration (ombudsman), set up to investigate allegations of torture during interrogation, found that although there had been some ill-treatment of detainees there was no evidence of physical brutality by either the British Army or the Royal Ulster Constabulary. Methods of interrogation were to be further examined by a committee of three Privy councillors under Lord Parker of Waddington. In the first three months of internment 882 suspects were arrested and 476 released.   (W. H. Ts.)

United Nations

Highlights of the year were the decisions to select a new secretary-general and to seat the People's Republic of China, and the attempts to settle the long-standing Middle East problems and to deal with the war between India and Pakistan.

Secretary-General. After the tragic death in Northern Rhodesia of Dag Hammarskjöld in September 1961, U Thant became UN secretary-general. On January 18, he announced that he had "no intention whatsoever" of serving beyond his present term, his second, which ended December 31. Despite delegates' persistent hopes that he might change his mind, he remained adamant. On September 16, he offered some valedictory thoughts to newsmen, stating that the drafters of the UN Charter "were overly obsessed with political and military conflict." He believed that it would be more useful to authorize the secretary-general to bring to UN attention "global threats to human well-being other than those to peace and security." He cited as examples his own warnings about the consequences of excessive population growth and a deteriorating environment.

By the time the 26th General Assembly opened on September 21 under the presidency of Adam Malik of Indonesia (*see* BIOGRAPHY), the search for a successor to U Thant had narrowed to five present and former UN delegates: Hamilton Shirley Amerasinghe (Ceylon); Felipe Herrera (Chile), former president of the Inter-American Development Bank; Max Jakobson (Finland); Endalkachew Makonnen (Ethiopia); and Kurt Waldheim (Austria). A late addition was Argentine diplomat Carlos Ortiz de Rozas. The UN Charter requires the General Assembly to appoint the secretary-general from among candidates nominated by the Security Council, a procedure requiring the nominees to have the support of all five permanent council members. On December 21 Waldheim (*see* BIOGRAPHY), an Austrian career diplomat, was chosen by a vote of 11–1 with three abstentions. The General Assembly approved the selection by acclamation the next day. It later was revealed that Ortiz de Rozas had received 12 affirmative votes in the Security Council but had been vetoed by the Soviet Union.

Chinese Representation. U Thant's ten years at the UN were years of annual combat over the question of the representation of China. Beginning in 1961 the U.S. took the lead in having the assembly designate the matter an "important question," which, under article 18 of the Charter, subjected it to a two-thirds vote. This parliamentary tactic helped ensure that the Republic of China (Taiwan), led by Chiang Kai-shek, would keep its seats in both the assembly and the Security Council.

On August 2, U.S. Secretary of State William P. Rogers announced that the U.S. would support a resolution to seat Communist China in the UN. The U.S. remained firmly opposed, however, to ousting Chiang's government. It thus seemed a foregone conclusion from the time the assembly met that the People's Republic would occupy the Chinese seats before the year's end. What remained uncertain and what most of the assembly debate on this item dealt with was the place, if any, at the UN of Nationalist China.

The parliamentary strategy was similar to that of previous years, with the U.S. seeking to designate the issue "important," although this time with the idea not of keeping the Chinese Communists out but of keeping in the Chinese Nationalists. Since the Peking government repeatedly stated that it would not sit in a UN that still accorded a place to the Taiwan regime, the question was important in more than a technical, parliamentary sense. The U.S. argued, however, that expelling the Nationalists would set an unfortunate precedent for the world organization and observed, in addition, that Taiwan alone embraced a larger territory and more people than many other UN members.

Debate on the question began October 18 and sparked an unremitting search for votes by both sides. Some predicted that the four most recent members of the UN (Bahrain, Bhutan, and Qatar, admitted on September 21; and Oman, October 7) might even find themselves in a position to decide the question. In actual fact, when the vote came on October 25 it was quite decisive. The assembly first rejected the U.S.-sponsored "important question" resolution by 59–55 with 15 abstentions. It then went on to adopt a resolution sponsored by Albania, Tanzania, and others, calling for the assembly to "restore" the "lawful rights" of the People's Republic, to recognize its representatives as the only lawful representatives of China in the UN, and to expel "forthwith the representatives of Chiang Kai-shek." The vote was 76–35–17. All the permanent members of the Security Council, except the U.S. and Nationalist China, whose delegates withdrew from the Assembly Hall between the first and second votes, voted with the majority.

Middle East. In January, responding to a request of UN special representative Gunnar Jarring, both Egypt and Israel prepared memorandums outlining their respective positions on Middle East questions. Israel indicated that it would withdraw from territories beyond frontiers delineated in a future peace treaty, but not until it could sign a binding agreement with the Arabs. Egypt insisted that Israel had to withdraw from all Arab territory occupied in the 1967 war. It also suggested a possible UN peace-keeping force and envisaged demilitarized zones along its Israeli frontier.

The cease-fire between the two belligerents lapsed on February 4, but Egypt agreed to extend it for another 30 days in response both to an appeal on February 2 by U Thant and, possibly, to advance reports that the U.S. would (as it did February 4 and 12) undertake talks with the U.K., France, and the U.S.S.R. about guaranteeing a Middle East settlement. Egypt hoped that Big Four influence would lead Israel to withdraw from Arab territories, whereas Israel feared an "imposed" settlement and preferred direct talks with Arab powers.

Jarring asked Israel on February 8 to agree to withdraw completely from occupied Egyptian territory in exchange for security provided through demilitarized zones, special arrangements in the Sharm el-Sheik area, and the right freely to navigate through the Suez Canal. He simultaneously asked Egypt to commit itself to a peace arrangement with Israel based on Security Council Resolution 242 (1967) requiring "termination of all claims or states of belligerency and respect for and acknowledgment of the sovereignty, territorial integrity and political independence of every state in the area and their right to live in peace within secure and recognized boundaries free from threats or acts of force." It would be understood, Jarring added, that the refugee problems would eventually be settled justly.

Egypt was willing to accept these specifications,

Left, Nationalist Chinese Foreign Minister Chow Shu-kai leaves the UN General Assembly chamber on Oct. 25, 1971, prior to the vote on an Albanian resolution to seat Communist China. Right, the Tanzanian and Albanian delegations stand and applaud the defeat of a U.S. resolution requiring a two-thirds majority vote to expel Nationalist China from the UN.

but added that lasting peace was impossible unless Israel withdrew from all Arab land it occupied. Israel did not reply directly to the memorandum and criticized Jarring for making specific suggestions that, in its view, exceeded his mandate. Although Israel stated that the Egyptian reply opened the way for significant negotiations, it again ruled out total withdrawal from occupied territories. Israel later refused to accept an international peace-keeping force as an adequate guarantee of a political settlement with Egypt, as proposed by Rogers on March 16. On December 13, the General Assembly, by a vote of 79–7, with 36 abstentions, including the U.S., adopted an Egyptian-supported resolution calling on Israel to withdraw from occupied Egyptian territories and to "respond favourably" to Jarring's memorandum of February 8. Israel indicated in advance that it found the resolution unacceptable.

Discussions about clearing the Suez Canal and re-opening it took place in February and April, but these also foundered. Egypt wanted to station troops on the east bank, but Israel refused to withdraw any troops until after the parties had reached a binding agreement. Israel also asked for assurances that a reopened canal would be available for its shipping, but Egypt said that these rights would have to await a final settlement. Israel refused to commit itself to specific troop withdrawals, asking instead that Egypt formally end the state of war between them and agree to concrete guarantees and sanctions to support any canal arrangements ultimately arrived at. Each side in effect regarded as preconditions for negotiations concessions that the other side thought depended upon a final settlement.

India-Pakistan War. After several confusing days of border thrusts and counterthrusts, Indian and Pakistani forces opened full-scale hostilities on December 3, accusing each other of aggression. India called Pakistani troops in East Pakistan a "threat to our security" and considered its own military movements a means of "liberating" the Bengalis of East Pakistan. (In December 1970, the Bengali-supported Awami League won a national majority favouring autonomy for East Pakistan, but Pakistani Pres. Agha Muhammad Yahya Khan prevented the National Assembly from convening on March 1. Bengali riots and strikes ensued, and on March 25 Yahya Khan ordered West Pakistani troops into East Pakistan to suppress them. This caused more than nine million Bengali

refugees to flee over the border into India to escape harassment, jail, or possible death.)

Pakistan on November 29 requested UN observers to examine the border clashes with India, but U Thant relayed the request to the president of the Security Council, apparently unwilling to act on his own initiative and preferring action by a major UN organ in the matter. For about a week, council members privately discussed the usefulness of a formal meeting, but events impelled nine members to call the council into session on December 4. Because of two Soviet vetoes on December 5, the council was unable to adopt a resolution calling for a cease-fire. Nor was the U.S.S.R. able to command a majority for its own draft resolution, which asked Pakistan to "take measures to cease all acts of violence," without calling for either a cease-fire by India or for an Indian withdrawal.

Somalia on December 6 proposed shifting the issue to the General Assembly under the "Uniting for Peace" procedure adopted in 1950 to allow the UN to function despite council paralysis. On December 7, the assembly, by a vote of 104–11, with 10 abstentions, adopted a resolution similar to the one that the U.S. had proposed in the council. It asked both parties "to take forthwith all measures for an immediate cease-fire and withdrawal of their armed forces" from each other's territory and urged that "efforts be intensified in order to bring about . . . conditions necessary for the voluntary return of the East Pakistan refugees to their homes." Pakistan, the U.S., and China voted in favour of the assembly resolution; India, the U.S.S.R., and other Eastern European countries against.

Meanwhile, on December 6 India recognized as independent the Bengali state of Bangla Desh. On December 9 Pakistan accepted the cease-fire on condition that India do so also, but India delayed its response. On December 13 the Security Council was again prevented by a Soviet veto from adopting a resolution calling for a cease-fire and mutual troop withdrawal, and on December 17 Pakistan accepted unconditionally a cease-fire imposed by India after complete victory over Pakistani forces in the east. On December 21, the Security Council demanded (13–0–2, the U.S.S.R. and Poland abstaining) a "durable cease-fire" and called for India and Pakistani forces to pull back within their own frontiers "as soon as practicable."

(R. N. S.)

UNESCO. In 1971 UNESCO celebrated the 25th anniversary of its founding on Nov. 4, 1946, membership having grown from 44 to 125. One of the most important educational events of the year was the convening of the third regional conference of ministers of education and ministers responsible for economic planning in Asia. The meeting examined progress in reaching targets for educational development in UNESCO's 18 Asian member states and recommended changes or adaptations in such targets for the future, in view of the region's high population growth.

There was agreement that whereas the 1960s had been a decade of quantitative expansion in education, in the 1970s priority would have to be given to the better mobilization of human resources through concern with the quality of education, including new content and curricula, more modern teacher training and methods of teaching, and more efficient use of school buildings.

Continued, and increasing, support was given during the year to programs promoting science in the less developed countries, especially in the training of scientists. As international intercommunication was indispensable for scientists and researchers, UNESCO convened at its Paris headquarters in October an intergovernmental conference to discuss the establishment of a World Science Information System—UNISIST. Attended by 300 participants representing 83 nations and 40 international organizations, the meeting unanimously approved the project, which was to seek UNESCO's General Conference approval at the end of 1972. (R. D. A. G.)

Table I. Member States of the United Nations
Dec. 31, 1971

Afghanistan	Denmark*	Laos	Saudi Arabia*
Albania	Dominican Rep.*	Lebanon*	Senegal
Algeria	Ecuador*	Lesotho	Sierra Leone
Argentina*	Egypt* (United	Liberia*	Singapore
Australia*	Arab Republic)	Libya	Somalia
Austria	El Salvador*	Luxembourg*	South Africa*
Bahrain	Equatorial Guinea	Malagasy Rep.	Spain
Barbados	Ethiopia*	Malawi	Sudan
Belgium*	Fiji	Malaysia	Swaziland
Belorussia*	Finland	Maldives	Sweden
Bhutan	France*	Mali	Syria*
Bolivia*	Gabon	Malta	Tanzania
Botswana	Gambia, The	Mauritania	Thailand
Brazil*	Ghana	Mauritius	Togo
Bulgaria	Greece*	Mexico*	Trinidad and
Burma	Guatemala*	Mongolia	Tobago
Burundi	Guinea	Morocco	Tunisia
Cambodia (Khmer	Guyana	Nepal	Turkey*
Rep.)	Haiti*	Netherlands*	Uganda
Cameroon	Honduras*	New Zealand*	Ukraine*
Canada*	Hungary	Nicaragua*	U.S.S.R.*
Central African	Iceland	Niger	United Arab
Rep.	India*	Nigeria	Emirates
Ceylon	Indonesia	Norway*	United Kingdom*
Chad	Iran*	Oman	United States*
Chile*	Iraq*	Pakistan	Upper Volta
China*	Ireland	Panama*	Uruguay*
Colombia*	Israel	Paraguay*	Venezuela*
Congo	Italy	Peru*	Yemen, (Aden)
Congo (Zaire)	Ivory Coast	Philippines*	Yemen, (San'a')
Costa Rica*	Jamaica	Poland*	Yugoslavia*
Cuba*	Japan	Portugal	Zambia
Cyprus	Jordan	Qatar	
Czechoslovakia*	Kenya	Romania	
Dahomey	Kuwait	Rwanda	

*Signatories to original charter.

Table II. Council Membership
Years indicate date membership expires

Country	Security Council	Economic and Social Council	Trusteeship Council
China	Permanent	1974	Permanent
France	Permanent	1972	Permanent
U.S.S.R.	Permanent	1974*	Permanent
United Kingdom	Permanent	1974*	Permanent
United States	Permanent	1973	Permanent†
Argentina	1972		
Australia			
Belgium	1972		
Bolivia		1974	
Brazil		1972	
Burundi		1974	
Ceylon		1972	
Chile		1974	
Congo (Zaire)		1973	
Finland		1974	
Ghana		1972	
Guinea	1973		
Greece		1972	
Haiti		1973	
Hungary		1973	
India	1973		
Italy	1972	1972	
Japan	1972	1974	
Kenya		1972	
Lebanon		1973	
Malagasy Rep.		1973	
Malaysia		1973	
New Zealand		1973	
Niger		1973	
Panama	1973		
Peru		1972	
Poland		1974	
Somalia	1972		
Sudan	1973		
Tunisia		1972	
Yugoslavia	1973		

*Reelected.
†Administering authority.

United States

The United States of America is a federal republic composed of 50 states, 49 of which are in North America and one of which consists of the Hawaiian Islands. Area: 3,615,122 sq.mi. (9,363,123 sq.km.), including 78,267 sq.mi. of inland water but excluding the 60,306 sq.mi. of the Great Lakes that lie within U.S. boundaries. Pop. (1971 est.): 207,180,000, including (1970) white 87.3%; Negro 11.1%. Language: English. Religion (1963 est.): Protestant 64,435,000; Roman Catholic 42,877,000; Jewish 5,365,000; Orthodox 2.8 million. Cap.: Washington, D.C. (pop., 1970, 756,-510). Largest city: New York (pop., 1970, 7,895,563). President in 1971, Richard Milhous Nixon.

Abrupt changes in the nation's economic and foreign policies put the United States on a new course both at home and abroad in 1971. Long on record as opposed to government control of the economy, President Nixon (see BIOGRAPHY) introduced a comprehensive federal program to hold down wage, price, and rent increases in order to combat inflation. At the same time, he initiated measures to redress the adverse U.S. balance of payments—an effort that led, at the end of the year, to devaluation of the dollar.

The president's new departures in foreign policy were no less startling. His decision to resume at least limited relations with Communist China led directly to that country's admission to the UN and ended two decades of implacable Sino-U.S. hostility. News of Nixon's plans to visit Peking, coupled with the subsequent announcement of his New Economic Policy, created apprehension among the allies and trading partners of the U.S. Accordingly, the president arranged a series of top-level meetings with foreign leaders, including a projected visit to Moscow in 1972.

The Nixon administration's relations with Congress improved considerably in 1971, although little was done to achieve the "six great goals" of the New American Revolution outlined in the president's January 22 state of the union message. The goals proposed by Nixon were welfare reform; full prosperity in peacetime; restoration and enhancement of the environment; improved health care; strengthening of state and local governments through revenue sharing; and reorganization of the federal government. The president explained that he was asking "not simply for more new programs in the old framework, but to change the framework itself—to reform the entire structure of American government so we can make it

A march led by the Rev. Carl McIntire in Washington, D.C., supports a proposed amendment that would allow voluntary prayer in public schools. The House of Representatives voted in November 1971 to kill the amendment.

again fully responsive to the needs and the wishes of the American people."

As it turned out, foreign rather than domestic issues constituted the major concern of Congress in 1971. One of the most hotly debated pieces of legislation was the Mansfield amendment, introduced by Senate majority leader Mike Mansfield (Dem., Mont.), which set a fixed date for the withdrawal of U.S. forces from Indochina. Passed twice by the Senate, the amendment was watered down in House-Senate conference both times, only to appear a third time as a rider to a foreign aid bill. It finally was rejected by the House on December 16. Earlier in the year, another Mansfield amendment also created controversy. Offered as part of the military draft bill, it would have reduced the number of U.S. troops in Europe from 300,000 to 150,000. After a week of debate, it was defeated on the Senate floor.

The biggest surprise of the first session of the 92nd Congress was the Senate's vote on October 29 to kill the $2.9 billion foreign aid program proposed for fiscal 1972. The defeat was engineered by an unusual

Demonstrators protesting the war in Vietnam lie on the steps of the state capitol in Lincoln, Neb., on Oct. 13, 1971.

coalition—conservatives who saw the program as a giant giveaway and liberals who felt that it placed too much emphasis on military assistance. Nixon called the rejection of the program an irresponsible and dangerous action. By the end of the session, however, it was clear that foreign aid was not as dead as it had appeared to be earlier. The Senate divided the foreign aid package into an economic assistance bill and a military assistance bill—an approach proposed by Nixon the previous April—and passed both by wide margins. The House repassed its version of the original foreign aid bill and took it to conference with the two new Senate bills. When the conferees disagreed on the bill's rider, the Mansfield amendment on Indochina troop withdrawal, both houses passed continuing resolutions extending aid at existing levels into early 1972. A compromise authorization bill was agreed upon, and the Senate passed it before adjourning. The House delayed action until 1972.

On the domestic front, Congress approved a one-year extension (through April 1973) of the Economic Stabilization Act of 1970, under which the president may impose wage, price, and rent controls. Congress also cleared the president's tax bill, cutting personal and business taxes over a period of three years in an effort to stimulate the economy. Among its major provisions, the bill repealed the 7% automobile excise tax, gave business a 7% investment tax credit, and raised the personal income tax exemption from $650 in 1970 to $675 in 1971 and $750 in 1972. Nixon signed the bill only after House-Senate conferees had removed a provision establishing federal financing for the 1972 presidential election campaign. He had threatened to veto the measure if the provision were not deleted.

In other action, Congress approved a new military draft bill, a $250 million loan to the ailing Lockheed Aircraft Corp., and an end to the supersonic transport (SST) subsidy. All of these developments overshadowed traditional social service issues, as most of the president's domestic recommendations were bogged down in committee for most of the year. But Congress did clear a bill appropriating more than $1 billion to fight cancer and another establishing day-care centres for children of working parents. Nixon vetoed the day-care bill on the ground that it would tend to weaken the family structure. He had previously vetoed two other bills—one providing $5.7 billion for public works acceleration and regional development, and one raising benefits for certain retired District of Columbia municipal employees. The vetoes were upheld in all three cases.

Nixon had been embarrassed and angered when the Senate, in 1969 and 1970, rejected two successive nominees to fill a vacant Supreme Court seat. In 1971, two of the president's three major appointees encountered opposition in the Senate, but all were confirmed. William H. Rehnquist (*see* BIOGRAPHY) and Lewis F. Powell, Jr. (*see* BIOGRAPHY), were nominated to the Supreme Court by Nixon on October 21 to fill the seats previously held by Hugo L. Black and John M. Harlan (*see* OBITUARIES). Powell, a Richmond lawyer, drew little opposition from the legal profession and was confirmed on December 6 by an 89 to 1 vote. Rehnquist had a more difficult time. As an assistant attorney general, he was involved in the Justice Department's handling of May 1971 protest demonstrations in Washington, D.C., and liberals asserted that he was insensitive to the rights of dissenters. After a short-lived filibuster, Rehnquist won

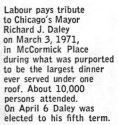

Labour pays tribute
to Chicago's Mayor
Richard J. Daley
on March 3, 1971,
in McCormick Place
during what was purported
to be the largest dinner
ever served under one
roof. About 10,000
persons attended.
On April 6 Daley was
elected to his fifth term.

UPI COMPIX

Senate confirmation by a 68–26 vote on December 10.

The toughest confirmation battle involved Earl L. Butz (*see* BIOGRAPHY), nominated to replace Clifford M. Hardin as secretary of agriculture. Butz found himself caught in the economic discontent gripping farmers and their representatives in Congress in a lean year for agriculture. His close ties to corporate farming interests made many members of Congress fear that he would be unwilling to use government policy to protect the small family farmer. Although the nomination put many Midwestern Republicans in the uncomfortable position of choosing between loyalty to Nixon and the wishes of their large farmer constituencies, Butz was confirmed by 51–44 with only four Republican senators voting against him.

Foreign Affairs. President Nixon provided a hint of things to come in his February 25 message to Congress on foreign policy. The United States, he said, was "at the end of an era" in its relations with other countries. "The postwar order of international relations—the configuration of power that emerged from the Second World War—is gone," he added. "With it are gone the conditions which have determined the assumptions and practice of United States foreign policy since 1945."

Despite that statement few persons would have guessed that Nixon would announce, as he did on July 15, that he planned to go to Peking before May 1972, "to seek the normalization of relations" between the U.S. and China and "to exchange views on questions of concern to the two sides." Nixon revealed that arrangements for his trip had been worked out a few days earlier in secret talks between Chinese Premier Chou En-lai and presidential assistant Henry A. Kissinger in the Chinese capital.

Further details of the Nixon visit were announced in Washington and Peking on November 29. It was revealed that the China trip would begin Feb. 21, 1972, and include visits to Shanghai and Hangchow as well as to Peking. The president, Kissinger said, was scheduled to meet with both Chou and Communist Party Chairman Mao Tse-tung; their discussions were to be of "a free-wheeling nature" so as to permit either side to raise any topic it considered urgent.

Kissinger said that the "major thrust" of the talks would be on bilateral issues, and that "no agreement will be made about third-party problems" but that third-party issues could be broached if either side "considers something of crucial importance." He stressed that the trip was not expected to result in establishment of formal diplomatic relations between the U.S. and China. Neither was it likely to resolve the differences between Peking and Taiwan nor put an end to the war in Southeast Asia. "We're not sentimental about this," Kissinger said. "We recognize that the People's Republic is led by highly principled men whose principles are diametrically opposed to ours."

News of Nixon's plans to visit Peking was followed on August 2 by Secretary of State William P. Rogers' announcement that the U.S. would, for the first time, "support action at the General Assembly this fall calling for seating the People's Republic of [Mainland] China." On the other hand, he said, this country would "oppose any action to expel the Republic of China [Taiwan] or otherwise deprive it of representation in the United Nations." The UN General Assembly voted on October 25 to seat the People's Republic— but the resolution provided also for the expulsion "forthwith" of the Republic of China. Two days later, presidential press secretary Ronald L. Ziegler said that Nixon had condemned the cheering and dancing of delegates after the UN vote as a "shocking demonstration" of "undisguised glee" and "personal animosity" toward the U.S.

At a White House news conference on October 12, Nixon disclosed that he would visit the Soviet Union "in the latter part of May 1972" for discussions with Soviet leaders on "all major issues, with a view toward further improving . . . bilateral relations and enhancing the prospects of world peace." Nixon emphasized that his visit to Moscow had no connection with his visit to Peking. "Neither trip is being taken for the purpose of exploiting what differences may exist between the two nations," he said. "Neither is being taken at the expense of any other nation."

Evidence of improved Soviet-American relations was provided by two agreements on preventing nuclear accidents and on modernizing the Washington-Moscow "hot line" for emergency messages. The first pact obliged each party to notify the other "in the event of detection by missile warning system of unidentified objects" or "an accidental, unauthorized or any other unexplained incident involving a possible detonation of a nuclear weapon which could create a risk of outbreak of nuclear war." The "hot line" accord was to replace the existing line with a satellite that would provide instantaneous voice and teletype communication. At the signing ceremony in Washington, September 30, Rogers noted that "considerable progress" had been made in the U.S.-Soviet strategic arms limitation talks (SALT), but that "much remains to be done." Foreign Minister Andrei A. Gromyko, who signed the pacts for the Soviet Union, said: "The agreements signed today do not yet solve in any way the substance of the problem of limiting strategic armaments. This task is still outstanding."

In addition to the Peking and Moscow visits, Nixon arranged a series of bilateral meetings with major U.S. allies. The itinerary included talks with Prime Minister Pierre Elliott Trudeau of Canada in Washington on December 6; with Pres. Georges Pompidou of France in the Azores, December 13–14, and with Premier Marcello Caetano of Portugal during that time; with Prime Minister Edward Heath of Britain in Bermuda, December 20–21; with Chancellor Willy Brandt of West Germany in Key Biscayne, Fla., December 28–29; and with Prime Minister Eisaku Sato of Japan in San Clemente, Calif., Jan. 6–7, 1972. These consultations, Kissinger explained on November 30, would be undertaken to assure U.S. allies that their vital interests would not be threatened by Nixon's discussions in Peking and Moscow. "While we cannot promise them a veto," Kissinger said, "we would take it extremely seriously and we would expect not to take actions which our allies would consider threatening their vital concerns."

The president's diplomatic initiatives had the effect of drawing attention away from the war in Indochina, which appeared to be winding down in 1971. Nixon announced on April 7 that he intended to withdraw 100,-000 U.S. troops from Vietnam between May 1 and December 1 and that "American involvement in this war is coming to an end." On November 12, he ordered a further withdrawal of 45,000 troops by Feb. 1, 1972—at which time the number of U.S. military personnel in South Vietnam would be down to 139,000. As for future withdrawals, the next announcement would be made before February 1, Nixon said, and would be based on (1) the level of enemy activity, particularly the infiltration rate; (2) progress of the vietnamization program; and (3) progress "that may have been made" on gaining release of U.S. prisoners

of war and obtaining a cease-fire "for all of Southeast Asia." Late in December the war flared up again; the U.S. made its heaviest bombing attacks in three years on military targets in North Vietnam in retaliation for actions by Hanoi that the U.S. claimed violated the 1968 bombing halt agreement.

The U.S. was involved only indirectly in the brief war that broke out between India and Pakistan in December. On December 6 Washington suspended $87.6 million in development loans to India, charging that it was the "main aggressor" in the conflict. The State Department said that in a meeting the same day between Nixon and congressional leaders the president pledged that the U.S. would adhere to "absolute neutrality" and not become "physically involved in any way" in the fighting. India's swift victory in the conflict led to second-guessing about the wisdom of U.S. policy; many observers felt that American influence on the subcontinent had been substantially reduced because Washington clearly had sympathized with a losing and now dismembered country.

Domestic Affairs. Nixon's New Economic Policy (NEP) was the major event on the U.S. domestic scene in 1971, and it had wide repercussions abroad as well. Nixon announced without warning on August 15 that he was ordering an immediate 90-day freeze on wages, prices, and rents and was ending the traditional convertibility of the dollar into gold, in effect freeing the dollar for devaluation against other currencies. These were the two major points in a program that included a 10% surcharge on dutiable imports, a $4.7 billion reduction in federal expenditures, a reduction in federal personnel, and a request for congressional action to end automobile excise taxes and enact tax incentives for industry. The wage-price freeze was the first to be imposed in the U.S. since the ceiling ordered by Pres. Harry Truman in 1951 to combat inflation generated by the Korean War.

Phase Two of the NEP was unveiled in October. In a nationwide television address on October 7, Nixon asserted that the freeze had been "remarkably successful" because the American people had "shown a willingness to cooperate in the campaign against in-

continued on page 719

UNITED STATES

Education. (1970–71) Primary (including preprimary), pupils 36.8 million, teachers 1,261,-000; secondary and vocational, pupils 14.8 million, teachers 1,014,000; higher (including junior colleges and teacher-training colleges), students 7.6 million, teaching staff 593,000.

Finance. Monetary unit: U.S. dollar, with a par value of U.S. $2.40 to £1 sterling and a free rate (Sept. 27, 1971) of U.S. $2.48 to £1 sterling. Gold, SDRs, and foreign exchange, official: (September 1971) $11,560,000,000; (September 1970) $13,580,000,000. Federal budget (1970–71 est.): revenue $202,103,000,000; expenditure $200,771,000,000. Gross national product: (1970) $974.1 billion; (1969) $929.1 billion. Money supply: (June 1971) $221.8 billion; (June 1970) $198.7 billion. Cost of living (1963 = 100): (June 1971) 133; (June 1970) 126.

Foreign Trade. (1970) Imports $39,952,000,-000; exports (excluding $565 million military aid) $42,659,000,000. Import sources: Canada 28%; Japan 15%; West Germany 8%; U.K. 5%. Export destinations: Canada 21%; Japan 11%; West Germany 6%; U.K. 6%. Main exports: machinery 27%; chemicals 9%; motor vehicles 8%; cereals 6%; aircraft 5%.

Transport and Communications. Roads (1969) 5,971,160 km. (including 48,807 km. expressways). Motor vehicles in use (1970): passenger 89,861,000; commercial 17,870,987. Railways: (1968) 336,400 km.; traffic (1970)

17,400,000,000 passenger-km., freight 1,117,270,-000,000 net ton-km. Air traffic (1970): 211,-459,000,000 passenger-km. (including internal services, 171,602,544,000 passenger-km. in 1969); freight 7,298,847,000 net ton-km. (including internal services, 4,506,165,000 net ton-km. in 1969). Inland waterways: freight traffic (1969) 442,228,000,000 ton-km. (including 168,-240,000,000 ton-km. on Great Lakes system). Shipping (1970): merchant vessels 100 gross tons and over 2,983; gross tonnage 18,463,207; ships entered (including Great Lakes international traffic; 1969): vessels totaling 177,860,000 net registered tons; goods loaded (1970) 218,570,-000 metric tons, unloaded 291,792,000 metric tons. Telephones (Jan. 1970) 115,222,000. Radio receivers (1970) 290 million. Television receivers (Jan. 1970) 88.3 million.

Agriculture. Production (in 000; metric tons; 1970; 1969 in parentheses): corn 104,393 (116,401); wheat 37,516 (39,734); oats 13,201 (13,790); barley 8,937 (9,222); rye 979 (802); rice 3,758 (4,120); linseed 761 (892); sorghum 17,706 (18,982); soybeans 30,910 (30,653); dry beans 816 (857); dry peas 179 (230); peanuts 1,355 (1,145); potatoes 14,740 (14,151); sweet potatoes (1969) 665, (1968) 616; sugar, raw value 5,624, (5,483); apples 2,880 (3,063); pears 491 (646); oranges 8,025 (7,658); grapefruit 2,240 (1,984); lemons 717 (664); grapes (1969) 3,536, (1968) 3,220; raisins 177 (228);

cotton, lint 2,213 (2,179); wool 40 (41); beef and veal 10,087 (9,888); pork 6,090 (5,873); milk 53,268 (52,773); butter 517 (512); cheese 998 (909); eggs 4,114 (4,053); timber (cu.m.; 1969): softwood 247,200, (1968) 253,000; hardwood 89,000, (1968) 84,300; fish catch (1969) 2,495, (1968) 2,442. Livestock (in 000; Jan. 1971): cattle 114,568; sheep 19,560; horses (Jan. 1970) c. 7,700; pigs 67,540; chickens 442,-783.

Industry. Index of production (1963 = 100): (1970) 139, (1969) 145; mining (1970) 123, (1969) 120; manufacturing (1970) 139, (1969) 146; electricity, gas, and water (1970) 171, (1969) 159; construction (1970) 104, (1969) 111. Unemployment: (1970) 4.9%; (1969) 3.5%. Fuel and power (in 000; metric tons; 1970): coal and lignite 546,972; crude oil 475,-088; natural gas (cu.m.) 620,338,000; electricity (kw-hr.) 1,638,010,000. Production (in 000; metric tons; 1970): iron ore (55–60% metal content) 90,569; pig iron 83,010; crude steel 119,-138; cement 67,728; newsprint 3,045; sulfuric acid 26,442; caustic soda 9,140; phosphate rock 35,143; nitrogenous fertilizers (N content; 1969–70) 7,632; plastics and resins 8,148; synthetic rubber 2,232; passenger cars (units) 6,546; commercial vehicles (units) 1,693. Merchant vessels launched (100 gross tons and over; 1970) 338,-000 gross tons. New dwelling units started (1970) 1,467,000.

CONRAD, REGISTER & TRIBUNE SYNDICATE

THE VANISHING RIGHT OF PRIVACY

By Robert Sherrill

The wilderness of the New World was, the historians tell us, pushed back and settled and then pushed back again by people who "kept to themselves," who enjoyed privacy and who felt that any neighbour closer than ten miles was practically an intruder. And because such areas commonly attract people who prefer to forget the past, the code of the frontier, especially in the Old West, discouraged (often on penalty of violence) unnecessary inquiries into a man's private life and his background.

If those attitudes were a mark of the nation's youth, then the year 1971 indicated as never before the approach of middle age. It was becoming clear that privacy—or what Justice Louis Brandeis called "the most comprehensive of rights and the right most valued by civilized men," which is "the right to be let alone" —would henceforth be virtually unobtainable.

This outlook developed in part, of course, from the tendency among Americans to pack into urban areas, elbow to elbow. But the most invidious intrusion into the life of the individual was coming from governmental and business investigators, cooperating in the construction of what Sen. Sam J. Ervin, Jr. (Washington's most vigorous critic of the trend), called "a dossier society." Skeletons that used to be in closets were now in files, officially indexed.

Having downgraded the frontier's ideals of liberty and privacy, it was only fitting that the new urban, commercial society impose ideals (loyalty, efficiency, honesty) that it could measure from outside the individual and against an artificial, consensus scale. Does the citizen belong to "dangerous" or "constructive" organizations? Does he spend his spare time in such a way as to increase or decrease (boozing? or bowling?) his work performance? Does he pay his bills? And it was also fitting that a technology-oriented society bring the latest prying and compiling devices into the process—telephone wiretaps, bugs (hidden microphones), and computer data banks.

Snooping's Seal of Approval. In this respect 1971 was very much into the new era, with the tone coming from the very top of the political hierarchy. To set more rigid standards of patriotism, Pres. Richard Nixon revived the Subversive Activities Control Board, which had been all but defunct for 20 years, and gave it new powers to investigate individuals and organizations for "subversive" traits. The SACB was expected to compile a list of taboo organizations; anyone who belonged to them or who was even suspected of having "sympathetic association" with people whom the SACB considered dangerously unorthodox would be blackballed from government employment (many private employers also were expected to use the list). Atty. Gen. John Mitchell denounced the federal courts for denying him carte blanche wiretapping powers against anyone he considered a potential "domestic subversive"; he conceded that innocent people would be hurt in his wiretap sweep, but he said that couldn't be helped. (The rate of official wiretapping increased 100% between 1969 and 1970.) And Assistant Atty. Gen. Robert Mardian indicated in testimony before Congress that the administration was considering a loyalty purge among government employees. To keep "terrorist revolutionists"—he did not define the phrase— off the payroll, said Mardian, they were thinking also of running a

preemployment FBI investigation on all supervisory personnel.

These public developments were in perfect harmony with other activities which the government would have preferred to keep secret. The State Department's Passport Office admitted reluctantly, under questioning from newsmen, that it did have a secret, computerized "lookout list" of 250,000 names; when people on that list apply for a passport, the Passport Office tips off certain officials. Sen. Edmund Muskie disclosed that the FBI had been caught infiltrating the ecology movement. Senator Ervin's Constitutional Rights Subcommittee held hearings that elaborately revealed—or re-revealed, since some of the material had first come to light in 1970—that for several years more than a thousand military spies had been putting together dossiers on 25 million civilians—all kinds: businessmen, teachers, students, ecologists, black militants, civil rights demonstrators, birth-control advocates. There was much more rhyme than reason to their spying routine. Sen. Eugene McCarthy's phone had been tapped at the 1968 Democratic convention, for example; the military agents seriously recorded in McCarthy's dossier that he had made a call to "a known leftist organization" to see if medical help was needed for some of the wounded demonstrators.

If a shy American could find any comfort in the year's disclosures, it was in learning that government snooping did have this democratic quality—the eyes behind the two-way mirrors were looking at senators and other important people and at the relatives of important people, as well as at ordinary citizens. When a mischievous group of dissenters stole records from the Media, Pa., FBI office and sent them to various newspapers, the public learned that federal agents had been keeping dossiers not only on a Boy Scout leader, tourists, and professors but also on the college-age daughter of Rep. Henry Reuss, an ideologically moderate and influential member of congressional banking committees. Rep. Hale Boggs, majority leader of the House, complained that the FBI had tapped his telephone and that he knew of at least three other members of Congress who had been subjected to similar harassment. After first denying that they had ever put any member of Congress under surveillance, both the Justice Department and the FBI admitted that hidden microphones had been used to record conversations between Rep. John Dowdy of Texas and an FBI informant.

Knowing they are in such notable company may be especially comforting to federal employees, whose dossiers already over-

---

Robert Sherrill is a Washington correspondent and the author of The Accidental President *and* Gothic Politics in the Deep South.

flow with job profile and personality tests containing such questions as "Do you think there is anything wrong with your sex organs?" and "Do you think Jesus Christ was a greater man than Abraham Lincoln?" In 1971 Senator Ervin uncovered a new test, with more urbane questions, such as "Do you cross your legs and if so which one goes on top?" and "Do you bite or cut off the end of a cigar?"

Dossiers Unlimited. Outwardly slapstick some of the prying may seem, but experts warn that there is nothing at all funny about what is happening. Arthur R. Miller, whose *The Assault on Privacy* (University of Michigan Press, 1971) is the most authoritative survey of the scope and impact of surveillance in the U.S., points out that already the average adult is the subject of 10 to 20 dossiers in government and private files, many of them filled with bizarre, inaccurate, vengeful, and irrelevant data, which never will be discarded.

"Each time a citizen files a tax return, applies for life insurance or credit card, seeks government benefits, or interviews for a job," says Miller, "a dossier is opened under his name and an informational profile on him is sketched." And it will live as long as he does. One need not be a revolutionary or a sexual deviant to wind up with a permanent dossier in the FBI files. The *New York Times* reported that the FBI compiled a "lifetime profile" on a 35-year-old hospital attendant whose only brush with the law occurred in 1954, a breach of the peace for which he was fined $5.

Putting together ten dossiers per adult would not be difficult from the government's files alone. Nine out of ten workers have records at the Social Security Administration. The Internal Revenue Service has the tax records of 75 million citizens. The Civil Service Commission controls the files on 10 million people who have tried to get government jobs since 1939, plus 1.5 million who are filed away as suspected subversives. The FBI's computerized National Crime Information Center reportedly has more than 1.7 million personal files and 195 million sets of fingerprints. The Pentagon has files on 25 million persons, including 7 million on whom "security, loyalty, criminal and other types of investigations" have been run, and including especially 14,000 who are marked for detention if ever an insurrection occurs. The Department of Transportation has the names of 2.6 million Americans who did not pass their driving tests or whose licenses were revoked. The Veterans Administration has dossiers on more than 13.5 million veterans who have drawn benefits. And on and on around the bureaucracy, but always skimming lightly, for as Miller says, "Even now only the extremities of a vast, subterranean information structure may be visible."

Beyond the bureaucracy there are the watchdogs of patriotism in Congress—the House Internal Security Committee (formerly the House Un-American Activities Committee) and the Senate Internal Security Committee, each with its files crammed with the names of individuals and organizations deemed suspect if not downright dangerous.

And beyond the federal government is the impressive web of commercial investigation, led by such groups as the Associated Credit Bureaus of America, largest of the trade associations, which has records on about 100 million persons and steadily supplements its information from 2,100 member credit bureaus. Among the "investigatory" type agencies, the largest and perhaps the most aggressive is the Retail Credit Company of Atlanta, whose 7,000 inspectors operating out of 1,225 offices are not at all reluctant to give their final opinion about a credit applicant's psyche and character after chatting with the subject's neighbours and fellow workers for half an hour. If they conclude that a youth's long hair should be equated with the probable consumption of pot, the family's auto insurance may be canceled.

Big Brother Grows Up. To civil libertarians, the existence of any one of these surveillance operations—executive branch, congressional, or private—without adequate control by the general public seems a sinister matter. But they do not operate singly. They are intricately tied together, which means that gossip, rumour, wild presumption, libel, and fact mix together and wash back and forth between government law-enforcement agencies, private law-enforcement agencies, credit bureaus, and business concerns in such volume as to defy control.

Although federal law specifically prohibits the FBI from circulating information obtained by telephone taps, the FBI does, nevertheless, provide this and other secret information to selected congressional committees, including the HISC and the SISC, and they in turn have been known to slip the information to favoured outsiders. The FBI also supplies arrest records and other confidential information about individuals to some insurance companies and banks. Occasionally, too, the FBI releases secret data for no apparent reason but revenge; when a TWA pilot criticized the FBI's handling of an airplane hijacking incident, J. Edgar Hoover released confidential records to TWA's board chairman to show that the pilot had had trouble when he was in the Air Force. Not to be outdone in this swapping, airlines permit federal and state sleuths to examine their computer data to see who traveled where, with whom, and what hotels they stayed in.

At that stratum of government and industry where dossiers and data banks have a life of their own, the quality of the material contained in the files seems to matter very little, even though the use of the material may be critical to an individual's reputation and career. Military surveillance agents (many of whose files were inherited by the FBI) commonly categorized a subject as "Communist" or "non-Communist" on no more conclusive evidence than the photo of a rally. Robert E. Jordan III, the Army's general counsel, acknowledged that "most of it [the surveillance data] was garbage," but this garbage is still in government files. Of much the same quality is the data accumulated by credit bureaus, put together from newspaper clips, plus a scavenging of public records (arrests, births, deaths, lawsuits), plus neighbourhood chitchat and employers' judgments. In 1969, FBI and Internal Revenue Service agents paid 50,000 visits to credit bureaus to get that kind of information.

As for the antisubversive congressional committees, they, too, rely on gossip, rumour, clippings. In 1971 the SISC inherited material that will fit in perfectly. These were the Van Deman files. Col. Ralph Van Deman retired from the Army in 1929, and until his death in 1952 he and his wife collected information on 250,000 individuals and organizations whom the Van Demans considered to be subversive. This impressive compilation of one couple's prejudices was turned over to Sen. James Eastland of Mississippi, chairman of the SISC. If he uses the material as he has used other "raw" material in the past, the names of people whose patriotism did not measure up to the standard set by an army officer will find their way into the *Congressional Record* from time to time.

To many observers, the most chilling thing about the developing dossier society is the quality of anarchy. No one controls the world of surveillance; there are no rules, no accepted code of conduct, no arbitrator, and apparently no penalties for wrongdoing. There is even a vast amount of confusion about how many computers are already riddling the citizen's privacy. Sen. William Proxmire of Wisconsin said in May 1971 that his Economy in Government Subcommittee had found 5,277 computer systems in the government, but eight months earlier Rep. Frank Horton of New York, a member of the Special Subcommittee on Invasion of Privacy, said the executive branch had over 10,000 computers.

Top Pentagon officials acknowledged they were ignorant of the existence of four computerized data banks stuffed with goodies about civilian "suspects"; later it turned out that the military was operating still another surveillance ring without the knowledge of civilian officials. The Justice Department had condoned the same type of freedom among its sleuths. Assistant Attorney General Mardian admitted that there are no specific, regular guidelines for FBI agents to follow in their campaign against college dissenters, black militants, and New Left political activists. Anything goes. Informants as young as 18 have been recruited; so have the relatives of suspects.

The Secret Service has been equally industrious in recruiting

flation." The program of wage and price restraint would be continued after the end of the freeze, he said, and he announced new administrative machinery for Phase Two—a Price Commission, a Pay Board, and a Government Committee on Interest and Dividends. Moreover, the Cost of Living Council established in Phase One (the 90-day freeze) of the stabilization program would continue to operate under the chairmanship of Secretary of the Treasury John B. Connally, Jr.

On the day the president spoke, the White House issued an explanation of the Phase Two program. It stated that the Cost of Living Council had proposed an interim goal of 2–3% annual inflation rate by the end of 1972—about half the rate prevailing before the freeze. In addition, it disclosed that a Committee on Health Services and a Committee on State and Local Government Cooperation would be set up to assist the Cost of Living Council in its work. Members of the various Phase Two bodies were appointed by Nixon later in the month.

While Americans generally took the 90-day freeze

and Phase Two in stride, foreign countries were alarmed by the implications of the 10% import surcharge and the new nonconvertibility of the dollar into gold. The international monetary system, which for a quarter-century had hinged on U.S. readiness to exchange dollars for gold at the rate of $35 an ounce, seemed in danger of drifting into chaos. Then, after meeting with Pompidou in the Azores, Nixon announced on December 14 that the U.S. was prepared to devalue the dollar by a small but undetermined amount as part of an international agreement to realign the rates of major world currencies.

Only four days later, representatives of the world's ten leading non-Communist industrial nations announced agreement on a new set of exchange rates after two days of talks in Washington. The Group of Ten concluded that the dollar would be devalued by 7.89% in terms of gold, the West German mark would be revalued upward by 4.6%, and the Japanese yen by 8%. Other currencies were revalued in smaller amounts, but the net effect was a dollar devaluation of nearly 12%. The realignment of exchange rates was expected to produce, within three years, an improve-

informants, encouraging civil servants to report the names of any citizens who by telephone or letter indicate they are "malcontents," who persist in "seeking redress for imagined grievances," or who sound as though they would be willing to "embarrass" the president or other government leaders. To some critics, this description of a "suspect" sounds very much like the average citizen who has been frustrated in dealing with the government. The Secret Service does not look tolerantly upon disgruntled Americans; all names of this kind are filed away, apparently without distinction, among those of potential assassins and persons who have been convicted of actually making physical threats against the president.

The same kind of overlapping criteria—by which philosophical dissenters are lumped with bomb throwers—is found in the files of the Department of Justice Interdivisional Information Unit, whose 14,000 dossiers include members of the American Nazi Party, members of the Ku Klux Klan, opponents of the war in Vietnam, outspoken advocates of higher welfare payments, and elected officials who condone civil rights protest marches—the only commonality being that the "suspects" believe strongly in something.

A Future with No Hiding Place? Efforts to turn back the dossier and data-bank tide so far have been futile. They also have been weak and defensive. There is legislation now in Congress, but not moving, that would require some federal agencies, on request, to tell a citizen what they have on him and to permit him to file supplementary material correcting his profile—more or less the same provisions as those of the Fair Credit Reporting Act of 1971, which applies to credit bureau files. But how many Americans would suspect, say, that the Federal Housing Administration had a card describing their drinking habits? And how many would know how to go about discovering the existence of that card, or what to do about it if they did find out? Aside from the impossibility of counteracting a government program on a case-by-case basis, there is still the question: Isn't there more to privacy than an accurate dossier? If government snoops became perfectly accurate, a citizen might still prefer, in Justice William O. Douglas' words, "to select for himself the time and circumstances when he will share his secrets with others and decide the extent of that sharing."

Expansion, the first impulse of government, will afflict surveillance until Congress not only forbids the collecting of new material but also forces the disgorging of much of the data already stored. Congress has never seriously considered legislation that would weed out the more offensive files and prohibit their

being filled again; it gets no shoves from the tolerant electorate, which seems perfectly content to accept the assurance of Assistant Atty. Gen. (later Supreme Court Justice) William H. Rehnquist that "self-discipline on the part of the executive branch will provide an answer to virtually all of the legitimate complaints against the excesses of information-gathering."

The significant enthusiasm and energy in this quarrel over the right to privacy comes from the other side, brought together by special interests that would like to widen the access to information about a person's beliefs and private conduct. Early in 1971 the Defense Department's Industry Advisory Council met in executive session with Pentagon officials to urge that the government supply defense industrialists with FBI and other law-enforcement data that would help them spot potential troublemakers on the assembly line. If the government refused to divulge this information, said Mark Shepherd, Jr., president of Texas Instruments Inc., "industry may in effect have to establish an undercover organization of its own in order to protect itself."

Shepherd's proposal, supported by the other 23 defense industrialists and financiers in the IAC, also won the backing of Maj. Gen. Lloyd B. Ramsey, the Army's provost marshal general, who warned the group of "worse things to come"—things like "dissension among the work forces." Wider and deeper and more personal surveillance, he said, was necessary to protect industry.

Wider and deeper surveillance is the very thing the Office of Management and Budget proposed in the form of a National Data Bank, linking together all the executive branch computers and pouring into a central office the tax, census, military, educational, criminal, and business data that trail behind every person in America as he moves through the maze of citizenship. So far the OMB has been rebuffed in its request for the formal approval of Congress, but some believe the bank is already operating on the sly.

Supposing the intruders should have their way entirely, what will be the upshot of it all? Among civil libertarians who have been the closest observers of this trend, it is easy to get a dire answer. Ralph Nader is convinced that citizens "can be reduced to a new form of computer-indentured slavery." And Senator Ervin, who is normally sparing of pessimism, warns that "instant black-listing, rapid cross-country exchange of dossiers, million-name master indexes, and scientific surveillance can easily become the order of the political day. Government would know all about the individual citizen, his habits, his livelihood, his thoughts, his aspirations, his hopes, and his fears. Such a society will not be free."

Pres. Richard Nixon
greets enthusiastic
admirers on May 25, 1971,
in Mobile, Ala.,
where he attended
a ceremony opening
construction of the
Tennessee-Tombigbee
Waterway.

WIDE WORLD

ment of about $9 billion in the U.S. balance of payments—an amount roughly equal to the 1971 U.S. deficit in trade, tourism, and long-term investment. For its part, the U.S. consented to remove its 10% surcharge on imports and a "buy-American" clause in the new 7% investment tax credit.

The interrelated issues of government intelligence and information practices received considerable attention in 1971. In the first half of the year, the FBI and its director, J. Edgar Hoover, were accused by several members of Congress and others of monitoring the activities of persons not involved in or suspected of any crime. A prime source of material for these charges was provided in some of the 1,200 documents stolen from the bureau's Media, Pa., office in March. A self-styled Citizens' Commission to Investigate the FBI, which claimed credit for the burglary, distributed copies of the documents, a few at a time, to selected newspapers and members of Congress.

The first set of stolen documents to be made public dealt with investigations of students, blacks, and New Left groups. Among the 14 items in the set were an order from Hoover to investigate all student groups "organized to project the demands of black students" and a paper noting the plans of an Idaho Boy Scout leader to take his troop to visit the Soviet Union. The document that attracted the most attention, however, was a newsletter from the FBI's Philadelphia office. Increased interviewing of persons identified with the New Left was necessary, the newsletter said, because "it will enhance the paranoia endemic in these circles and will further serve to get the point across that there is an FBI agent behind every mailbox." Some of those interviewed, moreover, "will be overcome with the overwhelming personalities of the contacting agents and volunteer to tell all—perhaps on a continuing basis."

A second, more far-reaching controversy involved publication of the Pentagon papers. At issue was the publication, first by the *New York Times* and later by several other newspapers, of excerpts from a 7,000-page "History of the United States Decision-Making Process on Vietnam Policy" commissioned by Robert S. McNamara when he was secretary of defense under Pres. Lyndon B. Johnson. The study was classified as "top secret-sensitive" and consisted of a critique of U.S. Indochina policy up to 1968, plus texts of relevant documents.

Much of the ensuing uproar centred on the "top secret" label the study carried and, by extension, on the integrity of the classification system itself. Nixon administration officials contended that disclosure of the documents was not only unauthorized but also

harmful to the defense and diplomatic interests of the U.S. Press executives generally took the position that the study dealt with events long past and thus constituted a historical treatise that the public was entitled to read. The information that appeared in print, they further asserted, was not damaging to national interests; at most, it was embarrassing to those involved in making Vietnam policy.

Legal action initiated by the Justice Department interrupted the publication in four newspapers of articles quoting from the Pentagon papers. A flurry of appeals followed, culminating in a 6-to-3 decision by the U.S. Supreme Court on June 30 upholding the right of the *New York Times* and the *Washington Post* to resume publication of their respective series. Restraining orders against the *St. Louis Post-Dispatch* and the *Boston Globe* were lifted by federal district judges the same day. Although the Supreme Court was more divided than its 6-to-3 margin of decision would indicate, it generally agreed with the newspapers that the First Amendment ruled out prior censorship of the press.

Having lost its battle to block publication of the Pentagon papers, the government prepared to prosecute the man accused of distributing them to the press, Daniel Ellsberg (*see* BIOGRAPHY), a former analyst for the Rand Corporation and one of the authors of the study. A federal grand jury in Los Angeles indicted Ellsberg June 28 on charges of violating the Espionage Act and of stealing government property. Surrendering to the U.S. attorney in Boston the same day, Ellsberg said: "I did this clearly at my own jeopardy and I am prepared to answer to all the consequences of these decisions." Nevertheless, he pleaded not guilty before a federal district judge in Los Angeles on August 16. (*See* PUBLISHING.)

The explosive conditions inside the nation's prisons were dramatized in 1971 by a number of violent incidents. Forty-three persons died at the Attica Correctional Facility in Attica, N.Y., when 1,500 state troopers, sheriff's deputies, and prison guards staged an air and ground assault to put down an uprising by 1,200 inmates. The dead included 34 prisoners and 9 guards and civilian employees. Most of the prisoners killed in the onslaught died from the attackers' gunfire. Early reports by prison officials said that most of the slain hostages died when convicts slashed their throats; other hostages were said to have been beaten and stabbed to death. However, the report was contradicted when a medical examiner said that official autopsies showed the nine hostages had died of gunshot wounds. New York State Commissioner of Corrections Russell G. Oswald later confirmed the autopsy findings.

In an earlier incident three prisoners and three prison guards were killed during an escape attempt

The 26th Amendment to the Constitution was ratified by the required 38 states during 1971. Ohio's legislature was the 38th to ratify, doing so on June 30. The amendment was certified by Pres. Richard Nixon in a White House ceremony on July 5. The text of the amendment:

Article XXVI—1. The right of citizens of the United States, who are eighteen years of age or older, to vote shall not be denied or abridged by the United States or by any State on account of age.

2. The Congress shall have the power to enforce this article by appropriate legislation.

at the California State Prison at San Quentin. According to official accounts, black militant George Jackson, who had acquired fame as one of the three "Soledad Brothers," was shot to death as he dashed across the prison yard. After order was restored, the bodies of the three guards and of two white prisoners were found in Jackson's cellblock. California authorities later said they were looking for Stephen M. Bingham, a 29-year-old lawyer, for questioning about the gun carried by Jackson in the break. Bingham was believed to be the last person to visit Jackson before he attempted to escape. (*See* PRISONS AND PENOLOGY.)

With one major exception, the pace of antiwar protests slowed markedly in 1971. The year's chief demonstration against the war occurred in Washington, D.C., in late April and early May. The scheduled two weeks of antiwar activities remained peaceful until May 3, when leaders of the Mayday Tribe threatened to bring activity in the capital to a halt by blocking streets and bridges. Although some disruption of traffic occurred, the demonstrators fell far short of their announced goal. More than 7,000 were detained in mass arrests that were sharply criticized by civil libertarians. (RI. W.)

ENCYCLOPÆDIA BRITANNICA FILMS. *The Industrial Revolution—Beginnings in the United States* (1968); *Midwest—Heartland of the Nation* (1968); *Produce—From Farm to Market* (1968); *Heritage in Black* (1969); *The Pacific West* (1969); *The Rise of Labor* (1969); *The South: Roots of the Urban Crisis* (1969); *Chicano from the Southwest* (1970); *The Industrial Worker* (1970); *Linda and Billy Ray from Appalachia* (1970); *The Mississippi System—Waterway of Commerce* (1970); *The Presidency—Search for a Candidate* (1970); *The Rise of Big Business* (1970); *The Rise of the American City* (1970); *An Essay on War* (1971); *The Great Lakes* (1971); *Jesse from Mississippi* (1971); *Johnny from Fort Apache* (1971); *The Progressive Era* (1971).

Upper Volta

A republic of West Africa, Upper Volta is bordered by Mali, Niger, Dahomey, Togo, Ghana, and Ivory Coast. Area: 105,870 sq.mi. (274,200 sq.km.). Pop. (1970 est.): 5,485,981. Cap. and largest city: Ouagadougou (pop., 1970 est., 110,000). Language: French (official). Religion: animist; Muslim and Christian minorities. President in 1971, Gen. Sangoule Lamizana; premier from February 13, Gérard Kango Ouedraogo.

The military regime that had been in power since 1966 showed signs in 1971 of a desire to hasten Upper Volta's return to civilian rule. With persistent and strict austerity policies the military government had

---

UPPER VOLTA

Education. (1968–69) Primary, pupils 99,827, teachers (including preprimary) 2,292; secondary, pupils 8,117, teachers 432; vocational, pupils 1,298, teachers (1967–68) 106; teacher training (1967–68), students 1,114, teachers 35; higher, students 122, teaching staff (1967–68) 17.

Finance. Monetary unit: CFA franc, with a parity of CFA Fr. 50 to the French franc (CFA Fr. 277.71 = U.S. $1; CFA Fr. 666.60 = £1 sterling) and a free rate (Sept. 27, 1971) of CFA Fr. 276.50 to U.S. $1 (CFA Fr. 685.75 = £1). Budget (total; 1970 est.) balanced at CFA Fr. 9,757,000,000.

Foreign Trade. (1970) Imports CFA Fr. 12,960,-000,000; exports CFA Fr. 5,060,000,000. Import sources: France 45%; Ivory Coast 11%; West Germany 6%; U.S. 5%. Export destinations: Ivory Coast 34%; France 12%; Ghana 10%; Italy 9%. Main exports: livestock 31%; cotton 26%; oilseeds 26%.

---

managed to improve the financial situation of the country, left on the verge of bankruptcy by former president Maurice Yaméogo. In February, President Lamizana appointed Gérard Kango Ouedraogo premier, a step regarded as marking a definite stage in the gradual return to normal constitutional government.

According to the terms of the 1970 constitution, Lamizana would remain in power until 1975. However, the military retained only five portfolios in the new Cabinet appointed by Ouedraogo, and from midyear the new premier took an active part in the government.

In October, Lamizana paid an official visit to France, where he had talks with Pres. Georges Pompidou. During his visit Lamizana stressed the importance to his country of French cooperation and aid and succeeded in obtaining a significant increase in French financial and economic assistance. Other topics for discussion included the development of the valleys of the three Volta rivers and the creation of a centre for specialized higher education at Ouagadougou.

(PH. D.)

Uruguay

A republic of South America, Uruguay is on the Atlantic Ocean and is bounded by Brazil and Argentina. Area: 68,536 sq.mi. (177,508 sq.km.). Pop. (1971 est.): 2,921,000, including white 89%; mestizo 10%. Cap. and largest city: Montevideo (pop., 1967, 1,-280,000). Language: Spanish. Religion: mainly Roman Catholic. President in 1971, Jorge Pacheco Areco.

Political activity was dominated again in 1971 by the long-standing conflict between the executive branch and legislature over methods of suppressing the Tupamaro guerrillas. Censure motions by the legislature on the special security measures imposed in June 1969 forced many Cabinet reshuffles and ministerial resignations. In January, following the guerrilla kidnapping of the British ambassador, Geoffrey Jackson, President Pacheco requested the suspension of individual constitutional guarantees for 90 days, but the legislature authorized only a 40-day suspension. Then in July the legislature voted to annul the security measures. These were reimposed by presidential decree, but the legislature almost succeeded in impeaching the president for this action.

On February 21 the Tupamaros freed a Brazilian diplomat, Aloysio Dias Gomide, after 206 days in captivity, when his wife paid a ransom of between $250,000 and $650,000. On September 6, to the government's great embarrassment, 106 guerrillas escaped from the Punta Carretas prison via a tunnel. Included in their number were the founder of the Tupamaros, Raúl Sendic, and his two lieutenants, Jorge Manera Lluveras and Julio Marenales Saenz. The British ambassador was soon after "amnestied" by the Tupamaros and released.

Following the establishment by the government of a centralized executive council to run secondary education in place of "suspect" committees that had been elected by the teaching staffs, Congress declared the move unconstitutional and called for the reinstatement of the original committees. Children supported the committees by staging sit-ins, demonstrations, and occupations of schools, and the government replied by supporting a rightist "Uruguayan Youth on

Uruguay's Chamber of Deputies voted on July 23, 1971, to impeach Pres. Jorge Pacheco Areco but failed to obtain the two-thirds majority necessary for his immediate removal.
KEYSTONE

Universalist Church: *see* Religion

Universities: *see* Education

Uranium: *see* Mining

Urban Affairs: *see* Cities and Urban Affairs

WIDE WORLD

Two helicopters crash,
killing eight onlookers,
along the banks
of Río de la Plata
near Montevideo during
festivities celebrating
the Uruguayan Navy's
154th anniversary
on Nov. 14, 1971.

Guard." When it was discovered that one clash between schoolchildren and a group of adults had been provoked by a police inspector, the minister of the interior, Santiago de Brum Carbajal, resigned.

Presidential elections were held on November 28 after much maneuvering by splinter groups. The traditional political picture showed a marked change with the emergence of a left-wing alliance known as the Frente Amplio (Broad Front), led by Gen. Liber Seregni, whose platform included land reform, na-

tionalization of the banks, and government control of the export industries, similar to the policies of the Marxist government in Chile. In the election the Frente Amplio received less than 19% of the votes. President Pacheco failed to win a simultaneous plebiscite on a constitutional amendment that would have allowed him to succeed himself in office, but his protégé in the Colorado Party, Juan María Bordaberry (*see* BIOGRAPHY), seemed to have narrowly defeated the Blanco Party candidate, Wilson Ferreira Aldunate. The Blanco Party, however, stated that the handling of the count "does not merit the confidence of the party" and asked the Army to supervise a recount, which began on December 6.

On the economic front government policy continued to aim at a realistic balance between monetary stability and growth. The official growth forecast for 1971 was 5% (1970, 4.5%); cattle production continued to increase though crop harvests were expected to decline. The meat-packing and motor-vehicle industries showed significant rises, although production in other sectors remained stagnant.   (J. J. SM.)

Vatican City State

This independent sovereignty is surrounded by but not part of Rome. As a state with territorial limits, it is properly distinguished from the Holy See, which constitutes the worldwide administrative and legislative body for the Roman Catholic Church. The area of Vatican City is 108.7 ac. (44 ha.). Pop. (1971 est.): 648. As sovereign pontiff, Paul VI is the chief of state. Vatican City is administered by a pontifical commission of five cardinals, of which the secretary of state, Jean Cardinal Villot, is president.

The growth of contacts with Eastern Europe was marked by two important visits to the Vatican—those of the Soviet foreign minister, Andrei Gromyko, in November 1970 and of Marshal Tito of Yugoslavia in March 1971. The visit (postponed from 1970) of the Yugoslav chief of state was in several respects the crowning achievement of the policy of détente undertaken by the Vatican and Belgrade to renew normal relations. With Moscow things did not go as well; Archbishop Agostino Casaroli, chief of the Vatican diplomatic staff, visited the Soviet capital in February, but he was unable to bring back from the U.S.S.R. the desired assurances concerning the fate of the Catholic Church there.

Inconclusive agreements were reached with Czechoslovakia, Hungary, and Poland during the year. Negotiations with Hungary and personal pleas from Pope Paul led to the return to Rome in September of Jozsef Cardinal Mindszenty (*see* BIOGRAPHY), a voluntary prisoner in the U.S. embassy in Budapest since the Hungarian uprising of 1956.

Other notable events of the year were the visit of Emperor Haile Selassie of Ethiopia to the pope (the two had already met in Geneva in 1969); the Holy See's adherence to the nuclear nonproliferation treaty; its decision to seek representation in the European Economic Community; and the pope's reiterated calls for peace in the Middle East and aid to the victims of the disturbances in East Pakistan.

(Mx. B.)

See also Religion.

URUGUAY

Education. (1968–69) Primary, pupils 369,816, teachers 13,095; secondary, pupils 118,082, teachers 9,715; vocational, pupils 35,648, teachers 3,048; teacher training, students 6,963; higher, students 18,-650, teaching staff (1963–64) 2,182.

Finance. Monetary unit: peso, with an official rate of 250 pesos to U.S. \$1 (600 pesos = £1 sterling) and a free rate (Oct. 18, 1971) of 620 pesos to £1. Gold, SDRs, and foreign exchange, official: (June 1971) U.S. \$175 million; (June 1970) U.S. \$195 million. Budget (1969 est.): revenue 46,383,000,000 pesos; expenditure 52,288,000,000 pesos. Gross national product: (1968) 376,744,000,000 pesos; (1967) 164,476,000,000 pesos. Money supply: (Dec. 1970) 89,333,000,000 pesos; (Dec. 1969) 76,695,000,000 pesos. Cost of living (Montevideo; 1963 = 100): (June 1971) 2,792; (June 1970) 2,310.

Foreign Trade. (1970) Imports U.S. \$232.8 million; exports U.S. \$232.7 million. Import sources (1969): U.S. 14%; Brazil 13%; West Germany 11%; Argentina 10%; U.K. 6%; Kuwait 6%; Spain 5%. Export destinations (1969): U.K. 13%; Italy 10%; West Germany 10%; Spain 8%; Netherlands 7%; U.S. 7%; Brazil 5%. Main exports: meat 38%; wool 31%; hides and skins 10%.

Transport and Communications. Roads (1968) c. 42,000 km. (including c. 5,000 km. with improved surface). Motor vehicles in use (1969): passenger 195,600; commercial (including buses) 83,000. Railways (1969) 2,975 km. Air traffic (1970): 78.2 million passenger-km.; freight 220,000 net ton-km. Shipping (1970): merchant vessels 100 gross tons and over 41; gross tonnage 140,657. Telephones (Jan. 1970) 206,600. Radio receivers (Dec. 1969) 1,080,-000. Television receivers (Dec. 1969) 220,000.

Agriculture. Production (in 000; metric tons; 1970; 1969 in parentheses): wheat 388 (403); barley 50 (41); oats c. 62 (60); sweet potatoes (1969) c. 81, (1968) c. 81; corn 139 (129); sorghum 35 (51); linseed 81 (56); sunflower seed 65 (63); rice 142 (134); sugar, raw value (1970–71) c. 55, (1969–70) 45; oranges c. 60 (c. 60); wine c. 91 (c. 91); wool c. 44 (47); beef and veal c. 380 (352). Livestock (in 000; May 1970): cattle c. 8,500; sheep c. 21,800; horses c. 430; pigs c. 370; chickens c. 7,800.

Industry. Production (in 000; metric tons; 1969): cement 467; limestone 741; electricity (excluding most industrial production; kw-hr.) 2,026,000.

Venezuela

A republic of northern South America, Venezuela is bounded by Colombia, Brazil, Guyana, and the Caribbean Sea. Area: 352,143 sq.mi. (912,050 sq.km.). Pop. (1970 est.): 10,399,000, including mestizo 69%; white 20%; Negro 9%; Indian 2%. Cap. and largest city: Caracas (metro. pop., 1970 est., 2,175,438). Language: Spanish. Religion: predominantly Roman Catholic. President in 1971, Rafael Caldera.

The deployment of government resources and the role of foreign investment in the economy were the key political issues in Venezuela in 1971. The Colombian border problem took on a new significance during the year, while for the economy the signature of service contracts by Shell, Occidental, and Mobil oil companies heralded a new phase of production in the petroleum sector.

In 1970 the government had come under severe criticism for its direction and control of the use of public funds. Recognizing that there was room for improvement in this respect, Finance Minister Pedro Tinoco introduced a number of corrective measures that included: the establishment of a public expenditures commission; new guidelines for the autonomous institutions to ensure better use of their resources; and the introduction of an administrative reform program covering all governmental institutions.

The new banking law passed late in 1970 was the first of a series of measures designed to provide a new framework for foreign investors in Venezuela. It stipulated that banks with foreign ownership of more than 20% no longer could accept savings deposits, issue negotiable deposit certificates, or sell foreign exchange acquired from the Banco Central. Moreover, their deposits could not exceed six times their capital and reserves, compared with a limit of eight times capital and reserves for local banks. This was followed by a bill to place the domestic oil-products market completely under the control of the state oil company, Corporación Venezolana del Petróleo. The government also established a committee to define the role of private capital in Venezuela's future economic development, and promulgated the oil reversion and gas nationalization laws.

The oil reversion law allowed the government to take over within three years the underdeveloped parts of oil concessions held by foreign companies, to assume ownership of foreign companies' oil-producing and processing equipment on the expiration of their concessions, and to evaluate and control the use of the assets to be handed over. The gas nationalization law provided for state retention of gas obtained from hydrocarbon deposits and stated that companies formed to process and transport the gas must be Venezuelan-owned unless special laws were passed to cover individual cases.

Many saw in these developments a reflection of the general trend toward economic nationalism in Latin America, the oil reversion and gas nationalization laws in particular provoking a wave of criticism. In a midyear speech, however, the finance minister emphasized that while foreign investment would be excluded from a small sector of the economy, it would be actively encouraged in others; all foreign investors would be assured of the repatriation of capital, profits, and interest, and of fair compensation in case of expropriation. Regarding the oil reversion law, he stated that the original agreement, signed some 30 years earlier, had stipulated that oil-company installations would be handed over to the state on the expiration of a concession; the new law merely provided an unequivocal definition ensuring that Venezuela inherited useful assets and allowing the companies a fair return on their investments.

The problem of the border with Colombia, especially in the oil-rich Gulf of Venezuela, remained dormant for much of the year while negotiations took place in Rome. Then in early October it was reported that two Venezuelan newspapers had published secret defense documents revealing the country's military preparedness and plan of action for any eventual conflict with its neighbour. At about the same time the Swedish government was reported unwilling to sell fighter planes to Venezuela, and shortly afterward the talks in Rome ended without agreement. Both governments attempted to play down the issue, however, agreeing to resume talks at a later date.

As expected, Venezuela's economic growth rate in 1970 (5–6%) exceeded that of 1969 (3.5%), due to increases in production of 3.1% for petroleum, 6.2% for finance and commerce, 7.2% for manufacturing,

VENEZUELA

Education. (1968–69) Primary, pupils 1,602,433, teachers 48,382; secondary, pupils 254,513, teachers 11,649; vocational (including teacher training), pupils 139,821, teachers 7,249; higher (including 8 universities; 1967–68), students 58,747, teaching staff 5,717.

Finance. Monetary unit: bolívar, with an official selling rate of 4.50 bolívares to U.S. $1 (10.80 bolívares = £1 sterling) and a free rate (Sept. 27, 1971) of 11.13 bolívares to £1. Gold, SDRs, and foreign exchange, central bank: (June 1971) U.S. $1,089,000,-000; (June 1970) U.S. $892 million. Budget (1970 est.) balanced at 9,886,000,000 bolívares. Gross national product: (1968) 41,156,000,000 bolívares; (1967) 37,990,000,000 bolívares. Money supply: (May 1971) 7,131,000,000 bolívares; (May 1970) 6,543,000,000 bolívares. Cost of living (Caracas; 1963 = 100): (June 1971) 115; (June 1970) 111.

Foreign Trade. Imports (f.o.b.; 1969) 6,838,000,-000 bolívares; exports (1970) 11,580,000,000 bolívares. Import sources: U.S. 49%; West Germany 9%; Japan 7%; U.K. 5%; Italy 5%; Canada 5%. Export destinations (1969): U.S. 28%; Netherlands Antilles 20%; Canada 12%; Puerto Rico 6%; U.K. 5%; Trinidad and Tobago 5%. Main export crude oil and petroleum products 90%.

Transport and Communications. Roads (1969) 39,591 km. (including 495 km. expressways). Motor vehicles in use (1969): passenger 562,370; commercial 90,938. Railways (1969): 475 km.; traffic 29 million passenger-km., freight 10 million net ton-km. Air traffic (1970): 1,178,000,000 passenger-km.; freight 62,140,000 net ton-km. Shipping (1970): merchant vessels 100 gross tons and over 96; gross tonnage 392,576. Telephones (Dec. 1969) 376,945. Radio receivers (Dec. 1969) 1,685,000. Television receivers (Dec. 1968) 700,000.

Agriculture. Production (in 000; metric tons; 1970; 1969 in parentheses): corn 710 (670); rice 226 (244); sesame c. 83 (83); sweet potatoes (1969) 118, (1968) 115; cassava (1969) 310, (1968) 341; dry beans c. 50 (46); coffee c. 61 (61); tobacco c. 13 (9); cocoa (1970–71) 26, (1969–70) 26; bananas (1969) 948, (1968) 949; oranges c. 180 (170); sugar, raw value (1970–71) c. 475, (1969–70) 450; cotton, lint c. 14 (15); beef and veal c. 220 (195). Livestock (in 000; 1969–70): cattle 8,360; pigs 2,150; sheep 101; horses 423; asses c. 495; poultry c. 17,700.

Industry. Production (in 000; metric tons; 1970): crude oil 194,094; natural gas (cu.m.) 8,979,000; petroleum products (1969) 59,297; iron ore (62% metal content) 22,000; cement (1969) 2,140; gold (troy oz.; 1969) 19; diamonds (metric carats; 1969) 194; electricity (kw-hr.; 1969) c. 11,000,000.

12% for construction, 4.7% for transport and communications, 13.1% for electric energy, and 14% for iron ore. Petroleum production was 2.2% lower in the first nine months of 1971 than in the corresponding period of 1970, and the growth in the gross domestic product over the year was not expected to exceed that achieved in 1970.

Service contracts for oil development in the southern Lake Maracaibo area were finally signed by Shell, Occidental, and Mobil, after more than a year of negotiation. They required the companies to explore a given tract of land for three years at their own expense and gave the state almost 90% of any eventual profits. Meanwhile, Venezuela's economic diversification effort proceeded with the launching of a new agricultural development program, the signature of an 850 million bolívar contract between Siderurgia de Orinoco (SIDOR) and a Belgian-West German consortium for the construction of a rolled-products plant, and the presentation to Congress of a new capital market law.

The Comprehensive Agricultural Development Program initiated in 1970 was designed to raise the living standards and farm output of 63,000 low-income rural families in four major regions. The Inter-American Development Bank granted a loan of $75 million for the project, the total cost of which was reported to be approximately $181.3 million.

(Ro. E. S.)

A nurse peers into the crib of an 18-month-old gorilla being treated for a blood disorder at the zoo infirmary in Cincinnati, O

UPI COMPIX

Veterinary Medicine

The two major changes in the worldwide animal disease situation during 1971 were the outbreaks of Venezuelan equine encephalomyelitis (VEE) in Texas and of African swine fever in Cuba. Neither had ever occurred in the U.S., and considerable concern was expressed over the real or potential threat they posed to the highly susceptible equine and swine populations. A substantial number of horses had been vaccinated against the eastern and western strains of encephalomyelitis, but this conferred no protection against VEE.

VEE was first identified as a separate disease in Venezuela in 1935. It had spread to Central America by 1969 and to Mexico in 1970, where some 10,000 horses, donkeys, and burros died by the summer of 1971. More than 3,300 persons were affected, but Mexican health officials denied reports that up to 30 had died. The disease appeared in southern Texas in late June, and before the end of July had affected more than 2,000 horses, of which an estimated 800 to 1,000 died. All three strains of the virus are transmissible to man, the resulting disease being termed sleeping sickness because of the lethargy it produces, and in Texas there were 78 confirmed cases of VEE (but no deaths) in persons.

In mid-July the U.S. secretary of agriculture declared the VEE outbreak a national emergency, thus enabling the transfer of $5 million from other Department of Agriculture funds for use in combating it. An experimental vaccine developed at Ft. Detrick, Md., as a potential countermeasure in biological warfare had been tested in South and Central America, but its use in the U.S. had not been permitted because the risk of establishing the disease had not been fully assessed. With other exotic animal diseases, such as foot-and-mouth disease of cattle, the official policy had been eradication by slaughter, but this approach

was considered ill-advised for VEE, and within a week it was decided to vaccinate all horses that might be at risk.

Beginning in Texas and extending as far as California and Florida, more than two million horses in 19 states and the District of Columbia were vaccinated during a two-month period. A commercial vaccine was licensed and marketed, and the U.S. Animal Health Association, representing all state veterinarians, urged that all horses in the country be protected. Meanwhile, all horses in the affected and high-risk areas were put under quarantine, and several nations, including Canada and the U.K., placed an embargo on horses from the U.S. The immediate effect was to disrupt racing schedules.

Another approach to control was eradication of the mosquito vector by aerial spraying. By late July some 2.2 million ac. in Texas had been sprayed with insecticide, and a total area of more than 6 million ac., including parts of Louisiana, was projected. Together with vaccination and additional sanitary precautions, these measures appeared to have the disease under good control by early fall.

African swine fever had never been reported in the Western Hemisphere until June 1971, when an outbreak in Cuba was attributed to virus in meat brought from Europe. By late July some 30,000 hogs had been slaughtered in an attempt to control the disease, and plans calling for depopulation of all swine in the province of Havana were announced. As in earlier outbreaks in Italy and Spain, the mortality rate among affected hogs was high—said to be 100%—and because of its proximity there was great concern among U.S. livestock disease officials.

The disease resembles a virulent form of hog cholera (termed swine fever in Europe) and a mistake or delay in diagnosis would be costly since all swine in countries where it had not appeared would be highly susceptible. No vaccine had been developed to prevent the disease, which can be spread by virus in pork products or on clothing, thus prompting customs officials to perform even more rigid inspection at all U.S. ports of entry.

Canine brucellosis, caused by a bacterium similar to the one that causes abortion in cattle and undulant fever in man, was recently described as a separate disease of dogs in the U.S. At first it was thought to be confined to a few breeding kennels, but blood tests of dogs from pounds and dealers during the year indicated that it was widespread and a potential source of mild infection in persons. Among dogs the bacterium produces abortion in females and a chronic generalized infection in males.

Newcastle disease, a widespread fatal viral infection of poultry and ornamental birds, reached epizootic proportions in Britain. In the U.S. major outbreaks occurred in four states, and the USDA suspended entry permits for poultry products from 16 countries. Marek's disease of chickens, a form of leukemia caused by a virus like that of shingles and cold sores in man, posed a major threat in several countries. Losses in the U.S. had reached some $200 million a year. USDA veterinary scientists discovered that an "orphan" herpes virus of turkeys—so called because it produced no known disease—fully protected adult chickens but was somewhat less effective in young broilers. More recently, a sulfone compound similar to one used for treating human leprosy was found effective when used as a feed additive in extremely low concentrations.

(J. F. Ss.)

South Vietnamese soldiers, landing from helicopters at Mai Loc, South Vietnam, on Jan. 31, 1971, begin to march along Route 9 to Khe Sanh.
WIDE WORLD

Vietnam

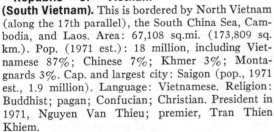

A country comprising the easternmost part of the Indochinese Peninsula, Vietnam was divided de facto into two republics on July 21, 1954.

Republic of Vietnam (South Vietnam). This is bordered by North Vietnam (along the 17th parallel), the South China Sea, Cambodia, and Laos. Area: 67,108 sq.mi. (173,809 sq. km.). Pop. (1971 est.): 18 million, including Vietnamese 87%; Chinese 7%; Khmer 3%; Montagnards 3%. Cap. and largest city: Saigon (pop., 1971 est., 1.9 million). Language: Vietnamese. Religion: Buddhist; pagan; Confucian; Christian. President in 1971, Nguyen Van Thieu; premier, Tran Thien Khiem.

An extended period of relative political stability that had covered the past several years was broken in 1971 by a general election in which the political strategy of President Thieu (see BIOGRAPHY) left him unopposed for a second term. Although the balloting was a mere referendum on Thieu's leadership, it produced a heavy voter turnout that belied the growing discontent and war-weariness of the South Vietnamese people. For them the year ended with a sense of resignation and little chance for political or military alternatives. Although conditions seemed ripe for an internal crisis, Thieu's controls over the military and the bureaucracy, plus the inability of the dissidents and the disaffected to mount sustained and effective opposition within the ostensibly democratic political system, placed the president in a near-dictatorial position.

With U.S. forces withdrawing from the country at a steady rate under the program of vietnamization, government troops provided most of the security under an umbrella of U.S. air and artillery support. The inability (or prudence) of the North Vietnamese and Viet Cong to mount large-scale military action postponed any battles in which the government's assumption of primary defense responsibilities would be tested. In 1971 the main action was initiated by the South Vietnamese, with the battleground in neighbouring Laos.

On February 8, South Vietnam announced the launching of Operation Lam Son 719, a heavy, multiunit incursion into the southern Laotian panhandle. This area had long been under Communist control and was used as a staging and logistics base for operations within South Vietnam. The stated objective of the South Vietnamese operation was to destroy the North Vietnamese supply routes along the Ho Chi Minh Trail, upsetting Hanoi's plans for further offensive action and thus permitting the safe and con-

VIETNAM: Republic

Education. (1968–69) Primary, pupils 2,083,642, teachers 36,078; secondary, pupils 556,916, teachers 14,177; vocational, pupils 13,651, teachers 582; teacher training, students 3,466, teachers 64; higher, students 39,515, teaching staff 1,253.

Finance. Monetary unit: piastre, with an official exchange rate of 118 piastres to U.S. $1 (283 piastres = £1 sterling), a parallel market rate (for exports and some imports) of 275 piastres to U.S. $1 (660 piastres = £1), and a free rate (Sept. 27, 1971) of 682 piastres to £1. Gold, SDRs, and foreign exchange, central bank: (June 1971) U.S. $188 million; (June 1970) U.S. $199 million. Budget (1969 actual): revenue 158,110,000,000 piastres; expenditure 158.7 billion piastres. Money supply: (April 1971) 182,020,000,000 piastres; (April 1970) 150,510,000,000 piastres. Cost of living (Saigon; 1963 = 100): (June 1971) 683; (June 1970) 580.

Foreign Trade. (1970) Imports 44,031,600,000 piastres; exports 915.7 million piastres. Import sources: U.S. 47%; Japan 14%; Taiwan 8%; France 6%; Singapore 6%. Export destinations: France 48%; Japan 13%; West Germany 8%; Hong Kong 7%; U.K. 6%; Singapore 5%. Main export rubber 77%.

Transport and Communications. Roads (1970) 21,143 km. Motor vehicles in use (1970): passenger 57,112; commercial (including buses) 29,906. Railways: (1969) 1,278 km.; traffic (1970) 83 million passenger-km., freight 53 million net ton-km. Air traffic (1970): 641.4 million passenger-km.; freight 5,198,000 net ton-km. Telephones (Dec. 1969) 36,150. Radio receivers (Dec. 1969) 1.3 million. Television receivers (Dec. 1969) 373,000.

Agriculture. Production (in 000; metric tons; 1970; 1969 in parentheses): rice 5,716 (5,115); sweet potatoes (1969) 237, (1968) 235; cassava (1969) 233, (1968) 260; peanuts c. 34 (34); dry beans c. 28 (c. 22); rubber c. 28 (28); tea c. 5 (4.9); coffee c. 3.6 (3.6); fish catch (1969) 464, (1968) 410. Livestock (in 000; 1969–70): cattle c. 930; buffalo c. 620; pigs 3,772.

Industry. Production (in 000; metric tons; 1969): cement 247; salt 118; cotton yarn 7.6; woven cotton fabrics (m.) 61,000; electricity (excluding most industrial production; kw-hr.) 1,042,000.

VIETNAM: Democratic Republic

Education. (1966–67) Primary and secondary, pupils 4,517,600, teachers 86,495; vocational, pupils 101,880, teachers 4,194; higher (including University of Hanoi), students 48,402, teaching staff 5,004.

Finance and Trade. Monetary unit: dong, with (Sept. 27, 1971) an official exchange rate of 3.50 dong to U.S. $1 (8.83 dong = £1 sterling) and a tourist rate of 5.52 dong to U.S. $1 (13.24 dong = £1). Budget (1963) balanced at 1,779,288,000 dong. Foreign trade (1965): imports c. 530 million dong; exports c. 290 million dong (85% with China, U.S.S.R., and Eastern European countries).

Transport. Roads (1965) c. 9,000 km. Railways (1969) c. 780 km.

Agriculture. Production (in 000; metric tons; 1969; 1968 in parentheses): rice c. 4,900 (c. 4,920); corn c. 240 (c. 230); sweet potatoes c. 900 (c. 830); cassava c. 700 (c. 700); peanuts c. 45 (c. 42); dry beans c. 15 (c. 15); tobacco c. 4 (c. 4); tea c. 2.7 (c. 2.7). Livestock (in 000; 1969–70): buffalo c. 1,830; cattle c. 865; pigs c. 6,600.

Industry. Production (in 000; metric tons; 1969): coal c. 3,200; apatite ore c. 1,200; salt c. 150; cement c. 500; cotton fabrics (m.; 1964) 105,200; paper (1964) 19; electricity (kw-hr.; 1964) 548,000.

Above, a Communist attack on March 28, 1971, at U.S. Fire Base Mary Ann in South Vietnam killed 33 American soldiers. Below, a Vietnamese woman passes a campaign poster in Saigon showing Pres. Nguyen Van Thieu (left) and his running mate, Tran Van Huong, the only slate in the October 3 election.

tinuing withdrawal of U.S. forces from South Vietnam. U.S. ground units were not involved in the operation. As many as 20,000 government troops were used in the thrust at any one time, most of them highly trained elite forces operating under extensive U.S. air and artillery support.

A month after the drive began, U.S. Pres. Richard Nixon labeled it successful enough to guarantee that U.S. troop withdrawals could be continued through the end of the year. For the South Vietnamese forces inside Laos, however, it was a bruising, sometimes humiliating series of battles with a determined, well-equipped enemy. North Vietnamese resistance was described by U.S. Secretary of Defense Melvin Laird as "tremendously vicious and violent."

On March 24 the drive into Laos was terminated. The South Vietnamese forces suffered heavy losses with some virtually wiped out as effective battle units. Official government losses announced by Saigon included 1,160 killed in action, 4,271 wounded, and 240 missing (casualties thus represented an acknowledged 28% of the committed force).

According to the South Vietnamese government, 13,812 enemy soldiers were killed during the operation. Saigon also claimed that the incursion force destroyed or captured 100 enemy tanks, nearly 300 vehicles, 176,000 tons of ammunition, 6,500 weapons, and more than 65 million gallons of gasoline. While some of the claims were considered suspect, it was evident that the North Vietnamese would be hard pressed to resupply their forces in South Vietnam, especially while still being subjected to intensive raids by U.S. B-52 strategic bombers.

Assessments of Lam Son 719 varied. It was, clearly, a controversial operation. Detractors described it as a rout of the South Vietnamese, who did not penetrate as deeply as planned, could not retain possession of key objectives, and failed to destroy as much enemy matériel and supplies as had been hoped. Others insisted that the operation succeeded in inflicting appreciable damage on the North Vietnamese before the spring monsoon and consequently forestalled future large-scale enemy attacks in the still contested areas within the northernmost provinces of South Vietnam. In the sense that the situation below the demilitarized zone became more secure, with less need for U.S. combat power, the operation did succeed, facilitating the continuation of U.S. troop pullout. South Vietnamese military officers, however, did not conceal their view that the costly price of the operation in casualties and dispirited troop morale was exceptionally high. President Thieu came under

personal attack from some in his usually loyal officer corps for approving the incursion, one of the few instances in which the military seriously challenged the president's leadership.

Other South Vietnamese questioned Thieu for a multitude of other reasons, and their dissatisfaction became manifest in the elections on August 29 for the lower house of the National Assembly. The reconstituted legislature was to have 159 seats, 22 more than the previous body. Only 40 deputies won reelection, and 22 of them were members of the opposition. Seventy-nine assemblymen were defeated.

The National Assembly generally had been considered to be a rubber stamp for the president, and the large election day turnout (78.5% of the registered voters) was interpreted as a repudiation of this role. This was coupled with public disgust at various widely reported but rarely investigated scandals, petty profiteering involving legislators, and what appeared to be growing resentment of overall government policy. As a party, the biggest gains were registered by the militant religious-political An Quang Buddhists, who became the strongest force against President Thieu.

The presidential election was held on October 3. It became controversial when Thieu forced through the legislature an election reform bill that had the ultimate effect of eliminating all opposition. Although it was obvious that the restrictive measure made it extremely difficult for aspirants to qualify, Thieu had assumed there would be at least three others challenging him: Vice-Pres. Nguyen Cao Ky, former Gen. Duong Van Minh, and a candidate of the coalition opposition. The operative clause in the new law required that anyone seeking nomination for the presidency could be qualified only by collecting the endorsement of at least 40 deputies and senators, or 100 city and provincial councillors. Most of the eligible endorsers were pro government, and the simple arithmetic of winning eligibility discouraged opposition. General Minh termed the election reform measure unconstitutional.

Vice-President Ky, whose political relations with Thieu had not been warm since their alliance of convenience and national unity began in 1967, predictably broke with the president in announcing his candidacy. Ky received the endorsement of 102 councillors as required, but the signatures of 40 of them were not certified by the government because it claimed those local officials had previously endorsed Thieu. Ky thus was eliminated from the race. He called the action completely illegal. The Supreme Court considered the case on appeal and reinstated Ky's candidacy, saying it viewed the government's ruling on disqualification as "not in good form." At this point, Ky declared the court's ruling was even more illegal than the original decision to rule him off the ticket. He refused to run. Instead, he proposed that both Thieu and he resign and that new elections be held within 60 days under the administration of a caretaker government.

After Ky's invalidation as a candidate but prior to the Supreme Court's overruling decision, Minh had decided to withdraw from the race. His nomination had been accepted after he filed endorsement signatures of 16 senators and 28 deputies, which were not challenged. He chose to bow out of the race ostensibly because of instructions allegedly sent by the Thieu government to provincial officials on rigging the balloting to ensure Thieu's reelection. It was known, however, that Minh felt his chances of winning the election were virtually nil without Ky as a third candidate to siphon off some of the military and civil service support that Thieu would be expected to monopolize without Ky's name on the ballot.

With Minh out of the race, and Ky refusing to be reinstated as a candidate, Thieu was without opposition. A fourth candidate had failed to submit endorsements of any kind and was, in any event, never considered to be a serious challenger.

Thieu's uncontested race for a second term was a matter of considerable embarrassment to the U.S. government. One of its oft-repeated purposes for being involved militarily in South Vietnam was to "insure the Vietnamese a choice in their elected officials through democratic methods." Washington had hoped the South Vietnamese would conduct free and fair elections, after which it would be easier to justify the massive involvement and permit withdrawal with a declaration that its mission had been completed.

Considerable pressure was exerted upon Thieu by the U.S. ambassador in Saigon, Ellsworth Bunker, to permit someone to run against him. Bunker also attempted to talk Minh and Ky into remaining in the race. Thieu's only concession was to announce that the balloting would be a referendum: "I would like to use this election to ask the people whether they still have confidence in me and my policies. If they do, I will accept another four-year term. If not, I will resign." An outcome in which he received less than half the votes cast would be considered by him to be a decision of no confidence. He said anyone opposing him could render his ballot invalid in thousands of different ways.

Thieu's uncompromising position led to bitterness, frustration, and sometimes violent protest. Students in Saigon, Da Nang, and Hue staged demonstrations that were aimed at opposing Thieu but that, increasingly, acquired a marked anti-American flavour as well. Scores of U.S. vehicles were burned in the weeks prior to the election. Joining in the anti-Thieu protests were disabled veterans, three of whom burned themselves to death.

On election day itself extensive violence was launched by the North Vietnamese and Viet Cong. Communist action was reported at its highest level in more than 18 months. There were 92 separate shellings and ground attacks on government positions, six times the daily average. Communist long-range gunners rained shells indiscriminately on practically every large South Vietnamese city, including Saigon.

Despite the level of enemy action and the disorders against a one-man presidential race, the October 3 election turnout was surprisingly high. Final official figures showed that 87.7%, or 6,331,918 of the eligible voters, cast ballots. Of those voting, Thieu won the support of 94%. Only 356,900 ballots were declared invalid, presumably spoiled intentionally to indicate opposition to Thieu. He carried the heavily populated Mekong Delta easily, capturing 97.7% of the total vote there, but he fared less well in Saigon (83.8%), Da Nang (74.4%), and Hue (64.3%).

Vice-President Ky declared that in the election there had been "brazen rigging beyond imagination." He was joined by other anti-Thieu forces in similar charges. The Senate, however, voted 37 to 8 against establishing a commission to investigate the charges. Three weeks after the balloting, the Supreme Court ruled the election legal.

During the year, the U.S. continued withdrawing its ground combat forces and sizable air units from South Vietnam, in line with President Nixon's statement of September 16 that the main U.S. objective "is to end the American involvement just as soon as that is consistent with our overall goal, which is a South Vietnam able to defend itself against a Communist takeover and which includes, from our standpoint, our primary interest in obtaining the release of our POWs." In November Nixon announced that U.S. troop strength in South Vietnam would be reduced to 139,000 by the end of January 1972. This contrasted with the peak level of 543,000 in April 1969.

The pace of vietnamization was slowed down by the

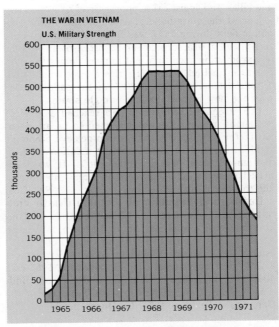

THE WAR IN VIETNAM
U.S. Military Strength

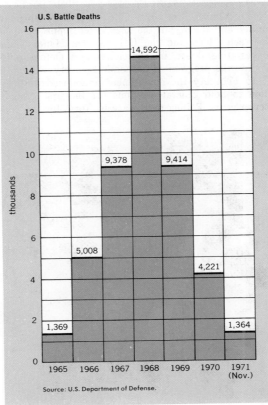

U.S. Battle Deaths

Source: U.S. Department of Defense.

limited ability of the South Vietnamese to absorb high levels of difficult-to-maintain modern weapons. This was particularly obvious in aircraft. Five of every six helicopter missions flown during 1971 were piloted by Americans.

South Vietnamese military strength remained at a level of 1.1 million men, with the regulars backed up by regional and popular forces totaling 520,000. Even with the withdrawal of U.S. (as well as South Korean, Australian, New Zealand, and Thai) units, the South Vietnamese would enjoy a seemingly superior numerical position, confronting an enemy force of 240,-000 (including 100,000 North Vietnamese regulars, 40,000 Viet Cong main force troops, and 100,000 guerrillas and logistical support forces).

One of the more hopeful developments in the economic field during 1971 was South Vietnam's ability to achieve a rice surplus for export. Not since 1963 had production been sufficient to meet domestic needs. It was estimated that 1971's rice output would total 6 million tons, with about 20% of the paddy seeded with the new higher yielding miracle strains.

U.S. economic aid, which had reached a level of $750 million annually, was expected to be an essential factor if South Vietnam was to achieve economic stabilization and recover from the inflationary, production-crippling period of the 1960s. It was estimated it might take ten years of large-scale foreign aid to realize that objective.   (Ro. Go.)

Democratic Republic of Vietnam (North Vietnam). This is bordered by China, the Gulf of Tonkin, the South China Sea, South Vietnam, and Laos. Area: 63,360 sq.mi. (164,103 sq.km.). Pop. (1970 est.): 19.9 million, including (1960) Vietnamese 85.1%. Cap. and largest city: Hanoi (pop., 1965 est., 500,000). Language: Vietnamese. Religion: Buddhist; pagan; Confucian; Christian. Secretary of the Communist Party in 1971, Le Duan; president, Ton Duc Thang; premier, Pham Van Dong.

The de-escalation of the war gave little respite to North Vietnam in 1971. The leadership remained united and stable, but the unexpected rapprochement between China and the U.S. worried Hanoi, while devastating floods in September and October disrupted the program of economic recovery.

In February the government announced its decision to hold general elections for the first time in seven years. Polling took place in April, for the peo-

ple's councils as well as for the fourth National Assembly, and 99.8% of the electorate was reported to have voted. There were 529 candidates running for 420 seats.

The first session of the new National Assembly was held in June. In a move described as showing the stability of the leadership, the Assembly reelected 83-year-old Pres. Ton Duc Thang along with Premier Pham Van Dong, National Assembly Chairman Truong Chinh, and Vice-Premier and Defense Minister Vo Nguyen Giap. This meant continuation of the collective leadership provided by the triumvirate that had held the reins of power in Hanoi since the death of Ho Chi Minh: the party's first secretary Le Duan, Pham Van Dong, and Truong Chinh.

The reelected leadership immediately made it clear that it would carry on both the war and the Paris peace talks as before. The premier said: "Our stand on an overall solution to the Vietnam issue remains undiscussed at Paris because the other side wants the war to drag out and keeps going after the mirage of a military victory."

There were signs that Hanoi was genuinely worried about the possibility of the China-U.S. thaw leading to an Indochina deal behind its back. It lost no time in pointing out that the destiny of Vietnam is decided by the Vietnamese. It appeared that Hanoi was perhaps more disgusted at the prospect of being betrayed by China than at what it called President Nixon's attempts to divide the Communist world. In a reference believed to be intended for China as well as the U.S., it said the time when a big power can bully a small country had ended for good.

Several summit-level contacts between the Chinese and the North Vietnamese followed. China hastened to state publicly that there was no question of its seeking a deal with the U.S. After a visit to Peking by the North Vietnamese special adviser at the Paris peace talks, Le Duc Tho, China specifically condemned the idea of an international conference on Indochina similar to the 1954 Geneva conference and emphasized that the unconditional withdrawal of U.S. troops was a precondition to any solution of the Indochina problem.

In September Chinese Vice-Premier Li Hsien-nien arrived in Hanoi at the head of a commercial, economic, and military delegation to sign an aid agreement with North Vietnam for 1972; two others had already been signed during the year. Five days after the departure of the Chinese, Soviet Pres. Nikolai V. Podgorny arrived and pledged total support to "the valiant Vietnamese people who are taking the lead in the liberation movement of the Indochinese people."

For a time in February it appeared that North Vietnam's campaign in Indochina had suddenly run into one of the biggest hurdles it had faced so far. The nation's resources were strained to the utmost when South Vietnam with active U.S. support mounted a massive invasion of southern Laos aimed at cutting off the Ho Chi Minh Trail. The incursion fizzled out in the face of determined Communist resistance, but some crack North Vietnamese divisions were believed to have suffered heavy casualties.

In the wake of the Laos invasion, South Vietnam's President Thieu said that an invasion of North Vietnam itself was only a matter of time. This provoked Hanoi's chief peace negotiator in Paris, Xuan Thuy, to protest that the Nixon administration was preparing to attack North Vietnam. Otherwise Hanoi ignored Saigon's threat, which never materialized.

North Vietnamese peasants work to widen the Red River and create irrigation canals in Thai Binh Province. In a crash economic program, young peasants are assigned to work in industrial projects at home.

THE "NEW YORK TIMES"

There were hopes of a more positive contact between the North and the South in May when Saigon agreed to release 570 disabled war prisoners under terms laid down by Hanoi, which included a sea rendezvous under Red Cross flags and a 24-hour ceasefire. Soon after the agreement, however, Saigon officials said all but 13 of the prisoners had refused to return to North Vietnam. Denouncing this as an example of "odious treachery of the U.S. and Saigon administration," Hanoi called off the deal.

For the most part, Hanoi's attitude to the U.S. remained tough throughout 1971. Hostilities between the two countries intensified late in December when the U.S. subjected strategic targets in the North to the heaviest bombing since the agreement to halt such attacks in November 1968. In response to North Vietnam's protestations that the U.S. was breaking the agreement, Washington accused Hanoi of previously violating the accord by firing on U.S. planes that were over the Ho Chi Minh Trail in Laos and by engaging in a massive buildup of war supplies.

For all its preoccupation with the war effort and peace negotiations, Hanoi's economic reconstruction program seemed to have reached a "Great Leap Forward" stage. Early in the year visitors reported a calculated shift of emphasis, with young men and women of military conscription age being assigned to development work. In August there were reports that consumer goods were more abundant, people were dressed more gaily, and brigades of architects and engineers were being trained. A month later, however, an unexpected natural calamity disrupted the country.

Hanoi described the floods of September and October as unprecedented over the past 70 or 80 years. It was believed they caused more damage to the country than three years of U.S. bombing. Among the worst-hit areas was the heavily populated Red River basin north of Hanoi. The main rice-producing areas were flooded. Also destroyed were some coal mines, railways, roads, electric cables, and houses. South Vietnam's surprise offer of aid to help flood victims was described by Hanoi's official news agency as "a perfidious trick used by Thieu to scrape up the wealth of our countrymen in the South."

The floods undoubtedly put a severe strain on the economy and at least temporarily reversed the encouraging trend set by two good harvests. All hopes of 1971 being a record year like 1970 were washed away. However, emergency measures such as planting rapidly maturing rice and turning playgrounds and office compounds over to cultivation were expected to reduce the period of agricultural recovery.

(T. J. S. G.)

See also Defense.

Vital Statistics

A conference of significance for vital and health statistics was the 38th meeting of the International Statistical Institute (ISI), held in Washington, D.C., in August 1971. Over 475 participants from 53 countries attended. One important topic on the program was the measurement of population growth in less developed countries. The ISI, whose members are leaders in the fields of mathematical, economic, demographic, and social statistics, would hold its next meeting in Vienna in 1973.

The International Training Program of the National

Center for Health Statistics (NCHS) of the U.S. Public Health Service enrolled 24 students from 17 countries for training in measurement of population change. Objectives of the program, initiated in 1965 to help less developed countries cope effectively with population problems, were to provide a thorough grounding in birth and death registration methods and procedures; training in developing sample registration areas for making current estimates of population change while extending the vital statistics system; and support for family-planning activities through study of evaluation procedures, with emphasis on record forms, data collection and analysis, and evaluative studies. Fifteen of the participants were sponsored by the UN; the others were financed by the U.S. Agency for International Development.

Birth Statistics. The birthrate in the U.S. rose slightly in 1970, thereby continuing the upward trend that began the previous year. In 1970 the provisional rate was 18.2 births per 1,000 population, or 3% higher than the rate of 17.7 in 1969. A pause in the upturn occurred in the first part of 1971 as some declines were reported. Data for the 12 months ended August 1971 showed a rate about 2% lower than for the comparable period ended August 1970. The provisional number of births was 3,718,000 for calendar 1970.

As a result of high birthrates in the late 1940s and 1950s, the population of women in the childbearing ages was estimated to have increased 2% between 1969 and 1970; further yearly increases were anticipated, especially in the 20–29-year age group where fertility is highest. Therefore it appeared that the number of births would grow larger in the next few years, even though age-specific birthrates for some age groups did not increase. Such factors as development of new contraceptives, changes in desired family size, and changes in laws and practices for abortion compounded the difficulties of predicting the trend of the birthrate. A new Family Growth Survey being planned for 1972 by the NCHS Division of Vital Statistics, involving biennial interviews with a nationwide sample of married women in the childbearing ages, would provide a range of data needed to interpret current trends.

The fertility rate for 1970 was 87.6 births per 1,000 women 15–44 years old, or slightly higher than the 1969 rate of 85.8. These rates were, however, considerably below the levels of the late 1950s and early 1960s. Final data for 1968, the latest year available for the U.S., showed that the fertility rate for nonwhites was 41% higher than for whites. The official estimate of the proportion of illegitimate births, also for 1968, was 9.7% of all live births. Natural increase, *i.e.,* the excess of births over deaths, added 1,797,000 persons to the U.S. population during 1970, as against 1,655,000 in 1969. The rates of natural increase for 1970 and 1969, respectively, were 8.8 and 8.2 persons per 1,000 population. Birth statistics for the U.S., as well as data on marriages, divorces, and deaths, were compiled by the National Center for Health Statistics.

Approximations of the birthrates for China, India, and Pakistan were made by the UN from the scanty data available. Allowing for uncertainty about geographic boundaries, wide differences in criteria for reporting live births, and other imponderables, the estimated average birthrates per 1,000 population in 1965–70 were China 33.1; India 42.8; and Pakistan 50.9. The rate for Taiwan rose from 25.6 in 1969 to 28.1 in 1970. In contrast to the relatively high rates for both China and Taiwan, that for Japan, where birth registration is complete, rose from 13.7 in 1966

Virgin Islands:
see Dependent States

Table I. Birthrates and Death Rates per 1,000 Population and Infant Mortality per 1,000 Live Births in Selected Countries, 1970*

Country	Birth-rate	Death rate	Infant mortality	Country	Birth-rate	Death rate	Infant mortality
Africa				Romania	21.1	9.6	49.5
Egypt	36.9†	15.0	118.0†	Spain	19.8	8.6	27.8
Kenya	17.7	3.9	53.7	Sweden	13.6	9.9	13.1§
Mauritius	27.3	7.8	57.6	Switzerland	15.9	9.0	15.4†
Tunisia	37.4	10.5†	74.3‡	United Kingdom	16.2	11.8	18.6†
Asia				England & Wales	16.0	11.7	17.9
Cyprus	21.3	6.8	25.7	N. Ireland	21.1	10.9	22.7
Hong Kong	18.9	5.1	19.6	Scotland	16.8	12.3	21.1†
Israel	27.0	7.0	23.6	Yugoslavia	17.6	8.9	56.3†
Japan	18.9	6.9	13.1	North America			
Kuwait	61.1†	5.9†	35.9§	Canada†	17.5	7.3	19.3
Lebanon	27.3	4.1	13.6‡	Dominican Republic†	37.1	6.5	61.9
Philippines	24.6	6.3	67.2	El Salvador	39.8	9.9	66.9
Singapore	23.3	5.3	19.8	Guatemala§	43.5	16.3	92.0
Taiwan	28.1	5.1	17.5†	Jamaica	32.9	7.1	32.3
Europe				Mexico	41.3	9.2	67.4
Austria	15.1	13.2	25.9	Panama	36.4	6.7	38.1
Belgium	14.7	12.4	21.7†	Puerto Rico†	26.2	6.6	28.2
Bulgaria	16.3	9.1	30.5†	Trinidad & Tobago	20.3†	6.7†	36.6§
Czechoslovakia	15.8	11.4	22.9†	United States	18.2	9.4	19.8
Denmark	14.4	9.8	14.8†	Oceania			
Finland	13.7	9.5	12.5	American Samoa	32.1	5.0	31.1
France	16.7	10.6	15.1	Australia	20.5	9.0	17.9
Germany, East	13.9	14.1	20.0†	Fiji	29.9	4.7	18.5
Germany, West‖	13.3	11.6	23.5	French Polynesia	45.7§	9.1§	52.4¶
Greece†	17.4	8.1	31.8	Nauru§	32.2	8.3	51.8
Hungary	14.7	11.6	35.7	New Zealand	22.1	8.8	16.7
Iceland†	20.7	7.1	11.7	Western Samoa	32.9	3.8	19.4
Ireland	21.8	11.5	19.2	South America			
Italy	16.8	9.7	29.2	Chile§	26.6	9.0	91.6
Luxembourg	13.0	12.2	24.9	Ecuador§	39.6	10.8	86.1
Netherlands	18.4	8.4	12.7	Paraguay	33.4	5.3	35.6
Norway	16.2	9.8	13.7§	Uruguay	21.3†	9.1†	53.9§
Poland	16.7	8.1	33.1	Venezuela	39.5§	6.8†	46.2§
Portugal	18.0	9.7	58.0	U.S.S.R.	17.5	8.2	24.4

*Registered births and deaths only. §1968.
†1969. ‖Not including West Berlin.
‡1960. ¶1967.

Sources: United Nations, *Population and Vital Statistics Report* (July 1, 1971).

(a poor year for baby girls according to folklore) to 19.3 in 1967, declined to 18.3 in 1969, and rose slightly to 18.9 in 1970. In the Americas the highest rates were reported by El Salvador (39.8), Guatemala (43.5), Mexico (41.3), Ecuador (39.6 in 1968), and Venezuela (39.5). Meaningful data for the East and Central African countries were not available.

Death Statistics. Mortality in the U.S. continued to decline in 1970 and the first part of 1971, according to provisional data. The crude death rate for 1970 was 9.4 per 1,000 population, compared with 9.5 in 1969. The rate of 9.3 for the 12 months ended August 1971 was also lower than that of 9.4 for the comparable period of 1969–70. The number of deaths in 1970 was 1,921,000, or roughly 5,000 more than in 1969. (Even with a larger number of deaths, the death rate may decline as a result of increased population. However, there appeared to have been some improvement in the health picture insofar as the death rate reflected it.)

The five leading causes of death for the U.S. in 1970 and estimated death rates are shown below. Each of these causes had the same rank in 1970 as in 1969. Small decreases occurred in 1970 in the rates for diseases of the heart, cerebrovascular diseases, and accidents. The death rate for influenza and pneumonia went down 12%. On the other hand, the rate for malignant neoplasms (cancer) rose 1%.

Cause of death	Estimated death rate per 100,000 population
All causes	940.4
Diseases of the heart	360.3
Malignant neoplasms, including neoplasms of lymphatic and hematopoietic tissues	162.0
Cerebrovascular diseases	101.7
Accidents	54.2
Influenza and pneumonia	30.5
All other causes	231.8

Transportation accident death rates for the common modes of travel, estimated by the National Safety

Council, showed the relative risk of death in the U.S. for passengers. After allowance was made for the number of occupants of the vehicles and the mileage traveled, the death rate for passenger automobiles and taxis on streets and highways (2.20 for 1968–70) was ten times that for buses (0.20). Travel on turnpikes was far less hazardous than on other roadways. Safest of all were railway passenger trains (0.09); next came scheduled airlines (0.13) and buses.

The crude death rate for some European countries rose between 1969 and 1970. Czechoslovakia, Denmark, Hungary, and the Netherlands were among those reporting increased mortality, as shown in Table I. By contrast, the provisional rates for France, Italy, Portugal, Romania, Spain, Sweden, and Yugoslavia declined appreciably, despite influenza in some areas. The rate for England and Wales fell from 11.8 to 11.7, although influenza was epidemic in early 1970.

Infant and Maternal Mortality. A highlight in U.S. vital statistics was the continued decline in the infant mortality rate. In 1970 it went down to 19.8 infant deaths per 1,000 live births, falling below 20 for the first time. The comparable rate for 1969 was 20.7. The decline continued into 1971, as provisional figures for the 12 months ended in August showed a rate of 19.5 vis-à-vis 20.1 for the corresponding period a year earlier. There were approximately 73,700 deaths of infants under one year of age in 1970. The neonatal mortality rate (infants under 28 days old) was 14.9, 3% lower than in 1969; the postneonatal mortality rate (28 days through 11 months) was 4.9, 9% lower than the 1969 estimate. The lowest infant mortality rates, as shown in Table I, were those of Japan, the Scandinavian countries, France, and the Netherlands. The rate for the U.S.S.R., though less comprehensive than rates for most English-speaking countries in terms of what it included as infant deaths, declined from 26.4 in 1968 to 24.4 in 1970. Rates for Latin-American countries continued to be quite high.

Maternal mortality in the U.S. apparently decreased between 1969 and 1970. The estimated rates for complications of pregnancy, childbirth, and the period immediately following birth for 1969 and 1970, respectively, were 27.4 and 24.7 deaths per 100,000 live births. In 1968, when the rate for all women was 24.5 per 100,000 live births, the rate for white women was 16.6, compared with 63.6 for nonwhite mothers. Death rates for maternal conditions per 100,000 females for the few countries using the eighth revision of the International Classification of Diseases in 1968 were relatively low for Australia, France, England and Wales, and Northern Ireland. Among the lowest rates was that for Scotland.

Expectation of Life. Babies born in the U.S. in 1970 could be expected to live, on the average, 70.8 years, the highest life expectancy ever attained there. In 1968, the latest year for which data were tabulated by sex, life expectancy for both sexes was 70.2 years; for males it was 66.6 and for females, 74. (Expectation of life at birth is the average number of years that an infant could be expected to live if the age-specific death rates observed during the year of his birth were to prevail throughout his lifetime.) As Table II indicates, life expectancy was much the same among the inhabitants of the various English-speaking countries. The figure for the U.S.S.R. (70 years for the total population in 1967–68) was close to that for the U.S.

Marriage and Divorce. Marriages in the U.S. and the marriage rate changed very little during the early part of 1971 as compared with 1970. Only 1% more

Table II. Life Expectancy at Birth, in Years, for Selected Countries			
Country	Period	Male	Female
Africa			
Burundi	1965	35.0	38.5
Egypt	1960	51.6	53.8
Liberia	1962	36.1	38.6
Nigeria	1965–66	37.2	36.7
Upper Volta	1960–61	32.1	31.1
Asia			
Cambodia	1958–59	44.2	43.3
Hong Kong	1968	66.7	73.3
India	1951–60	41.9	40.6
Israel	1969	69.2	72.8
Japan	1968	69.1	74.3
Jordan	1959–63	52.6	52.0
Korea, South	1955–60	51.1	53.7
Pakistan	1962	53.7	48.8
Taiwan	1965	65.8	70.4
Thailand	1960	53.6	58.7
Europe			
Albania	1965–66	64.9	67.0
Austria	1969	66.5	73.3
Belgium	1959–63	67.7	73.5
Bulgaria	1965–67	68.8	72.7
Czechoslovakia	1966	67.3	73.6
Denmark	1967–68	70.6	75.4
Finland	1961–65	65.4	72.6
France	1968	68.0	75.5
Germany, East	1965–66	68.7	73.7
Germany, West*	1966–68	67.6	73.6
Greece	1960–62	67.5	70.7
Hungary	1964	67.0	71.8
Iceland	1961–65	70.8	76.2
Ireland	1960–62	68.1	71.9
Italy	1960–62	67.2	72.3
Netherlands	1968	71.0	76.4
Norway	1961–65	71.0	76.0
Poland	1965–66	66.9	72.8
Portugal	1959–62	60.7	66.4
Romania	1964–67	66.5	70.5
Spain	1960	67.3	71.9
Sweden	1967	71.9	76.5
Switzerland	1958–63	68.7	74.1
United Kingdom			
England and Wales	1967–69	68.7	74.9
Northern Ireland	1967–69	68.3	73.7
Scotland	1967–69	67.1	73.2
Yugoslavia	1966–67	64.7	69.0
North America			
Barbados	1959–61	62.7	67.4
Canada	1965–67	68.8	75.2
Costa Rica	1962–64	61.9	64.8
Guatemala	1963–65	48.3	49.7
Mexico	1965–70	61.0	63.7
Panama	1960–61	57.6	60.9
Puerto Rico	1959–61	67.1	71.9
United States	1968	66.6	74.0
Oceania			
Australia	1960–62	67.9	74.2
New Zealand	1960–62	68.4	73.8
South America			
Argentina	1959–61	63.1	68.9
Chile	1960–61	54.4	59.9
Peru	1960–65	52.6	55.5
Surinam	1963	62.5	66.7
Uruguay	1963–64	65.5	71.6
U.S.S.R.	1967–68	65.0	74.0

*Not including West Berlin.
Source: United Nations, *Demographic Yearbook* (1970).

marriages were reported in the 12 months ended August 1971 than in the comparable period ended August 1970. The provisional marriage rate was the same for both periods, namely 10.6 per 1,000 population. The provisional national total of marriages in 1970 was 2,179,000, or more than in any other year except 1946. After a period of decline through the 1950s, the rate increased gradually through the '60s, but the relative annual increases after 1968 were smaller each year than earlier in the decade. Growth of the young adult population was the primary factor in the rise of the marriage rate in the 1960s.

In 1970 marriages increased in the northeastern, southern, and western regions of the U.S., with the West showing the largest increment over 1969. In the north central region a decrease of about 1% was reported. Brides in 1969 had a median age of 21.6 years, whereas the median for grooms was 23.5. Between 1963 and 1969 the median age at first marriage went up from 20.3 to 20.6 for brides, but down from 22.5 to 22.4 for grooms.

Many European countries had marriage rates for 1969 in the range of 7–8.9 per 1,000 population. An exception was Sweden, where the rate declined from 7.2 in 1967 to 6.6 in 1968 and 6 in 1969. Among the highest rates were those for Australia, New Zealand, Japan, and the U.S. The lowest rates were those for the Central and South American countries, which reported fewer than 7 marriages per 1,000 population. In countries where the number of consensual marriages is large, the rates based on recorded marriages are correspondingly low.

Countries	Range of marriage rates per 1,000 population, 1969
Colombia*, Dominican Republic, El Salvador	Less than 5
Argentina†, Ireland, Panama, Sweden, Trinidad and Tobago, Venezuela†	5–6.9
Austria, Belgium, Canada, Chile*, Czechoslovakia, Poland, Portugal, East* and West Germany, France, Greece, Italy, Mexico, Norway*, Spain, U.S.S.R.*, United Kingdom	7–8.9
Australia‡, Israel‡, Japan‡, New Zealand‡, Puerto Rico‡, United States‡	9–10.9

*1968 data.
†1967 data.
‡1970 estimates.
Sources: United Nations *Demographic Yearbook* (1969) and UN *Monthly Bulletin of Statistics*.

Divorces and the divorce rate in the U.S. continued to increase in 1970 and the first eight months of 1971, though the rate of increase in 1971 was less than in 1967–70. The national estimate of divorces and annulments granted in 1970 was 715,000, an all-time peak and 12% greater than the total of 639,000 in 1969. The divorce rate was 3.5 per 1,000 population, second only to the 4.3 rate of 1946. Detailed divorce data in the U.S. are limited to those states with central, statewide registration, regular reporting, and a standard record form giving the characteristics of couples granted divorces. The median duration of marriage prior to divorce or annulment for a group of 28 states was 6.9 years in 1969.

Divorce rates for countries other than the U.S. were comparatively low, except for the U.S.S.R. where the rate rose, after divorce laws were eased, to 1.6 per 1,000 population in 1966 and 2.7 in 1967 and 1968. In Canada the rate was 0.5 in 1968; in Australia, New Zealand, and England and Wales it was between 0.8 and 1. The Divorce Reform Act that became effective in England in January 1971 was expected to increase divorces markedly. Rates for Austria (1.3), Czechoslovakia (1.7), Sweden (1.4), and Yugoslavia (1) were slightly higher than those of other European countries having legal provision for divorce.

(E. H. HA.)

See also Populations and Areas.

Western Samoa

A constitutional monarchy and member of the Commonwealth of Nations, Western Samoa is an island group in the South Pacific Ocean, about 1,600 mi. E of New Zealand and 2,200 mi. S of Hawaii. Area: 1,136 sq.mi. (2,942 sq.km.), with two major islands, Savai'i (662 sq.mi.) and Upolu (435 sq.mi.), and seven smaller islands. Pop. (1971 est.): 148,565. Cap. and largest city: Apia (pop., 1971 est., 30,593). Language: Samoan and English. Religion: about 80% Protestant, 20% Roman Catholic. Head of state (*O le Ao o le Malo*) in 1971, Malietoa Tanumafili II; prime minister, Tupua Tamasese Lealofi IV.

The government embarked on its second five-year development plan in 1971. Deficit budgeting and a substantially oversubscribed National Development

Loan provided capital. New Zealand offered a grant totaling NZ$1.2 million to continue educational, administrative, and technical assistance and to help finance capital works. The first New Zealand aid mission discussed projects that might be suitably assisted from the Colombo Plan allocation, extended in 1970 to include the South Pacific. The New Zealand government approved a grant of NZ$45,000 for the design and redevelopment of Apia hospital. The U.K. offered an interest-free loan for the purchase of British materials and equipment. Loans for a pilot beef project and a feasibility study for a hydroelectricity scheme were provided by the Asian Development Bank. Volunteer service from abroad relieved the shortage of trained manpower. (My. B. B.)

WESTERN SAMOA
Education. (1968) Primary, pupils 26,261; secondary, pupils 9,058; primary and secondary, teachers 1,174; vocational, pupils 92, teachers 9; teacher training, students 250, teachers 20.
Finance and Trade. Monetary unit: Western Samoan dollar (thaler), with a par value of WS$0.71 to U.S. $1 (WS$1.71 = £1 sterling) and a free rate (Sept. 27, 1971) of *c.* WS$0.69 to U.S. $1. Budget (1971 est.): revenue WS$6,478,000; expenditure WS$7,037,000. Foreign trade (1970): imports WS$9,-791,000; exports WS$3,391,000. Import sources: New Zealand 32%; Australia 16%; U.S. 14%; Japan 10%; U.K. 8%. Export destinations: New Zealand 47%; Netherlands 18%; West Germany 13%; U.S. 7%; U.K. 5%; Norway 5%. Main exports: copra 40%; cocoa 31%; bananas 16%.

Words and Meanings, New

In 1971 advances in space exploration brought still more new words into the language. Apollo 15 astronauts examined the lunar terrain, or **lurain,** and collected specimens of the moon's rock, or **regolith.** Astronomers investigating the varying periodicity of pulsars discovered unanticipated **spin-ups** and **spin-downs,** and coined the term **glitches** for both changes. Meanwhile, a strange eight-wheeled electric trolley known as **Lunokhod I,** or "moon walker," explored the surface of the moon under remote control from scientists on earth. Electric rockets or **ion thrusters** offered the best techniques for long space journeys. **Secant,** the mathematicians' "cutting" line, acquired an additional meaning when applied to an electronic device that could be fitted to an aircraft to signal the propinquity of other aircraft in time to avoid disaster.

The connotation of **pollution** (etymologically "letting loose") was certainly extended when used to include aircraft noise, and **environmental pollution** came to cover every conceivable form of defilement. One new and potent detector of atmospheric pollution was **lidar,** a kind of light-radar, strictly laser detection and ranging. It registered atmospheric impurities by bouncing back laser beams from smoke particles, water droplets, and gas molecules, and measured their intensity by means of a **photomultiplier.**

The film card or microfiche was further developed to produce the **microbook,** a film card bearing the image of up to a thousand pages. Moreover, computers grew smaller and smaller. **Multipurpose minicomputers,** it was predicted, would soon become part of the furniture of every reputable business house. Was there really such a thing as **machine intelligence?** Programming a computer to play chess seemed to point in that direction, and there was even talk of a **technetronic society,** a variation on the theme of Marshall McLuhan's **electronic village.** Electric vibration detectors, or subterranean **geophones,** first used by the Apollo 14 astronauts on the moon, proved useful in protecting Stonehenge and other monuments from disfigurement by vandals.

Liveliness in word creation was especially manifest in the formation of derivatives expressing fresh nuances and refinements of meaning. **Activism,** for instance, echoing the German *Aktivismus,* indicated a particular type of activity that (aside from its philosophical implications) indicated the doctrine and practice of vigorous action or involvement to achieve political ends. **Confidentiality** became closely associated with confidence in the legal sense of Latin *fidentia,* as of something held in trust, and referred more particularly to the safeguarding of secret information and the protection of individual privacy. **Criticalese,** modeled on **journalese,** proved a useful term to describe the style and jargon adopted by professional critics. **Deviance** was something more circumscribed than deviation. Applied to persons, it denoted the quality of being deviant in behaviour, whereas deviation signified any departure from the norm. **Informatics** (borrowed from the Soviets) became a comprehensive expression embracing every species of information retrieval. **Societal,** an important epithet in social and environmental studies, referred specifically to relations between human beings living in a community.

Many portmanteau words or blends were too frivolous to last, but **atomitats,** or atomic habitats, were being built in deadly earnest. **Reprographic,** pertaining to reproduction photography, covered the whole area of photocopying and mechanical duplication. The prefix **tele-,** in addition to its Greek signification "far off, remote," came to be short for television. A **teleplay** was one written especially for the magic box, and **telegenic,** synonymous with **videogenic** (both adjectives modeled on **photogenic**), denoted that indefinable and highly desirable quality possessed by persons who looked good on the television screen. **Agitprop** (Russian *agitatsiya propaganda*) was sometimes employed without Communistic undertones. **Guestimate,** for guesswork estimate, probably went up in status. It even appeared in official memoranda. Another blend that had apparently come to stay was the verb to **splurge,** signifying to indulge in a spending spree and to be ostentatiously extravagant. Was it a blend of splash and surge? Nobody could be sure.

At the reverse end of the verbal spectrum, polysyllabic neo-Hellenisms made their more impressive entry, especially compounds of three components like **endosymbiont, geobiology, neuropsychiatry,** and **nucleosynthesis.** In striking contrast, there appeared Anglo-Saxon neologisms like **spin-off** for by-product. Even in formal reports, an assembly of high-level experts, convened to solve problems and originate ideas, was called a **think-tank.**

A silent and almost unnoticed importation from the Romance languages was the use of the suffix **-phone** to denote speakers of a particular language, irrespective of nationality. For example, **Francophone Africa** was used as a neat and unambiguous label for all the French-speaking people of that continent. The most notable abbreviations were **demo** for demonstration and **lib** for liberation, the latter only in **women's lib.** As an abbreviation for vegetables on the menu, **veg** remained somewhat marginal.

continued on page 734

The words, phrases, and other forms listed below achieved some currency in the information media during 1971. This list has been prepared by the permanent editorial staff of G. & C. Merriam Company, Springfield, Mass., publishers of *Webster's Third New International Dictionary* and a subsidiary of Encyclopædia Britannica, Inc.

Afro-Saxon *n* : a Negro who accepts the values of white society

ageism *or* **agism** *n* : prejudice or discrimination against elderly people

air art *n* : art consisting of inflatable plastic forms

antinatalist *n* : an advocate of population control—**antinatalist** *adj*

body language *n* : the gestures and mannerisms by which a person unwittingly communicates his feelings to others

brawn drain *n* **1** : the migration of unskilled workers from their native country in order to secure employment **2** : the migration of amateur athletes from their native country in order to accept substantial college scholarships

bundled *adj* : having equipment (as a computer) and supporting services included in a single price—compare UNBUNDLED

cache *n, specif* : a high-speed auxiliary memory for a computer

cherrypick *vb* : to register new voters in an area where they are likely to be of the registrar's own party

cherry reds *n pl* : hobnailed boots with steel toes

chunnel *n* : a railway tunnel that passes under a channel of water

clean *adj, specif* **1** : free from drug addiction **2** : being without drugs in one's possession

cluttervision *n* : a diluted effect from seeing TV commercials for several different products within a relatively short period (as a half hour)

cold rodder *n* : one who races snowmobiles

condomarinium *n* : a condominium whose units are luxury boats instead of apartments

crazies *n pl* : apolitical radicals who behave irrationally and often destructively

creepy-bopper *n* : a preteen-ager who is an ardent fan of monster movies

Custerism *n* : bravado displayed in a last-ditch situation

desexegration *n* : the elimination of separate male and female fashions in favor of the unisex look

drop shop *n* : a dry-cleaning shop that sends its customers' clothes elsewhere to be cleaned

earth art *n* : art consisting of an environmental object (as a field or hill) that is modified by the artist—**earth artist** *n*

ecocide *n* **1** : the willful destruction of the natural environment **2** : a usually chemical agent that destroys all life in a particular environment (as a lake)

ecofreak *n* : an ecology zealot

flock shooting *n* : the aiming of a sales promotion toward a wide consumer market

fragging *n* : the throwing of a fragmentation grenade at one's own overly aggressive military leader

gasbaggery *n* : meaningless verbosity <political *gasbaggery*>

glasphalt *n* : a mixture of asphalt and crushed glass used to surface roads

grasshopper *n, specif* : one who smokes marijuana

gross out *vb* : to offend or insult someone by the use of obscenities or crudities

hot line *n, specif* : telephone service by which usually unidentified callers can talk confidentially about personal problems to a sympathetic listener

hot pants *n pl* : very short shorts

imploit *vb* : to take measures that will offset the exploitation of natural resources—**imploitation** *n*—**imploiter** *n*

instant mail *n* : a subscriber service that transmits facsimile letters, documents, or photographs over telephone lines

Isro *n* : an Afro hairstyle worn by Jewish youths

Jesus Freak *n* : a member of a fundamentalist youth group whose life-style includes communal living, Bible study, street preaching, and abstinence from drugs

job action *n* : a temporary refusal (as by policemen) to work as a means of enforcing compliance with demands

job bank *n* : a computerized job placement service for the unemployed

juvenician *n* : a physician who specializes in adolescent medicine

kiddielash *or* **kidlash** *n* : a negative reaction against young political activists and protesters

lip printing *n* : the using of the impression of the lips on a surface as a means of identification

longage *n* : SURPLUS <a teacher ∼>

maxi-bopper *n* : a middle-aged person who dresses in the current fashions of young people

musicotechnocrat *n* : a specialist in the electronic production or modification of music

night minister *n* : a clergyman who seeks out and helps people (as derelicts and prostitutes) who frequent the streets at night

no-knock *adj* : authorized to enter and search a private residence without announcing oneself

parajudge *n* : a paraprofessional court official who decides minor cases (as traffic offenses, loitering, and drunkenness) in order to free a judge for serious cases

pop wine *n* : wine artificially flavored with fruit juice

quadplex *n* : a building that contains four separate apartments

right on *interj*—used to express hearty approval especially of a statement or position

sexism *n* : prejudice or discrimination against women—**sexist** *adj or n*

shuck *vb* **1** : DECEIVE **2** : SWINDLE—**shuck** *n*

sky-hitching *n* : travel by securing free rides on airplanes

snopolo *n* : polo played in the snow by players on snowmobiles

soul jockey *n* : a Negro disc jockey who regularly plays soul music

spear block *vb* : to block a football opponent by ramming him with one's head—**spear blocking** *n*

stagflation *n* : inflation characterized by stagnant consumer demand and severe wage-price inflation

street worker *n* : an adult who seeks out and tries to help local teen-agers who are in or are headed for trouble

stun gun *n* : a pistol-sized gun that fires small wood pellets

suedehead *n, chiefly Brit* : a rowdy whose hair is cut very short

telediagnosis *n* : the diagnosis of physical or mental ailments through televised intercommunication between doctor and patient

transatlantese *n* : English marked by a mixture of British and American idioms

transsex *vb* : to change one's sex

trash *vb, specif* : to vandalize (as commercial or government buildings) especially as an act of protest <five stores were *trashed* during the riot> —**trasher** *n*

triple, *n, specif* : a system of betting on races in which the bettor must pick the first, second, and third horses in this sequence in a specified race in order to win

tripsit *vb* : to act as companion to a person under the influence of LSD

unbundled *adj* : having equipment (as a computer) and supporting services separately priced—compare BUNDLED

up front *adv* : in advance <actors demanding $1 million *up front*>

urbicidal *adj* : destructive to cities

vamp *vb, specif* : to put under arrest—usually used with *on*

vegeburger *n* : a sandwich containing vegetable protein as a meat substitute

water bed *n* : a bed whose mattress is a plastic bag filled with water—called also *aqua bed*

watercycling *n* : the sport of operating a pedal boat

workaholic *n* : an employee who works harder and longer than required so as to avoid being laid off—**workaholism** *n*

workfare *n* : a welfare program designed to encourage people to work

continued from page 732

Yemen, People's Democratic Republic of

In spite of numerous protests in the public press and elsewhere, **hopefully** gained ground as an attitudinal or sentence-modifying adverb meaning "as is to be hoped" or "if our hopes are fulfilled." The new use clearly emanated from the German *hoffentlich* (older *hoffen-lich,* the dental being phonetically intrusive) either through American Yiddish or by way of Pennsylvania Dutch. For the time being, it showed no signs of superseding the primary sense "full of hope and expectation" (German *hoffnungsreich* or *hoffnungsvoll*), as in that oft-quoted peroration to Robert Louis Stevenson's *El Dorado:* "To travel hopefully is a better thing than to arrive, and the true success is to labour."

Another more subtle innovation was **non-event,** signifying an incident that turned out "in the event" to be of no significance whatever, however much it had been previously apprehended as a thing of enormous importance. A **gubbin** was a new nickname for an electronic boffin or backroom boy. **Timely** became an **in-word.** Another novel in-word was **mismatch,** applied without opprobrium to any kind of unworkable or unsuitable union. The deverbative noun **mix** threatened to oust **mixture** completely. Among colloquial words that rose unexpectedly in dignity were **hunch** and **ploy.** A **hunch** came to mean any kind of immediate knowledge, intuition, or presentiment. A **ploy** (aphetic form of **employ**) came to denote any kind of stratagem or artifice, especially in sport or debate, by which one might gain an advantage over an opponent.   (SI. P.)

Yemen, People's Democratic Republic of

A people's republic in the southern coastal region of the Arabian Peninsula, Yemen (Aden) is bordered by Yemen (San'a'), Saudi Arabia, and Oman. Area: 112,000 sq.mi. (290,000 sq.km.). Pop. (1970 est.): 1,436,000. National cap. and largest city: Aden (pop., 1970 est., 250,000); administrative cap.: Madinat ash-Shab. Language: Arabic. Religion: Muslim. Chairman of the Presidential Council in 1971, Salem Ali Rubayyi; prime ministers, Muhammad Ali Haitham and, from August 2, Ali Nasir Muhammad Husani.

YEMEN, PEOPLE'S DEMOCRATIC
REPUBLIC OF
Education. (1967–68) Primary, pupils 56,267, teachers 1,941; secondary, pupils 17,659, teachers 803; vocational, pupils 232, teachers 32; teacher training, students 294, teachers 38.
  Finance and Trade. Monetary unit: Yemen dinar, at par with the pound sterling (1 dinar = U.S. $2.40) and with a free rate (Sept. 27, 1971) of c. U.S. $2.48 to 1 dinar. Budgets (1968–69): revenue 11 million dinars; expenditure 18 million dinars. Foreign trade (1970): imports 83,760,000 dinars; exports 60.8 million dinars. Import sources: Iran 18%; Kuwait 13%; Japan 11%; Trucial States 5%; U.K. 5%. Export destinations: U.K. 25%; Japan 14%; Thailand 9%; Australia 6%; South Africa 6%; Spain 5%; Yemen (San'a') 5%. Main exports: petroleum products 74%; ship's bunker oil 7%.
  Agriculture. Production (in 000; metric tons; 1970; 1969 in parentheses): millet and sorghum c. 75 (81); dates c. 8 (c. 8); cotton, lint 2 (7). Livestock (in 000; 1969–70): cattle c. 90; sheep c. 210; goats c. 850; camels c. 41.
  Industry. Production (in 000; metric tons; 1969): salt 63; petroleum products 5,890; electricity (kw-hr.) 180,000.

During 1971 Yemen (Aden) maintained its leftist and anti-Western policies in the face of internal and external opposition from several quarters. The regime made some attempt to broaden its base through reconciliation with other nationalist elements—notably the former Front for the Liberation of South Yemen (FLOSY)—but with little success, although two senior FLOSY members agreed to return to Aden.

On April 15 the formation was announced of a 101-member Provisional Supreme People's Council as the country's highest legislative body, with representatives of workers, peasants, youth, and women. Its task was to draft laws for the election of a permanent council at the end of the year. On August 1 the three-man Presidential Council resigned. When it was re-formed, Salem Ali Rubayyi remained chairman, but Ali Nasir Muhammad Husani, the former defense minister, replaced Muhammad Ali Haitham as a member. On August 2 Husani also replaced Haitham as prime minister. The country's severe economic difficulties, caused by the continued closure of the Suez Canal, were partly alleviated by aid from Kuwait, Egypt, China, the U.S.S.R., and several Eastern European countries. There were signs of Sino-Soviet rivalry for influence as the Chinese undertook extensive construction of roads and bridges.   (P. MD.)

Yemen Arab Republic

A republic situated in the southwestern coastal region of the Arabian Peninsula, Yemen (San'a') is bounded by Yemen (Aden), Saudi Arabia, and the Red Sea. Area: 75,290 sq.mi. (195,000 sq.km.). Pop. (1970 est.): 6.5 million. Cap. and largest city: San'a' (pop., late 1960s est., 125,093). Language: Arabic. Religion: Muslim. President in 1971, Qadi Abdul Rahman al-Iryani; premiers, Mohsin al-Aini until February 25, Ahmad Muhammad Noman from May 1 to July 20, Gen. Hassan al-Amri from August 24 to August 29, and Mohsin al-Aini from September 18.

The ending of the civil war in 1970 led to a general improvement in Yemen's diplomatic position in 1971. British and Saudi ambassadors to San'a' were appointed in January and an Iranian ambassador in February. In January it was announced that winter rains had alleviated the worst effects of the three-year drought, but the economic situation remained critical. On February 25 Premier Mohsin al-Aini resigned to enable a caretaker government to supervise

YEMEN ARAB REPUBLIC
Education. (1967–68) Primary, pupils 66,830, teachers 1,499; secondary, pupils 2,718, teachers 115; teacher training, students 221, teaching staff (1965–66) 5.
  Finance and Trade. Monetary unit: riyal, with an official exchange rate (Oct. 27, 1971) of 5 riyals to U.S. $1 (13 riyals = £1 sterling). Budget (1968–69) balanced at 102.2 million riyals. Foreign trade (1966): imports 56,815,000 riyals; exports 7,303,000 riyals. Main exports: coffee, hides and skins, salt, cotton.
  Agriculture. Production (in 000; metric tons; 1969; 1968 in parentheses): millet and sorghum c. 450 (c. 450); wheat c. 15 (c. 15); dates c. 60 (c. 60); coffee c. 3.6 (c. 4.2); cotton, lint c. 1 (c. 1). Livestock (in 000; March 1970): cattle c. 1,350; sheep c. 12,300; camels c. 58.

elections to the Consultative Council. Of the council's 150 members, 30 were appointed by the president and the remainder elected by popular vote in March.

On April 21 the five-man Presidential Council resigned, and it was agreed that in the future it should have only three members. Former premier Ahmad Muhammad Noman was asked to form a government on May 1, but he resigned on July 20, saying he was unable to shoulder the burdens of Yemen's finances. On August 24 Gen. Hassan al-Amri, commander in chief of the armed forces, formed a new government, but he resigned on August 29 and was exiled from Yemen following a dispute in which he personally shot a Yemeni photographer. The victim, not realizing he was speaking to the premier, had refused to get off a telephone line. Mohsin al-Aini formed a government on September 18. (P. MD.)

Yugoslavia

A federal socialist republic, Yugoslavia is bordered by Italy, Austria, Hungary, Romania, Bulgaria, Greece, and Albania. Area: 98,766 sq. mi. (255,804 sq.km.). Pop. (1971): 20,504,516. Cap. and largest city: Belgrade (pop., 1971, 741,613). Language: Serbo-Croatian, Slovenian, and Macedonian. Religion (1953): Orthodox 41.4%; Roman Catholic 31.8%; Muslim 12.3%. President of the republic and secretary-general of the League of Communists in 1971, Marshal Tito (Josip Broz); presidents of the Federal Executive Council (premiers), Mitja Ribicic and, from July 30, Dzemal Bijedic.

The adoption by the Federal Assembly in Belgrade of 20 major and several minor constitutional amendments as part of a fundamental reform of Yugoslavia's entire federal structure was the main event of 1971. Relations with the U.S.S.R. improved toward the end of the year, despite Yugoslavia's rapprochement with China, while its links with Western countries continued to develop.

Disagreements between Serbian and Croatian leaders in February and March about the position of the big banks and trading corporations in Belgrade and the status of the autonomous province of Kosovo

within Serbia culminated in accusations of bad faith and intrigue. On April 6 the Croatian Communist Party's Central Committee accused the federal foreign ministry and security service of spreading false rumours about Croat leaders' alleged links with pro-Soviet Croat émigré groups in West Germany. The assassination of the Yugoslav ambassador in Sweden by two young Croat extremists on April 7 (he died on April 15) heightened the tension in Yugoslavia. Liberal Communist circles feared that the assassination could be used as a pretext by conservative forces to sabotage federal reform. The situation calmed down after a meeting of top party leaders from all the republics at President Tito's island residence of Brioni (April 28–30), where Tito obtained a promise that direct polemics would cease. He also obtained a unanimous endorsement of the draft constitutional amendments.

On June 30 all five chambers of the Federal Assembly in Belgrade adopted the amendments to the 1963 constitution. The federal government retained responsibility for defense, foreign affairs, and broad economic policy including development. All other powers, including the power to initiate investment projects, were transferred to the republics and municipalities. Heading the Yugoslav state was a collective presidency of 22 members (three from each republic and two each from Vojvodina and Kosovo, Yugoslavia's autonomous provinces). Within this presidency, each republic had a right to veto decisions that were against its national interest. On July 29 the Federal Assembly endorsed all the selected members of the collective presidency. The Assembly elected the 79-year-old Marshal Tito as president of the republic and first chairman of the new presidency for a further five years. It also elected a new federal government under Dzemal Bijedic.

The new government was obliged to give its immediate attention to the rapidly deteriorating economic situation. Following Yugoslavia's devaluation of the dinar on January 23, exports had risen by only 6.3% during the first nine months of the year, while imports were 21% higher than in the corresponding period of 1970. In November inflation was running at the rate of 17% annually and demand was 6% higher than available supplies. On December 17 the dinar was devalued a second time, by 13.33% in relation to the U.S. dollar (17 dinars = $1).

Marshal Tito, president since 1953, was elected to a sixth term by the Yugoslav Federal Assembly on July 29, 1971.
CAMERA PRESS—PICTORIAL PARADE

YUGOSLAVIA

Education. (1968–69) Primary, pupils 2,875,075, teachers 113,908; secondary, pupils 183,193, teachers 9,673; vocational, pupils 481,396, teachers 15,975; teacher training, students 24,233, teachers 1,333; higher (including 8 universities), students 231,444, teaching staff (1967–68) 15,950.

Finance. Monetary unit: dinar, with a par value (following devaluation of Jan. 23, 1971) of 15 dinars to U.S. $1 (36 dinars = £1 sterling) and a free rate (Oct. 11, 1971) of 38 dinars to £1. Gold, SDRs, and foreign exchange, central bank: (June 1971) U.S. $203 million; (June 1970) U.S. $217 million. Budget (1969 est.): revenue 21,854,000,000 dinars; expenditure 21,492,000,000 dinars. Gross material product: (1968) 112.2 billion dinars; (1967) 103.7 billion dinars. Money supply: (May 1971) 39,110,000,000 dinars; (May 1970) 34,660,000,000 dinars. Cost of living (1963 = 100): (June 1971) 302; (June 1970) 253.

Foreign Trade. (1970) Imports 26.7 billion dinars; exports 18.4 billion dinars. Import sources: West Germany 20%; Italy 13%; U.S.S.R. 13%; U.K. 6%; U.S. 6%; Austria 5%; Czechoslovakia 5%. Export destinations:

Italy 15%; U.S.S.R. 14%; West Germany 12%; U.K. 6%; U.S. 5%; Czechoslovakia 5%. Main exports: machinery 11%; nonferrous metals 11%; meat 7%; ships and boats 8%; chemicals 6%; clothing 5%; textile yarns and fabrics 5%. Tourism: visitors (1969) 4,746,300; gross receipts U.S. $243 million.

Transport and Communications. Roads. (1969) 99,435 km. Motor vehicles in use (1969): passenger 562,509; commercial 95,318. Railways: (1969) 10,456 km.; traffic (1970) 10,940,000,000 passenger-km., freight 18,741,000,000 net ton-km. Air traffic (1970): 757 million passenger-km.; freight 6,760,000 net ton-km. Shipping (1970): merchant vessels 100 gross tons and over 348; gross tonnage 1,515,563. Telephones (Dec. 1969) 622,939. Radio receivers (Dec. 1969) 3,320,000. Television receivers (Dec. 1969) 1,546,000.

Agriculture. Production (in 000; metric tons; 1970; 1969 in parentheses): wheat (including spelt) 3,795 (4,882); barley 402 (459); oats 309 (308); rye 127 (135); corn 6,961 (7,821); potatoes 2,964 (3,144); sunflower seed 271 (390); sugar, raw value (1970–71) 385, (1969–

70) 514; dry beans 189 (192); onions (1969) 212, (1968) 203; tomatoes (1969) 328, (1968) 323; plums (1969) 1,292, (1968) 721; apples c. 300 (483); pears c. 90 (111); olives c. 13 (7); figs (1969) 20, (1968) 20; wine 539 (706); tobacco c. 48 (47); beef and veal c. 290 (275); pork c. 300 (287); timber (cu.m.; 1968) 17,000, (1967) 17,400; fish catch (1969) 44, (1968) 45. Livestock (in 000; Jan. 1970): cattle 5,029; sheep 8,974; pigs 5,544; horses 1,076; chickens 36,566.

Industry. Fuel and power (in 000; metric tons; 1970): coal 651; lignite 27,779; crude oil 2,852; natural gas (cu.m.) 977,000; manufactured gas (cu.m.) 98,000; electricity (kw-hr.) 26,022,000. Production (in 000; metric tons; 1970): cement 4,398; iron ore (35% metal content) 3,697; pig iron 1,374; crude steel 2,226; bauxite 2,100; antimony ore (metal content; 1969) 2.1; chrome ore (oxide content; 1969) 9.6; manganese ore (metal content; 1969) 5.6; aluminum 47; copper 89; lead 97; zinc 65; sulfuric acid 746; cotton yarn 102; wool yarn 38; wood pulp (1969) 500; newsprint 75; other paper (1969) 530.

The slow pace of the reform of the foreign trade system provoked bitterness in Croatia, which earned 40% of Yugoslavia's total foreign exchange income but was allowed to retain only a small proportion of it. On December 1 Tito attacked Croat party leaders for allowing a strike of Zagreb University students and called for a purge of "antisocialist" and "nationalist" elements. The resignation under pressure of three Croatian party leaders on December 12 was followed by disturbances in Zagreb and a purge of the Croatian party.

President Tito's visit to Italy in March marked the end of the brief quarrel over the status of some of the territories awarded to Yugoslavia after World War II. His visit to Pope Paul VI at the Vatican on March 29 demonstrated the satisfactory state of relations between Yugoslavia and the Roman Catholic Church. Relations with the U.S.S.R., Bulgaria, and Hungary worsened in the summer. In June and July the Yugoslav press criticized Moscow for supporting anti-Tito Yugoslav refugees in the U.S.S.R. and Western Europe. In turn, the visit to Peking of Yugoslavia's foreign minister, Mirko Tepavac, in June provoked criticism from the Warsaw Pact press. News of maneuvers by Warsaw Pact armies in southern Hungary in the summer and signs of increasing Soviet pressure against Romania led to close consultations between Romania and Yugoslavia in August (Tito also had talks with Pres. Nicolae Ceausescu of Romania in November). Yugoslavia emphasized its readiness to defend itself by announcing that it would hold its biggest ever defense exercises in October. In September, Leonid I. Brezhnev, the Soviet party leader, paid a three-day visit to Yugoslavia during which he reaffirmed, with some significant qualifications, Yugoslavia's right to its "independent road to socialism."

In October–November, Tito visited India, Iran, Egypt, Canada, and the United States, where his nonaligned foreign policy met with full support from Pres. Richard M. Nixon. The U.S. government undertook to help double Yugoslavia's exports to the U.S., which in 1971 were worth $100 million, and also supported private U.S. capital investment in Yugoslavia. (K. F. Cv.)

Zambia

A republic and a member of the Commonwealth of Nations, Zambia is bounded by Tanzania, Malawi, Mozambique, Rhodesia, South West Africa, Angola, and the Congo (Kinshasa). Area: 290,586 sq.mi. (752,614 sq.km.). Pop. (1969): 4,054,000, of whom about 99% are Africans. Cap.: Lusaka (pop., 1969, 238,200). Language: English and Bantu. Religion: predominantly animist; Europeans are Christian. President in 1971, Kenneth Kaunda.

At the Commonwealth meeting of heads of state and of government in Singapore in January 1971, President Kaunda asked all members to sign a declaration denouncing racism and promising to deny any assistance to nations practicing it. In the forefront of his mind was the possibility that Britain might supply arms to South Africa. In April the South African prime minister, B. J. Vorster (*see* BIOGRAPHY), carried the dispute into the Zambian camp by announcing that Kaunda had asked him for aid against military aggression from Rhodesia or Portuguese Africa. The Zambian government hotly denied the accusation.

The president had additional problems on the home front. Since independence, the economy had declined. Zambia's dependence on copper as an export revenue earner was increasing at the same time that the price of copper was slumping to a dangerously low £412 per ton from £748 in the first half of 1970. Urbanization and the departure of South African commercial farmers had caused a decline in corn production, and the situation was not helped by the temporary delaying of supplies by the Portuguese in reprisal for the death of a number of people kidnapped from Mozambique. So serious did the situation become that the government agreed to buy corn from Rhodesia in spite of the sanctions in operation against that country.

In January Kaunda decided to set up a commission of inquiry to investigate charges of tribal bias in the government. This was followed in May by an all-out attack on tribalism by the president during the United National Independence Party (UNIP) conference. Kaunda stated first that the system whereby members of UNIP's central committee were virtually assured of a Cabinet post was to be abolished. He then induced the conference to approve a new constitution for the party that would ensure the election of its central committee on a national and not on a tribal basis. Following the publication in June of the findings of the judicial inquiry into tribalism, the president dismissed three ministers.

In August Simon Kapwepwe, former vice-president of Zambia, resigned as minister of local government and culture and announced the formation of a new opposition United Progressive Party (UPP), which would press for an immediate general election. He claimed that the aim of the party was to stamp out capitalism in Zambia. In September the government detained 75 of the key members of the UPP, although Kapwepwe himself was not arrested. (K. I.)

ZAMBIA
Education. (1968) Primary, pupils 609,490, teachers 11,986; secondary, pupils 42,388, teachers 1,917; vocational, pupils 2,174; teacher training, students 2,180, teachers 172; higher, students 871, teaching staff 148.
Finance. Monetary unit: kwacha, with a par value of 0.71 kwacha to U.S. $1 (1.71 kwachas = £1 sterling) and a free rate (Sept. 27, 1971) of 0.69 kwacha to U.S. $1. Gold and foreign exchange, central bank: (June 1971): U.S. $362.5 million; (June 1970) U.S. $554.4 million. Budget (1970 est.): revenue 334 million kwachas (including mineral royalties and taxes); expenditure 244 million kwachas. Gross national product: (1968) 919.5 million kwachas; (1967) 840.5 million kwachas. Cost of living (1963 = 100): (March 1971) 157; (March 1970) 146.
Foreign Trade. (1970) Imports 358.6 million kwachas; exports 714.9 million kwachas. Import sources (1969): South Africa 23%; U.K. 23%; U.S. 10%; Japan 7%; Rhodesia 7%. Export destinations (1969): U.K. 26%; Japan 24%; West Germany 13%; Italy 10%; France 9%. Main export copper 95%.
Transport and Communications. Roads (1969) 34,653 km. Motor vehicles in use (1968): passenger 48,200; commercial (including buses) 25,800. Railways (1968) 1,045 km. Construction of a 1,600-km. railway linking Zambia with Dar es Salaam in Tanzania began in 1970. Air traffic (1969): 138,140,000 passenger-km.; freight 3,338,000 net ton-km. Telephones (Dec. 1969) 51,958. Radio receivers (Dec. 1969) 55,000. Television receivers (Dec. 1969) 20,000.
Agriculture. Production (in 000; metric tons; 1970; 1969 in parentheses): corn c. 550 (c. 655); peanuts c. 100 (c. 74); cassava (1969) c. 162, (1968) c. 160; tobacco 5 (5.3). Livestock (in 000; 1969–70): cattle c. 1,350; sheep c. 37; goats c. 187; pigs c. 92.
Industry. Production (in 000; metric tons; 1970): copper 580; zinc 53; lead 27; manganese ore (metal content; 1968) 13; electricity (kw-hr.) 693,000.

Zanzibar:
see Tanzania

Zinc:
see Mining

Zoology:
see Life Sciences

United States Statistical Supplement

Developments in the states in 1971

Frustration in federal-state relations, tragedy in prisons, and rising costs of public welfare coupled with taxpayer reluctance to pay for them were outstanding concerns of state governments of the United States in 1971. Financial pressures reflecting social needs preoccupied the states. These resulted in demands on their part for larger federal payments to them and produced another round of tax increases by numerous states.

The requisite number of state legislatures ratified the 26th Amendment to the U.S. Constitution to put it into effect, extending the 18-year-old vote to all elections. Conflict then emerged over rights of students to vote in college towns. Adding to concerns in several states were financial scandals and charges of conflicts of interest involving present or past state officials or legislators. At the same time, various states acted to strengthen governmental organization.

Problems of providing for educational systems were greatly to the fore. Action to safeguard the environment was not as widespread as in 1970 but included important measures.

Forty-nine states had regular legislative sessions, and more than 20 held special sessions. Significant legislation resulted in many fields.

Party Strengths. Twenty-nine governors were Democrats in 1971 and 21 Republicans. In November the election of a Democrat in Kentucky to succeed a Republican made the prospective Democratic majority 30 to 20 for 1972. Democrats had the edge in all of four major regions except the Northeast, where six Republicans were in governors' offices as against three Democrats.

Democrats held majorities in both legislative chambers of 23 states in 1971, as compared with 16 in which Republicans held two-house majorities. But in contrast to the division among governors, the Republican legislative score in the North, overall, was stronger than the Democrats'.

Traditionally, southern Democrats have been classified differently from those of the North. To a considerable extent that continued to be the case. But it was a fading distinction, as was particularly apparent at the gubernatorial level. An increasing number of governors in the 11 states of the Old Confederacy were widely considered a "new breed"—moderates on racial matters, relatively progressive on others.

18-Year-Old Vote. At the start of the year confusion on voting rights confronted the states. The Supreme Court in December had upheld a 1970 act of Congress lowering the voting age to 18 insofar as the law applied to federal elections but ruled against its application to state and local elections. Without extremely rapid action to change state constitutions or the U.S. Constitution so that 18 would be the voting age in all elections, chaotic conditions at the polls could be foreseen. Only three states provided for voting at 18, only six others at 19 or 20.

The problem was solved by the 26th Amendment to the U.S. Constitution qualifying voting at 18 in all elections. By overwhelming margins Congress cleared the amendment in March. In record time it received ratifications from the 38 states required to make it effective. In all cases ratification was by legislatures. Ohio's legislature was the 38th to approve, on June 30.

Town and Gown. Quickly, however, ratification of the amendment added fuel to another controversy: Were students to be permitted to vote in their college towns if these were not the towns of their parents? The question was not new, but the 18-year-old vote gave it far more portent. In many college towns old residents and officeholders feared that college students could outnumber other voters, turn local incumbents out, perhaps adopt bond issues that would burden taxpayers for years. Advocates of the students, on the other hand, asserted that to force them to refrain from voting unless able and willing to return to their parents' localities to vote, or arrange for absentee voting, was discriminatory, provided they could meet the requirements for registration that applied to other citizens.

In one response to this situation, the New York legislature passed a law that was expected to make it more difficult or impossible for most students to vote in their college towns. The California Supreme Court, however, ruled that it would abridge the rights of minors to compel them to travel to their parents' districts to register and vote or to register and vote as absentees; registrars might question a citizen as to his true domicile, but the questioning should not be based on his age or occupation alone. The Michigan Supreme Court and a U.S. district court in Ohio issued comparable rulings. There was litigation on the issue in numerous states.

In almost half the states election authorities other than courts, in most cases attorneys general, issued or expressed opinions on the subject up to autumn. More than half of these appeared to support, in general, the constitutional rights of students to register and vote in their college towns provided they could meet registration requirements for other citizens. The remainder appeared to oppose such voting or hedged their views.

Obviously, murkiness remained, not only among states but within states, on this 1971 version of the centuries-old town-and-gown issue. Even where there were clear rulings by courts or attorneys general, leeway could remain for college-town election officials to challenge or bar students' votes.

Federal-State Relations. Proposals for sharing federal revenues with the states and local governments and demands for welfare reform dominated federal-state relations. Pres. Richard M. Nixon called for both in January and thereby set off wide-ranging debate.

Speaking for revenue sharing, he submitted that "we have made the federal government so strong it grows muscle-bound and the states and localities so weak they approach impotence." Related to revenue and certain other goals, he asked Congress to open the way to "a new American revolution" in which power would be "turned back to the people" and government at all levels would be "refreshed and renewed."

Nixon had asked the previous Congress for revenue sharing, but his program this year was much bigger. It included "general revenue sharing," which would approximate $5 billion in the first year of operation, and $11 billion in "special revenue sharing." The latter would combine $1 billion of new money with $10 billion to be taken from a very large number of existing grant-in-aid programs and allocated in half a dozen block grants to states and localities for specified but broad purposes.

It was the $5 billion general program that received most attention. As proposed, it would increase automatically after the first year with the rise of U.S. personal taxable income. The money would be distributed to the states on the basis of their populations adjusted by the extent to which each had realized on its own tax resources. If a state reached an agreed formula with its localities for division of the funds, it would receive 100% of its potential allocation. Otherwise, it would receive 10% less and divide it under a federal formula expected to mean, as a nationwide average, about a 50–50 split between the states and the localities. Washington would attach no strings on use of the money, though there would be procedures to guard against fraud and civil rights discrimination.

In general, state governmental support for the proposal was strong. The National Governors' Conference upheld revenue sharing, as before. Other bodies of legislators and officials backed it. Some 13 legislatures, seeking to force the issue, even asked Congress to call a constitutional convention on revenue sharing.

The Advisory Commission on Intergovernmental Relations—comprising members from Congress, the national administration, state and local governments, and the public—renewed its support for the principle. Linked with it, the ACIR proposed that federal income tax payers be allowed substantial credit for state and local income tax payments—a move designed to encourage more state taxation of income.

Large opposition, nevertheless, quickly bore down on revenue sharing. The most influential single opponent to general sharing was Rep. Wilbur D. Mills (Dem., Ark.), chairman of the House Ways and Means Committee. There also was strong labor opposition to the plan. Big city spokesmen, desiring some form of revenue sharing, were glad that the new project would give the cities a larger share than the president's earlier proposal would have done, but feared that the $11 billion grant consolidation would cost the cities money. Advocates of the poor greatly doubted that the plan was directed to their needs, and guardians of civil rights wanted much stronger provisions against racial discrimination.

In addition, lack of confidence in state and local governmental ability to make best use of the money produced much opposition. One writer, citing state-local shortcomings and emphasizing national responsibilities, concluded that revenue sharing was not a revolution but a counterrevolution.

On November 30 Mills introduced legislation for a substitute plan, quite different from the president's. He proposed a five-year program, not permanent, providing grants of $3.5 billion a year to local governments for specified though broad purposes, the distribution to be based in part on the numbers of low-income families; and $1.8 billion a year to states, the amounts based on how much they themselves raised from income taxes—except that states without income taxes would receive some funds.

The issue went over to 1972.

In June the House of Representatives for the second time in two years passed a welfare reform bill that had as its principal innovation a federally guaranteed income for poor families. The broad proposal was a new version of a plan the president had placed before the last Congress, where the resulting bill died in the Senate. Despite overwhelmingly favorable House majorities both years, the 1971 measure again met Senate roadblocks. At the year-end it had not been reported out of the Senate Finance Committee.

For the states, the stakes were large. Not only would enactment bring a significant immediate decrease in their share of welfare payments; many regarded the reform bill hopefully as a step toward full federal take-over of all welfare costs. The National Governors' Conference and other state bodies renewed their calls for such a federal assumption, as did the Advisory Commission on Intergovernmental Relations. And numerous critics who opposed revenue sharing looked favorably on complete federal shouldering of the welfare load.

Finance. State budgets were at record highs, in keeping with a continuing pattern as populations and costs of services increase. At least 30 of the legislatures increased taxes. New personal income taxes were voted by the Pennsylvania and Rhode Island sessions and both personal and corporate income taxes by Ohio's. Florida's voters overwhelmingly approved a constitutional amendment in November authorizing a corporation income tax. Maine's voters refused to repeal its personal and corporate income tax. The Connecticut legislature earlier adopted a personal income tax, but repealed it following a public outcry, and substituted a revenue package including increase of the general sales tax from 5 to 6.5%, making it the highest such rate for any state. California's legislature for the first time required withholding of income taxes on its residents.

The Minnesota, New York, Tennessee, and Texas legislatures also increased general sales tax rates. Items subject to sales taxes were broadened or rates raised on selected items in Alabama, Connecticut, Florida, and West Virginia. Tennessee added a gross receipts tax on wholesalers. Personal income tax rates were raised in Arkansas, California, Delaware, Iowa, Massachusetts, Michigan, Minnesota, Montana, North Dakota, and Wisconsin. Increases in corporate income taxes were voted in California, Delaware, Iowa, Michigan, Minnesota, Montana, New Hampshire, New York, North Dakota, Tennessee, and Wisconsin.

Legislatures raised taxes on motor fuel in Connecticut, Delaware, Florida, Georgia, Maine, Massachusetts, New Hampshire, and Vermont—also in Alabama on diesel fuel only, and in Alaska on watercraft fuel; on designated alcoholic beverages in Delaware, Idaho, Iowa, Kansas, Oklahoma, and Texas; and on cigarettes in sixteen states.

State tax collections in the 1971 fiscal year totaled $51.5 billion, up 7.3% from the 1970 figure. Of the new total, $15.5 billion was from general sales and gross receipts taxes; $14.1 billion from selective sales taxes; $10.1 billion from individual income taxes; $3.4 billion from corporation net income taxes; and $5 billion from motor vehicle and other licenses.

Data compiled in 1971 showed that state revenue from all sources reached $88.9 billion in fiscal 1970, up 14.6% from the preceding year. General revenue (excluding state liquor store and insurance trust revenue) was $77.8 billion, up 15.5%. Total state expenditure was $85.1 billion. General expenditure, excluding outlays of the liquor stores and insurance trust systems, totaled $77.6 billion, 14.2% above the year before. Of general revenue, 61.7% came from state taxes, 12.3% from charges and miscellaneous revenue—including education charges; and 24.8%—$19.3 billion—from the federal government.

The largest state outlays were $30.9 billion for education, $13.5 billion for highways, and $13.2 billion for public welfare.

Administrative Structures, Powers. Several legislatures took important steps to consolidate state executive departments or provide central administrative offices or extend governors' powers in other ways. Reform in those directions has inched forward over the years, in the face of entrenched interests that resist change.

Reorganization measures of 1971 included extensive consolidation of agencies in Arkansas and North Carolina and the groundwork for broad consolidation in Maine. Georgia's governor was given new powers for executive reorganization. New agencies or departments for administrative or financial control or both were set up in Vermont, Wyoming, Missouri, and South Dakota. The governor of North Dakota received authority to appoint a majority of the members of many boards.

Legislatures raised salaries of executives or administrative staff or both in various states, including Illinois, Indiana, Maine, Missouri, Nevada, New Mexico, and Utah.

A National Center for State Courts was established, with a board of directors comprising judges of state appellate and trial courts, to seek improvement in administration of justice, promote research and training for the courts, and help other organizations working in this field.

Legislative Systems. Legislative reapportionment was a major concern in consequence of the 1970 census and past court requirements for representation on the basis of one-man, one-vote. By mid-autumn redistricting plans had been adopted for 29 legislatures—19 by their own action, 10 by other bodies. Not all were final. In several cases courts ruled legislatures' self-apportionments unconstitutional because of excessive population deviations among districts. Court challenges to reapportionments had been lodged in some 16 states.

The Indiana and Wisconsin legislatures established annual legislative sessions, as permitted by past voter action. This raised to 33 the number of legislatures with annual sessions, as compared with 26 in 1970 and six in 1947. (In New Hampshire, which was reported after the November 1970 election among states voting for annual sessions, a recount showed that the proposal fell short of the two-thirds majority needed.)

Several legislatures raised their members' salaries or expense allowances.

Much attention went to a study and rating of the 50 legislatures by the Citizens Conference on State Legislatures, a private organization with foundation support. Without attempting to measure the legislatures' products, its study gauged their procedures, rules, and operations. Using a series of criteria, the conference rated the California, New York, and Illinois legislatures at the top, in that order. The corresponding three from the bottom up were those of Alabama, Wyoming, and Delaware. A relatively high ranking, it was indicated, was hardly grounds for complacency. The study said that across the board legislatures "stand high on the list of institutions that need reform."

Ethics. The year produced more than its share of state scandals and conflicts of interest. Illinois and Texas were headliners, but other states competed.

As 1971 began, Illinois reverberated over the marvelous shoe boxes of Paul Powell, late secretary of state and downstate Democratic leader. Powell, who used to say in campaigns that he could "smell the meat a-cookin'," died suddenly in October 1970. Late in December the public learned that some $800,000 in cash had been found in shoe boxes, a bowling bag, and envelopes in the closet of his unpretentious two-room quarters in a Springfield hotel. By early January his estate was estimated at close to $3 million, although he had grown up poor and always remained a close man with his money. Ties with racetracks, trucking, banking, and insurance concerns were some of the links credited for his wealth. By May volumes had appeared in the press on his known and suspected activities.

Soon another scandal fascinated Illinois. According to evidence to a federal grand jury, politicians had made large profits from stock they bought at bargain prices in state-regulated racetracks. On December 15 the best known figure involved, Otto Kerner (Dem.), governor from 1961 to 1968, now a U.S. Court of Appeals judge, was indicted by a federal grand jury, together with three officials of his gubernatorial administration and an associate of one of them. It was charged that they conspired to obtain $356,-000 in racetrack stock for $70,158 and that the transaction constituted a bribe to influence racetrack regulation. In 17 counts against Kerner, the indictment charged him with bribery, perjury, income tax evasion, mail fraud and conspiracy. It alleged that he evaded $84,129 in 1966 income taxes.

Texas politics earlier seethed over repercussions of the collapse of a multimillion dollar insurance and banking operation headed by Frank W. Sharp, Houston real estate magnate. According to the Securities and Exchange Commission, Gov. Preston Smith and Dr. Elmer Baum, who resigned in October as state Democratic chairman, each made a $62,500 profit on stock in a Sharp life insurance company which they bought in 1969 with money loaned by a Sharp bank. Other politicians also had bought the stock on such loans. In June Sharp was fined $5,000 and received a suspended jail sentence after pleading guilty in federal court to making a false entry in bank records and selling unregistered securities. Subsequent developments included indictments in September of the Speaker of the Texas House of Representatives, another Democratic legislator, and several others in government employment or private life on charges connected with Sharp's activities.

Through most of 1971 Democrats monopolized the political trouble from the Sharp affair. In October, however, following public pressure based on his connections with Sharp, Will R. Wilson, Jr., an assistant at-

torney general in the Nixon administration, resigned, explaining that he wished to spare the administration embarrassment. Wilson, a former Democratic attorney general of Texas, now a Republican, was a lawyer for Sharp before going to the Justice Department, and had obtained a number of loans from Sharp interests.

Elsewhere, developments included the indictment of several New Jersey state politicians; a renewed crusade against corruption in Alabama by the editor of the *Montgomery Advertiser and Journal*, winner of a 1970 Pulitzer Prize for exposing a state prison system scandal; testimony before a congressional committee by the governor and other officials of Florida that federal law enforcement assistance funds were misspent by the state during the preceding administration; and a 12-year prison sentence for a former governor of West Virginia for bribing a federal jury foreman in 1968.

During the year a few legislative bodies adopted measures, varying in scope, on governmental ethics.

Education. Potentially much the most far-reaching development for shaping state education systems was a California Supreme Court ruling on August 30 and subsequent action in two courts elsewhere. In the case of California the court held that the state's system of public school financing, based primarily on local property taxes, violated the U.S. Constitution's requirement of equal protection under the law because of imbalances in amounts raised by rich as against poor communities. These, it found, made the quality of a child's education "a function of the wealth of his parents and neighbors." It directed a lower court to hold hearings on how the inequities could be corrected. Meantime, property taxes were unaffected. But as the California system is similar to that of most states, the implications of the opinion, if upheld nationally, were very large.

In October a federal judge in Minnesota ruled that its school financing system was unconstitutional because of inequities. He held that the level of spending for a child's education should not be a function of wealth other than the wealth of the whole state. On December 23 a three-judge federal court in Texas declared that its public school financing, based in important degree on the local property tax, was unconstitutional because it discriminated against children of poor communities and violated the equal protection guarantee. It ordered the legislature to take action to remedy this situation within two years or face a court solution.

Nor had these rulings come in a vacuum. The Advisory Commission on Intergovernmental Relations had called for substantial state takeover of education costs "to remove that major drag on the property tax and to equalize educational opportunity" throughout a state. It pointed out early in the year that the governors of Michigan and Minnesota had called for such a solution. Pressures for much more federal aid to schools also mounted during the year.

Nationwide, it was estimated as of 1970–71 that about 52% of revenue for public elementary and secondary schools came from the localities, 41% from the states, and 7% from the federal government.

Under Maryland legislation in 1971 the state assumed the full cost of public school construction.

State aid to parochial schools sustained a heavy setback in June when the U.S. Supreme Court declared, 8 to 1, that state programs to reimburse church-related schools for instruction, even in nonreligious subjects, was unconstitutional on the basis of the First Amendment. Some 36 states had adopted aid programs of varying kinds, from provisions for busing and free lunches to salary aids for teachers. The instructional salary provisions, at least, were directly hit by the decision. At the same time the court by a 5 to 4 margin upheld federal payments to construct academic buildings at private colleges, including church-related colleges.

Subsequently, federal, state, and church officials sought means of alleviating the prospects of parochial schools.

Problems of racial integration of schools, including busing for that purpose, received much attention in state governments. Here, however, the 1971 arenas were above all the federal courts, the Nixon administration, and local school districts.

Increased state appropriations for education were general.

Welfare. Burgeoning costs of public welfare, high rates of unemployment, straitened state treasuries, and taxpayer resistance to paying more brought critical welfare impasses in many states. Widespread retrenchment resulted, halting or reversing the expansion of a decade. By mid-August a nationwide tally indicated that 19 or more legislatures had reduced welfare benefits in 1971; other states were considering it.

Legislatures adopted varied forms of welfare trimming. Executive departments initiated others. Several legislatures—including those of Connecticut, Hawaii, New York, and Rhode Island—voted one-year residency requirements for eligibility to welfare payments, despite the Supreme Court's ruling in 1969 that residency requirements for welfare elsewhere were unconstitutional. The Illinois legislature also passed a one-year requirement but the governor vetoed it, then moved to cut welfare costs in other ways. In July and August federal courts held the Connecticut and New York residency laws unconstitutional. New York's session also adopted other measures to tighten welfare. California's legislature—although balking at the governor's original legislative proposals that would have slashed welfare and "Medi-Cal" by an estimated $800 million—adopted measures expected to save some $250 million in those categories.

By legislation or voter action, Alabama, Florida, Idaho, Kentucky, Maine, and New Jersey reduced taxes for the elderly, and Pennsylvania established a lottery to produce tax relief for them.

Mental Health. There was one mental health development of nationwide importance. A three-judge federal court in October ordered Pennsylvania to provide free public education for all its retarded children. It held that all children can benefit from education and have a right to it. Gov. Milton J. Shapp praised the ruling, and his administration agreed to the court's order, which was issued as a consent decree. Champions of retarded children declared the decision would prove a landmark in establishing a nationwide right of retarded children to free education.

Prisons. A fatal clash at California's San Quentin Prison and the bloodiest prison tragedy of American history at New York's Attica Correctional Facility drove home to millions that conditions were at a critical stage in the penal system.

At San Quentin three inmates and three guards were killed on August 21. A guard shot one of them, George Jackson—a nationally prominent black militant—in an armed attempt at escape, according to prison officials, and convicts murdered three guards and two white inmates.

At Attica on September 13, an assault force of state troopers aided by sheriff's deputies and guards stormed and recaptured the state prison from rebelling inmates who had held it more than four days. Forty-three men were killed or fatally injured: nine guards or other employees and 30 prisoners at the time of the assault; three inmates earlier, presumably at the hands of convicts; and one guard who died of injuries sustained early in the revolt. The dead guards and employees were among some 38 the prisoners had held hostage.

After the storming of the prison, correctional officials first said the nine hostages killed, or some of them, were murdered by convicts, wielding knives or beating them. Autopsies later showed that all nine died of bullet wounds; it was assumed that these were sustained in the fusillade of gunfire by law enforcement personnel retaking the prison. State authorities ordered the recapture after protracted negotiations in which they agreed to many demands of convict leaders for prison reforms but rejected what they regarded as impossible conditions. Following the event, a series of state and federal investigations began.

Late in November inmates of New Jersey's Rahway State Prison seized the warden and five guards, whom they released some 24 hours later after Gov. William T. Cahill promised to consider prisoners' grievances. The hostages had received relatively minor injuries, including stab wounds sustained by the warden in the initial melee between convicts and guards. The warden reported that thereafter he had good treatment.

The year brought lesser prison disorders elsewhere. Included were upheavals in state prisons of Idaho, Florida, Illinois, again in New Jersey, and work stoppages in two Massachusetts institutions.

Aware of perilous conditions in most state prisons, authorities pointed to many causes. "Correctional" institutions, it was recognized, did not correct, a great many were overcrowded, staffs were poorly trained, food and facilities left much to be desired, work programs were deficient. Drug addiction sometimes added to tension among convicts. Moreover, particularly in large urban states, experts pointed to racial and cultural polarization between many prisoners and guards. Penologists had long declared that prisons for inmates from large cities should be in or near the cities. Instead, large numbers are in or near small towns, largely white in population. That was the case at Attica, a rural town of 2,800, with a prison whose inmates were 85% black and Puerto Rican.

One of the needs, authorities agreed, was more money for prisons. But when money was not forthcoming for welfare requirements, few expected adequate state funds for prisons.

Yet some progress was made. There was evidence that prisons in recent years had been making distinctly less use of the most severe disciplines, although abuses and brutalities continued to be reported. Training of guards has increased. The attorney general of Pennsylvania in 1971 announced an impressive "Bill of Rights" for prisoners, in line with a United Nations prison code. Mississippi's legislature acted to end its armed trusty system in 1974—a system charged with much brutality. Perhaps the most extensive change was effected administratively in the Washington State Prison at Walla Walla, where the prisoners have written and adopted a constitution and elected a resident governmental council, and where other liberalizing reforms have been adopted.

Drugs. The trend, notable in 1970, to cut marijuana penalties was widened in 1971 by legislation in several states, including Colorado, Idaho, Illinois, Indiana, Florida, Massachusetts, Missouri, and Nevada. More states acted to expand or ease access to treatment for drug addiction. Sixteen legislatures adopted the Uniform Controlled Substances Act, proposed by the National Conference of Commissioners on Uniform State Laws. It seeks a coordinated system of drug control and, without prescribing penalties, sets forth prohibited activities.

The Environment. State action to protect the environment fell off from 1970's record pace, but there were advances, some of them broad. More than a third of the legislatures enacted programs for two or more categories of environmental protection. Pennsylvania's voters approved a constitutional guarantee of the right to pure water and air, and those of New Mexico declared preservation of the environment a right to be preserved by the legislature.

Lobbyists, mainly for industrial interests, sought to curb legislation, particularly proposals to limit phosphates in detergents or to control litter-producing containers, but also some more general measures. They were largely successful against detergent and container bills. Yet acts to limit phosphates after stipulated dates were adopted in several states, including Connecticut, Indiana, Maine, and New York. Oregon's legislature adopted a bill effective in October 1972 requiring deposits on beer and soft-drink containers and prohibiting metal pull-tab tops.

Conflicts with industry on such potential sources of pollution as refineries and power developments continued. Delaware legislation, adopted in the face of much business opposition, barred heavy industry from that state's coastlines. Some new laws were passed to regulate strip mining.

A *New York Times* survey showed in December that several states in 1971 reduced or eliminated representation of regulated interests on state pollution control boards, and indicated that several of 32 states with such representation on boards were moving toward similar action in 1972.

Consumer Protection. Much controversy centered on proposals for no-fault automobile insurance, under varied versions

of which one's own insurance company pays him medical costs, lost wages, and perhaps certain other costs resulting from an accident, within limits, regardless of who was to blame for it. A U.S. Department of Transportation study indicated need for a nationwide no-fault system and favored federal legislation for national standards in it; unpublished recommendations of the study group were reported to call for such standards to take effect within a specified time in any state that failed to enact them. The national administration, however, while supporting the no-fault principle, wished to leave it to action by the states rather than Congress at this stage.

Up to autumn the legislatures of Delaware, Florida, Illinois, and Oregon passed some version of no-fault in 1971. Massachusetts did so in 1970. But nationwide, economic interests gave proposals for state laws a rough time. Many bills were killed or held up. Lawyers and some of the insurance companies set up roadblocks. Interests of trial lawyers were greatly involved, as no-fault stood to cost them millions in fees. With relatively little state action forthcoming, and with criticism by consumer advocates that much of the legislation enacted was inadequate, there was continued sentiment in Congress for federal legislation. Meantime, the National Conference of Commissioners on Uniform State Laws and the Council of State Governments were cooperating to develop a model no-fault law for submission to the states.

In other areas of consumer protection, state initiatives were more successful. In Arkansas, Idaho, Indiana, North Carolina, Oregon, and South Dakota broad acts were adopted which, as a rule, banned a range of fraudulent or deceptive practices.

Legislation was passed in Arizona, Colorado, and Minnesota to protect installment buyers. Colorado, Indiana, Missouri, South Dakota, and Wyoming acts gave people who buy from door-to-door salesmen a cooling-off period, usually three days, in which to cancel contracts.

Other Developments. Pennsylvania's voters approved a constitutional amendment prohibiting abridgment of rights because of sex, and the Delaware, Indiana, Texas, and Washington legislatures forbade various types of discrimination on account of sex. Several legislatures increased rights of youth. Michigan and Vermont gave them basically full legal rights at 18, including those of making legal contracts and drinking alcoholic beverages. North Carolina and Washington reduced the age of majority to 18 but not the right to buy liquor.

Highway safety legislation included implied consent laws in Mississippi, Montana, Wyoming, and Illinois providing for chemical tests to determine intoxication of drivers; with Illinois' action, all states now have such laws.

FRANK SMOTHERS

*Journalist; formerly
Director of Publications
Council of State Governments*

Area and Population

Area and population of the states

State	AREA in sq.mi. Total	AREA in sq.mi. Inland water*	RESIDENT POPULATION April 1, 1960, census	RESIDENT POPULATION April 1, 1970	Percent increase 1960-70
Alabama	51,609	549	3,266,740	3,444,165	5.4
Alaska	586,400	15,335	226,167	302,173	33.6
Arizona	113,909	334	1,302,161	1,772,482	36.1
Arkansas	53,104	605	1,786,272	1,923,295	7.7
California	158,693	2,120	15,717,204	19,953,134	27.0
Colorado	104,247	363	1,753,947	2,207,259	25.8
Connecticut	5,009	110	2,535,234	3,032,217	19.6
Delaware	2,057	79	446,292	548,104	22.8
District of Columbia	69	8	763,956	756,510	−1.0
Florida	58,560	4,308	4,951,560	6,789,443	37.1
Georgia	58,876	602	3,943,116	4,589,575	16.4
Hawaii	6,424	9	632,772	769,913	21.7
Idaho	83,557	849	667,191	713,008	6.9
Illinois	56,400	470	10,081,158	11,113,976	10.2
Indiana	36,291	106	4,662,498	5,193,669	11.4
Iowa	56,290	258	2,757,537	2,825,041	2.4
Kansas	82,264	216	2,178,611	2,249,071	3.2
Kentucky	40,395	532	3,038,156	3,219,311	6.0
Louisiana	48,523	3,417	3,257,022	3,643,180	11.9
Maine	33,215	2,203	969,265	993,663	2.5
Maryland	10,577	703	3,100,689	3,922,399	26.5
Massachusetts	8,257	390	5,148,578	5,689,170	10.5
Michigan	58,216	1,197	7,823,194	8,875,083	13.4
Minnesota	84,068	4,059	3,413,864	3,805,069	11.5
Mississippi	47,716	493	2,178,141	2,216,912	1.8
Missouri	69,686	548	4,319,813	4,677,399	8.3
Montana	147,138	1,402	674,767	694,409	2.9
Nebraska	77,227	615	1,411,330	1,483,791	5.1
Nevada	110,540	752	285,278	488,738	71.3
New Hampshire	9,304	290	606,921	737,681	21.5
New Jersey	7,836	315	6,066,782	7,168,164	18.2
New Mexico	121,666	156	951,023	1,016,000	6.8
New York	49,576	1,637	16,782,304	18,190,740	8.4
North Carolina	52,712	3,645	4,556,155	5,082,059	11.5
North Dakota	70,665	1,208	632,446	617,761	−2.3
Ohio	41,222	250	9,706,397	10,652,017	9.7
Oklahoma	69,919	1,032	2,328,284	2,559,253	9.9
Oregon	96,981	733	1,768,687	2,091,385	18.2
Pennsylvania	45,333	326	11,319,366	11,793,909	4.2
Rhode Island	1,214	156	859,488	949,723	10.5
South Carolina	31,055	783	2,382,594	2,590,516	8.7
South Dakota	77,047	669	680,514	666,257	−2.1
Tennessee	42,244	482	3,567,089	3,924,164	10.0
Texas	267,338	4,499	9,579,677	11,196,730	16.9
Utah	84,916	2,577	890,627	1,059,273	18.9
Vermont	9,609	333	389,881	444,732	14.1
Virginia	40,815	977	3,966,949	4,648,494	17.2
Washington	68,192	1,483	2,853,214	3,409,169	19.5
West Virginia	24,181	102	1,860,421	1,744,237	−6.2
Wisconsin	56,154	1,449	3,951,777	4,417,933	11.8
Wyoming	97,914	503	330,066	332,416	0.7
TOTAL U.S.	3,615,210	66,237	179,323,175	203,184,772	13.3

*Does not include the Great Lakes and coastal waters. Percentages are based on unrounded numbers. ‡Provisional.
Source: U.S. Department of Commerc e, Bureau of the Census.

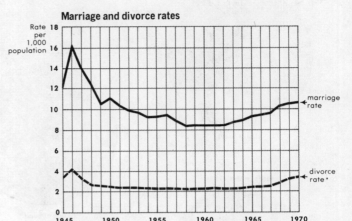

Marriage and divorce rates

All rates are based on population excluding Armed Forces abroad, except 1945-46 divorce rates which include Armed Forces abroad.
*Includes annulments.
Source: U.S. Department of Health, Education, and Welfare, Public Health Service, *Monthly Vital Statistics Report.*

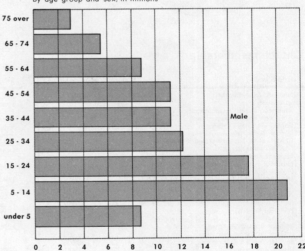

Population distribution, 1970

By age group and sex, in millions

Male

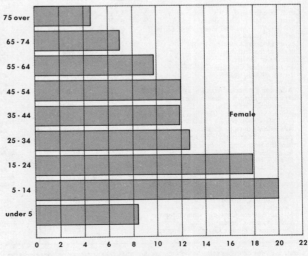

Female

Source: U.S. Department of Commerce, Bureau of the Census.

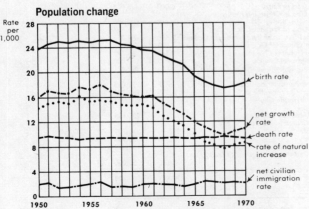

Population change

birth rate
net growth rate
death rate
rate of natural increase
net civilian immigration rate

Source: U.S. Department of Commerce, Bureau of the Census.

Characteristics of families
March 1970

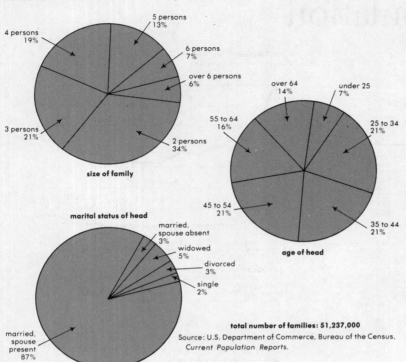

size of family

- 5 persons 13%
- 4 persons 19%
- 6 persons 7%
- over 6 persons 6%
- 3 persons 21%
- 2 persons 34%

age of head

- over 64 14%
- under 25 7%
- 55 to 64 16%
- 25 to 34 21%
- 45 to 54 21%
- 35 to 44 21%

marital status of head

- married, spouse absent 3%
- widowed 5%
- divorced 3%
- single 2%
- married, spouse present 87%

total number of families: 51,237,000

Source: U.S. Department of Commerce, Bureau of the Census, *Current Population Reports.*

Largest cities

City	Total area in sq. mi.	Population 1970 census	Mayor
Atlanta, Ga.	136.0	496,973	Sam Massell, Jr.
Baltimore, Md.	91.9	905,759	Thomas J. D'Alesandro III
Boston, Mass.	47.8	641,071	Kevin H. White
Buffalo, N.Y.	42.7	462,768	Frank A. Sedita
Chicago, Ill.	227.2	3,366,957	Richard J. Daley
Cincinnati, Ohio	78.5	452,524	Willis D. Gradison, Jr.
Cleveland, Ohio	76.0	750,903	Ralph J. Perk
Columbus, Ohio	144.8	539,677	M. E. Sensenbrenner
Dallas, Tex.	296.9	844,401	Wes Wise
Denver, Colo.	101.7	514,678	William H. McNichols, Jr.
Detroit, Mich.	140.0	1,511,482	Roman S. Gribbs
Houston, Tex.	446.9	1,232,802	Louie Welch
Indianapolis, Ind.	388.0	744,624	Richard G. Lugar
Kansas City, Mo.	316.0	507,087	Charles B. Wheeler
Los Angeles, Calif.	463.7	2,816,061	Sam W. Yorty
Memphis, Tenn.	217.4	623,530	Henry Loeb
Milwaukee, Wis.	95.8	717,099	Henry W. Maier
Minneapolis, Minn.	58.7	434,400	Charles Stenvig
Newark, N.J.	23.6	382,417	Kenneth A. Gibson
New Orleans, La.	363.5	593,471	Moon Landrieu
New York, N.Y.	320.0	7,867,760	John V. Lindsay
Philadelphia, Pa.	129.7	1,948,609	Frank L. Rizzo
Phoenix, Ariz.	254.9	581,562	John D. Driggs
Pittsburgh, Pa.	55.2	520,117	Peter F. Flaherty
St. Louis, Mo.	61.0	622,236	Alfonso J. Cervantes
San Antonio, Tex.	194.9	654,173	John Gatti
San Diego, Calif.	319.4	696,769	Frank E. Curran
San Francisco, Calif.	47.0	715,674	Joseph L. Alioto
Seattle, Wash.	91.6	530,831	Wesley C. Uhlman
Washington, D.C.	61.0	756,510	Walter E. Washington

Source: City planning departments.

Church membership

Religious body	Total clergy	Inclusive membership
Adventists, Seventh-day	3,341	420,419
Baptist Bodies		
American Baptist Association	3,312	790,000
American Baptist Convention	6,307	1,472,478
Baptist General Conference	919	103,955
Baptist Missionary Association of America	2,000	187,246
Conservative Baptist Association of America	...	300,000
Free Will Baptists	2,300	186,136
General Baptists (General Association of)	1,115	65,000
National Baptist Convention of America	28,574	2,668,799
National Baptist Convention, U.S.A., Inc.	27,500	5,500,000
National Baptist Evangelical Life and Soul Saving Assembly of U.S.A.	137	57,674
National Primitive Baptist Convention, Inc.	597	1,523,000
North American Baptist General Conference	441	54,997
Primitive Baptists	...	72,000
Progressive National Baptist Convention	863	521,692
Regular Baptist Churches, General Association of	...	210,000
Southern Baptist Convention	...	11,628,032
United Baptists	1,100	63,641
United Free Will Baptist Church	784	100,000
Brethren (German Baptists)		
Church of the Brethren	2,030	182,614
Buddhist Churches of America	101	100,000
Christian and Missionary Alliance	1,189	112,519
Christian Church (Disciples of Christ)	6,970	1,424,479
Christian Churches and Churches of Christ	5,987	1,020,751
Christian Congregation	265	50,801
Church of God (Anderson, Ind.)	2,793	150,198
Church of the Nazarene	6,585	383,284
Churches of Christ	6,200	2,400,000
Congregational Christian Churches, National Association of	458	85,000
Eastern Churches		
Albanian Orthodox Archdiocese in America	23	62,000
American Carpatho-Russian Orthodox Greek Catholic Church	65	106,900
Antiochian Orthodox Christian Archdiocese of New York and all North America	110	100,000
Armenian Apostolic Church of America	37	125,000
Armenian Church of North America, Diocese of the (including Diocese of California)	71	300,000
Bulgarian Eastern Orthodox Church	13	86,000
Greek Orthodox Archdiocese of North and South America	650	1,950,000
Orthodox Church in America	362	1,000,000
Romanian Orthodox Episcopate of America	50	50,000
Russian Orthodox Church in the U.S.A., Patriarchal Parishes of the	98	152,973
Russian Orthodox Church Outside Russia	168	55,000
Serbian Eastern Orthodox Church for the U.S.A. and Canada	64	65,000
Ukrainian Orthodox Church in America	131	87,475

Religious body	Total clergy	Inclusive membership
Episcopal Church	11,355	3,285,826
Evangelical Covenant Church of America	650	67,441
Evangelical Free Church of America	...	70,490
Friends United Meeting	548	67,785
Independent Fundamental Churches of America	1,197	111,611
Jehovah's Witnesses	None	388,920
Jewish Congregations	6,400	5,870,000
Latter Day Saints		
Church of Jesus Christ of Latter-day Saints	15,921	2,073,146
Reorganized Church of Jesus Christ of Latter Day Saints	13,720	152,670
Lutherans		
American Lutheran Church	6,103	2,543,293
Lutheran Church in America	7,328	3,106,844
Lutheran Church—Missouri Synod	6,866	2,788,536
Wisconsin Evangelical Lutheran Synod	938	381,321
Mennonite Church	2,335	88,522
Methodists		
African Methodist Episcopal Church	7,089	1,166,301
African Methodist Episcopal Zion Church	5,500	940,000
Christian Methodist Episcopal Church	2,259	466,718
Free Methodist Church of North America	1,750	64,901
United Methodist Church	34,561	10,671,774
Moravian Church in America	227	59,257
North American Old Roman Catholic Church	107	59,121
Pentecostal Assemblies		
Apostolic Overcoming Holy Church of God	350	75,000
Assemblies of God	11,912	1,064,631
Church of God	2,737	75,890
Church of God (Cleveland, Tenn.)	7,359	272,276
Church of God in Christ	6,000	425,000
Church of God in Christ, International (Evanston, Ill. Body)	1,465	500,000
Church of God of Prophecy	...	51,527
International Church of the Foursquare Gospel	2,690	89,215
Pentecostal Church of God of America	1,325	115,000
Pentecostal Holiness Church	2,546	66,778
United Pentecostal Church	2,445	250,000
Polish National Catholic Church of America	144	282,411
Presbyterians		
Cumberland Presbyterian Church	717	92,025
Presbyterian Church in the U.S.	4,595	958,195
United Presbyterian Church in the U.S.A.	13,151	3,087,213
Reformed Bodies		
Christian Reformed Church	964	285,628
Reformed Church in America	1,307	367,606
Roman Catholic Church	58,510	48,214,729
Salvation Army	5,190	326,934
Spiritualists, International General Assembly	...	164,072
Triumph the Church and Kingdom of God in Christ	1,370	55,090
Unitarian Universalist Association	868	265,408
United Church of Christ	10,121	1,960,608
Wesleyan Church	2,925	84,499

Table includes churches reporting a membership of 50,000 or more and represents the latest information available.
Source: National Council of Churches, *Yearbook of American Churches, 1972.*

(C.H.J.)

The Economy

Farms and farm income

State	Number of farms 1971*	Land in farms 1971* in 000 acres	Crops	Livestock and products	Government payments	Realized net income per farm 1970
			CASH INCOME, 1970, IN $000			
			Farm marketings			
Alabama	84,000	14,500	207,059	534,547	79,463	$ 3,510
Alaska	310	1,835†	1,168	3,108	84	1,484
Arizona	5,800	43,200	274,117	373,227	51,950	26,803
Arkansas	74,000	17,900	507,154	566,281	87,747	4,864
California	56,000	36,600	2,665,921	1,790,167	131,937	16,321
Colorado	30,000	39,000	259,828	921,689	68,035	5,745
Connecticut	4,600	600	63,967	102,871	773	10,184
Delaware	3,600	690	48,857	98,440	1,652	12,446
Florida	34,000	16,200	871,956	395,644	18,490	13,042
Georgia	76,000	17,000	433,992	710,612	83,621	5,451
Hawaii	4,300	2,340	170,365	41,097	11,115	18,604
Idaho	28,200	15,500	359,658	304,337	47,952	7,738
Illinois	124,000	29,300	1,400,799	1,298,782	166,644	6,169
Indiana	97,000	17,700	714,483	838,149	111,046	5,506
Iowa	139,000	34,400	1,073,289	2,856,412	235,815	8,481
Kansas	86,000	49,900	550,687	1,223,200	227,639	4,877
Kentucky	120,000	16,700	408,039	513,744	45,800	3,613
Louisiana	52,000	12,200	372,933	275,667	55,105	5,466
Maine	9,700	2,300	92,291	162,128	1,667	7,307
Maryland	18,000	3,200	125,726	267,853	7,986	6,877
Massachusetts	6,200	720	81,904	86,693	619	7,145
Michigan	85,000	13,000	412,834	482,568	65,698	2,858
Minnesota	122,000	32,000	642,761	1,373,087	151,773	5,104
Mississippi	93,000	17,400	398,643	513,168	146,500	4,650
Missouri	141,000	33,000	431,666	1,128,560	153,919	3,904
Montana	25,800	67,100	193,056	365,990	85,361	7,174
Nebraska	71,000	48,100	570,418	1,445,488	203,007	8,136
Nevada	2,000	9,000	14,571	65,975	2,080	9,330
New Hampshire	3,500	720	12,931	41,496	548	1,667
New Jersey	8,400	990	152,838	96,920	4,292	7,084
New Mexico	13,200	48,000	90,663	369,937	43,091	11,433
New York	57,000	11,500	302,248	815,015	22,009	5,925
North Carolina	156,000	16,000	918,823	625,072	59,682	4,628
North Dakota	41,000	42,000	417,374	263,914	167,239	5,056
Ohio	111,000	17,300	555,366	768,127	89,613	3,502
Oklahoma	90,000	37,100	234,366	824,051	117,951	3,337
Oregon	39,500	20,900	293,791	268,127	23,112	2,954
Pennsylvania	73,000	10,550	262,925	777,152	25,159	4,447
Rhode Island	900	90	10,194	10,659	72	3,917
South Carolina	51,000	8,200	261,700	180,337	54,434	3,571
South Dakota	45,500	45,500	200,464	811,484	91,698	7,800
Tennessee	125,000	15,400	268,760	438,083	70,985	2,202
Texas	185,000	145,000	1,191,116	1,945,745	543,156	6,579
Utah	14,500	13,400	42,956	182,469	11,144	3,724
Vermont	7,100	2,200	15,108	147,984	1,380	6,900
Virginia	71,000	11,400	261,801	334,692	20,011	2,795
Washington	45,000	18,000	501,493	291,086	57,888	5,431
West Virginia	28,000	5,000	26,608	84,486	3,588	748
Wisconsin	110,000	20,200	231,017	1,379,087	51,656	5,069
Wyoming	8,200	37,000	35,190	199,940	15,185	5,396
Total U.S.	2,876,310	1,117,835	19,635,874	29,595,347	3,717,371	5,374

*Preliminary. †Exclusive of grazing land leased from the U.S. Government, Alaska farmland totals about 70,000 acres.
Source: U.S. Department of Agriculture, Economics Research Service.

Livestock on farms

State	1960	1971	All cattle	Hogs, pigs	Sheep, lambs	Chickens	Turkeys	All cattle	Hogs, pigs	Sheep, lambs	Chickens	Turkeys
	AGGREGATE VALUE OF 5 SPECIES, IN $000		NUMBER, IN 000 HEAD, 1971					VALUE, IN $000, 1971				
Alabama	188,198	340,727	1,973	1,110	5.9	19,300	0.6	295,950	24,420	89	20,265	3
Alaska	...	3,213	9	1.1	27	26	...	2,340	75	743	55	...
Arizona	138,231	226,359†	1,289	79	506	1,373	77.6*	212,685	1,975	10,120	1,579	442*
Arkansas	158,292	318,807	1,787	392	8	24,018	113	285,920	8,232	128	24,018	509
California	733,873	1,142,409	4,771	165	1,264	54,865	1,227	1,025,765	5,033	37,920	65,838	7,853
Colorado	338,813	679,020	3,516	352	1,229	2,052	83	632,880	8,272	35,027	2,360	481
Connecticut	41,548	43,120	119	9.5	4.8	4,949	5	33,320	271	91	9,403	35
Delaware	11,199	10,442	32	46	2.1	895	4	8,000	1,081	39	1,298	24
Florida	184,463	335,432†	1,864	374	5.6	17,099	77.6*	307,560	8,976	87	18,809	442*
Georgia	180,505	407,018	2,002	2,065	5.5	40,091	188	310,310	51,625	99	44,100	884
Hawaii	...	50,487	249	58	...	1,370	...	44,820	3,132	...	2,535	...
Idaho	212,296	366,144†	1,735	171	773	1,139	77.6*	338,325	3,762	22,804	1,253	442*
Illinois	704,261	761,468	3,245	7,468	317	10,969	31	567,875	175,498	5,865	12,066	164
Indiana	397,221	497,060	1,937	5,129	251	18,504	40	348,660	120,532	4,518	23,130	220
Iowa	1,200,620	1,763,270	7,403	16,322	797	16,780	137	1,332,540	391,728	17,136	20,975	891
Kansas	586,828	1,182,068	6,618	2,202	328	4,635	38	1,125,060	46,242	6,396	4,172	198
Kentucky	305,185	526,737	2,859	1,734	88	4,151	5	486,030	34,680	1,848	4,151	28
Louisiana	201,423	294,361	1,705	259	23	4,850	3	281,325	6,346	368	6,305	17
Maine	39,353	47,229	141	10	15	8,459	...	33,135	305	255	13,534	...
Maryland	92,172	109,849	430	221	20	2,035	10	101,050	5,304	380	3,053	62
Massachusetts	44,421	39,425	114	89	8.1	2,831	19.3	31,350	2,537	162	5,237	139
Michigan	312,427	381,263	1,527	819	251	8,166	102	343,575	20,066	5,271	11,841	510
Minnesota	670,758	911,149†	3,998	3,692	504	13,584	1,057*	799,600	84,916	10,332	16,301	5,074*
Mississippi	226,717	438,801	2,537	632	16	15,329	2	405,920	14,220	256	18,395	10
Missouri	603,332	1,001,454	4,989	5,120	272	9,284	274	873,075	112,640	5,576	8,820	1,343
Montana	354,483	658,758†	3,104	221	1,142	1,400	77.6*	620,800	5,304	30,834	1,820	442*
Nebraska	732,337	1,263,450	6,457	3,691	370	6,296	101	1,162,260	86,739	7,955	5,981	515
Nevada	821,192	124,668	657	13	206	23	...	118,260	299	6,077	32	...
New Hampshire	21,937	21,133	71	12	5.3	1,801	4.1	17,750	360	111	2,882	30
New Jersey	75,553	48,888	125	121	8.5	4,451	10	37,500	3,570	191	7,567	60
New Mexico	181,582	254,206†	1,372	60	799	1,340	77.6*	233,240	1,380	17,978	1,608	442*
New York	486,348	554,873	1,848	101	98	13,417	33	526,680	3,030	2,156	22,809	198
North Carolina	147,463	243,827	1,081	2,031	16	22,680	743	167,555	48,744	296	23,814	3,418
North Dakota	272,321	446,336	2,190	425	368	1,288	25	427,050	9,988	7,728	1,417	153
Ohio	416,831	513,077	2,200	2,838	693	13,320	191	418,000	63,855	14,207	15,984	1,031
Oklahoma	415,872	856,759	5,085	506	122	3,490	55	839,025	11,385	2,562	3,490	297
Oregon	207,397	319,064	1,609	122	479	3,277	220	297,665	3,050	12,933	4,096	1,320
Pennsylvania	436,839	527,971	1,763	674	160	19,119	166	476,010	17,861	3,520	29,634	946
Rhode Island	6,453	4,732	12	10	1.8	460	0.8	3,540	255	34	897	6
South Carolina	72,952	124,898	661	633	1.5	7,989	239	99,150	14,559	32	9,986	1,171
South Dakota	517,669	935,622	4,498	2,009	1,121	5,694	14	854,620	47,212	27,465	6,263	62
Tennessee	252,512	433,432	2,354	1,111	35	7,377	10	400,180	24,442	648	8,115	47
Texas	1,249,699	2,138,620	12,578	1,419	3,789	17,267	1,747	2,012,480	31,928	66,308	18,994	8,910
Utah	125,650	200,606	840	59	1,058	1,760	120	163,800	1,328	32,798	1,936	744
Vermont	81,388	96,533	351	6	6.2	764	0.5	94,770	177	130	1,452	4
Virginia	213,161	293,174	1,489	817	176	6,418	252	260,575	19,608	3,784	8,023	1,184
Washington	183,221	278,918	1,285	96	144	6,344	46	263,425	2,688	3,960	8,564	281
West Virginia	77,171	87,095	470	76	155	1,653	68	79,900	1,862	3,023	1,984	326
Wisconsin	812,721	1,120,160†	4,158	1,932	151	8,204	1,057*	1,060,290	46,368	3,247	10,255	5,074*
Wyoming	209,784	335,387†	1,461	38	1,734	197	77.6*	284,895	817	49,419	256	442*
TOTAL U.S.	15,944,672	23,765,015	114,568	67,540	19,560	442,783	7,462	21,146,490	1,578,677	462,906	537,352	39,590

Data are for Jan. 1 of years reported except for hog and pig values which are for Dec. 1 of previous year. *Data combined for Minnesota and Wisconsin, Arizona, Florida, Idaho, Montana, New Mexico, and Wyoming to avoid disclosing individual operations.
†Excludes turkeys. Source: U.S. Department of Agriculture, Statistical Reporting Service, Livestock and Poultry Inventory.

Principal crops
of the United States, 1970

State	Corn, grain (bu.)		Hay (tons)		Soybeans for beans (bu.)		Wheat (bu.)		Tobacco (lbs.)		Cotton lint (bales)		Sorghum grain (bu.)		Potatoes (cwt.)	
	Amount produced in 000	Value in $000	Amount produced in 000	Value in $000	Amount produced in 000	Value in $000	Amount produced in 000	Value in $000	Amount produced in 000	Value in $000	Amount produced in 000	Value in $000	Amount produced in 000	Value in $000	Amount produced in 000	Value in $000
TOTAL U.S.	4,109,792	5,478,958	127,899	3,072,213	1,135,769	2,203,958	1,378,464	1,870,428	1,905,751	1,376,157	10,270	1,155,347	697,050	784,989	324,861	711,651
Ala.	12,535	19,805	791	22,544	14,312	40,074	...	...	...	...	510	57,375	...	...	...	...
Alaska	...	...	10,500	788	...	...	...	...	...	...	...	...	...	...	105	643
Ariz.	...	...	1,318	40,858	...	...	...	...	...	...	489	59,025	12,670	17,485	...	...
Ark.	...	...	1,348	31,004	97,043	276,573	10,725	13,192	...	...	1,075	120,938	...	...	...	...
Calif.	...	...	7,744	229,333	...	...	68,944	83,407	...	...	1,165	145,726	...	...	29,760	29,893
Colo.	31,872	41,115	3,364	82,418	...	...	...	...	...	...	...	...	...	...	13,590	24,183
Conn.	...	...	203	8,120	...	...	...	...	7,884	23,697	...	...	...	...	1,127	3,043
Del.	13,690	19,987	76	2,698	3,402	9,866	...	...	...	...	...	...	...	...	1,512	3,599
Fla.	8,050	12,880	...	...	...	...	...	...	28,923	30,712	...	...	...	...	...	...
Ga.	44,206	71,172	...	...	11,880	34,452	...	...	133,305	102,390	290	31,175	...	...	...	...
Hawaii	...	...	...	...	...	...	...	...	...	...	...	...	...	...	...	...
Ida.	...	...	3,957	85,076	...	...	42,734	59,069	...	...	...	...	...	...	73,195	144,350
Ill.	744,884	1,020,491	3,378	82,761	212,815	606,523	35,748	46,472	...	...	...	...	...	...	...	...
Ind.	371,998	502,197	2,204	56,202	104,297	292,032	29,799	39,037	...	...	...	...	...	...	...	...
Iowa	859,140	1,099,699	6,910	138,200	186,624	522,547	...	...	...	...	...	...	2,368	2,463	...	...
Kan.	79,670	103,571	4,102	96,397	15,075	40,703	299,013	382,737	...	...	...	...	145,960	159,096	...	...
Ky.	49,400	75,088	3,059	87,182	15,066	42,185	6,120	8,078	411,201	288,829	...	...	...	...	...	...
La.	...	...	...	...	37,890	108,243	...	...	...	...	530	59,625	...	...	...	...
Me.	...	...	408	13,872	...	...	...	...	...	...	...	...	...	...	35,700	64,260
Md.	40,172	59,053	735	23,520	5,112	14,825	4,181	5,477	27,040	20,307	...	...	...	...	...	...
Mass.	...	...	239	9,082	...	...	...	...	3,230	10,192	...	...	...	...	1,046	2,929
Mich.	114,076	148,299	3,260	71,720	13,624	38,147	22,035	31,069	...	...	...	...	...	...	...	...
Minn.	390,490	472,493	8,155	159,023	82,919	228,027	22,882	37,731	...	...	...	...	...	...	...	...
Miss.	6,944	10,833	1,061	27,056	56,064	162,586	...	...	...	...	1,635	179,850	...	...	...	...
Mo.	173,057	242,280	5,535	127,305	90,896	254,509	31,222	39,652	...	...	225	25,875	...	...	...	...
Mont.	...	...	4,112	92,520	...	...	85,167	115,928	...	...	...	...	...	...	1,388	4,442
Neb.	367,275	466,439	6,237	130,977	17,864	49,126	97,204	119,561	...	...	...	...	76,449	81,036	...	...
Nev.	...	...	834	22,101	...	...	810	1,116	...	...	...	...	...	...	184	515
N.H.	...	...	204	7,548	...	...	...	...	...	...	...	...	...	...	3,207	8,499
N.J.	5,070	7,656	331	12,909	...	...	...	...	...	...	...	...	...	...	...	...
N.M.	...	...	1,044	30,798	...	...	5,520	7,452	...	...	135	17,184	17,499	20,124	...	...
N.Y.	22,041	32,180	5,798	159,445	...	...	...	...	...	...	...	...	...	...	16,861	42,416
N.C.	67,250	102,893	602	20,769	21,024	60,970	...	...	814,603	583,932	...	...	...	...	...	...
N.D.	...	...	4,414	68,417	...	...	152,826	235,446	...	...	...	...	...	...	...	...
Ohio	232,078	313,305	2,913	72,825	69,483	198,027	35,927	51,016	...	...	...	...	...	...	...	...
Okla.	...	...	2,806	74,359	...	...	98,202	128,645	...	...	185	18,963	23,306	26,336	...	...
Ore.	...	...	2,369	60,410	...	...	30,216	44,706	...	...	...	...	...	...	16,056	29,893
Penn.	80,155	118,629	4,396	131,880	...	...	9,834	13,768	...	...	...	...	...	...	8,280	21,528
R.I.	...	...	25	1,075	...	...	...	...	...	...	...	...	...	...	1,323	3,572
S.C.	10,854	17,041	378	11,529	20,439	59,273	...	...	141,075	101,292	215	24,188	...	...	...	...
S.D.	102,336	123,827	5,795	104,310	...	...	2,835	59,154	...	...	...	...	...	...	...	...
Tenn.	22,760	34,823	2,036	60,062	28,267	77,734	...	...	117,864	80,355	390	43,875	...	...	...	...
Tex.	...	...	4,037	106,981	...	...	54,408	70,730	...	...	3,247	351,440	329,616	369,170	...	...
Utah	...	...	1,592	39,004	...	...	5,976	8,281	...	...	...	...	...	...	1,088	2,829
Vt.	...	...	904	30,736	...	...	...	...	...	...	...	...	...	...	240	696
Va.	31,144	46,093	1,778	61,341	6,441	18,679	...	...	126,015	87,437	...	...	...	...	...	...
Wash.	...	...	2,335	59,543	...	...	100,731	149,081	...	...	...	...	...	...	33,590	53,474
W. Va.	3,120	4,555	873	27,500	...	...	462	651	3,145	2,217	...	...	...	...	...	...
Wis.	143,520	193,752	10,601	196,119	3,213	8,836	...	...	...	...	...	...	...	...	12,768	31,703
Wyo.	...	...	1,853	44,472	...	...	6,259	7,409	...	...	...	...	...	...	...	...

Data cover production of leading states only.
Source: U.S. Department of Agriculture, Statistical Reporting Service, Crop Reporting Board, *Crop Production and Crop Values*, December 1970.

Commercial fishing
principal species caught

Species	QUANTITY in 000 lb.		
	1960	1965	1970
TOTAL	4,942,229	4,776,766	4,883,600
Menhaden	2,018,263	1,726,089	1,813,800
Salmon	235,447	326,871	396,700
Tuna	298,203	318,895	393,000
Shrimps	249,452	243,645	368,100
Crabs	221,681	335,407	268,500
Flounder	127,048	180,121	122,000
Herring, sea	239,018	110,293	87,500
Whitings	111,602	82,574	45,000
Ocean perch	150,275	111,960	55,300
Haddock	118,697	133,892	26,900
Clams	49,572	70,849	89,200
Cod	45,753	46,201	52,900
Jack mackerel	75,137	66,856	47,200
Oysters	60,010	54,688	50,600
Lobsters, Northern	31,168	30,246	32,700
Mullet	40,839	41,392	31,200
Halibut	51,202	40,825	34,700
Scup	49,229	35,870	10,600

Source: U.S. Department of Commerce, National Marine Fisheries Service, *Fisheries of the United States, 1970.*

Lumber production
in millions of board feet

Kind of wood	1965	1967	1969*	Kind of wood	1965	1967	1969*
Hardwoods	7,306	7,430	7,316	Softwoods	29,295	27,311	28,281
Ash	141	149	145	Cedar	633	586	567
Basswood	87	77	73	Douglas fir	8,783	7,822	8,027
Beech	182	163	176	Hemlock	2,576	2,257	1,918
Birch	109	99	88	Ponderosa pine	3,776	3,583	3,719
Cottonwood and aspen	198	202	202	Redwood	1,087	939	1,077
Elm	206	200	189	Southern yellow pine	6,628	6,511	7,243
Maple	786	715	691	Spruce	641	686	807
Oak	3,356	3,424	3,415	Sugar pine	464	495	487
Sweet (red and sap) gum	387	385	384	White fir	2,422	2,116	2,093
Tupelo and black gum	385	344	327	White pine	1,151	1,085	1,060
Yellow poplar	681	666	668	Other softwoods	1,134	1,231	1,283
Other hardwoods†	788	1,006	958	TOTAL	36,601	34,741	35,597

*Preliminary. †Includes estimate for western hardwoods not specified. Source: U.S. Department of Commerce, Bureau of the Census, *Current Industrial Reports;* and U.S. Department of Agriculture, Forest Service.

Principal minerals produced

in the United States and each state

Mineral (unit of production)	1960 Quantity	1960 Value in $000	1970 Quantity	1970 Value in $000
UNITED STATES		18,032,000		29,088,717
Mineral fuels		12,142,000		19,405,928
Petroleum, crude (000 42-gal. bbl.)	2,574,933	7,420,181	3,371,751	10,426,680
Natural gas (000,000 cu.ft.)	12,771,038	1,789,970	21,920,642	3,745,680
Coal (000 short tons)				
Bituminous and lignite*	415,512	1,950,425	602,932	3,772,622
Pennsylvania anthracite	18,817	147,116	9,729	105,341
Natural-gas liquids (000 gal.)				
Natural gasoline and cycle products	5,842,507	416,819	8,664,810	603,024
Liquefied petroleum gases	8,444,074	391,566	16,783,662	672,088
Nonmetallic minerals, except fuels		3,868,000		5,768,480
Stone† (000 short tons)	616,784	952,555	874,512	1,474,917
Cement				
Portland (000 376-lb. bbl.)	321,646	1,089,134	390,461	1,298,232
Masonry (000 280-lb. bbl.)			21,275	67,537
Natural and slag (000 376-lb. bbl.)			§	§
Sand and gravel (000 short tons)	709,792	720,432	943,941	1,115,705
Salt (000 short tons)	25,479	161,140	45,804	303,523
Lime (000 short tons)	12,935	172,731	19,749	286,155
Clays (000 short tons)	49,069	162,411	54,853	267,912
Phosphate rock (000 short tons)	19,620	117,041	38,739	203,218
Sulfur, Frasch-process mines (000 long tons)	5,003	115,494	6,419	151,779
Boron minerals (000 short tons)	641	47,550	1,041	86,827
Potassium salts, K_2O equivalent (000 short tons)	2,638	89,676	2,729	98,123
Metals		2,022,000		3,914,309
Copper, recoverable (000 short tons)	1,080	693,468	1,720	1,984,484
Iron ore, usable (000 long tons)	82,963	724,131	87,176	941,739
Molybdenum, content of concentrate (000 lb.)	69,941	87,406	110,381	190,077
Lead, recoverable (000 short tons)	247	57,722	572	178,609
Zinc, recoverable (000 short tons)	435	112,365	534	163,650
Uranium (recoverable U_3O_8) (000 lb.)	7,970‡	152,188‡	24,682	149,464
Silver, recoverable (000 troy oz.)	30,766	27,846	45,005	79,696
Gold (troy oz.)	1,666,772	58,336	1,743,322	63,439
Alabama [21]		221,802		323,199
Coal, bituminous (000 short tons)	13,011	92,439	20,560	166,262
Cement†				
Portland (000 376-lb. bbl.)	12,931	42,706	16,053	58,715
Masonry (000 280-lb. bbl.)			2,402	
Stone (000 short tons)	13,503	19,970	19,903	38,965
Petroleum, crude (000 42-gal. bbl.)	7,329	§	7,263	20,627
Lime (000 short tons)	536	6,593	749	10,286
Clays† (000 short tons)	1,840	2,170	2,748	8,213
Sand and gravel (000 short tons)	4,359	4,759	6,725	8,144
Iron ore, usable (000 long tons)	4,068	23,511	§	§
Alaska [20]		21,860		338,271
Petroleum, crude (000 42-gal. bbl.)	559	1,230	83,616	251,684
Sand and gravel (000 short tons)	6,013	5,483	25,825	41,092
Natural gas (000,000 cu.ft.)	246	30	111,576	27,448
Arizona [5]		417,225		1,166,767
Copper, recoverable (000 short tons)	346	345,784	918	1,059 277
Molybdenum (000 lb.)	4,359	5,211	15,672	26,700
Sand and gravel (000 short tons)	14,490	14,235	17,822	19,804
Silver, recoverable (000 troy oz.)	4,775	4,322	7,330	12,981
Stone (000 short tons)	4,249	5,107	3,511	7,094
Petroleum, crude (000 42-gal. bbl.)	73	§	1,784	5,281
Arkansas [27]		159,519		225,622
Petroleum, crude (000 42-gal. bbl.)	30,117	83,424	18,035	51,760
Natural gas (000,000 cu.ft.)	55,451	6,599	181,351	29,560
Bauxite (000 long tons)	1,932	20,469	1,869	26,293
Stone (000 short tons)	10,939	13,555	15,284	22,786
Sand and gravel (000 short tons)	8,192	10,262	13,301	16,036
California [3]		1,422,087		1,897,084
Petroleum, crude (000 42-gal. bbl.)	305,352	751,166	372,191	945,365
Natural gas (000,000 cu.ft.)	517,535	138,182	649,117	208,367
Sand and gravel (000 short tons)	87,679	107,503	140,259	174,221
Cement (000 376-lb. bbl.)	39,712†	128,826†	49,499	173,126
Boron minerals (000 short tons)	641	47,550	1,041	86,827
Stone (000 short tons)	33,075	49,842	46,399	66,950
Natural-gas liquids‖ (000 gal.)	1,203,035	83,978	799,848	54,484
Salt, common (000 short tons)	1,443	§	1,656	14,407
Lime (000 short tons)	345	5,628	572	9,911
Mercury (76-lb. flasks)	18,764	3,955	18,593	7,582
Colorado [18]		345,418		390,988
Molybdenum (000 lb.)	51,615	65,448	§	§
Petroleum, crude (000 42-gal. bbl.)	47,469	137,660	24,723	78,619
Coal, bituminous (000 short tons)	3,607	21,090	6,025	35,243
Sand and gravel (000 short tons)	19,053	16,882	22,261	24,190
Zinc, recoverable (000 short tons)	31	8,070	57	17,370
Uranium (recoverable U_3O_8) (000 lb.)	1,150‡	23,462‡	2,727	15,832
Natural gas (000,000 cu.ft.)	107,404	12,781	105,804	15,553
Connecticut [45]		15,353		28,383
Stone (000 short tons)	5,057	8,313	8,338	16,915
Sand and gravel (000 short tons)	6,575	5,960	6,765	9,202
Delaware [50]		989		1,615
Sand and gravel (000 short tons)	1,084	907	1,565	1,603
Florida [23]		180,286		300,042
Phosphate rock (000 long tons)	12,321	82,530	§	§
Stone† (000 short tons)	27,629	37,419	43,089	61,302
Clays (000 short tons)	252†	6,357†	872	12,661
Sand and gravel (000 short tons)	6,757	5,559	12,482	12,254
Titanium concentrate (000 short tons)	286	7,489	§	§
Georgia [29]		92,305		203,225
Clays (000 short tons)	3,519	40,160	5,684	110,149
Stone (000 short tons)	14,297	37,033	26,635	59,200
Sand and gravel (000 short tons)	3,338	3,047	3,667	4,437

Mineral (unit of production)	1960 Quantity	1960 Value in $000	1970 Quantity	1970 Value in $000
Hawaii [44]		9,367		28,965
Stone (000 short tons)	3,535	6,443	6,332	15,538
Cement (000 376-lb. bbl.)	113	571	2,162	10,334
Idaho [32]		57,606		119,748
Silver, recoverable (000 troy oz.)	13,647	12,351	19,115	33,849
Lead, recoverable (000 short tons)	43	10,040	61	19,121
Zinc, recoverable (000 short tons)	37	9,495	41	12,578
Phosphate rock (000 long tons)	2,177	11,044	§	§
Sand and gravel (000 short tons)	7,088	6,594	12,953	10,022
Illinois [11]		589,874		688,697
Coal, bituminous (000 short tons)	45,977	184,087	65,119	320,705
Petroleum, crude (000 42-gal. bbl.)	77,341	228,929	43,747	141,994
Stone (000 short tons)	41,721	55,593	55,776	86,502
Sand and gravel (000 short tons)	33,138	36,255	43,926	60,155
Cement				
Portland (000 376-lb. bbl.)	9,139	30,732	7,946	27,126
Masonry (000 280-lb. bbl.)			508	
Natural-gas liquids (000 gal.)	374,862	21,254		
Fluorspar (000 short tons)	134	6,936	148	8,637
Indiana [25]		210,932		255,786
Coal, bituminous (000 short tons)	15,538	61,570	22,263	102,371
Stone (000 short tons)	18,956	34,920	25,818	45,215
Cement, portland (000 376-lb. bbl.)	14,052†	48,310†	§	§
Sand and gravel (000 short tons)	20,752	18,377	23,476	25,796
Petroleum, crude (000 42-gal. bbl.)	12,054	35,439	7,487	23,958
Iowa [31]		99,319		120,822
Cement				
Portland (000 376-lb. bbl.)	12,517	44,204	12,744	47,190
Masonry (000 280-lb. bbl.)			520	
Stone (000 short tons)	23,185	30,321	25,305	41,119
Sand and gravel (000 short tons)	14,692	13,516	21,058	20,642
Gypsum (000 short tons)	1,283	5,428	1,136	4,223
Kansas [16]		486,534		586,161
Petroleum, crude (000 42-gal. bbl.)	113,453	329,014	84,853	277,469
Natural gas (000,000 cu.ft.)	634,410	74,226	899,955	125,994
Natural-gas liquids‖ (000 gal.)	243,138	13,037	1,149,246	45,214
Helium‖ (000,000 cu.ft.)	21,696	350	2,963	40,914
Cement				
Portland (000 376-lb. bbl.)	8,162	26,373	9,197	29,206
Masonry (000 280-lb. bbl.)			328	
Stone (000 short tons)	11,814†	15,031†	15,161	22,406
Salt (000 short tons)	1,213	14,109	§	§
Kentucky [9]		414,553		847,465
Coal, bituminous (000 short tons)	66,846	282,395	125,305	711,163
Stone (000 short tons)	15,810	21,493	29,310	45,358
Petroleum, crude (000 42-gal. bbl.)	21,147	60,268	11,575	36,461
Sand and gravel (000 short tons)	5,113	5,763	8,760	10,474
Natural gas (000,000 cu.ft.)	75,329	18,380	77,892	19,161
Louisiana [2]		1,990,895		5,182,617
Petroleum, crude (000 42-gal. bbl.)	400,832	1,258,138	906,907	3,061,558
Natural gas (000,000 cu.ft.)	2,988,414	511,019	7,788,276	1,583,137
Natural-gas liquids				
Natural gasoline (000 gal.)	875,567	66,214	2,374,092	174,637
Petroleum gases, liquefied (000 gal.)	606,023	28,147	3,376,170	138,267
Sulfur, Frasch-process mines (000 long tons)	2,256	52,639	3,618	89,489
Salt (000 short tons)	4,792	21,959	13,584	64,854
Sand and gravel (000 short tons)	14,319	19,106	18,155	22,363
Maine [47]		14,108		23,780
Sand and gravel (000 short tons)	9,833	3,892	12,971	6,888
Stone (000 short tons)	1,012	3,851	1,041	3,682
Copper (000 short tons)	—	—	3	3,120
Maryland [37]		57,697		88,216
Stone (000 short tons)	7,944	16,962	16,051	32,783
Sand and gravel (000 short tons)	10,076	13,221	12,951	20,434
Coal, bituminous (000 short tons)	748	2,799	1,615	1,433
Massachusetts [43]		28,245		50,360
Stone (000 short tons)	5,247	12,782	8,136	24,349
Sand and gravel (000 short tons)	14,789	13,013	17,925	22,244
Michigan [12]		437,598		670,729
Iron ore, usable (000 long tons)	10,792	95,791	13,100	168,958
Cement				
Portland (000 376-lb. bbl.)	22,361	77,694	29,813	106,272
Masonry (000 280-lb. bbl.)			1,519	
Copper, recoverable (000 short tons)	56	36,199	68	77,945
Sand and gravel (000 short tons)	46,910	39,304	53,092	54,646
Salt (000 short tons)	4,088	33,759	4,899	49,963
Stone (000 short tons)	31,256	32,274	41,687	49,501
Magnesium compounds, MgO equivalent (000 short tons)	§	§	412	38,050
Petroleum, crude (000 42-gal. bbl.)	15,899	46,266	11,693	36,246
Lime (000 short tons)	1,177	15,730	1,538	21,355
Minnesota [13]		515,521		640,127
Iron ore, usable (000 long tons)	54,723	470,874	54,791	571,488
Sand and gravel (000 short tons)	30,302	24,611	46,851	38,802
Stone (000 short tons)	4,234	10,034	4,618	19,432
Manganiferous ore (000 short tons)	441	§	321	§
Mississippi [26]		199,210		249,973
Petroleum, crude (000 42-gal. bbl.)	51,673	146,235	65,119	194,706
Natural gas (000,000 cu.ft.)	172,478	32,426	126,031	23,190
Sand and gravel (000 short tons)	6,181	5,568	10,859	11,950
Missouri [17]		162,244		392,997
Lead, recoverable (000 short tons)	112	26,196	422	131,751
Cement				
Portland (000 376-lb. bbl.)	12,183	42,330	§	§
Masonry (000 280-lb. bbl.)				
Stone (000 short tons)	27,180	37,878	39,726	57,285
Iron ore, usable (000 long tons)	365	3,760	2,612	38,100

Principal minerals produced (continued)

Mineral (unit of production)	1960 Quantity	1960 Value in $000	1970 Quantity	1970 Value in $000
Missouri (continued)				
Coal, bituminous (000 short tons)	2,890	12,450	4,447	19,526
Zinc, recoverable (000 short tons)	3	728	51	15,540
Sand and gravel (000 short tons)	10,207	11,601	12,446	15,379
Montana [22]		179,406		313,015
Copper, recoverable (000 short tons)	92	59,046	120	138,955
Petroleum, crude (000 42-gal. bbl.)	30,240	72,878	37,879	105,403
Sand and gravel (000 short tons)	12,589	11,657	19,275	20,249
Silver, recoverable (000 troy ozs.)	3,607	3,265	4,304	7,622
Stone (000 short tons)	1,183	1,576	6,501	6,896
Nebraska [39]		103,942		72,657
Petroleum, crude (000 42-gal. bbl.)	23,825	68,378	11,451	35,384
Sand and gravel (000 short tons)	10,876	8,746	12,232	12,974
Stone (000 short tons)	3,336	5,651	4,265	7,378
Natural gas (000,000 cu. ft.)	15,258	2,670	5,991	1,024
Nevada [30]		80,892		186,349
Copper, recoverable (000 short tons)	77	49,754	107	123,118
Gold (troy oz.)	58,187	2,037	408,144	17,472
Sand and gravel (000 short tons)	4,085	5,224	8,574	9,819
Mercury (76-lb. flasks)	7,821	1,648	4,916	2,005
Gypsum (000 short tons)	802	2,721	451	1,457
New Hampshire [48]		5,439		8,730
Sand and gravel (000 short tons)	6,621	3,687	6,529	4,753
Stone (000 short tons)	104	594	397	3,924
New Jersey [36]		56,469		89,281
Stone (000 short tons)	10,202	22,814	15,164	40,677
Sand and gravel (000 short tons)	11,594	19,511	16,732	31,571
Zinc, recoverable (000 short tons)	—	—	29	8,788
Clays (000 short tons)	664	1,597	262	990
New Mexico [8]		653,766		1,060,358
Petroleum, crude (000 42-gal. bbl.)	107,380	305,895	128,184	410,320
Copper, recoverable (000 short tons)	67	43,199	166	191,885
Natural gas (000,000 cu. ft.)	798,928	85,485	1,138,980	162,874
Potash, K₂O equivalent (000 short tons)	2,440	82,645	2,390	85,877
Uranium (U₃O₈) (000 lb.)	3,793‡	61,827‡	11,574	69,970
Natural-gas liquids‖ (000 gal.)	966,783	49,200	1,531,015	62,772
Coal, bituminous (000 short tons)	295	1,747	7,361	21,249
New York [24]		260,922		299,564
Stone (000 short tons)	29,802	46,955	37,616	68,118
Salt (000 short tons)	4,008	30,763	5,990	47,254
Sand and gravel (000 short tons)	30,687	35,152	35,537	38,839
Zinc, recoverable (000 short tons)	66	17,122	59	17,947
North Carolina [33]		45,096		98,365
Stone (000 short tons)	14,721	23,296	30,363	54,121
Sand and gravel (000 short tons)	8,801	7,453	12,772	13,277
Feldspar (000 long tons)	271	2,781	345	5,173
Clays† (000 short tons)	2,476	1,548	3,318	3,102
Mica, scrap (000 short tons)	47	1,100	64	1,457
North Dakota [34]		78,378		96,047
Petroleum, crude (000 42-gal. bbl.)	21,992	59,598	21,998	67,107
Coal, lignite (000 short tons)	2,525	5,790	5,639	11,009
Sand and gravel (000 short tons)	8,648	6,904	8,090	6,336
Natural gas (000,000 cu. ft.)	19,483	2,221	34,889	5,722
Natural-gas liquids (000 gal.)	§	§	98,448	4,320
Ohio [14]		406,142		612,166
Coal, bituminous (000 short tons)	33,957	130,877	55,351	262,390
Stone (000 short tons)	35,856	59,479	47,244	81,506
Lime (000 short tons)	3,117	44,403	3,951	61,197
Sand and gravel (000 short tons)	37,943	44,979	42,069	57,506
Salt (000 short tons)	3,108	24,149	5,329	47,498
Cement				
Portland (000 376-lb. bbl.) }	17,480	61,478	11,752 }	43,113
Masonry (000 280-lb. bbl.) }			3,116 }	
Petroleum, crude (000 42-gal. bbl.)	5,405	16,053	9,864	32,914
Natural gas (000,000 cu.ft.)	36,074	8,477	52,113	14,123
Clays (000 short tons)	5,165	14,325	3,920	10,100
Oklahoma [6]		782,579		1,137,267
Petroleum, crude (000 42-gal. bbl.)	192,913	563,306	223,574	712,419
Natural gas (000,000 cu.ft.)	824,266	98,088	1,594,943	248,811
Natural-gas liquids				
Natural gasoline (000 gal.)	531,995	33,074	622,146	39,933
Petroleum gases, liquefied (000 gal.)	762,258	32,409	1,177,218	52,975
Stone (000 short tons)	14,054†	16,098†	18,177	23,701
Coal, bituminous (000 short tons)	1,342	9,113	2,427	15,211
Oregon [40]		55,772		68,101
Sand and gravel (000 short tons)	17,673	16,170	17,532	25,978
Stone (000 short tons)	16,913	19,721	13,439	20,948
Nickel, content of ore (000 short tons)	13	5,246	16	§
Lime (000 short tons)	§	§	96	1,777
Pennsylvania [7]		838,146		1,096,053
Coal				
Bituminous (000 short tons)	65,425	345,971	80,491	585,057
Anthracite (000 short tons)	18,817	147,116	9,729	105,341
Cement				
Portland (000 376-lb. bbl.) }	38,320	131,763	40,909 }	129,424
Masonry (000 280-lb. bbl.) }			2,804 }	

Mineral (unit of production)	1960 Quantity	1960 Value in $000	1970 Quantity	1970 Value in $000
Pennsylvania (continued)				
Stone (000 short tons)	42,136	74,168	66,241	120,187
Sand and gravel (000 short tons)	13,011	21,204	18,504	33,915
Lime (000 short tons)	1,120	16,277	1,887	29,279
Natural gas (000,000 cu.ft.)	113,928	36,229	76,841	21,439
Petroleum, crude (000 42-gal. bbl.)	6,009	27,341	4,093	18,500
Rhode Island [49]		5,727		
Sand and gravel (000 short tons)	1,535	1,355 }	§	4,386
Stone (000 short tons)	1,810	4,372 }		
South Carolina [42]		30,987		56,384
Stone (000 short tons)	7,327	10,593	9,710	15,154
Clays (000 short tons)	1,297	6,201	1,974	9,878
Sand and gravel (000 short tons)	3,029	3,048	5,864	7,766
South Dakota [41]		47,675		61,576
Gold (troy oz.)	554,771	19,417	578,716	21,059
Sand and gravel (000 short tons)	13,548	9,359	16,556	16,656
Stone (000 short tons)	3,149	7,909	1,979	13,375
Tennessee [28]		145,538		220,465
Stone (000 short tons)	20,074	29,942	35,374	50,013
Coal, bituminous (000 short tons)	5,930	21,154	8,737	40,372
Zinc, recoverable (000 short tons)	91	23,579	118	36,233
Cement				
Portland (000 376-lb. bbl.) }	8,246	27,384	8,878 }	32,581
Masonry (000 280-lb. bbl.) }			969 }	
Copper, recoverable (000 short tons)	13	8,168	16	17,928
Phosphate rock (000 short tons)	2,172	15,424		
Sand and gravel (000 short tons)	6,293	7,655	6,715	10,639
Texas [1]		4,126,419		6,402,462
Petroleum, crude (000 42-gal. bbl.)	927,479	2,748,735	1,249,697	4,104,005
Natural gas (000,000 cu.ft.)	5,892,704	665,876	8,357,716	1,203,511
Natural-gas liquids				
Natural gasoline (000 gal.)	2,880,906	207,583	4,095,462	284,871
Petroleum gases, liquefied (000 gal.)	4,476,142	200,478	8,575,434	334,850
Cement				
Portland (000 376-lb. bbl.) }	23,365	76,577	33,967 }	126,729
Masonry (000 280-lb. bbl.) }			3,769 }	
Stone (000 short tons)	39,029	45,088	45,552	64,422
Sulfur, Frasch-process mines (000 long tons)	2,747	62,855	2,801	62,290
Sand and gravel (000 short tons)	29,844	30,754	31,438	46,362
Salt (000 short tons)	4,756	18,222	10,184	45,000
Lime (000 short tons)	821	9,087	1,673	24,427
Helium‖ (000 cu.ft.)	120,921	2,044	1,257	16,124
Utah [15]		432,712		606,093
Copper, recoverable (000 short tons)	218	139,987	296	341,282
Petroleum, crude (000 42-gal. bbl.)	37,594	103,008	23,370	65,603
Coal, bituminous (000 short tons)	4,955	31,458	4,733	34,472
Gold (troy oz.)	368,255	12,889	408,029	14,848
Lead, recoverable (000 short tons)	39	9,219	45	14,175
Iron ore, usable (000 long tons)	3,334	23,862	1,990	13,837
Silver, recoverable (000 troy ounces)	4,783	4,329	6,030	10,678
Sand and gravel (000 short tons)	6,848	6,182	12,010	10,439
Vermont [46]		22,903		27,843
Stone (000 short tons)	2,114	17,444	1,514	19,088
Sand and gravel (000 short tons)	1,809	1,218	4,046	4,122
Virginia [19]		208,880		374,321
Coal, bituminous (000 short tons)	27,838	122,723	35,016	246,181
Stone (000 short tons)	19,358	33,019	35,415	60,477
Sand and gravel (000 short tons)	7,666	11,432	11,126	15,229
Lime (000 short tons)	711	8,028	1,046	14,090
Zinc, recoverable (000 short tons)	20	5,142	18	5,534
Washington [35]		72,404		90,922
Sand and gravel (000 short tons)	25,594	19,459	25,089	27,902
Cement				
Portland (000 376-lb. bbl.) }	§	§	6,495 }	24,990
Masonry (000 280-lb. bbl.) }			41 }	
Stone (000 short tons)	13,897	15,796	13,701	19,100
Zinc, recoverable (000 short tons)	21	5,500	12	3,663
Lead, recoverable (000 short tons)	8	1,808	7	2,119
West Virginia [4]		722,628		1,285,364
Coal (000 short tons)	118,944	597,222	144,072	1,142,245
Natural gas (000,000 cu.ft.)	208,757	54,694	242,052	61,583
Natural-gas liquids (000 gal.)	353,085	18,040	§	§
Stone (000 short tons)	8,001	14,001	9,740†	16,722†
Petroleum, crude (000 42-gal. bbl.)	2,300	9,361	3,124	11,871
Sand and gravel (000 short tons)	4,506	9,802	4,396	11,473
Wisconsin [38]		78,760		87,670
Sand and gravel (000 short tons)	35,681	25,648	41,103	35,107
Stone (000 short tons)	16,486	22,302	17,577	25,167
Zinc, recoverable (000 short tons)	18	4,750	21	6,322
Wyoming [10]		439,256		705,533
Petroleum, crude (000 42-gal. bbl.)	133,910	336,114	160,345	469,811
Natural gas (000,000 cu.ft.)	181,610	21,793	338,520	49,762
Uranium (U₃O₈) (000 lb.)	1,357‡	27,387‡	6,346	38,768
Coal, bituminous (000 short tons)	2,024	6,992	7,772	24,423
Iron ore, usable (000 long tons)	§	§		
Clays (000 short tons)	788	9,571	1,950	18,829
Natural-gas liquids‖ (000 gal.)	192,888	9,814	300,426	14,557

Figure in brackets is the rank of the states by value of 1969 mineral production. Boldface type indicates the state that leads in value of production for that mineral.
Production is measured by mine shipments, sales, or marketable production (including consumption by producers).

*Includes small quantity of anthracite mined in states other than Pennsylvania.
†Excludes certain varieties. ‡Short tons of uranium ore. §Figure withheld to avoid disclosing confidential data. ‖For cement, portland and masonry figures combined; for helium, grade A and crude figures combined; for natural-gas liquids, natural gasoline, cycle products, and liquefied petroleum gases combined.
Source: U.S. Department of the Interior, Bureau of Mines.

(F. H. Sκ.)

National income

June 30, 1971

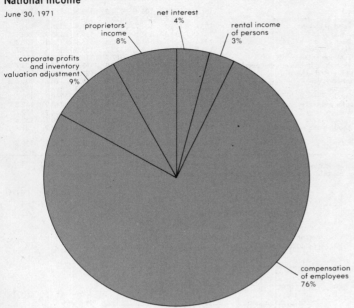

proprietors' income 8%

net interest 4%

rental income of persons 3%

corporate profits and inventory valuation adjustment 9%

compensation of employees 76%

Source: U.S. Department of Commerce, Office of Business Economics, *Survey of Current Business.*

New building construction

Constant values, in billion dollars

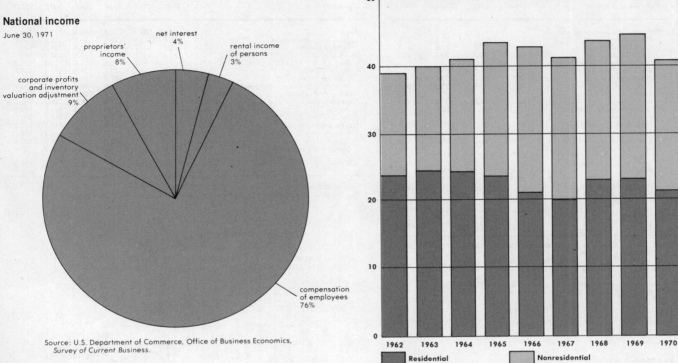

	Residential	Nonresidential

1962 1963 1964 1965 1966 1967 1968 1969 1970

Source: U.S. Department of Commerce, Bureau of Domestic Commerce, *Construction Review.*

Personal income per capita

State	1955	1960	1965	1970
United States	$1,876	$2,215	$2,765	$3,910
Alabama	1,233	1,488	1,923	2,828
Alaska	2,275	2,846	3,214	4,676
Arizona	1,677	2,032	2,400	3,542
Arkansas	1,142	1,372	1,839	2,742
California	2,313	2,710	3,274	4,469
Colorado	1,814	2,275	2,723	3,751
Connecticut	2,414	2,807	3,455	4,807
Delaware	2,519	2,757	3,346	4,233
District of Columbia	2,483	3,017	3,694	5,519
Florida	1,620	1,950	2,450	3,584
Georgia	1,375	1,639	2,171	3,277
Hawaii	1,837	2,369	2,863	4,530
Idaho	1,539	1,849	2,409	3,206
Illinois	2,243	2,650	3,304	4,516
Indiana	1,894	2,188	2,860	3,773
Iowa	1,608	1,986	2,741	3,714
Kansas	1,732	2,161	2,678	3,804
Kentucky	1,329	1,574	2,058	3,060
Louisiana	1,396	1,655	2,084	3,065
Maine	1,551	1,844	2,309	3,243
Maryland	1,994	2,343	3,027	4,247
Massachusetts	2,026	2,459	3,072	4,294
Michigan	2,183	2,324	3,052	4,043
Minnesota	1,729	2,116	2,683	3,793
Mississippi	1,020	1,205	1,615	2,561
Missouri	1,802	2,115	2,662	3,659
Montana	1,852	2,037	2,455	3,381
Nebraska	1,595	2,110	2,643	3,700
Nevada	2,549	2,856	3,320	4,544
New Hampshire	1,765	2,143	2,581	3,608
New Jersey	2,306	2,708	3,260	4,539
New Mexico	1,504	1,890	2,240	3,044
New York	2,283	2,746	3,296	4,797
North Carolina	1,313	1,561	2,054	3,188
North Dakota	1,379	1,715	2,311	2,937
Ohio	2,081	2,334	2,859	3,983
Oklahoma	1,507	1,861	2,303	3,269
Oregon	1,928	2,235	2,771	3,700
Pennsylvania	1,889	2,242	2,755	3,893
Rhode Island	1,961	2,211	2,819	3,920
South Carolina	1,181	1,377	1,852	2,908
South Dakota	1,293	1,782	2,220	3,182
Tennessee	1,281	1,543	2,047	3,051
Texas	1,667	1,925	2,360	3,515
Utah	1,625	1,968	2,379	3,210
Vermont	1,464	1,841	2,377	3,491
Virginia	1,571	1,841	2,422	3,586
Washington	2,038	2,349	2,913	3,993
West Virginia	1,326	1,594	2,029	2,929
Wisconsin	1,816	2,175	2,733	3,722
Wyoming	1,857	2,263	2,570	3,420

Source: U.S. Department of Commerce, Office of Business Economics, *Survey of Current Business.*

Personal consumption expenditures

in billions of dollars

Type of expenditure	1966	1967	1968	1969	1970
Food, beverages, tobacco	115.4	117.7	125.1	132.6	142.9
Clothing, accessories, personal care	56.6	59.6	64.5	69.5	72.4
Housing	67.1	71.8	77.3	84.0	91.2
Household operation	66.7	70.5	76.2	81.6	85.6
Medical care expenses	31.3	34.5	37.8	42.4	47.3
Personal business	24.0	26.2	29.5	33.3	35.5
Transportation	59.6	62.6	72.0	78.0	77.9
Recreation	28.7	30.8	33.6	36.3	39.0
Private education and research	6.7	7.6	8.7	9.6	10.4
Religious and welfare activities	6.5	6.9	7.6	8.1	8.8
Foreign travel and other, net	3.4	3.9	3.8	4.2	4.8
TOTAL	466.0	492.1	536.1	579.6	615.8

Source: U.S. Department of Commerce, Office of Business Economics, *Survey of Current Business.*

Family income levels

percent distribution, by region

1969 income level	Total U.S.	Northeast	N. Central	South	West
Under $1,000	1.6	1.2	1.2	2.3	1.5
$ 1,000 to $ 1,499	1.3	0.7	1.0	2.3	0.8
$ 1,500 to $ 1,999	1.8	1.1	1.5	3.0	1.4
$ 2,000 to $ 2,499	2.4	1.8	2.1	3.3	2.1
$ 2,500 to $ 2,999	2.2	2.0	2.0	2.8	1.7
$ 3,000 to $ 3,499	2.6	2.1	2.3	3.3	2.4
$ 3,500 to $ 3,999	2.7	2.2	2.5	3.4	2.3
$ 4,000 to $ 4,999	5.4	4.8	4.8	6.6	4.8
$ 5,000 to $ 5,999	5.9	5.5	4.9	7.4	5.6
$ 6,000 to $ 6,999	6.4	5.9	5.9	7.5	5.8
$ 7,000 to $ 7,999	7.3	7.6	7.2	7.2	7.1
$ 8,000 to $ 8,999	7.4	7.6	7.3	7.3	7.5
$ 9,000 to $ 9,999	7.0	7.4	7.2	6.8	6.6
$10,000 to $11,999	13.0	14.2	14.4	10.9	12.7
$12,000 to $14,999	13.7	14.2	15.6	11.0	14.6
$15,000 to $24,999	15.6	17.8	16.3	12.1	17.7
$25,000 to $49,999	3.2	3.4	3.3	2.2	4.8
$50,000 and over	0.4	0.5	0.5	0.4	0.5
Median income	$9,433	$10,018	$10,020	$8,105	$10,037
Number of families	51,237,000	12,373,000	14,358,000	15,770,000	8,736,000

Percentages do not add to 100 because of rounding.
Source: U.S. Department of Commerce, Bureau of the Census, *Current Population Reports.*

Retail food prices

in cents per pound, except as indicated

Commodity and unit	1950	1960	1965	1971*
Cereals and bakery products				
Flour, wheat	9.8	11.1	11.6	12.0
Corn flakes (12 oz.)	18.5	25.8	28.9	34.3
Bread, white	14.3	20.3	20.9	25.0
Meats, poultry, and fish				
Steak, round	93.6	105.5	108.4	137.2
Hamburger	56.6	52.4	50.8	67.8
Pork chops, center cut	75.4	85.8	97.3	106.5
Bacon, sliced	63.7	65.5	81.3	79.5
Frying chickens	59.5	42.7	39.0	40.8
Ocean perch, fillet, frozen	...	47.4	52.7	72.7
Dairy products				
Milk, fresh (grocery) (qt.)	19.3	24.7	47.3	58.8
Butter	72.9	74.9	75.4	87.8
Cheese, Am. process†	51.8	34.3	37.7	52.5
Fruits and vegetables				
Apples	12.0	16.2‡	17.8	23.5
Oranges, size 200 (doz.)	49.3	74.8	77.8	87.5
Potatoes	4.6	7.2	9.4	8.4
Tomatoes	24.3	31.6	34.3	52.1
Peas, green, No. 303 can	...	20.7	23.7	26.4
Other				
Eggs, Grade A, large (doz.)	60.4	57.3	52.7	53.6
Margarine	30.8	26.9	27.9	32.5
Sugar	9.7	11.6	11.8	13.5
Coffee§	79.4	75.3	83.3	93.7

Prior to 1965, data exclude Alaska and Hawaii. *April, 1971. †1 lb. before 1960, ½ lb. thereafter. ‡11-month average. §Beginning 1960, vacuum pack can only.
Source: U.S. Department of Commerce, Bureau of the Census, *Statistical Abstract of the United States*. Data compiled by the U.S. Department of Labor, Bureau of Labor Statistics, *Retail Food Prices by Cities* and *Estimated Retail Food Prices by Cities*.

Average employee earnings

March figures

Industry	AVERAGE WEEKLY EARNINGS		AVERAGE HOURLY EARNINGS	
	1968	1971	1968	1971
MANUFACTURING				
Durable goods	$129.68	$151.50	$3.14	$3.75
Ordnance and accessories	133.95	157.59	3.22	3.77
Lumber and wood products	100.50	123.11	2.50	3.07
Furniture and fixtures	98.42	112.29	2.43	2.85
Stone, clay, and glass products	119.19	147.80	2.90	3.57
Primary metal industries	146.23	168.50	3.49	4.13
Fabricated metal products	128.44	146.40	3.11	3.66
Nonelectrical machinery	140.86	159.17	3.33	3.93
Electrical equipment and supplies	115.49	137.76	2.88	3.47
Transportation equipment	151.62	182.96	3.61	4.43
Instruments and related products	119.66	137.76	2.94	3.47
Nondurable goods	106.79	124.87	2.69	3.21
Food and kindred products	111.08	133.27	2.77	3.34
Tobacco manufactures	92.01	114.82	2.48	3.12
Textile mill products	89.84	102.77	2.17	2.55
Apparel and related products	80.15	87.54	2.19	2.48
Paper and allied products	125.93	149.34	2.97	3.59
Printing and publishing	130.64	153.38	3.42	4.09
Chemicals and allied products	132.70	158.98	3.19	3.84
Petroleum and coal products	154.24	187.26	3.69	4.48
Rubber and plastics products	117.14	132.47	2.85	3.32
Leather and leather products	85.25	96.09	2.22	2.59
NONMANUFACTURING				
Metal mining	136.37	166.69	3.31	3.95
Coal mining	152.59	192.92	3.74	4.74
Oil and gas extraction	132.62	156.14	3.15	3.70
Contract construction	154.94	204.42	4.28	5.51
Local and suburban transportation	118.56	145.25	2.85	3.56
Telephone communication	113.78	133.82	2.91	3.44
Electric, gas, and sanitary services	145.55	179.24	3.55	4.34
Wholesale trade	119.80	141.81	3.01	3.59
Retail trade	72.93	84.33	2.12	2.54
Hotels, tourist courts, and motels*	58.68	71.11	1.63	2.11

*Excludes tips.
Source: U.S. Department of Labor, Bureau of Labor Statistics, *Employment and Earnings*.

Consumer prices by commodity groups

1957–59 = 100

Commodity	1960	1962	1964	1966	1968	1970	1971*
Food	101.4	103.6	106.4	114.2	119.3	132.4	134.3
Food away from home	105.5	110.7	115.2	123.2	136.3	155.4	160.8
Food at home	100.6	102.2	104.7	112.6	115.9	127.7	128.7
Housing	103.1	104.8	107.2	111.1	119.1	135.9	140.1
Rent	103.1	105.7	107.8	110.4	115.1	123.8	127.8
Home ownership	103.7	105.6	109.1	115.7	127.0	154.5	158.7
Fuel and utilities	104.5	106.1	107.3	107.7	110.4	117.3	123.5
Household furnishings and operation	101.5	101.5	102.8	105.0	113.0	122.7	125.7
Apparel and upkeep	102.2	103.6	105.7	109.6	120.1	132.4	135.0
Transportation	103.8	107.2	109.3	112.7	119.6	130.6	136.4
Private	103.2	105.9	107.9	111.0	117.3	126.5	132.0
Public	107.0	115.4	119.0	125.8	138.2	169.7	178.6
Health and recreation	105.4	109.4	113.6	119.0	130.0	143.9	149.2
Medical care	108.1	114.2	119.4	127.7	145.0	164.9	172.7
Personal care	104.1	106.5	109.2	112.2	120.3	130.7	133.6
Reading and recreation	104.9	109.6	114.1	117.1	125.7	136.2	141.4
All items	103.1	105.4	108.1	113.1	121.2	135.3	139.2

*Four-month average.
Source: U.S. Department of Labor, Bureau of Labor Statistics, *Monthly Labor Review*.

Unemployment trends

quarterly averages, seasonally adjusted

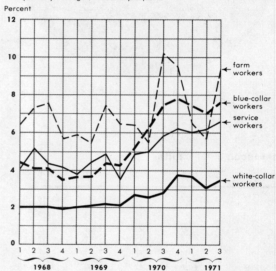

Source: U.S. Department of Labor, Bureau of Labor Statistics, *Monthly Labor Review*.

Consumer prices in selected cities, 1969

1957-59 = 100, except as noted

Standard Metropolitan Statistical Area	Food	Housing	Apparel and upkeep	Medical care	Transportation	All items
Average*	125.5	126.7	127.1	155.0	124.2	127.7
Atlanta	123.8	129.5	127.0	155.2	119.3	126.7
Baltimore	128.8	125.2	131.6	168.5	126.1	128.3
Boston	129.3	133.8	127.7	160.0	130.2	131.8
Chicago†	127.2	120.8	121.3	162.6	125.0	124.9
Cincinnati	122.1	119.1	130.9	164.8	124.2	124.6
Cleveland	123.2	121.8	125.5	174.5	126.8	126.3
Detroit	124.3	124.4	123.6	165.6	122.9	127.1
Honolulu‡	117.4	121.9	115.7	129.5	108.0	117.0
Houston	126.9	125.7	126.0	145.6	120.9	127.0
Kansas City	129.4	123.8	134.5	161.2	127.7	130.1
Los Angeles–Long Beach	122.6	132.2	124.5	149.9	128.3	128.0
Milwaukee	125.2	120.5	126.0	148.0	120.5	123.6
Minneapolis–St. Paul	123.7	127.0	123.8	161.2	123.1	127.4
New York†	127.1	130.8	133.3	161.5	127.3	131.8
Philadelphia	125.5	125.9	133.6	165.0	134.1	128.9
Pittsburgh	122.4	126.2	129.7	161.4	126.2	127.0
St. Louis§	129.5	121.5	127.3	147.8	125.0	127.5
San Diego§	117.0	118.5	112.7	122.9	109.1	115.1
San Francisco–Oakland	123.8	139.4	130.7	153.0	124.4	131.1
Seattle	124.5	132.0	123.7	148.5	121.6	128.3
Washington, D.C.	129.5	125.0	134.7	177.7	125.3	129.5

Indexes measure time-to-time changes in price. They do not indicate whether it costs more to live in one area than in another. *1969; 56 cities. †Standard Consolidated Area. ‡December 1963 = 100. §February 1965 = 100.
Source: U.S. Department of Commerce, Bureau of the Census, *Statistical Abstract of the United States*. Data compiled by U.S. Department of Labor, Bureau of Labor Statistics *Monthly Labor Review*.

Stock market prices

1941-43 = 100

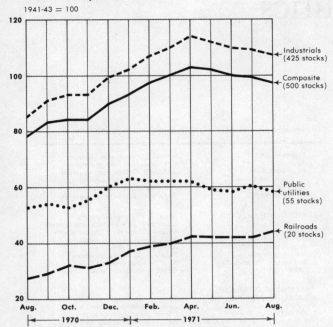

- Industrials (425 stocks)
- Composite (500 stocks)
- Public utilities (55 stocks)
- Railroads (20 stocks)

|—— 1970 ——|—— 1971 ——|

Source: U.S. Department of Commerce, Office of Business Economics, *Survey of Current Business*. Data compiled by Standard & Poor's Corporation.

Mortgage loan interest rates
conventional mortgages on single-family homes

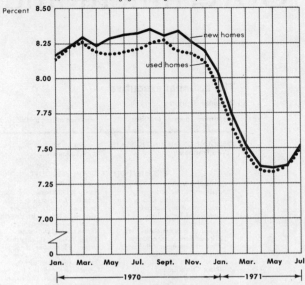

- new homes
- used homes

|—— 1970 ——|—— 1971 ——|

Source: U.S. Department of Commerce, Office of Business Economics, *Survey of Current Business*.

Residential rents

1967 = 100, except as indicated

Standard Metropolitan Statistical Area	1950	1955	1960	1965	1970
Atlanta, Ga.	76.1	89.3	94.2	96.9	109.9
Baltimore, Md.	73.1	84.1	93.1	97.6	106.9
Boston, Mass.	59.6	69.4	86.0	96.3	115.4
Chicago, Ill.-Northwestern Ind.	61.7	85.1	94.5	97.5	107.6
Cincinnati, Ohio	70.9	89.4	97.6	99.0	105.7
Cleveland, Ohio-Ky.	65.7	88.2	98.5	98.2	107.5
Dallas, Tex.	...	...	...	98.5	110.1
Detroit, Mich.	71.5	95.0	95.7	94.5	111.5
Honolulu, Hawaii	...	...	...	95.8	118.1
Houston, Tex.	89.2	97.5	97.7	97.7	106.9
Kansas City, Mo.-Kans.	75.1	92.5	96.5	98.8	106.3
Los Angeles-Long Beach, Calif.	69.5	85.0	90.9	97.8	111.9
Minneapolis-St. Paul, Minn.	65.0	83.9	93.1	97.9	114.2
New York, N.Y.-Northeastern N.J.	67.4	76.4	87.1	96.5	110.9
Philadelphia, Pa.-N.J.	73.9	81.8	91.3	96.9	112.5
Pittsburgh, Pa.	73.3	86.7	93.8	97.5	109.0
St. Louis, Mo.-Ill.	68.0	86.9	95.7	98.1	105.6
San Diego, Calif.	...	...	...	97.8	123.6
San Francisco-Oakland, Calif.	55.7	70.5	82.5	94.7	119.3
Seattle, Wash.	64.3	80.9	88.9	92.8	109.1
Washington, D.C.-Md.-Va.	71.9	82.6	88.6	96.9	109.4

Source: U.S. Department of Commerce, Bureau of the Census, *Statistical Abstract of the United States*. Data compiled by the U.S. Department of Labor, Bureau of Labor Statistics.

Homes with selected electrical appliances

number of wired homes in millions

Product	1953 Number	1953 Percent	1960 Number	1960 Percent	1965 Number	1965 Percent	1970 Number	1970 Percent
Total number of wired homes	42.3	100.0	50.6	100.0	56.4	100.0	62.7	100.0
Air conditioners, room	0.6	1.3	6.5	12.8	11.4	20.2	23.0	36.7
Bed coverings	3.6	8.6	10.8	21.3	18.3	32.4	29.8	47.5
Blenders	1.5	3.5	3.8	7.5	6.2	11.0	19.9	31.7
Can openers	...	...	...	...	11.1	19.7	27.1	43.2
Coffee makers	21.6	51.0	27.0	53.4	38.6	68.5	54.2	86.4
Dishwashers	1.3	3.0	3.2	6.3	6.7	11.8	14.9	23.7
Dryers, clothes*	1.5	3.6	9.0	17.8	13.7	24.2	25.3	40.3
Food disposers	1.4	3.3	4.8	9.5	7.6	13.5	14.4	22.9
Freezers	4.9	11.5	11.2	22.1	15.1	26.7	18.6	29.6
Fry pans	...	...	20.6	40.7	27.6	49.0	34.6	55.2
Irons	37.9	89.6	44.9	88.6	55.4	98.3	62.4	99.5
Mixers	12.6	29.7	27.0	53.4	39.7	70.4	51.2	81.7
Radios	43.7	96.2	50.0	96.1	55.2	97.9	62.5	99.7
Ranges								
Free-standing	}10.2	}24.1	{15.3	30.3	18.0	31.9	24.0	38.3
Built-in			{2.7	5.3	5.4	9.5	9.0	14.4
Refrigerators	37.8	89.2	49.6	98.0	56.0	99.3	62.6	99.8
Television								
Black and white	19.8	46.7	45.5	89.9	53.1	94.1	61.9	98.7
Color	—	—	...	...	2.9	5.1	24.0	38.2
Toasters	30.0	70.9	35.6	70.4	45.8	81.1	57.1	91.0
Vacuum cleaners	25.1	59.4	36.7	72.5	45.8	81.2	56.9	90.7
Washers, clothes	32.2	76.2	42.0	83.1	49.0	86.9	57.6	91.9

Data as of January 1. *Includes gas dryers.
Source: U.S. Department of Commerce, Bureau of the Census, *Statistical Abstract of the United States*. Data from *Merchandising Week*, Billboard Publications, Inc.

Medical care price indexes

1967 = 100

Year	Total medical care	Hospital daily service charges	Drugs and prescriptions	Physicians' fees	Obstetrical case	Tonsillectomy and adenoidectomy	Dentists' fees	Optometric examination and eye glasses
1950	53.7	28.9	88.5	55.2	51.2	60.7	63.9	73.5
1955	64.8	41.5	94.7	65.4	68.6	69.0	73.0	77.0
1960	79.1	56.3	104.5	77.0	79.4	80.3	82.1	85.1
1965	89.5	76.6	100.2	88.3	89.0	91.0	92.2	92.8
1966	93.4	84.0	100.5	93.4	93.0	94.9	95.2	95.3
1967	100.0	100.0	100.0	100.0	100.0	100.0	100.0	100.0
1968	106.1	113.2	100.2	105.6	105.2	104.9	105.5	103.2
1969	113.4	127.9	101.3	112.9	113.5	110.3	112.9	107.6
1970	120.6	143.9	103.6	121.4	121.8	117.1	119.4	113.5

Prior to 1965, data excludes Alaska and Hawaii. Source: U.S. Department of Commerce, Bureau of the Census, *Statistical Abstract of the United States*. Data compiled by the U.S. Department of Labor, Bureau of Labor Statistics, *Price Indexes for Selected Items and Groups, Annual Averages*.

Government and Politics

The national executive

December 31, 1971

Department, bureau, or office	Executive officer and official title
PRESIDENT OF THE UNITED STATES	Richard M. Nixon
Vice President	Spiro T. Agnew
EXECUTIVE OFFICE OF THE PRESIDENT	
Counsellor to the President	Robert H. Finch
Assistant, National Security	Henry A. Kissinger
Assistant, Domestic Affairs	John D. Ehrlichman
Management and Budget	George P. Shultz, director
Science and Technology	Edward E. David, Jr., director
Environmental Quality	Russell E. Train, chairman
Council of Economic Advisers	Herbert Stein, chairman
Office of Econ. Opportunity	Phillip V. Sanchez, director
Office of Consumer Affairs	Virginia H. Knauer, director
Drug Abuse Prevention	Jerome H. Jaffe, director
Cost of Living Council	Donald Rumsfeld, director
Price Commission	C. Jackson Grayson, Jr., chairman
Pay Board	George H. Boldt, chairman
Stabilization Office	Edward F. Preston, asst. comm., IRS
DEPARTMENT OF STATE	William P. Rogers, secretary
	John N. Irwin II, undersecretary
Political Affairs	U. Alexis Johnson, undersecretary
Educational and Cultural Affairs	John Richardson, Jr., asst. secretary
African Affairs	David D. Newsom, asst. secretary
Inter-American Affairs	Charles A. Meyer, asst. secretary
European Affairs	Martin J. Hillenbrand, asst. secy.
East Asian and Pacific Affairs	Marshall Green, asst. secretary
Near Eastern, South Asian Affairs	Joseph J. Sisco, asst. secretary
International Organization Affairs	Samuel DePalma. asst. secretary
DEPARTMENT OF THE TREASURY	John B. Connally, secretary
	Charles E. Walker, undersecretary
Monetary Affairs	Paul A. Volcker, undersecretary
Bureau of Customs	Myles J. Ambrose, commissioner
Bureau of Engraving and Printing	James A. Conlon, director
Bureau of the Mint	Mary T. Brooks, director
Internal Revenue Service	Johnnie M. Walters, commissioner
U.S. Savings Bonds Division	Elmer L. Rustad, national director
U.S. Secret Service	James J. Rowley, director
Office of the Treasurer	Romana Acosta Manuelo, treasurer
DEPARTMENT OF DEFENSE	Melvin R. Laird, secretary
	(vacancy) deputy secretary
Joint Chiefs of Staff	Adm. Thomas H. Moorer, chairman
Chief of Staff, U.S. Army	Gen. W. C. Westmoreland
Chief of Naval Operations	Adm. Elmo R. Zumwalt, Jr.
Chief of Staff, U.S. Air Force	Gen. John D. Ryan
Commandant, Marine Corps	Lieut. Gen. Robert E. Cushman, Jr.
Department of the Army	Robert F. Froehlke, secretary
	Kenneth E. BeLieu, undersecretary
Department of the Navy	John H. Chafee, secretary
	John W. Warner, undersecretary
Department of the Air Force	Robert C. Seamans, Jr., secretary
	John L. McLucas, undersecretary
DEPARTMENT OF JUSTICE	John N. Mitchell, attorney general
	R. G. Kleindienst, deputy atty. gen.
Solicitor General	Erwin N. Griswold
Federal Bureau of Investigation	J. Edgar Hoover, director
Bureau of Prisons	Norman A. Carlson, director
Narcotics, Dangerous Drugs	John E. Ingersoll, director
Immigration and Naturalization	Raymond F. Farrell, commissioner
DEPARTMENT OF THE INTERIOR	Rogers C. B. Morton, secretary
	William T. Pecora, undersecretary
Fish and Wildlife, and Parks	Nathaniel P. Reed, asst. secretary
National Park Service	George B. Hartzog, Jr., director
Mineral Resources	Hollis Dole, asst. secretary
Bureau of Mines	Elburt F. Osborn, director
Geological Survey	Vincent E. McKelvey, director
Public Land Management	Harrison Loesch, asst. secretary
Indian Affairs	Louis R. Bruce, commissioner
Bureau of Outdoor Recreation	G. Douglas Hofe, Jr., director
Water and Power Resources	James R. Smith, asst. secretary
DEPARTMENT OF AGRICULTURE	Earl L. Butz, secretary
	J. Phil Campbell, undersecretary
Rural Development, Conservation	Thomas K. Cowden, asst. secretary
Farmer Co-op Service	Eric Thor, administrator
Forest Service	Edward P. Cliff, chief
Rural Electrification	David W. Hamil, administrator
Soil Conservation Service	Kenneth E. Grant, administrator
International Affairs	Clarence D. Palmby, asst. secretary
DEPARTMENT OF COMMERCE	Maurice H. Stans, secretary
	James T. Lynn, undersecretary
Economic Development	Robert A. Podesta, asst. secretary
Domestic, Internat'l Business	Harold B. Scott, asst. secretary
Science and Technology	James H. Wakelin, Jr., asst. secretary

Department, bureau, or office	Executive officer and official title
Economic Affairs	Harold C. Passer, asst. secretary
Tourism	C. L. Washburn, asst. secretary
Maritime Affairs	Andrew E. Gibson, asst. secretary
Bureau of the Census	George Hay Brown, director
National Bureau of Standards	Lewis M. Branscomb, director
Patent Office	Donald W. Banner, commissioner
DEPARTMENT OF LABOR	James D. Hodgson, secretary
	Laurence H. Silberman, undersecretary
Manpower	Malcolm R. Lovell, Jr., asst. secretary
Labor-Management Relations	W. J. Usery, Jr., asst. secretary
Employment Standards	(vacancy) asst. secretary
Women's Bureau	Elizabeth D. Koontz, director
Employees' Compensation	John Ekeberg, director
Labor Statistics	Geoffrey H. Moore, commissioner
DEPARTMENT OF HEALTH, EDUCATION, AND WELFARE	Elliott L. Richardson, secretary
	John G. Veneman, undersecretary
Office for Civil Rights	J. Stanley Pottinger, director
Community and Field Services	Patricia Reilly Hitt, asst. secretary
Health and Scientific Affairs	Merlin K. Duval, Jr., asst. secretary
Food and Drug Administration	Charles C. Edwards, commissioner
Health Service, Mental Health	Vernon E. Wilson, administrator
National Institutes of Health	Robert Q. Marston, director
Planning and Evaluation	Lawrence H. Lynn, Jr., assistant secy.
Social, Rehabilitation Service	John D. Twiname, administrator
Social Security Administration	Robert M. Ball, commissioner
Office of Education	Sidney P. Marland, Jr., commissioner
DEPARTMENT OF HOUSING AND URBAN DEVELOPMENT	George W. Romney, secretary
	Richard C. Van Dusen, undersecretary
Community Planning, Management	Samuel C. Jackson, asst. secretary
Housing Production	Eugene A. Gulledge, asst. secretary
Community Development	Floyd H. Hyde, asst. secretary
Equal Opportunity	Samuel J. Simmons, asst. secretary
Research and Technology	Harold B. Finger, asst. secretary
DEPARTMENT OF TRANSPORTATION	John A. Volpe, secretary
	James M. Beggs, undersecretary
U.S. Coast Guard	Adm. Chester R. Bender, commandant
Federal Aviation Administration	John H. Shaffer, administrator
Federal Highway Administration	Francis C. Turner, administrator
Federal Railroad Administration	John W. Ingram, acting administrator
Urban Mass Transportation	Carlos C. Villarreal, administrator
St. Lawrence Seaway	David W. Oberlin, administrator
National Transportation Safety	John H. Reed, board chairman

INDEPENDENT OFFICES AND ESTABLISHMENTS

Department, bureau, or office	Executive officer and official title
ACTION	Joseph H. Blatchford, director-designate
Atomic Energy Commission	James R. Schlesinger, chairman
Civil Aeronautics Board	Secor D. Browne, chairman
Commission of Fine Arts	William Walton, chairman
District of Columbia	Walter E. Washington, commissioner
Environmental Protection Agency	William D. Ruckelshaus, director
Equal Employment Opportunity Commission	William H. Brown III, chairman
Export-Import Bank of the U.S.	Henry Kearns, pres. and chairman
Farm Credit Administration	Jonathan Davis, chairman
Federal Communications Comm.	Dean Burch, chairman
Federal Deposit Insurance Corp.	Frank Wille, chairman
Federal Maritime Commission	Helen Delich Bentley, chairman
Federal Power Commission	John N. Nassikas, chairman
Federal Reserve System	Arthur F. Burns, chairman
Federal Trade Commission	Miles W. Kirkpatrick, chairman
General Services Administration	Robert L. Kunzig, administrator
Indian Claims Commission	Jerome K. Kuykendall, chairman
Interstate Commerce Commission	George M. Stafford, chairman
National Aeronautics and Space Administration	James C. Fletcher, administrator
National Labor Relations Board	Edward B. Miller, chairman
National Science Foundation	H. Guyford Stever, director
Railroad Retirement Board	H. W. Habermeyer, chairman
Securities and Exchange Comm.	William J. Casey, chairman
Selective Service System	Curtis W. Tarr, director
Small Business Administration	Thomas S. Kleppe, administrator
Smithsonian Institution	S. Dillon Ripley, secretary
Tennessee Valley Authority	Aubrey J. Wagner, chairman
U.S. Civil Service Commission	Robert E. Hampton, chairman
U.S. Information Agency	Frank Shakespeare, director
U.S. Postal Service	Elmer T. Klassen, postmaster general
U.S. Tariff Commission	Catherine M. Bedell, commissioner
Veterans Administration	Donald E. Johnson, administrator

QUASI-OFFICIAL AGENCIES

Department, bureau, or office	Executive officer and official title
American National Red Cross	E. Roland Harriman, chairman
National Academy of Sciences	Philip Handler, president
National Academy of Engineering	Clarence H. Linder, president

State, district, name, and party

Ala.—1. Edwards, W. J. (R)
2. Dickinson, W. L. (R)
3. Andrews, George W. (D)*
4. Nichols, William (D)
5. Flowers, W. W. (D)
6. Buchanan, John H., Jr. (R)
7. Bevill, Tom (D)
8. Jones, Robert E., Jr. (D)
Alaska—Begich, Nick J. (D)
Ariz.—1. Rhodes, John J. (R)
2. Udall, Morris K. (D)
3. Steiger, Sam (R)
Ark.—1. Alexander, Bill (D)
2. Mills, Wilbur D. (D)
3. Hammerschmidt, J. P. (R)
4. Pryor, David (D)
Calif.—1. Clausen, Don H. (R)
2. Johnson, Harold T. (D)
3. Moss, John E. (D)
4. Leggett, Robert L. (D)
5. Burton, Phillip (D)
6. Mailliard, William S. (R)
7. Dellums, R. V. (D)
8. Miller, George P. (D)
9. Edwards, W. Donlon (D)
10. Gubser, Charles S. (R)
11. McCloskey, Paul N., Jr. (R)
12. Talcott, Burt L. (R)
13. Teague, Charles M. (R)
14. Waldie, Jerome R. (D)
15. McFall, John J. (D)
16. Sisk, B. F. (D)
17. Anderson, Glenn M. (D)
18. Mathias, Robert B. (R)
19. Holifield, Chet (D)
20. Smith, H. Allen (R)
21. Hawkins, Augustus F. (D)
22. Corman, James C. (D)
23. Clawson, Del M. (R)
24. Rousselot, John H. (R)
25. Wiggins, Charles (R)
26. Rees, Thomas (D)
27. Goldwater, Barry, Jr. (R)
28. Bell, Alphonzo (R)
29. Danielson, George E. (D)
30. Roybal, Edward R. (D)
31. Wilson, Charles H. (D)
32. Hosmer, Craig (R)
33. Pettis, Jerry (R)
34. Hanna, Richard T. (D)
35. Schmitz, John G. (R)
36. Wilson, Bob (R)
37. Van Deerlin, Lionel (D)
38. Veysey, Victor V. (R)
Colo.—1. McKevitt, James D. (R)
2. Brotzman, D. G. (R)
3. Evans, Frank (D)
4. Aspinall, Wayne N. (D)
Conn.—1. Cotter, William R. (D)
2. Steele, Robert H. (R)
3. Giaimo, Robert N. (D)
4. McKinney, Stewart B. (R)
5. Monagan, John S. (D)
6. Grasso, Ella T. (D)
Del.—duPont, Pierre S., IV (R)
Fla.—1. Sikes, Robert L. F. (D)
2. Fuqua, Don (D)
3. Bennett, Charles E. (D)
4. Chappell, William, Jr. (D)
5. Frey, Louis, Jr. (R)
6. Gibbons, Sam (D)
7. Haley, James A. (D)
8. Young, C. William (R)
9. Rogers, Paul G. (D)
10. Burke, J. Herbert (R)
11. Pepper, Claude (D)
12. Fascell, Dante B. (D)
Ga.—1. Hagan, G. Elliott (D)
2. Mathis, Dawson (D)
3. Brinkley, Jack (D)
4. Blackburn, B. B. (R)
5. Thompson, S. F. (R)
6. Flynt, J. J., Jr. (D)
7. Davis, John W. (D)
8. Stuckey, W. S., Jr. (D)
9. Landrum, Phil M. (D)
10. Stephens, Robert G., Jr. (D)
Hawaii—1. Matsunaga, Spark M. (D)
2. Mink, Patsy (D)
Ida.—1. McClure, James A. (R)
2. Hansen, Orval (R)
Ill.—1. Metcalfe, Ralph (D)
2. Mikva, Abner (D)
3. Murphy, Morgan (D)
4. Derwinski, Edward J. (R)
5. Kluczynski, John C. (D)
6. Collins, George W. (D)
7. Annunzio, Frank (D)
8. Rostenkowski, Dan (D)
9. Yates, Sidney R. (D)

State, district, name, and party

10. Collier, Harold R. (R)
11. Pucinski, Roman C. (D)
12. McClory, Robert (R)
13. Crane, Philip M. (R)
14. Erlenborn, J. N. (R)
15. †Vacancy
16. Anderson, John B. (R)
17. Arends, Leslie C. (R)
18. Michel, Robert H. (R)
19. Railsback, Thomas F. (R)
20. Findley, Paul (R)
21. Gray, Kenneth J. (D)
22. Springer, William L. (R)
23. Shipley, George E. (D)
24. Price, Melvin (D)
Ind.—1. Madden, Ray J. (D)
2. Landgrebe, Earl F. (R)
3. Brademas, John (D)
4. Roush, J. Edward (D)
5. Hillis, Elwood H. (R)
6. Bray, William G. (R)
7. Myers, John (R)
8. Zion, Roger (R)
9. Hamilton, L. H. (D)
10. Dennis, David (R)
11. Jacobs, A., Jr. (D)
Iowa—1. Schwengel, Fred (R)
2. Culver, J. C. (D)
3. Gross, H. R. (R)
4. Kyl, John H. (R)
5. Smith, Neal (D)
6. Mayne, Wiley (R)
7. Scherle, W. J. (R)
Kan.—1. Sebelius, Keith G. (R)
2. Roy, William R. (D)
3. Winn, Larry, Jr. (R)
4. Shriver, Garner E. (R)
5. Skubitz, Joseph (R)
Ky.—1. Stubblefield, Frank A. (D)
2. Natcher, William H. (D)
3. Mazzoli, Romano L. (D)
4. Snyder, Gene (R)
5. Carter, Tim L. (R)
6. Curlin, William P. Jr.‡ (D)
7. Perkins, Carl D. (D)
La.—1. Hébert, F. Edward (D)
2. Boggs, Hale (D)
3. Caffery, Patrick (D)
4. Waggonner, Joe D., Jr. (D)
5. Passman, Otto E. (D)
6. Rarick, John R. (D)
7. Edwards, Edwin W. (D)
8. Long, Speedy O. (D)
Me.—1. Kyros, Peter (D)
2. Hathaway, W. D. (D)
Md.—1. §Mills, William O. (R)
2. Long, Clarence D. (D)
3. Garmatz, Edward A. (D)
4. Sarbanes, Paul S. (D)
5. Hogan, Lawrence J. (R)
6. Byron, Goodloe E. (D)
7. Mitchell, Parren J. (D)
8. Gude, Gilbert (R)
Mass.—1. Conte, Silvio O. (R)
2. Boland, Edward P. (D)
3. Drinan, Robert F. (D)
4. Donohue, Harold D. (D)
5. Morse, F. Bradford (R)
6. Harrington, M. J. (D)
7. Macdonald, Torbert H. (D)
8. O'Neill, Thomas P., Jr. (D)
9. Hicks, Louise Day (D)
10. Heckler, Margaret (R)
11. Burke, James A. (D)
12. Keith, Hastings (R)
Mich.—1. Conyers, John, Jr. (D)
2. Esch, Marvin (R)
3. Brown, Garry E. (R)
4. Hutchinson, Edward (R)
5. Ford, Gerald R., Jr. (R)
6. Chamberlain, Charles E. (R)
7. Riegle, D. W., Jr. (R)
8. Harvey, James (R)
9. Vander Jagt, Guy (R)
10. Cederberg, Elford A. (R)
11. Ruppe, Philip (R)
12. O'Hara, James G. (D)
13. Diggs, Charles C., Jr. (D)
14. Nedzi, Lucien N. (D)
15. Ford, W. D. (D)
16. Dingell, John D. (D)
17. Griffiths, Martha W. (D)
18. Broomfield, William S. (R)
19. McDonald, J. H. (R)
Minn.—1. Quie, Albert H. (R)
2. Nelsen, Ancher (R)
3. Frenzel, William (R)
4. Karth, Joseph E. (D)
5. Fraser, Donald M. (D)

State, district, name, and party

6. Zwach, John M. (R)
7. Bergland, Bob S. (D)
8. Blatnik, John A. (D)
Miss.—1. Abernethy, Thomas G. (D)
2. Whitten, Jamie L. (D)
3. Griffin, Charles (D)
4. Montgomery, G. V. (D)
5. Colmer, William M. (D)
Mo.—1. Clay, William (D)
2. Symington, James W. (D)
3. Sullivan, Leonor K. (D)
4. Randall, William J. (D)
5. Bolling, Richard (D)
6. Hull, W. R., Jr. (D)
7. Hall, Durward G. (R)
8. Ichord, Richard H. (D)
9. Hungate, W. L. (D)
10. Burlison, Bill D. (D)
Mont.—1. Shoup, Richard G. (R)
2. Melcher, John (D)
Neb.—1. Thone, Charles (R)
2. McCollister, John Y. (R)
3. Martin, David (R)
Nev.—Baring, Walter S. (D)
N.H.—1. Wyman, Louis C. (R)
2. Cleveland, James C. (R)
N.J.—1. Hunt, John E. (R)
2. Sandman, Charles W., Jr. (R)
3. Howard, J. J. (D)
4. Thompson, Frank, Jr. (D)
5. Frelinghuysen, Peter, Jr. (R)
6. Forsythe, Edwin B. (R)
7. Widnall, William B. (R)
8. Roe, Robert A. (D)
9. Helstoski, Henry (D)
10. Rodino, Peter W., Jr. (D)
11. Minish, Joseph G. (D)
12. Dwyer, Florence P. (R)
13. Gallagher, Cornelius E. (D)
14. Daniels, Dominick V. (D)
15. Patten, Edward J. (D)
N.M.—1. Lujan, Manuel, Jr. (R)
2. Runnels, Harold L. (D)
N.Y.—1. Pike, Otis G. (D)
2. Grover, James R., Jr. (R)
3. Wolff, L. L. (D)
4. Wydler, John W. (R)
5. Lent, Norman F. (R)
6. Halpern, Seymour (R)
7. Addabbo, Joseph P. (D)
8. Rosenthal, Benjamin S. (D)
9. Delaney, James J. (D)
10. Celler, Emanuel (D)
11. Brasco, Frank J. (D)
12. Chisholm, Shirley (D)
13. Podell, B. L. (D)
14. Rooney, John J. (D)
15. Carey, Hugh L. (D)
16. Murphy, John M. (D)
17. Koch, Edward I. (D)
18. Rangel, Charles B. (D)
19. Abzug, Bella (D)
20. Ryan, William Fitts (D)
21. Badillo, Herman (D)
22. Scheuer, James (D)
23. Bingham, J. B. (D)
24. Biaggi, Mario (D)
25. Peyser, Peter A. (R)
26. Reid, Ogden R. (R)
27. Dow, John G. (D)
28. Fish, Hamilton, Jr. (R)
29. Stratton, Samuel S. (D)
30. King, Carleton J. (R)
31. McEwen, Robert (R)
32. Pirnie, Alexander (R)
33. Robison, Howard W. (R)
34. Terry, John H. (R)
35. Hanley, James M. (D)
36. Horton, Frank J. (R)
37. Conable, B., Jr. (R)
38. Hastings, James F. (R)
39. Kemp, Jack F. (R)
40. Smith, H. P., III (R)
41. Dulski, Thaddeus J. (D)
N.C.—1. Jones, Walter B. (D)
2. Fountain, L. H. (D)
3. Henderson, David N. (D)
4. Galifianakis, Nick (D)
5. Mizell, Wilmer (R)
6. Preyer, L. R. (D)
7. Lennon, Alton (D)
8. Ruth, Earl B. (R)
9. Jonas, Charles Raper (R)
10. Broyhill, James T. (R)
11. Taylor, Roy A. (D)
N.D.—1. Andrews, Mark (R)
2. Link, Arthur A. (D)
Ohio—1. Keating, William J. (R)
2. Clancy, Donald D. (R)
3. Whalen, Charles W., Jr. (R)

State, district, name, and party

4. McCulloch, William M. (R)
5. Latta, Delbert L. (R)
6. Harsha, William H., Jr. (R)
7. Brown, Clarence J., Jr. (R)
8. Betts, Jackson E. (R)
9. Ashley, Thomas L. (D)
10. Miller, Clarence E. (R)
11. Stanton, John W. (R)
12. Devine, Samuel L. (R)
13. Mosher, Charles A. (R)
14. Seiberling, John F., Jr. (D)
15. Wylie, Chalmers P. (R)
16. Bow, Frank T. (R)
17. Ashbrook, John M. (R)
18. Hays, Wayne L. (D)
19. Carney, Charles J. (D)
20. Stanton, James V. (D)
21. Stokes, Louis (D)
22. Vanik, Charles A. (D)
23. Minshall, William E. (R)
24. Powell, Walter E. (R)
Okla.—1. Belcher, Page (R)
2. Edmondson, Ed (D)
3. Albert, Carl (D)
4. Steed, Tom (D)
5. Jarman, John (D)
6. Camp, J. N. H. (R)
Ore.—1. Wyatt, Wendell (R)
2. Ullman, Al (D)
3. Green, Edith (D)
4. Dellenback, John R. (R)
Penn.—1. Barrett, William A. (D)
2. Nix, Robert N. C. (D)
3. Byrne, James A. (D)
4. Eilberg, Joshua (D)
5. Green, William J., III (D)
6. Yatron, Gus (D)
7. Williams, L. G. (R)
8. Biester, E. G., Jr. (R)
9. Ware, John H., III (R)
10. McDade, Joseph M. (R)
11. Flood, Daniel J. (D)
12. Whalley, J. Irving (R)
13. Coughlin, R. L. (R)
14. Moorhead, William S. (D)
15. Rooney, Fred B. (D)
16. Eshleman, Edwin D. (R)
17. Schneebeli, Herman T. (R)
18. ‖H. John Heinz III (R)
19. Goodling, George A. (R)
20. Gaydos, Joseph (D)
21. Dent, John H. (D)
22. Saylor, John P. (R)
23. Johnson, Albert W. (R)
24. Vigorito, J. P. (D)
25. Clark, Frank M. (D)
26. Morgan, Thomas E. (D)
27. ¶Vacancy
R.I.—1. St Germain, Fernand J. (D)
2. Tiernan, Robert O. (D)
S.C.—1. ♀Davis, Mendel (D)
2. Spence, Floyd D. (R)
3. Dorn, W. J. Bryan (D)
4. Mann, James R. (D)
5. Gettys, Thomas S. (D)
6. McMillan, John L. (D)
S.D.—1. Denholm, Frank E. (D)
2. Abourezk, James (D)
Tenn.—1. Quillen, James H. (R)
2. Duncan, John J. (R)
3. Baker, LaMar E. (R)
4. Evins, Joseph L. (D)
5. Fulton, Richard (D)
6. Anderson, W. R. (D)
7. Blanton, Ray (D)
8. Jones, Edward (D)
9. Kuykendall, Dan (R)
Tex.—1. Patman, Wright (D)
2. Dowdy, John (D)
3. Collins, James M. (R)
4. Roberts, Ray (D)
5. Cabell, Earle (D)
6. Teague, Olin E. (D)
7. Archer, William R. (R)
8. Eckhardt, Robert C. (D)
9. Brooks, Jack (D)
10. Pickle, J. J. (D)
11. Poage, W. R. (D)
12. Wright, James C., Jr. D).
13. Purcell, Graham (D)
14. Young, John (D)
15. de la Garza, E. (D)
16. White, Richard C. (D)
17. Burleson, Omar (D)
18. Price, Robert (R)
19. Mahon, George (D)
20. Gonzalez, Henry B. (D)
21. Fisher, O. C. (D)
22. Casey, Robert R. (D)
23. Kazen, Abraham, Jr. (D)

State, district, name, and party

Utah—1. McKay, Koln G. (D)
2. Lloyd, Sherman P. (R)
Vt.—δVacancy
Va.—1. Downing, Thomas N. (D)
2. Whitehurst, G. W. (R)
3. Satterfield, D. E., III (D)
4. Abbitt, Watkins M. (D)
5. Daniel, W. C. (D)
6. Poff, Richard H. (R)
7. Robinson, James K. (R)
8. Scott, William L. (R)
9. Wampler, William C. (R)
10. Broyhill, Joel T. (R)
Wash.—1. Pelly, Thomas M. (R)
2. Meeds, Lloyd (D)
3. Hansen, Julia Butler (D)
4. McCormack, Mike (D)
5. Foley, Thomas S. (D)
6. Hicks, Floyd V. (D)
7. Adams, B. (D)
W.Va.—1. Mollohan, R. H. (D)
2. Staggers, Harley O. (D)
3. Slack, John M., Jr. (D)
4. Hechler, Ken (D)
5. Kee, James (D)
Wis.—1. Aspin, Leslie (D)
2. Kastenmeier, Robert W. (D)
3. Thomson, Vernon W. (R)
4. Zablocki, Clement J. (D)
5. Reuss, Henry S. (D)
6. Steiger, William A. (R)
7. Obey, David R. (D)
8. Byrnes, John W. (R)
9. Davis, Glenn R. (R)
10. O'Konski, Alvin E. (R)
Wyo.—Roncalio, Teno (D)

Supreme Court

Chief Justice of the United States:
Warren Earl Burger
Associate Justices:
William O. Douglas
William J. Brennan, Jr.
Potter Stewart
Byron R. White
Thurgood Marshall
Harry A. Blackmun
Lewis F. Powell, Jr.*
William H. Rehnquist*

*Confirmed Dec. 1971.

*Died Dec. 25, 1971.
†Vacancy created by the resignation of Charlotte T. Reid, Oct. 7, 1971.
‡Sworn in Dec. 6, 1971, to fill vacancy created by the death of John C. Watts.
§Sworn in May 27, 1971, to fill vacancy created by the resignation of Rogers C. B. Morton.
‖Sworn in Nov. 4, 1971, to fill vacancy created by the death of Robert J. Corbett.
¶Vacancy created by the death of James G. Fulton, Oct. 6, 1971.
♀Sworn in April 27, 1971, to fill vacancy created by the death of L. Mendel Rivers.
δVacancy created by the resignation of Robert T. Stafford.

Senate

*Interim successor until Nov. 1972
 election to the late
 Richard B. Russell.
†Interim successor until Jan. 1972
 election to the late
 Winston L. Prouty.

Legislation
passed by Congress 1971

Act	House vote	Senate vote	Date of enactment
Debt Limit-Social Security HR 4690—Increased the temporary ceiling on the national debt to $430 billion from $395 billion; provided a 10% across-the-board increase in old-age, survivors and disability insurance benefits.	360–3 Yeas: D. 210, R. 150 Nays: D. 0, R. 3 March 16	76–0 Yeas: D. 39, R. 37 Nays: D. 0, R. 0 March 16	Signed March 17 PL 92-5
Wage-Price Controls HR 4246—Extended to April 30, 1972, the president's discretionary authority to impose controls on wages, prices, salaries, and rents.	Passed by Voice vote May 5	67–4 Yeas: D. 36, R. 31 Nays: D. 2, R. 2 May 3	Signed May 18 PL 92-15
Voting Age HR 4249—Sent to the states for ratification a constitutional amendment lowering the voting age in federal, state, and local elections to 18.	401–19 Yeas: D. 237, R. 162 Nays: D. 7, R. 12	94–0 Yeas: D. 51, R. 43 Nays: D. 0, R. 0	Signed June 22 Ratified June 30 PL 91-285
Emergency Employment S 31—Authorized $2.25 billion to provide public service employment at state and local levels.	343–14 Yeas: D. 206, R. 137 Nays: D. 6, R. 8 July 1	75–11 Yeas: D. 45, R. 30 Nays: D. 3, R. 8 June 29	Signed July 12 PL 92-54
Antipoverty S 2317—Authorized $4 billion to extend the Public Works and Economic Development Act of 1965, and the Appalachian Regional Development Act of 1965.	Passed by Voice vote July 28	Passed by Voice vote July 30	Signed Aug. 5 PL 92-65
Lockheed Loan Guarantee H 8432—Approved a $250-million federal loan guarantee for the Lockheed Aircraft Corp.	192–189 Yeas: D. 102, R. 90 Nays: D. 129, R. 60 July 30	49–48 Yeas: D. 22, R. 27 Nays: D. 31, R. 17 Aug. 2	Signed Aug. 9 PL 92-70
Military Draft Extension HR 6531—Extended the draft for two years, provided a $2.4 billion military pay increase, and called upon the president to set a time certain for Vietnam troop withdrawals if American prisoners of war were released.	293–99 Yeas: D. 146, R. 147 Nays: D. 84, R. 15 April 1	55–30 Yeas: D. 23, R. 32 Nays: D. 23, R. 7 Sept. 21	Signed Sept. 28 PL 92-129
Revenue Act of 1971 H 10947—Approved a 7% tax credit for investment, repealed the automobile excise tax, and increased personal exemption for 1972 to $750. Rider to bill enabled the taxpayer to specify $1 of his tax could go into a fund for financing presidential elections beginning in 1976.	321–75 Yeas: D. 163, R. 158 Nays: D. 66, R. 9 Dec. 9	71–6 Yeas: D. 36, R. 35 Nays: D. 4, R. 2 Dec. 9	Signed Dec. 10 PL 92-178
Alaska Claims H 10367—Gave Alaska's 55,000 natives $962.5 million and 40 million acres of land in settlement of their land claims.	307–60 Yeas: D. 198, R. 109 Nays: D. 15, R. 45 Dec. 14	Passed by Voice vote Dec. 14	Signed Dec. 18 PL 92-203
Economic Stabilization Act Extension S-2891—Approved a second one-year extension to April 30, 1973, of the president's authority to stabilize the economy.	Passed by Voice vote Dec. 14	Passed by Voice vote Dec. 14	Signed Dec. 22 PL 92-210
Cancer Act of 1971 S 1828—Authorized $1.59 billion for a three-year cancer research program.	Passed by Voice vote Dec. 9	85–0 Yeas: D. 46, R. 39 Nays: D. 0, R. 0	Signed Dec. 23 PL92-218

State executive officials
September 1, 1971

State	Governor	Lieutenant Governor	Secretary of State	Treasurer
Alabama	George Wallace(D)	Jere Beasley(D)	Mabel Amos(D)	Agnes Baggett(D)
Alaska	William Egan(D)	H. A. Boucher(D)	—	Ernest Garfield(R)
Arizona	Jack Williams(R)	—	Wesley Bolin(D)	Nancy Hall(D)
Arkansas	Dale Bumpers(D)	Robert Riley(D)	Kelly Bryant(D)	Ivy Baker Priest(R)
California	Ronald Reagan(R)	Ed Reinecke(R)	Edmund Brown, Jr.(D)	Palmer Burch(R)
Colorado	John Love(R)	John Vanderhoof(R)	Byron Anderson(D)	Robert Berdon(R)
Connecticut	Thomas Meskill(R)	T. Clark Hull(R)	Gloria Schaffer(D)	Emily Womach(D)
Delaware	Russell Peterson(R)	Eugene Bookhammer(R)	Eugene Bunting(R)	Thomas O'Malley(D)
Florida	Reubin Askew(D)	Tom Adams(D)	Richard Stone(D)	William Burson(D)
Georgia	James Earl Carter(D)	Lester Maddox(D)	Ben Fortson, Jr.(D)	
Hawaii	John Burns(D)	George Ariyoshi(D)		
Idaho	Cecil Andrus(D)	Jack Murphy(R)	Pete Cenarrusa(R)	Marjorie Ruth Moon(D)
Illinois	Richard Ogilvie(R)	Paul Simon(D)	John Lewis(R)	Alan Dixon(D)
Indiana	Edgar Whitcomb(R)	Richard Folz(R)	Larry Conrad(D)	Jack New(R)
Iowa	Robert Ray(R)	Roger Jepsen(R)	Melvin Synhorst(R)	Maurice Baringer(R)
Kansas	Robert Docking(D)	Reynolds Shultz(R)	Elwill Shanahan(R)	Walter Peery(R)
Kentucky	Louie Nunn(R)	Wendell Ford(D)	Kenneth Harper(R)	Thelma Stovall(D)
Louisiana	John McKeithen(D)	C. C. Aycock(D)	Wade Martin, Jr.(D)	Mary Evelyn Parker(D)
Maine	Kenneth Curtis(D)	—	Joseph Edgar(R)	Norman Ferguson(R)
Maryland	Marvin Mandel(D)	Blair Lee III(D)		John Leutkemeyer(D)
Massachusetts	Francis Sargent(R)	Donald Dwight(R)	John Davoren(D)	Robert Crane(D)
Michigan	William Milliken(R)	James Brickley(R)	Richard Austin(D)	Allison Green(R)
Minnesota	Wendell Anderson(DFL)	Rudolph Perpich(DFL)	Arlen Erdahl(R)	Val Bjornson(R)
Mississippi	John Bell Williams(D)	Charles Sullivan(D)	Heber Ladner(D)	Evelyn Gandy(D)
Missouri	Warren Hearnes(D)	William Morris(D)	James Kirkpatrick(D)	William Robinson(D)
Montana	Forrest Anderson(D)	Thomas Judge(D)	Frank Murray(D)	Alex Stephenson(R)
Nebraska	J. James Exon(D)	Frank Marsh(R)	Allen Beermann(R)	Wayne Swanson(R)
Nevada	Donal O'Callaghan(D)	Harry Reid(D)	John Koontz(D)	Michael Mirabelli(D)
New Hampshire	Walter Peterson(R)		Robert Stark(R)	Robert Flanders(R)
New Jersey	William Cahill(R)		Paul Sherwin(R)	Joseph McCrane, Jr.(R)
New Mexico	Bruce King(D)	Robert Mondragon(D)	Betty Fiorina(D)	Jesse Kornegay(D)
New York	Nelson Rockefeller(R)	Malcolm Wilson(R)	John Lomenzo(R)	Arthur Levitt(D)
North Carolina	Robert Scott(D)	H. Patrick Taylor, Jr.(D)	Thad Eure(D)	Edwin Gill(D)
North Dakota	William Guy(D)	Richard Larsen(R)	Ben Meier(R)	Bernice Asbridge(R)
Ohio	John Gilligan(D)	John Brown(R)	Ted Brown(R)	Gertrude Donahey(D)
Oklahoma	David Hall(D)	George Nigh(D)	John Rogers(D)	Leo Winters(D)
Oregon	Tom McCall(R)		Clay Meyers(R)	Robert Straub(D)
Pennsylvania	Milton Shapp(D)	Ernest Kline(D)	Joseph Kelley, Jr.(R)	Grace Sloan(D)
Rhode Island	Frank Licht(D)	J. Joseph Garrahy(D)	August LaFrance(D)	Raymond Hawksley(D)
South Carolina	John West(D)	Earle Morris, Jr.(D)	O. Frank Thornton(D)	Grady Patterson, Jr.(D)
South Dakota	Richard Kneip(D)	William Dougherty(D)	Alma Larson(R)	Neal Strand(R)
Tennessee	Winfield Dunn(R)	Frank Gorrell(D)	Joe Carr(D)	Charles Worley(D)
Texas	Preston Smith(D)	Ben Barnes(D)	Martin Dies, Jr.(D)	Jesse James(D)
Utah	Calvin Rampton(D)		Clyde Miller(D)	Golden Allen(R)
Vermont	Deane Davis(R)	John Burgess(R)	Richard Thomas(R)	Frank Davis(R)
Virginia	A. Linwood Holton(R)	J. Sargeant Reynolds(D)	Cynthia Newman(R)	Walter Craigie, Jr.(R)
Washington	Daniel Evans(R)	John Cherberg(D)	A. Ludlow Kramer(R)	Robert O'Brien(D)
West Virginia	Arch Moore, Jr.(R)		John D. Rockefeller IV(D)	John Kelly(D)
Wisconsin	Patrick Lucey(D)	Martin Schreiber(D)	Robert Zimmerman(D)	Charles Smith(D)
Wyoming	Stanley Hathaway(R)	—	Thyra Thomson(R)	James Griffith(R)

Party affiliations are indicated by (D) for Democrat, (R) for Republican, and (DFL) for Democratic Farmer Labor Party.
Source: State governments; The Council of State Governments.

Per capita state tax burden
Fiscal year 1970

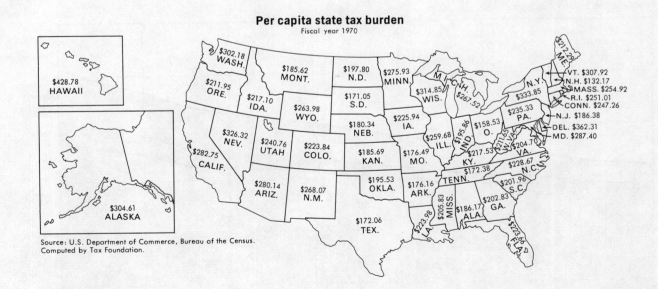

Source: U.S. Department of Commerce, Bureau of the Census.
Computed by Tax Foundation.

Federal tax burden

Fiscal year 1970

State	Amount*	Per capita	State	Amount*	Per capita	State	Amount*	Per capita	State	Amount*	Per capita
Connecticut	$ 3,828	$1,268	Ohio	$ 9,960	$922	Kansas	$1,850	$792	Idaho	$ 472	$654
Delaware	653	1,203	Pennsylvania	10,794	909	Wyoming	254	789	New Mexico	653	653
New York	21,299	1,156	Alaska	254	894	Iowa	2,195	784	North Dakota	399	645
Dist. of Columbia	925	1,152	New Hampshire	635	881	Texas	8,672	771	Tennessee	2,576	643
Illinois	12,137	1,092	Wisconsin	3,701	869	Virginia	3,592	765	South Dakota	417	629
New Jersey	7,747	1,077	Indiana	4,445	863	Vermont	327	740	Kentucky	1,996	614
Nevada	490	1,065	Hawaii	689	862	Arizona	1,252	735	North Carolina	3,211	613
California	20,718	1,059	Missouri	3,973	849	Montana	508	728	West Virginia	1,107	605
Maryland	3,991	1,054	Oregon	1,723	843	Maine	689	700	Alabama	2,014	567
Massachusetts	5,769	1,049	Colorado	1,723	815	Oklahoma	1,796	695	South Carolina	1,488	549
Michigan	8,672	983	Florida	5,207	814	Georgia	3,066	657	Arkansas	1,070	533
Rhode Island	871	950	Minnesota	3,030	814	Utah	689	656	Mississippi	1,070	451
Washington	3,193	933	Nebraska	1,161	796	Louisiana	2,467	655			

*In millions. Sources: U.S. Treasury Department and Tax Foundation, *Facts and Figures on Government Finances.*

Expenditures of all governments

Fiscal year 1970; million dollars

Function	Total	Federal	State	Local
Intergovernmental expenditure	*	23,257	28,892	633
Direct expenditure	332,985	184,933	56,163	91,889
General expenditure	275,017	143,685	48,749	82,582
National defense and international relations	84,253	84,253	—	—
Postal Service	7,722	7,722	—	—
Space research and technology	3,691	3,691	—	—
Education	55,771	3,053	13,780	38,938
Highways	16,746	319	11,044	5,383
Public welfare	17,517	2,837	8,203	6,477
Health and hospitals	13,587	3,919	4,788	4,880
Police and fire protection	6,927	409	688	5,830
Sewerage and sanitation	3,413	—	—	3,413
Natural resources	11,469	8,737	2,158	574
Housing and urban renewal	3,189	1,051	23	2,115
Air transportation	2,065	1,096	178	791
Water transport and terminals	1,904	1,460	173	271
Social insurance administration	1,790	1,021	767	2
Financial administration	3,284	1,254	1,022	1,007
Interest on general debt	18,411	14,037	1,499	2,875
Other	23,278	8,826	4,426	10,026
Utility expenditure	7,820	—	—	7,820
Liquor stores expenditure	1,627	—	1,404	223
Insurance trust expenditure	48,521	41,248	6,010	1,263
Total expenditure	332,985*	208,190	85,055	92,522

Detail may not add to totals because of rounding.
*Duplicative transactions between levels of government are excluded.
Source: U.S. Department of Commerce, Bureau of the Census, *Governmental Finances.*

Revenue of all governments

Fiscal year 1970; million dollars

Source	Total	Federal	State	Local
Intergovernmental revenue	*	—	20,248	29,525
Revenue from own sources	333,810	205,562	68,691	59,557
General revenue from own sources	272,480	163,582	57,507	51,392
Taxes	232,877	146,082	47,962	38,833
Property	34,054	—	1,092	32,963
Individual income	101,224	90,412	9,183	1,630
Corporation income	36,567	32,829	3,738	†
Sales and gross receipts	48,619	18,297	27,254	3,068
Customs duties	2,430	2,430	—	—
General sales, gross receipts	16,128	—	14,177	1,951
Motor fuel	10,100	3,776	6,283	41
Alcoholic beverages	6,208	4,726	1,420	62
Tobacco products	4,531	2,094	2,308	129
Public utilities	3,268	1,721	918	628
Other	5,954	3,550	2,147	257
Motor vehicle, operators license	2,904	—	2,728	176
Death and gift	4,640	3,644	996	‡
All other	4,868	900	2,971	997
Charges, miscellaneous revenue	39,603	17,500	9,545	12,558
Utility revenue	6,608	—	—	6,608
Liquor stores revenue	2,006	—	1,748	258
Insurance trust revenue	52,716	41,980	9,437	1,299
Total revenue	333,810*	205,562	88,939	89,082

Detail may not add to totals because of rounding.
*Duplicative transactions between levels of government are excluded.
†Minor amount included in individual income tax figures.
‡Minor amount included in "All other" taxes.
Source: U.S. Department of Commerce, Bureau of the Census, *Governmental Finances.*

Gross debt of all governments

In billion dollars; at end of fiscal years

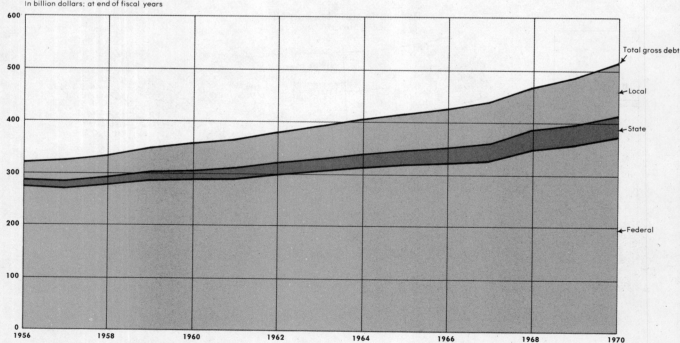

Source: U.S. Department of Commerce, Bureau of the Census; and Treasury Department. Data compiled by Tax Foundation, Inc.

Education

Federal funds supporting education

in thousand dollars

Funds	1968*	1969*	1970*	1971*
Supporting education in educational institutions	7,804,454	8,028,508	9,273,124	10,236,990
Grants, total	7,201,173	7,496,281	8,634,745	9,632,606
Elementary-secondary education	2,967,004	2,838,439	2,964,315	3,088,345
Higher education	3,262,988	3,369,489	4,029,327	4,328,278
Vocational-technical and continuing education (not classifiable by level)	971,181	1,288,353	1,641,103	2,215,983
Loans, total	603,281	532,227	638,379	604,384
Student loan program, National Defense Education Act	226,303	259,641	310,592	331,581
College facilities loans	376,978	272,586	327,787	272,803
Other funds for education and related activities	3,564,723	3,245,763	3,483,777	3,685,325
Applied research and development	1,142,350	1,188,349	1,253,083	1,293,000
School lunch and milk programs	543,845	597,700	651,100	680,800
Training of federal personnel	1,138,333	639,853	687,250	715,187
Library services	136,099	186,124	190,757	188,917
International education	272,008	278,135	268,155	292,255
Other	332,088	355,602	433,432	515,166

*Estimated data.
Source: U.S. Department of Health, Education, and Welfare, Office of Education, *Digest of Educational Statistics*.

Vocational education

	NUMBER OF STUDENTS		
Type of program	1964–65	1967–68	1969–70
Agriculture	887,529	851,158	852,983
Distributive occupations	333,342	574,785	529,365
Home economics	2,098,520	2,283,338	2,570,410
Trades and industry	1,087,807	1,628,542	1,906,133
Health occupations	66,772	140,987	198,044
Technical education	225,737	269,882	271,730
Office occupations	730,904	1,735,997	2,111,160
Total	5,430,611	7,533,986*	8,793,960†

Data refer to vocational programs receiving federal aid.
*Includes 49,297 enrollees not classified by type of program.
†Includes 354,135 enrollees not classified by type of program.
Source: U.S. Department of Health, Education, and Welfare, Office of Education, annual reports on vocational and technical education, and unpublished data.

Cost of attending college

in current dollars

	1961–62		1966–67		1971–72	
	Public	Private	Public	Private	Public	Private
Expenditure						
Tuition and required fees						
Universities	265	1,059	360	1,456	527	2,161
Other 4-year institutions	182	838	259	1,162	394	1,754
2-year institutions	88	537	121	845	174	1,351
Board rates						
Universities	433	500	490	548	616	672
Other 4-year institutions	409	464	417	490	491	594
2-year institutions	356	427	376	487	451	633
Charges for dormitory rooms						
Universities	249	323	321	452	456	664
Other 4-year institutions	197	268	271	355	400	512
2-year institutions	155	234	213	347	315	541

Data are for the entire academic year and are average charges per full-time resident degree-credit student.
Source: U.S. Department of Health, Education, and Welfare, Office of Education, *Digest of Educational Statistics*.

Universities and colleges

state statistics

	NUMBER OF INSTITUTIONS fall, 1970		Enroll-ment fall, 1970	EARNED DEGREES CONFERRED 1969–1970		
State	Total	Public		Bachelor's and first professional	Master's, except first professional	Doctor's
Alabama	49	29	102,707	13,281	2,344	221
Alaska	3	1	10,017	315	174	7
Arizona	18	14	110,106	8,028	2,825	383
Arkansas	21	10	51,639	7,478	1,159	124
California	199	112	1,255,732	70,989	19,467	3,175
Colorado	28	20	121,606	12,350	3,330	636
Connecticut	46	18	124,931	11,358	3,960	511
Delaware	7	3	23,850	1,533	364	60
District of Columbia	20	3	75,920	7,307	4,077	498
Florida	63	34	234,176	20,405	4,327	668
Georgia	62	28	126,191	14,670	3,278	345
Hawaii	7	1	36,510	2,612	1,017	53
Idaho	10	6	34,700	2,769	385	45
Illinois	132	44	453,573	40,703	12,712	1,884
Indiana	44	5	191,156	23,094	8,105	1,313
Iowa	51	15	108,312	14,838	2,244	620
Kansas	53	27	101,297	12,540	2,883	389
Kentucky	35	7	96,949	12,749	2,560	173
Louisiana	23	12	120,720	14,401	3,086	348
Maine	16	2	32,180	4,163	595	24
Maryland	47	23	148,557	12,858	3,012	576
Massachusetts	118	29	303,038	31,300	10,811	1,676
Michigan	90	42	394,095	36,703	12,043	1,577
Minnesota	57	25	159,076	18,825	2,582	546
Mississippi	42	24	73,128	8,972	1,433	178
Missouri	69	22	183,570	19,738	5,308	630
Montana	12	9	29,699	3,780	586	63
Nebraska	27	11	66,375	9,824	1,247	213
Nevada	4	3	12,960	1,006	222	11
New Hampshire	19	4	29,046	4,180	565	49
New Jersey	56	22	210,372	18,679	5,048	565
New Mexico	11	8	43,733	4,139	1,254	182
New York	219	74	776,608	70,998	26,811	3,292
North Carolina	97	52	171,577	19,252	3,216	634
North Dakota	12	9	30,484	3,904	703	86
Ohio	90	22	371,412	43,580	8,761	1,262
Oklahoma	36	24	109,542	12,416	2,892	484
Oregon	39	20	114,279	10,320	2,932	441
Pennsylvania	140	29	410,479	49,530	11,055	1,492
Rhode Island	13	3	45,087	4,793	1,072	187
South Carolina	45	21	70,230	8,068	769	115
South Dakota	17	7	30,731	4,684	899	63
Tennessee	56	16	135,499	16,730	3,054	452
Texas	123	71	438,548	42,251	8,489	1,241
Utah	13	9	79,144	8,990	1,827	413
Vermont	17	5	22,114	2,943	618	33
Virginia	61	28	149,217	14,401	2,564	306
Washington	39	27	180,397	14 960	2,964	466
West Virginia	22	11	63,230	8,154	1,179	143
Wisconsin	63	33	201,554	21,458	4,249	934
Wyoming	8	8	15,028	1,388	341	67
Total U. S.	2,549	1,082	8,481,081	824,407	207,398	29,854

All totals exclude data for service academies.
Source: U.S. Department of Health, Education, and Welfare, Office of Education.

Level of school completed

25 years old and over, by color

Level of school completed	April 1940	April 1950	April 1960	March 1969
Less than 5 years elementary school, percent:				
White	10.9	8.7	6.7	4.5
Nonwhite	41.8	31.4	23.5	15.2
4 years of high school or more, percent:				
White	26.1	35.5	43.2	56.3
Nonwhite	7.7	13.4	21.7	34.5
4 or more years of college, percent:				
White	4.9	6.4	8.1	11.2
Nonwhite	1.3	2.2	3.5	6.0
Median school years completed, percent:				
White	8.7	9.7	10.8	12.2
Nonwhite	5.7	6.9	8.2	9.8

Source: U.S. Department of Health, Education and Welfare, Office of Education, *Digest of Educational Statistics*. Data compiled by U.S. Department of Commerce, Bureau of the Census.

Public elementary and secondary schools

1970–71 estimates

State	Operating school districts	Instruction rooms in use	ENROLLMENT Elementary	ENROLLMENT Secondary	High school graduates	INSTRUCTIONAL STAFF Total*	Principals and supervisors	Teachers, elementary Total	Teachers, elementary Men	Teachers, secondary Total	Teachers, secondary Men	TEACHERS' AVERAGE ANNUAL SALARIES Elementary	TEACHERS' AVERAGE ANNUAL SALARIES Secondary
Alabama	124	—	426,209	378,996	45,900	34,667	1,641	16,145	941	16,881	6,504	$ 7,298	$ 7,451
Alaska	29	3,160	51,881	27,964	3,450	4,207	231	2,349	573	1,472	830	13,538	13,622
Arizona	292	17,881	304,585	134,939	22,500	21,028	830	13,545	3,390	5,778	3,494	9,000	9,950
Arkansas	386	19,085	252,046	211,274	26,200	20,969	730	9,638	658	10,033	4,635	6,550	6,779
California	1,070	174,900	2,864,287	1,768,911	294,100	204,000	12,000	112,000	22,724	72,000	50,882	10,620	11,654
Colorado	181	22,462	307,292	242,768	32,204	27,342	1,663	11,865	1,685	11,537	6,345	8,200	8,325
Connecticut	169	—	454,130	208,075	36,000	36,590	2,567	18,700	3,740	12,942	7,118	9,381	9,823
Delaware	26	5,449	73,590	59,155	7,500	6,795	375	3,024	499	3,010	1,739	9,598	9,963
District of Columbia	1	5,780	90,433	55,271	4,900	8,524	611	4,357	536	3,129	1,189	—	—
Florida	67	51,716	781,703	646,193	75,000	71,810	3,367	32,418	3,829	30,153	14,645	8,668	8,941
Georgia	189	45,176	705,347	393,554	58,730	50,001	2,582	28,489	2,352	18,930	7,602	7,582	8,068
Hawaii	1	7,546	102,251	78,390	10,700	9,059	655	4,565	275	3,093	1,361	10,120	10,200
Idaho	115	7,846	92,841	89,492	12,500	8,958	771	3,695	480	4,006	2,243	6,938	7,187
Illinois	1,171	90,897	1,499,554	857,082	133,400	113,805	3,820	64,845	12,569	42,940	23,406	9,900	10,600
Indiana	317	49,053	749,063	482,395	73,600	57,554	3,550	26,000	4,200	25,204	14,618	9,050	9,500
Iowa	454	29,266	373,701	286,403	45,683	37,233	1,665	17,039	1,537	14,804	8,960	8,756	9,493
Kansas	311	25,601	356,992	155,316	34,400	28,800	1,431	13,066	1,501	12,818	7,243	7,906	8,151
Kentucky	192	28,376	455,979	261,226	38,100	33,661	1,660	18,100	2,600	11,811	5,477	7,060	7,370
Louisiana	66	36,066	508,881	333,484	44,000	40,550	2,050	21,500	2,500	17,000	7,200	8,180	8,540
Maine	235	10,406	176,804	67,866	14,800	12,010	590	7,380	1,530	3,790	2,300	7,920	8,530
Maryland	24	34,374	523,725	392,519	48,394	45,960	2,781	21,201	2,438	19,610	9,276	9,980	10,212
Massachusetts	380	45,092	649,517	518,196	67,000	58,041	4,000	26,948	3,748	24,493	14,493	9,503	9,730
Michigan	618	92,083	1,227,734	952,965	127,000	100,287	5,500	41,744	5,957	51,543	26,555	10,500	10,800
Minnesota	613	39,754	489,232	431,607	64,000	49,820	2,580	21,500	3,130	23,440	14,940	9,000	9,520
Mississippi	150	21,977	312,093	222,302	28,000	24,704	1,166	12,270	1,060	10,263	4,730	5,911	6,134
Missouri	639	40,199	684,486	354,991	56,400	48,644	3,101	29,941	5,954	13,411	7,416	8,218	8,561
Montana	671	8,532	107,336	69,376	11,500	9,775	375	5,400	900	3,500	2,300	7,774	8,679
Nebraska	1,265	16,820	187,150	141,960	21,740	18,031	870	8,961	498	8,200	4,000	7,640	8,680
Nevada	17	5,015	74,116	53,434	6,000	5,748	313	2,782	494	2,304	1,370	9,411	9,646
New Hampshire	157	6,951	94,624	64,132	9,420	8,215	417	3,935	564	3,190	1,789	8,164	8,459
New Jersey	578	59,100	978,120	503,880	84,000	84,920	4,420	41,831	9,621	29,069	16,569	9,875	10,250
New Mexico	89	12,180	152,947	128,425	16,100	13,210	850	6,090	1,000	5,530	3,150	8,214	8,214
New York	737	139,699	1,922,161	1,554,855	190,000	208,622	16,768	91,918	14,431	86,217	45,609	10,700	11,100
North Carolina	152	52,918	835,739	356,448	69,700	54,778	2,663	33,322	4,517	16,243	6,504	8,110	8,290
North Dakota	356	8,055	91,275	55,738	10,588	7,566	313	4,480	805	2,529	1,720	6,740	7,620
Ohio	631	—	1,698,298	727,345	147,273	113,500	5,800	56,559	8,342	48,121	26,948	8,489	9,249
Oklahoma	665	28,963	350,004	276,952	37,500	30,000	1,499	14,810	2,450	13,374	8,317	7,260	7,500
Oregon	346	21,864	280,636	198,891	33,281	25,675	1,560	12,000	2,628	9,700	5,965	9,123	9,533
Pennsylvania	590	91,696	1,260,000	1,098,100	153,300	120,000	4,900	55,900	12,100	52,900	30,900	9,200	9,400
Rhode Island	40	7,539	111,157	76,933	11,010	10,081	520	4,538	638	4,450	2,536	9,425	9,460
South Carolina	93	25,656	393,319	244,481	37,500	31,700	1,350	15,300	1,000	12,700	4,300	6,850	7,275
South Dakota	270	7,718	87,852	78,453	11,100	9,707	474	5,950	713	2,913	1,893	6,300	7,800
Tennessee	147	33,967	571,224	328,669	49,500	39,284	1,775	21,200	2,460	14,250	5,950	7,130	7,800
Texas	1,179	118,644	1,577,800	1,262,100	147,400	134,600	7,112	64,600	7,750	57,300	28,100	8,184	8,437
Utah	40	11,467	165,492	138,510	19,100	13,111	760	5,850	1,111	5,500	3,465	8,020	8,130
Vermont	251	5,534	63,708	39,422	5,850	6,463	429	3,027	423	2,555	1,447	8,120	8,940
Virginia	130	49,000	682,644	396,110	59,500	54,125	3,325	29,500	2,950	21,300	8,400	8,400	9,000
Washington	320	34,988	442,618	375,094	51,500	39,810	2,900	17,480	3,600	15,900	6,100	9,180	9,940
West Virginia	55	16,514	221,780	177,751	26,200	18,885	1,730	8,760	830	7,865	3,490	7,600	8,000
Wisconsin	452	41,532	585,889	407,847	66,753	51,216	2,164	25,958	4,933	23,094	14,318	9,320	10,000
Wyoming	130	—	46,509	40,377	5,400	5,005	228	2,341	384	2,280	1,443	8,530	8,860
Total U.S.	18,181	1,864,300	27,496,754	18,406,617	2,685,676	2,269,046	125,432	1,124,816	175,548	915,075	491,784	9,025	9,540

Kindergartens are included in the elementary schools; junior high schools, in the secondary schools.
Enrollment data show cumulative count of pupils registered at any time during the school year in each state.
All dollar amounts for Alaska should be reduced by about 30% to make purchasing power generally more comparable to data reported for other areas.
*Includes librarians, guidance and psychological personnel, and related instructional workers.
Sources: U.S. Department of Health, Education, and Welfare, Office of Education, *Fall 1970 Statistics of Public Schools;*
National Education Association, Research Division, *Estimates of School Statistics, 1970–71* (Copyright 1970. All rights reserved. Used by permission).

Private elementary and secondary day schools

fall 1971 estimates

State	ENROLLMENT Elementary	ENROLLMENT Secondary	CLASSROOM TEACHERS Elementary	CLASSROOM TEACHERS Secondary	State	ENROLLMENT Elementary	ENROLLMENT Secondary	CLASSROOM TEACHERS Elementary	CLASSROOM TEACHERS Secondary
Alabama	17,100	8,800	760	560	Montana	10,100	3,800	430	270
Alaska	1,200	500	80	60	Nebraska	32,300	13,100	1,400	920
Arizona	17,100	7,700	770	550	Nevada	3,900	1,200	160	60
Arkansas	7,600	3,300	380	230	New Hampshire	22,100	11,000	940	870
California	307,200	101,800	12,390	6,510	New Jersey	242,200	71,100	8,790	4,570
Colorado	27,600	10,400	1,300	820	New Mexico	14,900	3,200	720	230
Connecticut	75,500	41,300	3,380	3,280	New York	639,900	197,200	24,100	11,590
Delaware	14,000	3,600	600	270	North Carolina	15,700	4,000	850	350
District of Columbia	13,600	8,100	660	590	North Dakota	10,300	4,200	530	250
Florida	79,000	30,200	3,620	2,090	Ohio	276,600	87,700	9,870	4,730
Georgia	18,500	10,000	1,020	820	Oklahoma	9,100	3,000	500	210
Hawaii	17,400	10,700	740	670	Oregon	24,800	8,800	1,070	610
Idaho	5,800	1,600	260	110	Pennsylvania	418,400	146,200	15,070	8,270
Illinois	367,700	114,700	13,720	6,240	Rhode Island	35,000	10,100	1,570	650
Indiana	97,200	26,200	3,930	1,570	South Carolina	15,500	5,900	910	440
Iowa	61,600	22,400	2,840	1,260	South Dakota	9,700	3,200	480	270
Kansas	33,100	9,900	1,570	660	Tennessee	21,600	12,800	1,240	1,000
Kentucky	54,800	21,100	2,450	1,370	Texas	87,200	23,800	4,550	1,740
Louisiana	97,300	31,600	4,270	1,890	Utah	3,300	1,000	140	80
Maine	15,500	10,000	750	810	Vermont	8,500	7,200	420	580
Maryland	96,200	31,200	4,090	2,310	Virginia	39,500	18,100	2,150	1,500
Massachusetts	162,900	71,700	6,620	4,330	Washington	38,200	14,400	1,640	910
Michigan	193,400	57,900	7,220	3,330	West Virginia	9,300	4,200	400	290
Minnesota	101,900	27,600	4,560	1,820	Wisconsin	186,600	38,300	8,120	2,420
Mississippi	15,200	4,900	840	360	Wyoming	2,700	400	140	20
Missouri	124,200	38,900	4,990	2,660	Total U.S.	4,200,000	1,400,000	170,000	88,000

Data exclude subcollegiate departments of institutions of higher education and residential schools for exceptional children.
Source: U.S. Department of Health, Education, and Welfare, Office of Education, *Digest of Educational Statistics.*

Universities and colleges

Selected list of four-year schools, 1971

Institution	Location	Year founded	Total students	Faculty	Bound library volumes	Endowment fund
ALABAMA						
Alabama A. & M. U.	Normal	1875	2,286	155	97,000	—
Alabama State U.	Montgomery	1874	2,524	106	123,000	—
Athens	Athens	1822	1,077	56	55,000	$1,379,016
Auburn U.	Auburn	1856	14,229	850	683,000	8,336,597
Birmingham-Southern	Birmingham	1856	1,040	85	97,000	6,694,000
Florence State U.	Florence	1873	3,235	145	105,000	—
Jacksonville State U.	Jacksonville	1883	5,645	249	200,000	—
Livingston U.	Livingston	1835	1,746	80	60,000	—
Samford U.	Birmingham	1842	2,663	175	240,476	3,134,661
Troy State U.	Troy	1887	3,750	139	40,000	250,000
Tuskegee Inst.	Tuskegee Institute	1881	2,918	253	186,552	15,417
U. of Alabama	University	1831	13,017	830	825,000	12,660,000
U. of Montevallo	Montevallo	1896	2,452	125	112,000	680,000
U. of South Alabama	Mobile	1963	5,221	232	145,000	101,000
ALASKA						
U. of Alaska	College	1917	2,265	170	250,000	1,918,000
ARIZONA						
Arizona State U.	Tempe	1885	23,341	1,013	927,000	787,000
Northern Arizona U.	Flagstaff	1899	9,100	420	280,000	3,000,000
U. of Arizona	Tucson	1885	25,827	1,753	1,608,348	3,906,272
ARKANSAS						
Ag., Mech. & Normal	Pine Bluff	1873	2,656	171	47,455	—
Arkansas Polytech.	Russellville	1909	2,497	111	62,078	—
Arkansas State U.	State University	1909	6,098	297	268,000	—
Harding	Searcy	1924	1,916	105	100,495	12,664
Henderson State	Arkadelphia	1929	3,350	140	120,000	—
Ouachita Baptist U.	Arkadelphia	1886	1,246	86	80,399	1,842,000
Southern State	Magnolia	1909	2,085	113	63,730	—
State Col. of Arkansas	Conway	1907	4,505	180	118,000	—
U. of Arkansas	Fayetteville	1871	10,800	780	560,000	—
U. of A. at Little Rock	Little Rock	1927	4,003	160	100,000	6,000,000
U. of A. at Monticello	College Heights	1909	1,873	100	50,000	—
CALIFORNIA						
Art Center Col. of Design	Los Angeles	1930	1,100	70	8,500	727,065
Biola	La Mirada	1908	1,444	84	100,000	—
California Arts & Crafts	Oakland	1907	1,562	84	20,000	87,000
California Inst. of Tech.	Pasadena	1891	1,512	654	221,860	107,545,000
California Lutheran	Thousand Oaks	1959	1,284	81	64,000	152,000
Cal. State, Bakersfield	Bakersfield	1965	1,023	77	—	. . .
Cal. State, Dominguez Hills	Dominguez Hills	1962	3,832	180	101,744	—
Cal. State at Fullerton	Fullerton	1959	14,149	629	336,277	—
Cal. State, Hayward	Hayward	1959	11,470	658	347,000	—
Cal. State, Long Beach	Long Beach	1949	27,536	1,150	445,000	—
Cal. State at Los Angeles	Los Angeles	1947	23,700	922	590,000	—
Cal. State, San Bernardino	San Bernardino	1967	2,316	121	140,000	—
Cal. State Polytech.	Pomona	1956	8,073	400	160,000	—
Cal. State Polytech.	San Luis Obispo	1901	12,386	716	320,000	—
Chapman	Orange	1861	3,519	270	77,000	1,120,000
Chico State	Chico	1887	10,110	560	295,000	1,426,000
Claremont Colleges	Claremont	—	4,520	332	687,409	63,164,808
Col. of Notre Dame	Belmont	1851	1,510	57	67,000	—
Fresno State	Fresno	1911	13,647	784	313,451	. . .
Golden Gate	San Francisco	1901	3,099	150	54,000	502,000
Humboldt State	Arcata	1913	5,570	340	135,737	—
Loma Linda U.	Riverside	1905	2,922	1,200	282,000	2,894,999
Loyola U.	Los Angeles	1911	3,657	179	290,000	2,999,400
‡Mt. St. Mary's	Los Angeles	1925	1,169	77	105,000	426,000
Naval Postgraduate Sch.	Monterey	1909	1,800	265	281,000	—
Northrop Inst. of Tech.	Inglewood	1942	1,982	106	126,000	370,000
Occidental	Los Angeles	1887	1,869	120	244,000	—
Pacific Union	Angwin	1882	1,981	135	87,000	—
Pasadena	Pasadena	1902	1,260	57	108,000	—
Pepperdine U.	Los Angeles	1937	2,430	140	100,000	2,500,000
Sacramento State	Sacramento	1947	16,808	740	250,000	—
San Diego State	San Diego	1897	25,572	1,575	680,000	—
San Fernando Valley State	Northridge	1958	22,500	1,450	500,000	—
San Francisco State	San Francisco	1899	17,600	1,018	429,000	204,445
San Jose State	San Jose	1857	24,574	1,200	542,000	450,000
Sonoma State	Rohnert Park	1960	3,833	225	120,000	—
Stanford U.	Stanford	1885	12,566	1,289	3,447,000	265,195,000
Stanislaus State	Turlock	1960	2,643	150	110,000	—
U. of California						
U. of C., Berkeley	Berkeley	1868	28,525	1,741	3,750,000	7,330,000
U. of C., Davis	Davis	1905	13,362	825	991,908	—
U. of C., Irvine	Irvine	1964	2,600	252	. . .	—
U. of C., Los Angeles	Los Angeles	1919	29,093	1,824	3,000,000	—
U. of C., Riverside	Riverside	1868	5,991	545	585,000	—
U. of C., San Diego	La Jolla	1912	4,838	450	. . .	—
U. of C., Santa Barbara	Santa Barbara	1944	13,644	722	800,000	—
U. of C., Santa Cruz	Santa Cruz	1965	3,772	324	325,000	—
U. of Pacific	Stockton	1851	5,064	425	243,735	5,018,000
U. of Redlands	Redlands	1907	1,993	135	171,000	13,750,000
U. of San Francisco	San Francisco	1855	6,831	320	312,000	3,160,000
U. of Santa Clara	Santa Clara	1851	5,983	282	277,000	11,866,758
U. of Southern California	Los Angeles	1880	20,593	1,908	1,393,698	37,218,160
West Coast U.	Los Angeles	1909	1,350	76	7,000	—
Whittier	Whittier	1901	2,226	127	90,000	4,500,000
Woodbury	Los Angeles	1884	2,143	76	16,000	—
COLORADO						
Adams State	Alamosa	1921	2,978	129	130,000	—
Colorado	Colorado Springs	1874	1,792	119	250,000	9,518,000
Colorado Sch. of Mines	Golden	1874	1,727	140	134,000	$ 410,000
Colorado State U.	Fort Collins	1870	17,047	784	700,000	1,291,651
Fort Lewis	Durango	1911	2,078	100	85,000	90,000
Regis	Denver	1877	1,424	86	85,000	750,000
Southern Colorado State	Pueblo	1933	7,367	310	120,000	—
†U.S. Air Force Academy	USAF Academy	1954	4,128	651	312,572	—
U. of Colorado	Boulder	1876	31,230	1,582	1,408,709	7,908,000
U. of Denver	Denver	1864	9,350	593	671,074	15,494,000
U. of Northern Colorado	Greeley	1890	10,547	459	316,000	175,000
Western State	Gunnison	1901	3,144	140	110,000	—
CONNECTICUT						
Central Connecticut State	New Britain	1849	12,496	556	184,820	—
Connecticut	New London	1911	1,767	178	265,000	6,913,780
Eastern Connecticut State	Willimantic	1889	2,022	120	70,000	—
†Fairfield U.	Fairfield	1942	3,148	180	102,000	—
Quinnipiac	Hamden	1929	2,936	160	70,000	—
Sacred Heart U.	Bridgeport	1963	2,074	81	60,000	—
Southern Connecticut St.	New Haven	1893	12,513	543	250,000	—
Trinity	Hartford	1823	1,875	156	485,000	17,404,000
U. of Bridgeport	Bridgeport	1927	8,938	402	191,000	4,500,000
U. of Connecticut	Storrs	1881	23,832	1,200	978,000	1,686,000
U. of Hartford	West Hartford	1877	9,605	401	170,000	4,611,000
U. of New Haven	West Haven	1920	4,713	264	65,000	100,000
Wesleyan U.	Middletown	1831	1,817	202	632,000	123,422,000
Western Connecticut St.	Danbury	1903	3,605	235	81,212	—
Yale U.	New Haven	1701	9,214	2,800	5,600,000	495,877,000
DELAWARE						
Delaware State	Dover	1891	1,669	85	72,000	106,000
U. of Delaware	Newark	1833	15,773	616	800,000	80,000,000
DISTRICT OF COLUMBIA						
American U.	Washington	1893	15,326	485	398,000	4,433,000
Catholic U. of America	Washington	1887	6,161	492	789,000	7,743,000
D. C. Teachers	Washington	1851	2,856	121	96,000	—
George Washington U.	Washington	1821	14,998	961	517,339	10,732,000
Georgetown U.	Washington	1789	8,074	591	704,000	25,534,000
Howard U.	Washington	1867	9,209	899	633,957	10,266,000
FLORIDA						
‡Barry	Miami	1940	1,260	96	74,000	169,000
Bethune-Cookman	Daytona Beach	1872	1,200	58	60,000	1,485,000
Florida A. & M. U.	Tallahassee	1887	4,543	274	196,000	—
Florida Atlantic U.	Boca Raton	1961	5,249	316	300,000	930,338
Florida Inst. of Tech.	Melbourne	1958	1,971	99	54,866	18,201
Florida Southern	Lakeland	1885	1,455	110	121,755	8,199,897
Florida State U.	Tallahassee	1857	15,513	1,150	872,025	84,000
Jacksonville U.	Jacksonville	1934	3,137	150	140,000	1,600,000
Rollins	Winter Park	1885	2,819	132	153,022	8,565,000
Stetson U.	DeLand	1883	2,864	132	201,569	5,728,754
U. of Florida	Gainesville	1853	22,255	2,424	1,500,000	5,600,000
U. of Miami	Coral Gables	1925	18,220	1,007	950,000	29,113,085
U. of South Florida	Tampa	1960	17,922	750	275,000	195,000
U. of Tampa	Tampa	1931	2,424	95	110,000	1,000,000
U. of West Florida	Pensacola	1963	3,206	222	277,000	—
GEORGIA						
Albany State	Albany	1903	1,942	135	54,000	—
Armstrong State	Savannah	1935	2,406	101	85,000	—
Augusta	Augusta	1925	2,672	93	91,000	—
Berry	Mount Berry	1926	1,044	71	72,000	11,263,893
Clark	Atlanta	1869	1,007	98	39,491	—
Emory U.	Atlanta	1836	5,126	758	927,542	84,674,060
Fort Valley State	Fort Valley	1895	2,247	105	91,000	85,442
Georgia	Milledgeville	1889	1,923	110	100,000	—
Georgia Inst. of Tech.	Atlanta	1885	7,113	469	560,000	2,329,000
Georgia Southern	Statesboro	1908	5,719	309	160,000	—
Georgia Southwestern	Americus	1926	2,416	135	53,000	—
Georgia State U.	Atlanta	1913	14,521	671	302,000	19,000
Mercer U.	Macon	1833	1,929	110	180,000	9,900,000
Morris Brown	Atlanta	1881	1,142	96	22,000	1,004,000
North Georgia	Dahlonega	1873	1,210	65	90,000	—
Oglethorpe	Atlanta	1835	1,042	46	39,000	1,700,000
Savannah State	Savannah	1890	2,331	91	72,000	—
U. of Georgia	Athens	1785	21,181	1,600	1,150,000	4,470,000
Valdosta State	Valdosta	1906	2,888	153	97,000	—
West Georgia	Carrollton	1933	5,503	284	112,000	—
GUAM						
U. of Guam	Agana	1952	2,349	184	81,000	—
HAWAII						
Church Col. of Hawaii	Laie	1955	1,307	70	75,000	56,000
U. of Hawaii	Honolulu	1907	21,090	1,364	722,290	795,000
IDAHO						
Boise State	Boise	1932	6,057	301	125,000	—
Idaho State U.	Pocatello	1901	6,436	279	200,000	45,000
Lewis-Clark State	Lewiston	1955	1,285	71	56,000	208,000
Northwest Nazarene	Nampa	1913	1,118	67	62,000	150,000
U. of Idaho	Moscow	1889	6,681	492	687,000	12,712,332

†Men's schools, ‡women's schools; the others are coeducational.

Universities and colleges (continued)

Institution	Location	Year founded	Total students	Faculty	Bound library volumes	Endowment fund
ILLINOIS						
Augustana	Rock Island	1860	2,072	97	151,000	$ 3,849,844
Aurora	Aurora	1893	1,282	59	65,000	289,500
Bradley U.	Peoria	1897	5,723	385	198,000	4,875
Chicago State	Chicago	1869	5,911	309	149,000	—
Concordia Teachers	River Forest	1864	1,465	110	96,000	450,000
De Paul U.	Chicago	1898	9,194	347	294,643	1,770,432
Eastern Illinois U.	Charleston	1895	8,652	522	209,000	—
Elmhurst	Elmhurst	1871	1,520	112	86,000	990,000
Illinois Inst. of Tech.	Chicago	1892	8,164	709	1,100,000	12,315,000
Illinois State U.	Normal	1857	17,549	1,289	475,000	—
Illinois Wesleyan U.	Bloomington	1850	1,693	125	100,000	5,362,000
Knox	Galesburg	1837	1,418	100	147,000	11,600,000
Lake Forest	Lake Forest	1857	1,365	100	120,000	7,930,000
Lewis	Lockport	1930	2,400	115	51,000	—
Loyola U.	Chicago	1870	14,469	920	550,000	17,871,000
Millikin U.	Decatur	1901	1,440	125	115,000	2,289,000
Monmouth	Monmouth	1853	1,320	81	125,000	2,300,000
‡Mundelein	Chicago	1930	1,245	73	82,000	392,934
National Col. of Ed.	Evanston	1886	2,599	81	68,000	628,000
North Park	Chicago	1891	1,422	81	124,000	1,654,000
Northeastern Illinois St.	Chicago	1869	8,409	420	170,295	—
Northern Illinois U.	DeKalb	1895	22,817	1,408	489,000	—
Northwestern U.	Evanston	1851	15,571	1,345	2,289,708	191,809,000
Olivet Nazarene	Kankakee	1907	1,844	98	80,000	57,000
Quincy	Quincy	1860	1,906	134	150,000	893,000
Rockford	Rockford	1847	1,433	120	74,000	3,100,000
Roosevelt U.	Chicago	1945	6,822	240	250,500	1,402,000
Rosary	River Forest	1901	1,237	95	125,000	700,000
Schools of the Art Inst.	Chicago	1866	1,500	83	89,000	3,408,000
Southern Illinois U.	Carbondale	1869	37,543	2,843	1,100,000	—
at Edwardsville	Edwardsville	1869	13,700	575	456,411	—
U. of Chicago	Chicago	1892	9,151	1,192	2,997,647	261,272,000
U. of Illinois	Urbana	1868	38,069	5,648	4,416,330	17,534,879
U. of I. at Chicago Circle	Chicago	...	18,996	1,457	368,032	—
Western Illinois U.	Macomb	1899	13,247	857	285,000	—
Wheaton	Wheaton	1860	1,948	145	155,000	10,775,000
INDIANA						
Anderson	Anderson	1917	1,803	106	112,000	527,000
Ball State U.	Muncie	1918	16,647	730	456,000	—
Butler U.	Indianapolis	1855	4,403	170	209,000	26,000,000
De Pauw U.	Greencastle	1837	2,370	162	293,383	14,821,000
Earlham	Richmond	1847	1,158	83	168,000	7,102,418
Goshen	Goshen	1894	1,283	76	105,000	307,000
Hanover	Hanover	1827	1,004	74	140,000	8,864,000
Indiana Central	Indianapolis	1902	2,456	86	64,000	1,113,000
Indiana State U.	Terre Haute	1865	13,533	806	462,000	572,000
Indiana U.	Bloomington	1820	58,566	2,934	3,054,000	10,600,000
Manchester	North Manchester	1889	1,510	83	106,000	1,600,000
Marian	Indianapolis	1851	1,008	80	75,000	120,000
Purdue U.	Lafayette	1869	38,827	2,203	1,000,000	19,200,000
Rose Polytech. Inst.	Terre Haute	1874	1,257	66	38,000	4,479,000
St. Francis	Fort Wayne	1890	2,228	75	66,000	—
St. Joseph	Rensselaer	1889	1,366	90	146,000	1,050,000
St. Mary's	Notre Dame	1844	1,652	118	114,380	896,000
‡Taylor U.	Upland	1846	1,426	79	89,000	765,000
Tri State	Angola	1884	1,845	110	74,000	761,000
U. of Evansville	Evansville	1854	5,353	227	120,000	3,350,000
U. of Notre Dame	Notre Dame	1842	8,156	745	924,000	60,000,000
†Valparaiso U.	Valparaiso	1859	4,651	263	220,000	2,085,000
IOWA						
Briar Cliff	Sioux City	1930	1,131	54	62,462	131,246
Central U. of Iowa	Pella	1853	1,230	86	79,000	1,293,282
Coe	Cedar Rapids	1851	1,108	80	124,009	7,404,144
Drake U.	Des Moines	1881	7,606	305	321,486	4,549,443
Graceland	Lamoni	1895	1,296	83	70,000	527,000
Grinnell	Grinnell	1846	1,261	112	190,000	10,589,000
Iowa State U.	Ames	1858	19,620	1,149	816,000	3,751,000
Loras	Dubuque	1839	1,500	98	180,000	—
Luther	Decorah	1861	2,025	122	176,000	1,782,000
Marycrest	Davenport	1939	1,062	67	80,000	336,000
Morningside	Sioux City	1894	1,336	75	100,000	2,654,000
Parsons	Fairfield	1875	1,669	73	131,000	653,000
U. of Dubuque	Dubuque	1852	1,308	75	156,000	3,075,265
U. of Iowa	Iowa City	1847	20,604	1,719	1,559,393	4,615,307
U. of Northern Iowa	Cedar Falls	1867	10,534	513	300,000	—
Upper Iowa U.	Fayette	1857	1,166	62	89,000	1,002,403
Wartburg	Waverly	1852	1,404	81	90,000	350,000
Westmar	La Mars	1890	1,074	68	76,000	712,000
KANSAS						
Fort Hays Kansas State	Hays	1902	5,442	226	225,000	615,996
Friends U.	Wichita	1898	1,005	59	50,000	950,000
Kansas State	Pittsburg	1903	5,679	311	322,000	452,000
Kansas State Teachers	Emporia	1863	6,982	300	320,000	1,000,000
Kansas State U.	Manhattan	1863	13,847	748	600,000	5,331,000
U. of Kansas	Lawrence	1866	19,393	1,119	1,600,000	32,740,119
Washburn U.	Topeka	1865	4,784	171	108,000	470,000
Wichita State U.	Wichita	1895	12,296	391	276,000	1,530,000
KENTUCKY						
Asbury	Wilmore	1890	1,044	69	69,000	5,100,000
Bellarmine-Ursuline	Louisville	1968	1,612	81	62,000	—
Berea	Berea	1855	1,399	111	166,000	43,000,000
Brescia	Owensboro	1925	1,017	61	50,000	300,000
Cumberland	Williamsburg	1889	1,742	63	54,000	915,000
Eastern Kentucky U.	Richmond	1906	9,602	490	340,000	—
Georgetown	Georgetown	1829	1,310	90	100,000	$1,604,156
Kentucky State	Frankfort	1886	1,754	101	67,000	—
Morehead State U.	Morehead	1922	6,030	325	230,000	—
Murray State U.	Murray	1922	7,053	378	250,000	—
Thomas More	Ft. Mitchell	1921	2,227	92	67,000	63,500
U. of Kentucky	Lexington	1865	16,201	1,330	1,000,000	639,000
U. of Louisville	Louisville	1798	9,668	800	598,000	9,647,161
Western Kentucky U.	Bowling Green	1906	10,737	517	425,000	312,000
LOUISIANA						
Centenary	Shreveport	1825	1,140	98	89,000	6,549,000
Grambling	Grambling	1901	3,674	198	84,285	201,160
Louisiana Tech U.	Ruston	1894	7,980	390	160,000	—
Louisiana St. U. System	Baton Rouge	1860	34,161	2,037	688,000	1,715,309
L.S.U. in Baton Rouge	Baton Rouge	1860	18,887	1,068	1,289,720	688,000
L.S.U. in New Orleans	New Orleans	1958	11,464	320	295,000	—
Loyola U.	New Orleans	1912	4,923	275	245,000	—
McNeese State	Lake Charles	1939	4,844	245	110,000	—
Northeast Louisiana U.	Monroe	1931	8,031	327	155,871	—
Northwestern State U.	Natchitoches	1884	5,947	320	170,000	—
Nicholls State U.	Thibodaux	1948	5,158	203	108,892	—
Southeastern La. U.	Hammond	1925	5,452	262	120,000	—
Tulane U.	New Orleans	1834	8,453	956	1,058,452	41,419,000
U. of Southwestern La.	Lafayette	1898	10,217	508	350,000	—
Xavier U.	New Orleans	1925	1,207	87	98,000	—
MAINE						
Bates	Lewiston	1864	1,129	84	145,889	10,274,473
Colby	Waterville	1813	1,561	120	300,000	17,140,444
U. of Maine	Orono	1865	8,315	658	450,000	6,501,000
U. of M. at Farmington	Farmington	1864	1,289	81	46,000	244,181
U. of M., Portland-Gorham	Portland	1957	9,227	215	231,000	—
MARYLAND						
Bowie State	Bowie	1867	2,297	75	60,000	—
Coppin State	Baltimore	1900	1,205	83	55,000	—
Frostburg State	Frostburg	1898	2,316	130	80,000	—
‡Goucher	Baltimore	1885	1,106	95	142,000	9,679,139
Johns Hopkins U.	Baltimore	1876	9,779	952	1,985,075	92,475,523
Loyola	Baltimore	1852	2,806	126	85,000	2,726,000
Morgan State	Baltimore	1867	4,900	259	120,000	—
Mt. St. Mary's	Emmitsburg	1808	1,129	87	80,000	570,000
Salisbury State	Salisbury	1925	1,535	71	98,000	—
Towson State	Baltimore	1866	6,247	377	138,000	—
†U.S. Naval Academy	Annapolis	1845	4,000	639	210,000	—
U. of Maryland	College Park	1807	54,129	4,784	1,191,218	10,407,000
Western Maryland	Westminster	1867	1,936	96	88,000	3,557,000
MASSACHUSETTS						
American International	Springfield	1885	1,894	100	87,000	969,000
†Amherst	Amherst	1821	1,221	141	438,000	72,000,000
Assumption	Worcester	1904	1,575	80	110,000	—
Babson	Babson Park	1919	1,657	42	51,000	5,000,000
Bentley	Waltham	1917	1,900	109	—	—
Boston	Chestnut Hill	1863	10,956	688	815,000	5,476,233
Boston State	Boston	1852	7,953	418	88,000	—
Boston U.	Boston	1869	25,124	2,700	755,500	20,515,000
Brandeis U.	Waltham	1947	2,286	340	416,000	19,859,000
Bridgewater State	Bridgewater	1840	3,303	216	70,000	—
Clark U.	Worcester	1887	3,212	260	300,000	11,500,000
Emerson	Boston	1880	1,625	130	40,000	224,317
‡Emmanuel	Boston	1919	1,449	110	86,217	—
Fitchburg State	Fitchburg	1894	2,348	170	68,946	—
Framingham State	Framingham	1839	4,090	146	85,000	—
Harvard U.	Cambridge	1636	14,967	8,041	8,279,000	733,060,000
‡Radcliffe	Cambridge	1879	1,244	—	166,245	24,458,289
†Holy Cross	Worcester	1843	2,493	200	280,000	5,000,000
Lowell State	Lowell	1894	2,288	151	75,000	—
Lowell Tech. Inst.	Lowell	1895	6,544	230	125,000	159,000
Mass. Inst. of Tech.	Cambridge	1861	7,799	982	1,221,000	158,515,000
Merrimack	North Andover	1947	2,036	122	65,000	420,000
‡Mt. Holyoke	South Hadley	1837	1,921	11	322,500	33,455,000
North Adams State	North Adams	1894	1,255	65	52,000	—
Northeastern U.	Boston	1898	35,542	1,158	295,000	24,682
Salem State	Salem	1854	5,989	212	71,000	—
‡Simmons	Boston	1899	2,216	304	143,000	9,754,000
‡Smith	Northampton	1871	2,542	240	770,000	50,050,800
Southeastern Mass. U.	North Dartmouth	1895	3,368	220	120,000	115,000
Springfield	Springfield	1885	2,644	112	100,000	5,376,959
Stonehill	North Easton	1948	1,658	75	68,000	—
Suffolk U.	Boston	1906	5,235	148	122,031	3,655,000
Tufts U.	Medford	1852	5,266	1,824	480,000	26,416,000
U. of Massachusetts	Amherst	1863	19,118	1,195	967,000	1,259,000
‡Wellesley	Wellesley	1870	1,796	192	480,000	84,602,000
Western New England	Springfield	1919	3,399	129	56,000	181,000
Westfield State	Westfield	1839	3,536	150	58,000	—
‡Wheaton	Norton	1834	1,142	103	143,000	5,807,000
Williams	Williamstown	1793	1,404	162	350,000	51,136,000
Worcester Polytech. Inst.,	Worcester	1865	2,341	170	94,000	24,700,000
Worcester State	Worcester	1874	3,858	168	91,000	—
MICHIGAN						
Adrian	Adrian	1859	1,562	97	88,000	2,500,000
Albion	Albion	1835	1,864	133	165,000	11,203,000
Alma	Alma	1886	1,358	75	84,000	2,426,050
Andrews U.	Berrien Springs	1874	2,061	167	234,548	466,000
Aquinas	Grand Rapids	1923	1,473	73	75,000	9,000
Calvin	Grand Rapids	1876	3,437	180	222,000	—

Institution	Location	Year founded	Total students	Faculty	Bound library volumes	Endowment fund
Central Michigan U.	Mt. Pleasant	1892	13,246	653	340,000	$ 143,000
Detroit Inst. of Tech.	Detroit	1891	1,125	75	50,000	100,250
Eastern Michigan U.	Ypsilanti	1849	19,965	774	316,000	472,000
Ferris State	Big Rapids	1884	8,439	400	192,568	—
General Motors Inst.	Flint	1919	3,034	230	30,000	—
Grand Valley State	Allendale	1960	3,301	139	120,000	638,285
Hillsdale	Hillsdale	1844	1,144	68	52,000	4,403,000
Hope	Holland	1866	2,071	139	135,000	2,200,000
Kalamazoo	Kalamazoo	1833	1,360	80	160,000	13,530,000
Lake Superior State	Sault Ste. Marie	1946	1,668	92	45,000	—
Lawrence Inst. of Tech.	Southfield	1932	4,333	110	40,000	—
Mercy	Detroit	1941	1,605	100	65,000	—
Michigan State U.	East Lansing	1855	40,511	2,561	1,638,000	9,882,000
Michigan Tech. U.	Houghton	1885	4,961	295	250,000	618,000
Northern Michigan U.	Marquette	1899	8,272	340	177,068	—
Oakland U.	Rochester	...	7,006	292	165,000	499,000
Saginaw Valley	University Center	1964	1,839	81	53,000	418,000
U. of Detroit	Detroit	1877	9,638	...	375,000	3,495,000
U. of Michigan	Ann Arbor	1817	39,661	3,069	4,256,597	61,187,000
Wayne State U.	Detroit	1868	35,655	1,650	1,277,000	3,539,100
Western Michigan U.	Kalamazoo	1903	21,713	1,030	692,000	40,000

MINNESOTA

Institution	Location	Year founded	Total students	Faculty	Bound library volumes	Endowment fund
Augsburg	Minneapolis	1869	1,697	101	113,000	538,000
Bemidji State	Bemidji	1913	4,823	283	179,000	—
Bethel	St. Paul	1871	1,107	72	65,000	262,000
Carleton	Northfield	1866	1,521	115	209,000	23,547,000
Concordia	Moorhead	1891	2,360	159	141,000	1,136,000
Gustavus Adolphus	St. Peter	1862	1,782	126	125,000	1,689,954
Hamline U.	St. Paul	1854	1,249	91	120,000	11,100,000
Macalester	St. Paul	1885	2,093	179	200,000	29,070,084
Mankato State	Mankato	1867	13,000	715	335,000	—
Moorhead State	Moorhead	1887	5,351	340	140,000	—
‡St. Catherine	St. Paul	1905	1,339	104	177,000	1,462,000
St. Cloud State	St. Cloud	1869	9,580	548	243,000	12,000
†St. John's U.	Collegeville	1857	1,604	123	220,000	5,768,000
St. Olaf	Northfield	1874	2,674	194	241,000	3,520,000
‡St. Teresa	Winona	1907	1,047	119	103,000	806,000
†St. Thomas	St. Paul	1885	2,500	138	150,000	6,700,000
U. of Minnesota	Minneapolis	1851	76,247	3,000	3,000,000	31,710,751
U. of M., Duluth	Duluth	1902	5,568	297	133,000	—
Winona State	Winona	1858	4,080	231	106,000	—

MISSISSIPPI

Institution	Location	Year founded	Total students	Faculty	Bound library volumes	Endowment fund
Alcorn A. & M.	Lorman	1871	2,520	120	65,000	—
Delta State	Cleveland	1924	2,535	117	75,000	—
Jackson State	Jackson	1877	4,665	254	80,000	—
Mississippi	Clinton	1826	2,372	108	125,000	2,188,000
‡Mississippi State	Columbus	1884	2,657	139	159,000	—
Mississippi State U.	State College	1878	8,955	592	366,000	466,270
Mississippi Valley State	Itta Bena	1946	2,497	158	43,000	—
U. of Mississippi	University	1848	7,376	446	490,000	1,543,415
U. of Southern Mississippi	Hattiesburg	1910	7,917	500	300,000	—

MISSOURI

Institution	Location	Year founded	Total students	Faculty	Bound library volumes	Endowment fund
Central Missouri State	Warrensburg	1871	12,610	550	275,000	—
Drury	Springfield	1873	2,390	161	109,000	3,597,000
Evangel	Springfield	1955	1,120	59	60,000	—
Harris Teachers	St. Louis	1857	1,344	70	44,000	—
Lincoln U.	Jefferson City	1866	2,411	134	91,000	—
Missouri Southern	Joplin	1949	3,185	120	67,000	—
Missouri Western	St. Joseph	1915	2,884	130	35,000	—
Northeast Missouri State	Kirksville	1867	6,270	232	150,000	—
Northwest Missouri State	Maryville	1905	5,530	260	125,000	—
Rockhurst	Kansas City	1910	2,469	142	88,000	1,023,022
St. Louis U.	St. Louis	1818	10,843	1,238	961,000	24,096,855
Southeast Missouri State	Cape Girardeau	1873	7,188	343	159,000	—
Southwest Baptist	Bolivar	1878	1,131	65	60,000	81,000
Southwest Missouri State	Springfield	1906	8,564	375	175,000	—
‡Stephens	Columbia	1833	2,141	168	95,000	2,100,000
U. of Missouri—Columbia	Columbia	1839	21,681	1,492	1,541,000	6,663,000
U. of M. at Kansas City	Kansas City	1929	9,515	623	418,000	5,391,000
U. of M. at Rolla	Rolla	1870	6,089	415	153,000	658,000
U. of M. at St. Louis	St. Louis	1963	9,681	347	165,000	2,000
Washington U.	St. Louis	1853	11,259	1,149	1,144,000	114,118,000
Webster	St. Louis	1915	1,545	75	30,000	—
‡William Woods	Fulton	1870	1,147	56	106,000	820,301

MONTANA

Institution	Location	Year founded	Total students	Faculty	Bound library volumes	Endowment fund
Carroll	Helena	1909	1,029	72	50,000	550,000
Eastern Montana	Billings	1927	3,771	154	122,000	—
Great Falls	Great Falls	1932	1,165	50	47,085	428,000
Montana State U.	Bozeman	1893	8,187	400	525,320	3,239,003
Northern Montana	Havre	1929	1,439	93	50,000	—
U. of Montana	Missoula	1893	8,393	489	525,000	1,521,000
Western Montana	Dillon	1883	1,072	49	42,000	—

NEBRASKA

Institution	Location	Year founded	Total students	Faculty	Bound library volumes	Endowment fund
Chadron State	Chadron	1911	2,469	95	96,501	—
Concordia Teachers	Seward	1894	1,685	115	71,000	116,000
Creighton U.	Omaha	1878	4,129	375	293,153	7,530,000
Kearney State	Kearney	1905	5,870	243	147,000	195,000
Nebraska Wesleyan U.	Lincoln	1887	1,119	110	100,000	3,622,000
Peru State	Peru	1867	1,117	50	90,000	65,000
U. of Nebraska	Lincoln	1869	20,810	1,020	1,000,000	10,386,000
U. of N. at Omaha	Omaha	1908	13,185	374	261,000	—
Wayne State	Wayne	1891	2,972	135	96,000	—

NEVADA

Institution	Location	Year founded	Total students	Faculty	Bound library volumes	Endowment fund
U. of Nevada—Las Vegas	Las Vegas	1964	5,782	202	214,661	—
U. of Nevada—Reno	Reno	1874	9,522	342	420,000	$ 4,252,000

NEW HAMPSHIRE

Institution	Location	Year founded	Total students	Faculty	Bound library volumes	Endowment fund
†Dartmouth	Hanover	1769	3,143	280	1,000,000	147,504,000
Franklin Pierce	Rindge	1962	1,043	74	31,000	66,000
Keene State	Keene	1909	2,014	125	80,000	—
New England	Henniker	1946	1,037	89	50,000	139,963
Plymouth State	Plymouth	1870	2,064	131	101,000	—
†St. Anselm's	Manchester	1889	1,615	141	90,000	—
U. of New Hampshire	Durham	1866	8,835	538	577,759	4,779,682

NEW JERSEY

Institution	Location	Year founded	Total students	Faculty	Bound library volumes	Endowment fund
Drew U.	Madison	1866	1,558	123	326,000	11,684,000
Fairleigh Dickinson U.	Rutherford	1941	20,111	878	370,000	10,680,674
Glassboro State	Glassboro	1923	10,123	366	175,000	—
Jersey City State	Jersey City	1927	9,247	475	100,000	—
Monmouth	West Long Branch	1933	6,128	232	125,000	1,331,056
Montclair State	Upper Montclair	1908	11,178	427	158,000	168,000
Newark Engineering	Newark	1881	6,429	315	71,000	197,000
Newark State	Union	1855	12,059	351	126,000	—
Paterson State	Wayne	1855	7,139	407	175,000	—
Princeton U.	Princeton	1746	5,025	778	2,567,000	254,080,584
Rider	Trenton	1865	5,665	205	200,000	3,229,735
St. Peter's	Jersey City	1872	4,600	197	110,000	500,000
Seton Hall U.	South Orange	1856	9,469	605	300,593	3,923,000
State U. of Rutgers	New Brunswick	1766	33,579	2,590	1,791,526	27,859,608
Stevens Inst. of Tech.	Hoboken	1870	2,650	201	83,000	39,000,000
Trenton State	Trenton	1855	13,000	355	200,000	—
Upsala	East Orange	1893	1,808	97	119,024	1,346,000

NEW MEXICO

Institution	Location	Year founded	Total students	Faculty	Bound library volumes	Endowment fund
Eastern New Mexico U.	Portales	1934	4,015	161	143,000	—
New Mexico Highlands U.	Las Vegas	1893	2,479	103	100,000	—
New Mexico State U.	Las Cruces	1889	8,155	336	305,000	2,192,000
Santa Fe	Santa Fe	1947	1,243	60	60,000	—
U. of Albuquerque	Albuquerque	1940	2,018	70	60,000	—
U. of New Mexico	Albuquerque	1889	18,061	561	759,000	11,126,000
Western New Mexico U.	Silver City	1893	1,425	65	75,000	—

NEW YORK

Institution	Location	Year founded	Total students	Faculty	Bound library volumes	Endowment fund
Adelphi U.	Garden City	1896	7,877	410	208,000	2,244,000
Alfred U.	Alfred	1857	2,130	172	175,000	5,593,000
Canisius	Buffalo	1870	3,912	281	150,000	1,638,476
City U. of New York	New York	1847	197,664	8,641	2,900,000	14,400,000
Bernard M. Baruch	New York	1968	10,003	459	82,000	—
Brooklyn	Brooklyn	1930	24,768	1,820	500,000	298,600
City	New York	1847	20,845	1,218	838,000	2,270,000
Herbert H. Lehman	Bronx	1931	11,899	815	201,210	1,609,680
Hunter	New York	1870	23,110	1,036	345,000	1,216,968
Queens	Flushing	1937	25,368	1,176	365,930	62,080
Richmond	Staten Island	1965	2,909	164	140,000	—
York	Flushing	1966	1,983	124	42,000	—
Clarkson Tech.	Potsdam	1895	2,688	187	96,000	3,930,000
Colgate U.	Hamilton	1819	2,250	172	263,000	23,551,000
Columbia U.	New York	1754	16,172	2,530	4,100,000	242,000,000
‡Barnard	New York	1889	1,950	144	120,000	19,252,365
Teachers	New York	1887	5,279	395	350,000	20,599,000
Cooper Union	New York	1859	1,104	168	86,173	29,902,572
Cornell U.	Ithaca	1865	16,163	2,100	3,600,000	221,050,079
‡D'Youville	Buffalo	1908	1,205	97	87,575	232,000
‡Elmira	Elmira	1855	1,183	79	103,000	3,300,000
†Fordham U.	Bronx	1841	12,591	560	886,674	5,062,000
Hartwick	Oneonta	1928	1,682	107	100,000	4,484,000
Hobart & William Smith	Geneva	1822	1,597	113	140,000	3,779,000
Hofstra U.	Hempstead	1935	12,760	532	474,000	7,073,377
Houghton	Houghton	1883	1,198	78	78,000	733,000
Iona	New Rochelle	1940	3,198	180	92,000	515,000
Ithaca	Ithaca	1892	3,900	260	160,000	340,000
Juilliard School, The	New York	1905	1,010	100	45,000	—
Le Moyne	Syracuse	1946	1,701	126	93,136	1,312,000
Long Island U.	Greenvale	1926	20,838	922	437,000	3,235,000
†Manhattan	Bronx	1853	4,409	255	140,000	1,806,000
‡Manhattanville	Purchase	1841	1,479	101	175,000	2,904,000
Marist	Poughkeepsie	1929	1,768	78	71,000	179,000
‡Marymount	Tarrytown	1918	1,066	82	81,000	—
Mercy	Dobbs Ferry	1950	1,263	78	61,000	13,000
‡Molloy	Rockville Centre	1955	1,137	86	52,000	24,000
‡Nazareth	Rochester	1924	1,462	89	115,000	3,382,706
‡New Rochelle	New Rochelle	1904	1,226	91	102,000	1,500,000
New School	New York	1919	15,000	490	70,000	—
New York Inst. of Tech.	Old Westbury	1955	4,919	370	92,000	500,000
New York U.	New York	1831	42,363	3,878	2,270,000	102,000,000
Niagara U.	Niagara University	1856	3,013	205	109,000	476,000
Pace	New York	1906	9,934	339	207,000	3,443,274
Polytechnic Inst.	Brooklyn	1854	4,097	333	210,000	6,400,000
Pratt Inst.	Brooklyn	1887	4,560	299	225,000	15,624,000
Rensselaer Polytech.	Troy	1824	5,102	474	193,000	67,357,000
Rochester Inst. of Tech.	Rochester	1829	12,751	735	135,000	21,000,000
‡Rosary Hill	Buffalo	1948	1,262	96	68,655	15,000
Russell Sage	Troy	1916	1,418	100	106,000	6,000,000
St. Bonaventure U.	St. Bonaventure	1859	2,575	170	156,181	400,000
St. Francis	Brooklyn	1884	2,505	100	75,000	405,000
St. John Fisher	Rochester	1948	1,350	75	70,000	650,000
St. John's U.	Jamaica	1870	13,207	565	448,000	1,031,000
St. Lawrence U.	Canton	1856	2,344	158	220,000	9,632,000
St. Rose	Albany	1920	1,390	92	86,000	397,465
Siena	Loudonville	1937	1,858	130	128,901	737,189

Universities and colleges (continued)

Institution	Location	Year founded	Total students	Faculty	Bound library volumes	Endowment fund
†Skidmore	Saratoga Springs	1911	1,663	162	140,000	$ 2,419,000
State U. of New York	Albany	1948	132,235	7,774	6,391,053	—
SUNY at Albany	Albany	1844	13,240	769	617,993	—
SUNY at Binghamton	Binghamton	1946	7,228	440	428,177	—
SUNY at Buffalo	Buffalo	1846	23,763	1,435	1,466,908	—
SUNY at Stony Brook	Stony Brook	1957	11,062	719	521,720	—
DownstateMedicalCtr.	Brooklyn	1858	1,142	252	336,871	—
State U. Colleges						
Brockport	Brockport	1867	8,330	383	198,064	—
Buffalo	Buffalo	1867	10,532	509	234,421	—
Cortland	Cortland	1868	5,092	303	183,295	—
Fredonia	Fredonia	1867	4,768	262	186,589	—
Geneseo	Geneseo	1871	5,408	300	226,996	—
New Paltz	New Paltz	1885	7,642	379	218,434	—
Oneonta	Oneonta	1887	5,582	341	227,662	—
Oswego	Oswego	1861	8,283	423	264,516	—
Plattsburgh	Plattsburgh	1889	5,226	290	176,659	—
Potsdam	Potsdam	1867	4,587	261	188,546	—
Agric. at Cornell U.	Ithaca	1904	3,368	173	405,317	—
Human Ecology at Cornell U.	Ithaca	1925	1,229	63	405,317	—
Forestry at Syracuse U.	Syracuse	1911	1,766	97	69,400	—
Syracuse U.	Syracuse	1870	22,080	1,230	1,450,737	53,543,500
Utica	Utica	1946	3,278	140	85,939	45,000
Union Col. & U.	Schenectady	1795	1,808	152	274,000	31,683,000
†U.S. Merchant Marine Acad.	Kings Point	1938	1,010	91	65,000	—
†U.S. Military Acad.	West Point	1802	3,894	549	300,000	—
U. of Rochester	Rochester	1850	8,679	1,744	1,200,000	85,500,000
Vassar	Poughkeepsie	1861	1,819	214	406,669	51,912,260
Wagner	Staten Island	1883	3,225	137	140,000	1,599,642
Yeshiva U.	New York	1886	5,356	1,850	500,000	3,500,000

NORTH CAROLINA

Institution	Location	Year founded	Total students	Faculty	Bound library volumes	Endowment fund
Appalachian State U.	Boone	1903	7,088	356	225,000	$ 700,000
Atlantic Christian	Wilson	1902	1,544	77	61,000	979,678
Campbell	Buie's Creek	1887	2,207	126	83,355	1,222,000
Catawba	Salisbury	1851	1,099	80	76,000	4,964,215
†Davidson	Davidson	1837	1,034	93	175,000	16,123,766
Duke U.	Durham	1838	8,113	1,053	2,129,000	76,219,588
East Carolina U.	Greenville	1907	10,028	610	384,518	113,345
Elizabeth City State U.	Elizabeth City	1891	1,011	72	62,000	—
Elon	Elon College	1889	1,715	97	76,520	1,546,000
Fayetteville State U.	Fayetteville	1877	1,425	90	69,187	—
Guilford	Greensboro	1837	1,705	104	140,000	4,007,357
High Point	High Point	1924	1,131	63	78,000	2,641,070
Johnson C. Smith U.	Charlotte	1867	1,137	73	87,000	857,538
Lenoir Rhyne	Hickory	1891	1,341	95	74,291	2,069,294
Mars Hill	Mars Hill	1856	1,494	90	70,000	750,000
‡Meredith	Raleigh	1891	1,109	64	55,581	1,468,000
N. Carolina A.&T. St. U.	Greensboro	1891	3,797	266	286,000	—
N. Carolina Central U.	Durham	1910	3,541	279	...	—
Pembroke State U.	Pembroke	1887	1,926	118	70,000	—
St. Augustine's	Raleigh	1867	1,041	76	25,000	479,000
Shaw U.	Raleigh	1865	1,203	81	45,000	525,000
U. of North Carolina	Chapel Hill	1795	45,023	4,078	3,002,450	18,289,051
N. Carolina St. U., Raleigh	Raleigh	1887	13,340	834	500,000	1,700,000
U. of N.C. at Chapel Hill	Chapel Hill	1789	17,438	2,853	1,722,768	20,230,000
U. of N.C. at Charlotte	Charlotte	1965	4,068	202	134,125	134,000
U. of N.C. at Greensboro	Greensboro	1891	6,703	452	467,000	—
U. of N.C. at Wilmington	Wilmington	1947	1,772	94	80,000	—
Wake Forest U.	Winston-Salem	1834	3,326	405	435,000	26,000,000
Western Carolina U.	Cullowhee	1889	5,178	285	100,000	217,242
Winston-Salem State U.	Winston-Salem	1892	1,405	113	79,686	276,507

NORTH DAKOTA

Institution	Location	Year founded	Total students	Faculty	Bound library volumes	Endowment fund
Dickinson State	Dickinson	1916	1,675	95	60,000	—
Minot State	Minot	1913	3,144	130	125,000	—
North Dakota State U.	Fargo	1890	6,785	340	265,000	2,874,000
U. of North Dakota	Grand Forks	1883	8,129	498	351,000	1,388,000
Valley City State	Valley City	1889	1,369	70	74,000	890,000

OHIO

Institution	Location	Year founded	Total students	Faculty	Bound library volumes	Endowment fund
Antioch	Yellow Springs	1852	2,170	115	190,000	5,653,299
Ashland	Ashland	1878	2,987	256	156,000	1,516,850
Baldwin-Wallace	Berea	1845	3,135	167	150,000	5,691,000
Bowling Green State U.	Bowling Green	1910	16,612	653	650,000	—
Capital U.	Columbus	1850	2,045	158	113,000	1,969,340
Case Western Reserve U.	Cleveland	1826	9,371	1,200	1,127,718	72,500,000
Central State U.	Wilberforce	1887	2,565	135	97,000	—
Cleveland State U.	Cleveland	1964	14,411	466	282,869	—
Defiance	Defiance	1850	1,137	77	65,000	1,004,832
Denison U.	Granville	1831	2,187	155	187,658	14,441,000
Findlay	Findlay	1882	1,258	63	60,000	761,183
Heidelberg	Tiffin	1850	1,301	107	103,329	4,307,512
Hiram	Hiram	1850	1,148	84	100,000	6,885,000
John Carroll U.	Cleveland	1886	4,062	214	260,000	3,954,574
Kent State U.	Kent	1910	29,808	1,385	800,000	—
Kenyon	Gambier	1824	1,138	97	182,000	8,000,000
Marietta	Marietta	1835	2,223	138	164,000	5,000,000
Miami U.	Oxford	1809	12,322	565	540,000	2,375,000
Mt. Union	Alliance	1846	1,268	95	140,000	4,500,000
Muskingum	New Concord	1837	1,373	108	125,000	7,049,000
Oberlin	Oberlin	1833	2,670	211	696,000	77,287,000
Ohio Northern U.	Ada	1871	2,201	168	100,290	3,561,685
Ohio State U.	Columbus	1870	50,547	5,088	2,397,126	27,308,000
Ohio U.	Athens	1804	20,317	802	534,000	1,234,597
Ohio Wesleyan U.	Delaware	1842	2,633	188	400,000	$ 9,518,000
Otterbein	Westerville	1847	1,427	96	92,000	2,485,604
Steubenville	Steubenville	1946	1,380	75	75,000	—
U. of Akron	Akron	1870	18,526	508	450,000	2,315,000
U. of Cincinnati	Cincinnati	1819	34,742	1,835	1,117,000	44,750,000
U. of Dayton	Dayton	1850	8,525	368	330,000	4,123,000
U. of Toledo	Toledo	1872	15,158	839	887,014	578,000
Wilberforce U.	Wilberforce	1856	1,182	46	39,864	103,517
Wittenberg U.	Springfield	1845	3,312	188	225,000	13,738,706
Wooster	Wooster	1866	1,806	150	199,000	14,000,000
Wright State U.	Dayton	1967	9,981	278	202,000	5,000
Xavier U.	Cincinnati	1831	6,139	205	174,693	2,923,000
Youngstown State U.	Youngstown	1908	15,030	627	210,000	—

OKLAHOMA

Institution	Location	Year founded	Total students	Faculty	Bound library volumes	Endowment fund
Bethany Nazarene	Bethany	1899	1,543	88	83,000	—
Central State U.	Edmond	1890	10,608	354	200,000	—
East Central State	Ada	1909	3,003	106	90,000	—
Langston U.	Langston	1897	1,110	63	110,000	—
Northeastern State	Tahlequah	1846	5,476	234	154,000	—
Northwestern State	Alva	1897	2,543	100	132,000	—
Oklahoma Baptist U.	Shawnee	1911	1,632	104	89,500	8,900,000
Oklahoma Christian	Oklahoma City	1950	1,125	35	60,000	1,200,000
Oklahoma City U.	Oklahoma City	1904	2,523	90	127,000	2,500,000
Oklahoma Panhandle St.	Goodwell	1909	1,341	65	52,422	—
Oklahoma State U.	Stillwater	1890	18,447	935	775,000	10,635
Phillips U.	Enid	1906	1,346	97	163,000	3,817,000
Southeastern State	Durant	1909	3,086	121	105,000	—
Southwestern State	Weatherford	1901	5,174	195	114,000	—
U. of Oklahoma	Norman	1890	21,486	1,075	1,275,033	28,676,513
U. of Tulsa	Tulsa	1894	6,567	318	350,000	9,000,000

OREGON

Institution	Location	Year founded	Total students	Faculty	Bound library volumes	Endowment fund
Eastern Oregon	La Grande	1929	1,724	111	78,000	—
Lewis and Clark	Portland	1867	2,188	112	125,821	2,835,102
Linfield	McMinnville	1849	1,067	74	67,000	2,600,000
Oregon Col. of Education	Monmouth	1856	3,946	215	101,000	—
Oregon State U.	Corvallis	1868	15,509	902	638,000	—
Oregon Technical Inst.	Klamath Falls	1947	1,483	132	30,000	—
Pacific U.	Forest Grove	1849	1,209	84	85,000	6,918,864
Portland State U.	Portland	1955	11,354	658	311,000	—
Reed	Portland	1908	1,305	102	209,000	5,901,000
Southern Oregon	Ashland	1926	4,646	258	175,000	—
U. of Oregon	Eugene	1872	15,301	896	1,307,022	3,536,166
U. of Portland	Portland	1901	1,959	131	135,000	724,000
Willamette U.	Salem	1842	1,714	117	140,074	10,312,286

PENNSYLVANIA

Institution	Location	Year founded	Total students	Faculty	Bound library volumes	Endowment fund
Albright	Reading	1856	1,535	117	126,000	2,890,000
Allegheny	Meadville	1815	1,680	122	199,813	8,031,000
Bloomsburg State	Bloomsburg	1839	4,603	290	220,000	—
‡Bryn Mawr	Bryn Mawr	1885	1,368	162	350,000	30,770,000
Bucknell U.	Lewisburg	1846	2,933	218	295,000	22,000,000
California State	California	1852	6,790	385	130,000	—
‡Carlow	Pittsburgh	1929	1,009	76	75,513	186,335
Carnegie-Mellon U.	Pittsburgh	1967	4,963	599	363,081	112,957,996
‡Chestnut Hill	Philadelphia	1924	1,038	78	83,781	601,000
Cheyney State	Cheyney	1837	2,300	210	95,000	—
Clarion State	Clarion	1866	4,166	284	200,000	—
Delaware Valley	Doylestown	1896	1,279	74	42,445	2,384,359
Dickinson	Carlisle	1773	1,642	109	193,056	11,385,501
Drexel U.	Philadelphia	1891	9,459	502	305,000	11,387,000
Duquesne U.	Pittsburgh	1878	8,080	389	313,888	—
East Stroudsburg State	East Stroudsburg	1893	3,362	246	185,000	—
Edinboro State	Edinboro	1857	6,851	442	200,000	523,000
Elizabethtown	Elizabethtown	1899	1,691	118	92,000	—
Franklin and Marshall	Lancaster	1787	2,795	161	205,000	10,854,000
Gannon	Erie	1944	3,869	203	98,000	586,000
Geneva	Beaver Falls	1848	1,642	89	84,944	3,360,001
Gettysburg	Gettysburg	1832	1,916	152	185,000	3,241,067
Grove City	Grove City	1876	2,038	117	115,000	4,867,000
‡Gwynedd-Mercy	Gwynedd Valley	1948	1,057	79	37,000	—
‡Immaculata	Immaculata	1920	1,506	80	92,000	262,000
Indiana U.	Indiana	1875	10,347	586	380,000	—
Juniata	Huntingdon	1876	1,179	90	118,000	4,449,000
King's	Wilkes-Barre	1946	2,381	112	114,000	590,000
Kutztown State	Kutztown	1866	4,891	266	110,000	—
Lafayette	Easton	1826	2,161	146	260,000	29,075,000
La Salle	Philadelphia	1863	6,681	265	166,711	3,340,000
Lehigh U.	Bethlehem	1865	5,149	390	545,000	35,492,000
Lincoln U.	Lincoln University	1854	1,027	98	131,000	1,571
Lock Haven State	Lock Haven	1870	2,436	176	204,389	—
Lycoming	Williamsport	1812	1,590	96	90,000	1,600,000
Mansfield State	Mansfield	1857	2,625	203	86,000	—
‡Marywood	Scranton	1915	2,214	125	106,834	310,353
Millersville State	Millersville	1855	5,900	330	175,000	—
Moravian	Bethlehem	1807	1,270	85	115,000	5,490,000
Muhlenberg	Allentown	1848	1,558	106	150,000	5,000,000
Pennsylvania State U.	University Park	1855	46,003	3,200	1,431,300	517,000
Philadelphia Col. of Art	Philadelphia	1876	1,629	80	30,000	1,000,000
Phila. Col. of Tex. & Sci.	Philadelphia	1884	1,511	74	30,000	2,184,000
PMC Colleges	Chester	1821	3,051	148	80,000	841,565
Point Park	Pittsburgh	1960	3,190	147	42,000	590,000
St. Francis	Loretto	1847	1,639	115	108,000	—
St. Joseph's	Philadelphia	1851	6,790	169	118,000	621,000
Shippensburg State	Shippensburg	1871	3,812	295	200,000	—
Slippery Rock State	Slippery Rock	1889	5,446	357	245,000	—
Susquehanna U.	Selinsgrove	1858	1,314	95	87,500	1,362,600
Swarthmore	Swarthmore	1864	1,163	130	350,000	33,748,000
Temple U.	Philadelphia	1884	32,973	2,489	975,149	7,052,348
Thiel	Greenville	1866	1,401	80	80,000	1,100,000
U. of Pennsylvania	Philadelphia	1740	19,577	2,175	2,271,000	158,847,000

Institution	Location	Year founded	Total students	Faculty	Bound library volumes	Endowment fund
U. of Pittsburgh	Pittsburgh	1787	26,980	1,775	1,428,605	$83,793,856
U. of Scranton	Scranton	1888	2,941	145	123,862	2,325,266
Ursinus	Collegeville	1869	1,926	98	99,000	6,537,000
Villanova U.	Villanova	1842	9,381	474	415,235	436,000
Waynesburg	Waynesburg	1849	1,080	67	90,000	2,000,000
West Chester State	West Chester	1812	6,554	481	250,000	—
Westminster	New Wilmington	1852	1,945	116	115,000	3,336,831
Wilkes	Wilkes-Barre	1933	3,176	190	105,000	3,750,000
York	York	1941	2,439	75	63,400	1,111,624

PUERTO RICO

Institution	Location	Year founded	Total students	Faculty	Bound library volumes	Endowment fund
Catholic U.	Ponce	1948	6,763	368	135,000	443,668
Inter American U.	San German	1912	10,001	336	182,745	970,000
U. of Puerto Rico	Rio Piedras	1903	42,516	2,785	2,078,000	61,000

RHODE ISLAND

Institution	Location	Year founded	Total students	Faculty	Bound library volumes	Endowment fund
Brown U.	Providence	1764	5,759	1,076	1,346,349	94,669,084
Bryant	Smithfield	1863	3,380	80	50,000	—
Providence	Providence	1917	3,840	220	141,780	1,365,005
Rhode Island	Providence	1854	4,203	299	135,000	—
Rhode Island Sch. of Design	Providence	1877	1,127	108	40,514	13,882,936
U. of Rhode Island	Kingston	1892	7,481	750	400,000	66,892

SOUTH CAROLINA

Institution	Location	Year founded	Total students	Faculty	Bound library volumes	Endowment fund
Benedict	Columbia	1870	1,340	79	50,000	451,112
†The Citadel	Charleston	1842	2,606	162	114,000	—
Clemson U.	Clemson	1889	8,038	540	450,000	661,000
Furman U.	Greenville	1826	2,011	140	164,000	8,773,000
South Carolina State	Orangeburg	1896	2,191	120	103,420	1,000,000
U. of South Carolina	Columbia	1801	13,558	780	1,000,000	2,019,887
‡Winthrop	Rock Hill	1886	3,910	190	270,260	—

SOUTH DAKOTA

Institution	Location	Year founded	Total students	Faculty	Bound library volumes	Endowment fund
Augustana	Sioux Falls	1860	2,178	139	93,100	877,000
Black Hills State	Spearfish	1883	2,869	114	55,000	411,865
Dakota State	Madison	1881	1,334	69	60,000	—
Northern State	Aberdeen	1901	3,410	158	135,000	—
S. Dakota Mines & Tech.	Rapid City	1885	1,752	137	100,000	525,000
South Dakota State U.	Brookings	1883	6,257	340	225,000	3,433,000
Southern State	Springfield	1881	1,044	82	68,000	647,373
U. of South Dakota	Vermillion	1882	5,072	400	254,000	—

TENNESSEE

Institution	Location	Year founded	Total students	Faculty	Bound library volumes	Endowment fund
Austin Peay State U.	Clarksville	1929	3,574	142	116,000	—
Carson-Newman	Jefferson City	1851	1,687	103	99,000	1,892,000
David Lipscomb	Nashville	1891	2,237	107	87,518	3,023,273
East Tennessee State U.	Johnson City	1911	9,798	495	295,000	—
Fisk U.	Nashville	1867	1,326	101	169,896	8,988,500
George Peabody	Nashville	1875	1,975	169	1,260,000	13,000,000
Lee	Cleveland	1918	1,111	52	47,639	795,118
Memphis State U.	Memphis	1909	18,780	646	460,000	143,591
Middle Tenn. State U.	Murfreesboro	1911	8,093	397	199,000	292,000
Southern Missionary	Collegedale	1892	1,352	110	56,000	—
Southwestern	Memphis	1848	1,058	96	125,000	6,737,000
Tennessee State U.	Nashville	1909	4,543	276	120,000	36,450,270
Tennessee Tech. U.	Cookeville	1915	6,377	294	325,000	—
U. of Tennessee	Knoxville	1794	30,771	2,897	1,075,000	4,646,000
U. of T. at Chattanooga	Chattanooga	1886	4,427	205	135,000	7,352,475
Vanderbilt U.	Nashville	1872	6,397	1,302	1,256,000	93,159,164

TEXAS

Institution	Location	Year founded	Total students	Faculty	Bound library volumes	Endowment fund
Abilene Christian	Abilene	1906	3,234	146	169,739	7,125,718
Angelo State U.	San Angelo	1928	3,883	138	88,233	—
Austin	Sherman	1849	1,102	88	114,000	8,600,000
Baylor U.	Waco	1845	6,123	335	520,000	24,000,000
Bishop	Dallas	1881	1,968	143	77,000	614,000
Dallas Baptist	Dallas	1898	1,452	75	60,000	350,000
East Texas State U.	Commerce	1889	8,720	417	430,000	—
Hardin-Simmons U.	Abilene	1891	1,729	100	188,689	5,000,000
Houston Baptist	Houston	1960	1,089	61	40,000	—
Howard Payne	Brownwood	1889	1,429	75	89,000	3,091,000
Incarnate Word	San Antonio	1881	1,321	117	85,981	1,004,651
Lamar U.	Beaumont	1923	10,874	416	231,409	282,707
McMurry	Abilene	1922	1,544	83	95,000	3,300,000
Midwestern U.	Wichita Falls	1922	4,308	150	123,000	—
North Texas State U.	Denton	1890	15,015	911	720,000	—
Our Lady of the Lake	San Antonio	1911	1,834	103	94,000	1,376,402
Pan American U.	Edinburg	1927	5,294	151	100,000	62,000
Prairie View A. & M.	Prairie View	1876	4,325	218	116,000	619,450
Rice U.	Houston	1891	3,163	450	550,000	—
St. Mary's U.	San Antonio	1852	4,211	127	170,000	833;184
Sam Houston State U.	Huntsville	1879	10,025	360	375,000	—
Southern Methodist U.	Dallas	1911	10,136	654	1,350,000	30,939,000
Southwest Texas State U.	San Marco	1899	9,940	336	264,500	35,000
Stephen F. Austin State U.	Nacogdoches	1923	9,614	387	390,000	—
Sul Ross State U.	Alpine	1920	2,800	125	153,000	—
Tarleton State	Stephenville	1899	2,976	130	110,000	—
Texas A. & M. U.	College Station	1876	14,316	1,049	650,000	4,232,000
Texas Arts & Ind. U.	Kingsville	1925	7,817	310	234,000	—
Texas Christian U.	Fort Worth	1873	6,433	386	713,000	25,548,000
Texas Southern U.	Houston	1947	5,530	215	191,000	54,000
Texas Tech U.	Lubbock	1923	20,008	950	761,907	1,487,652
Texas Wesleyan	Fort Worth	1891	1,760	78	88,000	—
‡Texas Woman's U.	Denton	1901	5,600	300	410,000	500,000
Trinity U.	San Antonio	1869	2,914	194	209,895	42,000,000
U. of Dallas	Irving	1956	1,359	95	80,000	7,500,000
U. of Houston	Houston	1927	25,582	776	600,000	6,130,000
U. of St. Thomas	Houston	1947	1,321	101	42,000	—

Institution	Location	Year founded	Total students	Faculty	Bound library volumes	Endowment fund
U. of Texas System	Austin	1883	67,313	3,514	3,260,285	$616,043,315
U. of Texas at Austin	Austin	1881	39,089	1,818	2,269,785	24,383,314
U. of Texas at Arlington	Arlington	1895	14,115	450	500,000	290,000
U. of Texas at El Paso	El Paso	1913	11,484	400	290,000	3,650,000
West Texas State U.	Canyon	1910	6,888	352	125,000	—

UTAH

Institution	Location	Year founded	Total students	Faculty	Bound library volumes	Endowment fund
Brigham Young U.	Provo	1875	25,021	1,129	1,000,000	38,491,856
Southern Utah State	Cedar City	1897	1,964	90	56,000	—
U. of Utah	Salt Lake City	1850	23,111	975	1,157,529	12,833,108
Utah State U.	Logan	1888	7,712	472	541,000	956,000
Weber State	Ogden	1889	10,373	372	164,439	68,000

VERMONT

Institution	Location	Year founded	Total students	Faculty	Bound library volumes	Endowment fund
Castleton State	Castleton	1867	1,268	76	36,000	8,500
Goddard	Plainfield	1938	1,344	92	45,000	—
Middlebury	Middlebury	1800	1,665	135	198,802	18,064,580
†Norwich U.	Northfield	1819	1,059	120	100,000	7,225,000
St. Michael's	Winooski	1903	1,273	102	63,000	400,000
U. of Vermont	Burlington	1791	6,845	908	500,000	14,100,000

VIRGINIA

Institution	Location	Year founded	Total students	Faculty	Bound library volumes	Endowment fund
Hampton Inst.	Hampton	1868	2,770	202	132,000	35,642,332
‡Hollins	Hollins College	1842	1,120	82	115,000	4,948,000
‡Longwood	Farmville	1839	2,234	158	120,000	—
Lynchburg	Lynchburg	1903	1,915	116	66,677	2,082,179
Madison	Harrisonburg	1908	4,162	266	156,694	—
Old Dominion U.	Norfolk	1930	9,471	441	191,000	—
‡Radford	Radford	1910	3,959	220	114,595	—
Roanoke	Salem	1842	1,399	77	85,000	1,839,620
U. of Richmond	Richmond	1830	4,682	245	200,000	52,022,000
U. of Virginia	Charlottesville	1819	10,852	1,120	1,618,249	64,248,806
‡Mary Washington	Fredericksburg	1908	2,017	147	208,949	59,500
George Mason	Fairfax	1957	2,390	135	60,000	—
Va. Commonwealth U.	Richmond	1838	14,211	1,034	257,287	7,036,075
†Virginia Military Inst.	Lexington	1839	1,163	124	187,700	7,973,000
Virginia Polytech. Inst.	Blacksburg	1872	9,427	934	485,000	875,000
Virginia State	Petersburg	1882	2,948	218	134,934	183,314
Virginia Union U.	Richmond	1865	1,280	79	67,000	1,490,000
†Washington & Lee U.	Lexington	1749	1,555	133	297,500	15,809,710
William & Mary	Williamsburg	1693	4,351	390	559,637	5,600,356

WASHINGTON

Institution	Location	Year founded	Total students	Faculty	Bound library volumes	Endowment fund
Central Washington St.	Ellensburg	1891	7,536	395	160,479	—
Eastern Washington St.	Cheney	1890	6,801	388	204,426	10 000
Gonzaga U.	Spokane	1887	2,776	210	201,000	—
Pacific Lutheran U.	Tacoma	1890	3,001	179	129,425	735,372
Seattle Pacific	Seattle	1891	2,014	116	84,000	71,750
Seattle U.	Seattle	1891	3,373	198	144,000	1,000,000
U. of Puget Sound	Tacoma	1888	3,822	168	142,857	6,700,000
U. of Washington	Seattle	1861	33,202	1,959	1,900,000	7,711,890
Walla Walla	College Place	1892	1,758	101	111,000	—
Washington State U.	Pullman	1890	14,520	720	900,000	45,121,000
Western Washington St.	Bellingham	1899	9,600	596	255,000	63,000
Whitman	Walla Walla	1859	1,105	80	170,000	13,646,000
Whitworth	Spokane	1890	1,535	76	63,830	—

WEST VIRGINIA

Institution	Location	Year founded	Total students	Faculty	Bound library volumes	Endowment fund
Bethany	Bethany	1840	1,089	69	104,000	8,188,000
Bluefield State	Bluefield	1895	1,316	67	54,800	—
Concord	Athens	1872	1,980	107	110,000	—
Fairmont State	Fairmont	1867	3,551	160	110,000	—
Glenville State	Glenville	1872	1,617	87	77,000	—
Marshall U.	Huntington	1837	8,945	385	190,000	—
Morris Harvey	Charleston	1888	3,123	98	65,000	2,350,000
Salem	Salem	1888	1,449	71	68,000	1,500,000
Shepherd	Shepherdstown	1871	1,876	101	69,000	—
West Liberty State	West Liberty	1837	4,047	182	80,000	—
W. Virginia Inst. of Tech.	Montgomery	1895	2,444	150	64,000	—
West Virginia State	Institute	1891	3,663	160	106,000	—
West Virginia U.	Morgantown	1867	15,127	1,244	1,025,780	136,200
West Virginia Wesleyan	Buckhannon	1890	1,761	105	95,000	2,238,312

WISCONSIN

Institution	Location	Year founded	Total students	Faculty	Bound library volumes	Endowment fund
Beloit	Beloit	1846	1,782	131	230,000	8,348,000
Carroll	Waukesha	1846	1,250	92	101,868	2,515,473
Carthage	Kenosha	1847	1,849	95	90,000	3,532,000
Lawrence U.	Appleton	1847	1,409	127	190,000	23,752,000
Marquette U.	Milwaukee	1864	10,678	756	550,000	7,412,000
Ripon	Ripon	1850	1,048	87	90,000	2,350,000
St. Norbert	West De Pere	1898	1,673	102	96,500	1,400,000
Stout State U.	Menomonie	1893	5,080	352	120,000	110,000
U. of Wisconsin	Madison	1848	67,874	2,861	3,403,000	45,052,030
U. of W.—Madison	Madison	1848	34,388	1,427	2,303,000	
U. of W.—Milwaukee	Milwaukee	1956	20,822	795	595,000	
W. S. U.—Eau Claire	Eau Claire	1916	8,288	509	180,000	—
W. S. U.—La Crosse	La Crosse	1909	7,248	442	250,000	—
W. S. U.—Oshkosh	Oshkosh	1871	11,549	675	285,000	—
W. S. U.—Platteville	Platteville	1866	4,813	350	185,000	—
W. S. U.—River Falls	River Falls	1874	4,152	270	165,000	—
W. S. U.—Stevens Point	Stevens Point	1894	8,734	489	195,000	—
W. S. U.—Superior	Superior	1896	3,053	230	155,000	367,826
W. S. U.—Whitewater	Whitewater	1868	9,721	554	260,000	—

WYOMING

Institution	Location	Year founded	Total students	Faculty	Bound library volumes	Endowment fund
U. of Wyoming	Laramie	1886	8,495	587	477,000	13,400,120

Health and Welfare

Health personnel and facilities

State	Physicians* December 31, 1970	Dentists* December, 1970	Nurses* 1966	Hospital facilities December 1, 1970 Hospitals	Hospital facilities December 1, 1970 Beds	Nursing homes, 1969 Facilities	Nursing homes, 1969 Beds
Alabama	3,061	1,180	5,912	121	14,075	194	12,543
Alaska	203	114	590	13	546	4	192
Arizona	2,539	865	5,862	57	6,331	77	5,221
Arkansas	1,767	655	2,609	89	7,745	201	13,015
California	38,031	13,489	58,694	543	74,096	2,856	107,872
Colorado	3,871	1,344	8,312	74	9,618	178	12,548
Connecticut	5,798	2,032	15,438	40	10,136	339	17,559
Delaware	730	240	2,098	7	1,840	35	1,471
Dist. of Columbia	2,883	737	3,662	14	5,451	113	2,478
Florida	10,437	3,731	21,760	166	27,143	339	24,957
Georgia	4,879	1,577	6,956	142	15,544	237	15,242
Hawaii	1,150	509	2,334	20	2,267	84	1,561
Idaho	671	358	1,954	48	2,894	50	3,171
Illinois	15,299	6,395	35,552	256	50,605	1,038	59,015
Indiana	5,274	2,321	12,829	112	20,208	492	26,643
Iowa	2,914	1,526	9,981	133	15,169	693	31,148
Kansas	2,601	1,084	6,895	145	11,641	435	17,638
Kentucky	3,261	1,274	6,297	107	12,241	310	13,675
Louisiana	4,323	1,457	6,758	131	15,105	186	12,044
Maine	1,097	447	4,051	47	4,215	280	5,891
Maryland	7,105	1,888	10,005	47	11,694	246	15,172
Massachusetts	11,727	4,094	28,743	138	25,246	911	40,049
Michigan	10,982	4,734	23,441	197	32,873	541	35,989
Minnesota	5,756	2,671	14,441	183	21,150	503	31,949
Mississippi	1,849	647	3,670	96	8,580	99	4,272
Missouri	5,994	2,405	11,291	119	21,393	505	28,731
Montana	722	375	2,483	55	3,661	79	3,014
Nebraska	1,711	966	4,730	100	8,966	270	12,593
Nevada	550	254	1,060	17	1,953	21	1,022
New Hampshire	1,034	363	3,521	31	2,959	127	3,982
New Jersey	10,390	4,554	24,942	107	24,878	529	26,964
New Mexico	1,133	364	2,511	39	3,437	52	2,451
New York	42,975	14,925	74,280	341	81,375	1,076	73,508
North Carolina	5,524	1,710	12,126	136	18,497	821	19,320
North Dakota	580	283	2,114	58	3,948	98	5,693
Ohio	14,106	5,240	32,649	195	41,081	1,132	52,399
Oklahoma	2,597	1,028	4,650	119	10,468	442	25,029
Oregon	3,021	1,636	6,814	81	8,402	291	14,714
Pennsylvania	17,876	6,739	45,809	238	53,296	759	50,903
Rhode Island	1,465	493	3,673	15	3,410	162	5,245
South Carolina	2,349	782	5,625	72	9,408	96	5,433
South Dakota	534	301	2,089	54	3,563	132	5,868
Tennessee	4,658	1,737	6,755	135	17,352	221	11,068
Texas	12,977	4,700	20,167	493	45,996	1,058	65,137
Utah	1,462	661	2,347	33	3,715	129	4,005
Vermont	832	217	1,836	20	2,002	104	2,751
Virginia	5,586	1,966	11,511	100	15,691	273	10,727
Washington	4,985	2,318	11,361	109	11,204	263	18,294
West Virginia	1,823	692	4,707	74	9,050	62	2,542
Wisconsin	5,320	2,634	14,084	154	22,156	472	30,025
Wyoming	333	167	1,209	27	1,822	31	1,478
TOTAL U.S.	298,745	112,879	613,188	5,848	836,096	19,646	994,211

*Excluding those in government service not allocated by state. Sources: American Medical Association, *Distribution of Physicians in the United States;* American Dental Association; American Nurses' Association; U.S. Department of Health, Education, and Welfare, Public Health Service.

Social insurance beneficiaries and benefits

State	OLD-AGE AND SURVIVORS INSURANCE Beneficiaries Jan. 1, 1971	OLD-AGE AND SURVIVORS INSURANCE Benefits for year ending Jan. 1 1971 (in 000)	DISABILITY INSURANCE Beneficiaries Jan. 1, 1971	DISABILITY INSURANCE Benefits for year ending Jan. 1 1971 (in 000)	Medicare* enrollment July 1, 1970	UNEMPLOYMENT INSURANCE STATE PROGRAMS Beneficiaries† June 1971	UNEMPLOYMENT INSURANCE STATE PROGRAMS Benefits for year ending June 30 1971 (in 000)
Alabama	399,364	$ 404,192	68,251	$ 69,330	329,343	16,839	$ 38,761
Alaska	11,136	13,183	1,218	1,365	6,662	4,524	13,779
Arizona	196,797	239,003	25,547	30,468	159,158	7,525	21,342
Arkansas	278,344	268,337	46,953	45,275	239,025	9,812	23,458
California	2,031,457	2,587,057	250,743	322,375	1,801,491	263,626	783,740
Colorado	212,792	254,279	21,557	24,932	190,032	4,236	14,748
Connecticut	321,731	456,897	24,929	33,515	288,852	79,818	199,453
Delaware	54,177	69,371	5,878	7,084	45,157	3,951	12,759
District of Columbia	69,881	80,516	8,039	9,106	68,827	6,257	16,028
Florida	1,066,649	1,293,270	104,168	121,840	936,595	24,177	47,282
Georgia	443,921	456,017	82,382	82,279	369,651	14,538	37,738
Hawaii	59,967	70,026	6,521	7,567	45,232	9,139	21,753
Idaho	84,019	98,583	9,043	10,450	69,309	3,608	10,771
Illinois	1,220,569	1,627,293	101,817	131,869	1,100,271	80,467	222,798
Indiana	584,949	749,684	55,615	68,461	495,653	27,495	73,492
Iowa	389,138	470,600	28,129	32,929	355,257	11,832	36,461
Kansas	290,739	348,922	21,323	25,091	268,794	12,597	41,443
Kentucky	401,770	417,552	70,025	67,930	342,878	14,692	38,815
Louisiana	358,801	372,836	70,601	67,267	306,687	25,006	60,264
Maine	136,035	160,090	13,680	14,892	120,640	9,723	24,403
Maryland	343,685	429,292	33,301	41,418	294,980	23,717	63,689
Massachusetts	673,597	906,349	53,891	67,035	635,927	89,052	240,438
Michigan	947,593	1,249,142	101,924	130,871	767,435	83,643	332,483
Minnesota	464,160	546,773	31,152	36,429	414,905	21,127	70,085
Mississippi	274,263	243,939	49,297	44,500	226,016	6,368	13,907
Missouri	614,821	730,871	64,442	72,838	562,274	29,232	83,583
Montana	83,600	$ 100,221	9,333	$ 10,523	69,994	3,037	$ 8,234
Nebraska	199,619	235,574	13,302	15,090	184,743	4,323	13,345
Nevada	38,369	50,557	4,481	5,883	31,722	6,100	15,547
New Hampshire	92,177	119,384	7,240	8,763	81,996	4,901	11,943
New Jersey	789,106	1,095,684	71,161	94,294	695,773	114,909	309,300
New Mexico	94,177	99,442	17,055	16,005	73,625	4,865	13,249
New York	2,177,388	3,034,061	200,486	260,892	1,970,332	212,241	635,978
North Carolina	540,788	555,729	82,706	84,281	418,374	28,527	57,099
North Dakota	80,504	88,667	6,407	6,314	67,981	1,647	5,864
Ohio	1,142,354	1,470,929	116,319	144,033	1,001,102	65,537	177,803
Oklahoma	323,508	362,169	43,953	47,100	298,769	14,040	26,439
Oregon	267,896	335,906	28,003	35,207	227,102	19,720	52,713
Pennsylvania	1,449,127	1,893,642	140,960	183,164	1,278,387	110,981	262,753
Rhode Island	115,939	152,919	11,541	14,233	105,197	13,987	39,813
South Carolina	257,194	259,313	49,578	49,720	194,732	14,432	31,787
South Dakota	94,066	103,953	7,231	7,476	81,559	770	2,859
Tennessee	459,550	471,675	69,083	70,070	389,454	24,090	57,714
Texas	1,142,942	1,259,553	134,035	142,112	993,761	37,610	80,423
Utah	93,202	115,879	8,814	10,416	77,616	5,294	14,175
Vermont	55,536	66,944	5,687	6,319	49,870	4,562	12,310
Virginia	443,965	486,931	66,731	71,317	367,890	9,502	22,500
Washington	377,204	481,652	35,106	44,713	324,636	66,217	236,900
West Virginia	245,116	274,624	56,384	62,087	199,791	8,594	17,123
Wisconsin	554,741	695,413	45,730	55,884	478,279	29,216	105,893
Wyoming	36,042	43,690	3,313	3,903	31,095	714	2,602
Total U.S.‡	23,563,634	28,796,378	2,664,995	3,067,002	20,490,908	1,688,817	4,757,839

*Includes hospital and/or medical insurance.
†Weekly average.
‡Includes data for American Samoa, Guam, Puerto Rico, Virgin Islands and for beneficiaries or enrollees living abroad for all categories except unemployment insurance state programs.
Source: U.S. Department of Health, Education, and Welfare, Social Security Administration.

Public assistance
June 1971

State	NUMBER OF RECIPIENTS					AVERAGE MONEY PAYMENTS				
	Old-age assistance	Aid to dependent children*	Aid to the permanently and totally disabled	Aid to the blind	General assistance	Old-age assistance	Aid to dependent children, per recipient	Aid to the permanently and totally disabled	Aid to the blind	General assistance
Alabama	115,000	147,000	17,600	1,900	110	$67.15	$15.50	$52.10	$69.85	$12.50
Alaska	1,900	10,700	1,100	110	740	130.10	69.65	173.65	174.55	36.45
Arizona	13,500	66,600	9,100	520	8,000	71.70	32.00	77.95	81.20	34.80
Arkansas	58,400	68,700	12,100	1,700	780	66.05	26.60	76.25	83.60	4.85
California	320,000	1,569,000	190,000	14,100	88,300	108.00	57.35	136.15	155.60	55.30
Colorado	32,000	99,300	12,200	240	4,600	74.30	52.20	82.70	91.25	80.50
Connecticut	8,300	106,000	8,300	260	25,200†	94.65	69.05	131.25	101.70	50.65
Delaware	2,500	27,700	1,700	380	7,700	74.60	35.55	132.80	106.80	31.95
Dist. of Columbia	3,900	73,300	9,000	220	2,700	85.00	55.40	100.15	102.90	104.90
Florida	58,200	290,000	22,200	21,300	20,700†	56.75	24.45	75.70	77.55	—
Georgia	91,000	287,000	38,200	3,200	2,700	54.20	28.15	65.45	70.15	26.85
Hawaii	2,500	35,000	2,000	74	9,700	96.30	71.60	139.75	136.55	68.60
Idaho	3,300	18,600	2,900	100	—	67.65	51.15	87.90	88.65	—
Illinois	34,600	607,000	56,300	1,700	78,200	60.50	58.30	95.25	96.25	82.80
Indiana	16,200	137,000	7,300	1,300	—	55.30	42.25	57.75	79.60	—
Iowa	22,400	78,000	3,200	1,900	8,300	125.30	52.90	151.75	66.90	—
Kansas	11,300	77,200	6,100	440	13,200	62.65	55.90	78.30	79.00	51.75
Kentucky	59,600	141,000	17,200	2,100	—	58.35	32.25	78.80	77.70	—
Louisiana	116,000	232,000	22,000	2,300	9,200	73.90	20.35	55.35	76.15	49.45
Maine	10,700	61,300	4,300	230	10,100	61.35	40.40	94.45	92.70	18.00
Maryland	8,900	175,000	17,800	360	11,200	65.20	43.20	88.55	98.80	85.10
Massachusetts	56,200	276,000	19,600	2,800	46,200	95.15	67.25	128.60	155.50	70.45
Michigan	41,000	419,000	33,200	1,500	101,000	79.25	62.95	108.00	108.75	59.95
Minnesota	18,200	110,000	13,100	850	13,900	77.80	72.15	91.00	100.85	46.65
Mississippi	77,800	144,000	24,800	2,100	1,700	54.25	13.45	65.05	65.80	14.20
Missouri	94,600	194,000	20,900	3,900	14,200	75.65	31.05	77.10	91.55	58.85
Montana	3,300	19,500	2,600	170	1,900	55.85	40.15	82.10	80.50	20.15
Nebraska	7,500	41,400	4,900	310	—	57.60	45.70	82.05	98.85	—
Nevada	2,900	17,800	—	160	—	71.75	32.05	—	96.30	—
New Hampshire	4,600	16,700	960	240	4,200	164.95	64.55	143.80	165.25	30.95
New Jersey	19,100	446,000	15,500	1,000	12,300	75.60	62.75	107.40	102.25	112.10
New Mexico	8,800	56,400	9,100	370	—	54.40	31.80	74.10	77.30	—
New York	109,000	1,269,000	111,000	3,800	215,000	95.10	66.95	129.30	121.30	65.75
North Carolina	34,900	159,000	29,900	4,500	3,800	68.05	31.60	79.40	87.50	12.30
North Dakota	3,700	13,600	2,400	79	630	90.20	58.70	99.85	104.50	15.45
Ohio	53,800	396,000	36,400	2,700	79,700	60.60	44.50	76.00	75.70	54.55
Oklahoma	69,200	111,000	23,400	1,300	2,300	69.40	38.30	76.10	109.20	9.15
Oregon	7,600	87,100	8,000	640	3,000	55.65	45.80	76.10	100.45	58.73
Pennsylvania	50,700	613,000	32,500	7,400	108,000	99.15	62.60	99.45	120.55	99.10
Rhode Island	4,000	47,500	4,200	120	12,500	55.65	54.75	92.40	88.20	45.45
South Carolina	18,400	82,300	11,600	1,200	170	48.50	19.70	56.45	120.75	31.65
South Dakota	3,800	19,200	1,500	110	990	61.25	48.15	69.80	90.15	11.75
Tennessee	50,400	180,000	27,100	1,700	4,700	49.70	29.70	68.35	70.50	10.25
Texas	233,000	383,000	25,700	4,000	—	52.25	29.85	66.95	78.20	—
Utah	2,900	40,500	4,900	160	960	60.60	50.15	79.45	104.35	63.00
Vermont	4,400	16,700	2,200	100	—	77.35	62.75	109.65	106.45	—
Virginia	13,700	130,000	9,700	1,200	9,400	67.35	47.80	83.50	89.10	56.55
Washington	20,100	146,000	22,100	460	5,200	63.05	56.15	95.45	87.30	64.80
West Virginia	11,900	95,700	11,700	540	2,400	77.75	27.10	64.45	69.90	13.10
Wisconsin	18,000	108,000	7,700	680	26,000	118.10	64.50	105.85	96.40	44.25
Wyoming	1,500	6,600	890	32	350	56.20	43.00	68.35	—	23.00
Total U.S.	2,035,200	9,952,400	978,150	79,555	971,930‡	$75.65§	$49.30§	$98.00§	$104.10§	$62.45§

*Includes children and parents or caretaker relatives in families in which these adults were included in determining amount of assistance.   †Estimated.
‡Excludes Idaho, Indiana, Kentucky, Nebraska, Nevada, New Mexico, and Vermont.   §Includes Guam, Puerto Rico, and the Virgin Islands.
Source: U.S. Department of Health, Education, and Welfare, Social Security Administration, *Social Security Bulletin.*

Vocational rehabilitation
year ending June 30, 1971

State	DISABLED PERSONS			State	DISABLED PERSONS		
	Number rehabilitated	Number in process of rehabilitation June 30	Total federal and state funds		Number rehabilitated	Number in process of rehabilitation June 30	Total federal and state funds
Alabama	6,877	14,666	$ 18,297,068	Montana	1,069	4,424	$ 2,600,873
Alaska	389	985	1,295,342	Nebraska	1,559	4,572	4,507,056
Arizona	1,841	3,787	6,549,049	Nevada	520	929	1,297,238
Arkansas	5,804	10,180	10,935,036	New Hampshire	588	1,534	2,327,048
California	14,430	30,801	40,324,880	New Jersey	8,744	14,577*	14,997,770
Colorado	2,967	6,606	6,761,769	New Mexico	1,099	2,323	4,303,572
Connecticut	2,425	5,722	5,175,586	New York	11,405	33,655	37,187,909
Delaware	716	1,229	1,369,744	North Carolina	13,144	22,983	23,881,562
Dist. of Columbia	3,432	4,675	5,380,903	North Dakota	1,213	3,163	2,626,580
Florida	12,277	25,498	23,332,170	Ohio	8,038	16,861	30,425,066
Georgia	11,512	19,553	20,824,428	Oklahoma	7,051	19,415	10,692,108
Hawaii	746	2,507	2,183,008	Oregon	1,700	5,623	6,411,396
Idaho	890	2,715	2,976,414	Pennsylvania	20,064	42,534	35,806,120
Illinois	14,001	21,494	22,238,161	Rhode Island	1,611	4,543	2,613,558
Indiana	2,714	9,072	12,750,587	South Carolina	9,688	18,943	13,999,157
Iowa	3,979	12,287	8,767,957	South Dakota	859	2,820	2,777,112
Kansas	1,555	3,095	7,188,230	Tennessee	6,641	15,179	18,602,333
Kentucky	9,832	11,263	14,985,340	Texas	17,905	40,140	43,500,085
Louisiana	5,431	18,410	17,064,373	Utah	2,231	7,022	4,216,058
Maine	846	1,762	3,590,266	Vermont	523	1,325	1,763,346
Maryland	8,014	13,860	10,401,590	Virginia	11,042	17,517	17,506,681
Massachusetts	4,475	8,909	12,906,491	Washington	3,242	8,746	8,634,373
Michigan	9,810	20,279	21,662,392	West Virginia	6,539	8,064	9,050,490
Minnesota	4,833	15,036	12,301,452	Wisconsin	9,284	19,587	13,337,340
Mississippi	5,079	8,914	13,987,728	Wyoming	467	936	1,280,672
Missouri	7,057	9,881	15,285,645	Total U. S.	288,158	600,601	$632,881,112

*Estimated.
Source: U. S. Department of Health, Education, and Welfare, Social and Rehabilitation Service.

Defense

Vietnam
U.S. armed forces and casualties

	1961	1962	1963	1964	1965	1966	1967	1968	1969	1970	1971*
Military forces	3,200	11,300	16,300	23,300	184,300	385,300	485,600	536,100	475,200	334,600	239,200
Army	2,100	7,900	10,100	14,700	116,800	239,400	319,500	359,800	331,100	249,600	190,500
Navy†	100	500	800	1,100	8,400	23,300	31,700	36,100	30,200	16,700	10,700
Marine Corps	—	500	800	900	38,200	69,200	78,000	81,400	55,100	25,100	500
Air Force	1,000	2,400	4,600	6,600	20,600	52,900	55,900	58,400	58,400	43,100	37,400
Coast Guard	—	—	—	—	300	500	500	400	400	100	100
Casualties‡											
Battle deaths	11	31	78	147	1,369	5,008	9,378	14,592	9,414	4,221	1,105
Killed	1	19	53	112	1,130	4,179	7,482	12,588	8,119	3,483	873
Died of wounds	—	1	5	6	87	517	981	1,636	1,170	556	132
Died while missing	10	11	20	28	151	309	911	367	120	180	99
Died while captured	—	—	—	1	1	3	4	1	5	2	1
Wounded, nonfatal											
Hospital care required	2	41	218	522	3,308	16,526	32,371	46,799	32,940	15,211	3,870
Hospital care not required	1	37	193	517	2,806	13,567	29,654	46,021	37,276	15,432	3,303

Data are for December 31 of years reported, except as indicated. *As of June 30. †Excludes personnel on ships off Vietnam shores.
‡Represents casualties from enemy action. Deaths exclude servicemen who died in accidents or from disease.
Source: U.S. Department of Defense.

National defense expenditures
in million dollars

Function	1962	1963	1964	1965	1966	1967	1968	1969	1970	1971
Department of defense—Military:										
Military personnel (including retired)	13,032	13,000	14,195	14,771	16,753	19,787	21,954	23,818	25,158	24,104
Operation and maintenance	11,594	11,874	11,932	12,349	14,710	19,000	20,578	22,227	21,500	19,650
Procurement	14,532	16,632	15,351	11,839	14,339	19,012	23,283	23,988	21,550	18,799
Research and development	6,319	6,376	7,021	6,236	6,259	7,160	7,747	7,457	7,300	7,382
Military construction and other	1,602	513	1,236	928	2,279	2,636	3,975	525	1,139	1,421
Deductions for offsetting receipts	—163	—251	—159	—150	—160	—138	—164	—135	—140	—163
Subtotal, Dept. of defense—Military	46,916	48,144	49,576	45,973	54,180	67,457	77,373	77,880	76,505	71,193
Atomic energy	2,806	2,758	2,764	2,625	2,403	2,264	2,466	2,450	2,461	2,411
Military assistance	1,337	1,406	1,209	1,125	1,003	858	654	789	495	600
Defense-related activities	92	24	172	136	— 62	— 17	139	260	119	— 51
Deductions for offsetting receipts	— 53	— 74	—130	—281	—738	—481	—116	—138	—150	—572
Total national defense	51,098	52,258	53,591	49,578	56,786	70,081	80,516	81,241	79,432	73,581

Source: Executive Office of the President, Bureau of the Budget, *The Budget in Brief*.

Armed forces personnel
as of June 30, 1971

Branch of service	Personnel on active duty* Officers	Personnel on active duty* Enlisted men	Reserve personnel† Officers	Reserve personnel† Enlisted men	Total military personnel
Army	148,950	974,860	76,747	636,727	1,837,284
Navy	74,782	548,466	23,363	109,873	756,484
Air Force	125,919	629,381	23,857	114,009	893,166
Marine Corps	21,765	190,604	3,763	44,953	261,085
Coast Guard	5,747	31,534	1,567	11,267	50,115
Total	377,163	2,374,845	129,297	916,829	3,798,134

*Includes cadets and officer candidates.
†Paid status only; excludes personnel on inactive reserve.
Sources: U.S. Department of Defense and U.S. Department of Transportation, United States Coast Guard.

Status of selective service draftees examined

Status	1950–1970* Number (000)	1950–1970* Percent	Number in thousands, 1970 Total	Number in thousands, 1970 White	Number in thousands, 1970 Non-white	Percent, 1970 Total	Percent, 1970 White	Percent, 1970 Non-white
Examined	15,245	100.0	1,017	905	112	100.0	100.0	100.0
Found acceptable	9,046	59.3	549	498	51	54.0	55.0	45.5
Disqualified	6,199	40.7	468	407	61	46.0	45.0	54.5
Medically disqualified only	3,499	23.0	380	355	25	37.4	39.2	22.3
Failed mental requirements only	2,158	14.2	63	35	28	6.2	3.9	25.0
Failed mental test only†	1,699	11.1	54	30	24	5.3	3.3	21.4
Trainability limited‡	459	3.0	9	5	4	0.9	0.6	3.6
Failed mental test and medically disqualified	366	2.4	15	9	6	1.5	1.0	5.4
Administratively disqualified	176	1.2	10	8	2	1.0	0.9	1.8

Based on results of preinduction examinations.
*1950 data are for July through December only.
†Examinees who failed minimum requirement on Armed Forces Qualification Test.
‡Examinees classified as mental group IV on basis of AFQT but who failed to meet additional aptitude area requirements.
Source: U.S. Department of Commerce, Bureau of the Census, *Statistical Abstract of the United States*. Data compiled by the Department of the Army, Office of the Surgeon General.

Law Enforcement

Public expenditures and employment for law enforcement

Expenditures (in 000,000)	1955	1960	1965	1969
All governments	2,231	3,349	4,573	7,340
Police protection	1,359	2,030	2,792	4,430
Judicial	409	597	748	1,449
Correction	463*	722*	1,033*	1,462
Federal government	206	291	377	800
Police protection	129	173	243	492
Judicial	49	74	75	238
Correction	28*	44*	59*	71
State governments	475	769	1,135	1,849
Police protection	139	245	348	621
Judicial	68	99	155	314
Correction	268*	425*	632*	914
Local governments	1,550	2,289	3,062	4,691
Police protection	1,091	1,612	2,201	3,317
Judicial	292	424	518	898
Correction	167*	253*	343*	477
Employees (in 000)				
Police protection, all governments	265	363	420	523
Federal	...	22	23	36
State	...	32	41	54
Local	244	309	357	432
Correction, all governments	...	...	117	142
Federal	...	...	3	5
State	...	...	71	86
Local	...	...	43	51

*Includes capital outlay.
Source: U.S. Department of Commerce, Bureau of the Census, *Statistical Abstract of the United States.*

Arrests, 1970

Offense charged	UNDER 18 Persons arrested	UNDER 18 Percent change from 1969	18 AND OVER Persons arrested	18 AND OVER Percent change from 1969	ALL AGES Persons arrested	ALL AGES Percent change from 1969
Murder and nonnegligent manslaughter	1,302	+18.4	10,640	+ 5.6	11,942	+ 6.9
Negligent manslaughter	219	−14.1	2,481	−13.1	2,700	−13.2
Forcible rape	2,986	+ 3.0	11,130	+ 0.8	14,116	+ 1.3
Robbery	28,275	+ 9.0	55,416	+10.2	83,691	+ 9.8
Aggravated assault	19,509	+ 4.6	95,723	+ 4.0	115,232	+ 4.1
Other assaults	48,758	+ 8.7	213,742	+ 3.5	262,500	+ 4.5
Burglary—breaking or entering	136,018	+ 1.5	125,672	+10.8	261,690	+ 5.8
Larceny—theft	289,053	+ 8.0	278,675	+18.4	567,728	+12.9
Auto theft	66,175	− 8.1	52,076	+ 2.6	118,251	− 3.7
Arson	5,159	− 0.5	3,438	+11.4	8,597	+ 4.0
Forgery, counterfeiting	4,246	+ 5.4	35,565	+12.6	39,811	+11.8
Fraud	2,882	− 3.6	63,583	+12.1	66,465	+11.3
Embezzlement	310	+26.0	7,221	+24.1	7,531	+24.2
Stolen property; buying, receiving, possessing	16,801	+18.1	39,260	+29.0	56,061	+25.5
Vandalism	73,870	− 2.8	28,354	+ 2.4	102,224	− 1.4
Weapons; carrying, possessing, etc.	15,937	+ 5.3	79,267	+ 8.9	95,204	+ 8.3
Prostitution, commercialized vice	1,097	+12.4	47,030	+ 0.1	48,127	+ 0.3
Sex offenses (except forcible rape and prostitution)	9,660	−10.7	36,503	− 6.4	46,163	− 7.3
Narcotic drug laws	73,139	+30.2	254,653	+48.5	327,792	+44.0
Gambling	1,592	− 4.7	80,878	+ 6.1	82,470	+ 5.9
Offenses against family and children	702	−10.9	45,905	− 2.6	46,607	− 2.7
Driving while intoxicated	4,054	+12.0	371,730	+12.0	375,784	+12.0
Liquor law violations	66,583	− 1.6	128,129	− 4.3	194,712	− 3.4
Drunkenness	36,999	−10.4	1,327,126	− 1.7	1,364,125	− 1.9
Disorderly conduct	115,308	− 0.3	428,619	− 4.8	543,927	− 3.9
Vagrancy	11,892	+ 7.9	83,610	− 9.5	95,502	− 7.7
All other offenses, except traffic	212,573	+ 7.0	511,860	+15.9	724,433	+13.1
Suspicion	18,182	−12.4	44,282	−38.6	62,464	−32.7
Curfew and loitering law violations	96,342	− 2.1	—	—	96,342	− 2.1
Runaways	162,961	+ 4.6	—	—	162,961	+ 4.6
Total arrests*	1,504,402	+ 3.9	4,418,286	+ 5.7	5,922,688	+ 5.2

Data are from 4,222 agencies reporting on 1970 population of 137,267,000.
*Excludes arrests for suspicion.
Source: U.S. Department of Justice, Federal Bureau of Investigation, *Uniform Crime Reports.*

Disposition of persons formally charged, 1970

Offense	Charged (held for prosecution)	Guilty As charged	Guilty Lesser Offense	Acquitted or dismissed	Referred to juvenile court
Total	2,602,511	63.3%	3.5%	15.2%	18.0%
Murder, nonnegligent manslaughter	3,585	35.2	20.1	34.3	10.4
Manslaughter by negligence	961	38.4	10.8	42.2	8.5
Forcible rape	4,915	27.7	15.6	34.8	21.9
Robbery	23,320	25.2	11.1	23.6	40.1
Aggravated assault	38,466	36.3	14.5	31.1	18.1
Burglary: breaking, entering	97,282	23.1	8.6	12.9	55.5
Larceny: theft	236,495	45.6	3.9	14.5	36.0
Auto theft	47,519	18.7	5.3	13.9	62.1
Other assaults	123,729	46.4	4.0	36.0	13.7
Arson	3,163	17.8	4.6	15.4	62.2
Forgery and counterfeiting	13,903	55.9	10.3	21.2	12.6
Fraud	28,133	65.4	4.3	26.8	3.5
Embezzlement	2,884	51.1	6.2	32.3	10.3
Stolen property; buying, receiving, possessing	20,043	36.6	6.7	21.3	35.4
Vandalism	35,320	24.8	1.4	19.9	53.8
Weapons; carrying, possessing, etc.	37,164	58.3	6.2	22.0	13.5
Prostitution, commercialized vice	11,818	67.5	2.7	27.2	2.6
Sex offenses (except forcible rape, prostitution)	19,278	51.9	7.9	21.2	18.9
Narcotic drug laws	93,583	40.6	5.9	25.1	28.4
Gambling	27,877	69.0	3.7	26.0	1.3
Offenses against family, children	22,919	55.1	2.9	29.1	12.9
Driving while intoxicated	177,846	75.8	15.4	7.9	0.8
Liquor laws	105,005	65.1	1.5	12.3	21.1
Drunkenness	803,823	91.5	0.3	6.7	1.5
Disorderly conduct	217,237	60.5	1.0	23.0	15.4
Vagrancy	29,606	68.2	0.9	23.9	7.1
All other offenses	376,637	48.4	1.5	16.8	33.2

Data are from 3,025 cities with a 1970 population of 68,897,000. Source: U.S. Department of Justice, Federal Bureau of Investigation, *Uniform Crime Reports.*

Crime rates per 100,000 population

Metropolitan area	MURDER* 1960	MURDER* 1970	FORCIBLE RAPE 1960	FORCIBLE RAPE 1970	ROBBERY 1960	ROBBERY 1970	AGGRAVATED ASSAULT 1960	AGGRAVATED ASSAULT 1970	BURGLARY 1960	BURGLARY 1970	LARCENY† 1960	LARCENY† 1970	AUTO THEFT 1960	AUTO THEFT 1970
Baltimore	7.2	13.2	8.5	34.9	56.5	564.4	132.1	**395.9**	424.7	1,351.4	319.2	1,309.1	245.6	701.0
Boston	1.8	4.4	5.2	14.8	29.4	136.2	28.4	95.0	313.5	1,053.9	203.0	809.9	262.8	983.9
Chicago	6.7	12.9	17.0	25.4	**237.5**	362.5	134.9	232.7	640.8	829.6	451.4	617.2	442.3	708.4
Cleveland	5.3	14.5	5.3	18.7	81.7	287.9	33.0	132.1	265.0	826.1	125.6	595.2	196.3	**1,208.1**
Detroit	5.1	14.7	14.6	31.1	130.6	648.5	159.6	222.5	746.3	1,986.3	303.8	1,488.2	256.1	757.6
Houston	**10.9**	**16.9**	16.1	27.1	53.7	335.3	149.9	183.2	877.8	1,532.1	312.3	757.6	261.7	740.6
Los Angeles–Long Beach	4.4	9.4	**29.0**	**50.0**	143.9	307.3	**199.1**	370.8	**1,200.9**	1,980.5	**657.3**	1,401.3	**444.3**	944.6
Minneapolis–St. Paul	1.8	2.6	3.9	16.8	62.5	178.6	19.0	88.6	585.7	1,198.4	345.2	1,146.1	258.2	614.7
Newark	3.8	9.5	12.7	20.5	95.4	333.1	121.0	182.1	663.5	1,315.4	411.9	952.6	332.7	666.8
New York	4.0	10.5	8.4	19.9	64.2	**664.8**	106.9	285.6	414.2	1,821.0	565.0	1,471.2	228.4	947.1
Philadelphia	4.8	9.3	16.5	15.2	62.3	173.3	119.4	123.4	430.3	754.0	184.7	470.0	135.9	534.1
Pittsburgh	2.4	4.4	10.6	14.0	47.9	145.1	340.0	108.1	354.9	695.5	212.6	526.1	261.4	537.0
St. Louis	5.7	14.8	17.4	34.4	152.8	279.5	133.0	202.7	785.9	1,458.2	350.7	736.2	279.7	840.2
San Francisco–Oakland	3.5	8.3	11.9	42.9	102.8	347.7	92.9	226.1	739.9	**2,163.7**	335.7	**1,583.4**	320.8	957.0
Washington, D.C.	6.9	11.4	10.2	23.0	67.3	503.5	183.6	232.0	455.1	1,432.5	270.8	1,141.4	192.6	766.8

Boldface type indicates highest rate for that crime among the listed metropolitan areas.
*Includes nonnegligent manslaughter. †$50 and over.
Source: U.S. Department of Justice, Federal Bureau of Investigation, *Uniform Crime Reports.*

Transport, Power, and Communication

Mineral fuels and electricity production

in trillion British thermal units

		MINERAL FUELS				ELECTRICITY*	
Year	Total production	Bituminous coal and lignite	Anthra-cite	Crude petroleum	Natural gas, wet (unprocessed)	Hydro-power	Nuclear power
1965	49,467	13,417	378	15,930	17,652	2,051	39
1966	51,741†	13,507†	329	16,925	18,894	2,029†	57†
1967	54,791†	13,904†	311	18,098	20,087	2,311†	80†
1968	56,545†	13,664†	291	18,593	21,548†	2,319†	130†
1969†	58,727	13,957	266	18,886	22,858	2,614	146
1970‡	61,994	15,001	247	19,744	24,154	2,617	231

The fuel equivalent of hydropower and nuclear power is calculated from the kilowatt-hours of power produced, converted to coal input equivalent, at the prevailing average pounds of coal per kilowatt-hour each year at central electric plants, using 12,000 BTU per pound. Average annual conversion factors for the mineral fuels are those used by the U.S. Bureau of Mines and for fossil fuel steam electric plants, the average national heat value calculated by the Federal Power Commission.
*Includes installations owned by manufacturing plants and mines, as well as government owned public utilities.   †Revised.   ‡Preliminary.
Source: U.S Department of Interior, Bureau of Mines.   (F. H. Sĸ.)

Railroads

years ending December 31

Item		1965	1967	1969
Number of operating companies*		372	370	361
Miles of road owned, first track†		211,384	209,292	207,005
Total miles operated		370,636	368,030	364,854
Number of locomotives in service		30,061	29,874	29,090
Number of passenger-train cars in service‡		20,022	17,822	12,630
Operating revenues	($000,000)	10,425	10,582	11,659
Operating expenses	($000,000)	8,003	8,359	9,209
Net income§	($000,000)	866	368‖	517‖
Passenger revenue	($000,000)	556	489	442
Passengers carried	(000,000)	306	304	302
Passenger-miles	(000,000)	17,454	15,264	12,214
Revenue per passenger-mile	(cents)	3.185	3.201	3.615
Average journey per passenger	(miles)	57.07	50.21	40.49
Freight revenue	($000,000)	9,037	9,329	10,538
Freight revenue-tons originated	(000,000)	1,479	1,498	1,558
Tons carried one mile	(000,000)	705,705	727,075	773,830
Revenue ton-miles per mile of road	(000)	3,121	3,238	3,457
Revenue per ton-mile	(cents)	1.281	1.283	1.362
Haul per ton				
U.S. as a system	(miles)	477.15	485.21	496.82
Individual railroad	(miles)	257.40	262.49	272.77
Revenue per ton				
U.S. as a system	(dollars)	6.11	6.23	6.77
Individual railroad	(dollars)	3.30	3.37	3.71
Average number of employees	(000)	655	624	590
Compensation of employees	($000,000)	4,887	5,026	5,451

All data are for Classes I and II.
*Includes unofficial companies.
†Includes lessors, proprietary and unofficial companies.
‡Includes switching and terminal companies.
§Includes lessors.
‖After extraordinary and prior period items.
Source: Interstate Commerce Commission.

Transportation

	ROAD AND STREET MILEAGE Jan. 1, 1971					AUTOMOBILES, TRUCKS, AND BUSES registrations, in 000, 1970				RAILROAD MILEAGE OWNED Jan. 1, 1970		AIRPORTS‡ Jan. 1, 1971		CIVIL AIRCRAFT Jan. 1, 1971	
				Rural mileage			Private and commercial								
State	Total*	Total surfaced	Municipal mileage	State controlled	Locally controlled	Total	Auto-mobiles	Trucks and buses	Publicly owned†	Total	Class 1	Total	Private	Total	Eligible
Alabama	78,872	70,188	11,527	19,828§	47,242	1,966	1,553	385	28	4,567	3,888	128	41	2,036	1,750
Alaska	7,272	3,799	774	4,399	1,511	139	93	41	5	20	—	708	211	2,970	2,551
Arizona	42,669	21,248	5,980	5,429	18,054	1,093	822	250	21	2,052	1,879	215	113	2,867	2,398
Arkansas	78,850	60,131	8,776	12,990	55,136	1,043	724	305	14	3,584	3,318	144	71	1,888	1,625
California	164,136	120,091	44,966	13,871	71,190	11,901	9,821	1,906	174	7,447	6,636	730	466	20,365	17,389
Colorado	82,315	50,563	7,311	8,314	66,639	1,442	1,092	324	26	3,510	3,393	209	134	2,563	2,325
Connecticut	18,407	18,264	13,026	1,514	3,867	1,733	1,527	184	22	688	633	78	65	1,336	1,157
Delaware	4,892	4,871	1,485	3,407§	—	313	261	47	5	287	—	26	23	435	378
District of Columbia	1,086	1,086	1,086	—	—	257	230	17	10	31	12	6	1	21	18
Florida	89,499	62,306	20,559	16,937	50,951	4,120	3,540	521	59	4,290	3,814	291	181	6,649	5,691
Georgia	99,995	68,883	14,883	15,456	68,545	2,584	2,060	496	28	5,436	3,807	202	97	3,433	3,070
Hawaii	3,529	3,342	988	807	1,643	405	355	43	7	—	—	59	35	312	260
Idaho	56,049	30,783	2,927	4,750	26,382	474	327	133	14	2,668	2,478	166	44	1,360	1,151
Illinois	129,942	123,495	27,428	13,272	89,242	5,238	4,539	643	56	10,868	9,091	599	520	6,554	5,759
Indiana	91,011	86,053	12,822	10,276	67,913	2,815	2,293	496	26	6,441	3,424	179	118	3,742	3,304
Iowa	112,119	105,466	12,884	8,980	90,228	1,790	1,381	378	31	8,127	7,866	236	134	2,905	2,576
Kansas	133,987	98,453	10,918	9,978	113,091	1,548	1,121	402	25	7,801	7,777	270	157	3,510	3,090
Kentucky	69,071	60,722	5,683	23,859§	39,093	1,763	1,370	370	23	3,518	3,097	69	22	1,147	1,044
Louisiana	52,845	48,382	10,787	14,200‖	27,572	1,742	1,358	360	24	3,793	3,482	221	152	2,538	2,251
Maine	21,356	19,761	2,401	10,955¶	7,838	515	405	104	6	1,679	1,523	139	96	735	633
Maryland	26,309	26,234	4,131	4,940	17,093	1,872	1,620	233	19	1,127	564	81	64	2,050	1,813
Massachusetts	29,074	28,420	21,647	1,210	6,168	2,575	2,301	241	33	1,462	1,258	118	92	2,237	1,997
Michigan	114,729	97,091	19,939	7,971	86,817	4,569	3,897	603	69	6,301	4,217	305	176	6,197	5,523
Minnesota	127,742	115,588	17,166	11,514	97,212	2,206	1,747	431	28	7,908	7,787	262	130	3,889	3,402
Mississippi	66,782	64,226	6,441	9,715	50,096	1,117	817	282	18	3,653	3,170	152	85	1,724	1,478
Missouri	115,261	107,633	15,236	30,006	69,345	2,408	1,883	501	24	6,355	5,726	286	188	3,393	2,957
Montana	78,276	41,417	2,344	11,834	53,593	485	311	164	10	4,925	4,888	179	64	1,527	1,388
Nebraska	100,445	76,138	6,591	9,523	83,797	974	707	251	16	5,498	5,496	259	177	1,904	1,710
Nevada	49,704	16,177	1,911	6,141§	41,651	355	262	80	13	1,635	1,474	102	51	1,051	915
New Hampshire	14,823	12,208	4,766	3,044	6,893	362	302	53	7	816	679	52	36	633	531
New Jersey	32,059	29,815	17,034	1,712	13,308	3,586	3,198	327	61	1,762	932	184	159	3,549	3,082
New Mexico	67,326	20,119	4,605	11,691	45,484	637	451	172	14	2,120	2,046	127	62	1,464	1,330
New York	105,753	101,608	23,032	14,417	68,269	6,718	5,968	648	102	5,662	4,743	414	350	5,906	5,073
North Carolina	86,019	78,319	13,868	70,355§		2,826	2,208	541	77	4,163	2,947	210	154	2,808	2,475
North Dakota	106,897	69,332	3,111	6,557	95,939	428	266	153	9	5,164	5,096	184	99	1,197	1,030
Ohio	108,926	107,255	23,402	16,867	68,657	5,975	5,290	628	57	7,884	4,564	447	346	6,659	5,876
Oklahoma	107,870	79,526	13,784	11,506	82,550	1,713	1,211	476	26	5,439	5,347	230	123	3,324	2,875
Oregon	95,063	59,846	6,249	9,019	35,351	1,369	1,107	233	29	3,075	2,774	221	124	2,874	2,440
Pennsylvania	115,167	96,031	23,874	44,146	46,425	5,819	5,040	716	63	8,444	5,595	475	408	5,184	4,471
Rhode Island	5,342	5,203	4,340	481	521	488	431	52	5	146	103	14	7	219	196
South Carolina	59,726	40,166	6,769	31,312	21,188	1,360	1,095	240	25	3,102	2,115	115	53	1,252	1,093
South Dakota	84,184	59,457	2,975	8,663	70,879	426	290	126	10	3,721	3,721	113	46	1,046	930
Tennessee	78,666	76,792	10,316	8,247	58,900	2,050	1,631	388	31	3,237	2,783	108	42	2,055	1,858
Texas	245,532	181,172	47,207	60,855	136,478	6,693	5,104	1,488	101	13,888	13,210	982	729	11,971	10,407
Utah	40,440	23,017	4,392	4,765	21,632	626	476	137	13	1,749	1,685	81	24	840	749
Vermont	14,464	12,502	978	2,534	10,757	229	189	36	4	770	325	44	31	267	238
Virginia	61,136	59,931	8,483	49,726§	829	2,263	1,875	343	45	3,932	3,278	185	136	2,164	1,920
Washington	75,098	62,059	9,950	11,135	39,463	2,102	1,605	453	44	4,931	4,815	240	135	4,126	3,463
West Virginia	35,499	26,583	3,580	31,332§		860	680	167	13	3,547	3,161	47	25	777	692
Wisconsin	103,232	97,277	14,056	10,764	78,338	2,218	1,851	328	39	5,970	5,675	256	155	3,052	2,608
Wyoming	40,636	17,434	1,282	5,798	20,944	247	157	84	6	1,812	1,805	80	39	677	605
Total U.S.	3,730,082	2,946,463	560,670	707,002	2,274,714	108,436	88,841	17,978	1,617	207,005	178,099	11,226	6,991	153,382	133,545

*Includes federally controlled rural roads.   †Excludes vehicles owned by military services.   ‡Includes seaplane bases, heliports, and military fields having joint civil-military use.
§Includes mileage of state-controlled county roads.   ‖Includes mileage designated as farm-to-market.   ¶Includes the state-aid system.

Sources: Interstate Commerce Commission; U.S. Department of Transportation, Federal Aviation Administration; Federal Highway Administration, Bureau of Public Roads.

Commerce of selected ports

1970 in thousands of short tons (cargo)

Port	FOREIGN		DOMESTIC		Port	FOREIGN		DOMESTIC	
	Imports	Exports	Receipts	Shipments		Imports	Exports	Receipts	Shipments
COASTAL PORTS					Gulf coast				
Atlantic coast					Tampa, Fla.	2,469	10,804	11,900	4,624
Portland, Me.	24,643	11	3,906	938	Mobile, Ala.	8,777	2,940	33	1,838
Salem, Mass.	939	—	305	1	New Orleans, La.	7,535	24,680	1,966	29,441
Boston, Mass.	9,014	816	13,196	2,006	Baton Rouge, La.	7,211	6,763	762	8,787
Providence, R.I.	2,389	287	6,106	496	Lake Charles, La.†	193	1,692	32	3,386
New Haven, Conn.	3,359	313	6,355	1,409	Galveston, Tex.	321	2,124	241	319
Bridgeport, Conn.	2,134	123	1,361	198	Texas City, Tex.	158	724	268	5,101
Norwalk, Conn.	—	—	1,056	—	Houston, Tex.	4,828	12,256	2,365	19,994
New York, N.Y. and N.J.	50,792	7,140	35,916	18,099	Corpus Christi, Tex.	3,986	2,867	139	12,711
Hempstead, N.Y.	—	—	1,821	2,326	Harbor Island, Tex.	—	1	—	4,498
Port Jefferson, N.Y.	721	—	3,436	176	Freeport, Tex.	8	1,116	118	1,049
Albany, N.Y.	1,954	345	3,129	—	Brazos Island, Tex.	1,845	477	—	1,443
Delaware River ports*	49,634	4,412	36,178	8,279	Beaumont, Tex.	102	3,515	629	15,597
Baltimore, Md.	20,480	9,375	5,233	1,586	Port Arthur, Tex.	316	1,818	3,329	10,391
Norfolk, Va.	6,120	35,549	2,213	728					
Newport News, Va.	605	13,906	1	17				ALL COMMERCE‡	
Wilmington, N.C.	1,915	217	2,320	208	**GREAT LAKES PORTS**			Receipts	Shipments
Charleston, S.C.	2,593	694	2,939	148					
Savannah, Ga.	2,736	1,398	1,809	140	Ashtabula, Ohio			6,303	5,598
Jacksonville, Fla.	4,576	1,340	3,663	606	Buffalo, N.Y.			14,301	716
Port Everglades, Fla.	2,708	172	5,804	604	Chicago, Ill.			15,588	11,302
Pacific coast					Cleveland, Ohio			21,772	965
Long Beach, Calif.	5,618	6,909	5,222	3,286	Conneaut, Ohio			7,966	7,569
Los Angeles, Calif.	4,811	4,909	5,923	6,009	Detroit, Mich.			29,183	1,753
San Francisco Bay area, Calif.	6,253	6,589	16,799	10,010	Duluth-Superior, Minn. and Wis.			3,683	39,075
Stockton, Calif.	55	1,172	167	35	Indiana Harbor, Ind.			12,148	5,222
Portland, Ore.	1,322	3,886	4,421	309	Lorain, Ohio			4,990	3,183
Longview, Wash.	452	3,117	675	197	Milwaukee, Wis.			5,066	1,905
Tacoma, Wash.	2,239	2,794	399	225	Sandusky, Ohio			47	4,986
Seattle, Wash.	2,655	1,685	2,174	875	Toledo, Ohio			7,128	24,412
Honolulu, Hawaii	1,498	132	3,974	2,465					

Data exclude purely local port traffic and commerce with ports on internal rivers and canals.
*Includes tributaries. †Includes Calcasieu River and Pass.
‡Includes both foreign and domestic shipping.
Source: U.S. Department of the Army, Corps of Engineers, *Waterborne Commerce of the United States.*

Communication facilities

State	Post offices July 1, 1971	RADIO STATIONS January 1, 1970		TV STATIONS March 1, 1971		TELEPHONES January 1, 1971		NEWSPAPERS					
								Daily		Weekly April 1, 1971		Sunday	
		AM	FM	Commer-cial	Educa-tional	Total	Residence	Number Feb. 1, 1971	Circulation Sept. 30, 1970	Number	Circulation	Number Feb. 1, 1971	Circulation Sept. 30, 1970
Alabama	675	134	51	16	9	1,562,800	1,169,900	22	714,647	106	388,146	15	626,034
Alaska	201	18	3	7	—	953,700	...	6	71,437	6	9,540	1	16,843
Arizona	216	59	15	11	2	953,700	656,000	13	439,696	56	141,453	5	361,735
Arkansas	710	84	35	6	1	858,900	641,200	35	426,467	124	271,499	11	329,701
California	1,171	231	145	48	9	13,305,500	9,367,700	126	5,688,923	433	5,092,540	38	4,825,414
Colorado	425	67	26	11	2	2,061,200	1,509,500	27	937,338	49	290,194	7	630,442
Connecticut	251	38	20	5	3	1,374,400	957,600	3	158,752	11	55,963	—	
Delaware	57	10	4	—	1	379,600	277,600	3	1,011,719	...	...	2	996,422
Dist. of Columbia	1	6	6	6	1	878,400	456,400	50	2,059,741	133	511,034	29	1,829,826
Florida	471	191	88	23	9	4,141,600	2,940,900	32	994,136	182	530,618	11	928,086
Georgia	660	169	57	16	10	2,413,000	1,742,700	5	235,378	2	17,127	2	187,048
Hawaii	80	25	4	10	2	...	...	15	179,995	57	104,611	5	143,116
Idaho	277	42	7	7	1	357,800	256,200	92	3,986,270	556	2,772,558	20	2,612,597
Illinois	1,299	121	92	23	5	7,110,000	5,120,000	80	1,688,749	194	466,634	19	1,148,518
Indiana	771	83	72	18	5	2,905,300	2,196,200	43	999,589	360	701,033	9	845,137
Iowa	975	73	35	13	2	1,624,800	1,242,800	50	657,904	246	453,578	15	445,272
Kansas	736	57	24	12	2	1,303,700	984,200	27	770,723	138	456,363	13	571,568
Kentucky	1,362	102	60	10	14	1,435,300	1,071,900	23	771,203	90	256,897	10	670,965
Louisiana	553	90	41	16	1	1,780,600	1,334,400	9	266,907	35	137,681	1	112,129
Maine	515	36	13	7	4	490,100	367,500	12	709,262	66	534,327	4	680,348
Maryland	433	52	31	6	1	2,482,200	1,787,600	47	2,392,717	145	851,495	8	1,616,286
Massachusetts	453	62	38	10	2	3,522,900	2,458,500	56	2,512,389	295	1,421,973	13	2,189,198
Michigan	888	124	76	20	4	5,134,700	3,826,800	30	1,116,865	321	674,766	7	991,640
Minnesota	892	83	39	13	4	2,247,900	1,677,000	20	323,327	99	236,514	8	228,307
Mississippi	491	99	34	9	1	891,400	676,200	52	1,760,188	281	642,344	14	1,173,169
Missouri	1,015	104	41	23	2	2,753,400	2,009,500	14	189,041	73	127,912	9	184,414
Montana	392	41	7	12	—	357,000	259,800	19	485,796	199	426,761	4	359,264
Nebraska	567	47	15	14	9	883,700	659,200	7	150,497	16	33,547	4	126,105
Nevada	99	20	8	7	1	333,000	207,500	9	165,267	33	101,937	1	54,609
New Hampshire	254	25	10	1	5	425,300	319,900	32	1,790,801	213	1,175,659	9	1,270,266
New Jersey	523	32	26	1	—	4,785,900	3,542,600	19	212,908	25	60,609	12	181,739
New Mexico	347	55	19	7	1	494,400	329,200	80	7,487,953	405	1,722,368	16	6,400,393
New York	1,651	157	91	30	8	12,415,600	8,492,400	48	1,264,720	135	467,331	19	921,079
North Carolina	798	195	71	17	6	2,384,500	1,755,400	10	187,903	91	163,635	3	105,973
North Dakota	483	27	11	12	1	321,000	237,300	96	3,535,338	263	1,414,318	19	2,321,687
Ohio	1,092	116	108	27	8	6,200,500	4,633,100	53	848,665	211	369,185	42	789,538
Oklahoma	665	64	35	10	3	1,469,200	1,060,200	22	663,046	93	309,737	5	534,190
Oregon	371	80	17	13	2	1,189,700	855,700	109	3,971,529	229	1,273,045	10	2,983,205
Pennsylvania	1,861	169	109	24	8	7,475,900	5,646,600	7	321,066	13	91,468	2	217,921
Rhode Island	59	15	7	3	1	530,700	387,100	17	563,467	77	235,752	7	440,176
South Carolina	401	101	37	11	5	1,167,500	865,200	12	170,916	146	200,680	4	121,464
South Dakota	438	29	6	10	4	334,500	255,900	32	1,127,679	123	384,371	14	946,056
Tennessee	609	139	61	16	5	1,947,300	1,442,800	112	3,243,507	490	1,179,733	83	3,149,720
Texas	1,579	285	122	50	6	6,328,600	4,606,100	5	260,451	50	109,222	4	257,053
Utah	231	31	10	3	4	595,600	430,300	9	116,327	13	26,778	—	
Vermont	296	18	4	2	4	235,600	167,600	32	1,010,944	109	484,257	13	721,744
Virginia	975	123	53	13	5	2,475,900	1,775,500	23	1,035,099	143	833,512	12	963,146
Washington	499	96	39	15	6	1,996,300	1,438,300	31	490,192	81	233,982	9	376,539
West Virginia	1,079	58	23	9	3	762,600	572,200	37	1,206,153	241	667,644	6	825,299
Wisconsin	802	97	74	17	3	2,370,100	1,728,000	9	74,863	29	62,275	3	48,948
Wyoming	182	29	1	3	—	195,900	137,300						
TOTAL U.S.	31,831	4,209	2,021	673	195	119,645,500	86,533,500	1,748*	62,107,527*	7,610†	29,422,487†	586*	49,216,602*

*Total has been adjusted to account for double listings of Covington, Ky. edition of an Ohio newspaper. †Excludes District of Columbia.
Sources: U.S. Post Office Department. Federal Communications Commission. Television Digest, Inc., *Television Factbook* (Copyright 1971. All rights reserved. Used by permission. American Telephone and Telegraph Co. The Editor & Publisher Co., Inc., *International Year Book* (Copyright 1971. All rights reserved. Used by permission.) American Newspaper Representatives, Inc.

Foreign Trade and Affairs

Major recipients of foreign assistance

in millions of dollars

Program and country	1965	1967	1969	1971*
Total	5,644	6,600	5,084	6,113
By program				
Economic assistance programs	4,335	5,120	4,067	4,632
Agency for International Development	2,033	2,253†	1,449†	1,700†
Loans	1,129	1,091	570	608
Grants	904	1,162	879	1,092
Food for Peace	1,370	976	1,242	1,150
Export-Import Bank long-term loans	360	1,338	724	1,349
Other economic programs‡	572	553	652	432
Military assistance programs	1,309	1,480	1,017	1,481
By country				
Africa				
Congo (Kinshasa)	27	47	13	31
Ethiopia	28	27	11	36
Ghana	3	37	39	22
Guinea	19	¶	33	12
Liberia	42	11	14	11
Morocco	36	52	50	58
Nigeria	35	18	58	35
Tunisia	50	54	42	47
Asia				
Afghanistan	31	32	23	15
Ceylon	4	10	31	16
India	698§	588	451	448
Indonesia	−1	58	249	187
Iran	91	181	170	360
Israel	70	12	75§	69
Japan	72	112	109	120
Jordan	46	64	14	17
Korea, South	355	331	451	381
Laos	48§	55§	50§	48‖
Pakistan	342§	234	86	96
Philippines	45	66	59	115
Ryukyu Islands	17	38	17	3
Taiwan	132	92	75	150
Thailand	78	82	36‖	18‖
Vietnam, South	542	541‖	349‖	550‖
Canada			6	64
Europe				
Greece	131	46	56	87
Italy	88	64	51	83
Spain	99	177	70	37
Turkey	118	118	109	203
United Kingdom	¶	407	100	13
Yugoslavia	87	12	27	31
Latin America				
Argentina	16	12	77	48
Bolivia	14	31	38	13
Brazil	287	286	50	179
Chile	138	290	112	−13
Colombia	38	145	135	108
Costa Rica	16	14	18	8
Dominican Republic	77	62	33	20
Ecuador	25	8	16	27
El Salvador	19	4	15	6
Guatemala	14	22	80	21
Jamaica	7	5	18	27
Mexico	105	102	18	31
Panama	24	36	18	14
Paraguay	10	6	18	14
Peru	43	39	33	20
Venezuela	47	45	8	23
Oceania				
Australia	19	242	182	146
Trust Territory of the Pacific Islands	18	24	40	63
Nonregional	345	520	620	640

Years ending June 30. Economic assistance data on net obligation and loan authorization basis, rather than expenditure basis. Military assistance data represent value of goods delivered. A minus figure indicates deobligations in excess of new obligations.
*Preliminary. †Excludes $43 million in 1967, $35 million in 1969 and $65 million in 1971 in Department of Defense reimbursements for grants to Vietnam.
‡Principal programs include contributions to international lending organizations and the Peace Corps. §Economic assistance only; military assistance data classified. Values are included in overall total. ‖Economic assistance only. Military assistance transferrred to the Department of Defense. ¶Less than $500,000.
Source: U.S. Department of State, Agency for International Development.

International investment position

in millions of dollars

Item	1960	1965	1970*
U.S. assets abroad	85,589	120,374	166,574
Nonliquid	66,230	103,156	149,714
Private	49,310	79,760	117,517
Long-term	44,497	71,375	104,693
Direct investments	31,865	49,474	78,090
Portfolio	12,632	21,901	26,603
Short-term	4,813	8,385	12,824
U.S. government	16,920	23,396	32,197
Long-term credits	14,028	20,200	29,699
Foreign currencies and other claims	2,892	3,196	2,498
Liquid	19,359	17,218	16,860
Private		1,768	2,373
U.S. monetary reserve assets	19,359	15,450	14,487
Gold	17,804	13,806	11,072
Special drawing rights	—	—	851
Convertible currencies	—	781	629
IMF gold tranche position	1,555	863	1,935
U.S. liabilities to foreigners	40,859	58,797	97,507
Nonliquid	19,830	29,224	50,466
Private	19,037	27,280	48,496
Long-term	18,418	26,315	44,758
Direct investments	6,910	8,797	13,209
Portfolio	11,508	17,518	31,549
Short-term	619	965	3,738
U.S. government	793	1,944	1,970
Liquid	21,029	29,573	47,041
To private foreigners	9,139	12,909	22,645
To foreign official agencies	11,890	16,664	24,396
Net international investment position	44,730	61,577	69,067

Estimates for end of year. *Preliminary.
Source: U.S. Department of Commerce, Office of Business Economics, *Survey of Current Business.*

Major commodities traded, 1970

in millions of dollars

Item	Total	Canada	American Republics	Western Europe*	Far East†	Other areas
Total exports	43,226	9,084	5,696	14,465	8,675	5,306
Agricultural commodities						
Grains and preparations‡	2,588	175	226	686	1,183	318
Fruits, nuts, and vegetables‡	584	224	51	212	67	30
Tobacco, unmanufactured	488	2	5	320	120	41
Soybeans	1,216	175	23	605	378	35
Cotton, excluding linters, waste	372	27	2	35	284	24
Non agricultural commodities						
Ores and scrap, metal	938	78	52	368	420	20
Coal, coke, and briquettes	1,044	212	75	312	412	33
Petroleum products	469	55	79	146	128	61
Chemicals	3,826	554	716	1,453	657	446
Machinery‖¶	11,632	2,506	1,836	3,914	1,805	1,571
Agricultural machines and tractors and parts¶	933	242	203	201	111	176
Other nonelectrical machinery‖	7,699	1,661	1,188	2,626	1,155	1,069
Electrical apparatus	3,000	603	445	1,087	540	325
Road motor vehicles‖ϙ	3,186	2,064	463	227	129	303
Automotive parts, nonmilitary	1,603	1,175	194	92	38	104
Aircraft, civilian, and parts for all aircraft	2,192	241	218	1,107	335	291
Pulp, paper, and manufactures	1,123	117	199	497	165	145
Metals and manufactures	2,978	630	469	1,181	427	271
Iron and steelmill productsδ	1,190	251	209	449	167	114
Textile yarn, fabrics, and made-up articles	603	140	78	180	85	120
Other	9,987	1,884	1,204	3,222	2,080	1,597
Total imports	39,963	11,091	4,779	11,175	9,277	3,641
Agricultural commodities						
Meat and preparations	1,014	77	214	241	4	478
Fruits, nuts, and vegetables	735	32	417	115	128	43
Coffee	1,160	—	769	§	41	350
Sugar	729	—	421	2	220	86
Nonagricultural commodities						
Alcoholic beverages	725	180	5	533	3	4
Pulp, paper, and manufactures	1,574	1,435	5	93	31	10
Ores and scrap, metal	1,149	513	291	24	34	287
Petroleum, crude and partly refined	1,449	654	445	17	53	280
Petroleum products	1,321	49	567	122	4	579
Chemicals	1,450	362	54	611	194	229
Machinery¶	5,374	1,264	157	2,132	1,781	40
Transport equipmentϙ	5,797	3,141	12	1,796	842	6
Automobiles, new	3,719	1,806	§	1,457	456	—
Iron and steelmill productsδ	1,954	194	39	785	912	24
Nonferrous base metals	1,502	636	289	216	256	105
Textile yarn, fabrics, and made-up articles	1,135	27	41	450	579	38
Fish, including shellfish	794	193	177	125	175	124
Other imports	12,101	2,334	876	3,913	4,020	958

*Includes Greece and Turkey. †Asia, excluding the Near East. ‡Includes shipments for relief by individuals and private agencies. §Less than $500,000. ‖Excludes "Special Category" commodities. ¶Includes parts for tractors reported under transport equipment. ϙExcludes parts for tractors. δExcludes pig iron. Source: U.S. Dept. of Commerce, Bureau of the Census, *Statistical Abstract of the United States.*
Data compiled by the U.S. Department of Commerce, Bureau of International Commerce.

CONTRIBUTORS

Initials and names of contributors to the Britannica Book of the Year *with the articles written by them. The arrangement is alphabetical by initials.*

A.D.Bu./El Salvador; Honduras
ALLEN D. BUSHONG. Associate Professor of Geography, University of South Carolina.

A.Dr./Industrial Review (*in part*)
ALFRED DAWBER. Textile consultant in all aspects of textile production. Specialized writer on textile, engineering, and electrical subjects.

Ad.T./Literature (*in part*)
ADRIEN THERIO. Professor of Lettres Françaises, University of Ottawa. Author of *L'Humour au Canada français; Soliloque en hommage à une femme.*

A.D.Wi./Sweden
ALAN DAVID WILSON. Assistant Editor, *Sweden Now.*

Ae.B./Literature (*in part*)
ANNIE J. M. BRIERRE. Literary Critic, *Les Nouvelles Littéraires; La Revue des Deux Mondes; France—U.S.A.* Author of *Ninon de Lenclos.*

A.F.D./Merchandising (*in part*)
ALTON F. DOODY. Professor of Marketing, College of Administrative Science, Ohio State University, and Vice-Chairman, Management Horizons, Inc. Author of *Retailing Management; Marketing in America: Settlement to Civil War* (vol. 1).

A.G./Malta
ALBERT GANADO. Lawyer, Malta.

A.G.A./Investment, International; Trade, International
ALAN GORDON ARMSTRONG. Lecturer, Department of Economics, University of Bristol.

A.G.Bl./Biography (*in part*)**; Music** (*in part*)
ALAN GEOFFREY BLYTH. Music Critic, London.

A.G.R./Religion (*in part*)
ARTHUR GUY REYNOLDS. Registrar and Associate Professor of Church History, Emmanuel College, Toronto.

A.J./Sailing
ADRIAN JARDINE. Company Director, and Public Relations consultant. Secretary, Guild of Yachting Writers.

A.J.A.M./Biography (*in part*)**; Turkey**
ANDREW JAMES ALEXANDER MANGO. Orientalist and broadcaster.

A.J.Z./European Unity
ARNOLD J. ZURCHER. Professor of Comparative Politics, Graduate School of Arts and Sciences, New York University.

Al.Ma./Engineering Projects (*in part*)
ALDO MARCELLO. Civil Engineer.

Al.Pa./Medicine (*in part*)
ALEXANDER PATON. Consultant Physician, Birmingham Hospital Group, Eng. Postgraduate Clinical Tutor, University of Birmingham, Eng.

A.P.Kl./Religion (*in part*)
ALFRED PAUL KLAUSLER. Executive Secretary, Associated Church Press; Religion Editor, Westinghouse Broadcasting Company. Author of *Censorship, Obscenity and Sex; Growth in Worship.*

A.R.A./Cricket
ARTHUR REX ALSTON. Broadcaster and Journalist. Author of *Taking the Air; Over to Rex Alston; Test Commentary; Watching Cricket.*

Ar.C.B./Indonesia
ARNOLD C. BRACKMAN. Author of *Indonesian Communism: A History; Southeast Asia's Second Front: The Power Struggle in the Malay Archipelago; The Communist Collapse in Indonesia.*

A.R.G.G./Australia; Biography (*in part*)**; Nauru**
ANTHONY ROYSTON GRANT GRIFFITHS. Lecturer in History, Flinders University of South Australia.

A.R.W./Panama
ALMON ROBERT WRIGHT. Retired Senior Historian, U.S. Department of State.

A.S./Museums and Galleries (*in part*)
ANDREW SZPAKOWSKI. Head, Section of Standards, Research and Museums, UNESCO, Paris.

A.Sd./Swimming
ALBERT SCHOENFIELD. Editor, *Swimming World.*

A.S.M./Medicine (*in part*)
ABRAHAM SAMUEL MARKOWITZ, M.D. Head, Department of Experimental Immunology, Hektoen Institute for Medical Research of the Cook County Hospital, Chicago.

A.Th./Libraries
ANTHONY THOMPSON. General Secretary, 1962–70, International Federation of Library Associations. Author of *Vocabularium Bibliothecarii; Library Buildings of Britain and Europe.*

A.Tl./Industrial Review (*in part*)
ARTHUR TATTERSALL. Textile Trade Expert and Statistician, Manchester, Eng.

A.W.Bs./Japan
ARDATH WALTER BURKS. Professor and Director, International Programs, Rutgers University, New Brunswick, N.J. Author of *The Government of Japan; East Asia: China, Korea, Japan.*

A.W.O./Nicaragua
ARDEN W. OHL. Instructor of Geography, Modesto (Calif.) Junior College.

Ay.K./Literature (*in part*)
(THOMAS) ANTHONY KERRIGAN. Editor and translator of *Selected Works* of Miguel de Unamuno (10 vol.). Author of *At the Front Door of the Atlantic.* Co-translator of *Selected Poems* of Pablo Neruda (1970).

B.Ar./Ireland
BRUCE ARNOLD. Free-lance Journalist and Writer, Dublin.

B.C.N./Fuel and Power (*in part*)
BRUCE CARLTON NETSCHERT. Vice President, National Economic Research Associates, Inc., Washington, D.C. Author of *The Future Supply of Oil and Gas.* Co-author of *Energy in the American Economy: 1850-1975.*

B.D./Biography (*in part*)
BRENDA DAVIES. Head of Information Department, British Film Institute.

Be.N./Track and Field Sports (*in part*)
BERT NELSON. Editor and Publisher, *Track and Field News.*

B.Gr./Music (*in part*)
BENNY GREEN. Jazz Critic, *Observer,* London; Record Reviewer, British Broadcasting Corporation. Author of *The Reluctant Art; Blame It on My Youth; 58 Minutes to London; Jazz Decade.* Contributor to *Encyclopedia of Jazz.*

B.L.Go./Religion (*in part*)
BRIAN LLEWELLYN GOLLAND. General Secretary, The General Assembly of Unitarian and Free Christian Churches, London.

B.S.Ka./Biography (*in part*)
BERNARD SOLOMON KATZ. Public Information Specialist with the U.S. Department of Defense.

C.C.O./Engineering Projects (*in part*)**; Industrial Review** (*in part*)
CARTER CLARKE OSTERBIND. Director, Bureau of Economic and Business Research, University of Florida. Editor, *Feasible Planning for Social Change in the Field of Aging.*

Cd.H./Religion (*in part*)
CLIFFORD HAIGH. Editor, *The Friend,* London.

C.E.N./Religion (*in part*)
C. EMIL NELSON. National Chief Secretary and Colonel, Salvation Army, U.S.A.

C.E.R./Timber
CHARLES EDGAR RANDALL. Assistant Editor, *Journal of Forestry.* Author of *Famous Trees; Our Forests.*

C.F.Sa./Finland
CARL FREDRIK SANDELIN. Foreign News Editor, Finnish News Agency. President, Society of Swedish-speaking Writers in Finland.

C.H.J./U.S. Supplement: *Church Membership Table.*
CONSTANT HERBERT JACQUET, JR. Director of Research Library and Research Associate, National Council of Churches. Editor, *Yearbook of American Churches.*

C.J.Ay./Motor Sports (*in part*)
CYRIL J. AYTON. Editor, *Motorcycle Sport,* London.

C.L.Be./Environment (*in part*)
CHARLES LEOFRIC BOYLE. Lieutenant-Colonel, R.A. (retd.). Chairman, Survival Service Commission, International Union for Conservation of Nature and Natural Resources, 1958–63; Secretary, Fauna Preservation Society, London, 1950–63.

C.L.F.W./Life Sciences (*in part*)
CHRISTOPHER LEONARD FRANK WOODCOCK. Lecturer on Biology and Associate in Electron Microscopy, Department of Biology, Harvard University.

C.M.Jo./Bowling and Lawn Bowls (*in part*)
CLARENCE MEDLYCOTT JONES. Editor, *World Bowls; Lawn Tennis.* Author of *Winning Bowls; The Watney Book of Bowls; Bowls: How to Become a Champion.* Co-author of *Tackle Bowls My Way; Bryant on Bowls.*

Co.L./Biography (*in part*)
COLIN LEGUM. Commonwealth Correspondent, *Observer*, London. Author of *Must We Lose Africa?; Bandung, Cairo and Accra; Congo Disaster; Pan-Africanism— A Short Political Guide*. Co-author of *Attitude to Africa; South Africa: Crisis for the West; The Bitter Choice*. Editor of *Africa —A Handbook to the Continent*.

Co.S./Commercial Policies
CONSTANT CHUNG-TSE SHIH. Counsellor, Trade Policy Department, General Agreement on Tariffs and Trade (GATT), Switz.

C.Th./Biography (*in part*)
CASSIE W. THOMPSON. Researcher, *Life* Magazine.

Cy.W./Industrial Review (*in part*)
CYRIL WEEDEN. Assistant Director, Glass Manufacturers' Federation, London.

D.A.F./Archaeology (*in part*)
DAVID A. FREDRICKSON. Associate Professor of Anthropology, Sonoma State College, Rohnert Park, Calif.

D.A.Ha./Engineering Projects (*in part*)
DAVID ALEXANDER HARRIES. Director and Chief Engineer, The Mitchell Construction Kinnear Moodie Group Ltd., London.

Da.J.R./Motion Pictures (*in part*)
DAVID JULIEN ROBINSON. Film Critic, *The Financial Times*. Author of *Buster Keaton; Hollywood in the Twenties; The Great Funnies—A History of Screen Comedy*.

Da.L.S./Environment (*in part*)
DAVID LAWRENCE SMITH. Staff member, Centre for Environmental Studies, London.

D.A.S.J./Employment, Wages, and Hours
DUDLEY ANTHONY STEPHENSON JACKSON. Research Officer, Department of Applied Economics, University of Cambridge; Fellow of St. Catharine's College, Cambridge.

D.B.J.F./Football (*in part*)
DAVID BROUGH JAMES FROST. Rugby Union Correspondent, *The Guardian*, London.

D.Bo./Biography (*in part*); **Netherlands**
DICK BOONSTRA. Member of the staff, Department of Political Science, Free University, Amsterdam.

D.D./Economics
DUDLEY DILLARD. Professor and Head, Department of Economics, University of Maryland. Author of *The Economics of John Maynard Keynes; Economic Development of the North Atlantic Community*.

D.F.C./Metallurgy
DONALD FREDERIC CLIFTON. Professor of Metallurgy, University of Idaho.

D.Fo./Migration, International (*in part*)
DAVID FOUQUET. Staff Writer, *Congressional Quarterly*.

D.H.Wo./Transportation (*in part*)
DAVID HUMPHREY WOOLLEY. Air Transport Editor, *Flight International*, London.

D.K.Da./Bolivia; Spain
DAVID KEITH DAVIES. Economic and Political Research Officer, Lloyds and Bolsa International Bank Ltd., London.

D.K.R.P./Sporting Record
DAVID KEMSLEY ROBIN PHILLIPS. Contributor, *World Sports*. Editor, *World Sports Olympic Games Report*. Co-compiler of *Guinness Book of Olympic Records*.

D.L.Bi./Insurance (*in part*)
DAVID LYNN BICKELHAUPT. Professor of Insurance, College of Administrative Science, Ohio State University. Author of *Transition to Multiple-Line Insurance Companies*. Co-author of *General Insurance*.

D.L.McE./Medicine (*in part*)
DONALD L. McELROY, D.D.S. Associate Dean, College of Dentistry, University of Illinois. Co-author of *Handbook of Oral Diagnosis and Treatment Planning*.

D.Me./Social Services (*in part*)
DAVID MICHAEL MAZIE. Associate of Carl T. Rowan, syndicated columnist. Free-lance writer.

D.M.L.F./Canada
DAVID M. L. FARR. Professor of History, Carleton University, Ottawa. Author of *The Colonial Office and Canada, 1867–1887; Two Democracies; The Canadian Experience*.

Do.B./Telecommunications (*in part*)
DON BYRNE. Washington correspondent, *Electronic Design* and *Microwaves*.

D.P.B./Industrial Review (*in part*)
DONALD P. BURKE. Senior Editor, *Chemical Week*.

D.R.J./Toys and Games
DAVID R. JAMES. Editor, *Toys International*, London.

Du.C./Crime (*in part*)
DUNCAN CHAPPELL. Professor of Criminal Justice, State University of New York at Albany. Author of *The Police and the Public in Australia and New Zealand*.

D.Ws./Communist Movement
DAVID LOUIS WILLIAMS. Assistant Professor of Government, Ohio University.

E.A.J.D./Transportation (*in part*)
ERNEST ALBERT JOHN DAVIES. Editor, *Traffic Engineering and Control* (monthly); *Roads and Their Traffic; Traffic Engineering Practice*.

E.B.Br./Religion (*in part*)
EDWIN BLAINE BRONNER. Professor of History and Curator of the Quaker Collection, Haverford College, Haverford, Pa. Author of *William Penn's Holy Experiment*. Editor, *American Quakers Today; An English View of American Quakerism*.

E.Di./Austria
ELFRIEDE DIRNBACHER. Austrian Civil Servant.

E.H.Ha./Vital Statistics
EVELYN HUNTINGTON HALPIN. Writer and consultant on vital statistics and accident prevention programs.

E.L.Cy./Medicine (*in part*)
EDWIN L. CROSBY, M.D. Executive President, American Hospital Association.

E.M.St./Medicine (*in part*)
E.M. STEINDLER, M.D. Assistant Director, Department of Mental Health, American Medical Association.

E.Na./Life Sciences (*in part*)
ERNEST NAYLOR. Professor of Marine Biology, University of Liverpool; Director, Marine Biological Laboratory, Port Erin, Isle of Man. Author of *British Marine Isopods*.

Er.As./Horse Racing (*in part*)
ERIC ARTHUR ASTROM. Executive Secretary, National Association of Canadian Race Tracks; Editor, *Track Talk* (the Association's publication).

E.W.M./Religion (*in part*)
ERIK W. MODEAN. Director, News Bureau, Lutheran Council in the U.S.A.

F.Br./Boxing
FRANK BUTLER. Sports Editor, *News of the World*, London.

F.G./Italy
FABIO GALVANO. London correspondent, *Epoca*, Milan.

F.H.Ka./Religion (*in part*)
FREDERIK HERMAN KAAN. Secretary of the Department of Cooperation and Witness, World Alliance of Reformed Churches (Presbyterian and Congregational), Geneva, Switz.

F.H.Li./Religion (*in part*)
FRANKLIN HAMLIN LITTELL. Professor, Department of Religion, Temple University, Philadelphia, Pa. Author of *The Origins of Sectarian Protestantism; From State Church to Pluralism*.

F.H.Sk./Fuel and Power (*in part*); **Mining** (*in part*); **U.S. Supplement:** *Mining Table; Power: Mineral Fuels Table*
FRANK H. SKELDING. President, AMDEC Corp. (mineral consultants).

F.J.C.R./Medicine (*in part*)
FRANCIS JOHN CALDWELL ROE. Research coordinator, Tobacco Research Council, London. Author of *Biology of Cancer; The Prevention of Cancer; Metabolic Aspects of Food Safety*.

F.J.Se./Medicine (*in part*)
FREDRICK J. STARE, M.D. Professor of Nutrition and Chairman, Department of Nutrition, Harvard School of Public Health. Author of *Eating For Good Health* and syndicated newspaper column "Food and Your Health."

F.P.P./Fairs and Shows
FREDERICK P. PITTERA. Chairman, International Exposition Consultants Co. Member, Board of Trustees, New York Institute of Technology. Member, Board of Governors, National Business and Professional Council. Author of *The Art and Science of International Fairs and Exhibitions; The Fairs of the United States and Canada*.

F.W.N./Medicine (*in part*)
FRANK W. NEWELL, M.D. Professor of Ophthalmology and Chairman, Department of Ophthalmology, The University of Chicago. Author of *Ophthalmology, Principles and Concepts*. Editor in chief, *American Journal of Ophthalmology*.

F.W.Rr./Meteorology
FRANCIS W. REICHELDERFER. Aeronautical and Marine Meteorology Consultant. Former Chief, Weather Bureau, U.S. Department of Commerce, Washington, D.C.

F.Wt./Biography (*in part*)
FRANK G. WRIGHT. Washington (D.C.) correspondent, *Minneapolis Tribune*.

G.A.A./Dominican Republic
GUSTAVO ARTHUR ANTONINI. Associate Professor, Center for Latin American Studies, University of Florida.

G.A.Po./Profits
GERALD A. POLLACK. Vice-President, First National City Bank, New York City. Author of *Perspectives on the U.S. International Financial Position*.

G.B.Sm./Philately and Numismatics (*in part*)
GLENN B. SMEDLEY. Governor, American Numismatic Association.

G.C./Literature (*in part*)
GIOVANNI CARSANIGA. Reader in Italian, University of Sussex, Eng.

G.C.Cu./Jamaica
GLORIA CLARE CUMPER. Chairman, Council of Voluntary Social Services; Member, Judicial Services Commission, Kingston, Jamaica.

G.C.Ho./Merchandising (*in part*)
GRAHAM CHARLES HOCKLEY. Lecturer, Department of Economics, University College, Cardiff. Author of *Monetary Policy and Public Finance.* Co-author of *The Wealth of the Nation: The Balance Sheet of the United Kingdom, 1957–61.*

G.C.L./Ethiopia
GEOFFREY CHARLES LAST. Adviser, Imperial Ethiopian Ministry of Education and Fine Arts, Addis Ababa. Author of *A Regional Survey of Africa; A Geography of Ethiopia.* Co-author of *A History of Ethiopia in Pictures.*

G.De./Advertising (*in part*)
GEOFFREY DEMPSEY. Manager, Overseas Department, J. Walter Thompson Co. Ltd., London.

Ge.We./Industrial Review (*in part*)
GEORGE WEBER. Editor in chief, *The Oil and Gas Journal.*

G.F.R./Industrial Review (*in part*)
GEORGE FRANK RAY. Senior Research Fellow, National Institute of Economic and Social Research, London.

Go.M./Industrial Review (*in part*)
GORDON MINNES. Secretary, Canadian Pulp and Paper Association.

G.P./Literature (*in part*)
GABRIEL PREIL. Writer. Hebrew and Yiddish poet. Author of *Israeli Poetry in Peace and War; Nof Shemesh Ukhfor* ("Landscape of Sun and Frost"); *Ner Mul Kokhavim* ("Candle Against the Stars"); *Mapat Erev* ("Map of Evening"); *Lieder* ("Poems"); *Haesh Vehadmama* ("The Fire and the Silence"); *Shirim* ("Poems").

G.U./Bhutan; Burma; Dependent States (*in part*)**; Nepal**
GOVINDAN UNNY. Agence France-Presse Special Correspondent for India, Nepal, and Ceylon.

Ha.E./Medicine (*in part*)
HAROLD ELLIS. Professor of Surgery, Westminster Medical School, University of London. Author of *Clinical Anatomy* (5th edition); *Anatomy for Anaesthetists* (2nd edition); *Lecture Notes in Surgery* (3rd edition); *Principles of Resuscitation; History of Bladder Stone.*

Ha.Fr./Contract Bridge
HAROLD FRANKLIN. Editor, *English Bridge Quarterly.* Bridge Correspondent, *Yorkshire Post; Yorkshire Evening Post.* Broadcaster. Author of *Best of Bridge on the Air.*

H.A.Ru./Medicine (*in part*)
HOWARD A. RUSK, M.D. Professor and Chairman, Department of Rehabilitation Medicine, New York University School of Medicine. Author of *Rehabilitation Medicine.*

H.B./Hockey (*in part*)**; Ice Skating; Skiing**
HOWARD BASS. Journalist and Broadcaster. Editor, *Winter Sports* annuals, Winter Sports Correspondent, *The Daily Telegraph,* London; *The Christian Science Monitor,* Boston; *Ski Racing,* Denver; *World Sports,* London. Author of *The Magic of Skiing; Winter Sports; International Encyclopaedia of Winter Sports.*

H.B.J./Government Finance (*in part*)
HELLA B. JUNZ. Senior Economist, Board of Governors of the U.S. Federal Reserve System.

H.C.Cl./Literature (*in part*)
HENRY CUMMINGS CAMPBELL. Chief Librarian, Toronto Public Library, Toronto.

H.Du./Historic Buildings
HIROSHI DAIFUKU. Chief, Section for the Development of the Cultural Heritage, UNESCO, Paris.

He.B.H./Food (*in part*)
HENRY BERNARD HAWLEY. Consultant, Human Nutrition and Food Science, Sherborne, Eng.

H.E.Ku./Life Sciences (*in part*)
HERBERT E. KUBITSCHEK. Senior Physicist, Division of Biological and Medical Research, Argonne National Laboratory. Author of *Introduction to Research with Continuous Cultures.*

H.Go./Chess
HARRY GOLOMBEK. British Chess Champion, 1947, 1949, and 1955. Chess Correspondent, *The Times* and *Observer,* London. Author of *Penguin Handbook on the Game of Chess; Modern Opening Chess Strategy.*

H.H.G./Medicine (*in part*)
HARRY H. GARNER, M.D. Chairman and Professor, Department of Psychiatry and Behavioral Science, Chicago Medical School. Author of *Psychotherapy: A Confrontation Problem-solving Technique.*

H.H.Sa./Propaganda
HOWLAND H. SARGEANT. President, Radio Liberty Committee. Author of *The Representation of the United States Abroad.*

Hi.S./Housing (*in part*)
HIDEHIKO SAZANAMI. Chief, Urban Facilities Research Group, Building Research Institute, Ministry of Construction, Tokyo. Author of *Housing in Metropolitan Areas.*

H.J.Kl./Prisons and Penology
HUGH JOHN KLARE. Head, Division of Penal and Criminological Questions, Council of Europe, Strasbourg, France.

H.L.En./Environment (*in part*)
HERBERT LEESON EDLIN. Publications Officer, Forestry Commission of Great Britain. Author of *Trees, Woods and Man; Wayside and Woodland Trees; Man and Plants; What Wood Is That?; Guide to Tree Planting and Cultivation.*

H.M.F.M./Industrial Review (*in part*)
HUGH MICHAEL FINER MALLETT. Editor, *Weekly Wool Chart,* Bradford, Eng.

Ho.S./Literature (*in part*)
HOWARD SERGEANT. Lecturer and writer. Editor of *Outposts,* Walton-on-Thames. Author of *The Cumberland Wordsworth; Tradition in the Making of Modern Poetry.*

H.R.Mo./Music (*in part*)
HAZEL ROMOLA MORGAN. Secretary to Editor, *Emi News,* E.M.I. Ltd., London.

H.R.Sh./Agriculture (*in part*)**; Food** (*in part*)**; U.S. Supplement:** *Principal Crops Table*
HARVEY R. SHERMAN. Environmental Policy Division, Congressional Research Service, Library of Congress.

H.Sa./Life Sciences (*in part*)
HAROLD SANDON. Formerly Professor of Zoology, University of Khartoum, Sudan. Author of *The Protozoan Fauna of the Soil; The Food of Protozoa; An Illustrated Guide to the Fresh-water Fishes of the Sudan; Essays on Protozoology.*

H.S.N./Fisheries
HAROLD STANLEY NOEL. Editor, *World Fishing,* London.

H.-T.Ch./China; Taiwan
HUNG-TI CHU. Expert in Far Eastern Affairs. UN Area Specialist and Chief of Asia-Africa Section and Trusteeship Council Section, 1946–67; Professor of Government, Texas Tech University, Lubbock, 1968–69.

H.Y.S.P./Biography (*in part*)**; India**
HOLENARASIPUR Y. SHARADA PRASAD. Director of Information, Prime Minister's Secretariat, New Delhi.

I.Fr./Life Sciences (*in part*)
IRWIN FRIDOVICH. Professor of Biochemistry, Duke University Medical Center, Durham, N.C.

I.H.M./Alcoholic Beverages (*in part*)
IRVING H. MARCUS. Publisher, *Wine Publications;* Columnist, *Wines and Vines.* Author of *Dictionary of Wine Terms; Lines About Wines; How to Test and Improve Your Wine Judging Ability.*

I.Ka./Mathematics
IRVING KAPLANSKY. George Herbert Mead Distinguished Service Professor, Department of Mathematics, The University of Chicago.

I.Pr./Stock Exchanges (*in part*)
IRVING PFEFFER. Professor of Insurance and Finance, Graduate School of Business Administration, University of California at Los Angeles. Author of *Insurance and Economic Theory; The Financing of Small Business.*

I.S.F./Development, Economic
IRVING S. FRIEDMAN. Economic Adviser to the President of the International Bank for Reconstruction and Development (1964–70). Author of *Exchange Controls and the International Monetary System; U.S. Foreign Economic Policy.*

ITU/Telecommunications (*in part*)
INTERNATIONAL TELECOMMUNICATION UNION, Geneva.

IULA/Cities and Urban Affairs (*in part*)
Research staff, International Union of Local Authorities, The Hague, Neth.

Ja.C.C./Life Sciences (*in part*)
JAMES CLINTON COPELAND. Associate Geneticist, Division of Biological and Medical Research, Argonne National Laboratory, Argonne, Ill.

Ja.E.M./Motor Sports (*in part*)
JAMES EDWARD MARTENHOFF. Boating Editor, *Miami* (Fla.) *Herald.* Author of *How to Buy a Better Boat; Handbook of Skin and Scuba Diving.*

J.Ag./Horse Racing (*in part*)
JOSEPH C. AGRELLA. Turf Editor, *Chicago Sun-Times.* Author of *Ten Commandments for Professional Handicapping.*

J.A.Kr./Chemistry (*in part*)
JAMES ALISTAIR KERR. Lecturer, University of Birmingham, Eng.

J.A.O'L./Biography (*in part*)
JEREMIAH ALOYSIUS O'LEARY. Latin America Correspondent, *Washington Evening Star,* Washington, D.C. Author of *Dominican Action—1965.*

Ja.R.E./Belgium
JAN ROBERT ENGELS. Editor, *Vooruitgang* (Quarterly of the Belgian Party for Freedom and Progress).

J.B.A./Religion (*in part*)
JACOB BERNARD AGUS. Professor of Rabbinics, Reconstructionist Rabbinical College, Philadelphia, Pa. Author of *The Evolution of Jewish Thought; Dialogue and Tradition.*

J.B.Be./Industrial Review (*in part*)**; Transportation** (*in part*)
JOHN BERESFORD BENTLEY. Editor, *Air-Cushion Vehicles.* Publisher, *Hoverfoil News.*

J.Be./Baseball (*in part*)
JACK BRICKHOUSE. Vice-President and Manager of Sports, WGN Continental Broadcasting Company.

J.B.Kr./Medicine (*in part*)
JOSEPH BARNETT KIRSNER, M.D. Deputy Dean for Medical Affairs and Chief of Staff, The University of Chicago School of Medicine.

J.B.St./Religion (*in part*)
J. BUROUGHS STOKES. Manager, Committees on Publication, The First Church of Christ, Scientist, Boston.

J.C.Y./Chemistry (*in part*)
JOHN COLIN YOUNG. Lecturer in Chemistry, University College of Wales.

Je.Ho./Basketball (*in part*);
Biography (*in part*); **Football** (*in part*)
JEROME HOLTZMAN. Sportswriter, *Chicago Sun-Times*. Columnist, *Sporting News*.

J.E.McK./Sociology
JAMES EDWARD McKEOWN. Professor of Sociology, University of Wisconsin-Parkside, Kenosha, Wis. Co-editor of *The Changing Metropolis*. Author of *Study Guide for Economics; Study Guide for Sociology*. Co-author of *A Study of Integrated Living in Chicago*.

Je.Wi./Medicine (*in part*)
JELIA C. WITSCHI. Assistant in Nutrition, Department of Nutrition, Harvard School of Public Health.

J.F.Ba./Biography (*in part*)
JOHN FREDERICK BARTON. Diplomatic Correspondent, United Press International, Washington, D.C.

J.F.Ss./Veterinary Medicine
J. FREDERICK SMITHCORS. Associate Editor, American Veterinary Publications, Inc., Santa Barbara, Calif. Author of *Evolution of the Veterinary Art; The American Veterinary Profession*.

J.G.S.M./Gardening (*in part*)
JOHN GRAHAM SCOTT MARSHALL. Horticultural Consultant.

J.H.Bo./Life Sciences (*in part*)
JEFFERY HUGH BOSWALL. Producer of Sound and Television Programs, British Broadcasting Corporation Natural History Unit, Bristol, Eng.

J.H.v.V./Consumer Affairs (*in part*)
JAN H. VAN VEEN. Executive Secretary, International Organization of Consumers Unions, Neth.

J.J.A./Bowling and Lawn Bowls (*in part*)
JOHN J. ARCHIBALD. Writer, the *St. Louis Post-Dispatch*. Author of *Bowling for Boys and Girls*.

J.J.Ac./Fuel and Power (*in part*)
JOSEPH JOHN ACCARDO. Washington Columnist.

J.J.Gm./Advertising (*in part*)
JARLATH JOHN GRAHAM. Editor, *Advertising Age*.

J.J.Sm./Paraguay; Peru; Uruguay
JOHN JERVIS SMITH. Research Officer, Economic Intelligence Department, Lloyds and Bolsa International Bank Ltd., London.

J.K./Biography (*in part*); **Israel**
JON KIMCHE. Expert on Middle East Affairs, *Evening Standard*, London. Author of *The Second Arab Awakening: The Middle East, 1914–1969*.

J.Ki./Museums and Galleries (*in part*)
JOSHUA B. KIND. Associate Professor of Art History, Northern Illinois University, De Kalb. Author of *Rouault; Titian*.

J.Kn./France
JEAN MARCEL KNECHT. Assistant Foreign Editor, *Le Monde*, Paris. Formerly Permanent Correspondent in Washington and Vice-President of the Association de la Presse Diplomatique Française.

J.K.R./Agriculture (*in part*)
JOHN KERR ROSE. Senior Specialist in Natural Resources and Conservation, Congressional Research Service, Library of Congress, Washington, D.C.

J.L.Re./Oceanography
JOSEPH LEE REID. Research Oceanographer, Scripps Institution of Oceanography, La Jolla, Calif. Author of *Intermediate Waters of the Pacific Ocean*.

J.Me./Religion (*in part*)
JOHN MEYENDORFF. Professor of Church History and Patristics, St. Vladimir's Seminary; Professor of History, Fordham University, New York City; Adjunct-Professor of Religion, Columbia University.

J.M.Ka./Religion (*in part*)
JOSEPH M. KITAGAWA. Professor of History of Religions and Dean of the Divinity School, The University of Chicago. Author of *Religions of the East; Religion in Japanese History*.

J.N.B./Religion (*in part*)
JOHN NICHOLLS BOOTH. Unitarian Universalist clergyman. Co-founder Japan Free Religious Association. Author of *The Quest for Preaching Power; Introducing Unitarian Universalism*.

Jn.M./Social Services (*in part*)
JOHN MOSS. Barrister-at-Law. Author of *Hadden's Health and Welfare Services Handbook*. Editor of *Local Government Law and Administration*.

J.No./Theatre (*in part*)
JULIUS NOVICK. Assistant Professor of English, New York University, New York City; Guest Lecturer, Drama Division of the Juilliard School. Dramatic Critic for the *Village Voice* and *The Humanist*. Contributor to *The Nation*; the *New York Times*. Author of *Beyond Broadway: The Quest for Permanent Theatres*.

Jo.A./Religion (*in part*)
JOSEPH ANDERSON. Assistant to the Council of Twelve Apostles, Church of Jesus Christ of Latter-day Saints (Mormons), Salt Lake City, Utah.

Jo.A.A./Libya
JOHN ANTHONY ALLAN. Lecturer in Geography, School of Oriental and African Studies, University of London.

Jo.A.K./New Zealand
JOHN ARNOLD KELLEHER. Editor, *The Dominion*, Wellington, N.Z.

Jo.B.W./Cycling
JOHN BORLAND WADLEY. Writer and Broadcaster on cycling. Author of *Tour de France 1970 and 1971*.

Jo.N./Mountaineering
JOHN NEILL. Head of Chemical Engineering Department, C. & W. Walker Ltd. Author of Climbers' Club Guides: *Cwm Silyn and Tremadoc, Snowdon South*; Alpine Club Guide: *Selected Climbs in the Pennine Alps*.

J.R.By./Rubber
J. R. BEATTY. Senior Research Associate, B.F. Goodrich Research Center, Brecksville, Ohio.

J.R.El./Medicine (*in part*)
JOHN ROGERS ELLIS, M.B.E. Physician, The London Hospital; Dean, London Hospital Medical College; Secretary, Association for the Study of Medical Education.

J.T.B./Motion Pictures (*in part*)
JOHN TEAL BOBBITT. Writer and Producer of Encyclopædia Britannica Films: *The Bill of Rights of the United States; The Congress; The Constitution of the United States; The Declaration of Independence by the Colonies; The Supreme Court*.

J.T.G./Psychology
JOHN T. GOODMAN. Associate Professor of Psychiatry, McMaster University, Hamilton, Ont.

Ju.W./Alcoholic Beverages (*in part*)
JULIUS WILE. Senior Vice-President, Julius Wile Sons & Co., Inc., New York City. Vice-President, New England Distillers, Inc., Teterboro, N.J. Vice-Chairman, Wine Conference of America. Lecturer on wines, School of Hotel Administration, Cornell University.

J.W.Ma./Alcoholic Beverages (*in part*)
JOHN WILLIAM MAHONEY. Director, Society of Friends of Wine, London. Author of *A Guide to Good Wine* (Introduction); *Wines; Spirits and Liqueurs; The Labelling of Wines and Spirits*.

Jy.L./Postal Services (*in part*)
JERRY LIPSON. Public information officer, Commission on Population Growth and the American Future, Washington, D.C.

K.de la B./Arctic Regions
KENNETH de la BARRE. Director, Montreal Office, Arctic Institute of North America.

K.F.C./Philately and Numismatics (*in part*)
KENNETH FRANCIS CHAPMAN. Editor, *Stamp Collecting*; Philatelic Correspondent, *The Times*, London. Author of *Good Stamp Collecting; Commonwealth Stamp Collecting*.

K.F.Cv./Biography (*in part*); **Yugoslavia**
KRSTO FRANJO CVIIĆ. Leader Writer and East European Specialist, *The Economist*, London.

K.G./Education (*in part*)
KENNETH G. GEHRET. Education Editor, *The Christian Science Monitor*.

K.H.W./Religion (*in part*)
KENNETH H. WOOD. Editor, *Advent The Review and Sabbath Herald*. Author of *Meditations for Moderns*. Co-author of *His Initials Were F.D.N.*

K.I./Congo, Democratic Republic of the; Dependent States (*in part*); **Equatorial Guinea; Kenya; Malawi; Rhodesia; Tanzania; Uganda; Zambia**
KENNETH INGHAM. Professor of History, University of Bristol, Eng. Author of *Reformers in India; A History of East Africa*.

K.K.Mi./Basketball (*in part*)
KEITH KIRKMAN MITCHELL. Lecturer, Department of Physical Education, Leeds University; Hon. General Secretary, Amateur Basket Ball Association.

K.L.O./Rowing
KEITH LANGFORD OSBORNE. Editor, *Rowing*, 1961–63. Hon. Editor, *British Rowing Almanack*, 1961–.

K.R.P./Literature (*in part*)
KARIN ROSAMUND PETHERICK. Crown Princess Louise Lecturer in Swedish, University College, London.

K.Sm./Albania; Biography (*in part*);
Bulgaria; Hungary; Intelligence Operations;
Mongolia; Poland; Political Parties;
Romania; Soviet Bloc Economies
KAZIMIERZ MACIEJ
SMOGORZEWSKI. Writer on contemporary
history. Founder and Editor, *Free Europe*,
London. Author of *The United States and
Great Britain; Poland's Access to the Sea*.

L.C.Ba./Industrial Review (*in part*)
LESLIE CHARLES BATEMAN.
Manager, Tariffs and Trade Regulations
Section, International Department,
British Steel Corporation, London.

L.C.Br./Housing (*in part*)
LEWIS CHARLES BRAITHWAITE.
Extramural Lecturer in Urban and
Environment Studies, University of
Birmingham, Eng.

L.Ch./Fuel and Power (*in part*)
LUCIEN CHALMEY. Adviser, Union
Internationale des Producteurs et
Distributeurs d'Énergie Électrique, Paris.

L.F.R.W./Afghanistan; Iran
LAURENCE FREDERIC RUSHBROOK
WILLIAMS. Fellow of All Souls College,
Oxford University, 1914–21; Professor
of Modern Indian History, Allahabad, India,
1914–19. Author of *India Under the Company
and the Crown; The State of Pakistan; What
About India?; Kutch in History and Legend*.
Editor of *Handbook to India, Pakistan,
Burma, and Ceylon*.

L.H./South Africa
LOUIS HOTZ. Formerly editorial writer,
the *Johannesburg (S.Af.) Star*. Co-author
and contributor to *The Jews in South Africa:
A History*.

L.H.Jo./Telecommunications (*in part*)
LAURENCE HENRY JOHN. Producer,
Science Unit, British Broadcasting
Corporation (radio).

L.Ke./Cooperatives
LOTTE KENT. Editor, *Cooperative News
Service*, International Cooperative Alliance,
London.

L.M.Gd./Antarctica
LAURENCE M. GOULD. Professor of
Geology, University of Arizona. Chairman,
Committee on Polar Research, National
Academy of Sciences. Author of *Cold:
The Record of an Antarctic Sledge Journey*.

L.M.M./Seismology
LEONARD M. MURPHY. Chief,
Seismology Division, Coast and Geodetic
Survey, Environmental Science Services
Administration, U.S. Department of
Commerce, Washington, D.C.

L.O.T./Biography (*in part*); **Tennis**
LANCELOT OLIVER TINGAY.
Lawn Tennis Correspondent, *The Daily
Telegraph*, London.

L.R.Bu./Education (*in part*)
LEONARD RALPH BUCKLEY.
Formerly Assistant Editor, *The Times
Educational Supplement*, London.

**M.A.K./Economy, World; Payments and
Reserves, International**
MIROSLAV A. KRIZ. Vice-President,
First National City Bank, New York
City. Author of *The Price of Gold; Gold in
World Monetary Affairs Today; Gold:
Barbarous Relic or Useful Instrument?*

Ma.Ka./Music (*in part*)
MAUD KARPELES. Hon. President,
International Folk Music Council, Kingston,
Ont. Author of *Cecil Sharp: His Life and
Works; Folk Songs from Newfoundland*.
Editor of *Journal of the International Folk
Music Council*, vol. i–xiii and xvi;
*English Folk Songs from the Southern
Appalachians* by Cecil Sharp.

M.B.Su./Biography (*in part*)
MARK BARRY SULLIVAN. Staff
Correspondent, Washington Bureau, *Time*
magazine. Contributor, Time-Life Library of
America series.

M.By./Transportation (*in part*)
MICHAEL BAILY. Shipping and
Transport Correspondent, *The Times*,
London.

M.C.G.I./Medicine (*in part*)
MARTIN C. G. ISRAËLS. Professor
of Clinical Hematology, University and
Royal Infirmary, Manchester. Author of
*Atlas of Bone Marrow Pathology; Diagnosis
and Treatment of Blood Diseases*.

M.C.MacD./Agriculture (*in part*);
Transportation (*in part*)
MALCOLM CHARLES MacDONALD.
Director, Econtel Research Ltd., London.
Editor, *Factual Series; Business
Cycle Series*.

M.Cs./Biography (*in part*)
MERCER M. CROSS. Political Editor,
Congressional Quarterly.

M.Ct./Laos
MAX COIFFAIT. Correspondent, Agence
France-Presse; *Time* magazine, Vientiane,
Laos.

M.Fd./Medicine (*in part*)
MAXWELL FINLAND, M.D.
Epidemiologist, Boston City Hospital. George
Richards Minot Professor Emeritus, Harvard
University.

M.F.F./Income, National
MICHAEL FREDERICK FULLER.
Lecturer in Economic and Social Statistics,
Eliot College, University of Kent at
Canterbury.

M.Fi./Medicine (*in part*)
MORRIS FISHBEIN. Editor of *Medical
World News*. Emeritus Professor, The
University of Chicago; University of Illinois,
College of Medicine. Author of *Modern Home
Remedies and How to Use Them; Handy
Home Medical Adviser; Concise Medical
Encyclopedia*.

M.F.S./Switzerland
MELANIE F. STAERK. Editor, *UNESCO
Press*, Swiss National Commission for
UNESCO.

M.L.N./Medicine (*in part*)
MURIEL LINA NEWHOUSE. Reader in
Occupational Medicine, London School of
Hygiene and Tropical Medicine.

**M.Mr./Botswana; Burundi;
Commonwealth of Nations; Dependent
States** (*in part*)**; Gambia, The; Ghana;
Lesotho; Maldives; Mauritius; Nigeria;
Rwanda; Sierra Leone; Swaziland**
MOLLY MORTIMER. Writer on
Commonwealth and International Affairs.
Author of *Trusteeship in Practice; Kenya*.

M.N.Y./Religion (*in part*)
M. NORVEL YOUNG. President,
Pepperdine University, Los Angeles. Editor,
Twentieth Century Christian and *Power for
Today*. Author of *Churches of Today*.

Mo.M./Greece
MARIO (S.) MODIANO. Athens
Correspondent, *The Times*, London.

M.Pan./Prices
MILIVOJE PANIĆ. Senior Economic
Adviser, National Economic Development
Office, London.

M.Pl./Industrial Review (*in part*)
MAURICE PLATT. Consulting Engineer.
Formerly Director of Engineering, Vauxhall
Motors, Ltd. Author of *Elements of
Automobile Engineering*.

M.Pu./Mexico
MANUEL PULGAR. Senior Economic
Research Officer, Lloyds and Bolsa
International Bank Ltd., London.

M.R.-R./Literature (*in part*)
MARCEL REICH-RANICKI. Literary
critic, *Die Zeit*. Author of *Deutsche Literatur
in West und Ost; Literarisches Leben in
Deutschland; Wer schreibt, proviziert;
Literatur der kleinen Schritte; Die
Ungeliebten; Lauter Verrisse*.

M.R.S./Astronautics
MITCHELL R. SHARPE. Science writer.
Author of *Living in Space: The Environment
of the Astronaut; Yuri Gagarin, First Man in
Space; Satellites and Probes, the Development
of Unmanned Space Flight*. Co-author of
Applied Astronautics; Basic Astronautics.

M.Sn./Literature (*in part*)
MOSHE STARKMAN. Essayist in Yiddish
and Hebrew, Bibliographer. President,
Yiddish P.E.N. Club, N.Y. Editor, *Hemshekh
Anthology of American Yiddish Poetry*.
Associate Editor, *Lexicon of Yiddish Literature*.

M.S.R./Biography (*in part*); **Malaysia;
Singapore**
MAHINDER SINGH RANDHAVA.
Sub-editor, *The Straits Times*, Kuala Lumpur,
Malaysia.

M.Ta./Medicine (*in part*)
MASUO TAKABE, M.D. Director,
Division of Communicable Diseases, World
Health Organization, Geneva.

M.Ty./Television and Radio (*in part*)
MICHAEL TYPE. Assistant Editor,
European Broadcasting Union, Geneva.

M.W.Wo./Religion (*in part*)
THE REV. MAX W. WOODWARD.
British Secretary, World Methodist
Council.

Mx.B./Vatican City State
MAX BERGERRE. Correspondent ANSA
for Vatican Affairs, Rome.

Mx.H./Biography (*in part*)
MAX HARRELSON. Chief of United
Nations Bureau, The Associated Press.

My.B.B./Fiji; Tonga; Western Samoa
MARY BEATRICE BOYD. Senior
Lecturer in History, Victoria University of
Wellington, N.Z.

N.A.So./Medicine (*in part*)
NICHOLAS ARTHUR SOTER, M.D.
Research Fellow in Dermatology, Harvard
Medical School.

N.Cr./Biography (*in part*); **Germany** (*in part*)
NORMAN CROSSLAND. Bonn
Correspondent, *The Guardian*, London.

N.D.McW./Track and Field Sports (*in part*)
NORRIS DEWAR McWHIRTER.
Television commentator, British Broadcasting
Corporation, London. Co-compiler, *Guinness
Book of Records*.

N.H.K./Religion (*in part*)
NATHAN HOMER KNORR. President,
Watch Tower Bible and Tract Society of
Pennsylvania.

N.Ma./Photography
NEVILLE FREDERIC MAUDE.
Consultant Editor, *British Journal of
Photography; Photo News Weekly*. Editor,
Photographic Processor. Author of *Take
Better Photos; Choosing a Camera*.

N.M.H./Law (*in part*)
NEVILLE MARCH HUNNINGS.
Senior Research Officer, British Institute of
International and Comparative Law,
London. Author of *Film Censors and the
Law*.

N.R.U./Commodities, Primary
NORMAN RICHARD URQUHART.
Assistant Vice-President, in charge of
Commodity Section, Economics
Department, First National City Bank,
New York City.

N.Si./Horse Racing (in part)
NOEL SIMPSON. Managing Director,
Sydney Bloodstock Proprietary Ltd.,
Sydney, Austr.

O.F.K./Biography (in part); Norway
OLE FERDINAND KNUDSEN.
Editor, Norway Exports, Oslo.

O.H.H./Guatemala
OSCAR H. HORST. Professor of
Geography, Western Michigan University.

O.K./Industrial Review (in part)
ORLAND BENJAMIN KILLIN.
Associate Professor of Industrial Education
and Technology, Eastern Washington State
College.

O.Me./Tourism (in part)
OLIVIER MOSSÉ. Marketing Specialist,
International Union of Official Travel
Organisations (IUOTO), Geneva.

O.Pl./Medicine (in part)
OGLESBY PAUL, M.D. Professor of
Medicine, Northwestern University Medical
School, Chicago.

Ot.P./Czechoslovakia; Union of Soviet
Socialist Republics
OTTO PICK. Visiting Professor of
International Relations, University of
Surrey; Director, Atlantic Information
Centre for Teachers, London.

O.Tr./Theatre (in part)
OSSIA TRILLING. Vice-President,
International Association of Theatre Critics.
Co-editor and contributor, International
Theatre. Contributor, The Times, London.

P.A.H./Religion (in part)
THE REV. PETER HEBBLETHWAITE,
S.J. Editor, The Month. Author of
Bernanos; The Council Fathers and Atheism;
Understanding the Synod. Editor of
Faith in Question; Talking with Unbelievers;
The Documents of Vatican II.

P.A.St./Astronomy
PETER ALBERT STRITTMATTER.
Staff member, Institute of Theoretical
Astronomy, Cambridge; Visiting Research
Associate, University of California,
San Diego.

Pa.T./Consumer Affairs (in part)
PAT TUCKER. Free-lance writer and
editor, Washington, D.C.

P.A.W.-T./Golf
PERCY AINSWORTH WARD-THOMAS.
Golf Correspondent, The Guardian,
Manchester.

P.Bs./Art Sales (in part)
PIERRE BERÈS. Managing Director,
Hermann Publishing Company, Paris.
Founder and Editor in Chief, Sciences. Expert
in rare books.

Pe.B./Drugs and Narcotics (in part)
PETER BEEDLE. Assistant Secretary,
Home Office, London.

P.F.Y./Mining (in part)
PAUL FREDERICK YOPES. Mining
Engineer, Bureau of Mines, U.S. Department
of the Interior, Washington, D.C.

P.Gl./Religion (in part)
PAUL GLIKSON. Secretary, Division of
Jewish Demography and Statistics, Institute
of Contemporary Jewry, The Hebrew
University, Israel.

Ph.D./Cameroon; Central African Republic;
Chad; Congo, People's Republic of the;
Dahomey (in part); Dependent States
(in part); Gabon (in part); Guinea; Ivory
Coast; Malagasy Republic; Mali;
Mauritania; Niger; Senegal; Togo;
Tunisia; Upper Volta
PHILIPPE DECRAENE. Member of
editorial staff, Le Monde, Paris. Editor in
Chief, Revue française d'Études politiques
africaines. Author of Le Panafricanisme;
Tableau des Partis Politiques Africains.

Ph.K./Biography (in part); Nobel Prizes;
Publishing (in part)
PHILIP KOPPER. Free-lance writer,
Washington, D.C.

P.Md./Biography (in part); Iraq; Jordan;
Kuwait; Lebanon; Middle East; Oman;
Saudi Arabia; Syria; United Arab Republic;
Yemen, People's Democratic Republic of;
Yemen Arab Republic
PETER (JOHN) MANSFIELD. Formerly
Middle East Correspondent, Sunday Times,
London. Free-lance writer on Middle East
affairs.

P.M.Ha./Cities and Urban Affairs (in part)
PHILIP MORRIS HAUSER. Professor
of Sociology and Director, Population
Research Center, The University of Chicago.
Editor of Urbanization in Latin
America.

P.M.Re./Industrial Review (in part)
PHILIP MORTON ROWE. Press Officer,
British Man-Made Fibres Federation,
Manchester.

Pr.K./Algeria; Biography (in part); Morocco;
Sudan
PETER KILNER. Editor, Arab Report
and Record.

P.Sh./Tourism (in part)
PETER SHACKLEFORD. Research
Officer, International Union of Official
Travel Organisations (IUOTO), Geneva.

P.Ss./Insurance (in part)
PERCY STEBBINGS. Insurance
Correspondent of Investors' Chronicle;
Post Magazine, London.

P.V.-P./Biography (in part)
PIERRE VIANSSON-PONTÉ. Political
News Editor, Le Monde, Paris. Author of Les
Gaullistes; The King and His Court.

P.W.Ga./Industrial Review (in part)
PETER WILLIAM GADDUM. Chairman,
H. T. Gaddum and Company Ltd., Silk
Merchants, Macclesfield, Cheshire, Eng.
President, International Silk Association.
Author of Silk—How and Where It Is
Produced.

P.Wi./Dance (in part)
PETER WILLIAMS. Editor, Dance and
Dancers.

P.W.Mi./Life Sciences (in part)
PETER WALLACE MILES. Professor of
Zoology, University of Zambia, Lusaka.

Ra.Pa./Philippines
RAFAEL PARGAS. National Geographic
Society, Washington, D.C.

Ra.R./Guyana; Trinidad and Tobago
RANDOLPH RICHARD RAWLINS.
Journalist and broadcaster. Tutor,
Extramural Department, University of the
West Indies, St. Augustine, Trinidad.

R.B.Gt./Medicine (in part)
ROBERT BENJAMIN GREENBLATT,
M.D. Professor and Chairman, Department
of Endocrinology, Medical College of
Georgia, Augusta. Author of Office
Endocrinology; The Hirsute Female; Ovulation.

R.B.Le./Colombia; Ecuador
RAYMOND BASIL LEWRY. Senior
Research Officer, Lloyds and Bolsa
International Bank Ltd., London.

R.C.Pe./Industrial Review (in part)
ROBIN CHARLES PENFOLD. Public
relations executive, Carl Byoir and
Associates Ltd., London. Author of A
Journalist's Guide to Plastics.

R.D.A.G./United Nations (in part)
RICHARD D. A. GREENOUGH. Chief
English writer, Press Division, UNESCO,
Paris. Author of Africa Prospect; Children's
Progress; Africa Calls.

R.d'E./Brazil
RAUL d'ECA. Formerly Fulbright Visiting
Lecturer on American History, University of
Minas Gerais, Belo Horizonte, Braz. Co-
author of Latin American History.

R.D.Ho./Andorra; Liechtenstein; Luxem-
bourg; Monaco; San Marino
ROBERT DAVID HODGSON.
The Geographer, U.S. Department of State,
Washington, D.C. Author of The Changing
Map of Africa.

R.E.E.H./Religion (in part)
REUBEN ELMORE ERNEST
HARKNESS. Emeritus Professor of History
of Christianity, Crozer Seminary, Chester,
Pa. Emeritus Professor of History of World
Religions, History of Christianity, Baptist
History, Ellen Cushing Junior College,
Bryn Mawr, Pa.

R.F.Mi./Philately and Numismatics (in part)
RICHARD F. MILLER, Professor of
English, Eastern Washington State College.

R.G.Bu./Medicine (in part)
RICHARD GEOFFREY BURWELL.
Professor of Orthopedics, Institute of
Orthopedics, London.

R.H./Literature (in part)
REIKO HATSUMI. Senior Editor, TBS
Britannica Ltd., Tokyo.

R.H.B./Medicine (in part)
ROWINE HAYES BROWN, M.D.
Associate Director of Pediatrics, Cook
County Hospital, Chicago.

R.H.Be./Hockey (in part)
RICHARD HERBERT BEDDOES.
Sports Columnist, Toronto Globe and Mail.

R.H.Tr./Stock Exchanges (in part)
ROBERT H. TRIGG. Manager,
Institutional Research, New York Stock
Exchange.

R.H.W.D./Literature (in part)
R. H. W. DILLARD. Associate Professor
of English, Hollins College, Va. Author of
The Day I Stopped Dreaming About
Barbara Steele and Other Poems (1966);
News of the Nile (1971).

R.Hy./Peace Movements
RICHARD HATHAWAY. Dean, Adult
Degree Program; Teaching Faculty, History
and International Studies, Goddard College,
Plainfield, Vt.; Member, Board of Editors,
Current.

Ri.W./Liberia; United States
RICHARD WORSNOP. Writer, Editorial
Research Reports, Washington, D.C.

R.J.B./Archaeology (in part)
ROBERT J. BRAIDWOOD. Professor of
Old World Prehistory, the Oriental
Institute and the Department of
Anthropology, The University of Chicago.

R.J.Fe./Motor Sports (in part)
ROBERT JOSEPH FENDELL. New
York Editor, Automotive News. Automobile
Columnist for Action. Scriptwriter for
Speed Sport News syndicated radio
series. Co-author, Encyclopedia of
Motor Racing Personalities.

R.J.Fo./Fuel and Power (*in part*)
ROBERT JOHN FOWELL. Lecturer, Department of Mining Engineering, University of Newcastle upon Tyne, Eng.

R.J.Le./Industrial Review (*in part*)
RICHARD JOHN LEDWITH. Consultant, The International Paint Company, Surrey, Eng.

R.J.Ra./Defense
ROBERT JOHN RANGER. Visiting Lecturer in Strategic Studies, Queen's University, Kingston, Ont.

R.L.F./Religion (*in part*)
ROBERT LOUIS FRIEDLY. Director, Office of Communication, Christian Church (Disciples of Christ), Indianapolis, Ind.

R.L.Hs./Hockey (*in part*)
RICHARD LYNTON HOLLANDS. Hockey Correspondent, *The Daily Telegraph*, London. Co-author of *Hockey*.

R.L.R./Religion (*in part*)
ROGER LEWIS ROBERTS. Editorial Consultant, *Church Times*, London.

R.L.Ro./Chile
ROBERT L. ROSS. President, Adela Development Corp., Washington, D.C.

R.M.Gn./Horse Racing (*in part*)
ROBERT MARSHALL GOODWIN. Assistant Editor, London, *Encyclopædia Britannica*.

Rn.C./Cuba; Haiti; Inter-American Affairs; Portugal
ROBIN CHAPMAN. Economic Research Officer, Lloyds and Bolsa International Bank Ltd., London.

R.N.S./United Nations (*in part*)
RICHARD N. SWIFT. Professor of Politics, New York University, New York City. Author of *International Law: Current and Classic.*

Ro.Ch./Engineering Projects (*in part*)
ROBERT CHAUSSIN. Government Civil Engineer, S.E.T.R.A. (Service d'études Techniques des Routes et Autoroutes), Bagneux, France.

Ro.E.S./Costa Rica; Venezuela
ROBERT EDWARD STENT. Economic and Political Research Officer, Lloyds and Bolsa International Bank Ltd., London.

Ro.Go./Vietnam (*in part*)
ROBERT GORALSKI. NBC News Pentagon Correspondent.

R.Pn./Alcoholic Beverages (*in part*)
RENÉ PROTIN. Director, International Vine and Wine Office, Paris.

R.R.No./Life Sciences (*in part*)
RONALD RICHARDS NOVALES. Professor of Biological Sciences, Northwestern University, Evanston, Ill. Member, Editorial Board, *American Zoologist.*

R.Sa./Environment (*in part*)
RICHARD SALTONSTALL, JR. Author of *Your Environment and What You Can Do About It.* Co-author of *Brown Out and Slow Down.*

R.S.Mi./Engineering Projects (*in part*)
RAYMOND SPENCER MILLARD. Deputy Director, Road Research Laboratory, Department of Environment, Crowthorne, Berkshire, Eng.

R.V.M./Religion (*in part*)
ROBERT V. MOSS. President, United Church of Christ, New York City; President, American Association of Theological Schools, 1966–68. Author of *The Life of Paul; We Believe; As Paul Sees Christ.*

R.W.Cr./Television and Radio (*in part*)
RUFUS WILLIAM CRATER. Editorial Director, *Broadcasting*, New York City.

R.W.Fe./Fuel and Power (*in part*)
RONALD WHITAKER FERRIER. Company Historian, British Petroleum.

R.W.Ko./Industrial Review (*in part*)
RICHARD WALTER KOVAN. Features Editor, *Nuclear Engineering International*, London.

R.W.Sm./Religion (*in part*)
REUBEN WILLIAM SMITH. Assistant Professor of Islamic History, The University of Chicago.

R.W.T./Religion (*in part*)
RONALD WILLIAM THOMSON. Assistant General Secretary, Baptist Union of Great Britain and Ireland. Author of *Heroes of the Baptist Church; William Carey; The Service of Our Lives; A Pocket History of the Baptists.*

S.Aa./Denmark
STENER AARSDAL. Economic Editor, *Børsen.* Press Officer, Chamber of Commerce, Copenhagen.

Sa.H./Literature (*in part*)
SAMUEL HAZO. Director, International Poetry Forum, and Professor, Duquesne University, Pittsburgh, Pa. Author of *Blood Rights; My Sons in God; The Quiet Wars.*

S.A.P./Ceylon
SIDNEY ARNOLD PAKEMAN. Historian. Author of *Ceylon.*

S.B.P./Physics
STUART BEAUMONT PALMER. Lecturer, Department of Applied Physics, University of Hull.

S.Bs./Literature (*in part*)
SALVADOR BARROS. Literary Critic, *Visión; El Día.* Lecturer in Latin American Literature, University of Mexico.

Se.H./Political Science
SERGE HURTIG. Director of Studies and Research, Fondation Nationale des Sciences Politiques; Professor, Paris Institute of Political Studies. Former Secretary-General, International Political Science Association.

S.E.S./Germany (*in part*)
STEPHAN E. SCHATTMANN. Economist, London.

S.F.Y./Drugs and Narcotics (*in part*)
STANLEY F. YOLLES, M.D. Professor and Chairman, Department of Psychiatry, Medical School, State University of New York, Stony Brook.

S.H.Co./Fashion and Dress (*in part*)
STANLEY HARRY COSTIN. London Correspondent, *Nykytekstiili* (Finland); *Textil Branschen* (Sweden).

Sh.P./Barbados; Dependent States (*in part*); **Migration, International** (*in part*); **Race Relations** (*in part*)
SHEILA CAFFYN PATTERSON. Research Fellow, Centre for Multi-Racial Studies, University of Sussex, Brighton. Author of *Colour and Culture in South Africa; The Last Trek; Dark Strangers; Immigrants in Industry.*

Si.P./Words and Meanings, New (*in part*)
SIMEON POTTER. Emeritus Professor of English Language and Philology, University of Liverpool. Author of *Our Language; Language in the Modern World; Modern Linguistics; Changing English.*

S.J.N./Geography
SALVATORE JOHN NATOLI. Educational Affairs Director, Association of American Geographers. Co-author of *Dictionary of Basic Geography.*

S.Ls./Biography (*in part*)
SOPHIE LANNES. Editorial Staff Member, *L'Express*, Paris.

S.Mi./Architecture; Art Exhibitions
SANDRA MILLIKIN. Architectural Historian.

S.M.Mc./Philosophy
STERLING M. McMURRIN. E. E. Ericksen Distinguished Professor and Dean of the Graduate School, University of Utah. Co-author of *A History of Philosophy.*

S.Pa./Furs
SANDY PARKER. Fur Editor, *Women's Wear Daily.*

S.S.G./Medicine (*in part*)
SYDNEY S. GELLIS, M.D. Professor and Chairman, Department of Pediatrics, Tufts University School of Medicine, Boston. Editor, *Year Book of Pediatrics.* Co-editor, *Current Pediatric Therapy.*

S.Tf./Television and Radio (*in part*)
SOL TAISHOFF. President, Editor and Publisher, *Broadcasting*, Washington, D.C.

St.F.B./Horse Racing (*in part*)
STANLEY F. BERGSTEIN. Executive Secretary, Harness Tracks of America Inc.; Vice-President, United States Trotting Association.

T.B.F./Medicine (*in part*)
THOMAS B. FITZPATRICK, M.D. Edward Wigglesworth Professor of Dermatology and Head, Department of Dermatology, Harvard Medical School; Chief, Dermatology Service, Massachusetts General Hospital, Boston. Co-editor, *Dermatology in General Medicine.*

T.C.J.C./Industrial Review (*in part*)
THOMAS CHARLES JOHN COGLE. Technical Editor, *Electrical Review*, London.

T.F.P./Race Relations (*in part*)
THOMAS FRASER PETTIGREW. Professor of Social Psychology, Harvard University. Author of *A Profile of the Negro American; Racially Separate or Together?*

T.J.S.G./Biography (*in part*); **Cambodia; Korea; Southeast Asia; Thailand** (*in part*); **Vietnam** (*in part*)
THAYIL JACOB SONY GEORGE. Assistant Editor, *Far Eastern Economic Review*, Hong Kong. Author of *Krishna Menon, a Biography.*

T.L.T.L./Medicine (*in part*)
THOMAS LOFTUS TOWNSHEND LEWIS. Obstetric Surgeon, Guy's Hospital; Surgeon, Queen Charlotte's Maternity Hospital; Surgeon, Chelsea Hospital for Women. Author of *Progress in Clinical Obstetrics and Gynaecology;* (jointly) *The Queen Charlotte's Textbook of Obstetrics.*

T.M.R./Savings and Investment
TADEUSZ MIECZYSLAW RYBCZYNSKI. Economist, Lazard Brothers, London.

Tm.S./Gardening (*in part*)
TOM STEVENSON. Garden Columnist, *Baltimore News American; Washington Post; Washington Post-Los Angeles Times News Service.* Author of *Pruning Guide for Trees, Shrubs and Vines; Lawn Guide; Gardening for the Beginner.*

To.S./Literature (*in part*)
TORBJØRN STØVERUD. W.P. Ker Senior Lecturer in Norwegian, University College, London.

T.R.Sh./Speleology
TREVOR ROYLE SHAW. Commander, Royal Navy. Vice-President, British Speleological Association.

T.R.T./Biography (*in part*)
TRUMAN R. TEMPLE. Information Officer, U.S. Atomic Energy Commission.

T.Sc./Alcoholic Beverages (*in part*)
TILMAN SCHMITT. Brewery Engineer.
Editor of *Brauwelt; Brauwissenschaft.*

T.Sw./Biography (*in part*); **Fashion and Dress**
(*in part*)
THELMA SWEETINBURGH. Paris
Fashion Correspondent for *International
Textiles* (Amsterdam) and the British Wool
Textile Industry.

T.W./Football (*in part*)
TREVOR WILLIAMSON. Sports
sub-editor, *The Daily Telegraph*, London.

T.W.Me./Engineering Projects (*in part*)
T. W. MERMEL. Assistant to
Commissioner for Research and Chief,
General Engineering Division, Bureau of
Reclamation, U.S. Department of the
Interior, Washington, D.C. Chairman,
Committee on World Register of Dams,
International Commission on Large Dams.
Author of *Register of Dams in the United
States.*

Va.K./Iceland
VALDIMAR KRISTINSSON. Editor of
Fjármálatidindi, Reykjavik.

V.F.Ra./Tobacco
VIVIAN FOSTER RAVEN. Editor,
Tobacco, London.

V.J.P./Cyprus
VERNON JOHN PARRY. Reader in
the History of the Near and Middle East,
School of Oriental and African Studies,
University of London. Contributor to *New
Cambridge Modern History; Cambridge
History of Islam; Encyclopaedia of Islam.*

V.L.A./Labour Unions
VICTOR LEONARD ALLEN. Reader
in Industrial Relations, University
of Leeds. Author of *Power in Trade
Unions; Trade Union Leadership; Trade
Unions and the Government; Militant Trade
Unionism; International Bibliography of
Trade Unionism.*

V.R.Lu./Somalia
VIRGINIA R. LULING. Social
Anthropologist.

V.W.P./Crime (*in part*); **Police** (*in part*)
VIRGIL W. PETERSON. Executive
Director, Chicago Crime Commission,
1942–70. Author of *Gambling—
Should It Be Legalized?; Barbarians in
Our Midst.*

W.A.E./Geology
WILFRED A. ELDERS. Associate
Professor of Geology, University of
California, Riverside.

W.A.Ha./Publishing (*in part*)
WILLIAM A. HACHTEN.
Professor, School of Journalism and Mass
Communication, University of Wisconsin.

W.A.Ka./Publishing (*in part*)
WILLIAM A. KATZ. Professor, School
of Library Science, State University of
New York. Author of *Introduction to
Reference Magazines for Libraries.*

Wa.Ls./Art Sales (*in part*)
WILMA LAWS. Journalist, London.
Member, International Association of Art
Critics.

W.B.Mi./Religion (*in part*)
WILLIAM B. MILLER. Manager,
Department of History, United
Presbyterian Church, U.S.A.

W.Bn./Argentina
WILLIAM BELTRÁN. Economic
Research Officer, Economic Intelligence
Department, Lloyds and Bolsa International
Bank Ltd., London.

W.B.Ri./Computers
WALLACE B. RILEY. Computers Editor,
Electronics magazine.

W.C.Bo./Biography (*in part*); **Motor Sports**
(*in part*)
WILLIAM CHARLES BODDY. Editor,
Motor Sport. Full Member, Guild of Motoring
Writers. Author of *The Story of Brooklands;
The 200 Mile Race; The World's Land Speed
Record; Continental Sports Cars; The Sports
Car Pocketbook; The Bugatti Story.*

W.D.E./Industrial Review (*in part*)
WILLIAM DUNLOP EWART. Editor
and Director, *Fairplay International
Shipping Journal*. Author of *Marine
Engines; Atomic Submarines; Hydrofoils
and Hovercraft; Building a Ship.*

W.D.Hd./Law (*in part*)
WILLIAM D. HAWKLAND. Professor
of Law, University of Illinois, Urbana.
Author of *Sales Under Uniform Commercial
Code; Cases on Bills and Notes; Commercial
Paper; Transactional Guide of the Uniform
Commercial Code; Cases on Sales and Security.*

W.D.McC./Money and Banking
WARREN D. McCLAM. Economist,
Bank for International Settlements,
Basel, Switz.

W.Ei./Populations and Areas (*in part*)
WARREN WOLFF EISENBERG.
Legislative Assistant to Rep. William J.
Green, Washington, D.C.

W.G.J./Literature (*in part*)
WALTON GLYN JONES. Reader in
Danish, University College, London.
Author of *Johannes Jørgensens modne ar;
Johannes Jörgensen; Denmark.*

WHO/Medicine (*in part*)
WORLD HEALTH ORGANIZATION,
Geneva.

W.H.Ta./Religion (*in part*)
WINSTON HOWARTH TAYLOR.
Director, Washington Office, Commission on
Public Relations and United Methodist
Information. Author of *Angels Don't Need
Public Relations; Ending Racial Segregation
in the Methodist Church; Toward an Inclusive
Church.*

W.H.Ts./Biography (*in part*); **Publishing**
(*in part*); **United Kingdom**
WILLIAM HARFORD THOMAS.
Managing Editor, *The Guardian*, London and
Manchester.

Wi.D./Television and Radio (*in part*)
WILLIAM I. DUNKERLEY, JR.
Assistant Secretary, American Radio
Relay League.

W.J.Bn./Medicine (*in part*)
WILLIAM J. BROWN, M.D. Chief,
Venereal Disease Branch, Center for
Disease Control, Atlanta, Ga.

W.Le./Government Finance (*in part*)
WILFRED LEWIS, JR. Chief Economist,
National Planning Association. Author of
*Federal Fiscal Policy in the Postwar
Recessions.*

W.L.We./ Literature (*in part*)
WILLIAM LESLIE WEBB. Literary
Editor, *The Guardian*, London and
Manchester.

W.M.Sa./Medicine (*in part*)
WILLIAM MASON SAMUELS.
Executive Director, Association of Schools
of Allied Health Professions, Washington,
D.C.

W.P./Religion (*in part*)
WILLIAM ASHWORTH PRATT.
Director, Salvation Army International
Information Services, London.

W.P.Ja./Industrial Review (*in part*)
W. PINCUS JASPERT. Technical
editorial consultant. European Editor,
North American Publishing Company,
Philadelphia, Pa. Member, Society of
Photographic Scientists and Engineers.
Editor of *Encyclopaedia of Type Faces.*

W.R.G./Anthropology
WALTER GOLDSCHMIDT. Professor
of Anthropology, University of California,
Los Angeles.

W.So./Africa
WALLACE SOKOLSKY. Associate
Professor, History Department, Bronx
Community College, the New School for
Social Research, New York University,
Division of Adult Education. Co-author of
*Contemporary Civilization; African
Nationalism in the Twentieth Century.*

W.Te./Dance (*in part*)
WALTER TERRY. Dance Critic, *Saturday
Review*. Author of *The Dance in America;
The Ballet Companion; Miss Ruth: The
"More Living Life" of Ruth St. Denis.*

Y.S./Bowling and Lawn Bowls (*in part*)
YRJÖ SARAHETE. Secretary,
Fédération Internationale des Quilleurs,
Helsinki, Fin.

Index

V

W

X

Y

Z

Printed in U.S.A. by R. R. Donnelley & Sons Company

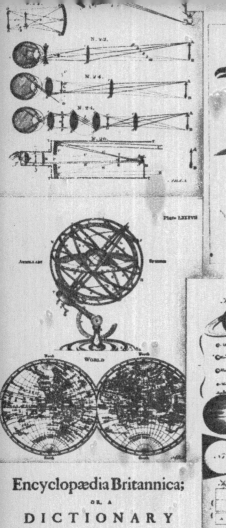

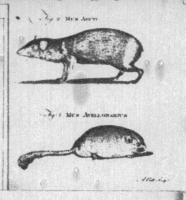

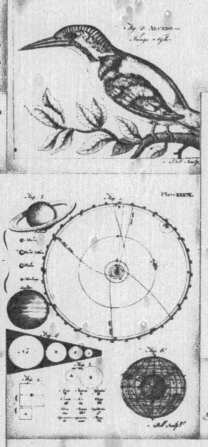

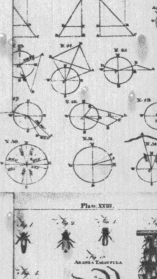

CONIC SECTIONS.

CONIC SECTIONS are curves lines formed by the interfection of a cone and plane.

If a cone be cut by a plane through the axis, the fection will be a triangle ABC.

ELLIPSE

HYPERBOLA

Description of Conic Sections as a Place.

PARABOLA.

Encyclopædia Britannica;

OR, A

DICTIONARY

OF

ARTS and SCIENCES,

COMPILED UPON A NEW PLAN.

IN WHICH

The different SCIENCES and ARTS are digested into
distinct Treatises or Systems;

AND

The various TECHNICAL TERMS, &c. are explained as they occur
in the order of the Alphabet.

ILLUSTRATED WITH ONE HUNDRED AND SIXTY COPPERPLATES.

By a SOCIETY *of* GENTLEMEN *in* SCOTLAND.

IN THREE VOLUMES.

VOL. I.

EDINBURGH:
Printed for A. BELL and C. MACFARQUHAR;
And sold by COLIN MACFARQUHAR, at his Printing-office, Nicolson-street.
M DCC LXXI.

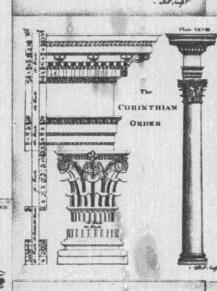

The
CORINTHIAN
ORDER

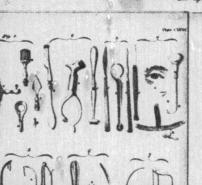

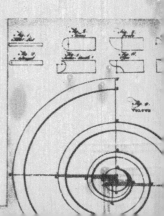